Praise for *Many Europes*

"I would describe this book as the book I have been waiting for."

AMANDA BAHR-EVOLA, Southern Illinois University Edwardsville

"I believe that this may well be the best Western civilization text so far. The book is well written, concise, and presents a picture of events that encourages readers to analyze historical events with an open mind."

MATTHEW D. SCHAFFER, Florence-Darlington Technical College

"I love this textbook. The writing style is descriptive, interesting and engaging, all while keeping the tone and content at a college level."

REANNE EICHELE, Pikes Peak Community College

"This text is a genuine rethinking, reordering and restating of the rise of Europe and, uniquely, different ways to approach the very concepts of Europe and the West."

WAYNE BOWEN, Southeast Missouri State University

"I would describe this book as fresh, innovative, and setting the trend for future Western civilization textbooks to acknowledge the diversity and complexity of Europe."

ANGELA L. ASH, Owensboro Community and Technical College

"The book takes a different approach to history, avoiding the same stagnant stories that those who have just graduated from high school already know—I do believe that it takes the boredom out of history and it brings history alive, which we should all strive to do."

MARY ANN BORDEN, Hudson Valley Community College

"The opening vignettes, the focus on individuals and their experiences, and the look at what historians do in the investigations section make this book better than the competition."

SUSAN G. THOMPSON, Northern Virginia Community College

"*Many Europes*' approach makes it more interesting and readable than other texts I have seen or used. I think that if there is a text that students might actually read and get something out of, this is it."

MICHAEL KENNEDY, High Point University

MANY EUROPES

CHOICE AND CHANCE IN WESTERN CIVILIZATION

Paul Edward Dutton

Simon Fraser University

Suzanne Marchand

Louisiana State University

Deborah Harkness

University of Southern California

MANY EUROPES, FIRST EDITION
Published by McGraw-Hill, a business unit of The McGraw-Hill Companies, Inc., 1221 Avenue of the Americas, New York, NY, 10020. Copyright © 2014 by The McGraw-Hill Companies, Inc. All rights reserved. Printed in the United States of America. No part of this publication may be reproduced or distributed in any form or by any means, or stored in a database or retrieval system, without the prior written consent of The McGraw-Hill Companies, Inc., including, but not limited to, in any network or other electronic storage or transmission, or broadcast for distance learning.

Some ancillaries, including electronic and print components, may not be available to customers outside the United States.

This book is printed on acid-free paper.

2 3 4 5 6 7 8 9 0 DOW/DOW 1 0 9 8 7 6 5 4

ISBN   978-0-07338545-7
MHID   0-07-338545-X

Senior Vice President, Products & Markets: *Kurt L. Strand*
Vice President, General Manager: *Michael Ryan*
Vice President, Content Production & Technology Services: *Kimberly Meriwether David*
Managing Director: *Gina Boedeker*
Director: *Matthew Busbridge*
Director of Development: *Rhona Robbin*
Managing Development Editor: *Nancy Crochiere*
Content Development Editors: *Betty Slack, David Chodoff, Karen Dubno*
Editorial Coordinator: *Kaelyn Schulz*
Digital Development: *Meghan Campbell; Denise Wright, Southern Editorial*
Digital Product Analyst: *John Brady*

Marketing Manager: *Stacy Ruel*
Director, Content Production: *Terri Schiesl*
Senior Production Editor: *Catherine Morris*
Senior Buyer: *Laura Fuller*
Design Manager: *Debra Kubiak*
Cover and Interior Designer: *Ellen Pettengell*
Senior Content Licensing Specialist: *John Leland*
Photo Researcher: *David Tietz/Editorial Image, LLC*
Connect Media Project Manager: *Sarah Hill*
OLC Media Project Manager: *Jennifer Barrick*
Typeface: *10/12 Palatino*
Compositor: *Thompson Type*
Printer: *R.R. Donnelley & Sons*

Cover Images: *(Top to bottom, left to right)* © Archives Charmet/The Bridgeman Art Library; © Clara Amit/AFP/Getty Images/Newscom; The Gallery Collection/Corbis; © Erich Lessing/Art Resource, NY; © Bridgeman-Giraudon/Art Resource, NY; © Guido Baviera/Grand Tour/Corbis; © Digital Vision/Punchstock; © Gianni Dagli Orti/The Art Archive at Art Resource, NY; © Gianni Dagli Orti/The Art Archive at Art Resource, NY; © Bettmann/Corbis; © Werner Forman/Corbis; © Mark Harris/The Image Bank/Getty Images; © G. Nimatallah/De Agostini Picture Library/Getty Images; AP Photo/Petros Giannakouris; © Ancient Art & Architecture Collection Ltd/Alamy; © SuperStock; AP Photo/Peter Kemp; © SuperStock; Haworth Art Gallery, Accrington, Lancashire, UK/The Bridgeman Art Library; © Gideon Mendel/In Pictures/Corbis; AP Photo; © Alliance Images/Alamy

All credits appearing on page C-1 are considered to be an extension of the copyright page.

Library of Congress Cataloging-in-Publication Data
Dutton, Paul Edward, 1952–
  Many Europes : choice and chance in Western civilization / Paul Dutton, Suzanne Marchand, Deborah Harkness.—1st ed.
  p. cm.
(vol. 1 : alk. paper)—ISBN 0-07-333050-7 (vol. 2 : alk. paper)—ISBN 0-07-333051-5 ([special vol]. : alk. paper) 1. Europe—Civilization—Textbooks. 2. Civilization, Western—History—Textbooks. I. Marchand, Suzanne L., 1961– II. Harkness, Deborah E., 1965– III. Title.
CB203.D88 2014
940—dc23
                                                                                                2012036126

www.mhhe.com

ABOUT THE AUTHORS

PAUL EDWARD DUTTON is the Jack and Nancy Farley University Professor in History at Simon Fraser University, where he teaches the survey of Western civilization. He holds a Ph.D. from the University of Toronto and a higher doctorate from the Pontifical Institute of Mediaeval Studies. He is the author, coauthor, or editor of eight books, including *The Politics of Dreaming in the Carolingian Empire* (Nebraska, 1994) and *Charlemagne's Mustache and Other Cultural Clusters of a Dark Age* (Palgrave, 2004), which was awarded the Margaret Wade Labarge Prize for best book in medieval studies. A Fellow of the Medieval Academy of America and the Royal Society of Canada, Dutton is also the creator and editor of three series with the University of Toronto Press that seek to help students deal with the periods before 1600 CE.

SUZANNE MARCHAND received her B.A. from the University of California–Berkeley, and her M.A. and Ph.D. from the University of Chicago. She taught European intellectual history at Princeton University and in 1999 moved to Louisiana State University, where she is professor of history. Marchand is the author of two books, *Down from Olympus: Archaeology and Philhellenism in Germany, 1750–1970* (Princeton, 1996) and *German Orientalism in the Age of Empire: Religion, Race and Scholarship* (Cambridge University Press, 2009), which was awarded the George Mosse Prize of the American Historical Association for best book in cultural and intellectual history in 2009. In addition, she has been the recipient of an ACLS Burckhardt Fellowship and an Atlas Grant from the LSU Board of Regents.

DEBORAH HARKNESS received her B.A. from Mount Holyoke College, her M.A. from Northwestern University, and her Ph.D. from the University of California–Davis. An historian of science and medicine from antiquity to the present, she is professor of history at the University of Southern California. Her published works include *John Dee's Conversations with Angels: Cabala, Alchemy, and the End of Nature* (Cambridge University Press, 1999) and *The Jewel House: Elizabethan London and the Scientific Revolution* (Yale University Press, 2007) and the novel *A Discovery of Witches* (Viking, 2011). Harkness has received fellowships from the Guggenheim Foundation, the National Science Foundation, and the National Humanities Center and in 2008 was awarded both the Pfizer Prize for best book in the history of science and the John Ben Snow Prize for best book in British studies.

iii

How *Many Europes* Guarantees Better Course Performance

Better prepared students

Imagine the dynamic class discussions you could have or lively lectures you could give if your students came to class prepared.

Enter McGraw-Hill's **LearnSmart,** the online adaptive learning system that guarantees that students come to class prepared. As part of McGraw-Hill's *Connect History* program, LearnSmart assesses students' knowledge of the chapter content and identifies gaps in understanding. Students come to class with a better grasp of the course material, resulting in more lively discussions and the freedom to lecture on what you think is important.

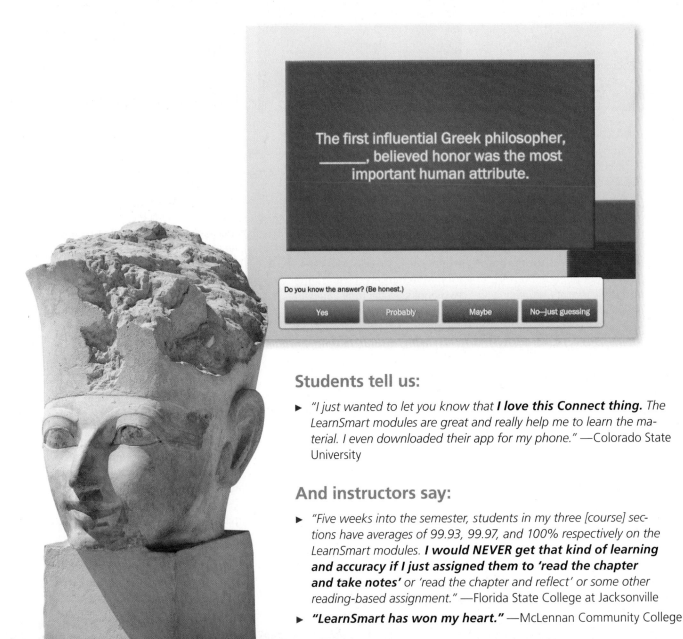

The first influential Greek philosopher, _____, believed honor was the most important human attribute.

Do you know the answer? (Be honest.)

| Yes | Probably | Maybe | No—Just guessing |

Students tell us:

▶ *"I just wanted to let you know that **I love this Connect thing.** The LearnSmart modules are great and really help me to learn the material. I even downloaded their app for my phone."* —Colorado State University

And instructors say:

▶ *"Five weeks into the semester, students in my three [course] sections have averages of 99.93, 99.97, and 100% respectively on the LearnSmart modules. **I would NEVER get that kind of learning and accuracy if I just assigned them to 'read the chapter and take notes'** or 'read the chapter and reflect' or some other reading-based assignment."* —Florida State College at Jacksonville

▶ ***"LearnSmart has won my heart."*** —McLennan Community College

Better critical thinking skills

Many Europes moves students beyond memorization of names and dates and promotes critical thinking:

▶ **Back to the Source** is a primary source exercise that can be assigned in Connect.

▶ Choose from **five to eight <u>additional</u> primary sources per chapter** that can be assigned as activities in Connect History, or added to your print text.

▶ **Connecting the Sources,** an activity that compares two primary sources, is available in Connect History.

▶ A primer activity on **"How to Analyze a Primary Source"** can be assigned in Connect History or added to the text.

▶ Vibrant maps showing topographic features include critical thinking questions, while the digital program provides a wealth of **map and geography activities.**

▶ **"Critical Missions"** digital activities place students in a pivotal moment in time, and ask them to develop an historical argument.

Better grades

Research shows that students' grades improve when using McGraw-Hill's Connect History and LearnSmart. Imagine being able to document this type of grade improvement through easily run reports.

Listen to instructors:

▶ *"My class that is **using Connect scored higher than any other class in my 25 years of teaching.**" —University of Colorado Denver*

▶ *"The students really love Connect. **They also got the best test scores on their first exam that I have ever seen in my teaching career.**" —Georgia Southern University*

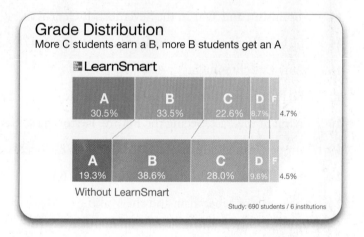

Grade Distribution
More C students earn a B, more B students get an A

LearnSmart

A	B	C	D	F
30.5%	33.5%	22.6%	8.7%	4.7%

A	B	C	D	F
19.3%	38.6%	28.0%	9.6%	4.5%

Without LearnSmart

Study: 690 students / 6 institutions

Many Europes: the digital and print program that Connects students to Success!

BRIEF CONTENTS

1   Preliminary to Western Civilization   2

2   Many Greeces   36

3   Hellenistic Ages: Achievements and Anxieties   70

4   The Roman Republic: Survival and Success   102

5   From Republic to Empire   132

6   The Slow Turn from Ancient to Medieval   162

7   The Early Middle Ages   196

8   The Romanesque Central Middle Ages   230

9   The Gothic High Middle Ages   260

10   The New World of the Late Middle Ages   292

11   The Northern Italian and European Renaissances   324

12   Europeans Take to the Oceans   356

13   The Religious Re-formation of Europe   386

14   Absolutism and War in the Seventeenth Century   420

15   The Old Regimes and Their Revolutions, 1600–1789   456

16   Many Enlightenments   490

17   The French Revolution and the Napoleonic Wars   524

18   Living in the Past, Seeing the Future: Restoration, Nationalism, and Industrialization, 1815–1850   558

19   Europe Unified, Europe Divided, 1850–1880   594

20   Imperialism and Resistance, 1820–1914   630

21   The Crisis of Liberalism and the Making of Mass Society, 1880–1914   664

22   The Great War   696

23   The Interwar Era: The Search for Stability   728

24   World War II   762

25   The Cold War and Decolonization, 1945–1989   798

26   Europe after 1989: One and Many   832

G-1   Glossary

R-1   References and Readings

N-1   Notes

C-1   Credits

I-1   Index

CONTENTS

Preface   xxii

Primary Sources and Maps   xxvi

1 PRELIMINARY TO WESTERN CIVILIZATION   2

Opening Vignette: The Murder of Ötzi,
the First European   3

The Long Dawning of Prehistory   6
    A Special Species?   6
    INVESTIGATING THE PAST: The New Prehistoric Past   7
    The Domestication of Animals   8
    Settling Down and the Birth of Agriculture   9
    The Domestication of Plants   9
    Mesolithic Europe   10
    The Indo-European Factor   11

The Emergence of Cities and Writing
in Mesopotamia   12
    Mesopotamia and the Appearance of Cities   13
    The Invention of Writing   14
    The Importance of Writing   14
    THINGS THAT REMAIN: Cracking Cuneiform   15
    Cities to Empires   16
    Mesopotamian Religion   17

The Lasting Stability of Ancient Egypt   18
    The Nile and Egyptian Agriculture   18
    Hieroglyphics and Egyptian Writing   19

The Dynasties Take Hold   20
Egyptian Religion   22
WHAT A DIFFERENCE A YEAR MAKES: C. 1350 BCE:
    Follow That Name   23
Living Ancient Egypt   23

An Age of Bronze Turns to Iron   24
    OTHER VOICES, OTHER VIEWS: The Might of Egypt Seen
        from Outside   25
    The Minoans   25
    The Mycenaean Greeks   26
    The Indo-European Hittites   27
    Sea Raiders Roil the Mediterranean   27
    The Advantages and Effects of Iron   27
    The Semitic Phoenicians   28

The Religious Breakout and Endurance
of the Hebrews   29
    The Formative Phase: From Abraham to Moses   29
    Hebrew Singularities: The Struggle for Authority   31
    Kings and Kingdoms   31
    Empires and Diaspora   32

Conclusion   32
    BACK TO THE SOURCE: The Venus of Hohle Fels   35

2 MANY GREECES   36

Opening Vignette: The Wanderings and Warnings
of Herodotus   37

Darkness Descends   39
    After the Mycenaean Collapse   39
    The Iron Age Arrives   40
    Homer, Whoever He Was   41
    Was the Greek Alphabet an Accident?   42

The Archaic Age Breakout   42
    The Olympic Games and Delphic Oracle   42
    Archaic Age Emigration: Homes away from Home   44
    Dirty Politics and Hesiod's Discontent   45
    Tyrants, Reformers, and Military Change   46
    Archaic Age Economies and Cultures   47

INVESTIGATING THE PAST: The Black Athena
    Controversy   50
The Conflicting Pulls of Pan-Hellenism and Polis-Centrism   51

The Persian Wars   51
    The Persian Empire   51
    Lydia and the Ionian Greeks   52
    The First Persian Invasion of Greece   53
    The Interwar Years   53
    The Second Invasion   54
    THINGS THAT REMAIN: Stuffing the Ostracism
        Urn for Themistocles   55

Mature and Major City-States   56
    Sparta, the Radical Polis   56

Corinth, the In-Between Polis   57
Thebes, the Federalizing Polis   57
Athens, the Democratic Polis   58
  OTHER VOICES, OTHER VIEWS: *The Greek Bubble*   59
Living on the Margins of the Greek Polis   59
The Peloponnesian War   60
The Delian League   60

Pericles and the Outbreak of the War   61
The Long Second Phase of the War   63
The Brief Golden Age of Athens   63
  WHAT A DIFFERENCE A YEAR MAKES: *405/404* BCE:
    The Unmaking of Imperial Athens   65
Conclusion   66
  BACK TO THE SOURCE: *The Perfect Athens of Pericles*   68

3 HELLENISTIC AGES   70
ACHIEVEMENTS AND ANXIETIES

*Opening Vignette: Alexander's Entombment
in Alexandria*   71
The First Hellenistic Age   74
The Many Greeces Stumble   74
The Rise of Philip of Macedon   75
The Great Orators Demosthenes and Isocrates Part Ways   75
  INVESTIGATING THE PAST: *Searching for Philip's Face*   76
Philip and the Macedonians Take Greece   76
The Assassination of Philip   77
The Cultural Turn from Classical to Hellenistic   77
From Poetry to Prose   77
Socrates the Charismatic Individualist   78
Plato as Hellenistic Thinker and Hellenizer   79
Aristotle the Great Particularist   80
Early Hellenistic Anxieties: Asclepius and Hippocrates   81
**The Opening of the Second Hellenistic Age:
Alexander's Wider World   82**
Greece after Philip's Assassination   82
Into Persia   83
To Egypt and Godhood   84
Lord of Asia   84
To the Indus   85
Arabia and Death   86

  WHAT A DIFFERENCE A YEAR MAKES: *323* BCE *and the Death
    of Alexander the Great*   87
The Hellenistic Kingdoms   87
Back to Earth   88
The Kingdom of Greater Greece   88
The Ptolemaic Kingdom of Egypt   88
The Seleucid Kingdom   88
The Outliers   89
  THINGS THAT REMAIN: *India's Hellenistic Royal Coins*   90
Living the Hellenistic Age   91
Hellenistic Civilization   91
The Greek Fact in a World of Many Peoples and Many
  Languages   92
  OTHER VOICES, OTHER VIEWS: *The Camel Trader's
    Complaint*   93
Greek Cities in Asia   94
Hellenistic Economies   94
Later Hellenistic Philosophy   95
Later Hellenistic Technology, Science, and Medicine   95
Hellenistic Religious Ferment   96
Alexandrian Literature   97
Hellenistic Art   97
Conclusion   99
  BACK TO THE SOURCE: *The Trial of Socrates*   101

4 THE ROMAN REPUBLIC   102
SURVIVAL AND SUCCESS

Opening Vignette: Polybius and the Romans   103
Early Stories, Early Days   105
The Etruscans and Prehistoric Italy   105

  THINGS THAT REMAIN: *The Pyrgi Tablets*   106
Early Rome   107
Archaic Roman Religion   109

The Early Roman Republic: Conflict and Stability   109
   The Beginnings of Republican Government   110
   The Senate   110
   The Orders of Roman Society   110
   The Roman Patriarchy: Fathers, Patricians, and Patrons   111
The Expansion of the Roman Republic   112
   WHAT A DIFFERENCE A YEAR MAKES: *386 BCE:*
     Rome or Roman Veii?   113
   Cleaning Up the Neighborhood   113
   Taking on the Latin League and the Samnites   114
   The Roman Army in the Early and Middle Republics   114
   Conflict with the Greeks in Southern Italy   115
Territorial Expansion and a Religion of War   115
   Reasons for the Republic's Territorial Expansion   115
   Roman Virtue and the Pursuit of Glory   117
   A Religion of War   118

Living the Religious Life: The Roman Calendar
   and Vestal Virgins   118
The Carthaginian Contest and the Middle
Republic   119
   The First Punic War   120
   The Second Punic War   122
   Rome Takes the War to Africa   123
   Rolling Up the Mediterranean Rim   123
   OTHER VOICES, OTHER VIEWS: *The Pleading of Perseus*   124
The Mature Republic   125
   Toward a Mediterranean Roman Economy   125
   Roman Literature of the Middle Republic   126
   INVESTIGATING THE PAST: *Fakes and Their Outings*   127
   The Year of Reckoning: 146 BCE   128
Conclusion   128
   BACK TO THE SOURCE: *Polybius on Roman
     Exceptionalism*   130

5 FROM REPUBLIC TO EMPIRE   132

Opening Vignette: Cicero Dies, Augustus Thrives   133
The Late Republic in Disarray   135
   Symptoms of Dysfunction   135
   The Reforming Gracchi Brothers   136
   INVESTIGATING THE PAST: *Roman Slavery
     by the Numbers*   137
   Jugurtha and Corruption   138
The Rise of the Great Consul Generals   138
   Gaius Marius Subverts the Senate   139
   The Italian and Mithridatic Wars   139
   Sulla, the Dictator   140
   The Strivers: Pompey, Cicero, and Catiline   141
   The Golden Age of Republican Literature   142
The Civil War and the Collapse of the Republic   142
   Caesar Forms a Powerful Consular Faction   142
   The Civil War   142
   The Murder of a Dictator   143
   The Official Triumvirate   144
   Antony and Cleopatra   144
   WHAT A DIFFERENCE A YEAR MAKES:
     Caesar's Big Break, 59–58 BCE   145

Augustus the Emperor   146
   The Great Transformation   147
   The Augustan Ideology of Order   147
   Dressing Rome in Marble   147
   Augustan Writers   149
   OTHER VOICES, OTHER VIEWS: *Inside Out, Outside In*   150
The Wider Culture of the Early Empire   151
   Roman Religion in the Early Empire   151
   Jews and Christians   152
   Living the Augustan Age   153
   Roman Women   154
   The Lives of the Lower Classes in Rome   155
   THINGS THAT REMAIN: *The Antikythera Device*   156
Toward an Empire That Worked   157
   The First Julio-Claudian Successors   157
   Claudius and Nero   157
   The Good Emperors   158
Conclusion   160
   BACK TO THE SOURCE: *The Accomplishments
     of Augustus*   161

6 THE SLOW TURN FROM ANCIENT TO MEDIEVAL 162

Opening Vignette: Theodora and Sidonius Confront the Old and the New 163

A Century of Imperial Anarchy 166
Late Imperial Society 166
Emperors Come and Go, Dozens of Them 166
The Empire's External Enemies 167

The Romanization of Christianity 168
Early Christianities: From Oral to Written 168
THINGS THAT REMAIN: *The Nag Hammadi Find* 169
Early Christian Thinkers and Greek Thought 170
Toward Orthodoxy 170
The Desert and Pillar Fathers and Mothers 170
State Persecution 171
Bishops and the Church Hierarchy 172

Diocletian's Renewal of the Roman Empire 172
Diocletian Restructures the Empire 172
Reforming the Economy 173
Restoring Roman Religion 175
Donatism and the Fallout from the Great Persecution 175
OTHER VOICES, OTHER VIEWS: *Saint Augustine on the Outside* 176

Constantine and the Christianization of the Roman Empire 177
Constantine's Conversion 177
WHAT A DIFFERENCE A YEAR MAKES: *312–313: Constantine's Big Turn* 178

Making a New Rome in Byzantium 179
Toward a State Religion 179
Julian Lapses 179
Institutional Growth of the Church 180

German Tribes Enter the Empire 180
The Visigoths Request Entrance 181
Imperial Strategies for Managing the Germans 182
The Sack of Rome in 410 183
Attila and the Huns 183
The End of the Empire in the West 183
INVESTIGATING THE PAST: *The Decline and Fall of the Roman Empire* 184

Germanic Kingdoms in the West 185
Vandals, Visigoths, and Ostrogoths 185
King Theoderic's Troubled Last Years 187
The Franks Take Control of Gaul 187
The Conversion of Clovis 187

Justinian's Reassertion of Roman Imperial Grandeur 188
The Emperor and Empress 188
The Reconquest 189
The Disastrous 540s: Dust-Veils and Disease 190
Living a Shrinking Urban Life 191

Conclusion 192
BACK TO THE SOURCE: *Constantine's Dream* 194

7 THE EARLY MIDDLE AGES 196

Opening Vignette: Charlemagne's Coronation 197

The Making of a New Western World 199
Monasticism Makes a Difference 199
Living the Monastic Life 200
Gregory the Great and the Papacy 201
Bishops as the Great Mediators 202
The Saints Come Marching In 203

Power at the Start of the Middle Ages 204
Germanic Kingship: Long Hair and the Privatization of Power 204
Living and Dying the Merovingian Way 205
Merovingian Power at the Political Turn 206
Islam Ascendant 206
The Eastern Roman Empire Becomes Byzantine 209

Carolingian House Building 210
The Carolingian Mayors 210
INVESTIGATING THE PAST: *Henri Pirenne and His Thesis* 211
Pepin the Short Unmakes the Merovingian Line 211
Charlemagne as Conqueror and King 213
Charlemagne, Father of Europe and Roman Emperor 214
Al-Andalus, a Hot Corner of European-Islamic Conflict 215

Carolingian Cultures: High, Low, and In-Between 216
Court Culture and Education 216
The Carolingian Church: Royal, Monastic, and Militant 218
THINGS THAT REMAIN: *The Past Preserved in Ice* 219
An Economy of Trade and a Shift to Silver 220
Living off the Land 220
Popular Beliefs 221

Disorder Returns to Europe   222
   The Woes of Louis the Pious   222
   Three Brothers and a Civil War   222
   WHAT A DIFFERENCE A YEAR MAKES:
     817: An Imperial Watershed   223
   The Vikings Raid Francia   224

OTHER VOICES, OTHER VIEWS: *Dhuoda Inside Out*   225
The Imperial End Game: Two Charleses, One Bald,
   One Fat   226
Conclusion   227
   BACK TO THE SOURCE: *Charlemagne as Family Man*   229

8 THE ROMANESQUE CENTRAL MIDDLE AGES   230

*Opening Vignette: The Last Judgment
of Gislebertus*   231
**In the Aftermath of the Collapse
of Carolingian Order**   234
   Vassalage and the Grounding of Power   234
   INVESTIGATING THE PAST: *To Use the "Feudal" -ism
     or Not*   236
   Local Lords and Castle Building   236
   An Ethic of Service   237
Imperial and Royal Power   238
   The Ottonian Moment in the Imperial Sun   238
   The First Millennium and the Delayed Second Coming   239
   OTHER VOICES, OTHER VIEWS: *An Ambassador's
     Purple Rage*   240
   The Stirrings of Stronger Monarchies in England
     and France   241
   The Royal Ideology of the Three Orders   243
Religious Corruption and Reform   244
   Cluny Begins Reforming Monasticism   244
   An Emperor and Church Reform   245

Pope Gregory VII and the Investiture Controversy   245
What Cost an Imperial Papacy?   247
Power Shifts at the Edges of Europe   247
   Byzantine Troubles and the Rise of the Seljuk Turks   248
   Norman Adventurers Take Sicily and Southern Italy   248
   William Conquers England   248
   THINGS THAT REMAIN: *The Many Mysteries
     of the Bayeux Tapestry*   249
   The Norman Restructuring of England   250
Europeans on the Move   250
   A Measure of Internal Peace Returns to Europe   250
   WHAT A DIFFERENCE A YEAR MAKES:
     1066: How Much Changed?   251
   Pilgrims Take to the Road   252
   Preconditions for Crusade   253
   Living the Material Surge of the European Economy   253
   The First Crusade   254
Conclusion   256
   BACK TO THE SOURCE: *A Pope Calls for Crusade*   258

9 THE GOTHIC HIGH MIDDLE AGES   260

*Opening Vignette: The Affair of Abelard
and Heloise*   261
A New World of Learning   264
   The Old Way of Learning   264
   The Tumult of the Schools   264
   INVESTIGATING THE PAST: *Lost or Found? The Love Letters
     of Heloise and Abelard*   265
   The Revitalization and Renewal of Monastic Learning   266
   Abbot Suger and the Birth of Gothic Architecture   267
   Bernard of Clairvaux and the Cistercians   268

Two Thirds and Two Fourths   269
   The Third Crusade   270
   Pope Innocent III   271
   The Fourth Crusade   271
   The Fourth Lateran Council   272
High Times for the Medieval Economy   272
   WHAT A DIFFERENCE A YEAR MAKES: *1215: A High Water
     Mark for the Middle Ages?*   273
   The Agricultural Base   273
   The Growth of Towns   274
   Guilds and Industry   274
   Communes and Urban Tensions   276

Dissent and Control, Church and State   276
  Dealing with Dissent   277
  The Mendicant Orders and the Inquisition   277
  State Development   278
  OTHER VOICES, OTHER VIEWS: *Mongol Relations*   279
  Rulers Respected, Feared, and Loved   280
The Medieval University   282
  The Passing of the Cathedral Schools   282
  Translating the Collected Wisdom of the West   283

THINGS THAT REMAIN: *How the Middle Ages Saved and
  Modern Technology Recovered Archimedes
  and Hyperides*   284
Birth of the University   285
The University of Paris   286
Living the Medieval University Life   287
Scholasticism and the Dumb Ox   287
The Gothic Peak   289
Conclusion   290
  BACK TO THE SOURCE: *The Existence of God*   291

10 THE NEW WORLD OF THE LATE MIDDLE AGES   292

*Opening Vignette: Yersinia Pestis Visits
a Monastery*   293
The Fourteenth Century Opens with Calamities   295
  The Arrival of a New Ice Age   295
  The Great Famine   297
  The Dire Impact of the Early-Fourteenth-Century
    Famine   298
  Not All Was Doom and Gloom   298
  Living the Great Famine   299
Church Captivity, Imperial Indirection,
and Chivalric War   299
  The Babylonian Captivity of the Papacy   299
  The Further Fragmentation of the Empire   300
  The Opening Act of the Hundred Years' War   301
  The Chivalric Ideal   302
  The Chivalric Code Meets Actual War   304
Yersinia Pestis Comes Calling   304
  The Arrival of the Plague   304
  OTHER VOICES, OTHER VIEWS: *The Plague Strikes
    Others*   305
  Transmission and Symptoms of the Disease   306
  THINGS THAT REMAIN: *Was Yersinia Pestis to Blame?*   307

The Spread of the Disease in Europe   308
What Could Europeans Have Done?   308
The Immediate Consequences   308
A Battered Society Responds   309
  Medical Implications   309
  Economic Adjustments   310
  Social Insurrection Spreads   310
  Remaking Religion: Personal Piety, Schism,
    and Conciliarism   311
  Critics of the Church: Wyclif, Hus, and Valla   313
The Late Medieval State   314
  A New World of Political Relations   314
  The Final Phase of the Hundred Years' War   315
  The Maid of Orléans   315
  New Medieval Monarchy   316
  The Fall of Constantinople   318
  WHAT A DIFFERENCE A YEAR MAKES: *1453: To Fall Asleep
    in Constantinople and Wake in Istanbul*   319
  INVESTIGATING THE PAST: *The Waning of the
    Middle Ages*   320
Conclusion   321
  BACK TO THE SOURCE: *Agnolo the Fat and the Plague*   323

11 THE NORTHERN ITALIAN AND EUROPEAN RENAISSANCES   324

*Opening Vignette: Petrarch, Cassandra,
and the Dying Boy*   325
Why Then, Why Italy?   328
  Geography, Politics, and Society on the Italian Peninsula   329

Rome: The Popes Return to Prominence   331
Living the High Life in Renaissance Rome   332
The Political Landscape of Florence   332
From Medici Munificence to Magnificence   333

The Bonfire of the Vanities   334

Machiavelli's Cold Eye   335

WHAT A DIFFERENCE A YEAR MAKES: *1527 and the Sack of Rome*   336

West and East in the Renaissance   336

Venice, City of Banks, Ships, and Republican Ease   337

The Colonial Reach of Venice   339

The Ottoman Empire as a Renaissance State   339

Renaissance Cosmopolitanism in Big Europe   340

Humanism and Individualism   341

The Humanist Course of Study   341

OTHER VOICES, OTHER VIEWS: *The Jewish Tradition in the Italian Renaissance*   342

Reading Classical Literature   343

Civic Humanism and a New Sense of History   343

Individualism   344

Italian Renaissance Art   345

Living Renaissance Art   345

The Early Renaissance: Ghiberti, Donatello, and Masaccio   346

The High Renaissance: Leonardo, Michelangelo, and Raphael   347

INVESTIGATING THE PAST: *Seeing the Renaissance in a New Light*   348

The Spread of Renaissance Ideas: The European Renaissance   349

Commerce and Urban Life in the European Renaissance   349

European Renaissance Art   350

The Print Revolution of the European Renaissance   351

THINGS THAT REMAIN: *Humanizing Print: Aldus Manutius*   352

Conclusion   353

BACK TO THE SOURCE: *Machiavelli's Crafty Prince*   355

12 EUROPEANS TAKE TO THE OCEANS   356

Opening Vignette: The Choice and Chance of Bernal Díaz   357

European Exploration before 1492   360

Western Fantasies, Western Wanderlust   361

Genoese Trade and Travel   361

THINGS THAT REMAIN: *Travelers' Tales*   362

Portugal's Big Breakout   362

Castile and the Contest for the Canaries   365

The Pursuit of Technological Advantage   366

West to Asia: Columbus's Voyages   366

Columbus's Early Years   366

The Search for Sponsors   367

To the Americas   368

WHAT A DIFFERENCE A YEAR MAKES: *1493–1494: The Columbian Exchange*   369

Later Voyages   369

The Atlantic Space Race   370

Amerigo's New Continents   371

Living on Board   372

Hernán Cortés and the Conquest of the Mexica Empire   372

Francisco Pizarro and the Conquest of the Inca Empire   374

The English and the French Enter the Race   374

Spanish Colonization and Its Critics   375

The Problems of Colonization   376

First Encounters   376

The Economic Impact of Spanish Colonization   377

Spanish Colonization and Conversion   378

Criticizing Spanish Conquests and Colonization: Las Casas   378

OTHER VOICES, OTHER VIEWS: *Fragments of the Native Narrative of the Conquest*   379

East to Asia: The Portuguese Venture   380

The Portuguese Reach Asia   380

INVESTIGATING THE PAST: *Alternative Junk History*   381

The Dutch and the English Arrive   382

A New Wave of Christianity Hits Asia   382

Conclusion   382

BACK TO THE SOURCE: *Picturing European Fantasies of the Americas*   385

13 THE RELIGIOUS RE-FORMATION OF EUROPE   386

Opening Vignette: Erasmus and Katharina von Bora Leave Monasticism Behind   387

The Protestant Re-Formation Begins   390

Martin the Monk   391

Luther and the Indulgence Controversy 392

THINGS THAT REMAIN: *Viewer Beware!* 393

Struggling with Rome 394

From Instituting to Living the Lutheran Faith 395

WHAT A DIFFERENCE A YEAR MAKES: *1521–1522: The Knights Rebel* 396

The Early Re-Formation of Church and State 397

Lutheran Princes 398

Huldrych Zwingli 399

OTHER VOICES, OTHER VIEWS: *Picture Wars* 400

Henry VIII Divorces the Catholic Church 401

John Calvin and the Religious Re-Formation of Geneva 402

Living a Religiously Re-formed Life in Calvin's Geneva 403

The Schmalkaldic League and Peace of Augsburg 404

The Radical Religious Re-Formation Splinters and Spreads 404

Anabaptism 405

Millenarians Make a Last Stand 405

Separatism and Peace: The Mennonites 406

The Catholic Reformation 406

An Order of Spiritual Soldiers: The Jesuits 407

Catholic Mysticism Connects 408

Reforming Popes and the Council of Trent 408

Welcome Back: The Baroque Embrace of Rome 409

The Wars of Religion 410

The French Wars of Religion 410

The Dutch Revolt and the Spanish in the Netherlands 413

Elizabeth I and the Spanish Armada 413

INVESTIGATING THE PAST: *The Mystery of the Unloaded Cannons* 415

Conclusion 416

BACK TO THE SOURCE: *A Call to Debate: The Ninety-Five Theses* 418

14 ABSOLUTISM AND WAR IN THE SEVENTEENTH CENTURY 420

Opening Vignette: Louis XIV, Sun King and State-Builder 421

The Many Torments of the Seventeenth Century 424

The Origins of Absolutism 424

INVESTIGATING THE PAST: *Weather and the Seventeenth-Century Crisis* 425

The Thirty Years' War 426

The Habsburg Empire Reacts to Protestantism's Spread 426

The Defenestration of Prague 526

The Bohemian Phase 427

The Danish and the Siege of Magdeburg 428

WHAT A DIFFERENCE A YEAR MAKES: *1631–1632: The Lion of the North and the Turning of the Tide* 429

The French Phase and the War's Bitter End 430

The Consequences of the Thirty Years' War 430

The Culture of the High Baroque 431

Theater 432

Art and Architecture 433

Music 433

Political Philosophy in the Age of Absolutism 434

Popular Culture in the Baroque Era 435

Living the Witch Craze 435

Absolutism Triumphant 436

France under Louis XIV and Louis XV 437

Absolutism and the Austrian Habsburgs 439

The Consolidation of Prussia 440

Russia: From Ivan the Terrible to Peter the Great 440

Incomplete Absolutisms: Spain, Poland, and Sweden 443

The Non-absolutist Exceptions: The Venetian and the Dutch Republics 444

The Venetians 445

The Dutch 445

OTHER VOICES, OTHER VIEWS: *The Ottoman Empire in the Seventeenth Century* 446

The Defeat of Absolutism in England 447

THINGS THAT REMAIN: *The King James Bible* 448

Charles I and the English Civil War 449

Trial and Regicide 450

The Commonwealth 451

England's Colonies 451

The Restoration 451

The Glorious Revolution 452

Conclusion 453

BACK TO THE SOURCE: *The Trial of King Charles I, 1649* 455

15 THE OLD REGIMES AND THEIR QUIET REVOLUTIONS, 1600–1789   456

Opening Vignette: Johann Böttger: Alchemist, Inventor, and Prisoner   457

A World of Legal Inequalities   460

The Social Hierarchies of the Old Regimes   460
   The Monarch   461
   The First Estate: Church and Clergy   462
   The Second Estate: The Nobility   464
   THINGS THAT REMAIN: *The Symphonies of Joseph Haydn and the Patronage of Nicholas Esterhazy*   465
   The Third Estate: Nothing and Everything   466

A World of Quiet Revolutions   471
   Revolutions in the Countryside   471
   The Commercial Revolution   473
   The Military Revolution   476
   The Seven Years' War: A Global War   478
   WHAT A DIFFERENCE A YEAR MAKES: *1762–1763: The Miracle of the House of Brandenburg*   479

Transforming the Heavens and the Human Mind: The Scientific Revolution   480
   OTHER VOICES, OTHER VIEWS: *The Black Hole of Calcutta*   481
   Doubt and the Scientific Method: Francis Bacon and René Descartes   482
   The Cosmological Revolution   482
   The Anatomical Revolution   484
   The Social Life of Science   485
   Women and the New Science   485
   INVESTIGATING THE PAST: *Maria Sibylla Merian, Scientist and Artist*   486

Conclusion   487
   BACK TO THE SOURCE: *Order Establishing a Consumption or Excise Tax in All Towns of Electoral and Mark Brandenburg (1667)*   489

16 MANY ENLIGHTENMENTS   490

Opening Vignette: Robinson Crusoe   491

Europe's Many Enlightenments   494

The Origins of Enlightened Thought   494

Enlightened Societies in the Dutch Republic and Great Britain   495
   The Dutch Republic   495
   England   496
   Scotland   498
   WHAT A DIFFERENCE A YEAR MAKES: *1745–1746: The Highlanders Revolt*   500

The French Enlightenment   501
   Montesquieu and Voltaire   501
   The French Enlightenment Comes of Age   503
   Denis Diderot and the French *Encyclopédie*   503
   Jean-Jacques Rousseau   504

Enlightened Absolutisms in Central and Eastern Europe   505
   Russia   506
   Prussia   507
   Austria   508

Cultural Enlightenments in Southern Europe   509
   Spain and Portugal   509

The Italian Enlightenment   509

Spreading the Enlightenments   510
   The Enlightened Novel   510
   Literature by and for Women   511
   The French *Encyclopédie*   511
   Pamphlets and Pornography   512
   Enlightened Travel   512
   Enlightened Gardening   513
   OTHER VOICES, OTHER VIEWS: *Enlightened Ethnography*   515
   Eating the Enlightenment   516
   Hearing the Enlightenment   516
   THINGS THAT REMAIN: *The Cookbook*   517

The Many Enlightenments and Their Consequences   518
   The Enlightenments and Religion   518
   INVESTIGATING THE PAST: *Did the Enlightenments Kill Christianity?*   519
   The Enlightenments and Politics   520

Conclusion   520
   BACK TO THE SOURCE: *Rousseau's* Emile   522

17 THE FRENCH REVOLUTION AND THE NAPOLEONIC WARS 524

Opening Vignette: Anne Louis Germaine Necker, Madame de Staël: One Woman's Revolution 525

Origins of the Revolution 528
Long-Term Causes 528
Short-Term Causes 529
The Revolution Begins 531

The Moderate Revolution, 1789–1791 532
From the Great Fear to the Constitution of 1791 532
The Revolution and the Church 534
The King and the Revolution 534
WHAT A DIFFERENCE A YEAR MAKES: *1791: The Flight to Varennes* 535
Toward the Radical Revolution 534

The Radical Revolution 537
The September Massacres 537
Montagnards and Girondins 537
The King's Execution 538
The Reign of Terror 539
The Revolution beyond France 539
Revolutionary Culture 541
The Thermidorian Reaction 543

The Directory 543

The Rise of Napoleon 543
Napoleon's Early Life and Military Career 543
INVESTIGATING THE PAST: *When Did the French Revolution End?* 544
Napoleon in Egypt 545
The 18th Brumaire 546

The Napoleonic Empire 546
In Search of Stability 546
OTHER VOICES, OTHER VIEWS: *Napoleon in Cairo* 547
The Grande Armée 549
THINGS THAT REMAIN: *The Legion of Honor and the Iron Cross* 550
Napoleon's Early Campaigns, 1805–1808 551
Napoleon's Fall 553
The French Occupations and the Origins of Modern Nationalism 554
The Napoleonic Wars, 1809–1815 554

Conclusion 555
BACK TO THE SOURCE: *Emmanuel-Joseph de Sieyès, "What Is the Third Estate?"* 557

18 LIVING IN THE PAST, SEEING THE FUTURE 558
RESTORATION, NATIONALISM, AND INDUSTRIALIZATION, 1815–1850

Opening Vignette: Alexis de Tocqueville, Aristocrat— and Liberal 559

The Congress of Vienna: Old Monarchies, New Borders 561
The Political Spectrum: Liberals, Radicals, and Conservatives 563
OTHER VOICES, OTHER VIEWS: *Meet the Utopians* 566

Reform, Recovery, and Religion after 1815 567
The Legal Spectrum: Rights and Freedoms—for Some 567
Economies, New and Old 568
WHAT A DIFFERENCE A YEAR MAKES: *1816–1817: The Year without a Summer* 569
Religious Reorganization and Revival 569

Nationalism Comes of Age 570
Inventing Modern Greece 570
THINGS THAT REMAIN: *The Elgin Marbles* 572

Belgium Is Born 573
Nationalist Projects That Failed: Poland, Germany, and Italy 574

Domestic Politics in the 1820s–1830s: From Revolution to Reaction 574
Revolution Returns: France, 1830 575
Reform without Revolution: England 575
Reaction without Reform: Russia 576

Restoration Culture 576
Romanticism: Mourning the Passing of the Past 577
Utilitarianism: Planning for the Future 579

The Industrial Revolution 580
Why Britain? 580
Why Textiles? 581
A Revolution in Gadgets 581

INVESTIGATING THE PAST: *Could Europe Have Become a China?*   582
A Revolution in Transportation   583
A Revolution in Capital   584
A Revolution in Labor   585
Manchester: City of the Future?   587
The Hungry Forties   588

A Return to Revolution   588
How Revolutions End   590
How Restorations End   591
Conclusion   591
BACK TO THE SOURCE: *Friedrich Engels,* The Condition of the Working Class in England *(1845)*   593

19 EUROPE UNIFIED, EUROPE DIVIDED, 1850–1880   594

Opening Vignette: The Rhine   595
After the Revolutions   597
Liberalism Triumphant   598
Liberalism's Foes   600
Capitalism Triumphant   600
Nationalism Triumphant   601
Liberal Modernization in Western Europe   601
Great Britain: The Liberal Empire   601
THINGS THAT REMAIN: *Patriotic Anthems*   602
France: The Bourgeois Empire of Napoleon III   603
Making Paris Modern   604
The Illiberal Empire: Russia   606
Living the Victorian Life   607
Class Society in the Liberal Era   607
The Victorian Household   608
Women at Home   608
A Life of Domestic Service   609
On Property: The Haves   609
On the Propertyless: The Have-Nots   610
The Culture of Positivism   611
Positivism and Liberal Order   611

Charles Darwin, Victorian Positivist   612
Realism in Literature   612
Realism and Impressionism in Painting   612
INVESTIGATING THE PAST: *Christianity and Evolutionary Theory in the Victorian Age*   613
Realism in Music   614
Remaking Metternich's Map   615
Breaking Old Maps: The Crimean War   615
Unifications and Their Makers   616
OTHER VOICES, OTHER VIEWS: *Abraham Lincoln and American Unification*   617
France and Germany after 1871: Wages of the Wars of Unification   621
WHAT A DIFFERENCE A YEAR MAKES: *1870–1871: The Franco-Prussian War*   622
Divided Europe   624
Reshaping Southeastern Europe   625
Austria Partitioned   626
Life and Identity after Unification   627
Conclusion   627
BACK TO THE SOURCE: *Manifesto of the Temporary Government of Macedonia, March 23, 1881*   629

20 IMPERIALISM AND RESISTANCE, 1820–1914   630

Opening Vignette: Cecil Rhodes, Colonizer and Oxford Man   631
European Empires: Old and New   633
The Old and the New Neo-Europes   634
The New World Closes, the First Wave Ends   634
The Second Wave: 1820–1860   635
The Motives of the Modern Colonizer: Profit, Prestige, and Progress   636

Back to the Old World: The British in India   636
Africa Beckons: The French in Algeria   637
OTHER VOICES, OTHER VIEWS: *The Europeanized Native*   638
Opening East Asia: The Opium Wars   639
Japan Opened—and Closed   640
Overland Empire: The Russians in the Caucasus   640
A Turning Point: The Indian Rebellion   642

Cultures of Empire   643
   Living the Empire: The Colonial Soldier   643
   The Civilizing Mission and the Missionary Impulse   644
   Imperialism and the Field Sciences   645
   THINGS THAT REMAIN: *George Everest, Surveyor General of India*   647
   The Imperial Exchange   648
   INVESTIGATING THE PAST: *The Imperial Origins of Modern European Identity*   649
   Race and Empire   650
The Third Wave: Consolidating Empires after 1860   650
   The Ottoman Power Vacuum   651

The Failing Chinese Empire   652
The Scramble for Africa   654
WHAT A DIFFERENCE A YEAR MAKES: *1870–1871: The South African Diamond Rush*   655
King Leopold Builds Himself an Empire   656
Carving up Africa   656
The New Resistance   658
   Resistance in German Colonies   658
   The Boxer Rebellion   659
   The Second Boer War   659
Conclusion   660
   BACK TO THE SOURCE: *The Casement Report*   662

21 THE CRISIS OF LIBERALISM AND THE MAKING OF MASS SOCIETY, 1880–1914   664

Opening Vignette: Sarah Bernhardt: Fin de Siècle Superstar   665
Living the Modern   667
   The Modern Experience   668
   The New Mobility   669
   The Fin de Siècle Metropolis   670
   Social Mobility— and Its Limits   672
   Women in Motion   672
The New Culture(s)   673
   Mass Culture   674
   Modernism—without the Masses   675
   OTHER VOICES, OTHER VIEWS: *Lourdes and the Mass Pilgrimage*   676
   Breaking with Conventions   677
   Modernism in the Sciences   678
The New Economies   679
   The Second Industrial Revolution   680
   THINGS THAT REMAIN: *The Department Store*   681

The Worker and the Second Industrial Revolution   682
The Social Question, Again   682
The New Politics   683
   Modern Society's Challenge to Liberalism   683
   Socialism and the Second International   683
   INVESTIGATING THE PAST: *Liberalism's Death in Hamburg*   684
   Moderate and Conservative Mass Parties   685
   The Russian Revolution of 1905   686
   Civil Strife Intensifies   686
   WHAT A DIFFERENCE A YEAR MAKES: *1904–1905: The Russo-Japanese War*   687
Racism, Hyper-nationalism, and the Collapse of Old Empires   688
   The New Anti-Semitism   688
   The New Ways of War   690
   The New Nationalism and the Old Empires   691
Conclusion   694
   BACK TO THE SOURCE: *Gustav Le Bon,* The Crowd   695

22 THE GREAT WAR   696

Opening Vignette: Gavrilo Princip, Terrorist   697
The Greatness of the Great War   699
What Caused the Great War?   700
   Entangling Alliances   700

Imperial and Continental Tensions   701
Balkan Uncertainty   701
The War Breaks Out   701
   What Did Total War Mean?   703

Fighting a Total War   704
Theaters of War   704

INVESTIGATING THE PAST: *Belgian Atrocities*   706

The New Technology and the Old   711
The New   712
. . . And the Old   713

Enabling the Fight: The Home Front   713
A Woman's War   714
Command Economies   715

The Russian Revolution   716
Origins of the Revolution   716
The February Revolution   716

WHAT A DIFFERENCE A YEAR MAKES: *1917–1918: The Russian Revolution*   717
The Bolsheviks Take Power   718

The October Revolution   718
The Bolsheviks Make Peace   718

How the War Ended   719
The End, at Last   719
The Spanish Flu   720

The Peace   721
THINGS THAT REMAIN: *War Memorials*   722
The Victors   723
The Losers   723
Of Greeks and Turks   724

OTHER VOICES, OTHER VIEWS: *Mustafa Kemal's War— and Peace*   725

Conclusion   726
BACK TO THE SOURCE: *Anna Eisenmenger:* Blockade: The Diary of an Austrian Middle-Class Woman 1914–1924   727

23 THE INTERWAR ERA   728
THE SEARCH FOR STABILITY

Opening Vignette: Alexandra Kollontai: The New Woman, Soviet Style   729

The Search for Stability   731

The Soviet Experiment   732
The Russian Civil Wars   732
Inventing a Communist State   734
Soviet Sticks and Carrots   735
Soviet Society in the 1930s   736

The Survival of Democracy in France and Britain   738
Stability through Safety Nets   738
Colonial Instabilities   738

OTHER VOICES, OTHER VIEWS: *Ho Chi Minh and Subhas Chandra Bose*   740

The Anti-democratic Right   742
Italy's Fascist Experiment   741
What Was Fascism?   742
The Weimar Republic and the Origins of the Nazi Party   742
Stabilization by Authoritarian Means: Eastern Europe in the 1920s and 1930s   744
Authoritarian States and Stateless People   746

The Body and the State   746
The New Woman—and the Old Family Structure   747
The New Man   747

Experimentation and Modernism in Interwar Culture   748
Art and Architecture   748

THINGS THAT REMAIN: *The Films of Sergei Eisenstein and Leni Riefenstahl*   749

Interwar Science, Philosophy, and Literature   750
Popular Culture   751

The Great Depression and the Radicalization of Politics   752
Hitler Becomes Chancellor   752
Hitler's "Little Men" in Power   752

WHAT A DIFFERENCE A YEAR MAKES: *The Economies of 1931–1932*   753
Enabling Dictatorship: The Reichstag Fire   754
Nazi Sticks and Carrots   754

INVESTIGATING THE PAST: *Victor Klemperer's Diaries*   756
Foreign Policy and Rearmament   757

Fascism Triumphant   757
The Spanish Civil War   758
The Anschluss   759

Conclusion   760
BACK TO THE SOURCE: *Benito Mussolini,* The Political and Social Doctrine of Fascism *(1932)*   761

24 WORLD WAR II 762

Opening Vignette: Winston Churchill, Imperial Warrior 763

Hitler's Preparations for War 766
Appeasement 766
Preparing for Racial Warfare 767
The Hitler-Stalin Pact 769

The War Begins: The Invasion of Poland and the Winter War 769
Hitler's New Order in Poland 769
INVESTIGATING THE PAST: *Sex and the Third Reich* 770
The Winter War 772

War in Europe and Northern Africa 772
Resources First: Norway 772
Breaking the Enigma Code 772
The Axis Triumphant 773
France Falls 773
Britain Alone, Yet Defiant 774
War in the Mediterranean 775

The World at War 777
The Other Axis Power: Japan's Triumphs in the Pacific 777
War in the Colonies 778
Operation Barbarossa 778
OTHER VOICES, OTHER VIEWS: *The Fall of Rangoon* 779

Life and Death in War-Torn Europe 780
WHAT A DIFFERENCE A YEAR MAKES: *The War in the East, June 1941–August 1942* 781
The "Final Solution to the Jewish Question" 782
Living and Dying in Auschwitz 784
Collaboration 784
Resistance 785
Slave Laborers 786
Women and the War 786
War Propaganda 787
Science and War 788

The End of the War 789
The Tide Turns 789
The Red Army and the Battle for Berlin 790
Ending the War in the Pacific 790
WHAT REMAINS NO MORE: *The Firebombing of Dresden* 791

Planning Europe's Future 792
Yalta and Potsdam 792
Postwar Justice 792
Displaced Persons 793

Conclusion 795
BACK TO THE SOURCE: *Joseph Stalin, Broadcast to the People of the Soviet Union, July 3, 1941* 796

25 THE COLD WAR AND DECOLONIZATION, 1945–1989 798

Opening Vignette: Erich Honecker, Communist Die-Hard 799

The Making of Two Europes 802
Making the Soviet Bloc 803
Remaking the Eastern European Economy 803
National Communism 804
Making Western Europe 805
Remaking the Western European Economy 805
Cold War Battleground: Berlin 806
The Making of Two Germanys 807

Eastern Europe after Stalin: The Thaw— and Its Limits 808
Khrushchev and the Hungarian Uprising of 1956 808
Communist Successes 809
The Prague Spring 810

The Brezhnev Era 810
Cracking Down on Poland 811

Western Europe: The New Prosperity 811
The Baby Boom 811
The Welfare State Comes of Age 812
Economic Integration and Prosperity 812
Southern Europe 813
Guest Workers 813

The End of European Imperialism 813
Decolonization in Asia and the Middle East 814
OTHER VOICES, OTHER VIEWS: *Encountering the Other in Vietnam and Afghanistan* 816
Decolonization in Africa 817

The Culture of the Cold War 818
Popular Culture 818

Elite Culture   818
WHAT A DIFFERENCE A YEAR MAKES: *1963–1964:
Beatlemania*   819
The Boom Years Are Over   820
1968   821
Christianity and the Cold War   821
Western Europe in the 1970s and 1980s   822
A Sexual Revolution?   823
THINGS THAT REMAIN: *The Washing Machine*   824
The Conservatives Return to Power   825
Communism under Pressure   825

Living Communism's Last Years   825
Glasnost and Perestroika   826
INVESTIGATING THE PAST: *Why Did Communism Fail?*   827
How the Cold War Ended   827
Poland and Hungary Break Free   828
The Fall of the Wall   828
The Velvet Revolution   829
Romania: Death of a Dictator   829
Conclusion   830
BACK TO THE SOURCE: *Ronald Reagan's Address
to the British Parliament, June 8, 1982*   831

26 EUROPE AFTER 1989: ONE AND MANY   833

*Opening Vignette: Bono, European
and World Citizen*   833
Who Is a European?   836
Remaking Central and Eastern Europe after 1989   838
German Reunification   838
The Soviet Union's Demise   838
THINGS THAT REMAIN: *Where Is the Berlin Wall Now?*   839
Living with Post-Communist Uncertainties   840
OTHER VOICES, OTHER VIEWS: *Post-Communist
Chechnya*   842
The Return of Nationalism   843
A Hot War after a Cold One: Yugoslavia   844
From Tito to Milošević   844
Sarajevo Holds Out   844
The Dayton Accords   846
Western Europe after the Fall of the Wall   846
Defining the Values of Post-1989 Europe   846
The European Union   849
The Eurozone and Its Walls   850

Global Citizenship   851
Consumerism, American Style   852
Football, European Style   853
The Communications Revolution   853
INVESTIGATING THE PAST: *The Arrival of the Digital Age*   854
Postmodernism   855
English, the New Lingua Franca?   855
Cultural Diversity Endures   856
Challenges Facing Europe Today   856
Relations with the United States   856
Political Corruption   857
The Challenge of Diversity   858
Assassinations, Terrorist Strikes, and Riots   858
A Dirty and Dangerous World: The Post–Cold War
Environment   859
Demographic Challenges   859
The Sovereign Debt Crisis   860
WHAT A DIFFERENCE A YEAR MAKES:
The Debt Crisis of 2010–2011   861
Conclusion   862
BACK TO THE SOURCE: *Two Views of Europe's Future*   864

Glossary   G-1

References and Readings   R-1

Notes   N-1

Credits   C-1

Index   I-1

PREFACE

AN INTERVIEW WITH THE AUTHORS

Q: Why "Many Europes"?

A: In historical terms, there never was a "single" Europe. The history of the European continent has always been one of many diverse peoples, languages, and regions, each seeking to survive, and striving to preserve and promote its own identity in the competitive world that was wider Europe. Diversity not unity, nations not empire, explain a great deal about the energy and dynamism of the history we study in Western civilization courses.

Q: Is this a new approach to Western civilization?

A: Absolutely. We think of it as an introduction to Western Civilization for a new generation, one that views "the West" as an important part of the world, but not the only part worth studying. With the growth of the world history course, we need to approach the history of the West in new ways and to search out what makes the many Europes different from the other great historical powers in Asia and the Middle East. One great difference is that the European continent rarely achieved the great and dominant empires that China and Islam did. Why, and is that important in accounting for the historical personality of the West? By looking at the strivings of the many Europes, its individuals and groups, we hope to present the Western civ experience in a vivid, fresh, and relevant way.

Q: You also invite students to think in terms of "Big Europe." How is that different?

A: Too many Western civilization textbooks focus almost exclusively on Britain, France, and Germany. In *Many Europes*, we made it our goal to stretch the boundaries, physical and intellectual, of Europe, integrating the vitally important, fascinating, and often blood-spattered histories of southern, central, and eastern Europe. Naturally, we also include the civilizations of Egypt, Islam, and Persia that have always been part of shaping what the many Europes could and could not be. All of them had a critical impact on the history and contours of Western civilization.

Q: Your subtitle is *Choice and Chance in Western Civilization*. Why did you choose those themes?

A: The subtitle reflects our fundamental conviction that people make history through their choices and their struggles to overcome particular problems and dilemmas. We believe that students engage best with history when they recognize that real human beings, whether in ancient Rome, medieval Byzantium, revolutionary France, or Nazi Germany, had to make difficult decisions while caught up in turbulent times, with a limited set of ideas and options available to them.

Q: That explains choice; what about chance?

A: Flesh and blood humans make history, but, as Karl Marx noted long ago, they cannot make it exactly as they wish. Chance intrudes—often in the form of external events such as dramatic or long-term weather changes, economic downturns, famines, and pandemic diseases that force people and societies to respond as best they can. Even Europe's most powerful rulers encountered unexpected forms of opposition within as well as outside their borders, and were compelled to change their plans. So, chance may matter as much as choice in shaping both individual lives and collective experiences.

Q: By "choice and chance," are you talking about the idea of contingency?

A: Exactly. Things didn't have to turn out the way they did. Surprising events, decisions, and actions of individuals and groups often turned the course of events in a new direction—for example, Constantine's unexpected embrace of Christianity and creation of a New Rome in Constantinople. We highlight the important idea of contingency with a feature in every chapter entitled "What a Difference a Year Makes." It gives students an understanding of how changeable history is, how pivotal some choices and some events were, in contrast to how inevitable it all seems when we view history backwards.

In *Many Europes*, we try to strike a balance between the micro and macro levels, choice and chance, but we seek always to emphasize *lived experience*, what it was like to be there, in a particular historical time. Context, in other words, is essential to outcomes, and we believe it a mistake to ride a wave of events without looking below the surface to the vast and sometimes ordinary forces at work generating change.

Q: Why is this idea of "lived experience" important?

A: Students can understand the choices made by individuals in the past only when we help them think themselves back into the historical and cultural contexts in which the actors lived—what it was like to be a Roman senator, an English peasant after the Norman Conquest, or a Victorian scullery maid. We can engage students in history by showing them how fascinating these stories are and why they still matter today, rather than overwhelming them with endless detail. So, we have selected illustrative and gripping human stories that reveal the past and its actors rather than offering an encyclopedic presentation of "one damned thing after another."

Q: How do primary sources fit into your program?

A: We are excited to offer instructors and students a rich portfolio of relevant and revealing primary sources to accompany the textbook. Not only have we included a primary source exercise at the end of each chapter, but we have also included a wide selection of additional primary source exercises tailored to our narrative in the associated digital program. The same choice of primary sources is available through McGraw-Hill's Create for instructors who want to customize their course materials with specific readings or even create their own reader.

Q: Is your narrative shorter than that of other "full-sized" Western civilization books?

A: Another of our departures from most other Western civilization texts involves making the narrative more concise. We have reduced the standard number of chapters from thirty to twenty-six, making it easier for instructors to cover the material in an average school year. In some cases, our chapter order reflects a compromise between chronological and thematic approaches to the subject. For the sake of student attention and a coherent presentation of historical phases, we separate early Rome and the mature Roman Republic from the collapse of the Republic and the Roman Empire, and treat the crusades as separate events and not as a single set of connected events. We also combine the material usually divided between chapters on the Industrial Revolution and on nation-building to emphasize the simultaneity of the two processes throughout most of Europe. This combination gives new punch to liberalism and nationalism, two forces that are alive in neo-versions today. But we have left room at the end of the book for a full chapter on Europe since 1989, recognizing that students today want and need to know about the developments and crises the continent has experienced since the end of the Cold War. We bring the story right up to the Eurocrisis, a development that helps us see clearly that even as economic integration, technological transformations, and cultural globalization have made life across the continent more uniform, the many-ness of Europe remains.

Q: What other unique features support student engagement?

A: Boxed features in each chapter ask students to think about the variety of ways in which history can be seen and done. In addition to "What a Difference a Year Makes," each chapter has a feature titled "Investigating the Past," which examines how historians work—how they use new evidence and approaches to throw fresh light on the past and historical mysteries.

Another feature, "Things That Remain," gives students a sense of the ways in which objects can open up the past to us and lead to valuable insights. Our explorations range from what new DNA testing can tell us about the plague that struck China, Islam, and Europe in the mid-fourteenth century, to a look at nineteenth-century Parisian department stores and the films of the great Russian director, Sergei Eisenstein.

We also include one last feature in each chapter, called "Other Voices, Other Views." It offers students other perspectives than those of the dominant voices of European history. Groups and individuals outside the main political and cultural centers of Europe had something to say about the prevailing narrative; they did not sit silently on the margins and watch it all happen without criticism and complaint. This feature seeks to hear them out, to give them back their compelling voices. Students are enriched, we believe, when they view events such as Roman imperialism, voyages of exploration, and World War II from different vantage points.

Q: Finally, why is your book different from others and do you do anything new?

A: Our emphases are certainly different. Grounding the narrative in people and their lived experience of transformative events; engaging students in a history that is not fixed but shaped by the decisions people made and the chance events that shaped their historical circumstances; and viewing Europe and the West as the special story of the competition between groups, regions, and peoples, with no one side dominating for long, make *Many Europes* a book about a history that is still unfolding, still full of tension and energy, still engaging from first to last, and its future unfixed.

And, yes, we hope to challenge instructors and students with new arguments, approaches, and ways to think about western history. We seek to engage readers in presenting to them the idea that ancient Greece drew its richness not from its unity, but from its manyness; we ask if the story of the Reformation might better be told not as one of reform but rather as one of the restructuring of religion across Europe. In the book's second half, we describe an early nineteenth century in which accelerating differences between western industrializing and eastern and southern rural regions made Europe a more diverse place than ever before. Our presentation of twentieth-century events focuses, unusually, on events in eastern and southeastern Europe where, we argue, the fates of nations and the fate of the continent as a whole were decided. Our readers need not agree with us, and we hope that they won't always do so, but we do sincerely hope that they will have stimulating discussions about the material itself by thinking about western history in new ways. The history of the many Europes and the West have earned our attention, mindfulness, and heightened engagement, for we are still living with it and within it.

Many Europes is all about CHOICE

We offer a wealth of tools to help you teach the course:

Primary Sources

Over 130 primary sources specifically tailored to this text by the authors are available through McGraw-Hill Create. You can customize the text with your own selections of primary source readings or even create your own separate reader. All sources have accompanying headnotes and critical thinking questions written by the authors.

In addition, all of these primary sources and questions are available as digitally assignable and assessable exercises in McGraw-Hill's Connect History.

How to Analyze a Primary Source Document

A brief, illustrated, five-page tutorial on how to read and analyze a primary source document can be bound into your text. Ask your sales rep for details on this Create customization.

The tutorial is also available as a video exercise in Connect. Your students watch the video and are prompted to pause and answer questions to test their understanding.

connect plus+—Online Assessment Exercises Tailored to *Many Europes*

Connect History is a highly interactive learning environment designed to help students connect to the historical tools and resources they will need to achieve success. Through engaging media and study resources, students improve their performance on exams and assignments. *Connect History* makes managing and completing assignments easier.

Connect Plus offers all this with the addition of an integrated, interactive e-book. The e-book optimized for the Web immerses students in a flexible, interactive environment. Assign e-book exercises to ensure your students are reading, or direct them to the embedded activities and multimedia for a more memorable and engaging homework assignment.

LearnSmart—Mapping Out a Personalized Study Plan for Students

LearnSmart, McGraw-Hill's adaptive learning system, helps assess student knowledge of course content and maps out a personalized study plan for success. Accessible within Connect, *LearnSmart* uses a series of adaptive questions to pinpoint the concepts students understand—and those they don't. The result is an online tool that helps students learn faster and study more efficiently and enables instructors to customize classroom lectures and activities to meet their students' needs.

Customize Your Text with Primary Sources through create

Design your ideal course materials with McGraw-Hill's Create: www.mcgrawhillcreate.com! Rearrange or omit chapters, combine material from other sources, choose your own primary sources from our Western civilization collection, and/or upload any other content you have written to make the perfect resource for your students. You can even personalize your book's appearance by selecting the cover and adding your name, school, and course information. When you order a Create book, you receive a complimentary review copy. Get a printed copy in 3 to 5 business days or an electronic copy (eComp) via e-mail in about an hour. Register today at www.mcgrawhillcreate.com, and craft your course resources to match the way you teach.

CourseSmart—an e-book version of your text

CourseSmart offers thousands of the most commonly adopted textbooks across hundreds of courses from a wide variety of higher education publishers. It is the only place for faculty to review and compare the full text of a textbook online, providing immediate access without the environmental impact of requesting a printed examination copy. At CourseSmart, students can save up to 50 percent off the cost of a printed book, reduce their impact on the environment, and gain access to powerful Web tools for learning, including full text search, notes and highlighting, and e-mail tools for sharing notes among classmates. Learn more at www.coursesmart.com.

Campus

McGraw-Hill Campus is the first-of-its-kind institutional service that provides faculty with true single sign-on access to all of McGraw-Hill's course content, digital tools, and other high-quality learning resources from any learning management system (LMS). This innovative offering allows for secure and deep integration and seamless access to any of our course solutions such as McGraw-Hill Connect, McGraw-Hill Create, McGraw-Hill LearnSmart, or Tegrity. McGraw-Hill Campus includes access to our entire content library, including e-books, assessment tools, presentation slides, and multimedia content, among other resources, providing faculty open and unlimited access to prepare for class, create tests/quizzes, develop lecture material, integrate interactive content, and much more.

Primary Sources

Primary Sources in the Print Text

Chapter 1: The Venus of Hohle Fels   35
Chapter 2: The Perfect Athens of Pericles   68
Chapter 3: The Trial of Socrates   101
Chapter 4: Polybius on Roman Exceptionalism   130
Chapter 5: The Accomplishments of Augustus   161
Chapter 6: Constantine's Dream   194
Chapter 7: Charlemagne as Family Man   229
Chapter 8: A Pope Calls for Crusade   258
Chapter 9: The Existence of God   291
Chapter 10: Agnolo the Fat and the Plague   323
Chapter 11: Machiavelli's Crafty Prince   355
Chapter 12: Picturing European Fantasies
of the Americas   385
Chapter 13: A Call to Debate: The Ninety-Five Theses   418
Chapter 14: The Trial of King Charles I, 1649   455
Chapter 15: Order Establishing a Consumption
or Excise Tax in All Towns of Electoral and Mark
Brandenburg (1667)   489
Chapter 16: Rousseau's *Emile*   522
Chapter 17: Emmanuel-Joseph Sieyès, "What Is the Third
Estate?"   557
Chapter 18: Friedrich Engels, *The Condition of the Working
Class in England* (1845)   593
Chapter 19: Manifesto of the Temporary Government of
Macedonia, March 23, 1881   629
Chapter 20: The Casement Report   662
Chapter 21: Gustave Le Bon, *The Crowd*   695
Chapter 22: Anna Eisenmenger, *Blockade: The Diary of an
Austrian Middle-Class Woman 1914–1924*   727
Chapter 23: Benito Mussolini, *The Political and Social Doctrine
of Fascism* (1932)   761
Chapter 24: Joseph Stalin, Broadcast to the People of the
Soviet Union, July 3, 1941   796
Chapter 25: Ronald Reagan's Address to the British
Parliament, June 8, 1982   831
Chapter 26: Two Views of Europe's Future: Angela Merkel
and Daniel Hannon   864

Primary Sources in Connect History and
Customizable through McGraw-Hill Create

* Indicates document is available in Connect only

Chapter 1
1. Two Early Law Codes
2. The Egyptian Book of the Dead
3. The Great Hymn to Aton
4. A Summary of Hebrew History and the Covenant
5. Two Versions of the Ten Commandments
6. The Song of Deborah

Chapter 2
1. The Shield of Achilles
2. Hesiod's Complaint
3. Herodotus on the 300 at Thermopylae
4. Plutarch on Lycurgus and His Reform of Spartan Life
5. Thucydides, The Melian Dialogue

Chapter 3
1. Demosthenes and Isocrates on Philip of Macedon
2. Xenophon, The Apology of Socrates to the Jury
3. Late-Fourth-Century BCE Witnesses to the Divine Cures
of Asclepius at Epidaurus*
4. Alexander's Hellenization of Asia according
to Plutarch*
5. An Egyptian Scribe Working for the Greeks*

Chapter 4
1. The Legend of the Foundation of Rome by Romulus and
Remus
2. Twelve Tables: Laws on Offenses and Damages
3. Polybius on the Destruction of Carthage in 146 BCE

Chapter 5
1. Catiline's Reasons for Revolution
2. Election Notices, Signs, and Graffiti at Pompeii
3. Pliny and Trajan on Christianity
4. Scenes of Imperial Life as Observed by a Roman Noble
5. Letters and Various Meditations of Marcus Aurelius

Chapter 6
1. Diocletian's Wage and Price Controls
2. The Edict of Milan, 313
3. The Nicene Creed
4. Cassiodorus, King Theoderic's Letters
5. The Demons Justinian and Theodora

Chapter 7
1. The Rule of Saint Benedict: A School for Monks
2. The Salic Law: A Compensatory Code for Living
3. The Donation of Constantine
4. Charlemagne as an International Figure
5. Are the Dogheads Human?
6. Dhuoda's Lament

Chapter 8
1. A Vassalage Oath
2. Fulbert of Chartres on the Obligations of Vassals
3. The Deaths of Oliver and Roland
4. The Dictation of the Pope (Dictatus papae)
5. A Lady Sings for the Return of Her Crusader

Chapter 9
1. Heloise's Second Letter of Complaint to Abelard*
2. Bernard of Chartres's Six Keys to Learning
3. Abelard's Yes and No, the Preface and Passages
4. The Mongol Correspondence
5. Magna Carta
6. Thomas Aquinas on the Nature and Domain of Sacred Doctrine

Chapter 10
1. Observations of the Plague
2. The Peasants' Revolt of 1381
3. Joan of Arc's Letter to the English Invaders and Her Trial*
4. George Sphrantzes and the Fall of Constantinople

Chapter 11
1. Petrarch's Ascent of the Windy Mountain
2. Laura Cereta's Defense of Wise Women
3. Vergerio on Education as a Moral Necessity
4. Pico's Oration on the Dignity of Man
5. Three Church Responses to the Art of Printing
6. Erasmus's Sayings

Chapter 12
1. John Mandeville at Court of Great Khan
2. Columbus's First Description of the Americas, 1493
3. Bernardino de Sahagún Account of the Taking of Tenochtitlan
4. Doña Marina, La Malinche: Native Help-Mate of Cortés
5. Montaigne's American Cannibals
6. Laws and Reactions to the Americas

Chapter 13
1. The Confrontation of Luther and Charles V at Worms
2. Luther on the Good Estate of Marriage
3. The Twelve Demands of the Peasants
4. Policing Calvin's Church
5. Queen Elizabeth I's Act of Supremacy
6. Charles V's Abdication

Chapter 14
1. James I Defends Absolutism
2. Luis Granada, "Meditations for Monday Morning"
3. The Trial of Jean Williford for Witchcraft in Faversham, Kent, in 1645
4. Hugo Grotius, The Freedom of the Seas
5. Thomas Hobbes, Leviathan
6. Jacques Bénigne Bossuet, Defense of Divine Right
7. The Absolutism of Peter the Great of Russia

Chapter 15
1. An Old Regime Clergyman Describes His Role
2. Dick Turpin, Highwayman
3. A Reformer Depicts the Condition of the Serfs in Eighteenth-Century Russia
4. The Job of a Slave Trader
5. Galileo on Science and the Bible

Chapter 16
1. Treatise of the Three Imposters
2. John Locke, Second Treatise of Government
3. Denis Diderot, "Christianity"
4. Joseph II of Austria's Decree on Religious Toleration
5. The Parlement of Paris Protests Royal Improvements
6. Johann Wolfgang von Goethe, Italian Journey
7. A German Traveler Reflects on the Causes of Cannibalism

Chapter 17
1. Declaration of the Rights of Man and Citizen
2. Declaration of the Rights of Woman
3. Robespierre Defends the Use of Terror in "Report on the Principles of Political Morality"
4. De Staël Describes Germany's Rustic Qualities in "On Germany"
5. Polish Commander and Revolutionary Tadeusz Kosciuszko Appeals to Polish Peasants in the "Polaniec Manifesto"
6. The British Ambassador Reports on the Disorder and the Initial Stages of the French Revolution in 1789
7. Napoleon Lays Out His View on the Church in Italy

Chapter 18
1. Alexander Ypsilantis, On Why the Greeks Should Fight for Faith and the Motherland*
2. Charles Fourier, A Utopian Plan for Saving the Planet*
3. Lord Byron, "Manfred"
4. A Parliamentary Report on Child Labor, 1832
5. Bentham, On Liberalism and Utility
6. Sándor Petőfi, Hungarian National Song
7. Karl Marx, The Communist Manifesto

Chapter 19
1. Anthony Trollope, The Way We Live Now
2. The Life of a London Prostitute
3. Impressionism and Realism: Contrasting Images*
4. Giuseppe Mazzini, On Italian Unification
5. Princess Victoria on Bismarck
6. "The Charge of the Light Brigade": A Heroic View of the Crimean War

Chapter 20
1. Cecil Rhodes Establishes the Rhodes Scholarships
2. Florentia Sale's Terrible Experiences in Afghanistan
3. The Indian Rebels Speak, 1857
4. The Last Days of David Livingstone in Africa
5. Charles Darwin, The Descent of Man
6. Ferdinand Fabri on Germany's Need for Colonies

Chapter 21

1. Modern Pilgrims Flock to Visit Holy Relics
2. Vladimir Lenin Advocates the Formation of a Revolutionary Elite
3. On Village Hygiene (1902)
4. Sigmund Freud, *The Interpretation of Dreams*
5. Émile Zola Accuses the French Government of Framing Alfred Dreyfus
6. Eduard Bernstein Endorses Democratic Socialism

Chapter 22

1. Emperor Franz Joseph and Emperor Wilhelm II Prepare for War
2. The Socialists Opt to Support the War, 1914
3. War Hysteria Grips an Austrian Novelist*
4. A Red Cross Doctor Reports from Serbia*
5. Women and the First World War*
6. Woodrow Wilson, Fourteen Points

Chapter 23

1. Alexandra Kollontai Proclaims the Russian Revolution a Victory for Women
2. Lenin on Electrification and Communism
3. Stalin Declares War on the Kulaks
4. Field Marshal Piłsudski Explains Why Democracy Has Failed in Poland
5. Hitler Begins Preparations for War, 1933
6. Robert Graves, *Goodbye to All That*
7. Walter Gropius on the Bauhaus Style

Chapter 24

1. Winston Churchill, Speeches on War
2. Adolf Hitler Warns the Jews, January 1939
3. A Survivor Describes the Siege of Leningrad
4. Himmler Stiffens the Resolve of the SS Murderers, October 1943
5. Voices from the French Resistance
6. Dwight D. Eisenhower, Memos on D-Day—Success or Failure

Chapter 25

1. Erich Honecker Praises the Achievements of East German Socialism, 1989*
2. The Soviet Union Condemns Titoism, 1948
3. Khrushchev, Secret Speech, February 25, 1956
4. East Germany Resolves to Build the Berlin Wall, August 12, 1961
5. Beatlemania
6. UN Declaration Against Colonialism, 1960
7. Frantz Fanon, Why Africa Should Not Imitate Europe*

Chapter 26

1. Genocide on Trial: The Case of Slobodan Milošević
2. Otto Schily, Changes in German Citizenship, 1999
3. Salman Rushdie, "Imagine No Heaven"
4. Damien Hirst, What Art Has Become*
5. Angela Merkel, "If the Euro Fails, Europe Fails . . ."

Maps

1.1 *Homo sapiens sapiens* on the Move   8
1.2 The Spread of the Indo-Europeans, 4000–1000 BCE   12
1.3 Mesopotamia, 3000–2000 BCE   13
1.4 Ancient Egypt and the Fertile Crescent   19
1.5 The Near East, c. 1450 BCE   26
1.6 The Eastern End of the Mediterranean in the First Millennium BCE   28
2.1 Archaic Age Greece, c. 800 BCE   43
2.2 Greek and Phoenician Emigration, c. 500 BCE   44
2.3 The Persian Empire and Lydia, c. 500 BCE   53
2.4 The Two Persian Wars, 490–479 BCE   54
2.5 Poleis and Regions of Southern Greece in the Fifth Century BCE   57
2.6 The Peloponnesian War, 431–404 BCE   62
3.1 Macedonian Expansion, 359–336 BCE   75
3.2 Alexander's Empire and March into Asia, 334–323 BCE   83
3.3 The Hellenistic Kingdoms in the Third Century BCE   89
4.1 Early Italy and Its Peoples, c. 500 BCE   107
4.2 Rome Takes Italy, 485–265 BCE   112
4.3 The Expanding Roman Republic, 264–44 BCE   120
4.4 The Campaigns of Hannibal and Scipio Africanus, 219–202 BCE   122
5.1 The Civil War of the Late Roman Republic, 49–45 BCE   143
5.2 The Imperial City of Rome in the Second Century CE   148
5.3 The Roman Empire to the Time of Trajan, 117 CE   159
6.1 External Enemies of the Roman Empire, c. 350   168
6.2 The Spread of Christian Communities in the Roman Empire, 33–311   171
6.3 Diocletian's Division of the Roman Empire by 304   174
6.4 Entry and Movement of German Tribes in the Roman Empire in the Fourth and Fifth Centuries   181
6.5 The Roman Empire by the Early Sixth Century   185
6.6 The Roman Empire of Justinian, 527–565   190
7.1 Spread of Islam to 750   207
7.2 Byzantine Empire, 8th Century   209
7.3 Charlemagne's Empire by 814   214

7.4 The Division of Carolingian Lands by the Treaty of Verdun, 843 224

8.1 Anglo-Saxon England, c. 900 241

8.2 Medieval Europe, c. 1000 242

8.3 The First Crusade, 1095–1099 255

9.1 Trade Routes and Fairs, c. 1100–1300 275

9.2 European State Development, c. 1100–1300 278

9.3 The Spread of Medieval Universities 283

10.1 Northern Europe, c. 1300 297

10.2 The Hundred Years' War, 1337–1453 302

10.3 Spread of the Plague, 1347–1350 306

10.4 The Reconquest of Spain, 900–1492, and Its Final Phase 318

11.1 Renaissance Italy, 1454 329

11.2 The Commercial and Cultural Reach of Venice in the Fifteenth Century 338

11.3 The Spread of the Ottoman Empire, 1326–1566 340

12.1 Portuguese and Spanish Overseas Exploration, 1450–1542 364

12.2 Native Peoples of the Americas in 1500 373

13.1 Charles V's Europe, 1519–1558 395

13.2 The Religious Make-up of the Many Europes by 1600 411

13.3 The Netherlands in 1609 413

14.1 The Thirty Years' War 427

14.2 Louis XIV's Annexations 438

14.3 Russian Expansion, Ivan to Peter the Great 441

14.4 The Ottoman and Venetian Empires, c. 1700 445

14.5 English Civil Wars 450

15.1 Europe, c. 1721 469

15.2 European Colonization and Commerce, c. 1650–1740 473

15.3 The Seven Years' War, 1756–1763 478

16.1 The Rising in Scotland and England, 1745–1746 499

16.2 The Partitions of Poland, 1772–1795 507

17.1 France's Sister Republics, 1792–1799 536

17.2 Napoleon's Campaign in Egypt, 1798–1799 546

17.3 Napoleon's Empire at Its Height, 1812 552

18.1 Europe after the Congress of Vienna, 1815 564

18.2 The Creation of Modern Greece, 1832–1913 573

18.3 Revolutions and Failed Revolts, 1820–1831 574

18.4 The First Industrial Revolution in Britain, c. 1760–1850 581

18.5 The Revolutions of 1848 589

19.1 Baron Haussmann's Rebuilding of Paris, 1853–1869 605

19.2 Italian Unification, 1859–1870 618

19.3 German Unification, 1863–1871 621

19.4 Europe after the Russo-Turkish Wars, 1878 626

20.1 Colonial South Africa, c. 1800–1914 632

20.2 Imperialism in Asia before the First World War 641

20.3 Russian and British Expansion in the Caucasus and Central Asia in the Nineteenth Century 654

20.4 The Scramble for Africa, 1885–1914 657

21.1 Railroads and Big Cities, c. 1914 671

21.2 Jewish Emigration, 1870–1914 689

21.3 Language Groups of the Austro-Hungarian Empire, c. 1914 692

21.4 Ottoman Territorial Losses, 1800–1914 693

22.1 World War I, 1914–1918 702

22.2 The Western Front during World War I 705

22.3 World War I in the Ottoman Empire 709

22.4 Patterns of Human Loss in World War I 721

22.5 Europe after the World War I Peace Treaties, c. 1923 724

23.1 Russian Revolution and Civil Wars, 1917–1921 733

23.2 The Middle East, 1920s–1930s 739

23.3 The Spanish Civil War, 1936–1939 758

24.1 Hitler's Europe, Annexations to 1939 767

24.2 World War II in the Pacific 780

24.3 Major Ghettoes and Concentration Camps, c. 1942 783

24.4 Patterns of Human Loss in World War II 793

25.1 Territorial Changes in Europe, 1945–1949 802

25.2 Cold War Europe, 1945–1949 806

25.3 Decolonization after World War II 814

26.1 The Breakup of the Soviet Union, 1991 841

26.2 The Breakup of Yugoslavia, 1991–1995 845

26.3 Income Inequalities in Europe 851

ACKNOWLEDGMENTS

Many Europes has been the work of many hands, so many that the authors can only mention a few here. We are grateful to all who played some part in bringing this book to completion. First we would like to thank Deborah Harkness who first conceived of this book, but withdrew midway through the project to pursue a trilogy of highly successful novels. The enthusiasm of the acquisitions editor Monica Eckman for our original proposal started us off in the right direction. Among those who have seen the project from start to finish, we would like most of all to thank our managing development editor Nancy Crochiere, who has overseen every step of the process, and done so with infinite skill, patience, and good humor over the last six years. We also owe enormous debts to the rest of the McGraw-Hill team, including the ever-inspiring Matthew Busbridge, director of products and markets; our excellent and indefatigable production team led by our senior production editor Catherine Morris; development editor Betty Slack and copyeditor Amy Marks; our extremely hardworking photo and map editors, David Chodoff, Karen Dubno, and David Tietz; and our permissions editor, Wesley Hall. Nancy's interns Melissa Henderson and Rebecca Crochiere also provided crucial assistance during the production process.

Suzanne Marchand's fabulous and beloved team of LSU grad students, Scott M. Berg, Wade Trosclair, and Jason M. Wolfe helped with many different aspects of *Many Europes'* second half, and should get credit for enhancing both the general form and the specific content of those chapters; Scott Berg and Jason Wolfe also did the lion's share of the work on the electronic primary source documents for Volume 2 that are available to instructors in both McGraw-Hill Connect and Create.

The authors would also to thank the many hardworking and meticulous reviewers of their chapters who prevented them from making a myriad of mistakes, small and large; and individually, we owe debts to the following scholars for reading chapters in their early stages: Courtney Booker, Jeffrey Herf, Anne-Marie Feenberg-Dibon, Natalie Fingerhut, Herbert L. Kessler, Christine Kooi, Paul F. Paskoff, Jonathan Sperber, and Victor Stater. The book depends heavily on the specialized scholarship of recent years; a selection of the most important of those works is listed in the bibliography and footnotes at the book's close; the authors hope that by citing this work directly that readers will be enticed to delve more deeply into those inspiring books and articles. Finally, the authors would like to thank our families, whose love and understanding has sustained us through the long process of writing and rewriting *Many Europes,* and who will, we hope, appreciate how much of their inspiration has gone into the final manuscript.

Academic Reviewers

Carl Abrams
Bob Jones University

Kathryn Amerson
Craven Community College

Stephen Andrews
Central New Mexico Community College

Angela Ash
Owensboro Community and Technical College

Amanda Bahr-Evola
Southern Illinois University Edwardsville

Thomas Behr
University of Houston

Mark Bocija
Columbus State Community College

Mary Ann Borden
Hudson Valley Community College

Wayne Bowen
Southeast Missouri State University

John Brackett
University of Cincinnati

Joy Branch
Southern Union State Community College

Bob Brennan
Cape Fear Community College

Robert Brown
Finger Lakes Community College

Harry Burgess
St. Clair County Community College

Paul Byrd
Des Moines Area Community College

Kevin Caldwell
Blue Ridge Community College

Celeste Chamberlain
Roosevelt University

Anthony Cheeseboro
Southern Illinois University Edwardsville

Karen Christianson
DePaul University

Mark Clark
University of Virginia's College at Wise

Michele Clouse
Ohio University

Lynda Coon
University of Arkansas

Eugene Cruz-Uribe
Northern Arizona University

Marion Deshmukh
George Mason University

Joanna Drell
University of Richmond

Ian Drummond
Gordon College

Eric Duchess
High Point University

Martin Ederer
Buffalo State College

Angela Edwards
Florence-Darlington Technical College

Reanne Eichele
Pikes Peak Community College

Elizabeth Elliot-Meisel
Creighton University

Paula Findlen
Stanford University

Rodger Fisher
Craven Community College

Benita Fox
Columbia Southern University

Carole Collier Frick
Southern Illinois University

Heather Fryer
Creighton University

Christopher Gehrz
Bethel University

Sylvia Gray
Portland Community College–Sylvania

Robert Greene
University of Montana

Timothy Hack
Salem Community College

Robert Harrison
Linn Benton Community College

Frances Jacobson
Tidewater Community College

Thomas Jennings
Stillman College and the University of Alabama

Leslie Johnson
Hudson Valley Community College

Lloyd Johnson
Campbell University

Michael Johnson
Northwest Arkansas Community College

Lars Jones
Florida Tech

Matthew Keith
The Ohio State University

John Kemp
Truckee Meadows Community College

Michael Kennedy
High Point University

Darin Kinsey
Florence-Darlington Technical College

Janilyn Kocher
Richland Community College

Tim Konhaus
Tidewater Community College

Andrew Larsen
Marquette University

Rachel Larsen
Bob Jones University

William J. Lipkin
Union County College

Wenxi Liu
Miami University–Middleton

Paul Douglas Lockhart
Wright State University

Jonathan Malmude
Saint Joseph's College of Maine

Art Marmorstein
Northern State University

Thomas Massey
Cape Fear Community College

Bruce McCord
Aiken Technical College

Edrene McKay
Northwest Arkansas Community College

Ashleigh McLean
Central New Mexico Community College

David McMahon
Kirkwood Community College

Jennifer McNabb
Western Illinois University

Elisa Miller
Rhode Island College

David Mock
Tallahassee Community College

Brandon Morgan
Central New Mexico Community College

Annette Morrow
Minnesota State University

Wyatt Moulds
Jones County Junior College

Samuel Mulberry
Bethel University

Shannon O'Bryan
Greenville Technical College

Lisa Ossian
Des Moines Area Community College

Troy Paddock
Southern Connecticut State University

Ronald Palmer
Jefferson Community College

Craig Pilant
County College of Morris

Ann Pond
Bishop State Community College

Michael Prahl
Hawkeye Community College

David Ramsey
Midlands Technical Community College

Eric Reisenauer
University of South Carolina–Sumter

William Robison
Southeastern Louisiana University

Patrice Ross
Columbus State Community College

Geri Ryder
Ocean County College

Matthew Schaffer
Florence-Darlington Technical College

Linda Breckstein Scherr
Mercer County Community College

Jessica Sheetz-Nguyen
University of Central Oklahoma

Heidi Sherman
University of Wisconsin Green Bay

Myron Silverman
Suffolk County Community College

David Stone
Kansas State University

John Taylor
Southern Illinois University

Emily Teipe
Fullerton College

Susan Thompson
Northern Virginia Community College

David Tompkins
University of Tennessee

Andrew Traver
Southeastern Louisiana University

Rebecca Woodham
Wallace Community College

Ian Worthington
University of Missouri–Columbia

Jackie Wright
Cossatot Community College of the University of Arkansas

Symposia Participants

Gisela Ables
Houston Community College

Donna Allen
Glendale Community College

Sal Anselmo
Delgado Community College

Simon Baatz
John Jay College

Mario A. J. Bennekin
Georgia Perimeter College

Manu Bhagavan
Hunter College

C. J. Bibus
Wharton County Junior College

Olwyn M. Blouet
Virginia State University

Michael Botson
Houston Community College

Patrick Brennan
Gulf Coast Community College

Cathy Briggs
Northwest Vista College

Brad Cartwright
University of Texas at El Paso

Roger Chan
Washington State University

Tamara Chaplin
University of Illinois at Urbana-Champaign

June Cheatham
Richland College

Karl Clark
Coastal Bend College

Bernard Comeau
Tacoma Community College

Charles Connell
Northern Arizona University

Kevin Davis
North Central Texas College

Michael Downs
Tarrant County College–Southeast

Laura Dunn
Brevard Community College

Arthur Durand
Metropolitan Community College

David Dzurec
University of Scranton

Amy Forss
Metropolitan Community College

Jim Good
Lone Star College–North Harris

R. David Goodman
Pratt Institute

Derrick Griffey
Gadsden State Community College

Wendy Gunderson
Colin County Community College

Debbie Hargis
Odessa College

John Hosler
Morgan State University

Lloyd Johnson
Campbell University

James Jones
Prairie View A&M University

Mark Jones
Central Connecticut State University

Sarah Jurenka
Bishop State Community College

Bill Kamil
Sinclair Community College

Philip Kaplan
University of North Florida

Stephen Katz
Philadelphia University

Carol A. Keller
San Antonio College

Greg Kelm
Dallas Baptist University

Michael Kinney
Calhoun Community College

Jessica Kovler
John Jay College

David Lansing
Ocean County College

Benjamin Lapp
Montclair State University

Lynn Lubamersky
Boise State University

Julian Madison
Southern Connecticut State University

David Marshall
Suffolk County Community College

Meredith R. Martin
Collin College

Linda McCabe
North Lake College

George Monahan
Suffolk County Community College

Michael J. Mullin
Augustana College

Tracy Musacchio
John Jay College

Mikal Nash
Essex County College

Sandy Norman
Florida Atlantic University

Michelle Novak
Houston Community College–Southeast

Veena Oldenburg
Baruch College

Troy Paddock
Southern Connecticut State University

Jessica Patton
Tarrant County College–Northwest

Edward Paulino
John Jay College

Valor Pickett
Northwest Arkansas Community College

Craig Pilant
County College of Morris

Sean Pollock
Wright State University

Michael Prahl
Hawkeye Community College

Robert Risko
Trinity Valley Community College

Esther Robinson
Lone Star College–Cyfair

Matthew Ruane
Florida Institute of Technology

Geri Ryder
Ocean County College

Linda Breckstein Scherr
Mercer County Community College

Susan Schmidt-Horning
St. John's University

Donna Scimeca
College of Staten Island

Jeffrey Smith
Lindenwood University

Rachel Standish
San Joaquin Delta College

Matthew Vaz
City College of New York

Roger Ward
Colin County Community College–Plano

Christian Warren
Brooklyn College

Don Whatley
Blinn College

Geoffrey Willbanks
Tyler Junior College

Scott M. Williams
Weatherford College

Carlton Wilson
North Carolina Central University

Chad Wooley
Tarrant County College

Connect Board of Advisors

Michael Downs
University of Texas–Arlington

Jim Halverson
Judson University

Reid Holland
Midlands Technical College

Stephen Katz
Rider University

David Komito
Eastern Oregon University

Wendy Sarti
Oakton Community College

Linda Scherr
Mercer County Community College

Eloy Zarate
Pasadena City College

Many Europes Board of Advisors

Kathryn Amerson
Craven Community College

Amanda Bahr-Evola
Southern Illinois University Edwardsville

Mary Ann Borden
Hudson Valley Community College

Wayne Bowen
Southeast Missouri State University

Joy Branch
Southern Union State Community College

Roger Fisher
Craven Community College

Frances Jacobson
Tidewater Community College

Brandon Morgan
Central New Mexico Community College

David Ramsey
Midlands Technical Community College

1

Cave Painting of Horses and Rhinoceros, Chauvet, France

PRELIMINARY TO WESTERN CIVILIZATION

The Long Dawning of Prehistory
A Special Species?
The Domestication of Animals
Settling Down and the Birth of Agriculture
The Domestication of Plants
Mesolithic Europe
The Indo-European Factor

The Emergence of Cities and Writing in Mesopotamia
Mesopotamia and the Appearance of Cities
The Invention of Writing
The Importance of Writing
Cities to Empires
Mesopotamian Religion

The Lasting Stability of Ancient Egypt
The Nile and Egyptian Agriculture
Hieroglyphics and Egyptian Writing

The Dynasties Take Hold
Egyptian Religion
Living Ancient Egypt

An Age of Bronze Turns to Iron
The Minoans
The Mycenaean Greeks
The Indo-European Hittites
Sea Raiders Roil the Mediterranean
The Advantages and Effects of Iron
The Semitic Phoenicians

The Religious Breakout and Endurance of the Hebrews
The Formative Phase: From Abraham to Moses
Hebrew Singularities: The Struggle for Authority
Kings and Kingdoms
Empires and Diaspora

Conclusion

THE MURDER OF ÖTZI, THE FIRST EUROPEAN In the late summer of 1991 in the high Alps, two German hikers stumbled upon the deep-frozen, mummified remains of Ötzi (named after the place where he was found), the first European we know in detail. Thanks to melting glaciers, other bodies preserved in ice have begun to reveal themselves. The bodies of three Austro-Hungarian soldiers from the First World War found on an Italian mountain in 2004 and the Iron Age bodies found in Europe's peat bogs are impressive human remains, but they can't compare with Ötzi, who died 5,300 years ago. The dynasties of Egypt had not yet been established, writing was just emerging in faraway Mesopotamia, and the agricultural breakthroughs of prehistory were just beginning to reap results in Mesopotamia and Egypt. Ötzi's case is a good place to begin our examination of western civilization because, though he did not belong to western civilization, he did belong to its long backstory.

He was forty-five years old, small at five foot three and 110 pounds, tattooed, and suitably dressed for the mountains (bearskin cap, grass cloak, coat, loincloth, leggings, and leather shoes). He was carrying a precious copper ax, stone knife, bow, quiver with arrows (only two of them tipped), and a pack loaded with necessities (dried berries and mushrooms, and some fire-starting materials). On the day he died he had eaten some mountain goat and deer meat, as well as some wheat, dried fruit, and tubers. Ötzi had lived a hard life, but he did well enough to make it to an advanced age before his misadventure in the Alps, and he did not die a natural death. Ötzi was murdered.

Why was he in the high Alps? Ötzi had lived his life in the area around Bolzano in northern Italy (across the mountains from the area of Innsbruck, Austria) and may, as a shepherd or hunter, have been a frequent visitor to the mountains, but that autumn 5,300 years ago Ötzi had a fatal encounter. Someone shot Ötzi in the back with an arrow, severing an artery. Ötzi's head was also crushed by a rock. This was no simple mountain mugging; the perpetrator left behind the murdered man's possessions, and someone removed the arrow shaft from his back. There Ötzi lay with the Alpine snows falling on him for 5,300 years.

Ötzi was a continental European, but Europe as a political and cultural entity would not exist for another four thousand years. The Austrian and Italian governments wrestled over who owned the corpse of the iceman (it was eventually

Ötzi A recent reconstruction of Ötzi, who died in the Alps c. 3300 BCE.

determined that he lay one hundred yards inside Italy), the irony being that those nations did not come into existence until five thousand years after Ötzi's death. In Ötzi's small

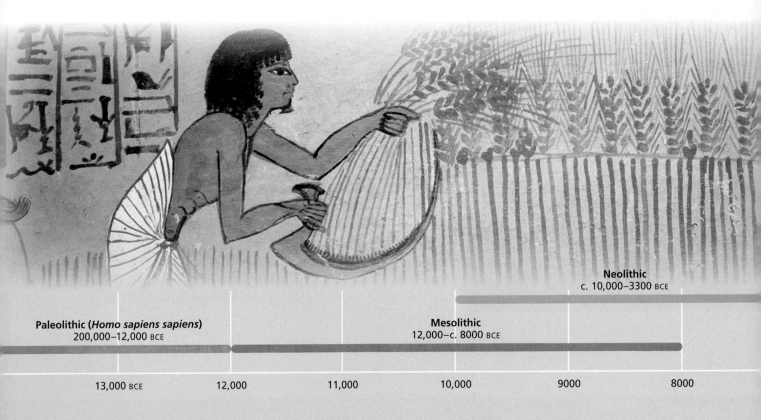

Neolithic
c. 10,000–3300 BCE

Paleolithic (*Homo sapiens sapiens*)
200,000–12,000 BCE

Mesolithic
12,000–c. 8000 BCE

| 13,000 BCE | 12,000 | 11,000 | 10,000 | 9000 | 8000 |

Alpine world, there were no governments, no law as we know it, no settled communities of any substantial size or duration, no systematic agriculture, no writing, no higher forms of thought (philosophy, theology, mathematics). Yet Ötzi carried a copper ax and wore excellent shoes that imply the existence of cooperative communities of people who could make specialized objects. He could not have tattooed himself fifty-seven times, including on his lower back and behind his knees. Ötzi had help. His very survival suggests the existence of organized life, but we would not likely call his a civilized life.

The elements that make civilization possible are four pairs of connected things: settled life (most often in cities) and a critical mass of people, sustainable agriculture and trade, government and law, writing and abstract thought. The Mesopotamian peoples possessed all of these civilizational pairs by the third millennium BCE: cities, a large population, a working agricultural system and active trade, leaders and laws, cursive (flowing) and then **cuneiform** (wedge-shaped) writing, written laws, religious texts, and the world's first literature. The Egyptians also perfected a settled agricultural life, a prosperous economy, political rule and law, and writing. Egypt achieved steady prosperity and an enduring stability that fueled economic development in the eastern Mediterranean world over several millennia, but Egyptian life was not driven by urban growth. A different, but successful model of civilized life was at work along the Nile River. The civilizational pairs were critical to spurring a higher form of human life, far beyond what Ötzi could have imagined. These were the preliminaries upon which western or European civilization was to root and grow.

The development of **civilization** with large cities as its defining feature would not have been possible without these preliminary pairs, but we should not define civilization too narrowly. One way to look at the early ancient world would be as a series of experiments in living under specific and often confining conditions. Civilizations are more than just small, isolated communities of people. They tend to be large and encompassing, impacting entire regions and neighboring lands. Many smaller, less developed, historical communities either proved to be dead ends or were integrated, willingly or by force, into larger historical enterprises.

We need not think that the rise of civilization was a universal good. With civilization came developments that may seem less good to us: the coalescing of power into great empires, large-scale organized warfare, systematic violence, and inequalities of persons (both material and legal) and sexes. Our view of early history is distorted by the particular historical lens through which we view it. Prehistoric and early historical sources are meager and often of an unfamiliar character, and the amount of

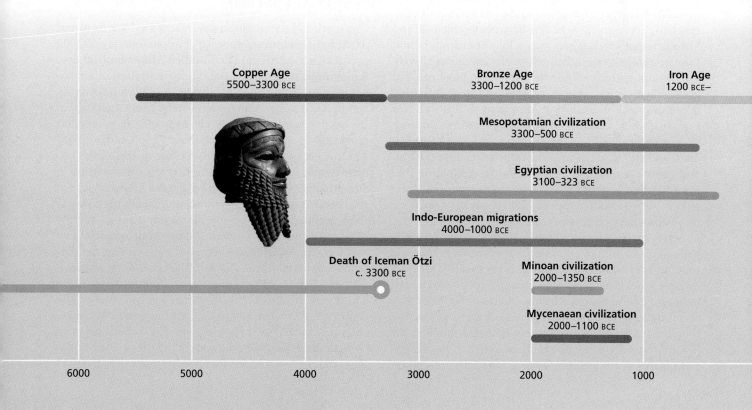

Copper Age
5500–3300 BCE

Bronze Age
3300–1200 BCE

Iron Age
1200 BCE–

Mesopotamian civilization
3300–500 BCE

Egyptian civilization
3100–323 BCE

Indo-European migrations
4000–1000 BCE

Death of Iceman Ötzi
c. 3300 BCE

Minoan civilization
2000–1350 BCE

Mycenaean civilization
2000–1100 BCE

6000   5000   4000   3000   2000   1000

time involved is comparatively huge (almost three thousand years), which has the effect of making time seem to rush by in the telling, loading us down with names and people we cannot know, know differently, or cannot afford to spend much time with. People and places seem to dash rapidly on and off the historical stage. We can try to correct for the historical distortion, but only a lengthier dedicated narrative, particularly of three thousand years of Egyptian history, could accomplish that. Here we intend to pursue only the main contours of early history.

The Long Dawning of Prehistory

Prehistory is typically thought of as that period before the invention of writing. The nature of what we know

Why is our knowledge of prehistory limited, and are there ways to overcome those limitations? How was agriculture critical to the first stirrings of civilization?

about the past changes with writing. Written records do more than simply supply specifics about the past; they personalize it, for at last named individuals grounded in place and time step forward. Prehistory, however, is not quite as prehistoric as we once thought, as the case of Ötzi shows us. Other kinds of records have begun to fill

in the prehistoric past, though they fall short of personalizing it. Yet new dating techniques have given prehistory needed contour and precision.

Early writing (the critical factor in setting the prehistory-history divide) has many limitations as a historical dividing point: its spottiness, limited range, slow gradual emergence and spread, and perilous state of preservation. Consequently the line between prehistoric and historic is not sharp. There was a long transition period from one stage to the other, which the invention of writing did not entirely eliminate. Moreover, most of what goes on in daily life is never recorded and so by definition is prehistorical or ahistorical (unrelated to history). Nor is prehistory an absolute chronological distinction, since prehistoric peoples have long existed alongside historical ones, and still do. Similarly, the opposition of prehistory and history should not be a qualitative distinction into primitive and sophisticated, given that some prehistoric cultures were strikingly sophisticated and many historical peoples have been remarkably primitive.

Since our species is roughly 200,000 years old, 97.5 percent of all human existence was spent in prehistoric time. In this book, our attention is necessarily focused on only a small portion of the human experience in both temporal and geographic terms. Many of the formative, social developments of our species occurred before the time covered here. But when and how did humans, an itinerant species, settle down, learn to live in hostile environments, learn to farm, learn to live with each other,

and learn to dominate others? Many of these formative changes occurred before records were kept.

Another issue we cannot afford to ignore is the pace of change (historical, social, and psychological). For almost 200,000 years, humans lived in small, scattered bands of itinerant hunters and gatherers, yet in the last 12,000 years the human population has exploded from 1–5 million humans in 10,000 BCE to perhaps 300–400 million people in 1 CE, and to 7 billion people by 2011 CE. It has been estimated that around 120 billion humans have existed, almost 6 percent of whom are alive at present. The geographic spread of humans now covers the globe, and in the past five thousand years we have gone from being the users of stone tools to a species that has landed men on the moon and unlocked the secrets of the atom. One cannot but notice that the pace of change has accelerated as we approach the present. As you go forward in this book, you will notice that the chapters treat shorter and shorter spans of time, which is itself a reflection of the increasing speed of historical change, of the expansion of the human population, and of its spatial reach. The historical record thickens not because of the passage of time, but because of the growth of the human population, the geographic spread of the species, and improved and richer record keeping. There was more change in the period from 8000 BCE to 3000 BCE than in the previous 190,000 years; more change (technological and material) between 1850 and 1950 CE than in the previous 500 years; and more change in the past six decades than in the previous century. Whether change itself at this accelerated pace is sustainable remains to be seen, but it does lead us back to our long, slow, formative beginning.

A Special Species?

Our species, *Homo sapiens sapiens*, reached its basic form (out of preceding hominid species) at approximately 200,000 (±50,000) BCE in Africa. The so-called **Mitochondrial Eve,** the common matrilineal (descending from the mother) ancestor of all living humans, lived 170,000 (±50,000) years ago in Africa. For some reason—most likely a change in the environment or climate—the early human population narrowed to a perilous point about 75,000–60,000 years ago in eastern Africa. A great cooling of the earth's climate caused by the massive eruption of a supervolcano in Sumatra 75,000 years ago probably made the survival of the species precarious. Every human male living today is the descendant (based on specific genetic traits) of a single man nicknamed the **Genetic Adam**; Mitochondrial Eve and Genetic Adam therefore never met—he was her distant descendant. About 75,000–60,000 years ago, anatomically modern humans began to move out of Africa (Map 1.1 on p. 8). By 40,000 (±10,000) BCE they had reached the continent of Europe, where they encountered a separate, older hominid species, *Homo sapiens neanderthalensis*.

Neanderthals had been resident in Europe, the Middle East, and northern Africa for a much longer time (500,000

The New Prehistoric Past

The division of prehistory into stone ages—Paleolithic (Old Stone, 2.5 million years ago to approximately 12,000 BCE), Mesolithic (Middle Stone, roughly 12,000–8000 BCE), and Neolithic (New Stone, 10,000–3300 BCE)—and metal ages (Copper, 5500–3300 BCE, and Bronze, 3300–1200 BCE) is convenient but deceptive. Neither the stone nor the metal ages are absolute divisions; they overlap and are only regionally meaningful. The Mesolithic and Neolithic periods arrived earlier in the Near East than they did in Europe or the Americas; so, too, did the metal ages. The old prehistoric categories housed a wide set of material, economic, and cultural traits associated with the development of human societies. These divisions were the constructions of thoughtful prehistorians and anthropologists, but they are highly subjective and somewhat contradictory. The peoples of both the late Paleolithic and Mesolithic periods were hunter-gatherers rather than farmers, but they were at different stages of development. Because no critical development in stone technology took place in the Mesolithic period, the stone (in Greek, *lithos*) element of its name may mislead. Stone technology, especially in the use and trade of polished stones such as obsidian, did improve in the Neolithic period. The Neolithic, in general, connotes the move to agricultural society along with the creation of pottery, polished axes, and new tools. The stone and metal ages are useful categories, but loaded ones lacking precision.

New dating techniques developed in the late twentieth century have revolutionized prehistoric studies. In 1947 the chemist Willard Libby discovered the basis for radiocarbon dating of organic materials. He showed that organic materials experience a steady and measurable loss of radioactive carbon-14, which is naturally present in plants because of photosynthesis, whereas carbon-12 remains in the same organic substances as an unchanging isotope and can be used as a basis for comparison. Because the half-life of radioactive carbon-14 is 5,730 years, radiocarbon testing calculates the proportion of carbon-14 against the fixed presence of carbon-12 to determine when an organic body (plant or animal) died. The technique is more complicated than it sounds and requires considerable expertise in measurement, but at last prehistorians had an objective way to determine dates in the past. The calibration of the date of each object may vary according to circumstances, but the margin of error for materials less than two thousand years old is now as little as ±40 years. Other dating techniques have since been discovered, and even human DNA contains information about the history of human bodies in relation to human populations over time.

The more exact dating of objects has revolutionized our understanding of the distant past, for the stone and metal ages were ideas shaped by theories of human development. Scientific, objective dating of the past has allowed a more reliable ordering of things and their cultures without an overlaying theory, allowing for a more exact comparative history, one not privileging literate early societies and cultural centers.

QUESTIONS | *Why bother to date and categorize the distant past into periods? What limitations and weaknesses are there to a more exact dating of the prehistoric past?*

or more years ago) but lost out in the competition for space and resources to modern humans about 25,000 (±5,000) years ago. Interbreeding between the two species apparently occurred before Neanderthal extinction, given that an estimated 2.5 percent of the DNA of today's non-African peoples comes from a Neanderthal source.

While the last major Ice Age still held its grip on much of Europe, European hunter-gatherers of the period from about 35,000 to 15,000 years ago began to produce objects with symbolic meaning. Though their population numbers were relatively low, they made carved bone flutes and small fertility or Venus figurines (see Back to the Source at the end of this chapter). Most wondrous of all are the great cave paintings at Chauvet and Lascaux in France, though there are less spectacular examples in northern Spain and southern Germany. The cave dwellers painted representations of animals (deer, goats, horses, rhinoceroses, bears, lions), some of them now extinct, such as the auroch (a wild bull); a few humans; and abstract signs, which may be the first rudimentary attempts to communicate through written signs. The style of the paintings is naturalistic, but the scenes lack scenery—no plants, clouds, or stars—just the essential animate and symbolic objects of the cave dwellers' economic and thought worlds. The material traces of these cave visitors ceased with the end of the Ice Age 10,000 years ago (approximately 8000 BCE).

The interest of Paleolithic peoples in art was not a product of genetic makeup or an evolutionary advance of the species. The achievements of human beings over the past 20,000 years have not been caused by bigger brains or better brain wiring but by shared and cumulative cultural advances. Humans have a special capacity among animals not just to learn new things (for even dogs can learn new tricks), but to teach that learning to their communities and pass it along to future generations. This species learning curve, the basic ability to expand and preserve accumulated knowledge, may help us to understand the rapid development of human societies. We keep, communicate, and transmit cultural, economic, and political knowledge. Not all the things that we learn and pass along survive or are good, but the species as a whole gathers advantageous knowledge and conveys it over time.

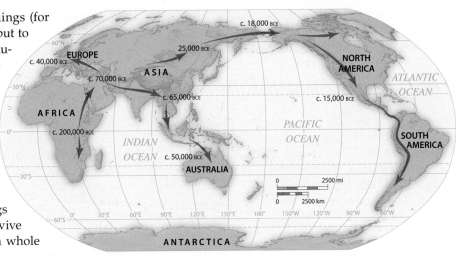

MAP 1.1 | *Homo sapiens sapiens* on the Move
Our species, *Homo sapiens sapiens,* arose in Africa about 200,000 BCE (±50,000 years). By about 75,000–60,000 BCE, groups of humans had moved out of Africa in several different waves, and by about 40,000 BCE, humans had reached Europe. ***What might explain the movement of early humans out of Africa? Where did they go? How fast or slow was the migration?***

The human imperatives to learn and convey vast amounts of information are species particular. Anatomically we are the same as people were 20,000 or 5,000 years ago. Ötzi is one of us. So how then did the dangerous, marginal human existence of the Genetic Adam or the iceman Ötzi lead to the successes of human civilization, with its vast increase in the size of the human population and its expanding pool of cultural and practical knowledge? Developments in social organization, the accumulation of useful knowledge, and success in preserving that knowledge over generations may come closest to accounting for human social, cultural, and historical development.

The engine driving evolutionary change is the external world. Unlike most species, which are products of particular environments and specially suited to their exacting demands, humans have the ability to overcome that limitation and dramatically widen their natural ecological niche by adapting themselves to survive hostile environments (with the wearing of specialized clothes, for instance) and by transforming environments (by diverting or damming a river, for instance) to suit their needs. Late Paleolithic men and women in Europe found a way with fire and clothing to survive and even thrive during an Ice Age.

The Domestication of Animals

Early human life was a constant struggle to secure food. Thus, one of the first great human transformations of the physical world was the domestication of animals and plants. Some animals were domesticated before plants, which is likely a reflection of the hunter-gatherer existence of early humans and their closeness to the animal world. Association with humans conveyed an advantage to certain animals, which were seeking their own survival.

The dog was the first domesticated animal. All dogs are descended from wolves. The DNA evidence suggests that canine descent began about 140,000 years ago and

that the more complete domestication of dogs did not occur until about 15,000 years ago in the Middle East. Later, in central China, domesticated dogs interbred again with wolves. Dog remains from as early as 12,000 BCE have been discovered in graves in the Middle East. The advantages of the relationship for people are clear: dogs are teachable and they can hunt, protect, serve as guard dogs, provide companionship, and also be eaten. The advantages of the relationship for dogs are protection from predators and a more secure food supply. Sheep were domesticated around 10,000 BCE in western Asia and goats at about the same time in the area of present-day Iran and Iraq. In all these cases, domestication led to temperament and physical changes in the domesticated species: dogs became adapted to the demands made upon their activity, sheep grew longer wool, and goats developed shorter horns. The nature of the domestication process is much debated. Did humans deliberately select preferred animals that then interbred and developed in a particular direction, or was natural selection at work, with the tamable species accommodating themselves to survival with humans and the human environment? In the latter scenario, certain naturally occurring genetic mutations might have conveyed advantages to animals living with or near humans, in which case a dependent evolutionary relationship developed.

The symbiotic relationship of domesticated animals and humans has been called co-evolution, for the domestication of animals (and plants) led to a form of domestication of humans. To care for, discipline, and tend to the needs of animals regularizes human behavior. Humans, in other words, change because of their contact with and care of animals. In the transformation of hunter-gatherers into settled peoples, the domestication of animals and plants was a step in the process of managing economic resources and regularizing a wandering life.

By 2500 BCE most of the animals upon which humans depend had been domesticated: pigs in western Asia about 7000 BCE, cattle in the eastern Sahara by 7000 BCE, chickens in the area of Thailand by 6000 BCE, horses in northern Kazakhstan as early as 5500 BCE, donkeys in northern Africa by 4000 BCE, silkworms in China by 3500 BCE, camels (both Bactrian and dromedaries) in southern Russia and Arabia by 3000 BCE, and honeybees in Egypt by 3000 BCE. The cat is a special case, because its economic use is less obvious. Cats were likely attracted to human communities by the rodents (mice and rats) that lived off human food, so they were tolerated as rodent-catchers. Some evidence suggests that cats domesticated themselves, which may explain their half-wild or independent natures. Descended from Middle Eastern wild cats, early domesticated cats were much larger than today's house pets. On Cyprus, a large domesticated cat was buried beside a grave around 9500 BCE. The Egyptians later bred smaller and tamer cats than the one found on Cyprus.

Settling Down and the Birth of Agriculture

Another great challenge for early humans was to stabilize their lives by securing greater safety. A purely nomadic life would have been a perilous, exhausting life. The simplest injury or illness could lead to abandonment and death. Seasonally, hunter-gatherer groups of prehistoric humans needed to find or make more permanent and fixed habitations. The hunter-gatherer people of Chauvet and Lascaux in France could not have painted their caves so delicately and extensively if they had not regularized, to some extent, their seasonal patterns. Yet it cannot have been easy for prehistoric peoples to settle down permanently. Much depended upon the availability of local food, water, and security, but they were still hunting and gathering peoples, often following wild herds of great migratory beasts. Semi-settled and settled life came before systematic agriculture, so that agriculture may be the result of settlement rather than the reverse. By about 10,000 BCE in the Middle East various Neolithic (or New Stone Age) peoples had begun to settle at places such as Jericho. In the beginning they were not farmers.

The fact of settlements, first seasonal and then permanent, had important implications for Neolithic peoples. Economic conditions needed to be regularized. Agriculture was one way to do that, even if hunting and gathering were still necessary. Trade with other communities offered the chance for people in one place to obtain things they lacked locally. The harvesting of wild crops may have been an accidental feature of early settlements. The chronology is striking: settlements first, the domestication of plants second and at a slower pace than habitation.

Living in more or less permanent villages and towns imposed new conditions and problems on Neolithic peoples. Life in a settled community depends on cooperation between people and codes of acceptable behavior. Settled life also introduced new divisions between people, the first of these being material. Settled peoples hold, and in some sense invented, the idea of private and fixed property; nomadic peoples have only what they can carry with them. But not all houses or settlements are equal; indeed, it is their very nature to be different and unequal. Settled peoples acquire and accumulate lands and goods—some more than others—so that settled life produces differences in wealth and status between people. **Sedentism** (settling down) produced its own particular problems: greater vulnerability to attack (enemies knew where settlements were); the spread of communicable diseases, since people lived in such close quarters to each other and might suffer the same environmental stresses (from polluted water, spoiled food, poor air quality); and the exhaustion of local resources (particularly the overuse of the same soil and water resources). Though settled peoples regularized the supply of food, their diet was less varied and perhaps less healthy than that of their hunter-gatherer predecessors. The size and height of settled men and women seems, as a result, to have shrunk.

Settlement and the occupation of residences was another great leap forward in the human drive to reshape the environment from one imposed by nature to one controlled by humans. The possibilities of material culture (goods, tools, houses) expanded significantly with settlement as did new skills associated with house-building and its materials (of mud, stone, and wood). Settled humans belong to house cultures; that is, houses not only are their creations, reflecting in their materials and design particular societies and individuals, but also shape humans and their relations with the world. Settled peoples created internal or house worlds, which hastened intellectual changes unknown to wandering peoples who knew animals and food sources, the moon and stars, topography and winds, but less about themselves than they did about a demanding external world. Settled life also changed the roles of the sexes, each beginning to specialize in specific activities that were different from those of their earlier wandering existence.

As the Ice Age was drawing to a close and glaciers were retreating, as early as 10,000 BCE, a series of villages began to appear in the Near East, especially in southern Turkey (Anatolia) in the area in the north of the so-called Fertile Crescent (an area curving from the Nile to the Tigris and Euphrates Rivers). People in these communities still hunted, but they also began to construct circular homes and to farm. The domestication of sheep and goats in the same area was probably not a coincidence, but these Neolithic farmers devoted themselves chiefly to the cultivation of grain crops, which made all the difference to regularizing life.

The Domestication of Plants

The domestication of plants lagged behind the domestication of animals but was put to better advantage by settled communities. Of most importance to the Near East settlements after 10,000 BCE was the domestication of einkorn wheat, emmer wheat, bread wheat, and barley. Wheat in its wild state is of little use to humans and difficult to digest, but in the dry summers of the Middle East wheat tended to produce larger seed pods. Were these selected by Neolithic humans or was wheat another example of a domesticate that did well by accommodating itself to human needs? Perhaps it was both. Under human cultivation, possibly by women farmers tending to the nearby fields, wheat lost its toxicity and produced larger yields and more manageable germination and growth cycles.

The results were significant. In the case of wheat, its cultivation and the great shift to carbohydrates in the human diet (including the focus on cultivating rice in China and maize in Mexico by 8000 BCE) allowed human beings to escape complete dependence on a nomadic gathering and hunting life. The domestication of goats and sheep made up for the protein lost from less hunting. The Near East success in farming spread west and east, to Europe, Egypt, and India. By 5000 BCE Greece, the Nile valley, and parts of Pakistan were growing the Near Eastern cereal crops. Some scholars have called this the **Agricultural Revolution of Prehistory.** Although it was a revolution in terms of radical change, it took millennia for these crops and farming skills to spread across Eurasia. Nor was this agricultural advance limited to grain crops. In the Near East fig trees were domesticated around 9000 BCE, and chickpeas, lentils, and peas by 7500 BCE. Farming led to the development of new tools, for grain crops need to be sown, harvested, and thrashed to separate the grains from their husks, and each of these stages required its own special technologies and techniques. By 6000 BCE ceramic pots were being produced at Jericho. A community of nearly a thousand rectangular houses at Çatal Hüyük in Anatolia flourished around the same time. Its residents farmed wheat, peas, and lentils; traded obsidian objects; and painted their houses with scenes of fertile women and bulls.

Mesolithic Europe

With the passing of the Ice Age, the continent of Europe entered its Mesolithic Age. As the ice retreated north, many of the migratory herd animals such as reindeer or caribou that European peoples had depended on moved north. The hunter-gatherer peoples turned to hunting smaller, solitary game and relied increasingly upon wild plants and fish. In

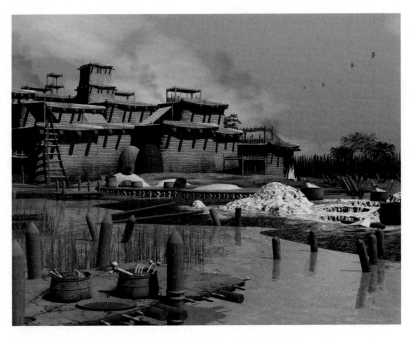

A Neolithic Settlement A reconstruction of the settlement of Çatal Hüyük in Anatolia. Settlements such as this one occurred before the domestication of plants.

their art they began to depict human subjects rather than herd animals. Farming came to the Mediterranean rim of southern Europe and spread slowly after 7000 BCE (on the day of his death, Ötzi had eaten some einkorn wheat), but it took three thousand years before farming spread across Europe. In Scandinavia there are nonagricultural settlement sites from 5000 BCE.

About that time, various peoples in Europe and the British Isles began erecting megaliths, giant stone and wood structures, many of them for religious reasons at grave sites. The most impressive of these is Stonehenge, erected about 2400–2200 BCE on the Salisbury Plain of southern England. Stonehenge contains a series of stand-

Stonehenge The Mesolithic stone circle on the Salisbury Plain of Wiltshire, England, was once the site of prehistoric religious rites.

ing stones called menhirs that may have been arranged to mark points in the solar calendar, particularly the summer solstice. An earlier funeral site called Bluehenge, because of its bluestones (brought from Wales), has been found nearby. Not far from Stonehenge was Woodhenge, and a causeway or marked footpath seems to have connected them. These **henges,** or earthenworks, were probably used to mark different ceremonies in the lives, health, and deaths of prehistoric Britons. On the Orkney Islands, off the coast of Scotland, the later Ring of Brodgar and other rings of stone also bear witness to related pagan belief systems and customs. These were impressive community structures, but the societies that built them were not higher civilizations. That Europe was well behind the Near East culturally and economically was a reflection of its climate; the warmer Fertile Crescent blossomed, while Europe remained chilly, its climate thawing slowly.

The Indo-European Factor

Almost three billion people today speak an Indo-European language. Linguists concluded long ago that these languages, because of their shared root-words and grammatical structures (the way their languages work), descend from a mother tongue called Proto Indo-European (Table 1.1). This language was spoken in the Pontic-Caspian area of Eurasia, in the steppes or prairie lands between and above the Black and Caspian Seas, between 4500 and 2200 BCE.

These peoples possessed a vocabulary for family members, animals, and material culture that in its root forms is common to its descendent languages. By examining the root vocabulary of Proto Indo-European, historical linguists have determined the historical and geographic setting of these peoples. For example, they had words for northern animals, but not southern ones, and for northern trees, but not for dates and palms. Their economy was pastoral, based on sheep and cattle herding in the area near the Dnieper River. The cave peoples of the late Paleolithic period had lived in matrilineal societies; the Indo-European herding cultures were patrilineal (descending from the father), perhaps as a result of the central importance of male cooperation in managing herds. As early as 5000 BCE they began to place themselves under

chiefs. At about the same time, they domesticated horses, and by 4200 BCE these peoples learned to ride horses.

The vast grassland of the Eurasian steppes was not a welcoming environment for humans, but the domestication of horses gave these peoples a way to expand space. They developed wheeled carts, which allowed them to be mobile and migratory. The Indo-European peoples were thus agents of cultural penetration and engagement; they encountered others, sometimes peacefully, often violently. The steppes served as a Eurasian land bridge, allowing these peoples to move south into areas of the Fertile Crescent, east into greater Asia, and southwest into Europe (Map 1.2). Between 4000 and 3800 BCE the weather in the steppes turned colder, glaciers advanced, and spring flooding was severe. Copper and Bronze Age warriors on horseback with wagons to carry their goods brought their culture to Anatolia between 3700 and 3500 BCE. Over the next thousand years, these peoples with their horses, technology, and political and social systems moved south, east, and west. This migration was neither sudden nor constantly violent. The very fact that the Indo-European language did not join itself to native languages but generally replaced them may suggest that its adoption was voluntary rather than compulsory. Resident populations may have adopted the foreign language because of its prestige, utility, and association with power. The dependent languages that developed can be dated roughly and suggest the order of contact with Proto Indo-European: Anatolian around 4000 BCE, Tocharian (in the area of northwestern China) around 3500 BCE, Celtic and Italic around 3000 BCE, Greek closer to 2500 BCE, and early Indo-Iranian (including Sanskrit) closer to 2000 BCE.

Though the Indo-Europeans have been misrepresented for racial and nationalist reasons as Aryans by the Nazis and others, they may best be thought of as several prehistoric peoples in the Dnieper-Danube area who shared a basic language and who, because of their use of wheeled carts and horses, were able to penetrate and influence developing lands to the south, east, and west of their homeland in the steppes. They not only introduced languages that replaced indigenous languages, but also influenced the political and religious values of these lands. Patriarchal societies with chiefs, horses, and a male sky-god came to predominate.

TABLE 1.1 | Shared Indo-European Words

ENGLISH	GERMAN	SPANISH	GREEK	LATIN	SANSKRIT
father	vater	padre	pater	pater	pitar
one	ein	uno	hen	unus	ekam
Sun	Sonne	sol	helios	sol	surya
King	König	rey	basileus	rex	raja
God	Gott	dios	theos	deus	devas

MAP 1.2 | The Spread of the Indo-Europeans, 4000–1000 BCE

From their original homeland in the area between the Black and Caspian Seas, groups of Indo-Europeans began, over several millennia, to spread south, east, and west, influencing the languages, cultures, political systems, and technologies of the lands they occupied. *How might the geography and climate of the area between the Black and Caspian Seas have promoted or even forced the movement of the Indo-Europeans? How do the language and technologies of the Indo-Europeans help us to track their migration and the impact they had on the lands they entered?*

The Emergence of Cities and Writing in Mesopotamia

The word *civilization* (from the Latin word *civilis* for things referring to a city, its citizens, and society) can mislead us into thinking that without cities or substantial settlements there can be no civilization. Around 3500 BCE the important thing was the establishment of farming communities, which arose not just in the Near East, but also around the world (perhaps the effect of the waning of the Ice Age): in the Indus Valley, China, Egypt, Mexico, Peru, and parts

Why was writing such an important human invention, and why did it first appear in Mesopotamia?

of southern Europe. These societies were often associated with great rivers such as the Nile. In many of these places, such as the Near East and Egypt, the emergence of complex societies occurred almost simultaneously. The histories of Near Eastern peoples (Mesopotamian, Egyptian, Minoan, Mycenaean, Hittite, Hebrew, and many others) are each deserving of extended independent study, but here we examine only briefly the larger picture and direction of the civilizations that emerged at the eastern end of the Mediterranean Sea and take note of their characters and contributions to laying down the preliminaries for the emergence of western civilization.

One of the issues we may wish to think about is why bigger was better and the predominant historical pattern of early history, which saw empires emerge from important cities and dominate and incorporate other cities and lands. This imperial impetus might be called the Mesopotamian model since it was followed by the great Mesopotamian powers—Akkadian, Babylonian, Hittite, Assyrian, and Persian. The same model did not take hold in Egypt. The particular geography of Mesopotamia may explain the pattern, but there were contributing causes for the imperial impetus: the growing complexity and expanding resources (both material and human) of Mesopotamian powers; the need to defend a vulnerable land against competitive rivals, both to overcome threats and to seize resources; the martial nature of warrior societies and their religions; and the unilateral power and dominance of all-powerful rulers who could, through an act of sheer will or individual drive, turn their societies toward singular goals such as conquest.

The historical players in the early history of the eastern Mediterranean can be divided into land empires (Akkadians, Babylonians, Hittites, Phrygians, and Assyrians) and the sea enterprises of the Minoans, Mycenaeans, and Phoenicians, which tended to be less imperial, more commercial, and somewhat remote from Mesopotamia. The particular nature of Mesopotamia, its problems and tensions, shaped the primary pattern and instabilities of early Near Eastern history.

Mesopotamia and the Appearance of Cities

In the Near East the earliest development occurred in the area the Greeks called Mesopotamia, the lands lying between the Tigris and Euphrates Rivers but stretching north into Anatolia and south to the Persian Gulf (Map 1.3). Settlements first appeared in Anatolia in the northern part of Mesopotamia between 10,000 and 7000 BCE. These urban developments coincided with the retreat of the glaciers in the northern hemisphere, leaving Mesopotamia a lusher region than it is today. In northern Mesopotamia, annual rainfall was sufficient to support crops. Southern Mesopotamia (Sumer proper) remained drier and depended on the Tigris and Euphrates Rivers to flood in the spring to moisten fields and maintain soil fertility. Sumer was at the mercy of its great rivers;

sometimes they did not flood, and sometimes they overflowed at the wrong time, washing away valuable soils and crops and drowning fields. As early as 5500 BCE, farmers began to manage the great, but unpredictable rivers to irrigate their fields and protect them from seasonal flooding. Lacking rocks in that part of Mesopotamia, these peoples constructed levees of earth and used tools made of hardened clay. Large-scale irrigation projects necessitated advanced planning, organization, and cooperation between groups of people. The particular needs of southern Mesopotamia may, thus, have led farming peoples to experiment with the first forms of large-scale cooperation for the general good. Governments followed, first civic and then royal and imperial.

By 3300 BCE, while Ötzi was dying on a European mountain, Uruk on the Euphrates had grown into a recognizable city with impressive temple structures, meandering roads, and thousands of houses. Its large size (a population estimated at over 50,000) was supported by an agricultural economy producing surpluses and by satellite or dependent villages. By the third millennium most Mesopotamians resided in cities. There were twenty or so prominent cities in southern Mesopotamia (Sumer), among them Eridu, Uruk, Kish, Shuruppak, Akkad, Ur, Nippur, Sippar, Assur, Nineveh, and Babylon. The landscape of Mesopotamia—with its openness to invasion,

MAP 1.3 | Mesopotamia, 3000–2000 BCE
The geography of Mesopotamia was dominated by two rivers, the Tigris and Euphrates. Mesopotamia could be reached by land, particularly from the west, since the land there was unobstructed by natural barriers such as mountains. *How did the geography of Mesopotamia shape the early history of the region? Why did so many important cities arise there, and why did they play such a critical role in the history of the region?*

rivers both dangerous and life-giving, fragile climate, and need for trade—may have made city living the best option for coping with a demanding environment. If the creation of cities and urban cultures was southern Mesopotamia's first great invention, writing was its second.

The Invention of Writing

Writing was a product of an urbanized society that wanted a way to record economic information. Not surprisingly, numbers probably came into existence before the creation of characters or word-signs. Before the full emergence of writing, early Mesopotamians had introduced marked clay tokens and stored them in round clay containers to facilitate and record transactions. At Uruk after 3300 BCE these tokens were replaced by a system employing abstract pictographs (pictures of things) with an indication of the number of objects involved. Ideographs (pictures of ideas or actions) supplemented the pictographic base. By the second millennium BCE, Mesopotamian scribes introduced signs for sounds (phonograms). They inscribed signs on wet clay, the only

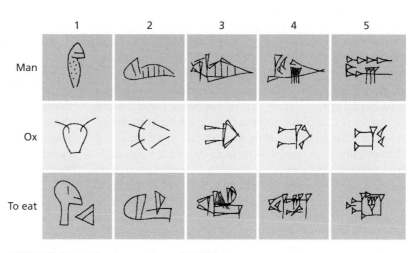

	1	2	3	4	5
Man					
Ox					
To eat					

FIGURE 1.1 | **The Invention of Writing**

widely available and inexpensive surface in Mesopotamia upon which to write. These clay tablets were then dried in the sun to form a fragile, perishable surface. To make a harder, more enduring surface for important records, the Mesopotamians heated or fired the inscribed clay tablets.

Mesopotamian scribes wrote in rows or columns left to right so as not to efface already inscribed signs with their right hands. After 3000 BCE, probably in order to write more quickly, scribes started to use a wedge-shaped stylus, which they pressed into the wet clay. This gave Sumerian writing an angularity and wedge-shaped look called cuneiform (from the Latin *cuneus,* or wedge). These inscriptions were more abstract in appearance and could be written and read only by trained scribes and priests (Figure 1.1).

Sumerian writing (both its original cursive form and later dominant cuneiform style) held sway for some 2,000 years in Mesopotamia and surrounding regions. Cuneiform writing was used to record a number of languages (Sumerian, old Persian, Semitic or Akkadian, and Elamite), making its modern decipherment difficult. The questions were two: what did the cuneiform signs mean, and what ancient language were they recording?

The Importance of Writing

The slow development of writing did not change the Mesopotamian world overnight, but it was a significant step in the establishment of civilization. Mesopotamian society still remained chiefly oral (as is our own). Writing became a specialized cultural tool, known and practiced by a select few. The differences between preliterate and literate societies are, however, considerable. In oral cultures, everything of importance to a group must be remembered or it is eventually lost. Ancient oral cultures developed cultural tools such as songs and encyclopedic poems that could be remembered and passed to the next generation, but oral poems are not fixed; they change from performance to performance. Moreover, there were limits on how much information could be packed into

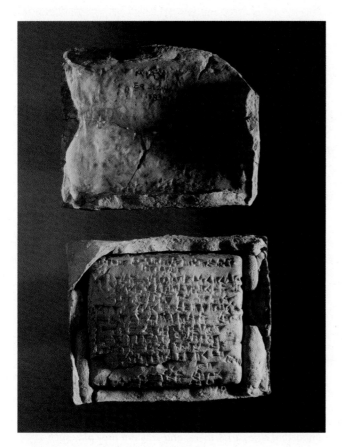

Cuneiform Clay Tablet A typical clay tablet with its clay envelope from Syria. The cuneiform or wedge-shaped writing on this clay tablet records the specifics of an inheritance.

Cracking Cuneiform

Thousands of inscribed clay tablets from the Near East survive, some in the older cursive script (3300–2500 BCE) and an even greater number of tablets in the cuneiform script (2500 BCE–75 CE). Rulers such as Ur-Nammu, Hammurabi, and the Persian Darius the Great left extensive records in their palaces. But cuneiform was so rich in symbols and conventions that recognizing it as a script and cracking its meaning was lost until the early seventeenth century CE when the great Persian capital of Persepolis was rediscovered and copies of these strange inscriptions were first published. Initially, scholars thought that these markings were purely decorative. Only in the eighteenth century did some scholars begin to realize that they were looking at a script, whose elements could be isolated and analyzed. Georg Grotefend, a German grammar school teacher, identified divisions between recognizable words and names in the inscriptions. Among the names he recognized were Darius and Xerxes. Grotefend did not crack cuneiform, but he did at long last establish that it was a form of writing.

In Iran, one remarkable late inscription had been carved high on a mountain at Behistun (modern Bisitun).

It was inscribed in three different forms of cuneiform (Old Persian, Babylonian, and Elamite) but was hard to read in its mountain setting. A nineteenth-century British adventurer, Henry Rawlinson, perched himself precariously on the mountainside to copy the inscription and hired an agile local boy to make plaster casts of the parts he could not reach. It took Rawlinson ten years to make a complete copy of the Behistun inscription, and not long afterward he was able to decode and translate Babylonian cuneiform writing. Unfortunately Rawlinson never explained how he had managed to crack one of the world's most complex scripts. He was a gifted linguist and knew many relevant old languages, which helped, but his awareness of the work of his predecessors and peers may explain both his breakthrough and his silence.[1]

QUESTIONS | *Why did writing first emerge in Mesopotamia? Why was the knowledge of such a widespread and long-lasting script lost, and what were the consequences of that loss?*

Rawlinson's Drawing of the Mountainside at Behistun

an oral song, and if the singer died before he could train an heir, the string of an oral tradition might be broken permanently.

Writing fixes information, absolving writers or their society from having to remember everything. Written records allow information to be stored and retrieved, hence, its economic and religious advantage. Writing produced, just as agriculture and permanent settlement had, new attitudes to the world and new forms of expression and behavior. Critical and rational thought depend, to some degree, on the reader's capacity to check information that lies beyond the spoken word. It is difficult in an oral and aural (hearing) world to verify what was previously said. Literacy fosters a sharper and more developed organization of thought. An awareness of different kinds of time—business, historical, and religious—depends on the existence of writing, for writing helps us to order events and transactions. The Mesopotamian merchant needed to know when and to whom he had traded his wheat and when the buyer was obliged to pay him in full. By moving away from an absolute reliance on memory, some Mesopotamians could preserve and arrange information, freeing their minds for other intellectual activities. Of course, something was lost as well, for oral societies are intimate and personal, sealed together by shared memories of events and stories. The song belongs to a community. By contrast, a written text is separable, belonging to individual readers, and can be put to a variety of selected purposes ranging from bills of sale to complex propaganda pieces such as royal inscriptions. In Mesopotamian society, writing was a tool that empowered priests and rulers. Writing was, in the beginning, concerned largely with economic information, but it proved to be just as useful in recording information about law, religion, and rulers.

Cities to Empires

By the third millennium BCE the developing cities of southern Mesopotamia established identities. Each had its own gods and rulers, often priests or priest-kings, and society was rigidly hierarchical. Kings, nobles, and priests, in that order, represented and had real power; soldiers, artisans, and farmers, in that order, represented the productive classes. Slaves stood at the bottom of society.

Southern Mesopotamian (Sumerian) cities varied in size from small (10,000 people or less) to very large (some with as many as 50,000–60,000 people). These city-states controlled a surrounding territory, including outlying villages. Their rulers were not all equal. Some were called lords, others governors, and others great ones (*lugals*). The *lugal* comes closest to being a king and ruled over the lords and governors of smaller dependent cities or communities. The *lugal*'s wife or *nin* (lady) also participated in public affairs. Their prominent partnership hints at the hereditary nature of the *lugal*'s dynastic claim to power. The *lugal*'s roles were many: religious, legal, and military. *Lugals* built complex palaces from which

they governed their kingdoms with the assistance of a palace government of servants and officials. They assembled armies composed of infantry and war chariots.

Agricultural Mesopotamia was a world at war, each city always on the watch for hostile moves by its neighbors, who were often only fifty or sixty miles away. The open geography of Mesopotamia made attack inevitable and sudden. The best long-term defensive strategy for any city was to conquer nearby aggressive cities. A stable balance of power between these cities was impossible to preserve; political instability was to be the Mesopotamian condition. The first city to shatter any rough balance of power and dominate many others was Kish, just south of present-day Baghdad. Around 2650 BCE the great city-state of Uruk, south of Kish, was led by Gilgamesh, whose exploits are remembered in a famous epic. If *The Epic of Gilgamesh* is to be trusted, Gilgamesh led Uruk in its conquest of much of Mesopotamia.

Over the coming centuries a series of city-states rose to dominance (Ur, Lagash, Elam, and Umma), before the rise of Sargon the Great. Sargon spoke a Semitic language and may have begun his rise in Kish as a servant of the king. Around 2350 BCE he overthrew the king of Umma and moved to consolidate all of Mesopotamia under his control. He founded a chief city at Agade or Akkad, after

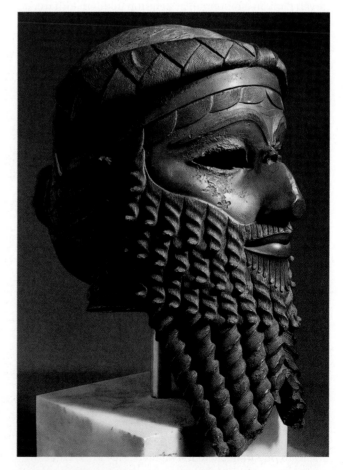

Sargon the Great A bronze bust of the founder of the Akkadian Empire of Mesopotamia.

which his Akkadian Empire is named. His was not a radical break with older southern Mesopotamian culture or governance, but in terms of its reach and prosperity Sargon and the Semitic Akkadians produced one of the first great empires of the ancient world. A century later, Sargon's grandson, Naram-Sin, declared himself and his ancestors gods and conquered territories throughout the Middle East (including Syria and Lebanon). The powerful Akkadian Empire dissolved after Naram-Sin's death.

Mesopotamia fell into a period of war between rival cities and faced a group of northern invaders known as Gutians, dragons from the mountains, as they were called in the south. By 2100 BCE, a ruler of Uruk drove the mountain men from Mesopotamia and was replaced by the famous Ur-Nammu, who created the last great southern Mesopotamian dynasty. It was Ur-Nammu who presided over the building of the famous **Ziggurat** (or temple structure) of Ur and laid down history's first law code, which survives in fragmentary form. Ur-Nammu's code specified payments rather than corporal punishments, even for many serious crimes.

By 2000 BCE the Ur dynasty had failed and Mesopotamia fell back into a period of wars between various cities that lasted almost two centuries. One of these warlike cities was Babylon on the Euphrates. Led by King Hammurabi (reigned c. 1790–1750 BCE), Babylon slowly conquered rival cities such as the fabled Mari with its immense palace of three hundred rooms and lush gardens. Hammurabi's Semitic or Akkadian language replaced Sumerian as the major language of Mesopotamia. Thousands of documents survive from Hammurabi's reign, but the most celebrated of these is his law code.

The **Code of Hammurabi** is not a set of universal laws, but rather specific decisions reached under Hammurabi's royal authority and useful to judges considering the disputes placed before them. The code was circulated on clay tablets and carved stone slabs or columns (stele). Half of the code, which contains almost three hundred legal decisions, concerns contract disputes and a third treats domestic matters. The Code of Hammurabi seems harsher than the Code of Ur-Nammu. Capital punishment was prescribed for a host of offenses, including adultery, robbery, incest, and kidnapping. If a matter could not be resolved from the evidence provided by witnesses, the accused was subjected to trial by ordeal or divine judgment. The accused was tossed into the river; the guilty sank, the innocent were able to swim to shore. Yet the presumption of innocence lies behind many of the cases in the document. The code drew sharp legal distinctions between nobles, commoners or dependents, and slaves, valuing the word and worth of nobles over the two lower orders. An individual who had physically harmed a noble was punished with the same injury, whereas an injured commoner could be paid compensation. The purpose of the code may have been less to set out a systematic law code than to demonstrate how a great ruler such as Hammurabi reached wise decisions and presided over a firm legal system.

Hammurabi Receives the Law On a stele containing his laws, the standing Hammurabi is shown receiving the laws or his authority from the sun god, thus indicating the divine origin and basis of his rulings.

After its peak under Hammurabi, Babylon prevailed until the Indo-European-speaking Hittites conquered it at the end of the sixteenth century BCE. Mesopotamia, surrounded by hostile peoples, was always susceptible to invasion because it lacked natural barriers to keep outsiders out.

Mesopotamian Religion

Prehistoric peoples doubtless had myths, legends, and religious beliefs of some complexity, but these are largely lost to us. The invention of writing in Mesopotamia marks the first sustained recording of religious belief, not its invention. Religious belief has always been part of the human condition, reflecting a desire to make sense of a mysterious world and to invest human existence with purpose.

The Mesopotamian peoples were polytheists (**polytheism** being the belief in many gods). They wanted to know about the nature of human existence and the gods, where and how humans live, what affects their lives, and how to appease the great forces that animate the world. They naturally thought of the earth as centered in Mesopotamia and ringed by its mountains and seas. Mesopotamians looked up to the sky and saw the home of heavenly bodies and looked down to the earth and imagined an underworld below it. The surface of the world, they thought, was alive with divine forces, in the water, in the air, and in living things. They conceived of a pantheon of gods, who were eternal and yet took human form. Thus, they offered their gods human food. Four principal gods, three males and a female (An, Enlil, Enki, and Ninhursag), created the world and represented the four elements: the ethereal sky, air, water, and earth. These four gods left their creation to their divine children (lesser gods, including the sun and moon) to administer. Mesopotamian religion was as hierarchical as society was. The gods were ranked and assigned numbers reflecting their importance and power.

The gods regulated human affairs. Wars, the destruction of cities, calamitous weather, and illness on earth were divine reckonings, and the lesser gods, the children of the great four, interfered with and haunted the world in which people lived. As agricultural peoples often are, the Mesopotamian peoples were convinced of the precarious and unpredictable state of the world: flooding rivers, droughts, disease, starvation, war, and early deaths seemed beyond their control, but not beyond the power of the capricious gods, whom the Mesopotamians sought to appease.

Agricultural prosperity paid for a class of priests and priestesses to serve the gods in their temples. People believed that the abundance of the land, the regular flow of the great rivers, and good weather depended on the favor of the gods, so Mesopotamian cities curried favor with the gods. Each city had its patron gods to whom it built temples and from whom it expected protection and prosperity in return. Inside these temples stood statues of the patron gods, whom the priestly class tended. Priests clothed the statues, sang hymns and prayers to the gods, and celebrated festivals in their honor. The people brought offerings for the gods, but it fell to the priests to prepare daily meals for the gods. Most Mesopotamians rarely if ever glimpsed the great statues.

Kings and powerful men allied themselves with the gods and eventually assumed a priestly function, subordinating the priestly class to state or palace needs. A southern Mesopotamian (Sumerian) king list (from the third millennium BCE) mixes divine kings, legendary kings, and real kings together as though they constituted a divinely sanctioned line. *The Epic of Gilgamesh* is not only the world's first great literary work, but also an example of the meshing of royal and religious persons. Gilgamesh, who was a real ruler of Uruk, is more god than man in the epic. He is also cruel, wanton, and tyrannical, but nevertheless a hero. Ancient heroes were not pleasant people one wanted to emulate, but rather tough superhuman figures beyond mortal reach. In the epic, Gilgamesh saves Uruk from destruction and tests the limits of human mortality. The epic gave Sumerians a look inside the divine forces that encircled their lives and determined their fates. People believed not that they would go to heaven or hell after death, but rather to an underworld. The living sent their deceased loved ones off to the lower world with the things they thought they would need there, but they interred their corpses below their houses so that the dead would not return to haunt the living world above.

The Mesopotamians shared a set of fundamental myths or religious stories. They believed that the gods were once so angry with humans that they had unleashed a great flood to drown the world, but some breakaway gods thought that the punishment was too severe, so they ordered a good man to build a boat to rescue representatives of humankind and animal life. The flood story alerts us that some portion of the Mesopotamian religious narrative became the common property of Near Eastern peoples: creation, a garden of Eden, an underworld (Hades, or Sheol for the Hebrews), the fall, a great flood, and a divinely favored people.

The Lasting Stability of Ancient Egypt

Mesopotamian and Egyptian civilization emerged at almost the same time, with Mesopotamia in advance by several centuries. The two shared one essential feature: dependence on a great river complex and, thus, on agriculture. Beyond that, they had little in common. Even their rivers were different. The Nile was predictable; the Tigris and the Euphrates fluctuated wildly.

What were the chief achievements of Egyptian civilization, and what critical role did ancient Egypt play in the Mediterranean world?

Egypt's landscape and configuration made it less vulnerable to invasion than borderless Mesopotamia. Ancient Egypt had a longitudinal shape with a short hundred-mile stretch of delta open to the Mediterranean and seven hundred miles of river surrounded by forbidding deserts east and west and blocked to incursion at its southern source by dangerous rapids and waterfalls. Egypt's geography left it isolated and protected from frequent turmoil (Map 1.4). As a result, Egypt was more politically stable, confident, and self-sufficient than Mesopotamia, so much so that it became tradition bound. Why change what worked? Ancient Egypt was permanent, prosperous, and civilized; its civilization was not driven by vibrant and restless cities vying for power and domination. Ancient Egypt's stability and generation of wealth were critical elements in spurring development in the Near East.

The Nile and Egyptian Agriculture

The Nile was fed by the snows and spring rains of central Africa. Every July, like clockwork, the Nile flooded its banks, inundating the surrounding soils of Egypt and depositing a layer of fertile black mud. By November the Nile receded and farmers were able to plant crops that matured in March and April. So essential was the rhythm of the Nile that Egyptians divided their seasons into flooding, planting, and harvesting times and called Egypt "the black land," since their lives depended on the beneficial mud and 12,000 square miles of productive riverside.

Though the habitable and productive part of the Nile valley was thin (a band 5–25 miles along the river), the delta area at the mouth of the river, where the Nile broke into a fan-shaped series of rivers, supplied a different ecology that supported a larger population. Prior to 3000 BCE, Lower Egypt (the delta area from Memphis to the sea) and Upper Egypt (the rest of the river) were separate.

At the end of the Ice Age, the area of Egypt was wetter than today but climatically unstable. The warming temperatures and spread of the Sahara Desert transformed Egypt. Once various hunting and gathering peoples had moved freely across northern Africa, but the stabilization of the desert surrounding the Nile changed that. Wandering peoples settled along the thinning band of arable land along the Nile. There they built houses made of reeds on higher land beyond the reach of the annual floods. These peoples fished and hunted along the river and began to grow grain crops (emmer wheat and barley), figs, and flax.

The Nile focus of Egypt shaped Egyptian civilization. The river, not roads, was Egypt's means of transport

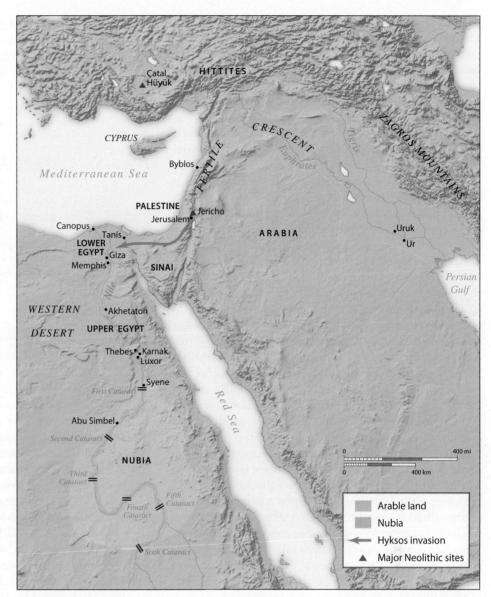

MAP 1.4 | Ancient Egypt and the Fertile Crescent

The Nile River lay at the heart of ancient Egypt. Its fertile banks stretched from Upper Egypt to Lower Egypt, ending in the fan-shaped delta where the Nile spilled into the Mediterranean Sea. The vast majority of the Egyptian population lived, farmed, and traveled along the Nile. Nubia contributed to shaping the culture of Upper Egypt, whereas Lower Egypt was early on in commercial contact with the lands along the eastern end of the Mediterranean and with Mesopotamia. *How was Egypt, unlike Mesopotamia, sheltered by natural barriers? What effect did such geography have on the history of Egypt? How was Egypt connected to the Mediterranean world and the Near East?*

and travel. Egypt was blessed with many more natural riches than Mesopotamia: Egypt possessed stone resources (for buildings and monuments), clay (for pottery and bricks), minerals (copper and gold), and semiprecious stones (turquoise, amethyst, and garnets). To obtain the few things it needed from outside, such as hard woods, Egypt had ample resources to trade.

Hieroglyphics and Egyptian Writing

Egyptian writing appeared around 3100 BCE, several centuries after Mesopotamian writing and different in character, but it is unlikely that it was an absolutely independent development. Word of the existence of writing in Mesopotamia, carried back by travelers and traders, may have spurred Egyptians to develop their own writing system. The Greeks called the Egyptian inscriptions they saw on stone monuments "sacred carvings" or **hieroglyphics,** but the term does not do full justice to the character of Egyptian writing or to the variety of surfaces on which Egyptians wrote.

Egyptian writing started with pictographs, as had Mesopotamian writing, and retained the appearance of picture writing, but from the beginning it also possessed signs for the sounds of consonants (phonograms). There are twenty-four of these consonantal signs. Hieroglyphics, however, remained a complex system that mixed together pictographs, phonograms, logographs (whole word signs), and ideographs, to which were added determinatives, small signs that gave a specific meaning or twist to standard signs.

Hieroglyphics, the original Egyptian script, continued in use for three millennia. Its more than seven hundred signs were painted on walls, carved into stone monuments, and written on other surfaces. As Egyptian society developed, hieroglyphics became something of a formal, monumental, and prestige script. For quicker, more common writing, the Egyptians developed two cursive scripts: hieratic (c. 2000 BCE), which came to be used largely to record religious documents, and demotic, a still more popular and even more cursive script, employed for business and private writing.

There may have been a material reason for the development of cursive scripts: the Egyptians' discovery of another writing surface, this one soft and pliable. Papyrus, from which we take our word *paper*, is made from the papyrus plant, a bulrush or native reed that grew along the banks of the Nile. A longitudinal layer of split papyrus stalks was laid down and on top of it a horizontal layer of stalks; the two layers were then pressed or gently beaten together, releasing the glue-like resin of the pith of the papyrus stalks, binding the layers together to make a soft organic surface that was dried and treated to receive ink. The resulting material, soft and paper-like, could be written upon with ink using a reed pen (*calamus*). Because scribes could write more quickly, or cursively, on papyrus rolls (made by gluing together papyrus sheets), both the hieratic and demotic scripts followed. Papyrus became the chief writing surface of the ancient world, and for thousands of years its supply remained Egyptian, another special benefit of the wondrous Nile.

The meaning of ancient Egyptian writing was lost by modern times, just as the meaning of cuneiform had been. The discovery of the Rosetta Stone (now in London's British Museum) in Egypt by Napoleon's soldiers led to its decipherment. The Rosetta Stone contains an inscription written in three scripts (hieroglyphic, demotic, and Greek) and eventually allowed Thomas Young of England and Jean François Champollion of France to crack the hieroglyphic code. It was soon realized that, for much of three millennia, writing in Egypt had been an essential tool in preserving and promoting power and tradition in dynastic, religious, and economic matters.

The Dynasties Take Hold

Before 3000 BCE Egypt had evolved from several dozen village-centered regions in the delta and along the Nile to the separate kingdoms of Upper Egypt (including the older kingdom of Nubia, formed by peoples from Sudan who were famous for their use of the bow) and Lower Egypt. Egypt's long dynastic history began when the

CHRONOLOGY	The Egyptian Dynasties and Kingdoms	
DYNASTIES	NAME/PERIOD	APPROXIMATE DATES BCE
I–II	Early Dynastic	3050–2647
III–VI	Old Kingdom	2647–2124
VII–XIa	First Intermediate	2124–2040
XIb–XIII	Middle Kingdom	2040–1648
XIV–XVII	Second Intermediate	1648–1540
XVIII–XX	New Kingdom	1540–1069
XXI–XXV	Third Intermediate	1069–664
XXVI	Saite	664–525
XXVII–XXXI	Late Dynastic	525–332

two kingdoms were united about 3000 BCE. Since writing had been introduced at about the same time, Egypt entered history literally and dynastically at the same time. Traditionally Egypt is thought to have had thirty-one dynasties over the next twenty-seven hundred years, a run that ended with Alexander the Great's conquest of Egypt in 332 BCE. Though ancient Egypt's long history is subject to many divisions and subdivisions, the most convenient is into the distinctive periods of unity achieved during the Old Kingdom (2647–2124 BCE), the Middle Kingdom (2040–1648 BCE), and the New Kingdom (1540–1069 BCE). Between the kingdoms were intermediate or transitional periods of instability and disorder.

The first transitional period is the Early Dynastic (3050–2647 BCE), and the first ruler of importance is Narmer, who is credited with uniting the two kingdoms. The first great piece of Egyptian art is the Palette of Narmer, now in Cairo's Egyptian Museum. The two-foot-high piece of slate served as a surface for the making of royal eye-paint. The two sides of the tablet show Narmer's unification of the two kingdoms. At the top on both sides, two human-faced bulls representing Hathor, goddess of love and sexual pleasure, frame a building and glyphs of Narmer's name. Narmer, wearing the White Crown of Upper Egypt, bestrides one side of the palette, his hand clutching a mace about to fall upon the head of a defeated enemy whose hair he grasps. Looking down upon the conquest of Narmer, the solar god Horus (here a falcon, but also a personification of Narmer) sits atop and so subdues a bed of papyrus reeds representing Lower Egypt. An attendant carries Narmer's sandals, while below the king's feet his enemies flee.

The obverse has four registers, the second showing Narmer, wearing the headdress of Lower Egypt, followed by his sandal-bearer and preceded by an official

The Palette of Narmer

and standard-bearers; the group marches toward ten enemy corpses, the head of each man tucked neatly between his legs for a "head count." The third and largest register, formed of exotic beasts with their trainers, was the surface on which eye makeup was mixed. The bottom register shows Narmer as a bull trampling the enemy. By the time the palette was made, around 3000 BCE, many of the features of Egyptian history, culture, and art were already fixed and would remain constant for three thousand years. Narmer is depicted as large, godlike, symbolically powerful, and deserving of all the credit for unifying Egypt and conquering its enemies. The representation of figures on the palette is two-dimensional but highly stylized. Each segment of the human form is shown in unmistakable outline but distorted to emphasize its essential perfection: fingers of equal length, eyes full and frontal though shown in profile, and legs shown in walking position while the chest is flat and frontal. These conventions of Egyptian art would change little for thousands of years not just because they were grid based and repeatable, but also because Egyptians and their allmighty rulers (popularly called pharaohs because they were so named in the Bible) wanted to portray stability and continuity, the virtues of Egyptian culture and of its life-giving Nile.

Written records are sparse for the predynastic period, but they increase dramatically for the stable Old Kingdom, which lasted almost five hundred years. The rulers of the Old Kingdom were extremely powerful and regarded as gods by their subjects. Old Kingdom rulers commanded the construction of pyramids in the desert to receive their bodies for the journey to the other world. Royal bodies were preserved carefully by mummification and entombed, surrounded by everything that these royal gods would need on their journey to the other world. The size of the great pyramids at Giza suggests just how prosperous and powerful kings were around 2600 BCE. A pyramid might take twenty or more years to build; involve thousands of workers, who were probably peasants (not slaves) brought to the site from their farms during flood season; and the transport of immense blocks of stone from distant places and then up earthen ramparts to their place in the pyramid. The cost of constructing huge pyramids may have weakened the Old Kingdom dynasties and empowered their nobles over the long run. The problem with a weakened dynasty was that ultimately, if the king was unable to maintain a strict control over the Nile's irrigation and agricultural production, famines and revolts followed. Smaller pyramids late in the Old Kingdom were a sign of dynastic breakdown.

The Middle Kingdom period saw a change not only of ruling families, but also of the core set of Egyptian beliefs. Ra, the chief god, was now joined by Amon, out of which a conjoint god called Amon-Ra was created. Royal culture had become so pervasive and persuasive that it moved down the social scale. During the weaker Middle Kingdom, many came to believe that all Egyptians might travel to the other world, not just their divine rulers. They gravitated to the worship of Osiris, the god of the netherworld who had been dismembered by Set, god of the desert and chaos. Osiris's wife (and sister) Isis reassembled her husband-brother's dismembered body. Thus Osiris, as a divine mummy and visitor to the other world, decided who deserved a splendid afterlife and who did not. Nobles and even common people (if wealthy) were mummified and placed inside elaborate coffins with the things they would need for their afterlife. The Egyptian *Book of the Dead* prepared the living for their encounter with Osiris at the moment of death. Though Middle Kingdom Egyptians were apparently confident that they could be taught how to pass over successfully, the netherworld's horrors made this a serious rite of passage, for if they failed Osiris's examination, they would be ripped apart by a monstrous god (a combination of a hippopotamus, a crocodile, and a lion), a death eater who consumed the unworthy dead.

Around 1730 BCE the Semitic Hyksos people, who possessed superior bows, horses, and chariots, invaded the weak Middle Kingdom. The Hyksos conformed to Egyptian traditions and never tried to rule all of Egypt but were finally driven out of Egypt in 1570 BCE. The dynamic rulers of the New Kingdom mastered the new technologies, hired mercenary armies, and subdued dissent within Egypt. New Kingdom rulers marched on other lands, including Mesopotamia, Nubia, and Syria. The Hyksos episode may have convinced these kings that Egypt was more secure if it attacked outsiders before they could attack Egypt; the result was an Egyptian Empire of tributary states. These new rulers built elaborate underground tombs as a strategy to avoid the grave robbers who had plundered the pyramids. The Egyptian Empire of the New Kingdom period was short lived. A radical ruler by the name of Amenhotep IV (r. 1353–1337 BCE) declared that there was only one god, Aton, the life force of the sun, and forbade all other worship. The abrupt religious change unsettled Egyptians, compelling the state to heighten its domestic military presence and to loosen control over its tributaries. By the 1250s a new line of military kings (the greatest of them the long-lived Ramses II) restored order.

Egyptian Religion

With the exception of Amenhotep IV's preference for one god, the Egyptians were thorough-going polytheists. Their complex pantheon of gods is difficult to understand. Beetles (scarabs), reptiles, mammals, plants, and stars were all regarded as divine, treated as gods, and represented in half-human forms. Thus, Anubis, a god

Akhenaton/Amenhotep IV, Nefertiti, and the One Sun God A relief of Akhenaton, his wife, and children basking under the life-giving rays of the sun god, Aton. Note the egg-shaped skulls of the couple's children, a physical feature of their royal line.

of the underworld, is shown as a jackal or a man with a jackal's head. The Egyptians joined or fused gods to create composite gods. Some gods were greater than others. Ra (or Re) was the sun god who was particularly worshipped in the Old Kingdom, in which he was regarded as the father of the gods and humans. He was often presented as a falcon. Apis was the sacred bull who was supposed to have given birth to another creator-god, Ptah. Thoth, god of wisdom, learning, and magic, was deemed the creator of speech and writing and served as the scribe of the gods. For this reason, writing always had divine sanction in Egypt; by contrast, the Mesopotamians believed that they had invented writing, which was therefore a human or lesser art.

Egyptian rulers presented themselves as gods. On Narmer's Palette, the god Horus was not just a solar deity, but also Narmer's protector and another form of the king. When kings died their heirs identified with Horus, whereas the dead king was associated with or became Osiris, who represented the fertility of Egypt and the other world. Rulers took the names of various gods as their own, thus claiming the divine functions of the gods of the sky, earth, and netherworld. Egyptians believed that rulers were their best link to the divine and embodied **Ma'at** (justice, truth, wisdom, and harmony), principles that insured peace and prosperity for the land. Even the Nile maintained its life-giving seasonal rhythm because the king was a god and the gods were at peace with Egypt. Thus, kings were credited with Egypt's successes in good times, but they were blamed if famines and failure struck. State power flowed from the divine king;

C. 1350 BCE: Follow That Name

In 1353 BCE Egypt was calm and abundant. King Amenhotep III had constructed the elaborate Temple of Luxor and added to the immense temple structure at Karnak, both in honor of Amon-Ra and his divine family. Amon-Ra, the chief creator-god of the Egyptians, stood at the center of state worship. Amenhotep III's successor, however, withdrew personal and state support from Amon-Ra, not only replacing the great god with another, but dismissing all the other gods. Radical change in ancient Egypt was so unusual that it is worth thinking about how and why this occurred.

Amenhotep IV succeeded his father and married (along with other wives) the alluring Nefertiti, who became his co-regent. Although he moved slowly at first, the new king developed a personal devotion to the god Aton, a solar deity or, rather, the life-giving energy of the sun. A few years into his reign, the king changed his name from Amenhotep (meaning, "Amon is satisfied") to Akhenaton ("devoted to Aton"). In this way he signaled to Egypt that he had transferred dynastic and state support from the cult of Amon-Ra to Aton. Some observers have suggested that he did this to undercut the traditional power of the Amon-Ra cult; its established and powerful priests; and the importance of the city of Thebes, where the old cult was enshrined. The "Great Hymn to Aton," however, makes it hard not to think that the king's worship of Aton was a deeply personal cosmic insight. Akhenaton built temples to Aton that let the sun's rays flow into his shrines and established a new capital named Akhetaton ("horizon of Aton"). If the king had stopped there, he might have met little resistance, but he soon ordered the destruction of images of, and forbade mention of, Amon-Ra and the multitude of other Egyptian gods. Akhenaton styled himself the sole earthly son of Aton, the one god, and invited Egyptians to worship Aton through him. Little of this was popular.

The transformation of Egyptian polytheism into a form of **monotheism** (the belief that there is but one god) or **henotheism** (a preference for one god while still allowing for the existence of other gods) might have taken hold and endured had it had a longer time to root and won dynastic and priestly support. But Akhenaton was succeeded by young King Tutankhaton (1336–1327 BCE), the famous King Tut, whose intact tomb was discovered by the English archaeologist Howard Carter in 1922 and whose dazzling treasures were sent on a world tour in the 1970s. King Tutankhaton was only eight or nine years old when he came to power. He was surrounded by powerful advisors who swayed the weak king back to traditional Egyptian religion. The king changed his name to Tutankhamon ("the living image of Amon"); was worshipped as a living god (or the personification of one); and relocated his court to Thebes, where the cult of Amon-Ra was restored to its former place of prestige and power. Egypt was back. Tradition had won out over dramatic change. Poor King Tutankhamon died before he was twenty, apparently of malaria and a broken leg that turned gangrenous.

QUESTIONS | *Why was Egypt so resistant to change? Why might Akhenaton have promoted monotheism or henotheism? Was this truly monotheism or simply a radical reorganization of religion to enhance the king's power?*

his officials, including the superintendents or viziers, derived their authority from the king and through him from the gods. The viziers managed an extensive organization of bureaucrats, tax-collectors, scribes, and priests.

Living Ancient Egypt

Egyptians viewed their rulers not only as divine, but also essential to the health of the land. Nobles, who owned vast estates and were extremely wealthy, maintained their favored status by the king's pleasure. Common people were relatively poor, but because of the bounty of the Nile they survived and accepted their lot. The range of common occupations was great, with farmers dominating; but there were house-builders, painters, artisans, jewelers, and merchants. There were few slaves, and these were mostly foreign men and women captured in wars.

Commoners were, by necessity and limited resources, monogamous; marriage for them consisted of starting a new home away from their parents. Nobles, however, might maintain harems of slave girls and concubines. Royal marriages differed from those of others in one significant aspect. To keep the dynastic line pure and connected to the gods, kings wished to remain unsullied by common blood. Royal brothers and sisters could and often did marry. For this reason, Egyptian queens, sharing in royal and divine blood, were more powerful than the royal women of Mesopotamia and several of them became rulers. The most important of these was Hatshepsut (1472–1458 BCE), who ruled in her own name

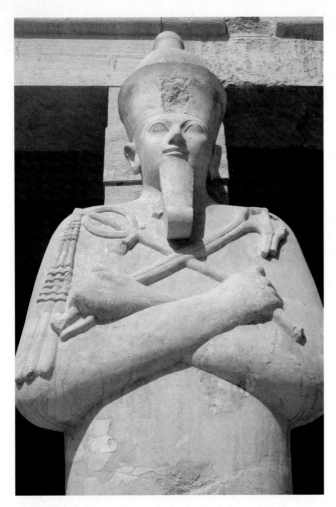

Bearded Hatshepsut On this formidable mortuary representation, the female king Hatshepsut wears, as do the other rulers in the sequence of statues, a royal beard to indicate her traditionalism, preeminence, and power as the ruler of Egypt.

Egyptian Harvesting Scene A painting of the harvesting of wheat, a tomb symbol of prosperity and the bounty of the Nile.

preoccupation with public presentation and the surface appearance of life. The image of unchanging perfection preserved on faces, bodies, paintings, pyramids, and tombs was cultivated for the sake of maintaining tradition and easing entry to the other world, but it was also a facade that hid harsher realities. The mummified remains of Egyptians tell a story of bodies that paid a heavy price for enduring a searing climate, of diseases that terminated lives early, and of teeth worn down over a lifetime from chewing foods laced with sand. The Egyptian experiment worked because of a successful and exacting mastery of the unique bounty of the Nile, and it worked as long as the Nile's price was paid.

as the "king of Upper and Lower Egypt and daughter of Ra." Official portraits depict her with a beard. Egyptian women had the right to own property in their own name. Noble women were educated and might become scribes and priestesses. Peasant women worked on farms alongside their husbands and were kept busy at other times making clothes, bearing children, and cooking.

The farmer's diet was a sparse one, based on drinking beer and eating bread, a few vegetables, and some protein in the form of fish and eggs. The noble diet was almost limitless: fancy fruits, deer, duck, cheese, butter, and honey. Nobles, however, might for religious reasons avoid eating pork and fish. The priests, who offered up banquets of rich food and drink to the gods three times a day, ate the unconsumed food and ended up with blocked arteries, high blood pressure, and premature heart attacks. So say their mummified remains.

Upper-class men and women wore wigs (men wore them over shaved heads), applied cosmetics to their faces, and applied perfumes, customs that reveal the Egyptian

An Age of Bronze Turns to Iron

The appearance of bronze (an alloy of copper and tin) was coincident with, but not the cause of the appearance of civilization in Mesopotamia and Egypt. As a metal, bronze was used to make luxury goods and armaments, not farm implements. Bronze suited an aristocratic age, but had limited uses for agricultural economies. The so-called Bronze Age ran from 3000 to 1200 BCE, when iron first appeared. The second millennium BCE belonged not only to Mesopotamia and Egypt, but also to a series of peoples in the eastern Mediterranean: the Minoans, Mycenaeans, Hittites, Phoenicians, and mysterious **Sea Raiders** (Map 1.5 on p. 26). The appearance of iron, a more useful metal than bronze, toward

> How can we account for the collapse of the eastern Mediterranean economy late in the second millennium BCE?

The Might of Egypt Seen from Outside

In the 1880s an old woman discovered a cache of some 380 clay-tablet letters in Egypt at Tell el-Amarna, once the site of Akhenaton's capital of Akhetaton. The letters belonged to the Egyptian royal archives and had been written in the Semitic Akkadian language (not Egyptian) in cuneiform characters (not hieroglyphics) by Canaanite and Palestinian scribes. The correspondence between Egyptian kings and Near Eastern rulers and their agents dates from the 1380s to the early 1350s BCE, during the reigns of Amenhotep III and his son Akhenaton. This concentrated collection of administrative correspondence bears witness to the international reach of ancient Egypt. Near Eastern rulers from the kingdoms of Babylonia, Mitanni, and Assyria wrote to the Egyptian kings offering their deep respect and seeking favors: gold, military support, protection from Egyptian mistreatment of foreign merchants, and Egyptian princesses to marry into their families. In return, they offered loyalty, service, and gifts. The language of ancient diplomacy is ornate. For instance, the ruler of Tyre, writing to Akhenaton, begins by saying that he has prostrated himself on the ground seven times before the king, calls himself the dirt under the feet of the sun god king, and praises the royal sun god's splendor in shining on his servants and dependent lands. He promises to preserve Tyre for Akhenaton until he can bless the city with a visit. Ninety percent of the letter is devoted to praising the Egyptian king's power and humbling the sender. Only in a final small passage does the ruler of Tyre pass along some insignificant news. Petty rulers were pleased to report on rebel and criminal activity, to accuse their rivals of treachery against the Egyptian dynasty, and to defend themselves against similar accusations.

One sequence of letters informed the Egyptian king that a certain Lab'aya ("the lion-like") in Palestine was threatening to seize the city of Megiddo (south of Tyre) and to compromise Egyptian interests. Lab'aya wrote to King Akhenaton to defend himself, accusing his accusers of undermining him and Egypt's interests. The Amarna archive suggests that Egypt's power and influence, its extensive wealth and military strength, elevated it to a position as the great arbiter of Near Eastern affairs, but its relative isolation left it prey to the complaints and neediness of a turbulent Mediterranean world. Power depends not just upon a solid command of information, which in the case of Lab'aya was a difficult matter of weighing self-interested, competing reports, but also upon a willingness to intervene decisively in foreign lands. This Egypt tried not to do.

QUESTIONS | *What cost did Egypt and the Near East bear because of Egypt's might? Was Egypt a paper tiger?*

---

the end of the second millennium BCE pushed eastern Mediterranean civilization in new directions.

The Minoans

Chiefly known from the palace ruins discovered on Crete by the archaeologist Arthur Evans, the Minoans were named after the legendary King Minos of Crete, the son of the god Zeus and Europa. By the start of the second millennium, Crete was enjoying the prosperity of the eastern Mediterranean world. It had few natural resources of its own, but its location in the eastern Mediterranean suited it to conduct sea trade. Aside from native olive oil, Crete chiefly supplied finished luxury goods such as ceramic pots and finished jewels to the outside world. Minoan merchants acquired metals, semiprecious stones, and raw resources from the lands ringing the Mediterranean and established trading outposts that allowed them, for a time, to dominate sea trade. The Minoans employed a writing system called Linear A that so far has not been convincingly deciphered.

Minoan rulers built great palace complexes on opposite sides of the island, at Knossos to the north and Phaistos to the south. The complexes were multipurpose centers where officials conducted the island's business, stored and distributed goods, and maintained rich palace cultures. The sites were not fortified, suggesting Crete's relative isolation and a period of relative calm in the eastern Mediterranean. We know of Minoan culture chiefly from its buildings and art, which includes ceramic pots, terracotta figurines of women, small bronze bull figures, jugs, and carved jewels. Most striking of all is the fresco from the palace of Knossos (c. 1500 BCE) of an acrobatic bull-leaping scene. Historians generally regard Cretan society at the time as remarkably sunny and peaceful, which was the way Arthur Evans wished to present the Minoans. The story of the labyrinth with its monstrous Minotaur, the product of Minos's wife coupling with a bull, which fed yearly on seven Greek maidens and seven Greek boys, undercuts that pleasant image. There is also some evidence that cannibalism was once practiced at Knossos. The Greeks remembered the Minoans as aggressive and cruel.

We have, however, only a limited and impressionistic knowledge of the Minoans. They were apparently polytheists, but their religious beliefs were more private and less state-sponsored than those of Mesopotamia and Egypt. Their cults remain largely mysterious, including their devotion to a snake priestess or goddess shown grasping a snake in each hand. Nor do we have a good sense of the social and political character of Minoan power, because it does not figure in Minoan art. Unlike the Mesopotamians and Egyptians, the Minoans did not create a cult of ruler-worship.

Events around 1400–1350 BCE brought Minoan civilization to an end. Many people, in their search for the legendary lost city of Atlantis, have wondered if an earthquake or volcanic event overwhelmed the Minoans. The island of Thera (today Santorini), a Minoan outpost north of Crete, was hard hit by a massive earthquake around 1600 BCE that produced a tsunami that crashed against the shores of Crete. But that disaster occurred well before the collapse of Minoan civilization. In the end, Minoan Crete seems to have been undone by external economic and military forces, for the eastern Mediterranean was becoming a dangerous sea by 1400 BCE. At about that time a new language and new artifacts began to appear on Crete. Linear A texts had been written in the unknown language of the Minoans, but a **Linear B** script (based on Linear A) replaced it, recording transactions in a form of archaic Greek. Certain objects such as large swords and chariots associated with the warlike Greek mainland also appeared. The Greeks had arrived.

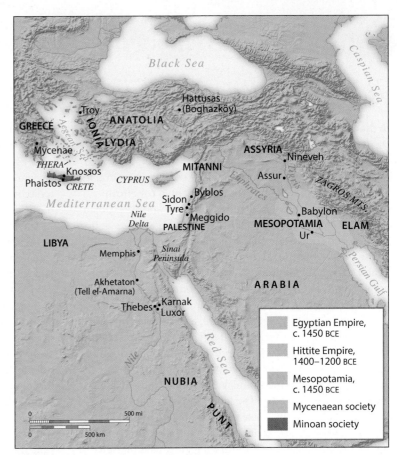

MAP 1.5 | The Near East, c. 1450 BCE
By 1450 BCE, the Near East was crowded with peoples and civilizations in competition with each other. *How did the presence of seas and deserts shape the development of civilization in the ancient Near East? Why might Crete have played a critical role in commerce and trade? Why was the eastern Mediterranean susceptible to piracy and conflict?*

The Mycenaean Greeks

After 2000 BCE, waves of Indo-European peoples began to migrate into the area of greater Greece. Mycenaean civilization was a widespread development in Greece that has been associated with the Peloponnesian city of Mycenae because of the nineteenth-century discoveries by the archaeologist Heinrich Schliemann. He discovered graves, dating from 1600 BCE to 1300 BCE, full of aristocratic objects and instruments of war. Unlike "peaceful" Crete, mainland Greece in the Bronze Age was a land of warriors and constant conflict. Mycenaean art is filled with scenes of war, and Mycenaean palaces, unlike those on Crete, were heavily fortified. Mycenaean sites of habitation were constructed on hilltops and surrounded by great stone walls. Contact with the Minoans had a formative effect on the Mycenaean Greeks. The adaptation of the Minoan Linear A script to Greek use in the form of Linear B is evidence of that influence, as is the development of Mycenaean pottery. After invading Crete, the Mycenaeans replaced the Minoans as traders in the

Bull-Leaping Scene from Knossos A Minoan fresco from the palace of Knossos on Crete that celebrates acrobatics and bull-leaping.

eastern Mediterranean and set up their own trading outposts. Trade and war, not farming, made the Mycenaeans wealthy, and that wealth can be measured by the rich grave goods found on mainland Greece.

The most memorable sequence of events of the Mycenaean Age was the so-called Trojan War, memorialized long afterward in Homer's *Iliad*. Troy, which dates from about 3000 BCE, was situated on the eastern shores of the Aegean Sea in Anatolia. The heavily fortified city of Troy, which was attacked many times, was inhabited by 5,000–10,000 Trojans, and besieged over many years by some 5,000 Mycenaeans who had crossed the Aegean in a hundred ships. Around 1200 BCE these Mycenaean Greeks destroyed the city. The Mycenaeans and their enemies took war to new levels of sophistication, in terms of both strategy and magnificent armor (bronze swords and spear tips, enclosed helmets, breast plates, body armor, and light wicker shields). Legend says that the Greeks eventually prevailed because of the clever deceit of the Trojan horse, which may have been a specially designed siege engine rather than a gift delivering Greek soldiers. The destruction of Troy was a sign of the troubles that came by sea to the eastern Mediterranean around 1200 BCE.

Reduced Mediterranean trade hurt the Mycenaean economy. But what may lie behind the unsettled conditions of mainland Greece was yet another series of Indo-European peoples penetrating Greece or moving south within Greece toward the sea. Among these Indo-European migrants were the Dorians, who preyed upon the established cities of Greece and overthrew their resident aristocratic societies. Mycenaean Greece came under attack from both land and sea after 1200 BCE. Around 1100 BCE Mycenae was sacked, and many Mycenaeans fled to Ionia, the safer shores of Asia Minor. The Mycenaean Age was over.

The Indo-European Hittites

Anatolia, at the northeastern end of the Mediterranean and lying along the northern frontier of Mesopotamia, was a hot spot of historical importance in the second millennium BCE. The Hittites, an Indo-European people from the north, moved into Anatolia around 2000 BCE and achieved political and linguistic dominance over the resident peoples. Many historians think that the Hittites dominated by inserting themselves into the area as a ruling elite with chariots, horses, superior political organization, and a richer language. The Hittites were quick to adopt local learning and cultural advances such as cuneiform writing and so have left us with thousands of written records. The Hittites established a kingdom that lasted for almost 500 years (c. 1650–1180 BCE), overcoming in time the non-Indo-European Hurrians, who controlled lands from Mesopotamia to Syria, and their Indo-European successors, the Mitanni. The Hittites also

fought the Egyptians to a standstill, preventing Egypt's annexation of Syria under Ramses II (r. 1279–1213 BCE).

The Hittites were polytheists, whose religious beliefs seem more Anatolian than Indo-European. Their gods were a quibbling lot constantly at war with each other and difficult to appease. The Hittites did produce a literature, but it is an eclectic body of writing, reflecting Hurrian and Mesopotamian myths. They also produced lists of the legendary deeds of their kings.

Sea Raiders Roil the Mediterranean

The Mycenaean Greeks' violent overthrow of the Minoans and Trojans was a symptom of the instability that overwhelmed the eastern Mediterranean and strongly suggests that Greeks were one of the mysterious Sea Raiders or Sea Peoples, though there are many candidates. Among the possible, suggested, and known raiders were various Indo-European groups, the Greeks, Hebrews, Philistines, Sicilians, and various others. It is likely, given the confusion of the records, that the Sea Raiders were several different peoples who participated in raiding during the turbulent last centuries of the second millennium BCE. The identity of the Sea Raiders may remain elusive, but their impact on the Near East was real, for these peoples did not just raid the coast: they penetrated inland, leaving ruined cities behind them. The Sea Raiders attacked Egypt during the reign of Ramses III (r. 1182–1151 BCE), but the king bragged that he had fortified the Nile delta with warships and walls and crushed the invaders. Nonetheless, the Sea Raiders ended the prospect of an expansive Egyptian Empire and were one of the reasons the eastern Mediterranean was a less-than-secure body of water by the end of the second millennium BCE. The Sea Raiders limited the Hittite supply line to the Mediterranean, leaving the overextended Hittite kingdom vulnerable to various hill peoples in Anatolia. As a negative force, undermining a stable economy and curtailing the Hittites, Egyptians, and Mycenaean Greeks, the raiders had a profound impact on early Mediterranean civilization, limiting its immediate growth and economic prospects. It is no accident that the Minoans, Mycenaeans, and Hittites all fell within a 250-year span, for the Sea Raiders preyed upon prosperity.

The Advantages and Effects of Iron

The Hittites were the first to manufacture iron, sometime around 1200 BCE in Anatolia. The discovery of iron came too late to save the Hittites, in part because early iron was brittle, could not be used to make sharp-edged weapons, and was expensive to produce. At first, iron was considered a luxury good more valuable than bronze. In 1327 BCE, King Tutankhamon was entombed with gold and iron daggers, as well as sixteen iron chisels, rare objects fit for a divine king. Iron was hard to find in its pure form and required a much higher melting temperature than bronze. By 1100 BCE, techniques for handling and improving the quality of iron began to spread throughout the western world. The cost of iron dropped dramatically, making iron tools possible. Iron spread not just geographically outward, but also socially downward. Bronze had belonged to aristocratic and warrior elites; iron would become a people's metal. Moreover, iron was a common trade good, and people in the early Iron Age were looking for goods to sell beyond their home regions. By contrast, the stable Egyptian agricultural system and the less stable, but still prosperous, Mesopotamian one never had a need for such extensive trade. The Phoenicians are an example of the success of Iron Age traders and the return of some economic stability to eastern Mediterranean civilization. The great changes to the eastern Mediterranean world—the fall of the Hittites, the disorder caused by the Sea Raiders, and the collapse of the economy—occurred before ironwork had been perfected. Iron was, however, to play a critical role in the economic recovery that began by 1000 BCE (Map 1.6).

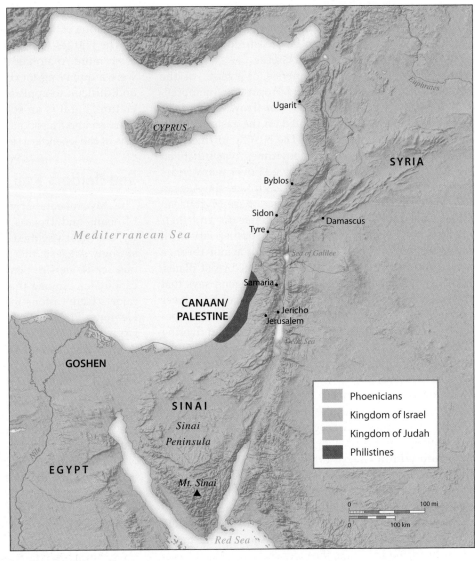

MAP 1.6 | The Eastern End of the Mediterranean in the First Millennium BCE
The kingdoms and peoples along the eastern coast of the Mediterranean were in close proximity to each other and vulnerable to attack and assimilation by each other and by the great empires of the Near East. *Why were the lands at the eastern end of the Mediterranean so crowded and prone to conflict? Why were these commercial peoples so vulnerable to attack?*

The Semitic Phoenicians

With the sea raids subsiding and iron economies and cultures spreading by the end of the second millennium, the eastern Mediterranean was ready for the rise of great trading powers. The fall of the Hittites not only left a power vacuum in Anatolia, which was filled by the Phrygians for the next five hundred years, but also left Syria vulnerable to rising powers. In the second millennium, the eastern end of the Mediterranean (the area today of Syria, Lebanon, Israel, and Gaza) was occupied by Semitic-speaking peoples including the Amorites and Canaanites, whose chief city was Ugarit. The Phoenicians, a Canaanite people known as the purple people (from the dark red dye for which they were renowned), inhabited the area that

is today Lebanon. Once the Sea Raiders ceased their banditry, the Phoenicians became the chief maritime traders on the Mediterranean. Rising to importance were prominent Phoenician cities, such as Sidon, Tyre, and Byblos (the great importer and exporter of Egyptian papyrus, from which the Greek word for book, *biblion*, derives).

Though purely mercantile peoples often have little lasting impact on civilization's major accomplishments, the Phoenicians did something critical. They adapted and spread a Canaanite writing system consisting of a Semitic alphabet of twenty-two characters, each of which represented a consonantal sound. The characters were originally pictographs; A or Aleph, for instance, represented an ox (Figure 1.2). By turning A upside down one can still see the ox's triangular head and horns: ∀.

The Phoenicians were famous for their glassware and beads. Their commercial ships were fitted with sails; their warships manned by oarsmen. The Phoenicians benefited from the growing prosperity of the eastern Mediterranean economy after 1000 BCE, but this part of the world remained a dangerous place to live and conduct business. The great empires of Assyria and Persia easily conquered Phoenicia in the first millennium. Only the Phoenician trading outpost and colony of Carthage retained its independence and vigor. Situated along the coast of northern Africa, Carthage lay just beyond the reach of the rising empires.

| North Semitic | | | Greek | | Etruscan | Latin | |
Early Phoenician	Early Hebrew	Phoenician	Early	Classical	Early	Early	Classical
K	K	X	A	A	A	A	A
9	9	9	8	B	8	B	B
1	1	1	1	Γ	1	C	
△	9	4	Δ	Δ	0	D	D

FIGURE 1.2 | Early Alphabet Characters

Source: Jerry H. Bentley, Herbert F. Ziegler, and Heather E. Streets-Salter, *Traditions and Encounters: A Brief Global History,* 2nd ed. (New York: McGraw-Hill, 2010), 22.

The Religious Breakout and Endurance of the Hebrews

They are all gone, all the civilizations, empires and kingdoms, and religions of early history—the ancient Mesopotamians, Egyptians, Minoans, Mycenaeans, Hittites, and Phoenicians—all except the Hebrew or Jewish people and their religion. They have endured in one form or another for over four thousand years, surviving one of the most dangerous regions of the world. How did they do it? One answer seems likely: that their religion and culture set them apart from the other peoples of the eastern Mediterranean world. The Hebrews abandoned the polytheism of their own early history and of all the other early civilizations of the Near East and Mediterranean world by making a pact or **covenant** with one God. That commitment prevented their complete absorption by any empire and the loss of their identity as a people.

Why and how did the Hebrews distinguish themselves from others and manage to endure?

Monotheism in its most rigorous form came slowly to the Hebrews. Their demanding beliefs bound them together as a people (ethnically, religiously, morally, and legally); politics did not. Political disunity haunted the Hebrews and left them prey to their many aggressive neighbors, but that political disunity, which is usually regarded as negative, may have played a positive role in the preservation of a culture and the endurance of a people, as did the mobility of the Hebrews. For political, economic, and religious reasons, Hebrews spread to other parts of the world, not so much to promote their religion, as to survive. They created the first great religion of a book, in their case the Hebrew Bible or Tanakh, consisting of the **Torah** (Genesis, Exodus, Leviticus, Numbers, and Deuteronomy), the Nev'im or Prophets, and Ketuvim or writings. These holy scriptures, composed over many centuries, record the sacred history of a people, although there is some question about their historical reliability. Yet Hebrew scripture remains the most detailed primary source we have of one people's experience of ancient Near Eastern history. The Hebrew Bible became the Old Testament of the Christian Bible and the monotheism of the Hebrews became the central belief of two other world religions, Christianity and Islam.

The Formative Phase: From Abraham to Moses

The Hebrew Bible supplies a detailed narrative of the history of the Jewish people, but we always need to

CHRONOLOGY The Hebrews

PERIODS AND PEOPLE	APPROXIMATE TIME BCE
Patriarchs	2000–1700
Moses and the Exodus from Egypt	1250
Judges	1200–1050
Reign of King Saul	1047–1007
Reign of King David	1000–970
Reign of King Solomon	968–922
Prophets	800
Babylonian Captivity	587

bear in mind that the Bible is not strictly speaking a historical source but rather a religious book, a sacred history. According to the Bible, Jewish history began with Abram, whose name God changed to Abraham ("father of many"). He departed from the Babylonian city of Ur sometime in the second millennium BCE. Biblical stories such as that of the great flood confirm a Mesopotamian origin for the earliest recollections of the Hebrews, who spoke a form of proto-Semitic, raised sheep, and were semi-nomadic residents of Mesopotamia. Abraham and his tribe may have begun their journey because of one of the frequent political disruptions that plagued Mesopotamia. Abraham, his son Isaac, and Isaac's son Jacob are known as patriarchs, each of whom found God and brought the Hebrews closer to fulfilling the divine plan. At this early stage not all the Hebrews were strict monotheists; it had always been possible within polytheism to prefer one god while allowing for the existence of other gods (henotheism). As late as the first millennium, Hebrews could still be found worshipping gods and goddesses such as El, Baal, and El's companion Asherah (a goddess represented as a tree). The Ten Commandments do not so much deny the existence of other gods, as place one God first in a special and direct relationship with the Hebrews. The patriarchs, however, vehemently denounced any worship of other gods by the Hebrews.

According to the Hebrew Bible, God struck a covenant or agreement with Abraham and the Hebrews, promising them that, after four centuries of tribulation and suffering, they would receive the lands between the Nile and the Euphrates as their own. For this promised land, God imposed circumcision upon his people as a sign of the special bond between them. Jacob was called an israel, a warrior for God, and to honor him the Hebrews took to calling themselves the children of Israel. Jacob's son Joseph was sold into slavery and sent to Egypt to begin a period of captivity for the Jews that may have begun as early as 1750 BCE. It was at this time that certain sources mention the existence of the Habiru or Hebrews ("the dusty ones") as a class of people performing manual labor in the great building campaigns of Ramses II. During the period of their captivity in Egypt, the Hebrews became manual laborers, farmers, and artisans, abandoning their earlier pastoralism. King Akhenaton's experiment with monotheism in Egypt and the Hebrew belief in one God were apparently unrelated.

Moses is a puzzling figure. His name seems Egyptian in origin, leading some biblical scholars to think that he was of Egyptian royal stock. The Hebrew Bible says that after his rescue as a baby from the bulrushes, Moses was reared by an Egyptian princess. After slaying an Egyptian master who was attacking a Hebrew slave, Moses fled to the Sinai Desert, where God spoke to him from a burning bush. There he learned from God that God's true name was YHWH, meaning "I am who I am." Though the Hebrew Bible generally does not give God's name fully in order to respect his mystery and sacredness, the Semitic peoples early on did not employ vowels in their consonantal writing system, so the expansion of the name has generally been rendered as Yahweh (Jehovah). The common expression *Hallelujah* thus means "Praise God" or "Praise Yah(weh)."

Moses led the Hebrews out of Egypt (the exodus) through the Land of Goshen (east of the Nile delta), across the Red Sea (the Sea of Reeds), south along the coast of the Sinai Peninsula, and then north along the Sinai coast toward Canaan. On Mount Sinai Moses received God's Law. God reinforced the covenant he had earlier made with the Hebrews, imposing upon them a special set of obligations and laws that set them apart from other peoples. There on Sinai, Moses received the Ten Commandments (the Decalogue) on two stone tablets, though the several records of these commandments vary in the number, order, and content of the commandments, perhaps suggesting later revision or interpretation.

God's renewal of the covenant with the Hebrews was a defining moment in Jewish religious history, for with it the Hebrews had their own legally based and religiously sanctioned legal and moral code, not unlike Hammurabi and the Mesopotamians before them. The Bible says that the Hebrews' exodus from Egypt took forty years, but numbers in the Bible are rarely trustworthy. Moses died before the Hebrews arrived in the promised land, a territory by then not defined as broadly as in God's original promise to his chosen people.

Led by Joshua, one of Moses's companions, the Hebrews invaded Canaan in a period known as that of the judges. The Bible provides different stories of the invasion. According to one, the invasion was a five-year military campaign by united Israelites, in which they conquered the city of Jericho, slaughtered and displaced the resident Canaanites, and laid siege to walled cities. In another account, various Hebrew tribes waged guerrilla warfare against Canaan over many years. One of the unexpected leaders of this conflict was Deborah. Dismayed by the direction of the war, she made a pact with the Hebrew general Barak to rally the Hebrews against the Canaanite forces in a battle in which the Israelites prevailed. Deborah's song (Judges 5, generally considered the oldest extant piece of the Hebrew Bible) celebrates not only the Hebrews' victory, but also the death of the Canaanite general Sisera at the hands of a Hebrew woman who, with trickery, promised to aid the fleeing general and then drove a tent peg into his skull. These were not pretty times, but the Hebrews settled Canaan, united only in their reverence for God and their sacred history. They stored the stone tablets containing the Ten Commandments in a sacred wooden box known as the Ark of the Covenant. To touch the Ark, even by accident, meant death, so sacred was the object. The Hebrew peoples took up farming and herding their flocks in Canaan and were firmly resident there by 1208 BCE, when an Egyptian king boasted that he had invaded Canaan and left Israel defeated.

Hebrew Seal from the Time of the First Temple A seal showing an archer and the inscription "for Hagab"—which dates to the time of the First Temple—was recently found in Jerusalem. Hagab is a name that appears in the Hebrew Bible.

Hebrew Singularities: The Struggle for Authority

To have survived their long exile, to have been delivered from Egypt, to have received through Moses the reconfirmation of their covenant with God, and to have been given the promised land of Israel all seemed to the Hebrews signs of God's continuing approval and protection. By this point in its history Judaism had arrived at its central beliefs: that God is singular, immaterial, and omnipotent; that God insists on the Jews' continued faithfulness; that God and the Hebrews are bound together by a covenant; and that to honor that covenant the Hebrews must scrupulously obey God's Law. The Hebrew belief that their relationship with God is singular, both religiously and historically, set them apart from other Near Eastern peoples and, at the same time, bound them together as a religious people.

Another of the singularities of the Hebrews was the scriptural basis of their religion. The Torah, the first five books of the Hebrew Bible, was a record not only of cosmic and historical origins, but one of laws, as well. The Torah was regarded as a divinely given code of instruction for living the covenant. The God the Hebrews meet there is a forbidding presence, one who delivers divine justice in the most exacting terms. Even the practical

human justice of "an eye for an eye, a tooth for a tooth" may seem extreme, but the same idea of equivalent penalties was present in Hammurabi's Code and served to curtail disproportionate punishment, preventing an escalation of violent revenge beyond the concerned parties. God's justice extends beyond punishment, for it also includes compassion for the downtrodden. Widows and orphans were to be protected and slaves to be saved from ill treatment. The entire Hebrew Bible was not brought together until late in the first millennium BCE in Israel, when most of the Bible's texts were written down. Certain key Jewish ideas emerged slowly over time: the hope of God's gift of a better future for a faithful people, the immortality of the soul, and the belief that there would be future resurrection.

Canaan—or Israel after the exodus—where these beliefs were maturing, was both a blessing as the promised land and a test for the Hebrews. Theirs was a totalized religion, one that governed all aspects of their lives. It specified dietary codes of permitted and forbidden (or clean and unclean) foods, mandated morality, and regulated religious observances such as the observance of the Sabbath and the practice of circumcision. A priestly class of religious authorities oversaw strict adherence to the terms of the covenant with God. But Canaan was an alluring land of milk and honey with a powerful native culture and delights that threatened to undermine strict religious observance. In the struggle to maintain religious uniformity and authority, prophets appeared in times of tribulation. They claimed that Israel suffered because the Israelites or their leaders had fallen away from strict obedience to God. A prophet was not so much one who predicted the future as a critic of evil times and evil ways. And troubles did arise repeatedly in the ancient Near East. In the 1050s BCE the Philistines, one of the Sea Raiders, invaded Canaan and attacked the Israelites, seized the Ark of the Covenant, and carried it away as a trophy.

Kings and Kingdoms

Though the Hebrews had a religious code that bound them together, they were divided into various tribes with different regional, familial, and political interests. The attack of the Philistines exposed the vulnerability of the Hebrews on the Canaanite coast of the eastern Mediterranean. According to their scriptures, the Hebrews asked the judge Samuel to approve a king. He chose the warrior Saul to lead Israel (r. 1047–1007 BCE). Unlike the Mesopotamians and Egyptians, the Israelites did not regard their kings as divine, but rather as men who had received divine approval to rule. The Hebrews consecrated their kings by anointing them with holy oil. Saul had some small success against the Philistines but was undermined by Samuel and a young warrior named David. Saul took his own life after a defeat by the Philistines, leaving the controversial young King David (r. 1000–970 BCE) to unite the Hebrew tribes.

David was, according to the Hebrew Bible, a bit of a rascal, who was prepared to sacrifice his people's interests to personal ones. He committed adultery with Bathsheba and secured the convenient death of her husband. But he was also an inspired leader and managed to capture Canaanite Jerusalem and make it his capital. He regained the Ark of Covenant and installed it in Jerusalem. Under his leadership, the Israelites expanded their territory to the southeast, but King David pressed the Hebrews hard for taxes and labor for his extensive building program, which made him at times an unpopular ruler. His son Solomon (who began his long reign c. 968 BCE) could be brutal and had a huge harem, but the Bible reveres him as a wise man and builder. The temple erected by Solomon was of Phoenician design and part of a grand palace complex. Solomon named twelve administrative units within Israel, taxed heavily, and forced men to do military service. By the end of the reigns of David and his son, Israel had a centralized royal government, a capital at Jerusalem, a temple that was the central institutional home of Judaism, and a larger kingdom. Jewish traders were now visiting Mesopotamia and Egypt, and Israel was producing iron for the new Iron Age.

After Solomon's death, the northern kingdom of Israel revolted against his son and the Hebrews were divided between a northern (Israel) and southern kingdom (Judah, from which come *Judaea* and *Jew*). These kingdoms were disrupted by dynastic disputes, foreign cultural influences, and biting prophetic criticism. The kingdom of Judah retained Jerusalem, emphasized the importance of the temple, and was rigorously monotheistic. The kingdom of Israel, which was under the commercial influence of the Phoenicians, was more prosperous. At about this time, the Hebrews adopted the Phoenician alphabet and began to write down the books that would comprise the Hebrew Bible.

Empires and Diaspora

Even if the Hebrews had remained politically united, it is unlikely that they would have been able to resist the rising empires of Assyria and Babylon. The Assyrians were a Semitic-speaking Mesopotamian people who devoted themselves to war. Their chief gods, Ishtar and Assur (after whom they were named), were gods of war, and the Assyrians introduced standing armies, improved weapons made of iron, and mounted soldiers. By the eighth

century BCE the Assyrians had conquered Damascus and began to harass the kingdoms of the Hebrews. They captured Samaria, the capital of Israel, around 722 BCE, killed or drove into exile the Hebrews who lived there, and abolished the northern kingdom. The southern kingdom capitulated, but in 701 BCE the Assyrians attacked Jerusalem, withdrawing only when paid. The Assyrians then turned their attention to Egypt and forced it into submission by the early seventh century BCE. As the overextended Assyrian Empire declined, the Hebrews resisted as best they could, but it was not until the Babylonians under Nebuchadnezzar (r. 605–562 BCE) crushed the Assyrians that the Hebrews saw their opportunity to revolt. When the plan was discovered, an angered Nebuchadnezzar marched on Jerusalem, violated the temple, and stripped it of its religious artifacts. Nebuchadnezzar transported back to Babylon many high-status Hebrews as his captives, beginning the so-called Babylonian Captivity of the Hebrews. When the Hebrews revolted again, Nebuchadnezzar destroyed the temple and displaced an even larger number of Hebrews. The prophet Jeremiah called upon the Hebrews to await the appearance of a messiah, an anointed ruler who would with justice and wisdom return Israel to its promised land.

The Assyrian and Babylonian attacks marked the beginning of the **Diaspora** or emigration of the Hebrews from Israel to other lands. The wanderings of the Jews may have strengthened rather than imperiled the Hebrews and their religion. Without the close presence of the temple to govern their lives, the exiled Hebrews turned to their sacred scriptures as a guide to preserving their special identity in lands of idolatrous and hostile others. The Hebrews had always understood suffering as something demanded of them by their God. The Book of Job tells of a man forced to lose his entire family and all his possessions and to undergo physical torment rather than forsake his God. Abraham faced the same dilemma when he was ordered by God to sacrifice his son Isaac. The overriding commitment of the Hebrews to the word of God, no matter the suffering and sacrifice asked of them, allowed the exiles to endure their condition, to preserve their unique identity, and to hope for the fulfillment and deliverance promised by their covenant with God. While the other civilizations of the early ancient world were overthrown and absorbed by greater cultural and political forces, the Hebrews because of their singular religious identity and core beliefs proved largely immune to assimilation and endured.

Conclusion

In late prehistory and early antiquity *Homo sapiens sapiens* became the dominant species of the globe. Nature played an important role, since if the weather had not changed with the retreat of the last Ice Age, it is hard to imagine the spread of the species and the change of human lifestyles

that occurred in the Fertile Crescent. That these changes were climate driven and not culturally or racially specific seems evident from the fact that they occurred not just in the Near East, but across the globe, in the Indus Valley, China, and the Americas. The geographic setting of the

Tigris and the Euphrates in Mesopotamia and the Nile valley in Egypt shaped the specific economies and cultures that developed there, one unstable, the other stable; one competitively creative, the other traditional and long-lasting. These two cultures were on almost the same developmental schedule, with Mesopotamia out in front by a few centuries. Geographic proximity was an important element in the spread of higher civilization, cross-fertilizing ideas and people. The particular geography of the eastern Mediterranean Sea played a role, allowing for easy contact among the peoples of Egypt, Anatolia, Iraq and Iran, and the island of Crete.

Contact and competition—military, cultural, and religious—among these peoples made the Near East a hotbed of historical development. Those who forced advantageous change reaped rewards. Egypt's model for continued success, based on tight control of the bounty of the Nile, encouraged it to keep things the same, to emphasize tradition and regularity; its art and political system were designed to perpetuate continuity, at least on the surface. The Hebrews discovered a similar model based on the radical religious idea that as a people they had an enduring contract with one God. That all-encompassing belief allowed them to survive while all other Near Eastern peoples changed into something else or disappeared.

Humans achieved civilization through their special ability to adapt to and alter various environments, their capacity to organize into groups, and their expanding accumulation of knowledge that was preserved and conveyed to future generations. In hindsight we can see that each of these contributed to making some human societies more sophisticated and successful than others.

The pairs of necessities for civilization (settled life and a critical mass of people, sustainable agriculture and trade, government and law, writing and abstract thought) came slowly in prehistory, compared to the pace of subsequent change, but they were critically important advances in the human experiment. Settlement and a sufficient mass of people were achieved in late prehistory, reaching a critical takeoff point in Mesopotamia in the fourth millennium BCE. Agriculture and trade produced the food and goods needed to support a growing and settled population. Law and government came early as well in the law codes of Ur-Nammu and Hammurabi and the religiously sanctioned laws of the Hebrews. Writing and abstract thought developed together and were spurred by the economic explosion of the same period. Writing gradually transformed the range and capacities of human thought and, perhaps more important, provided a way to break free of the limitations of individual and small-group memories and slow development, allowing human societies to preserve and convey information over generations and civilizations. Religious belief was a constant throughout early history, its dominant form being polytheism or the belief in many gods. Monotheism was at the time an outlier, but one with a future.

Government in early history took on many forms, but as eastern Mediterranean society thickened with peoples, resources, and skills, empires (Akkadian, Egyptian, Hittite, Assyrian) came to dominate, crushing, if they could, all rival powers before they were crushed. This imperial phase of early history, as brutal and sweeping as it might seem to us, contributed to the spread of ideas, peoples, and technologies around the eastern Mediterranean.

Critical Thinking Questions

1. Why are prehistory and early history particularly important to the human story?
2. Why were the Near East and the area at the eastern end of the Mediterranean Sea such early and turbulent sites for the emergence of civilizations?
3. What roles did chance and choice play in the rise and fall of various peoples and civilizations?

Provide specific examples and explain why they matter.
4. What historical patterns emerged in the period 3200–1000 BCE?
5. How "civilized" was early civilization?

Key Terms

cuneiform (p. 5)

civilization (p.5)

prehistory (p. 6)

Mitochondrial Eve (p. 6)

Genetic Adam (p. 6)

sedentism (p. 9)

Agricultural Revolution of Prehistory (p. 10)

henge (p. 11)

Ziggurat (p. 17)

Code of Hammurabi (p. 17)

polytheism (p. 17)

hieroglyphics (p. 19)

Ma'at (p. 22)

monotheism (p. 23)

henotheism (p. 23)

Sea Raiders (p. 24)

Linear B (p. 26)

covenant (p. 29)

Torah (p. 29)

diaspora (p. 32)

Primary Sources in connect

For information on Connect and the online resources available, go to **http://connect.mcgraw-hill.com**.

1. Two Early Law Codes
2. The Egyptian Book of the Dead
3. The Great Hymn to Aton
4. A Summary of Hebrew History and the Covenant
5. Two Versions of the Ten Commandments
6. The Song of Deborah

The Venus of Hohle Fels

The small (2.4 inches in height) carving of a female figure, made from a woolly mammoth's tusk, discovered in 2008 in Germany, has been dated to 40,000–35,000 BCE. The figurine belongs to a group of Paleolithic Venus figurines, most of which bear similar features. Some researchers have claimed that the Venus of Hohle Fels, because of its early date, is the oldest surviving piece of western and world "art."

The Venus Figurine of Hohle Fels

QUESTIONS | *What does the carver emphasize and why? Is the piece best thought of as art or as a cult object, one that chiefly had religious meaning? Why? Why does the figure lack a head but have a perforated knob at the top?*

2

The God Dionysus Delivering Grapevines and thus Viniculture to Greece on an Athenian Black-Figure Drinking Cup

MANY GREECES

Darkness Descends
    After the Mycenaean Collapse
    The Iron Age Arrives
    Homer, Whoever He Was
    Was the Greek Alphabet an
    Accident?

The Archaic Age Breakout
    The Olympic Games and Delphic
    Oracle
    Archaic Age Emigration: Homes
    away from Home
    Dirty Politics and Hesiod's
    Discontent
    Tyrants, Reformers, and Military
    Change
    Archaic Age Economies and
    Cultures
    The Conflicting Pulls of Pan-
    Hellenism and Polis-Centrism

The Persian Wars
    The Persian Empire

    Lydia and the Ionian Greeks
    The First Persian Invasion of Greece
    The Interwar Years
    The Second Invasion

Mature and Major City-States
    Sparta, the Radical Polis
    Corinth, the In-Between Polis
    Thebes, the Federalizing Polis
    Athens, the Democratic Polis
    Living on the Margins of the
    Greek Polis

The Peloponnesian War
    The Delian League
    Pericles and the Outbreak of the
    War
    The Long Second Phase of the War
    The Brief Golden Age of Athens

Conclusion

THE WANDERINGS AND WARNINGS OF HERODOTUS Herodotus (c. 484–425 BCE) of Halicarnassus (along the coast of Asia Minor) has been called the father of history and the father of lies. He was neither. He did write the world's first great narrative history and described his work as *historiai* or "inquiries," from which comes our term *history,* but he did not think of himself as a historian. The field of historical inquiry didn't exist at the time, and he didn't work from written records. Nor was he an especially notorious liar. He lived, after all, in the age of Pericles, the wily Athenian politician who so brilliantly and so often stretched the truth.

Herodotus was above all a marvelous storyteller. The great Greek battles of Marathon, Thermopylae, and Salamis are so vivid because of his stirring accounts of them. His histories are a strange and delightful mixture of inquiries: travelogues; ethnographies; anthropologies; and oral, religious, social, art, and sexual sketches. At times, his work has the prurient quality of a tabloid, revealing the private lives of the powerful. He tells us the story of the king of Lydia, who induced a minion to gaze secretly upon the naked body of his queen. The queen then compelled the voyeur to murder the king and assume his place since he had seen her whole.

Herodotus wrote to inform and entertain, to take the Greeks beyond the glorious imaginings of Homer into the strangeness of foreign lands and customs. Only from the outside, Herodotus may have thought, could the many Greeks see Greece whole. His history, however, constantly confirms that there was not one Greece, but many. Hundreds of city-states (**poleis;** singular, **polis**) existed within Greek lands (around 1,500 poleis have been identified in Greece and around the Mediterranean in the archaic and classical periods),[1] each with its own deep history and fiercely guarded independence. These small states had been at war with each other for centuries, and a great new war between them was building during Herodotus's stay in mid-fifth-century BCE Athens. He knew of the ancient grudges and feuds of these small states, of unforgotten slights and disgraces, and of their various plans to undermine and secure advantage over each other. The *raison d'être* of the people or nation (*ethnos*) of every city-state was to preserve its separate and autonomous existence against its many Greek enemies. In the midst of so many different Greeces, the most Herodotus could hope for was a united nations of Greece, but the many Greeces ruled the day, not the united nations.

Herodotus took his Greek audience on a grand tour of a world filled with peoples who lived dramatically different lives. Herodotus wanted to show the Greeks why the Persian Empire had invaded Greece and how freedom-loving Greeks had managed to thwart the imperial giant. To discover the background of Near Eastern history and the roots of the Persian invasions, Herodotus traveled to foreign lands, visited temples, saw pyramids, and questioned foreigners (through translators). He sifted stories and never hesitated to repeat a good one, even when he knew it to be untrue. His willingness not to privilege his own opinion or the truth makes him seem deceptively modern as he mixes together the real and the reported, the fanciful and the revealing.

Herodotus's style is lively, animated, and a comfortable one for us, as he digresses from the main story to explore some gripping house history, some tick in a king's life, or a bizarre local custom. He was intensely interested in people, their virtues and vices. But the reader only slowly becomes aware of Herodotus's systematic and categorical approach. He treats each foreign land in a similar way: its geography; animal life; and people and their origins, language, gods, customs, food, marital and sexual relations, and funeral rites. From Herodotus the Greeks learned fascinating things:

Herodotus, the Storyteller A marble bust of the author of the *Historiae*.

the Egyptian devotion to cats, fantastic animals such as crocodiles, and foreign customs such as the mummification of the dead and the strange information that Egyptian women urinated standing up, men while sitting down. He reports that in Scythia (the extreme north of cultural difference from Greece, while Egypt holds the extreme south) people told stories about men with goats' feet, people who sleep for a half a year every year, and a race of one-eyed men, but he dismisses these as fanciful stories. Herodotus was not just teaching the Greeks about foreigners, but explaining the many Greeces to the many Greeks.

In writing his large, wandering, and woolly book, Herodotus seduces us with his delightful entertainments, leading us away from seeing his deeper design. Geography matters a great deal to him. The continents of Europe, Asia, and Libya (Africa) belonged in his view to their resident peoples; lands and peoples are fitted together inseparably. The fatal Persian mistake was an immoderate violation of the natural and divine order of things by stepping outside of Asia. Herodotus thinks the same of people who breach the bounds of natural justice.

Herodotus neither feared nor despised foreigners; rather, he regarded the Lydians, Scythians, Egyptians, Babylonians, and Persians as living strange, but legitimate lives that were normal for them within their appointed places of abode. A message of warning lurks ever so softly in Herodotus's great entertainment. His audience was Greek, particularly the Athenians who were then caught up in their own immoderate imperial drive, which would lead to the disastrous Peloponnesian War, and his message of moderation to them was the lesson of the Persian Wars: that unbridled imperialism was an unnatural thing that threatened the freedom and established contours of Greece and its city-states. During the build-up to the war, the Spartans and Peloponnesians had been claiming much the same, that the Athenian drive for imperial dominance violated the legitimate and traditional rights of other freestanding, long-established Greek states. The weakness lay within the Athenians, as it had within Darius and the Persians; imperialism was an external sign of the internal failings of greed, pride, and poor judgment. Athens was on its way to becoming Persia, violating the appointed limits of Greek life. As quietly as he could, Herodotus warned the Athenians that their path would lead to defeat and destruction, and so it did.

❋ ❋ ❋ ❋

Ancient Greek history is a story of the many Greeces within Greece changing over time and space, polis by polis (or city-state by city-state), region by region, each place having a claim to be a freestanding end point of Greek history.

Classical Greek history of the fifth century BCE was the end product of the **Dark Age,** about which we know far too little, and the **Archaic Age,** which immediately preceded the **Classical Age.** The effect of Greece's geography and the depressed economic conditions of the Dark Age gave the individual city-sized areas of Greece the freedom and isolation to develop independent ways of life and governance. The broken landscape of Greece, with its many islands and rugged terrain, provided the isolated peoples of Greece the time and freedom from interference during the long Dark Age to develop autonomous traditions. The geography of Greece and the economic depression of the eastern Mediterranean world after 1200 BCE did not invite foreign occupation. The Hittites fell before they could turn their attention to Greece, and the Assyrians had richer targets in Phoenicia and Egypt.

The Greek city-states (poleis) in the Archaic and Classical Ages were fully formed and stubbornly independent. The great Greek problem was to preserve the freedom and autonomy of the poleis from those internal and external enemies who would create one Greece by conquering and uniting its separated parts. The Greek poleis faced major crises of unification twice in the fifth century BCE—first when the Persians twice invaded Greece and were resisted by an alliance of Greeks led by Athens and Sparta, and second in the Peloponnesian War when the Athenian drive for dominance provoked other poleis to resist. There were also hundreds of smaller conflicts as the poleis waged wars against each other and formed alliances of poleis to harass other poleis. The problem of cities, their freedom and independence, both made and unmade classical Greece. In the fifth century BCE in imperial Athens, in particular, one polis produced one of the most extraordinary moments of human civilization, a blossoming of the arts, of critical thought, and of a profound exploration of what it means to be human.

Darkness Descends

The Dark Age of Greece (1100–800 BCE) is the great unknown of Greek history. The age is so-called not because

How was the Dark Age of Greece primitive as well as cloaked in a fog of silence?

it was primitive (though it was that, at least in relative terms), but because the Greece of that period has left few material traces. There are no contemporary written sources and few pots or buildings to study. The period was relatively free of major conflicts, and little is known of minor local conflicts (and there were doubtless many). A lack of information should not, however, be equated with unimportance. Though we know little about the period, something significant was happening. The Greeks entered the Dark Age out of the heroic Bronze Age of Mycenaean warriors, but they emerged from it in the Archaic Age as a different Iron Age people with intense local identities and with their precious poleis in place.

After the Mycenaean Collapse

After Mycenae and other cities were attacked and destroyed around 1100 BCE, Mycenaean Bronze Age culture limped along and tried to adapt for almost a century. Burned and abandoned cities were resettled, but not along the same lines. Burial practices and pottery styles changed, but life continued. Greek traders tried for a time to maintain a presence in the economically depressed eastern Mediterranean and maintained some contact with Cyprus. But the contraction of the eastern Mediterranean economy meant that the Mycenaean economy of aggressive sea trade, Greek warrior elites, and fortified palaces was no longer sustainable. The movements of peoples such as the Indo-European Dorians within Greece in the 1200s and 1100s BCE, the displacement of the Mycenaean elite (some to Ionia, some to Attica), along with the deep economic downturn, all signaled that Greece was entering a period of sharp adjustment. Linear B writing disappeared entirely, large stone buildings were no longer erected, and wars of foreign conquest ceased. Greece turned from the public (elite governance, great palaces, regional wars, heroes, and aristocratic art) to the local and personal. Each person, family, and locality was forced to cope as best they could within the restricted conditions of life in the Dark Age: Greece moved from sea trading to farming, from elite rulers to community rule—or worse, no rule—and from connected cultures to isolated local cultures. It was a great age of forgetting. Dark Age Greeks knew that they had had a glorious past, as we know from Homer, but they had forgotten the conditions that had made the Mycenaean Age work.

The Iron Age Arrives

Cyprus made the conversion to iron implements and technology sooner than did mainland Greece, but by 1000 BCE iron was in wide use in Greece. Iron replaced bronze almost entirely and better suited the coming age. Virtually all the metal objects from this period uncovered in Athens are iron ones: swords, axes, knives, and dress ornaments. One of the new economic ventures of the age was the location and mining of iron ore. The problem was that in the straitened circumstances of the age, the Greeks mined the ore locally for domestic use, not for Mediterranean trade.

After the Mycenaeans, Greece remade itself locally. The movement of the Dorians can be determined by the spread of their particular dialect of Greek. They seized much of the best land, particularly in southern Greece, and began to farm. Greece at the time had few economic outlets. Each family produced from the land what it needed to survive. Families and their productive capacities remained the core of Dark Age society. Without the existence of larger governments or recognized systems of justice, each family protected its own. Blood feuds with other families were the result. Over the next several centuries, powerful extended families established themselves, encompassing related individuals in clans and tribes, and extended their property holdings and wealth. Indo-European peoples seem generally to have had kings at their head (as had the Mycenaeans), but in the Dark Age, these kings were little more than the nominal heads of villages. Power belonged to those with productive property who soon deemed themselves the best sort of people (nobles) or aristocrats. At first they advised the king, but in many places they removed him. When the Greek poleis emerged from the Dark Age, their kings were gone or severely reduced in power.

The polis began in the Dark Age as little more than the protective wall around a village or extended area. It bound together a village or collection of villages having a common defensible high spot or hilly area (an **acropolis**) and marketplace (*agora*). The early poleis were run by aristocratic or landholding elites. There were other peo-

Greek Dark Age
1100–800 BCE

Iron Age
1200 BCE–

1200 BCE   1100   1000   900   800

ples in the early poleis—slaves, workers, transients—but none of them were citizens. Property defined status and blood ties determined aristocratic standing and, consequently, citizenship. This polis development was largely absent in the Near East and may be attributed to the particular nature of the breakdown of the Greek world and its intense local isolation, community by community, in the wake of the Mycenaean collapse.

One question worth asking is why the Dark Age lasted so long in Greece, while Cyprus, Crete, and the Near East in general rebounded more quickly. Not until the ninth century BCE did Greece begin to show signs of building programs, the introduction of new death rituals, and the resumption of some forms of Mediterranean trade. Almost two centuries earlier, the Assyrians had established an empire committed to securing its borders. Assyria was uninterested in annexing Greece but slowly hemmed in the Phoenicians, who took more actively to the sea and around 800 BCE founded Carthage along the southern coast of the western Mediterranean. The Assyrians and Phoenicians created the conditions that provided Greece with the opportunity to break out of its depressed economic state. The Phoenicians, in particular, were agents of commercial and cultural contact in the late Dark Age. They brought their alphabet to Asia Minor and Greece, without which the poems of Homer could never have been recorded.

Homer, Whoever He Was

Almost everything about Homer and his poems, the *Iliad* and *Odyssey,* is controversial. The common opinion is that the blind poet of legend lived sometime between 850 BCE and 600 BCE, that he was a bard who dictated the verses about the dramatic events of the Mycenaean Age and its heroes: Hector and Achilles, Agamemnon and Helen, and lost Odysseus wandering the Mediterranean seeking a safe harbor and home. But was Homer blind? Was Homer one man or two (one poet for each poem)? Was there an author named Homer at all, and did he live around the time of the Trojan Wars or as late as the seventh century BCE?

Let us assume in the midst of these many uncertainties that someone like Homer lived around 750 BCE and was a Greek native of Ionia in Asia Minor (as detected in the diction of the poems). He was a transitional figure living at the end of the Dark Age and on the cusp of the new Archaic Age (800–500 BCE). The great epic poems, the *Iliad* and *Odyssey,* provide evidence of the cultural churning that preoccupied the Greeks during the Dark Age. Homer's stories derive from older oral ones about the preceding Mycenaean Age, and Homer was, at the very least, their recorder if he wasn't their author, though if so he was a genius at fashioning the long poetic narrative of the *Iliad* out of scattered Dark Age tales.

Homer might be thought of as the recipient, recorder, and inspired synthesizer of a long line of oral poems that had survived in changing form, from retelling to retelling, since 1200 BCE. As such the oral epic was a repository of cultural information, the living encyclopedia of a small society. Homer or the storytelling bards who repeated the poems of the Trojan War had mnemonic or remembering tricks that allowed them to perform the basic poems over and over again. Repeated lines and stock phrases such as "the wine-red sea" recur not so much for the sake of color or poetic effect as to keep the

Classical Age
500–404 BCE

Persian Wars
490–479 BCE

Wanderings
of Herodotus
c. 450 BCE

Archaic Age
800–500 BCE

Golden Age of Athens
479–404 BCE

Greek emigration
750–500 BCE

Peloponnesian War
431–404 BCE

Persian Empire
550–330 BCE

700   600   500   400   300

King Priam Asks for the Body of His Son The king (*center*) advised by Hermes (*right*) asks Achilles (*left*) to return the body of his son Hector, who lies at his feet, one of the events of the Trojan War recounted by Homer in the *Iliad*.

poem on track and to complete lines of verse during an active recitation.

Yet Homer's immediate predecessors were not Mycenaeans. Rather, they belonged to the Dark Age and could not avoid changing the received songs by inserting little pieces of themselves and their Dark Age values into the poems, even when they didn't square with the Mycenaean Age about which they were singing. The Mycenaean elite buried their dead in grand tombs; Homer's heroes are cremated, as people were during the Dark Age. Homer or his sources have forgotten the names and locations of the great Mycenaean cities and palaces. Thus, while the stories told by Homer describe the distant Mycenaean past, culturally they also reflect the Dark Age.

Was the Greek Alphabet an Accident?

Was Homer, whoever or whatever he was, even a writer? Some scholars have suggested something more radical: that Homer invented Greek writing, either by shaping the Greek alphabet to accommodate the needs of writing down the poems or that others had invented the Greek alphabet to record his poems. The idea is an intriguing one, but probably too good to be true. However the Greek alphabet came into being, its invention had a tremendous impact on Greece and the western world.

The Phoenicians spread their goods, some with Phoenician writing on them, around the eastern Mediterranean shoreline. The Phoenician alphabet consisted entirely of consonants. Though some exposure to the Phoenician alphabet had occurred as early as the ninth century BCE, the Greek alphabet, with characters

adapted to express vowels, appeared early in the eighth century BCE. With the addition of vowels, phonetic literacy was born; now, anything spoken could be expressed more or less exactly in writing and the reverse. Did someone or some group of people introduce this adaptation to accommodate the special needs of spoken Greek, or might it have been an accident? In other words, in the late Dark Age or early Archaic Age, did the Greek alphabet come about because the Greeks didn't fully understand the Phoenician one and so assigned vowels to various characters to make the alphabet more expressive and comprehensive? The task of copying down Homer's poems might have necessitated such a breakthrough, but little evidence exists to suppose that it did. The earliest Greek writing, aside from Homer's poems, is trivial: curses, official dedications, lists.

Phonetic literacy spread no more quickly or popularly than had Mesopotamian cuneiform writing millennia earlier. It did not change the Greek world overnight or fundamentally, but it did slowly transform its possibilities. The spread and preservation of the Homeric poems is proof of that. The Mycenaean tales that Homer drew upon were fluid oral objects that could not have been preserved in fixed form. Writing them down stabilized the poems as literary texts. The *Iliad* became the bible or world history of the Greeks, a shared inheritance of stories that showed the Hellenes (the Greeks) their deep past, helped to regularize the Greek language, and pushed them toward greater self-awareness and self-knowledge.

The Archaic Age Breakout

Late in the Dark Age, there were signs that Greece was reviving. Life was being reorganized at different rates city by city; aristocratic elites were in place; and customs, religion, and the economy were stabilizing. But the full effects of those gains did not become apparent until the Archaic Age. Tensions in the Archaic Age were acute, as seen in the farmer-poet Hesiod's complaints about the unfairness of his times. There were various attempts to relieve these tensions: from games and religious authority to tyranny and the forgiveness of debts.

Why does Archaic Age Greece matter?

The Olympic Games and Delphic Oracle

Traditionally the first fixed date of ancient Greece is 776 BCE when an all or *pan*-Hellenic festival was convened at Olympia in southern Greece. Far to the north the sanctuary of Zeus on Mount Olympus had long been a special site of sacrifice and reverence for the Greeks (Map 2.1). The Dark Age did not kill off Mycenaean religious beliefs so much as refashion them locally. As the population expanded and material resources improved in the Archaic Age, the Greeks began to emphasize the importance of temples as sites of worship. Inside these temples and sanctuaries stood cult statues of the Olympian gods (Zeus and company), to which people donated gifts such as small statues, jewelry, and precious metals.

Dark Age Greeks had held funeral games to honor the dead, but they were infrequent and irregular. To honor Zeus, Olympia in the Peloponnesus mounted festival games every four years. Athletes prepared for up to ten months to qualify for the games. No prize money was given, but athletes received great prestige for winning. The results of the Olympic Games were recorded, and the champions were celebrated as heroes by their cities. The emergence and importance of the Olympic Games in the eighth century BCE was a sign of the growing confidence of the various poleis and their aristocrats who wanted to reach outside their small cities for wider Greek acclaim.

The Olympic Games brought Greeks together in the shared pursuit of individual excellence (*arête*). The concept of *arête* underlined the commitment to aristocratic honor of the sort that brave heroes were expected to demonstrate in all aspects of their lives: on the field of battle, when facing the gods, and in their treatment of family and fellow aristocrats. Demonstrative outer excellence was more important than inner rightness. The other concept that defined the citizen ethos was that of **agon,** the belief that life was a constant struggle or competition. The Olympic Games made manifest the concepts of *arête* and *agon,* as the honorable outer virtue of the Greek competitor was tested publicly in competition before Zeus and the Greek world.

The sanctuary of the god Apollo at Delphi was built on a slope of Mount Parnassus just north of the Gulf of Corinth on the mainland. By the late eighth century BCE, individuals and community representatives from many parts of Greece traveled there to consult the Oracle. Greeks believed that Apollo communicated divine truths there through his priestess, the Pythia, commonly known as the Oracle. The priestess was generally a local woman of no special learning or prominence in society, but ancient stories that she was inspired by vapors and drug-induced ecstasy lack proof. Through the priestess the god delivered messages, often in a yes or no form, to specific questions. The Oracle was rarely controversial, but rather supplied divine approval for individual and community decisions already reached. On disputed matters, the Oracle's answers tended to be more elaborate and equivocal. The Oracle did not, strictly speaking, predict the future, but rather reinforced the leanings of the authority figures who sought the consultations. The petitioners came because they needed the Oracle's authority to sanction their official decisions. Since opinions on problems facing a community were often divided, the Oracle was called upon to resolve the division and offer a divine reason for moving forward.

MAP 2.1 | Archaic Age Greece, c. 800 BCE

Greece is a mountainous land surrounded by the sea and islands, and situated not far by sea from the coast of Asia Minor. *How did geography shape the history of Greece? Why were Crete and the islands of the Aegean Sea of such critical importance to Greece?*

Consulting the Oracle at Delphi Aegeus, the king of Athens, is shown consulting the Pythia, the priestess through whom the god Apollo spoke at Delphi.

MAP 2.2 | Greek and Phoenician Emigration, c. 500 BCE
In the first millennium BCE, both the Greeks and the Phoenicians settled coastal lands along the Mediterranean Sea. The Greeks also established settlements along the southern Black Sea. They called their colonies "homes away from home." *When and where did Greek emigration take place? Are there patterns to Greek and Phoenician settlements? What advantages and disadvantages, if any, did the settlements bring to mainland Greek cities?*

Delphi was, thus, like the Olympic Games, a physical and spiritual place where Greeks could step outside their small societies and local disputes to secure external approval for themselves and their communities. The important thing about these archaic Greek institutions was that they mediated local differences between rivals, for the Greeks were deeply divided, within their poleis and within greater Greece. Both Delphi and Olympia began to bind scattered and rancorous Archaic Age Greeks to a shared cultural world.

Archaic Age Emigration: Homes away from Home

The Greeks were used to migration. The Indo-European pattern was to settle and then pick up and move when necessary. There is little information, except from later self-serving classical reports, of any substantial Dark Age emigration to foreign lands. Greece was too poor at the time to support mass movements and was probably without the social pressures that forced emigration. The Archaic Age, however, witnessed widespread emigration and the establishment of Greek settlements outside Greece. The Phoenicians were also establishing settlements and outposts along the southern rim of

the Mediterranean, but the Greeks tended to stick to the northern coastline.

Some observers have called this movement one of *colonization,* but that term does not perfectly describe the Greek situation. The Greeks referred to these settlements as "homes away from home." Most of the settlements (in southern France, Italy, Asia Minor, Ionia, and northern Africa) were on the coastal lands of the northern and eastern Mediterranean and the Black Sea (Map 2.2). The settlers established Greek-like cities controlling hinterlands. Though these settlements might maintain some of the traditions and customs of their home cities, they were politically independent of their original homes. Around a hundred small settlements were established, some of which later became famous cities such as Marseilles, Naples, and Byzantium.

There was no single reason for these foreign settlements, but many were caused by crises at home such as feuds, lack of land and opportunity, population pressures, economic problems including famines, and the desire to establish trading posts. The building social tensions of Archaic Age poleis may lie behind many of the settlement ventures. Land and power at home were in the hands of aristocrats not willing to share. In many cases, all-male groups of settlers voluntarily left their homes, had specific destinations in mind, and seized the new land by driving out or murdering the previous male occupants and abducting their women. Some settlements, however, seem to have occurred peacefully, based on an alliance between the settling Greeks and the indigenous population.

Not all emigrants wanted to leave their homes. Some were forced to go, as they were at Thera, which compelled families with more than one son to send one brother to the new settlement of Cyrene. Death and the loss of property were the penalties hanging over the heads of those who refused to go. The home cities had trading and economic interests to pursue in these ventures, but those seem to have been secondary considerations. The reduction of the home city's population and the opportunity for the settlers to secure new lands were more important factors. As such, the settlement movement over several centuries served as a social release valve, relieving internal civic pressures. Home cities underwrote the costs of these settlement ventures (ships, resources, arms), but that was the end of their direct investment. Each new settlement had to survive on its own and lost much of its direct contact with the home city.

Each settlement experiment was different. Much depended on the character and culture of the home city, including whether the settlement was peaceful or violent, the nature of relations with the native population, the site's geography, and economic prospects. In some settlements there was a mixing of cultures (native and Greek), whereas in others Greek culture dominated. By the late Archaic Age, there was a general reinforcement in these homes away from home of Greekness or Greek values through central institutions such as temples, religious practices, language, and political customs. The new settlements were as likely to consult the Oracle at Delphi as were mainland Greek cities. War and conflict in the new lands also encouraged alliances with home cities and the aligning of political interests, often to the detriment of the settlement's autonomy. By 650 BCE, Greece had a diffuse presence on the northern and eastern rims of the Mediterranean Sea, which was a factor in the resumption of sea trade, the emergence of a greater sense of what it meant to be Greek, and the growing influence of the Greek presence in shaping the cultural character of the European continent.

Dirty Politics and Hesiod's Discontent

Hesiod lived in the eighth century BCE and wrote the *Theogony*, an account of the origins of the world of the Greek gods, and *Works and Days*, which principally concerns farming, farm labor, and the seasons. The two poems (some scholars believe that they were composed by two different poets) complement each other and constitute an Archaic Age circle of life that led from the gods

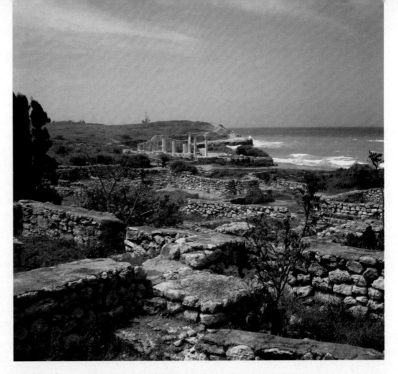

A Greek Settlement on the Black Sea During the period of emigration, Greek settlers established "homes away from home" in such distant locales as Chersonesus on the shores of the Black Sea.

on high down to human work and suffering. These were the poles of the Greek condition in the early Archaic Age.

According to Hesiod, humans had once lived in a golden age, free of strife and labor, growing fat and free of cares in a land abundant with fruit. Death came as a pleasant sleep. All was right with the upper and lower worlds, but the gods then fashioned a silver age that suited humans less, then one of bronze when men were at war, then another of frightening heroes, and finally an age of iron when men turned hard and mean. Hesiod belonged to the last age, but he wished that he had never been born or had died before entering an iron age so full of grief and suffering. Now all was ceaseless strife. His was an immoral, lying, and murdering age, in which children cheated their aged parents, and people died young from disease and want.

Works and Days is a moral poem pleading for justice in a wicked time. Hesiod begins his gloomy poem by calling upon Zeus to set right a broken world. He views Zeus and the gods as moderators, lifting up plains, lowering mountains, humbling powerful men, elevating the low. Strife and tears are the human condition, but strife is good for people, thrusting them into never-ending competition with each other, carpenter against carpenter, beggar against beggar, and brother against brother. Hesiod and his brother Perses, for whom he wrote *Works and Days,* had had a falling out over family property. They split their land, but, according to the poet, Perses with the compliance of a bribed judge had grabbed the better portion.

In the poem, Hesiod complains that the rich rule the world; in a just world the good man and his honest labor should suffice. To this end, he seeks to teach his brother and so his audience how to earn an honest living from the land: when to plow, plant, and harvest. He worries that Perses does not know how to survive except dishonestly. Hesiod longed for rulers who would render justice, and his poem cries out for fairness and for the fair resolution of disputes. *Works and Days* is not a farmer's almanac, then, but an editorial on a world that no longer valued honest labor and devotion to the land. Above all, the poem is a moral manual for a brother gone wrong; to teach him that the secret to survival is to respect the gods, to follow wise farming practices, and to dedicate himself to honest labor.

Inequalities and injustices that had been building over centuries reached a crisis point in the Archaic Age. Property may have been everything, but there was only so much land and it was held by too few people. The social tensions that permeate *Works and Days* are those also revealed by the emigration movement, the building militarism of the Archaic Age as groups of people violently seized the resources of others, and poleis that were becoming increasingly aggressive.

The Greek gods and the social and class rigor of Hesiod's age are not unconnected. With the elimination of powerful kings, Dark Age and early Archaic Age Greeks and their fledgling poleis fell under the tight control of aristocratic families. These landholders sought to justify their power and position by means other than just the possession of land. They not only claimed superior genealogy (thus allowing them to justify their families' hold on land and power), but also asserted that they were the descendants of gods and heroes.

The aristocrat's position in society, particularly as a coercive and controlling force, needed all the reinforcement he and his family could secure. It was expensive to be an aristocrat in the Archaic Age. The means of warfare were changing; horses were costly in a period when mounted warfare still mattered, and improved weapons made of iron were expensive. Helmets and body armor were necessary, but only a wealthy aristocrat could afford them. It was also costly to buy the support of subordinate groups within society and to secure the services of slaves. The needs of wealthy aristocrats sucked resources out of the economy on the backs of commoners, who tended to hold small or dependent farms. Small farmers fell perilously into recurring debt to their aristocratic patrons for seeds, tools, and land. The social tensions in Hesiod's world were real: between family members, between wealthy landowners and commoners, and between aristocrats. All the while small landholders like Hesiod complained that the prevailing distribution of resources and power was unfair.

Tyrants, Reformers, and Military Change

Hesiod's call for social justice was a symptom of a world in which the interests of the wealthy few and those who took advantage of a corrupt system predominated.

Emigration, recourse to the Delphic Oracle, religious institutions, and the composition of first assemblies in poleis were all Greek innovations that somewhat helped to ease internal tensions. But matters came to a head in the late seventh and early sixth centuries BCE, when across Greece social reformers and tyrants emerged to redress internal problems. The reformers were not seeking universal equality among classes and peoples. Rather, they were attempting to deal with the disgruntled, addressing complaints that the legal system was designed to serve aristocrats and protect their interests alone.

The social reformers were trying to fix a system under siege by repairing it in the least disruptive way. The rise of tyranny in the seventh and sixth centuries BCE was a more radical and successful repair. **Tyrants** were not despots in the modern sense, but autocrats who seized power by force. They thought of themselves as kings and sought to establish lasting dynasties. They appeared when competition between aristocratic families threatened to destroy a polis or when the polis was in conflict with another polis or with foreigners. Tyrants (in places such as Corinth, Sicyon, and Athens) offered military solutions and polis superiority, and could be tremendously popular with the nonaristocratic peoples of most poleis, who saw the tyrant as someone who might release them from the excessive demands made upon them or a foreign danger threatening their polis. In general the tyrants welcomed popular support, which they maintained by distributing wealth, sponsoring religious festivals, and promoting commerce. As a group, tyrants were reluctant to engage in foreign wars or conquest. They preferred to pacify their poleis rather than to militarize them.

Unlike kings who depend upon royal blood to continue their lines, the Greek tyrants tended to be charismatic individuals such as Peisistratus (d. 527 BCE) in Athens. Successful tyrants had few successors, and tyranny proved to be but a stage in the development of the Greek polis, not its final form. In a few places tyrants did manage to break the gridlock of forces that had seized Greece since the Dark Age, overriding entrenched aristocratic interests and devoting themselves to the good of the polis and their own political success.

There were as many types of poleis as there were poleis. Each one was unique, the product of the isolation of the Dark Age, the geographic separation forced upon it by the Greek landscape, particular settlement patterns, the timing of development, and other particularizing factors. For the Greeks, the polis was three things: a built-up physical place, a territory (the city plus its outlying lands), and a political community of citizens. Scholars have long tended to translate the term *polis* as "city-state," a term that is more appropriate for some larger poleis than for smaller ones with populations of less than 1,500 people. But in all cases the polis was more than a city in our terms and less than a state by modern standards. Even a small polis was an autonomous city with its own independent traditions, identity, and foreign relations. Ancient Greeks generally described themselves as Corinthians, Spartans, Megarans, and so on. A polis was not just a place but also its individualizing character, which described who its residents were.

Greece in the Archaic Age was filled with hundreds of poleis. Many of them had similar features such as an agora and an acropolis, but there were considerable differences as well: between coastal, island, and inland poleis, between southern poleis and northern ones, between home poleis and settlement poleis. The political identities of poleis were in a state of flux in the Archaic Age. Dominant aristocratic families controlled the poleis of the Dark Age and at the start of the Archaic Age. For a time these aristocrats were the only lawful citizens of most poleis. Most commoners, all women, slaves, and foreigners were excluded from citizenship and executive decision making. The law, as Hesiod complained, served nobles and their property interests. The Athenian Draco in the seventh century BCE set out a series of harsh laws with death penalties for many minor offenses (hence Draconian refers to an arbitrary, harsh, or cruel measure), but law did not bind the Greeks together since each polis had its own laws and legal procedures.

The pressure for inclusion within the political body of many poleis was building in the sixth century BCE, but there was little widespread recognition that all commoners or native-born males within a polis should be considered citizens. Some poleis (in places such as Athens, Kos, and Naxos) began to move toward more inclusive assemblies. These were not so much early democracies as they were a way to silence common complaints by allowing representatives of the lower classes to participate at some level in the political process and so to be parties to and tacit supporters of its decisions. Not just complaints about injustice, but also the changing military needs of Greece and its cities, and the growth of the population in a more prosperous Greece, began to give the non-nobles of many poleis a more prominent voice in city affairs.

The construction of the **demos** (masses, the people: free male native residents of a polis, non-noble, but of some standing and wealth) in places such as Athens paralleled the emergence of the **phalanx** as the basic fighting unit of most poleis. The soldier who stood in line with his fellows in the rectangular phalanx formation of infantry was called a **hoplite.** Hoplites were small farmers who presumably paid for their own equipment (spear, sword, shield, helmet, breastplate, and shin protectors). They were named after either the *hoplon,* the double-handled shield that was essential to the phalanx, or *hopla,* that is, all their military equipment. Shields were critical since they protected not only their bearers, but the men standing beside them in the phalanx. Great disgrace fell upon any soldier who dropped his shield during a battle, for it

Hoplite Formation A seventh-century BCE depiction on a jug, of Greek infantry in formation. Note the importance of the wicker shields of the hoplites.

jeopardized the men standing beside him and the integrity of the phalanx formation. The shield and the phalanx were egalitarian in nature; the hoplites fought as a unit of equals. Although Greek battles still featured a good deal of individual hand-to-hand combat, formation warfare now became common. Gone was the heroic mounted warfare described by Homer. Yet Archaic Age battles remained messy affairs in which the phalanx did not operate as a human tank mowing down the enemy. Hoplites often ran in disarray toward or away from the enemy, there were other participants besides the hoplites, and not all the hoplites were equally equipped or disciplined.

In this new age of warfare, poleis could not afford to exclude from politics the men who fought for them. Hoplites were men with property and some stake in the survival and success of the polis. Their voice may not have become louder or more insistent in the Archaic Age, but they were better placed to speak and to be heard by the late Archaic Age.

Archaic Age Economies and Cultures

There were as many economies and cultures in Greece as there were regions and poleis. There were agricultural innovations and new crops in the Archaic Age, but they were not enough to sustain growth. The advice that Hesiod offered in *Works and Days* was designed to maximize and safeguard agricultural productivity in a relatively static economic world. The Greek farmer still relied on basic crops such as olives, grapes, and wheat, but in Greece's varied landscape different kinds of wheat were grown and at different times of year in different regions. Greek farmers knew that they needed to transport their

Harvesting Olives The economies of the many Greek poleis were based chiefly on agriculture. In this pottery depiction, we see a four-man operation: one man in the tree shakes olives loose, two use sticks to hook and shake branches out of his reach, and a fourth farmer gathers the fallen fruit.

stamped with a seal. By 500 BCE, most Greek poleis were producing recognizable coins made of silver with both sides marked for identification. Some of these coins were designed for local use, since they were convenient items for the collection of taxes and the payment of debts, but by the end of the Archaic Age the coins of active trading poleis such as Corinth and Athens became common coinage in Mediterranean trade. Although coinage did not revolutionize the Greek economy, it marked Greece's re-entrance (or, at least, that of some of its poleis) in the sixth century BCE as a trading presence in the Mediterranean.

Just as the economy and coins were less Greek- than polis-centered, so was culture in its various forms. Greek poetry in the middle to late Archaic Age turned away from epic to choral and lyrical poetry. New meters were introduced and local poets such as Archilocus of Paros, Theogonis of Megara, and Sappho of the island of Lesbos explored new poetic voices. These poets spoke in the first person about personal crises and human emotions. Sappho's poems, in particular, are full of the subjective "I." Most of her poems are now lost, in part because of the blackening of her reputation by later periods. Sappho wrote on the labors of love between women, probably for a small audience of school girls. Her poetry in its highly refined lyric voice is not easy to unravel, but then we lack a sharp understanding of the context in which she was writing. These poems were not written for us, but for an audience in a different emotional and gendered space. Still, her poems carry universal themes. In one she writes that she would rather see the light step and lit face of Anactoria, who reminded her of Helen of Troy, than chariots and soldiers on the march.

The wise men of the Archaic Age have been much celebrated as scientists and philosophers, but they were neither. They were sages, chiefly from Ionia, who wrote few treatises but rather taught orally. They speculated on the cosmos and the place of humans in it. Many of them had been influenced by Asian work on mathematics, astronomy, and physics. Thus, another of the individualizing elements of Archaic Age culture was the intellectual differences between the overseas settlements and mainland Greece. The refined thought of the sages probably would not have been possible or been preserved without the emergence of the Greek alphabet, which had first appeared in Ionia. A new range of intellectual possibilities was emerging. Even the spread of coins may have set the sages to thinking about the problem of universals (for instance, of goodness apart from individual good things), for coins are standardized and representative items that have an abstract or universal meaning beyond the physical objects themselves.

Thales of Miletus held that water was the universal element out of which the earth originated. Anaximander of Miletus postulated that the world was generated out of an indefinite (or chaotic and boundless) space in which the contraries of hot and cold, wet and dry competed and eventually achieved balance. The important point is that Thales and Anaximander thought of the physical world

crops for sale. Hesiod, who was reluctant to travel by ship, nevertheless advised his brother when to load his produce on ships, what size those ships should be, and what season to sail. Transport by water was critical to the diffusion of goods within Greece and abroad.

In general, Greece needed to import foodstuffs rather than to export them. For food they traded olives and wine, silver, and large vessels (*amphorae*). The Phoenicians had opened up the western Mediterranean to trade, which brought Greek settlements such as Naples into larger trading networks. On their own, the Greeks also began to trade with Etruria in northern Italy in the eighth century BCE. Corinth, in particular, sold its goods to the Etruscans.

The leading edge of economic growth for the poleis was not agricultural, but commercial. Poleis began to discover the advantages of coined money. Greeks did not invent coins (the Lydians had), but they improved their design and circulation. By the early sixth century BCE, Greek cities were issuing irregular lumps of metal (generally made of electrum, an alloy of gold and silver) as a product of physical forces with consistent physical characteristics. Pythagoras of Samos was an Ionian who lived in Italy. His comprehensive and eclectic system was based on mathematical regularities (including the Pythagorean Theorem that the square of the length of the hypotenuse of a right angle triangle equals the sum of the squares of the lengths of the other two arms). Pythagoras was also interested in politics, personal codes of behavior, morality, and ideal societies. Heraclitus of Ephesus presented himself as an oracular sage. His aphorisms, or short sayings, were designed to provoke students to deeper reflection. He sought to uncover the underlying reasons of the cosmos as opposed to the surface realities we encounter. His well-remembered saying about the river never being the same (because it is always in flux) captures the essence of his challenge to probe beyond the surface to the underlying truth of things. For Heraclitus, the *logos* (word) or divine essence was the underlying force of things. In a complex poem, Parmenides of Elea went even further in presenting this phenomenal world as deceptive, the lie told by a goddess. He advised humans to search for the truths hidden to them. These Ionian Greek thinkers speculated freely and rationally with remarkable insight, but they were content to speculate rather than to prove their propositions; they remained religiously inclined teachers whose chosen goal was to encourage Greeks to think about the nature of the world and their place in it.

Archaic Age art was innovative. Stone temples were introduced at the beginning of the seventh century BCE, chiefly of the so-called Doric design. The Archaic Age was a world without palaces, so that these temples were the most enduring buildings of the era. Dark Age Greek pottery had lacked figural representation, but by the eighth century BCE pottery began to be adorned with figures. Each region or polis tended to have its own potters, some of whom late in the period began to place their names on the pots they produced. The figural scenes grew more sophisticated as the period proceeded. The sixth century BCE (not the fifth) was the golden age of Greek pottery. At Athens, in particular, a wide variety of pots used for both personal and funereal purposes was produced. Vase painters experimented with changing the background and figure colors (chiefly black and red).

Sculpture too changed in the Archaic Age. The Greeks were deeply impressed by Egyptian sculpture and by the mid-seventh century BCE had begun to produce their own statues called *kouroi* (*kouros* being a young man or boy; *kore*, a young woman or maiden). These figures were at first as rigid and unsmiling as Egyptian sculptures, but by the sixth century BCE they assumed a Greek character. To take but one example, around 550 BCE a young woman by the name of Phrasikleia died and her parents hired the artist Aristion of Paros to make her death statue. The large statue shows the young girl in a dress pulled to one side; adorned with a necklace, belt, and elaborate hair style; and holding a lotus blossom in her raised left hand. Originally the marble statue would have

Statue of Phrasikleia From late in the Archaic Age, the statue by Aristion of Paros reflects the influence of Egyptian statuary but with a Greek emphasis on individuality. The base contains an inscription in which the girl addresses those who chance to see her image.

been brightly painted. Phrasikleia smiles the "Archaic Smile," an expression difficult to decipher, but appropriate for one entering the other world. The statue stood on a base that bore a poem in which Phrasikleia spoke to those who chanced to see her statue. She says that she will now never marry but remain a maiden forever, bearing that name from the gods as her marker. The poem is integral to the statue, animating the young girl's claim to be remembered. By the last decades of the sixth century BCE, the freestanding nude young men of Greek statuary walk forward, one leg firmly before the other. They reveal musculature, anatomically exact bodies, and the knowing Archaic half-smile.

The Black Athena Controversy

The ancient Greeks were, quite rightly, proud of their cultural achievements. But how influenced were they by the ideas, religions, technologies, and art of others, the non-Greeks who inhabited the wider Mediterranean world? From the Romans to the present, many European and North American Grecophiles (people who love the Greeks) have celebrated ancient Greece's originality and creativity as though it had arisen in isolation. Some have even described the development of Greek art, democracy, philosophy, science, and history writing from the fifth and fourth centuries BCE as a "Greek Miracle," forgetting that the ancient Greeks lived in a wider world inhabited by other cultured peoples, including the Egyptians, Persians, Phoenicians, Hittites, and Hebrews. This neglect may have arisen from the European fear of Asian empires or by the belief that Greece's political and moral systems were so alien to Asian traditions that the Greeks could not have borrowed anything substantial from "the Orient" (a "baggy" term used to include all of the diverse civilizations of the Near and Middle East, and North Africa).

In 1987, a Cornell professor of political science, Martin Bernal, unleashed a storm when he launched an attack on classicists and the Grecophile tradition in a three-volume study, *Black Athena: The Afroasiatic Roots of Classical Civilizations.* In his first volume, Bernal claimed that the amnesia about Greece's debts had begun in the early nineteenth century, as Europeans, seeking to establish "Aryan" roots for their continent, had cut off Greece from the Orient, ridiculed those who revered the Egyptians, and downplayed Greek texts such as Herodotus's *Histories* that acknowledged borrowings. In Bernal's view, the Aryanizing of Greek antiquity after 1830 influenced generations of Europeans and Americans who were taught that they were the descendants of autonomous Greeks and that their cultures had nothing whatsoever to do with the cultures of the Orient. Bernal called the book *Black Athena* not to say that all of Greek culture had its origins in Egypt

Egyptian Statue of Ahmes-Nefertari

and the Near East, but rather to demonstrate just how impossible it had become for Europeans to think of the founders of European civilization having black or brown faces.

Volumes 2 (1991) and 3 (2006) of Bernal's trilogy attempted to prove that Greece's debts to the Orient were more substantial than classicists and archaeologists had been willing to admit. Classicists have on the whole rejected and disproved Bernal's specific evidence of connections and interconnections, but have acknowledged that a traditional European reading of antiquity may have underestimated Greece's borrowings from Babylonian science, Egyptian art, and Assyrian literature. They have come to agree that something like a "Mediterranean cultural community" surrounded the Greeks from Homeric times forward, and that the Greeks knew more about the worlds to their east and south than was once thought. Herodotus had explored the east with great avidity, and Plato in his *Timaeus* had reflected upon Egyptian antiquity. The Greeks incorporated aspects of Egyptian cults into their religious rituals, and Homer was apparently aware of Gilgamesh's exploits. To Bernal's surprise, the primary success of his work was among readers in the African American community, many of whom have seen *Black Athena* as a means to assert ancient Africa's cultural creativity and to remind Americans and Europeans of the influence of racial thought in shaping western ideas and cultural institutions. As ancient history, Bernal's books may be flawed, but as cultural criticism, they have challenged readers to confront the nature of received history, how it is shaped, by and for whom, and for what reasons.

QUESTIONS | *What are the dangers and advantages of radically rethinking history? What might Herodotus and Plato have said about this controversy? Can you think of other such culturally weighted and misleading characterizations of the past and the "historical other"?*

The Conflicting Pulls of Pan-Hellenism and Polis-Centrism

By the end of the Archaic Age, around 500 BCE, the Greeks were growing culturally more alike while remaining politically divided. This was to be both their curse and singular achievement. The things that united the Greeks in Greekness or Pan-Hellenism were many, but they were undercut by the ever-resilient identification of Greeks with their native poleis. Polis-centrism seems to win out, again and again, when one looks at the course of Greek history.

The Greeks spoke and wrote a common language, though local variations of dialect and pronunciation were substantial and a source of much fun for the comic poets. They shared the same polytheistic religion, with the same pantheon of gods, and a rich store of myths, but these were all subject to local emphasis and interpretation. Athens had Athena, who was not worshipped widely outside of areas of Athenian dominance. The Greeks shared religious rituals and forms of worship, specifically the common practice of sacrifice (vegetable and animal), but again subject to variation from polis to polis. The Oracle at Delphi came to be a common source of sanction for Greeks, and the Olympic Games brought the Greeks together every four years but in the individual pursuit of glory by the home athlete. The Greeks all had coins, though those were minted locally, thus reinforcing the polis-centrism of the age.

Archaic Age cultural and economic developments contributed to a new mobility. Bards and sages took their talents from city to city, thus homogenizing, cross-fertilizing, and spreading the accumulating knowledge and cultural advances of the age. Economic contact promoted economic and cultural interchange between poleis. But the lack of roads and the geographic isolation of many poleis inhibited movement within Greece. Moreover, the economic conditions of each polis were so different (with coastal poleis able to exploit sea trade opportunities, while landlocked poleis were forced to practice agriculture in traditional ways) that there was a growing disparity between poleis as the economy began to prosper in the late Archaic Age.

What the Archaic Age never overcame was the stubborn independence of each polis. Though political developments followed a similar path in many poleis, with their experiments with tyranny and the addition of citizen assemblies, each polis was different and in competition with others. The story of most of the ancient world and Greece in particular was the success of cities that stubbornly chose to cling to their independence, thus constantly raising the competitive stakes. Hesiod was right to characterize his world as an agonal or competitive place, in which every person was in competition with every other person. In Greece the polis was the engine driving this competition both internally and externally. The geography and resources of Mesopotamia had allowed its stronger cities to conquer neighboring cities and create empires. In Greece, for reasons geographic and historical, the poleis developed powerful identities, traditions, and interests that they protected fiercely against each other and imperial intrusion. The many Greeces were in constant contest, hundreds of little states at war with each other. It was unclear by 500 BCE if they could ever unite, for what reason, and what the cost of political unification would be.

The Persian Wars

The two Persian invasions of mainland Greece in 490 and 480–479 BCE were bracing experiences for the Greeks. Facing a common enemy, several Greek poleis made common cause in the defense of Greece. The odds were not good. The Persian Empire was the most powerful and aggressive power in the eastern Mediterranean at the time. The failure of the invasions may not have been all that important to Persia, but success and survival meant everything to the many Greeces.

> What lessons did the many Greeces learn from the Persian Wars, and how did the invasions unbalance the many Greeces? In what ways might it have been better if the Persian Empire had triumphed?

The Persian Empire

The Persians were an Indo-European people whose homeland was in the area of present-day Iran. They were originally subject to the Assyrian Empire, but around 550 BCE King Cyrus of Persia defeated the Assyrians to create a Persian Empire. He conquered and incorporated the Lydians, Mesopotamians, and Babylonians. Since the Babylonians had controlled Syria and Palestine, the Persian Empire annexed those lands as well. The Persian model of empire was more inclusive or, at least, tolerant than the Assyrian and Babylonian empires had been. Cyrus allowed the Hebrew captives of Babylon to return home, thus initiating the Second Temple period of Hebrew history, which flowered around 515 BCE, after Cyrus's death. Persian armies under Cyrus conquered territory all the way to the edge of India, but the king died in Scythia in 531 BCE. His son Cambyses (d. 522 BCE) invaded Egypt and was named king of Egypt. Cambyses's successor, Darius (r. 521–486 BCE), launched the first invasion of Greece.

The Persian Empire was different from anything the Greeks had experienced previously. The great king, as he was called, was chosen by the gods and his subjects were all considered his slaves, there to do his bidding and to die for him. The great king's absolute power was manifest in the majesty of his person and the low station of his subjects, who prostrated themselves on the ground when in his presence. The empire was tolerant of its incorporated parts, known as satrapies, each with its own

Lydia and the Ionian Greeks

Herodotus begins his account of the Persian Wars with the Lydians, for that was where the conflict began for the Greeks. Lydia controlled a coastal kingdom (c. 700–550 BCE) in western Asia Minor, where there were many Greek settlements such as Melitus, Ephesus, and nearby Halicarnassus (Herodotus's home). The Ionian Greeks and the Lydians lived well together. Lydia had pioneered the use of coins, experimented with musical styles, and exposed the Greeks to Asian learning. It was no accident that Ionia, which had stimulating contacts with the wider Near East, produced the great sages of the Archaic Age, rather than isolated mainland Greece.

King Cyrus had recognized that the Persian Empire needed clear access to the Mediterranean, and so early on he targeted King Croesus of Lydia and successfully incorporated Lydia and the Ionian Greek cities into his empire (Map 2.3). Many Ionian Greeks saw the historical change not as enslavement, but as an opportunity. Greek troops campaigned for King Darius and struck agreements where necessary with his officials. But Persian Lydia was a land filled with intrigue as the Ionian Greeks tried to balance the interests of their poleis against Persian demands. Some Ionians sought advantage by working directly for the Persians. Greeks took up official and servile positions at Persepolis, the Persian capital.

The Persian incorporation of Lydia, however, upset the political stability of the Ionian poleis, which fell under the control of local Greek tyrants who supported Darius. Cities from mainland Greece also began, somewhat naively, to interfere in Persian affairs through the Ionian poleis. The Persian conquest of Thrace, north of mainland Greece, and Persian overtures to Macedonia showed how dangerous it was to irritate or even interest Darius. The Ionian Greek tyrants were in a difficult position, since they could not easily please Darius and their poleis at the same time. When Aristagoras of Melitus failed to secure Persian backing, he urged the Ionians to overthrow their Persian-backed tyrants. The result was an Ionian revolt against the Persian system. Fearing that Persia would invade Lydia again and reinstall pro-Persian Greek tyrants, the Ionians sought help from mainland poleis. The Ionians assembled an impressive navy but were outnumbered and defeated in the eastern Mediterranean by a large Persian navy. The Persians then ruthlessly suppressed the Ionians and reincorporated Lydia into the empire.

Tribute Offered to the Persian Empire A procession of men representing subdued lands bears tribute to the Persian Empire on a relief from Persepolis. On the top level, Scythians bring cloth, bracelets, and a stallion; and on the bottom, Lydians bring objects such as vases and cups.

governor (**satrap**) who was directly subject to the great king. All was well in the empire so long as the conquered peoples and their representatives acknowledged the great king's absolute power and paid taxes. Because all regions contributed soldiers to the Persian Empire, it was able to throw huge international armies into any conflict. The king had a personal army of 10,000 Immortals (an elite force of Persian soldiers selected for their proven bravery and so called by Herodotus), who served as his imperial bodyguard.

The Persian Empire was a vast conglomerate, loosely governed and organized, but with a standard language (Aramaic), script (cuneiform), coinage, and impressive road network dominated by the Royal Road, which ran from Persia to Lydia. The Persians were devoted to the benevolent god Ahura Mazda, the god of fire, light, warmth, and purity. They also believed in the existence of malevolent gods and that all of life was a battle between the forces of good and bad, spirit and matter, light and dark. This dualistic religion was systematized by the prophet Zarathustra or Zoroaster in the eighth century BCE, and the religion was later called Zoroastrianism.

Like so many overextended empires, the Persian Empire began to experience troubles at its margins. Cyrus died fighting against the Scythians, and Darius just escaped with his life from another campaign against them. Darius led his troops into Thrace and made it a satrapy, but the problem of Greece was still pending.

The First Persian Invasion of Greece

The poleis of Greece were divided on what the Persian suppression of the Ionian Greeks meant for each of them. Sympathetic to the overthrow of tyranny in the Ionian poleis, democratic Athens encouraged Ionian resistance to Persia. Sparta and many of the cities of the Peloponnesus avoided involving their states in the foreign conflict, though they had long been hostile to Persia. Inside Greece, poleis continued to struggle against each other over a variety of matters, most of them unconnected to the Persian business. Athens had had a long-running conflict with the wealthy island-polis of Aegina, but when Aegina, which had a large navy, symbolically submitted to Persia, Athens rallied Sparta and Corinth to attack the island. Once defeated, Aegina acknowledged the error of its ways and agreed to support the anti-Persia policy of the victors. The danger all along had been that if Persia had the naval support of Aegina, it might easily overpower Greece.

Darius had many reasons to be infuriated by the interference of the Greek poleis in his affairs. Moreover, Greece seemed a natural territorial extension of his empire. The incorporation of Thrace in the 490s BCE was just the first step in this westward expansion. Darius may have thought Greece a particularly fragile target. His advisors told him that the Greeks foolishly and incessantly waged wars against each other. A Persian naval force was assembled and attacked Greece in 490 BCE (Map 2.4). With around 25,000 soldiers, the Persian force was extremely small by Persian standards. The Athenians asked Sparta for help, but it arrived too late to do any good. Ten thousand heavily armed Athenian hoplites engaged and defeated the lightly armed Persian force on the plains of Marathon, twenty-six miles from Athens. Several hundred Athenian soldiers died, but some six thousand Persians perished. The rest of the Persians returned to their ships and sailed home. The strange thing about the first Persian attack was how un-Persian it was. Darius did not try to overwhelm the enemy with a massive army and was not present to lead his army. Instead, the Persians fought one small battle in Greece and then retreated. Was Darius just testing the waters for a larger invasion, or had he seriously underestimated his opponents?

The Interwar Years

The battle of Marathon was of little importance to Persia but was critical to Greece, its survival, and its mood. The interwar years (489–481 BCE) were fluid ones, as poleis and politicians positioned themselves to reap the rewards of the triumph at Marathon and to take advantage of the still looming Persian threat. Athens crowed that it had saved all Greece and employed propaganda and warships against those poleis and its own citizens who had not fully supported the resistance to Persia. In these years Athens first introduced **ostracism,** a democratic technique for expelling from its midst dangerous individuals (often those accused of collaboration with the Persians). Some Athenians despised Themistocles, a prominent citizen and office-holder (a *strategos,* or popularly elected commander), who was leading a campaign to erect a powerful Athenian navy to resist any future Persian attack.

At Sparta, its nominal kings, who were Sparta's official agents for dealing with the external world, were carefully watched by citizens for any indication of Persian

MAP 2.3 | The Persian Empire and Lydia, c. 500 BCE
The Persian Empire stretched 3,000 km (1,864 miles) from east to west and had absorbed the kingdom of Lydia directly across the Aegean Sea from the Greek mainland. Encompassing Ionia, Lydia was home to many Greeks. *Why did the expansion of the Persian Empire threaten various Greek interests? Where was the heart of the Persian Empire? Why was Greece important to Persia's expansion? Why was Lydia a point of cultural and historical contact for Greece and Asia?*

sympathies. Sparta led the **Peloponnesian League** (a group of poleis committed to the interests of the Peloponnesus of Greece) in pursuing a policy during the interwar years of forcing Argos (a Peloponnesian city near Mycenae) to join the League, a plan that ultimately failed. Sparta's chief worry, as always, was that its vast servile population of agricultural workers would revolt. It realized that it needed to be able to dispatch an army for foreign conflicts without leaving its home territory or its Peloponnesian allies undefended and inclined to rebel or, worse, to join the Persians.

The Second Invasion

Persia did not return immediately to its Greek campaign because Egypt was in revolt and the great king Darius died. His son Xerxes, however, was not one to leave business unfinished. The Persian diplomatic campaign to separate further the divisive Greek poleis heated up in the interwar years. The Persians promised gentle treatment to poleis that cooperated, and many did, often because they were more worried about hostile neighboring poleis than about the Persians. Representatives of the Greek cities and leagues met at Corinth in 481 BCE, but they were struggling as well with their various polis disputes and could not decide whether to resist the Persians or who should lead the resistance. Almost a third of the poleis decided not to resist an invasion. Using persuasion and trickery, Themistocles managed to assemble a large Athenian navy to resist the coming invasion, but only the Spartans and Athenians were firmly committed to the cause. Much of this pro-Athenian story is told by Herodotus. Many smaller poleis realized that they had as much to fear from Sparta, Athens, and hostile neighboring poleis as they did from Persia.

The Second Persian War (480–479 BCE) had two military phases, the first on land, the second at sea (see Map 2.4). In the first, Xerxes led a large army of up to 300,000 soldiers by ship and land across the Hellespont into Europe, where it won a costly battle against a vastly outnumbered Spartan force of 300 under the command of

MAP 2.4 | The Two Persian Wars, 490–479 BCE

The First Persian War in 490 BCE was a fairly small raid that ended with the defeat of the Persians at Marathon near Athens. The Second Persian War was a major land and sea assault on Greece led by Xerxes. *Why was the First Persian War so different from the Second? Where and why did the tide turn for the opposing Greek forces in the Second Persian War?*

King Leonidas at Thermopylae. Xerxes invaded Athens, which had been largely abandoned by the Athenians, and ordered the destruction of the Acropolis. He left his army behind to take control of Greece, while he returned to Persia to tend to other business. The second phase of the war began after the great king departed. At sea, the Persian and the Athenian navies met indecisively several times, but the Athenians lured the Persian navy into a narrow body of water between Salamis and the mainland and defeated it decisively. In 479 BCE, the Spartans, the Athenians, and their allies defeated the remaining Persian army with its many Greek soldiers at Plataea.

The Persian Wars were over, but the aftermath proved to be more important than the wars. Herodotus's account captures the exhilaration of small but clever and determined Greece, led by Athens, overcoming a mighty foreign power that would have crushed Greece's freedom. The Athenian (and Spartan) triumph, however, reinforced the disunity of Greece, the independence of

Stuffing the Ostracism Urn for Themistocles

In the heated interwar years of the 480s BCE, the Athenian assembly of citizens either invented or actively began to employ the institution of ostracism to expel dangerous politicians from Athens for up to ten years. The procedure was so called because citizens cast into a large urn broken pieces of pottery (shards) or prepared ceramic pieces (known as ostraka) on which had been written the name of the person they wished to ostracize. Ostracism was not a trial with the presentation of evidence and jury deliberation, but an unpopularity contest. Over ten thousand ostraka survive, a near majority of which bear the name of Themistocles. The future hero of the Persian Wars was eventually ostracized in the 470s BCE, but he was always a controversial and polarizing Athenian politician. His popularity bred animosity among those dedicated to preventing the dominance of democracy by any individual. One writer left a little verse on his vote for Themistocles's expulsion, calling it Themistocles's just "reward."

Considerable physical information can be gathered from the ostraka, including the location of the ostraka, the number and composition of the votes, the nature of the pottery shards used, and whether they came from the same shattered pots. They also contain linguistic; paleographical (old writing); and historical information, including how names are spelled, how adept the writers were, as well as what names appear, how they are related to each other, and how people are identified.

One batch of ostraka is particularly intriguing: 191 ostraka, all bearing the name of Themistocles, were found discarded in a well on the Acropolis. The shards came from the same general pottery source and bear the inscriptions of only fourteen different scribes. Was this, then, an attempt to rig the expulsion of Themistocles by stuffing the voting urns with votes? The votes, however, were discarded unused. Given the low literacy rates and pride of Athenians, not every citizen voter could or would want to inscribe a shard personally. It seems likely that scribes, perhaps commissioned by the polis, had prepared shards with Themistocles's name on them in advance so that voters could simply pick up a prepared shard. In this case, the scribes had overestimated the need and so after the vote disposed of the unused ostraka. The irony is that Themistocles himself used ostracism successfully to rid himself of opponents or to silence them by means of the threat of expulsion. That his name appears so often on legitimate ostraka may be an indication of a general if unsuccessful pushback by his enemies in the 480s BCE.

Ostrakon Inscribed with the Name of Themistocles

QUESTIONS | *How do democracies manage dissent? Was ostracism a good or bad way to rid Athens of dangerous citizens? Why? How might such a process be abused?*

its many poleis, and the right of all poleis to continue to press for advantage within Greece by harassing their Greek neighbors, depriving them of independence just as Persia would have. Greece lacked a referee to settle disputes and enforce peace. Had Persia triumphed, it might have acted as an overriding force, preventing the poleis from attacking each other, just as it had for a time in Ionia. The outcome of the Persian Wars also left Greece with the Persian Empire as an external power to which individual poleis could appeal when seeking advantage over their Greek enemies. The Persian Wars, thus, con-

firmed the crippling polis-centrism of Greece. Greece had faced a similar crisis of knotted power during the Archaic Age when its aristocrats stifled progress, a crisis that was finally broken by the rise of tyrants who would be kings. Had it triumphed, Persia might have acted as a benevolent tyrant, albeit one demanding taxes and soldiers, to keep the peace in Greece and protect the poleis from one another.

The Persian Wars produced an upheaval in the Greek world, but of the wrong sort. Sparta and Athens, the leading poleis, were emboldened by their roles in fending off the Persians, but they had different visions. Sparta wanted to return to things as they were. Athens seized the opportunity to press the war against Persia even after its end because it had finally found a cause to trump the claims to independence of the other poleis. In the name of preserving the freedom of Greece, Athens was prepared to suppress the freedom of other poleis. Persia had given the Athenians the dangerous idea that only an empire could resist another empire.

Mature and Major City-States

Ancient Greek history can be divided in many ways. One way is to think that the Classical Age occupied the whole of the fifth century BCE. Another is to suppose that

What were the strengths and weaknesses of polis-centered Greece? What joined and what divided the many poleis?

it lasted only from the end of the Persian Wars in 479 BCE to the end of the Peloponnesian War in 404 BCE. The latter seventy-five-year period is often associated with the Golden Age of Athens, when Athens reached its cultural and material peak. Sparta, Corinth, and Thebes were also important poleis in the fifth century BCE, but Athens outpaced them all in innovation, invention, and aggression. But Athens, because of its cultural grandeur, its ambition, and its flood of words and images, has always commanded most of the historical attention. Since historians follow the evidence and so much of it exists for Athens, it is hard to look away, but look away we should in order to restore some balance to the many Greeces of classical Greece. The fifth century BCE is not the story of a single polis, but rather of the resilience of the many Greeces (Map 2.5).

Sparta, the Radical Polis

Each polis was unique, but some were more extreme experiments than others. Sparta was an unusual polis long before the fifth century BCE. The Spartans were Dorians and thus Indo-European latecomers to Greece who had settled in the Peloponnesus. Sparta began as a series of four villages far from the coast on the west bank of the Eurotas River. Sparta was a landlocked polis without easy access to the sea. At first it controlled an area of 700 square miles in which it subdued the local population, transforming some into *perioikoi* (the nearby ones), who lived as relatively free subjects of Sparta. The *perioikoi* were called upon to fight in Spartan wars but had little influence on its foreign policy.

Spartan history took a radical turn at the start of the eighth century BCE when Sparta conquered neighboring Messenia, annexed its fertile lands, expanded its landholdings to over 3,000 square miles, and enslaved the Messenians as agricultural slaves called **helots.** From that point on the Spartans were a small minority within the region of Laconia (the southern third of the Peloponnesus) and felt forced to regiment their own society rigidly to maintain stiff control over a huge slave population. At about this time the constitution of the legendary Lycurgus was instituted. This constitution should probably be thought of as a set of working principles rather than a written document. The Lycurgan code of life militarized Spartan society. Its manifest purpose was to focus Spartan society upon the all-important need to produce perfect soldiers. Spartan men did not work but instead dedicated themselves exclusively to the art of war. Children were examined after birth and those deemed weak or deformed were left to die. Boys left their parents at an early age and were raised with their peers in common barracks, learning to fight, to sharpen their cunning by stealing from the *perioikoi* and helots, to spy on the subjugated masses, and to endure bad weather and lack of food and water. Once the boys became men and were named citizens, they were granted properties that slaves worked on their behalf. At thirty years of age, Spartan men married, but they never spent much time at home with their wives. Spartan girls were encouraged to be physically strong in order to produce strong children, to defend the homeland, and to oversee their slaves and estates while their soldier-husbands were away.

The citizen-soldiers of Sparta were a band of equals, but there were other political elements within Spartan society. Sparta retained the vestigial remains of its monarchical beginning and so still had two nominal kings, who occasionally led armies. Spartan kings were not raised in barracks to be citizen-soldiers and so were not always a respected force within Spartan society, but they were Sparta's representatives to the external world. The five annually chosen *ephors* were in charge of the Spartan citizen assembly and seem to have run the state, but the presence of occasionally dynamic kings, two royal families, and quickly changing external and internal problems meant that Sparta was less solid and stable than it seemed to other Greek states.

Sparta remained a relatively isolated regime, suspicious of the outside world, and devoted constantly to keeping a tight grip on its large slave population. The Spartan state was, thus, anxious to secure peace in the Peloponnesus and formed a Peloponnesian League of other Peloponnesian poleis to ensure the cooperation of its neighbors. The other great problem faced by Sparta was its relative lack of citizen manpower. Sparta might have produced the most impressive warriors of the ancient world, but it was never able to put many men onto the field of battle. The five thousand Spartans who fought at Plataea at the end of the second Persian invasion formed Sparta's largest army on record. More typical were the three hundred Spartans who had taken on the Persians at Thermopylae.

The polis of Sparta was a radical Greek experiment, one created to deal with its particular vulnerabilities (a vast territory, lack of easy sea access, a huge enslaved population, and small citizen-army). Sparta's cultural production was meager and that made mostly by *perioikoi*. What Sparta produced were magnificent warriors, just not enough of them. From its weaknesses flowed Sparta's dedication to land warfare, its reluctance to involve itself in wars, its slowness to act, and its vigilance and constant concern to suppress its vast, but restless slaves, who several times revolted. It must have been a wretched life to live as a Spartan slave, but it was not easy to be a Spartan.

Corinth, the In-Between Polis

Corinth had many advantages. Located at the eastern edge of the Peloponnesus, it controlled the isthmus that joined the Peloponnesus to mainland Greece. With its walled control of the isthmus, it could shut down land travel between the Peloponnesus and the mainland, as it did during the Persian Wars. As such, the ancients thought that Corinth handcuffed Greece. Corinth had an impressive citadel from which to defend itself and possessed harbors on both sides of the isthmus. Though Corinth had little importance during the Mycenaean Age, Homer described it as a wealthy polis during the Dark Age. As a coastal city, fronting two gulfs, it assembled an impressive navy, traded widely, and produced impressive crafts and manufactured goods for transport by sea and land. In the seventh century BCE, a family of tyrants ruled the city, but Corinth returned to an oligarchic form of government (rule by the powerful few) in the sixth century BCE.

Corinth's unique position derived from its geographic location. It was the in-between polis, almost equally distant from Sparta and Athens, but able to mediate between and communicate with both. Everything was good for Corinth so long as Sparta and Athens were dedicated to the same policies. Indeed, Corinth and the two powerful cities shared an interest in subordinating the smaller cities that lay between them and Corinth. Thus, Corinth was one of the most desired allies in the various balance-of-power struggles the poleis waged with each other. But

MAP 2.5 | Poleis and Regions of Southern Greece in the Fifth Century BCE
Sparta was located in the region of Laconia in the Peloponnesus; Corinth, on the isthmus that linked the Peloponnesus to mainland Greece; Athens, in the region of Attica; and Thebes, to the north in Boeotia. These important poleis played critical roles in the Peloponnesian War. *What role did geography and circumstances play in making the poleis of Sparta, Corinth, Thebes, and Athens so different? What were the larger regional realities of Greece? Did any of the four major poleis have a distinct advantage over the others for geographic and developmental reasons? If so, why?*

what had worked during the Persian Wars did not work when Athens and the Peloponnesian League fell out in the fifth century BCE.

Thebes, the Federalizing Polis

Thebes was a very different sort of polis from Corinth. Located in northern Greece on fertile plains surrounded by small mountain chains, landlocked Thebes was the central polis of Boeotia. During Mycenaean times it had held a prominent place. Thebes and its twelve rival Boeotian poleis turned to agriculture in the Dark and Archaic Ages, but Thebes never conquered and suppressed surrounding peoples and poleis as the Spartans did, perhaps because the rich land of Boeotia was sufficient for all. Instead, Thebes and its Boeotian neighbors were, after many minor conflicts, forced to work toward a federation of interests. Thebes was somewhat exposed in the Boeotian plains, but by the sixth century BCE it had erected massive walls around the city. Thebes never had a tyrant but developed a stable **oligarchy** of propertied aristocrats who ran the city. Perhaps as many as a third of the city's male population, including all of its hoplites, were considered citizens of the polis.

The agricultural stability of Thebes led to political stability and freed Thebes from pursuing trade and imperial goals. The Persian invasions, however, placed Thebes in a delicate bind. Inside Thebes, a party of Persian sympathizers advocated cooperation with Persia. Thebes did send a force of five hundred soldiers to fight alongside the Spartans at Thermopylae, but after the defeat, Thebes submitted to Persia and sent troops to fight alongside the Persians at the battle of Plataea the next year. The Thebans were not alone. Herodotus estimated that Greek poleis sent around 50,000 soldiers to fight for the Persians on Greek soil. When the Persians were expelled from Greece, Athens and its Greek supporters punished Thebes both materially and rhetorically. For the next twenty years, Thebes largely withdrew from Greek affairs, licked its wounds, and repaired the physical damage to its city, but as the conflict between Sparta and Athens heated up in the fifth century BCE, Sparta allied itself with Thebes. Thebes maintained a vigorous culture of music, aristocratic male bonding, and the poetry of the Theban poet Pindar (c. 518–428 BCE), who celebrated athletes, the Olympic Games, and the concepts of *agon* and *arête*.

Athens, the Democratic Polis

The geography of Athens shaped its history, just as that of Sparta, Corinth, and Thebes had theirs. Mountains cup the city-site, providing it with a natural barrier that in ancient times was backed up by city walls. The defensible Acropolis of Athens was the organizing feature of the site and the one that made Athens a unified physical space. The hinterland of Attica, the large region around the city, was relatively fertile, producing wheat and olives, but the key economic feature of Athens was its access to the sea, not just at one harbor (the Piraeus), but over a long stretch of coastline sweeping around Attica and jutting out into the eastern Mediterranean. Attica, an area of around 1,000 square miles (the second largest territory after Sparta), contained valuable silver deposits. Athens did not suppress the farming peoples of Attica, but instead incorporated all free males of Attica as citizens. In general Athens was able to balance its moderate agricultural production with its industrial productivity (of pottery, in particular) and sea trade.

Even Athens could not surmount the economic depression of the Dark Age and emerged in the Archaic Age with the same aristocratic stranglehold that suffocated other poleis. In 630 BCE, the noble Cylon tried to impose his tyrannical rule on Athens, but failed. The statesman Solon, who was both a social and a legal reformer, became archon around 594 BCE. He attempted to deal with the mass of indebted people and the failing administration of the polis. The reforms that Solon instituted included relieving the debts of the poor. Debt relief lessened some of the social tensions that had been building in Attica.

Solon also broadened the participation of the different Athenian orders in the political system, so that the hoplites and others obtained a stronger voice in politics.

Aristocratic families still held most of the power, but between 545 BCE and 510 BCE, the tyrant Peisistratus and his son ruled Athens. Peisistratus governed by placating common Athenians, buying their support with games and grain, and maintaining the outward forms of Athenian government (the assembly, the council of the Areopagus or senate, and the legal system), while manipulating them to his advantage. The general effect of the long tyranny of Peisistratus and his son was to curtail the aristocracy's claim to rule Athens. Aristocrats were forced to become part of a city governed by a wider franchise. A brief civil war occurred in Athens after the fall of the last tyrant, as some aristocrats tried to regain their former power over the state.

The polis of Athens was made up of demes (*deme*, a specific population grouping). The urban area of Athens and its politics dominated Attica. Small cities such as Marathon preserved the equivalent of a civic government, but they were subordinate to the foreign policies and economic direction of Athens. Still the local attachments of people were to their local demes. The roots of Athenian democracy lay in the recognition that all free males with property were citizens of the polis (that is, of greater Athens). But the tension between the rural and urban, coastal and inland territories within Attica made Athenian democracy a vibrant, almost electric mix of peoples with various interests.

The great compromise between these competing elements within the Athenian political system occurred after the fall of the house of Peisistratus. Two aristocratic families were locked in a struggle for dominance. Cleisthenes of the Alcmaeonid family found himself on the losing side and so took the radical step of turning to the *demos* for support. He proposed that the polis should have a council of five hundred representatives divided into ten tribes, fifty representatives from each. Each tribe would be composed of thirds made up of scattered urban, coastal, and inland demes. There were many reasons—military, economic, and political—for creating individual tribes, but it is likely that the new system favored the family and interests of Cleisthenes. Despite its complicated composition, the council of five hundred achieved some representative balance. Its power, however, was offset by that of the popular assembly, which was made up of all free Athenian males of a certain age. The *demos* remained, however, a limited group of citizens that excluded women, foreigners, slaves, and others. Athenian democracy was never universal; it was highly qualified.

Although large numbers of citizen-males (perhaps as many as 40,000) might attend the Pynx, or assembly-place, no votes were registered. Citizens voted with their raised hands or shouted their approval or disapproval of proposals. In a system of limited checks and balances, the council qualified the assembly's motions, sometimes redefining, sometimes overturning them. The coun-

The Greek Bubble

There is a problem, rarely noticed, with ancient Greek history: we are trapped inside a Greek bubble, a torrent of words, seductive and persuasive, from inside Greece and virtually nothing from outside. This was partially the product of the extraordinary literary self-discovery of Greece in the fifth century BCE, but the Persians, Egyptians, Hebrews, and Lydians also wrote. Yet outsiders took little notice of Greeks or their doings. Old Persian documents for the period are choppy. There have been accidental findings at Persepolis and elsewhere of bureaucratic and administrative documents written in cuneiform from the fifth century BCE, but the Persian Empire was vast and no sustained attention was paid to Greece in its surviving records. Is this the result of the accidental nature of the survival of records or a comment on the marginality and unimportance of the Greeks? We have no right to expect a Persian Herodotus or Lydian Thucydides to spin a narrative web about the campaign failures of Darius and Xerxes, but the almost complete external neglect of the Greeks in the fifth century BCE raises questions about whether the Greeks were as important as they thought they were and about the reliability of reports from inside the bubble.

Perspective matters, but how in this case do we test the Greek narrative against other records? The historian Thucydides was pleased to report how the Athenians had almost wiped out Mytilene because it was merely contemplating revolt, but archaeological finds now confirm that the Mytileneans were planning a full-scale revolt. In this case, archaeology allows us to qualify one written account, but how do we correct or qualify the Greek record as a whole when we only have Greeks talking to or about each other? Both Pericles and Xerxes speak to us through the words of Greeks, but no Persian conveys Xerxes to us on his own terms. The story the Greeks tell is compelling and convincing, worrisomely so. Perhaps that is why the Greeks mark the beginning of western history; they constructed a captivating narrative that the Romans, when they learned to read and write, adopted without dissent, attaching their story to it as its continuation. Thus, Greece and Rome seem continuous and, as two connected points form a line, so western civilization assumed a direction and self-defining character.

QUESTIONS | *Why are one-sided accounts dangerous to our understanding of the past? Why might the Greek (or Athenian) bubble be a problem? How might we escape from it?*

cil, whose members tended to be more aristocratic and wealthy, acted, therefore, as a senate to the assembly's congress or lower house, reserving some legal matters as its proper jurisdiction. The assembly could be swayed by popular speakers or demagogues, which made it a dangerous but fertile body of popular opinion. Athenian politics produced sophisticated politicians who appealed to the emotions of the people.

Athenian democracy was an important constitutional advance in the Greek world, but it was so complex and so different from democracy today, which has near universal suffrage (or voting rights), that it should always be qualified as *Athenian* democracy. Indeed, all forms of government in the Greek world of the time contained a mixture of elements: oligarchic, democratic, and monarchical or tyrannical, but the nature of the mix mattered, and it varied from polis to polis.

Living on the Margins of the Greek Polis

Each polis had different sets of customs, rights, and peoples, which cannot easily be generalized. The first distinction in all poleis was between the free and the not-free. To be free did not, however, guarantee full political rights in a polis. Some free men were citizens, but not all. Foreigners almost everywhere had reduced rights, if they had rights at all. In Athens, a distinction was drawn between transient and resident foreigners (**metics**).

The most unfree people in the Greek world were slaves, who can be categorized as rural slaves and city slaves. Sparta and Argos had large populations of agricultural slaves, enslaved as entire peoples when their homelands were conquered and annexed. From such slavery of place and ethnicity there was little chance of escape or improvement. City slaves in Athens, which is thought to have had around 20,000 slaves in the fifth century BCE, were generally foreigners who had been captured in wars or purchased from foreign lands; these foreigners included Greeks who had been captured in various Greek conflicts. Slaves were considered to be living property that could be bought and sold on the open market. Slaves had few if any civil rights. In Athens, slaves performed hundreds of lowly tasks from household work to street cleaning, bearing water, and prostitution. Some owners rented out their slaves for manual labor. An owner might free his slave or the slave might purchase his freedom, but this was not common. Escape

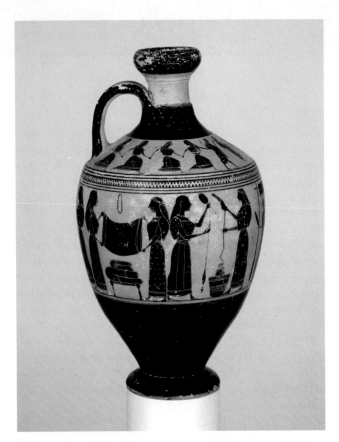

Wool Working and Weaving The oil flask shows various stages in the preparation of wool cloth by Greek women.

arose informally since merchants needed to acquire and dispose of goods and so required suppliers and buyers, and the means to convey goods. For Athenian merchants and foreigners, the purchase of goods and their delivery in Athens could span the Mediterranean and take many weeks or months. War was not beneficial to trade, merchant travel, or the transport of goods, but by the 430s BCE it seemed more and more likely, as Herodotus had suspected, that a great war was about to break out.

The Peloponnesian War

The Persian Wars had pushed the Greek poleis toward even greater efforts to preserve their independence from and advantages over one another. Even the Athenian drive to lead Greece against the next threat from Persia may be viewed as one of those strategies, leading to an Athenian imperialism that had both economic and political elements. After a half-century of amassing power and preserving a deceptive peace, Athens threatened the city-state system of Greece. The Peloponnesian cities led by Sparta finally had had enough and fought Athens in the long and disastrous Peloponnesian War (431–404 BCE), which broke the back of the old Greek order and undid classical Greece.

> How was the Peloponnesian War the natural result of ancient Greek history? Would there have been an Athenian Golden Age without Athenian imperialism?

The Delian League

The year after the retreat of the Persians after the battle of Plataea, Athens formed the **Delian League** (located on the island of Delos) of cities to continue to resist the Persians. The Spartans and the other members of the Peloponnesian League withdrew from the Persian Wars coalition, feeling that the war was over and their commitment fulfilled. The Spartans proposed that the Ionian Greeks should be brought back to Greece to avoid future conflict with Persia. The Delian League's mandate was the opposite: to liberate Ionia and its Greek settlements from Persian control. Each polis-member of the Delian League contributed ships, men, or money to the common cause. With these resources, the Delian League harassed the Persians in Asia Minor and in 448 BCE the Persian Empire was forced to free the Ionian Greeks from its direct control. In the meantime, however, the Delian League had become a vehicle for Athens to amass power and influence. Athens pressured member cities to support Athenian interests and to adopt Athenian-style democracy and values. The political and military leader of the pro-Delian, anti-Persian cause in Athens was Cimon. Under his leadership, Athens compelled the island of Euboea to join the league and conquered other Greek islands in the name of the Delian mandate. When the island of Naxos attempted to withdraw from the league, Athens attacked it.

was a risky proposition for most slaves, but slaves who worked in the mines, where the life expectancy was extremely low, were often prepared to risk torture and execution to escape their wretched condition. The Greeks did not question the legitimacy of slavery since they believed that nature had consigned the slave to slavery because of something inferior or tainted in the slave's nature. Many owners thought of the slave as a living possession like the family cow, but some Greek thinkers came to believe that free men demonstrated their nobility by the way they treated their slaves and women.

The status of women in Greek society varied from polis to polis. At Sparta, women were honored as the mothers of citizen-soldiers and as the keepers of houses and estates while the men were away at war. At Athens, free women stayed at home out of public view; they ran the household, managed the domestic slaves, and planned and made meals. Women of the courtesan class such as Pericles's Aspasia moved more freely in the polis and occupied a more dynamic role in public life. Athenian noble women had limited property and inheritance rights. The one area in which aristocratic women might enjoy a greater public role was in religious life.

Beyond the citizen life of Athenian free-born males in the Greek polis, other groups such as merchants and traders had limited political rights, but substantial economic freedom. Networks of commercial associations

CHRONOLOGY	Athens and Events Leading Up to and During the Peloponnesian War
DATE (BCE)	EVENT
478	Formation of the Delian League
459–456	Conflict with Corinth
456–431	Thirty Years' Peace
431–404	Peloponnesian War
Winter 431–430	Pericles's Funeral Oration
Summer 430	Plague strikes Athens
429	Death of Pericles
428–427	Revolt of Mytilene
421	Peace of Nicias
415	Males of Melos executed
415–413	Sicilian campaigns
411	Aristophanes's *Lysistrata*
405	Destruction of the Athenian fleet
404	Athens surrenders

Imperial Athens also established garrisons of soldiers in cities that contemplated secession from the league and planted representatives and spies in league cities. By the 450s BCE Athens was an empire in all but name and not a particularly pretty one at that.

Pericles and the Outbreak of the War

Pericles dominated Athenian politics for twenty years leading up to and through the first years of the Peloponnesian War. He was an aristocrat descended from two of the principal families of Athens; he opposed Cimon and his son-in-law, Thucydides, the historian of the war, who was ostracized in 443 BCE. Pericles has always seemed a charismatic politician: a powerful speaker, promoter of Athenian culture at the time of its greatest achievements, and colorful. The poets mocked him as a "squill-head" because his bulbous head resembled a sea-onion, but we cannot judge the deformity since in official portraits his head is covered by a helmet. He kept a foreign courtesan, Aspasia, as his mistress and treated her better than most Athenians treated their

The formation and activities of the Delian League did not sit well with the Peloponnesian League. Corinth, the in-between polis, was not at the time a member of either league, and had long had friendly relations with Athens based on their shared animosity toward the island of Aegina and the polis of Megara, which lay between them. After Athens campaigned successfully against both, Athens and Corinth were brought into direct contact without a buffer zone of shared enemies and interests. This produced what some historians have called a first Peloponnesian war between Corinth and Athens. In its drive for dominance, Athens pushed Corinth into the Peloponnesian camp. In 457 BCE, Sparta sent reinforcements to Boeotia to fend off Athenian aggression there. Thus, Thebes too was forced into the Peloponnesian camp, but Athens invaded Boeotia and subdued all its cities except Thebes. The conflict ended when the Peloponnesian and Delian Leagues signed a peace treaty in 456–455 BCE that was supposed to last for thirty years.

In 454 BCE, Athens removed any pretense that the Delian League was a company of equals by transferring its common treasury from Delos to Athens and no longer accepting men and ships as contributions, but only money dues from league members. Some of the money went toward civic improvements in Athens. To many of the Delian League members, it now seemed that they were paying tribute to Athens, not membership fees.

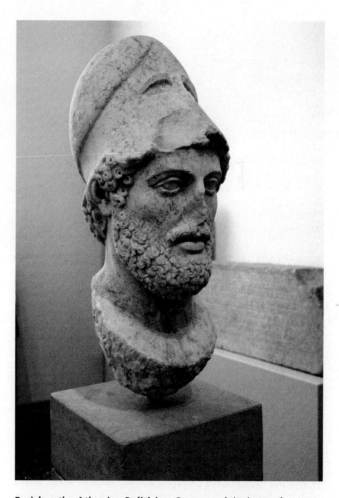

Pericles, the Athenian Politician On many of the busts of Pericles, he wears a war helmet, supposedly because his head was misshapen and the subject of ridicule. The wily politician did cultivate a particular public image of himself for democratic Athens.

MAP 2.6 | The Peloponnesian War, 431–404 BCE

During the Peloponnesian War, many Greek cities and regions struck up alliances with either Athens or the Peloponnesian League, headed by Sparta. *In geographic terms, where did the strength of Athens lie in the war? What of the Peloponnesian League? What role did the Aegean islands, the Greek cities in Ionia, and the Persian Empire play in the conflict, and why?*

wives. Like most successful politicians, Pericles, who regularly served as a *strategos,* pleased many audiences, but intensely irritated others. The Athenian *demos* held him in high esteem because he provided jobs, food, and diversions, and stroked their pride in their polis. Pericles served on the committees that oversaw the commissioning of Phidias's monumental statue of Athena and the completion of the Parthenon. Most Athenians cared chiefly about their prosperity and supported Pericles's active promotion of a hard-fisted, Athens-first imperialism that kept foreign monies flowing into the city. It was Pericles who moved the Delian treasury to Athens, and he opened up the treasury box for civic projects.

But could Athens afford Pericles or the drift toward war with Sparta? Pericles pursued an aggressive anti-Sparta policy, behind which lay his conviction that all the Athenian Empire had to do to triumph was to survive intact any conflict with the Peloponnesians. Pericles may have sensed how fragile Sparta was and hoped that it could not endure

an extended conflict. Sparta and the Peloponnesians held the higher moral ground, for they claimed to be interested only in liberating Greeks from the imposition of aggressive Athenian imperialism; they would preserve the polis status quo against Athenian tyranny. When the war finally broke out over Athenian interference with Sparta's allies, the Periclean policy was to withdraw the peoples of Attica behind the walls of Athens while the Spartans ravaged their lands. With the Spartan land force occupied, Athens sent its navies to ravage the coastlines of the Peloponnesus and Sparta's allies (Map 2.6).

In the first phase of the war, called the Archidamian War after the Spartan king Archidamus, Athens suffered minor setbacks. Pericles's famous *Funeral Oration,* as reconstructed by Thucydides, was occasioned by one such setback. Pericles's speech conjures up an image of Athenian civic perfection to the neglect of the bloodied war dead, men who had died violent and gruesome deaths. He laid out how Athens was superior to Sparta, but not everyone even in Athens trusted his message. (See Back to the Source at the end of this chapter.)

In 430 BCE, the people gathered inside the walls of Athens by the circumstances of the war suffered a horrendous outbreak of disease (most likely typhus, though some scholars have argued that it was an outbreak of bubonic plague), described in excruciating detail by Thucydides. Pericles died the next year, perhaps from the lingering effects of the disease. The Periclean strategy of sheltering the people of Attica inside defensible Athens created the crowded conditions that contributed to the outbreak and spread of the disease.

Sparta's allies, especially the Thebans and Corinthians, continued to hamper Athenian ambitions and weaken the resolve of Delian League member-states. In 427 BCE, when the Mytileneans of Lesbos contemplated revolt against the burden of being an Athenian ally, Athens ordered the slaughter of every male Mytilenean but had a change of heart, as related by Thucydides, and killed only one thousand, expelling the rest of the community from Lesbos and turning their land over to Athenians. Athens opened up another theater of war in Sicily, with mixed success. Neither side achieved a clear victory, and in 421 BCE they struck the Peace of Nicias, which was favorable to Athens inasmuch as the agreement seemed to recognize the Athenian Empire. Sparta asked for a promise that Athens would help defend it against its slaves, which was a sign of Sparta's continuing preoccupation with its domestic problems, but of little real value to the Peloponnesian League or its preservation of the polis system of Greece.

The Long Second Phase of the War

The Nicias accord did not produce a comfortable peace. Corinth and Thebes with its Boeotian neighbors refused to sign the treaty, and many of Sparta's Peloponnesian allies were unhappy with the terms of the peace. Various poleis jockeyed for power and position. Democratic Argos reemerged as a powerful rival of Athens and pursued its own dream of Greek dominance. Corinth joined an alliance with Argos, which made its own deal with Athens and then waged a war against Epidaurus. Sparta had lost the peace, and the Greek world was drifting again into petty polis conflicts that benefited the superior scheming of Athens. At last, in 418 BCE, Sparta reached a breaking point and marched against Argos, defeated it soundly, and forced it back under the Peloponnesian umbrella.

Stirring the pot in these affairs was the dynamic young Athenian politician and commander Alcibiades. Full of intrigue and complex schemes, he seemed to be everywhere. These were suspicious and dangerous times, and Athenian imperialism was at its most brutal, an indication that Athens could not tolerate the loss of any ally lest it lose them all. In 416 BCE, the island of Melos, an ally of Sparta, was seeking to remain neutral in the war, but Athens conquered the island, killed all the men, enslaved the women and children, and sent Athenian colonists to reoccupy the island. With actions such as the Melos murders, Athens won little respect or trust from its enemies and allies. At Alcibiades's prompting, Athens decided to take the war to Sicily, whose politics was dominated by Syracuse, a Spartan ally. Alcibiades was named one of the commanders of the fleet and set sail, but just as the war began Alcibiades was recalled to Athens to stand trial on charges of sacrilege and impiety. To avoid a sentence of death, Alcibiades deserted to Sparta and for several years served as an advisor to the Spartan campaign. The Athenian attack on Sicily was a disaster. The Athenian navy was destroyed, the Athenian commanders were executed, and as many as 40,000 Athenian soldiers were thrown into the quarries of Syracuse to die horrible deaths.

Despite the Sicilian disaster, Athens hung on, just barely. Its allies revolted whenever they could. Within Athens, an oligarchic faction vied for power and control of the war. The Spartans realized that to defeat Athens, it would need a naval force of its own. Lacking the funds to build a navy, Sparta turned to Persia. Sparta agreed to cease any interference in Ionia, thus recognizing Persia's claims on Lydia. The king of Persia lent naval support and financed the continuing Spartan war effort. In 405 BCE, the Spartan navy caught the Athenian fleet off the coast of Asia Minor and destroyed it. By autumn, Spartan troops were besieging Athens; the people of Attica were dying from starvation when Athens sued for peace.

The Peloponnesian League met in 404 BCE to decide the fate of Athens. Bitter Corinth and Thebes called for the complete destruction of the city. Sparta asked for much less: the removal of Athenian fortifications at the Piraeus or port of the city, the destruction of the long walls (north and south) that led from the port to the city, and the leveling of the great protective walls that surrounded the city. Athens agreed to remove its walls and defenses, to join the Peloponnesian League, to follow Sparta's decisions, to abandon democracy, to destroy all but twelve of its ships, to release its hold on dependent cities, and to confine its activities to Attica. The Athenian Empire was dead, but polis Athens survived.

The Brief Golden Age of Athens

The Persian Wars largely created and the Peloponnesian War killed the Golden Age of Athens (479–404 BCE), a short seventy-five years that produced one of the most splendid periods of human achievement. The Classical Age was not confined to Athens or to its Golden Age, but Athenian culture led the way, influenced wider Greek tastes, and set the standards. Athens was able to achieve so much culturally because of its democracy, imperial wealth, exposure to the wider world, and critical mass of people and ideas. A good part of its cultural achievement came from its imperial success, but with imperial failure came cultural decline.

All Athenian culture was, in one light, political. Athens produced gorgeous pottery, ceramics, bronze objects, and household items such as furniture that may seem apolitical, but even these cultural products reflected

The Acropolis of Athens with the Parthenon The Parthenon was erected on the highest point of the Acropolis and stood as a symbol of Athenian religious and civic virtue, and as a symbol of imperial might.

the bounty of imperial prosperity. Athenian ships and traders covered the Mediterranean, dependent poleis and bound allies were compelled to trade with Athens, and the tributary monies that poured into Athens fueled its economy. The same could be said, to a lesser degree, of Corinth, whose exquisite culture of fine buildings and sculptures was a product of its vigorous trading economy, but its culture was proudly Corinthian rather than aggressively imperial.

Athenian culture is infected with political issues. Its public building projects were a source of civic pride. The Temple of Athena (or Parthenon) on the Acropolis had originally been a public statement of the regime of Peisistratus, but in 480 BCE the Persians had set fire to the Acropolis. When Pericles took high office, he promoted the restoration of the Acropolis and financed it with silver taken from the treasury of the Delian League. The sculptor Phidias supervised the restoration, including the building of the large entranceway (the Propylaea), the construction of the temples of Erichtheus (an early king of Athens) and Athena Nike (or Victorious Athena), and the marvelous sculpted frieze of the Parthenon. The Panathenaea frieze ran for 175 yards around the Parthenon, showing a procession of hundreds of figures (gods, civic leaders, citizens, and musicians) coming to honor Athena Polias (Athena of the city) in a striking expression of the confident mood of democratic imperial Athens. Phidias also sculpted a massive ivory and gold-plated statue of the Virgin (*Parthenos*) Athena that could be seen by ships approaching the harbor. The temple complex of the Acropolis was a demonstration to the world of Athenian preeminence. The Parthenon was a graceful and exquisite statement of civic pride and Athenian stature; it was also propaganda paid for with imperial tribute.

Golden Age sculpture sought a perfection of form based on theories of almost mathematical precision about the symmetry, proportion, and balance of the human body in motion. The Athenian sculptor Myron's original works are lost, but later copies of his sculptures survive. His Discus Thrower captures the athlete in a convincing naturalistic pose at the moment of greatest back-

The Discus Thrower A Roman copy of the famous sculpture by Myron that is remarkable for its expression of classical ideals in both art and life.

405/404 BCE: The Unmaking of Imperial Athens

In 405 BCE, people were starving to death in Athens. The Spartans were at the city walls; the Athenian navy had been crushed and could no longer bring shipments of food to Athens. Although Thucydides seems to have survived the war, the surviving parts of his history do not extend to 404 BCE. He was, in any event, in exile in Thrace and would not have been able to supply personal details of the final fall of Athens. Thus, we lack a direct description of the changes that overtook Athens at the end, but we can infer them. The great walls and harbor fortifications that protected the city were torn down, which must have left Athenians feeling utterly exposed to their many enemies. Ships no longer pulled into the harbor with tribute and food from Athens's far-flung economic empire, which was dismantled quickly. The abundance of money that had funded Athenian culture dried up. Plays were no longer being mounted because there was no one, private or public, to pay for them. Employable artists and architects soon began leaving Athens for greener lands. The erection of great buildings, the mounting of plays, and the wickedness of Aristophanic comedies all stopped.

For the people crowded into Athens, the end of the war meant that the residents of Attica could now return to their homes, and the residents of Athens could reclaim their city. The population of greater Athens had been reduced by half during the war. Life in general and for some time to come was difficult in Athens, as it adjusted economically and politically to the new realities. Gone was the democratic constitution that had long governed Athens and the robust citizen debates of the war years. It was better to keep one's mouth shut in these years. A Spartan-backed faction, the Thirty Tyrants, ran the polis harshly. Yet it may have been the deprivations and extreme conditions of life in 404 BCE that made the Athenians so anxious to return to a better life. By 403 BCE, they were already plotting the removal of the tyrants and the restoration of their prosperity and democracy.

QUESTIONS | *Why was Athens unable to stop the disastrous Peloponnesian War that it had provoked? How disastrous was the Peloponnesian War on Athens, given its rather rapid recovery? Did the Peloponnesian War kill the Golden Age, or were other factors at work?*

ward tension and stillness as he prepares to swing his arm forward to release the discus. The athlete is not individualized, he is a perfected type; not a person, but an ideal. Classical art strove in Periclean Athens for elevated models of perfection. The discus thrower does not wince and is not bandaged. Sculpture was most often official or public art, as was Phidias's colossal gold and ivory statue of Zeus at Olympia, one of the Seven Wonders of the Ancient World, which was paid for by the poleis.

For introspection, Athenians went to the theater. Greek cities organized religious festivals, among them ones devoted to the non-Olympian, wine-god Dionysus. In Athens, at the festival of the Great Dionysia, competitions were held between a small number of comedies, tragedies, satyr plays, and poetry readings selected by the city officials for presentation. The plays, performed by men wearing masks, took place in a theater not only before an audience, but before a statue of the god Dionysus. At Athens, the festival became another opportunity for civic and political discourse. Though most of the tragedies were based on well-known myths about the gods, the great playwrights could turn these myths into opportunities to probe universal human problems and, under their guise, contemporary Athenian crises.

Aeschylus (525–456 BCE), the first great tragic playwright, fought in the Second Persian War and in 472 BCE presented the *Persians,* a drama about the recent invasion.

His *Oresteia* trilogy (*Agamemnon, Choephori, Eumenides*) examined not only the Trojan War, but also the triumph of civic justice over blood feuds. Aeschylus wrote seventy-three plays, only seven of which survive. Sophocles (497–405 BCE) is reputed to have written 123 plays, only 7 of which survive, among them the famous *Oedipus Rex.* His *Antigone* is a product of Periclean Athens at its height, and an open-ended exploration of civic power. In it the ruler Creon has, in the interests of civic justice, commanded that the body of Antigone's executed brother should be left unburied in defiance of the rites due to the dead. Antigone, driven by family pride and a sense of human dignity, risks all to bury her brother's body and, for her act, is condemned to be buried alive. Sophocles uses the story to explore individual and collective rights, the dangers of pride (*hubris*), and the nature of power. The play refuses to reveal which side is right, instead provoking the audience to think about the issues at stake. The last great, but least popular playwright was Euripides (c. 484–406 BCE), who wrote ninety-two plays, nineteen of which survive intact. His *Medea* may be the most famous and shocking of these, as to punish her husband Jason, Medea slaughters their children.

Though he was far from being the only comic poet, Aristophanes (c. 450–385 BCE), because eleven of his forty-four comedies have survived, dominates our view of Athenian comedy. Tragedy had its feet firmly placed in ancient myth and universal themes; comedy was current and not myth bound. Most of Aristophanes's surviving plays were written and presented during the Peloponnesian War. The outrageous *Lysistrata* concerns a congress of Greek women who decide to put an end to the war perpetrated by their husbands by withdrawing from sexual relations with them. With wicked asides, mock accents, jabs at recognizable politicians and current affairs, Aristophanes set his comedies at the center of the Athenian civic discourse as it whipped back and forth during the swings of the destructive war.

Athenian philosophy and science belong to the fourth century BCE and the Hellenistic Ages, but the writing of history asserted itself powerfully in the Golden Age.

Alongside Herodotus's long and digressive account of the Persian Wars stands Thucydides's impressive account of the Peloponnesian War. Thucydides, the exiled aristocrat and general, more analytically, but no less subjectively, probed the progress of the great war between the many Greeces. Unlike Herodotus, Thucydides used written sources and his personal observations of the war. He re-created the speeches of Pericles and others and wrote with seductive precision about events. Thucydides was not an admirer of the war, of Athens for causing it, or of the way Athens conducted it. For Thucydides, history was a contest for power and the calamitous Peloponnesian conflict a case study of its abuse and the dire consequences of bad policies.

Conclusion

The Peloponnesian War was not all bad news. It did push Athenians to ponder their place in the Greek world, the meaning of being citizens and human beings in times pushed to the extreme edges of experience, and the importance of history. Thucydides framed the war as one of bad human decisions, not as the playground of impish gods toying with errant humans. His account of the peoples of Attica fleeing their homes and fields for the safety of Athens and his heartrending description of the plague in Athens are studies in the war's profound impact on Athenians. Thucydides was rethinking the costs and benefits of Athenian imperialism or, as he framed it, the moral dilemma of the strong acting willfully and the weak being acted upon in ways they could not avoid. He showed his readers the stark underbelly of brute Athenian power but knew that the other actors—Sparta, Thebes, Corinth, and Argos—were just as bad.

Doubts about democracy were already spreading during the war. The Athenians had made democracy the issue by fusing it with their imperial policy and forcing their way of life upon others. In the Funeral Oration, Pericles stood at the center of proud and defiant Athens, but Socrates (469–399 BCE), the Athenian philosopher, and his circle of students doubted the wisdom of the Athenians. Indeed, some Athenians welcomed the oligarchy that Sparta imposed on them.

The Persians were for a time satisfied by the results of the war. Sparta returned to Persia what it had lost during the Persian Wars, thus sacrificing the future of the Ionian Greeks. The readiness of both sides in the conflict to entice the help of Persia to break the deadlock of power between them proved once again that the poleis of Greece thought mostly of advancing their own interests. Pan-Hellenism mattered much less than protecting one's own polis, and so Sparta turned to Persia to win the war.

Not all the victors prospered. More than ever, Sparta lacked soldiers and was spread too thin to control the conquered Athenian Empire for long. Corinth lost much

of its navy and was forced to subordinate its interests to those of Argos. Only Thebes and the Boeotians seem to have prospered after the war by feeding on the carrion of the Athenian Empire, looting Athenian dependencies and annexing neighboring poleis. The Peloponnesian War was not the triumph of the polis system that Sparta had promised; the Greek poleis were weaker after the war and never recovered their earlier dynamism and stubborn autonomy.

Herodotus had been right. He had warned Athens indirectly about the dangers of straying beyond its home and native land, just as the Persians had when they sought to conquer European Greece. Athenian imperialism was built on hubris, that fatal pride in its moral, intellectual, and military superiority so evident in Pericles's Funeral Oration. One might argue that the many Greeces could not have continued as they had for five hundred years, with hundreds of fiercely independent poleis scheming incessantly to weaken and dominate other poleis. The Greek poleis did not believe in the autonomy and independence of the polis; they believed in the autonomy and independence of their own.

The Persian Wars upset the delicate balance of independent poleis, transforming Sparta and Athens into super-poleis prepared to risk all. Sparta risked all to preserve its dominance over its Messenian helots and its traditional way of life; Athens risked all to create an empire and its culture flourished as a result. Ultimately the checks and balances of the Greek polis system were too great to be overcome by any one polis, for the poleis all existed within the limitations created by the Dark and Archaic Ages. Each polis had a fixed geographic environment, a deeply ingrained culture, and traditional adaptations to its circumstances or it could not have survived into the fifth century BCE. The great Athenian mistake was to think that it could rise above the stubborn balance of entrenched powers that had produced the polis system of the many Greeces. The Athenian Empire was the first of many empires that would fail in the West, most of them unable to overcome the intense cultural and political identities of the many regions of the continent of Europe. The failure of Athenian imperialism to dominate the many Greeces and the steep cost of the Peloponnesian War permanently weakened the polis system and the great poleis, leaving them vulnerable to higher orders of power. Something had to give and it did during the Hellenistic Ages that followed.

Critical Thinking Questions

1. Why and how did ancient Greece remain a history of the many Greeces rather than of one Greece?

2. What choices did individuals and their poleis make in events such as the Persian Wars and the Peloponnesian War that pushed their histories in one direction rather than another? Consider the cases of Sparta, Corinth, Thebes, and Athens.

3. How did the distant Dark Age shape the ages that followed and the essential character and limitations of ancient Greek history?

4. What role did chance or contingency play in shaping ancient Greek history? Consider such cases as the death of Darius after the brief First Persian War, the plague in Athens during the Peloponnesian War, and the recall of Alcibiades from the Sicilian campaign.

Key Terms

polis (plural, poleis) **(p. 38)**

Dark Age **(p. 39)**

Archaic Age **(p. 39)**

Classical Age **(p. 39)**

acropolis **(p. 40)**

agora **(p. 40)**

arête **(p. 43)**

agon **(p. 43)**

tyrants **(p. 46)**

demos **(p. 47)**

phalanx **(p. 47)**

hoplite **(p. 47)**

satrap **(p. 52)**

ostracism **(p. 53)**

Peloponnesian League **(p. 54)**

helots **(p. 56)**

oligarchy **(p. 57)**

metic **(p. 59)**

Delian League **(p. 60)**

hubris **(p. 65)**

Primary Sources in connect

For information on Connect and the online resources available, go to **http://connect.mcgraw-hill.com**.

1. **The Shield of Achilles**
2. **Hesiod's Complaint**
3. **Herodotus on the 300 at Thermopylae**
4. **Plutarch on Lycurgus and His Reform of Spartan Life**
5. **Thucydides, The Melian Dialogue**

The Perfect Athens of Pericles

The Peloponnesian War had barely begun when Pericles, the leading Athenian politician and architect of the war, spoke to the Athenians about their early losses and the excellence of their city and way of life. The *Funeral Oration* of Pericles is not a verbatim account of that address, but the reconstruction of it made by the Athenian historian Thucydides, who says that Pericles stood on a high platform at the gravesite and "spoke like this."

My first words shall be for our ancestors; for it is both just to them and seemly that on an occasion such as this our tribute of memory should be paid to them. For, dwelling always in this country, generation after generation in unchanging and unbroken succession, they have handed it down to us free by their exertions. So they are worthy of our praises; and still more are our fathers. For they enlarged the ancestral patrimony by the empire which we hold today and delivered it, not without labor, into the hands of our own generation; while it is we ourselves, those of us who are now in middle life, who consolidated our power throughout the greater part of the empire and secured the city's complete independence both in war and peace.

Of the battles which we and our fathers fought, whether in the winning of our power abroad or in bravely withstanding the warfare of the barbarians or Greeks at home, I do not wish to say more: they are too familiar to you all. I wish rather to set forth the spirit in which we faced them, and the constitution and manners with which we rose to greatness, and to pass from them to the dead; for I think it not unfitting that these things should be called to mind at today's solemnity, and expedient too that the whole gathering of citizens and strangers should listen to them.

For our government is not copied from those of our neighbors: we are an example to them rather than they to us. Our constitution is named a democracy, because it is not in the hands of the few but of the many. Our laws secure equal justice for all in their private disputes, and our public opinion welcomes and honors talent in every branch of achievement, not as a matter of privilege but on the grounds of excellence alone. And as we give free play to all in our public life, so we carry the same spirit into our daily relations with one another. We have no black looks or angry words for our neighbor if he enjoys himself in his own way, and we abstain from the little acts of pettiness which, though they leave no mark, yet cause annoyance to whoever notes them. Open and friendly in our private exchanges, in our public acts we keep strictly within the control of the law. We acknowledge the restraint of reverence; we are obedient to whoever is set in authority, and to the laws, more especially to those which offer protection to the oppressed and those unwritten ordinances whose transgression brings shame.

Yet ours is no work-a-day city only. No other city provides so many recreations for the spirit—contests and sacrifices all the year round, and beauty in our public buildings to cheer the heart and delight the eye day by day. Moreover, the city is so large and powerful that all the wealth of all the world flows in to her, so that our own Attic products seem no more homelike to us than the fruits of the labors of other nations.

Our military training too is different from our opponents'. The gates of our city are flung open to the world. We practice no periodic deportations, nor do we prevent our visitors from observing or discovering what an enemy might usefully apply to his own purposes. For our trust is placed not in the devices of material equipment, but in our own good spirits for battle.

So too with education. They toil from early boyhood in a laborious pursuit after courage, while we, free to live and wander as we please, march out none the less ready to face the same dangers. Here is the proof of my words. When the Spartans advance into our land, they do not come alone but with all their allies; but when we invade our neighbors we have little difficulty as a rule, even on foreign soil, in defeating men who are fighting for their own homes. Moreover, no enemy has ever met us at full strength, for we have our navy to attend to, and our soldiers are sent on service to many scattered possessions; but if they chance to encounter some portion of our forces and defeat a few of us, they boast that they have driven back our whole army, or, if they are defeated, that the victors were at full strength. Indeed, if we choose to face danger with an easy mind rather than with vigorous training, and to trust rather in native manliness than in state-made courage, the advantage lies with us; for we are spared all the weariness of practicing for future hardships, and when we find ourselves among them we are as brave as our plodding rivals. Here as elsewhere, then, the city sets an example which is deserving of admiration.

We are lovers of beauty without extravagance, and lovers of wisdom without unmanliness. Wealth to us is not mere material for vainglory but an opportunity for achievement; and poverty we think it no disgrace to acknowledge but a real degradation to make no effort to overcome. Our citizens attend to both public and private duties, and do not allow absorption in their own affairs to interfere with their knowledge of the city's. We differ from other states in regarding the man who holds aloof from public life not as "quiet" but as useless; we decide or debate, carefully and in person, all matters of policy, holding not that words and deeds go ill together, but that acts are foredoomed to failure when undertaken undiscussed. For we are noted for being at once adventurous in action and most reflective beforehand. Other men are bold in ignorance, while reflection will stop their onset. But the bravest are surely those who have the clearest vision of what is before them, glory and danger alike, and yet still go out to meet it.

In doing good, too, we are the exact opposite of the rest of mankind. We secure our friends not by accepting favors but by doing them. And so we are naturally more firm in our attachments: for we are anxious, as creditors, to cement by kind offices our relations with our friends. If they do not respond with the same warmness it is because they feel that their services will not be given spontaneously but only as the repayment of a debt. We are alone among mankind in doing men benefits, not from a consideration of self-interest, but in the fearless confidence of freedom. In a word I claim that our city as a whole is an education to Greece, and that her members yield to none, man by man, in independence of spirit, many-sidedness of attainment, and complete self-reliance in limbs and brain.

QUESTIONS | *How reliable is the Funeral Oration, given the re-creation of it by Thucydides? Why is Pericles so proud of Athenian imperialism? Is the speech fair to the Spartans and their Peloponnesian League allies? Why or why not?*

Source: Thucydides, *History of the Peloponnesian War* 2.36-41, trans. Alfred Zimmern, *The Greek Commonwealth* (Oxford: Clarendon Press, 1911), 196–200; revised.

3

The Hellenistic Theater at Epiduarus

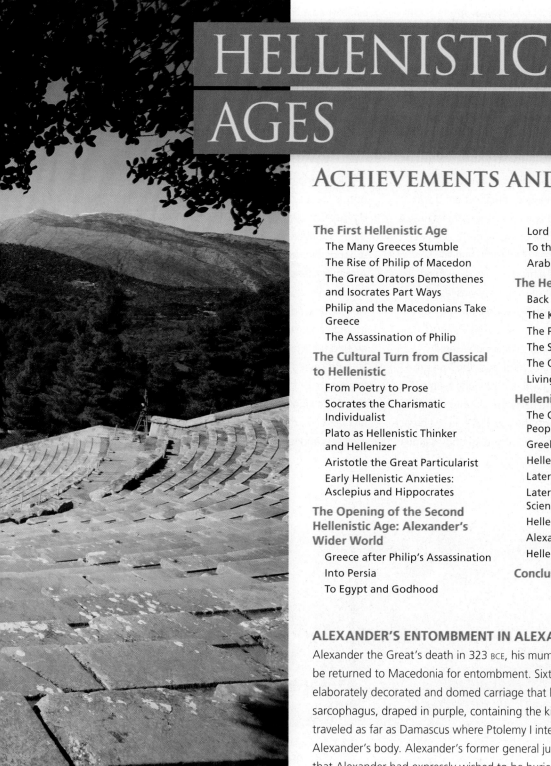

HELLENISTIC AGES

ACHIEVEMENTS AND ANXIETIES

The First Hellenistic Age
  The Many Greeces Stumble
  The Rise of Philip of Macedon
  The Great Orators Demosthenes
  and Isocrates Part Ways
  Philip and the Macedonians Take
  Greece
  The Assassination of Philip

**The Cultural Turn from Classical
to Hellenistic**
  From Poetry to Prose
  Socrates the Charismatic
  Individualist
  Plato as Hellenistic Thinker
  and Hellenizer
  Aristotle the Great Particularist
  Early Hellenistic Anxieties:
  Asclepius and Hippocrates

**The Opening of the Second
Hellenistic Age: Alexander's
Wider World**
  Greece after Philip's Assassination
  Into Persia
  To Egypt and Godhood

  Lord of Asia
  To the Indus
  Arabia and Death

The Hellenistic Kingdoms
  Back to Earth
  The Kingdom of Greater Greece
  The Ptolemaic Kingdom of Egypt
  The Seleucid Kingdom
  The Outliers
  Living the Hellenistic Age

Hellenistic Civilization
  The Greek Fact in a World of Many
  Peoples and Many Languages
  Greek Cities in Asia
  Hellenistic Economies
  Later Hellenistic Philosophy
  Later Hellenistic Technology,
  Science, and Medicine
  Hellenistic Religious Ferment
  Alexandrian Literature
  Hellenistic Art

Conclusion

ALEXANDER'S ENTOMBMENT IN ALEXANDRIA Two years after Alexander the Great's death in 323 BCE, his mummified body was ready to be returned to Macedonia for entombment. Sixty-four mules transported the elaborately decorated and domed carriage that housed the doubled golden sarcophagus, draped in purple, containing the king's body. The procession traveled as far as Damascus where Ptolemy I intercepted it and stole Alexander's body. Alexander's former general justified his theft by claiming that Alexander had expressly wished to be buried near the temple of Zeus Ammon at Siwah in Libya, though in fact Ptolemy redirected Alexander's coffin to Memphis in Egypt for entombment. Ptolemy probably planned all along for Alexander to be housed in Alexandria, but the city was still undergoing construction and Ptolemy was engaged in a deadly twenty-year struggle with the other claimants to Alexander's empire.

Finally it fell to Ptolemy's heirs to move Alexander's body to Alexandria, for Alexander was almost as important in death as he had been in life. Legitimacy and authority flowed from his physical presence, and Ptolemaic kings were entombed near Alexander. Over the centuries Roman emperors and tourists visited the tomb, whose gold was, for financial reasons, removed and replaced by glass (purportedly to better display Alexander). The Roman emperor Augustus is said to have asked for a private viewing, but when he bent down to kiss the emperor, he slipped and broke Alexander's nose. Since the third century CE, the site of Alexander's tomb has been lost, though many have searched for it, and still do.

The magnet of this show of a movable corpse, visiting emperors, and the royal pursuit of legitimacy was less Alexander's body than the city of Alexandria, the greatest of all Hellenistic cities, a hotbed of peoples, ideas, and religions for nearly a thousand years. Alexandria could boast of having one of the Seven Wonders of the Ancient World, the lighthouse at Pharos with a mirror at its summit to reflect the light of a fire some thirty miles out to sea and guide sailors safely to the harbor. The city also held the great temple of Sarapis (the Sarapeion); the Museum of Alexandria,

with its legendary library; a theater; a gymnasium; a forum; and the royal palace complex. The plan of the city, laid out by Alexander, was realized by Dinocrates of Rhodes. He established a Greek rectilinear grid-pattern of streets blocking out the residential areas and great public buildings that shaped the urban character of Alexandria. The most distinctive feature of the city was its two harbors, which the architect created by ordering the construction of a causeway, 600 feet wide, that ran almost a mile from the mainland to the island of Pharos, thus dividing the bay in two. A brackish lake on the southern side of Alexandria left the city nearly surrounded by water. Fresh water was piped to the city from the Nile.

Alexandria became a great commercial city and symbol of the vibrant cosmopolitanism of the **Hellenistic** or Greek-like Ages of the Near East. The Hellenic period that preceded them had been more narrowly Greek (not Greek-like) and grounded in the poleis of Greece and their defining natures. Alexandria was dramatically different. Throngs of traders, scholars, Jews, Syrians, royal officials, Greeks from all over the Hellenistic world, and natives brought the city alive, crowded its wide boulevards, and carried stories of the fabled city around the Mediterranean. In 271–270 BCE, a new Ptolemaic king processed through Alexandria in a magnificent parade. In advance of statues of the gods Dionysus and Priapus and of the divine kings Alexander and Ptolemy I, hundreds of exotic animals were driven: Asian sheep, Indian oxen, a white bear, panthers and leopards, a giraffe, and a rhinoceros. Behind the carts marched women personifying various Hellenistic cities. Next came a golden Bacchic staff 135 feet long, a silver lance 60 feet long, and a golden phallus 180 feet long topped with a gold star nine feet in circumference. If those symbols of fecundity and phallic

Death of Alexander the Great
323 BCE

Philip II conquers Greece
338 BCE

First Hellenistic Age
404–336 BCE

Persian Empire
550–330 BCE

500 BCE   450   400   350   300

The Harbor of Ancient Alexandria In this re-creation of the city of Alexandria as it might have looked late in Ptolemaic history, we see the two harbors of the city, separated by a causeway that runs to the island of Pharos. Just off the island stood the famous lighthouse and beyond it on the coastline of the city the royal quarter, with its own docks, and Alexandria's main port.

vigor were not enough to demonstrate Ptolemaic power, the 57,600 infantry and 23,200 cavalry who followed surely did. The Ptolemaic kingdom of Egypt, rich, proud, and Greek, achieved its luxury and cultural dynamism in a productive and pacified kingdom within a century after Alexander's death.

Alexandria was hardly typical of the Hellenistic Ages, but it did embody its central characteristics: maritime, urban, commercial, cosmopolitan, culturally Greek, and royal. Alexandria was also like the Hellenistic world in its newness; nothing quite like it had existed prior to the meteoric rise of the Macedonian kings. After the Peloponnesian War, Greece was forced to unite and to abandon its older commitment to independent poleis.

The passing of the Classical Age came quickly in the fourth century BCE in what can be thought of as a transitional period of the Late Classical or, as here, First Hellenistic Age (404–336 BCE), which ended with Philip of Macedon's death. The Second Hellenistic Age (335–30 BCE) began with Alexander's succession and march into Asia and ended when the Romans annexed the last of the Hellenistic kingdoms, Ptolemaic Egypt. The Greek

Second Hellenistic Age
335–30 BCE

Antigonid Kingdom of Greater Greece
306–168 BCE

Seleucid Kingdom
305–64 BCE

Ptolemaic Egypt
305–30 BCE

| 250 | 200 | 150 | 100 | 50 |

presence in and control of the eastern Mediterranean and large parts of the Near East and Asia would define the Hellenistic world. Alexander took Persia, Babylonia, Egypt, Phoenicia, and lands all the way to the western margins of India (today Pakistan). The Hellenistic kingdoms that arose after Alexander's early death consolidated Alexander's conquests and officially Hellenized or made them Greek-like. Yet the Greeks neither assimilated with the native populations and civilizations they conquered nor encouraged a deeper integration of peoples and cultures that might have permanently transformed the ancient world and so the West.

The First Hellenistic Age

After the fall of Athens at the end of the Peloponnesian War and end of the Classical Age in 404 BCE, the Greeks moved gradually into the first Hellenistic Age in the fourth century BCE. The Peloponnesian War had reconfirmed the fierce independence of the Greek city-states and, ironically, the necessity of imperial unity. The struggle between independence and empire continued but further destabilized the Greek poleis. In the first half of the fourth century BCE, the city-states of Sparta and Thebes competed to dominate Greece and the Persian Empire reemerged as a threat. Athens resumed some of its former glory and restored its battered democracy, but the emergence of the Macedonians under the inventive and determined Philip of Macedon brought the Athenian revival to an end. Philip took all of Greece before his own premature death at the hands of an assassin.

Why did Philip of Macedon succeed where so many others had failed in uniting Greece?

The Many Greeces Stumble

As a consequence of its calamitous loss in the Peloponnesian War, Athens was ruled briefly by a tyranny of thirty men, supported by a small garrison of Spartan troops. The Thirty Tyrants, who ruled harshly, were then replaced by a group of Ten Oligarchs, but in September 403 BCE the Athenians did away with oligarchy altogether and restored democracy. The cruelty of the brief period of tyrannical and then oligarchic rule made Athens long for the old days of prosperity and for a form of government central to its identity. Yet much had changed. The great Peloponnesian conflict had sapped the confidence of Athens and stripped away much of its economic empire and wealth.

Triumphant Sparta fared little better. Spartans thought that they had been called upon to defend not only Spartan independence, but also the freedom and autonomy of those Greek city-states that had fallen under Athenian dominance. Yet the outcome of the war led Sparta—against its best interests, which lay in isolation and the preservation of its limited resources of manpower—to at-

tempt to dominate the peace of Greece. Because of its lack of experience at imperial domination, victorious Sparta made a heavy-handed attempt to "pacify" Greece and imposed cruel tyrannies and oligarchies upon its defeated rivals. The deal that Sparta struck with Persia during the Peloponnesian War (financial resources to construct a navy in exchange for recognition of the Persian Empire's claim to Ionia) proved costly in the long run to both the Spartans and the Persians.

Greeks continued to be involved in Persian affairs. Cyrus the Younger, seeking to overthrow his brother Artaxerxes II, the great king of Persia, hired Greek hoplite mercenaries to help him make his claim for power. Among these Greek mercenaries was Xenophon, who wrote the *Anabasis,* an eyewitness account of the campaign and the retreat of 10,000 Greek mercenaries after Cyrus led them deep into Babylonia against his brother. When Cyrus was slain by his brother's forces, the Greeks were left leaderless deep inside Persia, but they rallied and made a daring return to Greece.

Sparta soon found itself at war with Persia. The march of the 10,000 may have wrongly convinced Sparta that Persia was weak and ripe for the taking. Sparta's war with Persia strained its resources and produced little. Moreover, Sparta's entanglements in Greece and Asia heightened tensions within Spartan society. A few Spartans had grown rich from Sparta's imperial ventures, but many citizens had become poorer and lost their citizenship rights. The anger of the newly disenfranchised led to a conspiracy against the established order in 397 BCE, but it was detected and suppressed. Three years later a naval venture of the Spartans at Cnidus off the coast of Asia Minor failed and the Spartans abandoned their Asian interests. Back in Greece, an alliance of Corinth, Thebes, Athens, and Argos allied against Sparta in the Corinthian War (395–387 BCE). Sparta won all the battles, but was unable to maintain its authority and slowly withdrew to its Peloponnesian homeland, where its power was now largely to be confined.

Following Sparta's retreat, the Athenians rebuilt the walls of their city, restored their navy, and re-established their maritime interests. Athens then allied with Persia against the Spartans, but it was Persia that imposed a peace of sorts upon Greece in 387 BCE at the end of the Corinthian War. Amid the shifting alliances of the early fourth century BCE, Athens also helped its old enemy Thebes to free itself from Spartan control. Thebes then made a play of its own over the next decade to assert not only its freedom from Sparta, but also its dominance in Greece. Thebes rejected the age-old claim of Sparta and Athens to be the two chief city-states of Greece. To the surprise of the ancient world, the outnumbered Thebans under their brilliant general Epaminondas defeated the Spartans at Leuctra in 371 BCE. The next year Epaminondas invaded Laconia. Sparta was in dire straits. Its citizen population was small and its older economic system of small land holdings was weak. Forced to relax its traditional way of life, Sparta continued to decline.

By the 360s BCE Thebes was in conflict with Athens, Sparta, and other Greek city-states. At the Battle of Mantinea in 362 BCE, Thebes prevailed, but Epaminondas was killed. With the great general dead, Theban dominance passed.

The Rise of Philip of Macedon

Watching the unfolding chaos in Greece was Philip of Macedon. Macedonia was a rough and fairly uncivilized part of greater Greece where blood feuds still destabilized society and the people spoke a dialect of Greek almost unrecognizable to the sophisticated Athenian ear. The Macedonians worshipped the wine god Dionysus and the royal dynasty claimed to be descended from the legendary heroes Achilles and Herakles (Hercules). Macedonian kings ruled both the civilized coastal areas of the Macedonian Sea north of Thessaly and the less civilized hill country of Illyria.

Philip was a member of the royal house but had spent his youth as a hostage in Thebes. There he had learned Theban military tactics and befriended Epaminondas. In 359 BCE, only twenty-four years old and back in Macedonia, Philip became the guardian of his nephew, the young Macedonian king. Philip moved quickly to remove his rivals and foreign threats. He refashioned the Macedonian army and moved against Thrace, whose great attraction was its gold mines. Before long Philip replaced his nephew, took the title of king, and set about subduing Macedonia.

Philip sought the impossible: to unite all of Greece under his control. Against him stood a resurgent Athens, again with a powerful navy, the prospect of internal problems at home in Macedonia, and the abiding threat posed by Persia. Philip, however, had cunning and immense ambition on his side. He professionalized the Macedonian army into a formidable force, tapping into the large manpower resources of the Macedonian tribes he had subdued. He perfected the Macedonian phalanx, a rectangular body of infantry armed with eighteen-foot-long pikes (called *sarissa*), rather than short spears, and flanked by an impressive cavalry that helped to turn the tide in battles. Philip waged an ancient version of total war. He was prepared to fight summer and winter, night and day, to surprise the enemy when he could, to chase down and kill fleeing enemies, and to employ siege engines to demolish city walls. With gold from his Thracian conquests, Philip had the financial resources to support extensive war. Of greatest advantage to him, however, was the continuing disunity of the Greek city-states to the south. Philip moved against his southern neighbors, and by 352 BCE the Macedonians were engaged in conflict in the Peloponnesus (Map 3.1).

MAP 3.1 | Macedonian Expansion, 359–336 BCE
Philip II consolidated Macedonia and then moved south into Greece, defeating the combined forces of those resisting his invasion at the Battle of Chaeronea. *What geographic and historical advantages and disadvantages did the kingdom of Macedonia have? Why was Philip's natural direction of Macedonian expansion south? Why was southern Greece such a prized possession for Philip?*

The Great Orators Demosthenes and Isocrates Part Ways

One of the first Athenians to become alarmed by Philip's aggression was the orator Demosthenes. His father, a prosperous Athenian furniture maker, died when Demosthenes was young. Inheriting little, he took up the study of oratory and the law. Since he had a weak voice, he reputedly trained his voice by filling his mouth with pebbles and made speeches in front of mirrors to perfect a rather flashy style of presentation. In time, he became a powerful orator in the Athenian assembly. Before other Athenians noticed, he labeled Philip an enemy of Athens, who must be stopped before it was too late. To this end, he wrote a series of speeches called the *Philippics* against the king of Macedonia. The Athenians admired the speeches but ignored the warning.

The orator Isocrates was older than Demosthenes and had seen the continuing chaos of Greek affairs and the failure of the autonomous city-state model of Greece.

Searching for Philip's Face

To his contemporaries, Philip of Macedon's body was a visual record of the many wounds that he had received in battle: his collarbone shattered by a lance, lame in his right leg, an arm permanently damaged, and, most striking of all, his right eye lost to an arrow. His consummate critic Demosthenes regarded these permanent disfigurements as visible signs of the king's lust for power. In 1977 the archaeologist Manolis Andronikos unearthed some unplundered tombs at Vergina near Aigai, where the Macedonian kings once held court. In one of the tombs were the shattered bones of a man (dated as between thirty-five and fifty-five years of age) and a younger woman. Philip died when he was forty-six and was cremated, but the bones of a body disposed of in that way survived and were entombed. The Macedonian tomb treasures, including sculptures and precious objects, were exhibited in the United States in the early 1980s. But were the skeletal remains of Tomb II Philip's? Circumstantial evidence suggested that they were. A Manchester, England, team confirmed the hypothesis; the damage to the skull was consistent with the reported injury to Philip's face. Two reconstructions of the face of the man circulated, one based on the assumption that the right eye had been untreated and a later one corrected according to Pliny the Elder's ancient report that Philip's doctor had so treated Philip's face after the loss of his eye that he was not disfigured. In the tomb a small ivory head of a bearded man bearing some similarity

First Reconstruction of Philip of Macedon's Head

to known coin portraits of Philip seemed to match the reconstructed face of the king. So far, so good. The world at long last had a "real" image of King Philip that made the past visible.

Investigating the past, however, is never quite that easy. Paleoanthropologist Antonis Bartsiokas pointed out that the male skull showed no dramatic damage and that the skeleton lacked evidence of Philip's other reported injuries. Other scholars argued that the objects found in Tomb II came from a period well after Philip's death. Who then was the man whose face was reconstructed? The current thinking is that it belongs to a son of Philip, Philip III Arrhidaeus, who was reportedly poisoned to death by the mother of Alexander the Great in 317 BCE. In the search for Philip's face, the interplay of bones and written records has been revealing. The identification and reconstruction of Philip's face were guided not by bones alone, but by reading the bones in the light of the information contained in written records. Making the distant dead more immediate to us is an admirable but elusive goal. In the end, however, words may win out, if we know how to read them.

QUESTIONS | *What is to be gained by knowing what celebrated historical figures looked like? What are the dangers? How should a truly scientific approach to historical facial reconstruction proceed?*

When Philip arrived in Greece, Isocrates wrote him a letter that circulated widely. In it, he called upon Philip to unite Greece and lead it against Persia. For Isocrates, the greatest threat to the future well-being of Greece came not from Philip, but from Persia. Demosthenes harkened back to the glories of the Golden Age and Athenian independence. Isocrates looked beyond Greece to the wider world and the rightful place of Greeks in it. In the two orators, we can dimly see the division into the old Greece and the new, Pericles and Alexander, the Hellenic and the Hellenistic.

Philip and the Macedonians Take Greece

By 352 BCE, Philip had amassed his forces in Thrace, just outside of Greece, and Athens was alarmed. Philip presented himself as a Greek and a friend of Athens, but few Athenians were reassured. The democrats of Athens had finally realized that absolute monarchs of Philip's kind should be regarded with suspicion. They formed alliances with other Greek peoples against Philip, but these ended in disaster. Philip took the city of Olynthus, destroyed it, and reduced its people to slavery. Athens opened negotiations with Philip and finally in 346 BCE struck a peace accord with him that lasted for five years. During those years, Philip insinuated himself into Greek affairs, becoming president of the great festival at Delphi, an archon of Thessaly, and a member of the great Greek council. Athens, however, remained wary and, after many intrigues against Philip's interests and the continual defamation of his claims and character by Demosthenes, provoked a war. The dispute was decided at the Battle of

Chaeronea in August 338 BCE. The Athenians, Thebans, Corinthians, and Phocians assembled a considerable army, but Philip had some 30,000 infantry and several thousand cavalry under the command of his son Alexander. Reports suggest that it was the cavalry that defeated the Theban line, which was critical to the Greek formation, and turned the battle into a Macedonian victory. Thousands of Athenians either died or were captured. Demosthenes was among those who fled.

Power over Greece now passed to the Macedonians. Philip punished Thebes for its treachery but still sought to pacify Athens. He returned the bodies of the fallen Athenians to their city, promised to free captured Athenians, and granted the city some of its traditional territories. Athens erected a statue to Philip, and even Demosthenes had to concede that Philip had treated Athens leniently. Philip established a Hellenic Confederacy that Athens and the other city-states were compelled to join. Sparta resisted, but Philip attacked Laconia and further reduced Sparta's already diminished territory. The Macedonians controlled the Confederacy and Philip soon announced his grand agenda to invade Persia, a plan that inspired few of the Confederacy's members. Philip allowed the Greek cities to remain relatively autonomous but positioned three Macedonian garrisons in Greece to keep the peace.

The Assassination of Philip

By 336 BCE, Philip had already sent an advance party into Asia Minor as a prelude to his Persian campaign. He had also married again, this time to a young noblewoman who might supply him with more heirs. He had married six times previously, including to Olympias, the dynamic mother of Alexander. Olympias and her son seem to have been worried by the implications of the new marriage and the prospect of more heirs to the throne, for they withdrew from the Macedonian court.

Philip's assassination, as with so many similar events in history, is a muddle of competing conspiracy theories, often created by contemporaries for their own advantage (to blame a rival, divert attention away from themselves, and so on). What we do know is that in October 336 BCE, Philip was killed by one of his bodyguards. The philosopher Aristotle claimed that the assassin was working out a personal grudge against the king, but the assassin killed the king at a wedding party and may not have acted alone. Several horses were waiting to carry the assassin(s) away. During his escape the assassin tripped before reaching his horse and was slain on the spot; the other bodyguards were cleared of involvement. A diviner was crucified for having identified good omens for a day that turned out so disastrously.

Philip's death pleased many. The Athenians awarded a crown to the assassin and Demosthenes rejoiced. The Persians, who knew of the planned invasion, doubtless thought that they had been spared the trouble of resisting Philip. Even Alexander and Olympias probably felt that their futures were more secure after Philip's death. Yet none of these reactions necessarily make any of these players party to the plot to assassinate Philip. His death may simply have been the result of a personal grievance, as Aristotle thought.

Philip has had the sad historical fate of being overshadowed by a brilliant son and dogged by the defamation of Demosthenes. Yet Philip shaped the Macedonian and Hellenistic future. After centuries of squabbling, the Greek city-states were finally forced to unite under his authority. Philip had fashioned the most powerful and dynamic army in Greece and pointed it toward Asia.

The Cultural Turn from Classical to Hellenistic

Before Alexander entered Asia, the culture of Greece was already turning away from the classical values of order, due proportion, perfection, and civic identity admired in the Athenian Golden Age. People began to doubt that answers could be found or that essential questions were worth asking. In the transition from classical Greek (Hellenic) to Hellenistic culture, particularism and individualism replaced the concentration on collective or universal human values that had characterized the culture of Golden Age Athens. In drama and comedy, philosophy, religion, and medicine, the thinkers of the post–Peloponnesian War era began to look in new directions, which better reflected the concerns of the new age.

Was Socrates a fish out of water or part of a great cultural turn and, if so, how and why?

From Poetry to Prose

The Peloponnesian War had undermined the confident certainties of the Athenians and the polis-centrism of the Greeks. The tragedy of classical Greek tragedy was that it did not outlive the great war. The complex social and historical conditions that had fostered tragedy and a rich civic life had changed. After the war, there was little surplus money or time to mount elaborate tragic plays, but the real reason may have been a lack of Athenian interest in examining themselves or their troubled times, as Socrates foresaw.

The last of the great tragic playwrights was Euripides (c. 485–406 BCE). He had rarely won the outright approval of the Athenian audiences that saw his plays. Late in his life, threatened with prosecution for impiety, Euripides abandoned Athens for the safer and more remunerative confines of the Macedonian court. There he wrote the *Bacchants,* in which the young rationalist Pentheus, who does not believe in the gods, is ripped limb from limb and eaten by his mother and the other bacchants (revelers and worshippers of the wine god) in ecstatic devotion to Dionysus. There is no escape for Pentheus; gods will be gods and will do as they wish. The *Bacchants* was not presented until after Euripides's death and would have disturbed an Athenian audience. The *Bacchants* led Athenians to a brutal place beyond civilization, the home of a non-Olympian, wine-soaked god, who was nonrational and willful. Euripides and the Athenians, battered by unending war, had come to doubt the underlying beliefs and structures of civilized life. Athens and its poets soon gave up on tragedy entirely.

Comedy faced the same dilemma. There were fewer resources available to costume the actors and little interest or courage under either an oligarchic regime or its fledgling democratic successor to poke fun at politicians on the great issues of the day. Like tragedy, Old Comedy disappeared, but it survived in the new forms of Middle and New Comedy. Aristophanes (c. 445–c. 385 BCE), the great wit of Old Comedy, was a transitional figure in the emergence of the new comedic art. He wrote only two plays over the last twenty years of his life after the fall of Athens. The *Parliament of Women* (*Ecclesiazusae*) from 392 BCE takes up a theme similar to that of his famous *Lysistrata,* rule by women and the common holding of property. The new play, however, lacked Aristophanes's former sparkle and wicked wit: there is no chorus and little that is bawdy or politically pointed in the play. His last play, *Plutus* (the god of riches), continued the playwright's late preoccupation with money. In this play about fickle fate and life's fundamental unfairness, wealth falls to the wrong people. Aristophanes reduced the characters to familiar types: an honest man, an old woman, her young lover, a funny god. In *Plutus* the outlines of New Comedy were emerging: absurd situations, stock characters, and harmless apolitical fun. It was this New Comedy that Menander (342–c. 291 BCE) would perfect. Though only one of his many plays, *The Grouch* (*Dyskolos*), survives intact, he was the acknowledged master of the form. Said one Byzantine critic, "Oh Menander, Oh life, which imitated which?" Hellenistic men and women found in New Comedy a domestic mirror to reflect their ordinary lives and the new realities and anxieties of the Hellenistic Ages in which they lived.

Socrates the Charismatic Individualist

He was plain to the point of ugliness—pug nosed, balding, squat—and proud of it. His background was undistinguished: his father was a stonemason and his mother, a midwife. Yet by force of personality and intellect Socrates (c. 470–399 BCE) became the western world's first great individualist. His individualism types him, as it did Euripides, as a transitional figure, one who lived in the Golden Age but died in and partly fashioned and reflected the newly forming Hellenistic one.

Scene of a Farce A fourth-century BCE image of a theater scene on a wine vessel. Hellenistic audiences loved these comedies of absurd domestic situations.

Socrates was a character so memorable that few could forget him. In a city-state dominated by collective civic values and sameness, Socrates stood out as different. He was a charismatic figure for many, a controversial one for most. He wrote nothing himself, though others talked about him a great deal. We learn about him through the writings of his students Xenophon and Plato, who recorded their subjective memories of him. In fact, we know more about him than we do about Plato. He fought with distinction on behalf of Athens in the Peloponnesian War, served as president of the Athenian assembly, and refused to carry out the order of the Thirty Tyrants to lead a just man to his execution.

He was already a controversial figure in 423 BCE when Aristophanes lampooned him in *The Clouds*. The Socrates of the play presides over a school, the Thinkery, that teaches students how to win arguments. In the play, Socrates is concerned chiefly with the natural world and cosmology, as the real Socrates once was, and descends from the heavens (or roof beams) in a basket. He doubts the gods and the certitude of any truth. In the play, an aged Athenian father wants his lay-about son to train at the school so that he can successfully argue his case against pressing creditors. The son, instead, turns his argument-twisting skills against his father, physically throttles him, fully justifies it, and offers to assault his mother in the same way. The alarmed father responds by burning down the Thinkery, sending Socrates fleeing in disgrace through the streets of Athens. Aristophanes's caricature presents Socrates as a clever teacher who believed in little, practiced a relativism whereby weaker arguments can defeat stronger ones, cast his spell over the impressionable young, overthrew family order, and disrespected the gods.

Socrates Socrates as portrayed in the third century BCE in Alexandria. He is squat, bald, and every inch an unforgettable character.

The real Socrates had street presence. Students and those who wished to discuss important ideas knew where to find him. He did not charge to impart wisdom and stoutly maintained that he had none or rather that his wisdom consisted in knowing how little he knew. Instead, he questioned those who claimed to know something, challenging their core assumptions and claims to expertise. The irony of studying Socrates is that we cannot put questions to the great questioner since we have only the reports of others about him, and we can be none too sure about those. There can be little doubt that he was a great individualist and openly questioned conventional thinking. He doubted the value of democracy, associated with rich young men, and trusted his own personal god (*daimon*) or inner voice. His critics and a public who had only heard of him thought, as did Aristophanes, that Socrates was a dangerous nuisance in Athens.

Little wonder that he was put on trial in 399 BCE. Athenian democracy had just been restored a few years earlier, and Socrates was charged with impiety for introducing new gods and for corrupting young minds. All Athens knew that some of his students had turned against Athens: Alcibiades had led the Sicilian misadventure and turned traitor, and Charmides and Critias had been among the Thirty Tyrants and had been executed

when their tyranny failed and democracy was restored. No friend of Athenian democracy, Socrates had the annoying habit of questioning all accepted truths in his pursuit of abstract moral truths: what is the "good" once all the things to which goodness is attached (such as a good meal, a good man, or a good idea) have been stripped away? The **Socratic method** of teaching consisted of asking questions and drawing forth answers from students and others. The method produced no positive answers but cleared away false assumptions. The technique was hard on those questioned, since it exposed their core convictions as unsound. At his trial, Socrates tried to use his method of close questioning to expose false Athenian assumptions about him and themselves. But his questions only further angered the jurors, who found him guilty. Even then the jury was prepared to let him escape into exile, as others had, but Socrates chose to drink poison and die, wishing until the end, as he said, to be a great gadfly pestering Athens. (See Back to the Source at the end of this chapter.)

Philosophy and science had not been native Athenian strengths during the Golden Age of the fifth century. They were, however, central to the Hellenistic Age. Socrates was shaped by the Golden Age, but in the difficult days at the end of the Peloponnesian War he had refused to act against his conscience when called upon to do so by the state. His radical individualism belonged not to the collective civic values of classical Athens, which he challenged, but to the emerging First Hellenistic Age. The relentless force of his method of examining and undermining accepted truths was hard for the average Athenian to bear, for in the end Socrates left them with less certainty—he stripped away their comfortable beliefs, leaving little in their place except a method leading to truth that few were brave enough to take up.

Plato as Hellenistic Thinker and Hellenizer

Plato (c. 429–347 BCE) was in many respects the exact opposite of his master Socrates: he was an aristocrat, wealthy, a voluminous writer, and founder of a school. His method and training, however, came from Socrates, but with one great difference. Although Socrates rigorously questioned accepted truths, he rarely if ever arrived at a satisfactory definition of the truth. Plato, as he aged and moved beyond his master, became a great synthesizer. In the logical sequence of the syllogism, consisting of a thesis, antithesis (its opposite), and synthesis (the resolution), Plato often arrived at the final step.

What we may not always fully appreciate in our study of his ideas is just how fine and supple a writer Plato was. It is he who brought Socrates alive for us. His re-creation of the trial, life, and thought of his master is utterly engaging, whereas Xenophon's description fails to reveal the epic dimension of Socrates's thought or personality. Most of Plato's twenty-six dialogues are not just philosophical discussions, but moving works of art filled with unforgettable characters and believable scenes of interaction between real people, with Socrates almost always at the center of the discourse.

Plato belonged primarily to the First Hellenistic Age, even though he may not seem to. His dialogues are set in the Golden Age of fifth-century BCE Athens, but he composed them in the fourth century BCE, well after the Peloponnesian War. Plato died not long before the Battle of Chaeronea in 338, when Philip of Macedon took control of Greece. Not only did Plato work in the new world being shaped by Greek instability and the rise of Philip and the Macedonians, but he had a more cosmopolitan focus than Socrates, who had preferred to remain in the streets of Athens. Though doubts linger about the so-called Letters of Plato, which claim that Plato visited places as distant as Egypt, he did visit Sicily several times to advise its Hellenistic tyrants.

Around 385 BCE, Plato established an Academy outside the walls of Athens. Though philosophical issues were discussed at the Academy, his school's primary mission was to train statesmen. Plato was much concerned with politics, with good rule and good rulers, topics taken up in the *Republic* and the *Laws,* two of his most famous works. His notion of the philosopher-king or wise ruler reveals something of Plato's concern with the problems of the transitional age in which he lived. Like Socrates, he was no lover of democracy. Plato believed that the state would be best ruled by a wise man. As such, the events in Sicily probably disappointed him since the tyrants he advised there were hardly paragons of wisdom and order; they stole, assassinated, and acted rashly in the pursuit of power. Plato's focus remained primarily fixed on the poleis of Greece, but his thought and actions were moving in new directions, as he does in the *Timaeus,* which includes a report on Egypt and its long history and treats the cosmos and natural history, employing mathematics to reveal the symphonic structure of the universe.

Though Plato's philosophy of the Ideas or Forms derived from Socrates's search for ethical abstractions such as the Good, it fitted the search for order and absolutes in the emerging Hellenistic Ages. In the *Republic,* he explained through the fable of the Cave the essence of his notion, one grounded in the Socratic search for the underlying truth of things. A man in a cave sees images cast on the wall and assumes that he is seeing real things when, in fact, all that he is seeing are images of the real things, not the things themselves. Similarly, in our daily lives, he thought, we mistake the things we sense (both material and conceptual) for realities. For Plato the Forms or Ideas are the real things: invisible to the senses but perceived by the mind as perfect, eternal, and divine. The material world obstructs our knowledge of truth, goodness, justice, and beauty. Thus Plato moves readers from the perceptible world to an unseen and imperceptible world that is perfect and true. That world lies beyond mere conjecture and opinion in the realm of knowledge and the mind.

Several attributes mark Plato as an early Hellenistic thinker: his interest in the wider Mediterranean, his preoccupation with the politics of rule by a single man rather than the people, and his drive to achieve resolution or synthesis in the pursuit of truth. He was an influential agent of Hellenization and had a formative impact on shaping the thought of the Hellenistic Age. Virtually everything he wrote has survived, which is a testament to the popularity of his dialogues and the importance accorded them in Alexandria. Even the stories of his travels, whether created or real, reinforce the image of him as a Hellenizer. Hebrews found in Plato's teachings a vehicle for explaining the theology of their Bible, notions of the soul, the divine, and the eternal beyond a material present. Cynics, Stoics, and the Romans received their impression of Socrates and their philosophical outlook from Plato, whose Academy lasted for almost a thousand years. Plato's writings became a touchstone not only of Hellenistic thought but of all western thought.

Aristotle the Great Particularist

Aristotle (384–322 BCE), born in the northern Greek city of Stagira, was the son of a physician who served the Macedonian king (Philip of Macedon's father) at Pella. Aristotle was orphaned early but apparently was reared at the Macedonian court and probably knew the young Philip. Amid the succession battles that disturbed that court, the seventeen-year-old Aristotle was sent to study at Plato's Academy, where he remained almost until the death of his master. The Macedonian invasion of Greece made Aristotle's presence in Athens difficult; he had Macedonian connections and sympathies not shared by Demosthenes and many Athenians. In 343 BCE, Philip invited Aristotle to tutor his son Alexander. As Plato had with the Sicilian tyrants, Aristotle accepted the challenge of shaping a young prince in the hope of producing a wise ruler. Full engagement in the politics of the mid-fourth century was, however, dangerous. One of Aristotle's patrons and mentors, Hermeias, who had married his sister, was captured, tortured to reveal the secrets of Philip, and crucified by the Persians. Throughout the war years, Aristotle remained in Macedonia. After Philip's triumph at Chaeronea, Aristotle returned to Athens and opened his own school at the Lyceum, where he remained until Alexander's death. At that time, Athens, venting its anti-Macedonian resentments, charged the philosopher with impiety. Aristotle left the city and died the next year.

Aristotle was more interested in natural philosophy or science than were Socrates and Plato. He had arrived at the Academy when Plato was away in Sicily for three years and gravitated toward the scientists studying there. Aristotle's family was originally connected with Ionia, the home of Greek science, and his father was a physician. Aristotle wrote dialogues early in his career, but they are now lost and he later abandoned the form and wrote purely expository treatises. Aristotle revered Plato but never slavishly followed his teachings. He seems never to have accepted the concept of the Ideas or Forms and urged Platonists to abandon the Cave and to settle down to the contemplation of the natural world.

Aristotle's early works such as the *Categories* and *Topics* take up the dialectical issue of how best to distinguish and describe things. He wrote on a wide range of topics: nature, physics, cosmology, animals (including their generation, movement, and respiration), meteorology, metaphysics, ethics, the soul, and literature. Unlike Plato, Aristotle sought to be comprehensive, systematically ordering a topic in all its details. His thought was primarily logical and analytical. In his orderly classification of particulars, Aristotle was the chief thinker of the First Hellenistic Age.

Aristotle was also a Hellenistic political thinker. He leaned toward Isocrates's view of a greater Greece. He was suspicious of Persia, supported the ambitions of Philip and Alexander, and looked to the triumph of Greek values throughout the wider world. His late work, the *Politics,* systematically examines the different constitutions of the city-states of Greece. Aristotle's political views changed with the times and, as an old man, he was hard pressed to keep up with the world Alexander was making. He may have been particularly perplexed by Alexander's blurring of the distinction between Greeks and barbarians. The latter he regarded as naturally suited to slavery. According to Aristotle, slaves were either slaves by convention (those forced into slavery by war and seizure) or by nature (those whose intellects lacked the capacity for human deliberation and so required a master to supply direction). He viewed human beings as social creatures who gather together in families and city-states based on complementary contributions to unified and useful human units. Although Aristotle believed that both men and women contributed as active and deliberative agents of the greater social good, he thought that men were more virtuous and contributed more to society because they could transform their deliberations into action. Aristotle died before finishing his great political treatise, but Alexander's career and premature death made all political thinking speculative by the 320s BCE.

Together Socrates, Plato, and Aristotle shaped the basics of Hellenistic Greek thought, including its promise and limitations. But Aristotle's practical concern with the particulars of the material world, with the single-man rule of kings and tyrants, and with analytical thought may have made him the one most representative of the thought of the emerging Hellenistic world.

Early Hellenistic Anxieties: Asclepius and Hippocrates

The Hellenistic Ages were a great period of religious belief, but one driven by individual needs. If the polis had once protected and defined a sense of community among city-state dwellers in Greece, Hellenistic men and women now needed to look after themselves, both materially and spiritually. The polis was not there to provide them with the same protection and sense of belonging. Kings and tyrants ruled huge territories and had their own compelling interests. Almost overnight the world had become vast and overwhelming for the Greeks. Hellenistic men and women often suffered from a feeling of alienation and loss, and so turned not just to philosophy, but to religion and medicine for individual relief and comfort.

At the end of Plato's *Phaedo*, Socrates asks his friend Crito to sacrifice a rooster to the god Asclepius on his behalf. They were Socrates's final words. Asclepius was a god of healing, whose cult became extremely popular in the Hellenistic Ages. Hundreds of shrines to him were erected, the most prominent ones at Epidaurus and Pergamum. Individuals sought to forge personal connections with the divine Asclepius. In times of personal crisis, the sick and needy slept in his temples in the hope that they would be visited by the god in their dreams and receive advice about how to cure their physical ailments and solve their spiritual crises. Believers paid tribute to the god and his healing gift with inscriptions placed on stele (standing stone tablets) outside the shrines. The remarkable testimonies left at Epidaurus tell of five-year pregnancies, children born walking and talking, and miraculous cures of the blind. These stories may surprise

Hippocrates or Asclepius Treating a Woman Both Hippocrates and Asclepius were legendary healers of the sick, so there should be little surprise that we can't be sure just which one is shown healing an ill woman on this Hellenistic relief. Both were heroes and exemplary physicians to the people of an age concerned about illness and physical well-being.

modern readers, who too often think of the ancient Greeks as supreme rationalists and their religion as one of harmless myths. But, despite the rise of sophisticated philosophies, the Greeks continued to hold irrational beliefs in their daily and religious lives that may have assumed increased importance and provided greater comfort in a searching and anxious age. The devotion to Asclepius may suggest just how needy and worried about themselves some Hellenistic men and women were.

The Hellenistic Ages were also a golden age of Greek medicine, but falling into two phases, an early one best represented by Hippocrates and a later one located in Alexandria. Hippocrates (c. 460 BCE–c. 377 BCE) and Socrates were contemporaries. Little is known about the most famous of ancient doctors. Though it is difficult to distinguish the genuine works of Hippocrates from those of his disciples and the various reworkings of his treatises at Alexandria, it seems beyond dispute that Hippocrates was the first scientific physician in that he looked for physical causes for physical ailments. He was, however, interested in the whole body as opposed to its particular problems. The followers of Hippocrates, however, found the Hellenistic Ages fertile ground for an active physical medicine to address the many physical complaints people had.

The Opening of the Second Hellenistic Age: Alexander's Wider World

The Greeks were not unfamiliar with Asia, the Middle East, and Africa, as the experiences of Herodotus and Xenophon prove. Contact with the Persian Empire had played a part in shaping the identities of the Greek poleis in territorial, cultural, and ethnic terms. Barbarians were, for the many Greeces, peoples who spoke a language that was not Greek and sounded like nonsense (*bar-bar-bar*). At the time of Philip of Macedon, the Persian Empire remained the one great threat to Greece's survival. Whereas the Greeks had exhausted themselves in the Peloponnesian War, the Persians had regained much of what they had lost in the Persian Wars. Yet there was still something fragile about the vast Persian Empire, as the Spartans had suspected. Alexander the Great would go to Persia to settle old scores but ended by conquering a great part of the Near East and Asia and created a new and wider world for the Greeks to inhabit.

How was the invasion of the eastern Mediterranean world, the Near East, and Asia more a reflection of Alexander's dynamism and drive than a Greek mission to conquer and civilize the "barbarian other"?

Greece after Philip's Assassination

Only twenty years old when his father Philip died, Alexander was already an accomplished soldier, having

DATE (BCE)	EVENT
336	The Assassination of Philip II
335	Destroys Thebes
334	Crosses Hellespont
334	Battle of Granicus River
Early 333	Visits Gordium
October 333	Battle of Issus
332	Takes Tyre in Phoenicia
Late 332	Reaches Egypt
331	Founds Alexandria
October 331	Battle of Gaugamela
330	Burning of Persepolis
330–325	Travels east
326	Crosses Indus River
324	Returns to Babylon
323	Dies after a royal banquet

distinguished himself at the Battle of Chaeronea, but his future was uncertain. If Philip had lived another decade or two, the importance of Alexander and his scheming mother would probably have passed. Persia would still have been invaded, but by Philip, who might well have limited his campaign to more achievable, short-term goals. Within Macedonian circles there were other claims to the Macedonian throne than just Alexander's. Invoking his right to avenge the death of his father, Alexander purged his enemies, and his mother Olympias arranged the murder of Philip's last wife and her child—they were roasted alive.

When Philip was assassinated, Greece thought that its Macedonian problem was over. Athens celebrated Philip's death but took little notice of young Alexander, repeating the mistake it had made earlier when it had ignored Philip's rise. Demosthenes, despite mourning the recent death of his wife, put on his finest clothes to parade through the streets of Athens in celebration of Philip's fall, but he should have known better. Neither the orator nor Greece had taken the measure of the ambitious young king who, within two years, suppressed a revolt against his rule by Thessaly, reasserted Macedonian control over Greece, and announced his intention to carry out his father's plan to invade Persia. Alexander first led

MAP 3.2 | Alexander's Empire and March into Asia, 334–323 BCE

In 334 BCE, with Greece secure, Alexander set out with his army for Persia, Egypt, and, finally, India. *How far did Alexander and his troops travel over a decade? What explains the chronology and direction of his conquests? Where did he stop his eastward march and why? Why was Arabia the next land he wished to conquer?*

a campaign against the Tribali near the Danube to avenge an attack that they had once made upon his father. The campaign was unnecessary, but it served as a training exercise for his troops and a demonstration of Alexander's leadership. Hardly was the little war over when Thebes, with the moral support of Athens and the financial support of the Persians, revolted against Alexander's rule. Alexander rushed to the scene, defeated the Thebans, and enslaved most of its population. He then utterly destroyed the polis, preserving only the poet Pindar's ancestral home. The example made of Thebes was a powerful deterrent to any future Greek resistance to Alexander's power. Greece was now subdued, and Persia awaited his arrival.

Into Persia

A more prudent man than Alexander might have delayed his march into Persia, might have married and produced an heir before leaving on a perilous campaign, and might have more firmly secured his political control of Greece. But Alexander was Alexander, a twenty-two-year-old

world winner who reputedly slept at night with a copy of Homer and a dagger beneath his pillow. Neither prudent politics nor ponderous reflection would deter him. He had a world to conquer, and his father had pointed him toward Persia.

Why Persia? The plan was Philip's, but both he and Alexander liked to claim that they were avenging Persia's assaults on Greece and the looting and burning of Athens during the Persian Wars. Alexander and his father were Hellenizing kings who saw the political advantages of placing themselves at the forefront of the Greek historical mission. Isocrates and others had maintained that Greece could never breathe easily as long as Persia, with its immense resources of men and money, threatened. Yet Alexander, like his father before him, was anxious to invade Persia for another, less noble reason. Alexander needed gold. The conquest of Greece had been costly for Philip, and his son had been forced to spend a great deal of money to keep his armies in the field and to buy support. Alexander needed not just glory, but gold from his Asian campaign (Map 3.2).

In 334 BCE, he assembled an army of almost 50,000 infantry and 6,000 cavalry, fewer than a quarter of them Macedonians. A sizable navy carried his army across the Hellespont. The young king was the first to step ashore, casting a spear into Asian soil, announcing symbolically that he intended to take Asia by force. Alexander's march into Asia also had a mythic dimension, since he repeated the symbolic deeds and religious dedications of the heroes and gods of the Greek past, particularly those of Herakles, as he went. His first battle was not with Darius III, the great king of Persia, but with one of his satraps (the governor of a region). The Persian army, which was slightly smaller than Alexander's, was divided almost equally between Persians and Greek mercenaries. On the day of the Battle of Granicus River, however, Alexander assembled only part of his army, less than 20,000 men. He led them across the river and into a battle that they won decisively. Then he turned to consolidating his hold on the coastal areas of the Persian Empire, including Ionia and Lydia. He did this in part to neutralize landing bases for the Persian fleet in the eastern Mediterranean, but lost his advantage by sending the Greek fleet home.

Alexander had still not engaged Darius, but he longed for that encounter. He marched into Phrygia in 333 BCE and headed for the capital city, Gordium. Legend said that it contained a wagon dedicated to Zeus and that whoever could untie the rope that knotted its yoke would rule all Asia. Alexander couldn't resist the challenge, but the knot was unmovable and so Alexander, not to be denied his destiny, severed the Gordian knot with his sword. Anyone could have done the same, but only Alexander dared to do so. Darius led a large army from Babylonia and engaged Alexander's forces at Issus in Cilicia. Though his army was outnumbered, Alexander concentrated his attack on Darius himself, which, as luck would have it, worked. Darius fled when the assault came too close and his huge army retreated in chaos. The Macedonians chased down thousands of Persian soldiers but failed to capture Darius. Alexander did seize Darius's rich baggage train and his family, which had been abandoned as the great king fled. Alexander treated them kindly, in essence replacing Darius as their protector and patron, and is supposed to have ordered them to learn Greek.

To Egypt and Godhood

Instead of pursuing Darius, Alexander moved along the coast westward to Syria, Lebanon, and the great prize of Egypt. He conquered Phoenicia out of fear that the Persians might attack him from behind, using Phoenicia as a base of operations. To avenge a grudge against the port city of Tyre, Alexander spent six months laying siege to the city. In the end, he destroyed much of the city, enslaved its population, and crucified thousands as a warning against resistance to his rule. He did much the same when Gaza refused to submit to him.

By 332 BCE, Alexander had reached Egypt, a land of endless fascination for the Greeks. Egypt was ancient, rich, and a home of the gods; it was also a distant and loose part of the greater Persian Empire. Egypt, pleased to be rid of Persian control, welcomed Alexander without a fight. He became its new king and honored the Egyptian gods. Throughout his invasion of Asia, Alexander was committed to establishing the evidence of his own divinity by exceeding what mere men could do and testing his own superhuman capacities. For this reason, he visited Siwah in Libya to consult the oracle of Zeus Ammon. There, at the famous oasis, Alexander entered the sanctuary where the priest addressed him as the son of Ra (Zeus to the Greeks). At last, Alexander thought, he had the proof of his personal divinity, which he had long been seeking. He was not merely the son of Philip, but the acknowledged son of the great god Zeus; ergo, he was a god. The god-king returned to the site of Alexandria, laid out the city, and set his architects and engineers to work. He also set about reorganizing the administration of Egypt, left garrisons in place, stationed a fleet of ships to guard the coast, and instituted a tax collection scheme. Then he retraced his steps to Persia and unfinished business.

Lord of Asia

Darius apparently made overtures toward Alexander, offering him territories west of the Euphrates and a daughter in marriage. But Alexander wanted more; he demanded Darius's outright surrender. Darius now knew that the impending battle was one for his empire and his life. He assembled a massive army, variously estimated as from 250,000 to 1,500,000 infantry and cavalry. Alexander's army consisted of 70,000 men. Moreover, this time Darius had no need for Greek mercenaries, but collected troops from his eastern lands. The battle took place at Gaugamela near a tributary of the Tigris River in 331 BCE. So large was Darius's army and so evident its formation that Alexander was able to plan his line of attack well in advance of the battle. His men withstood the charge of the Persian chariots, and eventually Alexander and the phalanx punched through the Persian front line and once again targeted Darius, who fled with Alexander in pursuit. Eventually Alexander halted the chase and led his men to Babylonia. Overjoyed to be free of Persian control, the Babylonians welcomed Alexander. The new lord of Asia retained the old Persian form of administrative control and moved on.

By the end of 331 BCE, Alexander and his troops were marching toward Susa and Persia proper. There he dined in Xerxes's palace, recovered ancient art removed from Greece during the Persian Wars, and took possession of the Persian treasury. But what Alexander wanted was Persepolis (Parsa), the great Persian capital, and so once again, after establishing a garrison of troops in Susa, he took to the road. Though the royal city surrendered to him, Alexander and his men had come for revenge and to settle the unfinished business of the Persian Wars of the previous century. They looted the city, assembling a vast array of riches. Alexander sent his gold on some seven

Alexander Turns the Great King of Persia A Pompeii mosaic captures the critical moment in the battle of Gaugamela in 331 BCE when Alexander, rushing forward on horseback on the left, forces the great king Darius to begin to turn his chariot around and to flee.

thousand camels to Susa for safekeeping. But the issue remained: what to do with the palace of Persepolis, now looted, but still a symbol of Persian greatness? Alexander was committed to two contradictory policies: the old commitment to avenge the burning of the Athenian Acropolis by destroying the symbol of Persian might and the new commitment to rule Asia with the support of the conquered Persians. The "accidental" destruction of the palace after a night of heavy Macedonian drinking satisfied both: the palace was destroyed, but Alexander, the lord of Asia, had not ordered its destruction and was said to have regretted the fire.

With the destruction of Persepolis, Alexander and his troops could have gone home with their goal achieved, but Darius was still on the run and plotting his return. In 330 BCE, Alexander's army set out to track him down. Darius was assembling a new army and hoped to reclaim his empire, but his support was weak in the far east of his empire and his reputation had suffered after the two defeats. With Alexander in hot pursuit, Darius's men overthrew the king and stabbed him to death. Alexander sent the body of the once great king back to Persepolis for a high state burial.

The Macedonians and Greeks may have thought that their daring adventure was now over, but Alexander wasn't finished just yet. Some troops did leave at that point, but the lord of Asia had the financial resources from his conquests to hire mercenaries to replace them and the foresight and practical need to begin training Asians for

his army. The Greek and Macedonian troops forced to remain with him tried to persuade him to halt his eastward march, but Alexander argued that the murderers of Darius were still at large, that the new empire needed protecting, and that the campaign would be conducted quickly.

To the Indus

Alexander wanted to extend his empire to the far east, to India, which Greek geographers had convinced him could form a natural eastern border for his empire. To rule his new lands with more authority and native acceptance, Alexander was already adopting Asian customs. He wore both Greek and Asian dress, donned an Asian crown, employed Asian bodyguards, and allowed his new subjects to bow or prostrate themselves before him. His Macedonian men thought that Alexander had gone native, and they resented the transformation of their king. At a banquet, a general named Cleitus insulted Alexander for his oriental leanings and praised Philip. The inebriated lord of all Asia ran the defenseless man through with a pike. Several plots against Alexander's life by his Macedonian men and once loyal supporters surfaced. He could no longer trust even his old guard, but still Alexander pushed forward.

Alexander pursued the men who had betrayed Darius into Afghanistan and there established yet another city named after himself, Kandahar. He marched his troops through the Hindu Kush into Bactria, crossed the Oxus River, and entered Sogdiana. The Macedonians were forced to fight their way forward and then to deal with resistance behind them. By the summer of 328 BCE, Alexander was preparing to march to India (to lands today a part of Pakistan). After conquering Bactria, he married the Bactrian princess Roxane, the daughter of one of the princes he had defeated. Alexander's men grumbled that the marriage to a conquered foreign woman was beneath him.

Of more irritation to the Greco-Macedonians was prostration before Alexander. As the lord of Asia, Alexander permitted ritual bowing and groveling at his feet as a standard Asian custom, but soon expected it of his Macedonian troops, probably because he thought that, for the good of his army, his soldiers should be treated equally. He also believed that prostration before him constituted public acceptance of his divinity. His Macedonian old guard declined to perform prostration and there the matter rested; the Asians treated him as a supreme lord, the Greeks as a Greek king. By late 326 BCE, Alexander had marched into India, heading toward the Indus River, fighting native peoples along the way. At a tributary of the Indus, the ruler of Taxila, Porus, amassed a considerable army containing hundreds of elephants to resist the invaders. The Battle of Hydaspes River was a monumental contest, but again Alexander prevailed. Alexander made Porus his subordinate and left him in control of most of his land. Bucephala, Alexander's favorite horse, died after the campaign and Alexander founded a new city there and named it after the horse. Alexander led his men farther east, but the monsoon season was upon them and local resistance was mounting.

At the Hyphasis River, his generals advised him that it was time to end the campaign. Facing a mutiny, Alexander relented, erected monuments to the gods to mark the end of his eastward advance, and ordered the construction of a fleet. Even in retreat, Alexander wanted to explore India to the sea and so he proposed that part of his army should sail south on the Hydaspes to the Indus and thence to the Indian Ocean. A great part of the army under General Nearchus took to boats. They saw whales; were attacked by hippopotamuses, which are fiercely territorial; and sailed west to rejoin Alexander.

Alexander and the rest of his army crossed the deadly Gedrosian Desert on their return to Persia. Back in Babylonia he found that his appointed governors had become corrupt and abusive in his absence; most of them had probably doubted that Alexander would ever return from his eastern adventure. He executed some, reprimanded others, and ordered all to disband their private armies. The lord of Asia returned to Persepolis and Susa, where he married almost a hundred of his Macedonian officers to Iranian noble women. He also recognized the older relationships of 10,000 of his men to Asian women as legal marriages. There too he married two Persian princesses, the daughters of the defeated Darius and the previous great king. All of these marriages were less idealistic (the joining of the races) than pragmatic political moves on Alexander's part. He did not need to unite the races (and no Asians were sent to Greece to marry Greeks); however, he did need to rule Asia with the support of the native population, did need Asians in his army, and did want to discourage native resentment to his rule. Alexander wanted Persia to remain subservient while he contemplated his next campaign.

Arabia and Death

In early 324 BCE, Alexander was planning a new campaign, this one against Arabia, whose riches and spices attracted him. Moreover, Arabia had not submitted, even symbolically, to Alexander, which served as a pretext for the campaign. His troops, however, were not enthusiastic about the venture and mutinied at Opis. He executed the principal plotters, made a speech, and sought omens but could not rally his men. When he began promoting Persian officers to replace the Macedonian resisters, his men relented. Still they had never embraced Alexander's Asian customs in dress or ritual or the integration of native peoples in his empire and army.

By 323 BCE, Alexander was back in Babylonia, tending to his empire and small outbreaks of disorder. He was also waiting on the preparation of the fleet that would support the invasion of Arabia and later Carthage. Alexander was also beset by problems back in Greece. Demosthenes was stirring up trouble once again but was put on trial and exiled from Athens. By May, Alexander's invasion of Arabia was ready, with all that that would mean for the subsequent history of the Mediterranean world. He held a banquet in June 323 BCE, at which he drank an inordinate amount of wine, collapsed, and died at only thirty-two years of age. The most likely cause of his death was alcohol poisoning complicated by malaria; a modern coroner might rule it a death by misadventure.

In a short thirteen years, Alexander had transformed the ancient world. He was not simply a conqueror who had marched almost 11,000 miles with his troops through some of the most hostile lands imaginable. Alexander deliberately set about carving out an empire. He overthrew old dynasties and empires, took new titles, and led the Greeks into lands, such as India, that they had not previously entered. He traveled with merchants because he was aware of the trading possibilities, founded Greek cities (dozens of them) as military outposts, and established Greek rule over the lands he conquered either with his own men and garrisons or through the subordination of local rulers who were willing to rule in his name. He was not, however, always a good manager of people or money. Had he lived longer, he would have expanded his conquests, but it is also likely that his empire, particularly at its distant margins, would have been difficult to hold.

What one can never avoid is Alexander's personality. It infects all our sources and was a product, in large part, of the man himself and the subsequent Roman portrayal of him. He drank too much, acted recklessly in moments

323 BCE and the Death of Alexander the Great

The effect of Alexander's death was immediate. The invasion of Arabia that he was on the verge of conducting was aborted. The more distant plan to attack Carthage and conquer all of the Mediterranean lands was forgotten, and resistance to Macedonian rule broke out in Greece. The wars of succession had begun. Had Alexander lived longer, he would most likely have conquered new lands. It is impossible to know whether the new campaigns he was planning would have lasted days or years; whether he would have been successful; and whether he could have held already conquered lands. Contemplating the *what ifs* of history can be stimulating but is ultimately a profitless pursuit. What can be said with some certainty is that Alexander's untimely death changed the course of ancient history. The year 322 BCE was very different from 323 BCE. The Macedonians went from conquering new lands to consolidating lands already conquered. They moved from the rule of one man over a vast empire to the rule of many Greek kings over discrete

Alexander the Great

territories within that empire. These lesser Greek rulers turned away from many of Alexander's practical policies such as integrating native peoples into the army. They did pursue Alexander's policies of co-opting native religions to support their reigns, but they ultimately grounded their legitimacy in Alexander whereas he had claimed a divine right to rule. His claim to rule rested ultimately on his conquest of foreign lands, whereas theirs rested on Alexander's conquests rather than their own. While Alexander pursued the new, his Hellenistic heirs settled down in established kingdoms and held on to the old. All of that came about when it did because Alexander one night decided to drink more than he should have.

QUESTIONS | *What impact does the "great man" or "great woman" have on history? Did Alexander change history or simply achieve what would have been achieved anyway?*

of drunkenness, and was vain and arbitrary to a fault. He was not just convinced of his divinity; he lived it, seeking out proofs such as breaking the Gordian knot to fulfill his divine destiny, retracing the steps of Herakles, and seeking out the oracle of Zeus Ammon in Libya. These actions were important not just to Alexander, but, at some level, to his men, who saw them as proofs of the specialness of their king. They never believed that Alexander was a god but accepted that he thought he was. Alexander was a brilliant general, motivated his men to do what seemed impossible, moved with determination and blinding speed against his enemies, was courageous to a fault, and inspired in executing battles. His greed for more land, money, and honor was a powerful force in driving his men beyond the limits of human endurance. None of this would have been possible had his father, Philip, not created the preconditions and possibilities that Alexander built upon. But Alexander was driven by the need to surpass Philip, to test himself against all that his father had accomplished, and to claim divinity in order to remake his origins. Philip conquered Greece; Alexander, a world.

Like Socrates, Alexander was one of a kind. He belonged to the Hellenistic Ages precisely because of his extreme individuality; his desire to explore new lands and to know new things; his cosmopolitan and interna-

tional interests; his engagement with Asian realities; his belief in rule by one divinely inspired man; and his commitment to trade, commerce, and a wider Greek world. He was also, of course, a dangerous megalomaniac who made hundreds of thousands suffer as a consequence. Alexander the Great may not be knowable, so exceptional were his ideas and person, so extraordinary were his accomplishments, and so mythologized and opaque the surviving sources, but it is hard to believe that any other person could have transformed a world as dramatically as he did and in so short a time. But in 323 BCE he was suddenly dead and the fate of his empire hung in the balance.

The Hellenistic Kingdoms

Alexander's legacy was a land mass, its future fuzzy and undetermined; an idea of a governable Greek civilization of the wider world, not yet tested or proved; and an image of himself, the great, golden boy-king and self-declared god. The realization of the Hellenistic world would not have been possible without his superhuman drive,

> **Why were the Hellenistic kingdoms and the retreat from Alexander's grandiose scheme of conquest necessary?**

but his ill-defined dream of an enduring empire was not achievable, at least not by any less driven, mere mortal. Those who followed him were realists who established viable dynastic kingdoms. Their Hellenistic kingdoms retreated from Alexander's boundless striving, but they endured for centuries.

Back to Earth

Despite the constant dangers in his life, Alexander had not planned to die. He was probably more surprised than anyone to realize that he could. He had made few if any plans for his succession, and there was no one who could succeed Alexander as another Alexander. His Macedonian soldiers had different ideas. Some wanted to choose a new leader, to take their fair share of the treasure on hand, and then to return to Greece. The great men closest to Alexander were not ready to abandon the empire that they had helped to create. These powerful men could not agree on who should be named king, though they did concede that Alexander's half-brother should take the title, at least temporarily, until Roxane, who was pregnant when her husband died, gave birth. Roxane delivered a boy who was named Alexander, but he and his mother were murdered in 311 BCE to end any prospect of the boy's elevation. In the world after Alexander the Great, the last thing any of the chief players wanted was the return of another Alexander.

The generals and established powers divided up Alexander's territory. They founded dynasties that took their legitimacy from Alexander and his conquests, for they were his warriors and had marched with him or had been granted power by him. A week after Alexander's death, the great men had decided upon the lands each would receive and immediately departed for them, accompanied by their share of the available army and treasure. For the next twenty years, these successors (*diadochi*) to Alexander fought a series of battles with one another to test their claims to Alexander's inheritance and to establish kingdoms: in greater Greece, Ptolemaic Egypt, and the Seleucid east (Map 3.3).

The Kingdom of Greater Greece

The most problematic of the three great Hellenistic blocks was Greece and Macedonia. It was the slowest of the royal areas to achieve stability and was always a difficult area to hold. Part of the problem was that it was the homeland of the Greeks and Macedonians and so a much desired kingdom; part, that it was as historically and geographically divided as ever. The main players in this contest were the Macedonians, lords of Greece since Philip's conquest. First there was Perdiccas, who had led Alexander's cavalry and who was with him at his death; then Cassander, whose father, Antipater, Alexander had appointed to run Macedonia in his absence; and finally, Antigonus the One-Eyed, who had been the governor of Phrygia at the time of Alexander's death.

Perdiccas tried to achieve supremacy early on, but things did not turn out well. How was he to achieve legitimacy? He thought of marrying the daughter of Alexander's mother Olympias, who was trying to hold onto some vestige of power and influence after her son's death. Perdiccas permitted Alexander's half-brother to be king but only as long as he wielded the power behind the throne. The Macedonians expected Perdiccas to secure Alexander's body for royal burial in Macedonia. Unfortunately for him, he lost Alexander's body and his own life in 320 BCE.

After the death of Antipater in 319 BCE, his son Cassander tried to take Macedonia, but he was opposed by Antigonus the One-Eyed. Alexander's infant son was nominally ruler, but Cassander had Roxane and the boy killed. There were a host of other claimants and players, but Antigonus finally rose above all of them. He and his son Demetrius, who are called the Antigonids, had wanted an Asian kingdom but settled for holding Greece and Macedonia, though not without considerable and continuing difficulty.

The Ptolemaic Kingdom of Egypt

Egypt fell to Ptolemy I, one of Alexander's generals. He was fortunate, for Egypt was a governable kingdom and one that was, if well managed, extremely wealthy. Egypt produced grain and papyrus, which the Mediterranean world wanted. Alexandria became the Hellenistic world's most important commercial and cultural city. Thus, the Ptolemies were able to attract the mercenary soldiers from Macedonia and Greece that they needed to oversee Egypt and protect it from the other kingdoms, particularly the powerful Seleucid kingdom.

Ptolemaic Egypt was royalist, highly bureaucratic, and aggressively commercial. The Ptolemies taxed almost all the activities and resources of their native subjects (land and agricultural production) and kept under their direct control considerable property, which was worked by Egyptians who held leases to the land. The king also maintained monopolies over mining ventures and salt-beds. Although the Ptolemies held lands outside Egypt and tried at various points to expand their portion of Alexander's wider empire, they succeeded in Egypt because they consolidated and secured their firm possession of a defined and productive kingdom. Steady wealth permitted Ptolemaic Egypt to remain militarily strong. It lasted the longest of the Hellenistic kingdoms, enduring for three centuries.

The Seleucid Kingdom

Seleucus I had been one of Alexander's commanders, and his kingdom was the largest of the successor kingdoms. In 312 BCE, Seleucus seized Babylonia, and by 303 BCE he controlled the eastern reaches of Alexander's empire and later still Syria. In theory, then, the Seleucid dynasty held an area from Damascus all the way to the Indus

MAP 3.3 | The Hellenistic Kingdoms in the Third Century BCE

After Alexander's death in 323 BCE, his empire gradually coalesced into three major kingdoms: the Antigonid kingdom of greater Greece, Ptolemaic Egypt, and the Seleucid kingdom of the Near East and western Asia. *How did geography determine the relative strengths and weaknesses of the three kingdoms? Which kingdom was likely to encounter the most problems and why? What lands did not fall easily into the three large kingdoms? Why did some lands quickly fall out of direct Greek control?*

River in India that contained well over 50 million people and dozens of important cities. The Seleucid kingdom was at its strongest at the start under Seleucus, but its size and complexity made it unsustainable. Distant parts of it began to fall away in the third century BCE. India could not be held, and everything east of the Caspian Sea fell to the Parthians in the mid-third century BCE. Moreover, the Seleucids were hard pressed by their Hellenistic rivals. The Ptolemies and Antigonids nibbled constantly at the Seleucid control of Asia Minor. The Seleucids were forced to pay their mercenaries with land, which over the long run left the dynasty pressed for cash. Yet the Seleucids had an impressive military machine, ambitious warrior rulers, and an army that employed elephants with impressive effect.

Alexander's eastern holdings proved, in cultural and logistical terms, to be too distant from the Macedonian heartland to maintain securely. Unlike Egypt with its one people and long tradition of being governed, the Seleucid kingdom was composed of many peoples: Babylonians, Persians, Bactrians, Arabs, Syrians, and

Jews. The one constant was Seleucid rule aided by its Greco-Macedonian ruling elite, but the centrifugal and ethnic forces pulling at the Seleucid center were too great to contain.

The Outliers

The three great Hellenistic kingdoms were not the whole of the Hellenistic political world. Various outlying regions and cities achieved some independence and viability, even if they had fallen away from Alexander's empire. Greek kings ruled in Bactria and parts of India on and off for several centuries. We know about them chiefly from coins and popular tales, for they had been cut off from the greater Greek narrative. Evidence of Greek cities with grid plans and Greek ornamentation in Afghanistan and Pakistan, however, suggest the continuing presence of Greek rulers in the east. Occasionally a Seleucid king such as Antiochus the Great raided Bactria and India, thus renewing efforts to reincorporate these outlying territories into the larger Hellenistic kingdoms. Demetrius I

India's Hellenistic Royal Coins

Coins are a remarkably enduring and useful historical resource. They carry information of several kinds: physical (the metals, their relative value, and quantity and dispersion), inscriptional (the names of rulers, their attributes, and occasionally a date), and iconographic (images of the ruler and various symbols). The range of information provided by coins is, however, limited. The images, postures, symbols, and inscriptions are often repeated, and the form is conservative and nondescript. Yet numismatics (the study of coins and medals) can supply, within its limits, a wealth of information. Some of it is quantitative in nature, for example, regarding metal content and worth, or the distribution of coins, their frequency, circulation, transport, and economic importance. Coins survive for a number of reasons. Physically they are small, hard, and made of metals that do not degrade easily. Coins experience different fates: many are hoarded, most circulate, and some are lost along the way. The monetary value of coins often exceeds

their metallic value, so that there is often little incentive to melt them down en masse.

The coins of Alexander the Great are extraordinary. His bust profile is nearly identical to that of the god Apollo. They also occur in a sequence that allows us to track the territorial and mythical claims of Alexander and his successors. The Hellenistic kingdoms, seeking legitimacy, early on favored coins depicting Alexander, his head covered by the skin of the Nemean lion (as in the Labors of Herakles) as a conqueror of eastern lands. One rare coin from the last years of Alexander's life shows him on horseback hurling a spear at King Porus of Taxila, who is fleeing on an elephant. Occasionally the Hellenistic kings portrayed Alexander with an elephant's skin draped over his head, since like the god Dionysus he was deemed the conqueror of India. Coins are also an invaluable source of information about the Hellenistic kings of India. Cut off from the wider Greek world, these kings are chiefly known by the coins they issued. One coin shows Demetrius I (r. 200–185 BCE) with an elephant-head headdress, signaling his possession of India. The reverse sides of these coins contain Greek inscriptions and the depiction of Greek gods. A large silver coin of Amyntas (r. c. 100–75 BCE) shows a king of India, otherwise unknown, wearing a helmet, while the reverse depicts Zeus and an inscription naming Amyntas as emperor and conqueror. The last coin of these lost Greek kings of India depicts Alexander the conqueror on the reverse. Alexander remained, as he had begun, the reason for a Hellenistic presence in India.

Silver Coin of Demetrius I with Elephant-Head Headdress

QUESTIONS | *How are coins, even now, both symbols of economic value and propaganda pieces? What are the strengths and weaknesses of coins as a historical source?*

(r. 200–185 BCE), the Greek ruler of Bactria, retook part of the Punjab region of present-day Pakistan. Demetrius was forced to recognize satraps and local kings who could rule in his name. Menander (c. 165–130 BCE) became a hero and philosopher-king of Indian legend in which he converts to Buddhism and controls lands as far away as the Ganges (well beyond Alexander's Greek footprint). Greeks ruled areas of western India and Afghanistan down until 55 BCE, but little is known about them.

Pergamum in Asia Minor near Smyrna was a fortress kingdom that soon shed Seleucid control. While the three major kingdoms dominated the Hellenistic world, Pergamum thrived by being small and defensible and by playing the great kingdoms off against each other.

Under the control of the Attalid kings, it became the richest of the minor kingdoms of Asia Minor. It produced silver, a range of luxury goods, and parchment (named after Pergamum), perhaps so that it did not have to rely on Ptolemaic Egypt's monopoly on papyrus production. In the second century BCE, Republican Rome annexed Pergamum and made it the control-center of its Asia Minor holdings.

Bithynia, another petty kingdom of Asia Minor, had been under the control of Persia until Alexander's conquest. Its Greek kings variously fell under the influence of the great Hellenistic blocks, but by the second century it was a viable kingdom and survived Roman annexation longer than Pergamum did. It was, however, pressed on two sides: to the east by Pontus and to the west by Rome. The kings of Pontus were also Greek and ruled there throughout the second century BCE. Pontus mounted a major resistance to Rome, but Republican Rome eventually prevailed after three sustained conflicts against the eastern territory. Bithynia became a Roman client-state and in 74 BCE a Roman province.

The outliers in the Hellenistic world testify to several things: the extent of Greek control of the rim of the eastern Mediterranean and the Near East and the inability of the great Hellenistic kingdoms to hold on to marginal areas. Rome eventually put an end to both the large and the small but should have been pleased that Alexander and his heirs had done so much to tame foreign lands and establish governments over a vast land mass. The process involved phases: the first, Alexander's conquests; the second, the practical Greek administration of these territories in discrete units, some of them huge, some of them small, by Hellenistic kings; and the third, Rome's eventual conquest of already packaged units fitted for foreign control.

Living in the Hellenistic Age

The nature and quality of life in the Hellenistic Age depended on when you lived, where, and who you were. To be a member of a royal family or to be associated closely with one brought riches and power. It was better to be Greek than native, better to live in a large city than a village, better to be a man than a woman, better to be an aristocrat than a merchant or sailor, better to be free than a slave, and so on. An urban life in a city such as Alexandria could be rich and rewarding. There were public entertainments, ample food, and economic prospects. But in Egypt, as we have seen, most people still worked on the land and dealt with greedy and rapacious landlords, who were often Greek. In principle, the Hellenistic king owned all the land by right of conquest, but in practice his friends and the rich held it outright and paid him taxes.

Even within the rigid hierarchy of the various groups in society, there were degrees of difference. Royal and aristocratic women were much better off, obviously, than lower-class women and slaves. Some royal women achieved positions of great prominence as benefactresses, as some inscriptions record. But, at the lower levels of society, infant girls were still abandoned and left to die or sold into slavery. Female infanticide and the always lower life expectancies of women in preindustrial societies kept the size of the female population below that of the males. A tomb inscription from the second century BCE describes Sokratea of Paros as a reputable woman, whom the goddess of childbirth (Erinys) had carried off during delivery, along with her unborn child. She had bled to death. This was a man's world, for the most part. In the fourth century BCE, a Greek rhetorician smugly said that the Greek male had mistresses to serve his pleasure, concubines to serve his person, and wives to supply legitimate offspring. In Egypt at least, marriage contracts granted couples common possession of their joint property and enjoined them to live in a faithful monogamous relationship. Since some Egyptian women could own property, they could and did become businesswomen, a privilege women did not share throughout the Hellenistic world.

Wealth was not spread evenly (it never is), but the divide between the rich and the poor in the Hellenistic kingdoms was immense. Complaint was common, but there were few revolts probably because the powerful were sensitive to any sign of unrest and found ways to pacify the lower classes with free wheat, games, and public entertainment. Some poor men drifted into the army, which exacerbated the recurrent problem of depopulation in many regions. So desperate for manpower were the Ptolemaic rulers of Egypt that by the second century BCE, they were recruiting Egyptian soldiers into their armies.

Slavery was a fact of this world. A fourth-century BCE treatise said that the most important possession was the human being and that the life of the slave had three aspects: work, punishment, and food. Food was necessary to produce work and punishment to keep slaves from becoming insolent and rebellious. The slave owner needed to balance carefully the three aspects to maximize and properly manage his property. Hellenistic aristocrats thought of slavery in economic rather than moral terms. The island of Delos had a large slave market that saw thousands of slaves bought and sold daily. Egypt did not require agricultural slaves, since it had its own native farm population and had relatively few domestic slaves, but it did need slaves for its gold mines in Nubia. A Greek historian described the scene at one such mine. The slaves were kept chained and worked day and night (since it was always night underground). Escape was nearly impossible and the care and feeding of the slaves minimal. These slaves were worked until they dropped dead and were replaced, all for the glittering gold that would adorn royal costumes, precious objects, and pay for mercenary soldiers. To enjoy the bounty of the Hellenistic Age, it always mattered who you were and where and when you were. That was, as we shall see, the camel trader's complaint about his lot in life.

Hellenistic Civilization

The spread of Greek culture (language, economy, art, religion, and thought) in the world carved out by Alexander had a profound effect on Roman and so western civilization. The critical sites for the diffusion of Greek culture were Hellenistic cities. Trade and taxes made up the principal language of interaction between the rulers and the native population of the conquered lands. Although there was some synthesis of Greek and foreign elements, Hellenistic culture at its leading edges was thoroughly

What were the key features and achievements of the Hellenistic Ages, and how did they differ from those of Golden Age Athens? What were the roles and fates of the native populations of the Hellenistic world?

Greek. In philosophy, science, religion, and art, the Hellenistic Greeks achieved remarkable things, but the limited nature of the Greek penetration of foreign lands and native cultures also set cultural, linguistic, and political limits upon the western future.

The Greek Fact in a World of Many Peoples and Many Languages

With the intrusion of the Greco-Macedonians into foreign lands that had their own languages and ancient traditions, Greek became the chief language of administration and trade. **Hellenization,** in its primary meaning, was the spread of the Greek language (and of the civilized customs associated with Greek culture). Native languages and cultures did not disappear. Instead, Greek was laid over them as the language of authority and interaction. But while Alexander and his successors, as the powerful often do, assumed that the conquered peoples (or, at least, their elite) should learn Greek, the Greeks as a whole never learned native tongues. The famous Rosetta Stone is an exceptional and revealing piece. It contains a decree of Egyptian priests marking the anniversary of the elevation of Ptolemy V to kingship in 196 BCE. The Rosetta Stone is remarkable because it is a bilingual tablet, containing the decree in Egyptian (in two scripts: hieroglyphic and the demotic or cursive form of the same language) and Greek. The Egyptian text is above the Greek, probably because the decree was written by Egyptians for Egyptians. Bilingualism was a native necessity, a Greek rarity, perhaps explaining why there aren't other Rosetta Stones. Since Greek was the learned and paramount language of the new world made by Alexander, native things might be translated into Greek, but Greek works were rarely translated into native languages. The Hebrew Bible (the Old Testament) was translated into Greek in a version called the Septuagint, not the *Iliad* into Hebrew.

The Greek language was changing, perhaps hastened by the Hellenistic world. Attic or Athenian Greek, which had dominated the Golden Age, was replaced by *koine*, the grammatically simpler form that became the common Greek of the Hellenistic Ages. *Koine* standardized Greek, eliminating regional variations, but picked up little from the native languages of the occupied lands aside from some local pronunciations and words for native objects not previously known to the Greeks. The Greek language may have remained relatively free from external influence, but Greek had a large impact on native languages such as Coptic, Syriac, and in time Latin. These native languages absorbed new vocabulary from Greek, testifying to the powerful presence of Greek in their worlds. Hebrew, in particular, absorbed a host of terms from Greek that rabbis employed to explain their sacred scriptures.

The Rosetta Stone Recovered from a wall in Egypt by Napoleon's soldiers, the stone provides parallel texts of an official Hellenistic proclamation in three scripts and two languages, from top to bottom: Egyptian hieroglyphics, Egyptian cursive or demotic, and Greek.

The agents of the diffusion of the Greek language were many: kings who established royal courts and distributed royal privileges; royal officials; Greek and Macedonian soldiers established in garrisons in the cities and distant regions of the kingdoms; and Greek traders. Yet the Hellenization (in the sense of learning Greek) of the native population was not promoted actively by the Greeks. Instead, it seems to have been more of a natural need for ambitious and commercially savvy natives. Positions of high power belonged to the Greco-Macedonians, and they did not need to learn native languages. Syrians and Egyptians complained that they were discriminated against because they were unable to Hellenize. Many Greeks looked down on natives. A woman in a Hellenistic poem dismissed the Egyptians as so many ants, and a Greek epigram circulating in the Hellenistic world said that one should thank the gods for being born a human not an animal, a man not a woman, and a Greek not a barbarian. Very few natives ever rose to positions of power and responsibility in the kingdoms. In the Seleucid kingdom of the third century, less than

The Camel Trader's Complaint

In regimes of foreign autocratic power, taxation, and economic exploitation, there are intermediaries between the ruling powers and the natives at the lower end of the scale. Such a world is revealed by the archives of officials at work in Ptolemaic Egypt. Apollonius was a financial officer serving Ptolemy II (Philadelphus) in the mid-third century BCE in Egypt. Zenon, an agent of Apollonius, preserved on papyrus the correspondence sent to his master by people requesting privileges, permissions, and assistance. In one case, Egyptian farmers wrote to complain that a Greek named Damis had taken away lands that Apollonius had leased to them. When they protested, Damis arrested three elders and forced them to renounce their rights. In their petition to Apollonius, the farmers complained about Damis, a wicked Egyptian scribe, and newcomers (Greek migrants), who knew nothing of Egyptian agriculture. The farmers traveled to Alexandria to submit their petition, but after waiting for twenty days they had exhausted their resources and become desperate; hence, their plea to Apollonius.

Even more plaintive is the letter that an unnamed camel merchant sent to Zenon in 256 or 255 BCE. He reminded Zenon that he had been left in Syria with Crotus, another of Apollonius's agents, to complete a transaction for some camels. He reported that Crotus had repeatedly refused to pay him, even though Zenon had ordered him to do so. The camel dealer, after waiting in vain for Zenon to return, finally left Syria and followed Zenon's order to travel to Philadelphia in Egypt and to report to one Jason. This Jason refused to pay the camel trader for nine months' work, though he did give him a clothing allowance and offered to pay him in cheap wine. The camel merchant complained that Crotus and Jason had disrespected him because he was a barbarian. He asked Zenon to order Crotus and Jason to pay him what he was owed and to stop using the fact that he didn't know Greek as an excuse for abusing him. The camel trader's plight was that of many natives in the Hellenistic kingdoms. They suffered from real discrimination, attributing it chiefly to their inability to speak Greek. Their view of the Hellenistic world was less than rosy; to them it seemed economically exploitative, linguistically divided, and culturally arrogant. The camel merchant's resentment against the established Greek order and its fundamental unfairness was probably common.

The High Life of the Hellenistic Elite A master reclining on a couch is waited on by a slave. The relationship between masters and slaves was not always as comfortable as this Ptolemaic relief would suggest. There were reports from the baths in Alexandria of incidents in which masters were doused with scalding water by their slaves. It is unlikely that all these incidents were accidents.

QUESTIONS | *What problems do obvious social and cultural inequities lead to? How might Zenon's role as intermediary and supervisor have softened the cultural and economic solitudes?*

2 percent of the native population held positions of power and prominence. Over time some of these barriers broke down and natives rose to positions of greater power, but such natives were completely Hellenized.

The Hellenistic Age was an age of movement and dislocation, which is reflected in its new comedies, which tell stories of shipwrecks and long-lost family members. The Greeks had left the smaller confined quarters of Greece for a wider world, but so did Phoenicians, Arabs, Ethiopians, and Etruscans. In this world on the move, travel on the Mediterranean Sea became more common, if no less dangerous. Many of the shipwrecks identified in the Mediterranean date from Hellenistic times. Traders moved from port to port, seeking spices from India and China, lumber from Europe, and ivory from Africa. Even peoples outside the Hellenistic world such as the Romans and Etruscans were forced to begin dealing in the Greek language if they were to play a part in the Hellenistic Age and its robust economy.

Greek Cities in Asia

The site of cultural diffusion was typically the Hellenistic city, where Greeks and other peoples mixed and interacted. Alexander founded dozens of cities (almost all of them named after him), though probably not as many as the seventy with which he was credited. He intended these cities to be military, strategic, and administrative centers for the control of the conquered lands. When he died, there were, however, relatively few Greeks and Macedonians in Asia. His Greco-Macedonian soldiers had not come to stay. They did their time, expected to be paid, and then hoped to return home. Mercenaries from Greece and Macedonia, Greek traders, royal officials, and learned men were attracted to Hellenistic cities over the next several centuries. Without this mix of peoples, Hellenistic rule and civilization would not have been sustainable.

Hellenistic cities varied in style and function from region to region. Some were centrally planned from the ground up; some developed alongside previously existing towns. Greco-Macedonians formed the ruling elite, but natives and slaves served the economic needs of the cities. A few cities such as Seleucia remained closed societies of Greeks. Few Greek women were among the original settlers of the Asian cities; soldiers took Asian wives, though in the later Hellenistic period, upper-class Greek citizens brought their wives and families with them. The central Greek institution of the Hellenistic city was the **gymnasium,** which was a place of recreation, exercise, education, and cultural exchange; gymnasia were generally exclusive institutions—all the Greek citizens of a city were expected to belong, but few others were allowed in. Other institutions such as assemblies and courts followed, depending on the size and function of the city. Egypt was unusual in not having been a land of many cities before the arrival of the Greeks. Alexandria was special; it became not only the chief city of Greek Egypt, but also the most dazzling city of the Hellenistic Age.

Hellenistic Economies

Hellenistic thinkers tended to divide economies into four types: royal, regional, urban, and domestic (the household). Yet throughout the fourth century BCE, the Hellenistic economy was a haphazard one that remains difficult to analyze. The circulation of silver coins, objects such as vessels (*amphorae*), and building campaigns provide evidence of the size and fluidity of various Hellenistic economies. By the third century BCE, for Egypt, there are enough written records for us to see roughly how one Hellenistic economy functioned.

Hellenistic economies were predominantly agricultural, but the landscape of this vast world was extremely variable. Terrain, soil quality, rainfall, and rivers varied from place to place. Whereas grain was the chief product, even in Greece, other crops such as olives, grapes, and beans were important foodstuffs. Some regions were more successful than others in growing things, and over the centuries these relative capabilities mattered. Egypt flourished economically, but Greece did less well. Land tenure was so variable within the Hellenistic kingdoms that it is hard to generalize, but at its core was the idea, as in Egypt, that the land belonged to the king by right of conquest.

No matter what was produced, if there was a surplus, it required transport: from rural areas to cities, from region to region, and from kingdom to kingdom. In the Hellenistic world, roads were less reliable than water transport and so camels in Egypt and Asia Minor were more common conveyors of goods than were wheeled carts, but they took their loads of surplus produce to rivers where they could be shipped to markets. Whereas roads were never a priority of Hellenistic development, harbors, docks, and warehouses were. Most goods of the macroeconomy passed through ports at some point. The volume of Mediterranean sea trade in the Second Hellenistic Age can be judged in relative terms by the number of Mediterranean sea wrecks that archaeologists have identified. The early Hellenistic period doubled the classical rates, but those rates almost tripled in the late Hellenistic period once the Carthaginians and Romans joined in. One of the great strengths of Hellenistic sea trade was its considerable reach, all the way to the Indian Ocean. The Hellenistic world was a conduit and market for the flow of luxury items, from Indian elephants and ivory to precious spices and gems.

The Hellenistic economies were money economies. Soldiers needed to be paid, and after Alexander, mints were established in most regions. Much of the gold that Alexander had seized from the Persian treasury at Persepolis later circulated as coin. In general, silver coins were the common currency. Kings taxed their subjects at rates as high as 35–40 percent; this excessive taxation allowed royal regimes to survive in a militaristic world in which they needed to employ and pay mercenary soldiers.

The Ptolemaic dynasty of Egypt was the most centralized and economically successful regime of the Hellenistic kingdoms. The Ptolemies took advantage of Egypt's fertile agricultural lands and of a native farming population that knew how to keep these lands productive. Egypt's surplus could be converted into cash with which to support the royal operation, obtain resources from outside Egypt, and hire mercenaries. By the third century BCE, however, lands were increasingly being turned over to Greeks in exchange for military service.

One of the casualties of the Hellenistic Age was the older polis ideal of the equality of citizens. The hoplite citizens

Pergamum A reconstruction of the dramatic setting of Pergamum with its Acropolis and extensive set of buildings neatly molded to the terrain of the site.

of Athens had fought for Athens and demanded a say in its politics and economy; Hellenistic kings hired their soldiers and controlled the dispensation of wealth. This encouraged men and women to think of their financial well-being not in civic terms, but personal ones. Some Hellenistic men and women grew fantastically wealthy. They became patrons of cities and people, acting like minor kings in dispensing wealth. The poor farmer and camel trader saw the polarization of wealth in the third century BCE as their lot, a condition from which they could rarely break free.

Later Hellenistic Philosophy

The schools of Plato and Aristotle continued in Athens throughout the Hellenistic Ages, but new movements appeared in Greece that concentrated on moral matters. The **Skeptics** doubted all knowledge, since they thought that humans simply lacked the ability to know reality or to determine truth—their doubtfulness was the doubtfulness of the Hellenistic Ages, a time when large geographic, ethnic, economic, and political realities seemed beyond comprehension.

The **Cynics** rejected the conventional Hellenistic world and dropped out of society. They spurned religious piety, reverence for kings and kingdoms, and all hypocrisy. In their place they taught doctrines of simplicity and self-sufficiency; theirs was an ancient form of a back-to-nature movement. People likened them to dogs (hence the name *Cynic,* from the Greek for dog) for their praise of simple and natural pleasures. The most famous Cynic was Diogenes, who was reputed to have lived in a barrel in fourth-century BCE Athens. Diogenes and his successors taught Hellenistic men and women how to cope

with the travails of life by denying the complexity, hypocrisy, and material exuberance of the day. The Cynics even avoided the conventions of philosophy and created no school of their own.

The **Stoics** appeared late in the fourth century BCE, in Athens. Their intellectual forebears were Socrates and the Cynics, but Zeno of Citium, the founder of Stoicism (from the Stoa, or porch, where he taught), advocated a philosophy of individual responsibility, individual action, and the pursuit of virtue. Though the Stoics thought that the material world and possessions were worthless, they thought that all men, from emperors down to slaves, should strive to do their best in all the things that they did or were forced to do. It was in virtuous activity, not achievement that individuals pursued the Stoic ideal. Stoics believed in living in harmony with Nature, which they thought had been established by divine wisdom and goodness. Whereas the Cynics had withdrawn from the civilized world, the Stoics believed in living in the world with all of its troubles and public responsibilities.

The **Epicureans**—named after Epicurus of Athens, who lived in the fourth century BCE—established a school in Athens that viewed the world quite differently from the Stoics. Epicurus thought that the world was a product of random combinations of atoms, and so a purely physical or material reality. For Epicurus and his followers, the universe lacked any underlying purpose or goodness. If morality was not divinely imbedded in the universe, as the Stoics believed, then humans were free to act for their own individual and material ends. At the same time, Epicurus sought to free humans from their physical chains by teaching them that the highest good was freedom from emotional turmoil. His school renounced

The World According to Eratosthenes A re-creation of the world map as proposed by the Alexandrian geographer.

simple hedonism, treasured friendship, and sought emotional equanimity. In its own way, Epicureanism was another response to the Hellenistic condition. The vast, alienating, material world was a fact, but the mind could free humans from the anguish it caused by recognizing it for what it was and seeking true happiness in being free of illusions about the world, living a quiet life, and treasuring friends and simple human pleasures.

Each of the distinctive philosophies that arose in the shadow cast by the philosophies of Socrates, Plato, and Aristotle were responses to the new Hellenistic world, its size and sheer complexity. The Skeptics denied its comprehensibility; the Cynics rejected its basic conventions and dropped out; and the Epicureans, recognizing the purposeless nature of the universe, withdrew from it to seek simpler human pleasures. Only the Stoics crafted a philosophy of engagement with the world based on individual virtuous action, but even they refused to embrace the pure energy and exuberance of the Hellenistic world.

Later Hellenistic Technology, Science, and Medicine

Greek technology, science, and medicine attained its greatest achievements in the Hellenistic world, chiefly in Ptolemaic Alexandria. The Second Hellenistic Age was one of great technological invention and advance: siege engines, water-powered machines such as organs and clocks, and automated devices that could move dolls, theaters, and calculating machines. Archimedes of Syracuse (287–212 BCE) was not just a brilliant mathematician, but a brilliant engineer. He is credited, for instance, with inventing a large screw-like device for conveying water from a river or pond onto fields for the irrigation of crops. His home city of Syracuse was defended by his machines.

In astronomy, Hellenistic advances were impressive. For example, at Alexandria, the third-century BCE geographer Eratosthenes of Cyrene calculated the circumference of the earth to within a reasonable margin of error. Whereas the *Geographika* of Eratosthenes approached the problem of the earth's land masses as a mathematical question, Theophrastus preferred a descriptive geography in his study of winds.

Aristarchus of Samos, another third-century BCE Alexandrian thinker, determined that the earth completes one rotation per day on an axis and circles the sun once a year. He proposed a **heliocentric** (sun-centered) **theory** of the relationship of the earth and planets, but, as so often in Hellenistic thought, the implications of such a daring idea were not followed up, partly because Hellenistic astronomers could not reconcile Aristarchus's theory with the observable progress of the constellations against the night sky. Nor did the radical implications of a heliocentric theory, which threatened to displace the earth from its central position in the universe, seem to worry Hellenistic men and women, since they probably never learned of the theory. It remained but another scientific speculation, and Alexandria produced many of those.

The mathematical concerns of the age reflected its preoccupation with space. Euclid's *Elements* of geometry, which was written around 300 BCE, concentrated on solids such as cones and spheres. Archimedes discovered calculus, and Heron of Alexandria, who worked in the first century BCE, introduced trigonometry.

The most important of the Hellenistic scientific advances were in medicine. In Egypt, with its long expertise in mummification, Ptolemaic scholars were permitted to dissect cadavers and so to explore the internal workings of the human body. In the third century BCE, Herophilus of Chalcedon and his students investigated the anatomical details of the nervous system, pulsation, the heart, and blood circulation. A contemporary said that Herophilus even dissected still living criminals, who had been condemned to death, to observe organs at work. Still, despite these daring investigations, the prevailing medical theory remained the older one of Hippocrates, that the body was subject to the four humors and that doctors were chiefly charged with restoring balance to the body.

Hellenistic Religious Ferment

When Alexander marched into Asia, he assumed that his gods were universal ones and that he would encounter and honor familiar gods wherever he went. What Alexander found, of course, were native religious beliefs that did not quite match Greek norms. Still, he and his advisors were ready to assume that, given the universal presence of the gods, the natives of Persia, India, and Egypt had the same gods as the Greeks but called them by different names and honored them in different ways. At Tyre, for instance, Alexander thought that the Phoenician god Melgart (or Melkart) was a form of Herakles. At Siwah, he regarded the Egyptian divinity Ammon as a manifestation of Zeus. Underlying polytheism was the idea that the divine was universal and omnipresent but that its manifestations (in place and form) were variable. Hellenistic kings were keen to claim some measure of religious authority by promoting and honoring local religious beliefs that in turn recognized their divinely sanctioned royal lines. Hence in Egypt, Alexander and his successors were recognized as kings and honored as gods.

What Alexander and the creation of a wider Hellenistic world had actually done was to set religion on the move. Not only did cultures collide when the Greco-Macedonians invaded foreign lands, but religions as well. Greek soldiers and traders became powerful agents of cross-fertilization in spreading religions that had previously been restricted regionally. The **mystery religions,** which had secret practices and rites of initiation, spread in this way. At the same time, the beliefs, practices, forms, and divinities of these religions often combined—a process called **syncreticism.** In this way, the Egyptian goddess Isis became an all-encompassing divinity: a great mother goddess, with many names and powers, and the ruler of the entire earth. She offered believers immortality and revealed to them the mysteries of the world. Ptolemy I wanted a central religious figure who could answer the needs of both the Greeks and Egyptians and so invented the god Sarapis (or Serapis). Associated with Memphis and the Egyptian god Osiris, Sarapis was seen as a native form of Helios (the sun) and Zeus—in statues he was bearded like Zeus and was regarded as the supreme god. The Hellenistic era thus forced on ancient religions, west and east, a period of intense fluidity of form and meaning; the top of traditional belief had been set spinning.

Alexandrian Literature

In the Hellenistic Age, Greek literature was an important cultural touchstone for the Greek minority set down in the midst of the vast native population of foreign lands. Hellenistic Greeks venerated Greek literature of the Classical Age. It reminded them of their connection to their Greek homeland and its golden past. Hellenistic kings were pleased to solidify that cultural connection and to outdo their rivals in proving who the better Greek was. Hence, Pergamum started its own library of parchment manuscripts as a way to rival the Ptolemies, but Alexandria outpaced all others. Ptolemy I and his successors were so anxious to collect texts that they insisted that all ships docking in Alexandria had to submit whatever books they had on board, which were then copied. The copy was given to the original owner; the original book entered the Ptolemaic collection. The royal library of Alexandria was probably confined at first to a portion of the Museum. The collection consisted of a half-million papyrus rolls (though probably closer to 100,000 books since each roll might contain only a small portion of a long work such as the *Iliad*), but before too long it exceeded the available space and an annex of texts was opened at the Sarapeion. Ptolemaic kings had probably been persuaded that knowledge was power and that books were the best way to acquire and retain knowledge and to preserve Greek culture. Indeed, some of the Ptolemies became writers, and one of the Seleucid kings wrote a poem about snake bites.

The mission of Alexandria's librarians was to collect and codify the masterpieces of Greek literature. Their tastes shaped some of what has survived of classical Greek literature. It was they who worked to collect the complete corpus of Plato's works, as well as those of Aristotle and the chief tragic playwrights (Aeschylus, Sophocles, and Euripides). Alexandria served as a funnel through which ancient Greek literature was channeled, defined, and preserved.

Alexandrian poets, under the weight of the classical Greek literary monuments collected and read at the library, became learned and allusive (referring by allusion to older literature). They were also brief, preferring epigrams to lengthy poems; their brevity was a product of living in the shadow of the massive collection of words in the library. What was left to be said needed to be said well, and said in few words. The librarian Callimachus is famous for his motto, much beloved by students: "Big Book, Big Evil." He wrote, however, many books and lists of his own, including a lengthy catalogue of the library's books, a list of abstruse words, a poem on the waterways and rivers of Europe, a volume on myths, and another on the habits of barbarians. He also invented different forms of verse, another recognition that the Greek greats of the past could not be equaled and so the Alexandrian poets needed to find new ways and means to say things.

Hellenistic Art

Hellenistic art departed from the earlier concerns of classical Greek art. It embraced the particular and the realistic, not the ideal and the perfect. The famous sculptures of the Venus de Milo and winged Victory of Samothrace, housed today at the Louvre in Paris, are Hellenistic pieces. Those two works are twisting, expressive, vibrant pieces that speak to the energy and dynamism of the Hellenistic Age. There had been a change in the nature of patronage, from classical civic commissions to art produced for Hellenistic kings and rich patrons. Not surprisingly, portraiture lay at the heart of Hellenistic art: on coins and

The Old Courtesan Hellenistic artists and patrons were interested in detailed character studies. This sculpture, with its emphasis on a particular type of person, an aged courtesan on her way to a wine festival, would have found no place in classical Greece, which wanted to see idealized, perfected human beings.

The Winged Victory of Samothrace The Winged Victory captures the dynamic energy and motion that Hellenistic artists emphasized.

tombs, in paintings and mosaics. The many busts of the philosophers Socrates, Plato, and Aristotle all come from the Hellenistic period. In keeping with Aristotle's drive for natural truths, Hellenistic art sought realizable and recognizable portraits of individuals. The mummy paintings from Fayoum in Egypt in the late Hellenistic period are portraits of real individuals, warts and all. Or take the example of the sculpture of the old market woman or courtesan on her way to a wine festival from the second century BCE. She is a stock type, as suited the concerns and conventions of Menander and New Comedy, but nonetheless a specific, highly realized example of a type and subject that would not have attracted sculptors or patrons of the Classical Age.

Hellenistic architecture and art, including religious statues, had a propagandistic feature and left a Greek impress upon occupied lands. Native art did not disappear—Egyptian temples continued to be erected in a native style—but it was overridden by Greek art. Hellenistic architecture makes a Greek statement. Though it was eclectic, employing different types of classical columns, its geographic dispersion, regional variation, and massiveness impressed itself upon the Asian and Mediterranean landscape. The extensive complex of buildings at Pergamum (a theater spilling down the hillside, a market place, temples, porticoes, and vaulted passages), neatly molded to the landscape of an Acropolis, reinforced the Hellenistic values of the Attalid royal dynasty that sponsored the building campaign. Alexander may have shown the Greeks a wider world, but it fell to rival Greek dynasties to give it shape and character.

Conclusion

The rise of the Macedonians and their conquest of Greece may seem, in hindsight, to have been destined to occur, but Philip and Alexander were extraordinary individuals whose like were not seen before or afterward. They subdued a Greece that still had bite, as Demosthenes demonstrated, and planned the invasion of Persia. Alexander conquered a vast world stretching from the Nile to the Indus, but it fell to his Greco-Macedonian successors to shape and govern it. Some of the Hellenistic kingdoms were more successful than others, but all participated in and promoted the Hellenization of the eastern Mediterranean, Asia Minor, and lands farther east. For almost three hundred years, Greek culture, Greek officials, and Greek kings dominated this vast territory. These Greek kingdoms were shrinking by the third century BCE and were not able to withstand the rise of more aggressive peoples, but their cultural imprint was long-lasting. Greek coins were being produced in western India in the first century BCE, and Etruscan traders and Roman Republicans learned Greek as the common language of the civilized peoples of the Mediterranean world. Yet Hellenistic civilization did not so much domesticate Asia as bring it under an umbrella of Greek government and culture.

Philip, Alexander, and the Hellenistic kings paved the way for Rome's rule of the greater Mediterranean world. Yet, by not penetrating deeply or integrating native cultures, the Hellenistic Age might be viewed as a lost opportunity to create a common Greco-Asian civilization, one that might have incorporated Egyptians and Syrians, Indians and Greeks in a shared world. The only way up and out of the conditions of ethnicity, language, and culture for most natives was to Hellenize, to become Greek, and even then it was hard to rise. Egyptians and Greeks possessed their own law codes and courts. Syrians who could not speak Greek were doomed to second-class status. Even those who did learn the language had a difficult time escaping their race.

The one people who did move in the Greek direction were the Jews, but Hellenization, which meant assimilation, proved to be both a blessing and a curse. Hellenization enriched Jewish culture and gave Jews a permanent foothold in western culture, but it divided the Jewish community over its divine mission and loss of identity. The pull in different directions of the Jewish temple and Greek gymnasium became an existential drama for Jews in the Hellenistic Ages and long afterward. The Seleucid king Antioch IV went so far as to suppress the temple in Jerusalem and to attempt to demolish Jewish identity, but the backlash was a Jewish war of resistance (described in Maccabees 1–2 of the Hebrew Bible) and a period of independence from Greek interference in the mid-second century BCE. The experience of the Jews may suggest that Hellenization, as one sided and limited as it was, might not have been able to accomplish much more than it did.

The Greeks had come to rule Alexander's empire as efficiently and successfully as they could, not to absorb, reform, or destroy native realities. Egypt remained Egypt and long outlived its Greek rulers. The Hellenistic legacy of cosmopolitanism, profound philosophies, religious ferment, scientific speculation, economic specialization, and worldly alienation had a lasting effect on the Romans and so upon western civilization. But it was Islam that would inherit most of the Hellenistic territories and much of the Hellenistic emphasis on city life, science, and mercantile enterprise.

Critical Thinking Questions

1. How were the two Hellenistic Ages different, and in what ways were they different from the preceding Classical Age?

2. What did Alexander want, and what choices did he make to achieve those ends?

3. How did the chance event of Alexander's premature death change the ancient world?

4. Why did the creation of the Hellenistic worlds produce among the many peoples it affected, particularly the Greeks, feelings of dislocation, alienation, and anxiety?

5. Why did Hellenistic culture and Hellenistic Greeks not assimilate with the cultures and peoples they governed? What was the ultimate cost of the Greek failure to integrate the Hellenistic world?

Key Terms

Hellenistic (p. 72)

Socratic method (p. 79)

Hellenization (p. 92)

koine (p. 92)

gymnasium (p. 94)

Skeptics (p. 95)

Cynics (p. 95)

Stoics (p. 95)

Epicureans (p. 95)

heliocentric theory (p. 96)

mystery religions (p. 97)

syncretism (p. 97)

Primary Sources in connect

For information on Connect and the online resources available, go to **http://connect.mcgraw-hill.com**.

1. **Demosthenes and Isocrates on Philip of Macedon**
2. **Xenophon, The Apology of Socrates to the Jury**
3. **Late-Fourth-Century BCE Witnesses to the Divine Curses of Asclepius at Epidaurus**
4. **Alexander's Hellenization of Asia according to Plutarch**
5. **An Egyptian Scribe Working for the Greeks**

The Trial of Socrates

In 399 BCE, three years after the restoration of democracy in Athens, Socrates was put on trial for allegedly not believing in the state gods, introducing his own god (or personal *daimon*), and for corrupting the young. Behind the prosecution may have been the worry by the democratic leaders of Athens that Socrates was antidemocratic and that some of his students, such as Critias and Alcibiades, emboldened by Socrates's teaching, had willfully harmed Athens. The young aristocrat Plato attended the trial and skillfully re-created Socrates's speech, much, we may suppose, as Thucydides had reconstructed Pericles's *Funeral Oration.* The jury of 501 Athenians first voted by a small majority of sixty to condemn the philosopher, but after Socrates, as was his right, again addressed the jury and advised them either to let him pay a small fine or to support him at public expense, the jury overwhelmingly condemned him to death.

How you, O Athenians, have been affected by my accusers, I cannot tell; but I know that they almost made me forget who I was—so persuasively did they speak; and yet they have hardly uttered a word of truth. . . .

I will begin at the beginning and ask what is the accusation which has given rise to the slander of me, and in fact has encouraged Meletus to prefer this charge against me. Well, what do the slanderers say? They shall be my prosecutors, and I will sum up their words in the affidavit: "Socrates is an evildoer, and strange person, who searches into things under the earth and in heaven, and he makes the worse appear the better cause; and he teaches the aforesaid doctrines to others." Such is the nature of the accusation: it is just what you have yourselves seen in the comedy of Aristophanes, who has introduced a man whom he calls Socrates, going about and saying that he walks in air, and talking a deal of nonsense concerning matters of which I do not pretend to know either much or little about, not that I mean to speak disparagingly of anyone who is a student of natural philosophy. I should be very sorry if Meletus could bring so grave a charge against me. But the simple truth is, Athenians, that I have nothing to do with physical speculations. . . .

There is another thing: young men of the richer classes, who have not much to do, come to me of their own accord; they like to hear the pretenders [those who claim to know something] examined, and they often imitate me, and proceed to examine others; there are plenty of persons, as they quickly discover, who think that they know something, but really know little or nothing; and then those who are examined by them instead of being angry with themselves are angry with me. That confounded Socrates, they say; that villainous misleader of youth! Then if somebody asks them why, what evil does he practice or teach, they do not know, and cannot tell. But in order that they may not appear to be at a loss, they repeat the ready-made charges that are used against all philosophers, about teaching things up in the clouds and under the earth, and having no gods, and making the worse appear the better cause. They do not like to confess that their pretense of knowledge has been detected, which is the truth; and as they are numerous and ambitious and energetic, and are drawn up in battle array and have persuasive tongues, they have filled your ears with their loud and inveterate calumnies. And this is the reason why my three accusers, Meletus and Anytus and Lycon, have set upon me. . . .

Men of Athens, I honor and love you, but I shall obey god rather than you, and while I have strength I shall never cease from the practice and teaching of philosophy, exhorting anyone whom I meet and saying to him after my manner: You, my friend, a citizen of the great and mighty and wise city of Athens, are you not ashamed of heaping up the greatest amount of money and honor and reputation, and caring so little about wisdom and truth and the greatest improvement of the soul, which you never regard or heed at all? And if the person with whom I am arguing, says Yes, but I do care, then I do not leave him or let him go at once, but I proceed to interrogate and examine him, and if I think that he has no virtue in him, but only says that he has, I reproach him with undervaluing the greater and overvaluing the lesser. . . . This is my teaching, and if this is the doctrine which corrupts youth, then I am a mischievous person. . . .

And now Athenians, I am not going to argue for my own sake, as you may think, but for yours, that you may not sin against god by condemning me, who am his gift to you. For if you kill me you will not easily find a successor to me, who, if I may use such a ludicrous figure of speech, am a sort of gadfly, given to the state by god; and the state is a great and noble steed who is tardy in his motions owing to his great size, and requires to be stirred into life. I am that gadfly which god has attached to the state, and all day long and in all places am always fastening upon you, arousing and persuading and reproaching you. You will not easily find another like me, and therefore I would advise you to spare me. I dare say that you may feel irritable (like a person who is suddenly awakened from sleep), and you may think that you might easily strike me dead as Anytus advises, and you would sleep on for the remainder of your lives, unless god in his care for you sent you another gadfly. . . .

QUESTIONS | *Why does Socrates think that he is being tried? Did he die a scapegoat for Athenian irritation at the end of the Peloponnesian War and its aftermath, a martyr to philosophical freedom and truth, or a stubborn old man who refused to placate his accusers? Explain. In what ways had Socrates here already stepped into the First Hellenistic Age?*

Source: B. Jowett, ed., *The Dialogues of Plato,* Vol. 1 (Oxford: Oxford University Press, 1920), 401–403, 406, 413–414; revised.

4

The Ruins of the Forum in Rome

THE ROMAN REPUBLIC

SURVIVAL AND SUCCESS

Early Stories, Early Days
The Etruscans and Prehistoric Italy
Early Rome
Archaic Roman Religion

The Early Roman Republic: Conflict and Stability
The Beginnings of Republican Government
The Senate
The Orders of Roman Society
The Roman Patriarchy: Fathers, Patricians, and Patrons

The Expansion of the Roman Republic
Cleaning Up the Neighborhood
Taking on the Latin League and the Samnites
The Roman Army in the Early and Middle Republics
Conflict with the Greeks in Southern Italy

Territorial Expansion and a Religion of War
Reasons for the Republic's Territorial Expansion

Roman Virtue and the Pursuit of Glory
A Religion of War
Living the Religious Life: The Roman Calendar and Vestal Virgins

The Carthaginian Contest and the Middle Republic
The First Punic War
The Second Punic War
Rome Takes the War to Africa
Rolling Up the Mediterranean Rim

The Mature Republic
Toward a Mediterranean Roman Economy
Roman Literature of the Middle Republic
The Year of Reckoning: 146 BCE

Conclusion

POLYBIUS AND THE ROMANS In 167 BCE, Polybius (c. 200–c. 118 BCE) was one of a thousand Greek hostages loaded onto ships for transport to Rome. He said that the experience left him on the edge of mental collapse. His fall from high places had been steep, for he had been a politician, diplomat, and officeholder in the Achaean League, of which his native city Megalopolis was a member. Rome accused Polybius and the other prisoners of committing treachery. None of them was ever brought to trial; instead, most of the captured Greeks languished unhappily for fifteen long years in Roman detention.

Polybius made the best of a bad situation. He made powerful friends and worked his way into the highest social circles. His forty-book history of the Republic of Rome, written in Greek, investigates how a single city conquered and brought under its power the Mediterranean world. Polybius was an eyewitness to great events. He saw the city of Carthage razed to the ground and its population sold into slavery at the end of the Third Punic War, and he visited the city of Corinth not long after Rome had destroyed it in 146 BCE.

Polybius committed himself to recording events and people as accurately as he could. "Truth," he wrote, "is to history what sight is to the living," for without truth history is only a meaningless distraction for fools, and Polybius was no fool. He was, however, an unabashed and amazed admirer of what Rome had accomplished. The historical question that drove him was how Rome did it. How did a single city subdue an entire world?

The Romans were geniuses at organization (both political and military) and survival. Surrounded by hostile peoples and cities, Rome found the means to match its times and circumstances. Guided by its **Senate,** Rome survived and prospered, perfecting the most successful of all forms of ancient government, the Roman Republic. The great challenges to its survival from the Etruscan, Latin, and Greek cities in Italy, and from Carthage and

Etruscan civilization
750–350 BCE

800 BCE   700   600   500

the Hellenistic kingdoms, led Rome along a path to the domination first of central Italy, then all of Italy, and finally the western Mediterranean and ancient world.

In this chapter, we examine the Roman Republic's rise to power prior to the middle of the second century BCE, when things began to fall apart. In religion, government, and war, the Roman Republic before 146 BCE achieved unparalleled stability and success. Like Polybius, we need to ask how and why the Romans succeeded when so many rival powers in Italy and the wider Mediterranean world wanted to crush it. What made Rome special?

Early Stories, Early Days

The earliest history of Rome is wrapped in legend. Later Romans knew little definite about it, and Polybius even less. The simple stories the Romans told about their beginnings are both charming and chilling. Horatius fighting nobly at the Bridge, Cincinnatus laying down his arms and returning to the plow he had dropped when Rome called him to war, and the geese that warned the Romans that Gallic invaders were violating the sacred precincts of their city are legends that describe a humble agricultural people and their core virtues.

Why were the Etruscans important to Mediterranean and Roman history?

Yet, according to a darker set of legends, the city of Rome began its history with rape (of a Vestal Virgin by a god), regicide (the murder of King Amulius), fratricide (of Remus by his brother Romulus), and mass abduction and violation (of the Sabine women). Such stories did not make for the most glorious of foundation myths. In compensation, imperial Romans would overlay this bumpy narrative with the story of Trojan warriors led by the gods to found Latin Italy and to lead Rome toward its divine destiny. To elevate their past, imperial Romans joined their history to that of the Greeks, fashioning a story of Greco-Roman continuity and the westward passage of civilization.

The Etruscans and Prehistoric Italy

Italy went through a series of stages—Neolithic, copper, and bronze. Evidence of the richness of Italy's prehistoric past is abundant: cave paintings in the south, Neolithic fertility idols, thousands of small stone structures on Sardinia, and rich gold and bronze objects from graves in the north in the area around Bologna. After 1000 BCE, northern Italy began to receive waves of immigrants coming from the north and east by land and sea. The invaders, including Indo-European Italic peoples such as the Samnites and Latins, slowly displaced the previous residents.

The Etruscans, one of these early peoples in northern Italy, were not Indo-Europeans, which we can tell from their language. Although the Etruscans (unlike the Italic peoples at the time) had a written language, it is still not fully understood. It falls into that class of written languages in which the script is known, but the language is not. Because the Etruscan script consists, with some modifications, of Greek capital letters, its more than 10,000 surviving inscriptions can be deciphered, if not read for precise and full meaning. Most Etruscan inscriptions are short and do not reveal the grammatical structure and specific workings of the language. Even several bilingual texts, the most famous being the gold Pyrgi Tablets with Phoenician and Etruscan parallel texts, are relatively short and have not yet led to the unraveling of the Etruscan language.

The problem of understanding the Etruscan language and culture is compounded by uncertainty about where the Etruscans came from. In the ancient world, opinion was divided about the origins of the Etruscans. Some believed that they were natives of Italy, others that they came from Mesopotamia, yet others that they were Lydians who fled their homeland during a famine. Some modern scholars suspected that they came from the island of Lemnos in Asia Minor. Recent DNA studies, though contested, point to Lydia (or western Turkey), as Herodotus had claimed, as the original home of the Etruscans.

What little we do know about the Etruscans confirms their historical importance. Tombs, gravesites,

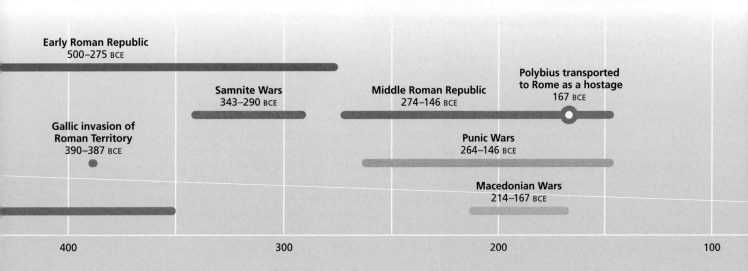

Early Roman Republic
500–275 BCE

Samnite Wars
343–290 BCE

Middle Roman Republic
274–146 BCE

Polybius transported to Rome as a hostage
167 BCE

Gallic invasion of Roman Territory
390–387 BCE

Punic Wars
264–146 BCE

Macedonian Wars
214–167 BCE

400   300   200   100

The Pyrgi Tablets

In 1964, three thin sheets of pressed gold, rolled up like a scroll, were unearthed during the excavation of a temple site at Pyrgi on the coast twenty-five miles northwest of Rome. Pyrgi served as a port for the Etruscan city of Cerveteri. The find immediately excited interest since the gold sheets were inscribed and two of them formed a pair, one sheet written in Etruscan, the other in Phoenician. The third sheet, containing a longer text than the other two, was also written in Etruscan. Found with the sheets were the nails with which they were once affixed to a surface in the temple. The nails are bronze but have golden heads to match the tablets, suggesting that the tablets were precious display objects.

Discovery of the tablets gave scholars the hope that at long last the Etruscan language had its Rosetta Stone, a parallel text in a known language (in this case Phoenician) that would allow philologists to break the Etruscan code. Sadly the situations are not the same. The Rosetta Stone

The Pyrgi Tablets

contains a long text reproduced in two different languages and three different scripts. The Pyrgi Tablets have a relatively short text in only two scripts and languages. Compounding the problem of deciphering Etruscan, the Phoenician and Etruscan texts are parallel and not literal translations of each other. Translation in the ancient world was rarely literal, a word-for-word reproduction in another language, but rather an adaptation of the spirit of the original, conveying its general meaning.

The Pyrgi Tablets honor, celebrate, and date a gift made by the Etruscan king of Caisra to a goddess. The hope that the Pyrgi Tablets would supply evidence of Etruscan-Carthaginian relations now also seems shaky. The Carthaginians and Etruscans did have formal dealings and entered into treaties with each other. Parallel texts of such a treaty might well prove to be a Rosetta Stone, but the Pyrgi Tablets are not that and they now seem not even to provide firm evidence of contact between the Etruscans and Carthaginians. After careful examination of the Phoenician text, the classical philologist Philip C. Schmitz concluded that the texts were not written in Carthaginian, but a Mediterranean dialect of Phoenician connected more closely to a form of the language used on Cyprus.

History is often a matter of small steps. Big breakthroughs such as the bonanza of a Rosetta Stone are rare. Still, one never knows what the ground might cough up tomorrow. In 1999, a bronze tablet with a long Etruscan inscription surfaced in Cortona, though it too has not as yet led to the long desired breakthrough.

QUESTIONS | *How is our view of the past shaped (or distorted) by knowing or not knowing a civilization's language? Why has the Etruscan language not been identified and fully understood?*

and inscriptions attest to their long presence in Etruria (Tuscany) and farther north in Italy. Etruscans established twelve chief city-states that, like the Greek city-states, shared linguistic, ethnic, cultural, and religious connections, but they were also fierce competitors with each other. By the seventh and sixth centuries BCE, some of these cities were actively trading with the Greeks, who sometimes dismissed them as pirates. The Romans later mocked the Etruscans as ineffectual warriors and their society as one given to debauchery and weakness, but

that was the condemnation of the winning side, whose existence had once been threatened by the Etruscans. The greatest Etruscan expert in the ancient world was the Roman emperor Claudius (r. 41–54 CE), who wrote a now-lost twenty-volume history of the Etruscans that was kept and read out annually in the Library of Alexandria. But by the emperor's time the Etruscans had largely lost their place and voice in history.

Yet, in the eighth century BCE, Etruscan cities were trading widely in minerals and artifacts. By 700 BCE,

Etruscan Warriors Bearing a Wounded Comrade The Etruscans were famous not only for their far-reaching trading networks and cultural sophistication, but also for being fierce warriors. Note in particular the fringed helmets with cats' ears, spears, and leather body armor.

Etruscan Women in Funeral Procession Here Etruscan women do a funeral dance around a corpse.

they had begun to colonize the middle parts of Italy, and the islands of Elba, Corsica, and Sardinia fell under their sway. Etruscan cities established trading and diplomatic contacts with the great Mediterranean powers, particularly with the Greeks and Carthaginians. Etruscan art reveals the influence of Greek art in both subject matter and style.

The Etruscan cities of early Italy played a critical role in exposing northern Italy to the cultural influences of the Mediterranean east, particularly to Greek art and the Greek alphabet. It was the Etruscans who transformed Rome into a city.

Early Rome

The Latins, an Indo-European people like the Greeks, migrated to central Italy and settled on the plains of Latium around 1000 BCE. The people who settled the seven hills of Rome around 900 BCE were one or several offshoots of these Latin peoples. Romans later fixed 753 BCE as the foundation date of their city, but archaeology suggests that nothing like a city existed on the site that early (Map 4.1).

Rome was located fifteen miles from the Mediterranean on the Tiber River. Located on the western side of Italy, Rome lay far from the Adriatic Sea and easy access by Greek and Phoenician ships. Tributaries of the Tiber River cut through the Latin plains and reach across much of the peninsula. A series of paths and later roads joined Rome to the rest of Italy. The site of Rome was a midpoint in Italy. To the north lay the Etruscans of Etruria and to the south other Latin peoples; beyond them were the Samnites of central Italy and farther south, various Greek settlements.

MAP 4.1 | Early Italy and Its Peoples, c. 500 BCE
Early Italy was crowded with different peoples. Rome was surrounded by powerful Etruscan cities; various tribes such as the Latins, Marsi, and Samnites; and farther south, Greek cities and the Carthaginian trading outposts in Sicily. *What advantages and disadvantages were there to Rome's location in Italy? How did the geographic setting of Rome dictate its development?*

Around 900 BCE, shepherds who grazed their flocks on the seven hills of Rome began building huts. By the mid-seventh century BCE, these settlements began to spread down the hills. The inhabitants of the area organized themselves by tribal or family groups called clans, which became a law unto themselves, protecting family members and assaulting others. Bands of mounted warriors raided other clans and neighboring territories, rustled cattle and livestock, and pursued private justice, seeking revenge for violence done to them. By controlling the means of force (a populous clan, weapons, and horses) and religious sanction, some families gained control over wide areas of the extended site and established their claims to priority and prominence. Rome was still not a city with a defined space, public laws, public spaces, or institutions. The Roman Forum (the central meeting place) began as a cattle market where people met to swap cows.

Legends speak of Roman kings, the first of whom was the legendary Romulus, whose name seems to be Etruscan in origin, but these early kings may have had a largely religious role. Only with the Etruscan phase of its early history in the sixth century BCE did Rome become what we would recognize as a city. The last three of Rome's legendary kings were Etruscans, and they transformed the site of Rome. It was not by accident that the name of the city of Rome (Ruma) comes from Etruscan. These kings encouraged migration (probably of their own people) to the new city, drained the marshes in the area of the Forum, and promoted religion by building temples to the gods. The first Roman art style is called Etrusco-Italic, one famous example being the statue of the she-wolf of Rome. Another effect of Rome's Etruscan period was that some basic political unity was forced on the scattered villages of the hillsides. The second of the three Etruscan kings, Servius Tullius, is credited with building a wall to outline a single urban space and mounting games and religious festivals to unite the dispersed population.

The economic impact of the sixth century BCE on Rome was considerable. One crude measure of Etruscan Rome's contact with the wider Mediterranean economy can be found in surviving pottery shards. Few Athenian pottery fragments have been found on the site of Rome before the Etruscans took control, but hundreds after they arrived. The economy of Rome and its hinterland remained primarily agricultural, but the Etruscans had extensive economic links with the Mediterranean world to which Etruscan Rome was exposed. Rome still lacked a money economy (that is, it had no coinage). Goods were paid for with cattle and sheep or chunks of copper.

The Etruscan contribution to Rome's political and religious formation was equally significant. The Etruscan kings introduced the Romans to **augury** (reading the will of the gods and signs of the future by studying the flight of birds) and **haruspicy** (reading entrails, particularly the livers, of animals). Even some central political symbols such as the **curule** or official chair of the **magistrate** (a representative of the people given the right to hold executive power), **fasces** (an ax and rods joined together to signify the magistrate's right to enforce physical punishment), purple toga, golden wreath, and ivory rod date from the Etruscan period. The Etruscans left Rome with an inheritance of religious, artistic, and political symbols and, above all, with a rudimentary city. Cities were not common in prehistoric Italy. Most of the peoples of central Italy lived in scattered clan-based societies, but the Etruscans, like the Greeks, organized their societies around cities.

The Etruscan rule of Rome ended around 500 BCE, though the legendary date of 510 or 509 BCE was the one given by the Romans. Roman aristocrats called on the help of another Etruscan chieftain or mercenary war lord to aid them in expelling their last Etruscan king, Tarquin the Proud. The Etruscans did not take their expulsion from Rome happily and, with the assistance of the king of the Etruscan city of Clevsin, they marched on Rome, whose weakest point of entry was the Sublician Bridge. The crossing was guarded, according to legend, by Horatius Cocles, who rallied the fleeing Romans to destroy the bridge. Soldiers dismantled the bridge behind him while Horatius fought on alone against the oncoming Etruscans. He then swam across the river to his grateful city. The story of Horatius at the Bridge was remembered by Romans as a model of the daring and dedication that good Romans owed to their city.

Though the Etruscan cities shared a language and general culture, they had little success in achieving

The She-Wolf of Rome Roman legend told how the she-wolf nursed Romulus and Remus. The Etrusco-Roman statue of the wolf dates from around 500 BCE, but the bouncing baby boys were added later in the Italian Renaissance to complete the scene.

greater Etruscan unity. Rome was on its way to becoming a fiercely independent city-state. Yet it escaped the Greek and Etruscan dilemma of failing to unite many rival independent city-states by becoming a city that dominated and incorporated surrounding lands and peoples; it found a way to become the power city without equal in the ancient world.

Archaic Roman Religion

Religion was central to Roman history and culture. As an Indo-European people, the Romans carried with them into Italy the rudiments of the polytheistic religion known to the Greeks. They possessed triads of great gods (Jupiter, Juno, and Mars—the Capitoline gods—and Jupiter, Mars, and Quirinus, a god of the early settlement of one of Rome's hills), but during Rome's earliest history no paintings, temples, or statues dotted the seven hills. Instead, Iron-Age Romans believed that vague divine forces (*numina*) animated their world. Driven by a need to survive a daunting physical world of huge boulders, disease-bearing marshes, and marauding wolves, the early Romans sought to appease the divine forces at work in their world. They turned to little gods of small things.

The *numina* attended everyday Roman life in all its mundane activities; separate gods were credited with overseeing birth, weaning, pubescence, and so on until death. Early Romans believed that, if they did not call on the right god at the right time and in the right way, they would not receive critical assistance from the gods. In a world of low life expectancies, crippling disease, violent neighbors, and sudden death, divine help was thought necessary. Rituals, as tried-and-true ways of invoking the gods, became customary.

The Etruscan kings in the sixth century BCE exposed the Romans to a more mature form of polytheism, one informed by Greek religious notions. Temples were built in Rome to great gods such as Jupiter who made the little divine forces of daily life seem puny. During the period of the Etruscan kings, Rome adopted some of the most Roman of its religious practices. The Etruscans were particularly alert to prodigies and portents, whether by reading lightning bolts or the livers of sacrificed animals.

At Rome under the kings there were two chief religious rites, the *inauguratio* and *auspicatus*. In the inauguration ceremony, the augur—a priest imbued with supernatural power—touched the king's head and so transmitted divine power. In the taking of the auspices (from which we derive the word *auspicious*), the flight of birds was studied for signs of the divine will. Romans recalled that, at the foundation of Rome, Romulus and Remus climbed their respective hills to look for birds in the sky to reveal which twin had the favor of the gods. Later the Roman Senate supervised the taking of the auspices since the rite foretold the fortune of the state.

The state also fixed the calendar and sanctioned the institutionalization of archaic religious practices presided over by **pontiffs** (high priests), colleges of priests,

The Haruspex Reads a Liver The winged god Calchas studies an animal liver to see what it portends for the future on the back of this Etruscan bronze mirror. Each section of the liver was divided into regions, and the haruspex examined them for any unusual signs or deformities.

and the Vestal Virgins. An older Roman religion of ritual purification and forbidding taboos was modified and institutionalized as the Republic matured.

The Early Roman Republic: Conflict and Stability

Polybius thought that the Roman Republic had a perfectly balanced form of mixed government, for the **consuls** (chief magistrates) represented the despotic or monarchic principle, the Senate the oligarchic or aristocratic, and the assembly of the people the democratic (see Back to the Source at the end of this chapter). But Polybius, writing late in the history of the Republic, did not realize how much the Early Republic (510–275 BCE) and its constitution had changed over the centuries. There never was a written constitution, and the Republic's rules and practices had evolved over time. For that reason, even terms such as *assembly, senate,* and *council* defy simple definition.

> How and why did the Early Roman Republic develop? How was its development different from that of other city-states in the ancient world?

The Beginnings of Republican Government

The Roman historian Livy (59 BCE–17 CE) thought that after the expulsion of its last king, Rome had developed a fully formed government designed to prevent the return of kingship. Royal power passed to a pair of consuls who held office for a single year. To choose magistrates to guide the state was a rejection of kingship. To divide power between the two guardians of the Republic, each of whom could veto the actions of the other, was designed to introduce a system of checks to prevent the omnipotence and willfulness of a single ruler. To limit the consuls' terms to a single year was intended to prevent the perpetuation of power in a single set of hands. The Romans granted their consuls extensive power (*imperium* or supreme power in both conducting wars and carrying out the law) as the military, religious, and judicial leaders of the city, but they sought to limit consular power.

Consuls, however, did not assume their high Republican roles until the middle of the fourth century BCE, long after the monarchy had been overthrown and following a critical transition to a new style of warfare and a shift in the social fabric of Rome. In the fifth century BCE, after the expulsion of its kings, aristocrats had first placed military power in the hands of horsemen (masters of the cavalry), supreme commanders, and **tribunes** of the people. For much of the fifth century BCE, Romans on horseback continued to carry out raids on their enemies.

What chiefly changed after 400 BCE was the emergence of the phalanx, whose use had been pioneered by the Greeks and Etruscans, as the chief body of warriors Rome put onto the field of battle. The phalanx was a rectangular formation of infantry in rows that moved as a unit against the enemy. The lower classes of Rome (*plebs*), who fought as infantry, came to play an increasingly important role in Roman affairs. Their representatives, the tribunes, had veto powers over Roman affairs. The Curiate Assembly, which had begun in royal times, was made up of thirty units that were supposed to represent all Roman citizens. Its function was to approve (or disapprove) by unit votes or acclamations all important decisions. The Centuriate Assembly came in Republican times to speak for soldiers and was organized like the army itself, by units of one hundred. To this early assembly fell the tasks of selecting consuls and approving wars.

The Roman constitution as such was a living set of unwritten practices and procedures, traditions and laws, always undergoing change as circumstances and customs warranted. The sheer complexity of Roman politics was the result of its various assemblies, the unfixed character of its unwritten constitution, its several classes of citizens, and its underlying conservative nature. Without a Senate to bind things together and steer a straight course, it is hard to imagine the Roman Republic becoming as successful as it proved to be. Rome's success belonged as much to its government as it did to its army and war.

The Senate

The Senate was technically a body of seniors (*senes*, meaning "old ones" in Latin) or **patricians,** men from the oldest, most well-established, and most distinguished Roman families. In royal times the Senate advised the king or sought to affect his will; in the mature Republic it became Rome's central institution. The early Senate was composed of patricians; they represented powerful families and lineages that had established themselves early on and found a way to monopolize power and prestige through an aristocratic code. The number of senators fluctuated over the centuries, but there were typically 300 for much of Republican history.

The Senate met irregularly and was called into session by the tribunes, who served as the chief operating officers of the Assembly of the People (Figure 4.1). Senate meetings were private, but representatives of the various assemblies were allowed to listen from outside the hall. The other assemblies soon found it best to follow the advice and direction of the Senate. The Senate's areas of particular concern were foreign affairs, domestic peace and order, state finance, and religion. During war and crises the Senate's power was enhanced since it made critical appointments, chose or approved a dictator (an official appointed during a time of crisis) for a fixed period of time, and controlled the purse. The Senate's institutional importance grew in the Early and Middle Republics precisely because of the increasing importance to Rome of war and conquest.

Rome was an oligarchy (rule by the privileged few) in which power was shared by a few men who were, theoretically, equals, but distinguishable by family ancestry, wealth, and achievement. In Rome, political power came to those from distinguished families who secured the support of their peers. Important decisions were supposed to be made by and within this closed group, and any aristocrat who appealed to the population at large for political support broke the code of aristocratic conduct and could be charged with rabble-rousing and executed.

The Orders of Roman Society

Roman society was divided into two chief citizen orders: the patricians (aristocrats) and **plebeians** (lower classes). The division was the result of timing and success. The aristocratic families had secured property and social stature, the means of violence (mounted raids), and the control of power and resources. The plebeians were divisible into two sorts, farmers and merchants, both of whom held a subordinate position within the Roman Republic. Before 450 BCE, plebeians were not even permitted to marry patricians.

The plebeians were always an essential part of the Roman state and had early on pressed for legal protection and political rights. Not only did they have their own assemblies and spokesmen, the tribunes, but when the consulship took on its full form in the fourth century BCE, one of the two consuls for each year was supposed to be a

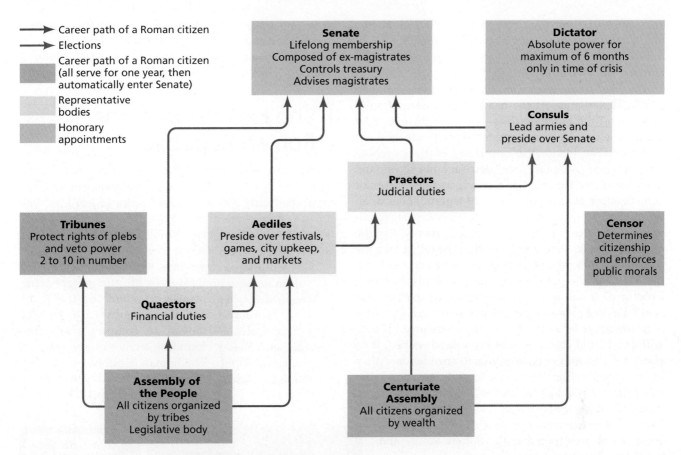

FIGURE 4.1 | Officers and Assemblies of the Roman Republic
The upward path of the Roman aristocrat toward the Senate and a consulship led through a number of offices and long years of service in the representative assemblies and high offices of the Republic.

plebeian. What has often been seen as a desperate struggle between the orders in the Republic (with the people on occasion threatening to withdraw their services, particularly as soldiers, from the state) may just have been politics as normally practiced by Roman citizens. Livy's famous statement that the *plebs* became a state within a state attests to how powerful and necessary lower-class citizens were to the success of Republican affairs.

The shift to infantry warfare made the common plebeian soldier the core military resource of the Republic and knocked the aristocracy off its high horse. As a result, aristocrats sought other ways to maintain preeminence within the state: by supervising religious rites, leading armies in conquest, using the Senate as a decision-making body, by **clientage** (by which an inferior citizen became the dependent or client of a superior), and by keeping plebeians in debt.

Although the plebeians were often unhappy with the way in which patrician power was exercised, they benefited from the material prosperity of an expanding Rome and that may have lessened social tensions in the Early Republic. Plebeians were prepared to fight for Rome because they profited materially from Rome's successes. The important thing for most common citizens was simple survival, and increased prosperity made for contented

citizens. The early patrician order was to a great extent a closed group, but ambitious plebeians placed considerable pressure on the aristocracy in general and the Senate in particular to address their concerns. Since plebeians could never be patricians, the social climbers among them were attracted by a newer concept of ranking, nobility, which recognized merit as well as wealth and birth. A noble was typically someone from a family who could count several consuls among his ancestors. This made the Senate and high office the goal of both aristocrats and ambitious plebeians and ensured that there was some fluidity within Roman society. War was one of the best places to demonstrate meritorious service to the state.

The Roman Patriarchy: Fathers, Patricians, and Patrons

The main operating unit of the Roman world was the extended family. The Romans had no simple word for a nuclear family but called their larger family units a *gens* or clan. The importance of birth and background is reflected in aristocratic names. In the Early Republic these names had two parts: a personal name such as Gaius (also written as Caius) and the family name. By the later republican period, aristocratic names often had three parts, such as Marcus (the personal or given name), Tullius (the family or clan name), and Cicero (a surname that might indicate either another given name or the branch of the family from which the individual derived).

The word *familia* referred to a household and included unrelated servants. At the head of these large family units stood the **paterfamilias**, who was the extended family's nominal father or master of the house, and the **materfamilias**, that mother or mistress of the household who managed the family's children, servants, slaves, and daily resources. The *paterfamilias* was generally the senior male member of the family, perhaps a grandfather or an uncle, and his powers and responsibilities were far reaching. In matters of politics and religion, he represented the family in public. On domestic matters, he might take the advice of the family as a whole in a quasi-counsel, but he alone had the power over whether family members lived or died and to whom they could be married. He could dissolve marriages, even ones between happy couples, whenever he chose. He could also divorce his own wife at will and compel her death if he so wished. If he chose to sell a son into slavery or to abandon and thus kill a newborn child, he had the legal right to do so. His *patria potestas* or paternal power was almost unfettered in law, if not carried to extremes all that often.

Male power, a legacy of Rome's Indo-European background, was rooted in the Roman family and extended throughout Roman society. In the Early Republic, patricians established rules or primitive laws, laying out what was permissible and what was forbidden for all. Plebeian families seem to have shared the same male model of organization but lobbied to reduce the right of their powerful superiors to render arbitrary decisions and sought to lessen the penalties for such things as debt. In the fifth century BCE they gained a codification of Roman laws on *Twelve Tables*, so called because the laws were posted in the Roman Forum on tablets made of wood or bronze. Although the fragments of the law code that survive may seem harsh to us, a fixed set of laws was less whimsical and biased in favor of arbitrary decisions by powerful patrician magistrates. The *Tables* treat predictable matters: rules for trials, debt and property, rights of the Roman father over family members, and crime.

A person who lacked a family or membership in one of the better families was forced by circumstances to seek out a patron for protection and support. The individual seeking the protection of a patron was called a client and the network of these extra-familial associations was called the institution of clientage. The relationship between patron and client involved an exchange of assistance for loyal service, the patron giving land, gifts, and money for the client's allegiance, service, and dependence. Clientage operated as an influential ordering force throughout most of Roman history. As an institution, it helped the disadvantaged and those without powerful families to bridge the divide that lay between them and the patri-

cians and nobles, whose help and influence they required for survival and advancement. Clientage relationships established long-lasting extra-familial bonds between the more and the less powerful in Roman society.

The Expansion of the Roman Republic

At the start of the fifth century BCE, when the Republic began its slow and steady territorial expansion, Rome controlled only 300–400 square miles of territory. The

Why was Rome so dedicated to war, conquest, and incorporating conquered territory? How did the commitment to conquest affect Roman institutions and the Roman population?

city was surrounded by hostile and ambitious peoples. After a series of military and diplomatic conflicts, it dominated and signed treaties with the neighboring peoples of Latium. Together Rome and these nearby Latin peoples moved to conquer other surrounding territories and peoples. The Roman Republic was aggressive and expansionary by both nature and need (Map 4.2).

MAP 4.2 | Rome Takes Italy, 485–265 BCE

Over two centuries, Rome slowly but steadily took control of Italy. ***What was the pattern of Rome's expansion in the Early Republic? What was left to do by 265 BCE?***

386 BCE: Rome or Roman Veii?

The invasion of the Gauls in 390 BCE and the capture and sack of Rome in 387 BCE struck the Roman people hard. So damaging was the assault that some Romans proposed abandoning their city and moving permanently to the recently conquered Etruscan city of Veii. Tribunes pushed for the move to Veii as early as 390 BCE, when the Gauls invaded Roman territory, and they increased their campaign after the sack. They argued that Rome was so destroyed that it could not be rebuilt. Much of the population favored the move. Many had already migrated to Veii and others were pouring in daily, hoping to find a new political and social beginning in Veii.

The critical issue for the Roman people was religious. They worried that the gods had deserted their city by permitting its violation. The conqueror of Veii, Marcus Furius Camillus, who served as consul and then dictator at the time of the Gallic crisis, was dead set against the move. Why, he said, should victorious Rome change places with vanquished Veii? Why should Romans abandon their gods and become exiles from their true home? In 390 BCE, the Senate rallied behind Camillus's call to stand by Rome, but he did grant the plebeians some of Veii's land. When the Gauls seized Rome in 387 BCE, the migration issue heated up again. Camillus drove out the last Gauls and immediately began to restore Rome's religious integrity. All the temples that had been polluted by the presence of the Gauls were purified, and Camillus called for games to honor Jupiter, who had permitted Rome's restoration. Tribunes, however, held mass meetings to urge the Roman people to abandon the city. At this juncture Camillus, surrounded by senators, addressed the people. Yes, he said, we ignored the dire

Apollo of Etruscan Veii, One of the Gods Supposed to Protect the City

warnings of the gods and neglected our religious duties and so suffered defeat and the capture of Rome, but we soon remembered our religious obligations, restored proper worship, and won back the favor of Jupiter. Why would we now in the midst of victory abandon our city? If we move to Veii and it is destroyed, will we move again and become forever wandering exiles? Rome's very success was connected to its urban place, to the beloved Tiber and hills of Rome, their ancestral traditions, and to the gods of the city. When Camillus finished his speech, the Senate voted to stay, rebuild the city, and rededicate itself to Rome's gods.

Had Camillus lost the argument, would there be a Roman history to write? Would the displacement of the population have cost Rome critical time in its territorial expansion and given one of its hostile neighbors an edge in the next war? If they had moved, would the Roman people have lost their conviction that they were superior to other peoples and that they were the darlings of the gods? Would the delicate and successful mix of political forces in Rome have become so unbalanced by a move to Veii that Rome would no longer have possessed the dynamism and determination that characterized its conquest of Italy? Rome's very future hung in the balance in 386 BCE, and it could have gone either way.

QUESTIONS | *Consider the case of Rome or Roman Veii. What role does contingency, or chance, play in history? If the Romans had abandoned their city in 386 BCE, what would have been their fate and historical importance? Would Rome's history have been essentially the same?*

Cleaning Up the Neighborhood

The chief threat to the Republic at the outset came from those Etruscans whose cities were located near Rome. Etruscan power was in decline by the end of the sixth century, and the expulsion of the last Etruscan king of Rome was a symptom of that decline. Etruscan interests were also suffering in the western Mediterranean. Both the Greeks and the Carthaginians were in stiff trading competition with them. The Greeks also had hold-

ings in northern Africa, Sicily, southern Italy, and Spain. Etruscans and Carthaginians joined together to resist them but lost a sea battle to the Greeks around 535 BCE. In 474 BCE, Greek forces destroyed an Etruscan fleet. With Etruscan power waning, the Romans were able, in the fourth century BCE, to pick off the disunited Etruscan cities one by one.

The Etruscan city of Veii lay only twelve miles from Rome along the Tiber. It was richer and more defensible than Rome. After a century of periodic hostility, diplomatic

DATE (BCE)	VICTORIES OVER . . .
340–338	The Latin League
343–290	The Samnites
282–272	Greek settlements of southern Italy
264–241	Carthage in the First Punic War
218–201	Carthage in the Second Punic War
212–211	Syracuse, Sicily
215–146	Macedonia and Greece
212–133	Spain
196–163	The Seleucid kingdom
149–146	Carthage in the Third Punic War

maneuvering, and a decade-long blockade, Rome finally conquered it around 396 BCE and annexed its territory. Roman soldiers stripped the city of its gods (that is, its statues and cult objects) and carried them back to Rome.

In 390–387 BCE, disaster struck Rome. A large band of Gauls (Celts) invaded northern Italy and defeated a Roman force fifteen miles from the city. In 387 BCE, the Gauls took the city of Rome and set fire to much of it, though some young Romans stayed behind to protect the citadel and a few patricians remained to protect their own properties. It was then that Juno's geese are supposed to have alerted the defenders to a creeping assault on the citadel of the city. Eventually the invaders were paid off and departed after sacking the city.

The Romans returned and repaired their city. Although many historians have downplayed the Gallic crisis, the Romans did not. The sack of Rome was a blow, however temporary, to Roman confidence. The incident does testify to the underlying resilience and determination of the city; Rome redoubled its efforts to remove by force its enemies from the neighborhood. Romans constructed a wall almost six miles long around the city and continued to take over nearby cities. In 351 BCE, Rome defeated the city of Tarchna, from which its own Etruscan kings had originally come, and the city of Caisra submitted to Rome's domination not long afterward. The Etruscan peoples to the north had also been hammered hard by the raiding Gauls, which left Rome the strongest city in northern Italy.

Taking on the Latin League and the Samnites

The Republic's next conflict was with the so-called Latin League, of which Rome had once been a part. Comprised of several dozen villages and tribes in the area of Latium near Rome, the league and Rome separated ways after the Gallic invasion. In 340–338 BCE, Rome successfully fought a brief war against these peoples and then disbanded the league. Rome's conquest of the Latin peoples and lands brought it into new conflicts in central Italy, particularly with the Samnites, a mountain tribe. In a series of three wars with the Samnites, fought between 343 and 290 BCE, Rome gained a measure of control over central Italy. It also gained a steady supply of Samnite slaves. The south of the Italian peninsula, however, remained a center of Greek influence and resistance to Roman hegemony.

One of Rome's advantages during these early wars was that its subordinate allies, the nearer Latin peoples, remained loyal. Rome struck treaties with its allies, stipulating what percentage of the war spoils each ally was to receive. During the Samnite wars and because of its continuing conflicts with the remaining Etruscan cities and the still dangerous Gauls, Rome restructured its army into mobile and efficient legions.

The Roman Army in the Early and Middle Republics

Rome's army and manner of conducting war was evolving constantly: from equestrian warfare to phalanxes and then legions. In the fourth century BCE, the Republic replaced the phalanx with the legion and doubled the size of its basic fighting unit to 5,000–6,000 men. The legion was broken into lines of maniples or rectangular blocks of unit formations that were spread across the field of action in thirty maniples, each containing about 150–200 soldiers. These units were under the command of a centurion and each possessed its own standard. Within the maniples the soldiers were sorted in horizontal lines according to their skill and experience.

To the enemy the legion seemed a solid and yet mobile fighting force. The maniples were assembled so that there were gaps between them, staggered so that the gaps in the front unit were filled in by the soldiers of the second line standing behind it. This open order assembly (unlike the solid phalanx) allowed a legion to cover more space and yet ensured that all its gaps were plugged.

As a battle was engaged, the javelin throwers at the front hurled their light spears at the enemy but then moved through the gaps between the maniples to be replaced by the front line of spearmen who hurled heavy spears when the enemy was within range. Once the spearmen had reached the enemy's front line, they tried to finish them off with short swords. At any stage of a battle, if the soldiers at the front were exhausted or making no progress, they could, on command, slip as a unit between the gaps between the maniples to be replaced by the fresh troops behind them. If the first and second lines both failed to win the skirmish, they would retreat through the gaps to a position behind the third line, which would then close ranks to fill all the remaining gaps, and the legion as a whole would retreat. The standards of the legion were kept with the third line, both to protect them and as a point of reference during any retreat.

The early Romans were skilled at laying siege to cities, but it was the legion that predominated during the period of expansion. Though the legion was a highly organized, hierarchically arranged, and successful fighting force, the Republic still lost many battles. Its legions had problems fighting under certain conditions: bad weather that might obscure sightlines, night battles, and charging elephants that threw the legionary formation into disarray. But Rome learned from its mistakes and was constantly adjusting its army formation and style of fighting to meet the changing conditions of war. The individual Roman legionary may not have been a better fighter than an Etruscan or Samnite soldier, but the Roman army was better disciplined and organized. Credit for its preparedness lay with the Roman Senate and its commitment to producing regular, rational warfare; to putting large numbers of men in the field under successful and ambitious generals; and to adjusting its military strategies according to need. Without a successful military machine, Republican Rome might not have survived.

Conflict with the Greeks in Southern Italy

In 280 BCE, Rome stood on the brink of ruling all Italy. The Greek colonies in southern Italy were all that stood in its way. After the conquest of the Samnites, Rome came into direct conflict with the powerful coastal city of Tarentum, a Greek foundation at the instep of the Italian boot. Tarentum, irked by Roman interference in its affairs and trade, asked the Hellenistic king Pyrrhus of Epirus (319–272 BCE) to come to its aid. In 280 BCE, the king arrived at Tarentum with 25,000 mercenary troops and some twenty elephants. Pyrrhus was an exceptional general and decisively defeated several Roman armies, in part because of his clever use of elephants to disrupt the front lines of the Roman legions he faced. The Roman Senate was reportedly on the verge of accepting his terms of settlement when the Carthaginians, eager to limit Greek influence in southern Italy, offered the Romans assistance. The conflict moved to Sicily where the Carthaginians had mercantile and political interests. Pyrrhus successfully invaded Sicily and came close to eliminating the Carthaginian presence on the island, but when he turned his troops back against the Romans his campaign stalled and he withdrew. For all his military success against the Romans, Pyrrhus could not afford to sustain the war; for this reason a **Pyrrhic Victory** is one that comes at too great a cost. The king's withdrawal left Rome in control of the south, where it now compelled the Greek cities to accept the presence of Roman troops.

At the end of the Early Republican period in 275 BCE, the Roman Republic controlled the entire Italian peninsula. Conquered peoples were enlisted either as Roman citizens or, more commonly, as allies (*foederati*). The Republic did not initially demand heavy taxes or tribute

from its allies, but rather loyalty and troops, both necessary to keep the Roman war machine running. The invasions by the Gauls and Pyrrhus reveal something else about Rome's success. Rome lost battles, but not wars. It was generally reluctant to settle with invaders except to buy time for their expulsion. By treating allied lands and people as part of its expanding territory, Rome gradually integrated Italy into a greater Roman cultural and historical entity. Roman roads, often built for military purposes, began to bind Italy together. Wider Rome became the condition of all Italy and the city of Rome its center of power. Economically, Italy was becoming an interdependent unit.

By 275 BCE, Rome controlled nearly 47,000 square miles of territory, an area larger than all of the Hellenistic kingdoms except the shrinking Seleucid kingdom. It is estimated that Italy had a population of around three million people, while the city of Rome had a male population of 300,000. Yet Rome had found the means and determination to dominate the whole peninsula.

Territorial Expansion and a Religion of War

How can we account for Rome's dramatic territorial expansion? It was not dramatic in terms of speed. It took the Romans two and a half centuries to conquer an area much smaller than Alexander the Great conquered in thirteen years. But Rome's expansion was dramatic in terms of the incorporation and integration of its conquests. Rome slowly made Italy Roman in a way that Alexander never made Asia Greek. A number of reasons might help to explain Rome's successful territorial expansion.

> What role did religion play in Roman life and the Roman state?

Reasons for the Republic's Territorial Expansion

HISTORICAL AND GEOGRAPHIC. The first reason for Rome's success lay in the historical and geographic nature of Italy. In 500 BCE, Rome had no master plan for subduing the ancient world. Indeed, in 387 BCE, whatever building confidence Romans had that they were a race pleasing to the gods was shaken by the Gallic invasion and sack of their city. Romans were motivated from their perilous early days by a basic drive to survive, which was a product of the unstable conditions of early Italy. Rome's geographic setting in Italy was of critical importance. It was to Rome's advantage not to be on the sea, but to have near access to it, and to be on the western side of Italy away from the hotter action in the Balkans and eastern Mediterranean.

Rome's location lay on a historical fault line in early Italy. Rome was located near the middle of Italy with powerful Etruscan cities around it and to the north and the fiercely independent Samnites and Greek cities to the south. Situated on a vulnerable, hilly site that was difficult to defend, Rome was surrounded by hostile peoples at a time when the most elemental conflicts were between tribes holding mountainous terrain and those dwelling on plains. Rome was forced to confront these various ethnic and linguistic groups that were each seeking to preserve their own way of life.

Rome's response was the obvious one: conquer or be conquered by the other aggressive peoples of Italy. The Republic of Rome realized that only by steadily defeating and incorporating its defeated enemies could it endure and thrive. Thus, it was the drive to survive in a hostile land that drove Rome to succeed.

TIMING. Chronology and chance also contributed to Rome's success. In the sixth century BCE, the city of Rome emerged and prospered under its Etruscan kings, but over the next two centuries it caught the various Etruscan cities in decline and disunity. The Latins and the other peoples of central Italy were in their own formative stages of development when they encountered Rome, while the city-states of Greece had more important business with the Persians in the east and with one another in Greece. The Greek settlements in southern Italy were at some distance from Rome. It was fortunate for Rome that Alexander the Great marched east, not west, and died young. While Carthage had the upper hand in the Mediterranean, it was a maritime power at a time when Rome's interests were land based. If an ill-favored wind had risen in the sixth or fifth centuries BCE, it might have blown Rome away, but aside from the Gallic gale of 390–387 BCE, that wind never blew.

STRUCTURAL. Another reason for Rome's success was structural. In a hostile environment, the Roman government institutionalized war. The Senate and Centuriate Assembly determined what the greatest threats to the city were and decided which wars to fight the next year and over the long term. It is striking that the Gauls, whose wanderings could not easily be predicted, were the one people to catch Rome by surprise and to do the greatest damage. Fixed and established powers with cities and territories to defend could be handled. In a world with city-states similar to its own and more decentralized clan-based powers, Rome's Senate proved a superior institution for managing external affairs and making war. In foreign affairs, Rome was opportunistic, signing treaties with some peoples while attacking others and then, in the coming years, turning the tables on its enemies. The Senate supplied justifications for these wars against its neighbors, often claiming that its motives were purely defensive, that Rome was threatened or that its rightful interests had been damaged by the enemy. Rome's centralization of power and decision making were simply superior to those of the decentralized and often disorganized peoples of Italy.

Moreover, in the fourth century, Rome improved its military techniques and restructured its army into the more efficient legion. Rome's system of war was tested on the field of battle and improved over several centuries. In short, the institutional structure of Rome led to a deliberate, rational commitment to warfare. Making war was Rome's chief function, yet Rome did not become a military state during the Republican period.

INCORPORATION. Another advantage to the Roman system, born of necessity, was the flexibility of its dealings with the other peoples of Italy. In the early days of the Republic, those peoples closest to the city of Rome were incorporated as full citizens. Other peoples farther away lacked full citizenship rights, unless they relocated to Rome, but could operate as Roman cities. They were thus reduced to the status of self-governing municipalities. Other Italian peoples agreed by way of treaties to submit to Rome as allies and to supply troops to Rome, but each of these peoples struck a different agreement with Rome and those agreements changed over time. The Samnites in the Apennine mountains of central Italy had resisted Rome so fiercely that many of them were enslaved and had their lands seized. But the Roman road system built for military reasons brought about the increasing circulation of peoples and goods, and led to further economic and social integration within Italy. Allied and conquered peoples supplied troops to Rome when so ordered and subordinated their external affairs to Rome and its central planning.

By 225 BCE, a million subordinate Italians had gained full Roman citizenship and, thus, enjoyed the benefits and protection of Roman law, though most were not given votes in Rome. One of the reasons Rome could not afford to surrender in war was that it would risk the collapse of its ally system, which depended on Rome continuing to hold the whole of its territory under the umbrella of its power. But Rome's flexible treatment of the Italian peoples also meant that not all of the Italian peoples or regions were equal, that resentments grew in some places, and that Rome would eventually have to resolve the uneven set of relationships it had with the peoples of Italy.

WEALTH GENERATION. Although survival may have been the earliest reason for Rome's wars of expansion, the conquerors' desire for material gain was always a factor. Land was the chief gain during expansion in Italy. Losing to Rome was not particularly pleasant and came at a cost not only to a territory's independence and cultural identity, but also to its real estate. Romans obtained and maintained vast and fertile villas throughout Italy. Often they took the best of any newly conquered land. Typically Rome expropriated something like a third of the land it conquered, unless it had made a treaty with the conquered that stipulated what land would be surrendered. Conquering armies also seized movable goods or riches during campaigns. By the Middle Republic, the enslavement of conquered peoples also generated immense wealth for Romans. Rome struck agreements with its allies to share the spoils of war.

ETHOS. The virtues that aristocratic Romans prized may also help to explain some part of the dynamics of Roman military success. Rome was always on a war footing and the Senate's chief business was foreign affairs or, to put it more bluntly, making war and dominating territory. In the whole of the fourth and third centuries BCE, there was hardly a year when Rome was not at war with some territory. Behind the generation of war there was a central ethos, or set of guiding beliefs.

Polybius believed that it was not by accident or without planning that the Romans sought and achieved dominion over the Mediterranean world. He thought that it was Rome's destiny. But, if we were able to ask a common Roman soldier or senator from 400 BCE whether he believed in the inevitability of Rome's conquest of the known world, he would probably have been astounded by the idea. There were too many enemies in the neighborhood and too many problems at home for them to take such a prospect seriously. Yet Rome slowly but surely swallowed a world. There was, at the time, no systematic ideology of conquest, no notion of Rome's responsibility to lift up a troubled and uncivilized world. That would come later, after the fact of expansion and the achievement of an effective empire. For much of the period of Republican expansion, Romans sought land, resources, and territorial integrity.

No abstract idea drove Rome to expand, but rather a set of immediate goals and Republican ideals. The reasons for Rome's expansion are complex, but the virtues that Republican patricians and nobles admired may have supplied the energy and competitive drive behind conquest.

Roman Virtue and the Pursuit of Glory

The Latin word *virtus,* from which English derives the word *virtue,* suggests the moral core of Rome's aristocratic elite. For Romans the word meant something closer to "manliness" since its root is *vir* or "man." A small constellation of virtues guided Roman males, both aristocrats and those wishing to secure noble standing. Among these were seriousness (*gravitas*), firmness of purpose (*constantia*), training (*disciplina*), hard work (*industria*), pious reverence toward the gods (*pietas*), simplicity of life (*frugalitas*), and fair dealing or trustworthiness (*fides*). The opposite of these virtues was exemplified by a man who was flippant and flighty, lazy and lacking a goal in life, self-indulgent, given to luxury, and untrustworthy.

The approval of the aristocratic group was all-important, for from it flowed stature and preeminence. But just as a group approved an individual's merits, it was another group—the individual's extended family—that benefited in terms of prestige and social standing. The Roman virtues were a set of ideal behaviors that were rewarded with "glory" or "glorious fame" (*gloria*). By battling nobly and even dying for the state on the field of battle, a man achieved a reputation of enduring magnificence that lifted him above others. He would be able to achieve such glorious renown, Romans believed, only if his life was well ordered and if he possessed in his very nature

the core virtues that the Romans prized. Sallust, the Late Republican historian, said that there was an intense competition for glory among Republican Romans. Each man wanted to achieve a military victory that would bring fame, respect, and wealth to his family and himself. The competition for glory fueled the Republican war machine as aristocrats lined up to lead armies into battle.

Immortality was the ultimate prize. Polybius describes in fascinating detail the honor paid to aristocrats who died gloriously in battle. Their bodies were carried into the Forum and propped up by the speaker's platform in the Senate as though they were about to listen to their praises being sung by a senator. The man's accomplishments and virtues were then described. The ritual created the impression that the man or his spirit was watching over the proceedings, enjoying the praise for his efforts on behalf of the Republic. When aristocratic males died, wax images of their faces were made. Great Roman families stored these death masks in cupboard shrines. On important occasions, such as the death of a noble Roman in battle, aristocrats donned the death masks of their relatives, dressed themselves in rank-appropriate togas, and marched in solemn procession to the Senate to listen to a speech in the dead man's praise. On such occasions the Senate was filled with the ghostly images of the gloriously deceased of the Republic, who were its real guardians. This was the company Roman nobles and aristocrats

A Roman Patrician Cradles the Busts of His Ancestors Ancient Romans worshipped their glorious ancestors and kept images and death masks of their glorious dead.

hoped to keep. Death masks reproduced the likeness of the dead with remarkable fidelity, which may help to explain the startling realism of Roman bust portraits.

Ancestor worship animated aristocratic Rome. A noble Roman's sense of place was grounded in his family's reputation and the chance that his own glorious deeds would contribute to the family's growing repute. The Roman military machine operated so successfully because it was driven by the individual's desire to excel inside a system of collective values. These men fought not just for money and land, and not for something as elusive and abstract as power, but for immortality. Glory overcame death. What invigorated Roman expansion, then, was a complex set of factors, not the least of which was a dynamic competition to achieve glory inside an aristocratic ethos that welcomed war.

A Religion of War

Religious beliefs and a warrior ethic meshed in the Republic. When waging war, Romans paid particular attention to pleasing the gods. They thought of war as a religious rite. In 340 BCE, a consul fighting the Latins encamped near Mount Vesuvius "devoted" himself. He had, in other words, decided to sacrifice himself to the gods so that Rome might win the battle. After dressing himself in a special toga for the occasion, he veiled his head and, while standing on a javelin, invoked a prayer and offered himself and the enemy to the gods. Trusting that death awaited him, he rode out alone against the enemy.

A counter-example is the case of the Roman general Publius Claudius Pulcher (consul in 249 BCE), who was insufficiently reverent during a naval battle in the Punic wars. On the eve of the battle, he called for the ritual feeding of the chickens, a traditional test of augury that would determine if the gods favored Rome. When the birds refused to cooperate, he had them thrown into the sea, saying that if they would not eat, they should drink. His fleet was destroyed and Romans understood why. The gods had been angered by an impious general who spurned their counsel.

The point was to get war right and, to do so, the gods needed to be on the Romans' side. The historian Livy said that the (legendary) king Ancus Marcius set down the religious rites of war. An envoy should first be sent to the frontier with his head covered in a veil. He would then proclaim aloud that he was the religiously commissioned herald of Rome, declare himself to the god Jupiter, and proclaim the righteousness of the Roman cause. He would then read out a list of Rome's demands, after which he was to step across the frontier boundary, proceed to the enemy's central square, and restate the demands. If satisfaction was not forthcoming within the sacred number of thirty-three days, the envoy would declare war and return to Rome to report to the Senate. Then the herald would return to the border carrying a spear bloodied from an animal sacrifice and hurl it into the enemy territory after singing another ritual prayer. It is unlikely that

Philip of Macedon or his son Alexander would have worried quite so much about religious rituals, but the Romans wanted not just to win wars but to enlist the gods, both their own and the enemy's, in their wars.

The *evocatio* or "calling out" was the religious rite by which the Romans summoned forth the gods of another city to their side. They were convinced that each city had its own protective deities. If those gods could not be persuaded to join them, it would not be possible to take the city. But first they needed to know the names of the gods they had to win over. Romans were careful not to publicize the secret name of Rome or the secret names of its protective gods. Once the names of the gods of a besieged city were known, the Romans would invoke them, promising to respect them and their temples, to offer sacrifices to them, and to treat them better than their besieged rulers had. When the Romans decided to destroy a city, a different ritual was performed. In those cases, the city was stripped of its gods and the people and properties were sacrificed to the gods. Such were the fates of Veii, Carthage, and Corinth.

Triumphs or triumphal processions through the streets of Rome by victorious generals were religious festivals. The Senate and people of Rome honored a general who had achieved a victory in which the enemy lost five thousand men or more. The general rode in a chariot through the streets of Rome, preceded by the spoils, animals, and people seized from the conquered land. At the end of the triumph the general dedicated a trophy of the armor and weapons of the defeated people to the temple of Jupiter Feretrius. With his face painted red, the victorious general wore a purple toga, sported a wreath on his head, and carried a scepter. The purpose of the triumph was to treat the successful general as if he were god for a day. The parade itself was as raucous and exuberant as urban parades for victorious sports teams today. In Rome virtually everything had a religious tinge and nothing more so than the conduct and success of war.

Living the Religious Life: The Roman Calendar and Vestal Virgins

As the Republic reaped success in war and the city of Rome grew, its religion matured and its old beliefs and practices were institutionalized. The older household gods and *numina* retained their force in the daily lives of most Romans, but the state itself increasingly sanctioned, systematized, and formalized religious practices, especially those that belonged to the public realm.

The old pre-Julian calendar may be the best witness to traditional Roman religion. On it the days of feasts, games, deities, and public business are intermeshed, suggesting how central religion was to public life. The Romans of the Middle Republic (274–146 BCE) paid scrupulous attention to the religious spheres of life, which may be what Polybius had in mind when he said that the Roman genius lay in its scrupulous attention to religion. Strict devotion to religious rites secured the approval of the gods and reinforced the Roman belief that its success came from satisfied gods. There were a variety of colleges and priests at work in Rome, the chief of whom was the **Pontifex Maximus,** who controlled the calendar and also exercised authority over the other priesthoods, including the Vestal Virgins.

The cult of Vesta may serve as an example of how religion functioned to integrate religion in daily life, and also of how Roman religion had evolved. The six Vestal Virgins were women of patrician stock of different ages, chosen by the Pontifex Maximus as young girls to serve a term of thirty years. They did not marry, and the penalty for not preserving their chastity was to be buried alive. They tended the holy fire and cult of Vesta, the goddess of the hearth. Vesta did not just represent the warmth of the hearth, but was the guardian of fire. Her cult stretched back to the distant hut age of Rome of the ninth to seventh centuries BCE, when keeping a fire alive could have made the difference between living and dying for the early shepherds and farmers of the Roman hills. As Vesta was the hearth, her cult in Rome was observed in a round building that was not a temple but a round hut. There was no statue of Vesta in the building, only an eternal fire tended constantly by the Vestal Virgins. If it died out, it was assumed that the goddess was angry because one of the Virgins had broken her vow of chastity. If identified, the unchaste woman was killed. At the very least, the Virgins were beaten and then they ritually rekindled the fire by rubbing sticks together as archaic Romans once had.

The religious festival of Vesta, the *Vestalia*, began on June 9 when the Virgins left their house in solemn procession to collect water from a holy spring. They were not allowed to set the water down as they returned to their ceremonial hut since the water would be polluted if it touched the earth. The Virgins used the sacred water to make holy cakes that were offered to Vesta. The *Vestalia* became a special festival day for the millers and bakers of Rome. On June 11 the Festival of Mothers or *Matralia* took place, when barefooted women entered the hut to visit the goddess. By June 15 the celebration of Vesta drew to a close. The Vestal Virgins swept the floor of their building and returned to their regular task of tending the flame.

The Virgins participated throughout the year in various other religious rites, many of them of special significance to women. The women's feast of the *Bona Dea* (the Good Goddess) was observed in December. On February 13, at the opening of the feast of the *Parentalia* to honor parents and ancestors, the senior Vestal Virgin gave a public libation to the ghosts of dead parents. The Vestal Virgins also processed with the other priesthoods of Rome in February as the city was purified. On March 1, the first day of the New Year in the old calendar, the Virgins offered some of their hair to the temple of Juno Lucina, goddess of women and childbirth. So that nothing would hinder the delivery of babies, Roman women loosened the knots on their garments and unbound their hair when giving birth. To assist in the unbinding, the

Virgins placed strands of their own hair on two old lotus trees in a sacred grove. On May 14 the Virgins proceeded with other priests to the Sublician Bridge over the Tiber where they cast thirty straw dolls into the river. This ceremony has been colorfully called the Drowning of the Dummies. Even the Romans were not sure what the ceremony signified, but it may have been a rite of purification that stretched back to archaic times and represented a symbolic form of human sacrifice.

The Vestal Virgins held an office that endured for over a thousand years until it was abolished by the emperor Gratian in 375 CE. They were at the peak of their importance during the Middle Republic. By then the agricultural rites of expiation and purification made less and less sense to urban Romans, but they were retained as a revered feature of traditional Rome, helping to bind together the archaic agricultural religion of traditional Rome and its complex calendar. What Romans and the state wanted from a cult was constant, rigorous attention; piety; and respect. Individuals need not worry about upsetting Vesta when the state ensured that the goddess was appeased by ritual observance. The Roman calendar was filled with dozens of such religious observances that gently governed their daily lives.

The Carthaginian Contest and the Middle Republic

Rome's spreading lines of conquest had brought it into conflict with a widening frontier of others who had their own lands, cultures, languages, and economic interests.

Why did Hannibal and the Carthaginians lose to Rome?

By the Middle Republic, Rome was bumping up against the interests of the great Mediterranean powers, particularly the Carthaginians and Hellenistic Greeks. Over several centuries Rome had perfected a style of fighting that had proven successful on land, but not yet at sea.

By 275 BCE, Roman Italy had taken solid shape. Pyrrhus had abandoned the Greek territories of Italy to Roman control, the Samnites had been suppressed, and the Etruscan cities had been incorporated. Internal tensions within the city of Rome were not pressing in the third century BCE because so many Roman citizens now profited from Rome's expansion, enjoying the resources and riches that came with conquest. Rome was on its way to becoming an imperial power. Each successful conquest increased the desire and need for more land and power. Moreover, because of its ally system, the manpower available to conduct wars increased with each conquest. Over the next two centuries, Rome engulfed a host of lands fronting the Mediterranean: Sicily, Sardinia, Corsica, Spain, Greece, northern Africa, and Asia Minor (Map 4.3). So quickly were the lands lying around the Mediterranean rim taken that Rome would have some difficulty managing its conquests and for a time it was

MAP 4.3 | The Expanding Roman Republic, 264–44 BCE
By the middle of the third century BCE, Rome was at war with its Mediterranean neighbors, first Carthage and then the Hellenistic kingdoms. *Why did Rome's conquest of Carthage lead naturally to conflict with the Hellenistic kingdoms? What advantages did controlling the Mediterranean Sea have for Rome's military and economic interests?*

not sure that it wanted to or needed to manage the wider Mediterranean world.

Rome's contest with Carthage played out over a century, but it was a fork in the road for western civilization. One way led to a Mediterranean world dominated by a combination of eastern Mediterranean civilizations (Phoenician, Semitic, and Hellenistic), and the other to the Roman Empire, the Middle Ages, and the West as we know it. At the outset it was far from clear which side would prevail and the consequences that would follow from Roman domination.

The First Punic War

Rome's first and most dramatic Mediterranean conflict was with Carthage, a city located just across from Sicily in northern Africa (near present-day Tunis in Tunisia). The Carthaginians were Phoenicians or red-skins. The traditional foundation date for Carthage was 814 BCE, when some colonists from Tyre sought to establish a port closer to Spain. The city had remained in the shadow of its

mother city until the seventh century BCE when Tyre had fallen under the control of a series of empires. Carthage, lying outside the reach of those powers, built a trading empire in the western Mediterranean that stretched from modern-day Libya to Gibraltar. Throughout the sixth and fifth centuries BCE, it continued to trade with and struggle against the economic interests of various Greek and Etruscan cities. For its part, Rome agreed not to impinge on Carthaginian trading zones, which included Sardinia, southern Italy, and Sicily. The power of Carthage reached its pinnacle in the third century BCE, when it took possession of Ptolemaic holdings along the coast of northern Africa and subdued outlying Berber tribes.

Carthage and Rome had different ways of dealing with conquered territories. Like most other ancient empires, Carthage subjugated conquered peoples and forced them to pay tribute, while Rome offered them allied status and asked for troops and participation in Roman wars. Consequently in its conflict with Rome, Carthage seldom had loyal allies, foreign friends, or permanently secure territories. Revolts within its own lands aggravated its contest with Rome. Although Carthage was primarily a sea power, it did practice agriculture on a large scale on vast plantations worked by slaves. The economic prosperity of Carthage came chiefly from the success of its maritime trade; few foreign ships dared to trade in the western Mediterranean or, indeed, ply its waters. Carthage had an effective trading monopoly, particularly once the Etruscans and Greeks ceased to compete with it. Its maritime enterprise was impressive and the harbor of Carthage had a great round house for docking and sheltering ships. The city was particularly proud of its navy, which was made up of citizen crews under veteran commanders.

The Carthaginian army was a different matter. It was largely comprised of mercenaries hired from neighboring conquered peoples such as the Numidians and Libyans. These troops fought under Carthaginian commanders who were hardened professionals. What favored Rome in the coming conflict with Carthage was the stability of its government and its greater financial and personnel resources; what worked against Rome was its lack of maritime experience.

As late as 279 BCE, Rome and Carthage had struck an agreement of mutual cooperation against Pyrrhus, whose invasion of southern Italy and Sicily threatened both their interests. Once Pyrrhus withdrew, the two cities clashed over Sicily. The city of Messina had fallen to a band of mercenaries known as Mamertines (named after Mars, the god of war), who had taken the city, killed all its men, seized its women, and carried out sporadic raids on the rest of the island. Both the Mamertines and King Hieron II of Syracuse (r. 270–215 BCE) sought to win the support of Rome to counterbalance Carthage's claim to trading rights and special political privileges on the island. In 264 BCE, two Roman legions took Messina, precipitating the First Punic (or Phoenician) War (264–241 BCE) with Carthage (Map 4.4).

Rome had a problem at the outset of the war. It had no navy. Polybius found it amazing that Rome dared to challenge the greatest of Mediterranean sea powers. If Rome had been content with its ground strength, it might have remained a second-rate power in the Mediterranean world and never have formed a Mediterranean empire. But by chance the Romans captured a Carthaginian ship and used it as a model to build its own navy. Within two months it had built sixty quinqueremes (single-decked ships with 50–60 oars, five men per oar) and twenty triremes (ships having three banks of oars, one rower per oar).

In its first naval action, Rome lost seventeen of its new ships, but it soon found a way to fight land battles at sea. Rome developed a grappling device called the *corvus* (that is, like the beak of a raven)

that was lowered onto the deck of an enemy ship to form a bridge over which soldiers could pass. At Mylae in 260 BCE the Roman navy surprised the Carthaginians, boarded their ships, and destroyed fifty of them. The Roman commander was given Rome's first naval triumph; Carthage crucified its commander for his failure to counter the new strategy. For three years Rome waged a series of successful sea battles against Carthage and then decided to take the fight to northern Africa, transporting 100,000 men there. By 255 BCE, Carthage had figured out how to deal with Rome's boarding tactic, but its navy was already a largely spent force in the war, and soon afterward Rome abandoned the use of its grappling hook. Rarely do new military inventions supply more than temporary advantage, though at the time that advantage may be decisive.

Ironically, although Carthage was a sea power, in this war it did better on land. It hired a Spartan strategist named Xanthippus, who put elephants in the front line of the Battle of Carthage in 255 BCE. They wreaked havoc with Rome's legions of disciplined soldiers. Rome also lost two fleets of ships to storms at sea. For the next thirteen years, the war was confined chiefly to Sicily. In 249 BCE, the two sides fought a great sea battle in which Rome lost 93 of its 120 ships. By 247 BCE, Rome's fortunes stood very low, but Rome refused to capitulate. Carthage sent its most capable general, Hamilcar Barca (the Blitz), to Sicily but failed to give him the men and money he needed to win the war. Rome built another navy, which in 242 BCE destroyed the merchant fleet of Carthage and threatened to starve the Carthaginian forces in western Sicily.

Carthage sued for peace in 241 BCE. The terms agreed to were at first moderate, but Rome soon broke that treaty, seized the Carthaginian islands of Corsica and Sardinia, and demanded an indemnity of 3,200 talents (the rough equivalent in daily wages of 75,000 years of

A Roman Warship A relief showing a Roman battleship with armed soldiers ready to engage in conflict.

labor). If the mercantile interests of Carthage suffered a severe setback, its pride was even more deeply wounded.

The Second Punic War

The Second Punic War (218–201 BCE) was in many ways the direct result of the first. Having lost a valuable part of its trading empire and been forced to pay a large sum of money to Rome, Carthage had trouble hiring mercenaries for its army. For three years it was forced to wage a campaign against its own disgruntled mercenaries and rebellious subjects in northern Africa. Rome seized the opportunity to invade other Carthaginian lands. Hamilcar Barca brought the war with the mercenaries to an end and then concentrated on expanding Carthaginian holdings in Spain. Rome, with its eye on Spain's mineral resources, grew suspicious of its enemy's activities there.

Hamilcar's eldest son, Hannibal (247–183/182 BCE), seized Saguntum, a Spanish city allied with Rome, in 218 BCE after an eight-month siege. Hannibal's plan was not just to irritate Rome, but to strike at its very heart. He conceived of an almost impossible scheme: to invade Italy. The Carthaginian navy had not yet fully recovered after the first war, and Rome controlled the waters around Italy. Thus, Hannibal set out to invade Italy by land. Behind his plan stood the hope that he could win over Rome's allies, leaving Rome to stand on its own.

In May 218 BCE, with about 50,000 infantry, some 9,000 cavalry, and 37 elephants, Hannibal began his expedition. There was some urgency to his march since Roman forces were rushing to cut off Hannibal's access to Italy, but his army arrived at the Rhône River a few days before the full Roman force and he managed to make the crossing. Behind him the Romans cut off the Carthaginian supply lines, so that Hannibal and his troops now had to live off the land. The lack of both land and sea support were to be important factors in the outcome of the war. By the time Hannibal's forces reached the Alps, the September snows had already begun to fall. The pass they took was treacherous, and they were assailed by Gallic mountain peoples who rolled rocks down on them. Many horses and men could not manage the narrow mountain ledges and plummeted to their deaths. Hannibal crossed the Alps in fifteen days, but he seems to have lost almost half his troops during the crossing (whether through reas-

MAP 4.4 | The Campaigns of Hannibal and Scipio Africanus, 219–202 BCE
The Second Punic War played out in Spain, Italy, and North Africa, with Hannibal winning in Italy and losing at Zama in northern Africa. *How did Rome respond to Hannibal's successful invasion of Italy? Where did Scipio campaign and why? Why did Hannibal fail and Rome prevail in the war?*

signment, death, or desertion is not clear), though he arrived with most of his elephants.

For the next fourteen years, Hannibal and his army ran loose in Italy, winning battle after battle and gaining effective control over the Po Valley. At the Battle of Lake Trasimene in 217 BCE, he surprised and destroyed a Roman army that thought that he had already departed for a march on Rome. At the Battle of Cannae the next year, some 70,000 Roman soldiers fell to Hannibal's forces. The Romans came to realize that they were not going to defeat Hannibal in open warfare and so the dictator Fabius, counting on Rome's substantial resources and Hannibal's lack of them, developed a strategy of delay (hence, the term *fabianism* refers to a delaying or gradualist approach). The tactic did buy Rome the time it needed to develop a bolder plan for inducing Hannibal to leave Italy, but it unnerved the people and Senate of Rome. Much of southern Italy and Sicily went over to Hannibal's side, as did some Italian peoples such as the Samnites, but in general Rome's allies held fast. For the next four years the Carthaginians roamed the countryside south of Rome.

Hannibal's plan to win over the Italian allies was not in the long run successful. He lacked the resources to buy support and protect his sympathizers, and living off the land meant that he antagonized many of the peoples he was seeking to separate from Rome. The Second Punic War was chiefly a contest over different systems of territorial expansion and the treatment of subjected peoples. The Carthaginians imposed; the Romans, particularly in Italy, partnered up. Rome's federation of Italian peoples prevailed in the Second Punic War because the Italian peoples feared not only Carthaginian oppression, but also the wrath of Rome for any evident disloyalty. Ultimately Hannibal, for all his brilliance as a general, discovered, as Pyrrhus had, that he could win battle after battle and still not win the war against Rome and its Italian allies.

Rome Takes the War to Africa

As the war continued and there seemed little chance of defeating Hannibal in Italy, Rome decided, as it had in the first war, to attack Carthage and its territories. In 212–211 BCE, it laid siege to Syracuse and, despite the defenses of Archimedes (c. 287–c. 212 BCE), the city fell. The Roman general ordered his soldiers not to kill the famous inventor, but something went wrong and—the pen not always being stronger than the sword—the old man was killed in his study.

Rome took Spain in 207 BCE and drove Hannibal's brother Hasdrubal into retreat. He attempted to join his brother in Italy, but his army was cut down. The Romans later hurled Hasdrubal's head as a hostile greeting into Hannibal's camp in southern Italy. Rome's ultimate strategy for removing Hannibal from Italy was to take the war to Carthage, so in 204 BCE it invaded northern Africa. Hannibal was recalled, abandoning his troops in Italy. At the Battle of Zama in 202 BCE, Hannibal's weak army was largely wiped out by the Roman force led by Scipio Africanus, who earned the title of The African for his success in the campaign. Carthage could no longer continue to resist and sued for peace. It agreed to restrict its territory to Africa, to destroy its fleet, and to pay the crushing indemnity of 10,000 talents. Hannibal escaped and found refuge and employment in the Hellenistic kingdoms, which still lay outside of Rome's control.

The lines of Rome's eventual defeat of Carthage were consistent: never to surrender to an occupying force, no matter how many battles were lost, and to employ its greater resources to outlast and outflank the enemy. Of critical importance was the fact that Rome's allies had by and large stuck with it; they were now part of the expanding Roman world and cannot have been comfortable with the idea of knuckling under to a foreign power as potentially oppressive as Carthage.

Rolling Up the Mediterranean Rim

At the end of the Second Carthaginian War, Rome did not annex Carthage, but it was now fully engaged in the Mediterranean world. Over the next fifty years it would move from policing part of it to controlling most of it. The strains on the Republic of such a large imperial expansion were never hidden to Rome. One day in 180 BCE, Cato the Elder rose in the Senate and lamented the state of Rome's Mediterranean enterprise. He noted that a three-man team was being sent to Bithynia (eastern Turkey) to check on Rome's eastern Mediterranean interests, but one of the men limped with gout, the second had had a roof tile fall on his head and was permanently dizzy, and the

third was widely thought to be the stupidest man in all of Rome. Cato wondered what would become of a legation that lacked feet, head, and intelligence. Cato was trying to alert the Senate to bow out of its familiar depths it now was in. Rome slowly realized that it was one thing to conquer a world, quite another to administer it.

The Senate had not been established to control other Mediterranean lands. Tensions between those who favored Roman isolationism and those who promoted expansion and imperialism often divided the Senate, but Rome found that it could no longer divorce itself from the world it had entered so forcefully. The logical conclusion to Roman expansion for purposes of survival was to keep on expanding in order to stabilize the world around its heartland. But every expansion brought new problems and the need for yet further expansion, and a widening set of problems. Prior to its wars with Carthage, Rome had had relatively little to do with the Mediterranean east. In between the two Punic wars, Rome waged a successful war against the Illyrians who lived in the Balkans along the Adriatic coast facing Italy. The Illyrian queen, Teuta, was forced to submit most of her territory to Rome.

By the start of the second century BCE, Rome was regularly receiving foreign diplomats, each seeking something from the powerful new player: protection, favor, or peaceful distance. The Senate, which controlled foreign affairs, considered it its prerogative to interfere in the name of Roman interests in the internal affairs of independent states. Underlying Rome's sense of superiority was its conviction that its people, government, and way of life were superior to those of these foreigners, almost all of whom lived under monarchs. Rome's old hatred of kings, its confidence in its own noble virtues, and its belief that the gods favored Rome continued to underlie its actions.

When Rome encountered the Hellenistic kingdoms, they were for the most part in a state of steady decline. The three great kingdoms of the period were that of Macedonia ruled by Philip V (r. 221–179 BCE), the Seleucid kingdom ruled by Antiochus III (r. 223–187 BCE), and the Ptolemaic kingdom of Egypt under Ptolemy V (r. 203–181 BCE). Philip and Antiochus were among the strongest sovereigns of their respective lines, but Ptolemy was a mere boy. When he came to power, Philip and Antiochus seized the Ptolemaic possessions lying outside of Egypt proper. Philip even struck a treaty with Hannibal when he was still roaming Italy. Rome could not forgive or forget such interference in its internal affairs during its time of crisis.

Despite the isolationists in the Senate, Rome declared war against Philip in 200 BCE. On the pretext of liberating the cities of Greece, Rome fought the so-called Second Macedonian War (200–196 BCE). The Roman general Flaminius led his legions to victory over the famed Macedonian phalanx at the Battle of Cynoscephalae in 197 BCE. Philip was allowed to retain Macedonia but had to surrender mainland Greece, where the Romans now stationed three garrisons of troops. Greece was nominally free but was to be "protected" by Rome for its own good.

The Pleading of Perseus

The list of Republican Rome's victims is long, but few of them speak directly to us in the sources. Slaves, lower-class women, eunuchs, jugglers, children, farm workers, sewer men, and water carriers all pass by us in silence. Yet it would not be right to assume that these people lacked an opinion about Rome just because it was not captured by our limited sources. What of the thoughts of the long line of peoples conquered by Rome? All of them had had their own histories, traditions, languages, and identities.

Perseus of Macedon

In the Roman histories of Livy, we do encounter the protests of the defeated. He occasionally gives "voice" to their complaints, but we need to be careful about these re-created speeches. Although some of the words were based on written sources, none of them should be thought of as direct speeches. Livy's historical art demanded that he make his narrative gripping, but the speeches he presents belong to rhetoric, not to verbatim records. Rome's victims seldom speak to us in their own uncensored words. Moreover, even Livy's speeches of the defeated belong to a discourse with the Romans and are not what the victims might have said if the Romans were not in the room.

Take the case of King Perseus of Macedonia as told by Livy. In 171 BCE, as his relations with Rome were deteriorating, Perseus met with a Roman commission sent to investigate his role in stirring up trouble. First he complained that his case was a good one, but that it was fundamentally unfair for him to have to plead it before men who were both his accusers and his judges. Moreover, he pointed out that since he was not a Roman citizen he was not protected by Roman law. It was unfair, he argued, for Rome to prosecute a king for behaving as a king and ruling his kingdom as he saw fit. Rome was interfering with his royal rule and questioning his every action when in fact he was acting within his royal rights and for the good of his kingdom.

Should he have to account for all his actions to a foreign power? As he finished his defense, he said that he realized that the commission would hear what it wanted to hear.

The commission carried his plea back to the Senate, where the majority still viewed Macedonia as its last great Mediterranean threat. Rome had so hedged in Perseus that he had little to lose by resistance. The king spoke to his army, reminding them of all the wrongs that Rome had done to him, his father, and Macedonia. Even now, he told them, the Romans were preparing an army to invade and enslave their land. The Romans would destroy kingship, disarm Macedonia, and lord it over an independent people. The army rallied to his cause with a roar of approval. By 168 BCE, Roman legions had defeated the vaunted Macedonian phalanx and King Perseus was on the run. He surrendered at Samothrace and was brought before the Roman general in such a state of shock that he was unable to utter a single word. All pleading was now past. Perseus was sent as a prisoner to Rome where he was forced to march in chains in the victorious general's triumphal parade. Perseus was imprisoned and died not long afterward.

All Perseus's pleading and maneuvering had not saved him from overthrow or the kingdom of Macedonia from Roman occupation, but his argument was a sound one. By what right did Rome interfere in Macedonian affairs, by what right did the Roman Senate undermine his kingship, and why did he have to play by Rome's rules? The Roman army answered, but that does not make Perseus's perspective as an outsider and humbled king any less valid.

QUESTIONS | *How can the historical record be balanced so that history's "losers" obtain a fair hearing? Was Perseus's complaint a legitimate one or just sour grapes? Why?*

Philip's defeat led Antiochus to try to put his own kingdom in order. In 196 BCE, he invaded Thrace and in 192 BCE crossed over into Greece, claiming, as had the Romans, to be liberating it. At Thermopylae the next year Antiochus was defeated in a battle in which Philip and the Macedonians fought on the Roman side. By 188 BCE, Antiochus met Rome's terms and abandoned his hopes of controlling Greece. He left the ruin of the Seleucid king-

dom to his son and marched east where he was killed by a rebellious mob as his troops sacked a temple.

Thus, by 190 BCE Philip had become a Roman client and collaborator, and by 188 BCE Antiochus had surrendered the last Seleucid hope of restoring Alexander's vast domain. Rome had subordinated two of the three great Hellenistic kingdoms, leaving only Ptolemaic Egypt unconquered, but in a state of semi-clientage. Yet it was probably not the

Roman Senate's intention to annex and absorb these lands, and its original idea was not to leave behind permanent garrisons. What turned Rome from the protector of Greece into its master was Greece's incessant squabbling.

Philip's heir, Perseus (r. 179–168 BCE), attempted to negotiate a perilous middle course; he sought to retain his kingdom's semi-independence while swearing loyalty to Rome. It was an approach destined to fail. The Third Macedonian War (171–167 BCE) broke out when Perseus's supporters rolled rocks down on a king friendly to Rome who was consulting the Oracle at Delphi. Whether it was the sacrilege or the diplomatic insult that irritated the Roman Senate, we do not know, but Rome was angry enough to approve another invasion. Perseus was captured and dragged back to Rome.

When Perseus died in 168 BCE, he was the last of the heirs of Alexander's successors to be king of Macedonia. Rome put an end to the line and partitioned the kingdom into four republics, each of which was to be separate from the others. After a failed Greek attempt to reunite the kingdom in 148 BCE, Rome turned Macedonia, Thessaly, and Epirus into a single Roman province under the rule of a Roman governor appointed by the Senate. Soon Illyria, Rhodes, and Pergamum were all brought under direct Roman rule.

The decisive showdown between the Romans and the Seleucid kingdom took place in 168 BCE. Antiochus IV (r. 215–163 BCE) invaded Egypt, which was partially protected by Rome, and the Roman Senate sent him an ultimatum to withdraw at once. He asked for time to consider his options, but the Roman general Popillius drew a line with his walking stick around the king and demanded to receive his answer before he left the circle. Antiochus capitulated to Rome, which now controlled Seleucid affairs just as it did those of Greece. Rome had rolled up the Mediterranean rim, though the nature of its control of various lands varied from place to place.

The Mature Republic

By the start of the second century BCE, Roman Italy was at peace and prosperous. With territorial expansion, Rome's economy achieved Mediterranean reach. Another reflection of Rome's growing sophistication was the emergence of Latin literature, though in its first flowering it developed under the influence of Greek literature. Below the impressive military, economic, and cultural successes of the mature Republic, tensions were building as Rome attempted to adapt to the full flush of imperial power and prosperity. The destruction of the ancient cities of Corinth and Carthage in 146 BCE was a symptom not only of Rome's excessive power, but also of the Republic's failure to cope with its ex-

What problems faced the Roman Republic in 146 BCE, after 350 years of expansion? Had it kept pace with the many changes it had brought about?

panded role in the Mediterranean world and its growing inability to balance the political and social strains at home.

Toward a Mediterranean Roman Economy

By the middle of the second century BCE, the Mediterranean was effectively a Roman sea. As Rome expanded its territory, so had its economy expanded; from a local agricultural economy with a small hinterland in 500 BCE to trade with the Etruscans and Latins by 350 BCE, from a regionalized Italian economy in 250 BCE to a western Mediterranean economy by 200 BCE, and finally by 150 BCE to a Mediterranean economy operating with provincial centers connected to the city of Rome. Long-distance trade along the Mediterranean was in full flow. Grain came to Rome from Sicily and northern Africa, minerals from Spain, and new slaves from the east. After the wars with the Macedonians, Greece supplied the best and most learned slaves, the ones most desired by rich Roman households.

Italian traders had been in the east before the Roman army. Roman merchants began to trade at Epirus and Pergamum in the third century BCE, long before those cities were conquered. By then Rome had its own formal and state-approved coinage. In 289 BCE, the Senate approved the establishment of a Roman mint. The encounter with Pyrrhus and the Carthaginians pushed Rome away from bronze coins to silver ones, the most important of these being the silver denarius, the basic coin of the Roman world. The shift occurred while Hannibal was occupying parts of Italy. As with so much else in Roman life, it may have been war rather than commerce that moved Rome in a new direction. Merchants benefited from the change, for the denarius was on par with the Attic drachma, which had long been the basic currency of the Greek world. The Carthaginians had provided the only currency resistance to the Greek standard and that was effectively removed after the first two Punic wars. By the late third century BCE, Roman merchants were trading in Alexandria and spurred the transport of goods along the Nile and across the Mediterranean to Italy. The city of Rome was an attractive market for both precious and bulk goods.

The Roman merchant had not just come to the east to trade; he often settled down, married a Greek woman, and achieved a prominent role in a Hellenistic city. Many served as representatives for commercial houses based in Rome. Although they lived nominally under local law, Italian traders could plead their cases under Roman law and often cultivated the local Roman governor to win privileged concessions. For this reason, Roman traders often remained in areas controlled by Rome and may not have been as adventurous as Hellenistic merchants. Greek traders tended to be more aggressive in the long-distance trade routes that connected the Mediterranean economy to India and China.

Rome's Mediterranean conquests may have been designed as much to eliminate economic rivals such as

Carthage as to eliminate territorial threats. The Senate was filled with men who had a keen eye for their families' economic gain. Provincial governors were particularly gifted at putting the pinch on local populations, whether by squeezing taxes out of them or by granting special commercial rights in exchange for a bribe. Governors liked to brag that they governed without accepting bribes, but their boasts suggest just how common bribery was.

The Roman Senate's control of economic policy was relatively unsophisticated. In 166 BCE, it did declare the Greek island of Delos a free port, one in which no taxes were levied on goods arriving or exiting the port. Delos thus became a funnel for goods moving east and west. After Rome took control of most of the Mediterranean rim, trade flourished. Romans, Greeks, Syrians, Jews, and Egyptians gathered in thriving cosmopolitan centers such as Delos to barter with one another and move goods.

Taxes were another measure of economic control. In the mature Republic the Romans generally taxed lightly immediately after conquests outside Italy, but then slowly brought conquered territories under the full weight of normal taxation. Cities longed for special exemptions and tax immunities, and all lived in fear of a new round of taxation. Rome operated a tax farming system, which was subject to excess. The Senate put the taxes for cities and regions up for bid, with the highest bidder winning the right to squeeze as much as he could from the designated area. The tax collector (or publican) became a hated figure, and, when riots broke out in the east against Roman authority, tax collectors, Roman merchants, and administrators were often the first to be slaughtered.

By the first century BCE, Rome depended on its eastern revenues. Roman senators knew that the eastern territories needed particular protection and attention since together they produced more revenue for Rome than all of its other holdings put together. Back in Italy, things were changing rapidly with the seizure of the Mediterranean rim. The importation of the people seized as slaves in the conquests destabilized the Italian countryside where large estates began to practice farming on a massive scale. Italy and certainly Rome had left behind its once humble agricultural origins to become the chief consumer of the precious goods and foodstuffs of a subject world. One of the things Rome consumed was culture.

Roman Literature of the Middle Republic

Latin literature had a surprisingly slow beginning even though Rome was surrounded by writing cultures. To the north and south were literate Etruscans and Greeks. Latin, like Greek, is an Indo-European language. Many early Italian peoples spoke related Italic languages; Latin was but one of these. The language of classical Latin written by the poets was, however, not the people's Latin of daily speech, the one scribbled on street and brothel walls. Latin, whether in its literary or popular forms, is an inflected language, which means that word endings convey the function of the words in the sentence and not word order as in English and German. One must often wait until hearing or reading the final word of a Latin sentence to understand the sentence's essential meaning.

Latin has not been important to the West because of any intrinsic superiority of the language itself, but because it was long the language of power and the powerful. Its influence was immense because it became the language of the lands that Rome conquered. From it evolved the Romance languages (Italian, Spanish, and French). As languages go, Latin is easily learned and has a moderately sized vocabulary. The Latin alphabet is based on the Etruscan (that is, the Greek) alphabet, with some adaptations. Roman numerals began as finger signs.

Few genuine inscriptions of archaic Latin remain, and no literature to speak of emerged until the third century BCE, when poets such as Livius Andronicus and Ennius began writing. Livius was a Greek captured in Tarentum around 272 BCE. In Rome he wrote in Latin, producing an adaptation of Homer's *Odyssey* and various plays. Sadly the work of these first poets survives only in fragments, but later Romans do not seem to have felt the loss deeply. Cicero claimed that much of it was unbearable beyond a single encounter.

Rome's first surviving literature is unmistakably Greek in inspiration, and that may have been its problem. The curmudgeonly Cato the Elder demeaned many Republican poets as mere vulgarizers and said that Rome had not conquered Greece in order to be infected by its culture. A certain culture shock did strike Rome in the third century BCE, after the capture of the Greek south and the importation of learned Greek slaves. But Greek comedy, in particular the new Hellenistic comedy of the fourth and third centuries BCE, met the Romans where

Roman Comedy on Stage A relief from Pompeii showing a Roman comedy. A boy provides musical accompaniment with pipes, the figures wear masks, their gestures are exaggerated, and the comedy is broad and cutting.

Fakes and Their Outings

Not everything is as it seems, particularly when we study the evidence of the past. For almost a century, the oldest Latin inscription was believed to be the one found on a golden pin called the Praeneste Fibula from the seventh century BCE. The inscription runs backward from right to left, contains a mixture of Greek and Latin characters, has continuous letters with midpoints to divide words, and possesses archaic-looking features such as "fhefhaked" for "fecit" ("made"). The inscription reads: "Manius made me for Numerius." When the pin surfaced around 1900 near Rome, many classical scholars, including the great Theodor Mommsen, thought it was genuine. We now know that the piece is a fake. In 1980, Margherita Guarducci, an Italian scholar, proved convincingly that virtually everything about the piece—its clumsy incision, acid-aged surface, metal composition, and "archaic" Latin—is wrong. Her work, along with that of the American historian Arthur E. Gordon, revealed the dodgy history of the piece. There were whispers early on that the Fibula was not genuine, but no one said so publicly or could prove it. Guarducci thinks that the Fibula was concocted by a shady Roman antiquities dealer and a failed German archaeologist. The motive of the former was probably to make money; that of the latter, a longing for professional respectability as the discoverer of the oldest piece of Latin yet known.

An even more complex cache of fakes was put together in the seventeenth century by a Tuscan boy named Curzio

Inghirami, who was in his late teens at the time. Catering to an Italian desire to know more about their ancient ancestors, Etruscan objects, and the Etruscan language, Curzio supplied a treasure trove. Since the Etruscan language was and remains mysterious, few dared to question forged documents that they could not read. To antique his forgeries, Curzio placed them in capsules made of mud, hair, and his own spit. Then, as an adult, he wrote elaborate books to explain the importance of the discoveries and to decode the texts. As happens so often in fraud cases, people found ways to give Curzio and the objects the benefit of doubt, arguing that he had been too young to have pulled off such a daring deception. Even the controversy that surrounded the forgeries enhanced their importance and Curzio's career as a philologist. Though not everyone believed in his discoveries, it was not until 1924 that forgery was proved.[1]

Forgeries haunt historians, who need always to question the legitimacy of the materials on which they work. Like all good confidence swindles, forged documents and objects appeal to the expectations, desires, and greed of buyers and true believers who expect that just such a thing should exist, must exist, and therefore, does exist. The fakers have many motives, among them the mercenary and the desire to trick the scholarly world. The damage done is substantial: the wasted years of scholars trying to make sense of a fake, the duping of the innocent, and the distortion of the past. Historians need to think critically and to be alert, for there are those who would rewrite the past by faking it.

The Praeneste Fibula

QUESTIONS | *In our digital age, with its mass of unchecked information and blurring of the line between opinion and fact, how should we proceed to weigh the truthfulness of things? How do historians and others detect fakes and frauds? What real damage did the fibula fakers and Curzio do?*

they lived and became immensely popular in its adapted form. The plays of the Greek Menander (c. 342–290 BCE) and his imitators, with their powerful sense of Hellenistic dislocation, were reworked for Roman audiences by Plautus and Terence, the two greatest Roman comic writers. Their plays are essentially situation comedies of the sort that audiences still enjoy.

Plautus (d. c. 184 BCE), whose full name means the "flat-footed clown," wrote 130 plays, 21 of which survive. His critics accused him of writing only for money, but he, ever the comedian, considered the criticism a compliment. His plays are filled with quick-witted, sly slaves; mistaken identities; twins; shipwrecks; angry fathers; wayward sons; and gorgeous girls as the love interests around whom his plays often circle. Plautus was a lively social critic, often mocking Rome's citizens: "Want to find a liar, go to the Assembly; a nasty braggart, show up at Venus's temple by the sewer; a fallen husband, try the basilica next door." Much of the delight to be found in his plays comes from their exaggeration and earthy humor. The situations are ridiculous and may have seemed strange and foreign to Romans. That strangeness, however, may have allowed Romans to laugh at Plautus's plays without feeling the sting too deeply. In Rome slaves did not dare to talk back to their masters, women strayed at their own peril, and boys who mocked their senile fathers risked death. But Romans could see all the improbabilities of an upside-down world on view in Plautus's comedies.

Terence (190–159 BCE) may not have been as much simple fun as Plautus, but he was the darling of the humanist circle that formed around Scipio Aemilianus, the grandson (by adoption) of Scipio Africanus. He too adapted the plays of Menander and his followers, but his Latin is more sophisticated and more quotable than Plautus's. Lines of Terence, such as "He whom the gods wish to destroy, they first drive mad" (which he adapted from Euripides's *Medea*) or "I am human; nothing human is foreign to me," cut off from their context and their Roman setting, may seem more universal to us than they did at the time. Behind Terence and Plautus one senses the wider and more cosmopolitan world that the Romans had come to occupy. Its immensity was such that a man might be separated from a brother in a shipwreck, twins might be separated at birth, and a father and a son in a large city might have their eyes on the same woman. Rome was maturing and its literature was growing up, rapidly.

The Year of Reckoning: 146 BCE

The year 146 BCE was a watershed, at least symbolically, in the transition of Rome from the Republic it had been for three and a half centuries to the quasi-empire it was becoming. Rome's exercise of imperial power had by 146 BCE become one of absolute military might, of impatience with resistance, and of fractured politics at home.

In that year, Rome utterly destroyed two famous ancient cities. In Greece the Achaean League under the leadership of Corinth rebelled. Rome responded by reducing Corinth, one of the ancient world's great cities, to ruins. Polybius claimed that he had seen the results with his own eyes: the smashed city with its great works of art torn off its walls and its statues toppled. He saw soldiers playing dice on paintings thrown onto the ground. One general seized art for his own collection, giving the rather stupid order to his soldiers that if they destroyed these unique works they would have to replace them.

In the same year, Rome also destroyed Carthage. The Third Punic War (149–146 BCE) was Hannibal's bitter legacy to his homeland. So formidable an opponent had Carthage and its great general been, that Rome could not face the thought of another threat from its old enemy. The peace after the second war had been so designed that Carthage was not even permitted the resources to defend itself against its northern African enemies. Its debt to Rome had been paid off, but some Roman senators had commercial interests that would benefit from the destruction of the city once and for all. Others for political reasons whipped up hysteria in Rome against the continued existence of Carthage. Cato the Elder liked to conclude his speeches to the Senate, no matter the topic, with the line *Delenda est Carthago*, "Carthage must be destroyed." On the pretext that Carthage had broken its treaty, Rome declared war.

The city of Carthage fell after a battle of six days. Its citizens were sold into slavery and the city razed to the ground. The old story about Rome salting the site of Carthage so that nothing would grow there would seem to be untrue since it was not long before Rome rebuilt a city on the same spot. As Carthage fell, the general Scipio Aemilianus told Polybius that, though it was a wondrous thing to see Carthage burn, he feared that someday someone might give the same order for Rome to be torched. Scipio should have been more worried about the Republic's present perils: the immorality and needlessness of the decisions that led to the destruction of Corinth and Carthage, the deep divisions and disorder within the Republic itself, and the very real prospect of imperial overreach.

Conclusion

The Roman Republic had a great run in its early and middle periods. In three and a half centuries it had gone from being an insignificant village of Iron-Age huts to the dominant power of the lands that rimmed the Mediterranean. Behind it in 146 BCE lay a long line of crushed enemies: the Sabines, the Latins, the Etruscans, the Samnites, the Greek cities of Italy, Carthage, and two of the three great Hellenistic kingdoms. None of this had happened by pure chance, but what drove Rome to conquer had changed and conquest had in turn changed Rome. What had begun as a matter of necessity and the need to survive in a hostile historical environment had become habit and finally license, the freedom to do as it pleased, the brutal might of Rome that Corinth and Carthage experienced at the moment of their destructions.

The Roman Republic, with its stiff, war-hungry Senate and supportive people, was the most successful government of its kind in all of ancient history. Other Italian cities of the Latins, Etruscans, and Greeks, and Mediterranean powers such as Carthage and the Hellenistic kingdoms were just as violent and ambitious, but Rome planned and fought more successfully than they did. Romans may have thought that it was their devotion to the gods or their noble virtues that were responsible for their string of successes, but it was more likely due to a complex set of factors, at the center of which stood its unusual government. The Romans waged war better than the others, made it a way of life and a way of religion.

Yet, at its end, the Middle Republic was faced with the consequences of its world-shaking success. The challenge that faced it was to see if its government could carry it to the next level, to the administrative control of an empire of vast holdings, to the curtailment of excess and corruption, and to the transformation of a city of expansion into one that fairly and confidently governed an incorporated whole. That challenge would fall to the Late Republic and other generations of Romans. The destruction of Corinth and Carthage did not bode well for the immediate future.

Even Polybius, so impressed by the Roman Republic's many accomplishments, knew that the goddess Fortune, who had for so long smiled on Rome, might turn against it. He was not, however, a historian of decline, but of success and the reasons for it. Unable or unwilling to analyze the symptoms of the Republic's growing disorder and corruption, Polybius failed to see that the wheel of Fortune had already begun her slow turn against the Republic he so admired.

Critical Thinking Questions

1. Looking back at their history, Romans were convinced that it was their destiny to dominate the Mediterranean world. What do the facts and patterns of Rome's expansion tell us?

2. Why was the Roman Republic so committed to conquest, and how did it balance its own internal division of peoples and interests?

3. How was Rome fortunate in the Early and Middle Republics, and what choices did the Romans make to achieve success? What did they sacrifice to succeed?

4. What might have stopped Rome's rise?

5. Why did the Senate become the preeminent Roman institution, and why was it so successful?

Key Terms

Senate (p. 104)
augury (p. 108)
haruspicy (p. 108)
curule (p. 108)
magistrate (p. 108)

fasces (p. 108)
numina (p. 109)
pontiffs (p. 109)
consuls (p. 109)
tribunes (p. 110)

patricians (p. 110)
plebeians (p. 110)
clientage (p. 111)
paterfamilias (p. 112)
materfamilias (p. 112)

patria potestas (p. 112)
Pyrrhic Victory (p. 115)
virtus (p. 117)
Pontifex Maximus (p. 119)

Primary Sources in Connect

For information on Connect and the online resources available, go to **http://connect.mcgraw-hill.com**.

1. **The Legend of the Foundation of Rome by Romulus and Remus**

2. **Twelve Tables: Laws on Offenses and Damages**

3. **Polybius on the Destruction of Carthage in 146 BCE**

Polybius on Roman Exceptionalism

Polybius (c. 200–c. 118 BCE) belongs to the rich line of ancient Greek historians that included Herodotus and Thucydides, but he has rarely been regarded as highly. Despite his commitment to honesty and to telling the historical truth, his literary style has not always appealed to readers. But his chief problem has probably been that in his greatest work he was a Greek writing admiringly about the Romans. As such, he applied Greek values and categories of analysis to a foreign land and its people. Whether his historical approach suited the Roman case or whether Polybius understood the essence of Rome, its people, and history are open questions.

Can anyone be so indifferent or idle as not to care to know by what means, and under what kind of polity, almost the whole inhabited world was conquered and brought under the dominion of the single city of Rome, and that, too, within a period of not quite fifty-three years (219–167 BCE)? Or who again can be so completely absorbed in other subjects of contemplation or study, as to think any of them superior in importance to the accurate understanding of an event for which the past affords no precedent?

We shall best show how marvelous and vast our subject is by comparing the most famous empires which preceded and which have been the favorite themes of historians, and measuring them against the superior greatness of Rome. . . .

As for the Roman constitution, it had three elements, each of them possessing sovereign powers; and their respective share of power in the whole state had been regulated with such a scrupulous regard to equality and equilibrium that no one could say for certain, not even a native, whether the constitution as a whole were an aristocracy or democracy or despotism. And no wonder, for if we confine our observation to the power of the consuls, we should be inclined to regard it as despotic; if on that of the Senate, as aristocratic; and if finally one looks at the power possessed by the people, it would seem a clear case of a democracy. . . .

The result of this power of the several estates for mutual help or harm is a union sufficiently firm for all emergencies, and a constitution than which it is impossible to find a better. For whenever any danger from without compels them to unite and work together, the strength which is developed by the state is so extraordinary that everything required is unfailingly carried out by the eager rivalry shown by all classes to devote their whole minds to the need of the hour and to secure that any determination come to should not fail for want of promptitude; while each individual works, privately and publicly alike, for the accomplishment of the business at hand. Accordingly, the peculiar constitution of the [Roman] state makes it irresistible and certain of obtaining whatever it determines to attempt. Nay, even when these external alarms are past, and the people are enjoying their good fortune and the fruits of their victories and, as usually happens, growing corrupted by flattery and idleness, show a tendency to violence and arrogance—it is in these circumstances, more than ever, that the constitution is seen to possess within itself the power of correcting abuses. For when any one of the three classes becomes puffed up and manifests an inclination to be contentious and unduly encroaching, the mutual interdependency of all three and the possibility of the pretensions of anyone being checked and thwarted by the others, must plainly check this tendency. And so the proper equilibrium is maintained by the impulsiveness of the one part being checked by its fear of the other. . . .

Again the Roman customs and principles regarding money transactions are better than those of the Carthaginians. In the view of the latter nothing is disgraceful that makes for gain. With the former nothing is more disgraceful than to receive bribes and to make profit by improper means. For they regard wealth obtained from unlawful transactions to be as much a subject of reproach as a fair profit from the most unquestioned source is one of commendation. A proof of the fact is this. The Carthaginians obtain office by open bribery, but among the Romans the penalty for it is death. With such a radical difference, therefore, between the rewards offered to virtue among the two peoples, it is natural that the ways adopted for obtaining them should be different also.

But the most important difference for the better which the Roman commonwealth appears to me to display is in their religious beliefs. For I conceive that what in other nations is looked upon as a reproach, I mean a scrupulous fear of the gods, is the very thing which keeps the Roman commonwealth together. To such an extraordinary height is this carried among them, both in private and public business, that nothing could exceed it. Many people might think this unaccountable, but in my opinion their object is to use it as a check upon the common people. If it were possible to form a state wholly of philosophers, such a custom would perhaps be unnecessary. But seeing that every multitude is fickle and full of lawless desires, unreasoning anger, and violent passion, the only resource is to keep them in check by mysterious terrors and scenic effects of this sort.

QUESTIONS | *Why was Polybius such an unabashed admirer of the Roman Republic? How does he account for Roman exceptionalism? How might his view of the Roman constitution be criticized? What proof does he supply of the moral and religious superiority of Rome?*

Source: The Histories of Polybius, trans. from the text of F. Hultsch by Evelyn S. Shuckburgh (London and New York: MacMillan and Co., 1889), Vol. 1, 1, 356, 360–361, 384–385; revised.

5

The Roman Aqueduct, the Pont du Gard, France

FROM REPUBLIC TO EMPIRE

The Late Republic in Disarray
Symptoms of Dysfunction
The Reforming Gracchi Brothers
Jugurtha and Corruption

The Rise of the Great Consul Generals
Gaius Marius Subverts the Senate
The Italian and Mithridatic Wars
Sulla, the Dictator
The Strivers: Pompey, Cicero, and Catiline
The Golden Age of Republican Literature

The Civil War and Collapse of the Republic
Caesar Forms a Powerful Consular Faction
The Civil War
The Murder of a Dictator
The Official Triumvirate
Antony and Cleopatra

Augustus the Emperor
The Great Transformation
The Augustan Ideology of Order
Dressing Rome in Marble
Augustan Writers

The Wider Culture of the Early Empire
Roman Religion in the Early Empire
Jews and Christians
Living the Augustan Age
Roman Women
The Lives of the Lower Classes in Rome

Toward an Empire That Worked
The First Julio-Claudian Successors
Claudius and Nero
The Good Emperors

Conclusion

CICERO DIES, AUGUSTUS THRIVES On a chilly December day in 43 BCE, Roman soldiers finally ran Cicero (106–43 BCE) to ground. He had been fleeing to the sea, carried on a litter by loyal slaves. His head was chopped off as he poked it through the drapes of his portable couch, and then his hands. The soldiers gathered up the bloody body parts and bore them back to the Roman Senate where the great orator had spent so much of his adult life defending the Republic. There they placed his remains above the speaker's platform as a reminder to all of the mortal danger of speaking and writing against those who were determined to overthrow the Senate's power to control Roman affairs. Cicero's plan to preserve the Roman Republic had failed. It was to be the last such attempt.

A half-century later, thanks to the political genius of Augustus (formerly Octavian), the empire was established and at peace. The once dominant and deliberative Senate was reduced to a body that chiefly executed the emperor's wishes. Outside his Mausoleum in Rome stood two bronze pillars inscribed with a long list of what Augustus called his "Accomplishments" (*Res Gestae*). He had, he said, liberated the Republic from tyranny, avenged the murder of his father, Julius Caesar, successfully waged domestic and foreign wars, restored religion, and brought peace to the Roman world (see Back to the Source at the end of the chapter). His résumé was boastful propaganda, but it was not untrue. Augustus did transform the Roman world, moving the massive weight of the Roman state under house control, the house being his own. After a century of Republican disorder and instability, Rome was now an empire, but the road there had been bumpy and bloody.

The apparent peace and glory of Augustan Rome should not obscure the difficulties of the first century CE, when some emperors were still waging a campaign against the Senate and a reactionary Republican old guard that refused to accept its loss of power. The violent struggle that continued between the Julio-Claudian emperors and Rome's aristocrats is not just the story of evil emperors such as Caligula and Nero, but the more profound transformation of one world into another, one form of government into another. Only in the second century CE would the imperial government established by Augustus truly take hold, but that imperial stability would not outlive the second century.

Cicero, whose fame endures, would not have been surprised by the brutal turn that imperial power took, but

Cicero

Augustus might have been disappointed that he had not once and for all solved Rome's problems and created a stable and lasting empire.

Historians have often told three stories of the transformation of the Republic into the Empire. The first is that of the dramatic end of the Late Republic (145–27 BCE); the second tells of the empire of Augustus and its awkward first century (27 BCE–96 CE); the third, that of the good emperors (96–180 CE). This transformation, however, may also be viewed, as we shall see in this chapter, as the single history of the transition from one form of stable

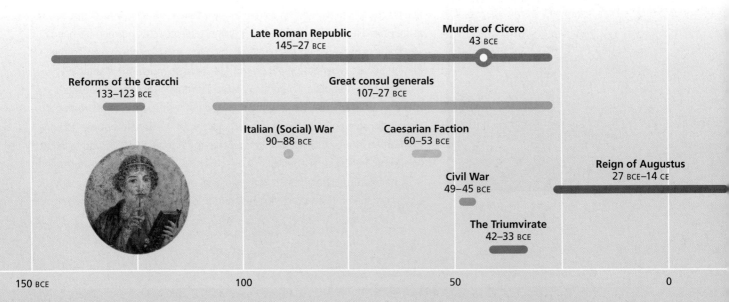

Late Roman Republic
145–27 BCE

Murder of Cicero
43 BCE

Reforms of the Gracchi
133–123 BCE

Great consul generals
107–27 BCE

Italian (Social) War
90–88 BCE

Caesarian Faction
60–53 BCE

Civil War
49–45 BCE

Reign of Augustus
27 BCE–14 CE

The Triumvirate
42–33 BCE

150 BCE   100   50   0

government at the end of the Middle Republic to another in the successful Roman Empire of the second century CE. To transform a form of government that had worked so well for so long was not done easily or quickly—hence, the violence and disorder, the intense rivalries, and the extreme rhetoric that characterize much of the period as the forces of conservatism and change struggled against each other.

The Late Republic in Disarray

In the Late Roman Republic the agreements and shared interests of the Roman peoples were breaking down. The Roman Republic was now three and a half centuries old and had been as successful as any government in the Mediterranean world. Yet what had worked for a city-state, surrounded by hostile forces in Italy and the western Mediterranean, worked less well for a Rome struggling to govern a vast territory. The Republic may have been too successful for its own good. Its form of government was still that of a single city with an intricate distribution of power among members of various privileged groups.

How did the Late Republic become unhinged?

By the middle of the second century BCE, many Roman citizens had begun to realize that Rome was already an empire in fact if not yet in name. Following the conquest of the Hellenistic kingdoms and the dramatic destruction of Corinth and Carthage in 146 BCE, Rome now needed to govern far-flung and foreign provinces with permanent armies. Conquest brought to the surface the underlying tensions of the Republic. Rome's government had been geared to conducting annual warfare close to home and the state had depended on war to reinforce a core set of virtues and rankings within society. Prolonged peace proved to be bad for the republican system, but so was maintaining a quasi-empire. The historian Polybius said that after Rome had been at peace for several years the population grew restless and so in 156 BCE the Senate manufactured a war "to refresh the martial way of life of its people."

Symptoms of Dysfunction

Like many governments and economies, then and now, Republican Rome depended on continual growth to thrive. It had neutralized internal tensions within society by externalizing them, encouraging the ambitious and disgruntled to seek their fortune and fame outside of Italy. By the middle of the second century BCE, Rome had transformed all of Italy and much of the Mediterranean world into relatively peaceful Roman territory. But contemporaries worried that the success of its conquests was corrupting Rome. Too much money, too many slaves, and too many exotic ideas were making their way to Rome.

There was also too much competition for too few political posts. To ascend the ladder of offices in Republican Rome was a laborious venture: the first rung on that ladder was the office of **quaestor** (magistrates and investigators: twenty positions), then **tribune** (representatives of the people: ten), **aedile** (magistrates of the people, guardians of public property: four), **praetor** (magistrates dealing with military and foreign affairs: eight), and finally, the

ulio-Claudian emperors
14–69 CE

Flavian emperors
69–96 CE

Five good emperors
96–180 CE

50 CE   100   150   200

highest office of all, **consul** (two). Each of these offices had an entry age, so that men of roughly the same age moved up the ladder together, always in competition, developing complicated political alliances and lingering resentments along the way. To attain the highest ranks of the state was becoming next to impossible for most aristocrats. Only two consuls were chosen each year, and the competition for those and lesser offices bred intense and often violent rivalries between individuals and their factions.

Another problem with the system was that it offered no pay. Although officeholders worked free for the state, they found ways to benefit personally from their appointments. The system of clientage, whereby powerful men or patrons protected and provided for their clients and dependents, reinforced factional loyalties. To be the client of a great man was to side with his political interests. Powerful aristocrats used their extensive wealth to fashion vast networks of influence and to manipulate the political process. This Roman oligarchy was the greatest of old boy networks. Blood, ancestry, and personal connections mattered in ways that we can barely grasp today.

So too did money, and there was too much of it as the Republic expanded to control all of Italy and most of the Mediterranean rim. Conquest brought tens of thousands of slaves into Italy, and their sale produced fantastic riches for the conquerors and altered social and economic affairs in the Republic. With more money came bribery, influence peddling, and extreme displays of wealth. The government tried to curtail corruption and extravagance, passing laws against conspicuous consumption by soldiers and provincial governors and restricting the number and frequency of triumphs for victorious generals. Senators condemned corruption and ostentation, but they could stop neither.

With the conquest of the eastern Mediterranean, new ideas and cultural influences—Athenian democracy, Greek learning, eastern mystery religions, Carthaginian agricultural practices—came to Italy, unsettling Rome's ancestral values. Foreign peoples were exposed to Roman values, but their own customs slowly influenced their conquerors. The most obvious case was that of the Greeks, but just as important was Spain, which would supply soldiers and emperors to the empire and eventually revitalize Rome in the second century CE.

Since Rome's success prior to 275 BCE had been a product of its core virtues and traditional means of governance, success in the wider Mediterranean world unbalanced those virtues and the government that was supposed to embody them. Because the Republic, like most governments, was built to endure and designed to eliminate attempts to change its fundamental nature, conflict was inevitable, particularly since the Roman Republic was stubbornly conservative. It was designed not to change. Not surprisingly the last century of the Republic was filled with turmoil and civil discord. The violence of the period was a symptom of political dysfunction, not its root cause.

Surveying their disordered world, contemporaries such as Cicero and the historian Sallust could not see that the Republic was giving way to something else.

They thought that they were witnessing the fall of Rome. Instead, the turmoil and dysfunction of the Senate and state produced a political genius in Augustus and an imperial form of government.

The Reforming Gracchi Brothers

There were early signs of trouble in the Late Republic. Military success had had a vast impact on Rome's economy, and not everyone benefited from the changes. Small free farmers in Italy found that they could no longer compete against large plantation-like estates (later called *latifundia*) worked by imported slaves. These small landholders often quit farming and drifted with their families to the city of Rome, whose size was increasing dramatically. The politics of the capital was changed by the presence of a mass of landless citizens always in need of food and entertainment. Soldiers returning home after long service discovered that their land had been seized. As well, some of the Italian peoples, who had been conquered by the expanding Republic, felt that they were getting a raw deal; they no longer wished to be merely Rome's allies and subordinates, but its citizens.

The story of the Gracchi brothers is the opening chapter of the final phase of the Republic. These two reformers may also have represented the last best chance for Rome to undertake the political changes necessary to preserve the Republic. Tiberius Gracchus (163–133 BCE) and Gaius Gracchus (154–121 BCE) were descendants of a distinguished aristocratic family that included Scipio Africanus, the conqueror of Hannibal.

Tiberius knew that something was wrong with Rome. Along with other Romans he had been shocked by a major slave revolt in Sicily in 135–132 BCE. Roman society had not yet learned how to manage its slave population, which was cruelly mistreated. Slaves who worked in mines and farms were beaten, chained, and held in pens at night. Cato the Elder, senator and landowner, thought it better to work slaves to death and replace them than to treat them humanely. The economic implications of slave labor were vast. With Italy's economy becoming more specialized, the slave revolt in Sicily cut off the secure flow of wheat to Rome.

As the supply and nature of labor changed, the citizen landholder who had once been the backbone of the Roman army was cut loose. These men still served in the army as conscripted troops, but now often lost the small parcels of land they held while they were away for long stretches of military service. Rome's military needs were changing as it was now necessary to station permanent garrisons of troops in distant places such as Greece. Tiberius Gracchus complained that the poor Roman soldier was styled the master of the world but had not a foot of ground to call his own.

Tiberius was not a rebel bent on the overthrow of the Republic. He did not advocate freeing slaves or improving their miserable lot. Nor was he an anarchist threatening the aristocratic order of Rome. Some scholars have wondered

Roman Slavery by the Numbers

How many slaves were there in Roman society, where did they come from, and did the economics and history of Roman slavery change over time? Historians such as Keith Bradley and Walter Scheidel have begun to break down the numbers of the Roman slave population. A quantitative approach to ancient slave demography (the statistical breakdown of population numbers) is not easy and involves the careful collection of scattered figures and a comparative extrapolation of them to obtain probable results. Unlike the African slave trade of the eighteenth and nineteenth centuries, with its detailed record of the slave traffic preserved in ship logs, sales accounts, and censuses, ancient sources are inconsistent and unsystematic. Ancient numbers are culled from narrative sources, legal records, and slave markets, but they are often large and suspiciously round. Nor do they always supply answers to basic questions: was the number of male and female slaves roughly equal, what percentage of slaves lived their entire lives enslaved, and what was the turnover of slaves in various regions and occupations?

Scheidel has drawn some conclusions based on the numbers that we do have. He estimates that over the millennium of Roman history, 100 million or more people were captured and sold as slaves. The circumstances of enslavement changed over time. During the territorial expansion of the Republic, Rome enslaved large numbers of conquered peoples: as many as 77,000 in the Third Samnite War (297–293 BCE), 100,000 during the First Punic War (264–241 BCE), and 150,000 from the taking of Epirus in 167 BCE. He estimates that in the space of less than a century, Republican Rome enslaved 700,000 conquered people. Ancient sources suggest that Caesar alone enslaved as many as a million people during his conquest of Gaul in the first century BCE.[1]

The enslavement of peoples was one of the chief causes of mobility, both geographic and social, within the Roman world. Italy received more slaves than other regions, with 15–25 percent of its population comprised of slaves. Areas such as Egypt had a lower figure (determined from census records) of around 7–10 percent, but only 15 percent of Egyptian households owned any slaves. The pace of enslavement by conquest slowed in the imperial period. Since Rome as an enslaving military and economic power depended on slave labor, how did it keep its slave numbers up? Scheidel reasons that if the average life expectancy of slaves was around twenty years, Rome would have needed 250–400,000 new slaves per year to replenish its slave pool. Conquest was not the only form of enslavement. Criminals were sometimes reduced to slavery, a man or woman might sell themselves or a child into slavery, and children abandoned to exposure by their parents could be recovered and enslaved. The principal source of new slaves, however, was biological. Scheidel thinks that perhaps 80 percent of the slave population in the empire was replaced by children born into slavery. The fertility of female slaves put up for sale was advertised. Although many older slaves were finally freed, female slaves were rarely freed until they passed menopause, their child-bearing years over, and their children legally fixed in servile condition.

Ancient slave numbers may be ragged and require deft handling, but they are chilling because they give us some idea of the scale of the institution of ancient slavery.

Roman Slave Collar The slave tag informs the finder of the slave to return him to his owner to collect a reward of one gold piece.

QUESTIONS | *Why were ancient societies so dependent on slave labor? How can historians overcome gaps in their sources? What are the strengths and weaknesses of quantitative history, particularly as applied to something as complicated as slavery?*

if he was influenced by ideas of Athenian democracy, but universal suffrage and equality were neither the point nor the effect of his reforms. Instead, he wished to return Rome to its ancient social contract, one that granted common citizens and soldiers their rightful place in Roman society.

When he became tribune of the people in 133 BCE, Tiberius put forward a land reform package to limit the size of state land that any individual could hold to three hundred acres. He proposed redistributing the recovered land among landless citizens. Many senators vehemently opposed the reform and persuaded another tribune to veto the bill. In response, Tiberius persuaded the Assembly of the People to remove yet another tribune from office and to vote in favor of an even stronger land reform bill.

A commission was set up to redistribute the land, but the Senate cut off its funds. Convinced that his land reform measures would be stalled by further obstruction, Tiberius took the radical step of standing for reelection as tribune. His opponents claimed that he was pandering to the people and seeking to set himself up as king. Many of his reforms and actions were unconstitutional, but then so was the Senate's response. An aroused senatorial mob hunted down Tiberius and his supporters, bludgeoning three hundred of them to death. Later Romans saw the murder of Tiberius as a turning point in their history. Roman blood had been spilled, the law trampled, and the landless lower classes of Rome emerged as a potentially powerful player in Roman politics, one to whom aristocrats seeking advantage could appeal. Tiberius was dead, but the Senate grudgingly allowed his land reform to proceed.

Ten years after the assassination, Gaius Gracchus, an even more radical reformer and populist than his brother, was elected tribune. He proceeded with his brother's land reforms and sought ways to curtail the Senate's power. Gaius wanted soldiers to be outfitted at state expense, and he worked to ensure the free and liberal distribution of grain within the city of Rome. He also wanted to establish Italian colonies overseas at places such as Carthage. His goal was to create a popular base for himself, while undermining the power and authority of the Senate. To do so he appealed to the **equestrians** (the knightly class just below the patrician senators), who were often wealthy and jealous of patrician and senatorial privileges. His most radical proposal was to grant full citizenship to Rome's Latin allies and partial citizenship to other Italian allies, which angered many citizens who feared losing their entrenched privileges and birthright.

Once again, the Senate decided to put a stop to social and political change. When Gaius failed to secure election as tribune for a third term in 121 BCE, the Senate moved to undo some of his legislation and canceled the colonization of Carthage. Gaius's supporters turned violent, but a consul imposed martial law. As many as three thousand of Gaius's people were slaughtered, and his own head (without the body, of course) was returned to the Senate for the bounty placed upon it.

The reform program of the Gracchi did not long outlive them, and their legacy was to leave Rome more socially and politically fractured. The people were not happy because grain prices were not fixed and the supply was uneven. Few soldiers ended up with plots of land to compensate them for their long service to the state. The Italian allies did not receive the citizenship they sought and their resentment rose. Most equestrians were no closer, after Gaius, to breaking the senatorial monopoly on power. The Senate was more determined than ever to fend off attacks on its traditional power. The city of Rome, whose size was increasing daily, remained a stew of alienated peoples overseen by a Senate that had shown that it was unwilling to entertain change.

Jugurtha and Corruption

The failed reforms of the Gracchi were soon left behind as a series of crises struck the Late Republic. The city of Rome was shaken by lawlessness and mob violence, and Romans became convinced that the gods were angry at them. The year 111 BCE was particularly dire. Two Vestal Virgins were found guilty of breaking their vows of chastity and were buried alive. Theaters were suspected of undermining morality and were censored. When consulted, the Sibyl, a prophetic female, ordered a drastic remedy: two Greeks and two Gauls were to be sacrificed to the gods. Finally, a great fire struck Rome, destroying much of the city.

There was also the persistent problem of Jugurtha, who ruled Numidia, a client-kingdom of Rome in North Africa (see Map 4.3). King Jugurtha, one of history's rascals, had risen to power by deceit and murder. Realizing that his actions had irritated Rome, he sent agents to bribe key senators. In the fateful year of 111 BCE, the Senate sent troops to pacify North Africa; Jugurtha bribed the consul in charge of the army. Ordered to Rome, Jugurtha apparently bribed a tribune and escaped having to testify before the Senate. While in Rome he arranged the murder of a rival to his throne. For the next five years, Jugurtha evaded his Roman reckoning by bribing as many Romans as he could.

The case of Jugurtha shows how corrupt the Republic had become. The Numidian king exploited Rome's factionalism and self-interested aristocrats, particularly in the Roman Senate. Individual ambition now trumped the old moral order.

The Rise of the Great Consul Generals

The Gracchi brothers had touched on many of the social and political strains within Rome, and the case of Jugurtha revealed how rampant corruption had become. Yet the greatest threat to the traditional Republic came, ironically, from the senators themselves. Rome elected two consuls each year, one

What role did individuals such as Marius, Cicero, and Pompey play in the final phase of the Republic?

of whom typically undertook military operations while the other remained in the Senate and city. In the old days, the consul generals had fought for family reputation and glory. By the Late Republic, powerful and ambitious men realized that the army and conquest promised more than just outstanding reputation; they brought power and profit. In seeking personal advantage, the great consul generals bent the Republic to the breaking point by subverting and bypassing the Senate.

Gaius Marius Subverts the Senate

Rome's war with Jugurtha continued until Gaius Marius (157–86 BCE), a man of middling birth and rank, and a former tribune, convinced the Senate to name him consul. His appointment was a sign of Rome's desperation to deal with the renegade Numidian king. It was highly unusual to elect a consul from outside the great families of senatorial rank. Marius sought the military advantages of the office of consul, for as consul a general gained not only a large army, but the chance to make vast wealth from the capture of slaves and loot. His aristocratic critics ridiculed him as a "new man," but he perceived more clearly than they did the new realities that were transforming the Late Republic.

His great innovation was to privatize or personalize the Roman army by binding soldiers and units to him personally through his power and wealth. He recruited soldiers from Rome's landless poor, who depended for their livelihood on his personal generosity or his ability to sway the government to grant them land or money. In this way, he established a deep source of personal power and extended the clientage system of personal patronage to the Roman army. In 105 BCE, after a series of successful battles, the Romans finally captured Jugurtha, who was handed over to Marius's representative, the young Sulla (137–78 BCE), who took credit for ending the war. The animosity between Marius and Sulla had begun. Jugurtha was chained and dragged back to Rome, where, unable to bribe the executioner, he was executed.

Marius found a more effective way than the Gracchi had to transform the Roman government, not by reforming it, but by subverting it. His populist thrust ushered in the phenomenon of the great consul generals of the Late Republic. Marius discovered that there was power in playing to the people of Rome, while manipulating and bypassing the Senate, whose standing and power were slowly slipping away. The degree and pace of change can be measured by the senatorial precedents that began to fall. Against all tradition, Marius was elected consul five straight times to deal with a series of military threats in Gaul, though in 100 BCE he was forced into exile when a riot broke out in Rome.

The Italian and Mithridatic Wars

The failure to extend citizenship to its Italian allies came back to bite Rome when the allies revolted in the Italian

The Italian Bull Gores the Roman Wolf A coin issued by Italia, the state set up by the Italian rebels in opposition to Rome during the Italian or Social War, does not disguise what the rebel state *wanted* to do to mighty Rome.

War (90–88 BCE), which is sometimes called the Social War (after the *socii* or allies). The rebellious allies were upset that they were no longer receiving their fair portion of the spoils of Rome's wars. Rome retained the allegiance of almost all its Latin allies, but the Marsi and Samnites of central Italy mounted stiff resistance. These peoples, who had never fully or willingly surrendered their identities and traditions, believed that Rome owed them for their recent loyalty. Moreover, they thought that citizenship would protect them from exploitation by corrupt Roman officials. The rebels established their own state called Italia that was to have a Senate and consuls. Italia began to mint its own coins and assembled an army of 100,000 men.

Rome recalled Marius to conduct the war but still lost a series of battles. Sulla was more successful, but what finally ended the Italian revolt was the Senate's offer of citizenship, first to those Italians who had remained loyal and then to all rebels who were prepared to rejoin Rome. The Samnites held out until the end, but eventually they too capitulated. With the end of the Italian War, the whole peninsula was integrated into the Roman state more effectively than it had been during the wars of expansion in the Middle Republic. The new Roman model permitted each region and city of Italy to retain its own identity as part of an expanding empire with the city of Rome as its capital and the Roman Senate as its great decision maker. Cicero said that there were now two fatherlands for all Romans, their natural homeland and Rome.

One of the reasons that Rome settled the Italian War so quickly was that Italia had sought help from Mithridates VI

(r. 120–63 BCE), the ruler of Pontus in Asia Minor. The king had extended his influence into the Aegean and had persuaded many Greeks, including the Athenians, to join him. Sulla was given command of an army to suppress Mithridates and set out on the campaign, but Marius had the order reversed and the command given to him. Sulla turned around his army and marched on Rome, breaking another long-standing tradition that Roman armies should not enter the city. Roman citizens were not pleased to be invaded and from their rooftops hurled stones down upon Sulla's army. The general replied by burning down their homes.

Events at this point became dizzying: Marius fled, Sulla restored order and set out again for the east, the people revolted in Rome, Marius returned and was elected consul again, and then died after first imposing, with his co-consul Cinna, a reign of terror on Rome. Sulla continued his campaign against Mithridates, retook Athens, brought Greece back into the Roman fold, and settled with the king, who surrendered the territories he had conquered.

Sulla, the Dictator

As Sulla marched home, Cinna was assassinated, the third consul to be killed in four years. In 82 BCE, Sulla reentered Rome with his army, which was illegal. He presented himself as Rome's liberator but quickly had himself named dictator and turned with a vengeance to eliminating his opponents. When one young senator pleaded with him to end the uncertainty about who was going to live or die, Sulla took him at his word and posted a list of proscriptions, a hit list. Sulla's list was both extensive and brutal; it included the names of 40 senators and 1,600 equestrians to be killed. Many of these men had been the supporters of Marius's regime, but some were murdered simply because they were wealthy and Sulla needed land and money to reward his troops.

Thousands of Romans died before Sulla felt sufficiently secure to begin restoring the Republic. He shored up the Senate's system of checks and balances so that no strong man like Marius (or, for that matter, himself) could again threaten it. He undid the last vestiges of the reforms of the Gracchi by limiting the power of tribunes and canceling the guarantee of grain to the people. Sulla was a law-and-order dictator and worked to reform the courts and to prosecute crime. Though he styled himself a conservative trying to restore Rome to its golden Republican past, Sulla was in reality one of the Republic's new military rulers, radically subverting the current Roman order. He used the Roman army to achieve power and advantage, overrode the Senate's directives, and shattered Roman traditions. Having restored the Republic, Sulla did something few expected: he retired.

Since 146 BCE a series of events had hammered Republican traditions and changed Rome forever. The Gracchi had both been murdered for attempting to reform the state; the case of Jugurtha revealed how cor-

rupt Rome had become; Marius, a "new man," had been repeatedly elected consul; the armies of Sulla, Marius, and Cinna had invaded the city; Marius became consul for a seventh time, this time without an election; and official death squads had operated in the city of Rome. The Republic, which had had a relatively stable history between 509 and 146 BCE, was now a cesspool of corruption, mob violence, and state-sponsored terror. An increasingly dysfunctional Senate seemed unable or unwilling to curb powerful aristocrats. Only foolish and stubborn traditionalists still thought that Rome could return to its old ways. Cicero was one of those; Julius Caesar (100–44 BCE) and Octavian (63 BCE–14 CE, later to be called Augustus) were not.

The Strivers: Pompey, Cicero, and Catiline

By the end of Sulla's rule, nearly all the symptoms of Republican stress were evident. Landless Romans and generals such as Marius forged new clientage bonds that left the conservative Senate more and more irrelevant. The new world order was being worked out in the violent streets, morning parlors where patrons met their clients, and wealthy villas of Rome where aristocrats supped together. The problem of an excess of money in the system had not been corrected. Moreover, there was a change in the collective value system. In the earlier Republic, few individuals had stood out above their fellows. Indeed, even the glorious few had wanted little more than the praise of the great corporation of the Senate and citizenry of Rome. The Late Republic was dominated by famous great men, all striving for individual power and wealth: Marius, Sulla, Pompey, Caesar, Octavian, and even the marginal strivers Cicero and Catiline, who were not generals. It was an age of great individuals, which was itself an indication of the drift away from the collective values of the earlier Republic.

The next great consul general after Sulla was Pompey (106–48 BCE), the golden boy of the Late Republic. The end of his career was as sad as its beginning was spectacular. Early on he attached himself to Sulla and, during the period of the proscriptions, was popularly called "the young butcher" for his success in hunting down Sulla's enemies. As a general, his military timing was perfect, and he had an uncanny talent for arriving on the scene of a recent kill. He made himself useful to the Senate during its many crises, including showing up in time to clean up the final remnants of the slave rebellion led by Spartacus.

Spartacus was a Thracian slave who had once served as an auxiliary soldier for Rome. In 73 BCE, he and a group of seventy-eight slaves rioted at a gladiatorial training camp. They camped near Mount Vesuvius south of Rome and began to attract other slaves seeking freedom, revenge, and wealth. Spartacus and his slave soldiers defeated nine Roman armies over two years. When Spartacus began to negotiate with Mediterranean pirates for passage out of Italy, the Senate sent one of Rome's wealthiest men, Crassus, who had little military experience, to lead six legions against the slaves. The slaves divided their forces and Crassus crushed each in turn. He crucified thousands of the rebellious slaves along the Appian Way leading to Rome. Pompey mopped up the remainder of the slave army as it fled north, and both he and Crassus were named consuls for 70 BCE.

The Senate found it all too easy in times of crisis to make exceptional military appointments: of Marius against Jugurtha and the Italians, Sulla against Mithridates, and Crassus against the slaves. These appointments shifted the balance of power away from the Senate to powerful military men, undercut the older competitive dynamic of the Republic in which many aristocrats had vied for military commands, and enriched those who were undermining the Senate's preeminence. The Senate reinforced the pattern when it commissioned Pompey by terms of an old law, the *Lex Gabinia*, to rid the Mediterranean Sea of the pirates who had been preying upon ships and inhibiting trade for years. Though the pirates were reputed to have a thousand ships and to operate out of scattered ports, Pompey eliminated them in a mere forty days in 67 BCE, destroying both their bases and ships. The commission gave Pompey extraordinary license over the entire Mediterranean and lands up to fifty miles from the sea.

Next the Senate appointed Pompey to resume the campaign against Mithridates VI that Sulla had ended on terms that did not fully satisfy Rome. Trapped inside his palace, Mithridates killed his family and himself rather than surrender. On his eastern campaign, Pompey extended Roman holdings to the Euphrates River and substantially increased Rome's annual revenues. So impressive were his accomplishments that some spoke of Pompey as a new Alexander and took to calling him Pompey the Great, but when he arrived back in Rome he was snubbed. The Senate refused to allot land to his soldiers, probably because many senators feared that Pompey would become another strongman like Sulla.

In the meantime, the Senate and Republic faced another crisis at home. Cicero, whose family belonged to the equestrian class, had distinguished himself as a lawyer and an orator. He slowly moved up the ladder of offices and finally achieved his dream job as consul for 63 BCE. In a vigorous campaign for election, Cicero beat the shady patrician, Catiline, who took his loss badly and stood again for election the next year during Cicero's term. Losing again, Catiline hatched a conspiracy to murder the consuls and take control of Rome. Cicero learned of the plot from spies and alerted the Senate. Catiline and his supporters, chiefly disgruntled aristocrats, fled Rome and began to raise an army among the poor veterans living in Etruria. Cicero and the Senate moved quickly to round up and execute Catiline and his fellow conspirators. Cicero believed that the suppression of the conspiracy was the greatest political achievement of his career. He thought that he had saved the Republic.

The case of Catiline is important, not because the plot was a real danger to the state, but because the actions of Catiline and his followers were symptomatic of the troubles of the Late Republic. These aristocratic rebels were broke and believed that their only way to secure riches was for one of them to become consul. With high office, Catiline could reward his friends and supporters, expropriate money from the provinces, and command an army on a campaign that would generate wealth. Catiline appealed to many of the disenfranchised elements of Roman society—bankrupt nobles, the needy lower classes, displaced soldiers, opportunistic provincials—but his rebellion failed and Cicero claimed the credit. As consul, Cicero made stirring speeches appealing for harmony between the orders, but he did little to address the underlying tensions and inequities of the faltering Republic.

The Golden Age of Republican Literature

Despite all the turmoil, or perhaps because of it, the last phase of the Republic was one of Rome's richest literary periods. Turbulent times often produce the liveliest expressions of human thought. Cicero and Julius Caesar were the greatest prose stylists of the age. The range of Cicero's writings is impressive. His letters to and from his friends survive in great number (nearly a thousand of them); so also do many of his legal addresses. His speeches against Catiline and Mark Antony are barbed masterpieces. His philosophical works may now strike readers as poor knock-offs of the deeper Greek philosophical thought of Plato and Aristotle, but Cicero served as a useful bridge between two cultural worlds. His works were, at the time, an effective Romanization of Greek thought.

The great poets of the age were Lucretius (c. 94–55 BCE) and Catullus (84–54 BCE). Lucretius, an Epicurean, wrote *On the Nature of Things,* which presents a gloomy theory of the world's atomic and material existence, but his central purpose was to allay the fears of his contemporaries about death. Catullus is a poet more at home with us since he wrote short poems about life and love, particularly about the girlfriend he called Lesbia (Clodia), the sister of one of the Late Republic's blackguards. We suffer along with the poet as Lesbia torments him and he moves from wanting to drown her in a thousand kisses to a state of high agitation:

> I hate and I love. You ask me how I manage it.
> I don't know, but I feel it and am a wreck.

Catullus died when he was thirty; he was every inch a Late Republican and was caught up in its turmoil. For a time he had opposed Caesar, before reconciling with him. His hatreds and loves, often of the same object at the same time, are spun in a web of sublime and captivating lyrical poetry.

Catullus and Cicero captured the emotional tenor of a deeply divided and confused age. They were not alone. Sallust's histories of the war with Jugurtha and Catiline's conspiracy are angry indictments of corruption. Cicero's lament over the death of his daughter and Catullus's agony over Lesbia's inconstancy reflect a period of Roman history that rested on a knife's edge of emotion.

Waiting just beyond the red hot eruption of the Late Republic lay the cool classicism of the Augustan poets and their politically careful poems, but then they were men without the freedom to speak their minds openly and confusedly. Catullus and Cicero probably enjoyed the exquisite agony of their loves and hatreds as free citizens of Republican Rome.

The Civil War and Collapse of the Republic

The Late Roman Republic was in trouble for a century before it finally collapsed. The Senate was no longer able to control the corruption, militarism, and rampant individualism of its own members. When the Senate finally saw the danger that one of the last great consul generals, Caesar, represented, it was too late. Civil war was the result. Although Caesar won the war against the Senate, he could not survive the uneasy peace of the still turbulent Republic and ruled for too short a time to transform the Roman state into a Roman empire.

Why was Caesar assassinated?

Caesar Forms a Powerful Consular Faction

Pompey's problems with the Senate forced him to turn to Caesar and together with Crassus they formed a powerful faction, the **Caesarian (or Consular) Faction**, sometimes mistakenly called the **First Triumvirate**, of three magnates bound together for political purposes. Each man did so out of individual and political necessity. Pompey wanted prestige for himself and land for his soldiers; Crassus sought tax advantages for himself and his supporters as well as a way to offset the extensive power and reputation of Pompey; and Caesar wished, in the short term, to receive a triumph for his campaigns in Spain and to become consul and, in the long term, to possess an army and new lands to conquer. Each of the men had grievances against a Senate that would not accede to their demands and vaunting ambitions. Their alliance was a private arrangement, a faction, and had no official power or legal standing on its own. Its power came when one of its members held the consulship and could swing benefits in their direction. Their plan to use the consulship was not unlike Catiline's, but it was handled more deftly by more powerful and better connected politicians.

Caesar himself was already a smooth political operator. As a senator he had won the support of the popular classes by mounting gladiatorial combats and widely distributing money and grain. Whereas Pompey sought alliances among the upper classes, Caesar counted on popular support in Rome just as Marius had once done. It was this alliance between Caesar and the people that would further marginalize the Senate and shape Caesarian or imperial politics.

Caesar became consul in 59 BCE, but he preferred to operate without the interference of the other consul, who largely withdrew from the scene. One wit claimed that the two consuls for the year were "Julius" and "Caesar." Others asserted openly that Caesar's actions were illegal, and many of them probably were. Like Marius and Sulla before him, Caesar subverted the traditional powers of the Senate for personal gain, the greatest of which was his own five-year proconsular appointment (one having the rights of a consul outside of Rome) as commander of the Roman armies of Illyria and then Gaul. He spent the next ten years carving out and stabilizing new territories in Gaul and Belgium for Rome, making himself rich and famous in the process. His written commentaries on his wars are elegant self-promotions that kept his name and deeds before the public.

With Caesar in Gaul, Pompey and Crassus quarreled in Rome, but together they successfully sought consulships for 55 BCE and each received territories to subdue. Pompey's province was Spain, where his military successes were modest ones. Crassus took command of a campaign in Syria but waged a disastrous war in which he lost seven legions and his head.

The Civil War

With Crassus dead, the faction dissolved. The two most powerful Romans, Pompey and Caesar, now stood against each other. Senators who had resented the presumption of Caesar's consular faction worked behind the scenes to separate the two men. Severing further the ties between them, Pompey's wife, Julia, who was Caesar's daughter, died in 54 BCE. The next year the Senate elected no consuls and for 52 BCE, for the first time in Republican history, chose only one consul, Pompey. He and the Senate now acted to limit Caesar's proconsular powers in Gaul. They also rejected Caesar's bid to become consul again. A sense of emergency gripped Rome as Caesar's command approached its official end. Would he give up his army peacefully, return to Rome, and face the charge of overstepping his authority? Or would he become a renegade? Early in 49 BCE the Senate declared martial law, put the Republic in the hands of Pompey, and sent two legions against Caesar's small force camped in the north (Map 5.1).

In January Caesar took the decisive decision to cross the Rubicon River, which marked the border between Gaul and Italy and, therefore, the legal limit of his authority to command an army. He entered Italy with a small army, thus provoking a civil war (49–45 BCE). Picking up small armies, veterans, and defectors along the way, Caesar's army grew as it marched south. In a panic and seeking more time to prepare, Pompey and much of the Senate fled Rome, but in their rush they

MAP 5.1 | The Civil War of the Late Roman Republic, 49–45 BCE
When Julius Caesar crossed the Rubicon River in 49 BCE, he ignited a civil war that spanned much of the Roman world. *Why was the civil war fought outside Italy? How methodical was Caesar in conducting the war? In what ways was this war an imperial war as much as a civil war?*

neglected to empty the Roman treasury before they departed. Caesar allowed the senatorial forces to flee across the Adriatic to Greece while he concentrated on securing control of Rome, Sardinia, Sicily, and Spain. In Greece Pompey managed to assemble an army of nine legions and was preparing to return to confront Caesar, when Caesar slipped across the Adriatic with half his troops. The other half was stranded in Italy, and Caesar was left short of men and supplies.

Though outnumbered two to one and lacking the naval forces Pompey commanded, Caesar's army defeated the senatorial army at the Battle of Pharsalus in July 48 BCE. Pompey and most of the senators fled the battle. Pompey fled all the way to Egypt, with Caesar in close pursuit. The Ptolemies greeted the defeated general by cutting off his head, preserving it in brine, and presenting it to Caesar when he arrived. Caesar was, by all reports, less than pleased. Throughout the civil war he had been generous to those he defeated. He welcomed back and forgave many senators, including Cicero, and likely would have received Pompey as well, probably

forcing him into retirement. Caesar spent the next three years mopping up the last of the resistance and delayed for nearly a year in Egypt where he apparently fathered a son by Cleopatra VII (69–30 BCE).

The Murder of a Dictator

Caesar returned to Rome in 45 BCE. He had already been named dictator for a ten-year term, but in 44 BCE his title was changed to dictator for life. He also held a series of other official titles: Pontifex Maximus (high priest), tribune, and consul. He fully intended to monopolize power in Rome. Indeed, he may for a moment have considered becoming a king like the Hellenistic monarchs, but in the end he came to regard his own name as its imperial equivalent: "I am not king, I am Caesar."

His legislative program was thin, but then he was only in Rome for a year and a half. During that short time, Caesar worked to improve the functioning of local government in Italy, found land for landless Romans in Gaul, and set about draining marshes to create yet more agricultural land. He replenished and expanded the ranks of the Senate and appointed all officeholders. He reformed the calendar, which by then was almost ninety days out of sequence with the seasons, and one of its months, July, was named after him.

He then made the mistake of a lifetime: he mistook official control of Rome and the Senate for absolute control, assumed that his victory at Pharsalus had decided once and for all the rightfulness and finality of his victory, and believed that those whom he had forgiven had accepted the new order. Those assumptions cost him his life.

The assassins who stabbed Caesar to death in the Senate on the Ides of March (March 15) 44 BCE had a variety of motives for their action. Some sixty senators were party to the plot. Cassius was the ringleader; Brutus, whose distant ancestor had reputedly dethroned the last Etruscan king, was its figurehead. Both had stood with Pompey and the senatorial side at Pharsalus, but Caesar had forgiven them. Some of the assassins were Caesar's own clients, officeholders, and friends, and many were "new men" whom Caesar had elevated to the Senate. The personal motives of these men suggest how dysfunctional the Senate had become.

The assassination was not an emotional outburst, but a carefully planned conspiracy. Caesar was scheduled to leave the capital in three days to take up a three-year campaign in the east and so the assassins acted before he could depart. Mark Antony (83–31 BCE), one of Caesar's loyalists, was kept in the dark about the plot. The various signs and rumors that were circulating did reach Caesar's ears, but he chose to ignore them. Someone slipped the dictator a note on his way to the Senate informing him of the plot, but he failed to read it and so was stabbed to death.

Whatever planning went into the murder, little thought was given to what to do afterward. The plotters assumed that Rome would be overjoyed to be rid of Caesar and to have its freedoms restored. They marched through the streets of Rome clutching their blood-stained daggers, proclaiming "Liberty!" When the Roman masses reacted with anger, the conspirators fled to safety. They had misjudged Caesar's popularity and the success of his patronage of the masses. They assumed that the Republic would return to its old ways without incident, and so left the dictator's body in the Senate house rather than dispose of it. The conspirators had not thought through the politics of assassination or how best to destroy Caesar's popularity.

The murder succeeded, but the Republic was already lost. It had been failing for a century.

The Official Triumvirate

Two days after the assassination, Mark Antony, who had already taken effective control of the Senate, spoke stirringly at the dictator's funeral. He reached a deal with the Senate whereby Caesar's acts were legitimized, but his murder was declared a patriotic and just deed by noble Romans. Antony deliberately obstructed the execution of Caesar's will, which called for the generous dis-

tribution of monies to the people of Rome and declared Caesar's posthumous adoption of Octavian as his son. The young man, who was the great-nephew of Caesar, sold personal properties to pay for the people's bequest; he already understood how essential the approval of the people of Rome was to his family's standing and the success of Caesarian politics. He also began to raise an army composed of Caesar's veterans.

Meanwhile Cicero began his last campaign to restore the Republic. He wrote a series of stinging orations called the Philippics (in imitation of Demosthenes's speeches against Philip of Macedon) against Antony. He did not hold back, calling Antony "a wine-soaked reprobate," so dissolute that he had once vomited in the Senate. Character assassination was part of the Senate's normal politics, but Cicero's attack on Antony was foolhardy, and he would pay for it dearly. The Senate sent a force against Antony and drove him north. It also refused the request of the young Octavian, then nineteen, to fill one of the consular vacancies. Octavian marched with his army on Rome, where the Senate felt compelled to elect Octavian consul, to acknowledge him as the legal son of Caesar, and to declare that Caesar's assassins were criminals.

Recognizing the strength of Antony and the fickleness of the Senate, Octavian established an official Triumvirate (42–33 BCE) with Antony and Lepidus, a former governor of Spain and ally of Caesar. **The Triumvirate** (sometimes mistakenly called the Second Triumvirate), unlike his father's faction, was given legal sanction by the Senate, which was aware that the Triumvirs possessed a large and threatening army. The official powers of the Triumvirate were extensive: a term of five years to straighten out the Republic and control over offices and taxation.

The Triumvirate declared Caesar a god, which enhanced its own legitimacy. It also introduced a Sulla-like list of proscriptions, with each Triumvir setting down the names of enemies to be killed. Cicero's name was high on Antony's list and so he was murdered that December day. Antony's wife at the time, Fulvia, is reputed to have pierced the dead orator's tongue with a hair pin in a fit of vengeful fury.

Antony and Octavian hunted down the assassins Cassius and Brutus, whose armies were defeated at Philippi in Macedonia in 42 BCE. After avenging Caesar's murder, the Triumvirs divided up areas of control within the empire: Lepidus took Africa, Antony the east (including Egypt), and Octavian the west (including Italy). While Antony campaigned in the east and began to court Cleopatra in Egypt, Octavian portrayed himself as the true Roman of the group. He concentrated on repairing a deeply divided and socially unstable Italy. On the surface he stood for justice, Roman religion, and Republican virtue.

Antony and Cleopatra

Like all three-legged stools the Triumvirate required all three legs to maintain its balance, and that was hard to achieve after the turmoil of Caesar's assassination. The

Caesar's Big Break, 59–58 BCE

Small pivotal moments may matter as much as big and famous ones, and Julius Caesar was a man of many moments when history might have turned in a different direction. Had he not crossed the Rubicon in 49 BCE; had he lost any of the important battles he fought over the last ten years of his life in Gaul or when outnumbered and facing Pompey and the senatorial forces in Greece; had he not gone to the Senate house the day he was assassinated and instead heeded the soothsayers and stayed home with his worried wife, the Roman world might have been different.

There was a moment, barely noticed at the time, when he did little and yet a world of possibilities opened for him. In 59 BCE, as he left the office of consul, Caesar was granted the governorship of Illyricum and Cisalpine Gaul (northern Italy). The appointment gave him the legal authority to have an army, but it lacked scope for a man of Caesar's ambitions. Those regions already lay firmly under Roman control, but Transalpine Gaul was different, an uncivilized land with an unconquered people and unfixed northern border. Its conquest was to be the critical turning point in Caesar's career. Bringing Gaul under Roman power was the finest accomplishment of his career. Success there brought him wealth and a loyal army of battle-hardened soldiers, but it also provoked the events that led to civil war. In the last five years of his absence from Rome, the opposition to Caesar rose in the Senate from the likes of Cato the Younger and Pompey, who sought to strip him of his army and extraordinary legal and military powers.

Those developments were, however, the result of an unexpected turn of events. Caesar was not supposed to assume the governorship of greater Gaul. Metellus Celer was already the legally appointed governor and he was famously fussy about senatorial rights. Cicero saw Metellus full of vim and vigor in the Senate one day in 59 BCE; three days later he was dead. Cicero suggested that his disreputable wife Clodia (Lesbia, later the girlfriend of Catullus) may have poisoned him to death. Though her brother Clodius was a partisan of Caesar, there is no evidence that Caesar plotted to deprive Metellus of his life or his governorship. Metellus may just have died naturally as middle-aged men sometimes do.

When Metellus died, the governorship of greater Gaul was handed to Caesar and it made his career. Caesar's conquest of Gaul led him to the Rubicon and Rome to civil war. Such are the twists of history. The Republic would have fallen anyway, even without Caesar, but it would have fallen in a different way and at a different time. History is the end result of millions of little decisions, actions, accidents, and, in this case, a mysterious and opportune death. Little historical things do matter. Rome's situation in 59 BCE, when Metellus was readying himself for the governorship of Gaul, was significantly different from what it became in 58 BCE, when Caesar began his great run.

QUESTION | *How do individual historical actors and the things that alter their lives matter in the larger scheme of history?*

A Fallen Gallic Helmet from the Site of One of Caesar's Victories in Gaul

Triumvirate first tottered under the weight placed on it and then collapsed when Octavian forced Lepidus to retire. Even Antony's marriage to Octavian's sister could not preserve their alliance once Cleopatra entered the scene. Cleopatra proved the perfect target for Octavian to attack. Reluctant to impugn the popular Mark Antony directly, Octavian's propaganda portrayed Antony as the captive of an evil Egyptian queen. Cleopatra was, in fact, Greek, fabulously wealthy, and charismatic. Romans despised her because she was both foreign and royal. They had despised kingship ever since driving the Etruscans out of Rome, and Cleopatra was the ruler of Egypt, a land that seemed to Romans to be full of exotic mystery and deadly intrigue. As the conflict between the two sides loomed, one of Antony's greatest problems was that few Roman soldiers were willing to fight for a foreign queen.

Cleopatra VII There are few reliable portraits of Cleopatra aside from her many and varying coin portraits, but this statue, though it lacks feet, bears a hieroglyphic cartouche on the upper right arm with her name.

its, among them his brilliance as a general and leader of men. Moreover, Antony had acted quickly and with skill after Caesar's assassination to win over the Roman masses and take control of Rome.

Did he fall into Cleopatra's trap, as Octavian's propaganda suggested, or was there a master plan behind his interest in her and Egypt? Antony had Hellenistic leanings. In his own religious propaganda in the east, he presented himself as Dionysus (or Osiris). After his failure to subdue Parthia in 36 BCE, Antony was even more dependent on Cleopatra and her Egyptian wealth for legitimacy and resources. In an elaborate ceremony in 34 BCE, Cleopatra, dressed as the goddess Isis, was named Queen of Kings, and Caesarion, her son by Caesar (though there were always doubts about the boy's paternity), was named King of Kings. Antony legitimized the children Cleopatra bore him, one named Alexander Helios (the Sun) and the other Cleopatra Selene (the Moon). Those names suggest Antony's Hellenistic ambitions, for he may have been attempting to graft his own line onto that of the existing Ptolemaic kingdom. Egypt was a wealthy and prosperous part of the Mediterranean world, and Antony may have hoped to establish an eastern kingdom to rival Octavian's Italy. On the other hand, Antony's Egyptian venture may just have been a colossal misjudgment. As melodramatic as the Antony and Cleopatra story may seem, its outcome mattered a great deal. If Antony had triumphed over Octavian, the Mediterranean world might have turned in a different direction.

The forces of Octavian and Antony met in a sea battle off Actium in Greece in 31 BCE. When Cleopatra fled during the fight, Antony chased after her and so lost the battle. They retreated to Egypt, where Antony committed suicide as Octavian closed in. Cleopatra did the same by the famous adder bite or, possibly, Octavian arranged for her death and made it seem self-inflicted. He ordered the execution of her son and heir Caesarion. Octavian now controlled the Roman world. He was thirty-two years old.

Augustus the Emperor

As successful as it had been as a conquering city-state, the Roman Republic was coming apart at the seams in the Late Republic. The regions and peoples of the Roman world were unsettled, but many of them wanted precisely what Octavian delivered: an end to disorder, disunity, and violence; in a word, peace. How he accomplished the great transformation of the Roman world from a dysfunctional Republic into an official empire is a story of structural changes to the Roman state and Octavian's personal political genius. The end result was the great "peace" that washed over the Mediterranean world under Octavian's (or Augustus's) watch, displaying itself in order and economic prosperity, classical monuments and words.

> **How did Augustus succeed in stabilizing Rome after Sulla and Caesar had failed?**

There is another way to view this elemental conflict. Mark Antony and Cleopatra were victims of Octavian's characterization of them. He and his propagandists depicted Antony as a boisterous boob, a big man who drank too much and was easily led astray by a wily foreigner working her foreign magic on an unsophisticated Roman. There is much to suggest that this picture is wrong. Julius Caesar himself had certainly seen Antony's many mer-

The Great Transformation

Few probably believed that Octavian would be able to restore Roman order. He settled his soldiers in Italy by buying land with the money he had taken from the captured Egyptian treasury, and he established a standing army over which he was the sole ruler. In this way, Octavian returned the Roman army to state control, which was now identical to his own. He created a **Praetorian Guard** of soldiers as his own imperial bodyguard. In 27 BCE, in a false and no doubt prearranged display of give and take, he offered to turn his official powers over to the Senate, which refused them. Instead, it asked him to assume proconsular powers over the empire for the next ten years. The Senate also bestowed on him the title of Augustus because he possessed *auctoritas* or authority over the state. For that reason, the starting date of the Roman Empire is usually set at 27 BCE, though for the Romans there was no sharp line between the end of the Republic and the start of the empire. Few probably realized that a new form of government had replaced the Republic.

Augustus succeeded where Caesar had not because of his relatively slow and sensitive reordering of the Roman world. Caesar was the greater general, but Augustus by far the greater politician. The list of his "Accomplishments" indicates how deliberate and categorical his mind was. He seemed to revive the Senate and Republic, while at the same time transforming their natures. From being a deliberating and advisory body, the Senate became one that executed the emperor's will. Under Augustus, the Senate lost its power over foreign, military, and financial affairs. Moreover, he created an inner council of senators that advised him directly rather than wait for the whole Senate to advise him. To win over the Romans and Italians, he encouraged their strong sense of place and superiority: Romans ruled; others served as incorporated subjects. Unlike Caesar, who forcibly brought about the collapse of the traditional Republic, Augustus promised his empire peace and prosperity.

The political brilliance of Augustus is evident. He seemed to restore the Republic and to reinforce old Roman virtues, but kept critical powers for himself, now sanctioned by the Senate. He polished the Senate's official sheen and ancient standing by increasing its size, but was quietly transforming it into a legislative agency of imperial power. He restructured the empire by dividing it into provinces, some under the control of the Senate, others under the control of the empire (that is, of himself and his family). Wealthy Egypt became an imperial province. Italy remained under the control of the Senate, but even there Augustus and his agents influenced policy decisions and administration. He directed affairs in the city of Rome by exercising his powers as tribune or through the prefect of the city, whom he appointed. Augustus kept the masses of the huge city content with entertainment for their diversion and bread for their stomachs.

Augustus controlled the senators and aristocratic elite by in essence making them his clients, while restoring their nominal dignity. Since his approval was necessary for the elevation of men to the Senate, they were effectively his men. In the case of any sign of senatorial independence or renegade legislation he could exercise his veto power as tribune. Still he presented himself as but one of the senators, though the first among equals (*primus inter pares*) or most eminent (*princeps*).

The Augustan Ideology of Order

Augustan ideology was seductive. As the Pontifex Maximus, he restored Roman religion by building new temples and encouraging a return to traditional religion. Augustus was a moral conservative, disapproving of the moral looseness of the Late Republic and its wild times. He banished his adopted daughter Julia for committing adultery. Though Augustus tried to curb excessive displays of luxury, the times were too good for extravagance to disappear entirely.

While much of Augustus's attention was devoted to the city of Rome and Italy, his peace was good for the empire as a whole. He reduced corruption in the provinces by more strictly controlling provincial appointments and by becoming the great patron of the local nobility of the empire. He also stabilized the empire as a contiguous territory and led the Roman army in its consolidation of Spain as an imperial province. Two permanent legions were stationed in Egypt. Where he could, he allowed local client kings to hold frontier areas, but not long after Herod the Great (r. 37–4 BCE) died, he made Judaea a province. Augustus extended Roman control over Gaul and parts of Germany, but in 9 CE a disaster struck. At the Teutoburg Forest three Roman legions were wiped out and their commander Varus felt compelled to commit suicide. It was a turning point in Rome's territorial ambitions since Germania was never to be as Romanized as Gaul.

Though Augustus himself was not a brilliant general, he found men who were, particularly Agrippa, and they remained loyal to him. Augustus ordered the creation of a state navy with bases on the eastern and western shores of Italy, and in Egypt. The standing army was one of almost thirty legions (perhaps as many as 250,000 men) spread throughout the empire, but mostly paid for by each province that housed them.

As successful and sure as was Augustus's reordering of Rome, there was a worm in this polished apple: the lack of a tradition of dynastic succession. While the emperor lived, all was well. Augustus was a second Romulus, another founder of Rome, and Rome did blossom (Map 5.2).

Dressing Rome in Marble

One of the functions of great patrons was to adorn cities with monuments. Augustus claimed that when he came to power, Rome was made of bricks, but he had left it dressed in marble. He boasted that he rebuilt eighty-two temples to the gods, and erected a Temple of Mars the Avenger to fulfill a pledge made at the Battle of Philippi. On the

MAP 5.2 | The Imperial City of Rome in the Second Century CE
The city of Rome had changed a great deal since the Middle Republic, as the patrons of the Late Republic and early imperial period left their mark on its design, architecture, and water supply.
How had the emperors of the first and second centuries left their mark on the city of Rome? What would a visitor to the city have been most struck by? How easy or difficult would it likely have been to move around Rome?

roofline of the pediment (the triangular shape at the top) of the temple were statues of Venus, Mars, and Fortune. Contemporaries thought that Mars looked remarkably like Augustus. Inside the Temple were statues of Mars, Venus, and the Deified Caesar, and in a side-room a colossal statue of Augustus standing over forty feet high. In general, the architecture of Augustan Rome was classical, but an eclectic blend of classical Greek and Hellenistic forms.

The emperor's drive to rebuild Rome spread to his advisors. Agrippa planned a new complex of buildings for the Field of Mars or War, including the Pantheon. Though the Pantheon as it exists today in Rome was rebuilt in the second century CE, it still reflects the high aspirations of Augustan Rome.

After the campaigns in Spain and Gaul, Augustus vowed to honor Peace, a goddess of concord, whom he either invented or institutionalized. To honor Augustus the Senate commissioned the erection of an Altar of Peace (*Ara Pacis*). The relief sculptures of the frieze running around the walls of the altar express Augustan ideology. The bottom layer presents a pleasant pastoral imagery of twisting vines, birds, and small animals; above it moves a parade of priests and dignitaries, including the imperial family. The

The Pantheon in Rome The interior of the Pantheon, originally constructed by Agrippa and later rebuilt, reflects the monumentality and sweep of Augustan architecture.

mood is somber, the figures dignified, the procession stately.

The Prima Porta statue of Augustus is probably a marble copy of a bronze original. The carved Augustus is larger than life (at six foot eight) and youthful. He is portrayed not only as a hero, but also as a barefooted god. A little Cupid rides a dolphin at his feet, a reminder that Caesar's family claimed to have descended from Venus, the mother of Cupid. The emperor's breastplate symbolically proclaims Augustus's victory over the Parthians. A bearded Parthian surrenders to the Roman army (represented by a single soldier) the standard that they had earlier seized. Above the two figures is a symbol of the spreading sky and below them Mother Earth with her cornucopia of bounty. To the bottom left is Apollo, to the bottom right Diana; to the left of the sky figure is the Sun and to the right Dawn empties dew from a jug while elbowing aside the Moon. On the breastplate the world rejoices at the dawning of the new age of Augustus and his cosmic triumph.

The Ara Pacis of Augustus Augustus's Altar of Peace was bestowed on him by the Senate. The altar, recovered in modern times from the Tiber River, is meant to express the pastoral calm of Augustan Rome. The stately procession of Augustus, his family, and the senators conveys the stability Augustus sought to return to Rome when he took charge.

The imperial art of the Augustan age is rich and highly symbolic, but there is a certain sameness to much of it. The hundreds of busts of Augustus that survive all seem remarkably alike: the youthful Augustus with his head slightly tilted to his right, an aquiline nose, wavy hair, and perfectly defined ears. There may once have been over twenty thousand such busts scattered throughout the empire in cities, homes of officials, and temples. These busts were mass produced by sculptors working from models with small protuberances that the artisan could measure with compasses to replicate the image as faithfully as possible.[2]

Roman art and architecture of the time was more than just Augustan, but his period and its pronounced tendencies toward classicism and imperial imagery marked a new phase in high Roman culture. Augustus's beautification of the city of Rome set a standard that radiated throughout the empire. Even the little towns of Pompeii and Herculaneum, destroyed by the volcanic eruption of Mount Vesuvius in 79 CE, lived and were buried in the shadow of its high standards. The drive to standardize and replicate images was an imperial and high cultural moment, though there was a world of common culture beyond its reach. Still Augustus knew how to communicate in both images and words his vision of the new Rome and his place atop it.

Augustan Writers

The three great Latin poets of the Augustan age, Virgil (70–19 BCE), Horace (65–8 BCE), and Ovid (43 BCE–18 CE),

Emperor Augustus The marble Prima Porta statue of Augustus.

Inside Out, Outside In

Empires produce both incorporation and alienation. While imperial systems tend to tolerate internal differences of language and customs as the cost of securing a unified whole, they struggle to balance a powerful imperial center and resistant marginal parts. That tension makes empires energetic and alert, but also anxious and adversarial.

Almost by definition, empires contain misfits. Among the insiders who found themselves on the outside of the Roman Empire was Ovid, the great poet of love. He had reveled in the high culture of Augustan Rome with its painted ladies, literary friends, fine dining, and imperial patrons. But in 8 CE he was exiled to Tomis, a dreary outpost on the Black Sea, at the very edge of Roman influence. Augustus was punishing him for the loose morality of his love poems and for some unspecified indiscretion. Ovid had apparently seen something he should not have. For eight long years until his death he languished in the frozen north far from the warmth of imperial Rome. Surrounded by people who knew no Latin and who lacked the basic refinements of civilization, he could not stop thinking of "Rome, home, my longing for old haunts, and that part of me that lingers in the city I have lost." The wailing poems that he wrote in exile in the hope that he would be recalled chart one distance between the center and periphery of Augustan Rome, and it was cold out there on the edge of the empire.

Ovid's complaint is deliciously literate, but many others forced unwillingly to be part of the empire did not write down their complaints. Yet their actions speak volumes. Slaves revolted and killed their masters, many poor men and women rioted when pushed or starving, and provinces waited for the opportunity to break free from Rome. No story is more eloquent or complicated than that of the Hebrews. Many Jews were pleased to see the Romans release Judaea from Hellenistic rule and so worked with their occupiers. Some Jews cooperated because in periods of toleration Rome respected their religion and way of life. But when Pompey stormed Jerusalem and desecrated the Temple in 63 BCE, Jewish resistance to Rome began in earnest. Cicero boasted that the gods had decided in Rome's favor since Jewish rites were not compatible with the great name of Rome or its ancestral customs. Jerusalem was now enslaved to Rome, he said. Few Jews saw it that way. The apocryphal Psalms of Solomon said that an alien enemy full of pride had laid waste to the land, killed women and children, and disrespected God. Portions of the Dead Sea Scrolls seem to refer to Pompey's invasion. The Jewish chronicler Josephus said that the Romans mercilessly tortured the Essenes, who probably deposited the scrolls in the caves of Quamram near the Dead Sea. The War Scroll curses Rome for bringing darkness down upon Israel. Over the next two centuries, the Jews revolted several times against their Roman occupiers, saw their Temple destroyed, and were banished from Jerusalem. The narrative of Jewish complaint against Rome provides powerful witness to what it meant for one group to be outsiders trapped under Roman rule and just how hot it was for them inside an empire of idolaters.

QUESTIONS | *What other external views of the Roman Empire would be valuable for us to encounter? Why?*

make a splendid, if all too neat, set of complementary bards. Each wrote in a different style and each explored different topics. Of the three, only Ovid was purely a product of the Augustan age, and he did not survive it well. Virgil and Horace had known the chaos of the Late Republic but flourished in the new world of imperial patronage.

Just as Augustus had a supreme military operative in Agrippa, he possessed a sophisticated political operative and cultural advisor in Maecenas (d. 8 BCE). As a wealthy patron, Maecenas gathered together a circle of poets that included Virgil and Horace. Virgil was born near Mantua to a gentleman farmer of the equestrian class whose land was seized after the battle of Philippi and handed over to returning soldiers. Virgil drifted into the employ of Maecenas and began writing the *Bucolics* (or *Eclogues*) about the joys of pastoral life. His patron suggested to the poet that he next write about Roman agriculture, which he did in the *Georgics*. Always a slow and measured versifier, Virgil spent seven years composing the work at the rate of about one line or seven words per day, a leisurely pace that would be the envy of many students today.

Virgil's crowning achievement was the epic *Aeneid*, which tells the story of the Trojan hero Aeneas fleeing from defeated Troy (as described in Homer's *Iliad*). Aeneas sails the Mediterranean with his men and, eventually, with the aid of the gods, establishes the Roman line. By fusing Greek and Roman myth and legend, Virgil gave epic dimension to the Augustan conceit that Rome was destined by the gods to achieve a world empire: "A boundless empire has been granted" to the Romans. The *Aeneid* is a stirring work, filled with images of great and moving humanity, but Virgil had some trouble finishing

Wounded Aeneas An imperial-period fresco of Aeneas, the great hero of Virgil's *Aeneid*, attended to by a doctor.

the great work. He left orders that if he died the unfinished poem should be destroyed. The emperor, whose vision of Rome's exceptionalism the epic celebrated, overruled that order and had the book published. The *Aeneid* ended up being, as it had begun, excellent Augustan propaganda, and so much more.

Horace was a different sort of poet. The son of a freedman, Horace wrote lighter barbed verse. He had fought on the side of Brutus in the civil war but returned home after the final defeat. Like Virgil, his family's property was seized after the battle of Philippi. "Gnawing poverty," he said, forced him to write poems. He too welcomed Augustan peace and patronage, composing a choral ode (*Carmen saeculare*) for the emperor. Yet he could be a stinging critic of himself and his times: "The wise man is just less than the great Jupiter, for he is rich, free, honored, and handsome, a king among kings and particularly well off, that is, until he catches a cold." Horace never fell into the trap of taking himself or Augustan pomp all that seriously.

Ovid was born too late to be part of the circle of Maecenas and did not write epic, which was ground already plowed by Virgil. Instead, he began by writing poems on the high life of a Rome now released from the worries of war and want. He said of the age of Augustus, "I like these times. They suit my way of life." He wrote poems about love, heroic lovers, cosmetics and how to apply them, strategies for seduction or, in modern par-

lance, how to get girls (*Ars Amatoria*), and the remedies for love, its breakups and pains. These light-hearted poems belong to that precious moment of peace and prosperity that stole over Rome with the end of civil discord, but before Augustus's higher moral code took hold. When it did, Ovid was banished from the city. His masterpiece, the *Metamorphoses*, describes the complex and surprising nature of mythical transformation. The work is filled with dozens of stories of humans changed into trees, birds, springs, and rocks. Ovid displays a special genius for destroying innocence. The poem ends with the **apotheosis** of Caesar, the transformation of a man into a god. That final cosmic change may have been the reason he took up the theme in the first place. Among the three great poets, Ovid was the one most enlivened by the Augustan age, but in the end he paid a heavy price for his own innocence.

For all their brilliance and creativity, Augustan writers were less free to express themselves than Catullus and Cicero had been in the chaotic Late Republic. Ovid said, now "Caesar is the state." The Augustan air was rich, but confined within a watchful palace.

The Wider Culture of the Early Empire

Imperial culture was more than just the high culture of imperial patronage. It was also the religion of the common man and his family and the daily lives of workers

> For whom was life good in the early empire? For whom was it bad?

and women, the poor and the enslaved. Great religious currents began to move through the Late Republic, transforming Rome's archaic religion into a more complex and cosmopolitan set of beliefs. Eastern mystery religions made inroads in the empire as did a new religion, Christianity. The daily lives of both common and elite Romans also changed as the city of Rome grew.

Roman Religion in the Early Empire

By the Late Republic, traditional Roman religion was, like much else, under pressure from the ideas encountered in Rome's spreading contact with the Mediterranean world. Official Rome had been dismayed when the cult of Bacchus or Dionysus, the wine-god, made a dramatic appearance in northern Italy late in the Republic. Soldiers, traders, and travelers from the Hellenistic east were carrying new religions back to Rome. These cults stood in stark contrast to older Roman religion, which was public, sober, and state-approved. Among the new cults were those of Cybele the Great Mother from Asia Minor, Isis from Egypt, and the Greek medical god Asclepius.

The Roman pantheon of gods, stuffed with divine forces, old gods and newcomers, was growing increasingly complex. Some Romans began to doubt the entire edifice of their religion. Cicero's treatises on divination and the gods demonstrated the weaknesses and absurdities of Roman polytheism: that it possessed no rational world principle, was devoid of morality, frequently seemed silly, and was far too utilitarian. *Do ut des,* "I give [a sacrifice] that you [O god] might give [to me in return]," was the working assumption of Romans who believed that an intimate, reciprocal, and rewarding relationship existed between people and gods.

There were practical strategies for dealing with the overgrown landscape of Roman religious beliefs. Each region, city, family, social class, and individual had a tendency to worship gods special to them without denying the existence of the other gods. They were in effect customizing and individualizing polytheism. Another way to rationalize complex religious forces was syncretism, the tendency to see one god in another or to join them together. On one level, Rome was engaged in rethinking and simplifying the divine; on another, Romans of the imperial age were spiritually needy, seeking forms of personal religion that were more intense, emotionally engaging, and satisfying. The rhetorician Aelius Aristides devoted himself, hypochondriac that he was, to the curative cult of Asclepius. When he received a dream from the god that he should not bathe, he declined to take a bath for the next five years. In a world of heightened emotional strains and personalized religion, many eastern mystery religions answered deeper and individual spiritual needs.

To some it seemed that a universal empire should have a universal form of religion. Polytheism was more a mode of religion than a single set of consistent beliefs and practices. Augustus responded by restoring traditional Roman religion and insisted on the timely celebration of the religious festivals of the Roman calendar.

The cult of the emperors began under Augustus. Though Caesar may have toyed with the idea of his personal and family divinity, Augustus personally promoted the idea that Caesar had become a god and insisted on describing himself as the son of the deified Julius. As politically shrewd as ever, Augustus refused to allow Italians to worship him, but when provincials, particularly the Egyptians, asked for permission to worship his genius (or divine spirit) it was granted. He could rationalize this as a policy that pleased easterners who were accustomed to believing that their rulers were divine.

The imperial cult belonged to the patron-client network of the Roman world. Provincial bosses and aspiring politicians were happy to treat emperors as divine, to erect statues and temples to them, and to encourage emperor worship, both to please their rulers and to control their own clients and subordinate peoples. The cult was probably never a deeply or emotionally satisfying one for the average believer, but it did serve as another layer of imperial presence throughout the empire. It is unlikely that sane emperors ever took their divinity seriously. The emperor Vespasian, one of the ancient world's great jok-ers, is supposed to have said as he was dying, "Oh dear, I think I'm becoming a god."

Jews and Christians

In the Late Republic only one religion, Judaism, stood aside from polytheism and its root assumptions. The God of Moses and the Jews was a jealous God who would not tolerate the worship of idols and other gods. Romans generally respected the antiquity of Judaism and the fact that it did not aggressively seek converts. In an exceptional move, they even exempted Jews from the obligation to worship the Roman gods or the emperor. Jews were able to take Roman names, to pursue a variety of professions, and to travel widely in the early empire.

One underlying tension in Judeo-Roman relations was a holdover from Hellenistic times. Many Jews had long been Hellenized, which many orthodox Jews regarded as an insult to their religion. Riots occasionally broke out between Jews and Greeks in eastern cities. These conflicts were often over which institution, the gymnasium or synagogue, should lie at the heart of civic and religious life. Official Rome disliked disruption within the empire and gradually became convinced that the Jews were politically divisive. The Jews in Jerusalem rebelled in 66 CE, which led the Romans over the next few years to wage a war of suppression. When he became emperor, Vespasian sent his son Titus to end the trouble. Titus took Jerusalem in 70 CE and all of Judaea in a brutal war in which the warriors and people of the fortress town of Masada took their own lives rather than surrender to Roman rule. Much of Jerusalem was destroyed and plundered in the war. The Arch of Titus (from 81 CE) in the Roman Forum depicts Titus's soldiers carrying back to Rome the holy goods removed from the Temple: the seven-armed candelabrum or menorah, silver trumpets, and table of the shewbread (the twelve loaves offered weekly in the Temple). The emperor Hadrian would eventually do worse, ordering the expulsion of the Jews from Jerusalem itself.

Looting the Jewish Temple Detail of a relief on the Arch of Titus in the Roman Forum that shows Roman soldiers bearing back to Rome the loot taken from Jerusalem and its temple.

Little noticed in the midst of these conflicts was the emergence of a new religion. Jesus of Nazareth was, according to the New Testament, born during the reign of Augustus and died during that of Tiberius (14–37 CE). His career was spent preaching in Judaea and Galilee about the kingdom of God to come and about the need for charity or love on earth. Christ, as he was called because of his identification with the messiah, was a Jew himself and his mission was largely confined to the Jews. Before his crucifixion, few Roman citizens took notice of him or his teachings. In the midst of turbulent Jewish events, Roman authorities largely missed the first stirrings of Christianity as a separate religion.

Saul of Tarsus or Paul (c. 10–67), the name he took after his dramatic conversion on the road to Damascus, taught that Christ's message was a universal one and he worked to free Christianity from the constraints of Jewish law and custom. His letter to the Corinthians from about 55 CE is thought to be one of the oldest documents in the New Testament. The growing missionary success of Paul and the apostles and their religion's growing separation from Judaism finally brought Christianity to the attention of Roman authorities. By then Christians had already reached the city of Rome and parts of the Greek east.

The Roman historian Tacitus (55–117) describes how the emperor Nero tried to blame the great fire that struck Rome in 64 CE on the "infamously depraved Christians." Tacitus supplies a potted history of Christ's career, viewing Christianity not as a religion but as a dangerous superstition and Christians as troublemakers. The few Romans who knew of Christianity regarded it as a new superstition and, therefore, by definition, not a true religion at all.

The Roman state in general charged Christians with being antisocial, with having, in Tacitus's phrase, a "hatred of humankind." Official Romans, always concerned about the danger of social upheaval, saw that Christianity was popular with the lower classes, the have-nots of the empire. To them Christians seemed treasonous since they would not cooperate with the state or follow its normal codes of conduct. They refused to worship the emperor or to undertake military service or civil office. Moreover, Christians withdrew from standard social relations, often rejecting their pagan parents and families in order to form new spiritual families. Romans regarded this as an assault on one of their core institutions. They were also bothered by the secretiveness of Christians, for Christianity was practiced not in public, but behind closed doors and in hidden places. No wonder that wild rumors circulated about the clandestine Christians: that they were cannibals (since they ate the Host or body of Christ), that they killed and cooked infants, that they participated in orgies (because they exchanged the kiss of peace and spoke constantly of love), and that they worshipped an ass. How, Roman aristocrats asked, could they honor a man, let alone a god, whom they had executed? Christians denied the very existence of the Roman gods and rejected the Roman way of life. For most Romans, Christianity was an insulting, antisocial, and dangerous superstition.

Despite the criminalization of Christianity and bouts of limited persecution, the new religion's role in the empire was negligible in its first two centuries. There were few Christian Roman officials, no Christian generals or emperors, and little official awareness of the religion. By the time of the good emperors of the second century, relations between Christians and Romans were a matter for bureaucratic disposal.

Living the Augustan Age

The city of Rome had a population of about one million people by the time of Augustus. Knowing that political stability depended on a peaceful capital, the emperor sought to ensure the quality of life in the city. To that end the people of Rome were supplied with free grain. A list of 200,000 recipients was under the control of the prefect of the city, often a senator, whom the emperor appointed. The prefect's primary job was to maintain law and order, particularly at the games and large assemblies. The prefect also oversaw fair prices for meat and was charged with putting out fires and maintaining soldiers who would act as a police force. As the people's tribune, Augustus was the chief civic protector and patron of the people, sponsoring games and entertainment.

To appreciate the tenor of ancient life, it would be helpful to try to reconstruct what a prosperous citizen's day might have been like in the city of Rome. To do that we have to scrape away many of the things with which we associate modern life. Romans had, for instance, a less precise awareness of time than we do. Their day was composed of twenty-four hours, but their hours ("hour" comes from the Latin *hora*) were variable throughout the year according to the amount of daylight: a summer daylight hour was longer than one in the winter. Romans had no way of telling time precisely. In the early Republican period a slave posted outside the Senate house announced when the sun was directly overhead. After conquering

Butcher Shop Sign A Roman butcher, Tiberius Julius Vitale, advertises his wares.

Greece, Rome imported the Greek sundial, but its markings were latitude specific. As a consequence, Romans told the time incorrectly for more than a century. Eventually, they fixed the problem and sundials spread throughout Italy, but sundials were a tricky way to tell time given the rotation of the earth and seasonal adjustments; they were also useless on cloudy days and at night. Eventually rich Romans had water clocks, which measured time by the regular passage of a flow of water.

In the city of Rome, the day for most people began at sunrise. The Roman bedroom was sparsely furnished with a couch, chair, bed, chest, mat, and chamber pot. The poet Martial claimed that one woke to the sound of carts in the street, school boys shouting, and the hammering of coppersmiths. Most citizens spent little time washing in the morning since they were likely to visit the baths later in the day. Breakfast was often just a drink of water. A rule of thumb in Europe, even today, is that the farther south you go, the more meager the breakfast.

Males often stopped at the barber's to be shaved, which could be excruciating. The Roman razor was, by our standards, a dull piece of iron. Martial claimed that one barber left him with a battered boxer's chin and lacking a piece of ear. There were remedies for nicks, but they seem more absurd than effective: a spider's web soaked in oil and vinegar was one popular cure.

The Roman matron rose at the same time as her husband but had probably spent the night in a separate bedroom. Some women had their hair layered in elaborate constructions by slaves, who were also charged with plucking out any gray hairs spotted in the process. Cosmetics, as we know from Ovid, would then be applied. Finally she donned her clothes, which included a brightly colored and voluminous dress.

Lunch was a light meal, followed by a siesta, baths, and a visit to the games. The main meal of the day was dinner. Aristocratic Romans reclined on couches so that, as one Christian critic said, their faces nearly fell into the food. The dinner couch was a three-sided piece of low-lying furniture (*triclinium*) set around a table so that slaves could efficiently serve the diners. The Romans did not have forks but chiefly used their fingers, knives, and spoons. Eating the great meal of the day was generally a messy but extravagant affair. Unwanted bits of food were thrown onto the floor to be retrieved by slaves. In the imperial period, floors often had mosaics depicting scattered bits of seafood and other remains, the better to hide the evening's droppings.

In Augustus's time M. Gavius Apicius wrote a cookbook that includes recipes for such delicacies as boiled ostrich, Numidian chicken, and stuffed dormouse. An essential ingredient of many meals was *garum,* a fish sauce made from the entrails of fish, salted and placed in the sun to age and ripen with the heat. The Romans had an elaborate network of wine-producing regions, but Roman wine may not have been as potable as modern wine; it was generally diluted with water. Since the Romans had no refined sugar in their diet, they suffered fewer cavities

The Roman Matron Aristocratic women went to great trouble to have their hair fixed in the latest styles, including this particularly elaborate bee-hive construction.

than we do. The skeletons found at Herculaneum, buried after the eruption of Mount Vesuvius, reveal excellent sets of teeth, though Romans were susceptible to gum disease, given their inattention to oral hygiene. After a hearty dinner eaten late in the evening, Romans retired to bed.

Roman Women

Roman upper-class women might be well educated, but they learned at home from tutors and did not go to a school. They could pursue rather independent social lives but were legally restricted by the male world in which they lived. Women had few independent legal rights and were legally the possessions of their fathers or husbands. Marriages were generally arranged, though women who had outlived several husbands were occasionally allowed to choose their next partner. Divorces were easy to obtain but favored the interests of the husband. The key issue was the disposition of the dowry or the goods and properties that the woman had brought with her into the marriage. Adultery was a one-way street: a guilty woman could be divorced; a man could freely indulge with women below his class without risking divorce or censure. Rape in Rome was treated in a bizarre fashion since the injured party was thought to be the woman's father or husband, whose property rights had been infringed.

A Woman Composing Her Thoughts In this painting from Pompeii, a woman, thought by some scholars to be Sappho, ponders her thoughts while holding a stylus to her lips and waxed tablets ready to be written upon.

Women were prized possessions because men outnumbered women in Rome. The average lifespan of the upper-class female was around 34.5 years; that of an upper-class man was 46 years. In preindustrial societies women tended to have low life expectancies, in part because of the primitive and unsanitary conditions of childbearing and because women unknowingly suffered from a lack of iron in their diets. Another factor in the reduced numbers of women was the selective infanticide of females, usually through exposure. Unwanted children were left at dumping sites to die or to be retrieved by strangers. Roman law mandated the rearing of all male children, except those who were deformed, but compelled families to rear only the first of any female children. This was a legacy of the agricultural past of the Early Republic.

The dynamic aristocratic women described in narrative sources lived lives of great, but exceptional privilege. The shift to dynastic rule under Augustus meant that the women of the imperial family became more politically and biologically important.

Lower-class women fell into three rough categories: free born but poor, prostitutes, and slaves. The average lifespan of poor women was about 20–25 years, which means that some lived into their forties and fifties, but many died as children and young women. Female slaves could not marry but could cohabit with another slave, their children being born into slavery as the property of their master.

The Lives of the Lower Classes in Rome

Below the golden glow of early imperial Rome—and it was a more prosperous city than all others in the empire—lay the dark dirty back street where the poor lived. The poor of Italy (displaced soldiers, farmers, and their families) drifted to Rome, where they were housed in apartment blocks called islands. Only the rich could own detached homes and villas in Rome itself. Because land was at a premium, apartment buildings grew taller, reaching heights of six floors. Since there were no elevators, the higher up one went the worse the apartment. These buildings were prone to catch fire, and so it was preferable to live close to the ground. Apartments were cold and drafty. Though the Romans knew how to make glass, they did not make window panes, insulated poorly, and had not perfected venting systems that would allow inhabitants to have fires safely.

Apartments also lacked running water. Although imperial Rome had a marvelous aqueduct system that by the second century CE was bringing over 200 million gallons of water to the city each day, much of the water was poorly distributed and ran into gutters and then into the Tiber. Water had to be carried from public wells to individual apartments and was probably not used for cleaning. As a result, apartments were filthy and full of bugs. Even worse were the dank, dark streets and alleys

A Roman Apartment Building A model of a Roman apartment block, called an island, from Ostia, the port of Rome.

The Antikythera Device

Greco-Roman technology chiefly consisted of large-scale war machines, water conveyances, construction tools, and agricultural implements. The Romans invented a harvester for collecting and threshing wheat in the field, but it did not catch on, probably because slave labor was cheaper and more efficient. War has long been an incentive to invention, and the peoples of the Mediterranean created deadly military machines: spring-loaded catapults, siege engines, tortoise rams, and Vitruvian wall drills. Archimedes is said to have built a device that could grasp the bows of enemy ships, hoist them into the air, and then release them to crash into the water.

Ancient small-scale technology did exist, but little of it has survived. In 1900, off the Greek island of Antikythera, sponge divers discovered a ship that had gone down around 85–60 BCE. The ship, likely built many years before that, may have been overloaded with precious objects, statues, and artifacts being sent to Rome. One small object was overlooked in the initial salvage operation: a mess of bronze pieces that had spilled out of a small wooden box, all much damaged by two millennia of sea currents and salt water.

The Antikythera Device Today

The object from which the pieces came was relatively thin (13″ × 6.7″ × 3.5″) and was housed in a wood casing with doors on two sides. Most remarkable, it had toothed gears (thirty of these survive) and inscriptions in Greek that arranged the calendar according to the months and Olympic games. After a century of speculation, most scholars agree that the device was a hand-operated astronomical calendar. Such mechanisms allowed the ancients to coordinate the solar and lunar calendars on a nineteen-year cycle, to plot the position of the planets, and to determine eclipses. Cicero's friend Posidonius constructed a clockwork-like sphere that would at every revolution reproduce the relative positions of the sun, moon, and planets.

Some scholars have claimed that the Antikythera device was an analog computer since, though it was hand operated, it was a device for performing calculations. Historians of science have been intrigued by the gears. It had long been assumed that no such machine with complex internal gears existed until the Middle Ages, but the small Antikythera mechanism suggests that the ancients had such devices. Why they did not have more of them, why these devices did not become widespread, and why technological advances did not follow a straight and continuous line forward are questions that belong to the study of the intellectual and social history of the ancient world. The medieval west would break through the barriers that held back all the ancient civilizations except China from making practical technological advances.

QUESTIONS | *How might the institution of slavery have inhibited the invention of labor-saving devices or made small machines elite playthings? If the Antikythera device was a calculating machine, what other uses might such machines have been put to in the ancient world? Why weren't they?*

of Rome into which little sunlight fell. There were public toilets, but the real toilet of Rome was the street. People who lived on the top floors of apartment buildings were in the habit of emptying their chamber pots onto the streets below. The poet Juvenal referred to this as the stinking rain of Rome, which often hit those walking below. To step into the street was to step into a running stream of filth. One crossed Roman streets, as can still be seen in Pompeii today, by stepping on raised stones, set so that cart wheels could navigate between them. A little gutter ran into the streets of Rome and there refuse was dumped and chamber pots emptied. This stinking river of effluent ran into Rome's vast sewage system, which emptied at the Cloaca Maxima, or great sewer mouth, into the Tiber. The pervasive smell of ancient Rome, from body odor, smoke, stinking fish sauce, and running sewage, would overwhelm our modern noses.

The Roman masses lived in this shadowy and putrid world. Most of them were part of family units that existed on the dole of free grain. The toll of daily violence, malnutrition, and disease was great. As miserable as was the life of the poor, the lives of urban, let alone industrial, slaves were even worse. Many slaves on farms and in the mines were viciously worked until they died. In the mines of Spain, slaves died by the thousands, whipped constantly to keep them moving rock. Petty cruelty toward slaves was common. Slave labor was more than just morally objectionable, for it led the Romans to economic dependence on servile labor. As a consequence, the Romans found it easier to employ slaves to do menial work than to invent domestic labor-saving devices.

Toward an Empire That Worked

Augustus had turned failing Republican Rome around and set it on a new, more peaceful and prosperous imperial course, but we do not need to accept the exaggerated boasts of his "Accomplishments," the splendor of marbled Rome, or the poems of his client bards that he had established an enduring Roman peace, the *Pax Romana.* Within his own family and much of the empire there was little Augustan peace.

What made the so-called good emperors good?

Augustus pacified Rome, lopped the head off of senatorial power, and replaced it with his own, but the transformation of the Republic into an empire was not finished. How was power to be passed to the next emperor? Augustus thought that his successor would come from his own family, but families are subject to unexpected twists and turns, his more than most. The four Julio-Claudian emperors who succeeded him were a mixed lot, two of them relatively competent and two others seeming disasters. After the short interregnum of the Flavian line of the emperor Vespasian, Rome saw the period of the so-called five good emperors, the most successful rulers in Roman imperial history. The long transformation of Rome from a Republic into a settled empire finally ended in the second century CE, but that successful empire lasted for a little less than a century.

The First Julio-Claudian Successors

The successors of Augustus, who sprang from his own extended family, are called the Julio-Claudians after the Julian and Claudian branches of his line and that of his wife Livia. There were four successors—Tiberius, Caligula, Claudius, and Nero—before power passed out of Augustus's family. The second century had good emperors. The first had a couple of notoriously bad ones. The paramount problem was that Augustus never solved the problem of imperial succession. His immediate successor was Tiberius (r. 14–37), the son of his wife Livia by a previous marriage. Almost all the other potential heirs had left the scene by means both fair and foul.

Tiberius was at first an efficient, if uninspired ruler, who did restore some of the Senate's powers, doing away, for instance, with Augustus's inner council of senators who reported to him rather than to the Senate. Before long he tired of the daily business of running the state and moved to the island of Capri. Tiberius still held all

CHRONOLOGY	Two Centuries of Imperial Rule, Bad and Good, After Augustus	
DYNASTY	**EMPEROR**	**DATES (CE)**
Julio-Claudians	Tiberius	14–37
	Caligula	37–41
	Claudius	41–54
	Nero	54–68
Flavians	Vespasian	69–79
	Titus	79–81
	Domitian	81–96
Nervan–Antonian (The Five Good Emperors)	Nerva	96–98
	Trajan	98–117
	Hadrian	117–138
	Antoninus Pius	138–161
	Marcus Aurelius	161–180

power in theory, but he delegated Roman affairs to a conniving soldier named Sejanus who was eventually murdered after one scandal too many.

Tiberius was succeeded in turn by the "monstrous" Caligula (r. 37–41). He began well enough and was at first popular, after the disorder of Tiberius's absentee reign, but he was, according to sources, deranged. He seduced his sisters, toyed with the idea of making his favorite horse a senator, and dedicated a shrine to himself in which he was worshipped as a god. Each day the clothes on his golden statue were changed to match those that he was wearing. The Praetorian Guard eventually assassinated Caligula and replaced him with his uncle Claudius.

Claudius and Nero

Claudius (r. 41–54) was so reviled as a stammering idiot that the philosopher and statesman Seneca (c. 1–65) wrote a satire known as *The Pumpkinification of Claudius the Clod.* Claudius was, however, a fairly good emperor. He devoted himself to the fair application of justice and good administration. During his reign, Rome conquered Britain, Mauretania, and Thrace. The biographer Suetonius and others claimed that he was poisoned by his wife so that her son Nero (r. 54–68) could assume the emperorship.

Nero's early years, when he was guided by his mother and advisors, were good ones and produced a renaissance of Roman literature and arts. The period's chief writers were Seneca, the epic poet Lucan (39–65), and Petronius (d. 65), Nero's arbiter of elegance and the author of the episodic *Satyricon.* After a failed plot against his life, Nero took vengeance on his advisors and killed off his men of letters. He forced Seneca to commit suicide, and Lucan and Petronius followed.

Nero perpetrated a series of acts that defy belief. He poisoned Claudius's son Britannicus, married Claudius's daughter and then had her executed, and kicked one of his mistresses to death. He tried many times to murder his own mother before succeeding. Nero styled himself a musician and went on a concert tour in the east during which stadium doors were locked until he had finished playing. Eventually Rome and its senators tired of him, and, as Roman soldiers closed in on him, he killed himself, and so fine an artist, he is supposed to have said at the end.

The characterization of the Julio-Claudian emperors as evil and their misdeeds as monstrous derives chiefly from later Roman authors such as Suetonius and Tacitus who lived in the next century in the civilized reigns of the good emperors and who wished to show that their emperors were superior to the wickedness and incompetence of their evil predecessors. It is more important to recognize the deeper structural changes at work in the early empire. Absolute and arbitrary power unhinged young and callow rulers, which was a predictable failure of newly assumed dynastic rule. These young rulers had not been trained to be prudent, judicious rulers. Tiberius and Claudius knew the politics of surviving in a dangerous family and moved cautiously; Caligula and Nero did not or could not. Yet the arbitrary manner in which all the Julio-Claudian emperors exercised power continued the assault upon the old Republican structures of government. The senators were cowed after fifty years of unpredictable and deadly Julian-Claudian rule. They dared not protest against emperors as willful as Caligula.

The Roman Empire, however, continued to perform fairly well during this period of transition. Political disruption was largely confined to the city of Rome and did not greatly disturb the fabric of the empire as a whole. The administrative systems established by Augustus worked well even while Caligula preened and Nero fiddled.

The transition from a fully functioning Republic to a fully functioning empire ran from 146 BCE straight through to the good emperors of the second century CE. It took the Romans a century to learn the art of empire and to accept and work under the rule of a single man. The weakest points of imperial rule were apparent. Not only was normal dynastic succession a fracture point, but so was the removal of an emperor by assassination. The army and Praetorian Guard remained the chief sources of organized violence. Provincial armies were in revolt against Nero when he took his life. The year 69 saw four generals claim to be emperor. Only the last of these, Vespasian (69–79), could hold onto power and replace the Julio-Claudian line with his own Flavian house. Vespasian and his two sons were military men. They built the Amphitheater or Colosseum, which still stands today, but they did not fundamentally restructure the Roman Empire. They did, however, signal that from then on the man who controlled the army had the best claim to be emperor.

The Good Emperors

When Domitian, the last and worst of the Flavian emperors, died in 96, the Senate selected his successor, an aged senator named Nerva (96–98). The Senate wanted not only one of its members to assume the imperial title,

but an old and childless man who would not rule for long and who would leave no dynastic heir. By luck as much as by design, Rome was to have five emperors in a row who were dedicated to the needs of the empire and not to their own whims or dynastic interests.

On the surface, there seemed to be an improved principle of succession, one based on merit rather than blood. Now the reigning emperor, rather than passing along the emperorship to a family member, adopted the man who seemed best suited to rule after his death. Adoption kept power within an artificial imperial family, giving legitimacy to a new ruler of already proven ability (chiefly in war) and solid political connections. The Romans thus found a way to overcome the inherent weakness of family rule by reaching outside the imperial family to recruit excellence. As rational as this development may seem, it was also partly accidental, since the next three emperors, Trajan (98–117), Hadrian (117–138), and Antoninus Pius (138–161), just happened to have no sons to succeed them and so in each case they selected a good man as their heir. Marcus Aurelius (161–180), the last of the good emperors, did, how-

Trajan at War The column in honor of Trajan's successful wars against Dacia is the greatest of Roman columns, spiraling upward with scenes of the emperor's campaigns, the daily activities of soldiers, and critical battles.

MAP 5.3 | The Roman Empire to the Time of Trajan, 117 CE

After Augustus defeated Antony and Cleopatra, he divided the Roman Empire into provinces. The emperor Trajan further extended the empire to its most-distant point. ***At its greatest size by 117 CE, did the Roman Empire make territorial sense? What natural and cultural boundaries prevented the Roman Empire from expanding much farther?***

ever, have a son, the dangerously incompetent Commodus, and he succeeded his father as all assumed that he would.

As a group the good emperors proved to be honest, capable, and conscientious men. All were deeply committed to dedicated service and to ruling more responsibly than their Julio-Claudian and Flavian predecessors. Trajan was, in many ways, the most successful of all the emperors. A gifted general, he expanded the Roman Empire to its greatest size, particularly by conquering territory in Dacia and Persia (Map 5.3). He was a competent administrator as his correspondence with Pliny the Younger reveals.

His successor, Hadrian, concentrated on integrating the empire and allowed some of Trajan's boundaries to collapse back inside natural borders for easier defense. He traveled to every part of the empire and promoted the standardization of Roman law, which by his time had become vast and often unworkable. He also did something unusual; he chose not only his own successor, Antoninus Pius, but also his successor's successor, Marcus Aurelius. This seemed to raise imperial succession to an even higher level of inspired planning.

Trajan and Hadrian, both born in Spain, were men of the empire, soldiers and, in Hadrian's case, an aesthete. Antoninus Pius was a bureaucrat and man of the city of Rome. His successor, Marcus Aurelius, was forced to fight a series of campaigns against the Germans along the northern borders of the empire. Marcus was also a philosopher-emperor, a dedicated Stoic, who left behind a precious, if melancholy book of *Meditations* written in Greek. Stoics believed in living in harmony with Nature, which they identified with reason itself. Roman Stoicism was concerned chiefly with ethics or the Stoic's place in the world. Stoicism prepared Marcus for a life of responsible service and clear-headed action, but he neither delighted in earthly success nor was disappointed in defeat. He did his duty. An empire ruled by a philosopher was relatively immune to corruption, excess, and indulgence at the top, but it is less obvious that a Stoic could rule with inspiration. Marcus's Stoicism was colored by his disdain for all human life, which he thought was trapped in unending flux and worldly distraction. He was a dedicated caretaker of the empire, but his view of life may not have encouraged him to rethink or renew the fragile human empire he ruled.

Conclusion

Was the Roman world better off in the second century CE than it had been three hundred years earlier? Perhaps not, but the Republic could not have lasted as it was. Built on tradition and cherished virtues, firm rules, a delicate balance of the orders of society, and a privileged aristocracy, the Republic had exerted its will upon the Mediterranean world through war and diplomacy. All the while its own house was springing leaks. It was unable to adjust to the various pressures to which it was subjected. The world outside the Senate was changing: religion was in flux, the city of Rome was growing at a rapid pace, and Italy was awash with money. The emergence of great consul generals from Marius through Caesar, each committed to using and subverting the Senate to advance their own interests, often with the support of the people of Rome, was both a cause and a symptom of the Republic's failure to adjust to new conditions.

Augustus found a way, perhaps the only one possible, to restructure Roman government and society. He did it by a sleight of hand, seeming to preserve the old Senate, while confidently slipping it under his personal control. The Augustan empire may have been the only way for Rome to survive the great crisis of the Late Republic, but much blood was spilled in the transformation of one form of government into another. Both Cicero and Julius Caesar paid the price, one for holding fast to a past that was impossible to sustain and the other for rushing to a revolutionary future before his peers were ready to accept it or him. Yet Caesar's assault on the old ways of governing Rome and its privileged oligarchy paved the way for Augustus's reformation of the Roman order. The Roman world after Augustus was a very different place, one subject to the weaknesses of all monarchies—bad rulers, troubled succession, vicious dynastic politics, arbitrary decisions, and assassination—but under Augustus and dutiful emperors it could be made to work.

The good emperors of the second century showed just how civilized and civilizing Rome could be. They gave the Roman Empire its greatest period of steady and sustained good government. The Mediterranean was a secure Roman lake for the transport of goods, urban life flourished within its limits, and prosperity was high. Borders were secure and rebellions few. But the good times were not to last, for just ahead in the third century lay disasters, economic depression, and the near collapse of imperial government.

Critical Thinking Questions

1. How might the Roman Republic have survived?
2. What larger shifts in society, culture, and history were moving the Late Republic in new directions?
3. What choices did Octavian/Augustus make in transforming Roman government? In other words, how and why did he undo the Republic?
4. Why was the Roman Empire such a seeming mess in its first century?
5. How and why was the second century CE Rome's best imperial period?
6. What was the central political or historical issue of the period 146 BCE–180 CE?

Key Terms

quaestor (p. 135)
tribune (p. 135)
aedile (p. 135)
praetor (p. 135)

consul (p. 136)
equestrians (p. 138)
Caesarian (or Consular) Faction (p. 142)

First Triumvirate (p. 142)
The Triumvirate (p. 144)
Praetorian Guard (p. 147)
apotheosis (p. 151)

Pax Romana (p. 157)
imperator (p. 161)

Primary Sources in connect

For information on Connect and the online resources available, go to **http://connect.mcgraw-hill.com**.

1. Catiline's Revolution
2. Election Notices, Signs, and Graffiti at Pompeii
3. Pliny and Trajan on Christianity
4. Scenes of Imperial Life as Observed by a Roman Noble
5. Letters and Various Meditations of Marcus Aurelius

The Accomplishments of Augustus

The emperor Augustus wrote the *Res Gestae* or record of his "Accomplishments" and deposited it with the Vestal Virgins with an order that it be displayed in front of his Mausoleum in Rome. The bronze pillars are lost but many copies of the list survive. Although the work is factual for the most part, it is also a clever piece of memorialization and propaganda.

Below is a copy of the accomplishments of the deified Augustus by which he brought the whole world under the empire of the Roman people, and of the moneys expended by him on the state and the Roman people, as inscribed on two bronze pillars set up in Rome.

1. At the age of nineteen, on my own initiative and at my own expense, I raised an army by means of which I liberated the Republic, which was oppressed by the tyranny of a faction. For which reason the Senate, with honorific decrees, made me a member of its order in the consulship of Gaius Pansa and Aulus Hirtius, giving me at the same time consular rank in voting, and granted me the *imperium*. It ordered me as propraetor, together with the consuls, to see to it that the state suffered no harm. Moreover, in the same year, when both consuls had fallen in the war, the people elected me consul and a triumvir for the settlement of the commonwealth.

2. Those who assassinated my father I drove into exile, avenging their crime by due process of law; and afterwards when they waged war against the state, I conquered them on the battlefield.

3. I waged many wars throughout the whole world by land and by sea, both civil and foreign, and when victorious I spared all citizens who sought pardon. Foreign peoples who could safely be pardoned I preferred to spare rather than extirpate. About 500,000 Roman citizens were under military oath to me. Of these, when their terms of service were ended, I settled in colonies or sent back to their own municipalities a little more than 300,000, and to all of these I allotted lands or granted money as rewards for military service. . . .

4. Twice I celebrated ovations, three times curule triumphs, and I was acclaimed **imperator** twenty-one times. When the Senate decreed additional triumphs to me, I declined them on four occasions. . . . In my triumphs there were led before my chariot nine kings or the children of kings. At the time I wrote this document, I had been consul thirteen times, and I was in the thirty-seventh year of my tribunician power.

12. . . . When I returned to Rome from Spain and Gaul in the consulship of Tiberius Nero and Publius Quintilius, after successfully settling the affairs of those provinces, the Senate, to commemorate my return, ordered an altar of the Augustan Peace [the Ara Pacis] to be consecrated in the Campus Martius, on which it decreed that the magistrates, priests, and Vestal Virgins should make an annual sacrifice.

13. The temple of Janus Quirinus, which our ancestors desired to be closed whenever peace with victory was secured by sea and by land throughout the entire empire of the Roman people, and which before I was born is recorded to have been closed only twice since the founding of the city, was during my principate three times ordered by the Senate to be closed.

15. To the Roman plebs I paid 300 sesterces apiece in accordance with the will of my father; and in my fifth consulship I gave each 400 sesterces in my own name out of the spoils of war. . . .

17. Four times I came to the assistance of the treasury with my own money, transferring to those in charge of the treasury 150,000,000 sesterces. . . .

20. . . . In my sixth consulship I repaired eighty-two temples of the gods in the city, in accordance with a resolution of the Senate, neglecting none which at that time required repair. In my seventh consulship I reconstructed the Flaminian Way from the city as far as Ariminum, and also all the bridges except the Mulvian and the Minucian.

21. On my own private land I built the temple of Mars Ultor and the Augustan Forum from the spoils of war. On ground bought for the most part from private owners I built the theater adjoining the temple of Apollo which was to be inscribed with the name of my son-in-law Marcus Marcellus. In the Capitol, in the temple of the deified Julius, in the temple of Apollo, in the temple of Vesta, and in the temple of Mars Ultor I consecrated gifts from the spoils of war which cost me about 100,000,000 sesterces. . . .

22. I gave a gladiatorial show three times in my own name, and five times in the names of my sons or grandsons; at these shows about 10,000 men fought. . . .

27. I added Egypt to the empire of the Roman people. . . .

34. In my sixth and seventh consulships, after I had put an end to the civil wars, having attained supreme power by universal consent, I transferred the state from my own power to the control of the Roman Senate and people. For this service of mine I received the title of Augustus by decree of the Senate, and the doorposts of my house were publicly decked with laurels, the civic crown was affixed over my doorway, and a golden shield was set up in the Julian Senate house, which, as the inscription on this shield testifies, the Roman Senate and people gave me in recognition of my valor, clemency, justice, and devotion. After that time I excelled all in authority, but I possessed no more power than others who were my colleagues in each magistracy.

35. When I held my thirteenth consulship, the Senate, the equestrian order, and the entire Roman people gave me the title of "father of the country" and decreed that this title should be inscribed in the vestibule of my house, in the Julian Senate house, and in the Augustan Forum on the pedestal of the chariot which was set up in my honor by decree of the Senate. At the time I wrote this document I was in my seventy-sixth year.

QUESTIONS | *How did Augustus wish to be remembered after death? Was the* Res Gestae *merely commemorative, or did it have a continuing political purpose? Where does Augustus bend the record of his achievements?*

Source: Roman Civilization. Sourcebook II: The Empire, ed. Naphtali Lewis and Meyer Reinhold (New York: Columbia University Press, 1955), 9–19.

The Empress Theodora with Retinue on a Mosaic at San Vitale, Ravenna, Italy

THE SLOW TURN FROM ANCIENT TO MEDIEVAL

A Century of Imperial Anarchy
  Late Imperial Society
  Emperors Come and Go, Dozens of Them
  The Empire's External Enemies
The Romanization of Christianity
  Early Christianities: From Oral to Written
  Early Christian Thinkers and Greek Thought
  Toward Orthodoxy
  The Desert and Pillar Fathers and Mothers
  State Persecution
  Bishops and the Church Hierarchy
Diocletian's Renewal of the Roman Empire
  Diocletian Restructures the Empire
  Reforming the Economy
  Restoring Roman Religion
  Donatism and the Fallout from the Great Persecution
Constantine and the Christianization of the Roman Empire
  Constantine's Conversion

  Making a New Rome in Byzantium
  Toward a State Religion
  Julian Lapses
  Institutional Growth of the Church
German Tribes Enter the Empire
  The Visigoths Request Entrance
  Imperial Strategies for Managing the Germans
  The Sack of Rome in 410
  Attila and the Huns
  The End of the Empire in the West
Germanic Kingdoms in the West
  Vandals, Visigoths, and Ostrogoths
  King Theoderic's Troubled Last Years
  The Franks Take Control of Gaul
  The Conversion of Clovis
Justinian's Reassertion of Roman Imperial Grandeur
  The Emperor and Empress
  The Reconquest
  The Disastrous 540s: Dust-Veils and Disease
  Living a Shrinking Urban Life
Conclusion

THEODORA AND SIDONIUS CONFRONT THE OLD AND THE NEW People whispered nasty things about her—that she was the low-born daughter of the bear-keeper of the Hippodrome, an actress and a prostitute, sexually promiscuous, a murderess—but in mosaics and sculptures she is magnificent, every inch the empress of Rome. Wrapped in precious purple gowns, her head heavy with jewels, and waited on by court women and eunuchs, Theodora wears her imperial majesty. Her social agenda and political influence on her husband, the emperor Justinian, were considerable and controversial. At one critical point Theodora shamed her husband into showing some backbone, facing down their enemies, and staying put rather than fleeing a mob of raging rioters in Constantinople. She said that she would rather die than give up being empress. Theodora's tenacity and Justinian's dreams of imperial glory were proof that the Roman Empire lived on, at least in the east, in the sixth century. In a golden imperial court, one could try to forget how much had changed in the wider Roman world.

A century earlier in the west, Sidonius Apollinaris (c. 430–479), a Gallo-Roman gentleman and poet, never could; he lived in an already transformed world. One day in the streets of his hometown of Lyons he bumped into a band of Germans. He saw a Frankish prince, dressed in silk, followed by a formidable band of his men. The poet was struck by their appearance, which was so unlike that of his fellow Roman citizens. Their feet and legs were covered by boots of rough hide, their knees and thighs were bare, and they wore bright green and red garments that left their forearms bare. Around their waists they wore studded belts made of fur. From their shoulders hung Frankish swords. In their left hands they clutched magnificent shields; in their right they held barbed lances and throwing axes.

This colorful, but unnerving scene provides a glimpse of a world undergoing radical transition. Theodora's world in the east was stubbornly imperial; Sidonius's in the west was a daily encounter with the other and with change. The Germans

A Frankish King The replica of the seal (now lost) of Childeric, father of Clovis. His long Frankish hair flows down onto his shoulders.

whom Sidonius encountered were no longer merely the slaves or mercenaries of the Roman state; they were warriors, marching freely through a Roman city, their long blond hair flowing, their capacity for violence on display for all to see.

Historical change may be never-ending, but some periods experience it more dramatically and discernibly than others. Around the Mediterranean Sea, political, ethnic, and religious

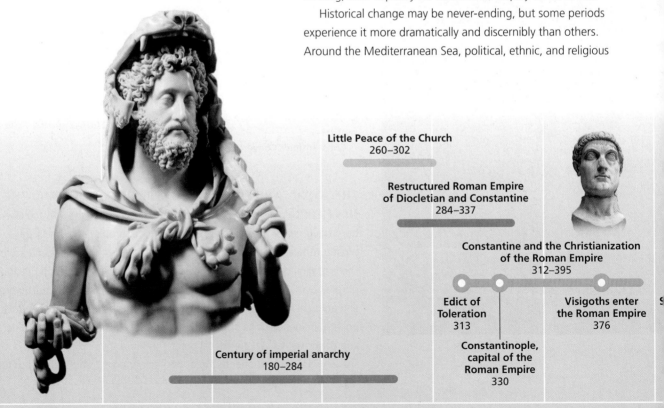

Little Peace of the Church
260–302

Restructured Roman Empire
of Diocletian and Constantine
284–337

Constantine and the Christianization
of the Roman Empire
312–395

Edict of
Toleration
313

Visigoths enter
the Roman Empire
376

Constantinople,
capital of the
Roman Empire
330

Century of imperial anarchy
180–284

100   200   300   400

change was unmistakable. The Germans Sidonius saw were one face of change; the monks who rejected ancient civilization and retreated into the deserts of Egypt were another; farmers and laborers bound by the fixed wages set by a reforming emperor felt its new strictures; and the old city of Rome, once the lamp of the world, bore the scars of change after its sack and abandonment. Theodora and Justinian ruled the Roman Empire from the magnificent city of Constantinople, but even they dreamed of restoring the empire to its former glory by reassembling its shattered pieces.

Historians have called the period from about 180 to 565 Late Antiquity, but that label claims too much for antiquity and too little for the emerging new world of the Middle Ages. It suggests continuity when, in fact, radical change was the disorder of the day. The period from the late second century to the mid-sixth century cannot be easily typed as one thing or the other; it was the age of the great turning of the late Roman world toward the Middle Ages, and its transitional quality needs to be recognized and preserved in all its messiness.

The three central ingredients that were to make the Early Middle Ages in the west—late Roman civilization, Christianity, and the Germans—were being brought together, often violently, inside the Roman Empire. All of them sought a lasting presence and a measure of authority within the changing Roman world. In these centuries, various voices competed for place and power, and cultural clashes such as the one Sidonius experienced were common.

The political, religious, economic, and cultural changes that occurred, particularly after 300, were profound and transformative. By the late fifth century the Mediterranean world that the Romans had built was much changed, its beliefs altered profoundly, its economy downsized, its religion remade, and its political and territorial organization unlike anything anyone could have imagined in 150. The empire suffered through its worst century of political instability since the Late Roman Republic. Christianity, once an illegal religion, became the official religion of the empire. The church assumed the mantle of the institutional home and voice of all Christians. East German tribes sought entrance into the empire, set themselves up as the new representatives and replacements of Roman authority, and established Germanic kingdoms inside the empire.

The eastern Roman Empire sealed itself off from the west but mounted one last futile attempt to reconstitute the whole empire. Thus, while the eastern Roman Empire, which much later came to be called the Byzantine Empire, continued to have a centralized imperial government, the west was in near free fall through centuries of decentralization. The period from the third to sixth centuries was one of the greatest ages of radical redirection in the history of western civilization. How did a civilization as old and established as the ancient west turn directions and emerge as something as starkly different as the medieval west? The changes came about gradually, in different regions at different times, and were cumulative. Sidonius's surprise at the sight of German warriors in the streets of Lyons was the surprise of the old world meeting the new, but the empress Theodora's pride was an indication that the idea of the Roman Empire, if not its former power and reach, would not go quietly.

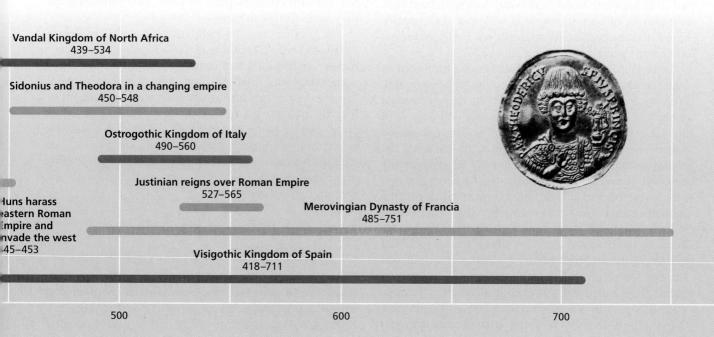

Vandal Kingdom of North Africa
439–534

Sidonius and Theodora in a changing empire
450–548

Ostrogothic Kingdom of Italy
490–560

Justinian reigns over Roman Empire
527–565

Merovingian Dynasty of Francia
485–751

Huns harass eastern Roman Empire and invade the west
445–453

Visigothic Kingdom of Spain
418–711

500   600   700

A Century of Imperial Anarchy

The events that slowly changed the Roman world began in the late second century and became apparent in the third, which was to be the first flash point of the new west. The Roman Empire underwent a century of imperial anarchy (180–284). The high Roman Empire of the second century with its good emperors and stable government could not last. That period of peace and prosperity had depended, in part, on a highly successful but partly accidental form of succession. When Marcus Aurelius died in 180, his natural son Commodus (r. 180–193) succeeded him, but Commodus was not, as imperial successors had been for almost a century, the best man for the job. Throughout the third century, an imperial system based on meritocracy gave way to a monarchical system of military tyrants.

Why did the Roman Empire experience its worst century since the Late Republic in the period 180–284?

Late Imperial Society

Maps of the Roman Empire that outline a vast mass of territory controlled by the Romans tend to mislead. The Roman Empire was more truly an empire of cities. Passing beyond the city and its hinterland with its thin layer of local temples, governors, gentry, and garrisons of soldiers, one entered a rough countryside peopled by sharp landlords, private armies, the rural poor, and bandits. The protagonist of Lucius Apuleius's dazzling novel, the *Golden Ass* (c. 180), is magically transformed into a donkey, captured by a band of robbers, and led into the brutal and uncivilized outer world that lay beyond the easy reach of urban justice and civilizing Roman order. Still this imperial world could work as long as the delicate balance of central order and widespread prosperity based on conquest, Mediterranean sea trade, and slave labor was maintained.

In the third century, that balance became unhinged as central authority began to falter and the economy to fail. With the accession of Commodus in 180, Rome entered a century of imperial disorder that would end only with the rise of the emperor Diocletian in 284. Throughout the century, new trends emerged, the principal one being the militarization of the empire. For most of Republican history and during the early empire, the Roman army had been an instrument of state power; now the state became an instrument of the Roman army, serving its needs and following its lead. Power was shifting from the city of Rome to the troubled frontiers where armies gathered to defend the empire's borders. Most of the century's emperors were generals from the provinces. Armies declared them emperors and murdered rival claimants. With this parade of army-made or barracks emperors, the empire became increasingly disunited as regional factions vied for power. The government of Rome, once the seat of senatorial power and resident emperors, fell under a military monarchy without the check of civilian law or an effective bureaucracy.

The social classes of the empire were also becoming increasingly polarized. A few aristocrats and soldiers became fabulously wealthy, but the lower classes endured hardship and the nagging threat of utter deprivation. Great landlords had incomes ten thousand times as great as those of their poor laborers. The empire underwent an economic crisis brought on by the expense of defending its borders and supporting its armies. At its edges, far from the Mediterranean, the Roman Empire was expensive to maintain. Though its roads were marvels of engineering, they were expensive to build and maintain. Moreover, it took much longer and cost more to move people and goods by road than it ever did to sail them around the Mediterranean.

The decline of the empire may well be traced back to the high cost of defending it. Excessive taxation placed pressures on an already overextended economy and began to warp economic and social relations. Roman coinage, which had maintained its value throughout the second century, was now steadily debased. A silver denarius from the time of Hadrian in the second century was a small solid silver piece; by the late third century the denarius had become a large silver-washed bronze disk with little metallic value. Debasement produced inflation and other pressures on the economy.

In more prosperous and peaceful times, Roman trade had been highly specialized, but with political disruption the flow of goods over long distances was interrupted and the Mediterranean economy was forced to downsize and localize. Regions that specialized in producing pots, sandals, or millstones suffered when they could not send their goods to distant locales and receive back salt, cloth, and olives in exchange. Regional economies shifted to the less efficient enterprise of producing most of what they needed close to home.

The population of the Mediterranean world had begun to fall, and would continue to do so for the next five centuries. Contributing to a struggling economy, there was a high degree of fiscal mismanagement and corruption. The good emperors had avoided the worst of such problems by maintaining an efficient centralized government and by either being good bureaucrats themselves or by appointing responsible stand-ins. With the new soldier emperors gone from Rome to the frontiers and provinces and constantly in need of money, much of that earlier civil vigilance disappeared.

Emperors Come and Go, Dozens of Them

Political and economic stability was hard to sustain when the turnover of emperors was so frequent and unsettling. In the half-century after Marcus Aurelius, Rome had nine emperors, only one of whom avoided

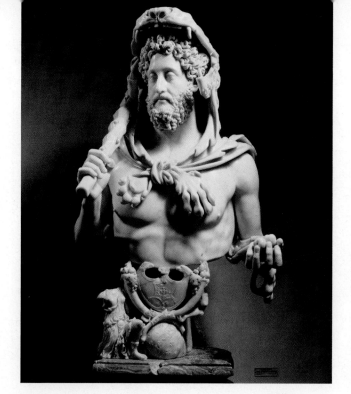

Emperor Commodus as Hercules A marble statue of Marcus Aurelius's son and heir as the mythological strongman Hercules. Commodus's flirtation with the gladiatorial life, extreme self-indulgence, and poor judgment eventually led to his assassination.

assassination. Commodus abandoned his father's defense of the Germanic frontier, put Praetorian prefects in effective control of the city of Rome, and styled himself a new Hercules. He was finally strangled to death when he offended Roman sensibilities by brazenly appearing in Rome as a gladiator-consul.

After a relatively brief spell of stability under Septimius Severus (r. 193–211), a military man who had risen to power on the arms of his soldiers, and his son Caracalla (r. 211–217), the empire slid even deeper into a long spell of disorder, at least at the top. The Severans had recognized the uneasy lie of the land. Before dying, while on a campaign against the Scots, Septimius advised his sons to make sure that they always kept their soldiers rich, and hence content, but he did not tell them how to respect each other. Caracalla had his brother Geta murdered and was himself killed while organizing an assault on the Parthians in Asia.

Over the next half-century, Roman armies advanced twenty-six imperial candidates, only one of whom died peacefully. Macrinus (r. 217–218), who conspired in the assassination of Caracalla, is a good example of how rickety the imperial house had become. He was from Africa, had a pierced ear, and was the first emperor who was not also a senator.

He lost the support of the army when he canceled a pay raise and was put to death after losing a battle at Antioch. To be emperor or, worse, a claimant to the throne in the middle of the third century was a crooked path to an unhappy end. In 238 alone, six men laid claim to be emperor.

The Empire's External Enemies

Not just the political order and economy were turning against Rome; so were its many external enemies. To the east, Persia threatened and to the north Germanic tribes continued to bother the border (Map 6.1). In 251, the Roman emperor Decius (r. 249–251) died battling the Goths. His successor Valerian (r. 253–260) was captured in the east, and the city of Antioch fell to the Persians. Various peoples from the continent, among them Saxons and Angles, began to cross over to Britain on longboats and to settle. Archaeological excavations have begun to reveal the patterns of these new settlements, often erected alongside native settlements, sometimes on top of them. A sign of the weakening confidence in Roman security, even at the center of the empire, was the massive wall that the emperor Aurelian (r. 270–275) ordered to be raised around the city of Rome. Only a century earlier, a Roman rhetorician had said that the eternal city had no need of walls since the empire itself was Rome's protective wall.

Amid the crumbling confidence in Rome's strength and security, the vestiges of high Roman culture in its late and sometimes exotic form persisted. Colorful mosaics adorned villa floors, and Septimius Severus built an enormous palace in Rome. His son constructed the baths named after him that still survive in impressive ruin. The great Roman jurist Ulpian compiled extensive collections of Roman laws and the Egyptian philosopher Plotinus (c. 205–270) propounded in Rome the ideas that comprise his *Enneads,* later compiled by his students. Plotinus was

Hunting Scenes from Late Rome The lavish style of Late Roman art is evident in this mosaic depiction: colorful clothes, violence, and men and animals in agitated motion.

MAP 6.1 | External Enemies of the Roman Empire, c. 350

Before the late fourth century, the Roman Empire had managed to keep the Germanic and Celtic tribes and other foreign peoples outside the empire. To the east, the Persian Empire was harassing Rome's borders. *How did the Roman Empire protect its borders? Could it keep the peoples gathering there forever outside the empire? What was the natural geographic weakness of the Late Roman Empire?*

a Neo-Platonist and believed that the One, an abstract, impersonal, immaterial, and intellectual force governed the universe.

The Romanization of Christianity

As the Roman world endured its difficult century of imperial anarchy and economic adjustment, Christians, who had not been taken seriously before, began to matter. To be a Christian was still illegal and punishable by death, but persecution was sporadic and depended on whether the emperor thought the Christians were a pressing problem. On a deeper level, a familiar pattern of the Roman encounter with alien religions was at work. In its long history, Rome had often rejected alien religions when first

> How and why did the various Christianities develop and spread in the second and third centuries?

encountered but, after a period of prohibition and bloodshed, slowly Romanized them until they became familiar and acceptable. Some observers thought that it was Rome's genius to take in all the world's gods and remake them as its own; such was the experience of Christianity, but with one great difference. Whereas the third century saw the Romanization of Christianity, the fourth would see the Christianization of the Roman Empire.

Early Christianities: From Oral to Written

Christianity was not in its early centuries a single set of beliefs represented by a single church. It might be more accurate to speak of christianities than Christianity during this period. As an underground religion in a world of slow travel and communication, it could not have been otherwise. Many of the books of the New Testament were circulating by the second century, including all of the Gospels (Matthew, Mark, Luke, and John), but the canon

The Nag Hammadi Find

In December 1945 an Egyptian peasant named Muhammad and his brother were digging for nitrate to fertilize their fields near a bend in the Nile River not far from the village of Nag Hammadi when they uncovered a jar containing a collection of ancient codices written on papyrus sheets. They were afraid at first to open the jar for fear that an evil spirit might be freed but eventually smashed it open and were surprised to see a cloud of golden specks drift into the air. They were disappointed to discover that there was no gold inside, only thirteen old codices. Muhammad carried the books home and left them outside. Needing some kindling the next morning, his mother gathered up some of the papyrus sheets and some straw to start a fire. We shall never know what was lost that morning. Over the following years the surviving books found buyers, and eventually scholars realized that Muhammad's find was an extraordinary collection of suppressed religious texts copied and buried in the fourth century.

The fifty-two books that survived are a strange lot: among them *The Gospel of Thomas, On the Origin of the World, Thunder: the Perfect Mind, The Concept of Our Great Power, The Thought of Norea,* and *The Interpretation of Knowledge.*[1] A few of the texts were already known, but most were new or contain fuller texts than previously known. The books are written in Coptic (Egyptian) but derive from texts once written in Greek. Most of them have been roughly classified as Gnostic texts, but that hardly describes them all or precisely. As scholars have worked on the texts over the past half-century, they have begun to appreciate just how complex and precious these books are, and how dangerous they might have seemed in the past. At the center of Gnostic belief was

A Nag Hammadi Codex Page from the Gospel of Thomas

the idea that this world, with its crimes, pain, and suffering, was not created by a good God, but by an evil one. This malevolent divinity had inserted himself between humans and the Invisible Spirit in order to work his mischief. But some humans (those who know, the Gnostics) have seen past this evil world, which most people mistake for a good creation by a good God, to the true nature of the Invisible Spirit who lies waiting beyond all the pain and suffering that the evil world visits on humans.

The collection may have been hidden because Bishop Athanasius of Alexandria sent a letter in 367 to the churches and monasteries of Egypt stipulating the contents of the New Testament and demanding that other texts lying outside the newly established canon should be purged. A monk (or group of them) at a nearby monastery may have decided that it was more prudent to hide their unorthodox library than to destroy it. The winds of orthodoxy had shifted many times; Athanasius himself was excommunicated five times. A monk may simply have hesitated to destroy books that might just be divine despite what his superiors now said. The Nag Hammadi texts open up a world of early Christian thought that was driven outside of the orthodox church's approved set of readings.

QUESTIONS | *Why were there so many varieties of Christianity in the early centuries of the religion, and how might the existence of so many different interpretations and practices have stimulated the development of Christian thought? Why did some texts become authoritative and others apocryphal? Why bury rather than destroy texts deemed dangerous?*

of authorized texts had not yet been fixed, in part because there were so many texts of varying degrees of authority in circulation and no authoritative ruling body to select and sanction a single collection of sacred texts.

As the voices and immediate presence of the apostles and their designates as the direct heirs of Jesus's mission

faded away by the end of the first century, written texts became increasingly important and circulated in portable **codex** or book form rather than in papyrus rolls. The move from oral to written authority continued throughout the third century and much of the fourth, shaping a Christian culture of texts and books.

Early Christian Thinkers and Greek Thought

While written texts were assuming greater importance, Christian thinkers began to engage their pagan critics and to work out the details of Christian theology. Many of these, including Justin Martyr (c. 100–165) and Origen of Alexandria (185–254), who was the greatest of the early Christian theologians, were heavily indebted to Greek philosophy, especially to Platonism. They tended to view problems of Christian theology in philosophical and rational terms, and their prose was shaped by their Greek rhetorical training. To refute learned pagan critics, early Christian thinkers sharpened the same dialectical skills of argumentation that their enemies employed.

This intertwining of Greek, Roman, and Christian thought was one feature of the Romanization of the Christian religion. As Christians adopted Greek ways of thinking and writing, learned pagans could begin to engage Christianity on familiar and rational terms. No matter how heated or sarcastic the debate between Christians and pagans became, they were talking.

Toward Orthodoxy

Even as they were debating their pagan critics, the great Christian apologists Irenaeus of Lyons (c. 130–c. 202) and Tertullian (169–240) were also confronting Christians who had different ideas and practices, particularly the **Gnostics.** They denounced these "others" as heretics, but it is important to recognize that orthodoxy or an established and sanctioned set of beliefs (and, therefore, its opposite, heresy) did not yet exist; the contest between the various christianities was precisely to determine which would be able to claim authoritative power and the right to define orthodox teaching, set the canon of Scripture, and specify Christian practices and customs.

There was a wide range of early Christian beliefs. The Ebionite Christians, for instance, believed that they were Jews and should hold fast to Jewish practices. Marcionite Christians maintained that they were Gentiles and should abandon Judaism and, hence, did not need the Old Testament or Hebrew Bible. In hindsight it may seem that these sects were unlikely to have created a universal religion, but at the time no one could be sure. The Gnostics (from the Greek *gnosis,* "knowledge") were elitists who held that only those few who possessed a deep and specialized understanding of the true state of the world were enlightened and so would be saved. The Gnostics set out Christianity's first systematic theologies, prompting others to reject them with systems of their own. Tertullian and Irenaeus vehemently rejected Gnostic teaching, but even they could not quite hold fast to a solid center that did not yet exist.

The total number of Christians within the Roman Empire remained relatively small throughout the third century, perhaps between 2 and 5 percent of the total population, but varying sharply between regions and between urban and rural populations (Map 6.2). The religion was stronger in the east than the west of the empire, and stronger in cities than in the countryside. Despite the small number of Christians, the sheer variety of Christian life and thought in the period is striking.

The Desert and Pillar Fathers and Mothers

Around 269 in Egypt, a well-off young man by the name of Anthony (251–356) happened to hear in a village church of Christ's injunction to rid oneself of all belongings and to follow him. Anthony was so moved by the message that he became one of the first of the desert fathers, a monk or hermit who disengaged from the urban life of the Roman world. He moved into the wilderness to battle temptation and the devil, and to concentrate exclusively on God. Women such as Mary of Egypt, a former prostitute, also retreated into the desert to cleanse themselves of earthly sin by renouncing the world and praising God.

A striking rupture in the urban life of Mediterranean civilization occurred when men and women began to abandon their homes and families to seek a closer bond with God. Since the rise of cities in the Near East and Greece, the ancients had thought of civilized life as city life with all its strengths and weaknesses. But by the third century many rich Romans were beginning to give up on cities, withdrawing to large self-sufficient estates (*latifundia*), where their security and prosperity could be ensured. While the rich withdrew from cities for material reasons, the desert fathers and mothers did so for spiritual ones; they rejected the material world of the city and instead opted for citizenship in heaven. Anthony and his fellow hermits simply walked away from urban life in pursuit of a more direct and intimate relationship with God. Theirs was not a back-to-nature movement or the pleasant pastoralism or love of rural life so admired by the ancients, but an active rejection of urban life and its state-supported structures. Cracks in the foundation of ancient civilization began to appear when Anthony and his followers came to regard the city with its shops, noise, and throngs of people as a distraction from religious life.

Pachomius (290–347) established monastic communities in Egypt that collected together hundreds of monks. This coenobitic (from *coenobium* or monastery) form of monasticism represented a commitment to organized and radical denial of the civilized world and of oneself. Less influential, but still typical of eastern monasticism, were the **stylites,** or pillar saints. Saint Simeon the Stylite (390–459) lived atop a pole in Syria for thirty-seven years. Local Christians gathered at the base of the pole seeking help and blessings from the saint. The point of living atop a pillar was so that the saint could be both among the people and apart from them at the same time. Perched between the divine and human worlds, the saint served

MAP 6.2 | **The Spread of Christian Communities in the Roman Empire, 33–311**

Before 311 CE, Christians tended to establish communities within large Roman cities, yet Christianity remained a minority religion within the empire until the fourth century. *Why would Christians gather in Roman cities rather than live quietly in the countryside? Where in the empire was the concentration of Christians greatest? What do the apostle Paul's travels reveal about the way in which early Christianity spread?*

as a model of steadfast devotion to God and as an active intermediary between separated worlds.

State Persecution

The disorder of the Roman Empire late in the second century and early in the third century may have allowed the various christianities to prosper. The beleaguered Roman state was unable to focus much attention on a small religious minority, even an illegal one that did not seem to be causing trouble. By the middle of the third century, however, as Rome's difficulties mounted, many Romans concluded that Rome was being punished for abandoning its gods. The waning Roman devotion to all the gods, they thought, led to divine retribution. The gods were not happy, and so Rome suffered, but it was Christians who paid the price. As Tertullian put it, whenever a natural disaster, plague, or famine struck, the first thought of the Romans was, send "the Christians to the

lion." By eliminating Christians, some Romans thought that their own devotion to the gods would once again, as in the golden past of the Republic, be pious, unanimous, and enduring. No longer would Rome be dragged down by those insulting the gods.

In 250, the emperor Decius issued an edict that established a commission to test the faith of Romans by commanding all to offer a sacrifice to the gods or to the emperor. The commission supplied certificates of pagan piety to those who passed the test of faith. Some Christians officially complied, while others found ways to avoid compliance. Some refused to hide their faith and so were executed. Decius's immediate successors continued the purge. The emperor Valerian ordered the seizure of Christian property: churches, cemeteries, and the land of rich Christians. But when Valerian died, the persecution again ceased. Without a strong imperial will, there could be no sustained persecution. The period from 260 to 302 is often called the Little Peace of the Church since,

The Good Shepherd of the Catacombs The good shepherd was a figure of Christ for early Christians as in this fresco from the catacombs of Rome.

during those forty-two years, Christianity was once again generally ignored by official Rome.

Bishops and the Church Hierarchy

By late in the third century, Christianity was a religion that had come to be represented by what we might call the Four Bs: bishop, book (the codex of Scripture, as opposed to oral culture, memory, tradition, and the papyrus roll), basilica (as opposed to the pagan temple or Jewish synagogue), and burial (as opposed to the pagan practice of cremation). The ecclesiastical structure of the universal church was being laid down. Bishops were in charge of the churches in larger cities and the areas around them. Many of these bishops claimed that their authority descended directly from the apostles. Some bishops had in the first century been in place as apostolic appointments before the New Testament was composed. By the third century that living line of direct apostolic sanction was dying out.

In its place there was a push to enhance the stature and power of all bishops by arguing that they stood in the living line of the apostles as their direct heirs. Although in principle bishops were supposed to be equal, the metropolitan bishops (later to be called archbishops) of the

imperial and provincial capitals of Antioch, Alexandria, and Rome towered above the rest. By the third century the city of Rome claimed universal authority. As the ancient capital of the empire and the site of some of Christianity's most dramatic events, including the martyrdoms of Peter and Paul, Rome had a certain claim to primacy, if not absolute supremacy. The single most important piece of evidence to bolster the church of Rome's claim to primacy was the so-called **Petrine authority.** In the Gospel of Matthew, Jesus tells the apostle Peter:

> you are Peter and upon this rock I will build my church, and the gates of hell shall not prevail against it. I will give you the keys to the kingdom of heaven. Whatever you bind on earth shall be bound in heaven; and whatever you loose on earth shall be loosed in heaven. (Matt. 16:18–19)

The passage (if genuine) may be one of Christ's few preserved puns, for in both Aramaic and Greek *Peter* means rock and, therefore, the passage could be understood as "You are a rock (Peter) and upon you I will build my church." It was the official doctrine of the church of Rome that this passage gave Peter, the first bishop of Rome, and his successors, the right and obligation to govern the whole church.

Some churchmen vigorously denied the Roman claim to superiority over other bishops. Other cities also claimed apostolic foundation. Alexandria maintained that its church had been founded by the apostles Peter and Mark. Both apostolic primacy and imperial importance made Antioch, Alexandria, and Rome rivals to lead the Christian church. Constantinople would later, as the new Rome, put in its claim for primacy at a church council in 381. Its claim was based, like that of the other three great metropolitan cities, on its stature as an imperial capital. As events would prove, however, it was not just the Petrine authority that determined Rome's ultimate success but the fall of the other great metropolitan cities. Two of them were overtaken by the rise of Islam in the seventh century, and Constantinople's claim to universality was an isolated one confined to the Greek east.

Diocletian's Renewal of the Roman Empire

After a century of imperial turmoil, the Roman Empire, if it was to continue, required a new direction and a firm

How did Diocletian restructure and in effect rescue the Roman Empire?

hand. The emperor Diocletian supplied both. He restructured the empire politically and geographically and attempted to end its economic and religious drift.

Diocletian Restructures the Empire

Diocletian (r. 284–305) was of undistinguished birth and from the province of Dalmatia. When the emperor whom he served was murdered, Diocletian with the support of the imperial army marched against the emperor's brother and was soon made emperor himself. His genius lay less in battle than in restructuring an empire that seemed almost ungovernable by the late third century. Realizing that the empire could no longer be ruled by one man and that the persistent problem of succession (as revealed by the fate of his many murdered predecessors) needed to be solved, Diocletian copied in the political sphere what the army had been doing to address regional disorder: he regionalized and compartmentalized imperial responsibilities and power. By so doing, he accepted and redirected the ongoing regionalization of Roman power, which had been gaining momentum throughout the third century.

By 286, Diocletian recognized that the general Maximian, whom he had earlier dispatched to Gaul to suppress a popular insurrection, was Augustus or emperor in the west as declared by his troops. Diocletian appointed two Caesars to serve under the two emperors. With this move, Diocletian created a **Tetrarchy** of four Roman rulers: two senior (Augusti) and two junior (Caesars), two in the east (one Augustus, one Caesar), and two in the west (one Augustus, one Caesar), each with his own territory to govern. Diocletian thus found a way to protect the empire from disorder by ensuring that if one emperor was assassinated, another already held the office, and his successor (the Caesar under him) was in place and ready to move against the rebels and assassins.

The Tetrarchy energized both the imperial and military systems since the new order rewarded merit (as the good emperors once had) and activism, and compartmentalized Rome's exercise of central power. Diocletian's real interest lay in the general reformation of Roman order. Seeing that the provinces were too large and bases for resistance to the emperors, he redrew the administrative map of the empire into ninety-six small provinces. Within these provinces and within the army he introduced new hierarchies of command. He also set his soldiers to work building fortifications. Diocletian held true to the Tetrarchy over which he maintained effective imperial control. When he finally decided to abdicate in 305, he forced his fellow Augustus to step down so that the junior emperors would succeed them as a matter of course.

One of the critical features of Diocletian's new empire was the recognition that its most natural dividing point was into east and west (Map 6.3). This division respected not only geography, but also the Greek and Latin cultures of the two dominant parts of the empire. Diocletian himself did not visit the city of Rome until shortly before his retirement; his own preferred center of operations was Nicomedia (today in modern Turkey). There his court adopted various eastern ceremonial features: the emperor was called Lord (*Dominus*) and revered openly as divine. Both advisors and petitioners knelt before him and kissed the hem of his robe as a sign of subservience. In Rome the Senate continued to operate under elected consuls, but in the emperor's eastern court a new set of officials was appointed, among them the count of sacred

The Tetrarchs Embrace On this porphyry sculpture at St. Mark's Basilica in Venice, the four tetrarchs are shown in pairs. In each pair an Augustus embraces a Caesar to show their common purpose and the nature of their relationship. Pairs of tetrarchs also signaled that one pair governed half the empire and the other pair the other half. In this way, both the eastern and western parts of the Roman Empire were alerted that each possessed its own duo of dedicated emperors.

gifts and the supervisor of the lord's bedchamber, who was a eunuch. Professional spies were also appointed, as befitted the tighter, more claustrophobic court Diocletian created.

Reforming the Economy

Diocletian introduced new fiscal measures to repair an economy struggling with inflation and a lack of productivity. All land was now to be taxed according to its size and relative worth, and labor was assessed according to its value to society. Local farm workers (*coloni*) were now bound to the land for life. Later this provision was extended to their heirs, thus freezing both the rural

MAP 6.3 | Diocletian's Division of the Roman Empire by 304

In 304, the emperor Diocletian divided the empire into four territories, each ruled by either an Augustus (senior emperor) or a Caesar (junior emperor). The most striking division, however, was into the Latin west and Greek east. *Why did Diocletian so divide the empire? Why had Ravenna in northern Italy become increasingly important? What part of the Roman Empire did the senior emperors occupy and why? What lands did the junior emperors, the Caesars, hold and why?*

Diocletian's Palace A reconstruction of Diocletian's seaside palace at Split in Croatia. The emperor Diocletian was already moving toward palace government, thus anticipating a medieval practice.

economy and its workers into place and station. In cities, workers who tried to run away to escape or improve their lot were forced both to remain and to pay the stipulated tax on their work. Little sense of freedom remained when much of the empire's population was held permanently in place with no chance of movement or advancement. Diocletian's attempt to revive a failing economy compromised the rights of Roman citizenship, including the freedom of movement and economic choice. Though restricting social mobility entirely was impossible, Diocletian's plan was an indication of the sharp needs of the state for steady income and of the stubbornness of a stagnant economy.

To combat inflation and the related problem of the falling value or depreciation of Roman coinage, Diocletian in 301 issued an edict to control wages and prices. But, given the looseness of the late Roman economy, this control of labor and goods could not succeed and was revoked eventually. The emperor also reformed the currency of the empire, in part by regulating the minting of coins. His successor, Constantine (285–337), reformed imperial currency further, introducing a new series of silver coins (*denarii*) and a gold coin (*solidus*). The efforts of both emperors to stabilize the empire's currency achieved some success.

Restoring Roman Religion

In religion, Diocletian attempted to restore a traditional set of beliefs. He was attracted to an older Roman religion of rank, devotion, and discipline. From the start of his rule he had been intolerant of other beliefs, banning the practices of astrology, alchemy, and Manichaeism (or religious dualism). Christianity, after the long interval of the Little Peace, seemed so comfortably rooted in Roman life that Diocletian ignored it for most of his rule. Indeed, from his palace in Nicomedia he could see a large Christian basilica looming in the distance. But in 303 he and the Caesar Galerius issued the first of several edicts against Christians. Diocletian probably thought, as his predecessors had, that Christianity threatened the spiritual and political unanimity of the Roman people. Just as he tried to standardize coinage, he wanted to standardize faith. He had a tidy mind and viewed religious pluralism as a threat to his reformed state. Galerius, the less prudent of the two eastern tetrarchs, was pushing for a more extreme response to religious dissonance in the east.

As their first act, Roman authorities assaulted the church of Nicomedia and made a point of destroying its sacred books, with which Christianity, as a religion of the book, was now identified. At first the persecution targeted Roman citizens and state officials who were Christians, then moved on to the Christian clergy, and finally to all believers. Yet, even then, the persecution seems to have been uneven; worse in the east than the west, worse in cities than in the countryside. Some areas such as Gaul and Britain experienced little if any persecution. After

CHRONOLOGY	The Religious Fourth Century
DATE	**EVENT**
303–311	The Great Persecution of Christians
300–320	Saint Anthony in the Desert
312	Constantine's Christian dream
313	Religious toleration proclaimed
325	Council of Nicaea
330	City of Byzantium (Constantinople) founded
361	The Emperor Julian lapsed
367	Canon of the New Testament fixed
387	Augustine baptized
390s	The Visigoths become Arian Christians
392	Theodosius bans paganism

Diocletian retired, Galerius continued the persecution until 311. Still, relatively few Christians were executed in most regions, perhaps fewer than five thousand.

But if the physical damage was relatively light, despite the horrific martyrdoms described by Eusebius of Caesarea in his history of the early church, the psychological damage ran deep. Christians had for several generations come to feel almost accepted within the empire; they had mistaken the lack of persecution for official toleration. They had begun to emerge from behind closed doors and private worship to attend church openly and to proclaim their faith publicly. Some of these Christians, not hardened by centuries of caution and an ideology that celebrated martyrdom, lapsed when put to the test. The social and ecclesiastical damage was profound.

Donatism and the Fallout from the Great Persecution

In northern Africa, **Donatism** (named after Donatus, a bishop of Carthage, who had led that region's resistance to restoring lapsed churchmen) began as a dispute over the damaged authority of churchmen, labeled as traitors, who had surrendered scriptures to their persecutors. The Donatists held that all churchmen who had committed such acts of betrayal and all the sacraments that they had administered were false. Saint Augustine (354–430) spent much of his career as a Christian bishop in northern Africa resisting the Donatists, who tried on several occasions to assassinate him. Augustine argued for a more

Saint Augustine on the Outside

Aurelius Augustinus, or Saint Augustine, had an immense impact on the shaping of medieval Christian thought. He wrote so much that readers have often wondered how one person could have written all that has been attributed to him. Once he became a bishop, he did have a stable of scribes to take down his thoughts. He was also an active and diligent bishop with many pastoral responsibilities and maintained an active correspondence with his many friends and sometimes enemies throughout the Roman world. Works such as *On Christian Doctrine, The Trinity,* and *The City of God* became statements of normative Christian doctrine. His episcopal concerns ranged from the good of marriage and the status of widows to the dangers of divination. He also found time to interpret Scripture, particularly in his study of the meaning of Genesis. He was also a controversialist, defending the orthodox faith against Manichaeans, Donatists, and Pelagians (who placed an emphasis on good works and free will). For all of this, he was deemed one of the doctors (teachers) of the church, whose teachings were considered orthodox and saintly.

There is another Augustine whom we think less about: Augustine the outsider and outlaw. Had he died in 385 when he was just thirty years old we might never have heard of him. From his *Confessions,* we know that, although he had been raised a Christian by his mother, Monica, he had for a time been more interested in Latin prose and poetry, the captivating sounds of Cicero, Virgil, and the pagan poets, than in Christ. When he was seventeen he went to Carthage to be educated, but as a teenager he was more excited by the alluring wickedness of the city: "I came to Carthage and there was overwhelmed by the sizzle of that frying-pan of lustful love. I was not yet in love but I wanted to love. . . ." Within a year he took a concubine and a year after that they had a son. The couple named their son Adeodatus ("given by God"), which may be an indication that his partner was a Christian, for Augustine had already begun to drift away from the faith of his mother. Like most Romans, Augustine was a materialist and he tried to understand God within the confines of

Aristotle's ten categories for describing *things*. His literal reading of the Bible and his exposure to his mother's devout Christianity were failures precisely because of his material approach to them. The Bible seemed to him, at the time, to be an unreasonable book.

Instead, he turned to the banned Manichaean religion because it promised an explanation for the existence of evil in the world and the underlying reasons for things. He went so far as to become a spokesman for the secretive religion and took pleasure in mocking simple Christians. For ten outlaw years he remained a Manichaean novice, deeply offending his mother, who barred him from her house. Had he died just before he turned forty when he sailed to Rome to become a professor of rhetoric, we might know him, if at all, as just another Manichaean preacher in Carthage. Augustine's world may have accepted official Constantinian Christianity, but a seething competition of alternative teachings and religions remained. The future saint experimented with an intellectually exciting, but illegal brand before it too disappointed him. He then turned his vast and energetic intellect to making Christianity and its Scriptures reasonable and to understanding his God as immaterial and transcendent. In the *Confessions* he looks inward to his own heart to discover the memories of his past that would reform his present life and outward to a perfect and transcendent God. In *The City of God* he follows the long hard story of Rome, its misunderstandings and great spiritual mistake, but ends with the saints and the power of a living God revealed in miracles still being worked in the present.

Augustine had come a long way from outlawry and from disappointing his pious mother.

QUESTIONS | *Why was the religious scene so unsettled in the third and fourth centuries? Why was Augustine's materialism an obstacle to his embrace of Christianity? How do Augustine's life and thought parallel the evolution of Christianity?*

inclusive and forgiving church against the rigorist, exclusive, and elitist one promoted by the Donatists.

Not only had Diocletian and Galerius powerfully reminded the Roman world that Christianity was illegal, but they had also sown seeds of dissension in Christianity that would take time to dislodge. In the early fourth century, Christianity remained a proscribed religion held by a minority of Romans. Yet the limited success of Diocletian's rigorous persecution of Christianity made it clear that the religion would not disappear from the Roman Empire. Other religions such as Mithraism, a soldier's religion, seemed, however, by the middle of the third century to have a better chance of eventual domination. But, then, something extraordinary happened.

Constantine and the Christianization of the Roman Empire

Two things make Constantine one of the west's most important historical actors: he recognized and supported Christianity, and he created a new capital for the empire in the east. Both were to be formative events in the shaping of western history for the next eleven hundred years and both turned the Roman Empire in a new, largely unexpected, medieval direction.

Why was Constantine such a powerful agent of change in Roman and western history?

Although much of the slow Romanization of Christianity occurred in the third century, the Christianization of the Roman Empire took place in the fourth. Tolerated in 313, Christianity became the state religion of the empire by the end of the century, and paganism was officially banned.

Constantine's Conversion

Despite Diocletian's plan for a stable succession after he and Maximian stepped down, the empire soon slipped into civil war. Constantine's father, one of the Caesars, died in 306, but his son was not named to replace him and so Constantine took control of his father's army in Britain. The wars of succession that followed suggest just how much the Tetrarchy had depended on Diocletian's dynamic control and not on the institution itself. In 312, at the Battle of the Milvian Bridge just outside of Rome, Constantine overcame his rival Maxentius. The next year he and another rival, Licinius, met at Milan and came to uneasy terms over their relative division of powers. Finally in 324 Constantine invaded the eastern empire and defeated and executed Licinius. Thus, after less than forty years of four-man rule, the empire once again had a single emperor.

A critical factor in Constantine's success was his religious conversion. Christians were still a fragile minority in the empire, and the events of the Great Persecution were still playing out in the east when Constantine marched on Rome. The illegal religion had been pushed underground once more, much of its property in the east had been seized, and its leaders and institutional structure had been undermined. Yet, at the Battle of the Milvian Bridge, Constantine and his troops fought under a Christian banner and called on Christ to help them achieve victory (see Back to the Source at the end of the chapter).

Constantine did not, however, proclaim Christianity the official religion of Rome in 312. In fact, he did not become a complete Christian himself, delaying baptism until he was on his deathbed twenty-five years later. The emperor, like many early Christians, believed that baptism washed away all one's sins and so was best delayed until a Christian took his last breath and so could die cleansed of all earthly sin. Constantine had much to repent since he had ordered the execution of one of his wives and his eldest son. But for much of his imperial career, Constantine was a Christian in all but name.

In 313, Constantine and Licinius did something more important, at least officially, than the famous Christian victory of the previous year. By the **Edict of Milan** the co-emperors proclaimed an edict of universal religious toleration by which Christians and others could now practice their religions openly and without state restraint. The emperors revoked all previous decrees against Christianity and ordered the return of all the property that had been seized from Christians both by the state and by private individuals.

Constantine's religious role in the western part of the empire was a delicate one. Most of the population was still pagan, and the emperor remained the chief priest of Roman religion. He allowed the cult of emperor worship to continue and sacrifices to the gods to be performed, and so fulfilled his official religious duties. Constantine presented himself as the emperor and spiritual leader of all Romans, pagan and Christian.

The general thrust of Constantine's religious beliefs, however, is evident. He and his family openly supported Christianity. His mother, Helena, built churches and promoted Christianity in Jerusalem, and Constantine financed the building of the great basilicas of Old St. Peter's and St. John Lateran in Rome. In many ways his most profound religious act was to transfer state patronage

Old St. Peter's Basilica A fresco from the sixteenth century of Old St. Peter's Basilica, which was replaced during the Italian Renaissance with the present St. Peter's.

312–313: Constantine's Big Turn

In the late summer of 312, few Christians or state officials, particularly in the eastern Roman Empire, would have predicted that Christianity was on the verge of an epochal breakthrough. Constantine's turn to Christianity on the eve of battle in October and his legalization of the religion four months later constituted one of the west's great and most unexpected turning points, and nothing about it was either inevitable or predictable. In 311, the worst of all the persecutions of the Christian cult was still proceeding in the eastern empire, and the religion was being driven underground once again. Constantine himself had had other dreams and other religious enthusiasms, some of them pagan, before the fateful one at the Milvian Bridge.

Roman pagans formed the vast majority of the population in 312. Their polytheism was warm and ancestral. They associated their gods with family, state, and success. For Mediterranean men and women, a true religion was never new; it was eternal and bound to the intimate passages of their personal and public lives. How could such a deep emotional attachment to a way of life and belief by millions of people change overnight? In short, it did not and need not have. Despite the rise of the great monotheisms (Judaism, Christianity, Islam) in the Middle East, Roman paganism might still have persisted openly and officially for a long time. By 312, Roman paganism was a thousand years old, and the sheer force of religious inertia might have maintained it for centuries.

But Constantine and his Christian advisors slowly moved the massive weight of old religious habits in a new direction. Imperial patronage and protection of the new religion were the sanctioning forces; church councils and local bishops were the instruments of transformation. Councils ruled against lukewarm converts who simply added Christ to the pantheon of all gods and continued to make sacrifices to pagan gods even after they had been baptized. Many of these new Christians of convenience were aware where promotion and advantage now lay. But Christian

The Colossal Head of Constantine Only the head, a hand, and several body parts of the colossal statue of Constantine in Rome now survive, but they are impressive reminders of how thoroughly Constantine impressed himself upon his Roman Empire.

morality began to transform pagan and popular culture. Constantine outlawed gladiatorial combat, which before long disappeared throughout the empire. His officials and priests reset the calendar of the Roman world, moving it from a cycle of pagan feasts and festivals to a Christian one. The gymnasium and baths, long the institutional centers of Greek and Roman civic life, soon ceded their central place to the church, which dispensed charity and served as a public gathering place. The Sibyls and oracles who had counseled the ancient world were replaced by saints and bishops. The transformation was not entirely peaceful. At the cult site of Didyma outside Miletus, local Christians tortured Apollo's priest and prophet into silence. But, in general, the remaking of the religious worldview of antiquity was surprisingly subtle and slow.

Still one can't but wonder what it was like for millions of Romans to fall asleep one night in 312 in a familiar world of old gods and family beliefs and to wake to the realization over the coming months and years that their world was moving in a new and unexpected direction. On the very edge of the great religious turn, provincial governors were executing Christians and seizing their property, while pagan philosophers were still making rational arguments against the cult. They would not have seen the rise of Christianity as inevitable, but simply as another stroke of bad luck, this one visited on them by an errant, ill-educated, and opportunistic emperor. Yet with Constantine their world changed and they along with it.

QUESTIONS | *Can history turn rapidly in new directions, or are large shifts in the predominant direction of a society gradual and only seem sudden? Explain. Why do we tend to associate large historical turns with spectacular events when so many complex historical factors are at work? Why was Constantine critical to the successful institutionalization of Christianity?*

from paganism to Christianity. For a thousand years, Romans had expressed their religious beliefs through inscriptions and in their worship of statues so imbued with the divine that they seemed, said Virgil, to breathe. These stones were proclamations of patronage and personal devotion to the gods. With the shift in official state support, the pagan stones of the ancient world began to fall silent and their breathing slowed.

Making a New Rome in Byzantium

The city of Rome was a problem for Constantine. It carried too much old baggage, was too pagan, and forced on him too many compromises with the old ways, both religious and political. But in the east, Constantine could create a new city of Rome and point the empire in a new religious and political direction.

The ancient city of Byzantium was located on the Bosporus Straits at the natural meeting point of Europe and Asia. It took its name from Byzas, the leader of the Greek settlers who had founded the site. The location had many defensive advantages because it could be fortified on both its land and sea sides. Merchants could travel out from it, west along the Mediterranean to Rome and east via the Black and Caspian Seas, or along land routes that led to the Silk Road and China. By the late third century the eastern part of the Roman world was also the most prosperous and Christian part of the empire.

After defeating Licinius, Constantine sent administrators and architects to the city. He had apparently concluded that the city of Rome was too difficult to defend and too pagan to serve as the administrative center of his new regime. For six years, Byzantium was fortified and redesigned and in 330 was officially proclaimed New Rome, though it quickly took on the name of Constantinople (the city of Constantine). We know it today as Istanbul in Turkey.

Constantinople was Rome with a difference. It was designed in the image of Rome and so had a Forum, a Senate house, a Hippodrome or Circus, and senatorial families transferred from Rome to the new capital. But Constantinople was to be a Christian city in which no new pagan temples were permitted. Though there was a patriarch or high churchman resident in the city and in nominal charge of the eastern church, the emperor was the effective head of the Christian religion in the east. His religious opinions and fancies mattered most of all.

Although some scholars date the start of the Byzantine Empire from the creation of Constantinople, eastern Romans still thought of themselves as citizens of the Roman Empire. Though it was Greek in nature and represented the Greek culture of the eastern Mediterranean, the eastern empire's official language for several centuries remained Latin. The people called themselves Romans and referred to their common Greek language as Romaic.

Toward a State Religion

As emperor, Constantine was called on to adjudicate disputes within the Christian church. He ruled against the Donatists and called a great church council that met at Nicaea in 325 to address the problem raised by Arius (260–336), a priest from Alexandria. Arius and his followers (called Arians) claimed that Christ was subsequent (since his human nature was created) to God the Father and his nature changeable, and therefore less divine. This doctrinal dispute roiled the church, particularly its eastern half, where there was a tendency to view God in **monophysite** or one-nature terms, that is, to view God the Father as unique and omnipotent. One could go nowhere in Constantinople, said one contemporary, without hearing shopkeepers and slaves debating the nature of Christ's person. Ask a baker for the price of bread, and he would instead tell you in no uncertain terms that the Son is subordinate to the Father.

Advising Constantine in the midst of this theological controversy were powerful churchmen, some opposed to **Arianism** (including the young Athanasius), others lukewarm to it (such as Eusebius, the emperor's biographer). The final decision of the council was the Nicene Creed. Though the Creed may sound more contractual than spiritual, the product of a committee wrestling over terminology and clauses, it became an official article of faith for the Christian church. Its central point of consensus was that Christ was "of the same substance" as the Father. But many of the fine points of Christ's nature and the Trinity (the Godhead with reference to its three persons, the Father, Son, and Holy Spirit) would continue to exercise Christian thinking for centuries to come. Still the Nicene Creed, as agreed to by the universal church, as represented by the bishops gathered together from the entire Roman Empire, set out a list of beliefs that, at a minimum, all Christians needed to hold.

Nicaea was a triumph of Constantine's religious authority. Eusebius said that the emperor had appeared before the council in a gorgeous purple robe adorned with gold and jewels and dazzled all by his presence. His costume may have sparkled, but his intellect did not. He changed his mind several times as the council wore on and did not always seem to understand the complex theological points at issue. But then Constantine's goal was to unify and govern the Roman Empire, and he may not have been all that interested in endless theological quibbling. Like others, he may just have been waiting to see which way the Christian winds were blowing. At Nicaea he finally chose the winning side. By the end of Constantine's reign, Christianity was not just tolerated; it was the preferred, patronized, protected, and defined religion of the empire and its emperors.

Julian Lapses

When Constantine died in 337 he was succeeded by his three natural sons, who murdered their rivals and had themselves declared Augusti. By 350, one of them, Constantius II (337–361), had overcome his brothers and relatives by assassination. A sarcastic contemporary said that he had only one virtue: he never wiped his nose or spat in public. In 355, Constantius raised his cousin Julian up as a new Caesar to fight against the Germans in the west.

Julian was a sensitive student of Greek philosophy and wrote a book called *The Beard-Hater*, in which he defended the long hair and beards worn by the pagan philosophers of old despite the fashion for a more clipped and clean-shaven look in his own time. Though raised a Christian, he renounced his faith in 361 and so is known as an **apostate.** Attentive to the administration of justice, property rights, and relieving the oppressed, he was a popular figure in the western empire.

Julian's popularity and military success against the Germans, however, roused suspicions about him at the imperial court. Faced with increasing imperial animosity and at the urging of his army, Julian rebelled against Constantius and marched on Constantinople. Before he arrived, the emperor died and Julian was left the sole emperor of all Rome. He now openly revealed his pagan beliefs, but he did not open a new round of persecution of Christians. Not only was Christianity too entrenched by then and his government filled with Christians too powerful to displace, but Julian's own religious beliefs belonged to an older learned polytheism that tended to be tolerant of other beliefs. Instead of persecuting Christians, he turned his energies against the Persians but was fatally wounded during a battle in 363 and died at thirty-one years of age. Julian's apostasy had not changed the Christian direction of the Roman state. By the mid-fourth century the Roman Empire was Christian and would remain so.

Institutional Growth of the Church

As the state embraced Christianity, the institution of the church was moving on a number of fronts to assume its official role in the new order. The number of bishops in Gaul increased from 26 to around 70 in the fourth century as the empire was officially Christianized. The canon of Scripture was set by late in the century; and apocryphal writings, those other gospels and secret teachings (including Gnostic writings), were labeled heretical and ordered destroyed. Throughout the empire the old aristocracy, though retaining elements of its older familial beliefs and pagan humanism, joined the Christian movement. In the west, heroic saintly figures such as Martin of Tours (316–397) took to the countryside to battle ingrained popular paganism. The church developed techniques for winning over the countryside, including a policy of accommodation. Christian churches, for instance, were erected on the sites of pagan holy places so that pagans might both see the triumph of Christianity and yet continue to associate those sites with their older aura of holiness. In battles against the entrenched paganisms of Gaul and other provinces, saints such as Martin came to represent a new set of heroic ideals based on charity, Christian compassion, and steely martyrdom. But the countryside of northern Europe was not to be completely converted for centuries. Pagan beliefs seemed to disappear from sight, but they persisted in small rituals, stubborn convictions, and village superstitions.

While Christians such as Martin were working from the bottom up converting local populations, the Roman state and church were working from the top down. The Trinity was accepted within the empire as a universal stan-dard in 381, and in 392 the emperor Theodosius (379–395) prohibited the practice of paganism and ordered all pagan temples closed. Theodosius led the general Christian suppression of paganism in the empire. He banned older rites of divination such as the reading of entrails and the flight of birds; abolished the celebration of pagan feasts and holidays, extinguished the perpetual fire of Vesta, and disbanded the Vestal Virgins and other pagan associations; and refused to restore the Altar of Victory in the Senate of Rome. At this twilight hour for the ancient gods in the late fourth century, a few learned men still evoked older pagan sensibilities, almost as a soft reaction to the hard Christianizing of the empire around them.

By 400, pure pagan culture was a thing of the past, best remembered by learned readers but fully lived by few. The Roman Empire had an official religion with all its parts in place. Christianity was to spread relatively easily inside the Roman Empire but with considerable difficulty outside it. That compatibility was the end result of the process of the Romanization of Christianity and the Christianization of Rome; the two, empire and religion, had grown together over the previous two centuries and were now inseparable.

German Tribes Enter the Empire

The name *German* (and from it Germania or Germany as the land of the Germans) was apparently derived from

Why and how did the Germanic tribes enter the Roman Empire?

a single early tribe and applied by extension to all the Teutonic peoples whom the Gauls and Romans encountered. Although some Romans thought that the word came from their own word for brother or sister (*germanus*), that derivation was farfetched; for most of their long contact the Romans had little feeling of fraternity with the Germanic peoples.

Germans had long been known to the Romans as part of the mix of peoples and cultures within the empire. Captured in wars, many had served as slaves and by the fourth century some were employed as mercenaries. What happened in the last quarter of the century, however, was something different and no longer on strictly Roman terms. Entire German tribes entered the empire as refugees, economic migrants, and invaders (Map 6.4). Those three different roles may help to explain the complexity of the German entry into the Roman Empire and to correct the common view of them as ferocious aggressors. Maps with large sweeping arrows of invading German tribes tend to mislead. So does the standard talk of a flood of **barbarians** pouring into the empire (it took half a century) and engulfing it (the German numbers were always relatively small). Such language does not do justice to the more subtle movement of peoples and the complex reasons for their entrance into the empire. Nor

MAP 6.4 | Entry and Movement of German Tribes in the Roman Empire in the Fourth and Fifth Centuries

In the late fourth century, various Germanic tribes began to move into the Roman Empire, at first with the permission of the emperors. *What does the route followed by the Visigoths reveal? Why and how did the Vandals end up in northern Africa? Is there a prevailing direction to these Germanic migrations? What role did the Huns play in forcing the movement of the German tribes?*

does the idea of a Germanic invasion take into account the Roman cooperation with their entrance and settlement inside the empire.

The various German peoples can be divided roughly into three basic groups: the Scandinavian peoples with whom the Romans had little contact; the west Germans comprising the Franks, Angles, and Saxons; and the east German Goths (Visigoths and Ostrogoths), Vandals, Lombards, and Burgundians. The east German tribes entered the empire; the west Germans, who would play a critical role in shaping the Middle Ages, lagged behind. Both the east and west Germans were warriors, hunters, farmers, and pastoralists, and both tended to wander as groups within the territories they occupied. Most of these tribes were small in number; even the largest do not seem to have had more than 50,000 to 100,000 men, women, and children. Still those were large numbers of people when one considers that no city in the western empire, with the exception of Rome, had that many residents.

The Germans did not want to destroy the Roman Empire; they probably never imagined that they could.

They took for granted the stability and superiority of the empire and wanted to partake of its benefits. The Roman frontier had long been a magnet for the Germans. They collected near its borders to seek employment as mercenaries, to trade with the Romans, and to secure Roman protection.

The Visigoths Request Entrance

By the second and third centuries the Germans had become a persistent problem for the Romans. Even Constantine was forced to take up arms against them. But the first tribe to enter the empire did not do so until the 370s and it was with the permission of an emperor. The Visigoths were an east German group, located around the Black Sea, that began to feel pressured by the Huns who were moving southeast into China and southwest toward the eastern border of the Roman Empire. Seeking protection, the Visigoths appealed to the emperor Valens (r. 364–378) in 376 for permission to cross the Danube and settle inside the empire. Not being in a good position to refuse them, Valens allowed them to enter. The emperor may have hoped that the Visigoths would settle peacefully and, in time, integrate into the Roman world as a subject people, but he was not particularly generous. He granted them poor land on which they could not support themselves. As well their agricultural practices and way of life did not allow them to adapt at once to a permanent settled life. The Visigoths also ran up against a corrupt Roman bureaucracy that exploited them. The Visigoths felt betrayed and took up arms.

They rebelled and on August 9, 378, the Visigoths defeated the Romans at Adrianople, not far from Constantinople. Though the overall size of the Roman army in the empire was huge (perhaps as many as half a million soldiers), it was spread thinly. The relatively small army that Valens put together to confront the Germans was cut down. The wounded emperor slipped away from the battle to take refuge in a cottage, which was burned down with him inside. The emperor Theodosius eventually struck a treaty with the Visigoths that permitted them to hold land as allies.

Imperial Strategies for Managing the Germans

The Romans thought that the safest barbarian (a term used by contemporaries to describe an uncivilized people who spoke an incomprehensible language) was a settled barbarian. The first imperial policy, then, was to settle them on land and keep them away from the Mediterranean Sea. Theodosius knew that as long as the Germans could be kept from the Mediterranean, the Roman way of life could continue without drastic disruption. His law code made it a capital crime to teach Germans how to build boats. As allies the Visigoths were accommodated, probably on state revenues, and so incorporated within the Roman state. This first Roman strategy of settling the German tribes inside the eastern empire proved to be disastrous. The Visigoths, though supposedly settled, turned to raiding. War had been one of their chief activities for centuries. Moreover, the German tribes knew that violence or just the threat of it was the surest way to win advantages from the Roman state.

The second imperial strategy was to deflect the Germans away from the eastern empire and to use them as a quasi-mercenary force to handle problems in the western empire, particularly to dislodge other Germans with whom the eastern empire was at odds. Thus, when Theodosius died in 395, his successor employed Alaric (d. 410) and the Visigoths to remove Stilicho, the Vandal general in charge of the Roman army of northern Italy, who was in imperial disfavor. For a decade Stilicho protected Italy against the Visigoths who attacked annually, but he was assassinated on imperial orders in 408.

The eastern Roman Empire had hit on what it thought was a winning strategy for managing the Germans inside the empire. The eastern empire decided that it would

The General Stilicho On this ivory diptych, the German general Stilicho stands on guard for Rome against the barbarian assaults on Italy. He is presented as a soldier, not as a senator or consul.

be best to have no resident Germanic tribes in the east and so encouraged or ordered them to go west, often to displace other Germans who were out of favor with the empire. The civilian population of Italy had long ago surrendered its military duties, thinking it better to let German mercenaries such as Stilicho fight on its behalf. Thus, independent east German tribes who had settled uncomfortably in the east were used as military and political instruments in the great Roman game to preserve the eastern empire and quiet the western front. Even if the result further destabilized the west, it was deemed a necessary, if desperate measure, to sacrifice the western empire to the greater good of maintaining a mostly German-free eastern empire. The cost of this scheme, however, was to accelerate the division of the empire into a relatively solid east and an increasingly fragile west.

The Sack of Rome in 410

The eastern imperial policy was a dangerous one since the east German tribes could be neither controlled nor contained once let loose in the west. Alaric and his Visigoths marched into Italy. They besieged Ravenna, by then the effective western imperial capital. Located on the Adriatic and therefore closer to Constantinople, Ravenna's rise also marked the final eclipse of the city of Rome as a center of imperial power. Alaric and the Visigoths next turned on Rome and attempted to starve it into submission. On August 23, 410, a gate was opened (reportedly by a slave) and for the next three days the Visigoths and many Roman slaves plundered the city, seizing what they could, overturning monuments, and setting fires.

On hearing of the sack of Rome, the old and weary Saint Jerome said that the very lamp of the world had gone out. Saint Augustine began writing the *City of God* in response to those pagans who claimed that the city had fallen because Rome had abandoned its gods. He argued instead that the fortune of the earthly city had always been variable and that the city of God (or better still "the state of God"), the kingdom of heaven, was the true home of the righteous. He was also apparently worried by the charge that it was *Christian* Germans who had sacked Rome and that it was Christianity itself that was bent on destroying Rome. Augustine countered that Christianity had limited the amount of damage done during the sack since the attackers had respected churches, nuns, and holy things.

The Visigoths were Christians. They had converted as a tribe to Christianity in the 390s at a time when Arianism was still in some vogue in the east. When the empire firmly returned to Nicaean orthodoxy, the Visigoths and the other east German tribes persisted in their Arianism even though by then it was deemed heretical. The east Germans may at some level have preferred Arian theology with its omnipotent God and human Christ over the intellectual complexities of the orthodox Trinity.

Everyone, including the Germans, knew that northern Africa was the grain basket of the empire, feeding the city of Rome and generating immense wealth. To take it was to control the supply lines of Rome's richest provinces. After sacking Rome, Alaric and his people headed south, but before securing ships and fair seas to carry them to Africa, Alaric died. A river in southern Italy was diverted from its course and the chief was buried in the river bed along with his treasure and the slaves who had dug his grave.

Another east German tribe, the Vandals, then crossed over the Rhine River into Gaul since the borders now had fewer Roman soldiers standing guard. For twenty years the Vandals settled in Aquitaine and Spain as Roman allies, but in 429 they captured an imperial fleet and sailed to northern Africa. They took control of the region and its wheat trade and impeded the flow of trade around the western Mediterranean. They also gained an infamous reputation as persecutors of orthodox Christians. In 455, a band of them sailed to Rome and sacked the eternal city.

Attila and the Huns

After putting pressure on the Visigoths and the area beyond the eastern empire in 375, the Huns, who were magnificent horsemen, dispersed back to their ancestral lands in the Asian steppes. In 434, Rua, the chief of the Huns, died and was succeeded by his two nephews, Bleda and Attila, who ruled together until 445, when Attila apparently murdered his brother. A Roman historian who saw Attila described him as short, broad shouldered, and flat nosed; his face was beardless, but he had angry, sunken eyes. So formidable a warrior was he that the emperor paid Attila 700 pounds of gold not to attack the eastern empire. Still, Attila and his Huns twice invaded Byzantine territories before turning west. In 452, the Huns invaded Gaul and Italy. They sacked Aquileia so thoroughly that poets hundreds of years later still sang of its unending ruin. After that the Huns attacked Milan, Pavia, and Rome.

Outside the walls of Rome, the pope is reputed to have urged Attila for the love of God to spare the city. Attila did withdraw, but some portion of the Roman church's treasury may have left with him. At the time Attila had his own problems: a famine and virulent disease (probably malaria) in northern Italy were making it difficult to continue the campaign. Attila died the next year after celebrating his wedding; contemporaries claimed that he had choked on his own drunken vomit, though it is more likely that Romans had arranged his assassination. The Roman state had plotted to assassinate him before, and failed. With Attila's death, the raids of the Huns on the Roman Empire ceased.

The End of the Empire in the West

The east German tribes soon drove out any remaining Huns and stood in effective control of the western empire. The Roman Senate in October 475 elected young Romulus Augustulus as emperor of the west, but the German mercenaries in Italy had other plans. They deposed the new emperor and chose as their king Odovacar, who, like Stilicho before him, was the German general of the imperial army in Italy. Odovacar asked the Senate to notify the eastern emperor that the west no longer needed an emperor. The eastern emperor would suffice and the Germans in Italy would serve in his place and in his name. This sequence of events effectively made Odovacar the first German king to rule Italy, but Italy officially remained part of the empire.

By 476, the Roman Empire was very different from what it had been even a century earlier. It had dwindled in size as distant provinces such as Britain had fallen out of Roman control. The city of Rome had been sacked twice, and other Roman cities in Gaul and northern Africa had suffered assaults. Even the Mediterranean was no longer a secure Roman sea. The empire continued in name in the west and in fact in the east, but various German peoples now controlled large parts of it in the west. Odovacar and his troops held northern Italy;

The Decline and Fall of the Roman Empire

One of the most enduring historical problems has been why the Roman Empire failed? It does no good to turn the question upside down and to ask the better question of why the Roman Republic and Empire lasted so long, for that still leaves the end problem unaddressed. Edward Gibbon was the first modern historian to pose the problem. The very title of his great work, *The History of the Decline and Fall of the Roman Empire* (published in three units in 1776, 1781, and 1788), contains a descriptive hypothesis as though it were a fact, that is, that the Roman Empire experienced a long slow decline and finally ended when Constantinople fell to the Ottoman Turks in 1453.

Gibbon thought he knew why: "the decline of Rome was the natural and inevitable effect of immoderate greatness. Prosperity ripened the principle of decay; the causes of destruction multiplied with the extent of conquest; and, as soon as time or accident had removed artificial supports, the stupendous fabric yielded to the pressure of its own weight." Roman historians themselves thought that the loss of Roman virtue was to blame. Greed, rampant vice, and angry gods undid the empire, but ancient historians were moralists whose goal was to reform the present and instruct the future. Modern historians have offered a variety of causes: territorial (an overextended empire, the rise of dynamic peoples on the margins, the militarization of the empire); economic (excessive taxation, the failure of the economy, inflation); material (lead poisoning, changing climate); structural (corruption and loss of power by the centralized state, the separation of civil and martial offices under Emperor Hadrian, the rise of soldier emperors), and many others.

The sheer complexity of the changing nature of the Roman state over eight hundred years defies any single or simple explanation. Important events or sequences of events can unbalance systems of government and life and lead to changes that produce yet other changes that ripple through time and space. The seeming solidity of large and complex historical phenomena such as empires may be deceptive since complexity produces interdependence and structural delicacy. A complicated machine can make intricate objects, but with a dropped gear, an interruption of power, or a wayward bolt, the thing can stop working altogether. Rome was not a machine, but there was something fragile about its greatness even in the second century. Multiple crises and underlying social and political changes produced responses that pushed Rome in new directions. But Rome did not so much fall as change. Historians can quantify some of those changes (how many books were being written, how many soldiers in the army, how many shiploads of grain, the worth of currency and goods), but historical decline remains a matter of perspective. Some people suffered, some prospered. Were outsiders (Persians, Germans, Africans), and subordinate insiders (conquered Greeks, Jews, slaves), better off or worse off as Rome changed?

What does Rome's historical fate mean for us? Are there lessons to be learned from Rome's end history? Gibbon's readers wanted to know just that and so at the end of Chapter 38 of the *Decline and Fall,* he inserted his "General Observations on the Fall of the Roman Empire in the West." He assured his contemporaries that all was well in their own world: "We may therefore acquiesce in the pleasing conclusion that every age of the world has increased, and still increases, the real wealth, the happiness, the knowledge, and perhaps the virtue, of the human race." His confidence in progress and his conviction that Rome's history was a specific case and not a universal pattern for the decline and fall of advanced societies was encouraging, but Gibbon and his contemporaries could not have anticipated the French Revolution and the rise of Napoleon, which lay only a few years in the future and shook the pleasing stability of the Europe that Gibbon had surveyed with such confidence.

QUESTIONS | *Why, in your opinion, did the Roman Empire decline or change for the worse, or did it? Does the case of Rome throw any light on current history, or are all histories unique?*

---

the Vandals occupied northern Africa; the Visigoths had drifted to and now controlled much of Spain; and the Burgundians took the Rhône Valley and controlled access to the western Alps.

The fourth century had seen the Christianization of the Roman Empire; the period between 376 and 476 saw the political Germanization of the western empire and northern Africa. As jarring as these changes seemed, even to contemporaries, there was something managed and still half-Roman about them. The east German tribes had entered the empire to benefit from its protection and prosperity, and they worked within the general contours of the existing imperial system. Not only had both the Visigoths and the Vandals negotiated their entrances into the empire, but they struck treaties with the state and extorted advantages from it just as powerful Roman citizens always had. The east Germans were Christians, but Arian Christians, which was a critical point of cultural difference.

By the end of the fifth century, the Roman Empire had changed, but it had not ended. Its center had shifted

MAP 6.5 | The Roman Empire by the Early Sixth Century
Although Constantinople was the capital, after Constantine, of the Roman Empire, by the early sixth century it exercised direct control chiefly over the eastern or Greek part. By 526, various Germanic tribes had established kingdoms inside the Roman Empire. ***Where and why did the Germans establish kingdoms? Who controlled the Roman Empire by the early sixth century?***

east to Constantinople, and a case could be made that the Germans inside the empire were acting within the framework of the shrinking Roman state. Living on Roman taxes and governing in the name of the emperor, they had been co-opted into the decaying Roman order.

Germanic Kingdoms in the West

With the end of the western empire and various German peoples settled inside the empire, the future of both the eastern and western parts of the Roman world was yet

> What did the German peoples inside the Roman Empire want, and how well did they play the great Roman game?

to be decided. The eastern empire had made the decision to save itself, even if it meant sacrificing effective power over the west. Each of the east German tribes inside the empire approached the problem of its survival in a different way, though they all shared simi-

lar problems and a similar final fate. One west German tribe, however, found a way to move forward.

Vandals, Visigoths, and Ostrogoths

The Vandals in northern Africa forced the Romans to recognize them as allies and were able to exert some control over parts of the western Mediterranean, but their hostility to orthodox Christianity meant that they never won over the local population. They were overthrown by imperial forces in the sixth century.

After the death of Alaric, the Roman emperor Honorius (r. 395–423) employed the Visigoths to attack other Germanic tribes. The Visigoths eventually set up a successful kingdom in Spain that survived until the early eighth century (Map 6.5). They persisted in their Arian faith until 589, when King Reccared converted to orthodox Christianity. The Visigoths lasted longer than the other east German kingdoms because they seem to have worked better with the Roman state and church, moved when necessary, and eventually joined the established Christian order.

The story of the Ostrogoths may be the most tragic of the German kingdoms, for under a dynamic ruler they pursued the enlightened rule of Italy. The Ostrogoths were an east German tribe of about 100,000 people, a quarter of whom were warriors. The emperor Zeno (474–491) was eager to remove Odovacar and his arrogant dominion over Italy and so, just as another emperor had sent Alaric and the Visigoths west to dislodge Stilicho, he sent the Ostrogoths west to overthrow Odovacar. They were led by Theoderic (453–526), the son of an Ostrogothic king. He had been sent as a boy to Constantinople as a hostage, was educated there, and became the first civilized barbarian king.

After Theoderic became fed up with the Roman policy of keeping the Germans off balance and poor, he led his men on several raids inside the eastern empire. The emperor Zeno decided that it was time to remove the dangerous Theoderic and the Ostrogoths and so sent them west in 489. For three years, Odovacar and his men held out in Ravenna against Theoderic's forces. When both sides were exhausted, the two leaders reached an agreement to share power, which didn't last much past dinner. Theoderic had Odovacar murdered at a banquet and took control of Italy.

Theoderic ruled Italy for the next thirty-three years. He was called *rex* or king but never clarified what he claimed to be king of, whether of the Romans in Italy or of his own people. He reigned in the name of the eastern emperor and dealt fairly and respectfully with the Roman Senate, which continued to meet. Each year, he nominated a candidate for consul. Since the right to issue laws still belonged to the Roman state, he only promulgated edicts. In the late imperial tradition of Diocletian he did wear purple, the imperial color, and permitted petitioners to prostrate themselves before him.

The Roman senator Cassiodorus worked for the Ostrogoths and wrote a series of letters for Theoderic that portray the king's dealings with the Romans in noble terms. Cassiodorus Romanized and idealized the king, but that may have been a reflection of Theoderic's own view of his role as a German king in Italy. He reminded the Romans that, though he was a barbarian, he was their protector against other barbarians, a role that Germans had by then long performed. He acted to protect the interests of Italy and the city of Rome, in particular. He secured a steady supply of food to the city and ordered the repair of the damage done by the Visigoths and Vandals.

Theoderic's policy was one of peaceful coexistence, not assimilation. Because the Ostrogoths and Romans were for the most part isolated from each other, the tensions between the occupiers and occupied were reduced. The only point on which Theoderic abandoned Ostrogothic tradition dramatically was by embracing Roman civil or property law over Ostrogothic law, which was based on a Germanic law code that specified fixed payments according to the worth of things damaged for both civil and

King Theoderic the Great On a gold medallion, the Ostrogothic king Theoderic is depicted as a German with long hair and mustache, but surrounded by Roman symbols.

criminal offenses. As a consequence of Theoderic's decision, the Ostrogothic law code is one of the few Germanic law codes that is now lost. The Ostrogoths, as an occupying military people, had their own military courts. The Romans, as a resident civilian population, were subject to civil courts.

Despite the cooperative regime, the divide between the Romans and the Germans was large. The Ostrogoths spoke a different language than the native population, and their appearance and dress were different. They wore their hair long and Theoderic sported a mustache. The Romans still generally despised Germans. The poet Sidonius claimed that they stank of garlic and greased their hair with butter.

In addition to the ethnic, linguistic, and cultural differences that separated the Ostrogoths and the Romans, so too did religion. Like other east Germanic peoples inside the empire, the Ostrogoths were Arian Christians. Although their religious beliefs were viewed as heretical in orthodox Italy, the Ostrogoths probably found that those beliefs and practices served as a useful hedge against assimilation. But, unlike the Vandals, Theoderic publicly promoted religious toleration. People, he thought, could not be compelled to believe against their will. As a consequence, he did not seize orthodox churches but began building his own Arian churches, several of which survive in Ravenna today. Despite his immersion in Italian affairs, the king had plans for a wider German world. He sought to influence parts of Gaul and Burgundy through a series of marriage alliances with other German tribes.

King Theoderic's Troubled Last Years

After the year 500, things began to go awry for Theoderic and the Ostrogoths. When Clovis, the king of the Franks, became an orthodox and not Arian Christian, the balance of power and authority in the west began to shift against the Arian Ostrogoths. Theoderic's dealings with the Romans became strained. In 523, worried that the Senate and emperor were conspiring against him and his people, he commanded the Romans not to bear arms. Next he ordered the arrest of the senator Boethius for colluding with the emperor. While in prison, Boethius wrote *The Consolation of Philosophy*, a dialogue in both prose and verse with Lady Philosophy on the nature of fortune. In 524, Boethius was executed.

The previous emperor, Zeno, may have been sympathetic to the Arians, but the new emperor, Justin (r. 518–527), viewed them as heretics and persecuted them openly. Theoderic ordered the pope to Constantinople to try to negotiate with the emperor and to put an end to the hostility. When the pope failed, he was arrested on his return to Italy. Theoderic's actions grew more desperate. He was planning a war against the orthodox Franks to the north and on August 30, 526, ordered that all orthodox churches in Italy should be surrendered to him. The next day he died of dysentery.

The future of the Early Middle Ages was not to lie with the east German tribes, but with the west Germans. Although religion had been a useful point of distinction for the Ostrogoths and the other east Germans as they tried to maintain their tribal identity in a sea of Romans, those religious differences also prevented the east Germans from becoming full members of the Roman world they occupied. Though the Visigoths, Vandals, and Ostrogoths had pursued different strategies for survival and success, each was unsuccessful in the end.

The Franks Take Control of Gaul

The Franks were a west German tribe that had received rights as Roman allies as early as the fourth century. There were two basic groups of Franks: the Salian Franks, who were located in the area around what is today Belgium, and the Ripuarian Franks farther north around the Rhine. The Franks were not attracted to the Mediterranean, as the east German tribes had been, and consequently received less attention from the Romans. The first Frankish leader of historical importance was Childeric (d. 481/482), a Salian Frank. Like other Frankish kings, his hair was uncut and flowed down onto his shoulders. This line of long-haired kings is known as the Merovingians, after Merovech, a legendary ancestor of the family.

When Clovis became king of the Franks on the death of his father, Childeric, he was only fifteen years old and in a precarious position. Frankish chiefs were the kings of a people, not a kingdom or territory, and they needed to win the support of their men by conducting successful raids and through the generous distribution of the spoils of war. Germanic kings were known as ring-givers since they bestowed on their men riches of gold and baubles. It was not royal blood so much as military success that kept a king in power.

The Salian Franks operated in Roman Gaul, where orthodox bishops had assumed active authority over the administration of their *civitates* (cities and their outlying areas). The Franks and the church maintained a cooperative relationship based on particular spheres of interest. The Franks conducted war, provided security of a sort, and controlled land and royal appointments. The church through its bishops supervised the faith and addressed the social needs of their communities with charity. Clovis began to take control of Christian Gaul and some of its most venerated Christian communities. In 486, when he was only twenty, Clovis moved against the old Roman and Christian cities of Soissons and Rheims. These conquests made it imperative for him to have good relations with the bishops of Gaul. The bishop of Rheims advised King Clovis to defer to his bishops and to heed their advice, for if he was on good terms with them, his province would remain strong.

The Conversion of Clovis

To orthodox Christians the Arians were heretics stubbornly clinging to falsehoods, lies that would lead both them and all whom they influenced to damnation. There was little point in talking to them. Pagans were a different matter; they were simply deluded and naive, polytheistic children who did not know better. For Christians, a pagan (*paganus*) was a rustic, uneducated and superstitious. Since, for their own historical and tribal reasons, the east Germanic tribes all remained faithful to Arianism, it became increasingly apparent to the Romans by the late fifth century that one of the pagan west German tribes would need to break the religious logjam.

The Franks, Angles, and Saxons were all pagans. None of the west German tribes had entered the Roman Empire during the time of Alaric or had encountered Arian missionaries in the eastern empire. The bishops of Gaul not only wanted good relations with Clovis, they also wanted to convert him to their faith, but Clovis was not an easy target. As a young prince, Clovis liked nothing better than to plunder churches and he was notoriously violent. In a dispute with one of his soldiers over who owned a piece of stolen church property, he ordered his men to line up before him. As he inspected the troops, Clovis singled out the man for having a dirty ax, hurled it to the ground, and when the man bent over to pick it up the king brought his own battle ax down on the man's skull, splitting him in two.

Clovis was under intense pressure from both Arians and orthodox Christians to convert to their form of faith. The young king had married an orthodox Christian named Clotild, a sincere believer who was pressured by bishops to persuade her husband to convert. It was a strategy employed by other bishops in the sixth century, but Clovis continued to waver, unsure where his advantage lay. Like Constantine, he finally converted on the eve of a battle sometime between 496 and 498. He too was looking for victory through religion, and the Roman church was pleased to support him, for their interest lay in having an orthodox king spread the faith through conquest, particularly over heretical lands and peoples. One bishop told the king that where he conquered, so did they.

The church's policy of converting the Germans depended on converting the king first. This was not popular, grassroots conversion, but top-down conversion. The tribe collectively converted with its leader. Three thousand of Clovis's men were baptized with him in Rheims. Clovis's conversion should not be thought of as insincere; rather, his religious beliefs were primitive or untrained. Even after conversion, Clovis's Christianity remained an amalgam of paganism and primitive Christianity. The Frankish people, without Clovis's fuller exposure to episcopal teaching, knew even less about their new religion. They were now nominally Christian, but their full conversion to Christianity would take centuries to achieve.

The political impact of Clovis's conversion was vast. By force of arms and with the sanction of the church, he defeated the Burgundians and Visigoths in Gaul and by 507 had united the cities of Gaul under his rule. In so doing, he changed the fundamental direction of the west. The various east German tribes felt the ground shift under them as they looked north and saw the success of Clovis, their orthodox Christian cousin. It was no wonder that Theoderic was planning to attack the Franks just before he died.

Clovis's triumph was not the end of Roman Gaul, but its last great flourish. The Salian Franks now controlled old Gallo-Roman territory. Agriculture based on grapes and olives still dominated in the south, huge villas remained, Roman amphitheaters in places such as Arles and Nîmes were still in use, and merchants from as far away as Syria and as near as Spain followed old trade routes into Gaul. Gallo-Roman civilization persisted, if in diminished form. The Salian Franks even continued Roman chancery or bureaucratic practices, and their documents were written on papyrus until the seventh century. Some historians believe that the Merovingians belong to the final phase of the ancient world since they still operated within the contours of the decaying empire, much as their east German cousins did.

Justinian's Reassertion of Roman Imperial Grandeur

In the eastern Roman Empire, events were unfolding that would remind the Mediterranean world that the empire still retained considerable power, even in the west. The emperor Justinian with his empress Theodora attempted to return the Roman Empire to its glory days by undoing the Germanic intrusion into northern Africa and the western empire, wiping out the Arian heresy, and making their reign a magnificent reassertion of imperial grandeur. Their bold attempt, however misguided and damaging, was to be critical to shaping the direction that the Middle Ages took.

> **What impact, good or bad, did Justinian's drive to restore and reassert the greatness of the Roman Empire have on Mediterranean and European civilization?**

The Emperor and Empress

Justinian (r. 527–565) was the last native Latin-speaking emperor of Constantine's Roman Empire and the last to dream of restoring it to its earlier glory. In 527, he was named co-emperor alongside his uncle Justin, an illiterate soldier and persecutor of Arians. Justinian had by that time already married Theodora (r. 527–548), a

The Emperor Justinian and Attendants On this mosaic, which faces the mosaic of Theodora in San Vitale, Ravenna, Justinian is accompanied by the Archbishop Maximianus and two priests to his left and two nobles and a group of soldiers, one with a Chi-Rho shield to Justinian's right. The general Belisarius may be the grizzled noble over his left shoulder. Neither Justinian nor Theodora ever visited Ravenna.

controversial and dynamic figure in her own right. As a lower-class woman, she was roundly despised by segments of the Roman nobility. Procopius of Caesarea, the secretary of General Belisarius and the chronicler of Justinian's many accomplishments, wrote a *Secret History (Anecdota)* in which he condemned Justinian and Theodora as rapacious monsters and murderers.

Regardless of her reputation, Theodora had courage and determination. In 532, a riot broke out in Constantinople between the Green and Blue racing supporters (Circus and political factions at the Hippodrome), the rough equivalent (with knives) of a modern soccer riot. Violence spilled over into the streets of the city and for three days the mob rampaged, setting buildings on fire and calling for a new emperor. Justinian was about to flee the city, according to Procopius, when Theodora shamed him into staying and fighting back. The generals Belisarius and Mundus attacked the mob and killed thousands. The emperor survived the crisis.

Theodora was also a social reformer, seeking basic rights for women in the empire. She worked against the trumped-up adultery charges that many men used to divorce their wives and to seize the property that these women had brought into their marriages. She campaigned for the prohibition of the sale of young girls for prostitution and purchased a palace where these abused children might be housed; she called it her House of Repentance. Procopius ignored her good deeds in his portrait, concentrating instead on the seedier side of her reputation.

After the riot, Justinian set about making fundamental changes to eastern Roman society. He ordered a great codification of Roman law. The quaestor Trebonian was assigned the task of sorting centuries of Roman legal precedents and imperial laws into a rational code of civil law. The *Corpus Juris Civilis* or Body of Civil Law consists of the Code, which contains imperial laws; the Digest (or examples) of Roman laws; and the Institutes, which is a textbook of Roman law. The New Laws (*Novellae*) contains laws from Justinian's own reign.

Justinian also ordered the repair of Constantinople and the construction of new buildings. The most famous of these is the church of Hagia Sophia ("holy wisdom"), which was dedicated in 537. Its interior was gilded, by one estimate, with over 300,000 pounds of gold. Its massive dome, which seems to float on air, was supported by new engineering techniques that allowed a round dome to be placed on top of a roughly square building, allowing light to pour into the massive space below from the rim of the dome.

The Reconquest

While Justinian's predecessors had been preoccupied with the eastern Roman frontier and the threat from Persia, Justinian dreamed instead of restoring the empire and retaking the west (Map 6.6). In 532, he struck an "endless peace" with the Persian ruler Chosroes I, which cost him

Hagia Sophia Justinian erected Hagia Sophia in Constantinople after the Nike rebellion. The huge church with its novel architectural features was covered with gold and decoration, but in 1453 was converted into a mosque.

11,000 pounds of gold. That left him free to turn his attention to the western empire, where he hoped to remove the Germans and stamp out their Arian heresy. He dispatched his young general, Belisarius, along with 20,000 troops to northern Africa to overthrow the Vandals, which happened relatively quickly. The persecuted orthodox Christian population, which had suffered under the harsh Vandal occupation, rallied to their Roman rescuers.

That easy victory convinced Justinian that he could reclaim control over the rest of the imperial rim of the Mediterranean. But wars drain treasuries, and Justinian was always in need of money to pay his mercenary armies. Behind Procopius's complaints about the greed of the emperor and empress lay the emperor's need to finance his expensive wars and extensive building campaigns. Justinian taxed heavily, imposing a heavy burden on the nobility and cities of the eastern empire.

In Italy the Ostrogothic succession was in dispute. To hold on to power, Theoderic's daughter, Amalasuntha,

MAP 6.6 | The Roman Empire of Justinian, 527–565

Over his long reign, the emperor Justinian attempted to restore the Roman Empire. ***Whom did Justinian seek to displace, why, and when? Why was his restoration of the old Roman Empire both a success and a failure?***

married her cousin Theodahad, but in 534 her husband had her strangled to death while she was taking a bath and declared himself king. Justinian used this event as a pretext for sending troops to Italy to reclaim his imperial rights. The Italian campaign was as difficult as the African one had been easy. General Belisarius was given fewer troops and the native population, for the most part content with the regime of the Ostrogoths, proved less cooperative. At one point, Belisarius and five thousand imperial soldiers were cooped up in Rome for a year as the Ostrogoths laid siege to it. From there the war descended into chaos and Belisarius was recalled.

Later Justinian managed to reassert his authority over Italy, and the adornment of Ravenna reflects that conquest. Justinian's representatives attempted to erase all traces of the presence of the Ostrogothic king from Ravenna and the west. Justinian's artisans even removed the mosaic images of Theoderic and his courtiers standing under arches of his palace, but their disembodied hands can still be seen in the mosaic as though grasping pillars, unwilling to leave.

The Disastrous 540s: Dust-Veils and Disease

The cost of Justinian's campaigns was considerable, and the reassertion of imperial authority over the west would not last. Despite Justinian's endless peace with Chosroes of Persia, by 540 the Persians had sacked Roman cities, including Antioch. The Ostrogoths under a new leader rallied. They took Milan, slaughtering all males and selling the women to the Burgundians. King Totila (r. 541–552) decided to level the city of Rome and began to tear down its walls and to burn the city. For one month the eternal city was virtually without inhabitants. Late in Justinian's reign, his Slavic frontier also began to crumble.

The natural world also seemed to turn against Justinian. In 535–536, a dust-veil, most likely caused by volcanic ash, shrouded the northern hemisphere, blocking solar radiation from reaching the earth. Procopius said that the sun shone weakly in 536, its rays dull. Another Roman contemporary said the sun dimmed for eighteen months and crops failed and the wine was bitter. The effect of the dust-veil was to cool not only Europe, but global temperatures in general, perhaps by as much as 4.5 degrees Fahrenheit (3 degrees Centigrade) between 535 and 555. Whether this climate event also made the population of Europe more susceptible to disease or set into motion a complex chain of factors contributing to the transmission of a particular bacillus is not known, but a deadly disease did strike the west a few years after the dust-veil first obscured the sun.

In 542, a pandemic known as Justinian's Plague struck Constantinople and the rest of the Roman Empire. The evidence so far suggests that the disease was the bubonic plague. At its height, Justinian's Plague was killing between 5,000 and 15,000 people a day in Constantinople alone, and it may have killed as many as 300,000 people in the city. The emperor himself fell ill but survived. The disease also reached Italy and recurred there and in various spots throughout the empire for several centuries before dying out.

The Clinging Hands of Theoderic and His Court After the conquest of Ravenna by Justinian's army, the mosaic decoration of Theoderic's church of San Apollinare Nuovo was reworked. Originally images of Theoderic and his courtiers had stood between the arches of the depicted palace, but they were removed, leaving only some of their hands clinging to columns as though unwilling to depart.

The economic impact of the dust-veil and disease on the empire, which had already been experiencing a sharp decline in population, was significant. Justinian still needed money to finance his wars and soldiers to fill his armies, but manpower became scarcer and more expensive to employ. Labor costs increased, while consumer demand for goods dropped. Whatever else the dust-veil and plague meant in terms of extensive human suffering and economic hardship, they did not enhance Justinian's already faltering scheme to restore the Roman Empire to its former integrity and glory.

Despite these setbacks, Justinian remained in power and worked to restabilize his empire. Italy was relatively secure by the mid-550s, the coastal regions of southern Spain were subdued, and northern Africa was in line by the end of the decade.

Living a Shrinking Urban Life

While Constantinople rebounded from the disastrous 540s, urban life throughout the rest of the empire entered a period of dramatic decline. Smaller cities supplied men and taxes to the Roman state, but did not thrive under a stagnant economy and incessant imperial demand. The once highly specialized economy of the Roman Empire, which had remained vigorous through the fourth century, was breaking down. Even the production of items

as simple as shoes, cloth, and pots to hold wine and oil had depended on a combination of regional production, transportation, and distribution within a secure empire, and an extensive series of urban markets. To impede even one of those links was to jeopardize an economic chain, and by 500 in the western empire all three were in a state of crisis. There were fewer consumers and producers, and the transportation and distribution of goods, whether across the Mediterranean or within regions occupied by the Germans, had been compromised. In the eastern empire, the economy, because of imperial security and its greater urban economic scale, was able to overcome many of these problems and remained relatively prosperous.

The east, however, was not without serious economic problems, one of those being caused by Constantinople itself. It seemed at times as though the very purpose of the eastern empire was to feed Constantinople, which sucked resources but supplied little in return. Taxation and religion, petty violence and bullying patrons were the constants of provincial life in the sixth century. Justinian's expensive imperial projects did more to distort than to stimulate the Roman economy.

Around the Mediterranean the population continued to fall as supply lines broke down and long-distance trade dried up. The maritime city of Ephesus, after fire and destruction in the early seventh century, was never rebuilt and its once vigorous harbor became clogged with silt. In Italy many towns and cities were abandoned in the fifth and sixth centuries and people moved to hilltop settlements that could be better defended. Even the city of Rome was not spared. For much of imperial history it had had a population of as many as a million people; by the mid-fifth century it probably had less than half that number. After Justinian's reconquest, the Ostrogothic ravages, the dust-veil, and the plague, the population of Rome fell to around 50,000 people. Other cities shrank inside their old Roman walls. The city life of the ancient Mediterranean, particularly in the west, was ebbing away in the century before the rise of Islam.

Conclusion

The restored Roman Empire that Justinian's heirs inherited was overcommitted and too dominated by one great city and its needs; it could not endure. Within seventy years, northern Africa and large portions of the Roman Middle East fell to Islam and the west broke away again. It might be argued that the effect of Justinian's reconquest and of the natural events that occurred during his reign left a blighted northern Africa and Middle East ready and waiting for the emergence of the dynamic new element that Islam proved to be. In the west, Justinian's legacy was just as disastrous. The new Germanic kingdoms of the Vandals, Visigoths, and Ostrogoths were enfeebled before they had fully developed. Justinian's drive to restore the old Roman Empire, which had been broken and drifting for centuries, only worked to destroy the incipient and dynamic new cultures stirring in the west and northern Africa. The west would have to wait several centuries for the appearance of a German leader as civilized and constructive as Theoderic had been. Justinian's western distraction and diffusion of resources had not materially benefited the east, which would soon see the rise of a new challenge to the surviving Roman Empire.

In many ways Rome lived on, though much diminished and deformed, throughout the sixth century. The east Germanic peoples had seen themselves as working within the Roman imperial system onto which they had grafted themselves. Even the Franks throughout the sixth century occupied a Gallo-Roman territory and by becoming orthodox Christians further integrated themselves into an existing order, one that still looked to the Mediterranean and to an underlying Roman economy of long-distance trade and international merchants.

The period from 180 to 565 marked the slow turn of the ancient world toward the medieval world it was becoming. The three main elements of the Early Middle Ages—late Roman civilization, Christianity, and the Germans—were all in place by its end, but their order of importance had shifted discernibly since Commodus's accession. Christianity, because of Constantine and his successors, moved in the fourth century from being a marginal and persecuted religion to the official belief system of the western world. The Germans, for so long a slave and mercenary element within the empire, now ran much of it. From a centralized Roman Empire with a single ruler (or four of them under the Tetrarchy), the west by 400 consisted of a centralized Roman Empire in the east and a decentralized or localized German west.

If there was one centralizing element in the whole of the old empire, it was Christianity, which had consolidated its presence in the empire, established an official church with a hierarchy of officers, and suppressed voices of difference and dissent. If religion defined the Middle Ages, giving it its distinctive character, then the Middle Ages officially arrived with Constantine. The Roman economy had lost much of its imperial fluidity as goods and people no longer moved across it with ease. There were fewer goods to trade and fewer markets to attract trade. In the west, the economy was already more medieval (highly localized and agricultural) than ancient (with an extensive sea trade and dispersion of goods). The Mediterranean Sea still remained a critical feature of the late Roman world; it was just no longer the dominant one. The Middle Ages didn't arrive everywhere at the same time; it came sooner to the west than the east. The presence of medieval ways was already evident in the west before the Roman Empire finally lost its great middle sea. When it did, western Europe turned inland and to a north bounded by the Atlantic. But the eastern Roman Empire was hardly static. It too was becoming more medieval, as its cities shrank, and its economy became more regionalized. The late Roman, proto-medieval world that stretched from the late second through to the sixth century was neither fish nor fowl, neither wholly Roman nor entirely medieval. It was a world in bumpy transition from one way of organizing and viewing the world to another. Much remained to be done before the Middle Ages overtook the west.

Critical Thinking Questions

1. What choices did late Roman emperors make to preserve the Roman Empire?

2. What roles did economics and outsiders play in the transformation of the late Roman world?

3. Why was religion such an important force in shaping change in the period 180 to 565?

4. What medieval traits were present in the period, where did they predominate, and why did they prevail?

5. What should we call the period from 180 to 565?

Key Terms

codex **(p. 169)**

Gnostics **(p. 170)**

stylites **(p. 170)**

Petrine authority **(p. 172)**

Tetrarchy **(p. 173)**

Donatism **(p. 175)**

Edict of Milan **(p. 177)**

monophysite **(p. 179)**

Arianism **(p. 179)**

apostate **(p. 180)**

barbarian **(p. 180)**

Primary Sources in connect

For information on Connect and the online resources available, go to **http://connect.mcgraw-hill.com**.

1. **Diocletian's Wage and Price Controls**

2. **The Edict of Milan, 313**

3. **The Nicene Creed**

4. **Cassiodorus, King Theoderic's Letters**

5. **The Demons Justinian and Theodora**

Constantine's Dream

The fourth-century ecclesiastical historian Eusebius presents Constantine as a ruler who received a critical dream in his rise to power. Eusebius does not clearly set the dream on the eve of Constantine's breakthrough battle at the Milvian Bridge in 312 against the rival imperial claimant Maxentius, but others were quick to associate the dream and the pivotal battle. Eusebius informs his readers that the report he is relaying came directly from Constantine's sworn and personal testimony, which he wholeheartedly accepted and made the pivotal event in Constantine's conversion and victory.

Knowing well that he would need more powerful aid than an army can supply because of the mischievous magical devices practised by the tyrant, he sought a god to aid him. He regarded the resources of soldiers and military numbers as secondary, for he thought that without the aid of a god these could achieve nothing; and he said that what comes from a god's assistance is irresistible and invincible. He therefore considered what kind of god he should adopt to aid him and, while he thought, a clear impression came to him, that of the many who had in the past aspired to government, those who had attached their personal hopes to many gods, and had cultivated them with drink-offerings, sacrifices, and dedications, had first been deceived by favorable predictions and oracles which promised welcome things, but then met an unwelcome end, nor did any god stand at their side to protect them from divinely directed disaster; only his own father had taken the opposite course to theirs by condemning their error, while he himself had throughout his life honored the God who transcends the universe, and had found him a savior and guardian of his empire and a provider of everything good. He judiciously considered these things for himself, and weighed well how those who had confided in a multitude of gods had run into multiple destruction, so that neither offspring nor shoot was left in them, no root, neither name nor memorial among mankind, whereas his father's god had bestowed on his father manifest and numerous tokens of his power. He also pondered carefully those who had already campaigned against the tyrant. They had assembled their forces with a multitude of gods and had come to a dismal end: one of them had retreated in disgrace without striking a blow, while the other had met a casual death by assassination in his own camp. He marshaled these arguments in his mind, and concluded that it was folly to go on with the vanity of the gods which do not exist, and to persist in error in the face of so much evidence, and he decided he should venerate his father's God alone.

This God he began to invoke in prayer, beseeching and imploring him to show him who he was, and to stretch out his right hand to assist him in his plans. As he made these prayers and earnest supplications there appeared to the emperor a most remarkable divine sign. If someone else had reported it, it would perhaps not be easy to accept; but since the victorious emperor himself told the story to the present writer a long while after, when I was privileged with his acquaintance and company, and confirmed it with oaths, who could hesitate to believe the account, especially when the time which followed provided the evidence for what he said?

About the time of the midday sun, when day was just turning, he said he saw with his own eyes, up in the sky and resting over the sun, a cross-shaped trophy formed from light, and a text attached to it which said, "By this conquer." Amazement at the spectacle seized both him and the whole company of soldiers which was then accompanying him on a campaign he was conducting somewhere, and witnessed the miracle.

He was, he said, wondering to himself what the manifestation might mean; then, while he meditated, and thought long and hard, night overtook him. Thereupon, as he slept, the Christ of God appeared to him with the sign which had appeared in the sky, and urged him to make himself a copy of the sign which had appeared in the sky, and to use this as protection against the attacks of the enemy. When the day came he arose and recounted the mysterious communication to his friends. Then he summoned goldsmiths and jewelers, sat down among them, and explained the shape of the sign, and gave them instructions about copying it in gold and precious stones.

This was something which the emperor himself once saw fit to let me also set my eyes on, God vouchsafing even this. It was constructed to the following design. A tall pole plated with gold had a transverse bar forming the shape of a cross. Up at the extreme top a wreath woven of precious stones and gold had been fastened. On it two letters, intimating by its first characters the name "Christ," formed the monogram of the savior's title, *rho* being intersected in the middle by *chi*. These letters the emperor also used to wear upon his helmet in later times. From the transverse bar, which was bisected by the pole, hung suspended a cloth, an imperial tapestry covered with a pattern of precious stones fastened together, which glittered with shafts of light, and interwoven with much gold, producing an impression of indescribable beauty on those who saw it. This banner then, attached to the bar, was given equal dimensions of length and breadth. But the upright pole, which extended upwards a long way from its lower end, below the trophy of the cross and near the top of the tapestry delineated, carried the golden head-and-shoulders portrait of the God-beloved emperor, and likewise of his sons. This saving sign was always used by the emperor for protection against every opposing and hostile force, and he commanded replicas of it to lead all his armies.

That was, however, somewhat later. At the time in question, stunned by the amazing vision, and determined to worship no other god than the one who had appeared, he summoned those expert in his words, and inquired who this god was, and what was the explanation of the vision which had appeared of the sign. They said that the god was the only begotten son of the one and only God, and that the sign which appeared was a token of immortality, and was an abiding trophy of the victory over death, which he had once won when he was present on earth. They began to teach him the reasons for his coming, explaining to him in detail the story of his self-accommodation to human conditions. He listened attentively to these accounts too, while he marveled at the divine manifestation which had been granted to his eyes; comparing the heavenly vision with the meaning of what was being said, he made up his mind, convinced that it was

God's own teaching that the knowledge of these things had come to him. He now decided personally to apply himself to the divinely inspired writings. Taking priests of God as his advisors, he also deemed it right to honor the God who had appeared to him with all due rights. Thereafter, fortified by good hopes in him, he finally set about extinguishing the menacing flames of tyranny.

QUESTIONS | *What did Constantine want in the midst of a campaign against his enemies? How had the roots of his conversion been laid? How did he verify and then proclaim his conversion? How might Romans have reacted to this conversion story?*

Source: Eusebius, Vita Constantini 1.27–32, ed. F. Winkelmann, trans. Averil Cameron and Stuart G. Hall, *Eusebius: Life of Constantine* (Oxford: Clarendon Press, 1999), 79–82. © Averil Cameron and Stuart G. Hall 1999. By permission of Oxford University Press.

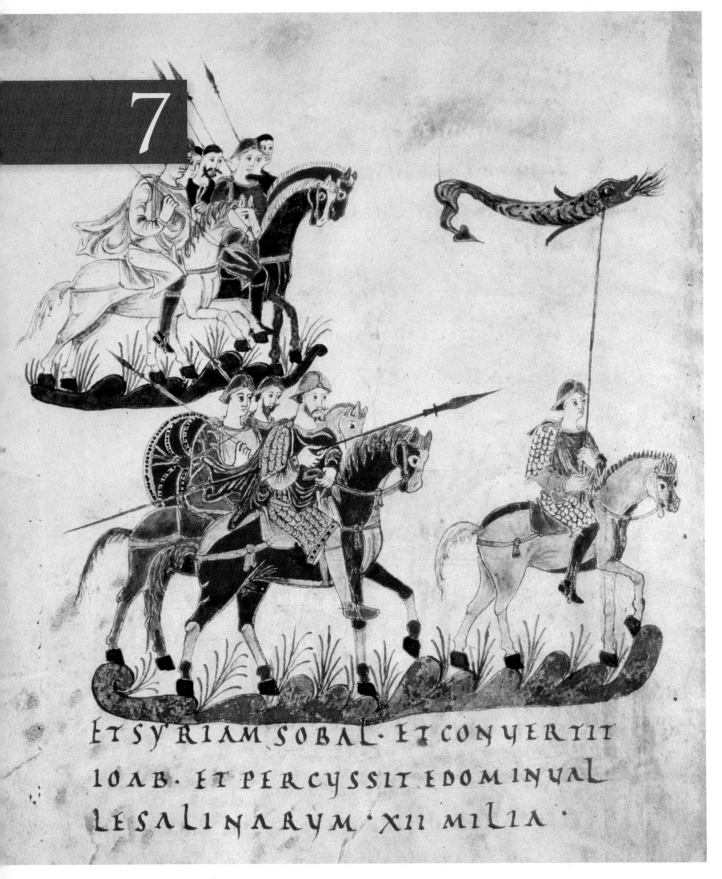

7

Cavalry Riding to War, Golden Psalter, c. 875

THE EARLY MIDDLE AGES

The Making of a New Western World

Monasticism Makes a Difference

Living the Monastic Life

Gregory the Great and the Papacy

Bishops as the Great Mediators

The Saints Come Marching In

Power at the Start of the Middle Ages

Germanic Kingship: Long Hair and the Privatization of Power

Living and Dying the Merovingian Way

Merovingian Power at the Political Turn

Islam Ascendant

The Eastern Roman Empire Becomes Byzantine

Carolingian House Building

The Carolingian Mayors

Pepin the Short Unmakes the Merovingian Line

Charlemagne as Conqueror and King

Charlemagne, Father of Europe and Roman Emperor

Al-Andalus, a Hot Corner of European-Islamic Conflict

Carolingian Cultures: High, Low, and In-Between

Court Culture and Education

The Carolingian Church: Royal, Monastic, and Militant

An Economy of Trade and a Shift to Silver

Living Off the Land

Popular Beliefs

Disorder Returns to Europe

The Woes of Louis the Pious

Three Brothers and a Civil War

The Vikings Raid Francia

The Imperial End Game: Two Charleses, One Bald, One Fat

Conclusion

CHARLEMAGNE'S CORONATION The year was 800, the day Christmas, the place Rome. Old St. Peter's basilica was dressed in its finest array and filled with a throng of worshippers. The men of the moment were a pope and a Frankish king; their marriage of interests was convenient, complex, and dangerous.

When Charlemagne (Charles the Great), a tall man with a sizable paunch, short hair, and mustache, entered St. Peter's, he fulfilled the aspirations of his courtiers, who thought that the time had come for the restoration of the Roman Empire under their illustrious king. Three long centuries had passed since Romulus Augustulus had been deposed as the last emperor of the west. Charlemagne embodied the hope of a new Christian imperial order.

The king traveled to Rome to render justice and restore a pope accused of corruption. Pope Leo III had been physically assaulted by his enemies and driven from Rome. Charlemagne's idea of right order was a practical one; his family had long committed itself to the Roman church and would not now abandon it to disorder, but something went wrong in Rome. Expecting to be rewarded with the largely honorific title of emperor, Charlemagne had dressed in an elegant Greek gown for the occasion. But Pope Leo had other ideas. He took charge of the proceedings and personally placed the imperial crown on Charlemagne's head. To some it seemed that the pope was making the king an emperor. No wonder that Charlemagne later regretted the event. He probably thought that his royal use of force in subduing hostile lands, conquering vast territories, delivering justice, and promoting Christendom made the imperial title a fitting recognition for his many achievements. Leo, as the living representative of Saint Peter and the chosen agent of God on earth, apparently believed that it was by papal intervention and his choice that Charlemagne was made the Roman emperor.

Charlemagne as Roman Emperor, Silver Denarius Image

❈ ❈ ❈ ❈

Whatever happened that day in Rome, Charlemagne's elevation to emperor marked the highest expression of restored order in a world that had long been without lasting stability. The conversion to orthodox Christianity of the Frankish king Clovis had begun the final process of integrating Rome and the Germans, southern and northern Europe, but the Merovingian kings squandered their power in family squabbles and fratricidal wars.

The Early Middle Ages in the west experienced the radical decentralization and disappearance of Roman power. The west returned to being a simpler agricultural society. When western Europe reached its point of greatest disorganization in the sixth century, it was religion, not royalty, that first began to reorder this chaotic world. Monks led the way. Monasticism, one of the great institutional creations of the Middle Ages, provided the Early Middle Ages with a form of religious stability that set a high example for society and helped it begin to reorder religious, economic, and even political life. By retreating from the world, monks grounded the external world in regularity and rationality. Saint Benedict's *Rule* for monks schooled the Early Middle Ages in the advantages of order, work, and economic and religious rationality.

Along with Saint Benedict, the other great religious man of the half millennium was Muhammad, the messenger of a set of divine mandates that inspired and

Merovingian Dynasty of Francia
485–751

450   500   550   600   650

directed the peoples of the Middle East, Near East, and northern Africa, that part of the Roman Empire that had been adrift in the late Roman world, devastated by the Vandals and Justinian's costly reconquest. The territorial spread of Islam undid once and for all the Roman hold on the Mediterranean as a secure body of water for the transport of goods and peoples. Islam reshaped the territorial outline of Europe, pushing the Roman Empire in the east to become a Byzantine Empire and the Roman Empire in the west away from the Mediterranean and north toward the Germanic kingdoms.

The Carolingians, after overthrowing the Merovingians, came closest to imposing on Europe an effective new order. The very idea of Europe as a territorial, cultural, and political whole took on its first rough form under Charlemagne and his court; and when Charlemagne became the Roman emperor in 800, he and the pope with their German-Christian alliance achieved a new vision of what the West might be.

The real genius of Charlemagne's reign lay in territorial conquest, the conversion of conquered peoples, and the educational and ecclesiastical reformation of Europe. Though his heirs would squander his hard-won stabilization of Europe and the empire would be lost, the Carolingian age proved to be a turning point in the fortunes of Europe, particularly its religious renewal, material prosperity, and intellectual drive. A working synthesis of the three main elements of the Early Middle Ages—Roman civilization, Christianity, and the Germans—was achieved in the Carolingian Empire.

The mid-ninth century, however, saw the breakdown of central authority, and Vikings began to harass the shores and riverways of Europe. By 900, disorder once again became the prevailing condition of European political and social life. Although it seemed on the surface that little had changed in four hundred years, almost everything had changed inside. An ancient way of viewing and acting in the world was gone and a medieval way had taken its place.

The Making of a New Western World

The first agents of the transformation and stabilization of the west were religious, and monks led the way. The *Rule of Saint Benedict* was a response and antidote to the disorder of the Early Middle Ages. High churchmen, particularly powerful, saint-loving bishops, mediated between various quarreling powers, while the popes of Rome, particularly Gregory the Great, attempted to set their own house in order; and the cult of the saints and their relics came to occupy a central place in popular religion.

> Why and how did religion play such a large role in the restructuring of western Europe after the decline of central Roman authority?

Monasticism Makes a Difference

Monasticism had its Christian beginnings in Egypt and Syria, but there hermits, desert fathers, and pole-sitters practiced forms of extreme denial of the world that relegated monasticism to the fringes of late Roman society. Early medieval monasticism in the west was a richly varied experiment in spiritual living and came in many forms, all of them committed to lasting as long as this world did and to finding ways to endure. Even the rugged monks of Ireland and northern England, who pursued solitary lives on isolated rocks washed by the cold waters of the north Atlantic, fashioned rules for living. Across

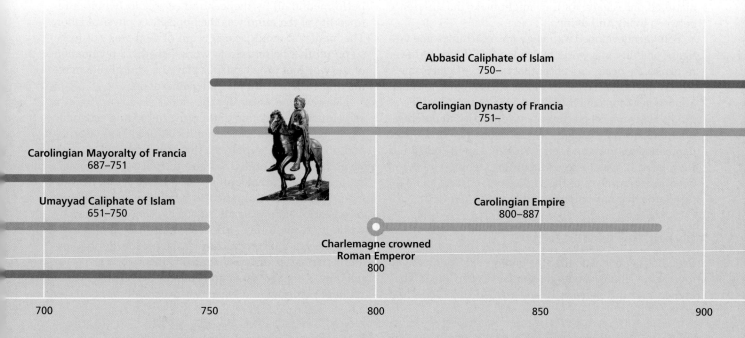

Abbasid Caliphate of Islam
750–

Carolingian Dynasty of Francia
751–

Carolingian Mayoralty of Francia
687–751

Umayyad Caliphate of Islam
651–750

Carolingian Empire
800–887

Charlemagne crowned
Roman Emperor
800

700   750   800   850   900

Europe, monks set out to save the world and themselves by dedicating themselves to God and to prayer, but they differed about how best to live a solitary, prayerful life.

In the midst of these many monasticisms, Benedict of Nursia (c. 480–543) supplied what became the normative form of monasticism for the western Middle Ages. When he was fourteen, Benedict renounced the world and set out to become a hermit. Although Theoderic and the Ostrogoths had temporarily reclaimed some political peace for Italy, Benedict's homeland, ravaged by war and economic collapse, was decentralizing rapidly. The population was in free fall and people were abandoning established cities in favor of hilltop settlements. Their world was shockingly poor and exposed.

Benedict settled in a cave south of Rome and there, alone, set out to test his devotion to God against the elements and the snares of the devil. It was a difficult life, both physically and emotionally. Benedict was a Roman with one foot already planted firmly in a Middle Ages of fragmented economic and political conditions and an overriding religious purpose. When the thought of a beautiful woman popped into his head, he hurled himself naked into a thicket of nettles and thorns to extinguish an interior fire with the blood of self-inflicted exterior pain.

As his reputation for extraordinary renunciation spread, Benedict attracted others seeking to abandon a wicked and distracting world. To them Benedict and his manner of life seemed the cure for what ailed the world. Benedict had powers that matched the needs of his disfigured society. In an age of material want and gnawing poverty, he was gifted at miraculously fixing things that to us would seem hardly worth the bother. He mended broken pots, located lost keys, dredged up iron tool heads from deep lakes, and moved huge boulders by prayer. His powers may have been heavenly, but they were applied to earthly ends, for Benedict and his monks lived not in golden imperial Rome, but in an Italy that had returned to a mostly metal-less age. The simplest things mattered once again, for they might make the difference between living and dying.

Benedict developed a strategy for returning some vestige of stability to a world that wondered if it would ever return to the peace and order that had once been Rome's. By 528, Benedict moved to Monte Cassino and founded a monastery for which (around 535) he wrote a *Rule* or guide. He emphasized constancy, regularity, and dedication to God over extreme forms of asceticism on the one hand and looseness and self-indulgence on the other. His *Rule*, he said, was to be a school for beginners to begin devoting themselves to the service of God, and so he set standards that most monks could satisfy.

Living the Monastic Life

Benedictine monastic life was communal. Monks lived together in a house under the guidance of an abbot. They owned nothing personally and turned their lives and bodies over to God. The monk's chief virtue was humility. He kept his hooded head down, not even looking other monks in the eye; and he dedicated himself to a regular round of daily prayer, chanting the Psalms during the seven holy services of each day. Monks swore obedience to their abbot, for they were spiritual brothers and the abbot was their father. The officials of the monastery included a porter or door-keeper, a sacristan or treasurer, a cellarer who kept the stores of food and wine, and later a prior who served as the abbot's chief assistant in administering the monastery. Hierarchy among the monks (indicated by the order in which they processed into church) was determined by the date on which each of them had entered the monastic life. Seniority of membership reinforced the idea that monasticism was a work of endurance, lasting until one was spiritually reborn in Christ at the moment of physical death.

A portion of the *Rule* was read out daily at mealtime, and for much of the day Benedictine monks observed a rule of silence; idle chatter would distract them from their steadfast devotion to God. So paramount was silence and attention to the holy words being read by one of the brothers that the Benedictines developed a set of hand-signs for communicating at the supper table in the refectory. To ask a brother for the plate of fish, the monk signed the fluttering motion of a fish's tail. Monks did speak at communal meetings called by the abbot to decide matters of importance to the monastery, but once the abbot had received their advice, his decisions were binding.

The divine work of the monk was the daily round of prayer, but manual labor was considered necessary and beneficial. Early medieval monks plowed fields, planted and reaped crops, built buildings, and made manuscripts. Benedict believed that idleness was an enemy of the soul and that physical labor was its remedy and a good thing in itself. In the ancient world, few had thought of manual labor as positive. It was servile, something done under compulsion by slaves and the working classes, and not performed at all by the leisured classes for whom a refined life of the mind was the opposite of physical labor. The medieval monk as a servant of God was not to be so proud that he refused to work. Benedict's revaluation of the worth of physical labor played a critical role in remaking ancient attitudes into medieval ones.

Labor was necessary for the monastery to survive as a self-sufficient economic unit. In the imploding economic world of the sixth and seventh centuries, monasteries had, in theory, to supply all that they required for survival. Labor was organized and purposive; the storage, rationing, and provisioning of food and drink, heating materials, and clothing had to be planned. Benedictine monasteries became small islands of economic efficiency while the work-a-day societies outside the monastery's walls knew a more haphazard economic life. By their example, monasteries demonstrated to their world the value not only of manual labor and collective enterprise, but of rational planning and expenditure as well. Monasteries became economic exemplars for surrounding communities. Despite being self-contained economic units, monasteries needed commodities such as salt and wine that they often could not supply from their own lands. They did not always acquire these on the open market, but through trade with other monasteries. Over time, monasteries acquired (generally as gifts) extensive properties, often geographically dispersed, from which they received income and resources. Monastic isolation from the world may have been a spiritual goal but was never economically or socially achievable. Important monasteries attracted the poor and the sick, who would gather at their gates in the hope of receiving charity, food, and miraculous cures.

Monasticism was the first great success story of the Early Middle Ages in the west—over three hundred new monasteries were founded in Francia (Frankish lands) alone in the seventh century—but its triumph was one of extreme localization, each monastery being a well-ordered and self-sufficient local organization. Not just the early medieval economy, but also learning benefited from the spread of monasticism. The emphasis in Benedict's *Rule* on daily reading and chanting meant that each monastery needed to train monks to read and write Latin and to supply them with books and scribal training. To learn Latin, particularly in northern Europe, monks used grammar books that were filled with classical citations as examples of good Latin, even though monks felt guilty about reading profane poetry and prose.

Early medieval monks copied their books on parchment (made from the skin of animals), a more durable surface than either the papyrus rolls of antiquity or modern paper. They chiefly reproduced the Bible and holy books, but they also made copies of the works of pagan antiquity. Without that copying, many of those texts (often written on perishable papyrus rolls) would have been lost. Benedictine monasticism institutionalized reading, writing, and the copying of books in a world that had lost much of its educational footing. To be learned or lettered in the Early Middle Ages became synonymous with being a monk.

The Benedictine monk was supposed to pray for four hours a day, to read for four hours a day, and to perform manual labor for five to six hours a day. This reading culture and the education of monks in Latin was one reason ancient culture and learning survived in the Middle Ages. It meant that the Middle Ages did not begin from scratch, but with a formal language of learning, books both religious and classical, and an educational anchor. That meant much to the survival and character of western civilization.

Gregory the Great and the Papacy

The early medieval papacy, at least prior to 750, was not the powerful institution that it would later become. With the breakdown of Roman order and the impoverishment of Italy, the pope in Rome was hardly more powerful

Gregory the Great and His Scribes The Holy Spirit, in the form of a dove, whispers divine words into the ear of Pope Gregory, who records the holy message and feeds off the divine inspiration. Below him, three monastic scribes copy down the saint's dictation. A ninth-century ivory book cover.

than most other metropolitan bishops. The Lombards, a Germanic people originally from Pannonia, moved into northern Italy in the late sixth century and waged war against the eastern Roman outposts of Justinian's reconquest. The Italian peoples were not particularly fond of the eastern imperial presence, which taxed heavily and held a set of eastern theological beliefs (on such things as the nature of Christ) that were at odds with the theology of the Roman church.

The Lombards, like other German tribes, entered Italy as Arian Christians, but in 680 they became orthodox Christians, a conversion that still did not lead the papacy to accept their presence in Italy. The popes claimed territory throughout Italy and so were often in conflict with the Lombard kings and their nobles, who controlled territories both north and south of Rome. The long-term policy of the papacy was to try to dislodge the Lombards from Italy. With its territorial problems, doctrinal conflicts with the eastern church, and local power struggles with powerful noble families in Rome, the papacy remained as fragile as Italy was.

Pope Gregory the Great (590–604), the most dynamic and influential of early medieval popes, straddled several worlds. He was a propertied Roman aristocrat, one of whose ancestors had been pope. In his mid-thirties, when he was both a senator and the prefect of the city, he defended Rome against a Lombard assault. After that he abandoned the secular world to become a monk and founded a series of monasteries. He was soon recruited by the pope to serve as an emissary to the court of the Roman emperor. For six years he resided in Constantinople, accomplishing little, before returning to Rome and his monastic career. Gregory was elected pope in 590. His concerns and powers were chiefly those of a late Roman aristocrat. He used his own wealth to pay for the army that defended the city, and he bought the food that sustained the refugees and poor dribbling into Rome. His power over the various kings and peoples of Europe was almost nonexistent, and the distant eastern emperor was of little help in defending or provisioning the west.

Gregory was an effective aristocrat and bishop of his immediate lands and people, but he also labored to make the papacy a moral force in the west, emphasizing humility and charity as papal ideals. He actively promoted monasticism, even supplying an account in his *Dialogues* of the life of Saint Benedict. He also wrote a *Pastoral Rule* that detailed how bishops should tend their flocks. His pen (as much as his service as pope) worked to shape the Early Middle Ages. He was an avid protector of papal property, striving to preserve Rome's claim to central Italy as a papal kingdom called the Patrimony of Saint Peter. He tried with limited success to exercise power over western bishops, but though they might defer to him on general and spiritual issues, they resisted his intervention in their local affairs.

Like other great administrators, Gregory seized on new opportunities when he saw them. He placed the papacy at the head of the continuing conversion of Europe. One day in the marketplace of Rome he saw some blond-haired boys being sold as slaves. On discovering that they were from Britain, he organized a mission to the island led by one of his own monks, Augustine (not the famous writer and northern African bishop), who knew little about England, including its languages. Augustine established his Roman mission at Canterbury and set about slowly Christianizing Britain.

Augustine of Canterbury took his orders from Rome. Pope Gregory ordered the division of England into two chief provinces with one metropolitan bishop in Canterbury and the other in the north at York. Each metropolitan bishop was to receive his appointment and authority in the form of the *pallium* (a mantle of white wool) directly from the pope. By the pope's authority, each metropolitan bishop consecrated twelve ordinary bishops. Thus, unlike the disorganized episcopal arrangements of continental Europe, the tighter ecclesiastical organization of England under Gregory the Great hints at a plan for organizing the church under tighter papal supervision.

Bishops as the Great Mediators

Bishops, rather than popes, were the essential ecclesiastical actors of the Early Middle Ages, mediating between the powerful, the church, and ordinary people. Given the intense localization of early medieval life, it could hardly have been otherwise. There were no capital cities, no centralized governments, and no effective means of quick and reliable communication. As Roman imperial government first shriveled and then disappeared from much of the west, bishops stepped in to act as the chief administrators of the shrinking and insecure cities of Europe. The extreme localization of life enhanced the power and standing of bishops.

One example is Gregory of Tours, who became the bishop of Tours in 573. Like most early medieval bishops, he was born into a rich, landed, aristocratic family. Thirteen previous bishops of Tours belonged to his family; only five did not. Episcopal dynasties were common in the west, but, although they worked to stabilize older aristocratic power, they threatened the independence of the church by placing it under the control of family monopolies.

A bishop's appointment was for life. Whereas the local count with whom he shared authority over a region might be replaced or transferred to another area, the bishop stayed put. The count's interests were those of the king and his own family, particularly the desire to profit from the land. The bishop had a higher, Christian calling as well as the duty of a late Roman patron to dispense charity and grant jobs and promotions. He was the center of what remained of the urban traditions of the west; his church organized religious festivals and so governed the rhythms of local life.

Gregory of Tours promoted justice and peace within his **diocese** (the area of the bishop's jurisdiction) and city. When two men in Tours were engaged in a blood feud, it was Gregory who gave one of the men the money needed to end the dispute. The interests of the Merovingian count, who was the official arbiter of justice, were largely mercenary and private; he would not have paid a thin denarius to settle a private dispute. What remained of any higher notion of the public good came to rest with the bishop, not the king or his count. The bishop and not the count looked after public works (the repair of cities and civic improvement projects). The count lived outside the city in a great villa and had little interest in maintaining a city if it cost him.

Gregory of Tours sought to be a good bishop. He oversaw the rebuilding of churches, including the cathedral of Tours, which had burned down before he took office. He tended to his flock as best he could, but when disease struck in 580, killing many children in his diocese, he confessed that he could do little more than weep. One wonders if the local count did even that. As bishop,

Gregory visited the various monasteries of his diocese and investigated their way of life and faith. He also acted on behalf of the church in Gaul. When a nun at the monastery of Saint Radegund in Poitiers planned, with a motley crew of cutthroats and fornicators (Bishop Gregory's characterization of them), to murder the abbess and assume her position, Gregory intervened to restore peace and order. He also carefully supervised the vast properties of his church and their hundreds of workers.

Gregory of Tours also resisted heresy, writing powerfully against Arians and other dissenters. Like Pope Gregory the Great, Gregory of Tours influenced the Middle Ages chiefly through his many writings, the most famous being the *History of the Franks,* which laid out the history of Merovingian Gaul during its first century. As the most learned men in Gaul, Gallo-Roman bishops served as advisors to the king and local nobles. Bishops bridged the divide between the German rulers of the land and the Gallo-Roman people, running interference between them, counseling the king on justice, and urging the Franks to live Christian lives.

The Saints Come Marching In

The role of Gregory of Tours and his fellow bishops as the keepers of the saints meant something to King Clovis and his quarrelsome clan. One indication of that royal respect is that kings and counts honored the right of sanctuary. No matter the crime, if men and women made their way to a church and were granted sanctuary, they were generally safe from forcible removal by secular authorities. In keeping with their relatively primitive conception of Christianity and their recognition of the necessity of the church and its bishops, Merovingian rulers were reluctant to anger the saints whose remains rested in churches. As an avid promoter of the saints, Gregory of Tours wrote several books about their lives and miracles. He and his fellow bishops promoted the cult of the saints because they saw the saints as a way to harness the energy of their people and to humble arrogant and aggressive rulers.

To understand the early medieval mind and the power of religion, we need to appreciate how important and alive the saints were to the Early Middle Ages. Saints (from the Latin *sancti,* "holy ones") and saintliness do not have the particular institutional presence and character in the Bible that they assumed in the Middle Ages. In a world of untreatable disease, looming starvation, greedy German nobles who were a law unto themselves, and lawlessness in the countryside of Europe, men and women wanted someone, anyone, to look out for them. Saints seemed to offer supernatural protection, a power of first and last resort for the anxious and suffering. In the Early Middle Ages, saintly status was conferred not by a papal commission, but by the general consensus of a community. If enough people thought that Christopher was a saint and were devoted to him, then Christopher was a saint, no matter that he was reputed to have been either a giant or a dog-headed man. Such cults were promoted by institutions and influential people for whom the saint was a celebrated wonder-worker.

Medieval Christians believed that the saints had risen into heaven to stand beside Christ, where they received prayers from the faithful and interceded on their behalf with God. Since the saints had done holy works and the martyrs had died for Christ, they had built up a repository of holy credits to draw on in heaven. People in Gregory of Tours's time thought of Christ as omnipotent, too distant and austere for the average person to reach directly. They did not yet think of his mother, the Virgin Mary, as a great intercessory figure, so the saint was a closer, more approachable, and more persuasive advocate for their needs. The power to intercede in the world was Christ's, but the saint had his ear.

The cult of the saints and their **relics** did not arise spontaneously. It was a belief cultivated and channeled by bishops. Ambrose, the bishop of Milan (374–397), was one of the first to promote the cult of the saints' relics. Relics are the remains left behind by the saints, generally their bones, but also objects such as clothes and books with which they had come into contact. Although Jesus, according to the Gospels, had wholly risen to heaven at the Ascension, the things he had touched such as the

The Remains of the Saints The skeleton of Saint Ambrose—with those of Saints Gervasius and Protasius flanking his—are on display in his cathedral in Milan. The architect of the cult of relics thus became a revered relic himself.

cross of the crucifixion were considered contact relics. In 386, Ambrose discovered the remains of the saints Gervasius and Protasius and duly installed them in his church in Milan, where they still rest. Later he sent relics to bishops in the north so that they might dedicate their churches to the saints; altars were consecrated with relics of the saints.

The cult of the saints and their relics emerged after the legalization of Christianity and the Christianization of the empire. Without the ideology of martyrdom, which had sustained the church during periods of persecution, the Christian faith, particularly in the west, seemed less purpose driven, the claims of holiness less obvious. The church promoted the saints as athletes of God and the west's new heroes, but the sanctity of living humans was difficult to determine. In an age of cooling faith, Bishop Ambrose found another way to refresh the passion of the faithful. By enshrining the remains of saints in his church, he localized and renewed holiness. People from near and far knew where they could find the divine and they could witness holiness in action.

Ambrose and the churchmen were convinced that the saints had not really died, but had been reborn in heaven. The saints were thought to be entirely present and powerful in their earthly remains, no matter how small the fragment. Thus early medieval men and women thought of dead saints as still alive and active in the world. The saints could, through their appeals to Christ, bring about the healing of the sick, the exorcism of the possessed, and the granting of grace to the remorseful. The miracles brought about through the saints were small signs for them that the miracle of Christ's resurrection was still at work in the world.

Promoting the cult of the saints and their relics gave bishops not just symbolic, but real power. By managing the cult, Ambrose, Gregory of Tours, and other bishops were able to bring the scattered holiness of the saints inside their cathedrals where they could present, guard, and direct it. The Merovingian kings knew where Saint Martin was; he was in Tours, and Bishop Gregory served as the intercessor to a saint who could intercede with God. Cathedrals that enshrined famous saints reaped financial gains from the pilgrims who sought out the saints, but profit may not have been the primary motive for promoting the cult of the saints. Rather, the bishops' goal was to bring a source of tangible divine power under their immediate control to enhance their own prestige and that of their cathedrals. Bishops were not always saintly men themselves. Gregory of Tours said that one of his predecessors had drunk himself into a state of dementia and death. Personal holiness was too great an aspiration for living men, even the two Gregories, pope and bishop, who managed properties and granted and sought earthly favors. It was much better for them to stand next to the holy, to offer themselves as the guardians and earthly representatives of the saints, than to claim saintliness for themselves.

In the fragmented and localized west, the cult of the saints, like monasticism and the power of bishops, was another indication of how the west was remaking itself institutionally and intellectually in the Early Middle Ages.

Power at the Start of the Middle Ages

Germanic kingship was very different from Roman imperial government. Built on different assumptions and actions, Germanic kingship met the needs of its time, supplying a simplified world with a simple form of military might and local power. Events in the Middle East, however, directly and indirectly transformed the lands and legacy of the Roman Empire. The rapid religious and territorial rise of Islam in the seventh century pushed the Roman Empire to become a Byzantine Empire in the east and fully medieval in the west, determining what those two parts of the old Roman Empire could be and could no longer be. By its territorial, cultural, and religious impact, Islam shaped the contours of the Middle Ages.

How did the organization and exercise of power differ in western Europe, the eastern Roman Empire, and Islam in the Early Middle Ages?

Germanic Kingship: Long Hair and the Privatization of Power

With the withering of Roman imperial power in the west, notions of the public good and public citizenship disappeared from the administration and countryside of Europe. In the ancient world, men and women had lived in a world of public streets, public baths, public games, and temples that opened onto public squares. As cities shrank in the fifth and sixth centuries, private villas and rural conditions reclaimed the medieval west. As the public person disappeared, so too did sophisticated notions of a state government operating with a senate, a bureaucracy, and a standing army; indeed, the state as such ceased to exist in the west.

The disappearance of the state did not mean that the Franks ruled without operating principles. Those principles just were no longer based on Roman law or the good of the people and Roman elite as they once had been. Every age may get not only the government that it deserves, but also the one that it needs under the prevailing conditions that it faces. In this case, that government had a mobile, not fixed, base of power commanded by a dominant source of authority, the most accomplished leader available, whose chief interest was in self-preservation and the control of whatever force he could assemble. Germanic kingship fulfilled the need for a specific form of control in the disordered fifth and sixth centuries.

The fundamental source of all authority was the king (*rex*), the chief who most successfully commanded a warband of men by winning its obedience through the careful exercise of brute force and timely reward. Around

500, the title of king carried fewer ideas of blood inheritance and divine sanction than it would later, connoting instead the successful general of an army. To maintain his dominance, the king needed to carry out successful military campaigns, seize territory, and distribute lands and wealth to his men. The members of a war-band were not interested in the public good or responsible government, but rather in the private interests of themselves and their families. Such self-interest may sound like a recipe for disaster, but instead it produced the most successful and realistic form of rule possible. The Germanic war-band was a dynamic, though unstable, unit driven to succeed in the subjugation of lands and peoples.

Early medieval Germanic kings were itinerant; they moved within their kingdoms and set up many palaces. Their mobility was not just a continuation of the older restless wanderings of the Germanic tribes, but a necessity in an age in which no single villa could long support the king and his retinue. The king's retinue would soon exhaust the resources of a place if it stayed too long. The essence of the palace was not a building but its resident king. Merovingian government was palace government, and its officials took titles that originally derived from their domestic functions in that palace operation: butlers, cup-bearers, stewards, constables, and grooms.

Germanic kings might hold kingdoms, but they had only a weak idea of a territorially defined kingdom with fixed borders. The king was more truly the king of a people than of a land. The Merovingian king was *rex Francorum*, the king of the Franks, not the king of Francia. These kings and their nobles thought of their property, both fixed (land) and movable (gold and wealth), as divisible among their heirs. When a king died, his kingdom was divided equally among his heirs. Armed conflict and assassinations often followed, leading Gallo-Romans to associate disorder and violence with their Frankish kings. Gregory of Tours did not understand that these wars were dynamic tests of merit that ensured that the strongest, cleverest, and most violent rulers rose to the top and imposed their will on the Frankish nobles and kingdom.

An example of the different cultural world of the Germans is the matter of their hair. Gregory of Tours says that when the Franks occupied Francia, they set up long-haired kings in every *civitas* (a district having a major city). Both male and female Germans prided themselves on keeping their hair long as a sign of their free status and ethnicity. Slaves were shorn and Roman free males generally kept their hair short. What was typical for the average free-born Frank was extreme in the case of their kings and members of the royal line. Scissors never touched their hair from the time of birth. When a king was overthrown, his hair was cut to humiliate him and to signal his reduced status. Gregory of Tours tells the heartrending story of two Merovingian kings who wished to remove two nephews from any chance of succeeding to power. The uncles sent a messenger to their own mother, the boys' grandmother and guardian. In one hand the agent carried a pair of scissors, in the other

a sword. The grandmother was forced to choose between having her grandchildren shorn or killed; she chose death for them since she preferred to see them dead rather than denied the chance to rule as kings. Such was the world of Frankish kingship, which Gregory of Tours, with his Gallo-Roman values and Roman sense of justice, could not completely comprehend.

Living and Dying the Merovingian Way

The Franks comprised a relatively small portion of the total population of Gaul, perhaps as many as 200,000 people in the midst of a Gallo-Roman population of about seven million. Noble Franks were buried with rich treasures of grave goods: belt buckles, purses, daggers, and jeweled swords. These burial plots were organized according to kin groups. The early Franks practiced polygyny (one man, several wives). Merovingian lords sought to exercise a monopoly over the available wombs, for this was a world in which, no matter how rich and powerful one was, wives frequently died in childbirth and few infants lived to adulthood. Infant mortality hovered around 50 to 60 percent.

The economy of early medieval Francia was almost exclusively agricultural. Farmers grew grain crops such as barley and raised domestic animals. Most tools were made of wood, as were most buildings. Artisans made luxury goods for the Frankish and Gallo-Roman elites, but there were few other markets for precious goods.

Frankish Ornament A jewel-encrusted Frankish brooch or clasp found in the tomb of a Merovingian woman who died in the mid-sixth century. The combination of animal imagery, rich decoration, gold, and cloisonné (poured enamel) was typical of Frankish ornament.

Some long-distance trade in bulk items such as slaves, salt, and spices still took place, and some prosperity did exist. Gregory of Tours reports that the merchants of Verdun were able to stand behind a loan of seven thousand gold pieces made by the Frankish king to their bishop.

Early medieval Francia was dominated by villages that were little more than a series of thatched huts marked off from the outside world by walls and hedge fences. The houses in these villages were small (6 × 6–12 feet), with approximately 50–60 square feet of floor space, but people were also relatively small, the average height for both sexes being around five feet.

Merovingian Power at the Political Turn

When Clovis died in 511, his four sons almost immediately began trying to kill one another. One of them, Theuderic, invited his brother Clothar to a meeting in order to assassinate him, but Clothar spotted the feet of assassins below a curtain and fled. Another of the sons died while fighting the Burgundians, who mounted his head on a pole. By 558, Clothar had by luck and design outlived his brothers and reunited the kingdom. King Clothar was ambitious, invading parts of Germany, but he died three years later. The kingdom was then divided between his four sons and the wars began again. Over the long run, these wars of succession shifted power to the nobles on whom the kings increasingly relied for support.

By the early seventh century, the strongest men in the land, Bishop Arnulf of Metz and Pepin of Landen, the mayor (or chief official) of the Merovingian palace (or government) of Austrasia (the eastern kingdom), became the founders of the Carolingian line. The marriage of their children joined their two lines. Arnulf and Pepin placed the Merovingian Clothar II (r. 613–629) on the throne. Thus, Clothar II and his son Dagobert (r. 629–639) were made kings by two nobles of the Carolingian house of Ripuarian (or Rhineland) Franks. Clothar and Dagobert were the last Merovingian kings to hold real power, and yet even they were already the creatures of their nobles. The year 613, thus, marked the great turn of the Merovingian house from independence and autonomy toward dependent status; the balance of power had swung in favor of their powerful nobles.

The case of Dagobert is revealing. Mocked in a French nursery rhyme as a feeble king who couldn't put on his own pants and was afraid of rabbits, he was, in fact, a warrior king, but his power and success were limited. He lost an important battle to the Slavs in 631 whereupon, with his nobles in Austrasia in revolt, he ceded effective control of the region to his mayor, Pepin of Landen. But though Dagobert was a less than dominant ruler of Francia, he was a better Christian than most of his predecessors. He was pious, heeded his bishops, and established the great royal monastery of St. Denis outside Paris, where he was buried in 639.

With the mayors of the palace, particularly the Pippinids or Arnulfings (both early names for the line that became the Carolingians), on the rise and Merovingian royal power in decline, the fate of Clovis's line was not promising by the mid-seventh century. At that very moment in the Middle East, a movement was stirring that would dramatically affect the shape and conditions of the Early Middle Ages east and west.

Islam Ascendant

In 610 a forty-year-old merchant of Mecca in Arabia began to receive messages from God, which the archangel Gabriel commanded him to recite in the name of God. Muhammad did not claim to be divine, but rather understood himself to be a prophet or messenger like Moses. Although Muhammad respected both Christians and Jews as peoples who knew God and had a great book of revealed (or divine) truth, he rejected the Christian conviction that Jesus was the son of God and thought that the Jews had forsaken God's message. A community (*Ummah*) of believers, the people of God, took shape around Muhammad and submitted itself to the will of

CHRONOLOGY	The Rise and Spread of Islam
DATE	**EVENT**
570	Birth of Muhammad in Mecca
622	Hejira
632	Death of Muhammad in Medina
632–634	Caliph Abu Bakr
634–644	Caliph Umar
636	Islam conquers Syria
638	Jerusalem conquered
641–642	Egypt conquered
644–656	Caliph Uthman
651	Persia conquered
656–661	Caliph Ali, son-in-law of the prophet
661–750	Umayyad Caliphate rules from Damascus
698	Carthage conquered
712	Samarkand and Sogdiana conquered
711–720	Most of Spain conquered
750–1258	Abbasid Caliphate rules from Baghdad

MAP 7.1 | Spread of Islam to 750

Within two centuries after Muhammad's death in 632, Islam had conquered the Near East, lands along the southern Mediterranean Sea, and parts of Asia. *What did the expansion of Islam mean for lands previously part of the Roman Empire? Why were the Byzantine Empire and Spain the doorways for Islam into continental Europe? What impact did the territorial dominance of the Mediterranean by Muslims have on the western economy? How might Islam have provided a critical link for the flow of goods east and west?*

God. The word *Islam* means submission to the will of God, and a *Muslim* is one who has submitted to the will of God.

For twelve years, Muhammad preached with limited success to the people of Mecca. Their paganism and stubbornness made Muhammad's revelations a tough sell in the dusty streets of the old city. In 622 Muhammad fled to Medina, an event called the **Hejira** that marks the beginning of Islamic chronology. Muhammad's messages from God were collected and written down in Arabic in the Qur'an (Koran) within twenty years after Muhammad's death in 632. Other testimonies and narratives about the prophet Muhammad, his life and sayings (called *hadiths*), that survive outside the Qur'an have been sifted for their trustworthiness and importance.

The basic teachings of Islam as found in the Qur'an are straightforward. The Five Pillars of Islam are as follows: (1) there is only one God and his name is Allah and he must be obeyed; (2) Muslims are obliged to pray five times a days (facing Mecca); (3) give charity; (4) fast during daylight hours of the (lunar) month of Ramadan each year; and (5) undergo a pilgrimage (*Hajj*) to Mecca once in a lifetime. Islam has implications for the state since it teaches that there is only one society under the will of God (theoc-

racy, or rule by God, is the result), and it follows a code of sacred law (*shari'ah*) determined by legal scholars based on the Qur'an, the traditions of Muhammad, community standards, and precedents. Thus, whereas Christian religious thought turned chiefly to matters of theology, Islamic thought would center primarily on God's law.

Islam's rapid spread shook the Middle East and the Mediterranean world (Map 7.1). By the time of Muhammad's death, Muslims dominated much of the Arabian Peninsula. The message of Islam overrode traditional tribal customs, directing not just the spiritual lives of Muslims, but most aspects of their interior and exterior lives. Tribal culture had been shame culture in which public honor and public shame were the chief elements of social reward and control. Islam subordinated human activity instead to God's judgment or law and the promise of rewards or punishment in the afterlife. In the shift from one to the other, Islam united diverse Arabian peoples under a common cause and shared set of beliefs. The Qur'an, as a book of law and rules, mediated cultural differences and divisions. Of the Qur'an's 114 suras (or individual chapters, organized from longest to shortest), some speak of the holy war (**jihad**) that Muhammad eventually led against the unbelievers, but jihad can also refer to an individual's personal calling to conform to God's will.

By uniting the Arabs and many of the Bedouin tribes of Arabia against the unbelievers inside the Arabian Peninsula and then against unbelievers outside, Muhammad not only spread the faith but pacified Arabia. After Muhammad's death, the first target of expansionary Islam was Syria, which was overrun in 636, when a Roman force was defeated at the Battle of Yarmouk. Jerusalem fell in 638; and most of Egypt, by 641. By 651, Persia was conquered; and northern Africa, all the way to Carthage, was taken by 698. Samarkand and Sogdiana had fallen by 712; and most of Spain, by 720. Thus, within a century of Muhammad's death, the southern part of the Mediterranean rim was in Muslim hands, and Islam had spread east into Asia and west into Europe. The big Europe of the old Roman Empire was shrinking fast.

Just as surprising as the relatively rapid spread of Islam was the permanence of the change to the western world. New military movements and the mobilization of peoples may help explain the success of the conquests, but it was the nature of Islam that fixed these lands firmly under Muslim control. The decadent old Roman cultures of northern Africa and the eastern Mediterranean quickly abandoned their older histories and beliefs. Many peoples long suppressed by the Roman Empire may have felt that the change was an improvement. Islam was tolerant of the other peoples of the book. Christians and Jews could continue to practice their own faith and retain their property. What Christians could not do was to convert Muslims, speak ill of Islam, or display the Christian cross. The effect of these regulations was to render churches such as the Christian church in Egypt (the Coptic Church) respected, but prevented from expanding. Non-Muslims had to accept an inferior or marginal status within Islam and pay tribute in place of the military service that Muslims rendered. Conversion to Islam offered some financial and social advantages to Christians and Jews, as well as the chance to assume public offices otherwise denied to them.

Not all went smoothly for Islam, however, since neither the Qur'an nor Muhammad had specified who should succeed him. Three rival factions emerged: those who wanted Ali, Muhammad's son-in-law and cousin, to assume control; the merchants of Mecca, who longed to see one of their number named; and Muhammad's early converts, who had supported him in Mecca and marched with him on Medina, and had their own candidate, Abu Bakr. The last group prevailed, and so for two years Abu Bakr (r. 632–634), called the caliph (successor), was the leader of Islam, and was succeeded by three other Rashidun ("rightly guided caliphs"), the companions of the prophet: Umar (r. 634–644), Uthman (r. 644–656), and Ali (r. 656–661).

Uthman's murder and disputed succession produced a schism within Islam that still endures. Although Ali was the revered son-in-law of the prophet, he was not supported by the whole Islamic community. A group known as the **Kharijites** withdrew their support from Ali and accused him of lacking an absolute trust in God's judgment.

The Great Mosque of Damascus Erected c. 700, the Great Mosque stands as a pinnacle of the cultural richness of Islam and the Umayyad Caliphate. In 750, the Abbasid Caliphate displaced the Umayyads and moved the capital of the Islamic world to Baghdad.

Theirs was an elitist view of Islam, in which only the purest and deeply committed believers should be counted within the Islamic community. As caliph, Ali labored under the charge of illegitimacy and was assassinated by a Kharijite follower in 661. For the Shi'a (or partisans of Ali), this was a dividing point in history. They maintain that Muhammad's authority flowed through Ali, the first imam (ruler), to his successor imams who possess divine inspiration and an inner or hidden knowledge of the Qur'an. They also believe that the twelfth or hidden imam, Muhammad al-Mahdi, did not die, but disappeared in 874 and is expected to return to render justice. Shi'as take the murder of Ali as a model of martyrdom and of the suffering that believers and rulers can expect in this life.

Shi'ism was and remains a prominent minority sect within Islam. The majority of Muslims are Sunnis who adhere to tradition (*sunnah*), and reject the elitism of the Kharijites and the exclusivity of descent followed by the Shi'as. Sunnis recognize the dominant caliphate tradition and tend to think of their rulers as human and temporal leaders with no particular divine connection, but who are supposed to act as defenders of the faith and caretakers of the law. Thus, Sunnis embrace the primacy of the Islamic community as a whole.

After Ali, the Umayyad Caliphate (661–750) moved the capital of the Islamic world from Medina to Damascus. The Umayyads were little interested in converting peoples within Islamic lands because the unconverted paid higher taxes. During this brilliant Arabic phase of Islamic culture, Muslims erected magnificent buildings in Damascus and Jerusalem.

MAP 7.2 | Byzantine Empire, 8th Century

By the eighth century, the Byzantine Empire was confined largely to southern Italy, Sicily, a scattering of lands in the eastern Mediterranean, and a large block of territory to the east of Constantinople. Those lands were divided into administrative units called themes. *What were the territorial strengths and weaknesses of the Byzantine Empire? Had the empire any room for expansion?*

The Eastern Roman Empire Becomes Byzantine

Seventy-five years after Justinian's death, Roman imperial fortunes were in eclipse. The Persians, Avars, and Muslims whittled away imperial territory. In the process, the eastern Roman Empire lost control of the Mediterranean, suffered a great military defeat to the Muslims, lost the rich lands of Syria and Egypt, and looked far across the Bosporus Straits to a world dominated by a new and dynamic religion with superior resources and manpower. The Romans resisted as best they could under the emperor Heraclius (r. 610–641), but he found that Constantinople had so neglected its provinces during its resistance to the Persians and Avars that few of its residents were willing to resist Muslim forces.

By the early eighth century, Muslim armies were attacking Asia Minor regularly, but failed to take Constantinople in 717–718. Following that successful resistance, the Roman east underwent a period of recovery and transformation. In effect, the eastern Roman Empire became what we think of as Byzantine because of the rise of Islam. The Byzantine identity was shaped and fixed by the events of the seventh and eighth centuries: it em-

braced a specific eastern orthodox form of Christianity, was thoroughly Greek with little Latin influence, and concentrated on Constantinople and the Greek northeast of the Mediterranean world without any realistic prospect of restoring the old Roman Empire (Map 7.2).

The emperor Leo III (r. 717–741) reorganized the empire so that it could defend itself against internal and external enemies. He taxed heavily, reorganized the army, and strengthened the walls of Constantinople. Leo also forced the Byzantines to rethink their religion. He was displeased by the importance that monasticism held in the Byzantine east and jealous of the tax privileges granted to its monasteries. He worked to bring the eastern church more firmly under his control, even overthrowing one patriarch of the eastern church.

During the difficult years of contraction, the Byzantine peoples had turned for reassurance to holy images, particularly of the Virgin Mary. Byzantine soldiers, to whom Leo looked for the defense of the empire, however, had their doubts. They suspected that they were so often defeated by their Muslim opponents because they worshipped graven images against God's law. The Byzantine peoples believed that the icon or image was a tangible connection to the divine, much as saints' relics functioned in the west. Leo, however, believed that the worship of icons diverted people from the true faith; he and his advisors knew that both the Old Testament and Islam spurned idols and graven images. In 726, Leo banned icons and declared that they should be destroyed. People revolted, and in the west the pope and a church council condemned the iconoclasts (image-breakers), excommunicating them. Yet Leo and his son, Constantine V (r. 740–745), persisted in their official policy of **iconoclasm.** Constantine persecuted the image worshippers with greater relish and more violence than his father had, but he was also a successful military leader, ordering regular attacks on the Muslims and conducting war against the Bulgarians and Slavs.

Byzantium survived its first great conflict with Islam, but the cost was great. With a reduced and still threatened territory, Byzantium was forced to militarize the state. Its official theological turn not only confounded the Byzantine peoples but drove a theological wedge between the east and west. Islam thus played a critical role in forcing Byzantium to redefine itself and forced the entire western world in directions it might not otherwise have gone.

The Iconoclasm Dispute The Byzantine Empire swung hard from official iconoclasm and the destruction of images to iconodulism or the veneration of images. In the ninth-century Chludov Psalter, an illustrator takes his revenge against the iconoclasts by mocking the crudity of the iconoclasts, one of whom is shown erasing a picture of Christ.

Carolingian House Building

The Carolingians went from being a successful Frankish family in the sixth century to the noble house that managed the Merovingian dynasty in the seventh and then pushed it aside in the mid-eighth century to set up its own royal dynasty. Fifty years later the Carolingians controlled an empire that dominated the medieval west. Their success and ultimate failure determined much of the territorial and cultural character of the Middle Ages: royal and Christian, papal and Germanic, learned and Latinate, multiregional and European.

How and why did the Carolingians replace the Merovingian royal line?

The Carolingian Mayors

Merovingian Gaul was divided into three rough areas: Austrasia (the east land of German speakers), Neustria (the new land of Vulgar or late Latin speakers), and Burgundy (stretching from Langres to the Mediterranean). Each area had its own mayor of the palace (*maior domo*) or chief executive officer acting on behalf of the king of that territory. In theory the difference between a king and his mayor was that the king possessed a legitimacy confirmed by his nobles or people and the mayor was a royal operative whose office derived its legitimacy from the king; in practice the question became who had effective power and could command the loyalty and service of the nobles of a kingdom. The mayors found that, as the Merovingian dynasty experienced periodic bouts of civil war, turmoil, and the reigns of young kings, their own importance as king-makers and power-brokers increased. Not only did the Merovingian kings need them more, but lesser nobles came to associate their own standing and privileges with the mayor rather than the king. Mayoral power grew in the late seventh and early eighth centuries under the so-called Do-Nothing (Merovingian) Kings of France whom historians once mocked as lazy, powerless, and nameless. The Merovingian royal condition may not have been fatal, but the Merovingian kings slowly lost power and property until little was left and their dynasty was overthrown.

The Carolingian family was nothing if not ambitious. Around 656 one of its mayors, Grimoald, tried to graft his own family onto the Merovingian family tree by banishing the rightful Merovingian prince and naming his own son as king. Other Frankish nobles rejected the rash move and put the mayor to death. Had Grimoald succeeded, the Merovingian line would have continued, but with a Carolingian intruder as the sitting Merovingian king. Grimoald's failure did not put a stop to the Carolingian rise. In 687, Pepin of Heristal defeated the non-Carolingian mayors of the other two palaces (of Neustria and Burgundy) and united the mayoralty, thus becoming the effective ruler of all Francia.

Henri Pirenne and His Thesis

If the recent past is difficult to unscramble, the distant past may seem at times largely unknowable. Whereas the historian studying modern history often has too many primary sources, the ancient and medieval historian frequently has too few. Professional historians are by nature cautious creatures, couching their statements about the past in "perhapses" and "maybes." They know all too well that a single new piece of evidence may lead to the radical revision of today's confident conclusions.

The last book of the Belgian historian Henri Pirenne makes a powerful case for direct speaking and bold thinking. Toward the end of a long life of careful, qualified scholarship on Belgian, urban, and medieval economic history, Pirenne laid down a daring new explanation for how the ancient world became the Middle Ages. He had just completed a draft of the book that became *Mohammed and Charlemagne* when he died. It was his habit, said his son, to write the first draft of a work just for himself; there he put down his ideas in their boldest form. It was that version of *Mohammed and Charlemagne* that his son and a former student, the medievalist F. Vercauteren, published in 1937.

The book put forward a daring thesis: that it was the rise of Islam that essentially made the medieval west. Pirenne observed that the effective loss of the Mediterranean Sea had brought an end to the ancient world, forcing western civilization northward and inland, and that Charlemagne with his northern capital in Aachen and his land-based empire was the end result. As Pirenne famously put it, "Charlemagne, without Mohammed, would be inconceivable." Pirenne's argument was based on economic evidence such as the lack of Byzantine coins in the west after 629 and the dramatic shift in the nature of European trade and settlement.

The beauty of Pirenne's thesis is its concision; its great weakness that the events and evidence it seeks to explain so simply are frustratingly complex. Almost from the day the book appeared, it aroused denial, qualification, and support from different quarters. Archaeologists such as Richard Hodges have wondered if the thesis actually fits the available evidence. Moreover, Michael McCormick, in his monumental *Origins of the European Economy: Communications and Commerce, AD 300–900* (2001), demonstrated that throughout the late Roman and early medieval periods both people and goods continued to travel east and west, south and north.

Still it is hard to deny Pirenne's essential observation that the Early Middle Ages moved away from the Mediterranean toward northern Europe or that the rise of Islam had irrevocably broken the hegemony of the classical world, whose ghost had lingered for so long and so grandly.

QUESTIONS | *How did the rise of Islam impact the West? Did it do so immediately or gradually? What are the advantages and disadvantages of making sweeping historical generalizations of the sort that Pirenne made in his last book?*

Pepin of Heristal's illegitimate son was Charles Martel, Charles "the Hammer" (d. 741), after whom the Carolingians (derived from *Carolus*) are named. With Charles Martel, the Carolingians entered on the road to kingship. He convened his own court of royal justice, issued decrees and laws, and assembled and led the royal army of nobles. He was as vigorous a warrior as his nickname suggests. In 732 (or 733) between Tours and Poitiers he stopped the forward advance into Francia of Muslims from Spain who were making their farthest northern incursion into Europe. That victory has probably been overrated as a turning point in European and Muslim fortunes since it coincided with changes in Spain and the Islamic world, but it did mark an end to Muslim expansion in the early medieval west. Charles Martel also led victorious campaigns into Bavaria and large parts of Germania, and made inroads into Saxony. He ruled with such confidence and relative autonomy that for a time he left the kingship vacant and ruled alone. Contemporaries called him a prince or petty king.

Pepin the Short Unmakes the Merovingian Line

When Charles Martel died in 741, Francia was divided between his two sons: Carloman became mayor of the palace of Austrasia; and Pepin the Short, mayor of the palace of Neustria. The division of Francia was now determined not by the heirs of the Merovingians, but by the interests of the Carolingian house. Although Charles Martel may not have needed a figurehead Merovingian ruler to buttress his power, his sons as fledgling mayors did, and so they elevated the obscure Merovingian Childeric III to be king (r. 743–751). Carloman and Pepin ruled in relative harmony, but in 747 Carloman retired to become a monk. Contemporaries claimed that his withdrawal was voluntary, but it was also convenient as it removed a key impediment to Pepin's drive to royal power.

But how could a new royal line be made or an old one unmade? Medieval theory maintained that God, not men, makes kings. As real Merovingian power and property were being stripped away by the mayors in the seventh century, the mayors had enhanced the religious prestige and divine standing of the Merovingian king as a way to enhance their own power as the representatives of royal authority. The title of king, which had held less real importance to the warrior Clovis, came to matter a great deal, and the long hair of the Merovingian kings took on an almost magical significance. The aura of the divine could be replaced only with another powerful set of royal symbols, this one more thoroughly Christian.

Why the Carolingians decided to take the final step of overthrowing and replacing a royal line with their own may not be a great mystery. Pepin took the final step because he could; he had the power and saw how it could be done. His father, Charles Martel, had shown him that the real ruler of Francia did not need a symbolic figurehead through whom to rule. Indeed, there was a certain danger in continuing to rule under a weak king since other nobles might seek to use the king or prop up a pretender as their own vehicle to power. To be king, rather than acting in the king's name, would bring Pepin additional protection and power, justifying his exercise of power and lifting his family above the other noble families of Francia with whom it had been competing. Kingship did not put an end to the struggle between the king and his nobles, but it gave the Carolingians a more direct way than the mayoralty to control the powerful nobles of Europe. It also gave them, if they managed it right, some protection against a dip in family fortunes.

The religious significance of the change was great. Kingship brought divine approval and divine protection. The church wanted more from its kings than the Merovingians had supplied. That the Carolingians had for so long been able to make and unmake kings suggested that they could unmake and make royal lines. By 751 a particular set of conditions and careful Carolingian engineering of the circumstances made it possible for Pepin the Short to justify overthrowing the old royal line. What chiefly distinguished the Carolingians from the Merovingians was their attitude toward the church and Christianity. As Clovis had outmaneuvered the other Germanic tribes by becoming an orthodox Christian, the Carolingians outmaneuvered the Merovingians by becoming better Christians. The education of Pepin's sons at St. Denis and Carloman's abandonment of the world for the monastery were examples of the Christian commitment of the Carolingians. Nor did the Carolingians assassinate each other, as the Merovingians had.

The piety and political interests of the Carolingians were not at odds, for they saw the advantages of Christianizing Europe. Charles Martel used the church in Francia, dispensed church offices, and treated church property as though it were his own. The Carolingians viewed the Christian church as a legitimate instrument of royal power. Believing that the kingdom should be uniformly Christian, they actively promoted missionary work inside the kingdom. With the sanction of the papacy, Carolingian rulers sponsored the English monk Boniface's mission to outlying areas of the kingdom. In the intersection of papal and Carolingian interests in converting northern Europe to Christianity, the Carolingian family and the papacy forged a supportive and codependent relationship.

Why did the papacy need the Carolingians? The papacy was still relatively weak and recognized that it needed a temporal protector. The popes hoped that with the right cultivation the distant Carolingians would thwart the Lombards and yet not directly threaten papal interests in Italy. Hence, the papacy and the Carolingians entered into an understanding about their complementary interests: kingship for the Carolingians, protection against its enemies for the papacy.

To overthrow the Merovingians, Pepin and his advisors moved on several fronts. Pepin reputedly sent the pope an official question: who should rule, the man who merely bore the name of king or the man who actually held the power? The pope answered in Pepin's favor. Yet the Merovingians were born royal; the Carolingians had to become royal. The Carolingians supplied what they lacked in royal blood by external sanction and signs: papal approval, public election, royal symbol, and religious rite.

In November 751 a Frankish assembly gathered at Soissons. Childeric III was deposed, his hair was shaved off, and he was confined to a monastery. In a parallel rite, Pepin was elected king by the Franks (that is, he was acclaimed by his nobles), anointed by Bishop Boniface, and raised to the throne by his nobles. Thus, with words and symbols the church and the Frankish aristocracy sanctioned Pepin's elevation. He was now king of the Franks. Clovis had not needed extraordinary signs and supports of divine and earthly approval; Pepin did. Pepin honored his commitment to the papacy when he crossed the Alps and attacked the Lombards in 755 and, with the **Donation of Pepin,** returned lands in central Italy to the pope's control. The new alliance freed the papacy from its nominal dependence on the Byzantine Empire for assistance and protection that it could no longer supply.

The overthrow and replacement of a royal line was a delicate moment in the early medieval west. Around 757 a papal cleric in Rome produced a document known as the Donation of Constantine, in which the emperor Constantine granted the popes control over the lands and peoples of the west. The appearance of this false document, which was not shown to be a forgery until the fifteenth century, hints at the jockeying for position that was taking place in the 750s as the Merovingians disappeared, the Carolingians took their place, the Byzantines were preoccupied with eastern problems, and the popes were plotting the fall of the Lombards and their absolute territorial control of central Italy. The Donation presented the papacy's claim to western territorial control and its rejection of any Byzantine imperial claims to the same since Constantine had surrendered them to the pope. In 754, Pope Stephen came north to visit King Pepin, and at St. Denis he blessed and anointed not only Pepin as king, but also his sons Charlemagne and Carloman. The ceremony of 751 had been about Pepin, but the one in 754 was about the sanctification of his entire dynasty. Pope Stephen blessed Bertrada, Pepin's wife and the mother of his sons, and proclaimed that the Frankish people should never, on pain of interdict and excommunication, presume to choose any king from outside of Pepin's family. Thus, Pepin secured papal approval for the permanent elevation of his dynasty to royal standing. The Carolingians were Christian kings approved and anointed by God through his earthly representative, the pope; their line was now sacred. A measure of stability had returned to Europe.

Charlemagne as Conqueror and King

Despite all their planning, the Carolingians could not escape the Germanic custom and curse of dividing up the kingdom among heirs on the death of the king. When Pepin the Short died in 768, his sons Charlemagne and Carloman succeeded to different parts of the kingdom, but there were persistent strains between the two. When Carloman died of natural causes in 771, Charlemagne became the sole ruler of all Francia.

Charlemagne conquered neighboring peoples to acquire their lands and wealth and to make them Christian. Between 768 and his death in 814, Charlemagne's armies fought a constant series of wars against the peoples of Europe. Each spring when there was enough grass on the ground for horses to graze, his army set out for war. Their destination was determined at an assembly called by the king during the winter or early spring. Carolingian armies fought throughout the summer months, often on several fronts, and returned home in the fall. Charlemagne conducted wars in this way for forty years. In that time he expanded the Carolingian kingdom into Aquitaine, Italy, Brittany, Hungary (the Avar lands), and Saxony. He also worked to secure buffer zones called Marches between Francia and the lands of the Slavs, Bretons, Danes, and Muslim Spain (Map 7.3).

Despite all this military activity, Charlemagne himself was not known as a great warrior; he led his army in only two battles of importance against the Saxons. The nature of Carolingian warfare was such that there were few open battles. Particularly gifted at organization, Charlemagne would put more men into the field than his enemy, who then most often chose to retreat, whereupon the Carolingian army would burn down their crops and homes. The enemy would then sue for peace, agree to pay tribute, and accept conversion to Christianity. Charlemagne's genius lay in planning wars and the en-

Equestrian Statue of a Carolingian King The small bronze statue was made during the time of King Charles the Bald, though it was probably a cult object meant to represent Charlemagne. The crowned king, dressed in Frankish clothes, holds a globe in his left hand and once held a sword or lance in his right.

forcement of the military obligations of his nobles and the Frankish peoples. Every free Frank who possessed 120 acres of land was obligated to fight in these wars, to appear when summoned by the king with the necessary arms and provisions to go to war for the length of the annual summer campaign. His vassals (dependents) and their vassals or men fought because they owed the king service for the land that they had received from him (a subject treated in Chapter 8).

Carolingian armies were smaller than ancient armies, used both infantry and a cavalry of knights who, unlike the ancients, used stirrups and thus could sit more firmly on their horses when running the enemy through with lances. Not particularly good at siege warfare, the Carolingian army was otherwise a formidable fighting force. One Byzantine observer spoke of the sheer pandemonium of fighting the Franks, for with reckless bravery the Franks thundered forth into battle seated on their heavy horses, the sound and confusion alone intimidating the enemy. Charlemagne's campaigns suggest just how deliberate he was in seeking to pacify the areas that bordered the Frankish kingdom and how stubborn he was in pursuing a goal. The campaign against the pagan Saxons lasted for thirty-two years, but in the end Saxony became part of the Carolingian Empire, Christian, and a critical part of medieval Europe.

Charlemagne was not content to take land; he sought to incorporate it within his Christian kingdom. The war against the Saxons was difficult because after each year's successful foray into Saxony, the Saxons would agree to accept religious conversion, Christian priests, and Carolingian outposts. When the Carolingian army returned to Francia, the Saxons would slaughter the Carolingians and priests left behind, and the Frankish army would be forced to return the next year. Charlemagne integrated conquered lands into the Carolingian territory by granting parcels of land to his men, who occupied it and whose presence stabilized a region; by subjecting conquered areas to Carolingian royal law; and by promoting the establishment of Christian churches and the Christianization of the population, by force if necessary.

Within his kingdom, Charlemagne was the effective head of the church, which he treated as an arm of government. He approved the appointments of bishops and regarded monasteries as an institutional part of his government. Since his kingdom was vast, controlling areas at the periphery was difficult. Charlemagne was an itinerant king, visiting various parts of the kingdom to administer justice. At its core, his government remained a palace operation, but by the late 790s he had established a permanent capital at Aachen in southern Germany. He employed royal officials called *missi dominici* (the lord's agents), who were sent out in pairs, one secular and one ecclesiastical agent, as traveling judges to administer justice in the name of the king. They often carried with them **capitularies,** royal laws issued in chapters (*capitula*) or itemized form by the king. These laws supplemented the various Germanic law codes that continued to hold force in most regions.

Charlemagne, Father of Europe and Roman Emperor

The idea of Europe, its character and territorial reality, took on its first rough form during Charlemagne's reign.

MAP 7.3 | **Charlemagne's Empire by 814**

Pepin the Short, before 768, and Charlemagne, before 814, expanded the size of the Carolingian kingdoms considerably and sealed their territory with Marches, or borderlands, and tributary peoples. ***What advantages and disadvantages did this land mass present to any potential rulers? How did Charlemagne try to administer such a large territory? What troubles did he and his heirs encounter?***

Europa was a figure from Greek mythology, a Phoenician woman or moon goddess who was seduced by Zeus in the form of a bull. Greek geographers had named the continent after her, but as a political reality Europe had had little force before the Carolingians. A Spanish chronicler in 754 called the troops of Charles Martel, who had defeated the Muslims at Tours/Poitiers, "Europeans" (*europenses*), the first known use of the term. A German annalist later identified Europe and the kingdom of Charlemagne as one and the same thing. Charlemagne's poets called him the "Father of Europe," "the glory of Europe," and the "shining light of Europe." The Europe that Charlemagne shaped was Christian, Latinate in learning and official language, universal in aspiration, and territorially complete (though having only a marginal presence in Spain, Poland, Hungary, and the Slavic lands, and no control over Scandinavia or the British Isles).

Charlemagne's courtiers, men like Alcuin (c. 732–804), the Anglo-Saxon teacher and deacon, came to the conclusion that a universal dominion with one faith and one king should be called an empire and its ruler an emperor. Just as Pepin the Short had looked to the papacy to "royalize" his family, Charlemagne looked south to Rome and the papacy to imperialize his preeminence. Such recognition depended on events and relative vulnerabilities. Just as one pope had wanted help against the Lombards when he agreed to recognize Pepin as king, so another pope needed help to remain on his papal throne when he crowned an emperor.

Charlemagne may have viewed the imperial title as an honorific, but it brought him more trouble than he had expected. The pope so engineered the actual ceremony that it looked to some, particularly in Rome, as if the pope had made an emperor and that it was his exclusive right to do so. Back home Charlemagne had to have his people swear their oaths to him again, now that he was emperor, lest there be some technical dispute about the legality of their earlier oaths to him as king. He may also not have fully foreseen the anger of the Greeks at the existence of another Roman emperor, for they already possessed a universal Roman emperor of their own. Not until 812 would Charlemagne secure their recognition of his new title, and even then the Byzantines qualified their recognition by calling Charlemagne the emperor of the Franks.

Still, for the first time in over three centuries, the west once again had its own emperor, but the idea of a western emperor and western empire would both frustrate and inspire Europe throughout the Middle Ages. The imperial title brought Charlemagne few additional powers. His courtiers and the church were pleased, for *empire* and *emperor* belonged to the realm of ideas, not to the realities of medieval politics. Yet Charlemagne's imperial title was a fitting symbol of the partnership of the Carolingians and the papacy and marked a new stage in the elevation of both partners. Thus, within fifty years, the Carolingians had moved from being a powerful noble family to the height of imperial majesty, and the papacy had inserted itself at the center of the medieval European identity and politics as the sanctioners of empire.

Al-Andalus, a Hot Corner of European-Islamic Conflict

When Charlemagne was delaying in Italy after becoming emperor, he received the gift of an elephant from the caliph Harun al-Rashid (r. 786–809). Harun (whose exotic court is the setting for *The Thousand and One Nights*) was the fifth caliph of the Abbasid Caliphate that overthrew the Umayyads in 750 and moved the capital of the Islamic world from Damascus to Baghdad. The Umayyads had provoked resistance in the widening Muslim world by their Arab-first policy. The Abbasid focus was more cosmopolitan, integrating Persians and other Muslims in its government, and the move to Baghdad symbolized the eastward shift of Islam away from its original Arabian heartland. The move east also compelled the Abbasids to accept, reluctantly, that hereditary Muslim rulers controlled distant regions such as Egypt, Syria, and Spain. It was probably that irritant that explains Harun's extraordinary coronation

gift to Charlemagne. Harun and the Abbasids longed for the overthrow of the Umayyad emirs (commanders) who held al-Andalus (Spain), and they hoped that their "friend" Charlemagne might rid them of that line of imposters.

Charlemagne and his father tried. Pepin the Short drove the Umayyads south of the Pyrenees; and in 778, at the invitation of the disgruntled emirs and provincial governors of Barcelona, Saragossa, and Huesca, Charlemagne invaded northern Spain. Finding little success, Charlemagne withdrew. As he and his troops, forced into a long line by the mountainous terrain, reached Roncesvalles, Christian Basques attacked the rear guard of the army and seized its baggage train, which carried some portion of Charlemagne's movable wealth. The embarrassing defeat, no matter how unimportant, passed before long from history into legend. The Carolingians remained committed to establishing a firm border or March in northern Spain to protect Europe from any further incursions from Muslim Spain and to offer some assistance to the Christians of northern Spain.

In 711–712, Umayyad armies had invaded Spain from northern Africa and over the next decade dislodged the Visigoths from the Iberian Peninsula and established al-Andalus, a Muslim province with its capital at Córdoba in the south on the Guadalquivir River. By the 720s, Muslim armies were making raids on Aquitaine, though Christians in northern Spain set up their own kingdom of Asturias north of the Ebro River. Even then, during this first phase of conquest, northern Spain was under Muslim control and Muslims made ambitious raids farther north, including the attack on Tours/Poitiers, where they were turned back by Charles Martel.

Andalusian society was made up of Muslims, Jews, and Christians; and its Muslim rulers were tolerant of the various faiths in Spain, in part because Muslims remained a minority population within Spain. Moreover, Spain's Muslim governors were trying to contain not provoke internal dissension, since they were under constant pressure from rival tribal and dynastic claims. In 755, the Umayyad Abd al-Rahman I was fleeing Abbasid Caliphate forces when he led his Berber troops across the Mediterranean to Granada and set himself up as the emir of al-Andalus. He slaughtered the reigning Abbasid emir and his men, and sent their body parts to Abbasid Baghdad as proof of his victory. Abd al-Rahman established a dynasty that successfully managed the various populations and powers in Spain for over a century.

The Carolingians, always concerned about their borderlands, slowly pushed the frontier between Francia and al-Andalus back to the Ebro River, and established a March between the two. At the very time Charlemagne was in communication with the caliph Harun al-Rashid, he commanded his son Louis the Pious to free Barcelona from Umayyad control, which happened in 801—not a bad reason for Harun's gift of an elephant, though the Carolingians made little further progress into the Iberian Peninsula.

Abd al-Rahman and his descendants transformed Córdoba into a cosmopolitan jewel of bazaars, bookshops, and magnificent architecture. In the 780s, the emir began the construction of the Great Mosque of Córdoba, which has hundreds of columns, horseshoe arches, and a surrounding orchard of orange trees. Al-Andalus was the last great holdout of the Umayyads against the Abbasid Caliphate, and Córdoba was designed to rival Abbasid Baghdad. Its libraries, institutions of higher learning, and vibrant cosmopolitan population surpassed in many areas Charlemagne's own cultural achievements and may have indirectly inspired a few of them.

The Great Mosque of Córdoba Córdoba was the jewel of al-Andalus (Muslim Spain), and its great mosque, with its hundreds of columns, was a magnificent architectural achievement. Some of its features may have made their way into Carolingian churches.

Carolingian Cultures: High, Low, and In-Between

The intersection point of the many Carolingian cultures—ecclesiastical, court, noble, ethnic, regional, and popular—was the church, in which all groups participated to varying degrees. Charlemagne and his advisors were the architects of an early medieval movement that has sometimes been called a renaissance, but that may be more appropriately thought of as a reformation of western Christian culture. Charlemagne emphasized the reform of church practices and education. To inform and enliven his kingship he established a vibrant court culture, while at the same time raising the standards of education among the clergy and monks throughout the realm. His investment in education paid dividends in subsequent generations as the Carolingian church achieved high standards of clerical practice and a thriving written culture of monks and clerics who wrote hundreds of books that laid down essential dogma and raised profound poetic, theological, and philosophical ideas. The Carolingians also created the basic print script that we still employ.

> **What were the chief characteristics and achievements of Carolingian culture?**

Court Culture and Education

Charlemagne began collecting foreign scholars for his court in the 780s. English, Italian, Irish, and Spanish scholars came to the king's court, creating an intimate international circle of learned men around their patron, the king. The Anglo-Saxon scholar Alcuin, whose inter-

ests included arithmetic, theology, poetry, letters, and Christian doctrine, became both the headmaster of the Carolingian court school and an advisor to the king. Court poets gave each other playful nicknames and called their king David after the Old Testament king. They circulated poems that poked fun at one another, ridiculed buffoonish nobles and drunken monks, and achieved moments of transporting warmth and spirituality. "Give sweet sleep to the brothers in this royal court for a dark power sends terrors that worry our sleep," wrote Alcuin. Royal poets spawned intense rivalries while trying to attract the attention of the king. Some of their controversies may amuse us today, particularly the one over whether darkness and nothingness are something or nothing and Ratramnus's later letter on the dog-headed people, but they do suggest the lively intellectual atmosphere of the royal court and Carolingian thought.

Almost all these learned men were churchmen; they served not just for the amusement of the king, but were his counselors and took on important church postings and state offices such as that of traveling judges or *missi dominici*. One who was not a churchman was Einhard, a Frank who was educated at the monastery of Fulda and later wrote the famous biography of Charlemagne (see Back to the Source at the end of the chapter). Einhard seems to have taken on the job of supervising the construction of Charlemagne's chapel complex. By the late 790s the king had a capital and chief palace at Aachen, and he was building an impressive church to adorn it. Like so much else, Charlemagne's chapel, which is octagonal in shape and furnished with materials removed from Ravenna, is an impressively solid building with a late Roman feel to it, yet its arches of alternating black

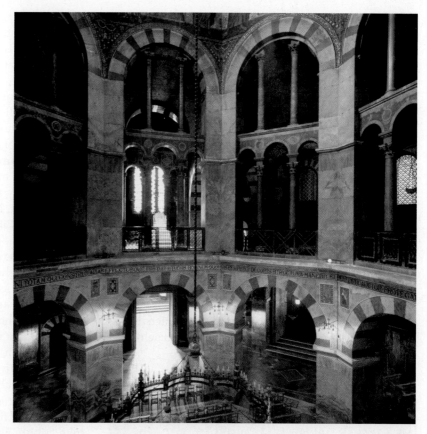

The Palace Chapel of Aachen In the 790s, Charlemagne began to erect a church at his capital in Aachen. The chapel is an impressively sturdy building with an octagonal shape, dome, central space, and heavy round arches. Charlemagne's throne is set on the second level, from which he could observe the service below.

and white stones remind one of the same feature in the Great Mosque of Córdoba.

The king was convinced that many monks and churchmen in Francia were poorly educated, for his advisors had noticed that the letters these churchmen sent to court were often poorly written and ungrammatical. Since such faults might lead to errors of religious expression and dangerous misunderstandings, Charlemagne ordered his abbots and bishops to establish schools to provide education to repair such deficiencies. This education of boys in the basics of Latin was far from universal, leaving out most of the poor and most women. Carolingian education was designed primarily to serve the needs of the church and government; still, some local village boys were educated in schools housed outside the precincts of the monastery. Charlemagne's emphasis on basic education led to several generations of highly literate churchmen and a few educated laymen and women. Charlemagne's educational reform reached few women since its primary goal was to train boys for the church and state.

Charlemagne, his courtiers, and monks were aware that the different scripts used in writing contributed to miscommunication and error. By the 790s a new or reformed script called **Caroline Minuscule** began to appear in Tours and other monasteries and to radiate out from the court itself. Caroline Minuscule is a small, regular script that maintains space between its simply shaped letters and emphasizes legibility; it is the basic print script found on this textbook page (the only real differences being the use of the tall s [ſ] and the lack of the dot over the letter *i* in Caroline Minuscule).

At the same time, Carolingian scholars, for whom Latin was a learned language and not the language spoken in their birth homes, began to reform early medieval Latin, returning it closer to the classical standards of

Caroline Minuscule As seen in this manuscript with its amusing portrait of the evangelist Matthew, Caroline Minuscule was the new script of small, regular, evenly spaced letters that was promoted by Charlemagne and his court. Caroline Minuscule became the main script used by medieval Europe until the twelfth century and was reintroduced as the standard Roman font in the Italian Renaissance.

writers such as Cicero. This Carolingian reform marked an important dividing point in the linguistic history of Europe. The medieval version of classical Latin became the official literary language of government, learning, and the written word, whereas the Romance languages (French, Italian, and Spanish) began as Latin but developed their own characteristics as popular, regional, spoken languages. Under Charlemagne, Carolingian humanists began to correct many ancient texts such as the Vulgate or Latin Bible and classical texts such as the works of Terence, Lucan, and Cicero, which had over the centuries of copying and recopying accumulated textual errors. The Carolingians also began to place primitive musical notations called neumes in the manuscripts of their prayers, a practice that assisted them in standardizing the singing of Gregorian Chant, which despite its name dates from after the time of Pope Gregory the Great.

The Carolingians also created some of the most splendid illuminated manuscripts of the Middle Ages. At Charlemagne's court, different groups of painters began to make deluxe Gospel books for the king. The differences between these manuscripts in style, use of color, and representation underline both the influence of antique models on court painters as well as the new and experimental nature of Charlemagne's court culture. After Charlemagne, manuscript illumination, like learned culture in general, was associated less with the royal court than with individual monasteries. Both the Ebo Gospels, with its painterly depictions of the evangelists and marginal scenes of everyday life, and the willowy line drawings of the famous Utrecht Psalter (a manuscript of the Psalms) were made near Rheims in the 830s. By the mid-ninth century the scriptorium (the place where scribes worked) of St. Martin of Tours was producing stunning one-volume Bibles called pandects for royal and noble patrons. In the First Bible of Charles the Bald, the painting of King David set in a blue cosmic egg, dancing nude beneath a light linen wrap to demonstrate his lack of pride before God, is a triumph of early medieval book art.

Learned Carolingian culture moved in phases: from the intense and intimate court culture of Charlemagne, to the brilliant writerly culture of Louis the Pious's reign, the mid-ninth century when dozens of writers associated with individual monasteries and cathedrals were at work, and finally to the slow tailing off of written culture in the last decades of the century, interrupted by the late brilliance of Charles the Bald's royal court. Ninth-century high culture was the result of Carolingian royal patronage but was dominated by churchmen. We know of very few lay writers and the three most prominent of these—Einhard, Nithard, and Dhuoda—all moved within the orbit of royal politics and Christian culture.

The Carolingian Church: Royal, Monastic, and Militant

Charlemagne's drive to reform Christian culture reflected his conviction that he was the guardian of the church in his empire. Bishops were the principal ecclesiastics in the Frankish church, but the king approved their appointments, employed them to serve the needs of his government, and sought their advice on the state of the kingdom, religion, and the Frankish people. He often appeared at church councils, and his capitularies frequently concerned ecclesiastical matters that would then work their way down to local parish priests and villages.

Despite the worldly authority of bishops, monasticism held spiritual primacy in the Carolingian world. The so-called three orders of Carolingian society were monks, priests, and laypeople. Monks, because of their closeness to God, stood first in the spiritual hierarchy. Charlemagne and his son Louis were particularly concerned to ensure that monasteries were regularly ordered and governed, for a corrupt monastery threatened to poison Carolingian relations with God since it was the monk who prayed for all. Under Charlemagne and Louis there was a drive to standardize Benedictine monasticism as the norm for the realm; Louis even sponsored a new and improved edition of the *Rule of Saint Benedict*.

David Dances Naked before God One of the masterpieces of Carolingian book art, this image from the First Bible of Charles the Bald called on King Charles to be as humble and respectful to God and his priests as was the Old Testament king. The four virtues are personified as women in the corners of the painting, and the king is surrounded by his four musicians and two guards.

The Past Preserved in Ice

Everything that exists exists in the present; the past itself is entirely gone. All that we know about the past we know from the slight record of it (for it is never the whole) that has somehow survived into the present. All historical evidence, whether the thoughts of Plato recorded in a dialogue, a monument such as Constantine's Arch, or the lyrics of a medieval drinking song, have survived in some concrete form, however altered, into the material present.

That does not mean that we will not find new records of the world's past of which we had been unaware. Such is the ice of Greenland. For thousands of years the snows that fell annually on Greenland captured and deposited atmospheric particles containing chemical traces of human and climate events. Between 1987 and 1993, scientists from the United States and Europe extracted a three-kilometer-long ice core from Greenland containing a record of 110,000 years of atmospheric activity. They analyzed the chemistry of the core's layers at 2.5-year intervals. Known events, such as the volcanic eruptions of Mount Vesuvius in 79 CE and Krakatoa in 1883, left physical traces in the form of sulfate deposits.

The volcanic record revealed in the ice has begun to produce striking results. Europe's weather during the first millennium CE was warmer and more stable than that of the second. The Early Middle Ages, particularly around 800, benefited from warmer temperatures and longer growing seasons, but was still hit by eight multiyear severe winters between 750 and 950 that correspond to major volcanic deposits in the Greenland ice core. Particles ejected by violent volcanic eruptions were carried into the jet stream and blocked the sun's rays from reaching the earth, producing colder weather and agricultural failure. In 763–764, volcanic activity produced a particularly cold winter in Europe: crops failed, people died from lack of bread, portions of the Black Sea froze solid, and a gigantic iceberg taller than its city walls struck the port of Constantinople. In 821–824, Carolingian Europe was hit by cold, wet summers and a harsh winter—again caused by some distant volcano—that killed animals, froze humans, and devastated the agricultural economy. The emperor Louis the Pious asked his people to pray for God's forgiveness.[1]

The vagaries of unseen volcanoes, darkened skies, cold weather, and poor harvests remind us that humans are not in complete control of their historical environment and, more positively, that there are still new records for us to find in our search to understand the human past in the physical present.

QUESTIONS | *What role does climate change play in history? What are the dangers of using climate explanations to account for specific historical phenomena such as the rise of Islam or the Viking raids?*

Carolingian kings demanded military service from their abbots and bishops, for the higher Carolingian clergy was a church militant. These men were almost always of noble stock. In promoting a candidate for the office of abbot, a bishop of Mainz listed the man's noble lineage and wide connections to the nobility, as though he needed to say little else to make the case for the candidate's suitability for high office. These noble prelates were raised as warriors, went to war, and fought in battles; simple monks and priests were forbidden to do so.

Frankish nobles shared a medieval aristocratic culture of manor management, control of their workers (serfs), disdain for the lower classes, and celebration of war and feats of bravery. They also shared a love of banquets, song, and drink, but Charlemagne and the church tried to curb the worst excesses of noble life. Charlemagne disapproved of public drunkenness, and his son frowned on the courtly amusements of jugglers and mimes and refused to smile in public. Since the abbots, bishops, and archbishops of Francia generally came from noble families, the nobility was well connected to the Frankish church and its basic mission; nobles often turned to churchmen to approve questionable marriages or to grant forgiveness when scandals surfaced.

Despite the integration of church and state, each preserved its own spheres of jurisdiction. Both belonged to the same general enterprise, yet the Carolingian state was not theocratic in the way that Islam was. The corporate or bodily character of medieval society meant that, in theory, each order had its own separate goals, duties, and areas of action, all pointing toward the common goal of pleasing God in the perfection of a Christian society. Yet, in reality, these orders constantly rubbed against each other, producing friction and frequent ruptures. Late in his life, as the abbot of St. Martin of Tours, Alcuin once found himself at one of these friction points when a criminal fled to his church and sought sanctuary. The emperor demanded that he surrender the man, which Alcuin, with some embarrassment, reluctantly did. But the common people of Tours rioted over the insult shown to their saint by men ready to invade his sacred precinct to retrieve the criminal. The complex interplay of groups in the Carolingian world meant that the various Carolingian societies rarely achieved lasting stability.

An Economy of Trade and a Shift to Silver

Carolingian civilization was for the most part river-valley civilization. Because northern Europe was covered by old and dense forests, Carolingian towns and cities lay along the natural clearings and available water supplied by rivers. The Roman road network still existed in parts of Gaul, but was often in a state of disrepair. Thus merchants found it easier to transport wheat and bulk goods along rivers than to travel over land. Towns and cities situated along rivers were, however, vulnerable to spring flooding and, by the mid-ninth century, to raids by the Vikings.

Carolingian trade was chiefly local, along rivers from town to town, although some evidence indicates that Carolingian Europe sent bulk goods such as wood, grain, and even slaves into the Mediterranean to Byzantine and Islamic lands in exchange for spices and precious metals. Primarily agricultural, the Carolingian economy was by the late eighth and early ninth centuries surprisingly successful. Carolingian agriculture benefited from the warmest temperatures in Europe for many centuries, giving it longer growing seasons and generally good harvests.

The wealth of the church, revealed by extensive church building and the creation and collection of precious religious objects, suggests just how successful the Carolingian economy was. The relative prosperity of the Carolingian Empire, both from its own agricultural economy and from the conquest of peoples such as the Avars, was a factor in attracting Viking raids.

Charlemagne moved Francia from a gold standard of coins to a silver one. Gold was hard to acquire in Europe, whereas the Carolingians possessed silver mines. Charlemagne and his successors established mints that regulated the production of coins. Whereas earlier Germans had once made payments in cattle, the Carolingians established a partial money economy with exact monetary amounts paid for many transactions. The fluctuating price of bread during times of scarcity, for instance, was recorded.

Living Off the Land

The Carolingian economy remained chiefly agricultural, with each area, village, and farm producing the crops and animals that grew best on its terrain. The rural economy was a **subsistence economy,** one producing just enough to meet its own needs, but it seems to have operated on a three-year scale of subsistence so that even if a village or region experienced crop failures over several years, it might still avoid starvation conditions.

Manorialism was a system in which the holder of the land, who had probably received the parcel of land from the king, lived in a manor house overlooking the land, which was farmed by dependent laborers with different rights and obligations (Figure 7.1). These workers came with the land as part of its fixed resources. They lived in a village and farmed plots of land allotted to them.

The Labors of the Months This Carolingian picture shows the activities of the months arranged over four panels left to right: January, a peasant warms his hands; February and March, lords practice falconry and the collection of small animals; April, a peasant collects the winter wheat and first fruits; May, a lord prepares the land for planting; June, plowing begins; July, hay is gathered; August and September, summer wheat is harvested, threshed, and winnowed; October, grapes are gathered; November and December, pigs are slaughtered.

These farm workers (sometimes called serfs or peasants) received a portion of the produce of their work, but owed the lord of the manor work on his property, other service, and dues. Depending on his legal status, a man might have to spend so many days of the week working on the lord's land and an extra amount of time planting and harvesting the lord's crops. His wife and children might owe the lord work in the manor house, time spent weaving cloth, and eggs from the family's chickens. The lord of the manor took on the roles of judge, mayor, and *paterfamilias* of the village.

Despite the rudimentary nature of the Carolingian rural economy, it was more rational than the Merovingian economy had been. Since the demands of kings and the church upon the land were heavy, the Carolingians kept inventories of properties and of the people who worked them. They knew how much each farm and worker should produce from the land. Carolingian innovations to farming benefited the Middle Ages and may explain the slow increase in the medieval population that started in the eighth century. The Carolingians used a heavier plow that was better suited than the light Mediterranean plow (or scratch stick) to turning over the heavy, moist soils of northern Europe. To pull this plow, they employed oxen or the heavy Carolingian horse. They introduced the so-called three-course system of agriculture in which they planted some strips of land in the fall with winter wheat that would ripen in the late spring, planted nearby strips in the spring with summer or fall wheat, and every third year left the strips of land in which the winter wheat had been harvested the previous year fallow for a full year. The next year they rotated their use of the land. The system increased the amount of land producing crops each year; spread the labor needed to farm the land over several seasons; ensured that crops were planted and harvested at different times of the year, thus safeguarding against calamitous crop failures caused by poor weather; and better preserved the fertility of the soil. Finally, the Carolingians promoted the use of water mills for grinding wheat to make bread, thus making integral use of machines as labor-saving devices.

These improvements contributed to the success of the Carolingian economy, but it remained an economy susceptible to shortages and famine. Monastic records report that some twenty-five years between 764 and 874 suffered serious shortages or short hungry seasons, generally in the late winter or early spring when, after a paltry harvest the previous fall, the surplus of grain had run out and the spring crop had not yet come up. Even then, Carolingian men and women knew how to forage for nuts and berries in the forest, kill a domestic animal (though that was not a good economic choice in most cases), kill one of the many half-domesticated pigs that roamed the forests, buy bread at inflated prices if they had the means, or turn to a local church or monastery for charity. During this 110-year period, deaths by starvation were reported in only 3 years. The real problem was that the Carolingian diet was excessively dependent on bread. The average monk may have eaten as much as three and a half to four pounds of bread per day. The heavy reliance on cereal crops had the effect of distending Carolingian stomachs so that when

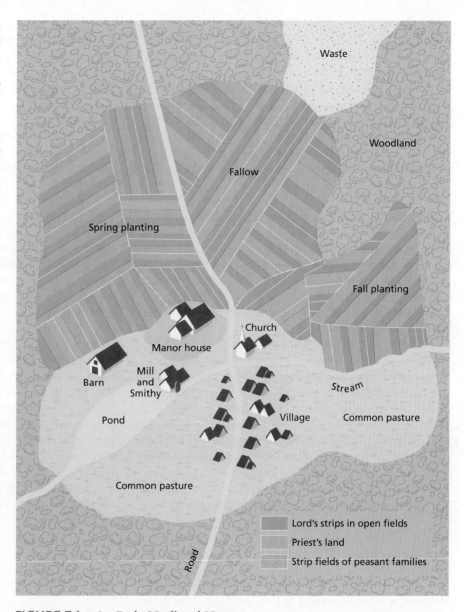

FIGURE 7.1 | An Early Medieval Manor

Medieval peasants or farm workers lived in villages on the lord's land. They went out each day to work the nearby fields for the lord; some peasants were allotted several strips of land for their own use, as were the miller and the blacksmith.

Source: Dennis Sherman and Joyce Salisbury, *The West in the World,* 4th ed. (New York: McGraw-Hill, 2011), 235.

bread was unavailable, Carolingian men and women became extremely hungry. It was a hard life, but a sustainable one; life expectancies were low, but the population was growing.

Popular Beliefs

We know something about the activities of the common people of the Carolingian Empire, but their thoughts largely escape us. Though these people do not speak directly to us, learned churchmen did occasionally report what the people thought, often to censure them. One night in the middle of the ninth century, a bishop was hard at work writing a sermon in his study when he heard a commotion outside. The moon was in eclipse and his parishioners had assembled to bring the moon back to life; some shattered plates, others shouted at the moon, and yet others shot arrows at it. They were apparently convinced that the moon was being attacked by a monster and needed help to rouse and defend itself. The next day in church the bishop explained the nature of a lunar eclipse and chided his flock for their superstition.

Many superstitions did exist in the Carolingian countryside. A bishop of Lyons said that everyone in his region, high and low, young and old, believed in weather wizards who could send hailstorms to destroy crops. He had also heard that people believed that in 810, when animals were dying in the kingdom, enemies of Charlemagne had come from southern Italy to poison the fields and waters of the empire. In these two cases, people were chiefly worried about two key elements of the Carolingian economy: crops and cattle. In a subsistence economy without crop insurance or protection from setbacks, Carolingian farmers worried about the weather and looming calamity.

Popular Carolingian culture sprang from the village and its fields, which defined the lives of the vast majority of the population. These people seldom traveled beyond the narrow confines of their villages, learned what little they knew from their parish priest, drank with him, suffered from aggravating diseases and farming accidents, and watched as their children died young and harvests failed. They did not lack shrewdness; survival demanded it. They had a practical knowledge of others in their small communities, knew the land, and tried to survive physically and mentally a difficult and often relatively short life.

Disorder Returns to Europe

After Charlemagne's impressive reign, the Carolingian dynasty quickly returned to the root Germanic problem of succession. Charlemagne's luck had been spectacular; he had outlived all his heirs but one and so escaped the problem of passing down a divided kingdom. His surviving son, Louis the Pious, was neither as fortunate nor as powerful as his father, and his commitment to an indivisible empire worsened the problem. Civil war ripped apart the realm, and by the end of the century the Carolingian line had self-destructed.

Why did the Carolingian Empire fail, or did it?

The Woes of Louis the Pious

In 813 Charlemagne summoned his only living legitimate son, Louis the Pious, from Aquitaine to Aachen where a great council was held. After days of discussion his advisors persuaded him to make Louis co-emperor. Charlemagne may not originally have intended to bequeath the imperial title, but with only Louis left he may have decided that no harm would be done. Louis has

often been criticized for not measuring up to his father's accomplishments, but the last years of Charlemagne's rule were already difficult ones for the empire. Charlemagne was in his sixties and no longer the active ruler he had been for much of his energetic career. He now remained in Aachen much of the time, soaking in hot springs and making the occasional hunting trip. In 810 when a Danish king threatened to invade Francia, Charlemagne personally assembled his army and set out on his last campaign, but his elephant died along the way and the old emperor suffered a dramatic fall from his horse.

Louis was a different ruler from his father, more attentive to the advice of his churchmen, more pious as his name suggests, and less committed to war and decisive command. The Carolingian church flourished during his reign with Benedictine monasticism leading the way, successful and learned churchmen advising him, and a supportive papacy. But in 817 Emperor Louis decided to name the eldest of his three living sons co-emperor and to make the other two kings, but subordinate to their brother. Only in this way, he believed, could the empire endure and remain united in faith. His younger sons were not happy. In 830 and then again in 833, all three sons revolted and tried to force their father to become a monk, a form of forced retirement and permanent imprisonment. Both times he sought restoration and reassumed his throne. The real problem behind these revolts was that many self-interested nobles believed that the Frankish kingdom should be divided equally among all the legitimate male heirs, but that notion clashed with the idea of an indivisible empire.

Three Brothers and a Civil War

When Louis died in 840, his eldest son, Lothar, immediately tried to impose his imperial will on his two younger surviving brothers, Louis the German and Charles the Bald, who was only seventeen at the time. A civil war broke out that pitted the younger brothers against their older brother. The Carolingians found themselves in a difficult moral and religious dilemma. It was one thing to kill pagan or heretical outsiders, quite another to wage war against Frankish Christians and your own blood. In a great battle at Fontenoy in 841, the younger brothers defeated Lothar. Two years later the three brothers agreed by the Treaty of Verdun to divide the Frankish territories into three parts (Map 7.4, p. 224).

The geography of the division was as much human as physical since the treaty framers were charged not just with dividing Europe into three viable kingdoms, but also with preserving the landholdings of the three brothers' men. Some European nations mark their beginning from the treaty because the rough outlines of France and Germany can be seen in the divided kingdom, but those national boundaries seem largely coincidental. Lothar's middle kingdom with its strangely elongated shape could not last, but the division allowed Lothar to separate his

817: An Imperial Watershed

Several sources describe the occasion in 813 when Charlemagne made his son, Louis the Pious, co-emperor. In one version, the father crowns his son; in another, Charlemagne invites Louis to retrieve the crown resting on an altar and to crown himself. There is a small world of difference between the two acts. What is certain in both is that the pope was not present and did not crown Louis co-emperor. The ceremony was a strictly Carolingian affair, not a papal production. The shadows of 800 and the papacy's claim to the right to make emperors may have worried Charlemagne to the end of his life.

Whatever doubts the old emperor had in transferring imperial power, his pious son had few. In 816 Louis arranged for the new pope, Stephen IV, to re-crown him em-peror in Rheims. That act reinforced the papal prerogative. What Louis did the next year proved to be a turning point in Carolingian fortunes. Louis was only thirty-nine years old at the time, but he had had a serious scare that spring. The wooden arcade that ran from the palace to the church in Aachen collapsed on him and his retinue, killing some nobles and leaving the emperor injured. Not long after the accident, Louis crowned his eldest son Lothar co-emperor, made his younger two sons kings, but subordinate to and dependent on their older brother, and marginalized his nephew, Bernard of Italy, on whom Charlemagne himself had bestowed the kingdom of Italy. Bernard and his sup-porters, who were still loyal to the deceased Charlemagne and his earlier territorial arrangements, revolted. Bernard surrendered, was blinded, and died, an event for which Louis later did penance. Worse was to follow. Louis's younger sons never accepted their subordination to Lothar. Louis himself remarried in 821 and bore a fourth legitimate son, Charles the Bald, and so tried to undo the provisions of 817 in order to find a fitting place for his youngest son in the realm. His first three sons revolted twice and de-posed their father.

The year 817 was a watershed both for Louis's reign and for the fortunes of his house. Louis had abandoned his father's imperial caution, probably for religious reasons. A universal Christian faith, he believed, should be contained within a united and enduring empire. But the idea of an indivisible empire clashed with the Germanic tradition of dividing lands equally among legitimate heirs. Louis's embrace of a primitive form of primogeniture (succession by the first-born male heir) also undercut older Frankish notions of the equality of heirs. Louis's plan in 817 was bold and radical. Had it succeeded it might have produced a stable and united imperial line and a different fate for the Carolingian Empire, but it did not work and perhaps never could have. From it came political turmoil, revolt, and civil war. By 818 the Carolingian world had political turbulence and failure in front of it. Stability lay in the past, and the memory of Charlemagne's golden reign cast a lengthening shadow over his heirs.

Louis the Pious in Letters The image of Louis the Pious set in Hrabanus Maurus's work on the Holy Cross is an example of "figured poetry." The letters make up an acrostic poem that can be read across or down and, to add yet more complexity, Louis's image (including the halo, headdress, shield, and cross) contains lines of verse that can be read separately. Louis, the most religious of Carolingian kings, has literally become a lettered man and something of a holy cipher.

QUESTIONS | *What is the difference between the two reports of Louis's coronation in 813? What was the essential Carolingian constitutional issue? How had the Roman Empire for a brief time overcome the problem of imperial and dynastic succession? Why was Louis the Pious's commitment to empire either a bold or a foolish idea?*

brothers and to hold the two imperial capitals of Rome and Aachen within his middle kingdom. Lothar clung tenaciously to his preeminence as emperor, even if the civil war had shown that he could not dominate his brothers by right of imperial title. The end result was that Europe was left with a nominal emperor whose power was scarcely more than that of his brother kings, all three of them operating in their territories as kings with relative autonomy.

The Vikings Raid Francia

Civil war and the general political confusion in northern Europe encouraged the **Northmen** (as the Carolingians called them) or **Vikings** (as we know them, from *vik*, meaning a bay or creek, from which their ships set out) to increase their raids on the continent. The Viking raiders were opportunists who seemed to know which areas of Europe and the Middle East were easiest and most profitable to strike. From late in Charlemagne's reign, various Scandinavian warriors, mostly Danes and Norwegians, began conducting raids on Ireland, northern England, and the western parts of the Carolingian Empire. The nature of these raids, which were often acts of piracy not supported by the pagan kings of Scandinavia, shifted over time.

The Scandinavians were Germanic peoples doing what the east and west Germans had done four centuries earlier, raiding more powerful and richer lands to the south. They could do so because of their superior sailing skills and ever larger ships. The Carolingian Empire was a land-based power without a navy. The early Viking raids were relatively small affairs. As violent and disruptive as these piratical

MAP 7.4 | **The Division of Carolingian Lands by the Treaty of Verdun, 843**

After the civil war of 840–843, the three living legitimate sons of Louis the Pious agreed to divide the Carolingian lands into three kingdoms. *Why did the emperor Lothar I take the middle kingdom? What problems was such an elongated kingdom likely to experience? Which of the three kingdoms was the most vulnerable in the disturbed conditions of the mid-ninth century? With what limitations were the treaty makers working?*

raids were, they probably did little substantial physical damage to the overall Carolingian agricultural economy.

In the first four decades of the ninth century, the Vikings attacked along the coastline of Francia and sailed up rivers, targeting monasteries and churches that were conveniently located along waterways. The pagan Vikings knew that churches held the greatest repositories of movable wealth in the form of gold and silver objects (chalices, plates, crosses). The Viking raids may actually have done the western European economy some good by recirculating wealth that had dead-ended in churches or that the Vikings had stolen from Islamic and Byzantine cities. Some Carolingian ports and trading centers such as Dorestad in northern Francia were struck repeatedly.

Carolingian accounts of the raids are often exaggerated. Churches and monasteries were the prime targets

A Viking Dragon-Head Found with the Viking ship buried at Oseberg c. 825, this post with its dragon-head was like those mounted on the prows of the Viking ships that raided the continent.

Dhuoda Inside Out

Dhuoda was a pious mother, a noble woman, and the wife of one of the ninth century's great rascals. She proudly recalled that she had married the noble Bernard of Septimania in Charlemagne's chapel at Aachen. Her world began to fall apart not long after that day, for her husband, Louis the Pious's chamberlain (or chief of staff), was accused of committing adultery with Empress Judith, the emperor's young second wife, and was driven from court. During the civil war between the sons of Louis the Pious, Bernard hid out in Aquitaine and Dhuoda, left behind near the Spanish March, raised money to aid him. Then came the greatest emotional crisis of her life. In 841 her fifteen-year-old son William was turned over to King Charles the Bald to ensure Bernard's good behavior and to regain some of the family's lost lands and privileges. The resourceful Dhuoda began to write a manual to help her son survive at the court of a hostile king and to teach him how to be a good Christian.

Her emotional pain was doubled since she had recently given birth to a second son, whose name she did not yet know. Bernard had sent the child into hiding before he was even baptized. Dhuoda urged William to share the manual with his baby brother when he was old enough to read. Beyond merely setting out the forms of proper Christian and noble behavior for William, she also pondered the state of her own soul and life. "Returning to Myself, I Mourn" is the title of one of the last chapters of her book. She feared that she would soon die and begged William to pray for her and their entire noble family, to pay off the debts she had incurred on Bernard's behalf, and to protect his brother. With her little book she hoped, from a distance, to bind together her dissolving and wounded family.

Dhuoda supplies us with a special perspective on Carolingian life and politics. She was, so far as we know, the only laywoman of the ninth century to write a book, and she speaks as a mother caught up in the great events of her time. Her view is unique since virtually all other Carolingian literature was shaped by royal patronage and interests, by the center not the edge. But Dhuoda speaks from the margins—of a distant territory, of an embattled family, and of her gender. She placed her noble family ahead of all other considerations except Christian ones. We do not know when she died, but if she lived long after finishing her manual she would have been devastated by the storm of destruction that swept over her family, for the king executed her husband and her son William when he was only twenty-four, after he had tried to assassinate the king. He had not, after all, heeded his mother's instructions on how to survive in a dangerous world and to do the impossible: to please God, his noble family, and the king, all at the same time.

QUESTIONS | *What role did women, both noble and common, play in the Frankish world? Make a case that Dhuoda was either an insider or an outsider. What is most remarkable about her situation?*

---

of the raiders, thus bringing the attackers and the people reporting on those attacks (monks and priests) into direct contact. No wonder that church reports of the raids are often hyperbolic and apocalyptic. Since these church reporters were convinced that nothing happened outside of God's will, they interpreted the Viking raiders as "the rod of God's wrath" and thought that the Carolingian kingdom and its leaders were being punished for their sins. A Carolingian farmer might have been somewhat less worried that the Vikings would attack him and his family since there was little reason for the Vikings to burn down fields of wheat. The Vikings lacked the manpower to wreak widespread devastation.

The Vikings did not bring down the Carolingian Empire; the Carolingians themselves did that with civil war and political division. But it would be wrong either to glorify the Vikings as blond-haired warriors sailing south in search of high-minded wars to test their manhood or to dismiss them as harmless visitors adventurously opening up a closed world. They were many things—farmers, fishers, traders—and not all Scandinavians were Vikings raiding the Carolingian Empire, the Byzantine Empire, or Islamic lands. But those who did were pirates and, in the medieval context, terrorists. Their attacks, which were hard to anticipate and thwart, sapped the confidence of Carolingian society and inflicted psychological damage, just as they were intended to. The raids were brutally violent, and the Vikings went out of their way to convince their victims that they were bloodthirsty and vicious. They were prepared to assassinate bishops in front of their congregations, to steal saints' relics and drop them into the Atlantic, to murder women and children, and to enslave victims, all to remove present and future resistance to their raids.

By the 840s various Viking groups realized that they could make better use of their time if they wintered over in Francia, often on an island, so that they could begin raiding early the next spring. By the 880s some had decided to seize territory in places such as Normandy (the land of the Northmen) and eventually to become Christians.

Other Viking groups had entered the Mediterranean, where they encountered and attacked Muslim lands; twice they attacked Constantinople. Another group of Vikings called the Rus made it to Russia and established settlements at Novgorod and Kiev. In England, the city of York fell to the Vikings; and the Danes occupied much of southwestern England.

Two other groups of raiders attacked the large Carolingian Empire. Saracens (Muslims) made sporadic raids on Italy and southern Francia in the ninth century, and late in the century the Magyars (Hungarians) began to attack along the empire's eastern frontier. None of these raids amounted to much. While churchmen moralized about the Viking attacks, Carolingian kings took a more practical view, striking deals with the Vikings to attack their Frankish rivals, granting them land when necessary, and paying them off when possible. These arrangements were part of a longer-term process of accommodation and integration. As well, Louis the Pious sent missionaries north to begin converting the Scandinavian peoples.

The Viking experience was not all bad for Europe: it shook the Carolingian Empire out of its comfortable complacency, introduced a dynamic force into a settled world, and forced various rulers to become more efficient in their handling and distribution of power. Eventually, in the tenth and eleventh centuries, the Vikings would be fully assimilated into Europe, becoming Christians and an energetic presence within medieval European society.

The Imperial End Game:
Two Charleses, One Bald, One Fat

The last two emperors of the Carolingian Empire were Charles the Bald and Charles the Fat. The bald one survived the civil war of the early 840s and went on to establish a viable kingdom in west Francia. Once the troubles with his brothers had settled down, he mounted a spirited resistance to the Viking raiders, establishing island outposts and barricades to prevent the Vikings from having free access to the river highways into his kingdom. He dreamed of reuniting his grandfather's empire, though it never happened. Yet on Christmas Day 875 the pope crowned him emperor.

Like his grandfather, Charles the Bald established a viable court school, his under the Irish master Eriugena (c. 810–c. 877; also known as John the Scot, *Scot* meaning "Irish" in the ninth century). Eriugena was the greatest thinker of the Carolingian age. He taught the liberal arts, including grammar and music; and wrote amusing poems, including drinking songs and a funeral epitaph for a despised bishop who was still very much alive: "the best thing he ever did was die." He also knew Greek and immersed himself in Neo-Platonic Christian books. From these he created a comprehensive Christian cosmology in his masterwork, the *Periphyseon* (meaning "about nature"). For Eriugena, Nature encompasses

An Audience with Charles the Bald The monks of the monastery of St. Martin of Tours are shown presenting the First Bible of Charles the Bald to the king c. 845. The scene is a complex court scene with the king seated on his throne and accompanied by his retainers as the monks present him with the Bible. The image is an active one as the monks move into position and different stages of the ceremony are depicted.

all, including God, and can be divided into four parts: (1) that which creates and is not created (God); (2) that which creates and is created (the ideas or first thoughts of God); (3) that which is created and does not create (creation, including humans); and (4) that which does not create and is not created (God as the point of return of all things). Eriugena's work may have reassured Charles the Bald and his contemporaries that beyond the chaos of the political present there was a cosmic plan sweeping humans toward a reunification with God at the end of time. Eriugena did not believe that a hell of physical punishment awaited sinners. All would return to God, even the pagan Vikings.

Despite the Irishman's enfolding view of history, human and divine, Charles the Bald's difficulties did not end when he became emperor. He invaded the eastern Frankish kingdom of his nephews and was beaten soundly. In 877 he marched into Italy to aid a beleaguered pope and died while retreating through the Alps.

One of his nephews, Charles the Fat, became emperor in 881, but he had few resources and little power in an overextended empire. Once again powerful nobles held the upper hand. The Vikings were besieging Paris in 887 when some east Frankish nobles deposed him. Charles the Fat was the last legitimate Carolingian emperor.

Thus, although the Carolingian hold on power in much of Europe lasted for two hundred years (687–887), the Carolingian Empire (800–887) came to an end after a mere eighty-eight years. The royal line itself would not be completely extinguished for some years, but the last Carolingian kings were hardly towers of strength. What is surprising is not that the Carolingian Empire had such a short run, but that the Carolingians were successful for so long. The difficult conditions of Europe (the vast and varied geography, lack of roads, poor communications, rural economy, and absence of a vibrant urban element) and the lack of reliable resources (no standing armies, few fortifications, no direct taxation, and a rather primitive form of government) make their accomplishments, particularly those of Charles Martel, Pepin the Short, and Charlemagne, seem all that much more remarkable. During the following centuries, Europe would turn away out of necessity from Charlemagne's model of a united European whole, but the Carolingian experiment in power and culture would ripple through the Middle Ages. Its achievements in learning, language, script, and agricultural innovation formed the basis on which the culture and economy of the Middle Ages would be built.

Conclusion

Some historians have called the period from 565 to 900 the crucible of the Middle Ages, an age in which the basic elements of the Middle Ages were being mixed and ground together to form a more stable amalgam. The Early Middle Ages was a formative period for western civilization; out of it came the basic contour and character of the Middle Ages. Religion and, in particular, monasticism were the early agents of that transformation. The Carolingian dynasty temporarily straightened out the politics of the age, transforming Germanic kingship into a royal rule based on Christian teaching and the institution of the church. The Carolingians hitched their fortune to the papacy, notions of a universal church and universal empire, and the value of Latin learning and the classical ideal. That Charlemagne's empire did not last long mattered less than its reformation of European society. The work of these proto-Europeans had a subterranean effect. Below the surface, Europe was being transformed into a defined space with a set of shared cultural traits and ideals.

Little of that transformation would have been possible without the parallel rise of Islam and the Carolingians. It would be wrong to say that Islam created the medieval west and Byzantium, but not by much. Islam removed from the west a great deal that had belonged to the Roman legacy, effectively forcing a form of redefinition on the eastern Roman Empire, which now became a Byzantine Empire, and leaving the rural west to find its way in a world without the Mediterranean Sea in play and without Byzantine interference. Charlemagne and the Carolingian Empire took up the challenge, forcing on continental Europe a set of cultural and religious standards and a loose political model of many Europes or regional realities inside a relatively weak imperial system. The long political and cultural redirection and identification of Europe had finished only its first phase when the Early Middle Ages came to a close.

Critical Thinking Questions

1. What events, cultural and political changes, and people are important to determining when the Middle Ages began?

2. Who were the most influential figures and what were the most influential forces at work in the Early Middle Ages?

3. Was religion the defining feature of the Early Middle Ages? If so, why? If not, what was?

4. How did the rise of Islam affect the many Europes, east and west, their contours and natures?

5. Was the Carolingian Empire an exceptional or a natural development of the post-Roman world? Why?

Key Terms

diocese **(p. 202)**

relics **(p. 203)**

Ummah **(p. 206)**

Hejira **(p. 207)**

shari'ah **(p. 207)**

jihad **(p. 207)**

Kharijites **(p. 208)**

iconoclasm **(p. 210)**

Donation of Pepin **(p. 212)**

missi dominici **(p. 214)**

capitularies **(p. 214)**

Caroline Minuscule **(p. 217)**

subsistence economy **(p. 220)**

manorialism **(p. 220)**

Vikings (Northmen) **(p. 224)**

Primary Sources in connect

For information on Connect and the online resources available, go to **http://connect.mcgraw-hill.com**.

1. **The Rule of Saint Benedict: A School for Monks**
2. **The Salic Law: A Compensatory Code for Living**
3. **The Donation of Constantine**
4. **Charlemagne as an International Figure**
5. **Are the Dogheads Human?**
6. **Dhuoda's Lament**

BACK TO THE SOURCE

Charlemagne as Family Man

Einhard, long a presence at Charlemagne's court, wrote a biography of the king about 826–827, just over a decade after Charlemagne's death. One of the things he claimed to know most about was the inner workings of Charlemagne's domestic life: his troubles with his brother and how he treated his mother, loved his children, and disregarded the scandalous behavior of his many daughters.

18. . . . [Charles] protected, increased the size of, and beautified his kingdom. Now I should begin at this point to speak of the character of his mind, his supreme steadfastness in good times and bad, and those other things that belong to his spiritual and domestic life.

After the death of his father [in 768], when he was sharing the kingdom with his brother [Carloman], he endured the pettiness and jealousy of his brother with such great patience that it seemed remarkable to all that he could not be provoked to anger by him. Then [in 770], at the urging of his mother [Bertrada], he married a daughter of Desiderius, the king of the Lombards, but for some unknown reason he sent her away after a year and took Hildegard [758–783], a Swabian woman of distinct nobility. She bore him three sons, namely Charles, Pepin, and Louis, and the same number of daughters, Rotrude, Bertha, and Gisela. He had three other daughters, Theoderada, Hiltrude, and Rothaide, two by his wife Fastrada, who was an eastern Frank [that is to say, German], and a third by some concubine, whose name now escapes me. When Fastrada died [in 794], [Charles] married Liutgard, an Alemannian woman, who bore no children. After her death [in 800], he took four concubines: Madelgard, who gave birth to a daughter by the name of Ruothilde; Gersvinda, a Saxon, by whom a daughter by the name of Adaltrude was born; Regina, who bore Drogo and Hugh; and Adallinda who gave him Theoderic.

[Charles's] mother, Bertrada, also spent her old age in great honor with him. He treated her with the greatest respect, to the point that there was never any trouble between them, except over the divorce of King Desiderius's daughter, whom he had married at her urging. She died [in 783], not long after Hildegard's death, but [had lived long enough] to have seen three grandsons and the same number of granddaughters in her son's house. [Charles] saw to it that she was buried with great honor in St. Denis, the same church where his father lay.

He had only one sister, whose name was Gisela. She had devoted herself to the religious life from the time she was a girl. As he had with his mother, he treated her with the greatest affection. She died a few years before him [in 810] in the monastery [of Chelles where she was abbess] in which she had spent her life.

19. [Charles] believed that his children, both his daughters and his sons, should be educated, first in the liberal arts, which he himself had studied. Then, he saw to it that when the boys had reached the right age they were trained to ride in the Frankish fashion, to fight, and to hunt. But he ordered his daughters to learn how to work with wool, how to spin and weave it, so that they might not grow dull from inactivity and [instead might] learn to value work and virtuous activity.

Out of all these children he lost only two sons and one daughter before he himself died: Charles, his eldest son [who died in 811], Pepin, whom he had set up as king of Italy [died in 810], and Rotrude, his eldest daughter, who [in 781] was engaged to Constantine, emperor of the Greeks [she died in 810]. Pepin left behind only one surviving son, Bernard [who died in 818], but five daughters: Adelhaid, Atula, Gundrada, Berthaid, and Theoderada. The king displayed a special token of affection toward his [grandchildren], since when his son [Pepin] died he saw to it that his grandson [Bernard] succeeded his father [as king of Italy] and he arranged for his granddaughters to be raised alongside his own daughters. Despite the surpassing greatness [of his spirit], he was deeply disturbed by the deaths of his sons and daughter, and his affection [toward his children], which was just as strong [a part of his character], drove him to tears.

When he was informed [in 796] of the death of Hadrian, the Roman pontiff, he cried so much that it was as if he had lost a brother or a deeply loved son, for he had thought of him as a special friend. [Charles] was, by nature, a good friend, for he made friends easily and firmly held on to them. Indeed, he treated with the greatest respect those he had bound closely to himself in a relationship of this sort.

He was so attentive to raising his sons and daughters, that when he was home he always ate his meals with them and when he traveled he always took them with him, his sons riding beside him, while his daughters followed behind. A special rearguard of his men was appointed to watch over them. Although his daughters were extremely beautiful women and were deeply loved by him, it is strange to have to report that he never wanted to give any of them away in marriage to anyone, whether it be to a Frankish noble or to a foreigner. Instead he kept them close beside him at home until his death, saying that he could not stand to be parted from their company. Although he was otherwise happy, this situation [that is, the affairs of his daughters] caused him no end of trouble. But he always acted as if there was no suspicion of any sexual scandal on their part or that any such rumor had already spread far and wide.

QUESTIONS | *What strengths and flaws does Einhard identify in the character of Charlemagne? Why does Einhard's account include so much about the children and so little about the wives? Why would Charlemagne not allow his daughters to marry? Why should any of that matter to Einhard or to history?*

Source: Einhard, *The Life of Charlemagne* 18–19, trans. Paul Edward Dutton, *Charlemagne's Courtier: The Complete Einhard* (Toronto: University of Toronto Press, 1998), 27–29.

8

"Gislebertus Made This." The Tympanum Sculpture of the Last Judgment, St. Lazare, Autun

THE ROMANESQUE
CENTRAL MIDDLE AGES

In the Aftermath of the Collapse of Carolingian Order
- Vassalage and the Grounding of Power
- Local Lords and Castle Building
- An Ethic of Service

Imperial and Royal Power
- The Ottonian Moment in the Imperial Sun
- The First Millennium and the Delayed Second Coming
- The Stirrings of Stronger Monarchies in England and France
- The Royal Ideology of the Three Orders

Religious Corruption and Reform
- Cluny Begins Reforming Monasticism
- An Emperor and Church Reform
- Pope Gregory VII and the Investiture Controversy
- What Cost an Imperial Papacy?

Power Shifts at the Edges of Europe
- Byzantine Troubles and the Rise of the Seljuk Turks
- Norman Adventurers Take Sicily and Southern Italy
- William Conquers England
- The Norman Restructuring of England

Europeans on the Move
- A Measure of Internal Peace Returns to Europe
- Pilgrims Take to the Road
- Preconditions for Crusade
- Living the Material Surge of the European Economy
- The First Crusade

Conclusion

THE LAST JUDGMENT OF GISLEBERTUS Anyone wishing to see the Romanesque Central Middle Ages (900–1100) could not do better than to spend some time with Gislebertus, a sculptor who worked in a number of churches in Burgundy at the start of the twelfth century. His finest work is to be seen in the cathedral of St. Lazare of Autun south of Paris. There he and a team of sculptors carved a series of stunning capitals. Some scenes are shocking: a demon hurtling at breakneck speed toward the ground; Judas being hung by howling demons who tug on the rope. Some are touchingly tender: Joseph leading a funny little donkey on which sits a perfectly peaceful Mary cradling her divine child; an angel reaching out delicately to wake the Magi (Wise Men) beatifically asleep below a blanket of dramatic swirling lines.

There are dozens of such capitals, many of them masterpieces, but the great **tympanum** sculptures placed above the doors of the church take us even closer to the Romanesque imagination. On the north portal, Gislebertus sculpted one of the first female nudes of the Middle Ages, a languorous Eve just before the Fall, casually reaching out to pluck the apple that will undo her and all of humankind. Above the west portal entrance to the church, Gislebertus mounted a monumental depiction of the Last Judgment. An inscription on the lintel (the horizontal piece above the door)

The Temptation of Eve

tells us that Gislebertus made (or, perhaps, that someone of that name sponsored or supervised) the piece. Christ as the final judge occupies the middle of the semicircular space, his arms stretched wide to encompass all. To his right are the saved, some already entering paradise where Mary holds court, others gazing with reverence upon Christ. To Christ's left, sinners are weighed on scales, while Satan and agitated demons herd the damned together for never-ending torment. Below Christ runs a carved frieze also divided right and left into the elect and the damned. There, with chilling effect, a pair of giant disembodied hands grasps the head of one sinner to haul him off to hell.

Gislebertus's genius lay in capturing the extremes of the Romanesque worldview: of light and dark, spirit and body, joy and horror. The Romanesque age was one that knew and experienced such extremes: the rough times around the year 1000 and the pursuit of peace, the slaughter of innocents in the temple at Jerusalem at the end of the First Crusade and the hushed silence of great monasteries, the resolute conquest of England and a flowering economy. In stone and on parchment, artists captured

the dynamic energy of the age. Romanesque figures are rarely static. They move, twisting and writhing in punishment, or elegantly bend upward to gaze upon the blessed. The uncertainties and charged energy of the tenth and eleventh centuries can be sensed in its agitated art.

Romanesque churches are stately if slightly dour constructions; hence, the need for lively adornment, sculptures and objects to enliven stern spaces. These were massive stone basilicas with round Roman arches (from which the name *Romanesque* derives), heavy walls, and

Romanesque Interior of St. Foy of Conques, Eleventh Century

FIGURE 8.1 | Cross-section of a Romanesque Cathedral

The vertical thrust of the vaults and narrow width of the nave give the Romanesque cathedral its stately and imposing presence.

Source: Adapted from *Romanesque: Architecture, Sculpture, Painting,* ed. Rolf Toman (Cologne: Koenemann, 1997), 27.

small windows. The main aisle of a Romanesque **nave** (the central longitudinal space, from the Latin *navis* for ship, so named because it resembles the upside-down hull of a ship) has two or three vertical levels: the first fixed by the arches, which create a tubular effect that draws believers toward the choir in the east end and the main altar, and move sideways through the side arches into parallel side aisles; the second is the gallery level above the arches; and the third, a clerestory level of windows above the gallery (Figure 8.1). These

immense buildings, whose physical footprint might occupy an entire city block, dwarfed the small wooden houses of townspeople that lay in their shadows. With bold lines and towers that seem to scratch the sky, Romanesque basilicas dominated their world. In northern Europe, Romanesque churches are often dark and gloomy inside, but in the south, awash with sunlight, their interiors are filled with light. The Romanesque style, which grew out of the rich range of Carolingian architectural experiments, was the first great pan-European style of architecture.

Architectural description fails to encompass what these churches meant to the people of the Middle Ages or how relatively poor farming communities could have erected such massive buildings. Romanesque **basilicas** served as the institutional, religious, and social centers of their communities and of western Europe as a whole. In them communities met, people were married, babies baptized, and funeral rites read. The decoration of these churches shaped the average person's visual understanding of the world. At Autun, Gislebertus and his team greeted Christians at the door of the cathedral with re-creations of the unseen world lying behind the flat and impoverished facade of the real world. By the eleventh century, Romanesque churches sported stained glass windows, trumeaus (the central columns of the portal) decorated with twisting saints and back-biting beasts, and delightfully strange capitals. Approaching the entranceway of an imposing cathedral such as Autun, people entered a world of stark opposites. It was almost as if a visual contract was being laid down before they entered. To set foot in a cathedral like Autun and to participate in the medieval Christian community was to accept a view of the world as one of sharp opposites. The life one lived would soon be examined by the great judge Christ and a final reckoning would be made: sinners would suffer for all eternity, gnawed by fiends, while the righteous would enter paradise and join the restful company of Mary and the saints. There was no avenue of escape, no other options on display.

The great story of the Central Middle Ages was how Europe once again transformed itself, turning away from the failed Carolingian imperial model (of a single family of strong kings and a universal emperor, court culture, dependent church, and rural economic realities) to the Europe that was emerging by the late eleventh century (with weaker kings, vibrant regional and national cultures, a formidable papal church claiming to lead all Christendom, burgeoning cities, and a resurgent European economy). The first great problem was how, in the aftermath of the Carolingian collapse, to redistribute

power. In a world in which central power had been shattered, power went to ground, becoming local and often brutal in vast **vassalage** networks. How would power that was so segmented and localized be re-collected by centralizing forces, or would it? What would bring about that centralization, and who would give Christendom a set of uniform values and purpose? Emperors and popes each thought that they should supply Christian Europe with the needed leadership and direction. By 1100, some answers were becoming evident. The popular First Crusade had been fought, a medieval Christian culture was in place, an imperial papacy had emerged, the economy was vibrant and growing, and Europe was ready to wrestle with the wider world.

In the Aftermath of the Collapse of Carolingian Order

At the end of the ninth century, Europe seemed to be falling back into political disorder and a new dark age, the name so long and so inappropriately applied to the Early Middle Ages. The collapse of the Carolingian Empire meant that authority and legitimacy were once again uncertain. Throughout Europe self-made, petty kings stepped into the political vacuum left by the Carolingians, but they exercised little power and could claim even less legitimacy.

Why was vassalage a natural vehicle for the reorganization of power in a decentralizing world?

Charlemagne's great cultural enterprise died with his house. His had been a royally sponsored court culture and educational enterprise, but when his dynasty failed, so did its cultural model. Writing fell off, dramatically. The tenth century had a fifth of the literary output of the ninth. Church building slowed or stopped altogether. The institutional church, which had benefited from royal supervision and resources, began a slow drift into disorganization and the corruption of standards, irregular practices, and spotty devotion. The papacy seemed a long way away in Italy, and it had its own problems now that its great protector, the Carolingian house, was gone. The economy of Europe, however, may not have suffered to the same degree since the population of Europe continued to creep upward. There were signs that a fundamental restructuring of Europe was taking place in the troubled tenth century.

Vassalage and the Grounding of Power

After the Carolingians, Europe entered a period of rapid decentralization. The most basic questions were who held power and by what means. In the seventh and eighth centuries the Carolingians had established contractual relations with lesser men. Although some scholars have called this institution *feudalism* (an early-modern term coined from the fief, or piece of land, that the lord gave to his subordinate), it is probably more accurate to call it vassalage.

A vassal was the sworn man of a more powerful individual. Vassalage was sealed by an oral contract in which the vassal publicly and orally swore allegiance (commended himself to the lord), did homage (demonstrated his subservience), and committed himself to perform military service on behalf of the lord. The vassal swore to be the lord's man. The lord in turn promised the vassal protection and granted or invested him with land (the fief) along with the people bound to that parcel of land. The public ceremony was formal, indeed holy since God was its real witness and oaths were often sworn on relics. The ceremony was a whole body experience with visual, oral, aural, and tactile elements. The rite was enacted before witnesses who watched as the inferior man knelt before the lord (or, on occasion, lady) and swore homage or fealty to him, while the lord cupped his hands around the outstretched hands of the vassal. The vassal received the lord's declaration of acceptance and pledge of protection and care; the lord then offered him a piece of land, often symbolized by a clump of earth or stick. By the physical ceremony, vassals were said to have become "men of mouths and hands." They and their lords had acted out their contract and bonding by means of reciprocal gestures. The land given (the **benefice**) was the property and resource that the vassal would use to sustain his service to the lord, provide for his family, and outfit himself and his dependents for armed conflict in the lord's service.

While vassalage properly refers to a military and political arrangement that was contractual and legal in nature,

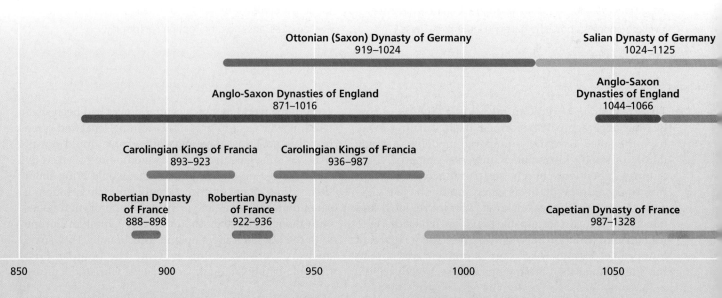

Ottonian (Saxon) Dynasty of Germany
919–1024

Salian Dynasty of Germany
1024–1125

Anglo-Saxon Dynasties of England
871–1016

Anglo-Saxon Dynasties of England
1044–1066

Carolingian Kings of Francia
893–923

Carolingian Kings of Francia
936–987

Capetian Dynasty of France
987–1328

Robertian Dynasty of France
888–898

Robertian Dynasty of France
922–936

850   900   950   1000   1050

A Lord and Vassal Publicly Make a Contract In this twelfth-century depiction, the lord clasps the hands of a standing man to make him his vassal. Typically the man would have knelt before the lord to demonstrate his subservience and the nature of their relationship; here, the vassal bends his knees. Notice the crowd of witnesses: an oral contract required a publicly witnessed ritual. The unsmiling demeanor of all suggests the seriousness of the ceremony.

manorialism (treated in Chapter 7) refers to an economic and social one that was not contractual in nature (that is, it was not formalized or witnessed), though it did involve obligations by both parties. Though ties of dependency may characterize both vassalage and manorialism (the man to his lord, and the worker or serf to the lord of the manor), the functions and purposes of the arrangements were different. Vassalage forged a contract between two free parties; manorialism was a noncontractual, already-existing set of arrangements between a propertied free man and his dependent workers to work the manor he held.

At its core vassalage concerned the alignment of power, for it sorted men into formalized power and resource relationships. Vassalage existed prior to the collapse of the Carolingian house. Before they became royal, the Carolingian family used vassalage-like contracts to bind men to them since they could not expect the allegiance of supporters and subjects that a king could command just by the fact of his sovereignty and standing. When they became a royal dynasty, the Carolingians were somewhat less supportive of vassalage because they could now command men's allegiance because all were subjects of the king. Yet they did not abolish vassalage; it still sorted power and property between men at levels below the king. Instead, the Carolingians tried to control vassalage to ensure that it did not impinge on their royal rights.

As the Carolingian dynasty began to lose power during the civil war and weakened further in the second half

Norman Dynasty of England 1066–1154

Gislebertus at work on Cathedral of Autun 1120–1135

1150   1200   1250   1300   1350

To Use the "Feudal" -ism or Not

All *-isms* (such as monasticism, manorialism, capitalism, humanism, and Marxism) have some value as terms, but they can easily mislead, enticing us to accept as actual wholes our own collections of often unrelated parts. Feudalism is an *-ism* to consider. The great nineteenth-century legal historian F. W. Maitland observed wryly that, should someone ask what feudalism was, one good answer would be that it was a seventeenth-century essay in comparative jurisprudence, by which he meant that feudalism was a legal invention of the early-modern era imposed by scholars on the medieval past. By the eighteenth century the idea of a medieval feudal system was used to describe the totality of medieval social and political relations.

Mid-twentieth-century medievalists tended to adopt either an exclusive or an inclusive understanding of feudalism. F. L. Ganshof confined "feudalism" to the military relationship between a lord and his vassal, who were tied together by the lord's gift of a fief (land) in exchange for military service from his vassal. Marc Bloch spoke in broader terms of a feudal society characterized by ties of dependency: lord and vassal, manor lord and serf, bishop and priest, abbot and monk, and so on. In a refreshing review of the topic in 1974, Elizabeth A. R. Brown advocated abandoning the term *feudalism* altogether since it is artificial and distorts the specifics of medieval power relationships. It is a fact that no medieval man or woman had any notion of feudalism *per se* or ever used the term. They knew oral contracts and obligations, understood what a fief was and what service was, but they doubtless

also knew that these social arrangements varied widely from place to place, time to time, individual to individual. The truth for them lay in the details. Specific contractual arrangements, not some overriding institution, determined the relations between people.

Many historians (though perhaps fewer economists) have begun to drop *feudalism* as a term, recognizing that the problem with the term will never be settled by having a better definition. They have rejected the argument that the term is a necessary simplification of complex social dealings suitable for students, who can more easily grasp the ordering of medieval power if it is sorted into a pleasant feudal pyramid. The problem with all *-isms* is that they box us in, forcing us to think of abstract wholes instead of detail and difference. In a major book in 1994, Susan Reynolds reexamined the entire subject and made a case for studying feudalism on its own terms. Whether or not we decide to use the term *feudalism*, it would be good when encountering all *-isms* to think critically about what they mean and how they may direct our thought away from the actual to convenient pigeon-holes.[1]

QUESTIONS | *What other -isms are there, and how accurate, convenient, or misleading are they? If Scotland, England before 1066, and freeholders throughout Europe were never a part of "feudalism," and if "feudal" relations were constantly changing and never the same in time or place, what case can still be made for employing the term feudalism?*

of the ninth century, Carolingian kings had increasing trouble ensuring that the vassalage arrangements their subjects were making with one another did not compromise royal power. Kings needed noble support during those difficult times and were pressured to grant their subjects special privileges, including making fiefs heritable so that the son of a vassal might under special circumstances hold his father's benefice after his father died. The danger was that once a benefice became an inheritance or a family holding, it ceased to be a freely given grant of land and position that a great lord exchanged for service, but rather was a traditional right that passed out of the king's or lord's direct dispensation.

Local Lords and Castle Building

With the disruption of the Viking attacks and the weakening of royal power, and its eventual collapse, powerful nobles assembled large numbers of dependent vassals

who recognized that their futures and livelihoods were better protected by local lords than by a distant king with decreasing power. Vassals did not always welcome their contractual dependency but were forced by the rearrangement and redistribution of power taking place to accept their inferiority. Vassalage represented the localization of power, its grounding, but it did not cause that localization. Nor did it fundamentally cause disorder, though it may have seemed that way to contemporaries. In the tenth and eleventh centuries, local lords came to dominate the countryside of Europe, particularly in the area of greater France, where disorder was greatest. There men with limited local power fell to fighting each other and victimizing others by blocking roads, waylaying travelers, handing out rough justice to the people of their lands, and exacting fines and fees. That might seem to make for a brutal and disordered society, but power had in fact found a principle of organization in local expressions of force. That fragmented power would not begin to flow back up to regional and centralizing forces until the eleventh and twelfth centuries.

With most of Europe lacking effective monarchies between 880 and 950, local lords filled a power vacuum. Vassalage, then, may be viewed as a necessary reordering of power in the countryside of Europe in response to the decline of central power. Local lords had already begun erecting fortifications by late in the ninth century. Kings such as Charles the Bald ordered their destruction, but the threat of Viking raids and attacks by their own aggressive neighbors made the lords' need for protective defenses paramount. Early on these structures were made of wood and stone and were generally situated on a prominent piece of land such as a hillock or rock outcropping. The **keep** (or *donjon,* "dominant point") was a stone tower erected on an elevated site within the fortification. The keep served not only as the lord's residence, but also as a place for his family and vassals to retreat when under severe attack. Around the castle were various earthworks and walls, encircled by a ditch or water-filled moat. The Normans in the tenth century built what are called Motte-and-Bailey castles, the motte being the mound of earth on which the keep was built and the bailey being the outer wall that surrounded the motte, keep, and a small parcel of land.

Castles later evolved into grand, often stylized medieval constructions of great size, but in the tenth and eleventh centuries, smaller sturdy fortifications represented the frontline of a struggle for power and survival. The local lord was oath-bound to protect his vassals and a castle did that, since its function was largely defensive. But the right to build castles and so to control territories was hotly contested. Greater lords and kings did not want their inferiors controlling pockets of territory they considered their own, to have castles with which to protect themselves when they should be relying on superior lords, or to assemble and protect armies of vassals who should rely on a greater lord. Great counts such as Fulk Nerra in Anjou spent considerable effort ringing their territories with castles and destroying the rogue castles of lesser men. Much of the tenth and eleventh centuries was taken up with a struggle between lesser and greater lords over who had the right to build and maintain castles, many of which were attacked and leveled as the chief point of contention in local power struggles.

An Ethic of Service

As an institution built on something as fragile as an oral contract, vassalage required extraordinary social and ideological support if it was to hold firm. An ideology of vassalage that glorified service and condemned disloyalty emerged. It was a system of values aimed downward, insisting on the faithfulness of vassals. Fulbert of Chartres's injunctions about the relations of lords and vassals are negative in nature, stressing the vassal's obligation not to injure his lord's interests, but largely ignore the lord's reciprocal obligations toward his vassal. An ethic of service put pressure on vassals to be subservient and to remain utterly faithful to their lords. A Carolingian capitulary had set out the grounds on which a vassal might break his oath, but the conditions were so exceptional that under most circumstances the contract was unbreakable. A vassal could break his oath if his lord sought to enslave him, plotted against his life, committed adultery with his wife, drew a sword to kill him, or failed to protect the vassal as he had promised.

The *Song of Roland* (*Chanson de Roland*) promotes this ideology of service. The core of the story concerns the ambush of Charlemagne's baggage train at Roncesvalles in 778, but the epic poem in Old French that was written down by 1100 reflects the social and political conditions of the tenth and eleventh centuries. The poem transforms the enemy from the mountainous Christian Basques into an international army of Muslims. The two main Christian warriors of the epic are brave Roland and wise Oliver. Both are good men who ride pell-mell into battle atop mighty steeds, slashing the enemy with great glistening, fabled swords. Charlemagne's men in the *Song* are impulsive, high-spirited warriors, all bicker and bite, proud and ready to fight wherever and whenever their lord commands. Roland is the bravest of them all, the best of the vassals, not because he is prudent—indeed, he injures Charlemagne's interests—but because of his utter, doglike loyalty.

A Motte-and-Bailey Castle A reconstruction of what a typical eleventh-century castle fortification might have looked like: an outer wall (bailey), moat or ditch, inner wall, interior space, and mound (motte) with a keep or sturdy castle at its summit.

The poem is like Roland and the values he embodies. It is active, not reflective; exterior, not interior. The lines of verse are broken into short, self-contained bursts of action that belonged to an age that knew intense episodes of isolated action. The poem's very style and rhythm are combative. At the end, as the battle turns against the outnumbered men at the rear, Oliver urges Roland to blow his horn to summon help. Roland refuses. He says that men must endure such burdens, suffer searing heat and freezing cold, sharp wounds and bloodied bodies for their lord. Roland will not consider damaging his reputation and so brings destruction upon himself and his fellow warriors. Only when the cause is lost and his death certain does Roland blow his horn to alert the king. No enemy fells him. Rather, in signaling the king, the exhausted warrior blows out his own brains, the blood gushing from his temples. He dies the perfect vassal's death.

As he dies, Roland lifts his gloved hand to the heavens, transferring his service from Charlemagne to God. In death, Roland becomes God's vassal. The *Song of Roland* puzzles modern readers. Wise Oliver would seem to us the better man; Roland is too proud, impulsive, and rash, but Roland is the hero of the poem because of his utter, unquestioning loyalty to his lord. Everything was forgiven because of his loyalty and bravery, even his stupidity and stubbornness. The *Song* sings not of kings (Charlemagne is two hundred years old, frail, and beset by bad dreams), but celebrates vassalage. But Roland, bound and restricted by the rules and obligations of being a vassal, is a prisoner of his condition and can find transcendent freedom only in action on the field of battle and in glorious death.

A second, simpler story makes the same point. Stephen of Bourbon recorded a medieval legend of a knight and his lady who left their infant son in a cradle in a castle room with a faithful greyhound as his guardian. A snake slithered into the room through an open window and was about to attack the baby. The dog leaped to the rescue, throttled the snake, spilling blood over the baby and himself in the fight, and then cast the snake out the window. Hearing the commotion, the noble couple rushed into the room. Seeing their baby covered in blood and blood around the dog's mouth, the knight killed the dog. When he later discovered the dead snake at the foot of the castle and realized that his son was uninjured, he understood that the dog had been protecting his son and deeply regretted having killed him.[2]

The death of the innocent greyhound reflects the ideals of the age, for the dog died the faithful servant of his lord, mortally wronged. Vassalage celebrated the silent, mis-

Roland Blows His Horn A thirteenth-century depiction of the vassal Roland blowing an oliphant or horn to alert King Charlemagne that he and the rear guard are under attack. In fact, in the *Song of Roland* the struggle to resist the pagan attack was already over and in blowing the horn Roland burst his temples and died.

understood, ever loyal, resolutely faithful servant. No matter the cause, he did his unwavering duty. An open wound of misunderstanding and victimhood belonged to vassals. It was the burden they bore for their service to a superior. The ideology of vassalage promoted the idea of self-sacrifice; Roland died and so, too, a loyal dog.

Imperial and Royal Power

Despite its weakened state, kingship remained, at least in principle, admired and sought after by many. Power in the Middle Ages may be viewed as the story of a continual contest for power between noble and royal interests. When one was up, the other was down. The struggle played out in small, gradual advances and retreats over decades. The empire and imperial title returned in the tenth century under the Ottonians (the dynasty named after Otto I the Great), but the Roman Empire of the Ottonians contained little more than parts of Germany and northern Italy. The Carolingian dream of an empire of all Europe was gone. All medieval empires after theirs were regionally restricted. The idea of empire persisted, but medieval empires were more royal than imperial in the world of real politics and power.

How did kingship find its footing again in the Romanesque Central Middle Ages?

The Ottonian Moment in the Imperial Sun

In 911, when the last Carolingian king of eastern Francia died, nobles recognized Conrad, the duke of Franconia, as king, but they gave him little support and often waged war against him. Though the Vikings had not done great damage to east Francia, the Magyars (Hungarians) continued to harass its eastern border. Conrad may not have been a strong king, but he did something remarkable as he lay dying. He lacked a son, and so in 919 he decided to pass the crown to Henry the Fowler, the duke of Saxony. As king, Henry labored to subdue his powerful German neighbors and used a nine-year truce with the Magyars to secure his own territory and build fortifications. At the Battle of Unstrut in 933 he defeated the Magyars and then turned his attention to the Danes, who soon sued for peace.

Otto I the Great (r. 936–973) succeeded his father in 936 and was crowned king at Aachen in Charlemagne's chapel. He resumed the campaign against his troublesome neighbors and in 955 at Lechfeld decisively defeated a force of Magyars, marking an end to their harassment. At the time of their defeat, the Magyars were already becoming a settled, agrarian, European people, and in the tenth century they became Christians.

Otto was drawn into Italian and papal affairs. In 960 Pope John XII begged him to rescue the papacy from the king of Italy, which Otto did, even though John was not the most admirable of medieval popes. His critics charged that Pope John had ordained a deacon in a stable; accepted money to ordain priests; committed adultery with four women (one of whom was his niece); turned the papal palace into a brothel; blinded his godfather; castrated a rival; and was an arsonist, a drunkard, and a gambler. Despite that defamation of the pope's character, Otto allowed John to crown him emperor and his wife Adelaide empress in 962, but Otto deposed the infamous pope the next year and spent several years sorting out papal affairs. Like Charlemagne, Otto considered both the safety and the integrity of the papacy and the church to be a critical part of his imperial mandate. The **Ottonian system** for managing the church extended to investing bishops and abbots with their offices, controlling the proprietary church (that is, having the lands of a church belong to a secular lord appointed by the king), and appointing secular operating officers of church lands.

Otto sought to open up relations with the Byzantines. He sent an ambassador, Liudprand of Cremona, to Constantinople to secure a Byzantine princess for his son to marry, thus hoping to further legitimize his own imperial dynasty. He eventually found a Greek bride for his son, Otto II (r. 973–983), but Otto II was forced to fight the Byzantines and Saracens in southern Italy and lost a critical battle there. Italy held other dangers for all the Germans, particularly from its malaria-infested swamps in the north. When Otto II died from malaria, he left his three-year-old son, Otto III, as his co-regent and heir (r. 983–1002). Otto III took control of the government in 994 when he was fourteen and became emperor in 996. Though Otto III ruled for only six years, his was one of the most precocious of medieval reigns. He modeled himself after Charlemagne, styling himself the restorer of the Roman Empire and placing the learned Gerbert

Emperor Otto Honored by His Empire The four chief provinces (represented as women) of the Ottonian Empire (Germania, Francia, Italia, and Alemannia) pay homage to the enthroned emperor. It is not certain which of the three Ottonian emperors is depicted.

of Aurillac on the papal throne as Pope Sylvester II (999–1003), but Otto died when he was twenty-one and was succeeded by his cousin Henry II (r. 1002–1024), who ruled the empire from Bamberg in Germany.

The Ottonians showed their debt not only to the lengthening shadow of Charlemagne, but also to a firm commitment to religious rigor, the restoration of the Roman Empire, and renewed contact with the Greek east.

The First Millennium and the Delayed Second Coming

Otto III's death in 1002 was just one of a series of calamities that worried Europe around the year 1000. Apocalyptic fears had been the background noise of western civilization since the rise of the Roman Empire, though official sources always firmly reminded Christians that only God knew when and how the world would end. A monk by the name of Raoul Glaber (also known as Rodulfus Glaber and Bald Ralph) compiled a chronicle that begins with the events around the year 1000: outbreaks of heresy, strange events, disease, famine, fire, and floods. Raoul's world was wrapped in symbols and signs, prodigies and portents with which he believed God was speaking to

An Ambassador's Purple Rage

Perspective is always particular and relative. Who does the seeing, when, from what angle, of what object, and to what end? Virtually all the documents that historians employ involve matters of perspective. No better demonstration of how changeable and tricky perspective can be comes from two contacts between east and west that occurred late in the tenth century.

Liudprand of Cremona (c. 920–972) visited Constantinople twice, but the reports of his two experiences are strikingly different. In 949 he went as a young man keen to learn Greek and found all things Byzantine wondrous. The emperor Constantine VII Porphyrogenitus received him graciously; housed, fed, and entertained him exquisitely; and flattered the young man with courtly attention. Liudprand was so embarrassed by the meanness of King Berengar II of Italy for whom he was carrying a letter full (as he said) of lies for the emperor, that he gave the emperor his own gifts in Berengar's name. Liudprand had brought Constantine four child-eunuchs as slaves. He was rewarded with imperial gifts and could not stop talking about the marvels he saw at the imperial court, the glorious buildings, and his own privileged reception.

Medieval Map of Constantinople

Twenty years later, in 968, he returned to Constantinople, this time as a legate of the emperor Otto the Great. By then, Liudprand had become the bishop of Cremona and Otto entrusted him with the delicate task of arranging for a Greek imperial bride to marry his son. Everything that could go wrong on a trip did go wrong this time. He was housed in drafty lodgings far from the imperial palace; had an awful, grumbling, penny-pinching landlord; and was forced to drink wretched wine full of pitch, pine juice, and plaster. From the start, he was received rudely and treated with humiliating disrespect by the Byzantines. He dealt chiefly with the emperor Nicephorus's brother Leo, who went out of his way to insult Otto and his ambassador. Even the eastern emperor, when he finally deigned to see Liudprand, treated him insultingly. At a state dinner, the ambassador was seated far from the emperor at the end of a table where the tablecloth had run out. Nicephorus baited Liudprand, telling him that westerners regarded their bellies as their gods, were given to drunkenness, and were not true Romans. Liudprand gave as good as he got, telling the emperor that the Romans (that is, Byzantines) should remember that Romulus was born of a whore and murdered his brother. He said that when in the west they wanted to insult someone they called him a Roman. The trip was all downhill from there, and as the ambassador was leaving the city with his mission a crashing failure, officials searched his bags and seized some purple imperial robes that they said no westerner had the right to export. Liudprand was outraged by the violation of his baggage and the suggestion that he was smuggling precious goods.

Why the stark difference between the two experiences? Almost everything had changed. In 949, Liudprand had been a young unthreatening westerner received by a generous host and shown the splendors of Constantinople. In 968, he was the official representative of a western emperor whom the Greeks regarded as an imposter. In the meantime, Liudprand had aged and as his standing in society had risen, so had his pride. The memory of his glorious first visit had probably raised unrealistic expectations about what he might expect on his return. His second account (*Tit for Tat*) was written for Emperor Otto, and Liudprand wanted to explain why his mission had failed. What better way to do that than to document the cruel treatment that he had received as Otto's legate. Perspective, in short, depends on particular historical, personal, and contextual circumstances, all of which had changed dramatically for Liudprand between his two trips to Constantinople.

QUESTIONS | *How should historians identify and handle matters of perspective when considering primary sources? Are both of Liudprand's accounts true, or in what way are they true?*

the world. Raoul was convinced that Satan would be loosed upon the world at the millennium, and so he collected evidence that the end was near as he attempted to read God's mind.

When the world didn't end, some learned men recalculated and came to the conclusion that the true millennium, the second coming of Christ, should occur around 1033, a thousand years after Christ's crucifixion. Raoul gathered the signs: the deaths of nobles, kings, emperors, and high churchmen; eclipses; and a famine with a horrific outbreak of cannibalism in 1033. Raoul was not alone in worrying about the end time. The French king had heard that it had rained blood in Aquitaine and asked the wise men of his realm to explain the event. When the world survived the 1030s, even Raoul noticed a new optimism at work in his world as it put on what he called "the white mantle of churches," that is, the freshly cut stone of the new Romanesque churches that were being erected. For some people, it was as if the western Christian world had survived some great test set by God and could now turn to new things.

Others were less sure. Raoul continued to collect signs of the times into the 1040s, trying to understand what God was telling them about the workings of divine history. The sculptor Gislebertus, at the end of the Romanesque Age, was still preoccupied by stark visions of final things.

The Stirrings of Stronger Monarchies in England and France

The Anglo-Saxon kingdoms of England were hit hard by various Viking attacks. The Danes occupied East Anglia in 869–870. Mercia fell to the invaders in 874, and Northumbria, including York, fell to Danish settlers two years later. A large portion of Wessex fell under Danish control during the same period. King Alfred the Great of Wessex (r. 871–899) and a small band of supporters were forced to travel through parts of his occupied kingdom at night. Over the next twenty years, Alfred slowly recovered his kingdom, reorganized Wessex, secured its defenses, and built a navy to resist the Danes (Map 8.1).

When Alfred died, Danes still inhabited parts of his kingdom and England, but Alfred's reign marked the beginnings of an Anglo-Saxon revival. As a learned man, patron of the church, and maker of laws, Alfred set a model for Anglo-Saxon kingship. Alfred was also an author and composed works in Old English. While continental Europe turned chiefly to Latin as its learned language for writing, Anglo-Saxon England had the earliest and most vigorous vernacular written tradition in Europe. By the reign of King Edgar (r. 959–975), much of England was under west Saxon (or Wessex) control and at relative peace.

Monarchy reasserted itself in England without a great deal of direct Carolingian or Ottonian influence. Anglo-Saxon kings established traditions for ruling that would

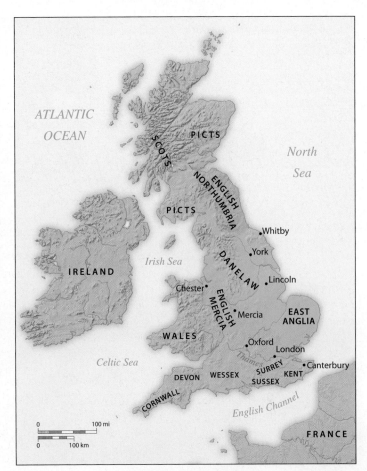

MAP 8.1 | Anglo-Saxon England, c. 900

At the end of the reign of Alfred the Great, southern England was under the control of Anglo-Saxon kings, but the rest of England was under Danish control (the Danelaw). *Why was Alfred's reign important? Why was England so divided and the Danes such a continuing threat?*

persist until the Norman Conquest in the eleventh century. The Danish occupation forced Alfred and his successors to make their governments more efficient. Older Anglo-Saxon divisions of the land were abandoned, and in their place, Alfred and his heirs introduced the hundreds (an area of approximately one hundred families), boroughs, and shires. To build his navy, Alfred ordered each three hundred hides (a hide being enough land to support a single family of dependent farmers) to pay for the construction of a ship. He and his successors insisted that their men do garrison duty, standing ready to thwart invaders.

The prestige and claims of Alfred and his royal line rested on their successful resistance to foreign occupation. There were fewer noble challenges to monarchy in England than on the continent. Nobles assembled at the Witenagemot or Witan (the supreme council), but it was filled with the king's advisors and its function was to carry out his will. Moreover, Alfred and his heirs had the support and sanction of the church. Anglo-Saxon kings did seek oaths of fealty from their subjects, but the institution of vassalage was absent. Royal law was enforced by thegns (king's agents) and shire reeves (sheriffs). The instrument of command was the royal writ,

MAP 8.2 | Medieval Europe, c. 1000

By the year 1000, Europe contained a number of weak kingdoms, a territorially limited empire, and lands held by Islamic powers. Even within these seemingly solid blocks, power remained fragmented. France was a fiction in that the area of royal control was limited to a small territory around Paris. **What are the geographic and historical reasons for Europe's fragmentation?**

short documents written in Anglo-Saxon (Old English), which began to appear in the early tenth century. Despite all the Anglo-Saxon successes, England experienced another round of Viking attacks starting about 980, and Cnut (d. 1035), the king of Denmark and Norway, became king of England. Thus Anglo-Saxon control of most of England lasted for just over a century before England was ruled by a foreign magnate.

The situation in France was almost the opposite of what occurred in Germany, in part because the Carolingian dynasty had held on longer in west Francia, despite having experienced more severe Viking invasions than other areas of the continent. Late in the ninth century, after Charles the Fat's fall, Odo, the count of Paris, declared himself king and Odo's son Robert held the title briefly before it returned to a Carolingian claimant. Between 936

and 987, the Robertians waited for their opportunity to reassert their claim to kingship. The Robertian Hugh the Great (d. 956) and other French nobles slowly whittled away at late Carolingian royal rights, lands, and offices. By the tenth century, the monarchy of Francia was impotent; these kings made no laws and could hardly rule. King Louis IV (r. 936–954) held only one fortified town, Laon. His vassals held far more property and power than he did. To travel outside his small royal realm, the king had to secure the permission of his nobles.

In 987, the last of the Carolingian kings of France died. Hugh Capet (r. 987–996), one of the sons of Hugh the Great, was elected and crowned king of France at Rheims, where he enjoyed the support of the archbishop, Adalberon. Hugh's power lay not in the royal title that his family (called the Capetians) now held, but in his might as lord (or suzerain) with an extensive network of vassals at his command. He dominated the territory between Paris and Orléans. Like most successful lords, Hugh and his line knew how limited their power was and how small the area of royal France was at the time. Throughout the eleventh century, the Capetians continued to lose land to the powerful dukes of Champagne and Burgundy. Hence, the Capetians moved slowly and cautiously in pressing their new royal claims, but kingship had time on its side (Map 8.2).

The Royal Ideology of the Three Orders

Whereas the institution of vassalage and the noble-military complex laid its ideological emphasis on faithful service, kings had their own persuasive ideology in the scheme of the three orders, which appeared when monarchy was at its weakest. In his Old English translation of Boethius (the Roman senator and philosopher executed by Theodoric), King Alfred asserted that, to rule, a king needed priests (*gebedmen*), warriors (*fyrdmen*), and workers (*weorcmen*). A century later, an Anglo-Saxon abbot explained that royalty rests on three supports: workers (*laboratores*), warriors (*bellatores*), and priests (*oratores*). All were necessary—the workers to provide sustenance for the kingdom, the warriors to protect it against invasion, and the priests to intercede with God—for the kingdom to function. The division into the three orders of those who work, those who fight, and those who pray lays out an interdependent trifunctional society, one that effectively limited women to two of the categories and included a class of people, the workers or farm laborers, who were not free. The king stands outside the orders, surmounting them.

In Francia, when royalty reached its lowest point, Adalberon, the archbishop of Rheims, who oversaw the elevation of Hugh Capet to kingship, advocated the same: a well-ordered society of those who work, those who fight, and those who pray. The assumption behind this ideology was not only that each order produced something good and necessary for society as a whole, but also that kingship was necessary to govern the parts of a harmonious whole. The thrust of the ideology from the king's perspective was to equalize the orders, each being necessary to the kingdom. Here the warriors did not dominate as they had seemed to in the *Song of Roland*.

Royal ideology could, however, produce nightmares. According to his physician, King Henry I of England in

King Henry I's Dream King Henry late in his reign is supposed to have dreamed of being attacked by peasants, knights, and bishops, which were the three orders of medieval society (those who work, those who fight, and those who pray). The nightmare suggested how greatly the king had upset the balance of the three orders in England.

the early twelfth century had a bad dream one night late in his life while visiting Normandy. He first envisioned a mob of peasants with their rustic tools rioting around him. The king awoke in a start as his guards fled. In a second sequence, the king dreamed that a host of soldiers dressed for war was threatening his life. He awoke screaming, grabbed his sword, and slashed at the air. In a third dream sequence, archbishops, bishops, and abbots approached the king with their staffs, complaining bitterly over his seizure of church property. The dream-story suggested that an aggressive king had upset the balance of the three orders and so a smoothly functioning kingdom.

The scheme of the three orders, which was later transformed into the idea of the Three Estates, was never descriptive of medieval society, which was infinitely more complex and varied. There were merchants, sailors, Jews, children, lepers, popes, outsiders, and many others whom it failed to include. The point of the ideology was rather to advocate a simplified scheme of medieval society's general shape and of the necessity of having a king to reign over its complementary parts. The ideology of the three orders did not concern itself with theology or God's sanction of kingship, but with the king's natural duty to rule over society if it was ever to achieve stability and perfect harmony.

Religious Corruption and Reform

If one way to view the Middle Ages is as a struggle for power between lords and kings, another way to understand it is as sequences of church corruption and reform.

What were the strengths and weaknesses of the imperial and papal views of church-state relations?

By the tenth century, the western church was in disarray. Fewer local and regional councils were held, local lords thought of the churches and monasteries in their territories as their property and a place to employ family members, and the education of priests and monks had declined dramatically. The call for reform came from the Cluniacs, but before long the papacy took charge and steered the reform of the church from the top down. By the end of the great reform period of the eleventh century, the papacy, and so western Christendom, had been transformed. An imperial papacy was the result, and the Middle Ages was never to be the same.

Cluny Begins Reforming Monasticism

Monasteries were always prone to corruption. Over time as abbots and monks interpreted the *Rule*, little changes grew into big changes and customary habits, loosening standards of rigor and practice. Some monasteries allowed women to live with their monastic husbands and others permitted a generous daily allotment of wine. Graver charges were made: that in some monasteries sodomy was common, that abbots bought their offices, and that monks were so uneducated that they could not say the Lord's Prayer. Small reform movements sprang up in areas of Germany and France in the tenth century, but none that compared to the scope and success of Cluny.

Cluny was a Benedictine monastery founded in Burgundy in 910 by Duke William of Aquitaine (thought to be the grandson of Dhuoda) and his wife.

William and Cluny's first abbot conceived of something special, a monastery that was not subject to a local bishop or lord, but nominally to the papacy. By this innovation, Cluny obtained independence and freedom from local interference, both lay and ecclesiastical. Cluny was a monastery with a central administration, a heavy regimen of daily prayer, and strict rules. Between 910 and 1109, Cluny had only six abbots, all of them dedicated reformers. When abbots, particularly laymen, wanted to reform their corrupt monasteries, they turned to Cluny to investigate and purge its vices. Odo, the second abbot of Cluny, was nicknamed the "digger" because of his ability to see into the hearts and wayward habits of the monks he visited. Many monasteries signed on to the Cluniac movement and in turn became reforming monasteries. By the twelfth century, Cluny had hundreds of dependent and associated monasteries, many of whose monks were Cluniacs who professed in person to the abbot of the mother house. By the eleventh century, Cluny was so powerful that contemporaries mocked its fourth abbot as "King Odilo."

What Cluny specialized in, aside from reform, was ritual observance, chant, and prayer. Its particular devotion to prayer struck a receptive chord with people, who had become convinced by the disordered and tumultuous times in which they lived that God's reckoning was about to fall. The best remedy they could see was to give land and wealth to Cluny, which stood closer to God than worldly sinners ever could. Cluny would not just pray for their souls, but would keep praying for them until doomsday. Cluny's rigor and steadfast attention to the eternal promised donors their best chance to reach the merciful ear and forgiveness of God. The land they gave

2. CLUNY (NO).

Cluny Re-imagined The third church of Cluny was a large Romanesque basilica erected 1088–1121. The building was almost entirely destroyed during the French Revolution. On the drawing, the principal features of the church are evident: two towers at the west end, long nave, distinct crossing with three towers to form a cross, and built-up east end (the choir) with radiating chapels around the apse.

was intended to ensure the security of Cluny, to remove it from the flux of the world so that the monks could keep on praying. Cluny's example and commitment to church reform had a powerful impact on the eleventh century and wider church reform.

An Emperor and Church Reform

In 1024, the Saxon line of the Ottonian emperors was succeeded by a line of four Salian (or Frankish) kings and emperors that also thought of the papacy and the German church as under its special care. Some scholars date the beginning of the so-called Holy Roman Empire from 1024, though others would date it from the time of Charlemagne in 800 or that of Otto I in 962. The name, however, may be no more than a convenient way to distinguish a medieval empire centered in Germany from the ancient Roman Empire. Under the Salian emperors, the Ottonian system of church control continued, though it was increasingly resented by many churchmen who thought that the church should be independent and self-governing. They pointed to corrupt practices within the church that compromised its purity and godliness, particularly clerical marriages and **simony** (the buying of ecclesiastical offices).

The emperor Henry III (r. 1046–1056) agreed that the church should be reformed, though his idea of church reform differed from the one held by most ecclesiastical reformers. Henry refused to accept gifts or favors for promoting individuals to clerical offices. Like his Ottonian predecessors, he viewed himself rather than the pope as the true guardian of the integrity of the church, especially since the popes seemed to be doing such a poor job of it.

The papacy's problems in the early eleventh century were many. Its power remained largely local. Even a learned and upright pope such as Sylvester II carried little authority outside Rome and papal lands. Many of his successors could not even claim respect for their spiritual authority. They were often the creatures of their noble families and the intense factional politics of Rome. The noble house of Tusculum had over time successfully placed three members of its family on the papal throne, but in 1045, another aristocratic family arranged the election of one of its own as pope. The problem was that Pope Benedict IX was still in office. Benedict abdicated in favor of another pope, but then withdrew his abdication. In 1046, with three men claiming to be pope, Emperor Henry intervened. He deposed all three popes and oversaw the election of a German cleric as Pope Clement II (1046–1047).

The emperor's interference angered some church reformers and the noble families of Rome, but an important group of reformers within the church applauded his efforts to save the papacy and church from itself. Peter Damian (d. 1072), a Cluniac monk and sharp critic of clerical sin, welcomed Henry's intervention. With the emperor's support, Clement's successor, Pope Leo IX (1048–1054), took charge of the movement to reform the church. In a dramatic meeting at the cathedral of Rheims in 1049, he placed the relics of Saint Remigius on the high altar and then called upon the collected bishops to swear that they had not bought their offices. The group panicked. Some slipped out of the meeting before speaking, some requested time to consider their answers, and others were reputed to have been so flustered that when they rose to speak no words issued from their lips. Pope Leo had made his point. The high church was infested with corruption, and it fell to the papacy to cleanse it.

Among the reformers gathered around Leo was Cardinal Humbert (d. 1061). Humbert wrote a treatise against simony and precipitated a crisis of relations with the eastern church. On a papal legation to Constantinople in 1054, he presented the expansive claims of the reforming papacy in favor of western ecclesiastical predominance and the supremacy of its doctrines. The eastern patriarch resisted, and each side excommunicated the other. The break of the Christian Church into a Roman Catholic western church and a Greek Orthodox eastern church created the **Great** (or **East-West**) **Schism** that was not repaired (at least formally) until 1965.

Pope Gregory VII and the Investiture Controversy

The papal reformers had just begun. Like so many revolutions, this one gained speed as it went. While the emperor Henry III lived, he was as much the patron of the reform movement as the pope. When he died in 1056 and was succeeded by his six-year-old son, who was under the supervision of his mother, the church reformers asserted their right to elect the pope without imperial interference. But, since Otto the Great, the emperors had claimed the right to nominate popes. Pope Nicholas II (1058–1061) and his reforming clergy wanted to be free not only of imperial control, but also of interference from the Roman nobility. They proposed that in the future popes should be elected by cardinal-bishops. The regent for the young king Henry IV (r. 1056–1106) reacted harshly and lobbied German bishops to reject the proposal. Thus, a few years after Henry III's death, a rupture opened between the interests of the empire and the papacy. The conflict forced the papacy to reach out to other Christian kingdoms for support against the empire and thus to become more European and to practice international politics. Pope Nicholas even began to cultivate the Normans as a vassal state and his protectors. The Normans, who had an infamous reputation and had invaded southern Italy and Sicily, had even captured Pope Leo and held him for ransom in 1053.

Into this maelstrom of shifting papal prerogatives and high ambitions came one of the most enigmatic of medieval personalities, the Italian monk Hildebrand. He had gone into exile with one of the popes deposed by Henry III, but quickly found himself working for the reforming popes. He was elected Pope Gregory VII (1073–1085), not by the cardinals as the reform agenda stipulated, but by the acclamation of the people and clergy of Rome. Gregory, after whom the reform movement is called Gregorian, was not just a dedicated reformer; he was a supremely stubborn one. Now that the papacy had more or less established its autonomy, Gregory set out to put his Catholic house in order. He pushed hard against priests being married and promoted the practice of absolute clerical celibacy. He denounced simony, as had his predecessors, but Gregory's signature reform concerned the lay investiture of ecclesiastical officeholders. For that reason, the Gregorian Reform is commonly called the **Investiture Controversy.**

The Ottonian emperors and their successors had insisted on their right to invest bishops with the symbols of their office, the ring and staff (crosier). To Christendom at large it may have seemed that by this act the emperor, king, or a local lord was granting the officeholder his position and authority, in effect making him bishop. To the emperors it was critical that they continue to reserve the right to approve, nominate, and appoint bishops. The Ottonian system of controlling the proprietary or propertied church depended on it and, indeed, at some level the emperor thought of himself as the equal of, or even superior to, the pope, both being appointed by God and both having a religious or priestly function. Throughout the empire, bishops appointed by the emperor had a vested interest in maintaining the emperor's right to choose and approve bishops. To the reformers, however, **lay investiture** seemed to represent the secular control of spiritual life.

Upon this issue rested the future of both the empire and the power of the reformed papacy and its control of the church. By pursuing church reform, the papacy became one of the first centralizing forces in Europe after the collapse of Carolingian order and the localization of power. Pope Gregory claimed that all archbishops must swear an oath of obedience to the papacy and receive their palliums (mantles) from the pope. Strictly speaking, some of Gregory's claims were not based on precedent and so were not reforms, but claims for new powers. In a document called the *Dictation of the Pope* (*Dictatus papae*) an extraordinary range of bald claims was made. The problem is that we are not entirely sure of the document's origins or purpose. One explanation might be that the *Dictation* is a set of research topics or talking points that awaited precedents and proofs from the papal archives. The document does, however, suggest just how high the revolutionary Pope Gregory aimed.

King Henry IV, not yet emperor, and Gregory struggled over the appointment of bishops. In the case of the church of Milan, each supported a different candidate. In 1075, Henry marched on Milan, drove out Gregory's candidate, and invested his own choice as archbishop. The pope threatened Henry with excommunication. Henry and his bishops responded by calling Hildebrand a false monk who was claiming unprecedented powers for himself and disturbing the peace of the church. Henry's bishops broke with the pope and no longer recognized his authority. Gregory responded by excommunicating the king and did something even more damaging; he released all Christians from the allegiance they had sworn to Henry and forbade them to serve the king. It was a brilliant stroke. Henry's German enemies almost at once began to plot against him.

King Henry realized that he had been outmaneuvered by Gregory, but he seems also to have understood that, now that the matter was a public spectacle, the contest was far from finished—it was check, not checkmate. Rebels were already waging war against Henry in Saxony when his magnates granted Henry one last chance. If he did not set things right with the pope and bring about an end to his excommunication, they would choose another king. Many of them wished Henry to fail and so tried to block any attempt he might make to communicate with Rome. Henry broke free and set out to track down Gregory to ask for forgiveness. The pope for his part tried valiantly to elude Henry and to get to Germany to attend the meeting where Henry was to be deposed. The weather intervened, however, and the pope was forced to take refuge from a snowstorm in the castle at Canossa in northern Italy. There Henry found him and for three days, dressed in sackcloth as a penitent, he stood barefoot in the snow outside the castle, begging for the pope to forgive him. Finally the pope relented and forgave Henry, readmitting him to the church and undoing his excommunication. Gregory's priestly obligation to forgive sinners had not allowed him to do otherwise, though it changed everything and was not in his political interest.

King Henry was now free to suppress his enemies in Germany. Angered that the pope had abandoned them,

Henry IV Seeks Forgiveness With Abbot Hugh of Cluny as his witness, Henry IV begs Abbess Matilda of Canossa to intercede with Pope Gregory VII to lift Henry's excommunication.

the rebels elected a new king to replace Henry. Gregory claimed that he had never restored Henry to kingship, but Henry acted as though he had. With a rebel king and Henry now both claiming royal authority, a conference was called at which the pope would decide between the two. Henry was not prepared to allow Pope Gregory to render a decision that would depose him, and so he worked to undermine the conference. Gregory, however, excommunicated the king again and this time sanctioned a replacement. Henry did the only thing he could; he declared the pope deposed and replaced him. At first no one paid much attention to that deposition, but things changed when Henry defeated the rebels in 1080 and the king appointed by the pope died in the battle. In 1084, Henry marched on Rome, and his chosen pope declared the king emperor. Gregory fled into exile to his Norman protectors and died the next year.

What Cost an Imperial Papacy?

The contest between the papacy and the German rulers was chiefly over the proper place of the church in the world: who governed it, on what basis, and to what end. Since Charlemagne and Otto the Great, German rulers had felt that they were the best and divinely sanctioned protectors of the church. The emperors had integrated the church into the operation of their governments, and they were not prepared to have a distant pope abolish their authority. Moreover, the emperors were not the source of corruption within the church, as the reformers charged, for the evidence suggests that rulers such as Charlemagne, Otto the Great, and Henry III had what they thought were the best interests of the church in mind. They rescued popes on numerous occasions, deposed bad and criminal popes, and appointed to episcopal office men who they thought were good for the church and shared an interest in the state and good government.

The controversy became a war of pamphlets and propaganda as both sides sought to justify their actions. The early church reformers had not been opposed to imperial oversight of the church because they realized that negligent popes had allowed the church to drift. By the late stages of the contest, however, the reformers were dedicated to removing all secular interference from the church. Pope Gregory tested the core of the issue: did God vest the pope with the singular responsibility of ruling the church or did he also appoint the emperor to watch over it? In the process of the Investiture Controversy and, despite Gregory's final failure to unseat an emperor, the popes claimed complete leadership over the church, but they also transformed the papacy into an international political player in Europe. The *Dictation* claimed that popes could depose emperors and that only popes had the right to wear imperial insignia (a right granted by the *Donation of Constantine*). The reforming papacy had become an imperial papacy. It sought a measure of control over the empire and kingdoms of Europe, developed an impressive bureaucracy, and called for and sanctioned wars. But popes

discovered, as Gregory VII did, that while they could recognize kings and make emperors, it was less easy to remove them. Gregory's papacy showed just how unsettling and intrusive a powerful and politicized papacy could be.

Finally, at Worms in 1122, an agreement or concordat was struck whereby another emperor renounced the imperial right to invest bishops with the symbols of their holy office, but was permitted to supervise their election and to invest them with their scepters, the symbols of their worldly power. The emperor thus retained some influence over the process of choosing bishops and retained an interest in one dimension of their power, but he ceded some of his religious rights over the church. The striking thing is that the kings of Christendom were not forced to surrender their own religious claim over their bishops and churches. The same contest over a king's right to control the church in his realm and the church's interest in defending its independence was waged several times over the following centuries. Kings held fast to the notion that they held a royal and religious power over the churches in their realms. Powerful churchmen and monarchs were bound to infringe on one another's authority for the simple reason that in the medieval world the church had become politicized and monarchy sanctified since kings believed that they too were sacred guardians of the church appointed by God.

The emperor Henry IV remained cut off from the official church as one excommunicated until he died. The contest with the papacy left Germany weaker than it would otherwise have been, for the emperor was left without firm control over his church and his status within Christendom remained religiously uncertain. It may not, in the long run, have been in the best interests of medieval Europe for popes and their supporters to undermine Christian kingship and emperorship. Still, the radical reform of the church, its reordering and cleansing, spilled over into local churches and local practices throughout western Europe. The church was well on its way to becoming a central player in the history of the Middle Ages; and Gregory VII had created, as his *Dictation* suggested, an imperial papacy. Although the reformers had begun by seeking a church free from worldly corruption, they ended with one that was politically engaged, centralized, and more in the world than ever.

Power Shifts at the Edges of Europe

Important power shifts occurred in the eleventh century at the territorial margins of Europe: in Byzantium, southern Italy, and England. The rise of the Seljuk Turks and their impact on the Islamic world and on Europe introduced another dynamic element into an increasingly aggressive period that was remaking the West. The Mediterranean

What did the Norman adventurers want, and what was the effect of their various conquests?

Sea and southern Europe reentered western European history and England rejoined continental history when the Norman William the Conqueror took England.

Byzantine Troubles and the Rise of the Seljuk Turks

The Byzantine Empire had a rough mid-eleventh century. The Macedonian dynasty that had, with many ups and downs, distinguished itself in the ninth and tenth centuries in war, the cultivation of the arts, relative religious stability, the adoption of the Eastern Orthodox faith by the Kievan Rus, and a secure front against Islam, came undone after the death of the emperor Basil II (the Bulgar Slayer) in 1025. Problems of imperial succession, riots, earthquakes, and disease beset the empire. The Great Schism of the universal church occurred just when the empire was weak and almost leaderless as the Macedonian dynasty reached its end. A Russian prince crossed the Danube and invaded Byzantine territories in the 1040s, and various Byzantine generals, backed by provincial strongmen, revolted.

Worse still for the Byzantine Empire was the rise of the Seljuk Turks who set out to conquer Islamic and Byzantine lands. The Turks consolidated their control of Persia, and in 1055 the general Toghril Beg (r. 1038–1063) seized Baghdad and was named sultan. The Seljuk Turks reinvigorated Islam, bringing a new religious commitment to territorial expansion and the suppression of infidels. The late eleventh century was an age of fervent intellectual development under the Seljuks. The Persian poet Omar Khayyam wrote his famous quatrains and al-Ghazali, another Persian, was at work on *The Incoherence of the Philosophers,* his critique of Islamic philosophers who had grown too dependent on Plato and Aristotle. There were resisters to the Seljuks, particularly the so-called Assassins, an assassination cult that broke off from the Ismaili sect of Shi'a Muslims. They targeted the Seljuks, who had been persecuting them.

The sultan Alp Arslan (r. 1063–1072) waged campaigns against portions of the Byzantine Empire. At the Battle of Manzikert in 1071, the sultan demolished a Byzantine army and captured the Byzantine emperor. The Seljuks seized Armenia and regained Antioch.

Norman Adventurers Take Sicily and Southern Italy

While Byzantine lands were falling to the Seljuk Turks in the east, they were failing in the west, as well. The Byzantine Empire still claimed parts of southern Italy, particularly Calabria, but it was an unfixed territory with shifting allegiances. Opportunistic Normans first hired themselves out as mercenaries to local lords and by 1029 had been granted land as payment for their service. Other Normans infiltrated the area, and by the 1040s they were plotting to divide up the region of Apulia in southern Italy. The nastiest of the Norman chiefs, Robert Guiscard, nicknamed the "Cunning One," and Richard of Aversa, forced themselves on the area. Pope Nicholas II granted them Calabria, Apulia, Sicily, and Capua as papal fiefs. The Norman adventurers, thus, found a reforming papacy ready, for its own political reasons, to give them legal sanction.

The Norman dukes attacked Byzantine and Muslim outposts in southern Italy. Robert seized the Byzantine city of Bari in 1071 and continued his conquest of Sicily, which was subject to three quarrelsome Muslim emirs. Messina was taken in 1061 and Palermo in 1072. Sicily would not become a Norman kingdom until 1130, but the Norman presence in the south signaled a shift in the balance of power in favor of an energized and increasingly aggressive western Europe. As the Byzantine Empire withered under Muslim attack, the Norman adventurers in southern Italy showed that western-led war had reached the Mediterranean.

William Conquers England

Early in the eleventh century, Aethelred (meaning "noble counsel") II (r. 978–1016), but called the Unready (*unred* meaning "without counsel"), married Emma, the daughter of the duke of Normandy. Aethelred was all too ready to murder his Danish retainers and noble hostages, including the Danish king's sister, but less than ready to defend England when the Danish king Swein invaded and drove Aethelred into exile. Swein's son, Cnut, ruled England until 1035. After Cnut, with a civil war raging in Denmark, the Anglo-Saxons supported Edward the Confessor (r. 1042–1066), the son of Aethelred and Emma, as their new king. But Edward had no children, and in the 1050s the men wanting to succeed him began to make their preparations. Among them was Edward's cousin, William, the duke of Normandy, to whom Edward was said to have promised the crown. Godwin, the earl of Wessex, had long opposed Edward. After Godwin's death, his son Harold amassed considerable lands and powers and laid claim to the throne. Unfortunately for Harold, he became a prisoner of William when he accidentally strayed into Norman territory. To win his freedom, Harold was forced to swear homage to William and to agree to support the duke's case as the rightful successor to Edward.

Edward the Confessor died early in 1066, and the Witan crowned Harold king. The king of Norway, Harald Hardrada, threatened to invade England to press his claims and Duke William was finalizing his planned invasion. William accused his vassal Harold of betraying his oath to support his lord. William secured the support of the pope for his claim to the throne and, most important of all, he assembled some eight thousand Norman soldiers to cross the Channel and invade England. In the meantime, Harald Hardrada landed in northern England

The Many Mysteries of the Bayeux Tapestry

The first mystery of the Bayeux Tapestry is its popular name, since it is not a tapestry, but an embroidery. The work is 230 feet long and 20 inches high with a main panel of narration and running margins filled with small scenes and details, some decorative, particularly in the top band, and some, typically in the bottom margin, serving as decoration and commentary on the main narrative above. The work is named after Bayeux, where the cloth has been located since at least the Late Middle Ages.[3]

The second great mystery is how the Bayeux Tapestry has survived. Great stone churches and palaces have crumbled and disappeared, precious metalwork has been melted down, and most of the clothwork of the Middle Ages has turned to dust, but the Bayeux Tapestry survives, and in relatively good condition. There were many moments when the work might have disappeared. The first mention of the work's existence in the cathedral of Bayeux occurs in an inventory of 1476. It was not mentioned again until the eighteenth century, when it was displayed for a week each year in the religious calendar. During the French Revolution, the Bayeux Tapestry briefly served as a covering for a wagon-load of military equipment. When Napoleon was contemplating an invasion of England, he ordered the work to be publicly displayed. During World War II, the Nazis, who were planning to invade England and who identified with the Normans as a Nordic people, moved it to the basement of the Louvre. Paris fell to the Allies before the work could be transported to Berlin as Hitler had ordered, where its survival would have been endangered. If history didn't destroy the Bayeux Tapestry, moths and other natural causes easily could have, but against long odds the embroidered cloth has survived.

The other mysteries of the Bayeux Tapestry are many. For whom was it made? By whom? When? Opinion varies, but many scholars believe that the piece was commissioned by William the Conqueror's half-brother Odo, the bishop of Bayeux and a combatant at Hastings. The work was probably made in England by Anglo-Saxon women following a design. The work presents the Norman victory but shows William's troops brutally burning down buildings and pillaging, and shows the doomed King Harold nobly crowned. The Bayeux Tapestry has Latin inscriptions, which are simple labels that identify and locate scenes but do not explain events. The work announces King Harold's death, but two men are shown being killed—one with the outline of an arrow penetrating his eye and the other on the ground being hacked to death. Are both Harold? The last seven feet or so of the cloth are missing. Did these missing seven feet of cloth show William being crowned as the termination of the story? The work has little religious content and yet was preserved by a cathedral. Some of the marginal illustrations are obscene, yet the work was displayed in a church. Lastly, what are we to make of the mystery woman Ælfgyva? She stands with a cleric who is shown slapping her face while below her in the bottom border a nude man dances. Who is Ælfgyva? What part does she play in the story of the conquest? Is the marginal scene of the nude man a comment on her story or utterly unrelated? None of these questions has been answered satisfactorily. Ælfgyva is a reminder to us not to dismiss the Bayeux Tapestry as a cartoon, but rather to meet it on its many different levels: as a reflection of medieval thought, a medieval way of presenting history, and a piece of captivating medieval secular art.

Ælfgyva Slapped by Priest on the Bayeux Tapestry

QUESTIONS | *Why are cartoons and caricatures so often political in spirit? How might the Bayeux Tapestry be medieval propaganda? If so, why is its meaning so unclear?*

but was defeated decisively by King Harold at the Battle of Stamford Bridge near York. Duke William landed in the south four days after Stamford and Harold rushed down to meet the invading force. They met at the Battle of Hastings, where Harold and his brothers died on the field of battle.

That single battle cleared away all the immediate rival claimants to the throne except William. England's future had been decided by fewer than 15,000 soldiers. William the Conqueror was crowned king at the Romanesque Westminster Abbey (since replaced) on Christmas 1066.

The Norman Restructuring of England

Hardly was the battlefield at Hastings cleared when William began to legitimize his conquest and assert his authority over his new kingdom. He founded Battle Abbey on the site of his victory to thank God for his blessing that day. It took William years to overcome resistance to his conquest, from both Anglo-Saxons in the north of England and Vikings. William respected Anglo-Saxon law as it had existed before the conquest, but he set out to rule England in Norman fashion. Thus, he built castles and imposed upon England a continental form of vassalage. He regarded all the land of England as his royal property by right of conquest and redistributed much of it upon receiving oaths of allegiance. Less than 10 percent of England remained in the hands of the old Anglo-Saxon nobility. Toward the end of his reign, he commanded a great accounting of the properties of his kingdom. A chronicler complained that the king wanted to know everything he owned, right down to the last ox, cow, and pig. William's great reckoning known as the **Domesday Book,** which is now to be seen in several volumes in the Tower of London, was modeled on continental inventories of lay and ecclesiastical property. The book remains a treasure trove of information on the social history of England at the time.

William's hostile takeover did not please most Anglo-Saxons, who thought of their country as occupied by French foreigners. Revolts broke out in reaction to William's usurpation and brutality. In 1069–1070, the king savagely suppressed a rebellion in the archdiocese of York. William imposed a ruling class of French and Norman barons and subordinated Anglo-Saxons to inferior places in his government and across the land. His continental aristocrats, for social and economic reasons, reduced the Anglo-Saxon lower classes of England to a stricter servile condition. William took control of the forests of England, as was the custom on the continent, and denied English commoners their traditional right to enter and use the forests. The king's court replaced the Witan, and local lords' courts administered justice. Below the surface, however, as the Domesday Book reveals, the underlying nature of private and public life in England remained Anglo-Saxon. The Normans retained the division of the land into shires and hundreds, continued to employ sheriffs, and issued writs.

William also regarded the English church as his church, one that was reformed as the Norman church had been. Out went clerical marriage, simony, and bad bishops. William began to replace Anglo-Saxon bishops with continental clerics and reorganized the episcopal map of England, moving some episcopal seats from small towns to more prominent places. William's spirit of church reform belonged to the ideals of the emperor Henry III, not to the radical claims of Pope Gregory VII. The Conqueror agreed to pay the papal tax called Peter's Pence, but never swore fealty to the pope as Gregory requested. With William's conquest, England for better or worse joined the main course of European history.

Europeans on the Move

The Middle Ages was never static; people, individually and collectively, traveled to and settled in new places.

Why did the First Crusade occur?

Servile farm workers bound to the land and service to their lords might never have traveled farther than twenty miles from their birthplaces in a lifetime, but many people did. Merchants, Jews, clerics, pilgrims, scholars, and soldiers traveled vast distances, even in the Early and Central Middle Ages. There were conditions, of course, that inhibited travel: invasions by the Vikings and Magyars, the loss of open control of the Mediterranean Sea to Muslims, local lords who did not permit travel through their lands, intermittent wars, lack of good roads, heavy forests, and the lack of an infrastructure to support travel (no hotels, instruments of credit, safety or security). In the eleventh century, many of these inhibiting conditions began to change.

As power slowly flowed upward, the intense localisms of the tenth and early eleventh centuries began to break down. People in the west began to move about more often and more freely. The late eleventh century might be thought of as a critical takeoff point for European mobility and outreach.

A Measure of Internal Peace Returns to Europe

Even the grim chronicler Raoul Glaber noticed that, after 1035, Europe seemed a more vigorous place. Churches were being built, and people were on the move. It was not the passing of the millennium of Christ's birth or death that caused that revival, but changing political and social conditions. For one thing, the invasions had fallen off, and the Scandinavian peoples had become Christian. Although it was a great age of castle building and local lords and, therefore, of internal wars, forces both religious and political were working to stabilize Europe.

Before the papacy began to reform the church, various bishops and church councils were already acting to suppress local violence. Late in the tenth century, churchmen began to promote the **Peace of God,** a movement aimed

1066: How Much Changed?

The year 1066 may mark a great sea change in English and European political history, but the year could have turned out very differently than it did. William the Conqueror, for all his planning and industry, arrived in southern England with fewer forces than King Harold could command, didn't know the lie of the land as well as his opponent, and in fact didn't know who his enemy would be. If King Harold had lost at Stamford Bridge, William would have been forced to fight against Harald Hardrada. But King Harold won a stunning victory and set out at once to confront William. Had Harold delayed, raised more troops, or even rested the ones he brought with him, all might have turned out differently. Even then the Battle of Hastings was close. During the battle, a rumor spread that William had been killed. With his troops in retreat, William entered the fray, lured Harold's infantry off a piece of commanding land where they were prevailing, and his troops killed King Harold, thus giving William a spectacular win.

The battle was a decisive turning point. For one thing, it marked the end of any real Viking threat to the fortunes of Europe, Harald Hardrada being the last Scandinavian leader to threaten England. As well, the Norman use of horses signaled a change in the nature of medieval warfare for England. The Anglo-Saxon reliance on infantry had proven itself inferior to mounted knights. The Anglo-Saxon nobility was pushed aside and replaced by a continental nobility made up of Normans, French, and Bretons. For the rest of the Middle Ages, English kings would have continental cultural and property interests that often entangled England in continental wars that it had previously avoided.

What did all of this mean to common people? There are those who doubt that the decisions of the great affect little people at all and who believe that social history is real history and political history but a superstructure that doesn't penetrate the main fabric of society. The Norman Conquest is a test case. Imagine a common farm worker living in a village like Dorchester on Thames near Oxford. His immediate lord and his lord's greater lord were replaced by Normans who soon increased the demands they made upon him and his family. They demanded more work, more dues, and a tighter interpretation of his legal standing and relations to the manor lord. He was no longer able to venture into the forests to hunt small game. He and his wife thought of their new lords as foreigners, who spoke a foreign tongue and mangled English when they spoke it at all. The local court was now more imposing and introduced trials by ordeal for cases that could not be resolved in any other way.

Moreover, Dorchester lost its bishop. The new king transferred the episcopal see to Lincoln far to the north.

Change didn't happen overnight, but 1066 represented a turning point in English life for serfs, the old nobility, the English language, justice, tenure, and religion. By the 1070s, even commoners would have begun to realize how much had changed, all because their impatient Anglo-Saxon king had fallen on the field of battle to a band of horse-riding, French-speaking, foreign nobles.

QUESTIONS | *How and why do big events impact little or ordinary people? Why was the Battle of Hastings important?*

King Harold's Death on the Bayeux Tapestry The inscription states that Harold here dies, but is he the man to the left who seems to have received an arrow to his eye, the fallen knight being butchered on the right, both of them, or neither of them?

at curbing the violence of local lords against innocents (farmers, women, and children). The Peace of God sought to extend the church's protection to society's defenseless by threatening to excommunicate violators.

The **Truce of God** extended the same policy to cover the violence done by knights and vassals to each other. The church specified certain times of the year such as Lent and certain days of the week such as Sunday and then Friday on which warriors were not to attack each other. Cluny extended these Peace and Truce rules to all of its monastic lands.

As stronger kings and greater magnates amassed power, they sought to suppress the quarreling of lesser lords and knights in the countryside of northern Europe. Those efforts helped to bring a measure of internal peace to Europe.

Pilgrims Take to the Road

Pilgrimage to holy places has always been a feature of religious experience. In the ancient world and the modern, people have been prepared to travel great distances under difficult circumstances to experience the holy. By the late ninth century, the disruption of the Vikings in the north and Muslim raids in the south and the breakdown of central authority had made the conditions for long-distance pilgrimages to holy sites such as Jerusalem difficult. A Frankish monk by the name of Bernard undertook such a pilgrimage to the Holy Land in 867. In southern Italy, he and his two companions took passage on a ship transporting hundreds of slaves to Alexandria. When the ship docked, however, the captain extorted money from the monk before he would let him disembark. Though Bernard had secured letters of identification and security from Muslim officials in southern Italy, he found himself having to pay to proceed and once was thrown in jail until he agreed to settle accounts. Nevertheless, Bernard visited the Holy Land with relative ease and saw places (or so he believed) associated with Christ's life and death. His experience on the return trip was less than happy, and he complained about how difficult it was to pass through Christian lands with different lords and kings in dispute with each other. He wrote that it had been easier and safer to travel in Muslim territories than in Christian Europe.

Bernard's account of his trip is similar to many medieval pilgrimage records, which emphasize the hardships endured in the name of God on the outward-bound trip, the holy sites seen, and then a lightly described uneventful return. A pilgrimage was a series of physical and spiritual hardships on the way to a holy destination. Though these pilgrimages are often described as individual tests, they almost always occurred in traveling parties, often of considerable size.

Pilgrimages were not all the same or undertaken for the same reasons. There were pilgrimages of penance, pilgrimages to imitate the life of Christ and its hardships, pil-

Pilgrims Set Out on Their Journey Two pilgrims follow Christ on their journey from Emmaus on this Romanesque stone relief that served as an emblem for the pilgrimage to St. James of Compostela.

grimages to honor vows, pilgrimages for medical reasons, and, less often, pilgrimages as punishments imposed by the church. Pilgrimage changed over time according to historical circumstances. In the late ninth and tenth centuries, when conditions were disordered and dangerous, shorter-distance pilgrimages within Francia were more common. In a world with poor medical care, saints' relics were the draw. People suffered from a bewildering range of ailments: demonic possession, involuntary spasms, crippled limbs, blindness, and deafness. Some traveled by boat to visit the relics housed in Einhard's church in Germany; others rode, walked, or crawled. The sick and poor gathered in great crowds seeking cures from the saints and charity from Christians. Carolingian and Romanesque churches were designed not just to house relics, but to invoke internal pilgrimages within their interiors. Chapels, which contained relics, radiated off the nave and choir of these churches. The visitor could make a mini-pilgrimage from chapel to chapel, saint to saint within the safe confines of a church.

Trips to the Holy Land became somewhat easier and safer in the late tenth and early eleventh centuries. After Stephen I, the king of Hungary (r. 997–1038), converted to Christianity and the Byzantines rewon the city of

Antioch from Muslims, the overland route to the Holy Land opened up and was considered to be safer than the sea route. The weakening of the Umayyad Caliphate in northern Spain meant that travelers could pass unmolested from southern France to Santiago of Compostela where the remains of Saint James (from *Sant* or Saint and *Iago* or James), the supposed brother of Jesus, were said to be kept. Monasteries and hospices began catering to the crowds of pilgrims on their way to Santiago along the great pilgrimage roads of France and Spain. Holy travel and pilgrim commerce not only spurred a revival of trade and monasticism, giving some monasteries a particular economic and spiritual function, but also made Europe more interconnected. Cluny and its daughter houses promoted and facilitated pilgrimage. With profound awareness of their sinful state, Christians in the tenth and eleventh centuries saw pilgrimage as a form of release. We know of one female sinner who visited Vézelay in France, entered the great Romanesque church under its forbidding tympanum sculpture, and placed a list of her sins on the high altar, whereupon they were forgiven. Some bishops advised members of their flocks to make pilgrimages to Santiago and perform penance for their sins.

Preconditions for Crusade

After 1035, European society became more aware of itself as a Christian community and of those inside and out who were "other." As the church reformed its doctrines and practices, Christians became aware of those who were different. The Great Schism between the eastern and western churches was one sign of an aggressive new definition of western doctrinal orthodoxy. In territorial terms, the Norman attack on the Byzantines and Muslim powers of southern Italy and Sicily was also an attack upon the "other." In northern Spain, a similar drive to retake lands from the Muslims was under way.

The reforming church also began to identify those whose beliefs did not meet orthodox standards. Shortly after the year 1000, a number of popular heresies sprang up in Europe. Some of these "heretics" were anti-materialists who believed in holding property in common, spurned marriage and the sacraments, and refused to eat meat. One such sect broke out at Orléans in northern France in 1028. Two of the so-called heretics maintained that they were just following a simpler understanding of God's power and rejected the "fictions of carnal men written down on the skins of dead animals [parchment]." They were tried, stripped of their clerical vestments, and burned to death. Another example is the case of the peasant Eon. When he went to mass one day, he heard the priest intone in Latin *"per eundem . . . Jesum Christum"* [through Jesus Christ himself]. Hearing these words, Eon thought that he had been named in the service and so concluded that he was Jesus. He went through the countryside preaching until the authorities silenced him. As the church formalized its doctrines, it identified

those who held heterodox beliefs and sought either to reincorporate them or to remove them from the body of true believers. This stage in the doctrinal centralization of Europe was similar to the territorial centralizations occurring in the same period.

Living the Material Surge of the European Economy

Perhaps the greatest precondition for crusade was material. Both crusade and cultural revival depended on an economic surge that was transforming the material basis of European society in the eleventh and twelfth centuries, for neither war nor advanced thought can occur in a material vacuum. By the late eleventh century, Europe was an increasingly prosperous society. For one thing, Europe's climate was improving. Climatologists have identified a **Medieval Warm Period** that stretched from 775 to 1275, reaching a climatic optimum in the late eleventh and early twelfth centuries. The evidence for this warming climate is indicated by longer, warmer growing seasons as measured by tree rings and tree lines pushing farther north and farther up mountainsides. The Domesday Book records vineyards in England, and English monasteries such as Glastonbury were producing wines, which suggest the existence of higher temperatures. In a predominantly agricultural economy, warmer weather benefited areas with fertile fields such as France. The surpluses generated by the agricultural economy help to explain how the great burst of church building in the eleventh century was financed.

Improving weather and more bountiful agriculture may also have had something to do with a changing attitude toward nature. In the Early Middle Ages, men and women had tended to think of nature as dark and foreboding, a threatening presence in daily life. Now poets began to sing of gentle south winds and to speak of *Natura* (nature) as a goddess. Late in the Romanesque Central Middle Ages, the notion took hold that nature was a resource, a good given to humans by God for their benefit and exploitation. From that shift in attitudes from nature as a hostile "other" to nature as a good, God-given resource may derive many western attitudes (positive and negative) toward nature and the place of human beings in it or above it.

The eleventh and twelfth centuries were centuries of exciting invention. Anna Comnena, the Byzantine historian and daughter of the eastern emperor Alexius I, made the astute observation that the Franks (westerners) were obsessed with gadgets. Mills of different types now dotted the European countryside. By 1120, England had over five thousand watermills; windmills appeared late in the twelfth century. These mills were often controlled by lords who charged their dependent farm workers to grind their wheat. Europe was turning from an almost exclusively woodworking culture to one of ironworkers and stonecutters. The erection of massive stone buildings required complex machinery to cut and raise to great heights stones weighing as much as a ton. New developments in armor, castle building, and plumbing appeared.

Thanks to improvements in agriculture and economic production, the health of many Europeans improved, which led to an increased birth rate. The population grew dramatically. Estimates suggest that Europe's population may have risen from 40 million people in 1000 to as many as 48 million in 1100 and to 60 million in 1200, thus a roughly 50 percent growth in two centuries. By the mid-twelfth century, Paris may have had as many as 30,000 people; Rome, 35,000; and London, 40,000. Throughout the Early Middle Ages, Europe had been predominantly rural. Now it had a vigorous urban dimension as well, which spurred trade since rural areas now had markets for the sale of the foodstuffs and resources that only they could supply. Europe also saw the return of a money economy in the eleventh century. In 900, England had only ten mints, but by 1100, it had over seventy. The greater use of money and an expanding commercial base stimulated a shift toward arithmetical and rational thought among the merchant and burgher (prosperous townsmen) classes of the towns and cities of Europe.

Much of the dramatic demographic upsurge occurred in France, the Netherlands, northern Italy, and southern Germany, but marginal areas such as Hungary, northern England, Ireland, Scotland, and Poland saw only small population increases. Some internal colonization took place, and new towns were founded, often not located on rivers. New lands were being cleared and marginal agricultural lands brought into production. Monks moved into "wilderness" areas that previously had been deemed unsuitable for easy human habitation. In the Netherlands and Flanders, land was being recovered from the sea as marshes were drained and dikes built.

The production of surpluses and the return of limited peace may also help to explain the growth in population, but it may also have produced the conditions for more internal violence. The period between 1050 and 1150 witnessed the emergence of a youth culture with an excess of young men without obvious positions and employment. Young nobles were trained to fight and to seek adventure, but most were not destined to inherit land or title, at least not in greater France, where the practice of **primogeniture** (passage of land and title to the eldest son) had taken hold. So not only were there more people to go on pilgrimage to distant places, wandering scholars, and traveling merchants, but also young warriors looking for wars and a fitting place in an increasingly competitive and crowded world.

The First Crusade

Pilgrimages by land to the Holy Land were relatively easy until the 1060s, in part because of the Byzantine success in regaining part of Syria. Various Islamic groups were at war with one another in the area, so that there was for a time no general policy prohibiting travelers from reach-

CHRONOLOGY Dating the First Crusade

DATE	EVENT
1096	Failure of the Peasants' Crusade
1096	Crusaders assemble at Constantinople
1097	Crusaders cross the Bosporus Straits; take Nicaea
1098	Crusaders stall at Antioch; find the Holy Lance
1098	Crusaders capture Antioch
1099	Crusaders capture Jerusalem; Kingdom of Jerusalem established

ing Jerusalem. In the late 1060s and early 1070s, however, the Seljuk Turks finally placed most of the Holy Land under their control and imposed a stricter version of Islam, one that distrusted infidels. Western Europe began to hear rumors of the persecution of Christian pilgrims in the Holy Land, and Pope Gregory VII regretted that the Holy Land had fallen into pagan (as Muslims were portrayed at the time) hands. He planned a campaign of 50,000 warriors to liberate the Holy Sepulcher (the church site of Christ's temporary tomb after the crucifixion) in Jerusalem. Thus did the idea of crusade first occur to a pope who was trying to secure his universal leadership of Christendom. His political difficulties and death denied him his dream of liberating the Holy Land, but the right to call for a crusade became a papal prerogative just as was its right to crown emperors. When popes called for and mounted crusades, a militant imperial papacy sought to demonstrate its leadership of all of Christian Europe.

The Byzantine Empire may not have fully appreciated the dynamics of the unfolding western crusade, but it played a critical role in the process. By the last quarter of the eleventh century, the Byzantine Empire had seen its gains in Syria rolled back by the Turks and its buffer zone against Islam once again gone. The eastern emperor Alexius I (r. 1081–1118) wanted to employ western knights, the Franks, to assist him in regaining Christian lands and cities in the east and to protect Constantinople. He sought mercenaries, but instead got western warriors with a religious mission and territorial aims of their own.

At the Council of Clermont in 1095, Pope Urban II (1088–1099) gave an inflammatory speech to a gathering of bishops, abbots, and Frankish nobles. He invited them to put away their petty squabbles with each other, to enter upon the road to the Holy Sepulcher, and to liberate the Holy Land from the wicked race polluting it. His language was harsh and unforgiving, designed to stir his knightly listeners to hatred of the enemy and to free holy places from their desecrators. An unclean nation, he said, was engaged in destroying Christian churches and desecrating altars. Pagans were enslaving and torturing

MAP 8.3 | The First Crusade, 1095–1099

The First Crusade began with Pope Urban II's call for a crusade to the Holy Land in 1095 at Clermont, France, and ended four years later with the conquest of Jerusalem. *What were the staging points of the crusade? Why did the crusaders follow a land route to the Holy Land?*

Christians and raping Christian women. His appeal to Christians was religious, for he spoke of crusade (from the French word for "cross") and called on the Franks to think of their adventure as an armed pilgrimage. They were to travel with the sign of the cross on their foreheads and to return home with it on their backs as a sign of fulfillment. Crusaders were promised a plenary or full indulgence (or remission) for their sins, the right to keep the land they conquered, and the postponement of the debts they owed at home (see Back to the Source at the end of the chapter).

The pope did more than just announce a crusade to rewin the holy land; he actively promoted the idea. He went on a speaking tour in France to stir up support. Popular preachers, with colorful names such as Walter the Penniless, also began to preach crusade. One of these preachers, Peter the Hermit, led a throng of people toward the Holy Land on the so-called Peasants' Crusade, but it lacked official sanction and these common crusaders and their families were slaughtered long before they arrived. In Europe, popular movements at the time also led to the persecution of Jews as a dangerous "other" in

their midst. As the rhetoric rose, **pogroms** against the Jews were carried out in various European cities. The idea of crusade immediately struck Europe as an exciting adventure. The motives of the crusaders were many and mixed. Some went for religious reasons, others for material gain, others for a military adventure, and yet others because crusade opened up possibilities for advancement that Europe denied them. By 1096, thousands of western crusaders began to assemble outside the walls of Constantinople, ready to march to Jerusalem (Map 8.3). The Byzantine emperor Alexius was surprised by the size and fervor of the mob of armed Franks and was not prepared to let them pass until they swore an oath of fealty to him. By 1097, the western crusaders had crossed over the Bosporus Straits and quickly took the city of Nicaea, which they turned over to the emperor Alexius.

As the crusaders proceeded, they established the first of four crusader states at Edessa. At Antioch, the crusade stalled when the city would not surrender and the siege became protracted. The chroniclers report that it was at this point of despair that crusaders discovered the holy lance that pierced Christ's side while he was on the cross.

It apparently did not bother the crusaders that they could have seen another holy lance in Constantinople. They expected to find physical evidence of Christ in the land that he had once walked. The miraculous discovery, no matter how convenient its finding, re-inspired the crusaders, who captured Antioch in June 1098 and slaughtered all its male inhabitants. The crusaders did not reach Jerusalem until 1099 and broke through the walls of the Holy Sepulcher on June 15. One of the historians who was present claimed that 10,000 Muslims (men, women, and children) were slaughtered inside the temple. The conquerors then pillaged the city of Jerusalem. As brutal as the conquest was, for many it was also a moment of high religious fervor. They believed that they had restored the holiest of holies (the Holy Sepulcher) to Christian hands.

A kingdom of Jerusalem was established. Most crusaders, however, had not come to stay, and gradually small groups began to make their way home. Before leaving they went on tours of the Holy Land, took dips in the Jordan River, gathered palm branches, and collected seashells in Galilee. Then, like other pilgrims, they wended their way home to anxious loved ones. One of the problems with all the crusades was that too few crusaders wished to remain in the conquered lands. The crusader kingdoms were ruled from the top by a Christian minority that built magnificent castles such as Krak des Chevaliers in Syria, but that remained distant and defensive in the conquered lands. The First Crusade was a popular crusade, reflecting the growing dynamism of a resurgent west, its internal energy and tensions. Crusade was, in part, a safety valve releasing European demographic and social pressures onto the external world. It was also a vehicle promoted by the papacy for reinforcing European and papal identity. That same burst of energy

Jerusalem during the Crusades A map of Jerusalem from Robert the Monk's chronicle of the First Crusade.

was also at work in the building of magnificent cathedrals such as the one that Gislebertus adorned at Autun, in rousing martial epics such as the *Song of Roland,* and in the revival of culture that was redefining Europe.

Conclusion

At the end of the Romanesque Central Middle Ages of the tenth and eleventh centuries, medieval Europe stood on the brink of assuming its most refined form. Cluniac monasticism and a reformed papacy had redirected the purposes and efficiency of the medieval church, which was now more centralized, rigorous, and powerful. An imperial papacy believed that at some level it was in command of Christian Europe, even to the point of overthrowing emperors, establishing vassal states, demanding the fealty of kings and all Christians, and calling for holy war. At a popular level, religion had become the spiritual heart and motive force of Europe. Driven by religious fervor, men and women went on great pilgrimages to distant places, turned over their property as bequests to monasteries, and prayed for their eternal salvation. They visited massive new cathedrals such as the one built at Autun, and on its exterior and interior they saw high Christian art such as Gislebertus's unforgettable scenes of the life of Christ, the Last Judgment,

and the horrifying figures of the demons who haunted their nightmares. The church offered them a glimpse of another and truer world.

Royal and imperial power had been relatively weak in the tenth century after the fall of the Carolingians. Local lords and their vassals stepped in to take what power they could throughout Europe in this period of decentralization. The Ottonian emperors may have shaped their power along Carolingian lines, but empire was a diminished thing after Charlemagne, since its territorial command of Europe was limited. But by the eleventh century, power was once again returning to central authorities. The Anglo-Saxon kings of England and the Capetian kings of France showed that royal power had a future beyond the ideology of the three orders, which they had emphasized when kingship was weakest. In the late eleventh century, territory and power in Europe and the Middle East was still in flux, but the state changes in southern Italy, Byzantium, Islam, and England established the territorial conditions for the High Middle Ages. The First Crusade was the product of a reinvigorated and aggressive Europe and a sign that medieval Europe was reaching its mature, most developed, and dangerous form. Gislebertus, the sculptor of the portal of the forking path to paradise and hell at Autun, would not have been surprised. He knew something of the extremes of the human condition and reflected the Romanesque Age's restless energy and its preoccupation with the light and dark sides of the European imagination.

Critical Thinking Questions

1. How and why did the Middle Ages change direction in the tenth and eleventh centuries?

2. What impact did the disordered conditions of life in the Central Middle Ages have on people and their attitudes toward the world and their place in it?

3. What were the big events of the period, and how did they change Europe?

4. Why did so much of the historical action of the Central Middle Ages occur on the edges of Europe?

5. What choices did people such as vassals, pilgrims, Otto the Great, Pope Gregory VII, King Henry IV, and William the Conqueror make, and why did they matter?

Key Terms

tympanum (p. 232)

nave (p. 233)

basilica (p. 233)

vassalage (p. 233)

benefice (p. 234)

keep (p. 237)

Ottonian system (p. 239)

simony (p. 245)

Great (East-West) Schism (p. 245)

Investiture Controversy (p. 246)

lay investiture (p. 246)

Domesday Book (p. 250)

Peace of God (p. 250)

Truce of God (p. 252)

Medieval Warm Period (p. 253)

primogeniture (p. 254)

pogrom (p. 255)

Primary Sources in connect

For information on Connect and the online resources available, go to http://connect.mcgraw-hill.com.

1. A Vassalage Oath

2. Fulbert of Chartres on the Obligations of Vassals

3. The Deaths of Oliver and Roland

4. The Dictation of the Pope (*Dictatus papae*)

5. A Lady Sings for the Return of Her Crusader

A Pope Calls for Crusade

In November 1095 at Clermont in France, Pope Urban II presided over a council of high churchmen and various princes from France and Germany. In a public square he addressed the assembled people. Five versions of the speech survive. The one presented below comes from the work of Robert the Monk, who wrote his account early in the twelfth century, but Robert may have been a witness to Urban's call for crusade.

Oh, race of Franks, race from across the mountains, race chosen and loved by God—as shines in many of your works—set apart from all nations by the situation of your country, as well as by your Catholic faith and the honor of the holy church! To you our discourse is addressed and for you our exhortation is intended. We wish you to know what a grievous cause has led us to your country, what peril threatening you and all the faithful has brought us here.

From the confines of Jerusalem and the city of Constantinople a horrible tale has gone forth and often been brought to our ears, namely, that a race from the kingdom of the Persians, an accursed race, a race utterly alienated from God, a generation indeed that has not directed its heart and has not entrusted its spirit to God, has invaded the lands of those Christians and has depopulated them by sword, pillage, and fire; it has led away some captives into its own country, and some it has destroyed by cruel torture; it has entirely destroyed churches of God or appropriated them for the rites of its own religion. They destroy altars after having defiled them with their uncleanness. They circumcise Christians and the blood of circumcision they either spread upon the altars or pour into the vases of the baptismal font. When they wish to torture people with a degrading death, they perforate their navels, drag forth the end of their intestines, and affix it to a stake; then with flogging they lead the victim around until their innards gush forth and the victims fall flat on the ground. Others they bind to a post and pierce with arrows. Others they compel to extend their necks and then, attacking them with naked swords, attempt to cut through their necks with a single blow. What shall I say of the abominable rape of women? To speak of it would be worse than to be silent. The kingdom of the Greeks is now dismembered by them and deprived of a territory so vast in extent that it cannot be traversed in a march of two months. On whom, therefore, falls the task of avenging these wrongs and of recovering this territory incumbent, if not you? You, upon whom above other nations God has conferred remarkable glory in arms, great courage, great energy, and strength to humble the hairy scalps of those who resist you.

Let the deeds of your ancestors move you and incite your minds to brave achievements; the glory and greatness of King Charlemagne, his son Louis, and your other kings, who have destroyed the kingdoms of the pagans, and have extended in these lands the territory of the holy church. Let the holy sepulcher of the Lord our Savior, which is possessed by unclean nations, especially incite you, and the holy places which are now treated with baseness and irreverently polluted with their filthiness. Oh, most valiant soldiers and descendants of invincible ancestors, do not be degenerate, but recall the valor of your ancestors.

But if you are hindered by love of children, parents, and wives, remember what the Lord says in the Gospel, "he that loveth father or mother more than me, is not worthy of me." "Every one that hath forsaken houses, or brethren, or sisters, or father, or mother, or wife, or children, or lands for my name's sake shall receive a hundred-fold and shall inherit everlasting life." Let none of your possessions detain you, no concern for your family affairs, since this land that you inhabit, shut in on all sides by the seas and surrounded by mountain peaks, is too narrow for your large population; nor does it abound in riches; and it furnishes scarcely food enough for its cultivators. So it is that you murder one another, that you wage war, and that frequently you perish by mutual wounds. Therefore, let hatred depart from among you, let your quarrels end, let wars cease, and let all dissensions and controversies slumber. Enter upon the road to the Holy Sepulcher; wrest that land from a wicked race and subject it to yourselves. That land which as Scripture says "floweth with milk and honey," was given by God to the children of Israel to hold.

Jerusalem is the navel of the world; the land is fruitful above others, like another paradise of delights. This the Redeemer of the human race made illustrious by his advent, beautified by residence, consecrated by his suffering, redeemed by death, and glorified by his burial. The royal city, therefore, situated at the center of the world, is now held captive by his enemies and is in subjection to those who do not know God and to the worship of the heathens. Jerusalem seeks, therefore, and desires to be liberated, and does not cease to implore you to come to her aid. From you especially she asks for relief, because as we have already said, God has conferred upon you above all nations great glory in arms. Accordingly undertake this journey for the remission of your sins, with the assurance of the imperishable glory of the kingdom of Heaven.

When Pope Urban had said these and many similar things in his polished speech, he so moved to one purpose the thoughts of all present that they cried out, "It is the will of God! It is the will of God!" When the venerable Roman pontiff heard that, with eyes uplifted to heaven, he gave thanks to God and with his hands commanding silence said:

Most beloved brethren, today is manifest in you what the Lord says in the Gospel, "Where two or three are gathered together in my name there am I in the midst of them." Unless the Lord God had been present in your spirits, all of you would not have uttered the same cry. For, although the cry issued from numerous mouths, the source of the cry was singular. Therefore I say to you that God, who implanted this in your chests, has drawn it forth from you. Let this then be your war-cry in combat, because these words were given to you by God. When you are making an armed attack upon the enemy, let this one shout be raised by all the soldiers of God: It is the will of God! It is the will of God!

And we do not command or advise that the old or feeble, or those unfit to bear arms, undertake this journey; nor should women set out at all without their husbands or brothers or legal guardians. For such [women] would be more of a hindrance than aid, more of a burden than advantage. Let the rich aid the poor; and, according to their wealth, let them take with them experienced soldiers. Priests and clerics of any order are not to go without the consent of their bishops; for this journey would profit them nothing if they went without the permission of those. Also, it is not fitting that laymen should enter upon the pilgrimage without the blessing of their priests.

Whoever, therefore, shall commit to this holy pilgrimage and make his vow to God to that effect and shall offer himself to him as a living sacrifice acceptable unto God, shall wear the sign of the cross of the Lord on his forehead or on his chest. When he has fulfilled his vow and wishes to return, let him place the cross on his back between his shoulders. By that two-fold action he will fulfill the precept of the Lord as he commands in the Gospel, "He that taketh not the cross and followeth after me, is not worthy of me.

QUESTIONS | *Why might the speech and the First Crusade be viewed as the conclusion or culmination of the Romanesque Central Middle Ages, its tensions and aspirations? Why did Pope Urban sponsor a crusade? How did he excite the passion of the crowd? How did he justify the proposed attack upon a foreign land?*

Source: "The Speech of Pope Urban II at Clermont," trans. Dana C. Munro, *American Historical Review* 11 (1906), 231–242; revised.

9

Interior of St. Denis

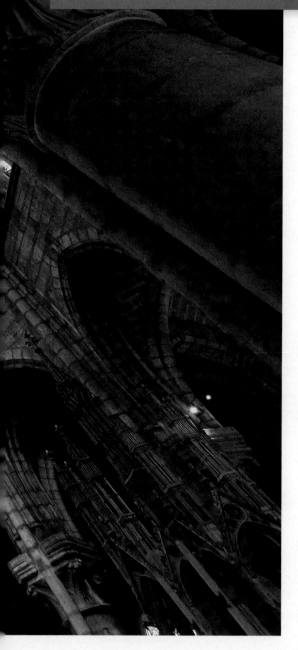

THE GOTHIC HIGH MIDDLE AGES

A New World of Learning
   The Old Way of Learning
   The Tumult of the Schools
   The Revitalization and Renewal
   of Monastic Learning
   Abbot Suger and the Birth
   of Gothic Architecture
   Bernard of Clairvaux
   and the Cistercians

Two Thirds and Two Fourths
   The Third Crusade
   Pope Innocent III
   The Fourth Crusade
   The Fourth Lateran Council

**High Times for the
Medieval Economy**
   The Agricultural Base
   The Growth of Towns
   Guilds and Industry
   Communes and Urban Tensions

**Dissent and Control, Church
and State**
   Dealing with Dissent
   The Mendicant Orders
   and the Inquisition
   State Development
   Rulers Respected, Feared,
   and Loved

The Medieval University
   The Passing of the Cathedral
   Schools
   Translating the Collected Wisdom
   of the West
   Birth of the University
   The University of Paris
   Living the Medieval University Life
   Scholasticism and the Dumb Ox
   The Gothic Peak

Conclusion

THE AFFAIR OF ABELARD AND HELOISE The affair of Abelard and Heloise was not only a great scandal; it flouted the conventions of the ordered society the High Middle Ages was laying down. Abelard was in his thirties, Heloise in her late teens or early twenties when they became lovers. He had been employed as her private tutor because of his towering reputation and sterling character. Bloated with pride, he set out to seduce his student. Intimate reading soon led to whispers of love. Eventually her uncle Fulbert caught the two of them. She may already have been pregnant. To protect himself against her enraged uncle (since to hurt him would be to endanger her), Abelard sent his lover to stay with his family in Brittany, where she gave birth to their son. With his reputation in danger of ruin, Abelard resolved to marry Heloise, but secretly so that he could continue to hold his clerical teaching post. Heloise argued vigorously against marriage, preferring "love over marriage, freedom over bondage." If the Roman emperor himself had offered her marriage, she said, she would still rather be her lover's whore than empress of the whole world. They did marry, but Fulbert remained resentful, and so Abelard spirited Heloise away to the monastery where she had been educated. Uncle Fulbert, a church deacon, furious over his public disgrace, sent henchmen to castrate Abelard, the violator of his niece. After that cruel cut and the public humiliation of it, Abelard became a monk and compelled Heloise to become a nun.

The melodrama of their passionate affair should not cause us to lose sight of what these two extraordinary individuals have to tell us about the Gothic High Middle Ages, particularly about the great intellectual and institutional achievements the age made. Education led the way and so we need to spend time in this chapter following the path that led from cathedral schools to universities, from Abelard to Aquinas, and that produced a remarkable confidence in the human capacity to know the world.

The Romanesque Central Middle Ages, after its bumpy start and troubles managing rapid growth and political and religious upheaval, had longed for reform, order, and rules. The High Middle Ages sought to perfect a form of Christian society best reflected in soaring Gothic cathedrals, rigorously

rational scholastic thought, universities, representative assemblies, and powerful kings and popes. The heavy weight of authority, of centralized power and ecclesiastical bureaucracy, Aristotelian logic and synthetic thought, great wealth and a flourishing economy produced before long a backlash of popular, learned, and religious resistance.

Abelard and Heloise were among the first to test the strictures of a society striving for order and high purpose. Their unconventionality was challenge enough. They named their son Astralabe, a strange name since an astrolabe was a mechanical instrument for plotting the stars. Their careers were highly unusual. Abelard was a fiery wandering master of logic who shattered conventional forms of thinking and captured the imagination of a generation of students who flocked to Paris and wilderness retreats to hear him lecture. To his students he seemed a young prince slicing through the stale thoughts of the old masters and the dead weight of authoritative teaching. He was almost always in trouble: with his fellow masters, with church authorities, with the abbot of his monastery, and with a living saint.

Abelard's calamities continued after his affair with Heloise ended. His ecclesiastical enemies pursued him for two

Norman Dynasty of England
1066–1154

Capetian Dynasty of France
987–1328

Affair of Abelard and Heloise
1116–1117

1000   1050   1100   1150

decades. To escape them, he retreated to the countryside, but students sought him out, begging him to continue to impart his new style of reasoning. In a moment of despair, he even dreamed of escaping to Islamic Spain, where he might be allowed to think in respectful peace. The core of his revolutionary method was to question received wisdom and tradition in a logical and systematic way: "Ask not who said a thing, but what is said," he advised his son. Twice the church put Abelard on trial for his teachings; at the first, a few years after the affair with Heloise had turned sour, the authorities forced Abelard to burn one of his books and confined him to a monastery. After the second, the pope excommunicated him.

Heloise was as remarkable as Abelard. Trained in a monastery school, she wanted something unheard of for a woman of her time: she wanted to be a writer and philosopher. Even as a young woman she was reputed to be the most learned woman in all of France, but Heloise had few options. She probably could not marry well for social reasons, and there were few occupations or opportunities for learned women outside of the church. Eventually she became a much admired abbess. Her letters of unrequited love and complaint to Abelard are supple and demanding. She had a gift Abelard lacked for penetrating the emotional and intellectual core of life. She never forgot Abelard, their physical and emotional bond preoccupying her thoughts about her place in the world until the day she died.

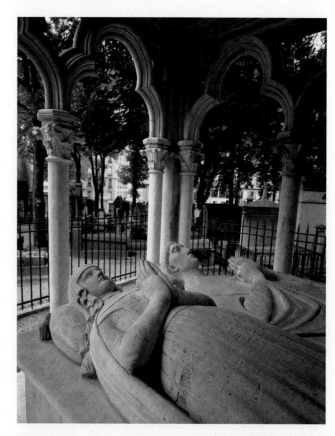

Tomb of Heloise and Abelard in Père Lachaise, Paris The remains of the controversial couple were not moved to Paris until the nineteenth century. Today there is still disagreement about where their remains are buried.

The robust intellectual searching of the early twelfth century gave way in the thirteenth century to a society that was often crowded, restrictive, and repressive. Yet its accomplishments were many: the creation of universities, scholasticism, soaring Gothic cathedrals, and the greatest systematic thinker of the Middle Ages. Thomas Aquinas became the common doctor and leading intellectual light of the Middle Ages. His life was hardly a quiet one, but his logically rigorous philosophy represented a peak of high medieval thought.

Habsburg Dynasty of Germany
1250–

Latin Empire of
Constantinople
1204–1261

Hohenstaufen Dynasty of Germany
1138–1268

Plantagenet Dynasty of England
1154–1399

1250   1300   1350   1400

Life in Paris and other European cities was crowded by the thirteenth century. Despite disastrous crusades, strong monarchs emerged once again, and the most powerful pope of the Middle Ages, Innocent III, reformed church practice, sanctioned new religious orders, and played politics at the highest level. Enemies of the established order resisted what they deemed to be an increasingly repressive and misguided society. The thirteenth century was prosperous, urban, and intellectually vibrant, but there were signs that the medieval world (or one form of it) was reaching its limits.

A New World of Learning

Abelard was a product of the cathedral schools of greater France, which laid down the foundations of the High Middle Ages and European intellectual life. This great movement, sometimes called the Twelfth-Century Renaissance, was dynamic, humanistic, and controversial, producing at its leading edge an engagement with the world through dialectic or logic, and was succeeded by the rise of the universities and the triumph of scholasticism. The intellectual history of the age can, thus, be roughly divided into its cathedral school and university phases. Self-reflection, classicism or humanism, and a pronounced individualism characterize the first phase; limited scope but logical rigor and soaring achievement, the second.

What was the old way of learning, and what was wrong with it by the early twelfth century?

The Old Way of Learning

By the late eleventh century, stale air hung over the monastic schools that had dominated western education for six centuries. Monastic education, like life in the Early Middle Ages, was highly localized. Each monastery set its own educational standards and practices, which were chiefly religious in nature. Monastic learning and the monastic ideal (of a permanently enclosed religious life in a monastery) tended to keep scholars and books closeted in relative isolation. Travel remained difficult. In the late tenth century, a scholar from Rheims wanted to travel to Chartres to study medicine. The distance is a mere 120 miles, but the journey proved an arduous undertaking of missed roads, dying horses, injured travelers, and dilapidated bridges.

In France, things did not improve much over the next fifty years. The monk Guibert of Nogent claimed that there were so few teachers in northern France around 1060 that his noble mother bribed a tutor to leave a relative's family to teach her young son. Although this teacher was the only one available, he was poorly educated. He could not teach the boy what he himself did not understand and used to beat and berate the boy. One day Guibert's mother told her son that she could not stand to see his little body bruised all black and blue. If he wished to abandon his studies and become a knight (as the less dangerous occupation), she would support him. The plucky little boy told his mother that he would rather die on the spot than give up studying to become a cleric (or clerk). He went to a nearby monastery, where he learned Latin and began to write. His abbot, however, disapproved of young monks writing, and so Guibert was forced to write at night in secret.

Great learning still lingered in many monasteries, and outstanding monastic scholars such as Anselm of Bec (or Canterbury) wrote treatises to prove the existence of God. But too many scholar-monks were bound by a rigid older tradition of scriptural commentary and the interpretation of the symbols they saw in their texts and the world. A symbolist mode of thinking dominated the old way of learning.

Monks mumbled as they read and were said to "eat" their books, that is, they read out loud and ingested the contents of entire books as they tried to make them part of their very being. Their reading was a whole body experience of chanting and swaying that belonged to an older, primarily oral culture that knew only a few great books that needed to be learned in their entireties. It was a style of reading and thinking that was about to change, as was the large, plain, early medieval book.

The Tumult of the Schools

From 1075 to 1175, the leading educational institution of Europe was the cathedral school. Such schools had existed earlier, but they now flourished as the population grew and expanding cities surrounded their old cathedrals. The townspeople of these vibrant small cities sought places to educate their sons in Latin and the liberal arts of the **trivium** (grammar, rhetoric, and logic) and the **quadrivium** (mathematics, geometry, astronomy, and music). Bernard, the master of the cathedral school of Chartres, was reputedly so gifted a teacher that he could teach boys, even dull ones, how to read and write Latin within a year. The curriculum relied heavily on memorization and recitation. Each day, students recited passages learned the previous day. Bernard not only taught boys Latin prose and poetry, but also sought to instill moral values. Though he worked by encouraging his students, he occasionally, like other twelfth-century masters, flogged those who failed to meet his high standards.

By the first quarter of the twelfth century, prominent cathedral schools with famous masters became magnets attracting students from far and wide. The masters were formidable figures: stern, impressive in their learning, and prone to humble any student or fellow master who dared to challenge them. Abelard likened the educational atmosphere of the time to a war in which the old masters defended their citadels against new ideas and brash young rivals. But cathedral schools were the leading edge of change, benefiting from a society in which the roads were now open and safer to travel, there was a sufficient material surplus to allow a few young men the

Lost or Found? The Love Letters of Heloise and Abelard

In his account of his troubles, Abelard confesses that one of the reasons he seduced the highly educated Heloise was that she was someone with whom he could exchange letters when they were separated, writing things to each other that they dared not say in person. Some of his love songs, he recalled, became popular and were long sung by those pursuing lives of pleasure. Did the two lovers send each other love letters, and if so, what happened to them? Abelard and Heloise exchanged another set of letters called "the personal letters" twenty years after the end of their affair. The authenticity of the personal letters was a subject of some doubt in the late twentieth century, but that doubt seemed to have subsided by 2000 when a new controversy broke out. In 1999, Constant J. Mews, a leading Abelard expert, published *The Lost Love Letters of Heloise and Abelard.* Twenty-five years earlier, Ewald Könsgen had published a Latin edition of 113 love letters and poems and wondered (with a question mark in the title of the book) if these might be the lost love letters of Heloise and Abelard. Mews removed the question mark with a sustained historical, textual, and circumstantial argument that the letters were, indeed, the missing love letters of the famous couple.

The attribution is not without difficulties. There is no twelfth-century manuscript evidence of the letters. The love letters were copied by a fifteenth-century Cistercian monk who was interested in them initially because of their elaborate salutations (Man: "To his most brilliant star"; Woman: "To a shining lamp and city set upon a mountaintop"). The greater problem is that neither of the letter-writers addresses the other by name. Still the couple in the letters had as many ups and downs in their relationship as Abelard and Heloise did in theirs: breakups, hurt feelings, and solidarity against their detractors. They share events and cultural characteristics that might well fit with Abelard and Heloise. Although many prominent medievalists accepted the attribution as certain or probable, others have doubted it. Jan Ziolkowski carefully compared the Latin of the Man's letters against the known writings of Abelard and came to the conclusion, based on a comparison of verse techniques, prose rhythms, and word use, that Abelard could not be the author of the love letters. Mews observed, in response, that the special conception of "love" developed in the letters is one that Abelard alone went on to develop further in his works, as though he (or he and Heloise) owned the idea.[1] The attribution of the love letters to Heloise and Abelard still awaits consensus, but then a quarter of a century ago so did the personal letters. That dust-up seems to have died down as the leading edge of the controversial careers of Heloise and Abelard has moved forward to the new brouhaha over the love letters. In their lives and in the scholarship about them, controversy has always dogged the two lovers. Abelard, at least, might have been pleased, for he believed that it was only through the presentation of contraries, argument, and analysis that true understanding could be achieved.

QUESTIONS | *Why was a celebrity culture, at least in modern terms, not possible in the Middle Ages? Why were Abelard and Heloise so controversial? Did Abelard just have a contrary nature, or was there something about his time that was inherently controversial? Why? How does the comparison and contrast of ideas lead to intellectual progress?*

luxury of obtaining a higher education, and larger towns and small cities that looked to cathedrals to educate boys. Part of the appeal of these schools was the star quality of upstart masters such as Abelard.

Abelard and other daring masters worked less by exposition than by questioning received wisdom. Abelard's *Sic et Non* (*Yes and No*) is an extraordinary example of the method. He collected contradictory authoritative statements by the fathers of the church and a few from the Bible and set them beside each other to demonstrate their differences. He chose not to resolve those differences but demonstrated that the authorities were in disagreement and, following the dialectical method, left it to the reader to engage and resolve the differences.

Anselm, the master of the cathedral school of Laon, with whom Abelard tangled, systematically amassed and sorted through the vast body of scriptural interpretation. In his evening meetings with senior students, Anselm also explored various issues that they might expect later as parish priests to hear from their flocks: could a man marry his longtime lover, what was to be done when a child died before receiving baptism, and how should the claims of some women that they had sexual intercourse with demons (the *incubi*) be handled? These question-and-answer sessions were one place where the higher learning of the schools touched a wider world of domestic concerns.

Around 1125, William of Conches, a young master of Chartres, produced a textbook he baldly called *Philosophy,* a summary of what could reasonably be said about the world. His approach was based not on scientific experiment or observation, but on reason and intelligent book learning. In opposing his monastic critics, who trusted in what the Bible and sacred teachings had to say about the natural world, William doubted that God was a capricious bender of the rules of nature. He cited the case of peasants who believed that God could make a calf from a tree trunk. God could do that, of course, says William, but has he ever actually done so? William's was a twelfth-century version of Albert Einstein's quip that God doesn't play dice with the universe. William's attitude, in medieval terms, was scientific, for he respected creation as a physical phenomenon and the human capacity (also given by God) to understand it. Nature, for him, was regular and followed established rules and patterns. William's book reflected a new attitude toward the material universe, its rational causes and processes. Not surprisingly, that attitude landed him in trouble with certain monks and conservative elements within the church, since he seemed to have put reason ahead of doctrinal or church authority. Like Abelard and Anselm of Laon, William of Conches belonged to the great rethinking of the medieval world that was transforming twelfth-century thought.

John of Salisbury from England was one of William's students and a **humanist** (in medieval terms, one with an interest in the classics, Latin eloquence, and human affairs). John went on to write on papal politics, the doings of kings and courtiers, and the tumultuous world of the cathedral schools. When as a young man in 1136 he had arrived in Paris, he found dozens of teachers on such subjects as logic under whom he could study. A critical mass of intellectuals had gathered there to argue with each other and collectively work toward a rational explanation of the world, one in which the created world rationally reflected the divine will. The masters were confident that their logical methods (of ordered and systematic investigations and reasoning) would make sense of the world as it was and that these methods, if applied systematically, would restore the proper place of human beings in the cosmos. The masters fought with and ridiculed each other but established a high medieval confidence in the "knowability" of the world.

The Revitalization and Renewal of Monastic Learning

In the early twelfth century, the exciting new worldview of the masters began to revitalize even the monastic schools. Heloise herself was a product of the monastic school of Argenteuil, where she had imbibed classical

Hildegard Receiving a Vision Here a molten light pours into Hildegard in visionary rapture while a monk (in an adjoining space or room) takes down her description of the vision and a nun tends to her.

and medieval learning, learned Latin poetry, and become a twelfth-century humanist in her own right. Women were excluded from the cathedral schools, but many religious women continued to pursue scholarly work in monasteries. The parents of Hildegard of Bingen had surrendered her as a child to the religious life. She became a Benedictine nun in Germany and eventually an abbess. She wrote works on natural history, medicine, and theology; corresponded with popes and famous men and women; and went on speaking tours. Most startling were the visions that informed her spiritual life. Some people have speculated that Hildegard's visionary experiences, which she illustrated and which came to her while she was conscious, were caused by migraine headaches. Others claim that they should be taken as reflections of her intense and expressive personality. Hildegard believed them to be divine.

At Paris, the monk Hugh of St. Victor showed just how high a reformed monastic education could aim if informed by the new learning. In his *Didascalicon* (meaning "things instructional"), Hugh laid out the essential importance of reading and a program for learning the sum total of things. For Hugh and his contemporaries, human knowledge as well as the human image had been shattered by the Fall of humankind. Twelfth-century men and women were attempting to restore human knowledge to its original state before the Fall, reassembling and ordering all the knowledge that God had once given them. Hugh and the masters thus undertook a great project to restore the human image and human mind to their pristine state through modern learning.

Abbot Suger and the Birth of Gothic Architecture

In 1122, the monk Suger became the abbot of St. Denis, the ancient royal monastery just outside Paris. The kings of France were buried at St. Denis, which also preserved the symbols of the monarchy, including the Oriflamme or banner under which the French kings fought. Suger's goal was to enhance St. Denis's standing as the royal abbey of France and so enthusiastically supported the Capetian king, Louis VI (the Fat), and wrote an account of his deeds. Louis was reputedly so large that he required a crane to help him mount his horse. Suger zealously promoted the interests of his large king and proud abbey, no matter the cost to others. To gain more property for his monastery, he expelled the nuns of Argenteuil, including Heloise, claiming both that he had charters proving that their property originally belonged to St. Denis and that the nuns were leading immoral lives. His case had little basis on either count, but he obtained the land. With Heloise now homeless, Abelard turned over his own small and poorly funded monastery, the Paraclete, to Heloise and her displaced sisters. Suger thus changed the course of the lives of the famous lovers, bringing them back together again, for Heloise became a successful abbess and administrator and Abelard spent much of his later life devoted to the Paraclete's interests, writing a rule for Heloise's convent as well as a book of hymns.

In his account of his efforts on behalf of St. Denis, Suger describes collecting and restoring its precious objects, managing its properties, and rebuilding the church. St. Denis was old, parts of it having been constructed in the Merovingian and Carolingian periods. To restore and expand the church, Suger planned to rebuild the west facade and narthex (entranceway). He discovered that he lacked the necessary stone columns for the job. Having determined that old columns from the ancient palaces and baths of Rome might serve his purpose, he hoped to transport them from Rome to Paris. After years of planning, he found that he could obtain the same stone columns from a nearby quarry. He also required wooden beams but was told that none large enough were available. Suger personally led an excursion into a local forest, found trees of the right size, and supervised the harvesting. Suger's dynamism is an indication of the energy and purpose driving twelfth-century Europe.

The product of this determination and industry was a massive new west end for St. Denis, with heavy wall buttresses, three large portals with statues, and a central tympanum scene of the Last Judgment. The west end of St. Denis delights the eye with its organized presentation of elements, vibrant tympanum, and colorful rose window. As impressive as the exterior was, St. Denis becomes even more dramatic on the inside, for Suger's vision inspired an architectural revolution. He wanted to flood the church with colored light pouring in through large stained-glass windows. In his reading, he had been struck by the doctrines of light and transcendence in the writings of the Neo-Platonist writer now known as Pseudo-Dionysius, who was thought at the time to be the Denis the Areopagite mentioned in the New Testament and the patron saint of his church. When Abelard after his castration became a monk of St. Denis, he questioned the association of St. Denis with Denis the Areopagite, which forced him to flee the monastery and its angry monks. Suger had no such doubts about the divine origins of the abbey or his own inspiration.

To achieve Suger's spiritual goals, the masons of St. Denis were the first to introduce the basic elements of Gothic architecture: the use of buttresses (attached and later on flying buttresses), which supported the lateral or horizontal pressure on the external walls, and pointed arches, which conveyed the downward vertical pressure of the weight of the walls and roof to the earth. The Romanesque round arch was heavy and squat in order to bear the great weight of a heavy stone building, and Romanesque walls had to be heavy to support the immense load. With the pointed arch and the better flow of pressure downward, walls absorbed less downward pressure and so could be made higher and opened up with larger windows, allowing more light to enter sacred spaces. Finally, instead of Romanesque barrel vaults (essentially a series of round arches), the masons of St. Denis created ribbed vaults, which allowed the weight and stresses of a large stone building to be collected and transferred down to the ground. The interior of Suger's church pinches upward and achieves a heightened sense of verticality.

Some of these Gothic features had been pioneered in Muslim buildings and in various Norman churches, but at St. Denis they were brought together to achieve the beginnings of a new architectural style that we know as Gothic. Strangely, in his account of his administration of St. Denis, Suger says not a word about these specific developments. His attention was fixed not on the technical details, but on the end result: the desire to build a taller, light-filled building that would honor God, concentrate the divine light, and sparkle for France and its savvy, self-promoting abbot.

Romanesque remained the main architectural style of Europe, but the new Gothic style would be at first a royal Capetian or Île-de-France (Parisian) style that was refined over the next century and spread across Europe. The finest example of the high or mature Gothic style in France is to be found in the cathedral of Chartres. Its older Romanesque cathedral had caught fire in June 1193, and immediately a campaign was carried out between 1193 and 1250 to build a state-of-the-art cathedral to replace it. The finished cathedral contains the classic elements of High Gothic: rich sculptural programs at its

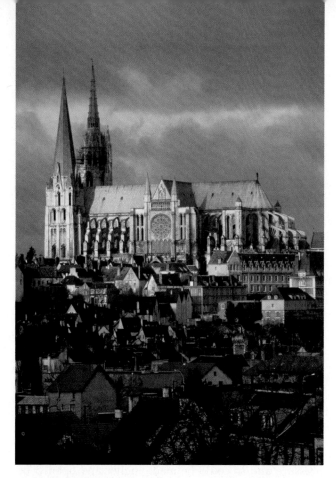

Chartres Cathedral With its asymmetrical towers, mature Gothic style, rich stained-glass windows, elongated figural statues, and dramatic natural setting, the cathedral of Chartres has often been considered the high point of Gothic architecture.

main portals, pointed arches, flying buttresses, and a complex vaulting system that allowed for greater light to shine into the cathedral through stunning stained-glass windows (Figure 9.1).

Bernard of Clairvaux and the Cistercians

By the mid-twelfth century, a chill had settled over the cathedral schools of France. The church opened up prosecutions of three masters (Abelard; William of Conches; and Gilbert of Poitiers, the bishop of Poitiers) for teachings that endangered the Catholic faith. Bernard of Clairvaux was involved in all three cases. He so stage-managed the case against Abelard in 1141 that the master didn't stand a chance; he was condemned before he could defend himself. The case against Gilbert's complex teachings collapsed and the one against William never got off the ground.

Bernard should not be judged solely on the basis of these repressions of intellectual "heretics." He was the conscience of his age, a charismatic religious leader whose career touched many of the formative events of the twelfth century. Bernard was a Cistercian, a reforming monastic movement that took shape in Burgundy at

the monastery of Cîteaux at the end of the eleventh century. There a group of monks devoted themselves to a simpler form of monastic life, one not encumbered by the excessive and time-consuming prayers and rituals of the Cluniacs. The Cistercians rejected pomp and ceremony, riches and city-living. Instead, they set out for the wilderness, erecting plain monasteries in out-of-the-way places and devoting themselves to charity and manual labor. Eventually, the Cistercians would have hundreds of monastic houses throughout Europe, but in the first half of the twelfth century, the Cistercian monastic movement was finding its footing and Bernard of Clairvaux was its spiritual voice and guide.

Bernard was austere, even condemning the fancies of Romanesque decoration of the sort that Gislebertus had carved at Autun. Bernard wondered what depictions of fabulous creatures and bizarre scenes had to do with a contemplative monastic life. He asked why monasteries were decorated with sculptures of obscene monkeys, lions and tigers, warring soldiers, multiheaded creatures, fish with mammalian heads, and creatures half-horse and half-goat. He objected to the distracting quality of such fanciful art. Monks could spend the whole day gazing upon these entertainments carved in stone rather than reading the Bible. The Cistercians turned away from Romanesque decoration toward simpler unadorned churches and manuscripts.

In addition to spurning artistic fantasies and learned heresies, Bernard was dismayed by the rise of popular heresies. In the 1140s in Cologne a number of heretics claimed that they led a more apostolic life than did the representatives of the Catholic Church; they ate no meat, embraced poverty, and altered the practices of the official church. Bernard attempted to refute their teachings by restating Catholic truths as simply as he could, for he thought that the wayward should be brought back to the true faith by argument and persuasion. A mob in Cologne was less patient and burned some of the heretics to death. Bernard was moderate and forgiving, but his righteousness belonged to an increasingly repressive church. As the number and variety of unorthodox beliefs swelled in an ever more complex society—or became more apparent to increasingly vigilant religious authorities—the church turned from persuasion to coercion.

Bernard stood deep within the power structures of his age, and one of his followers became pope. As a powerful speaker and writer, Bernard was called on to preach against heresy and to defend the church. In 1144, the crusader kingdom of Edessa fell to the Seljuk Turks. At the pope's request, Bernard called for a Second Crusade (1146–1149). Though the fervor for crusade had cooled in Europe, Bernard's oratorical magic galvanized Europe to take up the cross once again. After Bernard delivered a stirring sermon in Vézelay in northern France, thousands of people assembled to retake the Holy Land. Castles emptied and women were left without husbands, said Bernard. He roused the nobility and royalty of Europe to go on crusade. In Germany, crusade fever and popular preaching

Spire

Transept

Apse

Flying buttress

Rose window

Tympanum

West portal

Nave

Pointed arch

Rose window

South portal

FIGURE 9.1 | **Principal Features of a Gothic Cathedral (Chartres)**

spilled over into attacks on Jews. Bernard tried to put a stop to the persecution, but many Jews were massacred. The Second Crusade was a disaster of disorganization and royal rivalries that soon failed. In the end, Bernard regretted his role in calling for so disastrous an undertaking and denounced the folly of the Second Crusade.

Despite that disaster, Bernard of Clairvaux played a critical public role in fortifying the Catholic Church by bolstering its core spiritual values (particularly by his devotion to the cult of Mary) and orthodox character in the midst of an expanding, prosperous, and contentious world.

Two Thirds and Two Fourths

The Third Crusade proved to be no more successful than the Second, but under the powerful stewardship

> Why might Innocent III have been the most powerful and imperial of medieval popes?

of Pope Innocent III (1198–1216), the Catholic Church reached the summit of its political power in the Middle Ages. The range of Innocent's activity—interfering in the politics of his day, correcting

CHRONOLOGY	Early-Thirteenth-Century Church Events
DATE	EVENT
1198	Innocent III becomes pope
1200	University of Paris receives its royal charter
1204	Fourth Crusade takes Constantinople
1208	England placed under interdict
1209	Establishment of the Franciscan Order
1209–1229	Cathar (or Albigensian) Crusade
1215	Fourth Lateran Council
1216	Establishment of the Dominican Order
1231	The beginning of the Inquisition
1244	Thomas Aquinas becomes a Dominican friar

kings and emperors, shaping Catholic doctrine in the Fourth Lateran Council, and promoting crusade—was a high water mark for the medieval church. Yet the Fourth Crusade led to the capture of Constantinople and shattered the hope of reconciling the eastern and western churches.

The Third Crusade

What the First Crusade had brought about with spontaneous and popular enthusiasm, the second and subsequent crusades could achieve only with great difficulty. When new crusaders arrived in the Holy Land, they found that the first crusaders and their successors, who had remained there to manage the crusader states, had survived by settling into a state of peaceful coexistence with the Muslim population. Many of the old crusaders had come to see the virtues of Islamic life, and all of them understood that they could not rule these foreign lands without the acquiescence of the native population. The new crusaders were almost as distant from the heirs of the first crusaders as they were from the resident Muslim population.

The Islamic world became more united by the end of the twelfth century. Saladin came to power as the ruler of Egypt and Syria in 1174. This inspired warrior retook the city of Jerusalem in 1187 and overthrew the Latin Kingdom of Jerusalem. Europe was once again called to war in a Third Crusade (1189–1192). The Holy Roman emperor, Frederick Barbarossa (so called for his red beard), set out for the east in 1189, but his army was destroyed and he died while fording a river. Richard the Lionheart, king of England, and Philip II Augustus, king of France (r. 1180–1223), had more luck and retook Acre and Jaffa, but the two warrior kings were locked in a personal contest for power and land in greater France and rarely cooperated. Complicating their relations was the fact that Richard as the duke of Normandy was the vassal of Philip. Eventually Philip withdrew from the crusade and once home attacked Richard's continental holdings. Worse for King Richard, on his way home from the crusade, he was captured by a duke of Austria and held for ransom by the emperor Henry VI.

The Third Crusade ended as had the Second, in disunity and disaster. The religious motives and popularity of the First Crusade had been replaced by grudging royal commitments to the pope to take up crusade and by stubborn European economic and territorial interests. The Christian presence in the Holy Land continued to shrink.

Richard the Lionheart and Saladin Joust In this fantasy, Richard and Saladin face each other as chivalric heroes. No wars were settled in this way, though many knights wished they could be.

Pope Innocent III

In 1198, Lothario di Segni was thirty-seven years old, a cardinal and canon lawyer, when he was elected pope and took the name Innocent III. Italy was in turmoil, and the emperor Henry VI had just died. The Investiture Controversy had succeeded in establishing not just the reform of the church, but also the doctrine of the **papal plenitude of power,** that is, that the pope had unlimited or absolute power. The imperial papacy's claim to extensive powers over Christian Europe had been exercised fitfully by Innocent's predecessors. Gregory VII's reign had ended in exile, but Urban II and his successors had marshaled Europe for three crusades. Two of those crusades failed miserably, and heresy in Europe was thought to be on the rise. Innocent moved against corruption within the church, particularly **pluralism**

Pope Innocent III A thirteenth-century fresco portrait of the most powerful of medieval popes.

or the holding of several offices at once (as, for instance, when one man was bishop over several episcopal sees at the same time). Despite the difficult times, Innocent became the strongest, though not the most other-worldly of medieval popes. One of his chief goals was to secure control of central Italy and a strong papal state.

Innocent was a brilliant papal politician. He secured the succession of the four-year-old Frederick II as king of Sicily and forced several European monarchs to become papal vassals. Innocent crowned the new king of Aragon in Rome and tried to overthrow the king of Norway. When the pope and King John of England disagreed over the appointment of a new archbishop of Canterbury in 1208, Innocent placed England under **interdict,** effectively closing the church in England. Sacraments were offered only to the sick and dying. When King John seized church properties and bishops fled the kingdom, Innocent responded by excommunicating the king and invited the French king to invade England. To restore his standing, John surrendered his kingdom to the papacy and received it back as a papal fief. King John was also forced to grant the church a series of freedoms from royal interference. In this contest of wills, Pope Innocent prevailed because he was the more astute politician.

Innocent's papacy was the end result of the Investiture Controversy with its claims of extensive papal power over all Christendom and, therefore, over the monarchs and emperors who claimed to rule it. Under Innocent, the medieval imperial papacy achieved its fullest expression, but it was not to go unchallenged.

The Fourth Crusade

If the Second and Third Crusades were small disasters, the Fourth Crusade (1198–1204) was an outright crime, an international mugging in the European daylight. At the start of the First Crusade there had been a delicate moment when the Byzantine emperor was worried that the crusaders gathered outside the walls of Constantinople might attack his city rather than pass by it peacefully on their way to the Holy Land. The Fourth Crusade led to the feared conquest of Constantinople and the Byzantine Empire by western crusaders.

In the second half of the twelfth century, many Latin traders resided in Constantinople, but in 1182 many of them had been massacred by the Greeks. A succession of incompetent and often corrupt emperors reigned in the east, but Constantinople, however chaotic and dangerous, remained the most fabulous city in all of Christendom, and its wealth attracted the predatory. Early in his reign, Pope Innocent had sent legates to Constantinople to urge the eastern emperor to end the Great Schism of the church by acknowledging the supremacy of the pope in Rome. Innocent played a dangerous game, even threatening the Byzantine emperor with a forcible solution to the disunity of the church if he did not conform. In the meantime a new crusade to liberate the Holy Land, called for by Pope Innocent, was being planned in the west, financed in part by the doge (chief official) of Venice. In 1195, a claimant to the Byzantine throne named Alexius promised the crusaders that if they elevated him to the throne, he would pay off the debt owed to the Venetians, provide the crusaders with money to campaign in Egypt, and reunite the eastern and western churches.

A number of western interests thus came to focus on Constantinople early in the thirteenth century. In June 1203, western ships sailed within sight of the walls of the grand old city. An assault on the city might still have been avoided, but the religious, dynastic, and commercial disputes were too great. When a wall of the city was breached, the emperor fled the city and the crusaders waited to be paid. When the newly installed emperor Alexius and his

The Fourth Lateran Council

In 1215, at Pope Innocent's command, a great council of the church was convened in Rome. Some thirteen hundred church officials gathered, along with spokesmen for the various monarchs of Europe. The council considered the sorry state of the crusading movement and the threat to the church posed by heretics, but it was its codification of church practices that was to have lasting significance.

Under Innocent's direct guidance, the prelates of the Fourth Lateran Council set about binding the Catholic Church to clear rules and tighter conduct. The council condemned heresy and stipulated how heretics were to be identified and prosecuted. Even though the Greek church was, after the Fourth Crusade, more compliant, the council condemned any remaining resistance to papal primacy.

Innocent's great council worried that the church was under assault from the forces of a changing world and far too loose for its own good. The council regulated standards for the high medieval church. It established tighter qualifications for the priesthood, often framed in negative terms: no irrational feasting or breaking of celibacy by priests, no drinking, no hunting, no pub crawling, no trials by ordeal overseen by churchmen, and no surgery performed by priests. The council mandated the election of bishops, set stricter monastic standards, and specified and justified papal taxes on the clergy. All Christians over eight years old were to confess once a year and receive communion, generally at Easter, or be excommunicated from the church. Marriage was confirmed as a sacrament, and restrictions were imposed on who could be married (dependent on the relatedness of the couple) and under what conditions.

The council also served as an arbiter of high politics in Christian lands, confirming the elevation of Frederick II as Holy Roman emperor and settling scores with the nobles of southern France who sympathized with heretics. In some cases, the nobles' lands were to be removed from their possession until they complied with the church; and in others, transferred to their conquerors. The Fourth Lateran Council was Innocent's attempt to establish the Catholic Church as a universal church in fact as well as theory.

Christians and Moors Battle over Spain A thirteenth-century depiction of Christians and Moors (Muslims) at war in Spain. The reconquest of Spain spanned centuries but was over by 1492.

father could not find the funds needed to satisfy the assembled attackers, they were deposed and Alexius was strangled to death. At the urging of the doge of Venice, the crusaders continued the attack on Constantinople. On April 12, 1204, two ships financed by Latin bishops took two of the city's towers; a week later Constantinople fell to the wayward western crusaders. For three days they ran riot in the city, burning and looting. Many of the precious objects that Constantine and the Romans had transferred to the city centuries before were seized and sent west, among them the four ancient copper horses that were mounted on St. Mark's Basilica in Venice.

In short order, the western crusaders established a Latin Empire of Constantinople in the east that lasted until 1261. In the west, Pope Innocent publicly condemned the crusaders for their shocking seizure of Constantinople and the diversion of the Fourth Crusade from its mission to reclaim the Holy Land. He realized that the capture of Constantinople would make the reunification of the churches more difficult, but he eventually came to accept that the new Latin Empire in the east was a judgment of God and a miracle. The Byzantines lamented the fall of their city and regarded the crusaders as the agents of the Anti-Christ. Once again the dream of reuniting all of Christendom under one faith had been dashed.

High Times for the Medieval Economy

The medieval economy was working about as well as it could by the thirteenth century, at least in lands such as

> How did population growth in the High Middle Ages begin to transform Europe?

France, which sustained a large and growing population. By nearly every indicator—food production, population growth, urbanization, industry, and trade—the economy was flourishing. Growth, however, produces tensions and it did so in Europe, particularly between towns and villages, burghers and nobles.

1215: A High Water Mark for the Middle Ages?

The year 1215 was an extraordinary one, filled with events that determined the direction the Late Middle Ages would take. King Alfonso VIII of Spain died the previous year, not long after opening the long campaign to expel the Muslims from Spain. The Latin emperor of Byzantium, Henry of Flanders, died the next year after uniting the four provinces of his eastern empire. Simon IV de Montfort was leading the crusade (backed by the pope) against the Cathars of southern France and in 1215 was named the count of Toulouse; in May he entered his city.

For Pope Innocent III the year was a busy one. He forced Frederick II to agree to go on crusade and was raising monies for a Fifth Crusade. Though he had called for a great council of Christians two years earlier, the Fourth Lateran Council did not meet until November 1215. Among those attending the council was Saint Dominic, whose order of preachers was confirmed the next year. Innocent had approved the order of the Friars Minor or Franciscans in 1209. Together these mendicant (begging) orders would transform the "street-presence" of Catholicism in Europe. Innocent III died the next year.

Gothic architecture had not yet reached its pinnacle, but many of its finest examples were under construction in 1215. The cathedral of Laon was complete; Sens was largely finished but had been damaged by a fire; much of Noyon stood, and its west facade was being erected; the west facade of Notre Dame of Paris was being erected; and Chartres was partially built by 1215, but its choir and buttresses had not yet been executed. Thus, had one visited any of the great cities of France in 1215, one would have seen massive Gothic cathedrals rising up with fresh pale stone, seen huge cranes lifting stones into place, heard the sound of hammers, and watched as hundreds of workers climbed about on scaffolding.

In 1214, Philip Augustus, the king of France, won the battle of Bouvines against English troops and forced King John of England to depart from Normandy. Philip's famous grandson, Louis IX (known to us as Saint Louis), was born that year. In defeat and disgrace, King John returned home to deal with his angry church, irritated magnates, and anxious people. On June 15, 1215, at Runnymede he capitulated to his rebellious barons and signed the Magna Carta, which restricted the king's arbitrary royal powers. At Aachen in Germany, in Charlemagne's chapel, on July 15, Frederick II was crowned emperor and a few days later oversaw the transfer of Charlemagne's corpse to a gold and silver sarcophagus, even throwing off his imperial robes and driving nails into the new tomb. The year 1215 was a remarkable one for the Middle Ages. What would the High Middle Ages have been without great Gothic cathedrals, friars, the powerful church of Innocent III and his great council, the removal of the Cathars, the continuing Christian reconquest of Spain, or King John's comeuppance?

QUESTIONS | *What other years might be considered historically more important than others? Was the year 1215, with its remarkable events, a pinnacle and, therefore, a turning point for the High Middle Ages? Why or why not?*

The Agricultural Base

At its base, the medieval economy of the High Middle Ages remained rooted in the countryside and in agricultural production, now in its most perfected medieval form. Most of the agricultural techniques in use had been introduced in the Early Middle Ages, but now the horse rather than the ox was used in many places to increase the speed and quality of plowing. Lords and their workers, who pressed north and east in search of new arable lands, extended western Europe's unfixed borders. Inside Europe, marginal lands were brought into production as marshes were drained and tidal areas reclaimed from the sea, particularly along the coast of the Netherlands, Germany, and England. Europe was getting bigger by the day. As the forests were cut back, new villages and towns appeared. By the twelfth century, northern Europe had a clear agricultural advantage over southern Europe, which had less arable land, poorer soil, and less water. The great Medieval Warm Period (775–1275) brought higher temperatures and longer growing seasons to northern Europe but may have made agricultural conditions in the south worse.

In the great growing season of the High Middle Ages, France benefited more than any other region of Europe. Its population grew to about twenty million people, roughly six times the size of England and two and a half times the size of Italy. The population of northern France would not surpass its high medieval peak until modern industrial times. An increase in population, however, need not mean an increase in the physical well-being of individuals. The average serf or peasant was still lucky to survive into his or her late twenties, and their children continued to die in high numbers. Deforestation, expanding towns, and rivers used as the carriers of waste materials had environmental consequences, producing floods, local pollution, and disease. Many of the outlying lands brought under cultivation were marginal for a reason; they possessed poor soil that was quickly exhausted from overuse and poor land management. The population increase in Europe was a product of an agricultural system that had achieved its highest medieval form, but by 1275 the economy was beginning to experience difficulties.

Farmers remained the backbone of the economic world of the High Middle Ages and were recognized as an essential part of the social and economic fabric of society. Their legal standing, however, varied from place to place and individual to individual. Some agricultural workers were free and others servile and entirely dependent on their lords for sustenance and legal standing. The lord, or *seignior,* viewed the farmers who worked for him as his dependents. Upon them he imposed duties of labor and taxes, and even had some control over their personal lives.

The effect of such tight and exploitative overlordship in places such as northern France bound the peasantry together as a group living with common conditions, interests, and grievances. One group of farm workers held by a royal monastery of Paris resented that the king had, with a stroke of his pen in 1178, reduced them to servility. They carried their complaint to the pope in Rome, who recognized their free status. The papacy could not, however, enforce its opinion and, by 1226, the peasant community had capitulated. Its drive to achieve freedom was finally purchased twenty years later with an agreement to pay an annual tribute to the king. Peasants understood that their lot was not fixed, but negotiable. They turned to popes and kings for relief and demands for justice. Higher authorities, who were involved in building power bases of their own, helped occasionally, but their own serfs could look to few higher authorities for assistance.

The Growth of Towns

Towns and small cities flourished in the High Middle Ages. Small cities such as Bruges and Cologne reached populations of around 30,000 people. Paris grew to at least 75,000 to 100,000 residents by 1300 and may have been almost twice that size. In Italy, mercantile cities such as Venice and Florence had around 90,000 people by the early fourteenth century. Kings and magnates had an interest in promoting towns and cities in their realms since they lay outside the direct control of nobles or could be dislodged from their control. Magnates such as the duke of

Poland actively promoted the foundation of new cities as engines of economic activity.

Medieval towns were mixed or complex economic centers closely connected to nearby villages. Many towns continued to operate as large villages, in which farming was still practiced on plots of land around the town and many residents went out to work on local fields just as early medieval villagers had. Towns and small cities of the High Middle Ages increasingly imported and exported goods, and served as depots for the storage and distribution of goods. Many towns, particularly those in the textile trade in Flanders, specialized in specific industries. Northern traders moved from a base of operations in some city out to other towns, villages, or into the Mediterranean Sea and Slavic lands, areas long traveled by Byzantine traders. The in-home or **cottage industries** that had existed in medieval villages moved to towns where larger enterprises could be maintained. Medieval towns and cities also offered financial services, particularly the lending and investment of money.

Guilds and Industry

In early medieval villages, women had worked not only on the land with their families, but also in cottage industries producing clothes and other local necessities. In the High Middle Ages, associations of craftsmen called **guilds** were formed to control production. These associations largely excluded women from membership or, if they were allowed in, denied them official roles. Guilds

The Blessings of Good Government Ambrogio Lorenzetti's mural (1337–1339) in Siena, Italy, of the benefits of city living, peace, and good government.

MAP 9.1 | Trade Routes and Fairs, c. 1100–1300
This map highlights the principal trading areas and routes for the flow of goods in the High Middle Ages. The system was more complex than shown here. **How did trade and commerce work to integrate Europe, or did it? How was trade a point of international contact?**

controlled production, divided workers into masters and apprentices, and set prices and the terms of trade. Most large towns had guilds that made cloth, shoes, parchment, and furniture. Although the guild system guaranteed the quality of the goods produced, it was economically and socially rigid. The guild system suppressed competition. Long-serving apprentices often had little chance of becoming masters and were forced to accept low wages to sustain themselves and their families.

Not only craftsmen, but professional groups formed guild-like associations. Italian city-states established hierarchies of guilds in which professions such as the notaries were ranked higher than the craft guilds. Merchants and universities would imitate the basic system of masters and apprentices to control the terms and conditions of production within their spheres of activity.

The scale of industry in the High Middle Ages could be impressive. In Ghent, 5,200 men worked to produce cloth. In Paris, 130 different guilds looked after every-

thing from the building trade and leather goods to making manuscript books. One could judge the size and development of a town by the number and variety of its guilds and professions and the range of goods and services supplied. Towns in which the chief guilds supplied horsemen and farmers with equipment such as stirrups, bridles, harnesses, and yokes defined an economy as local and serving the needs of farmers. Moneylenders and financial guilds tended to prevail in port cities, where traders and seamen gathered and active maritime trade networks operated.

In some sectors, Europe's agricultural production was so large that traders needed to transport their goods over great distances to find markets (Map 9.1). In good years, England exported fifteen million pounds of unprocessed wool. French vineyards supplied millions of barrels of wine to Europe. By the thirteenth century, Italian port cities were picking up bulk goods from England and Flanders for transport and trade in the wider

Mediterranean. An improved road network facilitated trade, encouraging local producers to send their goods to large markets such as Paris and London, where they might connect with long-distance trade networks. These roads, which served chiefly as surfaces for two- and four-wheeled carts pulled by horses, mules, and donkeys, were rarely paved or planked. A wheeled cart might cover only ten miles per day, and ground transport could add as much as a third to the cost of goods. It was faster and cheaper to send goods by boat.

By 1300, the European economy was operating about as well as it could, sustaining in fertile areas such as France a dense medieval population, spreading goods throughout Europe and reaching the Mediterranean, Baltic, and Slavic frontiers. Traders from Venice, Pisa, and Genoa could be found in all major ports and were helping to restore a wider world of Mediterranean trade. Annual fairs in Champagne and elsewhere provided opportunities for traders and purchasers to collect at specific times of the year. More sophisticated commercial contracts and loan structures developed. Some shipping contracts specified late fees, which were actually interest charges disguised to avoid church prohibitions against practicing **usury** (charging interest on loans). Another method for circumventing rules against making a profit was to accept payment in a currency other than the one the contract specified. Capitalists and traders found ways to overcome economic obstacles. Complex trading networks arose along the North Sea and the Baltic, where the Hanseatic League of trading centers was forming.

Communes and Urban Tensions

During this period of rapid urban growth and economic development, tensions surfaced as towns attempted to extend their control over the surrounding countryside. One point of conflict centered on transport and travel. Traders wanted free access to roads and bridges, but wherever they could local lords and villages imposed tolls on passage through their lands or across their bridges. Tolls were one of the only ways in which the countryside and local nobility could derive economic benefit from prosperous towns. Early in the thirteenth century, the town of Toulouse waged a small war against local country lords and their "excessive" tolls. Forming an integrated economy meant sorting out which was the dominant force and which the subservient one in each region; the answer varied from place to place, region to region. In Flanders, the towns won; in parts of England and France, the countryside often did.

Towns were also grappling with the tensions caused by rapid internal growth. At the start of the twelfth century, towns in northern France were hotbeds of tension between residents and the prevailing powers. A few years after Abelard went to Laon to study under Master Anselm, a murderous communal riot broke out. The burghers, merchants, and priests of the town bridled under the arbitrary rule of their bishop and local nobles, who imposed arbitrary taxes and subjected them to indignities. Even the king, when he visited his royal town, was forced to pay various fees. The disgruntled residents of Laon formed a **commune,** to which at first the bishop, under some pressure, agreed. When the bishop finally dissolved the bonds of the association and broke his previous promises, the shopkeepers closed their shops, fearing that the bishop and nobles would plunder their goods. Some of the angered townsmen then conspired to murder the bishop. When he went to church one Sunday, one of them, thinking it was time to begin the riot, began to chant, "commune, commune." The riot lasted for days. The conspirators murdered the bishop, hacking off his legs and leaving his corpse to rot in the street, where it was rescued by Master Anselm. Other aristocrats and associates of the prelate tried to flee, but many were hunted down and murdered by the mob.

Laon was not the only town to form a commune. Burghers and merchants established communes in a number of northern French towns, as well as in the Netherlands and northern Italy. During the twelfth and thirteenth centuries, towns struggled to govern themselves, often with the support of the king. Towns established laws that stipulated residents' freedom from tolls but their subjection to town taxes, their right to dispose of their property, and their willingness to abide by established laws. Towns and small cities set out their rights in charters to ensure their relative freedom from noble and church interference. By the late thirteenth century, however, some Italian city-states, which had been self-governing republics, began to fall under the control of local lords (*signori*).

As towns and small cities were asserting their rights in the High Middle Ages, villages were often left behind, their prosperity reduced and any hope of independence gone. The economic centralization of Europe produced winners and losers. The countryside of Europe, ironically, became more exclusively agricultural than it had been in the Early and Central Middle Ages because large towns monopolized nonagricultural production and cottage industries in villages could not easily compete.

Dissent and Control, Church and State

After the Investiture Controversy, the new imperial papacy sought to eradicate ideas and practices not sanctioned by the reformed church. As medieval society became more vigorous and urban and people traveled greater distances, new ideas about religious life inevitably emerged, many of them in reaction to a church that was seen as too powerful and worldly. At the same time, medieval states were becoming more centralized and controlling, but their development was uneven.

> Why did the ordered society of the High Middle Ages produce so much complaint and outright resistance from common people, learned "heretics," and religious dissenters?

Dealing with Dissent

Popular culture mocked an increasingly prosperous and bureaucratic church. In the Gospel of Silver Mark, a widely circulating parody, a poor man approaches the gates of the papal palace, begging for mercy, but is sent away. He was told that he could not enter until he had surrendered his last dime. When he sold his only cloak, the cardinals counted it as nothing and sent him away again. Yet a fat priest, who had committed murder and greased all the right palms with cash, was welcomed by the pope, who advised his cardinals to take from their flocks as he did from his, which was to make mock of the golden rule to do unto others as you would have them do unto you.

In the twelfth and thirteenth centuries, groups critical of the church attracted official attention. The Poor Men of Lyons or Waldensians (their leader was Peter Waldo) rejected a propertied church and corrupt clergy, and advocated the relief of the poor. They were also antipapal, which was to doom their movement. By Pope Innocent III's reign, the popes led an aggressive campaign to identify and condemn those such as the Waldensians who were critical of the church. The church labeled them heretics.

Most of the heresies that arose in the High Middle Ages were anticlerical and antipapal. The Patarines in northern Italy repudiated clerical marriages and simony, the same as the reforming popes had, but their leader, Arnold of Brescia, went further, arguing that the church should not own any property.

The strongest of the dissenting movements was the one associated with the Cathars or Albigensians (named after the city of Albi in southern France). Centered in southern France and northern Italy, Catharism flourished among the prosperous middle class in towns. Cathars were not Catholic Christians, but Manichaeans. These dualists believed that the world was divided into forces of good (light) and evil (darkness), which were at constant war with one another. They believed that all things material, including flesh and the world, were evil. In its most extreme stages, Cathars practiced total asceticism or self-denial, right down to ritual starvation. The Cathars rejected Catholic norms: the sacraments, marriage, and reproduction. They avoided all consumption of flesh, preferring to eat foods such as melons and honey, which they thought were produced asexually. The movement was structured so that only its leaders, the good men or "perfected ones," starved themselves to death.

Pope Innocent sponsored an internal crusade against the Cathars (1209–1229). He first sent missionaries into Languedoc in southern France to try to win back the faithful to the church. When that failed, he gave the noble warrior Simon IV de Montfort license to proceed against the Cathar heretics. Simon did just that, but he and his

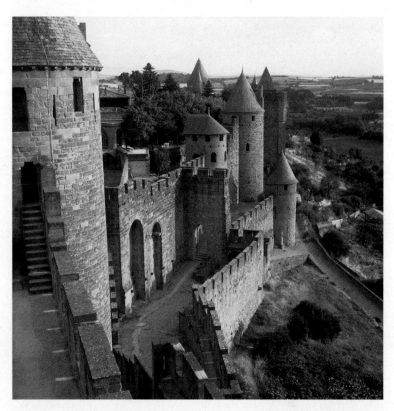

The Walled City of Carcassonne Southern France was troubled in the thirteenth century by outbreaks of heresy, frequent wars, and political disruption, which also struck the walled medieval city of Carcassonne. The small, enclosed city, which still stands, was forced at one point to expel its Cathar citizens.

men also wanted to uproot the nobility of southern France, which was sympathetic to the good men, and to seize their lands. Ultimately, Catharism was destroyed.

The situation of Jews in Europe deteriorated in the thirteenth century. Not only had crusade fever engendered attacks on Jews, but the new theological rigor of the west meant that Jews were often thought of as "other" and enemies of Christ. After the Fourth Lateran Council, most European Jews were forced to wear signs of their faith: symbols, special hats, or particular clothes. In England there was a campaign to cancel debts owed to Jews, and in 1182 King Philip Augustus of France expelled all Jews from France, in large part to seize their European assets.

The Mendicant Orders and the Inquisition

The official church was not without its own popular religious movements and the means to resist heresies through persuasion rather than violence. In the early thirteenth century, two men emerged with new missions: Saints Francis and Dominic. They established movements of **mendicant** or begging friars (so named after the Latin, *fratres,* for brothers), who devoted themselves to the Roman Church, the papacy, the poor, and the sick (especially lepers). The mendicants preached and begged in the cities of Europe, and practiced absolute poverty. The

MAP 9.2 | **European State Development, c. 1100–1300**

By the High Middle Ages, Europe was filled with states that had various degrees of power and command over their regions and borders and different ways of organizing themselves. The Holy Roman Empire may seem large and dominant on this map but was in reality relatively weak and only in loose control of its vast territory. *Why was Europe so regionally divided? Which forms of government prevailed? Where and why?*

friars fitted the needs of high medieval society. Unlike monks who were cloistered in monasteries, the mendicants were mobile and responded better to the new urban realities of the thirteenth century. They were a visible and vocal presence on the streets of European cities. Pope Innocent recognized the legitimacy of the Franciscans, and his successor recognized the Dominicans (the order of preachers). The Dominicans, in particular, devoted themselves to teaching and were to be key agents in the investigation of heresy. Their goal as educators was to bring about the end of heresy by identifying, correcting, and enlightening wayward Christians.

One papal complaint was that the investigation of heretics, which often fell to local episcopal courts, was too lax. Various rulers in France attempted to set up **inquisitions** of the Cathars, but Pope Gregory IX (1227–1241) decided to formalize the process. He appointed Dominican friars as inquisitors to examine, under the watchful eye of a papal legate, the Cathar sympathizers of southern France. At Toulouse the inquisition took on its high medi-

eval form, including secret accusations, torture, and the keeping of meticulous records of the interviews of suspects. From the standpoint of the church, the purpose of an inquisition was to restore balance and rectitude to the Christian religious body either by reincorporating those who had strayed from the orthodox faith or by cutting them off (by death) from the faithful before they contaminated the entire body. Much blood was spilled and many lives ruined in the process.

State Development

Europe was politically and territorially segmented in the High Middle Ages (Map 9.2), and state development differed in three basic areas. In the first, England after the Conquest and France after 1100 developed strong monarchies. In the second, Germany and Italy were internally divided and power there was fragmented. In Germany the decisive factors for fragmentation were of long standing: a Holy Roman emperor with claims to extensive

Mongol Relations

Before the merchant family the Polos (Marco, his father Niccolò, and uncle Maffeo) ventured to the Far East in the 1260s and 1270s, Europeans had already made official contact with the Mongol Empire. Twelfth-century stories of Prester John, a Christian king in the east, the supposed heir of the Magi, may have fueled western fascination with the mysterious East, but in the thirteenth century there were real relations brought on by war and religion. Genghis Khan and his heirs pressed not only into China, but also along the edges of eastern Europe, ravaging parts of Hungary and Russia. Pope Innocent IV was alarmed and sought to open negotiations with the Mongols. In June 1245 in Lyons, the pope called together a council that decided to send a party of Franciscans, led by Lawrence of Portugal and Giovanni di Piano Carpini, on a long and difficult journey to the Mongol court. They carried letters for the khan, whose name the pope and his emissaries did not know at the time. The papal party set out immediately after the council, reached Kiev by early 1246, and six months later were at the Mongol court to witness the elevation of the new Mongol khan (Küyük, the grandson of Genghis). They presented their letters to the khan and received a letter to take back to the pope. They arrived back in Lyons by late 1248. The letters they carried both to and from the Mongols were worlds apart.

The pope's first letter is a complex discourse on Christianity that is so layered in European thought and technical language that it may have been difficult for its recipients in Asia to understand. The letter did, however, introduce the pope's emissaries and asked for the khan to protect them and to listen to what they had to say. The pope's second letter, also written before the mission set off, was an unequivocal assertion of Catholic supremacy and judgment. In it Pope Innocent condemned the Mongol invasions of Christian and other lands

Küyük Khan

and called on the khan to stop the slaughter lest he suffer in hell for the savagery his people committed on earth. Carpini, in his impersonal account of the journey, reports that after they had presented the court with the letters he was asked whether his pope understood the Russian, Saracen (Arabic), or Mongol languages. The Franciscans suggested that the khan's court should reply in Mongol and that they would translate it into Latin and supply the pope with both versions. The Mongol court's secretaries insisted on interpreting the khan's letter to them and then carefully checked the rendering of it into Latin to make sure that there were no errors that might cause trouble or misunderstanding. The khan's letter survives in both Latin and Persian (the original is in the Vatican Library). The pope was probably not pleased by the khan's letter, but then neither was the khan by the pope's two letters. The great khan demanded that the pope and his princes come and submit to him. He claimed not to have understood the pope's letters about either religion or the Mongol conquests. He had conquered peoples because of their impudence and charged the pope with the same offense. Moreover, he was the emperor of all peoples and the success of the Mongol conquests was proof of God's approval. If the pope chose not to submit to him, he should know that he would be the khan's enemy and should expect war. The religious disagreements between the pope and the khan were profound. The khan rejected propositions not found in the letters (and so, perhaps, conveyed orally by the Franciscans) that the khan be baptized, become a Nestorian Christian (an eastern form of Christianity that had reached India), or an ascetic. The khan denied the pope's claim to speak for God and convey his judgment. Instead, the great khan claimed that Genghis Khan and his successors were the ones who had been sent by God.

Long-distance disagreements, filtered through several languages and worlds of cultural difference, made the perspectives of the western pope and eastern khan sharply different, but the papacy sent other delegations of Franciscans to talk to the Mongols and to collect information. Thirty years later the Polos would, more successfully, speak a different language, the language of trade and mutual advantage, which was somewhat more accommodating.

QUESTIONS | *Why is war in some cases a first form of communication? Was the papal mission to the Mongols a good idea or not? Why? How deep was the cultural chasm between far east and far west? Why might those cultural differences have been largely official and not societal?*

powers, strong magnates, and papal interference. In Italy the situation was different: a resident and intrusive papacy, imperial claims, and stronger urban and local traditions. The third area of special state development was the imperial papacy, which reached its apex under Innocent III but struggled after that. At the end of the thirteenth century, Pope Boniface VIII aggressively extended the claims of the papacy, but he met strong resistance from powerful secular forces. Princes were now often stronger than popes.

The mechanisms of state control improved in the High Middle Ages. A more sophisticated bureaucracy assisted the drive toward centralization and control. In France and England, noble interests were increasingly subordinated to royal ones. The concept of real boundaries to a kingdom began to emerge, at least in England and France. Systems of taxation also improved. By the thirteenth century, Europe may still not have achieved any sharp sense of state, but the conditions for that conception were emerging. Politics remained primarily dynastic, and thinking about the state (as in Thomas Aquinas's *On Kingship*) remained God centered and religious in purpose. The duty of a prince was not to achieve the practical and necessary, but to do the religiously right thing. Real rulers, as opposed to ideal ones, knew how to serve their own political interests. Pope Innocent and Frederick II with their new sense of political possibilities played the game at a more calculating level, but they had to deal with the intricate city-states, chiefly republics, that were developing in Italy. City-states such as Venice not only managed their own territories and internal urban affairs, but also operated as if they were fully autonomous European states on the international stage.

The high medieval state was still conceived of as a corporate body or incorporated entity. John of Salisbury likened the various groups of society to parts of a body: the king was the head, the priesthood the soul, soldiers the breast, tax collectors the intestines, and farmers the feet. As rudimentary as this scheme may seem, its effect was to treat the state as a living body of interdependent parts, each of which had its proper place and function. John also began to explore the limits of kingship, the most controversial being the removal of a tyrant. John granted that the king deserved the support of his subjects, but only so long as he obeyed God and his commandments. Should he wage war against God, then he would be, by definition, a tyrant who should be removed from office, by force if necessary. Thus John proposed a doctrine of tyrannicide (the murder of a tyrant) and not regicide (the murder of a king), since a ruler who attacked God no longer ruled by divine right or rightfully held the title and office of king.

By the early thirteenth century, some limitations on kingship were being formulated in England. After his capitulation to Pope Innocent III, King John faced the resistance of his barons, who resented his many attempts to raise monies and to levy demands upon them. At Runnymede in 1215, he finally relented, issuing the **Magna Carta,** or Great Charter (to distinguish it from a smaller one), which provided a series of guarantees to the magnates and people of England that delimited what the king could demand of his people and powerful lords. The document may not have been the groundbreaking constitutional charter some once thought that it was, but it did set down rules about taxation, property rights, and limits on the king's power. The king was no longer allowed to tinker with or undo legitimate inheritances, to allow his agents to seize the property or goods of any man without fair payment, or to override the law of the land in pursuit of royal interests.

The monarchies of France, England, and to a lesser degree Spain were not yet states in the modern sense of the term, but they were on their way toward statehood in having defined territories and representative assemblies of the king and the powerful of the land. Spanish kings met with their knights and lords in an assembly called the *cortes,* where they decided on united action and settled disputes. By the end of the thirteenth century, Spanish rulers accepted that they required the support of their people, as expressed in the *cortes,* to make general laws for all. What mattered was who was included in the assemblies. In England, each borough was able to send two representatives to its assembly or parliament, which had developed out of the older Anglo-Saxon Witan. France attempted to widen the franchise even further, including not only lords and church prelates, but also representatives from hundreds of villages and towns. These assemblies were limited bodies, since they met irregularly and at the will of the king. As promising as the assembly movement was across Europe in the thirteenth century, it may also be seen as just another tool for the centralization of the state under powerful monarchs. In the Late Middle Ages, these assemblies would generally weaken.

Rulers Respected, Feared, and Loved

To learn about a period and place there may be no better way to measure its ideals than to see which rulers it admired and despised, and why. The medieval Christian ideal (as found stated explicitly in early medieval political treatises) was that a ruler should be loved and feared, just as God was. The hard realities of ruling meant that few high medieval rulers could achieve both and survive.

Consider the case of Henry II, king of England (r. 1154–1189), who was respected but not loved. After the death of William the Conqueror, England had lived precariously on the edge of civil war and rebellion as the church, the great barons, and the people were upset over new taxes and royal demands. During his long reign, Henry II put down regional resistance to England in Scotland and Wales, reorganized English government by improving the quality and jurisdiction of royal officials, regularized royal revenues, and insisted on the rule of law, both royal and common. Trial by ordeal was slowly replaced by the collection and weighing of evidence by juries.

Henry was a canny and successful king, but he was not loved—not by his subjects, not by the church, and not by his family. He spent the majority of his reign outside the realm, but he had organized his kingdom so well that it could run without him being physically present. As duke of Normandy and the husband of Eleanor of Aquitaine, he was a powerful continental lord and presided over the so-called Angevin Empire. The curse hanging over the Angevin (or Plantagenet) Empire was dynastic dispute, and Eleanor and Henry were a quarrelsome couple. Their three sons—Richard (the Lionheart), Geoffrey, and John—sided with their mother and their continental land holdings. They joined with their mother in supporting the French against Henry, who overcame their rebellion and in 1174 imprisoned Eleanor.

Henry's conflict with his old friend Thomas Beckett belonged to the final stages of the papal reform of the church, for Henry thought of the church in England as under his care and control. But Thomas, whom the king appointed archbishop of Canterbury, fought hard for church rights and resisted royal interference in church affairs. John of Salisbury was present when Thomas was murdered in his cathedral by noble supporters of the king, who thought that they were ridding their king of an impolitic and rebellious enemy. In the eyes of the church and people, Thomas Beckett was a martyr and they blamed the king for his murder, but Henry took the necessary steps to repair his reputation and his culpable soul. He performed penance, was scourged, and gained papal absolution for the murder, but the church found it hard to love and embrace Henry, who treated the church as just another player in the game of royal politics.

Though Henry achieved a united England, promoted royal justice and a more efficient government, balanced the financial books, and maintained his continental possessions, few wept when he died on the continent after an unsuccessful campaign against the king of France and his own son Richard. Henry was shrewd, competent, and better for England, but the heart of the age belonged to the swashbuckling Richard, the noble crusader, who succeeded him.

Richard the Lionheart spent less than a half year of his decade in power (r. 1189–1199) in England, preferred France, probably couldn't speak English, had rebelled against his father, and exhausted the English treasury filled by his father. But Richard was larger than life and apparently much loved by the people. It is not hard to see

Eleanor of Aquitaine and Her Royal Family In a damaged mural from the chapel of St. Radegonde, Chinon, France, Queen Eleanor and her daughter Joanna (in the center) ride behind King Henry II of England and in front of two retainers or guards. The meaning of the mural is uncertain. Some scholars have suggested that it shows Eleanor being led into captivity by her husband, others that she has just been released from house arrest, and yet others that it is just a magnificent procession of the royal Plantagenet family.

why. He was famously generous and charming, reputedly handsome and courageous, and every inch the ideal chivalrous king. Moreover, by treating England as an afterthought in his international career, Richard had not aroused many grievances against him within English society. Richard's popularity and neglect of active government were possible only because his father, Henry, had demanded so much and ruled England so well.

Few knew what to make of Frederick II: some were amazed by the *stupor mundi* (the wonder of the world), who stunned the High Middle Ages with his novel behavior; some were horrified. His father was the emperor Henry VI, his grandfathers Roger of Sicily and Frederick Barbarossa. When he was three years old, his father died and a year later Frederick was named the king of Sicily. When his mother died the next year, Pope Innocent III became the boy-king's guardian. Sicily was a crucible of Arabic, Christian, Italian, and Norman influences, and the young Frederick became a proto-renaissance man: he wrote a scientific book on falconry, planned castles and canals, spoke several languages, and dreamed of restoring the empire. At age fourteen, and finally free from the pope's control, he became the ruling king of Sicily. By age eighteen he was king of the Romans, and at twenty-six he became emperor of the Holy Roman Empire. What stunned Europe was his extraordinary behavior. He reclaimed Jerusalem not by war, but through negotiation and marriage, challenged a hostile papacy, started the

University of Naples, collected exotic animals, promoted science, doubted the truths of established religions, and allowed Muslims to settle and openly practice their faith in Sicily. No wonder people of the time either praised or feared him. The papacy portrayed him as an Anti-Christ and a heretic, and excommunicated him several times because of the unorthodox way in which he retook Jerusalem. Enemies of the papacy rejoiced over Frederick's resistance to Rome, believing that he would free the church from its unholy worldliness and return it to a state of apostolic poverty. Thirteenth-century men and women projected many hopes and fears onto Frederick II, for he showed them a future different from the one that the papacy had so carefully constructed for the High Middle Ages.

Frederick II occupied the dark imagination of Europe. Saint Louis, the king of France, fulfilled its Christian aspiration for a good and lovable king. Louis became king of France on his father's death in 1226 but did not take control of the kingdom until 1234. Twice he went on crusade (the Seventh and Eighth Crusades), and despite their futile outcomes, he was admired greatly for his devotion to the Christian cause. His capture by Egyptians in 1250 shocked Europe, but he was ransomed for an enormous amount of money. For four years he remained in the Holy Land, repairing castles and improving the standing and defense of the Christians there. At home, Louis ruled a Christian state at the peak of its power and wealth. He could do almost no wrong. He was a devoted servant of Christianity, buying precious relics for France and building impressive churches. Like Pope Innocent IV, Louis sent emissaries east to meet the great Mongol khan; he thought that it was his duty as a Christian king to convert pagan kings. Even his support of the inquisition and the persecution of the Jews—seizing property to pay for his crusades and ordering the destruction of Jewish holy books—seemed to his age to be the just deeds of a true son of the church. He died a "good death" in 1270 while he was on his second crusade, and his remains were returned to St. Denis for burial. While he lived, Louis was already considered to be a holy ruler. In death he became a saint.

For the Middle Ages, Louis was a perfect Christian king, loved, but not particularly feared unless you were a Jew with property or holy books, a heretic, or a Muslim in the Holy Land. Richard the Lionheart was much admired and loved, but he was an absent and irresponsible ruler. Frederick II stunned his age with his audacity and daring, but he was little loved and much feared. Yet he personified a vision of a different sort of Europe, one not dominated by religion and the high medieval papacy, but his politics brought Europe little peace and may have doomed Germany to its long division of powers and principalities. Henry II of England was respected, but little loved by his family or country, and yet he transformed England into a better kingdom, one governed by law, order, and a strong monarchy. Yet his claim to properties in greater France meant that England would continue to be dragged into continental wars that were of royal and not necessarily English concern, as his son King John discovered.

The Medieval University

Like the monastery and representative assemblies (parliaments), the university was an institution invented and shaped by the Middle Ages. Institutions should not be thought of as buildings, but as sets of rules and customs that help specialized societies preserve authoritative cultures from generation to generation. Institutions work to overcome the limitation of mortal life, ensuring continuity across time. With written and unwritten rules, linked offices and officers, the goal of institutions is to persist, carrying out specific functions for the general good of a society.

> Why did the Middle Ages, and not some other period, create the institution of the university?

Neither the Greeks nor the Romans had found a suitable, broadly based institutional receptacle for higher learning. Plato's Academy was too elitist and unstructured. Roman aristocrats had largely privatized higher education in a tutorial system. Yet eight hundred years ago in Salerno, Bologna, Paris, Montpellier, Oxford, and Cambridge, masters were lecturing to university students and still do. The university had no exact moment of birth and there was no one individual who created it, but there were reasons for the university's emergence and persistence (Map 9.3).

The Passing of the Cathedral Schools

The great cathedral schools led by the likes of Bernard of Chartres and Abelard in the first half of the twelfth century could not cope with the demands of society or the reorganization of knowledge in the second. Instead of an advanced student seeking out a master, wherever he might be located, in order to learn a specific discipline, it became more efficient for students to move to educational centers that contained many masters. By the mid-twelfth century, Paris was already becoming one of those central meeting points for masters and students.

The University of Paris grew out of the school operated by the cathedral of Notre Dame. By 1200, Paris was four or five times the size of Chartres, and the older cathedral schools, no matter how distinguished, could not compete. Moreover, cathedral schools depended on the prestige of their great masters to draw students, but, as Abelard's case shows, respect for old authoritative teaching was under intense pressure. Adelard of Bath, an adventurous English scholar of the early twelfth century, quipped that authority had a wax nose that could be twisted. Students were restless for new ways to learn and new masters to learn from.

When asked by their father what they did at their cathedral school, two students at Chartres characterized their experience in less than elevated terms: "We make glosses; we owe money." Such an education was based on a master pronouncing upon a text, but there were few texts available to comment on. Bernard of Chartres apparently owned twenty-four volumes, which was a large personal library

MAP 9.3 | The Spread of Medieval Universities

The institution of the university spread throughout Europe after the rise of the original six: Salerno, Bologna, Paris, Montpellier, Oxford, and Cambridge. *Why did universities become so popular so quickly? Which regions and periods saw the greatest growth in the number of universities and why?*

for the time. The technique of glossing (essentially making notes in the margins of a book) was the product of an educational world based on a few core texts that received intensive study. By the mid-twelfth century, students were impatient with this older style of learning. Like Abelard and William of Conches, they wanted to know the reasons for things. Part of Abelard's popularity was that he made his subjects clear, not obtuse and rarefied, and subject to reason. He was also wickedly funny. Ambitious masters began to gather where the students were, often in larger centers such as Paris, and there offered instruction for a fee.

Translating the Collected Wisdom of the West

Students and their teachers wanted new and better books. By the middle of the twelfth century, the texts

that had sustained five hundred years of medieval education began to be displaced by a new generation of books, though they arrived too late for Abelard to put them to use. The vast store of ancient wisdom had been divided and localized by the breakdown of Roman order. The Latin works of Rome had fallen to western Europe; 90 percent of the ancient Latin texts that have survived had been copied and preserved by the Carolingians. The Greek works survived in the monasteries and schools of Byzantium. Between 700 and 900, Islamic and Middle Eastern scholars assiduously translated (into a variety of languages) and studied the Greek remains. By 1100, it was still unclear which of these three players (western Europe, Byzantium, or Islam) would attempt to unite the mass of ancient learning. Since Byzantine and Muslim scholars showed no abiding interest in Latin texts, it was likely, though not inevitable, that the Latin west would

How the Middle Ages Saved and Modern Technology Recovered Archimedes and Hyperides

On April 14, 1229, with the Byzantine Empire under the control of the Latins and Jerusalem once again in Muslim hands, Ioannes Myronas closed the book he had just made, a palimpsest, or book made by writing overtop an old one. His creation may be a testimony to the hard times on which the empire had fallen, for Ioannes was desperate for parchment. To save the cost of purchasing parchment or because it was unavailable, he took several manuscripts, already several centuries old but no longer in much demand, and pulled them apart. He laboriously removed the previous writing, scraping off and erasing the old lettering, turned the large pages sideways, folded them, and began copying a series of Greek prayers. The humble little prayer book he produced ended up at the monastery of St. Sabas in the Holy Land, where it remained until the early twentieth century, when it was transported to Istanbul, then Paris, and other places. The palimpsest shows centuries of use and misuse (candle wax stains, pages missing, mold, and fire damage), but the book survived because it served a purpose and contained holy words. In making the prayer book, Ioannes had inadvertently saved some of the rarest texts of the ancient world.

The lower text (the one that was written over) of the palimpsest contains pages from the lost works of the great mathematician Archimedes and lost speeches of the ancient orator Hyperides. These ancient texts could hardly be read: portions of the lower text lay hidden under the binding and some pages had been painted over with fake illuminations by a modern forger. The modern owner of the palimpsest turned the damaged book over (for purposes of conservation and investigation) to the Walters Art Gallery in Baltimore, which organized a team of philologists, classicists, and scientists to recover the lost texts. Using multispectral analysis (essentially subjecting the surface of the parchment pages to different frequencies of light) and breaking down the information by algorithms and computer analysis, the team was slowly able to read the ancient texts lying beneath the prayers, all the while preserving both the lower text (the ancient texts) and the upper text (the Byzantine Greek prayers) of the palimpsest. A nineteenth-century German editor of Archimedes had studied the codex and made a first edition, but his eyes could only see so much; modern technology and experts finally freed the ancient texts from their damaged pages.

Yet the words of the ancients might not have survived at all if a medieval scribe had not recycled what he probably thought were useless texts written on perfectly good parchment and secured their survival by filling the palimpsest with holy words.[3]

QUESTIONS | *In our digital age, how might we be in danger of losing the information contained on paper pages? Why would a Christian scribe have written over precious ancient texts?*

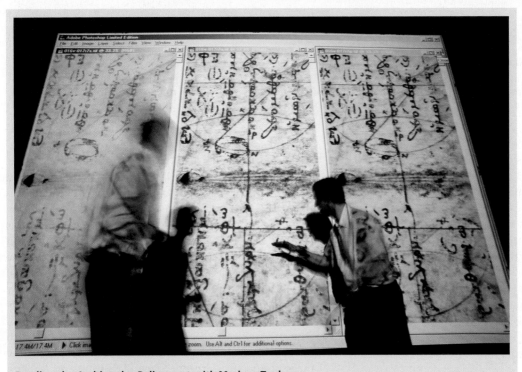

Reading the Archimedes Palimpsest with Modern Tools

stir itself to the task of understanding the surviving knowledge of the ancients.

The cultural acquisition and appropriation of the ancient library was part of the same aggressive drive that led the Christian west to wage the First Crusade, for by the twelfth century the Latin west had become militarily aggressive and culturally acquisitive. Translation centers were the cultural parallel to crusade.

In 1085, the cosmopolitan city of Toledo in Spain, with its rich Muslim and Jewish cultures, fell to Christian conquerors. By the early twelfth century, Toledo was an established center of translation, where scholars such as Adelard of Bath, Dominic Gundisalvi, and John of Spain began translating Greek and Arabic works into Latin. Gerard of Cremona translated numerous works, including those of the ancient geographer Ptolemy, Aristotle, Euclid, Hippocrates, and Galen. Another translation center opened in Palermo in Sicily.

A massive influx of new books poured into Europe between 1150 and 1250, undermining the old liberal arts curriculum of the cathedral schools and altering the fundamental character of western thought and its methods of inquiry. By 1250, the majority of Aristotle's treatises were available to the Latin west. The Middle Ages may have had an inherent bias in favor of Platonism and the idea that this world is a mere appearance behind which lie its invisible real forms and essences, but its encounter with Aristotle, with his logical methods and scientific interests, pushed higher education in a new direction. By 1255, the *Timaeus,* Plato's great work of cosmology, which had been partially available in Latin since the Early Middle Ages, was removed from the curriculum of the University of Paris. Plato's thought did not disappear, but instead went underground, finding an outlet in popular vernacular works such as Jean de Meun's *Roman de la Rose* (*Romance of the Rose*) before finally resurfacing in the Florentine Renaissance reclamation of Plato in the fifteenth century.

The creation of the university was a corporate response to the need to integrate and make sense of the mass of ancient knowledge, particularly the works of Aristotle that were flooding the west. Without the new texts, particularly those of Aristotle, Hippocrates and Galen, and Justinian's *Digest,* the thought of Thomas Aquinas, advanced medical studies at Montpellier and Salerno, and legal studies at Bologna—indeed, the very existence of **scholasticism** and the universities—would have been unlikely. The task of the university, then as now, is to systematize and synthesize information, though the modern university emphasizes the creation of new knowledge while the medieval one was tasked with understanding older book learning.

The book itself also underwent a dramatic transformation between 1150 and 1250. The large early medieval codex that monastic readers consulted in restricted libraries gradually gave way to smaller, portable books made from thinner parchment. Caroline Minuscule, the regular and highly legible script that filled medieval manuscripts from the ninth century to the twelfth, was replaced by the small, cursive, highly abbreviated Gothic script; more words could now be squeezed onto a page. The slow munching and mumbling of words by monks as they sought to ingest whole books gave way to quick, silent, and searching reading by a wider range of readers. The book became a source of information, a tool, not a part of one's being. The high medieval book became easier to use, taking on those formal characteristics with which we associate books today: title pages, tables of contents, chapters with titles, running heads, paragraphs, diagrams, and indices. Those features attest to a new scholastic way of reading in a world with many more books and a flood of information that needed sorting and easier access. The High Middle Ages invented the essential organization and properties of the modern book.[2]

Birth of the University

The institution of the medieval university was not created by any one person, country, or place. Four famous universities appeared in the years between 1175 and 1200: Salerno, Bologna, Paris, and Oxford. Cambridge University began slightly later, when some Oxford scholars left their university in protest after two students were hanged for murder. The first universities had different educational emphases. Salerno concentrated on medicine, Bologna on law, and Oxford and Paris on arts and theology. Each was a response to the mass of new information that needed to be explored.

The university at Bologna grew out of the need to make sense of Roman civil law. For most of the Middle Ages, Justinian's great *Corpus of Civil Law* had been lost, but around 1076 the *Digest* was rediscovered in Italy and studied intensively. The rapid growth of towns and trade made the need for civil law, with its emphasis on property rights, pressing. In the early twelfth century, Irnerius wrote an influential commentary on the *Corpus* that laid down the basis for the systematic study of Roman law. By the mid-twelfth century, canon (church) law at Bologna assumed a place almost equal to the study of civil law. Gratian's *Decretum* became the core textbook of canon law. Bologna supplied canon lawyers to the church for the rest of the Middle Ages.

By 1158, the emperor Frederick Barbarossa had conferred a set of special rights and privileges upon the schools of Bologna. These protections were needed to safeguard the developing university from the local town, which often preyed on the students and masters, forcing them to pay exorbitant rents for rooms and charging excessively for food and transport. As a term, *university* does not refer to universal knowledge, but rather to *"universitas societas magistrorum discipulorumque,"* that is, "the university is an association [or guild] of masters and students." They stood, in other words, as a small society of students and teaching clerics apart from the lay townspeople. At Bologna and elsewhere the university assumed a corporate identity.

Protection against exploitation by the town may have been the first reason for incorporation, but each university developed its own identity. Bologna was thought of as a students' university. There the professors were closely regulated and monitored. The town did not want its masters to leave and so enforced covenants against their free movement, including compelling masters to leave a deposit before they left Bologna to guarantee their return. As early as 1193, the students at Bologna set up a student union, which defined the nature of their contract with the masters. Instruction was a service contract setting the terms for the buying and selling of knowledge. At Bologna, professors were not permitted to miss classes without the corporation's prior approval and were fined if they failed to lecture to at least five students. The professor at Bologna was required to begin his lecture when a bell rang and to finish when the next bell sounded, and he was not allowed to skip over important subjects or squeeze them in at the end of his lecture.

Medieval masters may have needed curtailment. They could be extremely arrogant. They feigned nobility, wore elaborate gowns and gold rings, and sat on elaborate elevated thrones. Students occasionally mocked them. At one university a statute prohibited students from throwing stones at their professors during lecture, even if they missed. Since professors lacked secure employment and depended on student fees to survive, they needed to please both the corporation and their students. Many of them grumbled that their students were poor payers, eager to receive instruction, but never to pay for it. When the mendicant friars, particularly the Dominicans, began teaching in Paris, it caused considerable controversy, since the friars taught for free and thus threatened to undermine the guild-like system of the corporation.

The medieval professor was a product of the system, having obtained a teaching license, which was the first of the university degrees. A master of arts degree (the M.A.) was awarded at the end of six years of instruction and the acceptance of a masterwork. The new master joined the teachers' guild and swore to uphold the statutes of the university. He was then placed on his throne, held a book of Aristotle in his hands, was invested with a ring, and was kissed by his fellow masters. This rite of passage from student to master allowed the new master to teach the liberal arts.

The University of Paris

Unlike at Bologna, masters at the University of Paris held the upper hand. The university developed out of the cathedral school of Notre Dame, which was under the direct control of its chancellor. By the second half of the twelfth century, Paris was growing rapidly, as was its student population. By 1200, students may have formed 10 percent of the city's population; perhaps there were as many as 2,000 to 4,000 students. Tensions were inevitable,

The Medieval Classroom At the University of Bologna, a master lectures from his high throne while students pay varying degrees of attention to his instruction. Although the third student in the first row may seem to our eyes to be a woman, it is highly unlikely that the artist meant to depict a female because women were excluded from the medieval university.

particularly in the Île de la Cité area around the cathedral. These tensions often led to town-gown fights. In 1200, a tavern brawl broke out after some German students imbibed too much wine, misbehaved in their search for more to drink, and were attacked by locals, leaving some of the students dead. In the wake of that incident, a royal charter conceded that students stood outside lay courts and lay justice. The scholars of Paris welcomed the king's recognition of their relative autonomy.

The faculty of arts at Paris comprised almost two-thirds of the student population in the thirteenth century. The masters of arts soon developed a corporate identity for their institution and resisted the chancellor's interference. The university was divided into four "nations" of students—French, Norman, Picard, and English-German—each with its own proctor or supervisor. These nations bandied words and blows with each other. The medieval university seethed with various tensions—between the local town and the corporation, students and teachers, church authorities and the university, and various groups of students.

By the mid-twelfth century, logic and philosophy began to displace the study of grammar (in its wider medieval meaning of philology or textual studies), which had been at the core of the cathedral school curriculum. Instruction was in Latin, which was an artificial and learned language for all. By the thirteenth century, the works of Aristotle had replaced many classical texts, including the ancient poets. At Oxford and Paris, students read and commented on the logical works of Aristotle, the grammatical works of Priscian and Donatus, and Aristotle's *Ethics* and natural treatises. Examinations were oral and tension-filled. Some study manuals with sample examination questions and pertinent topics survive. Students likened their examinations to the Last Judgment. On occasion, students simply froze, unable to respond. At Bologna, one student became so flustered during his oral exam that he reminded the gathered witnesses, who hurled abuse at him, of a bleating goat.

Living the Medieval University Life

Student life was distinctive. All the students at the medieval university were male, many of them from the lower gentry and upwardly mobile middle class. They started their university years as young as age thirteen or fourteen. They were called clerks (*clerici*), though they were not priests. They underwent a symbolic haircut (tonsure) and at some institutions were compelled to wear long black gowns. Most universities prohibited the wearing of extravagant dress by students: no pointed shoes, ballooning sleeves, or bright stockings. Students lived in residences under the supervision of a master, but strict rules were enforced. Students late for breakfast received only bread. The house kitchen was off-limits. They could not bring friends to their residence to eat and drink, nor could they have women in their rooms or assault servants. Poor students had their own residences.

Classes were held in rented rooms or a church and began as early as 5 or 6 a.m. Students sat on wooden benches or the floor and took notes on waxed tablets, from which they might later make a good or, at least, more organized record of the lecture on parchment. The greatest hindrance to learning was the limited access to books. Manuscripts were expensive to buy, and libraries were out of bounds to undergraduates. At the University of Paris, a stationer authorized by the university would rent portions of texts for students to copy.

Two themes dominated medieval university life: poverty and drink. Paris was expensive, and lecture fees needed paying. Masters realized that if their students could not convince their parents and patrons to keep the funds flowing, they would go unpaid, and so they taught their students how to write begging letters. Said one master: "Let us take as our topic today that a poor but deserving student has to write home to his mother for the funds he needs . . . ."

Most medieval university students may have been earnest and hard working, but it is often the others whom we hear about in the regulations. These wilder students apparently loved to play dice and to fence. In Bologna, one student pulled a sword on another during a lecture. In Germany, freshmen (*beani*) were hazed to rid them of their rusticity, but university regulations prohibited the tormentors from insulting, yelling at, harassing, drenching with urine, or defiling with dust and filth their fellow students.

University students, then as now, live in a transitional state, caught between the mature workaday life of the career that awaits and their younger days at home. Medieval students found themselves in relatively large cities such as Paris, which observers called a paradise

Poor Students Receiving Charity Poor university students received clothes, shoes, food, and shelter from charitable churches and religious orders so that they might pursue their education.

of delights, but uncertain who they were or where they were headed. A profound feeling of alienation haunts the poems and drinking songs of the clerks. The most gifted of these, the Archpoet, prays in his confession to die with a tankard by his side with angels looking down upon him and singing joyously, "Let God keep company with this mighty drinker."

Scholasticism and the Dumb Ox

Scholasticism is the general term for the intellectual movement of university thinkers (the schoolmen) of the period between 1150 and 1350. They applied a highly refined form of logical reasoning or disputation to understanding revelation. Many Christian thinkers had from the beginning sought the same, but at the medieval university, especially in Paris, the pursuit took on a particular methodological and intellectual rigor. The intellectual explorations of the early-twelfth-century cathedral school masters had been individually and intellectually more daring, but they had often lacked a concentrated focus and method. Thirteenth-century scholastic thought was narrower, but a more exact synthesis of Christian thought, and the greatest of its thinkers, was the "Dumb Ox," Thomas Aquinas.

The curriculum at the University of Paris moved away from the liberal arts and its concentration on grammar, rhetoric, and the classics. Twelfth-century humanism gave way in the thirteenth century to the logical synthesis of complex doctrines. Dialectic (or logic), one of the liberal arts, took over, displacing even scientific and mathematical inquiry. As a consequence, the Latin written by the university doctors lacks the eloquence and charm of twelfth-century writers such as Bernard of Clairvaux, Suger of St. Denis, Hildegard of Bingen, and Heloise. Instead, university doctors wrote tight logical arguments without flourishes or, for the most part, personality. The beauty of scholasticism lay in the quality of its reasoning, not its prose.

Theology had always been the queen (or summit) of medieval inquiry, but she now pushed aside the subdisciplines, including philosophy. This did not happen quickly. The thought of Augustine and medieval Platonism remained strong, but the influx of Aristotelian and other ancient texts slowly changed the direction of university attention. Aristotle's texts did not arrive all in one piece or at one time. In the late twelfth and early thirteenth centuries, his works were known chiefly through translations from Arabic commentaries such as those by Persian philosopher Avicenna (Ibn Sina, 988–1037), which were colored by Neo-Platonic ideas. Thinkers of this transitional period still viewed Aristotle through a Platonist lens that allowed them to align Aristotle with Augustine, though with some difficulty. To some, Aristotle already seemed a threat and for a time his books were banned from the curriculum.

Early in the thirteenth century, medieval thinkers did not yet have a firm grasp of Aristotle's own works. It fell to the mid-thirteenth century and to the Dominicans to rediscover the genuine Aristotle. William of Moerbeke, a Dominican friar from Flanders, translated for Thomas Aquinas such works as Aristotle's *Politics* and *Economics* from Greek. Other translators such as Herman of Carinthia had translated such works as Aristotle's *Nicomachean Ethics* and *Poetics* by the mid-thirteenth century. With these texts, Thomas Aquinas could begin his great synthesis of scholastic thought, Aristotelian in method, Christian in purpose.

Thomas Aquinas was born near Aquino (between Naples and Rome). His noble family sent Thomas as a boy to be trained at Monte Cassino. His family may have hoped that he would someday obtain a high church office, but when the emperor Frederick II expelled the monks in 1239, Thomas moved to the newly established University of Naples. Mendicant friars were a vigorous presence in the city and were actively recruiting university students. In 1244, Thomas chose to become a Dominican friar, much to the shock of his brothers, who kidnapped him and, in a medieval version of deprogramming, kept him cut off from his order and profession for a year in the hope that he would renounce his Dominican vow. When he finally secured his release, Thomas went to Cologne to study under the famous scholastic thinker, Albert the Great. Thomas was teaching at Paris by the 1250s, but when the

mendicants' role at the university was disputed, Thomas left for Italy, not returning until 1269. He soon found himself embroiled in controversy when he challenged the so-called Latin Averroists. The Averroists (followers of Averroës or Ibn Rushd, the Arabic interpreter of Aristotle) chose to concentrate on the study of Aristotle and generally placed reason above faith, even above Christian authority. On the other side, Thomas was attacked by conservative Augustinian theologians for granting too much scope to reason and Aristotle and not enough to faith. Thus, Thomas stood between the intellectual progressives and traditionalists or left and right of his day.

Little is known about Thomas's personal life. He was reputedly very fat and given to long silences, prompting one wit to call him "the Dumb Ox." He was apparently slow to anger and gentle in the classroom. His handwriting (the so-called *littera inintelligibilis*, "incomprehensible handwriting") was almost unreadable except by his personal scribes; Thomas wrote with his left hand and writing with a quill pen was difficult for the left-handed.

Thomas is best known for his two *Summae* (*Summa contra Gentiles* and *Summa Theologica*), the massive summaries of his thought, but he also wrote commentaries on the works of Aristotle and Pseudo-Dionysius, expositions on Scripture, short philosophical works, and hymns (see Back to the Source at the end of the chapter). Thomas Aquinas was, above all, a great synthesizer who set himself the task of applying logical reasoning to a Christian understanding of the revealed world. He resolved the vexing problem of the relationship between faith and reason that had preoccupied medieval thought. In his time, the issue was playing out in Paris. Siger of Brabant and the Latin Averroists sought primarily to understand the physical world, not God's miracles, and to treat what was natural in a natural way. Opposing this sufficiency-of-reason school of thought was the great Franciscan thinker Bonaventure, who emphasized the primacy of faith over reason. Bonaventure subordinated philosophy to divine truth. Thomas essentially synthesized these two positions, treating philosophical issues philosophically and theological ones theologically. For Thomas, there was no conflict between faith and reason. One did not intrude on the other, but rather they complemented each other.

Paris in the 1270s was a hotbed of rancorous dispute. Certain contested propositions by the Aristotelian schoolmen, among them several by Thomas, were challenged and finally condemned in 1277. Thomas had, however, already left the scene. In 1273, he had a mystical experience or, perhaps, suffered a neurological incident and wrote no more. He apparently confessed to a friend that all that he had written now seemed to him to be but straw compared to the revelation of the unseen he had experienced. He died the next year. Eventually Thomas's thought became not only the accepted standard for scholasticism, but for the Catholic Church. One reflection of that is to be found in the *Divine Comedy* of Dante Alighieri, which has a scholastic rather than humanist bent. Thomas occupies a high and glorious place in Dante's Paradise.

The Gothic Peak

Scholars have long seen a similarity between scholastic thought and Gothic architecture: both were perfected syntheses and rational demonstrations of elevated truths. One can easily see that high Gothic architecture makes visual sense. The eye follows ribbed columns upward until they run into ribbed vaults; on the exterior of the church, flying buttresses rise from the ground to meet and support the external stone walls of the nave and choir. Unlike most architecture, Gothic cathedrals show us how they work, displaying both the skeleton and body or, in medieval terms, form and substance. The scholastic arguments of Thomas Aquinas are demonstrations that proceed from theses, overcome objections (antitheses), and are resolved in syntheses. There is a solid structure of demonstrated connections in both Gothic architecture and scholastic thought, a systematic ordering of parts leading to a truthful summit.

Yet the likeness of scholasticism and Gothic architecture cannot strictly be true. Medieval masons were not university trained, and scholastic thinkers did not receive their education from ribbed vaults. Both were relatively closed systems, building off previous developments in their fields and extending their possibilities. They did, however, share the general desire of the Gothic High Middle Ages to perfect itself, to demonstrate its reasons or how it worked, and to bring particular forms to their logical conclusions and highest state of accomplishment. By the late thirteenth century, each had also begun to discover its limits, but this was true of the High Middle Ages as a whole.

One way to measure the progress of Gothic architecture is to follow its chronological search for height. The crown or summits of the vaults reached 81 feet at the Cathedral of Sens in the 1140s; 116 feet at the Cathedral of Chartres in the 1220s; 137 feet at the Cathedral of Amiens in the 1230s; and finally, 157 feet at Beauvais, when the choir collapsed in a windstorm in 1284, putting an end to the Gothic search for ever-higher buildings. Gothic architecture was by then already turning away from the high style of the Cathedral of Chartres. The Rayonnant (radiant) style of Gothic emphasized instead the penetra-

The Light-Filled Interior of St. Chapelle Built by Saint Louis, the king of France, St. Chapelle is a late style of Gothic architecture known as Rayonnant. At St. Chapelle, the walls seem made of glass, the dimensions of the church intimate, and the overall effect that of a precious architectural container for the king's collection of relics.

tion of light, with the surface walls reduced to a lattice of glass. Saint Louis sponsored the construction of St. Chapelle in Paris as the holy receptacle for his collection of precious relics. With its intimate dimensions, lacelike windows, and interior washed with colored light, St. Chapelle is a radiant reliquary.

Gothic churches were still being erected in 1300, but the Gothic high style and purpose had found their limits and were slowly losing direction or, rather, moving off in new directions. So too was medieval thought. Scholasticism was to play itself out in the fourteenth century in a set of logical extremes.

Conclusion

During the Gothic High Middle Ages, Europe achieved remarkable things in thought, religion, architecture, education, and state development. The age saw the rise of institutions such as representative (or parliamentary) assemblies and universities that have been enduring legacies of the West. The economic vigor of the period led to increased population and the growth of vibrant cities such as Paris, Venice, Florence, and London. In intellectual life, the exciting and rambunctious twelfth-century cathedral schools gave way to thirteenth-century universities, Abelard to Aquinas, pioneering thought to scholastic synthesis. The High Middle Ages perfected the codex as the most efficient means for presenting and rationally organizing information in a book form designed for the eye rather than the ear. Massive Romanesque cathedrals were succeeded by soaring Gothic cathedrals as the leading architectural style of Europe.

Yet, for all its many accomplishments, the High Middle Ages was far from placid, and its pursuit of perfection and power did not go uncontested. The centralized and bureaucratic powerhouse of the Catholic Church, best represented by Pope Innocent III, incited a stubborn resistance from sovereigns such as Frederick II, who sought to curb the church's state power and its self-proclaimed religious right to govern Christendom. Religious sects, labeled by the church as heretical, charged that the church was too worldly and material. Popes called for crusades against both external and internal enemies of the church. One of these captured the Byzantine Empire, but all of them were questionable exercises and produced little of lasting worth. For the papacy, the point was not so much to win these wars as to preserve the right to call them and, by so doing, to unite Christendom and its secular leaders under church authority.

The heavy weight of a reformed and authoritarian church and of stronger monarchs in places such as France and England produced a backlash that made Europe at its high medieval peak an aggressive and antagonistic society of rival forces. The perfection of a Christian medieval society, particularly in the thirteenth century, was a powerful illusion that could probably never have been sustained much beyond its already towering achievements. A storm was coming.

Critical Thinking Questions

1. How was the High Middle Ages different from the Early and Central Middle Ages?

2. Why were medieval crusades after the First Crusade so problematic?

3. Why did dynamic individuals and individuality become so prominent in the period, and how were they offset by powerful collective and conservative forces?

4. How did women do in the High Middle Ages? What choices did they have?

5. In what ways is the modern university an institution that still reflects its medieval origins?

Key Terms

trivium (p. 264)

quadrivium (p. 264)

humanist (p. 266)

papal plenitude of power (p. 271)

pluralism (p. 271)

interdict (p. 271)

cottage industries (p. 274)

guild (p. 274)

usury (p. 276)

commune (p. 276)

mendicants (p. 277)

inquisition (p. 278)

Magna Carta (p. 280)

scholasticism (p. 285)

Primary Sources in connect

For information on Connect and the online resources available, go to http://connect.mcgraw-hill.com.

1. **Heloise's Second Letter of Complaint to Abelard**

2. **Bernard of Chartres's Six Keys to Learning**

3. **Abelard's Yes and No, the Preface and Passages**

4. **The Mongol Correspondence**

5. **Magna Carta**

6. **Thomas Aquinas on the Nature and Domain of Sacred Doctrine**

The Existence of God

In his *Summa Theologica,* the scholastic philosopher Thomas Aquinas, a Dominican friar, set out five proofs for the existence of God. Both the arguments and the method he uses owe much to Aristotle. For Aquinas, reason and Christianity were not at odds, but rather complemented each other, as we see in his presentation of the five proofs, which begin with particular antitheses or objections before moving to proofs and answers to the objections.

Third Article: Whether God Exists

Objection 1: It seems that God does not exist; because if one of two contraries be infinite, the other would be altogether destroyed. But the name God means that he is infinite goodness. If, therefore, God existed, there would be no evil discoverable; but there is evil in the world. Therefore God does not exist.

Objection 2: Further, it is superfluous to suppose that what can be accounted for by a few principles has been produced by many. But it seems that everything we see in the world can be accounted for by other principles, supposing God did not exist. For all natural things can be reduced to one principle, which is human reason or will. Therefore there is no need to suppose God's existence.

I answer that: The existence of God can be proved in five ways: The first and more manifest way is the argument from motion. It is certain and evident to our senses, that in the world some things are in motion.... [Now], whatever is moved must be moved by another. If that by which it is moved be itself moved, then this also must needs be moved by another, and that by another again. But this cannot go on to infinity, because then there would be no first mover, and, consequently, no other mover, seeing that subsequent movers move only inasmuch as they are moved by the first mover; as the staff moves only because it is moved by the hand. Therefore it is necessary to arrive at a first, moved by no other; and this everyone understands to be God.

The second way is from the nature of efficient [or productive] cause. In the world of sensible things we find there is an order of efficient causes. There is no case known (neither is it, indeed, possible) in which a thing is found to be the efficient cause of itself; for so it would be prior to itself, which is impossible. Now in efficient causes it is not possible to go on to infinity, because in all efficient causes following in order, the first is the cause of the intermediate cause and the intermediate is the cause of the ultimate cause, whether the intermediate cause can be several or one only. Now to take away the cause is to take away the effect. Therefore, if there be no first cause among efficient causes, there will be no ultimate, nor any intermediate cause.... Therefore, it is necessary to admit a first efficient cause, to which everyone gives the name of God.

The third way is taken from possibility and necessity, and runs thus. We find in nature things that are possible to be and not to be, since they are found to be born and to die, and consequently they are possible to be and not to be. But it is impossible for these always to exist, for that which is possible not to be at some time is not. Therefore, if everything is possible not to be, then at one time there could have been nothing in existence. Now, if this is true, even now

there would be nothing in existence, because that which does not exist only begins to exist by something already existing. Therefore, if at one time nothing was in existence, it would have been impossible for anything to have begun to exist; and thus even now nothing would be in existence, which is clearly false. Therefore, not all beings are merely possible, but there must exist something the existence of which is necessary. But every necessary thing either has its necessity caused by another, or not. Now, it is impossible to go on to infinity in necessary things which have their necessity caused by another, as has been already proved in regard to efficient causes. Therefore, we must admit the existence of some being having of itself its own necessity, and not receiving it from another, but rather causing in others their necessity. This all men speak of as God.

The fourth way is taken from the gradation to be found in things. Among beings there are some more and some less good, true, noble, and the like. But "more" and "less" are predicated of different things, according as they resemble in their different ways something which is the maximum, as a thing is said to be hotter according as it more nearly resembles that which is hottest. There is then something which is truest, something best, something noblest, and, consequently, something which is most being; for those things that are greatest in truth are greatest in being.... Therefore, there must also be something which is to all beings the cause of their being, goodness, and every other perfection. And this we call God.

The fifth way is taken from the governance of the world. We see that things which lack knowledge, such as natural bodies, act for an end, and this is evident from their acting always, or nearly always, in the same way, so as to obtain the best result. Hence it is plain that they achieve their end, not fortuitously, but designedly. Now whatever lacks knowledge cannot move toward an end, unless it be directed by some being endowed with knowledge and intelligence; as the arrow is directed by the archer. Therefore some intelligent being exists by whom all natural things are directed to their end. And this being we call God.

Reply to Objection 1: As Augustine says: "Since God is the highest good, he would not allow any evil to exist in his works, unless his omnipotence and goodness were such as to bring good even out of evil." This is part of the infinite goodness of God; that he should allow evil to exist, and out of it produce good.

Reply to Objection 2: Since nature works for a determinate end under the direction of a higher agent, whatever is done by nature must be traced back to God, as to its first cause.... For all things that are changeable and capable of defect must be traced back to an immovable and self-necessary first principle, as was shown in the body of this Article.

QUESTIONS | *What are the five proofs for the existence of God? Can they be reduced to one argument? What is Thomas's method of argumentation? How convincing are the proofs for the existence of God?*

Source: Thomas Aquinas, *Summa Theologica,* ed. Anton C. Pegis, *Basic Writings of Saint Thomas Aquinas,* Vol. 1 (Indianapolis, IN: Hackett, 1997), 21–24.

10

Alabaster Mourners from the Tomb of John the Fearless, Burgundian, Fifteenth Century

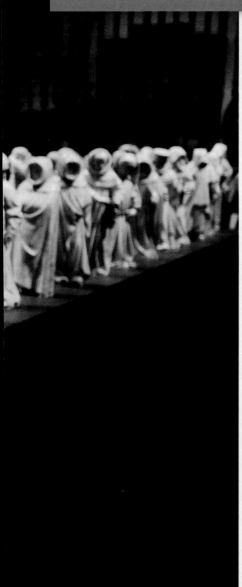

THE NEW WORLD OF THE LATE MIDDLE AGES

The Fourteenth Century Opens with Calamities
  The Arrival of a New Ice Age
  The Great Famine
  The Dire Impact of the Early-Fourteenth-Century Famine
  Not All Was Doom and Gloom
  Living the Great Famine

Church Captivity, Imperial Indirection, and Chivalric War
  The Babylonian Captivity of the Papacy
  The Further Fragmentation of the Empire
  The Opening Act of the Hundred Years' War
  The Chivalric Ideal
  The Chivalric Code Meets Actual War

Yersinia Pestis Comes Calling
  The Arrival of the Plague
  Transmission and Symptoms of the Disease

The Spread of the Disease in Europe
What Could Europeans Have Done?
The Immediate Consequences

A Battered Society Responds
  Medical Implications
  Economic Adjustments
  Social Insurrection Spreads
  Remaking Religion: Personal Piety, Schism, and Conciliarism
  Critics of the Church: Wyclif, Hus, and Valla

The Late Medieval State
  A New World of Political Relations
  The Final Phase of the Hundred Years' War
  The Maid of Orléans
  New Medieval Monarchy
  The Fall of Constantinople

Conclusion

YERSINIA PESTIS VISITS A MONASTERY No one saw her or even knew that she existed, but they felt her effects. She was one of the dominant actors of the Late Middle Ages (1300–1500), ruining families, undermining faith, and fracturing medieval confidence that the world was knowable and perfectible. Yersinia Pestis is a strange little lady, a rod-shaped bacterium adapted to surviving in ground-squirrel populations around the globe. On occasion, she leaves her preferred host and begins a long migration through less welcoming hosts, whom she tends to kill in staggering numbers. The loss of her host means that Yersinia must soon find another or die. Tiny Yersinia began her long and strange voyage in the 1330s. Setting out from the steppes of central Asia, she traveled by flea and rodent, caravan, wagon, and boat, until she arrived in China, the Middle East, and the shores of Europe, where she wreaked such storied havoc that the very idea of plague still haunts the human imagination.

Late in 1348, Yersinia came calling at the Carthusian monastery of Montrieux in France, home to thirty-six monks, including Gherardo, the brother of Petrarch. After the woman Gherardo had loved from a distance died in Avignon, he abandoned the world and became a monk. Gherardo was lucky not to play host to little Yersinia, who has the annoying habit of killing almost everyone she comes into contact with, but his brother monks did. The prior urged the monks to flee, but only the prior himself fled. Gherardo was determined to stay where God had put him. The monks soon fell ill and started dying. Gherardo buried them one after the other, sometimes three or more a day, as they succumbed to Yersinia's deadly charm. Finally, only he and the monastery's dog were left alive. With his canine companion, Gherardo guarded the monastery by night and rested by day until summer came and he could begin making plans to restore and repopulate Montrieux.

***Yersinia pestis* Bacteria**

The plague did not kill off the Middle Ages, but Yersinia played a critical role in shaping its final act. A single crisis rarely destroys a civilization, but a sequence of disasters can compromise the delicate web of a complex interconnected world. Fourteenth-century Europe was hammered by a series of calamitous events, some of its own making, most not. The weather turned bad with the onset of the Little Ice Age; a Great Famine indirectly brought about the deaths of millions of people and weakened the generation that survived; wars, including the poorly named Hundred Years' War, unnerved Europeans; the papacy confused already shaken western Christendom further when it abandoned Rome for Avignon and later split into several rival popes; and the bubonic plague devastated a once comfortable world. The impact of these calamities was quick and far-reaching: insurrection, the reordering of society, the transfer of land and the redirection of its use; the reshaping of religious beliefs; and the

Capetian Dynasty of France
987–1328

Spanish Reconquest of Iberian Peninsula
900–1492

900   1000   1100   1200

replacement of royal houses and whole political orders. The many Europes that emerged in the mid-fifteenth century were different from those of the High Middle Ages. The world of the Late Middle Ages was, in many ways, made anew, and it set the conditions for the radical developments to come in the ensuing centuries.

The Fourteenth Century Opens with Calamities

There were already signs late in the thirteenth century that the High Middle Ages was in trouble, but the first crisis of the fourteenth century could hardly have been foreseen: the weather turned cold and wet, and famine followed. One crisis did not necessarily cause the other, but Europe was soon shaken from the pleasant high medieval confidence and prosperity that it had enjoyed for two centuries.

> **Which was worse for medieval Europe, the onset of the Little Ice Age or the Great Famine? Why?**

The Arrival of a New Ice Age

The Medieval Warm Period had stretched from the late eighth century to the late thirteenth, achieving its peak (the climatic optimum) in the period 1075–1125. By the second half of the thirteenth century, colder weather returned to the North Atlantic. Sediment cores taken from the coastal areas of Greenland reveal that the climate

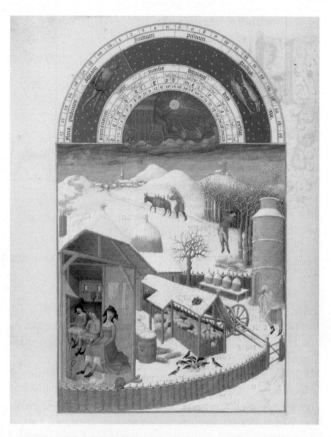

Winter in the Late Middle Ages The depiction of the winter month of February in *Les Très Riches Heures du Duc de Berry* does not look all that harsh, but at the time the miniature was being produced in 1416 the Little Ice Age was well under way in the northern hemisphere.

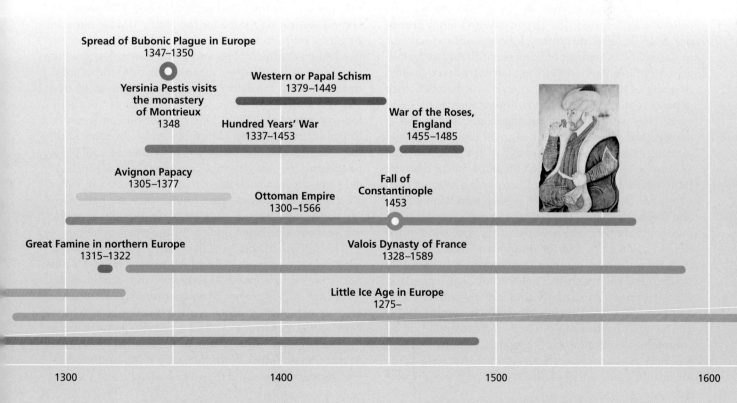

Spread of Bubonic Plague in Europe
1347–1350

Yersinia Pestis visits the monastery of Montrieux
1348

Western or Papal Schism
1379–1449

Hundred Years' War
1337–1453

War of the Roses, England
1455–1485

Avignon Papacy
1305–1377

Ottoman Empire
1300–1566

Fall of Constantinople
1453

Great Famine in northern Europe
1315–1322

Valois Dynasty of France
1328–1589

Little Ice Age in Europe
1275–

1300   1400   1500   1600

of the northern hemisphere had been relatively mild and warm between 900 and 1200, but was followed by particularly cold weather between 1270 and 1370. The fourteenth century was the coldest century of the millennium in Greenland. Climatologists call this period a **Little Ice Age**, a term based on the advance of the globe's ice. After centuries of retreat, Swiss glaciers began to move down the valleys of the Alps, and other glaciers across Europe advanced. The Little Ice Age might still be the world's prevailing climatic condition were it not for

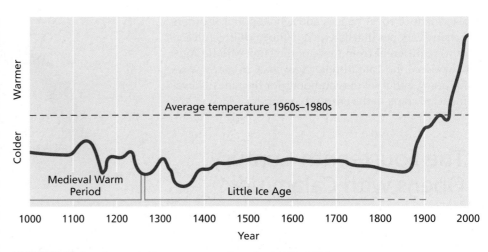

FIGURE 10.1 | **Smooth Temperature Graph, 1000–2000**

Source: Adapted from Eugene Linden, *The Winds of Change: Climate, Weather, and the Destruction of Civilization* (New York: Simon & Schuster, 2006), 75.

the rapid climate change or global warming that began in the twentieth century and continues to accelerate in the twenty-first (Figure 10.1).

The gentler North Atlantic climate of the Medieval Warm Period had made possible the extensive travels of the Scandinavian raiders known as the Vikings. During the Warm Period, arctic ice packs were confined to the far north. By the late tenth century, Scandinavians had migrated to Iceland and from there set out for and established communities in Greenland and a temporary outpost on the tip of Newfoundland in North America. In the mid-fourteenth century, as the weather worsened, Greenland lost contact with Iceland. At the same time, Icelanders generally abandoned growing cereal crops. On the lands lying along the fjords of Greenland, the colonies suffered a general collapse. By about 1360, the western colony was deserted; the larger eastern colony disappeared in the fifteenth century, leaving no Scandinavians in Greenland. A number of factors contributed to the failure of the Greenland settlements. Greenlanders persisted in many of their Scandinavian economic habits, which depended on cereal crops and animals such as pigs and cows. They were apparently unable to adjust to changing climatic and economic conditions, and the growing cold probably inhibited their access to fish in the open ocean. They were less well adapted to life in the north than the Inuit, who were replacing the Dorset as the resident population of the arctic region of the western hemisphere, and whom the Norse encountered in open battles in the fourteenth century. The reasons for the shriveling of the Iceland community and the disappearance of the Norse from Greenland are complex, but the worsening weather undermined their marginal hold on survival. Greenland experienced ten particularly cold winters between 1343 and 1355, the last year being the coldest in centuries.

The effect of the Little Ice Age on continental Europe is more difficult to measure. England suffered through a period of economic retraction in the first half of the fourteenth century that seems to have been made worse

by the turn in the weather. The arable land of Norway shrank in the Late Middle Ages and half of its farms were deserted, again something that had multiple causes, one of which was the weather. Farms in Denmark, particularly those in Jutland, were abandoned. A decrease in population may explain some of these land desertions, but it is striking that northern Europe suffered so dramatically in a time of cooling temperatures. In a subsistence agricultural system with low crop yields, even small changes in climate conditions can make marginal lands unproductive.

Europe experienced bad weather in the early fourteenth century. A series of cold winters struck between 1310 and 1330, with the second coldest winters of the entire Middle Ages occurring between 1320 and 1330. The rain-soaked summers between 1310 and 1320 were the second wettest on record for the entire Middle Ages. In England, mills on the usually placid Avon River became blocked by floating debris and broke down. The growth of oak trees (studied by means of dendrochronology, determined by measuring the annual growth of tree rings) reinforces the same conclusion, that of unusually low growth in the 1320s. Bad weather hit Scandinavia, England, and France in 1315, followed by the rainy summer of 1316, and the bitterly cold winter of 1317–1318, deepening the severity of a prolonged agricultural crisis. One chronicler claimed that it had been the worst weather in a thousand years, and he may not have been far wrong. A German contemporary thought that the whole world was being undone by inclement weather.

The Little Ice Age, like all weather patterns, varied from region to region, hemisphere to hemisphere. It did not strike everywhere in exactly the same way or at the same time. Europe seems to have suffered from the Little Ice Age earlier than other continents. Nor is it easy to draw out larger historical and economic patterns from the turn in the weather, but it is striking that in the Late Middle Ages, France, with its fertile fields and productive agriculture, was not to be the economic and cultural powerhouse that it had been during the High Middle Ages. The proto-industrial economy of Germany, which had superior mining and manufacturing capacity, gained more prominence in the Late Middle Ages, and northern Italy, which escaped some of the direst aspects of the Little Ice Age and had an economy based on short- and long-distance trade and mercantile interests, flourished. Several hypotheses are, of course, possible: that the Little Ice Age provoked a crisis in the agricultural economy of the Late Middle Ages, that it contributed to an underlying weakness in an economy that was already in crisis, that it was a marginal factor, or that it was no factor at all.

The Great Famine

Europe north of the Alps was struck hard by famine between 1315 and 1322, perhaps contributing to the deaths of four to five million people in a population that was then in excess of thirty million people in the north (Map 10.1). Severe bouts of famine can have long-lasting effects, altering economic and social relations over space and time, but it is hard to gauge their causes and long-term impact, partly because they are so entangled with other events.

The **Great Famine** that struck northern Europe came about for a number of linked reasons. The first of these was probably the poor weather that pushed parts of Europe over the edge of successful subsistence. For the economy to fall so hard and so fast into a crisis of agricultural production suggests that it was already close to the edge by 1300. Crop yields had been falling for years in France. The high medieval population in some places such as northern France was excessive, given the new economic conditions. The population had grown to unsustainable levels partly because of the good weather of the Medieval Warm Period, which had lasted for so long and had allowed for the gradual perfection of a particular form of economic activity. Marginal lands had been brought into production when times were good and the population growing, but those same lands failed to deliver in bad times and many were abandoned in the fourteenth century. As with all medieval shortages, the slowness and inefficiency of transport meant that regions that were still fairly bountiful could not easily supply

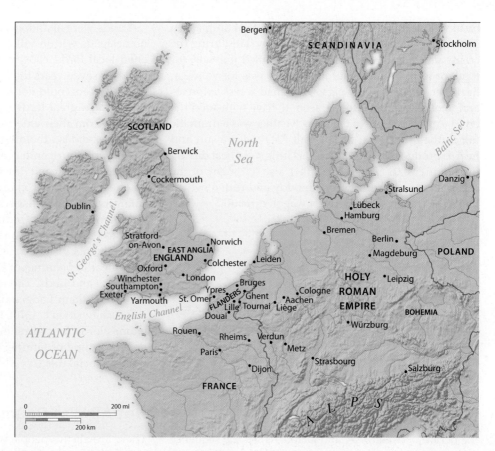

MAP 10.1 | Northern Europe, c. 1300
The Great Famine struck the heavily populated areas of northern Europe. *Given the regional scope of the Great Famine, what sort of economic problem was it? What does the Great Famine reveal about the European economy, and how might the bout of scarcity been dealt with?*

suffering areas in times of dire need. Europe was not well interconnected economically. Just as in Greenland, the farming population, long used to a form of agriculture that had worked well in good times, could not adapt immediately to an unbroken sequence of seasonal disasters, and the Great Famine was seven bad years long.

Beginning in 1315, crop failures were extensive. England experienced agricultural catastrophe over several years. Contemporaries spoke of water-logged fields and rains washing away good soils. It can take thousands of years for nature to produce (and, therefore, replace) fertile top soils. Yields were already low, rarely above ten to one (that is ten seeds produced for every one sown) and more typically five or four to one. At Winchester in England in the crisis years, productivity fell below three to one; elsewhere it fell as low as two to one. Such low rates of return left barely enough seed, after consumption needs were met, to replant the fields the next year. In East Anglia, yields in the crisis years fell 20–30 percent below the yields of previous decades. At some places in France, harvests dropped by as much as 50 percent. Not just grain crops, but viniculture also collapsed. The year 1316 was famous for producing no wine.

During the famine years, humans suffered, but so did their animals. A lack of hay and fodder left many domestic animals weak and susceptible to disease, which did break out, leading to a remarkable die-off of animals in 1317–1318. Sheep flocks in England fell by half during the crisis, and many older animals were killed (for sale, for food, or to preserve what fodder there was for younger, healthier animals). Only pigs, which had access to forests and to other marginal foods, seem to have withstood the crisis. Another result of the rainy weather was a dramatic fall in the production of salt. Salt flats require sun and heat to produce salt, and there was little solar heat during the famine years. The wet weather also left many of the dirt roads of northern Europe muddy and rutted, which made the transport of goods by wagon difficult.

The Dire Impact of the Early-Fourteenth-Century Famine

The mortality caused by the Great Famine is difficult to measure. Death rates varied over northern Europe during the Great Famine, depending on the resources and resilience of local economies, but there is no escaping how serious a crisis it was. English parish figures for 1315–1318 suggest a mortality rate of 15 percent. Flanders lost nearly 10 percent of its population in 1316 alone. In the small city of Ypres (with a population under 30,000), city officials kept a running tally of weekly mortality for the period between May and October 1316: the sequence started off with weekly deaths of 54, 173, 146, and 101, but by late summer had reached weekly rates of 158, 172, 190, and 191, before closing out October with 115, 37, 27, and 15. Close to three thousand people (or 10 percent of the population) died in Ypres that awful year. Nearby Bruges, with a slightly larger population, lost two thousand people.

The price of grain rose dramatically during the famine years, reaching its highest price since the twelfth century. Even though consumption dropped because much of the population lacked the means to pay the elevated cost, grain prices continued to rise. Some scholars have speculated that the price for cereal crops in France may have risen by as much as 800 percent during 1315–1317. A dramatic rise in prices also occurred in Flanders, Germany, and England. Grain riots broke out as people blamed grain sellers and speculators. A riot broke out in Douai in northern France in 1322 when two women harangued people in the market-square to take up arms against those hoarding grain. People pillaged granaries and burghers' homes, looking for hidden grain. For a time, the grain rioters took control of Douai.

During the worst famine years there were reports of atrocities (always difficult to confirm) such as cannibalism and the eating of corpses and children (with shades of the Hansel and Gretel fairy tale). In the countryside and towns and villages of northern Europe, vast numbers of beggars haunted the streets. By 1316–1317, the poor were dying in the streets of Europe in astonishing numbers. One witness remarked how hard it was to listen to the wailing of the poor, homeless and starving, writhing in agony in Europe's streets.

Lands were abandoned, whole villages deserted, and homesteads within villages vacated. The famine weakened local lords, especially those with small holdings, since for seven years their lands produced little and their farm workers could not render the service and dues they owed. Even great lords had problems generating much income from their extensive lands in the famine years. Centuries-old landholding patterns began to break down in the early fourteenth century as lords lost revenue and workers to death and desertion.

The attitude of the church and people to the economic calamity was moralistic, for they tended to see God's judgment in the unfolding disaster. Rains were likened to biblical floods and starvation to Old Testament punishments visited upon a sinful people. There was a good deal of blaming: of Jews, of those who hoarded, of burghers and lords. The most striking indictment came later in William Langland's long allegorical poem, *Piers Plowman* (written c. 1370), in which the character Hunger blames lords for not relieving the suffering of the poor during a time of famine; they failed to fulfill their appointed social role.

Not All Was Doom and Gloom

There are always people who prosper in times of adversity, and there are those who prevent things from becoming worse than they already are. The church responded to the breakout of famine by trying its best to relieve suffering. There are some indications, however, that by 1317 some monasteries and churches could no longer cope with the demands on their resources, which were also in crises of production. In some cases, princes, local lords, and cities responded to the lack of food by increasing their own charitable outlays, trying to control prices, and seeking to obtain foreign grain. Some places were better situated to deal with famine than others. Bruges, for instance, may have suffered less than Ypres because it was better connected to long-distance trade routes and could import what it could not produce locally.

An unexpected result of the Great Famine was the settlement of new lands. The poor were not entirely passive in the face of the disaster. Many took to the road in search of food and livelihood. Some of them, particularly from Germany, moved to Poland and Bohemia as part of a mass migration driven by hunger. It could also be argued that the Great Famine forced deeper and beneficial adjustments upon the economy as marginal lands fell out of production and agricultural efficiencies were forced on the lands that remained in production. By 1325, older and familiar crop yields returned and the medieval economy regained much of its old stride.

Areas that had not suffered from the weather crisis to the same extent as northern Europe or been struck by famine conditions—such as northern Italy, northern Spain, and southern France—may have benefited from the economic crisis to gain an advantage over the rest of Europe.

They sold or traded their grain surpluses to northern Europe at exorbitant rates. Italy's early-fourteenth-century prosperity and mercantile dynamism may not, then, have been just the product of hard work and ingenuity, but also of opportunism and good fortune.

Living the Great Famine

Most victims of the Great Famine did not die of starvation, but from diseases that overcame them in their weakened state. Lacking bread, many of the poor began to consume what contemporaries called strange diets, a miscellany of available edibles: earth, insects and worms, spoiled grains, clothing, diseased animals and birds, bark, grasses, leaves, and things that we can hardly imagine. These strange diets further weakened people and left them vulnerable to disease and severe malnutrition. Dehydration and severe diarrhea accompany slow starvation, and outbreaks of disease did follow the famine. Observers reported that pestilence broke out in Germany in 1315 and that people died quickly, another indication that they were already severely weakened by hunger.

The Great Famine was probably harder on nursing infants, young children, and the old than it was on young adults. Birth rates fell over the period 1315–1322. The young people who survived the famine were on the whole permanently weakened by the famine years of their youth. Developmentally impaired, they would have had weak immune systems, poor bone development, and smaller bodies than other generations. Thus, while the malnourishment of northern Europe between 1315 and 1322 passed and normal dietary intake returned by the mid-1320s, it was a weakened generation that made its way through time toward another rendezvous with calamity. A child born in 1315 was in his early thirties when the plague arrived. Many northern Europeans who were above the age of twenty-five when the disease hit northern Europe between 1347 and 1350 had survived the Great Famine, but many from that famine generation, wounded by the damage done to their development during the hungry years, had bodies that were less able to resist Yersinia Pestis.

Church Captivity, Imperial Indirection, and Chivalric War

The European world did not grind to a stop when the first of the fourteenth-century crises struck; it adjusted. There were still problems of church and state to address, a papal church in distress, and the code of aristocratic conduct known as chivalry reached its absurd end as it came up against the reality of actual war in the Late Middle Ages.

Why did medieval Europe seem to be flying apart and losing its central convictions in the fourteenth century?

The Babylonian Captivity of the Papacy

The powerful medieval church achieved by Pope Innocent III was in some trouble as the fourteenth century opened. Pope Boniface VIII (1294–1303) and King Philip IV (the Fair, r. 1285–1314) of France were locked in a fierce struggle over the wealth and control of the French church. Boniface sought to stop the French crown from taxing the French clergy, which he considered his own resource pool. In his papal **bull** (a public letter or proclamation) *Clericis laicos*, Boniface threatened to excommunicate any layman who taxed the clergy. The king responded by prohibiting the removal of monies from his kingdom by the church. To assert his rights and his irritation with a meddlesome cleric, Philip in 1301 arrested the bishop of Pamiers on a charge of high treason. In response, the next year, Pope Boniface issued the bull *Unam sanctam* in which he declared the absolute supremacy of the papacy over all Christendom. Philip decided to bring Boniface to trial on a host of charges, including his improper election as pope. In 1303, Boniface retreated to his hometown of Anagni and was composing a bull that would have excommunicated Philip and freed his subjects from their allegiance to the king. Philip's men intervened and seized the pope in Anagni on September 7, but Boniface's fellow townsmen rose up in outrage over the insult to their pope. They rescued Pope Boniface and spirited him away to Rome, where he reportedly died in a state of delirium in mid-October.

Boniface's successor tried to bring peace to the church, but served for only two years before he was succeeded by Pope Clement V (1305–1314), who moved the papacy and the governance of the church to Avignon in southern France (technically outside the royal realm), where they remained from 1305 to 1377. Popes had previously lived outside of Italy for extended periods, but the Avignon residency was exceptional for the length of the papacy's absence from Italy and the predominance of the French in papal affairs. Clement was from Gascony, an area of southwestern France above Spain. His Curia (the papal court of officials, tribunals, and assemblies), however, was divided between those who supported King Philip and those who still defended the policies of Pope Boniface. Clement and his successors chose to side with the French king.

Pope Clement even went along with the French king's campaign to dissolve the order of the Knights Templar. The order of the Poor Fellow-Soldiers of Christ and of the Temple of Solomon had been founded after the First Crusade as a military and charitable order to protect pilgrims visiting the Holy Land. The Knights Templar gained a reputation as formidable warriors but were also recognized for being particularly skilled at managing the charitable donations they received. They became the managers of a large financial and property enterprise, but that became a problem for them by the early fourteenth century. Not only did the order lose its central purpose as the crusade movement withered, but worse, King Philip was heavily in its debt and accused the order of holding secret and criminal ceremonies and perpetrating obscene and illegitimate acts such as spitting on the cross. It was whispered that the Knights practiced idolatry, held heretical beliefs, participated in sexual crimes, and were corrupt in their handling of donations. With the pope's support, Philip ordered the arrest of the Templar leaders, had them tortured, forced them to confess to false charges, and burned them at the stake. The king's assault on the Knights left him free of his debt to the order, which the pope disbanded in 1312, turning its property over to another order. In this case, the French state and the Avignon church cooperated in a two-pronged attack on an illustrious arm of the Catholic Church.

The Palace of the Popes in Avignon Despite the impressive solidity of the magnificent papal palace in southern France, the Avignon popes insisted that their residence there was temporary.

To many observers, it seemed that the Avignon papacy was an agent of the French king. Though a magnificent papal palace was erected in Avignon, the papal residence there was regarded as temporary. Public opinion was never favorable to the Avignon papacy. In Italy, people widely considered the Avignon popes to be corrupt French puppets. To call the period of the papal residence in Avignon, as critics did, the "Babylonian Captivity of the Church" was to censure the worldliness and temporal subordination of the Avignon church. Some blamed Pope Boniface for this sad state of church affairs. The poet Dante placed Boniface deep in the *Inferno* among the simoniacs (those who had paid for their offices) for sowing confusion in the church, and many Italians lamented that Rome was bereft of its rightful holy father. The Avignon period brought the fourteenth-century papacy into disrepute and undercut its claim that it commanded a universal church.

The Further Fragmentation of the Empire

The so-called Holy Roman Empire ("so-called" because, as Voltaire later observed, it was neither holy, nor Roman, nor an empire) continued in the fourteenth century to be weighed down by its many territorial claims and obligations. The emperors were dragged continually into Italian affairs and territorial disputes that lay well outside their legitimate German interests. Each emperor had to be elected. Efforts to establish a strict hereditary principle of imperial succession had failed. Frederick II (r. 1220, the date of his papal crowning, to 1250) and the emperors who followed him all had to earn acclamation, a costly and divisive waste of energy and resources. Each new imperial family also had to begin anew since there

was little continuity between reigns, governmental agencies, or record keeping. When Rudolf of Habsburg (r. 1273–1291) was elected emperor in 1273, he had little more territorial reach and resources than his rival German princes. There was almost no fixed imperial land for the emperors to draw upon for funds, yet they had few other sources of revenue. Rudolf, however, successfully extended his properties to the east. When he died, the electors of Germany, anxious not to further empower his family, elected the relatively weak Adolf of Nassau, who conducted a series of unprofitable wars, as his successor.

The electors kept the empire in a constant state of weakness for much of the fourteenth century by disputing elections, choosing new imperial families to succeed to imperial power, and placing restrictions on imperial action. The popes and the French monarchy also contributed to the destabilization of the imperial system by supporting rulers they thought would support them. The great game of fourteenth-century politics was to see who could best keep the emperor and empire weak and in line. In 1313, when two men claimed to be emperor, the pope excommunicated one of them, Lewis of Bavaria, in the interests of promoting a pro-French candidate. Lewis prevailed but did not achieve much beyond establishing a lively imperial court at Munich attended by Marsilius of Padua, who challenged papal authority in his *Defender of the Peace,* and William of Ockham, the last great scholastic philosopher.

Between 1273 and 1400, the empire had ten emperors (from six different dynasties), five of them never crowned, and two of them anti-emperors or rival claimants. The election of Charles IV (Wenceslas) of Bohemia in 1346 brought some regularity to the electoral process, though not wholly in the emperor's favor. In 1356, Charles issued the **Golden Bull,** an edict meant to straighten out the constitutional complexities of the empire, particularly those governing the relations of the emperor and the seven electors, who were the archchancellors of Trier, Cologne, and Mainz, and four great regional princes. The Golden Bull (called so because of its golden seal) recognized that the right to elect an emperor belonged to the seven German prince-electors, whose own lands were fixed, their autonomy and independence acknowledged, and any offense against them deemed treason. By the Golden Bull, other powerful groups in Germany were in effect subordinated to the interests of the emperor and electors, and the pope's role in the choice and approval of an emperor was sidelined.

Charles was not just emperor, but also the king of Bohemia, and though he was ineffective as the first, he accomplished much as the second. With Prague as his capital, Charles encouraged Czech migration there and founded a university. With the consent of the pope, Charles established Prague as a metropolitan or an archiepiscopal see and rebuilt its cathedral. He established a court culture that attracted European luminaries. Charles's imperial reign, though less than successful, signaled the increasing importance of eastern territories to the empire.

The Opening Act of the Hundred Years' War

Since it lasted 116 years and was not one war, but a series of prolonged skirmishes punctuated by extended truces and periods of long inactivity, the **Hundred Years' War** (1337–1453) is poorly and misleadingly named. The underlying reason for the war was the old claim the English crown had on continental lands, but there were a host of irritants, often of long standing, between the two sides. William the Conqueror, Henry II, and their heirs had set this sad table, but by the early fourteenth century the English kings controlled little of wider France. In fact, they held only a part of Gascony, where England had commercial interests. As the century opened, King Philip IV of France and King Edward I (r. 1272–1307) of England were at war over Gascony. That conflict ended inconclusively in 1303. Both kingdoms were also seeking to control the fate of Flanders, where the English traded their wool. When King Charles IV (r. 1322–1328) of France died without leaving a son as heir, King Edward III (r. 1327–1377) of England laid claim to the French throne, since he was descended from the French royal family on his mother's side. The French responded by denying that inheritance could pass through the female line and crowned Philip VI (of Valois) king (r. 1328–1350). Edward bided his time, but in 1337 he renewed his claim to the French throne and invaded. There were, at the time, a dizzying number of irritants between France and England. Both were seeking to extend their influence and control over the Low Countries and Flanders, and both had different and competing claims to the duchy of Brittany. Ships were being attacked in the English Channel. Perhaps the greatest provocation was Edward's claim to the right to confiscate Gascony.

CHRONOLOGY	Over a Hundred Years of Ups and Downs
DATE	**EVENT**
1337	King Edward III of England invades France
1346	English triumph at Crécy
1356	English forces led by the Black Prince win at Poitiers
1360	Treaty of Brétigny acknowledges English control of Aquitaine and Calais
1415	English under Henry V win at Agincourt
1420	King Henry V named heir to the French crown
1422	King Henry V dies; Henry VI becomes king of England and France
1429	Joan of Arc rescues Orléans
1431	Joan of Arc executed
1435	By Treaty of Arras, Burgundy agrees to support France
1453	English defeat in Bordeaux
1453	The Hundred Years' War ends

King Philip was a flashy, chivalrous knight, but not much of a warrior in the field. He and his barons thought that France, which had over three times the population of England and, despite the Great Famine, was still relatively rich, would have no problem handling the English invaders. But Edward had both military strategy and technological superiority on his side. He paid for support where he could and starved obstinate towns into submission (Map 10.2). By 1346, he was outside the walls of Paris, and the first decisive battle in the conflict came at Crécy in the same year. The French attempted to dislodge the English from a strong position on the field of battle at Crécy, but the English moved the wings of their army around the assaulting force and shot at them with deadly longbows from three sides. The French relied on their crossbows, but the English archers could fire their longbows three times as rapidly as the French and from farther away and, thus, safely out of the range of France's crossbow bolts. The French defeat at Crécy did not end the war, which limped lazily on for years. King Philip died in 1350.

The English invasion of France in 1356 was two pronged: one army moved against Normandy, while Edward, the prince of Wales, called the Black Prince (by chroniclers after his death because of his black sword or coat of arms), invaded Aquitaine. At Poitiers, the Black Prince was outnumbered, but the French made a rash attack

MAP 10.2 | The Hundred Years' War, 1337–1453

The Hundred Years' War between England and France had many phases and hot spots of activity over the length of the protracted conflict. *Why did two of the critical battles in the war occur in the north in areas outside of France? Why were Orléans and Poitiers important strategic sites for the English and French? What was peculiar about Joan of Arc's geographic origins, given her prominent historical role in the war?*

and were defeated. Worse, the French king, John II, was captured and held for ransom by the English. By the Treaty of Brétigny of 1360, the French agreed to ransom back their king and granted the English control over much of Aquitaine and the trading city of Calais. With that treaty, the Hundred Years' War turned temporarily quiet, but the underlying problem of the English claim to French lands and the French king's insistence that the English king held those lands as his vassal remained.

The Chivalric Ideal

On the evening after the Battle of Poitiers, the Black Prince wined and dined the captured French king and his knights. The Prince himself served the French at their own high table and refused to sit with King John, not because he was his prisoner, but because he was so distinguished. The Black Prince, full of courtesy and flowery French, told the king not to despair; he had acted with great skill and bravery in battle and Edward's father would surely treat him with friendship and honor, as far as circumstances

The Battle of Crécy Here the more numerous French are shown employing crossbows against the English with their longbows. In reality, the English archers fired a volley of arrows from considerable distance at an opposing army, trusting that some arrows would find their targets.

would allow. The French knights whispered to each other that the Black Prince was truly noble and destined to achieve great things. These men shared a chivalric ideal that may seem to us reckless, the very opposite of realistic politics and their own best interests. King John was taken to England and held for ransom. When the French finally raised part of the huge sum demanded, the king was released and the duke of Anjou took his place as a hostage and security for the remainder. Breaking his oath, the duke escaped from detention and returned to France. King John's chivalric pride was hurt and his family shamed by this betrayal of the chivalric code, so the French king freely returned to England, to confinement, and to his eventual death.

Chivalry is a term with many meanings, but the root of the word comes from the French *cheval* (horse), the *chevalier* being a horseman or knight. Chivalry refers in part to the code of conduct espoused by these horsemen. Elements of chivalry were already present in rituals of vassalage and the *Song of Roland*, but they were codified, transformed, and stylized in the High and Late Middle Ages into something more formalized. Knighthood had always allowed powerful men to distinguish themselves from the other classes of society, particularly the lower classes and clergy. Knightly power was essentially that of coercion—the fist, the sword, and the abrupt and arbitrary use of violence to intimidate others. The war horse with its mounted rider was an intimidating elevation of elite power; it was large, expensive, and frightening. In the Central Middle Ages, the knight was a brutal warrior with few redeeming social virtues or higher ideals. Chivalry did not so much tame the rough knight as lift him into a society of those who espoused a set of ideals that defined them as superior to others. Knights belonged to a rarefied elite of the socially superior, who had their own models, symbols, and rituals.

Of course, what distinguished these knights in the first place was their violent occupation. They were warriors who delighted in killing the enemy and not just their equals, but little people. They burned down villages and did not always think twice about running through women and children with their swords. They needed special skills to do even that. Boys began training when young for the demanding job of being a knight. Outfitted in increasingly heavy and impregnable armor (which could weigh between 40 and 150 pounds depending on the style and metal used), knights sat on rushing war steeds and wielded a variety of heavy weapons (swords, lances, battle axes).

In the Central Middle Ages (and probably throughout much of the Late Middle Ages), knights were exalted robbers on the hunt for plunder. As the conditions of life changed in the twelfth century and the great age of castle contests and crusades began to subside, knights needed a higher purpose, which their poets were pleased to supply. The vernacular poets of Provence in southern France were the first to give chivalric meaning and glory to the knight's role. In their idealized portraits, the knight was not a thug; he was a man with a pure and holy purpose.

He was dubbed a knight by a superior, who in this way transmitted elevated status to his man. In chivalric times, the church even viewed dubbing as a form of sacrament, the Christianized bonding of an elite, one that included the knights' families, in a closed aristocratic circle.

The poets set other goals for this horse nobility. The knight no longer robbed, but pursued a great quest against long odds for an unobtainable, but singular object such as the Holy Grail (thought to be the cup Christ drank from at the Last Supper) or the idealized perfect woman. In moving from the *Song of Roland* to the romances of the poet Chrétien de Troyes and the troubadour (or wandering) poet-musicians, we move inside. Roland and his band lived in a world of exterior earthly action. Chrétien's knights live a more interior life in their own minds, imagining the noble deeds they will do. From these literary roots came the romantic imagination, and chivalry was its higher code.

Knights of the Late Middle Ages lived in domesticating societies that counted courtesy and manners within the group as their defining traits, hence, the Black Prince's deferential and dignified treatment of the captured French king. Both the captor and captured were defined and joined by acts of courtesy and respect. This knightly set of values was based on idealized models: King Arthur and his court, Charlemagne and his paladins, and the mythical and mythologized strivers of the past (Hercules, Alexander, and Caesar). These were exemplary heroes constructed by court literature and deemed fit to be imitated. As the chivalric code was refined, heraldic tokens such as coats of arms, colors, and symbols were invented

Siege of the Castle of Love Even love was seen in chivalric terms on this fourteenth-century ivory carving on the back of a mirror. Here women try to thwart the besieging warriors.

and highly refined distinctions and rituals within chivalric society laid down. The tournament and pageants became the place where the relative equals of this closed aristocratic society met and tested themselves in jousting against each other and in displays of pomp. Their families, particularly the ladies of the court, came to watch and test themselves against each other. The language of chivalry and courtly love was, for the most part, French. The high ideals of chivalry and courtly love may have belonged more to books than the real world, but the ennobling of a class of women may also have helped free the Middle Ages from some of its older misogynistic baggage, which had associated women with temptation, danger, and destruction.

The Chivalric Code Meets Actual War

By the fourteenth century, chivalry had begun to lose much of its luster in society and its effectiveness in war. Cannons and gunpowder, against which the mightiest knight was no match, appeared in Europe in the 1320s. But the knight was already susceptible to arrows and crossbow bolts. Common English bowmen had felled many a knight at both Crécy and Poitiers. The tactical advantage of the English at both battles was precisely the coordination of their cavalry and infantry. Knights might dream of settling contests, as they did at tournaments, with clean contests between two equals, but that was no way to settle a war. Great knights agreed upon when they would fight, where, and how, and they labored to make sure that all the conditions were fair for both sides. But the conditions of war are rarely fair and courteous. At Crécy the English had the better lie of the land and took advantage of it. Shaped by their chivalric pride and bravery, the French knights acted rashly at Crécy and Poitiers. But their military technology was no match for the longbow, and they launched their attack at the wrong time and from a poor position on the field. War, like most human activities, is a learning experience. With heavier armor and better placement of its troops, the French eventually learned to overcome the deficiencies of chivalric warfare. They developed a more systematic plan for capturing castles and fortified towns by employing explosives to undermine walls and ramparts.

Chivalric ideals were one of the causes of the opening of the Hundred Years' War, but the English had already begun to move beyond chivalry. The Black Prince, the courteous victor at Crécy, was not content with glorious combat between equals. He destroyed villages and burned crops to weaken French resistance to his campaigns. He massacred people in large numbers in French cities and leveled exorbitant taxes on conquered lands. No dreamy knight was the Black Prince, but rather a warrior committed to winning wars by means both fair and foul. Moreover, the turn to mercenary armies made war not a matter of glorious contests between knights, but one filled with companies of paid adventurers and outright murderers.

The sign that chivalry was on the wane came not so much from the field of battle as from the intrusive control of chivalry by kings. King Edward III founded the Order of the Garter (c. 1348). This order and the Order of the Golden Fleece, founded in 1430, not only collected knights into royally sanctioned societies, but also turned them away from the chivalric ideal of the solitary and individual quest toward collective patriotism for king and country.

What also began to undermine chivalry was disastrous war itself. The Hundred Years' War was not a particularly noble affair and that soured many people on the ideal of chivalric adventure. Kings banned judicial duels, the last of which were fought in the fourteenth century.[1] By the fifteenth century, chivalry was much criticized and afterward became a figure of fun for writers such as Miguel de Cervantes in his picaresque novel, *Don Quixote de la Mancha*. Yet a residue of chivalry was implanted in the western moral code in the form of gentlemanly manners, conventions of romantic love, and rules for the conduct of war.

Yersinia Pestis Comes Calling

Twenty-five years after the Great Famine, plague came to Europe. The Little Ice Age may have in some way created the conditions that disrupted the life cycle of Yersinia Pestis and its host population and set it on the move. The conjunction of climate change and plague may, in other words, be more than just coincidence. The impact of the plague on the Middle Ages was, in conjunction with the other fourteenth-century calamities, immense.

Why did the plague hit Europe so hard?

The Arrival of the Plague

Medieval Europe may have been particularly susceptible to the plague. Its cities, built of wood, were often cramped, dirty, and rat infested. Frequent wars had unnerved the population and upset social stability, and its people were malnourished and many of them in northern Europe had been developmentally disadvantaged by the effects of the Great Famine. None of those reasons, however, may have mattered as much as the fact that Europeans had not been exposed to the plague since the early eighth century, when the last small outbreaks of Justinian's Plague petered out in depopulated northern Italy. European peoples had not been exposed to the plague for six hundred years and possessed no natural resistance to it when it arrived. Europe was virgin territory for Yersinia.

The fourteenth-century plague was not an epidemic, but a more dangerous **pandemic** (an outbreak of communicable disease extending over many regions and involving high mortality) that began in the 1320s in the Asian steppes and moved east into China and west toward

The Plague Strikes Others

The plague pandemic of the mid-fourteenth century struck not just Europe, but Asia, Africa, and the Middle East, as well. Some historians have speculated that it was the Mongols who spread the disease, allowing Yersinia to escape its home in the central Asian steppes. The Mongols had opened up long-distance trade routes (as explored by the Polos) that not only brought foreign peoples into closer contact, but also exposed them to alien diseases. An interconnected world is always more susceptible to all things communicable (ideas, religions, goods, economic crises, and pathogens). The plague spread across late Yüan China in the 1330s, killing 13–30 million people, yet little official attention and few records were devoted to the disease. In China the plague was not an epochal event, perhaps because the Chinese had previously been exposed

Arabic Medical Consultation

to the bubonic plague and it had settled into being, as it would eventually become in Europe, an endemic, permanent disease presence, killing chiefly the young. Those who argue that the plague undid the Mongol dynasty's control of China and led to the rise of the Sung Dynasty may have been overly impressed by the impact the plague had on European society.

The plague also swept through the Islamic world, killing as many as 40 million people. A hundred people a day were dying in Damascus in June 1348. In Europe, the disease tended to intensify the religious devotion and fear of most people; but many Muslims viewed the plague as a form of martyrdom for the faithful and as punishment for the unfaithful. Yet the Muslim reaction to the swelling sickness was hardly passive. Muslim physicians supplied theories about the disease and advised practical measures for resisting it: avoid contact with those who have contracted the disease; get plenty of fresh air, good food and drink, and lots of sleep; and avoid excessive exertion. Doctors were advised to bleed people who did contract the disease and to open sores surgically once they were ready to release their poison, which seems to have been good medical advice.

Abū Hafs 'Umar Ibn al-Wardī was a Muslim scholar living in Aleppo in Palestine when the plague arrived. He had heard through the vast Islamic grapevine that the disease was coming. It had ravaged India and China, moved through Persia, and killed people in Cairo before it came to Palestine. Al-Wardī presents the plague as a frightful visitor, doing its deadly work like a silkworm, a lion, and a king swaggering upon his throne. Al-Wardī contracted the disease in 1349. His reaction to the disease in general was fatalistic, as it was for many Muslims, who refused to flee from a disease that God had sent. Muslims did not generally view the plague as a civilization-ending event, though it did tremendous damage in Islamic lands.

QUESTIONS | *Why do new diseases often lead to irrational explanations for them among the general population? What are the typical responses to a new contagion? How and why did the plague strike Islam and Europe differently—materially, spiritually, and historically?*

Europe. It was not called the **Black Death** until the sixteenth century. Medieval men and women commonly referred to it as a plague (from the Latin *plaga,* meaning "blow"). By the late 1330s, Europe had already begun to hear rumors of a dread contagion on the loose in Asia,

and over the next decade, the disease passed in a complex way from Asia to Europe. As many as thirty million people died in China alone by the late fourteenth century. The disease also hit Islamic lands as the pandemic spread westward.

MAP 10.3 | **Spread of the Plague, 1347–1350**

The plague moved in what look like waves, south to north, to cover Europe over a four-year period, 1347–1350. *Where and why does the wave pattern seem to break down? Why were some years and seasons more dangerous for human populations than others? What can we infer from the wave pattern about humans spreading the disease and how they were moving about?*

By the 1340s, Yersinia Pestis had reached centers where Europeans traded with Asia (Map 10.3). Here the bacterium found a new host, the Italian sea trader. Medieval chroniclers had a good story of the first European outbreak of the plague. They claimed that a Tartar (Mongol) lord, besieging some Genoese merchants at Kaffa (or Caffa) in the Crimea, ordered that the plague-infected corpses of his men should be catapulted into the enemy's encampment. When the merchants started dying, they fled to their boats and headed back to Italy, carrying the plague with them. Although the story seems too good to be true, merchant ships probably did carry the disease to Europe. By 1347, Constantinople experienced an outbreak of the plague, which then spread around the Mediterranean. A Genoese merchant fleet docked at Messina in Sicily in October 1347; port authorities recognized that these were plague ships and barred the sail-

ors from entry into the city. Nonetheless, within a month Sicily was laid low by the plague.

Transmission and Symptoms of the Disease

How then did these ships infect Sicily, if indeed they did? Yersinia is an efficient traveler. She typically infects fleas that live on rodents, and rats such as the black rat (*Rattus rattus*) are good at surviving on boats and climbing down ropes. Hence they are sometimes called ship rats. Yersinia can travel on old clothes and lie dormant for months until awakened into activity when conditions improve. So something left these ships or arrived in Sicily by similar means.

The infecting agent is the flea, for as it becomes filled with the plague bacillus, its esophagus becomes clogged.

Was Yersinia Pestis to Blame?

The pathogen that infected China, Islamic lands, Byzantium, and Europe in the fourteenth century has been assumed to be Yersinia Pestis since the Swiss bacteriologist Alexandre Yersin first identified the bacterium and disease in 1894, but scientific confirmation was lacking. In the past, the identification of historical diseases has depended almost entirely on contemporary descriptions of symptoms, and these can be variously interpreted. Even the swellings associated with bubonic plague, as described by medieval contemporaries, might be attributed to other diseases such as typhus. In the 1990s, a French team began to investigate whether DNA might resolve the matter. Led by Michel Drancourt, the team retrieved dental pulp from the teeth of people who were supposed to have died from the plague in the sixteenth and eighteenth centuries

Treating Plague Victims A doctor lances a bubo on the neck of a woman while a man shows the swelling below his armpit to the doctors, and a young boy indicates that he suffers from the same ailment.

and to have been buried in plague pits in Lambesc and Marseilles, France. The French team believed that they had found DNA evidence of the presence of septicemic plague. A later French team, led by Didier Raoult, identified the traces of Yersinia in the DNA extracted from the dental pulp of three fourteenth-century victims of the plague in Montpellier. A German team achieved similar results working with the DNA of some sixteenth-century Bavarian plague victims, but an English team working with English "plague victims" was unable to replicate those results in their extraction and analysis of medieval DNA.

The matter of whether Yersinia was to blame for the fourteenth-century plague still lacked uncontroverted physical proof. This did not mean that Yersinia was not responsible, but that the scientific proof of her role was not yet definitively established. Other evidence still pointed to Yersinia: fourteenth-century paintings that show swellings on the necks and armpits of victims, descriptions such as the one by Agnolo the Fat of Siena that victims "swell under the armpits and in the groin area" or by Gui de Chauliac, the pope's physician, who described both the bubonic and pneumonic forms of the disease and himself contracted the disease. Finally, in 2010, a team of European paleopathologists, working with seventy-six medieval skeletons from France, Germany, Italy, and the Netherlands, announced that they had positively identified the presence of Yersinia Pestis in the DNA samples that they had gathered.

QUESTIONS | *What are the inherent flaws of historical descriptions of diseases? Why do scientists and historians, even in an age of DNA analysis, need each other in order to resolve the diagnosis of historical diseases?*

In trying to clear itself of the infection, it bites its host and thus transmits Yersinia to a new host. When the host rodent dies, its colony of 25–30 fleas moves to another available warm body. Although neither rats nor humans are the preferred host of the fleas, an infected and hostless flea is not choosey about its next residence. It too is trying to survive.

Since the disease was finally identified in the late nineteenth century after a massive outbreak of plague in India, we know that the disease takes on three basic forms. Bubonic plague (transmitted directly by an infected flea) is the most common form and so named because of the buboes or swellings of the lymph nodes in

the armpits, groins, and necks of its human victims. This form of the infection lasts about a week and 50 to 60 percent of the infected die. Pneumonic plague is transmitted from human to human by infected air and surfaces, much as a common cold is. In this less common form of the disease, the incubation period is three days, and 95 to 100 percent of all victims die. The rarest form of the disease is septicemic plague, in which Yersinia directly infects the bloodstream of its victims and kills all of them in short order.

What is still not completely understood are the microbiological details of the transmission of the disease in fourteenth-century Europe. Both bubonic and pneumonic plague probably played a part, but the death rates seem very high and the means of transmission are not perfectly clear. Did Yersinia mutate into a particularly virulent form in fourteenth-century Europe; did the pneumonic form of the disease predominate and speed transmission, overcoming the winter lethargy of the carrier fleas; or was Yersinia the same and the European population and its resistance to this specific disease just weak?

The Spread of the Disease in Europe

By early 1348, outbreaks of the disease struck the major port cities of Italy. The disease leaped from port to port and then worked its way inland and north at a rate of about five to ten miles per day. At Florence, the great banking city, the disease was particularly virulent, killing perhaps half the population, or 45,000 people out of 90,000, over its six-month run there. The disease arrived in the port city of Marseilles in February 1348, killing approximately 50,000 people. At Montpellier, 40,000 people died; at Narbonne, 25,000. In papal Avignon, four hundred people were dying each day early in the year. One graveyard in Avignon received 11,000 corpses in six weeks. One out of every three cardinals died, and seven thousand houses were abandoned. Paris was hit in the late spring of 1348, and late in the year plague reached Britain, with London being hit near the end of the year. The disease spread through late 1348 and early 1349 up the valleys of Europe, jumping from large center to large center before working its way back to infect rural districts.

The disease generally quieted down during the colder winter months, but in 1349 Yersinia again began to move north in Europe and by 1349–1350 had reached Scandinavia. In its initial four-year run, something like 35 to 40 percent of Europe's population died, probably 25–35 million people. Pope Clement VI's agents put the total death count at 23,840,000, which seems a reasonable minimal figure for the mortality caused by the plague.

What Could Europeans Have Done?

Could anything have been done? It is unlikely. Given that the disease was not identified until 1894, medieval men and women knew nothing of the transmission of the disease from bacillus to flea, rat, and human. The chain of the disease can be broken at the outset if rats and their fleas are absent and unavailable to serve as the hosts of Yersinia. Or, as the comedian Mel Brooks said, the problem with the Black Death was "Too many rats, not enough cats." Contemporaries did not note any large-scale die-off of diseased rats, which should have occurred, but their silence is hardly surprising since their attention was on dying humans, and sick animals often seek out concealed places to convalesce or die.

Some outlying regions such as Poland and Bohemia, without extensive merchant trade, were largely spared. Cities such as Milan, Liège, and Nuremberg escaped severe outbreaks of the disease, but there were probably

particular reasons involving the absence of infected rats. At Milan (where the death rate was close to 15 percent), a ruthless policy of quarantine was imposed. When plague victims appeared, they and their families were walled up inside their homes, though it is unlikely that this would have effectively quarantined Yersinia, the rat flea, or the rat. It was much better for people to abandon infected areas, particularly towns. Giovanni Boccaccio's *Decameron* recounts the stories of a group of men and women who flee plague-stricken Florence for the countryside.

Medieval men and women had many theories about the origins of the disease: that it had been set loose by a meteor, an earthquake that released pestilential air from subterranean vaults, or a perverse conjunction of the stars. They were looking for a macro-explanation for a micro-event, the pernicious work of invisible Yersinia. Medieval people generally viewed the plague as caused by pestilential air and so were advised to burn special, aromatic woods and herbs to ward off the foul air. Some physicians prescribed special potions according to the wealth of their clients: drinkable gold for the rich, garlic-based concoctions for the poor. The University of Paris went further, ordering students and faculty to observe a moderate lifestyle: no exercise, bathing, or sex.

Medieval doctors could do little and were heavily blamed for their ineffectiveness. Some contemporaries accused them of gouging money from the sick for cures that did not work; others charged that doctors abandoned their patients when they fell ill. Doctors seem to have died in greater numbers than other groups in society, which suggests their greater exposure to the ill, but even so they were criticized. Many people doubted the usefulness of doctors, who in general seemed unable to save themselves.

The Immediate Consequences

As the plague moved through communities and across Europe, there were immediate consequences. In many places, the rituals accompanying dying and death broke down. How does one grieve when so many people are dying and you yourself might die? There was a general reluctance to handle diseased bodies, and often too few people were left living to bury the dead. Men of the lower classes were often hired to bury the dead, but their rates of death were likely as high as if not higher than those of the wealthy. In many places, the death bells stopped ringing altogether since death was no longer a special event to be solemnized, and the church bells would have been ringing all day and night, further disturbing the infirm.

As with the Great Famine, people blamed human agents for producing the crisis. A widespread rumor charged that Jews had poisoned wells and the air, and many Jews were massacred. It did not matter to panic-stricken people—swept up in a moment of intense fear and irrationality—that Jews were dying from the disease in the same numbers as other segments of the population. Pope Clement VI banned such persecution and tried to enforce it by excommunicating the persecutors of Jews.

In the short term, there were practical problems to deal with: abandoned houses, the collapse of family units, orphaned children, and the critical breakdown of institutions (city governments, cathedral operations, monasteries). Gherardo's experience at the Carthusian monastery at Montrieux is a stark example of how bad it could get. Not only did he bury his dead brothers, but he was forced to protect the monastery against thieves, for some people were taking advantage of the breakdown of social order for personal gain.

The plague devastated families. Agnolo the Fat of Siena buried his five children (see Back to the Source at the end of the chapter). In Florence, where marriage ties were intricately complex and negotiated over many years and involved complex social standing and property issues, new family matches had to be made among survivors and property rights worked out. At its simplest level, new social bonds needed to be established in this contracting society.

The immediate response of many people to the plague was to live for today. Boccaccio noted that many people thought that the best response to the death-bringing plague was to treat it as a gigantic joke, to drink much, enjoy life, and to surrender to one's desires. Promiscuity was common. In fact, birth rates in the immediate aftermath of the plague were higher than normal, as though a biological response to sudden population decline. At the other extreme were those who turned antisocial, sealing themselves off from others in self-enforced social quarantine. Herein lay the roots of the reported abandonment of the sick and the unburied dead, for many medieval men and women were convinced (rightly in some cases) that this disease was a matter of person-to-person contagion. The pope was quarantined to prevent him from having contact with infected people. Others fled infected cities as quickly as they could, which was an understandable response to the plague, though a seemingly heartless one.

The impact of the plague on Europeans' psyche was immediate. Contemporaries observed that a cloud of anxiety hung over communities as they received rumors of the approaching disease. When it arrived and family units and social order broke down, the damage was worse than imagined. The ideals of Christian charity and love suffered. The plague seemed to encourage selfishness; why worry about others when you yourself might soon die? Agnolo the Fat simply said that so many died, people believed the world was coming to an end. But Dame Julian of Norwich, the English mystic, said, with the light of divine optimism, "alle shalle be wele."

The plague did engender a new spirit of energetic activism and opportunism among survivors, which some observers mistook for greed. A French friar who lived

Couples Amusing Each Other during the Plague The depiction of a scene from Boccaccio's *Decameron*, in which people fleeing plague-infested Florence seek to distract themselves from the dead and dying of northern Italy in 1348.

through the plague lamented that the survivors were a greedy and contentious lot, grasping for the goods freed up by the deaths of others. The plague cleared away not only people, but also physical, religious, and psychological space for the survivors to fill and exploit. The survivors were left to remake their world with a new set of attitudes and energies, and this new world did not reward passivity. The older medieval ideal of withdrawal from and contempt for the material world failed to meet the needs of a reordering society.

A Battered Society Responds

History is made by the living, not the dead, who are no longer historical actors. As tragic as the suffering and deaths of over 25 million people was, we need to examine the response of those who survived. The surprising thing is that many of them were better off once the plague subsided and society slowly began to remake itself.

How did Europe change after the great calamities?

Medical Implications

Many of those who survived the plague were actually better off, though they doubtless did not realize it at first. By successfully warding off the disease, many survivors now carried immunities against the plague. Human DNA is filled with what were once thought to be junk strands that seemed to have no immediate purpose. Many of those sequences are the remnants of previous body wars, biological battlefield adjustments of our ancestral DNA to fight off diseases encountered in the past, including the fourteenth-century plague. Europeans needed that protection since the plague was not finished with them just yet. In 1361–1362, the plague returned again, this time infecting children born after the first outbreak. After that, Yersinia Pestis became a frequent visitor, coming back uninvited almost every decade, often attacking the young. The population of Europe flat-lined for the rest of the Middle Ages and would not begin a slow upward trend until the late fifteenth century.

Even as the plague struck, some cities took measures to control the disease. In 1348 at Pistoia, not far from Florence, the people's council issued a set of statutes to deal with the disease: limiting the travel of Pistoians outside of their city, particularly to plague-stricken places; controlling the importation of cloth from outside; setting stipulations regarding the handling and transport of the dead, burials, and funerals; and imposing restrictions on the handling of meat and general assembly. The measures constituted a policy of civic quarantine that attempted to restrict Pistoia's contact with a diseased world.

Economic Adjustments

If Europe had been overpopulated in 1300, famine and plague quickly solved that problem. In the countryside, better lands became available to the reduced population of survivors. Farm workers now had more fertile lands available to them, and some became wealthy as a result. Even if they did not obtain better land, their labor was still worth more than it had been before.

With the workforce of Europe reduced by at least a third in four years, those who survived the plague were potentially better off than they had been in the crowded and competitive pre-plague world. Recognizing that their labor was more valuable, city workers sought an increase in wages or a change in the conditions of their work. Cloth workers in Flanders wanted to work fewer hours than they had before the plague and asked for fixed hours. Some scholars claim that a growing awareness of the conditions of work gave rise in western Europe to ideas of merchants' and workers' time and to more sophisticated ideas about the economic value of time and labor. Rapid adjustments in the market forces of the economy played out in the reordering of the economy across Europe in the period 1350–1375.

In the countryside of Europe, farm workers discovered quickly that the balance of power between them and their lords had shifted in their favor. Some insisted on a strict observance of their customary rights, which lords had tended to disregard, or a reduction of the dues (both of service and money) that they owed to their lords. Many took the opportunity to flee farms since towns offered them a steady wage for their work. Wage earners benefited from the plague's reduction of the population, but those with fixed resources such as lords and monks did less well. They had to pay their farm workers more for their labor and received less work from them at a time when the price and demand for agricultural goods was fluctuating. Some manor accounts in England show that a plowman in 1347 was paid 2 shillings for a week's work; in 1349, 7 shillings per week; and by 1350, 10 shillings 6 pence a week. This represented a 500 percent increase in weekly wages in just three years.

Social Insurrection Spreads

Local lords resented the inflation of labor costs. In 1351, the English Parliament passed the Statute of Laborers, which sought to restore the old economic order by fixing wages at pre-plague rates. The act had little success. Serfdom itself was fading in the face of the new economic realities. Although the European world now had fewer people, it still had the same amount of hard money at its disposal, which meant that almost overnight survivors had to pay more for goods. But the disruption of production (due to the random death of workers, lords, and owners) meant that the supply of goods was radically uneven. An inflationary spiral took hold in the 1350s. If the working people who survived had done well after the great initial die-off, by the late 1350s lords and kings were trying to return the genie of social and economic change to its bottle.

Kings still needed, on occasion, to raise extraordinary monies. In 1358, to ransom King John of France, the French royal family raised the taxes on farmers and local lords, and increased rents in the area north of Paris. Peasants revolted in an uprising called the **Jacquerie,** named after the caricature of a good peasant, Jacques Bonhomme (Jack the "good guy"). These fellows were far from good and soon began attacking their lords, pillaging, raping, and roasting them alive. French aristocrats were shocked since they believed that coercive power was their divine right, not that of their inferiors. They viewed the Jacquerie uprising as a satanic plot to overthrow God's appointed social order. Around the same time, a rich merchant in Paris led a campaign by merchants to seize the dauphin (French heir) and the royal treasury. Aristocratic armies suppressed both insurrections with great brutality.

In England, a peasants' revolt erupted in 1381. Three times between 1371 and 1381, the English king had imposed a poll or head tax on his subjects. The last imposition sparked a rebellion. In the wealthy western part of the kingdom, Wat Tyler and John Ball led the resistance, questioning the very authority of their lords. The memorable motto of the rebels was:

> When Adam delved [dug] and Eve span [spun],
>   Who was then the gentleman?

The rebels questioned the arbitrary and unnatural nature of social classes, for at creation Adam and Eve had lived in a simple world without social distinctions and inequalities. The rebels had some successes, but they were almost as violent as their aristocratic oppressors, and murdered the archbishop of Canterbury. Before agreeing to return to their homes, they compelled the young king, Richard II (r. 1377–1399), to make some concessions to their demands for justice and tax relief. The king, however, broke his word and the rebellion was suppressed violently.

In Italy, a revolt by the Ciompi (wool carders or combers) broke out in 1378. Other revolts by the lower classes broke out in almost every region of Europe, all of them symptomatic of the restructuring of medieval society. None of the insurrections was successful in their immediate aims in the fourteenth century, but all were a product of the raised expectations of the lower classes, who did not want to lose the gains they had made after the plague. The lower classes were not starving; downtrodden and emaciated people rarely have the energy or resources to revolt. In the second half of the fourteenth century, prosperous peasants jealously protected their rights against the weakened authorities who were trying to reclaim their previous powers and social primacy.

Towns recovered more quickly from the economic impact of the plague than the countryside of Europe, in part because they could replace lost workers with farmers now ready to become wage earners. Indeed, the plague may have spurred the increased urbanization of Europe or, at least, the balance of power shifted from the rural to the urban after the plague. Yet the plague had hit towns harder than the countryside. Town councils and guilds became more restrictive and jealous of their privileges, not more open. It was an understandable reaction to all the breakages: of contracts, covenants, and economic security.

Although one element of town life became more restrictive and conservative, the plague promoted a new spirit of economic activism among most survivors. The plague broke the lock on innovation and venture economics that had kept the medieval economy conservative and sustainable. In Germany, new mining ventures opened up in the late fourteenth century. With reduced markets, some industries widened their reach to pursue the entire market, not just luxury markets. Thus, in England there was a mass production of cloth and in Flanders the production of cheaper fabric for a wider market of consumers. Europeans also began to look to innovations and inventions in shipbuilding, navigation, and armaments, as they began to reach outside the European world for other individual, economic, and national advantages.

Massacre of Rebellious Peasants The French soldiers of the dauphin are depicted slaughtering rebels in 1358 by throwing the dead or wounded into the Seine River, which flows through Paris.

Remaking Religion: Personal Piety, Schism, and Conciliarism

The crises of the first half of the fourteenth century hit organized religion hard. Institutional religion had been as helpless as any group in society to deal with the devastation of the plague and may have suffered more than other groups because of its emphasis on community living. All of Gherardo's brothers at the monastery of Montrieux died. In Exeter and Norwich, over half the priests succumbed to the disease; in Barcelona, over 60 percent died. Some elements of the institutional church tried to respond to the needs of believers during the plague years. Many dioceses lacked priests because so many had died, fled, or taken up safer and more rewarding posts in the private chapels of the wealthy. As a result, extraordinary measures were needed. The church responded as well as it could. The bishop of Bath and Wells permitted laymen and laywomen to hear the confessions of the dying and to administer sacraments.

Following the first outbreak of the plague in 1347–1350, various penitential groups interpreted the disease as a sign of God's anger at a sinful world. Their response was not so much anti-institutional as extra-institutional; they were still believers but sought to appease God outside the confines of institutional religion. The **Flagellants** (from *flagella*, "whip") paraded through the streets and countryside of Europe, whipping themselves to atone for their sins and those of humankind and to imitate Christ's suffering. The Flagellants were not sanctioned by religious authorities. Instead, they reflected and focused a shifting set of popular anxieties: the widespread conviction that the world was evil and God was punishing it, that the world was ending (millenarianism), and that the established church and priesthood had lost God's favor. The more immediate the plague and the more devastating its results, the more intense the Flagellant movement was. When the plague subsided, the Flagellant movement quieted down.

Many people in the Late Middle Ages began to turn away from organized religion and toward expressions of personal piety. In England, aristocrats built elaborate private chapels, both so that they would not have to practice their religion with commoners and to establish a more direct relationship with God. Rising levels of urban literacy created a market for personal Books of Hours (prayer books) and Psalters (collections of the Psalms), evidence of the growing privatization or personalization of religion. The rise of powerful spiritual women such as Catherine of Siena (1347–1380) suggests something of the intensity of later medieval spirituality. Catherine drove herself into states of spiritual ecstasy by extreme asceticism, particularly extreme fasting, for which she won the admiration of popes and common people. The unsettled conditions of the Late Middle Ages led many to want a more intense and intimate relationship with God than the established church could supply or contain.

There were many collective responses to the new world of religion after the plague, but the new way preferred simplicity of faith over elaborate ritual. Lay brothers and sisters formed societies outside the formal church to live in imitation of Christ and to practice charity. Gerhard Groote's Brethren of the Common Life (founded in 1384) explored a new form of personalized devotion, the *devotio moderna,* that emphasized individual education, piety, and commitment to God that depended little upon the sacraments and other standards of the Catholic Church. The most famous manual of the age was Thomas à Kempis's *Imitation of Christ* (c. 1418), which sought to establish a direct and personal contact between the believer and Christ.

Religious fervor found new expression in popular culture. It was, for instance, but a short distance from the late medieval doctrine of transubstantiation (that the bread and wine of the Eucharist were transformed in all but appearance into the substance of the body and blood of Christ) to the cult of the body of Christ (*corpus Christi*) and the many medieval blood cults that entranced the Late Middle Ages.[2]

King Death Triumphs A fifteenth-century Italian fresco shows a king, bishops, monks, and others bowing down before King Death, humbly acknowledging his victory over them, and offering him gifts. The bottom panel shows a parade of the skeletal dead leading the living to their ultimate end.

One popular enthusiasm involved reimagining and re-enacting the experience of the plague. The dance of death (*danse macabre*) was first performed in 1348 to ward off the disease. By the 1370s, frenzied dancers began to appear in many parts of Europe, dancing to bagpipes and drums until they dropped and were trampled by other dancers. Their herky-jerky, rattling dance may have been meant to imitate the symptoms of dying plague victims, who were then trod upon as though to stamp out the disease. By the late fourteenth century, the dance of death had been transformed into a morality play, a reminder that the disease felled all without distinction: popes, kings, monks, women, and children. The church took up that message as a reminder to all that life was short, death random, and eternity long, but that had not been the dance's original meaning, which may instead have signaled the triumph over the plague by its anxious survivors.

Early in 1377, Pope Gregory XI brought an end to the papacy's self-enforced exile in Avignon and returned to

Rome. He died the next year and the cardinals, under pressure from the Roman people, elected Pope Urban VI (1378–1389). Of low birth and stubborn temperament, Urban ran afoul of many cardinals and, worse, of the French king, Charles V, who was unhappy to see the papacy decamp from greater France. Before long, the king's party among the cardinals declared Urban deposed and elected the bishop of Cambrai as Pope Clement VII (1379–1394); he returned to Avignon. The rival popes each appointed their own cardinals. The so-called **Western (or Papal) Schism** of rival claimants to be pope lasted long after the deaths of Urban and Clement. A church council held at Pisa in 1409 declared the two popes of the rival papal parties to be heretics, which led to the election of a third pope. At the Council of Constance (1414–1417), all three popes were deposed and Pope Martin V (1417–1431) was elected in an attempt to end the schism. After he died, his successor Eugenius IV (1431–1447) fell out with the conciliarists, who with support of the king of France elected an **anti-pope** (one elected in opposition to a pope duly elected by church law and custom), Felix V, who did not step down until 1449. Not until the Council of Basel (1431–1449) did the Western Schism end, with the election of Pope Nicholas V (1447–1455).

The Avignon period and the Western Schism made the Catholic Church a source of confusion to Christendom. The pope was no longer the universal representative of God, as Pope Innocent III had vigorously claimed in word and deed. Instead, for almost seventy years, rival popes and their supporters divided Christendom along political lines. The schism divided not just popes and regions of Europe, but diocese and parishes, as well. Many episcopal sees had two bishops during the schism, each appointed by a rival pope, thus forcing individual believers to pick sides. The one ray of light amidst papal division was the **conciliar movement,** which held that a general council of the church, not the pope, had the authority to set the standards for proper governance for the church and Christian behavior. The Council of Constance, in particular, elevated the claims of the powers of general councils dangerously high. The council claimed to receive its powers directly from Christ and demanded obedience from all, including the pope. It maintained that it had the right to repair schisms and to reform the church and all its members. But conciliarism also contributed to division. The Council of Basel had elected and supported the anti-pope Felix. Conciliarism finally foundered on one key issue: it remained the pope's prerogative to call universal councils of the church and, after the Western Schism ended, popes were wary of calling councils, whose principal power seemed to be to depose popes.

Critics of the Church: Wyclif, Hus, and Valla

The Roman Catholic Church was still the most powerful institutional presence in Christian Europe, but Pope Boniface VIII's misadventures, the papal retreat to Avignon, the Western Schism of the papal church, and the general questioning of the usefulness of institutional religion after the calamities of the fourteenth century left Europe religiously uncertain and the church adrift. Many critics charged that the papacy itself was the problem, though the society in which the church operated had changed and a universal church may no longer have been able to meet the needs of so many divergent European communities.

The English theorist John Wyclif (c. 1324–1384) called into question some of the fundamental tenets of the late medieval Roman Catholic Church, including the need for the seven sacraments. Before the plague hit, Wyclif had been studying scholastic philosophy at Oxford University, but scholastic philosophy had lost much of its steam by Wyclif's day. In the thirteenth and fourteenth centuries, scholasticism turned away from the drive toward synthesis of the Dominican friar Thomas Aquinas and toward **nominalism,** which holds that universals are mere names and have no real existence. The Franciscan friar Duns Scotus (1266–1308), the subtle doctor, thought that God was so remote that human reason was insufficient for understanding him. The dunce (from Duns) cap was a caricature of his obtuse students. Another Franciscan, William of Ockham (1280–1349), was a nominalist who thought that the human mind could understand only this world and should not unnecessarily multiply nonexistent entities. This principle, widely known as Ockham's Razor, argues that, all things being equal, the simplest explanation is generally the best one. Scholasticism was still the prevailing mode of academic thought in Wyclif's time, but the plague hit the universities and their thinkers hard, and Ockham may even have died from the plague. Eclecticism crept into post-plague thought. It was neither as purpose driven nor as logically rigorous as it had been in the High Middle Ages. Humanists such as Petrarch were already rejecting scholasticism as arid and moving in new directions, away from substance (truth) to form (style). Others were moving toward mysticism.

Wyclif himself was a dabbler. Heavily influenced by Ockham, he still rejected nominalism. His inclination was to study the sciences and mathematics, but he took up theology and played politics (even attending the Hundred Years' War peace council held at Bruges in 1374 as an English representative). He denied that England should have to pay the papal tax on its lands as agreed to earlier by King John. Wyclif criticized the Avignon papacy and the claim that the pope held both spiritual and worldly power. Wyclif wanted the church and clergy to be less worldly and to embrace apostolic poverty. Although some elements within the state supported him, the English church was horrified by his teaching and condemned many of his propositions. Wyclif also translated the Bible into English and turned to a strict literalism in his interpretation of the Bible. He denied, for instance, that the pope was the head of the church, since

Christ was, and he supported the mendicant friars, but attacked monasticism. He was blamed for stirring up the peasants who revolted in 1381, though he criticized them and their materialist goals. Despite a church council that condemned his teachings in 1382, King Richard II and the English Parliament would not allow Wyclif's condemnation as a heretic. His supporters, called **Lollards** (idlers) by their Catholic critics, continued to propagate his works and theological views throughout much of the fifteenth century. Wyclif's attack on the existing church was, in many ways, a fundamental rethinking of the nature and purpose of the established church.

In Bohemia, the conditions were more favorable for the emergence of an early national (or Bohemian) church set in resistance to Rome. The emperor Charles IV's creation of Prague as a Czech town, with its own cathedral (and, thus, free of control by the episcopal see of Mainz) and university (with a Bohemian focus) established the basis for the rise of a Czech church. Jan Hus was a student of theology at the university of Prague and there first encountered the doctrines of Wyclif. During the Western Schism, Hus, now the rector of the university, supported the conciliarists, but his archbishop excommunicated Hus and prohibited him from preaching. Hus and his followers were critics of a corrupt clergy, a temporal papacy, and a wealthy church. Hus appealed to poor Czechs, long subject to Germans and to heavy church taxation. Like Wyclif, he believed in the primacy of the Bible, even subordinating the established church to its teaching. In 1415, with the promise of safe conduct, Hus attended the Council of Constance, was put on trial, and condemned when he would not recant his teachings unless they were in opposition to the Bible. He was found guilty of heresy and burned to death. In Bohemia, a Hussite church (with married priests, services in the vernacular tongue, and unadorned churches) developed in opposition to the Roman church. The Hussite national church was not suppressed for many years.

Resistance to the papal church of Rome came not only from national religious movements, but also from princely quarters. In the 1440s, Lorenzo Valla, an Italian humanist, was in the employ of Alfonso I, the king of Aragon, Sicily, and Naples. Alfonso was waging a campaign against the pope over the possession of Italian lands, which led his employee Lorenzo to examine one of the central documents of the medieval Catholic Church. By the terms of the so-called Donation of Constantine and widely accepted in the Middle Ages as legitimate, the emperor Constantine, at the moment of his conversion to Christianity, had bestowed upon Pope Sylvester and his heirs the lands of the western empire as well as

Jan Hus Burned at the Stake The Council of Constance in 1415 revoked its pledge of safe conduct to the Bohemian reformer and ordered his execution.

extensive rights over the west. Lorenzo made a critical (though hardly disinterested or perfectly objective) examination of the document and found that it contained anachronisms, barbaric Latin, statements that did not square with known history or geography, improper dating, and internal inconsistencies. Lorenzo dismissed the papal document as a forgery, and not a very good one at that, thus removing another prop that had supported the claims of the imperial papacy of the Middle Ages.

The Roman church as headed by the pope was much challenged by the new forces of the Late Middle Ages, at a time when there was a general crisis of confidence in institutional religion. The church, however, was not the only institution to feel the effects of the upheavals of the fourteenth century.

The Late Medieval State

The crises of the first half of the fourteenth century did not immediately alter the medieval state, but the conditions produced by those crises disrupted the delicate balance of late medieval society. The crises and accompanying social upheavals undermined the high medieval confidence in a corporate state of cooperative units.

> **What signs of redirection and renewal are evident in the fifteenth century?**

A New World of Political Relations

The crises struck hard at the institution of kingship, or perhaps the royal dynasties of the High Middle Ages had just naturally begun to fail, as all dynasties eventually do.

The Hundred Years' War was a product, in part, of the Capetian failure to put a dynamic heir on the throne. The English War of the Roses came about because two rival dynasties (Lancaster and York) laid claim to the throne. In France, England, Castile, Portugal, Naples, Hungary, and Poland, the monarchs by 1450 were not the direct descendants of the monarchs who had been in place in 1300.

The pressures on kingship increased as society changed. Fiscal pressures rose as a result of the many wars that states were engaged in, for wars were more expensive to wage in the Late Middle Ages. Kings found that mercenaries were more available and reliable soldiers than their nobles, but also more expensive. A settled nobility, hit hard by the economic downturn of the first half of the fourteenth century, when its landed resources were unreliable and underworked, could not be counted upon. Given the lack of manpower, lords preferred to pay the king in money rather than men (an arrangement sometimes called bastard feudalism). Kings welcomed the exchange because mercenary armies of adventurers were more professional and directly dependent on the royal purse and person. The nature of warfare was also changing as cannons and guns became more common, though costly. Castles could no longer resist battery in an age of cannon shot.

While war was becoming more expensive to wage, royal revenues were falling. Kings had previously relied on revenues from their own domains, but as with the nobles' landed resources, royal estates were producing less money after the great depopulation of 1315–1350. Kings could tax their subjects, but they found that they could do so only on an extraordinary and irregular basis. To ask for consent from representative assemblies was to admit some dependence on nobles for their approval of royal action, which kings wished to avoid. Assemblies always wanted something in exchange for their consent, most often the redress of some old grievance.

The late medieval nobility was a particularly troublesome class for the king. They were deeply dissatisfied with how their fortunes had fallen and sought the restoration of their old rights and privileges. The brutality of the suppression of the various popular insurrections across Europe suggests just how angry a class the nobles had become. One of their greatest complaints was that kings no longer needed them as they once had. Thus the corporate ideal of cooperative orders of farmers, aristocratic lords, priests, and others that had sustained the High Middle Ages had been damaged irreparably in the fourteenth century. The orders occupied a world of fluid social relations by 1400, one that had been scarcely imaginable in 1300.

The Final Phase of the Hundred Years' War

When King Edward III of England died in 1377 and was succeeded by the boy-king Richard II, it may have seemed that the war between France and England could be brought to a close, but the French monarchy was unlucky in the extreme. The French king Charles V (the Wise; r. 1364–1380) died prematurely and was succeeded by a son, Charles VI (r. 1380–1422), who was incompetent, quarrelsome, and at times incapacitated by mental illness. Complicating the French resistance to the English was a civil war (1407–1435) in greater France between the Burgundians and Armagnacs (a French faction that supported the dauphin). Both sides in that conflict sought to ally with the English in order to control the French throne. Eventually the martial king Henry V of England (r. 1413–1422) renewed the Hundred Years' War with considerable zest, and at the Battle of Agincourt in 1415 his outnumbered forces defeated the French. English archers and poor French strategy once again determined the day. Eventually the French struck a deal with Henry whereby the dauphin Charles, the son of Charles VI, was deposed. Henry was named the regent and heir to the French throne and married the French king's daughter, Catherine. In 1420, Henry set about claiming his territory, including Paris, by force.

The Maid of Orléans

Although disinherited by treaty, the dauphin Charles led the resistance to the English and Burgundians. The dauphin was popular in certain quarters, but his resources were limited, his position perilous, and his legitimacy in doubt. France, occupied by English and French opponents, was in disarray—plunder, rape, and devastation destabilized France—and people fled, if they could, to walled towns. Charles had been declared king but had not been crowned and was deeply aware of the many challenges to his royal standing. The city of Orléans was under siege by the English when Joan of Arc (c. 1412–1431) came to the rescue. Joan was a peasant girl from the village of Domrémy who had begun to receive visions commanding her to save Orléans and assist the dauphin, Charles. After an interview with Charles, in which she confirmed his rightful claims, and an examination by his theologians, she was given permission to accompany the French army to the besieged city. In March 1429, she sent a remarkable letter to the king of England and the duke of Bedford, his chief operative in France. She denied them the right to hold France and declared that she had been appointed by God to reclaim the blood royal for France. She warned that if the English did not leave France, she would have them executed. Dressed in soldier's armor, Joan successfully led the relief of Orléans in May.

The next stage of her mandate from God was to ensure that Charles VII was crowned at Rheims, which against long odds and English resistance occurred in July. She next hoped to reclaim Paris for her king, but Charles stupidly accepted a Burgundian truce and postponed the attack. Against her king's wishes, Joan went to Paris anyway, but the attempt to take the occupied city failed. At Compiègne, Joan was captured by the Burgundians and sold to the English, who put her on trial in Rouen as a

Joan of Arc the Soldier By most accounts, Joan insisted on dressing as a soldier and participating in relieving the siege of Orléans in 1429. She was later executed for heresy by the English, who cited cross-dressing as a sign of her heretical depravity and stubbornness.

heretic. Her cross-dressing was deemed particularly perverse and a sign of heretical stubbornness. She was not yet twenty years old when she was put to death at the stake on May 30, 1431. Her last word was "*Jhesu*." Her ashes were cast into the Seine, lest people collect her bones as relics.

Whatever else the strange short career of Joan of Arc means, it speaks to the emergence of a deeply patriotic and royalist sentiment in France. Joan had demonstrated that the king, no matter how weak a sovereign, was sacred. The king belonged to France and France to the king, and in Joan's thought God had appointed them for each other. Joan's mission was a religious one; she was the virgin sent by God to rescue France from foreign oppression and corruption. She became a national heroine and, much later, was declared a saint.

The Hundred Years' War wore down after Joan's death, not because of her, but because it was becoming clear that the English could not hold France. The cost was too dear and popular acceptance of foreign rule impossible. In 1435 by the Treaty of Arras, Burgundy finally moved to support the French rather than the English side, which changed the balance of power. The French may never have rallied as enthusiastically as Joan did to Charles VII, but they knew that the English were worse.

King Charles finally became more decisive. He took Paris, entered a new truce with the English, and slowly began to recover French lands from the foreigners. In 1453, after an English defeat at Bordeaux, the Hundred Years' War ended fittingly without any treaty or truce. All the truces, treaties, and breathing spaces had prolonged the war, allowing the equally matched parties to recover and fight decade after decade under different actors. In 1456, a French high court annulled the original condemnation of Joan of Arc as a heretic and Charles set about repairing his exhausted kingdom.

New Medieval Monarchy

Charles VII may have started badly, but by the end he led the way for the new monarchs of Europe. Relying on good advisors, he instituted fiscal, military, and administrative reforms of the state. The king alone was permitted to call up and pay troops. He established a standing army by stationing garrisons of soldiers in provincial towns. A paid army meant that the king had to raise taxes on a regular basis, so Charles instituted a permanent tax in France. Indeed, the king let the assembly of the Estates General of France lapse. Many minor nobility now looked to the king for employment.

King Charles had limited success in kick-starting the economy, but the prosperous career of Jacques Coeur (c. 1400–1456) in Bourges shows just how much could be achieved. Coeur began as a silversmith but won royal favor and took charge of the royal mint in Bourges. He parlayed his role as a royal minter into that of a merchant-trader and assembled his own navy, which supplied France from the Mediterranean. Coeur was skilled at the new financial techniques pioneered in Italy such as double-entry bookkeeping and kept careful track of his venture capital, expenses, and income. He made himself indispensable to King Charles as a wealthy financier and advisor on both domestic and diplomatic matters, for which he and his family were ennobled. Though he was every inch the new-style official that the new monarchs promoted, Jacques Coeur in the end was undone by his success and the chicanery of Charles. The king and so many nobles owed Coeur money that the easiest solution for King Charles and his court nobles was to arrange the fall of the mighty money man. Charges of corruption and treason were laid, Coeur was imprisoned and condemned. He escaped but died in exile outside France.

Western monarchs in the mid-fifteenth century were less and less inclined to rely on their nobles. They established more rewarding relationships with towns and filled their bureaucracies with military counselors, lawyers, and merchant-traders such as Jacques Coeur. In so doing, they found a way to centralize authority under their control, and, as Jacques Coeur discovered, the king's new officials and friends were easier to use and dispense with than the old nobility ever was.

France continued its state reform under King Louis XI (the Spider King; r. 1461–1483). Louis was known to be particularly crafty, patiently waiting for his enemies to fall into the traps he had prepared for them. When Duke Charles the Bold rashly died in battle in 1477, Louis annexed the Duchy of Burgundy, thus removing a powerful thorn in the side of medieval French kings and their control of greater France. During the reign of Louis's son, Charles VIII (r. 1483–1498), France was involved in a series of Italian conflicts that pushed the French state toward a more efficient, but also more expensive bureaucracy. France could afford the cost of expanded government, being in much better economic shape by the last half of the fifteenth century. By 1400, several thousand French villages had been abandoned because of famine, war, and disease, but in the period 1450–1500, bountiful harvests returned and the Hundred Years' War was no longer a steady drain on the treasury.

Between 1455 and 1485, England was divided by the War of the Roses, the white rose representing the House of York and the red rose the House of Lancaster; those memorable designations were created later by Tudor historians. At the Battle of Bosworth Field in 1485, the Lancastrian Henry Tudor defeated the unpopular Richard III and founded the Tudor dynasty as King Henry VII (r. 1485–1509). Henry was in desperate need of money, but his subjects expected him to "live of his own." Henry set about discovering ways to amass money that did not lead through Parliament. He increased the royal domain, took charge of custom revenues, resurrected old taxes, charged fees for royal services, and assigned fines for the administration of justice. These monies went straight into the royal accounts. Henry was particularly gifted at squeezing money out of his nobles, often on some trumped-up charge of disloyalty or some manufactured scandal. To do so, he required an instrument of royal investigation and so employed the Court of the Star Chamber to examine, discipline, and break the landed gentry that opposed him. Henry loathed, as the Tudors generally would, the expense of foreign wars, which was the lesson of England's long entanglement on the continent.

In the late fifteenth century, Spain at last achieved unity. The Iberian Peninsula was composed of three basic areas: Portugal, with 1.5 million people; Castile (including Léon and Navarre), with a population of 8 million; and the area of Aragon (Catalonia, Aragon, and Valencia), with approximately 1 million people.

In October 1469, Isabella, heir to the throne of Castile, married Ferdinand, heir to the thrones of Sicily and Aragon. It was an almost impossible marriage to pull off. Because the ruling king of Castile, Henry IV (the Impotent), had no heir, he reluctantly agreed for a time to support the elevation of Isabella, his half-brother's sister, against the wishes of his own nobles. The marriage ceremony of Isabella and Ferdinand took place in Toledo under the most unlikely circumstances. King Henry had withdrawn his consent, and a forged papal document permitting the marriage mysteriously appeared. To get to Toledo, Ferdinand dressed as a mule-driver to slip by those seeking to stop the marriage. The king subse-

quently condemned the marriage, denied that Isabella was his legitimate heir, and chose another. Yet Isabella hung on, and after King Henry's death in 1474, she was quickly crowned queen.

Castilian nobles, fearing that the marriage would lead to the unification of the Spanish kingdoms, revolted, leading to a decade of civil war. Instead of immediately imposing unification upon Spain, Isabella and Ferdinand set about securing their borders. Between 1482 and 1492, they initiated the conquest of the Moors in Granada. This completed the long reconquest (*reconquista*) of Spain that had stretched over many centuries (Map 10.4).

As part of their campaign to purify Spain and make it entirely Christian, Ferdinand and Isabella in 1492 expelled Spain's Jewish population. By 1502, Muslims who would not convert were expelled, as well. The king and queen employed the Spanish church to bring about unity of faith in Spain and introduced the Spanish Inquisition as a national instrument of inquiry.

Isabella was a powerful sovereign in her own right and retained control of Castile. It may not be a coincidence that it was at this time in Spain that the game of chess took on its modern form. The game had long been played in European and Islamic lands, often with no queen piece or a queen with little power. During Isabella's reign, the queen piece finally became the most powerful and dominant player on the board.[3]

The Coerced Baptism of Muslim Women A wood panel decoration from an altar depicts Muslim women in Granada undergoing baptism after the success of the reconquest of Spain by Ferdinand and Isabella.

The splintered states of the Holy Roman Empire and the city-states of Italy are treated in subsequent chapters, but the late medieval monarchs of France, England, and Spain were already pointing the way toward the new methods and goals of late medieval government and increasing their intense competition with each other for resources and land. They did this by securing new forms of revenue, employing new-style officials, bureaucratizing their governments, arranging strategic marriage alliances, bypassing or subordinating their nobles, and supporting new international ventures outside of Europe.

The Fall of Constantinople

The decline of the Byzantine Empire transformed Europe and the historical and geographic setting it occupied. For eleven hundred years the eastern Roman Empire had been an enduring counterpoint to western Europe, supplying it with economic, intellectual, and theological stimulation. The existence of Constantinople in the east was a hard fact during times when western Europe seemed adrift and dangerously unstable. But the emergence of the Ottoman Turks, particularly under Beyazit I Yilderim (the Lightning), had stripped Byzantium of its empire, including Greece, and left it with only Constantinople. Beyazit was on the verge of taking the city in 1402 when he was forced to withdraw his forces to engage Tamerlane (Timur the Lame), a Mongol Muslim, who had conquered Baghdad and Damascus the previous year. At the Battle of Ankara, Tamerlane defeated and captured Beyazit. Constantinople survived a little longer, then, not because of its internal resources but because of external forces beyond its control.

Early in his reign, the Turkish sultan Mahomet II (r. 1451–1481) resumed the assault on the great city. Complicating matters, the attempt of the Roman Catholic Church to enforce a union of the eastern and western churches remained unpopular in Constantinople. Many Byzantine Christians believed that the sultan would respect their orthodox beliefs in ways that the pope would

MAP 10.4 | The Reconquest of Spain, 900–1492, and Its Final Phase
The Christian reconquest of Spain spanned almost six centuries, concluding with the retaking of Granada by Ferdinand and Isabella and the expulsion in 1502 of all Muslims who would not convert to Christianity. *Why had Muslim Granada been able to hold on so long? How was the Christianization of Spain part of a larger European movement of consolidation? Why did Ferdinand and Isabella make reconquest such a critical part of their consolidation of Spain?*

not. The emperor Constantine XI was able to secure the service of few western soldiers to defend his city. In April 1453, Mahomet assembled over 80,000 soldiers and some three hundred ships outside the city's famous double walls. Constantine had only 8,000 men (3,000 of them westerners) to defend his city. Moreover, Mahomet brought an immense cannon to bear on the walls of the city, which soon crumbled, and he blocked any relief supplies from entering the city. In late May, his troops poured through the breaches and the emperor Constantine was killed in the fighting. Constantinople was ransacked and renamed Istanbul, and the famous Hagia Sophia, built by Justinian, was made a mosque. Istanbul became the capital of the Turkish or Ottoman Empire.

For westerners, the fall of Constantinople seemed a second fall of Rome, but they did not have long to lament its passing. The rise of a powerful Ottoman block to its east had the effect of enclosing, redefining, and balkanizing Europe. Europe's outlet to the east was now cut off, economically, territorially, and psychologically. Overseas exploration to the west would be the result.

1453: To Fall Asleep in Constantinople and Wake in Istanbul

There are two stories of Constantinople's fall: one Greek, the other Muslim. One is a story of death and destruction, slavery and forced dispersion, the loss of church and pride of place. The other is a story of proud achievement, of the green banners of Islam and the red banners of the sultan being unfurled in a city that had resisted the Islamic world for eight hundred years, but was now the brightest jewel in the resplendent Ottoman crown.

The city of Constantinople fell to Mahomet II Fatih (the Conqueror) on May 29, 1453, and for the Greeks of Constantine's city, everything changed overnight. Some 4,000 defenders of the city were killed, and nearly 30,000 Greek residents were captured and enslaved. Within days, long lines of chained Greeks were paraded through their former city and shipped to slave markets in Islamic lands. Among them was George Sphrantzes, an imperial of-

ficial and former Byzantine governor. He was eventually ransomed in September, but his wife and children were enslaved to a Turkish family before being purchased by a high Turkish official, who eventually sold the children to the sultan. After a few years, George was able to ransom his wife, but his two captive children died in the sultan's seraglio (harem), his daughter from disease and his son John executed by the sultan because he had been plotting Mahomet's murder. The fate of George and his family was probably similar to that of many rich and powerful Byzantines—a story of broken families, dispersion, and loss. Greek officials and scholars fled to the west, seeking what employment they could find. The story of lower-class Constantinopolitans was one of a horrific fall into foreign servility, silence, and oblivion.

If the world of the Christian Greek residents of Constantinople was upended overnight, so too was that of the Turks of the new Istanbul, but their half of history's hourglass was now on top. The great city was quickly "Islamicized." Churches were turned into mosques, which became the new organizing centers of the city renamed Istanbul. A minaret was erected within days at Hagia Sophia. The sultan encouraged traders, including the Italians, to set up shop in the city and sought to internationalize the city, forcing some of his subject peoples to relocate there and trying to attract others from outside to his new capital. Twenty-five years after the conquest, the city was twice as populous as it had been in 1453. Muslim Turk families now made up half the city's population, Greek households a quarter of the civilian population. In the days after the conquest not all the Greeks were sold into slavery. The sultan claimed a fifth of the captives, perhaps as many as six thousand Greeks, as his own and settled them in a part of the city that would become a Greek quarter. He also allowed those Greeks who had fled the city before it fell and, therefore, had not resisted him, to return to repossess their property. Mahomet approved a new patriarch for the Greek church and proved himself to be a benevolent ruler, who was interested in Greek and Persian poetry and was proud to establish a quasi-Byzantine court to rival those of European rulers.

Sultan Mahomet II

QUESTIONS | *In what ways is history merely a story of winners and losers? Constantinople fell, but how was its place in the Greek identity preserved?*

The Waning of the Middle Ages

What makes historical works classics may not make them great works of history. Historical classics share common features; they capture the imagination of readers by breaking out of the boxes that others inhabit and they create an unforgettable image and understanding of a period. They are also controversial. They endure as books read by the generations because they demand engagement, discussion, and debate. Classics are rarely definitive studies, for the fate of many definitive works is to be absorbed into the accepted interpretation of a period. Classics are books that we return to again and again; they keep kicking.

Johan Huizinga's *Waning of the Middle Ages* is one such classic. It has gone through numerous editions and translations since its initial publication in 1919. Its arresting opening (in Fritz Hopman's translation) is gripping: "To the world when it was half a thousand years younger, the outlines of all things seemed more clearly marked than to us. The contrast between suffering and joy, between adversity and happiness, appeared more striking. All experience had yet to the minds of men the directness and absoluteness of the pleasure and pain of child-life." What follows in Huizinga's book is an impressionistic study of the violent tenor of late medieval life, its pessimisms, chivalric and heroic ideals, visions of life and death, religious sensibilities, and the movement from a symbolic to realistic imagination. The tableau Huizinga lays before us is sweeping and sensuous; his Late Middle Ages in the north is overripe, reeking of the rot of final things.

Professional historians were not pleased. Huizinga's book, they thought, was too beautiful, too topical and imagistic to be historically true. They noted that Huizinga had a weak sense of historical change and chronology; that his book was actually about Burgundian society, not the whole of northern Europe in the Late Middle Ages; that he ignored politics, the economy, and the mass of people who did not participate in high culture. His was a cultural history designed to evoke the sensibility of the Late Middle Ages, not the reasons it had become that way. In North America, the book became a classic college text when Hopman's translation appeared in an Anchor paperback version in 1954, but that version reduced the number of chapters, eliminated much of the original, and was based on the French translation of the work and not the final Dutch edition. To repair those flaws and give Huizinga fuller voice, Rodney J. Payton and Ulrich Mammitzsch brought out a complete retranslation (but of the second edition of the work) in 1996 under the title *The Autumn of the Middle Ages.*

A work that continues to attract so much attention and to provoke so much discussion qualifies as a classic. It is not a book that leaves readers unmoved. Huizinga's view of the Late Middle Ages—that it had its own voice and natural ending—seemed to speak to the modern world. So did J. R. R. Tolkien's *The Lord of the Rings* (1954–1956). Tolkien saw the Middle Ages as a rejection of so much that he disliked about the modern world: mechanization, democratization, and materialization. Yet Tolkien's sprawling three novels are hardly an accurate re-creation of the Middle Ages. There is nothing like the Catholic Church in the Middle-earth of the wizard Gandalf and the Hobbits Frodo and Sam. Huizinga and Tolkien, to different degrees, present us with quasi-medieval worlds, whose very point is to make us think about the world we live in through the lens of its opposite.

QUESTIONS | *Is the Middle Ages the opposite of the modern world? Why or why not? Why is the Middle Ages the subject of so many modern projections and fantasies in popular culture (movies, novels, and music)?*

Conclusion

Just as there is no consensus on when the Middle Ages began, there is little consensus on when it ended. The Middle Ages ended not with any single event, but rather with a series of fundamental changes: the educational changes that occurred in the fifteenth century during the Italian Renaissance, the fall of Constantinople, the invention and spread of the printed book after 1450, overseas exploration in the fifteenth and sixteenth centuries, and the religious re-formation of western Christendom in the sixteenth century. The most popular view may be that the fifteenth-century developments in northern Italy were the bridge to an early-modern age that saw the loosening of the church's stranglehold on medieval Europe. Others might look to the fall of Constantinople in 1453 as removing one of the critical features of the Middle Ages, a Christian eastern empire in place since the emperor Constantine's day. As such, the rise and fall of Constantinople might be viewed as bookends enclosing the Middle Ages. The arrival of the printing press in the 1450s removed another key feature of the Middle Ages: the parchment manuscript. Others look to 1517–1520, when Luther and his movement of protest fractured the Catholic Church's hold on Europe, but Christianity would remain the predominant religion of Europe.

Questions of periodization are never easy to resolve, but they do force us to think about what was essential to a period. The beginning and end of a period are likely to be fuzzier than its core, when it was essentially itself in its most developed form.

There can be little doubt that the crises that overtook Europe in the fourteenth century brought about change and produced a new world in the Late Middle Ages. The onset of the Little Ice age, the desperate times of the Great Famine, and the disaster of the plague undermined some of the main achievements of high medieval civilization. If the building campaign of a great Gothic cathedral was not finished by the early fourteenth century, it would not likely be completed for centuries. The loss of resources and people in the first half of the fourteenth century sapped the energy and dynamism of high medieval civilization. The survivors of the calamities, however, did not surrender; they adapted. Not all the changes happened on the same time scale. Workers in the cities and farms of Europe were sensitive to economic changes and responded quickly to new opportunities. A generation later, workers and peasants revolted against measures to claw back their gains. Royalty was relatively slow to react to the new conditions of life, but by the late fifteenth century, kings were back on top, transforming monarchy into a more dynamic and self-sufficient force. Along the way, customs and practices that had defined the medieval order were transformed or ended. The French king's move to impose permanent taxation was one of those, since the Middle Ages had begun with and had long relied on an exchange of land for service.

The church too was changing. The imperial papacy created by Gregory VII and the Investiture Controversy had its last moment of great pretense early in the fourteenth century under Pope Boniface VIII, but he died in retreat, painfully aware of the limits to his power. The Avignon papacy, the Western Schism with its rival papal claimants, and the stirrings of national churches in Bohemia and England were all symptoms of a papal church beleaguered. In the aftermath of crises of climate, sustenance, and disease came a reworking of religion that turned gradually from institutional answers to personal and private ones. Religion was, if anything, more important after the crises, even if the papal church was weaker than it had been in the High Middle Ages.

Little Yersinia and her companions Cold and Hunger cut Europe to the quick, forcing it in new directions—political, economic, and religious—that would have been inconceivable seventy-five years earlier. From this great shattering of medieval direction and confidence came the great trifurcation of European history into the Northern Italian and European Renaissances, overseas exploration, and religious re-formation, which we take up in Chapters 11–13. Those historical developments had their roots in the new world of the Late Middle Ages and would be responses and reactions to its many troubles and surprising achievements in fashioning many new Europes.

Critical Thinking Questions

1. How did the elements of chance and choice play out in the fourteenth century as people dealt with calamity and change?

2. Which groups in society were hit hardest by calamity and changing circumstances?

3. Why was the Hundred Years' War such a prolonged and fruitless set of conflicts?

4. How did religion change between 1300 and 1450?

5. How and why did the period 1300–1450 either kill off the Middle Ages or refashion it?

Key Terms

Little Ice Age **(p. 296)**

Great Famine **(p. 297)**

bull **(p. 299)**

Unam sanctam **(p. 299)**

Golden Bull **(p. 300)**

Hundred Years' War **(p. 301)**

chivalry **(p. 303)**

pandemic **(p. 304)**

Black Death **(p. 305)**

Jacquerie **(p. 310)**

Flagellants **(p. 311)**

devotio moderna **(p. 312)**

Western (Papal) Schism
  (p. 313)

anti-pope **(p. 313)**

conciliar movement **(p. 313)**

nominalism **(p. 313)**

Lollards (idlers) **(p. 314)**

Primary Sources in connect

For information on Connect and the online resources available, go to **http://connect.mcgraw-hill.com**.

1. **Observations of the Plague**

2. **The Peasants' Revolt of 1831**

3. **Joan of Arc's Letter to the English Invaders and Her Trial**

4. **George Sphrantzes and the Fall of Constantinople**

Agnolo the Fat and the Plague

Agnolo di Tura, called the Fat, was an eyewitness to the destruction the plague visited on Siena and his own family in 1348. Agnolo was a man on the way up in Sienese society. Though his origins were in the lower classes, his wife Nicoluccia came from a higher station and never let him forget it. Together they had five children, but his wife and children died, along with some 80,000 other Sienese when the plague struck according to Agnolo. At different points in his life, Agnolo worked as a shoemaker, tax collector, and chronicler. His account of the plague's destruction is part of his larger chronicle (*Cronica Maggiore*) of Siena from 1300 to 1351, which he based partly on official documents and partly on his own observations.

The mortality began in Siena in May [1348]. It was a cruel and horrible thing; and I do not know where to begin to tell of the cruelty and the pitiless ways. It seemed to almost everyone that one became stupefied by seeing the pain. And it is impossible for the human tongue to recount the awful thing. Indeed, one who did not see such horribleness can be called blessed. And the victims died almost immediately. They would swell beneath their armpits and in their groins, and fall over dead while talking. Father abandoned child, wife husband, one brother another; for this illness seemed to strike through breath and sight. And so they died. And none could be found to bury the dead for money or friendship. Members of a household brought their dead to a ditch as best they could, without priest, without divine offices. Nor did the death bell sound. And in many places in Siena great pits were dug and piled deep with the multitude of the dead. And they died by the hundreds both day and night, and all were thrown in those ditches and covered over with earth. And as soon as those ditches were filled more were dug.

And I, Agnolo di Tura, called the Fat, buried my five children with my own hands. And there were also those who were so sparsely covered with earth that the dogs dragged them forth and devoured many bodies throughout the city. There was no one who wept for any death, for all awaited death. And so many died that all believed that it was the end of the world. And no medicine or any other defense availed. And the lords selected three citizens who received a thousand gold florins from the commune of Siena that they were to spend on the poor sick and to bury the poor dead. And it was all so horrible that I, the writer, cannot think of it and so will not continue. This situation continued until September, and it would take too long to write of it. And it is found that at this time there died in Siena 36,000 persons twenty years of age or less, and the aged and other people [died]

to a total of 52,000 in all in Siena. And in the suburbs of Siena 28,000 persons died; so that in all it is found that in the city and suburbs of Siena 80,000 persons died. Thus at this time Siena and its suburbs had more than 30,000 men, and there remained in Siena [alone] less than 10,000 men. And those that survived were like persons distraught and almost without feeling. And many walls and other things were abandoned, and all the mines of silver, gold, and copper that existed in Sienese territory were abandoned as is seen; for in the countryside . . . many more people died, many lands and villages were abandoned, and no one remained there. I will not write of the cruelty that there was in the countryside, of the wolves and wild beasts that ate the poorly buried corpses, and of other cruelties that would be too painful to those who read of them. . . .

The city of Siena seemed almost uninhabited for almost no one was found in the city. And then, when the pestilence abated, all who survived gave themselves over to pleasures: monks, priests, nuns, and lay men and women all enjoyed themselves, and none worried about spending and gambling. And everyone thought himself rich because he had escaped and regained the world, and no one knew how to allow himself to do nothing. . . .

At this time in Siena the great and noble project of enlarging the cathedral of Siena that had begun a few years earlier was abandoned. . . .

After the pestilence the Sienese appointed two judges and three non-Sienese notaries whose task it was to handle the wills that had been made at that time. And so they searched them out and found them. . . .

1349: after the great pestilence of the past year each person lived according to his own caprice, and everyone tended to seek pleasure in eating and drinking, hunting, catching birds and gaming. And all money had fallen into the hands of the *nouveaux riches*.

QUESTIONS | *How is Agnolo's account enhanced or compromised by his personal experience and individual losses? What symptoms of the disease did he detect? Based on the numbers he provides, who suffered most from the disease, the young or the old, city dwellers or country folk?*

Source: Translated by William M. Bowsky, in William M. Bowsky, *The Black Death*, 1st ed., pp. 13–14. © 1971 Wadsworth, a part of Cengage Learning, Inc. Reproduced by permission. www.cengage.com/permissions

11

Gentile Bellini, *The Procession in St. Mark's Square,* Venice

THE NORTHERN ITALIAN AND EUROPEAN RENAISSANCES

Why Then, Why Italy?
Geography, Politics, and Society on the Italian Peninsula
Rome: The Popes Return to Prominence
Living the High Life in Renaissance Rome
The Political Landscape of Florence
From Medici Munificence to Magnificence
The Bonfire of the Vanities
Machiavelli's Cold Eye

West and East in the Renaissance
Venice, City of Banks, Ships, and Republican Ease
The Colonial Reach of Venice
The Ottoman Empire as a Renaissance State
Renaissance Cosmopolitanism in Big Europe

Humanism and Individualism
The Humanist Course of Study

Reading Classical Literature
Civic Humanism and a New Sense of History
Individualism

Italian Renaissance Art
Living Renaissance Art
The Early Renaissance: Ghiberti, Donatello, and Masaccio
The High Renaissance: Leonardo, Michelangelo, and Raphael

The Spread of Renaissance Ideas: The European Renaissance
Commerce and Urban Life in the European Renaissance
European Renaissance Art
The Print Revolution of the European Renaissance

Conclusion

PETRARCH, CASSANDRA, AND THE DYING BOY On the morning of April 26, 1336, Petrarch set out to climb Mont Ventoux ("windy mountain"), the tallest mountain in southern France. From there he could, with a sweep of his eyes, see France, Italy, and toward Spain. He wanted to imitate the ancient king who had climbed Mount Haemus. Petrarch (Francesco Petrarcha; 1304–1374) was the progenitor of humanism and the **Italian Renaissance** rethinking of Europe's past and present. He was also a complex and contradictory character. He spent his formative years and early career as a creature of the Avignon papacy, but longed for Italy and its golden past. He was a cleric and chaplain, but he idealized from a distance the sublime Laura, a young woman whom he first saw in church in 1327 and about whom he wrote elegant love poetry in Italian. He wrote often about Laura yet bore illegitimate children with women about whom we know next to nothing.

Petrarch's ascent of Mont Ventoux was also full of contradictions. He chose his brother, the monk Gherardo, as his boon companion for the climb, but they took servants with them to do the heavy lifting. Petrarch presents the climb as an allegory of the soul's ascent. The problem was that he kept losing his way, descending into valleys, while his religious brother made the easier and straighter ascent. At the summit, Petrarch opened a copy of Saint Augustine's *Confessions,* where his eye fell upon a passage criticizing those who admire tall mountains, vast seas, and the stars, but forget themselves. He descended the mountain in a blue funk, refusing to speak to the others and blaming himself for his love of the material world. Petrarch was torn between this world and a higher one, the present and the distant past, between activity (*negotium,* meaning the daily business of life) and contemplation (as the result of ease, *otium*). Convinced that his own age reeked of corruption and fallen standards, Petrarch admired the superior men of ancient Rome, the superior government of the Roman Republic, and the superior art and writing of the classical past. He had that rare gift of inspiring others to take up his cause, in this case rethinking the assumptions of his age.

If Petrarch was the father of humanism, Cassandra Fedele and Laura Cereta were his intellectual and spiritual daughters. In 1556, the Republic of Venice requested that the ninety-one-year-old humanist Cassandra Fedele (1465–1558) give a public address in honor of the visiting Queen of Poland. Cassandra was an internationally renowned scholar. From the age of twelve, she had studied philosophy and the natural

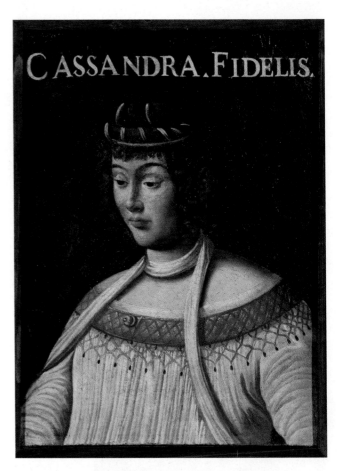

Cassandra Fedele A portrait of the humanist of Venice by an unknown artist.

Petrarch climbs Mount Ventoux
1336

Ottoman Empire
1300–1566

Angevin Dynasty in Naples
1285–1435

Visconti Dynasty in Milan
1278–1447

1250   1300   1350   1400

sciences and knew classical literature intimately. At the age of twenty-two, though barred as a woman from attending university, Cassandra addressed her cousin's graduating class at the University of Padua on the subject of the value of the arts and sciences, a speech that was published many times during her lifetime. At a time when women were expected to either marry or become nuns, she chose to marry a physician, and moved to the island of Crete, which brought her close to the Ottoman Empire and the vestiges of Greek civilization. Angelo Poliziano, the Tuscan poet, praised her to his patron, Lorenzo de' Medici, for her great beauty and fluent command of Greek and Latin. Two years after making her address to the Polish queen, Cassandra died and was given a Venetian state funeral. Cassandra Fedele lived the Renaissance, its opportunities and limitations. She and Laura Cereta were the heirs of Petrarch's humanist movement, but they knew how hard it was to pursue advanced learning in a world that still constrained women to familiar roles. The Italian Renaissance, as lived by Petrarch and Cassandra, was not revolutionary. It was transitional, a world in-between, not quite modern, but not entirely medieval either. The Renaissance was working its own slow, cerebral, and distinctly human way toward something new.

We can visualize this world in transition in a painting by Gentile Bellini. It shows the great square outside of Saint Mark's Cathedral in Venice on April 25, 1444. At the leading edge of the painting we see a procession through the square. The previous day, a wealthy merchant had taken his son to the square, but the boy had fallen down and fractured his skull. He lingered on the edge of death. The next day the brothers of the Confraternity of Saint John, dressed in white, mounted a ritual procession for the soul and recovery of the boy. The brothers bore a relic of the True Cross, while the father, shown in the painting in a brilliant red gown, knelt down in solemn prayer to Saint Mark to save his son. Much of the scene remains medieval (the belief in relics, miraculous cures, religious orders, and prayers to saints), but other elements in the painting seem strangely new: flags fluttering with the civic pride of Venice, citizens milling about in the square oblivious to the ritual taking place in their presence, men and women in idle conversation, and the looming cathedral and ducal palace (to the right). Even to paint the drama of civic life reflected something of the new urban vigor and attitudes toward life and its cultural possibilities that were animating life in the great cities of northern Italy in the fifteenth century.

❉ ❉ ❉ ❉

Any mention of the Renaissance conjures up images of the fascinating notebooks of Leonardo da Vinci, of Michelangelo's gorgeous frescoes in the Sistine Chapel, and of the ruthless politics of the Medici and Borgia dynasties. The Italian Renaissance has long seemed a time of flashing genius, a rush of creativity, and shrewd decision-making. What has been less apparent is that during this glittering period poverty, famine, and disease remained pressing problems; creative men and women struggled to secure financial support from capricious

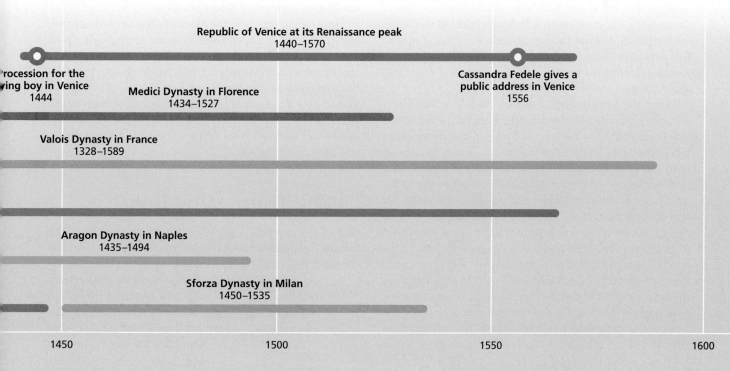

Republic of Venice at its Renaissance peak
1440–1570

Procession for the dying boy in Venice
1444

Medici Dynasty in Florence
1434–1527

Cassandra Fedele gives a public address in Venice
1556

Valois Dynasty in France
1328–1589

Aragon Dynasty in Naples
1435–1494

Sforza Dynasty in Milan
1450–1535

1450   1500   1550   1600

327

patrons; and relatively few extraordinary men (and only a handful of women) participated in the Renaissance in any meaningful way. The Italian Renaissance achieved remarkable things, but it did not represent a dramatic shift in political, social, or cultural attitudes. It took centuries before most people reaped the benefits of its emphasis on universal education, individual potential, and service to society. Among the privileged few who lived this high cultural moment, hard decisions had to be made: between old and new models of life, between family and the pursuit of individual fame, and between their Christian faith and the allure of ancient and pagan beliefs that was pulling people in different directions.

The Italian Renaissance presented some men and women with a series of choices and opportunities to re-imagine the world. A new approach to scholarship and the arts was emerging, one that privileged the distant classical past as a golden age. The result was a form of scholarship known as Renaissance humanism that emphasized the study of the Latin and Greek languages and literatures. In the Renaissance, medieval Christianity as developed over a thousand years (with its emphasis on collective values, humility, and steadfast devotion) remained a powerful shaper of attitudes and actions, but alongside it was a growing emphasis on the importance of the individual in society and of human activity in the world, a drive that began after the plague and the crises of the fourteenth century had shaken the otherworldliness of the High Middle Ages. Caught between the classical and Christian pasts, and between traditional religious beliefs and a new secular emphasis on living in the moment, men and women in the Renaissance were forced to decide how best to move forward. Petrarch's confusion on Mount Ventoux was the confusion of someone torn between the competing ideas and impulses of the age, not sure which way to turn, but fully aware that there were choices, good and bad, to be made. Nor was everyone making the same choices. Petrarch rejected medieval scholasticism, but his brother became a medieval monk. Scholars, intellectuals, politicians, princes, and artists were exploring different ways of living and thinking about the past and the present.

What the Renaissance was (and was not) has been a subject of intense debate and scrutiny ever since nineteenth-century historians took up the descriptive label. The term *renaissance* (meaning rebirth) had been used earlier by the Italian artist and writer Giorgio Vasari to describe contemporary efforts to return to the artistic glories of the classical past. Examples of ancient art and architecture, often revealing a dazzling mastery of design, perspective, and anatomy, were being recovered from the earth in Italy and dredged from the sea. These newly found works contrasted sharply with the iconic imagery of medieval art and led Vasari to conclude that the arts had been in decline since Roman times and were only beginning to regain their former glory.

Vasari's impression of the rebirth of the arts was shared among scholars, who felt the same way about their rediscovery of classical literature. They knew that many works by Greek philosophers and Roman humanists had been lost sight of over the centuries, and that their knowledge of the classical Latin and Greek languages was limited. As Greek scholars and theologians fled the crumbling Byzantine Empire in advance of the Muslim armies of the expanding Ottoman Empire, they carried with them to Italy previously unknown and un-studied texts. Western scholars, like its artists, felt that they were recovering a lost golden age through these precious manuscripts. The study of ancient languages and literatures was tackled with enthusiasm as scholars began the arduous work of translating and deciphering those texts. Cassandra Fedele could speak with pride of the University of Padua as a place where the liberal arts were once again flourishing as they had in ancient Athens. For Cassandra, the past had become present.

Despite the feeling of rebirth among artists and intellectuals, it was not until the nineteenth century that the term *Renaissance* was capitalized and used by historians as a shorthand description for an entire age. The most well-known proponent of the Renaissance was the Swiss historian Jacob Burckhardt, who saw fifteenth-century Italy as a turning point between the darkness of the Middle Ages (the time between the classical past and the Renaissance) and the bright light of modernity. Today few historians see the Renaissance as a radical rupture with the Middle Ages. Nor do they see the Middle Ages as dark, backward, and superstitious. Despite the changes in the way that historians now use the term, Renaissance has remained a widely used label to designate the period from as early as 1350 to as late as 1650, with its core in fifteenth-century Italy, the so-called Quattrocento (the 1400s). The term has its problems, since the Renaissance has no firm starting or ending dates, unfurls at different moments in different parts of Europe, and was experienced fully by only a small, elite segment of the population.

Here we explore how the Northern Italian Renaissance and the wider European Renaissance were made up of a series of small developments between the fourteenth and the sixteenth centuries. Touching on geography, politics, international relations, scholarship, and the arts, we look at how the choices made by men and women of the period shaped an identity based on a return to ancient ideals and fostered new attitudes toward politics, texts, education, and the world.

Why Then, Why Italy?

One of the most difficult questions to answer about the Italian Renaissance is why the preoccupation with the classical past and the associated sense of rebirth came

Why did the Italian Renaissance occur when and where it did?

to the foreground of intellectual, cultural, and political life when it did in the northern Italian peninsula? Burckhardt argued that the Renaissance began on the peninsula because "Italy began to teem with person-alities," implying that a fortuitous convergence of gifted people in one place was sufficient to explain the changes. Historians are no longer satisfied with that explanation, which seems to take the effects of the Renaissance for its cause; they prefer instead to emphasize the specific and local conditions that fostered the Italian Renaissance.

Some general causes can be identified. The crises of the Late Middle Ages in the first half of the four-teenth century changed Europe, and some of those changes benefited northern Italy. Though Italy was hit hard by the plague, it escaped the poor weather and famine that struck northern Europe. Moreover, threats to the relative stability and prosperity of northern Italy were few in the period from 1350 to 1493. The papacy, which for much of the Middle Ages had constrained the freedom of development and action in Italy, was weakened by the plague, its residence outside of Italy, and the Western or Papal Schism of the Late Middle Ages. Italian cities found that they could, for a time, operate without much papal interference. The German or Holy Roman Empire was also for much of this time weak and un-able to interfere in Italian affairs. French kings were busy trying to deal with English invaders, restless nobles, and their own wobbly reigns, all of which left some parts of Italy time to trade and prosper. Cities in the north flourished.

Geography, Politics, and Society on the Italian Peninsula

The Italy of Petrarch and Cassandra was not a single state, but a diverse region where different languages and dialects were spoken, with different calendars used and different political systems in place. The one thing that distinguished Italy from the rest of Europe in the fourteenth century was the predominance of cities (Map 11.1). Northern Italy was more urban than the rest of Europe, including southern Italy. By 1300, twenty-three northern and central Italian cities had populations over 20,000. The mid-century plague reduced the population of Europe, but left northern Italy still relatively populous. By 1550, forty Italian cities had populations in excess of 10,000 people. Rome had a population of around 45,000; Florence, 60,000; and Venice, 160,000.

Northern Renaissance Italy was dotted with indepen-dent city-states (the chief of which were Florence, Venice, Rome, and Milan) where wealth and power were increas-ingly in the hands of urban elites who, unlike their noble superiors, required relative peace and stability with rival states in order to foster trade and economic development. The peninsula boasted a higher rate of literacy than other parts of Europe at the time, and urban men and women increasingly viewed education as a way to achieve indi-vidual glory and to rise to greater heights of prosperity. By the fifteenth century, vernacular education in Italian

MAP 11.1 | Renaissance Italy, 1454

At the height of the Northern Italian Renaissance, Italy was divided into republics (such as Florence and Venice), a duchy (Milan), and the Papal States cutting across the peninsula. The Kingdom of Naples dominated the south. *Why did Renaissance Italy separate into the advanced city-states of the north and the more traditional monarchy of the south? What geographic advantages did Venice have? Why was Milan vulnerable to attack and invasion? Why could this balance of powers in Italy not last?*

dialects flourished in classrooms dedicated to educating urban boys and girls in the mathematical and linguis-tic skills necessary to thrive in the competitive world of business and trade. The city-states of northern Italy were known throughout Europe for their well-developed trad-ing networks, conspicuous consumption, and craftsmen skilled in producing luxury goods such as silk, glass beads, and paintings. This combination of social, eco-nomic, and political factors was particular to the region and casts light on why Vasari believed that his age was one of transformation, fueled by intense competition be-tween cities and between people.

Although many differences existed on the penin-sula, the region shared some common geographic and historical features. Throughout the peninsula there are steep hills, deep valleys with rivers running through them, and ancient ruins. These features had long been there, of course, but were to prove critical to the devel-oping Renaissance. The hills, for example, made Italian states easier to defend militarily. Cities and towns were almost always built on hills, which afforded a good view of advancing armies and also a clear vantage point from which to shoot at the approaching enemy. The most notable exceptions to this rule were Venice with its lagoon layout and Florence, which was built along one of the peninsula's prominent river valleys. River valleys, which offered more fertile soil and arable land than the adjacent hillsides, were necessary to towns built on craggy overlooks. Valleys provided towns with food and water; their rivers served as transportation arteries leading from the Mediterranean Sea to the Italian interior. The ancient ruins of the peninsula did not offer Italians of the fifteenth century anything that was tangibly beneficial; instead, they grounded Italians in deep history. Italians shared a conviction that they were part of a glorious past, the evidence for which lay all around them. During the Renaissance, many Italians believed that they should play a unique role as the caretakers and interpreters of classical and Christian history.

Despite these common features and concerns, strong regional differences existed within the peninsula. The most important dividing line was—and still is—the one that exists between the north and the south. In the Renaissance, this dividing line was most apparent politically. The Italian peninsula had inherited two chief governmental styles from the medieval period: hereditary kingdoms (such as those found in most of Europe), which were located primarily in the south, and communes, which were found chiefly in the north. Kingdoms were dominated by hereditary elites that provided military power in exchange for economic support in the form of tax revenues and the right to receive a portion of agricultural goods.

Communes consisted of groups of local, powerful men who governed the northern states, many of which were based in a city. During the early medieval period, communes were relatively small, being made up of only about 200–300 individuals in a given area. Between 1198 and 1250, middling landowners, merchants, shopkeepers, and members of trade guilds began to play a larger role in the political life of communes. The growing governing class of these cities produced larger communal bureaucracies and the need to pay city officials whose full-time occupation was to run the government. Expanding communes also led to a growing sense of what is known in Italy as *campanilismo,* the love of the bell-tower of one's birthplace, which can be understood as civic pride and identity. After 1250, many communes began to fall under the influence of powerful local families. Within families and between powerful families there were frequent feuds and murders as ambitious people sought supreme power for themselves. Only one medieval commune, Venice, managed to escape this fate and transformed its commune into an enduring republican form of government.

After years of interference from foreign powers that sought to manipulate the region's political fragmentation to their own advantage, the Italian peninsula emerged in the fifteenth century as a conglomeration of strong

The Mercantile and Maritime Prosperity of Venice A ship is being loaded with grain at the port of Venice. The painting by Ambrogio Lorenzetti in the mid-fourteenth century depicts the miracles of Saint Nicholas, who was reputed to have miraculously filled the holds of ships.

independent states. Most Italian states of the time were anchored by flourishing cities—whether it was the Kingdom of Naples of the south; the Papal States that surrounded Rome; the republics of Siena, Florence, Genoa, Lucca, and Venice; or the duchies and counties of Ferrara, Savoy, Milan, and Mantua. Although much of the power base of western Europe still depended on landholding and an economy based on agriculture, the states of the Italian peninsula were coming to depend increasingly on urban centers and their ability to engage in commerce and trade. Italy's merchant economy meant that the states of the peninsula were wealthy by European standards. Surplus wealth was spent on ambitious building projects; on commissions for literary and artistic works; and on territorial expansion through advantageous marriages, diplomacy, and warfare.

The peninsula's dependence on trade for economic survival meant that political leaders needed to keep their desire to make war for territorial gain in balance with their interest in maintaining peace and order to facilitate mercantile activity. Because Italian political elites enjoyed the benefits of both peace and war, they cultivated civic behaviors unlike those of the traditional medieval nobility. These included reading, writing, and debating artistic merit and new ideas. One Florentine historian, Matteo Palmieri, viewed the Italian elite as participating in a new kind of army, one outfitted with pens and paintbrushes rather than swords. Palmieri was grateful that he had been born into an age that was so full of hope and already rejoicing in a greater army of gifted noble souls than the world had seen in a thousand years. Despite the fourteenth-century plague or, perhaps, because of it, Italian elites embraced the future, convinced that they had survived the worst calamity in history and were poised on the brink of a new and wonderful flowering of cultural and historical achievement.

Examining three Renaissance cities and their different styles of political leadership should help highlight what made the Italian peninsula so suited to the growth of Renaissance ideas and ideals. There were many important Italian cities (including, among others, Milan, Naples, Siena, and Urbino) in the fifteenth century, but Rome, Florence, and Venice (to be treated in the next section) stood out to contemporaries and later historians as striking examples of Renaissance politics and culture in action.

Rome: The Popes Return to Prominence

In the medieval period, the ancient city of Rome had always been considered the center of the Papal States, which sprawled diagonally across the middle of the Italian peninsula. Rome was special among the cities of the Italian Renaissance because of its defining relationship with antiquity and the institution of the Catholic Church and papacy. Medieval and Renaissance popes were temporal as well as spiritual leaders, and they depended on the income and power they drew from the Papal States to maintain their relative political autonomy. The Papal States in Italy provided Renaissance popes with agricultural crops, tenants, armies, and merchant enclaves that could be relied on to support and sustain the papacy and its centers of bureaucratic and administrative power at the Vatican and in Rome.

Though smaller than other Renaissance cities, Rome underwent enormous change during the Renaissance. The papacy's removal to Avignon in the fourteenth century had caused Rome's population to decline markedly as hundreds of clerics left the city along with their entourages. A small number of lawyers, doctors, and merchants remained to carve out lives for themselves in Rome, but otherwise there was little industry or commerce. Consequently, by the beginning of the fifteenth century, Rome had a population of only about 25,000 individuals, the majority of whom were still associated with the church.

As the schism of the papacy wound down after 1417, most Europeans probably thought that the city was beyond saving. At that time, gang warfare was rampant between the rival Orsini, Frangipani, and Colonna families; innocent people could not walk the streets for fear of being robbed or murdered; and the artists and minor clergy members who had accompanied the papacy into southern France were only beginning to trickle back to the city in search of patrons and commissions. What was needed to turn the city's fortunes around was the return to prominence of energetic and dynamic popes.

The pope was vitally important to Rome and the center of the peninsula not only as the spiritual leader of the Catholic Church, but also as the temporal ruler of the Papal States. The ideal pope, from the point of view of the city of Rome, was someone present, pragmatic, and sophisticated. The best popes were shrewd politicians who could negotiate and coexist with the Roman nobility, while handling the administrative needs of church and state. The Renaissance popes who guided Rome back to a position of prominence cut splendid, princely figures by supporting art and architecture. Such worldly popes were a boon for Rome. The church, however, often paid the price when its leaders seemed less concerned with spiritual life than with European politics and world affairs.

The first pope to return the papacy permanently to Rome was Martin V (1417–1431), whose abilities as a statesman made it possible for him to repair some of the damage done to Rome and the Papal States during the long Avignon absence and troublesome schism. A native Roman and a member of the powerful Colonna family, he was ideally suited to manage the city's difficult political climate, even though charges of nepotism threatened to bring about his ruin on more than one occasion. Martin thought that Rome could and should reestablish itself as one of Europe's premier cities by becoming a center for the arts and scholarship. His successor Pope Eugenius IV (1431–1447) was an important opponent of the Council of Basel and of conciliarism in general.

Nicholas V (1447–1455), the first post-schism pope, followed Martin's lead by focusing on the renovation of Rome. One of his pet projects was to establish a grand papal library. By 1481, the Vatican Library had one of the largest collections of books in the west with over 3,500 volumes. Pope Nicholas commissioned scribes to copy special editions of rare texts, which were then bound in distinctive red bindings closed with silver clasps. For all his interest in architecture and scholarship, Nicholas also proved to be a strong political leader. He survived an attempted coup during the Porcari Conspiracy of 1453, when native Romans tried to restore the ancient republican form of government to the Papal States. His successors were a mixed lot. Pope Pius II (1458–1464, born Aeneas Silvius Piccolomini), who while in office wrote an account of his life, was learned and committed to the good of the church. But Pope Sixtus IV (1471–1484) was plagued by charges of gross corruption and of being more interested in indulging in political intrigue than in looking after the church.

Pope Alexander VI (1492–1503) possessed elements of both predecessors. Like Pius II, he was a great promoter of education and learning. But like the pontificate of Sixtus IV, his was overshadowed by his colorful personal life and dynastic scheming. Born into the noble Spanish-Italian Borgia family, Alexander was always an outsider in Rome. His position worsened when he tried to use his church office to place members of his family in positions of power and influence throughout Europe. His publicly acknowledged mistress, Vannozza Catanei, bore him four children, including the infamous Cesare and Lucrezia. Cesare Borgia (1476–1507) made the pope's family name synonymous with greed, treachery, and murder. Cesare was rumored to have arranged more than 250 murders in the city of Rome, including those of his elder brother and his sister's second husband. Made an unlikely cardinal at the age of fourteen through his father's political maneuverings, Cesare ultimately left the church to take a more active role in family politics and was eventually assassinated.

Popes such as Martin V, Nicholas V, and Alexander VI focused new attention (both positive and negative) on Rome, and the city began to revive. Tourism, industry, trade, and banking began to thrive, bringing new economic opportunities and wealth to Romans. Pilgrims flooded into the city each spring to visit the center of western Christianity, leading to housing shortages, inflation, and epidemic disease. Despite these pressing urban problems, Pope Nicholas declared a "Jubilee Year" in 1450 to encourage still more pilgrims to visit Rome. Over 100,000 people flooded into the city, so many that the balustrades of the main bridge over the Tiber collapsed and over two hundred people were trampled to death or fell into the river and drowned.

Living the High Life in Renaissance Rome

In addition to the tourists, clergymen, and bankers, Rome had a thriving entertainment industry, and chief among it were the courtesans, who were famed for their refined tastes and great beauty. Many of these women adopted classical names and saw themselves as heirs to the ancient Roman tradition of imperial courtesans. During the pontificate of Alexander, Roman courtesans experienced their own golden age of prominence and patronage, holding elaborate salons and posing for famous artists. One of the most popular and famous courtesans of the period was Imperia, who lived like a princess. She had a palatial home filled with carpets from the east, embroidered gold tapestries, and antiquities discovered in Roman soil. Imperia was exceptionally successful, and her notoriety and that of other courtesans made them a famous or infamous feature of Roman life. Evidence suggests that in 1500 as much as a tenth of the city's population was made up of courtesans, prostitutes, and their operatives. By 1566, so large a proportion of the city's population was connected to the prostitution trade, and so much of the city's taxable wealth was tied up in the leisure industry, that it proved difficult for reform-minded popes to dislodge the courtesans without risking the collapse of the urban economy.

The Political Landscape of Florence

Rome was unique on the Italian peninsula because of its association with the classical and Christian pasts, but Florence stood out during the fifteenth century because of its vigorous mercantile activity and enormous wealth. One contemporary observed that a Florentine who was not a merchant had no standing or respect among his fellow citizens. To be rich in Florence was to be honorable and powerful, and nowhere in Renaissance Europe was the desire to acquire wealth more pronounced.

Florence's rulers tried to maintain a delicate balance between urban professionals, craftsmen, and businessmen, who brought economic power and prestige to the city, and the hereditary nobility of the region. Throughout the medieval period, Florence struggled to check the development of family factions such as those that were found among the Roman nobility, but political instability was the norm. Around 1300, Dante said that Florence was like a sick woman, tossing and turning on her plush bed, unable to find a comfortable position in which to lie. During times of crisis, Florence's government became more oligarchic as wealthy merchants and nobles worked to preserve the republic in the face of an increasingly frustrated and anxious populace. Despite the growing influence of noble families and prominent individuals on Florentine politics, the city's life was still dominated in the fifteenth century by the twenty-one guilds that oversaw all business dealings. Among them were seven major guilds (led by the lawyers, wool-makers, and bankers) and fourteen minor guilds. Although the guilds dominated political and economic life in Florence, 75 percent of the city's population did not belong to any guild at all.

Florence's oligarchic government was led by a nine-member committee called the *Signoria*. All members of the city guilds who were male and over thirty years of age were eligible to serve on the *Signoria* for a two-month term. Each person on the *Signoria* was selected at random from among guild members, their names picked out of a leather bag. During a two-month term of service, the members of the *Signoria* moved into the central Palazzo della Signoria in Florence so that they could be available at any hour for city business; they also received a paid salary to keep them from being distracted by their own business concerns and enjoyed the assistance of a dedicated staff. There were two chief problems with the *Signoria*. First, like most representative bodies, the quality of the *Signoria* and its ability to rule varied widely, depending on its members. Second, although the process seemed democratic, in reality the most prominent and wealthy Florentine families were able to keep the names of eligible men out of the bags, rigging the selection process to ensure that their own people were chosen to serve.

The Medici family rose to prominence due to its place among the urban elite and prominent role in the *Signoria*. The patriarch of the family, Giovanni di Bicci de' Medici, belonged to the powerful wool and banking guilds; he built his family's vast fortune first on the cloth trade and then on the careful management and investment of the profits. Giovanni founded the Medici bank in Florence, and it eventually had bank offices in most of the important cities of Europe, including Rome, Venice, Naples, London, Bruges, Geneva, and Paris. Giovanni de' Medici's friendship with the anti-pope John XXIII established the family as the papacy's bankers for decades. With the papacy's money in hand, the Medici were able to invest it at a profit for themselves rather than its depositor. The Medici and Florence were at the forefront of the formative development of banking. Using Arabic numerals (rather than the more clumsy Roman numerals), bankers in Florence were better able to keep track of money, profits and losses, and investments. They also were among the first to use double-entry bookkeeping (as first described by Luca Pacioli), a system that records transactions as credits and debits on different sides of the ledger or book.

The Medici Dynasty and Its Cultural Clients In Botticelli's painting *The Adoration of the Magi* (1475), the Medici and their cultural and political circle are active participants in the scene. Three Medici have taken on the roles of the magi: Cosimo de' Medici (long dead) as the old magus kneeling before Mary, Piero de' Medici as the second magus in red cloak kneeling at the center, Giovanni de' Medici as the third magus in white kneeling to his right, and Lorenzo de' Medici standing with the red and black garment. The artist may be the figure in yellow at the far right.

The Medici success in business led to its political prominence in Florence. As a non-noble family, the Medici were viewed as upstarts by Florence's hereditary elites, but the Medici proved that it was possible for people to rise above the conditions of their birth. The Medici accomplished that by amassing power based on their wealth and shrewd political deals rather than on hereditary power.

From Medici Munificence to Magnificence

In addition to advancing a new style of rule, the Medici staunchly supported Renaissance cultural and intellectual pursuits, and under their influence the city of Florence came to be one of Italy's leading centers of scholarship and the arts. The first member of the family to achieve civic prominence was Cosimo de' Medici (1389–1464), the wealthiest man in Florence. Educated at a local monastery, Cosimo was particularly adept at foreign languages, being fluent in German, French, and Latin. He also had some mastery of Hebrew, Greek, and Arabic, leading Pope Pius II to describe him condescendingly as "more

lettered than merchants usually are." When Cosimo began exercising his authority in 1434, the *Signoria* was in disarray and the city was slipping into decline. Cosimo stepped into the void and began to supervise the government of Florence, using his money to exert his influence over Florentine society. He excelled in the arts of negotiation, preferring to buy support or to manipulate events behind the scenes rather than to wage showy, but expensive, wars. His support came from the loyalty of his power base among ordinary citizens, whose allegiance he cultivated by implementing a policy of upward mobility, promoting members of the lower orders into positions of power rather than relying on the hereditary nobility.

Cosimo de' Medici was the most powerful and wealthiest man in Florence, but he maintained a modest and reserved demeanor. His approach to leadership was based on munificence: he was generous with his money and influence, not only among his family, but also among Florentine society at large. His style of rule was therefore strikingly different from that of the hereditary nobility, because he preferred to work within the existing political system of Florence to achieve his objectives, rather than undermining it. No one in Florence, however, doubted who was in charge.

Cosimo's grandson, Lorenzo de' Medici (1440–1492), known as "the Magnificent," rose to power in 1469 after

The Fortunes and Misfortunes of the Medici Family in Florence

DATE	EVENT
1300s	Medici family members active in the wool-makers' guild
1396–1400	Medici involved in political plots, banned from political activity
c. 1397	Giovanni di Bicci de' Medici founds the Medici bank in Florence
1434–1464	Cosimo de' Medici, son of Giovanni, runs bank, governs Florence
1464–1469	Piero I de' Medici, son of Cosimo, an invalid often ill with gout
1469–1491	Lorenzo I de' Medici, son of Piero, neglects bank, governs Florence
1478	Pazzi Conspiracy attempts to assassinate Lorenzo, kills his brother
1490–1497	Savonarola in Florence
1492–1494	Piero II de' Medici, son of Lorenzo
1494	Medici bank goes out of business
1494	Bonfire of the Vanities in the central square of Florence
1494–1512	Medici expelled from Florence
1513	Machiavelli, in exile, writes *The Prince*
1523–1535	Giulio de' Medici, nephew of Lorenzo, becomes Pope Clement VII

his father Piero's death. As a child, Lorenzo had been intellectually precocious and showed from an early age the diplomatic and political skill for which his grandfather Cosimo had been so famous. From the age of fifteen, Lorenzo conducted diplomatic missions for his father and participated in the backroom politics of Florence. Lorenzo was not, however, as keen to respect and follow tradition as his grandfather had been, and his unusual marriage to a woman not of Florentine birth, the Roman noblewoman Clarice Orsini, proved to be a diplomatic and public relations disaster. Lorenzo had hoped that his alliance with the Orsini family would secure his family's fortunes with Rome and the papacy, hopes that were dashed when the scheming Pope Sixtus IV backed the leaders of the Pazzi Conspiracy in 1478. The Pazzi sought to overthrow the Medici family by assassinating Lorenzo, but succeeded only in assassinating his brother and unleashing Medici anger upon the conspirators and the church that had supported them. Though this sequence of events forced

Florence and Rome into bitter hostility for years, it did not hurt Lorenzo's status in the city, and by the time of his death he was regarded as the virtual king of Florence.

The Bonfire of the Vanities

Lorenzo, for all his ostentation, was neither as charismatic nor as capable as Cosimo had been. He was unable to see the value of munificence as a political strategy and turned instead to showy magnificence as a way to impress Florentines and achieve greater influence over the political life of the city. Lorenzo's showiness ultimately turned the tide of public opinion against the Medici and contributed to the rise of an unlikely, but spellbinding religious adversary, Girolamo Savonarola. A physician's grandson and the son of a failed merchant, Savonarola had attended the University of Ferrara before becoming a Dominican friar. The Dominicans or "hounds of the Lord," as they were known in the Renaissance, helped Savonarola to craft an image of himself as a knight fighting in the service of Christ. Savonarola prepared for this life by studying biblical and medieval scholastic texts and preaching to growing audiences. Women, in particular, were drawn to his sermons, despite Savonarola's belief that women should play only a minor role in religious life. He also attracted intellectuals such as the young Pico della Mirandola and the artist Sandro Botticelli, who gave up painting as a result. In 1485, Savonarola revealed that he had been given the gift of prophecy and had been called upon to preach a message of penitence and reform to the people. At the suggestion of a leading humanist who was under Savonarola's intellectual and spiritual spell, Lorenzo made a critical mistake and chose to summon the friar to Florence in 1490. In Florence, Savonarola developed a loyal following called the *Piagnoni* ("the snivelers" or "big cry babies") because of their constant weeping over the fate of the world.

On a chilly winter day in December 1494, Savonarola declared that the Florentines had been chosen by God to receive salvation, but his claim came at the expense of the autocratic regime of the Medici family. Clandestine meetings between Savonarola and the land-hungry French king, Charles VIII, led to the elaborately engineered expulsion and enforced exile of the Medici family.

Savonarola's own star was already in decline when he convinced his followers to burn their books, paintings, cosmetics, and Florence's famous luxury goods in the main governmental square, the Piazza della Signoria. The event became known as the **Bonfire of the Vanities,** a vivid conflagration that consumed the idle material trappings of exuberant Florentine life. But in the spring of 1497, the youth of Florence, tired of Savonarola's efforts to stamp out the urban pleasures of drinking and gambling, rioted in the streets. Sensing that the winds were blowing against the Dominican preacher, Pope Alexander VI excommunicated Savonarola just nine days after the riot. Arrested by an angry mob, he was tortured and burned alive in the same piazza where he had presided over the bonfire. Florence, again a functioning republic, soon returned to its typical style of politics and self-promotion and the Savonarola episode seemed but a bad dream.

Machiavelli's Cold Eye

The political theorist Niccolò Machiavelli (1469–1527) served as the second chancellor (or secretary) of Florence under the Medici (of whom he could be critical) and as an ambassador to France for the restored Republic of Florence after the fall of the Medici. He also worked to improve the Florentine militia, but when the republican government of Florence was overthrown in 1512, he found himself out of work, and was arrested and tortured. In prison, he was dropped six times on a rope tied to his wrists, which were bound behind his back. Later he retreated to his country estate, where in 1513 he wrote the infamous *The Prince,* in which, with a calculating and cold eye, he describes and praises the often ruthless political style of the Medici and lauds the shrewdness of Cesare Borgia. *The Prince* so shocked contemporaries for its candor, cold-bloodedness, and seeming amorality that some people thought it a satire.

The Bonfire of Savonarola In the same square where the Bonfire of the Vanities happened, the Dominican friar Savonarola and two of his Dominican supporters were executed by the citizens of Florence in 1498. The three men were hung first and then the pyre was set aflame, both to send them to hell and to eliminate their bodies lest relics remain. The men carrying bundles of wood to the fire underline the public support for the execution.

Medieval political treatises had been devoted to teaching future princes how to be good and pleasing to God. Machiavelli wanted to teach princes how to survive and operate successfully without reference to what was right or pleasing to God. Medieval political theorists assumed the existence of evil, but preached the good and godly. Machiavelli assumed the existence of human political realities and advised princes how to manage them. His political examples are chiefly ancient and modern (with few medieval), but they do include the non-Christian Ottomans. Machiavelli was a strikingly systematic political thinker, as he proceeded logically toward provable conclusions, but he was also a man of his time: he believed that comets foretell the future, that history is cyclical, and that infantry armies composed of citizens, as in the Roman Republic, were the most effective military force. He also dreamed of the unification of Italy and dedicated his work to a younger generation of the Medici in the hope that they would emulate the family's great rulers,

Niccolò Machiavelli Diplomat, statesman, and political theorist, Machiavelli was also a politician in Florence and advocated such schemes as a republican militia made up of citizens.

1527 and the Sack of Rome

For almost two hundred years, the Italian peninsula was free of direct foreign interference and invasion, which meant that its small city-states were, in relative terms, evenly matched and free to explore their commercial, cultural, and political opportunities. Ludovico Sforza, the regent of Milan, observed in early 1494 that Italy was like a duck pond, in which each duck swims in circles, unconcerned with the other ducks: the Venetians hide, the Florentines joust, the Milanese hunt, the pope makes cardinals, and the king creates counts. He feared the ruin that would fall on all if they did not awaken from their self-centered sleep. For twenty years, various cities such as Naples, Milan, and Florence had suffered from severe political instability. By destabilizing Florence and its resident rulers, the Savonarola affair was one of the events that invited foreign intrusion. Savonarola looked to the intervention of the French to tip the balance of power in Italy in his favor. In September 1494, King Charles VIII of France did just that. With an army of 32,000 men, he crossed the Alps and marched on Naples, which he took in February. Not the peoples of Italy, but other European countries rose in resistance, forming a Holy League to expel the French invader. A year later, Charles was back in France, driven out of Italy by disease and the armies of the emperor and king of Spain. But the door had been opened to foreign interference, and for the next thirty years Italy was a playground for contests between the French and Spanish. In 1499, King Louis XII of France laid claim to Milan and seized it from the Sforza dynasty and Ferdinand of Aragon took southern Italy, so that by 1500 the French dominated the north and the Spanish the south of Italy.

No wonder Machiavelli viewed politics in such coldly realistic terms. Artists deserted Florence for more peaceful and prosperous cities. Botticelli left an inscription from 1500 on his painting of the *Mystic Nativity,* which he said he had completed in Italy's time of troubles, likening the age to the one predicted by Revelation when the devil would be loosed upon the world. Italy's troubles after the foreign invasion of 1494 were ones that revealed the fundamental weakness of small states in a world of new and more powerful European monarchs, and there was no easy fix. By the early sixteenth century, Rome was the chief patron of the arts in Italy. Leonardo and Raphael had worked there under papal commission, and Michelangelo had finished painting the ceiling of the Sistine Chapel by 1512. The 1520s was a trying time for Italy: disease, famine, and the sack of cities such as Genoa, Milan, Naples, and Florence. Worse befell Rome. In 1527, in a dispute with the French king and the pope, the emperor Charles V ordered the taking of Rome. The troops that did so, poorly paid and refusing to follow orders, ransacked Rome, burned down buildings, murdered thousands, held cardinals and rich Romans for ransom, and tortured others to reveal where their money was hidden. The economy of the city collapsed, the pope fled into exile, and the brutalized population of Rome fell by half over the next several years. It was the end of Rome's cultural renaissance and, in some ways, a symbol that the Italian Renaissance was finished, since Italy could no longer manage its own affairs.

QUESTIONS | *How did the situation of Renaissance Italy parallel that of classical Greece, in both its cultural achievements and its political vulnerabilities? Did the Italian Renaissance end in 1494 or 1527, or had it already transformed into something else?*

restore Medici power, and, perhaps, return Machiavelli to government once again (see Back to the Source at the end of the chapter).

West and East in the Renaissance

One of Cosimo de' Medici's most significant political triumphs came in 1439, when he successfully lobbied to have a General Council of the Roman Catholic and Greek or Eastern Orthodox Churches meet in Florence. Four centuries of doctrinal differences and historical friction had kept apart these two branches of the Christian church (in the Great or East-West Schism), but with the Muslim Ottoman Empire gaining strength in the eastern Mediterranean, reconciliation seemed prudent and no one was better at high and low negotiations than Cosimo.

Why was Venice special?

The eastern ambassadors and clergymen from the Byzantine Empire made a lasting impression on Florence. Emperor John Paleologus, the Eastern Orthodox patriarch Joseph II, and over seven hundred delegates with long, impressive beards, opulent clothes, and complicated headdresses walked the city's streets with their African and Mongol servants in tow. The artists Gentile da Fabriano and Benozzo Gozzoli painted images of the exotic visitors on canvases and frescoes, where they appear

Cosmopolitan Headgear Benozzo Gozzoli's painting *Procession of the Magi* (1459) shows a variety of different head coverings, including the eastern headdress of the three bearded magi. The artist is the figure wearing the turban with an inscription.

as the Magi from the east, bringing gifts to the infant Christ. When a doctrinal compromise was finally brokered between the leaders of the two Christian churches in the summer of 1439, it was trumpeted as reuniting east and west. "Let the heavens rejoice and the earth exult," Patriarch Joseph proclaimed, "for the wall that divided the western and eastern churches has fallen." The religious divide had not, of course, been repaired and the council did not prevent the fall of Constantinople in 1453, but the proclamation sounded good and awakened deeper cultural interest, east and west.

Western Europe had long been fascinated by the exotic wonders of the East. Crusaders brought back stories of Constantinople's wealth and of strange spices and aromatic foods unknown in Basel, Florence, and London. Soldiers returned to the West with silks, relics, and a taste for sugar. The fifteenth-century Italian Renaissance also recognized that the East possessed an unrivaled knowledge of ancient Greek culture, which was important to its own growing critical appreciation of classical civilization. Eastern clothing, food, and literature were fashionable in the Renaissance, so much so that Pope Alexander VI had his son and daughter painted wearing Turkish costumes. Despite the attraction of things eastern to those in the

west, the relationship between east and west was tense, with deep ideological and theological divisions and memories of a troubled past, particularly the imposition of the Latin Empire of Constantinople in the thirteenth century. These tensions, however, should not obscure the strong economic ties and regular social contacts that persisted, despite struggles over belief and territory.

Venice, City of Banks, Ships, and Republican Ease

Venice played a critical role in connecting east and west, both commercially and culturally. Venice's singularity came from its geographic location and status as the only true republic in Italy. Known as *La Serenissima* ("the most serene one"), Venice steadfastly resisted the pressures of invading armies and navies, and the territorial ambitions of nearby despotic leaders, without giving in to the lure of being ruled by a single, charismatic figure. As a result of its republican ease, Venice had no popes or Medici princes to engage our historical attention.

During the High Middle Ages and the Renaissance, Venice evolved from a relatively small and remote urban enclave on a lagoon into a bustling gateway between west and east with colonies that extended across the Adriatic and into the Mediterranean (Map 11.2). The only medieval city of any significance not surrounded by walls, Venice was instead encircled by waterways that were navigable but that shielded the city from direct armed attacks by military forces on horseback or on foot. Venice's position on the northeastern edge of Italy gave it the ability to participate in and eventually dominate Adriatic and Mediterranean trade. Its geographic location made Venice a cultural and economic force in European life.

The economic power of Venice was symbolized by its relatively stable currency, which enabled Renaissance merchants to trade money for goods in distant ports. More Venetian money was in circulation during the Renaissance than that of any other western European power, and from 1400 to 1460 the republic had more of its money in circulation than the kingdoms of England and France combined. A Venetian ducat was recognized throughout the Mediterranean world because the republic's government made sure that it always contained the same amount of precious metal. Venetian currency set the standard for most other currencies, and in 1425 Cairo debased its gold currency to bring it into line with that of Venice.

With so much money on hand, Venice had to devise new methods to store and protect it. Venice and not Florence was the first state in Europe to establish banks, which at first were seen simply as secure warehouses for money. Banks in fact take their name from the benches (*banchi*) set up in the center of Venice on the Rialto Bridge over the Grand Canal, where people with surplus cash to invest went to meet with individuals who had projects in need of funds. Once deals were struck, Venetians faced another problem: how to get those funds across the European continent or across the hazardous

MAP 11.2 | The Commercial and Cultural Reach of Venice in the Fifteenth Century

In the fifteenth century, the Republic of Venice reached commercially across the Mediterranean, trading with centers as far east as Tanais on the Sea of Azov. *Why did its geographic location enable Venice to dominate trade in the Mediterranean world? How did it support its trading operations? Why was Venice destined to be not just an aggressive trading state, but one that facilitated cultural exchanges?*

Mediterranean Sea. Because transporting cash was too dangerous, Venetian banks began to issue letters of credit to their clients. When Venetian merchants wished to import paper from China through middlemen in Syria without worrying about bandits or blockades, they carried letters of credit from a Venetian bank to a bank agent in Syria, who turned over the sum of money stipulated by the credit agreement.

Venice's trading success depended not only on the stability of the republic's currency, but also on its technical and military expertise as represented by another symbol of the city, the **Arsenal.** Located at the mouth of Venice's Grand Canal, the Arsenal equipped and repaired the republic's warships and its merchant vessels. During the Renaissance, the Arsenal had one of Europe's first industrial-style production lines, where hundreds of workers labored with saws, hammers, and brushes. The Arsenal featured prominently in the popular images of Venice. In the *Inferno,* Dante described it as a place of bubbling pitch and stifling heat. Inside the Arsenal, a warship could be completely built and outfitted in twenty-four hours, a remarkable achievement made pos-

sible because of the mobilization of a large number of skilled workers. Some five thousand workers were employed at the Arsenal at any given moment during the Renaissance, each one with specific skills. In one of the Arsenal's buildings, people made nothing but rope; in another, men and women made sails for the fleet.

The ships outfitted and repaired at the Arsenal were a point of Venetian pride and an example of Venetian ingenuity. The Venetians introduced the **galley** to western Europe, a unique vessel (between 120 and 150 feet long, carrying a crew of 100–200 men) employed for transporting cargo and conducting naval warfare. What made the galley special was its dual power system: it could travel under oar or sail power. When there was no wind or when the galley was leaving or entering a port, rowers propelled the ship forward. The majority of rowers on Venetian galleys were not slaves, but free men hired for the voyage. When the galley was farther out at sea and enjoying favorable winds, the oars were pulled in and the sails were raised.

The third symbol of Venice was the *Libro dell'Oro* (*Book of Gold*), a list of two hundred Venetian families compiled in 1297. The Venetians selected their political leaders from men over age twenty-five who could trace their lineage directly from one of the family names listed in the *Libro* and were therefore automatically accorded life-time membership in Venice's Great Council. The Great Council was used as a pool for constituting governmental subcommittees such as the Senate (which instituted policies), the College (which put Senate policies into action), and the Council of Ten (which oversaw Venice's security). Presiding over all these committees was the **doge,** the chief official selected to serve the republic for the remainder of his lifetime by a system so complicated that it was difficult for one family to control the process, although many old Venetian families managed to influence it. The doge's functions were largely ceremonial: he opened buildings, presided over Venetian ceremonies, and entertained visiting ambassadors. With a governmental apparatus so wide reaching and complex, Venice's political system limited the loopholes that could be exploited by a single family, as the Medici had done in Florence.

Venice's unique position, successful trade operations, and strong republican politics made careful diplomacy essential to the maintenance of Venetian serenity. Secure peace was as important to Venice's success in the world as its currency or the ships that departed from the Arsenal. In the Middle Ages, diplomacy had been a recognized but underused form of political interaction. Most nobles preferred to go to war rather than to sit and negotiate, and most medieval diplomatic negotiations came at the tail end of warfare when agreements had to be made about the division of territory and titles, and the marriage of noble children. Renaissance Venice preferred to exhaust diplomatic channels before undertaking a war. Ambassadors from Venice were among the first resident diplomats to take up positions at courts throughout Europe and the eastern Mediterranean. By 1500, virtually every royal court in Europe, northern Africa, and Asia Minor had a resident Venetian ambassador who attempted to keep the peace between the republic and its mercantile and military rivals.

In their own ways, Rome, Florence, and Venice were each archetypal Renaissance cities. Interested in the ancient past, intent on charting a new course for their city-states in European politics and culture, devoted to the Roman Catholic faith, intrigued by the cultural traditions of other peoples, and eager to participate in the new secular possibilities of trade, finance, and exploration, these cities were vital, vibrant, and competitive urban centers during a period of cultural and political transition.

The Colonial Reach of Venice

None of the great Renaissance city-states had greater geographic reach than Venice. It achieved security and prosperity by expanding its territorial holdings along the northeastern tip of the Italian peninsula, around the Adriatic coastline, and toward Asia Minor. Venice won many of those territories from the Ottoman Turks, who

had launched a campaign to extend their territories into western Europe. In 1414, Venice defeated an Ottoman army at Gallipoli and went on to conquer Morea, Cyprus, and Crete. Despite these victories, the republic of Venice was almost constantly in conflict with Ottoman forces in the fifteenth century and struggled to remain the preeminent power of the central Mediterranean and Adriatic Seas.

Renaissance Venice was also the port city through which most eastern goods, peoples, and ideas flowed west. Venice was the only European nation at the time with colonies, a string of small islands extending toward Asia Minor that, along with a block of territory at the very top of the peninsula, made up the maritime republic of Venice. Venice's colonies served important commercial and military functions, for they made it easier for the republic to protect vital sea lanes through which its goods and naval forces traveled. The colonies also made it easier to provision merchant and naval ships because they could dock at Venetian ports on their way east. Venice's early colonizing efforts, along with its long-standing relations with the Byzantine Empire and other political entities in the Adriatic, Black, and Mediterranean Seas, set the republic apart from the other states of Italy.

The Ottoman Empire as a Renaissance State

One of Venice's most important trading links was with the Ottoman Empire. The Ottomans, a frontier people, had established their power along the Aegean coast (Map 11.3). They absorbed different elements from the traditions of Islamic civilization, the Byzantine Empire based in Constantinople, and the Seljuk Empire of western Anatolia. Though officially rooted in the Muslim faith, the Ottomans tolerated other "peoples of the book"— Christians and Jews—living within their borders. They viewed the followers of Muhammad, Christ, and Moses as branches of a single family tree.

Still there were considerable differences in religious interpretation and historical mission between the West and East, and within their territories. Western Christian rulers had expelled or, in the case of Spain, were about to expel Jews and Muslims from their lands. The Ottomans had conquered Greece and imposed higher taxes on Jewish and Christian residents and barred Jews and Christians from wearing certain types of clothing and adornment. A case could be made that the Ottoman Empire was more cosmopolitan and tolerant than western Europe was at the time. The Ottomans, for instance, were willing to allow religious minorities to coexist with the Sunni Muslim majority, and they employed Jews and Christians to help them rule their multiethnic empire. It was not unusual to find Jews among the sultan's advisors, Christian merchants in Ottoman cities, or western military experts supplying tools and techniques to the Ottoman army and navy. Mahomet II hired Christians from Greece and from the Italian port cities of Venice and Genoa to build ships for his navy. A Hungarian engineer

MAP 11.3 | **The Spread of the Ottoman Empire, 1326–1566**

The Ottoman Empire was a powerful presence in the Mediterranean world, controlling access to the east and managing goods from Asia moving west. The effect on western Europeans was to block their own eastward movement, essentially boxing them in. The Ottomans arose in the shadow cast by Constantinople, first conquering lands that had belonged to the Byzantine Empire, then moving into the Middle East, northern Africa, and eastern Europe. *Why was the Byzantine Empire no match for the Ottomans, geographically or historically? How did Venice deal with the Ottoman presence? What was the likely long-term impact of the Ottoman Empire on the many Europes of the late fifteenth and early sixteenth centuries?*

provided Mahomet with the designs for the large cannon with which he took Constantinople in 1453. Mahomet, with his cosmopolitan city, foreign advisors, trade with Europe, interest in Greek culture, and ability to speak six languages, was in his own way a Renaissance prince.

Renaissance Cosmopolitanism in Big Europe

The cultural mixing and blending that was a hallmark of the Ottoman Empire affected western Europeans as well as the Turks. In the increasingly cosmopolitan world of the Mediterranean, it was not unusual for Italian princes and merchants to own slaves they had acquired through Venetian middlemen from Istanbul and other Ottoman ports. Both Cosimo de' Medici and his son, Giovanni de' Medici, purchased Circassian slaves in Venice to be their mistresses. Andrea Gritti, a Venetian nobleman who was elected doge in 1523, had a wife and son at home and four more sons in Istanbul who had been born to a faithful Turkish mistress who served as his official hostess and partner while he was conducting business and

diplomatic missions in the city. Merchants often lived for significant portions of their adult lives in eastern cities. One such merchant, Lorenzo Contarini, lived in Damascus in 1437, Beirut in 1440, and Syria between 1451 and 1455. Cosmopolitan contacts of this sort brought West and East closer together, expanding the cultural footprint of Europe.

An additional connection was made by Greek and Italian intellectuals. Scholars in the Byzantine Empire and Italy believed that they shared a tradition of Greek and Latin philosophy and letters that stretched back to antiquity. When Constantinople fell to the Ottoman Turks, Byzantine scholars were quick to lament what they viewed as the final collapse of Greek civilization. Some of them fled west with their rare manuscripts and fluent command of the Greek language, and were received warmly in Italy by a growing critical mass of humanist scholars.

Venice was the most exotic city in Europe. The city's cosmopolitan residents and their enormous wealth were celebrated in works of art and scholarship. Venetian architecture is the best example of its exotic, hybrid culture since it blends western European, Muslim, and Byzantine styles. The city's buildings often included minarets, towers, and elaborate decorative details. These buildings provided an exotic backdrop for the lavish public ceremonies and celebrations that glorified Venetian life and the republic. The diversity of Venetian life and commerce was enhanced by its large population of Jews. The Jews of Venice were known for their learning, their wealth, and their language skills, all of which were important attributes in a cosmopolitan center as rich as Venice's. Venetian Jews attended beautiful synagogues in the city, and even the doges visited them to hear the rabbis speak about education and faith.

Humanism and Individualism

The city-states of northern Italy established the material and political conditions for the Italian Renaissance. Its defining feature, however, has always seemed to be the remarkable flowering of high culture that occurred as a result of prosperity. Yet Petrarch, the father of humanism, began the movement outside Italy. The Middle Ages had always had a strong humanist tradition of interest in the Latin classics, most pronounced in the ninth and twelfth centuries, though that tradition was driven underground by the rise of universities and scholasticism in the thirteenth century. It was against the aridity of scholasticism—all syllogisms and *summae*—that Petrarch reacted so strongly. The first phase of the humanist movement in Italy was concerned with the recovery of the Latin classics, the ancient Roman past, and the perfection of superior (that is, classical) forms of Latin literary expression. The second, which took over after 1430, was more concerned with the recovery of the ancient Greek language and Greek classics, thus completing the agenda to recover the Greco-Roman past and to improve living humans in the light of Europe's towering classical past.

What was Italian Renaissance humanism, and how important and transformative was it?

The humanists were Renaissance scholars who prized a course of study based on the mastery of ancient languages; the close, unmediated reading of ancient texts (that is, without medieval glosses and commentaries); and the emulation of ancient literary, artistic, and philosophical models. Based on a deep and historicizing interest in the classical past, this set of interests came to be known as humanism or **Renaissance humanism.** Not only did the classical past shape Renaissance humanism, but Renaissance humanists shaped the classical past, giving it contour and definition. There was some pushback against the humanist agenda. One Franciscan friar stoutly denied that the fathers of the church had had any use for classical authors; the humanists dismissed such opponents as barbarians.

Along with **Renaissance individualism,** or the belief that human beings occupy a special place in the created world and are capable of extraordinary achievements, humanism supplied one of the foundational cornerstones of Renaissance cultural and intellectual life. While it is common to see the development of humanism and individualism in the West as a product of exchanges between the classical past and the Renaissance present, both humanism and individualism were also influenced by the interplay in the period between the West and the East and by new trends in European societies and Italian cities.

The Humanist Course of Study

Petrarch and his humanist friends hunted down copies of Latin authors such as Cicero that had long lain on the library shelves of Europe's monasteries. They plumbed the works of the great poets, Virgil, Horace, and Ovid, for stylistic leads and elevated forms of expression. Petrarch became so passionately attached to the eminent literary figures of classical Rome that he wrote a series of *Letters to the Ancient Dead* addressed to the likes of Cicero, Horace, Virgil, Homer, and other famous figures, in which he expressed his fervent wish that he had lived among them rather than in his own corrupt times. Humanism was more than just a literary agenda; it was a moral one. Petrarch and his humanist friends imitated Cicero's Latin prose, but after Cicero's *Letters to Atticus* were found and revealed Cicero to be less than perfect (crafty and equivocating politician that he was), Petrarch ceased to idolize Cicero, much to the dismay of his Ciceronian friends. Petrarch may have loved Rome's golden past, but he pushed his contemporaries toward a more critical and historically exact appreciation of that golden past.

The second (or Greek) phase of the humanist movement benefited from the arrival of Greek scholars in Italy in 1439 at the opening of the General Church Council in Florence, when learned Greeks appeared as part of the entourage surrounding the Byzantine emperor and the Eastern Orthodox patriarch. Eminent Greek scholars such as Basilius Bessarion (later a cardinal) and Georgius Gemistus Plethon became established figures in the intellectual and cultural circles of Renaissance Italy. It is hard for us to imagine the pure excitement aroused by the arrival of Greek scholars and Greek manuscripts in Italy, the intellectual ferment caused by the first lectures on Plato, or the eagerness that Italian scholars felt when they first caught a glimpse of a Greek text that had never before been seen in western Europe. Italian noblemen, politicians, scholars, and artists avidly followed each new development and responded enthusiastically to new courses of study concentrating on Greek language and literature. One young humanist in France spent three hours on his wedding day studying Greek, somewhat to the consternation of his bride. Cosimo de' Medici, after hearing Plethon lecture on Plato, was inspired to sink a considerable amount of his wealth into the foundation of a Platonic Academy in Florence. "I myself intend

The Jewish Tradition in the Italian Renaissance

In 1516, Venetian leaders decided to segregate the city's Jewish residents in a specific area known as the *geto nuovo* (meaning "the new foundry," where slag or metal waste was deposited). It is from this Venetian residential and industrial district that the West derived the word **ghetto,** meaning an area segregated by race or religion. Jews had been expelled from England, France, and Spain at various points in the Middle Ages. The decision to segregate Venice's Jewish residents, which was a milder form of those religious expulsions, came after centuries of toleration and inclusion and marked a change in the official treatment of Jews.

During the Renaissance, Jews could be found in cities throughout the Italian peninsula. The region's political fragmentation was helpful in establishing resilient Jewish communities because, even if they were expelled temporarily from one region, they were often welcomed by the next. The largest population of Jews in western Europe during the fifteenth century was in Rome, the center of Roman Catholicism, where they played a critical role in teaching Hebrew to church figures studying the Old Testament. After 1437, when the Medici came to power, Jews were welcomed back to Florence, where they remained prominent in banking circles so long as the Medici family remained in the city. Briefly expelled while Florence was under the influence of Savonarola, they returned again to the city with the Medici in 1512. In Venice, the Jewish population increased steadily throughout the fifteenth and sixteenth centuries.

Renaissance Jews led double lives, one among Italian Christians as bankers specializing in loaning capital to princes, politicians, and merchants and the other within their Jewish communities as teachers, scholars, and neighbors. Affluent Jewish banking families like the Volterras

of Florence became targets of hatred among their less prosperous Christian neighbors and faced an omnipresent risk of expulsion and resettlement. On the other hand, Renaissance Jews were avid travelers, who shuttled between Italy and the Holy Land, where they made pilgrimages to Jerusalem and visited sites of religious significance. Pilgrimages helped to balance their experiences as a disenfranchised and marginalized population within Europe, bringing them into contact with other Jews from Europe and the Middle East and with places of holy and spiritual importance to their religion.

In addition to appreciating their banking and mercantile expertise, learned Christians looked upon Renaissance Jews as a deeply learned people. Because Jews tended to know not only Hebrew, but also Latin and Arabic, they were able to communicate with both the ruling Muslim elite and the conquered Christian population in Muslim parts of Spain. Despite the Christian interest in the Jewish intellectual tradition, Jews were formally barred from attending the west's universities after the Council of Basel in 1434. These strictures were largely ignored by Italian schools. As early as 1409 a Jew, named Leone Bendiati, received his doctorate from the University of Padua. In the faculties of Italian universities, there were Jews who taught Hebrew, astronomy, medicine, and mathematics. One of the Italian Renaissance's most illustrious scholars, Giovanni Pico della Mirandola, learned Hebrew and the esoteric Jewish wisdom of the kabbalah at the University of Padua from Elia del Medigo (c. 1458–c. 1493). Del Medigo is an example of the intellectual versatility possessed by many Jewish scholars of the Renaissance. He was born on the island of Candia in the Venetian colony of Crete, and translated Greek works of Aristotle and the Arabic philosopher Averroës into Latin for Renaissance scholars. Fluent in Hebrew, Latin, Greek, and Arabic, he studied medicine along with the traditional teachings of his faith and may once have attended classes at the University of Padua. By 1480, Del Medigo had made a home in the nearby city of Venice, where he taught philosophy to the children of the Venetian elite. Del Medigo's life story exemplifies the contradictions of the Jewish experience in Renaissance Italy. Prized as an intellectual, but marginalized and vulnerable because of his faith, Del Medigo knew nobles, clerics, scholars, and poets but was never fully welcomed into Christian circles.

QUESTIONS | *What other groups were disadvantaged by the Italian Renaissance? Why might the opportunities for Jews have been better in cosmopolitan Renaissance Italy than in the rest of Europe?*

The Jewish Ghetto in Venice

to pursue immortality through such study," Cassandra Fedele wrote. Her imagination was stirred by the promise of humanism and the brave new world of classical texts that she was encountering.

While humanism emphasized the study of classical languages and literature, it also spurred renewed interest in European vernacular tongues. Three late medieval Florentines—Dante Alighieri, Petrarch, and Giovanni Boccaccio—all believed that their native Tuscan dialect possessed as much beauty and literary potential as any ancient language. Those three writers led the way in inspiring humanists to study both vernacular and classical literature. Dante wrote on the eloquence of the vernacular language, penned courtly love lyrics and the sweeping *Divine Comedy* in Italian, and published a polemical political treatise (*Monarchia*). Boccaccio knew Petrarch and was so inspired by his passion for antiquity that he set himself the task of learning Greek and collecting as many ancient manuscripts as he could.

The followers of Dante, Petrarch, and Boccaccio were particularly interested in what Cicero (106–43 BCE) had called the *studia humanitatis*: grammar, rhetoric, poetry, literature, and moral philosophy or ethics. By the fifteenth century, many people perceived the *studia humanitatis* as standing in sharp contrast to scholasticism and the intellectual curriculum of the medieval university, which combined the mastery of Aristotelian logic with the study of theology. Although scholasticism was also based on the study of ancient texts, the approach that medieval scholars took to those texts was not as historically sensitive as the one taken by the humanists, who regarded ancient texts as textual artifacts that needed to be carefully preserved and critically studied. The Renaissance recognized the historical otherness of ancient texts.

All humanists began their training with an intensive study of classical Latin, for without Latin it was impossible to read most modern or ancient texts, to correspond with scholars in other cities, or to compose the elaborate prose that was considered the hallmark of the educated individual. Renaissance humanists did not stop their language training with Latin, but proceeded to study the other two ancient languages of the Bible and classical world: Hebrew and Greek.

Reading Classical Literature

After learning ancient languages, a humanist might spend the remainder of his life reading and explicating classical texts. Manuscript hunters such as Poggio Bracciolini scoured old European monasteries and contacted refugees from Constantinople to obtain ancient texts for Renaissance humanist readers. In 1415 at Cluny, Bracciolini found several orations of Cicero that were believed to be lost, and the following year at St. Gall in Switzerland, Bracciolini found a complete manuscript of the Roman rhetorician Quintilian's *Education of an Orator,* which

became the Renaissance's most widely used rhetoric textbook. Bracciolini did more than just collect ancient manuscripts. As a humanist, he tried to determine whether they were authentic and to date them more precisely. This historical attitude toward texts became vital as more manuscripts entered into circulation and were systematically studied by humanists.

Hundreds of ancient texts were identified during the Renaissance, but none were more important than the works of the philosopher Plato, which had largely been unavailable to scholars in the medieval West. When Plethon attended the council of 1439, he reintroduced the works of the ancient philosopher to Italian audiences through his lectures. One of Plethon's most avid students was Marsilio Ficino, the small, hunch-backed son of Cosimo de' Medici's personal physician. Although his father had hoped that his son would follow in his footsteps and become a doctor, Ficino's wide-ranging intellect kept him from settling on one subject of study. When Ficino's brilliance came to Cosimo's attention, he employed Ficino in 1463 to translate all the recently recovered works of Plato from Greek into Latin in order to make them available to a wider audience. It took Ficino six years to complete the monumental task.

In recognition of Ficino's accomplishments and expertise, Cosimo put him in charge of the Platonic Academy he housed in a Medici villa outside Florence, where the humanist presided over scholarly conversations and entertained visiting philosophers, scholars, lawyers, businessmen, and poets. In 1474, Ficino published an influential synthesis of Platonic and Christian ideas, the *Platonic Theology,* in an attempt to find the hidden unity among the diverse ancient authors and opinions that were beginning to overwhelm humanist scholars. Ficino next turned from Plato to the works attributed to a legendary wise man known as Hermes Trismegistus. Hermetic texts blended ancient Egyptian, Neoplatonic, and early Christian ideas and reinforced Ficino's belief that there was a single, unified core of ideas in ancient philosophy and theology just waiting to be discovered.

Civic Humanism and a New Sense of History

Once Renaissance humanists had learned Latin, Greek, and maybe even some Hebrew and had steeped themselves in the texts that men such as Bracciolini and Ficino were making available, questions were raised about what humanists should do with their learning. Humanists were quick to respond that the *studia humanitatis* was meant to do more than just teach students more languages. The curriculum should also prepare ideal citizens, trained to be both eloquent and virtuous and to emulate the examples of heroic behavior from the classical past.

Fifteenth-century humanists applied their new learning to improving educational standards. Pier Paolo Vergerio in a series of books advocated a form of liberal education that balanced the grammatical and language skills of the teacher against the natural abilities and interests of students. He also emphasized physical education and thought about which sports or games would exercise which parts of the body. Vergerio was interested in developing the whole person and designed programs for those destined for a military life. At Mantua, Vittorino da Feltre established a school called the Casa Jocosa ("happy house") in 1423 that taught both rich and poor boys a rounded Renaissance educational program broken into three parts: religious training, classical learning, and military training. Vittorino was keen to demonstrate in a practical way that Christianity and the classics were not at odds. His was a Christian humanism.

The application of humanist thought to political and social problems is known as **civic humanism,** and it came to the fore as humanists gained confidence that ancient ideals might be used to reform and enlighten their communities. Their model for civic humanism was Cicero, who was thought to be the embodiment of virtuous dedication for the greater good. The chief civic humanist of the period was Leonardo Bruni. A Florentine from a modest family, Bruni studied at the University of Florence and became a language tutor in the Medici household. During his lifetime, he held a number of positions in the government and in each he was guided by his humanist ideas about what constituted the civic good. Bruni inspired his fellow Florentines to follow models of ancient literature to better craft their written and spoken work, pointing out that Cicero was important not only for what he said, but also for how he said it.

A new emphasis on the importance of recent history flowed from the *studia humanitatis* and civic humanism. Bruni wrote a *History of the Florentine People* (1442), modeled after the ancient histories of Livy, which explored the significance of both ancient and more recent political events. Bruni's book focuses on the machinations of actors motivated not by piety or the lack of it (as had often been the issue in medieval histories), but by their worldly pursuit of power, money, glory, and revenge. Humanist scholars of the Renaissance tended to exaggerate their distance from the Middle Ages and to disregard the debts they owed to their immediate predecessors. At the same time, they were sharply aware that a vast temporal and cultural gulf separated their world from that of the ancient Greeks and Romans. Whereas Christian scholars of the medieval period divided human history into two periods (the pagan world before the birth of Christ and the Christian era), Renaissance humanists divided history into three periods: a period of classical antiquity that ended with the sack of Rome in 410; a middle age (*medium aevum*) that stretched from the fall of the Roman Empire until the fourteenth or fifteenth cen-

tury; and the present, when the legacies of classical antiquity were being rediscovered and renewed.

With the humanists' new sense of history came problems of interpretation. They discovered evidence that ancient authors and philosophers had not always agreed and had not always been admirable human beings, and other evidence indicated that some ancient texts had been altered and corrupted over the centuries. Humanists, therefore, sought to return to the purest, oldest examples of the texts they were reading. This *ad fontes* spirit, which means, literally, a return "to the sources," informed the work of many Renaissance humanists, including Lorenzo Valla's investigation of the *Donation of Constantine* for his patron, King Alfonso. The pen and the humanist spirit of textual criticism produced a new sense of the importance of the learned individual in society. Humanism empowered humanists.

Individualism

Individualism, like *humanism*, is a term that can have many definitions. As used in relation to the Italian Renaissance, individualism refers not just to the older sense that humans occupied a central and important place in the created world between the divine world of the angels in heaven and the mindless life of the animals on earth, but also to the dynamic potential of individuals to grow, learn, and achieve. Vasari's treatment of Renaissance artists focused on individuals in the act of creating and accomplishing great things.

The development of Renaissance individualism is linked closely to another humanist from Florence, the nobleman Giovanni Pico della Mirandola. At age fourteen, Pico began his formal university studies at the University

Three Great Lights of Florentine Humanism A fresco depiction by Cosimo Rosselli of Pico della Mirandola (the wonder boy of the late Italian Renaissance), Marsilio Ficino (the Florentine Platonist), and Angelo Poliziano (the poet and classicist), three leading lights of the Florentine Renaissance, front and center in the painting.

of Bologna. Eventually, his interests led him to the Universities of Padua and Florence, where he met and became the pupil of Marsilio Ficino. Under Ficino's guidance, Pico became convinced by his teacher's belief that there was a philosophical unity behind ancient ideas that could unite pagan and Christian beliefs. Unlike Ficino, however, Pico believed that ancient Jewish and Islamic ideas should be included along with the theology and philosophy of ancient Greece, Rome, and Christianity. He began to study Hebrew and Arabic in an effort to expand the number of ancient texts he was able to consider. In 1486, his studies resulted in a remarkable, if pretentious, set of nine hundred theses about philosophy and theology known as the *Conclusiones,* which he wanted to debate in public in Rome. Church authorities prevented the event when they realized how sympathetic Pico was toward Jewish and Muslim philosophy and theology.

Pico wrote a brief treatise to accompany his nine hundred conclusions known as the *Oration on the Dignity of Man.* In the *Oration,* Pico argues that each individual is a creature of importance and dignity because each human being stands at a midpoint between the divine heavens and the corrupt earth. But, unlike all other creatures, humans have the God-given capacity for self-invention and unlimited self-development and self-realization. We are the only free agents of creation. For Italian Renaissance humanists, individualism meant that every person—and every intellect—was a precious part of the divine plan and should be cherished and nurtured. Cassandra Fedele, who shared Pico's appreciation of the power of individualism, maintained that every individual and not just the philosophers, but even the most ignorant man, recognized and admitted that reason is what separates humans from the animals. An individual's ability to maneuver between the world of the senses and the world of the intellect was seen by Pico, Cassandra, and other humanists as a gift that would lead humanity to a more moral way of life and to a greater understanding of the natural and divine worlds.

Italian Renaissance Art

Humanism was based on the study of languages and classical texts and individualism depended on a par-

What were the chief characteristics of Italian Renaissance art?

ticular application of human reason to life. Renaissance art was not so very different in capturing the tenor of the age, its underlying principles and purposes. The moment when God reaches out from heaven to touch the finger of Adam, as depicted in Michelangelo Buonarroti's fresco on the Sistine Chapel ceiling, is in harmony with Pico's belief in the dignity and importance of the individual. But we need to remember that Michelangelo's finely modeled human forms evoke the classical sculptures he had studied. Just as humanists admired ancient works of literature, so Renais-

sance artists sought to learn from and emulate classical works of art. To some of these artists, medieval painting and sculpture seemed stiff and one-dimensional when compared to lifelike classical art. The ancient mosaics, frescoes, and sculptures they admired were naturalistic and infused with classical ideas of due proportion, harmony, and symmetry. But Renaissance artists were not slavish imitators of ancient things. They had new ideas and made their art in new ways and with new techniques that were alien to the ancient world. Renaissance artists introduced four new ways of achieving their artistic visions: through the use of contrasting light and shadow (**chiaroscuro**) to shade figures and give them a sense of three-dimensionality; the mastery of **linear perspective,** which gave paintings a sense of depth; the use of paints that had an oil base; and the close, almost clinical observation of both the natural world and the human body. Nor were Renaissance artists overawed by the classical past. They thought that they could both equal and even surpass ancient monuments, which reflected the confidence of their Renaissance individualism.

Living Renaissance Art

Renaissance artists were not trained in universities or libraries, but in urban workshops where knowledge was handed down from master to apprentice according to the medieval craft tradition. Most Renaissance artists were of humble background, the sons of shopkeepers and artisans. Few peasants and few nobles made art. Michelangelo, coming from patrician stock, was an exception, and his family disapproved of his occupational choice. In Renaissance Italy, manual work was less valued than military service or scholarly pursuits, but a few great artists were seen as individuals of genius and talent and commanded handsome commissions and rewards. The emperor made Gentile Bellini of Venice, the painter of the procession for the dying boy in Venice, a count; and Raphael was led by the pope to believe that he would be made a cardinal. Most artists, however, were still regarded as mere artisans engaged in degrading manual labor, and some were considered social deviants. A fair number of them were. They acted out, some committing murders and assaults, as Benvenuto Cellini in his autobiography confessed that he had; and some had eccentric social habits. Donatello kept all his money in a basket hanging from the ceiling, allowing workers, friends, and family to take what they wanted.

What connected the historical and economic worlds of the Italian Renaissance with artists and the efflorescence of culture was patronage. Who paid for art, what did they want, and what was the relationship of the artist and the patron? The Middle Ages chiefly had religious and royal art because the church and kings commanded it. In northern Italy in the fifteenth century, with its prosperous cities, ambitious rulers, wealthy merchants, and civic and religious institutions, new patrons were in play. Vasari explained that to succeed in Florence, artists needed to be clever, critical, and competitive. They were in intense competition with each other for commissions and reliable patrons. Literary humanism was not strictly a paying proposition until the sixteenth century, but visual artists and makers of music sold their services and their creations. Yet at the end of his life, Donatello was destitute, until Piero de' Medici granted him a farm. Many artists had to deal with patrons who delayed payment. Both Raphael and Michelangelo were owed large sums of money by their patron-popes. A few artists did become rich and enjoyed paid positions within their patrons' households, but most were happy to settle for regular employment in a thriving workshop. As an apprentice, Michelangelo was paid 32 lire a year, at a time when a Florentine servant made 40 lire a year, a Venetian soldier 150 lire a year, a bank manager in Florence close to 600 lire a year, and a Venetian cardinal around 140,000 lire a year. Still it was not a bad salary for a fourteen-year-old boy just starting out on his career. It was, however, held against both the rich and the poor artist that they labored for financial gain, to which Leonardo responded, so did his patrons.

Artists were sought out by powerful patrons, including rulers such as Cosimo de' Medici, by Renaissance popes and church figures, by wealthy merchants, by cities, and by religious confraternities to paint commemorative portraits, design frescoes, and sculpt statues with elaborate allegorical themes using characters from classical literature and scenes from the Bible. As the most celebrated artists traveled to princely courts and between the rich cities of Florence, Rome, Milan, and Venice to consult on art commissions, their work began to command high prices and their status rose even higher in the eyes of their contemporaries. Owning a statue by Michelangelo or a painting by Raphael was considered a symbol of cultural refinement within princely circles. In contrast, we know the names of few medieval artists before the Late Middle Ages, little about their lives or the contours of their careers. Vasari's detailed and personalized biographies of artists reflect the Renaissance's cultural celebration of great art and its makers. A few of these artists became widely known and had outsized personalities. Michelangelo was known to be particularly prickly, once leaving Rome and the pope's employ because the pope's secretary had failed to grant him an instant audience with the pope. Leonardo was not much better, causing a scene in a bank one day when the clerk tried to pay him his monthly salary in small coins; he said he was no penny painter and quit working for his current patron.[1]

The Early Renaissance: Ghiberti, Donatello, and Masaccio

Some of the earliest artistic expressions of Renaissance ideas occurred in Florence. The wealthy Florentine elites saw commissioning art as a way to express their devotion to the church and to the republic, and entered into contracts with artists to complete public art projects to be displayed in the city's churches, public squares, and

Ghiberti's Gate of Paradise Scenes from the lives of Cain and Abel from the great bronze doors that Ghiberti made for the Baptistery of St. John, Florence.

government buildings. The city of Florence itself was a major patron of art, ordering works that would glorify and celebrate the city and its people.

Lorenzo Ghiberti achieved lasting fame when he won a contest to complete a massive set of decorated bronze doors for Florence's oldest building, the Baptistery of St. John. One set of doors had been completed by Andrea Pisano in 1329, but it was not until 1401 that the city announced that it was ready to commission the second set of doors. Seven artists competed for the honor, including distinguished artists with established reputations, but it was a relatively unknown twenty-one-year-old artist who received the commission. Ghiberti had impressed the judges with the vitality of his figures and the way that he made biblical stories come to dramatic life. Ghiberti established a workshop to train younger artists to help him in his work, but it still took over two decades before the twenty-eight bronze door panels were completed. Ghiberti was also a historian and an author committed to the ideals of humanism. He composed the first autobiography by an artist, a testament to his sense of the worth of the artist as an individual.

Donatello (c. 1386–1466) was one of Ghiberti's apprentices. Before going to work for Ghiberti, Donatello began as a goldsmith and excelled at low-relief carvings that were surprisingly lifelike. Donatello, like his master, was fascinated by history and traveled to Rome to engage in excavations of ancient ruins and detailed studies of surviving buildings such as the Pantheon. Donatello's most famous works are the five statues he carved for one of Florence's major landmarks, the Duomo's bell-tower. These five statues, especially those of the prophets Habacuc and Jeremiah, were modeled on statues of classical Roman orators, but have highly individualized faces and features. In 1430, Donatello was able to sculpt the first free-standing nude (a statue of the biblical hero David) since ancient times for his patron, Cosimo de' Medici.

Ghiberti and Donatello specialized in sculpture, but Florence was also home to many skilled painters. Chief among them in the early Renaissance was Masaccio, an artist famous for his frescoes. A devoted student of linear perspective, Masaccio was able to give rounded, three-dimensional forms to his human figures that made them appear strikingly realistic to early-fifteenth-century viewers. His most important commissions were religious, including the frescoes on the life of Saint Peter in the Brancacci family chapel in the church of Santa Maria del Carmine. Masaccio died a young man, his full potential unrealized, but he had a profound influence on later artists, including Leonardo, Michelangelo, and Raphael.

The High Renaissance: Leonardo, Michelangelo, and Raphael

As the fame of Florence's artists spread throughout the peninsula, along with word of their interest in classical models and their emphasis on the individual, Florentine artists were called upon by patrons outside the city who wanted to commission their work. Chief among those patrons were the popes, who commanded both resources and prestige. As a result, the next generation of Renaissance artists shuttled back and forth between Florence, Rome, and other Italian cities in search of commissions and new artistic opportunities.

Leonardo da Vinci (1452–1519) was born in a hillside town outside Florence, began his artistic career in the city, moved to Milan in 1482 to work for Ludovico Sforza, returned to Florence, worked again for the Sforza family in Milan, and then moved to Rome to work for the pope. He died in France in 1519, in service to his last patron, King Francis I. In every city, and with every patron, Leonardo showed an insatiable curiosity about the world around him. Everything from anatomy to engineering was a subject of interest to him, and his curiosity and ability to move easily between fields of study such as painting, sculpture, physiology, botany, armaments, and civic fortifications have made him the image of the archetypal "Renaissance Man." But Leonardo was far from a typical man of the Renaissance. For one thing, he did not receive a rigorous Renaissance education and never learned Latin and Greek, which hobbled his access to certain sophisticated circles of learning. Yet he has always

seemed an extraordinary example of what people are capable of achieving.

Leonardo's insatiable curiosity meant that he was not always an ideal employee. Renaissance princes and popes were accustomed to having their commissions completed on time and to their specifications. Leonardo left many projects unfinished, and his experiments with painting techniques often led to disastrous final results in frescoes (as in the case of his *Last Supper in Milan,* which began to deteriorate almost before the paint had dried). His constant search for something new to stimulate his active, brilliant mind made him restless and easily distracted. Despite these difficulties, Leonardo completed some of the most important and influential works of Renaissance art, including highly individualized portraits such as the *Mona Lisa* and paintings on religious themes such as the *Virgin of the Rocks,* which employed linear perspective and chiaroscuro painting techniques to great effect. He also left thousands of pages of notes written in his backward or mirror script,

Leonardo's Womb A page from Leonardo's notebooks on which he examined a fetus in the female womb and the nature of conception. Note Leonardo's distinctive backward or mirror writing, which as a left-handed writer he found easier to execute.

Seeing the Renaissance in a New Light

On the last day of December 1989, as television cameras whirled and photographers clicked, the world let out a collective gasp when one of the Renaissance's most cherished works of art, the frescoes of the Sistine Chapel ceiling at the Vatican, were publicly unveiled for the first time after a restoration program that began in 1981. Though work to restore the remaining frescoes on the walls of the chapel was not yet complete, the restored ceiling showed an image of Renaissance art that was very different from the subdued colors and shadowy chiaroscuro that centuries of visitors had known and come to love as they gazed sixty-five feet above the chapel floor at the details of the painted ceiling above. Bright colors, strong lines, and an almost garish use of oranges and greens characterized paintings that were very different from what students of the period had come to know and think about Michelangelo. They were seeing the Renaissance in an entirely new light, and they were not sure that they liked the result.

Michelangelo painted the frescoes that adorn the Vatican's Sistine Chapel between 1508 and 1512, and since that time they have become emblematic of the Italian Renaissance. Every inch of the ceiling is covered with images from the Old Testament, from the very first chapter of Genesis forward. Michelangelo did not lie on his back to paint the ceiling as popularly thought, but worked from a special scaffolding system that allowed him to reach over his head and lean back while painting. Still he complained that his sight never completely recovered from the experience. Michelangelo applied pigment to wet plaster, working quickly before the plaster dried and fixed the image.

Occasionally, he painted over or touched up the images that he had captured swiftly on the ceiling's surface. The pictures were large, bright, and colorful, painted to be seen by people standing far below on the chapel floor. As early as 1800, however, conditions inside the chapel had already obscured Michelangelo's masterpiece. Smoke from the candles used in religious ceremonies left a dull, sooty film on the walls and ceiling of the room. Leaky roof tiles let in water, which calcified into a hard, white crust in some places on the ceiling and stained others brown. Years of repair using varnishes and glue did damage, too, as the layers of later materials built up.

Not surprisingly, given the treasured status of the frescoes, an international team of conservation and art history experts was gathered to guide, supervise, and execute the project. They discussed and planned the restoration for three years between 1981 and 1984. Chemical analyses provided new insights into Michelangelo's fresco technique and revealed the extent of the damage. Once the work on the frescoes began, conservators worked on scaffolding that was modeled after Michelangelo's and made to fit into the support holes he had left in the walls so as to avoid further damage to the deteriorating ceiling.

The restoration of the Sistine ceiling frescoes was the subject of controversy from the moment the project was announced in 1981. One group of American art historians tried to halt the restoration process during its early stages, arguing that the layers of chiaroscuro that Michelangelo had applied to the frescoes were being removed. Others believed that Michelangelo had applied the layers of glue found on the ceiling's surface to deliberately tone down the bright pigments that he had applied to the wet plaster. Detractors hated the "ice-cream colors" revealed by the restoration and, though proponents of the restoration countered their claims by pointing out that the sophisticated coloration and brush techniques were monumental achievements, even today some people miss the older, more muted ceiling. Once the cameras had stopped rolling and the bright lights were turned off, however, the dimly lit chapel was far less garish than it had first appeared.

QUESTION | *What does the case of the restoration of Michelangelo's frescoes reveal about our expectations about the past and its art?*

Michelangelo's Painting of the Sistine Chapel Ceiling

which suggest the range of scientific and technical questions that interested him and of his extreme individualism.

Working in Florence and Rome at the same time as Leonardo was another great Renaissance artist, Michelangelo Buonarotti (1475–1564). Like Leonardo, Michelangelo was a man of wide-ranging interests and awe-inspiring talents. He could paint and sculpt, and was a talented architect, poet, and engineer. Michelangelo was born in Arezzo in Tuscany, and was trained as an artist in Florence before his talents were noticed and brought to the attention of Lorenzo de' Medici, who oversaw his education and introduced him to prominent philosophers and intellectuals such as Pico della Mirandola and Marsilio Ficino. In the first phase of his career, he divided his time between completing projects for patrons in Florence and Rome, such as the Pietá and the statue of David. In 1505, Pope Julius II invited Michelangelo to Rome, where he embarked on an ambitious fresco cycle for the Vatican's Sistine Chapel.

Despite Michelangelo's considerable success, the most popular artist of the age was his contemporary, Raphael (1483–1520). Born in Urbino, Raphael at the age of twenty-five was commissioned by Pope Julius II to paint frescoes in the Vatican palace. Raphael's frescoes focused on both classical and religious themes, and established him as a serious painter who adhered to his patron's artistic vision and fulfilled his contracts. In 1514, he was appointed the Vatican architect, and the following year was given responsibility for cataloguing and conserving the Vatican's growing collection of ancient Roman sculpture. The high style of Italian Renaissance art faded after the political troubles of the 1520s, succeeded by Mannerism and then Baroque, which turned away from the strict rules of classical proportion, moderation, perspective, and background.

The Spread of Renaissance Ideas: The European Renaissance

The Renaissance began in Italy, but by the late fifteenth century its ideals, interests, and techniques had touched many parts of Europe and transformed the movement into a European (or, as it is sometimes misleadingly called, northern) Renaissance. Renaissance ideas traveled outward along trade routes from Florence, Rome, and Venice; they spread between artists in Italy, the Netherlands, France, and Germany; and they were adopted when European princes and patrons began to see the advantages associated with a political toolbox that included force, diplomacy, espionage, and cultural competition. The reach of Renaissance values was extensive. Matthias Corvinus, the king of Hungary (r. 1458–1490), was not only a Renaissance ruler who eventually became the king of Bohemia and duke of Austria, but he also knew Italian, assembled Renaissance humanists at his court, established a vast library, and lived in a Renaissance palace. While the Italian Renaissance and its individual civic expressions served as models for other European rulers, countries, and kingdoms, the wider European Renaissance took on its own regional and continental flavors. Just as the unique conditions of the Italian region had shaped the Renaissance's primary motivations and expressions, other areas of Europe put their own distinctive stamp on these developments. The Renaissance proved to be a set of possibilities, interpreted differently in different places and times, but sharing a new, more critical and systematic way of doing things and viewing the world.

In general, the European Renaissance (which included significant developments in the arts, literature, and education in Germany, the Netherlands, England, France, and Spain) began to unfold at a later date than did the Italian Renaissance. Most historians detect an interest in humanism and individualism outside Italy as early as 1450, and underscore the importance that artists, church leaders, and noble patrons played in promoting Renaissance values and ideas. European artists, who traveled to Italy to study art and learn from Italian workshops, were particularly sensitive to the new changes they encountered and then carried home, where they affected and mixed with the native cultural styles of France, the Netherlands, and Germany. Despite similarities with the original Northern Italian Renaissance, the European Renaissance is often described as having a more overtly religious cast to it, as humanists outside of Italy applied the *ad fontes* spirit of humanism to the church and its texts, teachings, and doctrines. The wider European interest in commerce also made Europeans eager to explore how the beliefs in individualism and the tenets of their religious faith might work with and justify business and trade. The European Renaissance was, however, not merely an extension and adaptation of dominant Italian Renaissance ideas. It was a living and evolving expression of new ideas and tendencies that came to include Italy as one of many voices.

Commerce and Urban Life in the European Renaissance

As in Italy, much of the energy of the wider European Renaissance was associated with urban centers. In northern Europe, the chief Renaissance city was Bruges in Flanders, the capital city of the dukes of Burgundy. Bruges had become enormously wealthy through commerce and trade. The patronage opportunities provided by the Burgundian court and by the city's wealthy elites attracted artists and intellectuals from all over Europe. The traffic was in both directions. Italian artists and architects were in great demand, and Flemish artists traveled to the Italian peninsula to learn of the new artistic styles being developed there.

> What, where, and when was the European Renaissance? How and why did it differ from earlier cultural developments?

Bruges, like Florence, was a city associated with luxury goods, including textiles, wine, and spices. Trading companies from Genoa and Venice had long established merchant colonies that linked the Flemish port to the trade routes of the Mediterranean. From Bruges, Mediterranean goods flowed to the other cities in northern Europe, where they were traded for furs, fish, and grain. So much international trade took place in Bruges that currency exchanges and banks emerged early there and were run from its *Bourse* (exchange).

Fifteenth-century Bruges was home to the court of Philip the Good, the duke of Burgundy. An ally of King Henry V of England, Philip was known for his glittering court and chivalric ideals. Burgundian clothing styles, tapestries, metal goods, and jewelry set the standard for high fashion throughout Europe. The duke of Burgundy was known as a generous and discriminating patron who advanced the careers of important artists. He was also a scholar interested in the translation of classical texts and the production of literature in the Flemish vernacular. But the pinnacle of Bruges as a center of the European Renaissance passed after Philip's death.

Not only had the Duchy of Burgundy been annexed by France in 1477, but around 1500 the port of Bruges lost some of its navigability due to silting. As a consequence, large merchant and cargo ships looked elsewhere to dock and unload their cargoes. Antwerp and then Amsterdam became the ports of choice for ships from the Mediterranean. As money and trade went elsewhere, so too did the energy of the continuing European Renaissance.

European Renaissance Art

The artists of the European Renaissance absorbed stylistic elements from Italy, but they also made major new contributions to the development of western European art. The most significant of these developments was the formulation of oil-based paints. By blending pigments into linseed oil, instead of the egg white mixture used in previous centuries, Flemish artists were able to manipulate their paints over extended periods of time, adding layers of detail and subtle shading that made their works seem to shimmer with life. Oil paints were particularly revolutionary when it came to portraiture, as the new pigments were capable of capturing fine physiological details and could more effectively represent skin tones and fabrics.

Two important artists of the European Renaissance, Jan van Eyck (1395–1441) and Rogier van der Weyden (c. 1400–1464), exemplify the exchange of Renaissance ideas and demonstrate how Italian Renaissance concepts and techniques influenced and were influenced by other Europeans. Van Eyck was a court artist who served Duke Philip of Burgundy. In addition to painting important commissions for his patron, he also conducted diplomatic missions. Van Eyck traveled to the Iberian Peninsula to conduct wedding negotiations for his ruler and patron. He was a master of the use of the new Renais-

The Arnolfini Wedding Scene Jan van Eyck's oil painting on a wooden panel (1434) is the subject of endless interpretation. Is it even a wedding portrait as popularly thought? Though the woman may seem pregnant, all indications are that she is not. The mirror on the rear wall shows the couple in reverse and two mysterious figures in a doorway. The painting abounds with symbols: cast-off shoes, lap dog, and oranges on the window sill.

sance oil paints, specializing in painting religious works that included finely detailed portraits of his patrons. Van der Weyden also painted important religious commissions for patrons that included donor portraits. His work became well known in Italy after he traveled to Rome in 1450 to celebrate Pope Nicholas V's jubilee year. In Italy, he accepted the patronage of the Medici family and lectured on the use of oil paints. After Van der Weyden's death, his style influenced later Renaissance artists in the Netherlands, England, and Spain.

The portraits of Van der Weyden and Van Eyck, including the famous Arnolfini wedding portrait, with its enigmatic wall mirror, are vivid expressions of individualism. What made them so arresting was their detailed treatment of the human face and body. At the same time, Van Eyck and his successors lavished attention on the depiction of natural and manufactured objects. The juxtaposition of religious themes with individualized portraits and carefully rendered material objects became hallmarks of European Renaissance art.

The Print Revolution of the European Renaissance

Just as art and artists circulated in Renaissance Europe, so too did works of literature. Prior to 1450, these works were copied laboriously by hand onto parchment. Large books such as the Bible took hundreds of hours and hundreds of animal skins to manufacture. As a result, they were rare and expensive, and were locked away in private or church collections. Their content was also subject to variability because scribes (sometimes expert, sometimes incompetent) working for long hours were prone to make mistakes as they copied. Yet no real alternative to manual copying existed in the West.

Johann Gutenberg, a German gem-cutter and goldsmith, was not a humanist, but he had an idea that would shake the Late Middle Ages and European Renaissance. His "automatic writing" was a technique for producing medieval manuscripts more quickly and in greater number. As inventive and ambitious as Gutenberg was, he was not a particularly good businessman. In 1438, he and his partners invested their capital and industry in making 32,000 trinkets with small mirrors set in the middle to capture the holy rays of the saints' relics that would be on display the next year in Aachen. Unfortunately, Gutenberg and his partners had the year wrong. The Aachen relics would not be revealed to the public and pilgrims until 1440, and Gutenberg had invested his capital and energy a year too soon.

After the failed venture in manufacturing potential contact relics, Gutenberg returned to Mainz to work on what he called "mysterious" or "secret arts." These were techniques for printing text mechanically. Gutenberg may not have been a humanist, but he realized that there were now more readers in the cities of Europe and so a growing market for available and affordable books. His great achievement was to perfect a technology for the mass production of books. He invented little. The Chinese had already pioneered the use of rag paper (which was spread west by Islam), block printing, and the printing press. But the obstacle to printing in Europe was a character set that required a large number of small letters and signs that needed to be set, reset, and replaced when broken. Gutenberg, the metal worker, came up with a hand mold, a portable device for casting type on the spot. He and his workers also perfected the use of an olive or screw press, movable type, a suitable ink, and the alignment of characters so that they made the proper contact with the paper surface. By 1450, Gutenberg had already tried printing some small texts and a Latin grammar book for his humanist market. He then turned to the first great moment in the history of print: the production of his so-called 42-Line Bible. His majestic Bibles were large, the lettering dark and clear, and the text largely free of error. His stock of up to 180 Bibles (approximately 35–40 printed on parchment, the rest on paper) sold out almost immediately, but by 1455 Gutenberg was bankrupt, his equipment seized, and the secret of automatic writing let loose upon Europe.

What followed was a revolution in European communications. Fifty years after Gutenberg produced his great Bible, 250 cities in Europe had printing presses in operation. In 1440, there had not been a single printed book in Europe; by 1500, there were over six million. The books printed in that first fifty years are called **incunabula** (from the cradle or beginning). The industry and business of print transformed elements of the European economy. Soon gone were parchment makers and scribes (but not notaries); in their place were new trades and professions: typecasters, typesetters, book sellers, and book peddlers.

The intellectual impact was just as great. The scriptorium of the medieval monastery and stationers of the medieval university were replaced by the print shop as the center of intellectual exchange. Writers were freed from having to search out patronage since they could find printers and readers to support their work. By the late fifteenth century, people no longer needed to go to the few places where manuscripts were kept; the book traveled with them or to them. Now many readers could read the same book, and one reader could read many books. As a result of print culture, the author became a distinct individual; he or she was named on the title page, and all the readers of his book could refer to the same page and be relatively sure that they were discussing the same thing. The printed book produced a standardization of typeface, text layout, size, and format. The fixity of print made the post-Gutenberg world more intellectually exact. New forms of literature (autobiographies, advertisements, and broadsides) met people where they lived, intellectually and financially.

European Renaissance humanists such as the Dutchman Desiderius Erasmus; his English friend Thomas More, who wrote *Utopia*; and the French satirist Françoise Rabelais, who wrote the wickedly outrageous history of the giants Gargantua and Pantagruel, embraced the new printing technology to perfect their texts and to reach large European audiences. Erasmus prepared the first published edition of the Greek New Testament in 1516. Devoted to an *ad fontes* approach to reforming the Catholic Church and improving the text of the New Testament, Erasmus believed in restoring the church to its pure and spiritual foundations. His most famous work, *The Praise of Folly,* is a satire on both popular superstition and the abuses of traditional church practices. Not all of Erasmus's work was religious. He was fond of adages (even supplying some for the young man who would become King Henry VIII of England) and published a volume of sayings culled from his extensive reading of ancient, medieval, and Renaissance literature. These included phrases we still use today, such as "one step at a time" and "many hands make light work." Erasmus's interest in adages reflects the humanist preoccupation with education, as most of the sayings he collected were intended to teach children not only the classical vocabulary, but also valuable life lessons.

Humanizing Print: Aldus Manutius

Aldus Manutius came to Venice in 1490. He was a humanist and schoolteacher, but not a gifted writer. Yet he was sure that he could contribute to the humanist program. Above all, he wanted to make Greek classical texts available to an intelligent reading public and so spread humanist values. The printing press took some time to reach Italy. By 1465, a press run by German clerics was in operation in a monastery near Rome; later the printers moved their press to Rome and were printing several thousand books per year. These printers found themselves in conflict with the old scribal culture of Rome: with master scribes, stationers, and a church that wanted to retain authority over the spread of texts.

A generation later, Aldus Manutius was free of some of those concerns and was a sharper businessman than Gutenberg. He had taken careful steps in planning his intellectual and business enterprise in Venice before publishing his first book. He designed beautiful Greek and Latin typefaces for his books that were easier to read than Gutenberg's Gothic font. His Roman or Humanist typeface was designed after the model of Caroline Minuscule. He pioneered the use of a clean and clear Greek minuscule script and, most striking of all, an Italic form of Roman characters, which he had copied from the reformed book script perfected by a humanist copyist. The Italic script also saved paper because more characters could be printed on the page. Finally, in 1494 he was ready to go and began publishing, at first large handsome books of Aristotle and the Greek classics. He soon found, however, that the Greek books sold less well than the Latin classics and that large-format books sold less well than small books. Thus, he introduced small, pocket-size, portable books. His print run for most editions of the classics was between 1,000 and 4,000 copies, and he reprinted the bestsellers. His press became famous for the quality of its works and had its own logo, a dolphin curled around an anchor, meaning "hasten slowly." Authors such as Erasmus spent time in Venice working in Aldus's print shop to oversee their publications, and Thomas More praised the beauty and utility of Aldus's books. The books of his press, called Aldines, were so attractive that people thought them a good investment.

Thousands of these Aldine books survive today in the great libraries of the world, among them the British Library, Vatican Library, National Library of France in Paris, State Library in Munich, Library of Congress in Washington, and the university libraries of North America. With Aldus Manutius and his press, the age of the incunabula was over and the first age of printing, with its lightning changes and awkward moments, had passed. The book was now a modern thing and little different from the books that have been published for the past five hundred years. Aldus Manutius had spread the central texts and the new method for reading them (directly and in good editions) of the humanist agenda. He had humanized print and transformed the classics into obtainable commodities, blending together in one small package the intellectual and commercial faces of the Renaissance. The printed Aldine book was a masterpiece of art and materiality, classicism and commerce.

The Title Page of Aldus Manutius's Second Printing (1508) of ***The Adages of Erasmus***

QUESTIONS | *How does the history of print from Gutenberg to Aldus Manutius parallel our own awkward transition from print culture to digital media? What lessons can be learned from the print revolution? Why was Gutenberg almost destined to fail and someone like Aldus bound to perfect the art of printing? How did Aldus Manutius marry Renaissance values and the economics of publishing?*

Pieter Bruegel the Elder, *Netherlandish Proverbs* **(1559)** Several paintings by Bruegel surveyed the popular culture of his age.

The Dutch painter Pieter Bruegel the Elder (c. 1525–1569) also had a humanist agenda that reached down the social scale. In his painting *Netherlandish Proverbs,* he depicts over a hundred common proverbs and vernacular expressions such as "she can even tie the devil to a pillow," "patient as a lamb," "he fills the well after the calf has drowned," "he stoops to get on in the world," and "he has the world spinning on his thumb" (scenes running along the front from the far left of the painting). His delightful painting *Children's Games* shows hundred of children engaged in dozens of different games, but makes deeper humanist points about the stages of childhood, about the adult world that children imitate, and about the

darkness of city life and the light-filled world of nature, the world's innocent playground.

Humanism may have begun with a small group of learned men and women in Italy, but by the middle of the sixteenth century it had become a European phenomenon that reached out and into society. The Renaissance was a way of viewing the world in its messy splendor. The spreading Renaissance (with its shared belief in superior models, critical and systematic analysis, and the appreciation of cultural and linguistic particulars) made Europe more distinctly European, just as Christianity and the Middle Ages once had.

Conclusion

Between Petrarch and Cassandra Fedele, western Europe underwent a significant change of attitudes toward the ancient past, educational programs, politics and its methods (statecraft, diplomacy, espionage, and bureaucracy), and technology. Italy's cultural and intellectual

preoccupations with humanism and individualism spread through much of Europe. The visual and literary arts flourished, with new styles and techniques of painting and sculpting, the rise of vigorous vernacular literatures, a critical approach to classical texts and the classical past, and the wondrous spread of printed books. The Renaissance at its humanist core was a movement for intellectual, individual, and social improvement.

Events between 1494 and 1527 meant, however, that Italy would have to surrender its centrality to the movement. The independence and vigor of the Italian city-states was fatally compromised, and Italy and its Renaissance were drawn ever deeper into European affairs. The Italian Renaissance was absorbed into an overriding European Renaissance that by 1550 was fracturing at the seams; there was too much information, too many disagreements between various schools of thought, and too many regional and religious interests for it to hold together as a coherent movement. The next two stages of European history—overseas exploration and religious re-formation—were laced with humanist aspirations but would in the end move in very different directions. For one thing, the Renaissance had trumpeted the values of travel and new experiences, the acquisition of new knowl-

edge, and the discovery of new things. Petrarch ascended Mont Ventoux for spiritual and personal growth, but he was also climbing a tall mountain because no one had done so before (or for a long time), because the experience was worth having, and because he might learn something new about the world and himself. By the late fifteenth century, Europeans were looking beyond Europe and beyond the Ottoman imperial block to the east, which was territorially and spiritually suffocating Europe's lust for new lands, riches, and peoples to convert. Many church reformers of the sixteenth century—including Erasmus, More, and Rabelais—were humanists, intent on improving the church, just as they improved their old and corrupt texts. The European Renaissance and its Italian beginnings were not unconnected to the formative and fundamental changes that would remake and reform Europe in the sixteenth century. Above all, they drove the desire to make a better (or at least, different) world, no matter the cost to others.

Critical Thinking Questions

1. What was the Italian Renaissance a "rebirth" of? Does the label adequately cover the changes at work in fifteenth-century Italy? Why or why not?

2. What case can you make that the Italian and European Renaissances were still part of the Middle Ages?

3. Why did Renaissance art emerge and flourish? How big a departure was it from previous trends in art?

4. What did the Renaissances achieve, and what lasting effects did they have on European history?

Key Terms

Italian Renaissance (p. 325)

commune (p. 330)

Bonfire of the Vanities (p. 334)

Arsenal (p. 338)

galley (p. 338)

doge (p. 339)

Renaissance humanism (p. 341)

Renaissance individualism (p. 341)

ghetto (p. 342)

civic humanism (p. 344)

ad fontes (p. 344)

chiaroscuro (p. 345)

linear perspective (p. 345)

incunabula (p. 351)

Primary Sources in Connect

For information on Connect and the online resources available, go to **http://connect.mcgraw-hill.com**.

1. **Petrarch's Ascent of the Windy Mountain**

2. **Laura Cereta's Defense of Wise Women**

3. **Vergerio on Education as a Moral Necessity**

4. **Pico's Oration on the Dignity of Man**

5. **Three Church Responses to the Art of Printing**

6. **Erasmus's Sayings**

Machiavelli's Crafty Prince

Niccolò Machiavelli (1469–1527) was a contrary and contradictory character in his own time and has been a controversial one ever since. In 1513, he wrote the contrary and controversial *The Prince* for a junior line of the Medici.

Those Who Become Princes through Crime

... [I]n gaining a state by force, a conqueror must weigh carefully all the negative things he must do and then do them all at once so that he does not have to do them over and over again. By refraining from applying constant coercion, men will begin to feel safe and the prince will secure their loyalty through the rewards he bestows upon them. Any ruler who proceeds otherwise, because he is fearful or hesitant or because he follows poor counsel, will always need to have a dagger within reach. For he will never be sure of his subjects' support since their new wounds will always be fresh and they will never feel safe under him. The prince needs to impose all negative things at once, for the less often they are inflicted, the less they sting. Rewards, however, should be given in small doses, but often, so that they may be fully appreciated. And a prince needs to live alongside his subjects and in this way be aware of their thoughts so that no unexpected event, either positive or negative, should force him to alter his agenda. For when crises arise you will not have the opportunity to sway your subjects with cruelty, and any good you do to them will not help, since they will think that you were forced by circumstances and you will receive no appreciation whatsoever.

On Cruelty and Kindness

... A prince should always be careful not to believe too fervently or to act too openly, but he also should never seem timid or hesitant. He should moderate his actions with prudence and a human touch so that excessive trust does not lead him to take foolish risks or too little trust make him inflexible.

From this arises the question of whether it is better to be loved than feared, or the contrary. I would recommend that the prince should be both, but since it is hard to combine them, it is safer to be feared than loved, if one must choose between them. For it is true of men that they are ungrateful and fickle, full of deceit and double-dealing, absolute cowards who still remain greedy for their own advantage. While you pour rewards on them, they remain loyal and will offer you their blood, property, lives, and offspring, that is, so long as all danger is distant. But when danger draws close, they turn away from you. Any prince who relies entirely on their empty promises rather than finding his own means to protect himself will doubtless be destroyed. For any friendship that is bought rather than based on greatness and nobility of character is never true and cannot be cashed in when needed.

Moreover, men are not concerned about harming someone who seeks to be loved rather than feared, for love is bound by a voluntary obligation, which men, who are at the core rotten, are prepared to break whenever their own self-interest is in jeopardy. But fear always binds tightly because anxiety about punishment never disappears.

A prince, however, should make himself feared in such a way that, even though he may not have won the love of his subjects, he will have avoided incurring their hatred. Being feared but not hated is a good combination, so long as the prince keeps his hands off the property and the women of his subjects. If you must execute someone, insure that you do so only when there is an obvious reason and a proper justification for it. Above all, avoid seizing the property of others, for men would rather forget the deaths of their fathers than the loss of their inheritance. Indeed, there will never be any shortage of reasons for seizing people's property.... To return to the question of whether it is better to be loved or feared, I think that since men love by their own will but fear by the will of the prince, a prudent prince should always depend upon himself and not on the will of others. But he should, above all, seek only to avoid being hated, as I said above.

How a Prince Should Keep his Word

... A prince should be a fox so as to spot the traps set out for him and a lion to frighten the wolves. Those princes who only employ the lion's nature mistake their business. A prudent ruler, therefore, cannot and should not keep his promises when it is to his disadvantage or when the reasons that inclined him to make the promise have ceased to exist. If men were entirely good, this advice would be wrong, but since men are at their core rotten and will not stand by their promises to you, you similarly need not keep your promises to them. A prince never lacks legitimate reasons for breaking his promises. I could cite innumerable modern examples to show this.... Rulers who know how to act as foxes have always been the most successful. But the prince should also know how to disguise his character and to be a consummate hypocrite and a brazen liar, for men are so naïve and so governed by their immediate desires that the deceiver will always find a fool willing to allow himself to be duped....

A prince must appear to be thoroughly merciful, faithful, honest, kind, and pious. And it is especially necessary for the prince to seem to possess the last of these, since men generally judge more by what they see than by what they touch. Everyone sees what you appear to be, few know what you really are, and those few won't contradict the opinion of most men, who are protected by the majesty of the state. Since for the actions of everyone and particularly those of princes there is no court of appeal, we need to examine their outcomes. A prince should, therefore, boldly seize and maintain his state. His means will always be judged praiseworthy and will be lauded by all, for common people are constantly deceived by appearances and by outcomes, and in the world there are none but common people.

QUESTIONS | *What makes Machiavelli a product of the Northern Italian or European Renaissance? What does Machiavelli seek to achieve by advising the prince to be crafty, insincere, and entirely self-interested? What weapons does the prince have in his political toolkit?*

Source: The Historical, Political and Diplomatic Writings of Niccolò Machiavelli, trans. C. E. Detmold (Boston: J. R. Osgood, 1882), 51–52, 54–59; revised.

·S· graviel

12

℄ Vasquo da gama, ℈

EUROPEANS TAKE TO THE OCEANS

European Exploration before 1492
   Western Fantasies, Western Wanderlust
   Genoese Trade and Travel
   Portugal's Big Breakout
   Castile and the Contest for the Canaries
   The Pursuit of Technological Advantage

West to Asia: Columbus's Voyages
   Columbus's Early Years
   The Search for Sponsors
   To the Americas
   Later Voyages

The Atlantic Space Race
   Amerigo's New Continents
   Living on Board
   Hernán Cortés and the Conquest of the Mexica Empire

   Francisco Pizarro and the Conquest of the Inca Empire
   The English and the French Enter the Race

Spanish Colonization and Its Critics
   The Problems of Colonization
   First Encounters
   The Economic Impact of Spanish Colonization
   Spanish Colonization and Conversion
   Criticizing Spanish Conquests and Colonization: Las Casas

East to Asia: The Portuguese Venture
   The Portuguese Reach Asia
   The Dutch and the English Arrive
   A New Wave of Christianity Hits Asia

Conclusion

THE CHOICE AND CHANCE OF BERNAL DÍAZ Bernal Díaz del Castillo was born in the Spanish city of Medina del Campo around 1496, just a few years after Christopher Columbus landed unexpectedly on a cluster of islands in the present-day West Indies. At the age of nineteen, Díaz set sail for the Americas to make his fortune. As was so often the case among the adventurous young men who crowded onto the ships, his high hopes for the expedition were dashed by encounters with resistant native populations, mission mismanagement, and the general ignorance of local lands and customs. After making his first port-of-call in what today is Panama, Díaz tried to improve his prospects for financial success by starting over again in Cuba. In 1517, he undertook his first mission to the Yucatán coast, where he and his fellow soldiers encountered the Maya, an ancient people with a still prosperous and sophisticated culture. Dazzled by the potential riches of the Yucatán

◀ Vasco da Gama's Caravel under Sail

Peninsula, the Spanish soon organized expeditions to explore the region.

While there, prisoners and translators told the Spanish of an even richer civilization to the northwest. The lure was irresistible to the Spanish, and in 1519, under the brutal and gifted military commander Hernán Cortés, Díaz once again found himself under sail and headed to an unknown land of golden promise. Cortés's forces soon found themselves pitted against the powerful Mexica (Aztec, as the Spanish called it) Empire of Moctezuma (Montezuma). Cortés's hostile contact left the native population overcome by warfare and ravaged by disease, and brought about the collapse of the Mexica control over its far-flung territories in Mesoamerica. The Mexica Empire was effectively destroyed; the Spanish overseas empire secured.

Tenochtitlán, 1524 An early map of the large capital city of the Nahua or Aztecs in Mexico as it might have looked near first contact.

Díaz's life, and those of many European men and women of the time, was shaped by the challenges and opportunities that arose in the wake of Columbus's voyage of 1492. At the end of many weeks on the open sea, with a fleet of only three ships manned by less than a hundred men, Columbus had failed to find a direct route to the fabled lands of Japan for his expedition's Spanish sponsors. Instead,

Reign of Moctezuma
Mexica Empire
1509–1520

Reign of Louis XII, France
1498–1515

Reign of Henry VII, England
1485–1509

Reign of João (John) II, Portugal
1481–1495

Reign of Manuel I
1495–1521

Bernal Díaz del Castillo sets sa
for the Americas from Spa
151

Reign of Isabella and Ferdinand, Spain
1474–1516

1470   1480   1490   1500   1510

he came to a world previously unknown to Europeans. Thanks to a skillful propaganda campaign that began the moment Columbus wrote up his report for his royal backers in Spain, European contact with the Americas soon came to dominate the imaginations and aspirations of princes, merchant sailors, and ambitious young men throughout the West.

The Americas became a promised land for young Europeans forced to find their own way in the world. Díaz's family was old and honorable, but it was not wealthy. He could hardly rely on it for land or titles to make his fame and fortune. He had received some education, but not enough to think of becoming a humanist scholar, and he had no vocation for the priesthood. Díaz instead pinned his hopes for social advancement on a career as a **conquistador**, a soldier of fortune, in the Americas. His early hopes for an easy route to wealth and glory were crushed by the harsh conditions, poorly managed military engagements, and resistant native populations of the Americas. This was to become the common fate of many who explored and colonized the Americas, but the chance for gold and glory drew them irresistibly onward.

More than thirty years after arriving in Panama and Cuba, and after receiving an administrative post in Antigua Guatemala for his service to Cortés and the Spanish monarchs, Díaz wrote an account of his life in the Americas. His *True History of the Conquest of New Spain* is not easy for us to read five centuries after the 1519 attack on the Mexica Empire. In the Americas, Europeans encountered civilizations as ancient and complex as their own, but they seldom appreciated their rich histories, deeply rooted religious beliefs, complicated economic systems, or intricate political thought. Exploration led to the conquest and subjugation of the native peoples in the Caribbean, Mesoamerica, and North and South America. After enduring centuries of unflattering comparisons between their own culture and the wealthy and sophisticated cultures of the Far East and Middle East, Europeans were ready to assert the superiority of their civilization over that of native Americans. European overseas exploration was to prove a turning point in the West's relationship with the rest of the world.

�֍ �֍ ✖ ✖

The early modern explorations and conquests of Europeans are subjects of continuing controversy, and long have been. Mark Twain captured the mixed feelings many have about this transformative episode in European history when he said: "it was wonderful to find America—but it would have been more wonderful to miss it." What we can do, at the very least, is to be aware of the bias built in to the European records and perspectives on the experience, and to guard against blindly accepting European assumptions, terms, and frames of reference. For one thing, though it was the

explorers' language of description, the New World was not new and the Old World was not any older than the Americas. These terms are relative ones and have the potential to mislead. Nor were the Americas unknown. They were unknown to Europeans, just as Asia, Africa, and Europe were unknown to native Americans. Even the language of discovery seems misplaced: the Americas were not lost and so could not be found. Yet Europeans in the age of exploration were convinced that they had discovered unknown new worlds. Maps and books spoke of a *Mundus Novus* (New World) and the discovery of new

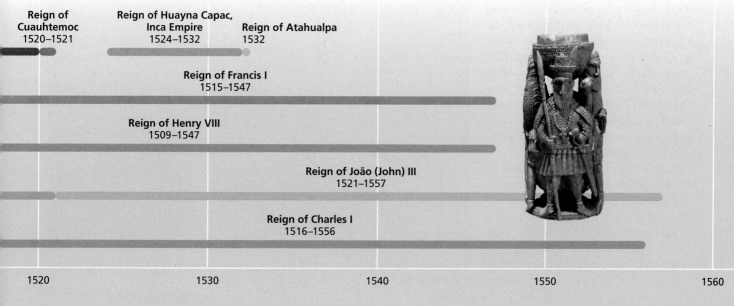

Reign of Cuauhtemoc
1520–1521

Reign of Huayna Capac, Inca Empire
1524–1532

Reign of Atahualpa
1532

Reign of Francis I
1515–1547

Reign of Henry VIII
1509–1547

Reign of João (John) III
1521–1557

Reign of Charles I
1516–1556

1520   1530   1540   1550   1560

things and new peoples. Talk of newness and discovery helped Europeans to conceptualize and deal with realities beyond their existing knowledge and expectations. But it is important for us to recognize that there was not a single European exploration, conquest, and colonization, but rather a series of explorations, conquests, and colonization movements by various Europeans in competition with each other in different areas and representing different interests. Europe was no more a unified block of interests than the Americas were a unified and single thing.

Nor were early modern Europeans the first or only explorers. Human beings are a migratory species. We have already seen the spread of *Homo sapiens sapiens* out of Africa, the movement of the Indo-Europeans and Germanic tribes, and the travels of the Muslims and Vikings in the Middle Ages. Several characteristics of the European experience in the late fifteenth and sixteenth centuries, however, set it apart from those of earlier migration movements:

- The late medieval and early modern movement of Europeans overseas covered a vast distance in a relatively brief interval of time. Within fifty years, the economic and political contours of the globe were sent in new and unanticipated directions.
- This was the first great transoceanic movement of peoples in recorded history, behind which stood a series of technological transformations and particular historical circumstances in Europe.
- Europeans and native Americans came into contact with lands and peoples outside their previous experience and knowledge and, as such, theirs was a meeting of utterly alien societies.
- The impact worked in both directions, slowly transforming the European and American peoples, their societies, histories, and economies.

These distinctions may highlight the extraordinary nature of European expansion, but not why it took place. The two main reasons typically given for European expansion are material (greed for gold and land) and religious (to convert or coerce others to Christianity), but a third may be more convincing and house the other two: that is, the intensely competitive character of late medieval and early modern Europe. This dynamic competitiveness was the result of the spirit of activism and opportunism that animated Europeans after the crises of the fourteenth century, the fracturing of high medieval certainties and traditional ways of living, and the vigor of Mediterranean mercantilism. Both China and Islam had more sophisticated and technologically advanced cultures, but it was the competitive

Europeans who took to the oceans in pursuit of advantage. European monarchs, rulers, merchants, and priests were locked in to contests for dominance over each other. The many Europes had taught them that lesson the hard way. Europe was **balkanized** or broken into dozens of small units of various sizes and importance (kingdoms, principalities, republics, cities, regions) in constant struggle with each other. At the personal level, individuals such as Gutenberg, Columbus, and Díaz were looking for their big break, gold and glory, by rising above their competitive contemporaries. This war of interests did not begin when Columbus set sail. It had been building throughout the fifteenth century and would continue throughout the early modern period.

European Exploration before 1492

As startling as Columbus's discovery of the Americas was to Europeans, his voyages were only the latest in a series of voyages of exploration in the Late Middle Ages. Knowledge acquired over centuries of maritime experience in the Mediterranean and near the North Atlantic came together with a desire to find a way to trade with Asia that did not require Ottoman middlemen, an interest in converting others to Christianity, and a political interest in expanding the territorial holdings of European kingdoms.

Why did Portugal and Castile send their ships outward into the Atlantic rather than inward to the Mediterranean?

Europeans had been building toward their Atlantic breakout from Europe for over a century. Extraordinary developments in navigation and technology made the

Fourteenth-Century Iberia and Africa The Catalan Atlas of 1375 set out what Europeans knew at the time of islands in the Atlantic and of northern Africa.

voyages possible. Columbus's journey across the Atlantic was preceded by decades of explorations of lands closer to Europe sponsored by princes, funded by merchants, and undertaken by adventurous mariners. For two centuries before 1492, Europeans had been undertaking voyages of exploration in the eastern Atlantic Ocean and along the coast of Africa in search of a route that would lead them to the Indian Ocean and Asia. Developments in ship-building technology made it possible for mariners to sail farther than ever before into uncharted seas and along unmapped coastlines. At the same time that the ideas and ideals of the two Renaissances were being developed, the knowledge and skills necessary for lengthy voyages across open seas were being developed in western Mediterranean cities such as Genoa, Lisbon, Barcelona, Valencia, and Cadiz. In the process, islands were encountered off the coast of northern Africa that provided opportunities for early colonial experiments that would shape what Columbus and his successors did in the Americas. The Canary Islands, in particular, proved to be a testing ground for European expansion and the struggle for advantage between rival powers and ambitious men.

Western Fantasies, Western Wanderlust

Europeans had long been fascinated by the exotic external world known to them through tales of strange peoples, monsters, and freaks of nature. Were they culturally (as well as historically) predisposed to explore and migrate? The Bible, with its accounts of the Near East, foreign lands, and wandering Hebrews, transported Christian Europeans to a world other than the one they inhabited. The various accounts of the adventures of the desert fathers took them into an Egyptian landscape filled with strange creatures such as crocodiles and hippopotamuses, and shape-shifting demons. Stories of this kind served as the fantasy literature of the Middle Ages. Added to this was the information about bizarre lands, pygmies, fire-breathing mountains, and stones that burned (phosphorous) that they could cull from reading Roman encyclopedias such as Pliny the Elder's *Natural History*. By the Early Middle Ages, fantastic tales of the wonders of India were in wide circulation. The Middle Ages and Northern Italian Renaissance were equally attracted to the exotic East, spawning their own stories such as the one of Prester John, the legendary Christian king in the east surrounded by hostile pagans (Muslims) and waiting to rejoin the Christian community in the west. There was a hunger in Europe for stories of distant travel to marvelous and dangerous places. Geography and history combined with myths and legends in popular chronicles and travelers' tales such as *The Travels of Sir John Mandeville*.

Genoese Trade and Travel

Beyond the eastern fantasies that fueled western wanderlust, there were real contacts with Asia in the Middle Ages.

In the thirteenth century, as we saw, Franciscan friars and merchant adventurers such as the Polos had reached the Mongol court. The fall of the Mongol dynasty, the closing down of long-distance travel routes, and the fourteenth-century plague that stunned European society and its economy meant that the late fourteenth century was no longer as conducive to long-distance travel. By the mid-fifteenth century, Europeans were once again on the move. The European economy had recovered and, indeed, there was more money for urban Europeans in particular to spend. Those who had never been able to afford luxury goods found that they could afford imported cloth or a packet of Asian spices. The European appetite for luxury goods grew in the plague's aftermath. Given the competition in the Mediterranean for control over shipping lanes and ports, the European need to find new trade routes and opportunities was acute. The Genoese, who tried to fill that demand, were among the most adventurous searchers for mercantile advantage. The first recorded attempt to reach Asia by a southern sea route was made by the Vivaldi brothers of the Italian maritime republic of Genoa in 1291, when their expedition attempted to round the coast of Africa. The brothers anticipated that it would take ten years to reach Japan. Somewhere off the northwestern coast of Africa the ships disappeared, and so entered travelers' lore, but the Vivaldis had planted the idea that Europeans might one day find a southern sea-route to the Far East.

Throughout the late medieval period, the Genoese won colonial outposts closer to home on islands in the eastern Mediterranean, such as Chios, and in the Black Sea near the Crimea. While much of Genoa's military and mercantile effort was directed eastward and in direct competition with Venice, its more westerly location meant that the Genoese were also attuned to developments in the Atlantic and were in competitive trading networks with Portugal, France, the Netherlands, and England. Genoa played a critical role in these northwestern European economies because, apart from agriculture, those economies were based largely on wool and cloth production. Through its colony on Chios, Genoa controlled the European supply of alum, a mineral substance used to fix dyes in cloth and to tan hides for leather goods. The substance was in high demand in countries where significant amounts of cloth were produced.

Always in a political and economic struggle with Venice over shipping lanes and access to Mediterranean ports of call, Genoa was dealt a severe blow in 1453 when Constantinople fell to the Ottomans. Though Chios remained a Genoese colony, Ottoman forces on the seas and within the lands that surrounded it made transporting alum to Europe an increasingly difficult and expensive operation. Alum was so important to the European economy that when it was discovered north of Rome, at Tolfa in 1462, the papacy proclaimed it a miracle. The Genoese moved quickly to monopolize the supply, but they had learned a lesson in economic diversification and began looking for ways to monopolize and control other commodities in other ports.

Travelers' Tales

While preparing for his first voyage across the Atlantic, Christopher Columbus repeatedly read a strange traveler's tale by John Mandeville that he hoped would give him some idea about where he was going and what he might encounter. Jehan de Mandeville (John Mandeville, as he is known in English) is the name attached to a compilation of travelers' tales drawn together between 1357 and 1371 as *The Travels of Sir John Mandeville.* Though the tales were written in Anglo-Norman French by a man who claimed to be an English knight, there is no evidence that John Mandeville ever existed, and these "autobiographical" tales were most likely elaborate fabrications. Nevertheless, they were thought to be true and became immensely popular among late medieval readers. Such tales were translated into dozens of European languages and dialects, and hundreds of manuscript copies of them survive. After the advent of print, the tales of John Mandeville and Marco Polo circulated widely.

Early travel accounts such as those ascribed to John Mandeville can give us important insights into the stories and experiences that shaped European attitudes toward different peoples and cultures, but they can be tricky to use. Some of the material in the early travel books is undoubtedly drawn from firsthand, eyewitness accounts of people, places, and events. But rumors and legends that might contain only a nugget of truth were imaginatively

John Mandeville as Portrayed in a Copy of His Tales

embellished in these books. Other tales about exotic people and faraway lands were completely fabricated to entertain listeners. Mandeville's supposed encounters with dog-headed men, Amazonian warriors, and a race of pygmies with giant slaves were based on ancient and medieval fables that had been passed down at European firesides for centuries.

As time passed and Europeans were no longer able to travel to Asia as they had under the Mongols, it became harder to sift the true from the false in various travelers' tales. Even so, the widespread interest in these stories demonstrates just how curious medieval and early modern Europeans were about the external world. As western Europeans took to the seas and explored the globe, their interest in ancient and medieval travelers' tales grew as they looked for guidance in interpreting what they saw and heard. It would be centuries before books such as *The Travels of Sir John Mandeville* were recognized as works of fiction. Until that time, they continued to shape European attitudes toward other peoples and cultures, and thus provide important clues as to why explorers and colonizers behaved as they did.

QUESTIONS | *What literature today serves the same function as did the late medieval travelers' tales? What is that function? How did such tales both reveal and shape European attitudes?*

The Genoese pioneered a trading strategy different from their Venetian rivals. Specifically, Genoa established small trading colonies in foreign ports that oversaw the procurement of raw materials rather than the acquisition or production of finished luxury goods for trade; it would then trade those raw resources in European markets. The republic turned its attention to purchasing or leasing mercury mines in Spain, iron mines on the island of Elba, and salt manufacturing operations on Ibiza. Although the Genoese colonies were not as large or strategically important as the long chain of Venetian colonies that ringed the Adriatic and extended into the eastern Mediterranean, they helped Europeans to appreciate the importance of controlling the resource trade.

Portugal's Big Breakout

By the fifteenth century, Europe was a small continent surrounded by Muslims and water (see Map 11.3, p. 340). One was a block, sealing Europe inside Europe; the other a watery avenue to a wider world. Just as the rise of Islam had shaped the European Middle Ages, so too did its territorial dominance of the Near East play a critical role in determining the direction of European expansion. The dramatic rise of the Ottoman Empire had blocked off the eastern Mediterranean and made the Silk Road to China and the Far East largely inaccessible to Europeans. Moreover, the rise of more aggressive monarchs in Europe in the Late Middle Ages meant

YEARS	EVENT
1405–1433	Chinese Admiral Zheng He surveys the Indian Ocean
1455–1487	Portuguese explore the African coastline from Cape Verde to the Cape of Good Hope
1492–1493	First voyage of Christopher Columbus reaches the Bahamas and Hispaniola
1493–1494	Second voyage of Columbus establishes settlement of La Isabella
1497	John Cabot reaches Newfoundland and Nova Scotia
1497–1499	Vasco da Gama rounds the Cape of Good Hope and enters the Indian Ocean
1498–1500	Third voyage of Columbus reaches Venezuela and Orinoco River
1499–1501	Amerigo Vespucci touches down in South America
1502–1504	Fourth voyage of Columbus surveys the coast of Central America
1513	Vasco de Balboa crosses Isthmus of Panama and sees the Pacific Ocean
1519	Hernán Cortés conquers the Mexica Empire
1519–1522	Ferdinand Magellan's expedition circumnavigates the globe
1531	Francisco Pizarro conquers the Inca Empire

that Europe was not an easy place in which to expand internally. The Hundred Years' War between France and England had shown how costly and destructive it was for one European country to claim territory from another. Yet European countries continued to hunger for growth and advantage, and were intensely competitive with each other. By the fifteenth century, it was becoming apparent that the only way to break out of the competitive gridlock of Europe was by seeking advantage outside of Europe by water, in effect by sailing away from Europe.

Portugal, a small land on the western shore of the Iberian Peninsula, is a revealing example of what drove European kingdoms to maritime exploration and territorial expansion (Map 12.1). Portugal was carved out of Muslim Spain when King Dom Afonso Henrique in 1147 employed western crusaders to assist him in capturing Lisbon. By the late thirteenth century, the territory of Portugal was fixed, with Muslims (Moors) and the Christian kingdoms of Léon, Castile, and Navarre as

its less-than-friendly neighbors in Iberia. There was little prospect of Portuguese expansion within the Iberian Peninsula and none whatsoever in Europe. Moreover, Portugal's physical setting was such that it lacked rich agricultural land; its economy depended on fishing and trade. Portugal's big breakout from its Iberian and European limitations would, therefore, have to be by sea and by aggressive trade. While Genoa cornered the European alum market and developed merchant colonies, the kingdom of Portugal set its sights on acquiring gold. Little gold was found in European mineral deposits, and most of the gold in circulation in Europe in the fifteenth century came by way of Muslim middlemen in cities on the north coast of Africa who drew on suppliers from western Africa. Loyal to the Ottoman Empire, the gold traders dealt with Europeans on increasingly unfavorable terms. The Portuguese hatched a plan to deal directly with western Africans. To do so, they had to increase their knowledge of the African coastline, make contacts with the resident peoples, and find safe and efficient ways to move gold from the African interior to the coast.

In 1415, Portugal conquered Ceuta, a strategically important port directly across the mouth of the Mediterranean from the Straits of Gibraltar. This gave the Portuguese two mercantile and strategic advantages it had lacked: direct access to the Mediterranean Sea and a territorial foothold on the continent of Africa. They soon took Tangier and established a permanent trading presence in northern Africa. With the aid of Muslim geographers, Portugal began to expand its knowledge of Africa, breaking out of the older Greek or Ptolemaic scheme of the world centered on the Mediterranean Sea. After Ceuta, the Portuguese began to explore and map the western coastline of Africa. Leading this exploration was Prince Dom Henrique (Henry the Navigator; 1394–1460). He trained navigators, ordered maps of the African coastline, and sent ships out each year to proceed farther south down the coast of Africa. In 1455, the Portuguese sailed past Cape Verde and saw that, beyond the Sahara Desert, Africa was lush and green. After the death of Henrique, the Portuguese continued to push south, reaching Benin by 1475 and reaching the southern tip of Africa (later called the Cape of Good Hope) in 1487–1488. Ten years later, Vasco da Gama (1460–1524) rounded Africa and headed for India. We will return to the eastward voyages of the Portuguese at the end of the chapter.

As they extended their knowledge of the African coast, the Portuguese established outposts to trade with local rulers. They traded horses, saddles, cloth, wine, salt, lead, and copper in exchange for gold to fuel their economy, spices and drugs to supply the luxury market, grain to feed their people, and slaves to provide labor. The Portuguese interest in acquiring slaves began as early as 1434, when they raided the Saharan coast, capturing and enslaving native Africans. Tensions with local rulers soon convinced the Portuguese that it was politically and economically more advantageous for them to trade

MAP 12.1 | Portuguese and Spanish Overseas Exploration, 1450–1542
This map shows only the significant "firsts" or breakthrough voyages that Europeans made to open up new territories overseas. Europeans made many other voyages overseas. *Why did the Portuguese and Spanish go in different directions? What results did the division of Tordesillas in 1494 have? What do the different settlement patterns of the Portuguese and Spanish suggest?*

European goods for slaves through African agents than to launch their own slave raids.

The African slaves who entered the European economy through the hands of Portuguese traders did not, for the most part, end their journey in Lisbon or another European city. Instead, they were transported to the Atlantic archipelagos of the Canary and Madeira Islands off the northwestern coast of Africa to work on the plantations and farms that European colonists were developing there.

Under King João (John) I (r. 1385–1433), the Portuguese focused their colonization efforts on the Madeira Islands. In 1417, to stave off Castilian plans to occupy the Canaries and Madeiras, King João sent one hundred settlers to the chief islands of Madeira and Porto Santo under the leadership of two minor Portuguese nobles and a longtime Italian resident of Portugal, Bartolomeu Perestrelo. The crown was able to exercise greater control over the islands after 1433, when King Duarte placed them under the supervision of his brother, Prince Henrique (Henry the Navigator).

An African View of the Portuguese An Edo or Benin carver depicted four Portuguese (two wealthy traders facing out) and their assistants (in profile) on this ivory salt cellar. The sculptor paid particular attention to the elaborate dress of the Portuguese traders. The salt cellar was probably a trade item meant for the traders or the Portuguese market.

The Portuguese were able to gain control over the Madeiras relatively quickly, for though the islands were fertile, they had been uninhabited. Portuguese settlers had to clear forests and establish irrigation systems before the islands could be planted with valuable crops such as grain and sugarcane, but there was no native population to overcome or enslave. By 1450, the Madeiras were producing a profitable amount of grain and flour, and after 1452, its sugarcane crops yielded enough to make a tidy sum for the Portuguese crown and investors. Planters there never relied heavily on slave labor for their agricultural work since the influx of cheap Portuguese laborers eager for a better life kept up with the demand for plantation workers. Given the profitable enterprises that were established on the islands, it is not surprising that the population grew dramatically, from 100 settlers in 1417 to as many as 800 by 1455, and to somewhere between 15,000 and 18,000 settlers and a small number of slaves by 1600.

In the fifteenth century, the Portuguese finally broke out of the restricted confines of Iberia and Europe, brought western Africa into a European trading network, and finally found a direct sea route to Asia. By doing so, they escaped the limitations imposed on them by crowded and competitive Iberia and Europe. In the Madeira Islands, they laid down a model for the exploitation of conquered lands through plantation agriculture. They also influenced the next generation of explorers, including Columbus.

Castile and the Contest for the Canaries

Portugal's most serious rival in Africa and the Atlantic islands was the kingdom of Castile, which dominated the Iberian Peninsula both geographically and politically. Castile had coastline on the Mediterranean and the Atlantic but shared the Iberian Peninsula with the kingdoms of Portugal, Aragon, Navarre, and Muslim-held Granada. Despite their relatively landlocked position, the Castilians were eager to explore new ways to enter into maritime trade and to best their Portuguese rivals (see Map 12.1).

Their first great struggle was over the Canary Islands, a set of volcanic islands (like the Azores and Madeiras) forming an archipelago off the western coast of Africa. Berbers had attempted to take the islands in the eleventh century but met resistance from the native inhabitants. The islanders (called Guanches) were a non-Muslim people of northern African origin who herded animals and farmed. Though the islands were known in classical antiquity, serious European interest in the Canary Islands did not begin until the fourteenth century. In 1341, ships from Lisbon, with a mixed European crew, landed on the islands. The Europeans attempted to communicate with the natives by sign language but were interested chiefly in sizing up these strange people and the wealth of the islands. They were particularly struck by the Guanches'

nakedness, strange diet, and lack of organized religion. The Portuguese brought back four islanders as proof of their landing.

The existence of the Canary Islands and their unknown people posed a problem for European thought. Who were these people, and why did neither the ancients nor the Bible talk about them? The Florentine writer Giovanni Boccaccio, struck by the pastoral simplicity of the Canary islanders, wrote a short treatise on the islands that was not published in his lifetime. Petrarch also wrote about the islanders, seeing them as masters of solitude because they were cut off from the rest of the world.

Portugal may have had first claim to the Canary Islands, but in 1402 Castile launched a force to conquer the islands. The Castilian efforts in the Canary Islands would set patterns of conquest, colonization, and economic organization that would shape their later practices in the Americas. Though the Portuguese established plantations on the Azores and Madeiras, those island chains were empty and open to Portuguese settlement. The residents of the Canary Islands, however, fought back and were able to use the rocky terrain of the islands to hide from and ambush any invaders. Prince Henrique had his own plans for securing control of the Canaries, but his attempts in 1422 and 1434 were futile. Not until 1479 did Portugal and Castile settle their dispute over who owned the islands; they decided to divide up the African islands. Portugal gained absolute possession of the Azores and Madeiras, and Castile took the Canaries. Castile spent much of the late fifteenth century trying to subdue the islands, but it was not until 1496, when the island of Tenerife finally fell, that the archipelago was entirely under Castilian control.

The Castilians viewed the native Guanches as a people who could be subjugated and sold into slavery or put to work on the sugarcane plantations that were being introduced on the islands. Over the fifteenth century, the relatively small population of Guanches was reduced substantially by warfare, capture, and slavery for those who resisted, and even further by the spread of the epidemic diseases carried by Europeans. As the native population shrank, slaves were brought back from Spain, from raids launched by the Castilians in northern Africa, and from Portuguese slave traders dealing in African slaves. Over time the enslaved labor force of natives was replaced by labor from the Iberian Peninsula, which was sufficient to keep the relatively small sugar plantations operational.

The Canary Islands proved to be a testing ground and template for the coming century of overseas explorations, conquests, and the establishment of settlements by Spain, Portugal, and the other exploration-sponsoring powers of Europe. Europeans may have had an intellectual interest in figuring out who these unknown peoples and places were, but their real interests were economic and competitive. There was a race to secure an advantage over their rivals by dominating territories previously unknown to Europeans and then to put them to economic use. To that end, the native population was turned into a subservient labor force and its religious well-being and security were ignored. The identity and culture of these residents was not a primary consideration in the larger scheme of exploration. Western war did some damage to the Canary islanders, but it was western diseases that destroyed them and their way of life. Native Americans would undergo much the same experience.

The Pursuit of Technological Advantage

As the Genoese, Portuguese, and Castilians were expanding their geographic knowledge of the Atlantic and the coast of Africa, they were also improving their navigational tools and skills. Changes in shipbuilding resulted in ships that were lighter, more resistant to damage, and faster. By the time Columbus set sail in 1492 for Japan, he could sail the open seas for a significant distance and period of time.

Prior to the fifteenth century, two basic kinds of ships were in use in Europe: galleys and round ships. Galleys were faster and powered primarily by oars, although they used sails when possible. They had small cargo areas, required large crews, and were heavy and slow. Round ships were short, wide, and powered by small triangular sails set on a single mast. They required only small crews but were almost entirely dependent on the prevailing wind conditions to achieve speed, and they were never very fast. Their sails were notoriously inefficient. Round ships often waited in port for months before the winds allowed them to depart.

To cross any large expanse of water, Europeans needed to blend the two styles into a single vessel that combined their strengths. First, larger, square sails replaced the smaller, triangular sails of the round ships; these were better at catching the wind. The new square sails, however, were incapable of filling completely in light winds, and by 1492, shipbuilders had developed a three-masted ship called a **carrack** that was rigged with both square and triangular sails to ensure that any hint of wind would be caught. These new ships still remained large, heavy, and hard to maneuver. Carracks were best employed as merchant vessels, since their holds could contain 100–200 tons and they required large crews to tend to the sails. The three-masted **caravel** required only a small crew, could hold 50–70 tons of cargo, and its sails could capture sufficient wind to power the light-hulled ship across the open seas with speed.

The challenge of steering vessels into unknown waters and along unknown shores demanded advanced navigational instruments and techniques. There were three essential navigational tools on fifteenth-century ships: the magnetic compass, the Portolan chart, and the astrolabe or quadrant. Pilots who knew how to use these instruments were critical to the success of any voyage. The earliest European compasses appeared in the twelfth century, following Arabic examples, and were little more than magne-

tized needles that pointed to true north and were mounted on a card painted with the four cardinal directions. Over time, the designs became more sophisticated, as demanded by wealthy merchants and venturesome princes.

Portolan charts showed navigable ports, landmarks, geographic features, and compass headings so that a pilot could plot his course with respect to the shoreline and his ship's position. These charts were of little use in the open seas where there were no fixed coastal reference points from which to take bearings. In the northern hemisphere, mariners used **astrolabes** (or the smaller quadrants) to steer on the open seas by the only fixed point available, the Pole Star. On clear nights, mariners used an astrolabe to calculate their latitude relative to their earlier positions on the voyage. Astrolabes measured the angle of the Pole Star relative to the horizon, but as Portuguese explorers moved south of the equator in their search for the southern tip of Africa, the Pole Star disappeared from view. Instead they used the astrolabe and the sun's position at noon relative to the horizon to approximate their position, and in 1500 they identified the southern equivalent of the Pole Star, the constellation known as the Southern Cross. This enabled more accurate calculations of position in the southern hemisphere and improved the accuracy of maps and charts.

Despite this progress, fifteenth-century mariners undertaking long voyages on unknown seas still had no easy way to calculate with accuracy their speed or to find their longitude (east-west position). Experienced mariners were adept at "dead reckoning," a method for calculating how fast a ship was traveling and in what direction based on a combination of observing the hull's progress through the water, noting each change of compass heading, and measuring the passage of time with an hourglass.

West to Asia: Columbus's Voyages

Christopher Columbus had an unlikely idea: to sail west to Asia. His passion and persistence convinced at least three patrons that he was not crazy, but might be on to something. His personal ambitions by pure luck matched the economic, territorial, and religious aspirations of Spanish monarchs who were in the full flush of success and ready to take a gamble on the Genoese mariner. Like most of the early explorers and administrators, Columbus was not a renaissance humanist, but a man of humble background and enormous ambition. His accidental landing in the Americas was an unexpected event that changed history.

Why was Columbus both a success and a failure?

Columbus's Early Years

Christopher Columbus's life prior to 1492 is shrouded in relative obscurity. Surviving evidence suggests that

Christopher Columbus Sebastiano del Piombo painted this portrait of the explorer thirteen years after Columbus's death in 1519, but it captures the majesty of the man in the full flush of his achievement.

he was born in the seafaring republic of Genoa around 1451. Columbus's father, Domenico, was a humble wool-weaver who, around 1439, opened a shop in Genoa, married Susanna Fontanarossa, and had four children.

Columbus spent his early years learning the skills that he would need to pursue his father's trade. During those years, Columbus received a rudimentary education at home and may have spent some time in a grammar school that taught the children of guild members in the city how to read and write. He was raised a Roman Catholic, though some historians have, with little evidence, argued that Columbus's family were *conversos*, Jews who had converted recently to Catholicism. By the time Columbus was twenty-one, he had entered the wool trade, but the pay was too poor for such an ambitious young man. To make more money, Columbus kept a tavern and picked up jobs in the harbor, serving on ships that traveled to England, Ireland, and the Genoese colony of Chios.

Around 1476, Columbus decided that he was more interested in a life at sea than a life spent in a wool shop in Genoa. He left for Portugal, determined to make his fortune and a name for himself. There he worked as an agent for a Genoese merchant; studied theories about the earth and seas; and began to learn languages, including Latin (which was essential for the study of cosmology and mathematics), the Castilian dialect spoken at the royal courts on the Iberian Peninsula (which was vital to win influential patrons), and Portuguese (the language of the mariners who worked on ships).

In 1478–1479, Columbus solidified his position in Portugal by marrying Felipa Moniz Perestrela, the daughter of Bartolomeu Perestrelo, the official from the Portuguese colony on the Madeira Islands. The marriage provided Columbus with access to the Perestrelo family's navigational papers. These included Portolan charts, wind readings taken on the open seas of the Atlantic, and detailed information about the African coastline. The Perestrelo family's court connections gave Columbus his first opportunity to put together and promote his plan for reaching Japan and China by sailing west across the Atlantic, rather than east through the Mediterranean or around Africa.

Columbus interviewed sailors, ship captains, and merchants about their experiences in the Atlantic. Much of the information he gathered was a mixture of myth and rumor, but from it he concluded that the earth was smaller than generally believed, that Asia extended thirty degrees of longitude farther east than it actually does, and that Japan was 1,500 miles east off the coast of the Asian mainland. The novelty of Columbus's theory, then, was not that the earth was round (something assumed by medieval men and women), but that the earth was smaller than generally believed and that Japan was much closer to the west coast of Europe than Europeans believed. If Columbus was right, it meant that a ship could reach Asia before it ran out of manpower and supplies. Not surprisingly, Columbus found little support for his radical and erroneous idea.

The Search for Sponsors

Despite the skepticism about his theory, Columbus stuck with it and promoted his plan tirelessly. He approached King João II (r. 1481–1495) of Portugal in search of funding for his venture, but the king's advisors warned against it. In 1485, still bitter over João's rejection, Columbus left Portugal for Spain. There he resumed interviewing mariners about their experiences in the Atlantic and sought out people who might endorse his theory about the size of the earth and the feasibility of a westward voyage to Japan. He also contacted King Henry VII of England with his idea for a westward voyage to Asia but received little encouragement at the young Tudor court. In Spain, however, Columbus gained the support of several Franciscan friars who served as middlemen between Italian merchants and the royal court of Isabella of Castile. In 1486, Isabella and Ferdinand agreed to provide Columbus with enough funds to plan his voyage, but not enough to set off across the Atlantic.

Six years later, Columbus was chafing to get under way and threatened to leave for France if he was not given the funding to outfit his ships. At that point, a combination of events and the intervention of an unlikely sponsor changed Columbus's prospects. The year was 1492 and Isabella and Ferdinand were elated by their victory over the Muslim armies at Granada. At that moment, Luis de Santangel, a Jewish *converso* and royal financial minister, offered to help finance the voyage. Luis convinced Isabella and Ferdinand that their victory over the Muslims would pale in comparison with converting the Japanese to Christianity. Buoyed by their success and relieved of the responsibility of financing the venture entirely by themselves, the monarchs released the funds and approved the voyage. Columbus hired a crew of fewer than a hundred men (all he could afford) and left the port of Palos in Spain in early August 1492 with a fleet of three ships, a carrack named the *Santa Maria* and two caravels named the *Niña* and *Pinta*. He headed first for the Canary Islands, but learned while there that the Portuguese had sent out a ship to arrest him. On September 8, he quickly left the Canaries, headed west into the Atlantic, and made landfall in the cluster of islands now known as the Bahamas on October 12, 1492. Columbus thought he had reached Japan, but he had actually entered a world unknown to western Europeans.

To the Americas

The impact of Columbus's landing would not be felt immediately, but after October 1492, the lives of Europeans and indigenous Americans were never to be quite the same. We have only Columbus's fragmentary accounts of these first encounters between Europeans and native Americans. The Taíno people whom the Spanish encountered in the Bahamas showed no hostility, and Columbus described them as beautiful, brown, naked, and poor. He thought that they had a temperament and nature that would make them ideal servants to Europeans. He also believed that it would be easy to convert them to Christianity because, in his eyes, they lacked any religion.

Today we know that the Taíno (which means "good" or "noble" in their own language) dominated the Caribbean region; five of their kingdoms stretched throughout the region. The Taíno were farmers, growing manioc (cassava), and fierce warriors who had a long-standing rivalry with the Carib peoples of South America and the Lesser Antilles. They had a complex religious and ceremonial life based on ancestral gods and a highly organized matrilineal society. None of their traditions would have been recognizable to the Europeans, who saw them as simple, childlike, and lacking in sophistication. Only two days after he made landfall, Columbus boasted that he could conquer the entire population with a force of only fifty men and govern them as he wished.

Columbus spent the next six months sailing around the Caribbean, exploring not only the Bahamas but the islands that we now call Hispaniola (the island divided today between the Dominican Republic and Haiti) and Cuba. Wherever he went, Columbus met with curious Taíno and exchanged European goods for a little gold, new foods, and other material tokens of his discovery. Columbus and his crew captured a few parrots and two dozen Taíno.

All were transported back to Spain in the spring of 1493. Fewer than a dozen Taíno survived the voyage, but they were the first in a long series of native Americans unwillingly or unwittingly taken to Europe to show investors and patrons what the territories had to offer.

From the start, Columbus and his crew were sizing up the economic, territorial, and religious potential of the Caribbean. As his boats sailed from island to island, Columbus made sure to stake the Spanish crown's claim to each, gave each island a Spanish name, and planted a cross on foreign soil. Since the Europeans and Taíno had languages unfamiliar to each other, sign language served in their place, but there was considerable misunderstanding between the natives and explorers. When natives on one island resisted his authority, Columbus showed them a crossbow and sword and indicated that he could kill them if he so chose. Columbus took the next aggressive step at Christmas and established a settlement of thirty-nine of his men on Hispaniola. He also left a cannon with his men. The *Santa Maria* had been wrecked on a reef, so he could not take all his crew back to Spain.

Columbus's effort to promote his explorations in Europe was not limited to the material objects and native peoples he brought back with him, for he knew that he had to launch a publicity campaign to explain why he had not reached Japan and the Asian mainland. He remained convinced for the rest of his life that he had been just about to do so; one more voyage and he would have been there. His rationalization began in earnest with the letter he wrote to his patron, Luis de Santangel, in which he described the "New World" as a paradise inhabited by peace-loving natives who had no knowledge of weapons, little suspicion of newcomers, and no objection to him flying the Spanish royal standard in their waters. This behavior seemed to prove that the native population welcomed the Spanish and accepted their rule. Columbus also described the richness and money-making potential of the land, which had fruit, flowers, singing birds, honey, gold mines, and spices. His account not only exaggerated, but also misrepresented, the true state of things, for little gold had been found in the islands he visited.

The letter to Santangel arrived in Spain before Columbus himself did in 1493, since he sent the letter when he docked in Lisbon to make repairs to his ship. The letter was translated into Latin and printed in various cities in Europe within months. When he arrived in Barcelona, word of his triumph had spread widely. Banquets, parades, and public baptisms of the surviving Taíno were staged in his honor. Ferdinand served as godfather to Spain's new Christian citizens. Columbus received a coat of arms and was appointed the admiral and governor of all the lands that he had encountered. Plans commenced immediately for a return voyage.

There was one little territorial problem that needed sorting out first. The Portuguese claimed that Columbus's discoveries belonged to Portugal. Ferdinand and Isabella submitted the question to the pope, who in May 1493,

1493–1494: The Columbian Exchange

When Columbus returned to the Americas in the fall of 1493, he led a far larger contingent than on the previous expedition. Nearly a thousand settlers returned with him, along with the animals and food needed to establish a colony. His second expedition, thus, kicked off what has become known as the **Columbian Exchange,** a long-term process of the two-way transfer of peoples, goods, diseases, and ideas between Europe and the Americas. The ecosystem and human geography of the Americas began to change, in some areas slowly, in others rapidly, after 1493.[1]

One of the most striking features of the exchange is that it was far from equitable. Over the long run, Europeans introduced more animals into the Americas (including cattle, horses, sheep, pigs, cats, and dogs) than they took back to Spain. Most of these animals were domesticated, and the native American populations that received them were traditional hunting societies. The introduction of domesticated animals disrupted ancient patterns and practices associated with hunting societies and led to the establishment of permanent tribal settlements. Native Americans introduced Europeans to the alpaca, llama, and turkey.

Though the animals of the Americas had a negligible impact on Europeans, the plant and food products they discovered brought much needed diversity to European agriculture and the European diet. New varieties of beans and nuts such as the cashew and peanut provided alternative sources of protein for Europeans. Foods that were rich in vitamins and minerals (avocados, peppers, pineapples, and tomatoes) were introduced to Europe, along with foods and agricultural products such as cocoa and tobacco that would become sensationally popular. Over the long run, corn (maize) and potatoes from the Americas became im-

A Nahua Farmer Cultivating Maize One of many drawings in the Florentine Codex that detail the popular culture of Mexico and Central America in the sixteenth century.

portant staples in Europe, serving as caloric alternatives to wheat and other grains.

The Columbian Exchange had more than one dark side, for Europeans unknowingly introduced deadly new diseases to the Americas. This biological imbalance was one of the chief **contact vulnerabilities** of native Americans when they encountered Europeans. Native American bodies had had no exposure for almost 20,000 years to European and Asian diseases. Beginning in 1492, these invisible colonizers did the work of a vast army when it came to weakening the defenses and reducing the numbers of the indigenous population. Malaria, cholera, and typhoid (diseases associated with poor hygiene) spread among native Americans. So too did viral diseases and pathogens such as influenza, the bubonic plague, and, the most deadly of all, smallpox. Native Americans had never been exposed to these diseases and that proved devastating. Though exact figures are difficult to calculate, it has been estimated that smallpox alone was responsible for hundreds of thousands of deaths during the initial decades of colonization. In exchange, the Europeans were exposed to a relatively small number of new diseases, including a tropical skin infection caused by spirochetes (yaws) and a strain of yellow fever. It was once thought that western Europeans were first exposed to syphilis in the Americas, but recent research on ancient and medieval burials has cast doubt on that assumption.

QUESTIONS | *How might the negative impact of foreign peoples have been softened? Why was the exchange between continents so uneven? What was the ecological impact of the Columbian Exchange on both Europe and the Americas?*

---

mere months after Columbus's return to Europe, divided the world from the North Pole to the South, 100 leagues (about 300 miles) west of the Azores. Everything to the west was assigned to Castile, to the east to Portugal. By the Treaty of Tordesillas in June 1494, the Portuguese and Spanish reset the dividing point as 370 leagues (approximately 1,000 miles) west of the Cape Verde Islands off Africa. This left the coast of Brazil, not yet identified,

lying within the Portuguese allotment, a claim they secured with force when Brazil was identified in 1500.

Later Voyages

Columbus's return to Spain in 1493 was the highpoint of his career. The final decade of his life would mire him in disappointment and controversy. He would be charged with fraud and incompetence as voyage after voyage failed to put Spain in contact with Japan. Columbus was a victim of his own grandiose promises.

Columbus returned to the Americas three times: in 1493, 1498, and 1502. The rationale for each voyage was the same and was based on Columbus's unwavering belief that he had reached the Spice Islands near Japan. He believed that it was simply a matter of time before he reached that fabled land and forged an all-important alliance with the Japanese emperor. If members of his crew suspected that they were not anywhere near Japan, they were never able to persuade Columbus.

In September 1493, Columbus left Spain with seventeen ships and over a thousand sailors and settlers. His crew this time was a more official one: with priests, friars, a physician, and an archdeacon whose royal authority rivaled Columbus's. He sailed around the Caribbean for over nine months, naming islands as he went. Columbus and his crew charted the locations of the Lesser Antilles, Greater Antilles, Virgin Islands, and Puerto Rico before returning to Hispaniola. There they returned to the settlement and fort established in 1492 and found that it had been violently demolished and his thirty-nine crewmen were all gone. As persistent as ever, Columbus established another short-lived settlement, named La Isabella after the queen. The second voyage confirmed the rumors Columbus had heard from the natives on his first visit that the Caribs were a fierce, violent people who practiced cannibalism. Modern archaeology suggests that these reports were probably true, though Europeans were quick to conclude that some of the natives that Columbus encountered were not just uncivilized, but subhuman animals. That conclusion became a further pretext for the violent conquest of native Americans, even though to natives the Spanish Inquisition might have seemed an equally barbarous ritual.

Columbus was an inspired explorer, but a poor administrator. The purpose of his second voyage was not just to find new territories, but to begin the process of the European domestication (through colonization and economic exploitation) of the Americas. The French essayist Michel de Montaigne later said that these new lands were so infantile that they needed to learn their ABCs. Spain kept close watch on its man in Hispaniola as he began to establish settlements. As governor, Columbus regarded the native population as mere labor, directed gold mining operations, and introduced taxation. As an explorer, Columbus remained disappointed that he had not yet located the Japanese islands that he had been seeking, worried about the outstanding costs of his voyages, and was driven to satisfy the demands of his sponsors and royal patrons. When he returned to Spain, complaints about his governorship of the colonies and his failure to find the Far East followed him home and kept him in Spain for four years trying to win over investors and skeptics.

Given the hesitations about Columbus's plans to return along his previous route, it is not surprising that the 1498 voyage involved only six ships. Once he reached his destination, the difficulties continued. Some of his crew mutinied. The settlers who had been left at La Isabella complained about the living conditions and the fact that this was not the land of plenty that they had been led to expect; and the indigenous population was quick to resist the Spanish once they realized that the visitors meant to stay. In spite of these problems, Columbus reached the South American mainland and began to explore the Orinoco River in what is now Venezuela. But the voyage was not judged a success, and on his return to Spain, Columbus was jailed on suspicion of fraud and mismanagement of the colony.

Columbus tried one last time, in 1502, to redeem his reputation by proving that he had found the Indies. Accompanied by his brother and son, Columbus took a fleet of four ships from Spain to Hispaniola. He narrowly avoided a hurricane that destroyed a fleet of Spanish galleons loaded down with cargo from the Americas. While looking for Japan, Columbus explored the coasts of the Honduras, Costa Rica, Nicaragua, and Panama. In Panama, natives told Columbus that gold could be found in the interior, as well as a navigable passage to another great body of water. It was the first hint that Columbus had of the Pacific Ocean, but he did not realize that this other ocean lay between him and his longed-for destination. Storms, native resistance, and an uncooperative Spanish governor on Hispaniola kept Columbus in the Caribbean until 1504, when he was rescued from the island of Jamaica, where he and his crew had been starving for months. He left the Americas that summer, never to return.

The Atlantic Space Race

Like Gutenberg, Columbus could not contain or control his breakthrough. Within a few years, European ships sponsored by European monarchs were regularly crossing the Atlantic. Columbus was convinced that he had reached the islands surrounding Japan, but his contemporaries were not. The explorers who followed in his wake also dreamed of finding territories and riches unknown to Europeans, but they, more practically, chose to exploit the existing resources of the Americas by establishing permanent settlements and profitable trading colonies for their kingdoms. This development sprang from the realization that if the lands Columbus reached in the western Atlantic were not the easternmost edge of Asia, they were still valuable, and offered a distinct territorial advantage for European kingdoms locked in intense competition with each other.

How did the nature of European overseas exploration evolve in the first half of the sixteenth century?

Exploration, conquest, and colonization of overseas lands also fulfilled the imperial aspirations of western monarchs. The Italian and European Renaissances had made them ever more aware of the greatness and dimensions of imperial Rome and that empires were greater things than the enfeebled Holy Roman Empire in their midst. Just as they were territorially blocked in Europe by their long established European neighbors, they were also imperially blocked by the existence of an ineffectual Holy Roman Empire sanctioned by the pope and Catholic Church. Most European monarchs could never be emperors of the many Europes, but they could be the emperors of vast European states that held overseas territories. Spain led the imperial way in the first phase of exploration. Its recent consolidation and unification of the Iberian Peninsula had convinced Ferdinand and Isabella that they already reigned over a multiregional and multicultural kingdom. Hence, it was not by accident that Columbus's voyage across the Atlantic was authorized only after the reconquest of Spain was complete. It was in fact the next logical step in imperial expansion to add other lands to Spain's holdings. England and France would, in Spain's immediate wake, follow the same tack, seeking to assemble empires built on the conquest and domination of overseas territories. In the process of creating empires, they would establish many Neo-Europes abroad, a New Spain here, a New France and New England there, each replicating overseas their own societies and state patterns.

Half an America The cartographer Jan ze Stobnicy's 1512 outline of the Americas depended on Martin Walseemüller's 1507 map. In both, South America was roughly filled in, but North America was still half a continent, not yet complete in the north or west. The large island lying to the west of Central America may be Baja California, not yet recognized as a peninsula. Maps of the sixteenth century gradually filled in the rest of the continent as more information became available.

Amerigo's New Continents

The Florentine Amerigo Vespucci (1454–1512) was the first to proclaim that the lands across the Atlantic were previously unknown continents. Though other explorers of the time called the landmasses and islands they encountered "the Indies" in an effort to conjure up images of the East while remaining vague about their precise identity, Vespucci's recognized that South America (and, later, North America) were separate landmasses unconnected to Asia.

Vespucci, like many of the early explorers, was a merchant and mariner who had a substantial knowledge of navigation and geography. He entered into the service of Ferdinand of Aragon and, between 1497 and 1502, participated in voyages that crisscrossed the ocean between present-day Cuba and Florida and explored the coastline of South America. As Vespucci and his company traveled farther south, he compared their findings with maps of India and realized that they far exceeded its possible coastline.

Like Columbus, Vespucci understood the benefits of publicity and patrons. He wrote letters to various princes to describe his adventures that were the basis for the stories of Vespucci's travels that were drawn together and published between 1502 and 1504. Vespucci's travel tales proved as popular as medieval accounts of voyages to strange and unknown lands and were translated into various European languages. As a self-publicist and popularizer, Vespucci was unrivaled. He titillated Europeans with stories of naked and promiscuous natives who wished to mate with Europeans and tales of South American cannibals. Many of the details of his accounts were either fanciful or fabricated, but he did not invent the American continents; he merely recognized their existence. Yet Vespucci had inserted himself into the narrative of the Americas, and in 1507 a German mapmaker, Martin Waldseemüller, named the previously unknown southern continent as America after the Latin form of Vespucci's first name.

Vespucci's publicity campaign paid off when Ferdinand of Aragon named him "pilot major." Along with the title and office came the responsibility for training Spanish pilots and mariners about geography, navigation, and the routes across the Atlantic. From a school set up in his home, Vespucci trained the next generation of Spanish mariners and explorers, including men who would explore the Pacific Ocean and circumnavigate the globe. Most of the men under Vespucci's guidance set out on their voyages of exploration to reach the Americas—not Japan—and to find other lands unknown to Europeans, and their "discoveries" kept coming. In 1513, Juan Ponce de León, searching for the fountain of youth for his aging king, Ferdinand, made contact with the Calusa natives of Florida. The same year, Vasco Núñez de Balboa crossed the Isthmus of Panama and gazed upon the Pacific Ocean. In 1530, Spaniards reached Baja California and the Spanish began their exploration of the western coastline of what would become the United States.

Living on Board

Exploration was a business for the tough of mind and body. Crews were typically paid by the month or with a share of the booty. On Columbus's first voyage, the ships' masters and pilots earned 2,000 maravedis a month; experienced sailors, half that much; and the inexperienced, a third. It hardly seems enough for what they endured. The ships were small (barely 70–80 feet long) and, except for a couple of bunks for Columbus and the masters, all the other sailors slept wherever they could find space, often in the hold with the ship's supplies or on some protected part of the deck. The deck was often preferable since after weeks at sea, the hold stank of rotting food and was infested with rats. The crew prayed and ate twice a day. Their diet consisted of meats such as pork preserved in brine or dried, salted fish such as sardines, beans, lentils, and olives. They drank poor wine diluted with water.

The length of a voyage was always uncertain. Columbus's initial crossing took a month; Ferdinand Magellan's (1480–1521) to Brazil, seventy days. Later in the Pacific, Magellan's small fleet was at sea for over a hundred days. One of the ship's company described the hunger the sailors experienced. He said that their biscuits had been reduced to worm-infested powder soaked with rat urine. They ate sawdust and the hardened ox hides used to cover the area under the mainmast, and thus were literally eating their ship. Rats were in high demand, but expensive since there was an active trade in captured rodents. Nearly the whole crew fell sick with scurvy from lack of vitamin C. Their joints ached and gums swelled and bled, so that they couldn't eat anything at all and soon died. The death toll on these voyages was horrendous. Vasco da Gama lost most of his men in 1499 to scurvy; Magellan lost 80 percent of his crew.

Magellan left Spain in 1519 with 239 men spread over five ships; one ship finally limped back to Spain in 1522 with eighteen survivors on board. Magellan was not among them; he died fighting in the Philippines the year before. In the thirty years after Columbus's first voyage, twelve explorer-captains died on their expeditions, due to storms, disappearances at sea, misadventures on land, and sickness. Balboa was beheaded for treason. Mutinies were common. Before his death, the Portuguese Magellan had been overthrown by the Spanish captains of his fleet, who charged that he was going to betray their Spanish mission to Portugal. Once he regained his ships, Magellan had forty of the mutineers executed.

Ships were tense environments and the seamen had much to worry about: leaking ships, whales, falling overboard, fierce storms, lack of food and water, disease, and what awaited them on shore in lands said to be filled with monsters and cannibals. If the grumbling sailor was disloyal or disrespectful, he faced a variety of punishments: keelhauling (being dragged under the boat), flogging, or worse. One of Magellan's masters was executed for sodomy. The sailors' suffering was nothing compared to that of the native peoples they invaded and infected, but living on board was grim and coarsening, and it may help explain why the European invaders dealt so roughly and unsympathetically with the native Americans they encountered. The sea had not trained them to be kind.

Hernán Cortés and the Conquest of the Mexica Empire

As Vespucci's mariners and explorers undertook extensive voyages to chart the coastlines of the Americas, they brought along with them soldiers and colonists to explore and settle the interior. These individuals encountered flourishing civilizations that at first welcomed and then resisted them (Map 12.2). Native Americans found themselves up against not only mounted men, guns, and armor, but also the microbes the men carried, which proved even more deadly. The first major Mesoamerican people to succumb to Spanish conquest were the Nahua, who were called Aztecs by the Spanish.

The Aztecs were a single tribe that had established the Mexica Empire in the fifteenth century through a triple alliance between three of its principal cities: Tenochtitlán, Tlacopan, and Texcoco, with Tenochtitlán eventually dominating the alliance. By the time that Cortés and his troops arrived in 1519, the Mexica Empire centered in Tenochtitlan included much of present-day Mexico. The first Spanish force to explore the Mexica Empire was led by Diego Velázquez, the governor of Cuba. Velázquez sent expeditionary forces into the Yucatán Peninsula and the Gulf of Mexico between 1516 and 1518 to gather information. They heard of a wealthy empire just beyond the Gulf. Velázquez selected Hernán Cortés to lead an expedition of exploration.

Cortés had left Spain after growing tired of his life as a lawyer and of the threats from the husband of a woman he had seduced. As a clerk in Cuba, he impressed Velázquez and had the necessary charisma to lead such an undertaking. In the winter of 1519, Cortés left Cuba to search for the Mexica Empire. He had only a few pieces of artillery; sixteen horsemen; and roughly four hundred soldiers recruited from the poorest white residents of Cuba, including young Bernal Díaz, who would later boast that he took part in 119 battles on the expedition.

Once on the Gulf coast of present-day Mexico, Cortés abandoned his mission of exploration in favor of conquering the Mexica Empire. Fearful that his troops would mutiny, he destroyed all but one of his ships so that they could not return to Cuba and notify Velázquez. On the lone surviving ship, Cortés sent a letter to the Spanish king, Charles I, to explain that he had decided to launch a "just war" against the tyrannical ruler of the Mexica peoples and his "ungodly ways." Stories of the Mexica practice of ritual human sacrifice and other non-European ways had already reached the ears of the conquistadors. To ensure that he had the king's full attention, Cortés included enticing references to the wealth of the Mexica Empire and the excellent prospects for converting the Mexica peoples to Christianity. Without waiting for a reply, Cortés set out for the capital city of the Mexica, Tenochtitlán, and began to look for local allies, whom he found among the Cempoalans and the Tlaxcalans.

Three months later, Cortés arrived in Tenochtitlán. The city was nearly two hundred years old when the Europeans arrived. The Spanish, on first seeing the capital compared its luxuries, elaborate canal system, and spectacular bridges to those of Venice, one of Europe's most glittering cities. The city had refinements equal to any in Europe, including aqueducts to deliver fresh water, craft workshops, schools, museums, zoos, a large aquarium, gardens, palaces, and religious temples. By 1521, the Europeans had sacked the city and most of it lay in ruin. Today the remains of Tenochtitlán lie below Mexico City.

The indigenous Mexica population greeted Cortés as the long-awaited descendent of the white-skinned god Quetzalcoatl, who was reputed to have departed in the tenth century, but who was destined to return from the east. The emperor Moctezuma viewed Cortés's arrival

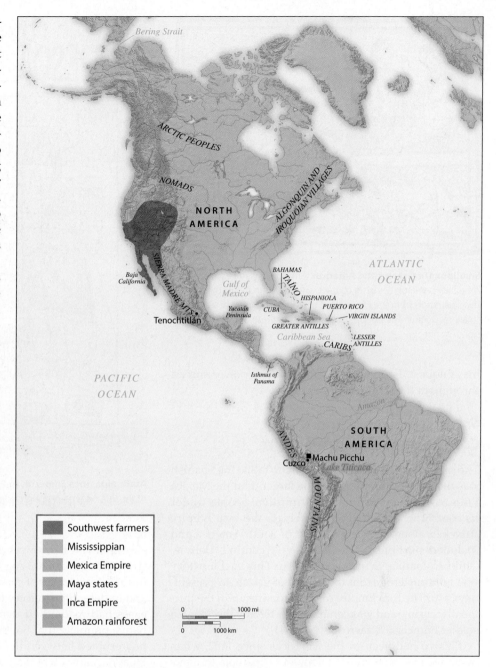

MAP 12.2 | Native Peoples of the Americas in 1500
When Columbus first reached the Bahamas, the native peoples of the Americas were geographically dispersed, spoke different languages, and had organized themselves in a variety of different ways. *How did geography separate native Americans from each other? Why did empires develop in Mexico, Central America, and South America, but not North America? Why were native American societies so vulnerable when they made contact with Europeans?*

as the fulfillment of that prophecy and lavished gifts on the Spanish forces. As with most Spanish expeditions, after a few weeks of relative courtesy, things began to fall apart. Cortés seized Moctezuma and held him as a prisoner. That act stunned the natives, who began to gather treasure throughout the empire to ransom their ruler. While still a prisoner, Moctezuma was struck on the head by a rock during a dispute between the Spanish and the indigenous population, who were protesting the

massacre of hundreds of unarmed Mexica. The insurrection was so severe that Cortés retreated to collect fresh troops. Cortés and his forces returned in 1521 and laid siege to Tenochtitlán, starving its citizens, already weakened by European diseases, into surrender. When Cortés entered the city, he razed all of its buildings. By 1540, the Spanish had constructed a capital for Spanish America, Mexico City, on the ruins of Tenochtitlán. Cortés received a title, wealth, and fame from the Spanish government for

Smallpox Devastates the Americas Smallpox ravaged native American communities after contact with the Spanish invaders. In this illustration from the Florentine Codex, a medicine man treats smallpox victims. The bubbles near mouths in these drawings are signs of speech.

his conquest. From Mexico City, Spanish power spread throughout the former Mexica Empire.

Francisco Pizarro and the Conquest of the Inca Empire

The second native American empire to fall to the Spanish was the Inca Empire. Territorially larger than the Mexica Empire, with an estimated 20 million people under its control when the Spanish arrived, the Inca Empire stretched along the western coast of South America and included portions of present-day Argentina, Bolivia, Chile, Colombia, Ecuador, and Peru. This vast territory was administered from the capital of Cuzco, in present-day Peru. The Inca Empire rose to prominence in the thirteenth century and was conquered in 1533 by the Spanish soldier Francisco Pizarro (c. 1474–1541).

Pizarro had been in the Americas since 1502, when he arrived at the Spanish colony of Hispaniola to make his name and fortune. Born into a minor Spanish noble family around 1474, Pizarro was illegitimate and therefore unable to succeed to his father's titles or lands. He was a second cousin to the famous Hernán Cortés, so it is not surprising that the path he chose was that of a conquistador. In 1522, Pizarro first learned from sailors of a powerful indigenous empire to the south of Hispaniola. He immediately decided that he would find the empire, conquer it, and claim the land and people for Spain. Four years later, Pizarro arrived at his destination and began to scout out the terrain and the people under the control of the emperor in Cuzco. After talking to locals, Pizarro realized that this empire was far grander than he had imagined and he returned to Spain to seek official approval for a military undertaking to conquer it.

Pizarro received the title of viceroy or governor of the soon-to-be-conquered territories and the funds to recruit

Atahualpa, Inca Emperor, in Prison Guaman Poma's drawing of Atahualpa under arrest with a Spanish guard watching over him.

a force of less than two hundred men. After six years of strategizing and planning, he returned to the Inca Empire in 1532. Two strokes of chance enabled his relatively small and underequipped force to succeed. First, European diseases had made their destructive passage through the native population of South America. Second, a civil war had erupted between the two sons of the Inca emperor, Huayna Capac, who had split the empire between them on his death. The Inca armies, with standing forces of well over 200,000 men, had been decimated by disease by the time that Atahualpa's forces finally overcame those of his brother, Huáscar. Atahualpa had little time to enjoy his victory, since he was captured by Pizarro's troops shortly after the civil war ended and became a puppet ruler acting on Spanish instructions. About a year later, after outliving his usefulness to Pizarro, Atahualpa was strangled to death and Spain took control of the empire.

The English and the French Enter the Race

While Spain quickly took the lead in exploring and colonizing the Americas, it soon had overseas rivals anxious to create empires and overseas Neo-Europes of their own. French and English monarchs were eager to enter the race for new territories, riches, and settlements. Though none of their efforts resulted in the collapse of indigenous empires, the French and English undertook to establish their own permanent colonies in North America.

Still smarting from his failure to hire Columbus before the Spanish did so, Henry VII turned to the Cabot family to take up overseas explorations for England. John Cabot (c. 1450–1498), like Columbus, was from the Italian peninsula, most probably from the region surrounding Venice. In 1490, he led his family to England, where he hoped to put his navigational expertise at the service of the new king. Cabot believed that he could find a northwest passage to Asia. In 1496, as the Spanish were busy exploring the south Atlantic, Henry VII supplied Cabot with five ships and the funds needed to explore the north Atlantic and to look for an alternative route to the Spice Islands and Japan. The fleet left England in the late spring of 1497 and by July had made landfall on the east coast of present-day Canada. Cabot mapped the coastline from Newfoundland to Nova Scotia and believed that he had arrived at the continent of Asia. He returned to England in August, was warmly received by the king, and was promptly given the funds for another attempt to reach Japan. Five more ships left England in 1498, but after a fierce storm, one ship was damaged so badly that it had to return to England. The other four ships continued west into the Atlantic and were never heard from again. Though he sponsored Cabot's voyages, Henry's real interest lay in assembling a fleet of merchant vessels that could be quickly refitted into small warships if England ever faced an attack from its traditional rival, France. As the monarch of an island nation, King Henry was one of the first European kings to appreciate the benefits of possessing a professional navy. He never fully realized his naval hopes, but he did make a fundamental investment in ships and maritime technology and England became a maritime power.

The French joined the European space race after Spain and England, but were driven by the same desire to secure new territories and riches, and to rival their traditional enemies. Under Francis I (r. 1515–1547), France ventured into the Americas. In 1524, the Italian explorer Giovanni da Verrazzano (c. 1485–c. 1528) surveyed the North American coastline between the Carolinas and Newfoundland, claiming Newfoundland for the French crown. Jacques Cartier (1491–1557), like John Cabot, came from a family of mariners. As a young man, Cartier took part in voyages to Brazil and Newfoundland. From the king, Cartier received the funding to embark on a voyage to find a northwest passage in 1534. During his first voyage, Cartier mapped the Gulf of St. Lawrence and portions of what are today Canada's Atlantic maritime provinces, traded with members of the Mi'kmaq people, and apprehended two Iroquois boys (the sons of a chief) to take back to France. One year later he returned and reached the St. Lawrence River, where the boys were reunited with their tribe. The French remained on the St. Lawrence through the winter, but disease and starvation took their toll. Iroquois medicines likely saved the eighty-five Frenchmen who survived, but many tensions remained between the two groups. That same winter, Cartier jotted down his impressions of native American society and tried to establish better diplomatic relations with the Iroquois. By the time he returned to France in 1536, he was convinced that what he called Canada (his misunderstanding of the Iroquois-Huron word *kanata*, for village, settlement, or meeting place) was a land previously unknown to Europeans. In 1541, Francis, dreaming of a colonial empire and of creating his own Neo-France or New France overseas, ordered the young nobleman Jean-François de la Roque de Roberval (c. 1500–1560) to establish a permanent settlement in Canada. Roberval hired Cartier to serve as the chief pilot for the first voyage, but his attempts to establish a permanent colony were not successful, and the colony was dissolved in 1543.

Spanish Colonization and Its Critics

The history of the European explorations, conquests, and settlements of the Americas was told chiefly by Europeans, and they most often cast it as a story of heroic triumph over difficult conditions and hostile pagan peoples. At the distance of five hundred years, it may seem that Europeans would inevitably succeed in their efforts to control and exploit the Americas because of their superior weaponry and technology, but the case of the tiny Canary Islands suggests otherwise. There a small resident population of Guanches had successfully resisted the periodic invasions of Muslims, Portuguese, and Castilians for almost five hundred years. In the Americas, during the first half century of exploration and warfare, Europeans did not know the immense land or its many different peoples. The Europeans had guns and iron, but they also had limited knowledge of the local conditions, no dependable food supply of their own, and relatively small numbers of men to send overseas. Yet they did succeed in conquering and colonizing the Americas.

> **Why did the Spanish turn to the colonization and economic exploitation of the Americas?**

Spain had to grapple first and most dramatically with the day-to-day problems of conquest and colonization. Facing enormous challenges and resistance from native Americans, the Spanish resorted to harsh and deadly means to conquer and then control the native populations through systematic colonization and economic exploitation. As the English and French also moved from exploration to colonization, the template established by Spain informed many of their early colonial ventures. Colonization was not without its critics in Europe and the Americas, and, as the problems mounted, Europeans began to question their treatment of native Americans.

The Problems of Colonization

The problems with colonization were many. Europeans boarded their ships with assumptions and expectations that were not well founded, but that shaped their behavior and actions in the Americas. Europeans had two models for the establishment of permanent settlements: the Italian/Portuguese and the Spanish. The Italian/Portuguese model had been pioneered by the Genoese and Venetians in the Mediterranean and the Portuguese along the coast of Africa. The Italian and Portuguese goal was primarily to locate potential markets and then to establish trading centers on the peripheries of a foreign land in order to gain access to its inland resources and trading networks. This less invasive approach led to the exploitation of local resources without making heavy investments of manpower, money, or military presence.

The Spanish method was rooted in the medieval reconquest of the Iberian Peninsula and the Spanish experience on the Canary Islands. The Spanish emphasized the systematic military takeover of a territory, followed by a division of lands and goods between the conquerors and the conquered, with the largest share going to the conquerors. This was a model of invasive or intrusive expansion that had the long-term goal of permanent settlements, rather than the short-term goals of trade and the exploitation of resources. Once the Spanish controlled most of a territory, however, they could begin the widespread and systematic exploitation of its resources, including labor and land.

These two models were applied by the Spanish, Portuguese, and Italians in the Mediterranean, Africa, and the Americas, and then adapted by the French and English. When Columbus set out for Japan in 1492, he had the Italian/Portuguese model in mind, since he was intent on reaching the court of the Japanese emperor and establishing trading and political relations. It was only after Columbus realized he had not yet reached the Japanese court that the Spanish model of conquest and colonization took over, and the desire for settlement and economic exploitation replaced that of diplomacy and trade with a partner.

The military expeditions that set out from Spain in the decades after Columbus, thus, had conquest and colonization as their primary goals. Evidence for this can be seen in the fact that the leaders of the expeditions were given the military rank of captain. The captain then put together a company of investors and participants to finance and make the voyage. As in an early modern army, the members of the company provided their own equipment and provisions in exchange for a share in the profits of conquest. Most were not military men, but came from a variety of backgrounds and social classes that included artisans, merchants, clergy, lesser nobility, urban and rural residents, and even freed blacks from Africa. During the first waves of conquest and colonization, little effort was made to ensure a diversity of skills and abilities among the company, which often led to disaster when few knew how to farm, shoe horses, or repair weapons.

First Encounters

When the Europeans met native Americans for the first time, they came into contact with the descendants of peoples who had migrated from Asia across the Bering Straits (either by an ice bridge or by boat) between 18,000 and 15,000 BCE. As they fanned out throughout the Americas, those peoples eventually formed more than 350 tribal groups speaking over 160 languages and possessing dozens of distinct cultures. The population of the Americas was isolated from Africa, Asia, and Europe, where people, diseases, goods, and technologies had been swapped back and forth for millennia. As a result, native American society prospered and developed without external continental contact or interference.

All of that began to change with the coming of the Europeans. The isolation of the native American population meant that they had no natural immunity to European diseases such as smallpox and plague. They also did not possess the iron and steel weapons that dominated warfare in Europe, Asia, and Africa. Native American encounters with Europeans set off an exchange of goods, microbes, and technologies unlike anything that either party had ever experienced. The debilitating effects of this exchange made it easier for Europeans to conquer and exploit the Americas. After the conquest of the Yucatán, the Mayan Chilam Bayam wrote that before the arrival of the Europeans there had been little sickness, no smallpox, no stomach ailments, no consumption (tuberculosis), and few headaches among the people. The arrival of the foreigners had changed everything, he said. In 1493, Columbus sent five hundred Arawak people back to Spain to serve as slaves. On the ship, disease spread rapidly in the crowded and filthy conditions in the cargo holds where the slaves were confined, and only five shivering captives arrived to be sold in the streets of Barcelona.

Once in the Americas the Spanish were usually met by a friendly and curious indigenous population that was used to treating visitors as guests, provided that there was no sign of hostility. During this first period of contact, the Spanish made careful surveys of the land and people to determine whether they represented a resource ripe for seizure. Within a few weeks or months, the Spanish would typically exhaust local food supplies and resources and begin helping themselves to food, women, and precious goods, and would soon wear out their welcome. At this point, the native people often turned against the Spanish, sometimes harshly, as on the island of Hispaniola when a coalition of tribal leaders joined forces to expel the Spaniards for a time. In most cases, however, the Spanish advantage in military technology (swords, guns, and cannons) allowed them to put down the uprisings and capture local tribal leaders, thereby compelling indigenous cooperation.

Although the Spanish approached their first encounters with native Americans with an eye to conquest and colonization, native Americans generally regarded the Europeans as visitors with whom they were prepared to trade. This was another of what might be called the contact vulnerabilities of native Americans. The tribal societies of the Americas expected that encounters with other peoples would provide opportunities for exchanging goods and ideas. Although warfare occurred between native peoples before Columbus and long after he was gone, there were also more peaceful cross-cultural exchanges.

Though the Europeans were not interested primarily in cultural exchanges with native Americans, exchanges nevertheless took place. In the first stages of European contact and conquest, few women accompanied the soldiers and administrators who traveled to the Americas. Many European men had both coerced and consensual relationships with native American women. Hernán Cortés's relationship with a Nahua woman known as La Malinche began when she helped him communicate with the Mexica people. She was fluent in a number of local languages and quickly learned Spanish. Diáz wrote with admiration of her beauty and intelligence, as well as her power and influence, and explained that La Malinche was of noble lineage but had been sold into slavery. La Malinche became Cortés's mistress and the mother of his son, Martin.

The mixing of European and native American blood happened across the Americas in the early modern period, but it was often unsettling. Europeans resorted to stereotypes and other tactics to demean natives in order to keep the two peoples and cultures distinct. Columbus, for example, believed that the indigenous population of the Caribbean spoke a form of Spanish and kept listening for familiar words, but other Europeans described native Americans as so strange that they seemed not to be human, which made it far easier to justify enslaving or murdering them. It did not help that the Caribs practiced cannibalism, which allowed some Europeans to see native Americans as less than civilized or even human. One telling example of the European struggle to cope with their encounters with native Americans is that they called all indigenous peoples

Malinche Meets Cortés Malinche became the mistress and interpreter of the conquistador Hernán Cortes, and the mother of his children.

"Indians," a single, familiar, and incorrect name that conveyed nothing of the diversity of peoples they encountered.

The Economic Impact of Spanish Colonization

When Europeans realized they were not in or anywhere near Japan, their priorities shifted to outright economic exploitation and religious conversion of lands and peoples. Once local resistance was crushed through a combination of military technology and disease, Europeans found institutionalized ways to coerce the indigenous population to engage in agriculture, pay tribute, and mine for precious minerals. In the Spanish colonies, native Americans were placed under the **encomienda system,** a modified vassalage relationship in which a Spanish settler was given, in the name of the king, trusteeship over a piece of land and its residents in exchange for the military enforcement of Spanish rule and a promise that the colonist would teach the indigenous peoples in his charge about Catholicism. It fell to the Spanish *encomendero* (trustee) to determine how best to make use of the land and people to benefit the Spanish crown's coffers and his own pocketbook. Initially, the grant of an encomienda was not supposed to involve more than three hundred native Americans, but in practice few encomiendas reached that size. Spain established the first encomienda in 1493 in Hispaniola; the system was not abolished until 1791.

In the eyes of the Spanish colonists, the encomienda system was not slavery because native Americans were given a choice to convert to Catholicism and, thus, could avoid being taken under the legal protection of an encomendero. In reality, however, the lines of communication and enforcement between Spain and its possessions were stretched thin, and the encomenderos were free to do what they liked with the land and the people on it with little interference. Widespread abuse of the system led to charges that it was nothing more than slavery. These charges were often made by clerics who visited the colonies and were horrified by the working conditions of native Americans and the lack of attention paid to their religious instruction.

Because of concerns over the breakdown of proper relationships between encomenderos and the indigenous population, the crown drew up two documents "to protect" native Americans. The *Requerimiento* (Requirement) of 1510 provided soldiers and settlers with a legally binding document that had to be read aloud to native Americans before any hostilities could ensue or any encomiendas could be established. Few native Americans, especially in newly conquered lands, knew enough Spanish to understand the document, which outlined the history of the creation, the establishment of the papacy, the rights of the Spanish crown in the Americas, and the people's need to recognize the authority of the pope and Spain. If the natives failed to agree to the terms of the *Requerimiento*, the Spanish were authorized to seize their lands and claim them for Spain, extract labor, and wage war on them if they resisted.

The Laws of Burgos were drawn up at the request of Ferdinand of Aragon in 1512. Designed to define proper government and treatment of the native Americans, the laws reduced the size of encomiendas, gave tribal chiefs rights and exempted them from certain types of work, and outlawed some forms of punishment. The laws, however, were never fully enforced because of the complexities of administering far-flung territories. The Laws of Burgos were rewritten and strengthened in the New Laws of 1542, which proposed a gradual abolishment of the encomienda system. But colonists, many of whom were encomenderos and saw that the laws would mean their economic destruction, rose up in revolt in Peru and resisted their implementation. The New Laws, as a consequence, were not enforced and the encomienda system remained in place.

Under the encomienda system, the native American population was further reduced by European diseases, harsh labor conditions, and brutal mistreatment. The tragic results of the land system, however, were dwarfed by those associated with the brutality of silver mining. The Americas were associated with gold and silver in the European imagination, and the silver mines of South America fed those dreams. The most famous mine site was the *Cerro Rico* ("rich mountain") of Potosí in present-day Bolivia. Between the middle of the sixteenth century and the end of the eighteenth century, more than 45,000 tons of pure silver were extracted from the site. Long hours of bone-crushing labor with picks and shovels, combined with the adverse effects of exposure to mercury, which native Americans amalgamated with crushed silver ore using their bare feet, led to such a precipitous decline in the population of the city that African slaves had to be imported to work the mines by 1608. More than 30,000 African slaves worked the Potosí mines before 1800.

Spanish Colonization and Conversion

The economic aspects of colonization were important to all concerned, but the religious beliefs of the native American population were a matter of special concern to the Spanish crown and the Catholic Church. With their hopes of making a strategic alliance with the Japanese against the Ottoman Turks fading, the Spanish focused on the opportunity to baptize thousands of new Catholics in the Americas. Though priests had accompanied Columbus and other early explorers, by 1500 church and crown officials recognized the need for an organized approach to establishing the faith in the conquered lands. The church responded by appointing bishops and priests to oversee the newly founded churches of the Spanish colonial territories, and by sending missionaries from the church's monastic orders to convert native Americans. The missionaries, unlike bishops and priests, tended to see themselves as independent of the local encomenderos and crown officials and were, therefore, more likely to try to meet native Americans on their own terms and to communicate with them in their own languages. They established schools in the colonies and often lived among the native Americans they sought to convert. Much of what is known about the life and customs of native American peoples comes to us through treatises such as Bernardino de Sahagún's *General History of the Things of New Spain*, which was based on the richly illustrated volume of Nahua accounts and drawings copied from his original reports and known today as the Florentine Codex.

The task of converting native Americans to Catholic Christianity during the first three decades of settlement was taken up by three religious orders: the Franciscan friars, the Dominican friars, and the Augustinian monks (canons). The first to arrive overseas in any significant number were the Franciscans, who entered Brazil with the Portuguese in 1500 and were active in Venezuela by 1508, Mexico by 1524, and California slightly later. The Dominicans began their work in Haiti in 1510 and came in considerable numbers after 1525. The Augustinians were the last of the three orders to arrive, in 1533.

The work of conversion was made easier because of the tendency of native Americans to adopt the religious systems of their conquerors. This was another of the contact vulnerabilities of native Americans. The Inca and Mexica Empires had practiced this form of cultural conquest alongside their own military conquests, and native Americans did not resist participating in the worship and rituals of the Catholic Church. A lack of resistance, however, is not the same thing as complete acceptance, and traditional Nahua beliefs persisted. Catholic missionaries often emphasized similarities between cultures, such as the Mexica belief in ritual sacrifice and a mother goddess, to help native Americans accept Christian beliefs in the power of the Eucharist and the Virgin Mary. The Virgin of Guadalupe, the iconic image of the Catholic Church in the Americas, shows how the indigenous and European religious traditions might blend together. When a newly baptized native American named Juan Diego Cuauhtlatoatzin saw a vision of the Virgin Mary on a hill outside Mexico City in 1531, the Virgin appeared with brown skin, spoke to him in the native language Nahuatl, and asked him to build an abbey on the spot. In the decade following Juan Diego's vision, the missionary campaign was widely successful and most native Americans joined the Catholic Church.

Criticizing Spanish Conquests and Colonization: Las Casas

As the encomienda system became entrenched and the evangelizing efforts of the missionaries continued, critical voices began to speak out against the abuses of colonization. Bartolommeo de Las Casas (1474–1566) was one of the most vocal critics of the Spanish colonial system, and he knew it intimately. A former encomendero who had come to the Americas in 1502, Las Casas became a leading European advocate for native Americans. In 1514, he heard a sermon by the Dominican Anton Montesano, who argued that participating in the encomienda system was a mortal sin. Three years later, Las Casas gave up

Fragments of the Native Narrative of the Conquest

Beginning in 1547, the Franciscan missionary Bernardino de Sahagún began drawing together Nahua accounts of the colonization of Mexico in an effort to preserve a detailed picture of native society from just before the conquest to the present. Sahagún knew the indigenous language, Nahuatl, and in 1558 he was encouraged to make a systematic study of the Nahua people to aid in conversion efforts. Between 1558 and 1569, he spoke to the oldest men and women he could find whose memories stretched back to the earliest years of the Spanish presence. Though Sahagún wrote down all the testimony, he had his Nahua students copy the stories into a trilingual work that included Nahua, Spanish, and Latin and over 1,800 illustrations. Sahagún later edited and in some cases censored the work of his students, and several of his abbreviated versions of the work survive. In 1580, a version of the work was compiled that included only the Spanish translation.

Given Sahagún's role in the production of the text, the Florentine Codex must be seen as a collaborative work. Nevertheless, it provides our best view of native American responses to the Spanish during the first months of encounter and conquest. According to the codex, the Nahua first viewed the Spanish as gods who had come from the heavens and appeared on the waters. Questions have been raised about whether the Nahua had that view initially or were influenced by later efforts by Cortés and other crown and church officials to make the transition between Mexica and Spanish rule seem as seamless as possible.

While the Florentine Codex is the best-known text that includes Nahua reactions to the conquest, scholars have over five hundred codices or partial codices to draw on for information about indigenous life before and during the early years of the

The Florentine Codex Depiction of Nahua Women Preparing a Banquet

encounter. Most were written after the conquest, but a few were made shortly before. That so many codices survive and continued to be made even after the Spanish conquest is in part because of the traditional role that the *tlacuilo* or codex painter played in Mesoamerican life. Four different writing systems had developed in Mesoamerica before the conquest, though the Spanish did not recognize that fact when weighing how civilized these peoples were. Before the Spanish arrived, the *tlacuilo* created volumes that outlined the Nahua calendar and depicted important rituals and ceremonies. Later, the Spanish added captions to these works to explain their meaning for a European audience. After the conquest, many of the codices that survive were dedicated to histories of the Mexica Empire and genealogies of important native families.

Today, these Nahua texts with many additions still survive, having passed through many hands. They stand in stark contrast to the fate of the Mayan codices in the Yucatán Peninsula in the sixteenth century, when whole libraries of volumes that described the history of the Mayan people for nearly a thousand years were destroyed deliberately. The final destruction of the Mayan codices in 1697 in Guatemala left scholars with so little information about the Maya and their culture that today we know far more about the Mexica Empire before and during the conquest than we do about the great Maya Empire.

QUESTIONS | *Why were the writings of and about native American societies dispensed with or destroyed? Given the circumstances under which those codices were produced and survived, can we trust them to provide useful insights into Mexica life and civilization? Why or why not?*

his land and began preaching against the enforced labor of native Americans. After his attempt at creating a new style of colonial government in northern South America failed, Las Casas went to Hispaniola and entered the Dominican order in 1522. As a Dominican, Las Casas believed that meaningful conversion was achieved through peaceful methods that respected native cultures and beliefs. His views were controversial, but they influenced the formulation of the New Laws of 1542.

Las Casas debated his views with Juan Ginés de Sepúlveda in the Spanish city of Valladolid in 1550–1551. Las Casas argued on behalf of the church and the crown that native Americans were a free and rational people who could be freely led to Christianity and that they should be treated no differently from other Catholics. Sepúlveda argued in support of the Spanish landowners of the colonies that native Americans were fitted by nature to be slaves and could be forced into dependent labor relationships by war and conquest. Enslaving them was not a sin, but in accordance with natural law, which was an early modern version of Aristotle's argument about the different conditions of peoples, some deserving to rule, some to serve. Both Las Casas and Sepúlveda later claimed victory, but no one won, certainly not the native Americans at the heart of the issue. There was no change in governmental policy or the encomienda system.

In 1552, Las Casas completed the work for which he is best known, *An Abbreviated Account of the Destruction of the Indies.* It is a far different account of the Spanish in the Americas from the one written by Bernal Díaz. For Las Casas, the Spanish perpetrated unspeakable cruelties against native Americans, who were treated not as children of God but as animals fit only for labor. He noted that by the time he arrived, Hispaniola was home to only 60,000 native Americans. He estimated that nearly three million natives had been killed by warfare or excessive labor in the encomienda system and the mines during the short period from 1492 to 1552. Who in the future, Las Casas wondered, would ever believe such a thing? Spanish arrogance and their victimization of native Americans became a theme that other colonizing powers such as France and England would embroider into the "Black Legend" of Spanish colonial excess. But England and France also found it difficult in North America to balance the needs of colonizers and the rights of the colonized.

East to Asia: The Portuguese Venture

The conquest of the Americas by Europeans was an accidental and world-changing event, but the original dream of finding a direct eastward route to Asia had, in fact, proceeded forward at the same time. The Portuguese reached the Indian Ocean in late 1497 and in the sixteenth century established a long-

Why was the Portuguese enterprise in Asia different from the Spanish program in the Americas?

lasting Asian trading network. They were followed by both the Dutch and the English, who came to dominate Asian trade in the seventeenth century and paved the way for a legacy of western colonialism, mercantilism, and imperialism in Asia.

The Portuguese Reach Asia

The Portuguese never accepted that the way to Asia was west across the Atlantic. They had, instead, resolutely and patiently continued their annual progress south along the coast of Africa until in December 1497 Vasco da Gama finally sailed around the Cape of Good Hope and sailed east into the Indian Ocean. His goal was to find those Christian princes who were thought to hold lands in the east and to acquire gold, spices, and jewels. He made his way up the eastern seaboard of Africa and by May 1498 had reached India. He had not expected to find established trading networks in the Indian Ocean, many of them controlled by Muslim traders. On their first entry into the Indian Ocean, the Portuguese had brought goods (wool garments and trinkets) that Asians found inferior and not worth acquiring. Da Gama did make contacts, acquired some spices, and lost two-thirds of his crew before turning around and sailing home, reaching Lisbon in late 1499. He returned with a large flotilla of ships in 1502 and this time brought military force to bear to begin monopolizing the trade in pepper, which was shipped back to Portugal for a handsome profit.

The Portuguese proceeded to set up trading outposts (*feitoria*) and fortifications around the Indian Ocean, which allowed them to maximize trade, undermine their rivals, and force trade deals. Some of these trading outposts remained in Portuguese hands for centuries. Goa in India was set up in 1510 and not reacquired by India until 1961. The Portuguese did not reach China until 1513 and were allowed to establish a trading base at Macao in 1556 (not surrendered until 1999) so that they could barter for silk cloth. The Portuguese monarchs divided their Asian trade interests into two enterprises: the *Carreira da India* for handling trade from Asia to Portugal and the *Estado da India* for trade within Asia. In Lisbon, a large dockyard and arsenal employed thousands to manage Asian trade as loaded ships came in and new ships were sent out to India. The king issued licenses and approved monopolies over the spice trade in pepper, nutmeg, and mace. Such was Portugal's dominance of the spice trade that Venice transferred its spice operations to Lisbon.

The impact of the Portuguese in the Indian Ocean was considerable, disrupting or severing older trading routes that had supplied the Venetians and, hence, Europeans with spices through the Ottoman Empire and Egypt. There was local resistance to Portugal's intrusion into old trading lanes. Traders in India were not pleased. In 1501 at Calicut, where the Portuguese had set up a trading post, Muslim traders rioted and were met with cannon fire from Portuguese ships. At the other end of this trading network stood the Mameluke rulers of Egypt, who

Alternative Junk History

The claim that the Portuguese reached New Zealand and Australia long before Captain Cook did in the late eighteenth century is possible, but virtually no evidence supports the claim that the Chinese in the early fifteenth century discovered Australia, New Zealand, Antarctica, and the Americas. Yet in 2003, Hu Jintao, the president of China, claimed before the Australian Parliament that the Chinese had been the first (that is, after aboriginal settlement) to visit Australia. It is true that in the early fifteenth century, during the Ming Empire, the eunuch admiral Zheng He commanded a fleet of junks that sailed west into the Indian Ocean and supplied reports on the Indian subcontinent to the Chinese emperor. There is no evidence, however, that Ming mariners sailed farther east or west or established settlements or trading posts far outside of China.

In 2002, Gavin Menzies set off a firestorm of controversy when he published *1421: The Year China Discovered the World*. In his sensational book, Menzies claims that during the reign of the emperor Zhu Di, Zheng He's fleet, captained by four eunuchs, discovered a host of lands while circumnavigating the globe. Historians universally panned the thesis, noting not only that no solid proof existed for such a claim, but also that Menzies had misunderstood or misrepresented maps, references, and archaeological and DNA evidence. The publisher referred to the work as an alternative history; the critics claimed it was a pure fiction. Over a million copies of the work were sold and *1421* became particularly popular in China, where it seemed to satisfy a longing for an early modern history to rival that of Europe.

History depends on evidence, context, and sound judgment, all of which seem to be lacking in *1421: The Year China Discovered the World*. Alternative history may not be history at all, but it does respond to other needs, both nationalistic and financial. In the case of Menzies's book, the publisher, Transworld, supplied a team of over one hundred people to produce and package a book that addressed that audience. When pressed about the lack of evidence to support the extraordinary claims in his book, Menzies and the publisher answered, as so often is the case for alternative histories, that there had been a conspiracy to destroy the evidence; that when Emperor Zhu Di died in 1424, the next emperor decided that it would be best not to endanger the Chinese economy by pursuing the discoveries and, thus, his bureaucrats systematically removed mention of Zheng He's extensive expedition from the official records. Menzies followed up the first book with the 2008 publication of *1434: The Year a Magnificent Chinese Fleet Sailed to Italy and Ignited the Renaissance*. It seemed not to matter to the author that 1434 was a little late to ignite a renaissance movement that was already well under way by then or that not a single Italian humanist, and they were an observant and loquacious crowd, described the arrival of the Chinese fleet. Alternative history can be fun and thought provoking, but it requires correct labeling so that bookstore clerks, at least, will know where to shelve new books when they arrive, whether in the history or fiction aisles.

QUESTIONS | *In our digital age, how can we best assess the various alternative histories that populate the Internet? What sort of evidence should we require to support new and extraordinary claims? Why is the idea of extensive Chinese exploration in the fifteenth century so appealing to some audiences?*

---

saw their trade with Europe drying up. They assembled a fleet of ships to evict the Portuguese from the Indian Ocean but were defeated decisively in the important naval battle of Diu Island in 1509. This event critically undermined the traditional Muslim role as the critical conveyors of jewels, spices, and gold from Asia to Europe.

Portugal defended its trade interests in the Indian Ocean but apparently never dreamed (as had the Spanish in the Americas) of conquering the old and established states that ringed the ocean. They had too few men and, perhaps more important, they lacked the military and disease advantage that the Spanish had possessed in the Americas. There simply weren't the same contact vulnerabilities between Asia and Europe that there were between the Americas and Europe. Though Asia had been cut off from easy access by Europeans for a century, Europe and Asia were effectively one military and disease pool, with no one side having a distinct advantage. That relative equality forced the Portuguese to tread more lightly, to negotiate, and to trade, much as Columbus imagined he would have done had he reached Japan. In fact, the Portuguese adapted to local conditions, often employing Muslim traders, with their local knowledge and command of different European and Asian languages, as pilots and emissaries to conduct negotiations for them. The Portuguese got to Asia first, which was a distinct advantage, but they never had the manpower or the resources to dominate Asia or to keep their European rivals out. Instead they traded, replacing the Muslim middlemen who had facilitated east-west trade in the

Indian Ocean for centuries. The Portuguese influenced but did not dominate or overwhelm the languages and cultures of the Asian peoples with whom they interacted. Asians came to call the Portuguese "hat men" because of their distinctive black head gear.

The Dutch and the English Arrive

Portugal's rivals first reached Asia by the westward or Pacific route. Ferdinand Magellan was Portuguese but worked for Spain. He sailed with five ships around the southern tip of South America in 1520 and then set out across the ocean that he named the Pacific (peaceful) Ocean. He died in a battle in 1521, but one of his ships made it back to Europe the next year. Though Portugal's European monopoly of trade with Asia was supposedly protected by terms of the world-dividing Treaty of Tordesillas of 1494, the terms of the treaty were undercut in 1580 when Philip II of Spain was also crowned king of Portugal. Instead of giving Spain the absolute right to dominate world trade, both American and Asian, Spain's many enemies seized the opportunity to establish their own trading interests in Asia.

Both England and the Dutch Republic in the early years of the seventeenth century sanctioned companies that were given monopoly trading rights to East Asia. The English and Dutch proved more aggressive and resourceful than the Portuguese in pressing their advantage in the Indian Ocean. The Dutch East India Company eventually out-hustled the English and Portuguese, took the East Indies (Indonesia), and gained a toehold in South Africa. The age of global mercantilism and imperial reach arrived in the seventeenth century.

A New Wave of Christianity Hits Asia

Asia has experienced many waves of Christian contact. In the early Christian period, India had small communities of Nestorian and Thomas Christians; and in the Middle Ages, China under the Mongols was exposed to the Franciscans and made contact with the medieval papacy and Christian traders such as the Polos. In the sixteenth century, as Europe's religious temperature rose, Catholics (not Protestants) began active missionary work in Asia. Magellan was given permission to baptize some natives in the Philippines in 1521. Later in the century, the Spanish found themselves locked in religious warfare with Muslims in the Philippines.

The Portuguese attempt to convert the peoples around the Indian Ocean was secondary to Portugal's economic interests. With the creation of the Jesuit order (see Chapter 13), however, the Christian effort by both the Spanish and the Portuguese intensified. The most famous of the missionaries was Francis Xavier (1506–1552), one of the founders of the Jesuit order. With the approval of the Portuguese king and his own appointment as a papal representative, Xavier set off for East Africa and India in 1541. Xavier worked from the top down by trying to convert kings, nobles, and powerful men, and was constantly on the move: from Mozambique to Goa, India; to the Spice Islands; and then to Indonesia. By 1549, he was in Japan where he tried to convert the emperor to Christianity. Unlike their experience in the Americas, the Christian missionaries to Asia encountered deeply entrenched and sophisticated organized religions (Islam, Buddhism, Hinduism, and Shinto) that were difficult to dislodge or replace. Xavier died of a raging fever on an island off the coast of mainland China in 1552.

| Conclusion

European overseas expansion changed the world. In some ways, this was the first great moment of a connected global history, for continents previously unknown to Europeans, Africans, and Asians were brought into play. The very notion of the Earth as a globe of scattered landmasses set in two chief bodies of water was born, a change in awareness that was being worked out visibly, line by line, on sixteenth-century maps.

Deep contact between continents separated by vast oceans would have happened anyway at some point in world history, with many of the same disastrous ecological and demographic results for the Americas, but it occurred in the late fifteenth century because of the competitive tensions at work in Europe and between Europeans, and because of the strange conviction of one Genoese explorer that the world was smaller than it actually is. By the late fifteenth century, Europeans found themselves hemmed in by the sea and surrounding Ottoman Muslim lands that blocked their way east.

Ambitious European countries could not find suitable outlets within Europe for their goals of expansion or their imperial aspirations. Locked into fierce struggles with each other for advantage, first Portugal and then Spain, England, and France, turned to the sea to break out of the territorial gridlock of Europe. The success of Islam in locking down the Middle East, Near East, and Asia forced Europeans to look south and west, whether along the coast of Africa or across the Atlantic. Within European society the same struggle for advancement and advantage was being played out between individuals such as Columbus, Vespucci, and Cortés, all of them looking for their chance to make their own breakthrough to wealth and fame and for royal patrons to fund their ambitious schemes. Middling men such as Bernal Díaz saw exploration as their way to move up in the world.

Once Columbus made contact with the Americas in the Caribbean and publicized the fact, others rushed to follow in his sea-steps. The pace of early exploration was furious, for within forty years of Columbus's landing, Europeans had mapped the coastline of the two Americas, circled South America, and sailed around the globe. The Portuguese at the same time had rounded Africa and sailed to India, China, and Japan. This was discovery not for the sake of new knowledge, but for economic and religious gain. Colonies with economic and religious goals began with Columbus's first voyage and were institutionalized as royal policy. In the Americas, Europeans had come not just to visit, but to stay, dominate, and exploit their possessions, to create Neo-Europes in their own image. In this, they pursued their national advantages and exported their European rivalries overseas. Spain profited more than the others in the short run, as the sixteenth century was to be its golden age, fed by South American gold and silver. The many Europes can seem the big winner of the overseas gambit, since they had extended their footprint over two more continents and escaped the narrow confines of their own small continent and their even smaller kingdoms. They had circumvented their effective containment by Islamic lands, thus gaining a huge advantage over their nearest neighbors in world domination. The European world further shifted its economic and political focus from the Mediterranean to the Atlantic and Pacific.

The balance sheet of European expansion can seem starkly unbalanced. The fall of two empires in the Americas, the disruption of patterns of existence that were thousands of years old, and the shocking loss of life in the Americas from disease, conquest, and economic enslavement make it seem that native America, with its hundreds of different peoples spread over two continents, was the passive victim of the invaders. The demographics of European expansion are shocking. When Columbus first visited Hispaniola there were about 100,000 residents; seventy-five years later, only 300 natives were left on the island. The native population of Mexico might have been as high as twenty-five million people in 1520 but had dropped precipitously to around one million people by 1600. These changes didn't happen overnight; native Americans made subtle accommodations and adaptations. Take the case of horses. Though horses had first evolved in the Americas, they had gone extinct long before the explorers arrived and the Spanish reintroduced them. Yet within a century many American peoples had made the horse the central animal of their cultures and economies.

If there were small gains for native Americans, there were large losses for some Europeans. Not every European country participated in overseas expansion. The Germans, most Italian city-states, the Dutch, and the Belgians did not enter the first rush of sixteenth-century exploration and spent much of the following centuries hankering for territorial holdings and empires of their own outside of Europe, but the big prizes in the west were already gone. Spain, the chief and most successful imperial dreamer in Europe, was, despite all the precious metals that poured into the country or, perhaps, because of them, bankrupt by the end of the sixteenth century. Even the Portuguese found that their domination of the spice trade was less lucrative than they might have hoped. The massive influx of gold and silver into Europe from the Americas distorted the European economy and led to a runaway inflationary spiral throughout most of the century. The price for goods in Spain had doubled from pre-exploration levels by 1560. Aside from the economic problems caused by expansion, the balance-of-power problems within Europe were made worse or more complicated by overseas expansion. The rivalries between European states had not been solved by expansion, just diffused to other arenas of engagement. Europeans now had more lands and conflicts to dispute and wage war over.

The most interesting impact of European expansion may have been intellectual. When Boccaccio and Petrarch wrote haltingly about the Canary Islands, they were in effect dealing with the European and Renaissance problem of authority versus firsthand experience. In its discovery and reverence for classical antiquity, the Italian Renaissance had erected a new realm of classical authority (based on ancient authors) to set beside the Christian one (based on the Bible), and these intellectual regimes threatened to inhibit Europeans from a more adventurous investigation of the world. The Americas challenged that fixity, for they needed to be dealt with on their own terms, a thing the bookish Columbus had trouble doing. In 1560, a Parisian lawyer said that it was astounding that classical authors had had no knowledge of the Americas. And in 1512 the Nuremberg geographer and humanist Johann Cochlaeus said, after reading of Vespucci's voyages, that whether his accounts were true or a lie, they had nothing to do with cosmography or history and were of no interest to geographers. Illustrious humanists such as Erasmus simply ignored the Americas. The Renaissance reinforcement of authority, albeit classical, would lead to some difficulty in certain quarters adjusting to new information not bound within familiar book covers.

The encounter with nonclassical and nonbiblical peoples in the Americas led to a category crisis. Where were these peoples to be placed on the human tree that descended from Adam and passed through Athens and Rome? A Portuguese adventurer, Antonio de Montezinos, in the seventeenth century proposed that he had located in Ecuador one of the ten lost tribes of ancient Israel, but the theory came late and was an indication that a century and a half after Columbus's contact, the peoples of the Americas were still difficult to fit into familiar European categories. Pico Mirandola's Renaissance flourish on the dignity of man meant little on the shores of the Bahamas, especially if explorers were disinclined to recognize that these others were fully human. Few explorers coped well with contact, regarding native Americans as childlike, uncivilized, promiscuous, and murderous primitives (see Back to the Source at the end of the chapter). Christian missionaries did better, for at least they saw the American peoples as human beings with souls to save and lives to reform, though they too participated in a form of exploitation, this time religious.

The Americas and their many peoples could not, however, be denied. They had to be dealt with by experience and observation. A cosmographer of the sixteenth century said that what he had to say about the Americas couldn't be learned in Salamanca, Bologna, or Paris. Christianity and Eurocentrism cushioned Europeans against the utter shock of new knowledge and new experience, layering perception with old and familiar ways of perceiving the world. But the Americas opened up the European imagination and knowledge bank to new possibilities and realities. Some boldly embraced the new. One Spaniard by midcentury proclaimed that contact with the Americas was the greatest event since the creation of the world. Another confidently claimed that the world had been opened up for the human race, by which he meant, opened up to Europeans. The very existence of the Americas and its unknown peoples expanded the European imagination. After reading of Vespucci's travels, Thomas More in his *Utopia* imagined a more perfect society existing somewhere across the sea far away from troubled Europe. But native Americans were neither primitive nor pure and did not exist in some state of innocence; they were themselves and that took longer to recognize and respect. Still, the Americas were that breath of fresh air that Europeans had long needed to extricate themselves from their old view of the world and their tired debates. The explorations that began with the Canary Islands and Columbus's first landing in the Bahamas shook Europe out of its comfortable medieval and renaissance restraints, confident and settled certainties, and territorial confinements. But Europe had another old, large, and lingering problem yet to resolve, and religion would be the great battleground of the early modern world.

Critical Thinking Questions

1. What is wrong with using unqualified terms such as *New World* and *Old World, Known World* and *Unknown World,* and *Discovery*?

2. What best explains the drive of Europeans to explore and colonize overseas?

3. What were the contact vulnerabilities of the Americas and the many Europes? Why did they exist, and what was the result?

4. Why was it so difficult for Europeans to conceptualize and deal with overseas realities?

5. How did overseas exploration and conquest change the explorers, the many Europes, and the world?

Key Terms

conquistador **(p. 359)**

balkanize **(p. 360)**

carrack **(p. 366)**

caravel **(p. 366)**

Portolan chart **(p. 366)**

astrolabe **(p. 366)**

converso **(p. 367)**

Columbian Exchange **(p. 369)**

contact vulnerabilities **(p. 369)**

encomienda system **(p. 377)**

Primary Sources in connect

For information on Connect and the online resources available, go to **http://connect.mcgraw-hill.com**.

1. **John Mandeville at the Court of the Great Khan**

2. **Columbus's First Description of the Americas, 1493**

3. **Bernardino de Sahagún's Account of the Taking of Tenochtitlán**

4. **Doña Marina, La Malinche: Native Help-Mate of Cortés**

5. **Montaigne's American Cannibals**

6. **Laws and Reactions to the Americas**

Picturing European Fantasies of the Americas

Within a few years of Columbus's landing in the Bahamas, European illustrators were already imagining the delights and horrors of the Americas, as seen in the two woodcuts below. The first fantasy, based on Columbus's account, shows King Ferdinand of Spain extending his approval of Columbus and his three ships as they land overseas on a tropical island paradise populated by scantily clad natives. The second woodcut (Augsburg, 1505) presents more of the dark than the light side of the Caribbean islanders, who are shown as promiscuous cannibals. Even by late in the sixteenth century, the Mannerist painter Paolo Farinati (1524–1606) of Verona still expressed something of the continuing European fantasy with the Americas and their strange peoples in his allegorical painting *America* (1595).

QUESTIONS | *Analyze the main elements of the three images. What European assumptions do they reveal? How are the native Americans imagined and portrayed? What has changed between the imaginings of the early woodcuts and Farinati's later painting? What does the painting imply? Why did Europeans indulge in these fantasies?*

13

TEMPLE DE LYON, NOMME´ PARADIS.

Jean Perrissin's Painting of the Calvinist Temple of Paradise, Lyons, France (1565)

THE RELIGIOUS RE-FORMATION OF EUROPE

The Protestant Religious Re-Formation Begins
Martin the Monk
Luther and the Indulgence Controversy
Struggling with Rome
From Instituting to Living the Lutheran Faith

The Early Re-Formation of Church and State
Lutheran Princes
Huldrych Zwingli
Henry VIII Divorces the Catholic Church
John Calvin and the Religious Re-Formation of Geneva
Living a Religiously Re-formed Life in Calvin's Geneva
The Schmalkaldic League and Peace of Augsburg

The Radical Religious Re-Formation Splinters and Spreads
Anabaptism

Millenarians Make a Last Stand
Separatism and Peace: The Mennonites

The Catholic Reformation
An Order of Spiritual Soldiers: The Jesuits
Catholic Mysticism Connects
Reforming Popes and the Council of Trent
Welcome Back: The Baroque Embrace of Rome

The Wars of Religion
The French Wars of Religion
The Dutch Revolt and the Spanish in the Netherlands
Elizabeth I and the Spanish Armada

Conclusion

ERASMUS AND KATHARINA VON BORA LEAVE MONASTICISM BEHIND Erasmus, the prince of humanists, was a self-made man. Born Herasmus Gerritszoon, he later took the first name of Desiderius and dropped the last name, which identified him as Gerard's son. As the illegitimate son of a young man who had abandoned him and his mother, Erasmus had little social standing and few worldly prospects, and so his family pushed him toward a religious life. After some training in the new devotion promoted by the Brothers of the Common Life, which was the rage in the Netherlands at the time, Erasmus was compelled to enter the monastic life. He had wanted to go to a university, but became instead an Augustinian monk (canon), and was often resentful, bored, and restless. Yet there were benefits to being a monk: conversation with other bright young monks, access to a decent library, and a superb training in Latin. His reputation as an accomplished

Portrait of Erasmus in 1517 by Quentin Metsys

Portrait of Katharina von Bora in 1528 by Lucas Cranach

Latinist helped him to convince his superiors to release him, for he had a job waiting as secretary to the bishop of Cambrai. Finally, Erasmus broke free from an enclosed life and was never again to be caged by what he came to view as the stifling, rigid, and conservative torments of monastic life. By 1500 he had published his first bestseller, *The Adages,* and became a humanist star, ever on the move from patron to

patron, always in search of a good meal, fine wine, and clever conversation with learned friends.

Erasmus was not alone in wanting to break free from the chains of monasticism. Other famous reformers of the sixteenth century abandoned the monastic life, among them both Martin Luther and his future wife, the noble Katharina von Bora. Katie, as Luther came to call her, had been raised from the age of

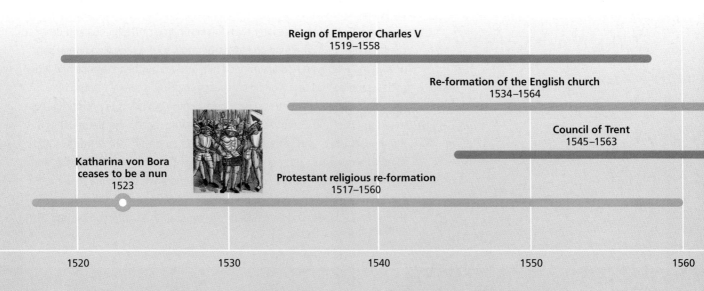

Reign of Emperor Charles V
1519–1558

Re-formation of the English church
1534–1564

Council of Trent
1545–1563

Katharina von Bora ceases to be a nun
1523

Protestant religious re-formation
1517–1560

1520   1530   1540   1550   1560

five in a convent, learning Latin and the basic teachings of the Roman Catholic Church: the need to do good works in pursuit of salvation, the spiritual necessity of celibacy, and the supremacy of the pope. But during the years of Katie's monastic confinement, people were beginning to question the nature of their religious beliefs. The Catholic monk and university professor Martin Luther was the most prominent of these, and his writings and ideas made their way into Katie's monastery. She and her sisters wrote to him about their growing doubts. With Luther's personal encouragement, Katie and eleven of her sister nuns decided that their path to salvation did not lie within the confines of a monastery or Roman Catholicism. They plotted to abandon the convent, break their monastic vows, and join Luther and his followers in the city of Wittenberg. On Easter eve 1523, under cover of darkness, the nuns crept out of their monastery. Following Luther's plan, they hid in the wagon of a fish merchant and were driven away from the monastery by a sympathetic city councilor. When the wagon pulled into the university town of Wittenberg, the students took note of the arrival of a "wagonload of vestal virgins . . . more eager for marriage than life." Two years later, after her first love match had failed, Katie married Martin Luther and became the wife of Europe's most controversial married cleric.

The abandonment of monasticism by the likes of Erasmus and Katharina von Bora was yet another sign that the Middle Ages was slipping away, just as the Fall of Constantinople and the replacement of the parchment medieval manuscript by the printed paper book had signaled its end. Ten years after Katie left the monastic life, King Henry VIII ordered the dissolution of the monasteries of England, seized monastic properties, and sent monks and nuns out into the world they had rejected. Since the Early Middle Ages, monasticism had been a central element of the Catholic Church and its claim to be in intimate and constant conversation with the divine. When nuns such as Katharina von Bora quit the monastery, broke their vows of chastity and obedience to the spiritual guidance of the Roman Catholic Church, and pinned their hopes for salvation on a radical new way of viewing and living a Christian life, their departure from the old ways was as revolutionary a social act as had been the hermit Anthony's abandonment of Roman city life for the desert in the third century. The religious life of Europe was being remade and Christianity re-formed.

� ✝ ✝ ✝

Though the period has typically been called the Reformation, that familiar term has lost some of its capacity to shock us into an appreciation of the radical and transformative nature of the remaking of European religion that occurred in the sixteenth century. As a label, *the Reformation* has many problems. By 1519, Luther was no longer interested in reforming the Catholic Church, but was determined to do away with it, replacing it with a different ordering of the relations between humans and the divine. Moreover, there were several reformations, not just the Lutheran or Protestant Reformation, but also a Radical Reformation and a Catholic Reformation. Only

Wars in the Netherlands
1566–1609

French Wars of Religion
1562–1598

1570   1580   1590   1610

the last of these consisted of the actual reformation of an existing church and not its replacement. Some scholars have, instead, called the Catholic Reformation a Counter Reformation, for to call it a Catholic Reformation is to assert that it was a preexisting movement, generated internally, and largely independent of Protestant criticism, whereas to call it a Counter Reformation is to suppose that Catholics reformed their church only in reaction to the Protestant Reformation. Some observers have wondered if the Protestant Reformation would be better called a revolution, since the effect of the radical rethinking of Christendom by Protestants was to overthrow an old religious order that had dominated western Europe for over a thousand years.

To treat the period as a re-formation, remaking, or re-founding of Christian institutions and beliefs is not, we hope, just to play with words, but an attempt to capture something of the active restructuring and fundamental reordering of Christianity that took place in the sixteenth century. For if "to reform" is to revise, correct, and improve something while leaving the thing itself still intact, "to re-form" is to shape something anew, to begin again from the ground up and put aside the old, which may legitimately be said of the Protestant approach to the establishment of new churches and new forms of Christianity based on the apostolic or early Christian church. The first formation of the church had taken place in that early period stretching from Christ's life to the emperor Diocletian's great persecution of the Christian Church. The second period began with Constantine's conversion and stretched through the Early Middle Ages, east and west. In that long period, the church took on its normative institutional and doctrinal form. The third great reform of the church, often called the Investiture Controversy or Gregorian Reform, was the restructuring of the church by the papacy in the eleventh and twelfth centuries. That reformation produced the Great Schism of the church into eastern and western churches, and was the last great reordering of the western church and of its sources of power and fundamental claims before the monumental events touched off by Martin Luther. The religious re-formation of Europe in the sixteenth century was one of the West's great turning points. It was turbulent, revolutionary, and lasting in effect.

The medieval church had rested on a set of fundamental beliefs and practices, at the heart of which lay the celebration of the Mass (as the reenactment of Christ's last supper). The Catholic faithful met in the physical and spiritual church under the supervision of a priest who acted as an essential intermediary between humans and God. The priest administered the granting of the sacraments to the faithful, for humans were regarded as deformed and sinful as a result of the Fall and so in need of sacramental remedies. Moreover, Christians required a priest to serve as an agent intervening with God to secure forgiveness and favor for them. The Catholic Church also held that **Purgatory** was a place between heaven and hell, where the sinful dead awaited the Last Judgment and welcomed the prayers of the living in the hope of securing release from everlasting torment and a prolonged period of punishment or purgatorial cleansing. On earth the pope was God's supreme representative, his archpriest, and the arbiter of all things concerning the faithful. Martin Luther and the Protestants would in time challenge each of these fundamental tenets of Catholicism, and by so doing create new churches, new sets of beliefs, and a re-formed idea of the essential meaning of Christianity. Protestants broke the back of the unity and universalism of the Roman Catholic Church.

At its most basic level, the religious re-formation of Europe was a struggle for authority that pitted individual faith against the Catholic Church's traditional and institutional monopoly over Scripture and religious practice. This crisis of authority had profound implications for religious and political life throughout the early modern period, and for the political and religious contours of the West. When the Catholic Church lost its institutional and religious monopoly, it was as though a dam had burst. Long pent-up ideas, frustrated spiritual desires, and political aspirations flooded forth, washing over the many Europes and into its many nooks and crannies.

The Protestant Religious Re-Formation Begins

The problems of the late medieval church and the new trends in medieval religion were many, as surveyed in Chapters 10 and 11: the profound impact of the plague and other crises; the Babylonian Captivity of the papacy in Avignon; the Western or Papal Schism, when multiple popes reigned at the same time; the rise of a vigorous conciliar movement; the emergence of a deeply felt lay piety less dependent on the institutional church; the turbulent national religious movements in England under John Wyclif and in Bohemia under Jan Hus; and the rise of humanism, with its critical examination of texts, both classical and religious. None of these disturbances, however, can account for the appearance and impact of Martin Luther (1483–1546), one of history's great radicals. They were rather the background noise against which he emerged. As a university professor of theology and a member of the Catholic clergy, Luther was an unlikely candidate to bring about the re-formation of the Christian religion. But his growing conviction that the pure message of Christ and Christianity had been perverted over the centuries by the existing church led him to a radical rethinking of salvation, of the individual's relationship to the divine, and of the essential purpose of the church. By 1600, Europe was dramatically different, at least religiously, from what it had been in 1517, when Luther accidentally sparked a revolution in Christian thought and practice.

Why couldn't Luther just go along with tradition and the age-old weight of church authority?

Thirty Years of Religious Turmoil

DATE	EVENT
1517	Martin Luther issues the Ninety-Five Theses
1518	Huldrych Zwingli begins to reform the Catholic Church in Zürich
1519	Charles V becomes emperor
1519–1521	Huldrych Zwingli establishes his own re-formed church in Zürich
1521	Luther refuses to recant his beliefs at the Diet of Worms
1522	The Knights' Revolt
1522	The sausage scandal in Zürich
1524–1525	Peasants' Revolt in Germany
1525	Luther marries the former nun Katharina von Bora
1525	Anabaptists publicly gather in Zürich
1529	Luther and Zwingli meet at Marburg and fail to unite their churches
1530s	Scandinavian kingdoms all join the Lutheran Church
1531	Zwingli dies in battle against the Catholics
1534	Henry VIII by the Act of Supremacy breaks from the Catholic Church
1535	Anabaptist Münster falls to Catholic forces
1540	Ignatius Loyola founds the Society of Jesus (Jesuits)
1541	John Calvin establishes his re-formed church in Geneva
1545–1547	The Council of Trent's first session
1547	Defeat of the Protestant Schmalkaldic League at the Battle of Mühlberg

Martin the Monk

Unlike the noble Katie, Martin Luther was of middle-class background. His father, Hans, the son of a successful farming family, became a prosperous miner in Saxony and married well. Hans dreamed of Martin becoming a lawyer and helping out their large family. To that end, Hans funded his son's education right through university. Like Erasmus, Luther was enrolled in schools established by the Brothers of the Common Life and dis-

tinguished himself as a student by his quickness and intelligence. In 1501, he entered Erfurt University to study secular law and thrived, earning his degree after a single year of study and continuing on to acquire his master's degree three years later.

He then began the advanced study of the law, but in July 1505 a sudden summer storm changed the direction of his life. Luther was very nearly struck by a bolt of lightning. Cold, wet, and frightened, he prayed to Saint Anne (the mother of the Virgin Mary), promising that if he lived he would dedicate his life to the church. Luther made good on his promise by entering the Augustinian monastic order. The world lost a lawyer that stormy day, but gained a religious revolutionary.

Unlike Erasmus and Katie, Luther willingly and with utter spiritual sincerity entered into the monastic life, and he proved to be a dedicated monk. He advanced to the priesthood and even traveled to Rome on behalf of his monastic order. Luther, however, was unsatisfied, for as a monk he was tormented by the worry that he was a wretched sinner who would never achieve salvation, not even by being the best monk that he could be. He did try, driving himself to religious extremes by abstaining from

The Young Martin Luther, 1520 Lucas Cranach's engraving of Luther early in his career, three years after the Ninety-Five Theses and a year before his confrontation with Emperor Charles V. Luther is still dressed as a monk, is tonsured, and has a look of righteous conviction that his supporters and opponents came to know well.

sleep and meals, and observing all-night prayer vigils. In 1511, his superiors, fearing for the health of their driven young monk, encouraged him to return to a life of scholarship and so sent him, still a monk, back to school.

Luther and the Indulgence Controversy

The Augustinians sent Luther to the new University of Wittenberg, which the elector of Saxony, Frederick the Wise, had proudly opened in 1508. There Luther became a professor of theology. Though a lifelong and devoted Catholic, Frederick was extremely proud and protective of his fledgling university and of its brilliant new professor. Luther soon established himself as the dominant voice of the university. His first target, however, was the curriculum, not religion. He led an assault on the older scholastic study of Aristotle and the schoolmen that lay at the core of the new university's curriculum. In early 1517, he released a less well-known set of Ninety-Seven Theses on curriculum reform, whose central conviction was that "Aristotle is to theology what darkness is to light." To a friend he explained that, when he was done, the study of the Bible and Augustine would have entirely displaced Aristotle. As a teacher, Luther was an inspired innovator. He stripped away medieval commentaries from the texts used by his students so that they could read Scripture afresh, unhindered by the erroneous interpretations of the past. Although Luther was indebted to humanist ideas about how to handle texts and the need to cut through textual complexities to rediscover original simple truths, he was never a humanist in spirit. His view of the world and of humankind was always too dark and pessimistic to have shared in humanist optimism about human potential and human capacities.

While he was earning a reputation at the university as a stirring teacher, Luther continued to worry about his own salvation. He discussed with his students the Catholic doctrine of salvation, which taught that faith, good works, and the confession of sins led to divine forgiveness. In an effort to answer his students' questions about the subject, Luther looked to early church teachings and the New Testament for guidance. He slowly came to believe that faith was a gift freely bestowed by God and that it might be a sign of salvation. Luther's ideas about salvation were not fully developed in 1517, but he was heading in a dangerous direction, for, according to the Catholic Church, faith alone was not sufficient for salvation. The believer also needed the Catholic Church and all that went with it (pope and priests, church and custom, sacraments and intercession). The matter soon came to a head.

One of the most popular forms of good works in Catholic Europe was the purchase of **indulgences.** Indulgences were believed to shave time off a sinner's sentence or lessen the severity of his or her punishment in Purgatory, the waiting room to heaven or hell, in exchange for a fee. Luther had been struck by the church's reliance on indulgence monies when he visited the Vatican in 1510, a year in which Michelangelo was hard at work painting the ceil-

ing of the Sistine Chapel. Indeed, the two are not unconnected, for Luther's great doubt about the existing church was rooted in his dismay over the opulence of the papacy and its drive (first by Julius II and then Leo X) to adorn the papal palace (including the Sistine Chapel) and St. Peter's Basilica. Michelangelo and Luther thus stood at opposite ends of the same papal imperative to beautify the Vatican, one as its client-painter, the other as its critic-priest.

Within Catholic theology, the sale of indulgences made perfect sense, for the sinner by purchasing an indulgence was performing a penitential act of repentance and restitution for his crimes, and Christ as a fount of limitless power could save whomever he wished, indeed the whole world if he so chose. Even if the sinner fell short of deserving to be saved, she might appeal to the intercession of Mary and the saints, who were believed to have done so much good in the world that their merits constituted a vast treasury of credits that could be expended on behalf of the penitent.

In 1517, the church enlisted a Dominican friar named Johann Tetzel to sell indulgences in Germany. Frederick the Wise, however, was himself a great collector of relics and saw the indulgence campaign as competition to his own fundraising plans. He banned the sale of indulgences in his territory, but students and citizens from Wittenberg were soon leaving the elector of Saxony's lands to purchase indulgences across the line. The purpose of this indulgence campaign was to help the pope finish his expensive renovations of papal Rome and to assist the Hohenzollerns, an ambitious noble family from Brandenburg, to secure the important archbishopric of Mainz for one of their own, Albrecht, who was already the archbishop of Magdeburg. The archbishopric of Mainz was a great prize since Mainz occupied a critical place in the selection and election of the Holy Roman emperor. Moreover, Albrecht was already deeply in debt to the Fugger banking family that was bankrolling his bid for the Mainz see and various other enterprises. The powerful players promoting the sale of indulgences in 1517 were not, however, crass hypocrites, since they also remained confident that the purchasers of indulgences would still obtain an earlier entry to heaven through their pious act.

Luther was perturbed that the students and citizens of Wittenberg were purchasing indulgences. He had questioned the indulgence trade before, but in 1517 he was still preoccupied by the curriculum reform he was spearheading at the university and may not have fully appreciated what a storm of controversy he was about to unleash. On October 31, 1517, he issued a list of Ninety-Five Theses against the sale of indulgences and other church abuses. We can no longer be sure that he posted these statements on the door of the cathedral in Wittenberg or that he expected a debate to follow, but the theses soon spread in printed form in both German and Latin versions. He also sent a copy to Archbishop Albrecht, who sent the contentious propositions to Rome for review. Within weeks, copies of Luther's Ninety-Five Theses had reached a wide audience in Europe, sparking a pamphlet war of words

Viewer Beware!

The satirical image of "Johann Tetzel, the Dominican Monk, with his Romish Sale of Indulgences," as the caption to the cartoon reads, has appeared in many surveys of western history. The image is a Protestant caricature of Tetzel's indulgence campaign. The pretentious friar sits on an ass, as Christ did on Palm Sunday, while a haloed dove hovers above his head and insects or small birds encircle it. Nestled in his left arm are fox-brushes (fox tails), a common symbol of deceit and double-dealing. In his right hand he rings bells to beckon penitents, who approach the heavy, locked money chest to deposit their coins in a pan and purchase forgiveness for their sins. The first approaching penitent may be a noble, since he wears boots and a sword, but the smaller figure being dragged forward is a poor barefooted peasant. The accompanying poem mocks, as Luther did

Caricature of Johann Tetzel Peddling Indulgences

in his Ninety-Five Theses, the idea that "The moment the money into the pan rings, the soul into heaven springs."

The great problem with this striking cartoon is that it is a secondary (or subsequent) source, not a primary (or contemporaneous) one. It did not appear in 1517 as a piece of Protestant propaganda during the Indulgence Controversy, but a hundred years later in Wittenberg as a broadsheet commemoration of Luther's protest against indulgences and the start of Luther's revolt against the Catholic Church.[1] For generations the drawing has worked to fix an image in student heads of the Protestant complaint against the crude sale of indulgences by Tetzel and the church. Yet how accurate is it? The caption calls Tetzel a monk and the caricature shows him as tonsured or balding, but in fact Johann Tetzel was a Dominican friar. In the Ninety-Five Theses, Luther never once mentioned Tetzel by name, and though he criticizes the outlandish claims of the indulgence sellers, Luther had bigger fish to fry. His propositions were more academic and abstract in nature, not the stuff of a personal drama between him and a fiery Dominican preacher. When we encounter icons of the past, we need to maintain a critical attitude, always questioning, particularly in our own electronic and imagistic age, whether what we are looking at is what it pretends to be. It matters historically whether the image of Tetzel atop an ass was contemporary propaganda and influenced Luther's contemporaries to turn against the Catholic Church and its sale of indulgences or was a later, distorted commemoration of the past.

QUESTIONS | *Why might historical images easily mislead us? What critical questions should we raise when examining them? Why are printed drawings and images from the early modern period particularly susceptible to misinterpretation?*

and images with the Dominicans, who felt obliged to defend their man Tetzel. Had the wider world and the religious parties simply ignored the theses of the obscure German professor from the little university, his critique of the church might have passed unnoticed, but this was the age of print, and a narrow academic argument soon became the opening sally in a religious revolution.

The strange thing about the Ninety-Five Theses is that they seem, with hindsight, not to be overly provocative (see Back to the Source at the end of the chapter). Luther

did lay into the pope and the papacy as an institution, calling on the pope to pay for St. Peter's Basilica out of his own extensive riches, and not the meager resources of the poor, but he held out the possibility that the extremes of the indulgence trade were the product of extreme preachers. He charged that the pope could not remit any punishments but those that he had imposed. Though Luther doubted the theology and efficacy of indulgences, it is striking how much Catholic teaching he still accepted. He qualified some assumptions about Purgatory, but still accepted its reality, as he did that of the saints and sacraments, penance and merit, and good works. Though it may have been but satirical posturing on his part, he presented himself as someone seeking to help the pope live and act within his rightful powers and religious limitations.

Struggling with Rome

Pope Leo returned Luther's theses to the Augustinian order to sort out internally. Luther still suspected that his criticism of the sale of indulgences could be contained within the existing framework of the Catholic Church and resolved in academic debate, so he agreed to attend an Augustinian convention in Heidelberg in the spring of 1518. There Luther planned to discuss his criticisms with his fellow monks and reduced his ninety-five propositions to a more manageable list of twenty-eight, chiefly on the subject of grace. When Luther arrived and presented his ideas, his fellow Augustinians cheered him, but his Dominican critics remained sullen, resentful over the attack on one of their own, and opposed to the implications of Luther's theological impertinence.

In Rome, as reports filtered in from Germany about the slow pace of indulgence sales and the swelling impact of Luther's protest, Pope Leo X became concerned. He ordered Luther to report to Rome by August 1518 to present in person his objections to the sale of indulgences. Unsure whether to obey the order, Luther sought out Frederick the Wise for guidance. Frederick was assured by his private chaplain that the professor was not a heretic but was simply trying to bring the Catholic Church into proper alignment with Christian teachings. Concerned that the pope might not share this opinion, Frederick advised Luther to remain in Wittenberg.

In October in Augsburg, Luther did meet with the pope's representative, Cardinal Thomas Cajetan, a Dominican scholar, who found the professor brash and stubborn. At about this time, not finding a sympathetic ear within the official church, Luther came to his most critical theological insight after reading the letters of Saint Paul, that it was "by faith alone" (*sola fide*), as a pure gift of God, that believers live and are righteous. Christians can do nothing to achieve salvation by their own merit, he thought; no good work could win them their way to heaven. At this point, Luther turned away from the authority of the church and its doctrine of good works to the primacy of faith as encountered in the Bible. "By Scripture alone" (*sola scriptura*), he concluded, and not from church tradition or through its priests, was the word of God to be known. "By grace alone" (*sola gratia*), which was a pure gift of God, was the believer saved. Luther and his followers held that humankind was so fallen, so sinful, that it could do nothing to achieve salvation on its own. The human will was simply too weak to achieve salvation; only God's intervening grace could save humans. These core insights were to undermine the Catholic Church and its doctrinal foundations. Luther's radical theology made the church unnecessary and, indeed, an obstacle blocking Christians from the truth.

In 1519, with the support of the Hohenzollerns, a new Holy Roman emperor was elected. As Luther's arguments were hardening, the nineteen-year-old Habsburg Spanish king, Charles I, became the emperor Charles V. His was an unenviable lot, for he suddenly had vast and difficult territories to govern and faced in the north the stirrings of the new religious movement that was rapidly taking concrete form (Map 13.1). Charles's problem, like that of all overcommitted people, was that it was difficult to do any one thing well when you have too many things to do, and Charles was dragged from one crisis to the next over the forty years of his tumultuous reign.

Luther, who was still just an outspoken member of the Catholic clergy, was challenged by an ambitious professor named Johann Eck to a traditional academic debate in Leipzig on the idea of salvation. In the debate, Eck attacked Luther for his criticism of the papacy and forced Luther to defend Jan Hus, even though a council had executed Hus for heresy. In this way, Eck trapped Luther into revealing his animosity toward the entire Catholic Church, both to the papacy and to its councils. In the aftermath of Leipzig, Eck crafted the formal papal bull *Exsurge Domine*, in June 1520, giving Luther sixty days to recant his heretical beliefs or face excommunication. Luther publicly burned the papal bull, the treatises of his opponent Eck, and the legal documents drawn up against him.

Luther then went on the offensive, taking his case to a wider public. In short order in 1520, he produced three concise works that spread quickly in print and that constituted a frontal attack on the Catholic Church. In the first, *The Address to the Christian Nobility of the German Nation*, he presented the pope as the Anti-Christ interfering with the administration of the empire and the clergy as the destroyers of the Christian church. For Luther, all people, not just clerics, could establish a direct relationship with God. He spoke of ordinary worshippers as belonging to "a priesthood of all believers" that bore the responsibility for seeing that the church was set on the right path. In the second pamphlet, *The Babylonian Captivity of the Church*, Luther continued his assault on the papal and priestly perversion of the Christ's message and church. Here he rejected four of the Catholic Church's seven sacraments (confirmation, marriage, the taking of holy orders, and last rites), leaving only baptism, the Eucharist, and penance as sanctioned by Scripture. Finally, in his treatise *On Christian Liberty*, which was addressed to Pope Leo X, Luther returned to his argument that good works, merits, and indulgences do not lead to salvation, only faith does. With the publication of these tracts, Luther went around the established church to address Germans and Christians at large. The German monk now stood so far beyond the Catholic Church that he was unable to reenter.

Luther's pamphlets finally made it clear to the pope and emperor that something had to be done about the rogue monk. Leo X signed the orders to excommunicate Luther and passed them to Charles to enforce. The young emperor found himself in a difficult spot, caught between the pope and Frederick the Wise of Saxony, Luther's protector

MAP 13.1 | Charles V's Europe, 1519–1558

The Holy Roman Empire and Habsburg lands were not the same, but Charles V's empire consisted of both. Together they made him the preeminent ruler in the first half of the sixteenth century, but one whose lands were scattered and troublesome, each having its own demands and interests. In addition, the Ottoman Empire was encroaching from the east and the Valois kings of France were bothersome in the west. The locations of many of the emperor's battles during his long reign are marked on the map. *Why was Charles V's inheritance of such a vast territory a mixed blessing? What sense can be made of the timing of the various battles and areas of conflict? How did Charles's political and territorial problems affect the attention he paid to religious problems?*

and the emperor's potential military ally. Charles tried to reach a compromise by calling an imperial meeting (diet) in the city of Worms. On April 17, 1521, Luther appeared at the diet and was asked to recant his heretical beliefs. Luther asked for a recess. The next day, he refused to revoke his belief in salvation through faith alone and spoke the famous words "Here I stand. I can not do otherwise."

From Instituting to Living the Lutheran Faith

After Luther held fast to his religious principles at Worms, the emperor issued an Edict of Worms (1521) that declared Martin Luther an outlaw. Added to the pope's earlier excommunication decree, this declaration made Luther a pariah in the eyes of both church and state. The

terms of the edict made it illegal for anyone within the empire to aid Luther and his followers, or to buy, sell, read, preserve, or print any of Luther's writings. If the threat of civil penalties was not enough to deter them, Luther's excommunication placed at risk the immortal soul of anyone who offered him shelter. But Charles had been as good as his word at Worms; he respected the terms of the safe conduct that he had granted to Luther and allowed him to leave Worms in peace. Frederick the Wise engineered a mock arrest of Luther and sent his controversial professor to the castle of Wartburg in Saxony, where for ten months, while northern Europe seethed with religious turmoil, Luther remained out of harm's way and beyond the emperor's reach.

While in hiding, Luther worked on a new, vernacular translation of the New Testament (the Old Testament

1521–1522: The Knights Rebel

By 1521, Martin Luther had powerful enemies in the pope and the emperor. Though he had begun by criticizing the church from within as a monk and had been supported by his university, his Augustinian order, and the elector of Saxony, his position as a critical insider vanished at the Diet of Worms. By 1522, Luther's ideas were being used by others to attack the political and religious establishment. The stakes surrounding Luther's actions were high. When Luther attacked the church, he had not only explicitly questioned the pope's religious powers, but also implicitly called into doubt the secular powers of the pope and earthly princes. By standing up to the emperor at Worms, he had snubbed his nose at Europe's most powerful leader (at least in theory and symbol) and protector of the faith. The pope and emperor were forced to take Luther's stubborn resistance as a political as well as religious threat to their authority. Early modern Europeans had little awareness of the concept of a loyal opposition, and that made it imperative for political authorities to silence dissent before it spread.

Charles's worst fears about the explosive connections between political rebellion and religious criticism were realized in 1522 with the outbreak of the Knights' Revolt. One of the most avid proponents of what has been called "swash-buckle reform" (the use of the sword to bring about religious change) was Franz von Sickingen. Sickingen was a member of the traditional landed nobility of the Holy Roman Empire and had seen the fortunes of his family decline while those of the merchant classes rose. To make ends meet, Sickingen used military force to extort payments and trade agreements from those families and

cities unfortunate enough to fall under his power. He was outlawed for these extortions in 1515 and later turned to Luther's ideas. Sickingen believed that Luther's criticisms of the established church would further weaken European institutions such as property holding. He also believed that Luther's doctrines contained a criticism of the mercantile culture of buying and selling that had undermined his family's traditional privileges.

Sickingen gathered supporters, many of them aristocrats also disgruntled over their loss of standing and angry at the church. They attacked the city of Trier in 1522. To defend itself against the marauding knights, the city hired Philip of Hesse, a supporter of Luther, who did not want to see Luther's religious movement linked to political and social violence. The city's forces drove Sickingen from Trier; his soldiers fled to their own estates, where they were hunted down and dispatched.

The political establishment had won the day, but the damage was done. Many people who were sympathetic to Luther's criticisms of the church drew back from the new religion out of fear that the Knights' Revolt was just the beginning of a flood of insurrection. Politics and religion, which had been uneasy bedfellows for centuries, became even more tightly connected in the minds of early modern Europeans after Martin Luther refused to bend to the wills of an emperor and a pope.

QUESTIONS | *Why do revolutions so often take on a life of their own and soon spin out of control? Why and how did Luther's stand at the Diet of Worms encourage political and social rebellion?*

translation came later). Luther's translation of the Bible was to have a formative influence on shaping the German language. He made his version of the Bible consistent with his Augustinian and Protestant interpretation of the text. As well, Luther began to assemble the pieces that would serve as the theological foundation for the Lutheran Church. To do so, he adopted the *ad fontes,* or back to the source spirit of humanistic textual analysis, and closely examined Scripture to be sure that his new church was in agreement with the ideals practiced by Christ and the Apostles.

One of Luther's goals for his new church was to offer worshippers a greater sense of spiritual connection with God. For Luther, one of the essential ways to achieve this connection was through re-formed church services and a Bible that was in the common language. Reading and

listening to the word of God in German, rather than Latin, advanced lay spirituality, Luther argued, and further diminished the Catholic distinctions between the laity and the clergy. The Lutheran Church would have ministers, who would be thought of as members of the congregation, not priests. Luther argued that all worshippers should receive both bread and wine in the Eucharistic ceremony. The new practice departed from Catholic custom, which taught that the wine, as transformed into Christ's blood, was too spiritual to give to the laity and so was offered only to the clergy. For Luther the idea of a "priesthood of all believers" meant that the faithful would not need intermediaries such as priests or saints to help them communicate with God. In Luther's new church, every worshipper was capable of speaking directly with God without an intervening agent, whether human or institutional.

While these doctrines were important to formulating the theology of the new Lutheran Church, Luther knew that he needed to address clerical and church abuses when he established the guidelines for his new religion. To reinforce the idea that a person's faith was all that was truly important to God and to achieving salvation, Luther simplified church rituals and ornamentation, removing images of saints from churches and their feast days from the official church calendar. He discouraged the collection of relics and declared that neither indulgences nor good works had any value in achieving salvation. Luther also reduced further the number of legitimate sacraments from three to two, leaving only baptism and the Eucharist in place. Luther also opposed the Catholic Church's belief that the priest, by saying the holy words of consecration in the Mass, completely transformed the bread and wine of the Lord's Supper into the body and blood of Christ. Luther replaced this Eucharistic doctrine known as transubstantiation with the idea that the substance of the bread and wine coexisted with or alongside the presence of Christ's body and blood.

Luther also doubted the value of a monastic life and a celibate clergy. He did not believe that ascetic or celibate lives were any holier than other forms of faithful living, and in fact monks and celibates were living unnecessary and unnatural lives. As a result, he argued against monastic orders like his own that had served as spiritual bedrocks of the Catholic tradition. Luther believed that the clergy should be out among the laity, teaching and preaching the word of God, not praying in isolated monastic cells. Since they were no closer to God than any other believer, monks should abandon their monasteries and rejoin the congregation of the faithful, the very argument that he made to Katie and her sister nuns. For Luther, the Catholic priests' vows of celibacy ignored God's instruction to be fruitful and multiply. Instead, Luther argued for the importance of a married clergy that could, through the example set by their households, promote Christian beliefs and principles. For him, marriage was a Christian good that established a decent, friendly, charming, and necessary relationship between man and woman.

Luther put his beliefs in a married clergy and the importance of the family into practice when he married Katharina von Bora in 1525. Their household grew over the years to include their own six children, the children of relatives, and Luther's students who boarded with the family to provide extra income. Ever the good Protestant wife, Katie treated the sick, brewed and sold beer, and involved herself in the day-to-day business of running an early modern household of considerable size.

Within Lutheran families, discipline and order were seen as the cornerstones not only of virtuous private lives, but also of virtuous public lives. Lutheran communities called for all people to live without sin within the boundaries of acceptable collective moral behavior. The best way to enforce these ideals was through the institution of the family. A strict hierarchy of father/master, mother/ mistress, children, and servants was observed to help promote personal virtue and civic righteousness. Within Protestant families, age was superior to youth, masters to servants, and men to women. Despite this hierarchy of power, the mistress of a household, as the second in command, bore considerable responsibility, and many women were drawn to the Lutheran Church because of the relative autonomy and respect it promised them.

The Early Re-Formation of Church and State

By the time Luther emerged from his castle retreat, the religious revolution he had started was spinning out of control as dissidents and radicals emerged from the cracks now evident in the vast facade of the Catholic Church. In 1521, there were already incidents of idol smashing as the old tokens of the Catholic Church were being torn down and destroyed. In 1522, the so-called Zwickau prophets began to show up in Wittenberg, claiming to speak directly to God. As Wittenberg reeled from incidents of idol smashing and social riots, Frederick insisted that Luther return from his castle hideout in Wartburg to restore order. Luther returned, banished the false prophets, and worked to stabilize Wittenberg. The speed of the unfolding events brought out Luther's own social and political conservatism, alerting him to the pressing need to establish his re-formed church. Though he had unleashed the forces of religious heterodoxy and divergence, he did not intend to license the free play of religious thought and experiment in Europe.

How did the existence of many Europes and the political divisions of the early sixteenth century save Luther and Protestantism from being silenced and suppressed?

By 1522, Luther was trying as hard as he could to control and direct the religious forces he had loosed on northern Europe, giving definition to his true religion, and casting out all those ideas and people who refused to remain within its ever-tightening definition of the faith. He did not intend to test the wild world of religious ideas seething outside Saxony, except in print; he rarely left the comfortable confines of re-formed Wittenberg. His most immediate problem was how to ensure the survival and success of the Lutheran Church. For Jan Hus and the Hussites in Bohemia, that part of their religious program had turned out badly. Luther and Lutheranism needed to find a better way. Support from the elector of Saxony and deference to political authority were Luther's critical starting points in securing secular support for his religious movement.

As Lutheranism grew and gained a wider following, problems arose regarding the relationship between church and state. Nobles and other powerful people in the Holy Roman Empire began to convert to the new religion but were placing themselves on a collision course with the empire and the papacy. In addition, new religious leaders such as Huldrych Zwingli and John Calvin challenged not only Catholic Church teachings, but also Luther's ideas, and moved to establish their own churches. Finally, the interest in national churches shared by many of the new monarchs bore unexpected fruit when Henry VIII of England broke with the Catholic Church to clear his way to divorce and remarriage. By the middle of the century, the relationship between church and state was explosive.

Lutheran Princes

In the years following the Diet of Worms, Luther found a way to combine his religious radicalism with political conservatism; he never revolted against his immediate worldly masters in Germany. But princely conversions to Lutheranism in Germany were complicated by the princes' continuing commitments to Emperor Charles V. Some of Luther's earliest princely followers came, therefore, from Scandinavia. Unencumbered by political alliances with the Catholic emperor, Gustavus Vasa of Sweden (r. 1523–1560), Frederick I of Denmark (r. 1523–1533), and Christian III of Denmark (r. 1534–1559) established national Lutheran churches in the 1530s. Through Christian III's efforts, the Lutheran faith was also taken up by Norway, which made Scandinavia staunchly Lutheran by the 1540s.

The adoption of Lutheranism was more problematic in the Holy Roman Empire. One of the earliest setbacks occurred when the Peasants' War broke out in Germany in 1524. Some historians have seen the earlier Knights' Revolt as a dress rehearsal for this much lengthier and bloodier revolt. In the Peasants' War, the rebels were peasants who had been suffering under the financial burdens of paying not only local taxes, but also imperial and papal taxes. New taxes were imposed on beer and wine and even on slaughtering one's own farm animals for food.

In 1524, peasants in the Black Forest rebelled against their overlord by declaring that they would not pay tithes or taxes to him, nor would they honor their traditional obligation to work his land. The peasants stopped working and began to gather supporters. As they did, the conflict began to spread through southern Germany. A radical mystic and former follower of Luther, Thomas Müntzer, who had become frustrated with the slow pace of Lutheranism, aligned himself with the peasants and encouraged them to see themselves as God's chosen ones in a war of the godly against the godless. Müntzer was looking to the end of time and saw the peasant uprising in apocalyptic terms. The peasants' actual grievances were a complex mixture and confusion of social and religious complaints. They sought an end to serfdom and tithes, freedom from oppressive lords and their punishments, a lifting of restrictions on hunting and fishing, the right to choose their own pastors, and to have them preach to them only the Gospels, clearly and without human additions or doctrines. Luther was at first sympathetic to the peasants, but he soon realized that their goals were not

The Peasants Protest Most copies of The Twelve Articles, which was reprinted dozens of times in the early months of the rebellion, were confiscated and destroyed. This image from a rare copy of the pamphlet depicts the peasants sympathetically, but determined and armed to the teeth.

ones of religious improvement, but of social revolution. In the spring of 1525, large peasant armies seized lands, burned castles, and looted churches and monasteries that stood in their path. In May 1525, Luther urged European authorities, both Catholic and Protestant, to put down the revolt by any means: "let all who can, strike, slay, and stab them, in secret or in public, remembering that nothing is more poisonous, harmful, or devilish than a rebel." Luther, the religious rebel, saw no contradiction here; his political sympathies lay on the side of order and established secular power. Some 70–80 thousand peasants were slaughtered in 1525.

Despite this unsettling incident, German princes continued to convert to Luther's church, and by 1526 the emperor Charles V once again found himself in a difficult situation. He needed the support of the German princes to fight an expensive war against the Ottoman Turks, who were threatening to invade Hungary and Austria. When the urgency of the problem required the emperor to recognize the fact of Protestantism, Charles convened an imperial diet in the town of Speyer in 1526. He intended to use the diet to reinforce the terms of the Edict of Worms, but the gathering instead called for a general church council to meet and discuss the issue of religion in the empire. The Diet of Speyer decided that until the council could meet, a degree of religious toleration and coexistence should be granted to the princes so that every state could continue to exist, govern itself, and follow its own religion if it believed that it could be justified before God and the emperor. The decree not only postponed the implementation of the Edict of Worms, but also gave many princes the opportunity to adopt the new religion. After the diet, the rulers of eight regions and eight cities in Germany quickly adopted Protestantism as their official religion.

Three years later, Charles was back at a newly convened diet in Speyer (1529). Imperial armies had failed to halt the Ottoman advance on Hungary, and the Ottomans were now threatening Vienna. This time the extreme crisis encouraged representatives of the emperor to take a harder stance against Luther's new religion. The decisions made at the first Diet of Speyer to delay the implementation of the Edict of Worms and permit religious diversity in the empire were overturned at the second in favor of a stricter enforcement of the Edict of Worms. The Lutheran princes protested against these reversals, earning themselves the name **Protestants,** which followers of all branches of the re-formed Christian faith have held ever since. The Protestant princes joined together to defend themselves against the attack on their religious beliefs and adopted the motto "The word of God remains forever" to link their protests to the authority of Scripture, on which the Lutheran Church rested.

Huldrych Zwingli

The thirteen cantons (small territorial divisions) of the Swiss Confederation fared no better than the empire did in achieving religious compromise and stability. A Catholic priest and religious radical, Huldrych Zwingli, propelled the region into religious war. Educated at the Universities of Vienna and Basel, Zwingli developed ideas of church reform that were based on the principles of Christian humanism, especially those of Erasmus. He thought that both the church and the state could and should be reformed and renewed in conformity with the Bible. His study of the Bible led him to a series of radical conclusions. The words that Christ spoke at the Last Supper ("this is my body" and "this is my blood") were, he came to believe, purely symbolic and did not connote the transubstantiation of the bread into Christ's body or the wine into his blood. He also determined that it was wrong and unnecessary to venerate the saints, to display images, to sing in church, or for priests to remain celibate.

By 1518, Zwingli had carried his message of reform to the city of Zürich. Although still a Catholic priest, Zwingli was by 1521 an increasingly vocal critic of the church, which placed him in opposition to his bishop and to the officials of the Holy Roman Empire. Matters reached a crisis point in 1522, when Zwingli's followers violated the Catholic prohibition against eating meat during Lent, the forty-day period of fasting and prayer before Easter. Since they could find no evidence in the Bible to support that Catholic custom, Zwingli's disciples divided up and ate two smoked sausages in public during Lent, though Zwingli himself refrained. In the aftermath of the sausage scandal that ensued, Zwingli provoked an even greater outcry when he revealed that he had married a young widow named Anna Reinhard earlier that year. He petitioned city officials to abolish a celibate clergy and to start down the path toward constituting a new church. Zwingli had passed quickly from Catholic reformer to church re-former. No longer content to work within the Catholic system, he was ready to establish a new church based on a different set of practices and beliefs, all of them grounded directly in the Bible. The Catholic Church responded by sending officials to Zürich to silence Zwingli. In 1523, city officials held a public debate to consider Zürich's religious future and Zwingli's fate. They decided that Zwingli should be allowed to continue preaching in the city and that all priests should confine themselves to preaching the Bible.

News of Zwingli's victory in Zürich and the city council's support of re-forming religion soon spread to the other urban cantons. Officials in Bern and Basel welcomed the precedent Zürich had set in taking control of its own religious affairs. They also approved of Zwingli's idea of a lived faith, in which believers followed in the footsteps of Christ and modeled their lives after his. Urban leaders promoted both re-formed teaching and preaching as a way to build a more cohesive and unified society.

Despite Zwingli's popularity in the Swiss cities, the countryside remained Catholic and loyal to the emperor. Concerned about the threat of religious and civil war, Zwingli reached out to Luther and his followers to form an alliance of religiously re-formed Swiss and German cities. The two men met in the city of Marburg in 1529, along with other prominent Protestants. At the Marburg Colloquy, they found that they shared a great deal in common, but their radically different beliefs concerning the Eucharist were irreconcilable. Zwingli remained convinced that Christ's words at the Last Supper were symbolic, whereas Luther maintained that the body and blood of Christ were present along with the bread and wine. Zwingli, like Luther, could hardly keep up with the moving frontline of Protestant development, and many of his supporters after Marburg charged that he had turned soft and was not ready to follow his conscience or Scripture all the way.

Without support from the Lutherans in Germany, the threat of religious war between Catholics and Protestants in the Swiss Confederation drew closer. The war broke out in October 1531, but the Protestant armies were no match for the Catholic forces supported by the emperor. Zwingli was wounded in battle, and when the Catholic army discovered him they executed, dismembered, and burned him as a heretic, scattering his ashes in the wind.

Picture Wars

The experiences of both Luther and Zwingli demonstrate the important role that cities and the printing press played in the spread of new religious ideas. By 1523, almost four hundred editions of Luther's various treatises were in circulation in northern Europe. Early modern cities such as Wittenberg and Zürich were crowded and vibrant. Even though the number of residents in an early modern city may seem relatively small by modern standards, population densities were comparable. Tens of thousands of people clustered into urban spaces that were often confined to a few square miles. In such a restricted environment, new ideas spread quickly, not only in print, but also through the networks of gossip.

These cities often possessed many literate citizens. Printers were active in most European cities by the 1520s, and printing presses spread new ideas and images rapidly. Urban schools, many established by craft and trade guilds, provided basic education to the city's children, who could then take advantage of books, broadsides, and cartoons. Available for relatively small sums of money, printed works tended to be written in the vernacular. Not everyone, of course, could read even the vernacular, but religious pamphlets often relied more on pictures than words to convey their messages.

The Protestant images below seek in cartoon form to capture the differences between Catholic and Protestant worship. On the right side of the first image, a group of men and women of all ages with a few children is shown listening with some degree of distraction to a well-fed Catholic priest wearing splendid robes while many of them work their rosary beads. On the left side, people share copies of the Bible while the simply dressed Protestant minister speaks from a plain pulpit with an open Bible before him. The contrast between the two scenes was meant to inspire debate and discussion. The cartoon invites the viewer to choose the better form of worship. In the middle of the cartoon, an elderly man with outstretched arms seems by his gesture to invite the viewer to pick one side.

Although this cartoon is relatively sophisticated and understated, many were not. They were crude caricatures and lampoons of the other side. This was, after all, a contest for souls and the ultimate reward for choosing rightly was a better chance to enter heaven. In this picture war, re-formers understood the power of such images to demean the Roman Catholic Church. In the broadsheet below, the pope is depicted in the act of selling indulgences. The pope sits on a plump pillow on his throne while surrounded by bishops and a cardinal as he signs a stack of indulgences. A woman seems to be bribing a Catholic priest. Before the pope, simple Catholics count out money to purchase their chance at salvation. The line of those waiting to purchase the indulgence includes the poor and old, whose needs stand in sharp contrast to the hale and hearty clerics tending to the pope and not the faithful. The mockery of the piece is obvious in the image of the dog defecating below the pope.

QUESTIONS | *How did the combination of visual culture and the printing press help spread Protestant ideas, and what were the dangers of using cartoons to spread the message?*

Woodcut Image of the Pope as Moneychanger and Indulgence Seller, 1521, by Lucas Cranach

Woodcut Image of Rival Church Services, 1529, by Hans Sachs, Nuremberg

Martin Luther, on hearing of Zwingli's gruesome death, was rumored to have said, "He got what he deserved." It was not the finest moment of either re-former.

Henry VIII Divorces the Catholic Church

The divisions between Catholic and Protestant and between church and state were complicated further when the pious Catholic monarch, Henry VIII of England (r. 1509–1547), decided to divorce his first wife and so the Catholic Church. Few could have foreseen that Henry would be the first prominent monarch to break with Rome. He was on record as despising the religiously rebellious Luther and had lined up behind the emperor and other princes against the new religion, but as so often before in Europe dynastic interests overrode religious ones. At the time, Henry was married to Catherine of Aragon, the daughter of the Catholic monarchs Ferdinand and Isabella of Spain. But Henry feared that, if he passed his throne to a woman (in this case, his daughter Mary), another civil war would erupt in England. He wanted a son, and so began the great Tudor melodrama that would transfix England for the rest of the century. The melodrama was created both by religious division and by the king's reckless fickleness and extreme power. By 1526, Henry had his eye on a preferred partner, Anne Boleyn, a young English woman with aristocratic connections, French manners, a sharp tongue, and Protestant leanings.

Divorce or, more commonly, the annulment of a marriage was not impossible in the early modern Catholic Church, but ending a marriage to the aunt of the Catholic emperor Charles V was next to impossible, especially since imperial armies had sacked Rome in 1527 and were still occupying the city. The pope's freedom to act was more limited than usual. Catherine herself refused to give way to her husband's demand for an annulment of their marriage. Had she but relented all might have been different, but Catherine as the last child of Ferdinand and Isabella of Spain was a woman of considerable pride and determination. Moreover, Charles and the pope were annoyed that Henry had declined to participate in the campaign against the Ottoman Turks. Thus, despite Henry's earnest pleas for the pope to annul his marriage to Catherine, Pope Clement VII refused. The English king relied on the advice of his chief religious and legal advisor, Cardinal Thomas Wolsey, and continued to press for an annulment on the grounds that he and Catherine should never have been granted a papal dispensation to marry in the first place since the Spanish princess had previously been married to the king's older brother, Prince Arthur. Not only was Pope Clement poorly placed at the time to resist Emperor Charles's wishes in the matter, but he was also reluctant to admit, given Luther's recent attack on papal authority and the institution of the papacy, that the earlier papal dispensation had been a mistake.

In 1529, Henry dismissed Cardinal Wolsey and soon turned to officials who might arrange his divorce. Thomas Cromwell (1485–1540) concerned himself with the legal and political side of the matter, and Thomas Cranmer, a Catholic cleric, with the religious side. Both men wanted to curb abuses in the English church, as well as to advance their own careers and to protect England from foreign political interference. Together, they advocated an approach to the problem of the divorce that would use English common law and the English legal system to annul the marriage, rather than relying on a Roman Catholic court or the approval of foreign powers. To make their case, they argued that England was an empire and, therefore, that its ruler could have no superior, not even the pope.

While the English Parliament heard the king's case against his marriage to Catherine, Anne Boleyn, who had been holding the king at arm's length for over five years, finally became his mistress. The couple was secretly married in January 1533 when it was clear that she was pregnant. The marriage technically made the king a bigamist, since he was now married to two women at the same time. Henry pressured Parliament to resolve the matter quickly, and in May 1533 English church courts pronounced the king's marriage to Catherine invalid. The king then married the visibly pregnant Anne Boleyn in a lavish ceremony; she was crowned queen within weeks.

In September 1533, King Henry and Queen Anne announced the birth of their daughter, Elizabeth. It was not the dynastic outcome that Henry had hoped for, but there was no going back since English law was in the process of making the Church of England (the Anglican Church) a separate religious entity with the monarch, Emperor Henry VIII, as its "supreme head." The **Act of Supremacy** that passed in 1534 established the king and succeeding monarchs as the supreme religious authorities of the English empire, with the full right to determine church doctrine and practice. In the first weeks of 1535, Parliament passed the Treason Act, which made it a capital crime punishable by death for anyone to fail to uphold the Act of Supremacy.

Even the king's closest advisors were not spared the consequences of the Treason Act. Sir Thomas More (1478–1535), who had earlier been one of Henry's chief advisors, refused to swear an oath supporting the Act of Supremacy. King Henry could not allow his notable subjects to disobey him and disrespect his new religious authority, so More was put on trial. The verdict was never in doubt. More was found guilty of treason and beheaded at the Tower of London in July 1535.

With the passage of the Act of Supremacy, it fell to the king in name and his advisors in fact to shape the new English church. Cromwell handled the political and governmental fallout. He realized that he could smooth the ruffled feathers of the nobility and wealthy merchants with money and so devised a plan to dissolve England's monasteries and friaries, and redistribute the vacated property and monastic wealth to the king and his supporters. Between 1536 and 1540, about one-third of the land in England, which previously had been held and managed by the Catholic Church, was turned over to private individuals who built great houses on it and paid taxes to the

Henry VIII and Charles V in Conference before the Pope An Italian artist created this scene of Henry VIII in discussion with the newly crowned Emperor Charles V (*seated*) under the watchful eyes of Pope Leo X. The date seems to be about 1520, when Charles and Leo were pressing Henry to support their stand against Luther. In 1521, the pope declared Henry a defender of the faith for his denunciation of Luther. Some scholars have portrayed this painting as a debate between the English king and emperor over Henry's request to annul his marriage to Queen Catherine of Aragon, but that seems unlikely if not impossible.

king rather than to the pope. Henry dissolved England's monasteries, but he did little to replace their charitable and community functions. No wonder so many Tudor beggars (often former monastic dependents) gathered in cities such as London; they now had no other place to go to seek local charitable relief. With the overthrow of old practices, traditional English religion was unsettled and believers were confused about what to believe. Cranmer responded by instituting new church doctrines and practices, but his drive to establish the new Anglican Church was compromised by the king's own religious conservatism. Henry personally disapproved of married clergy and remained for a time a great admirer of churches with statues, beautiful music, and other adornments of Catholicism. The result was an English church that was cut loose from Rome, but not fully re-formed either. Henry did agree eventually to supply parish churches with William Tyndale's English translation of the Bible, which may have done more than anything else to sever the English church from the old

order, since English men and women could now read and hear the Bible in their own tongue. Not until the reign of Edward VI, the son of Henry and Jane Seymour, would the English church take a firm turn toward re-formed religion with Cranmer's *Book of Common Prayer,* the removal of images from churches, and the lifting of prohibitions against clerical marriage.

John Calvin and the Religious Re-Formation of Geneva

One of the problems facing the Protestant Re-Formation was that few religious re-formers had taken the time to think through the political implications of radical religious change until they were well on their way to overthrowing old institutions and establishing new churches. John Calvin (1509–1564) and the Swiss city of Geneva were different, but then Calvin was a second-generation re-former and subtle theorist. He was the first Protestant leader to work out ideas about the relationship of church and state in a systematic, lucid, and persuasive fashion.

Calvin was born to a family of urban merchants and professionals who placed a premium on education. He was sent to study at the University of Paris, where he was steeped in the ideas of the European Renaissance. Initially, Calvin expressed an interest in theology, but his father felt that a career in the law would better advance the family's fortunes, given the religious turbulence of the age. Like Luther, Calvin dutifully followed his father's wishes, at least until his father died in 1531. Calvin then returned to the university to embark on a humanistic program of language education and religious study. After hearing a friend lecture on Luther's doctrine of justification by faith alone, Calvin had an overwhelming religious conversion and a year later was forced to flee Paris as a recognized re-former. Paris was rocked at the time by the so-called affair of the placards, in which a group of students broke into the king's palace and scrawled Protestant slogans and cartoons on Francis I's bedroom door. Outraged by this assault on his royal dignity and authority, King Francis clamped down on Protestants and Calvin fled to the re-formed Swiss city of Basel.

In Basel, Calvin began work on his masterwork of theology, the *Institutes of the Christian Religion* (first published in 1536). Calvin was only twenty-six when the treatise appeared, but it established him as one of the leading religious thinkers in Europe and he would continue to refine and extend the work until 1559. In the *Institutes,* Calvin set out his belief in the importance of preaching and adherence to the two sacraments of baptism and the Eucharist. He believed that the body and blood of Christ were spiritually present in the bread and wine of the communion service, but that they were not physically present, as believed by Catholics. Calvin's formulation could not, however, be reconciled with Luther's formula and would keep their churches apart. As a consequence, Protestantism was never to be a single church, but then the revolt against the monolithic Catholic Church was always pluralistic in nature. Each movement against the Catholic Church had developed separately in a specific location and under the leadership of a charismatic individual. The result was not just many Europes, but many religions inside the many Europes, each having its own teachings and separate histories.

In the *Institutes*, Calvin set out his belief in the majesty and authority of God, urging his readers not to focus on feelings of their unworthiness in the face of God's total power, but instead to concentrate on God's love for all his creation. One way that God expressed this love was in a finely tuned master plan that would guide the world until the end of time. Calvin urged people to put their faith in God's plan and to accept that they could never know what was in store for them. According to Calvin, God had already determined who had been elected for salvation and who would be damned. There was no way of knowing with certainty which future awaited an individual, though possessing faith might be an indication that you were in the right camp. Thus, Calvin's followers looked to the quality and depth of their faith for signs, no matter how small, that they were among the elect. Material success (such as a thriving business) and spiritual rectitude (such as resisting temptation) were taken by some people as indications of election, even though these indications were not a specific part of Calvin's theology.

In the same year that the first edition of Calvin's *Institutes* appeared, he visited Geneva and, at the request of one of the city's ministers, began to sketch out how government and religious life could be joined into a single institutional framework that would oversee matters of faith and civic affairs. Geneva was at the time a city of some 16,000 rambunctious inhabitants who had driven out their local bishop. No wonder, then, that Calvin believed that the power to excommunicate citizens who would not follow church standards was critical to re-forming the city, but officials balked at the demand. When, in 1538, Calvin refused to administer the Eucharist during Easter services on the grounds that some Genevans were not worthy to receive it, the city expelled him. He traveled to Strasbourg, where he was impressed by the New Testament–style unification of church and government taking place there under the leadership of the Protestant Martin Bucer. While there, Calvin married, but as a second-generation re-former, his marriage did not raise even a ripple of interest. Meanwhile, without strong religious leadership, Geneva began to experience difficulties, just as Wittenberg had when Luther was hiding in his castle. Attendance at church services declined and moral infractions were on the rise. In 1541, city officials invited Calvin to return, granting him sweeping powers to establish a church that would constitute a godly society.

Living a Religiously Re-formed Life in Calvin's Geneva

With the *Ecclesiastical Ordinances*, Calvin shaped a church in Geneva with the power to discipline its members through a variety of methods, including excommunication. Calvin divided the ministry of the church into pastors, who preached and looked after the needs of the flock, doctors who taught, elders who disciplined, and deacons who oversaw charity and counseled Christian love among believers. A combination of church officials and elected members of the laity formed a court called the Consistory to hear charges and levy punishments for infractions that ranged from public lewdness to bad business deals to violent crime. Calvin's Geneva banned dancing, ribald song, and superstition. Perhaps it was for this reason that one sixteenth-century artist painted Calvin as something of a cold fish, his head assembled of skinned chickens and dead fish.

Nonetheless, Protestants from all over Europe were soon flooding into Geneva to witness "the most perfect school of Christ on earth." Geneva became a center of Protestant thought and a model of how re-formed religion and civic life could be joined together to promote law, order, and Christian principles. But all was not peaceful in Geneva. Calvin's program was demanding; he was particularly on guard against idolatry, even forbidding reverence for the Virgin Mary as a form of idolatry. Two to three witches a year were burned to death in re-formed Geneva, and in 1553, Calvin saw to it that the bold thinker Michael Servetus, who was visiting the city, was burned to death. Calvin saw Servetus as a competitor and heretic, and, like Luther, he was determined to keep a tight rein on thought that fell outside the boundaries of his re-formed church. Despite the bracing morality of Geneva, the city cared for the sick and elderly and possessed a first-rate university that spread Calvin's ideas across Europe. Geneva was clean, orderly, charitable, and worked, just as Calvin's thought did, and that may have been advertisement enough of the high standards that re-formed religion might achieve.

The Schmalkaldic League and Peace of Augsburg

With the many Europes fracturing further along religious and political fault lines, the emperor Charles V had no choice but to convene further imperial assemblies in an attempt to stem the tide of the spreading Protestant re-formation of the church and to keep the empire from disintegrating entirely. At the Diet of Augsburg in 1530, Charles assured the Lutheran princes that all men would be heard fairly. In keeping with that conciliatory overture, the Protestant prince John of Saxony asked Philip Melanchthon, one of Luther's disciples, to draw up a statement of the Lutheran faith that came to be known as the Augsburg Confession. It set out Luther's theological views clearly and concisely. But the Augsburg Confession also gave Charles and the Catholic Church a clear target. The emperor commissioned Johann Eck, the man who had first labeled Luther a heretic, to write the report now known as the *Confutation*, which supported the traditional doctrines and teachings of the Catholic Church.

Giuseppe Arcimboldo, *The Lawyer* (1566) Arcimboldo is famous for his paintings of figures constructed of familiar objects. Here he caricatures the lawyer as one with books for guts, legal documents for his neck fringe, a face made of poultry parts, the mouth of a fish, and the beard of a fish tail. Calvin, as a lawyer and disapproving Protestant, has been suggested as the subject of the painting.

more to broker an agreement that would make it possible for Protestants and Catholics to live together within the empire. The resulting treaty between Protestant and Catholic powers in the empire, known as the **Peace of Augsburg,** acknowledged that there were two permissible forms of religious observance. Although the Peace of Augsburg succeeded in bringing peace to the empire for a time, two of its conditions caused further instability. First, under the terms of the treaty, it was agreed that the religion of the ruler would determine the religion of his or her state (*cuius regio, eius religio*; "his region, his religion"). But this meant that a region's religion could flip back and forth between Lutherans and Catholics in a few short years, depending on the faith and longevity of its ruler. Second, the Peace of Augsburg did not include Calvinism as a religious option, though Calvinism was by that time the most popular of the Protestant faiths. The exclusion of Calvinism from the agreement led to more warfare in the empire and beyond.

The Radical Religious Re-Formation Splinters and Spreads

As Luther, Zwingli, and Calvin consolidated their followers into distinct churches with carefully outlined beliefs

> **What was the Radical Re-Formation, and why was it a natural consequence of the Protestant revolution?**

and practices, some individuals, drawn to the exciting freedom of remaking and reorganizing their religious beliefs, continued to move forward. These radical re-formers represented the frontline of the advancing religious re-formation of the many Europes, but they soon found themselves outside both the old Catholic Church and the new Protestant churches, and spurned by all. Instead of subordinating their beliefs to the new churches, these radical re-formers formed into small Protestant sects, which were radical experiments in living and thinking.

Fundamental to the beliefs of the radical Protestant sects were notions of perfection and separation from the unbelieving, errant others. To stay true to God's word, Protestant sectarians felt the need to withdraw from what they saw as a coercive state and from church laws that forced people to accept religious beliefs and practices sanctioned by the established churches. Instead, the radical re-formers believed in an entirely voluntary church in which membership was a matter of private choice and conscience.

These radical groups believed that separatism and voluntary religion should lead to the complete separation of church and state. Only within such a framework could true religious freedom be achieved and the religious and political entanglements that had crippled Europe fade away. The beliefs of the sectarians were for the most part

After his initial attempt to be tolerant and conciliatory, Charles was exasperated by the continuing stubbornness of all parties and decided that he had no choice but to insist that Protestants in the empire accept the *Confutation.*

In response to Charles's decision, the Lutheran princes established the Schmalkaldic League in the winter of 1531 to ensure the safety and security of Protestants within the empire. The purpose of the alliance was chiefly military. Eleven Protestant cities in the empire and eight Protestant princes promised to offer military assistance to one another in the event that any one of them was attacked for religious reasons. The alliance was put to the test in the Schmalkaldic Wars (1546–1547), when the emperor led armies into the field to do battle with the League. Despite their defeat at the Battle of Mühlberg in 1547, members of the Schmalkaldic League regrouped with the unlikely assistance of the Catholic king of France, Henry II (r. 1547–1559), who had no wish to see the emperor resolve his serious problems in Germany.

By 1550, few in Europe would have thought that politics and religion or church and state were separate. Experiences in the empire and in England had demonstrated that decisions regarding religion were deeply political. In 1555, Charles returned to Augsburg to try once peaceful and unthreatening, but they offended most mainline Protestants and Catholics, who thought that the sects were anarchic, antisocial, and a refuge for dangerous fanatics and revolutionaries. The various sects drew followers from the lowest orders of society, many of whom were happy to separate from the mainstream of a society that had not been kind to them. They lived in the hope that the present religious turmoil might one day cease and leave them at peace with their God.

Anabaptism

If the chief dividing point among the major church reformers, Luther, Zwingli, and Calvin, had been over the nature of the Eucharist, the principal disagreement between them and the radical re-formers was over baptism. In his careful review of the biblical precedents for the sacraments, Luther had realized that there was no support for infant baptism anywhere in the Bible. He nonetheless believed that, since everyone should be a Christian and a full member of the religion, it was necessary for all to be baptized as infants. Zwingli and Calvin believed the same; for mainline Protestants it was one matter where Scripture did not win out over tradition. In Wittenberg, the Zwickau prophets, having tested the sacraments against Scripture, were already speaking against the baptism of infants. For Luther, Zwingli, and Calvin, the issue smacked of runaway radicalism. For the radical re-formers, infant baptism was not justified biblically, was not a voluntary act (since infants could not make such a choice of their own free will), and was forced on all by the coercive establishment.

In 1525, in Zwingli's Zürich, a group of the most fervent re-formers collected together in public and began to baptize each other. Protestant church authorities, including Zwingli, were outraged. They labeled the radicals rebaptizers or **Anabaptists** and passed legislation against the practice of re-baptism. Four of the Anabaptists were drowned, death by water being considered a fitting punishment for their particular form of dissidence. One problem that Catholics and mainline Protestants had with re-baptism was that it seemed to insult the power of Christ, who was thought to have acted once already in the baptism of the child, which should be sufficient. God had no need of "do-overs." Another problem was that re-baptism seemed to set some individuals outside the normal congregation of Christians, as a twice-baptized elite.

One of the radical enthusiasts for adult baptism in Zürich that day in 1525 was Conrad Grebel, a well-educated humanist. As the number of Grebel's followers increased, he began to refine Anabaptist thought and practice based on a literal reading of Scripture. Grebel's group advocated a return to a simple, biblical pattern of life involving agricultural work and simple church services in private homes. They withdrew into disciplined communities that stood apart from the rest of early modern society, calling their religious fellows "Brethren" and subjecting Brethren to a policing of community behavior

known as the "ban." Within Anabaptist communities, all other forms of religious discipline or governmental control were shunned, and the Brethren would not take oaths of office, swear fealty, or bear arms on behalf of the state.

Millenarians Make a Last Stand

Within Anabaptism, there were even more radical elements. The religious re-formation was, as so many revolutions do, spinning out of control and moving toward disaster. The most radical of the re-formers may have wanted just that, to bring on the very destruction that the book of Revelation had promised. Some Anabaptist sects viewed their actions and the persecutions they were suffering as signals that the end of the world was near and a new time of peace and prosperity at hand. This belief, known as **millenarianism,** was fueled by the increasingly volatile religious and political persecutions within the empire.

The center for millenarian religious belief in the mid-sixteenth century was the German city of Münster. The city had first appointed Lutheran ministers to preach in its churches in 1532. Protestants flocked to the city as a religious safe-haven. Among them were the followers of a Dutch baker named Jan Matthys, who believed that he was the reincarnation of Enoch, a biblical figure come to usher in the end of days. Matthys preached that his followers should take up the sword of righteousness against the ungodly, and he proclaimed that Münster was "the city of God" and would become the "New Jerusalem." In Münster, some of his more enthusiastic followers, on learning of his prophecy, removed their clothes in order to stand naked before God's final judgment, and ran through the streets warning people of Christ's return. Once Matthys entered the city, all those who accepted him as a prophet were re-baptized, private property was abolished, and new laws were struck. Anyone who would not follow Matthys's Anabaptist and millenarian beliefs and would not willingly leave the city was evicted forcibly.

Catholics and conservative Protestants, outraged by Matthys and the extreme radicalization of Münster, laid siege to the city as though it threatened to infect other Christian communities. Matthys's followers were so convinced that the end of days was at hand, one young woman came to believe she was called upon to imitate the biblical heroine Judith, who had saved her city by slaying the invading general Holofernes. This new Judith believed that she must assassinate the former Catholic bishop of Münster. She walked straight into the hands of the enemy, was tortured, confessed, and then beheaded.

Despite extreme incidents of this kind, the Catholic-Protestant army was unable to oust Matthys from Münster until the prophet had a vision that persuaded him to do battle with the former bishop of the city. Matthys believed that God would protect him from musket fire. He was wrong, dying in the battle, and Jan Beukels (John of Leiden), one of Matthys's men, took over. To reassure the faithful of his calling, he too ran naked through the streets, fell into a trance, and proclaimed that he was a

The Execution of Jan Beukels The Anabaptist rulers of Münster were defeated in 1536 and their leaders, including Jan Beukels, were hung in cages from the church of St. Lambert as a message to the radical reformers and millenarians of their fate.

new prophet and the king of Zion. Beukels instituted even more radical measures, including the institution of polygamy. He led the way, taking sixteen wives (including Matthys's widow), but he had one beheaded for talking back to him. Finally, after sixteen months of protracted warfare, the besieging armies conquered Münster in 1535 and tortured and executed its Anabaptist leaders, hanging their corpses in iron cages as a warning to all that Münster was not the New Jerusalem and its Anabaptist leaders were frauds and false prophets of the end of time.

Separatism and Peace: The Mennonites

Münster gave Anabaptism a bad name that was hardly fair, for sectarian movements, by their very nature, always have many different faces and group beliefs. One successful form of Anabaptism was pioneered by Menno Simons, a man of genuine faith and deep piety. Born in the Netherlands, Menno served as a Catholic parish priest for over a decade. In 1527, he heard shocking reports of

the torture and execution of an Anabaptist in Holland. Menno consulted the Bible and, like Grebel, he could find no passages that supported infant baptism. Despite his conviction that there was nothing sinful about adult baptism, he was hesitant to abandon his Catholic training. When Menno heard tales about what the Catholic and Protestant armies were doing to Anabaptists, he was ashamed that so many were willing to die for their belief in adult baptism while he remained silent.

In October 1536, Menno was re-baptized and became an Anabaptist preacher, spreading the message of separatism and peace among the faithful. Menno set out his ideas about adult baptism and pacifism in two books, *Christian Baptism* (1539) and the *Foundations of Christian Doctrine* (1540). Menno also advocated the literal reading of the Bible, telling his followers, "the children of peace," that Scripture did not need interpretation, just obedience.

Anabaptism took so many forms, including the Family of Love in England, the Netherlands, and Germany, which followed eclectic spiritual and mystical practices, that it is not possible to detail them all here. Anabaptism survived not just because of enlightened leaders such as Menno Simons, Hans Huth in Germany, or Jacob Hutter in Moravia, but because its vibrant sectarianism allowed small separated groups of believers to hunker down against the violent storms blowing against them from a hostile external world. Yet, their separation from the outside world also meant that the Anabaptists would remain within relatively small, tightly bound groups that stood outside of normative society and the established religions. The events at Münster, however, became an excuse for European authorities to damn all the radical reformers as evil and deserving of destruction.

The Catholic Reformation

The Catholic Church dismissed Luther's early complaints as baseless criticisms that would never amount to much and viewed his refusal to recant at Worms as evidence

How did the Catholic Church fight back, and why did it take so long?

of his stubbornness and heresy. But the church found it difficult to remain untouched by calls for reform. Indeed, Catholic figures such as Erasmus had long worked from

the inside to reform the church. As more reformers (including Henry VIII, Zwingli, and Calvin) parted with the church, Catholic clerics began to worry about the church's survival. As the number of Protestants in Europe grew, deciding how to respond to the challenges of religious diversity became a pressing issue within the Catholic Church. The Peace of Augsburg presented one solution in the form of political alliances and agreements. Such measures, however, did not address demands for spiritual reform or answer calls for the reform of existing church abuses such as indulgences. When the church began to seek for ways to address these issues, it found that reformation and consolidation were its most effective responses.

An Order of Spiritual Soldiers: The Jesuits

One of the most striking Catholic developments was the founding of the Jesuit order in 1540. For the next two and a half centuries the Jesuits would be a controversial organization in western Europe, admired and feared by many. The Jesuits, as highly educated and engaged Catholics, served as the spiritual soldiers of the Catholic Reformation, seeking to convert non-Christians and always ready to resist Protestant critics.

The order's founder, Ignatius Loyola (1491–1556), was born into an aristocratic Spanish family and became a soldier. While recuperating from wounds suffered in battle in 1521, Loyola contemplated the life and sufferings of Jesus and the saints, and experienced a surge of renewed faith. His was the vision of a chivalric knight, with Mary as the lady he would seek in a Christian quest, waging war against the Devil and his minions who wanted to keep him from his divine lady. Loyola was convinced that his quest could be fulfilled only within the Catholic Church and with the support of its leader, the pope. His appointed mission in God's great plan was to convert Muslims in the Holy Land to Christianity. Loyola traveled to Jerusalem to spread his ideas among the Catholic faithful there, but he found little support in that cosmopolitan city, long exposed to the ebb and flow of religious fervor.

At the age of thirty-four, Loyola decided to educate himself. To learn Latin, he entered a class of boys to begin his language training. Within three years, Loyola knew enough to be admitted to the University of Paris, the preeminent theological university of Catholic Europe. Loyola spent seven years there, perfecting his command of Latin and reading the spiritual teachings of the Catholic tradition. He assembled a band of followers from his fellow students, all of whom were captivated by his idea of converting Muslims to Christianity and following the orders of the pope.

In 1534, Loyola and six of his friends dedicated their lives to missionary work in the Holy Land. Frustrated by their inability to get to Jerusalem, the men traveled to Rome to offer their services directly to the pope. While waiting for an audience with the pope, Loyola and his band began to work among the sick and poor in Rome. Their activities brought them to the attention of Pope Paul III, who agreed to establish them as a holy order under the name the **Society of Jesus.**

The Society of Jesus (or Jesuits as they have come to be known) was envisioned as a small brotherhood of around sixty men who would perform charitable works on behalf of the papacy. Quickly, the Jesuits became so popular and so powerful that they exceeded those modest expectations. One explanation for their success was the respect that many Catholics had for the rigor of Jesuit training. Each Jesuit "client" underwent a program of intense contemplation supervised by a single Jesuit advisor. This program of contemplation and education, which might extend over a decade or more, fostered a spiritual awakening of the sort described in Loyola's own "Spiritual Exercises." By 1550 almost all Catholic states had at least one leading figure who had been trained in the "Spiritual Exercises."

As the number of Jesuit supporters grew, Loyola and his advisors drew up a set of guidelines called the *Constitutions* that set the standards for the order. Those who wanted to join had to undergo a two-year period of probation to test their faith, during which time they did menial work for the sick and prisoners, underwent a pilgrimage, received extensive theological training to become a priest, and passed a second test of their faith. By 1556, more than a thousand men were interested in becoming Jesuits, but there were still only forty-three full members. Those forty-three men operated like a military order in their efficiency, their emphasis on obedience, and their strict adherence to the instructions of their leader (called a general) and the pope. Some Jesuits took up Loyola's initial interest in conversion and became missionaries to the distant continents of the Americas and Asia. Other Jesuits became educators and established

Jesuit Missionaries in China The Jesuits made a spirited attempt to convert Asians to Catholicism; it was one of their central mandates as set out by the founder of the Society of Jesus, Ignatius Loyola.

a Jesuit college (Collegio Romano) in Rome to promote learning and the formal study of theology.

Catholic Mysticism Connects

The logical and educated rigor of the Jesuits was one expression of the Catholic Church's reform and renewal; another was the rise of a Catholic mysticism that captured the popular imagination. In the religious confusion of the mid-sixteenth century, many people wondered amid all the religious noise what God truly wanted. The mystic cut through all uncertainty to make direct contact with the divine. Ignatius Loyola's own mystical experience was far from unique among sixteenth-century Catholics. The ecstatic visions of people such as Teresa of Ávila (1515–1582) and John of the Cross (1542–1591) inspired a popular renewal of Catholicism, for God was speaking to the world through Catholic religious men and women, approving of the Catholic life and institutions, the lives and sanctity of monks and nuns, and the holiness of a celibate life.

Teresa of Ávila had a Jewish background but was raised within the Christian church. Plagued by chronic illness after entering a Carmelite convent at the age of twenty, Teresa experienced ecstatic visions during her sufferings. When spiritual advisors suggested that her visions might be more diabolical than divine, she tested her faith by fasting and scourging her body. Gradually, she became convinced that she was receiving messages from God and, between 1559 and 1561, she experienced repeated visions of the suffering Christ. The motto associated with her, "Lord, either let me suffer or let me die," captures the close connection between pain and spirituality in Teresa's mysticism. To suffer was to be Christian and God's beloved. In 1562, she established a reformed Carmelite convent that observed strict vows of poverty and celibacy. As a symbol of their poverty and humility, the nuns wore nothing on their feet, and when church officials granted Teresa permission to found a new order of nuns in 1567 they were called Discalced Carmelites, or shoeless Carmelites.

One year later, in 1568, another Spanish mystic, John of the Cross, founded a parallel, male order of Discalced Carmelite monks in Ávila. Influenced by Teresa's example, John of the Cross was drawn to both the strictness of the order and its emphasis on suffering. In late 1577, he was jailed by senior members of the Carmelite order who did not approve of Teresa of Ávila's order. Imprisoned and tortured for a period of nearly nine months, John of the Cross experienced religious ecstasy through his suffering. During his imprisonment, he wrote one of the great works of Catholic mysticism, *The Spiritual Canticle,* on paper that was secretly passed to him by one of his jailers. Today, John of the Cross's poetry and his writings on the progress of the soul toward salvation, such as *The Dark Night of the Soul,* are considered among the finest examples of Catholic Reformation spirituality as well as landmarks of Spanish literature.

CHRONOLOGY	Popes in an Age of Religious Change	
DATES	**POPE**
1492–1503	Pope Alexander VI
1503	Pope Pius III
1503–1513	Pope Julius II
1513–1521	Pope Leo X
1522–1523	Pope Adrian VI
1523–1534	Pope Clement VII
1534–1549	Pope Paul III

Reforming Popes and the Council of Trent

Along with new religious orders and the emergence of higher educational standards and ecstatic mysticism, the vitality of the Catholic Church was evident in the reform agenda of the popes and the doctrinal decisions made by the Council of Trent (1545–1563). Though he did not live to see the council's final work, Pope Paul III led the drive to reform and consolidate the Catholic Church.

Paul was born into one of Italy's wealthiest and most aristocratic families. He experienced a spiritual awakening late in life and was ordained a priest only in his fifties. Sixty-six years old when he became pope, he turned quickly to the matter of reforming the Catholic Church. Paul's plan was to reestablish papal authority by rationalizing Catholic doctrine and fostering a healthy College of Cardinals to assist the papacy. He reestablished the Roman Inquisition in 1542 to combat the spread of heresy and gave the investigative body wide-ranging powers to act against persons suspected of heresy.

The pope's most important decision came in 1536, when he decided to call a general church council to address church discipline, administration, and spirituality. His goal, he said, was to reform the Catholic Church in both its head and its parts. After years of delicate negotiations about who should attend the meeting and where it would be held, the council finally met in 1545 to discuss clerical abuses and to draw hard and fast lines between acceptable and unacceptable religious beliefs and practices. The Council of Trent transformed Catholic doctrines (or teachings) into Catholic dogmas (sanctioned and necessary tenets), thus making any reconciliation with Protestant beliefs that much more difficult.

The council confirmed that both faith and good works were necessary for salvation, that both tradition and Scripture were valid as the sources of the Catholic faith, that Thomas Aquinas's teachings were normative, that the seven holy sacraments were the conduits of grace, that the doctrine of transubstantiation was a true description of what happened to the bread and wine in the Mass, and that the need for clerical celibacy was paramount. The council also refused to do away with indulgences and re-affirmed the authority of the Vulgate Bible as translated by Saint Jerome, despite its imperfections.

Between 1562 and 1563, under the influence of the French crown and French clerics, the Council of Trent reconvened. Efforts were made to extend the precisely defined teachings of the church to Catholic practices. The religious life of the laity became the focus of delibera-tions, and church discipline was strengthened by placing more emphasis on the role of bishops in Catholic reform. After the council, bishops were expected to serve as mid-dle managers responsible for seeing that priests kept in regular contact with the laity and were better trained and more effective. Trent's resolutions had a vast impact on standardizing Catholic belief and practice. A priest now had to supervise a Christian marriage, and the confes-sion box became standard. At Trent the Catholic Church regained its moral and institutional footing, and the in-quisition worked to eliminate dissent within the church.

In 1562, the Council of Trent also began to deal with the issue of print culture and how the Catholic Church should handle the heretical religious works flooding Europe from Protestant printers and urban centers. The church had finally realized how important printed works had been in disseminating the ideas of Luther and the Protestants. In 1559, the pope had authorized the Roman Inquisition to compile an index of prohib-ited books (*Index Librorum Prohibitorum,* known simply as the *Index*). The *Index* banned the publication, possession, and reading of scores of books, including all vernacu-lar Bibles and any works written by leading Protestants such as Luther, Calvin, Zwingli, and Henry VIII. Even some works of Erasmus were forbidden. The Council of Trent recognized that the 1559 *Index* had been too restric-tive and reformulated the *Index* to allow for a greater degree of freedom for publishers, authors, and readers. The works of heretics such as Luther and Calvin, how-ever, remained on the prohibited list. Published in 1564, the *Tridentine Index* served as a model for the subsequent forty editions of the *Index* and gave censors guidelines to follow in weighing orthodox and harmful publications. The final authorized version of the *Index* appeared in 1948, but in 1966 the *Index* was abolished by papal decree.

Welcome Back:
The Baroque Embrace of Rome

The Council of Trent asserted that images were useful in promoting the faith, particularly to illiterate, com-mon Christians. Protestants had gone in the other di-rection. Worried about idolatry and artistic distraction, Protestants had stripped their churches bare of symbol and visual delight. By the late sixteenth century, with their confident reassertion of traditionalism, Catholic churches embraced not only their old symbols and art,

but also a new artistic and architectural style known as **Baroque.** The word *Baroque* originally suggested the deformed and tortured. New Catholic churches were sumptuously adorned, golden monuments that not only impressed a visually impoverished age, but also demon-strated a renewed Catholic confidence. Baroque churches were filled with thundering organ music, rich liturgy, and ceremonies that overwhelmed the senses of the faithful. Baroque art may be the most remarkable and vibrant cel-ebration of resurgent Catholicism, standing in stark con-trast to the iconoclastic spirit of plain Protestant churches devoid of images and often of transporting music.

If classical art was an art of restrained observation and simplicity, Baroque is its opposite, an overly rich feast, sensuous and expressive, full of electric energy. In Rome, Caravaggio (1573–1610) found many church patrons for his dramatic scenes of the lives of Christ and the apostles, but he also shocked them with the liberties he took with the holy. The Carmelite sisters of Santa Maria in Rome had commissioned him to paint *The Death of the Virgin*, but were shocked by what they got, a painting showing a bloated corpse in a frumpy and disheveled red dress, her feet bare, fingers fat, face a sickly greenish yellow. It was rumored to be a portrait of the drowned corpse of a

Caravaggio's *Death of the Virgin* (1605) Caravaggio's life and paintings are colorful Baroque dramas.

prostitute. Yet the painting is utterly engaging, for it is (except for the thin halo encircling Mary's head) a thoroughly human scene of a very human death. Only the stunned apostles looking on and Mary Magdalene weeping in sorrow alert us to the importance of the event, but that was Caravaggio's point: that the divine story is a human one and the Gospels live in the present. The shocked sisters did not see it that way and refused the painting.

The Roman painter Artemisia Gentileschi (1593–c. 1653) was influenced deeply by Caravaggio's sense of drama and his play of light and shadow. Her painting of *Judith and Her Maidservant with the Head of Holofernes* captures the same sense of heightened drama and high intrigue. Judith, with the sword still in her hand and a servant stuffing the assassinated man's severed head into a sack, looks off canvas at something hidden from our eyes.

Gian Lorenzo Bernini (1598–1680) worked on the exterior and interior of St. Peter's Basilica, including the shimmering Throne of St. Peter. His sculpture of the *Ecstasy of Saint Teresa of Ávila* takes us deep into the sensuous ecstasy of a woman who knew spasms of the divine. The sculpture has not a still moment, as Teresa swoons and her gown swirls in rippling waves that envelop the viewer in her transporting passion. Such art simply refuses to leave the viewer unmoved and unengaged.

Early Baroque captured the great drama of the Catholic view of the world as a lived experience, for both the human and the divine. By the seventeenth century, Catholicism was back and on demanding display. Opulent Catholic churches were a sensuous answer to plain reformed churches and Baroque paintings, rich, colorful, and filled with bodies in motion and unfolding dramas, answered pointed, but shallow Protestant cartoons. Protestant complaint may in the end have animated the Catholic Church, giving it the "other" against which it could rediscover its doctrinal and spiritual confidence; Baroque art and architecture embraced those already inside the church, and those returning.

Bernini's *Ecstasy of Saint Teresa of Ávila* The sensuous rippling folds of the saint's garment reflect the high energy and sheer passion of Baroque art and its drive to engage the emotions of observers.

political and social revolts. By the second half of the sixteenth century, with the religious situation across Europe becoming more varied and complex, religious warfare broke out in France, the Netherlands, and England. Religion had become a complicating factor in the relations of states.

The French Wars of Religion

Between 1560 and 1600, France was beset by a series of conflicts known as the French Wars of Religion. These struggles brought destruction and disorder to a once prosperous kingdom, ushered in social and economic change, and pushed the French monarchy into a period of decline.

The French monarchy already had problems. The king's traditional power base had been limited to a small area around present-day Paris, while the competitive French nobility controlled the remainder of the country. A series of strong monarchs, especially Louis XII and his successor Francis I, had made strides in consolidating power and prestige. Thanks to them, France was better

The Wars of Religion

As religion and politics became ever more entwined in the first half of the sixteenth century, struggles over religious authority often became indistinguishable from struggles over political authority (Map 13.2). The Knights' Revolt of 1522 and the Peasants' War of 1525 were early, ominous signs of how religious protests could turn into

Why did wars over religion dominate the second half of the sixteenth century, and what did Europe learn from them?

able to engage in an expensive military campaign in Italy, where the French army fought against both the emperor and the Spanish crown. In matters of religion, the French kings had been able to manage the growing number of French Protestants, nearly a million of them by 1560, who were largely followers of John Calvin. Called **Huguenots** (a term of derision whose etymology remains uncertain), these Protestants clustered in towns and urban centers prior to 1560, and their religious views were not seen as a serious threat to the stability or authority of France. The Huguenots, however, were never a uniform group but ranged from royal supporters to extreme Calvinists. That variability was a common feature of Protestantism. Divisions and differences existed not only between Protestant churches such as the Lutheran and Calvinist, but also within Protestant religions, wherein different groups viewed their religion and its essentials in different ways. England would experience a similar fluidity of Protestant belief and practice.

In 1559, the French king, Henry II, died during a jousting accident. The event brought home the fragility of royal authority, for while Henry had been a popular king with a string of military and political successes to his credit, when he died his eldest son, Francis, was only fifteen years old. His mother Catherine de' Medici stepped forward to take an active role in government. Tensions between the French nobility and the Italian queen mother escalated as the guardianship of her other children became a matter of dispute and rivalry. Catherine, isolated at court, complained that there was no one whom she could trust.

Her son Francis II died in 1560, after less than a year of rule, and was succeeded by his ten-year-old brother Charles IX. Catherine, determined not to be pushed aside by the nobility, managed to secure the control of her son's political actions by assuming the position of regent, giving her the power to govern in his name until he was ready to rule. From this moment on, the French Wars of

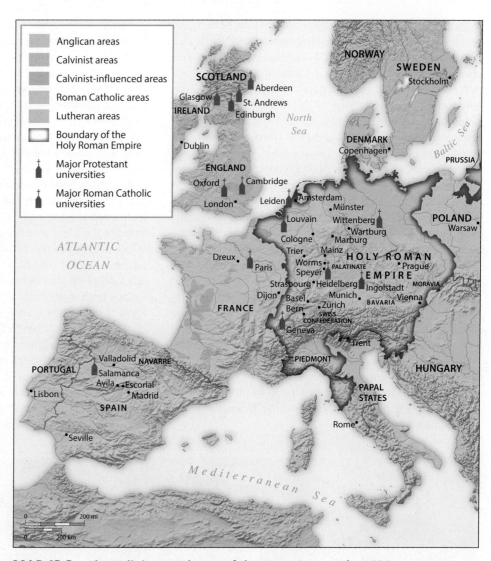

MAP 13.2 | The Religious Make-up of the Many Europes by 1600
By the end of the sixteenth century, the many religions of the many Europes were more or less fixed and immovable. Catholicism may seem to have remained territorially dominant, but Calvinism was a presence in many states, and Lutheranism prevailed in a solid block in the far north. *What might explain the nature of the territorial spread of the re-formed religions? What areas remained free of Protestantism? Why?*

Religion took shape within a shifting balance of power between the queen regent and three powerful noble families: the Montmorencies (Protestants), the Guise (Catholics), and the Bourbons (Protestants).

Amid these perfect conditions for a civil and religious war, armed hostilities broke out in 1562 and were not resolved until 1598. A series of seven wars were waged over the three and a half decades, each one a combination of family feuds, struggles for authority, and various religious conflicts. Catherine showed her preference for conciliation over war by issuing an edict in January 1562 that promoted a policy of religious coexistence between Catholics and Huguenots and gave Protestants the right to worship openly and to hold religious assemblies. Her efforts were not well received, however, and war dragged on as the Guise family opposed vigorously any move toward religious toleration.

In 1572, the growing intensity of the Wars of Religion reached a new peak when Huguenots and Catholics flooded in to Paris for the St. Bartholomew's Day celebration of the marriage that Catherine had arranged between her daughter, Margaret of Valois, and Henry, the son of King Anthony of Navarre. Following the ceremony, Admiral Coligny of the Montmorency family was shot while walking home from the royal palace. Huguenots rushed to the wounded man's side, and King Charles IX issued an official proclamation against the would-be assassins. Many people believed that the Guise family had plotted the attack, but some suspected that Catherine herself was involved. Protestants demanded retribution and Catherine, no longer willing to be conciliatory, convinced her son that the only solution was to do away with all the Huguenot leaders who remained in Paris. The king's Swiss guards were given a list of potential targets, blockaded the streets and city gates so that no one could escape, and began massacring Huguenots. Admiral Coligny was one of the estimated two thousand Protestant men, women, and children who were killed in Paris before the St. Bartholomew's Day Massacre ran its course. As news spread of the situation in Paris, Protestants in other towns in France were also massacred. Estimates are that another three thousand Protestants were killed.

The St. Bartholomew's Day Massacre was a religious, political, and diplomatic disaster for France. Protestant leaders throughout Europe were outraged by the persecution, and even Tsar Ivan IV ("Ivan the Terrible") of Russia spoke out on behalf of the murdered Huguenots. The French Wars of Religion were not resolved until Catherine de' Medici and all her sons were dead and the crown passed into the hands of her son-in-law, Henry III of Navarre. In 1589, he became King Henry IV of France. Born and raised a Protestant, Henry put aside his religious upbringing and converted to Catholicism in 1593 to bring stability and peace to his still largely Catholic country. "Paris," Henry is purported to have said, "is worth a Mass." In 1598, Henry brought the wars to a close through the **Edict of Nantes,** which set out the conditions under which Huguenots and Catholics could coexist within France. The terms of the edict differentiated between loyalty to the crown and religious faith, essentially acknowledging the existence of a loyal other within French society. It also restored certain civil rights to the French Protestants, including the right to practice their religion openly and the right to hold public offices formerly restricted to Catholics. In 1562, the enthusiasm for Catherine de' Medici's much milder edict had been lukewarm, but by 1598, after the massacre, the French people were tired of religious conflict and willing to agree to the terms of the new edict.

Saint Bartholomew's Day Massacre On the day of the saint, August 24, 1572, Swiss guards were ordered by King Charles IX to begin rounding up and murdering the Huguenots, or French Protestants, who had assembled in Paris for a royal wedding. Two thousand were slaughtered in and around Paris, and another three thousand in France in an event that shocked Europe.

The Dutch Revolt and the Spanish in the Netherlands

North of France, religious warfare broke out between Catholics and Protestants in 1566. In the Spanish Netherlands, Philip II of Spain ruled a profitable conglomeration of commercial cities that provided a stable source of income for the maintenance of his extensive empire. The seventeen distinct provinces under Philip's control, including present-day Belgium, Luxembourg, and the Netherlands, had a variety of populations with many different religious beliefs. In addition to Catholicism, the people of the Spanish Netherlands were drawn to various Anabaptist sects, Calvinism, and Lutheranism. After years of debilitating tax policies, war broke out when Philip tried to oust Calvinism from the provinces. Devout Calvinists responded by destroying statues, paintings, and other ornaments in Catholic churches. Philip sent the Spanish duke of Alva north with an army of more than ten thousand troops to put down the Dutch revolt.

The Dutch resisted the military campaign of the Spanish to impose religious standards on the provinces. William the Silent, the prince of Orange, organized rebellious Dutch citizens in the northern provinces. In the North Sea, experienced Dutch mariners harassed the Spanish navy and laid siege to the Spanish army stationed on the coast. William's goal was to unify the Netherlands under a single Dutch ruler. After years of warfare, he seemed to have achieved his goal when Philip II agreed to the terms of the Pacification of Ghent in 1576. Philip had recalled the militaristic duke of Alva in 1573, but one of his later replacements, the duke of Parma (as much a politician as a warrior), managed to undermine William's delicate coalitions. In 1579, the northern and southern provinces split along religious lines. In the largely Catholic south, the Union of Arras was formed under Spanish rule. In the primarily Protestant north, William's Union of Utrecht was established to oppose both Catholicism and the power of Philip.

War between the Union of Utrecht and the Union of Arras went on for decades, fueled by funding and military assistance from Protestant England as well as Catholic Spain, which supplied troops and resources along the so-called Spanish Road. In 1609, the two regions of the Netherlands reached a formal truce that all but recognized the independence of the seven northern Protestant provinces as the United Provinces. With the powerful merchant cities of Amsterdam, Rotterdam, and Utrecht within its borders, the United Provinces became known as the Dutch Republic (Map 13.3).

Elizabeth I and the Spanish Armada

Philip II of Spain, not content with an empire that stretched from the west coast of South and Central America to the

MAP 13.3 | The Netherlands in 1609
After religion, politics, and Spanish interference divided the Low Countries into a number of different interests and religions, the long conflict in the Netherlands led to their further division into a Protestant north and Catholic south, each with its own political and religious configuration. *How were William the Silent and his supporters in the north able to fend off the mighty Spanish Empire? What made the north a more difficult area for the Spanish to control? Which area was likely to be more prosperous, at least in the short run?*

kingdom of Naples in the east, Sicily in the south, and the Netherlands in the north, set his sights on adding England to his possessions. England had seen its share of religious turmoil in the years following the death of Henry VIII, as the Protestant boy-king Edward VI (r. 1547–1553) tried to promote a mixture of moderate Lutheran and stricter Calvinist forms of worship among the English people. Edward's brief reign was followed by that of his Catholic half-sister, Mary I (unfairly called "Bloody Mary" by her Protestant critics; r. 1553–1558), who attempted to return England to the authority of the pope and the Catholic Church. Nearly three hundred people were executed for their religious beliefs during her reign. Philip got a taste of what it might be like to rule over England when he married Mary in 1554. Their marriage was childless, however, and on Mary's death the throne passed to her half-sister Elizabeth I (r. 1558–1603), the daughter of Henry VIII and Anne Boleyn. Yet Mary's short and somewhat abrupt reign created the conditions that set up Elizabeth's successful one. For if Mary was less than subtle in her religious maneuvers, Elizabeth was full of subtlety and sensitivity in her political and religious actions, and the Protestants of England were ready after Mary's harsh reign for the return of a religious sympathizer and more politically adept and intelligent sovereign.

Elizabeth remains one of the most enigmatic and skilled political figures in western history. She inherited her father's temper and his shrewd ability to pick ministers capable of implementing royal policies and her mother's interest in re-formed religion. Elizabeth was intellectually gifted, superbly educated, and vain. That combination of talents and weaknesses proved to be effective when it came to managing her unruly aristocrats, the country's growing financial and religious crises, and dangerous foreign diplomacy. Elizabeth remained an unmarried ruler at a time when marriage was considered to be a diplomatic and dynastic necessity, vital to good government, and critical to the peaceful transfer of power from one generation to the next.

Elizabeth's reluctance to take hard stands was most evident in her early religious policies, when she was trying to heal the deep religious divisions that had been created during the reigns of her brother and sister. She famously said "there is but one God, the rest is a mere dispute about trifles." In 1559, Elizabeth instituted a new Parliamentary Act of Supremacy (known as the Elizabethan religious settlement) that made her the "supreme governor" of the English church. The Act of Uniformity, which put the English Book of Common Prayer back in churches and restored vernacular worship, followed shortly thereafter. The growing power of Calvinism, which had proven to be disruptive in the empire and in France, undermined Elizabeth's efforts, as did the threat posed to her by her Catholic cousin Mary Stuart, queen of Scots. Mary was Elizabeth's obvious heir and when she fled Scotland after a Calvinist coup in 1568, she turned to Elizabeth for help. In the 1560s the Scottish lowlands had taken up the religious re-formation of the church as promoted by John Calvin, driven out a Catholic French occupying force, and overthrown the Catholic Church and its clergy. Mary left her young son behind in the hands of the Calvinists when she sought exile in England. Elizabeth placed Mary under castle arrest and kept her confined for more than two decades, which angered Mary's Catholic sympathizers.

In the 1580s, a cluster of problems and challenges shattered Elizabeth's careful efforts to bring about religious peace. First, Elizabeth turned a blind eye when English mariners such as Sir Francis Drake and Sir Walter Raleigh seized Philip's Spanish ships returning from the Americas loaded with treasure. Their piracy fattened their own pockets, as well as the English treasury, but the Spanish king viewed the raids as a form of warfare against Spain. Second, Elizabeth had formally agreed by the Treaty of Nonsuch in 1585 to give military assistance to the Dutch Revolt. In exchange for specific territories in the Netherlands, Elizabeth provided troops and supplies to help drive the Spanish out of the region. Not surprisingly, Philip saw this commitment as a tacit declaration of war. Finally, in 1587, Elizabeth put Mary on trial and executed her for treason. Mary had been the focal point for numerous conspiracies to overthrow and assassinate Elizabeth. Queen Elizabeth's ministers finally convinced her that Mary must be eliminated. When the ax fell, Philip declared that Elizabeth was making war not only on Spain, but also on Catholicism, for she had killed one of God's anointed.

Philip's response to the events of the 1580s was to assemble an enormous armada of ships and troops to invade England, oust Elizabeth from the throne, and stamp out Protestantism in England. As preparations began and the sound of shipbuilding filled the air along the coast of Spain and Portugal, intelligence filtered back to England about the size of the planned invasion. England prepared for the invasion, daunted by the prospect of a military engagement with Europe's wealthiest and most powerful Catholic nation.

The king of Spain increasingly saw the battle not as one between Spain and England, but as one between good and evil, Catholic and Protestant. As such, he believed that he was waging a just and holy war against heresy and an illegitimate monarch. When his fleet took

The Armada Portrait of Queen Elizabeth I Elizabeth is empress and ruler of the seas in this portrait. She rests her right hand on a globe, her hand taking possession of the Americas, and above her hand rests the imperial crown. Behind her are scenes of the English fireships ready to attack the Spanish Armada on the left and Spanish ships driven by the divine wind onto the English coast on the right.

The Mystery of the Unloaded Cannons

To better understand why the Spanish scheme to invade England failed in 1588, historians and archaeologists have investigated the artifacts recovered from the sunken Spanish ships. When the Spanish Armada began to falter against the English navy, part of the Spanish fleet tried to sail the long way home around Scotland and Ireland. In the process, many ships were wrecked along the Scottish and Irish coasts. Treasure-hunters in pursuit of Spanish gold and other artifacts have over the years violated many of these sunken remains. The Spanish ship *San Juan de Sicilia,* for instance, sank in muddy waters off the coast of Scotland and would have been preserved perfectly had not treasure-seeking divers ripped open what remained of the hull looking for doubloons and other valuable antiquities. A Neapolitan ship, the *Girona,* remained undetected off the Irish coast near Antrim until 1967, when divers began to bring up jewelry and gold that had fallen from the hull to the ocean floor.

Still, some Armada wrecks have provided historians and archaeologists with unexpected insights into why the Spanish may have lost their naval encounter with the English. One such ship, *La Trinidad Valencera,* was a Venetian merchant vessel that had been requisitioned by the Spanish navy and outfitted to transport soldiers, horses, and guns between Spain and England. One of the Armada's largest ships, *La Trinidad* carried twenty-eight enormous bronze guns into battle, making it one of the Armada's most heavily armed ships. Along with its great bronze guns, the ship had four more cannons on board, and carried just under eighty mariners and around three hundred Neapolitan and Spanish soldiers. After engaging with the English off the southern coast, *La Trinidad* sailed around

northern Scotland and was shipwrecked in a storm off the north coast of Ireland. Most of the men on board made it to the Irish coast before the boat split and sank. The majority of the soldiers were killed, but thirty-two survivors made it to Scotland and from there set sail for France.

The ship's hull was not discovered until 1971. Although few items of value were found on the sunken ship, the ship's guns were still intact. The remains of *La Trinidad* reveal that the historical belief that the Spanish had been beaten despite their superior guns was a myth. When the ship's bronze guns were recovered, they were found unloaded despite Philip's orders that all guns should be kept ready for action at all times. Why the twenty-eight large bronze cannons on board were not ready for use remained a mystery, and that mystery deepened when a set of large wooden wheels unattached to any other equipment were also found in the wrecked ship.

Historians and archaeologists went back to the archives with their findings, reexamining the detailed lists of what was put on each ship and the instructions Philip gave regarding the use of the guns. What they discovered was that the magnificent cannons placed on *La Trinidad* were not meant for use at sea. They were there to support the land invasion of England. *La Trinidad* may have been one of the Armada's largest and most heavily armed ships, but its vast store of weapons was cargo rather than weapons to be used in the sea battle.

QUESTIONS | *What were Philip's many motives for attacking England? Why were England and Elizabeth lucky to survive the onslaught? Why did England's success in the encounter matter?*

to the seas in 1588, it was neither as large nor as well equipped as he had hoped, but Philip felt that God was on his side and victory certain. A combination of mismanagement, unforeseen bad weather, and the inherent disadvantage that heavy, Spanish warships had when sailing in unfamiliar, coastal waters against smaller, more maneuverable English vessels proved to be disastrous for the Spanish Armada. Many Spanish ships fell victim to English cannons and fire-ships (old fishing and merchant vessels that were set on fire and rammed into the Spanish fleet) before a powerful storm struck. They simply could not turn quickly enough to avoid the oncoming fire-ships. The duke of Parma failed to meet up with the Spanish fleet and then the storm hit, dashing many of the Spanish ships against the English coastline.

After the Armada's spectacular and unexpected loss, England emerged as a powerful naval power in the Atlantic. Medals were struck to celebrate the victory, many of them bearing the inscription "Jehovah blew with His wind and they were scattered." The medals also depict English people kneeling and praying to God for his intervention and divine guidance. Protestants in Europe hailed the English victory as proof that a "Protestant wind" was blowing so fiercely that the old Catholic powers such as Spain would be swept away. Philip made the best of things by blaming the weather, saying that he had sent his ships against the English, not the elements. Spain recovered economically and militarily from the events of 1588, and Philip continued to dream of launching other invasion attempts in the 1590s.

Conclusion

Chapters 11–13 explored how the many different Europes left the Middle Ages and began to fashion an early modern world. The Italian and European Renaissances developed a form of critical thinking about texts and history that undermined the great weight of authority that had lain so heavily on traditional Europe. Overseas exploration ended the economic and geographic isolation of Europeans, for there were other worlds out there beyond Europe, Africa, and Asia, worlds unknown to the ancients and the Bible, facts and economic chances beyond the long accepted ones. Finally, religious re-formation broke the fragile block of religious unity that had dominated the west for a millennium. The early modern world that emerged in the sixteenth century was the result of these crises of authority, knowledge, and religious uniformity, each crisis necessitating a rethinking of European assumptions about the world. Europe's new outlook was not so much a matter of fresh confidence as it was a product of competing certainties, political divisions, and European instabilities.

Though we have separated out these great unburdenings of tradition and authority (textual, geographic, and religious), we need to remember that they were happening at the same time and probably seemed utterly entangled and bewildering to contemporaries. A woman living in Cologne in 1519 might in the same year have seen a map showing Amerigo Vespucci's outlandish claim of the existence of new continents in the west; have first read some passages of Erasmus's *Praise of Folly*, illustrated with funny pictures by Holbein; and heard her husband mention something about an upstart monk somewhere up north challenging the pope and the Catholic Church. She would most likely have felt queasy by the sudden shock to her intellectual assumptions. Early modernity brought not just an awareness of change, but also the unsettling realization that nothing would ever be quite the same again, that change was the new normal condition for all, and that Europe's peculiarity was internal division and fierce competitiveness between its parts.

What separated Europe from the great empires of the Ottoman Turks and the Ming Dynasty in China was precisely the failure of empires in the Middle Ages (Carolingian, Ottonian, Holy Roman, and Byzantine) to dominate Europe. Medieval empires in the West were fractured, limited enterprises, never able to control either big or little Europe. Europeans shared a common culture but were politically, religiously, and linguistically divided. The passing of the Middle Ages and the arrival of intellectual instability, religious difference, and entrenched political divisions made Europe an energetic and aggressive force in the early modern world.

With the Catholic Church already changing by the Late Middle Ages and early sixteenth centuries, few

would have predicted that the actions of an Augustinian monk in a small university town in Germany might be enough to threaten its survival. Yet the ideas of Martin Luther, spread with the assistance of the printing press, regional religious fervor, and political divisions, changed European political and religious life profoundly. Many people in the many Europes were ready for Luther or someone very much like him to appear and shake the old establishment. Luther loosened the bonds that had fastened Europe to the official church, freeing up religious objectors across northern Europe to experiment with the creation and institution of new forms of Christianity. By 1600, Europe was no longer a single religious landmass, but a swamp punctuated by islands of different beliefs. Religion still mattered, but it mattered in different ways and within a century it would matter even less.

The cost of religious change was considerable. In 1556, the emperor Charles V, worn out by thirty years of religious and political controversy, resigned his high office in some despair. By the late sixteenth century, the lines drawn by the Protestants and a resurgent Catholic Church had hardened, doctrine had become dogma at Trent, and kings and princes were prepared to send their armies to defend whatever religion they preferred. Europe was divided further into fixed religious and political positions. The emperor Charles paid the price of that great fracturing and might be seen, in his divided commitments and varied regional powers, as every inch the much compromised and confused early modern European ruler. The great achievement of the religious re-formation of Europe in the sixteenth century remains the introduction into Europe of religious diversity and institutional change. The Catholic Church could no longer dominate the life and thought of Europe, if it ever had. The cost of religious revolution was so great that some observers have wondered if it was worth the calamities of spiritual division and anxiety, the blood spilled, and the wars that followed Luther's stubborn stand against the established church.[2] But something was gained: dramatic religious change had come to the many Europes. The imperial papacy was finished; Europe's incorporation under the papal banner had been broken. The age of the monks was over, the papacy reduced to a regional power, and the many Europes were, for better or worse, shaping an early modern world. As such, Europe's sixteenth-century experience intellectually, geographically, and religiously was not just one of religious re-formation, but of the re-formation of Europe into something more modern and familiar, *modern* and *familiar* because we still live with its economic, intellectual, religious, and political consequences.

Critical Thinking Questions

1. What was the tipping point that tumbled Luther's protest into a full-blown European religious revolution?

2. Which of the so-called Reformations was a genuine reformation of established religion, and why?

3. Had religion become a matter of free choice for most Europeans in the sixteenth century, and why did they make the choices they did?

4. What did the religious turmoil of the sixteenth century cost Europe? What did Europe gain? Was it worth it?

Key Terms

Purgatory (p. 390)

indulgence (p. 392)

Protestant (p. 399)

Act of Supremacy (p. 402)

Peace of Augsburg (p. 404)

Anabaptists (p. 405)

millenarianism (p. 405)

Society of Jesus (Jesuits) (p. 407)

Baroque (p. 409)

Huguenots (p. 411)

Edict of Nantes (p. 412)

Primary Sources in connect

For information on Connect and the online resources available, go to http://connect.mcgraw-hill.com.

1. The Confrontation of Luther and Charles V at Worms

2. Martin Luther on the Good Estate of Marriage

3. The Twelve Demands of the Peasants

4. Policing Calvin's Church

5. Queen Elizabeth I's Act of Supremacy

6. Charles V's Abdication

A Call to Debate: The Ninety-Five Theses

Luther released the Ninety-Five Theses on October 31, 1517. How he did so is a subject of some controversy. No formal debate followed, though that was the stated intention of issuing such a list of contentions. Instead, the Ninety-Five Theses were soon circulating in published form in Latin and German and set off a firestorm of opinion.

Out of love and zeal for truth and the desire to bring it to light, the following theses will be publicly discussed at Wittenberg under the chairmanship of the reverend father Martin Luther, master of arts and sacred theology and regularly appointed lecturer on these subjects at that place. He requests that those who cannot be present to debate orally with us will do so by letter.

In the name of our Lord Jesus Christ. Amen.

1. When our lord and master Jesus Christ said, "Repent" (Matt. 4:17), he willed the entire life of believers to be one of repentance.

2. This word cannot be understood as referring to the sacrament of penance, that is, confession and satisfaction as administered by the clergy.

3. Yet it does not mean solely inner repentance; such inner repentance is worthless unless it produces various outward mortifications of the flesh.

4. The penalty of sin remains as long as the hatred of self, that is, true inner repentance, until our entrance into the kingdom of heaven.

5. The pope neither desires nor is able to remit any penalties except those imposed by his own authority or that of the canons.

6. The pope cannot remit any guilt except by declaring and showing that it has been remitted by God; or, to be sure, by remitting guilt in cases reserved to his judgment. If his right to grant remission in these cases were disregarded, the guilt would certainly remain unforgiven.

7. The penitential canons are imposed only on the living, and, according to the canons themselves, nothing should be imposed on the dying.

8. Therefore the Holy Spirit through the pope is kind to us insofar as the pope in his decrees always makes exception of the article of death and of necessity.

18. Furthermore, it does not seem proved, either by reason or Scripture, that souls in purgatory are outside the state of merit, that is, unable to grow in love.

19. Nor does it seem proved that souls in purgatory, at least not all of them, are certain and assured of their own salvation, even if we ourselves may be entirely certain of it.

20. Therefore the pope, when he uses the words "plenary remission of all penalties," does not actually mean "all penalties," but only those imposed by himself.

21. Those indulgence preachers are in error who say that a man is absolved from every penalty and saved by papal indulgences.

22. As a matter of fact, the pope remits to souls in purgatory no penalty which, according to canon law, they should have paid in life.

23. If remission of all penalties whatsoever could be granted to anyone at all, certainly it would be granted only to the most perfect, that is, to very few.

24. For this reason most people are necessarily deceived by that indiscriminate and high-sounding promise of release from penalty.

25. That power which the pope has in general over purgatory corresponds to the power which any bishop or curate has in a particular way in his own diocese or parish.

26. The pope does very well when he grants remission to souls in purgatory, not by the power of the keys, which he does not have, but by way of intercession for them.

27. They preach only human doctrines who say that as soon as the money clinks into the money chest, the soul flies out of purgatory.

28. It is certain that when money clinks in the money chest, greed and avarice can be increased; but when the church intercedes, the result is in the hands of God alone.

32. Those who believe that they are certain of their salvation because they have indulgence letters will be eternally damned, together with their teachers.

33. Men must especially be on their guard against those who say that the pope's pardons are that inestimable gift of God by which man is reconciled to him.

36. Any truly repentant Christian has a right to full remission of penalty and guilt, even without indulgence letters.

42. Christians are to be taught that the pope does not intend that the buying of indulgences should in any way be compared with works of mercy.

43. Christians are to be taught that he who gives to the poor or lends money to the needy does a better deed than he who buys indulgences.

46. Christians are to be taught that unless they have more than they need, they must reserve enough for their family needs and by no means squander it on indulgences.

50. Christians are to be taught that if the pope knew the exactions of the indulgence preachers, he would rather that the basilica of St. Peter were burned to ashes than built up with the skin, flesh, and bones of his sheep.

51. Christians are to be taught that the pope would and should wish to give of his own money, even though he had to sell the basilica of St. Peter, to many of those from whom certain hawkers of indulgences cajole money.

69. Bishops and curates are bound to admit the commissaries of papal indulgences with all reverence.

70. But they are much more bound to strain their eyes and ears lest these men preach their own dreams instead of what the pope has commissioned.

71. Let him who speaks against the truth concerning papal indulgences be anathema and accursed;

72. But let him who guards against the lust and license of the indulgence preachers be blessed.

81. This unbridled preaching of indulgences makes it difficult even for learned men to rescue the reverence which is due the pope from slander or from the shrewd questions of the laity.

82. Such as: "Why does not the pope empty purgatory for the sake of holy love and dire need of the souls that are there if he redeems an infinite number of souls for the sake of miserable money with which to build a church?"

86. Again, "Why does not the pope, whose wealth is today greater than the wealth of the richest Crassus, build this one basilica of St. Peter with his own money rather than with the money of poor believers?"

90. To repress these very sharp arguments of the laity by force alone, and not to resolve them by giving reasons, is to expose the church and the pope to the ridicule of their enemies and to make Christians unhappy.

91. If, therefore, indulgences were preached according to the spirit and intention of the pope, all these doubts would be readily resolved. Indeed, they would not exist.

94. Christians should be exhorted to be diligent in following Christ their head through penalties, death, and hell;

95. And thus be confident entering into heaven through many tribulations rather than through the false security of peace (Acts 14:22).

QUESTIONS | *Into what categories might the theses be separated? How does Luther define and, therefore, limit papal power? At this point, did Luther still subscribe to the fundamentals of Catholic belief? What are his specific complaints against indulgences?*

Source: Career of the Reformer: I, Luther's Works, XXXI, ed. Harold J. Grimm (Philadelphia: Fortress Press, 1957), 25–33.

14

Perspective View of Louis XIV's Grand Palace Complex at Versailles

ABSOLUTISM AND WAR IN THE SEVENTEENTH CENTURY

The Many Torments of the Seventeenth Century

The Origins of Absolutism

The Thirty Years' War
The Habsburg Empire Reacts to Protestantism's Spread
The Defenestration of Prague
The Bohemian Phase
The Danish and the Siege of Magdeburg
The French Phase and the War's Bitter End
The Consequences of the Thirty Years' War

The Culture of the High Baroque
Theater
Art and Architecture
Music
Political Philosophy in the Age of Absolutism
Popular Culture in the Baroque Era
Living the Witch Craze

Absolutism Triumphant
France under Louis XIV and Louis XV

Absolutism and the Austrian Habsburgs
The Consolidation of Prussia
Russia: From Ivan the Terrible to Peter the Great
Incomplete Absolutisms: Spain, Poland, and Sweden

The Non-absolutist Exceptions: The Venetian and the Dutch Republics
The Venetians
The Dutch

The Defeat of Absolutism in England
Charles I and the English Civil War
Trial and Regicide
The Commonwealth
England's Colonies
The Restoration
The Glorious Revolution

Conclusion

LOUIS XIV, SUN KING AND STATE-BUILDER Louis XIV of the house of Bourbon was a man of large appetites. Indeed, the autopsy after the French king's death in 1715 found that his stomach was twice normal size. Louis had a taste not only for rich food, but also for war, work, and glory—and he firmly believed himself to be the man whom God had appointed to rule France and to make it great. His subjects, too, believed him virtually all-powerful; every day hundreds of people lined up to tell the king their troubles, or to petition him for favors. His mere touch was thought to cure the skin infection known as scrofula. Having taken the throne during a period of religious, economic, and political turmoil in France, Louis never wavered in his belief that France's greatness depended on his taking complete command of his kingdom. Throughout his life, he exulted in and cultivated his semi-divine status; but at the same time he devoted his enormous energies into making himself the embodiment of a new kind of state, one with its own increasing appetite for power.

This new state would be one with a centralized army and bureaucracy, one that respected and defended the Catholic Church, but ultimately set limits on its power and would not go to war over religion alone. It would be one in which the monarch collected his own taxes and chose his own advisors—even if most of them remained nobles—rather than one in which the king had to depend on powerful aristocrats to fill his coffers and provide him with soldiers. And above all, it would be a state that kept order. Louis would never forget the terrifying and chaotic world of his childhood, as France itself nearly collapsed in the wake of the horrific Thirty Years' War and the ensuing civil conflict known as the Fronde. He would do his all to be sure that his kingdom never fell prey to such disorder again.

During his long life, Louis pursued the aim of state-building. He worked hard to prevent the spread of Protestantism, believing religious disunity to be an offense against God and an incitement to civil war. Louis worked very hard, often rising early and retiring late to hear petitions and to attend to paperwork, by no means responsibilities a modern-minded monarch could ignore. He waged wars to advance France's interests and sent out surveyors and spies to find out what was happening in the provinces; he spent a great deal of time hunting, attending masses, and giving parties at his fabulous palace complex at Versailles—but such public appearances, too, were political acts, essential to demonstrating the grandeur and graciousness of the king. He may never have uttered the famous phrase, *"L'état c'est moi!"* ("The state? That's me!"), but on his deathbed in 1715, he did say, perhaps with more hope than confidence: "I am going, but the state

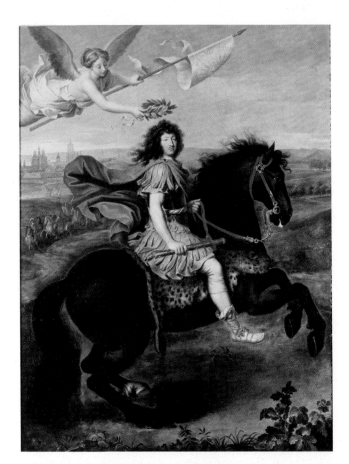

The Warrior King Louis XIV loved to see himself depicted in classical garb. Here the king—mounted to demonstrate his suitability for military leadership—is crowned by the winged goddess of fame.

will remain forever. . . ." Crowned in an era of chaos, it was the quest for permanent security and order that defined the absolute reign of Louis XIV.

Louis liked to portray himself as the Sun King, around which all of France revolved, but he was eager for Europe,

Dutch Revolt
1566–1609

Dutch Revolt
1621–1648

Thirty Years' War
1618–1648

English Civil War
1642–1648

Reign of Louis XIV
1643–1715

1550   1575   1600   1625   1650

or indeed the world, to revolve around him as well. From the 1670s on, he regularly made war with neighboring states and succeeded in adding some territory to France, though at the cost of hundreds of thousands of lives and a mounting state debt. He set about formalizing French colonial domination over areas in North America, the Caribbean, and Southeast Asia where French traders had established toeholds. Louis's brand of absolute monarchy succeeded, by and large, in stabilizing and modernizing France. But this form of modernization also had its costs, and not just in money and soldiers' lives. During his reign, some two hundred men and women were imprisoned in the Paris prison and armory known as the Bastille for writing, printing, or selling books critical of the church or of royal tyranny, and he allowed church officials to persecute heretics, witches, Protestants, and even nonconformist Catholics known as Jansenists. Louis would leave an absolutist state, but also a troubled legacy, to his heirs.

Louis was by no means alone in perceiving his age as one teetering on the brink of chaos. The seventeenth century—and especially the period before about 1675— was characterized by political upheaval and by intense human misery, in which extreme weather, war, famine, and disease took the lives of millions, and religious passions and prophecies drove people to persecute their neighbors or flee their neighborhoods. In the midst of this misery, however, some Europeans were also finding new opportunities. The Ottoman threat in the East declined at last after the Turks made one last attempt to take Vienna in 1683; this opened up new opportunities for Austrian, Swedish, and Russian enlargement. The older trading networks of the Baltic and Mediterranean Seas, such as the Hanseatic League and the Venetian Empire, were forced to make way for new sea powers, such as the Dutch and the English. The opening up of Spanish and Portuguese, and then Dutch, French, and English trade with Asia and with the Atlantic world expanded the merchant elite and brought new wealth into urban trading centers. The Dutch and English proved particularly adept at developing small industries to refine new products like sugar, tobacco, and copper. In these places, too, landowners began to produce goods for market rather than for consumption at home. Controlling the dynamic forces of increasing commerce, specialized manufacturing, and a widening market became yet another challenge for Europe's rulers.

Europe's kings and kingdoms dealt with these crises and opportunities in different ways, and their choices mattered. Louis XIV's absolutist solution to the crises of the seventeenth century was not the only one available. The Dutch and the English, to give two important exceptions, chose other routes, resulting in the development of crucial models of religious toleration and republican citizenship in the Dutch Republic, and of parliamentary governance and the protection of individual rights in England. But building a modern, centralized state would prove essential in the face of the seventeenth century's new challenges. Those who wanted to retain their power would need large armies, extensive and well-tapped tax

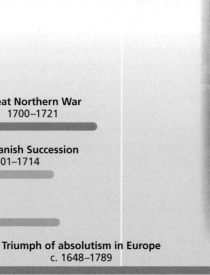

Great Northern War
1700–1721

War of Spanish Succession
1701–1714

Triumph of absolutism in Europe
c. 1648–1789

1700   1725   1750   1775   1800

bases, and stomachs strong enough to endure and overcome the sufferings and the often-violent discontents of their peoples. The seventeenth century saw the birth of many modern institutions, including the centralized state, but we cannot forget that these transformations were not inevitable and that they arrived in the midst of religious chaos and political upheaval. Building stable states in such an age—whether absolutist monarchies, republics, or constitutional monarchies—as Louis XIV well knew, was a gigantic task—and one that even he feared might never be done.

The Many Torments of the Seventeenth Century

If we were to attempt to catalogue the torments seventeenth-century Europeans suffered, we would have to start with the Thirty Years' War (1618–1648).

What forms of hardship and conflict did Europeans endure in the seventeenth century? Even if we take the lowest estimates of its disastrous consequences—the reduction of 20 percent of the population of central Europe—this still makes the Thirty Years' War the most murderous of Europe's conflicts ever. By no means was it the century's only war; there were multiple civil wars, and conflict over royal succession led to several grand-scale wars both in the seventeenth and in the eighteenth century.

Then there were the more generalized forms of misery. The large influx of Spanish New World silver made for serious, continuing inflation, which reduced peasants' real incomes below subsistence levels and spread hunger throughout the continent. There were disastrous harvests in 1660–1663, 1675–1679, 1693–1694, and 1708–1709; in France in 1692–1694, some 2.8 million people, or about 15 percent of the population, died of starvation and malnutrition. Disease cut down those who managed to find enough to eat. In 1665–1666, the plague rampaged through London, killing more than 80,000 of the city's 500,000 inhabitants. The suffering of Londoners was increased the next year by a devastating fire, which destroyed much of the medieval city center. But plague struck elsewhere, too, as did cholera, typhus, and smallpox.

Disaster and chaos were so widespread that many Europeans concluded the world was coming to an end. During the height of the Fronde, a Parisian judge wrote: "If one ever had to believe in the Last Judgment, I believe it is happening right now."[1] In 1666 (calculated by Bible readers to be the year of the Anti-Christ), several would-be Messiahs gathered large followings. Some Europeans blamed witches for crop failures and epidemics, and witch-burning became commonplace, especially in central Europe. In some places, peasants and townspeople turned their anger on tax collectors, exploitative landowners, or hoarders, making for a series of rebellions through-

out the continent—though virtually all of these ended with the massacring of rebels, rather than with reforms.

Unquestionably, the combination of hunger, anger, war, political instability, disease, and religious extremism justifies historians speaking of a "crisis of the seventeenth century" for Europe. But the fact that the century brought famines, droughts, and terrible epidemics to places such as Egypt, Mexico, and China has spurred some scholars to wonder if the chaos had at least some of its roots in something more universal: the weather. Whatever the causes of this crisis, the suffering and conflict it entailed contributed greatly to the elaboration of a new form of kingship: **absolutism.**

The Origins of Absolutism

In the medieval world, to be a king was in theory to be raised above the other nobles of the realm by divine sanction. In practice, however, a medieval king remained merely the top-ranking noble in

How did absolutism differ from previous forms of kingship in Europe? his kingdom. When one king died, his heir needed to be formally elected or at least acclaimed by the other nobles before he could sit comfortably on his throne. In some cases, when a royal line was broken, the nobles chose a new monarch from among their number. Kings depended on their fellow nobles to see that the laws were carried out and the taxes collected, and to raise armies for them when they wanted to go to war. The king was supposed to consult his people, and especially his fellow nobles, about matters of importance to the realm. For that purpose, medieval states had developed various sorts of advisory assemblies, made up mostly of nobles, which met from time to time, at the king's pleasure. In Poland, this body was called the Sejm; in France, it was the Estates General. Spain had several assemblies, the most important of which was called the Cortes. These assemblies had various rights, but they did not have the right to overrule the king. Only in England did Parliament really have the power to resist the king's will, especially in matters of taxation.

In the sixteenth century, kings began to see assemblies as obstructions and well-armed nobles as threats, and they began a series of moves designed to centralize power and to ensure the succession of their direct heirs to Europe's many thrones. Some kings claimed that God alone—and *not* the kingdom's other nobles or advisory assemblies—had given them the **divine right** to rule. In the seventeenth century, in the wake of the grueling Thirty Years' War, many kings moved to do away with the assemblies and disarm nobles in favor of state-funded, standing armies. Kings also cut into noble power by allowing wealthy men of lower rank to buy offices that came with titles, or by appointing bureaucrats and foreigners to help them run the kingdom. These innovations distributed power upward, to the king, making him less

Weather and the Seventeenth-Century Crisis

Historians have long described the seventeenth century as a century of crisis. Not only did it see an unprecedented number of bloody wars and civil conflicts, but it was also a century of famines and epidemic diseases, in Europe and across the world. All in all, the century saw levels of mortality of epic proportions.

What caused all this misery? Contemporaries identified a series of very cold winters and crop-destroying droughts as part of the problem, but scholars have recently acquired more comprehensive and accurate means by which to measure the extent to which climate change afflicted the people of the seventeenth century. Combining studies of ice cores, tree rings, pollens, and glacial debris with reports from contemporaries, scientists are now able to show that the seventeenth century was abnormally cold and dry in many places, while floods raged in others. They discovered that the era saw the lowest level of solar activity in two millennia, and that a series of eruptions threw volcanic dust into the atmosphere, further reducing the amount of solar energy that reached the earth. The result was that Europe was, on average, two degrees colder during the seventeenth century than it had been in the sixteenth century, and the growing season was shortened by three to four weeks. In addition, the El Niño effect—which brings floods to Central and South America, and drought to Asia and Europe, on average every five years—struck more frequently in the middle years of the seventeenth century. The result was severe climatic instability, summers blighted by freak frosts, and winters so cold that even the Egyptians took to wearing fur coats. Weather conditions were undoubtedly responsible for many of the famines and contributed to the numbers of plague deaths, but did weather *cause* the political turmoil of the seventeenth century?

That, of course, is quite a different question, and it is the one that the highly respected historian of the era, Geoffrey Parker, is now asking. In a recent essay, Parker suggests that we take more seriously than before the linkages between bad weather and rebellion. We can, he argues, be sure that rising bread or rice prices sparked rebellions in Portugal in 1637, in Catalonia in 1640, in Ireland in 1641, and in Japan in 1642. Other revolts, such as that of the Scots in 1637, were certainly couched in religious terms, but were given urgency by a preceding series of terrible harvests and the resulting scarcity of food. The intransigence of absolutist rulers and the circulation of pamphlets complaining about both political and economic conditions or prophesying imminent apocalypse added the fuel necessary to turn complaints into rebellions. It is instructive, Parker points out, that many of these rebellions began in early summer, the period before the new harvest when the stores from the last year's crop typically ran low. Parker be-

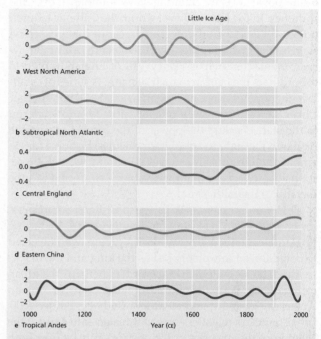

FIGURE 14.1 | **Estimated Relative Temperature Variations during the Past Thousand Years**

Note the dip in temperature in the middle of the seventeenth century in all regions. ***Does this evidence support Geoffrey Parker's theory that the weather was a major factor in causing the crises of the seventeenth century?***

Source: Adapted from Michael E. Mann, "Little Ice Age," in *Encyclopedia of Global Environmental Change,* Vol. 1: *The Earth System,* ed. Michael C. MacCracken and John S. Perry (Chichester, U.K.: Wiley, 2002), 504–509.

lieves that the increases in atmospheric volcanic ash and in El Niño effects "triggered or fatally exacerbated major political upheavals,"[2] and he argues that it is about time historians take climate change seriously in explaining why the seventeenth century saw such pervasive and widespread challenges to authority.

Parker's work is clearly shaped by recent discussion of climate change, but it poses important questions about how we see the past, and about the kinds of sources historians use. Even if some historians will not accept causal linkages between weather and political crises, Parker has put together convincing evidence that environmental factors did play an important part in destabilizing regimes across the world.

QUESTIONS | *How did weather affect European societies in the seventeenth century? Do you think weather can have an effect on politics?*

responsive and less beholden to his nobles, who were no longer able to check his "absolute" power. As we will see, England—where Parliament's powers were protected in law—was one of very few European kingdoms able to resist the advent of absolutism.

Another means by which kings sought to establish absolute power was by claiming state dominance over the churches. In the late medieval world, the Catholic Church possessed wealth and power in excess of that possessed even by the greatest kings. In the sixteenth century, however, monarchs such as Henry VIII of England opted to subordinate the church to their dictates. A series of established churches arose as monarchs made one or another Christian sect the state's official faith. Tying the clergy to the state checked the power of the former, giving the monarch the right to appoint (or dismiss) bishops, for example, though this also meant monarchs were to be responsible for seeing that their subjects conformed to the dictates of the faith.

This was no easy task in the post-Reformation era, for Christendom had split, and many states, including England, contained large minority groups who objected to being forced to worship just as the king and the majority did. The Holy Roman emperor had perhaps the greatest challenge here, for by tradition the emperor was an Austrian Habsburg and an ardent Catholic. But by 1600, Protestantism's relentless spread threatened to make it the religion of the majority of the empire's inhabitants. Both the Austrian Habsburgs and their Spanish relatives (for a Habsburg also ruled in Spain after Charles V divided his kingdom in 1556) already believed Protestantism to be a loathsome heresy; now they began to fear that it would undermine the already precarious stability of the empire, and of its semiautonomous kingdoms. Their attempt to reverse the Reformation and to move in the direction of absolutism sparked the greatest war of the seventeenth century.

The Thirty Years' War

The series of conflicts that historians have dubbed the Thirty Years' War were sparked by several sources of intra-European hostility: the unfinished business of religious re-formation; the monarchs' drift toward absolutism; and a changing balance of power, which raised some rulers' hopes that they might use the opportunity to seize someone else's spoils. Among the causes, too, was a long smoldering dispute in one corner of the Spanish Habsburg Empire: the Netherlands.

> **What factors led to the Thirty Years' War? What were the political, diplomatic, and religious results of the war?**

The Habsburg Empire Reacts to Protestantism's Spread

As we saw in Chapter 13, the Spanish Habsburg king Philip II, heir to the western and New World domains possessed by Charles V, had tried his best to suppress what became both a religious revolt and a trade war in the Netherlands. From the 1570s through the 1590s, Philip sent army after army up the Spanish Road, the land route to the Netherlands that passed along the French border (Map 14.1). But the Dutch opened their dikes and flooded the fields and sent well-trained militiamen to beat down waterlogged Spanish troops.

While Philip II and his successor Philip III (r. 1598–1621) struggled to deal with the Dutch Revolt, the Austrian Habsburgs dealt with the Reformation's fallout in their domains. They had some success; in the decades after the Council of Trent, Catholic reformers managed to bring most Poles back to the Catholic fold. But in other places, Protestantism was making serious gains: by the end of the sixteenth century, the majority of the nobles in Hungary, Saxony, Brandenburg, Bohemia, and the Habsburgs' home province, Austria, had become Protestants. Terrified, the Habsburg emperors ennobled Catholic state servants and gave them land, enlarging the Catholic nobility. Pioneering their own absolutist methods, they began also to build a centralized, stable Catholic bureaucracy, which some believed was designed to spy on and undermine the Protestant nobility.

By the 1610s, the Peace of Augsburg had come to seem fragile or outdated, in part because everyone continued to believe that there was only one true church—and that was the one to which the believer adhered. Large numbers of Catholics believed Protestantism to be the work of the devil, and most Protestants believed the pope to be the Anti-Christ. No one wanted to compromise, and the result was war without mercy and seemingly without end.

The Defenestration of Prague

Frederick V (r. 1610–1623), a Calvinist and prince of a western German state called the Palatinate, was one of those who feared that the Reformation might be overturned. He also believed that imperial, Catholic conspirators were out to take away the autonomy and traditional privileges of German noblemen like himself. That is to say, he feared both the reinstatement of Catholicism and absolutism—and he believed he was divinely appointed to stop both of these trains before they left the station. Others shared those fears, most notably Bohemian Protestant nobles, who were forced to accept the Catholic Habsburg prince Ferdinand as king of Bohemia in 1617. After his coronation, rather than working to reconcile the Protestant nobles, Ferdinand returned to the imperial capital of Vienna, and left Bohemia in the hands of hardline Catholic regents. In response, on May 23, 1618, some passionately Protestant nobles staged a confrontation at the royal palace in Prague and threw two of Ferdinand's regents out an upper-story window. The men survived, thanks to having landed in a huge dung heap. But the incident, known as the Defenestration of Prague, incited both Frederick V and Ferdinand II (who became Holy Roman Emperor Ferdinand II in 1619) to action, touching off what

MAP 14.1 | The Thirty Years' War

The Thirty Years' War was fought primarily on the territory of the Holy Roman Empire. **Study the patterns of conflict on this map. Why was France able to recover from these wars so much more quickly than the German states?**

is known as the Bohemian Phase of the Thirty Years' War. Not for the first, nor for the last time in European history, a confrontation between a handful of hardcore believers provoked a world-altering conflict.

The Bohemian Phase

The Bohemian militants moved to form an independent government and conscripted every tenth peasant and every eighth town dweller to form a makeshift army. They rejected Ferdinand as king and elected Frederick V of the Palatinate instead, hoping that Frederick's marriage to the daughter of James I of England would bring England and perhaps other enemies of the empire into the fight on their side. The Bohemian army gained support from Austrian and Hungarian Protestants, though James I remained unmoved. In 1619, 42,000 Protestant troops laid siege to Vienna, but could not sustain it, as their ranks were decimated by disease and lack of food. With his back against the wall, Emperor Ferdinand II bribed Austrian nobles

and negotiated for support from the Poles, Bavarians, and Spanish to muster a formidable army.

In early November 1620, a force of 27,000 imperial troops routed a Bohemian army of about 15,000 at White Mountain. They drove the Protestants back to Prague, where stragglers were put to the sword. Imperial officers rounded up rebels, including as many of the defenestrators as could be found, seized their property, and executed twenty-eight of them in Prague's Town Square. Twelve heads, two hands, and one tongue were posted on the city gates, where they remained for more than a decade. Known as the Blood Court, this was in fact one of the *least* bloody reprisals in this grisly war, but it deeply angered the Bohemians, who immediately turned the barbaric acts into propaganda for the Protestant cause.

Of greater general significance for the history of central Europe was what happened next: determined to stamp out religious disunity, in 1621 Ferdinand II ordered all Calvinists (those who were not serfs bound to the land) to leave Bohemia; the serfs he forced to convert to

CHRONOLOGY	Key Events in the Thirty Years' War
DATE	**EVENT**
1618	Defenestration of Prague
1620	Battle of White Mountain
1631	Siege of Magdeburg
1631	Battle of Breitenfeld
1632	Battle of Lützen
1635	France entered war
1648	Peace of Westphalia

Catholicism in mass ceremonies. About 20 percent of the population fled, including most of the nobility. Austrian, Bavarian, and Hungarian Lutherans were treated more leniently, but they too were bullied or bribed to convert. In effect, the Bohemian war reversed the course of the Reformation in eastern central Europe.

The Danish and the Siege of Magdeburg

Emboldened by the Habsburgs' victory in central Europe, the Spanish monarchy renewed its war against the Dutch, seizing Frederick's former kingdom, the strategically important Palatinate, in 1624. Fearing Protestantism would be wiped off the map, Denmark entered the conflict, promising to lead and fund the fragmented Protestant cause. After 1625, England, now under Charles I, also began to funnel money to the Protestants, and sent a few troops as well. Meanwhile, the Catholic Bohemian general Albrecht von Wallenstein took over the rebuilding of the imperial army, creating an effective fighting force of 110,000 men by 1628. The soldiers, for the most part mercenaries or conscripts, received little in the way of supplies and were expected to live chiefly off booty and provisions provided by local populations. More accurately stated, the soldiers were invited to plunder—and plunder they did, especially when they were hungry or their salaries were long overdue.

In May 1631, imperial armies overran the Protestant stronghold of Magdeburg. Though the imperial commander Count Tilly tried to halt the plundering, he lost control as a fire swept the city and soldiers rampaged, raped, and robbed for days. Approximately 20,000 civilians and defending soldiers died, most of them in the fire; their bodies had to be thrown in the river, as the remaining 450 inhabitants of the town had neither the strength nor space to bury them. Nor did they have sufficient wealth to rebuild the town, much of which was still rubble nearly one hundred years later. The Siege of Magdeburg made excellent propaganda for the Protestant side, and its horrors—inflated even beyond the grisly realities—helped push more Protestant allies to take an active role in the cause.

The victories of the imperial armies and events like the Siege of Magdeburg alarmed the Swedish king Gustavus Adolphus (r. 1611–1632), a pious Protestant, as well as Louis XIII of France, who, despite being a Catholic king, had no desire to see the Holy Roman Empire dominate the entire continent. Gustavus Adolphus II was already in Pomerania (see Map 14.1) with his formidable Swedish troops; he had arrived in 1630, intending to protect his own territories and perhaps to acquire new ones. After Magdeburg, the French agreed to a large subsidy for Gustavus Adolphus's army, thereby avoiding sending in troops themselves, and in 1631, the Swedes entered the war on the Protestant side. The Swedish king's energy in recruiting allies and his brilliant battlefield tactics helped turn the tide of the war

Massacre at Magdeburg In May 1631, imperial troops (here depicted bearing the double-headed eagle banner of the Habsburg's monarchy) overran the Protestant stronghold of Magdeburg. Hungry, unpaid, and frustrated by the long siege, Habsburg troops pillaged and burned the city, killing most of its inhabitants and creating useful propaganda for the Protestant cause.

1631–1632: *The Lion of the North and the Turning of the Tide*

For the Protestant side, prospects in the war were poor when Gustavus Adolphus II of Sweden led his troops into the conflict in early 1631. Many Protestant leaders had tried to take command of the Protestant side, including Frederick V and Christian IV of Denmark. Gustavus Adolphus outshone them all, in part because his victories turned the tide dramatically in 1631–1632, and in part because the tactics he employed would provide models for the military revolution to come (see Chapter 15).

Gustavus Adolphus was an ambitious ruler, but so were many of his contemporaries and rivals. More important, he was a savvy military strategist. He had studied Roman and Dutch tactics, and he knew how to use the mobility of his troops to his best advantage. He had been involved in previous conflicts, and he knew the value of motivated and well-trained soldiers. He was also a good propagandist, using the horrors of Magdeburg and his own swagger to convince some neutral German princes to enter the war on his side, though others hesitated, unwilling to commit themselves to war against the powerful empire. At the Battle of Breitenfeld in 1631, the Swedish king decisively defeated an imperial army of about 37,000 men, killing more than 7,000. The empire's military leader, Count Tilly, was wounded and his army diminished to nearly 13,000 after his troops fled the field in disarray. In an era of mercenary soldiers and no prisoner of war camps, Gustavus Adolphus simply forced the more than nine thousand prisoners he had taken to join his army instead.

After the battle was over, Protestant propagandists claimed that the Swede's victory at Breitenfeld was divine retribution for Magdeburg. To some, Gustavus Adolphus, now sweeping down into southern Germany, was a Goth who would sack Rome and restore German liberties; others simply called him the Lion of the North. His charisma counted for much, but the enhanced skills and firepower of his army actually delivered the victory. While the armies of the previous century had relied on pikes and swords, Swedish forces bristled with muskets and cannons, and yet demonstrated far greater mobility than the much larger imperial armies arrayed against them. The Swedish commander trained his musketeers so that they could reload and replace one another to fire a continuous barrage. Though his cannons fired standard-sized balls, state-of-the-art engineering made them lightweight and easier to move. Following the battle at Breitenfeld, the Swedish commander marched with what was, for his day, lightning speed, establishing strategic bases and linking together German allies. He swept across the German states to the Rhine and invaded Bavaria, covering nearly one thousand miles in one year.

In the chaos of the Battle of Lützen in 1632, Gustavus Adolphus strayed from his command post into a fierce cavalry battle and was shot. He fell from his horse and was stabbed repeatedly. Looters eager for trophies unceremoniously stripped the king's body. His Protestant forces fought on, losing thousands in the battle, but the imperial armies retreated first, and the Protestants claimed the field. But the Swedish king's death left the Protestant cause without an effective leader and it lost momentum; the Protestants badly needed the French support they received after 1635. Had the Lion of the North not joined the war in 1631, the imperial cause might have been victorious, and all of continental Europe might have been returned to the Catholic fold.

QUESTION | *How did Gustavus Adolphus's brief participation in the Thirty Years' War make a difference?*

Gustavus Adolphus II This image commemorates the Swedish king's victory at the Battle of Breitenfeld, 1631.

at a moment when the empire seemed poised to win the war and wipe out Protestantism's remaining strongholds on the continent.

The French Phase and the War's Bitter End

Gustavus Adolphus's victories at Breitenfeld and Lützen prevented a Protestant defeat in 1631, but by 1635 the empire again appeared to be winning, although it too had lost its most charismatic leader. In 1634, Wallenstein was accused of treason and murdered by Austrian agents. Once again alarmed at the prospect of being encircled by the Spanish and Austrian Habsburgs, the French now applied all their resources to the conflict. Louis XIII and his chief minister, Cardinal Richelieu, opened a new round of office-selling and tax levies to enlarge and modernize the French army, and these troops were launched against the imperial armies in the Rhine region while the Swedes fought on in the east and the Dutch harried Spanish ships at sea.

This phase of the war, in particular, was rife with atrocities, committed by both sides, as ravenous and rapacious armies crisscrossed the countryside. Soldiers hanged children and elderly people from trees and roasted peasants over fires until they divulged the hiding places of their valuables. Women were raped, and men had their genitals cut off; horrible forms of torture were invented such as the "Swedish draught," in which robbers forced wood, sand, and feces down the throats of their victims. The war's savagery was worst in central Europe, where the main battlefields lay, but the spinoff civil wars that followed brought horrors to Ireland, Spain, and France, as well. Famine and disease, even more deadly than the conflicts themselves, took a terrible toll. In central Europe and in Spain, the population declined by 20 percent overall, and some places lost 40 percent or more of their prewar inhabitants.

By 1644, Europe's kingdoms were collapsing under the strains of war. The Portuguese and the Catalonians revolted against their greatly weakened Spanish overlords. The Portuguese took back their independence relatively quickly, but bloody fighting in Catalonia continued for some time. The Scots and then the Irish staged their own revolts against Charles I's policies, plunging the British Isles into civil war in 1642. After the death of Louis XIII in 1643, France too, as we have seen, faced internal crisis as well as bankruptcy. It remained only for the exhausted parties to work out a settlement. Negotiations between the various parties were finally concluded in the Peace of Westphalia in 1648.

The Consequences of the Thirty Years' War

The Peace of Westphalia did little to change the outward shape of Europe's states. Sweden gained some new territory and the Dutch Republic was guaranteed its independence, but otherwise, borders changed little. What mattered most were the *religious* provisions of the Peace, which in turn had major political consequences, especially for the Habsburgs. The Peace reiterated the right of the princes of the Holy Roman Empire to choose the religion of their states—and Calvinism was finally recognized alongside Catholicism and Lutheranism. Thus, although the Habsburgs moved toward absolutism in their Austrian lands and succeeded in reconverting Bohemia and parts of Hungary, the Holy Roman Empire remained a federation with a relatively weak emperor nominally in charge of a religiously disunited patchwork of more than three hundred mutually suspicious states. Religious and political disunity would make economic recovery in central Europe even more difficult in the decades to follow.

The Thirty Years' War also bankrupted and dramatically weakened Spain, the greatest power of the sixteenth century. Although the Spanish retained control of the southern Netherlands and its vast empire in the Americas, most of the once formidable Spanish army had died or deserted. Its ranks were now staffed by foreign mercenaries, drunks, and severely wounded men. Civil wars and rule by incompetent kings further damaged Spain in the second half of the seventeenth century.

The Thirty Years' War persuaded statesmen that the quest to impose one true faith on all of Europe was fruitless,

The Horrors of War Mercenary soldiers on both sides of the Thirty Years' War committed atrocities against civilians, often in the process of stealing their horses, livestock, and valuables. Hanging a few villagers (of all ages) from centrally positioned trees was a popular means to scare others into handing over their property.

and after 1648, European states would never again go to war for primarily religious reasons. But the Peace of Westphalia also established another important principle: Christians who belonged to denominations other than that of their prince or king would be allowed to practice their faith in public (according to local restrictions) and in private as they wished.

Although rulers and clerics did not always honor this principle—Louis XIV, for example, officially outlawed Protestantism in France in 1685—it laid the foundations for embryonic forms of religious toleration. Instead of killing "heretics" or driving out Christian minorities, kings began to use other means to coerce their subjects into attending the established church. People did not give up their dislike, or even hatred, toward those who practiced other faiths—and the Peace did not apply at all to Jews, Muslims, individuals accused of being witches, or nonbelievers. But rulers themselves largely stopped using violent means to enforce religious uniformity, especially after some realized that toning down religious strife contributed to political stability and helped the state to attract skilled dissenters to settle inside its borders. They turned their attention, instead, to protecting their domains by building up large and well-equipped armies and by cultivating sufficient splendor to distract at least some of their subjects from the misery around them.

The High Baroque No building so exemplified the Baroque as did Gian Lorenzo Bernini's new St. Peter's Basilica in Rome, completed in 1626. The Baroque style used shafts of light, heavy ornamentation, and grand-scale, symbolic sculptures to give religious and royal spaces a feeling of sacred presence and historical grandeur.

The Culture of the High Baroque

The cultural world of the seventeenth century reflected both apocalyptic sentiments and absolutist aspirations. The early Baroque culture of the later sixteenth century continued, characterized by sensuous extravagance on the one hand and gruesome portrayals of human suffering on the other. Writers and artists continued to draw on stories from the classical and Christian traditions even when they wanted to say new things. In ornate Catholic masterworks such as St. Peter's Basilica in Rome or the Cathedral of St. Gallen in Switzerland, architects, sculptors, and painters created colorful frescoes, gilded rays of light, and row upon row of marble saints and cherubs to

How did artists and writers deal with the political, religious, and social strife of the seventeenth century?

remind church-goers of the majesty of the divine—and the terrible suffering of even the saintly on earth. Calvinist sermons, similarly, featured dramatic depictions of earthly torments and warnings about the coming end of the world. Calvinist church interiors, however, were whitewashed to prevent parishioners from committing the sin of idolatry. In both Catholic and Protestant Europe, the late Baroque culture continued to revolve around religious themes. But over the course of the seventeenth century, absolutist state patronage and new commercial wealth began to expand Europeans' cultural portfolio, and to focus at least some attention on more worldly concerns.

The transformations under way in cultural life over the course of the seventeenth century reflect the shifting of power and wealth from south to north and from a predominately church-centered to a predominately court-centered world. At the beginning of the sixteenth century, the global cultural power was the Catholic Church. For theologians, scholars and poets, Latin works remained central at least until the mid-seventeenth century. But over the course of the seventeenth century, more and more works were being published in vernacular languages. Of these, at first Italian and then Spanish dominated, the former the language of the Renaissance, the latter spoken by officials and commercial tradespeople in the Netherlands, the Americas, and the Philippines. The Italian states continued to produce great painters, such as the widely revered Bolognese cousins Annibale, Ludovico, and Agostino Carracci; scientists and scholars, such as Galileo Galilei (see Chapter 15); and architects, such as Gian Lorenzo Bernini, who designed the new St. Peter's Basilica in Rome. And wealthy Spaniards, especially the Spanish kings, poured their New World silver

Diego Velázquez, Portrait of Pope Innocent X (c. 1650) This beautiful painting of a wily and powerful pope is one of the most acclaimed portraits of all time. Like his Dutch contemporary Rembrandt van Rijn, Velázquez frequently used dark backgrounds to focus viewers' attention on the psychological complexity of his subjects' faces.

grew in northern Europe, English and especially French works began to attract attention. Willing and able to invest large sums in patronizing artists, dramatists, scholars, and architects, the French monarchy and aristocracy, by the seventeenth century's close, made French culture *the* model for sophistication, elegance, and good taste.

Theater

Throughout Europe, the development of court cultures made possible the expansion of the repertoire of medieval sacred dramas. Princes hired actors to play for themselves and their noble friends, and some localities agreed to allow street performances or even the building of public playhouses. Writers began to compose a rich variety of plays, usually taking their subjects from either classical antiquity or from the Middle Ages, but infusing their work with the powerful and often violent emotions of their day. It was not unusual for Baroque plays to end with piles of dead bodies on the stage or with the sudden intervention of angels, devils, or God himself, though humble people also made their way into the plays of Lope de Vega and the great English writer and actor William Shakespeare (1564–1616). Like Shakespeare and Lope de Vega, many playwrights were accomplished poets and used intricately crafted language to depict these dramatic events. This was particularly true of the great French playwrights of the age, Jean Racine and Pierre Corneille; their work set the standards for beautiful writing in French for centuries to come.

For English speakers, Shakespeare was undoubtedly the master playwright of the seventeenth century, though he died not long after its opening, in 1616. His magnificent tragedies, comedies, and history plays continue to be performed and reinterpreted today, but in his day, Shakespeare was addressing on stage some of his age's greatest anxieties. Would there be a stable succession to the throne, and would the monarch be both brave and honorable? These questions were posed, for example, in *Hamlet* and *King Lear*, and in his sequence of plays on the Wars of the Roses and the Tudor monarchs, *Richard II*, *Henry IV* (two plays), *Henry V*, *Henry VI* (three plays), and *Richard III*. Several of the plays deal with Scottish subjects or with the difficulties faced by English kings in uniting the nobility, issues highly relevant to both Elizabeth I and her successor, James I. Shakespeare's plays also reveal much about the problems of lesser people of the period, from the struggle of servants to be treated with human dignity in *The Tempest* to the torments suffered by young lovers seeking to cross political lines in *Romeo and Juliet*. Similarly, the prejudices of the age are reflected in the subjugation of headstrong women in *The Taming of the Shrew* and the humbling of greedy Jews in *The Merchant of Venice*. Of course, Shakespeare's reach extended far beyond political commentary. His insight into the human condition derives in part from the fact that he inhabited a dangerous and uncertain world full of dramatic political and private tragedies but one also characterized by new opportunities and experiences.

into patronizing both Italian and Spanish artists, scholars, and churches. Spanish devotionals such as Luis de Granada's *Book of Prayer and Meditation* animated Catholic culture. The poetry and plays of Félix Arturo Lope de Vega treated historical, mythological, and humble subjects and were widely read and imitated. Spanish painters such as Diego Velázquez produced psychologically insightful portraits of Spanish courtiers, including in his depictions their pet dogs and the dwarves they kept for their entertainment.

The late Baroque period also saw the flourishing of eastern European cultures. The Holy Roman Emperor Rudolf II (r. 1576–1612) created an extravagant collection of paintings, gemstones, live animals, and scientific devices, housing them in his huge palace in Prague. He collected scholars, too, paying them to do their work at his court and if possible to help him in occult pursuits, such as finding the philosopher's stone. Even after the Thirty Years' War, the Habsburgs continued to build and furnish lavish Baroque residences and places of worship in the major cities of their grand empire. In Poland-Lithuania, Krakow, one of the great Gothic cities, continued to be renowned for its beauty and wealth even though King Sigismund III of the house of Vasa moved the capital to Warsaw in 1596.

But as economic and military power began to shift from south to north, and from east to west, so too did cultural supremacy. As urban populations and literacy

Numerous seventeenth-century writers made their mark by composing epic poems or the first novels since Roman times. The earliest of these novels were Spanish, the most famous being Miguel de Cervantes's *Don Quixote*, published serially between 1607 and 1615. The story tracks the adventures of Don Quixote, a would-be conquistador, whose imagination far outstrips his abilities. Instead of crusading against the Moors or conquering the peoples of the Americas, he tilts against windmills. Cervantes presents the Spanish noble knight (hidalgo) as a man of great aspirations, but no practical sense. Quixote, like his fellow Spanish nobles, is too haughty to engage in any sort of labor and survives only thanks to his able and jovial servant, Sancho Panza. In many ways, *Don Quixote* predicts the decline of Spain as its nobles continue to live in the dream world of sixteenth-century conquests and fritter away their riches in pursuit of antiquated ideals.

Another of the period's great novels, *The Adventures of Simplicius Simplicissimus* (1668), by the German writer H. J. C. von Grimmelshausen, comments even more directly on current events. The novel follows the career of another sort of simpleton, not a nobleman like Don Quixote, but an ordinary peasant, during the Thirty Years' War. In the first pages, Simplicius's farm is overrun by marauding soldiers who rape and kill his mother and sister. The peasant survives by hiding with a hermit in a forest until he is nearly murdered by another group of soldiers and forced to join the army. Simplicius learns what it is to be a mercenary—to be a merciless thief and an unprincipled man who works for whomever pays best—and learns that there is no justice, and perhaps no rhyme or reason, in this world.

In his great epic poem *Paradise Lost* (1667), the blind Puritan poet John Milton recast events in the book of Genesis in ways that reflected the moral anguish experienced by many of his contemporaries. In the poem, Satan, the fallen angel, denounces God for rejecting him and for allowing terrible evils to torment humankind. Adam accepts his expulsion from Eden and the inevitable toil and suffering that will now be humankind's lot. *Paradise Lost* demonstrates the extent to which Milton and his contemporaries worried about God's responsibility for the evils and hardships experienced by his earthly children. Readers of the poem often came away convinced not of God's ultimate justice, as Milton wished them to, but resentful of God's cruelty toward both of his creatures, Satan and Adam.

Art and Architecture

The Baroque was an age of enormous canvases and cavernous churches, of dramatic frescoes and gargantuan sculptures of monarchs, religious figures, and historical heroes—but also of new depictions of everyday life and of Europe's new commodities. It was an age of great court painters, as monarchs commissioned portraits that depicted their power and wealth. The Flemish painters Peter Paul Rubens and Anthony Van Dyck, for example, composed hundreds of canvases to be hung in French, Spanish, Italian, and British palaces. These often over-sized and dramatically colored paintings frequently employed mythological and religious symbolism to enhance the splendor of the monarchies or to depict the painful agonies of the human condition.

Baroque artists also created vast numbers of religious pieces. They produced sculpted tombs and jewel-studded chalices by the hundreds of thousands. Southern European and Flemish Catholic painters such as Rubens tended to stick with a highly colorful palette and with fleshy renderings of biblical scenes. Protestant artists in the north, notably Rembrandt van Rijn, favored a more somber style, but still produced painting after painting depicting the crucifixion and scenes from the Old Testament.

Some Dutch painters, such as Jan Vermeer, began to paint scenes of ordinary people, illustrating that non-nobles, too, like Vermeer's *Girl Reading a Letter by an Open Window* (c. 1659), could be beautiful to contemplate. Many of these images also came with a moral message. *The Dissolute Household* (1664) by Dutch artist Jan Steen shows what happens to family life when the elders give in to drink and neglect their work. Still-life painting also became fashionable, and the art market teemed with depictions of breakfast tables groaning with fish, wine, fruit, and flowers.

Baroque architecture appealed greatly to royal and clerical patrons, for its theatrical spaces and rich decoration offered ideal settings for hierarchical court rituals and religious services in an era in which monarchs and the clergy were eager to display their wealth and power. There are magnificent examples of such architecture not only in Bernini's Rome, and in Austria, where the court architect Johann Bernhard Fischer von Erlach built his ornate and eclectic masterpieces, but also in the colonies, in Spanish Mexico and Peru, and in Portuguese-dominated Goa. The more humble urban dwellings of Amsterdam and London, such as those depicted in the works of Vermeer and Steen, remind us that there was a new, non-noble architecture evolving as well, one whose inhabitants happily did without Baroque splendor and put their money into private comfort rather than into display.

Music

While Europeans continued, as they always had, to sing and make music in the streets, at village festivals, and in their homes, the polished compositions of the Baroque era remained tied to the church or the court. Music in this era was not meant to make the composer famous, but rather to glorify God or the royal patron. In central Europe's German-speaking states, for example, musicians composed mostly sacred music, as did the great organist Dieter Buxtehude and the late Baroque sensation, Johann Sebastian Bach. Bach was famed for his complicated fugues and his exquisite organ music. As monarchs expanded their courts, chamber music, or music made by small groups of well-trained musicians, came into fashion, and kings hired court composers to compose new chamber pieces. As court composer for Louis XIV of France, Jean-Baptiste Lully produced numerous ballets, operas, and pastorals, as well as church music.

The real center of innovation, however, was Italy. Here in 1607 Claudio Monteverdi composed the first opera, *Orpheus*. By rewriting the myth of the Greek god of music, Orpheus, Monteverdi demonstrated the power and beauty of music itself. Another great Italian musician, Antonio Vivaldi was born a generation after Monteverdi's death. Vivaldi, a virtuoso violinist and composer, worked to develop harmony and counterpoint, in so doing laying the foundations of polyphonic music. Vivaldi produced more than seven hundred works, including operas, concertos, sonatas, and cantatas. Among his best-known works is the violin concerto "The Four Seasons" (1725).

Political Philosophy in the Age of Absolutism

If music and art reflected the rising importance of secular society, political and moral philosophers in the age of absolutism also gradually began to move away from theology and to develop new ideas about the proper nature and practice of statecraft. Most of those who wrote on politics or law in this era continued to be close readers of traditional texts, the works of classical antiquity and the Bible, but some began to read these in new ways. Speculating on the right way to run a state was a dangerous business in most places, especially when intellectuals called into question traditional practices or the privileges of the king, aristocracy, or church. Thus, most of the new ideas came from places where individuals were able to discuss proper governance with relative freedom: the Netherlands and England. Discussions of citizenship, natural law, religious freedom, and what would be called "the social contract" emerged primarily from these relatively free centers. But as the examples here demonstrate, by no means did even these thinkers agree on how the states of the present and future should be ruled.

In the Dutch Republic, the humanist Hugo Grotius found in the work of the Roman orator Cicero a basis for arguing that humans could discover a series of **natural laws** that defined the good society. These laws preserved what Cicero called "the tranquility and happiness of human life" and ensured the safety of the states' citizens. Natural laws stood above laws made by humans and by religious authorities. Drawing on these ideas, Grotius argued for limitations on the power of human laws (that is, those made by particular kings and states). These, he said, should only ensure safety and order and should not coerce citizens in matters of religious belief. Grotius

Jan Steen, The Dissolute Household (1665) This humorous Dutch painting teaches middle-class virtues by depicting improper behavior. Here, the (probably inebriated) parents sleep while the children run the household, the dog eats off the table, and valuable books, musical instruments, and dishes, including a spilled glass of wine, are strewn carelessly across the floor. The only intelligent creature in the picture is the monkey, who seems to be recording the scene with a quill pen.

also argued that universally valid natural laws governed warfare and established the freedom of the seas. Again, the laws of nature were more permanent and persuasive than those made by any particular king or state.

The arguments from nature that Grotius used laid the foundations for what would later be called human rights and international law. A few, more radical thinkers found in Roman republican texts an appreciation for the idea of the freedom and equality of citizens within the state, something that contrasted directly with absolutist ideas. With the help of Jewish scholars, some Protestant Bible-readers also concluded that God disapproved of worldly kings. Both of these streams fed an attack on absolutist tyranny that helped launch the English Civil Wars and would be most clearly articulated in the work of the English champion of popular sovereignty and individual liberty, John Locke (see Chapter 16).

But these were dangerous and heretical lines of inquiry, even in England and the Dutch Republic. The ideas of the Englishman Thomas Hobbes (1588–1679) were closer to the ways in which the monarchs of the day thought about proper governance. Horrified by England's political turmoil and the brutality of the Thirty Years' War, Hobbes plunged backward to humankind's beginnings, asking what human societies looked like before monarchs had emerged as rulers. In his masterwork, *Leviathan* (1651), Hobbes argued that in humans' original state of nature, there had been nothing but ceaseless warfare. In Hobbes's pessimistic view, the human condition, human nature itself, was endless selfishness, "a war of all against all." Desperate for peace, humans had agreed to a "social contract," according to which they would obey an absolute ruler, one who could end this conflict and impose order. Hobbes valued order above all, and *Leviathan* was frequently used to justify absolutism as the only means to establish peace. His work, however, contained subtleties and insights that ranged well beyond such political uses and initiated a long series of conversations about human nature and the origins and nature of the social contract between rulers and the ruled.

Popular Culture in the Baroque Era

The cultural world beyond the court and the church was necessarily limited by the fact that for most people life remained, as Hobbes put it, "nasty, brutish and short." There were ceaseless burials and outpourings of religious invective. For readers—of which there were an increasing number, especially in urban areas in the north and west—there were an increasing number of books, some of them inexpensive and adorned with woodcuts. Many of the bestsellers were older religious works; by 1700, Granada's *Book of Prayer and Meditation* (1564) had gone through more than one hundred editions. John Foxe's *Book of Martyrs* (1563) continued to attract large numbers of Protestant readers who found in it lurid stories about Catholic persecutions of religious reformers. In 1678 the English preacher and writer John Bunyan published *Pilgrim's Progress*, an allegorical tale tracing the sufferings of a Christian Everyman as he searches for deliverance, loaded down with his heavy burden of human sin. Not all popular reading, however, was religious. There were joke books, including *Six Varieties of Fart* in French, and books describing how to play games or tell fortunes. Peasants purchased almanacs that advised them on when to plant as well as when to make love; early newssheets and pamphlets circulated widely, describing—usually in highly partisan ways—the latest Catholic or Protestant atrocities, or giving humble people instructions on how to recognize one of the scariest threats to their well being: witchcraft.

Living the Witch Craze

A central feature of both popular and elite culture in the Baroque era was simultaneous fear of and fascination with witchcraft. Since antiquity, many Europeans had believed in some sort of magic or sorcery; this was a convenient way to explain accidents, coincidences, or bad luck. In an age of radical religious conflict, a veritable witch craze seized Europe, and between about 1550 and 1750, hundreds of thousands of people were tried as witches and as many as 50,000 executed in Europe and the Americas. The means to identify the heresy of witchcraft came from a handbook composed by two Dominican priests, *The Malleus Maleficarum* (*The Hammer of Witches*). Printed in 1486, the book's influence spread,

especially as the religious warfare and economic disasters of the sixteenth and seventeenth centuries tore apart communities. By 1669, when *The Hammer of Witches* was in its twenty-ninth edition, most Europeans had come to believe that witchcraft was a real and dangerous social and religious problem.

What was it like to live through this witch craze? Suspicions that a witch was at work usually began with a frightening and inexplicable event—a freak hailstorm or the sudden death of an infant. Evildoers were charged with everything from desecrating the host to raising armies of mice, from cursing cows that then sickened and died to causing sudden storms that destroyed crops. A large majority of the accused were women, especially midwives, healers, and those burdensome to the community such as elderly widows. Children and male misfits, including religious nonconformists, were also accused of witchcraft. The accused were handed over to local religious or regional officials, who used *The Hammer of Witches* or other manuals to identify suspects and try them—often using various means of torture. There were some standard accusations: witches consorted with the devil, participated in satanic and sacrilegious rituals, or sold their souls in order to obtain special powers. Sometimes local officials hired "witch-smellers," but usually they could rely on villagers to denounce their neighbors. Some of the accused began to confess that they had participated in nocturnal rides with Satan; Sabbath-eve orgies; black masses; and the cursing of crops, cows, and children. Often open to the public, trials of witches were high drama and could excite both participants and spectators to frenzy. Fearful of allowing the devil's servants to inflict more damage and mindful of the Bible's commandments ("Thou shalt not suffer a witch to live"; Exodus 22:18), both the elite and the peasantry were eager to rid their communities of witches: a single witch endangered everyone. Most Europeans were not revolted by watching witches hanged, drowned, strangled, or burned at the stake, but felt justified in protecting their property, their families, and their souls from Satan's power.

What was it like to be accused of practicing witchcraft or sorcery? Undoubtedly it was terrifying and personally devastating. Most of the accusers were one's neighbors, or in the case of the midwives, one's employers. Establishing innocence was next to impossible when the crime was one committed at a distance: how could a person show that he or she had not cursed a baby or caused lightning to strike? Some accused witches believed in magical powers themselves and feared they had caused the evils with which they were charged. Many confessed at trial, under torture or in hopes of a lighter sentence. Some named accomplices, which could lead to mass accusations and executions. Catharina Schmid, a seventy-four-year-old widow from a small village in southern Germany, tried to resist. Accused first of inflicting madness upon a young girl and of killing a neighbor and her six children, Catharina was subsequently charged with every other misfortune her town had suffered and of sharing her bed with both her daughter and the devil. Catharina tried to tell the court that her neighbor's husband was a violent drunkard, that his children died of abuse and hunger, and that the animals she was accused of killing were struck down by God, in punishment for their owners' sinfulness. But the court persisted, interrogating her twelve times over eight months. Her torturers applied thumbscrews and cut out a "devil's mark" (probably a mole) on her thigh; she was whipped and vinegar poured into her wounds. She maintained her innocence until she finally broke, and confessed that she had been seduced by the devil and inflicted harm on her neighbors and their property. She insisted on her daughter's innocence, but both were executed anyway. Catharina was strangled, then her body was burned at the stake, with bags of gunpowder tied around her neck as an additional, symbolic punishment for having been so stubborn.[3]

Executing Witches This image from a seventeenth-century book depicts the hanging of four witches in England in 1649. The individual marked "D" is said to be a witch-finder, who is being paid for his services.

Of course, trying and executing supposed witches did nothing to ward off the plague or to prevent hailstorms. In some regions, the witch craze itself caused instability as well as injustice. Gradually, in different places at different times, higher-level courts began to intervene to end torture and decriminalize witchcraft, establishing noncapital penalties. The end to witchcraft persecution tended to follow increases in prosperity and in feelings of security. Accordingly, it both started and ended later in central and eastern Europe, where effective state structures and rising incomes arrived more slowly. Executions ended as early as 1603 in the Netherlands and were largely over in France by 1670, but large numbers of witches continued to be burned in central Europe. Catharina Schmid died in 1746; in Poland, the last witch was executed as late as 1776.

Absolutism Triumphant

If trying and executing witches was a popular means to explain and eradicate the evils of the day, European monarchs recognized that it would take more than this to deal

Where did Absolutism prevail, and where was it less successful?

with the period's dangers and opportunities. To prevent renewed civil war, to protect themselves against expansionist neighboring states, and to invest in overseas adventures, they would need more power and more money, and more latitude to use both as they wished. Thus, after 1648, monarchs from Spain to Russia with quite different personalities and quite different kingdoms continued early absolutist attempts to stabilize their houses—and in doing so built family dynasties: the Bourbons in France, the Vasas in Sweden and Poland-Lithuania, the Stuarts in England, the Hohenzollerns in Brandenburg,

the Romanovs in Russia, and the Habsburgs in Austria and Spain. All also sought to guarantee the succession of their heirs and to develop centralized bureaucracies, standing armies, efficient systems of taxation, and established churches, in the process taking away (to a greater or lesser degree) the independent power and wealth of the kingdom's nobility and the clergy.

Of course, kings and queens needed help to turn Europe's decentralized, rural economies into centralized and efficient providers of income for the state. So they turned to well-educated, hard-working ministers, men whose job it was to impose some sort of uniform system on the kingdom in order to move power and money from the provinces to the capital. Favorite ministers such as the duke of Olivares in Spain or Cardinal Richelieu in France appointed their friends and family members—whom Richelieu aptly called his "creatures"—to important offices. Kings rewarded loyal supporters or members of their own religions with titles, creating a group of new nobles and bureaucrats who depended on royal or ministerial favor. Kings in need of cash also began to tax more extensively and to sell privileges, such as the right to collect taxes in a particular locality, or offices, such as sheriff of a certain town. The older nobility despised both the selling of offices and the ennobling of ministers and loyal bureaucrats, as they saw both as means by which their own privileges and clout were threatened.

As this suggests, not everyone in the kingdom liked absolutist innovations, and in some places, nobles had considerable powers of resistance. In fact, despite monarchs' best efforts, nobles everywhere retained most of their privileges and most of the kingdom's wealth down to 1789. By establishing state churches, monarchs exerted new control over the clergy, but the churches continued to extract the tithe, to censor publications, and to exert independent dominion over enormous tracts of land.

Local conditions shaped the kind of absolute power each king acquired—and the degree to which the nobility was able to protect its traditional powers. In western states such as the Netherlands, England, and France, medieval law codes gave nobles an unimaginable variety of special privileges and rights to sue over them. In France, Louis XIII refused to call his representative assembly, the **Estates General,** into session after 1613, and his son Louis XIV continued the practice of ruling without such a council. But the French kings could not disband the local law courts known as **parlements,** some of which continued to voice their objections to royal policies. By contrast, in eastern Europe, Prussian and Russian monarchs had fewer legal limitations on their power. They used more force to consolidate their states and gave their nobles more control over their serfs. Louis XIV's France may have been the archetypical absolutist state, but absolutism was *more* absolute in the East.

France under Louis XIV and Louis XV

France's gains in the Peace of Westphalia were minimal, especially in view of the enormous costs of the war. Land taxes, for example, had tripled between 1635 and 1648. France's nobles had long chafed under the rule of Louis XIII (who died in 1643) and his chief minister Cardinal Richelieu, whom they blamed for raising taxes without calling an Estates General. They despised Louis's practice of appointing **intendants,** officials who fanned out across France to see that taxes were collected properly and that nobles did as the Crown instructed. Not surprisingly, local nobles who wanted to protect their privileges and their local power bases despised the intendants, who epitomized the king's absolutist leanings. In 1648, a civil war known as the **Fronde** (for the *frondeurs,* or those who slung mud at officials' carriages) terrified the young and as yet uncrowned Louis XIV, who afterward made it his mission to ensure that such a challenge to the house of Bourbon never happened again. He expanded the number of intendants, widened their powers, and took to heart the advice of his chief minister Cardinal Mazarin: "it is up to you to become the most glorious king that has ever been." He pursued this goal partly through the expansion and use of his army; partly through building a centralized, religiously united state; and partly through seeking to extend French power in the world (see Map 15.2, p. 473).

In 1663, Louis made New France—all French holdings in North America—into a province of France. The next year, he claimed the Caribbean island of Hispaniola and established a French East India Company to monopolize what would prove to be a very rich trade in Caribbean sugar. He oversaw the founding of the first French outposts in India, at Chandernagore and Pondicherry, and in general pushed forward the extension of French trade down the African coast, along the Atlantic seaboard, and into the Indian Ocean. Acting as his own chief minister after the death of Mazarin in 1661, Louis instituted a census so that he could better survey and more efficiently

tax his subjects. To show that he was just as forward-thinking and generous a king as was Britain's Charles II, he founded a French Academy of Sciences on the model of Britain's Royal Society. Determined to ensure France's stability as well as to enhance his own glory, Louis seized every opportunity to build state power and prosperity.

The great palace complex at **Versailles,** just eleven miles outside of Paris, is the quintessential embodiment of Louis's ambitions for France, and for himself. Building began on the site of Louis XIII's hunting lodge in 1661 and continued for decades thereafter. Louis XIV added lavish buildings to the complex after the conclusion of each of his wars, hiring the most modern architects and artists to create spectacular surroundings for himself and his court. In 1682, he made Versailles the monarchy's official place of business, meaning that all petitioners and nobles who wanted to influence high politics would have to make their way to a palace that reflected Louis's power in every possible way. Visitors could not avoid seeing their king endlessly represented as the Greek sun god Apollo or the Roman god of war Mars. The carefully manicured gardens of Versailles, complete with trick fountains, became world famous, as did the ornate decoration of vast rooms such as the Hall of Mirrors.

LOUIS XIV, ABSOLUTIST WARRIOR. By the 1670s, Louis had established absolutist rule at home, but he was eager to add luster to his image by conquering new territories. For this monarch, true glory was won the old-fashioned way: through victory on the battlefield. Moving in 1672 to push the Spanish back from the French border by attacking the Spanish Netherlands, Louis threw himself into a series of wars with Spain, Sweden, England, and the Dutch Republic, all of which tried to prevent France from making a bid for continental hegemony. Fighting continued periodically from the 1670s through the 1690s, during which time Louis's huge army frequently behaved badly, burning and plundering Dutch and German towns along the Rhine, and creating lasting hatred for the French in both the Netherlands and the German states.

At first, Louis was victorious. He conquered and annexed a number of Rhine basin cities and the provinces of Alsace and Lorraine, incorporating the many German-speakers of this rich region into his empire (Map 14.2). Churches that had been converted for Protestant use, such as the cathedral in Strasbourg, reverted to offering Catholic mass. Evidently Louis cared little that his campaigns plunged France into debt or that the new taxes he imposed generated deep resentment among his subjects. For soon afterward he initiated a new war, one that would prove even more debilitating than the last.

The cause of Louis's next war was the succession to the Spanish throne of a Bourbon prince (as the Habsburg king Charles II had died childless), who in 1700 took the title Philip V of Spain. On his ascension, Philip renounced his right to inherit the French crown as well, but then Louis XIV, worried about his own succession, began to talk of revoking this promise. Outraged, the Austrians took up arms, and the English and the Dutch, equally concerned about the prospect of a single ruler uniting the kingdoms of France and Spain, joined the Habsburg side. Together they fought Louis XIV in the long-lasting War of the Spanish Succession (1701–1714). The army arrayed against the French featured colorful, brilliant commanders such as John Churchill, duke of Marlborough, and Prince Eugene of Savoy, but even they had trouble with Louis's now formidable forces. Marlborough's efforts at the Battle of Blenheim in 1704 and at Malplaquet in 1709 kept the French from marching into the Spanish Netherlands, but at a horrific cost. At Malplaquet alone more than 20,000 of Marlborough's soldiers were killed or wounded, whereas the French casualties were half as great.

In 1713–1714, three peace treaties (the Treaty of Utrecht, the Treaty of Rastatt, and the Treaty of Baden) ended the war, giving the French a partial victory. They were permitted to put a Bourbon king, who took the title Philip V, on the Spanish throne. But they were not permitted to unite the crowns or to take control of Spain's overseas colonies. The real winners in the war were the Austrians and the English. The Austrians obtained Spanish possessions in the Netherlands and Italy, and the English received Gibraltar and Minorca. French hopes of expanding further east were dashed. Louis XIV died two years later, in 1715, proud of the glorious state he had built and seemingly untroubled by the debts and difficulties he was passing on to his heirs.

By the time of Louis's death, France had plenty of problems, some of them brought on by Louis's wars, others by his religious policies. To fund the wars, the king had imposed direct taxes on both nobles and commoners. His relentless conscription of soldiers had made him greatly unpopular with the commoners, and the nobles resented his selling of offices to wealthy members of the middle class and his refusal to listen to noble coun-

MAP 14.2 | Louis XIV's Annexations
Louis XIV spent much of his reign waging war to extend France's borders and to demonstrate his glory. *Why was Louis XIV able to seize this territory after 1648?*

selors. His religious policies also drew criticism, within France and beyond. Under the influence of his pious second wife, Madame de Maintenon, Louis had grown less open minded; the court's lavish parties became fewer and more sedate; and the classical nude statues in the gardens of Versailles received fig leaves. More important, in 1685 Louis made Protestantism illegal in France by issuing the Revocation of the Edict of Nantes, thereby defying pledges France had made in the Peace of Westphalia to permit the peaceful practice of Protestantism. Louis's action, meant to shore up Catholic unity, made him unpopular among intellectuals who had come to value religious freedom in the wake of the Thirty Years' War. It also proved an economic blunder, for revoking the Edict drove many skilled and well-educated Protestants to leave France and to settle instead in the Dutch Republic, in Protestant Prussia, or in Britain's North American colonies.

LOUIS XV. When the Sun King finally died, his only remaining heir was his five-year-old great-grandson. Control of the kingdom was given to a cousin, the duke of Orléans, whose irresponsible investments caused enormous economic turmoil. The regency lasted until 1723, when the thirteen-year-old Louis XV took the throne, but by that time complaints about the court's corruption and the weakness of the state were rife. Louis XV continued the domestic policies of his great-grandfather, selling offices to favorites and spending lavishly on his court; he embroiled France in the Seven Years' War (1756–1763; see Chapter 15), which resulted in the loss of most of France's overseas possessions. Louis's subjects generally disapproved of the company he kept. Everyone knew that his beautiful mistress, Madame de Pompadour, had been a courtesan, and rumor had it that she wasted all the kingdom's money and told the king how to run the state. Throughout his long reign (1715–1774), Louis did not call the Estates General into session, and he had a series of confrontations with the regional parlements. Louis XV did nothing about the nation's debt, which continued to grow. He did not have the Sun King's interest in building the state or his taste for battle. Thus, he did not increase French absolutist rule so much as give it an increasingly bad name.

Absolutism and the Austrian Habsburgs

To France's southeast lay the Holy Roman Empire, where, as we have seen, the Thirty Years' War broke the Habsburgs' attempts to overturn religious pluralism. But the Habsburgs did not break the emperors' desire to consolidate power, at least in Austria, Slovenia, and pieces of what are today Italy and southern Germany—lands where the Habsburgs were hereditary, as opposed to elected rulers. The Habsburgs were successful in large part; in the course of a series of wars with the Ottoman Empire, they gradually built up a modern army and won back all of Hungary. Although the emperors' religious policies were erratic—sometimes Catholicism was forcibly imposed, sometimes Protestants left in peace—the

The Ottomans Besiege Vienna, 1683 In what turned out to be the Ottomans' last attempt to seize the Habsburg capital city, troops surrounded Vienna. The intervention of Bavarian and Polish troops, commanded by Jan Sobieski, as well as Ottoman mistakes, saved the city. Depicted on the left is the war tent of Ottoman commander Kara Mustapha, which Sobieski, after the battle, took back to Krakow as one of his prizes.

state did manage to claim a considerable amount of power over the church. Although economic modernization was halting—serfdom continued on the land, and the late-arriving idea of becoming an overseas trading power never bore fruit—during the long reign of Maria Theresa (r. 1740–1780), the Habsburg monarchy had largely succeeded in creating an absolutist state.

Crucial in creating backing for Habsburg absolutism were the wars against the "infidel" Turks, who had conquered large swathes of central Europe in the sixteenth century. The Habsburgs tried to push them back in 1663, but failed; in 1683, a huge Turkish army took the offensive, advancing rapidly to the gates of Vienna. The Ottoman commander Kara Mustapha set siege to the city—cannon balls struck the great St. Matthias Church (and can still be seen there today). After two months of fierce fighting, the Austrian army was relieved by the arrival of forces commanded by the charismatic Polish king Jan Sobieski, who later claimed that he had saved central European Christendom. Sobieski did assist in forcing the retreat of the Turkish forces, and he took back to Poland numerous reminders of his victory, including the stirrup of Mustapha, which today hangs at the foot of a revered Gothic crucifix in Krakow's main cathedral.

The defeat of the Turks in 1683 became a boasting point not only for Sobieski but also for the Austrians, especially in light of the wars that followed, in which first the city of Buda and then the rest of Hungary was conquered. By 1718, the eastern Habsburgs had conquered far more territory than had Louis XIV (compare Map 14.1 on p. 427 and Map 15.1 on p. 469). But swallowing Hungary, a nation with a powerful and proud aristocracy of its own, put Austria's digestion to the test, and the Habsburgs never managed to bring this territory fully under absolutist control. The same could be said, to a lesser extent, of the Italian, Flemish, and Croatian nobles. Austria's position between the powerful French in the west and the Turks and increasingly powerful Russians in the east also meant that the empire had to negotiate with others. When Emperor Charles VI (r. 1711–1740) sought to ensure the succession of his daughter, Maria Theresa, he was compelled to make a series of compromises, including giving up an Austrian East India Company based in the Austrian Netherlands. The modernizing policies of Maria Theresa and her son Joseph II (see Chapter 16) would have to go forward without the extra income and influence other states procured by promoting commerce and colonization overseas.

The Consolidation of Prussia

In 1640, when Frederick William, prince of the house of Hohenzollern, became ruler of Brandenburg, his small, land-locked state was occupied by the Swedes and in chaos. Frederick William was an elector—that is, he possessed one of the seven votes required to confirm the appointment of a Holy Roman emperor—but otherwise he was hardly a powerful man. Brandenburg suffered much in the Thirty Years' War, though officially it fought on the Protestant side for only a few years during the conflict. Much more devastating than the battles were the troops quartered there, who robbed, murdered, and spread disease throughout the territory. Perhaps half of the population died during the wars, and marauders burned and pillaged thousands of farmsteads and small towns.

The experience convinced Frederick William that only a powerful military of his own could secure his state, and he began raising taxes and building one as soon as possible. From 3,000 men at arms in 1641–1642, he built a standing army of 38,000 by the 1670s, a force big enough to allow him to push back the Swedes and the Poles on his borders. He built fortifications and founded a cadet school to train his officers in the latest tactics, and he supplied his troops with modern, standardized weaponry. Because his reforms were expensive and usurped some of the powers of the nobility, he created a General War Commissariat to collect taxes and recruit soldiers for the state. During his reign, he also increased the size of his state, adding noncontiguous territory in the west as well as a chunk of Poland-Lithuania. These acquisitions gave his heirs both a window on the west and a foothold in the east.

To manage this transformation, Frederick William, subsequently known as the Great Elector, had to battle his nobles, and in this struggle he scored his greatest successes. As elsewhere, there were terrific battles over taxes,

but he prevailed, compelling his nobles to submit to new taxes without the consent of representative assemblies. A Calvinist in a state populated largely by Lutherans, he put many of his co-religionists into the administration and began hiring talented commoners. As compensation, he gave landowning nobles a free hand to exploit their serfs.

The Great Elector died in 1688, leaving to his son and successor, Frederick, the second-largest territory in the Holy Roman Empire (after Austria) and a large modernized army. When the Habsburgs needed allies to fight Louis XIV, Frederick's price was that the emperor should allow Prussia to become a kingdom, and in 1701 he got his wish. As king in Prussia, Frederick I (r. 1701–1713) continued his father's military build-up and administrative reforms, but also tried his hand at emulating the French monarch. He spent twice the annual revenue on his coronation and brought famous painters, musicians, scholars, and cooks to the Prussian court.

Frederick I's son, Frederick William I (r. 1713–1740), was revolted by his father's fancy tastes and the corruption in the court. Immediately upon his accession to the throne, Frederick William I dismissed the musicians and the chocolatier, diverting the money to his first love, the army. He embarked on a vigorous new expansion of the military, and he saw that all officers and men were well drilled. He loved nothing more than to watch their drills from his palace windows.

Frederick William I was a man of many contradictions. A devoted Calvinist, he prayed fervently but showed no mercy to soldiers or state officials, who could be publicly garroted for dereliction of duty. He instituted rigorous examinations for state bureaucrats but chose as friends heavy-drinking, uneducated Prussian aristocrats known as **Junkers.** His son, the future Frederick II ("the Great"), like Peter the Great's son Alexei (see below), also tried to run away from a father whose idea of preparing his heir for kingship amounted to psychological and physical torture. Frederick, unlike Alexei, survived and once again overhauled Prussian court culture. But he too would continue what had now become a Prussian tradition of putting the army at the core of state-building.

Russia: From Ivan the Terrible to Peter the Great

Russian absolutism began with Ivan III ("the Great"; r. 1462–1505), a Muscovite prince who, with the backing of the powerful monasteries, established hegemony over the medieval center of Novgorod. Ivan brought Italian artists to Moscow to rebuild the monastery-fortress-palace complex known as the Kremlin, to which they added a bell-tower whose bells were to mimic the music of the heavens and to warn Muscovites when invaders approached.

Ivan the Great's successor Ivan IV ("the Terrible"; r. 1533–1584) built a standing army, made war in all directions, and extended Muscovy's holdings further than any other prince of his day (Map 14.3). He combined

MAP 14.3 | Russian Expansion, Ivan the Terrible to Peter the Great

After 1584, Russia's czars expanded the size of their empire to make it the largest on earth. *Compare the size of absolutist Russia's annexations to those of France (see Map 14.2). Why were the Russians able to take so much more land than the French?*

Byzantine and absolutist ideas to proclaim Moscow a third Rome and himself czar ("Caesar") of a grand new Russian empire.

Ivan the Terrible made grand plans for modernizing his state, though some of this modernization was also strongly inflected by Ivan's Russian Orthodox piety, by having been beaten as a child, and by his belief that he was divinely appointed to rule. To celebrate his victory over the (Muslim) Khanate of Kazan in 1556, he patronized the building of St. Basil's Cathedral in the Kremlin, which featured a new, Russian style, characterized by elaborate wood-carving and onion-shaped domes. He extended special trading privileges to the Dutch, the Prussians, and the English, though he did so mostly to have friends on the borders of his longtime Lutheran and Catholic enemies, the Swedes and the Poles. He hired many Germans from the Baltic region to staff his military and bureaucracy and rewarded them handsomely. In

1566, Ivan created a national representative assembly, the Zemsky Sobor, not because the czar wanted more advice from delegates, but because he needed help in extracting taxes from his subjects. In the main, he relied on monks and priests to help him formulate policies, and remained suspicious of his nobles, known as boyars. In the 1570s, Ivan set about breaking the boyars' power in ways much more violent than, but parallel to, Louis XIV's attempts to curb noble privileges a century later.

Ivan's modernizing plans entailed such enormous amounts of violence and so much warfare that eventually his kingdom was thrown into chaos. His wars with Poland-Lithuania lasted for decades and devastated the western sector of his kingdom. His hired thugs oversaw forced recruitments and mass murders in areas thought to be potentially disloyal. Novgorod in particular suffered, and Ivan reputedly had some of his boyar enemies roasted to death in a huge frying pan. In a fit of pique,

Ivan executed the highest official in the Russian Orthodox Church, the metropolitan bishop of Moscow. In 1581, he pummeled his pregnant daughter-in-law, causing her to miscarry, and beat his eldest son and heir to death. Although he broke the political power of the boyars, he gave Muscovites and military men huge tracts of land in the newly conquered east and south, and he allowed landowners unchecked power over their serfs. He took away what mobility serfs had previously possessed, instituting a more exploitative second serfdom (see Chapter 15) throughout the Russian Empire. He allowed Moscow's one printing press to be destroyed a year after it arrived, a symbol of his desire to be Russia's one and only modernizer—and master.

Ivan was succeeded by his son, the simple-minded Fyodor I, who left governance in the hands of his brother-in-law, Boris Godonuv. When Fyodor died in 1598, the Zemsky Sobor elected Boris czar, but his election did not end disputes over the throne. Russia suffered a prolonged period of civil war known as the Time of Troubles (1604–1613), during which the Swedes and Poles sought to seize chunks of the czarist empire. Michael Romanov (r. 1613–1645), who was crowned czar in 1613, finally ensured stability but only by signing unfavorable peace treaties with the Swedes and Poles in 1618–1619, just as the Thirty Years' War was beginning in central Europe.

Russia endured another period of crisis between 1682 and 1689, the result of uncertainty about the succession, a revolt by the nobles, and renewed threats from neighboring Swedes and Poles. This was the context in which one of Russia's most powerful czars, Peter I ("the Great"; r. 1689–1725) took the throne. Peter was the first of Russia's rulers to visit western Europe, and he modeled himself partly after Louis XIV—but there was much of Ivan IV in his behavior, as well. During his travels, Peter learned Dutch, which allowed him to communicate with the commercial men of the Baltic rim and spurred his desire to modernize his empire along western lines. He recognized the need to speed up modernization after Russia was humiliated by Sweden in the first battles of the Great Northern War (1700–1721). Acting, as was his wont, quickly and without consulting his boyars, Peter imported English, German, Italian, and Dutch experts to help him reform shipbuilding and arms manufacture. In 1703 he also began building a new Russian capital, St. Petersburg, on boggy but strategically important land seized from the Swedes. Building his "window on the west" required massive amounts of serf labor and suffering—tens of thousands of whom died in the disease-ridden climate—and the importation of hundreds of western architects

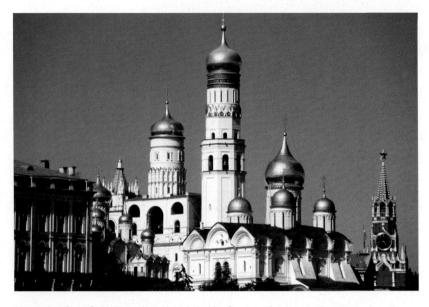

The Splendor of the Kremlin Already by the fourteenth century, the Muscovite princes were adding their residences and churches to the medieval fortress complex known as the Kremlin. This image shows Ivan the Great's Bell Tower, completed in 1508 and long Russia's tallest building, and to the right, the Cathedral of the Assumption, where Russian czars were crowned. Note the distinctive onion-shaped domes, one of the signature features of Russian Orthodox architecture.

and craftsmen. But Peter wanted St. Petersburg to be a modern capital and Baltic commercial port for Russia, and as absolute ruler, he made sure that he got his wish.

Peter's powers as czar allowed him to subdue his nobles as western monarchs could not. In 1722, Peter simply eliminated the boyars' titles and instructed them that henceforth, to hold any rank, they would have to serve the state in some fashion. Male children from noble families were sent to cadet schools and then assigned to jobs in the military or bureaucracy. Peter's introduction of the Table of Ranks not only broke the independent power of the nobility, but also provided the czar with the much-needed educated personnel he needed to modernize his state. Nor did Peter spare his family. Peter treated his son, Alexei, with such cruelty that he tried to run away. On his return, Alexei was tortured, probably at Peter's orders, and died.

Peter's cultural policy was a violent parody of that of the Sun King. Rather than simply bribing his nobles to come to his new capital, Peter compelled a thousand nobles to move to St. Petersburg, where they were to build homes at their own expense but designed by Peter's architects. He ordered them to come to his court and to drink with him as long as he desired, and he insisted that all his nobles wear western dress and cut off their beards. The consolation for his nobles was that those who remained on their land were allowed to act as absolute rulers with respect to their own serfs—and that the distances between St. Petersburg and many parts of the empire were enormous, and communications slow. Peter was the most successful of all Europe's monarchs in establishing his absolute rule, but his subjects paid a heavy price for his brand of modernization.

Incomplete Absolutisms: Spain, Poland, and Sweden

In Spain, Poland, and Sweden, for different reasons, monarchs were not as successful in establishing absolutist regimes.

SPAIN. Spain, in many ways, had had its absolutist era too early, during the reign of Philip II (r. 1556–1598). Philip had tried to overrule the Cortes and to subdue nobles unhappy with Habsburg overlordship. He had seen his share of warfare—against the Ottomans, against the French, against the Dutch, and disastrously, against the English, who destroyed his Armada in 1588. He presided over the golden age of Spanish cultural production, patronizing great religious painters such as the Greek painter known as El Greco and the Italian master of color, Titian. In some ways anticipating Louis XIV, he built an enormous palace for himself outside of Madrid—though Philip's El Escorial, finished in 1584, was built according to descriptions of Solomon's Temple, and intended to be a center for Catholic Reformation learning rather than an aristocratic playground. Its austere furnishings and enormous collection of religious art and manuscripts reflected its housing of a monarch who compared himself to the biblical king David, and not to the sun. Philip II was a king who devoted himself to serving and patronizing the church in Rome, rather than one, like Louis XIV, who insisted on keeping the church under his own, secular, control.

Already saddled with debt when he inherited his kingdom in 1556, Philip II was happy to promote silver mining in the Americas, but this early silver rush promoted inflation in Europe and hardships for peasants who could not afford to pay higher food prices. By the time Philip's reign ended, his many wars had further bankrupted the kingdom. The Thirty Years' War completed the eclipse of Spain's Golden Age. Once again, the kingdom declared bankruptcy and now also faced demographic decline—disease and endless conscriptions had decimated the population, and in 1640, civil war broke out in the province of Catalonia, a response to the high-handedness of the court in Madrid.

After 1648, Spain did not recover as rapidly or thoroughly as the French. A problematic succession to the throne and a powerful and deeply conservative landowning elite hampered attempts at reinstituting absolutist rule. The Catholic Church remained more powerful in Spain than elsewhere and nimbly resisted attempts to curb its influence. When the Bourbon king Philip V (r. 1700–1724) took the throne, he attempted to implement French absolutist models with some success, but by this time, Spain had already lost the Spanish Netherlands and southern Italy to Austria. It still held huge territories in the Americas, but its silver mines were playing out, and gradually its trading routes fell into the hands of the Dutch, English, and French. Without money or new military conquests, the Spanish Bourbons never managed to

fully break the resistance of the church and the landed nobles to their modernizing projects or their attempts to institute absolutist rule.

POLAND. Polish nobles, similarly, worked hard to protect their privileges and their tax revenues from centralizing forces. When called on to fight—as they often were in this era—the Poles did so effectively, but once the threat to their lands or enticement to conquer more territory was over, the Polish nobles resumed squabbling with one another. The situation was made worse by the fact that the king was, according to tradition, elected by Poland's representative assembly, the Sejm, and had to be an outsider. These conditions meant that the king was beholden to the great nobles in the Sejm and could not force them to agree to new taxes.

Kings elected from the Swedish house of Vasa (such as Sigismund III, r. 1587–1632; and Wladyslaw IV, r. 1632–1648) were patrons of the arts and successful military leaders, but after Wladyslaw's death in 1648, the kingdom suffered a series of invasions—most notably by the Swedes—and internal crises. As we have seen, a heroic moment came in 1683 when Jan Sobieski (r. 1674–1696) helped defeat the Ottomans before the gates of Vienna. But Sobieski's army could not be held together. The troops went home, and the Sejm refused to raise taxes to fund improvements, meaning that Poland could not build a powerful standing army or efficient centralized bureaucracy. Without an absolutist monarch, Poland could not modernize and eventually fell prey to its stronger neighbors. By 1720 it was living under the shadow of Peter the Great's expanding realm to its east, and the rising power of the Prussians to the north and west.

SWEDEN. At the time he took the Swedish throne, the Vasa king Charles XI (r. 1660–1697) could boast a large empire, stretching from Norway (then ruled by the Danes) to the Estonian city of Riga. Charles wrestled with large landowners to force them to hand over some of their huge estates and built an effective bureaucracy and a modernized army on the proceeds. In 1700, just after Charles's death, a united Polish, Danish, and Russian army attacked Sweden in the hopes of divvying up this rich kingdom. But the would-be partitioning powers ran into a buzzsaw in the form of the seventeen-year-old Charles XII (r. 1697–1718), who built on his father's absolutist achievements to create a Swedish military machine. With Dutch and English help, he defeated the Danes and then turned on the Russians, inflicting a humiliating defeat on the army of Peter the Great at the Battle of Narva in November 1700. In 1706 he compelled the Poles, too, to stand down. In this first stage of the long-lasting Great Northern War (1700–1721), Charles XII displayed his bravery, charisma, and stamina—but also his extravagant ambitions. In 1707 he invaded Russia, boasting that he would drive Peter the Great from his throne, and chop up the czar's empire into "petty princedoms."

Horrified by his army's failure at Narva, Peter I had begun rebuilding his own army, borrowing western European expertise. By 1709, when the Russians met Charles XII's Swedish troops at Poltava (see Map 14.3), the Russians were ready. Charles, for the first time, suffered a major defeat. After escaping to the Ottoman Empire, he tried, unsuccessfully, to get the Turks to help him battle the Russians. He returned home in 1714, riding more than nine hundred miles in two weeks' time, to find his war-weary nation broke and his nobility angry. But Charles, whose identity as a king and a man had been forged by ceaseless warfare, could not resist going to war once more, this time against the Danes in Norway. Here he was shot in 1718, perhaps by one of his own soldiers.[4]

After Charles XII's death, the Swedes made a series of peace agreements with their enemies, the result of which was the demise of Sweden as a great power. Weary of war and of charismatic absolutism, Swedish nobles compelled Queen Ulrika, who succeeded her brother Charles, to adopt a constitution that gave Sweden's representative assembly, the Riksdag, power almost equivalent to that of Parliament in England. If Polish absolutism was thwarted by the state's failure to build an army and produce a charismatic king, Swedish absolutism was killed by a flamboyant king who cared about nothing but military glory and was willing to squander the kingdom's resources on battles that, in the end, he could not win.

The Non-absolutist Exceptions: The Venetian and the Dutch Republics

Some of Europe's smaller states were never tempted to make themselves into absolutist monarchies. These included Swiss states, such as Geneva, where John Calvin had established a Calvinist republic, and several Italian and Dalmatian city-states, such as Florence and Dubrovnik. The most prominent, however, were two states that used their extensive commercial networks to make possible, at least for a time, their survival in an increasingly absolutist world: the Venetian and the Dutch republics. The differing fates of these two commercial republics demonstrate that adapting to the seventeenth century's challenges was not just a matter of choosing one or another form of government, but of developing the state as such.

What role did commerce play in the Dutch and Venetian Republics?

Venice, City of Commerce This painting of St. Mark's Square by Antonio Canaletto depicts an ordinary day in the life of this cosmopolitan city, as residents hang out laundry and well-dressed men and women meet to discuss business or to exchange gossip in the square. Close inspection of the image would also reveal a series of stalls lined up in front of the cathedral, some of them tended by turban-wearing Ottoman silk merchants.

MAP 14.4 | The Ottoman and Venetian Empires, c. 1700

After 1683 the Ottoman and Venetian Empires began to decrease in size, though the Ottomans remained powerful until 1918. The orange shading here indicates areas that belonged to the Venetians but were lost to the Ottomans between 1686 and 1715; the green shading indicates areas that were once Ottoman territory but were lost to the Habsburgs and Russians between 1683 and 1815. *How did the Ottoman losses of territory suggest that the balance of power in Europe had begun to shift away from the Mediterranean Sea?*

The Venetians

Venice entered the seventeenth century as an already formidable trading empire and exited it still powerful, but in decline. Though the Venetians continued to battle the Ottomans in the Mediterranean throughout the century, they stayed out of the Thirty Years' War and avoided the civil wars that devastated their neighbors. Thus Venice weathered the seventeenth century with its medieval institutions intact. These included its quasi-republican government, with its Great Council and an elected Doge as head of state. Its prosperity allowed the city to support a large number of painters, musicians, and architects, as well as skilled shipbuilders and craftsmen. In its famous St. Mark's Square, vendors of luxury goods—including Ottoman traders—congregated to sell their wares.

Yet infighting among the great families and the prosperity that allowed them to resist change prevented the Venetians from making timely reforms. The Venetians did not venture into the Atlantic or modernize their navy. They did not build an army, found a stock exchange, or create a state bank. Venice remained a Mediterranean power in an era in which influence and wealth was shifting to the Atlantic and the North Sea. Enjoying relatively good times while others suffered repeated crises and then falling off the pace as the absolutist states recovered, the Venetians experienced the seventeenth century in ways that paralleled the experience of their much-differently governed rivals, the Ottomans.

In 1660 the Venetians lost the important island of Crete to the Ottomans; they took part of the Greek mainland in 1699, but lost it again a few years later (see Map 14.4). By the 1720s, Venice itself was still wealthy and its culture rich, but its empire had receded and it no longer posed an expansionary threat.

The Dutch

In the 1579 split of the provinces of the Spanish Netherlands, the southern, largely Catholic Union of Arras got most of the large estates and most of the landowning nobility. The northern, officially Calvinist United

The Ottoman Empire in the Seventeenth Century

For the Ottomans, as for their neighbors, the seventeenth century was one of virtually uninterrupted warfare and internal unrest. The century opened and closed with a series of wars against the Habsburgs. In between, there were conflicts with the Venetians, the Poles, and the Russians. For the most part, the Ottomans won their external wars, but waging them, once again, required the increasing of taxes, something local leaders and landowners resented. Waging wars also increased Ottoman dependence on the class of warriors known as the Janissaries. Janissaries were Christian boys, forced or bribed to convert to Islam and to serve the state. This was the sultan's way of getting around arming his nobles, and of creating an elite loyal only to the central state. But the Janissaries had to be paid, and when, in the seventeenth century, the sultans occasionally tried to debase the currency to raise extra cash, they staged a series of destabilizing revolts. Thus, the Ottomans had good reason to think that a move toward absolutism—the building of a centralized bureaucracy and army and the increasing of central-state control over the economy—might be advisable.

In 1656, factional fighting and a Janissary uprising threw Istanbul into a state of anarchy. In response, Sultan Mehmed IV (r. 1648–1687) appointed Koprülü Mehmed as grand vizier (chief minister) and gave him dictatorial powers. Over the next fifty years, the Koprülü family would monopolize the office of grand vizier and use it to subdue the Janissaries and take territory for the sultan in both the Mediterranean and central Europe. By 1683 the Ottoman Empire reached the summit of its territorial influence. Although the Ottomans were pushed back from Vienna

for the last time that year, it still took several decades before Ottoman decline was noticeable to anyone but Ottoman intellectuals, some of whom had been predicting it since the mid-sixteenth century.

Ottoman absolutist reforms never fully succeeded. Though the Koprülü reforms helped defuse internal threats, over the next centuries the Ottomans' external enemies multiplied and gained in strength. Why did the reforms fail? In some ways the sultan, like the Russian czar, already had too much arbitrary power, and Mehmed's successors had no qualms about having anyone assassinated who displeased them, including viziers, Janissaries, and wives. The custom of retaining many wives presented sultans with the problem of too many possible heirs rather than too few. The result was continuous and sometimes murderous intrigue in the section of the palace called the harem, where the sultan's wives and children lived. On the other hand, like the Holy Roman emperors, the Ottoman sultans were too weak. Their empires were too decentralized and local privileges too strong; there were some older practices, such as provincial governors' power over local economic matters, that no sultan had the will or power to change. The combination of Russian-style arbitrariness and Habsburg-style weakness put the sultans at risk. In 1703, for example, Sultan Mustafa II (r. 1695–1703) was deposed by Janissaries who disapproved of a peace treaty he had signed with the infidel Habsburgs.

Ottoman absolutism, on the French, Russian, or Prussian model, did not take hold, but the Ottomans' decentralization actually gave them flexibility in dealing with internal factions. They did not found overseas colonies, but older forms of trade and tributary arrangements continued to provide relative prosperity to their subjects. Though battered by the long war with the Habsburgs that ended the century (1683–1699) and the even longer wars with their Persian rivals to the east, the Ottomans in 1700 still controlled an empire that embraced the eastern Mediterranean. Although they did not undertake long sea voyages, such as around the Horn of Africa or across the Atlantic to the New World, they were making a tidy profit on the luxury trades in the Mediterranean. Before his toppling, Mustafa II reigned over a population of some 30 million people and lodged in one of the finest palaces in the world, the Topkapi Palace in Istanbul. The Ottoman Empire did not follow the state-building model of some of its neighbors to the west, but it would prove longer lasting than many of Europe's absolutist kingdoms.

The Sultan's Court Just as in western Europe, the Ottoman sultan daily received visitors and petitioners, some of whom had traveled very long distances to seek his assistance or patronage, or to bring him tribute and gifts.

QUESTION | *What characteristics of the Ottoman Empire prevented the development here of French-style absolutism?*

Provinces of the Netherlands got many centers of trade, including the increasingly important port of Amsterdam. As a small, densely urbanized, and heavily commercial state more similar to Venice or Genoa than to France or Poland, the United Provinces had no need for a monarch to break down traditional privileges or to raise taxes in order to form a modern army and build a modern state bureaucracy. Thus, the United Provinces modernized in another way, one that fit the state's unique geographic and demographic profile.

Clamoring for independence and unwilling to bend to Spanish rule, the United Provinces began to call itself the Dutch Republic. It adopted a novel form of governance in which each of the seven provinces elected delegates to a federal States General. Each province also elected an executive officer, but in times of war, these executive officers were subordinate to a single military commander called a *stadtholder*. Often the *stadtholder* came from the house of Orange-Nassau, as had the great sixteenth-century hero, William of Orange. But Dutch republicans resisted attempts to make the office hereditary. Only the provinces' wealthiest men were permitted to vote, but still, this right made the United Provinces a republic, a somewhat singular form of government in the seventeenth century. After the Peace of Westphalia gave the United Provinces full independence, the Dutch retained this form of governance along with a tradition of religious toleration they had developed in response to the persecutions going on in their neighboring states. This policy of toleration, though far from perfect, meant that exiles and heretics from elsewhere streamed into the Dutch Republic. Eager to work and to live comfortably, the newcomers were also willing to contribute to their new communities by serving in local militias or by donating to new civic institutions such as orphanages and workhouses for the unemployed. The Dutch were notoriously intolerant toward people who broke God's laws, such as prostitutes and gamblers, because they did not perform what the Dutch called honest work.

Modernization in the United Provinces was driven chiefly by geographic circumstances: proximity to the sea and a shortage of arable land. Centuries earlier the Dutch had pioneered the draining of marshes and the building of canals. In the seventeenth century, state-backed loans allowed ordinary citizens to pour more capital into these projects, yielding new land for cultivation and accelerating the transport of goods. The Dutch built on Italian innovations to develop investment tools such as banks and joint stock companies, which provided ordinary citizens sufficient means to expand these activities and to make themselves Europe's richest citizens in the seventeenth century (see also Chapter 15).

The republican political system of the United Provinces did not prevent the Dutch from seeking to establish colonies of their own. On founding the Dutch East India Company in 1602, Dutch merchants quickly pushed their Portuguese rivals out of the islands that now form Indonesia (then known as the Dutch East Indies) and off the African coast. Setting up shop in new places, the Dutch quickly became the dominant traders in nutmeg, cloves, cinnamon, pepper, and salt. They soon added a lively trade in Caribbean sugar and African slaves, as well. And they established trading relationships with the Chinese and the Japanese and set up colonies in South Africa, New Amsterdam (now New York), the West Indies, and throughout Southeast Asia (see Map 15.2, p. 473). The Dutch Republic survived as a formidable military power into the eighteenth century despite growing rivalry with another up-and-coming commercial empire, England, where the struggle to stave off absolutism ended with the establishment of history-changing models of parliamentary governance and the protection of individual rights.

The Defeat of Absolutism in England

When Elizabeth I of England died in 1603, still wearing rouge and pearls, the crown passed to a man who was already a king, James VI of Scotland, son of Mary Stuart, queen of Scots. Known as the union of the crowns, this coupling of Scotland and England resulted in a double title for James. He would hereafter be James I and VI. In addition, the union of crowns put on the English throne a man who was a staunch Anglican and who had already produced two sons and a daughter, heirs who would secure the continuation of the Stuart line now that the Tudors had died out. James was nothing like his vain cousin Elizabeth. He drooled, wore threadbare clothes, and was terrified of water, which meant he rarely washed. If he was shabby, however, James was also endowed with a formidable intellect, and he took his mission to unite England and Scotland very seriously. He once leapt off his horse at the Scottish-English border and laid his body across it, hoping to prove that one king could indeed span two kingdoms.

Why did absolutism fail in England?

Like Holy Roman Emperor Ferdinand II, James, as ruler of England, Scotland, and Ireland, had to try to build a state in a period in which Protestantism, and especially radical new forms of it, were spreading like wildfire. Scotland was already heavily Presbyterian; in London, many merchants and skilled workers had become nonconformists, choosing not to conform to the rituals and beliefs of England's only legal religious institution, the Anglican Church. Some "godly" Anglicans—called Puritans by their critics—demanded the stripping away of the rituals and rich church furnishings that reminded them of Catholicism. James believed that God had appointed him to rule his domains and to protect his church, and he was not about to let Presbyterians or Puritans call the shots. But James did not, like Ferdinand, provoke a showdown with the firebrands, nor simply murder his opponents, as did Ivan the Terrible. Nor did he, like Louis XIII and XIV, refuse to consult his representative assembly. According to English

The King James Bible

Particularly eager to gain the king's favor were those Anglicans who wanted to strip the church of rituals and corruptions that reminded them all too much of Catholicism. They called themselves the godly; critics dubbed them Puritans. In pamphlets and public debates, they attacked "pomp-fed" and "dumb dog" priests as well as the 1552 *Book of Common Prayer,* the manual that prescribed the rituals of the Anglican Church. In 1603 they circulated a petition, in which they demanded reform and asked James to convene a council to discuss religious matters. James resented their attacks on his church, but instead of instead of locking them up, he opted for an unusual approach to peacemaking: he commissioned a new translation of the Bible.

The Bible project began with a conference in December 1603, attended, at James's request, not by "brainsick and heady preachers," but by serious scholars representing both Puritan and orthodox Anglican points of view.[5] At the conference, James denounced the Geneva Bible, the English translation made by Calvinist exiles in the 1550s. Favored by Presbyterians and Puritans, the Geneva Bible was antiroyalist and anticlerical. It made scathing references to tyrants and provided extensive marginal notes so that individual readers could understand the text without needing clergymen to interpret it for them. Of course, the Bible translation used in the Anglican Church, the Bishops' Bible of 1568, was also partisan. It featured a frontispiece depicting Elizabeth and her bishops as the source of religious authority in the kingdom; its language was awkward and frequently obscure.

James was no Puritan, but he recognized that the Bishops' Bible did nothing to bring discerning Christians into the Anglican fold. Thus, his company of fifty-four scholars spent years stitching together and reworking existing translations to produce a Bible worthy of their king. Subsequently known as the King James Version, this Bible combined the clarity of the Geneva translation—without the footnotes—with poetic phrasings intended to highlight God's majesty and authority. This was a Bible meant to defang Puritan critics, but also to unify James's subjects in common reverence for the majesty of God and the poetic power of the scriptures. By examining a short passage from Psalm 23, we can see how much James's translators depended on the Geneva Bible—and how much less elegant the Bishop's Bible sounds to the ear. We can also see how subtle changes in the King James Version make it the most poetic of the three:

King James Bible
The Lord is my shepherd; I shall not want. He maketh me to lie down in green pastures: he leadeth me beside the still waters. He restoreth my soul: he leadeth me in the paths of righteousness for his name's sake.

Geneva Bible
The Lord is my shepherd, I shall not want. He maketh me to rest in green pasture and leadeth me by the still waters. He restoreth my soul, and leadeth me in the paths of righteousness for his name's sake.

Bishops' Bible
God is my shepheard; therefore I can lack nothing. He will cause myself to repose me in a pasture full of grass, and he will lead me unto calm waters. He will convert my soul and will bring me forth into the paths of righteousness for his name's sake.

Completed in 1611, the King James Bible did not become every Englishman's Bible; even after James prohibited the publishing of the Geneva Bible in 1616 and made the King James Version the only Authorized Version of the Bible in English, Puritans and Presbyterians continued to smuggle the Genevan version in from Holland and Switzerland. But the King James Bible was used for centuries in the Church of England and by generations of English-speaking writers, poets, politicians, and theologians throughout the world. It is the source for numerous idioms still used in everyday conversation, including "by the skin of his teeth," "no rest for the wicked," and "a fly in the ointment." The King James Bible has become a nearly invisible part of the language and heritage of English speakers, in England and abroad. We forget too easily that for King James, this synthetic, poetic translation of the scriptures was a political act, meant to shore up the king's authority—and to make peace.

Episode 7. Part II. THE TRANSLATORS PRESENTING BIBLE TO JAMES I.

King James Gets His Bible In 1611, the scholars charged by King James I of England with the task of producing a new, authorized Bible in English completed their work and presented to their patron what would now be known as the King James Version of the Scriptures. This version of the Bible would thereafter exert an enormous impact on the English language and on English literature.

QUESTIONS | *Why did King James order a new version of the Bible? How did it differ from its predecessors?*

law, he *had* to get Parliament's consent in matters of taxation. Instead, James chose a moderate course, mollifying moderate and peaceful nonconformists and persecuting or forcing into exile only the most radical critics of the church. Thus, in the very first year of his reign, he took as his motto "blessed are the peacemakers," a motto he would try to employ in the religious as well as the political realm.

Wily and hardworking, James kept the peace even as war exploded on the continent, and political and religious tensions mounted at home. By the 1620s, however, it was clear that James's ambivalent policies had both emboldened and further radicalized critics of the church and king. On his ascent to the throne, James's son Charles I (r. 1625–1649) would learn that his father's peacemaking had not wiped out differences between Scots and Englishmen, between Puritans and Anglicans, or between parliamentarians and the crown. In fact, all now claimed the right to be consulted about how the kingdom should be run.

Charles I and the English Civil War

The year 1625, Charles I's first as king, was a rough one. He ascended the throne during an outbreak of plague, and, having immediately plunged the country into war against Spain, he saw the army's first campaign fail miserably. He married the same year, but his queen, the Catholic sister of Louis XIII, Henrietta Marie, proved hugely unpopular. The next years were equally rocky. Each time he asked for a war subsidy, Parliament protested bitterly before finally giving in. During one standoff, Charles lectured them: "Remember that Parliaments are altogether in my power for their calling, sitting, and dissolution. Therefore, as I find the fruits of them good or evil, they are to continue or not. . . ."[6] Members of the House of Commons, in particular, balked at Charles's high-handed manner, as well as his imprisonment of those who refused to pay the new taxes. In 1628 the House of Commons issued a Petition of Right, insisting on its traditional privilege to approve taxes and objecting to Charles's imposition of something akin to martial law. Charles accepted the Petition with ill grace and in 1629 decided that he would no longer do battle with Parliament, but rule alone.

The period of Charles I's so-called Personal Rule lasted from 1629 until 1641 and was marked by religious as well as political strife. Charles's attempt to reform local government seemed intrusive to rural nobles; his ship tax—England's first yearly tax on income—outraged city dwellers. His appointment of William Laud, a high church Anglican, as archbishop of Canterbury in 1633, provoked further outrage. Laud liked stained glass, candles, and rich vestments, proof to some of the "godly" that he was in league with the Anti-Christ, the pope. The real problem was not only that Laud liked these things, but also that he moved to force all Anglican communities in England, Scotland, and Ireland to worship in the way he did. The reaction was fierce, but even more violent was Presbyterian reaction to Laud's attempt to im-

pose a new, Anglican prayer book on Scotland in 1637. When the Scottish archbishop tried to hold mass according to the new book at St. Giles Cathedral in Edinburgh, a riot erupted, and the archbishop narrowly escaped with his life. The Scots banded together and in 1638 signed a National Covenant, swearing to defend the Presbyterian Church to the death—some signed with their own blood. In 1639 they marched to the English border.

Charles called out an army, which, though badly paid, managed to halt the Scots and convince them to call a truce. The king feared the truce would not last and desperately needed money. Finally, in April 1640 he was forced to call Parliament to fund the raising of a new army. Parliament refused, insisting that reforms come first. After only three weeks in session, Charles dissolved what became known as the short Parliament and called another. The next batch of deputies proved equally intent on reform and demanded that Charles ensure the regular meeting of Parliaments, remove his evil councilors, and end Laud's reforms. At first Charles seemed amenable to these demands, even allowing Laud to be imprisoned in the Tower of London. Emboldened, Puritans demanded even more reform; some sought to purify the churches by shattering their stained glass and painting over Baroque murals.

Reacting to this militant Protestantism and centuries of Anglican persecution, the Irish rose in rebellion in March 1641. Releasing pent-up hostilities, Irish rioters savagely set upon their Protestant overlords, massacring an estimated 12,000 people; rumors circulated that 500,000 were dead. Fear of a Catholic invasion swept England, causing townsfolk to hide in caves and women to suffer miscarriages. In the chaos, Charles moved to head off a supposed plot to imprison his Catholic wife, Henrietta. He charged five key figures of Parliament with treason and sought to lock them up. These actions convinced the reformers that the king was about to reverse course and destroy Parliament's newly won power. As London turned against him, the king found he had to flee his own capital city. Leading Puritan parliamentarians seized control of the army, and Charles was left to raise his own troops among conformist Anglicans and nobles loyal to the throne.

Civil war between the parliamentary and the royalist or "cavalier" armies erupted in the summer of 1642. The royalists long held sway in the north and west, while the parliamentarians commanded the south and east, including the city of London (Map 14.5). The parliamentary army was better organized and in command of more resources than the king's forces, and boasted skillful and charismatic leaders, the most important of whom was a country gentleman named Oliver Cromwell (1599–1658). As in the Thirty Years' War, soldiers on both sides often relied on looting and pillaging for survival and spent a great deal of time laying siege to one another's cities, but also fought with swords, poleaxes, and matchlocks at close range. By 1644 the tide was turning in Parliament's favor. The queen, with her sons Charles and James, escaped to France. In 1646, after the battle of Naseby, Cromwell's army captured the king.

Trial and Regicide

Parliamentary forces were now faced with a dilemma: what should be done with the king? Charles, they believed, had become a tyrant, rather than a benevolent father, to his people. But he would not admit that that was so. As a captive, he continued to insist on his right to rule, and for two years, royalists tried numerous tricks to rescue him. Many members of Parliament hoped to compel the king to negotiate a settlement, but Cromwell and the army wanted to secure their achievements. For them, the only option was regicide, the killing of the king. But the trick was to do it without drawing sympathy for his cause. "This is not a thing done in a corner," Cromwell insisted. There would have to be a trial.

The trial of King Charles I was a first in European history. Never before had a people made their ruler subordinate to the law, nor was it easy to get Parliament to vote to try His Majesty (see Back to the Source at the end of the

Controlled by the parliamentarians, beginning of 1645

Controlled by the royalists, beginning of 1645

Conquered by the parliamentarians, 1645

★ Battle sites

MAP 14.5 | English Civil Wars

This map shows the areas of parliamentary strength as the war began to turn in its favor in 1645. Note that London, by far the richest and most populated city, is easily inside parliamentary territory. *Why did Charles I look to the more rural west of England and Wales for supporters?*

chapter). The military had to surround the chambers and allow in only the delegates who would be sure to vote their way. Charles never admitted Parliament's right to try him, and in the end, only twenty-six members condemned him to death and signed his death warrant.

On the morning of January 30, 1649, Charles was marched from the chambers in which he had been imprisoned to his execution. As it was a very cold day, Charles wore an extra shirt so that he would not shiver before the crowds that gathered to watch in front of Whitehall Palace, the king's major residence. With drums beating, Charles stepped onto the scaffold. Pushing his long hair under a nightcap, he lay his head on the block. One blow of the executioner's heavy axe sufficed to sever the king's head from his body. As was customary, the executioner held up the severed head for the spectators to see it. By most accounts, the crowd greeted the sight with a mighty groan. Parliament, acting in the name of the people of England, had killed their king. Absolutism, to the degree it existed in seventeenth-century England, was dead, and England was declared a republic, or commonwealth.

Absolutism on Trial This contemporary image of the trial of Charles I depicts the courtroom, with the judges facing the viewer (the chief judge in the center). The king faces the court, still wearing his hat, which he refuses to remove.

DATE	EVENT
1629–1641	Personal Rule
1642–1648	English Civil War
1649	Charles I executed
1660	Charles II restored
1685–1689	Rule of James II
1688–1689	Glorious Revolution

The Commonwealth

In the wake of Charles's death, the parliamentarians had to deal with schisms in their own ranks, with renewed violence in Ireland, and with royalists on the Scottish border. Cromwell, who emerged as leader of the movement, dealt with the trouble in Ireland by force. His army massacred thousands, and he kept the peace by settling demobilized troops there, much to the cost of Irish Catholics. Eventually, he cleared the royalists from Scotland, too, sending Charles I's son—who was already calling himself Charles II—into exile in France.

Cromwell found schism within his own ranks harder to deal with. He abolished the monarchy—assuming the role of Lord Protector of the Commonwealth in 1653—and ended Anglicanism's dominance as the established religion. He allowed for a certain amount of religious toleration and even invited Jews to settle in England for the first time in four hundred years. But some of his supporters wanted more radical religious and political reform. Some wanted to make England a grand-scale Geneva, under the rule of the godly. Others, called Levelers, wanted to abolish property qualifications and give all men the vote. Some went so far as to support the redistribution of all property to make all Englishmen truly equal. Cromwell managed to crush the Levelers, but the godly proved more intractable. Parliament enacted a series of godly provisions: immoral acts, such as playing cards or celebrating Christmas, were banned, and adultery and blasphemy were to be punished with death (though few were actually sentenced). But new and more radical sects—such as the Adamites, who insisted on going naked, as Adam did—seemed to appear daily, and to find backers in Parliament. When Cromwell and the army could take no more, they locked the House of Commons and Cromwell pocketed the key, announcing that God made him do it.

England's Colonies

Cromwell and his backers were concerned not only about religion, but also about the English economy, and in 1651 the Commonwealth passed the Navigation Acts, which required that all goods imported from Europe or the Americas arrive in the British Isles on English ships. This legislation was targeted at the Dutch, who were profiting greatly from the carrying trade, and it resulted in a great windfall for English shippers, who now had a monopoly on the increasingly lucrative trade in sugar, slaves, and other commodities (see Chapter 15). Not surprisingly, the Navigation Acts incited a series of trade wars between the English and the Dutch between 1652 and 1674, during which the English seized New Amsterdam and renamed it New York.

Beginning in 1620, Puritan settlers had founded English colonies along North America's Atlantic seaboard, and other English and Scots settlers gradually followed them. Both England's kings and its Lord Protector saw colonial expansion as a good idea, and over the course of the seventeenth century, England's rulers provided the financial backing and occasional military assistance that allowed its traders and planters to lay claim to more and more territory in present-day New England, Canada, and the Caribbean. Increasingly these colonies become neo-Englands, sharing the language, religion, and culture of the mother country, but without enjoying the right to representation in Parliament. Although in terms of domestic policies Cromwell's Commonwealth could not have been more different from the absolute monarchy of Louis XIV, both regimes recognized that long-distance trade and colonization would be fundamental to building powerful new states for the future.

In 1658, Oliver Cromwell died. Parliament honored the Lord Protector's desire to have his son Richard succeed him, but Richard proved an ineffectual leader. Moreover, he could not find a lender to finance the enormous debts incurred in the course of the civil wars. In spring 1660, a group of leading figures decided that restoring the Stuart Dynasty was the only practical option, and they invited Charles I's eldest son (also named Charles) to return from French exile and make England a monarchy once more.

The Restoration

On May 8, 1660, cheering crowds greeted Charles II and his younger brother James as they paraded through the streets of London on their way to Whitehall Palace. Charles moved quickly to assure those hostile to his return that he would forgive and forget past differences if he could have their loyalty in the future, and he avenged himself only on the regicides, who were rounded up and executed. Oliver Cromwell had already died, but his body was symbolically hanged and his severed head displayed over the entrance to the House of Parliament. Charles II (r. 1660–1685) reestablished the Church of England and called a new Parliament, this one well stocked with cavaliers. Unwilling to unleash a new civil war, he did not, however, try to impose religious uniformity or political absolutism, as had his father. He filled his court with his mistresses rather than with Bible-translators, but ominously, too, with Catholics, including his brother James, next in line for the throne. This would not have mattered had Charles II sired a legitimate, Protestant heir. But he did not, and by the later 1670s the succession question began to disturb the restoration settlement.

Charles understood that the nation was dead set against having another Catholic king. The memory of the siege of Magdeburg was still fresh, and his subjects, especially the Puritans and Presbyterians, were terrified that a Catholic ruler might undo the English Reformation. But he believed his Stuart line had been appointed by God to take the throne, and thus he refused to go along with Parliament's desire to exclude James from the succession.

In the course of the raging debates over this question, known as the Exclusion Crisis, the first real political parties developed. Those who opposed James and wished to have Parliament choose a new king were called **Whigs.** Those who made the case for James's legitimate succession were called **Tories.** Both terms were derogatory, but telling. *Tory* was a term originally used to describe Irish bandits, who were of course Catholic. Tories were staunch backers of the king and the Anglican Church, whom opponents wanted to portray as closet Catholics. The term *Whig* was also originally a derogatory term, used for Scottish bandits, especially those of fanatical

Presbyterian beliefs. Whigs were in many ways the descendants of the moderate parliamentarians of the civil war era and were usually proponents of parliamentary sovereignty. Most despised Catholicism and thought Anglicanism dangerously "popish." A combination of political and religious allegiances, then, laid the foundations for the party politics of England long after the English Civil War had ended.

The Glorious Revolution

After dissolving several pro-exclusion Parliaments, Charles prevailed and James did succeed to the throne in 1685, in part on the expectation that one of his Protestant daughters (Mary and Anne) would take the throne when he died. But his succession was not without violence. Soon after his coronation, James had to use his army to crush an attempted Protestant coup, and in the aftermath ordered three hundred gentry executed and eight hundred conspirators sent to the West Indies as serfs. Then, worried about the stability of his regime, he began to promote Catholics to positions of power in the army, judiciary, and Parliament. Both Tories and Whigs resented these actions, but the breaking point came when James's second wife, who was Catholic, produced a male heir

Note: Names in blue indicate which members of the family took the English throne.

FIGURE 14.2 | The House of Stuart

This figure shows how the English crown descended through the Stuart line, and finally passed to the Hanoverians after the death of Queen Anne in 1714. **Which of these monarchs did not die in office?**

in 1688. The baby, James Edward Stuart, signaled that a line of Catholic kings would now rule England, a situation both Tories and Whigs found intolerable. Leaders in Parliament sent out feelers to the Dutch prince William of Orange and his wife Mary, James's eldest daughter and a Protestant, both of whom could claim to be next in line for the English throne. They were willing to seize the moment, and in late 1688, William landed in England, commencing the largely bloodless coup known as the Glorious Revolution.

James II and his supporters fled first to Scotland, his grandfather's homeland, and then to France. William and Mary agreed to a Bill of Rights in which they consented to call elections for Parliament regularly and to allow their subjects to petition them without fearing persecution for their opinions. Hereafter, they promised, the English king or queen would not interfere with the operation of the law, nor impose taxes without Parliament's assent. The provisions of the English Bill of Rights amounted to an agreement on the part of the monarchy to share power with Parliament—a move diametrically opposed to absolutist doctrine. Moreover, the monarchs agreed to tie the hands of their heirs in religious matters. At Parliament's insistence, Catholics were banned from the succession.

The Church of England remained the established church, and its members retained privileged status in society, but Puritans and Presbyterians were allowed to worship as they pleased.

Under William and Mary, political stability was established without resort to absolutist measures. The monarchs allowed a virtually free press to flourish. They agreed to abide by laws made by Parliament and refrained from persecuting their political opponents—with the exception of Irish or colonial subjects who demanded home rule. All these measures gave English subjects—especially those who were Protestant, male, and middle class or above—a much greater measure of individual liberty and prosperity than could be enjoyed by other Europeans at the time. Stabilization achieved by sharing power with Parliament was so successful that even though neither William and Mary, nor Mary's sister Anne I (r. 1702–1714), produced children to inherit the throne, the crown passed to a German (Protestant) descendant of James I, George I of the house of Hanover (r. 1714–1727), without any whisper of a new rebellion. Absolutism was defeated, though monarchy, the Church of England, and the aristocracy remained firmly in control.

Conclusion

The seventeenth century was an era of terrible wars and catastrophes, of witch hunts, civil wars, and famines. At the center of the century, responsible for much of the chaos, was the disastrous Thirty Years' War, which carried away perhaps a quarter of the population of central Europe and Spain and bankrupted governments across the continent. It destabilized regimes, generating civil wars in England, Spain, and France. Although the Peace of Westphalia of 1648 resulted in few territorial changes, it marked a great change in the attitude of European sovereigns toward the re-formation of the church. The war proved that Europeans would have to live in a Christendom divided among Catholics, Lutherans, Calvinists, and other sects. Never again would Europeans engage in grand-scale warfare for primarily religious ends.

In response to the Thirty Years' War, and to the other crises of the century, many monarchs attempted to consolidate and centralize their states; their successes and failure contributed much to changes in the continent's balance of power. Though often brutal, these absolutist regimes were often modernizing ones, able to raise armies and taxes more efficiently. France, for example, by 1700 could boast Europe's largest army and a network of overseas colonies, and Louis XIV's Versailles, whose elaborately patterned gardens and glittering Hall of Mirrors reflected the glory and orderly kingdom of the Sun King, had begun to eclipse even Baroque Rome. Those who aspired to establish absolutism but lacked the economic power or will to modernize, as in Spain, fell off the pace, as did formerly powerful kingdoms such as Sweden and Poland-Lithuania, both battered, like Spain, by long periods of warfare. Meanwhile, absolutist Russia and Prussia began to build their own empires in the east. But lacking access to Atlantic ports, neither developed the commercial and colonial economies that, by 1700, had begun to yield rich profits to the Dutch, the English, and the French.

A few states managed to both modernize and avoid absolutism, as did England, which quickly became an economic powerhouse and a political model for reform-minded people on the continent. On the whole, Europe's states in the north and west, especially the Netherlands, England, and France, ended the century with a greater share of European power, influence, and prosperity than they had had in 1600, in part because they had begun to exploit their opportunities to trade and colonize in the rest of the world. The crises of the seventeenth century had changed Europe's balance of power internally and globally and opened the way for new opportunities as well as new tensions in the decades ahead.

Critical Thinking Questions

1. What challenges and opportunities did European monarchs face in the seventeenth century?

2. In what ways did the Thirty Years' War alter the course of European history? Did it resolve any dilemmas or disputes? Could you pick a winner, or is it more accurate to say that all sides lost more than they gained?

3. Compare and contrast the absolutist regimes of Louis XIV in France and Charles I in England with the regimes of Fredrick William II of Prussia and Peter the Great of Russia. Where was absolutism more "absolute"?

Key Terms

absolutism **(p. 424)**

divine right **(p. 424)**

natural law **(p. 434)**

Estates General **(p. 437)**

parlements **(p. 437)**

intendants **(p. 437)**

Fronde **(p. 437)**

Versailles **(p. 437)**

Junkers **(p. 440)**

Whig **(p. 452)**

Tory **(p. 452)**

Primary Sources in Connect

1. **James I Defends Absolutism**

2. **Luis Granada, "Meditations for Monday Morning"**

3. **The Trial of Jean Williford for Witchcraft in Faversham, Kent, in 1645**

4. **Hugo Grotius, *The Freedom of the Seas***

5. **Thomas Hobbes, *Leviathan***

6. **Jacques Bossuet Defends Divine Right**

7. **The Absolutism of Peter the Great of Russia**

The Trial of King Charles I, 1649

In January 1649, the remaining members of the Long Parliament accused Charles I of treason. Even before the outbreak of the civil wars, they argued, he had put himself above the law and had become a tyrant, and in so doing, he had provoked cruel and bloody wars. Not willing to make Charles a martyr, the parliamentarians decided that they would try the king before Parliament, sitting as the kingdom's highest court of justice. Brought before them, Charles denied that Parliament, or any earthly court, had the right to try him. On being seated the king refused to take off his hat (signifying he had no respect for the court or his prosecutor, Parliament's lord president, John Bradshaw) or to enter a plea to the charges against him.[7]

King: I would know by what power I am called hither . . . and when I know what lawful authority, I shall answer. Remember I am your king, your lawful king, and what sins you bring upon your heads, and the judgment of God upon this land; think well upon it, I say, think well upon it, before you go further from one sin to a greater; therefore let me know by what lawful authority I am seated here, and I shall not be unwilling to answer. In the meantime, I shall not betray my trust; I have a trust committed to me by God, by old and lawful descent; I will not betray it, to answer to a new unlawful authority. . . .

Lord President: If you had been pleased to have observed what was hinted to you by the Court, at your first coming hither, you would have known by what authority; which authority requires you, in the name of the people of England, of which you are elected king, to answer them.

King: No. Sir, I deny that.

Lord President: If you acknowledge not the authority of the Court, they must proceed.

King: I do tell them so: England was never an elective kingdom, but an hereditary kingdom, for near these thousand years; therefore let me know by what authority I am called hither. I do stand for more the Liberty of my people, than any here that come to be my pretended Judges; and therefore let me know by what lawful authority I am seated here, and I will answer it: otherwise I will not answer it. . . .

For the rest of that day, and the one following, the king refused to enter a plea. On January 27 the king entered the chambers to cries of "Execution! Justice! Execution!" but still declined to acknowledge the court's jurisdiction. The weary lord president offered a long speech before reading the sentence. Here is a segment of that speech:

Lord President: Sir, you have held yourself, and let fall such language, as if you had been in no way subject to the law, or that the law had not been your superior. Sir, the Court is very sensible of it, and I hope so are all the understanding people of England, that the law is your superior; that you ought to have ruled according to the law; you ought to have [done] so. Sir, I know very well your pretence hath been that you have done so; but, Sir, the difference hath been who shall be the expositors of this law: Sir, whether you and your party, out of courts of justice, shall take upon them to expound law, or the courts of justice, who are the expounders? Nay, the Sovereign and the High Court of Justice, the Parliament of England, that are not only the highest expounders, but the sole makers of the law? Sir, for you to set yourself with your single judgment, and those that adhere unto you, to set yourself against the highest Court of Justice, that is not law. Sir, as the law is your Superior, so truly, Sir, there is something that is superior to the law, and that is indeed the Parent or Author of the Law, and that is the people of England. . . . Sir, the Charge hath called you Tyrant, a Traitor, a Murderer, and a Public Enemy to the Commonwealth of England. . . .

King: Ha!

Lord President: Truly Sir, We have been told "Rex est dum bene regit, Tyrannus qui populum opprimit":* And if that be the definition of a Tyrant, then see how you come short of it in your actions. . . .

Charles still refused to acknowledge either Parliament's right to try him or the truth of the charges—how could a divinely appointed monarch be charged with treason by his people? Thus, the high court simply silenced him, and sentenced him to death.

QUESTIONS | *How does Charles in this episode reveal his pretentions to be an absolute monarch? On what grounds did the lord president claim Charles could be tried by this court?*

Source: State Trials, ed. H. L. Stephens (London, 1899), 371–380.

*He is a king while he rules well, and a tyrant if he oppresses the people.

15

Spring Plowing, a Ritual of Rural Life under the Old Regimes

THE OLD REGIMES AND THEIR
QUIET REVOLUTIONS, 1600–1789

A World of Legal Inequalities

**The Social Hierarchies
of the Old Regimes**

The Monarch

The First Estate: Church and Clergy

The Second Estate: The Nobility

The Third Estate: Nothing and
Everything

A World of Quiet Revolutions

Revolutions in the Countryside

The Commercial Revolution

The Military Revolution

The Seven Years' War:
A Global War

**Transforming the Heavens
and the Human Mind:
The Scientific Revolution**

Doubt and the Scientific Method:
Francis Bacon and René Descartes

The Cosmological Revolution

The Anatomical Revolution

The Social Life of Science

Women and the New Science

Conclusion

JOHANN BÖTTGER: ALCHEMIST, INVENTOR, AND PRISONER

Born in 1682, Johann Böttger grew up around gold. One of his grandfathers had been a master goldsmith; another was the overseer of the mint in the town of Magdeburg, where Böttger's father was employed. Not surprisingly, the young Böttger demonstrated an interest in chemistry, a field still very much dominated by experimenters interested in solving practical problems, such as how to work metals and how to create colorful fabric dyes. No one in his day would have dreamed of sending someone of Böttger's social standing to a university to study something called "science." Universities were for the nobility or for those who wanted to pursue careers in the church. Instead, Böttger's stepfather chose a suitable career for his stepson, apprenticing him at age fourteen to an apothecary. He began the process of learning to be a master apothecary but never finished. In 1701, Böttger made one of the few boasts likely to draw the attention of an absolutist monarch to the work of a mere apothecary's apprentice: he claimed that he could manufacture gold.[1]

In an age of princes desperate to build their armies and enhance their prestige with lavish displays of wealth, the ability to perform **alchemy**—to turn base metals into gold—was a highly attractive talent. News of Böttger's boast traveled fast, and soon the luxury-loving Prussian king Frederick I wanted the humble apprentice to appear at his court. Fearing punishment for fraud, Böttger ran away. But he immediately landed himself a job, and virtual life-imprisonment, with a neighboring king equally eager to own the secret to making gold, Augustus the Strong, elector of Saxony and king of Poland.

Augustus supplied Böttger with helpers, furnaces, food, and various kinds of ingredients, in the hopes that he might manufacture a "philosopher's stone," the substance through which, it was thought, metal must pass to be changed into gold. When experiment after experiment failed, Böttger tried to escape, but was captured and confined to a workshop in the medieval palace of Meissen, a short distance from Saxony's capital city, Dresden. There the chemist

The King Learns a Scientific Secret In this melodramatic reimagining of a scene from Johann Böttger's life, the humble apothecary's apprentice explains to his patron, Augustus the Strong, king of Saxony, how to make porcelain, nicknamed "white gold." The painting portrays the event as having occurred in Böttger's attic workshop, where he was kept prisoner, lest he be tempted to share this valuable secret.

Military revolution
c. 1550–1715

Scientific revolution
c. 1550–1750

Portuguese, Spanish slave trade
c. 1500–1715

Agricultural revolution
c. 1500–

1500   1550   1600

wisely turned his attention to yet another mystery of the day: how to make the delicate hard-paste porcelain that so many Europeans were then importing from China and Japan. Augustus was obsessed with porcelain and already owned a vast collection of vases, tea cups, and plates, elegantly molded and decorated with brilliant enamel glazes. Böttger spent several years trying to discover the recipe for making porcelain—all the while confined to his workshop, lest he share his secrets with another prince. Finally, in 1709, he succeeded, thereby not only satisfying Augustus's vast desires, but also allowing Saxony to profit from sales of porcelain to other luxury-hungry princes and nobles. Meissen porcelain became so popular and profitable that it earned the nickname "white gold."

The rigors of his imprisonment, exposure to mercury and other dangerous substances, and overindulgence in drink, his one means of escape, ruined Böttger's health. He died just after his thirty-seventh birthday. He was, for his day, a great scientist—it took others decades to replicate his findings. His work contributed to a major shift in the luxury trade, as Europeans began to produce their own porcelain instead of buying it from East Asia. He was also unusual for his day in having adopted a profession other than the one chosen for him by his parents; and perhaps he might have lived a happier life, after all, as an apothecary. For even as the man who developed the recipe for white gold, Böttger was no free agent and had no rights other than those his king wished to bestow on him. He was a man living in, and contributing to, long processes we call the commercial, proto-industrial, and scientific revolutions. But his life was shaped too by the limitations on social mobility, intellectual activity, and economic opportunity set by the hierarchical era in which he lived.

In the wake of the French Revolution of 1789, Europeans would look back at the period between roughly 1600 and 1800 and see France, in particular, as a stagnant society, an **Old Regime.** Here we apply this term to all of Europe, but also pluralize it, both to capture the commonalities in early modern social structure and to underline the persistence of regional and political differences between Europe's Old Regimes. We do not accept the postrevolutionary claim that these societies were static—though, as this chapter shows, for the most part they did remain local and rural ones. Most people who experienced the era of the Old Regimes worked on the land and died without traveling farther than five miles from home. Their world was held in place by a strict social structure, in which privileges and

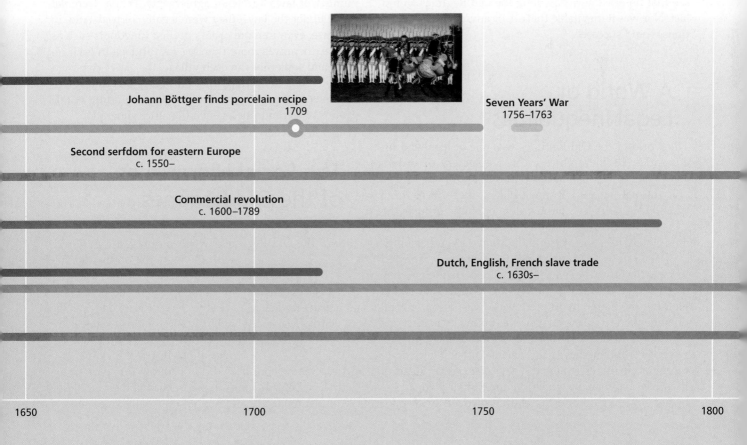

Johann Böttger finds porcelain recipe
1709

Seven Years' War
1756–1763

Second serfdom for eastern Europe
c. 1550–

Commercial revolution
c. 1600–1789

Dutch, English, French slave trade
c. 1630s–

1650   1700   1750   1800

inequalities were fixed in law, and few believed that their lives could or should be much different from those of their grandparents. Change, after all, was likely to be for the worse. Kings might lose their thrones, nobles might lose their privileges, and peasants might starve or find their sons conscripted for new wars. The majority were hesitant to adopt new forms of thinking. Even as what was called the new science began to spread, most Europeans continued to view nature and the heavens as subject to God's commands or whims, and humankind's chances of increasing the store of knowledge as slim, at best. Especially before enlightened ideas began to spread in the later eighteenth century (see Chapter 16), most Europeans looked at the world as a zero-sum game, one they feared losing perhaps even more than they desired to win.

Even as many of Böttger's contemporaries continued to follow traditional patterns of work and belief, several movements had started—agricultural, proto-industrial, commercial, military, and scientific—that would prove transformative enough to be called revolutions. Some regions, such as England and the Dutch Republic, which possessed the advantages of easy access to shipping routes, stable governments, and some measure of religious toleration and social mobility, were particularly active in spawning these revolutions. Looking at this era in retrospect, we might see it as an increasingly rapid downhill race, with the brakes—in the form of traditional practices inscribed in law and traditional understandings of the world based on ancient and biblical authorities—screeching madly all the way. But to experience this period as individuals like Böttger lived it is to see that no one knew how long the Old Regimes would last. Nor was it inevitable that all, or any, of these revolutions would succeed.

A World of Legal Inequalities

The world of the Old Regimes was one of legalized inequalities. Its hierarchies created a **society of orders** based on birth and fixed in law.

How did contracts work to maintain the social order of the Old Regimes? In most places, there were three basic orders or status groups: the nobility, the clergy, and everyone else. Individuals—whether kings or peasants—were not expected to leave the order into which they were born, though they might move upward or downward within that order. Holding the hierarchy in place was a vast array of legal documents. Virtually everyone was bound by at least one contract, and many by more than one. Some contracts were very old, medieval agreements; others were more recent or newly renegotiated. They covered every part of life, from baptism, in which the individual pledged his or her soul to God and the church pledged to care for

the individual's soul, to the grave—for some landowners were obliged to pay for their servants' funerals and some servants had to pay to bury their masters. Contracts between kings and nobles could exempt nobles from paying taxes or gave them the right to tax or work their social inferiors; in exchange, the nobles pledged to fight for the king when necessary, to recognize his heirs as his successors, and to help in governing the kingdom. Contracts bound peasants to serve their lords (or seigneurs, in French). Such **seigneurial dues** or obligations might include shearing the lord's sheep or building roads on his estate. Even among the peasantry, brides-to-be signed marriage contracts with their spouses, stipulating how dowries could and could not be spent. Nobles contracted with beekeepers, musicians, cooks, falcon-trainers, and coachmen to obtain their services in exchange for salaries and various other perks. When a man died, his heirs typically swore an oath to the lord before a court of law, reconfirming the provisions of the family's contract. Thus, the next generation was obliged to live under the same contracts that bound their forefathers.

There were hundreds of thousands of other sorts of contracts, all of them with slightly different provisions: one group of cobblers might sign a contract to set up shop in a particular town, in exchange for the town's agreement that this guild of cobblers would have monopoly rights on the making of shoes within the city limits. People argued—or sued one another—constantly over subjects such as whose sheep were permitted to graze on certain hillsides. Thus, the world of the Old Regimes was not a lawless society, but a society regulated by a vast number of laws and legal agreements. People were *not* equal under the law—they were legally *unequal*. And, in any case, even in more or less unified kingdoms such as France, there was more than *one* law. In fact, in each region, and sometimes in each village, the "law" consisted of a plethora of overlapping and highly inequitable obligations and privileges, many of them binding whole groups or communities, generation after generation.

The Social Hierarchies of the Old Regimes

These laws, critically, held in place the basic social structure of the Old Regimes, which resembled a pyramid, with the monarch on the top, followed by society's three "estates," or status groups. The first estate was the clergy, the second was the nobility, and the third estate comprised all those who lacked the special privileges of the other two groups. Some countries did not follow this pattern exactly. The English, for example, beheaded their would-be absolutist monarch, and had an unusually large class of

What were the obligations and privileges of the king and the clergy under the Old Regimes?

The Royal Hunt During the period of the Old Regimes, kings and other aristocrats spent lavishly on dogs, horses, guns, and other accessories to be used in the hunt, a pastime that, since the medieval period, symbolized the noble status of the participants.

"gentlemen" who owned land and could vote, but did not have the same sorts of noble privileges held by French or Prussian aristocrats. The Dutch had no king, but rather a *stadtholder,* who oversaw national defense during wartime. But even these states possessed social hierarchies comparable, in some respects, to those deeply ingrained in the absolutist states.

The Monarch

At the top of the Old Regimes' social hierarchy was the monarch. To be a monarch meant to be the sole ruler of a state, usually by hereditary right, and as we saw in Chapter 14, the monarchs of this era definitely believed that as God's earthly representatives it was their job to wield power and display majesty as they alone saw fit.

In many respects, the period between 1600 and 1789 was the best time in European history to be a king or queen. Although most monarchs spent the era struggling continuously—and sometimes violently—with their nobles in the hopes of centralizing and modernizing their states, many enjoyed unprecedented wealth, bodily comforts, cultural enrichment, deference, and power. Having absolute power meant that monarchs could do virtually anything they dared—they *were* the law, after all, though they were in principle restrained by God's commandments and in practice restrained by what their nobles and the clergy deemed tolerable. Some, like the Russian czars, frequently disregarded existing contracts and used

violence regularly to put down peasant uprisings or stifle their opponents. Others, like the English monarchs after James II, used violence sparingly and generally honored legal agreements. Monarchs could raise taxes as long as their nobles were willing either to pay or to allow the king's tax collectors to operate in their regions. Rulers could declare wars and insist that their subjects fund and fight them, for as long as the king wished to fight and as long as the money and men held out. Though they were supposed to provide moral leadership, monarchs often took lovers and sired—as did Charles II of England—numerous illegitimate children.

Kings and queens could get away with strange behavior. Queen Christina of Sweden, the daughter of Gustavus Adolphus II, developed a passion for art and learning and a distaste for governance. She locked herself in her rooms for three years before abdicating and fleeing Sweden—dressed as a man—for Rome. There she converted to Catholicism and attempted first to make herself the queen of Naples and then the queen of Poland. Philip V of Spain suffered bouts of depression during which he refused to leave his bed and lay in his own excrement for days. King George III of England endured fits of madness in which he spoke to trees.

THE KING AT WORK—AND AT PLAY. Although some monarchs of the period were mentally ill, incompetent, or inattentive, other rulers of the era took guiding the state as their somber duty. Louis XIV interested himself in all aspects of the governance of France and worked extremely hard. So did Maria Theresa of Austria and Frederick the Great of Prussia, who prided himself on never taking a vacation. In an era that saw the building up of modern armies, bureaucracies, and commercial economies, those rulers who did not work hard often inflicted long-term harm on their states.

But it was also the job of the king to play. Monarchs had to show that they lived nobly, and they had to exhibit their refined taste and power of patronage to Europe's other rulers. They established academies of art and of the sciences; they hired painters to decorate their palaces; and they brought intellectuals and skilled artisans to their courts to write histories, to forge fabulous pieces of armor, to bake elaborate pastries, and to explain the latest scientific discoveries. They established theaters, organized concerts, and sponsored extravagant balls. But their favorite, and most meaningful, pastime was an activity that today seems completely irrelevant to governance: the hunt.

THE HUNT. Monarchs certainly had business to conduct. They received all manner of petitions from their subjects, served as the highest court of appeal, and doled out favors and offices. But the typical European monarch of this period spent a great deal less effort in running his or her kingdom than in pursuing its wildlife. The period between 1648 and 1789 was the great era of the royal hunt, in which sovereigns spent vast quantities of time and treasure on specially bred falcons, horses, and hounds, not to mention on gamekeepers and hunting lodges. In his later years, Louis XIV hunted as many as 140 days per year; Louis XV hunted at least 3 days per week; and Louis XVI, despite growing turmoil in his kingdom, hunted every other day. Virtually any animal was fair game, including wolves, hares, herons and other large birds, wild boar, and foxes. But stag hunting remained the most prestigious. The antlered male deer had long been rumored to have semimagical qualities, to retain eternal youth, and to possess remarkable sexual powers; to kill one was to achieve a symbolic victory over the "king of the forest." Monarchs set aside huge tracts of land with specially cut roads and devised elaborate procedures for stag hunting. At the feasts that followed the hunt, cooks worked up hundreds of recipes for venison to show off the king's conquest over nature.

Other blood sports were also popular with monarchs and their courts. The Prussians and Saxons perfected fox tossing, in which the gamekeeper placed a fox in the center of a blanket, and courtiers holding the blanket's edges tossed the fox until it died. Hares, badgers, and even wildcats were also tossed. Horseracing and cockfighting were also popular. The breeding of animals for hunting, racing, and fighting gave Europeans practical experience in genetics and produced a market for purebred animals, particularly horses and hounds.[2]

BEING KING HAS ITS DOWNSIDES. Being a monarch certainly beat occupying every other position in early modern society, but the post came with its own duties and dangers. Most European monarchs had no choice in their marriage partners; often they were engaged from childhood to the son or daughter of another royal household. Engagements were based not on compatibility— even in religion—but purely on the basis of the state's diplomatic imperatives. Many a Habsburg married a near relation to keep power in the family. For example, at age fifteen, Margaret Theresa, princess of Spain, was married to her uncle and cousin Leopold I, the Holy Roman emperor. It was pure accident that the couple got along. Monarchs also had to spend their lives in the public eye. Louis XIV made his levée, or getting out of bed, into an elaborate ritual, attended by a hundred or more of his courtiers. Sometimes the rumor mill accused kings and queens of terrible things: in the 1750s, rumors flew that Louis XV was having Parisian children kidnapped and murdered so that he could bathe his gouty toes in their blood. And occasionally monarchs were themselves murdered, as were Charles I, Czar Peter III, and eventually Louis XVI.

THE MONARCH AND THE CHURCHES. One way absolute monarchs could make themselves unpopular with some of their subjects was to interfere in the religious policies of their states. Sometimes monarchs acted subtly by appointing bishops and other high clergymen whose ideas they favored. At other times their interference might be more drastic, such as expelling religious dissenters from their realms, as did Louis XVI in 1685. As time went on, monarchs began inviting religious groups that were unwelcome elsewhere to live in their domains. They had learned from the Dutch that dissenters were often highly skilled and hard-working individuals who could make important economic contributions to their new homes. Modernizing monarchs also increasingly sought to close monasteries where more praying than efficient working went on, and to limit the number of religious holidays, during which time their tax-paying subjects feasted rather than labored in the fields and workshops. In moving toward secular state control of institutions and in liberalizing religious policy, Europe's eighteenth-century monarchs increasingly came into conflict with the first estate, the clergy, whose traditional job was to attend to the nation's spiritual welfare.

The First Estate: Church and Clergy

Members of the European clergy belonged to a privileged elite, set apart from the laity by having officially taken religious orders or having been ordained as priests or ministers. Ordained clergy members—whether Lutheran, Calvinist, Catholic, Eastern Orthodox, or Jewish—formed a small minority of the population, probably no more than 1–2 percent in most places, though in some areas there were many more monks and nuns. Those clerics who shared the faith of the ruler were exempted from most taxes and were for the most part subject to their own laws, which meant that churches had to act themselves to root out corrupt priests or monks who kept concubines. Higher clerics had frequent access to and sometimes powerful influence over monarchs, especially in the seventeenth century, and played an important role in schooling, cultural patronage, and censorship.

Most countries had an established church, which meant that the king and all his subjects officially belonged to that church and were bound to support it by tithing or paying other taxes. Officially, the Peace of Westphalia obliged those who had signed it to allow members of Christian sects other than the established ones to live in peace, but in practice dissenters or nonconformists as well as Jews faced a battery of discriminatory practices, including additional taxes. They were also obliged to practice their faiths only in private and, for the most part, were barred from serving in the army or in consultative assemblies.

In return for their privileges, clergy members were supposed to pray for the king and his people. As in the past, the care of souls was their principal work, but just as the churches were much more than spiritual institutions, so too were the lives of clergy members in the era shaped by the political and economic changes going on in the wider society.

Lavish Lifestyles of the Higher Clergy As this engraving of Cardinal Mazarin suggests, many high-ranking members of the clergy lived in their own palaces, surrounded by extensive collections of books, sculptures, and scientific instruments. Mazarin, like many others, was a notable patron of the arts and sciences.

LIVING THE CLERICAL LIFE. All of early modern society was structured hierarchically and according to birth. Clerics were no exception—though occasionally men of lower birth could rise to positions of some wealth and influence. At the top of the Catholic hierarchy were men of aristocratic lineage, who enjoyed enormous incomes; a few noble women enjoyed comfortable lives as abbesses. At the bottom of the first estate were priests posted to small villages and impoverished widows who took religious orders as a means to avoid starvation. Those who were accepted into orders usually did not starve, and generally the church taught them to read. But they did not rise dramatically in society.

In the seventeenth century, those at the top of the first estate enjoyed a considerable amount of influence. Archbishop Laud in England and Cardinal Richelieu in France, for example, held positions of great political power. The clergy's political clout tended to diminish over time, as monarchs increasingly turned to secular bureaucrats to help them run their states. Though many kings and queens succeeded in appropriating some of their lands and income, on the whole churches in the period 1600–1789 enjoyed considerable economic prosperity. Most established churches were permitted to collect a **tithe,** that is, a 10 percent tax on income. Sometimes the tithe

was paid in kind, sometimes in cash, and some payments turned out to be more than 10 percent. Churches also collected rent from land they owned, which amounted to a large share of European property as a whole. In Bavaria, the church owned as much as 30 percent of the land. Church holdings were worked by monks and nuns, or by peasants under seigneurial obligations to the clergy. In eastern Europe, churches owned serfs. Extracting tithes and rents did not endear the clergy to the people, especially during years of poor harvests, and after reformers began to complain about the luxurious lifestyles of the higher clergy members. The lower clerics too had cause to complain, given that much of the church's income was not redistributed fairly to cover their needs.

The large number of magnificent sanctuaries and monasteries built throughout Europe during the period demonstrate both the cultural and the economic power of the first estate. Representative examples are the late Baroque cathedral of St. Gallen, Switzerland, or the monastery-palace at Mafra, Portugal. The churches patronized painters, architects, and musicians of the first quality, and many clergymen could afford lavish robes and jewel-studded chalices, reliquaries, and bibles. Churches also supplied charity to the sick, the indigent, and the orphaned and provided social services, such as baptism, marriage, and burial, for people of every rank.

The clergy's main job was to ensure that parishioners performed their religious duties. In the decades before the 1750s, parishioners typically fulfilled their obligations to attend mass; they also participated in scores of processions to honor the saints, to mourn the dead, or to visit local shrines. But they did not necessarily perform these duties with the seriousness the clergy tried to promote. One frustrated village priest in central France reported: "All sorts of people who attend the service out of habit or decency—the drunken, the non-devout, the lazy—position themselves behind the [baptismal] fonts, lean against them, or use them as cover so they can talk during the divine service."[3] The duty to hold people to their religious obligations grew more challenging over time, as urban and secular entertainments multiplied and the fear of persecution or damnation waned. By the later eighteenth century, many men were not attending services with any regularity, prompting considerable alarm among the clergy. Women continued to attend and were particularly inspired by some of the period's reformist movements, which emphasized individual piety and the doing of charitable deeds.

CHALLENGES FROM WITHIN. Perhaps the greatest challenge for the clergy in this era came from within the churches. In the eighteenth century in particular, several sects arose within the established churches, among them Methodism in England, Pietism in some northern German states, and Jansenism in France. Religious reform was the goal of each of these sects; all wanted to involve the individual believer more directly and emotionally in the church services.

John Wesley (1702–1791), the English founder of **Methodism,** believed that the Anglican Church of England was neglecting the poor and failing to speak directly to ordinary sinners. He advocated the use of nonordained, lay preachers to spread Christ's message, and he promoted the conducting of open-air services for those who were not moved by learned sermons delivered in stuffy churches. The Anglicans protested, and Wesley, not wanting to make a full break with the church in which his father and brother were priests, compromised. Methodist pastors, too, were to be ordained members of the Church of England—but the church could not deny Wesley's insistence that going out to the people had sparked mass religious revival, not only in England but in the American colonies as well.

Pietism in the German-speaking states and **Jansenism** in France, too, emphasized the need for more personal and active forms of faith among members of the established church. These movements continued to grow over the eighteenth century, involving increasing numbers of aristocrats and well-off members of the third estate. Viewing Jansenism as a threat to the king's ability to dictate religious policy, Louis XIV and Louis XV both tried to stamp out the movement, but discovered that too many of their influential subjects had already accepted reformist ideas. The clergy, too, had to learn to live with at least some degree of internal dissent.

Despite these challenges, the clergy continued to play a central role in the spiritual and cultural lives of Europeans. The cycle of church festivals—from Christmas and Epiphany through Easter and Pentecost—still structured most people's calendars, and the clergy was needed to maintain the long-standing customs and culture of most Europeans. In eastern and southern Europe, Russian, Greek, and Serbian Orthodox prelates remained key members of their societies, often serving as political and cultural as well as spiritual leaders. In Europe's Jewish communities, rabbis were vital as teachers and as spokesmen for the community. If this was a good time to be a king, it was also a good time to be a member of the higher clergy.

The Second Estate: The Nobility

To be a noble in this era meant that one was a member of a noble family; at some point in the past, one's ancestors had been granted legal privileges that set one apart from the rest. Nobles had the legal right to be called by their titles, such as the duke of Bedford or the marquis de Sade, and to pass their titles and their estates down to their heirs. They could carry swords, a reminder that their main duty, from medieval times, had been to fight for the king. To be a noble did not necessarily mean that one was rich or powerful, although some, such as the Russian Sheremetevs, were; by the later eighteenth century, this family owned nearly two million acres of land and approximately a million serfs. Other nobles were so poor that they had to till their own land. Their privileges, inscribed in legal documents or patents, gave them a variety of rights, including, for many, exemption from taxes; some jobs, military offices, and special schools were reserved for them alone. Depending on his patent, a noble could insist on being seated in the church's front pews or on standing near the king at court (how near depended on how old and important a title one held), or he could force his peasants to "beat the woods" to flush out animals for his hunt.

To be a noble entailed obligations as well as privileges. Some larger landowners owned villages or towns, and acted as the only employer for the whole region. Even landowners who spent most of their time in their city houses in London or Vienna were expected to serve in some way as "fathers" to the "little people." Some were responsible and decent "fathers" who fed the "little people" in times of dearth; others ruthlessly foreclosed on peasants behind on their rents. Nobles were often obliged to carry out the king's business, to draft labor to build his roads, to find soldiers to fill his army, to collect taxes to fill his coffers. Their peasants expected them to provide protection from foreign invaders, to give them work to do, and to provide them sustenance in times of want. Nobles were expected always to behave nobly and to protect their family's honor. Because labor was considered incompatible with elevated social status, nobles were expected not to work—and especially not to work with their hands. In some cases, nobles were forbidden from engaging in trade, and although absolutist monarchs gradually

The Symphonies of Joseph Haydn and the Patronage of Nicholas Esterhazy

Austrian-born Joseph Haydn was, legally speaking, a nobody. The son of a wheelwright, he had shown early talent as a singer and then landed a job as a court composer with a Bohemian nobleman, but when the nobleman died, Haydn was dismissed. Fortunately for him—and for the history of music—in 1761 he obtained a position with the Hungarian nobleman Nicholas Esterhazy at his sumptuous "Hungarian Versailles," Eszterháza.[4] The Esterhazy family was one of the richest in Hungary and one of the most noble: members of the family had served as military leaders in the Habsburgs' many wars with the Ottoman Turks in the seventeenth century and had been rewarded with land and titles as the Ottomans withdrew from the Hungarian plain. Although the Esterhazys had numerous palaces, Eszterháza was Nicholas's favorite, and he furnished its 120 rooms with tapestries, indoor fountains, and crystal chandeliers. The grounds included an opera house, a game preserve, and a lavish puppet-house, whose scenery could be changed more than thirty times during a performance. To operate such a huge estate and show it off to his many guests, Nicholas hired a vast number of servants, lawyers, artisans, security guards, cooks, tax collectors, and musicians. As music master at Eszterháza, Haydn was a servant, and like other house servants, he wore a uniform that marked him as an employee of the house of Esterhazy. He was not quite the prisoner Johann Böttger became, but neither was he free to compose on his own: when Prince Esterhazy wanted music, it was Haydn's job to supply it, whenever and in whatever form the prince desired.

Haydn worked very hard at Eszterháza; he composed music—including more than ninety symphonies—for an endless stream of birthdays, fireworks celebrations, balls, and semipublic concerts. He rehearsed the Esterhazy's huge contingent of musicians and conducted performances nearly every day. To please the prince, he composed all manner of musical pieces, including chamber music, sonatas, dances, and piano variations. The prince was very lucky to have such an industrious and talented court composer. By the same token, Haydn was fortunate to work for a prince who could afford a large orchestra. Had he been forced to take a job as a church organist, Haydn probably would not have been able to experiment with the symphonic sound he achieved in pieces such as his Mourning Symphony no. 44. Haydn's connection with the Esterhazys also granted him entrance into the Viennese music scene, where he met and inspired the younger Wolfgang Amadeus Mozart.

Haydn's fame spread across Europe, but still he continued to wear the uniform that marked him as a servant of the prince. When Prince Nicholas died in 1790, Haydn was rewarded with a handsome pension. He then made his way to England, where he was free to compose and to market his services to the highest bidder, but he eventually returned to the more secure world of Esterhazy patronage. The story of Haydn and of Eszterháza reminds us that even the musical compositions of this era owed much to the social circumstances in which they were created. In their richness as well as in their number, Haydn's symphonies preserve aspects of the noble life that today everyone can enjoy.

QUESTION | *How might Haydn's music have been different if he had been employed by the church rather than by the Esterhazy family?*

Joseph Haydn, Employee Here Joseph Haydn, left, conducts an orchestra of uniform-wearing musicians during a performance of his opera *The Unexpected Encounter* at the Esterhazy family's estate at Eszterháza in 1775. The opera was written and staged in honor of the visit of a high-ranking member of the Habsburg family.

did away with those prohibitions, many nobles continued to think of commerce as a dirty business, suitably only for grossly ambitious commoners. The "noble" response to an insult to one's family was to challenge the offender to a duel. Although monarchs across Europe tried to outlaw dueling, thousands of these confrontations occurred every year, even into the nineteenth century.

Nobles derived their income and status chiefly from land and from the people who worked for them; the larger the number of servants and peasants dependent on the lord, the more impressive and self-sufficient the estate. Some grand seigneurs employed hundreds or even thousands of workers on their estates: gardeners, butlers, stable boys, and scullery maids, as well as higher-level employees such as doctors, musicians, and estate overseers. But over time, money became more and more necessary to demonstrate one's status. In fact, kings themselves increasingly sold noble titles to rich commoners, a practice that infuriated the established nobility. Gradually, nobles began to convert their property and obligations owed them into cash, which they could use to buy luxury goods they could not produce on their estates, such as lace and porcelain dinnerware, and any number of other showy appurtenances, including horses, hounds, carriages, opera boxes, brocade dresses, wigs, and jewelry. They wasted huge sums on frivolous—but flashy—entertainments. At a dinner given by Count Brühl of Saxony in 1746 the table groaned under the weight of an eight-foot-tall replica of the fountain in Rome's Piazza Navona, which sprayed real rose-water. But some of the nobility's expenditures, too, went into cultural products of long-lasting beauty and value.

By the mid-eighteenth century, many of even the wealthiest nobles were in debt, and took to borrowing money even from their own employees, some of whom looked upon these interest-bearing loans as good investments. At a time when commoners were regularly imprisoned for debts, nobles—like monarchs—were able to spend far beyond their means. Bankruptcy might force a noble family to sell its jewels or marry daughters to rich commoners, but its privileges were inalienable and remained intact.

Even in absolutist states, nobles were not without a voice, and they complained loudly about real or suspected infringements upon their privileges. Under Louis XIV, French nobles with older titles complained about the selling of offices to rich commoners, but by the middle of the eighteenth century, high and lucrative positions in the military and bureaucracy were even more dominated by nobles than they had been a half-century earlier, even though nobles made up only 1 percent of the population of France. In Prussia, Frederick the Great reversed his father's policy of promoting commoners and instead appointed nobles to administrative jobs and military posts. Conditions were somewhat different in England. There were so few English lords (only 145 "peers of the realm" sat in the House of Lords in 1685, at a time when England's population was nearing five million inhabitants) that they could not possibly dominate all the po-

sitions. Thus, lower-ranking gentlemen found more opportunities to gain positions of influence. But even in England, the privileged few—less than 5 percent of the population—monopolized power throughout the eighteenth century. Although they complained about the Old Regimes, the nobility, like the clergy, would in the end be very sorry to see them go.

If the nobility made up less than 5 percent and the clergy just 1–2 percent of the population of Europe's states, that left the vast majority of Europeans in the unprivileged class, or the third estate. Though united by its common lack of privileges, the third estate was even more diverse in its occupations and obligations than the other two.

The Third Estate: Nothing and Everything

In 1789, the clergyman Emmanuel-Joseph Sieyès published an important pamphlet which posed the following questions:

> What is the Third Estate? Everything.
> What has it been up to now in the political order? Nothing.
> What does it want? To be something.

Sieyès was arguing that this order of persons—who did virtually all the work of the kingdom and yet had no special privileges—was nothing in the eyes of the king and the law. Strictly speaking this was not true. Some artisans, for example, had privileges to produce certain goods, and even peasants could sue if their traditional rights were infringed (though the chances that they would win were slim). Furthermore, this nonprivileged group contained myriad different types, from sharecropping Italian peasants to wealthy German master goldsmiths, from destitute Polish widows to rich (but untitled) French wine merchants. Local laws and customs protected some of these people; others lived or died at the pleasure of their seigneurs. What all had in common was that the privileged classes could *legally* command them to do things. As long as the privileged did not exceed their patents, members of the third estate could do nothing about it.

TAXPAYERS WITHOUT A VOICE. Above all, as Sieyès underscored, the third estate comprised the nations' taxpayers. Insofar as this diverse group had a set of common complaints, those complaints were generally about the unfair tax burden they were compelled to bear. Taxes and tolls in the Old Regimes came in a dizzying array, from the hated taxes on salt to taxes on land, tobacco, and wine; some countries taxed houses by the number of windows or chimneys. The tithe paid to the church was a kind of tax, extracted in some cases by professional tithe-lords; so too were road or bridge tolls and duties on glass or paper. The taxes were used to build up the army; to pay for the king's palaces, hunts, and mistresses; and, sometimes, to pay for the improvement of public thoroughfares or buildings in the towns (see Back to the Source at the end of the chapter).

In France, the nobility, clergy, and many city dwellers were exempt from the *taille,* the basic tax on land assessed by the king. The king decided how much he wanted and then divided this amount into provincial chunks. Tax farmers, a much hated breed of royal official, told villages how much they had to pay. Individuals who could not pay were imprisoned, and richer peasants or villagers had to make up the difference. Other countries had slightly different systems, but nowhere, with the partial exception of England and the Dutch Republic, did the third estate at home or the colonized subjects abroad have any voice in or vote on the levying or manner of collecting taxes. During the eighteenth century, as warfare and bureaucracies grew more and more costly, the tax burden on the third estate increased, squeezing those already at subsistence level even further and making the better-off resentful. Whereas the first and second estates could pressure the king to reduce their taxes or could themselves raise their rates, the third estate and the colonized continued to suffer taxation without representation.

The Third Estate at Work This painting depicts a busy day of commercial activity at the port of Marseilles in southern France. Note the diversity of the crowd, and of the products being loaded and unloaded from ships and mules; at center right a nobleman is carried through the area in a litter.

TOWNS AND TOWNSPEOPLE. Early modern cities and towns often had privileges and traditions of their own, and the minority of Europeans who inhabited them had quite different lives than those living on the land. On the whole, towns were dirty and dangerous, and life expectancy in them was often lower than it was in the countryside. But they also offered diversions and opportunities not available to those living on the land, and after about 1715, they began to attract new inhabitants, and to grow appreciably in size.

In 1600, Europe's towns and cities were uncomfortable and often hazardous places to live. All were overcrowded and most of them stank, especially in summer. Chamber pots were emptied from open windows; rats, pigs, and dogs lived and died in often unpaved streets. Most cities were walled, to allow for easier defense—and the taxation of goods entering the city's gates—but the walls also made the cities within death-traps when they were besieged or overrun by invaders. In some central European and Italian cities, walled sections known as ghettoes were reserved for Jews, who were locked in at night and on Christian holidays. The mostly wooden buildings were always in danger of fire. A huge conflagration destroyed most of central London in 1666, only a year after the city had been visited, once again, by the plague. Infectious diseases, including cholera and typhus, struck cities especially hard. Merchants and tradesmen inhabited the towns, but so did people escaping from one or another form of persecution, such as religious dissenters, debtors, or runaway serfs who—according to tradition—were entitled to their freedom if they managed to survive a year and a day in the town. Other residents included widows, orphans, prostitutes, and drunks seeking charity from passersby, or quietly starving to death in the streets.

After 1715 the sieges, sackings, and epidemics of the plague that made the towns so dangerous in the seventeenth century became less frequent, and towns began to prosper and to attract opportunity-seeking new residents. Some came for what the Puritans called "ungodly" entertainments, such as the theaters, where aristocrats might rub shoulders with pickpockets, whores, and street rowdies. The number of pubs in seventeenth-century London topped a thousand and the number of brothels probably followed close behind. Street entertainment in Paris included tooth-pulling and the singing of bawdy ballads about figures at court. But a more important draw than the diversions were the opportunities that burgeoning towns and cities offered for people hoping to make or remake themselves. Townspeople tended to be less heavily taxed than peasant farmers, and social hierarchies were not so fixed. There were new jobs to be had on the docks in Liverpool, Marseilles, and Amsterdam, or in the expanding number of workshops, where the artisans were the kings.

ARTISANS. Among those who thrived in the towns were the artisans, members of the third estate who developed a hierarchical system of their own, ranging from lowly apprentices—like the young Johann Böttger—to more experienced journeymen, and, at the pinnacle, the masters. An artisan was not just any worker but rather a skilled laborer, whose aptitude was certified by induction into a guild. The guilds were organizations of laborers who contracted with towns or cities to produce certain commodities, such as shoes or cutlery; by law, the guild members then monopolized that trade. Only members of the cobblers' guild of Erfurt, for example, could produce shoes for that German town. To join a guild, a craftsman had to serve as an unpaid apprentice with a master craftsman for a certain amount of time, then work as a journeyman, moving from master to master and learning each one's techniques, which were often considered trade secrets. The journeyman then had to produce a masterpiece of his own—an elaborate saddle, for example, to join the saddlers' guild—and pay a large fee. If accepted into the guild by the other members, he too became a master and could legally ply his trade and employ apprentices in his turn. In some places, women could belong to guilds, but they were increas-

ingly pushed out by men eager to monopolize the relatively high wages and unwilling to serve apprenticeships under female masters.

In the early modern era, Europe teemed with guilds; there were guilds for tailors, bakers, paper makers, silk weavers, and apothecaries, among many others. Some guilds were large: for example, an estimated 945 credentialed wigmakers were operating in Paris in 1770.[5] A small town, by contrast, might have only a handful of licensed guildsmen. The guilds constricted the labor market and tried to keep their secrets—such as how to make paper from rags or how to weave silk brocade—from passing into the hands of non–guild members. But the guilds endured, as they benefited both the towns and the laborers. For the towns, contracting with the guilds provided some sort of quality control in the production of goods. For guildsmen, the system guaranteed decent wages and low competition, and the guild itself served as a sort of social club and even a primitive lobbying organization.

THE URBAN POOR. Towns housed many people besides guild members. There were day laborers, many of whom resented the guilds' monopolization of the higher-paying jobs. Early modern towns also teemed with homeless, poor people, who made up as much as one-quarter of the population of Paris, Cologne, and Berlin. London had fewer, proportionally, but still about one-eighth in 1796. The poor depended on charity, chiefly from churches, though some Dutch cities set up workhouses for them, where debtors, drunks, petty thieves, and prostitutes were sent to do menial labor until they had proved themselves productive members of society. Though some of Europe's urban poor might have worked up from destitution to more comfortable lives, many, probably most, did not. Even as towns were becoming increasingly dynamic places, they continued to be places of suffering for those on the lower end of the social scale.

SERFS AND PEASANTS. Though the urban population swelled in the eighteenth century, before (and long after) 1789, the vast majority of Europeans were rural farmers. Just as with town dwellers, there was diversity in this group. Some peasants owned or rented relatively large and prosperous plots of land, or supplemented their farming income with some kind of trade or lucrative local office. Other peasants were bound by ancient contracts to perform various services for the lord and depended on him for subsistence; either side could buy out or renegotiate these contracts, though doing so was harder for the peasants than for the lord. If a peasant's eldest son took over his father's land, the other children could move or take up other professions—*if* that is, they could afford to purchase land elsewhere or obtain proper training.

Serfs differed from peasants by being bound to the land, not to the landowner. They and their families were obliged to till this land and not allowed to move; those who attempted to escape were caught and returned. Although **serfdom** had, for the most part, been tempered and

An Unusual Guild Artisans fashioned all sorts of products in their workshops, including church bells. Note that although women had been pushed out of many artisanal guilds by the mid-eighteenth century, in this shop, women are performing the prestigious craft of bell making.

MAP 15.1 | Europe, c. 1721

The second serfdom affected Europe east of Vienna, where states were larger and the agricultural and commercial revolutions took hold much later. **Which regions of Europe were positioned to take advantage of the development of Atlantic trade?**

transformed in western Europe in the later Middle Ages, the practice continued in eastern Europe (Map 15.1). In fact, in the sixteenth and seventeenth centuries, landowners sought to increase their control over their serfs, in order to produce more grain at a time of rising food prices. Thus, serfs in Poland-Lithuania, Russia, Hungary, and other eastern lands were made to stay on their lands and to work even more days for the lord. When the state seized church lands, and with them, the churches' serfs, it sold the serfs to nobles, who obtained even greater power over these laborers. Known as the **second serfdom,** this reinforcement of the medieval economic order in eastern European deprived serfs of even the modest set of choices available to western peasants and slowed down the East's development of market-oriented production and urban commerce.

Throughout the seventeenth and eighteenth centuries, the poorest peasants and serfs faced the perpetual danger of starvation. Rising food prices meant that they ate less meat and more bread or gruel than their high medieval ancestors. Even in years of good harvests, most peasants consumed a limited array of foods, virtually all of which were grown nearby. Many drank more beer and wine than fresh water; fermented drinks were less likely to make one sick than stagnant well-water. When bad weather damaged the harvest, peasants suffered. Poor relief was spotty; seigneurs were greedy or strapped themselves. Even when the central state cared enough to wish to feed the hungry, the poor condition of the roads and the high cost of transport made sending grain to famine-stricken areas virtually impossible. The introduction of the hardy and nourishing potato was the best thing that happened to many German and Irish peasants in the eighteenth century, but as the nineteenth century showed, potato crops too could fail and leave their cultivators to starve.

Given the number of wars, famines, and epidemics of the seventeenth century, life expectancy remained low, generally about thirty-two years, though a person who made it to age twenty-one might live to be sixty. Around 1750, life expectancies began to lengthen, and the death rate among children began to fall, producing something of a population boom by 1800. Many factors accounted for the population increase, including the disappearance of the plague in western, though not central, Europe as well as advances in commerce and science that contributed to rising wealth and longevity. Better medicine was not the cause of the population boom. In spite of advances in understanding the human body, trained doctors were few and people continued to credit old-fashioned cures like eating stewed owls to cure toothache or shaving one's head and strapping pig's eyes to it to treat forgetfulness.

Peasants' lives differed greatly, depending on where they lived. Generally, peasants in northern and western Europe had more rights and resources than those in the east and south. Workers on estates in Spain and central Italy, for example, were essentially still serfs, whereas peasants in England, the Dutch Republic, and the western German states could move freely and owed few, if any, seigneurial dues. In France, peasants typically could move or marry, but owed fees and labor of various sorts to their lords; the *corvée*, for example, obliged many to build roads when and where the seigneur wanted them built. There were also free peasants, who owned their own land, some of them at least moderately prosperous.

Eastern serfs, on the other hand, were typically bound by the *robot*, the duty to work the lord's land for several days a week. They often had to pay fees to finance the lord's wedding or funeral; serfs in Hungary might have to pay to ransom the lord from Turkish captivity. Landowners could force serfs to marry or could order whippings, and in some cases, they had the right to impose the death penalty. Serfs could be sent to serve in the army, where the death rate was notoriously high. In Russia, even "free" peasants were bound by the decisions of the village commune, which saw that land was parceled out equally—but its restrictions discouraged individual initiative and kept all more or less equally poor.

REVOLTS AND RESISTANCE. Peasants had some ability to resist their betters. Some had ancient legal contracts on the basis of which they could, and often did, sue. There were also regular peasant uprisings, most of them small and short lived, but some, like the revolts that shook Russia in the 1760s and 1770s, were far more threatening. In these years, serfs responded angrily to Czarina Catherine II's deepening of the second serfdom. The most serious of the uprisings was the one led by former soldier Emelyan Pugachev. In 1773, Catherine promised Pugachev's followers freedom from serfdom, taxation, and conscription; he offered land, food, and arms to those who would support him. Tens of thousands of serfs and nomadic tribesmen did, and for a year Pugachev's army looted, tortured, and murdered nearly three thou-

Emelyan Pugachev, Serf Rebel In 1773–1774, Pugachev incited tens of thousands of serfs to revolt against Czarina Catherine the Great and other great landowners. This image depicts him in the metal cage in which he was sent to Moscow, where he was publicly beheaded.

sand landowners, clergymen, and officials across a wide area of the Don River basin. Imperial troops finally put down the revolt and beheaded Pugachev, but the memory of this attempt to overthrow Russian absolutism and the serf-driven economy on which it was built continued to terrify landowners and officials for generations.

Peasant uprisings were usually occasioned by rising bread prices or poor harvests, or by the landowners' attempts to introduce new taxes or work rules. Often the revolts did cause the lords to provide more bread or to back off on new rules, but the uprisings did not result in any wide-ranging reforms or abolition of preexisting contracts. A more successful form of resistance lay in pretense: peasants pretended not to have heard of new requirements or taxes, or engaged in foot-dragging when compelled to work for the master rather than for themselves. Peasants expended no great effort to perform their compulsory *robot* labor; they would show up for duty late, having exhausted themselves and their animals tilling their own plots first. They would drag out their jobs as much as possible, or send to work the weakest animals and members of the workforce, causing frustrated estate managers to resort to the whip in order to make the *robots* even slightly productive. For serfs bound to the land, these were the only options; for those who could move, however, there was another choice: hitting the road.

LIVING ON THE ROAD. When times grew tough on the farm, peasants not bound to the land often took to the road to sell their labor elsewhere. France teemed with migrant laborers who made yearly trips from poor mountain regions in the Pyrenees to central France, for example, to aid in the harvest. Joining them on the road were an increasing number of well-heeled travelers, tradesmen, and private postmen; dissenters displaced by religious persecution; and debtors, draft dodgers, and criminals fleeing the law. Already strapped communities feared opening their doors to more indigent people, so towns often passed laws allowing townspeople to whip vagrants and to lock beggars in the stocks. Some migrants who had begun as honest laborers turned to banditry as a last resort, making traveling the good roads even more dangerous than sailing the pirate-infested Mediterranean. Highwaymen such as Dick Turpin, who committed a spate of robberies on the roads radiating outward from London in the 1730s, became legendary figures, heroes to the little people who didn't mind seeing the rich deprived of their goods.

Many of the folktales of the period involve individuals taking to the road to seek their fortunes or to escape some terrible fate at home. Not surprisingly, they faced new dangers in their travels. The stories often portray the dangers as magical ones: giants, witches, and talking animals. In reality, the road's dangers were more prosaic: starvation, wild animals, or officials, who delighted in displaying captured highwaymen's heads on pikes planted along the very roadsides where they had plied their trades. Petty thieves often received harsh punishments: floggings, branding, deportation, or impressment for naval service, which was frequently a delayed death sentence. Greater crimes, including inciting riot, armed robbery, and piracy, were punished by hanging, or some variety of death by torture, such as drawing and quartering, burning at the stake, or being broken on the wheel.

The lives of individuals in the Old Regimes' society of orders depended greatly on the accident of birth. Those who were born with privileges could usually live and travel in comfort; those who were not struggled to survive, whether in the towns, in the countryside, or on the road. The severe limitation of most individuals' options by this system of legalized inequalities made this world resistant to change. But in some places, quietly, deep transformations were under way.

A World of Quiet Revolutions

Even while contracts, traditions, and poverty maintained the social framework of the Old Regimes, several long-term

How did Europe's quiet revolutions disrupt the Old Regimes' society of orders?

transformations—revolutions, we may call them—in agriculture, proto-industrialization, commerce, and military organization—were quietly transforming this world.

The most basic and probably the most widely influential of these revolutions was the one under way on the land.

Revolutions in the Countryside

Locating and dating the beginning of what has been called Europe's agricultural revolution is difficult. It began first in smaller countries with large populations such as England and the Dutch Republic, when farmers beset by land shortages, soil exhaustion, low yields, and the destruction of fields by grazing livestock began to enclose their land with hedges or fences or to seek new crops to add to their traditional rotation. By the later seventeenth century, this process, known as enclosure, was well under way in England. Here prosperous landowners were able to obtain seats in the House of Commons and then pass legislation authorizing them to enclose what had once been "common" land. This meant, however, that peasants who had subsisted by pasturing animals or gathering wood on the commons were now forced from the land.

Enclosure was less frequent elsewhere, because neither peasants nor nobles were eager to modify traditional agreements, and wealthy landowners did not have sufficient political clout to pass legislation favorable to their interests. In Spanish-controlled central Italy, for example, powerful sheep owners retained the right to drive millions of animals over rich farmland every year, making enclosure impossible. To combat soil exhaustion, some farmers introduced nitrogen-restoring crops, such as peas, turnips, clover, or the potato. But here, too, change seemed frightening. Although reform-minded landowners and monarchs such as Frederick the Great trumpeted the virtues of calorie-rich potatoes, Russian, Italian, and French peasants refused to plant them, insisting that potatoes caused leprosy or cholera and, moreover, that they had not been mentioned in the Bible.

Even in the absence of enclosure or new crops, Europe's population began to grow. During the eighteenth century, the Habsburg Empire doubled in population, from 9 to 18 million, as did the German states (to 20 million); France's population rose from 18 to 26 million, making it the second largest state in Europe after Russia, with 44 million. European peasants and town dwellers began to divide and specialize their labor, and to work longer and harder. Rising populations meant that more hands could be spared to devote themselves to spinning and weaving at home or to selling vegetables or baked goods in the town square. Landholders tested out new crops when and where they were able and began to grow food to sell at market, rather than simply to consume on the farm. Workers increased their productivity so that they could buy the commodities made newly available by the revolution in commerce, including tea, cotton cloth, and sugar. Town dwellers in particular plowed money into tableware, increasingly made of ceramics rather than wood or pewter. Gradually, if they were able, rural dwellers began to accumulate material comforts as well. Over time, more and more Europeans—especially in western states—produced for the marketplace rather than solely for self-sufficiency. They purchased more, too—not only goods they needed, but also small luxuries for which they worked and saved.

PROTO-INDUSTRIALIZATION. The demand for small luxuries in turn fed the need for laborers to produce and sell them. As the eighteenth century opened, European towns, predominately in the north and west, began to teem with new shops and workshops, producing and selling things like buttons, saucepans, and silk ribbons. The goods most Europeans purchased were not the same as those produced for the very rich at court. The rich still wanted one-of-a-kind objects—goblets inlaid with pearls or paintings by Renaissance masters; the new consumers wanted goods that provided comfort and conveyed respectability. They were willing to buy cotton dresses, even if these did not last as long as garments made of wool, for they could be made to fit the latest fashion and were easier to wash. The finest porcelain, whether imported from China or made at home, remained out of their reach, but the richest members of the third estate in Dutch, English, Scottish, French, and some western German towns could

Enclosure's Lasting Imprint This twenty-first-century image from the Lake District in England illustrates the impact the enclosure movement made on the land. The stone walls standing here were built many centuries ago to demarcate private plots of land and to keep grazing animals from ruining neighbors' crops.

afford table settings of Delftware, the blue and white pottery from the Dutch town of Delft, or the durable crockery known as stoneware. Increasingly, households owned not just bedsteads and tables, but kitchen cupboards and bedroom dressers as well. Women purchased curtains, hats, and wallpaper, and men purchased wigs, watches, and military uniforms decorated in gold braid.

The production of these goods required more laborers than the guilds were able to provide, and labor specialization meant that workers did not need to be especially skilled to make some of these goods. We can call this development *proto-industrialization* because most of these workshops remained small and employed part-time manual laborers, not steam-powered machines, to produce their goods. Ironically, additional signs of the industrial revolution to come could also be found far from the towns and cities, in the peasant-populated countryside.

COTTAGE INDUSTRIES. Textiles, especially lighter-weight fabrics such as linen and cotton, were particularly important to the proto-industrializing world. As raw cotton began to reach England and the Dutch Republic, first from India and then from the southern United States, a new system of production developed that challenged the monopolies of the weavers' guilds. Known as the cottage system, this method began with merchants distributing raw cotton to workers outside guild-controlled cities. Rural or small town dwellers spun and wove the cotton, then returned the finished cloth to merchants who paid them by the piece. This system worked well especially for women weavers who could spin thread while watching children or in between other household tasks. Because female cottage weavers charged less for their labor than did the guildsmen, the cloth they made could be sold more cheaply and to a larger circle of consumers. Women also broke into the largely male-dominated tailoring trade in this period, especially with the appearance of new fashions for women, such as the mantua, a lightweight half-jacket usually made of colorful linen or cotton.

The proto-industrial revolution involved relatively little in the way of new mechanical devices. This was not the era of mass production of identical goods, and "factories," such as they were, remained small. Transporting larger or breakable commodities over long distances remained difficult, and in some places the guild system continued to function, preventing new producers from entering the marketplace. Thus, proto-industrialization was centered in England and the Dutch Republic, where distances were relatively short, urbanization most dense, and the agricultural revolution most advanced. On the whole, in central and southern Europe, cities were too few, distances too long, and capital too difficult to come

MAP 15.2 | European Colonization and Commerce, c. 1650–1740
This map shows the outposts established by western European states during the commercial revolution. As time passed, Atlantic trade, especially throughout the Caribbean Islands, grew increasingly profitable. **Which European nations were largely left out of this new trading system? Why?**

by for proto-industrialization to make much headway. But even in these places, the sumptuary laws that had once prohibited commoners from wearing gold, silks, or wigs had lapsed, and for those with access to some cash or credit, the array of choices expanded greatly between 1600 and 1789. This expansion of choice has everything to do with another, closely related, quiet revolution—this one in commerce.

The Commercial Revolution

If it is hard to date the agricultural revolution of the early modern era, fixing a starting moment for the commercial revolution is equally difficult. Europeans had been involved in overseas trade for millennia, from the ancient Greeks and Romans to the medieval Venetians in the Mediterranean. What made commercial developments after about 1600 revolutionary was not so much vast differences in the way trade was managed as it was the rising quantity of goods traded and the expanding power of the European nations that traded them (Map 15.2).

One of the most important preparatory developments for this commercial revolution was the shifting of the European economy's center of gravity from the Mediterranean to the Atlantic. Already in the sixteenth century, the Italian powerhouses of Genoa, Venice, and Milan were losing market share; the exports of these three states fell by more than 75 percent during the sev-

enteenth century. Ottoman trade through the Balkan and Mediterranean ports of Cairo and Smyrna was still flourishing. But the action was shifting to the north and west, as the English, French, and Dutch began establishing colonial outposts and enlarging their fleets. South American gold and silver had made the Spanish and Portuguese rich, but the colonial opportunities and financial innovations of the Dutch and English allowed them to take the leading role in the revolutionary developments of the seventeenth century.

NEW FORMS OF FINANCE. Among the difficulties faced by merchants in the early seventeenth century was the borrowing, banking, and exchanging of money. Although the Catholic Church had officially abolished the sin of usury (lending at interest) in 1517, making it a bit easier for Europeans to borrow money, many Europeans continued to look upon money-lending as sinful, and most nobles could not engage in the practice or risk losing their titles. In much of eastern Europe and in court circles, many lenders were Jews, who had long served as pseudo-bankers, which made them unpopular when hard times coincided with the due date for loans. In most of Europe, it remained nearly impossible for individuals outside of the privileged elite to obtain loans. The most peasants could hope for might be the delaying of tax payments or seigneurial dues, or the provision of small amounts of charity from their lords or from the churches when they faced starvation. If they earned more money than they needed at the moment, they had nowhere to keep it safely. Both merchants trading overseas and little people at home needed a bank.

Here the Dutch led the way, first by turning provinces and cities into proto-banks, into which investors could put money and receive a profit in return and from which smallholders could obtain loans to be used for draining land for farming, ship-building, or buying houses. People were in effect buying government debt, debt that rose precipitously as the wars of the seventeenth century ravaged the continent. In 1609, Dutch businessmen officially founded the Bank of Amsterdam. Like all successful early-modern banks, it was backed by the government, and for a long time, it offered the easiest credit and most secure deposits in all of Europe. Like the Bank of Amsterdam, the Bank of England (founded in 1694) profited by helping to finance warfare as well as trade. The English profited handsomely, for example, by financing Prussia's fight in the Seven Years' War.

The Stock Exchange, Amsterdam In this busy space, seventeenth-century Dutch traders sold shares in some of the first joint-stock companies, including the state-chartered Dutch East India Company.

The English and the Dutch also founded the first **chartered companies.** These were special companies chartered or protected by the state, in which investors could buy individual shares. The first of these were the English East India Company (founded in 1600) and the Dutch East India Company (founded in 1602). States chartered only one such company to trade in a designated part of the world (for example, England had only one Virginia Company and one West Africa Company), which gave these companies a monopoly on trade in those regions. State backing and monopoly privileges made it possible for chartered companies to offer limited liability, which meant that the investor risked only the amount he or she put into buying shares. The chartered company was one kind of joint-stock company—in which investors joined together to back a particular enterprise—and soon the public was being offered stocks of other kinds as well.

Stock markets popped up in Amsterdam, London, Paris, and Frankfurt. But trading on the early modern exchanges remained risky. Some Dutch investors lost their shirts in the tulip craze of 1636–1637, in which speculators drove up prices for tulip bulbs far beyond reason. A bigger crash on the French market occurred in 1720, when prices for colonial shares plummeted suddenly. This crash made French investors wary of state-backed initiatives, and in consequence the French did not found a national bank until much later. In response, some businesses arose to temper risk. In the eighteenth century, for example, Dutch and English firms offering marine insurance evolved, making it possible for investors to back sixteen-month trading trips to India or Indonesia without fear that one shipwreck would entail financial disaster.

Stock markets, banks, and marine insurance generated new capital for western European endeavors. In central Europe and Russia, where such institutions were missing, commerce developed more slowly. Governments here were slow to charter companies and did not back loans to the nonelite. Because most wealth was held in the form of land (which rarely changed hands), capital for new ventures was extremely hard to come by. This was the result, in part, of these nations' expansion over land, rather than overseas, and of the imposition of the second serfdom, which kept people and wealth tied to land. Over time, such institutions would evolve in the East, but their slow development highlights the extent to which, by 1750, Europe was a continent not just of many kingdoms and cultures, but of many economies as well.

MERCANTILISM. The new forms of finance that developed chiefly in the Dutch Republic and England laid the foundations for the economic system known as capitalism, in which exchange between persons operates in an unrestricted marketplace, and wealth in the form of money (or capital) is ceaselessly reinvested to spur more production. But in the early modern period, Europe's markets were not free: they were restricted by the legal inequalities of the Old Regimes, and by the monarchs' favorite economic philosophy: mercantilism. The policy, first outlined by Louis XIV's minister of finance Jean-Baptiste Colbert, was simple: the state should export more than it imported. This would keep hard currency flowing in to, rather than out of, the king's coffers. Colbert's plans called for tariffs to dampen consumers' desires to buy imported goods and the establishment of colonies to be exploited exclusively by the parent country. Colonies should produce what the colonizing country could not, and they should be prohibited from trading with other nations. The goal of mercantilism was national self-sufficiency in all things, the very opposite of the global free marketplace.

Colbert's policies originated in the wake of the Thirty Years' War, when states desperately needed hard currency to build their armies. Pressed by the need to pay for fortifications, armaments, and soldiers, other monarchs saw the value in mercantilist policies and adopted them in one way or another. They chartered monopolistic trading companies, such as the Dutch East India Company, and gave the companies both monetary and military assistance to establish trading posts and colonies. They sponsored the development of industries, like porcelain manufacture, at home, so that their subjects could buy local, rather than imported, dinnerware. They hired scholars to investigate how to grow pineapples in Sweden or tulips in France and commissioned spies to steal other people's trade secrets. And monarchs imposed taxes on trade, which proved lucrative. By the 1780s, taxes on alcohol, sugar, tobacco, and tea amounted to 60 percent of Britain's public revenue. But taxation also had consequences, for attempts to enforce these taxes in the colonies also encouraged the flourishing of the greatest tax-evaders: pirates and smugglers.

PIRACY AND SMUGGLING.

Already in the early days of Spanish colonization, pirates and semiauthorized buccaneers such as Francis Drake preyed on ships carrying the mineral riches of the Americas back to Europe. The commercial revolution produced a veritable boom in piracy and smuggling; for one thing, there were simply more goods to steal and to smuggle. Pirates came in many guises and nationalities. Ottoman pirates captured European ships and sold their crews as slaves. European buccaneers, among them the Dutchman Laurens de Graaf, organized their own armies and specialized in sacking coastal towns. Conditions were so poor for sailors on early modern British merchant and naval ships that many sailors willingly turned pirate in hopes of earning a decent wage and a share of the captured rum.

Smuggling also thrived. The high taxes imposed by mercantilist policymakers made smuggling attractive, and often lucrative; for example, the American revolutionary John Hancock made a tidy fortune smuggling tea and rum to avoid paying British taxes on these commodities. In France, one of the most frequently smuggled commodities was salt, which was subject to the enormously unpopular gabelle, the tax on salt, imposed at various levels across the kingdom. Salt was not hard to smuggle; it was relatively lightweight and compact, and prices varied so much from region to region that smugglers could make a fine profit by traveling only a short distance with their

goods. Thousands, perhaps tens of thousands, of people made a living smuggling salt in eighteenth-century France, even enlisting dogs to carry salt across tariffs borders. Royal agents then trained their hounds to sniff out the salt carriers.

As far as governments and state-backed companies like the Dutch East India Company were concerned, smugglers and pirates were criminals. Sadly, Europeans in this period did not see as equally criminal the trade in a "commodity" we now find morally abhorrent: slaves.

THE SLAVE TRADE.

The Atlantic slave trade began with Spanish use of African laborers on proto-plantations in the Canary Islands (see Chapter 12). Spanish and Portuguese conquests in the Americas led to the decimation of native populations through disease and warfare. One of the consequences of this appalling event was a labor shortage, which led Europeans to attempt to apply the Canary Island system to the Americas. By the late sixteenth century, Europeans were seeking to break in to West African slave markets (Africa had been supplying slaves to the Muslim societies of northeastern Africa and the eastern Mediterranean for centuries) to supply labor for Spanish mining and plantation agriculture.

Spanish and Portuguese slave traders began by making deals with powerful African kings, trading European weapons and ammunition for prisoners taken in African tribal conflicts or raids. In the 1630s, the Dutch West India Company forced its way in to this market, capturing Portuguese West African ports, and by 1642 had become the dominant slave traders. Still, slave numbers remained relatively low, estimated at 13,000 people exported per year between 1650 and 1675 and a little more than double that figure for 1675–1700. Most of these slaves were sent to Brazil and to the sugar plantations in the Caribbean. But then the numbers skyrocketed. By 1780, some 80,000 Africans a year were being shipped across the Atlantic. Soaring numbers reflected not only rising demands for sugar, but also the Africans' horrific death rate. As many as one in four died on the "middle passage" across the Atlantic from Africa to the Americas. Slaves who survived and reached the sugar fields of the Americas could not expect to survive more than seven years of torturous work, cruel treatment, stifling heat, and rampant disease.

Brutality and inhumane treatment characterized the whole of the slave trade. The process began in Africa, where African slave-traders bought or kidnapped men, women, and children. Bound in chains, slaves were then branded and loaded onto overcrowded and disease-ridden boats; the middle passage to the Americas often took weeks. North and South American slaves were not simply prisoners for life, but their descendants were also declared to be the property of their masters. Families could be separated and their members sold to different owners. Unlike serfs, slaves had no tradition-sanctioned expectations that their masters might protect or feed them in hard times. Slaves had no rights; they could not sue in court when they felt the master had gone too far, as peasants sometimes did.

But criticisms of the slave trade were rare until the later eighteenth century, and rare too were depictions of its cruelty until that time, though traders, state officials, and colonists were well aware of the huge human toll that underpinned their profits. Instead, most Europeans, if they thought about the slave trade at all, wrote it off as a necessary evil, or one justified by biblical passages said to condemn Noah's son Ham—blackened by his sins—to enslavement.

The slave trade was one—immoral, but legal—means by which Europeans in the seventeenth and eighteenth centuries instigated the development of an increasingly global commercial economy. To be sure, some parts of Europe, such as the Habsburg lands and Russia, participated very little in the new commerce—in part because their men of business lacked good ports and access to liquid capital. Many rural Europeans continued to live and work as their ancestors had done, except that they were increasingly called on to fund and to fight for their king, rather than their local lords. This change was the outcome in large part of yet another of the Old Regimes' transformative developments, the military revolution.

"Seasoning" Slaves in the Caribbean In this scene from one of the Caribbean islands, a white master orders one of his slaves to beat another—perhaps the man being whipped has just arrived on the ship sailing out to sea, and is being "welcomed" to the cruel world of sugar plantation society.

The Military Revolution

We cannot fully understand either the rise of nation-states or the expansion of European power abroad without paying careful attention to the profound change in early modern war-making known as the military revolution. This slow-growing revolution transformed the states that had to bear the enormous costs of its implementation. It also transformed Europe's relationship with the rest of the world, as Europe exported abroad a particular sort of violence in which the object was to kill enemies and seize territories rather than capture slaves, force conversions, or extract ransoms.[6] This sort of violence was generated by the relatively small size and proximity of hostile kingdoms and by the need to bombard stone-fortified castles and city walls in order to win wars. To do so, states needed firepower, and it was above all the development of unprecedented firepower that marked Europe's military revolution.

FORTIFICATIONS, ARMAMENTS, AND CHANGING TACTICS. Siege warfare using cannons had already been in use for centuries when the Italians, in the late Renaissance era, began to build angled bastions to provide for better defense. This style, which allowed defenders to attack besiegers from the sides, was widely imitated, as European leaders recognized that strategically placed strings of such fortifications were essential to protect their territories. Between 1529 and 1572, the Dutch built more than twenty-five miles of fortified works, which they used to their advantage in their battles with their Spanish overlords. These bastions and walls were enormously expensive, and extracting sufficient tax money to build them and garrison them with troops proved to be one of the absolutist monarchs' biggest headaches.

Late medieval Europeans had possessed firearms, but their fat and heavy pistols were notoriously hard to load correctly and even more difficult to aim; the rate of misfire was much higher than that of skilled archers. Pikemen massed together in square formations had been used to defend against cavalry. Gradually, however, advances in ballistics and artillery design made firearms and cannons more reliable and forceful, and armies began to reduce the numbers of their pikemen and cavalry and increase their firepower. Matchlock muskets came first, but each powder charge had to be lighted, so firing in damp or rainy weather was difficult. Far better were flintlock muskets in which a piece of flint created the spark needed to fire the gun. By the 1620s, the flintlock musket was the weapon of choice for foot soldiers, though the cavalry still carried swords, and many brigades still contained archers and pikemen.

The Dutch were perhaps the first to recognize the virtues of training soldiers to fire in formation and to use weapons of a standard size and caliber. Counts Maurice and William of Nassau, who commanded the Dutch army in the 1590s, were inspired by their study of Roman military techniques to develop the idea of **volley-firing.** Instead of creating squares of pikemen fifty deep, they advocated lines of musketmen only ten deep, able to deliver a continuous barrage across a wider territory; the cavalry could be deployed on the flanks. Drills allowed commanders like Gustavus Adolphus of Sweden to change tactics and redeploy men quickly and also increased the speed of reloading. On entering the Thirty Years' War in 1631, Swedish troops astonished fellow Europeans by their furious pace of reloading; they were able to deliver continuous fire with a line of musketeers only six deep, each man able to reload and fire in less than two minutes.

Cannons were invaluable in siege operation, but they were extremely heavy and hard to transport, as well as expensive to manufacture. Gustavus Adolphus was once again an innovator. Taking some lessons from the Dutch, he provided his troops with standard-sized cannons of relatively lightweight brass, innovations that contributed greatly to the Swedes' remarkable mobility. As we saw in Chapter 14, Gustavus Adolphus's army was sensationally successful in the battles they fought in 1631–1632. By the 1650s, all European states were importing or seeking to imitate Swedish training and tactics and the advanced technology incorporated in Swedish guns.

Already in the fifteenth century, Europeans were carrying one or two cannons aboard their ships; the Portuguese used cannons to terrify hostile traders in the Indian Ocean, and the Venetians may have used as many as 1,815 against the Turks' 750 cannons in the Battle of Lepanto in 1571. But in the seventeenth century, Europeans embarked on a frenzied naval build-up, developing new warships with purpose-built gun ports and breech-loading (rather than muzzle-loading) cannons. England's new ships managed to defeat the Spanish Armada in 1588, but the Dutch navy developed the faster forty-gun frigate, which did even more damage to the Spanish fleet in subsequent naval battles. The French began building up their navy as well. By the end of the seventeenth century, England, the Netherlands, and France had hundreds of warships, equipped with thousands of cannons, which they used not only in naval battles with one another, but also to seize port cities across the world.

THE STANDING ARMY. Violence was perpetual and virtually inescapable in early modern Europe. Collectively, the states of Europe experienced fewer than ten years of peace in the sixteenth century, and only four years of peace in the seventeenth century. Some of these were smaller skirmishes, but some, like the War of the Spanish Succession, were large-scale conflicts. The frequency and the increasing scale of battles led to one of the period's most important innovations: the standing army.

In the seventeenth century, Europe's monarchs began to recognize the virtues of having troops always ready on hand, prepared to fight, and in the pay of the central state, rather than owing allegiance to provincial lords. The Romans provided an important model, but the modern standing army has its beginnings in the sixteenth-century armies of the Spanish, French, and Austrians. These powers were at war so often and in so many theaters during that century that they gradually developed permanent forces. They needed not only soldiers in the

field, but also soldiers to garrison their many outposts. The Spanish stationed troops all along the Spanish Road, whereas the Austrians garrisoned troops to guard the long border with the Ottomans. These forces were always insufficient for their needs, and mercenaries were hired regularly, especially during major conflicts.

After the Thirty Years' War, the numbers of soldiers in Europe's armies swelled. The Brandenburgian-Prussians had only 3,000 soldiers in 1648, but standing forces of 40,000 by the end of the seventeenth century, and 80,000 by 1740. During wartime many more recruits were fielded. France, the military powerhouse of the late seventeenth century, put 135,000 men into battle in 1667 and sent more than 400,000 to fight in the War of the Spanish Succession in the early 1700s.

A relatively small state, Prussia developed a large army. Whereas other states aimed at recruiting one soldier for every hundred civilians, Frederick the Great aimed for a ratio of 1:30. His conscription system, known as the canton system, drafted a certain number of trainees from each district, or canton. Draftees, nobles as well as men from the third estate, spent a year in training and then were placed into the reserves, which meant that they could return to their jobs and, in peacetime, spent only a few weeks a year on maneuvers. In this way, Frederick filled three-quarters of his ranks with native Prussians at a time when other armies still hired many more foreign mercenaries or scraped the bottom of the social barrel, drafting convicts or drunkards.

THE COSTS OF WAR. The wars of the seventeenth and eighteenth centuries cost the European nations hundreds of thousands of lives. They also cost an enormous amount of money. In addition to fortifications, arms, and salaries, states increasingly paid for standard-issue uniforms and for provisions. Eighteenth-century states at least tried to feed their troops rather than simply assuming they could scavenge for themselves. Louis XIV spent some 75 percent of state income on war between 1700 and 1715, whereas Peter the Great devoted a whopping 85 percent of his funds to military expenditures. Spanish expenses were so great that the crown declared bankruptcy in 1557, 1607, 1627, and 1647 and faced regular mutinies by unpaid soldiers. Even shorter wars, like the War of the Austrian Succession (1740–1748), destroyed the participants' economies and drove up the kings' debts.

Absolutist governments were, in essence, war machines. In the increasingly competitive colonial and mercantile world of the mid-eighteenth century, states discovered that it was essential to have an army, and if possible a navy, to defend their territory, at home and abroad. Winning wars and claiming territory was no longer about asserting religious authority but rather about settling succession questions or about establishing secular economic dominance, which could be turned into military power. The Seven Years' War, the most important conflict of the pre-1789 era, shows the extent to which fighting and winning wars with one's neighbors had become the means

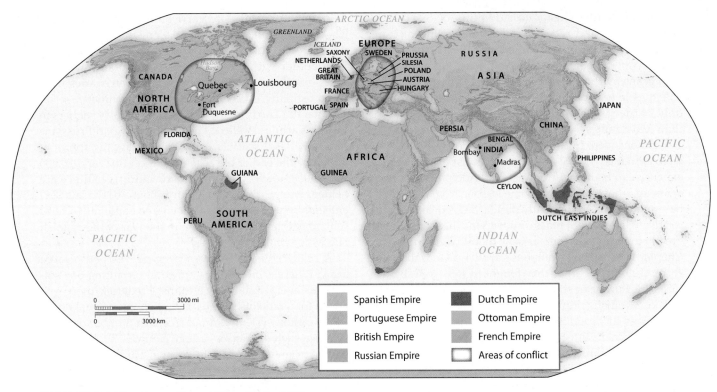

MAP 15.3 | The Seven Years' War, 1756–1763

The Seven Years' War has been called the first global war because its theaters ranged across Europe, North America, and South Asia.
Why would naval power have been very important in this war?

by which European states, and not just their rulers, established their place in the hierarchy of great powers.

The Seven Years' War: A Global War

The Seven Years' War was in essence two wars, and it is fitting that it goes by two names: the Seven Years' War for the European theater, and the French and Indian War for the brutal colonial war in North America. There was also significant fighting in India, where the French lost all but one of their colonial outposts, opening the way for the British to conquer the subcontinent piece by piece over the next eighty years (Map 15.3).

The causes of the war lay in Spanish, French, and Austrian attempts to preserve their great-power status and in Prussian and British attempts to extend their political and economic control. For Prussia, the aim was expansion in Europe, to be achieved by gaining territory in the south and east. For Britain, the aim was mercantile dominance in the Atlantic and Indian Oceans. The Seven Years' War was prefaced by rash action on the part of Frederick the Great of Prussia: in 1740, he seized the rich province of Silesia (see Map 15.1) from the Austrians. It was a gamble; the Austrians were by far the larger and richer state. But for the next eight years, they were preoccupied with the War of the Austrian Succession (over the ascent of Empress Maria Theresa to the Habsburg throne). Frederick got to keep Silesia, and in 1748 he enraged the Austrians again by signing a defensive treaty with the British.

Frederick's impertinence with respect to the house of Habsburg provoked Maria Theresa into allying with Austria's former rival, France, and with Russia, an action that completed what has been called the diplomatic revolution. Frederick then preemptively attacked Saxony, hoping to force it into an alliance, and seized all of its assets, including the famous porcelain factory at Meissen. He also found the molds used for minting Polish coins—for in 1756, Augustus III, elector of Saxony, was also king of Poland—and promptly used them to mint more money, thereby buying himself more soldiers and supplies. This act had its own consequences: by debasing the Polish currency, Frederick further weakened the kingdom of Poland, making it ripe for partition in the 1770s.

The Seven Years' War, like the earlier Thirty Years' War, was fought on battlefields throughout central Europe, though the professionalism of the new armies meant that this time far fewer civilians were affected. The numbers who died from disease, exposure, or starvation were also much fewer, though plenty of towns were plundered and many civilians victimized. Over time, the participants were compelled to further modernize their armies. Even Russia, which had not previously felt the full effects of the military revolution, now worked hard to field well-trained, well-armed troops. As Russian and Austrian armies swarmed into Frederick's territory, Prussia teetered on the brink of collapse. In 1762, Frederick despaired and even contemplated suicide. And then something happened that changed the course of history.

1762–1763: The Miracle of the House of Brandenburg

On January 5, 1762, the Russian czarina Elizabeth died. Elizabeth had despised Frederick the Great and had joined the Seven Years' War in the hope of extinguishing his ambitions in central Europe. But the next in the line for the Romanov throne, her nephew Czar Peter III, was of a quite different disposition. Peter III idolized Frederick and considered himself a friend of the Prussians. By February, Peter III announced that Russia was getting out of the war, making an alliance with Prussia, and returning its conquered territory to the Prussians. As far as Peter was concerned, Frederick could have Silesia. By May, the Russians and the Prussians had signed an official peace treaty. The Austrians had lost one of their major allies—one of the few that were not completely bankrupt and exhausted by the war. Emboldened, Frederick returned to the offensive, hoping now to use Russian armies to help him gain new territory.

But he too was to experience sudden changes of fortune. In July, Peter III was placed under house arrest, and his wife Catherine took the throne, proclaiming herself Czarina Catherine II. Two weeks later, Peter was dead,

having succumbed to what his wife unconvincingly described as "severe colic" following a "hemorrhoidal attack." Although a German princess, Catherine had devoted herself to serving her adopted kingdom's interests, and she now renounced Russia's alliance with Prussia. Meanwhile, Prussia's other ally, Britain, had turned its attention to the war in North America and India. Even Frederick realized it was time to make peace, and in February 1763, after months of negotiations, the Prussians and Austrians signed the Peace of Hubertusburg. A separate peace agreement, the Treaty of Paris, was concluded by France, Great Britain, and Spain.

The Peace of Hubertusburg did not make sweeping territorial changes on the continent. But it did confirm Frederick's hold on Silesia and Prussia's status as an up-and-coming continental power, a remarkable development, considering how close Frederick and Prussia had come to obliteration just a year earlier. Strategically located Silesia, rich in raw materials, was a prize, and Frederick had twice defeated the Habsburgs to gain it. Finally, the military build-up pursued by the house of Brandenburg since the Thirty Years' War was paying off. Frederick II could now legitimately claim the title "Frederick the Great," rather than, as he might have been called, "Frederick the Failure." As historian Franz Szabo writes, "Austria's failure to reduce Prussia to the status of just another middle-sized German principality was thus a fatal crossroad in Germany history,"[7] marking the beginnings of Austria's loss of clout in the region and the rise of Prussia as a force to be reckoned with in central European power politics.

Prussia's Military Revolution Completed In this image, Frederick II of Prussia ("the Great") reviews the Hesse Guard. Note that the soldiers no longer wear armor, and have been issued identical uniforms and weapons, unlike the mercenary soldiers of the Thirty Years' War.

QUESTION | *How much credit does Frederick deserve for Prussia's successes in the Seven Years' War?*

WAR IN NORTH AMERICA AND THE CARIBBEAN. In North America, the French and Indian War erupted first in the Ohio Valley, where British and French settlers and traders claimed territory for their respective countries. Both sides quickly drew their Native American allies into the fray, and soon a full-fledged war broke out that would involve Spain, the Caribbean colonies, and even colonies in the South Pacific before it was over.

The British were in the position of power for most of the war, led by the statesman William Pitt (1708–1778).

When England and France declared war on each other in 1756, Pitt's objective was simply to conquer Canada. When repeated English victories tipped the war decisively in Britain's favor in 1758, Pitt expanded his operations. His first target was the West Indies, where the French were rivals in the lucrative sugar trade. Pitt knew that the best way to knock the French to their knees was to attack not the plantations, but their slave trading outposts in West Africa so that they would have no new slaves to work on the plantations. After accomplishing that, it was relatively easy for British forces to take the islands of Guadeloupe in 1759 and Martinique in 1762.

Once the British had control of these islands in the West Indies, they turned to the Spanish, who entered the war on the French side in 1762. British troops attacked the major Spanish ports of Havana in the Caribbean and Manila in the Pacific and quickly seized them. All sides were now physically and financially exhausted, and ready to discuss peace.

THE SEVEN YEARS' WAR IN INDIA. French and British merchants had been establishing trading outposts on the Indian subcontinent since the seventeenth century, pushing out Portuguese and Dutch traders who had established bases there even earlier. Working as agents of the British and French East India Companies, European traders sought to increase their power and influence by trying to ally themselves with either India's Mughal Empire or with local princes. In the early eighteenth century, very few European men, and almost no European women, were willing to travel to India, so the trading companies depended on local people to staff their company armies and to help them understand local markets and power structures. When British and French interests came into conflict, just as they had in the Ohio Valley, both enrolled local allies and hired soldiers to fight for their side.

Some Indian leaders agreed to alliances in order to make war against internal enemies or in the hopes of eventually pushing all the Europeans out of their territory. Seeing the British preparing for war in 1756, the Mughal governor of Bengal, Siraj al-Dawlah, attacked Fort William, the British outpost near Calcutta. He overran the fort and imprisoned its defenders in an underground cell whose horrors became legendary when the story of the Black Hole of Calcutta reached English readers. But the British retook Bengal after the Battle of Plassey in 1757.

After Plassey, the French were driven from Bengal; the British then pushed them out of Madras and in 1760 blockaded the last French settlement at Pondicherry. Eventually, the French surrendered, ending the war favorably for the British in this theater as well.

THE PEACE TREATIES AND THE ADVENT OF THE GREAT POWERS. The Seven Years' War in Europe was brought to a conclusion by the Peace of Paris (concluded between the French and British) and the Peace of Hubertusburg (concluded between the Austrians and Prussians), both signed in 1763. The Peace of Hubertusburg affirmed Prussia's right to keep Silesia and confirmed Prussia's status as now one of the **great powers** of Europe, but no territory changed hands. The Peace of Paris, on the other hand, called for major redistributions of *colonial* territory. The English agreed to give Martinique, Guadeloupe, and Pondicherry back to the French and Manila, Havana, and parts of Louisiana back to the Spanish. But the English awarded themselves important trading hubs and naval stations, taking the island of Grenada, the slave trading station in Senegal, Florida, and the South Asian trading hub of Bengal. They now assumed naval and mercantile supremacy in the Caribbean as well as in the Atlantic and Indian Oceans. And they secured the biggest prize, all of Canada, though at the time few recognized its potential. The French writer Voltaire claimed his nation had lost, at most, "a few acres of snow."

The agricultural, commercial, and military revolutions contributed much to the global scope as well as to the destructiveness of the Seven Years' War. Hundreds of thousands of lives were lost, worldwide, in the conflict, and enormous sums were spent by all the states involved. The consequences of those debts alone were considerable: Britain's attempt to recover some of its expenditures by making the colonies pay for their own defense would result in the imposition of onerous new taxes on tea and stamps, actions that bred colonial resentment and galvanized revolutionary sentiment. More broadly speaking, the Seven Years' War confirmed that the powers that had fielded the largest armies—Britain, France, Russia, Prussia, and Austria—had become the great powers of the day. Although the Dutch, Portuguese, Spanish, Ottoman Turks, and Venetians remained important trading powers or allies, they had fallen to the status of second-class powers. The machinations of the five great powers would define Europe's destiny for the next two centuries, and beyond.

Transforming the Heavens and the Human Mind: The Scientific Revolution

The scientific revolution, like the quiet revolutions in agriculture, commerce, and the military surveyed earlier, was not a sudden event but a long process. This process, however, was linked more closely to the changes in worldview made possible by the Renaissance and Reformation than to political events or economic developments. Much more than the other revolutions, it was initiated by a few people—those who wanted to understand how nature worked and who were willing to place more trust in their own observations and

In what ways did scientific skepticism provoke advances in the study of the heavens and of the body?

The Black Hole of Calcutta

The one firsthand account of the Black Hole of Calcutta we possess was written by J. Z. Holwell, an East India Company official who experienced the Mughal victory at Fort William and survived his underground imprisonment. According to Holwell, Siraj al-Dawlah rounded up 146 defenders of the fort, 69 Europeans—a few Dutchmen as well as English soldiers—and 77 Indian mercenaries, and threw them all into an earthen pit, which measured no more than eighteen square feet. It was mid-June, and the pit was fiery hot. The prisoners were so crammed together that the door could scarcely be forced shut. People rushed for the tiny, barred windows, trampling one another for air. The weak and the wounded died quickly of heat stroke or

The Indignities of the Black Hole Like the many other melodramatic images that circulated throughout Great Britain, this reimagining of the scene was based on J. Z. Holwell's account of the Black Hole of Calcutta. We will probably never know how much Holwell embroidered the truth to highlight the suffering of the Europeans at the hands of their Indian captors.

suffocation. The guards brought water, but most of it was spilt as the prisoners fought one another for a sip. Holwell claimed that the Muslim captors were taunting them deliberately. One prisoner was reduced to sucking perspiration from Holwell's shirt to relieve his thirst. Holwell's account described the breakdown of civilization in the prison, and the longing for death that seized the sufferers:

By half an hour past eleven the much greater number of those still living were in a state of delirium, the others quite ungovernable. . . . Every insult that could be devised against the guard . . . were repeated to provoke the guard to fire upon us, every man rushing tumultuously towards the windows with eager hopes of meeting the first shot. Then a general prayer to heaven to hasten the approach of the flames to the right and left of us, to put a period to our misery. But these failing, those whose strength and spirits were quite exhausted, laid themselves down and expired quietly upon their fellows.[8]

By morning, 123 of the captives were dead. The remaining few were shackled and crawled, feverish and covered with boils, to new quarters. They were freed when the British retook the territory later in the war.

Holwell's narrative created a sensation in England and a taste for further captivity narratives—stories of men and women taken as captives, either by Muslim pirates in the Mediterranean or in the brutal and difficult wars the East India Company fought in India in the 1770s and 1780s. The captivity narratives underscored how vulnerable and weak British forces remained and, like Holwell's Black Hole account, emphasized the brutishness of the behavior of non-Christian leaders, while omitting or downplaying European violence against indigenous peoples. Muslim leaders were stereotyped as oriental despots, men who loved luxury and treated their underlings and foreigners cruelly. Subtly or not so subtly these narratives justified British conquest: as an act of civilization, India should be colonized, for its own good.

In recent years some historians have challenged Holwell's narrative of the Black Hole. Just how much did he sensationalize the story? Although there is no reason to think he invented the Black Hole story out of whole cloth, he may well have exaggerated the numbers or the suffering of his fellow Europeans—and, in so doing, helped create stereotypes that would last for many generations to come.

QUESTION | *How do you think English readers back home might have reacted to the story of the Black Hole?*

calculations than in the accumulated wisdom of the ages contained in classical treatises and in the Bible. These scholars did not intend to revolutionize thinking about nature, nor were they enemies of religion. But in seeking to answer particular questions, they increasingly felt emboldened to doubt what older authorities had claimed, and to seek their own solutions. These solutions would eat away at the Old Regimes' structures of authority and hierarchical and biblical understandings of the world.

Doubt and the Scientific Method: Francis Bacon and René Descartes

In many respects, the scientific revolution began with doubts—doubts the Polish astronomer Nicolaus Copernicus expressed about the earth's being the center of the universe, and doubts the Italian physician Andreas Vesalius had about medieval approaches to medicine. Two of the greatest contributors to the new sorts of investigation launched by the scientific revolution were great doubters: the English scholar Francis Bacon (1561–1626) and the French philosopher René Descartes (1596–1650).

Bacon was a well-traveled lawyer who lost his seat in Parliament after being convicted of corruption in 1621. Perhaps he had lined his pockets—in the era of James I, doing so was hardly exceptional—but in other matters Bacon was extremely self-critical. In his scholarly work he refuted the notion that philosophy alone could deal adequately with the complexities of nature. Inquirers needed to start not with certainties, but with doubts, for it was all too common that those who began with truths forced facts to fit their claims. "People prefer to believe what they prefer to be true," he claimed.

Bacon promoted the inductive method of reasoning, which moved from observed particulars to substantiated generalities. The inductive method upheld the importance of the senses in natural philosophy—particularly the role of the eyes in observation—and bolstered the authority of experiments. Hypotheses and hands-on inquiries into nature had to be designed carefully to guard against tricks the senses played. Above all, investigators must reject any preconceived notions and doubt results achieved as a result of a single experiment. Only by beginning with doubt, Bacon wrote, could one hope to reach something like truth. Bacon's challenges to older forms of thought, articulated especially in his treatise on logic, *New Instrument of Science* (1620), laid the foundations for what we know today as the scientific method, according to which hypotheses must be tested empirically in optimal and reproducible conditions before researchers are allowed to offer any secure conclusions.

Like Bacon, Descartes was concerned about reaching certainty about nature, but he proposed an alternative methodology. Even in his school days, Descartes distrusted his teachers' claims and used the excuse of poor health to spend hours in bed meditating while others were in the chapel at prayer. He volunteered to fight for the Holy Roman Empire in the Thirty Years' War and did

see some conflict, but then retired in 1621 and spent the next years living mostly in the Dutch Republic, where, together with like-minded scholars, he pursued high-level studies of philosophy, mathematics, and the sciences. By 1637, he was ready to write *Discourse on the Method of Rightly Conducting One's Reason and Seeking Truth in the Sciences,* in which he rejected Baconian testing as an unreliable basis for trustworthy scientific principles. Given that knowledge was a human product, the knower should start with his certainty that he himself must be a thinking being: "I think, therefore, I am." This truth could then be the starting point for deducing a great deal about the human mind and its products, including mathematics, logic, and the sciences. Descartes' **rationalism** contrasted sharply with Bacon's **empiricism,** but both would be instrumental in challenging older views of nature based on classical treatises and readings of Scripture.

The Cosmological Revolution

Even before Bacon and Descartes began seeking new methods for scientific inquiry, Nicolaus Copernicus (1473–1543) grew tired of the complex mathematical calculations needed to maintain the medieval view of the heavens. Copernicus, the son of a Polish copper merchant, had learned to make these astronomical calculations at the University of Cracow but had also undertaken a wide-ranging humanistic course of studies at the Universities of Bologna and Padua. When he returned to the north in 1503, he took a job as a priest and doctor in the cathedral town of Frauenberg in East Prussia. He continued his studies of the heavens but increasingly despaired of the complicated mathematics needed to reconcile the traditional belief that the heavens were uniform, perfect, and unchanging with observations that showed planets to be moving at different speeds. Eventually he discovered that the simplest solution was to remove the earth from the center of the cosmos and replace it with the sun. In 1514, Copernicus set out his hypothesis in a small manuscript called *The Little Commentary,* but not until 1543 did he publish his theories in full, in a treatise titled *On the Revolutions of the Heavenly Spheres.*

Copernicus died the same year that *On the Revolutions* was published. Outside the world of astronomers, the general population took very little notice of the work. After all, there was absolutely no direct evidence to support any of Copernicus's theories, and his treatises were technical and mathematical—not light reading by any means. Daily experience seemed to confirm that it was the sun that moved while the earth remained fixed, and no one could come up with an experiment or test that would prove otherwise. Although a few astronomers found his ideas interesting, little credence was given to them until the mathematician Johannes Kepler (1571–1630) accepted Copernicus's hypothesis that placed the sun at the center of the cosmos. In the *New Astronomy* of 1609, Kepler laid out two laws of planetary motion— that planets move in elliptical, not circular, orbits, and that each planet sweeps out equal areas of the elliptical orbit in equal times.

But it was the Medici family's court mathematician, Galileo Galilei (1564–1642), and ironically the church authorities who disapproved of his efforts, who pushed the work of Copernicus and Kepler to the forefront of science in the beginning of the seventeenth century. Support from the wealthy Medicis gave Galileo fame and influence, which he used to promote Copernicus's ideas. Galileo's first defense of Copernicus appeared in his *Letters on Sunspots* (1613), in which he argued publicly with a prominent Jesuit astronomer about the nature of the heavens. The heavens, Galileo claimed, obeyed the same laws of physics as did the earth. This position outraged the clergy, who insisted that God's realm could not be bound by laws that humans had derived merely from observing the sky with a telescope. They pointed out biblical passages in which the earth stood still and accused Galileo of suggesting that he was right and the Scriptures were wrong.

In response, Galileo boldly published an open *Letter to the Grand Duchess Christina* (1615) in which he asked his Medici patrons to consider biblical passages that appeared to contradict human observation. These passages, Galileo argued, should be interpreted metaphorically. They were written, he claimed, to explain Christian ideas "to the shallow minds of the common people." The church did not miss his implication that natural scientists, reading what Galileo called "the book of nature," could produce better knowledge than did theologians reading the holy book. In 1616, the pope denounced Copernicus's theories as "philosophically foolish" and heretical. Galileo was warned privately against presenting Copernican ideas as scientific fact. Instead, he was told, he should present them only as a hypothesis that could not be proven.

From 1616 to 1632, Galileo retreated into his teaching and continued to study the heavens for evidence to support the Copernican system. When a friend and former student, Maffeo Barberini, was elected Pope Urban VIII, Galileo felt that he might have a chance to persuade the church about the truth of Copernicus's ideas. The two met in Rome, and Galileo felt encouraged to present his ideas in print. In *Dialogue Concerning the Two Chief World Systems* (1632), he presented a discussion of astronomy between a Copernican astronomer, an Aristotelian philosopher named Simplicius ("the simpleton"), and a skeptical middleman waiting to be persuaded about which theory was correct. Galileo filled Simplicius's remarks with some of the defenses of Aristotelian astronomy that Pope Urban VIII had shared with him during their meeting, and though the work had been approved by church censors, Urban condemned it. Galileo was accused of violating the instructions he was given in 1616 regarding the theories of Copernicus and was put on trial for heresy. After years of suspicion, inquiry, and questioning by the Inquisition, the seventy-year-old Galileo recanted his scientific beliefs in June 1633. His experiences became

widely known in Europe's scholarly community, some of whose members rallied to his defense and called for a greater separation between faith and science.

Galileo died in 1642, the same year that another great student of the heavens, Sir Isaac Newton (1642–1727), was born. Newton spent his boyhood reading and making mechanical toys, and at age eighteen, he finally persuaded his mother that he would not make a good gentleman farmer. He studied at Cambridge between 1661 and 1665 but had to return home when plague struck the university town. Back home, he turned his mind to a set of questions about the natural world that would lay the groundwork for his later work in physics, optics, alchemy, and mathematics.

The first question Newton worried over was why the moon didn't fall like an apple did, since it had no visible means of support to hold it up in the sky. Newton decided that the moon was falling, but it was also moving forward, motions that propelled the moon around the earth. He also wondered why a ray of light, which appeared to be white, produced colors when it passed through a prism. By grinding his own lenses and prisms, Newton was able to distinguish rays of strikingly different colors, rather than the merged rainbow that had been seen earlier. In 1666, Newton reached the conclusion that white light is made up of all the colors in the rainbow.

In the next decades, Newton worked—largely without recognition—on a number of projects. He developed his ideas about "fluxions" or differential calculus, which attempted to solve the problem of analyzing curved paths like elliptical orbits. In response to a series of particularly bright comets that crossed European skies in 1664, 1680, and 1682, Newton formulated his theory of universal gravitation; comets, he explained, recurred on predictable elliptical orbits shaped by gravity's pull. He put together his findings in a landmark treatise, *The Mathematical Principles of Natural Philosophy* (1687), best known by its shorthand Latin title, *Principia*.

In the *Principia*, Newton used the Latin word *gravitas* or weight to describe the force that we call gravity and described the universal law that made gravity work on the earth as well as in the heavens. Other philosophers had blurred the distinctions between the heavens and the earth, but Newton, by proposing a single system of physics that was consistent throughout the created world, showed why the ancient distinction was meaningless. Newton formulated three universal laws of motion that depended on gravity and determined the motion of everything from falling apples to heavenly bodies. Newton's contemporaries saw the *Principia* as the summit of the new science, a work that finally made all the old forms of calculation obsolete and made it seem likely that all the world's mysteries, uncertainties, and inequities might, in time, be eliminated by secular investigators, rather than being perpetuated by clergymen or kings.

Newton was pleased by the amount of acclaim garnered by the *Principia*, but to him it was only part of a larger set of scientific investigations. While students of nature throughout the world read the *Principia* with awe and amazement, Newton was poring over biblical chronologies, looking for evidence about how the world might eventually come to an end in the Apocalypse and for proof that the Old Testament's history of the earth could be squared with the new science. Newton also became interested in alchemy, which he believed would help him understand the universal principles of cohesion that held the world together. Like Johann Böttger, the great Newton spent a considerable amount of time attempting to turn base metals into gold. In fact, autopsies suggest that Newton may have been killed by lead poisoning from alchemical experiments. That both Newton and Böttger dabbled in alchemy tells us much about how hard it was to tell, even in the mid-eighteenth century, what was science and what was fantasy. But it is also telling that both men turned to experiment rather than to books to pursue their dreams.

The Anatomical Revolution

Experimentation would also make crucial contributions to the study and treatment of the human body. Like many other branches of learning in early modern Europe, medicine was a field in which theoretical knowledge, derived from the ancients, was seen as more worthy of cultivation than practical, hands-on knowledge of the type acquired by guildsmen through apprenticeship. By the early sixteenth century, however, physicians had begun to discover new knowledge about the body from their firsthand experiences.

In the generation after Copernicus, Andreas Vesalius (1514–1564) leveled the first serious blows against the prevailing anatomical tradition in Europe. Born in Brussels, Vesalius experienced his first human dissections as an observant student at the University of Paris. In these dissections, the physician never touched the body, but stood on a raised platform above the body and read aloud from the works of the long-trusted Roman anatomist Galen while the surgeon pointed to specific parts of anatomy that were being revealed by his knife. Vesalius became convinced while witnessing these dissections that the human body was understood only imperfectly and that Galen may have been wrong in some of his anatomical knowledge. Vesalius then embarked on his own studies of the human body using corpses that he and his friends stole from public executions and smuggled into their rooms for hasty dissections. From one of these corpses, Vesalius reconstructed a human skeleton, which he used to better understand the body's structure. In 1543, he issued *On the Fabric of the Human Body*, one of the classic texts of the scientific revolution, which became a standard work and convinced physicians across Europe to make their own dissections.

Among those he inspired was the young English physician William Harvey (1578–1657), who would challenge Galen's beliefs about the role that the heart, kidney, and lungs played in the human body. After years of work at

The Body's Secrets Explained This image from William Harvey's *On the Circulation of the Blood* (1628) illustrates the location of the veins and the pressure points in the human arm. Surgeons often referred to Harvey's diagrams as they performed their dissections.

London's St. Bartholomew's Hospital, Harvey moved beyond Galen's conception of the heart as the transfer station for human blood to describe the entire circulatory system. Supporters of Galen's traditional medicine attacked Harvey's findings in *On the Circulation of the Blood* (1628), fearing that Harvey's new theories would undermine centuries of therapeutic medicine based on bloodletting. Early modern physicians believed that the body's inability to consume all the blood it produced resulted in congestion and advocated blood-letting as a way to restore health by reducing that congestion. Harvey's theory that blood was not consumed but instead circulated throughout the body would necessitate an entirely new system of medical remedies and therapies.

In the eighteenth century, nonphysicians also worked to improve public health. Lady Mary Wortley Montagu, the wife of the British ambassador to the Ottoman Empire, adopted the Turkish practice of inoculating her family against smallpox by injecting fresh pus from smallpox victims under the skin. She then vigorously urged others to do the same. By the 1760s, Maria Theresa of Austria, Louis XVI of France, and Frederick the Great of Prussia were inoculating their families, and in the 1790s British

CHRONOLOGY | Key Texts of the Scientific Revolution

DATE	TEXT
1543	Nicolaus Copernicus, *On the Revolution of Heavenly Spheres*
1543	Andreas Vesalius, *On the Fabric of the Human Body in Seven Books*
1620	Francis Bacon, *New Instrument of Science*
1628	William Harvey, *On the Circulation of the Blood*
1632	Galileo Galilei, *Dialogue Concerning the Two Chief World Systems*
1637	René Descartes, *Discourse on the Method of Rightly Conducting One's Reason and Seeking Truth in the Sciences*
1679	Maria Sibylla Merian, *Wonderful Transformation and Singular Flower-Food of Caterpillars*
1687	Isaac Newton, *The Mathematical Principles of Natural Philosophy*

physician Edward Jenner perfected a safer vaccination using the milder cowpox virus. Doctors continued to bleed their patients, and sterilization and anesthesia—other than rum—were still unknown. But Europeans were increasingly confident that new ideas could reduce the death toll, and they no longer shuddered at the idea of dissecting cadavers or trying new cures.

The Social Life of Science

The scientific revolution was not made in laboratories or, for the most part, in universities. Instead, the scientists who produced these revolutionary ideas and discoveries worked in dusty studies, in busy cities, or in palace apartments provided to them by aristocratic patrons. They consulted instrument-makers and philosophers. But increasingly natural scientists sought out the company of men like themselves, who were particularly devoted to experimenting and deriving new knowledge, and some began to urge their princely patrons to found state-supported scientific societies, along the lines of the Medicis' Florentine Academy or Rome's Academy of the Lynx, to which Galileo belonged. In 1661, a group of twelve English scholars petitioned King Charles II, and in 1662 he agreed to serve as official patron of the Royal Society of London, which met weekly for members to perform experiments and to discuss their efforts to understand nature. Their investigations ranged widely. During a three-week period in 1663, the Royal Society started a history of the weather, commissioned a new set of thermometers, made an artificial eye, considered how to best make glass coverings to protect portraits, removed and reattached a piece of skin on a dog, built an air pump to measure the force of gunpowder, and studied a fly under a microscope.

In 1666, a similarly ambitious scientific academy was founded in France. Unlike England's Royal Society, the Académie Royale des Sciences was established specifically to foster the state's interests through scientific research, namely to improve maps, sailing charts, and navigation. Louis XIV and his minister of finances, Jean-Baptiste Colbert, were determined to rival England's Royal Society in prestige and intellectual power, and they invited fifteen carefully chosen scientists to constitute the new society. With the king's full support, Académie members started large-scale, ambitious projects such as mapping all of France and solving the problem of how to establish longitude at sea. These projects required large staffs of trained assistants, whose work was overseen by a senior figure, usually one stationed in Paris. In this way the French academy pioneered the modern form of organizing scientific inquiry by positioning a primary investigator at the pinnacle of a team of usually younger experimenters and collectors of data.

Scholars who lived near one another could meet in the academies, but most sharing of ideas occurred through correspondence. In the early modern era, as roads and the post improved, so did the frequency and number of exchanges. Historians have termed these evolving correspondence networks the Republic of Letters, as exchanges between scholars increasingly crossed religious and political borders and created friendships and collaborative endeavors between individuals who treated one another more or less as equals. Many of the most important figures in the seventeenth century participated in these correspondence networks. René Descartes, for example, kept up an active correspondence with other scholars, including the French mathematician Marin Mersenne, who was such an active letter-writer that he earned the nickname "the mailbox of Europe."

Women and the New Science

With a few exceptions, women interested in science were barred from studying or teaching in universities and from belonging to the new academies, but correspondence networks provided them opportunities to participate in debates and discussions. Descartes corresponded with Princess Elisabeth of Bohemia and Queen Christina of Sweden, both of whom had formidable intellects and educations. Some women, like Maria Winkelmann Kirch, received scientific educations at home and then worked together with their husbands. Maria's husband, Gottfried Kirch, was a highly respected astronomer and calendar-maker in Berlin. Maria not only helped him amass data for his calendars, but also performed her own observations, in the course of which she recorded a new comet—though Gottfried was the one to get credit for the discovery. After Gottfried's death, the Berlin Academy of Sciences refused to allow Maria to continue making calendars for their use, but Maria did find a private patron

Maria Sibylla Merian, Scientist and Artist

Until recently, no one would have thought to include the artisanal painter Maria Sibylla Merian in accounts of the scientific revolution. Yet, as recent scholarship has shown, Merian was probably more typical of early naturalists than was someone like Isaac Newton, who spent relatively little time in the world of commerce and no time in Britain's colonies. Born in 1647 in Frankfurt, one of the liveliest commercial cities of German-speaking Europe, Merian grew up in the household of her Dutch stepfather, a renowned painter of flowers. From him she learned to examine closely and to sketch from life. As a young woman, she filled her home with flowers and with jars full of caterpillars, butterflies, and moths. Closely observing her subjects, she witnessed the changing of caterpillars into butterflies, a transformation the leading scientists of the day did not yet understand clearly. She married and gave birth to two daughters, but continued painting and collecting specimens. Her first book, *The New Book of Flowers* (1675), was a traditional, beautiful book of flower patterns for other artisans to copy, but her second publication, *Wonderful Transformation and Singular Flower-Food of Caterpillars . . . Painted from Life and Engraved in Copper* (1679), had another purpose: displaying the developmental stages and particular feeding habits of the caterpillar. Like the other naturalists of her day, Merian relied on her observations and wanted her book to display her learning as well as her artistic talent.

A religious woman, Merian believed that the transformations of the caterpillar exemplified God's attention to all aspects of his creation. In fact, her religious devotion led her to leave her husband and live, together with her daughters, in an austere Pietist community in the Netherlands for several years. Eventually she left the community and in 1686 moved to the great artistic, commercial, and scientific city of Amsterdam. In this teeming and tolerant port city, Merian set up shop as a painter and conversed with other female artists and artisans, as well as with individuals of many different religious backgrounds. But her longing to see and learn more was still unsatisfied, and in 1699 she set sail for the Dutch West India Company colony of Surinam in South America, taking along her younger daughter and fellow artist Dorothea Marie.

In Surinam, the two women discovered bird-eating tarantulas, enormous moths, and bugs never before seen in Europe. They sketched insects and flowers, often using slaves to help collect specimens. In the later seventeenth century, the Dutch West India Company was profiting hugely from selling slaves to the sugar plantations in the Caribbean and along the South American coast. Merian did not object to slavery or the slave trade, though she thought the Dutch planters in the colony were overly concerned about making money, and she criticized them for not appreciating the splendors of the natural world around them.

Maria eventually contracted a severe case of malaria and returned to Amsterdam, where she continued to paint and published *Metamorphoses of the Insects of Surinam* (1705). After her death in 1717, her sketchbook was stolen by a Russian doctor, and her daughter was hired by Peter the Great to paint objects in his collection. Dorothea Marie worked hard to keep her mother's images in print, and plates from the flower book, especially, were copied by many porcelain painters and embroiderers. In decades to come, male scholars would ridicule Merian's work and compound errors in her books by stuffing new editions with additional misinformation or poor translations of her words. Not until the 1970s, when the Soviet Union published some of her original materials, could her status as both artist and scientist be recovered. Thanks to recent work on the history of women in science we can now appreciate how very daring and innovative Maria Sibylla Merian was and how much she belongs to the world of early observational science.

Science Can Be Beautiful Produced by Merian in 1705, this illustration of the metamorphosis of the *Thysania agrippina* caterpillar into a butterfly is as much a contribution to science as it is a work of art.

QUESTIONS | *Was Maria Sibylla Merian a scientist in seventeenth-century terms? If not, why was she not recognized as such?*

who allowed her to work in his observatory. Maria also trained her son, Christfried, and her two daughters in astronomy. In 1716, Christfried became director of the Berlin Academy's observatory.

Maria Kirch was not allowed to study at any university—then again, her husband had not gone to university either, but had learned his science on the job, working up from apprentice to master just as other early modern guild members did in his day. Much science was learned in this way, by women as well as by men, and much of what we call the scientific revolution was produced by people who practiced science as a trade or a pastime. Lady Montagu, the champion of smallpox vaccination, surely belongs to this broader range of science-makers. So, too, do the many now-forgotten midwives who possessed deep and rich knowledge of herbal cures and birthing practices,

and the adventurous Maria Sibylla Merian, who made her contributions to science while practicing a seemingly unrelated trade: painting flowers.

Over the course of the eighteenth century, scientific activity became more expensive and time-consuming and involved an increasing number of gadgets, experiments, and calculations. The world of artisanal science in which Maria Sibylla Merian thrived did not disappear, but was pushed increasingly into the background. Patronage flowed chiefly to (male) members of the academies. But women continued to be vital contributors backstage, helping their husbands and fathers with experiments, or sharing with their male colleagues the knowledge they had gained as midwives, healers, or collectors. They too learned to look at nature in new ways, and in so doing, ensured that the scientific revolution would succeed.

Conclusion

Although the revolutions of the early modern period were largely gradual and unobtrusive, by the later eighteenth century they were nonetheless transforming Europe's western kingdoms. Agriculture, commerce, military matters, and the very conceptions people held about the body and the cosmos—all of these looked very different in 1720 than they had in 1600. And yet, in that year, even in wealthy and relatively progressive Saxony, a man like Johann Böttger could be held prisoner by a prince who wanted him to perform a kind of magic. By 1789, the quiet revolutions described in this chapter had furthered damaged the authority of the Old Regimes, but even in many parts of northwestern Europe, legal inequalities and traditional worldviews held on.

The quiet revolutions came more haltingly to central and southeastern Europe, slowed down by the second serfdom and relatively small number of urban hubs

from which ideas could circulate to wider populations. Although absolutist monarchs in these areas attempted periodically to impose sweeping changes, poor roads, poor soil, low rates of literacy, and little access to capital kept most cities small and most regional economies dependent on serf and peasant labor. In these centuries, southwestern Europe remained rich and relatively urbanized. Its inhabitants had contributed a great deal to the new science and to the commercial and military revolutions. But the southern kingdoms did not really embrace the new agriculture, nor profit from the now booming Atlantic trade. The economic and political diversity of Europe's regions would come into play time and again over the next centuries, but crucial advances in the development of Europe's diverse forms of modern life began here, in the simultaneously static and revolutionary world of the Old Regimes.

Critical Thinking Questions

1. What sorts of choices did a typical French peasant have in c. 1700? How was his or her life different from that of the typical Russian peasant, and the typical English gentleman?

2. Which of the quiet revolutions discussed in this chapter do you believe contributed the most to undermining the society of orders of the early seventeenth century? Why?

3. Compare and contrast the lives of the three non-privileged people featured in this chapter: Johann Böttger, Joseph Haydn, and Maria Sibylla Merian. What do their lives tell us about the possibilities for social mobility during this period?

Key Terms

alchemy (p. 457)

Old Regime(s) (p. 459)

society of orders (p. 460)

seigneurial dues (p. 460)

tithe (p. 463)

Methodism (p. 464)

Pietism (p. 464)

Jansenism (p. 464)

taille (p. 467)   *corvée* (p. 470)   chartered (joint-stock)   great powers (p. 480)
serfdom (p. 468)   *robot* (p. 470)   companies (p. 474)   rationalism (p. 482)
second serfdom (p. 469)   volley-firing (p. 476)   empiricism (p. 482)

Primary Sources in connect

For information on Connect and the online resources available, go to **http://connect.mcgraw-hill.com**.

1. **An Old Regime Clergyman Describes His Role**
2. **Dick Turpin, Highwayman**
3. **A Reformer Depicts the Condition of the Serfs in Eighteenth-Century Russia**
4. **The Job of a Slave Trader**
5. **Galileo on Science and the Bible**

Order Establishing a Consumption or Excise Tax in All Towns of Electoral and Mark Brandenburg (1667)

In this document, Frederick William, the Great Elector of Prussia, declares that all his domains shall pay a new tax to support town improvements. Note how very precisely goods were taxed. As was typical in the Old Regimes, particularities had to be specified. The Elector was eager for all to pay this tax and for it not to fall exclusively on the poor—though because this was a tax on consumer goods, it surely fell most heavily on those who devoted the majority of their income to food and drink. To make sense of the tax amounts, consider that in Prussia 30 groschen (or 360 pfennigs) made up 1 thaler—and a peasant or servant would only rarely earn 12 thalers a year. Note also that soldiers could be used to extract the tax, and the elector expected a report on what taxes had been collected from each town. "Tun" here refers to a barrel or cask.

We, Frederick William, by grace of God Margrave in Brandenburg, Chamberlain of the Holy Roman Empire and Elector, etc., in Prussia, etc.:

Do hereby proclaim and give notice to all and sundry: Inasmuch as most lively representations have on various occasions been made to Us concerning the poor and needy condition of Our towns in Our Electorate and Mark of Brandenburg, and We have accordingly considered all kinds of ways and means to restore them and to save them from final ruin and complete destruction, it has seemed to Us that it would be particularly conducive to the improvement of their condition and promotion of their prosperity if the public burdens were somewhat more evenly distributed, not all laid only on the poor, nor levied exclusively on land and houses, for which purpose we can think of no means more convenient and equitable than the introduction of a fixed and moderate excise, toward which all inhabitants without distinction shall contribute, each contributing much or little, according to whether his consumption is large or small.

1. And it is therefore, firstly, Our most gracious and strict will and command that as from the first of June, by which date the Patent can be brought to the public notice in all towns of Our Electoral Mark of Brandenburg . . . and similarly, so far as brewing is concerned, in all alehouses and breweries that engage in the sale of beer in cloisters, liberties, suburbs, villages and hamlets, the following tax shall be placed on the commodities hereafter specified. . .

4. Local wines
Local wines pressed on the spot or dispatched from the country into a town, per tun (to be paid by the buyer): 6 groschen
The same wine drawn from the cask: 9 groschen
Foreign wines such as Guben or Meissen wines, per tun: 10 groschen
5. Brandy
Home-distilled, per quart: 6 groschen
Rhenish, Polish, and other foreign brandy, per quart: 9 groschen
7. Meat slaughtered in a public slaughterhouse
Per ox so slaughtered and exposed for sale by the butcher: 1 thaler
Per cow: 15 groschen
Per hog: 6 groschen
Per sheep: 2 groschen
Per calf: 2 groschen

Young lamb or goat: 1 groschen
8. Slaughtered domestically
Per ox: 12 groschen
Per cow: 7 groschen, 6 pfennigs
Per hog fattened: 3 groschen
Per hog unfattened: 1 groschen, 6 pfennigs
Sheep: 1 groschen
Suckling young lamb or goat: 6 pfennigs
9. Cattle
Per milch cow (annually): 6 groschen
Per 25 sheep or goats milch or for breeding: 6 groschen
10. Salt
Per tun: 4 groschen
. . .

6. For the rest, no person whatsoever, whether resident in noble manors, Colleges, Episcopal liberties . . . in suburbs or outlying districts, whether he be cleric or noble, employee of the Court or army, higher or lower official, or of any other quality, shall under any pretext whatever, be exempt from this tax.

8. And the magistrates of each locality shall pay due heed and attention that the innkeepers, slaughterers, bakers, and handworkers do not make this small excise a pretext to raise their prices excessively, and shall fix equitable prices and see that they are observed.

9. All towns are to render to Us quarterly a true account of what this excise has yielded, in order that we may issue further instructions how and in what way the yield from it is to be applied to the welfare and best interests of the town, for which purpose alone it is to be used, and not touched in any other way or employed for any other purpose.

. . .

11. We hereby graciously and strictly command all Our Governors, Commanders, and others in places where garrisons are kept or Our soldiers quartered to render all assistance to magistrates and excise employees and not to permit anything conducive to the diminution or evasion of the excise. Given under Our Hand and Electoral Seal in Our residence in Colln on the Spree, April 15, 1667.
Frederick William

QUESTIONS | *How does this document demonstrate the complicated economic world of the Old Regimes? Does this seem an efficient way to raise revenue for town improvements? Why or why not?*

Source: *The Habsburg and Hohenzollern Dynasties in the Seventeenth and Eighteenth Centuries*, ed. C. A. Macartney (New York: Harper & Row, 1970), 253–258.

MANY ENLIGHTENMENTS

Europe's Many Enlightenments

The Origins of Enlightened Thought

Enlightened Societies in the Dutch Republic and Great Britain
  The Dutch Republic
  England
  Scotland

The French Enlightenment
  Montesquieu and Voltaire
  The French Enlightenment Comes of Age
  Denis Diderot and the French *Encyclopédie*
  Jean-Jacques Rousseau

Enlightened Absolutisms in Central Europe
  Russia
  Prussia
  Austria

Cultural Enlightenments in Southern Europe
  Spain and Portugal
  The Italian Enlightenment

Spreading the Enlightenments
  The Enlightened Novel
  Literature by and for Women
  The French *Encyclopédie*
  Pamphlets and Pornography
  Enlightened Travel
  Enlightened Gardening
  Eating the Enlightenment
  Hearing the Enlightenment

The Many Enlightenments and Their Consequences
  The Enlightenments and Religion
  The Enlightenments and Politics

Conclusion

ROBINSON CRUSOE In 1719, English readers acquired a new hero, an ordinary fellow named Robinson Crusoe. Robinson was the creation of Daniel Defoe (1660–1731), a religious dissenter who had been involved in various branches of the new commerce and been bankrupted by it more than once. Defoe's Crusoe was based loosely on a real-life model: that of the Scottish sailor Alexander Selkirk, who had survived four years of isolation on an uninhabited island by taming goats and enclosing a wild vegetable garden. Inspired by Selkirk's story, Defoe made his hero set out to sea to seek his fortune, and then stranded him on a deserted island for a full twenty-eight years. *Robinson Crusoe* has been called the first novel in English, for it is the first detailed account of the daily life of an ordinary man—not a prince, not a warrior, not a figure from history, mythology, or the Bible—but it is more than one man's story. It is also an investigation of the human soul, a celebration of human reason, and a subtle critique of the intolerant and idle aristocratic world in which Defoe lived.

◀ The Salon: Creating a Cultural World outside the Court and Church

The character Robinson Crusoe, though he is fictional, reveals much about enlightened values. Crusoe is daring; ignoring his father's advice to stay and be satisfied with the condition into which he was born, he leaves England. He makes a tidy sum in the slave trade, but then is captured by Muslim pirates and becomes a slave himself—a condition he finds impossible to endure. Crusoe, who has no practical skills, no understanding of himself, and no authentic religious faith, uses his reason to escape. He then finds himself stranded alone on a Caribbean island with only a Bible, a couple of guns, a little rum, and a few tools. Through trial and error he learns to do useful things: to house and clothe himself, to raise goats, and to grow corn. His material needs are met, though he continually seeks ways to improve and enlarge his

Robinson Crusoe's Island It was on this uninhabited island off the coast of Chile that the Scottish sailor Alexander Selkirk spent four lonely years until his rescue in 1709. Selkirk's tale of the resourcefulness that allowed him to survive in the wilderness would inspire Daniel Defoe to write the great novel of the early Enlightenment, *Robinson Crusoe*.

property. He comes to know God only after nature—by way of an earthquake, a flood, and his own illness—prompts him to pray. He then takes to reading the Bible, which satisfies his spiritual needs. After more than two decades of longing for human companionship, he rescues a Caribbean cannibal from being eaten by enemy tribesmen. Crusoe dubs the

cannibal "Friday," makes him his servant, and converts him to his brand of Protestantism. A few months later, he frees other captives and allows them to retain their paganism or Catholicism. Crusoe becomes the king of his island community for a brief time, and makes everyone work and live in the simple, rational way he had done for so many years.

Robinson Crusoe published
1719

Dutch Enlightenment
c. 1670–1789

| 1670 | 1680 | 1690 | 1700 | 1710 | 1720 | 1730 |

Once they obtain a boat, Crusoe and his crew sail away. The island has taught him all the lessons he needed; Crusoe has become an enlightened man.

Crusoe became enlightened by learning from nature, listening to his senses, and using his reason. Other than his Bible, he has no other authorities to consult, but he finds he doesn't need them. Having escaped from society's corrupting influences, he has become a productive rather than an idle member of society. Although he loathes and fears the cannibals and clearly considers them inferior even to the European Catholics who visit his island, he learns to love Friday and to practice a grudging sort of religious toleration. By the end of the book, Crusoe is rich, though restless after his return to civilization. He has succeeded in uncovering the natural laws of society, as so many Enlightened thinkers wished to do, but realizes that remaking Europe as he remade his island will be much more than a twenty-eight-year task.

Robinson Crusoe tells us much about the kind of human beings Enlightenment thinkers wanted their societies to create—and about their grand hopes that new kinds of humans *could* be created. These new humans would be people who did not have to rely on authorities, on other people, or even on God. They would be free from economic dependence, from social conventions, and from superstitious beliefs. They would consult their own reason and learn by observing nature; they would control their desires, consume moderately, and work hard to enhance the productivity of the land. Crusoe's actions also tell us much about Enlightenment thinkers' tendency to consider European values as the only rational ones and to regard other people as savages or children in need of reform and instruction. The fact that Defoe had to leave his hero on a deserted island for nearly thirty years suggests just how very hard it would be to divorce Europeans from their old beliefs and social conventions.

❄❅❄❅

Many, perhaps most, Europeans of the seventeenth and early eighteenth centuries feared change, doubting that it could bring improvement, for societies or for individuals. Things should be done as one's grandmother and grandfather had done them, and as God, speaking through clergymen, wanted them done. Even though plenty of quiet revolutions were under way by the eighteenth century, no one thought they might upend the system of social, economic, and political privileges that defined early modern European societies. What made such radical change thinkable were the intellectual and cultural developments of the period between about 1689 and 1789, which the French called "the century of light" and we conventionally refer to as the Enlightenment. These developments were not applauded by all. Many entrenched aristocrats and clerics in Europe fought hard to prevent the new ideas from spreading. Nevertheless, the Enlightenment did spread, generating new forms, including the novel and the French *Encyclopédie*, and appearing in diverse aspects of everyday experience, such as gardening and eating. By shining sometimes harsh new light on the social, political, and cultural worlds of the Old Regimes,

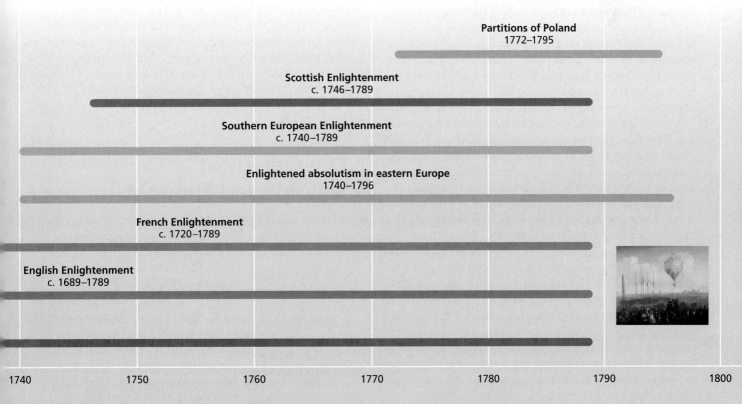

Partitions of Poland
1772–1795

Scottish Enlightenment
c. 1746–1789

Southern European Enlightenment
c. 1740–1789

Enlightened absolutism in eastern Europe
1740–1796

French Enlightenment
c. 1720–1789

English Enlightenment
c. 1689–1789

| 1740 | 1750 | 1760 | 1770 | 1780 | 1790 | 1800 |

Enlightenment thought provided Europeans with the capacity to look critically at their own society and the hope that modern individuals could change their lives, and perhaps even the whole world, for the better.

Europe's Many Enlightenments

Enlightenment is a catch-all term that covers the many attempts at rethinking religion, society, and human nature between about 1689 and 1789. The century that began with England's Glorious Revolution and ended with the outbreak of the French Revolution was in political and economic affairs an eventful one, marked by absolutist warfare and the expansion of commerce and colonization.

What did it mean to believe in enlightenment? Why did new hopes for improvement take so many different forms across the continent?

The second half of the century saw considerable population growth and a proto-industrial takeoff, at least in the northwest. Culturally, this century was perhaps even more eventful. The cultural changes of this era made possible the careers of daring innovators such as Defoe or his countryman John Locke, whose ideas provided the torch that allowed many Europeans to see their lives and their communities in a new light.

Of course, not all Europeans read the works of enlightened thinkers; most Europeans still could not read at all. But some of the ideas of the Dutch, Scottish, German, and English Enlightenments did trickle down to ordinary readers, in simplified and often distorted forms. Enlightened ideas also made their way into Spain and Russia, into Ottoman-held Greece and Habsburg Austria, mixing in each context with local conditions and complaints. Criticisms of religious authorities and new ideas about how to make music, grow crops, and spin cotton came from lower- and middle-class people as well as from upper-class iconoclasts and inventors. Collectively, these ideas contributed to Europeans' spreading self-confidence, which allowed individuals to try new things and trust their own reason and senses rather than the received wisdom of traditional authorities. "Dare to know!" was the Enlightenment's motto, the German philosopher Immanuel Kant claimed in 1784. Kant was right: fundamentally, to believe in enlightenment was to believe that knowing or trying new things would enhance the human capacity for self-improvement.

But if "daring to know" lay at the heart of the Enlightenment, the forms that new daring took differed greatly across Europe's regions, as did the pace at which new ideas were received, accepted, and put into practice. In western states such as the Dutch Republic, England, Scotland, and France, enlightened ideas tended to be generated by people of middling wealth and status, men and women who had profited from the commercial revolution or were excited by the new science. Here, we can speak of enlightened societies, where dense urban networks, high rates of literacy, relative religious toleration, the existence of a moderately wealthy third estate, and regular exposure to overseas goods and ideas made possible an earlier and more broadly based sharing of new ideas and the pioneering of many modern forms of thought. In the west, France was to play a particularly important role during the eighteenth century. The reason for this was that France generated a great number of innovative thinkers during a period in which its rulers remained Old Regime absolutists; that the French Enlightenment transpired in a Catholic nation—where the clergy played a more prominent role than was the case in England or the Dutch Republic—also made this Enlightenment more directly threatening to the ruling elite.

In eastern Europe, by contrast, enlightenment was for the most part a top-down affair: new ideas were introduced by rulers such as Frederick the Great of Prussia or Joseph II of Austria, figures who wanted to rule (or make war) more efficiently. These enlightened absolutists did transform their state bureaucracies; check the power of the churches; and patronize innovative scholars, artists, and musicians. But especially in the most easterly states—Russia, for example—state censorship plus poverty and low levels of literacy prevented enlightened ideas from traveling very far down the social scale. In southern Europe, too, the political power and popularity of the Catholic Church silenced most radical critics, though Italian cities such as Rome, Florence, and Venice remained rich cultural centers.

If we can say, with Kant, that enlightenment was about "daring to know," or daring to believe that change for the better might be possible, we must recognize that certain kinds of daring were more or less possible for Europeans, depending on the political, social, and economic conditions into which they were born. This chapter is called "Many Enlightenments" because, though there was one general movement, one "century of light," Europeans experienced the period very differently and in ways that would fundamentally shape the many cultures and polities of what would become, after the French Revolution, modern Europe.

The Origins of Enlightened Thought

Historically speaking, the Enlightenment's faith in the possibility of individual and social improvement grew out of a general revulsion toward the religiously inspired warfare

How did the quiet revolutions of the Old Regimes, especially the scientific revolution, lay the foundations for the Enlightenment?

of the sixteenth and seventeenth centuries along with a new openness to the world made possible by the commercial, scientific, and military revolutions. The commercial revolution made at least some Europeans richer and exposed them to new goods and lands. The military revolution promoted technological innovation and the development of bureaucracies; some of these new bureaucracies practiced **meritocracy,** the hiring of individuals based on their talents rather than on their birth. Absolutism, too, made a contribution, by beginning to break down the old system of aristocratic and clerical privileges and by centralizing and rationalizing the power of the state.

The scientific revolution played an especially important role in fostering enlightened thought. In showing that classical writers and church teachings could be wrong and that more rigorous methods of experimentation could lead to *new* truths about the human body, the stars, and the movement of matter, the new science made a critical contribution. Galileo and Newton had shown that nature was consistent, that its laws applied to the heavens and the earth, to England and to China, to the lives of peasants and the lives of kings. Even freaks of nature such as two-headed calves or earthquakes could be explained and did not have to be chalked up to the extraordinary intervention of God in the world or to witchcraft. Meanwhile, Christian humanists and radical religious thinkers asked daring questions about the Bible and about the outmoded, intolerant, or irrational policies of their state churches. Finally, political philosophers such as Hugo Grotius and Thomas Hobbes convinced their contemporaries that people who were not monarchs could speculate about the natural laws of statecraft. That eighteenth-century Europeans could "dare to know" owed a great deal to the willingness of these thinkers to risk their careers and sometimes their lives in the pursuit of ideas.

The Enlightenment is one of the great examples in history of a movement made by individuals, some of whose works are still regularly read and remembered, while others have faded into obscurity. Everywhere it was individuals who made the Enlightenment happen, whether by developing a new theory of proper state governance or by imposing new edicts of toleration or by composing new forms of music. Broadly speaking, these individuals shared many values, including the commitment to courageous use of one's reason, the longing to find universal laws, and the desire to improve the human condition. But these individuals were of different types and worked in places that offered different opportunities and constraints. Improvement was more thinkable and more feasible in some places than others, and the ways in which enlightened ideas did, or did not, permeate each of these places would shape the ways in which each of Europe's states passed into the revolutionary era and the modern world.

Enlightened Societies in the Dutch Republic and Great Britain

Enlightened ways of thinking came earlier and were more pervasive in the Dutch Republic, the British Isles, a few Italian and Swiss city-states, and France, places

> **What conditions and circumstances in the Dutch Republic, England, and Scotland fostered the development of enlightened thought?**

where the scientific, military, agricultural, and commercial revolutions had created a relatively large, geographically concentrated, and well-educated elite, composed of nobles and clerics but also of well-to-do members of the third estate. The latter increasingly sought to distinguish themselves from poorer members of their estate, describing themselves as **bourgeois** (denoting their usual residence in *bourgs,* or market towns). Where this sort of elite evolved, enlightened ideas spread easily from the middling classes upward and downward, creating an ever-widening band of shared conceptions—or at least shared debates. This broader elite was instrumental in the creation of what is known as **the public sphere,** the virtual world in which individuals from different regions, status groups, and religious backgrounds speak to one another, and to society at large, on subjects of mutual interest. Although cultural exchange before the late seventeenth century remained largely private, between elite individuals who knew one another personally or, as in the Republic of Letters, corresponded with one another directly, the development of a public sphere made possible a different kind of cultural world, one conducive to the spread of Enlightenment values. One of the first places to move from private to public conversations was the nation that was, from the sixteenth century, unique in so many ways: the Dutch Republic.

The Dutch Republic

In previous chapters we explored the unique political system, commercial efflorescence, and tradition of religious toleration of the Dutch Republic. All these factors help explain the vital role played by the Dutch in laying the foundations for enlightened thought already in the seventeenth century. From the 1550s to the 1790s, many exiles, including English Puritans and Bohemian Protestants, made the Dutch Republic their home. Here individuals dared to write and experiment in ways they could not imagine doing elsewhere. Here Hugo Grotius wrote on natural law and on the freedom of the seas, and Jan Steen and other artists produced some of the first paintings devoted to scenes of ordinary people engaged in ordinary affairs (see Chapter 14). Steen was able to sell paintings to ordinary consumers, for the Dutch had the first public art market in Europe. After 1648, the Republic was home to Baruch Spinoza, whose radical views would have condemned him to the stake in other parts of Europe. The Huguenot Pierre Bayle fled France to come to the Netherlands, where he wrote his *Historical and Critical Dictionary* (1695), a highly original work full of caustic remarks about the France of Louis XIV. In the late seventeenth century, Maria Sibylla Merian worked here, as did John Locke. Even the Russian czar Peter the Great recognized one of the Dutch Republic's great lessons: that a little bit of toleration and the promotion of cosmopolitan commerce attracted to one's shores the most talented of entrepreneurs and the most innovative thinkers.

The Dutch, as we have seen, were innovators in military thinking and shipbuilding, in canal building and the formation of joint-stock companies. They were experts, too, in the growing of exotic flowers, the making of telescopes, and still-life painting. Their universities enrolled students eager to study Asian languages and human anatomy. Dutch publishing houses churned out publications in many languages, making it possible for French and German radicals to smuggle banned books into their homelands. In all these ways, the Dutch drew new people into conversation with one another, inviting individuals who had been strangers to join a series of public conversations.

Baruch Spinoza (1632–1677), the most radical philosopher of his day, lived and worked in Amsterdam. Spinoza was a highly unorthodox Jewish philosopher and mathematician, isolated even from the Dutch Jewish community by his radical views. He worked as a lens grinder by day and a philosopher by night. In his *Theologico-Political Treatise* (1670), he described the world as pure matter and free will as an illusion. For Spinoza, God and Nature boiled down to the same thing—the universe's creative force. In his mind, the Christian Bible was a fiction, whose absurd claims flew in the face of natural laws. Spinoza's *Treatise* was quickly placed on the papal index of prohibited books, and the Dutch also disallowed further publication of his work during his lifetime. Such a radical stance was more than even the Dutch could tolerate.

Banning Spinoza's work did not, however, keep his ideas from spreading. *The Treatise of the Three Imposters,* an anonymous pamphlet probably written around 1688, but circulating mostly after 1711, claimed that Moses, Jesus, and Muhammad were all deceivers, who bamboozled their followers into believing their versions of dogma. The anonymous author drew heavily on Spinoza's ideas, insisting that the only true way to understand God was the rational one, that is, through studying nature. The New Testament, by contrast, was "nothing but a tissue of dreamings which ignorance brought into fashion, which interest maintains, and which tyranny protects." No man in his sense, the *Treatise* concluded, can believe in God, Spirit, or Devils. "All of these big words have been forged only to dazzle or intimidate the vulgar."[1] This pamphlet, like Spinoza's own work, remained banned across Europe throughout the eighteenth century, but contraband versions circulated un-

A Dutch Dissection In 1632, the young painter Rembrandt immortalized a dissection performed before Amsterdam's Guild of Surgeons by the leading anatomist Dr. Nicholaes Tulp. Tulp here exhibits the dissected arm of his subject—probably a deceased criminal—while referring to an open book, probably Vesalius's 1534 *On the Fabric of the Human Body.*

derground, challenging intellectuals to defend their religious beliefs and preparing people to think that, although Scripture and church rituals might be good for the soul, more permanent and universal truths were to be found by studying nature and consulting one's reason.

England

The English Enlightenment, like the Dutch, contributed much early on. Like the Netherlands, England also could boast relative religious toleration and a thriving commercial economy. The overturning of absolutism and the establishment of parliamentary sovereignty made early modern England a model for reformers on the continent. Many critics of the Old Regimes looked to English law to formulate their views on *rights,* an unusual concept in a world in which individuals were used to being described as subjects with *duties* and with or without *privileges,* and not as citizens with equal protections under the law. They admired, too, England's increasingly powerful House of Commons, whose delegates were elected by the citizenry. Finally, England's increasing wealth and its relatively uncensored press appealed to those who felt deprived of the opportunity to rise in the world or to express themselves as they wished.

In the seventeenth and early eighteenth centuries, the English were indeed innovators. They shared with the Dutch the claim to having developed joint-stock companies and stock markets. England was home to the first royal academy of sciences (the Royal Society of London) and to many leading scientists, including Isaac Newton. Although they borrowed the idea of opening public coffee houses from the Ottomans and the Viennese, the English made visiting the coffee house central to the exchange of political and commercial information, especially in metropolitan London, which by 1750 was Europe's largest city, with a population of more than 750,000.

The English also led the way in newspaper publishing, novel writing, the making of nautical instruments, cotton spinning, and the insurance industry. Along with the Dutch, they also led the world in the slave trade, a much more nefarious form of exchange. By the end of the eighteenth century, however, it was also in England that campaigns to abolish slavery were most active, and the English were first to permanently abolish the slave trade in 1807, though the practice continued in English colonies until 1833 and in the now independent United States until 1863.

England produced many important writers after 1689, including novelists such as Defoe. Its most important enlightened thinker was John Locke (1632–1704), whose father had served in Cromwell's army. The young Locke trained to be a doctor, and kept abreast of the new science all his life. But in the 1660s he entered politics, as a Whig. He stood for Parliament and won election to the House of Commons but had to flee England during the Exclusion Crisis (see Chapter 14) because of his outspoken opposition to the crowning of James II. In the 1680s, he settled in the Dutch Republic, where he had ample time to travel, read, and meet with other victims of religious and political intolerance. There he began his writing career in earnest. Though he waited to publish his work until after the Glorious Revolution—and even then published much of it anonymously—Locke's mature thinking took shape during this period of exile and political turmoil.

Upon his return to England in 1688, Locke immediately began to publish a slew of path-breaking works. In "A Letter Concerning Toleration" (1689), he argued that natural law gave individuals the right to practice their faith as they wished, undisturbed by the authorities or by their neighbors. Only if worshippers broke civil laws should the state intervene. In his brief "Letter," a reaction both to Louis XIV's revocation of the Edict of Nantes in 1685 and to England's recent religious conflicts, Locke articulated the key arguments for the principle of the separation of church and state. Even Locke had some caveats: he did not think Catholics, Muslims, or Jews should be allowed full citizenship, as he feared they were beholden

Conversations at the Coffee House Customers at London's coffee houses met to discuss business and to catch up on the latest news. Because they were public institutions, coffee houses allowed both business associates and strangers to interact briefly, without needing an introduction to a private home.

to foreign powers and thus considered themselves bound by other laws. In his day, however, the idea that the state should not meddle in religious affairs was a remarkably progressive one, and one no state ventured to implement until Thomas Jefferson enshrined it in the Constitution of the United States.

Next (in 1690) came Locke's theory of mind, *An Essay on Human Understanding.* This book served as a fundamental resource for Enlightenment philosophy, for it proposed that knowledge needed to be put on a new basis. Much of what currently passed for knowledge, Locke contended, was in fact superstition or unfounded claims: people wrongly believed that their ideas had come from God or from reliable ancient traditions. Not so, Locke argued. Rather, every person was born as a blank slate (**tabula rasa**) and came to understand the world through his or her senses. Like Sir Francis Bacon (see Chapter 15), Locke was a great believer in experiments: only through the process of testing their ideas against nature could individuals discover real, usable truths. Thus, individuals in the here and now must test conventional ideas and throw out those that could not be substantiated. One of the revolutionary aspects of Locke's *Essay on Human Understanding* was the notion that old claims could no longer be considered true unless they were tested anew by modern people. The idea held profound implications for biblical scholars as well as for political activists.

Politics proper was the subject of Locke's most influential work, the *Two Treatises of Government,* published anonymously in 1690. Even though William and Mary had by this time agreed to share sovereignty with Parliament, Locke rightly feared that his defense of government by and for the people was still too radical for many Europeans. In the "First Treatise," Locke confined himself to combating the claims of Europe's absolutist monarchs that God had given them, uniquely, dominion over the earth. The "Second Treatise" began with a thought experiment: what were human societies like in the "state of nature," that is, before recorded history? Using examples from the Old Testament and from European encounters with the indigenous peoples of the Americas, Locke claimed that people had formed civil societies of their own free will, not through warfare, as Thomas Hobbes had claimed, or by God's appointment of a king. They had voluntarily created **social contracts,** giving up some of their natural freedoms in order to impose laws on themselves, for those laws ensured that they could live in stable communities, at peace with one another. But those contracts, Locke argued, were binding only as long as they served the common good. If the king violated the contract by placing himself above the law, the people had the right to rebel and form a new social contract. Locke was the first philosopher to put individual rights, rather than privileges and obligations, at the core of his political philosophy, and thus many describe him as the first modern political theorist.

Locke's arguments in the "Second Treatise" clearly were intended to legitimize the overthrow of James II in the Glorious Revolution—but they also had much wider applicability. Locke knew that Europe was chock full of absolutist rulers and that advocating their overthrow was a dangerous business. He did not advocate rebellion against law-abiding monarchs or the egalitarian redistribution of wealth. On the contrary, another of his major arguments in the "Second Treatise" was that social contracts existed to protect individuals' property. Property, Locke thought, gave people a form of freedom and independence (for those who are dependent on others for basic necessities cannot make free choices), and thus those who seize property unlawfully are to be considered tyrants. A man of modest income and tastes, Locke did not approve of aristocratic extravagances and disapproved of those who owned land but did not work to make it fruitful. He was not, however, a socialist, nor did he advocate universal suffrage. Although he believed women should have more rights than were accorded to them at the time, he still thought that the people who ran the government should be middle- and upper-class Protestant men. In this way, he was very much a man of his time, but still the first founding father of the interlinked political, social, and economic worldview that the nineteenth century would call liberalism (see Chapter 18).

Scotland

The Scottish Parliament was not particularly pleased by the Glorious Revolution of 1688–1689. After all, a Scottish line of kings had been deposed. Moreover, as English commercial activity blossomed in the later seventeenth century, the kingdom's highly profitable overseas trade remained tightly controlled by English shippers thanks to the Navigation Acts (see Chapter 14). Scottish businessmen and politicians resented these restrictions, and wanted very much to share in the fruits of a highly profitable trade in commodities such as slaves, sugar, and cotton textiles. The 1707 Act of Union provided a solution to this Scottish-English antagonism. The act called for the Scots to give up their separate provincial parliament in Edinburgh, while the English opened English and colonial markets to Scottish merchants. By uniting these two states, the act created what would henceforth be known as the United Kingdom of Great Britain.

The Act of Union exchanged Scottish political independence for a share in England's booming colonial trade, which included the shipping of slaves to the New World. The act especially profited the southernmost or Lowlands part of Scotland, where the land was best and where the port cities of Edinburgh and Glasgow are situated (Map 16.1). Here, a civic-minded elite, composed heavily of Presbyterian men, dedicated itself to commerce and to economic modernization. Lowlanders founded organizations such as the Honorable Society of Improvers in the Knowledge of Agriculture, where men could share their ideas about production—still largely agricultural, as the society's title suggests—and debate means by which their communities, as well as the human race at large, could be improved.

Over time, the Lowlanders' world diverged more and more from that of the **Highlanders,** their fellow countrymen to the north. Most Highlanders were Catholic pastoral farmers whose first loyalties were to their clan lords. Many still wore kilts and spoke Gaelic, the Celtic language they shared with the Irish. The Act of Union had no benefits for them; on the contrary, they saw it as the selling of Scotland's independence for English gold. In the debacle known as **the Forty-Five,** the Highlanders, led by James II's grandson, Charles Edward Stuart, marched on London in what proved to be a vain attempt to turn back the clock." (See Map 16.1.)

After the Forty-Five, Lowland Scots turned their backs on the past and put their faith in the future. They had good reason to do so: by 1750, rents were rising across the British Isles. Linen and iron industries had begun to prosper, and trade with the colonies in commodities such as cattle and tobacco had expanded greatly. Blankets, rugs, curtains, china, and copper wares, once reserved for the rich, now made their way down the social scale. Fortunes were made in the manufacture of nails and buttons, the tobacco trade, and the saucepan industry; some mass-produced clothing, candles, and furniture were now available to the expanding middling classes. This world also produced the path-breaking philosophy of David Hume and his friend Adam Smith, who drew on the experience of his "nation of shopkeepers" to create the new science of political economy.

ADAM SMITH. When the Forty-Five broke out, Adam Smith (1723–1790) was studying ancient philosophy at

Oxford. No fan of the Highlanders' cause, Smith waited until the following year to return to Scotland, hoping to contribute to his nation's advancement through enlightened learning and the encouragement of commerce. In 1763, Smith accepted a position as a private tutor. This allowed him to travel with his pupil, in particular to France, where he was most impressed by a group of economic theorists known as the physiocrats. The physiocrats believed in rationalizing the economy, first by making agriculture more productive and second by freeing the marketplace from restrictions. They coined the expression *laissez faire*, which meant that people should be allowed to pursue their own interests without being restricted by guild rules, special privileges, or mercantilist policies. *Laissez faire* later became synonymous with free trade, but here it was a battle cry in the fight against the inefficiencies and inequalities of the Old Regimes. Smith returned to Scotland in 1766, where, thanks to the Act of Union, mercantile commerce was producing more wealth than ever before. Ironically, Smith's major treatise in defense of free trade took shape just at the moment mercantilist profits were making Lowland Scots rich and intellectual life in Scotland lively.

Smith's *An Inquiry into the Nature and Causes of the Wealth of Nations* (1776) was a work of moral philosophy as well as the first attempt to discover the laws of economic behavior. Smith believed that when we pursue our own happiness, we naturally promote the happiness of others; this is the case in the marketplace as well as in the moral sphere. Smith argued that states should not interfere with nature or with human nature; they should not attempt to limit trade (by imposing taxes and tariffs) or to force production (as the Swedish did by attempting to grow pineapples in Scandinavia). Rather, people should cultivate or make what suits them best and then seek to exchange this with others who are acting in the same way, thereby maximizing the happiness of all. Smith advocated what he called the division of labor to achieve greater efficiency in production. Instead of one pin-maker making a whole pin, several workers should divide up the jobs involved, thus saving time and making pins more affordable for all (for an image of a pin-making workshop in Smith's day, see the section "Spreading the Enlightenments," later in this chapter).

Smith believed that the market, if allowed to operate freely, would itself regulate the quantity and prices of goods, but for this to happen, old, unnatural restrictions had to be removed. Doing away with guilds would allow all who wished to produce pins or shoes to do so, and competition between producers would force prices down to their natural level, making goods more accessible. Leaving everything up to the market, or to nature—Smith thought the two interchangeable—would produce the utopian outcome he advocated in his book's opening

MAP 16.1 | The Rising in Scotland and England, 1745–1746
This map shows the route traveled by Charles Edward Stuart ("Bonnie Prince Charlie") from his landing at Moldart to the defeat of his Jacobite army at Culloden. ***Bonnie Prince Charlie chose to land in the Scottish Highlands because he (rightly) expected the support for his uprising would be strongest there. What problems did landing so far to the north pose for his bid to reclaim the English throne?***

Source: Geoffrey Plank, *Rebellion and Savagery* (Philadelphia: University of Pennsylvania Press, 2005), 2.

pages: universal opulence, or, as he put it, a Europe in which "a workman, even of the lowest and poorest order, if he is frugal and industrious, may enjoy a greater share of the necessaries and conveniences of life than it is possible for any savage to acquire."[2]

Smith's most memorable image in *Wealth of Nations* was that of the "invisible hand," the completely natural process by which the free market distributed goods, jobs, and profits. But Smith did not think that this invisible hand would be impeded by the imposition of some taxes. Taxes, he thought, were needed to provide for defense, elementary schooling, roads, and even for the glory of the monarch. Nor did he defend the rich of his day against the poor: he despised some of the biggest capitalist enterprises of his day, including the East India Companies, in part because they were state-licensed monopolies, and he worried that the division of labor might create citizens whose minds were numbed by repetitive work. For

1745–1746: The Highlanders Revolt

In emphasizing the changes introduced by the Enlightenment, we often fail to understand the resistance that enlightened ideas encountered and the fact that some Europeans stood to lose by their importation. The Scottish Highlanders opposed what others called enlightened advances, such as the Glorious Revolution and the rise of Lowland commerce, recognizing that these developments endangered their privileges, autonomy, and traditional way of life. They did not accept William and Mary as legitimate rulers, but continued to regard James II, a Scot and a Catholic, and his descendants as the rightful heirs to the English throne. To their sorrow, James, who was living in exile in Paris, died in 1701, but Highland Jacobites (supporters of James; *Iacob* is a Latin form of "James") staged an uprising in 1715 in the hopes of putting his son, James Edward Stuart, in power. The uprising erupted into a full-scale war in Scotland, pitting English troops against Highland clan armies. Most Lowlanders stayed home, unwilling to side with Highlanders whom they increasingly viewed as backward, barbaric, and lacking any enlightened virtues.

Gradually, James Edward Stuart, living comfortably in France, gave up his bid for restoration, but the Highlanders continued to pine for the Stuarts' return. In 1745, they got their wish. James's impetuous son, Charles Edward Stuart, bought a boat and sailed from France with twelve loyal followers. Landing in northern Scotland in July 1745, he rallied a considerable number of Highlanders to his cause. In six weeks' time, the dashing young man, known as Bonnie Prince Charlie, conquered all of Scotland, striking fear into the hearts of Englishmen and Lowland Scots.

Charles Edward Stuart James II's grandson—known to his supporters as Bonnie Prince Charlie—became a hero to Scottish Highlanders after he invaded Scotland and England in what proved to be a vain attempt to reclaim the English throne.

Bonnie Prince Charlie, full of ill-advised confidence, then ordered a march on England. In early December 1745, it looked as if he might attack London and overthrow the Hanoverian king George II, but confusion in his ranks, his lack of money, and a quickly raised English army undermined the Jacobite revolution. Bonnie Prince Charlie's campaign ended at the Battle of Culloden in northwestern Scotland on April 16, 1746, where an estimated two thousand Jacobites were slaughtered; no more than two dozen Englishmen lost their lives. Bonnie Prince Charlie escaped and hid with supporters for a few months before sailing back to France in September 1746. Other participants in the Forty-Five were severely punished for their sedition. The Highlands were "pacified," as the English put it; large numbers of clansmen were hanged, drawn and quartered, or sent into exile. Repressive measures included the banning of the traditional kilt, the outlawing of Gaelic, and the garrisoning of English troops throughout the Highlands to ensure the loyalty of the clans.

The defeat of the Highlanders in the Forty-Five had several important consequences for Scotland and Scottish intellectual life. The Highlanders would never again threaten the Lowlands, and Scottish nationalism became a sentimental cultural movement, captured most notably in the poetry of Robert Burns and the Gothic novels of Sir Walter Scott. Yet, the Forty-Five also served to strengthen the hand of those who sought solutions to Scotland's woes in economic improvement and the propagation of secular civic virtues. Pragmatic Lowland Scots could now see no future in cultivating a Celtic identity, but neither did these men of action as well as ideas, landed property, and commercial interests, want to see themselves merely as Englishmen with peculiar accents. Their solution was to develop a kind of universalist perspective, a forward-looking, rather than nostalgic, system for self-improvement. The Scottish Enlightenment of the mid-eighteenth century, more than anything else, was about the development of a language of secular civic morality freed from the backwardness of Highland traditions. Its emphasis on moderation, self-control, universal laws, and pragmatic community-building must be seen in light of Scotland's brush with civil war in the Forty-Five.

QUESTION | *How did the defeat of the Forty-Five change the course of Scottish history?*

Smith, opulence was what later generations might describe as middle-class comfort, not late-capitalist conspicuous consumption—and the former is what he wanted all to share. His *Wealth of Nations* was not a celebration of how the market actually functioned in his day, but an optimistic portrayal of what it *should* look like. By portraying the economy as an independent sphere of human activity, one perhaps even more important than politics, Smith laid the foundations for the study of economics as we know it today.

DAVID HUME. Smith was not, of course, the only Scottish philosopher of his age. Probably the most radical and the most renowned among them was David Hume (1711–1776). He was perhaps also the most persecuted. The first of Hume's path-breaking inquiries into the nature of the human mind was *A Treatise of Human Nature* (1737). According to Hume, all systems of philosophy were false, and adherence to any school was a form of superstition. The only way to establish truths about human nature or about the world was to present irrefutable empirical evidence, obtained through observation, experimentation, and data collection. Even then, he argued, it was always possible for human reason itself to be wrong and for our so-called sciences to require revision. Some scholarly readers—including the German philosopher Immanuel Kant—were deeply troubled by Hume's skepticism about the ability of human beings to know the world in any secure way, but Hume's view that the sciences should always be open to self-criticism and to new forms of experimentation laid the foundations for modern scientific thinking.

Hume's religious ideas were even more radical. Taking a step beyond Galileo's suggestion that the Bible's truths might be metaphorical ones, Hume challenged the New Testament's reports of miracles on the grounds that miracles violated the laws of nature. The apostles, he wrote, must have been deceived by appearances. In *The Natural History of Religion* (1757), he argued that all religions began not as the result of a divine revelation, but as prerational responses to natural phenomena—fear or awe, for example, inspired by a thunderstorm or an earthquake. Responses to natural phenomena led the first human societies to develop polytheistic forms of worship. Later, reason prompted societies to adopt moral values and monotheism, which made for more unified and productive communities. Religion had its social functions, then, but to continue to believe in religious precepts once reason and science came along was to hold on to superstitions in the face of real evidence. "Ignorance is the mother of Devotion," Hume wrote. Hume's religious works gave him a reputation as an atheist and prevented him from getting an academic post in Presbyterian Scotland, but he persuaded many readers that religion and miracles belonged to an early stage of mental development that had now been superseded. With Adam Smith, David Hume believed that human societies were evolving toward greater rationality and happiness, but they had some distance to go to reach those goals.

The French Enlightenment

The peculiarities, and the peculiar power, of the French Enlightenment were the result of the tension between France's openness to new ideas and the resistance of its ruling orders to change. By 1750, in the British Isles and the Dutch Republic, absolutism had been defeated, relative religious toleration had been established, and urban and commercial culture was providing new outlets for bourgeois citizens to get out from under aristocratic dominance. In France, by contrast, although absolutism had weakened the church and the aristocracy, these entities still had plenty of clout, and they used it chiefly to resist social, cultural, and economic change. During his very long reign (1721–1774), Louis XV employed a vast array of censors and police spies to harass those who challenged his authority or that of the Catholic Church. Although this censorship was not terribly effective in keeping criticism from circulating, it did restrict the freedom of the public sphere. Resistance to new ideas also made many intellectuals despise both the king's government and the Catholic clergy, and cease attempting to acquire royal or clerical patronage for their works.

> What factors made the French Enlightenment so prominent?

Instead, French intellectuals turned increasingly to private or illicit sources to support their work. Many aspiring writers found patrons in liberal aristocrats, especially female aristocrats who invited them to circulate among their friends and other intellectuals at private gatherings known as **salons.** French critics of the church or state were also able to sell their works in an increasingly lively market, some of it operating underground in order to evade the censors. Thus, even though French Enlightenment thought spread partly through private salons and partly through banned books, a relatively wide public did gain access to new ideas. By the time Louis XVI took the throne in 1774, French thought had become so powerful and diverse that many people associated enlightenment with France itself.

Montesquieu and Voltaire

Two figures stand out among the first generation of French Enlightenment thinkers: Charles de Secondat, the baron de Montesquieu; and François Marie Arouet, who adopted the pen name of Voltaire. Montesquieu and Voltaire were two of France's early *philosophes*, a term better rendered in English as "literary men of ideas" than as "philosophers." Both were admirers of Locke and of the English political system, but had quite different personalities. Born in 1689,

Montesquieu was an aristocrat and a genteel, erudite critic of his society; Voltaire, born just five years later, was not a nobleman, but the son of a successful lawyer. He proved to be a maverick, with a violent temper and a vicious wit. Both Frenchmen were more literary and long-winded than was Locke. Although Montesquieu's first acclaimed work, *The Persian Letters* (1721), was relatively brief, his 1748 *Spirit of the Laws* ran to thousands of pages. Voltaire published more than two thousand works in many genres—from short stories and plays to polemics on religious and political topics. Along with Locke, Montesquieu and Voltaire knew the political world of their day from the inside. Montesquieu was a member of the parlement of Bordeaux and an intimate of many of Louis XV's courtiers; Voltaire was patronized and consulted by the rulers of France, Prussia, and Russia. If Locke provided many of the ideas that would shape modern political theories, Montesquieu and Voltaire added the wit and worldliness that made the Old Regimes seem ridiculous and obsolete.

Montesquieu's *Persian Letters* was a strange sort of political critique, but it proved to be a hugely popular and effective one. The book was written as a series of letters exchanged between two visitors from the Persian Empire to the French court during the last years of Louis XIV's reign and the first turbulent years of the regency that followed. The writers of the *Letters* marvel at the strange habits of the world of Versailles. Montesquieu's criticisms are rather veiled, but the visitors clearly find Louis high-handed and his courtiers a spoiled bunch. They find the post–Sun King era much worse, as court intrigue and stock swindles create chaos. In the end, the Persians return home with eye-opening experiences about other ways of governing, other customs, and other religious practices. Montesquieu, who published the *Letters* under a pseudonym, does not advise that the Persians adopt the practices of the French, or vice versa. His point is simply that one learns a great deal about oneself—including about the absurdities of time-honored customs and forms of persecution—by seeing oneself from another's perspective.

Montesquieu followed *The Persian Letters*, the bestseller of its day, with *Considerations on the Causes of the Greatness of the Romans and Their Decline* (1734), a book that clearly suggested the French, after the "greatness" of Louis XIV, were also on the road to ruin. He traveled and began collecting information for his masterpiece, *Spirit of the Laws*. In this comparative work, Montesquieu surveyed the range of human political institutions. He presumed, as did Locke, that governments were made by people, but they were made, he claimed, in response to the climate, customs, and character of each group. The hot and dry conditions that he claimed characterized China, for example, contributed to the rise of what he called oriental despotism, under which the docile and unimaginative people were dominated by the despot who controlled the water. In Switzerland, the high mountains made for small, isolated communities, which organized themselves naturally into republics. Montesquieu praised the

English parliamentary system for its tolerance and inclusiveness and for having developed the idea of checks and balances that prohibited any one branch of the government from usurping too much power. He was openly critical of Catholic religious intolerance and of the Jesuits. Consequently, *Spirit of the Laws* was put on the pope's index of prohibited books and briefly outlawed in France. Montesquieu's aim was not to undermine the church, but to outline the natural laws that made states flourish or decline. In this way, he contributed to founding the discipline we know today as political science.

Like Montesquieu, Voltaire admired England's constitutional monarchy and despised the French clergy and court, whose members he thought corrupt and ignorant. Voltaire was no democrat; indeed, he believed that the little people, like their betters, were greedy, weak, and stupid. He happily accepted patronage from Louis XV, exchanged letters with Catherine the Great of Russia, and lived for three years with Frederick the Great of Prussia in his palace outside Berlin.

Religion, not politics, got Voltaire into trouble. Voltaire did believe in God, but in a purely rational God who was essentially just the creator of the universe and whom individuals came to know by observing nature and history, rather than by reading Christian scriptures. Indeed, Voltaire thought the Christian Bible was full of absurd, narrow-minded, and mean-spirited ideas. Far too much blood had already been spilled in trying to impose these absurdities on other people, he insisted, and he called on his contemporaries to abandon attempts at converting others. He insisted that modern society should "*Ecrasez l'infâme,*" that is, "crush the infamous thing," by which he meant destroy the Old Regimes' religious establishments, including the pope and all the clergy, theology and theologians, and all the rites, garments, proscriptions, tithes, and privileges that religious authorities propagated. In this way, he believed, Europe could rid itself of superstition, irrationality, corruption, and intellectual cowardice, vices he believed were propagated chiefly by the Catholic Church. These views made Voltaire one of the leading champions of **deism,** the belief in the existence of a non-denominational God, who reveals himself only in nature, rather than in any sect's scriptures.

For Voltaire, only things that were universally true were in fact true. Not surprisingly, then, both he, and his highly educated lover, Madame de Châtelet, idolized Isaac Newton. Madame de Châtelet even undertook the laborious task of translating Newton's *Principia* into French. Newton's universal laws of mathematics and physics were the model of what a good truth looked like to the French *philosophe,* who once wrote: "There are no sects in geometry," meaning that any true religion would have to be one on which everyone in the world would agree, just as all agree that a triangle must have three sides. Voltaire's identification of the true with the universal and the rational reveals much about the essence of the high Enlightenment and its tendency to assume that what its members considered

Voltaire Meets His Match Voltaire penned thousands of pages during his long career, but he was also admired widely for his brilliance in conversation. Here he is pictured conversing intimately with his beloved Madame de Châtelet, who was herself widely admired for her intellect.

rational and true should replace the backward and irrational ideas that people had held for centuries. Voltaire's desire to make human institutions more equitable and just was admirable, but there is also a high-handedness to enlightened philosophers such as Voltaire, who thought that everyone should see the world as they did.

One cannot do justice to Voltaire without appreciating his wit. His best-known essays and stories were his satirical ones, in which he caricatured his contemporaries to demonstrate just how ignorant and silly they could be. In *Zadig* (1748), a short story set in ancient Babylon, Voltaire made fun of clerical disputes in his day by describing a raging battle between Zoroastrian priests over whether one properly entered the temple with the right or the left foot first. Zadig, Voltaire's rational hero and alter ego, solves the bitter dispute by declaring that everyone should jump over the temple threshold with both feet. In his darker satire *Candide* (1759), Voltaire parodied enlightened optimists who claimed that they were living in "the best of all possible worlds." On the contrary, *Candide* depicts a world so riddled with corruption and ignorance that the innocent hero can hope to find sanity only by "cultivating his own garden," that is, retreating from the "best world" as much as possible.

Voltaire's relationship to the privileged and powerful in his day was mixed. Abhorred by the clergy, he was frequently jailed, censored, or forced into exile at their request. Some monarchs appreciated his intelligence and his criticisms of the churches and the nobility, but they dispensed with his advice when it did not suit their views. By the time of his death in 1778, Voltaire was rich and famous, but by that time many other Frenchmen were seeking to live by their pens—or just by their wits—and a host of writers across central and southern Europe were churning out critical essays, histories, and plays. All of them looked to Voltaire, and usually to Montesquieu and Locke as well, as the Columbuses who had opened up the new world of enlightened thought.

The French Enlightenment Comes of Age

Born, respectively, in 1689 and 1694, Montesquieu and Voltaire were old enough to remember the era of Louis XIV and to have experienced as adults the persecutions of the 1720s and 1730s. This was not the case for the next generation of French thinkers, who came of age in the 1740s and after, as clerical influence began to recede and as Louis XV's military blunders and political intransigence opened the way for new forms of criticism. This second generation still suffered from imprisonment and exile, but they could also count on a wider pool of patrons and readers. An increasing number of well-educated women organized salon conversations, and an increasing number of bourgeois or even lower-class writers from towns outside the metropole flocked to Paris to seek interlocutors. Many ended up writing or reporting for whoever would pay them, including the chiefs of police, who hired young critics to spy on their colleagues. Some of them wrote treatises on agriculture; others composed pornographic novels. For all, Paris offered a high-profile stage on which one could shine—or fail—and by mid-century, its vibrancy and diversity made it the envy of enlightened thinkers around the world. Yet for those who feared or loathed Enlightenment criticism, the radicalism of some Parisian intellectuals also made the city synonymous with ungodliness or sexual scandals.

Denis Diderot and the French *Encyclopédie*

One of the key French figures identified with Paris was Denis Diderot, a provincial nobody who made his career with his wit and his never-ceasing pen. Diderot came to Paris in 1728 and gradually captivated conversation-hungry nobles with his wit. The sorts of stories he might have told in elite salons can be seen in his risqué novel *The Indiscreet Jewels* (1748). By turning a special ring, the novel's main character makes the courtiers' genitalia report on their recent sexual encounters. Diderot undertook a series of other projects and odd writing jobs before settling down to edit the *Encyclopédie*, a huge undertaking since he wrote many of the entries himself. Like many members of his generation, Diderot made himself an expert on a vast number of subjects, from painting to politics, and conversed not only with aristocrats and his fellow enlighteners, but also with tradesmen of all sorts, from whom he hoped to learn about "the useful sciences." He was thrown in jail periodically, but managed to inspire and instruct a large number of correspondents, friends, and readers in Paris and beyond.

Jean-Jacques Rousseau

Jean-Jacques Rousseau (1712–1778) was born and spent his early years in the Swiss city-state of Geneva, and throughout his life he remained proud of his origins in that Calvinist republic. He did not make it to Paris until 1742, and once there he remained for a time a poor and unknown music copyist. Gradually he made his way to the salons, but unlike Diderot, Rousseau did not care for them, preferring heart-to-heart conversations, especially with aristocratic women. He quickly developed a reputation for insisting on genuineness of feeling and simplicity in dress and manners.

Rousseau's essays, including "Discourse on the Origin of Inequality" (1756), enhanced his reputation for contrariness. In the essay, Rousseau created the figure of the noble savage, the man who, unlike modern men, retained his God-given independence of mind and bodily strength. By contrast, modern people had become slaves to fashion, Rousseau argued, and had lost touch with authentic feelings and freedoms. Rousseau insisted that the origins of the social inequalities that characterized his world could be traced to one moment in human history: the moment at which the first person claimed a piece of property for his own. The claiming of private property, Rousseau argued, was theft, for God had given the world to all men. Worse, those who had committed this original sin had grown rich and established themselves and their families as masters over others for all time. Rousseau was not daring enough to recommend abolishing all private property or overthrowing the aristocracy, but his treatise gave future readers (including Karl Marx) fuel for revolutionary thought.

Rousseau returned to Geneva in 1754 and spent the next six years writing three very different treatises, each of which left deep and lasting marks on the history of ideas. The first of these was *Julie, or The New Heloise* (1761), a philosophy of modern morals disguised as a rewriting of the love story of Heloise and Abelard, the medieval cleric castrated after he impregnated his pupil Heloise. Next came *The Social Contract* (1762), Rousseau's contribution to debates about the proper way to form a government. Finally, in the spring of 1762, Rousseau published *Emile,* a blend of educational treatise and novel. Each of these works was original in its own way, but all were sketches of an ideal future much different from the world Rousseau inhabited.

By late 1762, *Julie* was a sensational success—but *The Social Contract* and *Emile* had been banned by the authori-

Jean-Jacques Rousseau: Honest Man In his autobiographical *Confessions,* Jean-Jacques Rousseau claimed that there had never been a man so honest about his faults as was he. That may have been true, but Rousseau also found fault with many aspects of European society.

ties, not only in France, but in Geneva as well. *Julie* did not lack scandalous content; it was a passion-packed love story, one in which the heroine makes love to a man her parents will not allow her to marry, but afterward denies her love and accepts an arranged marriage. Living in unpretentious circumstances on the shores of Lake Geneva, Julie also provides a new model for female virtue: unlike the Parisian salon hostesses Rousseau knew, she dresses and dines simply and rears and educates her children. Readers loved the novel. One wrote to Rousseau, longing "to throw my arms around you and to thank you a thousand times for the delicious tears that you wrung out of me."[3]

The Social Contract was a wholly different sort of book. In it Rousseau continued the Enlightenment's search for the natural laws that guided the forming of societies. Like Locke, Rousseau claimed that a social contract underlies all states, one that can be dissolved if the rulers become tyrannical. But Rousseau emphasized more than had Locke the sovereignty of the people, who were to be involved directly in the making of all laws. *The Social Contract* opens with the ringing lines: "Man is born free, but he is everywhere in chains," one of many lines that would appeal to liberals and revolutionaries across the world. *The Social Contract* was one of few enlightened treatises to actually recommend democracy as a form of government. Yet what offended the censors in both Geneva and France was not Rousseau's politics, but rather his insistence that state religions bred hypocrisy, for the only real religions were private beliefs of the heart.

Statements about religion in *Emile* got Rousseau in trouble once again, provoking authorities to kick him out of France and to ban his books across the continent. What had Rousseau said in *Emile* that so annoyed the authorities? He had said, first of all, that children should not be taught catechisms, for this just taught them to repeat meaningless phrases at a time they could not possibly hope to make their own decisions about their beliefs. Further, children should not be taught religion directly at all; once they reached maturity, they would, instead, be able to deduce the high probability of God's existence by observing nature's order and bounty. Emile, the protagonist, receives a wholly natural and individualized education; he learns to be independent of all social conventions and to engage only in useful pursuits. He reasons his way through life, and his reason provides him sufficient trust in God. Because he avoids the church, the court, and the big city, and instead enjoys the wholesome food, air, and labor available in the countryside, Emile is able to become a virtuous, autonomous, free man. In the book's final chapter, Rousseau provides his Genevan-French version of Robinson Crusoe with a mate, Sophie, who is supposed to be his ideal companion—but in no way his equal (see Back to the Source at the end of the chapter).

Rousseau championed a kind of republicanism for Geneva, but he was notoriously vague about political affairs in France. He criticized the aristocracy, but even his denunciations of salon ladies who refused to breast-feed their babies were nothing compared to the more scandalous literature others began to publish in his lifetime. Nonetheless, the French authorities forbade him from returning to Paris, and by 1765, he felt sufficiently persecuted even in Geneva that he sailed to England, where he took up residence with David Hume. Eventually, he returned to France, settling in the French countryside and marrying his longtime mistress, the washerwoman Thérèse le Vasseur. Though *Emile* and *The Social Contract* remained banned, *Julie* continued to be popular. Even Queen Marie Antoinette visited the philosopher's grave and established her own rustic farm at Versailles so that she and her elegant friends could cultivate Rousseau's virtues, or at least enjoy their delicious tears.

Enlightened Absolutisms in Central and Eastern Europe

In the Dutch Republic, England, Scotland, and France, most enlightened thinking and writing occurred outside the royal courts, sponsored by the new commercial elite or by aristocrats with sufficient independence from the court and clergy to pay for new ideas. In central Europe, however, the churches retained more of their privileges and power, as did the nobles, who still owned most of the land. Urban centers were few and far between, and the commercial elite remained relatively poor. All these factors impeded the development of a flourishing public sphere. Those who did champion at least some enlightened ideas were the monarchs themselves, for some of these men and women recognized that the new ideas might be useful for modernizing their kingdoms and curbing the power of the clergy and aristocracy. Monarchs here also encouraged the spread of enlightenment throughout the state bureaucracy. On the whole, reformers accepted the notion that if modern ideas were to come to Eastern Europe, they would have to be imposed from the top. They might have been right; but by committing themselves to serving the state and adopting a top-down model of modernization, eastern enlightened thinkers made the further spread of "light" dangerously dependent on the will of monarchs, rather than on the rights and desires of the public at large.

Absolutism was in part a means of modernizing, one driven especially by the military revolution. Building the power of the central state, creating a rationalized tax structure, establishing a more efficient labor force, and centralizing control of trade were all reforms compatible with the Enlightenment's emphasis on reason, universality, and

> **Why was enlightenment in central Europe primarily a top-down affair?**

CHRONOLOGY	Key Texts of the Enlightenment
DATE	**TEXT**
1670	Baruch Spinoza, *Theologico-Political Treatise*
1690	John Locke, *An Essay on Human Understanding* and *Two Treatises of Government*
1737	David Hume, *A Treatise of Human Nature*
1748	Montesquieu, *Spirit of the Laws*
1751–1772	Denis Diderot and Jean d'Alembert, *Encyclopédie*
1759	Voltaire, *Candide*
1761–1762	Jean-Jacques Rousseau, *The Social Contract*, *Julie*, and *Emile*
1764	Cesare Beccaria, *On Crimes and Punishments*
1776	Adam Smith, *Wealth of Nations*
1781	Immanuel Kant, *Critique of Pure Reason*

utility, even if the chief reason for these reforms was to enhance the state's war-making power. Many eighteenth-century monarchs introduced free elementary education, limited or abolished the use of torture, and pushed agricultural reforms. Some created state examinations to ensure a better-educated bureaucracy, and others tried to reform and simplify systems of justice. These reforms were driven not only by humanitarian concerns, but also by practical ambitions. Rulers such as Joseph II of Austria adopted enlightened ideas in part because they believed that happier and wealthier workers would strengthen the state. Moreover, these rulers tended to believe their subjects were too childlike to enlighten themselves, and, probably rightly, they believed that most nobles and clergymen were too resistant to enlightened change to be partners in reform. Thus, in central and eastern Europe, the Enlightenment was much more "top down" than "bottom up." This part of Europe was home to what has come to be called **enlightened absolutism**—rational reform without political power-sharing.

Russia

Russia's Enlightenment came early but never spread below the highest levels of court society; Russia was the most absolutist of enlightened absolutisms. Peter I ("the Great"), whom we met in Chapter 14, did not call Ivan III's Zemsky Sobor into session but undertook on his own the modernization of Russia. He modernized the Russian military and the Russian alphabet, completed the first census, and founded new colleges to transform uneducated nobles into efficient state servants. At the cost of hundreds of thousands of serf lives, he built a whole new capital city to be his "window on the West," at St. Petersburg, and established there an Academy of Sciences and a royal art collection. On the new city's outskirts, he built his own version of Versailles, which he called Petershof. Like many other enlightened absolutists, he attacked the privileges of the Orthodox Church, for whose rituals and hierarchies Peter had little but contempt. He even attempted to ban facial hair in his empire, believing that beards were a sign of barbarism and backwardness.

Peter died in 1725, and his inept successors added little until the German-born princess Catherine II acceded to the throne in 1762. Subsequently known as Catherine the Great, this determined ruler continued Peter's westernizing campaign. She spoke fluent French as well as German; corresponded with *philosophes*; and wrote her own educational manual, plays, and poetry. She displayed her enormous collection of western artworks at her Winter Palace in St. Petersburg and enticed western scholars, artists, and writers to come to live at her court. Waging war against the Ottoman Empire, she won the Crimea and access to the Black Sea as well as control of four rivers critical to furthering Russian economic and political penetration of southeastern Europe: the Dniester, the Don, the Dnieper, and the Bug (Map 16.2).

Absolutism, Russian Style Catherine II, czarina of Russia, was an avid reader of enlightened literature and significantly diminished the wealth and power of the Russian Orthodox Church. But her modernizing efforts did not include the abolition of serfdom.

Catherine thought that religion, even Islam, was a good way to pacify frontier territory. Her 1773 edict, "Toleration of All Faiths," allowed Muslims free practice of their faith and the right to build mosques. She was less tolerant in her treatment of Jews, the first large population of which fell under Russian dominion after the partitions of Poland in 1772, 1793, and 1795. Catherine gave up trying to force the Jews to convert, but made all of those who lacked a special permit reside in what after 1791 was called the Pale of Settlement, where they were subjected to discriminatory policies and taxes, and sometimes made the targets of popular violence. Catherine also attacked the privileges of the Russian Orthodox Church. She seized control of its lands and excluded religious instruction from schooling, further reducing the wealth and power of the clergy.

Neither Peter nor Catherine contemplated abolishing serfdom, for to do so would have provoked a revolt on the part of the nobles, most of whom continued to live on their rural estates in sublime ignorance of the westernizing ferment under way in St. Petersburg. Thus, no real agricultural revolution took place in Russia, and at a time of rapidly rising literacy in the West, most Russians remained illiterate.

When Catherine died in 1796, St. Petersburg had become a center of enlightened activity, but the vast expanses of the Russian Empire remained largely untouched by the modernizing efforts of nearly a century of enlightened absolutist leadership.

Prussia

Like his predecessors, Frederick II ("the Great") of Prussia took good care of his army. But Frederick also put considerable effort into improving the land his army conquered. During his long reign (1740–1786), he drained swampy territory and cleared forests in East Prussia, making it possible to resettle some 300,000 subjects from his crowded western territories to the newly annexed eastern ones. He modernized the Prussian bureaucracy and largely dismantled religious persecution and censorship, creating an environment in which a Prussian Enlightenment could flourish. Frederick, indeed, despised organized religion. In 1750, he invited Voltaire, Europe's most noteworthy heretic, to live at Sanssouci, Frederick's palace on the outskirts of Berlin. But he had no intention of sharing power with anyone and once told Voltaire, "I view my subjects as a herd of stags on some noble's estate . . . their only function is to reproduce and fill the space."[4]

Frederick's Prussia was an important, but not an exclusive, generator of something new in the eighteenth century: a body of literary and scholarly works written in German, rather than in French or Latin. Although many people, including Frederick himself, continued speaking in French at court, a wave of mid-century authors wrote in German, the language of most ordinary people. About one-third of the books published in 1700 were still in Latin. By 1780, only one-tenth remained in that language. Many German authors also took inspiration from the Lutheran nonconformist movement called Pietism, which emphasized such noncourtly attitudes as simplicity, individual virtue, and introspection. One of those authors was the philosopher Emmanuel Kant.

MAP 16.2 | The Partitions of Poland, 1772–1795

In the later eighteenth century, Poland ceased to be an independent kingdom as its neighbors divided up Polish territory in three successive partitions. This enlarged the Russian, Austrian, and Prussian states, giving each more territory. Now the expansionist designs of these three powers would have to be redirected to the south or to the west. **In what ways did the partitioning of Poland create shifts in the balance of power?**

IMMANUEL KANT. In addition to having an enlightened ruler, Prussia was home to Germany's most important Enlightenment philosopher, Immanuel Kant (1724–1804). As professor at the University of Königsberg, the young Kant devoted himself chiefly to the natural sciences—until he read the work of David Hume. Hume's skepticism terrified him, for it suggested that there was no secure way for humans to know the world. How then, Kant agonized, could there be true science? In his *Critique of Pure Reason* (1781), Kant sought to answer Hume by arguing that the security of our knowledge lies not in the world *out there*, but in the rational faculties that we all share; we can create knowledge that is true *for us*. Kant followed his groundbreaking book with a *Critique of Practical Reason* (1788), which showed how humans use introspection, rather than logic, to derive moral laws. Another work, the *Critique of Judgment* (1790), tried to bridge science and morals and show how the contemplation of nature could lead humans to subjective, but not scientific, certainty about the existence of God. By emphasizing subjective reasoning, Kant's third *Critique* charted a course many would follow from the Enlightenment's belief in universal laws to Romanticism's emphasis on individual experience.

THE GERMAN ENLIGHTENMENT BEYOND PRUSSIA.
Kant was a principal, but not the only creator of the German Enlightenment, and not all enlightened German thinkers were Prussians. The dramatist and philosopher Gotthold Ephraim Lessing was born in Saxony and traveled extensively. His most famous play, *Nathan the Wise* (1779), went further than any of his contemporaries in urging toleration for Muslims and Jews. *Nathan* was inspired in part by Lessing's friendship with Moses Mendelssohn, the great figure of the German-Jewish Enlightenment who wrote widely in support of blending faith and reason. Mendelssohn encouraged Jews to assimilate into enlightened society, though his critics and his Christian friends misconstrued his message as urging his fellow Jews to give up their religion entirely. Mendelssohn was born in the small state of Anhalt-Dessau, but spent most of his adult life in Berlin.

Johann Gottfried Herder studied with Kant, though he never gave up his career as a Lutheran pastor for a post as a university philosopher. Instead, Herder wrote essays on the religions of the ancient East and on the beauties of central European folk songs and customs. The former helped strip the Old Testament of its specialness, and the latter helped fuel Czech and Hungarian nationalism. Born in Prussia, Herder spent much of his time in the town of Weimar, ruled by Duchess Anna Amalia (r. 1758–1775), a great lover of music, poetry, and books, and her equally enlightened successors. Weimar was also home to the great poets Johann Wolfgang von Goethe and Friedrich Schiller, who, like Kant and Herder, wrote works that championed both enlightened and romantic values.

Herder was one of the few German thinkers to hope that social improvement would come from the wider society rather than from the state—and even he was not optimistic that real change might happen anytime soon. The Enlightenment certainly reached more German speakers than Russian ones, and Weimar and Berlin became hotbeds of enlightened activity. But on the whole, enlightenment came late and from above to the German states, and most Germans remained skeptical that the movement would truly improve their lives or free them from their obligations, even when they were fortunate enough to have as their sovereign an Anna Amalia, or a Joseph II, the most enthusiastic proponent of enlightenment ever to rule the Habsburg lands.

Austria

As a young man, Joseph, crown prince and then coregent of Austria, dreamed of curtailing the privileges of the Habsburg nobility and using the money they spent on lavish costumes to improve conditions for all his subjects. He opposed religious intolerance and, even more vehemently, clerics meddling in politics. He paid for the composition of new musical works and read French literature, at least of the moderate and nonlibelous sort. But if Frederick the Great had to wait for his father's death to overhaul Prussia, Joseph had to endure many years of coregency with his mother, Maria Theresa, before he could reform the Habsburg monarchy.

Maria Theresa (r. 1740–1780) was no ordinary mother: she was a highly intelligent, opinionated, and hardworking sovereign and was used to getting her way. She furnished her palace at Schönbrunn with the latest Chinese porcelain and began the process of modernizing the Austrian bureaucracy. She insisted that elementary education should be universal so that her subjects would be both better Christians and better workers. But this ardent believer in her divine right to rule would never have dreamed of corresponding with a *philosophe*. As long as she lived, Maria Theresa kept a lid on Joseph's more radical ideas for overhauling the empire. Only after her death could Joseph begin to reform a regime whose list of banned books was longer than that of the pope.

On becoming emperor in his own right, Joseph II (r. 1780–1790) introduced a large degree of religious toleration for non-Catholic Christians and even for Jews. He allowed virtual freedom of the press, and he reformed and enlarged the bureaucracy to make governance more efficient and to take it, as much as possible, out of the hands of the local aristocrats. More radically, he took steps to dismantle serfdom in the Habsburg lands. In a pastoral letter issued to his officials in 1783, Joseph claimed:

> I have weakened the influences resulting from prejudices and old, deep-rooted habits by means of Enlightenment, and combated them with proofs; I have tried to imbue every official of the state with the love I feel for the general weal and with zeal to serve it . . . [since] all the provinces of the Monarchy form only a single whole and thus can have only one purpose, . . . in all of them nationality and religion must make no difference, and as brothers in one Monarchy all should set to work equally in order to be useful to one another.[5]

Joseph was speaking to his officials in the language of the Enlightenment, celebrating Austria's escape from prejudices and old habits and its adoption of utility and universal brotherhood; however, the language of "father knows best" also appears in the letter. That language was not well received in the Habsburg lands, where each province had jealously preserved its own customs, languages, and laws. Joseph believed that there was "only one good" for his kingdom and that he already knew what that was. Valuing efficiency and utility over anything that might be called democracy, in 1784 he decreed that his whole bureaucracy, whether located in the Austrian Netherlands (today's Belgium) or in Hungary, should produce documents in one language, German. He would continue to appoint non-Germans to high-ranking roles, but they would have to speak German and enforce laws that would be made chiefly in Vienna by the German-speaking elite. The Hungarians refused, insisting on using Latin, and opponents of Habsburg absolutism in Belgium took to speaking Flemish, which before 1784 had been a dying language. Entrenched nobles and clergy members, too, did not think that taking away their power was the proper way to improve the empire. Hungarian aristocrats made impossible Joseph's attempts to abolish serfdom in much of the empire, and the Catholic clergy vehemently opposed his attempts to do away with all monasteries that did not perform useful functions.

After five years of frenzied attempts at reform, Joseph had to admit defeat or, at least, little progress. When he died in 1790, some people were even calling him a despot. Convinced that his was the only rational and right way to think about the world, Joseph had sought reforms he thought beneficial, but he had also expected far too much change, far too fast, and had failed to listen to and compromise with his critics. Unquestionably, Joseph succeeded in introducing enlightened ideas into the Habsburg lands, and his religious reforms, in particular, proved long lasting. His insistence to his empire that "I don't need your permission to do good" also laid the foundations for local elites in the empire to strike back and to insist that doing good was a matter of perspective.

Cultural Enlightenments in Southern Europe

The Enlightenment in southern Europe presents a mixed picture: in Spain and Portugal, most attempts at reform came from above, whereas in some of the Italian city-states, ideas and innovations were shared across a wider, commercial and noble, elite. In all these areas, the Enlightenment did not really challenge the power of rural elites or of the Catholic Church. But in some Italian cities, such as Venice, Rome, and Naples, a long tradition of artistic excellence and musical innovation continued and made a powerful cultural impact on the many northern visitors who came to enjoy Italian art, antiquities, music, and theater. Philosophy, history, and the natural sciences continued to thrive, but the southern European Enlightenment was especially important for the arts and for inspiring a return to Greek and Roman styles known as **neoclassicism,** a style whose simplicity and focus on the human form echoed the Enlightenment's broader admiration for rational thought and natural laws.

> **What forms did enlightenment take in southern Europe?**

Spain and Portugal

The Enlightenment in Spain and Portugal was largely another top-down affair. Borrowing reformist ideas from elsewhere, several enlightened absolutist monarchs made efforts to improve their territories. None of them, however, was as determined to make reforms as Joseph II, and none of them could muster equal courage to face down nobles and clergymen, who on the whole opposed change. Although a few cities, such as Lisbon and Seville, were home to wealthy bourgeois men of commerce as well as to enlightened nobles, in rural areas peasants remained virtually enserfed and illiterate, as in eastern Europe. The power of the papacy in these deeply Catholic regions also made the introduction of religious toleration here difficult. The Spanish and Portuguese crowns continued to profit from overseas colonies, though by the later eighteenth century, trading power and political influence had shifted away from the Mediterranean to northern commercial centers such as Glasgow and London.

The Italian Enlightenment

Since medieval times, Italian city-states such as Florence and Venice had been cultural centers, and even as their wealth and power declined, these cities remained home to wealthy men of commerce and liberal aristocrats eager to patronize the arts and sciences. Although Venice had lost its empire by 1718, it remained an active trading port and home to artists such as Giovanni Battista Tiepolo, who painted ceilings for princes all over Europe. Naples was Europe's third largest city, boasting a population of more than 350,000 by 1800 and stunning late Baroque architecture. From Naples, travelers could easily visit Pompeii, where some of the first modern archaeological excavations were attempted, or Mount Vesuvius, to which early geologists flocked. Florence had fallen on harder times, but remained a lively city.

In Milan, Cesare Beccaria read Montesquieu and developed his own ideas on enlightened statecraft. In his path-breaking treatise, *On Crimes and Punishments* (1764), Beccaria proposed that justice should be rational and humane. In most Old Regime systems, arrested persons were presumed guilty. Beccaria argued instead that defendants should be presumed innocent and that evidence was needed to prove their guilt. Beccaria's arguments, including his opposition to torture and to the death penalty, were admired widely by enlightened thinkers throughout Europe.

Although eighteenth-century Rome remained the center of Catholic Christendom, the Eternal City also played an important role in the making of enlightened culture. Northern European intellectuals, both Catholics and Protestants, began to make their way to Rome to see its classical remains. Rome became the highlight of "the grand tour," the city-to-city travel that wealthy fathers organized for their sons, to familiarize them with Europe's diverse culture and to improve their tastes. In Rome, young aristocrats visited the pope's enormous collection of classical sculptures or purchased their own statues to adorn their mansions back home. Those who were serious about classicism might have purchased beautifully engraved volumes such as *The Antiquities of Athens* (1762), written and illustrated by English architects James Stuart and Nicholas Revett, or *The History of Ancient Art* (1764), by the German archaeologist and art critic Johann Winckelmann, which laid the foundations for the scholarly disciplines of classical archaeology and art history. The scholarship and the glorious illustrations produced by these scholars made their way quickly into European parlors in the form of neoclassical furniture and clocks, paintings, and wallpapers.

But if Italy and art remained joined at the hip, music also remained vibrant here. Italy was opera central, the place where most composers and librettists were trained and the place where the most famous opera houses flourished. In the eighteenth century, operas became fully staged (not just sung) performances, some of them serious and tragic, others comic. They featured highly paid soloists, including *castrati,* castrated men whose voices could reach high notes otherwise possible only for women. Italy was so central to the music of the Enlightenment that even in France, England, and the German-speaking states, operas performed in anything other than Italian were the exception, and most princes insisted on hiring Italians to be their court composers.

Musical compositions and styles, like neoclassical designs, spread quickly from Italy throughout Europe, spawning new experiments in turn. New ideas and new forms spread as well, crossing religious, political, and linguistic borders, and offering many Europeans an expanded range of choices in how to see and experience the world.

Goethe's Grand Tour In 1786–1787, the German poet Johann Wolfgang von Goethe made a life-changing visit to Italy. As his travel diary describes, Goethe returned to damp and straitlaced northern Europe transformed by his year among the beautiful women, artistic communities, and classical ruins of Italy.

Spreading the Enlightenments

While each European country had a slightly different enlightened experience, the increasing pace and scope of literacy, commercial interaction, and cultural activity gradually made new ideas accessible to others. New forms of literature, new methods of travel, new kinds of gardening, and new ways of eating all became part of a shared cosmopolitan culture that reflected, in various ways, many of the ideas of the Enlightenment.

> **What forms did enlightenment take as it spread across Europe?**

The Enlightened Novel

One of the most striking of the new literary forms was the novel, the form discussed at the beginning of this chapter. Daniel Defoe's *Robinson Crusoe,* the story of the daily adventures of an ordinary man, was the first modern novel. The heroine of Defoe's next novel, *Moll Flanders* (1722), is a lower-class con artist, seductress, and thief who finds happiness only after being sent to the American colonies. Samuel Richardson expanded the novel form to explore the psychological aspects of his characters. His novel *Pamela; Or, Virtue Rewarded* (1740), is the life story of a virtuous serving girl who manages to resist a young nobleman's attempts to seduce her. Richardson's *Clarissa* (1748) told the story of a more dramatic trial of female virtue; the heroine is deceived into living in a brothel and is raped by the villain, Robert Lovelace, but refuses Lovelace's offer of marriage and dies of mental anguish, spiritually pure despite her ruined virtue.

Critics charged that both *Pamela* and *Clarissa* corrupted their huge and heavily female readership even as they pretended to laud virtue. Rousseau's *Julie* (another novel about an ordinary woman whose virtue is tested) came with a preface that acknowledged that those who read novels had already lost their pureness of heart. But audiences could not stop reading, and by the century's end, printing presses across Europe were printing novels in large quantities.

What marked the novel as an enlightened phenomenon was its accessibility and its characteristic themes. Novels were written in prose, not in verse, and in vernacular languages; they were meant to be read in private, rather than aloud, as was common for poems or religious writings. Readers did not need to have extensive education in the classics to understand them. Rather than telling tales of warriors, kings, or mythical figures, many novels described young people thwarted in love by their parents' need for cash or status, or the wanderings of middle-class poets and travelers. Some novels, such as Rousseau's *Julie,* were meant to be critical of the aristocracy of the day; others, including *Robinson Crusoe,* invoked natural theology. *Tom Jones* (1749), by the English novelist Henry Fielding, celebrated cross-class marriages. Novels helped spread some enlightened values by putting them in story form and making it acceptable for writers to lavish ink and attention on the troubles of ordinary people.

Literature by and for Women

Women proved to be some of the most voracious consumers of novels, but in the eighteenth century, they also became prolific producers of fiction and other works intended to be read by women. Though there had always been well-educated aristocratic women, now the ranks of reading and writing women expanded enormously. As early as the beginning of the century, journals exclusively for women began to appear sporadically in England. By the middle of the century, journals such as *The Ladies Monthly* in England and the *Journal des Dames* in France demonstrated that a market for women's periodical literature had been fully established. Women began to write their own novels and also—like Rousseau—educational treatises. By the century's end, numerous female intellectuals were publishing their work. The novels of the English writer Jane Austen, for example, dramatized the trials experienced by women with small dowries in finding suitable wealthy and sensible husbands.

The career of the English author Mary Wollstonecraft tells us much about the expanding possibilities for women writers in the eighteenth century. Wollstonecraft's evolution as a writer was not an easy one. As a girl, she resented the superior education of her brothers, and as a young woman, she found she was often shut out of conversations about philosophy or literature, even though her knowledge was greater than that of the men who excluded her. She accepted odd jobs as a governess, an editorial gofer, and a ghostwriter, before finally setting up her own school for girls near London in 1784. Two years later she published the educational treatise *Thoughts on the Education of Daughters,* and in 1788 she enjoyed moderate success with the semiautobiographical novel, *Mary.* Wollstonecraft then went on to write her much more famous political and social polemics, the *Vindication of the Rights of Man* (1790) and the *Vindication of the Rights of Woman* (1792).

Both works were endorsements of the revolution in France, but the second was something more as well. In the *Vindication of the Rights of Woman,* Wollstonecraft challenged Rousseau's claims about the proper education of the female sex. Women spent too much of their time trying to ensnare men with their beauty, both before and after marriage, she argued. Instead, they should cultivate their reason and the purity of their hearts and seek marriages based on true friendship. Within such marriages, women would ideally be free to spend time rearing children, rather than wasting time primping themselves in order to hold their husbands or attract new lovers. Only when such virtuous households replaced female intrigue and vanity would truly rational societies flourish. Radical in her personal as well as her political life, Wollstonecraft conceived two children out of wedlock and died giving birth to the second. This second child received her mother's name, Mary, and later married the poet Percy Bysshe Shelley. Like her mother, Mary Shelley was a writer, and in 1817 she authored *Frankenstein,* a novel that, ironically, turned the Enlightenment's desire to create new human beings into the world's most famous horror story.

The Enlightenment opened some doors for women such as Mary Wollstonecraft, but Wollstonecraft's own writing and other novelists' ideas about female virtue also closed off potential avenues for female advancement. They did so by ardently recommending a kind of female virtue that depended on women tending their children and avoiding the society of men other than their husbands. Frequently these novelists held up as ideals pious women modeled on Richardson's Clarissa, or mothers who put their all into child-rearing, as in the case of Rousseau's Julie. In this way, Enlightenment literature, for and often by women, might be said to have laid the foundations for the idea of **separate spheres** of male and female virtue. According to this idea, respectable women were to devote themselves to creating virtuous homes, while men looked after business in the wider world. Mary Wollstonecraft certainly did not intend to keep women out of the widening public sphere, nor was this the aim of most of these novelists, but the development of the idea of separate spheres ironically owes much to the consequences of the enlightened thinkers' attempts to create a more virtuous society.

The French *Encyclopédie*

Another attempt to create a more rational and virtuous society was made in a wholly different way. In 1745, two young *philosophes,* Denis Diderot and Jean D'Alembert, set about revising one of the first English encyclopedias, but quickly decided that much more than a basic reference work was needed. Their French *Encyclopédie* would instead be a compendium of all the branches of human knowledge, made accessible to all. No longer would ideas, and especially useful ideas, be the exclusive property of one class, one guild, or one religious sect. Carefully drawn illustrations would help explain topics such as "Pin-Making" or "Infantry Maneuvers." Radical thinkers themselves, the two friends commissioned articles from radical friends, but also from artisans with hands-on expertise. Many essays were submitted anonymously, to protect the authors from the wrath of the religious or royal authorities, or the outrage of the guilds. Some essays did contain radical content. Diderot's entry on "Political Authority" claimed that absolute power was illegitimate and that the state's proper function was to cultivate the happiness of the people. The real radicalism of the *Encyclopédie*, however, lay in its attempt to give every reader access to whatever knowledge they wanted or needed to improve their minds and their lives.

The *Encyclopédie*'s first volume appeared in 1751, and it was an immediate success. Although the original volumes were costly, by 1752 the project had acquired more than four thousand subscribers, even though in that year the French crown condemned the work for corrupting public morals and undermining religious faith. Diderot's papers were confiscated, but then returned, since the court decided that suppressing the project would simply be too difficult and controversial. Volumes continued to appear, mostly because Diderot kept up a furious pace of writing and editing, taking in stride periodic police raids on his house. He continued to work even after the crown once again banned the work in 1759. When Diderot finished the *Encyclopédie* in 1765, it had seventeen volumes. An additional eleven volumes of illustrations followed by 1772, as did a battery of inexpensive editions. By this time, the *Encyclopédie* was being read in St. Petersburg and in Philadelphia and by readers from the barely literate to the members of the French Academy. By no means was the *Encyclopédie* the only voluminous reference work created in the eighteenth century. To give just one example, Samuel Johnson's *A Dictionary of the English Language* exceeded 2,300 pages, and 42,000 entries.

Pamphlets and Pornography

Another characteristic form of enlightened discourse was the pamphlet, a short publication sold for a small charge.[6] The genre predated the eighteenth century, but it flourished as more and more writers and readers entered the market for print. Some pamphlets, *The Treatise of the Three Imposters,* for example, were very radical. But others defended the status quo. Pamphlets were especially prominent in places with little censorship. When Joseph II allowed press freedoms after his accession in 1780, his subjects unleashed what became known as a "pamphlet flood," as thousands of essays on every conceivable subject threatened to bury Viennese readers in print.

The Encyclopédie Shows How to Make a Pin This illustration from the French *Encyclopédie* shows a pin-making shop and the tools necessary for this trade. Some guildsmen regarded the sharing of this sort of information with the public as the unveiling of their trade secrets.

In France, the market for religiously radical or scandal-mongering pamphlets and books expanded as the century went on. In a society that had no way to check the power of the king, clergy, and nobility, telling scandalous stories allowed the little people to express their disdain for those in the higher ranks. Thus, despite heavy censorship and an active police force, pornographic and libelous pamphlets were everywhere by the 1770s. Cash-strapped peddlers carried books printed in Switzerland over the Alps; illegal booksellers stashed copies of works such as *The Private Life of Louis XV* (1781) in coat pockets and hollowed-out wine barrels. Publications circulated accusing Queen Marie Antoinette of holding orgies in her chambers and attacking priests for keeping mistresses. Stories and "news" (whether accurate or not) also circulated orally, sometimes in the form of satirical lyrics set to familiar tunes. Pornographic images made the rounds. The cheapness of the pamphlets and the wide circulation of these scandalous stories made it possible to spread criticism of France's Old Regime even to those who could not read.

Enlightened Travel

Enlightened ideas spread beyond writing to several interconnected fields of activity that touched the lives of many Europeans in various ways. One such activity was travel. For centuries, Europeans had ventured abroad on pilgrimages, to flee poverty or religious persecution, and to spread the word of God. There had been traders, imperial officials, soldiers, and missionaries in Asia and the Americas since at least the late fifteenth century. But as European empires and commercial relations stretched around the globe, the nature of travel changed. Travel became less risky as well-armed European ships exerted more and more control over coastal regions in the Americas, Africa, and South Asia. Mediterranean and Indian Ocean pirates were gradually put out of business, and more accurate compasses and maps increased the speed and safety of overseas voyages. By the early eighteenth century, many more Europeans had taken to the oceans and highways, some combining commercial or military ventures with the goal of satisfying their own curiosity or of collecting scientific specimens or artistic treasures.

By the later eighteenth century, skilled observers were at work recording the pathways of comets, collecting plant specimens in Southeast Asia, and seeking to capture Australian kangaroos. In the 1780s, European spectators thrilled to the sight of the first hot-air balloons. Travel and collecting were addictive pursuits, for individuals as well as states, both of which might profit from the discovery of a new variety of tea or the acquisition of ancient manuscripts. As Asian states, in particular, declined in wealth and power relative to European nations, Europeans found it increasingly easy to extract plants, manuscripts, and ideas from those areas. New groups of missionaries also fanned out across the continents, settling in places where they were tolerated, fleeing when local leaders turned hostile. We can envision the spreading of a vast net across the oceans and continents, its weave ever more dense and its catch ever greater. The information and inspiration caught in such a virtual net fueled comparisons and extended curiosity, but the process also reinforced a sense that the Europeans knew best and that the data and materials they brought back existed to be put to their uses.

Enlightened Gardening

Plants were among the things Europeans brought back from their travels. The importation of plants for nutritional, aesthetic, and scientific purposes was nothing new. Contact with the Americas had put Europeans in touch with species they did not know, such as tobacco and the tomato. In the seventeenth century, the Dutch de-

A Crowd-Pleasing Innovation One of the many novelties of the enlightened era was the hot-air balloon. Although the French pioneered ballooning, British crowds were also eager to see how the new contraption worked.

veloped flower markets and hothouses in order to cultivate exotic, decorative species such as tulips and orchids. Apothecaries, doctors, and midwives all studied botany, and apothecary guilds often planted their medicinal botanical gardens. Yet a new sort of gardening evolved as the eighteenth century dawned and as the commercial and scientific revolution hastened the dispersal of seeds and plants. The English developed the most ardent passion for collecting and cultivating and conceived of the art of displaying plants.[7]

The key early publication was Philip Miller's *Gardeners Dictionary* (1731), a complete, alphabetical listing of all plants being grown in Britain, with easy-to-follow instructions in English (rather than Latin or French) on how to cultivate each one. Miller was not an academic, but the son of a nurseryman with extensive hands-on experience as the head gardener at the Chelsea Physic Garden owned by London's Society of Apothecaries. He was also a tireless correspondent, one tied in to a large international network of plant collectors and university-trained botanists. Miller had no time for traditional advice about planting according to cycles of the moon, but he was willing to learn from the Dutch how to build hothouses and to compare specimens with local gardeners of all classes. By observation, Miller discovered the key role that insects play in plant pollination. He produced England's first coconuts, hibiscus, and camphor trees. Miller's *Dictionary* sold to scholars, nobles, middling gentlemen, and artisanal gardeners, making accessible to all the knowledge he had gained by plunging his hands directly into the soil.

Miller influenced gardening in yet another way. Aristocratic estates and royal palaces had long featured formal gardens, where idle nobles might stroll. The French in particular were famed for their geometrically designed plantings. But Miller, in the *Dictionary,* argued that plants "should appear accidental, as in a natural Wood," rather than pruned and styled to look like sculptures.[8] This view appealed greatly to Robert James Petre, a very rich nobleman who in the 1730s landscaped his great estate at Thorndon according to Miller's dictates. Rather than pruning his trees and shrubs into elaborate shapes, Petre juxtaposed trees with different shades of bark and leaves, and those which flowered at different times; he created winding paths through his forests in which visitors could contemplate nature's noble wildness and then suddenly come upon a striking vista or artfully placed classical ruin. Petre's designs at Thorndon inspired numerous other English and continental aristocrats to cultivate what came to be known as the English garden, which many preferred to French formal gardens precisely because they seemed more natural. The most famous of these is Kew Gardens, in London, where one can still see the Chinese-style pagoda, built in 1761 to charm the visitors.

The Enlightened Garden Kew Gardens profited from patronage from the English royal family and expanded greatly after the 1770s. Many travelers brought exotic plants and seeds back from their journeys to be propagated at Kew.

The emphasis that Petre put on the diversity of species also encouraged the practice of collecting and sharing seeds and specimens. Botanists and gardeners were discovering and trading thousands of new plants, but they kept running into a vexing problem: there was no internationally agreed-upon system of naming and classification. The one person confident that he could solve this problem was the Swedish scholar Carolus Linnaeus, a man with a passion for classification and the grand ambition of imposing order on all of God's creation. The son of a gardener, Linnaeus profited from his travels and his patrons, including the director of the Dutch East India Company, who hired the Swede to tend his hothouses and organize his huge collection of exotic plants. Linnaeus benefited from his contact with Miller, who sent him endless numbers of specimens for his growing collection. In his 1735 *Systemae Naturae,* Linnaeus proposed a bold and extremely simple means of classifying plants according to their number of male and female organs (pistils and stamen); each would be known by a Latin genus and species name. New finds could be easily classified and added to the system. For several decades, Linnaeus's sys-

tem was controversial, especially because it was based explicitly on sexual organs. In 1758, the pope denounced Linnaeus's licentious language and banned the books of a man some said was styling himself as a second Adam. But by this time, Linnaeus had published another, huge work classifying 7,700 species of plants (*Species Plantarum,* 1753), and scholars as well as amateur collectors had recognized the virtues of his system and largely accepted it.

Linnaeus's system did not end the drive to find new species. On the contrary, the mania for finding and cultivating new plants raged with even greater intensity in the eighteenth century's second half. The mania seized the young nobleman Sir Joseph Banks, who happily agreed to put up his own money to be taken along with the English mariner Captain James Cook on his first voyage. Cook was supposed to ferry astronomers to the South Pacific to observe the transit of Venus for the Royal Society, but he also had a secret mission: to explore a recently sighted landmass to the west of New Zealand, a landmass that turned out to be Australia. Banks shipped out in 1768, together with a student of Linnaeus, four servants, and the artist Sydney Parkinson, who would die of dysentery on the trip home. The expedition returned three years later with a collection of 30,000 specimens, including 1,400 new species, and more than a thousand of Parkinson's ethnographic and botanical drawings. Cook would return twice to the South Pacific to collect more information; his third voyage would be his last, however, as Hawaiian islanders accused his men of offending their gods and murdered Cook and many of his shipmates as they fled for their boats. Banks himself made no more voyages, but became England's greatest patron of the sciences in the dawning age of empire. By the time of his death in 1820, English botanizing had become a respected science, a big business, and a popular pastime.

Enlightened Ethnography

Carolus Linnaeus's mania for classifying involved him in a series of debates about how to understand human as well as botanical diversity. In 1735, using classical texts and travelers' reports, he identified several species within the genus *Homo,* including *Homo sapiens* and *Homo troglodytes,* a creature he knew only from hearsay and that turned out to be an orangutan. He then broke *Homo sapiens* into five groups based both on physical traits, such as skin color, and on social factors. Europeans, light skinned and governed by laws, clearly came off better than Africans, dark skinned and governed only by whim. As travelers penetrated more deeply into Asia, Africa, and the South Pacific, they failed to find the tailed men or the giants earlier voyagers claimed to have seen, but European naturalists did not give up Linnaeus's goal to provide a scientific explanation for differences among groups of humans.

The eighteenth century's ways of coming to grips with human diversity reveal both the best and the worst of the Enlightenment. Most writers emphasized the unity of the human race, and many explained racial and cultural differences as products of climate, which in no way added up to the inferiority of one group or another. Robinson Crusoe, though horrified by the naked savages he encountered, nonetheless came to love his converted servant Friday and to view pagan rituals as primitive forms of Christian sacraments. Rousseau elevated respect for non-European tribesmen by describing them as noble savages, strong and independent-minded people living in harmony with nature, quite unlike the overly civilized Parisians he despised. When a European ship first visited the island of Tahiti in 1767, the sailors believed they had encountered Rousseau's noble savages and came home singing the praises of the beautiful women and fragrant flowers they found in this version of the Garden of Eden. Some philosophers criticized those who presumed non-Christians were eternally damned simply because they had been born in places where the Gospels were unknown. All these arguments diminished differences between the world's peoples and encouraged policies of tolerance toward other cultures.

Yet most Enlightenment thinkers also believed that European cultures were best, that Europeans' skin color and facial features were most beautiful, and that their

Illustrating the Other This image of a heavily tattooed Maori man was made by the artist Sydney Parkinson, who accompanied Captain Cook on his first voyage to the South Seas. In his diary, Parkinson described the warriors as "disfigured in a very strange manner," but portrayed this individual in quite a sympathetic way.

Christian religion was the one true faith. Although some people disapproved of violent methods of conversion or of colonial conquest, in general they thought that Europeanization and modernization were good things that everyone on earth should strive to attain. Many writers, including David Hume, adopted a stage-theory of human evolution, according to which some customs and religions, such as the worship of many gods or animal sacrifice, characterized lower levels of development. Europeans involved in the slave trade or in colonial affairs justified conquering, imprisoning, and selling other humans by insisting that darker-skinned peoples needed European masters to "civilize" them. Thinkers who championed reason, as did Immanuel Kant, could still think and say terrible things about the inferiority of Africans or Native Americans.

By the 1790s, the first true physical anthropologist, Johann Friedrich Blumenbach, was using cranial size and skin color to divide humankind into five races. He assigned each race a color: Ethiopians (Africans; the black race), Mongolians (Asians; the yellow race), Americans (Native Americans; the red race), Caucasians (Europeans; the white race), and Malayans (Southeast Asians; the brown race) based almost exclusively on cranial size, hair type, and skin color. Blumenbach did not believe that the darker races were inferior, but his classification scheme promoted the notion that race was indelibly inscribed on the body. The longer that Caucasians spent in tropical climates and black slaves spent in the Americas without major changes in their skin color or culture, the more that Europeans came to believe that race was a biological, and not a changeable, factor. Similarly, discussions about male and female traits and the proper spheres of activity for men and women increasingly tended to emphasize deep, biological differences between the sexes. Many enlightened thinkers championed the unity of humankind as part of their program to root out the intolerance, superstition, and system of privileges characteristic of the Old Regimes; but in elaborating racial differences, they only replaced those evils with new forms of intolerance and privilege.

QUESTION | *How did enlightened thinking in ethnography produce positive and negative views of other humans?*

Eating the Enlightenment

Increased travel and the cultivation of new plants affected even the European dinner table. The culinary habits of elite Europeans have never been stagnant, but in the later seventeenth and early eighteenth centuries, they underwent a virtual revolution.[9] Cooks of the late Renaissance and Baroque eras still believed in using pungent spices, often mixing sweet and sour tastes, such as nutmeg and vinegar, or sugar and meat stock. Large and heavy game, including boar and venison, a part of the aristocratic culture of the hunt, were highly prized. Sauces made of mixed exotic spices demonstrated the head of household's wealth and prestige. Vegetables were chiefly for days of fasting. Those who could afford to show off did, serving their guests whole roasted peacocks, gigantic pies from which live song birds emerged once sliced, and roasts decorated with gold leaf. Cooks in this world were locally trained artisans. Cooking was a valued trade, but not yet an art, and no one nationality determined fine cuisine, though perhaps the Italians—closest to the spice traders of the Islamic world—had the early edge.

The commercial revolution brought new variety to the elite European table. By the early eighteenth century, there were far more different kinds of foods available and at cheaper prices. Sugar, in particular, had fallen drastically in price. Using glass jars and heavy fertilizer, English and Dutch gardeners were able to produce tropical fruits and vegetables out of season. Cooks, especially pastry chefs, became something like artists, creating whole fields of flowers made of sugar and marzipan. French chefs, acclaimed for their sauces, took the lead in creating new delicacies, and nobles across the continent increasingly felt they had to have a French cook directing their kitchens.

The complexity and costliness of these forms of cuisine generated another reaction, as some people decided that foreign or highly decorative food was unnatural. Those who argued for reforming the kitchen and the garden insisted that complicated recipes and expensive ingredients wasted time and money. They preferred lighter and more naturally flavored fare to heavier, mixed-spice dishes. Smaller and more numerous and various dishes replaced the giant pies and boars' heads. Coffee at the meal's end allowed guests to recover from their wine-induced stupor and attend to the conversation. The whole culture of dining changed as hosts gave up seating guests according to rank and arranged their friends so that all could converse and share the same dishes. Intimate dinner parties began to replace the more courtly banquets, and detailed cookbooks hit the market, simplifying the craft of food preparation for bourgeois cooks.

Of course, those who were able to "eat the Enlightenment" remained a small, if growing, portion of the population, concentrated in the richest areas of eighteenth-century Europe: Great Britain (excluding Ireland), France, the Dutch Republic, and the western and southern German territories. Among the peasantry and the small-town dwellers, eating the Enlightenment was about as far-fetched an idea as was reading Newton's *Principia*. In fact, most people's diets became less diverse and rich in calories during the seventeenth century, when many, especially in central Europe, died of starvation. By the eighteenth century, famine became less frequent, but malnutrition was pervasive. Bread became an even more crucial staple than before, given that it provided the most calories for the least cash. Peasants ate a great deal of soup, but their soup contained little meat and a limited number of root vegetables. Ordinary people who lived in cities and towns could profit from expanding markets and increasing division of labor to buy inexpensive ready-made meals; most people who did not live on isolated estates bought bread from bakeries rather than baking it themselves, but their incomes allowed them very little choice. Focusing on eating calls attention to the Enlightenments' limits. They changed and improved some people's lives, but they certainly did not transform life for all.

Hearing the Enlightenment

Before the eighteenth century, music, whether sung or played on homemade instruments, was central to both popular and elite European culture, but most people's musical experience remained, like their diets, dependent on local traditions and limited in variety. Although ordinary people commonly sang in the fields and the streets, to pass the time or to entertain one another, more elaborate music was generally restricted to the churches or the courts and performed at the pleasure of the nobles or the clergy. Most composers, such as Johann Sebastian Bach or Joseph Haydn, worked for aristocrats or for the churches. For the most part, Baroque music was made to accompany social events or singers; it was supposed to please its audiences, but not to draw attention to itself.

During the Enlightenment, concerts and operas gradually opened their doors to a wider public. Venice was the first city to build a public opera house, but soon other states followed, allowing urban dwellers the opportunity to hear more secular music than ever before. Departing from Italian traditions, French and Austro-German composers grew more daring, adding more instruments and unfamiliar harmonies in order to engage the individual listener's ears, mind, and emotions. Increasingly, audiences began to pay closer attention to the music. By the 1780s, it was not uncommon for concert goers to be moved to tears by music performed not just for the king or for God, but addressed to the individual soul.

MOZART. Wolfgang Amadeus Mozart, a musical child prodigy, was one of those whose music compelled audiences to listen more closely. As a young man, Mozart spent nearly four formative years studying music in Italy, then worked in Salzburg (as a court musician), Paris, and Munich before settling in Vienna, all the while composing a vast array of concertos, sonatas, and string quartets, many of which departed from traditional form and instrumentation. In 1782, after finishing an opera

The Cookbook

Between 1739 and 1761, the French chef François Menon worked hard to convince his countrymen to adopt what he called *nouvelle cuisine,* a new, simpler, and more natural style of cooking that emphasized authentic flavors and healthy eating.[10] He produced nine books on the culinary arts, among them *The Bourgeois Cook,* first published in 1746 and reprinted many times afterward. *The Bourgeois Cook* addressed itself forthrightly to nonaristocratic, or bourgeois, households, where the kitchen would be run not by a male chef overseeing a dozen or more staff, but rather by one (usually female) cook. Adapting recipes to make them easier to execute and less dependent on costly or rare ingredients, Menon contributed to the Enlightenment's war on artifice and its insistence on utility. Food should be healthful, he insisted, whether one was a prince or a humble town dweller. Menon had no doubt that his way of preparing meals, since it was both perfectly natural and rational, was the right way for everyone, everywhere, to cook.

There had been French cookbooks before Menon's, perhaps most notably François Massialot's *Cooking for Royalty and for the Bourgeois* (1702), which offered step-by-step methods of food preparation and instructed cooks to use seasonal, local produce. In early enlightened style, Massialot presented cooking as a systematic craft. The chef was above all the master of a series of basic techniques, such as making a stock, which laid the foundations for

many different dishes. Massialot's dishes remained quite complicated, however, and not suitable for bourgeois households. Menon offered an even more rational approach to cooking, breaking down beef into its principal parts and explaining which pigeons were best in which dishes. He avoided detailed recipes for venison (a favorite of the Baroque table), "because it is little used among the bourgeois," but offered extensive recipes for vegetables and dishes made with eggs, fish, rabbit, and fowl, which he thought light and healthful. He recommended using fresh herbs and seasonal produce. Many of his recipes contained exact measurements, and the book came with a helpful index. Like the *Encyclopédie,* Menon's cookbook was designed to share what had once been guild secrets with the public at large. Judging by the book's many reprintings, the author succeeded in the endeavor.

If we examine one of Menon's recipes, this one for "Duck à la Béarnaise," perhaps we can see just how much our modern cookbooks owe to the Enlightenment.

Set to boil a little bouillon, a half-glass of white wine, a bunch of parsley, scallions, thyme, laurel, basil, and two cloves. Put this [mixture] in a casserole with seven or eight onions cut in pieces and add a little butter; put this on the fire and stir often just until [the onions] take on some color. Add a good pinch of flour, moistened with the juice of the duck, cook the onion and reduce the sauce; skim off the fat and add to it a drop of vinegar. Serve this over the duck.[11]

Of course, not all of Menon's recipes were so simple. There were fancier dishes (described as royal or sultan style) and regional variations (described as English, Turkish, or country style). Menon's cookbook, like those today, was probably used more on feast days or days when the family entertained guests than for everyday cooking. It could not be used by everyone, for even its moderately priced ingredients remained out of reach for the poor, and it would probably have been difficult for those who did not live near urban markets to obtain the fresh meat and vegetables his recipes required. *The Bourgeois Cook* tells us a great deal about how tastes were changing during the Enlightenment—and about the ways in which certain ideas, such as simplicity, utility, rationality, and accessibility, were able to move from the salon to the kitchen, and back again.

QUESTION | *How did enlightened thinking transform European cooking?*

An Enlightened Breakfast This beautiful still life by the French painter Jean Chardin depicts a light breakfast of the sort a bourgeois cook might offer: a simple but delicious brioche, accompanied by a few biscuits, a small decanter of wine, and fresh fruit.

in German (*The Abduction from the Seraglio*) for Emperor Joseph II, Mozart earned Europe's esteem. He went on to write several works with enlightened themes, including *The Marriage of Figaro,* a grand opera that featured a servant as the hero. Another of his operas, *Don Giovanni,* featured an aristocratic playboy who sells his soul to the devil. But Mozart's greatest contribution lay in the nature of the music itself. In their form, his works were perfectly balanced and elegant in their simplicity. This quality made his music seem both rational and natural, the musical equivalent of artistic neoclassicism. Indeed, along with the works of Haydn and those of the young Ludwig van Beethoven, Mozart's music came to be seen as the epitome of classical music.

MUSIC AND THE PUBLIC. Mozart composed for Joseph II—but he also composed for a wider public, one that did not have to wait for an invitation to court but that could pay to attend public performances. Although the first public opera house was established in Venice in 1637, it took nearly a century for houses to open in northern cities. Opera also became more popular as enlightened composers introduced nonreligious, often comic, storylines. Public concerts, in which trained musicians performed well-known pieces, also began in the eighteenth century, as did the forming of singing clubs. Europeans' musical diet expanded, and a broader section of the population was able to enjoy cultural products that had once been available only in private palaces.

Mozart in Italy This painting depicts the young Wolfgang Amadeus Mozart and his father, Leopold, seated at the harpsichord (*left*), making music at the famous home of Sir William Hamilton in Naples. Posted to Italy as British ambassador to the Kingdom of Naples, Hamilton amused himself by studying volcanoes and collecting antiquities, such as those from early excavations at Pompeii, exhibited here in his drawing room. The Mozarts came to visit in 1770, the year Wolfgang Amadeus's first opera was performed in Milan; he was fourteen.

The Many Enlightenments and Their Consequences

Without question, the Enlightenments changed European culture and did damage to the legitimacy and authority of the Old Regimes. But how much, really, changed? Here we assess the impact of the Enlightenments on the two major spheres in which the Old Regimes exercised power: religion and politics.

How did the Enlightenment affect the religious and political institutions of the Old Regimes?

The Enlightenments and Religion

In the sphere of religion, Europe's Enlightenments had pronounced and transformative effects. The challenges posed by the new science and by increased circulation of social criticism prompted rulers and laypeople alike to rethink their attitudes toward the church and toward religion itself. Church-going, especially by men and especially in western Europe, declined over the course of the century. Theology faculties at universities began to lose their prominence to the philosophical faculties, where scholars pursued secular philosophy and natural science.

Everywhere, secular power was eating away at clerical power and privilege. Monarchs who had once proudly called themselves defenders of the faith now closed useless monasteries and cloisters, subordinated the clergy to state control, and banned the Jesuits, the religious order that most explicitly followed the directions of the pope. Many schools run by the clergy were closed and replaced by secular schools funded by the state. Deism, the conviction that God had made the universe but no longer played a role in it, appealed very much to critics of Christian intolerance, such as Voltaire or Thomas Jefferson in America. By the mid-eighteenth century, Frederick the Great said of Christianity that it was "an old metaphysical fiction, stuffed with fables, contradictions and absurdities; it was spawned in the fevered imagination of the Orientals, and then spread to our Europe, where some fanatics espoused it, where some intriguers pretended to be convinced by it and where some imbeciles actually believed it."[12] Although there is considerable dispute about whether the Enlightenment was fundamentally antireligious, there is

Did the Enlightenments Kill Christianity?

In 2001, the historian Jonathan Israel published *Radical Enlightenment,* which focused attention on the radical philosopher Baruch Spinoza and his many followers, many of whom published their work anonymously or circulated it through underground channels. They were not invited to salons, nor did they correspond with enlightened monarchs. For most, the subject they cared about was not politics but religion. The anonymous author of *The Treatise of the Three Imposters* wanted to vent his outrage that conniving clergymen had sown superstition and discord among men. Others sought to rationalize and reform Christianity to root out errors and to end Christian persecution of people of other faiths. Some became outright materialists, people who did not believe in the immortality of the soul or the existence of any sort of God. For Israel, these radicals are heroes, brave individuals who risked their personal safety to fight the good fight for secular society and human rights. They were the *authentic* voice of the Enlightenment, he maintained, against whom the more moderate reformers such as Montesquieu, Locke, and even Rousseau seem pale and cowardly wallflowers.

Scholars on the whole welcomed Israel's book, but some felt the need to qualify some of his claims, especially his argument that the radicals possessed the true voice of the Enlightenment. In his 2004 book, *The Religious Enlightenment,* the eighteenth-century specialist David Sorkin offered a contrasting view, insisting that enlightened ideas were fully compatible with a moderate approach to religious reform. Sorkin argued that throughout Europe, moderates constituted the majority of enlightened thinkers.

Jonathan Sheehan, in his work *The Enlightenment Bible* (2005), largely seconds Sorkin's claims. Although Sheehan agrees with Israel that radical religious thinkers and biblical critics abounded in the later seventeenth and early eighteenth centuries, he also claims that most of these writers were able to reconcile reason and religion. They produced hundreds of new translations and editions of the Bible with that goal in mind; scholars now offered rational explanations for Moses's parting of the Red Sea and for Jesus's raising of the dead Lazarus, but they did not cease being Christians. The Enlightenment diminished the Bible's status as an unerring account of the history of the true religion, Sheehan argues, but the Bible remained a central part for European cultural life for centuries to come.

But it is perhaps Derek Beales's book about Catholic monasteries, *Prosperity and Plunder* (2003), that most challenges Israel's picture of the eighteenth century as one of de-Christianization. Beales describes the huge monastic building projects of the era, such as the great Baroque abbey at Melk in Austria, and the vast expansion of smaller monasteries. There were at least 15,000 monasteries and 10,000 convents on the continent in 1750, a huge number for a supposedly secularizing population. In the Italian states, but also in Portugal, Spain, and France, eighteenth-century men and women committed themselves to the religious life in great numbers. In Naples alone there were more than two hundred monasteries and convents, housing about 10,500 monks and nuns; this meant that about one person in every thirty-six belonged to a religious order. Many of these institutions were small, but some were enormous, and rich: monasteries may have owned as much as one-fourth of the real estate in Paris, and nearly as much of the rich agricultural land in western Austria. The Russian Orthodox Trinity Monastery of St. Sergius near Moscow owned 106,000 serfs. Moreover, continuing unabated were religious pilgrimages to view the Spanish kings' most sacred relic, a feather from Archangel Gabriel's wing, housed in the royal palace known as the Escorial; or the Black Virgin at the Mariazell Basilica in Austria. Beales concludes that in many places, the eighteenth century marks the triumph of the Catholic Reformation rather than the demise of European Christendom.

These books give us a much deeper sense of the variety of religious and antireligious perspectives of the eighteenth century. The atheism of the very few had little impact on the many. Still, biblical criticism and attacks on clerical prejudice and corruption could often shape opinion among the decision makers in Europe's courts. The question comes down to a matter of timing: did Enlightenment critiques permanently damage faith, or did they simply inspire some Christians to rethink their beliefs?

Whereas in previous generations, the key question about the Enlightenment had to do with its contributions to the French Revolution, now it seems the central question is to what extent the Enlightenment killed Christian faith, in the long if not the short run. The debate over this question continues to unfold.

QUESTION | *In what ways did the Enlightenment present a radical challenge to religion?*

no question that the movement put an end to a world in which people were neither allowed nor expected to ask questions about their faith.

The Enlightenments and Politics

If the Enlightenments transformed—but did not destroy—religious life across Europe, their consequences for politics were more mixed. Most scholars would agree that many enlightened themes (the universality of natural laws, the need to free human reason from superstition, and the irrationality of the Old Regimes' system of privileges) contributed to launching the American and French Revolutions. But enlightened ideas did not cause the revolutions. If many revolutionary leaders read Montesquieu, Locke, and Rousseau, by no means did all of Rousseau's admirers become revolutionaries; certainly Marie Antoinette did not. Nor was revolution the goal for all those who applied the ideals of reason or naturalness to cooking or gardening, or of those who read about pin-making in the *Encyclopédie*. Most enlightened thinkers were merely seeking reform or improvement. Even those who wrote scandalous pamphlets aimed less at revolution than at rooting out the courtly corruption that surrounded a potentially benevolent king.

The cases of enlightened absolutism discussed in this chapter demonstrate that the new ideas could be used to modernize states from the top down. These attempts at modernization changed the power structures in these states, especially by whittling away the privileges of the landed nobility and the clergy and by increasing the power of the bureaucracies. But these reforms neither gave ordinary people political power, nor provoked them to revolt. As a method of Enlightenment, the top-down model also had mixed success. Some rulers, like Frederick the Great of Prussia, made important strides in promoting merit, religious toleration, and bureaucratic efficiency. Others, like Joseph II, one of the most committed of enlightened rulers, had little success in trimming the power of provincial nobles. In Russia, Peter the Great and Catherine the Great failed to make much headway in economic modernization, and neither was willing to take the important step of abolishing serfdom. Although they cultivated new ideas at court, for most Russians, their "greatness" lay less in spreading enlightened ideas than in employing a reformed military to enlarge imperial Russia at the expense of its neighbors.

The Enlightenments also had ambivalent social effects. In many places, enlightened rationalization and the spread of literacy opened up the possibility for new kinds of individual advancement. The bourgeoisie, that well-to-do sector of the third estate, expanded, especially in western states, but also in Prussia, where it was composed heavily of bureaucrats employed by the state. Some ambitious men of Robinson Crusoe's sort did dare to try new careers, and increasingly found they were not alone. Others, too, wanted to improve their circumstances, to read and write new books, to hear music in public opera houses. Some women yearned to participate in the expanding public sphere, and some, like Mary Wollstonecraft, managed to do so, though not on equal terms.

Yet enlightened changes that were thrilling to some also threatened traditional ways of life. Communal privileges and artisanal production suffered as enclosure and the new division of labor broke down the older rural economy. Reforms may have increased food production, but they did not result in the universal opulence for which Adam Smith had hoped. Artisans put up considerable resistance to change, as did the nobles and the clergy. In many places, these powerful groups managed to protect their privileges. In rural eastern and southern Europe, in particular, things changed very little. In the Scottish Highlands, things changed for the worse. All in all, the Enlightenments did make a difference to the lives of many, perhaps most Europeans; but they did not improve everyone's lot, or change everyone's mind.

❘ Conclusion

Enlightened ideas altered the way many Europeans lived and the way they thought about nature, society, and themselves. Over the course of the eighteenth century, many Europeans adopted a critical attitude toward ancient and clerical authorities, and learned to love new sorts of reading materials and musical experience. Some people, at least, began to consciously pursue new rights and liberties and to believe that they could catalog every plant and every human racial type. By no means did the Enlightenment reach into every corner of the European continent, and by no means did it always pose radical threats to the political and religious institutions of the Old Regimes. In some places, indeed, top-down reforms were engineered to strengthen states and to concentrate power rather than to share it. But enlightened ideas did not have to be pervasive or explicitly revolutionary to make a difference. Simply offering some new ways to cook or to garden gave an expanding sector of the population experience in choosing how to live and the daring to make changes in old routines. By 1789, a much wider European public had been convinced that human improvement was possible, not just on imaginary islands as in *Robinson Crusoe,* but by dint of hard work in the present.

Critical Thinking Questions

1. Why did Europe's Enlightenments take so many different forms?

2. Which Enlightenments were the most transformative? Why?

3. What difference did it make to European culture that information and ideas—like music, travelogues, novels, and cookbooks—could now circulate beyond the nobility and clergy, in the public sphere?

Key Terms

Enlightenment **(p. 494)**

meritocracy **(p. 495)**

bourgeois **(p. 495)**

the public sphere **(p. 495)**

tabula rasa **(p. 497)**

social contract **(p. 498)**

Highlanders **(p. 498)**

the Forty-Five **(p. 498)**

laissez faire **(p. 499)**

salons **(p. 501)**

philosophes **(p. 501)**

deism **(p. 502)**

enlightened absolutism **(p. 506)**

neoclassicism **(p. 509)**

separate spheres **(p. 511)**

Primary Sources in Connect

For information on Connect and the online resources available, go to **http://connect.mcgraw-hill.com**.

1. *Treatise of the Three Imposters*
2. John Locke, *Second Treatise of Government*
3. Denis Diderot, "Christianity"
4. Joseph II of Austria's Decree on Religious Toleration

5. The Parlement of Paris Protests Royal Improvements
6. Johann Wolfgang von Goethe, *Italian Journey*
7. A German Traveler Reflects on the Causes of Cannibalism

Rousseau's Emile

Rousseau's *Emile* (1761) is part educational manual, part novel. It describes how young men are to be raised in order to develop their natural and individual talents, and to free them from dependency on other men or on conventional opinions. In Book V, however, Rousseau gives Emile, his version of Robinson Crusoe, a mate (Sophie) who is to be educated in quite a different way. In the following passages, Rousseau spells out how "natural" gender differences and society's needs require that Sophie not receive an equal opportunity to develop an independent mind.

Sophie ought to be a woman as Emile is a man—that is to say, she ought to have everything which suits the constitution of her species and her sex in order to fill her place in the physical and moral order. Let us begin, then, by examining the similarities and differences of her sex and ours . . . .

The only thing we know with certainty is that everything man and woman have in common belongs to the species, and that everything which distinguishes them belongs to the sex . . . . This conclusion is evident to the senses; it is in agreement with our experience; and it shows how vain are the disputes as to whether one of the two sexes is superior or whether they are equal—as though each, in fulfilling nature's ends according to its own particular purpose, were thereby less perfect than if it resembled the other more! In what they have in common, they are equal. Where they differ, they are not comparable. A perfect woman and a perfect man ought not to resemble each other in mind any more than in looks . . . .

In the union of the sexes each contributes equally to the common aim, but not in the same way. From this diversity arises the first assignable difference in the moral relations of the two sexes. One ought to be active and strong, the other passive and weak. One must necessarily will and be able; it suffices that the other put up little resistance . . . .

Once this principle is established, it follows that woman is made specially to please man. If man ought to please her in turn, it is due to a less direct necessity. His merit is in his power; he pleases by the sole fact of his strength. This is not the law of love, I agree. But that of nature, prior to love itself . . . .

To cultivate man's qualities in women and to neglect those which are proper to them is obviously to work to their detriment. Crafty women see this too well to be duped by it . . . . Does it follow that [Sophie] ought to be raised in ignorance of everything and limited to the housekeeping functions alone? Will man turn his companion into his servant? Will be deprive himself of the greatest charm of society with her? In order to make her more subject, will he prevent her from feeling anything, from knowing anything? . . . Surely not. It is not thus that nature has spoken in giving women such agreeable and nimble minds. On the contrary, nature wants them to think, to judge, to love, to know, to cultivate their minds as well as their looks. These are the weapons nature gives them to take the place of the strength they lack and to direct ours. They ought to learn many things but only those that are suitable for them to know.

Whether I consider the particular purpose of the fair sex, whether I observe its inclinations, whether I consider its duties, all join equally in indicating to me the form of education that suits it. Woman and man are made for one another, but their mutual dependence is not equal. Men depend on women because of their desires; women depend on men because of both their desires and their needs.

. . . By the very law of nature women are at the mercy of men's judgments, as much for their sake as for that of their children. It is not enough that they be pretty; they must please. It is not enough for they to be temperate; they must be recognized as such. Their honor is not only in their conduct but in their reputation; and it is not possible that a woman who consents to be regarded as disreputable can ever be decent. When a man acts well, he depends only on himself and can brave public judgment; but when a woman acts well, she has accomplished only half of her task, and what is thought of her is no less important to her than what she actually is. From this it follows that the system of woman's education ought to be contrary in this respect to the system of our education. Opinion is the grave of virtue among men and its throne among women.

QUESTIONS | *In what ways does Rousseau think men and women are—and must remain—different from one another? What in his view should the object of female education be?*

Source: Jean-Jacques Rousseau, *Emile, or, On Education,* trans. Allan Bloom (New York: Basic Books, 1979), 357–58, 364–65.

N'AYANT PU ME CORROMPRE

ILS M'ONT ASSASSINÉ

THE FRENCH REVOLUTION AND THE NAPOLEONIC WARS

Origins of the Revolution
  Long-Term Causes
  Short-Term Causes
  The Revolution Begins

The Moderate Revolution, 1789–1791
  From the Great Fear to the Constitution of 1791
  The Revolution and the Church
  The King and the Revolution
  Toward the Radical Revolution

The Radical Revolution
  The September Massacres
  Montagnards and Girondins
  The King's Execution
  The Reign of Terror
  The Revolution beyond France
  Revolutionary Culture

The Thermidorean Reaction
The Directory

The Rise of Napoleon
  Napoleon's Early Life and Military Career
  Napoleon in Egypt
  The 18th Brumaire

The Napoleonic Empire
  In Search of Stability
  The Grande Armée
  Napoleon's Early Campaigns, 1805–1808

Napoleon's Fall
  The French Occupations and the Origins of Modern Nationalism
  The Napoleonic Wars, 1809–1815

Conclusion

ANNE LOUISE GERMAINE NECKER, MADAME DE STAËL: ONE WOMAN'S REVOLUTION Perhaps Anne Louise Germaine Necker (1766–1817) was predestined to live her life on the political cutting edge. Her parents certainly did. Her Swiss father, Jacques Necker, finance minister for Louis XVI, proposed major structural reforms in France's agricultural and taxation policies; his sacking, on July 11, 1789, helped precipitate the Parisian riot that led to the fall of the Bastille. Germaine's mother, Suzanne Curchod, who presided over one of the most celebrated salons in Paris, was even more committed to enlightened values than her husband. But it was Germaine herself, unhappily married at age twenty to a Swedish diplomat, the Baron de Staël, who greeted the coming of the French Revolution with the greatest delight.

By this time, Germaine de Staël had already authored a popular book praising Rousseau's ideas about civic and individual virtue, and in the summer of 1789 she hoped for a revolution that would replace France's corrupt

◀ Death of a Revolutionary: The Jacobin Jean Paul Marat Assassinated in His Bath and inefficient Old Regime with a virtuous constitutional monarchy based on a new social contract. She got her revolution and even her constitutional monarchy, but the course of political events soon raced beyond her dreams. By September 1792, neither birth, nor wealth, nor enlightened ideas could protect Germaine de Staël from a new regime that equated aristocrats and clergy with treason. She fled to Switzerland, recognizing more clearly than ever before how much difference political change makes in the lives of even the most privileged individuals.

Madame de Staël spent the next two years in Switzerland and England, writing both fiction and political commentaries and running her own salon. She befriended and in some cases conducted romances with other exiled proponents of the moderate revolution. She returned to France in 1797 and hailed the young Napoleon as the savior of the Republic, but she disapproved of Napoleon's self-promotion to consul for life and his compromises with the pope, and said so. In 1803 Napoleon barred de Staël from living in Paris. During her exile she traveled through several German states, where she was captivated by the virtues and ancient traditions of German townspeople and the dark beauty of the German forests. These travels and her contempt for Napoleon's tyrannical behavior led her to write *On Germany* (1810), a book that helped shape German nationalism. She also wrote short stories and novels, including *Corinne, or Italy* (1807), which featured a talented, self-aware heroine quite unlike

Madame de Staël at Her Writing Desk The author of many books and a vast number of letters to friends all over Europe, Germaine Necker, Madame de Staël, is pictured here wearing a simple gown of the sort Rousseau would have approved.

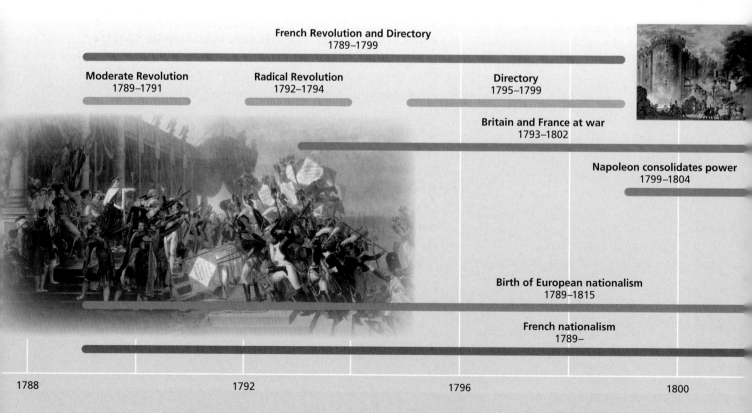

French Revolution and Directory
1789–1799

Moderate Revolution
1789–1791

Radical Revolution
1792–1794

Directory
1795–1799

Britain and France at war
1793–1802

Napoleon consolidates power
1799–1804

Birth of European nationalism
1789–1815

French nationalism
1789–

1788   1792   1796   1800

the virtuous martyrs of enlightened novels such as *Pamela* and *Julie*. *Corinne* praised English values and bemoaned Napoleon's high-handed treatment of the Italians. In both *On Germany* and *Corinne,* Germaine de Staël criticized Napoleonic tyranny without demanding a return either to the Old Regimes or to the radical revolution. She remained a proponent of moderate revolution, even as events had long since consigned moderation to history's dustbin.

Madame de Staël returned to Paris in 1814 and promptly set up a new salon. This one made trouble, too, for the restored Louis XVIII, whom Staël loathed, and she began a campaign for a liberal, constitutional monarchy that would culminate in the Revolution of 1830. Stael would not live to see that revolution, for she died rather fittingly on July 14, 1817, precisely twenty-eight years after the storming of the Bastille. Staël's life, like that of many of her European contemporaries, had been profoundly shaped by the Revolution's twists and turns; by no means was she alone in carrying those experiences to her grave.

❊ ❊ ❊ ❊

Like the revolutions surveyed in Chapter 15, the French Revolution undermined the Old Regimes, but it did so in a series of sharp, swift strokes rather than as the result of long-term transformations. This was a political and social revolution, one that changed the structure of government and abolished the legal inequalities on which early modern society rested. Although individuals such as Robespierre, de Staël, and Napoleon exerted enormous influence over the course of events, humble people also participated in political life as never before. Politics was no longer a matter exclusively for kings, nobles, and clergymen, but something that involved and affected everyone in France and, as French ideas and armies fanned out across the continent, in Europe as well.

This was revolution in its truest sense. Accordingly, it carried out its transformations much more quickly, and with much greater violence, than the Enlightenment and the military, commercial, agricultural, and scientific revolutions that preceded it, or the industrial revolution that coincided with and continued after it. For these reasons, the French Revolution is usually seen as the great event that inaugurated the modern world: by breaking decisively with the Old Regimes, this revolution laid the foundations for a society based on individual liberties, human rights, the protection of property, economic opportunity, and the sovereignty of the people, even if these foundations remained, for many years to come, little more than guidelines for the new world being born.

The French were not the first to stage a political revolution. The American Revolution of 1775–1783 inspired some European reformers to advertise more broadly the virtues of political liberty and individual rights, but it did not strike a blow to the Old Regimes' heart, as did the French Revolution of 1789. In its first year, the French

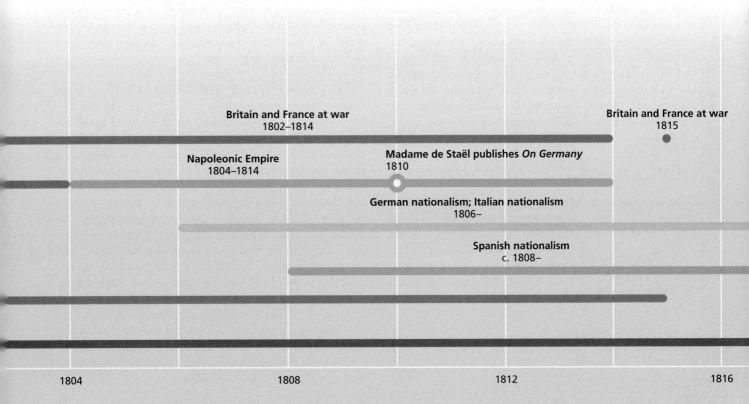

Britain and France at war
1802–1814

Britain and France at war
1815

Napoleonic Empire
1804–1814

Madame de Staël publishes *On Germany*
1810

German nationalism; Italian nationalism
1806–

Spanish nationalism
c. 1808–

1804   1808   1812   1816

Revolution dismantled absolutist France's system of legal inequalities. In its second year, the Revolution made further assaults on privileges and traditional beliefs, assaults that began to create a lively counterrevolution both at home and abroad. In the next three years (1791–1794), the Revolution grew ever more radical. Spurred on by fears that the Revolution would be reversed by backward-looking forces and by the wars that broke out on the French frontiers, radicals executed the king and established a republic. But the wars continued until 1799, when, seeking greater stability as well as military victory, France allowed the ambitious general Napoleon Bonaparte to seize power. He would go on to rule as emperor of the French after 1804 and conquer most of the European continent before his final defeat at the Battle of Waterloo in 1815.

This chapter tells the story of that Revolution, from its outbreak to Robespierre's fall and Napoleon's rise, a story that is fascinating in its unfolding and enormously consequential not just for European history, but for global history as well. It also treats the revolutionary and Napoleonic wars in rich detail. Although these wars were thoroughly political events, they had economic and religious aspects, as well. Between 1791 and 1815, European armies fought some 713 battles. It was not only the spread of revolutionary ideas, but also this experience of long, bloody, and expensive warfare that transformed Old Regimes across the continent. Together, these events speeded up the military, commercial, industrial, and agricultural revolutions already under way, and conveyed new ideas to people all across Europe. They ensured that revolution born in one country sparked enormous changes, even if in many places Napoleonic conflict and occupation eventually stifled reform and threw power back into the lap of nobles, clergymen, and kings. The French Revolution and the Napoleonic Wars were the great events in European history between the Reformation and the First World War because these events, like Martin Luther's revolt and the international conflicts of 1914–1918 reshaped the lives of virtually all Europeans in one way or another. For a time, Europe's many states and regions all shared in the same experiences, though by no means did they all emerge with the same liberties or the same scars.

Origins of the Revolution

Since the event itself, historians have speculated about the origins of the French Revolution and found them in both long- and short-term processes. If the long-term causes

What causes and events precipitated the French Revolution?

led the French to desire structural changes of some sort, the short-term causes shaped the exact course the Revolution would take.

Long-Term Causes

Before 1789, opposition to France's Old Regime came in different forms, depending on the position each critic held in the kingdom. Whereas the first two estates resented the monarchy for the modernizing aspects of absolutism (the breaking down of privileges, commercial expansion, increasing central state expenditure and taxation, bureaucratic centralization, and the opening of careers to talented commoners), the third estate, and especially the town- and city-dwelling bourgeoisie, wanted modernization to move more swiftly. The latter, in particular, were emboldened by enlightened ideas to participate in discussions about how the nation should be governed. The successful revolution in Great Britain's American thirteen colonies gave them further encouragement to pursue goals such as free speech and equality under the law.

DISSATISFACTION WITH ABSOLUTISM. Ironically, one of the most powerful forms of opposition came from within the tiny Second Estate: over the course of the later seventeenth and eighteenth centuries, the nobility had grown increasingly discontented with absolutist attempts at centralization. The nobles resented the king's attempts to build a bureaucracy staffed with talented, but perhaps non-noble men of his own choosing. They also felt that processes like the commercial revolution and the military revolution—which increased taxes, a few of which they did pay—were eating away at their privileges, and they did not want to be forced to pay more taxes in order to deal with the nation's rising burden of debt. The Catholic clergy, too, thought the monarchy was taking away too much of its taxing power and failing to curb the spread of dangerous enlightened ideas. Especially after the monarchy displayed its vulnerabilities by losing so much colonial territory in the Seven Years' War and by expending so much cash and blood to help the colonists in the American Revolution, the upper estates became vocal in their opposition to French absolutism. These two estates believed the solution was to turn the clock backward. A less modern France would, in their view, be a happier and more stable state.

DISSATISFACTIONS OF THE THIRD ESTATE. If anger toward the monarchy grew gradually among the first two estates, the various members of the third estate became increasingly dissatisfied with an economic and political system in which modernization was proceeding erratically. Depending on their positions in the economy, members of the Third Estate regarded this modernization differently. Peasants disliked new systems of farming that called for them to give up old privileges, like the right to pasture animals or gather wood on common land, and artisans opposed the development of the new cottage industries, which undercut the guilds' control of the labor market. Like the first and second estates, peasants and artisans basically wanted their own privileges restored—but they would definitely have liked to see the privileges of the nobility and clergy to collect taxes and tithes destroyed. Other members of the third estate, especially the bourgeoisie, by contrast, wanted to do away with a system of legal inequalities that kept them from

A faut esperer q'eu se jeu la Finira bentot

The Burdens of the Third Estates This caricature shows the view widespread in 1789 that the nobility and the clergy were idle parasites whose comfortable lifestyles were paid for by the hard work of the third estate.

participating in governance, taxed them disproportionately, and limited their access to certain jobs. This group wanted *more* modernization rather than less. If they diverged on this issue, however, members of the third estate were united in believing that they were overtaxed, and that the other two estates had grown fat and corrupt while the third worked to keep the nation afloat. In general, members of the third estate did not blame the king directly, as the nobility and clergy sometimes did. Rather, they saw him as a father who would rectify the situation if they could just get his ear.

THE ENLIGHTENMENT. Among the long-term causes of the Revolution, then, were aristocratic and clerical dissatisfaction with the absolutist monarchy, and the third estate's dissatisfaction with modernization and resentment toward the other estates. The Enlightenment played a major role in provoking French subjects to give voice to their dissatisfactions, and in generating hope that change could create a better, more equitable and open society. It is difficult to assess exactly how much the Enlightenment contributed to the Revolution's outbreak, but the works of writers such as Locke, Rousseau, and

Voltaire shaped a great deal of revolutionary rhetoric as well as much of the legislation passed by revolutionary governments. Enlightened ideas turned long-brewing grievances into plans to remake society and gave contemporaries confidence that they could, and should, try to change the world for the better.

THE AMERICAN REVOLUTION. In 1776, the largest and most successful neo-Europe, Britain's thirteen colonies, declared its independence from King George III's empire. Although the background to this revolt and the trajectory of the wars that followed lie beyond the confines of this book, it is important to recall the significance of this event for European history proper. Thomas Jefferson's Declaration of Independence articulated a series of enlightened principles that rang in European as well as American ears: all men are created equal and should be equal before the law; governments derive their legitimacy from the consent of the governed; all are endowed by their creator with unalienable rights to life, liberty, and the pursuit of happiness. No kings' subjects should be subjected to arbitrary justice and tyrannical governance, or told what they could trade, or taxed without their agreement; when such things occurred, the people had the right to rebel. It was quite startling in the 1770s, and long after then as well, for the colonized to rise up against their masters. Even more startling was that the Americans—with French backing—managed to win their war of independence. The success of the American Revolution owed a great deal to its occurring not in Europe, but thousands of miles overseas. But America's achievement of freedom and the establishment of a republic with an enlightened constitution gave Europeans eager for change hope that liberty and equality (at least for white, middle- and upper-class men) might lie in their future as well.

Short-Term Causes

How did long-simmering dissatisfactions and enlightened hopes turn into a full-scale assault on France's Old Regime in 1789? The short-term causes of the Revolution are not completely disconnected from the long-term causes. One short-term cause, the debt crisis, for example, was very much linked to France's extremely costly investment in supporting the American Revolution. A second short-term cause, the inflaming of political passions through print, had its origins in enlightened discourse. A third, the sharp increase in bread prices occasioned by the bad weather of 1788–1789, was something new, though the fact that hungry subjects blamed greedy nobles and clerics had much to do with long-term grievances. A final short-term cause for the Revolution's outbreak was the indecisiveness of Louis XVI, who did not succeed in stifling any complaints or solving anyone's problems and allowed all these things—a debt crisis, a political debate, and a series of bread riots—to fuse with one another and ignite a revolution.

THE DEBT CRISIS. Since the days of Louis XIV France had been spending beyond its means, and with no state bank, the crown had borrowed heavily and at high interest from Swiss bankers and from its own tax farmers. Bankrolling the American Revolution to spite France's traditional enemy, Britain, might have been satisfying, but it also brought the French government to the brink of collapse. A budgetary crisis began in 1787, when interest payments on the national debt reached 50 percent of the state's income and the French could find no one willing to lend more money. French finance minister Jacques Necker, Germaine de Staël's father, concluded that only new taxes on all landowners could save the situation, but when Louis called the nobles in for consultation, they refused to agree to further erosion of their privileges by having to pay the same taxes as those owed by members of the third estate.

By the summer of 1788, the situation was desperate. The old system of taxation would simply not yield enough money, but to change the system Louis had to call France's long-abandoned national representative assembly, the Estates General, back into session, a momentous step for an absolutist king. The Estates had last met in 1614, but Louis had no choice. In the fall of 1788, the king instructed each of France's provinces to elect one delegate for each estate. The delegates were to assemble the next spring in Paris, though it remained unclear how voting would proceed once the new Estates General assembled. Would the old system, in which each estate was collectively entitled to one vote, still prevail, even though the third estate so vastly outnumbered the other two? Or rather, should every delegate now be allowed to vote separately?

TWO TEXTS THAT CHANGED HISTORY. As the French began to ask these questions, printed pamphlets began to circulate, heightening public awareness of the crisis. Two important texts appeared, both of which helped enflame revolutionary sentiment. The first was a series of reports commissioned by the government, the *cahiers de doléances* (*grievance notebooks*). As elections for the Estates General commenced, note-takers were sent to each of France's provinces to collect complaints and compile them in notebooks, one for each estate, for the use of the Estates General. The idea was to gather information about conditions in each region, but the process also allowed people of all walks of life to speak about what was wrong with the kingdom. Some members of the third estate complained about excessive taxes; some complained about ruthless seigneurs, who charged exorbitant fees for the use of baking ovens or who abused their roles as local judges to steal the peasants' land. Nobles complained about the selling of offices to commoners. Impoverished clergymen lamented their inability to relieve the suffering of their flocks. All urged the king and the Estates General to do something as soon as possible to fix their problems.

The second important text was Emmanuel-Joseph Sieyès's pamphlet, "What Is the Third Estate?" written and published in the winter of 1788–1789 (see Back to the

Source at the end of the chapter). In the essay, Sieyès, an enlightened clergyman, insisted that the third estate was the nation and, as such, deserved to have its voice heard. Recognizing that the third estate was far larger than the other two and that the clergy and nobility contained reform-minded delegates, Sieyès argued that in the Estates General, each delegate—rather than each estate—should have a vote. Sieyès did not pull his punches; he denounced the idleness and the parasitism of the first two estates and insisted that all three estates should bear taxes equally and be equal in the eyes of the law. "Freedom does not derive from privileges," he wrote. "It derives from the rights of citizens—and these rights belong to all. If the aristocrats try to repress the People at the expense of that very freedom of which they prove themselves unworthy, the Third Estate will dare challenge their right."[1] In 1788, these were fighting words, and Sieyès's propositions and criticisms helped shape the debates that continued through that spring and into the eventful summer of 1789.

HARSH WEATHER, EXPENSIVE BREAD. The third major short-term cause was the bad winter of 1788–1789. While the cahiers were being collected and debates were raging over representation in the Estates General, the weather turned from bad to worse. In July 1788, freak hailstorms destroyed crops all over France. Drought followed the storms and made the situation worse; then came the winter of 1788–1789, the coldest in eighty years. Waterways froze, depriving boatmen of jobs and merchants of supplies; mills couldn't turn, and prices for both firewood and grain soared. This turn of events was disastrous for a population that lived on the edge of subsistence—especially as bread, their all-important foodstuff, cost more and more to procure.

Bread was the staple of the large majority of eighteenth-century Frenchmen. Most families of four survived on two four-pound loaves a day, each of which cost about 10 sous a loaf in 1787, a time when average wages ranged between 20 and 40 sous a day. By February 1789, the price was exceeding 15 sous a loaf, and people were becoming desperately hungry. With approximately 40 percent of the population living at subsistence level, every small price increase drove more people to the brink of starvation. By the spring of 1789, many urban-dwellers were spending all their wages just to buy bread. As usual in times of dearth, some townspeople took to the streets, rioting in front of bakeries or grain merchants' shops; rural folk took to the road, some of them spreading rumors that the nobles were hoarding grain and trying to starve the people into submission. The "little people" eagerly exchanged information and speculated about what would happen once the Estates General convened, hoping their delegates would convince the king to do something about their plight.

THE INDECISION OF LOUIS XVI. The final short-term cause of the Revolution's outbreak was the king's inability to make up his mind, either about the structure of the Estates General or about which voices in the kingdom to listen to. He remained, formally speaking, an absolute monarch. By law, he did not need to listen to anybody, but his finance minister, Jacques Necker, was pressing him to make crucial economic reforms, and he needed to give some direction to the Estates General now that he had called it into session. When the Estates General finally convened in Paris on May 5, 1789, the king still had not made a decision on how voting would proceed. As the credentials of the delegates were certified, fierce debates broke out both between and within the estates. Everyone waited for Louis XVI to appear at the meeting hall. Rumors flew that he would contract new loans or disband the body. Then Louis's son died, and grief drove the royal family to retreat to Versailles, where Louis could hunt in solitude. Six weeks passed, during which bread prices soared, tension in the streets of France's cities grew, and the king chased stags in the forests around Versailles.

The Revolution Begins

Exasperated by the stalemate, on June 17, 1789, the delegates of the Third Estate voted to call themselves the **National Assembly**—a sure sign they had adopted Sieyès's claim that the third estate was itself the nation. There was still no word from the king, and the newly constituted Assembly panicked when, on June 20, they arrived at the meeting hall to find it locked and guarded by soldiers. The hall was being prepared for the long-awaited royal session, but no one had informed the delegates of the third estate. They concluded quickly that the Estates General was being dissolved and that new taxes would be imposed without their consent. In defiance, delegates of the third estate, along with some renegade clergymen and nobles, reconvened at a nearby indoor tennis court. Those in attendance took an oath—subsequently known as the **Tennis Court Oath**—that the group would not disband until they had given France its first constitution.

Louis XVI finally proposed his reforms, but they did nothing about the system of privileges, and the National Assembly rejected them. The king made plans to dissolve the Assembly by force, but the French Guards, a key policing unit, refused to act to contain the Paris crowds gathering in the streets. On July 11, Louis dismissed Necker, hoping to install an antireformist cabinet, but the next day, a mob gathered to protest the popular finance minister's dismissal. Protestors stormed into a wax museum and stole a bust of Necker, which they paraded through the streets on the end of a pike as orators denounced the evils of the aristocracy, the clergy, and the grain-hoarders. The French Guards joined the rioters and helped to pillage gun shops. As thousands of Parisians swarmed into the streets and armed clashes with police began, it became clear that this was more than an ordinary riot.

When night fell, Parisians began to attack symbolic institutions of the Old Regime. They burned toll-gates around the city and attacked the headquarters of the tax farmers. The next morning, July 13, they attacked the abbey of Saint Lazare, which was being used both as a prison and as a grain depot. Attempting to avoid massive bloodshed and perhaps fearing desertions, Louis XVI withheld bringing in the army. The following morning, July 14, crowds, including soldiers who had deserted their posts, attacked the Invalides, the military veterans' hospital set up by Louis XIV. There they took a number of cannons and small arms, but they had no powder, and so they turned next to the Bastille, the prison and arsenal at the city's center.

Surrounded by angry rioters, the Bastille's guards opened fire, killing nearly one hundred members of the crowd. Unable to repel the mob, the guards finally surrendered their powder, their seven prisoners, and their commandant. The commandant was spit upon and beaten severely, then killed by a hailstorm of bayonets, knives, fists, and rocks when he dared to kick one of his captors in the groin. He was then decapitated with a pocketknife, and his head, put on a pike, was paraded grandly by the

The Fall of the Bastille The assault on the Bastille prison of July 14, 1789, by a mob of Parisian civilians was not previously planned, but its success set the stage for the unfolding of the French Revolution. Bastille Day (July 14) remains France's most important national holiday.

crowd. Over the next few days, several more Parisian officials were decapitated and their heads paraded; the archbishop of Paris was nearly lynched. Realizing that he could not trust his army, Louis was forced to make concessions. He promised not to disband the National Assembly, restored Necker as finance minister, and made the leader of the third estate mayor of Paris. The Marquis de Lafayette, a hero of the American Revolution, became commander of the National Guard, the new citizens' militia. Louis was cheered when he pinned a tricolor cockade to his chest—the white representing the Bourbons, the red and blue representing the city of Paris. These gestures convinced Parisians that the king had in some way joined the Revolution and would act quickly to correct abuses in his kingdom.

The Moderate Revolution, 1789–1791

In reality, the king was no fan of the National Assembly and no friend of the Parisian rioters. He had simply lost control of the course of events, and was stalling for time until he could decide how to proceed. In the meantime, however, the people of France had time to think about what *kind* of revolution they wanted to carry forward. Would it be an attempt to attain political liberty and equal opportunity under the law or an attempt to establish economic and social equality as well? From the beginning, the French were divided on this question, and this distinction largely reflects the two different stages between which the Revolution passed, the moderate phase—lasting roughly from the summer of 1789 until the summer and fall of 1791—and the radical revolution—lasting from early 1792 until the Terror subsided after July 1794. The moderate legal and political revolution of 1789–1791 laid the foundations for the radical social revolution of 1792–1794, and its accomplishments would be the most lasting, though by no means the most memorable, achievements of the era.

What did the moderate revolution achieve?

From the Great Fear to the Constitution of 1791

After the fall of the Bastille, the members of the National Assembly began to read through the cahiers of the third estate in preparation for writing a new constitution. The vast catalog they found of seigneurial abuses made a big impact, especially as news began to trickle in from the countryside. Spurred by hunger and emboldened by Louis XVI's concessions, peasants were sacking and burning manor houses and grain depots and, in some cases, murdering nobles and grain merchants. In fact, there were relatively few of these attacks, but in the tense atmosphere of mid-summer Paris, rumors circulated that everywhere armies of brigands were on the march, creating what has become known as the Great Fear.

Not only nobles, but also wealthy property owners grew more and more concerned that a nationwide radical peasant uprising might be under way. Some nobles packed their valuables and left France. Most of these wealthy emigrants, known as **émigrés,** settled in nearby countries—Austria, the German states, or England—and many joined pressure groups and volunteer armies, intent on using their influence and wealth to end and reverse the Revolution as soon as the opportunity arose.

THE AUGUST DECREES. In the National Assembly, emotions ran high as delegates sought to curb the violence and address the cahiers' complaints by proposing more and more reforms. The climax came on August 4, when speaker after speaker—including property owners, nobles, and clergy—rose to denounce legal privileges of all kinds, from salt taxes to the corvée. The session lasted long into the night, and when it was over the National Assembly had abolished all of France's legal privileges. This was one of the revolutionary era's first grand displays of emotional, crowd-pleasing oratory, but it would certainly not be the last.

In the sober light of day, the Assembly worked out these provisions, creating the Decrees of August 10–11, which did away with personal servitude, seigneurial dues, special rights for towns, and the tithe. Taxes were to be levied equitably; no offices were to be sold. The delegates reorganized France's administrative system, replacing the uneven patchwork of 130 religious units (dioceses) with 83 secular departments of more or less equal size. Peasants were not given the right to take land from their lords or freed from paying rent; landlords were to be compensated for the loss of seigneurial dues. The Catholic Church was perhaps the biggest loser. It lost the right to collect the tithe, and though some sort of state support for the clergy was envisioned, no promises were made.

THE DECLARATION OF THE RIGHTS OF MAN. As August came to an end, the delegates composed a document that formulated even more clearly the break from the Old Regime. The Declaration of the Rights of Man, drafted chiefly by the Marquis de Lafayette, borrowed some of its language from the American Declaration of Independence and from the Enlightenment. The document opened with a claim that signaled the end of the Old Regime: "Article 1: Men are born and remain free and equal in rights. Social distinctions can be based only on public utility." Article 3 declared, "The source of all sovereignty resides essentially in the nation," and Article 9 proclaimed that "Every man is presumed innocent until he has been found guilty." Articles 10 and 11 guaranteed freedom of religion and freedom of speech for the French people. Article 13 declared that taxes "must be shared equally among all the citizens in proportion to their means." Though Louis refused to sign the August Decrees or to officially accept the Declaration, it was clear now that a permanent social change, shaped around the principles of equality and liberty, was taking place.

Hoping that somehow this would all blow over, Louis and his family retreated to Versailles, where he continued to indulge his passion for hunting. By October, however, bread prices were still high, the debt crisis remained unresolved, and new rumors reached France's central marketplace that the National Assembly was to be dissolved by force. Enraged by the king's inaction, a large group of female vendors marched the eleven miles from Paris to Versailles, intending to make Louis return to Paris to see the plight of his subjects. Accompanying them was a regiment of the newly formed National Guard. Arriving on the afternoon of October 6, the now hungry and bedraggled women and the armed guards terrified the king and queen. In a skirmish between the king's bodyguards and the National Guards, one of the guards and two royal bodyguards were killed. After the heads of the bodyguards were cut off and mounted on pikes, the king agreed to return to Paris, where he signed the August Decrees. Following this second victory of the people, sentiment in favor of the Revolution swelled, and crowds gathered to swear allegiance to the Assembly and to the Revolution. Throughout France patriotic societies and clubs were formed to discuss how best the nation might implement and expand its revolutionary reforms.

All the clubs claimed to support the Revolution and to love France, the *patrie* (fatherland), but already some clubs were more radical than others in their vision of what the Revolution should accomplish. Two of the most important radical clubs were based in Paris: the Cordeliers' Club and the **Jacobin Club.** Both contained members of the National Assembly, and men who had spent many an hour in salon discussions of enlightened ideas. Many club members were young men like the provincial lawyer and devoted reader of Rousseau, Maximilien Robespierre (1758–1794), thrilled by the prospect of remaking the world in accordance with their ideas and capable of fiery oratory. In the hothouse atmosphere of the Jacobin club, Robespierre developed a fanatical dedication to destroying all remnants of France's Old Regime and to replacing the monarchy with an incorruptible republic based on democratic virtue. In 1789 the clubs were small and their anticlericalism and republican ideas atypical, even among delegates in the Assembly. Over time, however, events would push the clubs to the forefront of the Revolution.

DEALING WITH THE DEBT. Enthusiasm for the new liberties surged, but bread prices remained high, and in the countryside, peasants continued to attack manor houses; some aristocrats and clergymen fled the country, becoming exiles in Britain, Austria, or Prussia. The National Assembly tried to address the debt crisis with a tactic that might have been borrowed from any one of Europe's enlightened absolutists: milking the church.

CHRONOLOGY	Key Events of the French Revolution
DATE	**EVENT**
June 1789	Tennis Court Oath
July 14, 1789	The fall of the Bastille
August 1789	Declaration of the Rights of Man
December 1790	Civil Constitution of the Clergy approved by Louis XVI
May 1791	Constitution of 1791
September 2–7, 1792	September Massacres
September 22, 1792	Convention declared France a republic; beginning of the revolutionary calendar
January 21, 1793	Louis XVI executed
August 1793	*Levée en masse* proclaimed by the Convention
September 17 and 29, 1793	Convention passed Law of Suspects and the General Maximum
July 27, 1794 (9 Thermidor)	Robespierre guillotined
August 22, 1795 (5 Fructidor)	Constitution of 1795 created the Directory
November 9, 1799 (18 Brumaire)	Napoleon staged coup against the Directory
April 1802	Napoleonic Concordat ended revolutionary persecution of the church; Constitution of the Year X made Napoleon consul for life

In October 1789, the Assembly voted to dissolve all religious orders other than those dedicated to education, hospital care, and poor relief; monks and nuns who devoted themselves merely to the "useless" tasks of prayer or contemplation were to be turned out of their monasteries, and no new religious vows were to be taken. A month later the Assembly seized all church property, and in March 1790 declared it for sale to the highest bidder. This sale was linked to the issuing of France's first national paper currency, the **assignat,** backed by the properties newly confiscated by the state. This solution to the debt problem proved to be only a temporary fix. The assignats quickly lost value as the state printed more and more to offset the purchase of imported grain and the hoarding of coins. By spring 1792, the assignat had lost 40 percent of its value.

The Revolution and the Church

A combination of factors generated the revolutionaries' attack on the church: outrage at clerical corruption, Enlightenment-spawned criticism of Catholicism's irrationality, and the need to find new sources of income to return France to fiscal stability. Reforming the church was a widely popular cause; selling off church property appealed to those with sufficient cash to buy land. Making Protestants and then Jews full citizens (in December 1789 and September 1791, respectively) appealed to the enlightened elite, though not necessarily to provincial Catholics.

The abolition of the tithe and the seizing of church property necessitated some sort of state support for the clergy, but bitter divisions emerged in developing a new system of support. The Constituent Assembly, dominated by members of the third estate, wanted to be sure that state money was spent responsibly and that members of the clergy did not spread antirevolutionary ideas to their flocks. They decided that all clergy members, including Protestant pastors, should be made to swear an oath of loyalty to the state, in exchange for which they would receive a salary. Many Catholic clergy found this requirement offensive, for it meant that they were to put loyalty to the state above their commitments to God and to the church, headed by the pope in Rome. Louis XVI refused to sign the legislation requiring the oath, known as the **Civil Constitution of the Clergy,** for many months, but finally approved it in late December 1790. Almost immediately, the Constituent Assembly had the beginnings of a counterrevolution on its hands.

Eventually only about 54 percent of the lower clergy swore the oath of loyalty. That number includes anticlerical Paris. In some rural districts, the figure was as low as 15 percent. The overwhelming majority of the higher clergy—bishops and archbishops—refused to sign. That left the Assembly with a difficult question: what to do with priests and nuns who refused to swear the oath? Those who refused, known as refractories, had their salaries suspended, but some of them were popular local figures, and their parishioners refused to allow them to be replaced. Some members of the clergy took to oration themselves, proclaiming that the revolutionaries were empowering Protestants and destroying the church as a whole. To silence them and to force compliance with the oath, the Constituent Assembly gradually applied more and more force, imprisoning or exiling troublemakers. Revolutionaries increasingly feared that refractory priests, monks, and nuns would conspire with outsiders to bring down the revolutionary government; Catholic leaders feared the assembly would outlaw religious belief entirely. By late 1791, a cycle had begun in which episodes of persecution of refractory clergy led to counterrevolutionary violence, which in turn led to more persecution—and more violence.

The King and the Revolution

During this eventful two-year period of the moderate revolution, Louis XVI remained king of France. Only a small minority of radical republicans could even conceive of toppling him from the throne. Sometimes Louis seemed to concede decision-making power to the revolutionaries; at other times he refused to do the Assembly's bidding. He stalled endlessly on the Civil Constitution of the Clergy and put off again and again the signing of the Constitution presented to him in June 1791. As a stream of French nobles and clergymen left the country, the revolutionaries began more and more to fear that Louis might be in touch with his exiled friends, many of them working hard to get the Austrians, Prussians, or the English to make war on revolutionary France.

Had Louis acted decisively at this moment and signed the Constitution and the Civil Constitution of the Clergy—as William and Mary of England had signed the Bill of Rights and agreed to share sovereignty with Parliament in 1689—perhaps the radicalization of the revolution might have been prevented or diminished. By mid-1791, the moderate revolution had accomplished a great deal. French absolutism was abolished, the Old Regime's system of privileges dismantled, the church's secular power destroyed, a constitutional monarchy created, and equality under the law established. Instead of accepting these changes, Louis XVI made another fateful decision in the summer of 1791: he decided to try to escape.

Toward the Radical Revolution

The king's attempt to flee the country failed, and he was marched back to France by his own subjects. In the ensuing months he found himself increasingly irrelevant as his subjects pledged their allegiance either to counterrevolutionary movements or to more radical forms of revolution.

THE VENDÉE. On July 14, 1791, the second anniversary of the fall of the Bastille, Louis consented at last to sign the new Constitution, which required him to share power with the Assembly—though he retained the right to a veto that suspended legislation for a full six years. Again, he could have made the best of this constitutional monarchy and attempted to drown out the ever-louder voices of the radical Jacobins by agreeing to moderate reforms. Encouraged by a joint declaration of the Prussians and Austrians to protect the French monarchy and by the outbreak of counterrevolutionary violence in the Vendée, a coastal region southwest of Paris, in October 1791 (Map 17.1), he refused to make his peace with the revolutionaries.

In November 1791, the king vetoed a bill that would have confiscated the property of all émigrés who did not return to France within three months. Then he vetoed a law that stripped refractory priests of their pensions and declared them subject to trial for treason. He did not, however, renounce the Assembly or attempt another escape, but settled in to wait, perhaps hoping that

1791: The Flight to Varennes

By the summer of 1791, many French people had enthusiastically embraced the Revolution.[2] Some were frustrated that the king had not clearly committed himself to the cause of reform, but Louis XVI remained king of France, and only the most radical republicans thought of dispensing with him entirely. The Constituent Assembly still hoped he would sign the new constitution, and people preferred to blame noble conspirators, greedy priests, or even the queen rather than accusing the king of hostility to the little people of France. The Assembly had even put his picture on the assignat.

The king himself, however, had begun to fear for his safety and that of his family. Noble advisors, most notably the queen's friend and possibly her lover, the Swedish noble Axel Fersen, had been urging him for months to leave Paris, the center of Jacobin agitation. In mid-June, the king finally agreed to put one of Fersen's plans into action. At about midnight on June 21, 1791, the royal couple, lightly disguised and accompanied by their three children, the king's sister, and several nursemaids, piled into three coaches and headed for the border of the Austrian Netherlands. The plan was to rendezvous with royalist military officers, supported by German mercenaries. The king later said that he was bound only for the fortifications at Malmédy, where his family would be safe from the Paris mob. There is, however, little question that Louis was intending to join the émigré armies forming on France's border and make war on revolutionary France.

Though on a normal day, some two thousand Parisians worked in the Tuileries Palace, the king managed to leave undetected. But by morning, the news began to spread that a counterrevolutionary conspiracy was under way. The royal family's absence was discovered and the German soldiers had been spotted. Rumors raged that forces were being marshaled for a counterrevolutionary strike at the Assembly. In the meantime, the king had been recognized—thanks to his picture on the assignat—by Jean-Baptiste Drouet, the manager of a relay post, where the royal carriages had changed horses. Drouet's story quickly reached local members of the National Guard, who rallied to scatter the cavalry guarding the coaches from the rear. Drouet was sent on to the next town to warn the people to stop the king. He caught up to the party at the town of Varennes at about noon on June 21, and a courier from Paris arrived shortly afterward, bringing the Constituent Assembly's demand that the king return to the capital. As news spread, people from the region converged on Varennes, shouting "Long live the Nation! Long live the King! Back to Paris!" Louis wisely refused his armed escort's offer to use force, as six thousand guardsmen soon mustered to march alongside the royal carriages on their return trip. As the family retraced its journey, more and more little people joined the parade, armed with pitchforks, axes, and sticks. Celebrations broke out, with people cheering the cracking of the conspiracy and the avoidance of civil war.

Upon his humiliating capture and return to Paris, Louis XVI agreed to sign and swear loyalty to the Constitution of 1791, but his attempted flight to Varennes did his reputation irreparable damage. For one thing, he had shown that the Jacobins were right: there *were* royalist conspiracies afoot to use the king to undermine the Revolution. The Jacobins lost no time in circulating a petition calling Louis "an ungrateful traitor" and demanding that he be deposed. But Louis had made even his supporters cautious about trusting him, and his correspondence was now watched carefully. From now on, every move he made to protect nobles or clergymen from revolutionary justice was rumored to be part of a new conspiracy against the nation. Especially after counterrevolutionary violence began in earnest in late 1791, the Jacobins began to insist that the monarchy was fanning the flames in order to restore the Old Regime by force. The extraordinary events of 1791, along with the actions and inactions of King Louis XVI, had destroyed all possibility that the French Revolution might end with a constitutional monarchy—rather than in Jacobin-led terror.

Flight to Varennes Large crowds gathered to see Louis XVI and his family escorted back to Paris after their attempted flight to Varennes.

QUESTIONS | *What factors led Louis XVI to flee his own country? Putting yourself in the king's shoes, would you have also fled?*

MAP 17.1 | France's Sister Republics, 1792–1799

This map shows the expansion of revolutionary France, and the sister republics founded in the wake of the revolutionary army's conquests. It also depicts the regions where counterrevolutionary sentiment was most powerful in the years 1791–1794. ***At what point, do you think, would France's monarchical neighbors have been right to fear that the Revolution was spreading?***

Legend:
- French Republic at 1792
- Annexed to France 1792–1795
- Sister republics
- Areas of counterrevolutionary activity 1791–1794

the Prussians and Austrians would act on their pledge and invade France. Again, his indecision was fatal. While he took no action, radicals spread the rumor that he was plotting this invasion himself.

THE SANS-CULOTTES. The king's vetoes coincided with a new phase of economic hardship. To address unemployment, the National Assembly in March 1791 abolished trade guilds. But workers then began to band together to try to raise wages, provoking the moderate delegate Isaac René Guy Le Chapelier to propose a

law forbidding workers' organizations and strikes. The Assembly approved, and from mid-1791 until 1864, the Le Chapelier Law remained in force. This infuriated Parisian workers, some of whom began calling themselves **sans-culottes,** signaling their affiliation with working-class men who wore long trousers rather than the short breeches (culottes; *sans* meaning "without") and tights worn by the nobility. As the value of the assignat fell and bread prices rose again, the sans-culottes began to rally against the Assembly, finding a voice in Paris's local district councils known as sections.

In the sections, revolutionary language grew increasingly anticlerical, antiaristocratic, and democratic. They believed that equality meant not just equal legal rights but the leveling of the economic playing field. Unlike the Jacobin leadership, the sans-culottes had little rhetorical polish, but they used the threat of mob action to pressure the Assembly to listen to the demands of the ordinary people. What they cared about was the price of bread, unemployment, clerical corruption, and inequalities in wealth. Their insistence on addressing these social issues, rather than limiting their concern to legal and political reforms, and the threat of mob violence they wielded in Paris, France's decision-making center, made them crucial to the stoking of the fires of the radical revolution.

THE WARS. Most important in radicalizing the Revolution were the external wars. Urged on by orators who insisted that Habsburg support for the émigrés put the Revolution in grave danger, the Assembly declared war on Austria in April 1792. Skirmishes on France's borders broke out, led by exiles trying to end the Revolution and supported by Prussian and Austrian troops. By summer, the anti-revolutionaries were deep within France and threatened to burn all of Paris if the king and queen were harmed. For the radicals, this declaration confirmed that the Bourbons were at the center of a counterrevolutionary conspiracy. They convinced the Assembly to declare martial law and to mobilize the city to fight both the invaders and those who might side with them, such as the refractory clergy and remaining aristocrats. Orators began to invoke a new principle, fraternity, which called on Frenchmen to honor their obligations to their brother citizens. On August 10, radicals renounced the king and attacked the palace itself. Six hundred members of the king's guard were butchered and the royal family had to seek the protection of the Assembly. Deciding that the time had come to dissolve the monarchy, the Assembly locked the royal family in a medieval fortress. The Assembly also abolished itself and ordered new elections for delegates to frame a constitution for France's first republic.

The Radical Revolution

The dissolution of the monarchy set the stage for the radical revolution, the period between fall 1792 and late summer 1794, during which sans-culottes and Jacobin radicals pressed for greater social and economic equality and faster and more violent suppression of the "enemies of the revolution." In the course of this revolution, the counterrevolution would explode, and many more of Europe's monarchs would lend support to the Austrians in what became known as the War of the First Coalition (1792–1798). This stage of the Revolution generated the most memorable experiments in democratization and de-Christianization, but

What factors contributed to the radicalization of the Revolution?

it also unleashed a new sort of purely political violence known as the Terror.

The September Massacres

The violent events of August 10, 1792, left France in an uproar. Panic increased when rumors reached Paris on September 2 that the fortress at Verdun had fallen and the Prussians were marching on the capital. Mobs of radicalized Parisians invaded the prisons, where, over five bloody days, they slaughtered between 1,100 and 1,400 counterrevolutionary "traitors," most of them refractory priests and nuns. In the end, the rumors from Verdun proved false, and a French victory at Valmy that month prevented the feared Prussian march on Paris. The August coup and the September Massacres, however, doomed the possibility that the Revolution might have a moderate end. Instead, the Jacobins got what they wanted: the abolition of the monarchy and more war against the internal and external enemies of revolutionary France.

On September 22, 1792, Louis XVI was stripped of the throne his family had held since the late sixteenth century, and France became a republic. The National Assembly dissolved itself ahead of elections to seat delegates to a new constitutional convention, which would be charged with the task of outlining the framework for the new republic. These elections were the first in European history to be conducted on the basis of universal manhood suffrage; all adult men were considered equal under the law, and all were entitled to vote. Although women were deeply involved in revolutionary politics—many belonged to patriotic clubs and many more participated in both revolutionary and counterrevolutionary riots—they were not considered members of the political nation and thus were not allowed to vote. Some clubs, including the Jacobins, actively discouraged women from participating in political activities, just one of the ways in which even the radicals failed to establish full liberty, equality, and fraternity.

Many "little people," indeed, believed that the Assembly had done nothing to address their sufferings. As the newly elected **Convention** began to deliberate in October 1792, a new wave of grain riots and attacks on manor houses erupted. In Paris, the sans-culottes staged riots and demonstrations calling for reducing bread prices and putting the unemployed back to work. All these forces created havoc in the Convention, as one faction pursued the support of the sans-culottes, and others found themselves unwilling or unable to keep pace with the further radicalization of the Revolution.

Montagnards and Girondins

Within the Convention, a radical faction known as the Mountain formed, led by members of the Cordeliers and Jacobin Clubs. Members of the Mountain—or Montagnards—took their seats on the steep, left-hand side of the chamber, creating an association ever afterward of radical politics and "the left." On the right sat a motley crowd of men known as the Girondins, many of whom came from the southern French region known as the Gironde. The Girondins staunchly supported the moderate revolution of 1789–1791. When the Convention put the king on trial for treason in December 1792, he was convicted by a vote of 745 to 29, with only a few brave souls opposing the majority. The vote to sentence the king to death was considerably closer, 361 to 360, with many Girondins opposed to this radical move. After the king's execution, these "right-wing" revolutionaries came under increasing suspicion. In the spring of 1793, they were denounced by radical orators and purged from the Convention. Over the next six months, most would themselves face execution, one of the foremost examples of the Revolution nourishing and then eating its own children.

The King's Execution

Louis XVI, now known as Citizen Capet, lost his head on January 21, 1793. In the week before his execution, he read David Hume's account of the execution of Charles I of England, who had bravely faced the axe almost precisely 144 years before.[3] By all accounts, Louis was equally regal on the trip to the gallows, though his demise entailed putting his head into a newfangled revolutionary invention, the guillotine. The idea for a mechanical murderer had been conceived in 1791 by a revolutionary doctor, Dr. Guillotine, whose intent was to extend to all the noble privilege of death by one swift chop (previously common criminals faced more agonizing forms of torture or the noose). Perhaps the device spared Louis from additional suffering, but the enlightened invention did not diminish the radicals' increasing taste for blood. After the king's death, the guillotine was set up in the Place Louis XV, now renamed Place de la Revolution, where it was used to dispatch more and more enemies of the Revolution.

The king's execution unleashed a new wave of revolutionary enthusiasm and violence. It also prompted a sluggish English government to announce it would join efforts to contain the French. The Convention declared war on England on February 1, 1793, and immediately called for the conscription of 300,000 men, some of whom were needed on the frontiers, while others were needed to put down the continuing internal counterrevolutionary insurrections, especially in the

Vendée. Some young patriots eagerly signed on to serve the Revolution, but others rioted or fled, joining gangs of brigands who made intermittent guerrilla attacks on revolutionary forces. In April, the Convention appointed a nine-man **Committee of Public Safety** to oversee the war effort and to choose the members of the Revolutionary Tribunal, a panel of judges who tried people accused of political crimes. Tribunals set up in the provinces, similarly, sent many to their deaths with perfunctory hearings.

Some anti-revolutionaries resorted to extreme measures as well. On July 13, 1793, Charlotte Corday, a passionate opponent of the Revolution, tricked her way into the apartment of one of the most outspoken Jacobins, Jean-Paul Marat, and stuck a dagger into his heart as he soaked in his bathtub. The Convention dubbed him a revolutionary martyr, and the artist Jacques-Louis David painted a chilling tribute to the radical Marat, giving him qualities reminiscent of the traditional images of Christ's descent from the cross.

In the summer of 1793, under pressure from the sans-culottes and the sections, the Convention ratified a new constitution, one that envisioned new kinds of democratic governance and social equality. French citizens were guaranteed the right to public education and public assistance. But the document never came into force because, Convention members insisted, France needed first to win its wars against its foreign enemies. Decimated by the emigration of noble officers and by social upheaval, the army desperately needed more men. Thus, the deputies adopted another radical measure: a national draft, known as the *levée en masse*. This measure required every

Execution of Louis XVI In less than four years' time, Louis XVI had lost control of his absolutist state and been found guilty of treason against the French people. In January 1793, he was executed in the same "enlightened" manner used for all other enemies of the Revolution: by guillotine.

unmarried French male between the ages of eighteen and twenty-five to report for military duty immediately and to serve until the republic's enemies had been driven from French soil. Women and children were supposed to help by making tents and clothes; old men were enjoined to "betake themselves to public squares in order to inspire courage in the soldiers and to preach hatred of kings and the unity of the Republic."[4] In a year's time, the *levée en masse* netted France an army of 1.2 million, many of them eager to do the Convention's bidding, but it also created new bands of draft-dodging outlaws.

Frustrated by their inability to pacify the country and angered that all of Europe now seemed to be against them, the revolutionaries began to fear new conspiracies. To add to the Convention's headaches, bread prices were again soaring and the sans-culottes were screaming for price controls and the punishment of hoarders and speculators. By September 1793, the Convention had killed the king, purged the moderates, and forced tens of thousands of nobles and clergy into exile, but the radicals still saw enemies of the Revolution everywhere. The only option, the radicals concluded, was terror.

The Reign of Terror

In September 1793, the Convention passed a series of laws that laid the foundations for what came to be called the **Reign of Terror** or **"the Terror."** A revolutionary army was created to deal with hoarders, recalcitrant priests, and any nobles still inhabiting France—they were now denounced as conspirators and "reptiles who corrupt everything they touch,"[5] no matter what their politics. Radical new legislation was passed, and the revolutionary tribunals worked overtime to condemn and execute as quickly as possible enemies they feared were hell-bent on starving the little people and returning them to the "slavery" of the Old Regime. Robespierre, now president of a twelve-man Committee of Public Safety, insisted that "Terror is nothing but prompt, severe, inflexible justice; it is therefore an emanation of virtue."[6] Bloody it might be, but this sort of virtuous terror, Robespierre concluded, was crucial to wipe out threats to France's newfound equality, liberty, and fraternity.

THE LAW OF SUSPECTS. The central piece of legislation was the Law of Suspects, which permitted arrest of "those who by their conduct, associations, talk, or writings have shown themselves to be partisans of tyranny or federalism, and enemies of liberty."[7] The Committee of Public Safety assumed broad new domestic powers to enforce the new law and used it to purge France of those whose behavior suggested they might someday oppose the Revolution, even if the state could produce no evidence that they had been involved in conspiracies. All nobles and clergy members were now suspects and liable to imprisonment, if not death. The Convention forbade the wearing of clerical garb, the ringing of church bells, and the celebration of mass. Offenders were either shot

by firing squads or hanged from lampposts by marauding mobs of revolutionaries. "À la lanterne!" ("To the lamppost!") became a terrifying call to murder.

THE GENERAL MAXIMUM. The Law of Suspects allowed the radical revolutionaries to carry out the Terror with at least the trappings of legality, but just as important for the unfolding of the radical revolution was the economic legislation passed in September 1793. To placate the sections, Robespierre pushed through a measure setting a maximum price on bread. Local price ceilings had been set before, but the so-called **General Maximum** now stipulated that those caught selling bread above the maximum price or hoarding grain—that is, refusing to sell grain to the government at the set price—would be considered enemies of the state and thus subject to trial and execution. This provision alone immediately put Paris at odds with rural peasants, who wanted to hold out for higher market prices. Pressed by hungry Parisian mobs, the Convention sent revolutionary troops to the countryside to extract grain from supposed conspirators.

For the next nine months, from September 1793 until July 1794, terror was indeed "the order of the day." Some 16,000 "enemies of the revolution" were guillotined, and perhaps another 12,000 died in prison awaiting trial. Mobile, patriotic lynch mobs imposed extensive vigilante justice throughout the provinces. Civilians accused of siding with the counterrevolution were summarily executed. Soldiers enforcing the Maximum or the *levée en masse* frequently pillaged churches or manor homes for their own private gain and sometimes committed atrocities, such as lashing hoarders together with chains and drowning them in provincial rivers. In the Vendée, as many as 200,000 inhabitants may have been killed in the brutal civil wars. One visitor to Lyons in January 1794 reported:

> whole ranges of houses, always the most handsome, burnt. The churches, convents, and all the dwellings of the former patricians were in ruins. When I came to the guillotine, the blood of those who had been executed a few hours beforehand was still running in the street. . . . I said to a group of sans-culottes . . . that it would be decent to clear away all this human blood. Why should it be cleared? One of them said to me. It's the blood of aristocrats and rebels. The dogs should lick it up.[8]

In these conditions, it is scarcely a surprise that a song that began as the signature tune for a regiment of revolutionary soldiers from Marseilles, *The Marseillaise,* became the revolutionary national anthem. The song urged true patriots to fight to the death against "vile despots" and "traitors" whose fondest wish was to reenslave the people or to slit their throats. It became popular with radicals across Europe in the decades to come.

The Revolution beyond France

As the Terror raged across France, the Convention's armies swept into the Austrian Netherlands where émigré,

Prussian, and Austrian troops had been threatening an invasion. In 1794, French armies overran and annexed the Austrian Netherlands, home to so many real and supposed counterrevolutionaries. When they conquered the venerable Dutch Republic the next year, revolutionaries replaced it with a sister state under French control that they dubbed the Batavian Republic. In Italy, too, several sister republics were founded after French conquests in the 1790s.

Once the battles were won, however, the Convention faced the next question: what to do with occupied territories? One revolutionary slogan described French occupation policy as "War on the castles, peace to the cottages!" Indeed, in the Austrian Netherlands as elsewhere the revolutionary armies did intend to do away with other peoples' Old Regimes as they had done away with their own. In some places, the French were greeted by local Jacobins and reformers who were eager to use the occupation to do away with the system of privileges in their own backyards, but these reformers also wanted some degree of local autonomy and resented French economic policy, which was to extract as many resources—including food, horses, gold, and conscripts—from the territories as possible.

The French often imposed their anti-Christian policies more harshly than locals were able to stomach, and the revolutionary armies offended by pillaging churches, monasteries, and town halls. Everywhere ill-provisioned armies requisitioned supplies—then paid their bills in ever more worthless assignats. The sister republics of the Netherlands, Italy, and Switzerland were in fact ruled by the French, much to the dissatisfaction even of local republicans. They didn't last long, thanks to the renewal of warfare and the rise of Napoleon, but they were significant in breaking the continuity of the Old Regimes and in spreading ideas conservatives would find hard to root out.

POLAND. For non-French monarchs and nobles, more worrying were the spinoff rebellions inspired by the French revolutionaries' successes. In the spring of 1794, rebellion rose among the Poles, whose kingdom had recently been partitioned among the Austrians, Russians, and Prussians. The revolt was led by the enlightened military leader and hero of the American Revolution, Tadeusz Kosciuszko (1746–1817), and a group of Warsaw Jacobins. The revolutionaries succeeded in forcing the Russians to leave Warsaw, and Kosciuszko declared an end to serfdom in the new Poland. Prussian, Austrian, and Russian troops rallied quickly, and in October 1794, the Russians retook Warsaw, killing between 10,000 and 20,000 Poles in a single day. Kosciuszko was imprisoned, but later pardoned by the czar. He settled in France, but never gave up advocating for a free and independent Poland—and his countrymen never gave up resenting Russian rule.

IRELAND. In 1796, poor harvests and rising anger against their English Anglican overlords led some Irish radicals to attempt their own revolution. They sought assistance from revolutionary France, but the meager help they received was of little use, as the English brought in tens of thousands of soldiers, armed with cannons. The death toll in 1798 amounted to 30,000, in just over three months of bloody engagement. Among the dead was Wolfe Tone, leader of the Irish revolutionaries, who slit his own throat after he had been captured in battle. Despite the brevity of this revolutionary struggle, Ireland's bid for independence—and England's brutality in snuffing it out—would not be forgotten by later generations of Irish republicans, and Wolfe Tone, like Tadeusz Kosciuszko, would be hailed as a martyr to the cause of national independence.

SAINT DOMINGUE. Even more terrifying to all Europeans—including many Jacobins—was the grand-scale revolt that broke out on the French colony of Saint Domingue (later known as Haiti), on the Caribbean island of Hispaniola. This was a different sort of revolution, one that challenged a regime based on racial as well as social privilege. It began with the agitation of the island's free blacks, who fought for, and in mid-1791 finally won, the right to citizenship from the Constituent Assembly. Perhaps the French government in Paris was ready for racial equality, but the white plantation owners in Saint Domingue were not. They refused to implement the new policy. In response, free blacks sought backing from the slaves, who rose en masse. Some 100,000 had joined the rebellion by August 1791. Brutal fighting and bloody reprisals spread across the island, and the

Revolution in Saint Domingue The fighting on Saint Domingue involved battling the tropical elements, including mosquito-born yellow fever. This image shows Toussaint L'Ouverture (*center*) fending off a French charge; L'Ouverture proved very savvy in using the island's geography—and the susceptibility of the foreigners to disease—to his own advantage.

Spanish marched in, hoping to seize the chaotic territory for themselves. The British, trying to make trouble for the French, also sent troops.

In an effort to placate the rebels, the Convention in 1794 freed the slaves; this action convinced Toussaint L'Ouverture (1743–1803), a former slave who had emerged as a leader of the rebellion, to side with the French Republic. Eventually, L'Ouverture pushed back the Spanish and defeated the British, but he insisted on autonomy from France and made himself governor for life. In 1801, Napoleon, who was now first consul of France, demanded the return of the lucrative colony. He sent French troops to the island, most of whom perished of yellow fever, but L'Ouverture was captured and died in a French prison. The struggle continued until Napoleon finally tired of it in 1803, and on January 1, 1804, Saint Domingue became the independent Republic of Haiti and the only state in the Americas run by people of African heritage.

The long struggle had cost as many as 100,000 lives. The success of this revolution terrified not only European monarchs, who did not want their sources of cheap sugar, rum, and coffee cut off, but also American and Brazilian planters, who had much reason to fear that their slaves, too, might want the freedoms promised to all men by the French Revolution.

Revolutionary Culture

How can we explain this outburst of revolutionary sentiment and revolutionary violence in France and beyond? To do so, we need to understand that the revolutionaries increasingly believed that it was their mission and their right to remake society from the ground up. Especially from 1792 forward, the word *virtue* was on everyone's lips, especially those in the circle of Robespierre and Marat, men who preached both democratic idealism and terror to achieve their ends. Implementing revolutionary virtue meant much more than just abolishing privileges or granting all individuals equal rights and freedoms; it meant that everyone was required to pledge themselves wholeheartedly to the Revolution, and to rooting out monarchical corruption of all sorts. Old habits and loyalties had to be broken, and new ones put in their place.

Almost as soon as the Bastille fell, revolutionary patriots began to look for ways to celebrate the new and replace the old. Some of these were not altogether new, like the liberty trees that were planted to celebrate the rebirth of the French nation. In some parts of France, the planting of trees had long been a traditional means of celebrating deliverance from famine or plague. The tricolor cockade, which Louis XVI donned in 1789, was patriotic but not necessarily revolutionary. A much more radical gesture was the wearing of the Phrygian cap, a sort of baggy stocking cap copied from statues of freed Roman slaves. By 1792, the wearing of the cap was associated with the sans-culottes and radical revolution. The sans-culottes also insisted on addressing one another in the familiar form *tu* rather than *vous* to affirm their commit-

Sans-Culotte Wearing the Phrygian Cap The sans-culottes (men without short pants) frequently signaled their dedication to the radical revolution by wearing the Phrygian cap, copied from statues of freed Roman slaves. They were also often pictured with weapons, suggesting their willingness to fight for their principles.

ment to fraternity. According to the Convention, noble titles were abolished, and all people were to call one another "citizen."

Perhaps the most far-reaching attempt at cultural overhaul was the Convention's attempt to change the calendar. The body declared September 22, 1792, the day the monarchy was abolished, as day 1 of year 1; all the rest was prehistory. The idea was not only to mark the beginning of the republic, but also to do away with a division of time based on the birth of Christ and the church calendar. The new calendar was based instead on reason and nature. Each of the twelve months was divided into three weeks of ten days, the last of which was a rest day. The five leftover days were designated revolutionary festival days. Sundays were eliminated, and months were renamed for the seasons to which they corresponded. Thus, the period corresponding roughly to the old November was renamed Brumaire, the month of fog; and Thermidor, the hot month, replaced the old July. In 1799, the French also sought to rationalize weights and measures by introducing the metric system, in which distances and weights are denominated in units of ten. Although the revolutionary calendar would fall out of use during the Napoleonic period, the metric system survived and is now used by all of

BRUMAIRE
25 Octobre. *Le Soleil entre au Signe du Scorpion.*

Avant la fin du Jour, la prudente Bergère
De crainte que la Brume égarre son troupeau,
De presse de rentrer, portant le foible agneau
& le bois ramassé pour une bonne Mère

A Paris chez l'Editeur rue de Sorbonne N.º 384   *Déposé à la Bibliothèque Nationale*

Image from a Revolutionary Calendar This image celebrating the month of Brumaire (roughly, the month of fog, corresponding to our mid-October to mid-November) demonstrates the Convention's attempt to associate time with nature's seasons, rather than with events in the Christian calendar. Other months included Thermidor (the hot month, roughly mid-July to mid-August), and Fructidor (the month of fruit), which followed directly after Thermidor.

Europe's countries and former colonies, with the exception of the United States.

A more aggressive but less popular change was the Convention's attempt to replace Christianity with a new secular and rational form of religion. During the Terror and for many years afterward, priests, even those who had sworn the oath of loyalty to the state, were forbidden to say mass or to wear clerical dress. Clerics who remained in France were ordered to renounce their vows and to marry. Churches were closed, and vandalizing them was encouraged. Those who hid chalices or vestments to protect them from looters could be condemned by the tribunals. Robespierre thought, however, the people needed some sort of religion to replace the old one. He thus created the Cult of the Supreme Being, a kind of deist creator God who had no son and authorized no scriptures. In the spring of 1794, Robespierre staged a great festival to inaugurate the cult, but most people recognized the celebration for the farce that it was, and ru-

mors flew that Robespierre hoped to make himself the Revolution's god.

The Revolution unleashed visionary projects of all sorts, from political theory to painting. The great neoclassical artist Jacques Louis David painted a series of revolutionary martyrs, the most renowned of which is his fabulous painting of Marat (see p. 524). David himself was a Jacobin close to Robespierre, voted for the execution of the king, and endorsed the murder of numerous other suspects. He would go on, however, to paint for Napoleon as well, creating the most memorable canvases depicting Napoleon's rewarding of his troops (see p. 549) and his coronation as emperor in 1804. Other visionaries included the political theorist the Marquis de Condorcet, a Girondin member of the Convention who was forced into hiding during the Terror. While in hiding he wrote his most famous work, *Sketch for a Historical Picture of the Progress of the Human Spirit* (1795), in which he expressed his firm belief in the inevitability of humankind's progression toward utopian conditions of equality and happiness. In fact, Condorcet did not live to see his masterpiece published, as he died in prison, in March 1794.

Some radical plans for remaking society had only moderate or temporary effects. A Society of Friends of the Blacks, formed in 1788, pressed for the abolition of slavery in the French colonies. Although the society had some influence in revolutionary circles, the Convention abolished slavery in 1794 only in an attempt to contain the Haitian rebellion. Moreover, slavery in French colonies was reinstated under the Consulate and not ended until 1848. Even less successful were attempts to establish equality for women. Women participated actively in both revolutionary and counterrevolutionary movements, and many were guillotined or shot for their political views. In 1791, fired up by the revolutionary principles of liberty, equality, and fraternity, the Girondin actress and activist Olympe de Gouges composed the Declaration of Rights of Woman and the Female Citizen, which claimed that women, too, should be considered citizens and have the opportunity to take on any job or office for which they were qualified. De Gouges also proclaimed women's rights to sue for divorce and child support, but this proposal was rejected out of hand by both Jacobin and Girondin leaders who had no intention of extending citizenship to women. Disillusioned with the Revolution, De Gouges volunteered to defend Louis XVI at his trial and was guillotined with other members of the Girondin elite in November 1793. Revolutionary governments did give women the right to divorce, but Napoleon rescinded this right.

But if the Revolution produced visionaries, it also galvanized the ideas of conservative opponents of radical change. In response to the events of 1789–1790, the English statesman Edmund Burke wrote *Reflections on the Revolution in France* (1790), an eloquent prediction that imposing abstract ideas such as equality would lead to violence. Burke's treatise was translated widely and read throughout the world, subsequently becoming one of the founding works of conservative thought.

The Thermidorian Reaction

Obsessed with purifying France and urged on to more violence by Paris mobs, Robespierre had repeatedly purged the Convention and overseen the execution of thousands of enemies of the people. On June 10, 1794 (22 Prairial), he urged the passage of more legislation that shortened tribunal trials and made death the only penalty. The new laws brought more victims to the guillotine—some 1,515 in Paris in June and July alone. The intensification of the violence made some Convention delegates fear for their own safety. Robespierre, they felt, was becoming the very sort of tyrant the Constitution of 1793 said should be destroyed by free men. Thus, on 9 Thermidor, Robespierre himself was condemned to death and dispatched to the guillotine. Eighty more defenders of the Terror followed in the next twenty-four hours, but after this **Thermidorian reaction,** revolutionary violence slowed. In the next month, only six Parisians were executed; the Law of 22 Prairial was repealed, and many of those arrested under the Law of Suspects were freed from prison. The Committee of Public Safety gave up its domestic powers, though it continued to oversee the war effort and diplomacy. Had the Revolution finally ended?

The Directory

After Thermidor, revolutionary violence did abate. Hoping to establish stability at home in order to win its wars abroad, the Convention implemented a new constitution. This document created a two-chamber legislature, a lower Council of Five Hundred and an upper Council of Elders. Members of both chambers were to be elected, but only taxpayers were able to vote. The Convention also passed the Law of Two-Thirds, specifying that the new councils had to retain two-thirds of the members of the Convention. Because the framers of the new constitution believed that the Terror had been produced, in part, by young, single men, the 250 members of the Council of Elders had to be over age forty and married or widowed. Executive power was vested in the **Directory,** consisting of five directors, nominated by the lower house and approved by the upper house. One of the most prominent directors was Emmanuel-Joseph Sieyès, the author of "What Is the Third Estate?" who had managed to survive the Terror. France was still a republic, but it was no longer a fully democratic one. Nor could anyone be sure that this republic would survive.

Similarly, no one was sure that the republic would win its wars. After 1793, when a young Corsican commander named Napoleon Bonaparte seized the port of Toulon near Marseilles from English and Spanish control, the wars went reasonably well and allowed the French both to procure needed supplies and to repair and enhance patriotic sentiment. In 1795, France made peace with Prussia and Spain, though Britain rejected the terms. The British government under Prime Minister William Pitt mounted an ill-planned campaign to invade northwestern France

and join ranks with the counterrevolutionary forces operating there, but the landing at Quiberon Bay proved to be a fiasco, and the French won the day. Wisely appointing Napoleon to lead an invasion of northern Italy against the Austrians, the Directory benefited from his stunning successes in 1796–1797, which compelled the Austrians to end the War of the First Coalition and sign the Treaty of Campo Formio in October 1797. According to this treaty, France took possession of the Austrian Netherlands and northeastern Italy. The once-great Venetian Empire collapsed, and Austria took possession of Venetia and Dalmatia. Only one year later, however, after Napoleon's departure for Egypt, France's enemies regrouped and commenced the War of the Second Coalition (1798–1802).

By 1799, the Directory, still dominated by republicans, was facing new threats at home. While Jacobins agitated for a return to the Constitution of 1793, counterrevolutionaries sought to punish their persecutors or reinstall monarchy in France. Harvests continued to be poor, and the value of the assignat plunged to 8 percent of its original worth, then fell again. In 1799, as new elections threatened to sweep Jacobins into office, Sieyès and other republicans began to fear a return to revolutionary radicalism. Few expected that the man to deal the death blow to the fragile government would be its own military hero: Napoleon.

The Rise of Napoleon

The Directory saw its role as protecting the Revolution's gains by retreating from extremism—but this was by no means easy in a nation divided from within and at war with its neighbors. It took a military leader, Napoleon Bonaparte, to pacify and unite France, something he accomplished through force, negotiations with the church, and the fighting of more wars. A minor nobleman who owed his career to chance and to the opportunities the Revolution opened for talented men to rise, Napoleon put an end to revolutionary democracy but exemplified and championed some of the principles of 1789.

> How did Napoleon Bonaparte take advantage of the new opportunities provided by the Revolution?

Napoleon's Early Life and Military Career

Technically speaking, Napoleone di Buonaparte (1769–1821) was born a Frenchman, but only barely. His birthplace, the island of Corsica, belonged to the medieval sea empire of the city of Genoa until 1755, when it declared itself an independent republic. This declaration of independence did not stop the Genoese from selling the island to France in 1768. The sale enraged Napoleone's father, Carlo Buonaparte, a relatively poor aristocrat with a little land, a law practice, and eight children. The young Napoleone, the second of the four sons, grew up sharing his father's anti-French prejudices and speaking not

When Did the French Revolution End?

Brief accounts of the French Revolution often stop the story at Thermidor, leaving the impression that at this point, everyone knew the Revolution was over and Napoleon's rise was inevitable. In his book *Ending the French Revolution: Violence, Justice, and Repression from the Terror to Napoleon,* historian Howard G. Brown suggests that stopping the story at Thermidor overlooks the tumultuous course of events that occurred just after July 1794. Brown argues that revolutions end only when the new regime is structurally secure, and that was certainly not the case in France until 1801–1802, the year that Bonaparte silenced parliamentary opposition, created relative religious peace by signing the Concordat with the pope, and mustered enough power to stamp out popular resistance. If analyzing the interplay of ideas and material conditions offers a way to understand the outbreak of revolution, Brown shows that understanding how a revolution ends requires considering the relationships among the state, the justice system, and the army.

Brown begins by describing the Directory's difficulties in stopping outbursts of violence, from both the royalist right and the Jacobin left. The amnesty issued by the Directory in 1795, pardoning "acts purely related to the Revolution," did not clarify the difference, Brown says, between "what had been politically necessary and what had been criminally gratuitous."[9] Extremists went unpunished, and émigrés and priests returned in droves, many of them eager to repossess their properties and their churches. The gains of the moderate revolution, not to mention the anticlericalism and the democracy of the radical revolution, continued to be contested. Moreover, the civilian police were overstretched, and the army, poorly provisioned and needed outside as well as inside France, was unable to pacify parts of western and southern France, where brigands robbed and murdered travelers on the highways, and armed bands accosted peasants and townspeople. The bandits included the "chauffeurs," who placed their victims' feet over fires until they revealed the location of their valuables. The Directory meted out hundreds of death sentences, especially after a royalist coup attempt in September 1797, but had to rely more and more on military tribunals and military intervention to keep the nation from collapsing into civil war.

When Napoleon overthrew the Directory in late 1799, he did so to save a republic already at war from a possible return to revolution. Napoleon made himself first consul and won the War of the Second Coalition. But military victory alone could not solve the problem of brigandage in the west. Guerrilla bands, composed of royalists, draft dodgers, and highwaymen, continued to attack property owners and travelers; they did not hesitate to murder policemen and rob tax collectors. In 1800, Napoleon sent in more soldiers to aid the overstretched police. He authorized the immediate execution of armed opponents of the regime and even the burning of some villages to warn civilians against aiding the rebels. Symbolic executions of counterrevolutionaries, robbers, and their accomplices in city squares, usually staged by military firing squads, demonstrated that the regime meant business. Combined with the Concordat, which took away the leading cause of antirevolutionary sentiment by allowing Catholics to practice their faith freely once more, Napoleon's militarized repression of his remaining opponents in western France finally snuffed out the counterrevolution.

But if the counterrevolution died in 1802, what about the Revolution itself? Many revolutionary accomplishments were reversed in that year. The Concordat reestablished Catholicism as France's state religion (albeit without restoring the church's property), and Napoleon purged the legislative body of any remaining opponents and made himself consul for life. In effect, France now had both a church and a king again. Political battles between monarchists and Jacobins continued throughout the nineteenth century, the former losing their momentum only when the last direct Bourbon heir died in 1883. If French conservatives never ceased to cite the Terror as a warning against anarchy, French leftists never ceased to champion the Constitutions of 1791 and 1793 and to accuse their opponents of wishing to return to the feudal world of the Old Regime. The Revolution might be said to have ended in 1802, but its memory lived long afterward.

QUESTIONS | *How do we determine when a revolution ends? Does it end when change stops spreading to new groups, or when a stable state establishes a monopoly on violence? Explain.*

French but his parents' Corsican language. He would continue to speak French with a strong Corsican accent throughout this life.

The family took advantage of the Old Regime's perks, which included scholarships for the sons of impoverished nobles to attend military training schools. At age

nine, Napoleon was sent to school on the French mainland, where he learned French and bested his classmates in mathematics, history, and geography. In 1784, he went on to the École Militaire in Paris, where he felt very much the poor outsider among sons of far wealthier noble families. The young Buonaparte worked hard at military

Napoleon at Marengo In his Italian campaigns, Napoleon made himself hugely popular with his men by providing courageous leadership, and by encouraging them to live off the land. He won the loyalty of young men of talent—like himself—by promoting them swiftly, regardless of their social and economic backgrounds.

school and finished his training in a single year rather than the usual three. Upon his graduation at age sixteen, he took up a commission in an artillery regiment in southern France and then spent an additional, important year perfecting his skills in a special school for artillery officers. Had there been no French Revolution in his lifetime, he would have remained a minor officer in Louis XVI's army—he would not have been, as Sieyès said of the third estate, "nothing." However, he would not have been Napoleon I, emperor of the French, either.

But things turned out differently for Napoleon. After the outbreak of Revolution in the summer of 1789, his beloved Corsicans were made full citizens of France, and eventually his whole family settled in France and simplified their name to Bonaparte. Napoleon took his place in the revolutionary army, and began to apply his expertise in the deployment of firepower. Thanks to his strategic brilliance, the French won the port of Toulon in 1793, and Napoleon was appointed artillery commander of the French army in northern Italy. Here, the young commander's daring assaults on the Austrians and his concern for his men made him hugely popular—and ultimately victorious. A string of victories compelled the Austrians to sign the Treaty of Campo Formio in the fall of 1797, ending the first, glorious chapter of Napoleon's revolutionary career.

The Directory, however, remained at war with the British. Eager for more military glory, Napoleon planned, then reluctantly abandoned, a seaborne invasion of England—the French navy was simply too weak for the job. In secret, he concocted another means by which he hoped to bring Great Britain to its knees.

Napoleon in Egypt

In the spring of 1798, Napoleon left France with 52,000 soldiers and sailors—and a team of 151 scholars, all of them admirers of the young general. Once they had embarked, he told them where they were going: Egypt. Napoleon hoped that by conquering Egypt he would not only complete France's mastery of the Mediterranean, but also bring Britain to the bargaining table by threatening to invade India. While Napoleon's soldiers assaulted Egypt, an Ottoman vassal state ruled by a separate dynasty of warriors known as Mamluks, the scholars were to collect data and objects relating to both modern and ancient Egypt.

Arriving in Alexandria on July 1, the French were shocked to find a poor fishing village on the site of the renowned ancient city. Blaming Egypt's decline on the Ottomans, they marched on, but had difficulty living off the land, as local peasants withheld food and spoiled the wells. Within three weeks, Napoleon had defeated a poorly armed Mamluk force at the Battle of the Pyramids and entered Cairo, where once again the French expected to be greeted as liberators. As in other occupied cities and regions, however, the French soon wore out their welcome.

While Napoleon dealt with the resistance of Cairenes, a British fleet commanded by Admiral Horatio Nelson snuck up from behind and destroyed most of Napoleon's ships anchored at Aboukir Bay (Map 17.2). Despite having no naval support, Napoleon pressed on into Syria. French forces made slow progress, suffering from an outbreak of plague at Jaffa and mauled by fierce Syrian and Ottoman resistance. At Jaffa, unwilling to leave behind sufficient troops to serve as prison guards, Napoleon had some 2,500 captives executed by forcing them into the sea, where those who did not drown were shot by firing squads, a violation of conventional European codes of military conduct. Hearing that the French armies were collapsing in Italy and Germany, Napoleon secretly set sail for France in August 1799, taking with him the scholars and their treasures, but not his troops. Having won one last battle before his departure, he returned to Paris claiming victory, though both he and the soldiers he left behind knew the French were dangerously overstretched. In 1801, a British expeditionary force trounced the last French troops, and France's Egyptian adventure was at an end.

The scholars who Napoleon took to Egypt collected enormous amounts of information and artifacts and made hundreds of detailed drawings. Their most important prize, found near the town of Rosetta, was a stone inscribed with the same text in three languages, eventually enabling European scholars, for the first time since antiquity, to read hieroglyphics. In peace negotiations, the British claimed the Rosetta Stone but allowed the other artifacts to go to the Louvre, now no longer a royal palace but a public museum.

The Egyptian expedition proved to be a cultural triumph, and despite military disaster, Napoleon managed to present his efforts as heroic. Abandoning his troops may have been less than noble, but by doing so, he was able to return to Paris just at the right time and, with the right credentials, to launch his political career.

The 18th Brumaire

In 1796–1797, Napoleon's victories in Italy had helped to save the republic. In 1799, he knocked the last nail into its coffin. After less than a year of peace, the Directory had returned to war with the Austrians, and in Italy its sister republics were facing collapse. Sieyès, now one of the directors, went looking for a strong man to stage a coup against his own government—and found Napoleon. Napoleon agreed to Sieyè's plan and convinced his troops that the councils were full of conspirators trying to destroy France's power. On 18 Brumaire, in the year 8, or November 9, 1799, Napoleon's forces surrounded the council chambers and forced the councils to disband. Sieyès had planned to head up a three-man consulate and gradually ease Napoleon out of the picture, but from the first, Napoleon took charge. He quickly made himself first consul and then the only consul. In 1802, he nominated himself consul for life. In a plebiscite (popular vote) on this nomination, French voters overwhelmingly approved. The seizure of power that began on 18 Brumaire was completed in 1804, when Napoleon dissolved the consulate and crowned himself emperor of the French.

The Napoleonic Empire

Napoleon rose to power by anything but democratic means, yet he subsequently became wildly popular in France. His popularity was due in part to his military victories,

MAP 17.2 | Napoleon's Campaign in Egypt, 1798–1799

This map shows the progress of Napoleon's campaign in Egypt, beginning with his landing near Alexandria in early July 1798. *Why do you suppose Napoleon lost this territory, after his initial successes and the capture of the Egyptian capital, Cairo?*

What was the nature of Napoleon's rule after 1804?

a second string of which began in 1801. Napoleon made France a formidable empire, one that at its greatest reached from the Atlantic in the west to the borders of the Russian Empire in the east. If the Revolution had ignited popular patriotism, Napoleon created French nationalism. Just as important were Napoleon's domestic reforms, which sought to preserve some of the gains of the moderate revolution without opening the door to the polarization of the radical revolution. Most of all, Napoleon could not have accomplished any of these things without first establishing internal stability.

In Search of Stability

One of Napoleon's least famous measures was nonetheless crucial. In 1800, soon after becoming consul, he set up a national bank for France and managed to stabilize the new franc, which replaced the now-hated assignat. The twenty-franc coin was actually called a Napoleon. The consul

Napoleon in Cairo

How were the revolutionary wars experienced from the side of those fighting against the French? To answer this question, historian Juan Cole examined the reactions of the Cairenes, the inhabitants of Cairo, a city with a population of more than a million, in the book *Napoleon's Egypt.* In the wake of their victory over the Mamluks at the Battle of the Pyramids, Napoleon's troops entered the city on July 24, 1798, planning to turn Cairo into the capital of a new Egyptian republic.

On his arrival in Egypt, Napoleon issued a proclamation to the citizens, claiming that the French, like the Egyptians, were Muslims (in the sense that both parties believed in one God) and meant their religion no harm, but had come to liberate them from Mamluk corruption and tyranny. The proclamation instructed Egyptians to show their support for the French "liberators" by wearing the tricolor cockade and flying the tricolor flag. French printing presses produced thousands of copies of this proclamation, translated awkwardly into Arabic by one of Napoleon's scholars.

Egypt had not prospered under Mamluk rule, so some Cairenes might have believed the French propaganda or even welcomed a change of regime. Most, however, found the French claims and commands outrageous or silly. The Cairene historian Abd al-Rahman al-Jabarti noted that the French had recently killed priests as well as their king and displayed manners—such as allowing their women to wear revealing clothing—very much contrary to Muslim practices. Other Egyptians found it hard to respect clean-shaved

French infantrymen, for in this culture, only slaves and underage boys lacked beards. They resented having their valuables seized, their food requisitioned, and their women tampered with by lonely or violent soldiers. Enraged at French pretenses, the Ottoman sultan declared *jihad,* or mandatory religious war, against the Napoleonic invaders.

In early August, Napoleon sent part of his army to chase the Mamluk army in its retreat toward Syria, leaving some 20,000 Frenchmen in Cairo to pacify and reform the capital city. French military engineers demolished gates within Cairo to allow for the passage of traffic and troops. To the Cairenes, removal of the gates meant that their neighborhoods were now accessible to more strangers and thieves. French officials also imposed heavy new taxes. Because the Ottoman Empire imposed certain kinds of taxes only on subordinate populations such as Jews and Christian Armenians, Egyptians interpreted these taxes as a form of intentional humiliation. Merchants in particular objected and appealed to the clerics, especially those connected with al-Azhar, a prestigious mosque and school.

On October 21, 1798, the city exploded. Clerics at al-Azhar called on the population to "remove this dishonor and take our revenge on [the French infidels]."[10] Cairene rebels armed themselves with clubs and hammers and built barricades to blockade French troops; the French responded with cannons and rifles. Crowds beheaded engineers who had torn down their gates and paraded their heads around the city. French merchants and local women who had sold their favors to soldiers were also attacked. When Napoleon, on maneuvers outside the city, heard the news, he ordered troops to surround the area around al-Azhar and to commence shelling. When French troops entered, according to al-Jabarti, they intentionally destroyed copies of the Qur'an and desecrated the mosque, urinating and spitting in it.

When the riot was finally put down after two days of violence, insurgents were rounded up and executed. Estimates for Cairene deaths run to approximately 3,300; the French death toll was much lower, probably between 250 and 800—though Napoleon boasted later that he had lost only twenty-one men. The city was pacified, but anti-French sentiments intensified. After Napoleon's departure, an Egyptian assassinated the leader of the French forces in Cairo, and the French troops that managed to survive disease, difficulty, and more warfare were lucky that after their surrender to British and Ottoman forces in 1801, Britain organized their safe passage back to France. In a very short time, the liberators had become the enemy.

The French Suppress the Riots in Cairo This highly dramatic representation of the French crackdown in Cairo draws on European stereotypes of the Middle East (see the richly adorned, turbaned man on the right) and features, absurdly, a nude Caireine rebel in the foreground. But it does accurately depict the mixed ethnicities of those who stood against the French invaders, and the ferocity of the hand-to-hand combat in the city's streets.

QUESTION | *Why did the Cairenes come to despise the French, who claimed they had come to Egypt as liberators?*

sent out highly efficient tax collectors and by 1802 had repaid the national debt. When in 1803 Napoleon wanted more money to build up his army, he sold France's huge Louisiana territory to the United States for $15 million, or about 3 cents per acre. He calculated that Louisiana was too far from France to exploit without a powerful navy. Thus did Napoleon ensure France's financial stability, without which he could not have stayed in power so long, nor waged so many long-lasting wars, but at the cost of giving up France's largest overseas colony.

Having stabilized France's economy, Napoleon was also eager to stabilize the political system. He used his army to ruthlessly put down political enemies and criminal bands in the west, where there was still considerable brigandage. He also purged what remained of the councils, now called the legislative body, and censored his critics; some, like Madame de Staël, he sent into exile. Royalists made some attempts to assassinate him, and his defenders could argue that he made himself emperor to head off attempts to restore the Bourbons to the throne. But he enraged Europe's monarchs by ordering the murder of a Bourbon prince vacationing at a German spa, provoking them to join together to battle France once more in the War of the Third Coalition (1803–1806).

Largely a self-made man, Napoleon refused to restore the Old Regimes' social hierarchies. Legally, all Frenchmen were now equal. He urged émigrés to return to France, and many did so, but they did not get their titles or privileges back. Peasants who had purchased or seized land belonging to the nobility or church were allowed to keep it. Napoleon did not really trust the émigrés, but neither did he trust former Jacobins and sans-culottes. Those he favored were chiefly military officers who had served with him in Italy and Egypt, and members of his family. In staffing his empire, he put his brothers and sisters on Europe's thrones, much to the discontent of the local populations.

His social policy was something of a compromise between revolutionary meritocracy and Old Regime favoritism. Those who profited most were members of the military and wealthier members of the third estate. The ideals of liberty and equality were compromised, and fraternity was taken to mean that all should devote themselves to serving Napoleon's France.

THE CONCORDAT. Perhaps Napoleon's most successful act of stabilization occurred in the sphere of religion. In 1801 Napoleon opened negotiations with Pope Pius VII in the hopes of pacifying resistance to his regime both in France itself and in occupied areas such as the deeply Catholic Austrian Netherlands and Rhineland regions. In 1802 the pope agreed to sign a **Concordat,** an agreement that made Catholicism once again the official religion of the French. The Concordat allowed bishops—even refractory ones—to reclaim their places in the church hierarchy. But Protestants and Jews were also permitted to worship freely, and bishops could be seated only if they renounced their claims on nationalized church property. The clergy were obliged to pledge obedience to the state. By Easter 1802, the ringing of church bells was legal once more, and Napoleon attended a mass at Notre Dame Cathedral in Paris. The Concordat, more than any other act, dissipated counterrevolutionary opposition to Napoleon's regime—though it also enraged refractories, who saw it as betrayal of their years of resistance, as well as former radicals, who saw it as selling out of the great accomplishments of the Revolution.

If the Concordat was something of a victory for the pope, Napoleon's later regime tended more toward humiliation. Napoleon compelled Pope Pius VII to attend his coronation as emperor in 1804, but insisted on crowning himself and his queen rather than, as in previous royal coronations, allowing the pope to do the honors. After the coronation, relations between the pope and the emperor deteriorated. In 1808, French armies overran Rome, and Pius VII was taken captive. He would not be released until 1814.

NAPOLEON, ENLIGHTENED DESPOT? In many respects, Napoleon was a product of the Enlightenment. He was an advocate of rationalization, statistics-keeping, map-making, and administration. In some ways, these preferences constituted a continuity with the absolutist past, but they also reflected the Revolution's mania for uniformity and universalization. Also in the absolutist tradition was Napoleon's enthusiasm for increasing the nation's glory by feats of artistic grandeur or scientific discovery. He planned to overhaul Paris, to make it an even more impressive imperial city, but managed only to install the Arc de Triomphe and to add treasures, pilfered from occupied territories, to the museum in the Louvre. Many of his projects remained unfinished, but he did complete one grand feat of universalization: the creation of the **Napoleonic Code.**

In drafting a new, national civil law for France, Napoleon was inspired by the ancient Romans. He wanted to do away with that vast mass of legal privileges that bound the French during the Old Regime and substitute a single law to apply to all his citizens, one that would be valid throughout France and its colonies. The Napoleonic Code was to be a means to prevent the return of feudal justice and to integrate the empire. Napoleon claimed that the civil code was his greatest achievement, more important than any of his battles, a claim that proved to be true. It laid the foundations for a new society, based on property, not on inherited privilege, and was imitated across Europe in the decades to come.

The Napoleonic Code accomplished a number of important goals. It established the equality of all men before the law and outlawed both arbitrary, revolutionary justice and old-fashioned seigneurial justice. It standardized contractual relations and protected property. It did, however, rescind some of the rights given to women in the Constitutions of 1791 and 1793; it was now almost impossible for women to obtain a divorce. Women also lost some of their rights to independent ownership of property. Legally, they were treated like children and subjected to paternal authority.

Was Napoleon an enlightened despot? The term seems to fit. Within France, there were no checks on his power, especially after 1804. Yet he was not satisfied with the Old Regime's status quo; he wanted to reform, centralize, and modernize France. If he acted as an enlightened despot at home, abroad he was that and something more: a conqueror.

The Grande Armée

Napoleon is rightly remembered as a military genius, a man with numerous tactical tricks up his sleeve and the courage to try them. However, it took much more than one man's genius for France to conquer all of Europe. First, it took luck. Despite fighting in more than seventy battles, some on the front lines, Napoleon was wounded only twice. He also survived imprisonment after Thermidor and numerous assassination attempts. Second, Napoleon had the good fortune to surround himself with extraordinary talented colleagues and subordinates. Credit for this goes partly to him, since he gave them their commands, but also to the unprecedented opportunities offered by the Revolution. Finally, success in these wars owed much to the lessons revolutionary France learned from the American Revolution, which included the deployment of an army of citizens, united in what was thought to be the cause of liberty and the defense of their nation.

Louis XVI's army remained largely under the command of nobles, some of whom were proficient officers, but many were not. After 1789, and especially after the beheading of the king, thousands of noble officers had emigrated, resigned, or been thrown in prison; the Convention considered many others unreliable. Thus, there was considerable opportunity, suddenly, for talented men in the ranks to rise. In 1793, Napoleon himself rose from captain to brigadier general in a mere eight weeks.

The *levée en masse* called by the Convention in August 1793 swept into the army many revolutionary patriots who were proud to fight for the Revolution, as well as for France, and the revolutionary armies were increasingly led by young men of extraordinary talent, of whom Napoleon was one. The army became a bastion of patriotism and commitment to at least moderate revolutionary goals—many soldiers were keen to spread revolutionary liberty, equality, and fraternity to other parts of Europe. As the revolutionary and then Napoleonic armies traveled eastward, they were joined by thousands of volunteers from other European nations, as well as by troops conscripted from occupied areas, ultimately creating a multinational (but not mercenary) fighting force.

Napoleon Distributing the Eagle Standards Three days after being crowned emperor, Napoleon staged a Roman-style ceremony in which he distributed standards topped with an eagle to each of France's regional regiments. Jacques-Louis David's painting commemorating the event shows Napoleon offering a Roman salute to his men, and charging them to defend the eagles with their lives.

The Legion of Honor and the Iron Cross

From age nine, Napoleon inhabited a military world and excelled in it. Throughout his life, he felt most comfortable among soldiers. He had risen in the ranks swiftly, thanks in part to revolutionary opportunities, but also due to his own hard work, daring, and genius. He always allowed, and sometimes encouraged, his men to take booty and provisions from occupied areas, and in 1802, he found a new way to reward his men and build patriotism in the ranks: he created a new kind of club, one to which he appointed only those who had performed extraordinary service to the nation.

Under the Old Regime, military decorations and special orders had been reserved for the Catholic aristocracy. Napoleon's nominees for the "Legion of Honor," by contrast, received their reward regardless of their social standing, religion, or political opinions. Some who received it were Polish or Italian recruits. The five ranks within the order ranged from knight at the lowest level to grand eagle at the top; the award came with a stipend and a decoration. Perhaps even more remarkable than the creation of an order based on merit alone was the provision that allowed the Legion of Honor to be awarded to civilian patriots as well as to soldiers—though in practice, the bulk of the decorations went to the latter. Between 1802 and 1814, Napoleon awarded some 38,000 memberships to the Legion of Honor. Only four thousand went to civilians. He himself always wore "the grand eagle" and had the artist David paint the occasion on which he distributed the first eagles to other soldier-heroes.

Prussia had possessed a similar order, known as the *Pour le Mérite,* since 1740, when Frederick the Great reconfigured an older award in order to thank those who had helped him seize Silesia. The decoration for the *Pour le Mérite* is a blue cross with gold eagles positioned between the arms of the cross; it is popularly known as the Blue Max. Gold oak leaves were added in 1813 to signify loyalty to the fatherland, and many new memberships were awarded to

Wynton Marsalis, Member of the Legion of Honor The military decoration that Napoleon created to recognize men who had performed extraordinary services to the French nation was also awarded to non-Frenchmen, and to meritorious civilians. Among those holding this special rank is the great American musician Wynton Marsalis.

those who redeemed Prussia's military reputation after its humiliating losses in 1806. When the Prussians, along with the Russians and Austrians, began chasing Napoleon's Grande Armée back to France in 1813, Prussian King Frederick Wilhelm III announced the issuing of the Iron Cross, the first Prussian military decoration to be awarded to men of all ranks. It was a "time of iron" for Prussia, the king proclaimed, and all soldiers who displayed extraordinary courage should be honored with the simple, Teutonic-style medal. In 1814, a Queen Louise Medal appeared to honor women who had thrown their energy behind Prussia's war effort. All women, including Jews and non-noble women, were eligible. The Blue Max and the Order of Louise would continue to be awarded to special individuals. The Iron Cross became the symbol of valor and patriotism for the Prussians and validated the German army's "romance of itself" during the First and Second World Wars. After 1945, it became the emblem of the West German army.

Napoleon found other ways of honoring his most distinguished comrades, such as promoting them to the Imperial Guard, or awarding them the rank of marshal of France. He bestowed this new rank on men who had demonstrated their brilliance in battle, regardless of their social standing or their political inclinations. Of the twenty-six marshals that Napoleon appointed, the majority came from humble roots. The awarding of these distinctions and rewards helped Napoleon secure the loyalty of his troops, who retained their powerful commitments to France, to the Grande Armée, and to Napoleon himself, throughout long years of almost constant fighting. But the power and appeal of an award attainable, in theory, by any individual, also made the Legion of Honor—and its Prussian equivalents—enduring symbols of patriotism.

QUESTION | *Why was rewarding men for merit so important to Napoleon?*

By the mid-1790s, the revolutionary army was a formidable one. But as Napoleon observed, it was also filled with untrained men who often went long periods without proper armaments, pay, and provisions. Napoleon motivated his men by promising them rich booty and pleased his financially strapped civilian masters in Paris by implementing a policy of "making war pay for war," extracting provisions and rewards for his men from the countryside. Once in power, he implemented a series of military reforms that transformed the revolutionary army into France's **Grande Armée.** He began a stringent program of training, and although he maintained his policy of allowing troops to live off the land and claim booty, he also increased France's production of armaments and supplies and tried to ensure that the army was well fed. He organized his troops into corps, which could essentially function as independent armies; restructured the chain of command, centralizing power in himself; and rationalized conscription, so that fewer men escaped the recruiters. He oversaw the design of new uniforms and made major investments in industry and manufacturing to increase the production of weapons and supplies. He set up a special Imperial Guard, for distinguished soldiers of any rank and any nationality, and in 1802 began awarding a new medal, the Legion of Honor, for bravery. As one historian of the period has noted, he understood that what motivated the soldiers in the long run was not patriotism, but "the army's romance of itself, expressed by symbols and legends."[11] Napoleon enhanced that romance in ways that may have outstripped even his heroes, Julius Caesar and Alexander the Great.

Napoleon's Early Campaigns, 1805–1808

Napoleon made the Grande Armée the most modern army in Europe, and motivated it to win decisive battles. He had made peace with the Austrians in 1801 and with the British in 1802, thus ending the War of the Second Coalition. But after he made himself emperor and king of Italy in 1804, the British, Austrians, and Russians formed the Third Coalition to contain French power. The coalition scored a major victory when British admiral Lord Nelson defeated the French navy at the Battle of Trafalgar in 1805, ending all chance of a French invasion of England and reasserting Britain's mastery of the seas. But the land war went the other way. Marching very fast, the Grande Armée reached the Austrian border three weeks before the Austrians expected them to reach it, and cut them off from Russian troops advancing to their aid. Once the Austrians were surrounded, the Russians retreated to the north, leaving the road to Vienna open. Napoleon took it and on November 15, 1805, Napoleon entered the Habsburgs' capital unopposed.

THE DEFEAT OF AUSTRIA AND PRUSSIA. In response, early in 1806 the Holy Roman Empire simply folded, as the Habsburgs feared that Napoleon might want to add the title of Holy Roman emperor to his list. Remarkably, few mourned the passing of the centuries-old central European Empire—another sign that the Old Regimes had lost their symbolic power as well as their practical utility. But rather than settling in to enjoy courtly life in Vienna, Napoleon then proceeded north, chasing the Austro-Russian army until it turned to fight at Austerlitz. Leaving the high ground to the Austrians

and Russians, Napoleon had a large unit of his Grande Armée march undetected up the poorly defended high ground and split the Austro-Russian army. The Battle of Austerlitz would be one of Napoleon's greatest victories. The Austrians surrendered, and the remainder of the Russian army retreated in disarray into Poland.

The Prussians had stayed neutral in 1805, but French actions, including marching through Prussian territory on the way to Austria, angered the Prussians enough to declare war in 1806. Napoleon designed an elaborate plan to destroy the Prussian army near the town of Jena, but on the morning of October 14, 1806, the main Prussian army began to withdraw northward. While the main French force destroyed the Prussian rear guard, a small French force at Auerstedt held off the old army of Frederick the Great, which, on hearing the news from Jena, retreated from the field. Both Jena and Auerstedt were decisive French victories, and Prussian units surrendered seemingly everywhere. The Grande Armée marched into Berlin through the Brandenburg Gate. On top of the gate stood a goddess of victory in a horse-drawn chariot, which Napoleon promptly had taken down and sent to Paris.

The French then pursued the Prussians eastward, rallying Polish troops to their cause by hinting that the French would restore Poland's independence from the partitioning powers (Austria, Russia, and Prussia). The remaining Prussian troops linked up with a Russian army in East Prussia, engaging the French at the Battle of Eylau. At Friedland in the summer of 1807, the Russians had their backs to a river; Russian casualties numbered 30,000 to 11,000 French. This French victory forced Czar Alexander I to the bargaining table on a specially made raft in the middle of the Niemen River on the Polish-Russian border, where the czar and Napoleon met to sign the Treaty of Tilsit on July 7, 1807.

The terms of the Treaty of Tilsit required Alexander I to join France's economic embargo on Britain, thus making Russia an ally of France against Great Britain. The Prussians were the big losers. They were saddled with heavy reparations payments and forfeited more than a third of their territory. This territory was used to make up the new Grand Duchy of Warsaw, a reward to the many Polish patriots who served in the Grande Armée. Even more humiliating, the Prussians had to reduce their army to 42,000 men—who were, moreover, to serve the French—and to provide quarter for thousands of French occupying troops. Napoleon was now master of virtually the whole of the European continent (see Map 17.3).

THE CONTINENTAL SYSTEM. Great Britain, the constant thorn in Napoleon's side, had still not been subdued. Napoleon planned to invade England, but recognized that French naval power was too weak, especially after Trafalgar. He settled instead on economic strangulation. By creating the **Continental System,** a kind of continental free trade zone from which all British imports were barred, the French emperor hoped that he

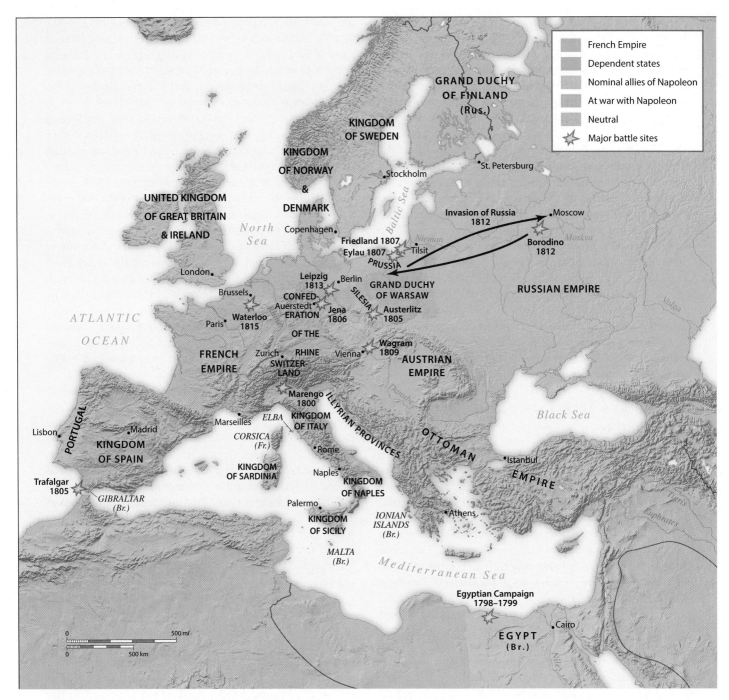

MAP 17.3 | Napoleon's Empire at Its Height, 1812

This map shows which states Napoleon had conquered, annexed, or made dependent on the French Empire at the time he launched his invasion of Russia in 1812. *Why was the continuation of Spanish resistance so great a problem for Napoleon when he invaded Russia?*

could bring Prime Minister Pitt to the bargaining table. But Napoleon's forte was offensive land battles, not economic warfare. The Continental System proved not only difficult to enforce but also unpopular with the occupied nations and with the Russians. Most problematic was Portugal, which retained its independence and an alliance with Great Britain. British goods continued to pour into its ports until Napoleon decided, in late 1807, to close this loophole by sending 25,000 soldiers across Spain to subdue the Portuguese.

THE SPANISH "ULCER." Spain had officially allied itself to France in 1796, but after the Battle of Trafalgar in 1805, Spain began to entertain the idea of switching to the British side. Eager to ensure Spanish loyalty and to impose reforms on the still largely feudal state, in 1808 Napoleon manipulated the Bourbon king of Spain to abdicate his throne and reshuffled the monarchies under his control. He gave Spain to his brother Joseph and passed Joseph's previous post as king of Naples on to his brother-in-law, the daring cavalry commander, Joachim

Murat. Joseph announced his intention to put in place liberal reforms, including disbanding the Inquisition and closing many convents and monasteries. Some Spanish liberals approved of these measures, but the population in general despised French high-handedness, and on May 2, 1808, Madrid exploded in rebellion. Murat put it down with great savagery, summarily executing hundreds of civilians on May 3.

But putting down this uprising did not diminish Spanish resistance; moreover, a Portuguese and British force, led by Sir Arthur Wellesley (later awarded the title of duke of Wellington) invaded from Portugal, harrying French forces. To fight what became known as the Peninsular War (1808–1814), the French were forced to seize food and horses, to quarter their men in Spanish villages, and to conscript Spanish soldiers. They also took a considerable amount of war booty, including many artistic masterworks from churches and monasteries. All these measures were highly unpopular and led to a guerrilla campaign against Napoleon's troops. Despite sending in more and more troops, Napoleon could not mend his Spanish "ulcer." The Austrians took note, and by mid-1809, war broke out in central Europe once again.

Goya, Execution of Spanish Rebels in 1808 This famous painting by the Spanish painter Francisco Goya immortalized those executed by the French after the May 2 uprising in Madrid.

speaking administrators and sometimes military force to impose enlightened reforms on their populations, insisting that the French way was the only rational way to modernize.

Napoleon's Fall

By 1809, many Europeans were wearying of French occupation, which had become increasingly onerous as Napoleon moved to extract more treasure and impose more reforms. Napoleon's mistrust of government by the people led him to replace republics abroad with kingdoms and to appoint his family members and closest military friends to these thrones. Ignoring the long-standing tradition of republicanism in the Netherlands, Napoleon first made his brother Louis king of Holland, and when that didn't work, he simply annexed the Netherlands to France. Brother Jerome became the king of the new state of Westphalia; his sisters, too, received kingdoms, and on his birth, Napoleon's son was named king of Rome. Many of these Bonapartist regimes used French-

What role did French hegemony play in the development of European nationalism?

CHRONOLOGY	Key Events of the Napoleonic Era
DATE	**EVENT**
1798	Napoleon's Egyptian campaign
1799	Napoleon overthrows the Directory
1800	Bank of France established
1802	Concordat with the pope comes into force
1804	First Napoleonic Code published; Napoleon crowns himself emperor (December 2)
1805	Battle of Trafalgar destroys French fleet
1806	Holy Roman Empire abolished
1812	Napoleon invades Russia (June 24)
1813	Battle of the Nations at Leipzig
1814	Napoleon abdicates and goes into exile at Elba
1815	Napoleon loses the Battle of Waterloo, ending his "Hundred Days" comeback

The French Occupations and the Origins of Modern Nationalism

Reaction to French occupation and overlordship shaped Europe's future even before the wars were over. The more the French tried to impose their civil code, their Continental system, and their supposedly superior language, the more the individual nations grew nostalgic for their local languages, customs, and governments. In Prussia and the other German states, even members of the third estate who had welcomed Napoleon as a liberator began to look upon him as a tyrant. Once again, taxation was a big issue, for the French extracted heavy taxes from the little people the Revolution was supposed to benefit. People began to think more fondly of their German, Spanish, or Dutch folksongs and traditions, and to commit themselves to forcing Napoleon and the Grande Armée off their native soil.

The imposition of French rule, then, laid the foundations for nineteenth-century nationalism. Everywhere, French occupation unintentionally spread Sieyès's idea that the people, not just the king and nobility, formed the nation. Patriotism had certainly existed before Napoleon built his empire, but now individuals committed themselves not to a specific king or native town, but to Spain, Germany, or even Italy, larger entities composed of ordinary people linked by a common history and often (though not always) speaking the same language. In Berlin, students began to dream of a new, united Germany, one that would field an army strong enough to force all French-speakers back across the Rhine. It is telling that one great historian of modern Germany opened his book with the phrase "In the beginning was Napoleon."[12]

Napoleon seems not to have understood this dynamic at all. Perhaps he thought time would heal all wounds, and he certainly believed that modernization, French-style, was medicine that all of Europe's backward monarchies needed to swallow. He brashly predicted that Spanish hatred for the French would disappear once they recognized that the laws of France were wiser, more liberal, and more suited to the present than "the old customs of the Inquisition." But the hatred did not disappear, and the wars were by no means over.

The Napoleonic Wars, 1809–1815

In the short term, Napoleon managed to stifle discontent through conquest. When the Austrians returned to the field in 1809, Napoleon massed even bigger armies to defeat them at the Battle of Wagram, near Vienna. At Wagram, on July 5–6, 1809, more than 320,000 troops faced off, the largest battle in European history to that time. Napoleon won, but at the cost of about 35,000 men. This French victory essentially ended conflict, except in Spain, for the next few years, as all the combatants turned to rebuilding their armies. The British and the Prussians, in particular, undertook large-scale reforms to modernize their forces.

In 1809 Napoleon divorced his beloved wife Josephine Beauharnais and married Marie Louise, a Habsburg princess. The point was not only to secure his standing among European royalty, but also to produce an heir, as Josephine had experienced early menopause. In 1811, Marie Louise gave birth to François Charles Joseph Bonaparte, nicknamed the eaglet. But producing an heir with Habsburg blood would not be enough to sustain the empire, especially when, in 1812, Czar Alexander I wearied of his alliance with the French.

THE INVASION OF RUSSIA. Alexander had good reason to be unhappy. Not only was the Continental system interfering with Russian trade, but the czar also vehemently opposed France's support for the Poles, traditional enemies of the Russians. Napoleon recognized that relations were fraying and began to plan for a grand invasion of Russia. By now, he had conquered so much territory that he saw himself as a modern version of Alexander the Great and on several occasions spoke of wishing to extend his conquests all the way to India. Even some of his ministers worried that the emperor had gone mad. But such was Napoleon's charisma, and his luck so far, that no one dared to suggest that marching the Grande Armée all the way to Moscow was likely to end in an appalling catastrophe.

On June 24, 1812, Napoleon crossed the Niemen River into Russia with an army of approximately 600,000 troops, only about half of them Frenchmen. The Russian army retreated rather than marching to meet him, but the French faced opposition from the elements, made particularly severe by the fact that the villages and countryside had been destroyed ahead of the army, a "scorched-earth" tactic Russian defenders would use against their enemies numerous times in the future. After one hugely bloody battle on the Moskva River, at Borodino, Napoleon broke through, and on September 14, the Grande Armée entered Moscow. The czar refused to sign a treaty, and the Russian army retreated to the east. Moscow's residents set fire to the city, hoping to prevent the French from staying a long time. Not having planned for a winter war, Napoleon did not want to go deeper into Russia to give chase and tried to broker a peace. On October 19, he could wait no longer and the French troops evacuated Moscow and headed for home. Most of them would never get there.

October and November 1812 proved horribly cold; temperatures are thought to have reached as low as −40° F. Supplies ran out, disease raged, and Russian partisans torched villages before the French arrived. Even a smaller army could not have lived off the land in these conditions. Russian troops harried the French army, taking as many as 200,000 men prisoner. By the time Napoleon crossed the Niemen again on December 16, he had only 30,000 left of the 600,000 soldiers he started with. Word traveled fast: the opportunity to strike at a weakened emperor had come.

THE END OF NAPOLEON'S REIGN. Although originally reluctant to break with the still powerful Napoleon and to ally with the Russians, the Prussians joined the westward-marching Russians and were able to drive the remnants of the Grande Armée into the kingdom of Saxony, one of Napoleon's German puppet states. During a summer armistice, Napoleon called up more—and younger—conscripts to rebuild his army, but this Grande Armée was much more inexperienced than the last. With the French off their territory, the Prussians rebuilt their army, half of which now consisted of a conscripted, mostly middle-class militia. By the time the armistice expired in fall, the Austrians had decided to join the fight against Napoleon.

The Retreat from Russia This contemporary rendering of Napoleon's retreat from Russia shows the disorder of the Grande Armée, some of whose desperate soldiers drown as they flee from the Russian forces. In fact, typhus and the terrible Russian winter were chiefly to blame for the decimation of the French forces.

After wearing down the Grande Armée in Saxony, the Prussians, Russians, and Austrians allied converged on and nearly encircled the town of Leipzig, where Napoleon attempted to make a stand. In three days—October 16–19, 1813—more than 90,000 men were killed in what was afterward known as the Battle of the Nations, in recognition of the many different nationalities that fought there, on both sides.

The Grande Armée was forced to retreat. Napoleon sought to rally his troops against an invasion of France, but he could not hold off the Allies. In an attempt to save a Bonaparte dynasty, on April 6, 1814, Napoleon abdicated in favor of his son, but the Allies refused to consider such a proposition. They turned instead to Louis XVI's brother, who was pleased to ascend the throne as Louis XVIII of France. Napoleon was exiled to Elba, a small island just off the Italian coast near Corsica, and banned from returning to France. After ten months of exile, however, he heard that the French had grown discontented with the new regime. He escaped his captors and on March 1, 1815, he landed on the southern coast near Cannes. As he made his way to Paris, discontented

Frenchmen armed themselves and rallied to their former emperor. By March 20, he was in Paris again, where huge crowds greeted the beginning of what would be a brief "Hundred Days" of return to Napoleonic rule.

Not surprisingly, the Allies did not look sympathetically on Napoleon's return to power, though the reinstated French emperor promised peace. Accepting that the Allies intended to invade France again, Napoleon decided to strike first and attempted to knock out the British and Prussian armies in Belgium. After separating the Prussians from the British in early skirmishes, Napoleon and his army engaged the British at Waterloo. At one point, it looked as if the French might defeat the British forces under the command of the duke of Wellington, but the Prussians made a surprise reappearance. The allied armies closed in and routed the exhausted French. Once again Napoleon was forced to abdicate and this time was sentenced to prison on St. Helena, a volcanic island off the coast of western Africa, where he died in 1821. The Allies scheduled a grand peace conference in Vienna for later that year, hoping then to fulfill everyone's hopes for a postrevolutionary, post-Napoleonic Europe.

Conclusion

The Revolutionary era brought new actors onto the stage and made the breaking of the Old Regimes' power thinkable. The French, American, and Haitian Revolutions inspired a wave of uprisings across the globe, including a series of rebellions against Spanish colonial rule in the Americas. Weakened by the Napoleonic experience, the

Spanish could mount only feeble resistance, and first Colombia (1819) and then Mexico (1821) established independence. A wave of revolutions, led by Simón Bolívar, Latin America's Bonaparte, liberated Venezuela, Ecuador, and Peru. The Ottoman Empire, too, faced a series of nationalist struggles for liberation, beginning with the successful quests for autonomy by the Serbs (1804) and the Greeks (1821–1829), and ending with an unsuccessful bid by the Egyptians (1839). To a large extent, the German and Italian movements for national unification have their origins in the experiences of Napoleonic occupation, and the reforms of the era that succeeded in breaking down many aspects of Old Regime provincialism.

The Revolution itself did make some lasting changes and left lasting aspirations, even though some of these were not realized in France or elsewhere for many years to come. France abolished its system of legal inequalities, modernized its army, and received a new civil code, to mention just a few transformations. The Austrians and Prussians ended feudal serfdom in 1807, in the wake of defeat by Napoleon's armies and in the effort to win the loyalty of citizens to fight for the nation. The concept of popular sovereignty—and with it, national pride—spread across the continent, and some who later called themselves socialists would not forget the sans-culottes' campaigns for full political and economic equality. Liberty, equality, and fraternity had not been fully achieved, even by the radical revolutionaries, and certainly not by Napoleon, but the clergy, nobility, and kings had been compelled to concede much by a series of political revolutions that gave force and voice to the quieter revolutionary forces under way long before 1789.

Critical Thinking Questions

1. Could Louis XVI have prevented the Revolution, or at least have moderated its course? What might he have done differently?

2. It has often been said that the Revolution "ate its own children." What does this mean, and why did this Revolution prove so destructive, even for those who supported change in 1789?

3. It what ways was Napoleon a product of the Enlightenment and the Revolution? How did his reign open the way—intentionally and unintentionally—for a new age?

Key Terms

National Assembly **(p. 531)**
Tennis Court Oath **(p. 531)**
émigré **(p. 532)**
Jacobin Club **(p. 533)**
assignat **(p. 533)**

Civil Constitution of the Clergy **(p. 534)**
sans-culottes **(p. 536)**
Convention **(p. 537)**
Committee of Public Safety **(p. 538)**

Reign of Terror ("the Terror") **(p. 539)**
General Maximum **(p. 539)**
Thermidorian reaction **(p. 543)**
Directory **(p. 543)**

Concordat **(p. 548)**
Napoleonic Code **(p. 548)**
Grande Armée **(p. 551)**
Continental System **(p. 551)**

Primary Sources in connect

For information on Connect and the online resources available, go to **http://connect.mcgraw-hill.com**.

1. **Declaration of the Rights of Man and Citizen**

2. **Declaration of the Rights of Woman**

3. **Robespierre Defends the Use of Terror in "Report on the Principles of Political Morality"**

4. **De Staël Describes Germany's Rustic Qualities in "On Germany"**

5. **Polish Commander and Revolutionary Tadeusz Kosciuszko Appeals to Polish Peasants in the "Polaniec Manifesto"**

6. **The British Ambassador Reports on the Disorder and the Initial Stages of the French Revolution in 1789**

7. **Napoleon Lays Out His View on the Church in Italy**

Emmanuel-Joseph Sieyès, "What Is the Third Estate?"

In January 1789, the antiaristocratic clergyman Emmanuel-Joseph Sieyès published a pamphlet, "What Is the Third Estate?," which gave powerful expression to commoners' resentments toward the Old Regimes' system of legal inequalities. Written in the midst of discussions of how to constitute a new Estates General and how to save France from bankruptcy, Sieyès's pamphlet was instrumental in popularizing the enlightened principle that all citizens should enjoy equal rights.

The plan of this book is fairly simple. We must ask ourselves three questions.

What is the Third Estate? *Everything.*

What has it been until now in the political order? *Nothing.*

What does it want to be? *Something.*

Chapter 1. The Third Estate Is a Complete Nation

. . . Who is bold enough to maintain that the Third Estate does not contain within itself everything needful to constitute a complete nation? It is like a strong and robust man with one arm still in chains. If the privileged order were removed, the nation would not be something less but something more. What then is the Third Estate? All; but an "all" that is fettered and oppressed. What would it be without the privileged order? It would be all; but free and flourishing. Nothing will go well without the Third Estate; everything would go considerably better without the two others. . . .

Chapter 2. What Has the Third Estate Been Until Now? *Nothing*

. . . the nation as a whole cannot be free, nor can any of its separate orders, unless the Third Estate is free. Freedom does not derive from privileges. It derives from the rights of citizens—and these rights belong to all. . . . By Third Estate is meant all the citizens who belong to the common order. Anybody who holds a legal privilege of any kind deserts the common order, stands as an exception to the common laws and, consequently, does not belong to the Third Estate. As we have already said, a nation is made one by virtue of common laws and common representation. It is indisputably only too true that in France a man who is protected only by the common laws is a nobody; whoever

is totally unprivileged must submit to every form on contempt, insult and humiliation. To avoid being completely crushed, what must the unlucky non-privileged person do? He has to attach himself by all kinds of contemptible actions to some magnate; he prostitutes his principles and human dignity for the possibility of claiming, in his need, the protection of a *somebody.* . . .

Chapter 6. What Remains to Be Done.

. . . The Third Estate must now see the direction in which both thought and action are moving, and realize that its sole hope lies in its own intelligence and courage. Reason and justice are on its side; the least it must do is to assure itself of their full support. No, it is too late to work for the conciliation of all parties. What sort of an agreement could one hope for between the energy of the oppressed and the rage of the oppressors? . . .

Among a people used to servitude, truth can be left to sleep; but if you attract the attention of the People, if you tell it to choose between truth and error, its mind clings to truth naturally as healthy eyes turn towards the light. And, light, in morals, cannot spread to any extent without, willy-nilly, leading to equity. . . .

While the aristocrats talk of their honor but pursue their self-interest, the Third Estate, i.e. the nation, will develop its virtue, for if corporate interest is egotism, national interest is virtue. . . . There was once a time when the Third Estate was in bondage and the nobility was everything. Now the Third Estate is everything and nobility is only a word.

QUESTIONS | *Why does Sieyès think the third estate really is the nation? Why does he think that the society of orders prevents the development of true virtue?*

Source: Emmanuel-Joseph Sieyès, *What Is the Third Estate?* trans. M. Blondel, ed. S. E. Finer (New York: Praeger, 1964), 51–2, 56–7, 59, 61, 142–3, 145.

LIVING IN THE PAST, SEEING THE FUTURE

RESTORATION, NATIONALISM, AND INDUSTRIALIZATION, 1815–1850

The Congress of Vienna: Old Monarchies, New Borders
  The Political Spectrum: Liberals, Radicals, Conservatives

Reform, Recovery, and Religion after 1815
  The Legal Spectrum: Rights and Freedoms—for Some
  Economies, Old and New
  Religious Reorganization and Revival

Nationalism Comes of Age
  Inventing Modern Greece
  Belgium Is Born
  National Projects that Failed: Poland, Germany, and Italy

Domestic Politics in the 1820s–1830s: From Revolution to Reaction
  Revolution Returns: France, 1830
  Reform without Revolution: England
  Reaction without Reform: Russia

Restoration Culture
  Romanticism: Mourning the Passing of the Past
  Utilitarianism: Planning for the Future

The Industrial Revolution
  Why Britain?
  Why Textiles?
  A Revolution in Gadgets
  A Revolution in Transportation
  A Revolution in Capital
  A Revolution in Labor
  Manchester: City of the Future?

The Hungry Forties
  A Return to Revolution
  How Revolutions End
  How Restorations End

Conclusion

ALEXIS DE TOCQUEVILLE, ARISTOCRAT—AND LIBERAL The French political philosopher Alexis de Tocqueville (1805–1859) was only ten years old in 1815, but he developed a much more profound understanding of the revolutionary era and its consequences than most of those who had lived through it. His family, minor nobles, had opposed the Revolution.

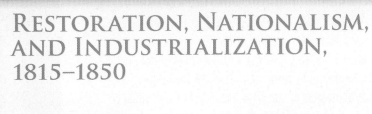

◀ The Old Technology, and the New: An Eighteenth-Century Warship Hauled Away by a Steam-Powered Tug

Revolutionaries had guillotined his maternal grandfather; his uncle, the writer François-René de Chateaubriand, had been cast into exile; and his parents had been imprisoned. Tocqueville's pious mother and royalist father welcomed the restoration of the French monarchy, and his father became one of the highest-ranking bureaucrats in post-Napoleonic France. Despite his parentage the young Alexis doubted that the revolutionary genie could be put back into the bottle, and by age twenty, he himself was in full rebellion. He abandoned his mother's conservative Catholicism, married a nonaristocratic Englishwoman, and began to champion individual liberties, equality under the law, and a free market. Born of conservative stock, Tocqueville had become a liberal.

Being a liberal in Tocqueville's day meant seeking to reestablish, through legal means, the liberties sought by French moderates in 1789–1791. It also meant rejecting the radical projects of social equalization through violence, as attempted in 1792–1794. After the restoration of the conservative monarchies in 1815, liberals in most places were shut out of power, though Tocqueville, thanks to his brilliant mind and noble birth, did serve as a legislator. In 1831–1832, he visited the United States and wrote a widely acclaimed study of the young democracy's unique political and social structures. But it took another sixteen years—and another revolution in France—before Tocqueville got his chance to apply his ideas to his own country. The aristocratic liberal was thrilled to help write a constitution for the Second French Republic, founded in 1848—but his contentment proved short lived. A mere three years later, he was briefly jailed when he opposed the attempts of President Louis Napoleon (nephew and imitator of the great Napoleon) to seize dictatorial power. Once again, Tocqueville was brought face to face with the excesses of revolution and the past's immense powers of revenge.

Tocqueville understood both the power of the past and the appeal of visions of the future. Among his writings, the two most important are *Democracy in America* (1835), and *The Old Regime and the French Revolution* (1856), an analysis of the origins and significance of France's break with the past in 1789. In *Democracy in America,* Tocqueville examined the remarkable changes under way in the America of populist president Andrew Jackson, where common men could vote, the frontier offered every emigrant a new chance, and restrictions on commerce were being eliminated. Tocqueville admired American individualism and ambition, but also feared that the new democracy's semieducated and materialistic citizenry posed a potential threat to the European cultural traditions he believed exemplified civilization.

Alexis de Tocqueville Alexis de Tocqueville was enough of a nobleman to have had his portrait painted as a young man, but he was a political liberal at heart.

Democracy in America was an attempt to envision a postaristocratic future, for Europe as well as for the new United States. *The Old Regime and the French Revolution,* by contrast, was concerned with the past. In it Tocqueville showed that the Revolution was not so revolutionary. Indeed, it had merely completed what absolutism had begun: the strengthening of the state at the expense of the church and aristocracies. Writing in the aftermath of the failure of the 1848 revolutions, Tocqueville expressed doubt that revolutions resulted in constructive change. Perhaps, he concluded, the only hope was incremental political reform and expansion in the number of property owners. Otherwise, societies ended in culture-destroying chaos (as in the Terror) or in law-trampling tyranny (as in Napoleon's rise to power).

Tocqueville devoted most of his brainpower to attempting to understand the political consequences of the eighteenth century's two great revolutions, the American and the French. He witnessed the beginnings of yet another revolution under way in at least some parts of Europe during his time: the industrial one. In 1835, he visited the city of Manchester in England, where mechanized textile production was most advanced, and was horrified by what he saw. In his diary, he contrasted the massive new productive possibilities being unleashed by industrial labor with the dehumanizing nature of new forms of work. "From this filthy sewer pure gold flows. Here humanity attains its most complete development and its most brutish; here civilization works its miracles, and civilized man is turned back almost into a savage."[1] Tocqueville saw Manchester as a specifically English problem, not a western or European one; he spent little time analyzing the Industrial Revolution because he—unlike his younger contemporary Karl Marx—could not imagine that *this* revolution would change Europe as profoundly as had the political revolutions that preceded it. But here he was wrong. In its own way, and at different rates in different nations, the Industrial Revolution would contribute just as much to the breaking down of the world of Tocqueville's parents as the political revolutions the great French liberal understood so well.

In this chapter we examine both political revolution and industrialization and consider the political, economic, social, and cultural consequences of each. The political experiments of the revolutionary era generated new visions of how society should be organized, but the Terror and the Napoleonic Wars led most Europeans to long for peace and for nonviolent forms of change. In many places, the Revolution had swept away the legalized inequalities of the Old Regimes. By no means had even Europe's western states become democratic—that was why American democracy seemed so strange to Tocqueville. But significant changes had occurred. In the wake of the Napoleonic Wars, in the places in which the commercial and agricultural revolutions had gone deepest—Britain and the Netherlands—and where French revolutionary influence had been most powerful—France, the Netherlands, northern Italy, and the western German states—new wealth and new liberties created a gradually widening middle class of citizens, as well as a reform-minded aristocracy.

In western Europe, the same sorts of people who had adopted enlightened ideas about improvement and the Revolution's belief in the power of the people, embraced the liberal worldview of Tocqueville and expressed an even stronger faith in civilization's inevitable progress. Elsewhere, especially in southern and eastern Europe, it was harder to believe in progress; constitutional governance, industrial production, and the collapse of aristocratic power remained simply visions. Nobles, who had retained most landed wealth and political clout, had less incentive to embrace liberal ideas, and ordinary people had fewer opportunities to change their traditional patterns of life. Even after 1848, Hungarian peasants, for example, remained virtually enserfed by their landlords and far too poor to buy their own land. Ordinary Sicilians could only dream of rights or of railroads.

The Europe that emerged from the common experience of the Revolution and Napoleon's wars became a continent more varied in its forms of governance, its legal and economic systems, and its ways of life than at any time since the fall of Rome. Across this diverse landmass, people had to grapple with the enduring power of the past even as they developed new visions of the future. The contrast and competition generated by the coexistence of so many Europes, past and future, would produce sensational new dynamisms—and equally dramatic disappointments.

The Congress of Vienna: Old Monarchies, New Borders

After the initial defeat of Napoleon in 1814, the victorious powers, Britain, Prussia, Austria, and Russia, sent high-ranking delegates to Vienna to decide how to reconstitute a war-torn continent. Negotiations were halted for several months during Napoleon's Hundred Days (see Chapter 17), but in 1815, once the French leader had been packed off to the rocky island of St. Helena, they began again. The delegates had many demands and desires, but could agree on three major goals: France had to be disarmed and contained; the revolutionary spirit it had unleashed had to be put back into the bottle; and finally, power in Europe needed to be balanced in order to prevent the outbreak of another devastating war. Led by the conservative Austrian foreign minister Clemens von Metternich, the delegates agreed to form a **Concert of Europe** that would meet from time to time to concert or coordinate efforts to preserve this balance of power and collectively suppress revolution. In Vienna, Metternich, who was known as the coachman of Europe for his ability to crack his whip and force others to do his bidding, also tried to suppress the genie of nationalism Napoleon had inadvertently conjured, and to restore the kings and provincial lords the Revolution had banished. For a time, his efforts succeeded, at the cost, however, of considerable repression and discontent among liberals such as Tocqueville, as well as among Jacobins and other radicals.

First, the **Congress of Vienna** attended to the containment of France. Hoping that restoring the Bourbon

> How did conservative delegates at the Congress of Vienna try to turn the clock back to 1788?

monarchy would keep both nationalism and revolution at bay, the delegates put Louis XVI's brother, who took the title Louis XVIII (r. 1814–1824), on the French throne. They also created some larger states on France's borders. Hoping to keep the French out of the Rhineland, the Congress merged the French-occupied territories of the Austrian Netherlands and the Dutch Republic, creating a new Kingdom of the Netherlands (Map 18.1, p. 564). The Holy Roman Empire was not revived, but many of the small German principalities disappeared into a larger-pieced patchwork of thirty-nine states. Prussia was allowed to swallow up the Rhineland and take almost half of Saxony, which gave it far more power and resources than ever before, though it was still yoked to and overseen by the Austrian Habsburgs, who dominated a loosely united political entity now called the German Confederation.

Metternich was a monarchist and an aristocrat, but less a conservative ideologue than a man who championed stability and order above all else. His recipe for stability beyond France was to restore dynastic control over multinational empires and to create a "balance of power" such that no European state became too strong—or too weak to deal with its own domestic opponents. By no means was this a popular solution. Many German liberals, in Prussia and elsewhere, disliked a solution that put them under the Habsburgs' thumbs. Similarly, few Italians cheered when the Austrians added to their domains even more territory in Dalmatia and in northern and central Italy. Although most of Poland became a

united kingdom, with an army, a constitutional charter, and a parliament, it was not an independent kingdom, but one ruled by the Russian czar. The Russians also took control of Bessarabia (from the Ottoman Empire) and Finland (from Sweden).

Frustration with the new arrangements led to numerous campaigns to alter the map, some of which, like the Poles' many attempts to overthrow Russian domination, were destined to perpetual failure. Eventually, Greeks, Belgians, Italians, Germans, and Bulgarians managed to carve out their own nation-states by the end of the nineteenth century—doing so, remarkably, without unleashing another pan-European war. Despised as it was by so many, Metternich's map charted the course for a century of such reduced warfare that, proportionate to the population, approximately seven times fewer people died in conflicts in the nineteenth century than in the eighteenth.

Metternich believed that creating stability was a matter of balancing power. His Russian contemporary, Czar Alexander I, by contrast, thought that a return to political and social order could be based only on the restoration of the churches. In 1815, Alexander pressed his fellow monarchs to sign a "Holy Alliance," a united front concerned with restoring religious institutions and beliefs to Europe after the critiques of enlightened thinkers and the assaults on the churches by revolutionaries and Napoleonic bureaucrats. Most European rulers signed, with the exception of the English and the Pope, who refused to ally himself with Protestants, but the Alliance was largely a

Restoration of the monarchies
1815–1848

Liberal nationalists attempt
to create new states
1821–1831

Belgium is born
1830

Greek War of Independence
1821–1832

Polish
independen•
thwarted
1830–1831

Failed Decembrist revolt in Russia
1825

Industrial Revolution
1760–1850

Britain
1760–

1810   1815   1820   1825   1830

fiction, and it collapsed after Alexander's death in 1825. Within nations, too, although the established churches did get back some of their privileges, they did not recover most of the wealth, power, and prestige they had lost during the Enlightenment and revolutionary period. Nor did the censors, in most places, do a very effective job of prohibiting criticisms of the clergy or scriptures from circulating. Similarly, although some noble titles and privileges were restored, many Europeans now began to associate themselves with political or nationalist movements rather than or in addition to their place in the system of privileges or specific religious identities.

The Political Spectrum: Liberals, Radicals, and Conservatives

One of the most important consequences of the French Revolution was its language: the Declaration of the Rights of Man and Napoleon's armies had spread through Europe the concepts of liberty, equality, and fraternity as well as the seeds of nationalism. Even if the conservatives returned to power and monarchs returned to their thrones, the Revolution's ideas and its experiments in governance were not forgotten, and both liberals and radicals drew on this recent history in their demands for reform. In fact, we can map the post-1815 political spectrum according to the way various movements reacted to the events of 1789: liberals applauded the destruction of Old Regime privileges and estates but opposed further radicalization; radi-

cals thought the constitutional monarchy and protections of property achieved in 1789 did not go far enough; and conservatives thought 1789 itself was an abomination. But the political perspectives of the period were made up of more than views on the Revolution, and as the meanings of the terms *liberal, radical,* and *conservative* have changed so much in the post-1945 era, we need to look a little more closely at what it meant to belong to these political camps in the years 1815–1850. For example, each of the three main political orientations can be characterized by specific stands on major issues of the period (Table 18.1).

THE LIBERALS. In the early nineteenth century, to be a **liberal** was to believe in many of the principles of the Enlightenment articulated by John Locke and Emmanuel-Joseph Sieyès (see Chapters 16 and 17). Liberals promoted equality (at least for adult males) before the law and believed that having a constitution and an elected assembly was an important means to protect political and religious liberties. They believed in the sovereignty of the people—though liberals typically argued that, because owning property ensured a citizen's intellectual and economic independence, only property owners should be allowed to vote or to hold office. For liberals, then, "the people" meant a limited number of men; non-European men in colonized territories were also excluded. Most liberals also believed that an inherited, albeit constitutional, monarchy was necessary to balance and temper the decisions of the state's elected bodies. Having absorbed the Enlightenment's

Reactionary rule of Nicholas I in Russia
1825–1855

Tocqueville publishes
Democracy in America
1835

Return to revolutions
1830–1851

July Monarchy in France
1830–1848

1848 revolutions suppressed
1848–1851

Belgium, France, German states
1830–

| 1835 | 1840 | 1845 | 1850 | 1855 |

MAP 18.1 | Europe after the Congress of Vienna, 1815

This is the map Klemens von Metternich and the other representatives of the restored monarchies imposed on Europe after the defeat of Napoleon at Waterloo. *Why did the Congress allow Prussia and the Kingdom of the Netherlands to grow? Note the large number of small states in the German Confederation and on the Italian peninsula. Why didn't the Austrian chancellor want to create a united Germany and a united Italy?*

critique of the established churches, many liberals regarded the clergy as their greatest enemies, responsible for spreading superstition and intolerance, and destroying individuality by their willingness to impose church teachings on all. Liberals regularly pressed their governments to replace churchmen in official positions and in schools with secular officials and teachers.

Some liberals were interested chiefly in economic policies. To the ideas advocated by political liberals, those who

backed economic liberalism added principles such as those articulated by Adam Smith (see Chapter 16). Economic liberals argued that removing barriers such as guilds, monopolies, and the continent's crazy quilt of local tariffs and taxes from the market would offer new prosperity to all. But they did not believe in the equalizing of fortunes or in regulating bread prices. Although some were concerned about the overworking or endangering of workers, they did not want either states or workers themselves to interfere in

TABLE 18.1 | The Political Spectrum, 1815–1850

CONSERVATISM	LIBERALISM	RADICALISM
Monarchy	Constitutional monarchy	Republic
No voting	Limited franchise	Universal suffrage
Privileges (according to birth)	Meritocracy	Meritocracy
Market restricted in favor of landowner	Free market	Market restricted in favor of lower classes
Some more equal than others	Equal rights	Equal rights
State religion	Religious toleration or secularization	Anticlericalism; sometimes atheism
Property protected by custom	Property protected by law	Property equalized
Against all revolutions	In favor of political revolution, such as 1688, 1789, 1840, 1848	Revolution must go farther than politics

the workings of the free market. For both political and economic liberals—positions that often coincided—the fundamental ideas were those of liberty and self-regulation. In their view, freeing the individual and the market from feudal and mercantile constraints was the best recipe for general prosperity and happiness, for creating a form of civilization that would be the envy of the world. But as their radical critics recognized, the liberty of the liberals was available only to the property-owning classes and, in most nations, to the wealthiest property owners.

THE RADICALS. Often defining themselves as republicans, early-nineteenth-century political radicals detested the restored regimes. They wanted, instead, to see states in the hands of "the people," which for them meant all adult males. Some radicals agitated for workers' rights and higher wages, whereas others were willing to return to revolutionary violence in the name of removing the monarchs and replacing them with republics. Political radicals tended to be deeply anticlerical, and some of them, like Karl Marx (1818–1883) and Friedrich Engels (1820–1895), believed that religion itself was, in Marx's famous words, "the opiate of the masses." Many radicals, though, were content to champion enlightened Christianity in some form—or to invent their own, humanitarian sects.

Economic radicalism frequently grew out of political radicalism, as it became clear that changes in the law without changes in the distribution of wealth did little to give the people power. To these social critics, it seemed abundantly clear that the rich were getting richer at the expense of the poor. To some extent they were right: real wages for both workers and peasants did fall for most of the century's first half.

Economic radicals developed a variety of schemes to remedy these inequities. Those who advocated equalizing incomes so that all had enough to eat were generally called **socialists.** Socialists came in various shapes and drew on the radical Enlightenments dreams of perfecting mankind

as well as on ideas articulated by the sans-culottes. Some championed the idea of worker-owned factories or farms in which profits were shared; others wanted to make women citizens or even to abolish marriage, ideas that horrified both liberals and most political radicals. And some, whom Karl Marx later dubbed "utopian socialists," believed that universal harmony could come about without bloody revolution, simply by reorganizing the world.

Utopian socialists had good insights into the distortions of the market, but their fanciful solutions made many people wary of joining the movement. In the 1840s, a more radical communist movement began to take shape. One of the leading theoreticians of this movement was Friedrich Engels, whose father had sent him to the northern city of Manchester to run his textile mill. Unable to endure his job, Engels resigned and wrote a vehement denunciation of the horrors of industrial society, *The Condition of the Working Class in England* (see Back to the Source at the end of the chapter).

Engels's book prompted the philosopher turned radical journalist Karl Marx to seek out and form what would be a lifelong partnership with its author. Together, Marx and Engels framed what they called scientific socialism or **communism,** which identified the laws of capitalism. According to these laws, capital accumulation would inevitably pit economic groups or classes against one another until the whole world was divided into the industrial working class on the one hand, and the land owners and factory owners (whom Marx and Engels called the bourgeoisie) on the other. Religion, nationalism, and political reform, they argued, did not help the working class in the long run, but were simply delusions. Finally, the working class, or **proletariat,** would stage a revolution against the bourgeoisie and establish a classless society, without religion, nation-states, or private property. In the 1840s, there were very few communists, and Marx and Engels were social outcasts with little influence even in socialist circles. But their ideas, products of this period

Meet the Utopians

The radicals in early-nineteenth-century Europe were definitely odd men—and women—out, and some of them had distinctly odd ideas. Quite a number of these individuals hailed from the urban elites. They were not underprivileged, but rather people with either iconoclastic political and religious views or strong social consciences. Among them was Barthélemy Prosper Enfantin, a banker's son who joined the early socialist movement. Enfantin supported women's emancipation, denounced "the tyranny of marriage," and praised the virtues of free love. In 1833, French officials sought to break up his movement on the grounds that it posed a threat to public morality. Enfantin cut his losses and took a group of disciples to Egypt, where they pushed another utopian project: the building of a Suez Canal, hoping to link the West and East in universal harmony. Enfantin could not persuade Egypt's ruler, Mehmed Ali, to undertake this project, but he did inspire Ferdinand

de Lesseps, who would later oversee the building of just such a canal—for the purposes, however, of increasing, rather than decreasing, capitalist competition.

Many critics accused Enfantin of trying to create an alternative religion, of which he was pope, or as he put it "the father." There were, however, many other radicals for whom freeing individuals from conventional marital and moral arrangements was crucial if society was really to be changed. One such individual was Charles Fourier. Perhaps it was his ability to put together an early critique of the market economy with a vision of a new form of family or community that made Fourier one of the most influential visionary radicals of the pre-1848 era. Working as a stockbroker in the late eighteenth century, Fourier came to hate the kind of market exchanges Adam Smith loved. For Fourier, wage work and the division of labor meant that producers neither used nor ate what they made and thus felt alienated from their work. In the new economy, he perceived, individuals were losing their integrity and curiosity, and life was losing its diverse pleasures. Just after 1800, he began to sketch out a form of utopian community that would take advantage of the efficiencies of the division of labor and at the same time rescue workers from the evils of "civilization." By organizing a series of phalanxes, each composed of some eight hundred complementary personality types, and by having workers rotate almost hourly through jobs, Fourier thought, people could be ensured diverse, interesting lives. At the same time, they would produce goods for the use of the phalanx community, or as it was called by Russian radical descendants of Fourier, the collective farm. People could produce food efficiently, but consume it locally. No one who worked would have to starve.

Fourier was as strange a duck as Enfantin—he believed that once his visions were realized, the earth's delight would cause the polar ice cap to melt and the seas to turn to lemonade. Marx and Engels borrowed much from Fourier, but also ridiculed his fantastic plans by calling his movement utopian socialism. But the social critiques and the utopian plans of these radicals reveal something that liberals such as Tocqueville refused to confront: for some Europeans, political liberty was not enough. Real social change, for them, required remaking both the world of work and the world of love.

Barthélemy Prosper Enfantin, Visionary Like the other radical reformers that Marx and Engels called "utopian" socialists, Prosper Enfantin believed that by liberating love from what he called "the tyranny of marriage," humankind could prepare itself for a new era of universal happiness.

QUESTION | *Why did Fourier think that abolishing the market would solve all of society's problems?*

of grand disappointments, and equally grand visions, would have enormous consequences for Europe and for the world in the twentieth century.

Usually urban dwellers, the radicals cultivated supporters in Europe's growing western cities. Chased by censors and policemen, they stood on soap-boxes to give speeches or handed out illegal, revolution-inciting pamphlets (such as Marx and Engels's *Communist Manifesto* of 1848). They paid little attention to peasants, and often saw them as profiteers who kept bread prices high. Peasants, in turn, usually had little time for movements that sought to fix grain prices and empower urban atheists. What they wanted was land, and to protect what privileges they still had from further erosion. In this way, ironically, they had much in common with the champions of the Old Regimes, the conservatives.

THE CONSERVATIVES. In contrast to the liberals and the radicals, **conservatives** rejected the idea that "the people," however construed, should rule. To allow this would result in instability and disaster. Conservatives distrusted men of commerce as well as urban workers and despised radicals as well as the mob of city dwellers who listened to their orations. They themselves tended not to orate. Since they held virtually all the power, they had no need to engage in debate and no respect for the opinions expressed in the wider public sphere.

In his *Reflections on the Revolution in France* (1790), Edmund Burke articulated the basic principles of nineteenth-century conservatism. Burke insisted that the ideas of the Enlightenment had given people the notion that it was possible to completely remake the world, according to their abstract and utopian plans (see Chapter 17). In fact, Burke argued, states were not social contracts, but organic entities which, like plants, could not be uprooted without disastrous consequences. Conservatives applied this idea to economic and religious spheres, as well as to political life. Conservatives saw commerce, as a whole, as a crude form of seeking wealth. They preferred traditional agriculture, in which production was largely for home use. Similarly, religious institutions should not be tampered with. The churches had long enforced proper moral behavior, including deference to one's betters, and should continue to do so. It was better to remain in one's appointed station and preferably on one's rural estate than to experiment with dangerous new things, like railroads, constitutions, and secular schools. As the Revolution and Terror had shown, attempts to leap forward or suddenly upward were likely to end in disaster.

Reform, Recovery, and Religion after 1815

For many Europeans, the legal and land reforms that came with the Enlightenment, the Revolution, and the Napoleonic occupations were significant and far reaching and laid the basis for a new kind of state: the secular nation-state, based on equality before the law (at least for men), expanding suffrage, religious toleration, the free movement of laborers, and the sharing of ideas in a (relatively, at least) uncensored public sphere. Creating such states in the early nineteenth century was a halting and uneven process, hardly touching the Russian Empire, for example. Movement in this direction happened earliest and went farthest in France, western Germany, Switzerland, the Kingdom of the Netherlands, and northern Italy, widening already existing differences with southern and eastern European nations. It was in this northwestern sector of the continent that Europeans moved most swiftly into the brave new civilization whose ambivalent qualities Tocqueville had charted.

> How did eastern and western Europeans grapple with the legacies of the French Revolution and the Napoleonic Wars?

The Legal Spectrum: Rights and Freedoms—for Some

Even where legal reforms took hold after 1815, liberals and radicals had to fight a series of battles to ensure their constitutionally guaranteed rights and liberties, to extend the powers of elected assemblies, and to expand the electorate that selected delegates. The fitful achievement of these aims before 1850 can be viewed in terms that make it seem either a glass half full or a glass half empty. Major reforms were achieved in some places—but only because some wealthy and well-born individuals were convinced change was essential, and because some middle- and lower-class leaders were willing to risk jail, exile, or worse to agitate for new liberties. In other places, and especially in central, eastern, and southern Europe, rights and freedoms remained restricted in part because fewer members of the elite felt inclined to undertake reforms, and fewer "little people" had the education or economic wherewithal to commit themselves to political protests.

WESTERN EUROPE. West of the Rhine, the liberals' glasses were increasingly full. Suffrage did expand, slowly, in France and England after 1830, alongside the expansion of commerce. In both places, as well as in western Germany and the Netherlands, an ever-increasing number of liberals were elected to local offices or hired as state bureaucrats, injecting moderate reformist perspectives into governance.

Religious freedoms were extended gradually. After the Dublin lawyer Daniel O'Connell won election to Parliament in County Clare, Ireland, the British government agreed to grant Catholic emancipation in 1829. This agreement allowed Catholics to take offices in the civil service and military and to be seated as members of Parliament, but it also increased the property qualifications for Catholic voters. Jews were allowed to become citizens in France in 1791 and in the French-occupied Netherlands in 1796, as well as in several German provinces between

1808 and 1814. But in Prussia their rights were restricted again after 1819, and many Christian Europeans remained very suspicious, if not hostile, toward both the assimilated and the religiously active Jews in their midst.

The English Bill of Rights had essentially done away with censorship in 1689, and during the Enlightenment, popular pamphlets and banned books had managed to escape many continental censors. The young United States guaranteed freedoms of speech and of the press in the Bill of Rights, and ratified and added to the U.S. Constitution in 1791; the French constitution of the same year similarly ensured the right to free speech. Subsequent French regimes, however, would not be so liberal, and censorship would continue in France into the post-1871 period, though it was often spotty and ineffective. Norway offered press freedom in 1814, as did Belgium and Switzerland in 1830. Although not everyone in these territories could yet enjoy these freedoms, the gradual achievement of them gave many people hope that the old world of inequality and privilege would indeed gradually disappear.

CENTRAL, EASTERN, AND SOUTHERN EUROPE. In eastern Europe, such hopes seemed far-fetched, to say the least. In Russia, serfs remained bound to the land and to their overlords until 1861, and many still labored under the whip. The Enlightened absolutist Joseph II officially abolished serfdom in his Austrian domains in 1781–1785, but he failed to impose his reforms on his Hungarian lands. In eastern Prussia too, after 1815, many peasants remained landless, and still owed feudal dues. Worse, during the Restoration era, landlords began to chip away at their peasants' cherished rights to use common lands and forests for pasturing animals or for foraging for food and fuel; and artisanal guilds continued to be powerful in eastern cities and towns. This meant that peasants here were struggling to maintain older ways of life, and the well-to-do remained noble landowners with little access to capital and little interest in reform.

In eastern and southern Europe, too, aside from Prussia and German-speaking Austria, literacy rates remained low. Nonetheless, the restored regimes came down hard on would-be nationalists and liberal proponents of free trade and secularization. Metternich's regime remained in force until 1848, catching numerous radicals in its claws. The situation in Russia was much worse. There the press was rigorously controlled, and Nicholas I's aggressive police force broke up potentially troublesome student and social groups. The steady stream of liberal exiles fleeing to the West or risking imprisonment in Siberian camps proved that the Russian nobility was not ready even to listen to proposals for change.

Economies, New and Old

Economic recovery and reorganization in the wake of the Napoleonic Wars took time. The wars and especially Napoleon's Continental System had disrupted trade but

The Hay Harvest, Russia, c. 1825 As industrialization began in northwestern Europe, Russia retained its rural economy, with much of the agricultural labor still performed by serfs.

had also created some new opportunities. The blockade that had prevented inexpensive English textiles and New World sugar from reaching the continent had, in turn, encouraged the development of small-scale linen and beet sugar industries in central Europe and cotton production in Belgium. But once restrictions on cheaper British cotton and New World cane sugar were lifted, many continental producers could not compete and had to close shop. The blockade completed the demise of Dutch commercial power and gave Great Britain, with its powerful navy, modern textile mills, and stable banking system, the opening to develop global economic dominance.

After 1815, the continent's economies were restarted largely on older rather than newer models, as nobles sought to return peasants to tilling the land and artisans only gradually and grudgingly adapted to new machines. In fact, *the* great source of conflict in rural Europe after 1815 was not low wages or poor factory conditions, but peasant anger about the landlords' increasing restriction of rights to use the forests. Rural dwellers in upland regions had long used the forests for hunting, wood gathering, and scavenging for acorns, berries, and mushrooms to supplement their own diets and those of their animals. But landlords in the Restoration era, wanting to put forest resources to their own ends, increasingly tried to restrict peasants' access to the forests. In 1848, violence over this issue would surge, as peasants assaulted officials who chopped down the oaks whose acorns the "little people"

1816–1817: The Year without a Summer

One of the preindustrial patterns to repeat itself in the post-Napoleonic world came in the form of famine, which struck the western hemisphere generally in the wake of the terrible weather events of 1816–1817.[2] The winter of 1815–1816 was unusually cold and wet, but worse, so was the following summer. Freak hailstorms finished off crops that had managed to ripen in the fields, and warm weather days were all too few. Grain prices began to rise, exacerbated by the dislocations that ensued as Napoleon's blockades were lifted and soldiers straggled back to their homes. Food shortages struck nearly everyone, but there was real famine in Ireland, Switzerland, and the Habsburg lands. Poor nutrition in the Balkans contributed to the spread of bubonic plague in that region, though the disease did not spread to western Europe as in the 1340s.

As the price of bread rose beyond the level most could pay, local officials began to note upticks in the number of vagrants and an increase in crime. Bread riots and the looting of grain supplies became everyday occurrences. In England in the spring of 1816, mobs carrying flags reading "Bread or Blood" demanded the setting of a maximum price for bread; hungry men and women plundered mills and bakeries and set fire to grain dealers' homes. There were major riots in Toulouse (France), Glasgow (Scotland), Limerick (Ireland), Catalonia (Spain), Bruges (Belgium), Tunis (northern Africa), and Christiana (Norway). Customs wars erupted between areas trying to prevent grain exports to areas where demand and prices were higher. In some places, especially in the German territories, Jews, some of whom earned their livings as cattle dealers, money-lenders, or grain merchants, were blamed for exorbitant prices or unpayable debts. This course of events—poor harvest followed by attacks on traditional representatives of

the subsistence economy and demands for a just price for bread—was hardly different than it had been a hundred years earlier, during the famine of 1709–1710, or two decades before, in 1788–1789, but this time improved transportation and states' greater abilities to provide aid made the actual death toll much less.

This story would repeat itself, in many ways, in the 1840s. Even later in the century, years of bad harvests would unleash suffering and, in some areas, famine. The revolutionary era did not ensure equal access to food, nor did the rise of capitalism solve the problem of provisioning the poor. It was actually rather difficult to push extra laborers off the land, as even the British discovered, and continental Europe in particular would remain a primarily agricultural region for decades. Thus, as the historian Niall Fergusson has argued, for most Europeans in the first half of the nineteenth century, the weather remained more important than the business cycle.[3] But the crisis also demonstrated that trade barriers and poor communication made for greater vulnerability and inefficiency. It certainly contributed to growing support for legislation such as the Prussian customs law of 1818, which created a free market for 10.5 million Germans, and laid the foundations for the *Zollverein,* the central European free-trade zone that strengthened the economies of many German states. The "year without a summer," as 1816–1817 has been termed, was yet another moment in which both the traditions of the past and the lessons for the future were simultaneously present.

QUESTION | *Why, for so many nineteenth-century Europeans, was the weather more important than the business cycle?*

---

relied on for pig-fodder and, in emergencies, to fill their stomachs.[4] This clash over forest resources is perhaps not the standard view of the nineteenth-century European economy—for that, see the section on Manchester later in this chapter. But it characterizes the still perilous and premodern economic circumstances in which most Europeans in this era lived, and those in which, in years of hardship such as 1816–1817, many of them died.

Religious Reorganization and Revival

In religious matters, too, we must beware assuming that the past was past and that the secular future promoted by the Jacobins had already arrived. The late Enlightenment and the Revolutionary eras had taken their toll on the

reputation of the clergy, on their income streams, and on their numbers—revolutionaries had murdered at least two thousand French priests, nuns, and monks, and disbanded many religious orders. But antireligious, as opposed to anticlerical, campaigns had never been popular, and many were relieved when, in his 1801 Concordat, Napoleon allowed the reopening of the churches. After his defeat, the clergy regained some of their lost clout—though they did not get back most of their land. Some embraced new prospects, setting sail for the colonies or adopting their sermons to urban audiences. Others assumed a defensive position, hoping to prevent the further erosion of their power and influence.

For the most part, they were not disappointed. Most Europeans after 1815 continued to be practicing

Christians. Neither the pious peasants of northern France nor the Eastern Orthodox Greeks gave up their beliefs, even when railroads and paper money finally reached them. People talked and read about religion all the time; the majority of university students still studied theology. A series of religious revivals commenced in the 1830s, as charismatic missionaries took to offering more emotional and personalized forms of faith. Methodism, which could claim only about 59,000 communicants in 1790, by 1850 had nearly 600,000 British followers. Though it became harder and harder to get men to go to church, women attended regularly, attracted, perhaps, by the enhanced role given to the Virgin Mary by Restoration-era Catholicism, or by the expanding role of Christian charitable work for middle-class women.

Revolutionary France had been the first to establish nonchurch, civil marriages in 1792. Napoleon continued the practice and spread it throughout his empire, though many restored regimes reversed his policies. England legalized civil marriage in 1836, enabling people to marry without a clergyman presiding. This permitted French and British men and women of different faiths (or no faith at all) to marry, although such marriages often caused considerable pain to the families concerned. Elsewhere, mixed couples had to convince a clergyman to preside at their weddings. Before 1848, there were still plenty of places where religious minorities faced *legal* restrictions on where they could live, what occupations they could hold, and how they practiced their faiths. Until 1917, Russian Jews were allowed permanent residence only in the Pale of Settlement in Russia's northwestern territory. Simply to visit St. Petersburg, a Jew had to present a special visa. There were deep hostilities—to say the least—between Catholics and Protestants in Ireland; and in the Balkans, tensions among Muslims, Christians, and Jews intensified throughout the nineteenth century. In some places, especially in western countries, a secular and tolerant future was in sight. But for most people, Europe's religious and conflict-ridden past lived on.

Nationalism Comes of Age

French patriotism—and the equally powerful Spanish, German, and Italian patriotisms that arose in response to Napoleonic occupation—left an enduring and revolution-inspiring legacy in the form of **nationalism.** The origins of nationalism stretch back at least into the eighteenth century, when people began to think that a nation must be more than the king and his courtly and clerical advisors. Instead, enlightened thinkers, such as Sieyès, J. G. Herder, and Adam Smith, argued the nation should be defined as the whole productive population of the state, united by a common culture and (usually) a common language (see Chapters 16 and 17). The mid-eighteenth-century revolt against the use of Latin or

How did the rise of liberal nationalism challenge the restored monarchies?

French as courtly, learned languages contributed to this movement, as those who spoke what had been seen as peasant languages, such as German, Romanian, Finnish, or Czech, began writing and teaching in those languages.

Nationalism, in the first years after Waterloo, was a movement confined largely to educated liberals and radicals. Even so, those who ruled multiethnic empires—such as the Russians, Ottomans, and Austrian Habsburgs—were rightly concerned about its spread. The Austrians found themselves besieged by a variety of nationalists, among them Germans, Hungarians, and Italians. The Russians put down numerous uprisings in Poland. As the czarist regime extended its control over minority ethnic groups in the Caucasus region and in central Asia, it brought into its empire a vast number of new nationalities whose loyalties it would have to buy or tame. Despite censorship and crackdowns, however, the Concert of Europe could not prevent people from increasingly thinking in nationalist terms.

One reason conservatives could not contain the spread of nationalism was that the centralization and rationalization of power had become indispensable for modern states. Starting in the period of absolutism, state bureaucracies had increasingly taken over functions the nobility and clergy had once served. Central states mustered and supplied armies, and local governments administered the education and justice systems. As the nineteenth century progressed, many states became major investors in infrastructure, building roads and ports, financing railways, and organizing postal and telegraph linkages in a way that continued absolutist practices but expanded them exponentially. Even where a unified or an independent state did not yet exist—as in Italy or the Czech lands—huge increases in the production of books, pamphlets, and newspapers expanded individuals' sense of being connected to other speakers of their language and sharpened their understanding of the social and ethnic hierarchies that disadvantaged members of their group. It is no wonder that the literate, at least, began to think of themselves as Frenchmen—or as Germans or Greeks—rather than as inhabitants of the Vendée or subjects of the duke of Hessen.

As states expanded their functions and as literacy spread, nationalism struck deeper roots into the middle and then lower classes. By the century's second half, when some conservatives gave up trying to repress it, nationalism had become inextricably bound up with European modernization and central to the way Europeans defined themselves. This shift created ever-increasing tensions within the multiethnic states in which most lived.

Inventing Modern Greece

Most early quests for nationhood were suppressed, but in the western portion of the Ottoman Empire, Greek nationalists did manage—with some help—to carve out a new nation-state. The Greek case is instructive not only because it was one of the few national causes to succeed in the pre-1848 era, but also because it was so clearly an invented, or reinvented nation, one *created* by the actions and ideas of individuals and by a series of contingent events. It is fully possible that modern Greece *might not* have won statehood in the 1820s, or that the new state might have looked very different, geographically, culturally, and politically. Focusing on Greece allows us to see how much of the formation of modern European nations was not foreordained, but the result of actions taken by individuals, and of historical coincidences.

During the Napoleonic Wars, the territory that is now modern Greece was still under Ottoman rule. But Greeks too had been exposed to enlightened and revolutionary ideas, thanks to contacts with Italian intellectuals or with Greeks who had settled in places like Paris, Vienna, and Budapest. Some cosmopolitan Greeks, like the Paris-based translator and intellectual Adamantios Koraes (1748–1833), began to dream of staging their own revolution, which would liberate Christian Greece from Ottoman "barbarism" and allow it to reestablish linkages with its glorious classical past. In 1803, Koraes made the case for Greek national independence in an inspiring speech that was widely circulated and won the backing of wealthy Greek merchants as well as many European intellectuals. Greeks at home and abroad formed a secret society, the Society of Friends, and swore an oath to serve their "sacred and suffering country," while Koraes pushed forward the creation of a purified Greek language, based on ancient Greek, as a means to unify all the Greeks, many of whom spoke mutually unintelligible dialects. The new Greek state made Koraes's version of Greek, called Katharevousa, the national language: culturally speaking, modern Greece has its origin in Koraes's Parisian dreams.

But the Greeks were not the only inhabitants of the Balkans who longed for independence from the Ottoman Empire. The Serbs, for example, had attempted a revolt in 1804, but their efforts had been repressed violently. Violence in Serbia continued sporadically until the Serbs gained limited autonomy in 1815. Ethnic Bulgarians and Romanians—Orthodox Christians like the Greeks and Serbs—also chafed under Ottoman rule, and some of the first revolutionary planners conceived their revolt as a general, Balkan-wide uprising. But the Romanian-Greek leader Alexander Ypsilantis failed to get Romanian or Serbian peasants to join a multiethnic rebellion. Thus, Ypsilantis, more by default than by design, began a "Greek" revolt against the Ottomans in 1821.

The Greek War of Independence succeeded not only because a large number of Greeks—many of them simple shepherds or farmers—were passionately committed to the cause, but also because other Europeans joined the fight. For elite Britons, Germans, Italians, and Frenchmen who had been schooled to appreciate classical culture and neoclassical art, ancient Greece had come to signify the foundation of European civilization. The British romantic poet Percy Bysshe Shelley wrote: "We are all Greeks—our literature, our religion, our arts have their root in Greece." Although Shelley was considerably more pro-Greek and more politically radical than most Europeans, this sort of rhetoric resounded powerfully. It won over thousands of

European volunteers, who flocked to Greece to fight for the revival of what the poet George Gordon, Lord Byron, in his world-famous poetic travel narrative *Childe Harold's Pilgrimage* (1818), called "the glory that was Greece."

To dispel the notion that nineteenth-century conflicts were neat and gentlemanly affairs, it is worth mentioning that the Greek War of Independence was marked by atrocities committed on both sides. Those of the Ottoman Turks—such as the massacre of the entire Greek population of the island of Chios in 1822—received great press coverage in Christian western Europe. The stories were part of a powerful propaganda campaign designed to whip up fear of "oriental" barbarism and appeal to "civilized" Europeans to support the Greek cause. But the Europeans who went to Greece knew that the Greeks had committed atrocities too and that they were internally divided and jealous of one another. Many came back home disillusioned, sure that whatever the new Greece

Eugene Delacroix, *Greece Expiring on the Ruins of Missolonghi* (1827) In 1826, after a long siege, Ottoman forces finally overran the Greek town of Missolonghi (where Lord Byron himself had died in 1824), avenging themselves on the Greeks by executing several thousand men and selling the women and children into slavery. Delacroix's painting was meant to call Europe's attention to the plight of the Greeks.

The Elgin Marbles

Who owns "the glory that was Greece"? Is the legacy of classical Athens something that Europeans possess equally, or do the Greeks—despite their early medieval transformation into the Christian Byzantine Empire and their long period under Ottoman rule—have unique title to it? The ownership question continues to be a difficult one in the case of Greek monuments, some of them acquired before the creation of the state of modern Greece and lovingly tended by elite connoisseurs, from the pope to the kings of Bavaria. In the case of the large collection of marble sculptures and frieze fragments taken from the Parthenon in Athens by Thomas Bruce, Lord Elgin, between 1801 and 1812, the debate over rightful ownership has been going on for nearly two hundred years and shows no sign of flagging.

We can be sure there were Greeks who lamented Elgin's plunder, but it was another English lord—Byron—whose critique of the Scottish Elgin first caught the public eye. Elgin's removal of the sculptures from the temple of Pallas Athena, Byron claimed, was a shameful act that wrenched these great relics from their ancient birthplace. In his highly popular epic poem *Childe Harold's Pilgrimage*, Byron enjoined his countrymen to curse Elgin, "the last, the worst, dull spoiler" of Greece's treasures.

Elgin replied that he had found the Parthenon in a state of total neglect and that, by taking the works of art, he had saved them from further damage or destruction.

In fact, Elgin—as British ambassador in Istanbul and, like Byron, a lover of all things Greek—had sought Ottoman permission first to copy and then to acquire the marble sculptures at just the right time, in 1799. The Ottomans expressed their gratitude to the British for helping push Napoleon out of Egypt by letting Elgin take some pagan Greek art—works of little consequence to the Muslim sultan. And Elgin had suffered in the acquisition of the monuments: during his time in Istanbul, he lost part of his nose to an infection, and when he was interned by the French on his way home to England, his rich wife journeyed ahead of him and began an affair that led to their divorce in 1808. Moreover, when Elgin first arrived home with the pediments, many connoisseurs had sniffed at the stripped down, archaic style of the frieze. Used to more delicate neoclassical forms, many regarded Elgin's authentically archaic marbles as ugly, and when the British Museum bought the treasures from Elgin in 1816, the governing board refused to pay him anything close to what he had spent on acquiring and storing the artifacts. Gradually tastes changed, but Elgin never got out of debt or lived down Byron's criticism.

Today there is no more reverently displayed monument in the British Museum than the Elgin Marbles—nor are any other of the museum's monuments so controversial. In the 1980s, after Greece joined the European Union, a new campaign began to return the marbles to the acropolis. For the Greeks, the British Museum's retention of the marbles seems to suggest that the former are not civilized enough to take care of these artistic treasures; the British insist that the sculptures were obtained legally and have become an essential part of the museum's collection and of British culture as well. In 2009, the Greeks completed a lavish new museum on the acropolis with a spectacular glass room specially designed to hold the marbles, hoping that Britain would at last return artifacts they insist are a vital part of their national patrimony. To whom do the Elgin Marbles really belong? The question is still an open one.

The Elgin Marbles Today, the Elgin marbles remain one of the most celebrated and carefully tended treasures in London's British Museum.

QUESTIONS | *Should the British return the Elgin Marbles? Why or why not?*

might be, it would never match the idealized glory of ancient Athens.

At first, the European governments stayed out of the fight. Metternich even forbade public discussion of the Greek war in the central European press. But volunteers continued to join the cause. Byron sailed to Greece in 1824—and promptly died of fever in the western Greek stronghold of Missolonghi. His death and reports of Ottoman atrocities committed when Missolonghi fell in 1826 inspired others to come to the aid of the Greeks. But more importantly, the Russians decided it was to their advantage to have the Greeks defeat the Ottomans, and the British and French, fearful that Russia's intervention would give Russia too much influence in the region, joined too. Together, the British, French, and Russians bottled up the Ottoman navy at Navarino in 1827, and when the Turkish commander Ibrahim Pasha refused to sign an armistice, they destroyed most of the Turkish fleet.

The war ended in 1829, but not until 1832 was a secure government formed for the new Greek state. Greece won its independence from the Ottomans, but the Great Powers made the Greeks choose a non-Greek of royal blood for their king, and they drew the new map, one that left many Greek speakers outside the new borders (Map 18.2). The new king, Otto, was from Bavaria and was deeply disliked by most of his Greek subjects, but he continued to rule until he was thrown out in a bloodless coup in 1864. He was replaced by a more likable Danish king, George I, who took the trouble to learn to speak Greek (Koraes's Katharevousa, of course).

MAP 18.2 | The Creation of Modern Greece, 1832–1913

The modern state of Greece was gradually carved out of the territory of the Ottoman Empire. *Compare the original Greek state won from the Ottomans in 1832 to the larger region in which Greek speakers lived. Does this map help you understand why the Greeks felt for so long that their nation-building attempts were unfinished? Imagine that you are an Ottoman Turk. How would you have reacted to the process of Greek nation-building?*

Belgium Is Born

Besides Greece, the other successful nationalist revolt of the nineteenth-century's first half occurred in the Kingdom of the Netherlands. Here, Congress of Vienna delegates had lumped together the territory that had once been the Spanish Netherlands (present-day Belgium and Luxembourg) with the Dutch Republic (today, the Netherlands), and given the crown to a Dutch king. In the 1820s, textile factories in the south and west suffered when cheaper British cotton goods flooded the market, and unemployment soared. In addition, many of the inhabitants of this southern, mostly French-speaking, and Catholic territory chafed under Dutch Protestant control. Infected by nationalist rhetoric and inspired by the July Revolution unfolding simultaneously in France, the discontented called for the creation of an independent state. They had to fight for it, and there were bloody battles as King Wilhelm I of the Netherlands tried to restore order.

But King Wilhelm failed, in part because Europe's monarchs refused his appeal for assistance. In their view, Belgian independence, like Greek independence, was permissible because it did not threaten to take territories from Russia, Austria, Britain, or Prussia. But the Great Powers insisted that Belgium must have a king and that he must have mixed loyalties. The man chosen was

Leopold I, a German prince-ling who was married to Princess Charlotte, the second in line for the British throne. To be sure that no one tried to conquer the small but strategically important state, in 1839 the Great Powers signed the Treaty of London, guaranteeing Belgian neutrality—a guarantee that the Belgians would invoke in 1914.

Nationalist Projects That Failed: Poland, Germany, and Italy

The Greeks succeeded, at least in part, in establishing a unified nation in the 1820s, but other attempts at nation-forming failed. In 1815, as we have seen, the Austrian Hapsburgs were allowed to claim Lombardy, Venetia, and the Dalmatian coast as their prizes, whereas control of the Italian states was returned to the pope and conservative princes. These moves angered Italian liberals and nationalists, who immediately began organizing secret societies dedicated to undermining these regimes. One of the most prominent of these societies was known as the Carbonari, or "charcoal burners," for those who swore allegiance to the group received a charcoal mark on their foreheads. The ardent nationalist Giuseppe Mazzini joined the Carbonari, but their ineffectualness eventually led him to organize his own nationalist group, "Young Italy," and to seek support for his cause abroad. Mazzini planned numerous (failed) uprisings against the Austrians, but always managed to slip through his jailers' hands. Other radicals were not so lucky. The Carbonari leader Ciro Menotti, for example, was hanged by the Austrians in Modena in 1831.

Nationalist movements in central and eastern Europe were also snuffed out. In the German states, Metternich forbade the student associations that had begun to champion the idea of uniting the smaller states. He despised and discouraged the work of liberal intellectuals like the brothers Jacob and Wilhelm Grimm, who collected folktales and archaic works in order to demonstrate the common cultural heritage of all German speakers. Using folk culture and language, they were inventing a unified Germany long before one existed on the map. The

MAP 18.3 | Revolutions and Failed Revolts, 1820–1831
Between 1820 and 1831, civil conflicts in Europe were widespread. *In what ways were the civil conflicts the fallout from the Congress of Vienna's map-making endeavors? Which of these revolts succeeded, and which failed?*

Grimm brothers held professorships at the University of Göttingen, in the state of Hanover, for a time, but were fired in 1837 for their liberal views. They did not suffer nearly as much as did Polish nationalists, however. Here, a November 1830 revolt led by nationalist nobles precipitated a Russian invasion, and a brief Russo-Polish War in which tens of thousands of Poles died, fled, or were sent to prison colonies in Siberia (Map 18.3).

Domestic Politics in the 1820s–1830s: From Revolution to Reaction

Considering all the factors described earlier—the (geographically uneven) evolution of a new political spectrum and of new nation-states, the overlapping of old and new economies, and the reorganizing of Europe's religious life—it is scarcely surprising that the 1820s

Which nations experienced a return to revolution in the 1820s and 1830s?

and 1830s would be a time of upheaval. This upheaval, however, took varying forms. Having surveyed the new nationalist projects that were launched in this era, we now examine domestic changes of differing kinds in three of Europe's largest kingdoms: France, England, and Russia.

Revolution Returns: France, 1830

By the later 1820s, France, home of the Revolution of 1789, was again seething with discontent. Louis XVIII had offered a constitution, had agreed to retain Napoleon's civil code (see Chapter 17) and had promised not to give property back to exiled aristocrats. But Charles X (r. 1824–1830), who succeeded Louis, became increasingly reactionary. Former soldiers, small farmers, and merchants who owed their rise from poverty to the revolutionary or Napoleonic governments looked on with horror as Charles appointed increasingly conservative ministers and censors. When he issued the July Ordinances in 1830, sending home the Chamber of Deputies and limiting the suffrage so that only about 20,000 of the richest Frenchmen could vote, both liberals and radicals had had enough. Demonstrators filled the streets of Paris, waving the tricolor flag and barricading major thoroughfares against the king's army.

The July Revolution in France, 1830 In July 1830, discontented French liberals and radicals joined together to compel King Charles X to abdicate in favor of a monarch who promised political and economic reforms, Louis Philippe of the House of Orléans. Here, a revolutionary standing atop a barricade celebrates the victory by brandishing the tricolor flag.

Charles X tried to abdicate in favor of another Bourbon, his nine-year-old grandson Henri, comte de Chambord, but the liberals insisted that their new constitutional monarch should be Louis Philippe of the French royal house of Orléans. Louis Philippe agreed to expand the suffrage slightly—allowing wealthy middle-class men to vote for the legislature—and to adopt the tricolor flag, the symbol of the moderate revolution. He took the title "king of the French," rather than king of France, suggesting that his rule depended on something like the social contract that enlightened reformers had championed.

The July Monarchy, as his regime came to be called, did not do away with the nobility or even with those who remained loyal to the Bourbon monarchs, but did support entrepreneurship and economic modernization. It also promoted national education and moderate forms of advancement based on merit for lawyers, military officers, and other professionals. Louis Philippe did not hesitate to call out the army when republicans or workers rose to protest his regime, and his prime minister François Guizot advised those who wanted to gain more social or political influence simply to "Enrich yourselves!"

Reform without Revolution: England

In Britain, voters elected delegates to the House of Commons, which during the eighteenth century gradually became the place where most of the nation's key political decisions were made. The leading party in the Commons got to choose the nation's prime minister, though the king or queen had to approve the candidate. The House of Lords (whose members inherited their seats) could veto legislation passed by the Commons, but could not initiate their own. Only Protestant men with a relatively large income were allowed to vote in elections; this meant that government represented the interests of only about 3 percent of the population. During the later period of the reign of George III (r. 1760–1820) and the reign of his spendthrift son George IV (r. 1820–1830), popular pressure grew to enlarge the electorate. Finally, under William IV (r. 1830–1837), Parliament passed the Great Reform Act of 1832, which gave the vote to a larger number of male property owners, but more importantly reformed voting procedures to increase the power of urban areas where liberalism was strong.

Britain had taken another step toward democratic governance, and middle-class liberals now won seats in the Commons and in town councils. But many radicals were disappointed that the bill did not enfranchise more Britons—and still left out most working-class men. They hoped that more reform might follow the ascent to the throne of William IV's eighteen-year-old niece, Victoria, in 1837. In 1838, those who wanted more reform drew up a document they called the Peoples' Charter in which they made six demands: universal manhood suffrage, salaries for members of Parliament, a secret ballot, annual elections, equal electoral districts, and abolition of property qualifications for members of the House of Commons. Three times—in 1839, 1842, and 1848—the supporters of the Charter, known as the Chartists, circulated a petition to put the Charter before Parliament. On its last round, according to one Chartist, the petition boasted nearly six million signatures, though probably fewer than half of these were authentic.

In general, Victoria favored the liberals and disliked the conservatives. But she also despised the radicals and thought the lower classes too ignorant, uncouth, and economically dependent to deserve the vote. After her marriage to the reform-minded Prince Albert of Saxe-Coburg, Victoria and Albert championed education and charity, but also condoned the suppression of radicalism. Chartists were arrested regularly and sometimes participated in violent strikes that were put down even more violently by police. When, in the revolutionary spring of 1848, some 20,000 Chartists assembled in London to present their petition for a third time, they were met by 100,000 constables mustered specially for the occasion and cheered on by the city's middle-class liberals. Parliament again refused to consider the Charter. Perhaps because the middling classes had been brought into governance, Britain escaped revolution, and after 1848, **Chartism** fizzled, to be replaced, ultimately, by other forms of working-class radicalism.

The Failed Decembrist Revolt in Russia In 1825, high-ranking Russian officers tried to prevent the accession of the arch-conservative Prince Nicholas to the throne. Their plot was discovered, and Nicholas called out guards loyal to himself to arrest and execute the reform-minded officers.

Reaction without Reform: Russia

In 1825, Europe's most reactionary regime, the Russian Empire, faced an internal challenge. After the death of Alexander I, the force behind the Holy Alliance, reform-seeking Russian military officers attempted to convince their garrisons not to swear loyalty to the next in line for the throne, Nicholas I (r. 1825–1855). Some of these men had fought Napoleon's armies in western Europe and had seen there a world without serfdom and with relative freedom of speech. These Decembrists, as they were called, knew that Nicholas would never bring such reforms to Russia. But their plot, the Decembrist revolt, was discovered. Nicholas I took the throne, crushed the revolt, and cracked down on the press. His trust in the elite destroyed, he established a political police force, devoted to spying on and persecuting political enemies of the regime. Nicholas believed Russia needed an authoritarian father to manage its enormous and diverse territories and tried to impose Russian orthodox Christianity and the Russian language on all his subjects. Even though literacy rates in Russia were much lower than elsewhere in Europe, censorship was much more extensive and crippled the free exchange of ideas. Ordinary Russians, even serfs, were rewarded for

denouncing persons who sympathized with the Poles or who criticized the regime. Nicholas so distrusted university students that they were required to have special haircuts so that in case of a riot, police could arrest them first.

In a way, Nicholas was right to suspect the students: in university circles, and among intellectuals living chiefly in St. Petersburg, liberal ideas *had* begun to circulate, albeit secretly. These people began to think that what Russia needed most was to embrace western ideas of the sort championed by the French in 1789. Russia, they thought, should look to the West for inspiration. But these westernizers faced opposition from a group that began to be called "slavophiles," people who believed that Russia should embrace its easternness, its distinctive Slavic culture, language, and heritage. Slavophiles typically championed Russian orthodox Christianity and argued that Russia should make itself the center of a Slavic empire, one that included the Balkans and a re-Slavicized Istanbul rather than imitating that of the Europeans. Russian intellectuals—both those for and those against westernizing—were among the first to invoke the concept of western civilization, by which they meant the liberal ideas and institutions whose realization even in Europe's westernmost regions was still incomplete.

Restoration Culture

Like the social world around it, the Restoration cultural world looked both backward and forward. It did not lose

How did Restoration culture reflect the period's contradictory tendencies?

touch with the past; in fact, this was the great age of history writing and of national histories. Nor did those we would now call social scientists give up on enlightened desires to find laws of human behavior; among students of political economy, especially, the search for laws continued. But writers and scholars also celebrated individuality and emotion, mystery, and sublimity.

Two worldviews, one major and one minor but both equally important, characterize the Restoration era. These two worldviews, romanticism and utilitarianism, were attempts to negotiate the often treacherous waters of the Restoration era, and both combined revolutionary elements and more conservative tendencies.

Romanticism: Mourning the Passing of the Past

Romanticism was a philosophical, literary, artistic, and musical movement that both clung to the past and reveled in visions of the future. Essentially an aesthetic reaction to the changes under way in European culture and society, romanticism substituted internal means to reshape humanity for the external means of social transformation tried by political revolutionaries. Thus, the Romantics' starting point was generally the individual, and they championed poetic geniuses, such as Lord Byron, whose creative talents allowed them to transcend

Contemplation and Solitude Among the Ruins This image, by the German artist Caspar David Friedrich, captures many of the preoccupations of the Romantics. Here, a well-dressed, solitary man contemplates a sunset from his perch inside a ruined Gothic church.

Baroque forms. But the Romantics also feared that, in the course of revolutionary changes, individuals had lost the integral relationships with one another, with God, and with nature that had provided stability and wholeness for so many centuries. Romanticism was thus an ambivalent movement, one that mourned breaking with the past—as seen in its painters' fascination with ruins—while it also celebrated the overcoming of conventions. Romantics found living in the modern age tormenting and, at the same time, seemed to revel in their own torments.

The sources of romanticism lie in the eighteenth century, in the loneliness of Robinson Crusoe and in Rousseau's celebration of wild and untamed nature (see Chapter 16). Central too was Kant's emphasis on subjective judgment in his 1790 *Critique of Judgment*. Here, too, he described the key romantic concept of the sublime. To experience the sublime was to confront something that was not merely beautiful, but that also awed or even terrified the spectator with its grandeur and power, such as a vast ocean, or an unscalable mountain peak. Worshipping the sublime in nature or in art was one way in which the Romantics differentiated themselves from their enlightened predecessors who had championed order, intelligibility, balance, and light. The Romantics, by contrast, loved disorder, mystery, violence, excess, and darkness. In their view, the Enlightenment's admiration for reason had given short shrift to the emotions. Many Romantics were fascinated by suffering and by grand crimes, such as Prometheus's theft of fire from the gods or Satan's rebellion against God. Indeed, grief, sorrow, pain, and woe are so central to romanticism that the whole philosophy has been summed up as *Weltschmerz*, the sense of the whole world in pain.

ROMANTICISM IN LITERATURE. Romanticism reached its full expression in literature, especially in poetry. The German poet Friedrich Schiller argued that mere words or concepts do not do justice to life; they address only the mind and do not engage the all-important emotions. One must go beyond rational discourse and speak to the feelings—acknowledging all the while that all of nature's secrets or the true content of other peoples' hearts may never be known. Central to romantic poetry was this kind of post-Enlightenment despair—about the possibility of true and lasting love, about reason's capacity to provide full knowledge of the world, and about humankind's ability to force nature to do its bidding.

But characteristic too of the Romantics was the desire never to give up the search for essential truths. In fact, they described the individual's very nature as that of the eternal seeker. The romantic poet Friedrich Hölderlin captured this idea in a line from his prose poem *Hyperion*: "No action, no thought can reach the extent of your desire. That is the glory of man: that nothing ever suffices."[5] The protagonist in Johann Wolfgang von Goethe's epic poem *Faust* epitomizes this ceaseless quest—Faust so desperately desires superhuman knowledge that he is willing to sell his soul to the devil to get it. Romantic literature is full of quests to find or rescue a beloved soul-mate and of suicides instigated by the failure of those quests. The theme of the untimely death of the hero, as in Alexander Pushkin's Russian epic *Eugene Onegin,* or the heroine, as in François-René de Chateaubriand's *Atala* or Germaine de Staël's *Corinne,* is omnipresent. The reader is called upon to shed tears for the demise of these extraordinary individuals, even when they, like Faust, or the brilliant poetess Corinne, have transgressed normal moral boundaries.

Several poets captured the very essence of romanticism: Byron, Shelley, John Keats, and William Wordsworth in England; Schiller, Goethe, and Hölderlin in the German states. They took inspiration from ancient Greek poetry—especially the Homeric epics—and from several nonwestern pieces, the Indian drama *Sakuntala* and the Persian love poetry of Sa'di. Leading Romantic novelists included the Scotsman Sir Walter Scott, author of *Ivanhoe,* and the Frenchmen Victor Hugo and Alexandre Dumas, authors of *Les Miserables* and *The Count of Monte Cristo,* respectively. In each of these works, the novelist used the historical setting to provoke readers to think about the worlds that were being lost in the process of modernization. Most of the Romantics were no friends of the Old Regimes, but neither were they entirely comfortable with modernizing processes. Like Tocqueville, they were perceptive enough to see some aspects of the future—the coming of mechanization and the rising importance of natural science—but they did not necessarily approve.

ROMANTICISM IN ART AND MUSIC. The same might be said of romanticism in painting and in music. Artists and musicians used themes similar to those described previously: the sublime but untamed power of nature, the sufferings of the misunderstood poet or the unrequited lover, the passing of time and the losses incurred as a result. Caspar David Friedrich, the great German Romantic painter, specialized in painting ruins; in his work the feeling of sadness and loss at the destruction of human handiwork is compensated for by the sense that nature is simply taking back its own. Friedrich's other paintings dramatize the loneliness of the individual, whose face the viewer does not see and to whom nature refuses to reveal itself entirely, or they document nature's violent majesty, which overwhelms humankind's spiritual imagination. Similarly, the English painter John Martin created masterful scenes of rocky crevasses of the apocalyptic end of ancient civilizations.

Music, some claimed, proved to be the art form most suitable to the Romantic imagination, for it could evoke emotion and spirituality without running up against the problem of how to represent these fleeting and internally felt sensations. Romantic composers appreciated the neoclassical elegance of works by Mozart and Haydn, but ventured farther away from conventional rules for composition. The symphonies and sonatas of Ludwig van Beethoven and the intimate nocturnes of the Polish composer Friedrich Chopin sought to express internal human

Franz Liszt, Virtuoso The Hungarian pianist and composer Franz Liszt was renowned throughout Europe for his ability to perform extremely complex pieces with great passion. His recitals played so powerfully on the emotions that numerous women fainted and had to be carried out of his performances.

passions by using dissonance and dramatic variations in tone, pace, and style. Some of these pieces—many of them very difficult to play correctly—were performed by court musicians, but increasingly audiences wanted to hear bravura performances, and a few self-promoting soloists, like Niccolò Paganini and Franz Liszt, became wildly popular throughout Europe.

In an age after the collapse of courtly entertainments, but before the era of sound recordings, the early to mid-nineteenth century was a great period for opera. Some of the most famous composers of the period, including Giacomo Meyerbeer, Carl Maria von Weber, and Hector Berlioz, adapted Romantic poems or plays to their music. Others drew on folklore or national epic poetry to create narratives that more or less made sense. Audiences demanded, and got, fewer religious works and more pieces with catchy tunes and lots of swooning, grieving, or fighting. In some cases, composers snuck liberal or nationalist themes into their pieces, inspiring audiences to denounce the authorities or even to riot. The chorus sung by Hebrew slaves in Giuseppe Verdi's *Nabucco* was widely interpreted as a call to Italian nationalists to overthrow Austrian oppression, and the motto "Viva Verdi" was used not only to praise the anticlerical, liberal nationalist composer, but also to demonstrate support for the unification of Italy under Victor Emanuel, king of Piedmont ("Viva **Vittorio Emanuele, Re d'Italia!**").

PHILOSOPHICAL ROMANTICISM AND THE IDEA OF WESTERN CIVILIZATION.
The American literary scholar M. H. Abrams famously described the typical Romantic narrative, in philosophy as in literature, as that of the *necessary* expulsion from the Garden of Eden. According to Romantic accounts, humankind *must* stray from God and home and travel the long road of experience in order to earn its return to Paradise as a mature, self-conscious species. The writings of G. F. W. Hegel (1770–1831), Prussia's most famous philosopher of the 1810s and 1820s, partook of this narrative, but not of the emotionalism of Romantic literature and music. His school of thought is known as idealism, because for Hegel, the world had to have first been thought by a being he called the Absolute Spirit before it could exist in reality. For Hegel, the task of philosophy was to describe the evolution of this Spirit as it embodied itself in human reason and then gradually realized itself in history. The Spirit could not realize itself, Hegel argued, without engaging in what he called dialectical conflict, in which, as in an argument, a thesis is stated, then contradicted, and finally a synthesis of two positions is found. These conflicts might be painful, but for Hegel they were necessary. Like Edmund Burke, he believed that the development of both thought and social relations had to evolve organically and that attempts to skip steps would lead to irrational speculation and violence. Only at the end of a very long series of conflicts would the Absolute Spirit and human reason be fully at one with one another, and humankind could, metaphorically, return to the Garden, fully rational, fully developed, and fully at peace.

Hegel's idealism was deeply historical, but it also partook of the Enlightenment's racial hierarchies and his own liberal and Christian prejudices against the non-European world. European rational thought, legal and political equality (at least for the upper classes), neoclassical and romantic cultural achievements, and bourgeois values defined civilization itself, in contrast to which all the other cultures were backward. In particular, Hegel claimed, Asian cultures had declined and become irrational and despotic. It was the turn of Europe (especially, in his view, Prussia) to guide progress in the future. Hegel's philosophy and similar liberal philosophies championed an idealized view of Europe that hardly reflected the continent's many diverse cultures. But this worldview laid the foundations both for a powerful vision of what civilization should be and for a kind of hubris that would justify European expansionism to come.

Utilitarianism: Planning for the Future

Utilitarianism was a less developed and less artistically resonant philosophy than was romanticism, but its impact in some spheres was more pronounced. It was cen-

tral, for example, in the tradition of political-economic thinking pioneered by Adam Smith and carried forward by the English pastor Thomas Malthus (1766–1834). In 1798, in response to the miseries created by this changing economy, Malthus wrote an *Essay on the Principle of Population* in which he pictured the European economy as a zero-sum game. Population, he claimed, grew exponentially and thus would always outstrip the production of food, which increased only arithmetically. Thus, Malthus claimed, either nature or God (for Malthus they were essentially the same) would be compelled to eliminate excess mouths; offering the poor relief or reducing the price of bread would simply increase the number of those who would have to suffer. Malthus did not mean to be hardhearted; he meant to offer a realistic analysis and a useful one. His theories, however, would be used to justify the curtailing of charity for the needy.

Malthus still believed in God, but in the next generation of thinkers, utilitarianism became a secular moral philosophy. It stated that the good should be defined not according to traditional Christian ideas, but simply as that which benefited the most people. Its foremost proponent, Jeremy Bentham (1748–1832), thought religion did more harm than good, inflicting "unprofitable suffering" and "imposing useless deprivations" on individuals, as well as "creating a particular class of persons incurably opposed to the interests of humanity" (that is, the clergy).[6] Rather than looking to God or older authorities for guidance, societies in Bentham's view should simply follow what he called "the greatest happiness principle" and seek to maximize happiness and minimize pain.

A radical English lawyer with an abiding interest in politics and economics, Bentham wrote many pamphlets advocating what he saw as more sensible approaches to social policy, all of them aimed at improving material conditions for the majority and expanding freedoms for the persecuted. Long before most of his contemporaries—even his radical ones—he supported women's rights and prison reform, the abolition of slavery, and the decriminalization of homosexuality. Although he published his critiques of religion under a pseudonym, his atheism was well known, and the wish he expressed in his will—that his body be preserved in a wooden display case rather than buried—was honored. Bentham's "Auto Icon" can still be seen at University College, London.

Bentham's close friend and disciple James Mill (1773–1836) brought together utilitarian ideas and historical analysis. Mill also brought people together, founding the Political Economy Club in 1821. Club members did not agree on everything, but they held in common a commitment to liberal reform and the pursuit of the good for the greatest number. Implicitly this might have been a radical idea; but their opposition to taking revolutionary action and their commitment to letting the market gradually "raise all boats," as Smith had suggested it would, undercut their political radicalism. Utilitarianism ended up being applied mostly in the economic rather than the political sector and tended to excuse liberal hardheartedness with respect to the poor rather than encourage grand-scale social reorganization. The one place utilitarianism did sanction change was in India, where it was used to justify the rationalization and Anglicization of Indian culture and society, "for its own good."

James Mill's son, John Stuart Mill (1806–1873), was a child prodigy who inherited his father's commitments to political economy and to furthering individual liberties. As a member of Parliament, John Stuart Mill pushed for rights to be extended to all, including women. In his most famous publication, *On Liberty* (1851), Mill insisted on the individual's right to think or act in any way he or she chooses, as long as others are not harmed, and argued that healthy societies were those that allowed unpopular opinions to be aired. One of Mill's friends called *On Liberty* "the chief textbook of Freedom of Discussion," and indeed it has become a canonical statement of liberal philosophy. His message boiled down to the necessity that the state should leave people—and markets—alone. It is perhaps poetic justice that only five people were present to see Mill buried in 1873.

If the Romantics dwelt, even wallowed, in the past, the utilitarians put all their faith in the eventual achievement of happiness. John Stuart Mill, indeed, once quoted what he took to be a characteristic statement of Jeremy Bentham's: "Take me forward, I entreat you, to the future—do not let me go back to the past."[7] Living in England, the utilitarians were well positioned to envision the future—for there, unlike on the continent, it was ever more obvious that another kind of revolution had taken hold—and opened with it a whole new way of life.

The Industrial Revolution

Together with the French Revolution, the process we term the **Industrial Revolution** marks the onset of modern times. Although it was a gradually occurring and unevenly experienced development rather than an event, in the end it proved more transformative than either the French or the American Revolutions. The Industrial Revolution laid the foundations for nineteenth-century European colonization as well as for the destructiveness of the great wars of the twentieth century and for the continuing imbalances between western and nonwestern wealth and power in the twenty-first century. Yet it is perhaps the hardest of any revolution to explain. It is a revolution that built on the quieter revolutions of the Old Regimes, but other factors also contributed to it: the population boom of the later eighteenth century; revolutions in transportation and communications; the end of serfdom; advances in mining and metalworking; legal revolutions such as the breaking of guild monopolies or the churches' rights to declare holidays; and ecological events, such as soil exhaustion and deforestation, which

Where and how did the Industrial Revolution begin?

forced peasants to seek work in the towns. Indeed, we can say that the Industrial Revolution was at least three revolutions rolled into one: a revolution in technology, a revolution in capital, and a revolution in labor. What, then, catalyzed such a transformation? We can say only that the causes of the Industrial Revolution were many and that no single factor is by itself sufficient to explain what happened.

Complicating the matter is the difficult question of *when* the Industrial Revolution occurred. Nowhere did it happen overnight. It was hardly even on the horizon when Adam Smith published *Wealth of Nations* in 1776. At that time, even in Britain, Smith was still—to his distress—living in an agricultural and mercantile economy, one in which very small amounts of capital were being put into manufacturing while comparatively large sums were being invested in land. By the time Alexis de Tocqueville visited Manchester in 1830, however, all three factors—technology, capital investment, and labor—had transformed Britain in ways Smith could not have predicted. But these transformations were not at all visible in Greece or Portugal or Russian Poland at the time. As in the case of the military and commercial revolutions and of the Enlightenment, the Industrial Revolution developed and spread unevenly across Europe's many diverse regions.

Why Britain?

In many respects, the easiest question to answer about the Industrial Revolution is the *where* question: historians agree that it began in Britain, especially in the coal-rich, textile-producing regions of northern England. Here there was a concentrated population of preindustrial laborers, who already had some useful skills and were no longer needed to tend the land. These workers found employment in small factories outfitted with new machines. In northern England in particular there were easy-to-reach coal deposits, as well as a network of waterways, vital to powering waterwheels and moving supplies (Map 18.4). Britain's leading role in the commercial revolution had left it with a privileged position in the world economy, modest amounts of surplus capital, and the world's most stable currency. Together with what the world historian Kenneth Pomeranz has called "the ecological windfall" provided by Britain's unique access to the New World, this combination of technology, capital, and labor freed Britain from the constraints to industrial development posed by shortages of land and energy and made it home to the Industrial Revolution.

Cultural factors also contributed to making Britain home to this revolution. British society did not, on the whole, condemn the making of money or the taking of risks. The British market was not free, but it was less regulated, and those regulations were evaded more easily, than was the case on the continent. British taxes were high, but neither confiscatory nor arbitrary, as in parts of Italy and Spain. The British Isles were also home to numerous skilled and curious tinkerers, people who had training as shipbuilders, clockmakers, printers, and miners, or who served as instrument makers. But its guild systems were weak, and competition helped increase efficiency and lower costs of production. And finally, Britain had a few more upwardly mobile consumers, women and men who wanted to improve their lot by taking risks, moving house, and deferring spending in order to save for luxuries like tobacco, tea, travel, books—and new clothes.

Why Textiles?

After the *where* question, perhaps the easiest question to answer about the Industrial Revolution is the *what* question: What did the Industrial Revolution produce? Although later in the nineteenth century iron and steel became almost synonymous with industrial development, the most significant and symbolic products of the early Industrial Revolution were textiles. The manufacturing of fabrics traditionally used in Europe—wool, linen, and silk—was speeded up and improved greatly in the period between 1760 and 1830. Far more important, however, was cotton, the cloth whose light weight, cheap cost, and colorful patterns made it *the* most desirable material for nineteenth-century coats and dresses, curtains, and overalls. By the eighteenth century's end, cotton had become inexpensive and abundant, thanks to increased production worldwide, especially in the U.S. South, where the reduction in its cost resulted from better land management and the use of slave labor. Cotton was easier to spin than linen or wool and easier to weave than silk; it could also be dyed and easily washed. To understand the Industrial Revolution, we must understand the evolution of cotton production, for clothes, in more ways than one, made nineteenth-century industrial society.

In the eighteenth century and long into the nineteenth century, most textiles were produced through the "cottage" system, in which spinning and weaving were done by individual workers in their homes (see Chapter 15). This system worked well for women weavers who could spin thread at home while watching children or in between other household tasks, and for peasant producers who could work part time. But it was not particularly efficient, especially as entrepreneurs applied mechanization and steam power to the production process. The gradual increase in the size and cost of machinery eventually made the concentration of labor, capital, and resources in factories the most efficient and cost-effective means of producing textiles and created a new model of manufacturing.

The production of cheaper, lighter, and more easily washable cloth also contributed greatly to revolutions in fashion and in marketing, as middle-class consumers got used to the idea of changing their clothes with the seasons and either buying ready-made clothing, or, after the

MAP 18.4 | The First Industrial Revolution in Britain, c. 1760–1850

This map shows the location of coalfields, major population centers, industrial areas, and major rail lines in Britain before about 1850. *How does this map help us understand why Britain was the first European country to industrialize?*

1840s, purchasing their own sewing machines to run up a new dress. Key in the process of cotton manufacture was what the English added: the application to spinning and weaving of the new machines.

A Revolution in Gadgets

The British historian T. S. Ashton once boiled down the essence of the Industrial Revolution to the "wave of gadgets" that swept England after 1760. Indeed, new machines were a crucial element in provoking economic and cultural change. In the eighteenth century, European, especially British, metalworkers developed the skills to produce these new gadgets and, more important, to improve them over time. Already in 1712, the English engineer Thomas Newcomen had made a steam engine that could be used to pump water from mines. But Newcomen's engine could not be turned to other productive uses until James Watt developed the separate condenser (patented in 1769, produced in 1775).

Could Europe Have Become a China?

For many years, scholars interested in what was known as the preindustrial, developing world asked the question: why didn't China (or Kenya or India) have an industrial revolution like the one Europe experienced in the nineteenth century? This question presupposed that the right and natural way for societies to modernize was the way Europe, and especially Britain, had done it, and that every nation that had not followed this path lacked something—ingenuity, proper institutions, or social, political, and legal conditions—that Europe possessed. As we have already noted, Europe's diversity should preclude such generalizations. This line of argument usually assumed, too, that by about 1760, Europe was already far richer and more advanced in pre-industrial manufacturing than was Asia or Africa, and that it used its own resources and resourcefulness to give it an industrial head-start. Recently, however, the world historian Kenneth Pomeranz has called into question the notion that Europe's industrial primacy was inevitable. He observed that in the eighteenth century, Europe and China were in many ways rather similar. Noting that both Britain and the Yangtze delta (areas with comparable eighteenth-century economies) were already short of land and of fuels (especially timber), Pomeranz, in his landmark study *The Great Divergence* (2001) turned the traditional question around to ask, why didn't Europe become a China?

His answer was that Europe, and especially Britain, benefited after 1780, and especially after 1815, from what he called the "ecological windfall" provided by access to North American, Caribbean, and Asian markets. Even after American independence, Britain continued to lean heavily on imports—particularly cotton and sugar—from its colonies and former colonies. By 1815, Britain was import-ing more than 100 million pounds of cotton per year from the Americas; by 1830, the figure was 263 million pounds. By the 1860s, large amounts of cotton were also being produced in India and Egypt. Much of this cotton was produced very cheaply, as it was grown on large plantations where slaves or indentured servants did the work. Buying cheap cotton on the world market, especially as transportation costs fell with the arrival of steamships and railroads, allowed British mill owners to enlarge their businesses and hire more workers as the population boomed. Meanwhile, in the Yangtze delta, a similar population boom was put to work in more intensive forms of agriculture—and limited sources of wood, water, and coal made it difficult to mechanize production. Thus, access to agricultural zones in the Americas and Asia rescued Britain from a developmental path that it might have followed, one oriented to labor-intensive production for home use—a path that would have made Britain a China.

Pomeranz did not discount British or European exceptionalism. He acknowledged that Britain was far ahead in the invention of gadgets, an aspect of industrialization emphasized by other scholars. Pomeranz noted as well the importance in Britain of the earlier agricultural and commercial revolutions. But in focusing on the "ecological relief" that Europe, and particularly Britain, got from exploiting its relationship to the New World at a crucial moment in global history, Pomeranz has succeeded in making us rethink the Industrial Revolution from a fascinating new environmental and global perspective.

QUESTION | *What factors allowed the Industrial Revolution to happen in England, rather than in China?*

Meanwhile, other tinkerers sought a means to hasten the spinning of thread, a process that took at least four times as long as weaving. In 1764, John Hargreaves invented the spinning jenny, a large-scale spinning wheel that allowed a worker to spin onto eight spindles simultaneously. Richard Arkwright's water frame, patented in 1769, used power from a waterwheel to spin thread quickly—but Arkwright's frame spun onto only one spindle at a time. Combining the two inventions was Samuel Crompton's "mule," essentially a water-powered spinning jenny, invented in 1779. Finally, in 1803, the mule was converted for use with steam power. By end of the nineteenth century, a mule could produce thread 200 to 300 times as fast as by hand. These power-driven mules were the gadgets around which were built the infamous "satanic mills" of Manchester—and of Barmen, in western Germany, and Lowell, Massachusetts, to name just a few of the Industrial Revolution's major sites.

There were, of course, other important technological innovations. The 1784 development of the "puddling and rolling" method of iron production allowed pig iron, the product that came out of blast furnaces, to be converted into the wrought iron that industries could use. The British inventor Joseph Bramah, a carpenter by trade, turned his skills to improving flush toilet design (1778). In 1784, he patented a lock so difficult to pick that not until 1851 did someone succeed in opening it without the proper key. His most important invention was the hydraulic press (1795), which could be used in many ways, including for the stamping of iron, and, in modified form, for the pumping of beer in pubs.

One technological change often led to others. Steam applied to ships and then to wagons on rails laid the foundation for the huge leap forward in transportation made possible by the 1830s. The invention of steamships and especially railroads pushed forward the development of numerous other innovations. Interest in technological improvements snowballed over time. In the early eighteenth century, a relatively small number of craftsmen or small landowners were interested in improvements, but by the 1850s there were 1,020 associations for technology and scientific knowledge in Britain with at least 200,000 members. Elsewhere, too, the cascade of new technologies—from the development of bleaching powder (1798) to the first successful sewing machine (1846)—inspired refinements and new inventions. As steam power replaced less predictable and less efficient human, animal, wind, and water power, transportation and communication became easier and less costly. Elite consumers across the world could now buy, steal, or copy these innovations, and adapt them to local uses.

The development of industrial commodities was not always smooth, nor was it always a successful enterprise. Many technologies were tried that didn't take or didn't work, and many inventors didn't succeed. The Mouchot brothers' mechanized bakery of 1847, powered by dogs running on a treadmill, never caught on.[8] There were numerous other attempts to mechanize the production of bread—that all-important commodity—including the invention of machines that supposedly reduced the usual nine-hour process of bread making to a few minutes—

The Spinning Jenny Invented in 1764, the spinning jenny allowed textile workers to speed up production by winding thread simultaneously onto eight or more spindles.

invariably with major consequences for the bread's taste. The introduction of yeasts with shorter rising periods speeded up the production of bread so that bakers needed four and a half hours, rather than nine hours, to produce their loaves. But the mechanization of bread making never really caught on, and most Europeans today still buy bread from bakeries, not from supermarkets.

A Revolution in Transportation

The iron horse, or railway engine, proved to be the most consequential innovation of the Industrial Revolution's gadgets. It too was the product of decades of tinkering, as horse-drawn mining wagons evolved gradually into steam-powered carriages on rails. Disasters often occurred, as when one of the foremost boosters of the Manchester line was run over by his own train. But once the completion of the Manchester-Liverpool line in 1830 demonstrated the efficiency of railway travel, the technology caught on like wildfire. Railroads offered considerable advantages over canal boats and coaches: they could carry much heavier freight and soon achieved speeds much beyond what boats and coaches could manage. By 1836, a trip from London to Edinburgh, which took the coach (in good weather) at least ten days, had been cut to less than two. The speed of travel continued to increase, and by 1850 some express trains could reach speeds of fifty miles per hour, far faster than any human had traveled in history.

The new experience was thrilling to many, terrifying to some, but to all a sign that the world had changed. Each time a railroad line reached a new town there were celebrations; possessing a railway station meant, in some

CHRONOLOGY	Key Gadgets of the First Industrial Revolution
DATE	**GADGET**
1712	Thomas Newcomen's steam engine
1764	James Hargreaves's spinning jenny
1769	James Watt's steam engine
1769	Richard Arkwright's water frame
1779	Samuel Crompton's mule
1795	Joseph Bramah's hydraulic press
1829	George Stephenson's Rocket

way, that the community had been brought into the modern age and made part of a new, interlinked set of markets and workplaces. Drastically reducing the cost of transportation for raw materials, consumer goods, and people, the railroad widened middle-class Europeans' horizons, allowing them to escape the dangers of the older highways and to think about such previously aristocratic luxuries as traveling for pleasure or purchasing goods made in faraway places. National and international marketplaces evolved as the pace of commerce increased. Of course, for the very poor and for those whose towns were *not* on the railroad, as was the case for virtually all of southern and eastern Europe in this period, the iron horse was merely a rumor—or a catastrophe, for some cottage industries were put out of business by competitors lucky enough to enjoy a nearby rail line.

A quick glance at the map of railroad building before 1850 documents Britain's industrial edge in the period before 1850 (see Map 18.4 for Britain; Map 21.1, p. 671, for Europe). Britain also led the way in follow-up developments, such as the telegraph system—essential to tell train operators when other trains were on the track ahead—and the glass and iron railway station, an efficient way to cover large spaces cheaply. The railways brought with them new habits, such as commuting long distances to work, and sea-bathing for the masses. They encouraged the publishing of cheaper and easier-to-read newspapers and the construction of railway bookstalls and restaurants, the first of the new businesses to wrap themselves around the stations rather than, as formerly, around churches and market squares. Calculating and standardizing the departures of trains made necessary the possession of accurate pocket watches and, in the United States, the development of time zones in order to predict the time a train leaving Boston might arrive in St. Louis.

The building of railways led to all sorts of improvements in the making of iron and the engineering of bridges, and to new sorts of blood, sweat, and tears for the poorly paid laborers hired to blast through mountains and lay rails across marshes and prairies. The factor that held back the swifter development of railway routes, however, was not a lack of innovative ideas or the difficulty of finding qualified engineers and willing workers, but the short supply of something very basic to industrial capitalism: money.

Europe's First Railroad Line As this 1834 drawing shows, the Manchester-Liverpool line, opened in 1830, was immediately put to use not only for carrying passengers (first class in the top row, and second class in the next one), but also for freight and (on the bottom row) livestock.

A Revolution in Capital

Inventors and enterprising landowners needed capital—although until railway production got under way, a very little often sufficed to produce a new gadget or even to get a factory started. The first factories were usually built in the countryside, near sources of running water, and were quite small, employing just a handful of workers. The division of labor according to task in these enterprises made production more efficient; they were, in essence, modified craft workshops. Operating such a business did not, at first, require a whole new system of financing. Most grew gradually, as modest profits were plowed back into modest enterprises. But mechanization and economies of scale soon changed the game, at least in textile production. The Welsh entrepreneur Robert Owen, for example, borrowed £100 to start his first factory in Manchester in 1789. In 1800, he bought a mill in New Lanark, Scotland, and by 1810, he was rich enough to launch his pet project: a communal manufacturing village.

In 1790 or in 1815 or even in 1830, the only place where the financial system was sophisticated and stable enough to make such investments was Britain. Only in Britain did private investors, rather than the state, finance infrastructural projects, like the building of canals, roads, and railways. On the continent, after the demise of the Dutch Republic, financial institutions were not yet able or willing to lend large sums to entrepreneurs. Only in the 1850s and 1860s did continental Europeans begin to devise new means to raise very large sums, by way of government-backed securities and investment banks, large-scale private companies, and huge new public investments in the building of roads, harbors, armies, and railroads. Having the hard currency to buy steam-powered "mules" or to hire more wage-workers was essential to pushing the Industrial Revolution forward, but for much of the early nineteenth century, the amounts invested in industrial production remained modest. It took time to convince non-Britons to invest in manufacturing, rather than to sink their capital into the traditional form of wealth: land.

It also took time to convince people that capital should be allowed to flow freely from nation to nation and that trade barriers made for inefficient economies. Products of the age of mercantilism, European states and statesmen still believed in the necessity of tariffs of some kind to protect their industries and to keep hard currency from leaving home. But gradually, the idea of free trade began to gain supporters. The English, predictably, were the biggest boosters, but others followed. Seeing how the patchwork of tariffs extracted by each of the small German states crippled their trading possibilities, German liberals, in the later 1820s and 1830s, pushed to expand what they called the *Zollverein*, or free-trade zone. The *Zollverein*, which included Prussia but not heavily protectionist Austria, would indeed boost the economies of the region and provide a partial blueprint for the unified German state created in 1871.

A Revolution in Labor

Most historians agree that one of the factors that contributed to Britain's rapid industrialization was its large population of free labor, resulting from the agricultural and commercial revolutions, increasing life expectancy, and the rising population over the course of the eighteenth and nineteenth centuries. England's population is estimated to have grown from less than 6 million in 1700 to about 8.5 million in 1800, but over the next fifty years the population grew by 100 percent, to over 17 million. Many of these people tried to stay on the land, saved from starvation only by the passage of the first Poor Law of 1795. But the new wage subsidies may also have given unemployed workers the courage to leave the land and seek employment in the new factories.

Many of those who took jobs in factories had formerly been employed in preindustrial cottage production, which was concentrated in northern England and southern Scotland. For them, spinning and weaving were familiar jobs. But as more and more expensive machinery was introduced, both their working and nonworking lives underwent a transformation whose magnitude was unprecedented in history. Unlike people or animals, machines did not tire or need to eat. Seasons did not matter to machines, nor did holidays. Machines might break down, but they could be quickly repaired or thrown away and replaced with identical models. Delighted with the machinery's new efficiency and productivity, owners wanted them operated continuously and increasingly wanted workers to behave like their machines, never to tire or need to be fed or cared for.

In the towns and cities where factories sprang up, everyday life changed dramatically. Gone, quite suddenly, were traditional rhythms of life, in which the seasons dictated when work was done and most economies were local, limited in their offerings, and based on barter. With the guilds now broken, workplace discipline centered increasingly on keeping expensive machinery operational. Gone were the old landlords, who confiscated most of the land's produce; dominated the social, religious, and cultural life of the region; and called the political shots. But gone too was the era in which tradition dictated that landowners allow their tenants to use common pastures or forests for foraging, and that they feed the little people in times of want.

In place of the seasons, there were punch-clocks and gas lighting. As people increasingly worked for wages paid at an hourly rate, the seasons became meaningless and time-telling—something unnecessary for most peasants—became critical. The new masters were different, many of them less well-born and harder working than the old landlords. The bigger the business, the more likely it was that owners would rarely be seen on the factory floor; even the middle managers increasingly lived in districts distant from those of the workers. Pay and conditions were determined less by local conditions than by international prices and markets—or so workers were told. Women and children, who had always worked on the land, also streamed into the mills and mines, and only gradually were the appalling conditions of their labor and their very long working hours regulated.

THE SHIFT TO WAGE WORK. Where industrialization set in, people no longer ate what they produced. Now they had to use their wages to buy food. Whereas previously they had depended on the weather and the soil for good harvests, and sometimes suffered famine when nature turned cruel, now they depended on constant employment. Wages for most industrial workers remained at subsistence levels for the first half of the nineteenth century. When there were market downturns, as in 1825–1826, 1836–1837, 1839–1842, and 1846–1848, workers were thrown out of work and risked starvation. Still, most managed to eke out a living. Those who did starve in large numbers in the nineteenth century were not urban industrial workers, but rural peasants who had the ill fortune to live in nonindustrialized countries such as Russia or Ireland.

It would be a mistake to romanticize farm labor, which involved back-breaking hauling, mind-numbing hoeing, and the multiple discomforts of living in the same hut with cows, chickens, and pigs. But industrial work also had its horrors. Dividing up tasks made work highly repetitive and tedious; operating machines was often dangerous, especially when workers were sleepy, sick, or hung-over. Coal miners in the early nineteenth century faced horrific conditions in unstable mine shafts. If young workers survived the hot, hard labor on the coal faces, by early middle age their lungs were destroyed by toxic coal dust.

The combination of wage work and repetitive, clock-regulated labor created a new kind of leisure pursuit for the working class; the inclination to drink to get drunk, to use one's few precious off-hours to drown one's sorrows. Gin, rather than beer, became the favorite Saturday night drink, much to the consternation of many middle-class reformers—and lower-class wives.

WOMEN AND INDUSTRIALIZATION. Living the Industrial Revolution presented new challenges for women. In the early modern period, women had for the most part been kept out of the skilled trades, a phenomenon reinforced by the guild system, which usually licensed only men to make pins or to weave cloth. Women had always worked at home, spinning, sewing, cooking, tending animals, working in fields, and raising children, and had often run or helped run shops or market stalls. The cottage system had increased women's participation in cloth production and allowed them to fit textile production into their busy lives; it had already challenged and begun to break down guild privileges. But the advent of machine production further transformed this system. Now relatively unskilled laborers could be put to work tending spinning mules or working power looms. Employers often sought out women and child workers because their small fingers were ideal for delicate work like threading machines, and because they could get away with paying them far less than men for their work.

With a factory job, a woman, single or married, might be able to achieve financial independence—except that husbands were legally entitled to take their wives' wages (and not vice versa), and women were almost never paid enough to survive on without other family wages. Moreover, women were expected to clothe, feed, and care for children. The rare man who helped in the household was labeled a "molly" and ridiculed by his peers.

The declining wages and status of skilled workers had other effects on women. A journeyman's career had always begun with a period of adolescent carousing and hard drinking before he became a master and was able to marry. But as guilds fell apart and fewer masters were needed, artisans married or started families anyway, without giving up their bachelor habits. The opening of new pubs and the organization of new men's clubs or proto–trade unions gave them opportunities to hang out with their workmates—and to spend their families' precious paychecks. More than one working-class woman sang ballads like this one:

> I am forc'd to get up in the morn,
> And labor and toil the whole day,
> Then at night I have supper to get,
> And the bairns to get out of the way,
> My husband to fetch from the alehouse
> And to put him to bed when I go
> A woman can ne'er be at rest,
> When once she is joined to a man.[9]

Many women suffered far worse, including threats, beatings, and stabbings when their mates came home drunk, depressed, or out of sorts. Domestic violence was not limited to the working classes, of course; men abused women—and women occasionally abused men—to win

The Satanic Mines One of the most vital jobs in the industrializing economy was the mining of coal, which was needed to power the new steam engines. But this form of wage work was also terribly dangerous, especially for the women and children often compelled to transport the heavy coal up fiery hot, airless, and slippery underground passages.

family arguments and to establish control in the household, over money, sex, or behavior. But industrialization put strains on the traditional role of the man in the house and seems to have aggravated domestic violence, especially among skilled workers. Ironically, in textile-working families, where men were accustomed to working alongside women at home or in small factories, domestic abuse does not seem to have been nearly as common as it was among cobblers, carpenters, and tailors.

Manchester: City of the Future?

In the 1770s, Manchester was a middle-sized town of about 24,000, in the middle of farming country in Lancashire, where the putting-out system had also been highly developed in the eighteenth century. Not far from the coast, it was just over thirty miles from the busy port of Liverpool, through which came many Irish immigrants and European emigrants, as well as raw materials from the Americas and India. Manchester lay at the confluence of the Irk and Irwell Rivers, both of which were used to power the early mills. Also nearby was an extensive set of coalfields—important in an era in which carrying heavy coal long distances was impractical. The first factories sprang up in the last decades of the eighteenth century and by 1815 already employed several thousand cotton workers. The real expansion of production came after 1820—in the next ten years, Manchester's population alone (not counting nearby towns) grew by almost 45 percent.

Manchester grew, however, in a completely unplanned and unregulated way. The only areas to which thought was given were the new suburbs and downtown areas where the merchants and mill owners worked and lived. Outlying suburbs and main streets connecting suburbs to downtown were clean and neat, allowing middle-class inhabitants to go to and from work without ever encountering the working-class districts. In working-class areas, thousands of new tenants were crammed into existing homes. New mills were built on the rivers without any thought to regulating water usage or pollution. Consequently, those waterways became fetid stews of sewage, dead animals, and factory waste.

Many onlookers realized something strange, new, and rather scary was happening in Manchester, and some came to see what the new world would look like. Most were horrified by the contrasts they saw between the rich

Nineteenth-Century Manchester This panoramic view of Manchester in the nineteenth century nicely depicts the smokestack rising next to the church tower, and the heavily polluted River Irk flowing into this wholly unromantic industrial city.

and the working poor, between, to return to Tocqueville's terms, gold and excrement. "What a place!" one traveler exclaimed, "the entrance to hell realized."[10] In 1833, reformers succeeded in pushing the Factory Act through Parliament. This first piece of effective factory legislation outlawed the employment of children under age nine in the textile industry, limited to twelve the hours that children aged fourteen to eighteen could work, and provided for regular inspection of factories. But conditions did not improve appreciably. Scores of visitors portrayed the city as a horrific inferno, to which all industrial society would sooner or later be condemned. Charles Dickens used what he saw in Manchester to create the fictional hard-hearted factory owners and the destitute members of the working class who populate his novels such as *Hard Times* and *Oliver Twist*. But the question remained, what should be done about hell, especially when it was so very profitable for its overseers?

Utilitarianism had no answer to this question. Manchester, unlike most places in the pre-1848 period, was governed by wealthy liberals with utilitarian perspectives, and their solution to the social question was essentially time. In time, they believed, self-regulation would put the market right, and individuals practicing self-regulation would eventually prosper. In time, housing shortages would disappear, and market cycles would stabilize. These liberals had supported the Great Reform Act of 1832 but feared further expansion of the suffrage, and thereafter their liberalism was chiefly economic in nature. Manchester liberals were strong critics of the so-called Corn Laws, which were tariffs on grain. They wanted to reduce bread prices so that subsistence wages paid to workers could be reduced and textile prices slashed, allowing exporters to sell more overseas. They took a leading role in the Anti-Corn-law League, a political pressure group that succeeded in abolishing these tariffs in 1846, something that effectively gave Britain "free trade."

Manchester liberals also backed the New Poor Law of 1834. This provision ended wage subsidies in favor of a requirement that those who wanted relief would have to enter state workhouses. The workhouse was a last-ditch resort where family members were separated and conditions were kept unpleasant and punitive. As Dickens suggested in *A Christmas Carol,* only hardhearted misers like Ebenezer Scrooge could believe the workhouse was an answer to the problems of the industrial poor. But the liberals viewed slow reform and individual effort as far better than handouts, and it took many decades for Britain, not to mention the rest of Europe, to address the social question by developing an effective social safety net.

Manchester also became home to a large number of radicals, individuals who believed that the market would *never* regulate itself, and that this machine-driven hell would simply destroy working people. Between 1811 and 1816, Luddites—named after their leader Ned Ludd—staged numerous acts of machine-breaking in Manchester, hoping to return control of textile production to artisans. Machine-breaking was not the only form of protest. In 1819, after a year of bad harvests, a group of mostly artisans gathered on St. Peter's field outside Manchester to advocate both political and economic reforms. The assembly was meant to be a peaceful one, but local guardsmen sent in to contain it panicked and began to fire, killing eleven workers and injuring many more. Parallels were drawn to the recent slaughter at Waterloo, and the incident became known as the Peterloo massacre.

The memory of Peterloo was long; scenes of the riot were reproduced on scarves, lockets, and tobacco cases, and radicals continued to celebrate the anniversary each August 16. But there were many other assemblies, strikes, and riots, some provoked by Chartists and some by disputes on the factory floor. Often police broke up the demonstrations, and the ringleaders were jailed and fired from their jobs. Working-class agitation in Manchester peaked in the summer of 1842, when hunger and high bread prices provoked strikes. This series of disturbances was called the Plug Plot Riots, because working people stopped work by pulling plugs out of factory boilers. The Plug Plot Riots involved over 50,000 workers and frightened the factory owners, though the violence was minor. The workers, having won nothing, had to return to their jobs after a few months of protesting. Friedrich Engels arrived in Manchester just after the riots had ended. It is no wonder that, seeing Manchester at the height of its productivity and the condition of the working class at its lowest point, Engels saw in Manchester not only a premonition of industrial hell, but also a vision of the revolutionary apocalypse to follow.

The Hungry Forties

The Plug Plot Riots were by no means the only disturbances of the 1840s. In fact, tension and unrest increased during the decade, especially in the wake of the poor harvests and economic downturns of 1845–1847. As in 1816, the weather contributed. Poor harvests in 1842–1843 created localized hardships that widened into large-scale crises by 1845. In that year, blight struck potatoes, a crop that had become vital to the diets of many German and Irish peasants. In 1845, one-third of the Irish crop was lost. In 1846, three-quarters of Ireland's potatoes rotted in the fields, leaving little to plant the next year. As prices rose, people took out new loans and stopped buying the factories' goods. The grain harvest in 1846 was also miserably low, and anger rose against the landlords who had closed off forests to hunting and foraging. In the German states, people blamed Jews, who were overrepresented among rural money-lenders; in Ireland, they blamed the English, who had limited the imports and exports of their quasi-colony and refused to intervene, arguing that increased diligence, workhouses, and private charity should take care of the problem.

> How and why did revolution return to Europe in the later 1840s?

On the continent, many towns and cities did respond, opening soup kitchens and pushing down grain prices. Thanks to public assistance and the good harvest of 1847, famine was averted. This was not the case in Ireland, where an estimated one million people perished and two million abandoned their homes to seek better lives abroad. The Irish potato famine was a special case, aggravated by the nation's dependence on this single crop. But everywhere fear, suspicion, and unstable conditions continued, both in cities and in the countryside. It would not have required an especially perceptive observer to guess that revolution was on the horizon.

A Return to Revolution

Revolution, however, did not break out where misery was worst—namely in Ireland—perhaps because the police force there numbered 13,000, fourteen times the size per capita as that of Prussia. Nor did it break out where industrialization was most advanced, in northern England. Remarkably, revolutionary agitation began first in southern Italy and was inspired by the election of a new, liberal-minded pope, Pius IX, in 1846. Pius IX immediately freed hundreds of political prisoners and instigated political and economic reforms in his domains. These actions triggered rioting next door, in the Kingdom of the Two Sicilies. In January 1848, King Ferdinand II was forced to offer his people a constitution. Ominously, the king did not trust the army to put down insurgents.

Similarly, in France, Louis Philippe was unable to trust his soldiers when crowds filled the streets and stormed the parliament demanding the resignation of the prime minister. It took just two days of barricade building and urban unrest for Louis Philippe to step down, and on February 24, the Parisian protestors proclaimed France a republic. In elections to the new assembly, the people (all adult males, at least) chose their representatives, among them Alexis de Tocqueville. In a matter of weeks, two powerful restored regimes had been toppled, and their opponents—liberal and radical—were in command.

All eyes were now on France, which radicals hoped would resume its role as instigator of revolution. Thanks to improved communications, news of the July Monarchy's collapse spread rapidly. Revolution broke out in Munich on March 4, and by March 18, protestors had mounted the barricades in Vienna, Budapest, Milan, Cracow, Venice, and Berlin (Map 18.5). There were triumphant speeches—many of them reported in the newssheets—by longtime proponents of revolution such as the Italian nationalist Giuseppe Mazzini and the Hungarian liberal Lajos Kossuth. Leaders of the restored governments could not stop the protestors,

MAP 18.5 | The Revolutions of 1848

Major uprisings took place throughout the European continent in the revolutionary year 1848.
Compare this map with Map 18.3. Which of the revolutions of 1848 happened in places that had already been embroiled in conflict in the 1820s and 1830s? Why do you think 1848 brought new revolutions back to the same places?

and desperate to keep order—and their heads—they fired unpopular conservative ministers and promised to grant civil liberties. Metternich was forced out of office and, fearing for his life, fled the Habsburg capital. The German princes agreed to allow the election of delegates to a constitutional convention, and by May the Frankfurt National Assembly began deliberating about what sort of a German nation it should frame. What became known as "the springtime of peoples" seemed infectious. All across the continent, from the Atlantic coast to the Ukraine, those who had suffered under the Restoration proclaimed the dawning of a new day.

The peoples' spring was not a bloodless event: in addition to peasant violence aimed at landlords, impoverished weavers took revenge on market-cornering merchants, Austrian soldiers battled Italian nationalists, and hungry townsfolk assaulted tax collectors. Boatmen and wagon owners fired on steamships and broke up railway tracks, and peasants angered by restrictions on their use of forests set fire to forestry officials' homes and offices. In urbanizing areas, there were strikes and as-

saults on recently arrived laborers, who were seen to be usurping the locals' jobs. Radicals flew the tricolor flag or, in some places, the plain red socialist flag. In the eastern European countryside, peasants raided manor houses and beat feudal landlords in their own, long-delayed version of the Great Fear (see Chapter 17).

The Communist Manifesto, published by Karl Marx and Friedrich Engels in early 1848, was just one of many manifestos written at the time, but its demands were far too radical for most of the 1848 revolutionaries. Most revolutionaries did not seek to dislodge the monarchy, much less the industrial bourgeoisie as a class. Outside of France, few people had heard of socialism, not to mention communism. Most demands for political reform were liberal demands: constitutional governance and expansion of the suffrage. Among those whose primary complaints were economic, many were peasants hoping to end the suffering they had endured under landlords. Some revolutionary action had anti-modernizing aims, such as the desire to keep artisanal jobs and communal farming techniques in the face of mechanization and

The Revolution of 1848 in Hungary This image depicts the Hungarian nationalist poet Sándor Petőfi declaiming his famous "Song of the Hungarians" before a cheering crowd. Standing to his right is the Hungarian nationalist hero, Lajos Kossuth.

market-oriented agriculture. And some of it, such as the war launched by the northern Italians against Austrian overlordship in 1848, was nationalist in character. No one was sure how the call for revolution would end—for the many and diverse people of Europe had many and divergent grievances, and finding a stable new order that satisfied liberals and radicals, students and artisans, Hungarian liberal nationalists and Polish Catholic peasants would be a tall order, indeed.

How Revolutions End

In fact, the revolutions ended in a remarkable and—for the revolutionaries—disillusioning return of the conservative regimes. Their return to power resulted partly from the application of force and partly from the incompatibility of the peoples' dreams. We could perhaps date the beginning of the end to Pope Pius IX's change of heart, in April 1848. Having been forced to flee the Vatican when Rome declared itself a republic in March 1848 and horrified by the outbreak of hostilities against the Austrians, in April 1848 the pope denounced what

the liberals were naming a war of liberation and called for good Catholics to support the restoration of authority.

THE JUNE DAYS. More important in curtailing revolutionary fervor were the so-called June Days in Paris, which demonstrated quite clearly the incompatibility of the liberal and radical factions in France's newly created Second Republic. As the spring passed, the liberals increasingly tired of the costly, market-restricting policies they had put in place to please the radicals. On June 23, the liberals decreed the closing of the Paris workshops, state-run agencies that had been created in the wake of the February Revolution to provide work for unemployed Parisians. In response, radical Parisians took to the barricades—only to have the liberals then call out the civilian militia against them. In three days of bloody battles, about 1,000 soldiers and between 5,000 and 15,000 rebels were killed. One eyewitness wrote later, "The atrocities committed by the victors make me shiver."[11] Of the 15,000 prisoners brought before the war court, 5,000 were deported to Algeria, others remained in prison, and still others went into exile. In another ominous move in December 1848, the French elected Louis-Napoleon Bonaparte, nephew of the great Napoleon, as president of the Second Republic. The new president had once championed Italian nationalism, but in June 1849, he sent in French troops to restore papal authority in central Italy.

ITALY AND AUSTRIA.

ITALY AND AUSTRIA. While the French liberals were eradicating their rivals in the June Days, an Austrian army put down the revolution in Prague, and soon thereafter, Italian nationalists, led by King Charles Albert of Piedmont-Sardinia, fell back before Habsburg troops. Accepting responsibility for the defeat, Charles Albert abdicated in favor of his son, Victor Emmanuel II (r. 1849–1861), and went into exile. He was far from being the only exile. The charismatic republican leader Giuseppi Garibaldi fled to South America, where he and his wife Anita fought for revolutionary causes and Garibaldi began to wear a red shirt and a poncho, in honor of the Latin American rebels. At least 15,000 other refugees fled Austrian Venetia and Lombardy, settling in Piedmont, where some concentrated on making money while others devoted themselves to stirring up another war against Austria.

In Vienna, Austrian forces restored Habsburg rule, though the mentally impaired emperor Ferdinand I abdicated in favor of his nephew, Franz Joseph I (r. 1848–1916). Several more serious uprisings had to be quelled in the Italian states, however, and the Austrians had to call on Russian forces to help them mop up the opposition in the Hungarian lands, which continued until October 1849. Now it was the rebels, such as Kossuth, who had to flee. During his years in exile, Kossuth became the darling of British and American liberals and a close friend of Mazzini.

THE GERMAN STATES. In the meantime, the revolution in the German states, which was supposed to lead to the creation of a united and constitutionally governed German nation, had stalled. The Frankfurt Assembly had not been able to agree on whether to create a "big" Germany that included the German-Austrian lands (and with a Catholic majority), or a "small" Germany, dominated by Protestant Prussia. The collapse of the revolution in Austria made the big Germany solution unviable, and in November, the Prussian prime minister put an end to debate by sending deputies home and simply imposing a constitution on Prussia. The Frankfurt Assembly issued an alternative, more liberal constitution and of-

fered the Prussian king, Friedrich Wilhelm IV, the crown of a small Germany. But Friedrich Wilhelm refused to accept a crown that, he claimed, smelled of revolution and of the gutter. Democrats and nationalists—whose causes now increasingly overlapped—mounted the barricades once more. Prussian troops stamped out the fighting but could not prevent the spread of nationalist rhetoric and sentiment, one of the many inadvertent legacies of 1848.

How Restorations End

The monarchies on the continent were restored to power once more—though not until 1851 did France's authoritarian president, Louis-Napoleon, proclaim himself Emperor Napoleon III. But some concessions stood. There was no question, now, of restoring legal inequalities; rural people had demonstrated all too forcefully their unwillingness to stand for that. Liberals, and even a number of conservatives, realized that modernizing the agricultural economy was crucial. The civil liberties granted could be curtailed, and for a time they were, especially in central Europe. It took a long time for censorship to be fully relaxed, and in Austria, martial law continued into the 1850s. Nicholas I's Russia, the great foe of revolution, saw precious little liberalization, even after the reactionary czar's death in 1855.

But most nation-states now had constitutions and elected assemblies, and even if the suffrage in many places remained quite limited, wealthy liberals and ambitious entrepreneurs did get elected, and conservatives turned to modernizing bureaucrats and professionals to help them cope with the industrial and commercial revolutions. Slowly—more slowly in rural areas and in eastern and southern Europe—these new men pushed through legislation or policies that achieved many of the aims of the liberals in 1848: the reduction of trade barriers; the opening of positions of power to middle-class men; expansion of the suffrage; reduction of the role of the church in state affairs; and the freedom to form associations, to speak one's mind in public, and to practice one's religion in peace. Not all these freedoms were won, and few of them were fully honored, but by the 1860s, Europe was a much more liberal place than it had been in 1847. It was also a place being transformed by an Industrial Revolution whose pace increased markedly after the 1840s. The glass now, at least for liberals, was half-full. The question remained, however, how many rights and how much prosperity would they be willing to share.

Conclusion

Less than forty-five years separate the Congress of Vienna from the date of Tocqueville's death in 1859. But these few decades saw the transformation of European society, culture, and politics. Even where political revolu-

tions failed—as did most in this period—reforms helped widen the suffrage, expand choices and opportunities, and offer new freedoms, at least for the middle classes. Inspired by these transformations, liberal intellectuals claimed that Europe—and its neo-European satellite states—was charting the right sort of "civilized" future for mankind. As we have seen, however, political conditions differed enormously across Europe's states. So too did the degree to which industrialization took hold differ. But in some respects the liberals were right. By the 1840s, liberal ideas, as well as textile mills, railways, and mass-produced newspapers, were transforming the continent and the world. Soon those who dreamed of national unification or of the achievement of social harmony without conflicts, like Koraes or Fourier, would seem quaint. Even the savvy Tocqueville would find that the days of aristocratic liberalism too had passed.

Critical Thinking Questions

1. Which Europeans were best positioned to "see the future" in the early nineteenth century? Which were still primarily "living in the past"?

2. What made liberal nationalism a revolutionary force in this era?

3. How did the Industrial Revolution transform the everyday lives of British and northern European men and women?

Key Terms

Concert of Europe **(p. 561)**

Congress of Vienna **(p. 561)**

liberal (liberalism) **(p. 563)**

socialist (socialism) **(p. 565)**

communism **(p. 565)**

proletariat **(p. 565)**

conservative (conservatism) **(p. 567)**

Zollverein **(p. 569)**

nationalism **(p. 570)**

Chartism **(p. 576)**

romanticism **(p. 577)**

utilitarianism **(p. 579)**

Industrial Revolution **(p. 580)**

Primary Sources in Connect

For information on Connect and the online resources available, go to **http://connect.mcgraw-hill.com**.

1. **Alexander Ypsilantis, On Why the Greeks Should Fight for Faith and the Motherland**

2. **Charles Fourier, A Utopian Plan for Saving the Planet**

3. **Lord Byron, "Manfred"**

4. **A Parliamentary Report on Child Labor, 1832**

5. **Bentham, On Liberalism and Utility**

6. **Sándor Petőfi, Hungarian National Song**

7. **Karl Marx, *The Communist Manifesto***

Friedrich Engels, The Condition of the Working Class in England *(1845)*

In 1845, after a nearly two-year stint as a manager in his father's textile mill in Manchester, England, Friedrich Engels published *The Condition of the Working Class in England,* a vehement attack on industrial society. Engels insisted that "the industrial revolution is of the same importance for England as the political revolution for France" and predicted that the capitalist class's exploitation of the industrial working class (the proletariat) would generate a revolution of its own, in comparison to which the Reign of Terror would seem child's play. The young journalist and philosopher Karl Marx was so moved by Engels's book that he insisted on meeting its author. By late 1845, the two radicals had become fast friends and would continue to work and write together until Marx's death in 1883. The following passage illustrates both what conditions were like in "liberal" Manchester in the 1840s and Engels's certainty that it was not the fault of individual workers, but of the capitalist system, that there was so much suffering to be seen.

Every great city has one or more slums, where the working-class is crowded together. True, poverty often dwells in hidden alleys close to the palaces of the rich; but, in general, a separate territory has been assigned to it, where, removed from the sight of the happier classes, it may struggle along as it can. These slums are pretty equally arranged in all the great towns of England, the worst houses in the worst quarters of the towns; usually one- or two-storied cottages in long rows, perhaps with cellars used as dwellings, almost always irregularly built. These houses of three or four rooms and a kitchen form, throughout England, some parts of London excepted, the general dwellings of the working-class. The streets are generally unpaved, rough, dirty, filled with vegetable and animal refuse, without sewers or gutters, but supplied with foul, stagnant pools instead. Moreover, ventilation is impeded by the bad, confused method of building of the whole quarter, and since many human beings here live crowded into a small space, the atmosphere that prevails in these working-men's quarters may readily be imagined. Further, the streets serve as drying grounds in fine weather; lines are stretched across from house to house, and hung with wet clothing. . . .

[L]et us follow the English officials, who occasionally stray thither, into one or two of these workingmen's homes.

On the occasion of an inquest held Nov. 16th, 1843, by Mr. Carter, coroner for Surrey, upon the body of Ann Galway, aged 45 years, the newspapers related the following particulars concerning the deceased: She had lived at No. 5 White Lion Court, Bermondsey Street, London, with her husband and a nineteen-year-old son in a little room, in which neither a bedstead nor any other furniture was to be seen. She lay dead beside her son upon a heap of feathers which were scattered over her almost naked body, there being neither sheet nor coverlet. The feathers stuck so fast over the whole body that the physician could not examine the corpse until it was cleansed, and then found it starved and scarred from the bites of vermin. Part of the floor of the room was torn up, and the hole used by the family as a privy.

On Monday, Jan. 15th, 1844, two boys were brought before the police magistrate because, being in a starving condition, they had stolen and immediately devoured a half-cooked calf's foot from a shop. The magistrate felt called upon to investigate the case further, and received the following details from the policeman: The mother of the two boys was the widow of an ex-soldier, afterwards policeman, and had had a very hard time since the death of her husband, to provide for her nine children. She lived at No. 2 Pool's Place, Quaker Court, Spitalfields, in the utmost poverty. When the policeman came to her, he found her with six of her children literally huddled together in a little back room, with no furniture but two old rush-bottomed chairs with the seats gone, a small table with two legs broken, a broken cup, and a small dish. On the hearth was scarcely a spark of fire, and in one corner lay as many old rags as would fill a woman's apron, which served the whole family as a bed. For bed clothing they had only their scanty day clothing. The poor woman told him that she had been forced to sell her bedstead the year before to buy food. Her bedding she had pawned with the victualler for food. In short, everything had gone for food. The magistrate ordered the woman a considerable provision from the poor-box.

I am far from asserting that all London working-people live in such want as the foregoing . . . families. I know very well that ten are somewhat better off, where one is so totally trodden under foot by society; but I assert that thousands of industrious and worthy people— far worthier and more to be respected than the rich of London—do find themselves in a condition unworthy of human beings; and that every proletarian, everyone, without exception, is exposed to a similar fate without any fault of his own and in spite of every possible effort.

QUESTIONS | *Read Engels's last paragraph closely. Does this paragraph make you feel more or less sympathy for the poor of Manchester? Does it make you feel more or less confident in liberal promises that, in time, all would profit from the Industrial Revolution?*

Source: Friedrich Engels, *The Condition of the Working Class in England in 1844,* trans. Florence Kelley Wischnewetzky (London: Swann Sonnenschein & Co., 1892), 26, 29–31.

19

After the Battle of Sedan: Napoleon III (the Loser) and Otto von Bismarck (the Winner) Discuss Terms

EUROPE UNIFIED,
EUROPE DIVIDED, 1850–1880

After the Revolutions
    Liberalism Triumphant
    Liberalism's Foes
    Capitalism Triumphant
    Nationalism Triumphant

**Liberal Modernization
in Western Europe**
    Great Britain: The Liberal Empire
    France: The Bourgeois Empire
    of Napoleon III
    Making Paris Modern
    The Illiberal Empire: Russia

Living the Victorian Life
    Class Society in the Liberal Era
    The Victorian Household
    Women at Home
    A Life of Domestic Service
    On Property: The Haves
    On the Propertyless: The Have Nots

The Culture of Positivism
    Positivism and Liberal Order
    Charles Darwin, Victorian Positivist
    Realism in Literature
    Realism and Impressionism
    in Painting
    Realism in Music

Remaking Metternich's Map
    Breaking Old Maps: The
    Crimean War
    Unifications and Their Makers
    France and Germany after 1871:
    Wages of the Wars of Unification

Divided Europe
    Reshaping Southeastern Europe
    Austria Partitioned
    Life and Identity after Unification

Conclusion

THE RHINE Rising in the Swiss Alps and running approximately 820 miles to the North Sea, the Rhine River flows through areas that are now some of the continent's most prosperous regions—western Germany, northern France, and the Rhine delta cities of Rotterdam and Utrecht. For centuries, this corridor and its main thoroughfare, the Spanish Road, linked Habsburg holdings in Spain and northern Italy with the Holy Roman Empire's domains in Flanders. Though many a monarch sought to conquer the Rhine valley, none were able to hold it very long. Life along the Rhine was a multicultural experience, as fishermen, traders, porters, and smugglers crossed and re-crossed the river. Speaking whatever language worked best, these riverbank dwellers were more attached to their villages or regions than to the larger nations within whose borders they officially resided. The river was the subject of romantic poems, such as Heinrich Heine's tribute to the mythical Rhine maiden "Lorelei," but its periodic floods also made it dangerous to those who lived on its shores. Meandering through wide plains and coursing around literally thousands of small islands, the early modern Rhine had not one, but many moods, shapes, and functions, and the regions that bordered it owed their character more to the river than to the inland capital cities that claimed ownership over them.

There were riches to be extracted from rivers—and not just the gold immortalized by Richard Wagner's opera *Das Rheingold,* which premiered in 1869, on the eve of the river's political transformation. If the river's scenic snags could be cleared and its unruly floods contained, its would-be modernizing masters thought, the Rhine might offer swift commercial transport as well as a natural defensive border. Controlling the river and patrolling its banks had been attempted in the past, but as historian David Blackbourn has shown, it took the self-confidence, capital, and heavy equipment of the nineteenth century to make a full-scale assault on the Rhine.[1]

As early as 1809, the German engineer Johann Gottfried Tulla developed a grand-scale plan for straightening and taming the Rhine—though even Tulla vastly underestimated the capital, political maneuvering, and management skills needed to organize this mammoth project. He died in the 1870s, before his vision was finally realized, thanks to the cooperation of German, French, Dutch, and Belgian bureaucrats, surveyors, and statesmen, the expenditure of vast sums, and the lives of many workers. In the course of the project, engineers significantly shortened the river, removed thousands of islands, and built hundreds of miles of dikes. The new Rhine was a much swifter, straighter river, one conducive to greater commercial efficiency and even to better health, as the draining of swampy areas reduced the

Rhine Landscape, c. 1850 This painting depicts a Romantic Rhine, its banks dotted with scenic towns and ruined castles. It also depicts a wide and peaceful river, but in many places the pre-industrial Rhine was wilder and difficult to navigate.

The Rhine River, c. 1880

incidence of malaria in the Rhineland. The Rhine in 1880 was a much different river than it had been in 1800, or even in 1850—just as the continent through which it ran had been thoroughly transformed.

Along the Rhine's banks, lifestyles too were changing as inhabitants were increasingly called on to identify themselves as loyal citizens of France, Germany, Belgium, or the Netherlands. As customs officials, schools, and policemen became more and more concerned with delineating borders, individuals were pressed to give up their regional identity in favor of a national one. Joining these larger entities gave people access to wider commercial networks, state-sponsored schools, and better-managed bureaucracies. There were, however, losses as well. Small villages and fisheries were sacrificed in the pursuit of greater efficiency and larger profits. Many species of fish and fauna in the Rhine basin were depleted and some even forced into extinction. Rectification did not tame the Rhine. Periodic floods continued throughout the nineteenth and twentieth centuries and still occur today. Nor did the streamlining of the river and the reordering of its borderlands make it a less dangerous place. In 1871, the brief but brutal Franco-Prussian War ended with the newly united Germany taking from France two multicultural Rhineland provinces, Alsace and Lorraine. Deeply angered, the French swore to retrieve the provinces, and both sides began arming themselves for a new, surely grander, war. The two industrial powers that had been most enriched by their joint efforts to correct the river now sought to master it for themselves.

Like the lives of those who dwelt along the Rhine, the lives of Europeans on other parts of the continent were transformed by the dynamic processes of industrialization and nation-building in the mid-nineteenth century. Though many had been disappointed and disillusioned by the failure of the 1848 revolutions, Europe's expanding economies now offered new opportunities, especially for those with some education, mobility, or capital. An acceleration of railroad building, machine production, and global trade, as well as the advent of new forms of banking and credit, made possible new forms of commerce and consumption. The expansion of state bureaucracies, the managerial classes, and the secular professions such as law, medicine, and teaching again increased the number of middle-class consumers, many of them political and economic liberals. These bourgeois liberals, with the help of modern-minded aristocrats such as Tocqueville, built up national institutions including armies, central bureaucracies, public schools, and museums. These institutions in turn made individuals feel more powerfully linked to their nation-states, and indebted to them, for protection, guidance, edification, and liberation of various kinds. Political revolution had been forestalled or at least delayed. But Europe teemed with ambitious individuals eager to remake themselves and their nations, or even, as in the case of Tulla and his colleagues, to master nature itself.

Mid-nineteenth-century transformations presented Europeans with both opportunities and challenges. During this period, most European states embarked on massive projects of modernization, seeking to link their inhabitants together literally through the building of roads, railways, and telegraph lines, and figuratively through the cultivation of loyalty to the nation-state. Liberals, or former conservatives who adopted liberal ideas, usually led the way, but economic conditions and political institutions varied widely in each of Europe's states, and each state chose a different path toward modernization. Further political and geographic reordering took place as Piedmont and Prussia pursued grand projects of overhauling Metternich's map, while the great multiethnic Habsburg and Ottoman Empires suffered fragmentation. Modernizing officials, such as the French city-planner Georges Haussmann or the Piedmontese prime minister Camillo Benso, count of Cavour, played significant roles in these developments. Others—including Victorian servants, Rhine ferrymen, and the poor city-dwellers whose homes Haussmann destroyed—paid heavy prices. For them, the modernizing processes were less dreams than nightmares.

After the Revolutions

What do the people do when their revolutions fail? What options do elites have after they put down a popular insurrection? The collapse of the revolutions of 1848 left Europeans in various states of limbo. Although monarchs returned to most thrones, there was a pervasive sense that the Restoration regimes could not go on ruling as they had done. For several years after the revolutions' defeat, most monarchical regimes kept a tight lid on reform. Governments developed new police forces and bureaucracies to watch over uneasy populations, and conservative clerics helped suppress dangerous ideas. But especially in northwestern Europe, the economic and political power of the old aristocracies was ebbing away; social mobility, industrial commerce, urbanization, and the development of bureaucracies ate away at the privileges and lifestyles of the old elite.

Gradually, most nations relaxed censorship and allowed private associations or even new political parties to form. Even though many radicals remained in exile, waiting for their day to dawn, old-style conservatives such as Metternich and his Habsburg prince, Ferdinand I, could not simply return to their old court-centered cultures. After 1848, all of Europe's monarchs, with the exception

How did liberalism change after the 1848 revolutions?

of the Russian czars, felt they needed to cultivate at least some measure of public support and invest in some kinds of industrial modernization. Even they recognized that the postrevolutionary world called for more inclusive styles of governance and more nationally focused forms of life.

In the post-1848 period, Europeans to the north and east of the Rhine also began to agitate for new rights: to vote, to assemble freely, to criticize their governments or religious leaders with much greater impunity, to choose a career or religion, or to choose not to attend church. Larger numbers than ever before married across religious lines or chose jobs other than those their parents practiced; literacy increased, though levels in the east and south still lagged behind those reached in western European nations. Some ambitious Danes, Poles, and Germans left the farm for the city, or left Europe for good, taking their skills, customs, and ideas to the neo-Europes in North and South America, Australia, and New Zealand—though many remained tillers of the land, their work still driven by the seasons and the quest to survive.

But if throughout Europe, choice was no longer limited by legal privileges, a new means of dividing society evolved: class, or distinction based exclusively on income. Although nineteenth-century society offered individuals more choice and more freedom, those choices and freedoms were far more abundant for those lucky enough to belong to the upper or middling classes. Children born to working-class or peasant parents were far less likely than

their middle-class contemporaries to enjoy the fruits of liberalism's triumphs.

Liberalism Triumphant

By the later 1850s, liberalism was making a comeback as many of Europe's monarchs decided they could not resurrect a system built on aristocratic privileges and fragmented economic power. The savvy ones among them realized that to survive they would have to build strong, centralized states and accept economic modernization in some form. Railroads, telegraphs, and the popular press were there to stay. So too was the idea of the nation-state. Wily and opportunistic leaders such as Napoleon III, Camillo di Cavour, and Otto von Bismarck saw the handwriting on the wall and embraced the new forces of capitalist expansion, national consolidation, and bureaucratic centralization. In England, Whigs began calling themselves Liberals after 1839 (and Tories renamed themselves Conservatives). Liberalism became such a popular force that a former Tory, Henry John Temple, Lord Palmerston, actually became a liberal and, under that party's name, served twice as prime minister, from 1855 to 1858 and again from 1859 to 1865.

By no means did liberals *rule* in every country. In fact, only in Great Britain did they remain the national governing party for very long, and even there, ingrained habits of deferring to the aristocracy led voters to continue to elect conservative nobles. In rural areas especially, aristocratic

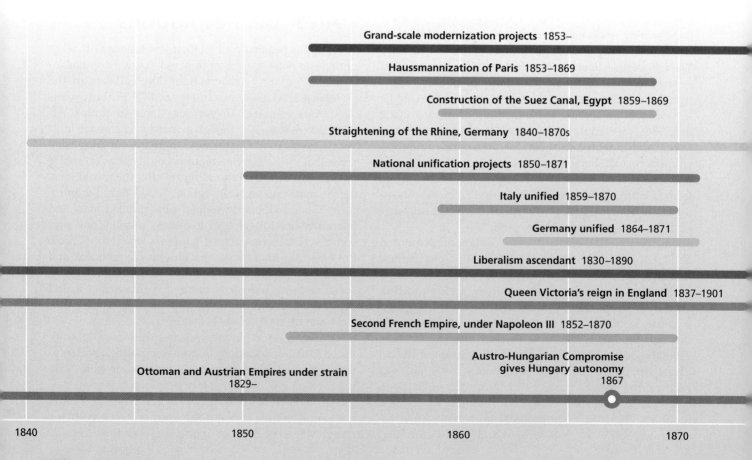

Grand-scale modernization projects 1853–

Haussmannization of Paris 1853–1869

Construction of the Suez Canal, Egypt 1859–1869

Straightening of the Rhine, Germany 1840–1870s

National unification projects 1850–1871

Italy unified 1859–1870

Germany unified 1864–1871

Liberalism ascendant 1830–1890

Queen Victoria's reign in England 1837–1901

Second French Empire, under Napoleon III 1852–1870

Austro-Hungarian Compromise gives Hungary autonomy 1867

Ottoman and Austrian Empires under strain 1829–

| 1840 | 1850 | 1860 | 1870 |

landowners continued to dominate the scene. But liberals were making headway, taking on prominent roles in France, Austria, Belgium, and the new states of Germany and Italy, and minor ones elsewhere. Perhaps more important, liberals began to play dominant roles in local governance, as mayors, city managers, councilmen, and judges. Moreover, as textile and iron production soared and coal mining and banking expanded, men of commerce tended increasingly toward liberal policies, which championed reason, individual liberty, and the rule of law, and favored an expanded and less restricted market over conservative or provincial restraints on trade.

In the post-1850 period, political and economic liberalism often went hand in hand. British liberal prime minister William Gladstone, for example, pushed for limits on governmental expenditures, the expansion of free-trade policies, and the 1884 Reform Act, which gave six million more Britons the vote. Many liberals continued to fight for the extension of rights, the expansion of public education, and the improvement of urban conditions for the lower classes. Yet there were also middle-class liberals who backed away either from free trade or from their former allies among the radicals and members of the working classes. Just as the radicals

A Jewish Textile Merchant Joins the Ruling Class, 1887 In 1836, Valentin Manheimer came to Berlin and started a women's clothing business. Despite his Jewish faith, his mid-century success in textile manufacturing made him a respected member of society and a councilor to the emperor on commercial matters. He was wealthy and influential enough by the 1880s to hire the court painter Anton von Werner to paint this portrait of his family on the occasion of his seventieth birthday.

remembered the treason of the middle-class liberals in events such as the June Days (see Chapter 18), after 1848, some liberals grew more and more fearful of working-class radicalization. Insisting that those who wanted new

Serbia, Bulgaria, and Romania gain independence from Ottomans 1878

1880   1890   1900   1910

liberties should earn them, by pulling themselves up by their own bootstraps, right-wing liberals were hesitant to expand the suffrage to those presumed too poor or ignorant to govern themselves properly—just as the imperialists among them would emphasize colonized peoples' need for European guidance.

If inherited privileges and titles no longer (in most places) gave individuals the legal right to rule, most Europeans, and even most liberals, believed that economic class *did* matter and that the lower classes had not yet earned the right to hold power. The liberalism of these right-wingers could easily shade over into conservative defense of the status quo and sanction the creation of new barriers to prevent industrial society's dynamism from undermining the ruling elite they had just joined.

Liberalism's Foes

The liberals were, in many places, the pacesetting group, but they were by no means unopposed. Their most vocal opponents were the radicals, who had championed the revolutions of 1848 but had been left out of governance thereafter. But it was from the conservatives that the liberals had to wrest power.

THE RADICALS. When the post-1848 crackdowns began, a large number of radicals went into exile to avoid imprisonment or execution. The exiles needed time to work through their disillusionment with revolutions gone wrong and the betrayal of their various dreams, whether for national unification, the abolition of poverty, or capitalism's overthrow. Many radicals concluded that their alliances with the liberals had been wrongheaded. In the future, they would have to go it alone, to form working-class organizations and parties to fight not just the aristocratic elite, but the middle classes as well, for their fair share of power and wealth. As the liberals acquired more social, economic, and political clout, the radicals moved increasingly into the camp of their critics—and foes.

CONSERVATIVES IN EASTERN EUROPE AND RUSSIA. The radicals were worrying, but, especially in eastern Europe and Russia, liberals continued to battle powerful enemies from those on other end of the spectrum, the conservatives. Conservative aristocrats, like the landed nobles (Junkers) in Prussia and the big landlords in the Hungarian crown lands, retained a considerable amount of domestic power. In Russia, although Czar Alexander II (r. 1855–1881) liberated the serfs in 1861, the nobility retained mastery over an impoverished peasantry. Despite the rise of a small class of critical intellectuals and a handful of enterprising men of commerce, Russia remained an agrarian, autocratic power. Aspiring to acquire new influence on the continent and full dominance over what it considered to be its territories in Central Asia, Russia in the mid-nineteenth century was a dynamic power, but neither an industrial nor a liberal one.

CLERICAL CONSERVATIVISM. Liberals also found themselves opposed by a reenergized conservative clergy, Catholic and Protestant. While political opposition to the Restoration regimes had been building in the 1840s, a religious revival had begun, one that called believers to return to the churches and to reject the secularizing processes under way. The Prussian king Friedrich Wilhelm IV (r. 1840–1858) had overseen a theological and cultural move to the right. After 1848, the Prussians would permit the conservative clergy to help them suppress revolutionary ideas. The Catholic Church, badly damaged by the French Revolution, also had begun to recover by the 1840s, organizing a series of huge outdoor rallies to appeal, in more modern ways, to believers. The hardly pious reign of Napoleon III (r. 1852–1870) witnessed a remarkable Catholic religious revival. Between 1853 and 1870, gifts and legacies restored much of the wealth and some of the property the church had lost during the revolution. Thousands joined religious orders. In France alone, the number of nuns quadrupled to 140,000, and the number of monks rose from 3,000 to 24,000.

The churches aggressively, and for the most part successfully, fought liberal plans to secularize all elementary education and opposed attempts to legalize civil marriage and divorce proceedings. In 1864, the once-liberal Pope Pius IX issued a Syllabus of Errors in which he rejected a raft of modern "mistakes," including Protestantism, freedom of speech, divorce, socialism, secular education, and modern progress. There were, of course, liberal churches and liberal believers, too, those who argued that faith could be reconciled with progress, science, and secular governance. But the more that liberals pushed an aggressive set of worldly reforms and ideals and the more that their lifestyles suggested indifference toward Christian norms and values, the more the clergy took up a critical posture toward them. Old Christendom divided along yet another set of lines.

Capitalism Triumphant

One of the things both conservatives and radicals could agree to dislike was capitalism, the economic system based on free markets and Adam Smith's laws of supply and demand. During the period of enlightened absolutism, capitalism already had begun to eat away at mercantilism, guild restrictions, and local, subsistence-based economies. After 1789, revolutionary upheaval and early industrialization made global trade, production for the market, wage work, and the division of labor all the more widespread. More people literally had more money in their pockets, thanks in part to the California Gold Rush (beginning in 1849), which quadrupled the world's gold supply and allowed for much new liquidity. Inspired by capitalism's triumphs, liberals after 1848 eagerly defended an economic system that for many individuals (especially for the already affluent or for those who combined both ambition and good luck) offered new opportunities to work, invest, and consume with fewer restrictions than ever before.

Many would-be entrepreneurs, however, lacked sufficient capital to expand their businesses. In the century's second half, European governments made bold and sometimes reckless attempts to found banks so that individual deposits could be used to float larger loans to growing businesses. As governments began printing small bills in large numbers, paper currency came into the hands of many who had never held it before. East Elbian landowners as well as workers in the Meissen porcelain factory were forced to produce what the markets wanted and to sell at prices anonymous consumers, hundreds or thousands of miles away, were willing to pay. As Marx and Engels noted in their later work, more and more Europeans—as well as colonized peoples—were being pulled into the capitalist economy, whether they liked it or not.

Nationalism Triumphant

Another way in which liberalism did succeed, even in eastern and southern Europe, was in convincing people that **nation-states,** rather than multinational empires, were the proper form of political organization for modern Europeans. Liberals had long wanted nation-states, sovereign entities in which aristocratic and provincial privileges would be destroyed and the rights of the people recognized. But after 1848, it became increasingly clear to conservatives as well that nation-states were the most efficient forms for industrial and capitalist modernization, just as absolutism once had been the most useful means to modernize the Old Regimes. National patriotism, too, surged in response to the expansion of literacy and the knitting together of regions by railroads, industrial markets, and new bureaucracies. It was also enhanced by liberal orators, whose flowery speeches were reported in the press, by poems, such as Byron's tributes to Greece, and by popular songs, some of which evolved into a new phenomenon, the patriotic anthem.

Patriotic songs made the process of uniting all German or all French speakers seem easy and natural. But once the making of new nations got under way, it became clear that enormous effort, and in many cases force, would be needed to make new borders—and by no means did all of these succeed. Europe's three great multinational states—the Ottoman, Russian, and Austrian Empires—and Britain's dominion over Ireland continued, despite attempts to fragment these entities along ethnic or linguistic lines. Some mid-century nationalists were ambitious, crafty, and ruthless enough to carry out the Herculean task of remaking Metternich's map, but in so doing, they abandoned many of the liberals' other ideals and provoked new tensions between nation-states. If nationalism and liberalism went together for much of the nineteenth century, leaders like Prussia's Otto von Bismarck would show that patriotism could also be manipulated to serve illiberal ends.

Liberal Modernization in Western Europe

For those inhabiting states such as England or France, where the task of nation formation had already been accomplished, further modernization came more swiftly, though by no means without its

> How did modernization unite and divide citizens in Great Britain and France after 1848?

perils. Although the states took separate paths, by the later nineteenth century, the strong traditions of enlightened thought, political reform (or revolution), and increasing commercial and industrial wealth made these two nations exemplary of what it meant to be a modern, civilized European state—part of which also involved seizing and exploiting a non-European empire (see Chapter 20). In this period, when people referred to Europe or the West what they really meant was Great Britain and France, where, it was felt, the future of civilization was on view. If these two nations' histories were by no means typical of the evolution of all European states, their innovations and achievements were admired by advocates of modernization worldwide.

Great Britain: The Liberal Empire

Britain was in many ways the nation most apart in nineteenth-century Europe. The first to industrialize and the possessor of the largest navy and most lucrative empire, it was also one of the few nations to avoid revolution in 1848. Separated from the rest of Europe by the English Channel, Britain also had older, stronger traditions of property protection, civil rights, and parliamentary governance. Thanks to the abolition of the Corn Laws in 1846, it was also the only nation that really engaged in free trade. Britain's advanced manufacturing, exploitation of its colonies, access to capital, and willingness to use force to open new markets combined to encourage pervasive belief in commerce.

Although the Great Reform Act of 1832 did not greatly increase suffrage, the 1867 and 1884 Reform Acts enfranchised more than 60 percent of adult men; women remained excluded. Catholics were permitted to run for public office after 1829 and Jews after 1845, although in practice, it took much longer for either the lower classes or the minority religious groups to acquire meaningful representation in Parliament. Benjamin Disraeli, the conservative who served as prime minister briefly in 1868 and again from 1874 to 1880, was a convert from Judaism to Anglicanism. That a convert could become socially acceptable enough to become prime minister was proof that English society was becoming more tolerant; that Disraeli had to endure anti-Semitic remarks throughout his life was proof that many social prejudices remained.

The mid-nineteenth century was the great era of British liberalism. Representative of the era was William Ewart

Patriotic Anthems

Patriotic songs were not invented in the nineteenth century. Musicians throughout history have written pieces in praise of kings and queens, and many a poet has composed verses glorifying the deeds of leaders and heroes. In fact, some of the songs that would later become national anthems were composed in the eighteenth century. The English "God Save the King" seems to have first been printed in 1744 and first sung by London crowds in support of King George II, during his campaign to suppress the Scottish uprising in 1745 (see Chapter 16). The original version of the piece that later became the French national anthem, "The Marseillaise," was first sung by revolutionary troops marching north from Marseilles in 1792 to help the Convention suppress the counterrevolutionaries. It was meant to be a battle song; the words call the people to arms, to avenge themselves against traitors, bloodthirsty tyrants, and foreign enemies. The Convention adopted it as France's national anthem in 1795—but subsequent French rulers, including Napoleon, the restored Bourbons, and Napoleon III, all banned it and chose other anthems. "The Marseillaise" did not die; radicals up and down the Rhine, and as far away as Poland and Russia, continued to sing it throughout the nineteenth century as a means of demonstrating their contempt for authority. In 1917, Russian revolutionaries were still using it to rally their supporters against the czar.

What finally made "The Marseillaise" France's official national anthem was the coming to power of the country's Third Republic and especially that republic's ferocious hatred of the new Germany, the nation that had defeated them in the Franco-Prussia War of 1870–1871, and taken as its prize the Rhine provinces of Alsace and Lorraine. Now there was once again a foreign enemy against which to take up arms, and the French, right and left, were united in their zeal for vengeance against this foe. The fact that France was no longer a monarchy also made it easier for the French to sing about killing tyrants—though this was perhaps still a bit worrying to the upper classes. The song was banned again by the Nazis and France's collaborating government after 1940. Their prohibition on singing it simply made the French resistance love it still more.

The German patriotic hymn "The Watch on the Rhine" also became a favorite as a result of national tensions. It was composed in 1840, when fears were raised that French armies, like those of the revolutionary era, would cross the river and seize territory from Prussia on its eastern banks. The song was revived in 1870, when a French invasion was again in the offing. After Prussia's victory in the Franco-Prussian War of 1871, singing it became a conventional means of expressing love for the fatherland—and contempt for the French. It was not the national anthem, however. Until 1918, the Prussian anthem was "Hail Thee in Victor's Laurels," a not particularly popular tribute to the monarch,

sung to the melody of "God Save the King." In 1922, the moderate Weimar Republic replaced "Hail Thee" with "The Song of the Germans," a much more pacific hymn. But "The Watch on the Rhine" ideally captures the growing nationalist tensions of the mid-nineteenth century and beyond. It is no surprise that in the classic 1943 movie *Casablanca,* a group of Nazis in a crowded Moroccan bar proudly sing the anthem of 1840, proclaiming the Rhine their own. Nor is it a surprise that a Swedish resistance leader, unable to endure this exhibition of German patriotism, stands up and convinces the mostly French crowd to drown out "The Watch on the Rhine" by singing "The Marseillaise."

The Marseillaise
Arise, children of the Fatherland,
The day of glory has arrived!
Against us of the bloody banner
Of tyranny is raised, (*repeat*)
Do you hear, in the countryside,
The roar of those ferocious soldiers?
They're coming right into our arms
To cut the throats of our sons and women!
To arms, citizens,
Form your battalions,
Let's march, let's march!
That an impure blood
Waters our furrows!
What does this horde of slaves,
Of traitors and conjured kings want?
For whom are these vile chains,
These long-prepared irons? (*repeat*)
Frenchmen, for us, ah! What outrage
What fury it must arouse!
It is us they dare plan
To return to the old slavery!

The Watch on the Rhine
The call resounds like thunder's crash
Like clashing swords and waves that dash
The Rhine, the Rhine, the German Rhine
Who will protect our Rhine?
Dear Fatherland, you shall not fear
Firm and true, the watch stands here!

A hundred thousand hear the cry
Their eyes are lifted high
The German youth devoutly stands
He guards the holy borderlands
Dear Fatherland, you shall not fear
Firm and true, the watch stands here![2]

QUESTION | *What does the adoption of patriotic anthems tell us about the changing character of nationalism during this period?*

Gladstone, who served as prime minister four times between 1868 and 1894. Before 1848, Gladstone had been a conservative with a strong reformist streak; his two major passions were free trade and the rehabilitation of London's prostitutes. By the 1860s he had parted company with the conservatives and become a leading liberal, pushing for extension of the franchise, reform in the army and civil service, and a reduction in the size and cost of government. He would later support Irish home rule and denounce those he saw as intolerant tyrants, including the pope, the Ottoman sultan, and his archenemy, Disraeli. An impressive orator, Gladstone was notorious for making long speeches, in Parliament and to huge audiences in the provinces, some of them lasting more than four hours. Somehow, in addition to dipping his fingers in so many political pots, Gladstone also managed to write a book about Homer, father eight children, and pen some 50,000 letters. He is but one indication that the English during the long reign of Queen Victoria (r. 1837–1901)—often portrayed as prudish, stuffy, and uninteresting—were neither simple nor boring nor entirely predictable individuals.

Queen Victoria at Work After Albert's death, Victoria grew fond of his former stable master, John Brown, and then of her Indian servant, Abdul Karim, who traveled with the queen and attended her while she worked.

The same could be said for their queen. Though Victoria continued to be queen of England, Ireland, Scotland, and Wales and became empress of India in 1877, after the death of her husband, Prince Albert, in 1861, she spent more than a decade in seclusion, allowing her prime ministers to run the state. A strong-willed individual, Victoria never remarried and wore black for the remainder of her life. Unlike many of her royal predecessors, she was abstemious and hard working, intelligent and uninterested in court intrigue; unlike most other post-1848 monarchs, especially in eastern Europe, she was content to rule as a constitutional monarch and symbolic figurehead. A number of Irish nationalists, anarchists, and radical republicans made attempts to assassinate her, but she was, on the whole, a popular queen. In 1897, she celebrated her sixtieth year on the throne with extensive festivities; Victoria's "Diamond Jubilee" was a grand celebration of Britain's uniqueness and its unique monarch.

France: The Bourgeois Empire of Napoleon III

If Victoria exemplified many middle-class Victorian values, mid-century France also obtained, by unusual means, a ruler who suited his place and time, Louis Napoleon Bonaparte. On the strength of his family name and his liberal credentials, Louis Napoleon was elected president of the Second Republic in December 1848. For two years following, he continued to rule together with the National Assembly. But in December 1851, delegates in the National Assembly wanted him out, to be replaced either by a new president or a restored king from the Bourbon or Orléans line. Rather than be put out of office, Louis Napoleon staged a coup against the Second Republic. He called for a referendum to alter the French constitution so that he could remain in office. Convincing peasants and lower-middle-class workers that he alone stood above the numerous factions, he won the referendum—and the right to remain in office—in a landslide. A year later, another referendum dissolved the Second Republic in favor of a Second Empire, and Louis Napoleon became Napoleon III, emperor of the French.

Napoleon III would seek to imitate many of his uncle's authoritarian tactics and aspire to the latter's cultural and military achievements. It is both to his credit, and to his detriment, that he was neither as strong willed and ruthless, nor as innovative and talented as his ancestor. Moreover, the times were different. The first Napoleon rose to power in the midst of political revolution and grand-scale European warfare. When Napoleon III seized his throne the revolutions to be reckoned with were chiefly economic and social ones. The third Napoleon had to make compromises—and in so doing, created the conditions for French modernization—of a unique sort.

Both Napoleons, however, were quite good at playing the nationalist card, and at rallying the people behind their governments, at least for a time. Napoleon I accomplished these goals by waging wars in Europe; Napoleon III played to the masses by trying some new tricks. He maintained universal male suffrage; championed modernization, progress, and French nationalism; and sought to expand French colonial holdings overseas. He pushed through free-trade legislation, invested heavily in public works and railroads, and in the 1860s made it legal for workers to form labor unions and even to go out on strike.

Napoleon III longed to move France forward by rising above the parties and even above the classes. In some ways, he remained a liberal, making it his task to curb the power of autocratic Austria and Russia—to the benefit, of course, of France. Like many contemporary entrepreneurs, he was ambitious and sometimes reckless. "[H]is mind is as full of schemes as a warren is full of rabbits," Lord Palmerston once commented. Some of his schemes succeeded, but others backfired. The Crimean War (see later in this chapter) netted him an alliance with Great Britain; by going to war with Austria over Italian territory in 1859 he won Nice and Savoy for France. But wars to assert French influence in Mexico (1862–1867) and Korea (1866) and the Franco-Prussian War of 1870–1871 were all boondoggles. By the time his regime ended, Napoleon III had grown fat and developed gout and hemorrhoids. Those of his enemies who did not simply loathe him for the nepotism, high-handedness, and corruption of his government thought him a buffoon. The popular press denounced him regularly for his incompetence, overspending, and failure to represent the people as a whole. Seen in 1851 as the man to unify France, by 1869 his country was again seriously divided, and virtually no one thought him capable of fixing the situation. But Napoleon III's reign—which one historian has described as "authoritarianism with a social conscience"[3]—had left its mark on France, and especially on Paris.

Making Paris Modern

Napoleon III's longest-lasting contribution to French and European history was the modernizing overhaul of Paris that the emperor set in motion in 1853. He began the process by hiring the energetic and hygiene-obsessed administrator, Baron Georges Haussmann (1809–1891), to serve as Paris's city manager. Haussmann set to work immediately and over the next sixteen years not only gave Paris a facelift, but also thoroughly refurbished the city's infrastructure, which made the capital into a flourishing commercial center, a consumers' paradise, and a tourist mecca. His work had its costs—lower-class workers were pushed out of central-city dwellings to suburban slums, and the French treasury was depleted to the tune of $15 billion in today's figures. But Haussmann's new, widened streets and underground sewers, his glass and iron train stations, and his public parks made Paris the

modern city it is today, united by rapid transportation and the cultural monuments of the city center—and divided by class and access to centralized power.

UNITING A MODERN CITY. Haussmann's accomplishments can be understood only if we know something about Paris before 1853. Culturally and politically it was a great city, but an overcrowded, difficult to negotiate, and unhealthy one as well. Like other early-nineteenth-century cities, Paris had suffered an acute housing shortage before Haussmann's arrival. It had also endured terrible cholera epidemics in 1832 and 1849, brought on by the use of the River Seine as both sewer and source for drinking water. Building in the downtown area had been going on, virtually unregulated, since the Middle Ages. As a result, it was difficult to get to public monuments and places of business, such as the central market at Les Halles. Foot and carriage traffic was perpetually snarled.

Narrow streets had been a political problem for French rulers in 1789, 1830, and in 1848, when rebels had thrown up barricades made of cobblestones, wagons, and wooden planks to prevent the kings' armies from suppressing unruly districts. Napoleon III wanted the streets broadened to make Paris a glittering modern capital, its neighborhoods united behind its new emperor. Haussmann wanted to clean up Paris and quarantine its dangerous elements, ensuring that both epidemics and revolution were rendered obsolete. Remarkably, both would succeed, making mid-nineteenth-century Paris the classic liberal city.

Haussmann accomplished this first major project of urban renewal not by building new monuments, but by destroying what he took to be old clutter, cutting grand new boulevards through Paris's inner city (Map 19.1). Along new boulevards like the Rue de Rivoli, he built

Paris under Construction This image shows the grand scale of Haussmann's construction project in the city center. In the background is the most lavish of the new buildings, the Paris Opera.

luxury apartments, luring the wealthy back into the city center, where, by 1870, 20,000 cafés had opened to serve them. The boulevards were wide enough to be shared by strolling shoppers and commercial traffic and too wide for radicals to block with barricades. Railroads could now carry passengers into the city's new downtown stations. By 1869, the glass and iron Gare St. Lazare was serving some 13,254,000 travelers a year, many of them provincial commuters.

Haussmann's widened arteries allowed traffic and consumers to flow into the city, but he also had plans for the space underneath those new streets. Eager to improve the city's water supply, Haussmann oversaw the building of a grand network of pipes and aqueducts that linked Paris to springs several miles distant, thereby avoiding having to draw water from the Seine. He built some 560,625 meters of sewer lines, enlarging and clearing out the waste disposal system such that the Paris sewers became a tourist attraction, drawing visitors who toured them on barges. Haussmann also believed that cities should have green spaces, public parks that reduced congestion and offered inhabitants places to enjoy nature (rather than to contemplate revolution). In 1850, Paris boasted 47 acres of city parks; by 1869, Haussmann had created 4,500 acres of green space, including huge parks on the city's fringe, the Bois du Boulogne and the Bois de Vincennes. The parks—once royal hunting grounds—became pleasure spots for all Parisians to enjoy on their days off.

MAP 19.1 | Baron Haussmann's Rebuilding of Paris, 1853–1869
Under the direction of Napoleon III, Baron Georges Haussmann undertook the modernization of Paris. Haussmann cut grand new boulevards through the narrow streets of the medieval city and built new sewer lines, parks, aqueducts, and railway stations. ***What do Haussmann's projects tell us about what was happening to European society in the mid-nineteenth century?***

THE DIVIDED CITY. Haussmann and his master, Napoleon III, meant to create a unified capital city, open and oriented to commerce and consumption. But their ambitious project proved hugely expensive. By 1870, Paris's municipal debt was so great that 44 percent of the city's budget had to be used to pay off the interest. The city's renovations would not be fully paid for until 1929. Moreover, Haussmann's efforts had at least as many critics as boosters in the 1850s and 1860s, for in clearing away the old clutter, the demolition teams disrupted older economic patterns and neighborhood cultures. More pointedly, they destroyed many people's homes. On the central Île de la Cité alone, some 15,000 inhabitants were displaced, and elsewhere thousands more were compelled to move. Many of the less fortunate could not afford the higher rents for the fancy new apartments built over their old neighborhoods and were forced to move out to the outskirts of town. Increasingly, the poor were concentrated in gritty suburbs, out of sight of the bourgeois but, as voices of protest grew more strident, definitely not forgotten by the more fearful liberals and monarchists. Although many workers had supported Napoleon III at the beginning of his reign, some could not forgive the emperor for destroying *their* Paris and denounced him for selling it to the financiers and property developers. They would seek to take the city back when French leaders abandoned it, briefly, in 1871.

THE NINETEENTH-CENTURY CITY. Paris was by no means the only city undergoing transformation in this era. In many places, medieval city walls were being knocked down to allow for expansion of the city and the quickening pace of commerce. In Vienna, the grand *Ringstrasse* was laid out on the ground previously occupied by city walls, and this great oblong boulevard became the location for fashionable apartments and the public institutions dear to the bourgeois liberals such as the Parliament building, city hall, and public museums. Just as in Paris, in Vienna new working-class districts arose to take in those dispossessed or priced out of downtown. In London, too, neighborhoods began to be segregated more rigidly by class, and the poor to be moved farther away from the elegant neighborhoods and governmental buildings. The rise of rapid transportation networks like London's Underground (first opened in 1863) would link together neighborhoods, but simultaneously allow workers to commute from longer distances.

European cities were growing: by 1870, Paris had 1.8 million inhabitants and London more than 3 million; the port city of Hamburg had 290,000. Mid-sized towns were expanding too, especially where, as in the Rhine region, there was factory work to be had. Towns along railway lines tended to prosper; those left off the network dwindled in size and significance. Yet even as late as 1866, peasants still comprised nearly 70 percent of the French population. The fraction was about the same in the German states, despite the economic boom and huge waves of overseas emigration that siphoned off 1.3 million German speakers between 1845 and 1858 and another million in 1864–1873. The overwhelming majority of southern and eastern Europeans, in Greece, Spain, Italy, Romania, Austria-Hungary, and Russia, still lived peasant lifestyles, largely unchanged from the lives their great-grandparents had lived, with the important exception that many now knew about and longed for the superior amenities and opportunities available to townspeople. Although some nineteenth-century Europeans, like the trendsetters in metropolitan London, enjoyed the modern lifestyles of the Parisian bourgeoisie, for most people, this world remained a distant dream, or merely a rumor.

The Illiberal Empire: Russia

One of the places where liberalism, capitalism, and even modern urban lifestyles were largely distant dreams was Russia, ruled until 1855 by the reactionary czar Nicholas I. Nicholas was proud of Russia's role in shutting down the 1848 revolutions and continued to believe autocratic rule right and proper for his state. But his bureaucracy was thoroughly corrupt and inefficient, and some members of the westernizing elite clamored for the abolition of serfdom.

When Nicholas's successor, Alexander II (r. 1855–1881), took the throne in 1855, he showed himself favorable at least in part to the westernizers. Alexander immediately set in motion the emancipation of the serfs, though the final legislation did not come into force until 1861. He encouraged railroad building and reformed the army,

making it possible to conscript men of all classes. He also oversaw the creation of provincial representative assemblies with taxing powers, called *zemstvos*. The *zemstvos* were dominated by the nobility, but did manage to take over previously neglected tasks such as the building of public roads, schools, and hospitals. Alexander II also relaxed censorship and encouraged parents to send children to schools and universities, although the number of men in the army far surpassed the number of children in schools, and it was in the army that most Russian men learned to read. Overall, between the 1860s and 1890, Russian literacy rates rose from about 7 percent to about 30 percent of the population.

But Alexander was no liberal, and many of his modernizing reforms showed themselves to be too little too late. Serfs, though officially freed, were compelled to pay landowners for the land their families had worked for generations. Loan rates were so high that most had to agree to fifty-year mortgages, essentially binding them, again, to work the land for the landowners' benefit. Their plight resembled in many ways that of former slaves in the U.S. South, many of whom became poor sharecroppers without land of their own. As the former serfs had no incentive to work hard or modernize their farming techniques, Russian agriculture stagnated, making it harder for the nation to support an industrial revolution.

Alexander also came to regret some of his reforms, perhaps most especially his educational reforms. In the 1860s and 1870s, the universities expanded their function as incubators of radical sentiment. Students were disappointed that reforms had not gone farther and discouraged by the plight of former serfs. Some turned to socialism and attempted to spread revolutionary ideas to the peasantry. This campaign, known as "going to the people," was a dismal failure. The peasants did not want the advice of student philosophers, and the authorities exiled student activists to Siberia (from which, however, most returned alive, to fight another day).

In response to failure and repression, the most radical opponents of the czar turned to anarchism. This philosophy preached that all governments should be abolished, and anarchists adopted terrorist tactics. In 1881, one of these groups, the People's Will, successfully organized a bombing that killed Alexander II. The result of the assassination, however, was that an even more reactionary czar, Alexander III, came to the throne. Alexander III (r. 1881–1897) did his best to stamp out radicalism and keep the old nobility happy. He also undertook a campaign of "Russification," forcing the ethnic minorities in the empire to speak Russian, and unleashed a series of beatings, village burnings, and pillaging known as pogroms against the inhabitants of the Jewish Pale, whom he suspected of being anti-Russian and potentially revolutionary. Not surprisingly, there were numerous attempts on his life, including a foiled assassination plot in 1892 that ended with the execution of Alexander Ulyanov, the brother of Vladimir Lenin.

Although the period from the 1850s to the 1880s was a high point in Russian literary production, with Fyodor Dostoevsky, Ivan Turgenev, and Leo Tolstoy publishing their masterpieces in this era, and although the period did see some reform, Russia did not witness the triumph of either liberalism or capitalism. The czars demonstrated their lack of respect for private property by abolishing serfdom in a stroke and at the same time failing to give the land to the former serfs; they had to bribe nobles to invest in railways and refused to create a national parliament or a constitution. Technically speaking, after emancipation all men were equal under the law, but in practice nobles were preferred in all things. Russia was modernizing and adopting some western ideas; but by no means were the czar's subjects living what, farther to the west, we have come to call the Victorian life.

Living the Victorian Life

In his 1875 novel *The Way We Live Now*, Anthony Trollope satirized the corruptions of **Victorian** capitalism and

How did class society evolve during the Victorian era?

Victorian love. In both matters of money and matters of the heart, people were living differently and, in his view, more dangerously, than ever before. One of the great realist writers, Trollope saw clearly that even in Britain's smaller towns, life had been changed by the diminishing power of the aristocracy. The coming of the railroads and the availability of cheaper, more exotic, and more plentiful goods belonged to an age in which individuals increasingly sought their own freedoms and fortunes. His novels also track the new forms that romance was taking. The utopians' dreams of transforming the family had not materialized, but more couples were crossing class or religious lines to marry, and the idea of marrying for love increasingly supplanted the custom of parent-arranged marriages. Trollope, like other realist writers such as Gustave Flaubert, was perhaps best at describing the new

world of possessions, clothing, and household decoration, and the ways in which their owners lived among, and sometimes for, their increasing collections of things.

Compared to their ancestors and to their neighbors in southern and eastern Europe, British and other northern European consumers were enjoying real increases in wages by 1850. Some, predictably, threw it away on sinful pleasures or piled up shady paper fortunes rather than becoming responsible property owners, a behavior that Trollope caricatured in the villain of *The Way We Live Now*, Augustus Melmotte.

Trollope's Melmotte epitomizes all the evils of modern capitalism, as well as respectable society's fear of foreigners and upstarts. A financier of mysterious, foreign ancestry, whose wife is Jewish, Melmotte is rumored to have been involved in swindles on the continent, but his enormous wealth makes London society grudgingly accept him. His scheme to sell investors forged railway stocks makes him even richer; he obtains a seat in Parliament and a country estate—but his neighbors continue to see him as uncultured and untrustworthy. Eventually his fraud is discovered, and he loses his fortune and poisons himself.

Melmotte was a fraud. But in caricaturing this rapacious financier, Trollope also reminded his readers that it was unsightly to make grand attempts at social climbing. Melmotte could not escape his foreignness and the fact that his money was newly accumulated. His manners, ambitions, and way of speaking betrayed him, just as a servant girl with a lower-class accent and dirty fingernails could scarcely hope to be invited to an aristocratic ball. Victorian society clearly offered more people more opportunities and choices than any European society had offered in the past, but its progressive tendencies were also tempered by lingering prejudices against foreigners, Jews, and Catholics, and by class distinctions that many people found impossible to overcome.

Class Society in the Liberal Era

Class lines were drawn with great rigidity in Britain, but were appearing throughout the rest of Europe as well. As rights were expanded, class mattered more, and as consumer economies grew, Europeans were increasingly conscious that it was income, not birth, that divided the fortunate and influential from the unlucky and powerless. But whereas privileges, under the Old Regimes, had been a matter of law and specified in legal patents (see Chapter 15), class was harder to document. Class could easily be seen, however—in the cut of a neighbor's clothes—or heard—in English spoken with a working-class accent or in German pronounced by native-speaking Poles. Individuals could occasionally escape their families' histories and fall or rise, in class terms, from the positions their parents held—though it was not so easy to gain acceptance to the upper classes, as the example of Melmotte demonstrates, and it was considered a scandal for a wealthy gentleman to fall in love with the family cook and a disaster if he opted to marry her. Even within the lower classes, distinctions existed between the respectable poor, who held steady jobs and kept away from strong drink, gambling, and prostitution, and those who fell below this barrier into the ranks of the disreputable *and* deprived.

Many people thought that with middle-class status came moral qualities, such as sobriety, industriousness, prudence, and marital fidelity. There were numerous ways to demonstrate the widely coveted quality of middle-class respectability, and just as many ways to fail to live up to the norms of good society. It was thought to be a mark of having risen out of the laboring classes for the wife to stay at home and to work in her separate sphere, cleaning and keeping the house, rather than to labor in the fields, factories, or shops. The ability to send one's children to school, rather than to keep them at home to work, was another sign of middle-class rank, as was having sufficient leisure time to join a singing club or a temperance union. For Karl Marx, to be bourgeois was no compliment. But for many Europeans, becoming a respectable citizen (or subject) was an enormous accomplishment, and one the successful were willing to defend with great energy. Just as new national consciousness, the development of urban cultures, and the spread of industrial economies were making Europeans more like one another, class lines were evolving to divide them.

The Victorian Household

For most Europeans, the struggle was not, as it was for Melmotte, to join the upper class, but to leave behind poverty and manual labor for a position in the middling ranks.[4] Those who could escape subsistence existence set their sights on larger accommodations and on employing others to help with the housework and cooking. Others used their surplus money for theater tickets, bets on horse races, home furnishings, fashionable clothing, or a more varied diet. Middle-class families often spent most lavishly on drawing rooms and parties for their friends, hoping to project a luxurious existence, whatever their actual means. Wherever possible, Victorian families also tried to segregate children from adults and servants from masters, seeking to keep everyone in his or her proper place. By mid-century, it was becoming customary for servants to wear uniforms, to keep them from using *their* new income to dress like their employers.

ARTIFICIAL LIGHTING. As Judith Flanders describes in her excellent book *Inside the Victorian Home*, one of the great series of changes in Victorian life came with the addition of gas lighting, first to upper-crust and then to more middling homes and businesses. Common in middle-class London households by 1816, gas lines had reached small English towns by 1850. On the continent, artificial lighting spread more slowly. Gas allowed for a much widened scope of nighttime pursuits; museums, theaters, and shops could now greatly extend their opening hours, and close work like sewing could continue after dark or

be accomplished even in badly lighted interiors. But gas was a mixed blessing; it could also cause explosions or headaches when used improperly, and it made city grime much more visible, propelling forward an obsession with domestic cleanliness and, in turn, the homemaker's desire for help in the perpetual war against dirt.

CLEANLINESS. Cleanliness, said to be next to godliness, was highly prized by Victorians, and housekeepers who let themselves, their homes, or their children fall below respectable standards were seen as moral failures. Keeping up the appearance of respectability was especially important for families recently risen from the lower classes, but even aristocrats needed continually to demonstrate that they still deserved deference. Cleanliness and respectability were increasingly tied to the consumer marketplace. As standards rose and the number of possessions increased, it took more and more brushes, chemicals, and hours of manual labor to run a middle-class home. Most families could afford only one, usually female "maid of all work." The lady of the house had to do the rest herself.

TASTE. Officially, husbands owned all the property, but women were expected to run the household. Middle-class respectability demanded that one's home be more than clean; its public spaces also had to demonstrate taste. As styles began to change more quickly and as some incomes permitted people to choose new curtains, hats, or decorative knickknacks on a regular basis, keeping up with fashion trends became increasingly desirable. The result was, on the one hand, a vast expansion of the market in fancy textiles, china, umbrellas, and scrub brushes, and on the other, increasing pressure on Victorians' pocketbooks.

Women at Home

Though the British were, for most of the nineteenth century, ruled by a queen whose consort, Prince Albert, had no official power and died young, the Victorians tended to frown on women who made themselves too public (indeed, a "public woman" was one way of describing a prostitute). Victoria had tried to portray herself as a dutiful wife and mother, even when she was actively presiding over the state. Her contemporaries were taught to confine their ambitions to the private realm. Though lower-class and lower-middle-class women continued to toil in factories, shops, and upper-class households, the ideal for middle-class women was to marry and to inhabit their own, well-tended homes.

The happy ending of the Victorian novel, in which the respectable young woman marries an eligible bachelor for love, was not necessarily an easy task. In years of high emigration, in which men in large numbers set sail for the Americas or the colonies, about 10 percent of women could not expect to find a partner and therefore failed to meet the ideal of virtuous homemaker. In an era that idolized nuclear families, the livelihoods of single women were particularly precarious. As young women they could be employed as nursemaids, governesses, shopgirls, or cooks, but as they aged they faced great financial uncertainty, as well as uncomfortable social lives lived in *someone else's* home.

Idealized in fiction, staying at home was not necessarily conducive to good health. Even middle-class homes were often poorly heated and badly ventilated, and it was common for rooms to be painted with lead paint or to be adorned with wallpaper, some of which was treated with arsenic. Unattended ladies could go out to call on one another, walk or ride through the parks, or, as the century wore on, shop in fashionable districts. Women's movements were, however, limited by neighborhood, by season, and by the extreme rarity of public lavatories for ladies. It was not respectable to frequent lower-class areas, to go out after dark, or to use privies designed for the use of men.

A Life of Domestic Service

Trollope's strength lay in his depictions of upper- and middle-class English society, rural and urban. He was not so good at depicting the lives of the men and women who made genteel Victorian life possible, namely, the servants. These individuals often worked as hard as, or harder than, contemporaries in the factories. The housemaid's day typically began at 6 a.m. and did not end until 10 p.m. Breaks were few, and perks strictly limited. Most Victorian householders believed that servants should not be spoiled or given opportunities to pilfer the owner's property. Food, soap, and free time were strictly rationed, and the silver and liquor carefully inventoried and locked away by the lady of the house. Much of the servants' work was hard labor—scouring heavy cooking pots, hauling large vessels of water, scrubbing floors, shoveling coal—and was done in badly ventilated kitchens or dark, cold upstairs rooms.

By 1851, one person in six in the city of London was in domestic service. Some of these were workhouse children who earned little more than their keep. In wealthier households, labor was divided, allowing the cook to focus on preparing meals, the scullery maids to clean up after her, the housemaids to take over the endless dusting, floor washing, bed airing, and fireplace sweeping, and the nursemaid or governess to look after the children. Whoever got stuck with the laundry landed a mammoth job, usually undertaken on Mondays. Laundering included boiling, soaking, scrubbing, and wringing out clothes, generally through two washes and four backbreaking rinses, followed by starching, drying, ironing, and sometimes stitching together pieces of clothing that had to be dismantled in order to wash them properly. But most households could not afford a washerwoman as well as housemaids, scullery maids, and governesses; thus, many tasks fell to the "maid of all work" and the lady of the house, who must often have felt it ironic that keeping house was considered genteel rather than manual labor.

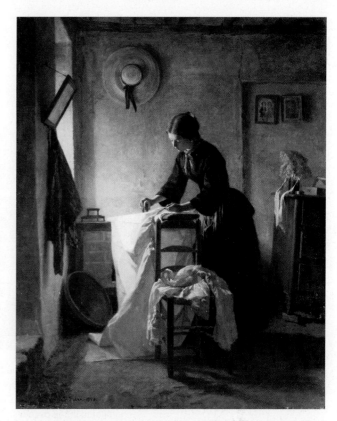

The Laundress One of the most time-consuming and exhausting tasks performed by domestic servants was the laundry.

On Property: The Haves

Although owning property was, increasingly, the ticket to (male) suffrage and even influence, Victorians did not want to invest all their income in land or houses. They also wanted to possess a rapidly expanded selection of consumer items, from paintings to tea tables, from oyster forks to tennis racquets. The number and diversity of foodstuffs, tableware, and textiles available for purchase in 1870 would have shocked even a worldly shopper of the 1770s. Indeed, the recipes in the cookbooks of the era used a much greater number and variety of ingredients than did the bourgeois cookbooks of the Enlightenment or than most cooks do today. Our imaginary 1770 visitor would also have been surprised by the mid-nineteenth century's low prices for foreign-produced commodities such as sugar, tea, tobacco, and chocolate, their affordability the product of Britain's imperial and economic dominance. Living a consumerist life was becoming feasible for a larger number of people, but given the vast number of new commodities for sale, individuals now faced the question, *which* things should one buy? How did one know what the latest fashions or innovations were?

One could, of course, be led by an increasing array of magazines, advertisements, and books, like *Mrs. Beeton's Book of Household Management* (1859) or Charles L. Eastlake's *Hints on Household Taste* (1868). One could also window-shop—as plate-glass windows came into production—or scrutinize the drawing rooms of one's friends. Or one could attend an international exhibition, the first of which was the great Crystal Palace Exhibition of 1851.

Planned by Prince Albert to celebrate the progress of the civilized world, the Crystal Palace Exhibition attracted more than six million visitors and would be imitated in succeeding decades by French, Austrian, and American "world" exhibitions. Set in an enormous park, the Crystal Palace itself was a remarkable feat of both engineering and callousness. Modeled on contemporary greenhouses, the outer structure was made up of 956,000 square feet of leaded-glass panels, all hand blown by glassmakers, whose craft was notoriously life-shortening. The Palace housed some 13,000 exhibits from around the world, designed to show off the bounty produced by the civilized, industrial world, as well as a circus and a dog show. Guests were attracted in particular by displays of manufactured goods and the new machines, including the recently developed flush lavatories, which some 827,000 (or 14 percent) of visitors paid to try.

Visitors took away different things from the exhibition. Some were transported by the light, height, and grandeur of the glass and iron structure itself. Others took away a patriotic message, believing the exhibits demonstrated the superiority of British industries. Some probably found in the "backwardness" of the exhibits of the colonized countries reason to believe in the justness of imperial expansion. Others may have been impressed by the machinery and its promise of easing work for all. But the Crystal Palace's exhibitions were not representative of the realities of most peoples' lives, and the people who operated the machines—the industrial workers—could scarcely afford the time off and train ticket needed to make a visit. Nor could the average factory laborer afford to devote time and income to furnishing tasteful modern homes. The Crystal Palace did not put on display their poverty; nor were victims of industrial accidents, workhouse orphans, or prostitutes exhibited. The Crystal Palace reflected, perhaps, the sides of progress that Prince Albert and the respectable Victorians wanted to see. It did not, of course, reflect the whole story.

On the Propertyless: The Have-Nots

Machine production, efficiencies of scale, and the exploitation of colonial markets and workers put some new commodities within the reach of working-class

The Crystal Palace The Crystal Palace Exhibition attracted middle-class visitors from across Britain and the world. Both the idea of inviting nations from around the world to exhibit their "civilized" achievements and the glass and iron architecture of the "palace" would be widely imitated in the decades to come.

English consumers. Even in the very poor home described by the reformer Elizabeth Gaskell in her novel *Mary Barton* (1848), there are a few niceties—a lacquered tea-tray, potted geraniums, a cupboard full of crockery and glassware. Early in the novel, when company comes, the daughter Mary dashes out to get ham, eggs, rum, tea, and fresh milk. But this scene occurs *before* Mary's mother dies and her factory-employed father loses his job. He then sinks his scanty pocket change into opium, and Mary very nearly starves. As this fictional—but intentionally realistic—episode demonstrates, those with steady work were able to afford more possessions and better food. The problem was that industrial work was rarely steady, and the margin between starving and modest success very thin. One might have property, or goodies, one day and have none the next.

This era saw some improvements in workers' rights and working conditions, particularly in Britain. Earlier attempts had been made to regulate the working hours of children and female laborers, but not until 1870 were serious efforts made to shorten their workweeks. In 1874, legislation officially limited textile workers' shifts to nine and a half hours; in 1878, that limit was applied to all workers. Two years later, compulsory education was mandated for children under ten. Some children managed to escape factory exploitation in this way; but many parents still needed the income, and schooling was put off until the family could make ends meet. Reformers such as Gladstone and Gaskell called attention to the plight of the workers, and organizations such as the Young Men's Christian Association (YMCA; founded in 1844) were formed in the hopes of providing workers wholesome, affordable entertainments. Legislation and reform efforts helped relieve some of the worst evils of early industrial society—in some places—by the 1880s. But limitations on the exploitation of workers and provisions for the have-nots were few, and outside Britain, they arrived even later, or not at all.

Then, too, there were new torments. The increased burning of coal took a terrible toll on the lungs of those who lived near or worked in the factories. The rising demand for plate glass put even more glassmakers at risk of dying from lead poisoning. Hatmakers who regularly used mercury to produce felt suffered from symptoms that mimicked premature senility, a historical reality that makes the Mad Hatter in Lewis Carroll's *Alice's Adventures in Wonderland* (1865) appear less whimsical and more pitiable. Perhaps worst was the reality that one had to have steady work to keep from sliding lower on the social scale, and losing one's grasp on what Disraeli called "the greasy pole." This was a world without safety nets, and the danger of falling was very real.

Thus, even in the midst of a booming industrial economy like that of Britain, there was also *downward* mobility, as families like the Bartons and the Melmottes knew very well. Small manufacturers were undersold by larger producers, large landowners incurred steeper costs and greater debt as grain prices fell, artisanal weavers were replaced by the "satanic mills," and midwives lost status and income to the increasingly male and increasingly professionalized medical doctors. Bankers went bust, and shop girls' indiscretions doomed them to lives of misery, poverty, and finally, prostitution. These people were also living the Victorian life.

The Culture of Positivism

Mid-nineteenth-century culture reflected nineteenth-century life—especially as the middle and upper classes experienced it. It was characterized both by a boisterous self-confidence and by a persistent fear of over-reaching, of allowing too much individualism, too much money, too much speculation, or too much novelty to destroy the progress in the arts and sciences most Europeans believed they were making. The high culture of the era was less utopian and emotional than that of the romantic generation, and more oriented to hard work—carefully researched realist novels and exhaustive dictionaries were perhaps the most characteristic products of mid-nineteenth-century culture. Across a range of genres, intellectuals showed an inclination to turn their backs on the Enlightenment's hopes for mankind's improvement in favor of using scientific approaches to capture objective realities. The emphasis on empirical data collection, description, and ordering did not mean these scholars, artists, and writers were uncritical. Many, like the French novelist Honoré de Balzac and the French painter Edouard Manet, used realism to indict a society they saw as corrupt and heartless. But their works reflected less a longing for change than a post-romantic positivist view of the world, one laid out most fully by the French philosopher-scientist-sociologist Auguste Comte.

In what ways did positivism represent a rejection of romanticism?

Positivism and Liberal Order

Chronologically, Comte (1798–1857) belongs more properly to the late romantic period than to the Victorian age, but he developed his philosophy of **positivism** in the 1820s as an antidote to romantic speculation and revolutionary politics. Like other proponents of the scientific method, Comte believed that all knowledge came through the senses and that, in the course of time, empirical sciences could be developed to derive laws for both nature and social interaction. He also believed in a hierarchy of the sciences, with the simpler natural sciences forming the foundations of human knowledge, upon which the more complicated social and moral sciences could be built. Hoping that these sciences could succeed in improving the human condition where politics or religion had failed, Comte concocted a grand system according to which real, lasting knowledge replaced speculation.

In this antiromantic philosophy, scholars were supposed to put aside the big, unanswerable questions—like the true nature of human beings or the existence of God—in favor of describing, computing, and organizing things that were observable. Despite his rhetoric, however, Comte had a tendency to range beyond the facts and, by the 1840s, had invented his own religion of humanity. Comte's religion, his critics said, amounted to Catholicism without Christianity, in which science replaced divine scripture and Comte himself assumed the role of pope.

Comte was considered a crackpot by some of those who knew him best, and few members of his generation actually believed in either his system or his religion. Nevertheless, Comte's passion for facts and for order typified the era and found echoes in the works of other influential thinkers such as the British philosopher and social scientist Herbert Spencer, whose work on the evolution of biological and social organisms was widely read in Europe, America, and the developing world. Even Karl Marx agreed that the era of romanticism, idealism, and utopianism was dead and wrote *Das Kapital*, a three-volume, nonspeculative and scientific analysis of the laws of the bourgeois economy to prove, he hoped beyond question, the inevitability of capitalism's collapse. Marx's analysis was so detailed that he completed only the first volume of the work (published in 1867). His friend and collaborator Friedrich Engels completed and published the other two volumes in 1885 and 1894.

Positivism was a philosophy of sorting, describing, and ordering rather than explaining things and in this way suited the Victorian world of perpetually increasing information and objects. This was a world in which ladies were encouraged to keep household accounts and detailed inventories in pre-printed books, debt and disorder being equally unpalatable to the Victorian mind. It was in this era that censuses were instituted, library catalogs initiated, and, in 1861, a massive "Archaeological Survey of India" begun. The classification systems for animals, minerals, and plants developed by Carolus Linnaeus in the eighteenth century had to be enormously expanded as samples, skeletons, and seeds flooded European museums and laboratories. As art museums expanded, new techniques needed to be developed simply to date and authenticate artworks and to label items before they were put on display or joined the crush in the storeroom. In its broad sense, positivism was simply a philosophy driven by the need to contain disorder, and the hope that one day, all things would fall into place, and subject themselves to that great liberal ideal, the rule of law.

Charles Darwin, Victorian Positivist

One of the great law-seekers of the mid-nineteenth century was the English naturalist Charles Darwin (1809–1882). Darwin was a typical positivist. Throughout his life he remained a fanatical collector of facts, observations, fossils, sketches, and ideas about animals. He began his endeavors as a beetle collector and reader of travelogues even before he sailed to South America and the Pacific aboard *The Beagle* in 1831. During his four-year voyage, following in the enlightened tradition of Joseph Banks (see Chapter 16), Darwin recorded a vast amount of information in his notebooks. In 1838, he had something of a revelation as he read Thomas Malthus's *An Essay on the Principle of Population* (1798), in which the clergyman described as a law the inevitability that populations rise faster than food supply and, thus, that individuals must struggle to survive. Applying this law to his notebook data, Darwin worked out what was distinctive about his theory: the idea that species are not fixed, but evolve over time, and that evolution is powered by **natural selection,** the competitive process by which some individual animals or plants live to pass on their traits, and others do not.

Darwin did not ask *why* this happened, and in *On the Origin of Species* (1859), he even declined to explain what his theory implied for human evolution. In his much later *The Descent of Man* (1871), he did try to apply his principles to human societies, following Comte's recommendation that scientists work up from lower to higher forms. In *The Descent of Man*, Darwin also explored the ideas of sexual selection and sexual dimorphism, which helped him explain in evolutionary terms the differences between the "higher" and "lower" races, and between men and women. Darwin was a quintessential Victorian—and one of the most consequential elaborators of scientific positivism of his age.

Realism in Literature

In some respects, literature and the fine arts as well as science partook of the positivist mindset. In literature, the genre known as **realism** was all the rage. Rather than setting their novels in exotic places or in distant historical eras, writers described their own world and their own unexalted contemporaries. In France, Honoré de Balzac laid out a whole series of human types on the model of a Linnaean zoological table. In his multivolume *Human Comedy* (1830–1850), Balzac sought to sketch the whole range of class-bound behaviors he saw around him, from those of the still arrogant but cash-strapped aristocracy to those of the ridiculously idealistic bohemian poets. The English writer Charles Dickens (1812–1870) displayed similar inclinations in his novels, although with greater attention to the plight of the poor. Dickens resisted the use of romantic scenery in favor of setting novels like *Oliver Twist* (1837–1839) in sooty, congested cities. Realist writers tried to avoid high diction and romantic emotionalism or even made fun of these flowery forms of expression.

The master of literary realism was French novelist Gustave Flaubert (1821–1880), who once said that his great ambition was to write a novel about nothing. In *Madame Bovary* (1857), he dissected the life of a provincial nobody, whose romantic affair and suicide—caused by her debts rather than by her shame—were entirely banal. Pretending to be only description, realism could certainly serve as a social critique, of bourgeois morals, as in Flaubert, or of factory labor, as in Dickens, but it was also an art form, an attempt to capture, and immortalize, its world in ink.

Realism and Impressionism in Painting

The same could be said of painting in this era. Interest in grand panoramas and romantic landscapes gradually gave way to a focus on contemporary ways of life. Some depictions of the new society were critical, as were Gustave Courbet's paintings of stone breakers or Adolf Menzel's tribute to the victims of the 1848 revolutions. Others were not. The mid-nineteenth century was the great era of genre painting, the depiction of everyday and often sentimental scenes, and artists such as the German Carl Spitzweg flourished by painting gently humorous or sentimental images of the middle-class public. The experimental painters known as the impressionists could fit in to either camp. Although the academies of art rejected their style of painting, known as **Impressionism,** most impressionists were not particularly radical in their politics. Some, like Pierre-Auguste Renoir, ended up paying tribute in paint to the new bourgeois cultures of Paris and the provinces. Others, like Edouard Manet, were suspicious of the new class and produced critical images such as *Olympia*, in which a prostitute looks defiantly at a presumably male viewer.

The impressionists were above all artists, but their specific style of painting derived from their desire to translate some of the new sciences into oil. The idea, for innovators

Christianity and Evolutionary Theory in the Victorian Age

Charles Darwin was a very important figure in mid-nineteenth-century science, but he was by no means the only proponent of evolutionary theory. For many years Darwin has been depicted as a lonely revolutionary and the man who completed the Enlightenment's destruction of Christianity in Europe. But in recent decades, historians of science have been recovering the cultural and theological context in which Darwin penned *On the Origin of Species.* What they have found is that the debate over evolution neither began nor ended with Darwin. As historian James Secord has shown, it was another book, *Vestiges of the Natural History of Creation,* that acquainted Victorian society with the idea that the universe, the earth, and all plants and animals were not created once and in their fixed forms by God but rather were the products of evolutionary processes.[5]

Vestiges appeared anonymously in 1844, because its author, the Scottish journalist Robert Chambers, feared that the free-thinking book would damage his reputation as a respectable gentleman. He was right: the book horrified the clergy and provoked intense debate among scientists. The very public debate that ensued, in newspapers, journals, and popular lectures, made for sensational sales. Victorians of all descriptions discussed the work, from Victoria and Albert to the working women and men who picked up copies of the paperback edition. This debate was so intense and so bitter that Darwin's theory of evolution, wisely labeled a hypothesis and not a natural law, seemed, by contrast, hardly controversial. Moreover, Darwin's multitude of observed facts, as well as his careful explanation of natural selection, made *On the Origin of Species* appear to be respectable and acceptable science, rather than—like Chambers's book—"infidel philosophy." In the 1860s, two of Darwin's defenders, the naturalists Thomas Huxley and Alfred Russel Wallace, applied the ideas of Chambers and Darwin to human beings—and in so doing put themselves on the front lines of the new, often venomous disputes that ensued. By the time Darwin wrote *The Descent of Man,* the most passionate phase of that debate was already ending.

But that does not mean that Darwin had won or that science had triumphed over faith. Working from another direction, another historian of science, Peter J. Bowler, has shown that it was fully possible for mid-nineteenth-century readers to find different things in Darwin's texts and to combine Darwinism and Christian faith. Reading a book about natural history, particularly one like *On the Origin of Species,* which said almost nothing about the origins of humans, did not cause Christian belief to crumble. As another historian has argued, it makes little sense to think "that Victorian intellectuals lost their faith as the rest of us lose umbrellas."[6] Although churchgoing declined during the nineteenth century, this trend began in the eighteenth century and had more to do with rising urbanization, mobility, dissent within the churches, and the decline of clerical power (caused in part by enlightened absolutism) than it did with any scientific theories. Even after Darwin's death, theology did not die. Neither evolutionary biology, nor radical critiques of biblical scriptures by philosophers, philologists, and geologists, could kill it. In mid-nineteenth-century Germany, fully one in six books published was a work of theology, and other national readerships probably devoured roughly the same diet. And why not? Theologians remained respected intellectuals, and there were still plenty of parsonages or priesthoods available to them at a time when natural science was only gradually becoming a real profession. As late as the 1850s, Secord reminds us, parents must have seen choosing a career in science as just about as risky and disreputable as joining the circus.

Long after *Origin,* Darwin's theory of natural selection remained one of many versions of evolutionary thinking. Many leading scientists continued to believe that Darwin's statements could be reconciled with those of the French biologist Jean-Baptist Lamarck, who believed in the inheritance of acquired characteristics. Others flirted with eugenic ideas, hoping to use what they knew about natural selection to breed healthier, smarter, and more "fit" human beings. Some applied versions of evolutionary theory to the history of human societies, arguing for the necessary and predictable triumph of Christian monotheism over other world religions—or for the logical, unavoidable victory of socialism over capitalism. In the nineteenth century, evolutionism was much bigger than Darwin, and science was by no means an uncontroversial set of practices and ideas.

QUESTION | *Did evolutionary theory simply extend the challenges to Christian doctrine posed by the radical Enlightenment (Chapter 16), or did it pose a new threat?*

like Claude Monet, was to paint light and the way it reflected from objects onto the human retina. It took some time for Victorian-era viewers to get used to what many thought was simply sloppy brushwork, but perhaps artists found it easier to move away from older conventions of representation because a new medium had arrived to mirror reality: photography. Invented in 1839, the creation of images of the world using chemicals and glass plates rapidly became faster and easier for amateurs to use, and less expensive. By the 1850s, middle-class individuals

Edouard Manet, _A Bar at the Folies-Bergère_ This impressionist masterpiece performs a visual trick: the viewer seems to see the waitress and her reflection at the same time. Manet also captures the loneliness of the working woman: she seems melancholy while all around her the wealthy theater-goers are enjoying their evening of leisure.

could have their portraits taken; by the 1870s, social reformers, world travelers, and archaeologists were using photographs to document what they saw. Europeans gained greater exposure to images of all kinds as enormous panorama displays traveled from town to town, entrepreneurs sold stereoscopic viewing machines, and more and more journals and newspapers printed lithographs or photos.

Realism in Music

In music, some composers followed their contemporaries in art and literature and attempted to write realistic operas or impressionistic tone poems. Grand opera continued to flourish, and many operas told stories that reflected current social issues. Based on a novel by Alexandre Dumas, Giuseppe Verdi's _La Traviata_ ("The Woman Who Strayed") told the story of a nobleman who falls in love with a courtesan. Desperate to protect the family name and fortune, the nobleman's father per-

suades the courtesan to leave her lover. The lover later returns to the courtesan's bedside only to find her dying of tuberculosis, the cause of much working-class suffering at the time. Dramatizing the lingering taboos surrounding cross-class relationships and making heroes of the lovers, rather than the tradition-protecting father, _La Traviata_ was immensely popular across Europe.

But realism was not the only style composers chose at mid-century. In Germany, Richard Wagner (1813–1883) rejected French and Italian cultural styles, which he claimed were contaminated by "the Jewish spirit." Wagner turned instead to Teutonic and Norse mythological themes for his operas, hoping in this way to plumb the depths of the human, and especially German, psyche. Using shocking dissonances and eliminating frivolous solos, Wagner composed lengthy, intensely serious music dramas that thrilled, or revolted, his contemporaries. He despised conventional opera-house culture, in which the lights stayed on so that audience members could talk with and look at their neighbors. Wagner insisted on darkening and silencing the theater so that listeners would watch his operas in a sort of trance. In this way, he believed, the powerful sensuality of works like *Tristan and Isolde* and *Parsifal* would transport them beyond their humdrum lives into a realm of deeper understanding of life's mysteries. For decades Wagner's music was highly controversial, but by the time he died in 1883 his influence on European composers (including Verdi) was pervasive. Wagner's combination of musical modernism and musical nationalism (and anti-Semitism) would make him a major force in European cultural history long after his passing.

Richard Wagner In 1870, Wagner married the daughter of one of his musical idols, Franz Liszt. Here Wagner is pictured with his wife Cosima, the gray-haired Liszt, and one of Wagner's own disciples. Wagner stands underneath a portrait of his favorite philosopher, Arthur Schopenhauer, whose pessimistic philosophy the German composer did much to popularize.

Remaking Metternich's Map

While impressionists, realists, and Wagnerians were seeking new ways of representing mid-nineteenth-century society, others were imagining

> How were German and Italian leaders able to transform Europe's map?

a new *geography* for Europe. Maps, of course, are human inventions, imposed on the landscape, and at various times societies feel the artificiality of those inventions and seek to change them. The maps made by the people of this period were not preordained. After the collapse of Napoleon's empire and the revolutions of 1830 and 1848, things *could* have been put back together in different ways. Just as engineers, fishermen, and statesmen fought to give the Rhine its modern shape, so too was the shaping of modern European nation-states and economies a contest, one in which some people and some maps won—and others lost out.

As we have seen, the French Revolutionary Wars forced the remaking of the map of Europe. Even the Congress of Vienna had been unable to restore all prerevolutionary borders. In the Italian and German states, nationalists and modernizers called for the creation of larger states, hoping to replace the continent's patchwork of political and economic systems with rationalized rights for the people and modernized markets. By contrast, in territories dominated by the Ottoman, Russian, and Habsburg Empires, Czech, Polish, Hungarian, Bulgarian, and Ukrainian nationalists sought to form *smaller* states, hoping thereby to get out from under the thumb of monarchs and nobles who still clung to the restored Old Regimes.

The period between 1850 and 1890 was an era of things falling apart and things being put together in new ways.

But in fact, not all nationalists managed to achieve their dreams in this era. Many of the nationality groups in eastern and southeastern Europe would need the help of the devastating Great War of 1914–1918 to really remake Metternich's map.

Breaking Old Maps: The Crimean War

For the unifications of Italy and Germany to succeed, the map-making ability of one other state had to be destroyed. That state was Metternich's old base camp, the Austrian Empire. In the 1850s, the Habsburgs still ruled over vast territories and wielded considerable political and military clout, though they had had to accept Russian help to put down the Hungarian uprising of 1849. But their multinational empire faced considerable difficulties in the era of triumphant liberalism, nationalism, and capitalism. First, centralization was hampered by an array of old privileges and by the increasing desire of other national groups in the empire to obtain economic, political, and cultural influence equal to that of the German ruling elite. Second, the rural character and long-lasting power of landed nobles in the eastern half of the empire made industrial development difficult. As other states grew stronger and pressures within the Austrian Empire mounted, it became increasingly clear that the Habsburgs could no longer manage the continental balance of power.

But if the Austrian Empire was becoming increasingly vulnerable, it was even more obvious that the neighboring multiethnic state, the Ottoman Empire, was in disarray. After losing control over Greece and Serbia (see Chapter 18), the Ottomans had also been forced to give Egypt virtual autonomy after 1839. Reforms in the 1830s helped, but the Ottoman Empire remained economically underdeveloped with respect to western European states and soon found itself deeply in debt to them. Concerned European diplomats began to discuss what might happen if the Empire should collapse entirely. Liberals especially feared that Russia, that bastion of reaction, would fill vacuums left by the Ottomans' retreat and become even more powerful. It was anxieties about this **Eastern Question** that provoked the outbreak of the mid-century's major international conflict: the Crimean War.

Scutari Hospital during the Crimean War After hearing horrific reports about conditions at this major field hospital, the British sent a team of nurses, including Florence Nightingale, to remedy the situation. Nightingale's team worked hard to improve sanitation, but still many more soldiers sent to Scutari died of disease and infections than of wounds received in battle.

The British, French, and Russians all contributed to destabilizing the balance of power after 1850. The British were meddling in the internal affairs of the Greeks, Egyptians, and Ottomans and extending their influence in Asia. To demonstrate his supposed global influence, Napoleon III claimed France's right to protect Christians in the Holy Land. His claim enraged the Russians, who insisted that the Ottomans reiterate the czar's rights to protect Orthodox Christians. To emphasize the point, they then occupied Ottoman territories in what would later be called Romania, home to many Orthodox Christians.

The Ottomans declared war in October 1853, but would have been too weak to prevail had not the British and French joined their side in December 1854. The British used their naval power to bottle up the Russians in the Baltic and Black Seas, and the British, French, and Piedmontese sent troops into the Crimean peninsula (see Map 19.4). More than 500,000 on the Russian and perhaps as many as 400,000 on the Ottoman-Allied side did not return. For the first time, the railroad and telegraph were put to military use, and the Russians used new, industrially produced explosives to power underwater mines. The British also sent newspaper correspondents and medical personnel, including a team of thirty-eight nurses headed by Florence Nightingale, to the main field hospital at Scutari, near Istanbul. Nightingale's exemplary battlefield service, fundraising abilities, and heroization in the press helped popularize nursing as a profession for women, even though conditions at Scutari continued to be grim.

The Crimean War was horribly bloody for its era and was notable afterward for the large numbers who died of disease, the many military blunders committed, and the changes in international relations that it ushered in. Although the Ottomans won the war, frustrating Russia's expansionist ambitions, their dependence on Western help was telling. Furthermore, Austria's refusal to support its former Russian ally caused a rift between these two supporters of imperial authority. Unsure of Russian support on its eastern flank, the Austrians now were left alone to face threats from Italian, German, or Hungarian nationalists. Naturally, this offered new opportunities to those eager to exploit them. Opportunity was what both Otto von Bismarck (1815–1898) and Camillo di Cavour (1810–1861), the great champions of unification, thrived on, the former insisting in one of his humbler moments that individuals were able only to "leap in and catch hold of [God's] coat-tail and be dragged along as far as may be."[7]

Unifications and Their Makers

The two major unifications of the nineteenth century's second half, that of Italy and of Germany, were accomplished by leaders who had not been devoted to the idea of nation-state building at the outset of their careers and who were much more pragmatic antirevolutionaries than romantic ideologues. Both Cavour and Bismarck opposed the revolutions of 1848 and came to champion their national causes largely because they thought that by unifying their states from above, they could prevent them from falling into the hands of republican radicals. It is striking that Cavour and Bismarck put their plans into action at the same time that President Abraham Lincoln was struggling to keep the United States together. In his own way, Lincoln too waged a war of unification: but it

Abraham Lincoln and American Unification

Abraham Lincoln, too, had problems with national unity. But whereas his Italian and German contemporaries, Camillo di Cavour and Otto von Bismarck, exploited changes in the balance of power to create new states where none had existed before, Lincoln's mission was to prevent the dissolution of what had been a united nation. Lincoln's task was also complicated by the fact that he was trying to hold together a democracy, whereas the others were seeking to expand kingdoms. Lincoln did prevail, but at the cost of more than 650,000 lives, more than twice the number who died in the Italian and German conflicts combined.

In 1860, Lincoln's United States bore some interesting similarities to the German and Italian states. In the United States, as in Italy and Germany, industrial development was concentrated in the North, whereas the southern regions devoted themselves chiefly to agriculture. But the U.S. South was not particularly poor or commercially underdeveloped, as was southern Italy. Like the North, it was home to both Protestant and Catholic Christians, with a few Jews mixed in; north and south were not divided on religious lines, as in Germany. In the United States, the big difference between the two sections was not language, religion, or wealth, but the fact that the southern states permitted slave-holding, and the northern states did not. Nor was slavery merely an incidental part of southern culture and the southern economy. Although most white southerners did not own even a single slave, and very few owned large numbers, slavery underwrote the prosperity, the culture, and even the self-image of southerners. Slave labor made it possible to grow cash crops like cotton, sugar, and rice cheaply, increasing the salability of southern goods on world markets.

By 1861, when Lincoln took office, white southerners were accustomed to prospering from slave labor and to seeing themselves as the rightful masters or "fathers" of inferior African Americans. After many earlier battles with northern abolitionists, these white southerners had come to see the block of slaveholding states as the political entity that preserved their honor, their prosperity, and their way of life. Whereas Bismarck and Cavour had to convince people who had lived in small kingdoms to feel love and loyalty for bigger, stronger, and wealthier nation-states, Lincoln had to fight against people who already felt a kind of patriotism for a wealthy and powerful entity, the South, and to force them to adopt values and governance from an entity they viewed as foreign and hostile. And fight they did, with everything they had, in a war that turned out to be much longer and much more destructive than anyone had anticipated and that left the defeated resentful and defiant for generations to come.

Lincoln was no aristocrat, as were Bismarck and Cavour. In European terms, he was a political radical. He believed in popular sovereignty and championed "government by, for, and of the people." He could not afford spa vacations, and he had no land on which to try out agricultural experiments. He was a hard-working, self-taught country lawyer who could tell popular stories as well as deliver eloquent speeches. Cavour, by contrast, was slick and sly, and Bismarck was a brilliant bully. Lincoln could be pragmatic; although he felt strongly about the issue, he did not promise to end slavery in his election campaign of 1860, and when he issued the Emancipation Proclamation in 1863, the document applied almost exclusively to territories over which his government had no control. But he was not an opportunist. He did not willingly provoke war, as did Cavour and Bismarck, but once it began, he refused to accept anything but the South's unconditional surrender to unification on his terms. That made the American Civil War far and away the bloodiest of the nineteenth century's wars of unification—and Lincoln one of the best-loved, but also one of the most hated, presidents in American history.

Lincoln Visiting the Union Camp at Antietam, 1862 Unlike Cavour and Bismarck, Abraham Lincoln had come from humble roots, and never wore fancy sashes, or military decorations. He felt the devastation and grief of his war of unification more keenly as well.

QUESTIONS | *Compare this description of Lincoln with the depictions of Bismarck and Cavour in the remainder of the chapter. How are these individuals different? What do these differences tell you about the differences between American and European politics in the age of nationalism?*

was a very different conflict, and Lincoln, every inch a man of the people, was a very different sort of man.

Through clever diplomacy and the waging of strategic wars, Cavour and Bismarck managed to forge new and powerful nations out of quite diverse pieces of territory. But these pragmatic unions remained torn by internal strife and caused neighboring states considerable anxiety.

ITALIAN UNIFICATION. As we saw in Chapter 18, the campaign for Italian unification, led by Giuseppe Mazzini, was squelched in 1849, after Austrian troops defeated the army organized by Charles Albert of Piedmont-Sardinia, and forced him to abdicate in favor of his son, Victor Emmanuel II. Under Victor Emmanuel, Piedmont-Sardinia emerged as the most liberal and prosperous of the Italian-speaking states. It announced its arrival on the world stage by joining the British and French in the Crimean War. Piedmontese writers continued to produce and export nationalist propaganda, and Piedmont also produced pro-capitalist landowners like Camillo di Cavour, for whom the Italian nationalists' call for *Risorgimento* (revival) meant moderate, deliberate modernization from above, not mass mobilization from below.

Cavour was in many respects a classic liberal: he had read the works of Jeremy Bentham and admired the French liberal François Guizot. As a landowner, he experimented with modern methods to increase crop yields. He supported lowering tariffs and building railroads, removing clerical privileges and guild restrictions, limiting royal authority, and enhancing the freedom of the press. But he was willing to sacrifice any and all of these principles at various times in his career, especially when he thought it strategically necessary to preserve his position as prime minister of Piedmont, which he had received in 1851. Cavour's genius for intrigue was notorious, and he was not above spreading misinformation when it suited his purpose. In 1859, he so vexed Victor Emmanuel by telling him his mistress was engaging in orgies with other men that the king nearly challenged his own prime minister to a duel. And yet, it was Cavour's wily diplomacy that created a much greater kingdom for Victor Emmanuel, for it was the king of Piedmont-Sardinia who in 1861 became the first king of Italy.

How Cavour accomplished this task deserves some scrutiny, as the knitting together of the territories that became Italy was neither foreordained nor particularly rational. In the 1850s, the Italian peninsula was a patchwork of states, from the Bourbon-ruled Kingdom of the Two Sicilies in the south to Savoy and Nice near the Swiss and French borders. The pope ruled the areas around Rome, and the Austrian Habsburgs still controlled the large provinces of Venetia and Lombardy to the north (Map 19.2). Most of these people did not consider themselves Italians or even speak Italian. In the province of Sardinia in Cavour's backyard, many people spoke Catalan. Many people in the Austrian-dominated areas spoke German, and in Savoy, they spoke French. Cavour himself long believed that the Sicilians spoke Arabic.[8] They might well

MAP 19.2 | Italian Unification, 1859–1870

This map shows the process by which the Italian states were united to form modern Italy. ***Why did it take so long for Italy to become a unified state? What similarities do you see?***

have done so, for all he knew. Even on the eve of unification, Cavour had never traveled as far south as Tuscany. Throughout his life, Cavour himself spoke better French than Italian; the former was his native tongue.

If the Italian peninsula was a linguistic patchwork, economic conditions were equally disparate. Whereas Sicily and Sardinia remained essentially feudal, agricultural lands, Piedmont was being crisscrossed by railroads and telegraph lines. What it meant, then, to unify Italy was really to *create* Italy—when and where the opportunity arose to do so.

Cavour began his aim of unification by bribing Napoleon III to help him drive the Austrians out of Lombardy—the reward for the French was to be Savoy and Nice. In 1859, Cavour provoked war with the Habsburgs, and French armies helped the Piedmontese take Lombardy and agreed to allow several other states to join the new confederation. In 1860, France and Piedmont signed the Treaty of Turin, giving Victor Emmanuel Tuscany, Parma, Modena, and the Romagna. Napoleon III received Savoy and Nice, as promised. Northern and central Italy had now been unified, but Venetia, the Papal States, and the Kingdom of the Two Sicilies remained outside the union.

Fortunately for Cavour, a rebellion in the latter territory over taxes and bread prices erupted in 1860. Giuseppe Garibaldi, one of the most popular leaders of the 1848 revolutions, saw this revolt as his opportunity to do his bit for the cause of unification. Unlike Cavour, Garibaldi was a passionate, *republican* nationalist, who had spent his time in exile fighting with South American rebels. Suspicious of Garibaldi's radical views, Cavour hesitated to bankroll his efforts. Thus, Garibaldi had a makeshift army of only one thousand radical followers—many of them wearing Garibaldi's trademark red shirt—with which to invade Sicily in 1860. The population, however, greeted Garibaldi as a liberator and helped drive out the Bourbons. Fired with the idea of joining south and north, the ragtag army then marched northward.

Civil war between the southern republican army under Garibaldi and the liberal monarchist factions behind Cavour was averted when Garibaldi agreed to give way and accept Victor Emmanuel as his king. Victor Emmanuel was crowned king of Italy in March 1861—even though Italy as we know it today was still incomplete. Austria kept Venetia until 1866, when the Italians took advantage of the Prussian victory in the Austro-Prussian War to seize the territory. When French troops protecting the Vatican left Rome to fight *their* war against the Prussians in 1870, the city of Rome, too, was annexed, completing the new Italian state.

GERMAN UNIFICATION. For the most part, the Prussians spent the 1850s and early 1860s engaged in economic build-up. As agricultural production became much more efficient, Prussians and other Germans began a period of rapid industrialization. But many, including the Prussian nobleman Otto von Bismarck, watched carefully as Italian unification progressed. Bismarck, who was appointed to the powerful position of chancellor by Kaiser Wilhelm I in 1862, had some of the same problems that Cavour faced. Although he disapproved of liberal nationalism, Bismarck wanted to free Prussia from Austrian

Giuseppe Garibaldi, Republican Hero After his years fighting with South American rebels, Garibaldi continued to wear a red shirt and poncho to signify that his heart lay with the people.

CHRONOLOGY	Key Events in the Unifications of Germany and Italy
DATE	**EVENT**
1859	Austria loses Lombardy to Piedmont-Sardinia
1860	Garibaldi invades Sicily
1861	Victor Emmanuel crowned king of Italy
1862	Bismarck appointed chancellor of Prussia
1866	Austria loses Venetia to Italy, and loses the Austro-Prussian War
1866	Prussia creates the North German Confederation
1870–1871	Franco-Prussian War; Rome incorporated into Italy
1871	German Empire proclaimed

domination in the German Confederation. Once he resolved that the way to do it was to deploy nationalism to his own ends and to create an independent Germany, he had to put together diverse territories with different economic interests. He also had to force provincial elites to make way for a centralizing and modernizing state, to be run, as was the new Italy, by the royal house and bureaucracy of one northern state, in this case, Prussia.

Bismarck also sought to unite peoples with different languages. Although German speakers predominated, there were French speakers in Alsace and Lorraine, Polish speakers in East Prussia, and Danish speakers in Schleswig and Holstein. A greater difficulty for the Prussians would be the incorporation into one state of both Protestants and a very large minority of Catholics. Bismarck sought to accomplish unification by using many of the same tactics as did Cavour: strategic warfare, with limited aims; cunning and sometimes deceptive diplomacy; and the pragmatic exploitation of opportunities. Both had stolen the ideas of national unification and economic modernization from the playbook of left-wing republicans. But Bismarck, who had the good fortune to live longer, was even more successful in building a state that could join the club of the great European powers.

THE EMBARRASSMENT AT OLMÜTZ.
The tale of German unification begins with an embarrassment. In 1850, the Prussians made a move to dissolve the Austria-dominated German Confederation in favor of a federation headed by the Prussians. The Austrians, with Russian backing, threatened war, and the Prussians, their military too weak to face Habsburg troops, were forced to sign the Treaty of Olmütz, which essentially reconstituted the German Confederation of 1815. Olmütz was deeply humiliating for conservative Prussians, proud of their military traditions, and inspired first the Prussian king Friedrich Wilhelm IV and then his successor, Wilhelm I, to push hard to strengthen the Prussian army.

To do that, however, they needed funding from the parliamentary body created in the wake of the 1848 revolutions, the Prussian *Landtag*. By the late 1850s, the *Landtag* was full of wealthy liberals, men who despised the old aristocratic Junker elite and who wanted to see economic policy modernized, clerical influence over schooling and the press ended, and the rule of law enforced on all. These liberal delegates balked when Wilhelm I tried to force through lavish funding for an army that delegates feared might become an instrument of domestic repression. To break the liberals' resistance, in 1862 Wilhelm called in a new chancellor, a Prussian Junker noted for his powerful antirevolutionary rhetoric, but also—like Cavour—eager to drag his state into the modern economy: Otto von Bismarck. In his first speech to the *Landtag*, Bismarck chastised the liberals for thinking that German unification would be achieved by "majority votes and parliamentary resolutions." Instead, Bismarck maintained, the task would require "blood and iron"—battles and advanced

industrialization. The Iron Chancellor, as Bismarck was known, did not mention but certainly believed that it would also take autocratic leadership willing to risk lives and fortunes to build a new central European powerhouse.

REALPOLITIK.
Otto von Bismarck was a unique individual. A pious Protestant, he was willing to renounce his allies, deceive his friends, provoke wars, and lock up (Catholic) clergymen when he thought the situation required doing so. An exceptionally cultivated aristocrat and masterful rhetorician, he also told coarse jokes and enjoyed shooting porpoises. Bismarck's policies all along were shaped by what one disillusioned liberal had called *Realpolitik:* the banishing of ideals, philosophies, and friendships in favor of the exploitation of opportunities. Bismarck employed *Realpolitik* in domestic as well as international politics. In 1866, he followed the lead of Napoleon III and pushed through universal suffrage in national elections for males over the age of twenty-five in the North German Confederation. He would extend it to the whole of the new German Empire in 1871. He did this not because he believed the people should rule but because he thought he could thereby steal the liberals' thunder and defuse their criticism. This was cynical, pragmatic *Realpolitik*—and it worked.

BISMARCK'S WARS OF UNIFICATION.
In a rather Darwinian way, Bismarck believed that the preservation of Prussian power and the power of the aristocracy within Prussia would be achieved only by struggle and expansion. But to expand, he needed a modern army. Although the liberals refused to grant him more funding, he collected taxes illegally to finance military build-up. Then, to the liberals' embarrassment, he set about using this army to pursue a policy of enlarging the state, along the lines of the "small German" solution proposed by Protestant nationalists in the Frankfurt Parliament of 1848.

Bismarck was fortunate that his tenure coincided with an economic and demographic boom in the German states. By 1866, Prussia had 19 million inhabitants (to Austria's 33 million) and stood to gain 20 million more if it could unite with the other states with which it was linked by the *Zollverein*. This expansion gave him the "iron"—including the vital railroad linkages—as well as the "blood" with which to launch his expansionist campaign. In 1864, the Iron Chancellor provoked the first in a series of conflicts, this one with the Danish monarchy over the provinces of Schleswig and Holstein. The two nations went to war, and Prussia's revamped army easily rolled over the Danes. Seeing their long-cherished project of national unification now succeeding, most of the liberals became vigorous supporters of Bismarck's plans.

In 1866, the chancellor again made war, this time against Austria, to prevent that state from standing in the way of the Prussian steamroller. Most Europeans failed to predict not only the outcome of this war, but its brevity. In just three weeks, the Prussian army chased the

Austrians to the village of Sadowa near the Elbe, where they captured 44,000 soldiers and put the remaining 196,000 to flight. The Italians seized the opportunity to send their own army into Venetia, forcing the Austrians to give up Lombardy (Map 19.3). The Hungarians were emboldened to ask for semiautonomy in the Austro-Prussian War's aftermath, and in the Compromise of 1867, they got it.

In Paris, Napoleon III now recognized that a dangerous new power had risen on his flank and considered making war on Prussia right away to grab the industrialized Ruhr valley and the wealthy cities of Cologne, Koblenz, and Düsseldorf on the German side of the Rhine. He also hoped to prevent the large, prosperous, and well-armed states of Bavaria, Saxony, and Württemberg from uniting with Prussia. Napoleon III's well-founded fears, along with Bismarck's unfulfilled ambitions, drove France and Prussia closer and closer to the brink of war in 1867–1870.

Bismarck manufactured a diplomatic crisis when, in early 1870, a prince from the Prussian house of Hohenzollern was offered the Spanish throne. The French haughtily insisted that the Prussian royal family relinquish all claims to the post. Wilhelm I, on vacation at a spa in Ems, sent the French emperor a semiconciliatory telegram, but Bismarck edited Wilhelm's words to make the telegram sound more bellicose. The chancellor then leaked what became known as the Ems Telegram to the French press, provoking French nationalists to demand war. Comparing Napoleon III to his famous ancestor, Germans forecast a French invasion, and choruses of "The Watch on the Rhine" broke out across the North German Confederation. The French declared war on July 19, 1870, and by early August, hundreds of thousands of troops were in the field. Bismarck's Danish and Austrian antagonists eventually, if grudg-

MAP 19.3 | German Unification, 1863–1871

This map shows how the old patchwork of the German Confederation gave way to the unified Germany by 1871. *Is this the "big Germany" or the "little Germany" solution? How might Germany's neighbors have felt about the creation of such a large state in the middle of Europe?*

ingly, accepted the results of his wars of unification. But the Franco-Prussian War would create a very long-lasting enmity between the two most powerful and industrialized nations on the continent.

France and Germany after 1871: Wages of the Wars of Unification

The Franco-Prussian War reshaped the way both Europeans and non-Europeans viewed the two powers. The

1870–1871: The Franco-Prussian War

Surveying newspapers and diplomatic correspondence in the summer of 1869, one might have suspected a war was coming.[9] Along the Rhine, however, business was going on as usual, as fishermen, tourists, and barge traffic moved up and down the river, and between cities that might administratively have been French, Prussian, Belgian, or Dutch, but had, as yet, little real association with any of these nations. That would change in the wake of Bismarck's bloodiest war.

The Prussians had prepared for this war. Under chief of general staff Helmuth von Moltke, the Prussian army had planned for conflict, ensuring it had railroad lines, food supplies, good maps, and well-drilled, disciplined troops ready to fight. The Prussians had even issued oval identifying discs to be worn by soldiers—the first dog tags—so that casualties could be easily identified and families informed. The French had made none of these preparations, counting on its seasoned (if often tipsy) troops and superior marksmanship to win the war. Believing that it would take the Prussians a full seven weeks to mobilize, the French were shocked to find 320,000 Prussians deployed on the border a little more than two weeks after war was declared. The French delayed their attack too long, and from mid-August on, the Prussians were the ones pushing forward. Most of the war was fought on what was then French territory, another blow for the French army, which had been supplied only with maps of the enemy's terrain.

As they had done in Austria, the Prussians moved very fast and worked hard to encircle their opponents, capturing hundreds of thousands of prisoners. The most famous of these was Emperor Napoleon III himself, who was captured at the Battle of Sedan on September 2. But over the course of the war, the Prussians took nearly a half-million French soldiers prisoner. French republicans seized the moment, declared the Second Empire dead, and proclaimed a new government, the Third Republic of France. As the Prussians marched on Haussmann's newly transformed Paris, however, the leaders of this new government abandoned the capital to direct the war effort from the city of Tours to the southwest. Their departure left the capital city largely undefended and cut off from supplies.

The remaining French troops in the field were also hungry, angry at their leaders, and hopelessly disorganized. But to the surprise of the Prussians, they continued to fight

German Unification Completed in France In January 1871, Prussian king Wilhelm I was crowned emperor of the newly united Germany. Embarrassingly for the French, he was crowned in a ceremony in Versailles's Hall of Mirrors, in which Chancellor Otto von Bismarck (here in white dress uniform) also featured prominently.

for France, led by three commanders who understood how to wage an irregular war: Marshal Achille Bazaine, whose experience lay in waging counterinsurgent warfare in Mexico; Charles Bourbaki, the son of Greek immigrants; and the great republican guerrilla Giuseppe Garibaldi, who arrived with Italian troops to help the French in mid-October. Thanks to their leadership and to the resistance of the French population, the French continued to harass Prussian troops through the beginning of 1871 and to burn into German memory the image of the *franc-tireur,* or guerrilla-citizen. But by mid-January, the game was up. The French surrendered and signed a punitive peace, requiring them to pay reparations and to allow the Germans to annex the Rhine provinces of Alsace and Lorraine. They were humiliated further by the Germans' decision to crown Emperor Wilhelm I at Louis XIV's Versailles palace.

The Franco-Prussian War lasted less than six months, but killed some 117,000 soldiers of the North German Confederation and its allies. Nearly 139,000 Frenchmen lost their lives. Though many of them could hardly be called professional soldiers, they were not mercenaries, but men who clearly understood that they were fighting for their nation. Prussian officers had taken care to drum into new recruits their duty to protect the fatherland against external enemies and the importance of military discipline in the face of threats to their individual lives. Evidently, the lessons hit home, for the Prussian army, in particular, showed itself remarkably willing to make sacrifices for the nation's sake. In shock, and perhaps delight, a drummer boy wounded in one of the first battles yelled: "My God, my God! I'm dying for our Fatherland!"

Wilhelm I, Bismarck, and Moltke became the new Germany's first *national* heroes, and September 2, the anniversary of the capture of Napoleon III, became a German *national* holiday, known as Sedan Day. On the Rhine's western banks, the war left a deep scar on the French psyche, as well as a longing for revenge and the reunification of France, which would have long-lasting political and cultural consequences. The valleys and plains of the Rhine valley had become part of two national—and antagonistic—histories, both with even bloodier futures before them.

QUESTIONS | *Why did the French lose this war? How did losing it to the Germans affect the French national psyche?*

easily defeated French were forced to agree to pay five billion gold francs in reparations and to hand over the rich, multiethnic Rhineland provinces of Alsace and Lorraine. France, the great threat to the balance of power in the Napoleonic era, now appeared defanged and perhaps even degenerate. Germany, by contrast, had demonstrated its previously underrated military and industrial power. Joining the great powers belatedly, it now seemed to have a bright, but perhaps dangerous, national future. But the war and its conclusion also had powerful *domestic* consequences both in France and the new German Empire. United internally by the war, both were also divided internally by political, economic, religious, and regional differences.

FRANCE: CIVIL UNREST AND REVENGE. After Sedan, Napoleon III was eventually released from German captivity and permitted to abdicate and go into exile in England, where he died. His abdication left a provisional government, headed by right-wing liberals and monarchists, in charge. But as German troops closed in on Paris in September 1871, the leaders, along with many wealthy property owners, abandoned the capital city. Most of the army was redeployed to continue the fight elsewhere, and the city's defense was entrusted to the national guard. Paris was left without leadership, and the Prussian army cut off commerce into the city, which had not been provisioned to withstand a siege. During the four-month siege, conditions grew so severe that butchers offered rats for sale and the beloved elephants of the capital city's zoo were slaughtered for meat. As right-wing liberals and monarchists negotiated a harsh peace with the Germans, Parisians grew furious with a government that seemed unable and unwilling to do anything to relieve their suffering.

THE PARIS COMMUNE. After the Germans retreated in February 1871, France's fledgling government—the Third Republic—began recovery efforts, but the liberals and monarchists who comprised it had little sympathy for the now radicalized workers and national guards who had defended Paris. When in early March, Adolphe Thiers, the head of the new French government, sent troops into Paris to repossess some cannons, an angry crowd seized two officers and executed them. Thiers then ordered the *French* army to march on Paris. The Parisian radicals responded by declaring themselves subject only to the governance of an entity they called the Paris Commune. The communards seized control of Paris, touching off a French civil war.

Compared with the essentially liberal, laissez-faire policies of Napoleon III's regime, the Commune's social reforms were indeed revolutionary. They included the establishment of nurseries for working mothers, the creation of a new system for labor protection like the workshop system of 1848, the recognition of women's labor unions, and the abolition of night baking—a measure quite obviously pushed through by the city's bakery employees. The Commune's radicalism could not be reconciled with the much more conservative values and practices of France's rural areas and smaller cities—and, of course, no one could envision France without its capital city. On May 21, 1871, French troops stormed the city and suppressed the Commune. The guillotine was returned to service and operated night and day to dispatch the enemies of the Third Republic. At least 25,000 Parisians died in the bloody mop-up that followed. Over 35,000 were jailed, and of these, more than 10,000 were sent to the penal colony of New Caledonia in the South Pacific.

This incident created a greater gap between the bourgeoisie and the working classes than had the events of June 1848. The Third Republic was quite hostile to working-class interests, and in the following years, radical socialists and anarchists sought to overturn the republic. In 1889, conservatives and liberals came perilously close to endorsing a coup by a charismatic army officer, Georges Ernest Boulanger, to push their political agenda. At the last moment, however, Boulanger lost heart, and the Third Republic staggered on, without another would-be Napoleon to unite them.

But if France after 1871 was divided by class and by political allegiances, the events of that year also created a set of common worries. A sense of national exhaustion swept over the French, and many writers, artists, and pundits expressed warnings about the degeneration or decadence

SUMMARY EXECUTIONS IN PARIS—SHOOTING DOWN COMMUNIST PRISONERS.

Communard Prisoners Executed in Paris After the fall of the Paris Commune, French troops executed thousands of rebels, some by firing squad and some by guillotine.

of France—caused by an assortment of maladies, ranging from alcoholism to urban anomie, and a variety of public enemies, from pacifist priests to syphilis-spreading prostitutes. This sense of malaise fueled innovations in the arts and social sciences, as well as a sword-rattling nationalism that underwrote reinvigorated imperialist policies. Unable to show its muscle on the continent, France now attempted to display its virility in colonial holdings in Algeria and Morocco. In the 1890s, France—once the great "revolutionary" power—formed an alliance with Europe's most reactionary state, imperial Russia. The purpose both shared was clear: containing the now alarmingly well-armed and prosperous German Empire.

GERMANY: UNBALANCING THE BALANCE OF POWER. If France after 1871 experienced considerable instability and internal dissention, the same can be said of its opponent, imperial Germany. In Germany the forging of national unity by war and under conservative Prussian-Protestant auspices meant that liberalism was never truly triumphant there. In the wake of the wars of unification, it was painfully obvious that the full economic, cultural, and spiritual integration of all Germans remained a distant prospect. In Alsace and Lorraine, for example, at least 5 percent of the population emigrated rather than agreeing to become German citizens. Many other French speakers despised the new regime and refused to consider themselves Germans.

Yet the most pressing immediate problem for Bismarck was not linguistic, but religious conflict. Protestants held a majority in the new Germany, but there remained a large Catholic minority, concentrated in the southern and western regions, whose loyalty to the new Berlin-centered regime was weak. Beginning in 1872, Bismarck and the Protestant liberals who had been strong backers of his unification program staged a *Kulturkampf* (literally, a "culture war") against the Catholics, seeking to root out practices and loyalties the regime considered backward and unpatriotic. The Jesuit order was expelled from the new Germany, and efforts were made to establish state control over the appointment of clergy, the financing of church activities, and the education of both clerics and parishioners. These actions were much more than a propaganda campaign. On several occasions, the army was used to force Catholic crowds to hand over illegally chosen priests, some 1,800 of whom were exiled or jailed.

But the *Kulturkampf* was ultimately unsuccessful, as was the simultaneous outlawing of the socialist parties in 1878, in the hopes that radicalism could be stamped out. By the mid-1880s, far from being destroyed as a political force, German Catholics had joined together to back the Catholic Center Party and to form hundreds of new Catholic civic organizations. The German socialists, too, gained increasing support among members of the working classes. In 1890, Kaiser Wilhelm II relented and legalized the **SPD (*Sozialdemokratische Partei Deutschlands*),** which soon became Europe's largest

socialist party. Conflicting goals provoked titanic political battles, as the socialist movement grew in the cities, while the landed Prussian aristocracy (the Junkers) tried to hold on to its traditional power.

While Bismarck tried unsuccessfully to crush his opponents, he also worked to outmaneuver his former friends. He had relied on an alliance between Protestant liberals and conservatives to bring about unification. After unification, he continued his tactical attempts to impose reforms from above, thereby forcing the liberals to do things his way. In 1883, Bismarck oversaw passage of a health insurance law. An accident insurance law and laws providing for disability and old-age pensions followed in 1884 and 1889. Though Bismarck's reforms did not cover everyone, industrial workers and low-level employees did benefit. Meanwhile, the older landed aristocracy and the new industrialists profited from newly increased tariffs. In 1884, Bismarck capitulated to pressure groups demanding that Germany join the race for colonies, but he still insisted that the German Empire should stay out of the complicated conflicts in southeastern Europe and retain its alliance with Austria-Hungary.

If the final years of Bismarck's service began to look distinctly post-liberal, German policy grew even less progressive when Wilhelm II became emperor in 1888. A disappointment to his liberal mother—a daughter of Britain's Queen Victoria—Wilhelm cared little for the moderate politics of his father Friedrich III, preferring instead his grandfather Wilhelm I's predilection for the Prussian military tradition. Wilhelm II was a man of violent tempers and far-flung passions. Bismarck once said of him, "The Emperor is like a balloon—if one did not hold him fast on a string, he would go one knows whither."[10] In one of his rages, he dismissed the Iron Chancellor, the master of balance of power politics, and embarked on an erratic diplomatic course. Under Wilhelm's reign, balancing power became an old-fashioned aspiration, replaced by a new and more virulent form of German nationalism and imperialist ambition.

Bismarck had not wanted to impose harsh peace terms on the French following the German victory in the Franco-Prussian War. That was the doing of Wilhelm I, Moltke, and the army. But neither had Bismarck made any attempt to reform the imperial constitution to restrain the power of the emperor and the military, neither of which was subject to any civilian oversight. Once France and Russia had formed an alliance, the German military began not merely to fear the encirclement of Germany by hostile and more populous powers, but even to plan for a double-fronted war.

Divided Europe

The unification processes in Italy and Germany were successful, though costly. There were other statesmen and populist factions who sought nationhood for their people

The Bulgarian Horrors This image depicts the massacre at Batak, an incident in which irregular Ottoman troops reacted to the town's declaration of independence by murdering between 3,000 and 5,000 civilians. The atrocities committed here, including rapes and decapitations, were widely reported and sensationalized in the western European press.

What challenges did national unification projects pose for the multiethnic empires of central and southeastern Europe?

but failed to achieve it. The Poles are one good example. Despite staging uprisings in 1830, 1846, 1848, and 1863 and the organization of many underground nationalist parties and newspapers, in the era before the First World War, the Poles never managed to free themselves from Russian, Austrian, and Prussian overlordship and create an independent Polish state.

Greece provides another example. Although the Greeks won independence from the Ottomans in the 1820s, many Greek speakers were left out of the newly created state, and some Greek nationalists dreamed of recapturing Constantinople, the long-lost capital of the Byzantine Empire. In the next decades, the Greeks continued to chip away at Ottoman territory, adding Thessaly to their domain in 1881. Sometimes Greek uprisings, such as one in Crete in 1866, failed. In 1895–1897, terrible partisan warfare again erupted on the island. This time, bands of Greek rebels hid in mountain passes to attack Muslim officials and civilians. The Muslim population of

the island was decimated in the bloody fighting. Britain, France, Italy, and Russia intervened, proclaiming Crete an independent republic, but the Greeks remained unsatisfied until after the Balkan Wars, when the island was allowed to join Greece. Even then, some Greeks continued to dream of reconstituting Byzantium.

Reshaping Southeastern Europe

Greek unification was realized at the cost of the Ottomans; the same could be said of nationalist agitation in other parts of southeastern Europe. In 1876, Bulgarian Christian nationalists rose against their Ottoman overlords. Fearful of losing more territory, the Ottomans responded swiftly, killing and in some cases mutilating between 3,000 and 12,000 Bulgarians, many of them civilians. The outcry in the European press was deafening. The British were so outraged at reports of what were called the Bulgarian Horrors that they refused to come to the aid of the Turks when war broke out between the Ottoman and Russian Empires in 1877. The Russians marched into Bulgaria, and Bulgarian radicals took advantage of their presence to

MAP 19.4 | Europe after the Russo-Turkish Wars, 1878

This map shows the route taken by British, French, and Piedmontese troops on their way to intervene in the Crimean War in 1853–1854, and the political changes in the Balkans and southeastern Europe since the Congress of Vienna (compare this map with Map 18.1). Although western intervention had saved the Ottoman Empire from great losses in 1853–1854, the Russo-Turkish War of 1877–1878 had compelled the Ottomans to give full independence to Romania and Bulgaria. Fearing that those two states would fall under Russian influence, the Austro-Hungarian Empire also moved in 1878 to occupy a former Ottoman province, Bosnia-Herzegovina (they would annex it in 1908). Still, the Ottomans retained control of a considerable amount of territory in the Balkans, including Macedonia, Albania, and the island of Crete, lost only in 1913.
Note the sizes of the three great multinational overland empires (Ottoman Empire, Austria-Hungary, and Russian Empire) and their relations to the Mediterranean Sea. How does this help to explain the increasing number of quarrels over Balkan territory?

avenge themselves on local Turks, committing their own horrors, though these were little discussed in Europe. In 1878, the Russians defeated the Ottomans, and as part of the settlement, Bulgaria, Romania, Bosnia, and Serbia were carved out of the Ottoman domains. The Treaty of San Stefano left the Ottomans with a sliver of Balkan territory, much to the disappointment of Greeks—who wanted to enlarge their state—and Macedonians and Albanians, who now wanted their own nations (Map. 19.4 and Back to the Source at the end of the chapter).

Austria Partitioned

In Metternich's own homeland, centrifugal forces were also at work. In 1867, the Hungarians seized the oppor-

tunity of Austria's defeat in the Austro-Prussian War to compel Franz Josef to sign a compromise agreement, according to which the Hungarian crown lands were given virtual autonomy from the Austrian ruling house. Austria thus effectively became a dual monarchy. The reorganized and renamed Austro-Hungarian Empire now shared only an emperor (Franz Josef) and a minister for war and diplomatic affairs. The Hungarian Diet—dissolved in 1849—was reconstituted, and the ethnic Magyars were allowed to impose their will on the minority groups in their territories. But many Hungarian nationalists were still unsatisfied, and the Hungarians' new rights simply increased the dissatisfaction of the Czech, Croatian, and Southern Slav nationalists, all of whom thought they deserved compromises of their own.

It is difficult to say if the repeated and large-scale geographic adjustments in southeastern Europe and the Balkans made anyone happy. France, Britain, Germany, and Austria-Hungary all worried about the expansion of Russian influence; the Ottomans worried about the extension of Greek and Austrian dominions, as well as relations with British-controlled Egypt and Russian-influenced Persia. The Croatians, in particular, chafed under Hungarian dominion. Bosnia-Herzegovina was occupied by the Austro-Hungarians in 1878, then annexed in 1908. These moves upset the Russians and infuriated the Serbs, especially those who now came under Austrian rule. From 1876 on, numerous episodes of small-scale ethnic cleansing would erupt in these territories as minority groups fled attempts by newly empowered ethnic majorities to consolidate their hold. Even those who had won national autonomy firmly believed that the new map would—and should—be subject to further, and probably violent, change.

Life and Identity after Unification

What was it like to live the unification process? For those who fought with Garibaldi or who cheered on Bismarck's armies, it was surely an exciting time. Wars were won (or lost) swiftly and, until the Franco-Prussian War, with relatively few casualties. A freer and cheaper press covered developments breathlessly. Inspiring, if less revolutionary, speeches were made in parliaments and on the streets. For those who had championed liberal causes in 1848, unification was at least a partial victory; for those who had not, unification without social or political revolution was perhaps the best they could hope for. Both German and Italian liberals could hope that their economies might now be modernized sufficiently to compete with those of the British and French. At least in the case of the Germans, this hope was realized. For those who had resented being second- or third-rate powers, becoming part of a bigger state now presented the possibility of new forms of glory, including perhaps the acquisition of overseas markets and colonies—although Cavour, and for a time Bismarck, remained uninterested in pushing beyond continental conquests. Unquestionably, unifications intensified and deepened nationalism in Italy and Germany—and, ironically, also intensified national feelings of their neighbors, many of whom felt threatened by the new powers.

Yet contemporary testimonies and subsequent events also demonstrate that for many, unification did not immediately make Sicilians into Italians, or Bavarians into Germans. Many people continued to speak minority languages and to identify themselves with their provinces or towns rather than with the central state. Economic, regional, and social differences still mattered; enormous tensions continued between the increasingly business-oriented northern Italian cities and the semifeudal economies of Sicily and Naples. Indeed, calls for the dissolution of Italy are still heard today. In newly unified Germany, religious tensions ran so high that Bismarck and the Prussian liberals waged a *Kulturkampf* against their Catholic fellow citizens in the 1870s. Provincial loyalty and hostility to Prussia remained strong enough that, following Germany's defeat in World War I, Bavaria and the Rhineland both seriously considered seceding once more. Even within Prussia, major regional and economic differences continued to matter. In the 1860s, Rhineland Prussians still looked down on the hicks from Brandenburg's rural eastern marshes, referring to their supposed brothers as *Stinkpreussen*. It would take a long time for the easterners' distinctive odor to fade.

Conclusion

Europe in the mid-nineteenth century underwent grand-scale processes of economic, cultural, and political transformation, reshaping national borders, domestic social relations, and peoples' lives. New states were unified in this era, and old ones divided; cities were reshaped, and women's roles redefined. Science, literature, and art took on the challenges of comprehending and reordering the many new facets of European experience. In succeeding chapters we examine how the modernizing processes like the taming of the Rhine and the rebuilding of Paris accelerated—and how those left out of this new order plotted their revenge.

Critical Thinking Questions

1. In what ways did the economic, social, and political changes of the mid-century divide Europeans? Which changes made their worlds more similar, and more distinctively modern, than those of their parents and grandparents?

2. Why did national unification succeed in Germany and Italy, but not in Poland or Macedonia (see Back to the Source)?

3. What factors made the Victorian age so much different in Russia than in Great Britain?

Key Terms

nation-state **(p. 601)**

Victorian **(p. 607)**

positivism **(p. 611)**

natural selection **(p. 612)**

realism **(p. 612)**

Impressionism **(p. 612)**

Eastern Question **(p. 616)**

Risorgimento **(p. 618)**

Realpolitik **(p. 620)**

Kulturkampf **(p. 624)**

SPD (*Sozialdemokratische Partei Deutschlands*) **(p. 624)**

Primary Sources in connect®

For information on Connect and the online resources available, go to **http://connect.mcgraw-hill.com**.

1. Anthony Trollope, *The Way We Live Now*
2. The Life of a London Prostitute
3. Impressionism and Realism: Contrasting Images
4. Giuseppe Mazzini, On Italian Unification
5. Princess Victoria on Bismarck
6. "The Charge of the Light Brigade": A Heroic View of the Crimean War

Manifesto of the Temporary Government of Macedonia, March 23, 1881

Not every nationality group in Europe got its own unified, autonomous state. The following document was issued by a group of Macedonian radicals, who were at the time seething with anger at other Europeans. In the wake of Russia's victory in the Russo-Turkish War (1877–1878), the (Christian) Macedonians had hoped to be given an independent state or at the least to have their territory joined to that of (Christian) Bulgaria (see Map 19.4). But the European powers had given Macedonia back to the Sultan instead. In response, some of the leading nationalists went into exile in Bulgaria, where they issued the following call to arms to their countrymen across the border. Note here their use of the militaristic patriotic rhetoric increasingly common in the later nineteenth century and their invocation of Macedonia's historical greatness as a call for the population to restore national freedom and pride.

Macedonians,

Once upon a time our dear fatherland Macedonia was one of the most glorious countries. And the Macedonian people, by building on the foundations of their military skills, with their victorious phalanxes and the wisdom of Aristotle civilized humanity and Asia. But our fatherland, once so glorious, is today at the threshold of annihilation because of our mistakes and because we have forgotten our origins. Alien and dubious peoples want to take possession of our country and destroy our nation that, shining with such a light, cannot and will not ever fall. Macedonia has become like a widow, tragically deserted by her sons. She no longer holds the flag once carried in triumph by the victorious Macedonian armies. She is today nothing more than a geographic notion. Conspirators roaming through our country have given her deadly poisons and have dug a grave for her. These plotters are the gravediggers of the great and glorious fatherland; these are the same [traitors] who seek to dismember her or allow the entry of the victorious Austro-Hungarian troops. By replacing one yoke with another the regeneration of Macedonia will become impossible and our nationality will disappear. The moment is critical for Macedonia: it is about her life or death.

True Macedonians, loyal children of the fatherland! Will you tolerate the fall of our dear country? Look at her, bound in slavery and covered by wounds made by the surrounding peoples. Look at her and behold the heavy chains put by the sultan. Powerless and weeping, our beloved Macedonia, our dear fatherland addresses you. "You my loyal children; you that are my inheritors after Aristotle and Alexander the Great, you in whose veins Macedonian blood runs, do not leave me dying but help me . . . here are my terrible bloody wounds, here are my heavy chains: break them, heal my wounds; make sure that on the flag I raise will be written: Macedonia one and united! Do so boldly, chase from your country those murderers who carry the flag of discord and introduce passions of separation and divide you, my children, into countless nationalities; gathering around the flag of Macedonia, as your only national sign, raise it high up, make this glorious flag ready and then [shout] unanimously:

Long live the Macedonian people, love live Macedonia!

The voice of our country does exist, freedom does exist—that cherished legacy of the peoples. To proclaim these words means to call the noble hearts to rush up and fight in order to help you, obtaining that sacred freedom absent from our dear fatherland for so many centuries.

Macedonians, remember our origin and do not give it up!

QUESTIONS | *The authors refer to those who seek to "introduce passions of separation and divide you, my children, into countless nationalities" as murderers. Shouldn't the authors themselves be seen as sowing murderous discord within the multiethnic Ottoman Empire? Why do they think they should be seen as liberators of Macedonia, rather than as murderers of the Ottoman Empire?*

Source: "Two Macedonian Manifestos," trans. Nikola Iordanovski in Discourses of Collective Identity in Central and Southeast Europe (1770–1945), Vol. 2: National Romanticism—The Formation of National Movements, ed. Balázs Trencsényi and Michal Kopeček (Budapest: Central European University Press, 2007), 484–485.

Board Game Celebrating the Exploits of Livingstone and Stanley For those who experienced directly the imperial carving up of Africa, it was anything but a game.

IMPERIALISM AND RESISTANCE, 1820–1914

European Empires: Old and New
> The Old and the New Neo-Europes
> The New World Closes, the First Wave Ends

The Second Wave: 1820–1860
> The Motives of the Modern Colonizer: Profit, Prestige, and Progress
> Back to the Old World: The British in India
> Africa Beckons: The French in Algeria
> Opening East Asia: The Opium Wars
> Japan Opened—and Closed
> Overland Empire: The Russians in the Caucasus
> A Turning Point: The Indian Rebellion

Cultures of Empire
> Living the Empire: The Colonial Soldier
> The Civilizing Mission and the Missionary Impulse

Imperialism and the Field Sciences
> The Imperial Exchange
> Race and Empire

The Third Wave: Consolidating Empires after 1860
> The Ottoman Power Vacuum
> The Failing Chinese Empire
> The Scramble for Africa
> King Leopold Builds Himself an Empire
> Carving up Africa

The New Resistance
> Resistance in German Colonies
> The Boxer Rebellion
> The Second Boer War

Conclusion

CECIL RHODES, COLONIZER AND OXFORD MAN In late 1871, eighteen-year-old Cecil Rhodes followed his elder brother Herbert to a dusty, remote region of South Africa just annexed by the British Empire. Cecil Rhodes's great ambition was to study at Oxford University, where he hoped to gain entrance into the British elite. But as the son of a village parson he first needed to earn money to cover his university costs; he also needed to prepare for Oxford's rigorous entrance exams in Greek and Latin. He had tried his hand at cotton farming the previous year in another part of South Africa, but Herbert, seeking adventure, convinced his brother that the area just renamed Kimberley (after British colonial minister Lord Kimberley) offered better prospects. Cecil Rhodes was just one of 50,000 Europeans and Africans who descended on Kimberley in the fall of 1871, for by then it was widely known that the area was rich in a much-desired colonial commodity: diamonds.

Rhodes came to Kimberley by ox-cart, bringing with him Greek and Latin textbooks to study at night. The brothers put back-breaking labor into mining on the hot, barren plain and made some money; then they sold their Kimberley shares for stock in what Rhodes called a "nice little mine" next door, known as the de Beers mine. Herbert left to follow another rush but died when his tent caught fire. Cecil stayed, cramming for his Latin exams by night and by day inhabiting a world characterized by dangerous mining conditions, the exploitation of African laborers, drinking, and gambling. The de Beers mine proved rich in diamonds, but Rhodes still had his sights set on Oxford. He was admitted in 1873 and spent the next eight years finishing his degree there, while also managing his increasingly complicated holdings in South Africa.

Rhodes loved Oxford, but

MAP 20.1 | Colonial South Africa, c. 1800–1914
This map shows the location of major gold and diamond deposits in South Africa as well as the areas settled by Dutch farmers (Boers). Note the path taken by these settlers into the Transvaal region as British colonists pushed them out after 1830 (the Great Trek). The areas in green were incorporated into the Union of South Africa in 1910. **Note the location of the major gold and diamond mines. What effect do you think these locations had on relationships between the British, the Boers, and the native Africans?**

not because it made him a scholar—it did not. At Oxford he learned to think himself a true gentleman, fit to rule large chunks of the world. Here he could sip sherry and discuss Virgil and forget for a time the South African hell that made his civilized life possible.

Rhodes read Darwin at Oxford, but more important, he also read a forgotten book called *The Martyrdom of Man*, which claimed that the time had come for Europe to do away with "slavish and oriental" Christianity and insisted that the superiority of the English race suited it to impose European-style progress on "savage" nations. In 1877, Rhodes wrote, "I contend that we are the first race in the world, and that the more of the world we inhabit, the better it is for the human race." By this time, he was not only thinking of Africa; he wanted to recover the United States for Britain as well. He knew violence would be necessary "to crush all disloyalty and every movement for the severance of the Empire." But

he believed that, in the end, humankind would profit: there would be peace between nations and general prosperity, and the whole world would come to appreciate the advantages of having the British as their masters.

By 1887, Rhodes's De Beers Diamond Company had become the sole owner of the "nice little mine" in which Rhodes began his excavations. He then maneuvered people and capital to obtain a controlling share in the larger Kimberley mine next door, making him enormously wealthy. Rhodes proceeded to invest in gold mines and railway shares, and as European powers scrambled to divide up Africa, he pressed Britain to seize as much territory as possible (Map 20.1). He stood for prime minister of Britain's Cape Colony in 1890, largely to protect his investments, and won the post; now he could pursue his grand imperial dreams. He floated the idea that his nation might link South Africa with Britain's recently acquired Egyptian holdings, creating a "Cape to

Cecil Rhodes Rhodes lived in two worlds: in Oxford, he sipped sherry and discussed the classics; in South Africa, he was the ruthless, rugged owner of a diamond mine, and the instigator of brutal imperial wars.

Cairo" empire running the length of eastern Africa. Then, with the consent of imperial officials, he launched two brutal wars against Matabele tribesmen (1893–1894, 1896–1897) to seize land that Queen Victoria agreed to call Rhodesia.

Rhodes involved himself in more intrigue in the later 1890s, playing a key role in inciting the Boer Wars, and becoming one of the richest men in the world. But his health had never been good, and before his death (at age forty-eight), he made a will in which he asked that his fortune be used to endow scholarships for athletic, energetic, *and* intelligent young men to go to Oxford and learn to be leaders and advocates of British values around the world. In endowing the Rhodes Scholarships, Cecil Rhodes wanted people to remember British imperialism's "gentlemanly" ambitions and outward appearances and to forget the greed, blood, and racism that characterized its practice, and Rhodes's own life.[1]

As Rhodes knew well, for as long as there have been written records, there have also been empires—states that use their superior political and economic power to force other peoples into dependent status. Empires are attractive to rulers because, when they operate as designed, they allow the parent country to extract resources and tribute from subordinate states without having to live in a constant state of war with them. But there were new elements to the British imperial endeavor by the time Rhodes signed on to it. What was different about this nineteenth-century imperialism—especially in its third and most intense phase (1860–1914)—was its increasing intensity and global reach, and the fact that some Europeans now had both the ambition and the power to make over the world in their own images.

The new imperialism also took on extensive cultural ambitions. Like Rhodes, many colonizers wanted to bring their versions of civilization and progress to the rest of the world. Their efforts spread both enlightened ideas and exploitative practices around the world, provoking varying degrees of opposition. The globalized and yet unequal world we inhabit today is a product of these processes of imperial competition and conquest and of indigenous acceptance and resistance.

Not all European states—much less all Europeans—participated directly in colonial conquest. Some, including the peoples of the Balkans (see Chapter 19), were immersed in their own nation-building struggles. Others—like the textile workers in Manchester—had little time to devote to thinking about overseas empires, though the economy in which they worked was increasingly linked to that of the colonial world. The imperialism of the second and third waves was chiefly the work of the elites in the western European nations in which the

quiet revolutions of the Old Regimes (agricultural, military, scientific, and protoindustrial) had gone the farthest: Great Britain, France, and the Netherlands. But others followed their lead—or, like the Russians, worked ever more industriously to extend their empires over land. By choosing to use their new economic and military power to create vast modern empires and by seeking to justify them as western, civilizing ventures, the imperial powers changed the course of both European and world history.

European Empires: Old and New

It was not irrational for Cecil Rhodes, or for anyone else in the nineteenth century, to want to build an empire.

> Which European nations engaged most heavily in overseas colonization before the nineteenth century?

Empires allow the dominant states to export *their* commercial and cultural goods—including their religious beliefs—while picking and choosing what to borrow (or steal) from dependent areas. Perhaps the easiest way to build an empire was to conquer one's neighboring states, and throughout history, from the time of the Assyrian Empire to that of Hitler's Germany, states have gone that route. But states have also experimented over time with other forms of domination: the settling of overseas colonies and the exertion of commercial control over faraway ports of call. Europeans—*some* Europeans—had taken to the oceans already in the fifteenth century. Their colonial successes, especially in the Americas, provided them with the commercial experience, increased wealth, and ambitious expectations that inspired them to look to the rest of the world when New World revolutionaries slammed their doors.

The Old and the New Neo-Europes

Since the fall of Rome, many a European monarch has dreamed of establishing a great empire on the continent—Charlemagne, Louis XIV of France, and Charles XII of Sweden were just three of those who made moves in this direction. But their well-armed continental neighbors and rival factions in their own states made these dreams impossible. Once cut off from the eastern Mediterranean trade by the fall of Constantinople and the rise of the Venetian Empire, Spanish and Portuguese voyagers happened upon rich territories in the Americas. They were able to exploit and colonize these lands because war and disease had destroyed a large proportion of the original population. Here, Spanish and Portuguese settlers, and later English, French, and Scandinavian groups, established what we have called **neo-Europes,** settlements where European ideas, languages, and customs took firm root. Examples include the British colonies in North America and Spanish-ruled Mexico. Many of these colonies, including the hugely profitable Caribbean settlements, imported millions of African slaves to do heavy labor and became extremely profitable. The new opportunities these territories offered—combined with religious persecution at home—encouraged many Europeans to settle the new areas.

In these neo-Europes, European settlers (at this stage, most of them men) frequently mixed with local, slave, or free black populations, creating children who were called **creoles,** that is, of mixed European and non-European ancestry. Creoles and settlers often continued to speak European languages and to practice as Catholics or Presbyterians. Having left Spain or Scotland, some settlers found a renewed appreciation for their homelands abroad. Creoles, particularly those with white or lighter skins, often boasted of their European heritage, using this as a means to demonstrate their own cultural or intellectual superiority.

In Asia and Africa, where populations remained stable and states and extensive commercial networks existed already, Europeans could not, during the first wave, establish neo-Europes. They entered as trading partners and kept largely to their coastal stations. Neither could they impose their cultures, but rather had to adapt to local conditions and learn local languages or live in small enclaves. Only in the later nineteenth century, when Europeans developed superior firepower, perfected tropical medicines, increased the speed of communications, and intensified capitalist competition, would they attempt to turn these continents, too, into neo-Europes.

The New World Closes, the First Wave Ends

Beginning in the late eighteenth century, some of the New World neo-Europes grew unruly and too difficult to manage from afar. The first great shock was the American colonists' success in throwing off British overlordship in the American War of Independence (1775–1783). Inspired by the French Revolution, the island of San Domingue

First Opium War in China
1839–1842

Imperialism: First Wave
1490s–1800

Imperialism: Second Wave
c. 1820–1860

1500   1800   1810   1820   1830   1840   1850

(Haiti) staged its own successful revolution against French control (Chapter 17), and soon thereafter, in 1803, Napoleon gave up trying to defend the vast territory of Louisiana, selling it to the United States. Taking advantage of the weakening of the Iberian states during the Napoleonic Wars, creole populations in South and Central America demanded their independence, and eventually established their own autonomous states. During the next century, the United States would extend its own empire, pushing farther westward and—as Native American communities were forcibly resettled and their resistance destroyed—claiming that America's "manifest destiny" was to link sea to shining sea. In 1823, U.S. president James Monroe issued the warning that became known as the **Monroe Doctrine,** which stipulated that Europeans were to keep their hands off the western hemisphere, in exchange for which the Americans would not interfere with European colonies elsewhere.

In many ways, this closing off of the Americas to colonial activity recalled the closing off of the eastern Mediterranean in 1453, after the fall of Constantinople. Older forms of imperial extraction in the Americas ended, and the race to find new markets and resources shifted. The British, French, and Dutch turned their attention to coastal outposts in the East Indies and to Southeast Asia, and states began to put new political and military muscle at the disposal of chartered companies such as the Dutch East India Company; considerable force, as well as persuasion, was often necessary to suppress local resistance to the extension of European trading power. In this era, Europeans began to claim that they came as civilizers, as conveyors of enlightened ideas and commercial prosperity, rather than simply as mercantilist traders. Gradually, a new sort of colonialism took the place of the old, one that would be linked powerfully to the processes of modernization and nation-building going on at home.

The Second Wave: 1820–1860

The closing off of the Atlantic world coincided with the tumultuous era of the French Revolution and the Napoleonic Wars. The wars left all parties exhausted and impoverished; thus, it took some time for most nations to recover sufficiently to think about new adventures abroad. Spain, Portugal, and the Netherlands had their hands full simply defending the territories they had acquired in earlier eras—and the first two found even this a challenge, as their colonies successively declared independence or fell to other imperial powers.

> How did the colonialism of the second wave differ from that of the first?

Great Britain stands out as the power whose economy—and ambitions—recovered most quickly. Although it had lost its American colonies, Britain emerged from the Napoleonic Wars with the world's most powerful navy, most extensive and profitable merchant fleet, most stable and flexible capital markets, and most developed industrial centers. With the help of British soldiers, the **British East India Company (BEIC)** had also managed to hang on to and extend its most lucrative commercial colony in Asia, Bengal. As the BEIC, backed by the British state and army, successively conquered the rest of the subcontinent, British India became a much-admired model for making the transition from mercantile to modern colonialism.

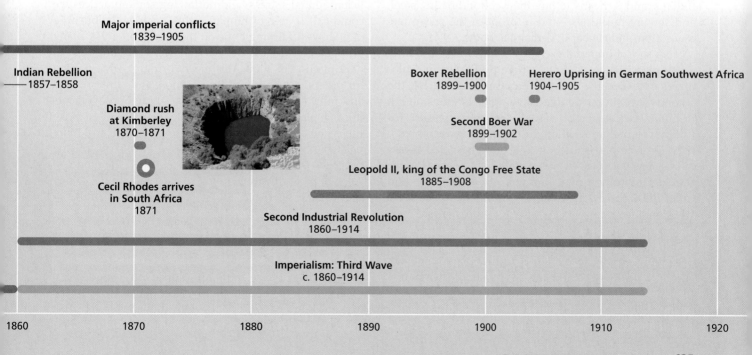

Major imperial conflicts
1839–1905

Indian Rebellion
——1857–1858

Boxer Rebellion
1899–1900

Herero Uprising in German Southwest Africa
1904–1905

Diamond rush at Kimberley
1870–1871

Second Boer War
1899–1902

Cecil Rhodes arrives in South Africa
1871

Leopold II, king of the Congo Free State
1885–1908

Second Industrial Revolution
1860–1914

Imperialism: Third Wave
c. 1860–1914

1860   1870   1880   1890   1900   1910   1920

Despite Napoleon's defeat, the French also recovered sufficiently to begin looking abroad by the late 1820s. They turned first to northern and western Africa and then to Southeast Asia, where the Dutch also began refurbishing their older commercial colonies, now seeking to fully control trading networks, not simply profit from them. Europe's largest land-based empire, Russia, acted in similar ways, moving to exert more direct forms of control in the region of the Caucasus. All the imperial powers, old and new, continental and overseas, faced resistance, though often it was poorly organized and did not pose much of a threat to European traders. That changed in 1857, when a violent and widespread rebellion against British rule in South Asia shocked the colonizers, and provoked the further intensification of modern colonizing methods.

The Motives of the Modern Colonizer: Profit, Prestige, and Progress

Early-modern, mercantile colonies in Bengal or Indonesia existed to provide investors with profits (and their states with tax revenues). Although there was some national pride at stake, before the nineteenth century companies and states were willing to give up unprofitable colonies from time to time or to sell overseas territory when they needed capital for continental endeavors—as Napoleon did with French Louisiana. During the second and third waves, profit making continued to be a major motivation for empire builders, and many investors—like Rhodes—made their fortunes in what was essentially the old way: by extracting natural resources from colonized territories. But central in motivating modern colonialism was more than extraction: this quest was also driven by the desire to find and monopolize markets for the finished goods the industrializing nations were now producing in abundance. Businessmen and officials expressed high hopes that eventually they could force the Chinese, Indians, and Africans to buy their cotton textiles, steel, and sewing machines—and to produce the cheap tea, raw cotton, and rubber in demand at home.

This sort of imperial exchange really worked in only a few places, such as India, where profits for the colonizers exceeded the costs of imperial rule. During the second wave, in particular, some officials wily enough to make the calculation actually resisted pressure for full-on colonial annexation. In the mid-nineteenth century, for example, British officials often hesitated before taking new colonies—it was usually far cheaper to give the administration over to a chartered company and to let the Royal Niger Company or Rhodes's De Beers Diamond Company keep order, while British merchants profited. The Russians, too, balked at the idea of exerting full control over a militarily powerless Persia, preferring simply to exploit it indirectly. As one wit summed up Russia's attitude, "Why should we marry the lady, when we can have her without the ceremony?"[2]

Yet by the later nineteenth century, through formal or informal colonization, the Russians had created an enormous empire and were ready to take advantage of the continued weakening of the neighboring Ottoman Empire and to move more aggressively westward into Europe. The British were busily unbalancing Metternich's balance of power by creating abroad an "empire on which the sun never sets." Having already toppled the Mughal Empire in India, they seemed poised to fill the vacuum being created as China's Qing Empire began to fragment. Envious of these nations' success and fearful that they would carve up the globe and leave nothing for the rest, other European states began to claim overseas colonies or to seek new territory on the continent for themselves. In the last decades before the First World War, the grim realities of empire—high costs, bloody warfare, increasing tensions between settlers and locals—mattered less than the conviction that having an empire would ensure the nation's economic flourishing—and its international prestige.

The nations that joined the race for colonies last—especially the Germans and Italians—did so less for financial profit than to show that they, too, were great powers, willing and able to build their own neo-Europes abroad. Indeed, their colonies, like many other modern settlements, did not turn a profit at all. Instead, they proved a net drain on the state budgets, above all because of costly wars and the reality that the colonized remained too poor to buy European goods. But the Germans in particular determined that they too deserved their "place in the sun." As the Germans seized several colonies in Africa and began furiously building up their navy, global tensions increased. At home, nationalist resentments and hatreds grew, even as colonizers abroad sang the praises of a supposedly singular, peaceable, and enduring European civilization.

Colonizers of the second and third waves often claimed that theirs was a civilizing mission: they were working for the good of others, helping them modernize their infrastructures, breaking up exploitative and inefficient feudal estates, and outlawing some practices we could call abuses of human rights, such as the burning of widows. Claiming to be on the side of progress, many Europeans really did believe they were bringing light to dark places. For some, this meant bringing Christianity; for others, it meant building schools and clinics, roads and railways. Europeans did make these improvements in some places—though they made them chiefly to make European domination easier, more profitable, and more palatable. Seeking profits and prestige, but also promising progress, the British, above all, established the model of colonial modernization, doing so especially in the colony they came to cherish as the "jewel in the crown": India.

Back to the Old World: The British in India

Britain did not take India all at once, but conquered it piecemeal, and there certainly were setbacks, as in the Mysore Wars of 1767–1799, when thousands of British soldiers, more than half of them native Indian troops, or **sepoys,** were killed, and thousands more taken captive. The charismatic leader of the resistance in Mysore, Tipu Sultan, was not defeated until 1799, and then the BEIC's armies advanced on the Maratha Confederacy, completing its destruction in 1804. These battles could not have been won without the use of semi-enslaved poor white soldiers, deals cut with Indian leaders, and a vast number of sepoys. They would not even have been waged except that India seemed to offer excellent prospects for colonial exploitation and new markets for what was becoming a flood of industrialized products, especially textiles.

But there was another dimension to British imperial efforts: the utilitarian historian and influential member of Parliament Thomas Macaulay (1800–1859) and other statesmen believed they were bringing civilization to India and ending the abuses, superstitions, and disparities pervasive under *its* Old Regime, including the caste system and the inefficient land-management system of the elites. In 1813, Parliament allocated funds to build public schools in India, hoping to produce, as Macaulay described, "a class of persons, Indian in blood and colour, but English in taste, in opinion, in morals and in intellect."[3] Missionaries were permitted to settle in India and officials worked hard to make India into a kind of neo-England, something they, like Macaulay, believed was for India's own good.

By 1833, the BEIC controlled most of the subcontinent, and in this year, the company's function changed officially: it lost its trading monopoly, in favor of the now fashionable doctrine of free trade, and began to act as the governing body of Britain's Indian holdings instead. Company officials introduced aggressive, utilitarian measures designed to bring civilization—English style—to India, and for a time were exuberantly confident that through these measures they could make India a neo-England. Anglicization would, in their view, benefit the Indians, who would ultimately be thankful that local religious practices, customs, law, and leadership had been replaced with English institutions, and who might ultimately become civilized enough to earn national autonomy. But to Macaulay and other liberals back home, civilizing India also seemed a more efficient way to enrich the home country: "To trade with civilized men," Macaulay wrote, "is infinitely more profitable than to govern savages."[4]

Because India could boast only about 45,000 British inhabitants in the 1830s, as compared to 150 million South Asians, implanting Christian capitalism had to be done

An East India Company Official and His Indian Employees This late-eighteenth-century image shows a British East India Company official traveling by elephant. He is escorted by three lower-ranking British officials, and a large company of Indian subordinates and sepoys.

with local help. Princes who agreed to abide by Britain's rules could retain at least some of their power over their former subjects and help the English collect their taxes. Decades of contact with the BEIC had produced a class of soldiers, officials, and men of commerce, many of whose members were of mixed Anglo-Indian heritage. On the whole, these men had profited from British rule. These *babus*, as they were called by their detractors, as well as the vast army of sepoys, made it possible for the British to establish a relatively stable and unified subcontinent by the 1840s—though some pockets of resistance remained. British liberals saw these at least partly Anglicized Indians as promising (but not yet mature) teenagers, junior officers who could help them complete the Europeanizing of India and continue to enjoy its fruits without additional expense.

Africa Beckons: The French in Algeria

By the later 1820s, the British had largely pacified India and were reaping handsome profits in the bargain. They were also sending settlers to their Cape Colony at the tip of South Africa (acquired in 1815) and, in the process, putting pressure on the Dutch farmers (**Boers**) already residing there. For the most part, however, Europeans had lost interest in sub-Saharan Africa. Trade in slaves, Africa's most lucrative commodity, had been banned by the British in 1807, though others carried it on much longer. Until the 1860s, the Royal Navy's Preventative Squadron prowled the coastline; it seized a few illegal slave ships and returned the captives to West African ports. Still, mosquito-borne malaria, and the tsetse fly—especially deadly for European horses—discouraged Europeans

The Europeanized Native

In Europe's colonies, most inhabitants were treated—as were lower-class Europeans in most nations—as subjects rather than as citizens, as people who were to follow orders, not as people expected to make laws for themselves. But educated and well-connected natives were as essential to maintaining European rule as were the usually poor and often ostracized individuals who were hired to police their own territories.

Those who wished to rise in the colonized world usually had to play by the colonizers' rules and to agree to adopt at least some significant aspects of their culture. The French, for example, offered some Algerians citizenship after 1865, but only if they rejected Islam and learned French (and, of course, only if they were male). Colonial subjects who made their way through elite French-speaking schools might be counted as *évolués*, or evolved persons, meaning that their contact with European culture had pushed them up the evolutionary scale a notch. Especially talented *évolués* such as the Senegalese politician Lamine Guèye (1891–1968) were even sent to Paris to obtain law degrees, in the hope they would return home to the French colonies (as Guèye did) and help impose France's will on the locals. In this latter hope, the French were sorely disappointed, as Guèye, on his return to Africa in 1921, founded the first socialist party in Senegal and, during a long career in politics, pushed hard for the erasure of France's color line and the equality of Africans under French law.

Lamine Guèye and Fellow Postcolonial Leaders In this 1963 photo, Lamine Guèye (*left*) and Senegalese president and literary figure Leopold Senghor (*right*) meet with the younger president of Dahomey, Hubert Maga (*center*). All three *évolués* grew up in French colonies, but later became leaders of independent African states.

Like the lower classes, colonial subjects were presumed to be unfit to govern themselves. But additionally, racial differences between subjects and overlords made it almost impossible for white Europeans to imagine that their colonial subjects would ever develop intelligence and moral virtues equal to those of their masters. Especially after the Indian Mutiny, the British took a dim view of the possibilities for the darker races to evolve. The westernized Indians (the *babus*) anointed as mediators and torch-bearers in the 1830s were ridiculed in the 1860s as brown persons attempting to pass themselves off as Englishmen. Clubs, restaurants, and churches were increasingly segregated, and relations between European men and local women driven underground. The moment at which the colonized world might be judged to have come of age was put off indefinitely. British colonial officials, writes the historian Bernard Porter, "found themselves in the embarrassing position of a manager who had trained up a man to run the firm with him, and then decided he could do the job on his own, and wanted a clerk instead."[5]

By the end of the nineteenth century, the number of these clerks was growing rapidly. So too was their discontent with the high-handedness of the colonial regimes. Many had begun their careers as loyal servants. During the Boer War, the future Indian leader Mohandas Gandhi organized an ambulance corps, and in 1906, Gandhi helped the British quash an African uprising in South Africa. Some had studied abroad or been exposed to socialist, abolitionist, or radical missionary literature that criticized European exploitation. Others had contact with indigenous cultural and religious movements, such as the Hindu revivalist movement in India or the Egyptian nationalist movement, which rejected Europe's civilizing mission as a whole.

By the time the twentieth century opened, many subjects felt betrayed by those who had promised them more autonomy and progress and less repression and condescension than they had received. Some began to regret the extent to which their adoption of European manners and ideas had made them strangers in their own lands. But they had learned to use European values to expose and criticize the unsightly realities of colonialism. It would be Europeanized natives, *babus* and *évolués* such as Gandhi and Guèye, who would lead the fight for reform or for full independence in the decades to come.

QUESTION | *Why might* babus *and* évolués *be especially inclined to join anticolonial movements?*

from attempting to seize new territory in southern Africa until late in the nineteenth century.

Northern Africa, too—nominally under the control of the Ottoman Empire—long resisted European colonization. A British colony had been founded at Tangier (Morocco) in 1661, but proved too costly and difficult to defend and was abandoned in 1683. North African pirates continued to ply the waters throughout the eighteenth century, and in the eastern Mediterranean, the Venetians, Greeks, and Ottomans dominated the trade. British and French commercial activity had shifted, in the meantime, away from the Mediterranean and toward the Atlantic.

In fact, it was less the prospect of riches than the need for national prestige that convinced France's Charles X to attempt to return to the idea of conquests in northern Africa. In 1827, he sent an expeditionary force to what is now Algeria. It took nearly three years for the French to gain control of the capital city, Algiers, by which time Charles had been forced to abdicate. His successor, Louis Philippe, expanded the campaign to conquer the northern African hinterland, a campaign that continued for the remainder of *his* administration. In 1831, he authorized the creation of the French Foreign Legion, in order to raise troops for Algeria, and throughout the 1830s and 1840s, the Legion and the French army together waged a series of brutal campaigns to pacify the territory.

Algerian resistance was fierce and long lasting. Abd al-Quadir (1808–1883), a Sufi scholar and *shaykh,* led the efforts to drive out the French. Al-Quadir called for guerrilla tactics to harry French troops and deployed religious rhetoric, including calls to engage in holy war, to rally Muslims to his cause. Finally defeated in 1847, al-Quadir was exiled to France—while, in a parallel movement, Parisian radicals arrested during the June Days of 1848 were sent to Algeria. In an interesting twist of fate, al-Quadir helped rescue many Christians during religious riots in Damascus in 1860, for which he received France's highest military decoration, the Legion of Honor.

Long after 1847, Algeria remained restive, and the French stationed troops there to prevent the revival of resistance. In 1848, the Second Republic declared Algeria officially part of France and gave it representation in the National Assembly. But it was careful to put both governance and the economy in the hands of land-hungry French settlers, known as *colons,* many of whom were eager to exploit their superior status. The Arab majority could not vote, and the better jobs were given to local, lighter-skinned Berbers, who were thought to be more capable of being civilized. As in India, the European language of the colonizers—in this case, French—was taught in schools on the presumption that transferring European culture was the only means by which Algerians could evolve into a higher civilization. But even those Algerians who converted to Christianity and graduated from elite schools were never fully equal to the *colons.* The whole model of uplift relied on a permanent, paternalist model, in which Muslim Arab children never quite grew up and never inherited the farm.

Abd al-Quadir, Islamic Scholar and Resistance Fighter This portrait of al-Quadir was probably taken in Paris, after the defeat of his Algerian resistance movement in 1847.

Opening East Asia: The Opium Wars

If establishing a toehold in Algeria was difficult, breaking into Chinese markets before the 1830s seemed nearly impossible. The Chinese economy remained vibrant, and Chinese exporters were profiting handsomely from trading in tea, a commodity that had become less a luxury than a necessity for British consumers. As Chinese markets and ports were officially closed to foreigners, British merchants wishing to trade in tea had to break with cherished mercantile practices and pay hard currency, as well as bribes, to extract the commodity from the Chinese. They were happy to discover another commodity that Chinese consumers wanted, but one that could not be provided legally by Chinese traders: opium. British planters in India could be induced to grow opium poppies, which could then be used as a kind of surrogate currency to purchase tea in China. Thus, against the express prohibitions of the Chinese emperor, a covert trade in tea and opium gathered steam. By the late 1830s, British traders were shipping some 20,000 crates of Bengali opium into China each year.

FIRST OPIUM WAR. Concerned both about the erosion of his control over commerce and about the rising number of opium addicts, in 1839 the Chinese emperor appointed a vigilant new official, Lin Zexu, to stop the trade through Canton, the one port city accessible to Europeans. Lin began confiscating and destroying the drug and closing Chinese markets to English goods. Outraged merchants pressured the British government to send an army, and in 1840, British gunboats arrived, manned in part by Indian recruits. A short war, subsequently known as the First Opium War, ensued. British steamships bombarded coastal towns and sailed up the Yangtze River into the interior.

TREATY OF NANJING. In 1842, the Chinese agreed to sign the Treaty of Nanjing, which established a number of **treaty ports** open to British trade. The treaty also granted Britain formal authority over the island of Hong Kong (which the British retained until 1997) and established the right of **extraterritoriality** for Europeans, which meant that British citizens living and working in China would be subject not to Chinese law or tried in Chinese courts, but subject only to British justice. Extraterritoriality was a provision Europeans regularly extracted from their colonial or semicolonial territories, and one that local populations greatly resented.

THE SECOND OPIUM WAR AND THE TREATY OF TIANJIN. Nearly two decades later, expanding European commercial ambitions led to a Second Opium War (1856–1860), in which Britain was aided by France, Russia, and the United States. During this conflict, the Chinese kidnapped and tortured British diplomats, and another Lord Elgin—the son of the Elgin who brought the Parthenon Marbles to London—ordered troops to burn the Imperial Summer Palace in Beijing. Distracted by the homegrown civil war known as the Taiping Rebellion (1850–1864), in 1860 the Qing Emperor signed the Treaty of Tianjin, legalizing two previously banned European imports (Christianity and opium) and expanding Britain's number of treaty ports. The treaty also granted the British the right to travel into the Chinese interior and forbade Chinese officials from referring to Queen Victoria's government or its subjects as barbarians. Shortly thereafter, the Chinese also gave the Russians a huge chunk of territory in the north, where the Russians would rapidly build the ice-free port of Vladivostok.

SPHERES OF INFLUENCE. Greatly encouraged by their successes, the Europeans mapped out **spheres of influences** in China and also began the process of extending and formalizing colonial rule in Southeast Asia (Map 20.2). With a cheap source of tea now ensured, British tea consumption rose from 1.5 pounds per person per year in the 1840s to 5.7 pounds in the 1890s. Consumers, however, preferred the even cheaper Indian teas, and the China trade lapsed. Opium, controlled by a government monopoly, continued to be highly profitable, providing the second greatest source of Indian revenue after the land tax. Some Chinese port cities, like Shanghai,

boomed; but clearly European traders and consumers benefited most from forcing the Chinese to engage in free trade.

Japan Opened—and Closed

This lesson was not lost on the Americans, and in 1853, American naval ships under Commodore Matthew Perry sailed to Japan to force this nation, too, to open its markets to foreign trade. Over the next five years, other western powers also demanded and received trade treaties and extraterritorial rights. But in the 1860s, a civil war ended the rule of the Tokugawa shogunate and restored the emperor, thus opening an age of Meiji, or enlightened, rule. Those who supported the Meiji Restoration had particularly disliked the shogunate's military weakness and capitulation to American, British, and French demands for special trading privileges. As they consolidated their hold on power after 1868, Japanese nationalists sought to preserve the nobility's control over Japanese society and to acquire the national power needed to overturn unequal foreign treaties.

In the 1870s, the Japanese began to borrow, selectively and on their terms, from Europe. They adopted Prussian models, sending Japanese students to the University of Berlin and bringing Prussian doctors, educational reformers, and especially military tacticians to Japan. Japanese modernizers modeled their constitution of 1891 on that of the Prussians and began importing large quantities of weapons from the German armaments maker Alfred Krupp. By the turn of the century, Japan had built its own industrial economy. It sent its European advisors home and began asserting itself as an imperial power in the Pacific. Although the European powers continued to believe that only the "white races" could modernize, Japan, stealing pages from the Prussian playbook, would prove them wrong.

Overland Empire: The Russians in the Caucasus

Already in the 1740s, Russian settlers had sought to leap the Pacific Ocean and settle in what is now the state of Alaska. Chiefly seeking otter pelts, these settlers tried to conquer and enslave the local Aleut population—but, as usual in the New World, it was disease that decimated the native population and made room for foreign settlements. The Russians held territory in Alaska until 1867, but the colony had ceased to be profitable long before as a result of American and Canadian competition for trapping rights and the near extinction of the fur-bearing mammals in the area.

For the Russians, empire in the Far East was attractive; but regions closer to the Mediterranean were much more alluring. Catherine the Great had been active in seeking to extend the Russian Empire southward, into Central Asia and the Balkans, in the hopes of securing Black Sea ports. She and her successors dreamed of eventually

MAP 20.2 | Imperialism in Asia before the First World War

The dates indicated are those of conquest by European powers. *Which powers were first to claim territory in Asia? Which controlled the largest amount of territory by the end of the nineteenth century?*

seizing Istanbul and with it access to the Mediterranean. Her primary method of conquest had been to cut deals with local potentates or simply to redraw borders as a means to incorporate smaller kingdoms into the vast, but lightly policed, Russian Empire. Between the 1820s and 1860s, however, especially in the Caucasus region, tactics changed, as Russian officials attempted to modernize the region and exploit its rich resources more efficiently.

In 1821, the Black Sea region called New Russia was put under the control of Mikhail Vorontsov, a highly energetic governor-general who modernized the port cities of Odessa and Sevastopol. He was then put in charge of the Caucasus, which he sought to pacify with a combination of institution-building and military force. The state's investment in building theaters, libraries, and schools paid off, convincing urban elites to buy in to Russian plans. The extremely bloody military expeditions into rural areas, by contrast, simply galvanized Muslim and Circassian resistance in the mountains and forests of Dagestan and Chechnya (see Map 20.3 on p. 654). The capture of one rebel stronghold in the summer of 1845, for example, cost the lives of two Russian generals, almost two hundred Russian officers, and more than three

thousand soldiers. The Muslim leader Shamil was finally defeated in 1859—and even then the Russians did not dare execute their longtime enemy, but settled him in a large, comfortable country house near Moscow. His coreligionists did not fare so well, as Muslims were forced out of the Crimea and northwestern Caucasus and resettled in the Ottoman Empire.

The Circassians, a Christian people native to the Caucasus region, suffered a similar fate between 1860 and 1864. Some of them were terrorized into finding new homes on the plains to the north or in Ottoman Anatolia; others were simply murdered by Russian troops. Large numbers of refugees died en route of disease or deprivation. Many more Muslims were expelled, resulting in the displacement or death of perhaps as many as two million Caucasians between 1859 and the conclusion of the Russo-Turkish War in 1878 in one of the first, and least discussed, episodes of modern ethnic cleansing.

In fictional depictions of life in the Caucasus such as Mikhail Lermontov's *A Hero of Our Time* (1840) and Leo Tolstoy's *Hadji Murad* (written 1896–1904), Russia's leading novelists acknowledged that this kind of conquest did no good, either for the natives or for the souls of the conquerors. In fact, even these extreme measures did not fully pacify the mountainous region, which would continue to provide fierce and numerous anti-Russian resistance fighters for generations to come, demonstrating that colonization over land could be just as difficult—and perhaps even more bloody—than imperial endeavors across the seas.

A Turning Point: The Indian Rebellion

The British, French, and Russian empires were not easily established. But perhaps even more difficult than acquiring territory was the on-the-ground job of ruling. In many places, resistance and counterinsurgency continued for decades, and governments back home were usually unwilling to spend much on colonial administration and defense. In fact, the ideal colony of the time was the one that paid for its own pacification—an ideal realized by few colonies in the nineteenth century, with the critical exception of India. Indeed, India, hugely profitable, held by an army of only about 275,000, a mere 45,500 of whom were Europeans, seemed to be *the* great colonial success story before 1857. And perhaps that is why the Indian Rebellion of 1857 proved such a painful wake-up call.

The rebellion was sparked by the British attempt to introduce standardization, with typical disregard for local religious sensitivities. In early 1857, rumors spread through the army that the cartridges for the new rifles issued by the East India Company had been coated with the fat of cows (sacred to Hindus) and pigs (which Muslims view as unclean animals). To troops who were ordered to bite off the tops of these cartridges in order to load their weapons, these contaminations were abominable. In May, eighty-five recruits were sentenced to ten years' hard labor for refusing to use the cartridges, and one leading objector was court-martialed and hanged. This new instance of British contempt for local people and customs proved the spark that ignited mutiny across northern India. Not all

Shamil Meets with the Russians, 1837 Here the Muslim leader of the resistance to Russian imperialism in the Caucasus region discusses terms with the invaders. Talks soon broke down, however, leading to decades of guerilla warfare and savage repression in the area that is now Chechnya and Dagestan.

Indians joined the revolt, and British control was never seriously in question, but it still took a year and a half to snuff out. British India would never be the same.

The revolt was most powerful in the army and in areas where rural landlords felt aggrieved by high-handed

The Indian Rebellion This image, made during the rebellion, shows an encampment of sepoy soldiers readying themselves for battle. The sepoys are flying a red and green flag, meant to symbolize the unity of Hindus and Muslims by combining their symbolic colors.

British policies, but it lacked organized leadership and a coherent set of objectives. Still, the fighting was brutal, and civilians were also attacked. Rebels murdered women and children in the settlement of Kanpur, and the British press teemed with reports of white women raped by "Moors." British troops committed atrocities as well: they sewed Muslim prisoners into pigskins, then sent them to the gallows or shot them from cannons; and one commander ordered Indian prisoners to lick up the blood of their victims.

After the rebellion, the British Parliament took over the administration of India. New, more direct forms of rule were imposed, including reform of the police and judicial systems. Once the country was stabilized, new investment poured in. A huge campaign of railroad building began. Whereas India had had less than 300 miles of track in 1857, 25,000 miles had been built by 1900 to increase trade and to allow for the swifter mobilization of soldiers, should rebellion threaten again. Significantly, too, arguments advanced earlier by conservatives—that liberal cultural reforms were too aggressive and had created instability—now won the day, and Britain adopted a much more deliberate, much less optimistic, policy of reform.

Some liberals who had believed they were bringing light to India felt betrayed and swore that the Indians were incorrigible and could not be fully civilized. Upper-crust colonial officials adopted an even more feudal attitude toward their "white man's burden." More British women ventured to India to prevent their husbands' corruption by contact with native women and cultures, and the colonizers' social lives and diets were segregated from those of their Indian neighbors as faster transportation made possible the importation of British clothing, food, and home furnishings. But settlers did not forget the terrors of the mutiny, and many Indians, too, would continue to carry with them a strong sense of betrayal.

Cultures of Empire

During the second wave of colonization, the projects of empire building involved relatively few people from a handful of European nations.

How did imperialism transform both European and colonial cultures? The third wave changed that, to some extent, as many more nations and many more individuals engaged in colonial endeavors. By 1914, indirectly at least, colonialism had begun to shape the experience not only of many Europeans, but also of many non-Europeans. Colonial exploitation provided the raw materials for western Europe's increasing affluence, even as it transformed—and often devastated—the economies, cultures, and environments of the colonized. But this is a good place to remind ourselves that Europe as a continent did not colonize anyone and that it continued to be home to non-imperial Switzerland as well as to eagerly imperial Britain. Even in the imperial nations, statesmen and busi-

nessmen cared more about domestic and European politics and trade than about the empire; the British worried more about rebellion in Ireland than in India.

If not every nation was imperial, or imperial in the same way, this also holds true for the inhabitants of each state. Even in Britain, some people knew and cared a great deal more about the empire than others. Cecil Rhodes, for example, owed virtually everything to his exploitation of South African diamonds and spent years experiencing the reality of empire abroad. The typical domestic servant, by contrast, had little knowledge of South Africa or India—even though she might dress her mistress in diamonds or drink Chinese tea during her breaks. And she certainly knew less about the sordid and exploitative sides of colonialism on the ground than did Rhodes or the women of Algeria. Here we examine the degrees and varieties of imperial experience and cultural transfer, beginning with an examination of what it was like to live the imperial age for the Europeans most directly involved in the process: soldiers and missionaries.

Living the Empire: The Colonial Soldier

What has often been called nineteenth-century Europe's **long peace,** the long pause in intercontinental warfare between 1815 and 1914, overlooks the fact that this period was rife with persistent, bloody, and expensive wars in Europe's colonial territories. The extension of colonial control beyond the older commercial models was a violent process, as had already been demonstrated by the Spanish, French, and British colonizing efforts in the Americas. Wars were fought in vastly different geographic areas, from the northern African deserts to the Alaskan islands, from the jungles of Southeast Asia to the mountaintops of Tibet. The conflicts were instigated by opportunity-seeking businessmen and settlers, or by politicians in Paris or St. Petersburg, but they were fought by hundreds of thousands of European soldiers, cajoled or conscripted into service, and by millions of non-Europeans who were either paid or made to help the residents of a tiny continent subdue the rest of the world.

The life of a colonial soldier, whether or not he was European born, was not easy. Men enlisted to escape debt or poverty at home or to seek adventure abroad. But many, if not most, did not return home at all, as tours of duty were generally very long (twelve years in the British East India Company Army; twenty-one years were required to earn a pension), and the death rate for soldiers abroad was appallingly high. For northern Europeans, the heat of colonial climates and the insects were hard to bear. Diseases such as cholera and dysentery killed many, especially in the West Indies and Southeast Asia. Just getting to India alive was something of a feat. Before 1790, the death rate of white soldiers en route to India was higher even than that of African slaves transported across the Atlantic. Disease took a terrible toll elsewhere as well. Europeans stationed on the west coast of Africa in 1824–1826 died at a rate of nearly 67 percent per year.

Many soldiers were poorly educated, indigent, and young, some as young as fourteen, or in the navy, even younger. Ireland, that endless pool of cheap labor, supplied a large number of British colonial soldiers. Colonial forces usually enjoyed little freedom of movement, and before the 1830s, British soldiers who attempted to desert or disobeyed orders were subjected to severe corporal punishments, including flogging. Soldiers often faced enemies whose fighting power their superiors had greatly underestimated; colonial intelligence was notoriously poor. Troops of colonial soldiers raised to help rule their own countries, such as the sepoys in India, or to subdue other ones for the Europeans, such as the Africans used to police the West Indies, suffered similar tortures and perils and were often given the worst and most dangerous assignments.

For European and sepoy soldiers, the only certainty about food rations was that they would be inadequate. Housing, health care, and sanitation were generally atrocious. Sometimes states ran out of money, and troops went for long stretches without pay. Such incidents provoked desertion, mutinies, and a black market trade in guns, intelligence, and supplies. Between battles there was typically nothing to do but drink, gamble, and dream of home. Elite Europeans remained, in general, contemptuous of their usually lower-class soldiery, and only in the later nineteenth century did governments begin to supply garrisons with newspapers, books, and other diversions. It has been said that without the additional inducement of large quantities of alcohol, used both for inspiration and as a reward, Europe's empires would never have been won.

The Civilizing Mission and the Missionary Impulse

Nineteenth-century empires secured themselves first of all by force. But, as historian Linda Colley puts it, "Successful military machismo and conquests were never enough."[6] More than the empire builders of past centuries, nineteenth-century Europeans wanted to reassure themselves that they were also virtuous and heroic, that they *deserved* to rule. The second and third waves of colonialism brought ever more soldiers, entrepreneurs, and bureaucrats to the colonies, but with them came large numbers of "civilizers" as well, including doctors, teachers, engineers, and their wives, all of them hoping to bring Europe's light to dark places. Foremost among these emissaries of European culture were the missionaries.

The Bible tells Christians that it is their duty to preach the gospel to non-Christians, and since the medieval period some Europeans have believed it was their duty to be missionaries for the faith. After 1492, many Catholic priests and monks crossed the Atlantic, seeking to convert the remaining natives. Using a combination of coercion (including the Inquisition) and persuasion, they succeeded in transplanting Catholicism to the Americas—though

native believers blended local traditions into their rituals. Jesuit priests had also been active in China and South Asia since the sixteenth century, but had made relatively few converts. In fact, the reports and documents these priests sent back to Rome and Paris did much to familiarize European intellectuals with Chinese and Indian religions and traditions and might be said to have had a bigger cultural impact on Europeans of the early Enlightenment era than Catholicism had on the South Asians or the Chinese.

Enlightenment ideas and the gradual, if uneven, spread of wealth, literacy, and industrial technology from the later eighteenth century on added to Europeans' confidence that they knew what was best for the rest. At just about the same time, evangelical revivals such as Methodism and Pietism swept the continent (see Chapter 15), provoking the creation of Protestant missionary societies in America and Britain, but also in Switzerland, the German states, and the Netherlands. The founding of colonies, as well as the concessions the weakening Chinese and Ottoman Empires were forced to make, gave missionaries more space to work, and by 1900, some 18,000 Protestant missionaries were living in colonial settlements around the globe. Many settled into remote areas where they founded clinics and schools, and some became beloved members of communities where they worked hard to care for both the souls and the bodies of their flocks. Often the Europeans in a particular locality stuck together, allowing into their inner circle only white people who spoke English or French. But some, such as the German missionary Karl Gützlaff, eagerly learned local languages and adopted local customs.

THE DISAPPOINTMENTS OF KARL GÜTZLAFF. Karl Gützlaff (1803–1851) ardently believed it was his duty to bring the light of Christ to Asia. During his years in Singapore, Bangkok, and Hong Kong in the 1820s–1840s, Gützlaff attempted translations of the Bible into Thai and Chinese and, together with his first wife, composed a Cambodian dictionary. He also published a magazine in Chinese, wore Chinese dress, and gave himself a Chinese name, Gūo Shila. Gützlaff surely invested his time and energy in these endeavors because he thought doing so would likely net him more converts. But he also learned a great deal about Chinese culture from his students. He came to trust the Chinese missionaries he trained so much that he was devastated by revelations that some of them had lied to him about the number of their converts and that they resold his New Testaments for profit. He died in 1851, shortly after learning that he had not really made them neo-Europeans, after all.

Missionaries had various relationships with European traders and colonial officials in the territories where they worked. Some colluded with entrepreneurs to exploit the natives economically, justifying their actions by arguing that work would civilize the natives. Others were vehement opponents of slavery and the slave trade, and some sought to protect the natives from exploitation by colonial rulers and ruthless businessmen. A few, inadvertently, provoked international incidents by getting into tight spots and provoking their own countrymen to come to their aid.

DR. LIVINGSTONE, LOST AND FOUND. David Livingstone (1813–1873) was one of the latter. An English missionary who went to Africa to work against the slave trade, he became increasingly famous in the 1850s for his forays into geography. Undertaking a daring trek across Africa, Livingstone was of the first Europeans to cross the Kalahari Desert and to see the natural wonder that natives called Mosi-oa-Tunya, which he dubbed Victoria Falls. He returned to Britain and in 1857 published a stirring account of his adventures and his good works in *Missionary Travels and Researches in South Africa*. The book sold 70,000 copies within a few months of its publication and made Livingstone a scientific, as well as humanitarian, hero. New expeditions took him to southeastern Africa in 1858 and then in 1865 to central Africa—for Livingstone longed, first, to solve the hotly debated question of the sources of the Nile and, second, to continue his work to stop Arab slave trading in the region.

During the next year, Livingstone's letters home were published in London newspapers—but then they suddenly stopped. In 1869, the enterprising publisher of *The New York Herald* sent the reporter Henry Morton Stanley (1841–1904) to Africa to find Livingstone. After a nearly two-year search, Stanley *did* find his man, at Ujiji, on the shores of Lake Tanganyika. Stanley reportedly greeted the ailing missionary with the diffident words, "Dr. Livingstone, I presume?" The story was a sensation; Stanley became a celebrity. But Livingstone refused to leave Africa, having not yet found the Nile's sources, and died there in 1873. His loyal servants carried his body through one thousand miles of Central African jungle to the coast, where it was shipped to Westminster Abbey for burial. Stanley returned to Africa many times thereafter, and his explorations and maps would be the means by which the carving up of sub-Saharan Africa was completed.

The activities of Gützlaff and Livingstone were not typical of all missionaries, most of whom did not aspire to grand scholarly feats. Gützlaff made some converts, but his successes were modest, more modest it turned out than even he thought. After many years of missionary work, Livingstone seems to have converted only one man, and even this conversion was questionable. His antislavery publications drew new attention among the British public, but he did nothing concrete to abolish the trade, and in the course of his explorations, he occasionally had to depend on Arab slave traders to provide him porters or to show him the way through jungles. Yet the careers of both Gützlaff and Livingstone produced some noteworthy results. Both men provided Europeans with new information about foreign places and cultures, information that could be used to aid in conversion or in partitioning and exploitation. Through their scholarly and

Henry Stanley, Explorer and Agent of Empire After finding Livingstone, Stanley returned repeatedly to sub-Saharan Africa, combining travel with reconnaissance for his employer, King Leopold II of Belgium. Here he poses with one of the many Africans—young and old—upon whom he relied for assistance.

humanitarian works, they allowed Europeans to feel they were bringing culture to dark places. Unintentionally, too, they drove wedges into these worlds that permitted the pouring in of other, more ambitious, conquerors, and the development of more extensive and mutually transformative forms of cultural transfer.

Imperialism and the Field Sciences

The imperial era was one of rapid, intensive development in the humanities and sciences and the huge expansion of European zoos, botanical gardens, libraries, and museums. The field sciences—geography, geology, archaeology, botany, zoology, anthropology, and paleontology—benefited greatly, as access to new territories and increasing wealth made it possible for European scientists to collect specimens on a vast new scale. Modeling their efforts on the expeditions of James Cook to the South Pacific and on Napoleon's treasure-trawling in Egypt, travelers and collectors fanned out all over the globe, seeking to bring home specimens, artifacts, and information—not, they said, to enrich themselves, but for the sake of science.

GEOGRAPHY.
Geography was perhaps the most obvious scholarly beneficiary of the age of imperialism. Describing and mapping the earth's surface was a very old pursuit, but in the nineteenth century geography became suddenly much more popular—and much more politically significant. While many earlier geographers had worked essentially in libraries, the drive for new knowledge and the yearning to go places no European had gone before gave birth to a new breed. The role of traveler or explorer had often overlapped with that of the geographer, but this overlap now increased dramatically as Europeans set their sights on mapping the *whole world,* including all the areas of the African and Asian interiors that had previously been off-limits to Europeans. The French Société de Geographie was founded in 1821; the German Gesellschaft für Erdkunde followed in 1828; and Britain's Royal Geographical Society, in 1830. Smaller, more popular geographic societies and publications sprang up across Europe. Cartographers set sail for the most remote of places, hoping to fill in "blank spaces" still left on the map and, by so doing, make their contribution to science before it was too late.

This urgency to get somewhere first, to make the first map, seized Europeans in the wake of competitions between the English explorers Richard Burton and John Hanning Speke to find the sources of the Nile in the 1860s. It continued at least until 1909, when American Robert Peary gleefully announced, in a telegraph to *The New York Times,* "Stars and Stripes nailed to the North Pole." But there were many more such races, for example, the highly contested and controversial attempts to map the Himalayas and to reach the closed city of Lhasa, capital of Tibet. Some individuals made careers, and even fortunes, by getting somewhere first. Henry Stanley was one; others included the Swede Sven Hedin, the first European to cross the treacherous Taklamakan Desert in southwestern China. Most of these endeavors involved reckless behavior on the part of the explorer-geographer, considerable amounts of assistance from local guides, and immense suffering on the part of both humans and pack animals.

Newspapermen, who decided exploration made fine copy, promoted these races. Adventurers made significant profits by relating their stories to packed public lecture halls all over the world. Hedin was feted in Japan, met U.S. president Theodore Roosevelt and Russian czar Alexander II, and became a particular favorite of the king of Sweden. Geographer-explorers, such as Livingstone, Stanley, and Hedin, also became authors of bestselling accounts of their exotic adventures, which were especially popular with young boys. But the explorers' stories also provided information, vast quantities of it, as evidenced by the massive atlases and scientific reports produced in the nineteenth century. Some of the information was simply gap-filling factoids, but much of it served practical purposes, for those who wanted to find coal deposits or lay down railroad lines. The *China Atlas* created by German geographer Ferdinand von Richthofen, for example, was useful for both purposes. The Survey of India, similarly, was a colonial as well as a scientific endeavor. As the surveyors understood, if one wanted to rule a territory, one needed first of all to have good maps.

BOTANY, ZOOLOGY, AND ARCHAEOLOGY.
Thanks to the newly available information about earth's surfaces, the science of geography earned new prestige and popularity, but it was not the only science to benefit from Europe's new access to the world. Botany and zoology also became high specialized and highly competitive fields as scholars and collectors searched to find new species. Seeds for useful tropical commodities, such as rubber or cinchona bark (from which quinine, used to treat malaria, was made), could be transplanted. So too could ornamental plants, such as rhododendrons, be made to travel; native to the Himalayas, rhododendrons became enormously popular in England, and the rhododendron exhibit remains one of the highlights of London's Kew Gardens.

Another former royal botanical garden, the Parisian Jardin des Plantes, displayed exotic animals. Zarafa, the first giraffe to reach Europe in modern times, was put on display there after her sensational 550-mile walk from Marseilles to Paris in 1827. All over Europe, zoos opened to display the nation's collection of rare species and to allow German, French, Dutch, Italian, and Swedish scholars to study exotic creatures (and to dissect and stuff them once they died). Circuses and traveling wild animal shows also trafficked heavily in exotic creatures and sometimes featured displays of African, Asian, or Native American human beings as well. Big-game hunters coveted the empires' animals; there was little more symbolically imperial than the British passion for the tiger hunt.

Museums of natural history originally served chiefly as laboratories for zoologists and biologists, who crammed them full of every obtainable species of bird and badger. But gradually and with the help of armies of taxidermists, these museums began displaying nature's global diversity to the public. In the process, scholars and museum curators learned enormous amounts about animal behaviors, diets, and habitats. The European public, too, was offered access to increasing amounts of knowledge about the world and its creatures, just as some of them—including the Tasmanian wolf—were becoming extinct. But the curators' zeal for bagging a new specimen also created markets for rare animals, and the new information allowed trackers to trap them more easily. We can easily trace the beginnings of the endangerment of many exotic animals to this era of rapacious colonial collecting.

The archaeological races, similarly, were concerned with the acquisition of new knowledge, and they too were fueled by European museums' hunger for impressive, unique possessions. Especially after mid-century, the Louvre, the British Museum, and the German Royal

George Everest, Surveyor General of India

When we hear accounts of heroic or tragic attempts to scale Mount Everest, the world's highest mountain, how many of us think about its namesake, George Everest?[7] Trained, like Napoleon Bonaparte, as an artillery officer, George Everest (1790–1866) did not make his mark on the British Empire by winning battles. Instead, as surveyor general of India, he played a crucial role in making the maps that statesmen, tax collectors, and other army officers used to exert authority over the entire Indian subcontinent. The mountain peak, named in his honor by his successor as surveyor general in 1865, is only a fragmentary and rather misleading reminder of Everest's role in world history, for he was not a climber but a mathematically skilled surveyor whose great aspiration was to cover all of British India with triangles.

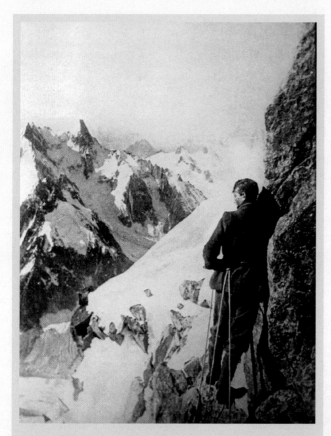

Mount Everest This image from the 1924 Royal Geographical Society's Everest expedition depicts the rugged geography and extreme climatic conditions that have made studying and mapping the Himalayas such a challenging but alluring endeavor since Europeans began their surveying work in the mid-nineteenth century.

Everest did not invent the idea of triangulation, imagining and then measuring straight lines through high points to create a chain of interlocking triangles whose angles and other sides can then be calculated. But as colonial India's surveyor general between 1830 and 1843, he was instrumental in pushing forward the scientific mapping not just of regions, but also of the subcontinent as a whole. The Great Trigonometrical Survey (GTS, later renamed the Survey of India) took decades—much longer than Everest's lifetime—and cost far more money than the British government wanted to pay. Nor was the project popular among Indians. Many surveyors were attacked, as villagers feared (rightly) that the more information the British had, the more tax revenues and other services they would want to extract. But Everest believed that he was making a critical contribution to science, and that it befit "the rulers of possessions so vast and important" (the BEIC) to fund his work properly.

One of the reasons Everest wanted funding from the BEIC was to pay the Indians upon whom the GTS depended to carry out its work. Surveying took time, and it took people to do the math. The survey could not be done entirely by British officers, who were too expensive and too thin on the ground. Everest insisted that English soldiers were unsuitable; they could not stand the climate, and they drank too much. Sepoys could not serve because most were illiterate. Everest favored instead Anglo-Indian creoles, whom he described, condescendingly, as "an acute and clever race . . . of whom the great defect is a proneness to falsehood, chiefly attributed to their native education." In fact, many of the GTS's workhorses were just such men, attractive because they were both literate and cheap to employ. Some were recruited directly from the orphanage at Madras, having been left there when their soldier-fathers and native mothers died or abandoned them. None of these men, or the Indian calculators who worked at their sides, had mountains named after them or received British knighthoods, as did Everest in 1861. When we need hear of Mount Everest, perhaps we should reflect a bit more on the long and demanding years of surveying and calculating that made up Everest's career—and of all the Anglo-Indian and Indian fieldworkers who helped make his survey both a scientific and an imperial achievement.

QUESTION | *What role do maps play in the imposition of empire?*

Museums engaged in campaigns to bring home large artifacts that were the archaeological equivalent of obtaining a giraffe or mapping a blank space. London's Elgin Marbles (see Chapter 18) were joined by the great winged bulls from Nineveh, excavated by A. H. Layard in 1849. The Louvre could boast a fabulous Egyptian collection as well as the Venus de Milo. In 1878, the German Museums managed to transport the huge Hellenistic Pergamon Altar from the Ottoman coast. Heinrich Schliemann, the excavator of Troy and of Mycenae, became a hero, and books about his discoveries sold as widely as those of Livingstone. The number and variety of excavations that followed in the twenty-five years after Schliemann's death in 1890 stagger the imagination and range from Flinders Petrie's careful digs in Palestine to the rapacious ripping away of Buddhist murals from cave walls all over western China by emissaries from the great imperial powers: France, Britain, Germany, Russia, and even Japan.

Archaeological discoveries yielded huge numbers of artifacts, and insofar as the museums were big enough to display all this material, the European public gained access to a wealth of knowledge about the history of civilizations beyond Europe. Connoisseurs began to appreciate authentic Chinese vases, and art historians to look sympathetically, for the first time, at African carvings and Indian sculpture. Europeans learned to appreciate oriental carpets; in 1893 the South Kensington Museum paid the equivalent of $314,000 in today's money for a sixteenth-century Persian carpet. In Munich in 1910, an eighty-room blockbuster exhibit of Islamic art attracted more than 600,000 visitors, among them some of Europe's leading artists. But many artifacts were purchased at rock-bottom prices, when Chinese or Persian owners were desperate to sell, and some monuments were destroyed during all-too-hasty excavations. In a very short period, much of the non-western world's cultural heritage was spirited away to Berlin, London, Paris, and Boston. Here, again, imperial science had its benefits, and its costs.

The Imperial Exchange

If civilizing the world involved Christianizing it and making it available for scientific knowledge, this also meant bringing non-westerners European goods and exchanging them for Asian and African commodities. Historians beginning with Alfred Crosby have emphasized the importance of what Crosby called the Columbian exchange, the transferring and transplanting of European ideas to the Americas, and of American commodities and customs to Europe, in the period after Columbus's voyages.[8] But of equal importance is what might be called the **imperial exchange,** the huge, two-directional traffic in goods and ideas that transformed both Europe and the colonial world over the course of the nineteenth and early twentieth centuries. Cotton cloth, gin, railroads, industrial machinery, and weapons made their way out of Europe, while diamonds, rubber, rhododendrons, tea, and oriental carpets made their way in. Many other goods were in motion as well, including material things, such as Singer sewing machines, synthetic dyes, dates, ivory, and palm oil; and more abstract goods, such as bureaucratic rationality and Buddhist contemplation—and perhaps even the definition of European identity itself.

As they were exchanged, commodities were put to new uses. Singer sewing machines were used to make saris; palm oil used for cooking in the Niger delta was used to lubricate machines in Britain. The Ottoman sultan sought to ingratiate himself with Muslims by building a railroad to Mecca, allowing pilgrims to more easily accomplish the hadj. Europeans were the primary beneficiaries of the imperial exchange, but many ordinary Asians and some Africans, too, profited from new forms of cultural hybridity, and from European investments in

Singer Sewing Machines, around the World Eager to advertise its global sales, the Singer Sewing Machine Company issued a series of cards showing natives of various countries using the machines in their local settings. The reverse side of the cards gave short, often condescending, descriptions of these settings in English, betraying the reality that the cards were meant to be read by English speakers, especially those in the United States and Great Britain.

The Imperial Origins of Modern European Identity

Among the central themes of this book is that there have always been many Europes. The successful resistance of Europe's inhabitants to efforts to bring the continent under the control of one empire meant that no single player has been able to impose a definition of what it means to be a European. Ever battling one another on the continent, the inhabitants of the European landmass, it might be said, most clearly espoused a collective identity on those occasions in which they found themselves *outside* of Europe, during the Crusades against the Seljuk Turks, for example, or in missionary or commercial outposts in the Americas, Asia, or Africa. European-ness, that is, may be a product of *leaving* Europe, literally or figuratively. As a collective identity, it was chiefly produced from the outside in.

If this is the case, it stands to reason that the age of empire, and of mass emigration and increasing intercontinental travel, would have had a powerful impact on the creation of modern European identity. In 1978, the literary scholar (and native of Palestine) Edward Said put forward a compelling version of this claim. According to Said, *European* came into being as a meaningful collective identity at about the time the British and French started establishing overseas colonies in Asia, that is, about 1770. Belonging to Europe, or to the West (thereby including the first neo-Europes), simply meant *not* belonging to the Orient or to the East.[9] Although Said's argument discounts

the importance of earlier colonial efforts—of the Spanish and Portuguese in the Americas, for example—it does make sense to think that this era was highly significant in the formation of the modern idea of European-ness. The Google Ngram viewer, which correlates data from thousands of titles, provides an interesting picture of the use of the term *European* in British English, which gives additional credence to Said's periodization (see Figure 20.1).

Definitions of European-ness have always varied. Europeans never have, and probably never will, agree *completely* on what Europe is, where its borders lie, and what it should stand for. But by the nineteenth century, most people's definition of Europe blended older conceptions of Christendom with a selection of ideals born of the quiet revolutions and the western European Enlightenment. This should not be surprising given that the settlers and colonizers of the period were largely products of the western nations—Britain, France, and the Netherlands—where both secularization and the quiet revolutions had gone the farthest. Most of the colonizers remained Christians, but most were also proponents of liberal ideals and middle- or upper-class forms of consumption. We should not forget, however, that the ideals and lifestyles these people championed as "European" did not correspond to the lived reality of many of the continent's inhabitants. The nineteenth-century ideal, for example, did not dwell on Russian serfdom or the agrarian poverty and illiteracy common in southern Italy, Spain, the Balkans, and eastern Europe. Few spoke of child labor or the Irish potato famine. The ideal came in most handy abroad and not at home, where Germans and Frenchmen, to cite just one example, were perfectly aware of how much they did, and did not, share. And too many of those Europeans who championed the ideal treated it as if it were the whole reality and used it as a means to judge and condemn non-European cultures as backward and in need of "civilization."

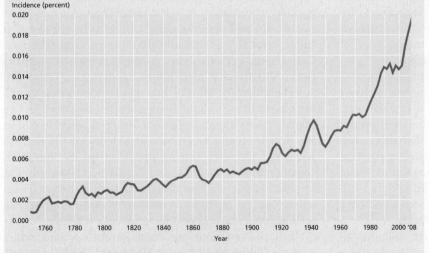

Incidence (percent)

FIGURE 20.1. | The Rise of European Identity

This graph, created using the Google Ngram Viewer, shows the rising incidence of the term *European* in British English over the period 1780–2008. The Ngram Viewer draws its data from thousands of books published each year, and thus provides an interesting glimpse at the usage of particular words over time. For example, in 1840, the word "European" represented just under .004% of all words used in the British English texts published in that year in the Google Books collection.

Source: Google Ngram Viewer, http://books.google.com/ngrams/graph?content=European&year_start=1780&year_end=2000&corpus=6&smoothing=3.

QUESTIONS | *Are there other identities (such as American or Californian) that might have been developed from the outside in? What else is involved in the making of an identity that relates to place?*

railroads, schools, clinics, and libraries, or from their employment in European enterprises. Many came to admire western liberal ideas: equality, the rule of law, meritocracy, free trade, popular sovereignty. But as the colonized learned to appreciate these values, they also recognized that, in the end, no matter what the law said, no matter what their merits or efforts, they and their European overlords could never be equals. The imperial exchange and the civilizing mission were tainted by a factor ever more in evidence: racial prejudice.

Race and Empire

As we have seen, the first neo-Europes were created in places where local populations had been decimated by warfare and disease, opening the way for settlement by white European emigrants. The colonies of the nineteenth century were different. For one thing, Asian and African natives had more immunity to European diseases. For another, many fewer Europeans, proportionally, were willing to settle in British-ruled Kenya or French Indochina. Indeed, many more chose to move to the now independent Americas than to settle in second- and third-wave colonies.

In response, in the early nineteenth century, British, French, and Dutch leaders envisioned creating neo-Europes populated by Asians and Africans or by individuals of mixed descent. In these decades, the mixing of races in the colonies was more or less taken for granted and not seen as a threat, either to the parent country or to the colony.

But the rise of native resistance—especially the Indian Rebellion of 1857—made Europeans anxious about the loyalty of those who were not entirely of European descent. Steeped in evolutionary thought, some began to worry that racial mixing might cause degeneracy. Increasingly, settlers were advised to keep their distance from the natives, and the production of mixed-blood or half-breed children was actively discouraged.

Thus, by the later nineteenth century, race was increasingly seen to dictate destiny, to destine a person to ruling or to being ruled. Many scientists as well as popular writers ratified this idea, claiming that some races were inferior and backward, and others superior and inherently suited to bearing the burden of civilizing the rest. Popularizers of Darwin's works elaborated theories known as **social Darwinism,** which argued, as Darwin did not, that cultures or races that won the struggle for existence had been chosen by nature, or by God, to rule the world.

Skin color now mattered far more than religious allegiance or language, and its shades were arrayed to form an evolutionary hierarchy: the blacker the skin, the less civilized the individual; the whiter the skin, the more the individual was obliged to take on the responsibilities of bringing progress to dark regions, a view subtly parodied by British writer Rudyard Kipling in his poem "The White Man's Burden" (1899). But racial inequality was far more than a scientific theory or a dodgy excuse for self-pity: it was the justification for the imposition and

continuation of European rule, and it was the barricade that prevented most Europeans from recognizing the injustices they were committing throughout the world.

The Third Wave: Consolidating Empires after 1860

In the period after 1857, racial thinking, increasing competition for markets and prestige, and the weakening of the Ottoman and Chinese Empires intensified and accelerated European imperial projects. As industrial output increased, entrepreneurs also sought new markets. The rise of commercial banking and the expansion of stock trading allowed firms to raise the necessary capital to plan big projects overseas such as the building of the Suez Canal or the establishment of a railway network in the Ottoman Empire. As the Ottoman and Chinese Empires lost control of their peripheral provinces, businessmen and statesmen found new spaces to exploit. What had been a staggered marathon, with nations stopping and starting at various points, now became an all-out sprint as new countries entered the race and as holding colonies—profitable or not—came to seem essential to being a great and properly modern power.

> Why was the third wave of colonization so much more violent than the previous two?

New "tools of empire," in the words of historian Daniel Headrick, also gave the imperialism of the third wave additional intensity.[10] After about 1860, thanks to new tools such as steamships and telegraph wires, people and information traveled faster than ever before in history. Instead of mail taking as long as a year to get to India, steamships, especially after the opening of the Suez Canal, could get it there in a couple of weeks. Military orders could arrive in mere hours, by way of the telegraph. An increasingly literate European population could now be informed about events across the globe. Just as Stanley's sensational stories about Africa began to run in the British press, foreign correspondents for the Reuters news service were setting up an office in Shanghai. Expanded news coverage and accelerated travel put the imperial powers in ever closer touch with their colonies and propelled attempts to exert ever greater cultural as well as economic and political influence abroad.

Perhaps even more important, Europe's second industrial revolution (see Chapter 21) brought with it innovations in medical and military technology. Most significant among medical improvements was the development of inexpensive quinine tablets, which allowed Europeans to pour into sub-Saharan Africa, a region previously too malaria-prone to permit extensive colonial intrusions. Among military innovations the breech-loading rifle, and later the Maxim gun, the world's first machine gun, proved most useful to colonizers. Increased firepower allowed Europeans more easily to seize territories or suppress resistance with small numbers of soldiers against much larger, but inexperienced and ill-provisioned local forces. It is estimated, for example, that in suppressing the Maji Maji Uprising in German East Africa in 1905, only about 15 Europeans died, together with 389 African soldiers in German employ, whereas as many as 300,000 Africans lost their lives.

In general, the story of imperialism after 1860 is one of the use of these tools of empire to create bigger and more closely monitored empires. It is also one of increasing inter-European competition and tension and of the race to fill power vacuums left by ailing empires (or, in the case of Africa, opened by quinine-equipped explorers). Perhaps it is not surprising that the "sick man" of biggest concern to Europeans was the one closest to home: the Ottoman Empire.

Mehmet Ali Receives a British Artist Mehmet Ali and his successors were happy to receive western visitors. David Roberts's reconstruction of his visit in 1839 shows Ali comfortably in charge in his palace in Alexandria.

The Ottoman Power Vacuum

Already in the 1830s, the once-inspiring Ottoman Empire seemed to be folding its once luxurious tents. Egypt and Tunisia had already become virtually independent kingdoms. Then the Greeks broke away, and the French nabbed Algeria. Moreover, the Ottomans were facing severe financial problems that reforms failed to solve. By the time of the Crimean War (see Chapter 19), the British and French had begun to worry about the Eastern Question and to fear that an Ottoman collapse would allow the reactionary Russians to extend their huge empire to the shores of the Mediterranean. European bankers began to loan the sultan and his regional governors large amounts of money. Western capital and capitalists flowed into the Ottoman Empire, but at a price. As in China, Europeans put pressure on the Ottomans to admit missionaries and to extend privileges to the Christian inhabitants of the empire. European involvement increased, and even though the Ottomans remained the overlords, the "sick man of the Balkans" grew increasingly dependent on his self-interested nursemaids.

EGYPT AND THE SUEZ CANAL. In Egypt, the local governor traditionally had considerable autonomy from Ottoman interference, and following Napoleon's retreat from Egypt in 1799, a new man, Mehmed Ali (r. 1805–1849) tried to make his territory fully independent. Ali

modernized the bureaucracy, instigated land reforms to encourage the production of cotton, and encouraged the development of textile and weapons manufacturing. Victorious in war against the Ottoman Empire, he got the Europeans to agree to support making his Egypt a hereditary monarchy; the new kings, or khedives, would retain only nominal ties to the Ottomans. But in his attempts to create a modern autonomous state, Ali also ran up a tremendous debt, held largely by British and French bankers.

To placate Egypt's creditors, Ali's successor khedive Ismail Pasha (r. 1863–1879) allowed the Suez Canal Company and French engineer Ferdinand Lesseps to build a hundred-mile shipping lane through Egyptian territory. Begun in 1859, the canal took ten years of hard labor to build. At least one million workers, most of them local Arabs, toiled to dig the canal, mostly by hand. The Suez Canal was a worldwide sensation when it opened in November 1869 and a boon particularly to the British, who could now avoid the long and perilous trip around the Cape of Good Hope and reach Indian ports much more swiftly.

But the canal did nothing to ease khedive Ismail's financial troubles, and in 1875 Britain bought his 44 percent share in the company, saving him from immediate bankruptcy, but also infringing further on Egypt's autonomy. The Ottomans could not help their semi-independent vassal state. They too were broke and hemorrhaging more territory. After the Russian victory in the Russo-Turkish War of 1877–1878, the British began to fear that the Ottomans might collapse entirely, leaving Istanbul, and perhaps even the canal, in the hands of the anything but liberal czarist empire. Western investors also began to fear that the Ottomans would go broke and fail to repay their substantial loans. In 1881, they forced the sultan to create the Ottoman Public Debt Administration, an entity that owned the debt in the forms of bonds and also received the right to various kinds of customs and taxes. The French also seized the opportunity to establish control of the nominally Ottoman territory of Tunisia.

When in 1882 Egyptian army officers staged a coup against the next khedive, intending to establish a state free from European meddling, the British had even more reason to fear that the canal might fall into unfriendly hands. The French too were worried, for they knew that the religiously inspired leader Mehmed Ahmad, known as the Mahdi, was organizing anticolonial resistance next door, in the Sudan, and they feared that the Egyptian rebellion would bring a fanatical Muslim regime to power in the region. The French threatened to invade—but the liberal British prime minister Gladstone beat them to the punch. Defeating the rebels by 1882, Gladstone found himself in possession of a new territory. Rather than annex Egypt, however, he declared Egypt a protectorate, withdrew British troops, and left the khedive in charge.

The British meant for the khedive to sit quietly and ignore the Mahdists, but the Egyptian leader had his own ideas (and fears) and sent an Egyptian army out to defeat the Mahdi. In 1884, the Egyptians were surrounded and nearing destruction when the zealous Christian general George Gordon decided, on his own initiative, to save them. Having spent a quarter-century fighting wars and intriguing in Africa and Asia and having earned the thanks of the Chinese emperor for his help in suppressing the Taiping Rebellion, "Chinese" Gordon was a popular hero—and self-important enough to believe that he personally could defend the Sudanese capital, Khartoum. In fact, he couldn't, and he was killed by the Mahdi's forces on January 22, 1885. Gladstone had no intention of intervening again, but a decade later the popular press spurred a hyper-imperialist conservative leadership to take revenge on Gordon's killers. In 1898, the British sent out a heavily armed Nile expedition under Horatio Kitchener to retake Khartoum. Kitchener got the revenge the British public wanted, using Britain's modern weapons to kill some 11,000 Mahdists, as against only 48 Anglo-Egyptians, at the battle of Omdurman. Gordon's body was ceremoniously retrieved and reburied, and monuments to his memory were erected all over Britain.

FASHODA. By the 1890s, the British had recognized that protecting Egypt was going to be a longer-term engagement than had initially been foreseen, and Egyptian anticolonial nationalism, too, had begun to grow. To add even more tension to the situation, the French gradually became more and more concerned about Britain's presence in Egypt and the Sudan, all too near to France's northern African territories. Kitchener's Nile expedition was the final straw, and in September 1898, the French sent their own expedition via a different route to the

southern Sudan to prevent further British inroads. The two armies met at Fashoda in the southern Sudan, and only a last-minute agreement on the borders of British and French protectorates prevented war between the two great European powers. As usual, the agreement was made without consulting the Sudanese.

Elsewhere, too, the vacuum left by Ottoman retreat attracted self-interested stabilizers. In 1908, for example, the Austrians officially annexed the province of Bosnia-Herzegovina, hoping to forestall its seizure by the Russians or the Serbs. Although the Austrians poured in cash in the hopes of modernizing and pacifying this territory, their new subjects—and especially the Bosnian Serbs—resented being handed over to a new set of colonizers. Here, as in ethnically mixed areas of the Ottoman Empire such as Macedonia and Palestine, the more the "sick man" suffered, the more radicals began to dream of finally getting their own states.

The Failing Chinese Empire

The First and Second Opium Wars weakened the Qing dynasty of China, and the homegrown Taiping Rebellion damaged it even further. All these conflicts made it difficult for the Chinese to continue to control their border regions, including Southeast Asia, whose rulers the Chinese had long treated as vassals. The concessions China made in the Treaty of Nanjing brought many more foreign traders to China's shores and European settlers into the treaty ports. By 1890, Shanghai, in particular, had a sizable population of foreigners. Embroiled in pacifying the Taiping Rebellion, the Qing could not do much to prevent the Dutch and French from extending their toeholds in Southeast Asia or to curtail Russian and British influence in Central Asia. Indeed, the once-mighty Chinese Empire could not even slow the rise of tiny but industrializing Japan, whose navy grew powerful enough to defeat the Chinese in 1895. Like the failing Ottoman Empire, the weakening of the Qing opened up new opportunities for both local and overseas powers to exploit.

DUTCH AND FRENCH IMPERIALISM IN EAST ASIA. In Southeast Asia and Indonesia, the French and the Dutch sought to exploit Qing weakness—though to do so, they found themselves embroiled in long-lasting wars with local peoples. In 1862, the French established themselves in the southern part of present-day Vietnam. The northern provinces, however, proved hard to subdue. As the French pushed northward after 1883, the Chinese joined the fight to keep the French out of what they considered to be *their* imperial domains. Fighting in the Sino-French War of 1884–1885 was vicious. Both sides committed atrocities, and antiforeigner riots broke out in China. But the French prevailed, leaving China, which had been the major power in the region, to be carved up further by the Japanese. The French then swiftly succeeded in conquering present-day Laos and Cambodia, creating a huge Southeast Asian empire (known as Indochina) that would not fall until after the Second World War (see Map 20.2).

In the territories collectively known as the Dutch East Indies, the Dutch sought to extend their commercial hegemony, the origins of which dated to the late sixteenth century. Using divide-and-rule tactics, the Dutch pitted small kingdoms against one another to their own benefit. But throughout the archipelago, the Dutch also had to fight to establish control. A series of bloody wars in Sumatra and Java in the 1820s and 1830s opened the way for more invasive colonization, including reorganizing the island's agricultural production to suit the Europeans. Aceh and Bali continued to resist, and here, as in the Caucasus and in Algeria, Islam became the glue that bound together anticolonial rebellions. In 1859, in their own version of the Opium Wars, the Dutch claimed a monopoly on opium trading and landed 3,500 troops in Bali to force open shipping lanes. The Dutch assault proved less successful than the British one. The Balinese retreated behind fortifications, and six hours later, nearly 250 invaders were dead—half of them Europeans, the other half Indonesians and Africans.

Eventually, deals were struck that allowed at least indirect Dutch control over most of the islands. In 1908, however, another major revolt broke out in Bali when the Dutch tried once again to enforce their opium monopoly. This time modern weapons proved decisive. Dutch bullets killed the revolt's symbolic leader, the Rajah of Klungkung. His palace was burned, and his wives committed ritual suicide. In Aceh, at least 50,000 natives died in the war that raged from 1873 to 1904; guerrillas regularly destroyed sections of the single-track Aceh Tramway the colonizers built to connect the ports with Dutch military outposts. The Dutch finally succeeded by buying off some chieftains and burning down villages that they suspected harbored guerrilla fighters. The man responsible for these policies, J. B. van Heutsz, earned acclaim as the "Pacificator of Aceh" and became a popular hero in the Netherlands.

These conflicts overlapped with the Netherlands' imposition of the so-called Ethical Policy (1901), which increased efforts to educate the population and to modernize health care and agricultural production. Although never fully safe from guerrilla attacks, the Aceh Tramway accelerated the transport of people and goods. The long-lasting Dutch presence on the islands created a large population of mixed ethnicity in Indonesia. Much of the local administration and policing was delegated to Indonesians, who were not, however, treated as equals by white Dutch officials and settlers.

The Pacificator of Aceh This postcard depicts the Dutch colonial leader J. B. van Heutsz with his staff outside the Indonesian guerrilla stronghold of Batu Iliq in the province of Aceh. In 1901, Heutsz and his troops finally succeeded in liquidating resistance in this region, making it possible to extend the Aceh Tramway through the area.

THE GREAT GAME. Ottoman and Chinese decline combined with Britain's increasing defensiveness of India resulted in a series of Russian and British intrigues and skirmishes in Central Asia, dubbed "the Great Game" by Rudyard Kipling. Already in 1839, a British army had been sent into Afghanistan to prevent the emir of Kabul both from fraternizing with the Russians and from extending his territory to the northwest (territory the British would claim for themselves in the Anglo-Sikh Wars of 1845–1846 and 1848–1849). At first the British were successful; the emir fled, and settlers began to arrive. But Afghani resentment at their second-class treatment provoked a rebellion, and in 1842, some 16,500 British soldiers and civilians were forced to evacuate the capital. Most perished, but about 120 captives survived, including the formidable Lady Florentia Sale, who had accompanied her officer husband to Afghanistan. Lady Sale's account of her nine months of captivity, *A Journal of the Disasters in Afghanistan* (1843), became a bestseller and was quoted in Parliament. Evidently Lady Sale's sufferings weren't enough to prevent the British from trying again, and an army composed largely of Indian troops invaded in 1878. In 1881, the British were forced to evacuate once again, and the territory was never formally subdued.

The Russians, meanwhile, were trying to formalize control over the Central Asian khanates, which Czar Peter the Great had claimed but never fully realized. Russia put down a rebellion among the Kazakhs in battles that lasted from 1837 to 1846, and then in 1865–1867 seized Tashkent and Samarkand, laying the foundations for the annexed province of Russian Turkestan (see Map 20.3). Between 1881 and 1885, the Russians conquered the Transcaspian region and reduced the local emirs to the

MAP 20.3 | Russian and British Expansion in the Caucasus and Central Asia in the Nineteenth Century

Beginning in the 1820s, the Russian Empire tried to subdue the mountainous Caucasus region—located between the Black and Caspian Seas. This region was very difficult to conquer, due in part to the mountainous terrain and in part to the fierce resistance of local groups. To protect this never fully pacified territory, the Russians continued to expand to the east, seizing Central Asian territory. To protect their own colonial "jewel," the British, in the later nineteenth century, also undertook several campaigns to expand their holdings in Central Asia. *How does this map demonstrate Russia's contribution to the race for colonies, even though it did not seek new territories overseas?*

status of dependent vassals. Russia also exerted increasing economic and political control over Persia, though it did not attempt to annex it. Like the Dutch in Indonesia, the Russians encouraged development in their colonies, especially the planting of cotton in Turkestan and Transcaspia. Because this territory was contiguous with their older empire, they also built railroads to link this part of the empire to Moscow and St. Petersburg.

The toeholds established by the Russians and British in Central Asia offered them the opportunity to launch geographic expeditions and spying missions directed at one-upping the other. But none of these maneuvers was significant, in terms of numbers of men involved, and for many, including Kipling, it seemed more like a game than incipient war. Even territories that were formally taken—such as Turkestan by the Russians, Burma and Baluchistan by the British—remained thinly administered. But tensions in Central Asia contributed to everyone's sense that the race was tightening and that when all

the neutral territories were conquered, it would remain only for the colonizing powers to fight it out.

The Scramble for Africa

In the early modern period, European slave traders had set up outposts along the coasts of sub-Saharan Africa, but had rarely sought to enter the interior. Not only did diseases ravage those not seasoned to the climate and local pathogens, but the tsetse flies feasted on European horses, killing them quickly. The opening of the Suez Canal offered Europeans much easier access to eastern Africa (where previously South Asians had dominated international trade), and Stanley's finding of Livingstone sparked new interest in settling the African interior, especially now that travelers could dose themselves with life-saving quinine. A third event, the South African diamond rush of 1870–1871, prompted new interest in the mineral wealth of tropical Africa, and demonstrated just

1870–1871: The South African Diamond Rush

Until 1870, South Africa hardly rated a mention in the European news.[11] The territory seemed too remote, poor, and hot for Europeans to bother with. The British bought the Cape Colony at the southern tip of Africa from the Dutch in 1815, driving the Dutch-speaking Boers across the dry plains where they could raise sheep. Their inroads into the territory of the Zulus and other African tribesmen provoked a series of vicious interracial battles that ended with the establishment of two Boer Republics, the Orange Free State and the Transvaal. But few in Europe took notice even when, in 1867, a young Dutch settler found a shiny stone on the banks of the Vaal River and an amateur mineralogist in a nearby town recognized it as a diamond. Some local speculators descended on the region, especially after a shepherd sold a trader a "pebble" that proved to be an eighty-three-carat diamond (subsequently named the Star of South Africa).

In the winter of 1870–1871, more diamonds were found near the Vaal in an area where the boundaries between the British Cape Colony and the Boer Transvaal were uncertain. Prospectors began buying up land and pitching tents on the hot, barren plains around the major site of the strike, Colesberg Kopje (see Map 20.1). Land prices skyrocketed, and shops and saloons sprang up to profit from the miners' obsessions and passions. By late 1871, there were 50,000 prospectors at Colesberg Kopje, one of whom was Cecil Rhodes. The British acted quickly to seize and annex the territory, renaming Colesberg Kopje Kimberley—after Lord Kimberley, Britain's colonial minister—and began issuing claims. And then the South African diamond rush began in earnest.

The Great Hole of Kimberley Today, diamond mining has moved to other locations, but the Great Hole of Kimberley remains to remind us of the nineteenth century's brutal assault on the land.

The diamond rush laid the foundations for both the economic exploitation and the modernization of South Africa and for future conflicts between British and Dutch settlers. Miners spent their new riches to buy more mines, more laborers, and more machines, quickly converting the once rural landscape into an industrial wasteland. Their funds also went to the building of railroads, so vital to the transport of modern commodities, all over South Africa. But the diamond rush, and the gold rush that followed it in the 1880s, also provoked hostilities between the British and the Dutch Boers. The Dutch increasingly feared being swallowed up into the British Empire, something they opposed, in part, because Britain had outlawed slavery in its colonies, and Boer farmers had long practiced the enslavement of African laborers. In 1877, the British did attempt to annex the resource-rich Transvaal, provoking the first of two Boer Wars.

The diamond rush made a difference, perhaps most of all, to the Africans, for it transformed both labor patterns and the environments in which they lived. During the rush, Africans in large numbers were hired by white claims-holders to do the hard labor in the mines. Driven to desperation by drought and by settlers' seizure of their lands, they signed contracts that amounted to indentured servitude. To prevent them from taking away the diamonds they unearthed, laborers were strip-searched and, in some cases, forced to work in the nude. Should Africans ever forget these abuses, the landscape itself reminds them of the ravages of the diamond rush. By 1872, Kimberley's many shafts had collapsed into one, leaving what was called the Big Hole. It was 230 feet deep in 1877 and was subsequently mined to 3,500 feet. It now covers forty-two acres and is partially filled with water. The region around the Big Hole is still very much devoted to, and dependent on, diamond mines.

The diamond rush made diamonds, like many other commodities caught up in the imperial exchange, integral parts of European culture. Vastly increasing the supply caused prices to fall, making diamond jewelry much more affordable to consumers back home. As mining continued in the Big Hole, more and more European women acquired South African diamonds. The events of 1870–1871 made a difference in their lives, too, even though they unfolded thousands of miles away.

QUESTIONS | *Do you view this picture of the Big Hole differently now that you know how it was made? What does this landscape tell you about colonialism in the nineteenth century?*

how quickly news now spread and how competition between Europeans for colonial resources could transform a region—virtually overnight.

On the heels of the diamond rush came the Banking Crisis of 1873, in which the Austrian stock market crashed and numerous Austrian banks failed. Worldwide, prices fell and nations—except Great Britain—moved to increase tariffs to protect their own producers. Merchants and manufacturers of heavy industrial products such as steam-powered machinery, steel rails, and weapons scoured the world for new markets and sources of cheap raw materials such as coal and iron ore. But the person most responsible for inciting what would be called the **scramble for Africa** was not a banker, a merchant, or even a diamond-miner, but rather a man who already had a kingdom of his own: King Leopold II of Belgium.

King Leopold Builds Himself an Empire

Since his ascent to the throne in 1865, Leopold II had been obsessed with the idea of colonization, a sure way, he believed, to obtain glory and riches for his recently founded state. Unfortunately for Leopold, however, Belgium was a constitutional monarchy, and the Belgian parliament refused to endorse his schemes. Like many stay-at-home Europeans at mid-century, the parliament's members thought full-on colonization created more diplomatic headaches and more budgetary red ink than it provided benefits to the state. Tired of waiting for parliament to change its mind, and inspired by Henry Stanley's exploits, Leopold decided in 1876 to set his own game in motion. He convened an International Geographical Conference in Brussels. At the conference, he proposed the founding of an international society to create operational posts for scientific, medical, and missionary work in Africa. Once elected as the new society's president, Leopold positioned himself as the leader of the crusade to bring civilization to Africa. As one of his first acts, he hired Stanley, the most famous Africa explorer of the day, to explore the Congo more fully and to establish trading stations along the river. Stanley agreed, and together the two set about opening up the sub-Saharan interior to civilization—and to exploitation.

The Congo was little explored before Stanley found Livingstone at Ujiji in 1871, but since that time, rival exploring parties had made inroads. The French and the Portuguese were also establishing trading stations and making ominous noises about claiming the region for themselves. The British backed Portuguese claims, provoking a diplomatic crisis. Hoping both to obtain maximum colonial territory and to avoid a European war to get it, all parties agreed to meet in Berlin to find a solution to the Congo crisis.

Carving up Africa

Before the Berlin Conference began in November 1884, the Germans had not participated in the race for colonies, having other pressing domestic matters to deal with. Iron Chancellor Bismarck had long opposed entangling Germany in battles abroad, once declaring: "Here is Russia and here . . . is France, and we're in the middle. That is my map of Africa." Seen as a neutral party at the Berlin Conference, Bismarck managed to broker a deal, and everybody got a share. No Africans were invited to the Berlin Conference. As usual in colonial endeavors, the maps were made by Europeans, without the input of those who inhabited the territory in question (Map 20.4). This practice would lay the foundations for all sorts of ethnic, religious, and economic strife in the decades to come.

The results of the Berlin Conference were the following: the French received a large chunk of territory to the north (now the Central African Republic and Congo-Brazzaville); in 1895 they would formally consolidate their holdings to the west, calling the immense colony French West Africa. The Portuguese received a large territory to the southwest of the Congo and inland from ports established long before by Portuguese slave traders (present-day Angola). The British confirmed their hold on the Nile area and the Darfur region in Sudan. In the end, the Germans decided to take their cut, a wedge to the west of the Congo basin, which would expand to become German Southwest Africa (now Namibia). They also took Togo and Cameroon. Later they would seize German East Africa (now Burundi, Rwanda, and parts of Tanzania) as well. Leopold II was

Congo Atrocities This image of African amputees was published by the American writer Mark Twain, in his 1905 pamphlet accusing King Leopold II of permitting atrocities to be committed in the Congo Free State.

permitted to take on the role of king-sovereign of a huge Congo Free State, whose borders were drawn by Stanley. Leopold's position was to be completely independent from his role as the king of Belgium, and he pledged to administer the territory as a free-trade zone, open to all interested (European) parties.

Leopold's free-trade zone was quickly divided into two areas, one given over to exploitation by the king-sovereign's administration, and the other divided between two huge rubber companies, also working on the state's behalf. Land on which elephants or rubber plants were found was confiscated, and the natives were forced to pay taxes in ivory or rubber. A British investigating committee in 1904 reported gruesome atrocities; those who could not meet their quotas were starved, flogged, or had limbs cut off. Violence against civilians was so great, the report showed, that residents fled the territory, deserting many once-flourishing towns and trading posts (see Back to the Source at the end of the chapter). It is no accident that the English novelist Joseph Conrad chose the Congo Free State as the setting for his novella about a power-mad European ivory merchant or that he titled it *Heart of Darkness*.

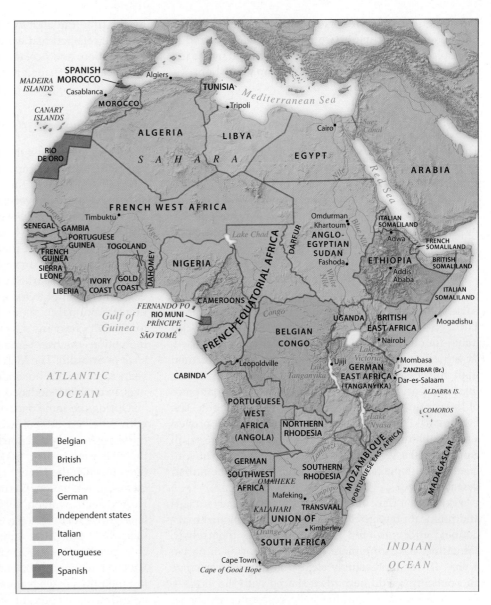

MAP 20.4 | The Scramble for Africa, 1885–1914

This map shows the location of European colonies in Africa. Note that the dates for the taking of these colonies fall mostly between 1885 and 1914. *Which European nations did not participate in the carving up of Africa?*

For Leopold II, the Congo Free State proved profitable. In 1893, sales of ivory and rubber in Antwerp brought in the equivalent of $1 million, at a time in which a factory worker might hope to earn just about a dollar a day. By 1908, the Congo was generating $12 million in exports and buying $4 million in imports from Belgium. Leopold kept most of this money for himself, using some of it to beautify Brussels, hoping to rival nearby Paris. Though shocking atrocities had, by this time, been widely documented, Leopold refused to instigate reforms even when pressed by his own government in Brussels. Finally, in 1908 the Belgian parliament succeeded in seizing control of Congo. Though the worst atrocities were stopped, exploitation and European rule continued, and the territory did not gain its independence until 1960. Only in 1966 did the

Congolese finally erase Leopold from *their* map, changing the name of the capital city from Leopoldville to Kinshasa.

Colonial endeavors in Africa after the Berlin Conference were far more invasive and exploitative than earlier undertakings. Although slave traders had established outposts on the African coasts during the period of commercial colonialism, few Europeans had dared to settle inland. Now traders and state officials attempted to seize land and set up mines and plantations in the interior. Missionaries were allowed to settle in villages throughout the African interior and to coax or bribe local children to attend their schools. Forced off their lands by war, drought, or outright theft, Africans were compelled to work for the Europeans, building roads, harvesting rubber and ivory, or mining copper, gold, and diamonds.

Older, more mixed forms of agriculture and animal tending, as well as trading networks, were damaged, and in some places whole ecosystems were destroyed by the imposition of European-owned, single-crop plantations.

The New Resistance

The scramble for Africa did not stop until virtually the whole continent was swallowed up. Whereas Europeans controlled only 11 percent of the territory in 1875, this figure was 90 percent by 1902, and by 1914 only two African states remained independent: Ethiopia and Liberia. But gorging is not good for the digestion, and European regimes and private companies that sought to extend control into the African interior were met with a new wave of resistance. The new, would-be imperial powers—Germany and Italy—found conquering new territories especially hard. In Ethiopia, for example, Emperor Menelik II, armed with European guns, managed to destroy an invading Italian army at Adwa in 1896, preventing that piece of the continent from falling into European hands. The Ethiopians' triumph inspired Africans just as it proved a national humiliation for the Italians. In 1936, Mussolini would wage a second, this time successful, war of conquest in Ethiopia, as a means of revenge for the Italian defeat at Adwa.

> How did the colonialism of the third wave create more powerful forms of resistance?

Fearful that they might lose the economic advantages and political prestige colonies offered, the colonizers redoubled efforts to bind their territories to themselves, sometimes by trying more conciliatory forms of native policy. It was increasingly clear that more governance and policing would have to be shared with the locals—force alone simply couldn't keep resistance in check, and sending large armies of Europeans to Africa or Asia was expensive and unpopular at home. New policies included offering more power, or perks, to indigenous leaders, and new attempts to spur European-style development in the colonies, by building new roads, schools, churches, railway stations, theaters, and hospitals. More European women made their way to colonial territories, both to reduce the threat of racial mixing and to serve as colonial intermediaries, educating native women in proper housekeeping, child rearing, and sanitation.

But if some nations hoped to make the colonies over in their own image to pacify them—making them Christian, capitalist, civilized nations—these plans usually crashed on the rocks of cost and were carried out only in limited fashion, for parliaments back home were unwilling to pay for so much transformation. Promises that colonial subjects would gain access to modern institutions and technologies, be made partners in ruling, and be offered a share in the new prosperity were for the most part never realized, creating a large gap between the rhetoric of the civilizing mission and the reality of colonial rule.

By the time the First World War broke out, many colonial subjects had had enough experience of subjugation, exploitation, and broken promises to be heartily sick of European governance, and some had become active supporters of home rule.

Resistance in German Colonies

The Germans entered the colonial race late, and from the beginning, their attempts to obtain what colonial lobbyists called "a place in the sun" met with considerable resistance. The first governor of German East Africa, Carl Peters, applied such brutality in extending his territory in the 1890s that the Reichstag fired him. But the equally exploitative policies of the next regime created powerful discontent among African inhabitants. In 1905, a huge uprising broke out, sparked by drought and resistance to the Germans' attempt to force farmers to grow cotton rather than traditional food crops. The rebels turned to magic to combat Germany's technological advantages, brewing potions that were supposed to turn bullets into water (*maji* in Swahili). The Maji Maji Uprising took nearly two years to stamp out, but ended, like most third-wave uprisings, in terrible bloodshed, especially for the colonized.

During the same period, the Germans also were faced with rebellion in southwestern Africa, as the nomadic cattle-raising peoples known as the Herero rebelled against the increasing confiscation of their lands by German settlers. In 1904, the Herero captured a few German settlements; in retaliation, German troops killed about 55,000 Herero men, women, and children, then seized their land, drove them into the Omaheke desert, and poisoned their wells. Survivors were crammed into disease-ridden concentration camps, where many more perished. Some 80,000 Herero and 20,000 of the neighboring Nama people lost their lives in what amounted to a genocidal campaign; an estimated 80 percent of the Herero and 50 percent of the Nama were killed. The German official report stated

CHRONOLOGY	Key Episodes of Resistance to Imperialism	
DATE	**EVENT**
1779–1784	Mysore Wars
1830–1847	Algerian resistance
1839–1842	First Opium War
1845–1859	Shamil's resistance in Chechnya
1856–1859	Second Opium War
1857	Indian Rebellion
1899–1900	Boxer Rebellion
1905	Maji Maji Uprising

triumphantly, and ominously, "Like a wounded beast the enemy was tracked down from one water-hole to the next until finally he became the victim of his own environment. The arid Omaheke was to complete what the German army had begun: extermination of the Herero nation."[12]

In the wake of these uprisings, the Reichstag—now containing a considerable number of socialist deputies—insisted on reforms. The colonial office was made independent and given a more moderate chief, and a version of the Dutch Ethical Policy was put into practice. But the other colonizers, especially the British, turned an ever more wary eye on Germany, as agitation for more colonies and a bigger navy grew. And there was no winning of African hearts and minds in the offing for the Germans: force alone would keep resistance at bay.

The Boxer Rebellion

Elsewhere, too, there were signs that colonialism's assault on indigenous economies, religions, and forms of leadership was beginning to produce a powerful backlash. In Egypt, anticolonial nationalists began to organize, setting their sights on overthrowing the puppet khedive. In India, the swadeshi (self-sufficiency) movement of 1905–1908 sought to promote homemade products, especially textiles, as a means of breaking British control over the Indian economy and reminding Indians of the specialness of their own craft traditions. Following the Second Opium War, the Qing dynasty of China attempted to impose on itself a self-strengthening movement, essentially an attempt to industrialize and modernize the country by adopting European methods and inviting in European investors. But when the Japanese defeated the Qing in a very brief war in 1895–1896, it was clear that this movement had failed. The Germans seized the opportunity to extort a long-term lease over a piece of the Shandong Peninsula, and the British, similarly, forced Chinese endorsement of a ninety-nine-year lease of Hong Kong. European missionaries poured in and were given increasingly favorable treatment by the unpopular Empress Dowager Cixi. In response, a large number of Chinese patriots turned against the Qing, looking instead to secret martial arts organizations for leadership. In 1899, galvanized by the Society of Righteous and Harmonious Fists, or Boxers, anticolonial nationalists took matters into their own hands.

The Boxers abhorred the weakness of the Qing and what they believed to be its slavish imitation of European ideas and its catering to the interests of the inhabitants of the foreign-dominated trading ports. In their assaults on towns and cities, they targeted missionaries and Chinese converts whom they believed to be destroying traditional Chinese religion, and railroads they thought to be destroying traditional Chinese trade. They attacked foreign merchants and the soldiers who protected them and murdered the German ambassador. Violence spread across the country quickly, and by 1900, the Qing had lost control. Frustrated by the dynasty's inability to put down the rebellion, all the would-be colonizers of China (Russia, Japan, Britain, Germany, France, and even the United States) sent troops. Together they subdued the countryside and bested the rebels in the hotly contested city of Beijing; both sides committed atrocities against civilians. Repeating the familiar insistence that colonies should pay for their own defense, the foreign powers assessed a penalty of $326 million on China, an indemnity against their expenditures and the losses of European property and life. Attempts to pay reparations (which continued until suspended in 1939) further weakened China, making it vulnerable to new attacks and intensifying nationalist sentiment and popular hostility against the Chinese court. The Chinese nationalists' overthrow of the Qing in 1911 was something of a preemptory strike against the probability that China would be, as the patriots feared, "carved up like a melon" by foreign powers.

The Second Boer War

In the 1870s and 1880s, the discovery of diamonds and then of gold in South Africa renewed conflicts over land between Boers, English settlers, and African natives. The British move to annex the Transvaal region in 1877 had been repulsed in the First Boer War (1880–1881). But the British had not given up claims to this mineral-rich land. In 1895, Cecil Rhodes, the prime minister of Britain's Cape

The Second Boer War This posed image of Boer guerrilla fighters illustrates the ruggedness of those who managed to fight off British troops for so long.

Colony, and his friend Leander Starr Jameson plotted to incite a rebellion in the Transvaal, into which the South African Britons could then intervene. They sent five hundred raiders over the border, but the so-called Jameson Raid did not spark an uprising, and the plot was discovered. The attempt to provoke a war with the Boers made Britain look bad—but that was child's play compared to the disasters of 1899–1900.

The long predicted second war between the Boers and the Brits finally broke out on October 11, 1899, and at first cheers went up throughout Britain. South African whites volunteered, as did many native Africans, who hoped that fighting on the British side would win them improved treatment after the war was won. War correspondents and illustrators descended on the battlefields in droves. Thanks to the new profitability of the popular press and to the increasing speed of international communications, the Second Boer War proved to be the most intensively covered and best illustrated war to date. It is estimated that in the first six months of 1900 alone, four London newspapers printed some 1,303 photographs and 868 drawings of the war, excluding portraits of those killed or wounded and sentimental scenes of soldiers leaving or returning home. Young Winston Churchill rushed to the field as one of these journalists, but decided to join the fight and was lucky enough to survive it.

When the South African town of Mafeking was freed from besieging Boers in the spring of 1900, pub-goers and middle-class clerks throughout England filled the streets to cheer the British commander, Colonel Robert Baden-Powell (1857–1941). Baden-Powell had used not only African soldiers, but also Mafeking boys in his endeavors; organizing the latter would prove inspirational to the man who would go on to found the Boy Scouts in 1907. But the thrill of holding Mafeking was short lived, as were hopes for a short war and one more civilized than previous colonial conflicts. Reports published by the increasingly omnivorous press showed British military recruits to fall short of adventure-novel standards: they were not tall and debonair, but short and malnourished.

Led by their wily president, Paul Kruger, and rich enough to afford European weapons, the Boers proved tough opponents. Using the terrain to their advantage, they engaged in highly successful forms of guerrilla warfare rather than coming out into the open battlefield. Many members of the British public began to despair of their leaders, who seemed not to have prepared for a war that observers (including Rhodes) had seen coming since 1895.

Despite a massive propaganda campaign and a huge advantage in numbers at arms, it took the British more than two years to defeat the Boers. The effort required the deployment of nearly 450,000 soldiers (from Britain and its colonies) and cost the equivalent of a whopping $974 million. Moreover, thanks to increased press coverage, the British public got a close, and stomach-turning, look at colonial warfare. Frustrated by their lack of progress against Boer guerrillas, soldiers in British uniforms had burned crops and fields; to prevent local people from aiding the guerrilla fighters they confined civilians, including women and children, to concentration camps. In those camps, liberal journalists reported, thousands died of malnutrition, thirst, and disease. This was a dirty war, but unlike many of those equally dirty conflicts before it, the British public now knew the gruesome details and felt uneasy, particularly as the Boers, though uncouth, were still white Europeans, and the Africans were, by and large, innocent bystanders.

After the Second Boer War, Britain continued to gobble up territory, and in 1909 joined its South African holdings, including Rhodesia, to form the Union of South Africa. Many Britons began to worry about German colonial and naval expansion and to notice the rapid rise in German and American industrial output. For their parts, the Germans, Italians, and Japanese grew increasingly resentful that so many of the world's resource-rich territories had already been claimed by Britain, the Netherlands, and France. Colonial rivalries were by no means the only spark that fueled the fires of the First World War: but they contributed a great deal to stoking the flames.

Conclusion

The Boxer Rebellion, the Herero Uprising, and the Boer Wars were bloody and costly, but afterward the European powers clung even more tightly to their holdings. Colonizing had become the mark of being a modern power—and a civilized one—even though anti-imperialists such as the young Mohandas Gandhi, living in South Africa during the Boer War, became increasingly aware that, for those on the receiving end, European civilization could seem uncomfortably close to barbarism.

For the colonized, decades—and in some cases, centuries—of forced economic and political dependence

destroyed local markets, traditional forms of authority, and even local customs and belief systems. But imperialism transformed Europe too—some states and people directly, some indirectly—by means of colonial warfare, relentless international competition, and the imperial exchange. Imperialist ventures produced a world that was much more interlinked and hybrid in its economic and cultural systems than ever before. It was more civilized, in European terms; but it was also more exploitative, more racially stratified, and more likely to be drawn into a global, industrialized conflict.

Critical Thinking Questions

1. Why was the race for colonies so much more competitive and aggressive in the later nineteenth century than in the earlier nineteenth century?

2. Trace the history of resistance to colonization from the first wave to the third wave.

3. How did colonialism shape the perception of *Europe* and *European* throughout the world?

Key Terms

neo-Europes **(p. 634)**

creoles **(p. 634)**

Monroe Doctrine **(p. 635)**

British East India Company (BEIC) **(p. 635)**

sepoys **(p. 637)**

Boers **(p. 637)**

treaty ports **(p. 640)**

extraterritoriality **(p. 640)**

spheres of influence **(p. 640)**

long peace **(p. 643)**

imperial exchange **(p. 648)**

social Darwinism **(p. 650)**

scramble for Africa **(p. 656)**

Primary Sources in connect

For information on Connect and the online resources available, go to **http://connect.mcgraw-hill.com**.

1. **Cecil Rhodes Establishes the Rhodes Scholarships**

2. **Florentia Sale's Terrible Experiences in Afghanistan**

3. **The Indian Rebels Speak, 1857**

4. **The Last Days of David Livingstone in Africa**

5. **Charles Darwin, *The Descent of Man***

6. **Friedrich Fabri on Germany's Need for Colonies**

The Casement Report

In 1903, the British House of Commons sent Roger Casement (1864–1916), an Irish-born diplomat based in Central Africa, to investigate widespread reports of atrocities being committed in the Congo Free State. After traveling to many villages in the region, Casement produced a scathing, sixty-page report that included many firsthand accounts of murders, whippings, rapes, and amputations committed by soldiers employed by King Leopold II or by employees of the rubber planters in the region. The report led to the rapid increase of European groups devoted to ending or at least reforming colonial practices. Casement himself later became a radical supporter of Irish home rule and was executed by the British government in 1916 for treason.

I have the honour to submit my Report on my recent journey on the Upper Congo.

. . . [T]he region visited was one of the most central in the Congo State. . . . Moreover, I was enabled, by visiting this district, to contrast its present day state with the condition in which I had known it some sixteen years ago . . . and I was thus able to institute a comparison between a state of affairs I had myself seen when the natives lived their own savage lives in anarchic and disorderly communities, uncontrolled by Europeans, and that created by more than a decade of very energetic European intervention . . . by Belgian officials in introducing their methods of rule over one of the most savage regions of Africa.

. . . [A] fleet of steamers . . . navigate the main river and its principal affluents at fixed intervals. Regular means of communication are thus afforded to some of the most inaccessible parts of Central Africa. A railway, excellently constructed in view of the difficulties to be encountered, now connects the ocean ports with Stanley Pool, over a tract of difficult country, which formerly offered to the weary traveller on foot many obstacles to be overcome and many days of great bodily fatigue. . . .

The people have not easily accommodated themselves to the altered conditions of life brought about by European government in their midst. Where formerly they were accustomed to take long voyages down to Stanley Pool to sell slaves, ivory, dried fish, or other local products . . . they find themselves today debarred from all such activity. While the suppression of an open form of slave dealing has been an undoubted gain, much that was not reprehensible in native life has disappeared along with it. . . .

[I] visited two large villages in the interior . . . wherein I found that fully half the population now consisted of refugees. . . . I saw and questioned several groups of these people. . . . They went on to declare, when asked why they had fled (their district), that they had endured such ill-treatment at the hands of the government officials and the government soldiers in their own [district] that life had become

intolerable, that nothing had remained for them at home but to be killed for failure to bring in a certain amount of rubber or to die from starvation or exposure in their attempts to satisfy the demands made upon them. . . .

. . . [O]n the 25th [of] July (1903) [we] reached Lukolela, where I spent two days. This district had, when I visited it in 1887, numbered fully 5,000 people; today the population is given, after a careful enumeration, at less than 600. The reasons given me for their decline in numbers were similar to those furnished elsewhere, [namely], sleeping-sickness, general ill-health, insufficiency of food, and the methods employed to obtain labour from them by local officials and the exactions levied upon them.

. . . A careful investigation of the conditions of native life around [Lake Mantumba] confirmed the truth of the statements made to me that the great decrease in population, the dirty and ill-kept towns, and the complete absence of goats, sheep, or fowls—once very plentiful in this country—were to be attributed above all else to the continued effort made during many years to compel the natives to work India-rubber. Large bodies of native troops had formerly been quartered in the district, and the punitive measures undertaken to his end had endured for a considerable period. During the course of these operations there had been much loss of life, accompanied, I fear, by a somewhat general mutilation of the dead, as proof that the soldiers had done their duty.

. . . Two cases [of mutilation] came to my actual notice while I was at the lake. One, a young man, both of whose hands had been beaten off with the butt ends of rifles against a tree, the other a young lad of 11 or 12 years of age, whose right hand was cut off at the wrist. . . . In both these cases the government soldiers had been accompanied by white officers whose names were given to me. Of six natives (one a girl, three little boys, one youth, and one old woman) who had been mutilated in this way . . . all except one were dead at the date of my visit.

QUESTIONS | *How can you tell that this report was written by an official in the employ of a colonial state? Would this report have stirred you to join an anticolonial or humanitarian organization? Why or why not?*

Source: Peter Singleton-Gates and Maurice Girodias, *The Black Diaries: An Account of Roger Casement's Life and Times with a Collection of His Diaries and Public Writings* (New York: Grove Press, 1959), 96–100.

21

Russians Cheer the Czar's Reforms, October 1905

THE CRISIS OF LIBERALISM AND THE MAKING OF MASS SOCIETY, 1880–1914

Living the Modern
The Modern Experience
The New Mobility
The Fin de Siècle Metropolis
Social Mobility—and Its Limits
Women in Motion

The New Culture(s)
Mass Culture
Modernism—without the Masses
Breaking with Conventions
Modernism in the Sciences

The New Economies
The Second Industrial Revolution
The Worker and the Second Industrial Revolution
The Social Question, Again

The New Politics
Modern Society's Challenge to Liberalism
Socialism and the Second International
Moderate and Conservative Mass Parties
The Russian Revolution of 1905
Civil Strife Intensifies

Racism, Hyper-nationalism, and the Collapse of Old Empires
The New Anti-Semitism
The New Ways of War
The New Nationalism and the Old Empires

Conclusion

SARAH BERNHARDT: FIN DE SIÈCLE SUPERSTAR Actress Sarah Bernhardt should probably be considered Europe's first media superstar— and sex goddess.[1] But her notoriety cannot be understood apart from the diverse and volatile cultural world she inhabited. The illegitimate daughter of a Jewish courtesan, Bernhardt became famous in the 1860s for her entrancing performances in such high-tone dramas as *Iphigenia* by the seventeenth-century playwright Jean Racine. Over the next five decades, Bernhardt's appearance in ever more sexualized and melodramatic roles gave her additional notoriety and allure. Audiences turned out especially to see her death scenes—which she performed nightly with tremendous charisma.

Bernhardt's death scenes may have been powerful, but the French actress was very much alive to the opportunities her age offered. In the 1880s, she allowed Thomas Alva Edison to record her "golden voice" on his recently invented phonograph, and by the 1910s, a woman who had starred in classical tragedies was performing in silent films and in vaudeville shows, alongside juggling acts, minstrels in blackface, and talking cockatoos. Perhaps

Sarah Bernhardt as Cleopatra In one of her most famous stage roles, the French superstar actress Sarah Bernhardt played Cleopatra, the Egyptian queen. Playwright Victorien Sardou's version of the story offered "the divine Sarah" plenty of opportunity for sexualized acting and melodramatic dying.

the most novel aspect of her performances was the breadth of her appeal. On the stage at the Comédie-Française and in her wildly successful whistle-stop tours of Europe and the United States, the actress popularly known as "the divine Sarah" enthralled millions of fans.

Sarah Bernhardt was hardly typical of her age. In fact, she lived at the extreme end of what was tolerable to most "respectable" Europeans. Unwilling to be bossed around by others, she bought a theater and set up her own artistic studio. Her widely publicized personal life was anything but the Victorian ideal. She had affairs, one rather openly with a woman, and bore an illegitimate son. Her sexuality and ethnic and religious identities, in fact, were highly complicated. In some of her most acclaimed roles, she cross-dressed, playing Hamlet or Napoleon's son the "eagle." Often cast as an oriental seductress, she was also acclaimed for her portrayal of the great French heroine, Joan of Arc. She was a practicing Catholic, but caricatures always highlighted her Jewish ancestry. Her success, which brought her riches as well as worldwide renown, did not erase her public's prejudice against Jews or against women who ran their own affairs.

Hyper-nationalism c. 1871–1914

Mass European emigration 1871–1914

Second Industrial Revolution 1860s–

| 1860 | 1865 | 1870 | 1875 | 1880 | 1885 |

Sarah Bernhardt's life and fame illustrate that in the late nineteenth century we enter a new age, one in which a decidedly un-Victorian actress could gain global popularity, even as hyper-nationalist and racist movements arose in reaction to the cosmopolitan and diverse lifestyles "the divine Sarah" represented.

The century's end would see the appearance of many new forms: new forms of industrial capitalism, new mass movements in politics, and new forms of cultural experimentation. It was a period of contradictions in which new, more racially charged forms of nationalism and imperialism appeared at the same time Europeans were experiencing unprecedented social and physical mobility. This era would see the formation of mass political movements such as socialism and the emergence of "life reform" programs such as vegetarianism. Europeans were richer, relatively speaking, than ever before—but that relative wealth made the plight of those left in poverty seem more desperate and unjust. The mixture of these contradictory forces and the new scale and speed on which life was lived made Europe before World War I a dangerous, daring, and innovative place—a place where a dangerous, daring, and innovative woman like Sarah Bernhardt could take the public by storm.

Living the Modern

It is not possible, of course, to single out one particular date and say of it, on that day, Europeans awoke to discover they had suddenly become modern. But the period

What were the major features of modern mass society in Europe?

just after the Franco-Prussian War of 1870–1871, the very years in which Sarah Bernhardt earned her fame, may be considered as marking the opening of a new, fully modern, era in European cultural, political, and economic life. Those who lived through this era also called it the **fin de siècle** or, literally, the century's end. This term caught on for Europeans precisely because, by 1900, most urban and even rural people felt that a slower, more stable, and more predictable era was ending, and another, faster-moving one was beginning. Artists and writers would call it the modern era and insist that it represented a real and permanent break with the traditions and ideas of the past.

Modernity meant different things to different people. For some, modernity meant hope—for more social mobility, for better working and living conditions, for new forms of entertainment and governance more responsive to the needs and desires of *all* citizens. For others, modernity seemed threatening. It meant industrial strikes, vicious competition between businesses, rising tensions within old empires, the destruction of older ways of life, and the composition of music and art that sought not to please, but to act as, in the words of the Russian Futurist poets, "a

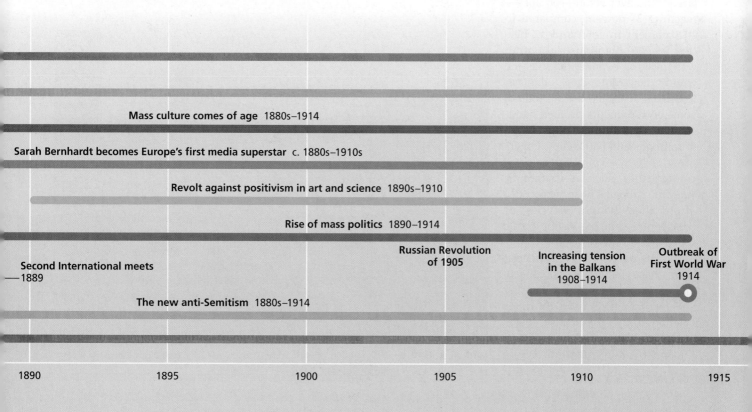

Mass culture comes of age 1880s–1914

Sarah Bernhardt becomes Europe's first media superstar c. 1880s–1910s

Revolt against positivism in art and science 1890s–1910

Rise of mass politics 1890–1914

Russian Revolution of 1905

Increasing tension in the Balkans 1908–1914

Outbreak of First World War 1914

Second International meets —1889

The new anti-Semitism 1880s–1914

1890   1895   1900   1905   1910   1915

slap in the face of public taste." It was a contentious era, in part because more people now were able to express their dreams, fears, and visions of the good society and in part because these dreams, fears, and visions were not easily reconcilable with liberal society as it had been constituted. Living the modern was about living with conflict, unpredictability, and difference—and few would be able to adjust to it as easily as did "the divine Sarah."

The Modern Experience

Europeans did not agree on what it meant to be modern, nor did they all celebrate the coming of the modern. But most did feel that a break with the past was under way, whether that break was in economic life, political relations, or architecture. What felt different was, first of all, the new scale on which life was being lived. More people than ever before in European history were living in big cities, voting in elections, and perusing newspapers. Buildings, ships, and factory workplaces were bigger than ever. Second, people, goods, and ideas could travel faster than ever before, by railway and steamship, by means of mass-circulated newspapers and magazines, by telegraph and telephone. Finally, especially for the affluent, the variety of possible experiences had increased at a rate unprecedented in history. By the 1880s, middle-class Europeans could visit the Holy Land or read Russian novels in translation; they could ride bicycles or buy ready-made furniture. By 1910, they could drive cars or see movies, experiences their parents could scarcely imagine.

At the nineteenth century's end, Europe was booming, in more ways than one. Demographically speaking, Europe's share of the world's population in 1900 was larger than ever before—or since—reaching 24 percent, compared to 20.8 percent in 1850 and 12 percent in 2000. Its industrial output was growing exponentially as the world's demand for steel, oil, glass, fertilizers, soap, and textiles soared. Some entrepreneurs profited handsomely from the frenetic building of railroads and battleships. Others grew rich by exploiting colonial commodities, such as diamonds, tea, and rubber. Those who could afford them bought bicycles, or later, motor cars, increasing traffic speed and urban congestion.

For the people who experienced them, these changes in scale, speed, and variety were both exhilarating and terrifying. As usual in times of change, there would be losers as well as winners in the course of European modernization. While Sarah Bernhardt rocketed to star-

dom, the older culture of street performances faded. As Singer sewing machines took the world by storm, tailoring businesses suffered. The pace at which new ways were replacing the old also differed greatly, being swiftest and most pronounced for urban dwellers, especially those in western rather than southern, eastern, or southeastern Europe. Even still-agrarian Russia began to industrialize, and in 1905, both workers and peasants rose in rebellion against the czarist government. Change in one sphere—such as the economy—did not necessarily mean change in all, but everywhere rapid and widespread changes unsettled mid-century hierarchies, institutions, and expectations.

The beginnings of this rapid change date to about the 1870s, as continental Europe began to adjust to German unification and its consequences (see Chapter 19). At the same time, a wave of new technologies, communications linkages, and investment practices laid the foundations for what has been called the second industrial revolution. The first experiment in socialist governance, the Paris Commune (January–May 1871), and its bloody repression by an army under *liberal* control marks another sort of watershed, as radicals learned not to trust liberals even in republican France. The banking crisis of 1873 opened a new era in economic relations, one in which there were more booms and busts, and in which larger entities, including large-scale manufacturers and labor unions, tried to constrain the free market to serve their own interests. Finally, after 1870, the real wages of Europeans began to rise, mortality rates fell, and as cities added mass transport systems, sewers, and parks, living conditions improved. Suffrage—at least for men—continued to expand, making it possible for reformers, especially

London, c. 1910 By 1910, London's streets were crowded not only with pedestrians and horse-drawn wagons, but also with buses and private motor cars.

in cities, to push through new legislation. Censorship largely disappeared (except in Russia), and labor unions and socialist parties were legalized.

But many people found the pace of social change far too slow to suit their expectations, and most members of the working classes did not feel that the decision making had been satisfactorily democratized, nor did they believe that the new wealth was being distributed fairly. As they were keenly aware, Europe's monarchs and old aristocracy, as well as the now well-established liberals, wanted to keep power concentrated in their hands. Some gave up on Europe entirely. From the 1870s, we can date the opening of the age of what historian Alfred Crosby called "the Caucasian tsunami," during which nearly 30 million Europeans migrated abroad.[2] Others joined one of the new political parties—socialist, anarchist, Christian socialist, and right-wing nationalist—all of which worked to mobilize new voters *against* Europe's political establishments. Increasingly, liberals and conservatives had to face up to the fact that a new era of mass politics was dawning—and that it would prove increasingly difficult for the elite few to determine the futures of their states.

Culturally the 1870s saw the development of new ideas and technologies, including the first real alternative to the steam engine, the four-stroke gas engine (1876); the telephone (also 1876); and the incandescent lamp (1879). Typewriters came onto the market, and with them, gradually, a whole new, largely female, workforce of typists, and above them, scores of male middle-managers. Thanks to both the increasing size of armies and the expansion of public schooling, literacy rates soared. Thanks to technological improvements and the curtailing of censorship, books and newspapers became relatively cheaper, more diverse, and more accessible.

Spectator sports were born in this decade. The first professional baseball league was formed in the United States, and the first international soccer match (between England and Scotland) was played. Though he would become famous only later, German philosopher Friedrich Nietzsche in the 1870s mounted his first assaults on idealist philosophy and bourgeois values. Scientists began to admit that the operations of the world were more uncertain than they had previously thought; painters and writers began to veer away from realism in order to understand human emotions and irrational drives. The decades that followed would see even greater dynamism, diversity, and forms of mobility so novel and far-reaching as to permanently destabilize the states, families, and social hierarchies of the mid-nineteenth century.

The New Mobility

One striking aspect of the world of the fin de siècle was the new mobility many Europeans could now enjoy—although this mobility was often occasioned by economic necessity and created new anxieties. The period of enhanced mobility opened with the coming of the rail-

roads and the famine years of the 1840s, but it peaked in the decades before the First World War. The causes of this new mobility were multiple: they included falling prices for agricultural products, which made factory work look more lucrative; the expansion of large-scale manufacturing and its concentration near ports or other transportation hubs; the greater affordability of means of transportation; and finally, rising expectations, which allowed Europeans to dream of lives of plenty and personal fulfillment beyond their hometowns.

GOODBYE, EUROPE. Emigration from Europe was the most dramatic form of this new mobility, and the number of migrants increased exponentially at the fin de siècle. Whereas some 9 million people left Europe between 1845 and 1875, three times that many (27.6 million) emigrated between 1871 and 1891, an average of 1.38 million per year (Figure 21.1). This annual figure held steady between 1891 and 1914, though by this time, Ireland and Germany were sending proportionally many fewer, and Italy and Scotland sending many more. Many of the migrants set sail for the United States, where they hoped to share in the universal prosperity promised by steamship company propagandists. Some did prosper, among them Austrian emigrant Joseph Pulitzer, who made a fortune in newspaper publishing by appealing to the common reader and engaging in ruthless battles over circulation. Many migrants, however, ended up working for starvation wages and living in overcrowded slums in New York, New Orleans, or Chicago, hoping that their children, at least, would enjoy better lives.

America's economy certainly profited from the seemingly endless number of eager European laborers willing to work for low wages, and their diversity contributed to the making of America's cultural melting pot. But between 1871 and 1914, some 4.5 million Europeans also moved to Argentina in search of a better life. Another 4.6 million went to Canada, and 2 million landed in Australia and New Zealand. One and one-half million settlers, many of them French speakers, set out for northern Africa, and more than two million Russians moved from western Russia to the Siberian hinterland between 1900 and 1914. All these migrants brought European traditions, ideas, and practices to their new homelands.

HELLO, PARIS, LONDON, BERLIN. The Caucasian tsunami described previously represented the largest population movement across oceans in history, and it shaped the modern development of neo-Europes such as the United States and Canada. But equally or even more important for shaping culture back home in Europe were processes of *internal* migration, as peasants and villagers moved in droves to the booming and expanding cities (Map 21.1). There they became wage earners, rather than farmers who bartered for supplies or lived off their own produce. With their wages, the new arrivals increasingly bought inexpensive mass-produced clothing, railway tickets, and

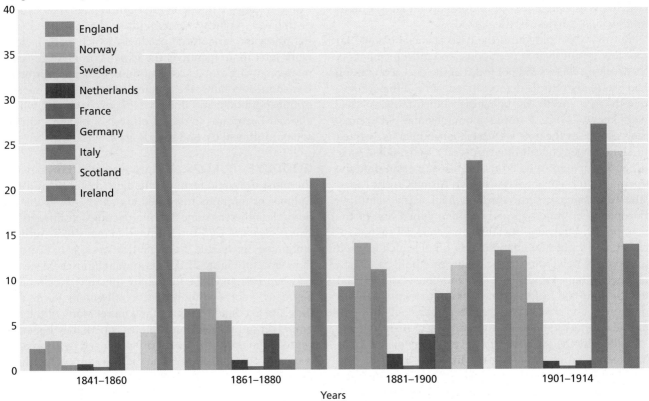

Emigration rate per 1,000

Legend:
- England
- Norway
- Sweden
- Netherlands
- France
- Germany
- Italy
- Scotland
- Ireland

Years: 1841–1860, 1861–1880, 1881–1900, 1901–1914

FIGURE 21.1 | Average Rates of European Emigration, 1841–1914

This bar graph represents the annual emigration rate per thousand individuals who emigrated from select European nations between the 1840s and the outbreak of the First World War. Thus, between 1841 and 1860, an average of about thirty-four individuals per thousand members of the Irish population emigrated to other countries. Although the numbers are impressive, as many as 40 percent of these individuals eventually returned to Europe.

Source: Synthesized by Jason M. Wolfe from Dudley Baines, *Immigration from Europe, 1815–1930* (Cambridge: Cambridge University Press, 1995), 2–4; and Charlotte Erickson, *Emigration from Europe, 1815–1914* (London: Adam & Charles Black, 1976), 27–29.

newspapers, each purchase contributing to the specialization of the economy, the mechanization of manufacturing, and the building of mass, urbanized societies.

The Fin de Siècle Metropolis

In the last decades of the nineteenth century, some rather sleepy small cities transformed themselves overnight into teeming metropolitan hubs. Berlin experienced extraordinary growth, its population expanding from about 420,000 in 1850 to more than 2 million by 1905. By 1900, nine European cities had populations over a million; the largest was London, with a whopping 4.2 million by 1891, up from 1.9 million in 1841. That figure represented between one-fifth and one-sixth of Britain's entire population. Although other nations were not nearly so intensively urban, London's expansion signaled a Europe-wide trend: the shifting of the population, and with it much of the states' economic and political power, from the countryside to the now-bustling cities.

Fin de siècle cities were by no means paradises, where all people lived together harmoniously. Instead, the cities were increasingly class segregated, as lower-class residents were concentrated in dilapidated old buildings, often near smoky factories or polluted rivers. The less affluent were forced to settle in working-class suburbs on the edge of town. White-collar workers, meanwhile, bought row houses or fashionable flats, and the wealthy bought villas in increasingly segregated neighborhoods far away from dirty factories or crowded slums. In 1900, in most cities, only the very wealthy could afford to have porcelain bathtubs, electricity, and telephones—but middle-class residents were beginning to enjoy amenities such as running water and regular trash pickups. Everywhere, the poor were the last to be hooked up to the public sewers or electric grids. Their unsanitary quarters made them more susceptible to disease, and the hesitancy of the municipal authorities to improve conditions contributed heavily to their exasperation with mid-century laissez-faire liberalism.

Urban dwellers at the fin de siècle consumed more food per capita and in many places enjoyed easier access to clean water than had their forebears. But it is not certain that levels of nutrition or hygiene improved markedly. There remained little in the way of regulation, and mass-marketed foodstuffs were regularly adulterated to

MAP 21.1 | Railroads and Big Cities, c. 1914

Western Europe's rail network expanded greatly between 1870 and 1914, just when many of its cities were also growing rapidly. This map shows areas of high industrialization as well as cities with a population that had exceeded one million by 1914. *Which areas developed an extensive rail network only after 1870? What does this map tell you about the relationships among industrialization, urbanization, and railroad building?*

reduce production costs. Coffee beans were made from clay or paste mixed with burnt sugar; and all manner of additives, including the leaves and berries of the poisonous belladonna plant, were used to reduce the cost of beer production. In southern Germany, inspectors found that egg noodles had been made by mixing cheap dough with picric acid and urine to give the noodles a yellow coloring; gypsum and chalk were added to flour to make white bread cheaper to produce. Tampering with foodstuffs became so common—and occasionally even lethal—that by the century's end, nations began to set up investigating units and pass laws to restrain the practice.

In the later nineteenth century, states also began to build public bathing facilities and toilets in urban areas, but they never managed to build enough. Only the very elite

had running *hot* water in their homes. Most city dwellers still depended on public fountains or urban water-sellers or took their water from polluted rivers and ports. Many people still feared that bathing more than once a month would cause illness; some continued to raise chickens or pigs in their urban backyards. Infectious diseases, especially tuberculosis, were rampant in factory towns, where air pollution intensified their effects. Of course, lower-class inhabitants could not afford to buy fresh foods, install bathtubs, or take spa vacations to cure their lungs; as usual, the poor bore the brunt of the city's new evils.

Mass transportation made the creation of big cities and distant suburbs possible, and over the course of the century's last decades, innovations in mass transport were nothing short of miraculous. By the 1880s, train travel between cities had become efficient and inexpensive, at least in northern Europe. Within cities, the horse-drawn omnibus came first, followed by electrified trams and then underground subway systems. The first of its kind, the London Underground was able to carry 30,000 people on its first day of operation in 1863, and by 1880 it was carrying 40 million riders a year. The Paris Métro opened in 1900 and the Berlin U-bahn in 1902—but other systems were slower to develop. The Moscow metro opened only in 1933, and construction on the Milan metro did not begin until 1957. Where they did appear, these systems could move tens of thousands of people per day.

These new transport systems had accompanying cultural effects, such as the erecting of newsstands near station stops and the production of newspapers in tabloid formats that could be read easily on trains. At least in theory, mass transit allowed persons who inhabited many different neighborhoods to share the same city, though in fact the upper classes continued to prefer private conveyances and to stick to their districts. Lower-class workers (other than the omnipresent servants) were made to feel uncomfortable and unwelcome in exclusive areas such as London's Belgravia or Berlin's Grünewald.

Mass transportation extended over larger areas as well. As steamship travel became more affordable, more and more Europeans ventured abroad, not just as emigrants or colonial settlers, but also as tourists. Taking advantage of their new wealth and their superior political and economic positions as colonizers, European travelers packed their bags for Egypt, India, and South America, often taking with them the handy new travel guides published by the Karl Baedeker Press. Many English travelers opted for the package tours offered by Thomas Cook, founder of the first modern tourist agency. European archaeologists and zoologists eagerly seized the new opportunities, dragging home to Europe even more exotic monuments and animals to stock museums and zoos. Travel writers had to venture even farther to interest armchair readers. Those who did were able to tour the world as celebrities. Thanks to his adventures in Tibet and the Taklamakan Desert, the Swede Sven Hedin did become internationally famous. His books earned huge royalties in England, Germany, the United States, and Japan.

If Europeans could move more freely throughout the world, the world was also coming to western Europe. After 1881 a wave of eastern European Jews moved not only into central Europe's bigger cities, but also to London, where they established Yiddish-speaking districts, shops, and theaters. Elite students from the Ottoman Empire, Japan, and India came to Heidelberg or Paris to learn European sciences and arts; some picked up socialist ideas as well. There was also considerable traffic between Europe and other parts of the world at the lower end of the social scale; every port city teemed with sailors from far-flung parts. One American visitor to the White Swan pub in London was horrified to see "scores of women of all countries and shades of colour . . . dancing with Danes, Americans, Swedes, Spaniards, Russians, Negroes, Chinese, Malays, Italians and Portuguese in one hell-medley of abomination."[3] This variety may have scandalized the American, though he could have seen the same in the dance halls of New York or San Francisco. But it also testified to just how much the new mobility was reshaping European experience at home.

Social Mobility—and Its Limits

In addition to physical mobility, the fin de siècle also brought increases in social mobility. New access to education, mass transit, and print media allowed many of those who had once lived rather isolated lives to move in circles previously closed to them. As new jobs opened up for state bureaucrats, middle-level managers, doctors, lawyers, and bankers, the middle class expanded, though artisans and small shopkeepers, their jobs threatened by the new department stores and mass-producing industries, also worried about *downward* mobility. The new opportunities for mobility were concentrated in the cities, whereas in rural areas, the aristocratic elite employed modern forms of financing, marketing, and political lobbying to turn older forms of landed wealth and noble dominance into leading positions in Europe's evolving class society.

The new social mobility was built, in part, on education, something even the absolutist monarchs had realized was crucial for modernizing their societies. Nation-states too recognized that public education was vital in building a productive workforce and a loyal citizenry. Even conservatives could, in the end, be persuaded that education might be useful in making the lower classes obedient servants and God-fearing Christians (for many elementary schools were still operated by the churches). Accordingly, state governments increasingly required children to attend elementary school and to learn to read and write the national language. By the fin de siècle, most children under the age of twelve were expected to attend school for at least part of the day.

Some children from working-class families delighted in the books and ideas available to them in the public schools, and a few managed to move up in the world. The number of students attending secondary schools and universities increased. But many children, especially in rural eastern and southern Europe, learned little more than basic literacy (if that) before they were pushed out into the labor force. Secondary education remained limited to the middle and upper classes and heavily based on the learning of classical languages, despite the advances made in some places by advocates of more utilitarian forms of schooling. The dawn of the age of mass public education opened the way for some social mobility, but the impact of education in this period should not be overestimated. Learning remained very much dependent on a person's class.

Women in Motion

Women's mobility had always been more circumscribed than that of their husbands and brothers. But the new economy and new forms of transportation offered women a few opportunities to try new lifestyles. The rise of factory labor meant that lower-class women, increasingly, were not working in their homes, but on the shop floor. Their new jobs gave them some independence, but women remained largely responsible for the household labor, cooking, shopping, cleaning, sewing, and child care. Some younger (and usually single) women could obtain jobs in the growing cities as salesclerks, typists, nurses, or waitresses and dispose of their own income, though their wages, lower than those of men in comparable jobs, usually did not give them much to dispose of. A lucky few who had been allowed to pursue their educations managed to land jobs as journalists, teachers, or even doctors, but they were usually restricted to writing about, teaching, and treating other women.

Perhaps even more important in the long run were the increasing number of middle-class housewives whose husbands' rising paychecks allowed them *not* to work. These women were able to devote themselves to activities such as prison reform, temperance, and urban renewal, or forms of self-improvement such as reading, organizing singing groups, or writing local histories. Their indefatigable efforts in recruiting volunteers, drawing attention to unmet needs, stimulating civic spirit, and keeping all sorts of local institutions running would make these women indispensible in the making of modern, urban societies.

The women most impatient to participate fully in the changing world around them were the **suffragettes,** the female activists who sought to win the vote for women now that virtually all men had that right. By 1910, women had won important rights in Britain, France, and Germany, including the right to divorce their husbands, to own property in their own names, and to attend universities. But they still could not vote. Lack of this right inspired many women to join suffrage campaigns, most of them peaceful. The Women's Social and Political Union, founded by British suffragette Emmeline Pankhurst (1858–1928) in 1903, however, rejected rhetoric in favor of more militant tactics. Members of the union chained themselves to the visitors' gallery in the House of Commons, set fire to politicians' houses, and used acid to burn "Votes for Women" into the grass on golf courses. The result was equally violent treatment by police, who threw protestors into jail and force-fed those who attempted hunger strikes.

Male society did not, on the whole, look favorably on suffragettes or on women who pursued higher edu-

The Typing Pool, 1907 By the turn of the century, typewriters were in widespread use, and more women than ever before were being hired as secretaries and typists, displacing the male clerks and scribes who had performed most of the (handwritten) office work of the past.

cation and permanent careers. Some alarmists warned that educating women was the first step in destroying the family; others insisted that women could not study the sciences because their brains were inherently irrational. Brilliant scholars such as Marie Curie (1867–1934), who shared the Nobel Prize for chemistry with her husband Pierre and took his chair at the Collège de France when he died, proved these claims baseless. In women's lives, as in many other aspects of European society, the volatility and dynamism of the fin de siècle created both new opportunities and new anxieties, new kinds of diversity that to some were exhilarating—and to others terrifying.

The New Culture(s)

There is no dispute that the cultural world of the fin de siècle offered novelty in many forms. Culture in an era that now self-consciously called itself modern was both much more richly varied and more accessible to Europeans than ever before. What *modern* meant was in dispute then and continues to be disputed now, but we can focus on two essentially different kinds of cultural modern*ism*. First, this period saw the emergence of a truly mass culture, the making and sharing of cultural forms and practices designed to be accessible and appealing to a wide audience of consumers. Second, and partly in reaction to the rise of mass culture, was the birth of

Why did popular culture come of age at the fin de siècle?

cultural forms that writers and artists called **avant-garde** ("ahead of the rest"). Whether by intention or not, avant-garde culture appealed to those who liked to be on what we would call the cutting edge or who disdained the pedestrian tastes of the masses.

It is possible here to offer only a brief survey of cultural developments, which range from the beginnings of modern spectator sports to the philosophy of Friedrich Nietzsche. Modern culture—mass and elite—was born simultaneously, and even though its practitioners and consumers were often quite different, these individuals inhabited the same rapidly industrializing and urbanizing world, one in which liberalism, with its belief in the rational individual and its fear of the masses, was increasingly coming under fire. Just as some places in Europe had been little touched by liberalism, some were little affected by cultural modernization. Rural areas in southern and eastern countries were again largely left out. But the scale and speed of changes under way did eventually bring newspapers and circuses to consumers far from the avant-garde cities.

Mass Culture

There had always been "popular" culture outside the courts, universities, and high church circles, but until the mid-to-late nineteenth century, popular culture remained a relatively undeveloped sphere for one important reason: there wasn't much money in it. But as printing and paper costs fell and as literacy rates soared, as more and more governments allowed for freer presses, and as cities grew, the print market boomed. Culture could now be made accessible to the masses, and it could be sold for a profit. Publishers learned quickly that scandal sold papers, and newspapers began to feature sensational stories about love affairs, round-the-world travels, and murder trials. In 1888, for example, the newspaper coverage of the mutilation of Jack the Ripper's victims was so graphic that tabloids today would hesitate to print the same details.

Founded in 1896, *The Daily Mail* of London made another concession to readers with lower levels of literacy and less time to peruse the papers: it put world news in bulletin form. Its price, a half-penny, also appealed so greatly that the first issue sold nearly 400,000 copies, and the *Mail* soon began to wield wide political influence. The print market also expanded in terms of its diversity as periodicals began to cater to specialized readerships, such as Czech nationalists or German women living abroad. Books and journals were now published specifically for working-class readers and also for children and young adults. Boys' adventure stories, like Rider Haggard's *King Solomon's Mines* (1885), sold especially well, as did religious literature aimed at the lower classes.

Of course, mass culture was not exclusively a reading culture. There were also new opportunities to enjoy music and the visual arts. Once private courtly affairs, concerts were now much more widely accessible and ticket prices

Marie Lloyd The music hall entertainer Marie Lloyd became so popular that some of her signature songs were marketed as sheet music.

affordable for most people. Pianos became more affordable, and sales of popular sheet music soared. The working classes tended to prefer lighter fare, offered in their neighborhoods in the form of music hall or public house (pub) entertainment. This was a booming industry by 1910—though many of its greater performers' names are no longer known to us. One of those who did earn widespread acclaim was Marie Lloyd (1870–1922), the daughter of a poor artificial flower maker. Her captivating performances in working-class venues made her a music hall star at sixteen, and she was earning about $3,000 a week before she was twenty. Despite being an alcoholic with a notoriously foul mouth and terrible taste in men, Marie Lloyd, the lower-class equivalent of Sarah Bernhardt, was well known and even well respected. At her death, the great poet T. S. Eliot paid tribute to her "genius."

The visual arts, too, became more accessible to people of lesser means. Many first experienced painting by visiting one of the panorama displays available in European cities and towns by the 1860s. New museums opened their doors to wider audiences and offered free days for those who could not afford the entrance fees. But the big changes in visual culture undoubtedly came with the development of dry plate photography in the 1880s. This innovation reduced exposure time to seconds, making it possible for photographs to capture more lifelike expressions and events. As it became less expensive to print photographs and colored plates, popular publications like Germany's *Art for All* could send their readers colored reproductions, suitable for framing.

The final and most impressive development in fin de siècle mass culture was the motion picture. Brothers Auguste and Louis Lumière screened ten short films for a paying audience in Paris in December 1895. After this first experiment, the genre took off quickly. By 1912, London had five hundred cinemas, Berlin had three hundred; even more provincial Budapest could boast ninety-two theaters showing films. Some middle-class viewers found the films too indecent or frivolous, but soon discovered that their sons and daughters loved them. Sarah Bernhardt made the leap into films quite early, appearing in her first in 1900. She would continue to make films even after the amputation of her right leg in 1915. Indeed, she was filming a movie, *La Voyante* (*The Fortune Teller*), when she died in 1923.

Arnold Böcklin, *The Isle of the Dead* (1883) In this endlessly reproduced symbolist painting, the combination of a mythological theme and a surreal rendering of Mediterranean scenery invited viewers to contemplate the elemental mystery of death. Sigmund Freud and Vladimir Lenin each had a copy.

We are used to seeing fin de siècle popular culture as predominately secular and urban, and indeed many producers of films and newspapers targeted audiences of these kinds. But we often overlook the fact that a majority of Europeans remained believing Christians and, in most places, remained rural dwellers, even as the new cities boomed. At the fin de siècle, these people too began to be drawn into broader movements of various kinds. They joined national religious organizations and read mass-marketed devotional books, the descendants of Luis de Granada's *Book of Prayer and Meditation*. And in new numbers they undertook a much older form of travel: the pilgrimage.

Modernism—without the Masses

To generalize about the innovative and largely elitist culture of the fin de siècle is risky, but the period did see something like a return to early-nineteenth-century romanticism—without, however, the naiveté that characterized much of that earlier form. **Modernism** in the arts and sciences was a movement that acknowledged the deep power of subconscious drives and the limitations humans faced in obtaining direct knowledge of the world. It also sought to find abstractions and an internationally understandable language to tame these deeper forces and make communication and science possible nonetheless.

Modernism demanded that artists, writers, and scientists break away from traditions of the past that were no longer applicable or relevant and seek bold new forms of expression, even if that meant their work would not seem beautiful or accessible to the wider public of the present.

Some writers, artists, and musicians also abandoned realism and impressionism for styles such as symbolism or art nouveau. **Art nouveau** ("new art") featured stylized organic forms rather than forms rendered according to the increasingly hackneyed laws of perspective. It was favored especially by artists working in the minor arts, such as glass-making, jewelry making, interior decorating, and poster and book design. Another popular artistic style of the period was **symbolism,** in which artists used symbols or mythological figures to imply hidden psychological meanings or mysteries. Whereas the romantics of the early nineteenth century had hoped that eventually one could solve the riddles of the sphinx, for symbolist painters of the late nineteenth century, such as Gustave Moreau (1826–1898), the sphinx represented the eternally mysterious and bisexual core of human existence. The beauty to be contemplated in these forms and images was neither rational nor strictly natural; the mythologizing in them was meant to draw viewers out of their historical context to reflect on universal themes—human beings' sexual instincts, the rituals invented to tame death's pain.

As European power in the world reached its zenith, artists and writers began to worry that it could not last and that excessive consumption, pleasure seeking, and pride would lead to disaster. In his novel *The Picture of Dorian Gray* (1890), Oscar Wilde (1854–1900) allowed his decadent aristocrat, Dorian Gray, briefly to escape the banality of everyday life into a life of vice, but in the end, Gray meets disaster. There is a powerful sense of foreboding in virtually all the later plays of Norwegian

Lourdes and the Mass Pilgrimage

We have learned to see late-nineteenth-century European society as a predominately secular one, characterized by socialism and steel production. But how secular was this society? If we look closely, considerable evidence indicates that religious sentiment was still alive and well. Many of the new political parties called themselves Christian socialists, and many broad-based civic associations, such as the Young Men's Christian Association (YMCA), acknowledged their roots in religious communities. Some religious confraternities were huge—the Confraternity of the Immaculate Heart of Mary, founded in Paris in 1836, is said to have had more than a million members in 1880. Religious books continued to outsell secular ones. But perhaps the most striking proof that not all Europeans had given up on faith comes from the revitalization of a much older form of Catholic piety in the century's last decades: the pilgrimage.

Catholic Christians had never ceased making pilgrimages to holy sites, though the practice had been disrupted by the enlightened absolutists, French revolutionaries, and liberal nationalists, who discouraged public exhibitions of piety. Liberals, especially Protestant liberals, tended to be anticlerical and considered popular devotional practices like the worship of saints or the veneration of relics to be superstitious and antimodern. The Catholic Church had suffered considerable decline in its status after 1789. It had lost most of its land in France, and many of its priests, monks, and nuns had been persecuted or even executed. In 1870, the pope had been forced to cede control of the city of Rome, his last piece of secular territory, to the newly founded Italian kingdom. In France the archbishop of Paris had been murdered during the period of the Commune's radical rule, and in Germany the *Kulturkampf* sought to break the clergy's loyalty to Rome and the lay Catholics' loyalty to the pope in the name of modernization and German patriotism. But even as liberals succeeded in secularizing many of Europe's formal institutions, a wave of popular religiosity surged up from beneath, giving the lie to the liberals' contention that they represented "the people" as a whole. The new forms of faith tended to emphasize emotions—suffering, love, and sorrow—over doctrine, and appealed most powerfully to women, which may explain why the Virgin Mary played so central a role in inciting a new set of pilgrimages.

The Virgin Mary Appears at Lourdes, c. 1890 This popular representation of the Virgin Mary appearing to the humble peasant girl Bernadette Soubiros in the grotto near Lourdes was one of millions produced after Lourdes became a mass pilgrimage site in the later 1870s.

As in earlier times, the pilgrims of the late nineteenth century set off to visit places where visions or miraculous healings had taken place. There was no shortage of such sites in the heavily Catholic Rhineland region or in the Pyrenees Mountains, where in 1858 the most widely publicized and controversial of such visions occurred. The seer in this case was a very young, poor, and rather sickly girl, Bernadette Soubiros, daughter of an uncaring mother and a father who worked as a rag collector. Bernadette saw eighteen visions of the Virgin Mary in a mountain grotto; the apparition instructed the girl to build a chapel there, near a healing spring.

As historian Ruth Harris describes in her study titled *Lourdes* (1999), fourteen-year-old Bernadette did not back down on her claims, despite being questioned by the police and several prosecutors, all of whom tried to get her to retract her story. Even some members of the clergy were dubious. Some feared being ridiculed in the press for having fallen for a little girl's fantasies. Others feared that the laity was becoming dangerously independent from church teachings and practices. Despite the authorities' attempts to close off the grotto, people came, hoping to see the Virgin Mary themselves, longing for miraculous cures. Eventually, the authorities gave in, and in 1876, some 35 bishops, 5,000 priests, and 100,000 lay Catholics were on hand to witness the consecration of a statue to the Virgin at Lourdes. A new road, connecting the site to the railway, was built and a complex of buildings arose, making it possible for large numbers of pilgrims to visit Lourdes, to partake of its healing waters, and to purchase souvenirs of their visit. The age of mass pilgrimages had begun.

Bernadette was by no means the only person of her age to see visions, nor were all mass pilgrimages Marian ones. In 1891, two million visitors traveled to Trier—many of them by train—to see the Holy Coat, said to be the seamless garment worn by Christ before his crucifixion. And, with the cheapening of transportation and the completion of rail lines to Mecca and Medina, Muslim participation in the hadj also soared. The same technology and social forces that made possible the development and spread of international socialism made possible the revival of the pilgrimage.

QUESTION | *What does the story of Lourdes tell us about secularization in the nineteenth century?*

dramatist Henrik Ibsen (1828–1906), a foreboding that comes from the sense that liberal values will end not in social harmony, but in disaster. Like the composer Richard Wagner, and the Russian novelist Fyodor Dostoyevsky, Ibsen was enormously popular with the generation of writers and artists who came of age at the fin de siècle. None of them believed in progress, and all were sure individuals would commit reckless, irrational acts simply to establish the existence of free will. It was at the fin de siècle, too, that western Europeans discovered the non-European elegance of the work of Indian poet and novelist Rabindranath Tagore, who won the Nobel Prize in Literature in 1910. Voices and critiques from Europe's periphery now seemed particularly timely, and their challenges to liberal, Eurocentric ways of thinking profoundly inspiring, as well as troubling.

Like creative geniuses in all eras, fin de siècle writers spent a great deal of time criticizing the work of the generation before their own, whose realism they saw as superficial description dressed up as literature. Impressionism and realism failed to explore the depth and irrational elements of human self-consciousness, the new generation complained. European conventions and the banalities of the marketplace were preventing westerners from experiencing life in its most elemental and truest forms. The answer, for some, was to escape to distant and supposedly exotic places, as did the poet Arthur Rimbaud (1854–1891) and the painter Paul Gauguin (1848–1903). Leaving behind poetic stardom, his lover poet Paul Verlaine, and a dissolute life, laced with hashish and absinthe, Rimbaud left Europe in 1876 for Java. He subsequently settled in northern Africa, where he took an Ethiopian mistress and abandoned writing poems about his torments in favor of trading coffee. Gauguin had already abandoned impressionism and naturalistic color and form before he set sail in 1891 for Tahiti. Like many Europeans before him, Gauguin hoped to find in Tahiti the lost Eden that modern Europe had completely forgotten. He sought to strip himself and his art of "everything that is artificial and conventional." Indeed, he would find not only love, but also inspiration in his encounters with Tahitian women and Tahitian traditional arts and crafts. Perhaps Rimbaud and Gauguin would have been gratified by the success their creations enjoyed in Europe, but neither of them ever came home. Real life, they believed, was elsewhere.

Breaking with Conventions

Unlike Rimbaud and Gauguin, most writers, artists, and musicians did not leave Europe, but simply attempted to escape old forms. Painters Pablo Picasso and Wassily Kandinsky sought to abandon the laws of perspective; Picasso's pioneering *Les Demoiselles d'Avignon* (1907), for example, depicted its female subjects as if viewed through shattered bits of glass. The inspiration for their faces came from the African masks Picasso (1881–1973) saw in Paris's ethnographic museum. Modernist ar-

Pablo Picasso, *Les Demoiselles d'Avignon* (1907) In this painting, Picasso broke with the long tradition of treating the canvas as a window, with the figures drawn using conventions of perspectival drawing. Instead, Picasso treated the canvas as a two-dimensional surface. In his attempt to capture the raw and tragic lives of these sex workers, Picasso was inspired by African masks.

chitects stripped historicizing decoration from their buildings, proclaiming, as did Austrian architect Adolf Loos, "ornament is crime!" It was wrong, he claimed, to obscure the function and modern origin of buildings by trying to disguise them as Gothic churches or Greek temples. Loos's German contemporaries, Peter Behrens and Walter Gropius, agreed. Between 1911 and 1913, Gropius (1883–1969) designed and built the Fagus Factory, which manufactured shoe lasts, using glass curtain walls to unite the building's exterior and interior and to provide a lighter, airier workspace for employees. Modernist architects were more inclined than any other group of artists to embrace that most modern of fixtures, the machine. Most others found machines inhumane and uninspiring—with the exception of the Italian and Russian Futurists, small groups of poets and painters who tried to make their work sing with the steam trains and evoke the speed of shiny new race cars.

In poetry, both realism and Victorian high diction gave way to interior dialogues and attempts to evoke the mythological and mysterious. The Irish poet and playwright William Butler Yeats drew on ancient Gaelic poems as well as Japanese dramas in the attempt to stretch the boundaries of representation. French poets such as Rimbaud and Verlaine tried to cultivate synesthesia, the mixing together of the senses. In Germany, the symbolist poet Stefan George had his poems printed in a typeface modeled on his own esoteric style of handwriting. In literature, too, writers began to experiment with time and space, breaking away from the conventions of realism. French writer Marcel Proust's *Swann's Way* (1913) narrated the contents of a young man's memory—as it related to tales of another, aristocratic, man's love life; *Swann's Way* would prove the first of the seven novels Proust (1871–1922) called *In Search of Lost Time.*

Although still enraptured by the pioneering work of Richard Wagner (see Chapter 19), musical composers strayed further and further from traditional tonal harmonies, drawing on the work of modernist contemporaries in literature and philosophy and provoking controversy even among elite connoisseurs. Austrian composer Richard Strauss (1864–1949) shocked his countrymen with the futuristic dissonances in his tone poems such as *Thus Spake Zarathustra* (1896), a work inspired by the philosopher Friedrich Nietzsche. The decadent themes of Strauss's opera *Salomé* (1905)—in which the leading lady exults in kissing the dead lips of John the Baptist—were also highly controversial. Strauss's *Salomé* was inspired by Oscar Wilde's play of the same name. Similarly, a symbolist poem by Stephane Mallarmé inspired French composer Claude Debussy (1862–1918) to write "Prelude to the Afternoon of a Faun." When the handsome Russian ballet dancer Alexander Nijinsky danced the piece barefooted and with overtly sexualized gestures in Paris in 1912, the performance caused a sensation and a revolution in ballet. The harsh dissonance of Russian composer Ivan Stravinsky's primitivist tone poem, *Rite of Spring,* provoked a riot on its premiere in Paris in 1913.

Modernism in the Sciences

The juxtaposition of the coming of mass society and the neo-romanticism of the fin de siècle made for watershed developments in the fledgling social sciences. Positivism, with its optimistic hopes for perfecting society through the application of universal laws, was rejected increasingly in favor of the analysis of irrational behaviors. In his pioneering work, *Suicide* (1897), French sociologist Émile Durkheim (1858–1917) suggested that increased rates of suicide in the modern West had their origin in urban, industrial *anomie,* or alienation. Durkheim's later work sought in other ways to comprehend what modern society had lost, focusing on religions and rituals that had created the glue holding together pre-modern societies. Sociologist Gustave Le Bon (1841–1931) also studied a phenomenon of particular interest at the fin de siècle: the behavior of crowds. Le Bon lamented the loss of individual reasoning powers that occurred in crowds, but his analy-

Walter Gropius, the Fagus Factory Completed in 1913, this innovative factory building displayed architect Walter Gropius's desire to remove decorative clutter and to allow natural light to penetrate to the structure's interior.

sis of the power of charismatic leaders to galvanize mob action fascinated the readers of his day. Like his younger Austrian and German counterparts, Sigmund Freud and Max Weber, Le Bon was essentially a political liberal, but his interest in subconscious processes marks him as a man of the fin de siècle (see Back to the Source at the end of the chapter). Weber (1864–1920) would be remembered for calling modern bureaucratic and technocratic society an "iron cage." Offering a glimpse of modern society's undersides, the new social scientists reminded their contemporaries that modernization had both its limits and its dangers.

Freud (1856–1939) did not consider himself a social scientist, but rather a doctor—a healer—of a quite new type. Concluding around 1900 that psychological disorders could be neither understood nor cured by purely medical means, Freud began to explore dreams as the means by which individuals might come to grips with their subconscious fears and desires. He concluded that early sexual fantasies—including the young boy's desire to replace his father (the Oedipus complex)—and subsequent attempts to repress them created psychic distress. Like the avant-garde artists, Freud offended his bourgeois contemporaries by plunging beneath the smooth surface of rational behavior to identify powerful and perhaps untamable forces operating below.

In philosophy, mathematics, and the natural sciences, rationalism and positivism gave way during the fin de siècle to various forms of neo-romanticism or postpositivist thinking. French philosopher Henri Bergson (1859–1941) argued that the brain did not operate according to strict principles of logic. Memory, for example, was a fluid force, not something that one could describe in an equation, but it was often more powerful than reason.

Similarly, Bergson argued, time, as humans actually experienced it, was often much different than time as measured by clocks. Following his lead, biologists sought to understand nonmechanical, instinctive, and creative forces that underlay the secrets of experience and organic life. Scientists began to examine memory and dreams, sexual desire, and telepathy, hoping to find rigorous ways to describe and perhaps tame these "irrational" forces.

The fin de siècle also saw breakthroughs in bacteriology and genetics. The French chemist Louis Pasteur (1822–1895) developed vaccines for rabies and anthrax and a process for heating milk and wine (subsequently known as pasteurization) to prevent the growth of bacteria. The British surgeon Joseph Lister showed how to use carbolic acid to sterilize medical equipment, a procedure that rapidly reduced the number of doctor-inflicted infections. Though completed decades earlier, the pioneering work of Austrian botanist Gregor Mendel in genetics became widely known after 1902. His work contributed to the breeding of better crops and to eugenic dreams of breeding "better" people.

In physics, Max Planck, Niels Bohr, and Albert Einstein laid the foundations for relativity theory. Their work destroyed the classic Newtonian physics on which the natural sciences had rested since the seventeenth century and offered new ways of conceptualizing the movement of light and matter. Perhaps most important, their work suggested that the universe is not completely continuous and fully knowable. We can never have the complete certainty about its workings that the positivists hoped we could ascertain by means of more and more experiments. The best we can obtain is *probable* understandings of the operations of the natural world. Although the new physics was little known and not at all understood outside of a small circle before 1918, it very much reflected the modernism of the fin de siècle.

The philosophers who became most influential among the avant-garde were Arthur Schopenhauer and Friedrich Nietzsche. Schopenhauer, who died in 1860, long before he achieved popularity, claimed that the world was a mere illusion, produced by individual consciousness. Informed by Buddhist philosophy, he argued that the only release from the pain of individuation lay in renouncing the world of representation or in aesthetic contemplation. As a young man, Friedrich Nietzsche (1844–1900) was briefly impressed by this pessimistic philosophy, but by the later 1870s was preaching heroic self-fashioning instead. In his *Thus Spake Zarathustra* (1883), Nietzsche gave the world a prophet of the new, life-embracing individualism he championed.

Behind all moral philosophies, including Christianity, Nietzsche claimed, lay a "will to power." This was also the case for quests for scientific truth. In his view, understanding this will to power was the means to establish a philosophy that ranged "beyond good and evil." Many of Nietzsche's contemporaries accused him of moral relativism. Nietzsche has also been accused of championing "the blond beast" over and against racially inferior others, especially Jews, but most scholars now agree that Nietzsche's most egregious statements about race were later additions by his racist sister and brother-in-law. Nevertheless, Nietzsche's works, such as *On the Genealogy of Morals* (1887), seem to romanticize a social Darwinist worldview in which the strong defeat the weak and humankind is better off for it. Though Nietzsche went mad in 1889 and died in 1900, his philosophy was well suited to an age in which the rapid pace of change seemed likely to leave all of bourgeois society's values—reason, science, the free market, Christian brotherhood, and the rule of law—in the dustbin.

The New Economies

To understand why tensions and anxieties mounted so high during an era of relative prosperity, we must examine the changes in the economies of Europe. Europe's economies were booming in the late nineteenth century. With deeper imperial and commercial penetration of non-European markets came an unprecedented leap in global investments and exchanges. Businesses grew larger, often eating up competitors and suppliers along the way, and as the need for greater amounts of capital increased, banks became even more indispensable to commercial success. Entrepreneurs producing the same product, such as rye or coal, banded together to form **cartels,** powerful organizations that could fix prices and drive rival competitors out of business. There were fortunes to be made in heavy industrial products, such as steel and oil, and in consumer goods, such as soap and chocolate bars. Railroads were being built not only in Europe and North America, but also in Africa and in the Ottoman Empire. The market for tropical commodities such as rubber and diamonds boomed—to the profit of European buyers and the terrible suffering of African laborers.

> **What made the economic situation of the fin de siècle distinctive?**

Some people made their fortunes dishonestly. As a series of scandals showed, big capitalists were happy to pay off politicians to support their interests, and numerous leaders enriched themselves by accepting bribes. The crash of the Viennese stock market in May 1873 exposed the kickbacks and favors that linked the minister of commerce, the liberal party's parliamentary leader, and railroad builders. It also showed that speculators could be punished for blind confidence in the free market. There was much new money to be made, but also a great deal of money to be *lost* in this global economy, and those who saw their fortunes crumble often gave up on economic liberalism for good.

Some of the biggest losers were agricultural producers. Two major factors—the linking of the Ukrainian and U.S. midwestern breadbaskets to urban marketplaces; and the expansion and improvement of farming in the Americas, southern Africa, and Southeast Asia—pushed grain prices down, ruining the fortunes of numerous European landowners. Peasants flocked to the cities and factories seeking work; older aristocratic families sought advantageous marriages with the manufacturing elite. Meanwhile, skilled artisans lost status and numbers as machines began to take over some of their jobs. Abandoning the family farm, with its steady rhythms and traditional values, put people at risk of becoming economically or psychologically rootless and susceptible to new forms of oppression or poverty. Mass production—the making of identical things in huge quantities—affected not only the items being produced, but the bodies and lives of the producers as well.

Harvest in the Ukraine, 1880s Whereas western Europeans increasingly moved to cities to take jobs in the industrializing economy, in eastern Europe many peasants continued to work in the fields as their ancestors had done. Thanks to accelerated means of transportation, however, the wheat being harvested here could now be transported to markets far away.

The Second Industrial Revolution

By 1870s, communications and transportation networks had become fast and predictable enough to allow for the exploitation of efficiencies of scale and of new, more sophisticated, and specialized technologies. Bigger businesses formed, in steelmaking and chemicals, in machine production, and in consumer products. Steel was the metal of the era. It was more adaptable than iron and new processes for producing it, and doing so cheaply, meant that it could now be used in building ships, tall buildings, typewriters, and harvesting machines. Prices for machinery fell. Engineers developed ways to produce high-voltage alternating current, allowing electricity for homes and factories to be generated in central power plants. Once the new oil-burning engines had been installed in cars, trucks, and ships, the pace of commerce could be accelerated again—and again.

As noted in Chapter 18, the first Industrial Revolution had an uneven impact in Europe. Its home and heartland was England, and it soon spread to the Netherlands, northern France, and the German Rhineland. The **second industrial revolution,** similarly, did not occur everywhere at the same time, and its dependence on a more skilled workforce and on new technologies meant that it was especially pronounced not just in Britain, but also in the United States and in the newly united German Empire. By 1914, the United States, Britain, and Germany were still producing two-thirds of the world's industrial output—but Britain, which in 1870 had been responsible for 32 percent of the output, was now producing only 14 percent, Germany's share had risen from 13 percent to 16 percent, and the United States had surged from 23 percent to 36 percent of total production. Russia industrialized very late, but steel production and railroad building were progressing very rapidly there by 1910. In Russia, as elsewhere, one of the liveliest sectors of the industrial economy was the production of weapons, battleships, and rail lines for military purposes. Everyone recognized that war would break out, sooner or later, and no one wanted to be left behind in what became an industrial arms race.

The second industrial revolution wasn't only about metals and machines. It was also about consumer goods. By 1900, the largest industrial operations in Britain were branded, packaged products such as Lever Brothers soap and Cadbury chocolates. U.S. businesses also invested in consumer products, and as early as the 1880s, mechanized canning was being used to produce nationally and internationally distributed products such as Campbell's soup and Borden's condensed milk. The United States was also highly successful in patenting and producing smaller, household machines. By 1913, demand for Singer sewing machines was so great that the company set up factories all over the world and was issuing sets of trading cards that featured women in local costumes proudly showing off their identical Singer machines.

As competition grew fiercer, both in global and in domestic markets, free trade, one of the great causes of mid-nineteenth-century liberals, began to lose its luster. Producers big and small grew disenchanted with supply-and-demand mechanisms and sought to circumvent them. Big industrialists, such as German armaments' manufacturer Alfred Krupp, attempted to create monopolies in the name of improving efficiency and, of course, profits. Farmers created cooperatives to fix prices and protect themselves from the market's volatility. Some states took over ownership of privately owned land, rail lines, telegraph networks, utilities, and roads to coordinate the development of communications and transportation systems. With the exception of Britain, few nations had fully embraced free trade and some now raised

The Department Store

One of the late nineteenth century's commercial innovations is still very much with us: the department store.[4] This new and much larger enterprise began to appear in big cities such as Paris, London, and Chicago in the 1840s and 1850s, but had its heyday in the years just before the First World War. It evolved from haberdashery shops, which sold a variety of dry goods such as lingerie, cloth, gloves, and umbrellas. By the 1840s, one of the new department stores, the Ville de Paris, was employing 150 workers and seeking to carve out its place in the market by selling high volume at low prices. Women were allowed to shop freely, and advertisements were circulated to draw in new customers. As time passed, the trend toward larger concerns increased, and store owners began to build grand new shopping palaces to please the largely female crowds who flocked to them. In New York City, Macy's added home furnishings, toys, and books to its offerings, and separate departments

began to evolve within each store, each with specially trained salesclerks. Textiles, either in the form of bulk cloth or as ready-to-wear clothing, remained, as they do now, the department stores' mainstay, a tribute to the long-lasting appeal of that central product of the Industrial Revolution.

In the department store, the intertwining of the histories of mass production and mass consumption is evident. As factories increased in size and speed of production, the price of goods fell, allowing more consumers to buy more goods. The advent of the department store also led to changes in the labor force. As goods sold in department stores were increasingly mass produced and purchased at cheaper prices from large factories, skilled artisans and small shopkeepers suffered. The stores offered more white-collar jobs to men and women. By 1910, the largest Parisian department store, Le Bon Marché, employed some 3,150 men and 1,350 women. These were desirable jobs for young people fleeing hard times on provincial farms—but they were not easy ones. Female salesclerks were treated very much like domestic servants. They were required to wear plain black clothing so as not to distract the customers from the goods to be sold. As revealed in the well-researched novel *The Ladies' Paradise* (1883), by Émile Zola, salesclerks' low wages often inclined them to take additional jobs, such as sewing, or in desperation, prostitution, to make ends meet.

One of the surviving shopping palaces of the fin de siècle is the Galeries Lafayette in Paris, founded in 1893. The store was built in the wake of Baron Haussmann's rebuilding of Paris (see Chapter 19), near the fashionable opera house and the busy St. Lazare train station. In 1906, the store's owners decided to make a splash by redesigning the interior to remind customers of an oriental bazaar. Artists known for their work in the art nouveau style were hired and designed an elaborate, five-floor, ninety-six-department emporium, complete with escalators and a neo-Byzantine glass dome, thirty-three meters high. This beautiful dome has been restored and can still be enjoyed by tourists and shoppers, who can hope to visit it for many years to come—for the Galeries Lafayette has now been classified as an historic monument. A mostly female staff still serves a mostly female clientele. But working conditions and wages have improved, and the store now belongs to a global franchise. Department stores such as The Galeries Lafayette were products of the second industrial revolution, but they must continue to evolve along with the European economy.

QUESTION | *What does the coming of the department store indicate about the European economy at the fin de siècle?*

The Splendor of Shopping The elegant dome built for the Galeries Lafayette in Paris transformed a department store into a "palace" or even a "cathedral" of commerce.

tariffs further to protect local industries. Capitalism was flourishing, but the market was anything but free.

The Worker and the Second Industrial Revolution

What was it like to be a worker in this era? Although trade union pressures and reformist legislation called attention to and in some instances curtailed the worst abuses, workers in this era still spent long hours on the job, often in unsafe and unsanitary workplaces. Some places prohibited child labor, but it continued, legally or not, in many industries. Industrial accidents continued to be commonplace, in coal mines and in meatpacking plants. With the opening of the new cafés and department stores, lower-class young women could seek employment in more comfortable surroundings than the textile factories but still suffered abuse.

Statistics suggest that inequalities in income between rich and poor declined between about 1870 and 1914. But many workers did not experience significant changes in their fortunes, or they began to expect more and better sharing of what was, quite obviously, more wealth. Crowded more closely together in big cities and exposed to other people's doings in the mass press, workers could compare their situations more directly with those of others. Political orators and radical newspapermen drew additional attention to injustices. Even children who had to work rolling cigars or ironing clothes began to feel resentful that their contemporaries had been allowed to stay in school, while they joined the workforce. In many places, the working classes became impatient with what seemed an all too static social hierarchy in an era of pervasive change.

The Social Question, Again

In Europe's towns and cities, economic change and the enormous profits being made by some forced the long-simmering social question (see Chapter 18) to the fore. Although real wages were rising, they were not rising fast enough to forestall the hardening of a class system that the poor found almost impossible to escape. Liberal doctrine said that this was not supposed to happen. According to Adam Smith and his successors, the increasing division of labor and the free operation of the market were supposed to allow "all boats to rise." Why was this not happening? Why were many workers still living at essentially subsistence wages, while owners ate roast beef in their private clubs? How long would it be before workers could enjoy the new prosperity? Would political leaders ever take the concerns of the workers to heart, or were they simply puppets of the industrialists? Emboldened to ask such questions, Europeans at the fin de siècle now blamed not only the capitalists, but also liberal political leaders for what seemed all too little progress toward social justice.

The social question had never been an exclusively economic one, but at the fin de siècle, the combination of rising expectations and expanding suffrage ensured that the distribution of Europe's new prosperity would be the great political issue of the day. In this context, new forms of working-class politics took hold across Europe. Some workers joined socialist or communist movements, which promoted the overthrow of capitalism. Others, usually skilled workers with reformist rather than radical goals, joined trade unions, which were the modern descendants of the guilds. In the unions, workers in particular industries banded together to try to pressure management for higher wages and better working conditions. By 1905, unions could claim 3 million members in Britain, 1.5 million in Germany, and 1 million in France—though these figures look much more modest in light of these nations' total populations (about 38 million for Britain, 56 million for Germany, and 38 million for France). Labor unions were instrumental in pressing for better pay, shorter working hours, and safer workplaces, at least for a few skilled workers. Many labor union leaders would make their way into politics and work avidly for further reforms.

The most dramatic way in which workers tried to call attention to their plight was by organizing strikes. There had been peasant revolts and workplace violence in Europe for centuries; England, in particular, had seen large industrial strikes in the 1840s. But by the 1880s, strikes were becoming much more frequent and larger. As both cities and factories grew in size, workers were more concentrated and more easily able to band together to stop work. Most of these stoppages were small and nonviolent, but some were very large. In the London Dock Strike of 1889, for example, some 10,000 protestors and 2,000 policemen gathered in a rally at Trafalgar Square in London on Sunday, November 13. Some strikes, like this one, did turn violent, as police or soldiers tried to disband crowds with horses, truncheons, and sometimes bullets. But workers, urged on by radical orators, increasingly stood their ground and defended their right to strike. When after the Dock Strike rally one ordinary worker died of his wounds, a huge funeral parade was organized to honor him, and perhaps as many as 100,000 people turned out to watch the procession and hear the speeches.

Unlike most work stoppages, the Dock Strike was ultimately successful, in part because supporters of the cause raised money to sustain workers' families during the five-week strike. Poorly paid dock workers ended up receiving slightly increased wages. Despite the eruption of massive strikes across the French coalfields in the 1880s and 1890s, little was done to relieve the poverty of the miners and the terrible conditions under which they labored. Disillusioned organizers realized that unless workers across all industries could be joined together, real progress was unlikely to be made. Frustrated with piecemeal efforts and liberal foot-dragging, many concluded that the older parties and established authorities had to go. It was time for the people to speak.

London Dock Strike On September 7, 1889, the popular British newspaper *The Graphic* devoted its front page to the London Dock Strike. The image on top depicts an orator addressing the workers outside the padlocked entrance to the docks; the lower image shows the workers' relief committee issuing coupons for striking workers to use to buy food.

| The New Politics

In examining changes in the lives of Europeans at the century's end, it is impossible to separate politics from

Why did liberalism fail at the fin de siècle?

economics; mass production and mass politics were deeply intertwined. Both of these aspects of European modernization brought with them social benefits, but they also created unforeseen conflicts. Speeding up and mechanizing production made some people richer, but destroyed the livelihoods of skilled workers. The expansion of the franchise offered the vote to many more men, but the proliferation of parties often made it impossible for major reformist legislation to pass. The consequences were mixed, and each nation developed its own versions of economic and political modernity. But everywhere, the combination of mass production and mass politics made political liberalism and its economic counterpart, laissez-faire capitalism, difficult to sustain.

Modern Society's Challenge to Liberalism

Liberalism, the mid-nineteenth-century commitment to the free market, individual reason, and the gradual expansion of political rights, was one of the casualties of the fin de siècle's dynamism. It suffered because it now seemed a far too narrow and exclusionary basis on which to build an industrial society and because the working classes had tired of waiting for their superiors to hand them the better wages and enhanced political influence they believed they deserved. Liberalism failed too because large-scale capitalism, aggressive overseas imperial ventures, and mass political mobilization were incompatible with its values and its experience, most of which lay in operating slower economies and managing smaller and less diverse groups of people. Liberal city managers simply couldn't deal with externalities like building metros or creating municipal sewer systems, or grand-scale threats to public safety, such as the cholera epidemic that struck the city of Hamburg in 1892.

Not all newly enfranchised voters chose radical options; a significant portion of lower- and lower-middle-class voters were horrified by the violence, atheism, pacifism, or property-seizure proposed by the radicals, and joined moderate or right-wing movements instead. But certainly the most striking departure from nineteenth-century liberalism was the advent of a diverse, but determined, socialist movement that insisted that solving the social question was *the* great political issue of the present, and the future.

Socialism and the Second International

By the century's end, radical visions of a society that had transcended capitalism, private property, and elite rule had been in circulation for some decades. Before the 1870s, socialism had been illegal in most of Europe, though officials in different nations treated it differently. Repression was most severe in Russia, where czarist officials regularly sent radicals off to work camps on the northeastern frontier. In 1849, the Russian novelist Fyodor Dostoyevsky had been treated to a mock execution and then sent to a Siberian prison camp simply for belonging to a circle of intellectuals drawn to the works of utopian socialist Charles Fourier. In western Europe, officials and police locked up agitators who they believed might provoke strikes or urban riots, but they usually did not molest peaceful organizers and writers. One of these (at least theoretically) peaceful organizations was the very small International Working Men's Organization, put together by Karl Marx and Friedrich Engels in 1864 with the intent of uniting the workers of all nations to fight for revolution. Nationalism, however, killed the

Liberalism's Death in Hamburg

One of the most striking accounts of the crisis of liberalism comes from the pen of historian Richard Evans, whose *Death in Hamburg* (1987) describes the challenges posed to Hamburg's liberal elite by the cholera epidemic of 1892. Evans describes in detail how this important port city had come to be ruled by a relatively small number of commercial businessmen, who fought aggressively to make Hamburg competitive in the new global economy. As was the case in many central European cities, the city fathers of Hamburg were not aristocrats, but they were elected on the basis of a narrow franchise, for only moderately well-off property owners could vote in local elections.

Unlike some more progressive European civic leaders, the Hamburg liberals neglected to undertake general municipal improvements such as building a sewer or adding a filtration system to improve the city's water supply. In the 1890s, most residents still depended on public pumps or took their water from polluted canals, into which people also threw trash, dung, and dead dogs. The port of Hamburg brought much wealth to the city, but the crucial human contributors to the city's commercial success—sailors and dock workers—were housed in terrible slums, around which developed a seedy and dangerous red light district. There were few amenities, such as public baths, or police. Hamburg epitomized a laissez-faire, liberal economy.

The cholera epidemic of 1892 was one of the last to strike the European continent, but it hit Hamburg hard. Doctors were slow to diagnose the disease, as vomiting and diarrhea were by no means uncommon in a citizenry accustomed to bad water and adulterated food. By August 19, some medical authorities had identified the presence of infectious disease in the port area and were calling it cholera.

Rumors began to fly and residents panicked; some 12,000 people left town on August 22–23 alone. But eager not to disrupt trade, the Hamburg authorities waited for six days before warning citizens that the disease was abroad and that their drinking water was unsafe. In the meantime, hot weather allowed the disease to spread through the central water supply. Thousands of people were infected. Between August 26 and September 2, about one thousand new cases of cholera were reported each day, and the disease continued to take a heavy toll all through September. By mid-November, the epidemic was over, but nearly 17,000 Hamburgers had contracted cholera, and 8,600 had died.

The uniqueness of Hamburg's fate was underscored by the fact that no other western European city suffered a major epidemic that year. In the weeks after the dying began, journalists, as well as the social democrats, took out their anger on the liberal authorities, who at first tried to cover up the number of deaths. Anger was increased by the fact that dealing with the epidemic, once it had spread, was costly. Ships, barges, and boats were first quarantined, then had to be inspected and sanitized. There were disinfection squads and hospital workers to pay, and enormous losses as the number of visitors and railway traffic plummeted. In November, the Hamburg Social Democratic Party rallied 30,000 people to attend meetings, at which the liberal elite was denounced as incompetent. By 1896, suffrage had been extended to all Hamburg men, and they had voted the liberals out of office. In the face of a citywide crisis, old-fashioned patrician politics had failed. In Hamburg, liberalism was dead.

QUESTION | *How did the cholera epidemic of 1892 kill liberalism in Hamburg?*

First International at the time of the Franco-Prussian War. Not until the years just before Marx's death in 1883 did his works begin to circulate more widely and to win followers to the cause of revolutionary socialism.

Socialists came from many walks of life. There were intellectuals like the Polish journalist and philosopher Rosa Luxemburg and abused workers like the young Josef Stalin, who had worked in the Caucasus oil fields under police supervision by day and been locked in a barracks for eight hours during the night. Though they took heart from the expansion of trade unionism and the rising number of industrial strikes, socialists did not believe that real progress for the working classes could come without overthrowing capitalism itself. They claimed that only the complete abolition of private property and

the destruction of the bourgeois nation-states would solve the social question. To cure workers' alienation from the products of their labor and from one another, the whole system of divided labor and market exchange had to be overthrown violently. Like Marx, most socialists believed capitalism was already undermining itself and that the revolution was inevitable, sooner or later. But sooner or later was exactly the question that would plague the Second International.

REVOLUTIONARY OR DEMOCRATIC SOCIALISM?

The recognition that capitalism was a global phenomenon, which could be overthrown only by concerted, international effort, led to the refounding in 1889 of an international consortium of socialist parties, the Second

International Working Men's Organization. Modeled on the organization founded by Marx and Engels in 1864, the much more influential Second International sought to unite the working classes of Europe's many nations in the common pursuit of overthrowing capitalism and launching the era of proletarian rule. But the Second International was split between orthodox Marxists, who insisted that violent revolution was the only answer to the social question, and a position known as **revisionism.** Revisionists, such as the German socialist Eduard Bernstein, insisted that workers did not want revolution, but better wages and working conditions. He urged his colleagues to stand for election and fight for workers' rights *within* the existing system.

At the 1899 socialist party congress in Hanover, Bernstein's position was roundly attacked by orthodox socialists. The controversy led Russian Marxist Vladimir Lenin (1870–1924) to write his famous pamphlet "What Is to Be Done?" in which he argued that leaders like Bernstein were simply playing into the hands of the capitalists and that their reforms would ultimately do nothing to free the workers from their enslavement by the bourgeois class. Recognizing the problem Bernstein had identified—that the masses did not want a grand-scale revolution—Lenin declared that small groups of radical leaders would have to spark revolution, for the workers' own good. Published in 1902, "What Is to Be Done?" helped precipitate the Russian socialist movement's split into the more radical Bolsheviks and the more moderate Menshevik faction. Elsewhere, too, this debate divided the socialist movement into what came to be known as democratic socialists (revisionists) and communists (revolutionary socialists).

ANARCHISM. Even more radical than the revolutionary socialists were the anarchists, who proclaimed that since governments inevitably fell into the hands of the elite, they needed to be done away with entirely. **Anarchism** was a tiny movement, but it was a highly visible one, as a number of its backers undertook to achieve their ends through terror. The movement attracted followers in southern Italy, southern Spain, and Russia, all places where the state seemed wholly insensitive to the plight of its poorer citizens. Its emergence in Russia came in response to the czarist state's refusal to institute reforms (see Chapter 19). Young men, not surprisingly, formed its shock troops. Between 1881 and 1914, anarchists killed six heads of states, including Czar Alexander II of Russia, King Umberto I of Italy (1900), and King George of Greece (1913). Anarchists were famous for throwing bombs—but as they had no positive solutions to the ever-more pressing social question, they never attracted mass backing but remained a dangerous, fringe element.

Moderate and Conservative Mass Parties

The anarchists and socialists of the Second International may have rejected revisionism, but plenty of other political parties were eager to welcome more moderate voters. Many newly enfranchised voters became strong backers of what was known as municipal socialism, the move to tax more heavily in order to make large investments in metro systems, water supply, electric lighting, and similar projects that would benefit *all* the cities' residents, not just the inhabitants of the wealthier suburbs. This movement would increase city budgets enormously and give much new clout and patronage to city leaders such as the extremely popular mayor of Vienna, Karl Lueger, first elected in 1895.

Lueger's party called itself the Christian Socialist Party and gained support from small shopkeepers and service-sector workers as well as from the nonrevolutionary working classes. Lueger was no old-fashioned liberal politician, but a charismatic populist who rallied support by agreeing with the socialists that capitalism needed to be tempered. The way to do this, he argued, was not through revolution, but by taxing businesses and providing services to the little people. Like many other right-wing parties of the day, Lueger's Christian Socialists also played the anti-Semitic card, making the Jews the scapegoats for a supposed decline of morals in urban areas and for the economic hardships faced by lower-class Germans in modern society.

In heavily Catholic areas, **Christian socialism** took off after Pope Leo XIII (r. 1878–1903) issued his 1891 encyclical, *Rerum Novarum* (*Of New Things*) in 1891. In it, Leo insisted that "some opportune remedy must be found quickly for the misery and wretchedness pressing so unjustly on the majority of the working class." His fear was that the capitalism of the late nineteenth century was causing terrible suffering, unceasing conflict between workers and employers, and moral degradation. Even more frightening to the pontiff were the communists'

DATE	EVENT
1848	The *Communist Manifesto* is published
1864	International Working Men's Organization founded by Marx and Engels (First International)
1878	Bismarck bans Socialist Party in Germany (ban lifted in 1890)
1889	Second International Working Men's Organization founded
1900	British Labor Party founded
1902	Lenin publishes "What Is to Be Done?"
1905	Mass strikes after "Bloody Sunday" in Russia
1912	German Socialists become the largest party in the Reichstag

CHRONOLOGY Socialist Milestones

solutions: the abolition of all private property, the destruction of paternal authority, and the dissolution of the churches. Other means needed to be found to improve the lot of the lower classes before, in despair, they joined the atheistic socialists. The pope did not mean to provoke the founding of multiple Christian socialist parties in Belgium, France, Italy, and Germany as well as Austria, but these movements clearly showed the widespread desire for a nonrevolutionary, popular alternative to old-fashioned liberalism.

Some of the Christian socialist parties held conservative views on moral and religious issues such as the secularization of schools or the rights of women. They often appealed to rural voters, small shopkeepers, and artisans by denouncing the big, mass production industries that threatened their livelihoods. They often boasted of their patriotism, contrasting their national pride to the socialists' commitment to international brotherhood. Christian socialist parties, as well as mass parties emerging farther to the right, also often adopted anti-immigrant or anti-Semitic platforms.

These measures, too, reflected the right-wing parties' attempts to attract newly enfranchised supporters to their ranks. The British Conservative Party reached out beyond its traditional aristocratic base by pursuing a harder line against Irish home rule and against socialism. Britain's colonies became a point of national pride, and building up the navy to keep the Germans down and their own empire pacified constituted a major part of party propaganda. Even conservatism, long the ideology of the aristocracy, was becoming a mass movement.

The Russian Revolution of 1905

Despite all this political ferment, the only major revolution before the First World War occurred in the most illiberal of nations, imperial Russia. It came on quite suddenly and was provoked not by socialists or communists, but by the czarist state's broken promises and humiliating performance in a war against a supposedly less civilized, "oriental" power, Japan.

In December 1904, overworked and angry about the czarist state's performance in the Russo-Japanese War, laborers at the Putilov armaments factory in St. Petersburg went on strike. Soon workers all over the capital city joined them, shutting down electricity and transportation systems. Hoping to undermine revolutionaries' attempts to spread radicalism among the workers, the secret police encouraged a Russian Orthodox priest, Father Gapon, to meet with the workers. Father Gapon listened to the workers' grievances and together they drew up a petition requesting the creation of a democratically elected representative assembly for Russia, the passage of legislation limiting the working day to eight hours, and the setting of a minimum daily wage. On January 22, 1905, a group of some 200,000 men, women, and children assembled before the czar's Winter Palace, hoping their sovereign would recognize their sufferings and accept their petition. Regrettably,

the czar was not home, and the guards panicked. They fired into the crowd, killing or wounding as many as a thousand people. The news spread quickly, unleashing a wave of rioting. Father Gapon denounced the czar and fled abroad; the time for peaceful protests was over.

In the wake of "Bloody Sunday," liberals demanded more civil rights and a representative assembly. Radicals demanded a broader sharing of power and wealth. In St. Petersburg and Moscow, the radicals formed **soviets,** or elected councils within factories, to serve as the basis for a new kind of municipal government. The czar offered only token reforms—one of which, remarkably, was to call an Estates General, just as France's Louis XVI had done in 1789. The soviets declared a general strike, shutting down banks, railroads, newspapers, and businesses. In October, unable to govern, Czar Nicholas II was forced to offer some concessions, including the forming of the first Russian national parliament, the Duma.

But many Russians, especially the radicals, remained deeply unsatisfied. There had been no land reforms, no eight-hour day or minimum-wage legislation. In the provinces, peasant protests continued. Tired of waiting for land reform that never came, peasants burned manor houses and attacked landowners and state officials, causing the rural elite to beg the czar to restore order. Nicholas did his best, using the army, now finally back from the war with Japan, and putting much of rural Russia under martial law. Yet, as late as 1908, nearly two thousand officials were reported killed and another two thousand wounded in rural Russia. If the distribution of shares of power and wealth to all of the nation's producers was agonizingly slow elsewhere in Europe, in the Russian Empire, improvement was almost imperceptible—and its inhabitants were increasingly unwilling to wait.

Civil Strife Intensifies

Russia's 1905 revolution was perhaps the most dramatic moment of civil strife in Europe before 1914, but it was by no means the only one. Paris, as we have seen, experienced a bloodbath in the wake of the Franco-Prussian War. In Spain, during the so-called Tragic Week of Barcelona in July 1909, violence exploded as the masses seized the city, destroying twenty-two churches and thirty-four convents. Military forces suppressed the uprising with brutality, and numerous opponents of the government were executed. Anarchist and extreme nationalist groups planned, and sometimes pulled off, assassinations of political leaders. There were no wars between the great powers, but colonial violence intensified, and a series of smaller regional conflicts, including the Boer Wars, the Russo-Japanese War, and the Balkan Wars, destabilized individual states on the margins.

To complete our picture of rising domestic and international conflict and aggression, we must add a military arms race, and the uncertainty and ambitions generated by the declining power of the two great multinational states on Europe's eastern peripheries, the Ottoman and

1904–1905: The Russo-Japanese War

In 1904, few Europeans knew anything at all about Japan. Only a handful realized that it had become an industrial nation, one with modern universities and bureaucracies and a formidable army and navy. Even those who knew these things failed to understand how much the Japanese resented the Russian seizure of the warm-water port of Port Arthur, which they believed was rightfully theirs. Japanese anger surged when the Russians positioned themselves to seize Manchuria and Korea as the Chinese Empire fell into decay. They responded by attacking Port Arthur in February 1904.

The war that followed was a terrible shock to the Russians. The Imperial Japanese Navy bottled up the Russian fleet and began to destroy it. Then the Japanese landed ground troops, which occupied Korea and began to march on Manchuria. The Russians had few soldiers stationed in the Far East and had to bring reinforcements from the western part of their empire, thousands of miles away. As the Trans-Siberian Railway was still incomplete, this process was very slow indeed. Port Arthur on the Pacific coast fell to the Japanese in January 1905, and in February the Japanese army forced Russian soldiers to retreat from the strategically important city of Mukden. The Japanese won the final naval battles, and in May 1905 the Russians, now engulfed in revolution at home, sued for peace.

Japan's victory made not only the Russians, but all Europeans, realize that non-European nations could also modernize and industrialize. Europeans had to confront their belief that Asia was a place where social and economic change could not happen, and explain how it was that a people they described as "oriental" and categorized as decadent or backward were able to win a war against a "white" power. Not everyone agreed on what East Asian modernity would look like, but quite suddenly it seemed that Japan was the place to look for it. Japanese lacquer surged into vogue, and every newspaper wanted a story about Buddhism. Meanwhile, fearful racists in the United States lobbied for discriminatory legislation and the preemptive seizing of Pacific bases. East Asia, wrote the German doctor and ethnographer Erwin Baelz in August 1905, had appeared upon the world stage: "What happens in the Far East will not henceforward have an exclusively local interest, but will necessarily concern us in Europe as well. People here hardly realize the significance of this as yet, but they will learn it as time goes on."[5]

Baelz was quite right, but for reasons he probably did not contemplate. Another audience was observing Japan's victories: anticolonial intellectuals in the nonwestern world. For Indian, Persian, and Indonesian nationalists, Japan's victory suggested that western domination was not eternal and that Europe's own weapons could be turned against it. The first social scientist in Ethiopia encouraged his countrymen to follow Japan's model of modernization, and newborn babies in India were named after Japanese admirals. In 1904, modernity seemed to be the property of Europe and America alone, but one year later, there was another, nonwestern, way forward.

QUESTION | *Why were Europeans so shocked by the outcome of the Russo-Japanese War?*

The Russo-Japanese War This Japanese image celebrates the destruction of the bridge at Pulantien, Manchuria, by Japanese soldiers in 1904.

the Austro-Hungarian Empires. Politically, fin de siècle Europe resembled a pressure cooker. The only questions were where and when the pot would blow.

Racism, Hyper-nationalism, and the Collapse of Old Empires

In various ways, each of Europe's states and multinational empires struggled to deal with impatient new citizens and volatile economic circumstances. To rally newly

In what ways was late-nineteenth-century nationalism different from the nationalism of the pre-1848 era?

enfranchised voters, many politicians employed a new, more populist, and more conservative form of patriotism in which race increasingly played a role. The new nationalists defined their states and their interests *against* rather than *together with* other nation-states. They aspired to live in a world in which power was not balanced; rather, they wanted to *win* a continent-wide, or even a global, Darwinian struggle for existence.

In this era, new political alliances were born with the probability of a great European conflict in sight. At several points along the way, war was only narrowly averted. Many of these war crises involved quarrels over colonial territories among the countries that now called themselves the great powers (Germany, France, Great Britain, Austria-Hungary, and Russia). In 1905, for example, the German kaiser provoked a crisis by pronouncing himself in favor of independence for Morocco, a position selected to vex Britain and France, the colonial powers in the region. There were also bitter rivalries over territory in Europe itself. French propaganda called for revenge for the loss of the provinces of Alsace and Lorraine, which the French had forfeited to the Germans after the Franco-Prussian War. All these competitions and animosities led to a massive arms race between the nations, as the British built intimidating warships called dreadnoughts and the Germans trained millions of volunteers to follow the orders of Kaiser Wilhelm II (r. 1888–1918), whatever the cost—to civilians, the state treasury, or their bodies and souls.

In each of these nations, the problems of containing the new mobility and technology and of dealing with diversity and clashing interests recurred. Looking back on the period from later in the twentieth century, it seemed a golden age, one in which world war *was* averted and commerce between nations continued, on the whole, amicably. Yet disturbing processes were under way, and considerable tension and violence existed both within nations and in the colonial theaters. The fin de siècle's combination of new technology, mass mobilization, and intensified economic and imperial competitions set in motion deadly new dynamics, including the hardening of racial categories and enmities, especially the rise of anti-Semitism

throughout Europe as a mass, politicized movement. The same combination of factors also worked its destructive magic on Europe's multinational empires, Russia, Austria-Hungary, and above all, the Ottoman Empire.

The New Anti-Semitism

A religiously founded dislike of Jews was nothing new in Christian Europe in 1880. But what was new after 1880 was the conversion of older campaigns against Jews as religious enemies into attacks on Jews as racial and political enemies, people who simply by virtue of their biological heritage posed a threat to the majority population or the state. Anti-Semitism was one particularly virulent expression of a new sort of racist thinking. Increasingly, Jews were identified not by their practice of a different religion, but for their supposed ethnic characteristics. The infamous "Jewish nose" was made an indicator of one's belonging to the Semitic "race"—and even those practicing Christians with Jewish grandparents, like Sarah Bernhardt, were slandered ceaselessly on account of their Jewish "blood."

The sources of this new anti-Semitism lie not only in racial biology, but also in the economic instability of the fin de siècle, and European reaction to the westward migration of hundreds of thousands of eastern or Ashkenazi Jews, seeking to escape Russian **pogroms** (Map 21.2). Unlike western European Jews, many of whom had assimilated into local cultures, these eastern Jews often adhered to orthodox practices, wore the traditional long caftan or curled sideburns, and spoke Yiddish or Russian rather than German or Czech. Most were quite poor and tended to live together in dilapidated cheap housing in big cities. Their unusual appearance, traditional practices, and poverty made these Jews, in particular, the targets of claims that they were taking all the jobs, planning secret conspiracies against Christians, or even seeking to undermine the health and prosperity of the host population.

Jews had long been associated with exploitative capitalism, rationalism, and internationalism, and this made them especially vulnerable in an era in which liberalism was under siege and new forms of virulent nationalism were taking hold. The 1890s and 1900s also saw an upsurge in archaic forms of anti-Semitism, as a number of Jews were accused of ritually murdering Christian children and drinking their blood. Pogroms continued, especially in western Russia. Villages were burned and their inhabitants terrorized, but modern mechanisms were now used to further the cause. Mass political parties, such as the Polish National Democrats, used anti-Semitism to rally support from those who were seeking scapegoats for the economy's failings. Mass-circulated newspapers, such as Édouard Drumont's *La Libre Parole* (*The Free Word*), founded in 1892, devoted themselves to denouncing Jews. Publishers eagerly printed, in inexpensive editions, horrible anti-Semitic tracts, such as *The Protocols of the Elders of Zion*. The *Protocols*, which pretended to be the secret plans of the Jews to take over the world, was a crude forgery created by Russian anti-Semites about 1905, but it would become the foundation for long-lasting suspicion and hatred of the Jews throughout the western world.

THE DREYFUS AFFAIR.

Anti-Semitism was particularly widespread and violent in central and eastern Europe, where most of Europe's Jews resided. But other countries were not immune. Indeed, the most widely publicized and politically important case of Jewish persecution occurred in liberal France. There, the widest ranging public debate about the possibility for full assimilation of the Jews occurred. In the wake of the debate, one particularly important Jewish leader, Theodor Herzl (1860–1904), despaired of the future of the Jews in Europe and founded yet another mass movement: Zionism.

The debate in France was provoked by a treason trial. In 1894, Alfred Dreyfus (1859–1935), a Jewish captain in the French military and an Alsatian Jew, was accused by conservative officers of selling secrets to Germany. Dreyfus was convicted on scanty evidence, court-martialed, and sent to prison for life. Drumont's newspaper *La Libre Parole* was exultant, as were many royalists and right-wing members of the Catholic Church and the army—groups who generally disliked Jews and felt threatened by the growing number of radicals in the government. Their opponents, French left-liberals and left-wing intellectuals such as Émile Zola and Sarah Bernhardt, were impressed by Dreyfus's insistence on his innocence and pushed for a new investigation. In 1896, the chief of counterintelligence uncovered evidence pointing to the guilt of a deeply indebted aristocrat and showed that the documents used to convict Dreyfus were forgeries. The aristocrat was tried, but now that the honor of the military and judiciary was at stake, the two groups rallied forces and acquitted him, and it was the chief of counterintelligence who went to jail.

This series of events provoked a blizzard of denunciations from the liberal press, the most famous of which was

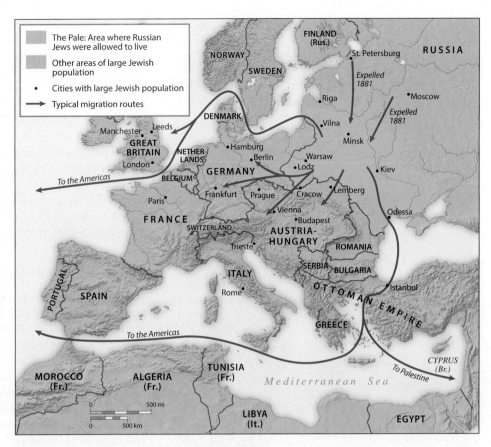

MAP 21.2 | Jewish Emigration, 1870–1914

This map shows the Pale of Settlement and other areas with a large Jewish population before 1914. Arrows indicate the direction of emigration from these areas, especially after the Russians unleashed a series of pogroms starting in 1881—though most Jews did not leave their home countries. The greater numbers and common language (Yiddish) as well as religious practices of the Jews of the Pale meant that community-building here had been much more extensive, and assimilation less prevalent than was the case among Jews in western European countries. Eastern Jews also tended to be poorer than western Jews, and to retain their older styles of dress. *Imagine the eastern Jews' reaction to a place like modern Paris or Vienna—how might they have felt in these new settings? How might urban Parisians or Viennese citizens have reacted to them?*

Zola's attack on the establishment, "*J'accuse*" ("I accuse"), published January 13, 1898, in Georges Clemenceau's newspaper *L'Aurore*. The edition sold its entire print-run of 300,000 copies in a matter of hours, and French readers were treated to a rhetorical tour de force in which Zola accused leading military and judicial officials of forgery, lying, and perverting the course of justice. It was a frontal assault on France's right-wing establishment, and it landed Zola in prison for libel.

The republicans rallied, and in the May 1898 elections, voters swept a radical majority into parliament, and a new official inquiry showed more documents to be forgeries. Right-wing anti-Dreyfusards denounced the Jews for trying to destroy the Republic. In response, the left organized rallies on Dreyfus's behalf. Newspapers around the world broadcast details of the "Affair." Prayers were said for Dreyfus in Jerusalem, and one rally in London's Hyde Park drew 50,000 demonstrators. After 1900, the Affair faded from public consciousness, driven off the front pages by

ERVL2927502   "Edouard Drumont – la France Juive ". Engraving by Godefroy Vintraut. Paris, musée Carnavalet. © Musée Carnavalet / Roger-Viollet / The
Image Works   NOTE: The copyright notice must include "The Image Works" DO NOT SHORTEN THE NAME OF THE COMPANY   Prior permission
required for all advertising & promotional use or use on consumer goods & derivative products.

Anti-Semitism in the French Press This cover of Édouard
Drumont's book *Jewish France* (1886) depicts a Christian crusader
striking down "Jewish France," caricatured as a modern Moses who
wears a German-style helmet and carries a bag of gold coins.

the Boer Wars, the Boxer Rebellion, and the Russo-Japanese
War. Dreyfus's full acquittal in 1906 came as something of
a quiet denouement. But the Dreyfus Affair exposed the
fault lines not only in France but throughout Europe, and
many assimilated Jews realized just how many of their fellow citizens still hated and feared them.

THE ORIGINS OF ZIONISM. Galvanized into action
by this realization was Theodor Herzl, an Austrian Jew
born in Budapest. Sent to Paris as a journalist to cover
the Affair, Herzl was shocked by the level of animosity
expressed by the anti-Dreyfusards and discouraged by
the lack of concern expressed by the liberals. Without
their own nation-state to push for their rights, Herzl
concluded, Jews were destined to be persecuted forever.
In 1896, Herzl published *The Jewish State,* a pamphlet in
which he argued that the Jews would not be safe unless
and until they obtained a nation-state of their own. Herzl
was not a religiously active Jew, and at the time of this
pamphlet, he thought the new state might be set up in
present-day Kenya or Cyprus. But a small movement of

more religiously oriented Jews was already under way
and called on Jews to return to Palestine. Soon Herzl
was convinced that **Zionism,** the return to the biblical Zion, was the only viable option. Though his efforts
to convince the Ottoman sultan to give Palestine to the
Jews were in vain, Russian Jews, in particular, began to
settle there. Between 1904 and 1914, some 40,000 mostly
eastern Jews settled in Palestine. This number, however,
amounted to only a fraction of the Jews who left eastern
Europe before the First World War—far more went to the
Americas, and in 1914, Jews constituted only about 8 percent of the population of Palestine. Although Zionism
was invented at the fin de siècle, it would take many
more decades for Herzl's successors to realize his vision.

The New Ways of War

Although there were no major conflicts among the great
powers between 1871 and 1914, there were numerous war
scares, and many discussions, in newspapers as well as
in secret meetings, about the big European conflict that
virtually everyone believed would eventually break
out. Competition over power on the continent and over
colonies abroad led the powers to worry more and more
about the size of their land armies and the sophistication
of their navies. Improvements in steel manufacturing
and in ballistics made possible the mass production of armaments, and technological innovations increased their
firepower and accuracy. From the 1890s on, Europe was
engaged in a fierce arms race. The French were first to develop a quick-firing 75-millimeter artillery piece that remained stationary after firing, which meant that the gun
did not need to be aimed before firing again. Developed
in 1896, France's new gun could also deliver shells accurately from a distance of seven kilometers (putting the
guns beyond the enemy's sight), and fire up to twenty
rounds a minute, four times the old rate of delivery.
Others immediately tried to imitate the technology, and
by 1905 all the great powers were investing considerable
time, energy, and money in producing their own quick-
firing artillery.

Enormous sums, indeed, were spent readying Europe
for wars—both the colonial wars they continued to fight
and the grand-scale continental war that planners predicted. Military budgets expanded, particularly after the
century's turn, as tensions over the Balkans mounted.
Nearly doubling their expenditures between 1904 and
1913, the Russians, on the war's eve, were spending about
$330 million on their army—a huge sum for a nation in
which impoverished peasants still formed a large majority. Germany, the fastest growing power of the period
and the one with the grandest aspirations, was spending $394 million, up from a mere $154 million in 1904. By
this time, the Russians could boast of a standing army
of 1.3 million; the German army reached 782,000 men.[6]
Under Kaiser Wilhelm II, a ruler eager to assert his nation's right to establish a great colonial empire (despite
having started after almost all of Asia and Africa had

been carved up), the Germans also engaged in a naval arms race with the British. The two sought to build larger and larger steel battleships, though the Germans never came close to rivaling Britain's dominance at sea. Though socialists in both countries complained about the enormous expenditures, and worried about the prospect of European workers being thrown into battle against one another—rather than against their common capitalist enemies—the build-up only intensified as time went on. No nation felt it could rest. Falling behind the others might well mean national defeat and disaster.

But, in yet another way, the fin de siècle also showed itself to be an era of contradictions. Though nations were planning for bigger conflicts, in a series of international agreements signed between 1864 and 1914, they also pledged themselves to the conduct of more civilized wars. In 1864, the Geneva Convention promised the humane treatment of prisoners. The Hague Convention on Land Warfare (1899) further committed signers of the document to refrain from using weapons such as poison gas and dumdum bullets that might injure civilian bystanders and from forcing civilians to serve as spies, hostages, or guides. Collective retribution against civilians was also forbidden. Although atrocities continued to be committed in the course of colonial warfare, a considerable number of Europeans publicly decried the cruel treatment of South Africans during the Boer Wars and the near genocide of the Herero people of German Southwest Africa. Again, grand aspirations—the "civilizing" of warfare—existed side by side with spiraling fears, in this case, fears of national annihilation.

The New Nationalism and the Old Empires

In the building of mass armies and the rising fears of national annihilation, we begin to see the emergence of a new kind of nationalism, one that is no longer of the liberal, reformist sort. Whereas liberal nationalists opposed the feudal economies and social privileges of the old regimes and at least in theory believed that all nations could live in harmony with one another, the new nationalists tended to be adversarial, contrasting their nation's needs and ambitions with those of others and rallying their people against foreigners or newcomers. Increasingly, one's membership in the nation was established not by residency or religion, but by one's first language or ethnicity, and national identity was reinforced by public school lessons, national holidays, and the popular press.

The new nationalists were well aware that Europe's map, especially in the east, was malleable, especially as nationality disputes and slow economic growth crippled the Ottoman and Austrian Empires. Rather than wanting to unite territories, as did the Italian and German nationalists of the 1850s and 1860s, the nationalists of the 1880s and 1890s wanted to break up old states in order to get their own. These activists—whose ranks included Czechs, Ukrainians, Serbs, and Poles in Austria-Hungary;

Arabs, Persians, and Greeks in the Ottoman Empire; and the Irish in the British Isles—resemble in many ways the anticolonial activists at work in the British, French, Dutch, and German Empires. Like their colleagues abroad, they had tired of waiting for the regimes above them to share power and were impatient for the opportunity to define their own modern destinies.

AUSTRIA-HUNGARY'S LAST DAYS. The Austro-Prussian and Franco-Prussian wars had a powerful effect on the territories known as the German Confederation. Bismarck's efforts had yielded a unified German Empire, but they had also allowed Hungarians in the Habsburg lands to achieve virtual self-rule within the newly christened Austro-Hungarian Empire (1867). Ceding so much autonomy to the Hungarians was important because it set up a whole series of other challenges to German-Habsburg overlordship. Austria-Hungary, populated by many different ethnic and religious groups, including Germans, Hungarians, Czechs, Poles, Ukrainians, Ruthenes, Jews, Croats, Serbs, and Italians, would find it difficult to contain the centripetal forces of nationalism as the century wore on (Map 21.3).

Emperor Franz Josef (r. 1848–1916) had signed a relatively liberal constitution in 1867 and did try to abide by it. Hoping to keep the empire together, he tried to balance the power of the different ethnic groups, though the Germans retained the upper hand. For example, Franz Josef made concessions to Czech nationalists, including the stipulation that public schools in heavily Czech areas such as Bohemia should offer instruction in Czech as well as German. Other groups, such as the Poles, Croatians, and Ukrainians, made similar demands, and in many areas, including the armed forces, the empire did function as a multilingual state. But Czech, Polish, Ukrainian, and Southern Slav resentment toward the German population was not only linguistic, but also socioeconomic. Whereas by 1904 only a third of German Austrians were employed in agriculture, half the Czechs, two-thirds of Poles, and over 90 percent of the Slavic-speaking Ruthenes still lived essentially peasant lifestyles. Germans dominated factory and handicraft industries and trade, as well as the civil service and white-collar jobs.

By the end of the nineteenth century, nationalists in all these regions had begun vigorous, and sometimes violent, campaigns to create their own autonomous states. There were fistfights between German and Czech delegates in the Austrian parliament. The Polish nationalist movement took a sharp turn away from liberal nationalism, adopting violence and hatred as weapons in their struggle for independence. As a leader of this movement wrote in 1902: "Patriotism based on love for one's own nation . . . is a patriotism good for that unrealized golden age when all social and national antagonisms will disappear. But such patriotism is ever more foreign to our civilized world. . . . Today's patriotism is associated with national antagonism."[7] At the same time, Slavic nationalists and their advocates in the Russian Empire began to insist on the commonalities all Slavs shared and to seek pan-Slavic alliances across national boundaries. They were answered, inevitably, by the formation of a Pan-German League, dedicated to promoting the interests of ethnic Germans, whether they resided in Germany, Austria-Hungary, Russia, or any other state. Nobody wanted to be a minority ethnic group anymore—nor, ominously, did the new nationalists plan to incorporate minorities into the future states they were dreaming up. The era of the multinational empire was coming to its end.

Pan-German and pan-Slavic movements were the most consequential for the Austrians and for Europe as a whole, but other pan-movements began in this era as well. One might call Zionism a pan-movement for Jews; a pan-African movement had begun to rally Africans of all nationalities to unite. A pan-

MAP 21.3 | Language Groups of the Austro-Hungarian Empire, c. 1914
A variety of language groups resided in the Austro-Hungarian Empire on the eve of the First World War. *Could the Austro-Hungarian Empire have been divided neatly into single-language nation-states? Which nationality groups were able to seek support from states on the borders of the empire?*

Asian movement was also beginning to take shape. The Ottoman sultan was a major supporter of an embryonic pan-Islamic movement—just as the Russian czar encouraged pan-Slavism. None of these movements were particularly well organized, and most historians do not think they were particularly influential—with the exception of pan-Germanism, which appealed powerfully to some young hotheads, such as Adolf Hitler. But what these movements suggest is that groups were beginning to think of themselves in grand racial terms, beyond the boundaries of the nations, and to look forward to a day when the old hierarchical and heterogeneous empires would crumble, and new, purer and more populist, ones would appear.

OTTOMAN APOCALYPSE. In southeastern Europe, new nationalist programs even more successfully ate away at the territory and power of a failing multinational empire, that of the Ottoman Turks. After the Russo-Turkish War, the Serbs, like the Bulgarians and Romanians, had obtained full independence from the Ottoman Empire. In 1882, Serbia replaced its princes with a monarch, Peter I. But the Kingdom of Serbia thought its borders too small. The Serbs lacked an outlet to the sea and many Serbs had been stranded in Bosnia, where they chafed under Austro-Hungarian rule. They saw the receding power of the Ottomans as an opportunity for

expansion (Map 21.4). The French and British regarded the Eastern Question as one in which they were entitled to meddle, for they did not want to see an Ottoman collapse result in Russian gains, or in Ottoman failure to pay back loans (see Chapter 19). Joined by the Russians, Austrians, and Germans, they also took advantage of the Ottoman Empire's weakness to send missionaries and men of commerce to the eastern Mediterranean, hoping to establish spheres of influence even in areas where they did not carve out colonial states, such as Egypt (under British control) or Tunisia (under French dominance).

Alarmed and angered by these events, some Ottoman Turks turned their resentment on the Christian minorities in their midst and began to see Greeks and Armenians as traitors, who would use Christian, European support to further erode the power and prestige of the traditional Turkish ruling class. In 1895, after a group of Armenians marched in Istanbul in favor of reforms, the city's residents turned on a population they believed should remain subordinate. In this incident and in several subsequent massacres, between 100,000 and 300,000 Armenians died. Another massacre occurred in 1909, in Adana in central Anatolia.

By this time, the Turks had developed a nationalist movement of their own. Turkish nationalism was born partly as a defense of Ottoman power and partly as a critique of the corrupt, indebted, and insufficiently

MAP 21.4 | Ottoman Territorial Losses, 1800–1914

This map illustrates the territorial losses experienced by the Ottoman Empire over the course of the nineteenth and early twentieth centuries.
Were critics of the empire correct in describing the Ottoman Empire as "the sick man of Europe"? Why or why not?

modernized sultanate. Most supporters of Turkish nationalism were not religiously motivated Muslims, but men who looked to secular, western states as models of proper development. Many of the leaders of the movement were army officers, who were eager to start winning, rather than losing, wars.

In 1908, the so-called Young Turks overthrew the sultan's government. Although the sultan was allowed to retain his title, running the state was entrusted to a secularizing, ethnically Turkish military elite. The Young Turks had little time to modernize before a series of new wars broke out. In 1911, the Italians seized the Ottoman provinces in northern Africa that now make up Libya, as well as the island of Rhodes. Then, in the first Balkan War (1912–1913), the Serbs, Bulgarians, and Greeks banded together to form the Balkan League and attacked the Turks.

The Balkan Wars The Balkan Wars proved to be the largest military engagements in Europe since the Franco-Prussian War. Here, two Turkish soldiers retreat after the Bulgarian victory over Ottoman forces in the Battle of Lüleburgaz in October–November 1912.

The Balkan League triumphed, but the victors fell out over who was to have the choice spoils of Albania and Macedonia. In 1913, the Bulgarians went to war with the Greeks and Serbs. In this second Balkan War, the Ottomans came in on the winning Serbo-Greek side and managed to reclaim the city of Adrianople (now Edirne) as well as part of Thrace.

The ethnic conflicts in the southeast and the Balkan Wars were in some ways continuous with previous developments. Just as French partisans had conducted a form of guerrilla warfare against the Prussian army in France in 1870–1871, so too in the Balkans did civilians and irregular militias operate outside the bounds of regular military conduct. There were harsh reprisals against civilians, and large sectors of the minority population were terrorized and compelled to leave their homes. The treatment of Muslims by the Greeks and Bulgarians, and even more powerfully the Italian attack on northern Africa, rallied Muslims to the cause of the Ottoman Empire, even as that empire was fragmenting. Radical nationalists, like the young Bosnian Serb Gavrilo Princip, volunteered to give their lives to help throw off the Austrian overlords. Elsewhere, radical German, French, and Italian nationalists were also calling for the expulsion of foreigners and the enlargement of their own states.

Conclusion

The roughly three decades that form the fin de siècle were years of extremely rapid change in Europe. Those changes—economic, political, and cultural—produced an enormously dynamic and diverse society, but also provoked heightened anxieties. New groups—workers, women, and minority ethnic groups—found it possible to participate in political and cultural life, although the wealthy and in some places the old nobility still held considerable power. Both political and economic liberalism came under fire as the masses tired of waiting for reform or for autonomous statehood. Some sought solutions in socialism—or in racist hyper-nationalism. There were, of course, moderate voices, those who tried to use diplomacy, reform, and reason to temper rising passions. But as the fin de siècle faded, these voices were hard to hear over the din of clanging machines, competing charismatic leaders, and sensation-seeking journalists. It was an exhilarating and terrifying age of tensions and transformations—but it would seem tame and placid for those Europeans who lived to see July 28, 1914, dawn.

Critical Thinking Questions

1. Why did the social question seem even more urgent than ever at the fin de siècle?

2. Why was liberalism losing its appeal in this era? What parties or causes were attracting new support?

3. What made so many people feel that they had suddenly been thrust into a modern age?

Key Terms

fin de siècle **(p. 667)**

suffragette **(p. 673)**

avant-garde **(p. 674)**

modernism **(p. 675)**

art nouveau **(p. 675)**

symbolism **(p. 675)**

anomie **(p. 678)**

cartel **(p. 679)**

second industrial revolution **(p. 680)**

revisionism (socialist) **(p. 685)**

anarchism **(p. 685)**

Christian socialism **(p. 685)**

soviets **(p. 686)**

pogrom **(p. 688)**

Zionism **(p. 690)**

Primary Sources in Connect

For information on Connect and the online resources available, go to **http://connect.mcgraw-hill.com**.

1. **Modern Pilgrims Flock to Visit Holy Relics**

2. **Vladimir Lenin Advocates the Formation of a Revolutionary Elite**

3. **On Village Hygiene (1902)**

4. **Sigmund Freud, *The Interpretation of Dreams***

5. **Émile Zola Accuses the French Government of Framing Alfred Dreyfus**

6. **Eduard Bernstein Endorses Democratic Socialism**

Gustave Le Bon, The Crowd

Gustave Le Bon (1841–1931) was a French liberal and a pioneer in the study of sociology and crowd psychology. His widely read study, *The Crowd,* appeared in 1896 and was read by Sigmund Freud, who found in it inspiration for examining the power of the unconscious. The book was also read by Benito Mussolini, Adolf Hitler, and Vladimir Lenin, men who would become the sort of leaders that Le Bon believed characteristic of the turn of the twentieth century. Le Bon, who also believed that racial characteristics determined national destinies, emphasizes the power of crowds to destroy liberal virtues such as individual rationality, willpower, and self-control. His leading example of the evils that attend the entry of the masses into politics is the era of Robespierre, the radical phase of the French Revolution.

Introduction: The Era of Crowds

Scarcely a century ago the traditional policy of European states and the rivalries of sovereigns were the principal factors that shaped events. The opinion of the masses scarcely counted, and most frequently indeed did not count at all. Today it is the traditions which used to obtain in politics, and the individual tendencies and rivalries of rulers which do not count; while, on the contrary, the voice of the masses has become preponderant. It is this voice that dictates their conduct to kings. . . . The destinies of nations are elaborated at present in the heart of the masses, and no longer in the councils of princes. . . .

Chapter 1: The General Characteristics of Crowds

Different causes determine the appearance of these characteristics peculiar to crowds, and not possessed by isolated individuals. The first is that the individual forming part of a crowd acquires, solely from numerical considerations, a sentiment of invincible power which allows him to yield to instincts which, had he been alone, he would perforce have kept under restraint. He will be the less disposed to check himself from the consideration that, a crowd being anonymous, and in consequence irresponsible, the sentiment of responsibility which always controls individuals disappears entirely. . . .

We see, then, that the disappearance of the conscious personality, the predominance of the unconscious personality, the turning by means of suggestion and contagion of feelings and ideas in an identical direction, the tendency to immediately transform the suggested ideas into acts; these, we see, are the principal characteristics of the individual forming part of a crowd. He is no longer himself, but has become an automaton who has ceased to be guided by his will.

Moreover, by the mere fact that he forms part of an organized crowd, a man descends several rungs in the ladder of civilization. Isolated, he may be a cultivated individual; in a crowd, he is a barbarian—that is, a creature acting by instinct. He possesses the spontaneity, the violence, the ferocity, and also the enthusiasm and heroism of primitive beings, whom he further tends to resemble by the facility with which he allows himself to be impressed by words and images . . . and to be induced to commit acts contrary to his most obvious interests and his best-known habits. An individual in a crowd is a grain of sand amid other grains of sand, which the wind stirs up at will.

Chapter 3: The Leaders of Crowds and their Means of Persuasion

A crowd is a servile flock that is incapable of ever doing without a master. The leader has most often started as one of the led. He has himself been hypnotized by the idea, whose apostle he has since become. It has taken possession of him to such a degree that everything outside it vanishes, and that every contrary opinion appears to him an error or a superstition. An example in point is Robespierre, hypnotized by the philosophical ideas of Rousseau, and employing the methods of the Inquisition to propagate them.

The leaders we speak of are more frequently men of action than thinkers. They are not gifted with keen foresight, nor could they be, as this quality generally conduces to doubt and inactivity. They are especially recruited from the ranks of those morbidly nervous, excitable, half-deranged persons who are bordering on madness. However absurd may be the idea they uphold or the goal they pursue, their convictions are so strong that all reasoning is lost upon them. Contempt and persecution do not affect them, or only serve to excite them the more. They sacrifice their personal interest, their family—everything. . . . The multitude is always ready to listen to the strong-willed man, who knows how to impose himself upon it. Men gathered in crowds lose all force of will, and turn instinctively to the person who possesses the quality they lack.

QUESTIONS | *How does Le Bon's work exemplify liberal fears about the coming of the age of mass politics? Would Le Bon's analysis describe the experience of the masses everywhere in Europe at the century's end? To which nations would it be most and least applicable?*

Source: Gustave Le Bon, *The Crowd: A Study of the Popular Mind,* 2nd ed. (Atlanta, Ga.: Cherokee Publishing, 1982), xv, 12–13, 113–114.

THE GREAT WAR

The Greatness of the Great War

What Caused the Great War?
Entangling Alliances
Imperial and Continental Tensions
Balkan Uncertainty

The War Breaks Out
What Did Total War Mean?
Fighting a Total War
Theaters of War

The New Technology and the Old
The New
. . . And the Old

**Enabling the Fight:
The Home Front**
A Woman's War
Command Economies

The Russian Revolution
Origins of the Revolution
The February Revolution
The Bolsheviks Take Power
The October Revolution
The Bolsheviks Make Peace

How the War Ended
The End, at Last
The Spanish Flu

The Peace
The Victors
The Losers
Of Greeks and Turks

Conclusion

GAVRILO PRINCIP, TERRORIST Gavrilo Princip (1894–1918) despised liberalism and what he saw as the semicolonial oppression of his native province, Bosnia-Herzegovina, by the German-dominated Austro-Hungarian Empire. A Bosnian of Serbian ethnicity, Princip and his schoolmates hated living in a multiethnic empire, one in which, despite liberal and reformist promises, the Germans seemed determined to make all the decisions and to hold on to all the power and wealth. Primarily peasants, the South Slavs, Princip claimed, were kept poor and treated like "cattle." The only way for his people to enjoy freedom and prosperity, he believed, was for them to break away from Austria-Hungary and establish their own nation-state. But Princip and his fellow pan-Slavs did not want to wait for a Cavour or a Bismarck to lead them. Instead, they spent their teenage years talking about committing heroic acts of violence. They so idolized Bogdan Zerajić, a twenty-four-year-old Serbian militant who had attempted to kill the governor of Bosnia-Herzegovina in 1910, that they took to tending his grave and repeating his motto, "Serbdom or death!" For these radicals, disgusted by high-handed Austrian attempts to "civilize" Bosnia, the time had come not only to remake Europe's map, but to kill the colonizing mapmakers.

Gavrilo Princip himself did not look like a man who would change the course of history. He was no Tocqueville, nor even a minor noble like

Otto Dix, *Flanders*

Napoleon. The few existing images of him show him dressed in the shabby coat and tie commonly worn by turn-of-the-century intellectuals. He frequented squalid cafés where angry young men read underground newspapers and revolutionary literature. Nineteen years old when he assassinated Austrian Archduke Franz Ferdinand and his wife, Sophia, on June 28, 1914, the Serbian citizen of Bosnia was pale and sickly, already suffering from the tuberculosis that would kill him a few years later. He had, in fact, been rejected by the Serbian government for service in the Balkan Wars because of his weak physical condition. But he had developed supreme confidence in his mission and willingness to go to extremes to make his mark on politics. After shooting the archduke and archduchess, he swallowed a cyanide pill (though he vomited it, nullifying its effects). He had intended to give his life for his cause. At his trial in October 1914, he declared, "I am not a criminal, because I destroyed that which was evil. I think that I am good."[1]

Princip's act of terrorism was not the first attempt by what we might call a colonized underling against one of Europe's multiethnic empires. Anarchists, revolutionaries, and radical nationalists had targeted many other leaders and had been themselves subjected to violence on the part of Europe's states. Princip's act proved to be the spark that set the Great War of 1914–1918 ablaze—for murdering the heir to the Austro-Hungarian throne was not something the Habsburgs, or their German allies, could countenance. But had Princip's bullets (like Zerajić's) failed to hit their target, surely some other incident would have sparked the war. What is telling about

Gavrilo Princip Arrested Having accomplished his mission of assassinating the archduke of Austria, the nineteen-year-old Gavrilo Princip was arrested by Serbian and Austrian police.

his life is that it was already, at such a young age, shaped by violent forms of mass nationalism and by the deep tensions between and within European nations at the fin de siècle. The war sparked by his act of terrorism would prove far longer and far more deadly than Princip or any of his contemporaries might have foreseen. But he was not alone in giving in to violent urges or in believing that mass warfare would give birth to peace and prosperity for all of those discontented with the failings of the liberal regimes and multinational empires. In this he would prove to be disastrously, tragically, mistaken.

Russian
Revolution
of 1905

European arms race
c. 1890–1914

Balkan Wars
1912–1913

| 1905 | 1906 | 1907 | 1908 | 1909 | 1910 | 1911 | 1912 | 19 |

At his trial, Princip divulged that he hadn't thought very far beyond the assassination. Somehow, he thought, his act would usher in the creation of a new Yugoslav state. And so it did: after more than four years of horrific warfare and at the cost of as many as 17 million civilian and military lives, 578,000 of them Serbian, the Austro-Hungarian Empire collapsed, and the southern Slavs got their own state of Yugoslavia. The assassin himself lived to see the war, but not the birth of the state for which he had risked his life. Though convicted of high treason, he, like the other four main conspirators, did not receive the death penalty because they were underage. Instead, Princip was interned in the Theresienstadt prison in Bohemia, where he died of tuberculosis in April 1918, sorry so many Serbs had suffered, but otherwise without remorse for his actions.

After the creation of an independent Yugoslavia in 1918, Sarajevo's historic Latin Bridge, where the young Serb had taken aim at the archduke, was renamed the Princip Bridge. But horrific wars in the 1990s destroyed what remained of southern Slav unity, and now the Latin Bridge has its old name back: the man who sparked the breakup of the Austro-Hungarian Empire is a hero no longer.

The Greatness of the Great War

Princip's terrorist act sparked a four-year global conflict. Participants in England called it the Great War. For the Germans, it was the *Weltkrieg*, or world war. What made the war great was its massive, unprecedented scale—for it involved many millions of men, women, and children, and its theaters of engagement ran from South Africa to Siberia, and from the waters around Australia to the Irish Sea. Military deaths alone totaled more than 9 million, most of them young men. Together with the Russian civil wars and the global influenza pandemic that spread on its heels, estimates of the death toll for the period 1914–1919 run as high as 50 million worldwide—and the war would leave at least another 21 million wounded men, as well as millions of widowed women and orphaned children, to suffer in its wake. This was truly *mass* warfare and *mass* death, the consequences, in some ways, of the rise of mass society, mass production, and hyper-nationalism traced in Chapter 21. To live this war meant to experience all these aspects of mass society at once. But it was surely the experience of mass death that made the most searing and enduring impression on the individuals who survived.

The advent of what would be described as the first total war had enormous sociopolitical and demographic consequences. The European nations called *everyone* to arms: men were to fight, women were to fill men's places in the workforce, and the elderly were to accept that food, medical assistance, transportation, and heating supplies would be shunted to the men at the front. Colonial subjects were also to fight or work to help their overlords win the war. Everyone was to sacrifice for the good of the state. But this mass mobilization also had important, ironic consequences, as all who answered the call felt they were owed recompense. Not only colonial subjects, but women and workers at home expected that their hard work would be recognized and their suffering redeemed. In some cases, the states did step in, providing special assistance to young mothers, pensions for war victims, or in some cases an expanded franchise. But when wartime and postwar governments were unwilling or unable to

What made the Great War "great"?

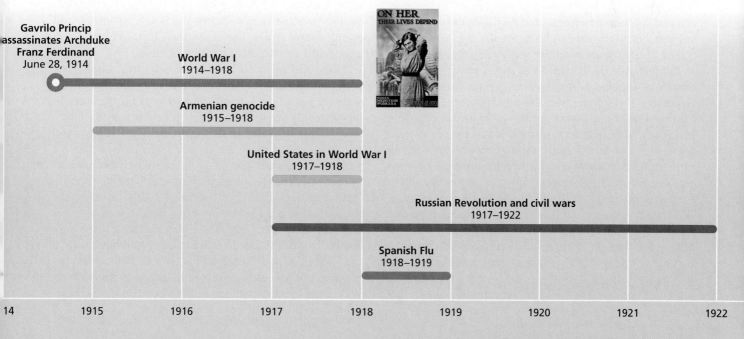

Gavrilo Princip assassinates Archduke Franz Ferdinand
June 28, 1914

World War I
1914–1918

Armenian genocide
1915–1918

United States in World War I
1917–1918

Russian Revolution and civil wars
1917–1922

Spanish Flu
1918–1919

ON HER THEIR LIVES DEPEND

14   1915   1916   1917   1918   1919   1920   1921   1922

offer what citizens considered sufficient compensation for their enormous sacrifices, everyone felt betrayed. The result was revolution, most notably in Russia, but elsewhere too, as authorities were discredited and bitterness, by 1918, was pervasive. Indeed, both the war and the interwar era that followed were marked by the states' more aggressive intervention into people's lives, in the hopes of taming the discontent created by mass mobilization and mass feelings of betrayal.

If the war was great in its scale and in its political consequences, it was also great in its far-reaching cultural consequences, not only for Europe and America, but also for the world as a whole. The brutality, duration, and enormous scope of the war undermined many Europeans' faith in progress—or in God—and made the return to lyric poetry, traditional Christianity, tonal music, and representational art seem artificial and empty. For many people, the war undermined the mantra of the imperial civilizing mission: that the superiority of European culture gave Europeans the right to rule others. The war also made activities previously considered sinful—swearing for men, drinking and smoking in public for women—more acceptable, but it also made Europeans less tolerant, especially of those seen as enemies of the nation. The carnage created by modern war machinery shocked many, but the war era also saw the intensified use of new forms of technology—such as radio and the airplane—whose nonmilitary cultural effects would be long lasting.

The Great War was also great in its diversity. It was not one war, but a combination of several kinds of war, fought over extremely varied terrain, and between combatants with different motivations, expectations, and tactics. In some places it was a trench war; elsewhere, a guerrilla war; and in still other places, it unleashed attempts at **ethnic cleansing.** In Russia it became both a revolutionary conflict and a civil war. Here we take the war's measure first by surveying its causes and then by examining the various fronts on which battles raged, moving from the best-known western front, to the eastern and southeastern fronts, and finally, to the crucial developments on the various home fronts.

For Europe, the Great War was surely *the* great event in modern history. It ended the lives of four enormous empires—Ottoman, Austro-Hungarian, Russian, and German—and accelerated the emergence of one neo-Europe, the United States, to the status of world power. Moreover, although each of the many Europes experienced the war in a slightly different way, virtually all of them found themselves thrown into the age of mass warfare, in which states were called on to mobilize their entire populations and individuals of all classes sacrificed themselves for the good of the nation. Europe and Europeans would never be the same. But the fact that both sides dragged their colonial empires into the conflict made this war perhaps *the* major event in *world* history as well. The way the war was fought—with terrible atrocities occurring not only on the continent, but in theaters on Europe's peripheries and beyond—and the com-

plicated and contested ways in which peace was made at the war's end both point to the global significance of the events of 1914–1918. For not only the basic Eurasian map we still live with but even the much more devastating Second World War that followed were in many ways outcomes of the Great War.

What Caused the Great War?

Great events need not always have equally great causes, but certainly the origins of the Great War are far deeper

> **What were the short-and long-term causes of the Great War?**

and more complicated than the story of Franz Ferdinand's assassination. Underlying the war was a very broad set of geopolitical, economic, and cultural clashes. Broadly speaking, they include a system of entangling alliances that obliged Europe's largest countries to come to the aid of their allies, long-standing but increasingly tense competition between nations over imperial holdings, and uncertainties about whether the balance of power could be maintained in light of the Ottoman Empire's weakening hold over the small and ethnically diverse states of the Balkans in an age of fierce nationalism.

Entangling Alliances

In the 1890s and 1900s, new competition between European states had led to the formation of a set of strategic alliances. The Germans and Austrians remained closely linked. A preliminary form of the Franco-Russian alliance was established in 1891 and finalized shortly thereafter. The Treaty of London (1839) bound the British to defend Belgium's neutrality, but no one was certain Britain would honor the treaty. The United States remained aloof, keeping watch over the two continents it considered its own backyard—North and South America—and eyeing events in the Pacific, as the Chinese Empire collapsed and a new power vacuum opened.

There had been no large-scale wars in Europe since 1815, but numerous smaller conflicts, imperial skirmishes, and war scares since the 1870s had kept European military officials busy. One of their most successful activities was the organizing of political pressure groups and the wringing of more tax dollars from parliaments for military expansion. The Germans, French, Russians, and British in particular engaged in an armaments race, resulting in the building of enormous battleships and the stockpiling of large numbers of new breech-loading rifles and quick-firing artillery. The Germans made plans for a war on two fronts, one in which they would have to fight the well-equipped French to the west as well as the numerous, but less industrialized Russians to the east. By 1914, the Germans were reaching (relatively speaking) peak strength, for the French army was still underfunded and ill trained, and the Russians had not yet fully recovered from the Russo-Japanese War and Revolution of 1905. After the assassination of the archduke, German emperor Wilhelm II agreed to support his ally in whatever measures it chose to take against the Serbs. German leaders hoped that Russia would not enter the war or at least that Britain would remain neutral. But if not, they were resigned to allow fate to take its course.

Imperial and Continental Tensions

As European nations exercised dominion over an ever-larger share of the earth's expanse, they increasingly came into conflict with one another and with the colonized peoples they sought to rule. Germany's late entrance into the race for colonies, on top of Emperor Wilhelm II's aggressive bluster, was especially important in destabilizing the balance of power between colonizers. But tensions had also arisen between the French and British in Africa and between the Dutch and French in Indonesia and Southeast Asia. The Russians and British were still engaged in disputes over territory in Central Asia. European nations' competition for colonies sowed mistrust even amongst allies. Once the war began, the colonies were mobilized and drawn into the war, intensifying the impact of this competition in various ways. But few Europeans would have been willing to fight a world war simply to gain more non-European territory. Colonial tensions were important, but were negotiated more easily than quarrels over territory and dominance on the continent of Europe itself.

Continental tensions were sharpest in eastern and southeastern Europe, ruled by the Ottoman and Austro-Hungarian Empires—both multiethnic and authoritarian states in which the radical nationalist movements and the beginnings of economic modernization had disrupted old patterns of rule. Both empires also had good reason to fear that the Russians, now industrializing quickly and eager to expand their influence farther west, might promote their demise or even seek to annex some of their territory.

As the leaders of these empires struggled to keep control, the other rising power, Germany, looked on with a mixture of anxiety and ambition. The Germans had recently established friendly relations with the Ottomans, whom they hoped would contain Russian expansionism. They did not want the Ottoman Empire to crumble, though they did hope to profit by being its friend. Nor could the Germans afford to let Austria-Hungary, its traditional continental ally, fall apart. By contrast, the Germans had many reasons to fear Russian industrialization and expansionism and to believe that weakening the Russians might be beneficial for a booming German economy and population. Before 1914, some ultra-nationalist Germans were already looking longingly at the breadbasket of the Ukraine and at sparsely settled western Russia. This struggle between the rising powers in eastern Europe, the Germans and the Russians, combined with the chaos created by the collapse of Austrian

Habsburg and Ottoman rule made the Balkans the powder keg that would set Europe ablaze.

Balkan Uncertainty

Over the course of the nineteenth and early twentieth centuries, bit by bit, the Ottomans had lost control over the Balkans. The Greeks, Serbs, Bulgarians, and Romanians had all established autonomous states, and the Austrians had annexed Bosnia. Following the Balkan Wars, the Ottomans lost even more territory—and an independent Albania had been created. But these outcomes satisfied none of the peoples involved. The Albanians hated their prince (and overthrew him in 1914); the Serbs wanted the seacoast that had been given to Albania; the Greeks, Bulgarians, and Romanians all thought they deserved *more* territory; and the Ottomans wanted their lost territories back. The Slavic inhabitants of Austrian Bosnia wanted a southern Slav state of their own, within or outside the framework of Austria-Hungary; the Hungarians and Czechs saw either of these options as detrimental to *their* interests. Everybody was unhappy, and heavily armed. The Bulgarians alone had mobilized more than 500,000 men for the Balkan Wars of 1912–1913. Perhaps most important, feelings were running too high, and trust between the great powers had fallen too low for anyone to believe that diplomacy would solve the many problems.

The War Breaks Out

The assassination of the archduke on June 28, 1914, led to a July Crisis in which leaders and military officials scrambled, some to make peace and others to mobilize for war. Diplomats and commanders were called back from their vacations, spas, and summer trips to deal with the crisis. Eager to save face and convinced that the Serbian government had backed Franz Ferdinand's assassination, the Austrians first sought Germany's assurance that it would join the fight, whether it was a limited war on Serbia or, as chief of the German general staff Helmuth von Moltke predicted, "a war which will annihilate the civilization of almost the whole of Europe for decades to come."[2] They received such an assurance on July 7, along with Wilhelm II's famous "blank check," permitting the Austrians to make war as they wished with their German allies at their side.

Still the Austrians delayed, waiting until July 23 to issue an ultimatum to the Serbs. Within two days, the Serbian state was to accept responsibility for the archduke's assassination, to suppress all anti-Austrian propaganda, to fire all civil servants who expressed anti-Austrian views, and to allow the Austrians to oversee the capture and punishment of anti-Austrian activists. Asked essentially to give up the autonomy of their state, the Serbs offered a cleverly worded list of concessions, but the Austrians would

How was the war on the western front different from the war elsewhere?

MAP 22.1 | World War I, 1914–1918

This map shows the states belonging to the Allied Powers and the Central Powers as well as the major battles during World War I. **Why was it so easy for the British and French to establish a blockade, preventing the Germans from receiving supplies by sea? Why was the front so much longer and broader in the east than in the west?**

accept nothing short of total capitulation. The Serbs began to mobilize on July 25, and their ally, Russian czar Nicholas II, recalled his reservists the next day. Although Wilhelm II got cold feet at the last minute and appealed to the czar to stop the war, his effort was half-hearted—and too late. On July 28, Austria declared war on Serbia and began bombarding Belgrade.

Knowing that speed was vital to success, the Germans mustered their army, sending the largest numbers to the west, where they hoped to win a swift victory before turning to fight the Russians. On August 1, German chancellor Theobald von Bethmann-Hollweg declared war on Russia and on August 2 issued another ultimatum, demanding Belgium's neutrality as German troops

marched across its territory on their way, presumably, to Paris. Belgium's king refused and turned to his British allies, who on August 4 declared war on the **Central Powers**—Germany and Austria-Hungary—joining the already allied Russians and French to form the **Entente.** The Ottoman Empire joined the war on the side of the Central Powers on October 31, 1914, and Bulgaria threw in its lot the following year. Italy and Greece joined the Entente in 1915 and 1917, respectively. The last major combatant to enter the war, the United States, declared war on the Central Powers in spring 1917. The scale of the conflict and the size of the armies involved ensured that this would be the bloodiest conflict in world history to date (Map 22.1).

What Did Total War Mean?

From the outset, this war took on qualities that have led many observers to call it a **total war**, in the sense that whole nations were immediately *expected* and whole populations (including colonial subjects) eventually *compelled* to contribute to the fight. Declarations of war in each of the major nations were greeted with enthusiasm so great that historians have described a "war hysteria" seizing Europeans, who flocked to volunteer for service. The general outpouring of patriotic sentiment testified to how pervasive nationalism had become. In Britain alone, nearly 500,000 men volunteered to fight in the war's first month; by this time, the Germans and Austrians already had 7.5 million men under arms, the Russians 6 million, and the French 4 million. Meanwhile, millions of civilians undertook the task of providing the troops with sufficient supplies to accomplish the widely anticipated feat of winning the war by Christmas.

Mass Mobilization In the Bavarian city of Munich, huge crowds turned out to cheer the start of the war. One of those caught waving his hat was the young Adolf Hitler, who volunteered immediately to serve in the German army.

But not everyone was keen on the war. Some had to be persuaded or even coerced into doing their bit for their country. Skeptical parties included Irish supporters of home rule, Christian pacifists, anarchists, and socialists. On the war's eve, the reactions of these internal opponents were unpredictable: would they call for a strike or resist mobilization? Everywhere, states locked up those they considered enemy aliens; some, such as the British suffragette Sylvia Pankhurst, were freed once they declared their support for the war. The most radical, including communists who refused to fight in what they called a capitalist proxy war, languished in prison. Living in exile in Switzerland, Vladimir Lenin almost welcomed the war. A Europe-wide conflict, he hoped, would destroy capitalism once and for all and prepare the ground for the social revolution to follow.

In fact, most internal critics sided with their home nations and voted to fund the war in national assemblies where they sat as delegates. In Germany, which boasted Europe's largest and best-organized socialist party, socialists chose nationalism over pacifism, signing on to Kaiser Wilhelm II's demand that the parties cease quarreling over domestic affairs until the war was won. In France, despite the assassination of the socialist leader Jean Jaurès by a right-wing nationalist on the eve of the war's outbreak, political leaders of all parties pledged themselves to a sacred partnership. In Great Britain, Irish members of Parliament agreed to postpone their campaign for home rule. Identification with nation-states had become so powerful that Germans, Frenchmen, and Britons of all classes and all political orientations threw themselves passionately into the fight. Russians even agreed to change the name of St. Petersburg to Petrograd, because "burg" sounded too German. During wartime, they insisted, Russia's capital city needed a truly Russian name.

At the outset, women enthusiastically supported the war, though like the rest of the civilian population, they surely had no conception of what would follow. There were already 1.1 million well-organized nurses in Germany in 1914, and nurses were mobilized quickly elsewhere. Women urged their husbands, sons, and lovers to enlist and proudly waved them off at train stations and ports. As one jaded writer had an officer comment in a short story published in 1918: "No general could have made us go if the women hadn't allowed us to be stacked on the trains, if they had screamed out they would never look at us again if we turned into murderers."[3]

What did total war mean? It meant, for one thing, the immediate harnessing of the economies of Europe for the purposes of supplying troops at the front with food, ammunition, horses, boots, and medical supplies. It meant the massive relocation of male laborers, depriving farms and many industries of their most able-bodied men. It meant the imposition of new forms of censorship—and the increasingly rapid flow and heightened sophistication of propaganda. In some areas, it meant the displacement, deportation, and internment of large numbers of civilians, a novel experience for most Europeans. Eventually, it meant that death or major injuries would afflict almost every European family. No one, male or female, rich or poor, young or old, would remain untouched by this war.

Fighting a Total War

Despite prewar romanticizing of soldierly chivalry or the morally cleansing impact of warfare, European wars had never been particularly civilized or uplifting. Even in the most recent and largest conflicts, the Franco-Prussian War (1870–1871), the Russo-Turkish War (1877–1878), and the Balkan Wars (1912–1913), civilians had been caught up in the violence. But the Great War, especially in Belgium and in the eastern and southeastern theaters, inflicted more extensive suffering than those localized conflicts. Germans, Russians, Austrians, and the residents of what is today Syria, for example, experienced shortages that bordered on famine in 1916–1918 because the Entente's naval blockades prevented foodstuffs from reaching them.

Like the imperial wars of the previous few decades, but unlike earlier European wars, this war was fought with machine guns and heavy artillery whose firepower had vastly increased since Prussia's cannons had fired on Paris in 1871. In fact, artillery would account for the majority of military deaths in this war and would produce distinctively new ways of dying: men blown out of their clothes and into nearby trees; soldiers of whom nothing was left but two hands clinging to barbed wire fencing; men buried alive in their trenches by shells they never saw coming. In some cases, artillery blasts were so powerful that there were no body parts left to send home.

There were many other gruesome ways to die in this war: from starvation and cold on the Russian front to dysentery or gangrene in makeshift hospitals; from gas poisoning in the Belgian trenches to typhus or hunger in eastern European cities and villages. For those who did not die as a direct result of the fighting, there were other torments—exile, epidemics, inflation, malnutrition, and grief. We will never really know how many millions, in total, perished on these offstage fronts.

In this war, Europeans thought of themselves as duty bound to serve their nations, and many believed they were fighting for civilization itself. Drawing the line between civilian and military personnel, and between fair and unfair ways of winning, proved especially difficult, making this war even more murderous than those that predated it. Already on August 5, Belgian officials had to remind militiamen to identify themselves openly and to plead with the civilians in Liège not to join in the fighting. The Germans saw *francs-tireurs*, or guerrillas, everywhere, and they burned numerous villages and conducted summary executions in reprisal. By early September, German troops had killed 6,000 and deported some 23,000 Belgian and French civilians; some of the latter remained in internment camps for the remainder of the war.

At the same time, on the eastern front, the Russian government ordered the deportation of many civilians, especially Jews, from the area that later became Poland,

for they feared these ill-treated subjects of the czar might be tempted to side with the Germans. In the late fall of 1914, the Ottoman army tried to force the Jews of Haifa onto ships or into the desert; and in the spring of 1915, irregular Ottoman forces swept through the Armenian areas of northern Anatolia, murdering men and driving women, children, and grandparents into wastelands where hundreds of thousands perished.

Many people considered chlorine gas, first used by the Germans at the Second Battle of Ypres in April 1915, and unrestricted submarine warfare, also a German tactic, to be inhumane innovations, as indeed they were. But the Germans pointed out that the latter tactic at least was vital to break through an Allied blockade that was starving civilians as well as military personnel. Given the prevailing racism, few Europeans worried that the Africans employed to carry arms and supplies into sub-Saharan war zones were dying en masse from malnutrition or that 43,000 Indians died and perhaps an additional 65,000 were wounded in fighting for the British Empire. But these offenses also belong on the balance sheet of the inhumanity of this war, a war that was supposed to "end all wars," but in fact did nothing of the kind.

Theaters of War

The Great War was great in its diversity. We cannot generalize about the theaters of war where the fighting occurred and still understand the nature—or natures—of this war, for in each region the geography, weaponry, supplies, and tactics, as well as the experiences of both combatants and civilians, were different. Nor can we generalize about the outcomes of the war, for the way in which the conflict unfolded in each theater contributed to the kind of peace each could expect when finally the war ground to a halt.

THE WESTERN FRONT. The more predictable part of the war unfolded on the western front, in Belgium and along the German-French border. Or this conflict *should* have been predictable, as all the military leaders of the day knew that the Germans would make a beeline for Paris, in the hopes that France could be defeated swiftly, as had been the case in 1870–1871. The German military's **Schlieffen Plan,** named after retired chief of staff Alfred von Schlieffen, called for the speediest possible rolling up of this front, to concentrate forces for the presumably much bigger fight in the east. It was a plan driven by geographic and demographic necessity and the German military's fear of encirclement—but it also called for the Germans to invade France by marching across neutral Belgium, a risky undertaking that might have as its consequence the entrance into the conflict of Belgium's protector, the British Empire (Map 22.2).

It was wishful thinking, on the part of the Germans, that the Belgians would allow them to occupy their territory and that the British, the world's greatest naval power, would choose not to declare war. The Germans had exaggerated, too, the advantages of taking the offensive, when in fact recent technological advances in weaponry chiefly benefited defenders. Everyone had seen how successful guerrilla warfare had been in imperial conflicts like the Boer Wars and in the Balkans. Nevertheless, most Europeans did not anticipate the course of the war in the west, which began with German atrocities committed against Belgian civilians and then, as the British joined the Entente on August 4, 1914, settled into a surreal, futile battle between exhausted and embittered trench-dwellers.

The war of the trenches began in earnest when French forces stopped the German advance thirty miles from Paris at the first Battle of the Marne, September 6–14, 1914. Halting the attempted sweep through northern France was crucial for the French. Not only did it prevent the Germans from laying siege to Paris—as they had done in 1870–1871—but it also gave the Russians time to mobilize, thereby rendering the Schlieffen Plan defunct. Germany now faced the dreaded, but long-predicted scenario: total war on two fronts. Nor could the German army make further headway into the marshy, forested territory. Along a front stretching nearly 250 miles, the Germans fell back to the Aisne River and its tributaries. On the eve of being sacked for having failed to carry out the plan, General Helmuth von Moltke gave the following critical orders: "The lines so reached, will be fortified and defended."[4] The French, too, dug in, and English troops arrived to help them. Trench warfare had begun.

In the next few months, frantic attempts to sweep around enemy lines to the north led to a trench-diggers' race to the sea. At the same time, to the south, there was a race to the Swiss border. No one won, and by 1914's end, a continuous line of trenches stretched some 475 miles, from neutral Switzerland to the North Sea. Eventually, both sides built three lines of trenches, one forward for mounting offensives; a middle trench for off-duty resting; and a rear trench for supplies and for the wounded waiting to be evacuated to hospitals. An estimated 25,000 miles of trenches were dug between 1914 and 1918—the equivalent length of a trench circling the earth. Requiring perpetual, backbreaking work to maintain, trenches offered little protection from the northern European climate, which was very cold in winter and often rainy in spring and fall. Every trench veteran would remember the mud, usually ankle-deep and often deeper. In the trenches, men

MAP 22.2 | The Western Front during World War I
The major fighting of World War I occurred on the territory of France and Belgium. This map shows the German invasion of France in 1914, according to the Schlieffen Plan. It also depicts other battle sites and the armistice line as of November 1918. *Considering the small amount of territory fought over for more than four years between 1914 and 1918, and the large number of casualties taken by all sides, what can you conclude about the nature of World War I?*

No-Man's Land: Ypres, 1917 Perpetual bombardment by heavy artillery reduced the land between the trenches to a post-apocalyptic wasteland.

Belgian Atrocities

Almost from the moment German armies crossed into Belgium in early August 1914, rumors about barbaric behavior began to circulate on both sides. The Germans publicized claims that supposedly neutral civilians were shooting their soldiers from church towers and poisoning requisitioned food. The Belgians claimed the Germans were raping nuns and nurses, cutting off children's hands, and burning hospitals and whole villages for enjoyment. Refugees flooding into France and Holland had horrific tales to tell, and the reality of Germanic barbarism seemed confirmed when on August 23 German troops summarily executed more than 600 civilians in Dinant and then proceeded to shell the beautiful medieval city of Louvain two days later. But the Germans countered with their own declaration, "Us, Barbarians?" in which they tried to show that Germany was in fact the most cultured nation in Europe.

The German denials did not silence the Belgians' claims that atrocities had been committed. The Allies recognized a good propaganda campaign when they saw one and eagerly spread images of German Huns attacking innocent western women and children in the hopes of stirring neutral nations, especially the United States, to enter the war on the side of the Entente. After the war, Belgian atrocities continued to be discussed widely. The Versailles Treaty called for the trial of all those responsible for "acts in violation of the laws and customs of wars"—including the kaiser. The left-liberal leaders of Weimar Germany adamantly opposed such trials and again denied the claims. In the end, only a few officers received light sentences for war crimes violations, and the former kaiser was left to enjoy his favorite pastime, chopping wood, in his comfortable Dutch exile.

When the Second World War ended, the Nazi atrocities were so vast that a few thousand bestial acts in Belgium in August 1914 seemed almost trivial. Trying to be objective about the Great War, historians outside of Belgium after 1945 tended to take the pacifists' line and either downplayed the significance of the atrocities or argued that propagandists had inflated them. In 2001, however, British scholars John Horne and Alan Kramer published *German Atrocities, 1914: A History of Denial,* a carefully researched study in which they used eyewitness testimony and German sources—

Belgian Atrocities This is just one of thousands of images of German soldiers committing atrocities during the first days of the Great War. In late August 1914, after German troops had seized the town of Dinant, Belgian citizens fired on the occupiers. The Germans retaliated by executing civilians and setting the town center ablaze.

soldiers' diaries and government documents—to show that many of the Belgian atrocity stories were likely true. Their study reveals that, under tremendous pressure to eliminate resistance and move fast, many German soldiers panicked at the least hint of civilian resistance and sought to wipe it out with brutal thoroughness. Exhausted and sometimes inebriated, troops also committed savage acts incommensurate with anything that might be interpreted as civilian provocation.

Crimes *were* committed in Belgium, but they were also committed elsewhere during the war. There is documentation of terrible savagery committed by Hungarian and Austrian troops in Serbia, for example, and by the Russians in Austrian Galicia. Above all, the Ottoman Empire's Armenian population experienced such brutality that many people call this episode an attempt at genocide. The question then is, why were the Belgian atrocities so much better publicized in the west than events in other theaters? During the war and afterward, Europeans knew more about Belgian atrocities because these incidents involved barbaric actions of one supposedly highly civilized population against another. As such, they became the fodder for propagandists, whose main audiences were in western Europe and the United States. These groups told the truth, but perhaps not the whole truth, namely, that atrocities were committed by many *other* armies, in the *other* theaters of the Great War. The world was invited to feel pity for Belgians, but not for those caught up in the conflicts in the east and southeast. The *other* Great War atrocities were not brought before the courts, nor even much discussed, resulting in Hitler's cynical comment, made, ominously, on the eve of his invasion of Poland in August 1939, "Who talks today about the annihilation of the Armenians?"

A century later, an important lesson is to be learned from studying the Belgian atrocities. Propaganda does sometimes convey real truths, but its single-minded focus on the sufferings of some and not of others may also tell us some harsh truths about ourselves.

QUESTIONS | *What constitutes an atrocity during wartime? Why are some atrocities more widely publicized than others?*

regularly suffered from lice, sleep deprivation, shellshock, and claustrophobia. Poison gas collected in the trenches, burning the lungs of those unable to get out quickly. Many felt that they were living in their own graves, and they were right. The trenches were home, too, to armies of rats, who feasted on hard bread—and dead bodies.

As deadly as the trenches were, however, it was even more deadly to go "over the top." This order, given repeatedly despite the continual failure of the tactic, involved rushing the enemies' trenches, often carrying more than sixty pounds of weapons and supplies on one's back. Both sides strung barbed wire across the no-man's-land between the trenches, a tactic that made offensives even more deadly for the attacker. The most futile attempt to go "over the top" occurred at the Battle of the Somme in 1916. After conducting an artillery bombardment that lasted a solid week, Entente commanders assumed that German machine gunners had been killed or forced to retreat and ordered a huge offensive. On July 1, 1916, the first day of the assault, 100,000 Britons were sent over the top, only to find that the Germans' deep trenches had protected their gunners. On that single day, 20,000 Britons were killed and 40,000 wounded. On the same day, Allied forces detonated nineteen mines beneath German lines; the combined force of the blast produced a crater ninety yards across and seventy feet deep. The explosion itself could be heard in London more than 120 miles away. Those unlucky enough to be close to the blast were simply vaporized.

The war in the west was one of attrition, not of decisive battles or startling encirclements. From fall 1914 to early spring 1918, engagements occurred in essentially the same fashion, with the first battles of Ypres and Champagne followed by second or even third ones—evidence that neither side ever gained much territory. The huge German offensive at Verdun, intended to "bleed the French white," begun in the spring of 1916, slowed briefly during the Allied offensive at the Somme in July, only to revive and continue into December. The four-month-long Somme offensive gained the Allies at most an eight-mile advance. When, exhausted, both sides ended their offensives, each had lost more than 600,000 men.

And still, there was no end in sight. Even the entrance of new participants did not seem to help. The Italians joined the Allies in May 1915, but quickly became involved in a terrible struggle with the Austrians for control of the southern Alps. These battles, fought on skis and from caves dug out of Europe's most rugged mountains, were so physically demanding and deadly that many soldiers posted here probably longed for the relative comforts of the trenches. Even the United States' entrance in April 1917 did not turn the tide immediately. Calculating the Allies' progress that summer, one pessimistic British officer estimated that if there were no further setbacks, the armies would reach the Rhine in 180 years.[5]

In the spring of 1918, after the Russians had been knocked out of the war by revolution at home, the Germans staged a massive offensive that almost allowed them to break the Allies' defensive lines in France—almost, but not quite. After that, the influx of fresh American troops began to take its toll on the Central Powers. It was only a matter of finishing the war of attrition, a phrase that can scarcely capture the lived reality of exhausted, battle-hardened, hungry troops battering one another until the Germans, grudgingly, finally conceded defeat.

THE EASTERN FRONT. The war on the eastern front was, from the outset, less scripted, territorially more wide-ranging, and just as brutal as the war in the west. Though less often described in detail than the war in the west, conflicts in the eastern theater would make a crucial difference not only in the war's outcome, but also in the postwar geography of central Europe. The war in the east began with one part of the Austrian army engaged in vicious fighting in Serbia, followed by the collapse of another Austrian division in the face of a rapid Russian advance. By early September 1914, 350,000 Austrians had been killed, captured, or wounded in Galicia. The Germans, however, had reversed an initial Russian surge, winning the Battle of Tannenberg in East Prussia—at the cost of 50,000 Russians killed and 92,000 prisoners taken. After securing East Prussia in the First Battle of the Masurian Lakes, the Germans succeeded in pushing the Russians back from Austria-Hungary's borders. Even so, 1914 ended with the eastern front stagnating along the Vistula River, bounded on the south by the Carpathian Mountains.

There were trenches in the east, but the war here was not primarily a trench war. Weather conditions made digging and living in holes in the ground much harder. Though there were periods of stagnation, the eastern front was marked by much more movement across large swatches of land, much of it plundered and burnt by retreating armies.

The victories of Tannenberg and the Masurian Lakes gave the two German commanders, Paul von Hindenburg and Erich von Ludendorff, hero status at home, and the military claimed occupied territory as its prize. Inspired by their early successes, Hindenburg and Ludendorff began to plan for the creation of an efficient and useful colony in conquered eastern lands. Presuming that local peoples were backward and fit only to do Germany's bidding, the Germans built an administrative apparatus in what is present-day Poland and Lithuania. The German regime intended to exploit laborers and destroy local culture in favor of forced Germanization. This military-utopian plan to subjugate the east and create *Lebensraum* ("living space") for the culturally superior population of the German Empire spurred Ludendorff, Hindenburg, and their right-wing backers to think that when they won the war, the Germans should be allowed to annex this territory as part of their reward.

The Russians also conducted a brutal war in the east, plundering as they entered new territory and burning villages and pushing out civilian inhabitants as they lost ground. Many of the civilians who suffered were themselves subjects of the czar—Poles and especially

Jews whom the Russian troops feared would prove treasonous. The Russians' scorched earth policy—which had been successful against Napoleon in 1812—sent a tidal wave of desperate refugees into the Russian interior and contributed greatly to the desperate conditions suffered by both noncombatants and troops in the east.

In the summer of 1915, the German and Austrian armies pushed the front eastward, into Russian-dominated Poland, but thereafter, major territorial gains ceased until early 1917. As Russia succumbed to first a liberal, then a communist revolution (see p. 716), the Central Powers surged eastward, and in February 1918, the communists signed a separate peace with the Central Powers at Brest-Litovsk, even though doing so meant the loss of a huge stretch of Russia's western territory.

The **Treaty of Brest-Litovsk** gave right-wing Germans grand dreams of an enormous empire in the east and minority groups in western Russia, such as the Armenians and Ukrainians, a brief opportunity to build autonomous states of their own. Freed finally from fighting a two-front war, the Germans immediately sent eastern troops to join the big spring offensive on the western front. When that effort failed, the Central Powers were forced to retreat and finally surrender. The combination of the Versailles peace treaties and the Russian civil wars snatched away Germany's gains and smothered the independence of Armenia and Ukraine. By raising and then dashing hopes, the Treaty of Brest-Litovsk and its aftermath created terrible bitterness in the east, which would smolder throughout the interwar era.

THE SOUTHEASTERN FRONTS. Divided into several theaters, the war in the southeast began with Austria-Hungary's invasion of Serbia. The consequences of the war there, including the breakup of the Ottoman Empire, the creation of Yugoslavia, and the issuing of the Balfour Declaration, were arguably just as important for world history as was Germany's defeat by the Entente.

The first months of the war in the Balkans were particularly bloody. Made overly confident by their presumption that the Serbs were nonwestern barbarians, the Austrians failed to take into account the Serbs' fierce patriotism, the army's experience during the Balkan Wars, and the small nation's nearly impassible mountain terrain. The Austro-Hungarian invasion of Serbia stalled quickly, and as in Belgium, troops accused civilians of sabotage. A contemporary observer estimated that Hungarian regiments murdered at least two thou-

Russian Soldiers Surrendering Their Arms By the time this photo was taken in January 1917, many Russian soldiers were thoroughly sick of fighting a war with poor provisions and outdated weaponry. By this time, too, many were unwilling to continue to fight for the czar.

sand Serbian civilians in September 1914 "under circumstances of the most revolting cruelty."[6] Civilians were disemboweled, women raped, eyes put out, and genitalia cut off. Even these measures failed to ensure quick victory in the Balkans, and finally in late 1915, the Germans and the Bulgarians joined the effort to finish the war in Serbia. They pushed their way through to the Albanian coast, but rather than surrender, the remnants of the Serbian army, together with King Peter and tens of thousands of civilians, attempted a treacherous crossing over the mountains to the sea. Perhaps as many as 200,000 perished on this march. Those who survived were evacuated to the Greek island of Corfu. With new equipment, the soldiers returned to Salonica, where they continued to battle Bulgarian forces for more than two years.

The Ottoman Empire joined the Central Powers in late October 1914, declaring jihad (holy war) on the Entente and hoping to rouse Muslims in Africa and Asia against Russian, British, and French rule. Initially, Ottoman armies succeeded in pushing into the multiethnic region of the Russian-held Caucasus Mountains, raising hopes among the pan-Turkish radicals that a vast territory rich in minerals might be reconquered for the Muslim empire. But in late December 1914, the Ottomans made a terrible mistake, advancing far into the snowbound mountains without supplies. The Russians took advantage of the extreme cold (reaching −33° F) and pushed back the invading forces at Sarikamish. As they retook territory, they discovered 30,000 frozen Turkish bodies around Sarikamish alone and captured almost as many prisoners. Of the 90,000 Turkish troops sent into Russia

MAP 22.3 | World War I in the Ottoman Empire

This map shows the major areas of conflict on the southeastern fronts and the locations of Armenian massacres during the Great War. ***Why did the location of Armenian settlements near the Russian border seem particularly dangerous to the Ottoman Turks?***

Map legend:
- Turkish borders after 1923
- Battle sites
- Sites of Armenian massacres
- Routes of death marches
- Railroads

in December, only 12,000 returned. Turkish propaganda urging Muslim subjects of the czar to join in the fight against him was largely unsuccessful, as most people preferred to wait and see how things came out. The propaganda did, however, unleash Russian terror against the predominately Muslim Azeris in what is now Georgia, causing the population of the Coruh Valley to fall from 52,000 to 7,000 in the spring of 1915 (Map 22.3).

Even more disastrous for the mixed population of civilians in the region, the retreat was a devastating blow to Ottoman pride. This retreat passed through Ottoman territory heavily populated by Armenians, who, like the Russians, were Orthodox Christians. For centuries, the Armenian minority population had paid extra taxes to the Ottomans and had been banned from certain positions, including service in the military. Yet they were, on the whole, wealthier than their Ottoman neighbors, many of whom resented the fact that their sons, and not Armenian young men, had been the ones to die in the Balkan Wars. Thus, as the Ottoman army retreated in spring 1915, rumors circulated that the Armenians were

siding with the Russians and seeking to sabotage the Turkish war effort.

In response to alleged acts of treason, special forces under the control of the zealous Turkish nationalist Behaeddin Shakir stirred up unrest in the Armenian towns of Van and Adana and then put the disorder down by massacring men and deporting noncombatants. The ways in which the deportations occurred suggest that they were intended to be death marches, as hundreds of thousands of women, children, and older people were forced to march out into the waterless wastelands with no provisions and no plans for resettlement. More than 100,000 Armenian refugees straggled into Syria and Lebanon, creating an enormous new need for orphanages and social services, as well as resentment among the local residents, for whom times were already tough. At least 800,000 and probably more than 1 million Armenian civilians perished in this cruel campaign.

Action farther to the south also demonstrated the war's brutality—both for those who would ultimately win and for those who would lose. In February 1915, an Ottoman expeditionary force attempted to attack the Suez Canal, Britain's swiftest route to India, its most populous and profitable colony. By approaching through the Sinai Desert, the Ottomans hoped to surprise British defenders, but failed and beat a chaotic retreat, losing thousands of men and camels.

Soon thereafter, however, the Ottomans turned the tables on the Allies, stopping their attempt to seize the Dardanelles Straits in order to open up a supply route to Russia across the Black Sea (see Map 22.3). Planned by First Lord of the Admiralty Winston Churchill, a campaign to invade and occupy the Gallipoli peninsula proved a disaster. When an initial naval assault failed, ground troops, composed largely of soldiers from Australia and New Zealand, were sent in. Ottoman troops fired down on the beaches,

Armenian Genocide Expelled from their homes, the Armenian men of fighting age were often shot, and women and children marched across deserts, where many perished from exhaustion, hunger, and thirst. Here refugees flee into Syria, 1915.

inflicting terrible casualties on the invaders, who tried again and again to break through with no luck. Finally, in December 1915, following floods and a freak blizzard, Entente soldiers were forced to withdraw, leaving much bitterness among the surviving Australians and New Zealanders, many of whom felt their dead comrades' lives had been wasted by Britain, supposedly their mother country.

The Entente may have had the worst of it in the early fighting in the south, but ultimately the Ottoman Empire would lose so decisively here that it would collapse before the armistice. In 1916, an Arab army loyal to the sharif of Mecca, Prince Hussein, began a revolt against the Ottomans in Arabia and Palestine. Egged on by the British and assisted by liaison officer Colonel T. E. Lawrence, subsequently known as Lawrence of Arabia, Hussein and the Arabs engaged in guerrilla activity behind the fronts, distracting large numbers of Turkish troops and raising hopes of an independent Arab state to be established at the war's end. The Jihad Declaration, issued at the war's outset, had as one of its major goals the enlisting of the Ottoman Empire's Arab population to fight beside their Turkish brethren. But the snowballing movement for Arab independence after 1916 showed that the Arabs had tired of fighting the Ottoman Empire's holy war. In yet another theater, an oppressed population wearied of the older authoritarian structures and signaled its readiness to remake the map.

Farther to the east, Egyptian-based Allied troops pushed eastward into Palestine, taking Jerusalem in December 1917. But it took nearly another year of fighting before the Allies could seize northern Palestine and force the Turkish commander, Mustafa Kemal, to lay down his arms and the German commander to flee Nazareth in his pajamas. In Mesopotamia, an Allied army heav-ily staffed by Indian troops fought Ottoman, Austrian, and German forces, making slow but sure progress. The Allies reached oil-rich Mosul by October 30, 1918, when the Turks finally bowed out of the war.

THE WAR IN THE COLONIES. Already in 1914, the Germans were calling the war a *Weltkrieg*, or world war, but only relatively recently have historians begun to appreciate just how powerfully this conflict shook and reshaped the world beyond Europe. Not only were colonial subjects compelled to fight or to labor on behalf of European combatants, so also were their economies and, in some cases, their social and political structures deeply affected by the conflict. The attitudes of non-Europeans also changed as a result of the war. The spectacle of the "civilized" peoples tearing one another apart made many members of the colonial world decide to seek alternative paths toward modernization.

Africa, the focus of so much European greed and the battleground for so many bloody skirmishes in the two decades preceding 1914, did not escape the war. One could even say that the war ended there with the surrender of the last German commander, Paul von Lettow-Vorbeck, at Abecorn in Northern Rhodesia on November 25, 1918. More than two million Africans served as soldiers, porters, or workers, and perhaps as many as 200,000 died in the conflict. Disease, especially malaria, was the biggest killer, as armies ranged over large territories and major battles were few. The African campaigns did not involve the heavy artillery characteristic of the western and eastern fronts, but focused rather on the taking of the strategic chokepoints colonial troops had defended: ports, river crossings, railroads, jungle clearings, and forts. Tactics included the burning of villages and the forced migration of civilians, the destruction of railways and other infrastructure, and the diversion of the population from food production. In Africa, as in Europe, the Great War was a total war.

But the war in Africa was also a colonial war, and in its midst, colonial aspirations and mentalities were on view. All the European combatants presumed, at the outset, that white European soldiers would fight more effectively than darker-skinned soldiers from Africa or Asia, and only the most pragmatic were willing to concede, even by the war's midpoint, that this simply was not true. In recruiting troops and requisitioning supplies, Europeans simply assumed the Africans would fight for their causes, but that the Europeans should get the spoils. When West Africa fell to the Allies in early 1916, French diplomat Georges Picot, who had not troubled to learn anything of the lands and peoples he was dividing, sat down with a pencil and carved up Germany's former colonies (Togoland and the Cameroons) between Britain and France. South Africa seized German Southwest Africa in July 1915 and did not allow present-day Namibia its independence until 1988. German East Africa was parceled out among Belgium, Portugal, and Britain.

In European eyes, the battles in Africa, so devastating to civilians as well as to the economies of Africa's territories, were simply sideshows, efforts to keep enemy troops engaged so that they could not concentrate forces on the western front. But their result was, for Africa, no trivial matter. A particularly astute and empathetic doctor with Lettow-Vorbeck's forces wrote in his diary as the war was ending: "Behind us we leave destroyed fields, ransacked magazines and, for the immediate future, starvation. We are no longer the agents of culture; our track is marked by death, plundering and evacuated villages, just like the progress of our own and enemy armies in the Thirty Years War."[7]

In East Asia the Japanese jumped first into the war, joining the Allied side on August 23, 1914, in recognition of their treaty obligations to the British. And the Japanese chiefly benefited from the war, their export trade booming during a period in which the Europeans' economies threw their all into war production. On joining the conflict, the Japanese seized a number of German holdings in the Pacific and even managed to force China, weakened by foreign attempts to seize spheres of influence and by the collapse of the Qing Empire in 1911, to sign a secret treaty. The Twenty One Demands, signed in 1915, gave the Japanese control over the Shandong Peninsula and Manchuria, territories they believed the Allies would let them keep as a reward for their support.

Though humiliated by having to concede regional supremacy to the Japanese, in 1917 the Chinese Republic

The War in Africa The Great War was also fought on African territory. All nations used native Africans in support roles, and some (the Germans and French) also used African soldiers in combat. Here, French Senegalese soldiers march triumphantly into the German colony of Cameroon.

joined the Allies, on the assumption that, if the Allies were victorious, German territory in China, especially the province of Jiaozhou on the Japanese-occupied Shandong Peninsula, would be returned to the Chinese. Again, contradictory Allied promises, or presumed promises, would generate feelings of betrayal when the war ended.

Approximately 200,000 young Chinese and Southeast Asian adults were dispatched to France on the understanding that they could study in France as long as they worked in the munitions factories—though most ended up working menial jobs rather than attending university courses. Some, like the Vietnamese dishwasher Ho Chi Minh, absorbed western political radicalism during their stays in the west. The East Asian front saw almost no land battles. The German colonies of Samoa and New Guinea capitulated quickly, though the Japanese lost 1,455 men storming the heavily fortified port of German-dominated Qingdao. After the outbreak of the Russian Revolution in February 1917, Japanese troops surged into Siberia, laying the foundations for expansionist dreams rather like those of the Germans in eastern Europe.

The New Technology and the Old

What helped make the Great War both a total and a global war was, above all, modern technology—that same combination of mass-produced machinery and newly harnessed energy sources that had provided so much of Europe's prewar prosperity. Wars have always speeded up experimentation and the production of new technologies, but the Great War,

Was the Great War the first modern technological war, or the last pre-modern war?

which began in an already highly industrialized age, would prove to be an especially high-tech war. But technology has never been the only factor in one side's victory over another, and on some battlegrounds, sophisticated machinery was either unavailable or unsuitable for effective use. Even the second industrial revolution had not given all Europeans access to the new technologies. In 1914, Europeans went to war with the armies—and the industrial societies—they had, which meant that mixed with the modern, plenty of age-old technologies were on display.

The New

Guns were, of course, the most omnipresent and deadly weapons in this war, and they came in all shapes and sizes, from the rifles tipped with bayonets carried by most soldiers to the super heavy cannons, which could throw a 1,400-pound shell up to 3500 yards (about two miles). Rapid-firing machine guns were mounted on zeppelins, planes, ships, submarines, and tanks. Guns of all types were manufactured in the millions by women, colonial subjects, and forced laborers, and carried across rivers and mountains by African bearers and Alpine skiers, or dragged by horses, camels, or the soldiers themselves through swamps and deserts. If the operation of guns was a relatively well-known art before the war, by the end it was virtually universal, at least for men between the ages of fifteen and fifty, many of whom also knew what it was like to be wounded by gunfire and to see their comrades' bodies shattered by artillery shells.

A newer weapon, poison gas, was first tried in October 1914, and chlorine gas was first used effectively by the Germans in the spring of 1915. Once inhaled, the gas burned the soldiers' lungs and internal organs, causing them to die of suffocation. But chlorine gas was difficult to discharge without harming one's own troops, and it dissipated relatively quickly. In 1916, mustard gas was introduced; unlike chlorine, it could be fired by shell and had long-lasting effects—it soaked into the soil and could cause its characteristic blisters on the skin or in the lungs weeks after its release. Gas probably killed only about 3 percent of those it affected, but many of those exposed to it would suffer from respiratory difficulties for the rest of their lives.

The frustrations of trench warfare stimulated technological innovation, and by war's end it was clear that two new vehicles would make entrenched fighting ultimately obsolete: the tank and the airplane. The tank or armored car was envisioned in 1914 as a means to get beyond the trenches, but making tanks usable in marshy, rugged Flanders and northern France proved expensive and difficult. They were used in only small numbers until the British Mark IV was perfected in 1917, and even then they made little real difference to the war's outcome.

Airplanes were first used in warfare in Italy's campaign against the Turks in Libya in 1911–1912. At first restricted to reconnaissance, airplanes had limited use until guns were added, and airborne fighting commenced. The German Fokker led the way in the development of fighter planes, followed by the French Nieuport 17 and British Sopwith Camel in 1917, which gave the Entente an equal chance in air battles. From early in the war, aerial bombing was used to target enemy rail lines and supply depots, and later the Germans used zeppelins to drop a few bombs on London. The air war was showy and had its heroes, like Manfred Freiherr von Richthofen, the German Red Baron, who reputedly shot down some eighty aircraft before being killed in April 1918. But the role that fliers played in reconnaissance was probably more important, for it allowed commanders, for the first time in history, to get a full, up-to-the-minute, picture of the troops and weapons arrayed against them. Like the first tanks, the increasingly sophisticated fighting planes signaled the opening of a new age of warfare, one in which trenches would become largely obsolete and civilian targets would be at greater risk. But in this war, the airplane was more intelligence instrument than battle-deciding weapon.

Despite the prestige and propaganda surrounding the build-up of the German and British navies before the Great War, sea battles were a relatively minor part of the conflict. The Imperial German Navy was not very large and easy to bottle up in the North Sea, though its ships were generally faster than those of the Allies and able to inflict some embarrassing early losses on the world-dominating British Royal Navy. But indirectly, sea power mattered a great deal, for it allowed the British to obtain supplies from their colonies and trading partners (especially the Americans) and to prevent the ferrying of supplies into German ports by imposing a highly effective blockade. Try as they would, the Germans could not break the blockade. Even their biggest and best effort to do so, at the Battle of Jutland off the Danish coast in mid-1916, failed. This defeat increased pressure on the kaiser's men to use their submarines or U-boats (the shorthand the Entente used for German *Unterseebooten*, or underwater boats) to run the blockade, and to do their own damage to British trade in the Atlantic.

Heavy use of submarines, however, got the Germans into terrible trouble. Prewar conventions for the conduct of war specified that neutral ships were not to be fired on and that noncombatant merchant ships were to be warned before being attacked. In 1915, a German U-boat sank the passenger liner *Lusitania*, causing the deaths of 1,201 civilians, 129 of them Americans. This was a propaganda disaster for those who hoped to keep the still-neutral United States out of the war. When in early 1917 the Germans decided to throw caution to the winds by declaring unrestricted submarine warfare as they sought a big breakthrough on the western front, the international outcry was fierce and spurred the Americans to join the fight.

Naval maneuvers had another unanticipated cultural consequence. Both before and during the war, naval officers were avid users of the relatively new technology of radio, which helped link ships to shore bases. Although military personnel employed radio exclusively for informational and intelligence-gathering purposes during the Great War, they contributed greatly to the perfecting of the technology. After the war's conclusion, radio would be adapted to important new political and commercial purposes.

. . . And the Old

It was a slightly older bit of technology that cemented America's decision to enter the war—the telegraph or, more accurately, the intercepted, transoceanic telegraph. Effective trans-Atlantic telegraph service had been available since 1866, and by 1900 a sophisticated telegraph network linked the great European capitals— and their journalists—to U.S. cities. Unluckily for the Germans, their direct cable to the United States was cut early in the war, making it difficult to give American readers the Central Powers' side of the story. Even more damaging was the British interception and deciphering of the so-called Zimmermann telegraph of January 16, 1917. In this message, German colonial secretary Arthur Zimmermann instructed the German ambassador in Mexico to seek Mexico's alliance with the Central Powers if the United States entered the war—and promised, in return, that Mexico could expect to reclaim territory in Texas, Arizona, and New Mexico. The deciphering of this message was a propaganda disaster for the Central Powers, for it created a tidal wave of anti-German sentiment in America. American leaders who had been sitting on the fence to this point now approved an alliance with the Entente, and by April 1917, U.S. troops were landing in France.

There was an even older piece of war technology whose use and abuse has rarely been commented upon: the horse. Though we think of the Great War as a particularly modern one and horses as belonging to the premodern age, horses and mules were *the* major means of conveyance for soldiers and civilian refugees alike during the conflict. This was especially so on the eastern and southeastern fronts, where railroad coverage was less dense, but even in the west, horses were indispensible. The only places they were not in heavy use were in the deserts, where camels were more practical, and in Africa, where they were particularly susceptible to the tsetse fly. Every nation had its cavalry—and that still meant horses, as tanks came into use only late in the war. Horses and mules were used to pull wagons, to drag artillery, and to convey the wounded to hospitals. They picked their way across Alpine and Albanian narrow mountain passes and slogged through the rutted, mud-holed roads of east-

Indispensable Technology: The Horse During the Great War, all nations continued to depend on horses to haul cargo as well as people and weapons. Of course, this meant that horses, too, died by the millions during the conflict.

ern Europe. Horses were called up in August 1914: some 600,000 for the Austrians, 715,000 for the Germans, and more than a million for the Russians. By mid-1916, the British had nearly 591,000 horses, 213,000 mules, 47,000 camels, and 11,000 oxen in service. Like humans, animals starved, froze, thirsted, and died, in staggering but unrecorded numbers. Millions, surely, were killed in the course of battles and retreats, and many too on the hungry home front. There are accounts of horses being attacked on the boulevards of Russia's Petrograd in 1916, starving inhabitants butchering and eating the animals on the spot. For Europe's horses, too, the war brought with it new forms of suffering, and death on an unprecedented scale.

Enabling the Fight: The Home Front

Unquestionably, life on any of the combat fronts was extremely hazardous and often short. But for many noncombatants, life on the home front was also difficult, debilitating, and perilous. The difficulties were different from those faced by direct combatants, which often led to misunderstandings. In the view of most frontline soldiers, the home front was not a front at all: life, they imagined, went on more or less as usual, while they were living in the subterranean hell of the western trenches or enduring the frostbitten terror of the eastern front. But those who spent the war at home felt they were fighting,

> **How did life on the home front change during the war?**

too—sacrificing good union jobs to work twelve-hour days in poorly maintained factories, sacrificing their leisure time, diverse diets, means of transport, and winter heat, not to mention family members lost at the front. Many could not even stay at home—for the war created millions of refugees fleeing the fighting, and economic incentives caused others to leave home. But wherever civilians fled, the war met them there—in the form of state-imposed economic controls and propaganda, in ration cards and censored mails. This omnipresent front was part of what it meant to be engaged in a total war.

The sufferings on the home front were particularly acute in central and southeastern Europe. Combined with decreased crop yields (because of labor shortages), the Allied ban on shipping through enemy ports created grain shortages throughout the region. Soldiers in the field were to be fed first, so shortages fell most directly and painfully on women, children, and other noncombatants at home, especially urban dwellers who could not grow their own food. In Vienna, Austria-Hungary's capital city, ration cards for bread and flour were issued as early as April 1915, followed by cards for sugar, milk, coffee, lard, potatoes, marmalade, and meat. By war's end, daily rations in Vienna allowed each consumer a mere 830 calories—explaining why, by one estimate, some 91 percent of children in the city were malnourished (see Back to the Source at the end of the chapter). Rationing also took its toll in Berlin and Petrograd, both of which saw an increasing number of protests and even riots over bread, led especially by women. Hungry, angry, and often grieving for lost husbands or sons, these women were among the first to tell state officials that they were fed up with sacrificing their bodies, families, and dreams for what increasingly seemed to be an endless and pointless war.

A Woman's War

But women were also essential enablers of the fight. In fall 1914, they had been just as eager as the men to do their all for their countries. As men marched off to the front, wives, sweethearts, sisters, and mothers volunteered in great numbers to serve as nurses, supply clerks, and intelligence officers. A few, including the Siberian patriot Yasha Bachkarova, even grabbed their guns. Bachkarova, incensed by the Russian infantry's tendency to retreat under fire, recruited 2,000 women to her Women's Death Battalion and exhorted them to hold trenches abandoned by their men on the Austrian front. Many more women went to work in the ever-expanding munitions industry, producing massive numbers of shells, rifles, landmines, helmets, and boots. The demand for labor was great. According to one estimate, by October 1918, between 2.5 and 3 million people were employed in making armaments just in Germany. Women took over traditionally male jobs such as those of streetcar conductor, doctor, and machinist, and became indispensable as clerks in

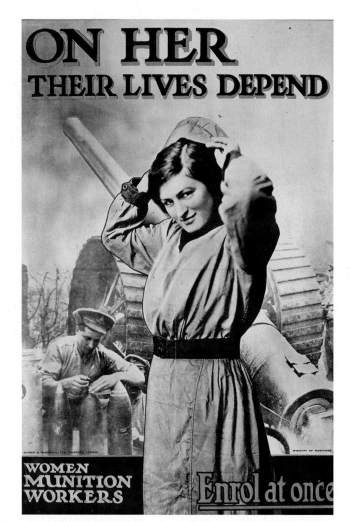

Women Workers in Demand As this British poster suggests, the conditions of total war demanded that everyone had a crucial job to perform to save the nation. All the belligerents needed female laborers to manufacture munitions as well as to fill in for men who had gone off to war.

European offices, though their pay remained far below that of men in the same jobs.

But the mobilization of women is not the only story and is in some respects misleading. Many working women *lost* their jobs as the war began, as many businesses were forced to close. As both private and public funds were channeled into the war effort, nonessential goods and services suffered. The textile industry was especially hard hit. In France, for example, 61 percent of female textile workers and 67 percent of garment makers lost their jobs. Domestic servants, too, were let go in large numbers. Thanks to the hardships of both the war and the postwar period, most would never regain their places.

Many of those who went to work in munitions did so for purely financial reasons; and their willingness to accept poor working conditions or to work longer hours was the result not only of patriotic commitment, but also of need. In rural areas, women had crops to tend, reap, and bring to market. However, despite the heroic efforts of women to cope and the employment of prisoners of war in agriculture, shortages of men on Europe's farms, especially in central Europe and Russia, created the conditions for price inflation, black marketeering, and shortfalls that would have extremely important social and political consequences.

Women also had households to run and children to tend to, even as charitable organizations counted largely on them to care for the indigent and wounded. Women were asked to volunteer for the Red Cross and to raid their children's piggybanks to buy war bonds, to keep a stiff upper lip (and not wear mourning clothes) despite losing sons and husbands. And though death in this war fell largely on young men—taking an appalling 22.7 percent of Serbian males of combat age—women were also often direct victims of the fighting: raped or murdered in areas where soldiers feared civilian resistance; forced to flee their homes in Belgium, Serbia, Anatolia, Poland, and Palestine; and abandoned to die from disease or malnutrition in Petrograd or Budapest.

The experience of war changed some women: they learned to drink or smoke, to navigate the cities on their own, and to do without men, or at least to make their own decisions without asking a husband, father, or brother for advice. The number of women writers and activists increased considerably during and after the war. They did not all agree on political matters, such as which political party best represented women's interests, or on social issues, such as whether birth control should be legal. But as the war ground on, women grew more and more critical of prewar structures of authority and more willing to voice their opinions in the public sphere. On the home front, too, there was no going back to spring 1914.

State officials did not specifically promise women anything in return for their sacrifices except national victory, but having shouldered so many burdens and taken on so many formerly male responsibilities, by war's end many women felt the state owed them something: the vote, perhaps, or a pension to sustain widows and the wounded through tough times; equal rights before the law, or simply enough to eat. In fact, the war's end drastically cut job opportunities for women. Despite the loss of so many male workers, women were sent home in droves. There were, however, some political rewards. Although women's suffrage had not been popular before the war, many states gave female citizens the vote afterward: Britain first in 1918, the United States, Germany, and the Soviet Union in 1919. Many members of the French left feared women would vote as their local priests told them, and French women would have to wait for another war's end to obtain full voting rights.

Command Economies

In 1914, Europe's economies were the richest and most diverse in the world, but even the wealthiest and best-organized states could not afford both guns and butter. Nor could basically liberal economies, built on free-market principles, cope with the demands of launching a total war. The war had to be financed in innovative ways, and the means by which goods were produced and requisitioned required the creation of new, centralized bureaucracies, able to compel producers not only to produce for the troops, but also to sell at the state's price. Though states varied in their approaches to the problem, most ended up with some form of command economy, in which—at least in theory—one central bureaucracy organized production, regulated money supply, and funneled goods first of all to the troops in the field.

Some measures of these command economies—such as food rationing in the cities and expropriation of grain from reluctant peasants—created anger and chaos, especially when, as was the case in Russia, corruption and incompetence plagued the system. Anger and chaos proved consequential enough, above all in the Russian case; but if we examine the long-term effects of the imposition of command economies in this period, we can also see that these policies contributed to the destruction of some businesses, including consumer-oriented ones such as the costume jewelry industry, starved by the reshuffling of the workforce and the sanctions placed on frivolous consumption. The command economies also contributed to the birth of new conspiracy theories to explain failures of supply or price rises in local areas. In general terms, the shift to command economies killed off what was left of economic liberalism, making the states, not the market, responsible for providing for Europe's citizens. And once the states got into the business of controlling the economies, consumers could blame *them*, and not just the vagaries of the marketplace, for hard times.

If in this way the war killed economic liberalism, it also provoked a monumental shift in Europe's economic position in the world. The wartime command economies all ended up borrowing far more than they could easily repay, much of it from the United States, which ended the war as the only major combatant (aside from Japan) still in the black. Whereas in 1914 the United States owed Europe $3.5 billion, by 1919 the Europeans were the debtors, to the tune of $12.5 billion, one of the most rapid and dramatic reversals of fortunes on record. In this way, the war greatly accelerated the rise of the largest neo-Europe to the status of leading world power, without the United States having to compromise on its commitment not to take any colonies of its own.

At home, wartime inflation had already eaten away all the increases in workers' wages that governments had been forced to concede during the conflict. But the removal of official price controls at the war's end made the situation far worse. Everybody's currency immediately lost value, in some cases precipitously. Middle-class people suffered from the erosion of their savings, and few now trusted the free market to allocate goods fairly or to protect the livelihoods of hard-working citizens.

The Russian Revolution

Wartime Russia offers the classic example of the collapse of civil peace as a result of the long-term strains of total war. Food shortages hit the Russians—many of them peasants with few resources to fall back on—especially hard, and the Russian government was particularly deaf to civilian complaints. The revolutions that broke out in Russia—for the virtually bloodless revolution of February 1917 was followed by a much more radical one in October of the same year—would lead to the establishment of the world's first communist nation. The state built by the Russian communists would be so unlike Europe's previous regimes that it would inspire some and horrify others. It would invent new pathways to modernization and inflict additional, brutal destruction on the population of eastern Europe. The Russian Revolution was a world-changing event, one that might not have happened at all had the czar not gone to war in 1914.

How did the Great War lay the foundations for the Russian Revolution?

Origins of the Revolution

As we saw in Chapter 19, industrialization, as well as economic and political reforms, came late to Russia and were far from complete in 1914. Many former serfs, nominally freed in 1861, were still effectively bound to the land by debts and farmed communally as had their forefathers. After the 1905 revolution, the czar had granted the nation a representative assembly, the Duma, and the right to form (nonrevolutionary) political parties, but these concessions had done little to empower, enrich, or pacify the citizenry at large. The autocracy had resisted liberal calls for reform for so long that the intelligentsia and even many members of the professional classes—lawyers, doctors, and teachers—sympathized with some of the radicals' ideas or even their revolutionary plans. Nevertheless, when the Great War began, all of Russia's radical parties were tiny, and almost no one, save perhaps the egomaniacal Lenin himself, would have predicted they would topple the czar.

In 1914, Nicholas II (r. 1897–1917) hurled his still incompletely modernized empire into a modern, industrial war. At first, Russians rallied to support the czar, but patriotism quickly gave way to frustration and anger. Debilitating shortages of ammunition, weapons, food, fuel, and even boots demoralized troops at the front, and at home, Russians wearied of the administration's bungling and corruption. Nicholas refused to recognize his subjects' sufferings or to offer political or economic reforms that would relieve their distress. Venturing out with the army, he left much of the state's governance to his wife, Alexandra, and her confidante Grigori Rasputin (c. 1869–1916). An illiterate faith-healer, Rasputin threw himself into court intrigue, accepting bribes and sexual favors and seeking to rid the court of his numerous enemies. Those enemies conspired to drown Rasputin in the Neva River in December 1916, but only after they had failed to poison, shoot, and beat him to death. Though corrupt and despised, Rasputin, like czardom itself, was hard to kill.

The February Revolution

By December 1916, the damage had been done. The Russian monarchy had been discredited, and the state was forced to send troops to put down mass strikes among forced laborers in central Asia. On the eastern and southeastern fronts, Russian casualties were horrific. As many as 1.8 million were dead by the end of 1917, another 2.8 million were wounded, and 2.4 million taken prisoner. Still there was no end in sight. Bread was in such short supply that the government began forcing peasants to sell it at low prices. Fearing their farms and villages would be stripped of food, and weary of fighting for the czar, peasant soldiers began to desert in large numbers.

By February 1917, Petrograd was seething. Nearing the end of its term, the Fourth Duma, hoping to push through reforms, petitioned the czar to continue its session, but he disbanded it instead. On February 18 (using the dates the Russians used at the time, from the old Russian calendar), workers in one section of the enormous Putilov munitions factory went out on strike, as they had in the run-up to the 1905 revolution. The strike spread. On February 22, the plant locked out 20,000 workers. In sympathy for the strikers, disorderly crowds filled the streets, demanding bread, better pay, and an end to the war. There were reports of mutinies aboard naval vessels, and armed deserters began to stream into the capital city. The police soon lost control of the city. By February 28, revolutionaries had seized the railway stations, commandeered artillery supplies, and even cut the military commander's telephone lines. Inspired by the experiments tried in 1905, workers' councils, or soviets, were organized within the factories to form the basis for a new kind of grassroots, workers' democracy.

Seeing no other solution, on March 2 Nicholas II abdicated in favor of his brother, Grand Duke Michael, and quietly accepted house arrest with his family outside Petrograd. Eventually the Romanovs were sent to Siberia, and then to Ekaterinberg in the Ural Mountains, where they were shot by revolutionaries in July 1918. Grand Duke Michael was no fool. He quickly declined the title of czar, thus ending, rather ignominiously, the three-centuries-old Romanov monarchy. But someone had to govern Russia, especially as the state was still at war, and several factions put themselves forward to fill the power vacuum. The most prominent group of the czar's opponents, led by the moderate socialist Alexander Kerensky (1881–1970), proclaimed itself the **provisional government.** But a second group insisted on participating in governance: the more radical Petrograd soviet, composed of workers, soldiers, and revolutionary intellectuals. For a time the moderates and the radicals shared power despite deep disagreements.

The Russian Revolution, 1917–1918

In January 1917, Vladimir Lenin was one of many hot-headed radical Russian propagandists scribbling in Swiss exile. In his native country, the number of battlefield casualties soared and the cities starved. Had a poll been taken, the czar's popularity would have been at an all-time low, but no one could have predicted the changes the next year would bring.

As eyewitnesses like the British nurse Frances Farmborough testified, the Bolshevik revolution of October 1917 overtook Russia with terrifying speed. Already by early November, Farmborough reported in her diary, gentlewomen in Moscow were disguising themselves as peasants to avoid being forced to sell their homes or perform menial tasks. Portraits of Lenin had begun to appear in the cities. The masses flocked to hear speeches denouncing war profiteers, heartless bureaucrats, and the idle rich. In Odessa, on December 16, Farmborough reported daily riots, in which "mobs were attacking the homes of the bourgeoisie, confiscating their possessions, arresting the owners and shooting all who resisted them. No one was safe. Entire families had fallen before the blind fury of the Marxist fanatics." Like a tidal wave, Bolshevism engulfed southern Europe and the front: "The trenches were emptied of Russian soldiers. . . . The whole of Russia was then at the mercy of the Communist Proletariat."[8] In scarcely a month's time, the autocratic old world had been swept away.

By January 1918, Farmborough was reporting that thousands had begun to flee the country. Czarist money was of no value, and Bolshevik tribunals—modeled on those of the French revolutionary terror—were beginning to persecute the enemies of the now clearly successful revolution. Rumors spread that infants would be taken from their mothers and reared in institutions, as wards of the state. All Orthodox church services had been abolished, she claimed, including Christian burials of the dead, and altars and icons were being smashed. "One wonders how these vandals dared to play such havoc," Farmborough wrote, "for are they not the same who, only a year ago, had been keenly and devoutly crossing themselves as the name of god the Father passed their lips? . . . It seems incredible that Lenin and Trotsky have in so short a time stamped out all that the Holy Orthodox faith had inculcated in the Russian soul through almost ten centuries."[9]

Unbeknownst to Farmborough, Lenin was making more big plans, for the collectivization of agriculture and the total elimination of the parasitical upper classes. Those who opposed his plans would be sent to work camps or gulags in Siberia or dealt with by Lenin's secret security force, known first as the Cheka (and later as the NKVD and then the KGB). Charged with protecting the revolution, these agencies were permitted to murder or imprison enemies of the state. No evidence was necessary, no recourse was possible. Created in December 1917, the secret police would characterize the Soviet state throughout its lifetime.

By January 1918, the enormous Russian Empire, the most reactionary and economically backward region of Eurasia, was declared to be the dominion of what Marx had called the proletariat, or the industrial working class, in what was the world's first Communist state. Of course, the Bolsheviks in early 1918 still had a long way to go to consolidate their hold over Russia's far-flung provinces—and would have to fight a devastating set of civil wars to do so. Still, a completely new world was being born, so different from the old that the word *revolution* scarcely does justice to the shock that Russians— and expatriots like Farmborough— experienced in 1917–1918.

QUESTION | *Compare the Russian revolutions of 1917 with the French moderate and radical revolutions of 1789–1791 and 1792–1794 (see Chapter 17). What similarities and differences do you observe?*

Lenin Triumphant, 1918 Here Lenin addresses a crowd gathered in Red Square outside the Kremlin to celebrate the first anniversary of the October Revolution.

Many soviet delegates wanted radical social reforms and an end to the war; the leaders of the provisional government, like so many moderate postrevolutionary regimes before them, wanted to introduce reforms more gradually, and believed themselves duty-bound to continue the war and to take back Russian land now occupied by German and Austrian armies.

The Bolsheviks Take Power

The collapse of the czarist regime had opened the way for the return to Russia of some of its most dangerous revolutionaries. The Germans seized the opportunity to stir up trouble on the enemy's home front by sending Lenin home from his Swiss exile aboard a sealed train. In this way, Lenin, the leader of the **Bolsheviks,**

"Long Live Equality and Brotherhood!" This Bolshevik propaganda poster calls on all Russians (including silhouetted figures representing sailors, soldiers, workers, Cossacks, workers, and middle-class men and women) to rally behind the revolution.

the most unflinching advocates of violent revolution, avoided being discovered and arrested by czarist officials. He arrived at the Finland Station in Petrograd in April 1917; the equally radical philosopher-organizer Leon Trotsky returned in May.

Although the name *Bolsheviks* meant "the party of the majority," in early 1917, the Bolsheviks were far from being the largest party. But this did not stop them from haranguing urban crowds, advocating the carrying out of a great social and economic revolution in Russia, one that would give Russians not liberty, fraternity, and equality, as the French revolutionaries of 1789 had promised, but "land, peace and bread." For Russia's peasants, hungry workers, and war-weary citizens, this slogan was extraordinarily appealing. The radicals made new recruits, especially in the big-city soviets. From a membership of fewer than 10,000 in February 1917, by October the Bolsheviks could boast some 350,000 members, most in the cities of Petrograd and Moscow. Still this was a small number in an empire of some 169 million. When the Bolshevik leaders decided the time was ripe for revolution, they took the state by strategic seizure of its urban institutions and communications networks, not by the consent of the governed.

The October Revolution

Between March and October 1917, the provisional government suffered numerous setbacks. A summer offensive against the Germans failed and led to an embarrassing retreat; troops began to desert. Alexander Kerensky, the leader of the provisional government, could provide no internal stability, and food shortages became ever more acute. Finally, on October 25 (on Russia's old calendar), ahead of general elections set for November, the Bolsheviks decided to make their move, storming the czar's Winter

Palace, which the provisional government had been using as a headquarters. Even more important, the Bolsheviks seized the railroad stations, the telegraph cables, and the printing presses. They allowed the November elections to go ahead, but when they received only 25 percent of the vote, against the 40 percent cast for the less radical Socialist Revolutionaries, the Bolsheviks refused to share power. They had finally managed to achieve the communist revolution Karl Marx had predicted so long before, and they were not about to cede power to those they saw as backers of old-fashioned bourgeois democracy.

The Bolsheviks Make Peace

Though they had promised to end the war immediately, the Bolsheviks were taken aback at the provisions of the Treaty of Brest-Litovsk. The treaty called for Russia's Baltic territories as well as most of the Ukraine and the Crimea to be lopped off, and Russian troops withdrawn from Finland and Transcaucasia. Despite the treaty's terms, German armies continued to move swiftly eastward, rolling up territory the size of France in present-day Ukraine, Belarus, and Georgia, and inspiring there the declaration of numerous independent states. By the time the Bolsheviks signed the treaty in March 1918, republics had been proclaimed in Finland, Ukraine, Moldavia, and Armenia. German, Turkish, and British troops all raced toward Baku, a Caspian Sea port city located at the foot of the Caucasus Mountains in the region of Azerbaijan, where oil was so plentiful it bubbled up in pools just outside the city.

Eventually the Bolsheviks seized Baku and incorporated Azerbaijan uneasily into the newly founded Union of Soviet Socialist Republics (USSR). When Germany and Austria lost the war, Russia would reclaim the economically desirable Ukrainian breadbasket and rich mining territory in the Don basin. Some Allied forces were sent to the Russian peripheries after the November armistice to try to prevent the Bolsheviks from retaking territory. Europeans and Americans, as well as the Japanese on Russia's eastern flank, worried that the USSR might send armies and revolutionary ideas deeper into Europe and Asia. Even as peace talks began, some soldiers were deployed to yet another front.

How the War Ended

Admitting defeat, or at least trying to stop the war, was something many Europeans wanted to do long before

Why was there so little joy or long-lasting satisfaction at the end of the war?

1918. But once a state goes to war, it is not so easy for it to stop the fighting, especially when its opponents do not want to make peace. Moreover, everyone, governments and citizens alike, wanted the war to end in a way they found satisfying. For the Irish, Poles, Armenians, and Arabs, the goal was independence; for the Germans, it was German domination in central Europe; and for France, it was the return of Alsace and Lorraine. Having sacrificed so much, nobody wanted to be poorer, nobody wanted to lose territory, and nobody wanted to have to pay for the messes they had made. But wars, especially wars of this magnitude, do not end this way. It would prove impossible for the moderate Germans who tried to end the war in 1916 to do so or for the Greeks, despite enormous opposition to the war, to get out once they entered in 1917.

The British stayed the course, despite an uprising in Ireland at Easter 1916, which the government suppressed with much bloodshed. But Britain could not, in the long run, stop the Irish independence movement, and once the war ended, the southern part of England's oldest colony had to be given home rule. The Canadians continued to fight for the king, but at the 1917 Battle of Vimy Ridge, Canadians led the charge that broke a deadlock and dampened German morale. That success has been credited with sparking the development of a Canadian nationalism that would make Canadians less willing to do England's bidding in the war's aftermath. The French also continued to fight, despite a massive mutiny on the western front in 1917, which was hushed up and suppressed by hundreds of summary executions. And so, despite a snowballing sense that the authorities had lost all their legitimacy and that the war was a disastrous boondoggle, Europeans fought on, forcing their non-European subordinates to do the same.

The End, at Last

For Russia, the Great War ended with the Treaty of Brest-Litovsk—though by no means was that the end of bloodshed for the czar's former subjects. In fact, between

seven and ten million Russians died in the civil wars and famines that followed the Russian Revolution, more than twice the number of Russian soldiers and civilians killed in 1914–1917. For the Germans, the Russian departure from the war was a godsend, for it allowed troops in the east to be sent westward for a last-ditch spring offensive. Though German troops were exhausted and reserves running low, and central European cities teemed with hungry and restive people, Hindenburg and Ludendorff hoped they could now deliver the masterstroke that would ensure victory with huge territorial gains in the east. In April 1918, they launched Operation Michael, a final, desperate attempt to break through French lines and threaten Paris. Although the campaign initially succeeded in pushing the front westward when its forward progress was halted, the Germans could not regroup. With its ranks decimated and no fresh recruits to call into action, the German army was finished. On August 8, British and French tanks overran the German lines at Amiens. On October 2, the Entente broke through the last major German defenses in the west, the so-called Hindenburg line, at Saint Quentin, opening the way for Allied troops at last to march toward German territory and claim their victory.

Seeing the writing on the wall, the Bulgarians, Ottomans, and Austrians all began to seek separate peace agreements, leaving the Germans to finish the war on their own. Recognizing the inevitable and fearing reports of mass desertions and mutinies at the fronts, Germany's civilian chancellor, Prince Max von Baden, also sent out peace feelers, despite Ludendorff's refusal to admit defeat. Prince Max also tried to convince Kaiser Wilhelm to abdicate, suggesting that, otherwise, revolution—like that recently witnessed in Russia—was imminent, but the ever-irresponsible Wilhelm II simply replied, "You sent out the armistice offer; you will also have to accept the conditions."[10] Rather than face defeat or his angry subjects, some of whom now joined communist uprisings, Wilhelm jumped on a train for neutral Holland, where he remained, comfortable but unapologetic, until his death in 1941. Ludendorff also evaded taking blame, insisting that German troops could not have been defeated militarily—the army must have been "stabbed in the back" by socialists, Jews, and women on the home front. This myth of home-front sabotage would become widespread and influential in right-wing circles after 1918. Prince Max resigned in favor of the moderate socialist Friedrich Ebert, and the armistice was made official on November 11, 1918.

There were celebrations around the world, particularly in the victorious nations. In Paris, London, New York, Rome, and Sydney, crowds cheered the end of the most devastating conflict the modern world had ever seen. But joy at the war's conclusion was tempered by the deep and virtually universal sorrow of survivors who had lost family and friends, and by the desire to demonstrate that those deaths had not been in vain (Figure 22.1 and Map 22.4).

World War I fatalities (millions)

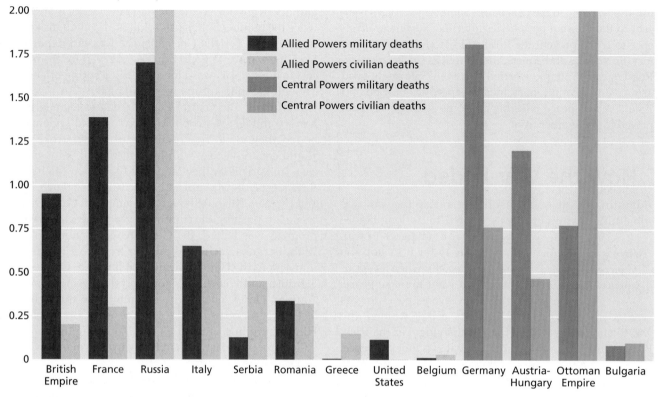

FIGURE 22.1 | World War I Fatality Rates

This bar graph shows the fatality rates for the Central Powers and for the Allies during World War I. It does not include fatalities caused by the influenza pandemic.

Source: Created by Jason M. Wolfe, based on data compiled by Scott Berg. For data sources see note for Map 22.4.

Postwar grief weighed heavily on many Europeans. But adding to their miseries was the fact that almost as soon as the armistice was declared, catastrophe struck in another form: influenza.

The Spanish Flu

We do not know precisely where the flu started, but its rapid spread undoubtedly was aided by the war's dispersal of both soldiers and civilians. It was first reported at Fort Riley, Kansas, in March 1918, but very quickly made its way to the front, where the flu may have contributed to the stalling out of the German spring offensive. The virus was quickly passed to the better-fed French and British troops as well. In May 1918 alone, 36,473 members of the British First Army were hospitalized. The disease spread like wildfire in Portugal and Greece, Hungary and South Africa, but became known as the Spanish flu because the Spanish press—uncensored because Spain remained a neutral nation—carried some of the first reports of the disease.

The effects on the soldiers in the spring and summer of 1918 were terrible, but the new strain that emerged in the fall of that year was far more deadly. In America the virus began to ravage army bases and then population centers in September 1918. Attacking especially the young and healthy, the influenza virus caused patients'

lungs to rupture; their noses, ears, and eye sockets to spurt blood; their bodies to turn blue or black from oxygen deficiency. People with no symptoms of illness in the afternoon could be dead by morning. Crowded troop trains left their stations full of healthy men only to arrive at their destinations loaded with dead bodies. In the particularly hard-hit city of Philadelphia, some 759 people died of the flu on October 10 alone. The morgue overflowed, and corpses backed up in homes where sick family members remained too weak to transport them. In Paris, some 1,500 people a week were dying of influenza in November 1918, while London lost more than 15,000 inhabitants that fall and winter. Economies that had managed to operate throughout the war threatened to break down entirely as hundreds of thousands of civilians and soldiers were too sick to staff telephone exchanges, police stations, and pharmacies.

An estimated 675,000 people perished of influenza in 1918–1919 in the United States alone. But this was a pandemic, and its terrible effects were felt in Gambia and Argentina, in neutral Switzerland, and in Japan. Regions with extensive contact with troops suffered most, as did India, where so many troops and laborers for the Allied war effort had been raised and where they returned after the war. Central European civilians, many of them malnourished, perished by the hundreds of thousands—those, that is, who had not already succumbed to typhus,

MAP 22.4 | Patterns of Human Loss in World War I

This map offers an overview of human losses, nation by nation, for the Great War. Losses include both civilian and military deaths.[11] **Which nations were hit hardest by the Great War?**

Legend: Fatalities by nation during WWI
- under 1%
- 1–3%
- 3–5%
- 5–10%
- over 10%
- Neutral nations

dysentery, or tuberculosis. Historian John M. Barry estimates the virus killed at least 50 million people worldwide (of a world population estimated at 1.8 billion), far in excess of the number of casualties of the war itself.[12] The flu's massive social, economic, and psychological effects are still insufficiently understood by historians, but the influenza epidemic provided an apocalyptic end to a disastrous war.

The Peace

The armistice brought with it the death of four empires: the German Reich and the multiethnic Austro-Hungarian, Ottoman, and Russian Empires. None of

Why did the victors have such trouble dealing with the war's aftermath?

the rulers of these empires had left a detailed plan for postwar— nor would such plans have been honored by those who succeeded them. During the war itself, many secret plans had been made for dividing up the spoils, but once the conflict ended, following through on these plans, many of them mutually contradictory, proved difficult, and in some cases they were no longer desirable. Elsewhere, facts on the ground helped shape the policies and state boundaries the peacemakers developed. The war's end spurred a series of attempted revolutions and counterrevolutions in Germany, Hungary, Italy, and Austria; pogroms in Poland; unrest in Ireland, India, and Egypt; and postrevolutionary civil

War Memorials

Among the most painful of postwar questions was this: how could the living pay proper tribute to the millions who had died? Both during and after the war, this was a pressing and highly charged problem for families and states all over the world—whether their side had won or lost the war. Everyone realized that remembering and commemorating the dead was crucial. But how could millions of men be offered suitable acknowledgment of their sacrifices?

There were both public and private means of commemoration. Private grieving came first, beginning as early as August 1914. Bad news came by telegram, letter, or personal visits from local officials or clergymen, but often the information offered was vague or faulty. Some families heard right away. Others, like the families of Australians killed at Gallipoli, did not know for weeks what had happened to their sons, brothers, and husbands. Bereaved families conveyed the news to others on printed death cards, which carried a picture of the deceased and a short account of his life and service. Though people tired of hearing funerary church bells, and by mid-war wearing traditional mourning dress began to seem ostentatious, we can be sure that the experience of mass death did not make the losing of one's own kin any easier. Throughout the war and afterward, private grieving continued and death never lost its sting.

It is hard to recover this world of private grief, which is rarely reflected in public monuments. Käthe Kollwitz's *The Grieving Parents,* a monument commemorating the loss of her son Peter in October 1914, however, speaks volumes. It took the Berlin artist some eighteen years after her son's death to finish the sculptures, which were set among the graves of young men in the Vladslo cemetery in Belgium. When it rains, the bowed heads of these suffering survivors seem to weep for their deceased child.

On the public side, from about 1915 on, all the combatant nations spent considerable time and effort erecting monuments to the dead. By the end of the war's first year, it was clear to the French government that the number of dead would be of such unprecedented magnitude that a dense network of military cemeteries would be needed to commemorate them. In 1916, the British too acknowledged the enormous scale of casualties and the new forms of bodily annihilation, by declaring that the war dead would not be brought home, but instead buried in British graveyards

The Tomb of the Unknown Soldier, Belgrade After the war, European nations built tombs to unknown soldiers, men who died in circumstances that prevented their bodies from being identified or buried properly. This tomb was built in the city first bombarded in July 1914: Belgrade, Serbia.

in France. So many remains were unidentifiable that to repatriate only identified bodies was thought to be discriminatory. And so began the tradition of commemorating the unknown soldier—the faceless victim of modern, mass warfare.

After the war, states designed and built cemeteries and monuments that tended to dignify sacrifice for the nation and to downplay the ugliness and brutality of modern warfare. Neoclassical designs were often used, both because Europeans of this generation thought the ancient world solemn and stately and because neoclassicism was a secular language—and monument designers were well aware that many of the dead were Jews, Muslims, Hindus, and atheists. Christian motifs, however, were still present, as is shown by two features erected in every British Great War cemetery: a Great War Stone, which was a sort of secularized altar, and a Cross of Sacrifice, on which was inscribed a verse from Ecclesiastes: "Their Name Liveth For Evermore." At Tannenberg the Germans erected a particularly nationalist monument, recalling the glories of the Teutonic knights. When Field Marshal Paul von Hindenberg died in 1934, the Nazis buried him on the site of his wartime triumph. Many of these memorials can still be visited today, though some, especially in eastern and southeastern Europe, fell victim to subsequent conflicts. The Tannenberg monument, for example, was destroyed after 1945 by the Soviets, who used materials from it to build the headquarters of the Communist Party in Warsaw.

QUESTION | *What do war memorials tell us about the experience of the Great War that usually doesn't appear in standard accounts of the war?*

Käthe Kollwitz, *The Grieving Parents* This powerful memorial, created by the artist Käthe Kollwitz in mourning for her son, stands in the cemetery for German soldiers in Vladslo, Belgium. When it rains, as it often does in this region, the figures seem to weep.

wars all across Russia. To make any sort of peace in such circumstances was a great challenge. But the victors had to try.

The Victors

From the moment the first peace conference opened in Paris on January 18, 1919, it was clear that even among the victors, there was no consensus on how to make a fair and lasting peace. The French and Belgians wanted to inflict punitive money payments, or reparations, on the Central Powers; the Italians wanted more territory than their fellow Allies were willing to give them; and the British wanted to secure their old colonies and if possible add strategically important and mineral-rich territories to their list. By signing a separate peace, the Russians had given up their rights to claim any spoils, but the Big Three—Britain, France, and the United States—would almost surely have tried to thwart Bolshevik participation anyway. The host of other minor Allies—the Greeks, Romanians, Poles, Japanese, and Serbs, not to mention the still stateless or subordinate Jews, Arabs, Armenians, Irish, and Indians—all had demands, but often these clashed or could not be realized without fearsome consequences—such as the unleashing of new wars.

Into this quagmire stepped U.S. president Woodrow Wilson. Many Europeans looked to Wilson, as president of the world's new economic powerhouse and as an outsider seeking no territorial rewards for his nation, to lead the way. On the whole, the peacemakers accepted his list of guidelines, known as the **Fourteen Points,** as the blueprint for the peace negotiations. Wilson was an idealist, and his Fourteen Points were meant to ensure lasting peace on the European continent by giving each ethnic group what he called the right to **national self-determination,** which meant the right to choose a political destiny as an independent nation or as a part of a multiethnic state. Having witnessed the persecution of ethnic groups such as the Armenians, Wilson also insisted that minority rights should be protected. He proposed the creation of an international body, the **League of Nations,** to protect these rights and to keep the peace in perpetuity. Eventually, five peace treaties would be signed (Table 22.1), all of them calling for the signatories to allow the League to negotiate future disputes.

The League of Nations seemed a promising solution to the problem of maintaining the global balance of power—at least until Wilson's own Congress refused to ratify the covenant of the League of Nations, and the United States retreated into isolationism. This left the world's most prosperous power out of the League and significantly weakened expectations that the new organization would be able to maintain the peace. Self-determination too was a noble idea, but it soon became evident that it was a totally unworkable one, especially for central and southeastern Europe, where multinational empires had collapsed, leaving a complex ethnic patchwork.

The principle of self-determination was not applied to the territories the Allies took from the former Ottoman Empire and the colonies they seized from Germany. Instead, to placate the anti-imperialist Americans, these territories were handed over to the League of Nations. The League, in turn, parceled out **mandates** of different types to the British and the French. The supervising, or mandatory, power, which was supposed to rule until such time as it decided that the inhabitants were ready for self-governance, had to promise to respect the rights of those it ruled and to protect ethnic and religious minorities within each territory. The League created three categories of mandates: the former Ottoman lands, which would be ready for independence first; some African countries, which would not be ready for autonomy for the foreseeable future; and some African nations and Pacific islands that probably would always remain mandates. The creation of the mandate system demonstrated that the war had not altered European racialist presumptions. Europeans still believed that the peoples of the Middle East, and especially the peoples of Africa and the Pacific, were not sufficiently "evolved" to allow them self-rule.

To Arabs and Jewish Zionists, both of whom believed the Entente had promised them independent states in exchange for their assistance during the war, the mandates created in Palestine, Syria, Iraq, and the Arab lands were crushing blows. The French remained unsatisfied with the level of reparations the Germans were asked to pay; and the British worried that France's passion for revenge would destabilize central Europe and pave the way for new conflicts. Even for the victors, this was a hard and often bitter peace (Map 22.5).

The Losers

Of course, among the most angry and bitter were the defeated powers. There was bitterness in Hungary, for the Treaty of Trianon required that state to relinquish almost two-thirds of its prewar territory. The Bulgarians considered the Treaty of Neuilly, which required the state to recognize Yugoslavia and to strip its army down to 20,000 men, a national catastrophe. The Austrians were so dissatisfied with the rump territory left to them in the Treaty of Saint Germain that even the socialists wanted to dissolve the new republic of Austria and annex it to Germany. The provisions of the Treaty of Sèvres were so unsatisfactory—and unenforceable—in the former lands of the Ottoman Empire that a series of partitioning wars soon rendered it wholly obsolete. The **Treaty of Versailles,** which the French forced the Germans to sign in the Hall of Mirrors (where France's humiliating loss of Alsace and Lorraine had been formalized in 1871) was bitterly resented in Germany. The representatives of the German Republic who were forced to sign it—since the generals and the kaiser refused to do so—were ever afterward tainted by their agreement to forfeit territory to the French and the Poles, to relinquish all overseas colonies,

MAP 22.5 | Europe after the World War I Peace Treaties, c. 1923

This map shows the territorial losses suffered by the Great War's losers: the Germans, Austrians, Russians, and Hungarians. **Describe what happened to Germany and Austria-Hungary. What new states existed in 1923 that did not exist in 1914? (Compare with Map 22.1.)**

TABLE 22.1 | The Peace Treaties

DEFEATED POWER	TREATY
Germany	Treaty of Versailles
Austria-Hungary	Treaty of Saint Germain
Ottoman Empire	Treaty of Sèvres
Bulgaria	Treaty of Neuilly
Hungary	Treaty of Trianon

to decimate and disarm the German military forces, and to pay colossal sums in reparations. The Germans also had to sign Paragraph 231, the infamous **war guilt clause,** in which they accepted blame for starting the war. Both the reparation payments, which contributed to

spiraling inflation in central Europe, and the war guilt clause made it very hard for the Germans to make peace with the postwar world.

Of Greeks and Turks

Peace was perhaps most fleeting in the Balkans, where the conflict had begun. Greek leaders seized the opportunity offered by the Ottoman Empire's collapse to realize their long-held dream of repossessing Istanbul and the Asia Minor coast. However, the Greek army's attempts to take their portion of Ottoman territory ended in catastrophe, as the Turkish army reorganized itself under the leadership of the nationalist hero Mustafa Kemal in 1919 and pushed the Greek army, as well as thousands of Greek and Armenian civilians, out of Asia Minor. In their wrath, the Turks destroyed several beautiful coastal

Mustafa Kemal's War—and Peace

Mustafa Kemal was born in 1881 to Turkish parents in the multiethnic city of Salonica, on the western fringe of the Ottoman Empire. He attended military school and became a politically active Young Turk, deeply critical of Ottoman corruption but a passionate advocate of Turkish nationalism. As a young officer, he fought bravely and with distinction in the Balkan Wars and in the Great War. At Gallipoli, he, not his German comrades, planned the successful repulsing of the Allies and rallied frightened and ill-equipped Ottoman troops to fight. In 1916, he again rallied demoralized troops to fight the Russians in the Caucasus. The next year he was in Syria, where he had to deal with the aftermath of the Syrian famine, the Arab revolt, and mass desertions as the Ottoman army collapsed. Raging against the incompetence of the Turkish generals in Istanbul, he was holding the line against further Allied incursions into Ottoman territory in Aleppo, Syria, when the war ended.

Mustafa Kemal (Atatürk) The Turkish war hero Mustafa Kemal in full dress uniform. Note that he was also awarded Germany's Iron Cross (pinned to his shirt, lower right).

But Mustafa Kemal was not done fighting. In early 1919, rumors coming out of Paris that independent states were being carved out of Ottoman domains for the Armenians, Kurds, Arabs, and Greeks horrified him, and he began to organize his own paramilitary Turkish resistance troops. Though demoralized by losing the war, the Turks were enraged when a Greek army landed at Smyrna (now Izmir) on

May 15, 1919, with the intention not just of keeping peace, but of seizing new territory. On May 19, Kemal landed at Samsun on the Black Sea, ready to repulse the Greeks. This date would prove a turning point in Turkish history, so important to Kemal that he later officially changed his birth date to May 19.

After three more years of failed diplomacy and intermittent warfare, Kemal's Turkish troops succeeded in pushing back the Greeks and in establishing the Turks as the masters of Asia Minor. The campaign ended in the brutal burning and occupation of the beautiful coastal city of Smyrna and the slaughtering of many of its Armenian and Greek citizens in 1922. In the wake of this act of ethnic cleansing, the new Turkish Republic was proclaimed, and Mustafa Kemal made its first president; he received, too, a new name: Atatürk, or father of the Turks. Both Kemal and his new state celebrated the glories of the Ottoman Empire, but both were actually products of the first modern global war—and the first, failed, attempt to secure global peace.

QUESTIONS | *How did Turkish nationalism contribute to the winning of the war and the constituting of a new Turkish state after World War I? What happened to Ottoman policy on minority groups as a result of this new sort of nationalism, exemplified by Mustafa Kemal?*

cities, including Smyrna, terrorizing fleeing citizens and murdering many of them.

In 1922, the Greek statesman Eleftherios Venizelos and Kemal saved the remainder of the Greek population in Turkey and the Turkish population living in Greece from the further escalation of intercommunal violence by arranging a population exchange. Some 1.2 million nominally Greek refugees, many of them Turkish speaking and most of them destitute, left Asia Minor for the Greek mainland, where a state of only 5.5 million had somehow to absorb them, while about 800,000 ethnic Turks passed in the opposite direction. Thus, the situation was stabilized not by the League of Nations, nor by agreements to protect minority rights, but by a state-sponsored form of ethnic cleansing, which dislodged approximately two million people from their homes, but may have prevented full-scale genocide. The new ethnic homogeneity of these two states, neither of them among the original belligerents, was yet another unintended consequence of the Great War—and the failed peace.

The Greek-Turkish population exchange marked the conclusion of one era of mass warfare, but it would not be long before a new era of mass violence, mass warfare, and genocide would be born.

Conclusion

We have seen the evolution of the citizen army from the time of Gustavus Adolphus in the Thirty Years' War to the French revolutionary armies of the end of the eighteenth century, to the rapidly expanded and heavily armed national armies of the early twentieth century. In 1914, the citizen-soldier, with the nation at his back, marched into warfare on a scale never before seen in Europe—and the war fought between the citizens of Europe's empires spread death and disruption not only across the continent, but across the world as well. The result of four and one-half years of fighting, much of it using weapons with unprecedented firepower, was not only the death of more than nine million men, but also the economic ruination of European nations and the discrediting and overthrow of many of its monarchies.

In Russia the war gave rise to a radical new form of governance, communism. In the Ottoman Empire, it gave an enormous boost to Zionism, Arab nationalism, and Turkish nationalism—and ultimately destroyed the Muslim empire that had once ruled most of the Mediterranean rim as well as large chunks of Anatolia. The peace treaties that attempted to clean up the mess envisioned a brave new world in which the self-determination of nations offered all nationality groups the opportunity to govern themselves and live peaceably with their neighbors. But there were, from the outset, many obstacles to realizing this vision. Europeans, who had done so much to expand voting rights, hasten technological progress, and extend to large sectors of the population public goods such as education, sanitation, and cultural enrichment, had now demonstrated that they could also wreak unprecedented destruction on themselves, and the rest of the world.

Critical Thinking Questions

1. What did it mean to fight a total war?

2. Could the war have been prevented, or ended earlier? If so, which individuals might have acted to stop the war, or to change its course?

3. Why is it important to understand the peculiarities of the war's western, eastern, southeastern, and colonial theaters?

4. How might the Great War have changed non-Europeans' view of the history of western civilization?

Key Terms

ethnic cleansing **(p. 700)**

Central Powers **(p. 702)**

Entente **(p. 702)**

total war **(p. 703)**

Schlieffen Plan **(p. 704)**

Treaty of Brest-Litovsk **(p. 708)**

provisional government **(p. 716)**

Bolsheviks **(p. 718)**

Fourteen Points **(p. 723)**

national self-determination **(p. 723)**

League of Nations **(p. 723)**

mandates (mandate system) **(p. 723)**

Treaty of Versailles **(p. 723)**

war guilt clause **(p. 724)**

Primary Sources in connect

For information on Connect and the online resources available, go to **http://connect.mcgraw-hill.com**.

1. **Emperor Franz Joseph and Emperor Wilhelm II Prepare for War**

2. **The Socialists Opt to Support the War, 1914**

3. **War Hysteria Grips an Austrian Novelist**

4. **A Red Cross Doctor Reports from Serbia**

5. **Women and the First World War**

6. **Woodrow Wilson, Fourteen Points**

Anna Eisenmenger, Blockade: The Diary of an Austrian Middle-Class Woman 1914–1924

The following passage from the diary of Anna Eisenmenger, a Viennese housewife, demonstrates how much the home front was transformed by the horrors of the Great War. Especially in eastern cities such as Vienna, the effects of the Allied blockade were keenly felt and resulted in terrible food shortages and malnutrition. Many, like Anna's son Karl (who had been sent home from the front with a head wound) were radicalized by the experience and eager, once the war was over, to overturn the empires that had made war on one another and in the process ruined so many lives. Eisenmenger wrote the following passage on November 8, 1918, three days before the armistice.

We housewives have during the last four years grown accustomed to standing in queues; we have also grown accustomed to being informed after hours of waiting that supplies are exhausted and that we can try again in a week's time with the pink card, section No. so-and-so; in the meantime, we are obliged to go home with empty hands and still emptier stomachs. These disappointments are the order of the day. Only very seldom do those who are sent away disappointed give cause for police intervention. . . . On the other hand, it happens more and more frequently that one of the pale, tired women who have been waiting in a queue for hours collapses from exhaustion and has to be taken away from the Food Center in an ambulance. The turbulent scenes which occurred today inside and outside the large market hall seemed to me perfectly natural. In my dejected mood the patient apathy with which we housewives endure all our domestic privation seemed to be blameworthy and incomprehensible. Karl immediately tried to profit by my state of mind to win me over to his communistic views: "Abolition of the present incapable bourgeois form of government, war on capitalism, war profiteers and exploiters of the starving people, etc." But my inherited bourgeois outlook made me see and fear in these familiar catchwords merely a provocation to fresh war and hatred. I protested immediately against Karl's introduction to communistic propaganda into my house. My own state of mind made me realize, however, how easy it must be to upset the moral equilibrium of whole classes of the population who have been forced out of their ordinary habits by this unhappy war and now fall an easy prey to the political alligator. . . .

The result of these four most terrible years I have ever experienced is, as regards my immediate family, consisting of eight persons, namely Victor, my husband, Karl, Otto and Ernst, my sons; Liesbeth, my daughter, Rudi, my son-in-law, and Wolfi, my grandson: 2 dead, 3 seriously wounded, 1 invalid. Out of eight people, six clawed by the devilish talons of war. Of these six, two torn from us forever (Victor and Otto). Of the remaining four: Erni, at 19 years of age, condemned to lifelong darkness through loss of his sight; Karl, with his moral equilibrium seriously disturbed as a result of his head-wound; Rudi, a poor helpless cripple owing to the loss of both legs; Liesbeth, his wife, suspected of tuberculosis as the result of insufficient nourishment. Wolfi at a tender age in constant danger of infection.

The eighth, myself, still in health, but nervously overstrained and in need of rest. Fully conscious of my heavy obligations, and firmly resolved to withstand the tempests of fate and, under these melancholy circumstances still to make the best of everything. I want to fill my dear invalids with resignation and courage to bear their fate. I want to try as far as possible to gather together the scanty remnants of their shattered lives and to make those lives worth living. I want to try, under these bitter, altered circumstances, to procure for them some meager joys, without which such terrible blows of fate could not be born for long, until time, that infallible though often cruelly relentless physician, has transformed even the most crushing losses into habit.

I lay aside my pen and fold my hands. "God Almighty! Give me strength to go on fighting for the happiness of my children!"

QUESTIONS | *What does Anna Eisenmenger's list of family tragedies tell us about the wider story of the war and its influence on European society? What special burdens did Anna bear because she was a wife and mother?*

Source: Anna Eisenmenger, excerpt from *Blockade: The Diary of an Austrian Middle-Class Woman 1914–1924,* in *Beyond the Home Front: Women's Autobiographical Writing of the Two World Wars,* ed. Yvonne M. Klein (New York: New York University Press, 1997), 120–122.

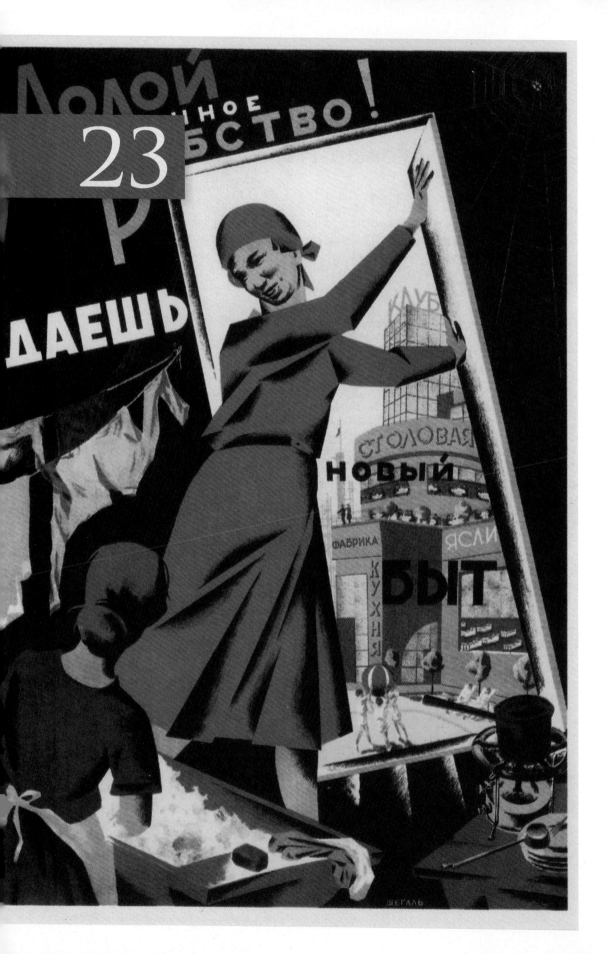

THE INTERWAR ERA

THE SEARCH FOR STABILITY

The Search for Stability

The Soviet Experiment
  The Russian Civil Wars
  Inventing a Communist State
  Soviet Sticks and Carrots
  Soviet Society in the 1930s

The Survival of Democracy in France and Britain
  Stability through Safety Nets
  Colonial Instabilities

The Anti-democratic Right
  Italy's Fascist Experiment
  What Was Fascism?
  The Weimar Republic and the Origins of the Nazi Party
  Stabilization by Authoritarian Means: Eastern Europe in the 1920s and 1930s
  Authoritarian States and Stateless People

The Body and the State
  The New Woman—and the Old Family Structure
  The New Man

Experimentation and Modernism in Interwar Culture
  Art and Architecture
  Interwar Science, Philosophy, and Literature
  Popular Culture

The Great Depression and the Radicalization of Politics
  Hitler Becomes Chancellor
  Hitler's "Little Men" in Power
  Enabling Dictatorship: The Reichstag Fire
  Nazi Sticks and Carrots
  Foreign Policy and Rearmament

Fascism Triumphant
  The Spanish Civil War
  The Anschluss

Conclusion

ALEXANDRA KOLLONTAI: THE NEW WOMAN, SOVIET STYLE

The bourgeois daughter of a Ukrainian noble father and a Finnish divorcée, Alexandra Kollontai (1872–1952) had enjoyed a privileged childhood and had married for love. But in the 1890s, that great decade of generational revolt, she began to immerse herself in communist literature. In 1896, a visit to the huge Kronholm textile works outside of St. Petersburg convinced her that she could not live a happy life while so many women workers remained enslaved. She left her husband and baby to study Marxist philosophy and to write books denouncing capitalist society, which she claimed made women slaves to men, both in the workplace and in the home. Kollontai was active during the Revolution of 1905 and in 1908 had to flee Russia. Vocally opposed

◀ The Soviet "Red" Woman Unveils the High-Tech (and Laundry-Free) Future

Alexandra Kollontai Born into a bourgeois family, Alexandra Kollontai was drawn to communism because she believed it was the only means by which to fully liberate women from the tyranny of men and the drudgery of housework. She would serve Lenin and Stalin faithfully, despite their authoritarian measures and their failures to put her ideas about reforming family relations into practice.

to the Great War, she returned to her native land after the February Revolution of 1917 and did her all to help Lenin seize power. Kollontai devoted herself to building a Bolshevik world—but in the process sacrificed to the cause many of her prewar hopes and dreams.

In the aftermath of the revolution, Kollontai worked feverishly to apply Marxist doctrine to women's issues, insisting that true socialist freedom required the dismantling of the bourgeois family. The most prominent female Bolshevik, Kollontai was made the first commissar for social welfare. She put into place new forms of state support for mothers and families and argued for the creation of central kitchens, communal child-care centers, and collective laundries to free women from the double burden of housework and work outside the home. She demanded that other women come to the aid of the Communist Party, denouncing as selfish or deluded those who wanted to spend their time dancing or attending church. In fact, the Bolsheviks were eager to bring women into the workplace and greatly expanded child care and education for women; divorces and abortions could be obtained much more easily in the Soviet Union than anywhere else in Europe, at least until Stalin began to reverse these policies in the mid-1930s. But male Communists were largely hostile to Kollontai's campaign for female sexual emancipation and put other priorities ahead of building collective laundries and child-care facilities; the double burden

Weimar Republic
1919–1933

Russian Revolution and Civil War
1917–1921

Alexandra Kollontai becomes ambassador to Norway
1922

World War I ends
1918

1915

1920

1925

of housework *and* work outside the home continued to fall heavily on Soviet women. As the new regime's lack of interest in women's issues became apparent, Kollontai began to air her disagreements with the party, but quickly found herself sidelined. In 1922, Lenin appointed her the world's first female ambassador (to Norway)—chiefly to remove her from the centers of Soviet power.

As ambassador, Kollontai faithfully and unflinchingly supported the Soviet regime; as both Lenin and Stalin saw it, her task was to negotiate trade treaties and neutralize opposition to communism, certainly not to criticize their regimes. She turned her feminism in literary directions, writing first a story of her life, titled *Autobiography of a Sexually Emancipated Communist Woman* (deeply censored in the USSR), and then a novel, *Red Love* (1927), in which one of the main characters opts to have a baby out of wedlock, but to have the state raise it so that she can continue her work for the party. Like Kollontai, this "Red" heroine was experimenting with new social and political arrangements

in the hopes of founding a more equitable postwar society. But the novel, like the autobiography, did not paint a realistic picture of the repressive and still-unequal world the Bolsheviks had created. It ended, for example, before the baby's birth and thus failed to follow the character as she struggled both to raise her child and to receive fair treatment by male party members.

In 1937, Kollontai denounced old Bolshevik friends after they had been tried and executed in Stalin's great purge of the party. Perhaps she was trying to save her former husband; but he too was deported to Siberia and reportedly shot as he got off the train. She continued to praise Stalin and Soviet social policy, concealing what she knew about the regime's brutality. Stalin must have found her useful as she, virtually alone among her generation of Bolsheviks, survived the purges to die of natural causes, at age eighty. Kollontai well knew, if she never dared to express it, that her own revolutionary dreams, like so many experiments of the interwar era, had ended in authoritarian nightmares.[1]

Alexandra Kollontai was only one of many Europeans of the interwar era to cheer the postwar fall of old monarchies and social structures—and one of the few, at least initially, to endorse the advent of a new dictatorship. The era opened with a great surge of hope, both in communist Russia and in western Europe's democracies, as the old empires, Ottoman, Russian, German, and Austro-Hungarian, collapsed. Though bitterness about the peace treaties and grieving for the dead continued, many people were ready to try new things, from communism to bob haircuts for women. Governments experimented with mass housing projects, and artists gravitated toward abstraction. But inventing and sustaining politi-

cal systems that could cope with the conflicts of the era tested even the most confident innovators.

The Search for Stability

The new borders created by the postwar peace treaties were extremely controversial. But economic recovery was an even more immediate and more troublesome problem. *All* of Europe's combatants had, to one degree or another, become debtor nations—in debt to the emerging

Why was it so hard for European leaders to establish stability after 1918?

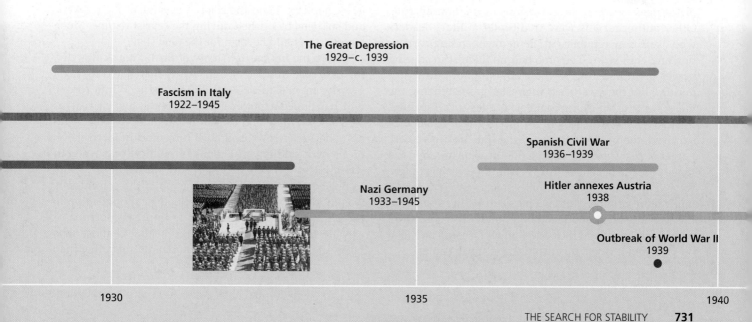

The Great Depression
1929–c. 1939

Fascism in Italy
1922–1945

Spanish Civil War
1936–1939

Nazi Germany
1933–1945

Hitler annexes Austria
1938

Outbreak of World War II
1939

1930

1935

1940

world power, the United States. Agricultural production had fallen off everywhere, inflation and black markets were omnipresent, and strikes and rallies burgeoned as workers ran out of patience with governing elites. States now had many disabled veterans, widows, and orphans to care for. France, Belgium, and the new states of Poland and Yugoslavia had significant war damages to repair; virtually all of Europe's cities had housing shortages. Everybody wanted some kind of stability, but the means by which they sought it were in many cases mutually exclusive, and only in a few places were democratic forms of compromise sufficiently fair or fast-working to satisfy populations that had tired of suffering in silence.

Under these circumstances, it is rather astonishing that the liberal democracies and market economies created in Europe after the war—some twenty in 1919—survived as long as they did, for democracies and market economies do not typically develop speedy and comprehensive solutions to political and economic problems. Indeed, one of the advantages of these systems is that, ideally, they allow solutions to emerge out of debate, compromise, and individual initiative—but the 1920s and 1930s were hardly ideal times. Nor were Europe's democracies flawless. Some were corrupt and served the interests only of the few. Others tried to force secularizing reforms on still-pious populations and resistant clergy. Only a few European states were sufficiently committed to democracy and capitalism and fortunate in their economic and geographic circumstances to hold on to these values throughout the interwar era; most were not. In such times, the lure of authoritarian solutions—in which one man or one party would simply tell everyone else what to do—was hard to resist.

Authoritarianism came in many different flavors. We can call Russian communism, along with Italian fascism and German Nazism, varieties of **totalitarianism,** for all three sought to establish the state's total domination over economic, political, cultural, and even private matters such as who one could marry or how (or even whether) one worshipped God. There were, however, considerable differences between these versions of totalitarian rule. Other authoritarians were traditional military leaders who overthrew republics in the name of ending corruption and civil strife. They too had no interest in sharing power or in listening to the complaints of ethnic minorities, but they were less interested in mobilizing the masses or in establishing complete mastery of all spheres.

Across the board, even in the places where democracy survived, the power and size of the state had increased. Larger states were now expected to provide an extended range of social benefits—from veterans' pensions to highways. For better and for worse, states now intervened much more routinely into people's private lives, attempting to create large and healthy populations whose work would help to rebuild the nation, and who could be called on to defend it when, inevitably, the next war came.

The Soviet Experiment

If the chaos and crises of the war's end made many Europeans long for stability, others, such as Alexandra Kollontai and Vladimir Lenin, used the opportunity to try daring new experiments. The most ambitious of these was the Russian Revolution, which resulted in the creation of an enormous, ideologically driven empire in the east. The revolution's success greatly emboldened the radical left not only in Europe but also in the rest of the world and correspondingly terrified and radicalized right-wing parties. The success of Soviet communism in modernizing the backward economy of the Russian Empire—and the Russians' evident desire to spread the revolution to other states—made the USSR both a model and a threat. To understand Europeans' hopes and fears, their great postwar appetite to try new things, and their even more powerful desire to impose order, we must first examine how the Russian Revolution gave way to the Soviet state and then see how this new regime dealt with the crises of the interwar period.

> For the people of the Soviet Union, what were the advantages and disadvantages of the new Communist economy?

The Russian Civil Wars

In November 1917, a handful of dedicated Marxist revolutionaries succeeded in toppling the provisional government headed by the moderate socialist Alexander Kerensky, which, together with a democratically elected Duma, had run the country after the abdication of Czar Nicholas II. The Bolsheviks' radical principles and uncompromising stance toward moderate reformers made what came next—prolonged, bloody, and bitter civil wars—all but inevitable. Born in the midst of the terrible brutality of the Great War, the Communist revolution and the regimes that perpetuated it never gave up the use of violence. They adopted the color red as their symbol, the color of the French revolutionaries' Phrygian caps (see Chapter 17) and the color, they said, of the workers' and soldiers' bloodshed during the czarist regime. Much blood, too, would be shed for the new state.

Before the ink on the Treaty of Brest-Litovsk was dry, the new Communist, or Red, Army marshaled by Leon Trotsky moved to destroy the opposing White forces, which included a motley group of liberals and czarists, as well as Ukrainian and central Asian independence fighters. The Red Army used both force and indoctrination on its own soldiers, as legions of political policemen or commissars were created to ensure the soldiers' loyalty to Bolshevik party doctrine. The job of the commissars was to identify and eliminate ideological opposition to the regime. They were allowed to imprison, torture, or execute "enemies of the revolution"—that is, those who believed in democracy, monarchy, or anything other than

MAP 23.1 | Russian Revolution and Civil Wars, 1917–1921

This map shows the relatively small, but crucial area of Russia in which the Bolsheviks first gained control and the incursions made by "White" armies and their supporters in the attempt to defeat the Bolsheviks during the civil wars. *Look at the names and relative sizes of the new "socialist republics" established within the Soviet Union by 1921 (S.S.R. stands for Soviet Socialist Republic). What has happened to the multiethnic empire of the czars? Which of the "republics" is likely to dominate the others?*

Bolshevism. Fired by hatred for the old czarist state as well as by the Bolsheviks' promises for the great workers' paradise to be established, the Red Army surged in size, numbering five million in 1919. In the meantime, peasants avenged themselves on their landlords and seized the land their families had tilled as serfs and sharecroppers for centuries.

Terrified that Communist revolution would spread, the United States, Great Britain, and France considered military action to thwart the Reds. In August 1918, 15,000 men were sent to protect the railways through Archangel, but by the end of 1919 they had departed, though a Japanese contingent seeking to push westward from Vladivostok stayed until 1922 (Map 23.1).

The anticommunist White Army was left to fight a series of brutal and devastating battles with Trotsky's Red Army; fighting was especially fierce in border regions— the Ukraine, Georgia, Azerbaijan, and Siberia. The Red Army forced its way into Finland and managed to secure some territory from that newly independent state. Seeking to take advantage of the confusion, the new state of Poland sought to push its borders eastward into

Belorussia. Initially the Red Army fell back but reorganized and threatened Warsaw. The conflict ended in 1921 with a victory and additional territory for Poland. During this bloody conflict, right-wing nationalists on both sides scapegoated and persecuted Jews unlucky enough to live in these territories.

All over the czar's former domains, the Russian civil wars brought with them new forms of terror and deprivation, especially for civilians. When supplies for the army and the cities ran short, the state declared a food dictatorship, which allowed Red Army soldiers to brutalize peasants reluctant to hand over their grain and animals. The White Army, too, did its share of murdering and pillaging. The result was chaos and mass starvation, especially in southwestern Russia. Approximately 10 million people died in the course of these wars, many of them from hunger and disease. In Ukraine and Belorussia, another 20 million were reduced to consuming acorns, sawdust, and, reportedly, one another. Their lives were saved by the massive western humanitarian campaign of 1921–1922 organized by the American engineer and future president Herbert Hoover, who hoped his efforts would save civilians from both starvation and Bolshevism. At first grateful, the communist leadership soon took to charging Hoover and the American Relief Administration with counterrevolutionary intentions.

Inventing a Communist State

Lenin definitely had *revolutionary* intentions and during the tumult of the civil wars put in place numerous new provisions and institutions designed to build the world's first communist state. Marx and Engels had said little about what should happen once a revolution had succeeded; thus, the Russian communists had to improvise. They started by repudiating the nation's $3.6 billion foreign debt; seizing control of all businesses, banks, and large estates; abolishing all legal restrictions on religious and ethnic minorities (including Jews); and allowing women the right to sue for divorce. In July 1918 a Bolshevik firing squad executed Czar Nicholas II, the czarina, and their children, making the Romanov dynasty's return to power impossible. All political parties other than the Communist Party were banned, and the former subjects of the czar, now made officially equal participants in the workers' state, were instructed to call one another comrade. Enemies of the new regime who fell into Bolshevik hands were tortured and killed by the secret police (the **Cheka**) or sent to the work and reeducation camps (**gulags**) in Siberia.

The Communist Party, headed by a five-man Politburo, ran the new state, but Lenin, the revolution's greatest hero, was clearly the key decision-maker. Lenin's state was officially a "Union of Soviet Socialist Republics," a name that reflected the Bolsheviks' promises that the provinces would be allowed considerable autonomy. Rhetoric aside, it soon became clear that the USSR would be run by Moscow (for Moscow) and the Communist Party, for the sake of building communism—as the party believed it should be built.

THE NEW ECONOMIC POLICY. During the civil wars, the Bolsheviks made some attempts to force peasants and herdsmen to join primitive collective farms, but this first effort at the dissolution of private property and the capitalist economy, known as **war communism,** foundered in the face of massive peasant resistance and mass starvation. To stabilize the economy and get the peasants producing again, Lenin in 1921 put in place a **New Economic Policy (NEP),** which he described as "one step backward to go two steps forward." Rather than nationalizing all property immediately, he accepted peasants' claims to lands seized during the revolution, sanctioning and expanding a class of property-owning farmers whom Stalin would later denounce as kulaks or "tight-fists." The NEP also allowed the private sector to revive, with the state retaining control over banking and large industry. Dentists, grocers, and other private businesses opened their doors again, and artists and writers felt safe in expressing themselves more freely. The result

was economic recovery and something of a Soviet cultural renaissance, at least for a time. Lenin never meant the NEP to last forever, but he did not live long enough to end it himself. After suffering several strokes, he died on January 21, 1924. In his honor, the great city of St. Petersburg, originally named after Peter the Great, and redubbed Petrograd in 1914, was renamed Leningrad. Lenin's passing led to a prolonged struggle between high-ranking party members, all of whom proclaimed themselves to be Lenin's handpicked successor. The man who emerged victorious, Joseph Stalin, was probably Lenin's least favorite of the rivals, but Stalin, like Lenin, was fully devoted to the project of building a modern—and totalitarian—communist state.

STALIN'S SEARCH FOR ORDER. Born in 1879, the son of a cobbler and an illiterate laundress, Iosif Vissarionovich Dzhugashvili grew up in Tbilisi, in the multi-ethnic province of Georgia. Hardship and persecution marked his early years. By the time he was thirty, he had been thrown out of a seminary, had joined a secret revolutionary group, and had escaped from a Siberian prison camp. Dzhugashvili, who took the name Stalin ("man of steel") in 1913, was a multitalented revolutionary, able to organize bank robberies, to contribute to debates about Marxist philosophy, and to repeatedly escape the clutches of the czarist police. Ruthless in his dedication to revolutionary ideas, he purged or outmaneuvered other long-serving Bolshevik leaders until, in 1927, he managed to reconsolidate Lenin's dictatorial powers. Still, throughout his life he continued to see threats everywhere—to Soviet communism and to his own leadership.

THE FIRST FIVE-YEAR PLAN: COLLECTIVIZATION. In 1928, Stalin put an end to the NEP and announced his first Five-Year Plan for Soviet industrialization. Characteristically, the Bolsheviks refused to wait for initiatives from below and instead insisted on the imposition of a new economy from above, planned and managed by party members. By no means ignorant of history, Stalin realized that an agricultural revolution would have to precede industrialization. He was incensed that in years of small harvests, including 1927, peasants withheld grain from the market, making it impossible for the state to provide urban workers with cheap bread. But rather than set a maximum price for grain, as had Robespierre (see Chapter 17), Stalin decided to engineer an agricultural revolution, if necessary by force.

Stalin's plan called for the collectivization of agriculture, plans for which resembled, in part, the utopian socialist Charles Fourier's phalanxes (see Chapter 18). **Collectivization** in Stalin's model meant the seizing of all privately held land by the state and the forced settlement of peasants and nomadic peoples on large-scale collective farms. Here, there was to be no free market; the state was to run the economy and to tell people where to live and what to grow. The state also gave each farm a quota to fulfill,

Stalin Promotes the Five-Year Plan This propaganda poster dated 1932 proclaims: "At the end of the Plan, the basis of collectivization must be completed." Stalin was willing to kill millions of people to accomplish as speedily as possible a communist version of the agricultural revolution in the USSR.

hoping in this way to increase efficiency and do away with hoarding and illegal trading. Peasants and herders resisted collectivization almost universally and responded by staging armed demonstrations and killing their livestock rather than handing it over to local party officials. Despite this resistance, party officials in 1930 announced that all farmland would be collectivized. There were more than 13,000 riots in 1930 alone. In response, Stalin issued a proclamation, "Dizzy with Success," in which he called collectivization a great success and yet quietly suspended the campaign for a short time to allow the economy to stabilize once more. Once some order was restored, he moved to finish the state's takeover of all privately owned land. Stalin and his henchmen labeled all sorts of people kulaks, including starving farmers who could not fulfill their grain quotas, and insisted that they should be destroyed as a class. Tribunals rather like those used in the French Terror of 1793–1794, but now on a much larger scale, condemned millions of kulaks to the gulag or forcibly resettled them on collective farms. Those who were not needed in the countryside were sent to work in huge new factories where quotas were set for the production

of steel, cement, and chemicals. Private businesses were seized, their owners bankrupted or murdered, and professionals (those who survived), such as doctors, teachers, or engineers, turned into employees of the state.

FAMINE IN THE UKRAINE. In 1931, Stalin avenged himself on Ukrainian resisters and nationalists by setting their grain quotas so high that peasants could not fulfill them, even by sacrificing their seed grain and starving their own families. By early 1932, the situation was desperate: there was no grain to sow, and mobs of weak men, women, and children were streaming into the cities, selling everything, even themselves, for crusts of bread. Annoyed by what he described as Ukrainian whining, Stalin insisted the quotas be filled and accused the starving peasants of trying to sabotage socialism. The Red Army was sent in to remove all grain from homes and barns. By spring 1933, people were dying at a rate of more than 10,000 per day, and episodes of cannibalism became commonplace. Parents killed and ate their children or instructed their children to eat them when they starved. And yet, during this period Stalin *exported* grain to other countries. This was a man-made, not a natural famine. Stalin's policies caused as many as nine million people to starve to death, rivaling the number of all combatant deaths in the Great War.

Soviet Sticks and Carrots

Unlike most of the totalitarian regimes, which directed violence at those identified as biological or political enemies of the nation, the Soviet state declared various *classes* of people to be state enemies. Along with the nobility, the bourgeoisie, and the kulaks, these enemies included people with contacts abroad (including stamp collectors and former Red Cross officials), members of religious groups, and people simply said to be anti-Soviet elements. Valuing loyalty over competence, the Soviet regime regularly murdered experienced engineers, intellectuals, and officers simply for thinking too independently. As a result, factories frequently produced shoddy goods. Even pro-communist poets and scholars were murdered, or like Kollontai, compelled to toe the party line.

THE GREAT TERROR. Because of his constant fears that he would be overthrown by his own advisors, Stalin purged the Communist Party, the army, the bureaucracy, and even his own inner circle, with the result that no one could be certain that he or she would not face a firing squad the next morning. Stalin expelled the theorist and Red Army leader Leon Trotsky, along with 1,500 sympathizers, from the party in 1927. Two years later, Trotsky was forced into exile; and in 1940 he was murdered in Mexico by Stalin's agents. In 1934, Stalin used the assassination of his close associate, the popular Leningrad party boss Sergei Kirov, to launch a campaign of persecution against the party itself, and against the armed forces, whose autonomy Stalin resented. Senior party members were subjected to show trials, in which they were forced to confess to supposed counterrevolutionary plots to undermine the Soviet state and economy. The numbers of arrests, denunciations, recantations, and executions peaked in 1936–1937 and even affected commissars and secret police. By 1938, nearly 700,000 were dead. By the time the Great Terror abated in 1938, the army had been purged so heavily that few experienced officers were left, even though another war was looming on the horizon.

Along with the kulaks, victims of the Great Terror were sentenced to hard labor in Stalin's gulags in Siberia. Forced to work as many as sixteen hours a day, many prisoners died in unsafe mines or in building roads and canals in subzero weather, without machinery, proper clothing or health care, or sufficient food. Estimates of the number of lives destroyed by Stalin range from 14 to 40 million for the years 1927–1953. For them, Soviet communism was an unmitigated disaster. But there were others who profited from the system or who believed so ardently in communism's future benefits for all that they found the Soviet experiment exhilarating.

SOVIET SUCCESS STORIES. By 1938, Soviet corrective labor camps held millions of inmates, at least a quarter of whom would not survive their captivity. But the Soviet regime was not all sticks; for some, it offered carrots. The Russian Empire had never been a prosperous place, and for many peasants, life on a collective farm or in an industrial city at least offered some insurance against famine and some access to education. Those who were lucky and toed the party line (or denounced those who did not) might be rewarded with a better ration card or an apartment in one of the massive new housing projects begun by the regime. In the new cities, former peasants were exposed to modern technologies unknown to

czarist-era peasants, such as movies, railroad and metro travel, and electric lighting. The end of the imperial nobility and the murder of so many intellectuals, military officers, industrialists, and party bureaucrats during the Great Terror had a bright side for those who escaped the purges: increased upward mobility. Although the system was plagued by incompetence, it was also full of people driven to improve their status and eager to obtain skills and education their parents had never dreamed of acquiring.

Soviet Society in the 1930s

Soviet propaganda endlessly told people that they were better off under communism, that they had escaped the oppression of the czarist empire and the decadence and inequities of bourgeois capitalist society. The working classes had been reborn, they were informed, and now had a new world to build, one better than that of the West. Having caused so much misery in shutting down the NEP, by the mid-1930s the Soviets could claim a significant victory. By severing its ties to capitalist economies and refusing to accept any outside investment, the Soviet Union proved to be one of the world's very few nations not to be debilitated by the Great Depression after 1929. By the mid-1930s the party was claiming that the era of severe hardships and shortages that had been necessary at first was ending. "Life has become better, comrades; life has become more cheerful," Stalin exulted in 1935, and his words were reiterated in songs, speeches, and banners across the country—and though people continued to stand endlessly in queues for shoes, clothes, and even bread, occasionally ordinary people could buy ice cream, champagne, or ketchup.

In the 1930s, special stores stocked with luxury goods such as dried fruit and cameras were created for extraordinary people—such as party officials and workers who surpassed their quotas—creating an elite of privileged comrades that flew in the face of communist claims to have created a classless society. Along with expanded access to education and increased upward mobility for loyal and lucky comrades, these measures did make some people feel that life had become more cheerful. But the Soviets also built loyalty to the regime by indoctrinating the generation born after the war and keeping it busy. One of its most successful organizations—still remembered fondly by many of its former members—was the Communist Youth League (Komsomol), which organized exercise groups, expeditions, entertainments, and community services for children and teenagers. Komsomol members were exhorted to be vigilant and vocal supporters of the regime and to denounce adults—including their own parents—who exhibited any sort of disloyalty.

WOMEN IN SOVIET SOCIETY. As Alexandra Kollontai repeatedly claimed, women's lives too were transformed by the Soviet regime—though the revolution did not change conditions as much as Kollontai had hoped.

CHRONOLOGY	Building Socialism in the Soviet Union
DATE	**EVENT**
1918–1921	War communism and civil war
1921–1927	New Economic Policy (NEP)
1924	Death of Lenin
1927	Stalin establishes dictatorial powers
1928	First Five-Year Plan announced; collectivization begins
1931–1933	Ukrainian famine
1936	Divorce and abortion restricted in Soviet Union
1936–1938	The Great Terror

At least initially, the communists favored measures that feminists had backed, legalizing divorce and abortion, and providing support for women and children. Many women were asked or forced to do heavy labor and pushed to dress and behave like their male comrades. "Red" women were expected to do their all to build communism and to sacrifice their bourgeois habits, including going to church and lavishing attention on their children and their appearances. Children, the party said, could be cared for collectively; communal living would create a society of equals. In fact, however, places in good schools and modern apartments were limited and often went only to high-ranking party members.

In the 1930s—in the wake of his wife's suicide—Stalin stepped back from some of the more ambitious attempts to remake the bourgeois family. Wanting to make up for his own decimation of the population through collectivization and terror, he outlawed abortion and made divorce more difficult to obtain. Propagandists like Kollontai continued to advertise the equal status of Soviet women, but in fact, patriarchal expectations prevented women from obtaining top jobs and continued to make them responsible for virtually all household duties.

Moscow, 1931 This unusual picture—unusual because cameras were rare and risky things for a Soviet citizen to possess, and because the slide is in color—illustrates an everyday event in the USSR: people lining up to buy food. Note the empty streets. In Moscow in 1931, only a few very high-ranking party members owned cars. Compare this image to the street scene of London on page 668 in Chapter 21.

SURVIVING THE SOVIET EXPERIMENT. Living—and surviving—in Stalinist Russia required using a new language and keeping silent about any dissatisfaction with the regime. Although the czarist secret police had been vigilant in censoring publications and chasing down potential troublemakers, they were in no way as thorough, as omniscient, or as brutal as the Cheka. Soviet citizens learned to be wary and to keep to the party line or to confine complaints to outdoor locations, where they could not be overheard. Even then complaining was risky, as close relatives and neighbors regularly denounced their friends and family, sometimes because they wanted to ingratiate themselves with the party, sometimes because they themselves were threatened with violence. The bureaucracy's endless and usually impossibly high quotas—and punishments for those who did not fulfill them—led plant managers and local officials to systematically lie about how much steel or grain was being produced and to insist the state's wildly utopian plans were being realized. The party heroicized workers who exceeded their quotas, such as the coal miner Alexei Stakhanov. "**Stakhanovites**" received perks including telephones, apartments, or bicycles, and were honored by the regime for their contributions to building communism. But most people knew that the old Russian proverb, "the tallest blade of grass is the first to be cut down," still applied; Stakhanovites generated at least as much resentment as admiration, and some were attacked by fellow workers for speeding up production lines.

Stalin's subjects learned to be careful about which party officials they backed, for some who were prominent one day, like Sergei Kirov or Leon Trotsky, could be labeled enemies of the revolution the next day. And people learned to read between the lines, rather than to trust publications such as *Pravda* ("Truth") and *Izvestia* ("Delivered Messages"), the two officially sanctioned Soviet newspapers. They had little choice, for all non-communist reading material was banned, and few foreigners were allowed to enter the country. Those who did come were largely fellow travelers, or Soviet sympathizers, to whom the whole system of sticks—including gulags, famines, and mass executions—were not mentioned.

MODERNIZATION MANAGED—AT A TERRIBLE PRICE. By handing complete control of the economy over to state planners and putting politics and the media in the hands of the party and the secret police, Stalin managed to turn an empire predominately of peasants into an industrialized nation. The Soviet Union's rapid industrialization and its highly effective propaganda machine convinced many outsiders that communism was a faster and better way to modernize than the laissez-faire path of market capitalism and liberal democracy pursued by Britain, France, and the United States. This view was especially widespread after the onset of the Great Depression, which did little damage in the Soviet Union, as it had broken its links with the financial markets in the West. But these sympathetic onlookers were largely deceived about realities inside the Soviet Union. Millions of innocent citizens lost their lives and livelihoods, but even those who survived suffered both physically and psychologically. Many had family members who were tortured or taken away, never to return; almost everyone's needs and desires were endlessly denied in the pursuit of "building communism in one country." Overconcentration on the production of a few industrial goods such as steel, cement, and hydroelectric power distorted the entire economy, while rapacious attempts to exploit raw materials devastated the environment. Soviet communism's radical experiment in modernizing and industrializing without a free market and without democratic institutions produced a state that maintained its stability and autonomy through the chaotic interwar era—but at a terrible cost.

The Survival of Democracy in France and Britain

Insofar as it was achieved, Soviet stability was the result of top-down initiatives and state-organized violence. The picture could not have been more different in interwar France and Britain, which saw considerable internal and external strife but did not give up on democratic governance. Having gone into World War I as democratically governed states, France and Britain did not face the same crises of legitimacy as did the autocratic states. They were lucky, too, that they were separated from the Soviet experiment by large landmasses, or in Britain's case, a body of water. Unlike the Habsburg Empire's successor states, they did not have to deal with the problem of matching ethnic minorities to new state borders, though England did have to deal with the Irish question, and both states faced major resistance to the continuation of colonial rule abroad.

> **How did Britain and France confront the difficulties of the interwar era, yet maintain democratic government?**

Yet democratic states faced many of the same acute economic problems as did authoritarian ones: huge war debts, high prices, food and housing shortages, agricultural depression, and friction between employers trying to master a turbulent market and discontented industrial laborers, many of whom now listened closely to socialist agitators. Both states also hosted right-wing movements. Although fascism was never particularly popular in Britain, conservative backers of empire such as Winston Churchill remained vocal and influential. In France, it

took the formation of a **Popular Front,** a union of leftist parties, to prevent French fascists from seizing power in the tumultuous 1930s.

Stability through Safety Nets

Tensions were worst in periods of real economic hardship, in the immediate aftermath of the war, and in the depths of the Great Depression. In Britain, a demonstration against high milk prices brought several hundred thousand Londoners into the streets in September 1919. In France, there were some 3,800 strikes, involving 2.6 million workers, in the years 1919–1920. Even more unrest came to France as the delayed effects of the Great Depression began to bite after 1931. In 1936, the state experienced some 16,000 strikes.

Behind these events were implicit demands for the state to intervene in the free market, to root out profiteering, and to ensure the home population of fair prices and fair wages. The states did intervene more often than they had done before the war, though a majority of voters resisted campaigns for radical change such as the nationalization of the coalfields or the railways. Leaders sought, therefore, to find ways to respond to at least a few working-class complaints rather than risk revolution. In 1919, workers in both states won the right to an eight-hour day. To placate the Labour Party, the British moved to build hundreds of thousands of council flats, replacing urban slums with inexpensive, state-funded apartments. The legislation passed by the French in 1936 went much further, establishing the right to strike, collective bargaining rights for laborers, across-the-board wage increases, and two weeks of paid vacation for all French workers. Both nations laid the foundations for the creation of modern welfare states, in which the government provides a safety net so that its citizens do not starve or gravitate toward the radical extremes.

Colonial Instabilities

Externally, both imperial nations faced challenges in their colonies, where the war had severely damaged their prestige and their pocketbooks. Woodrow Wilson's powerful appeal to self-determination and promises like the Balfour Declaration made during the war made it particularly difficult to justify the continuation of colonial rule after 1918. Britain and France had accepted mandates in Africa, the Middle East, and the Pacific from the League of Nations, meaning that they were supposed to ready each state for eventual independence (Map 23.2). In practice, none of the mandatory powers urged their quasi-colonies to prepare for self-rule. But the days of European dominance were numbered. Civilians in the colonies were encouraged to believe that, like the Czechs or Yugoslavs who now had their own states, they might soon see their hopes for national autonomy fulfilled.

These changes in expectations and the self-discrediting of the so-called civilized nations during the war made for more rather than less unrest in the colonies and in the new mandates. Once again, during a period of peace on the continent, wars raged in the colonies. These were usually short but intense and increasingly fought by the colonizers with local forces and with air power and tanks, in the hopes of conserving white lives. As before, force begat not docility but increasing resistance. This resistance led, in some places, to the granting of independent status or reform and, in others, to the radicalizing of the anticolonial movements.

Many colonial citizens had served their overlords during the war. Some had died in their service, while others had learned new skills. Almost the moment that an armistice was announced on the continent, colonies and dependences all over the world declared an end to civil peace. In January 1919, Irish nationalists proclaimed their island an independent republic and established an Irish Republican Army (IRA). They were opposed by British forces, but years of strikes, protests, and bloody guerrilla operations (and reprisals) finally forced England to declare a truce in mid-1921. In

MAP 23.2 | The Middle East, 1920s–1930s

After World War I, territories formerly belonging to the Ottoman Empire and the German Empire were entrusted to the League of Nations, which turned them over to the British or French as "mandates." Some of these territories resisted the transfer of power, and one—Egypt—managed to achieve independence during the interwar era. *By 1918, the Ottoman Empire's overlordship had become very unpopular in the Arab lands. How do you suppose the Arabs felt about the imposition of European governance after the war?*

January 1922, an Anglo-Irish Treaty created the Irish Free State. Composed of thirty-two counties, the new republic was obliged to allow each of these counties to opt out of the treaty, an option taken by six of the northern and heavily Protestant counties, which rejoined the United Kingdom as the province of Northern Ireland.

In Egypt the British faced student protests and attacks on British citizens in March 1919. For a time, British forces used martial law and aerial bombardment to keep the movement down, but finally decided that suppressing it was not worth the effort. In 1922, Egyptians celebrated their independence, though the British retained control of the Suez Canal and of Egyptian defensive forces. The British imposed a king (Faisal I) on Iraq, another multiethnic state cobbled together by the war's victors, but kept control of the region as a mandate until 1932, when general dissatisfaction with British meddling generated the creation of a semi-autonomous Iraq. Iran, occupied by

British and Russian forces late in the Great War, never became a mandate, but it too was ruled by a military man, Reza Shah Pahlavi, who came to power in 1921 and in 1925 made himself king.

Though Britain made concessions to colonials in Ireland, Egypt, and Iraq, it reestablished colonial hegemony in most places, including India, Burma, the Sudan, and Palestine. Each case was different, and methods for subduing colonial uprisings were mixed, ranging from enlargement of the native bureaucracy and educated elite to the use of machine guns on civilians. After a disastrous incident in which British troops fired into a crowded square, killing at least four hundred Indian civilians at Amritsar in 1919, the British tried other measures, including increasing press censorship and expanding the Indian officer corps (from 1,000 during the Great War to 16,000 by the 1930s). They were not above jailing or hanging their opponents, as the Indian leader Mohandas

Ho Chi Minh and Subhas Chandra Bose

Both the war—and the peace—deeply shook Europeans' faith in their old authorities and the free market and opened the way for radical and authoritarian solutions. But the crises of interwar European society may emerge into even clearer view when we examine them from the perspective of people in colonized territories. Here we spotlight two men who became radical anti-imperialists in the 1920s: Ho Chi Minh (1890–1964), a communist from the French colony of Vietnam, and Subhas Chandra Bose (1897–1945), a nationalist opponent of British rule in India. In the interwar period, both men became vehement opponents of imperialism and of European civilization as a whole, and both found new opportunities to experiment with new allies and new tactics in increasingly successful battles to disrupt colonial rule.

Both men had spent many years in Europe and watched closely as the Great War exposed the hypocrisies of the imperialist civilizing mission. Ho in particular had felt the

sting of racial prejudice. As a young man, he had traveled to France in search of opportunities. Despite having received a good education in colonial schools, he found employment only as a dishwasher in London and Paris. Inspired by the revival of working-class movements after 1918, he became a socialist. When delegates to the postwar peace conference descended on Paris, Ho submitted to Woodrow Wilson a petition for Vietnamese independence but never received a reply. Angered, he left for Moscow, where he joined the Comintern and sought an Asian revolution. In 1924, he set up a base to train Southeast Asian communists in southern China; some of these agents were sent into Vietnam to cause trouble for French authorities. Like many of his operatives, Ho spent time in jail, but this only hardened his resolve to overthrow all colonial regimes. He would continue to denounce the West, capitalism, and colonialism all through the 1920s and 1930s and fight both the Japanese and the Allies during World War II. After France reasserted colonial control over Vietnam in 1945, Ho provoked another war, one that would finally push the French out of Southeast Asia.

Bose studied philosophy at Cambridge in the years just after the Versailles Conference and the Amritsar Massacre. He was offered a job in the British Civil Service, but refused to serve the imperial government and returned to India, where he became a journalist and propagandist for Indian independence. He was imprisoned for anti-imperialist agitation but like Ho emerged more committed to his cause. Left leaning but not a communist, Bose organized mass rallies against the British, including one demanding the demolition of a monument mourning the fate of British victims of the Black Hole of Calcutta. He sought assistance from the Soviets, the Nazis, and the Japanese to defeat the British. In 1943, he organized Indian nationalist troops to help the Japanese liberate India from the Raj. His Indian National Army attacked from Burma but failed to spark the massive uprising within India he hoped for, and he died in a plane crash in August 1945, just as British power in India was collapsing.

Like Ho, Bose was an uncompromising hater of European civilization. Both had given up on reform and refused to listen to any promises from the West. From their perspective, the colonies could and should wait no longer for national self-determination; it was time to seize it by force.

QUESTION | *How did Ho Chi Minh and Subhas Chandra Bose exploit the instabilities of the interwar period to form violent anticolonial movements in Vietnam and India?*

Ho Chi Minh By the time this picture was taken, in about 1930, the Vietnamese radical Ho Chi Minh had become a communist, and a devout enemy of European colonialism.

Gandhi and the Burmese rebel Saya San discovered, respectively. But these tactics also failed to halt the formation of a mass movement in favor of Indian home rule.

The French attempted to snuff out opposition in Indochina, Syria, Algeria, and West Africa, using various combinations of air power, bribery, torture, censorship, and reform. The same was true of the Spanish, who faced a revolt in Morocco in 1920. The humiliating defeat of Spanish irregular forces by Moroccan insurgents near the town of Annual in 1921 contributed to the demise of the First Spanish Republic and its replacement by a military dictatorship in 1923. Ominously, some—such as Javanese who revolted against Dutch rule in 1926—began to turn to communist Russia for aid and encouragement. As an older generation of liberal nationalists gave way to a younger, more radical generation, anticolonial movements also gave up on democracy and liberal capitalism, and sought more authoritarian solutions.

The Anti-democratic Right

If the western democracies faced serious challenges in establishing stability in the colonies, in some places, unrest and corruption at home undermined the very project of democracy itself. Ominously, by the mid-1920s, military men, hardened by years of European and colonial warfare, had begun to play critical roles in governance. One by one, Europe's states either willingly gave up liberal democracy or were toppled. By 1938, only ten interwar democracies remained: England, Switzerland, France, Sweden, the Irish Free State, Finland, the Netherlands, Belgium, Denmark, and Czechoslovakia; six more of these would fall by mid-1940.

What made the radical right so appealing to so many in the interwar era?

The men who toppled these parliamentary regimes were of different sorts. Joseph Pilsudski in Poland and Miguel Primo de Rivera in Spain were traditional military leaders who overthrew republics in the name of ending corruption and civil strife. Elsewhere, a new form of authoritarianism known as **fascism** put into power leaders whose legitimacy rested on the support of the masses. Most famously, Adolf Hitler managed to seize control of Germany by legal means, but then used terror tactics to put a Nazi dictatorship in place.

Italy's Fascist Experiment

Although among the supposed victors, the Italians emerged from the Great War bankrupt and angry that their constitutional monarchy had not extracted more reparations and territory at the Versailles Conference. Beginning in March 1919, communist sympathizers launched a series of riots and strikes. For more than a year, both right- and left-wing thugs carried out political assassinations, terrifying the middle classes. In the meantime, inflation destroyed the value of the lira, Italy's national currency. Factions in the parliament were too polarized to push through reforms, and ordinary city dwellers as well as peasants began to long for a strong figure of authority to impose order. Benito Mussolini (1883–1945), a former journalist, saw the chaotic situation as an opportunity to seize power. Once a socialist, Mussolini during the war had rejected internationalism and joined the fledgling fascist movement, which also attracted many ruthless and corrupt local bosses.

In 1919, Mussolini consolidated his position as leader of the fascists, in part by preaching the use of violence to overcome what he called the decadence and weakness of Italian democracy. He reorganized the Arditi, a Great War paramilitary unit notorious for its love of violence, borrowing its signature black apparel for the new fascist shock troops he called the Black Shirts. The job of the Black Shirts was not to convince people with words, but to act, and they set about breaking up strikes, intimidating officials, and beating up Mussolini's opponents. Unlike liberal leaders who made their speeches in parliament, Mussolini used loudspeakers to address mass audiences in Italy's great piazzas. His speeches were not meant to explain his ideas, but to unite Italians behind his leadership, partly by impressing them with his charisma and partly by emphasizing the dangers of a communist revolution to scare property owners and pious Christians. He also ingratiated himself with King Victor Emmanuel III (r. 1900–1946), but could not extract from the king an appointment as prime minister. So Mussolini rallied his Black Shirts, and in October 1922, he staged a theatrical march on Rome, threatening violence if his demands were not met. The king, no great fan of democracy himself, capitulated, and Mussolini became prime minister of Italy on October 31, 1922.

Mussolini spent the next four years consolidating his power and shutting down the opposition. He forced opponents into exile or used the Black Shirts or the police to intimidate them. In 1924, fascist thugs murdered the leader of the socialist opposition, Giacomo Matteotti, who had dared to expose right-wing election fraud in parliamentary speeches just days before. In 1925, Mussolini officially outlawed the socialist party, and by late 1926, he had made himself the leader (Il Duce) of a fascist dictatorship.

As the charismatic head of what was now a totalitarian, one-party state, Mussolini tried to restart Italy's economy by exerting new state powers over the marketplace. A state-managed economy was supposed to provide for all Italians and end class conflict, though the appearance of social peace was chiefly the result of Il Duce having banned strikes and terrorized labor leaders. In 1929, the former socialist managed to get Pope Pius XI to legitimize his regime by signing the **Lateran Accords.** In these treaties, Mussolini agreed to make Catholicism the official religion of fascist Italy and gave the church full sovereignty over the territory surrounding the Vatican palace and St. Peter's (now called Vatican City). The pope pledged to remain neutral in international and domestic politics, though in practice the interwar church

Benito Mussolini By all accounts, Mussolini was a rousing orator as well as an expert organizer of thugs. For this 1925 speech, he enhanced his authority by wearing a fascist party uniform, onto which are pinned the military decorations he earned during World War I.

stability and heroism in the face of parliamentary paralysis, market dysfunction, and national humiliation. Communists tended to draw more support from industrial workers and urban dwellers, whereas fascists appealed to shopkeepers, peasants, businessmen, and white-collar workers. Women, as well as intellectuals, could be found on both sides. Both of these radical movements were aggressively expansionist. The communists sought to expand first by warfare in 1918–1920 and thereafter, secretly, by sending out agents of the Russian-sponsored Third Communist International (the **Comintern**), who were to spread communist ideas throughout Europe and the world. Nazism, born in the same chaotic postwar years, was a form of fascism to which early leaders such as Adolf Hitler and Hermann Göring added anti-Semitic racism and an even grander longing for military conquest.

Ultimately, however, there were major differences between fascism, an antidemocratic movement of the far *right,* and communism, an antidemocratic movement of the far *left.* For communists, a person's class was his or her most important characteristic, and overcoming class conflict was the goal of the good society. National, ethnic, and religious differences were of minor significance and should simply disappear. For fascists, however, class was insignificant. What mattered was one's devotion to enhancing the power and territory of the state. Private property and religious worship could be permitted as long as they didn't interfere with the nation's needs. Mussolini's ideas and actions taught Adolf Hitler much. But Hitler's Nazi movement would add to fascist authoritarianism and nationalism a powerful drive to racial purification, radical anti-Semitism, and a fanatical commitment to remaking Europe's map through war.

The Weimar Republic and the Origins of the Nazi Party

To understand the origins of Nazism, we need again to look at the conditions of the immediate postwar years. Germany, having lost the Great War, suffered terribly in the period between 1918 and 1923. Even after attempted revolutions in Berlin and Munich were put down in early 1919, street violence continued. Seeking a safer place to do their work, the framers of the new German constitution settled on the Saxon town of Weimar, once home to the enlightened German poets Friedrich Schiller and Johann Wolfgang von Goethe. The liberal, democratic constitution written at Weimar abolished the Prussian monarchy, replacing it with a president, a prime minister, and a parliament (Reichstag). The Weimar Republic, like postwar Italy, was deeply factionalized, hampering the lawmakers' ability to deal efficiently with the economic and political crises. Although the leaders of the new Weimar Republic had no choice but to sign the Versailles Treaty, many nationalists despised them for having agreed to the war guilt clause, the heavy reparations payments, and the surrender of Alsace, Lorraine, and the Polish Corridor.

clearly favored the fascists over the explicitly atheistic communists.

What Was Fascism?

The word *fascism* derives from the Latin *fasces,* meaning a bundle of sticks surrounding an ax. The name of the party, and its symbols, made it clear that the fascists were willing to use force to achieve their ends. Fascists, like the communists to the East, were completely uninterested in reforms or compromises. Instead, they dedicated themselves to destroying liberal democracy (to which the communists added the destruction of capitalism). Fascists refused to play politics as usual or to permit individuals to choose a party allegiance or place in the economy; the point was to get things done. Both fascists and communists—and Nazis, too—sought to mobilize the masses and to modernize the state through top-down planning. They appealed primarily to people who had no experience of democracy and capitalism or who craved

The Weaknesses of the Weimar Republic This famous 1927 cartoon from the popular magazine *Simplicissimus* captures one of the Weimar Republic's chief problems: very few of its citizens were enthusiastic about democracy. Here, an array of German types—a Catholic clergyman, an aristocrat, a paramilitary volunteer, two working-class men, a fat entrepreneur, an intellectual, and a Nazi—grudgingly spell out *Republik*. The caption reads: "They carry the firm's letters—but who embraces its spirit?"

Former soldiers hated the republic for agreeing to downsize the military, and many succumbed to the **"stab in the back" myth,** the rumor that the German army had not been defeated in battle but had been stabbed in the back by Jews and greedy speculators on the home front. Clerics thought the Weimar Republic was ungodly, socialists and communists thought it too kind to capitalists, and capitalists thought it too generous to socialists. Many of those who accepted it did so unenthusiastically, upholding the letter but not the spirit of its democratic constitution, and simply waiting for a chance to put *their* friends in power.

Violence in Germany was rampant, and political murders commonplace. City streets were full of demobilized soldiers who signed themselves up as voluntary shock troops (**Freikorps**), willing to put down communist uprisings or participate in right-wing coup attempts. The socialist and communist parties had their voluntary units and thugs as well, but the statistics show that the right-wing vigilantes were more active and less likely to be prosecuted, perhaps because stability-seeking officials feared communist revolution more than they did right-wing thuggery. Violence peaked, however, during periods of economic hardship in 1918–1920, 1922–1923, and 1930–1933, and so fully understanding the fatal weaknesses of the Weimar Republic requires a close look at its economy.

WEIMAR'S ECONOMIC WOES. Germany's war debts were enormous and were exacerbated by the massive printing of money during the war and at its conclusion. Its supplies of goods, and especially food, on the other hand, were very small. Not surprisingly, once the war ended, inflation set in immediately, and between 1918 and 1921, the mark slid from 4 to 75 to the dollar. Steep reparations payments to the French made the situation even worse, and by January 1, 1922, the mark stood at 7,000 to the dollar. Trying to get their fiscal house in order, the Germans stopped paying reparations, thus inciting the French—who had their own war debts to pay—to send troops to occupy the Ruhr mining district in January 1923. Outraged, the leaders of the Weimar Republic encouraged miners to put down their tools and even paid them not to produce for the French. As tension mounted in this critical industrial region, the mark went into free fall.

HYPERINFLATION. By July 1923, the mark had sunk to 160,000 to the dollar; by August, to one million to the dollar. People were paid every day and immediately rushed out to buy food before the currency dropped again. The savings of the middle class were wiped out, and people on fixed incomes began to suffer. One elderly man drew out his life savings of 100,000 marks from the bank and spent it all on a subway ticket. After riding around Berlin for several hours, he returned home, where he quietly starved to death. By November 1923 the mark had reached a low point of 1.3 trillion to the dollar, and people resorted to creating their own emergency currency or bartering for food and emergency supplies. Many of those who had supported the republic in 1918 now blamed democracy and capitalism for wiping out their savings and ruining their lives. The economic chaos radicalized right- and left-wing movements, and both sought to turn the popular anger and frustration toward the republic to their advantage.

NAZISM IS BORN. In the midst of Weimar's economic crisis, Adolf Hitler put himself on the political map for the first time. Born a subject of the Austro-Hungarian Empire in 1889, Hitler had been insignificant and unsuccessful in his early life. He had been refused admission to art school because he lacked talent in drawing human faces, and the Austrian Imperial Army rejected him in 1914 because he was too frail to bear arms. A Bavarian regiment had taken him, however, and given him the dangerous task of delivering messages between trenches. Hitler viewed his accidental survival in this dangerous job as proof that he was destined to greatness.

Hitler was one of a number of men who actually liked the Great War and was sorry when it was over. He was especially sorry about the *way* it ended; he swallowed and then spread to all who would listen to him the "stab in the back" myth, which blamed the war's loss on communists, civilian profiteers, and Jews. He loathed the peace treaties, which, in his view, sought to destroy Germans as a race. Once demobilized by the army, he immediately dedicated his life to fighting more wars: against Jews, against communists, and against the Weimar Republic. Hitler's war experience had given him an unshakeable belief in his own destiny; his immediate postwar experience gave him an apocalyptic conviction that Germany could survive only by completely destroying all of its enemies—including the racial others at home—with whom it could never live at peace. The combination of Hitler's megalomania and his apocalypticism made him a uniquely dangerous man.

Hitler was, however, still largely unknown in the early 1920s. In 1919, he joined the very small German Workers' Party, which in 1920 renamed itself the National Socialist Workers' Party (NSDAP), or Nazi Party. The early Nazi Party appealed to former soldiers who were not shy about using their fists, and quickly developed its own paramilitary wing, the SA (storm troopers). These men, who wore brown shirts in imitation of Mussolini's Black Shirts, were explicitly organized to beat up enemies and protect party leaders from other groups' thugs. The Nazi Party grew slowly at first. In 1923, it was just one of many small yet ungovernable organizations devoted to the destruction of the Weimar Republic. It recruited most heavily in Bavaria, rather than in Vienna or Berlin, where socialist city governments took power. The party grew as **hyperinflation** set in, and Hitler's stirring speeches radicalized fearful and resentful Germans.

THE BEER HALL PUTSCH. Party membership, along with Germany's economic travails, was growing by 1923, and Hitler thought perhaps the moment had come to stage his own march on Berlin—as Mussolini had marched on Rome the previous year. Initially Hitler hoped that Bavarian conservatives would back his plans, but eventually he grew tired of waiting and decided to initiate a coup himself. On November 8, 1923, he and about six hundred SA men surrounded the beer hall in downtown Munich, where the governor of Bavaria was making a speech. The Nazis kidnapped the governor, hoping to make him a collaborator, and announced they were planning to overthrow the Weimar Republic. They demanded that all patriotic Germans back them, seized control of municipal buildings, and tried to round up some prominent Jews. By the evening of the next day, however, the Bavarian army had the upper hand. Nineteen Nazis were killed, and Hitler and several other leaders were jailed. The whole Beer Hall Putsch episode was a fiasco, but in Nazi mythology it went down as a heroic crusade and, after 1933, those who participated were honored as "Old Fighters."

Sentenced to five years in prison, Hitler served only eight months and spent the time not repenting for his past sins, but writing *Mein Kampf* (*My Struggle*). In this semi-autobiographical rant, Hitler articulated the main ideas of **Nazism,** which included dedication to the rebuilding of German power and to the destruction of the enemies of the German folk, including Jews, Bolsheviks, capitalist exploiters, and liberals who had agreed to the Treaty of Versailles.

Meanwhile, the Weimar Republic stabilized, largely as a result of its acceptance of a plan developed by the American businessman Arthur Dawes. Under the Dawes Plan, the French evacuated the Ruhr, German reparation debts were rescheduled, and the way was cleared for American investment in Germany. In fact, the Dawes Plan relied on the issuing of American short-term loans that allowed the Germans to pay reparations to the French and British. The reparation payments, in turn, made it possible for the French and British to pay their war debts—to the Americans. The money flowed in circles—but at least it did flow, as long as the United States was willing and able to lend and the Germans were willing and able to pay.

Thanks to the Dawes Plan, middle-class confidence in the republic was restored, at least for a time, and street battles between radicals largely ceased. By the time *Mein Kampf* went to press in 1925, most Germans could muster little sympathy for the struggles of the Nazi corporal, and the book went largely unread until the 1930s when events made its themes, and its author, more popular than ever before.

Stabilization by Authoritarian Means: Eastern Europe in the 1920s and 1930s

The revolutions from the right that shook first Italy and then Germany were by no means exceptional. Economic crises, ethnic hatreds, and political radicalization threatened to topple states throughout central and southern Europe. Democracies were frail and market capitalism did not seem to work, or to work fast enough. Urbanization and modernization still lagged, the legacy of the second serfdom and the late arrival there of the agricultural and commercial revolutions. In the 1920s, stability was achieved largely by the creation of authoritarian states, led either by military men or by monarchs who sought to rule above the parties. Within the pervasive climate of political violence and economic chaos of the interwar years, millions of Europeans welcomed the imposition of order from above.

POLAND AND HUNGARY. Polish nationalist hero Józef Piłsudski (1867–1935) had won glory in leading the Polish effort to expel Soviet forces in 1919–1920 and then expanding Polish borders even farther into territory inhabited by Lithuanians (to the east) and Ukrainians (to the south). Expansion made the new Poland something more than the purely Polish, self-determined state Woodrow Wilson had envisioned. Indeed, Poles now made up only 69 percent of Poland's inhabitants. In addition to Ukrainians and Lithuanians, the new state incorporated Jews from the former Pale of Settlement, approximately 3.3 million of them by 1939. The new Poland was also home to as many as one million Germans, many of them from old Baltic landowning families and deeply unhappy with their new citizenship. Political fragmentation added to ethnic partisanship to make governing difficult. By 1925, thirty-two parties held seats in the Sejm, or Polish House of Commons. Frustration with factionalism led Piłsudski and the army to stage a coup in 1926. Piłsudski, who did not abolish the parliamentary system, ruled as a relatively tolerant military dictator until his death in 1935.

In Hungary, revolutionary forces led by Lenin's protégé Bela Kun founded the Hungarian Soviet Republic on March 21, 1919. It fell 133 days later, on August 1, but not before its attempts to nationalize land, requisition food in the countryside for the cities, and try its enemies before revolutionary tribunals roused the right wing to take its own violent measures. In the counterrevolution of 1919–1920, Hungarian troops under the leadership of the war hero Admiral Miklós Horthy (1868–1957) viciously attacked those it considered *its* enemies, including communists, socialists, and Jews. Though he was elected regent, Horthy retained the trappings of parliamentary democracy and constitutional law, but reduced the franchise to 27 percent of adults and restricted the powers of the Hungarian parliament. Horthy ruled a population diminished and angered by Hungary's peace treaty, the Treaty of Trianon, which stripped the nation of nearly three-fourths of its territory and two-thirds of its citizens. Once home to 18.2 million, the new kingdom without a king now had only 7.6 million inhabitants. The treaty moved nearly one-third of ethnic Hungarians—3.3 million people—to bordering states. So powerful was the desire to overturn the Trianon treaty that a prayer known as the National Credo was ritually invoked: "I believe in one God, one Fatherland, and the Resurrection of Hungary."[2]

BULGARIA, ROMANIA, AND YUGOSLAVIA.
In Bulgaria, deep resentment over the peace treaties, struggles between minority groups, and political polarization made for endemic violence. In 1923, a bloody military coup overthrew the left-leaning government of Alexander Stamboliiski; his assassins avenged themselves on a man they blamed for signing a shameful peace and for seeking to redistribute land by cutting off his head and sending it to Sofia in a biscuit tin. King Boris III (r. 1918–1943) did nothing and thereafter allowed General Ivan Vŭkov to unleash a counterrevolution that took the lives of tens of thousands of Bulgarian communists and other opponents of the regime. One observer, writing during its worst phase in 1939, lamented: "[V]illages burnt; girls raped; the wounded bayoneted; prisoners mutilated. Untried men, women, priests, teachers, schoolboys and girls, even babies were slaughtered by the hundreds. . . . The towns were purged of Left sympathizers, lorries [trucks] rumbling through the streets by night to take victims from their houses. From every village people 'disappeared' . . ."[3]

Romanian Fascists Worship the War Dead In this 1936 photo, the founder of Romania's Iron Guard, Corneliu Codreanu (*left*) and a colleague kneel among the bones of Romanian soldiers killed in World War I. The hypernationalism of the Iron Guard also expressed itself as concern for the peasantry and hostility toward Hungarians and Jews.

In Romania, wealthy liberals dominated in a constitutional monarchy run with little but contempt for the impoverished peasant masses. But by 1930, with the Great Depression eating away at everyone's economic security, peasants had begun to organize. The National Peasants' Party begged King Carol II (r. 1930–1940), who had been living with his mistress in Paris, to return. He did so and gradually usurped more and more of parliament's powers, though he did not abolish it entirely. In the meantime, the Depression and rising anti-Semitism led to the formation of a fascist movement, the Iron Guard, or Green Shirts, which won popularity among the peasantry by helping to build roads and bring in the harvest and by blaming Jews for the economic hardships of the people. In 1932, King Carol banned the Iron Guard and permitted the arrest of thousands of Iron Guard members, not because he wanted to defend democracy, which he also despised, but because he envied, loathed, and feared the charismatic Iron Guard founder Corneliu Codreanu. But the Iron Guard rebounded and launched vicious attacks on Jews and the Hungarian minority population; its popularity surged and it added an elite SA-like detachment, the Death Commandos. By 1938, mob violence against Jews and politically motivated killings had become so commonplace that King Carol took the final step into dictatorship and outlawed political activity. The police arrested Codreanu and thirteen of his fellow Green Shirts. After their execution, acid was poured over the corpses. The official report stated that the prisoners had been shot while trying to escape. Unfortunately for Carol, Codreanu became a martyr-hero, and the Iron Guards would force the king's abdication in 1940.

The new Yugoslavia was officially named the Kingdom of Serbs, Croats, and Slovenes—a name that vastly

DATE	EVENT
1920	Admiral Horthy overthrows Communist government in Hungary
1923	Alexander Stamboliiski overthrown in Bulgaria
1926	Józef Piłsudski stages coup in Poland
1929	Yugoslav constitution suspended and royal dictatorship established
1932	King Carol II returns to Romania; suppresses political opposition

oversimplified the ethnic complexities of the new state. The Serbs (43 percent) were the largest group in the new constitutional monarchy, and it was their king who was put on the new throne—but the population included Bosnian Muslims, Greeks, Gypsies, Jews, Hungarians, Macedonians, Romanians, Bulgars, and Albanians. The Croatians (25 percent) in particular chafed under Serbian dominance. Parliamentary sessions became screaming matches until 1928, when a radical Serbian delegate took out a revolver and shot four other delegates, including Stjepan Radić, a Croatian leader famous for his attempts to make crossethnic alliances. When Radić died of his wounds, ethnic violence resurged, and on January 6, 1929, King Alexander I (r. 1929–1934) suspended the constitution. The king renamed the state—it was now the Kingdom of Yugoslavia—and turned it into a dictatorship. King Alexander himself was assassinated in 1934 by a Macedonian radical.

CZECHOSLOVAKIA. The one supposed exception to these authoritarian states was the new Czechoslovakia, a state with the good fortune to have both a relatively developed industrial base and a strong and savvy liberal president, Tomáš Masaryk (in office 1919–1935). Czech art flourished, and Czechs turned out enough Pilsner beer and Skoda cars for export to make Czechoslovakia the world's tenth largest in industrial production. The Czechs did practice a form of democracy, but it too had repressive and manipulative qualities. Nationality and border issues plagued Czechoslovakia, in part because the Allies, trying to clip the power of the Germans and Hungarians, had made the new state's borders too wide. In fact, as Mussolini pointed out, the name of the state itself was deceptive: it should really have been "Czecho-Germano-Polono-Magyaro-Rutheno-Rumono-Slovakia." The German population in the industrialized Sudetenland was not a minority group at all; it was larger by some 500,000 than the Slovak population in the east. When Sudeten Germans protested their exclusion from Austria and joined in singing "The Watch on the Rhine" in March 1919, Czech police opened fire, killing

fifty-three and wounding eighty. Feeling very much victimized by the Czech Republic, Sudeten Germans continually expressed their desire to join their German friends and relatives in either Austria or Germany. Along with the Sudeten Germans, Hungarians, Poles, and Slovaks who chafed under Czech hegemony were also locked up regularly. Despite Czechoslovakia's relative successes, throughout the 1930s, virulent nationalisms and incipient fascist movements threatened to tear the state apart.

Authoritarian States and Stateless People

Throughout central and southeastern Europe, minority conflicts created enormous internal tensions, leading to the expulsion of some people and the persecution of others. Hundreds of thousands of Armenians and Jews, Germans and Hungarians, Bulgarians and Macedonians, fled their homes, as did millions of Russians who fled the revolution and ended up in all parts of the world. Because many refugees who took up new homes lacked legal papers, the League of Nations created the **Nansen passport**, travel papers issued by the league that allowed stateless people to find new homes and establish stable new lives. These passports were named for Fridtjof Nansen (1861–1930), the Norwegian humanitarian who devoted himself to the resettling of hundreds of thousands of Russian, Greek, Turkish, and Armenian refugees during the 1920s.

Even with a passport, finding a new home in the interwar era was difficult. Just about everywhere, economic hardships and increasing ethnic tensions provoked governments to close their borders. The traditional outlet to the United States was closed after the U.S. Congress passed legislation sharply restricting immigration. New work in the emerging field of racial science made white Europeans fear that racial interbreeding might corrupt and destroy their nations. Many people believed that the only healthy state was a pure state, one without minority populations who might reproduce too quickly or infect the majority population with communism or any number of degenerate symptoms. Many feared as well that their nations would not have enough of the right sort of men to fight the wars clearly to come. The racial thinking that had already structured Europeans' views of the colonial world now began to be applied much more extensively to Europeans themselves.

The Body and the State

Even before the Great War, many Europeans were worrying about their health—and more important, about the health of neighbors and fellow citizens. The French, in particular, feared that the decline in the birthrate that began in the later nineteenth century suggested the nation was degenerating rather than evolving, as was proper for a

What do the fascists' ideal body-types tell us about their political goals?

virile, fit state. Efforts were undertaken to improve public hygiene and to encourage the right sort of people to have babies. Especially in France, middle-class, white women were pushed to give up their professional aspirations and campaigns for suffrage and instead to do their duty for the nation by producing more children. In a few places, early supporters of racial hygiene, or eugenics, argued for confinement or sterilization of the physically or mentally disabled to prevent them from reproducing. Some health enthusiasts championed the clearing of slums or the forming of exercise clubs to improve national fitness.

The New Woman—and the Old Family Structure

In the 1920s, and especially in the 1930s, the trend toward state manipulation of its citizens' bodies accelerated enormously. Leaders were responding, in part, to the Great War's destabilizing effect on family structures and gender relations. During the long war, women had "worn the pants" for their families; they had taken new jobs, suffered terrible home-front hardships, and done without male heads of house. Their adjustment back to the purely private sphere was difficult—though a large number willingly gave up their jobs to accommodate men returning from the front. Yet women did not return eagerly to the provinces, already suffering agricultural depression, or to their parents' homes. Many sought new freedoms—even at rock-bottom wages—in burgeoning cities. The new woman of the 1920s, who smoked cigarettes in public, wore makeup, and kept her skirts short and her hair shorter, was a stereotype, but one that reflected a worldwide reality; China, too, had its "new women." These self-confident and often self-supporting women seemed to demand sexual, social, and political equality even when they did not campaign for it openly, and they greatly worried both men and conservative women who believed that dismantling traditional gender hierarchies would lead to moral chaos.

Thus a whole set of pressure groups and state policies blossomed in the interwar era whose desire was to improve the nation's fitness by returning women to the private sphere, where they would produce a healthy new generation of soldiers to replace the one that had been destroyed by the Great War. Reproduction was seen as central to the nation's ability to win a Darwinian struggle for survival. As Mussolini put it in 1928, "A nation exists not only because it has a history and territory, but because human masses reproduce from generation to generation. The alternative is servitude or the end."[4] States took action to curb abortion or outlaw the sale of contraceptives. The French began awarding medals to model mothers—those with ten children received a gold one, those with five a bronze—a practice the Nazis and Italian fascists emulated. Seizing the opportunity, florists and greeting-card manufacturers invented Mother's Day. But a majority of women, too, seem to have concluded that biology was indeed destiny and that the best possible future was

The Ideal Aryan Family This Nazi-era image is one of many idealizing motherhood and rural family life. Here, the blond, powerfully built mother nurses her fourth child. She is meant to be the complete opposite of the slender, urban "new woman" of the 1920s. The whole family is pictured as linked organically with the soil—only the Aryan-featured father wears shoes.

one in which women made their kitchens their kingdoms. Where they could vote, as in Weimar Germany, they voted overwhelmingly for Christian or nationalist parties, and by the early 1930s, in very large numbers for the Nazis. On the whole they did not, however, significantly increase their production of babies. When, by the mid-1930s, the Nazi economy reached full employment for men, women went back to work in large numbers.

The New Man

If women were exhorted and bribed to cultivate maternal values, an even stronger and more dangerous strain of state intervention sought to inject virility and purity into national populations. All authoritarian governments, and many socialist local leaders, urged their citizens to build up their bodies, through exercise and healthy living and eating. Those who were soft, sickly, or weak, or those who displayed "degenerate" lifestyles— homosexuals, prostitutes, gypsies, and drug addicts— were universally treated as dangers to the state, and in some cases sterilized to prevent *their* reproduction. Clubs for hiking, bicycling, mountain climbing, and exercising were hugely popular; some of the more zealous body-builders joined nudist clubs. The era's glorification of the ideal, male body is evident in the art produced by the Italian, German, and even Soviet states: gargantuan sculptures of half-nude workers and soldiers, stripped of their individuality, were made to show the masses what the new man of the future should look like. Ironically, these new men resembled most closely the classical ideal of the nineteenth-century middle class far more than they resembled the real leaders of the day, many of whom were short, dark haired, and distinctly lacking in beauty.

Those who did not resemble the new man suffered any number of new humiliations and persecutions. A semi-public gay culture began to emerge in some places; it was met with a barrage of homophobic literature proclaiming the degeneracy of homosexuality. Jews and gypsies, widely perceived as racially inferior to Europeans and likely to carry diseases, were eyed more suspiciously or subjected to violence. The mentally ill were increasingly institutionalized or sterilized. By 1936, seven European countries, including liberal Sweden and Nazi Germany, legalized sterilization, imposed largely on mental health patients. An increasingly loud group of writers expounded on the importance of genetics, informing their readers that breeding and purity of blood were scientifically legitimate ways to create stable and healthy nations.

Experimentation and Modernism in Interwar Culture

As in politics, the cultural realm of the interwar era was also marked by attempts to make a full break with the

What made the cultural world of the interwar period so vibrant?

past and to appeal to even larger and more educated audiences. Modern forms that had once been avant-garde now began to seem antiquated as experimentation pushed artists, writers, and musicians in new directions. The richness and variety of the music scene alone was astounding—its experimenters ranging from American jazz musicians to the French classical composer Erik Satie's furniture music, the unobtrusive style we now know as elevator music.

Perhaps even more astounding were the new ways this music could be delivered to the public: as live performances in theaters or cabarets; recorded on the now less expensive and more accessible phonograph records; and, miraculously, over the public airwaves, by way of radio. The same could be said for other art forms as well: paintings were now routinely photographed and reprinted; books circulated to much larger audiences than ever before; and, most impressively, theatrical performances could now be seen by millions in the form of feature-length films, to which sound was added in 1927 and full color in 1935. Made by the dozens in small studios all

over Europe, movies became the most experimental, as well as the most popular, of interwar art forms—and *the* premier modern means of spreading propaganda. At a time before television and when radios were still a luxury commodity, going to the movies was a popular and, for most people, an affordable pastime. The number of cinemas exploded; Germany had only 28 in 1913, but 245 in 1919, and more than 6,000 by 1933.

Art and Architecture

In art, the modernist challenge to old-fashioned, realistic, representational art had clearly won the day; artists who wanted to be innovators (though not necessarily those who wanted to appeal to popular taste) would need to keep pushing the envelope. Artists who had pioneered the new styles of cubism or expressionism before the war—such as Picasso and Kandinsky—now worked with more confidence and discovered others working on even more shocking projects. In 1918, the Russian artist Kasimir Malevich reached the limits of abstraction with his masterpiece *White on White,* just as, in Switzerland, a group of iconoclastic artists was inventing **Dada,** a self-consciously

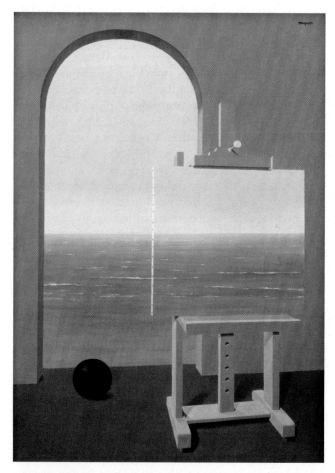

René Magritte, *The Human Condition* (1935) The Belgian Surrealist René Magritte regularly painted visual jokes, the meaning of which remains obscure. Does this painting tell us that the human condition is art (or nature), plus death (signified by the cannonball)? Magritte leaves it to the viewer to decide.

The Films of Sergei Eisenstein and Leni Riefenstahl

One way to attempt to understand what life was like in the 1920s and 1930s is to watch some of the movies of those decades. A new art form arose during the interwar era as directors sought to exploit the new technology to move far beyond the mere filming of theatrical scenes and incorporate mass politics into the cinema. The Russian communist filmmaker Sergei Eisenstein (1898–1948) used the technique of montage, in which careful editing led viewers to create storylines in their minds. In *October,* for example, scenes of moderate socialists making long speeches alternated with images of hands playing harps, suggesting that the moderates were simply wasting time in idle blather while the Bolsheviks were taking necessary action. In his masterpiece, *The Battleship Potemkin,* Eisenstein used montage to tug at viewers' heartstrings and to whip up their sympathies for the supposedly proto-communist mutiny of 1905, the subject on which he based the film. Close-ups show viewers the hard work performed by ordinary Russian sailors and the maggoty meat their superiors served them, underlining the injustices of the czarist regime. For the famous Odessa Steps sequence, Eisenstein filmed czarist troops firing on innocent women and children waiting for the battleship to dock. In the final segment a mother is shot and her body slumps against her baby's carriage, forcing it to plummet down the steps until, at the bottom, a shot of the innocent child is juxtaposed with images of a soldier raising a whip. Viewers are left to conclude that the child has been murdered by the heartless and oppressive czarist regime.

Eisenstein was a convinced communist, and his movies *Potemkin* and *October* could certainly be called propaganda; they certainly were not objective renderings of the mutiny of 1905 or of the Bolshevik assault on the Winter Palace in 1917. But he was also a filmmaker of real genius, and his movies are still widely admired by film directors and cinema historians of all political persuasions.

Eisenstein's counterpart on the right was Leni Riefenstahl (1902–2003), another filmmaker of genius—and another producer of highly influential propaganda. A woman working in a heavily male-dominated world, Riefenstahl had already made several of her own films

Leni Riefensthal's Greeks In this still photo from Riefenstahl's *Olympia,* a modern German athlete imitates the pose of an ancient Greek statue (see p. 64).

when propaganda minister Josef Goebbels hired her to film the Nuremberg Nazi Party rally of 1934. Riefenstahl's innovative camera work made her scenes of Hitler's plane descending over the medieval city and of massed crowds of Nazi supporters hailing the Führer even more striking. To get grand panoramas of the crowd, she stationed cameramen on high platforms at the rallies. The neoclassical platforms built by Albert Speer, Riefenstahl's contemporary, heightened the drama of the rally; massively oversized Greek columns served as a backdrop for parades and speeches. Riefenstahl also used neoclassical symbolism convincingly in the artistically revolutionary film *Olympia,* made to document the 1936 Olympics. *Olympia* begins with the transformation of classical sculptures into the perfect bodies of male athletes, mimicking the Third Reich's rhetoric about the importance of cultivating the purity of the Aryan body. The film also included remarkable innovations in sports photography, as Riefenstahl pioneered the use of underwater cameras for swimming events and cameras on rails to film track races. Unquestionably there was propagandistic content to these films; both featured Hitler making speeches before adoring masses and promoting Germany's return to power. But Riefenstahl never joined the Nazi Party, and, until her death at age 101 in 2003, she insisted that she was merely a filmmaker who undertook these projects simply to further her artistic career.

All authoritarian regimes used film during the interwar era to promote their ideas as well as to entertain the masses. Even the Nazis and Soviet communists made light comedies, though viewers usually had to sit through highly ideological newsreels before they could see the main fare. What the Nazis could not tolerate were Jewish directors and actors, of whom there were a large number in 1933. It was America's gain when directors such as Fritz Lang, director of the great expressionist film *Metropolis,* left the Reich and resettled in Hollywood.

QUESTION | *How do the symbolism and filming techniques used by filmmakers Sergei Eisenstein and Leni Riefenstahl serve as propaganda?*

absurd style of art and performance that was meant to mirror the nonsensical world of the day. Romanian sculptor Constantin Brancusi had rejected figural realism before the war, but his postwar works, such as *Bird in Space* (1924), secured his fame. The same could be said for the cut-out art of French painter Henri Matisse. Artists of many nationalities, including Max Ernst (German), Giorgio di Chirico (Italian), Salvador Dali (Spanish), and René Magritte (Belgian), worked in the genre known as surrealism: all these artists created a surreal feeling in their paintings by juxtaposing odd elements and by playing with painting's conventions.

For architects of the interwar era, modernism was even more natural—and in many respects, practical as well. One of the great challenges facing many European cities in the 1920s was providing enough lower-cost housing for those who continued to stream in from the countryside and home from the battlefronts. Because the cities, like most of their citizens, were short on cash, architects needed to build large complexes of many similar units on small budgets. Modern architecture, with its straight lines, was ideal for this purpose, as well as for the building of new infrastructures in the form of metro systems, highways, bridges, and stadiums. Left-leaning civic leaders oversaw the building of innovative housing complexes such as the Karl Marx-Hof in Vienna, which incorporated public kitchens and nurseries, in the hopes of creating communal living styles. Many of these ideas were transported to the Soviet Union, where architects built massive housing projects for workers. Often, however, the need to build cheaply led to the use of substandard materials and the omission of all pleasing elements of design.

Building shoddy boxes was never the intent of Germany's **Bauhaus** school, perhaps the foremost modernist movement in architecture, from which Ludwig Mies van der Rohe emerged. Like his counterpart in France, the Swiss-born Charles-Édouard Jeanneret, better known as Le Corbusier, Mies wanted to unify the minor and industrial arts with the fine arts and to marry *both* beauty and functionality. Unfortunately, many of their imitators chose cheapness and simplicity instead, creating the badly constructed and identical square boxes that would become even more numerous after the Second World War.

Interwar Science, Philosophy, and Literature

In science, philosophy, and literature, the interwar period saw the elaboration and expansion of modernism. Albert Einstein's theories of relativity predated the war's end, but in the 1920s he continued to refine them. His fellow physicists, Niels Bohr and Werner Heisenberg, developed quantum theory. In the social sciences, a new

Karl-Marx Hof Built by the socialist government of Vienna in the 1920s, this modernist housing complex was designed to provide inexpensive housing for workers and to encourage communal living.

generation of anthropologists spent years living among non-European peoples to understand their cultural structures. Political theorists meanwhile strove to understand the new European and American world of mass politics. Prewar work in sociology and psychology helped scholars to come to grips with phenomena such as the war hysteria of 1914 and the behavior of crowds in fascist Italy.

The most influential strains of philosophy in the interwar period were existentialism, Christian social thought, and Marxism. **Existentialism** emphasized the individual's role in defining for himself or herself the meaning of things in the world. Existentialists were found chiefly among professional philosophers, such as Jean-Paul Sartre (1905–1980) in France and Martin Heidegger (1889–1976) in Germany. Life in itself, they argued, was meaningless. Only real existing individuals gave things names and decided what significance to attach to them. Christian thinkers such as Paul Tillich (1896–1965) disputed such seemingly relativistic claims and insisted that only through God and his church could human beings find meaning and build lasting communities. Whereas Tillich lost his position and left Germany in 1933, Heidegger volunteered his services to the new Nazi regime. Sartre served briefly in the French army and associated himself with the French resistance.

Not only in Soviet Russia, but elsewhere too, philosophers now took Marx seriously and tried to use his writings to understand more than how to make a revolution. Marxist thinkers were materialists, meaning that they believed that all ideas were shaped by the material conditions that surrounded the thinker. Although this was the opposite of existentialist thought (in which thinking shaped reality) and entirely hostile to Christian perspectives, Marxist philosophy shared with the others the realization that there was no eternally and universally valid way of knowing the world. The war had killed the enlightened and liberal dream of universal knowledge.

The Great War did not kill poetry—the 1920s in particular were rich in poetic production, from the critical works of former soldiers, such as the Briton Robert Graves, to the love poems of Russian Boris Pasternak. The Russians in particular focused on poetry and short-story writing—in part because paper was in desperately short supply during the civil wars. Russian writer Isaak Babel produced brutally honest, apolitical poems about the horrors of the wars, whereas Vladimir Mayakovsky used his modernist talents to celebrate the glories of the new Soviet state. Anna Akhmatova's husband was murdered and she was denounced for producing bourgeois poetry during Lenin's last years, but Akhmatova continued to compose poetry in secret. The Anglo-American poet T. S. Eliot composed a series of poems on the general theme of postwar despair and modern soullessness, including *The Waste Land* (1922) and *The Hollow Men* (1925). Born in the United States like Eliot, Ezra Pound also made his career in Europe, especially in Italy. Admiring the profundity and simplicity of Chinese literature, Pound also developed a powerful contempt for modern technology, capitalism, and mass culture. Whereas Eliot ultimately found spiritual consolation in Anglican Christian faith, Pound found it in Italian fascism. He dedicated one edition of his *Cantos* to Mussolini and made radio broadcasts in favor of the Italian dictatorship.

Another of the leading writers of the interwar era, the German novelist Thomas Mann, also resorted to radio broadcasts in the 1930s and 1940s—but his broadcasts were denunciations of fascism and of Hitler's regime. Though Mann had been an outspoken German nationalist during the First World War, he became a staunch supporter of the Weimar regime in the 1920s. During this period, he completed one of his masterpieces, *The Magic Mountain* (1924), an account of the epic struggles between the forces of reason and unreason over the soul of an insignificant man—who ultimately throws himself into death's clutches by volunteering for infantry service in the Great War. Mann's novel dramatized Europe's postwar obsessions with health—for the novel is set in a Swiss sanatorium, where everyone suffers from some physical or psychological malady. Like two other great German novels of the era, Robert Musil's multivolume *The Man without Qualities* (1930–1933) and Hans Fallada's *Little Man, What Now?* (1932), Mann's novel also provided testimony that artists, like politicians, were now keenly interested in understanding that inscrutable entity, the ordinary man.

Popular Culture

In the interwar era, the ordinary man had new entertainment choices. In addition to older forms of cultural expression such as vaudeville, circuses, soccer, and pub entertainments, urban dwellers, in particular, could now listen to radio programming or see movies in a much-expanded network of inexpensive theaters. Moreover, though virtually all modernist ideas had been circulating

before the First World War, after 1918 modern design became more visible to all, as new buildings went up, newspaper circulation figures increased, and producers of mass consumer goods, such as radios, motor cars, and cutlery, adopted modern designs for ordinary household consumers. Tourism increased, especially for western European city dwellers. Cheaper fares for train travel drew the masses to beaches where, after 1936, they could slather on the first suntan lotion, L'Oréal's *Ambre Solaire*. Though both the Soviet Union and fascist governments kept wages low and sought to wring more productivity out of their workers, many state- or church-affiliated groups (outside of the USSR) sponsored inexpensive youth entertainments, including sporting events and holiday camps.

In the arts as in social life more generally, new forms did not completely crowd out older forms. Classical symphonies and operas continued to be composed and performed; some of the great performers of the age were classical soloists, such as Rudolf Serkin (piano) and Yehudi Menuhin (violin), or conductors, of whom Arturo Toscanini and Wilhelm Furtwängler were the most famous. These virtuosi coexisted with African American stars such as Josephine Baker and Duke Ellington, who brought jazz and swing to Europe, appealing especially to younger audiences. Although modernist painting reached its summit, middle-class publics continued to commission portraits and buy romantic landscape paintings. Writers such as Virginia Woolf and James Joyce stretched the boundaries of the novel to explore more deeply the subconscious. Yet their readers were few, especially in contrast to the wide readership enjoyed by writers of religious tracts, romance novels, adventure stories, and the newer genres of murder mystery and science fiction.

Class divisions remained apparent—the more respectable classes still favored classical music and great literature. But another division—between the generations—was emerging as well. After the war, many young people yearned to throw off the authorities and conventions that had governed their parents' generation. The English poet Robert Graves, who was badly wounded in the war, realized that the war had made him cynical about flowery poetry, the rhetoric of politicians, and the church's promises of heavenly rewards. "I found serious conversation with my parents all but impossible,"[5] Graves wrote in 1929. He reveled in dark humor and saw no reason not to write straightforwardly about the pleasures of sex and alcohol. What he meant by *Goodbye to All That*, the title of his autobiography, was goodbye to convention, propriety, patriarchal authority—and perhaps especially, goodbye to the innocence of childhood.

In Graves's world, a true youth culture was developing around new forms of music (jazz), new media (film, radio), new reading materials (magazines, comic books), and new public behaviors. Women, in particular, behaved differently, or at least young urban women did. Defying their parents' insistence that they remain cloistered at home before marriage, many sought out the society of other unmarried girls—or of young men. Sex came out into the open—at least among those determined to break old taboos and live fully modern lives. But there was something reckless about this modern life, as if its participants knew they had a limited time in which to enjoy freedom from conventions and the fruits of a recovering economy. *Goodbye to All That,* strikingly, was published in 1929, the year, in fact, that time ran out.

The Great Depression and the Radicalization of Politics

The bubble, financial and psychological, burst abruptly in the wake of the stock market crash of October 29, 1929.

What effect did the Great Depression have on Europe's remaining democracies? In truth, Europe's fragile stability of the 1920s had been built on American loans and American overseas investments. When these disappeared, European debtors— including virtually all of Europe's state governments—had to scramble to meet their payments. Germany, one of the biggest debtors, was the first of the major states to be hard-hit. Unemployment, which had been as low as 8 percent in 1928, climbed to more than 22 percent by 1930. To try to stem the crisis and save the mark, Chancellor Heinreich Brüning in mid-1930 pushed through a package of spending cuts and new taxes so controversial that the Reichstag erupted in fistfights. Brüning had to resort to emergency powers given to him by the Weimar Constitution to enforce the collection of taxes. His austerity measures did stabilize the currency and by late 1930 Germany could borrow from abroad at reasonable rates. But at home, consumption plunged, and unemployment and frustration continued to rise.

Governments everywhere tried to protect their economies by putting up trade barriers and devaluing their currencies. Both actions made exporting more difficult and resulted in unemployment and real wage reductions. Industrial firms increasingly replaced workers with less costly machines. In many places, agricultural workers suffered more than industrial workers. In the Netherlands, male farm workers' wages dropped by 25 percent between 1929 and 1933; in Hungary, the drop was 41 percent. Falling wages produced a downward spiral, as even those who managed to hold on to their jobs could not afford to consume as much as before. Inevitably, people blamed their leaders for their sufferings. As the slump continued or even worsened over the years, some Europeans gave up on capitalism and democracy and searched desperately for more comprehensive—and radical—solutions.

Hitler Becomes Chancellor

Terrified by bank collapses and rising unemployment, Germans of all sorts, but especially lower-middle-class men and women, gravitated toward the most radical of leaders. The Nazi share of the vote, a moderate 18 percent in 1930, more than doubled in the summer of 1932, to 37 percent, with communists taking 13 percent. Desperate voters turned to Paul von Hindenburg, who had been elected president of the republic in 1925, hoping that the old war hero might impose some sort of stability. But Hindenburg's post was largely honorary; he had to appoint a chancellor who could halt the Depression and control the chaotic Reichstag. A series of old-fashioned conservatives (including Brüning) failed, and so, on January 30, 1933, Hindenburg made the fateful decision of turning to the charismatic but, in his eyes, crude and impertinent leader of the Nazi Party, Adolf Hitler. Hindenburg intended to use Hitler to smash the left and then to push him out again. On the eve of Hitler's appointment, Hindenburg's conservative colleague Franz von Papen predicted: "Within two months we will have pushed Hitler so far into a corner that he'll squeak."[6] They were wrong; Hitler was indeed one of those "little people" whom the upper elite counted on manipulating; but this time he had masses of other "little people" ready to help him give Germany a radical political makeover.

Hitler's "Little Men" in Power

The first two years of Hitler's chancellorship were the most critical for the success of his future dictatorship. During that time, he managed not only to avoid being cornered, but also to destroy his political opponents and rivals in the party. In this endeavor, his old colleagues Hermann Göring and Heinrich Himmler were especially helpful. Appointed Prussian minister of the interior at the same time Hitler became chancellor, Göring immediately set about using the police to round up potential enemies of the regime. Himmler, a fanatical anti-Semite who would later oversee the Final Solution, seized the opportunity to expand his elite group of storm troopers, the SS, or Schutzsstaffeln (Security Guards). In March 1933, Hitler added two more key colleagues to his cabinet: Hjalmar Schacht and Josef Goebbels. Schacht was a brilliant economist as well as an ardent supporter of overturning the Versailles Treaty. As president of the Reichsbank and then minister of economics, he was instrumental in rescuing the German economy and engineering a massive rearmament campaign. Goebbels, one of the party's most skilled orators and rabble-rousers, took the title of Minister for Public Enlightenment and Propaganda. Even before Hitler became chancellor, Goebbels had proven his ability to use torch-lit marches, mass rallies, radio addresses, movies, and mass-circulated newspapers to the party's advantage. In his new position, he was responsible for controlling the media and for enhancing the image of the Führer, tasks he carried out with remarkable success. With the exception of Schacht, Hitler's point men were neither well born nor well educated. In normal times they would have remained insignificant men, but the early 1930s were not normal times, and the ruthlessness and ingenuity of these "little men" made them critical to Hitler's successful stabilization of the Nazi state.

The Economies of 1931–1932

Students of American history are familiar with the story of Black Tuesday, October 29, 1929, the day when the speculative boom of the roaring twenties ended with a steep fall in share prices. Prices continued to fall for two more weeks of "black" days, as panicking investors sold their shares for huge losses, some throwing themselves out of Wall Street windows in despair. The 1929 crash had immediate effects on Europe, as Germany, in particular, depended on American short-term loans. The effects are readily evident in figures for railway freight, a good measure of economic activity, which fell 20 percent between 1929 and 1930. Unemployment rose nine percentage points, to 22 percent, during the same time frame. But both the American and the German economies seemed to stabilize—at the very high cost of increased unemployment and deflation—by late 1930. Thus the bigger and more consequential story about the Great Depression may actually be the story of 1931–1932, the year in which a new round of bank failures and currency crises dashed the hopes of recovery.

The 1931–1932 story begins with the collapse of Austria's largest bank, the Creditanstalt, in May 1931. Europe's

strongest financial institutions, the Bank of England and Germany's national Reichsbank, could not afford a full bailout of the Creditanstalt, exposing the weakness of the financial system as a whole. Within thirty-six hours, foreign investors stripped the Reichsbank of 150 million marks in gold and foreign currency. On July 13, another large German bank failed, and the government declared a three-day bank holiday, preventing a run on the other banks. The stock market was shuttered for two months. Hungary and Romania experienced similar fates. And then on September 21, something momentous happened: Great Britain, the world's banker for more than two centuries, devalued the pound and slapped on new tariffs. Free trade—so long the great cause of economic liberals—was dead.

The abandonment of the gold standard threw all economies into chaos. All the European stock markets had to be closed. Most also separated their currencies from gold so that they could continue to export and pay off debts. Banks everywhere were under siege, and all nations tried more invasive methods of state control in a desperate effort to save the home economy. Consumption and trade slumped, causing declines in industrial production and increases in urban unemployment. Worst off were small farmers, for American overproduction of foodstuffs forced prices for their products to fall much more than prices for manufactured goods. Once again, farmers were squeezed by the price scissors, obtaining less for their produce and paying more for supplies and equipment. On one farm in Poland, peasants who could no longer afford lumber were forced to repurpose their wooden latrine to make a pigsty, a structure more vital to their livelihood. Many central European smallholders who had recently acquired their own land had to sell it again and return to sharecropping or seek work in the already overcrowded cities. Their poor understanding of market dynamics led many to believe the right-wing propaganda that blamed Jews and ineffectual liberals for the economic crisis.

Had the Great Depression ended in 1930, stability and confidence in the system could have been salvaged and the radicalization of the electorate avoided. But the new and deeper plunge of 1931 through early 1932 drove German unemployment up to 44 percent and railway freight down to 58 percent of 1929 levels—and a recovery by late 1932 came too late to undo the damage. Fed up with waiting for the market and republican governments to fix the problems, Germans gave up on democracy, and in central Europe, a generation of hungry, angry peasants longed for someone to rid them of Jewish merchants as well as liberal elites.

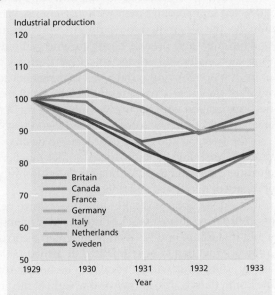

FIGURE 23.1 | Indexes of Total Industrial Production during the Depression of 1929–1933

This chart demonstrates the decline in European industrial output after the initial European economic collapse in 1929 (economies in 1929 = 100). Britain began a rebound in 1931, while the other European countries experienced a second fall, with the bottom reached in 1932.

Source: Created by Jason M. Wolfe based on data gathered from the following sources: Charles Kindelberger, *The World in Depression, 1929–1939* (Berkeley: University of California Press, 1986); and Organization for European Economic Co-operation, *Industrial Statistics, 1900–1957* (Paris; [s.n.], 1958).

QUESTION | *Would a worldwide economic recovery in 1931 have saved Germany and central Europe from political radicalization?*

Enabling Dictatorship: The Reichstag Fire

Once in power, the Nazis' first acts were to destroy freedom of the press, to eliminate parliamentary democracy, and to lock up or force into exile the most vocal anti-fascists, including communists, trade union leaders, and prominent liberal republicans, such as Thomas Mann and Albert Einstein. The Nazis lost no time. SA members immediately began destroying printing presses and arresting communists, and when on February 27 a Dutch Communist set fire to the Reichstag chambers, Hitler—intending to destroy parliamentary government anyway—seized the opportunity and gave himself emergency powers. On March 23, the Reichstag, whose non-Nazi members had largely been arrested or threatened with violence, approved the Enabling Act, which essentially transferred all power to the executive branch. By May, the trade unions had been broken, and in June all parties except the Nazi Party were disbanded. Leaders of the churches and universities either had agreed to collaborate with the regime or had been forced out. In much less time than it took Mussolini to achieve the same results in Italy, Germany's institutions had lost their autonomy and their independent voices. Germany was now a single-party dictatorship.

Nazi Sticks and Carrots

Like the Soviets, once in power the Nazis won support for their policies with a combination of carrots and sticks. The sticks came out right away, as Göring set about arresting labor leaders and communists. Jews were beaten and subject to being locked up if they resisted the regime in any way; by 1934, some of these "enemies of the Volk (people)" were sent to detention centers, including one at Dachau near Munich. In March 1933, Goebbels organized the burning of "leftist" and "decadent" books by university students in Berlin and a boycott of Jewish shops. In April, Jews, other than veterans of the Great War, were banned from serving in the military or civil service, supposedly to make jobs for Aryans, the Nazis' designation for people of pure Germanic ancestry.

Among the carrots were the films, rallies, firelight parades, and book burnings, in which party members and sympathizers delighted in displaying their numbers, their love for militarism, and their contempt for foreigners, pacifists, and decadent cultural critics. Particularly effective carrots were Hitler's dramatic fly-ins, followed by rousing patriotic speeches, some of them broadcast by radio across the nation. Many contemporaries have testified to the riveting quality of Hitler's rhetoric—and their delight at the way he thumbed his nose at the international community. But the Nazi regime also won backers by appearing to tackle the economic situation head on, and by seeking to please the "little men" rather than the rich. Using money appropriated by the last Weimar gov-

ernment, Hitler declared himself devoted to the struggle for work. He forced the labor unions to dissolve and replaced them with a German Labor Front that guaranteed (low) wages; men were put to work building the high-speed Autobahns and new housing developments. The new jobs and economic recovery generated by Hitler's government, however, were mostly the result of huge new investments in rearmament, one of the priorities of the Nazis once they took power.

The new stability—for Aryans—offered by the Nazis was partly the result of having the dangerous people now in power and having their opponents (Jews, communists, and some liberals) pushed out. The regime also sought to create something like an Aryan safety net, chiefly by compelling those who were marginally better off to help the less well off. The "winter help" program, for example, pressed Aryans with extra winter coats to donate them to needy Aryans. Families were encouraged to eat meatless meals to keep costly imports of beef low. Rather like the Soviet rewarding of Stakhanovites, the Germans encouraged workers to exceed their quotas through the "Joy through Work" campaign, which rewarded productive workers with spa vacations and similar perks. In fact, very few workers got the "joy"—but the regime happily reaped the rewards of the extra work.

THE NIGHT OF THE LONG KNIVES. The SA had been allowed to beat up its enemies with impunity and as a result attracted many young men with grievances. When, in mid-1934, the SA swelled to nearly three million men, Hitler, Himmler, and Göring began to worry about its size and its tendency to engage in *disorderly* street violence. Even more worrying, the SA's charismatic leader, Ernst Röhm (1887–1934), was making noises about merging his organization with the army, a move the conservative members of the armed forces opposed vigorously. On June 30, the Gestapo and SS were ordered to destroy the SA threat. Three days of coordinated, quiet murders—which Hitler preferred to pure thuggery—left Röhm and about ninety of his closest allies dead.

Hitler next set upon several of his conservative benefactors, murdering them as well. Shocked party members were told that Röhm and his men represented a corrupting influence that had to be eliminated. It helped Hitler's cause that Röhm was widely known to be homosexual. But the Röhm Putsch, also known as the Night of the Long Knives, was a daring and drastic act, perpetrated against individuals known to be party stalwarts, and it took a great deal of internal propaganda, including a lavish party rally at Nuremberg that fall, to cover over Hitler's purging of many of those who had helped him rise to power. Joseph Goebbels's major purpose of hiring filmmaker Leni Riefenstahl to document the Nuremberg rally was to demonstrate that the party remained united and committed to the common cause: one Volk, one Reich, one Führer. The title of Riefenstahl's film was *Triumph of the Will*: the will that had triumphed was that of Adolf Hitler.

LIVING NATIONAL SOCIALISM. What it was like to live national socialism in the first years of the Nazi regime depended very much on the individual's race and political views. For those who were ethnically German and politically moderate to right wing, the regime was hugely popular. All these people liked Hitler's willingness to end reparations and to seek the extension of Germany's living spaces, that is, if these goals could be achieved without provoking a war. Many supported shutting down what was seen to be an ineffectual democratic system, and many condoned violence against Jews and communists. Business owners approved of Hitler's harassment of revolutionaries and union leaders and eagerly lined up for state contracts to supply Germany's increasingly enormous appetite for weaponry. Eager to get the churches on board, Hitler signed a Concordat with the Vatican in July 1933, forcing the bishops to take an oath to the state and insisting that the clergy keep out of political affairs. In exchange, the church got a free hand in appointing clergy and support for Catholic schooling, which the Weimar Republic had refused to give. Some religious leaders, including Catholics, resisted being aligned with a party that was clearly hostile to religion and spoke out against the Reich's anti-Semitic policies. The Confessing Church, led by the Lutheran pastor Martin Niemöller, refused to accept Hitler's demand that the clergy of Jewish descent be defrocked. Niemöller would spend seven years in a concentration camp for his opposition to Nazism. But other Christian leaders applauded Hitler and his regime for destroying atheistic communism.

Thus, many middle-of-the-road, patriotic Germans found the regime deeply satisfying or at least liked many of Hitler's policies. Many in the international community looked on admiringly as well, chalking up Germany's relatively rapid recovery from the Great Depression to Hitler's nondemocratic efficiency and charisma. To view the regime in early 1938 was to see one that differed from the other authoritarian states around it only in its revived economic might, the explicitness of its anti-Semitism, and the size and the self-confidence of its military. If some of Germany's neighbors found the regime's rebound terrifying, others found it awe inspiring.

NAZI RACIAL POLICY. For those who felt the stick of Nazi policies, conditions were much different. The April

Hitler Energizes the Party Faithful In this photograph of the 1935 Nuremberg rally, Hitler, standing on a red-carpeted platform, addresses a well-organized and enthusiastic crowd of party members. Note in the foreground the bearers of the Nazi eagle standards, their design based on that of the Roman and Napoleonic armies (see p. 549 in Chapter 17).

1933 Law for the Restoration of the Professional Civil Service demonstrated that the Nazis were committed to cleansing non-Aryans from the state's payroll. Though two years passed before the Nazi regime pushed forward its policies of racial segregation and persecution, these early years plunged Germany's Jewish community into despair. The newspaper magnate Rudolf Mosse left the country immediately, but others, well aware of the long history of Jewish persecution in Europe, opted to stay, believing the Nazi regime would, sooner or later, either collapse or relent. Many people deemed Jewish by the regime did not practice the religion or had converted to Christianity; many felt more German than Jewish. Indeed, one of the regime's problems after April 1933 was deciding who counted as a Jew, in the face of so many who claimed they were not. To clarify the official position on this subject, Hitler announced to the party faithful at yet another Nuremberg rally that the time had come to implement a new set of laws for the protection of German Blood and German Honor, otherwise known as the Nuremberg Laws.

THE NUREMBERG LAWS. The decrees that Hitler laid out at Nuremberg were subsequently expanded and made more detailed so that the Reich bureaucracy could more effectively harass and restrict those deemed to be non-Aryans. These laws defined Jewishness not by religious affiliation or self-identification, but purely by biology. Individuals—regardless of gender, age, or profession—were identified as full Jews if they had

Victor Klemperer's Diaries

What did it feel like to be a Jew in Hitler's Germany? Why didn't all German Jews immediately pack their bags and move to France, Poland, or the United States? Historians have discussed these questions for decades, but a set of diaries by a Jewish scholar of French literature, Victor Klemperer (1881–1960), provides vivid insight into one individual's reactions to Hitler's policies as they unfolded day by day.[7] Born the child of a liberal rabbi in 1881, Klemperer had been baptized as a child and had married a Protestant in 1906. Though he was well aware that others (including his wife's family) considered him a Jew, he also considered himself a German and served on the western front in the Great War. In 1920, he was appointed chair of Romance languages at Dresden's Technical University. A great admirer of the French Enlightenment, he was also a supporter of the Weimar Republic, though not particularly politically active. Aged fifty-one at the time of Hitler's seizure of power, he was already keeping a diary and would continue to keep it all through the Nazi years, recording both personal and political events, including the Röhm Putsch, the passage of the Nuremberg Laws, and the annexation of Austria.

Klemperer's diary opens a window on the day-to-day experience of the regime's enemies, demonstrating what Klemperer frequently called the "mental illness" of both the Reich's fanatical supporters and those who pretended that nothing in Germany had changed. Particularly in its early years, the diary frequently repeated the refrain, "How much longer?" as Klemperer waits for someone to overthrow or assassinate Hitler or for Germans to come to their senses. Klemperer had grown up in a civilized European world in which Jews, it seemed, could be accepted as equal citizens, but by March 1933, he began to worry that this civilization had been a fiction. Rumors of Nazi atrocities began to reach him; the body of a communist arrived at the morgue with "fist-sized holes in the back, cotton wool stuffed into them. Official post mortem result: Cause of death, dysentery, which frequently causes premature 'death spots.'" Although he was cheered by

friends who stuck by him, he was shocked by ordinary people who bought the Führer's lies and cheered the Nazis' ruthlessness. He retained his job after the passage of the April 1933 Law on the Civil Service because he had served in the Great War, but his students, increasingly fearful or fanatical, melted away, and university budget cuts eliminated his job in early 1935, even before the enactment of the Nuremberg Laws.

Throughout the mid-1930s, Klemperer continued to hope that the persecutions would end, writing, "[I]t cannot go on like this much longer. And yet," he admits in September 1935, "it does go on and on." He tried to write his own book, on the eighteenth century—the great age of toleration and Enlightenment—and he collected notes for another study, on the absurdities of the language of the Third Reich, which let propagandists call the purging and militarization of university students "the reorganization of the student body" and magazine publishers to print articles titled "The Care of the German Cat," as if German cats required special tending. He noted the appearance of warlike phrases such as the Labor Front's "Struggle for Work" and silly abbreviations such as "Blubo," short for *Blut und Boden* (blood and soil). By 1936, he and his wife were suffering increasingly from depression and ill health, brought on in part by despair. The Anschluss (Hitler's annexation of Austria) finally led him to conclude that his self-perception as a German had always been a delusion: "How deeply Hitler's attitudes are rooted in the German people, how good the preparations were for his Aryan doctrine, how unbelievably I have deceived myself my whole life long, when I imagined myself to belong to Germany, and how completely homeless I am." That painful realization speaks volumes about the experience of central European Jews by 1938. The next seven years would bring disasters of a magnitude that Klemperer, even in his most despairing moments, could not foresee.

QUESTION | **What do Klemperer's diaries reveal about the Nazi stranglehold on German society?**

more than two Jewish grandparents. Those who had one or two grandparents who could be shown to have been born Jewish (including those who had converted to Christianity), were labeled *Mischlinge* or "mixed race persons" and could be reclassified as Germans only by submitting proof of their Aryan ancestry. Those the state deemed to be Jewish were now officially no longer Germans, but stateless people. Jews had no rights in the Third Reich: they could not serve in the army; they could

not vote (a right that had become meaningless anyway); and they could not hold positions in the state bureaucracy, which meant that many doctors, lawyers, university professors, and even postal officials lost their jobs. Jews were forbidden from using public facilities, including parks, libraries, and beaches; neither could they fly the national flag. Regulations on private lives were even more invasive: Jews were forbidden from marrying or having sexual relations with Aryans, and married mixed couples were encouraged to divorce. In 1936–1938, many more restrictions were passed, culminating in the requirement that all Jews must have "J" stamped on their passports (a demand insisted upon by Swiss officials, who wanted to limit Jewish immigration into Switzerland), the curtailment of Jewish freedom of movement, and the expulsion of Jews from public schools. On November 29, 1938, the regime even forbade Jews from owning carrier pigeons, fearing that the birds would be used to convey the news of Jews' persecution to sympathizers outside the state.

Anti-Semitism was hardly a German invention. Already in 1920, the Hungarians had passed a law declaring Jews to be members of a separate race, and in 1924, Romania deprived 100,000 Jews of citizenship. But Germany's laws were much more detailed and extensive than laws elsewhere, testimony to the ways in which Jews had been intimately involved in all parts of pre-Nazi society. The German laws encouraged some authoritarian, but previously not particularly anti-Semitic, states to follow suit. In 1935, the Polish Peasants' Party declared that Jews "cannot be assimilated and are a consciously alien nation within Poland." In 1938, Italy introduced its own racial legislation, including anti-Semitic laws that expelled Italian Jews from jobs in the universities and civil service. A new round of legal forms of persecution would come when Germany began to annex new territories, for wherever the Nazis went, they brought not only their thugs, but also their paper-pushing racists.

Nazi Humiliation of Jews, April 1933 Very soon after taking power, the Nazis demonstrated their eagerness to persecute ethnically Jewish Germans. In Leipzig, as this photo documents, people the Nazis deemed to be Jews were forced to scrub walls to remove communist and socialist graffiti. This exercise in public humiliation was also meant to demonstrate to the wider population the Nazis' claim that the Jews and the socialists belonged to a united group of enemies of the German people.

Foreign Policy and Rearmament

One thing was crystal clear to the Nazis and their supporters by January 1933: the legacies of the Versailles Treaty had to be erased. No longer would Germany tolerate restrictions that limited its army or reparation payments that depleted its treasury. No longer would Germans pretend to be contented with a far too confining set of living spaces, and no longer would they wait for permission from the international community to assert their will in the world. In late June 1933, Hitler made his first aggressive move on the international front when he suspended indefinitely Germany's repayment of its 19 billion mark foreign debt. At the same time, he secretly approved a vast new budget for rearming Germany: 35 billion marks were to be spent over eight years, a huge sum that amounted to nearly 10 percent of German gross domestic product, in an economy in which individual consumption was already very low.

No one was surprised when in October 1933 the Third Reich withdrew from the League of Nations, which the Weimar Republic had been allowed to join in 1925. Hitler officially repudiated the entire Versailles Treaty in 1935 and in 1936, stationing German troops in the demilitarized Rhineland against the Treaty's explicit prohibition. Hitler insisted the action was defensive, done in response to the signing of the Franco-Soviet mutual assistance pact of 1935, but what he was really defending was Germany's industrial heartland, the Ruhr Valley, which was now pumping out vast quantities of coal, steel, and munitions. In 1936, Hitler pushed through a revised budget that called for 9 billion marks, or about 25 percent of gross domestic product, to be spent on the military every year, the largest-ever peacetime armament spending in history. By 1939, military spending accounted for a shocking 80 percent of the goods and services purchased by the Reich. It was only a matter of time before all of these arms, and all of these soldiers, would be called to service.

Fascism Triumphant

Hitler's stabilization of the German economy and his bold assault on democratic values emboldened authoritarian regimes and movements. Mussolini, for one, took heart, but he also smelled a rival. In 1935, he decided that the time had come to display Italy's military prowess

How did Spain and Austria, too, become authoritarian states?

and to begin to build an empire. Avenging themselves on the African country that had embarrassed Italy at Adwa in 1896, Italian troops invaded Ethiopia in 1935. The brutal campaign involved saturation bombing and chemical weapons to subdue the Africans. Tens of thousands of Ethiopians died, along with three thousand Italians for the sake of salving Mussolini's pride. The next year, in fascist solidarity, Italy and Germany signed the Rome-Berlin Axis Pact and the Anti-Comintern Pact, to which Japan was a cosignatory. As the French left-wing parties rallied together to support a common president, Léon Blum, forming a Popular Front against fascism, the lines between left- and right-leaning nations came into sharp relief. The long and bloody Spanish Civil War would further crystallize these positions and initiate a dangerous new arms race.

MAP 23.3 | The Spanish Civil War, 1936–1939

This map shows the pattern of nationalist and republican attacks during the Spanish Civil War. *Where were the nationalists strongest in 1936? How did they use their early foothold in the southwest to squeeze the republicans and eventually take Madrid?*

The Spanish Civil War

Spain had already lost its first republic to the military dictatorship of Miguel Primo de Rivera in 1923. Primo de Rivera (1870–1930) had promised to root out the corruption and political bickering of the republic, but neither had disappeared by 1930. He had also used repressive measures to put down dissent among Catalonians and Basques (Spain too had its minority issues) and to squelch public debate. He tendered his resignation to King Alfonso XIII, who allowed elections to go forward. When republicans triumphed, the king also fled Spain. Although Alfonso did not abdicate the throne, his departure made way for the reestablishment of the Second Spanish Republic in 1931.

Written by anticlerical liberals and socialists, the constitution of the Second Spanish Republic called for full separation of church and state. Clerics were to be ousted from the schools, and church property was to be confiscated by the state. Some radicals celebrated the overturning of what they viewed as a Catholic cultural stranglehold on Spain by pillaging churches and inflicting violence on members of the clergy. The radicalization of the left provoked, in turn, the rise of various kinds of right-wing radicalism, including radical nationalism

(which included protection of the church as one of its pillars) and the development of a Spanish fascist movement known as the Falange. In 1933, these forces combined to elect a right-wing government to power—provoking, in turn, more left-wing radicalization. In October 1934, a huge miners' strike backed by anarchists and communists broke out in the northwestern province of Asturias (Map 23.3). To put down the strike, the government turned to General Francisco Franco, another man hardened by military experience in colonial Morocco. Franco saw the strike as an attempted Communist revolution and did not flinch when two thousand of the strikers were killed. In 1936, liberals banded together with the more radical left-wing parties, and narrowly won elections marked by political violence. This provoked the right to plan a coup, which began with a right-wing overthrow of the liberal government in Morocco. Landing near Seville, nationalist forces then launched a full assault on southern Spain, while other forces attacked the capital, Madrid, from nationalist-dominated northwestern Spain. By late summer 1936, Franco had taken charge of the nationalist forces (taking on the title of Generalissimo) and the Spanish Civil War had begun.

The Spanish Civil War was a bloody, three-year-long battle, in which both left and right committed terrible atrocities against civilians. Some 365,000 people were killed, about 130,000 of whom were summarily executed behind the lines. Although other European nations officially kept out of the war, both sides did receive support from outside forces, the nationalist-fascists from the Nazis and Italian fascists, the republicans from the Soviet communists. A number of republican sympathizers from Europe and the United States traveled to Spain to help the cause. But the left remained divided between anarchists, communists, and liberals, while the right rallied behind the leadership of Franco, who promoted himself as the defender of the church and the restorer of national greatness. He seized con-

The Spanish Civil War Led by veterans of colonial conflicts in North Africa, the Nationalist Army launched a semi-guerrilla insurgency against Spanish Republican forces. Here Nationalist soldiers stream toward Spain's capital city, Madrid, in November 1936.

trol of the Spanish fascist movement, and as he continued to mop up communist and republican resistance, he created a one-party state sustained by the secret police, rather like Mussolini's Italy. Several hundred thousand Spanish leftists fled into exile. Franco finished his war in 1939, but by then another one was clearly in the offing.

The Anschluss

Austria in February 1938 was relatively quiet, thanks in part to measures taken by its home-grown fascist leader Engelbert Dollfuss (1892–1934). Dollfuss had been appointed chancellor of the republic in 1932, a year of economic misery and political violence in Austria, as it was elsewhere. Dollfuss's particular problems included a rising tide of Nazi attacks on socialists and Jewish businesses as Austria's radical right wing increasingly blamed capitalism's malfunctioning on the Jews. Fearing the Austrian Nazis would stage a coup, Dollfuss banned the Nazi Party in June 1933. When another wave of violence erupted several months later, he banned the Socialist Party. By May 1934, the Austrian Republic was dead, and Dollfuss was ruling a one-party state modeled on Mussolini's Italy.

A major goal of Dollfuss's Austro-fascism was to defend Austrian autonomy against Hitler, who—like pan-Germans before him—had always seen German Austria as an integral part of the German Empire. Not surprisingly, it was an Austrian Nazi who assassinated Dollfuss in July 1934. But the pragmatic Hitler did not want to attempt an Anschluss, or union with Austria, just then.

Germany had not yet fully recovered from the Great Depression, and Hitler was still dealing with the fallout from the Röhm Putsch. Thus, a professor of political science, Kurt Schuschnigg, replaced Dollfuss as chancellor and—with Italy's backing—managed to keep Austria out of Hitler's embrace. No anti-Semite, Schuschnigg resisted efforts to pass racist legislation and made at least half-hearted attempts to suppress street violence against Jews. In 1936, Hitler assured the Austrian leader that he had no intention of compromising Austria's independence—but like all of Hitler's assurances, this one was a lie. Austria's Nazis kept up their pressure, and finally Schuschnigg, hoping to defeat violence with votes, scheduled a plebiscite on Austrian independence for March 13, 1938.

This was not to be. On March 12, Austrian Nazis staged a coup from within the state, and the German army crossed the border from the north. Two days later, Hitler entered Vienna to the tolling of church bells. Schuschnigg was arrested and sent to the concentration camp at Dachau. Brutal looting and pillaging of Jewish businesses and homes continued for several days. The Nazis released pent-up longings by humiliating Austria's Jewish community of approximately 220,000 people. Jewish women were compelled to scrub sidewalks and walls pro-Austrian graffiti off the street with bare hands and toothbrushes; other Jews were made to clean toilets or eat grass. The plebiscite now returned a more than 99 percent majority in favor of Anschluss, and Austria was incorporated into the Third Reich, solving, to most Austrians' satisfaction, one of the many problems of the interwar map.

Conclusion

In drafting the post–World War I peace treaties, the victors had attempted to "make the world safe for democracy." But that was a tall order, and in many cases, interwar democracies failed to provide the stability Europeans sought after the disastrous world war. The Soviet solution was not democracy, but communism. Lenin and Stalin managed to industrialize Russia and escaped the ravages of the Great Depression, but at the cost of instituting a totalitarian state and killing millions of their own comrades. Mussolini overturned parliamen-tary governance in Italy as early as 1922, and other authoritarian leaders followed suit. Thanks to the economic and political chaos of the early 1930s and the willingness of conservative elites to invite Hitler to take power, the Nazis seized control in Germany and began a program of rearmament and racial purification. Hitler's ruthless overturning of the Weimar constitution and the Versailles Treaty both terrified and impressed onlookers elsewhere, many of whom had already given up democracy.

Critical Thinking Questions

1. Why did democracy lose its appeal in so many places as the interwar era went on?

2. How many authoritarian regimes seized power by force, and how many came to power through legal means?

3. Would democracy have prevailed in Europe if the Great Depression had been only a short-term recession?

4. Why did this era produce so many charismatic leaders, and so much artistic experimentation?

Key Terms

totalitarianism **(p. 732)**

Cheka **(p. 734)**

gulag **(p. 734)**

war communism **(p. 734)**

New Economic Policy (NEP) **(p. 734)**

collectivization **(p. 734)**

Stakhanovite **(p. 737)**

Popular Front **(p. 738)**

fascism **(p. 741)**

Lateran Accords **(p. 741)**

Comintern **(p. 742)**

"stab in the back" myth **(p. 743)**

Freikorps **(p. 743)**

hyperinflation **(p. 744)**

Nazism **(p. 744)**

Nansen passport **(p. 746)**

Dada **(p. 748)**

Bauhaus **(p. 750)**

existentialism **(p. 750)**

Primary Sources in connect

For information on Connect and the online resources available, go to **http://connect.mcgraw-hill.com**.

1. **Alexandra Kollontai Proclaims the Russian Revolution a Victory for Women**

2. **Lenin on Electrification and Communism**

3. **Stalin Declares War on the Kulaks**

4. **Field Marshal Piłsudski Explains Why Democracy Has Failed in Poland**

5. **Hitler Begins Preparations for War, 1933**

6. **Robert Graves, *Goodbye to All That***

7. **Walter Gropius on the Bauhaus Style**

Benito Mussolini, The Political and Social Doctrine of Fascism (1932)

Ten years after the March on Rome, Italy's fascist dictator Benito Mussolini was still struggling to define the nature of fascism. Fascism, he argues in the following passage, is both a form of state power and a faith. It represents the rejection of liberal democracy and the will of once-humiliated nations to recover their strength and vitality. As such, it is the characteristic ideology of the twentieth century, just as liberalism was the characteristic ideology of the nineteenth century. Mussolini also acknowledges that fascism, in resting on the support of the loyalty of the masses, is also a very different form of governance than the absolutist monarchies that Europeans experienced before 1789.

Fascism combats the whole complex system of democratic ideology; and repudiates it, whether in its theoretical premises or in its practical application. Fascism denies that the majority, by the simple fact that it is a majority, can direct human society; it denies that numbers alone can govern by means of a periodical consultation, and it affirms the immutable, beneficial, and fruitful inequality of mankind, which can never be permanently leveled through the mere operation of a mechanical process such as universal suffrage. . . . This explains why Fascism, having first in 1922 (for reasons of expediency) assumed an attitude tending towards republicanism, renounced this point of view before the March to Rome. . . .

Fascism uses in its construction whatever elements in the Liberal, Social, or Democratic doctrines still have a living value; it maintains what may be called the certainties which we owe to history, but it rejects all the rest. . . . Political doctrines pass, but humanity remains; and it may rather be expected that this will be a century of Fascism. For if the nineteenth century was the century of individualism (Liberalism always signifying individualism) it may be expected that this will be the century of collectivism, and hence the century of the State. . . .

The Fascist State has drawn into itself even the economic activities of the nation, and through the corporative social and educational institutions created by it, its influence reaches every aspect of the national life and includes, framed in their respective organizations, all the political, economic, and spiritual forces of the nation. A State which reposes upon the support of millions of individuals who recognize its authority, are continually conscious of its power and are ready at once to serve it, is not the old tyrannical State of the medieval lord nor has it anything in common with the absolute governments either before or after 1789. The individual in the Fascist State is not annulled but rather multiplied, just in the same way that a soldier in a regiment is not diminished but rather increased by the number of his comrades. The Fascist State organizes the nation, but leaves a sufficient margin of liberty to the individual; the latter is deprived of all useless and possibly harmful freedom, but retains what is essential. . . .

The Fascist State is an embodied will to power and government; the Roman tradition is here an ideal of force in action. According to Fascism, government is not so much a thing to be expressed in territorial or military terms as in terms of morality and the spirit. It must be thought of as an empire—that is to say, a nation which directly or indirectly rules other nations, without the need for conquering a single square yard of territory. For Fascism, the growth of empire, that is to say the expansion of the nation, is an essential manifestation of vitality, and its opposite a sign of decadence. Peoples which are rising, or rising again after a period of decadence, are always imperialist: any renunciation is a sign of decay and of death.

Fascism is the doctrine best adapted to represent the tendencies and the aspiration of a people, like the people of Italy, who are rising again after many centuries of abasement and foreign servitude. But empire demands discipline, the coordination of all forces and a deeply felt sense of duty and sacrifice; this fact explains many aspects of the practical working of the regime, the character of many forces in the State, and the necessarily severe measures which must be taken against those who would oppose this spontaneous and inevitable movement of Italy in the 20th century, and would oppose it by recalling the outworn ideology of the nineteenth century . . . for never before has a nation stood more in need of authority, of direction, and of order. If every age has its own characteristic doctrine, there are a thousand signs which point to Fascism as the characteristic doctrine of our time. For if a doctrine must be a living thing, this is proved by the fact that Fascism has created a living faith; and that this faith is very powerful in the minds of men, is demonstrated by those who have suffered and died for it.

QUESTIONS | *In what ways was fascism—as Mussolini defines it—different from absolutism? What is the place of the individual in this sort of fascist state?*

Source: Benito Mussolini, "The Political and Social Doctrine of Fascism," *International Conciliation,* No. 306 (January 1935), 5–17.

24

WORLD WAR II

Hitler's Preparations for War
Appeasement
Preparing for Racial Warfare
The Hitler-Stalin Pact

The War Begins: The Invasion of Poland and the Winter War
Hitler's New Order in Poland
The Winter War

War in Europe and Northern Africa
Resources First: Norway
Breaking the Enigma Code
The Axis Triumphant
France Falls
Britain Alone, Yet Defiant
War in the Mediterranean

The World at War
The Other Axis Power: Japan's Triumphs in the Pacific
Anglo-American Cooperation
War in the Colonies
Operation Barbarossa

Life and Death in War-Torn Europe
The "Final Solution to the Jewish Question"
Living and Dying in Auschwitz
Collaboration
Resistance
Slave Laborers
Women and the War
War Propaganda
Science and War

The End of the War
The Tide Turns
The Red Army and the Battle for Berlin
Ending the War in the Pacific

Planning Europe's Future
Yalta and Potsdam
Postwar Justice
Displaced Persons

Conclusion

WINSTON CHURCHILL, IMPERIAL WARRIOR Winston Churchill liked war. It took him three tries to get into the Royal Military College Sandhurst. Like Cecil Rhodes, Churchill struggled with the Latin and Greek required for entry. But in 1894, Churchill did obtain a degree from this legendary training facility for officers of the British army. Then he set his sights on getting to the battlefield. Given that Britain was, rather remarkably, not engaged in colonial warfare at the time, Churchill had to begin by observing someone else's battlefield. In 1896, he took a job as a journalist so that he could observe the Cuban revolt against Spanish rule. Coming under fire for the first time on his twenty-first birthday, Churchill found the experience so exhilarating that he asked to be sent into colonial conflicts in India, Sudan, and South Africa, serving as both a soldier and a reporter and becoming a staunch proponent of British imperial policy and the perpetuation of white rule. He abandoned journalism to take a seat in Parliament in 1900, but continued to be keenly interested in warfare. His eagerness to get Britain into the Great War in 1914 inspired the historian

Mass Death and Personal Grief on the Eastern Front: Kerch, Ukraine, January 1942

A. G. Gardiner to write: "'Keep your eye on Churchill' should be the watchword of these days. Remember, he is a soldier first, last, and always. He will write his name big on our future. Let us take care he does not write it in blood."[1]

As first lord of the Admiralty, Churchill directed the Gallipoli campaign in 1915 (see Chapter 22). After this fiasco, Churchill was dismissed from his post and spent the rest of the war in obscurity. But his Great War experience did not destroy his conviction that war was the greatest decider of national destinies. Nor did it shake his faith in Britain's colonial civilizing mission. After Hitler's rise to power, Churchill, who remained a conservative member of Parliament, began a vigorous campaign for British rearmament. In November 1938, he sharply criticized Prime Minister Neville Chamberlain's decision to allow Hitler, the German Führer, to annex a swathe of Czech territory. Doing so was necessary, Chamberlain said, to prevent a war. By insisting that Hitler needed to be stopped right away, Churchill was very much in the minority, and most Britons still thought him an erratic warmonger, unsuited to govern Great Britain.

Public opinion turned in Churchill's direction after the Germans occupied Czechoslovakia in March 1939 and especially after war broke out on September 1, 1939. By the following April, the peace policy pursued by Chamberlain had been thoroughly discredited and, on May 10, 1940, Churchill took his place as prime minister. The bellicosity that Gardiner

Churchill Cheered at the Front Churchill frequently visited Allied troops in the field, reveling in the sense of being close to the battle zone. Here he is received warmly by British troops in northern Africa.

had once found so dangerous now seemed prophetic and vital to Britain's survival. On entering office, Churchill told Parliament: "I have nothing to offer but blood, toil, tears, and sweat" and for the next five years, in radio addresses and parliamentary speeches, that is what he demanded from his fellow citizens. In return, he gave them his blood, toil, tears, and sweat—and more: his enormous appetite for hard work, his rhetorical genius, his clever diplomacy, his indomitable courage, and his stubborn refusal to give up.

Japan at war in Asia and the Pacific
1937–1945

World War II in Europe
1939–1945

London Blitz
1940–1941

Winston Churchill
becomes prime minister
1940

1937

1939

1940

Churchill championed fighting at a time when Britain, Europe, and the world needed someone with determination and resolve to stand against that other war-making mastermind, Adolf Hitler. Churchill, born of a wealthy family, had little in common with the fanatical Austrian foot-soldier and racist rabble-rouser, nor were Churchill's methods anything like those of Hitler, for the British leader was waging a defensive, not an offensive war. It was Hitler, of course, who started the Second World War, and Hitler and the Nazis who planned and executed the genocide of the European Jews; it was Hitler and his Japanese Allies who committed most of the racially motivated atrocities (though some Axis collaborators and the Soviets, too, were guilty of terrible crimes). But Churchill was willing to pull out all the stops to get the United States into the war on his side and, once again, to exploit Britain's colonies to serve England's interests. Though he loathed communism and believed all Bolsheviks were "crocodiles," in 1941 he made an alliance with Joseph Stalin—for only such measures, he knew, could ensure Germany's defeat. The fiercest of nationalists, he presumed that fellow Britons would endure any sacrifice to defend the British Isles. As the fall of France loomed in late May 1940, he told his inner circle: "I am convinced that every man of you would rise up and tear me down from my place if I were for one moment to contemplate parley [negotiation] or surrender. If this long island story of ours is to end at last, let it end only when each one of us lies choking in his own blood upon the ground."

The image is gruesome, but the Second World War was one that had to be fought without contemplating surrender. Stalin's refusal to give up despite the Soviet Union's devastating losses of soldiers, civilians, and territory in 1941–1943 is further testimony that only the will to fight to the last kept the Nazis from conquering all of Europe, and their allies, the Japanese, from dominating the Pacific Rim. Yet for many, who lacked the resources and geographic advantages of Churchill or Stalin, the will to resist was not enough: this was a war of massive, mechanized forces, of brutalized and enslaved laborers, and of vast bureaucracies that coordinated new forms of violence against civilians. Many who gave their all did die, and even Churchill could not have won it on guts alone.

Churchill's side won the war—thanks to the fact that two critical allies, the USSR and the United States, joined and lent their colossal resources. Yet Churchill's personal determination and charisma mattered, too. Despite his age—he was nearly sixty-six when the war began—his energy during the conflict was boundless. Shuttling between the fronts and holding endless conferences with allies and neutral parties, he was in constant motion. Between fall 1939 and fall 1943, he logged more than 110,000 miles of travel. He reveled in visiting troops and hearing gunfire; to raise morale, he often led his audiences in singing popular songs. Whether traveling or at home, he worked relentlessly, spurred on by passionate hatred of the Nazis and by liberal doses of champagne. In May 1945, he had the satisfaction of seeing Hitler defeated. But by then he was already well aware that Stalin was poised to impose Soviet rule on eastern Europe, and that India, England's "jewel," would not tolerate colonial rule any longer. In 1946, it would be Winston Churchill who first warned the world that an "iron curtain" had fallen and a new, "cold" war had begun.

❉❉❉❉

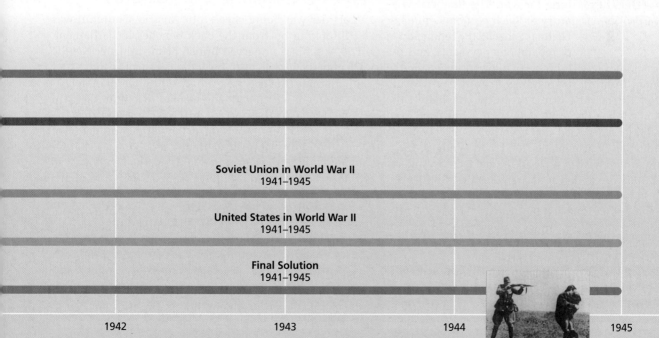

Soviet Union in World War II
1941–1945

United States in World War II
1941–1945

Final Solution
1941–1945

1942   1943   1944   1945

The war Churchill helped to win was not just a uniquely devastating and deadly one. It was also a genocidal war, and one that had revolutionary effects on Europe, Asia, and to a lesser extent, other continents. It was started by two major belligerents—Nazi Germany and Imperial Japan—but in its course, many other nations would aid in the victimization of their own inhabitants or those of neighboring territories.

Like the First World War, this one was many faceted, and each nation traveled its own path into the war and out of it. Some individuals caught in the war's path could choose to collaborate or resist; others were simply murdered by enemies who wanted to seize their property, to purify the race, or to exact revenge. Chance too played a major role in determining who lived or died. Some were saved by cloud cover that prevented one night's bombings; others died because their village was singled out for collective punishment. This war had its share of heroes, victims, and villains; some people combined all three roles. We can only comprehend the significance of this war by recognizing that in one way or another, it devastated and transformed all of Europe's ethnic, political, economic, and cultural landscapes. No corner of the continent experienced it in the same way, but neither was any corner left untouched by its terrible brutality.

Hitler's Preparations for War

Churchill's major foe, Adolf Hitler, was a man convinced that war was the only way to establish Germany's rightful dominance in Europe. Almost as soon as he obtained the chancellorship in 1933, Hitler began rebuilding his army and planning for war. The financial wizardry of Reich economic minister Hjalmar Schacht, the renunciation of reparations payments, and the expropriation of Jewish property allowed huge sums to be devoted to military spending. Together with army officials, Hitler and Göring carefully considered the Reich's needs for raw materials such as oil, iron, and rubber. Hitler concluded that even by vastly increasing the production of armaments, food, and synthetic fuels, Germany would have to seize additional territory and resources if it were to defeat its arch enemies, Bolshevism and world Jewry. Both men still believed that the starving home front had stabbed the army in the back in 1918, and thus also wanted to annex regions that would provide a reliable food supply for the Reich. In 1936, he developed a four-year economic plan whose secret intent was to make Germany ready for war in 1940. All other needs would be subordinated to this plan, and private industrialists were forced to produce for the military or

Why did Neville Chamberlain's "appeasement" of Adolf Hitler fail to prevent the outbreak of war?

have their businesses seized by the state. By 1938, 80 percent of Reich spending went to rearmament, reminiscent of the days of Frederick the Great when the state sector had been much smaller.[2]

What Hitler wanted from the next war was not only the defeat of communism and the supposed international Jewish conspiracy that underlay it, but a new order in Europe, one run by and for Aryans—the supposedly pure-blooded ancestors of the Germans, Scandinavians, and Brits. Hitler's new order had no room for democracies; those were weak, decadent, and cowardly. Instead, Hitler wanted to create authoritarian states, run by efficient, incorruptible, and racially fit men—Aryan women ought to remain in their homes, raising Aryan babies. The Germans stood at the top of this hierarchy; below them were other supposed Aryan peoples, followed by the Latin peoples (the French, Spanish, and Italians); at the bottom—though above the Jews—were the Slavs, who would have to give up their land and food and submit to being the lowliest of laborers or simply disappear.[3]

Although only a few Germans knew that Hitler was planning to launch an offensive war in 1940, they could hardly have failed to notice the military build-up. Some worried, but most rejoiced that Hitler had provided so many new jobs and that Germany was again a great military power. Some found Hitler's racial bigotry and the anti-Semitic legislation offensive, but others fell for the Nazis' claims that the Jews were to blame for Germany's ills. Many people cheerfully bought at cut-rate prices goods seized from Jews fleeing the country or forced to give up their homes and businesses. Fears that a new war might be in the offing increased after the Anschluss in March 1938. But even then, most Germans, like most other Europeans, did not want to believe that another world war was just around the corner.

Appeasement

As Hitler was being cheered in Austria, Churchill was still looking on from the back benches in Parliament. The Anschluss unnerved British prime minister Neville Chamberlain (1869–1940), but it did not surprise him. After all, German-Austria was inhabited by German speakers, many of whom had long wanted to join the German powerhouse to the north, and Hitler insisted that the League of Nations' provision on the self-determination of nations ought to apply to Germany, too. But it was harder to entertain Hitler's next demand: that he be allowed to annex the **Sudetenland,** the C-shaped belt of industrialized western Czechoslovakia on Germany's southern border (Map 24.1). This territory, too, was heavily populated by Germans—nearly three million of them—who had never wanted to be ruled by the Czech government. Chamberlain and French prime minister Edouard Daladier flew to Munich in September 1938 to discuss the issue with Hitler. Mussolini attended, but neither Eduard Beneš, the Czech president, nor Stalin, were invited to the conference. Chamberlain at least pretended to believe Hitler's promise that this would be his last annexation and stated that Britain should not go to war "because of a quarrel in a far-away country between people of whom we know nothing" and agreed to allow the Third Reich to swallow up the Sudetenland. Without apologizing to Beneš for handing over the richest and most productive part of his country to the Nazis, the British prime minister flew home, relieved to be able to assure his country of "peace in our time."

Churchill was enraged by Chamberlain's **appeasement** of the Nazi dictator, and his warnings that Nazis would not be satisfied with the annexation of German-speaking lands were confirmed when Hitler broke his promise and commanded German troops to seize the remainder of Czechoslovakia in March 1939. The Germans made the Czech lands a pseudo-colony; Slovakia was handed over to a puppet regime headed by the priest Jozef Tiso (1887–1947). The Hungarians were allowed to occupy the southern provinces, sealing Hungary's alliance with the **Axis Powers,** an alliance comprised of the

Germany in 1933

Remilitarized in 1936

Annexed in 1938

Satellite states in March 1939

Annexed to Germany in March 1939

Occupied by Germany in September 1939

Annexed by Germany in October 1939

Annexed by Soviet Union in November 1939

Annexed to Soviet Union in 1940

——— International boundaries, 1936

MAP 24.1 | Hitler's Europe, Annexations to 1939

This map shows the stages of Hitler's empire-building before the Second World War began, and the partitioning of Poland between the Nazis and the Soviets after the signing of the nonaggression pact just before the war's outbreak on September 1, 1939. Note the location of the Czech Sudetenland, heavily inhabited by ethnic Germans and given to Germany in the Munich agreements of September 1938. Note also the locations of Bromberg, one of the many areas in which Germans committed atrocities against Polish Jews in 1939, and of Katyn, where the Soviets brought thousands of Polish intellectuals for execution. *Looking at Hitler's gains as of March 1939, could you guess where he might next make war? Which nations were now most in danger?*

Germans, Japanese, Italians, Hungarians, Romanians, and Bulgarians. Hitler was now seizing territory inhabited by non-Germans, and the French and British moved to assure Poland, inevitably the Nazi dictator's next target, that they would not allow it to be gobbled up.

Preparing for Racial Warfare

By the spring of 1939, it was abundantly clear that the German dictator had his eye on other territories taken away from Germany at Versailles, namely, the Polish Corridor, the strip of Polish land running through Germany to the east, and Alsace-Lorraine in the west. It was clear, too, that Hitler was preparing for war to complete his central European empire. But his government's actions after the Munich Conference suggested that Hitler's regime harbored racial, as well as military, ambi-

tions. As the regime prepared for war with its external enemies, the Nazis developed increasingly violent methods for ridding the Aryan community of so-called internal enemies and unfit members.

THE NIGHT OF THE BROKEN GLASS. The annexation of Austria added another 200,000 Jews to the 200,000 Germans who had been classified as such under the Nuremberg Laws. Many of these Jews could not leave, as their livelihoods and bank accounts had been taken away and they could not afford the so-called flight tax now required of emigrants. So to rid itself of the Jewish population, Nazis turned to force. Using the pretext of the murder in Paris of a Nazi diplomat by a Polish Jew, Joseph Goebbels instigated an empire-wide pogrom on the night of November 9, 1938, the fifteenth anniversary of the failed Beer Hall Putsch (see Chapter 23).

In the course of the evening, the SA, together with civilian volunteers, burned synagogues and destroyed remaining Jewish-owned businesses. Some zealous thugs dragged Jews from their beds and beat them in the streets. At least ninety Jews were killed and thousands more were imprisoned, though most were later released. The Nazis referred to the action as the **Night of the Broken Glass** (*Reichskristallnacht*), covering up the violence against people by focusing on the number of shop windows broken. Protests about the violence came from Germans as well as from the international press; some high-ranking Nazis, including Hermann Göring, objected on the grounds that property the Reich might use profitably was being recklessly destroyed. The lesson the Nazis took from the Night of the Broken Glass was that confiscation of property should come first and violence applied afterward, preferably away from the view of sensitive citizens and the meddlesome foreign press.

Kristallnacht On the day after the Nazis terrorized and murdered Jewish civilians, and smashed or burned their shops and synagogues, pedestrians in Berlin continue their daily routines, seemingly unaffected by the violence.

Hitler was enraged by the international community's condemnation of his behavior. In a speech on January 30, 1939, the anniversary of his seizure of power, he blamed the Jews for the violent actions his regime was taking against them. Airing openly his fanatical and wholly baseless conviction that a worldwide Jewish conspiracy was plotting Germany's demise, he accused the Jews of threatening the peace (entirely his own doing) and made this ominous prediction or, in his terms, prophecy: "Should the world of Jewish finance succeed . . . in plunging humankind into yet another world war, the result will not be a Bolshevization of the earth and the victory of Jewry, but the destruction of the Jewish race in Europe." Vilifying the Jews, as was his custom, for being both money-grubbing capitalists and bloodthirsty communists, Hitler was putting the world on notice that the fate of the Jews would be closely bound up with the conduct and outcome of the now nearly inevitable world war.

THE NAZI EUTHANASIA CAMPAIGN (T-4). Since coming to power, the Nazis had sought to improve the "racial hygiene" of the German people, in part by forced sterilization of people with mental disabilities. Obsessed with having enough resources to feed and clothe the Aryan population, Hitler was eager to do away with "useless eaters" whose genes endangered the racial health of the community as a whole. In the summer of 1939, he approved a secret program of killing disabled children. At least five thousand were starved to death or given drug overdoses. Once the war started, the euthanasia program was expanded and dubbed **T-4** (for Tiergarten 4, the address of the staff office). German patients were shot, starved, poisoned with drugs, or gassed in vans. By autumn 1940, some 140,000 were dead. Relatives and

Catholic groups realized what the regime was up to, and protests were sufficiently vehement that the Nazis stopped official implementation of T-4 in early 1941. But throughout the war, the Nazis would continue to quietly murder people they considered unworthy of life and would apply many of their extermination techniques to the killing centers that began to spring up in the east only a few months later.

REPATRIATING GERMANS. The other side of the process of eliminating racial enemies was the attempt to populate the spreading Nazi empire with racial friends. Hitler was eager to welcome "home to the Reich" ethnic Germans who had taken up residence elsewhere in Europe. He first invited—and Mussolini compelled—thousands of Germans to leave northeastern Italy and settle in the territory of the Old Reich (Weimar Germany plus Austria). Then Hitler agreed with Hungarian dictator Miklós Horthy (1868–1957) to accept tens of thousands of Germans from Transylvania, and with Stalin to take 137,000 Germans from the Romanian territories that the Soviets annexed in 1941.

The Reich Resettlement Office, run by SS-chief Heinrich Himmler and his deputy Reinhard Heydrich (1904–1942), eagerly pushed Poles and Jews out of western Poland in the fall of 1939, making way for the settling of these Aryan farmers on newly Germanized land. They envisioned doing the same in the rest of eastern Europe, saving anyone deemed racially valuable and leaving the rest to flee, starve, or enslave themselves to the Germans. Married, middle-class, Aryan women, by contrast, were encouraged to have as many babies as possible, and Aryan women were officially prohibited from obtaining abortions. During the war, the Third Reich kidnapped an estimated 50,000 "racially valuable" children from other European nations, hoping to use them to improve the gene pool at home. Never before had biology, and with it sexuality, been so central to a conflict, and never had a regime brought the battlefield and the bedroom into such close and cruel contact.

The Hitler-Stalin Pact

Watching events unfold in the spring and summer of 1939, western Europeans felt a surge of fear—but surely nothing compared to what eastern Europeans experienced. Austria and Czechoslovakia had already been annexed; Poland was sure to be next. From Moscow, Stalin watched angrily as the Nazis tore away his buffer zone, and the western Europeans did nothing to stop them. As the Soviet leader saw it, the West surrendered the East to save itself from war. Stalin was also enraged by being cut out of the negotiations over Czechoslovakia and by the Poles' absolute refusal to allow Soviet troops on Polish soil, a stance that made an Anglo-Polish-Russian defensive alliance impossible. Stalin did not want to fight the Germans alone—he had just completed a fierce purging of the army, and Soviet industrialization was only beginning to catch up with western levels of production.

Nor did Hitler want to fight Stalin just yet. His experience in World War I taught him that German resources and manpower were not yet ready to win a war fought on both western and eastern fronts. Thus Nazi diplomats approached their Soviet counterparts with an astonishing proposition: a mutually beneficial nonaggression pact. The treaty between these two ideologically opposed nations, signed on August 23, 1939, shocked everyone at home and abroad. Europeans would have been even more shocked had they known about the secret provisions of the treaty, which allowed the Soviets a free hand in their sphere of influence, which included Finland, the Baltic nations, and the eastern half of Poland, in exchange for German dominion in central Europe and western Poland. Stalin rejoiced: "Hitler wants to trick us, but I think we've got the better of him." For his part, Hitler—who never met the Soviet dictator in person—believed *he* had got the upper hand. Indeed, the Nazis would benefit greatly from the pact, for the Soviet Union not only sent the Third Reich large quantities of needed supplies—including wheat, oil, and minerals—but also gave the Nazis time to build a much larger empire in both central and in western Europe.

The War Begins: The Invasion of Poland and the Winter War

Everyone, especially the Poles, knew that war was on the near horizon, and panic swept through Poland as the army mobilized and civilians made desperate at-

> **In what ways did the war in Poland herald the coming of a new kind of warfare?**

tempts to flee. When the Germans invaded Poland on September 1, 1939, France and Britain declared war. However, rather than sending troops to defend Poland, they readied themselves for the larger conflict that was sure to come. The Poles were left alone with their 313 tanks and 388 out-of-date planes to fight a David-and-Goliath struggle against 2,600 German tanks and 1,900 modern German aircraft. The Nazis chose not to march across the frontier to engage Polish forces, but began by using their high-tech weapons. They launched a massive air bombardment, destroying Poland's air force on the ground and strafing troops and civilians on the roadways. Warsaw, the Polish capital, was subjected to merciless bombing, and tanks rolled across the border at numerous points. David fought bravely, but Goliath won: the Poles were defeated in a **Blitzkrieg,** or a war of lightning speed, that lasted less than a month, though the Polish government and approximately 200,000 Polish soldiers managed to escape to Romania and then France to continue the fight.

During the campaign, the Soviets invaded from the east and claimed the eastern third of Poland for themselves. When the smoke cleared, Poland had been divided into three zones, two of them dominated by the Germans and one by the Soviets (see Map 24.1). The Soviets turned eastern Poland into a communist state, ruthlessly murdering class enemies and harvesting Polish labor and resources for their own purposes. The Germans designated central Poland, home to the majority of Poland's Jews, as the General Government, to be treated as a kind of slave colony, organized to produce food and supplies for the German war effort. The Germans simply annexed western Poland, the region that included the Polish Corridor. Poles were driven out, and ethnic Germans enticed to move in, claiming this territory as needed living space for the German master race.

Hitler's New Order in Poland

The first weeks of the Polish campaign made it clear to all that this was a new kind of war. For the Nazis, the occupation of western and central Poland in 1939–1940 served, in many ways, as a testing ground and a foreshadowing of what would be done on a much larger scale elsewhere.

DEPORTATION AND RESETTLEMENT. Germany's regular army (the Wehrmacht) entered Poland in September 1939 with the goal of defeating the Polish army. That was ordinary warfare, but what came next was not. In the wake of the Wehrmacht came units of the SS, whose mission was to destroy all enemies of the Nazi regime and to purify western Poland so that it could be settled by Germans once again. The SS carried out its orders enthusiastically, executing both Polish and Polish-Jewish leaders and educated persons to ensure that Poland would be reduced to slavery. Where peasants offered any

Sex and the Third Reich

For many years, it was widely believed that the Nazi regime was a prudish one with respect to sex. Hitler himself did not marry until almost the day he died, and then he married his Bavarian girlfriend, Eva Braun, whom many thought less precious to him than his dog, Blondi.

He and his minions endlessly attacked the immorality of decadent cities, supposedly packed with "new" women and male homosexuals. But as historian Dagmar Herzog has pointed out, the Nazis also expended a considerable amount of energy encouraging the right sort of people to have sex early and often. Here, too, they were not old-fashioned conservatives, but champions of a totalitarian way of life, in which the state dictated who had sex with whom and who lived to reproduce him- or herself—and who did not.[4]

Best known are the Nazis' attempts to prohibit sex that created more "racial enemies" or polluted Germany's supposedly pure bloodstream. Believing that "mongrelization" produced weak individuals with mixed loyalties, the Nazis were desperate to keep the races from intermixing. The Nuremberg Laws took clear aim at sexual practices, criminalizing relations between unmarried Jews and non-Jews; subsequently, the Nazis tried to break up marriages between the two as well. The regime sterilized the children of French African soldiers and German women, conceived during France's occupation of the Rhineland in 1923. They also sterilized or deported prostitutes, gypsies, and the mentally disabled, and they persecuted men suspected of homosexuality. These "racially unfit" persons suffered further persecution during the war, when they were deported to concentration camps, where tens of thousands were murdered alongside Jews, communists, and other enemies of the regime.

Less well known is the other side of the story of sexuality under Nazism: the Nazis' attempt to breed the right kind of people. As Herzog has shown, the Third Reich deliberately encouraged sex among unmarried young people, including members of the army and the labor front.

"Symbols for Protective Custody Prisoners in the Concentration Camps"
This poster instructs Nazi officials on which insignia are to be worn by which of Germany's "enemies." The vertical column reads: "Basic Color, Repeat Offender, Prisoner in Punishment Brigade, Jew." Horizontally, on the top, the categories are "Political [Enemy], Career Criminal, Emigrant, Bible Scholar [Jehovah's Witness], Homosexual, Asocial." On the bottom, the first row reads, "(Male) Race-Defiler; Female Race-Defiler; Potential Escapee; Prisoner Number," and the second, "Pole, Czech, Wehrmacht Member, Category Ia Prisoner."

Heinrich Himmler even set up a series of maternity homes for racially fit unwed mothers and wives of SS officers, and doctors were authorized to perform artificial insemination in the hopes of producing more Nordic Germans. A number of these homes were established in Norway, after the Nazi invasion, as well as in Germany, Poland, and the Ukraine. Aryan-looking children were sometimes taken away from their parents and sent to foster families in Germany. Himmler, who dabbled in the occult, circulated to his SS troops lists of good cemeteries in which to have sex, believing that babies conceived near the graves of Germanic heroes would inherit their superior courage and strength.

The Third Reich's attempts to dictate who had sex with whom frequently broke down. The army forbade soldiers from having sex with racially inferior people in the countries it occupied, but in the conditions of total war, many men ignored these orders and raped starving and desperate women who were already at death's door. German civilians had love affairs with foreign slave laborers. Concentration camp commanders took Jewish mistresses. As the war turned against them, many Germans adopted a motto that excused all behaviors: "Enjoy the war—the peace will be awful."

These attempts to regulate sex testify once again to the totalitarian aspects of the Third Reich and the degree to which World War II was, even more than World War I, a total war. Enlightened and liberal-minded Europeans had pushed for centuries to establish individuals' rights to choose their partners, but under the Nazi dictatorship, even sexual relations had become a matter for the state to approve or disallow. All too often their dictates succeeded, legitimizing sexual as well as physical violence against those the regime considered its racial enemies.

QUESTIONS | *Why did the Third Reich attempt to dictate sexual policies and practices? Why did these attempts fail?*

resistance, their villages were burned. The SS reveled in its opportunity to humiliate civilians. In Bromberg (Bydgoszcz), German occupiers locked Jews and Poles in the synagogue, refusing them access to restrooms; the prisoners were forced to wipe up their excrement with prayer shawls and the curtains that enclosed the synagogue's sacred space. Some Christian leaders, too, were eliminated: in one area of western Poland, 250 priests were arrested and 214 of them were shot. Approximately 17,000 Poles living in mental institutions were murdered, in part to carry out Nazi eugenic policy and in part to make space available to house the SS.

These actions provoked complaints from some professional soldiers, who disapproved of devoting so much energy to tormenting civilians and worried that the atrocities would result in bad press abroad. By the spring of 1940, the SS was ordered to focus attention instead on relocating Poles and Jews, harnessing all of Poland's assets, labor power, and resources to Germany's war economy, and preparing western Poland for German resettlement. Those expelled were often put to flight suddenly, forcing them to leave behind their clothing, livestock, and personal possessions. Teams of young German women were delegated to scrub and mop the dwellings, making them ready for their new inhabitants, many of them ethnic Germans shipped there from other parts of central and eastern Europe.

By June 1940, German atrocities in Poland were already widely known, and Winston Churchill was using Poland's fate to rally his countrymen. Referring to the Nazis' mass executions, he argued, "We may judge what our fate would be if we fell into their clutches." But, he added, from the same incidents "we may draw the force and inspiration to carry us forward on our journey and not to pause or rest till liberation is achieved and justice is done."[5] Churchill's words were, however, cold comfort for the Poles, who had now experienced a taste of what living under Hitler's new order would be like.

THE KATYN FOREST MASSACRE.

By this time, many Poles were experiencing horrors unknown to Churchill and the western press. At least initially, the Soviet regime in eastern Poland proved even more deadly than that of the Nazis. After the Red Army's invasion, the Soviet Secret Police (the Cheka, now called the NKVD) shot many Poles and deported hundreds of thousands of others to the Soviet interior, where they were placed in Stalin's gulags. In March 1940, Soviet leaders authorized the rounding up and shooting of 20,000 Polish military officers, teachers, and businessmen. The executions took place in secrecy in a heavily forested area known as Katyn, and the fate of these individuals was unknown until Nazi occupiers discovered a mass grave in 1943. Although the Poles suspected the Soviets had been the culprits, Stalin blamed the Nazis, and for many years, textbooks reported that the Germans had committed the massacre at Katyn. Not until 1990, after the collapse of Soviet power in eastern Europe, were documents released showing that the Russians were indeed to blame

for this atrocity. The Soviets committed similar atrocities following their invasion and occupation of Latvia, Lithuania, and Estonia in 1940–1941. In these areas, too, NKVD squads shot thousands of anti-communists, intellectuals, and would-be resisters, and deported hundreds of thousands to Siberian camps.

THE FATE OF THE POLISH JEWS.

As terrible anti-Semitic violence and legalized exploitation had been in Germany and Austria, the invasion of Poland made it clear that treatment of eastern European Jews would be far worse. Here the problem of numbers first really impressed the German bureaucracy with the logistical difficulty of making the Jews "disappear" from Europe, as Hitler wanted. It was one thing to drive out, imprison, brutalize, and vandalize the roughly 750,000 Jews who inhabited Germany and Austria in 1933; it was another to attempt such an operation in German-occupied Poland, whose Jewish population was nearly five times larger (about 3.3 million). Moreover, the pact with the Soviets made it impossible for the Nazis to simply force the Jews to flee eastward, and most Jews were far too poor to pay their passage to Palestine, England, or America—if indeed these nations would have let them in, for all had strict and small immigration quotas.

Eager to please their master, Hitler's bureaucrats in the General Government scrambled to find ways to make their territory "Jew free." After the fall of France in 1940, a plan was hatched to ship them to the French colony of Madagascar off the coast of southeastern Africa. But no one wanted to spend precious cash on the Jews—even to get rid of them—and in any event, the British navy controlled the seas. In 1940, there was still no "final solution to the Jewish question."

In the meantime, the Nazis decided to concentrate their enemies, the better to terrorize them. Jews were crowded into the poorest areas of Lublin, Lodz, Cracow, Warsaw, and other Polish cities. First barbed wire and then walls cordoned off the **ghettoes,** which grew increasingly cramped as new deportees arrived. Unable to work and without access to their savings, gardens, or property, ghettoized Jews had to be fed by their Nazi jailors, who resented every mouthful of bread or vial of medicine given to them. One calculation puts the rations for Jews in wartime Warsaw at 184 calories per day—compared with 634 for non-Jewish Poles and 2,310 for Germans. When malnutrition, poor sanitation, and overcrowding inevitably caused disease to spread, the Nazis blamed the contagion on the Jews and cut off all contact with outsiders.

THE WARSAW GHETTO.

Conditions in the Warsaw ghetto exemplified the sufferings endured by Polish Jews even before the extermination camps began their terrible work. By March 1941, some 450,000 Jews were living in the 1.5 square miles of the Warsaw ghetto; on average, each room was shared by 7.5 persons; by mid-1941, the average may have been as high as 13 persons per room. By June 1941, approximately 50 percent of the residents of the Warsaw ghetto were dying of hunger, and pedestrians regularly encountered corpses in the streets. In another year's time, about 100,000 had perished—but this death rate wasn't fast enough for the Germans. Solving the Jewish question would become even more challenging after the invasion of the Soviet Union and the Baltic states, which added millions more Jews to the Nazis' list of the condemned.

The Winter War

As the Nazis sought to impose their racial policies on Poland, the Soviets took aim at Finland, one of the few democracies to have survived the interwar era. Stalin wanted to control this neighboring territory—but he chose, for the Red Army, a most inopportune moment to attack the fiercely independent Finns. The invasion began on November 30, 1939, just as winter was setting in. Soviet troops had little experience in waging war in deep snow and dense forests, and despite their numbers, they suffered unexpectedly heavy casualties as the Finns used their knowledge of the terrain to stage surprisingly successful counterattacks. In just over three months of fighting, 27,000 Finns, and an astounding 258,000 Russians, lay dead or wounded. Yet Goliath eventually triumphed here as well, and on March 12, 1940, the Soviets proclaimed themselves victors of the Winter War. They quickly annexed some border zones, causing more than 420,000 Finns to flee westward in one of the first of the war's massive population relocations. The Finns would reopen the war against the USSR after the German invasion of the Soviet Union, in June 1941.

War in Europe and Northern Africa

For some months after the fall of Poland, the German war effort seemed to flag, and western Europeans, paying little attention to Stalin's annexations, furiously built

Why were the Nazis so successful in the first two years of the war?

up their armaments and worried about when and where the Nazis would next strike. For the **Allied Powers,** which now included Britain, France, and the Polish government in exile, the winter and spring of 1939–1940 felt like a "Phony War"—but in fact the period saw both an important victory for the Nazis and a crucial intelligence breakthrough for their opponents.

Resources First: Norway

Not for the last time, Hitler's attention to the location of natural resources vital to the nation's war effort dictated Germany's moves. In April 1940, German forces moved to secure the Danish coast, intending to launch an attack on Norway. Denmark was swiftly defeated and occupied. Here, Nazi occupiers treated the population with

far less brutality than they exhibited in Poland as Danes were considered Aryans, and the Nazis hoped to make Denmark a model colony. But the real prize was Norway, through which tons of vital Swedish iron ore flowed. The Germans also wanted to secure Norway's Atlantic ports in order to prevent the Allies from attacking or blockading German shipping in the Baltic Sea. On April 9, 1940, a Blitzkrieg on Norway began, shocking unprepared inhabitants and forcing the Norwegian royal family to flee. The Germans set up the Norwegian fascist Vidkun Quisling (1887–1945) as Norwegian prime minister, though many Norwegians refused to recognize him, and fifteen days later, Hitler replaced Quisling with a Nazi loyalist. Hitler's window on Britain and his iron ore supplies were secure.

Breaking the Enigma Code

In January 1940, French, Polish, and British intelligence experts, working together, achieved a breakthrough when they decoded one of Germany's Enigma keys. Invented at the end of World War I, the Enigma machine scrambled messages so thoroughly that the Germans were confident that their codes could not be broken. Deciphering these

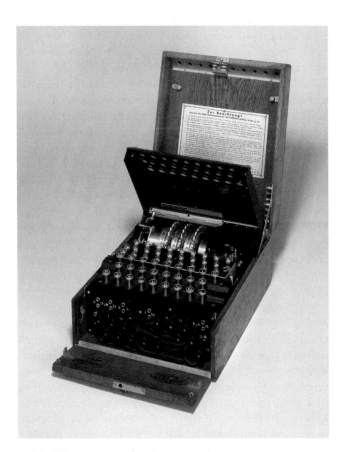

The Enigma Machine The Nazis counted on this message-scrambling machine to make their secret telegraphs undecipherable to Allied interceptors. Fortunately for the Allies, intelligence experts from France, Poland, and Britain decoded one of the Enigma keys in January 1940, and would soon gain access to the Nazis' supposedly secret plans.

messages remained difficult even after breaking the code, and it took some time before the Allies were able to intercept, read, and use German messages. But this first step laid the foundations for the vital intelligence work that would give the Allies advance notice of Hitler's plans.

The Axis Triumphant

The Phony War came to a sudden end with the German invasion of Belgium and the Netherlands on May 10, 1940. The intent was to launch two lightning-fast armies toward the main target of France, one along a northern trajectory through the Netherlands and another farther south through the rugged Belgian Ardennes Forest. The German plan worked even better than its creators had hoped. Overpowered on the ground and pounded from the air, the Netherlands and Belgium fell in rapid succession. German armored divisions swept through the French countryside with very light casualties and, by May 21, had reached the Atlantic. The German advance left a British expeditionary force, along with some French forces, cut off from the main body of the French army, and trapped against the English Channel coast. Luckily the Germans misjudged the numbers, thinking the expeditionary force numbered only 100,000 rather than nearly 400,000. Trying to conserve fuel for the final assault on the French, on May 24 German generals ordered a three-day halt.

Those precious hours allowed Churchill to engineer a courageous rescue: over nine days, a flotilla of naval vessels, privately owned sloops, fishing boats, and tugs whisked 225,000 British and 122,000 Allied troops off the beach at Dunkirk in northern France, even as German and British pilots engaged in a fierce air battle overhead. The Allies had to leave behind 38,000 vehicles, 90,000 rifles, 7,000 tons of ammunition, and 50,000 men, some of whom were summarily shot by German troops.

France Falls

The rescue at Dunkirk saved the Allied army, but it could not save France from occupation and partition. With German forces marching on Paris, mass panic engulfed the city. French leaders and refugees from other places fled; officials at the Foreign Ministry hurriedly tossed documents out the windows and burned them on the lawn below. Cars and wagonloads full of household goods threatened to run down fleeing pedestrians. French government officials decamped to northern Africa, from where, calling themselves "the Free French," they hoped to launch a counterattack. General Charles de Gaulle, who proclaimed himself head of the Free French forces, escaped to Britain. But the situation was hopeless. France surrendered on June 18. More than 1.5 million French soldiers were taken prisoner.

The Germans insisted on ruling northern France directly. Not only was this the more industrialized part of France, but the Germans also wanted to control France's Atlantic and Channel ports, vital for launching an assault on Britain. But Hitler allowed the French a moderate form of self-rule in the south—a government headed by the aged World War I hero Philippe Pétain (1856–1951), headquartered at the spa town of Vichy.

In exchange for collaborating with the Nazis, **Vichy France** was allowed to run its own internal affairs—but its military and diplomatic affairs were controlled by the Nazis, and its economic production was geared to satisfying the needs of the Germans. After war in northern Africa began in earnest, the Nazis increased the pressure on Vichy to do their bidding. By 1943, 40 percent of France's industrial production was dedicated to supplying Germany's needs, especially its need for submarines, planes, and communication cables.

Vichy's government was essentially conservative; Pétain substituted the phrase "work, family, fatherland," for the revolutionary motto "liberty, equality, fraternity," and evidently saw himself as something of an old-fashioned father, one who told his children exactly how to behave. Like the Nazis, he loathed Bolshevism and disliked democracy, but he was not willing to do everything the Germans wanted him to do. He refused to join the battle against Britain and made only perfunctory attempts to shut down Free French operations in northern Africa.

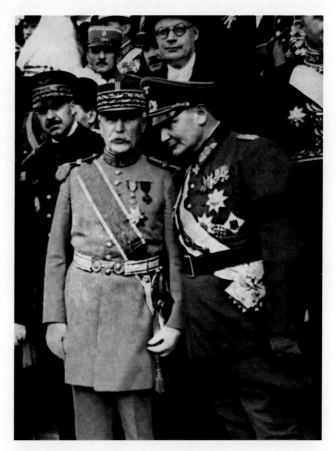

The French Collaborator Philippe Pétain Here Pétain (*center, foreground*), the deeply conservative Great War hero, converses with the Nazi leader Hermann Göring (right) at the funeral of Josef Piłsudski in 1935. After France's defeat in 1940, Pétain would accept the presidency of the collaboratist state of Vichy France.

But he oversaw the adoption of racial policies. The Vichy police helped identify, round up, and deport foreign Jews; some French Jews, too, were sent eastward to concentration camps. Pétain was only one of many collaborators in France, Belgium, and the Netherlands. Like others, he claimed that he had engaged in treachery only in order to save his nation from the terrors of direct German rule.

Britain Alone, Yet Defiant

By mid-summer 1940, the Germans had conquered and occupied Czechoslovakia, Poland, Belgium, the Netherlands, Denmark, Norway, and France. The Russians had defeated Finland and compelled Romania to hand over the province of Bessarabia. In July, the USSR swallowed up its own buffer zone, occupying Latvia, Lithuania, and Estonia. Governments sympathetic to the Nazis were now ruling Spain, Hungary, Romania, Bulgaria, and Italy. Only states on the periphery or ones guarded by high mountains (such as Sweden, Switzerland, and Turkey) were allowed to maintain their neutrality.

The resources at Hitler's command were breathtaking, and it is not surprising that many pragmatic Europeans, as well as those already favorable to fascism, agreed to play a role in Hitler's new order. Only Britain remained in the fight, though it brought with it the considerable wealth, manpower, and resources of its colonies, including India, and the neo-Europes it now called members of the Commonwealth, including Australia and Canada. Britain still possessed the world's most powerful navy, and the friendship of the world's largest and most prosperous economy, the United States. Britain desperately needed these allies, for it now faced threats in the Pacific as well as in Europe. Following the fall of France, the Japanese had seized French Indochina and signed on to the Axis Powers. They were now well placed to menace the British colonies of Burma and Malaya, as well as Britain's jewel in the crown, India. Worst of all, Churchill knew that Britain would be Hitler's next target.

THE BATTLE OF BRITAIN. On his celebratory visit to conquered Paris, Hitler visited Napoleon's tomb, perhaps knowing that he now confronted one of Napoleon's greatest difficulties: how to defeat Great Britain without an amphibious invasion. Hitler, unlike Napoleon, had an air force (the Luftwaffe), which he hoped would establish command of the skies and sow confusion and chaos before he attempted a naval invasion. Beginning in August 1940, Hitler's bombers targeted British military installations, aircraft factories, and port cities. Then he ordered the bombardment of inland cities and monuments, hoping that he could break the British will to resist.

Nearly 400,000 children were sent out of the cities to rural areas in the north to escape the bombardment; the evacuation saved the children's lives, but separated families. Aided by intelligence gained from decoded Enigma messages, British fighter pilots mounted a vigorous de-

fense and then began a counterattack, bombing military targets near Berlin for the first time on August 25 and continuing regularly thereafter. The counterattack led Hitler to focus his bombing on British cities, inflicting devastating damage on civilian lifestyles but taking some of the pressure off military installations. The British also began using radar effectively to locate incoming German aircraft, and British factories began churning out more planes. By October, Hitler quietly aborted his plans for a seaborne invasion, though the Luftwaffe and later V-1 flying bombs and V-2 rockets would torment the British population throughout the remainder of the war.

The nine months of most intense German bombardment of Britain, from August 1940 to May 1941, are known as "the Blitz," and would be Churchill's—and many said afterward, Britain's—finest hour, for both the prime minister and the people held out during a time in which the odds were very much against them. Everyone else was defeated; the United States maintained its neutrality, and the Soviet Union was bound by the Hitler-Stalin pact. For the Britons who experienced it, this hour was surely anything but fine—but their refusal to capitulate saved Europe from having to endure a long, Nazi-imposed, peace.

LIVING THE BLITZ. What was it like, night after night, to have to leave one's bed for a damp and crowded air raid cellar, to be in constant terror of being blown apart or buried in burning rubble, to visit a friend's apartment one day and wake the next morning to find her dead and her home in ruins?[26] To flee a shelter in flames, as did one working-class Londoner, and find that one's mother and eight-year-old daughter had been buried in the wreckage? While Winston Churchill emphasized the courage and defiance of the British, first-hand reports give us a sense of the fear, grief, exhaustion, and in some cases, exhilaration that Londoners experienced during a period in which an estimated 20,000 tons of explosives were dropped on the capital city, killing 15,000 and leaving at least 300,000 people homeless.

Because most of the raids occurred at night, when plane spotting was most difficult for antiaircraft battalions, millions of Britons learned to associate nightfall with danger and with the horrors and discomforts of hiding in basements, underground stations, and public shelters. Many, however, stuck it out at home, sleeping on mattresses in hallways away from windows. Whether they remained in their homes or sought safety in a shelter, people could be buried alive, crushed beneath possessions they thought too valuable to leave. Or they might be saved by freak coincidences, as was the young girl discovered unharmed (but naked) underneath her own bathtub. In the shelters, people gossiped, sang, cried, squashed the ever-present lice, and told stories. The next day, hordes of volunteers roamed the streets to pull people out of the rubble. With the government overwhelmed and unable to care for all the victims, individuals improvised. Firemen did what they could to extinguish fires;

bomb squads defused unexploded devices that had become lodged in back gardens or rooftops, at considerable peril to themselves. The owner of a bombed-out pie shop fashioned a makeshift oven, one good enough to produce 2,700 dinners the next day.

One social worker recalled seeing "Disheveled, half-dressed people wandering between the bombed house and the rest centre, salvaging bits and pieces, or trying to keep in touch with the scattered family. . . . A clergyman appeared and wandered about aimlessly, and someone played the piano." After a nearly eight-hour-long raid, one man recorded the cold, dull calm of early morning. "Through smoke, and a rain of charred paper, the sun was coming up. Pieces of human remains were being picked up and put into bins. Round the corner at the *Cross Keys*, with one wall blown into the bar, they were serving spirits as hard as they could go. . . . Everywhere people walked they crunched over rubble and broken glass. People were coming out of their homes with brooms to sweep it up."[7]

For some, especially adolescents, but also older men like Churchill, there was something exciting about the danger. They remembered the camaraderie in the basements and forgot the terrible smells, the lice, and the endless crying of babies. Some wanted to drink and be merry; others could not shake off their depression. The writer H. G. Wells refused to go to the shelter until he finished his lunch, saying to his hostess, "I'm enjoying a very good lunch. Why should I be disturbed by some wretched little barbarian adolescents in a machine?"[8] But others stampeded for a place in the public shelters. Their experience shows that danger and fear bring out different reactions in individuals, whatever their gender, age, or nationality.

All of the war's combatants could have learned a lesson from living the Blitz: terror bombing did not weaken resistance. In the meantime, Britain's factories began to produce thousands of new planes and munitions. They were aided by supplies sent by the United States. In January 1941, U.S. president Franklin Roosevelt pushed through Congress the **Lend-Lease Agreement** that allowed America to lend Britain vital armaments, with payments deferred until after the war. The Germans did considerable damage to Britain's Royal Air Force, to London, and to many other British cities and towns in 1940–1941. But the months of incessant bombing simply strengthened the British will to oppose German aggression. Hitler never gave up hoping he could destroy Britain from the air, and bombing raids continued throughout the war. By

The Blitz During the terrible nights of German aerial bombardment in 1940–1941, many Londoners sought shelter in underground "tube" stations.

spring 1941, however, that hope was fading, and the worst of the Blitz had passed.

War in the Mediterranean

By this time, Hitler was turning his attention to other matters, most importantly to his long-desired invasion of the Soviet Union. He knew it would be an epic battle and was accordingly readying the largest army in history to win it. Hitler's successes so far filled him with confidence—but they also went to Benito Mussolini's head. Without asking the Germans, in the fall of 1940, Mussolini launched two ill-fated invasions of his own. In September, he sent an army from the Italian colony of Libya into Egypt, hoping to capture the Suez Canal, and in October he landed troops in Italian-occupied Albania, with the intention of conquering Greece. The outraged Greeks formed a guerrilla army almost overnight and beat back the Italian advance, capturing two thousand Italian soldiers. The British response to the assault on Egypt, although delayed by the Battle of Britain, proved equally embarrassing for the Italians. A force of 36,000 British troops drove 75,000 Italians to retreat to Libya. Unwilling to expose Mussolini to ridicule or his southern flank to Allied invasion, in January 1941 Hitler made the decision to dedicate troops and resources to Libya and Albania to prevent double disaster for the Italians.

NORTHERN AFRICA. The man Hitler sent to northern Africa was tank commander Erwin Rommel (1891–1944), a veteran of the First World War and one of the heroes of the campaign in France. Courageous and charismatic, Rommel kept larger British forces at bay and launched counterattacks so impressive, even to his enemies, that he earned the nickname the Desert Fox. By the summer of 1942, Rommel had invaded Egypt and was poised to seize the canal and then to turn north, hoping eventually to link up with German troops sweeping through the Caucasus.

THE BALKANS. Rommel managed to tie up the Allies in northern Africa, long delaying their plans for invading Italy. But northern Africa was not the only Mediterranean theater the Germans, in early 1941, wished to close down. Greek resistance also had to be broken—but to get to Greece, the Germans needed the cooperation of its neighbors. Grudgingly and under pressure, the kings of Bulgaria and Yugoslavia agreed to join the Axis, though the Yugoslavs quickly overthrew their old king and installed seventeen-year-old King Peter on the throne. Peter promptly renounced the Axis alliance. In retribution, German bombers struck Belgrade, killing 17,000 civilians in a single day, Palm Sunday (April 6), 1941. Hungarian and Bulgarian armies were mustered and helped themselves to shares of Greece and Yugoslavia. By April 8, Salonika in northeast Greece was occupied, and in two weeks the Germans had conquered mainland Greece and forced 50,000 Allied soldiers to flee.

German occupiers immediately began stripping Greece, especially its capital city of Athens, of food and supplies that could be used in northern Africa or stockpiled for the invasion of the Soviet Union. Transportation networks were disrupted, and peasants, fearing officials would steal their grain, stopped supplying the cities. By June, workers in Athens were starving—but Hitler's mind was on the invasion of the Soviet Union, and he told the Italians that they would have to feed the Greeks. Mussolini, too, was indifferent to the fate of the Athenians and left approximately 40,000 inhabitants to starve in the fall and winter of 1941–1942. By 1943, some 250,000 Greeks overall had perished. The brutal occupation regimes of the Axis gave birth to mutually hostile communist and nationalist resistance movements, which would battle each other once the war finally ended. Although Greece's fate was unique in many respects, Greece was only one of many smaller nations whose history was forever transformed by having been caught up in this brutal war.[9]

In Yugoslavia, the Second World War had a different, and even more deadly, dynamic. Here, the German invasion ignited an ethnic civil war that would make pacifying the country impossible. King Peter's call to stand against the Nazis rallied many Serbs to the cause—for Peter was a Serb—but Croatian troops balked at joining the defense of a kingdom they believed treated them as second-class citizens. Their absence left gaping holes in the Yugoslav defenses. When the Germans plowed through them, the Serbs blamed the Croatians, and what became a civil war inside the world war began. The Germans happily gave over a part of their territory to the Croatian fascist league, the **Ustasha,** which used its new authority to achieve its own ends, one of which was to implement their plan to solve the Serbian question: a third of the community (two million strong) were to be murdered, a third expelled, and a final third converted to Croatian Catholicism and fascism. During the course of the war, the Ustasha, led by the Axis collaborator Ante Pavelić (1889–1959), killed at least 200,000 Serbs, carving an "S" on the bodies of some victims, who were then dumped into rivers. Others were tortured and murdered in camps such as the infamous Jasenovač (see Map 24.3 on p. 783). With the help of the Wehrmacht, the viciously racist Ustasha also murdered approximately 70,000 Jews and gypsies, leaving few members of those once-vibrant Balkan communities alive.

Opposing the Ustasha was a Serbian nationalist resistance force, which did not hesitate to commit murders and reprisals of its own, and a powerful communist resistance led by the wily half-Slovene, half-Croat Josef Broz, known as Tito (1892–1980). By the time Tito's communists liberated the country from the Germans in 1945, at least 10 percent of Yugoslavia's prewar population was dead, a statistic that puts it second only to Poland in the size of the native population that paid the ultimate price in the war (see Map 24.4, p. 793).

Yugoslavian Atrocities In this 1942 image taken at the notorious Jasenovač prison camp, a member of the Croatian fascist guards (Ustasha) poses with murdered Serbs and Jews. In the course of what became a brutal civil war, Serbian guerrillas committed atrocities as well.

DATE	EVENT
September 1938	Munich Conference
August 1939	Nazi-Soviet Nonaggression Pact
September 1939	Invasion of Poland
June 1940	France falls
June 1941	Operation Barbarossa
February 1943	Nazis defeated at Stalingrad
June 1944	D-Day landing in France
February 1945	Allied bombing of Dresden
May 1945	Nazi Germany defeated

The World at War

In mid-1941, Hitler was master of Europe—but elsewhere other players were altering the global chessboard. Most importantly, Japan was gobbling up territory in the hopes of building its own Asian empire. Concerned about the aggressive expansionism of both of these Axis Powers, in August 1941 Churchill and Roosevelt signed the Atlantic Charter. This document reiterated the Wilsonian "right of all peoples to choose the form of government under which they will live" and declared that changes in borders ought to occur only in accordance with "the freely expressed wishes of the peoples concerned." The rights of all people should be protected, and a "permanent system of general security" should be established to keep the peace. This was, in effect, a "statement of democratic war aims,"[10] and it would lay the foundations not only of the British-American alliance during World War II, but also of what would later be termed the "special relationship" between the two countries.

How was the war in the Pacific different from the war in Europe?

After the Japanese attack on Pearl Harbor, the United States entered the war, sending troops to fight both in the Pacific and in the European theaters. The Japanese also attacked Britain's colonies in Southeast Asia, successfully occupying Malaya and Burma, and threatening India. As the Nazis abandoned the Hitler-Stalin Pact and invaded Russia in July 1941, central and eastern Europe were drawn into what now became a truly global war.

The Other Axis Power: Japan's Triumphs in the Pacific

By the time Hitler had conquered Greece, the Japanese had their own successes to celebrate. Since the mid-1930s, Japan had been ruled by a small militaristic elite that had sworn loyalty to Emperor Hirohito (r. 1926–1989). Japan too had suffered from the Great Depression and was also confronting a population explosion that made its leaders, like Hitler, anxious to obtain living space. Japanese racists proclaimed the superiority of their ancestry over that of the other Asians. As they alone of other Asians had managed to modernize and to beat a great European power (the Russians, in the Russo-Japanese War), they believed they should be the ones to push western colonial powers out of the Pacific and become the region's leading power. Already in 1931, a formidable Japanese army had occupied the northern Chinese province of Manchuria, ignoring the protestations of the League of Nations. In 1937, Japanese troops poured into the Yangtze valley and attacked the capital city of the Chinese Republic, Nanjing. Here, soldiers unleashed ferocious violence, killing several hundred thousand Chinese civilians, in an episode subsequently known as the Rape of Nanjing. The Japanese invasion created an uneasy alliance between the ruling Chinese nationalists and their internal communist opponents, and what would be a long and brutal war between China and Japan commenced.

The Japanese initially intended to strike to the west, hoping to chip away at the Bolshevik empire. After the signing of the Hitler-Stalin Pact and the fall of France, they changed tactics and decided to seek living space and raw materials by seizing the British, French, and Dutch colonies of Southeast Asia instead. To woo the local populations of the region, they denounced the evils of the West and advertised the benefits of a "Great East Asian Co-Prosperity Sphere" in which Asians would together free themselves from western colonialism and seek prosperity for all. In fact, what the Japanese had in mind was an empire, in which the other, racially inferior Asians did as they were told, for the benefit of Japan. In summer 1940, Japan seized French Indochina (Vietnam and Cambodia) and then moved on to attack Indonesia, Thailand, Burma, Malaya, and the Philippines.

On December 7, 1941, the Japanese made what they hoped would be a decisive assault on the U.S. naval base at Pearl Harbor, Hawaii. That day would "live in infamy," President Franklin D. Roosevelt prophesied in his address to Congress and, via radio, to the nation—and indeed the unprovoked attack generated a groundswell of support for the president's decision to ask Congress for a declaration of war against Japan. The Lend-Lease Agreement, which provided Britain military supplies, had already propelled the ramping up of military production in the United States, but the build-up now began in earnest.

Despite Japan's small size, it had a modern military and a large empire from which to draw resources, and defeating this authoritarian state would take nearly four years of bruising naval and land warfare. The initial turning point came when, in an epic naval confrontation, the Americans stopped Japan's advance at the Battle of Midway in June 1942. But winning the war required reconquering the Pacific, island by island. American troops bore the brunt of defeating the Japanese at sea, but for the Europeans, too, the Pacific War had crucial long-term consequences.

War in the Colonies

The Pacific War differed from the European conflict in being, for the Americans, a heavily naval war. For the European powers, however, the uniqueness of the Pacific theater was that the war involved so many colonial subjects, both as combatants and as civilian victims. Elsewhere, Churchill was reluctant to arm black Africans—though not to force them to work in munitions factories or produce supplies for ships rounding the Cape. Many Africans did fight in the Free French armies, and the Belgian Congo was made to offer up copper, rubber, and soldiers, as well as uranium for atomic experiments. But in the Pacific, there were few Europeans, and, in addition to crucial assistance given by Australians and New Zealanders, the Allies were heavily dependent on the colonized populations to fill their armies and provide the resources needed to wage war. The Allies also looked for help from the Chinese, who were fighting their own war of liberation from Japanese domination. Though the Chinese did assist the Allies' cause, their efforts were hampered by terrible shortages of food and other supplies, and by division within the ranks between nationalist and communist factions.

In the Pacific, the Allies' determination to win "Europe first" meant that Southeast Asia was left largely on its own for several years, even as the Japanese moved from victory to victory. Their successes, and their anti-imperialist rhetoric, persuaded some local nationalists like Subhas Chandra Bose to back their cause. Churchill expected unquestioning loyalty from Britain's colonial subjects and also expected them to place all their resources at his disposal. He was infuriated by those who considered collaborating with Japan and by those who continued to press for rights and independence during the war. In India, he sanctioned the jailing of tens of thousands of supporters of Indian independence, including the pacifist leader Mohandas Gandhi. Gandhi, he wrote, "ought to be lain bound hand and foot at the gates of Delhi and then trampled on by an enormous elephant with the new Viceroy seated on his back."[11] In spite of Churchill's callousness, large numbers of Indians fought for Britain, and at least 36,000 died doing so. Incidents like the fall of Rangoon, Burma, in February 1942, however, illustrate the special kinds of suffering experienced by colonized peoples, many of whom were bitterly disillusioned by the actions of their supposedly more civilized masters.

In the Pacific, racial hatred contributed to the vehemence with which both sides sought to destroy enemies they considered subhuman. Thousands of Chinese, British, Australian, and American prisoners of war (POWs) suffered torture and death at the hands of their Japanese captors. Many civilian deaths were the unintended consequences of actions in the Pacific. The Allied effort to build the Burma Road, a zigzagging miracle of engineering that carried desperately needed supplies from India into China, succeeded at the cost of thousands of lives of local Chinese and Burmese forced laborers (Map 24.2). An estimated three million inhabitants of Bengal died in the famine of 1943–1944, which was caused in part by the cutting off of rice supplies from Burma and the requisitioning of grain for Britain's armies. There was famine in China, too, and conditions in the Chinese nationalist army were so horrific that the Chinese communists gained many new supporters simply by promising a full stomach and a clean bed of straw.

As was the case in Greece, those who experienced the torments of occupation did not forget them; they long remembered who had collaborated and profited from the war and who had resisted. Not only in China, but in many other places, these memories cast a rosy glow on regional communist parties, which seemed to offer an antidote to both fascism and European colonialism. In the Pacific, too, this merciless war transformed states, economies, and individuals, and its echoes resound even today.

Operation Barbarossa

Japan's war in the Pacific was one of unprecedented brutality, but its racial violence was exceeded by Hitler's war on the eastern front. On June 22, 1941, just one day after the 129th anniversary of Napoleon's invasion of Russia, Hitler launched Operation Barbarossa, named after the crusader king Frederick Barbarossa. Hoping to escape Napoleon's fate, Hitler had organized the largest military action in history: some 3.2 million soldiers swarmed across the border along a line that stretched nearly six hundred miles. The air assault was equally gigantic: on the first day alone, the Soviets lost 1,811 planes, and the Luftwaffe only 35. And behind the Wehrmacht were SS troops, eager to cleanse Germany's newly annexed **Lebensraum** ("living space") of Jews, Bolsheviks, and all others who exhibited resistance of any sort.

CHRONOLOGY	The War beyond Hitler
DATE	**EVENT**
October 1935	Mussolini invades Ethiopia
July 1937–August 1945	Japan at war in Asia
November 1939–March 1940	Russo-Finnish Winter War
October 1940	Mussolini invades Greece
October 1941–April 1945	Yugoslavia Partisan War
December 7, 1941	Japanese attack Pearl Harbor
Spring 1943–Fall 1944	Famine in Bengal
August 1945	Atomic bombs dropped on Japan

The Fall of Rangoon

Like the Nazis, the Japanese were very bad at cultivating and keeping their friends. They did find collaborators in Southeast Asia. In Burma, many local inhabitants craved independence and looked upon the Japanese as potential liberators. The territory had been conquered piecemeal by the British, beginning in 1824. Winston Churchill's father Randolph had instigated the war that completed conquest of the colony in 1886, but resistance to British rule had never been fully wiped out. Regard for the British would fall even lower when in December 1941 Japanese bombs began to fall on densely populated Rangoon.

As in Warsaw and Paris, aerial bombardment and the threat of invasion provoked panic in Rangoon. Common laborers, like the lower-caste Indian street cleaners, fled on foot, while the middle and upper classes thronged the ports, roads, and landing strips, desperately seeking to get their families and their property to the safest nearby country, in this case, India. The British colonial authorities gave priority to white Europeans, all too many of whom displayed a callous "save yourself" mentality in the face of the suffering of the hundreds of thousands of colonial sub-jects who had toiled for them for so long. After Rangoon fell on March 7, British troops withdrew swiftly over the mountain passes into northeastern India, ahead of a tidal wave of 600,000 civilians, many of whom sought to escape by the same route.

By the time these civilians reached the road, the monsoon rains had begun, and food and medical supplies were almost impossible to obtain. People could travel only a few miles a day, at most, through a seemingly endless sea of mud. Starving, some stripped poisonous fruit from roadside trees or fought over scraps of rotten food. Those too weak to complete the trek were trampled and left to drown in the mud. The Japanese continued their pursuit and were prevented from advancing into India only by the combined efforts of Burmese hill people, the Anglo-Indian Army, and monsoons, which made the roads just as impassable for them as they had been for the Burmese refugees.

As occupiers in Burma, the Japanese found willing collaborators among those who despised the British. They might have made more friends had they not refused to discuss postwar independence for the country and made it clear that Burma and the Burmese were now theirs to plunder and exploit. By the war's end, the Burmese were eager to throw out the Japanese, but they had not forgotten that their sufferings had been treated as a sideshow while the British battled Hitler in Europe and that so many of the colonizers had saved themselves while leaving their non-white servants, nursemaids, and friends behind to suffer. Though Churchill declared that he had not fought the war to lose the empire, his successors would have no choice. In 1948, Burma won its independence, and Rangoon rejoiced.[12]

QUESTION | *What did Churchill's war effort look like to the Burmese?*

The Japanese Enter Rangoon Local refugees make way for Japanese troops on their way to Burma in June 1942. The Japanese proved to be brutal occupiers.

Stalin had not expected Hitler to invade—or at least to invade so soon—and it took the Soviet leader days to absorb the news. In the meantime, German troops raced across Soviet Poland, western Russia, and the Baltic states, seemingly justifying Hitler's prediction that "We have only to kick in the door and the whole rotten structure will come crashing down." But already on June 23, quick-thinking Soviet officials began organizing the wholesale removal of more than 1,500 of western Russia's munitions and industrial factories, together with hundreds of thousands of workers, to locations beyond the Ural Mountains. Relocation on this scale was made possible by the dictatorship's complete ownership of the means of production and its ability to compel workers to do its bidding. By early 1942, these factories were beginning to turn out the colossal number of tanks, planes, and shells

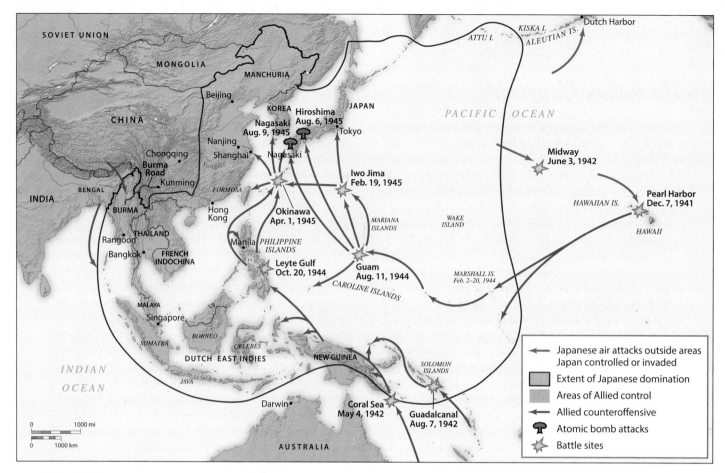

MAP 24.2 | World War II in the Pacific

By 1942, Japan had built a large empire by seizing land from the Chinese and from western colonizers in Southeast Asia. Many of its possessions were islands, which had to be defended by the Japanese navy. *In what ways did the Japanese Empire differ from Hitler's Empire? Follow the lines and dates of Allied attack. What does the slow progress toward Japan itself tell you about the difficulty of this "island-hopping" war?*

that the Red Army needed to retake its territory and to push on to Berlin in 1945.

Leningrad, like London, evacuated its children, but was quickly surrounded; refusing to surrender, Peter the Great's city was besieged for a staggering 872 days. In his first radio broadcast after the invasion, Stalin called on soldiers and civilians to wage a merciless guerrilla war against the German fascists or risk returning to czardom and slavery (see Back to the Source at the end of the chapter). In fact, the huge size of the Soviet state and the lightning pace of German conquest favored guerrilla warfare. Numerous partisan groups and some Jewish refugees were able to steal away into the forests and swamps of western Russia, where they cut telegraph wires or blew up railroad tracks. Yet these efforts were not enough to stop the German advance. In six months' time, German armies had conquered nearly a million square miles of Soviet territory and taken more than three million prisoners.

In Hitler's view, the USSR was populated almost exclusively by subhumans: communists, Slavs, Gypsies, and worst of all, millions of Jews—the lowest of the low. Thus, no mercy was to be shown to Russian soldiers or to Soviet

civilians. A handful of those considered "Aryan material" were exempted, and thousands of "racially valuable" women were sent back to the Reich to breed with noble Germans. Others were murdered on the spot or, like the Poles, turned into slave laborers. By August 1941, special commandos attached to the Wehrmacht known as **Einsatzgruppen** were killing people who were clearly not soldiers—including Jewish women and children.

Life and Death in War-Torn Europe

Why did this war generate so much violence against civilians, and drive so many ordinary citizens to act outside conventional moral boundaries?

Throughout this book, we have highlighted the choices that leaders, intellectuals, and individuals make as central to how European history unfolded. Perhaps in wartime those choices, like Stalin's decision to ally with Hitler in August 1939, or Roosevelt's decision to push for the Lend-Lease

The War in the East, June 1941–August 1942

The war in Poland; the aerial bombardments of London, Belgrade, and the Netherlands; and the brutal occupation policies implemented in France and Greece told the Allies a good deal about what sort of enemy they were fighting. Hitler, clearly, was determined to make the Germans the overlords and everyone else his slaves. It was also clear that Jews, who were being ever more concentrated, stripped of their belongings, and subjected to torture and hardship, were the regime's primary victims. But in the year that followed the invasion of the Soviet Union in June 1941, what had seemed a war of swift and brutal conquest revealed itself to be a war of genocidal butchery, which could be won only by sacrificing to it quantities of blood and iron unimaginable to the generation of Bismarck, Lincoln, and Cavour.

What changed the nature of the war was first of all the implementation of the "final solution," which had already been set in motion by the invasion of Poland and the forcing of millions of Jews into ghettoes. The second factor was the invasion of the Soviet Union, a massive campaign that required colossal increases in the supply of food and armaments. The planning for these grand-scale operations involved chilling calculations. It is telling, for example, that already in early 1941, German bureaucrats had crafted a Hunger Plan, according to which 30 million Soviets would have to starve, so that German troops and vital laborers could be fed. According to the Nazis' eugenic and apocalyptic logic, this sort of Malthusian plan had to be imposed on the peoples (and not just the armies) of eastern Europe—or the Jews and the Slavs would wipe out German civilization and forever contaminate the Germanic gene pool.

Thus, the war in the east would be different than the war in the west. Hitler publicly proclaimed that the Geneva Conventions, the series of agreements on humane treatment of POWs made in the nineteenth century, did not apply to Russia, and his administration urged the army in the east to live off the land. These were open invitations for more brutality against civilians and Soviet POWs. Of the 3.3 million prisoners captured before December 1941, 600,000 were labeled Bolshevik agitators and shot; the rest were allowed to starve, freeze to death, or collapse during

The Turning of the Tide at Stalingrad Surrounded at Stalingrad in February 1943, some 100,000 hungry and frostbitten soldiers of the German 6th Army were marched away from the battlefield and made Soviet prisoners of war. Only about 6,000 of these men survived to return home after the war's end.

endless forced marches. By January 1942, 2.25 million had died.

In response to these horrific losses, the Soviets massed battalion after battalion to throw into the fight; concentration camp inmates were made to fight, and blocking divisions formed of ardent communists were positioned just behind the front lines to shoot any of their own men who tried to flee the fighting. As the Germans advanced on Moscow, civilians were compelled to work nonstop to dig protective trenches and to man antiaircraft artillery.

In winter 1941, the weather and short supplies caused the Germans to halt before Moscow and to turn south, where Hitler hoped to seize Stalingrad, Stalin's namesake city, on the Volga River as well as the Soviet oilfields of the Caucasus. By August 1942, when German troops began their assault on Stalingrad, both dictators believed this would be the decisive battle in the east, and both threw everything they had into what would be an epic five-month battle, which the Soviets finally won, encircling the entire German 6th Army. No longer was this Blitzkrieg—now it was a war of survival, in which vast armies butchered one another and anyone who got in their way, along a front that ran from the Baltic Sea to the Caucasus.

If this was the year in which the Nazi-Soviet war of extermination commenced, it was also the year in which Hitler's hatred of the Jews became a full-fledged attempted genocide. The decision to kill Europe's Jews deliberately, rather than to force them to emigrate or to work or starve them to death, was made in the wake of the invasion of the Soviet Union, probably in August or September 1941, and confirmed at the Wannsee Conference in January 1942. By spring 1942, the extermination camps, including the most notorious at Auschwitz-Birkenau, were receiving Jews deported from the ghettoes of Warsaw, Lodz, and Lublin. By summer 1942, more than two million Jews were already dead, and millions more scheduled for destruction. An already brutal war had become a genocidal one—and there remained nearly three more horrific years still to fight before its end.

QUESTION | *How did the nature of the Second World War change after June 1941?*

Agreement in early 1941, seem even more critical to the course of events. But wars, especially wars in which great swathes of foreign territory are occupied by armies pursuing racial warfare, narrow people's choices greatly, and many people make moral choices they would not make in peacetime. Of course, the most consequential decision-maker in shaping the nature of this war was Adolf Hitler himself, for whom the world was made up of people who *had* to live and people who, therefore, *had* to die. But many others—and not just Germans—would decide to help Hitler carry out his racist and murderous crusade, while others would risk their lives to oppose his plans, or simply seek to survive in order to testify, afterward, to the crimes against humanity that he and his collaborators committed.

The "Final Solution to the Jewish Question"

Hitler had long wanted to make the Jews disappear from his Aryan Empire—and his henchmen worked diligently to drive them out of Germany and Austria, to take away their rights and property, to concentrate them and if possible starve them to death in Poland, and to isolate them from the non-Jewish population. By late 1939, many had already died, including at least seven thousand murdered by the SS in Poland. Many more succumbed to malnourishment and mistreatment in concentration camps. But in the wake of Operation Barbarossa—which made Hitler the overlord for millions more Russian, Polish, and Lithuanian Jews—attempts to exterminate the Jews as a race (later termed the **Holocaust**) began.

The Einsatzgruppen, operating just behind the front, typically forced their victims to dig their own trench graves, to sort their belongings for easier Nazi exploitation, and to remove their clothes before lining up on the edge of the trenches. SS-directed commandos then fired on them from point-blank range. The dead and dying fell backward into their mass graves, sparing the murderers from having to bury them. The work was thought so likely to traumatize German soldiers that whenever possible the Nazis delegated the murders to their eastern European collaborators or local policemen, many of whom had to stun themselves with alcohol to endure the screams, the pleading, and the splattering of blood, brains, and body parts. This was the pattern followed in the execution of nearly 34,000 Jews at Babi Yar, near Kiev, for example, in the fall of 1941.

German occupiers and their collaborators also punished partisan activities through reprisals against whole villages. This too entailed the shooting, bayoneting, lynching, or burning of men, women, and children by individual soldiers, SS men, or local police. Some two million Jews were killed in this way, in direct, face-to-face massacres.

But these face-to-face methods were not killing Jews fast enough for the Nazis' satisfaction, and they sometimes caused the perpetrators psychological distress. The T-4 program demonstrated another option, and as it happened, just as Operation Barbarossa began, the T-4

The Final Solution, Face to Face In this famous image, a member of the German Special Forces (Einsatzgruppen) takes aim at a Jewish woman, who tried to shield her child. Much of the violence of the Holocaust was of this type: individual perpetrators murdering individual victims at close range.

program in Germany was being officially dismantled (although, unofficially, murders continued), and men with experience in gassing the mentally handicapped were available for redeployment. They would help design the new camps, built specifically for extermination, on which began construction in October 1941. Most of the camps were located not in the old Reich, but in Poland, closer to the ghettoes and far away from prying eyes. One section of the huge labor camp at Auschwitz in southwestern Poland was converted to become the most notorious and deadly of the extermination camps.

Still, orders and the chain of command for solving the Jewish question had to be clarified. Thus, in January 1942, top Nazi officials met at a villa in the suburb of Wannsee near Berlin to lay explicit plans for what they called "the final solution to the Jewish question." As documents of the proceedings show, delegates at the Wannsee Conference were terrifyingly eager to get this job done efficiently and with as little expense and psychological harm to the German perpetrators as possible. Not least among the sinister individuals at Wannsee was Adolf Eichmann, a bureaucrat in Himmler's Resettlement Office whose job was to ensure that the trains taking the Jews to their deaths ran on time.

Eichmann was both a vehement anti-Semite and a terrifyingly efficient bureaucrat. His methods made possible the clearing of the ghettoes and concentration camps, which by 1942 stretched across the Nazi empire (Map 24.3). The process began with the selection of individuals—especially

MAP 24.3 | Major Ghettoes and Concentration Camps, c. 1942

This map shows the locations of the major ghettoes and the extermination camps in Poland and major mass murder sites in the Soviet Union. Note that one concentration camp in Yugoslavia is also indicated: Jasenovać, where Croatian fascists murdered at least 300,000 Serbs and Jews. *Why were so many of the major extermination camps located in the area the Nazis called the General Government?*

those not fit for hard labor—from ghettoes, camps, and occupied towns. Deportees were told to gather their most precious belongings and to report to officials. They were not told where they were going or what would happen to them once they reached their destinations. Selected men, women, and children were packed into boxcars for transport to the execution camps in the east. Although the trips might be as long as four days, the Nazis saw no reason to provision the trains with food, water, or restrooms. There were no windows and no rest stops—not even to unload and bury those who died during the journey.

When the trains reached the camps, SS officials and their henchmen seized anything the deportees had carried with them. Gold, foreign currency, and jewelry were sent to the state bank, to be used to purchase supplies to continue Germany's war. Other items, such as watches, wallets, shoes, and furs, were given to the SS or frontline troops as rewards for service or were sold at a discount to ethnic Germans. German dentists used gold teeth extracted from Jewish mouths to fill cavities in Aryan jaws. After the valuables were confiscated, SS men performed another selection, separating those who had special skills

or seemed young and strong from the rest, who were marked for immediate death. Divided by gender, these terrified and exhausted victims were told to hand over their suitcases and then to strip and allow their heads to be shaved. To the last, the camp guards kept up the deception that this sanitation process was simply the prelude to the victims' assignment to various kinds of labor, through which, it was implied, they would eventually earn some sort of freedom.

Naked and shivering, Jewish victims of all ages, class backgrounds, and nationalities were then herded into the showers. The doors to the shower rooms were locked, and from the shower heads insecticidal gas—Zyklon B—was piped in. Within minutes, the Nazis' enemies were suffocated; teams of selected Jews and other prisoners then carried out the bodies and hosed out the shower rooms for the next round of murders. Corpses were destroyed in incinerators which, at the peak of genocidal frenzy in 1942–1943, burned thousands a day but could not keep up with the pace of the executions. In his memoir, Primo Levi, an Italian Jew who survived the camps because of his training as a chemist, described the horrific smell of the flesh-burning incinerators at Auschwitz, which also spewed ash—and fragments of human bones—across the landscape.

Living and Dying in Auschwitz

The vast scale of the Nazi genocide boggles the mind, for Hitler hoped to exterminate *all* of Europe's 10 million Jews and then to kill or enslave the other "sub-humans" and "degenerates" in his domain. He succeeded in murdering some six million Jews. But the numbers do not tell us much about what it was like to be one of Hitler's victims. Most of those stories will never be told, as the victims died without being able to record their sufferings, but we do have some first-hand accounts, written by survivors. One of the most powerful is Primo Levi's memoir, originally titled *If This Be a Man* but now usually known by the title *Survival in Auschwitz.*

Survival in Auschwitz is a poignant and painful account of Levi's experiences. It exposes the Nazi presumption that their victims were *not* humans like themselves as a disastrous lie, one that allowed camp officials to treat inmates as something less than animals. In Levi's book, the prisoners display again and again their humanity and their individuality—though this does not mean that all are kind or sympathetic figures. Rather, the prisoners, for the most part, were driven by the will to survive, by the need for food, shelter, sleep, sex, or power over others. Even though they were reduced to near skeletons and dressed in rags, prisoners defined themselves by their skills, such as mending shoes, or by the generosity—or ferocity—they displayed toward other prisoners. These people were not saints, but they were *people,* and Levi offers a powerful condemnation of a regime that sought to deny and destroy their essential humanity.

Survival in Auschwitz describes the process of mechanized death at Auschwitz, but perhaps even more moving is Levi's account of how the selected few lived. Every moment was spent under the eyes of more or less sadistic guards, who beat and tortured their charges. Even during the harsh winter months, prisoners were made to stand for hours awaiting roll calls or more selections; inadequate rations of stale bread and soups made from thistles and rotten potatoes caused prisoners to fight, scheme, and dream about little other than having a full stomach. A complicated black market among the prisoners mediated the exchange of sex, skills, or cigarettes for the universal currency: bread. Those who befriended the guards or those who volunteered to perform the worst jobs, such as carrying bodies out of the gas chambers, survived more comfortably, doing so, however, by making moral compromises. Levi was lucky; he refused to compromise himself and lived to be liberated by the Russians in January 1945. But he could never shake the guilt for having survived Auschwitz, and although he pursued a successful career as a writer after the war, he had forever been robbed of his happiness. He died in 1987 in a fall from a third-story apartment that many people believe was suicide.

The Selected This haunting photo memorializes the faces of a group of Russian women and children who have been selected for death after getting off the train at Auschwitz.

The Auschwitz production line killed 1.1 million people in the course of just over three years of operations; another 2 million died in other execution camps, including Sobibor, Treblinka, and Chelmno. This mechanized form of murder was perhaps the most shocking—and the most unique—sort of violence perpetrated by the Nazis, and because it involved so many aspects of industrial civilization, it has become the most notorious of the evils of the Nazi regime. But the actual killing of real people was often far messier and less civilized. At least half of Hitler's victims died from starvation, disease, or exhaustion, or at the hands of executioners who shot at them from point-blank range or beat them to death with clubs. In some cases, the SS were helped by local people, eager to please their German overlords, to avenge themselves on neighbors they envied, or to abscond with Jewish property. The war and the final solution were German inventions, but they were carried out all over Europe with the assistance of many other Europeans.

Collaboration

To understand collaboration with the Axis Powers during World War II, we must remember that by 1939 or 1941, many people and many states had already gravitated toward authoritarianism. Some had experienced the horrors of Soviet rule; in the colonized world, many looked upon the French, British, or Dutch as their main oppressors. The speedy fall of the French Third Republic seemed to prove that democracy on the European continent was dead. In this world, many people found collaboration with German, Japanese, or Italian fascism an attractive option, especially when the Axis side was winning.

In Germany itself, Hitler ensured continued backing from his population by confiscating Jewish property and pillaging occupied nations. Convinced of the right-wing myth that the home front as well as the Jews had stabbed the army in the back at the end of the Great War, he was determined that during the war German civilians should not suffer hardships that would undermine their confidence in the regime. Thus, he allowed German soldiers on all fronts to confiscate or buy up at rock-bottom prices foodstuffs and luxury items and to ship them home, free of charge. Historian Götz Aly has shown that, by plundering racial enemies and occupied countries, the Nazis financed perhaps as much as two-thirds of their war effort and, at the same time, kept German families from suffering hardships until the last months of the war.[13] By making civilians co-beneficiaries of their criminal and genocidal regime, the Nazis effectively bought the silence and the complicity of the vast majority of German civilians.

Beyond Germany, collaborators came in many different shapes and sizes. Some, like Ante Pavelić in Croatia, volunteered to fight with the Nazis, sharing their vehement anti-Bolshevism and anti-Semitism. Others served as informers who told the police where resisters or Jews were hiding. Still others were suppliers who provided the war machine with its needs, often at a profit to themselves. Some people simply continued to do their jobs—whether as steel workers, rye farmers, or atomic physicists—and thereby contributed, to a greater or a lesser degree, to the Third Reich's vitality. The occupation regimes set up by the Germans in the Netherlands, Belgium, Greece, and Ukraine, and the puppet regimes in Croatia and Slovakia and other places needed local collaborators to make trains run on time and to feed and pacify the population. To a greater or lesser degree, the Nazis found they could depend on locals to do their bidding. Often higher-ranking individuals in the military or business world agreed to put aside their principles and then found themselves drawn ever deeper into a series of other moral and legal compromises. Collaborators followed many paths, some of which ended in the perpetrating of war crimes on behalf of regimes that were perfectly capable of sacrificing their friends when necessary. Others switched sides again when Axis fortunes waned.

Most famous among the collaborators was the Norwegian Vidkun Quisling, an anti-communist, anti-Semite who happily did his best to help the Nazis set up a puppet state in Norway. *Quisling* has become a byword for the weak-willed collaborator, of whom there were many—another example is Mohammed Amin al-Husseini (c. 1895–1974), the grand mufti (or protector of Muslim holy places) of Jerusalem, who wanted Hitler's help in destroying the Zionist movement and creating an Arab state in Palestine. But the more painful stories come from eastern Europe, where many collaborators saw the Germans as potential liberators. After all, many Ukrainians and Lithuanians, to mention only two nationality groups, had suffered terribly under Stalin's dictatorship. Many Hungarians and Bulgarians shared with their Nazi neighbors a great bitterness about the post-1918 peace treaties and preferred the Nazis in any event to the Soviets. The fall of France left Romania without western defenders. Fearful of being partitioned by the Russians, Romania too joined the Axis. These eastern European states were rewarded for allying with Hitler with territorial annexations and punished for their Axis alliances by the Soviets after the war's end.

Goebbels once described German policy with respect to occupied territories as "gingerbread and whippings." But it became quickly apparent that there were more of the latter than the former, especially in the east. Rather like the Napoleonic occupation regimes, but with far more brutality, German officials were unwilling to allow locals to develop their own forms of fascist rule and sought to exploit and extract each nation's natural resources and labor force for Germany's benefit alone. Quisling in Norway was only one of many local collaborators the Nazis pushed out in favor of installing German officials. In the Baltic, Poland, and eastern Europe, their cruelty and ruthlessness even outstripped that of Stalin, which is saying a great deal. In this way, the Nazis deprived themselves of support that might have turned the tide.

Nation by nation, collaborators differed in the degree to which they were willing and able to carry out the Nazis' final solution. Some of the most eager collaborators resided in Soviet-occupied territories such as Lithuania, Ukraine, and Belorussia, where already brutalized locals blamed Jews for their sufferings. In general, local police and militiamen were much more willing to deport Jewish refugees from other nations than local Jews. Some leaders, such as Horthy in Hungary, King Boris in Bulgaria, and even Mussolini, resisted turning over their Jews. Even Hitler's Slovakia puppet Josef Tiso stopped deportations in the summer of 1942. But Hitler overrode these decisions and put pressure on these regimes to deliver up their Jewish citizens. Even as the eastern front collapsed, he demanded that Slovakian and Hungarian Jews be eliminated. In this he succeeded, and in the last year of the war, some 500,000 Hungarian and 70,000 Slovakian Jews were sent to the camps. The Romanians did not allow the Germans to deport their Jews, but staged terrible pogroms themselves and sent their Jews to Romanian-run camps where hundreds of thousands died. Hitler's allies, the Italians, by contrast, in general protected their small community of assimilated Jews.

Resistance

If there were many opportunities and inducements for collaboration with Nazism, Italian fascism, or with the other regimes that supported the Axis Powers, there were also many forms of resistance mounted against them. It took great bravery—and sometimes great recklessness—to join the active resistance when the occupiers controlled virtually all the weapons, food, means of transport, newspapers, and radio stations, and exhibited daily their utter contempt for ordinary laws and human rights.

From 1933 forward, the Nazis had enemies within Germany itself and especially among those exiled from Germany—including communists, pacifists, liberals, aristocratic conservatives, and religious groups. Some brave individuals made it their duty to tell the truth about the evils of the regime. In 1942, Munich University students Hans and Sophie Scholl, informed by their friends' reports of atrocities on the eastern front, distributed leaflets

The White Rose This is one of the few images of the teenage resistance heroes who called themselves the White Rose. From the left, those pictured here are Hans Scholl, his sister Sophie Scholl, and their friend Christoph Probst. All three were guillotined by the Nazis in February 1943.

written by fellow members of the White Rose resistance group. The leaflets denounced Germans for their apathy, which enabled the fascist "brown horde" to commit crimes "unworthy of the human race." The Scholl siblings were arrested on February 18, 1943, found guilty of treason on February 22, and guillotined the same day. By this time, a few high-ranking members of the army and diplomatic corps, including Colonel Hennig von Treschow and Lieutenant Colonel Claus Schenk von Stauffenberg, were plotting to kill Hitler, but even their best attempt, known as Operation Valkyrie, narrowly failed in July 1944. Distantly implicated, Erwin Rommel was allowed to commit suicide. The other conspirators were hanged with piano wire.

As the Scholls knew all too well, resistance within Germany was weak, disorganized, and made little impact. The French resistance pulled off some daring operations, such as blowing up rail lines, but never attracted more than 5 percent of the adult population. The rugged terrain of Greece and Yugoslavia allowed large guerrilla movements to flourish in these lands, but the movements were bitterly divided among themselves. In the Soviet Union, German armies moved so rapidly across extensive territories that large pockets were left without effective supervision. Here renegade Red Army units, Jewish guerrillas, and Soviet resistance fighters on the run did their best to survive by hiding in forests. In Poland, the underground Home Army pulled off numerous daring operations. Jews in the Warsaw ghetto and in several concentration camps staged armed resistance, and forced laborers in many places slowed down production lines when possible. We will never know how many people performed quieter forms of resistance, such as hiding Jews or feeding underground fighters. But we do know that many put themselves in peril and sometimes suffered terrible consequences for minor acts of kindness. To give just one example, in 1942, a Christian Pole who had thrown a bag of bread over the walls of the Warsaw ghetto to ease the sufferings of the Jews was summarily shot by a Nazi guard.

Slave Laborers

One of the less appreciated aspects of Hitler's new order was its heavy dependence on slave and forced labor drawn from occupied nations. The scope of Hitler's forced labor pool was vast; by 1944, some 7.9 million laborers, representing all of Europe's nationality groups, were working in German territory. The use of these workers allowed the Germans to keep many middle-class women at home—though increasing numbers did join the workforce—and their near-starvation wages kept food prices down for Hitler's folk. This was again part of Hitler's strategy to keep the home front content while supplying the army with all it needed to win the war.

Laborers lived in camps, where they were subjected to starvation and whippings. If some had volunteered for service in order to eke out a living, none could have imagined how hard they would have to work and how terrible the conditions of that work would be. They were employed as munitions workers and coal miners, as boot makers and as doctors to other slave laborers. Their productivity often suffered as a result of their weakness from malnutrition or their beatings from guards. Many tried to escape, but even those who succeeded had difficulty surviving. In 1943, in an attempt to increase production and decrease "useless mouths," Nazi officials introduced "performance feeding," according to which only those who increased their quotas received adequate rations. Those who failed to make their quota lost their right to eat, often rendering them too weak to satisfy their masters. The death rate in the work camps was horrific, but the Nazis could not afford to kill too many of these laborers, for the war effort depended on them, especially in the final years of the conflict. In the winter of 1944–1945, when the Soviets overran labor camps in the east, German soldiers drove workers back to Germany on foot. During these death marches, thousands more died.

In the Pacific theater, the Japanese also employed vast numbers of slave laborers. Chinese and Korean civilians, in particular, were made to serve their Japanese masters. Among the Allies, Stalin used forced and slave labor; his gulags long predated the Nazi regime and would not be closed in 1945. The Soviets also seized laborers from territory occupied by their armies, including Poles, Latvians, Romanians, and Czechs, and put them to work in armaments factories. The western Allies depended on home-grown labor, whose wages were adequate but kept low, and on colonial laborers, who were paid far less, but not imprisoned or tortured. When the war ended, many of these workers were stranded far from home, in some cases homes that had been wiped off the map. Many never returned.

Women and the War

Many accounts of World War II mention women only in passing and only as victims of the Blitz or the final solution. Women certainly made up a huge share of the victims of the war, a much larger percentage than in the First World War, in which women suffered primarily from indirect causes, such as malnutrition, disease, and overwork. World War II brought violent death to the home front, and women were among the victims of the bombings, deportations, and reprisal killings. They were also subjected to sexual exploitation and violence. In all theaters and even in the concentration and forced labor camps, women were bribed or compelled to serve as prostitutes, for among the ruthless men who ran the war, it was widely agreed that men's morale depended on having sex on a regular basis.

But women in World War II were participants as well as victims. Women served in the front lines of the Red Army. An estimated 800,000 or more female volunteers served in army or partisan units and were especially important in air defense forces (Figure 24.1). Hundreds of thousands worked as laundresses, nurses, drivers, and doctors. Although the fascists tried to keep women at home, in practice, on both sides, women worked as switchboard operators, secretaries, translators, and photographers. Others insisted on being placed in more "masculine" jobs, such as repairing planes, welding, or driving trucks. Many urban women, especially teenage girls, were sent to rural areas to help bring in the all-important harvests. Some of these women shocked their relatives, who were still unused to seeing women wearing pants, and on the whole, European society continued to think of these forms of female labor as exceptional. Women continued to be paid far less than their male counterparts for equal work, even when they were their families' sole breadwinners.

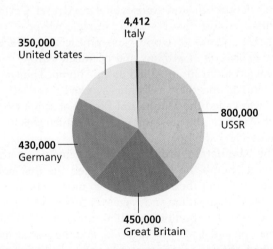

FIGURE 24.1 | Women's Mobilization in World War II
This pie chart shows the numbers of women mobilized for uniformed military service from select countries during the Second World War. Only the Soviet Union employed a significant number of women in active combat roles.

Source: Information synthesized by Jason M. Wolfe from the following sources: Joshua Goldstein, *War and Gender: How Gender Shapes the War System and Vice Versa* (Cambridge: Cambridge University Press, 2001); Campbell D'Ann, "Women in Combat: The World War II Experience in the United States, Great Britain, Germany, and the Soviet Union," *The Journal of Military History* 57 (April 1993): 301–323; and Maria Fraddosio, "The Fallen Hero: The Myth of Mussolini and Fascist Women in the Italian Social Republic," *Journal of Contemporary History* 31 (January 1996): 99–124.

Some women committed acts of terrible violence during the war. Perhaps 10 percent of the concentration camp guards were women, and women made up a larger percentage of the staff at the Ravensbrück camp near Berlin, which was designated especially for female laborers. Many female guards were trained at Ravensbrück and transferred to duty elsewhere. Like their male counterparts, female guards whipped inmates, selected people for extermination, and worked and starved prisoners to death. There were many other women living in and around the camps, working as sorters of goods, cooks, or laundresses, or living with husbands stationed in the east. They knew that Jews were being systematically murdered and that horrific experiments were being carried out on human beings, but they did not object. Some so loved the Führer and so feared the Red Army that they continued to support the regime until the bitter end. Joseph Goebbels's wife Magda, a passionate Nazi, insisted on staying in the bunker with Hitler during the regime's last days. As the Red Army approached Berlin, Magda convinced Joseph to commit double suicide, and to kill their six children as well. So powerful were racial and political ideologies in this war that even motherhood did not prevent some individuals from perpetrating barbaric acts.

War Propaganda

These ideologies did not simply float through the air . . . or did they? Except in the Soviet zone, where Stalin feared that radios would allow individuals access to noncommunist opinions, radio broadcasting was the most influential of the many propaganda weapons used during the war. For German audiences, Hitler was a riveting speaker, in person and on radio. Goebbels also knew how to impress and terrify listeners. Both hectored listeners ceaselessly about "the Jewish enemy" and the need for the German people to win the war or die. But the Allied side could boast even better communicators, including Churchill and Roosevelt, whose nationally broadcast "fireside chats" had been instrumental in preventing despair and radicalization during America's long-lasting Depression. The British Broadcasting Company (BBC) greatly expanded its activities during the war, each day churning out more than seventy news broadcasts that could be heard throughout the British Empire and in neutral nations. BBC broadcasters opted to offer more or less objective reporting of the war, hoping that doing so would convince neutral countries to fight on their side.

On the Allied side, American newscaster Edward R. Murrow reported from London during the Blitz. Murrow did his all to impress Americans with the horrors of aerial bombing and the bravery of ordinary Britons. He reported from rooftops so that his microphone could record the sound of the bombs and the antiaircraft fire and praised the "black-faced men with bloodshot eyes who were fighting fires and the girls who cradled the steering wheel of a heavy ambulance in their arms, the policeman who stands guard over that unexploded bomb down at

St. Paul's tonight." His reporting so effectively tugged at American heartstrings that a leading media critic wrote of him: "You burned the city of London in our houses. . . . You laid the dead of London at our doors and we knew the dead were our dead—were all men's dead. . . ."[14]

In addition to radio, all sides produced propaganda films and newsreels, as well as light comedies to amuse war-weary troops and civilians. Some films, like the Nazis' anti-Semitic *Jud Süss* (1940), were aimed exclusively at indoctrination. Others, like the American film *Casablanca* (1942), used a subtler appeal to support the Allied cause. All sides also repeatedly dropped leaflets on enemy cities, hoping to inspire civilians to surrender. Occasionally they dropped other items, including cigarettes, chocolate, and soap. After the fall of Java, the British dropped bags of Dutch East Indies' tea on the Netherlands, bearing the slogan "Holland will rise again!" They did not, naturally, drop the same morale-boosting messages on Java.

Josef Stalin did not approve of radios, but had his speeches broadcast from loudspeakers in towns and cities. Realizing that the communist slogans of the 1920s and 1930s would not suffice to rally Soviet citizens against Hitler's massive armies, Stalin began to incorporate older nationalist themes into his speeches and propaganda posters. Although communists had claimed for decades that national identities masked the real unity of the international proletariat, Stalin now urged his people to fight for Mother Russia. He made his peace with Russian Orthodox leaders and reopened the churches, hoping that religion, too, could be used to mobilize the population.

The evidence suggests that these were canny moves. Most Russians felt greater loyalty to Mother Russia and to the church than to the Soviet state apparatus. But Stalin's troops *were* fighting to preserve communism, as most of them realized, and many admirers of Stalin and the Red Army in the various European resistance movements would also adopt communism as an antidote to fascism. Stalin tried to present the Red Army as the liberator of eastern Europe, liberating not only from Nazi occupation, but also from the evils of western capitalism and corruption. Recognizing the power of patriotic rhetoric, he would allow huge monuments celebrating Mother Russia's triumphs to be erected after the war.

Science and War

We do not often think of wartime as providing the proper conditions for scientific advances. But in fact war has often acted as a great accelerator of, and sometimes an impetus to, innovation. In Chapter 22, we saw how World War I greatly enhanced developments in radio technology and in aeronautics. Even more clearly, World War II propelled innovation in spheres directly related to war production: the making of synthetic fuels, the production of sophisticated aircraft, the development of rockets, and the creation of atomic weapons. The combination of desperate need, enormously increased state funding, and the ability to mobilize resources, laborers, and talented minds for certain projects made it possible for scientific teams in the United States, Germany, Britain, and the USSR to make important discoveries, some of which contributed a great deal to the deadliness of the war.

MEDICAL EXPERIMENTS IN THE CONCENTRATION CAMPS. Before the Nazi era, Germans were rightly proud of their scholars and scientists, who led the world in many forms of research. During the Nazi era, many intellectuals of Jewish ancestry or of left-wing political orientation left Germany, a large number of them settling in Britain or the United States. Among those who did not leave, many willingly contributed their talents to the Third Reich; some even took advantage of the war and Germany's huge camp populations to advance their careers. Most notorious among the latter were the doctors who used prisoners for medical experiments, measuring, for example, how much atmospheric pressure the human body can stand. At Auschwitz, the infamous Dr. Josef Mengele experimented on sets of twins and murdered his "rabbits" when he had completed his tests. This dark chapter in German history demonstrated that even those considered scientific geniuses could commit crimes against humanity.

ATOMIC WEAPON DEVELOPMENT. The most important scientific research conducted during the war related to the secret production of atomic weapons. In 1938, scientists had discovered that splitting atoms could generate enormous power; the problem was figuring out how to harness this power in the form of a bomb or a rocket. Churchill and Roosevelt feared that German scientists would obtain such a "miracle weapon," and so in 1942, teams of world-class physicists, including many exiles from Germany and occupied Europe, were assembled to build an Allied atomic bomb. Thousands of scientists and their assistants worked frantically on what was called the **Manhattan Project** at secret labs in North America, the most important of which was in Los Alamos, New Mexico.

The Manhattan Project engineers never got their chance to bomb the Nazis; they tested the first bomb in July 1945 and then prepared two more, which were dropped on Hiroshima and Nagasaki, Japan, on August 6 and 9, 1945. The bombings killed more than 70,000 in Hiroshima and 40,000 in Nagasaki, and thousands more perished of their terrible wounds and of radiation sickness. The Manhattan Project forced the Japanese to surrender, but also unleashed a terrible new weapon of mass destruction on the world.

PENICILLIN. One important scientific development during the war had beneficial rather than destructive consequences. Penicillin, an antibiotic agent found in mold, had been identified and its use to cure infections known by 1929, but growing the mold colonies had been too slow to make it an effective medicine. In 1941, two British scientists brought their research to the United States, where they used spores from a moldy cantaloupe to increase production of the antibiotic. The new medicine was ready in large quantities to treat troops wounded during the terrible last year of the war. Mass-produced penicillin would be one of the war's few gifts to humanity.

The End of the War

For close observers, the changing nature of the war, as well as its ultimate outcome, could be discerned by the spring of 1942. For most of those engaged in the fight, there was still considerable confusion about what exactly was happening in the German-occupied east and uncertainty about how the Nazi war machine could be defeated. Here we can only sketch in broad strokes the military history of the conflict between the height of German conquest in late 1941 or early 1942 and the war's end in May 1945. What bears emphasizing is the almost incalculable cost of ending the war—in human lives, natural resources, and environmental degradation. How the war ended was fundamental to what kind of peace could, and would, be made.

How did the Allies rally to win the war?

The Tide Turns

The year 1942 saw colossal bloodletting on the eastern front, as the gigantic Soviet army struggled to prevent the Germans from seizing Moscow and Leningrad or from overrunning the oil fields of the Caucasus Mountains in the south. Stalin was desperate to turn back the German assault on Stalingrad, beginning in August 1942, to save his namesake city and keep control of the Volga River. He threw everything into this battle, refusing to evacuate troops even after the city was reduced to rubble. Hitler was equally resolute and refused to allow his generals to retreat or even to surrender after a Soviet offensive encircled the German 6th Army in November. Starving and frostbitten, the Germans continued to fight as the Red Army tightened the noose. Finally, in February 1943, after months of terrible house-to-house combat, during which some starving soldiers were reduced to cannibalism, the Soviets prevailed, taking some 90,000 Germans as POWs. The casualties were again staggering: the Axis lost more than 800,000 killed, captured, or wounded; the Soviet toll exceeded 1.1 million casualties.

The Soviets were now gaining the upper hand. Not only was the war being fought on their terrain and in weather familiar to them, but their population was much larger and their leadership even more callous about expending lives in the fight. By June 1942, the Soviet industrial base had been shifted eastward, behind the Ural Mountains, and began out-producing the Germans, at a ratio of three to one for small arms and four to one for tanks. By 1943, together with the United States, the USSR was producing aircraft at a rate unimaginable for the Germans. Although Hitler's favorite architect and newly appointed armaments minister Albert Speer now seized full control of the economy in order to escalate war production to new levels, after Stalingrad he, like many other Nazi officials, knew it would take a miracle for Germany to win what had become a war of both attrition and annihilation.

THE WAR IN NORTHERN AFRICA. Rommel's campaign in northern Africa was one of the bright spots for the Axis in 1942. But by late 1942, things began to go badly there when British general Bernard Montgomery succeeded in overrunning Rommel's stronghold at El Alamein, Egypt. By late June 1943, British and American forces had chased the Germans and Italians out of northern Africa, and the Allies were poised to invade Italy.

THE TANK BATTLE AT KURSK. At the same time, a new German offensive was mounted on Kursk in central Russia, with the aim of cutting behind and encircling Soviet forces advancing from Stalingrad. In this huge tank battle, 777,000 Germans attacked Soviet lines. This time, the German offensive was turned back—thanks to the mustering of 1.3 million Soviet soldiers. The Germans lost 50,000 men in two weeks and could not hold the line. The Soviets began a counterattack, one that would gradually force the Germans back across the vast territory they had conquered and "cleansed" in 1941–1943. Even though the tide had turned, the eastern front retained its reputation for being a meat grinder, where reprisals, deportations, and the savage mistreatment of POWs and civilians remained everyday affairs. For the Germans, some 84 percent of their losses came on the eastern front.

THE ALLIED INVASION OF ITALY. If the cost of the fighting in the east remained horrific, the Allies also found invading Italy (beginning in July 1943) no easy job. But they managed to win a number of bloody battles in Sicily, causing many Italians to lose confidence in Mussolini. King Victor Emmanuel III dismissed Il Duce on July 25, 1943, and put him in prison. Despite victories in southern Italy, Allied forces struggled to advance much farther due to the mountainous terrain. German forces rescued Mussolini and set him up as head of an Axis-supported regime in northern Italy.

D-DAY AND THE BATTLE OF THE BULGE. On June 6, 1944, the Allies were at last able to open up a true second front to relieve the Russians, who by this time had entered the former territory of Poland. After three months of strategic bombing designed to prevent the Nazis from further fortifying the area, on June 6, **D-Day,** Free French, British, Canadian, and American troops, under the command of U.S. general Dwight D. Eisenhower mounted the largest amphibious invasion in history. The huge increases in Soviet and American aircraft production made possible real Allied dominance in the air, which allowed for a successful landing of troops on the beaches of

Normandy, France, though fighting at Omaha Beach was especially fierce. Once ashore, Allied forces fought their way eastward, liberating Paris—with Charles de Gaulle leading the troops—on August 25.

The Allies suffered a setback when in December 1944 the Nazis mounted a surprise counterattack in the Ardennes Forest. This last-ditch German effort, known as the Battle of the Bulge, caught the Allies off guard and delayed their final breakthrough into German territory until March 1945. By this time, the Allies were bombing heavily throughout the Reich, and the Russians, who had launched a massive offensive a few weeks after the D-Day invasion, were rapidly advancing on Berlin, Hitler's capital city and the site of what everyone knew would be the final showdown.

The Red Army and the Battle for Berlin

From the tank battle at Kursk in mid-1943 onward, the Soviet Union pushed slowly but relentlessly into eastern Europe. The Red Army did halt, however, at Stalin's insistence, at the Vistula River near Warsaw in mid-July 1944. When news spread that an attempt on Hitler's life had been made, the underground resistance force known as the **Polish Home Army** rose in a desperate attempt to free their country. The Poles hoped that the Red Army would help them, but not seek to dictate Poland's fate after the peace. Unfortunately, Stalin understood Polish yearning for independence all too well and allowed the Home Army to be destroyed by German reinforcements. When the Germans had reduced Warsaw to rubble, the Soviets picked up their guns and continued their march westward.

Fighting in this final part of the war continued to be destructive and brutal, for the Germans were now desperate and the Russians eager for vengeance. The German retreat was complicated by streams of German civilians fleeing the Red Army and by the most ardent Nazis' desire to complete the final solution, despite the collapsing fronts. Camp guards were ordered to evacuate their prisoners and drive them westward for extermination; POWs and forced laborers were also transported from east to west. In these chaotic conditions, many of those who were already sick or starving were shot or simply left by the roadside to die.

As the Soviets advanced on Berlin, Hitler called on women, children, and the elderly to help defend the capital, a move that simply made the battle longer and more deadly. On April 28, 1945, Italian partisans captured Mussolini and his mistress Clara Petacci and hanged them. Two days later, on April 30, 1945, Hitler too gave up hoping for a miracle and shot himself in the bunker that he had made his headquarters; a loyal bodyguard burned his body. A few of his loyal followers imitated him; some, like Hermann Göring, sought to escape but were captured. Red Army soldiers raised the Soviet flag on the Reichstag, and on May 8, 1945, the Third Reich finally capitulated. The Allies demanded unconditional surrender

The Soviets Take Berlin This famous photo shows the raising of the Soviet hammer and sickle flag over the Reichstag in Berlin, on May 2, 1945. Note the devastated cityscape in the background. Nazi officials agreed to an unconditional surrender on May 7, and the war in Europe officially ended on May 8, 1945.

from the Germans, who thus had to agree to all the terms imposed on them.

By the time of the surrender, the Soviets had occupied most of eastern Europe, and the Allies had freed France, western Germany, part of Austria, and Greece. After the Germans evacuated Yugoslavia, fearful of being cut off as the Russians swept westward, Tito's partisans seized control of their territory before the Red Army could occupy it. Who liberated whom would matter deeply after the armistice.

Ending the War in the Pacific

Even after Germany's surrender, Japan continued to fight, and Britain and the United States now devoted their all to finishing the Pacific war as well. In late 1944, American victory in the Battle of Leyte Gulf cut off Japan from its oil supplies and inflicted irreparable damage on the Japanese navy. Still, the jungle fighting required to liberate the Philippines and Burma took a terrible toll on both soldiers and civilians. Battles on Japan's home islands of Iwo Jima and Okinawa, where the Japanese refused to surrender, ended with tens of thousands of casualties. The Allies estimated that the invasion of Japan necessary

The Firebombing of Dresden

In early February 1945, Dresden was a beautiful Baroque city on the Elbe River. More than 250,000 Germans lived there, many of them refugees from heavily bombed cities of the Ruhr or from the eastern front, where Russian troops were now terrorizing civilians. A handful of German Jews, including Victor Klemperer (see Chapter 23, p. 756), remained in the city and were scheduled for deportation on February 16. Although British and American bombers had increased their assaults on Germany after D-Day, Dresden remained one of fifteen major cities that had been spared.

Well known for its architectural splendor and artistic treasures, Dresden was not considered to have much strategic military value. By early 1945, however, the Allies, particularly Arthur "Bomber" Harris (1892–1984), the chief of the Royal Air Force Bomber Command, were eager to bring the war to the German people, and Churchill was eager to demonstrate to Stalin, on the eve of their meeting at Yalta (see p. 792), that he was helping relieve pressure on the eastern front. Harris thought terror bombing—as the Germans had used on Britain again and again—would finally persuade the civilian population to surrender. He also saw profit in disrupting transportation routes to complicate the movement of German troops. Some Allied officials pressed Harris to aim instead at Germany's synthetic oil factories, for they knew, thanks to deciphered Enigma messages, that the Reich was perilously short of oil. But after Berlin had again been raided on February 3—with the loss of some three thousand civilians—Germany still refused to concede defeat. Harris insisted that another target be tried, and now it was Dresden's turn.

Dresden Destroyed The British and American fire bombing raids of February 13–15, 1944, devastated the once-beautiful city of Dresden, where Augustus the Strong once housed his porcelain collections. Here, survivors line up to catch a streetcar, whose tracks have only just been cleared of rubble.

On the night of February 13, 1945, as Churchill was returning from Yalta, 796 British planes dropped more than 2,600 tons of incendiary devices on Dresden. The next morning, Ash Wednesday, American bombers dropped an additional 2,000 tons on the city. Usually, World War II bombers had trouble hitting their targets and devices often malfunctioned or the small fires they started were hastily extinguished by the residents. This time, however, everything went according to plan, and the two raids set off a firestorm that engulfed the central city. The unusually hot and gaseous fire created by the phosphorous bombs destroyed everything in its path, including women and children fleeing burning apartment buildings, tigers and horses belonging to the circus, paintings too large to remove from the King of Saxony's castle, and the castle itself. Eyewitnesses reported horrific scenes of streetcars passing by full of people on fire and of water reservoirs packed with people who had died of asphyxiation:

> From some of the debris poked arms, heads, legs, and shattered skulls. The static water-tanks were filled up to the top with dead human beings, with large pieces of masonry lying on top of that again. Most people looked as if they had been inflated, with large yellow and brown stains on their bodies. People whose clothes were still glowing. . . .[15]

In total, between 25,000 and 40,000 people were killed, though German estimates were at first much higher. The ensuing chaos saved Klemperer and 130 of his fellow Jews from deportation—though 40 were themselves victims of the firestorm. German morale was not broken. On the contrary, the raid played into the hands of Joseph Goebbels, who had long been insisting that an Allied peace would be one without mercy for German civilians.

Noting the slight strategic importance of the city and the large number of refugees killed in the raids, some on the Allied side felt uneasy about this incident. After the war, the firebombing of Dresden would become a major subject of debate, as German apologists and critics of Harris and Churchill would insist that this too was a war crime. Survivors, of course, did not forget the trauma they had experienced, and for decades the city, which fell into the Soviet zone after the war, remained an open wound. The East German government rebuilt the palaces where Augustus the Strong had displayed his famous porcelain and painting collections (see Chapter 15), and the famous opera house, but deliberately left the grand Church of Our Lady a pile of rubble in the city's center. Only after German reunification in 1990 was the church reconstructed. Dresden has restored some of its Baroque splendor—not because its past was preserved, but because the memory of the past refused to pass.

QUESTION | *Should the firebombing of Dresden be considered a war crime?*

to end the war would cost hundreds of thousands of lives. Invasion of Japan was rendered unnecessary by the dropping of atomic bombs on the cities of Hiroshima and Nagasaki; by the Soviet declaration of war on Japan on August 8, 1945; and by the invasion of Manchuria. Fearing the Red Army and more atomic attacks, Japan surrendered on August 15, 1945.

Planning Europe's Future

In late November 1943, following the Soviet victory at Kursk, Stalin, Churchill, and Roosevelt, the Big Three Allied leaders, met in Tehran, Iran, to discuss how to conduct the remainder of the war. Roosevelt and Churchill did not trust Stalin, and the feeling was mutual. Discussions of strategy—where to open the second front, whether to aid the Yugoslav partisans—evolved into discussions of postwar borders and spheres of influence. Churchill proposed partitioning Germany into several small, "cow-like" states, but was horrified when Stalin proposed shooting 50,000 Germans without trial as a form of collective punishment.

What difficulties did the victors face in making peace?

Yalta and Potsdam

These discussions were greatly expanded the next time the three met, at Yalta, a resort town on the Black Sea, in February 1945. The Allies agreed on a plan for disarming the aggressors and dividing Germany and Austria into zones of occupation. War criminals and leading Nazis were to be put on trial, and German citizens reeducated, so that Nazi ideology would no longer poison Europe. Stalin was enticed to sign a version of the Atlantic Charter, ensuring free elections and self-government for the peoples his armies had liberated. He also agreed that the USSR would join the United Nations, an international organization of states created in 1945 to take the place of the long-defunct League of Nations. But, by early March 1945, it was clear that Stalin had no intention of allowing the people of eastern Europe the right to self-determination. Six thousand Polish officers who had fought against the Nazis were arrested and many executed; thousands more, including Romanian workers and Polish teachers, were deported to labor camps. Later, Stalin would have at least 10,000 Russian POWs executed and many more imprisoned, fearing that they had been tainted by having served in "capitalist" eastern Europe.

Relations between the Allies were thoroughly poisoned by the time the leaders met again, this time at Potsdam just outside of devastated Berlin, between July 17 and August 2, 1945. Roosevelt had died that April, and the new U.S. president, Harry Truman, took his place at the Allied negotiating table. By this time, the war in Europe was over and the war in the Pacific was nearing its atomic end. Russian troops had liberated most of eastern Europe and showed no signs of leaving any time soon. Against the resistance of the Polish government in exile, Stalin insisted that he be given a chunk of eastern Poland and that the Poles be given the infamous Polish Corridor as well as additional territory in eastern Germany. The Allies agreed to the expulsion of ethnic Germans from the USSR and eastern and central Europe—a process already being implemented violently on the ground—and agreed to proceed with de-Nazification and the trials of war criminals.

Postwar Justice

The western Allies knew about the existence of the extermination camps already in 1942, but their horror increased as new details were learned. In a letter from July 1944, Churchill wrote: "There is no doubt that this [murder of the Jews] is probably the greatest and most horrific crime ever committed in the whole history of the world, and it has been done by scientific machinery by nominally civilized men in the name of a great state and one of the leading races of Europe. It is quite clear that all concerned in this crime who may fall into our hands, including the people who only obeyed orders by carrying out the butcheries, should be put to death after their association with the murders has been proved." The Russian, British, and American soldiers, who had liberated the survivors at Auschwitz, Dachau, Buchenwald, and Bergen-Belsen, had brought photographers and reporters with them. The images shocked the press, and Edward R. Murrow's moving broadcast from Dachau took listeners into the heart of the genocide, even though this camp was not nearly as deadly as those to the east, such as Auschwitz and Sobibor.

But it would be difficult to bring to justice all of those who had participated in what came to be called crimes against humanity. Some of the most guilty, including Hitler, Goebbels, and Himmler, had already taken their own lives. Others, like the notorious Nazi doctor Josef Mengele and the Croatian fascist Ante Pavelić, managed to flee. Every German and Austrian adult was required to submit documentation describing his or her level of collaboration with the regime, and for a time, those deemed major collaborators (such as members of the Waffen SS) were prohibited from voting or from being employed by the postwar bureaucracy. As a new Cold War between the Soviets and the western Allies set in, however, both sides wanted to turn their attention to the future, rather than dwell on the sins of the past, and most of these de-Nazification procedures were abandoned.

The most publicized part of postwar justice was the Trial of the Major War Criminals at Nuremberg, Germany, which began in November 1945. At the **Nuremberg Trials,** twenty-four of the highest-ranking Nazis were tried; two were acquitted and twelve received the death penalty. Other members of the Nazi elite, including Albert Speer, received long sentences. There were also trials of Nazi doctors and prison camp guards. In 1961, Israeli commandos captured Adolf Eichmann in

MAP 24.4 | Patterns of Human Loss in World War II

This map illustrates which nations suffered the greatest losses in World War II. The number of losses includes soldiers and civilians (including Jews murdered in the Holocaust).[16] **Compare and contrast the patterns of loss in World War II with those of World War I (see Map 22.4). What do the differences between the death tolls in Europe's western and eastern nations tell you about the nature of this war?**

Argentina and brought him to Israel, where he was tried and executed. Overall in western Germany, in the zones occupied by France, Britain, and the United States, some 200,000 people were arrested on suspicion of being Nazis; 5,153 were accused of war crimes, and 668 were condemned to death. In the Soviet zones, many more were targeted, and thousands were executed as Nazi collaborators, though some of these turned out simply to be people the new communist regimes wanted out of the way.

Beyond the official trials, in many localities civilians and especially members of the resistance movements satisfied their thirst for vengeance by lynching Germans, collaborators, or women accused of consorting with Nazi officials. Some of these women suffered the public humiliation of having their heads shaved and being marched through cities and towns. Throughout eastern Europe, Germans were forced to flee. Some 2.5 million Sudeten Germans were expelled by the new Czech government. Germans resettled in western Poland after 1939 fled back to Germany, and Poles in even larger numbers than before occupied their farms and villages. As a new wave of ethnic cleansing occurred, European states became less multiethnic than ever before.

Displaced Persons

When the war ended, many people, including concentration camp survivors, forced laborers, and POWs, found themselves far from home. Many had no home to go back to; tens of thousands of villages had been destroyed in the east, and cities in the west had been pummeled. Some eastern Europeans did not want to return to what were now Soviet-occupied zones. Transport was not easily available: ports were choked with sunken ships, most major bridges had been destroyed, and virtually all rail lines had been disabled. A huge network of displaced persons camps had to be set up, sometimes on sites where Nazi concentration camps had stood.

The Second World War devastated Europe—or to be more precise, it devastated *eastern* Europe and took a terrible toll on some areas in the west and south. Although Great Britain made crucial sacrifices and suffered grievous losses, it lost less than 1 percent of its population in this war—while Poland lost 18 percent, and the USSR upward of 15 percent (Map 24.4). Some western cities—Rotterdam, London, Palermo—suffered terrible destruction, but eastern Europe and Russia were hit even harder.

World War II fatalities (millions)

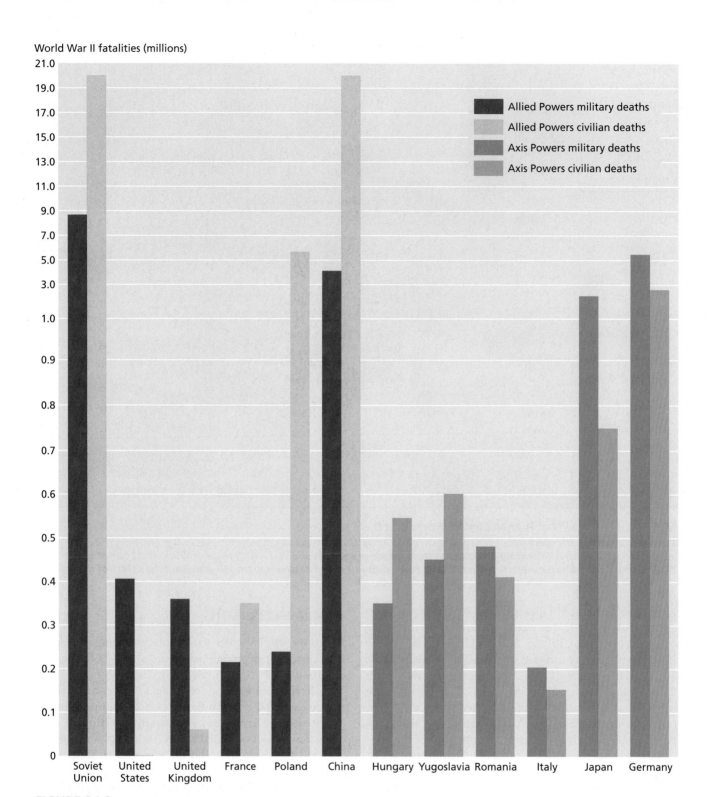

FIGURE 24.2 | **Fatality Rates in World War II**

This chart illustrates the very great differences in death toll for eastern and western Europe in World War II. Due to shifting borders, forced conscriptions, the continuation of violence after the war, and disagreements about the number of deaths in most countries, these numbers are necessarily rough estimates.

Figure created by Jason M. Wolfe, based on data compiled by Scott Berg and listed in the note for Map 24.4.

An estimated 70,000 Russian villages were destroyed, and little but piles of rubble remained where great cities such as Warsaw, Berlin, and Stalingrad once stood. Southeastern Europe also sustained considerable dam-age; Yugoslavia, Greece, and Hungary lost between 5 and 10 percent of their citizens in the conflict (Figure 24.2).

The war left as many as seventy million people dead, including six million Jews. This bloodiest conflict in human history saw the descent into genocide and barbarism of some of Europe's supposedly most civilized citizens. Cities, bridges, factories, churches, and schools were destroyed by the hundreds of thousands, and many survivors bore permanent physical and psychological scars. Hitler's new order was defeated, but eastern Europeans, in particular, paid a high price, as the Soviet Red Army settled in to stay, and a new, cold war began.

Conclusion

In a 1946 speech given in Fulton, Missouri, Winston Churchill warned that a Soviet **Iron Curtain** was descending across eastern Europe, from Stettin in the Baltic to Trieste in the Adriatic Sea. Beyond Europe, communist parties were growing and imperiling "Christian civilization." Churchill counseled that the West, the leadership of which had clearly now been placed in the hands of the United States, should confront the Russians directly and not seek appeasement of the sort that had been so disastrous in 1938. By the next year, 1947, Churchill was even more worried. Europe, he said, once the exporter of science, religion, and culture, had become "a rubble-heap, a charnel-house, a breeding ground of pestilence and hate." In his view, the only way to save the continent from communism and further disaster was to establish a united Europe, "where men of every country will think as much of being a European as of belonging to their native land, and wherever they go in this wide domain will truly feel 'Here I am at home.'" In these two speeches, Churchill demonstrated that in spite of all he had suffered and witnessed, he had not stopped fighting. But he realized, to his dismay, that the coming Cold War would prove a wholly different kind of conflict. He also acknowledged that Europe's fate was no longer in European hands; it was now up to the most powerful of the neo-Europes, the United States, to defend the values he prized as those of western civilization against the new superpower of the east, the Soviet Union.

Critical Thinking Questions

1. In what ways was World War II a more "total" war than World War I?

2. What decisions—on the part of either Allied or Axis leaders—changed the course of the war?

3. Why was the war so much more destructive in the East than in the West?

Key Terms

Sudetenland **(p. 766)**

appeasement **(p. 767)**

Axis Powers **(p. 767)**

Night of the Broken Glass **(p. 768)**

T-4 Program **(p. 768)**

Blitzkrieg **(p. 769)**

ghetto **(p. 771)**

Allied Powers **(p. 772)**

Vichy France **(p. 773)**

Lend-Lease Agreement **(p. 775)**

Ustasha **(p. 776)**

Lebensraum **(p. 778)**

Einsatzgruppen **(p. 780)**

Holocaust **(p. 782)**

Manhattan Project **(p. 788)**

D-Day **(p. 789)**

Polish Home Army **(p. 790)**

Nuremberg Trials **(p. 792)**

Iron Curtain **(p. 795)**

Primary Sources in connect

For information on Connect and the online resources available, go to **http://connect.mcgraw-hill.com**.

1. **Winston Churchill, Speeches on War**

2. **Adolf Hitler Warns the Jews, January 1939**

3. **A Survivor Describes the Siege of Leningrad**

4. **Himmler Stiffens the Resolve of the SS Murderers, October 1943**

5. **Voices from the French Resistance**

6. **Dwight D. Eisenhower, Memos on D-Day— Success or Failure**

Joseph Stalin, Broadcast to the People of the Soviet Union, July 3, 1941

In this radio broadcast, Stalin's first public pronouncement after the Nazi invasion of the USSR, the Soviet dictator called on all of the nationality groups in his empire to fight fascism "to the last drop of blood." Stalin calls on his people to "wage a ruthless fight" in what he clearly understands to be a vicious, total war in which the survival of the USSR is at stake.

Comrades! Citizens! Brothers and sisters! Men of our army and navy! I am addressing you, my friends!

. . . History shows that there are no invincible armies and never have been. Napoleon's army was considered invincible but it was beaten successively by Russian, English and German armies. Kaiser Wilhelm's German Army in the period of the first imperialist war was also considered invincible, but it was beaten several times by the Russian and Anglo-French forces and was finally smashed by the Anglo-French forces.

The same must be said of Hitler's German fascist army today. . . .

The enemy is cruel and implacable. He is out to seize our lands, watered with our sweat, to seize our grain and oil secured by our labor. He is out to restore the rule of landlords, to restore Tsarism, to destroy national culture and the national state existence of the Russians, Ukrainians, Byelo-Russians, Lithuanians, Letts, Esthonians [sic], Uzbeks, Tatars, Moldavians, Georgians, Armenians, Azerbaidzhanians [sic] and the other free people of the Soviet Union, to Germanize them, to convert them into the slaves of German princes and barons.

Thus the issue is one of life or death for the Soviet State, for the peoples of the USSR; the issue is whether the peoples of the Soviet Union shall remain free or fall into slavery. . . .

The peoples of the Soviet Union must rise against the enemy and defend their rights and their land. The Red Army, Red Navy and all citizens of the Soviet Union must defend every inch of Soviet soil, must fight to the last drop of blood for our towns and villages, must display the daring initiative and intelligence that are inherent in our people. . . .

We must strengthen the Red Army's rear, subordinating all our work to this cause. All our industries must be got to work with greater intensity to produce more rifles, machine-guns, artillery, bullets, shells, airplanes; we must organize the guarding of factories, power-stations, telephonic and telegraphic communications and arrange effective air raid precautions in all localities.

We must wage a ruthless fight against all disorganizers of the rear, deserters, panic-mongers, rumor-mongers; we must exterminate spies, diversionists and enemy parachutists, rendering rapid aid in all this to our destroyer battalions.

We must bear in mind that the enemy is crafty, unscrupulous, experienced in deception and the dissemination of false rumors. We must reckon with all this and not fall victim to provocation.

All who by their panic-mongering and cowardice hinder the work of defense, no matter who they are, must be immediately huled before the military tribunal. In case of forced retreat of Red Army units, all rolling stock must be evacuated, the enemy must not be left a single engine, a single railway car, not a single pound of grain or a gallon of fuel.

The collective farmers must drive off all their cattle, and turn over their grain to the safe-keeping of State authorities for transportation to the rear. All valuable property, including non-ferrous metals, grain and fuel which cannot be withdrawn, must without fail be destroyed.

In areas occupied by the enemy, guerrilla units, mounted and on foot, must be formed, diversionist groups must be organized to combat the enemy troops, to foment guerrilla warfare everywhere, to blow up bridges and roads, damage telephone and telegraph lines, set fire to forests, stores, transports.

In the occupied regions conditions must be made unbearable for the enemy and all his accomplices. They must be hounded and annihilated at every step, and all their measures frustrated.

This war with fascist Germany cannot be considered an ordinary war. It is not only a war between two armies, it is also a great war of the entire Soviet people against the German fascist forces.

The aim of this national war in defense of our country against the fascist oppressors is not only elimination of the danger hanging over our country, but also aid to all European peoples groaning under the yoke of German fascism.

In this war of liberation we shall not be alone. In this great war we shall have loyal allies in the peoples of Europe and America, including the German people who are enslaved by the Hitlerite despots. . . .

Comrades, our forces are numberless. The overweening enemy will soon learn this to his cost. Side by side with the Red Army many thousands of workers, collective farmers, intellectuals are rising to fight the enemy aggressor. The masses of our people will rise up in their millions.

The working people of Moscow and Leningrad have already commenced to form vast popular levies in support of the Red Army. Such popular levies must be raised in every city which is in danger of enemy invasion, all working people must be roused to defend our freedom, our honor, our country—in our patriotic war against German Fascism. . . .

All our forces for support of our heroic Red Army and our glorious Red Navy! All forces of the people—for the demolition of the enemy!

Forward, to our victory!

QUESTIONS | *How would you describe the rhetoric Stalin uses here to rally his people? What does the language he employs tell you about the nature of this war? Was Stalin correct that this was a war of survival for the USSR?*

Source: Soviet Russia Today (August 1941) Retrieved from ibiblio.org, www.ibiblio.org/pha/policy/1941/410703a.html.

Checkpoint Charlie, the Most Famous of Berlin's Crossing Points, Looking from West Berlin toward the East

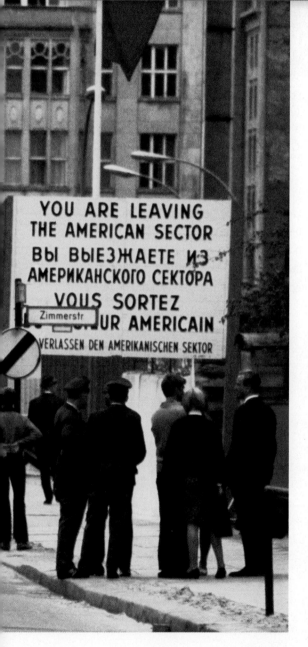

THE COLD WAR AND DECOLONIZATION, 1945–1989

The Making of Two Europes
  Making the Soviet Bloc
  Remaking the Eastern European Economy
  National Communism
  Making Western Europe
  Remaking the Western European Economy
  Cold War Battleground: Berlin
  The Making of Two Germanys

Eastern Europe after Stalin: The Thaw—and Its Limits
  Khrushchev and the Hungarian Uprising of 1956
  Communist Successes
  The Prague Spring
  The Brezhnev Era
  Cracking Down on Poland

Western Europe: The New Prosperity
  The Baby Boom
  The Welfare State Comes of Age
  Economic Integration and Prosperity
  Southern Europe
  Guest Workers

The End of European Imperialism
  Decolonization in Asia and the Middle East
  Decolonization in Africa

The Culture of the Cold War
  Popular Culture
  Elite Culture
  The Boom Years Are Over
  1968
  Christianity and the Cold War

Western Europe in the 1970s and 1980s
  A Sexual Revolution?
  The Conservatives Return to Power

Communism under Pressure
  Living Communism's Last Years
  Glasnost and Perestroika

How the Cold War Ended
  Poland and Hungary Break Free
  The Fall of the Wall
  The Velvet Revolution
  Romania: Death of a Dictator

Conclusion

ERICH HONECKER, COMMUNIST DIE-HARD Like Alexandra Kollontai, Erich Honecker (1912–1994) devoted his life to building a communist state. The son of a left-leaning coal miner, Honecker enrolled in the local communist Youth League, and in the fateful year of 1929, when he was seventeen years old, he joined Germany's Communist Party. He spent the next two years studying in Moscow, at the height of Stalin's collectivization. Honecker returned to Germany in 1931 and became a communist youth organizer. But in 1935 he was arrested by the Nazis and spent the next ten years in prison. Liberated by the Russians in 1945, he devoted himself to building a German communist state on the ruins of Hitler's empire. Honecker would do more than any other German to build and maintain communism in East Germany over the course of that nation's forty-year lifespan. He would prove one of the most tenacious defenders of "real-existing communism" even after communist East Germany ceased to exist in 1989.

Dedicated young Communists such as Honecker, many of whom had been persecuted by rightwing regimes during the interwar period, were instrumental in creating eastern Europe's new communist states. After 1945, backed by Soviet armies and agents, they wrested control from democratic socialists in the belief that only hard-line or uncompromising forms of communism would save their states from capitalism and democracy, which they blamed for allowing the fascists into power. For these young radicals, communism meant the empowerment of the working classes and the destruction of what they saw as oppressive and exploitative religious, political, and economic establishments. Although many eastern European Communists recognized that Stalin was a dangerous and dictatorial man, they hoped nonetheless that the Soviet leader would help them engineer the right kind of revolutions in their countries and then leave them to run those states. Stalin's postwar purges disillusioned some and destroyed others, but many, including Honecker, remained willing to work with Moscow and to call in Russian help when their own civilians got out of hand.

Erich Honecker Applauds East Germany's Thirtieth Birthday (1979) East German premier Erich Honecker (*right, foreground*) was much appreciated by Soviet officials, including Leonid Brezhnev (*left, foreground*), who found him eager to toe the party line and happy to turn out for parades and other official occasions, such as the German Democratic Republic's thirtieth anniversary.

Honecker was not East Germany's first communist leader. That role belonged to Walter Ulbricht (1893–1973), who had been a communist even longer than Honecker. Ulbricht oversaw the founding, in 1949, of the German Democratic Republic as a one-party communist state. He

Imposition of communist regimes in eastern Europe
1944–1948

Greek Civil War
1946–1949

Decolonization
c. 1950–c. 1970

World War II ends
1945

The Cold War
1945–1989

1940   1945   1950   1955   1960

set in motion the state takeover of all private businesses in East Germany and remained in power until 1971. To Honecker, who had been Ulbricht's loyal deputy, fell the task of keeping communism afloat after the first wave of post-fascist enthusiasm for the cause waned. To do so required tremendous political skill, ruthless commitment to the system, and the ability to tell whopping lies with a straight face. Honecker turned out to be eminently suited for the job.

As first secretary of the Central Committee of the Communist Party from 1971 to 1989, Honecker devoted much of his energy to propping up the East German economy, which was already sagging when he came into office. Ulbricht, like many other communist leaders of the older generation, understood modernization to mean central planning and heavy industrialization, but East German industries were already lagging behind those of the West. Knowing that the public, in the East just as in the West, wanted consumer goods—tastier food, refrigerators, and if possible, cars—Honecker set about organizing ingenious ways to buy both much-needed machines and much-desired luxuries from the West, even though East German ostmarks were not officially exchangeable for western hard currency. In the 1970s, he succeeded to some extent in placating consumers, especially Communist Party members, though people still had to wait a very long time for their appliances, especially for their Trabant cars.

But even that limited success came at a heavy price. Honecker relied on imports rather than remaking East German industry to meet new consumer demands. This policy consequently ran up a huge national debt to the capitalist West. Although he knew very well that the East German economy was steadily collapsing and that the distribution of the most-desired goods was unfair, Honecker never stopped proclaiming the superiority of communism over capitalism. Communism and the Eastern bloc lost the Cold War, but Honecker never officially recanted his beliefs. Only through his hypocritical and, in the end disastrous, dependence on western capital can we see his admission that his lifelong communist dreams had failed.[1]

In May 1945, Europe—especially eastern Europe—lay in ruins. Only about 10 percent of Germany's railroads were operational, a transportation nightmare that hampered the flight of ethnic Germans, some 12 million of whom were expelled from eastern Europe by the Red Army and new governments eager for vengeance. The German expellees joined the millions of slave laborers, demobilized soldiers, liberated camp inmates, and orphans in search of old homes or new lives. Many of these displaced persons were physically wounded and psychologically scarred, half starved, and grief stricken; many were homeless, some stateless. Fears that a nuclear World War III would soon devastate the planet abounded. In this climate, some Europeans declared that they had had enough of ideology and conflict and retreated into their private worlds, focusing on rebuilding their homes and family lives. Others sought to establish lasting peace and prosperity by working for major social and political reform—or for revolution.

In the war's immediate aftermath, many Europeans, particularly in central and southeastern Europe, found communism appealing. Stalin's USSR, they knew, had been instrumental in winning the war against fascism, and the Red Army had liberated their lands from the Nazis. Even before Hitler's ascent to power,

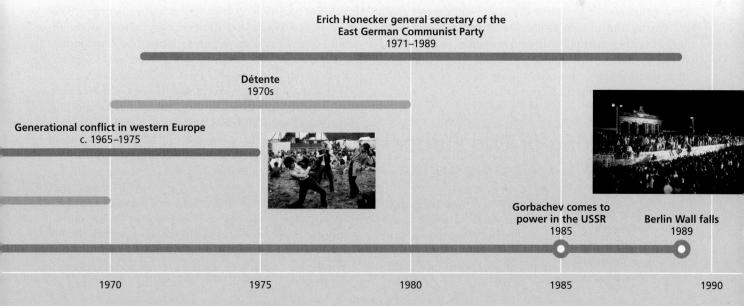

Erich Honecker general secretary of the East German Communist Party
1971–1989

Détente
1970s

Generational conflict in western Europe
c. 1965–1975

Gorbachev comes to power in the USSR
1985

Berlin Wall falls
1989

1970   1975   1980   1985   1990

communist parties in these areas had been large, and many communists had spent World War II in exile in the USSR, cementing their ties to the Soviet leadership. They now returned, determined to replace "bourgeois" governments with Communist states, which they called workers' democracies. This endeavor, they knew, was backed by the Soviet leadership, and they could count on support from the Soviet secret police (NKVD) and the Red Army when necessary. Stalin built himself a new communist buffer zone by seizing a large chunk of territory that had belonged to Poland, and by holding on to the once-independent republics of Estonia, Latvia, and Lithuania, which he had annexed in 1940 (Map 25.1). In the next four years, the Russians, together with local activists, would succeed in bringing all of eastern Europe into the communist fold.

There were also many communists in the western European states that had been liberated by the Allies (including the Netherlands, France, Italy, and Greece). But here there was no Red Army, and advocates for a return to the democratic and capitalist practices of the past got the upper hand. Still, these democracies were weak, and leaders quickly realized that they would need a powerful ally to prevent the return of extremism and to help establish political and economic stability. They turned to the now-nuclear superpower, the United States, which was just as determined to keep its half of Europe democratic and capitalist as was Stalin to bring his half into the Communist fold.

MAP 25.1 | **Territorial Changes in Europe, 1945–1949**
This map shows how eastern European territory was divided after World War II. It also indicates the year in which the Communists gained control of governments behind the Iron Curtain. The inset map shows the zones into which the city of Berlin was divided. ***Why did the "Iron Curtain" fall along these lines?***

The Making of Two Europes

In the tense years between 1945 and 1949, the two Europes would be wrenched apart by superpowers competing for their hearts, minds, and resources. U.S. political and financial backing helped western Europeans rebuild capitalism and parliamentary governance, while Soviet economic restructuring

How were the economies of both eastern and western Europe remade after World War II?

and military force managed to stabilize a series of new peoples' democracies in the East. The Americans acted vigorously to contain communism; the Soviets used propaganda to inoculate their citizens against contamination by a West they viewed as decadent and exploitative. The much-feared World War III never commenced, although plenty of smaller wars began as formerly colonized nations made bids for freedom, and some leaders looked for support from the mutually hostile entities or blocs.

For forty years after World War II, the **Cold War** was fought ideologically and in wars outside of Europe. For those who lived it, it was a tense and uncertain era, but also one in which Europeans gave up what had long been their most lethal practice: that of making war on one another. It was almost history in reverse: the huge military budgets states had sustained since absolutist times, and the grand, standing armies of the early twentieth century were abandoned. And since it was now up to the superpowers to supply military might, states, especially in the West, were able to turn their attention and their incomes to paying for a greatly expanded array of social services.[2] Over time, people grew used to living in a demilitarized and divided Europe—even while critics on both sides grew increasingly unsatisfied with some aspects of their societies. The abrupt end of the Cold War in 1989 surprised everyone. Some people, like Honecker, never recovered from the shock.

Enormous changes in European social, economic, and cultural life occurred during the Cold War. It was an era of many firsts. For the first time in history, Europe ceased to be a nation primarily of peasant farmers. For the first time, full-fledged **welfare states** emerged—in both the East and the West—to protect the elderly, the disabled, and the jobless from dying of poverty. For the first time, women obtained rights equal to men, though their pay, representation in democratic assemblies, and share in the housework continued to be unequal. As a result of the postwar baby boom, fertility rates rose briefly, but then began a steep decline. In both the Soviet and the Western blocs, individual states gave up a good deal of their sovereignty in attempts to prevent another war and to create large-scale, coordinated economies. For the first time since the early Middle Ages, Europe ceased to be a continent in which the majority were practicing Christians. Honecker's era was indeed a revolutionary one—though not at all as he hoped it would be.

Making the Soviet Bloc

The individual who played the largest role in the division of Europe was Joseph Stalin, who had always been suspicious of western intentions. He resented that it had taken the western Allies so long to open up a second front in Europe while his armies battled the Germans on the genocidal eastern front. After the war, he was determined to establish an eastern European buffer zone under his influence and to extract its materials and labor to rebuild the devastated Soviet Union. In territories occupied by the Soviets between 1939 and 1941, his secret police (NKVD) had subjected the people to terror, executions, and deportations. As the Red Army swept through eastern Europe in 1944–1945, Stalin authorized the deportation of many more civilians, most of them to be used as slave laborers in the East. By 1952, more than five million Russians and eastern Europeans had been sent to Soviet labor camps or colonies, where they endured backbreaking work regimes. Stalin also sent many members of the Hungarian, Bulgarian, and Romanian interwar elite to these camps, thus removing many potential opponents of the new communist states. Nearly a million, or one in ten, Hungarians were accused of opposition to the regime or collaboration with the Nazis and imprisoned, executed, or simply shot in prison and said to have disappeared.

As the war ended, the most urgent task for Stalin was to ensure that his people would be ready to take power when the Nazis pulled out. In Poland, he insisted that the Polish communists, and not the nationalist Polish government in exile, was the rightful government, and he backed campaigns to expand the Polish Communist Party and to terrorize its opponents until 1948, when his

Polish comrades took control of the state. Stalin provided similar backing for other communist insurgencies, such as the one in Czechoslovakia, which succeeded, and the one in Greece, which did not. After 1945, he allowed elections to be held, but ballots were by no means secret, and the NKVD (renamed the KGB in 1954) tapped phones, opened mail, and muzzled the independent media. Not surprisingly, communist parties gained more and more backers. In Hungary, for example, party membership rose from a mere 2,000 in late 1944 to an estimated 864,000 members in 1948. In places where the majority seemed to support socialism but not communism, as in East Germany, Stalin agreed to the creation of socialist unity parties. Once the communists had gained positions in these unity governments, they gradually forced out the moderates and enforced Stalinist policies, wiping out all other parties.

In 1947, Stalin replaced the old Comintern with a new organization called the Communist Information Bureau (Cominform), whose mission was to coordinate Soviet control over all of the world's communist movements. Through the combination of propaganda, trickery, and force, eastern European communists were able to complete their takeovers in Czechoslovakia, Hungary, Poland, Romania, and East Germany by 1948.

Remaking the Eastern European Economy

Fortunately for Stalin, Nazi occupation had furthered industrial development and centralized production and distribution in the Eastern bloc. He benefited from Nazi-sponsored industrialization in Czechoslovakia and Hungary and from the remarkable survival of about 80 percent of Germany's industrial plant. Dismantling some of these factories was one of his first orders of business, and the Soviets pilfered an estimated $14 billion worth of goods from the east—just about the same amount the United States was pouring into western Europe. Local communists also instituted land reforms popular with the working classes, breaking up large estates in eastern Germany and Hungary and giving the land to smallholders.

These reforms, however, were fleeting. In the 1950s, communist leaders reversed course and began efforts to collectivize agriculture in eastern Europe and the Balkans. This plan provoked considerable opposition, resulting in a new wave of kulaks being sent to Soviet prison camps—at least 80,000 Romanian smallholders suffered this fate. Collectivization, once again, did not succeed in increasing the food supply and, in 1951, had to be modified. In the places with some ability to resist Soviet plans—such as Poland and Yugoslavia—it was largely abandoned after Stalin's death in 1953.

Similarly, Soviet-style industrialization failed to benefit the buffer-zone states very much, as production focused only on the heavy goods Moscow wanted—steel, coal, and cement. As in the Soviet Union, Communist Party members could buy specialty goods from the West in shops available only to them, but other consumers had to make do with the goods offered in government-run stores. There were perpetual shortages of goods such as toilet paper, milk, and detergent, and people often had to stand in lines for hours to buy a single pound of coffee or a pair of shoes. State-dictated production, often accelerated to meet quotas without concern for workers' safety or environmental degradation, resulted in a high frequency of industrial accidents and heavily polluted skies and waterways. A considerable amount of industrial work was performed by slave laborers, imprisoned far from their homes and forced to work on projects such as Romania's Danube–Black Sea Canal. Here, hundreds of thousands of prisoners were compelled to dig with sticks or their hands; guards reportedly were encouraged to use violence against workers, tens of thousands of whom died as a result of cruel treatment, malnutrition, or exposure. Clearly, in the Soviet bloc, industrialization, not human welfare, was king.

Still, the eastern European economies did begin to recover, producing in relatively short time full employment and steady rates of growth. This was good enough for many people who were eager, after the horrors of the fascist era and the war, to return to some sort of normalcy, to work and raise families, and not to be involved in ideological or real battles. For them, the communists did have something to offer. There were jobs in the new economy and, for those who toed the party line, free schools, clinics, child care, and perhaps even new apartments, though many cities continued to have severe housing shortages. Education, both elementary and higher, was thoroughly Stalinized, but more people had access to it than ever before. In the interwar era, 50,000 Poles had been studying at the university level; in the postwar years, this number surged to 250,000.

indisputably long-term, loyal communists? The answer was the same one he used in the great purges in the Soviet Union in the 1930s: put the offenders on trial and force them to condemn themselves.

During the era of the postwar **show trials,** 1947–1953, hundreds of thousands of eastern Europeans fell victim to Stalin's desire to root out national communism. Some 200,000 people were arrested in Hungary, 180,000 in Romania, 136,000 in Czechoslovakia, and 80,000 in Albania. Most were sent to prisons and work camps without a trial, but trials were held for communist leaders who, Stalin feared, might want to adapt communist policies to their nation's economy or geography, or worse, to create communist regimes that were too economically or politically independent. Those tried were compelled, usually by torture, to admit that they were guilty of trying to sabotage their own regimes or had acted as spies and double agents for capitalist countries. All were found guilty, and some popular leaders were executed and erased from history. After Stalin's death, a few were "rehabilitated"—which meant, officially, that their friends and family could acknowledge that they had existed; a few who were lucky enough to have only been imprisoned, such as the Polish communist leader Władysław Gomułka (1905–1982), were graciously allowed to rejoin the party.

Even these show trials, however, could not do away with attempts to reform communism or to modify it to suit each nation's needs. After 1953, there would be some moderate successes: the Poles, for example, were able to prevent further collectivization and to keep open their Catholic churches. On the other hand, Latvia, Lithuania, Estonia, Ukraine, and Belorussia were absorbed into the USSR and subjected to intense Russification. There was little agitation for a return to democracy, in part because

National Communism

In 1944–1947, those targeted by the communists as enemies of the people were real or imagined collaborators with the Nazis, kulaks, monarchists, and liberal nationalists. In the years to follow, Stalin and his henchmen identified another brand of enemy: the Titoists, or national communists. Stalin resented the fact that the communist resistance leader Tito (Josef Broz) had been able to liberate Yugoslavia without Soviet help, and he resented even more Tito's efforts to create a communist state that was not aligned with the USSR. Stalin opted not to invade Tito's rugged terrain, but he was not about to allow similar forms of national communism to arise in his eastern European backyard. How was he to purge the party of men and women who were often heroes of the resistance and

Tito: The Nonaligned Communist Shown here in 1944, together with other members of the communist resistance, the half-Croatian, half-Slovene Josef Broz (Tito; *fourth from the left*) would emerge in 1945 as the leader of communist, but nonaligned, Yugoslavia.

the Nazis or the Soviets had already murdered or deported most of those who supported democracy during the interwar era. Furthermore, communist propaganda convinced many people that democracy was the doorway through which fascism and the Great Depression had entered. Finally, as noted earlier (see Chapter 23), many of eastern Europe's interwar democracies had been corrupt and ineffectual, and who wanted to go back to that? It would take forty years of communist misrule and refusal to reform to make the idea of returning to democracy popular again.

Making Western Europe

Although Stalin had been an indispensable ally, Winston Churchill had never trusted the Russians. Long before the war ended, he realized that the Soviets were positioning themselves to stage communist takeovers in the east, and perhaps in western Europe as well once Germany's defeat was ensured. By 1944, he realized that the Allies would not be able to prevent communist coups in the heart of Red Army–occupied central Europe, but he attempted to forestall similar revolutions in other border regions. He tried, ultimately unsuccessfully, to prevent the Polish communists from claiming to be the rightful heirs to Poland. He and his successors worked to prevent Stalin from seizing control of the Dardanelles Straits from Turkey. They sent money, arms, and men to Greece to stave off a communist victory in a conflict that by 1946 had become a civil war.

THE GREEK CIVIL WAR. Raging from 1946 to 1949, the Greek civil war killed more than 20,000 people and further devastated the Greek economy. The western powers were greatly relieved when the anticommunist nationalists won, keeping Greece, the birthplace of democracy, on the western side of the Iron Curtain. But in Greece, bitterness over the war and fear of a new communist insurgency led to the brutal treatment of former communists for decades, leaving bitterness and division between right- and left-wing parties even after full democracy was restored in 1971.

Other western European governments were also taking action, spying on and arresting leftist radicals whom they feared might stage communist takeovers. But such action required funds and personnel, and many policemen and spies had been compromised by collaborating with the fascists. Some former collaborators were allowed to stay on to provide expertise; but even more than intelligence, European states on the continent needed food and money to stabilize their economies. Although it meant continuing rationing at home, the British supplied food to the West Germans for nearly two years after the war's end in the hopes of keeping communism at bay. But by February 1947, Britain was teetering on the edge of bankruptcy and could no longer spearhead these efforts or provide funds needed to rebuild Europe and save it from radicalization. The torch was passed to Britain's main ally and the other original signatory of the Atlantic Charter, the United States.

THE TRUMAN DOCTRINE. President Harry Truman (1884–1972) cared deeply about Europe's stability and cared even more about containing the spread of communism. In March 1947, responding to the Greek civil war, to Soviet pressures on Turkey, and to inroads communists were making in eastern Europe, he issued a statement thereafter known as the **Truman Doctrine.** It was the policy of the United States, he proclaimed, "to support free people who are resisting attempted subjugation by armed minorities or by outside pressures." By this statement, Truman meant that it would now be U.S. policy to fight attempted communist takeovers. The United States adhered to this policy for many decades, supplying funds and sometimes arms to anticommunist forces all over the globe. For western European governments, the Truman Doctrine meant that the United States would not retreat into isolationism as it had after World War I and would support their efforts to fight communism.

COMPETING ALLIANCES. In 1948, talks between the western Europeans led to an attempt to create a defensive military alliance, but it was eventually concluded that this organization would not be meaningful without the participation of the United States. In 1949, the United States did agree to join, and in 1949, the **North Atlantic Treaty Organization (NATO)** was born. Its original members were the United States, Britain, Belgium, Canada, Denmark, France, Iceland, Italy, Luxembourg, the Netherlands, Norway, and Portugal. Greece and Turkey joined in 1952, West Germany in 1955, and Spain in 1982. By signing the treaty, these nations pledged mutual assistance should another member be attacked. States in the Soviet zone had already been allied informally, but in 1955 the Soviets announced the official founding of the **Warsaw Pact,** which bound Czechoslovakia, Romania, Bulgaria, Albania, Hungary, Poland, East Germany, and the USSR to mutual military assistance (Map 25.2). With the creation of this military alliance, the Iron Curtain had fully descended on Europe.

Remaking the Western European Economy

If the **Eastern bloc** was defined by its state-planned communist economies and its dependence on the Soviet Union, the Western bloc was defined by its dependence on the United States and its commitment to capitalism. The foundations for the revival of postwar capitalism were laid even before the war had ended. In 1944, at an international conference at Bretton Woods, New Hampshire, forty-four countries agreed to establish the International Monetary Fund (IMF), the World Bank, and a system of fixed exchange rates based on the price of gold in U.S. dollars. The stabilization of exchange rates enabled the nations that signed the agreement to engage in international trade without fearing—as so many had in 1930–1933—that their currencies would collapse and their banks fail; all now had hard, convertible currency. In many ways, these agreements established the basis for the unity and, in some places, the prosperity of the capitalist first world over that of the communist second world and the third world, composed of areas lacking the industrial might of either of the Cold War's emerging blocs.

The **Bretton Woods system** would help in the long run, but in 1947–1948, the economic situation on the continent and in Great Britain was grim. Terrified by a communist coup in Czechoslovakia in February 1948, two months later, on April 3, 1948, President Truman signed into law a bill to create the European Recovery Program, better known as the **Marshall Plan,** to deal with Europe's desperate need for economic aid. Named for its chief advocate, U.S. secretary of state George Marshall, the Marshall Plan funneled $13.3 billion into Europe, offering states the capital they needed to rebuild cities and transportation networks and to purchase goods on the world market. The plan, generous to Europe, also benefited the United States, as it helped stabilize capitalist and democratic states that became some of America's best trading partners and diplomatic allies. Marshall Plan aid was officially offered to eastern Europeans as well, but since recipients were required to participate in the western capitalist economy, Stalin refused to allow his satellite states to take the funds. In retaliation, in 1949, the Soviets formed the Council for Mutual Economic Assistance (COMECON), which organized trade and industry in the Eastern bloc but served the interests of the Soviet Union more than those of the member states.

Cold War Battleground: Berlin

The centerpiece of the remaking of eastern and western Europe was Germany, especially its capital city of Berlin. Although the city had been taken by the Red Army and

MAP 25.2 | Cold War Europe, 1945–1949

By the 1950s, most of Europe had been divided into Western and Eastern blocs. Only a few nations remained nonaligned, though many of these leaned heavily in one or another direction. Switzerland, Austria, and Ireland leaned in the western direction; the Soviets kept a close watch on the Finns; and Yugoslavia, though not formally a member of the Warsaw Pact and a communist nation, officially closed its borders to the West. ***Which European nations were members of NATO in 1955? Which nations opted for nonaligned status?***

lay in eastern Germany, well inside the Soviet zone of occupation, the Allies had insisted that Berlin also be divided into zones of occupation, one for each of the four official victors (Britain, France, the USSR, and the United States; see inset Map 25.1). For a time, movement between zones was largely unregulated, allowing approximately one million Germans to leave the Soviet zone for the western one between mid-1945 and mid-1946. But tensions over reparations mounted; the Soviets insisted on extracting more booty, while the Allies maintained that building a strong German economy was essential to Europe's recovery. Both sides erected new barriers and checkpoints between the zones.

By the spring of 1948, the western Allies had had enough of communist advances in central Europe and decided to act. On June 1, 1948, they announced plans to establish an independent western German state, and on June 21, they issued a new currency—the Deutschmark—for the planned state. On June 23, the Soviets countered the West's new deutsche mark with the Klebemark—old Nazi-era bills with new stamps hastily glued to the top—and attempted to make the Klebemark the currency for all Berlin. When the military government in West Berlin balked, the Soviets cut the rail lines linking West Berlin to West Germany and blocked the roads that western drivers had used to provision the city. The Soviets' idea was to hold what would soon be a starving West Berlin hostage until the Allies capitulated to their plans, which included taking more reparations and integrating the whole of Hitler's capital city into a now virtually separate East German state.

Unwilling to cede Berlin to Soviet control, the Allies began an airlift to supply food and medical supplies to West Berlin. Over the next year, Allied airmen flew 2.3 million tons of food into the western part of the city through Tempelhof Airport. Their efforts were not in vain. In May 1949, the Soviets wearied of the blockade and again allowed western trains and trucks to roll into the city. The issues that provoked the currency conflict and the airlift had not been resolved, but neither side wanted to solve the German question through renewed warfare. Thus, in May 1949, just after the lifting of the blockade, new borders were drawn, dividing Germany into two mutually hostile sovereign states and Berlin into two mutually hostile cities.

The Making of Two Germanys

In 1949, the Allied-occupied zones joined together to form the Federal Republic of Germany (FRG) in the West. The new democratic state, with a population of 49 million, established its capital in the Rhineland city of Bonn. Unlike the Weimar Republic, the new Federal Republic stuck with one leading party—the Christian Democratic Union (CDU)—and one chancellor—Konrad Adenauer—for a long time. Adenauer, the Catholic former mayor of Cologne and leader of the conservative CDU, held office from 1949 until his retirement, at age eighty-seven, in 1963. Also in 1949, Germany's Soviet-occupied regions formed the smaller German Democratic Republic (GDR), with 17 million inhabitants. The GDR proclaimed itself a socialist republic and built a new Palace of the Republic on the main square in Berlin where the emperor's palace had once stood. The man who took the helm of the GDR, Walter Ulbricht, was definitely Stalin's man. He quickly nationalized East German industry and readily agreed to purge from governance those whom Stalin considered dangerous elements.

Even after the founding of the FRG and the GDR, German borders were

CHRONOLOGY	The Making of Two Germanys
DATE	**EVENT**
1945	Germany defeated, divided into four occupied zones
1946	British and American zones merged
1947	Marshall Plan announced
1948	Western allies introduce the deutsche mark for western zones
1948–1949	Berlin airlift
1949	May: Federal Republic of Germany (West Germany) established
	October: German Democratic Republic (East Germany) established

relatively fluid, so much so that as many as three million East Germans, especially skilled workers and young people, left for the West as the communist regime settled in to stay. Eventually, however, the East Germans grew concerned about what increasingly amounted to a brain drain. In May 1952, Ulbricht received permission from Moscow to close the border between East and West Germany, although crossing the border in Berlin remained quite easy until 1961 when, during the night of August 12, the Soviets began building a wall all around the city's western zone. They claimed the wall was to keep western spies *out*, but in reality the wall—and the landmines, barbed wire, guards, and dogs that protected it—was meant to keep

Living with the Berlin Wall In this 1962 photo, a woman and her boyfriend stand on the western side of the wall in order to shout greetings to the woman's mother, now unable to leave East Berlin.

easterners *in.* Suddenly, families, streets, and even waterways were divided, as a real, cement and steel curtain descended, creating the most iconic and telling symbol of the Cold War.

Eastern Europe after Stalin: The Thaw—and Its Limits

In March 1953, an event that many had longed for occurred: Joseph Stalin died. In his last years, Stalin had

> **How did Stalin's death affect politics in the Soviet bloc?**

become increasingly doctrinaire, paranoid about opposition to his regime, and determined to extend his communist empire. Few were sorry to see him go—even many Party members felt he had gone too far in his persecutions. Thus, Stalin's death ushered in a thaw in Cold War politics and Soviet policy. The Soviet leadership immediately announced the release of some 1.2 million inmates from the gulags (though at least a million remained imprisoned). Hopes soared throughout the Soviet zone that the time had come for liberalization and perhaps for local leaders to obtain autonomous decision-making powers.

East Berliners were the first to react to news of Stalin's death—which was accompanied by an announcement that taxes, prices, and work quotas were going up. On June 16, disgruntled workers at a hospital construction site put down their tools and took to the streets. Soon many other East Berliners joined them, and strikes and rallies spread throughout East Germany. Perhaps as many as 400,000 workers joined the action, and calls went out for free elections as well as a reduction in production quotas. But the Russians were enraged by these protests, and by June 17, Soviet troops had been called in to restore order. Thousands of Germans were arrested, and at least 125 ringleaders were summarily executed. It was the first popular demand for reform in Soviet-dominated eastern Europe, and it was crushed.

Khrushchev and the Hungarian Uprising of 1956

Hope for reform revived in late February 1956, when Nikita Khrushchev, the new first secretary of the Communist Party, delivered a remarkable speech to the 20th Congress of the Communist Party of the Soviet Union. Khrushchev (1894–1971) was a staunch communist who had played important roles in Stalin's regime, but in his speech he acknowledged that Stalin had substituted a false "cult of personality" for

the true principles of the Russian Revolution. Contrasting Stalin to Lenin, Khrushchev condemned Stalin's purges and gave his audience an inkling of the scale of Stalin's persecutions. Although only elite party members were supposed to hear this speech, its contents quickly leaked out and spread throughout the communist bloc. Emboldened by the promise of more openness, workers in the Polish city of Poznán took to the streets, demanding better housing and food and higher wages. Polish party members insisted that Władysław Gomułka be restored to power, and the Russians consented. War was narrowly averted when Gomułka promised not to abandon communism or to take Poland out of the Warsaw Pact, and the Soviets agreed to increase wages, to free some 35,000 Polish political prisoners, and to allow Poland some economic independence.

Other Eastern bloc states, however, did not get off so lightly. In Budapest, demonstrations in support of Gomułka in October 1956 evolved into demands for reform in Hungary as well. The Hungarians wanted to return their own purged national communist, Imre Nagy (1896–1958), to power. Protests escalated after agitators pulled down the huge statue of Stalin in central Budapest. The Hungarian political police fired on the crowd, killing students and workers. In retaliation, protestors stormed police headquarters, killing everyone inside. Seeming to follow the Polish model, Khrushchev and the Soviets allowed Nagy to return to power, but balked when he announced that the Hungarians were planning to leave the Warsaw Pact. On November 4, the NKVD arrested Nagy and his

Hungary Rebels, 1956 The most powerfully symbolic act of the 1956 Hungarian Uprising was the toppling of the gigantic statue of Stalin in front of the National Theater in Budapest. Hungarians covered the statue with graffiti (including a prominent "W.C." for "water closet" or toilet, on Stalin's face), and then smashed it to bits. Only Stalin's boots were left—and can still be seen at an open-air museum of communist architecture outside of Budapest.

government and deported them to Romania, where they were imprisoned for more than a year, then tried and executed. In the meantime, Russian tanks roared into Budapest and crushed the remainder of the revolt with great severity. A new round of political purges followed, costing Hungary many lives, and sending 200,000 exiles fleeing across the Austrian border, bringing with them reports of Soviet terror that did much to discredit Khrushchev's "thaw" and communism in the West.

Communist Successes

The late 1950s brought some more hopeful news for supporters and those sympathetic to the communist worldview. In 1957, the Soviets launched into space *Sputnik,* the world's first artificial orbiting satellite; this achievement produced much boasting in the Eastern bloc and much concern in the West. The United States rushed to launch its own satellite, *Explorer I,* in January 1958 and later that year founded the National Aeronautics and Space Administration (NASA) to oversee the nation's civilian space program. The U.S. government poured money into programs to train scientists and engineers who could help the capitalist world win what came to be known as the space race. The Soviets managed to put the first man into outer space in 1961, but in 1969 the United States became the first and to date the only nation to plant its flag on the moon.

Communism itself enjoyed some major successes in the postwar era, beginning with the Chinese Revolution of 1949. Though Stalin and the Chinese communist leader Mao Zedong (1893–1976) disagreed about many things, having to contain a major communist threat in East Asia made life difficult for NATO and the western allies. Fidel Castro's communist coup in Cuba in 1959 and his alliance with the Soviets in 1961 gave the United States, in particular, even more reason to worry. Cuba was, after all, far closer to the United States than was Hungary or Poland. Fears escalated in October 1962 with the discovery that the Soviet Union was building bases on Cuba to house nuclear missiles that had the capacity to strike the United States. President John F. Kennedy (1917–1963) demanded that Khrushchev destroy the bases and remove the weapons. After a tense standoff, Khrushchev agreed, and Kennedy promised not to invade Cuba and to deactivate some of the missiles the United States had stationed in Turkey, within striking distance of the USSR. The Cuban missile crisis brought the world as close to nuclear war as it has ever come and illustrates once again the difference that individuals make in history. Had the negotiators been Stalin and Churchill, the outcome might have been a much more devastating one.

The Soviets cultivated allies in North Korea, Latin America, and the Middle East, but the enormous increase

The Great "Kitchen Debate" In 1959, Soviet premier Nikita Khrushchev (*center, left*) and U.S. vice president Richard Nixon (*center, right*) together visited an exhibit in Moscow meant to represent the typical American home. While Nixon tried to convince Khrushchev that capitalist furnishings made for more comfort and relieved the burdens of housewives, Khrushchev claimed that American goods were shoddily made and obtainable only by the rich. The "Kitchen Debate" was shown on both American and Soviet TV (though in the latter case, only late at night, and carefully edited).

in Soviet oil production and export in the 1950s and 1960s was perhaps of greater long-term importance to the endurance of Stalin's empire. Oil allowed the Soviet Union not only to become energy independent but also to make eastern Europeans dependent for their energy needs on the Soviets. With the profits from oil, the Soviets could retain their huge and costly army and provide civilians with their version of a social safety net and some consumer goods; without these profits, communism might have collapsed much earlier. For several decades, Soviet space programs and oil income allowed communists to claim they were building a stronger, healthier, more modern and just society than the one being produced in western Europe—though Soviet propagandists also took care to deny their citizens access to western newspapers, magazines, films, and radio and TV programs, so that citizens could not judge for themselves.

More goods and more propaganda helped stabilize communism in the 1950s and 1960s, but the Soviet bloc was never completely quiet. Periodic protests over labor and food were put down with brute force, and dissidents were perpetually silenced by censorship, imprisonment, or bribery. Many still longed for reform, but those outside the party leadership were powerless to engineer real change. People made do and learned to work, live, and raise families; some chose to collaborate with the system and some to resist it, but their choices were limited by the repressive one-party dictatorships under which they lived.

The Prague Spring

A major reform movement gathered steam in 1968 in Czechoslovakia when Alexander Dubček (1921–1992) came to power. Dubček became first secretary of the Czechoslovakian Communist Party in January 1968, and in April instituted a series of reforms that aimed at decentralizing and reorienting Czechoslovakia's underperforming industrial economy and offering new freedoms of speech and the press. Without criticizing Soviet-style communism, Dubček suggested that it was time for his state to move toward a style of government he called "socialism with a human face." His reforms unleashed a literary renaissance. Writers published plays and poems they had kept in secret drawers for many years; students founded newspapers and discussion groups and sought to import some of the 1960s fashion, music, and generational rhetoric popular on the western side of the Iron Curtain.

The Prague Spring On August 21, 1968, Warsaw Pact tanks rolled into Prague to end the period of Czech liberalization known as the Prague Spring.

Culture and criticism flourished during the spring and summer of 1968. Initially, the Soviets limited themselves to pressuring Dubček and his fellow communists from behind the scenes, but as the summer ended, they tired of negotiating. On August 21, an army of 200,000 Eastern bloc soldiers marched on Prague. Dubček was arrested, but allowed to remain in office until April 1969, when he was replaced with the hard-liner Gustav Husák. News and images depicting Czech students' largely passive resistance to the tanks and occupying forces caused many western governments, and even some communist leaders, to protest Soviet actions, but there would be no intervention in support of the Czechoslovakian dissidents. Some 300,000 Czechs risked being shot by armed border guards to leave the country. In despair at Russia's actions, one student, Jan Palach, set himself on fire in Prague's central Wenceslaus Square. Although his action accomplished nothing in the short run, in the longer term, Palach's act of defiance would remind his countrymen of those who had fought, suffered, and died for reform.

Reform was certainly not what the Czechs or other eastern Europeans got in the wake of the uprising known as the Prague Spring. Although fewer Czechs were murdered in 1968 than Hungarians in 1956, in Czechoslovakia the Soviets implemented a more thorough-going purge of civil society. Thousands were arrested and the entire intellectual elite, from accountants to zoologists, was purged of possible renegades and traitors. These highly skilled and educated individuals were sent to sweep out schoolrooms or to move dirt with tractors. Instead of modernizing the economy and preparing it for the kind of consumer revolution going on in the West, the Soviets froze the Czech economy in its industrial backwardness and eliminated a whole generation of skilled experts who were needed to run the nation's hospitals, schools, factories, and agricultural institutions. The playwright and leading dissident Václav Havel (1936–2011) was compelled to work in a brewery.

For many of those who had continued to hope for reform within the communist bloc, the Soviet crackdown in 1968 was a powerful wake-up call. Despite the occasional appearance of a Nagy, a Dubček, or a Khrushchev, Soviet communism simply would not allow reform. It had shown time after time that it had no human face. Although protests against its inhumane and economically disastrous policies could not be made openly, after 1968 many of those who wanted change now sought to subvert the system as a whole, or to "live in truth" as was Havel's motto, to counteract the party's systematic lies. The regimes' opponents began to talk about human rights and individual liberties, topics that could never be addressed within a socialist system.

The Brezhnev Era

In the fall of 1968, as the Soviets completed their crackdown in Czechoslovakia, the Soviet general secretary of the Communist Party, Leonid Brezhnev, defended their actions in a policy statement thereafter known as the **Brezhnev Doctrine.** According to Brezhnev, the movement of any socialist state in capitalist directions was "the common problem and concern of all socialist countries." The USSR's intervention in Czechoslovakia, Hungary, and East Germany to prevent deviation from its idea of communism, he was saying, was justified and would be repeated should any other states attempt economic or political reforms on their own. For eastern Europeans, this was a clear warning: no one was free to formulate their own versions of communist modernization.

In practice, this meant that the only forms of modernization implemented in eastern Europe were those developed by aging Soviet economic planners. For these men, modernization meant increasing the output of state-directed heavy industry. In the 1960s and early 1970s, some new attention was given to providing consumers with basic goods, such as housing and food, but in no way could the Soviet system offer the variety or quality of consumer goods available in western Europe. To make things worse, communist hard-liners like Brezhnev, who served as Soviet general secretary from 1964 until his death in 1982, purged intellectuals who might have helped build modern service and information technologies. Instead, Brezhnev relied on "apparatchiks," party-member bureaucrats who carried out their leaders' orders, no matter how absurd or ruthless, and in return were rewarded with the best apartments, access to western luxury goods, and the ability to travel outside the Eastern bloc.

Until the mid-1970s, the Soviet economy continued to grow, but Brezhnev's refusal to allow economic reforms began to take a toll. Gains in public health were offset by rising alcoholism and rising incidences of asthma and cancer, the latter two the result of environmental degradation. Brezhnev himself suffered several strokes and heart attacks, which reduced his working time and increased his dependence on drugs. The rest of his advisors were also over seventy, out of touch with civilians, and uninterested in their welfare. On the regime's lower levels, even the apparatchiks grew cynical about the system and began to exploit it. They found it increasingly easy to get away with corrupt practices as Brezhnev and his Politburo grew infirm and out of touch. Repression of dissidents continued, but usually now consisted of removing people from their jobs and harassing them, rather than killing them, as had been the case in Stalin's day. This allowed some critics, such as Havel, to emerge as moral models, and a few others, such as Lech Wałęsa (b. 1943) in Poland, to begin to build democratic movements that would eventually sweep away the communist regimes.

Cracking Down on Poland

In the summer of 1980, Polish workers at the Lenin Shipyard in Gdansk went on strike to protest rising food prices and to demand the right to organize a non-communist trade union. Polish officials refused permission to create a trade union but the workers, led by the electrician Lech Wałęsa, formed one secretly and named it **Solidarity.**

Soon Solidarity became a dissident movement as well, its members pressing for many of the same reforms the Czechs had wanted during the Prague Spring. Within a year, the union had 11 million members.

In December 1981, Polish prime minister Wojciech Jaruzelski (b. 1923), who had a previous history of dealing harshly with protestors, declared martial law, a tactic, he later claimed, to preempt a Russian crackdown. He was following the logic of the Brezhnev Doctrine, though recent research seems to suggest that by 1981 Brezhnev's government might have been too decrepit and too absorbed with the invasion of Afghanistan, to have sent tanks into Poland. In any event, Jaruzelski's crackdown sent some 10,000 Solidarity members to jail, but could not destroy the movement in the long run.

Western Europe: The New Prosperity

One power or one person did not dominate western Europe in the way that eastern Europe was dominated by the Soviet Union and Soviet premiers such as Stalin and Brezhnev, but western leaders were well aware of their military and economic dependence on the United States. Knowing that the U.S. military arsenal, which included nuclear weapons, defended them, western European states could essentially disarm, saving themselves money and sparing themselves the trouble of having to balance power on the continent. International institutions, such as NATO, the United Nations, and the World Bank, provided their own sorts of safety nets, assuring citizens that cross-border invasions would not be permitted, and that action would be taken to address major economic crises.

What factors accounted for western Europe's relatively swift recovery from WWII?

The Baby Boom

In the West, and to a lesser extent in the Eastern bloc, a postwar baby boom produced a huge rise in the European population, which increased from 264 million in 1940 to 320 million people by the early 1970s. This population explosion reduced the median age across the continent such that by 1960, more than one-third of the Finns, Dutch, and French were less than twenty years old. Death rates for both children and adults were also declining, thanks to the long peace, better nutrition, expanded access to medical care, the increasing use of antibiotic medicines, and childhood immunizations. This baby-boom generation of Europeans would have better access to education, energy, health care, jobs, mass transportation, and healthy food and water than any generation of Europeans before them. They would question many of their parents' conventions and beliefs, but they would also benefit greatly from the postwar world their parents built.

The baby boom, together with western Europeans' new prosperity, had significant cultural effects. Middle- and even lower-middle-class families could afford to keep their children out of the workforce into the late teenage years, and many more young people went to college. France had 150,000 university students in 1956; by 1968, this number swelled to 605,000. Young people also had more disposable income of their own to spend on clothes, music, and books of their own choosing. Heavily influenced by cultural developments in the United States, European teenagers developed a taste for rock 'n' roll and for blue jeans, much to the horror of their parents. But some, too, became deeply critical of America's role in the world, including its involvement in Vietnam and its stationing of nuclear missiles in western Europe. Although most baby boomers would not enjoy the Cold War, they would in fact have more freedom of choice and of expression than any European generation of the past.

The Welfare State Comes of Age

After the war, most western European states allowed voters to select their governments and to belong to a wide range of parties. In West Germany, citizens elected the conservative Konrad Adenauer to guide them through the rebuilding process. In France and Britain, left-wing governments took power directly after the war, but soon gave way to conservatives. In Great Britain, Winston Churchill returned for a new term as prime minister in 1951, serving until 1955. A series of other conservatives followed him until the ascension of the Labour deputy Harold Wilson in 1964. In France, war hero Charles de Gaulle returned to power in January 1959 and remained in office until 1969.

Determined to prevent another Great Depression, postwar governments in West Germany, Britain, and France, as well as in Austria, the Netherlands, and the Scandinavian countries, completed an evolution begun after World War I toward the founding of welfare states. Socialism's deep roots and continuing strength in Europe shaped a different sort of outlook on capitalism than was prevalent in the United States. Both conservatives and democratic socialists agreed to impose much higher rates of progressive taxation to finance new social welfare initiatives, such as guaranteed unemployment benefits, pensions, paid vacations, maternity leave, and subsidies to families with children. National health systems were created to provide free health services to all citizens, and states increased their support for museums, opera houses, and television and radio broadcasting in order to make culture, too, more widely accessible. Labor unions gained new powers to bargain for higher wages and better conditions.

In the postwar era, Europeans adopted a new conception of what it meant to be a citizen, one that underscored human rights rather than obligations to defend the state in times of war. In addition to voting rights, citizens were also entitled to decent health care and education, pensions for those injured in wars or on the job, and af-

fordable housing, food, transportation and information. The system in which these welfare states arose has been described as a **social market economy,** that is, a capitalist market cushioned by a social safety net.

By 1957, governments were spending four times more for social services than they had in 1930 and were taking over roles traditionally played by the clergy: performing marriages, and educating young children. For the first time, older Europeans could count on government-subsidized pensions and health care, and the unemployed were kept from starvation. Although disparities in income remained, the social question—how the better-off can prevent their fellow citizens from dying of poverty—seemed to have been answered.

Economic Integration and Prosperity

Movement toward western European economic integration laid another foundation for western prosperity. In 1950, French foreign minister Robert Schumann recognized that for France and the other western countries to prosper, they would need to move past the postwar desire to punish the Germans. In geopolitical terms, West Germany was vital to stopping the spread of communism; in economic terms, that region had always been vital to the continent's prosperity. Thus, Schumann pushed the French and other neighboring governments to reach out to the Germans and to form a common market in commodities desperately needed in the postwar period, coal and steel. The result was the European Coal and Steel Community (ECSC), composed of France, West Germany, the Netherlands, Belgium, Luxembourg, and Italy. The ECSC proved to be a trial run for much more extensive European economic cooperation. Six years later these same six nations signed the Treaty of Rome, which created the **European Economic Community (EEC),** often called the European Common Market.

The EEC dismantled customs barriers and agreed upon a common agricultural policy, guaranteeing that farmers in all six member nations would be paid the same amount for their produce. The EEC states hoped that linking their economies would end the threat of war on the European continent, create new efficiencies, and allow Europe to compete with the United States on the world market. This was an exclusive club, but nations that kept their budget deficits below 3 percent of gross domestic product could apply for entry.

The EEC's agricultural policy, which subsidized farm production as never before, generated a second agricultural revolution in the western European countryside, one of even greater magnitude than the one surveyed in Chapter 15. The use of new machinery, fertilizers, and pesticides resulted in a huge leap in agricultural productivity and a declining need for laborers on the land. In Italy, for example, 40 percent of the workforce was still employed on farms as late as 1950. Even in West Germany and France, nearly one person in four still worked the land. By 1977, only 16 percent of Italians, 7 percent of Germans, and

10 percent of Frenchmen were employed in agriculture. Europe had ceased to be a continent of farmers.

In northern Europe in particular, laborers no longer needed on the land streamed into the cities, where they found jobs in industry or in the growing service sector. Industrial production doubled between 1948 and 1951, and doubled again by 1960. Europe's exports surged, and prices for imported food and raw materials, mostly from the third world, fell. Real wages rose, and so many jobs were created that by the early 1960s Europe's northern states enjoyed more or less full employment. With their newfound prosperity, most people were now able to afford modern conveniences: indoor plumbing, refrigerators, and TV sets. Record numbers of people bought their first cars.

Southern Europe

Progress toward both affluence and democracy was slower in southern Europe. Despite its EEC member status, Italy, for example, lagged economically behind its neighbors to the north and suffered from political instability as governments rose and fell in rapid succession. Southern Italy remained largely rural, whereas northern Italians crowded into the cities of Milan and Turin. In 1960, when nearly all Germans, Brits, and Norwegians had water piped into their homes, that service was available to less than 40 percent of Italians and Greeks. Wages remained lower and fewer women worked outside the home in southern Europe.

Democracy, too, came later to this region than to northern Europe. In Spain, the military dictator Francisco Franco continued to reign until his death in November 1975—and the Spanish economy continued to lag behind the economies of countries north of the Pyrenees, though efforts were made at economic liberalization. In Portugal, the authoritarian Antonio Salazar held power from 1936 until he was removed by an only slightly less reactionary group of men in 1968; finally, a revolution led by the military catalyzed a transition to democracy in 1974. With western backing, the conservatives got the upper hand in the Greek civil war of 1945–1949, yet long afterward, Greece remained politically fragmented and economically underdeveloped. Elections scheduled for 1967 seemed likely to bring in a new, left-leaning government—but they never took place. Instead, a cadre of passionately anti-communist army officers staged a coup and installed a military dictatorship that lasted until 1974.

Guest Workers

The postwar agricultural revolution that transformed northern and western Europe came more slowly to central and southeastern Europe, where many people still lived on the land and many towns still lacked paved roads. Southern Europe, in particular, remained mostly rural and poor. Southerners knew, though, that better-paying jobs were to be found to the north, so many of them left

poorer regions, such as Kalamata, Greece, or Sardinia in southern Italy, or Alentejo in rural Portugal, to seek opportunity elsewhere. They either resettled in crowded cities in their own states, such as Athens, Milan, and Lisbon, or moved to other states in northern Europe. Foreshadowing a much larger wave of former colonial subjects streaming to Europe's cities, some 500,000 Afro-Caribbean immigrants moved to England in the 1950s. Those who went north largely took jobs in the construction sector, or as janitors, miners, cooks, or babysitters. From the first, these darker-skinned Europeans were considered guest workers and kept in low-paying, unskilled jobs; they were expected to return to their old homes, even after many years of guest work in their new ones.

By the late 1960s, guest workers from Turkey and from Europe's former colonies in Africa joined the migration to northern Europe. Europe needed inexpensive laborers and tolerated their cultural differences, but did not welcome them warmly and occasionally subjected them to racist abuse or violence. The migrants tended to live in inexpensive suburbs of Paris, Berlin, London, and other cities and were not offered citizenship. By the early 1970s, there were roughly 1.5 million Turkish, Italian, and Yugoslavian workers living in West Germany. Most of them sent money home, but settled in to stay. With the ending of European imperial rule in Asia, Africa, and the Middle East, many Pakistanis, Indonesians, Algerians, and West Africans also set sail for France, England, and the Netherlands in the hopes of finding secure employment. In general, those with darker skins and those who retained their Islamic beliefs assimilated less well into the population than did southern Europeans. Incidents of racial violence, however, remained relatively rare in Europe, even as postcolonial wars raged throughout the rest of the world.

The End of European Imperialism

In western Europe, new economic prosperity and new safety nets created relative stability and social peace throughout the 1950s and early 1960s. But, as usual, these

Why did 1945 mark the beginning of the end of European empires overseas?

costly programs were not offered in the West's colonial territories. Those territories, too, had become increasingly difficult and expensive to manage as modernization proceeded and as colonial citizens began to demand more rights. Many Indians, South Asians, and Africans had sacrificed and suffered during World War II and expected to be rewarded at least with independence after the war. Some leaders, such as Vietnam's Ho Chi Minh (see Chapter 23), had grown tired of waiting for reforms and sought to spark communist revolutions.

The European powers had become used to exploiting their colonies and were initially reluctant to give up the

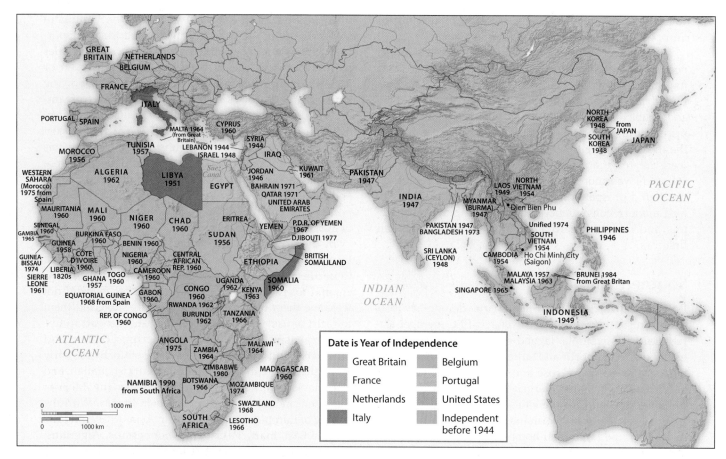

MAP 25.3 | **Decolonization after World War II**

In the decades after 1945, European colonialism experienced a collapse, strikingly apparent on this map. *Which nations achieved independence immediately after World War II (between 1945 and 1950), and which had to wait an additional twenty or more years?*

prestige, raw materials, and cheap labor these territories brought them. But they soon discovered that the costs of military engagement were more than their taxpayers were willing to sustain, and the costs of building modern infrastructure in the colonies were prohibitive. Thus, a series of developments took place that looked something like imperialism's "third wave" in reverse, as nations across Asia, the Middle East, and Africa sought to free themselves from European rule (Map 25.3). In some cases, the United States, fearing the further spread of communism, intervened in the process, as did the Russians and after 1949 the Chinese communists, hoping for the opposite outcome. As in the period of hyperimperialism, too, most Europeans enjoyed peace and increasing prosperity while their Cold War overlords took over the fighting, and in the colonial world, "hot" wars continued to rage.

Decolonization in Asia and the Middle East

As the war came to a close, Winston Churchill moved to reestablish British rule over Britain's colonies in Asia and the Middle East, not realizing the depth of local hostility to imperial rule. The French, too, hoped to regain colonies occupied by Japan in Indochina, and the Dutch spent

four fruitless years (1945–1949) trying to keep Indonesia from obtaining its independence. But World War II had weakened the European states, and strengthened the desire of colonial subjects to obtain independence—even at the cost of more violence.

INDIA AND PAKISTAN. Indians, on the whole, had remained loyal to Britain during the war, but leaders such as Mohandas Gandhi (1869–1948) took the opportunity to press for independence. In 1942, Gandhi launched the Quit India movement, hoping to force the British to grant India independence immediately. Churchill, who had no intention of giving up "the jewel in the crown," offended Indian and world opinion by jailing many members of Quit India, including Gandhi. Some were killed or injured by police, who used public floggings to subdue protestors. Although the Muslim leader Muhammad Ali Jinnah (1876–1948) did not join Quit India, he too was preparing for a British pullout. At first Jinnah had envisioned a joint Muslim-Hindu nation, but by the 1940s he was certain that India's minority Muslim population needed its own independent state.

As the war came to a close, mass protests against the reimposition of British rule convulsed the subcontinent. Churchill might have been willing to make the massive

Jawaharlal Nehru At this October 1947 rally, Nehru, the prime minister of the newly independent state of India, begged for an end to factional strife between Muslims and Hindus.

sacrifice of blood and treasure needed to subdue the opposition, but his successor Clement Attlee (1883–1967) was not. Attlee pulled British officials and troops out, agreeing, as he did so, to the creation of a separate Muslim state. The drawing of borders between this Muslim-dominated state (Pakistan) and India, in which Hindus formed the majority, led to massive population exchanges and communal violence in which at least a quarter of a million people died. Civil war in Pakistan resulted in the creation of a third independent state, Bangladesh, in 1971.

PALESTINE. The British Mandate in Palestine, established after World War I, had awkwardly balanced the needs and desires of Zionist Jews and local Palestinian Christians and Arabs. The Jews had long detested British limits on the number of Jews allowed to settle in the Mandate and were dismayed when the British continued these limitations even as Jewish survivors of the Holocaust begged to be allowed to emigrate. By 1945, the Zionists also believed that the time had come for the promise made in the Balfour Declaration of 1917, for the creation of a Jewish state, to be realized. But the Arabs of Palestine also believed that they had earned the right to independent statehood. Pressed from both sides, Britain announced in 1947 that it would return the Mandate to the United Nations in the hopes that this international body could work out a solution. The United Nations developed a plan to create two separate states, but before the plan could go into effect, Palestine descended into civil war between Zionists and Arabs, the latter backed by the other Muslim states in the region.

The Arab-Israeli War ended in 1949 with a peace favorable to the Israelis. As Jews from Europe poured into the new state of Israel, hundreds of thousands of Palestinians fled their homes; they and their descendants still live in refugee camps today. The city of Jerusalem was divided between Israel and Jordan until 1967, when, in what became known as the Six-Day War, the Israelis preempted an attack planned by the Arab nations and succeeded in claiming the West Bank of the Jordan River, the Sinai, the Golan Heights, and East Jerusalem. This postcolonial territory remains hotly contested today.

SOUTHEAST ASIA. In 1945, as the Japanese army withdrew from the French colony of Vietnam, the communist leader Ho Chi Minh proclaimed himself head of an independent Democratic Republic of Vietnam. As the French refused to recognize his government, he formed an army and in 1950 he received backing from China, which had just become a communist state. To fight Ho Chi Minh's communist insurgency, centered in North Vietnam, the French expended huge sums and many men. In 1954, they suffered an embarrassing setback at Dien Bien Phu, near Vietnam's border with Laos, after which they withdrew from Indochina, giving North Vietnam to the communists. In 1961, fearing that the whole region would fall into communist hands, American forces stepped in and again invested much blood and treasure in battling the insurgency. In 1973, the Americans too pulled out of Vietnam, humbling those who had believed the United States could contain communism wherever it threatened across the globe.

Two years later, the communists took the Vietnamese capital of Saigon, renaming it Ho Chi Minh City. After the fall of Saigon, communism spread throughout the region, to Laos and to Cambodia, where the ruthless Pol Pot (1925–1998) imposed Stalinist collectivization and terror. What had begun as an anticolonial struggle had become one of the most protracted, painful, and bloody conflicts of the Cold War.

KOREA. At the same time that Vietnam was descending into ideological civil war, Korea was facing new tensions. At the war's end, Korea, once a Japanese holding, had been occupied in the north, to the thirty-eighth parallel, by the Soviet Union, and in the south by the United States. Conflicts between the sectors grew deeper until in June 1950, soldiers from the communist North invaded the South. The United Nations condemned the attack and sent forces, under the command of the Pacific war hero General Douglas MacArthur (1880–1964), to repulse the attack. MacArthur did more. Pursuing the North Koreans, he pushed far beyond the thirty-eighth parallel. This enraged the Chinese, who wanted to see their North Korean comrades victorious, and they launched a counteroffensive, forcing the UN–South Korean army back to its starting place. The armistice, signed in 1953, made the thirty-eighth parallel the border between two mutually hostile new states and provided for a demilitarized zone

Encountering the Other in Vietnam and Afghanistan

In 1945, the Allies, using atomic bombs and massed tanks, had just won the bloodiest and most technologically advanced war in history. Yet, in the postwar era, Vietnam and Afghanistan managed to resist conquest by the world's superpowers, the Vietnamese withstanding the French and the Americans, and the Afghans holding out against the Soviets. In both cases, the conflicts dragged on much longer than expected, involving casualties that civilians at home increasingly found senseless and intolerable. In the end, both superpowers had to bow out, their self-confidence deeply damaged—and their former battle-fronts in chaos.

The Vietnam conflict shocked American troops and Americans at home. Americans were still rather inexperienced in colonial warfare, which Europeans had learned was always irregular, brutal, and difficult to bring to a conclusion. Americans were unfamiliar with the Vietnamese terrain and climate, while their opponents knew in detail how to use local resources and geography to their advantage. Using modern technology and armaments to wage the war, the Americans ended up killing civilians and blackening their reputation for fighting only good wars, but still could not isolate and destroy their opponents.

Vietnam vexed American troops and observers for a number of reasons. It was frustrating because superior weaponry could not win it and because those who gave aid and comfort to the communists, especially the Chinese, did not enter the war directly and so could not be attacked. The conflict in Vietnam was also a civil war, with many Vietnamese supporting the communists; it was not a clear case of fighting to prevent "subjugation by armed minorities or by outside pressures," as the Truman Doctrine stipulated. The longer the Americans were in the war, the less they seemed likely to win either the actual or ideological war, and the more Americans opposed sending young men to fight and die in what was increasingly seen as a quagmire. America's long engagement in Vietnam and its use of technology such as cluster bombs, napalm, and armed helicopters against guerrilla fighters and civilians convinced much of the colonial world that the United States was just another brutal imperialist power.

Soviet involvement in Afghanistan after 1979 was born of the same sort of pride—and rewarded with the same sort of humiliation. Leonid Brezhnev and his tiny cadre of elderly communists launched this quasi-colonial war, evidently believing that they could invade quickly and set up a puppet government to provide a base for further communist activity in the region. The Afghans, however, mounted a guerrilla resistance, killing more than two thousand Soviet soldiers a year and costing the USSR vast sums of resources. Again, technology and modern armaments failed to subdue a guerrilla army fighting on its own terrain. The United States secretly supplied resistance fighters, some of whom were nationalists while others were radical Islamists. Soviet censorship initially prevented citizens from protesting the unnecessary and bloody war, but by the mid-1980s, mothers of fallen or wounded soldiers began to voice their outrage at this Soviet quagmire.

Mikhail Gorbachev succeeded in pulling troops out of Afghanistan in 1989, but the Soviet reformer could not repair the damage done to the USSR's finances, to its citizens' confidence in the government's actions, and to its position in the world. Afghanistan descended into chaotic ethnic conflict, eventually falling into the hands of the Islamist Taliban in the mid-1990s.

QUESTIONS | *Why did the United States and the USSR find these wars so frustrating? Why, in the end, did these superpowers opt to retreat?*

Getting Out of Vietnam In this April 1975 photo, a U.S. cargo helicopter attempts to supply the United States' South Vietnamese allies. Afraid of being abandoned, South Vietnamese civilians attempted to climb aboard the helicopter and flee what now seemed to be a lost cause.

(DMZ) between them, a no-man's-land 160 miles long and about 2.5 miles wide. Korea remains divided there to this day, and the Korean DMZ still exists. There one can see the Cold War, in all its seriousness and with all its human consequences, being played out in microcosm.

Decolonization in Africa

In Africa, too, decolonization brought conflict. In the case of Egypt, it also called into being what became known as the nonaligned movement, something that appealed greatly to states not wishing to belong to either the western capitalist or the Soviet communist bloc. In 1955, a conference of independent African and Asian states in Bandung, Indonesia, celebrated the idea of nonalignment, inspiring states to choose not to make formal alliances with the first world (America and western Europe) or with the second world (the Soviet bloc), but to form their own, autonomous **Third World.** If African states succeeded in gaining political independence, however, achieving economic independence, and stability, would prove much more difficult.

THE SUEZ CRISIS AND THE RISE OF THE NON-ALIGNED MOVEMENT.
After he seized power in 1952, Egyptian president Gamal Abdel Nasser (1918–1970) made it clear that he was neither a communist nor a Muslim extremist nor a friend of the western colonial powers. He created a single-party authoritarian state based on Arab and Egyptian nationalism and insisted on its nonaligned status. An admirer of Tito in Yugoslavia, Nasser bitterly resented both blocs' attempts to use the rest of the world to fight their wars. He also despised the new state of Israel and wanted to arm Egypt to defend Arab rights in the region. When France and Britain refused to supply him with weapons or to finance the building of a huge new dam to control the Nile River, Nasser declared that Egypt, and not the Europeans, would now control the Suez Canal, the vital waterway between the Mediterranean and the ports of Asia.

Nasser's pronouncement struck the French and British in an especially vulnerable place. The British in particular depended on Middle Eastern oil. The Israelis were eager, too, to retain access to the canal. In October 1956, the French, British, and Israelis staged a brief attack on Cairo, but were made to back off by the Americans, who feared the Soviets would side with the Egyptians. The French and British did as they were told by their superpower ally, revealing, embarrassingly, that they were no longer able to do as they wished anywhere in the world.

Still, the situation remained tense and it took the intervention of Canadian diplomat Lester B. Pearson to avert a major war in the region. Pearson suggested that the United Nations send its first peacekeeping troops to the Suez to ensure the canal's neutrality. This solution prevented further bloodshed, and made Nasser a hero in Egypt and other Arab nations. His willingness to stand up to the European colonial powers set a precedent that many

other new nationalists throughout the Third World would follow. By the end of the 1950s, many nations on the North African rim, including Tunisia, Sudan, and Morocco, had declared themselves nonaligned, independent states.

ALGERIA.
Algeria, France's long-held North African colony, also made a bid for liberation in the 1950s. Contrary to the trend among imperialists in the second half of the twentieth century, France put up intense resistance. French troops had first invaded Algeria in 1827, and many French soldiers and merchants had settled there, living uneasily alongside the much larger Arab Muslim population. Until 1945, the French settlers held virtually all the economic and political power. After World War II, a few reforms attempted to adjust these inequities, but the reforms were too little too late. In 1954, the National Liberation Front, ready to fight for full independence, launched a revolt against the French government and the French settlers. Civil war raged. At home, French leftists opposed the war and denounced the French military, which responded to the terroristic tactics of the insurgents by committing atrocities of its own.

Psychiatrist Frantz Fanon, who was working at a psychiatric hospital in Algeria when the uprising began, insisted that violence was justified to free the colonized from the brutal domination of the West. A native of the French colony of Martinique, Fanon knew firsthand how difficult it remained for dark-skinned "évolués" (see Chapter 20) to find acceptance in French society. In his analysis of colonialism's evils, *The Wretched of the Earth* (1961), Fanon criticized Europe for inflicting so much suffering on its colonial subjects, while claiming to be the torchbearers of enlightened and humanitarian ideas. "Come, then, comrades," he wrote in the book's conclusion, "the European game has finally ended; we must find something different. We today can do everything, so long as we do not imitate Europe, so long as we are not obsessed by the desire to catch up with Europe." Fanon's book circulated widely, and served as a call to other proponents of the nonaligned movement to seek a third, non-European way of life.

The crisis in Algeria helped bring Charles de Gaulle back to power in France. The former general was able to rein in the army and begin a strategic pull-out. In 1962, he allowed the French to vote on Algerian independence, and they overwhelmingly approved of cutting the colony free. Many French settlers fled to France, even though most of their families had lived in Algeria for generations. Algeria itself became a military dictatorship.

SUB-SAHARAN AFRICA.
In the wake of independence movements elsewhere, sub-Saharan Africans also decided that the time had come to free themselves from their colonial overlords. In 1960, numerous colonies in West Africa gained independence, as did the Belgian Congo. Tanganyika (today Tanzania) and Kenya became sovereign states in 1961 and 1963, followed by Zambia (1964) and Botswana (1966). Many of the new nations,

however, remained economically dependent on the West, and many ended up with leaders who relied on force and bribery to govern weak states. As Fanon noted, decades of imperial rule had limited most African nations to supplying raw materials for the industrial powerhouses of Europe—it may take many more decades for African nations to escape their wretchedness.

The Culture of the Cold War

During the Cold War, the two great powers that dominated world politics, the United States and the USSR, also shaped cultural production in their respective blocs. The

> **How did Cold War culture reflect the politics of the Eastern and Western blocs?**

Soviets in particular worked hard to stomp out all "bourgeois" and "capitalist" ideas and to tout the communist party line. Western governments allowed far more freedom of expression, but some suppressed the work of communists or material they deemed blasphemous or sexually deviant.

Both blocs fostered new forms of fear—fear of nuclear war, fear of violent communist or capitalist takeovers, fear of being labeled abnormal or seditious. Some of these fears were justified; there were incidents, such as the Cuban missile crisis, when nuclear war was narrowly avoided. But often these fears were inflated or used to justify the imprisonment or persecution of innocent people. For example, in the East and occasionally in the West, state and medical officials sometimes condemned homosexuals or mentally ill people to penal institutions based on absurd claims that they threatened national security. The media helped whip up anxieties, publishing stories about how to build and stock bomb shelters and how to identify deviants. In the West in the 1950s, writers and actors suspected of being communists were blacklisted, which meant that no reputable newspapers or studios would risk hiring them. In the East, the secret police watched cultural figures closely. Those who toed the party line were rewarded with travel privileges and other perks; those who did not were forbidden to write, paint, or act—or locked away to prevent them from "poisoning" others.

During the early Cold War period, popular and elite culture developed quite differently, but by the later 1960s, some of the elite's experimentation and criticism of authorities went mainstream. Also by this time, two astonishing sociocultural transformations were taking place: for the first time ever women were claiming rights equal to those of men, and for the first time since the medieval era a majority of Europeans ceased to be practicing Christians.

Popular Culture

Differences between East and West were clearly visible in the heroes and heroines each bloc created for popular consumption. Western writers reveled in creating fictional spies, such as George Smiley, the British agent created by novelist John Le Carré, and James Bond, who first appeared in Ian Fleming's novels, and then in hugely popular movies such as *Dr. No* (1962), the first James Bond film. The USSR emphasized worker-heroes, humble men whose hard work helped build communist greatness. After *Sputnik,* the Soviets also championed astronauts such as Yuri Gagarin, the first man to orbit the earth, and Laika, the first dog in space.

America's booming film industry produced thousands of movies that were dubbed or subtitled and distributed all over the non-communist world. Though some, such as Stanley Kubrick's 1964 classic, *Dr. Strangelove,* contained political or social criticism, family-friendly fantasies such as *Lady and the Tramp, Peter Pan,* and *The Sound of Music* sold the most tickets. Gradually, more sex and more lower-class heroes, like those played by Marlon Brando, appeared on the screen. Actors and actresses such as James Dean, Marilyn Monroe, and Robert Redford became cultural icons, admired by even larger audiences than the millions that had acclaimed Sarah Bernhardt nearly a century before (see Chapter 21). Soviet movies were more overtly ideological, but here, too, love stories, action films, and comedies were what most people most wanted to watch.

Elite Culture

Like the popular culture of this era that sought either to heighten or to escape Cold War terrors, elite culture, too, either attacked political questions head on or tried to evade them entirely. Marxism attracted thinkers in both the East and the West, for it gave them tools with which to criticize their own societies and to interpret Europe's history. Especially in the later 1960s, many intellectuals in France, Italy, and West Germany adopted Marxist methods to understand the alienation of individuals in capitalist societies from their communities and the development of the West's culture industries.

In the postwar era, existentialism, the philosophical movement that depicted life as a series of unscripted and inherently meaningless moments (see Chapter 23), continued to be a dominant form of philosophy. But postwar thinkers also felt the need to comment on politics. Jean-Paul Sartre committed himself to Marxism, though he abandoned his faith in the Soviet system after the Hungarian invasion of 1956. Albert Camus, the French-Algerian author of *The Stranger* (1942), became an anarchist after being kicked out of the French Communist Party. Martin Heidegger's German-Jewish student and former lover Hannah Arendt settled in America, where she wrote her classic study, *The Origins of Totalitarianism* (1951), one of the first works to explore parallels between the Nazi and Italian fascists and the Russian communists. In her later study of the war crimes trial of the Nazi bureaucrat Adolf Eichmann (*Eichmann in Jerusalem,* 1961), Arendt denounced the paper-shufflers, like Eichmann, who allowed totalitarian regimes to function. That Eichmann had sent

1963–1964: Beatlemania

The new prosperity and the evolving welfare state freed baby boomers from having to supplement family income, allowing them to do new things during their teenage years. John Lennon and Paul McCartney decided to start a band. Lennon already had created one, called The Quarrymen, when at age seventeen he met fifteen-year-old Paul McCartney in 1957. In 1958, they added another fifteen-year-old, George Harrison, to their group. Adding and subtracting drummers and piano players, the group achieved a moderate success in their home town of Liverpool, England, the gritty industrial port through which so much of Manchester's textile trade and so many slaves and European emigrants had flowed in previous centuries. In 1962, the group, now known as The Beatles, signed on with Abbey Road Studios and added a permanent drummer, Ringo Starr. That year the group released "Love Me Do," which achieved a modest number 17 on the British charts. An album, *Please Please Me*, came out in early 1963 and by the end of the year had sold a million copies.

Something about The Beatles' music—and their youth—entranced British audiences, especially young women. Their early songs were not especially deep or meaningful; McCartney admitted that the words hardly mattered. What did matter was the sound, the beat, the large number of simple, singable songs. The Beatles were shocked by what happened when they went on tour in 1963. Screaming fans greeted them everywhere; in many places, the musicians had to be protected by police, some of whom used water cannons to contain the crowds. The second album, *With the Beatles,* flew off the shelves, and Abbey Road Studios received more than a million orders for the most popular of the hit singles, "I Want to Hold Your Hand," even before its release in October 1963. Beatlemania had begun.

By this time, The Beatles were already a sensation in their home country, but the band's producers hesitated before releasing this British music in America, where Elvis Presley, Chubby Checker, and The Shirelles dominated the music scene. The producers should not have worried. On February 7, 1964, The Beatles left a screaming mob at Heathrow Airport in London to fly across the Atlantic. That same month, an astonishing 40 percent of the American population tuned in to watch The Beatles' appearance on *The Ed Sullivan Show*—a tribute to the market's orientation to the new youth culture. Elvis Presley had appeared on this same program in 1956, to the consternation of conservatives, who found his hip gyrations provocative. The Beatles were far less threatening; they wore natty suits, did not dance, and sang innocent adolescent ballads such as "Help!"

The Beatles took America by storm, so much so that their arrival was described as a "British invasion." Here, too, police had to be called out to control screaming fans who threatened to trample one another in their efforts to get close to the still rather goofy young men with long, mop-like haircuts. "I Want to Hold Your Hand" sold more than 2.5 million copies in two weeks. The Beatles jetted off for concerts across the world, playing to crowds in Hong Kong, Australia, and the Netherlands. Beatlemania was now a worldwide phenomenon. Even behind the Iron Curtain, police began turning up contraband Beatles records.

Despite their successes, The Beatles opted for a dramatic change in style after they met folk singer Bob Dylan in August 1964. Dylan not only introduced them to marijuana, but also impressed them with his music of social protest. In response, The Beatles moved swiftly away from the pure pop ballads and dance tunes that had once made them famous. Lennon, in particular, gravitated toward countercultural ideas and lifestyles, but the whole band's transformation, along with changes in dress, was unmistakable by the time the album *Sgt. Pepper's Lonely Hearts Club Band* appeared in 1967. Some of the album's songs alluded to drug use ("Lucy in the Sky with Diamonds"); Indian gurus, Karl Marx, Sigmund Freud, and Bob Dylan, among other countercultural heroes, appeared on the album's cover. The Beatles' music was now much more sophisticated. Like the rest of the baby-boom generation, The Beatles grew up fast, exchanging the rather innocent-seeming Beatlemania days of the early 1960s for the psychedelic rock of Sgt. Pepper. Tragically, one Beatle left the stage without enjoying his middle age: John Lennon was murdered outside his New York apartment on December 8, 1980.

QUESTIONS | *How did Beatlemania both reflect and influence popular culture? How did changes in The Beatles' music reflect broader cultural changes?*

Beatlemania Wherever they toured, whether in England, the United States, or Germany, the Beatles were greeted by cheering crowds—and by screaming, or sobbing, female fans.

so many to their deaths without having to leave his desk represented, for Arendt, "the banality of evil" in its most modern form.

Another of the era's great philosophers, Michel Foucault, developed a distinct form of social and linguistic analysis. Foucault's works, including *The Birth of the Clinic* and *Madness and Civilization,* showed how new meanings for terms such as *madness* or *the body* had evolved in the modern era. Foucault claimed that these new meanings were attached to ever more invasive forms of power such as medical manuals and mental institutions, which dictated who was normal and punished those who were not. In many ways, Foucault's analysis of the repressiveness of western institutions echoed the criticisms that student radicals of the 1960s made of what they called "the establishment."

Abstract expressionism, a style of painting pioneered in the interwar era, flourished during the 1950s. Artists found it appealing because it dispensed with all political and religious symbolism and all historical or natural referents, allowing them to revel in color and pure forms. Leading abstract expressionists were the Americans Jackson Pollock, Barnett Newman, and Mark Rothko, but their style was picked up and spread across the globe. The Soviet elite, never renowned for its artistic taste, considered the style self-indulgent and nihilistic; on arriving at an exhibition of modern art in Moscow in 1962, an

angry Khrushchev declared: "A donkey could smear better than this with his tail."[3]

The Soviets also periodically condemned the modern music of Dmitri Shostakovich, Russia's greatest mid-century composer, despite Shostakovich's commitment to communism and his many attempts to contribute to Soviet propaganda efforts. They also imprisoned many modernist poets and writers and forced Boris Pasternak to refuse the Nobel Prize in Literature he was offered for his novel *Dr. Zhivago* in 1958. During the thaw, Khrushchev allowed Alexander Solzhenitsyn to publish his moving portrait of life in the gulag, *One Day in the Life of Ivan Denisovich* (1962), but the party could not stomach Solzhenitsyn's extensive history of the camps, *The Gulag Archipelago* (1973). It circulated only in illegal manuscripts known as *samizdat.* Eventually, Solzhenitsyn became so troublesome that the Soviets expelled him; in exile, he continued to criticize the regime and to prophesy its imminent collapse.

The relatively new medium of film attracted some of the most innovative minds of the post-1945 period. This was the great era of avant-garde film, in which directors such as Federico Fellini (Italian), Luis Buñuel (Spanish), Ingmar Bergman (Swedish), Alfred Hitchcock (English-American), and Jean-Luc Godard (French) built on foundations established in the interwar era. Though their styles were different, they shared a desire to use film as a form of art, using unusual camera angles or surreal juxtapositions of images to highlight the role of the filmmaker in framing what the viewer sees.

For several decades, avant-garde film and modernist literature went unseen and unread by middle-class Europeans, attracting chiefly intellectuals who thought of themselves as members of a counterculture. Like the earlier avant-garde, these artists and writers wanted to be ahead of the others, but to this desire they added deep objections to what they perceived as the stifling uniformity of mainstream postwar culture. Some dabbled in illegal drugs, others in leftist politics, psychoanalysis, vegetarianism, or jazz. This countercultural world expanded greatly with the coming of age of a new generation and the rise of new political concerns and lifestyle choices.

The Boom Years Are Over

By the mid-1960s, signs began to appear that the boom years were ending. There were fewer good jobs for an increasingly well-educated population, and people began to fear that the era of prosperity was coming to a close.

Now reaching maturity, the baby-boom generation was beginning to question its parents' tastes, values, and customs, as well as the political activities of the previous generation. Students demanded a more up-to-date and useful education and more say in university governance. Radical student leaders such as the West German Rudi Dutschke (1940–1979) claimed that fascism had not been defeated, but lived on in the institutions built by postwar conservatives. These claims were reasonable, as many institutions,

An Abstract Expressionist at Work This 1950 photograph depicts the American artist Jackson Pollock creating paintings that highlight color and texture rather than seeking to imitate nature.

such as the West German judiciary, had not been thoroughly de-Nazified, and very few Europeans had come to grips with the Holocaust and the many forms of collaboration that had underwritten Hitler's empire.

Some young people questioned their elders' participation in the horrors of World War II and the Holocaust and condemned the brutality and futility of their nations' bloody colonial wars. They protested the placing of nuclear missiles in Europe and the environmental degradation that threatened Europe as more factories were built and more fertilizers, pesticides, and fossil fuels were used and consumed. Feminist activists drew attention to glaring gender inequalities, denouncing regimes that did nothing to promote equal pay for equal work or the equality of the sexes in either the public or the private sphere.

"Hippie" Culture in the West The later 1960s and early 1970s marked the high point of intergenerational clashes and of "hippie" culture in western Europe and the United States. This image from the 1967 "love-in" at Woburn Abbey, England, could have been taken at any one of a number of grand outdoor concerts or antiwar rallies staged during those years.

1968

Globally, 1968 proved to be a year of student activism. Rallies against civil rights abuses and the Vietnam War in the United States sparked demonstrations of various sorts across the globe. On October 2, at least forty students demanding university reforms and protesting police brutality were massacred by governmental troops in Mexico City; the official explanation was suppression of a communist insurgency. As in 1848, ideas and tactics spread like wildfire, even reaching behind the Iron Curtain. In West Germany, the legacy of Nazism became a major topic; in Italy, the communist Party organized attacks on the state. In Northern Ireland, Catholic civil rights activists defied the Protestant government's ban on protest gatherings and rioted. So began "the Troubles"—thirty years of bombings, kidnappings, and murders perpetrated by both radical Protestants and radical Catholics.

In Paris, May 1968 proved an especially pivotal month. First, student unrest caused officials to close down the universities, then workers sympathetic to the students agreed to call a general strike as well. The police arrested or beat protestors, but ever larger and angrier crowds surged into the streets, in some places erecting new barricades and hurling paving stones, just as their ancestors had done in 1848. Eventually the police gave up and allowed students to occupy the universities and workers to take over some places of business. By mid-May, millions were on strike and hundreds of thousands rallied in the streets of Paris. The rioters issued two sorts of demands: the students wanted educational reform, while some radicals called for a complete remaking of capitalist, consumer society. In the end, President de Gaulle agreed to hold elections, which returned a huge majority for the conservatives. "La France profonde" (rural and small-town France) had no taste for revolution.

The protests in 1968 in Paris and elsewhere may not have had enormous short-term results, but over the longer run, they signaled the deep social changes under way in European society. A number of left-leaning governments came in to power in the later 1960s, universities made adjustments in response to students' grievances, and women's issues began—slowly—to receive a hearing. Alongside the more direct expressions of political and social discontent, too, a more general cultural and sexual revolution was under way. By the later 1960s, "hip" young people were removing their suits—as had the Beatles—and miniskirts and opting for jeans and t-shirts. Some experimented with drugs, or attended one of the many outdoor "love-ins" in which young people called on their elders to "Make Peace, Not War."

The baby-boom generation made a deep impact on the culture of the 1960s and 1970s, and especially in northern Europe, compromises were struck. The Americans did, eventually, end the war in Vietnam; universities were reformed and made more accessible; it became acceptable for women to wear pants. An East-West dialogue began on nuclear disarmament. These compromises laid the foundations for something like a western European thaw—a thaw that took place against the backdrop of another revolution, this one in the spiritual realm.

Christianity and the Cold War

In the immediate postwar period, western Europeans devoted some of their limited income to restoring damaged churches. Yet many of these churches quickly became museums rather than real places of worship. Once again, change occurred unevenly across the continent.

In some places, including communist Russia and some western cities, a majority of individuals had ceased being practicing Christians decades earlier. Elsewhere, in rural areas of southern Italy and the Republic of Ireland, long into the postwar period people continued to flock to their churches for baptisms, marriage ceremonies, and burials, and many of their children still attended religious schools. By the 1960s, however, real changes were obvious across the board. Religion had, for the most part, ceased to be a defining feature of European culture.

In eastern Europe, individuals did not have much choice. In Russia, although Russian Orthodoxy was not outlawed, priests and religious persons had been persecuted since the Revolution in 1917. Once communism took hold in eastern Europe, here too the free practice of religion came to an end. Most governments grudgingly allowed religious services to go on, but often harassed clergy members or church activists. From time to time, churches would be closed or spies sent to infiltrate the ranks of the faithful. Levels of persecution varied: in Poland, the Catholic Church was allowed to operate more or less freely and remained a central part of social life. In Albania, atheism was declared the state religion, and no religious services were permitted. In some places, religion was kept alive by being linked to dissent or to the national identities that communism was trying to suppress. In Lithuania, for example, retaining one's Roman Catholic faith was a way to keep one's distance from the Soviet Russian regime. Still, regular churchgoing was increasingly limited to grandmothers; their sons and daughters largely spent their Sundays at home.

In the West, other factors combined to result in deep declines in church attendance. Rapid urbanization contributed to this trend; rural areas had always been closer to their churches. Welfare states took over many of the functions of the old churches: elementary education, marriages, and burials were increasingly carried out by secular state authorities. The new leisure and consumer cultures provided entertainment for young people that proved more alluring than the church-organized youth leagues or social clubs of earlier decades. Finally, the horrors of the Second World War shook some Europeans' faith in God or in the churches, all too many of which had failed to protest or prevent crimes against humanity. The result was that by the 1980s, the vast majority of people under age sixty had stopped going to church. In Italy, churchgoers made up two-thirds of the population in the 1950s, but only one-third by the 1980s; by that time, less than 12 percent of Britons belonged to a church at all.

Recognizing that change was necessary, many denominations tried valiantly to adapt to new times. Even the Catholic Church, long a bastion of conservatism, called the **Second Vatican Council (Vatican II)** to reform both dogma and practice. Some 2,500 delegates met in Rome between October 1962 and December 1965, and made the most sweeping changes in the church since the Council of Trent in the sixteenth century. Criticizing old prejudices, the delegates declared that the Catholic Church would henceforth embrace religious freedom for all; it would work and meet together with leaders of other faiths to promote common, humanitarian goals. The Roman Catholic and Eastern Orthodox Churches, mutually hostile since 1054, could now engage one another in dialogue. To make the Catholic liturgy more accessible to contemporary Christians, Vatican II also allowed mass to be said in the vernacular, and soon thereafter the church insisted that priests give up the Latin mass. But these reforms did not turn the tide of European de-Christianization, even, ironically, as Christianity was gaining millions of new adherents beyond Europe in Africa and Asia.

In both eastern and western Europe, the absence of Jews, so many of whom had been murdered during the war, was palpable. Those who remained generally kept a low profile and only slowly gathered enough money and confidence to rebuild some of their historical synagogues. The largest synagogue in Europe, Budapest's Dohányi Synagogue, was restored to its original splendor only after the fall of communism in 1996 and now serves chiefly as a museum. In the 1970s, a few Russian Jews were allowed to leave the Soviet Union for Israel; after the fall of communism, they began emigrating in large numbers. At the same time, many emigrants and guest workers from Turkey and North Africa brought their faith with them, creating Muslim communities in Europe and in neo-Europes such as the United States, Canada, and Australia for the first time. Most received a cool, but usually not hostile, reception, and although anti-Semitism cannot be said to have disappeared (especially in eastern Europe), Europe became more religiously tolerant at the same time that it became a less religious society.

Western Europe in the 1970s and 1980s

The later 1960s saw a shift to the left in many countries. In Britain, the Labour Party formed its first government in thirteen years in 1964; in West Germany, the Social Democrat Willy Brandt took the chancellorship in 1969. Brandt was especially important in pressing for **détente,** or peaceful coexistence, with the communist East. Brandt also made an historic visit to Poland, where he knelt before the Warsaw ghetto memorial, and asked Jews and Poles for forgiveness for his nation's "million-fold crime." Other leaders also pursued the policy of détente, including U.S. president Richard Nixon, who negotiated with Leonid Brezhnev to reduce the number of nuclear missiles pointed at one another's countries. In 1972, Nixon and Brezhnev signed SALT I (Strategic Arms Limitation Treaty 1); SALT II was signed by Brezhnev and President

How did politics and gender relations change in western Europe after the upheavals of the 1960s?

Jimmy Carter in 1979, further easing tensions between the superpowers.

As fears of a nuclear World War III abated, western European governments devoted even more of their budgets to social services. State spending and workers' pay increased initially, but states' ability to sustain high rates of growth flagged after U.S. president Nixon took the United States off the gold standard in 1971. The dollar's value plunged, and the fixed exchange rates agreed on at the Bretton Woods Conference had to be abandoned. In 1973, the Organization of Petroleum Exporting Countries (OPEC) began restricting trade in oil, causing prices to rise drastically. Recession seemed imminent.

Partly in response, the EEC now moved toward closer integration, hoping to forestall a new depression. Britain joined in 1971, along with Denmark and Iceland; Greece, Spain, and Portugal came on board by 1986. Gradually, the EEC idea evolved beyond economic concerns as people envisioned political and legal unity for Europe as well, and the idea of a complete European Union was born (see Chapter 26). Transfer payments—from richer to poorer nations—and subsidies allowed southern Europe to rebuild its infrastructure and to experience a consumer revolution of its own. In the meantime, another seismic social revolution was under way, one that, though very slow to gestate, has transformed Europeans' private lives in far-reaching and unprecedented ways.

A Sexual Revolution?

Women had obtained the right to vote in Germany and Great Britain after World War I; French and Italian women finally obtained the same right in 1944 and 1946, respectively. But all over Europe, in the workplace and in the home, women were still treated very much as second-class citizens. Before 1965, most wives needed their husbands' permission to take a job and were the first to be laid off when companies faced hard times. The maternity leave provided by the states encouraged them to have children—and to be the ones to stay home to care for them. But the desire to earn their own wages or add to the family's income pulled more and more women into the workforce, taking jobs especially in the expanding service sector. Whereas in the 1950s approximately one in three women worked outside the home, by 1990, this figure was more like one in two—or a full 80 percent in Sweden, though in more traditional Portugal and Greece the figures remained at around 40 percent. Women's wages rose, but men still earned at least 20 percent more. Few women managed to break through glass ceilings and obtain the highest-status jobs in the bureaucracies, business, and academia.

In the 1970s and 1980s, for the first time in European history, women without crowns or noble titles began to play a significant role in politics. In 1979, Margaret Thatcher became Britain's first female prime minister, and by 1992, Iceland, Norway, France, and Poland had all had female leaders, at least briefly. Women's representation in

Margaret Thatcher Addresses Parliament Margaret Thatcher was Europe's first female prime minister, and a highly influential conservative politician. Attacking the size and expense of the postwar welfare state, Thatcher privatized some British businesses, reduced the power of the trade unions, and prevented Britain from linking its economy too closely with that of the European Union.

government increased dramatically in a few places, such as Sweden, where it reached 45 percent in the 1990s; elsewhere it remained much lower. In 1993, for example, only 6 percent of the delegates to France's National Assembly were women. Italy, Greece, Spain, and Portugal still await their first female prime ministers.

European women participated actively in the consumer and entertainment booms of the postwar era, donning miniskirts and buying their own Beatles' albums. As state-funded universities opened their doors to millions of new students, many more women, proportionally, were among them. Across the continent, the combination of liberalized divorce laws and the new availability of contraceptive pills and devices gave women more control over their bodies than ever before in human history. Even for those who did not work or study outside the home, another kind of liberation was on offer: liberation from the laundry.

The Washing Machine

For centuries, washing the family's clothing and linens has been women's work, undertaken either by domestic servants or by the lady of the house.[4] Until the postwar era, this was a backbreaking endeavor, involving heating large kettles and scrubbing or beating dirty clothes, wringing out heavy garments and hanging them out to dry, and finally ironing everything with a flatiron heated on a wood stove. These tasks were often done collectively, near streams or city pumps, or in wash houses, and could absorb an entire day—though many women used the opportunity to visit with their neighbors or to exchange stories or songs as they worked. The washing machine, invented in the early part of the century and common in middle-class American households by the 1930s, appeared in Europe in large numbers only in the 1950s and 1960s. Only then could middle-class European households afford them and find space and proper water and electrical hookups to make them usable. And by then, petroleum-based detergents had been developed to replace older soaps made from lye, ashes, and fats.

Liberation from Drudgery This advertisement for the Bendix washing machine promises women freedom from the rigors of laundering clothes, a job once assigned—when possible—to domestic servants (see Chapter 19).

At first, washing machines were extremely expensive—prices ran as high as 200,000 francs in 1950, nearly a year's salary for minimum-wage workers in France. But advertisers and women's magazines trumpeted the wonders of the labor-saving device. Moulinex, a French firm, appealed directly to female consumers' longing to give up their washtubs: "Moulinex liberates women," its advertising campaign declared. In fact, women *did* yearn for liberation from the laundry and saved or even took jobs in order to acquire the new machines. Over time prices fell and wages rose; credit plans allowed consumers to pay in installments, and more people acquired modern apartments for which the woman of the house, in particular, wanted modern appliances. Only 8 percent of western European households had a washing machine in 1954; but 57 percent had one in 1971, and in 1980, 80 percent of families owned a machine. Laundry could now be done speedily, and in the comfort, and privacy, of one's own home.

Into these machines was dumped another classically postwar product: detergent, first used extensively by the armies during World War II to launder uniforms without wasting precious fats. Unquestionably, detergent worked better than old soaps to remove dirt, but advertisers hyped this product, too, subtly convincing women that only those who purchased Persil—to use a famous West German brand of detergent—were really getting their clothes clean. Persil's campaign was so successful, in fact, that people who had been too easily cleared of charges of collaboration with the Nazis were described as "Persil-clean"—one quick wash, and their "brown shirts" had turned a nice, innocent white.

The washing machine and the new detergents did lighten the burden of housework. They did, however, also do away with the camaraderie and rituals that attended collective washing days; and the detergents have added greatly to the polluting of rivers and oceans. Nor did Moulinex, or any other household machine, actually liberate European women from housework, which still falls largely on their shoulders. But changes in women's lives in the postwar period cannot be understood without paying some attention to the introduction of an appliance we now take largely for granted.

QUESTION | *Is it coincidental that women began to earn new rights in the political arena at the same time that they began to enjoy at least some liberation from household drudgery?*

The Conservatives Return to Power

By the mid-1970s, Britain's national debt was soaring. High tax rates and inflation threatened to ruin the middle classes, and labor unions staged numerous strikes. Against this background, British voters turned out the Labour Party prime minister and voted in the Conservatives, led by the formidable Margaret Thatcher (b. 1925). Believing that Britain's economy was being strangled by too much state regulation and too many labor unions, Thatcher set about privatizing state-owned companies and breaking up some of the unions. She did not like the conciliatory stance toward eastern communism taken by Germany's Social Democrats in the 1970s, and said so. Like her American counterpart, Ronald Reagan (elected U.S. president in 1980), she did not believe communism would last forever, and she was eager to press for its collapse. Both Thatcher and Reagan were instrumental in reversing western policies of détente; like Thatcher, Reagan denounced the Soviet Union as an evil empire and worked to rebuild America's arsenal.

Thatcher was in many ways an old-fashioned nationalist. She involved Britain in a brief war with Argentina to recover the Falkland Islands in 1982, and though she did not want to see Britain leave the EEC, she thought the organization should stick to trade regulation and not evolve into a political body. She refused to allow Britain to unite its currency with that of the continent. Thus, Britain did not adopt the euro and preserved its pound sterling while a lso remaining a member of the European Union (EU).

In West Germany, the conservative Helmut Kohl (b. 1930) ascended to the chancellorship in 1982, just after Reagan and Thatcher entered office. He would last much longer than either, staying on as West German head of state until 1990 and then serving as chancellor of a reunited Germany from 1990 to 1998. Kohl allowed the United States to station missiles in West Germany, against fierce opposition from the left, but unlike Thatcher, he was not an aggressive proponent of the free market or an opponent of European integration. In fact, Kohl worked to create a partnership with the socialist François Mitterrand (1916–1996), who served as France's president from 1981 until 1995. Working together, Mitterrand and Kohl laid the foundations for further integration of Europe's economies and states.

Communism under Pressure

While a cadre of dynamic conservatives came to power in the West during the 1980s, an even more influential communist leader emerged in the Eastern bloc. Just as Joseph Stalin had been the individual most responsible for the division of Europe into Cold War blocs, Mikhail Gorbachev was the man most responsible for the fall of the Iron Curtain.

How did Gorbachev's attempts to reform Soviet policy contribute to the collapse of communism in eastern Europe?

When Gorbachev became Soviet premier in 1985, he was the youngest leader the communist bloc had seen for decades. Unlike most of his colleagues, Gorbachev had not been shaped by interwar battles with fascism. Born in 1931, he was too young even to have served in World War II. Instead, his formative experiences occurred chiefly during the years of Khrushchev's thaw. Gorbachev was able to rise through the party ranks because, unlike many of his contemporaries, he believed hard work and more reform could create a Russian version of socialism with a human face. He seems to have believed also that eastern Europeans, given autonomy from Soviet control, would *choose* to continue to live under the communist umbrella. In the late 1980s, he pushed through a series of monumental policies designed to make his reformist communist dreams come true. To his shock and chagrin, he succeeded in bringing down Soviet and eastern European communism and inciting the breakup of the Soviet Union itself.

In retrospect, Gorbachev may seem to have been a deluded optimist who thought that he could overcome the cynicism of his own party and restructure a dilapidated and deeply indebted economy. But even if another Brezhnev-like apparatchik had come to power on March 11, 1985, the Soviet Union would still have entered a crisis period. For one thing, oil prices and production were falling, just as costs for the Soviets' war in Afghanistan were increasing. The need for hard currency to buy western machinery rose as all of the Eastern bloc's industries gradually rusted away, and virtually everyone—with the exception of die-hards like Honecker and, in his way, Gorbachev—lost faith in the communist system.

Living Communism's Last Years

To those who lived in the Eastern bloc in the mid-1980s, communism had become something of a pathetic and malicious joke. Most people recognized that communism's claim to provide a better quality of life than that available to inhabitants of the western democracies was an empty one, and many knew that their hopes for reform were bound to be disappointed. Most households had radios and TVs—but there were few programs that people really enjoyed, except the jazz programs or the sitcoms from the West that the lucky few in border regions could sometimes tune in. Adults became accomplished interpreters of the daily propaganda sheets that served as newspapers. Private telephones were carefully restricted, and personal computers even more so; there were only 200,000 personal computers in the USSR in the early 1980s, at a time when there were already 25 million in the United States. People spent more time in one another's company than was the case in the West. They had no choice. A severe housing shortage meant that families had to wait ten or more years for an apartment—usually no more than three rooms—of their own.

In later years, some people would look back nostalgically to the 1960s and 1970s, a time when virtually everyone had a job, though most jobs were unsatisfying, and most workers did as little work as possible and pilfered goods and supplies for personal use. Everyone had access to (poor) health care and to (ideologically rigid) schools. There was enough food, but most people's diets were bland and tended to emphasize fatty meats and heavy bread. Women were in theory treated as equal to men, although in practice they rarely received equal treatment in the workplace or at home. Nonelites bitterly resented the privileges enjoyed by their supposed comrades—people who had become effectively a new aristocracy but still spouted Marxist-Leninist rhetoric about the glories of the workers' state. Many people agreed to spy on their neighbors, coworkers, or even family members in exchange for the many perks the states could offer. These acts of collaboration gave the state eyes and ears in virtually all public, and many private, places, and they made it difficult for individuals to trust even their closest friends.

In 1985, ordinary people did not know the system was about to collapse. Few were actively working to overthrow communism. Individuals put their energy into figuring out how to beat the system, how to buy western goods from the black market, how to use work-time to sleep, or how to enrich themselves. Virtually everyone had given up on making communism work better. Gorbachev was one of the very few who still believed reform was possible, but as his reforms snowballed, it became increasingly clear that the time for socialism with a human face had passed.

Glasnost and Perestroika

Once he had been appointed general secretary, Gorbachev immediately set about reforming the Soviet empire. He had to fix the economy—but to do so, he also had to mobilize the communist bureaucracy and the wider population and to convince a cynical public to trust him. He learned a valuable lesson when, in the spring of 1986, the nuclear reactor at Chernobyl in the Ukraine exploded, releasing one hundred times the radiation generated by the bombing of Hiroshima and Nagasaki. Some five million people in the Soviet Union and western Europe were exposed, including an estimated 30,000 Ukrainians who have since perished of thyroid cancer. Gorbachev said nothing until the western press broke the story—and he was then confronted with a public outraged at the party's continuing callousness toward its citizens. Unlike his predecessors who would have tried to cover up such a disaster, Gorbachev acknowledged that the catastrophe had happened and approved the evacuation of the area as well as huge investments to clean up the site, preventing an even greater tragedy from occurring.

From this experience Gorbachev learned that rebuilding the public's trust in the party required open discussion. Thus in 1986–1987,

he made it possible for citizens to discuss previously taboo subjects such as Stalin's deportations, the suffering of Soviet soldiers in the Afghan war, and widespread alcoholism. Official newspapers were allowed to print letters to the editor complaining about the Communist Party, and authorities stopped jamming western radio programs. Previously banned books such as *Dr. Zhivago* and *The Gulag Archipelago* were approved for publication.

Of Gorbachev's two major policies, **perestroika** (restructuring the economy) and **glasnost** (the opening up of the political debate), the latter was implemented more swiftly and effectively. Restructuring the economy was much harder, though Gorbachev did try to give businesses more autonomy from state control. One of his efforts at making the workforce more productive was to restrict purchases of alcohol, which could be bought only at state-run stores. This reform backfired, producing angry customers, a surge in the production of often toxic forms of moonshine, and a decrease in the state's income from alcohol sales.

Gorbachev was far more successful in his foreign policy efforts. Intelligent, affable, and interested in open discussions, he was so unlike his predecessors that he charmed western leaders. In 1987, he and U.S. president Ronald Reagan agreed to eliminate short- and medium-range nuclear missiles. Europeans applauded Gorbachev's downsizing of the Soviet army and his ending of the Afghan war in 1988. He began to speak about "the European house," suggesting that the Soviets might be willing to settle for peaceful habitation of only one part of it. Wherever he went, he charmed the media as well, which referred to him fondly as "Gorbi." He began to send clear signals to eastern European leaders that the Brezhnev era was over: they could initiate perestroika and glasnost for themselves.

The Time for Reforming Communism Runs Out After three days of extensive meetings with Soviet premier Mikhail Gorbachev (*right*), President Ronald Reagan was evidently tiring of the conversation. Indeed, by the time of this meeting in 1987, time was running out for Gorbachev, who was horrified to see the Soviet Union that he had tried to reform collapse in 1991.

Why Did Communism Fail?

Explaining the collapse of communism, and the astonishingly little violence that accompanied it, is no simple matter. External factors such as overspending on the war in Afghanistan and pressure to compete in the arms race with the United States helped weaken the Soviet Union. But much more important were the economic and internal factors that eroded support for the system as a whole.

By 1989, all eastern European states were in terrible debt to western creditors, even though officially they weren't supposed to borrow money from capitalist states. Most of their industrial plant was decaying, and they had purchased modern machines—available only from the West—in the attempt to make themselves competitive. This was one source of their indebtedness. Another was consumer goods, which were inferior or lacking in the Eastern bloc. The communist states had tried to supply at least some consumers with western goodies in the hopes of dampening political discontent.

But by 1988, eastern European indebtedness was running into the billions, and foreign currency stocks were depleted. The Soviets long postponed economic meltdown by treating the eastern European nations like colonies and by exploiting the oil reserves in the Caucasus; the latter, historian Steven Kotkin has argued, probably prevented the USSR from collapsing decades earlier.[5] Oil could be sold for hard currency or sold so cheaply at home that the decrepitude and inefficiencies of Soviet industries were masked. But state-planned agencies and aging leaders failed to invest oil revenues in the innovations that were transforming western markets: computer technology, advertising, and the development of a huge service sector. When the price and quantity of Soviet oil production fell in the mid-1980s, the Soviet economy entered its final crisis. Without sufficient money to either bribe or force people to keep communism afloat, the "evil empire" succumbed to the more powerful pressures of global capitalism.

Why didn't the fall of communism result in more violence? In 1988–1989, millions of eastern Europeans and Russians still belonged to the Communist Party, and the USSR still possessed Europe's largest army and an enormous stockpile of nuclear weapons. Why did hard-liners refrain from using force? Kotkin suggests that the party faithful had stopped believing that the West was itself an evil empire or that communism was the only way to ensure social justice and a good life. The Soviet system had become too corrupt, its economy too inefficient, and its leaders too elderly and out of touch for most to believe it could be reformed and saved—or even that it would mount a serious military effort to impose its ideas on Soviet satellite states. Communism failed, in large part, because people had lost faith in its messages and its promises, and ceased to fear the long arm of the Red Army and the Soviet secret police.

Failure to keep up culturally should also be counted as a cause of communist collapse. By the mid-1980s, western media and western goods had seeped through gaps in the Iron Curtain. Many easterners had heard recordings of Beatles songs or American jazz; many owned western blue jeans and t-shirts; many had heard Voice of America or BBC News broadcasts and preferred western culture to the austere, preachy, and prudish culture of the Eastern bloc. Younger consumers, in particular, wanted to see Hollywood films rather than educational and ideologically driven movies about heroic workers. They preferred The Beatles to the speeches of Erich Honecker, and who could blame them? By providing cultural variety as well as the security of the welfare state, by building peaceful alliances (in Europe), and by promoting capitalism and democracy, the West offered a more desirable model for modern social life.

QUESTIONS | *As discussed, both external and internal causes combined to bring down communism. Would communism have failed without one or the other? Why do you think so?*

"Gorbi" was no champion of either capitalism or bourgeois democracy, but his policies suggested that U.S. president Reagan's analysis of the Eastern bloc in 1982 had been correct: the Soviet planned economy could not keep up with global competition or even supply the needs of its people; governments "planted with bayonets" in eastern Europe had never fully taken root. (See Back to the Source at the end of the chapter.) Gorbachev introduced glasnost and perestroika as last-ditch resorts to save communism. But by this time, it was too late.

How the Cold War Ended

As British prime minister, Margaret Thatcher had persistently opposed the policy of détente, and insisted that communism could not endure. In 1987, her U.S. counterpart Ronald Reagan stood in front of Berlin's Brandenburg Gate and issued a challenge: "General Secretary Gorbachev, if you seek peace, if you

Was the fall of the Berlin Wall an accident?

seek prosperity for the Soviet Union and eastern Europe, if you seek liberalization, come here to this gate. Mr. Gorbachev, open this gate. Mr. Gorbachev, Mr. Gorbachev, tear down this wall!" By this time, Gorbachev's reforms had begun to take effect, but no one seriously believed that the Russian premier or the East German communist leadership would tear down the Berlin Wall. In a year's time, however, the prospects for realizing Reagan's demands looked more auspicious. On December 7, 1988, Gorbachev delivered a stunning speech to the United Nations. Though the full implications of the speech were vague, in it Gorbachev proclaimed that all peoples had the right to "freedom of choice," hinting that whatever Eastern bloc nations chose to do with this freedom, the Soviet Union would not interfere. Just as Gorbachev's hero Nikita Khrushchev had signaled the beginning of a post-Stalinist thaw in the mid-1950s, Gorbachev's UN address gave notice to eastern Europeans that the time had come to act.

Poland and Hungary Break Free

Realizing that Moscow would no longer underwrite communist rule, the Poles and Hungarians now devised peaceful means to incorporate non-communists into

their regimes. The Hungarian communists overthrew their longtime leader, replacing him with a reformer and a multiparty system. In Poland, when Solidarity members swept the June 1989 elections for parliament, the old communists tried to prevent them from taking control of the government. The wily Wojciech Jaruzelski, still prime minister, organized negotiations. Jaruzelski recognized that the time had come for the Polish communists to give up power, and in the end they did, without bloodshed or any new declarations of martial law. By 1990, Lech Wałęsa, the longtime leader of the Solidarity movement, had become president of the new Poland.

Changes in Poland and Hungary energized dissident groups and young people elsewhere in the Eastern bloc as well. Yet in East Germany, Romania, and Czechoslovakia, the Communist Party leadership continued to hope that reformist agitation could be suppressed. The events of November and December 1989 would demonstrate that here, too, communism had had its day.

The Fall of the Wall

By August 1989, thousands of East Germans opted to take "vacations" in Hungary, the liberalizing state next door, largely because the Hungarians had just announced that

The Wall Falls On the night of November 9, 1989, East Germans began scaling the Berlin Wall and streaming westward through checkpoints. Border guards, unsure of their orders, simply allowed the jubilant crowds to cross or even to chisel away parts of the wall.

they would not stop visitors from crossing the border into non-communist Austria. A big hole in the Iron Curtain opened and many unhappy easterners squeezed through it, most of them young, well educated, and uninterested in reforming communism. Their flight provoked a crisis in the East German leadership, and at last, after twenty-eight years in power, Erich Honecker lost his job as general secretary of the Communist Party. He was replaced by a reform-minded communist, but it was already too late. The regime floundered as dissenters began to organize rallies in favor of much greater change.

During a press conference on the evening of November 9, party leaders were asked about issuing travel permits and passports, something the state had controlled tightly. To the surprise of reporters and viewers, the party leaders announced that those who requested permission to travel would have their documents processed quickly, without careful political vetting. When was this new policy to go into force, reporters asked. Not really knowing what to answer, the interior minister blurted out: "At once, right away!" Though the party elite had not meant to open the floodgates, citizens in East Germany needed no further permission. Immediately they jumped on subways and into private cars and converged on the Berlin Wall, the great symbol of the division of East and West. Some students began climbing the wall; others took hammers and chisels to its formidable cement face.

Border guards awaited orders that never came to suppress the wall-jumpers, and so did not shoot, but stood and watched as the wall was breached. East German vehicles began driving boldly through checkpoints, without fear of being turned back. By midnight, West Berlin was full of East German revelers, and the next morning tens of thousands were entering the West, where West Germans greeted them with roses and chocolates. Television cameras recorded footage of young people sitting on the wall around the Brandenburg Gate, the very gate through which Napoleon's armies had passed triumphantly in 1806. For twenty-eight years, the wall had

stopped all from passing through that gate; now it was once again open.

The Velvet Revolution

The fall of the Berlin Wall was an occasion for jubilation in the West and for easterners longing to end the long, dreary, and repressive rule of the Communist Party. It was also the final signal to other Eastern bloc regimes and to their citizens that an era was ending. In Czechoslovakia, a rally held in January 1989 to commemorate the suicide of Jan Palach, the student who had set himself on fire to protest the suppression of the Prague Spring, ended with the jailing of dissidents, including the playwright Václav Havel. Hundreds of letters and petitions were sent to the government protesting this action and Havel was released in April, a first sign that popular pressure might sway the government.

But little liberalization occurred until after the Berlin Wall fell. In November, a series of night vigils in central Prague began. In these peaceful demonstrations, Czechs asked for new freedoms and an end to police brutality. Havel became the leader of the opposition and urged his fellow citizens to continue to exert nonviolent, moral pressure on the regime. Party leaders had to choose between violent crackdown and capitulation. Fearing that the army would not remain loyal, they handed over power to a "government of national understanding" and announced free elections—a transition so smooth it was termed a **velvet revolution.** By January 1, 1990, Havel, who had been in prison only a year before, was elected president of a free Czechoslovakia.

Romania: Death of a Dictator

Even as communist regimes toppled, the deeply corrupt Communist Party of Romania reelected longtime dictator Nicolae Ceauşescu (1918–1989) as secretary general, cheering him with sixty-seven standing ovations. In 1989, Romanians were among the poorest of all Europeans, but Ceauşescu was ridiculously rich. Romanians were compelled to work for the state on Sundays and holidays, but in return their food and fuel were strictly rationed so that Ceauşescu could export the remainder to the West. The hard currency that Romania received was used to reward the secret police and to pay for Ceauşescu's extravagant palaces, one of which had bathrooms with gold-plated toilet seats.

Discontent, however, was on the rise. In December 1989, the police fired on a crowd protesting the persecution of a clergyman in the mining town of Timisoara. Hundreds were killed. This time, news of the crackdown emboldened rather than intimidated Romanians. When Ceauşescu, speaking before a huge crowd in Bucharest, tried to blame the violence on fascists, the people cursed and booed him rather than offering him the standard ovation. Ceauşescu and his much-hated wife Elena fled the next day, as the army joined the demonstrators. More

CHRONOLOGY	Key Events in the Fall of Communism in Eastern Europe
DATE	**EVENT**
1980	Founding of Solidarity in Poland
1985	Gorbachev becomes leader of the Soviet Union
1988	December: Gorbachev gives UN speech hinting at noninterference in eastern Europe
1989	January: Hungary adopts liberal reforms May: Hungary opens border to Austria June: Solidarity wins first elections in Poland November: Berlin Wall falls December: Ceauşescu executed in Romania; Communist government falls in Czechoslovakia

than one thousand people were killed in the ensuing chaos. Soldiers located the fleeing couple and put them on trial, though Ceaușescu (like Charles I and Louis XVI before him) insisted that the court had no right to judge him. The Ceaușescus were found guilty and executed by a firing squad on Christmas Day, 1989. What followed was a battle between the army and the Romanian secret police. The army emerged victorious and promoted Ion Iliescu (b. 1930), a communist but an opponent of Ceaușescu. Iliescu was elected president in May 1990.

Conclusion

A series of communist collapses followed Mikhail Gorbachev's attempts at reform, bringing a dramatic and unexpected conclusion to a period that saw many other, quieter changes, such as the transformation of European agriculture, generational and sexual revolutions, and the large-scale abandoning of Christianity. Decades of unprecedented prosperity and of domestic peace made Europe a more desirable home than it had been since 1914, although living conditions in the west and the north continued to be considerably more comfortable than in the east and south. By 1989, Europe was barely recognizable to someone like Erich Honecker, born in 1912 and shaped by the horrors of the interwar era and World War II. As the twentieth century drew to a close, a new world was taking shape, one in which Honecker, and his fellow headliners, would have no place.

Critical Thinking Questions

1. How did eastern Europe become part of the Soviet bloc?

2. How did western European society change between 1945 and 1989? What role did the United States have in enabling these changes?

3. Did eastern and western Europe share any social and cultural trends, despite being politically divided and isolated from one another?

4. Why did communism fail in eastern Europe?

Key Terms

Cold War **(p. 802)**

welfare state **(p. 803)**

show trial **(p. 804)**

Truman Doctrine **(p. 805)**

North Atlantic Treaty Organization (NATO) **(p. 805)**

Warsaw Pact **(p. 805)**

Eastern bloc **(p. 805)**

Bretton Woods system **(p. 806)**

Marshall Plan **(p. 806)**

Brezhnev Doctrine **(p. 810)**

Solidarity **(p. 811)**

social market economy **(p. 812)**

European Economic Community (EEC) **(p. 812)**

third world **(p. 817)**

Second Vatican Council (Vatican II) **(p. 822)**

détente **(p. 822)**

perestroika **(p. 826)**

glasnost **(p. 826)**

velvet revolution **(p. 829)**

Primary Sources in connect

For information on Connect and the online resources available, go to **http://connect.mcgraw-hill.com**.

1. **Erich Honecker Praises the Achievements of East German Socialism, Oct. 1989**

2. **The Soviet Union Condemns Titoism, 1948**

3. **Khrushchev, Secret Speech, February 25, 1956**

4. **East Germany Resolves to Build the Berlin Wall, August 12, 1961**

5. **Beatlemania**

6. **UN Declaration Against Colonialism, 1960**

7. **Frantz Fanon, Why Africa Should Not Imitate Europe**

Ronald Reagan's Address to the British Parliament, June 8, 1982

U.S. president Ronald Reagan (1911–2004) was no friend of détente, the policy of peaceful coexistence with the Soviet Union. The USSR, he believed, was an "evil empire," but one destined to collapse because of its economic and moral failings. It was the duty of the West to keep up military pressure on the Soviets and to continue to advocate the values of democracy, to speak for what he called in this speech "the great civilized ideas: individual liberty, representative government, and the rule of law under God." In addition to typifying American Cold War rhetoric, this speech showcases Reagan's dislike for big government and his embrace of the "special relationship" between the Americans and the British in the wake of their World War II alliance.

We're approaching the end of a bloody century plagued by a terrible political invention—totalitarianism. Optimism comes less easily today, not because democracy is less vigorous, but because democracy's enemies have refined their instruments of repression. Yet optimism is in order, because day by day democracy is proving itself to be a not-at-all-fragile flower. From Stettin on the Baltic to Varna on the Black Sea, the regimes planted by totalitarianism have had more than 30 years to establish their legitimacy. But none—not one regime—has yet been able to risk free elections. Regimes planted by bayonets do not take root.

. . . In an ironic sense Karl Marx was right. We are witnessing today a great revolutionary crisis, a crisis where the demands of the economic order are conflicting directly with those of the political order. But the crisis is happening not in the free, non-Marxist West, but in the home of Marxist-Leninism, the Soviet Union. It is the Soviet Union that runs against the tide of history by denying human freedom and human dignity to its citizens. It also is in deep economic difficulty. . . . Over-centralized, with little or no incentives, year after year the Soviet system pours its best resource into the making of instruments of destruction. The constant shrinkage of economic growth combined with the growth of military production is putting a heavy strain on the Soviet people. What we see here is a political structure that no longer corresponds to its economic base, a society where productive forces are hampered by political ones.

. . . The decay of the Soviet experiment should come as no surprise to us. Wherever the comparisons have been made between free and closed societies—West Germany and East Germany, Austria and Czechoslovakia, Malaysia and Vietnam—it is the democratic countries that are prosperous and responsive to the needs of their people. And one of the simple but overwhelming facts of our time is this: Of all the millions of refugees we've seen in the modern world, their flight is always away from, not toward the Communist world. Today on the NATO line, our military forces face east to prevent a possible invasion. On the other side of the line, the Soviet forces also face east to prevent their people from leaving.

. . . In the Communist world as well, man's instinctive desire for freedom and self-determination surfaces again and again. To be sure, there are grim reminders of how brutally the police state attempts to snuff out this quest for self-rule—1953 in East Germany, 1956 in Hungary, 1968 in Czechoslovakia, 1981 in Poland. But the struggle continues in Poland. And we know that there are even those who strive and suffer for freedom within the confines of the Soviet Union itself. How we conduct ourselves here in the western democracies will determine whether this trend continues.

No, democracy is not a fragile flower. Still, it needs cultivating. If the rest of this century is to witness the gradual growth of freedom and democratic ideals, we must take actions to assist the campaign for democracy.

. . . Our military strength is a prerequisite to peace, but let it be clear we maintain this strength in the hope it will never be used, for the ultimate determinant in the struggle is now going—that's now going on in the world will not be bombs and rockets, but a test of wills and ideas, a trial of spiritual resolve, the values we hold, the beliefs we cherish, the ideals to which we are dedicated.

. . . [Winston Churchill] left us a message of hope for the future, as timely now as when he first uttered it, as opposition leader in the Commons nearly 27 years ago, when he said, "When we look back on all the perils through which we have passed and at the mighty foes that we have laid low and all the dark and deadly designs that we have frustrated, why should we fear for our future? We have," he said, "come safely through the worst." . . . [T]ogether, we too have come through the worst. Let us now begin a major effort to secure the best—a crusade for freedom that will engage the faith and fortitude of the next generation. For the sake of peace and justice, let us move toward a world in which all people are at last free to determine their own destiny.

QUESTIONS | *Why did Reagan think the West had cause to think that communism might soon collapse? What sorts of recommendations for western policy are suggested in this speech?*

Source: Retrieved from Miller Center, University of Virginia, http://millercenter.org/scripps/archive/speeches/detail/3408.

26

A New Panorama of Power: The European Parliament Buildings in Brussels

EUROPE AFTER 1989: ONE AND MANY

Who Is a European?

Remaking Central and Eastern Europe after 1989
   German Reunification
   The Soviet Union's Demise
   Living with Post-Communist Uncertainties
   The Return of Nationalism

A Hot War after a Cold One: Yugoslavia
   From Tito to Milošević
   Sarajevo Holds Out
   The Dayton Accords

Western Europe after the Fall of the Wall
   Defining the Values of Post-1989 Europe
   The European Union
   The Eurozone and Its Walls

Global Citizenship
   Consumerism, American Style
   Football, European Style
   The Communications Revolution
   Postmodernism
   English, the New Lingua Franca?
   Cultural Diversity Endures

Challenges Facing Europe Today
   Relations with the United States
   Political Corruption
   The Challenge of Diversity
   Assassinations, Terrorist Strikes, and Riots
   A Dirty and Dangerous World: The Post–Cold War Environment
   Demographic Challenges
   The Sovereign Debt Crisis

Conclusion

BONO, EUROPEAN AND WORLD CITIZEN The Irish rock singer Paul David Hewson (b. 1960), better known as Bono, has many fans. Bono, short for Bonavox ("beautiful voice" in Latin), helped found U2, a globally popular band, many of whose songs comment on the religious violence that convulsed Northern Ireland in the 1970s and 1980s. Bono considers himself very much an Irishman, but he has also performed numerous concerts for international relief organizations such as Amnesty International and has founded his own charity, ONE, to raise money to fight poverty and AIDS in Africa. Together with his wife, designer Ali Hewson, Bono started a clothing and accessory line whose proceeds are donated to people in need. In recognition of his charitable work abroad, Bono was knighted by Queen Elizabeth II and named person of the year (together with American software billionaires Bill and Melinda Gates) by *Time* magazine in 2005. On three different occasions, Bono has been nominated for the Nobel Peace Prize.

   Although many people find Bono's outspoken commitment to changing the world inspiring, Bono also has his critics. Some say he has used Irish and African suffering to make money, that he dodges taxes on his enormous income, or that he conveys the message that Africans cannot survive without European and American help. The Christian lyrics and Irish political commentaries in many of his songs make some people uncomfortable. Government officials are a bit nervous about his tendency to mix entertainment, politics, and fundraising. In October 2011, an advertisement made by ONE and calling on political leaders to do something about famine in Africa was banned in the United Kingdom for being overly political. Although he has reached middle age, Bono has not stopped trying new things, some of which benefit the world and some of which benefit mainly himself. His life and career so far reflect the complexity of Europe after 1989, a place where global factors as well as local histories continue to shape what it means to be a European.

Bono's career was shaped by Europe's history and especially by the rapid changes over the past few decades, but his own choices have also directed his path. Before the First World War, it would have been unlikely that his mother, an Irish Anglican, would have married his father, an Irish Catholic, or that Bono, raised in the Anglican Church, would have attended school with

Bono in Sarajevo, 1997 During the Yugoslav Wars, Bono sympathized deeply with the plight of the Sarajevans. He paid for the production of a documentary about civilian suffering in the city, and in 1995 wrote and performed a song, "Miss Sarajevo," inspired by the famous beauty pageant, in which the winner unfurled a banner reading "Don't Let Them Kill Us" (see p. 845). The singer visited Sarajevo just after the war's end, then returned in 1997 to perform a concert—the first world-famous performer to do so.

Catholics and Jews. These opportunities opened in the 1960s, and Bono's family took them. As a middle-class youth in the 1970s, Bono could afford to buy albums by the Beatles and the Rolling Stones. He started a band, rather than taking on

Globalization
1970s–present

1970   1975   1980   1985

an apprenticeship or shipping out to serve the British Empire, as had some of his Irish ancestors just a century before.

Yet Bono did not forget his country's past. The early U2 drew on Christian themes and Irish folk music to craft songs such as "Gloria," which contains the Latin refrain *"Gloria in te, Domine, Gloria exultate"* ("Glory to you, O Lord, Glory, exalt [him])." In 1987, Bono wrote "Sunday Bloody Sunday," which invokes the 1920 and 1972 incidents in which British troops clashed with Irish protestors. The original version of the song criticized the Irish Republican Army (IRA), the radical Catholic group committed to ending the Anglo-Protestant domination of Northern Ireland. Although the band revised the lyrics in an attempt to focus on the need for nonviolent solutions, the IRA remained outraged and tried to kidnap the singer. Nevertheless, Bono publicly condemned the organization for staging a bombing that killed twelve people in the town of Enniskillen, Northern Ireland, in November 1987.

U2's next collection, *The Joshua Tree,* was equally scathing about the evils of unbridled American capitalism. This album showcased Bono's blending of American folk music and blues with the Celtic and Christian music of U2's early years. It sold 300,000 copies in two days in Britain alone. *The Joshua Tree* made U2 *world* famous—not surprisingly, for its concerns were now much more than Irish or European ones. Bono was no longer addressing local concerns. In the 1990s, he did not write songs about the transition from communism to capitalism, a hot topic for poets and writers in eastern Europe after 1989, or about political corruption, indebtedness, and unemployment in southern Europe. But he did compose a song about the suffering and bravery of the citizens of Sarajevo during the Yugoslavian Wars of 1992–1996 ("Miss Sarajevo"). Thereafter, the singer began to focus on global issues. In 2001, he wrote "Walk On" about the dissident Burmese pacifist Buddhist Aung San Suu Kyi, and in 2005, he founded his charitable organization ONE committed to African, not European, relief.

But Bono remains a European. He has homes in Dublin and in France and is one of very few European performers today who openly acknowledges himself to be Christian. Bono believes that to be a European today, with all the economic privileges and historical baggage that entails, also obliges him to be a citizen of the world.

Bono's story reflects important aspects of Europe's development in recent years. First, it demonstrates the degree to which Europe is enmeshed in the global economy and the large impact Europe still has on global cultural affairs. His story also shows that Christianity remains a fact of European culture, though the explicit Latin phrases and biblical passages Bono deploys have mostly disappeared from Europe's elite and popular media. Bono's example shows that Europeans remain concerned about global issues such as third-world poverty, AIDS, political repression, and global climate change, sometimes paying more attention to these issues than European ones such as the continuing violence in the former Yugoslavia or Russian Chechnya.

In the wake of the collapse of communism, European states have been seeking to establish unprecedented forms of economic, judicial, and political unity. But many Europeans are not sure that they *want* more unity or will be able to sustain it in the face of so many conflicting regional, linguistic, and socioeconomic interests. Even though the term *European* is in ever greater use, and even though the western-oriented European Union (EU) increasingly

Expansion and crisis in the European Union
1992–2012

Maastricht Treaty
1992

Euro begins to circulate
2002

Eurozone crisis begins
2008

Armed conflict in Chechnya
1994–2005

Civil wars in the former Yugoslavia
1991–2000

Information revolution
1980–present

Bono named *Time* **magazine's Person of the Year**
2005

1995   2000   2005   2010

has defined the values that constitute "European-ness," there remain many different ways to be a European. Now, perhaps more than ever before, "European" is just one component of a person's hybrid identity, meaning that someone like Bono, who calls himself a European on the world stage, can also think of himself as a Catholic and an Irishman. In fact, the processes of European integration and expansion that accelerated so greatly in the 1990s and 2000s may prove to be a test of whether Europe is more than the sum of its parts and whether Germans and Greeks can rise above their national identities to be Europeans first and nationals second.

This is certainly possible. We know that nation-states are not eternal, and their full elaboration dates only to the nineteenth century (see Chapters 18 and 19). We also know that some Europeans, for example, participants in the seventeenth-century "republic of letters" (Chapter 15) and the eighteenth-century Enlightenments (Chapter 16), have long felt themselves part of a supernational entity, one that stood for some of the values the EU stands for today. But if one stream of European history feeds the river of integration, other tributaries run in the opposite direction. Rather like the Rhine River, profiled in Chapter 19, European integration can be broadened and deepened, but the landscape with all its particularities, and the river's old pathways, remain. And there is always the chance that a channeled and tamed river might at some point jump its banks. After all, Europe has never completely been one, but has developed in its own particular way as a result of its diversity, its "many-ness." Even in an age of integration and ever more **globalization**—in the form of the rapidly increasing availability of information, the ever-accelerating movement of peoples, goods, and ideas, and the changes to climate that affect all—Europeans will surely choose to retain in one form or another the diversity that has made their history so unique.

Who Is a European?

Many people across Europe and throughout the world welcomed the rapid and largely bloodless collapse of communism, though there were winners and losers in the process. But the fall of the Iron Curtain and the admission of Europe's formerly communist states into the EU posed a series of questions that had been tabled throughout the Cold War. During that time, it was possible to think of capitalist Europe, and especially the members of the European Economic Community, as "Europe" proper, and to create a super-continental identity that blended this Europe with the neo-Europes (especially the United States, Canada, and Australia, but also including postwar Japan and to some extent Latin America) to form "the West." Eastern European nations belonging to the Warsaw Pact and Turkey, which had been permitted to

What factors have made it urgent, after 1989, to define what it means to be a European?

join NATO, but not the European Economic Community, were considered part of "the East," and for the most part their European-ness forgotten. Even within the Eastern bloc, when people referred to Europe they often meant the continent's western half. But the fall of the Berlin Wall reopened the questions "where are Europe's borders?" and "who and what is a European?"

Another reason that these questions have become urgent is the enormous new wave of immigrants who have settled in Europe especially since the 1980s. For centuries, Europe exported its millions abroad, seeking religious and political freedoms and economic opportunities. Now millions of Asians and Africans, some of them former inhabitants of Europe's colonies, have begun to settle in Europe's nations, bringing with them religious and cultural traditions that sometimes clash with European ones. Many new immigrants have been slower than the guest workers of the 1960s and 1970s to assimilate into European society. Their larger numbers and the tightening of the labor market have meant that some of them form inward-looking communities and suffer disproportionately from unemployment. When the economy slumps, as in Ireland and southern Europe after 2008, the immigrants are the first to be laid off and often become the physical as well as the rhetorical targets of right-wing radicals. Are these inhabitants—many of whom do not possess full citizenship rights—Europeans? This question is still being hotly debated.

What is Europe now? A simple institutional definition would say that it is composed of the twenty-seven member states of the **European Union (EU).** But Switzerland, Norway, Iceland, Turkey, and Yugoslavia's successor states are not members, and most historians would agree that each of these states has been part of European history and has participated in extensive cultural exchange with the rest of Europe, for centuries. Some commentators, such as former German chancellor Helmut Kohl, have attempted a cultural definition. "Europe is more than just politics and the economy," Kohl claimed. "Above all, it represents a magnificent cultural heritage: classical antiquity, humanism, the Enlightenment and Christianity."[1] This definition captures many Europeans' sense of the *positive* aspects of the continent's history that bind them together—but there are endless exceptions to this rule: Scotland and eastern Germany were never conquered by the Romans, and Greece and Romania were long ruled by the Muslim Ottoman Empire. Even before its sixteenth-century religious re-formation, Europe's Christian population was never perfectly unified—Greek and Russian Orthodox believers maintained their faith in the East even when the Roman Catholic popes ruled in western Europe. As we have seen, too, there were many Enlightenments—some political, some cultural; some that spread outward from middle-class society; and some that were imposed from above. Moreover, Kohl's cheerful definition forgets that something else has made Europeans what they are today: the centuries of competition, rivalry, and conflict that made Europe a uniquely

Europeans of the Future This image features ninety-eight schoolchildren who inhabit the areas of London that hosted the 2012 Olympics. The children, aged six to sixteen, reflect the ethnic diversity of many European cities today.

diverse continent, but also, for a long time, a uniquely dangerous one as well. Finally, there are people today who have adopted European traditions and ideas (sometimes unwillingly, as a result of colonization) all across the globe—are they Europeans, too?

Perhaps the best we can do is to give Europe a simple geographic definition: the continent of Europe properly begins at the Ural Mountains in the east and runs west to Portugal and Ireland; its northern borders lie in the far reaches of Scandinavia and its southern boundaries stretch to the Greek islands and Gibraltar. Those who live within this geographic region—and plan to stay—are Europeans, or become so, by virtue of their commitment to the laws and values of the surrounding polities. But what are they committing themselves *to*? Here we might turn to the EU's Millennium Declaration of 1999, which states: "The Union's citizens are bound together by common values such as freedom, tolerance, equality, solidarity and cultural diversity." Building on this statement, we can identify some areas of common understanding. By and large, European-ness entails endorsement of what

we might call "capitalism with a human face," that is, the state permits a free market, but intervenes in it to provide basic services for all and to provide for the poor, sick, and unemployed. After a long and bloody history marked by persecutions and pogroms, Europeans have opted for a secular society. They have come to accept the necessity of protecting ethnic and religious minorities and equal rights for women and homosexuals. They have committed themselves to democracy, even though it can be messy and slow to deliver results. Moreover, Europeans have generally embraced cultural globalization, even when that means swallowing their pride and allowing Starbucks to sell cappuccinos in Italy and McDonald's to peddle burgers in Moscow's Red Square. These convictions are shared, more or less, by most of the continent's citizens.

Yet beneath this broad umbrella are many views of what democracy should look like, or what protections and rights should be shared with immigrants (many of whom are not officially citizens of the states in which they reside). Everyone might agree in theory that a social market economy is best, but implementing it—and paying for it—inevitably breeds dissent. Globalization brings some benefits—for some people—but also has costs, to local cultural integrity and to those who lose their jobs when their employers move their operations offshore. Moreover, even these shared values may fray in light of the challenges ahead, which include integrating increasingly diverse populations, dealing with climate change, and adjusting antiquated economies for survival in an age of global capitalist competition. The future of the EU is itself very much a topic of current debate. If we describe here some of the process through which eastern and western Europe moved toward integration after 1989, we should also remember that this process has not done away with the "many-ness" of Europe. The continent has made remarkable strides in the direction of unity in the past decades, but we can be sure that the diversity of Europe, and of Europeans, is here to stay.

Remaking Central and Eastern Europe after 1989

The year 1989–1990 was one of transformations. Poland, Hungary, and Czechoslovakia experienced remarkably swift and smooth overthrows of their communist regimes, and in Berlin, the wall that had divided the city for twenty-eight years was torn down. In Romania, the communist dictator Nicolae Ceauşescu and his wife Elena were murdered in a much bloodier coup. But what would come next? After decades of one-party rule and repeated purges of the non-communist elite, who would lead the states of eastern Europe? How could obsolete industries and planned economies, run by corrupt bureaucrats, be turned into profit-making ventures? If the first months after the fall of the Iron Curtain and the collapse of the USSR brought with them euphoria and optimism, the realities of post-communist society would make some easterners doubt that their lives had really been changed for the better.

> **What factors made German reunification possible?**

German Reunification

The first question that needed to be resolved in plotting Europe's post-communist future was the fate of the Germanys. Already in November 1989 some Germans, east and west, began to speak of reunifying their country, without appreciating just how different life had been for their counterparts on the other side of the wall. While the West had long enjoyed a free press, a working democracy, and considerable prosperity, the East had suffered censorship, dictatorship, and deprivation. In East Germany in 1989, 60 percent of dwellings still had no central heating and 33 percent had no indoor toilet. Spies were even more pervasive than people thought; as many as one of every seven people had at one time or another provided the party with information about their wives, friends, and coworkers. The secret police, the Stasi, had been much more numerous than the Nazi Gestapo.

Having been warned about the evils of capitalist society, many East Germans were initially hesitant about throwing themselves into the arms of the West. In late November 1989, even West German chancellor Helmut Kohl was predicting that reunification might take five years or more. In fact, less than a year later Kohl was celebrating the re-creation of a single German state.

Kohl's tentative approach was a response to fears voiced by Germany's World War II enemies, Britain, France, and the Soviet Union, that a reunited Germany would command too much power in Europe. Gorbachev did initially resist plans for a new Germany whose NATO membership would allow the stationing of troops on the Polish border, but capitulated in exchange for a payment of $8 billion plus an additional $2 billion in free loans. The Red Army occupation of East Germany ended, and hundreds of thousands of Soviet soldiers returned to their homes. The French received assurances that the Germans would bind themselves even more closely to the European Economic Community, adopting a common currency within a short time span. This agreement recognized the success of West Germany, which had the strongest economy within the EU. If Germany's first unification had been achieved through warfare, through blood and iron, as Bismarck said, this reunification can be said to have been achieved through purchase, one that resulted in a large bill for West German taxpayers.

By the end of 1989, the road to political reunion was clear. But economic union, as Chancellor Kohl recognized, needed to proceed even more rapidly. East Germans continued to stream westward in search of jobs and a better life, and the East German currency, the ostmark, lost more and more value. Although the official rate of exchange was at two to one, by January 1990, exchanges on the black market were running at twenty ostmarks to one deutsche mark. Kohl wanted to keep workers on the job in the East and to save nest eggs set aside by retirees; his plan for a currency union, which went into effect in June 1990, allowed ostmark holders a one-to-one exchange of up to 4,000 ostmarks per person (amounts above this figure could be exchanged two to one). This deal preserved East German purchasing power, though it also made employing East Germans expensive and drove up the cost of living in the east. Many easterners were simply laid off, and by 1991, industrial production in the east had fallen by two-thirds.

The Soviet Union's Demise

Under communism, most Soviet citizens gave up hope that positive changes in their lives could occur. Like peasants of the Old Regimes, they believed that change might take away the grim but stable lives they had built. Gorbachev's policies of perestroika and glasnost signaled that reform might be possible after all, and many

Where Is the Berlin Wall Now?

It is inaccurate to say that the Berlin Wall fell on the night of November 9, 1989. How could it have done so? The wall around West Berlin was about 100 miles in length, and in some parts of the city there were double walls, with a strip of mined no-man's-land in between. The western face of the wall was something of an outdoor gallery for graffiti artists, who had covered its downtown sections with colorful paintings and inscriptions, not because they loved the wall, but because they wanted to use its symbolic power to declare their opposition to war or their feelings about German history. The easterners had no such gallery; they were forbidden from writing, or paint-ing, or even approaching the dreary, gray wall on their side. On November 9 and succeeding days, most East Germans still passed through established check-points rather than scaling or knocking down sections of the twelve-foot-high wall; those who brought hacksaws or chisels to attack the concrete barrier did so mostly for symbolic reasons. Once the wall had been breached, its purpose (to keep East Germans from fleeing to the West) was lost and it became merely an obstruction, an eyesore, and a reminder of the evils that had befallen the city during the Cold War.

Once East German communism col-lapsed, hordes of "wall peckers" began carving out chunks of the wall to keep as souvenirs. Individuals, however, could never have torn down the whole of the wall, which had been built to withstand assault by armored tanks. In June 1990, the East German army began demolishing the wall at Bernauer Street, where an outdoor memorial now stands. Checkpoints between the two Germanys were abolished once East Germany adopted the West German deutsche mark in July of that year. It took military forces more than a year to complete the destruction, which included blasting through underground metro tunnels between city stations that had been sealed during the Cold War. Gradually the Berlin Wall disappeared from the landscape so completely that Berlin city officials decided to install colored paving stones to mark its previous path so that its history would not be erased entirely.

Today sections of the wall are stored in numerous Berlin museums, including the Allied Museum, which

You Too Can Own a Piece of the Wall When this picture was taken in 1990, fragments of the Berlin Wall were running at about $1 in Berlin's tourist shops. Today's shoppers can still buy one of these Cold War relics, together with a certificate of authenticity, though decorated pieces of the western side of the wall are now more costly (and probably less authentic).

documents the period of Allied occupa-tion in Berlin after 1945, and the Wall Museum at Checkpoint Charlie, the Cold War's most famous west-to-east cross-ing point. Sections of the wall are also on display in the United States, at CIA headquarters in Washington, D.C.; at the Microsoft Art Collection in Seattle; and at the presidential libraries of John F. Kennedy, Ronald Reagan, and Richard Nixon. Other European galleries also boast sections of the wall: they can be seen in the Vatican gardens in Rome; at the EU Parliament building in Brussels, Belgium; and in Schengen, Luxembourg, where the Schengen Agreements were signed in 1985. In each of these loca-tions, the wall's pieces continue to have a powerful meaning as symbols of past repression, of the triumph of freedom, and also, more quietly, of the victory of western capitalism.

Millions of small fragments of the massive wall were also taken home by private individuals, and sections of the wall, whether actual or fake, are still on sale today in Berlin's tourist shops. What these pieces mean to their owners is difficult to say; evidently some people see them as objects representing the victory of the West. Others simply want to show that they have visited Berlin or admire the colorful graffiti (few col-lect the plain gray sections of concrete that defined most of the wall during its existence). No one knows how many of these fragments are in private hands—millions, surely. But it is quite certain that more former westerners than easterners own pieces of the wall. Easterners on the whole want to forget the wall that trapped them in a dismal and repressive communist world. Some, who struggle to make ends meet in the post-communist, economy, are not convinced that the fall of the wall was such a magnificent event. Westerners accuse those who remain hesitant about embracing the newly united capitalist Germany of still hav-ing a "wall in the head," of not coming to grips with the fact that the wall and the Cold War belong to the past. They haven't forgotten the wall, but they don't want to possess a piece of it, either.

QUESTION | *What does it mean to own a piece of the Berlin Wall?*

Soviet republics were emboldened to seek independence for themselves by withdrawing from the Warsaw Pact. This process began with Lithuania's attempt to secede in January 1991. Soviet tanks rolled into the capital, Vilnius, and some civilians were killed. The Soviet economy, however, entered a period of severe crisis, and the tanks stopped rolling. One after another, the states of Latvia, Estonia, Armenia, Georgia, Moldavia, Ukraine, and Russia itself announced that they would seek autonomy. Gorbachev tried to prevent this fragmentation, but the republics refused to export food across their borders. As prices spiraled and the threat of violence grew, Gorbachev once again made a decision of monumental importance. Rather than deploying the Red Army to force the republics back into the USSR, he agreed to negotiate with them to form a new federal union.

The breakup of the Soviet Union was not bloodless. In some places, such as Georgia, Armenia, and Azerbaijan, there were attempts at ethnic cleansing as the new states established their borders. Had the Russians resisted the breakup, as the Serbs resisted the breakup of Yugoslavia, the collapse would have been far bloodier. Still, Gorbachev's decision damaged his popularity with the old guard at home. In August 1991, members of the army and the communist elite tried to mount a coup against Gorbachev's reformist government. Recent evidence suggests that Gorbachev may even have initially backed the plan—hoping to reassert the party's control of the state.[2] Claiming exhaustion, Gorbachev left Moscow for his vacation house in the Crimea; his departure offered the coup plotters an opportunity to seize power. When, evidently, Gorbachev got cold feet, the Soviet premier was put under house arrest, and members of the army and KGB surrounded the Moscow White House, where the Russian Republic had its headquarters.

BORIS YELTSIN TAKES CHARGE. The coup was thwarted by the president of the Russian Republic, Boris Yeltsin (1931–2007), who arrived at the Russian White House on a tank. His denunciation of the plotters, which was broadcast live on TV, rallied popular support and the coup leaders could not bring themselves to stage the kind of bloody crackdown Chinese communists had staged in their suppression of protests in Tiananmen Square in 1989. Gorbachev returned to Moscow, but Yeltsin was the man of the hour. He negotiated the creation of a federation of former Soviet Republics, dubbed the **Commonwealth of Independent States (CIS).** CIS members agreed to a common foreign policy and system of defense, but were allowed autonomy in other matters. Russia, by far the largest of the eleven-member CIS, remained dominant. The Baltic states were allowed to opt out entirely and to become independent states (Map 26.1).

THE CHECHEN WARS. The breakup of the USSR was especially painful for the Russians, so recently the overlords of both eastern Europe and heirs to the enormous czarist empire. After the collapse, Russia remained Europe's largest entity, in both size and population. It remained a multiethnic state, and one divided into numerous provinces, some of them far away from Moscow. But under Yeltsin, the Russian Republic committed itself to resisting further fragmentation. In 1994, Yeltsin turned his attention to Chechnya, a region within Russia heavily inhabited by an ethnic group known as Chechens. Since the nineteenth century, when the expansionist Russian Empire had set up Fort Grozny in their midst, the fiercely tribal Chechens, a largely Muslim people, had suffered Russian colonization and persecution. Almost from the start, the Russians had faced resistance from Muslim guerrilla commanders such as Shamil (see Chapter 20) and continuing resistance from the local population.

By 1994, Chechen leaders were pushing hard for national autonomy for Chechnya on the model of the other states that had left the Soviet Union in 1991. At this Yeltsin balked. Hoping to restore some of Russia's pride after the humiliating breakup of the Soviet Union, he launched what he boasted would be a "small victorious war" to destroy Chechnya's bid for independence. The result was not one but two vicious wars (1994–1996 and 1999–2005) and the deaths of thousands of Russians and tens of thousands of Chechens. Even after the formal end of hostilities in 2005, low-level warfare continued in the region. Chechnya is an example of what might have happened across eastern Europe and the USSR had a more aggressive attempt been made to suppress fragmentation by force.

Living with Post-Communist Uncertainties

The end of Soviet-sponsored dictatorships in eastern Europe and liberalizing measures in the Soviet Union were cause for celebration in much of Europe, but making the transition from communist one-party states to democratic rule was not easy. By 1989, few eastern Europeans had any memories of, much less any experience in, democratic rule. Imperial Russia had never been a democracy, and the 1917 revolution had transpired seventy years before. Almost no one was left who could remember the days of Kerensky's brief provisional government. Eastern Europe (except Czechoslovakia) had had little experience of democracy in the interwar era, and what experience it did have was rather grim. Moreover, the communist states had so thoroughly infiltrated their populations that very few people could claim to have entirely clean hands—and those who did had no experience in how to govern, how to operate a judicial system, or how to privatize and modernize industrial production. There were very few Havels and Wałesas, with exemplary records as dissidents and democrats. Who, then, would lead the fledgling states?

THE COMMUNISTS ARE STILL AMONG US. By and large, the answer was former communists. Although some effort was made to purge the worst offenders, these usually foundered, and many leading communists got off very lightly. In East Germany, people were allowed

MAP 26.1 | The Breakup of the Soviet Union, 1991

This map shows the division of the Soviet Union into autonomous states that vary greatly in size and population. Note the location of the province of Chechnya, which has been compelled to remain part of Russia. *Which states are most likely to look westward, to Europe, for cultural and economic assistance and inspiration? Which are more likely to look to the Islamic states in the south, or to China, for inspiration or trade?*

to see their Stasi files (records kept by the secret police), which led to some private soul searching—for example, when husbands had informed on wives, or priests on parishioners—but very few prosecutions or even public denunciations. Die-hard communist Erich Honecker (see Chapter 25) was jailed briefly but then whisked off to Russia and then Chile, where he died in 1994. The new Germany fired some judges and university professors and put on trial several border guards who had killed civilians trying to escape, but found it difficult to indict those officials who insisted that they could not be tried for actions that had been legal under the old system.

In Czechoslovakia, Václav Havel (1936–2011) became president, but an attempt to purge old communists ended with the indictment of mostly small fry rather than the communist leadership and had to be abandoned. After his retirement in 2003, Havel was replaced by the economist Václav Klaus, who admitted that he had never really been an anti-communist. In Poland, Lech Wałesa (b. 1943) lost his bid for reelection to the Polish presidency in 1995 to a former communist, though subsequent governments tended to be headed by conservative national-

ists. In Poland, as in Hungary, the old elites stayed on, but they did reform their states, making possible the dismantling of the security services, some economic growth, and the development of a more democratic and open—but increasingly nationalist—public sphere.

In Romania and Bulgaria, far less change occurred. In Romania, the Communist Ion Iliescu (b. 1930) took power after the coup. He did not move to make major changes to Romanian economic policy or to dismiss those who had served the Ceaușescu regime; police brutality continued. A confrontation between the government and people demanding reform in September 1991 resulted in the creation of a multiparty system, a market economy, and legislation that protected civil rights, but in practice, the communists remained the largest party and retained control of the media, facilitating Iliescu's reelection as president in 1992 and again in 2000. Romania remains one of the poorest nations in the EU, and one in which few former communist officials have been called to account for their crimes.

After Yeltsin's retirement in 2000, Russians elected as president Vladimir Putin (b. 1952), a former KGB officer

Post-Communist Chechnya

From the perspective of the Chechens, the collapse of communism delivered only misery. Life in this mountainous region of the Caucasus had never been easy. In the nineteenth century, the Russian Empire made war on the Chechens along with the other peoples of the Caucasus in an effort to seize their land. Worse came in 1944 when Stalin labeled the Chechens traitors and deported and dispersed the entire ethnic group across the Siberian plains. Those who survived to be allowed to return in 1957 committed themselves to staying on their ancestral land even in the face of continuing persecutions by the communist regime.

The First Chechen War began in 1994, when Russian federal troops invaded to prevent the region from establishing its independence. Opposition came from Chechen resistance fighters, many of whom were well armed and willing to use terror tactics. A brief cease-fire in 1996 was broken in 1999, ushering in the Second Chechen War. These conflicts were horrific, but in between them there were many bloody contests between various ethnic groups in Chechnya and between Chechen strongmen and their followers, and numerous acts of terrorism outside the region, in which some Russians and tens of thousands of Chechens were killed.

We can view these conflicts from the inside thanks to the work of the journalist Anna Politkovskaya, who committed herself to reporting from Chechnya despite the extreme hardships and dangers she endured. Politkovskaya recognized that this was not a conflict of good versus evil, or bad versus good guys. Although the Russians were the invaders and had the most machine guns, some Chechens joined in the murdering, kidnapping, and plundering of their neighbors. Some Russian soldiers, Politkovskaya showed, tried to report their fellows for burning villages or seizing civilians as hostages in order to extract ransom, but Russian officials turned a blind eye to rapes, senseless murders, and wanton destruction of people's property and lives. Politkovskaya's essays were long censored by the Russian media and largely ignored even by well-intentioned Europeans and Americans, who argued that they could not intervene in Russian domestic affairs. In 2006, Politkovskaya was herself murdered under suspicious circumstances.

But Politkovskaya did not mean her reporting to be purely political in nature. Her intent throughout was to document the terrible sufferings of the civilians who inhabited what she called "a small corner of hell."[3] And she showed, unquestionably, that from the perspective of Chechen civilians, the collapse of the Soviet Union was a disaster. The second war in particular cut Chechnya off from other regions in Russia as federal troops starved, strafed, and tortured civilians to make them give up their terrorists, a category into which fell both the guilty and the innocent. People were imprisoned for days in pits reminiscent of the Black Hole of Calcutta or had their fingers or toes amputated. Men and women with no link to the terrorists were routinely held hostage until the family or the village paid a ransom; both sexes endured rapes. Land mines claimed the lives of those who strayed off the roads, where numerous checkpoints allowed officials to extort money and goods from travelers. Many villages were burned, and constant bombing turned Grozny into a city of ruins in which desperately hungry people sought shelter. Grandmothers with starved bodies saved their paltry rations for their grandchildren; parents were tortured and dragged away before their children's eyes. Young men were beaten so brutally that their internal organs suffered damage; some joined paramilitary groups, some of them organized by Islamic extremists, wanting to inflict suffering on others before, inevitably, dying themselves.

A whole region has been so terrorized and starved that its people struggle not to victimize one another. As Politkovskaya argued, the young Chechens who managed to survive these persecutions will never forget how this supposedly democratic regime destroyed their childhoods, tortured and starved their bodies, and tormented their families. Chechens will remember the end of communism not as liberation, but as a headlong dive into hell.

Grozny, Summer 1996 The Chechen city of Grozny suffered terribly from the Chechen Wars of 1994–1996 and 1999–2000.

QUESTION | *What does the experience of Chechnya reveal about how the fall of communism played out in Europe?*

and communist official. Putin's staunch Russian nationalism and reputation as a strongman were enhanced by launching the Second Chechen War, but his popularity stemmed chiefly from his handling of the economy. Under Putin, many state businesses were sold, especially to his cronies. As oil prices soared, the Russian economy recovered, and some wealth trickled down to the urban middle classes. Putin was handily reelected in 2004 and, after his protégé Dmitry Medvedev acted as placeholder from 2008 to 2012, again in March 2012, despite having to endure several large-scale rallies denouncing his authoritarian style. But Putin has remained suspicious of western-style capitalism and contemptuous of democracy.

"CRONY" CAPITALISM. The reentrenchment of old communist elites in the political sphere has its parallels in the economic sphere as well. Markets cannot be created overnight, nor workers retrained, nor outdated industrial plants overhauled immediately—and after 1989, the process of replacing communism with capitalism proved difficult and all too likely to favor those with friends in high places. In part this was the result of western caution. Western capitalists invested some money in eastern businesses, especially in East Germany and the Czech Republic, but they tended to buy up viable, small-scale concerns and avoid collective farms and antiquated factories. Elsewhere they were wary of investing, especially because laws and institutions regulating the market and protecting property owners were, in many cases, nonexistent or regularly ignored.

That meant that those in the know, and those already close to the halls of power, managed to get hold of nations' mineral rights and valuable properties. In a few years' time, these "cronies" simply gobbled up the oil companies and fancy apartment buildings, the steel plants and the breweries. Get-rich-quick scams engineered by corrupt businessmen and former members of the security services tricked inexperienced members of the Romanian, Albanian, and Russian publics into investing their money—the "little people" lost their shirts while cash flowed to Mafia-like organizations. Those who profited from the fall of communism—in material terms at least—were often old communists, who formed a new oligarchy, whose many ties with the political elite (especially in Romania and the former USSR) allowed them to do as they pleased without fear of legal repercussions.

By the mid-1990s, this uneven and corrupt privatization had destroyed the command economy, but had not built a successful marketplace in its stead. Prices rose steeply—Ukraine had an annual inflation rate estimated at 5,371 percent in 1993[4]—and farm-to-city supply routes broke down. Yeltsin undertook what he called **shock therapy** to make a rapid transition from a communist to a market economy. The result was high inflation, high rates of unemployment, and the selling off of more state property to rich oligarchs. In 1998, Russia defaulted on its debt, and ordinary people lost their savings as the ruble was sharply devalued.

Here, as elsewhere in the former Eastern bloc, initial optimism about the fall of communism was replaced with skepticism about capitalism—partly because the kind of capitalism easterners got was one designed to profit the old guard. For some people, this led to a kind of nostalgia for communism's supposed good old days, in which workers were for the most part guaranteed jobs, even when they produced things no one wanted or simply stamped papers. By contrast, after the system's collapse, many people, especially the elderly and those who were state dependent, had no jobs at all. New goods were available in stores, but prices had risen even for basic supplies, and many easterners could not afford to enjoy the new products or to live comfortably. Benefits that people used to count on (free if imperfect health care; decent pensions; and cheap rents, movie tickets, and vodka) became unreliable or disappeared. Living the post-communist age was to find oneself in a world of new opportunities and choices, but new dangers and barriers as well.

Another consequence of the collapse of the Eastern bloc and of the disappearance of its repressive, though predictable, routines was that easterners were left wanting to join Europe, but feeling alienated from the West. Their income levels and past experiences were so very different, and some easterners found western individualism too predominant, its marketplaces too risky, and its sexual mores too permissive. Throwing off the Soviet yoke but not yet ready (or able) to become fully like the French or Spanish, eastern Europeans turned inward once more, embracing national traditions and identities that had been submerged since 1945.

The Return of Nationalism

During the Cold War, the communist leadership in the Eastern bloc had forbidden discussion of ethnic questions or the expression of nationalist sentiments. All workers were supposed to be comrades, committing themselves to building communism and leaving behind their prejudices and resentments. There was some intermarriage, and members of minority groups who were willing to toe the party line were often allowed to join the communist bureaucracy. But as the Chechen Wars showed, Europe's history of violence between ethnic groups, and especially events between 1914 and 1945, had not been forgotten. In fact, communism simply drove many of these tensions underground. When the Cold War ended, the taboo on national and ethnic questions suddenly lapsed.

In eastern Europe, nationalism was a good substitute for Soviet overlordship, and quite naturally people wished to celebrate once more the cultural and economic uniqueness of their states. This sort of nationalism was relatively free of the anti-Semitic or xenophobic tendencies of the interwar era, at least at first—in part for the tragic reason that the events of the twentieth century had reduced the size of minority populations in eastern European states from about 33 percent before World War I to about 3 percent in 1989. But new nationalists in Russia, such as Vladimir

Zhirinovsky, who developed a powerful following in the 1990s, were outspoken anti-Semites and xenophobes. Other former communists such as Putin or Slobodan Milošević in Yugoslavia adopted nationalist rhetoric as a means to win election in new times. If nationalism returned to eastern Europe in the 1990s, it did so in various guises and was sometimes tempered by the desire of the former Eastern bloc states to join the EU, whose members frowned upon expressions of extreme nationalism.

Czechoslovakia was one of the places where a return to nationalism was motivated chiefly by economic concerns—and where the solution proved to be a peaceful one. Once communism was gone, ethnic tensions revived between the predominantly Czech population in the western half of the state and the poorer, predominantly Slovakian population in the eastern half. For a time, Havel, now president, tried to keep the state together, but in 1992 he decided, instead, to opt for a "**velvet divorce**," in which Czechoslovakia split peacefully into two separate states, the Czech Republic and the Republic of Slovakia.

A Hot War after a Cold One: Yugoslavia

Why did ethnic violence occur in Yugoslavia? Elsewhere, the end of the Cold War and the return to nationalism had anything but a velvet ending. The most painful case was that of a state that had been awkwardly cobbled together from the start: Yugoslavia.

From Tito to Milošević

The origins of Yugoslavia's post-communist woes lay partly in its interwar conflicts and even more obviously in its experience during World War II (see Chapters 24 and 25). In 1945, the half-Slovene, half-Croatian Josef Broz (who took the name Tito) had made Yugoslavia a communist state, one in which ethnic tensions were defused by giving the separate republics (Croatia, Serbia, Bosnia, Slovenia, Montenegro, and Macedonia) within the Yugoslav federation additional autonomy and by banning all discussion of the ethnic violence of the past. Officially the state was called the Socialist Federal Republic of Yugoslavia (on the model of the Union of Soviet Socialist Republics). Within the republics of the federation, Yugoslav communists were supposed to forget about the past and work together toward a new state.

Slovenia, for example, remained ethnically homogeneous, but some communities did mix and intermarry, especially in Sarajevo, Bosnia's cosmopolitan capital. Large communities of Serbs lived in the republics of Croatia and Bosnia, and northern Serbia was home to many Croats. Although the province of Kosovo is especially sacred to the Serbs, it also contained a large Albanian population. The

Albanians, like the Bosnians, were Muslims, whereas the Serbs were Eastern Orthodox Christians and the Croats Catholics, though under communism no one was encouraged to practice their religions. But no one, it turned out, had forgotten to which group their families belonged or had forgotten Yugoslavia's recent history. Underground, powerful hatreds and painful memories persisted.

During his lifetime, Tito worked to prevent nationalist tensions from ripping Yugoslavia apart. After his death in 1980, his successors proved far less committed to Yugoslav unity than he had been. By this time, economic modernization was moving much more quickly in the westernmost provinces of Slovenia and Croatia than in the poorer regions of Serbia and Bosnia. In 1989, the communist turned Serbian nationalist, Slobodan Milošević (1941–2006), became president of the Serbian Republic as well as president of the Federal Republic of Yugoslavia. He inherited a huge debt and an annual inflation rate of more than 1,000 percent just as eastern European states, one after another, rushed to leave the Eastern bloc.

Playing to his Serbian brethren, Milošević suppressed the rights of the Albanian majority in Kosovo and of the Croatian minority in Serbia and moved to funnel national funds to federal bureaucrats (many of them Serbs). The Slovenes, who contributed far more to the national budget than they received in services, tired of this drain on their resources and in early 1991 declared their desire to secede from Yugoslavia. Milošević ordered the Yugoslav federal army to attack Slovenia, but gave up after a series of minor clashes and allowed Slovenia to declare its independence.

Sarajevo Holds Out

Milošević had a bigger problem to deal with, for in nearby Croatia the ardent nationalist and president of the Republic of Croatia, Franjo Tudjman, declared Croatia's intention to secede from the federation. In villages across Croatia, residents began to pressure members of the Serb minority to pack up and leave. When Serb families refused, they were subjected to vigilante violence and a process of ethnic cleansing began. Milošević and his fellow Serbs were outraged, and Milošević sent his Yugoslav federal army into Croatia. Armies clashed as ethnic cleansing continued, until a cease-fire was declared in late winter 1992, at which point the EU, pressed by the Germans, recognized the independence of Croatia. Milošević was not willing to accept that recognition, but faced a more worrying threat. In 1992, the Muslims and Croatians of Bosnia approved a referendum declaring their independence (Map 26.2).

The Serbian minority within Bosnia objected. Bosnian autonomy, after all, would have left them a weak minority in the new state. They declared war on their fellow Bosnians and obtained the backing of Milošević. Tudjman backed the Bosnian Croatians, and a brutal civil war erupted. The Croatians also turned against the Muslim Bosnians, hoping to annex as much of Bosnia to the new

Croatian state as possible. Paramilitary groups of thugs carried out much of the fighting in this war, and all sides practiced ethnic cleansing, driving civilians of opposing ethnic groups from their homes. Men were murdered and women were rounded up and forced into camps where they were systematically raped as a means of both physical and psychological torture. The Serbs were the worst offenders, for like the Russians in Chechnya they had the most weapons and the largest number of combatants. But Croatians and a few Muslims also committed atrocities against their former neighbors.

In the wake of the Holocaust, Europeans had declared that never again would genocide be tolerated. Nevertheless, reports that it was happening again abounded. Hundreds of thousands of refugees sought asylum in EU countries. As early as February 1992, the United Nations sent in peacekeeping troops, but they were not allowed to use their weapons and were unable to prevent further atrocities. An International War Crimes Tribunal was set up in The Hague in the Netherlands to try those who perpetrated crimes against humanity, but the tribunal could prosecute cases only when individual states cooperated and surrendered accused criminals to it.

In April 1992, Bosnian Serbs under the direction of the merciless commanders Radovan Karadžic and Radko Mladić surrounded the city of Sarajevo, hoping to starve it into submission. The siege of Sarajevo continued for almost four years, during which time food, water, and electricity only rarely made it through Serb lines. The city was shelled regularly, and snipers worked around the clock to pick off those who tried to go about their daily lives. Still, Sarajevans refused to surrender and managed to get the story of their suffering to the international media, despite the cutting of telephone lines, the murder of mailmen, and the poisoning of carrier pigeons. Finally, in the spring of 1995, U.S. president Bill Clinton convinced NATO to bomb Serbian outposts.

MAP 26.2 | The Breakup of Yugoslavia, 1991–1995
This map shows Yugoslavia's division into separate states as a result of the wars of 1991–1995. *Why was it so easy for Slovenia to separate itself from the Yugoslav federation, and so difficult for Bosnia to do so?*

Miss Sarajevo Beauty Contestants, 1993 At her crowning as Miss Besieged Sarajevo, seventeen-year-old Imela Nogić and her fellow finalists unfurled a banner reading "Don't Let Them Kill Us." This famous image was smuggled out of war-torn Yugoslavia and broadcast across the world. Among those touched by the photo was the Irish singer Bono, who composed a song, "Miss Sarajevo," in honor of the brave Sarajevans. The song also features a passage sung by the world's most famous opera singer at the time, Luciano Pavarotti.

CHRONOLOGY — Key Events in the Breakup of Yugoslavia

DATE	EVENT
1980	Death of Tito
1991	Slovenia declares independence
1992	Croatia's independence recognized
February 1992	The UN sends troops into Bosnia
April 1992–February 1996	Siege of Sarajevo
Spring 1995	NATO bombing of Serbia
November 1995	Dayton Accords signed
2006	Death of Milošević
2008	Kosovo declares independence

The Bosnia Serbs retaliated by taking UN peacekeepers hostage and then seizing Srebrenica, the town the UN had deemed a "safe zone," to which many Muslims had fled. The Serbs rounded up and murdered at least 7,400 unarmed men and boys, burying their remains in a mass grave beneath a soccer field. This massacre—the worst since the Second World War—pushed the UN and NATO to increase their involvement, forcing Milošević to withdraw support from the Bosnian Serbs.

The Dayton Accords

In November 1995, the United States oversaw the negotiation of the **Dayton Accords,** signed just outside Dayton, Ohio. According to these agreements, Bosnia was not divided up, but its regions were given some autonomy, and Serbs, Croatians, and Muslims were to share in its governance. An imperfect solution, the Dayton Accords nonetheless avoided a partition that would have rewarded the aggressors and rendered meaningless Sarajevo's costly resistance.

NATO forces were called upon to bomb Serbia proper again in 1999, when Milošević moved once again to suppress Albanian attempts at independence in the province of Kosovo. After a brief bombing campaign, Milošević capitulated and in Serbian elections in 2000 was removed from office and handed over to the War Crimes Tribunal in The Hague. He died in prison during his trial. After evading capture for many years, Radovan Karadžic and Radko Mladić finally had to face trial for crimes against humanity; neither expressed regret for his actions. With UN assistance, Kosovo declared independence in 2008. Serbia, hoping to win international favor and EU economic assistance, made no move to stop it, but remained deeply dissatisfied with the outcome.

Western Europe after the Fall of the Wall

After the fall of the Berlin Wall, western Europe, too, experienced something of an identity crisis. During the Cold War, western Europe had been defined chiefly by its desire to recover from—and never go back to—fascism and war and by its relationships with the United States. Spared the cost and potential conflicts involved in rebuilding their military forces, western states spent those saved tax dollars on building extensive welfare states. Individual national identities had not disappeared, but in the desire to get beyond the enmities that had resulted in two world wars, European politicians deliberately discouraged expressions of extreme patriotism. The provisions of the social welfare state—including extensive protections for unions and rights for laborers to bargain with business owners—cut to a minimum class conflict of the sort experienced at the end of the nineteenth century. But even as communism was collapsing, western European integration was proceeding, and immigration from non-European nations was increasing. All these developments contributed to an urgent need to define what Europe was, what held it together—and what made it different from the world's other polities, including the United States, Turkey, or China.

> What values did western Europeans commit themselves to after World War II, and especially after 1989?

Defining the Values of Post-1989 Europe

As European officials coped with German reunification, with the building of EU institutions, and with the incorporation of the former eastern European states into the EU, leaders worked hard to articulate a set of values that Europe, collectively, stands for. Broadly speaking, these are democracy, the social market economy, secularism, toleration of minorities, the protection of civil rights, and economic cooperation.

DEMOCRACY. After the defeat of fascism and Nazism in the Second World War, western Europeans had committed themselves to democracy. They are justly proud of this commitment, even though some states (such as Portugal and Spain) have adopted it only relatively recently. People are allowed to vote for the party of their choice, and when the electorate changes its mind, leaders step down from their posts peacefully. Many nations—including Britain, the Netherlands, Sweden, and Spain—still have monarchs, but real power (including the power to tax) is held by national parliaments and prime ministers. No one questions the sovereignty of the people—such a new idea in John Locke's time (Chapter 16). Indeed, the number of assemblies seems to be multiplying, as some nations devolve power from the national level, sharing it with regional assemblies. For example, to placate regional activists, Belgium in 1993 subdivided itself into three regions and gave each region a separate parliament (one Dutch speaking, one French speaking, and one German speaking). In 1997, British prime minister Tony Blair allowed Scotland, Northern Ireland, and Wales to vote in referenda on whether to reconstitute their own national parliaments. When all voted yes, he allowed elections to create such assemblies in 1998. **Devolution**—the process of passing power to regional assemblies—has given Britain's regions new symbolic power, though the power of the purse remains firmly rooted—at least for now—in the British Parliament in London.

In most places, there have been regular changes in governance, especially because the large number of parties means that no single party wins a majority of votes. Governments are often formed of coalitions, between conservatives and liberals, for example, or sometimes between moderate socialists and moderate conservatives. There are environmental parties and in some places communist parties. Recent years have seen the rise of right-wing parties, such as the National Front in France or the Freedom Party in the Netherlands, but these parties, too, when taken into the ruling coalition, have usually behaved according to democratic rules.

Of course, democracy sometimes can be subverted. In Italy, questions about the proper operation of democracy have been raised as a result of the longtime political dominance of Silvio Berlusconi, a former lounge singer who also owns much of Italy's media. In 2011, concerns were raised about the nondemocratic appointment of former bankers Mario Monti and Lucas Papademos to oversee the imposition of austerity measures in Italy and Greece (see p. 862). But these debates confirm the existence of a very deep and broad commitment to democracy in Europe.

THE SOCIAL MARKET ECONOMY. In the later 1970s and 1980s, conservatives, especially Margaret Thatcher in England, insisted on downsizing the state's role in the economy and began privatizing some business (for example, British Rail). By the 1990s, even some Labour and social democratic leaders, such as Tony Blair in England (prime minister 1997–2007) and Gerhard Schroeder in Germany (in office 1998–2005), were eager to trim back excessive spending and provide greater incentives for private ownership and competition. Thanks to Thatcher and to a lesser extent to Blair, Britain adopted a market model closer to that of the United States than that of Europe's continental states, and thanks to Kohl and Schroeder, Germany reduced some of its benefits. But even in these countries, leaders cannot imagine doing away with state-sponsored pensions and unemployment benefits, or with subsidies for museums, opera houses, universities, and orchestras. Education—at the lower and higher levels—is almost entirely state funded through-

out the continent, as is health care, and very few people would like to see this system dismantled and privatized. Europeans are happy with a system that ensures a considerable amount of job security (as long as one can find employment; by 2009, this was an increasing problem for young people and immigrants) and a safety net for the poor. Most western Europeans regard their social market economy as far superior to the more risk-friendly world of U.S. capitalism.

SECULARISM. A third pillar of western European identity is secularism. Already in the seventeenth century, some Europeans had begun to cultivate a secular, or nonreligious identity; absolutist monarchs and enlightened thinkers encouraged people to think of themselves as subjects of a centralizing state or as citizens of the world rather than exclusively as Christians. The French revolutionaries experimented with secularizing *everything*—including marriage and the calendar—but their actions were too radical for most Europeans at the time. In the nineteenth century, national identity, arguably, became the primary way in which Europeans identified themselves, though most continued to go to church and to think of Christianity as one of the virtues that separated "civilized" from "uncivilized" persons.

In western Europe, in particular, the nineteenth century saw the secularization of many institutions, such as schools, and the incorporation of non-Christians into the electorate, though many people still joined Christian socialist parties or attended parochial schools. Increasingly, religion was regarded as a private matter and relegated to the private sphere—even though hundreds of thousands continued to go to church or visit Lourdes (see Chapter 21). By the twentieth century, Europeans had learned to look to the state rather than the churches for social services, and after the horrors of the world wars, they were eager to have those states distribute services to citizens regardless of their faiths or ethnicities. The vast majority of Europeans assume that secular laws—including those that protect the civil rights of women—will and should take precedence over religious doctrines or traditional customs.

A commitment to secularism does not mean that Europe has entirely lost touch with the cultural and religious identity formed by its long Christian past, as the case of Bono makes clear. Christian holidays are still celebrated, and many Europeans still think of themselves as products of Christian heritage. Pope John Paul II (1978–2005), the first non-Italian pope in more than 450 years, was enormously popular in Europe, especially in his native Poland. His visit there in 1979 was instrumental in generating support for Solidarity's anti-communist campaigns, and he remains a hero there today. John Paul II also traveled extensively throughout the world, making visits to Egypt, Syria, Mexico, Armenia, Israel, and the Philippines, among other destinations, and his passing in 2005 was lamented throughout the world. During his reign, the Catholic Church was rocked by a series of sex scandals, involving priests' abuse of children; victims still feel that the high clergy have not done enough to apologize, and to make sure that abuses are prevented in the future, and some parishioners have left the church.

There remain states in which religion remains deeply imbedded in political culture. In Croatia, Catholicism—the religion of nearly 90 percent of its post-1996 inhabitants—has again become the state religion, and in Poland and the Irish Republic, Catholicism continues to be part of both politics and daily life. In discussions over a proposed EU constitution in 2003, the Poles refused to sign unless the document listed Christianity as one of Europe's founding principles. But they lost their case—in fact, the constitution was never passed—and subsequent statements tend to avoid mentioning Christianity. Most Europeans may feel themselves cultural Christians but, remembering their nations' histories of state-backed religious persecution, are hesitant to create official preferences for one religion above another.

The relatively recent influx of many immigrants with non-Christian backgrounds remains a challenge, in part because some immigrants do not wish to give up their religious identities, and in part because these non-Christians also tend to be Africans, South Asians, or people of Middle Eastern descent. Racism and religious prejudice often go hand in hand. But this influx of believers seems simply to have strengthened the conviction of culturally Christian Europeans that secularism should hold sway. In 2004, France banned Muslim women from wearing veils in schools, and in 2011, French president Nicolas Sarkozy extended this measure by outlawing the wearing of face-covering veils in public. Other states are contemplating similar measures. Although there were signs by 2012 that Christian church attendance is rising, it is safe to say that, for the foreseeable future, western Europe will remain a secular society—and a relatively tolerant one.

TOLERATION OF MINORITIES. If Europeans committed themselves to democracy and secularism after World War II, they also committed themselves to protecting the rights of minorities. As Chapter 25 showed, northern and western Europe in the postwar era had already become considerably more cosmopolitan because of the influx of guest workers from southern Europe and Turkey in the 1960s and 1970s. Many of these workers stayed and started families; their descendants learned the local language, joined ethnically mixed soccer teams, and attended European universities. But a new wave began in the 1990s, when western Europe began receiving not only a large number of political refugees, but also many people from its former colonies. In 1992, Germany received more than 400,000 applications for asylum, many of them from Yugoslavia, and to its credit, accepted most of them.

Pope John Paul II, Globetrotter Karol Wojtyła, who took the title John Paul II when he became pope in 1978, proved to be hugely popular, both in Europe and across the globe. John Paul II visited many countries never before accorded a papal visit, including South Africa, where he was greeted by President Nelson Mandela.

Other European states have also taken in many asylum-seekers in recent years, as well as an increasing number of Africans, Asians, and eastern Europeans seeking new homes. By 2012, some 20 million people from non-EU nations were living in Europe's twenty-seven states.

Across Europe the record of toleration varies. For the most part, newcomers are treated with decency, if not warmth, and many European countries fund language programs, youth centers, and job training. But right-wing thugs in many countries regularly harass and assault foreigners, especially those with darker skins. Right-wing parties regularly call for them to be sent back home or to be refused admission in the first place. More subtly, these immigrants face tremendous discrimination in the labor market and are usually hired only for the most unpleasant jobs, regardless of their levels of education. In many countries, immigrants are eligible to become full-fledged citizens if they meet certain legal requirements, but in most cases it takes many years, proof of steady employment, and learning a new language to become a citizen. Many newcomers cannot satisfy the criteria or fail to make the effort.

In 2005, in the Paris suburbs, heavily populated by poor immigrant families, anger about the lack of opportunities for non-white Frenchmen boiled over. A series of riots brought national and international attention to a problem that was not limited to France, but also plagues Germany, the Netherlands, and other nations. French president Sarkozy insisted on prosecuting the perpetrators of the riots, but later announced new programs for putting young immigrants to work. Sarkozy's actions typified

European policy today: insist on the rule of law, and then use state policy to address the problem. Whether state policies will be swift and comprehensive enough to drive forward assimilation and spread prosperity to blighted immigrant neighborhoods remains to be seen.

GENDER EQUALITY AND GAY RIGHTS. Chastened by the horrors of World War II, western Europeans pledged themselves to the protection of civil and human rights. Since 1989, the most important cases here have been attempts to increase gender equality and to establish gay rights. As birthrates have dropped, more women have joined the workforce, though many work part time and their wages continue to lag behind those of men. There are more women than ever before in national parliaments and local councils, but women are rarely appointed to the highest-level posts in the private sector. Only a small fraction of German corporate executives are women; the same is true in most other European states. Many of these countries have generous packages for maternity leave (up to three years in some cases), but this means that mothers are often passed over for managerial posts where their absence would be missed. Legally, women are entitled to hold any job in the EU, and culturally most Europeans agree that girls and women should be able to choose their sexual and marriage partners, have access to educational and job opportunities equal to those of men, and have the freedom to adopt birth control methods, including abortion. But, as most leaders would admit, full gender equality remains a distant prospect.

Adult prostitution is legal in western European nations (but illegal in eastern European states and Yugoslavia's successor states), and is regulated to various degrees. The fall of the Berlin Wall brought tourists seeking cheap sex to the former Eastern bloc, and a wave of eastern women to the West seeking employment as prostitutes. By about 2004, something like 70 percent of the EU's prostitutes were women from the former East.[5] Despite the efforts of humanitarian groups, thousands of eastern European women and girls are smuggled or trafficked across borders and made to serve as sex workers in the west. Thus, there have sometimes been conflicts between women asserting their right to earn money as sex workers, and EU officials trying to limit prostitution to protect the rights of women and children.

Initially, many Europeans reacted to the first reports on the HIV/AIDS virus by resorting to homophobic language. At the time (1981), Scotland and France had only just decriminalized homosexual acts, and many gay people remained terrified of coming out of the closet. But education and activism gradually helped to temper fears, and by the late 1980s, western governments were launching ads advocating toleration as well as informing both gays and heterosexuals about how to protect themselves against contracting the deadly disease.

The EU also committed itself to gay rights, and homosexual acts are officially legal throughout the EU. Twenty European nations allow same-sex civil unions and seven permit same-sex marriages. There is, however, a significant east-west difference; the former Eastern bloc states, with the exception of the Czech Republic and Hungary, prohibit same-sex marriages and partnerships. Many immigrants disagree with EU natives on this issue, as does the Catholic church. EU advocates contend that in extending rights to homosexuals they are carrying forward enlightened traditions of toleration and the expansion of human rights.

The European Union

Post-1989 identity in the west was shaped by commitments to democracy, the social market economy, secularism, tolerance, and civil rights—and European politicians have brought all these values into their discussions about the transition of the EU from a primarily economic association to one that also functions as a supranational political entity. The initial push for European integration, as we saw in Chapter 25, arose from the desire to move beyond the destructive nationalism that produced two world wars and to create in its place a European trading zone that could compete in the world economy. This movement was already well advanced by 1985 when five nations (West Germany, Belgium, Luxembourg, France, and the Netherlands) made a further push for cooperation by signing the **Schengen Agreements,** which envisioned doing away with border controls between their nations and allowing the free flow of people, capital, and goods. Although the Schengen Agreements could not be put into practice until 1997, by which time closer cooperation between nations had been orchestrated, they laid the foundations for the European Economic Community to become something more: a Europe without borders.

THE MAASTRICHT TREATY. The first major step in this direction was the signing of the Maastricht Treaty of 1992, which turned the European Economic Community, which was primarily an economic unit, into a European Union, in which nations would also coordinate their foreign policymaking and their criminal justice systems. The treaty envisioned a series of stages through which nations needed to pass on their way to joining the EU. First, the nation had to apply and be placed on a list of eligible nations; at the second stage, it needed to demonstrate its commitment to the rule of law, the protection of minorities, democratic governance, and human rights. By meeting these requirements, a state could gain status as an EU country. But to achieve membership in the more exclusive group of nations known as the **Eurozone,** the state's economy had to pass additional, stringent tests. To join this club, a state's budget deficits must not exceed 3 percent of gross domestic product (GDP), government debt cannot be more than 60 percent of GDP, and inflation rates have to remain close to those of surrounding nations. When these requirements have been met, the state is allowed to adopt the common European currency, the euro.

THE EURO. After the signing of the Maastricht Treaty, the EU finalized the details of its European monetary union. In 1999, the euro came into being as an electronic unit of exchange used across the EU. Actual coins and the paper euro bills came into circulation on January 1, 2002. The bills do not depict sites or heroes from any particular nation but are adorned with generic bridges on one side and gateways or windows on the other. Member nations are allowed to select designs for one side of the euro coins they issue, but they cannot deviate from the standard size or agreed-upon metal content, and the number of coins they mint is strictly regulated by an EU agency, the European Central Bank.

Not everyone wanted to join the EU or to adopt the euro. Norway and Switzerland declined to join the union. The United Kingdom, along with Sweden and Denmark, joined the EU but opted out of the common currency, even though their neighbor, the Republic of Ireland, did adopt the euro in 2002. Many of the nations that were allowed to join the EU after 1989 were unable to meet the stage-three economic criteria, and remain outside of the Eurozone. Although European leaders trumpeted the new currency, citizens of many states were sorry to see their local currencies disappear. Greeks had long known the drachma, and Germans, especially West Germans, were attached to the deutsche mark. More important were larger concerns about yoking together all of Europe's diverse economies. Though each state kept control of its banks, state spending, and budgetary policy, tying nations to the euro means that each state, to some degree, swims or sinks with the rest.

THE EU'S NEW MEMBERS. After the fall of the Berlin Wall, eastern European nations expressed their yearning to join the EU, hoping to ensure that they would not be drawn back into the Russian orbit and expecting that joining the union would be a ticket to new prosperity. In May 2004, the EU accepted into the union Poland, the Czech Republic, Hungary, Slovakia, Slovenia, the Baltic states (Latvia, Lithuania, and Estonia), and two Mediterranean islands, Malta and Cyprus. Romania and Bulgaria were allowed to join in 2007. Although Turkey had applied for membership far earlier, the EU states have constantly deferred a final decision on its entry. Turkey's poverty and record of human rights abuses remain issues to be resolved, and some Europeans remain uneasy about the prospect of moving the EU's borders so far to the east. Feeling spurned, Turkey has increasingly looked for other regional partners but has not given up entirely on joining the EU.

The Eastern bloc states see their future with Europe, but they cannot break all ties with the Soviet Union's suc-

The Euro Introduced as the single currency of the seventeen-country Eurozone in 2001, euro bills and coins feature common images of bridges and arches on one side, and designs selected by the various nations on the other. After 2008, divergences in levels of national debt and in economic performance among members of the Eurozone have made the future of the single currency uncertain.

cessor states. In particular, these states are dependent on Russia for virtually all their energy needs. The reality of this situation was brought home most notably in January 2009, when a dispute between Ukraine and Russia over a natural gas pipeline led to a severe reduction in energy supplies to Slovakia and Bulgaria. Another crisis in supply threatened Hungary in December of the same year. Though negotiations resolved these disputes, the incidents demonstrated how dependent eastern Europeans continue to be on infrastructure created during the Cold War.

Increasingly, the EU has become a political as well as an economic entity. For a time, most policies concerning subjects such as farming subsidies and environmental standards were made by the European Commission, made up of one member for each of the states and based in Brussels, Belgium. On January 1, 2009, the Lisbon Treaty went into force, giving the EU Parliament (composed of 754 members) many new lawmaking powers in areas such as agricultural and immigration policies; decisions of the EU Parliament are now binding for the separate states. Although the Lisbon Treaty made the process more democratic, critics worry that the separate nations have given up too much of their sovereignty to "foreigners" and to the Brussels bureaucracy. Recent financial crises have raised fears that the states have also given up too much of their ability to choose the right economic policies for their own citizens.

The Eurozone and Its Walls

By 2012, the EU comprised 502 million people living in twenty-seven states. But inequalities within the union remain (Map 26.3). Taxpayers in a few of these states (Germany, France, and the Netherlands) provide most of the funds transferred to poorer EU states. And, although EU members are officially entitled to a free and full exchange of labor and goods, many of the newer states may not allow more than a certain percentage of their population to work elsewhere. Some states that belong to the EU, such as the Czech Republic, Poland, Hungary, Bulgaria, and Romania, have not yet been fully admitted to the Eurozone. There are tremendous differences in the standards of living and the quality of social services between Germany and Latvia, and between the Netherlands and southern Italy. According to official measures, 35 percent of Bulgarians face severe "material deprivation," defined as lacking the means to afford such things as a washing machine, telephone, or TV, or the capacity to pay rent and utility bills. By contrast, according to official figures for 2010, only 4.5 percent of Germans and 1.3 percent of Swedes are "materially deprived."[6] Within European nations, immigrants from outside Europe are mostly in the same condition as the

MAP 26.3 | Income Inequalities in Europe

This map shows the relative wealth of Europe's states, based on GDP per capita in 2010. Note that many states in central Europe, as well as Yugoslavia's successor states, have incomes comparable to other non-European states in the Mediterranean region and the Middle East. *Which are Europe's poorest states? What factors would explain the divergence in income between western and eastern European states?*

CHRONOLOGY	Key Dates in the Forming of the EU
DATE	**EVENT**
1955	Treaty of Rome
1992	Treaty of Maastricht
1997	Schengen Agreements in force
2002	Euro adopted
2004	EU reaches 25 members
2009	Lisbon Treaty
2012	EU reaches 27 members

Bulgarians, making the ideal of European unity, while still admirable, a promise yet to be fulfilled. And then there are those who remain outside of the EU entirely, despite their desires to get in—the Ukrainians, for example, or the Turks. Despite the remarkable expansion of the EU, Europe still has its border zones, and its walls.

Global Citizenship

Europeans, especially those who live in larger cities and towns in the north and west, now participate actively in a global culture. They are passionate soccer fans, but they also watch American movies and sitcoms on TV. They eat McDonald's french fries and buy tennis shoes made in China. The Galeries Lafayette, one of France's first department stores, now has branches in Berlin and Dubai.

How have American-style capitalism and globalization influenced what it means to be European?

European fashion designers such as Yves Saint Laurent and Gucci market their merchandise all over the world. The Meissen porcelain factory founded by Johann Böttger (see Chapter 15) produces for the Chinese as well as for the German and European luxury trade. It is difficult to identify where exactly the artifacts of this global culture are being made. Products, people, and ideas travel and change so quickly that many goods belong not to one country, but to the world. It is important to note, however, that globalization is an effect of affluence; in poorer places there are fewer international retailers, fewer computers, and fewer people who have traveled by plane or eaten a Big Mac. Where governments and people are poorer, as in Bulgaria or Portugal, social services and infrastructure are less high tech and less adapted to the global information age.

Several factors continue to drive globalization forward. Capitalism is one, and having given up on communism, Europeans have decided that having a market economy is essential. But the idea of a completely free market makes Europeans profoundly nervous, for many people associate a free market with culture-killing forms of materialism or with the endangerment of the weak or the needy. Europeans also regularly associate excessive forms of capitalism with the United States, a nation whose exuberant consumer culture Europeans find both enviable and worrisome.

McItaly? After the Italian government permitted McDonald's to open a restaurant near the iconic Spanish Steps in Rome, many Italians complained that their culinary traditions and family-owned restaurants were being undermined by cheap and tasteless American fast food. In this 2010 photo, Italy's minister of agriculture Luca Zaia exhibits a burger he claimed was made exclusively from Italian ingredients.

Consumerism, American Style

During the interwar period, Europeans flocked to see American movies and during the Cold War, middle-class Europeans saved up to buy American-made washing machines, bluejeans, and records. After 1945, America was not just a political and military superpower, but a cultural and economic one, as well. While European filmmakers struggled, Hollywood churned out film after film, adapting them for use abroad with subtitles or dubbed dialogue. In 2000, American films accounted for more than 80 percent of box office receipts, though European films are widely considered to be more original and artistic and receive many film-festival prizes. American pop music has regularly topped the charts, rivaled only by British sensations such as the Beatles, the Rolling Stones, and, later, Bono's U2. Once TV caught on in the 1950s, American programming, again dubbed or subtitled, provided much-needed filler between nationally produced shows. Then the American fast-food industry hit.

In 1971, McDonald's restaurants opened in Munich and in Zaandam (near Amsterdam), as well as in Tokyo and Sydney, Australia. The world's largest McDonald's to date opened in 1986 in Rome, at the base of the historic Spanish Steps. Some Italians protested, arguing that the fast-food outlet destroyed the beauty of the place and that the standardized, bland food of McDonald's would destroy the sophisticated Italian palate. But the restaurant proved a huge success. In 1988, the communist world got to taste the Big Mac, as franchises opened in Belgrade, Yugoslavia, and Budapest. In 1990 and 1992, respectively, McDonald's came to Moscow and Beijing. Where McDonald's went, other American chains followed, populating European downtowns with Burger King and Dunkin' Donuts outlets, and, more recently, Starbucks cafés.

Although many European consumers welcomed American entertainment and chain stores, European intellectuals and business owners balked, fearing that Europeans would forget their rich cultural heritage and destroy the local businesses that kept money circulating at home. In response, individual nations moved to subsidize their own TV and film industries. European state support for opera, ballet, theater, classical music, and museums continues to be lavish by American standards. In 2002, for example, the cultural budget for the city of Berlin was approximately the same size as that of the U.S. National Endowment for the Arts.

In the competition for consumers, the best defense has been an offense: European businesses have retaliated by founding new branches of their own chain stores, such as the German supermarket giant Aldi and the British department store Marks and Spencer. The world's fifth largest corporation, Shell Oil Company—whose proper name is Royal Dutch Shell—has its headquarters in The Hague, and France's Carrefour group has nearly as many retail outlets across the globe as does Wal-Mart. European integration and the establishment of the euro have made Europe's economy stronger in world markets. The Germans, in particular, have developed a lively export trade with Asia and the rest of the world. Capitalist commerce, born in Europe in the seventeenth and eighteenth centuries, is by no means dead.

The mixed public and private response to the threat of **Americanization** is typical of European attitudes. Neither the state nor the market, most feel, could deal with such a big problem alone. European corporations compete in global markets, but are often required to invest heavily in culture at home. Taxes are high, but workers pay them to ensure the continuance of benefits such as universal health care, guaranteed pensions, and free public schools and cheap university education. Although Europeans differ according to their political outlooks—those on the left wanting the state to do more, those on the right wanting to leave more to market forces—most feel the United States is excessively dominated by private enterprise and by the desire for profit and that Europe cares more about social welfare, the arts, and the cultivation of individual fulfillment in nonmaterial ways.

Football, European Style

A defining feature of European culture linking it to the world is football (what Americans describe as soccer). For western and southern Europeans, in particular, football is an obsession. Sports pages in newspapers and television news focus heavily on the sport, and people throughout Europe are familiar not only with local players, but with the records and rosters of the leading clubs, which include Manchester United (England), Juventus (Italy), and FC Bayern (Germany). Whereas in the 1950s players usually played on local teams, now stars regularly sign lavish contracts with clubs in other nations. In 2009, for example, the Portuguese star striker Cristiano Ronaldo was paid an estimated 80 million euros to move from Manchester United to Real Madrid. Football has become something of a pan-European language. A recent *New York Times* article described a young Spaniard's difficulties in conveying his wishes to a German barber. Suddenly, he had an inspiration, and pointing to his head, simply said, "Cristiano Ronaldo." The barber immediately knew how to cut the young foreigner's hair.[7]

This is not to say that football makes only for friendships. There are bitter rivalries between clubs, violent incidents have occurred at matches, and more than a little corruption plagues the sport, on both the national and the international level. Fans—many of them working-class young men—regularly call out nationalist or racist insults to goad players on the pitch. This behavior led the world governing body, FIFA (Fédération Internationale de Football Association), to begin a campaign against racism in 2002 and in 2004 to issue a code of ethics, stating that "officials, players, and players' agents may not act in a discriminatory manner, especially with regard to ethnicity, race, culture, politics, religion, gender or language." FIFA has also attempted to give other continents where football is hugely popular—most notably South America and Africa—an equal opportunity to hold major competitions. In 2010, the World Cup competition was held in South Africa, and in 2014, it will be held in Brazil. In 2012, Ukraine and Poland cohosted the European championships, a sign that eastern Europe, too, has caught the football fever. Although many younger Americans play European football, and America now has a professional football league, soccer simply doesn't mean to Americans what it means to Europeans, who share this particular passion with the rest of the world.

The Communications Revolution

Another factor contributing to the globalization of Europe is the increasing speed and affordability of international communications and travel. Whereas once international telephone calls were too expensive for all but the rich and the business elite, cheap rates and Internet calling have reduced costs to almost zero, that is, for those who can afford computers and cell phones and who live in places

Football Fanaticism One thing that binds Europeans together, and links them to the nonwestern world, is their passion for football (soccer). Here, a huge crowd welcomes home the Spanish national team after its victory in the Euro 2012 championships, played in Poland and Ukraine.

The Arrival of the Digital Age

The history of human writing and reading is over five thousand years old, but the pace of change in the technologies that support them has been accelerating rapidly. The means of writing (by stylus, reed pen, quill pen, printing press, typewriter, all but the first with ink), the media or surfaces that receive writing (clay, papyrus, wax, parchment, and paper), and the form (tablet, scroll, and codex-book) underwent critical changes in the past, often in the move from one civilization or economy to another. All communications technologies impose on their users limitations and possibilities, both physical and cognitive, even in the digital age. In the early twenty-first century, the means is now the computer, the media are the stored electronic images displayed on a screen, and the form is almost infinite but bound by the restrictions of the screen surface.

The story of late-twentieth-century communications is one of the popularization of computer technology. The first personal computers appeared in the late 1970s and early 1980s. Computing power grew throughout the 1990s with the introduction of silicon chips and Pentium processors. By 1997, an IBM supercomputer nicknamed Deep Blue had defeated the world's reigning chess champion, Garry Kasparov of Russia, at his own infinitely complex game.

The new technology led to the electronic digitization of great masses of information by governments and companies such as Google, which set out in the first decade of the twenty-first century to digitize all the world's printed books. By 2007, well over 90 percent of the stored information of our species was in digital form accessible by computers. It is estimated that, by 2030, computers will be able to process 10,000 trillion electrical signals a second, the same number that flash through a human skull when a person is thinking. Will we then be able to download—or upload—a whole brain?[8]

The PCs of the 1970s could not "talk" to other computers. The World Wide Web—the invention of Tim Berners-Lee, of the European Organization for Nuclear Research in Geneva—went live in 1990. Soon people all over the globe were communicating with one another almost instantaneously by e-mail. The social networking site Facebook appeared in 2004 and within seven years had 750 million users.

It is too soon to know where all this is leading, but if the digital revolution is anything like previous communications developments, some outcomes can be anticipated. Businesses are being built, old technologies and their

Multitasking Cell phones have become common throughout Europe. Here, a London teenager texts while using her hula hoop, a now long-outdated form of entertainment. This photo was taken at a street fair to benefit victims of the London riots of 2011.

offshoots (stationery stores, book stores, printing presses) are shrinking or disappearing, professions such as the typewriter repairman and typesetter are being replaced by computer experts and programmers, and information storage has been transformed (from the university library as a repository of bound books and print journals to a multi-source site of old analog and new digital materials).

Communications changes in the past have been cumulative, that is, they have been added on to existing forms of communication. Despite the rise of text-messaging, we will still live most of the day in an oral culture, speaking to each other; and we will likely continue to write with our hands or at least, in the near future, learn that skill; and we will commit information (by finger or voice) into a print mode on a computer. Changes in the way we live are already evident. We read differently, often with less absorption. Around the world, cursive handwriting skills have been deteriorating with the increasing use of digital media and electronic keyboards, for to write by hand is a skill that requires constant physical exercise. The fate of past media—such as papyrus and parchment— suggests that paper may not persist as a surface.

All these changes have led Europeans and North Americans to worry about the death of the book or even the death of the author. Yet neither seems to be happening; more books are being published every year, and copyright laws still protect authors' ideas from theft, though copying and bootlegging words and music have become universal practices. What is occurring is a kind of democratization of culture, especially for those who can afford to own computers with web access and those who read and write English, the most-used computing language. The digital revolution has been both good and bad for European culture. Some never-heard voices can now contribute, but they are unlikely to be the voices of the immigrants and rural workers. And northern and western Europe, where both English and affluence are common, will likely be overrepresented with respect to the others.

QUESTIONS | *Does the accessibility of technology reflect other imbalances in European culture and economics? How so? What does digitization mean for western and world culture?*

with reliable service. The **digital revolution** is transforming European as well as world culture in striking ways and making possible new ways of engaging with people and texts as well as posing old questions about unequal access to power and influence.

Postmodernism

The dominant style of thought and design after 1989 has been that of the movement called **postmodernism,** a term that covers a wide range of eclectic ideas and activities. Essentially, postmodernists reject the ideal of objectivity, arguing that all realities are socially constructed and relative. For the postmodernist, no common style can be found to suit everyone; instead, postmodernists embrace the diversity of local cultures and consumers' appreciation for traditional designs or, in music, familiar harmonies. Postmodernism in Europe is best illustrated by architectural works, such as Germany's restored Reichstag building, completed in 1999. The British architect Norman Foster kept the outer shell of the nineteenth-century building, even though it had been damaged by the Reichstag fire of 1933 and by bombing during World War II. But to this he added an energy-efficient and transparent glass dome, meant to symbolize the new transparency of German democracy and its commitment to protecting the environment. The building now combines the old and new; it reminds Germans and tourists of Germany's troubled history but also celebrates reunified Germany's clearer skies.

Postmodernism, generously defined, has been pervasive in philosophy, where its chief role has been to show how knowledge is made by the knower. French thinkers, including Michel Foucault (see Chapter 25) and Jacques Derrida, have been particularly influential. Derrida, a philosopher who focused on the problem of reading, worked to destabilize our understanding of texts. According to him, no text, including the telephone directory, has a fixed meaning. We readers always construe them according to our interests and desires. Understanding that texts can be interpreted in an infinite number of ways, for Derrida, was the means by which to release the playful and creative energies of the present and to free readers to take what they wished from each of their encounters with texts. Derrida's "deconstructionism" thus laid down a foundational principle of postmodernism: there is more than one right answer, more than one TV channel to watch, more than one way to be modern. We live in a world of fragmented realities, audiences, and tastes, and individuals are free to cobble together bits and pieces of

The Reichstag Dome German and European Union flags fly over the Reichstag. Heavily destroyed by fire in 1933 and fighting during World War II, the Reichstag was long a ruin. After German unification, Germany's political capital was moved from Bonn back to Berlin, and the building refurbished and given a new, environmentally friendly and postmodern, glass dome.

disparate things and styles, without anyone insisting on consistency or universal truths.

The influence of postmodernist thought can be detected even in the most popular works. In many ways, British writer J. K. Rowling's wildly popular *Harry Potter* series of young adult novels merits inclusion in this category. Rowling set her seven-part story in the present, but many of the characters and the forms of magic they pursue are based on medieval or ancient models. Many German writers, such as W. G. Sebald and Günter Grass, incorporate and reflect on historical events in their fiction; the same can be said of the Anglo-Indian novelist Salman Rushdie, whose portrayal of the Prophet Muhammad in *The Satanic Verses* (1988) led the Islamic leaders of Iran to issue an order for his death.

Rushdie is by no means the only immigrant from Europe's former colonies to have brought his stories to the continent, further diversifying European culture. There are now Turkish writers publishing in German, West African writers producing novels in Paris, and Indonesian immigrants writing poetry in Dutch. Bollywood filmmakers work in India, producing films in Bengali, which are screened in Britain and Los Angeles as well as throughout Southeast Asia. European culture is increasingly becoming inseparable from global culture, even though much of what is most successfully dispersed across the world is literature, film, or scholarship produced in what has become something of a new *lingua franca*, English.

English, the New Lingua Franca?

The end of the Cold War and decolonization opened cultural borders not only between East and West, but between Europe and the rest of the world. Educated Europeans now read novels written by Egyptian, Chinese, and Latin

American authors; translations make it possible for those who read only French to read novels originally written in Czech or Swedish. But by far the most translated works are those originally written in English.

The last few years have seen a spectacular rise in the numbers of continental Europeans learning English as their second language. Before the seventeenth-century elite, Europeans used Latin as their lingua franca; for two or more centuries after that, French served as the language of international diplomacy and elegant conversation. In central Europe, German was spoken as a second or third language by those whose mother tongue was Czech, Yiddish, or Ukrainian. During the Cold War, many eastern European children were taught Russian, but after 1989, most now study English in school or pick up enough to use the Internet or understand pop music, most of which is produced in the United States or Great Britain. For natural scientists, in particular, English has become the new lingua franca, allowing them to collaborate on projects and to read one another's publications in international journals. But the study of Chinese is also on the rise, and Chinese speakers are in great demand in Europe's business community.

Cultural Diversity Endures

Enhanced global interconnectedness, the end of the Cold War, and the expansion of the airline industry has made it possible for scholars and businesspeople to travel easily and rapidly around the world. International and inter-European collaboration has made new ventures possible, in the cultural as well as the economic sphere. In 2008, the world's largest particle accelerator (the Hadron Collider) was built by the European Organization for Nuclear Research in an underground facility beneath the French-Swiss border. The price tag of 7.5 billion euros would have made the device unaffordable to any individual European nation, but by pooling funds, the Europeans have made it possible for their physicists to lead the way in basic research on the deep properties of matter that may shed new light on the origins of the universe.

The Hadron Collider offers an example of the advantages of European unity, but Europeans still inhabit their own cultural zones. Persistent localization remains true of those who live in relatively poor and rural areas such as southern Italy, Greece, Portugal, and the eastern European states. Greeks still learn how to play the instrument known as the bouzouki; the Irish still produce Celtic folk music. In small towns, German and Austrian men sit at the same table every night to drink beer with friends; Hungarians still frequent bathing houses, some of them originally built by the Ottomans. Such small towns may now have a Chinese or Thai restaurant, but their everyday eateries favor local foods: fresh pasta in Italy, fish in Scandinavia, and pierogi and cabbage in Poland. Despite the arrival of the digital age and the rising importance of English, culturally there remain many Europes.

Challenges Facing Europe Today

The fall of the Berlin Wall, German reunification, and EU expansion have opened a new chapter in European history. The Germans' wish to assure the world of their peaceful intentions, combined with the desire on the part of first southern nations and then eastern European nations to join the EU, have contributed to all these parties pulling in the direction of western Europe's ideals, as laid out so far in this chapter: all those who want to belong to the EU and to make it work pay at least lip service to their commitments to democracy, the social market economy, secularism, minority rights, and civil and human rights. But not all these states have managed to realize these ideals—and new developments, such as the rise of radical Islam and the worldwide recession that began in 2008, have posed new challenges even for those who did create functioning social market economies and tolerant polities. Other challenges include the problem of political corruption, the threat of terrorism, the need to find common solutions to environmental problems such as climate change, and demographic changes. After 2009, the sovereign (or national) debt crisis posed fundamental questions about the long-term survival of the Eurozone and of the EU itself.

> **What political, social, and economic challenges face Europe today?**

Relations with the United States

For European leaders, dealing with the United States has been challenging, especially after the 9/11 terrorist attacks and the beginning of the war against Iraq in 2003. Some states, most notably Great Britain and Poland, joined what U.S. president George W. Bush called "the coalition of the willing" and sent troops to assist in the invasions of Afghanistan and later Iraq. But others, such as Germany and France, disagreed openly with U.S. policy.

The Second Gulf War created hard feelings between the old Cold War partners. Western Europeans in particular criticized American unilateral intervention, the use of torture on suspected terrorists, and the extraordinary rendition of prisoners from the sites of their capture to states that allowed for aggressive interrogation. Americans, for their part, resented western Europeans' failure to support actions they believed to be in the collective interests of the West. But some liberals and conservatives in eastern Europe—including Polish president Aleksander Kwaśniewski and, at least initially, Václav Havel, did agree to send troops to join the coalition forces. Most outspoken in his support was British prime minister Tony Blair, who reaffirmed the British-American special relationship forged during World War II. Most outspoken against U.S. actions was Gerhard Schroeder, Germany's social democratic prime minister, whose disdain for American policy reflected that of many left-leaning Europeans.

American-European relationships have changed with Europe's increasing wealth. European investment in the United States now far outdistances American investment in the EU, and the EU has become a major trading bloc on the world stage. Once economic as well as military dependents, the Europeans have become to a certain extent economic rivals. Europeans and Americans disagree on many lifestyle issues: Europeans defend their social market economy, while Americans champion free markets; many Americans defend gun ownership rights, while most Europeans are appalled by the amount of gun violence Americans are willing to tolerate. Europeans tend to be more "green"; many more Americans attend church services. But, together with other neo-Europes such as Canada and Australia, Europe and the United States work closely together on many projects, including peacekeeping operations and human rights campaigns throughout the world, and drew somewhat closer together during the presidency of Barack Obama (beginning in 2008).

Political Corruption

Politics since 1989 has been marked by a series of corruption scandals. Italy's premier, Silvio Berlusconi, was put on trial for many kinds of corruption, but none of the charges stuck. The Italian Mafia continues to be extremely powerful throughout the country, especially in southern Italy. In Croatia, the reform-oriented leader Ivo Sanader, elected in 2003 to replace Franjo Tudjman, resigned suddenly in 2009; judicial proceedings showed that he had embezzled huge sums. Corruption in eastern and southern Europe not only continues to bleed many states of funds that could be put to productive use but also demoralizes citizens who increasingly feel that all politicians are seeking personal gain and that there is nothing they can do to clean up the mess. The records of Romania—whose parliament indicted its own president in 2007—and Bulgaria are particularly poor.

Where democracy is the weakest, however, is in the former USSR. In Ukraine, the communist Leonid Kuchma dominated affairs long after 1989. When his hand-picked successor was elected president in 2004, citizens occupied the central square of the capital city, Kiev, claiming widespread electoral fraud. The protestors wore orange ribbons to show their support for the candidate from whom, they claimed, the election had been stolen, and remarkably, the government bowed to both internal and external pressure and agreed to hold new elections. This time, the candidate backed by the **Orange Revolution,** Victor Yuschenko, won handily, and another backer of the Orange movement, the nationalist Yulia Timoshenko, in 2005 became the region's first female prime minister. She served again from 2007 to 2010, but has been thrown in prison numerous times by her political enemies, who accuse her of one or another sort of misdeed. Some of

Democracy in the Ukraine? Ukraine has now freed itself from Russian overlordship, and declared itself a democracy. But it still suffers from political corruption and human rights abuses. Here, a supporter of the former prime minister and Orange Revolution leader, Yulia Timoshenko, jailed by her opponents on what may be trumped-up charges, appeals for Timoshenko's release.

these accusations are surely concocted, but some are probably valid. Charged with abuse of power, tax evasion, and corruption in 2011, Timoshenko seems destined to spend many more years in jail—unless, of course, her allies take power and pardon her offenses.

In Russia, thanks to high oil revenues and citizens' lingering fear of the state apparatus, Vladimir Putin has remained the dominant political force, though in 2011–2012, some Russians took to the streets to protest his authoritarian style. Putin has jailed his political enemies, including Mikhail Khodorovsky, a former communist turned extremely wealthy crony capitalist. In 2003, Khodorovsky, already suspected of fraud in his dealings in the oil business, fell out with Putin and, after a lengthy trial, was sentenced to nine years in prison. While in jail he became something of a hero to the anti-Putin movement in the country, but it is unlikely he—like Timoshenko—will be set free, even when his sentence is up. Putin regularly criticizes U.S. policy in the world and plays on Russian nationalism to secure electoral victory; he reminds Russians, too, that economically they have been much better off under his leadership than they were under Boris Yeltsin's more democratic government. The journalist Thomas L. Friedman has described Putin's Russia as a "sort-of-but-not-really" capitalist democracy: "It's sort of a free market, but not really. It's sort of got the rule of law to protect businesses, but not really. It's sort of a European country, but not really. It has sort of a free press, but not really. Its cold war with America is sort of over, but not really. It's sort of trying to become something more than a petro-state, but not really."[9]

This description offers little hope that democracy and governmental reform in Russia will be achieved in the near future. But it suggests that Russia is perhaps *farther* along in adopting democratic ideals than other CIS states, such as Belarus. Here, president Alexander Luka-shenko has been elected three times since 2000; like Putin, he stabilized the economy, but he has crushed those who dare to protest his policies. He has also made anti-Semitic comments in public. In the other CIS states, too, authoritarian rule is the norm, and radical nationalism is on the rise. After 1991, these nations were told they should adopt the values other Europeans cherish as western ones—democracy, the rule of law, toleration, free market capitalism—and many of their citizens long for these ideals to become realities. But they still have a long way to go to do so—if, that is, their citizens and leaders decide to continue along these paths.

The Challenge of Diversity

In 2012, the twenty-seven countries of the EU contained a total population of 502 million. Of this total, a little more than 6 percent were foreign born—about 2 percent born in other EU countries and about 4 percent born outside the EU. These numbers do not seem all that large, but many members of immigrant communities were in fact born in Europe. They are second- or third-generation Frenchmen or Germans whose grandparents or parents came as guest workers many years before. A few manage to marry or assimilate into the larger population, but many find it difficult to do so or prefer to remain within their own separate communities. The children of immigrants typically do not have the opportunity to attend the best schools and many lack training for highly skilled and high-paying jobs. All these factors make it hard for them to escape suburban ghettoes and put them at risk of long-term unemployment, radicalization, or despair.

One of the foremost issues raised by continuing immigration is how a tolerant Europe will deal with a religion that its Christian ancestors considered anathema: Islam. A large number of migrants from Turkey, North Africa, and South Asia are Muslims, and a few follow strict dress codes for women, including the wearing of headscarves or full veils. Muslim women are also sometimes prohibited from dating or working as they would like. These are not attitudes that most Europeans share, and some states are moving in the direction of banning veils and setting up shelters for threatened or abused Muslim women.

In 2011, France prohibited face-covering veils on the grounds that hiding the individual's face made it impossible for that person's identity to be checked. Europeans worry too about the rise of a radical form of Islam known as Islamism that preaches hatred of the West and has provoked some terrorist attacks in Europe and beyond. Despite the minuscule number of these radicals, their presence makes Europeans worried about admitting more Muslim immigrants to their states.

Across the globe there are many more individuals who would like to be Europeans or, at least, to enjoy Europe's relative prosperity. In the nineteenth century, Europe sent wave after wave of emigrants to other parts of the world; now it is on the receiving end. Some immigrants are admitted legally, as political refugees or on work visas. Others arrive illegally, sailing from North Africa across the Mediterranean in rickety and overcrowded boats. Many are turned back, and some, tragically, die at sea. More would come if they could afford the passage and if the EU nations would admit them. They bring with them cultural diversity, but they are also, often, poor and unskilled, and some of their religious practices conflict with Europe's commitments to secularism and women's rights. European leaders will need to develop means by which to deal with cultural and religious diversity without overwhelming their social welfare systems or compromising their commitment to secular ideals.

Assassinations, Terrorist Strikes, and Riots

With the major exceptions of Chechnya and the former Yugoslavia, political violence since 1989 has been minimal, but some tragic events have occurred, especially after the beginning of the Iraq War in 2003. In 2004, radical Islamists loaded bombs onto commuter trains in Madrid, resulting in the deaths of nearly two hundred people. In that same year, Theo Van Gogh, a Dutch filmmaker who warned that Islamic suppression of women's rights, homophobia, and anti-Semitism threatened the Netherlands' long-standing traditions of tolerance, was brutally murdered by a Muslim extremist. On July 7, 2005, four suicide bombers attacked crowded buses and underground train stations in London, leaving fifty-two people dead and more than seven hundred injured. The culprits were young men with British citizenship, three of them of Pakistani and one of Jamaican descent. The incident drew attention to the rise of extremist Muslim groups within Britain, especially in poor suburbs where poverty and unemployment remain high.

In France, the deaths of two young men of North African descent in the fall of 2005 sparked three weeks of rioting in suburban slums throughout the country. Cars were set on fire and shops looted; nearly three thousand people were arrested and many were injured, though only one person died as a result of the violence. Like the 2005 bombings in London, these events drew attention to the plight of impoverished and unemployed young men, many of them of North African or Middle Eastern descent. Despite France's commitment to "liberty, fraternity and equality," these men claimed that France continued to discriminate against people of color.

Russia has been targeted by terrorists as a result of the ongoing conflicts in Chechnya and surrounding regions. In 2004, Muslim terrorists, led by the Chechen leader Shamil Basayev, seized over one thousand hostages at a school in Beslan, in Northern Ossetia. The Russians refused to capitulate to the terrorists' demands, which included an end to the Second Chechen War, and sent in tanks. The result was a shocking bloodbath in which more than 380 people died, many of them children. In 2010, two radicalized "black widows," Muslim women whose husbands were killed in clashes in the Caucasus region, blew themselves up on the Russian metro, killing forty civilians; and in January 2011, another suicide bomber killed thirty-five people at the airport in Moscow.

In response to immigration pressures and terrorist threats, some Europeans have adopted radical programs. In the Netherlands, the right-wing leader of the Freedom Party, Geert Wilders, compared the Quran to Hitler's *Mein Kampf* and advocated deporting all Muslim immigrants. In 2010 elections, his party received the third-largest share of the votes and was brought into the coalition government. In 2011, a Norwegian admirer of Wilders mounted a dual attack against what he insisted was Norway's overly tolerant attitude toward foreigners. He planted a car bomb outside the prime minister's office in Oslo and then stormed a meeting of young leaders of the Norwegian Labour Party with a machine gun, wishing to destroy both Muslims and others he deemed too tolerant. He killed seventy-seven people in total, the majority of them under the age of twenty-one.

The Norwegian attacks occurred just weeks before rioting broke out in London and other British cities in the late summer of 2011 in response to a police action that resulted in the shooting of a black Londoner. For five consecutive nights, young people from some of the poorer districts went on a rampage, burning cars, looting shops, and fighting with police. The riots were partially organized by instant messages sent on Blackberry cell phones. Unlike the simultaneously occurring demonstrations in the Arab world, known as the Arab Spring, the rioters in Britain seem not to have had political grievances. Although some of the perpetrators were immigrants or unemployed people, many were university graduates with jobs. These riots seem to have been generated by the longing to break the rules or by frustration that the path to success, for this generation, seemed increasingly beset with obstacles. Europe's leadership has not yet found a successful way to address these new social ruptures: a new generation's demoralization, the long-standing problem of immigrant integration, the persistent threat of terrorist attacks, and the radical rhetoric of extremists and reactionaries.

A Dirty and Dangerous World: The Post–Cold War Environment

Another challenge facing Europeans today is environmental sustainability. In the former Soviet bloc, the landscape and its inhabitants have suffered from hasty and careless industrialization. Many residents of the old industrial towns near the Ural Mountains suffer from terrible air and water pollution. Mining areas in the Ukraine were recklessly exploited for minerals, leaving the land denuded and full of dangerous caverns and pits. Deforestation and soil exhaustion remain major concerns. For decades, a huge Russian paper mill has been dumping chemicals into the world's deepest freshwater lake, Lake Baikal. The mill was closed briefly in 2008–2009, but has reopened, threatening the lake's unique species of fish, crustaceans, and plants. The region around Chernobyl, where the world's worst nuclear disaster occurred in 1986, remains uninhabitable by humans because of high levels of radioactivity. Animals have returned to the area in high numbers, however, and in 2007, Ukraine declared an area of nearly 200 square miles a wildlife sanctuary.

There are also many polluted places in eastern and western Europe. The situation is somewhat better in the old Western bloc in part because democratic governments, unlike communist ones, had to respond to citizen complaints. Green or environmental movements were already beginning in West Germany and Britain in the 1960s and have become part of the political landscape. But many problems remain. Romania, for example, faces multiple issues: one-tenth of its rivers are still so contaminated that they can support no life at all, and much of Romania's ground water contains dangerous toxins. The continuing use of coal and leaded gas worsens already-poor air quality. In Hungary in 2010 more than 35 million cubic feet of red sludge from an aluminum factory escaped from holding ponds and inundated homes and streams. Quick action prevented the contamination of the Danube River, but the spill showed that manufacturing in the east after the fall of communism remains a dangerous and dirty business.

Like the world's other citizens, Europeans are facing changing climate. The extremely hot summer and the extremely cold winter of 2011–2012 are just two events that point to new challenges in the future. Experiments in clean energy generation, such as incinerators in Denmark that turn trash into electricity, are under way, but they have yet to reduce Europe's dependence on fossil fuels.

Demographic Challenges

As recently as the 1860s, the average German woman gave birth to four or five children. Birthrates farther to the east and south were higher still. But, apart from the baby boom of the years immediately following 1945, European birthrates have been falling ever since. The new availability of contraceptive devices after the 1960s contributed much to this, but a precipitous drop has occurred in the east since communism's fall. As the younger and more optimistic section of the East German population streamed westward in 1989–1991, the birthrate for that region was cut in half. Rates in Ukraine and Romania fell by 30 percent, and by 2000, in Russia, the death rate was outstripping the birthrate by almost a million a year.

Recent figures show that the pattern holds across the EU—even in traditionally Catholic nations such as Poland and Italy, where the church officially prohibits contraception and abortion. In 2009, for every woman who passed through child-bearing years, an average of 1.3 children were born in Latvia, Portugal, and Germany; only a few European nations, including France, Ireland, and Iceland, managed to meet the rate of population replacement (26.1). Everywhere, the birthrate for immigrants far exceeds that of EU nationals; in the largest of the neo-Europes, the United States, the rate in 2012 stood at 2.05, buoyed up here, too, by higher rates in immigrant communities.

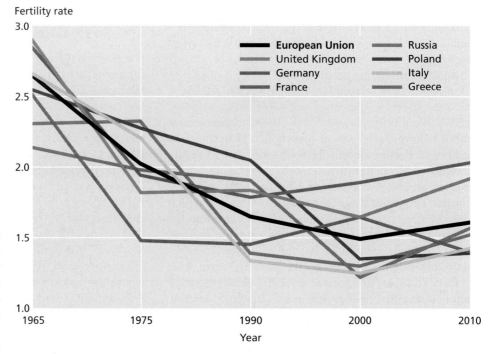

FIGURE 26.1 | Fertility Rates in Europe since the 1960s

Europe's fertility rate (the average number of children a women would have during her child-bearing years, condensed into any given year) has been declining since the 1960s. In the 2000s, the rate plunged below 2.1 children per women—the replacement rate. The recent recovery is in large part due to high birthrates among immigrant families.

Source: Created by Jason M. Wolfe. Data compiled by Scott Berg from Eurostat, the European Commission's official online statistics database; http://epp.eurostat.ec.europa.eu/tgm/table.do?tab=table&init=1&language=en&pcode=tsdde220&plugin=1.

Demographic decline is particularly pronounced in southern and eastern Europe, where citizens face uncertain economic prospects. In these nations, traditional family roles persist and men typically contribute little to child-rearing and housekeeping. Women who wish to remain in the workforce may be choosing not to marry or to have children for fear that most of the burden of child-raising will fall on their shoulders.

One of the problems that these falling numbers highlight is that even if states increase the number of immigrants they receive, it will be difficult for a declining number of younger workers to support an increasing number of retirees. Europe's population is living much longer nowadays; in 1914, life expectancy ranged between 40 and 50 years; in 2009, it stood at 76 years for men and 82 years for women, though rates for men are 13 years (and for women, 8 years) lower in the former Eastern bloc, especially in Russia, where alcoholism contributes significantly to a high death rate for middle-aged men. The median age of the population in 2009 was 40.6; it is projected to be 47.9 in 2060. During the postwar construction of welfare states, governments agreed to healthy pensions for people over age sixty-five (some of whom can retire in their late fifties, if they have sufficient years of service). As the population ages, the costs make perks like pensions, child and unemployment subsidies, inexpensive health care, and free schooling difficult to sustain. European nations are keenly aware that retirement ages, and if possible birthrates, will need to rise to maintain the social welfare states of the postwar era.

The Sovereign Debt Crisis

The latest and most pressing issue facing the EU is the **sovereign debt crisis** (euro crisis), the problem of debt accumulated by individual member nations. Although the Eurozone's seventeen states are linked by a common currency and monetary policy, each state retains economic sovereignty, that is, control over its own budget, benefits, and taxation rates. But each state is also obliged to meet the Eurozone criteria, including keeping budget deficits under 3 percent of GDP. Doing so was feasible in the relatively flush years of 1989–2007, but after the global economic downturn of 2008, states began spending more, including large sums to bail out wobbly banks.

In late 2009, a new Greek government admitted that its predecessor had fudged its budgetary numbers, and that the state's debt was not the 6–8 percent of GDP it had reported (already far above the Eurozone's 3 percent ceiling) but closer to 12 percent. This revelation provoked a

The Debt Crisis of 2010–2011

In the first months of 2010, Europeans were by and large optimistic about the future of their continent and their union of shared interests. The EU seemed to be recovering from the global downturn of 2008–2009, and the euro was hitting unprecedented highs against the U.S. dollar. In late 2009, Greece, which had not downsized its state sector in the 1980s or 1990s, revised its budget deficit numbers from 6–8 percent to 12 percent. This was a very bad sign for Greece, but no one panicked. The Eurozone as a whole seemed to be recovering from the downturn and would surely assist Greece in its fiscal and banking woes, despite the feeling of the Germans, in particular, that the Greeks should fix what they had broken.

In the spring of 2010, things began to change fast. A new Greek government came into office and promptly acknowledged that the Greek budget deficit was even higher than the revised figure of 12 percent; instead, the debt amounted to about 15 percent of GDP, far above the 3 percent level the Eurozone required. Given the situation, the state was having trouble borrowing money at all and was in danger of defaulting on its loans, many of which were held by French and German banks. Because Greece did not control its own currency, it could not simply inflate its way out of its difficulties, an option available to non-European countries such as the United States. In May 2010, the Eurozone nations agreed to float a 110-billion euro loan (about $150 billion U.S. dollars) for the Greeks on the condition that the government put austerity measures into place.

Those measures—such as cutting wages and jobs in the state sector, increasing taxes or collecting taxes from those who avoided paying them, and trimming benefits—were deeply unpopular in Greece, and sparked nationwide protests. In one demonstration in Athens, three people were killed and hundreds arrested. In the meantime, economists began inspecting the economies of neighboring nations and realized that several other Eurozone nations were also in trouble. Ireland received a loan to help it deal with its debt in November 2010, and Portugal received one in May 2011. By this time, however, it was clear that trouble was spreading, in part because other nations had tried to spend their way out of the 2008 fiscal crisis and in part because confidence in the Eurozone nations and their banks was falling. By the spring of 2011, what had begun as anxiety about Greece's relatively small economy had thrown open the question of the continued existence of the euro, and possibly the EU itself.

As the euro crisis deepened in the summer of 2011, differences between the Eurozone's national economies and resentments about these differences bubbled to the surface. The richer countries, primarily in northern Europe, felt they had already paid enough to bail out the Greeks and others and pointed angrily to a history of corrupt and inefficient Greek governments, which had frittered away large sums while also offering workers lavish benefits, despite low levels of productivity. The Greeks, for their part, expressed their frustration that they had never reached the full prosperity that joining the Eurozone had promised them and now had to endure high unemployment, salary reductions, and skyrocketing taxes and prices just to please the northerners. Some people looked back to the Second World War and complained that the Germans had never compensated the Greeks for the devastation inflicted by the Nazi occupation of Greece.

Although Greece's austerity measures had made little headway in closing the budget deficit, in July 2011 the EU nations decided on a second bailout package, valued at $157 billion. In announcing this measure, leaders made it clear that they were determined to save the euro, but also that they were terrified that the contagion would spread. Western European leaders originally adopted the euro with much fanfare, and eastern nations had pushed hard to gain entrance to the Eurozone. With the onset of the Greek debt crisis, Eurozone economic policy suddenly appeared dangerously exposed to the blunders of any one of its nations: it was compared to a car with seventeen steering wheels, something that makes it likely, sooner or later, to run off the road, imperiling all of its passengers. In 2010, few saw a Eurozone crash ahead; a year later, many were bracing for the impact.

The Eurocrisis in Greece In spring 2012, the Greek Communist Party draped huge banners on the acropolis in Athens reading in Greek and in rather awkward English: "Down with the Dictatorship of the Monopolies of the European Union." Although the most radical of the parties, the Communists were by no means alone in believing that the EU's leadership—especially the financially sound Germans—was dictating painful austerity measures, no matter the cost to the Greeks.

QUESTION | *How does the sovereign debt crisis illustrate the unequal distribution of wealth across Europe's states?*

panic—cutting the state's budget that much was simply not possible, and Greece was running out of lenders. Worse, it seemed that other countries, known by the acronym PIIGS (Portugal, Ireland, Italy, Greece, and Spain), might be in fiscal trouble as well; both in Ireland and in Spain, housing bubbles burst, leaving banks holding billions in bad loans. Borrowing became more expensive, and debts rose further, while budget cuts and low levels of consumption increased unemployment. European leaders, especially Nicolas Sarkozy of France and Angela Merkel of Germany, recognized that they had to restore confidence and trust in the European economy or risk undoing all the progress made toward European integration since the 1950s (see Back to the Source at the end of the chapter). The French and German leaders—both conservatives—worked together with the European Central Bank (ECB) to approve first one, and then a second, large bailout package for Greece (funded by the EU), and to boost the Central Bank's currency holdings so that it could loan more cash to the struggling states.

In return, Sarkozy, Merkel, and the ECB insisted that those who received bailouts and special loans implement austerity measures to get their budgetary houses back in order. In 2011, the Greek, Spanish, Portuguese, and Italian governments began imposing some of these austerity measures, leading to increased taxes and public sector layoffs; unemployment soared, leading to street protests. In Greece and Italy, popularly elected governments handed power over to the former bankers, Lucas Papademos and Mario Monti, who were given the tough job—rather like Jacques Necker in 1788 (see Chapter 17)—of raising taxes and trimming state spending in economies that were already faltering. Designed to streamline these economies, the effect was to sharply reduce consumer spending and growth, especially in southern Europe.

The imposition of austerity measures—demanded mostly by northerners and endured mostly by southerners—exposed regional economic disparities and provoked the expression of bitter, interregional, resentments. Unquestionably the southerners suffered more as a result of the debt crisis. Whereas unemployment in Germany in 2012 was about 4 percent, it was 25 percent in Spain (up from only 8 percent in 2007) and 24 percent in Greece. Youth unemployment was far worse: over 50 percent in Spain and a whopping 55 percent in Greece. These inequalities have provoked angry and sometimes derogatory statements from both northerners—who accuse the southerners of laziness and corruption—and southerners, who accuse the Germans, in particular, of reverting to the exploitative practices of the Nazi period. But even in northern states such as France and the Netherlands, austerity was unpopular, and governments seeking to impose cuts—including that of Nicolas Sarkozy—were ousted in the spring of 2012. In that year, as Greek austerity measures failed to produce little but the spiraling decline of Greece's ability to pay its debts, speculation rose about a Greek exit, or "Grexit" from the euro. A series of crises and corresponding European summits resulted in additional fiscal measures to help keep Greece in the Eurozone, but German pressure to continue austerity and reform even in the face of hard times continued.

In eastern Europe (aside from the former East Germany), EU improvements had only just begun when the economic crisis hit. It now seems unlikely that those countries seeking to join the EU will be admitted to the Eurozone without extensive proof that their debts can be controlled in both the short and long term. It has also become clear that joining the Eurozone has its downsides: in losing their own currency, nations lose some of their sovereignty and political autonomy, such as the ability to inflate their way out of debt crises, and must impose spending cuts and tax increases to please other member states. In fall 2012, Hungarian prime minister Victor Orban rejected a much-needed 15 billion euro loan from the International Monetary Fund because the Fund insisted on conditions opposed to Hungary's interests. Ironically, the intensely nationalist Orban chose to make the announcement that he would reject the offer on the social networking site Facebook—just another indication that it is now fully possible for Europeans to accept some aspects of globalization and to resist others.

The values that came to define post-1989 Europeanness are still cherished across the continent, but the challenges to their full realization, especially in the shadow of the sovereign debt crisis, abound. Can weaker and stronger national economies coexist within the Eurozone? Will member states agree to allow an increasing number of their laws to be made by the EU, rather than by national parliaments? Will tolerance prevail in the face of the rise of radical Islam? Will the social market economies survive global economic downturns? Europe's future, like that of the rest of the world, will be determined both by chance events we cannot foresee and by the choices today's Europeans make. We must hope that those choices are wise ones, informed by careful and critical reflections on a continental history marked by so much conflict on the one hand and the achievement of so many freedoms on the other.

Conclusion

Whether EU integration continues or stalls in the future, there will always be many Europes. What has made European history distinctive, in the end, is the series of never-ending struggles and exchanges between near neighbors that has played itself out on this continent. In ancient times, there were many Greeces, fiercely independent city-states that shared a general culture with one another but had their own histories to live, their own identities to preserve, and their own particular interests to pursue. This has been true, on the larger scale, of Europe's kingdoms and states ever since. Even the mighty Roman and Carolingian Empires were unable to overcome the intense regionalism characteristic of the continent. Long before the re-formation of the church split Christendom into mutually hostile religious enclaves, its landscape was dotted with warring kingdoms—and with the roads traveled by exiles, neutral brokers, and traders, who shared ideas and goods even during periods of the most intense conflict.

Beginning in the early modern era, European nations in competition and conversation with one another built empires on the continent or overseas, seeking to acquire territorial and financial resources that would elevate them above their neighbors. They learned, and extorted, much from these non-European interactions. The quieter revolutions of the era of the Old Regimes and the more powerful French and Industrial Revolutions were felt, in different ways, across the continent, and in their wake even more ambitious and aggressive but also more democratic and prosperous states arose. In the horrific wars of the twentieth century, Europeans destroyed much of the civilization they had created; and in the Cold War era, as a consequence, Europe was divided between new superpowers, both of whom were, at least in part, products of European history and culture.

In recent years, Europe has moved toward integration on many fronts, but its member states continue to demonstrate their resistance to homogeneity and their refusal to forget their divisive independent pasts. The many-Europes model did not vanish with the rise of the EU and may return with a vengeance if it fails. The modern identity of the peoples of Europe remains in flux. It will fall to them individually and collectively to decide what it means to be European or if it means much at all in a globalized world. Not everyone can be, or would wish to be, Bono, the world citizen; many people still seek to amass national or local power. In the wake of Europe's deep history of conflict, competition, and exchange, we can only imagine a future in which there remain many ways to be a European, and in which many Europes continue to thrive and contentedly live local lives.

Critical Thinking Questions

1. How does the Eurozone crisis beginning in 2008 reflect the fact that there are still many Europes?

2. Which long- and short-term historical developments help explain this diversity?

3. Trace the history of the movement of peoples from and to Europe since the late nineteenth century (see Chapter 21). What accounts for the fact that Europe is now a major destination for emigrants, whereas a little more than a century ago, a "Caucasian tsunami" took so many Europeans abroad?

4. As we have seen throughout this book, individual decision-makers (even in smaller states) matter very much in history. Choose several individuals—for example, Bono, Slobodan Milošević, Anna Politkovskaya, Vladimir Putin, Imela Nogić (Miss Sarajevo)—and explain how their decisions at critical moments changed the course of history.

Key Terms

globalization (p. 836)
European Union (EU) (p. 836)
Commonwealth of Independent States (CIS) (p. 840)

shock therapy (p. 843)
velvet divorce (p. 844)
Dayton Accords (p. 846)
devolution (p. 847)

Schengen Agreements (p. 849)
Eurozone (p. 849)
Americanization (p. 853)
digital revolution (p. 855)

postmodernism (p. 855)
Orange Revolution (p. 857)
sovereign debt crisis (euro crisis) (p. 860)

Primary Sources in connect

For information on Connect and the online resources available, go to **http://connect.mcgraw-hill.com**.

1. **Genocide on Trial: The Case of Slobodan Milošević**

2. **Otto Schily, Changes in German Citizenship, 1999**

3. **Salman Rushdie, "Imagine No Heaven"**

4. **Damien Hirst, What Art Has Become?**

Two Views of Europe's Future

The following passages exemplify the diversity of views about the future of Europe as seen by a proponent of further integration (German chancellor Angela Merkel) and a critic of EU policy (Daniel Hannan, a conservative member of the British Parliament). Merkel's speech was delivered to students at the College of Europe in Bruges, Belgium, on November 2, 2010, and lays out Germany's reasons for supporting the EU but also for insisting on fiscal discipline. Hannan's blog appeared a year later (November 14, 2011), after technocratic governments had taken power in Greece and Italy to deal with the deepening sovereign debt crisis.

Angela Merkel, Speech Opening the 61st Academic Year of the College of Europe

... We in the member states of the European Union are undergoing a process in which ever less is divided by borders. We can scarcely imagine any more how a Europe where nation states warred against one another for centuries could have existed. Students, let me say then that no other generation before you has been as able as you are to take advantage of the opportunities Europe offers. ...

Because we know how inestimably precious freedom and democracy are, we also see how the momentous changes of 1989–1990 have expanded our horizons. After 20 years, however, some things have come to be almost taken for granted in the freedom and democracy that a part of Europe once yearned for. Allow me to tell you that my generation—the first thirty-four years of my life were marked by lack of freedom, by despotism and dictatorship—changed massively in the years around 1989–1990. Suddenly we had the chance to live in freedom. This was not only the experience of those Germans living in eastern Germany—it was also a European experience. ...

We Germans know now that astonishingly great trust was placed in us during the era of German reunification. It wasn't just that the East Germans were courageous and Helmut Kohl was far-sighted. It was also the fact that the Chancellor of German unity was above all a person who was trusted in the world—in Europe and in the United States of America. We know how much trust we were granted. That's why we as the reunified Germany keep on trying to live up to this trust.

That's why it is apparent that Germany, Europe's largest economy, has a particular responsibility for our continent. I think we have particularly noticed this in the past two years, during the massive international financial and economic crisis. This spring, only a few months ago, we as the European Union stood on the brink of a precipice. Only through a considerable concerted effort was it possible to avert damage to the entire monetary union.

At that time I acted for Germany as the German Chancellor, but also a firm believer in Europe. Because I believe in Europe, I proposed that my parliament, the German Bundestag, take unusual and previously unimagined routes in order to help Greece and thus to ensure the stability of the eurozone as a whole. I was motivated to do so by the European project. This is the only reason why I decided to implement a short-term solution for the rescue package as well as ambitious reforms and strict austerity programmes for Greece and other countries. I faced severe criticism for this: For some it was too slow, for others too fast. But I believe it was the right thing, on the one hand, to insist that countries which caused such a crisis will have to take action themselves in the future and, on the other hand, to make clear that we bear a shared European responsibility. I think that today everyone in Europe agrees that on the whole this was the right way to bring Europe back from the brink of disaster. A great deal was at stake. This spring in the German Bundestag, our parliament, I said, "if the euro fails, Europe fails." That's why it's so incredibly important to secure the long-term stability of the monetary union so that we can continue to develop our visions of a shared Europe. ...

Of course there is always tremendous public debate when Europe is seeking the right way forward. It is my personal opinion that problems must not be swept under the rug. Harmony alone is not an end in itself for Europe. The key issue is that Europe must be built on a strong foundation. That's why we need a culture of stability and that's why we need shared values. That's why on Friday in the European Council we agreed on crucial new avenues, which also include sanctions in conjunction with the Stability Pact, and which will coordinate economic policy much more closely, and with which the member states cannot simply run up debts but rather must strive for economic strength and financial stability. ...

And now a final word to the members of the ... class assembled here today. ... What has made Europe strong—and we see this again and again—is this deep sense that the European Union is an amazing boon for us all. The Berlin Declaration on the fiftieth anniversary of the Treaties of Rome states that "we have united for the better." However much we may bicker and disagree on the details of what is best for Europe, this is something we must never forget. Europe is about rational thinking, Europe is about competition and the internal market, but Europe is also and will remain a matter of the heart. If during your studies here you experience Europe in both these senses, you will have spent your time very well indeed. ...

Source: Angela Merkel, speech given November 2, 2010, at the opening ceremony of the 61st academic year of the College of Europe; retrieved from http://www.bundesregierung.de/Content/EN/Reden/2010/2010-11-02-merkel-bruegge.html;jsessionid=99F51E8FB033E94652 011AF1BD24A76F.s2t2?nn=393812.

Daniel Hannan, The European Project Is Now Sustained by Coup

What we have witnessed is a coup d'état: bloodless and genteel, but a coup d'état none the less. In Athens and in Rome, elected prime ministers have been toppled in favour of Eurocrats—respectively a former Vice-President of the European Central Bank and a former European Commissioner. Both countries now have what are called "national governments," though they have been put together for the sole purpose of implementing policies that would be rejected in a general election.

Italy and Greece are satrapies of Brussels, just as surely as Bosnia or Kosovo. In its Balkan protectorates, the EU overtly favours technocracy as the antidote to "populism" (i.e., democracy). Left to themselves, the locals have a tendency to vote for parties that want ethnographic frontiers. The EU's solution is to rule through a series of appointed governors—diplomats (and the odd retired politician) in Bosnia, generals in Kosovo.

Now, like many previous empires, the EU is applying lessons learned through colonial administration to its metropolitan core. Politicians who lean too closely to what their voters want are removed....

The putsch is the logical culmination of the European scheme—though many Euro-idealists remain blind to that logic. The EU has always been an anti-democratic project. Lacking popular support, rejected in referendum after referendum, it depends on a tight-knit group of functionaries in the Commission and in the member states. Now, in a crisis, the democratic appurtenances and fripperies are discarded. Technocrats in Brussels deal directly with technocrats in Rome and Athens. The people are cut out altogether.

What's terrifying is that these "technocrats" caused the disaster in the first place. They decided that the survival of the euro mattered more than the prosperity of its constituent members; they presided over the rise in spending and debt; they deliberately overlooked the debt criteria when the euro was launched so as to admit Italy and Greece. Indeed the new Greek prime minister, Lucas Papademos, was running his country's central bank at the time.

In appointing these two Euro-apparatchiks, our masters are signalling in the clearest possible way that nothing will change. Closer integration matters more to them than freedom, more than prosperity, more than the rule of law, more than representative government itself.

Source: Daniel Hannan, "The European Project Is Now Sustained by Coup," blog for *The Telegraph,* November 14, 2011; retrieved from http://blogs.telegraph.co.uk/news/danielhannan/100117297/the-european-project-is-now-sustained-by-coup/; accessed 4/29/12.

QUESTIONS | *How do these contrasting perspectives demonstrate the persistence of "many Europes" even within the EU? What are the values Merkel and Hannan suggest are, or should be, shared by all Europeans?*

GLOSSARY

absolutism A form of government in the seventeenth and eighteenth centuries, in which the monarch had the right to rule without legal opposition to his or her authority.

acropolis The common defensible high spot or hilly area of a polis.

Act of Supremacy An English law passed by Parliament in 1534 that established the monarch as the supreme religious authority in the realm with the right to determine church doctrine and practice.

ad fontes The Italian Renaissance humanist drive to return to primary sources and to treat them critically.

aedile Magistrate of the people, guardian of public property.

agon The ancient Greek belief that life was a constant struggle or competition.

agora The marketplace of a polis.

Agricultural Revolution of Prehistory The birth and spread of agriculture 8000–5000 BCE.

alchemy The medieval study of chemistry, concerned primarily with turning base metals into gold.

Allied Powers The alliance of countries opposed to the Axis Powers during WWII, including the Soviet Union, Great Britain, and the United States.

Americanization The influence and presence of American products and practices, most notably mass consumerism, mass production, fast food, Coca-Cola, and Hollywood movies.

Anabaptists Members of a sectarian movement that emerged in the sixteenth century who believed in adult baptism.

anarchism A nineteenth- and early-twentieth-century ideology that viewed the state as a tool of bourgeois interests and thus rejected participation in parliamentary politics in favor of revolutionary action.

anomie The term used by sociologist Emile Durkheim to indicate alienation felt in impersonal modern industrial societies.

anti-pope One elected in opposition to a pope duly elected by church law and custom.

apostate One who lapses from the faith.

apotheosis The transformation of a man into a god.

appeasement The foreign policy of making concessions to satisfy an aggressor; used most notably by Great Britain and France in the late 1930s to avoid war with Nazi Germany.

Archaic Age The Greek period running from 800 BCE to 500 BCE.

arête The pursuit of individual excellence in ancient Greece.

Arianism The doctrine of Arius, a priest from Alexandria and his followers called Arians, who claimed that Christ was subsequent (since his human nature was created) to God the Father and therefore less divine.

Arsenal Located at the mouth of Venice's Grand Canal, the Arsenal equipped and repaired the republic's warships and its merchant vessels.

art nouveau Literally meaning "new art"; a movement in art, architecture, and design from the 1890s to 1914 that incorporated stylized natural forms.

assignat Paper money issued by the French Revolutionary government; replaced by the franc.

astrolabe A device used to measure the angle of the Pole Star relative to the horizon while at sea.

augury Reading the will of the gods and signs of the future by studying the flight of birds.

avant-garde Term meaning "ahead of the rest"; used by movements at the end of the nineteenth century celebrating art considered ahead of its time; associated with elitism and social radicalism.

Axis Powers World War II alliance among Germany, Italy, and Japan and other countries.

balkanize To divide an area such as the landmass of Europe into many rival powers, none able to dominate the others.

barbarian A term used by late Romans to describe the Germans as an uncivilized people who spoke an incomprehensible language and were uncivilized.

Baroque An art movement associated with the reformed Catholic Church that emphasized sumptuous, richly decorated churches and dramatic paintings and sculptures.

basilica A Christian church with a longitudinal axis formed by a nave and side aisles leading from an entranceway in the west to a choir and apse structure in the east.

Bauhaus School of architecture and industrial design that emerged in Germany in the 1920s. This new style insisted that modern buildings and furnishings should be both beautiful and useful.

benefice The land granted by a lord in exchange for the service and oath-bound loyalty of a vassal.

Black Death A term not used until the sixteenth century to describe the outbreak of the bubonic plague that struck Europe in the mid-fourteenth century.

Blitzkrieg A German term meaning "lightning war"; offensive military tactic used by Germany in World War II consisting of overwhelming a certain point in the enemy's defense with dive bombers, tanks, and motorized infantry, making it difficult for the enemy to repel the subsequent mass infantry attack.

Boers A Dutch word meaning farmers; used to describe settlers of Dutch extraction in South Africa.

Bolsheviks Russian communists led by Vladimir Lenin, who advocated a violent, immediate revolution to overthrow capitalism. The Bolsheviks toppled the provisional government in 1917 and became the founders of communism in the Soviet Union.

Bonfire of the Vanities In 1494 in Florence, the burning of books, paintings, cosmetics, and other material trifles as encouraged by Savonarola.

bourgeois Well-to-do members of the third estate, who usually resided in market towns (*bourgs*).

Bretton Woods system The economic framework signed in 1944 and put into effect after World War II in which the U.S. dollar served as the world's reserve currency, allowing international trade without extreme currency fluctuation. The World Bank and the International Monetary Fund were also established to facilitate economic growth and grant loans to countries for currency stabilization.

Brezhnev Doctrine Policy promulgated by Soviet premier Leonid Brezhnev stating that the Soviet Union had the right to intervene in its eastern European satellite states. It was used to justify Soviet suppression of the Prague Spring and other attempts at liberalization in the Eastern bloc.

British East India Company (BEIC) Founded in 1602, this state-chartered company was given monopoly trading rights in India. Between 1757 and 1858, the BEIC acted as a colonizing power in India.

bull A public letter or official proclamation issued by the pope.

Caesarian (or Consular) Faction Sometimes mistakenly called the First Triumvirate. Three magnates, Caesar, Pompey, and Crassus, joined together in an alliance without state sanction to seek power and advantage when one of them was consul, as occurred in 59 BCE when Caesar became consul.

capitularies Carolingian royal laws (pronouncements) issued in chapters (*capitula*) or itemized form by the king.

caravel A three-masted vessel that required a small crew and could hold 50–70 tons of cargo.

Caroline Minuscule A small, regular script that emerged during the reign of Charlemagne and was common in Europe until the twelfth century.

carrack A three-masted ship that was rigged with both square and triangular sails to catch any available wind; generally served as merchant vessels.

cartel An agreement among producers to coordinate prices, marketing, and production.

Central Powers The military alliance in World War I consisting of Germany, Austria-Hungary, Bulgaria, and the Ottoman Empire and opposed to the Entente.

chartered (joint-stock) companies Companies possessing a monopoly by the government and issuing stock to investors; established in the early seventeenth century by several nations (especially the English and Dutch) for the purpose of trade and exploration.

Chartism A reform movement among English workers and radicals that demanded universal suffrage and other political and social rights for the working classes.

Cheka The first of many Soviet secret police forces, charged with eliminating suspected enemies of the Bolsheviks through execution, internment in forced labor camps, and torture.

chiaroscuro The use of contrasting light and shadow in Italian Renaissance paintings to shade figures and give them an impression of three-dimensionality.

chivalry The code of conduct held by the elite warrior class or horsemen of medieval Europe.

Christian socialism A nineteenth-century mass political movement that sought to curb the excesses and inequalities of liberal capitalism, but opposed the idea of socialist revolution.

civic humanism The application of humanist thought to political and social problems, especially as humanists gained confidence that ancient ideals might be used to reform and enlighten their communities.

Civil Constitution of the Clergy Law passed by the National Assembly in 1790 turning the clergy into state employees and requiring the clergy to swear loyalty to the state.

civilization A higher organized form of historical and cultural life, often based on cities, and associated with settlements, a critical mass of people, agriculture, trade, government, law, writing, and abstract thought.

Classical Age Of ancient Greece, stretching from c. 500 to 404 BCE or the end of the Peloponnesian War.

clientage A Roman practice or institution under which an inferior citizen became the dependent or client of a superior. The patron expected loyal service from the client and provided the client with land, gifts, and money.

Code of Hammurabi A law code with nearly three hundred judgments issued by Hammurabi before 1750 BCE.

codex A book with pages bound between two covers as opposed to the papyrus roll.

Cold War Sustained ideological, economic, political, and military tension between the West, led by the United States, and the Communist bloc, led by the Soviet Union, from approximately 1945 to 1989.

collectivization Soviet policy starting in the late 1920s of replacing private farms with large cooperatives under state management.

Columbian Exchange The long-term, two-way transfer of peoples, goods, diseases, and ideas between Europe and the Americas.

Comintern International organization of communist parties directed from Moscow from 1919 to 1943.

Committee of Public Safety Board appointed by the convention to oversee the war effort and to choose members of the Revolutionary Tribunal, which tried suspected traitors; the *de facto* government in France during the Reign of Terror.

Commonwealth of Independent States (CIS) A loose association of former Soviet republics with the goal of coordinating trade and law enforcement.

commune In twelfth-century northern European towns, an association generally of burghers who agreed on local government, tolls, taxes, and the rights of townspeople. In the twelfth and thirteenth centuries in Italy, a form of government or city organization run by groups of citizens, at first by local, powerful, wealthy men and later with some degree of participation by middling landowners, merchants, shopkeepers, and members of trade guilds.

communism A revolutionary form of socialism, formulated by Karl Marx, that advocated overthrowing the bourgeoisie and industrial capitalism in order to give the proletariat ownership of the means of production.

Concert of Europe The intermittent efforts by Austria, Prussia, Russia, and France after the Congress of Vienna to cooperate in order to suppress revolution and keep peace in Europe.

conciliar movement A movement of high churchmen that held that a general council of the church, not the pope, had the authority to set the standards for proper governance for the church and Christian behavior.

Concordat A formal agreement between the papacy and a government regulating the affairs of the church.

Congress of Vienna The peace conference held in Vienna in 1814 and 1815 after Napoleon's defeat, at which the victorious powers (Britain, Austria, Russia, and Prussia) agreed to restore monarchies and cooperate to prevent future revolutions.

conquistador A term that refers to soldiers of fortune; conquerors, particularly of the Mexica and Inca Empires; or the leader of the forces leading those campaigns.

conservative (conservatism) An ideology that stressed order, traditional values, and the maintenance of aristocratic and clerical privileges; and opposed revolution and the implementation of liberal policies.

consuls Chief magistrates, a pair of whom were elected in the Roman Senate to hold office for a single year.

contact vulnerabilities The weak points (political, physical, cultural, etc.) exposed when alien peoples (e.g., native Americans and Europeans) came into contact for the first time in the fifteenth and sixteenth centuries.

Continental System Napoleon's embargo on British products from 1806 to 1814.

Convention Revolutionary government that followed the overthrow of Louis XVI. Ruling from September 1792 to November 1795, it was elected by universal manhood suffrage and marked by radical measures and excesses such as the Reign of Terror and de-Christianization.

converso A convert to Catholicism.

corvée The obligation of peasants to their lords to spend a few days making improvements, such as building roads.

cottage industries Sites of the in-home production of goods, often in villages.

covenant The binding agreement the ancient Hebrews made with God to abandon polytheism and follow but one god.

creoles People of mixed European and non-European ancestry.

cuneiform Wedge-shaped writing inscribed on wet clay tablets, stone, and other surfaces by the Mesopotamian peoples and others.

curule A throne or official chair of the Roman magistrate, adopted from the Etruscans.

Cynics Practitioners of Cynicism, a Hellenistic philosophy that rejected the conventional Hellenistic world and spurned religious piety, reverence for kings and kingdoms, and all hypocrisy.

Dada Artistic movement that emerged out of World War I, emphasizing silly forms and mirroring chaotic conditions in postwar society.

Dark Age The Greek period running from 1100 BCE to 800 BCE in which the Greeks left behind few material remains (buildings or artifacts).

Dayton Accords Peace agreement in 1995 ending the three-year-long war in the former Yugoslavia.

D-Day June 6, 1944; the opening day of the Allies' invasion of Nazi-occupied France.

deism Religious belief of the seventeenth and eighteenth centuries stating that God created the universe and established its laws of operation but did not subsequently intervene in its affairs or those of humans.

Delian League A league located initially on the island of Delos that was formed by Athens to resist any further aggression toward Greece by the Persian Empire.

demos Masses, or people; free male native residents, nonnoble, but of some standing and wealth in the Greek polis.

détente Term meaning "relaxation"; refers to the period of easing of tensions between the western powers and the Communist bloc in the 1970s.

devolution The process of passing power to regional assemblies, as practiced particularly by Great Britain in 1997–1998.

devotio moderna Emerging in late-fourteenth-century Europe, the new or modern form of devotion that emphasized individual education, piety, and commitment to God, rather than the sacraments and other standards of the Catholic Church.

diaspora The emigration or spread of the Hebrews from Israel to other lands.

digital revolution The rapid change in communications since the 1980s involving computers, cell phones, the Internet, and information storage, allowing unprecedented access to information and discourse among the world's peoples.

diocese The area of the bishop's jurisdiction.

Directory French government from November 1795 to November 1799 that replaced the Convention with a board of five directors to rule France. The Directory pulled back from the radicalism of the Convention and ended the Terror, but kept France at war, refused to restore the monarchy, and persecuted rebellious clergymen.

divine right The theory that rulers, usually monarchs, received their right to rule from God.

doge The chief official of the Venetian republic; served for his lifetime.

Domesday Book The record ordered by King William the Conqueror of all his royal property in England.

Donation of Pepin A gift of lands in central Italy to the Roman church by Pepin the Short.

Donatism The movement begun by Donatus, a bishop of Carthage, who had led the northern African resistance to restoring lapsed churchmen.

Eastern bloc Term used to describe the Soviet Union and its satellite communist regimes of eastern Europe.

Eastern Question Nineteenth-century discussion among the great powers about what to do about the Ottoman Empire, which seemed on the point of collapse.

Edict of Milan An edict of universal religious toleration proclaimed by the co-emperors Constantine and Licinius, by which Christians and others could now practice their religions openly and without state restraint, and receive back the properties seized by the Roman state.

Edict of Nantes King Henry IV's measure of 1598 that established the terms upon which the Huguenots (Protestants) and Catholics could coexist within France.

Einsatzgruppen A German term meaning "task forces"; German units of the SS assigned to go into occupied areas of the Soviet Union and kill Jews, communists, and partisans.

émigré One who has left the country, usually for political reasons. In the French Revolution, the term applied to nobles, clergymen, and other opponents of the Revolution who fled to foreign countries to organize a counterrevolution.

empiricism In science, the use of observation and experiments to draw conclusions.

encomienda system A system used by the Spanish in the Americas in which a Spanish settler was given, in the name of the king, trusteeship over a piece of land and its native residents in exchange for the military enforcement of Spanish rule and a promise that the colonist would teach the indigenous peoples in his charge about Catholicism.

enlightened absolutism The attempt by absolutist rulers in central and eastern Europe to impose some of the ideals of the Enlightenment on their populations.

Enlightenment Intellectual movement in the eighteenth century emphasizing reason and applying the laws of nature discovered in the scientific revolution to human societies.

Entente An informal "understanding" between Britain, France, and Russia before World War I. Used to describe the forces allied against the Central Powers in the war.

Epicureans Followers of the Hellenistic philosopher Epicurus of Athens, who thought that the world was a product of random combinations of atoms and without an underlying purpose or goodness. The Epicureans renounced simple hedonism, treasured friendship, and sought emotional tranquility.

equestrians In the Early Roman Republic, the name of men in the cavalry; later used to refer to the class of Romans below that of the senators.

Estates General The medieval representative assembly of France, dismissed in 1614 and recalled only in 1788. It consisted of three estates: (1) the clergy, (2) nobility, and (3) the rest. Such assemblies existed in various forms throughout Europe; known as Diets in the Holy Roman Empire, the Sejm in Poland, Zemsky Sobor in Russia, the Riksdag in Sweden, and Parliament in England.

ethnic cleansing The policy of murder, deportation, and violence against members of an ethnic group in order to clear a territory of its members.

European Economic Community (EEC) Association of western European states founded in 1957 to eliminate tariffs and take steps toward economic integration with the goal of economic prosperity and international peace.

European Union (EU) A confederation of twenty-seven European states with a single market; the successor organization to the European Economic Community.

Eurozone Currency union of seventeen states in the European Union that use the euro as its currency.

existentialism Twentieth-century philosophy that emerged out of World War I and remained popular until the 1960s. It asserted that individuals were responsible for finding meaning in a world that was meaningless and incoherent.

extraterritoriality The state of being exempted from local laws. Applied to Europeans in Asia in the nineteenth and early twentieth centuries, this provision extended the jurisdiction of European home laws to Europeans overseas.

fasces A Roman political symbol, an ax and rods joined together to signify the magistrate's right to enforce physical punishment.

Fascism A twentieth-century ideology, marked by dictatorship and militant nationalism, that rejected communism, conservatism, liberalism, and democracy. Fascists stressed the primacy of the nation and directed all resources to strengthening it.

fin de siècle French term meaning "end of the century." Refers to the cultural crisis at the end of the nineteenth century marked by increased mobility, mass politics, and the decline of certainty, positivism, and liberalism.

First Triumvirate See Caesarian (or Consular) Faction.

Flagellants After the outbreak of plague in fourteenth-century Europe, a movement of people who scourged or whipped themselves to appease the anger of God.

the Forty-Five The failed Jacobite Uprising of 1745, in which Charles Edward Stuart ("Bonnie Prince Charlie") landed in the Scottish Highlands and sparked an uprising to restore the Stuart Monarchy in Great Britain.

Fourteen Points Peace plans formulated by U.S. president Wilson as the basis for a new world order after World War I. Called for free trade, German evacuation of occupied territory, national self-determination, and the end of secret treaties.

Freikorps Right-wing paramilitary groups in Germany after World War I consisting of veterans pledging to fight Communist uprisings in Germany; formed the vanguard of the Nazi movement.

Fronde A series of rebellions by nobles from 1648 to 1653 against the French monarch and the development of a fully absolutist state. It ended with the victory of Louis XIV.

galley A Venetian vessel that could be propelled forward either by oars or by wind-filled sails.

General Maximum Law passed in 1793 by the French Convention establishing price controls on food.

Genetic Adam The common male ancestor of human males, who lived in Africa about 75,000–60,000 years ago.

ghetto An area segregated by race or religion; the term was coined after an area of Venice called the *geto nuovo*, where in 1516 Jews were segregated. Prior to implementation of the final solution in World War II, the Nazis concentrated Jews in ghettoes before deporting survivors to extermination camps.

glasnost Term meaning "openness"; part of Soviet premier Mikhail Gorbachev's reform program in the late 1980s to break the tradition of secrecy that had characterized Soviet political culture.

globalization A process, involving the rapid movement of capital, people, and technologies, in which the world's peoples, especially their market economies, are increasingly tied together in the global economy.

Gnostics Those who know; elitist early Christians who thought that they had secret knowledge of God and the ways of the universe.

Golden Bull Issued in 1356 by the emperor Charles IV, recognizing the right of the seven German prince-electors to elect the emperor (so-called because of its golden seal).

Grande Armée Napoleon's highly advanced army, which grew to almost 600,000 men before suffering heavy losses in Russia in 1812.

Great (East-West) Schism The rupture or division between the Christian churches east and west that occurred in 1054.

Great Famine The devastating famine that struck northern Europe between 1315 and 1322.

great powers The five European powers that fielded the largest armies during the Seven Years' War—Britain, France, Russia, Prussia, and Austria; these nations would dominate European politics until at least 1918.

guild An association of craftsmen that controlled production, divided workers into masters and apprentices, and set the prices and terms of trade for goods.

gulag Russian acronym for the system of forced-labor camps used in the Soviet Union to hold criminals, prisoners of war, and political prisoners until the Khrushchev era.

gymnasium A Greek institution of recreation, exercise, education, and cultural exchange.

haruspicy Reading the will of the gods and signs of the future by studying the entrails, particularly the livers, of animals.

Hejira Muhammad's flight in 622 from Mecca to Medina, an event that marks the beginning of Islamic chronology.

heliocentric theory The theory that the planets circle the sun, as proposed by Aristarchus of Samos in the third century BCE.

Hellenistic Those Greek-like traits, tendencies, and cultures of the period after the Classical Age, particularly as they appeared in the wider Greek world shaped by Philip II and his son Alexander the Great.

Hellenization The promotion and spread of the Greek language and the civilized customs associated with Greek culture.

helots Agricultural slaves of the Spartans.

henge Typically, a Neolithic earthenwork having a ditch and ring-shaped bank. Stonehenge, without a ditch, is atypical.

henotheism A preference for one god while still allowing for the existence of other gods.

hieroglyphics The oldest of three forms of ancient Egyptian writing, which the Greeks named "sacred carvings." Hieroglyphics, which were not understood in modern times until the nineteenth century, are a complex system of over seven hundred signs, including pictographic, phonographic, and ideographic elements.

Highlanders Residents of the Highlands in northern Scotland whose Celtic language, clan system, and Catholic religion made them distinct from the Presbyterian, commercially oriented Lowland Scots who inhabited regions closer to the English border.

Holocaust The systematic extermination of about six million Jews by Nazi Germany during World War II.

hoplite The soldier who served in the phalanx formation of infantry for a Greek polis.

hubris A Greek term for exaggerated or dangerous pride.

Huguenots French Protestants or Calvinists.

humanist In the Middle Ages, one with an interest in the classics, Latin eloquence, and human affairs.

Hundred Years' War Between 1337 and 1453, the war waged between France and England over England's claims on the kingdom of France.

hyperinflation Catastrophic rate of inflation, resulting in enormous price increases, such as that which occurred in Germany in 1923.

iconoclasm Icon breaking; the iconoclasts of the Byzantine world denied the veneration of images and sought to destroy icons.

imperator The title of a Roman military commander in the Republican period; used in the Roman Empire to refer to the general commander of the empire.

imperial exchange The exchange, between Europe and its colonies, of goods and ideas such as Christianity, weapons and industrial machinery, and diamonds, tea, rubber, and oriental carpets, resulting in cheap commodities for European consumers.

Impressionism The nineteenth-century school of painting that used thick brushstrokes and stressed the depiction of light.

incunabula The books printed in the first fifty years of printing, thus approximately between 1450 and 1500; *incunabula* means "from the cradle" or "beginning."

indulgence A Catholic device for the remission (through penance or its equivalent) of eternal punishments incurred through sin.

Industrial Revolution The cascade of economic and technological changes since the late eighteenth century that resulted in dramatically increased production using centralized factories, usually powered by machinery.

inquisition In the mid-thirteenth century, a process formalized by the papacy to investigate heretics and heretical belief.

intendants French officials, usually nonnobles, sent out to assert the will of the monarch in the provinces of France in the seventeenth and eighteenth centuries.

interdict The exclusion by the pope or a high ecclesiastic such as a bishop of a person, city, or kingdom from participating in or receiving the benefits of the Catholic religion.

Investiture Controversy The dispute that broke out during the pontificate of Gregory VII over the lay investiture of ecclesiastical officeholders, specifically bishops.

Iron Curtain Term first used by Winston Churchill in 1946 to describe the hardening divisions between the Soviet Union and the western powers after World War II. It became a metaphor to describe the division of western and eastern Europe during the Cold War.

Italian Renaissance The term *renaissance* literally means a "rebirth"; when applied to the Italian cultural movement of the fifteenth century, it means the rebirth or, more vaguely, the recovery of the glories of the classical world.

Jacobin Club Parisian political club that grew increasingly radical after 1789. The Jacobins dominated French politics in 1793 and 1794.

Jacquerie The peasants' revolt that broke out in France in 1358; named after the caricature of a good peasant, Jacques Bonhomme.

Jansenism A religious movement among seventeenth- and eighteenth-century Catholics that stressed salvation through faith and simpler, more emotional forms of worship.

jihad Holy war or an individual's personal calling to strive to conform to God's will.

Junkers Traditional landowning nobility in Prussia that exercised substantial political influence on the Prussian, and later German, monarchs.

keep A stone tower erected on an elevated site as part of a castle; it served as the lord's residence and the most defensible and sturdy part of the castle.

Kharijites "Those who walked out," a group that withdrew their support from the caliph Ali.

koine The grammatically simpler form of Greek that became the standard Greek of the Hellenistic Age.

Kulturkampf A German term meaning "culture war"; refers to Bismarck's battle against Catholicism in the 1870s in the newly unified Germany.

laissez-faire Literally, "let it be." An economic theory, developed during the Enlightenment, by which governments should not regulate or intervene in the economy, except to protect property and maintain public order.

Lateran Accords Agreement in 1929 between the papacy and Italy establishing Vatican City as a state and providing state support to Catholicism in Italy.

lay investiture The act by which laymen (lords, kings, emperors) invested bishops with the symbols of their religious offices.

League of Nations Organization of states established after World War I with the goal of resolving disputes through arbitration and maintaining peace.

Lebensraum A German term meaning "living space"; idea conceived before World War I and adopted by the Nazis, stating that Germans needed living space in the east and requiring that the racially inferior inhabitants living there should be killed, enslaved, or forced off the land.

Lend-Lease Agreement American program to supply the Allies in World War II from 1941 to 1945.

liberal (liberalism) An ideology, beginning in the nineteenth century, that stressed the freedom of individuals to use their natural rights. In economic terms, this meant little governmental interference. In the political sphere, liberals usually preferred monarchs constrained by written constitutions.

Linear B A script characterized by straight lines that was employed to write a form of archaic Greek on late Minoan Crete as well as in Mycenaean Greece.

linear perspective A system, based on geometry, used by Italian Renaissance artists to give painted figures a sense of depth.

Little Ice Age A period beginning around 1275–1300 in Europe, in which temperatures dropped and ice fields and glaciers advanced.

Lollards (idlers) A name used by Catholic critics to characterize the supporters of John Wyclif and his teachings on the nature of the church and Christian belief.

long peace The period between 1815 (Napoleonic Wars) and 1914 (First World War) in European history in which no large, general wars encompassing all of Europe broke out.

ma'at An ancient Egyptian principle embodying justice, truth, wisdom, and harmony.

magistrate A representative of the Roman people given the right to hold executive power.

Magna Carta A great charter issued in England in 1215 by King John that provided a series of guarantees to the magnates and people of England, delimiting what the king could demand of his people and powerful lords.

mandates (mandate system) Legal mechanism established in the post-1918 peace treaties by which the administrative functions of the former territories of the Ottoman and German Empires were transferred to the League of Nations, who then entrusted them to be ruled by Britain and France.

Manhattan Project Code name for the research project led by the United States to develop an atomic bomb during World War II.

manorialism An economic and social system in which the holder of the land lives in a manor house and supervises land farmed by dependent laborers.

Marshall Plan American aid package offered to Europe and accepted by western Europeans in 1948 to help rebuild Europe, establish free trade and stability, and combat the appeal of communism.

materfamilias The mother or mistress of the Roman household, who managed the family's children, servants, slaves, and daily resources.

Medieval Warm Period A period of warmer temperatures that stretched from 775 to 1275, reaching its peak in the late eleventh and early twelfth centuries.

mendicants Begging friars such as the Franciscans and Dominicans who devoted themselves to the Roman Catholic Church, the papacy, the poor, and the sick; preached and begged in the cities of Europe; and practiced absolute poverty.

meritocracy The practice of promoting or appointing individuals in government based on merits—such as skill, credentials, and ability—rather than on social status.

Methodism A Protestant sect, emerging out of Anglicanism in the eighteenth century, that stressed piety and preaching the gospel to the common people.

metic A resident foreigner of Athens.

millenarianism The belief that the end of the world is near and a new time of peace and prosperity at hand.

missi dominici Carolingian royal officials (agents of the lord) who were sent into the kingdom to administer the king's justice (traveling judges).

Mitochondrial Eve The common matrilineal (descending from the mother) ancestor of all living humans, who lived approximately 170,000 years ago in Africa.

modernism An umbrella term used to describe cultural and artistic developments from the late nineteenth century until the middle of the twentieth century. Stressed abstraction and universality but also uncertainty and the workings of the unconsciousness.

monophysite The view that God the Father had one, divine nature, and so was unique and omnipotent.

monotheism The religious belief that there is only one god.

Monroe Doctrine Proclamation by U.S. president James Monroe's administration and backed by Britain saying that the Western Hemisphere was off limits to colonization.

mystery religions Those religions that emerged in the Hellenistic world with secret practices and rites of initiation.

Nansen passport Travel papers issued by the League of Nations to refugees who had no homeland after World War I and the Russian Revolution, allowing them to settle in a country that accepted the passport.

Napoleonic Code The name used for the legal codes introduced by Napoleon in 1804, 1806, 1807, and 1808, which imposed a single civil law on France and French-occupied territories. The code outlawed privileges based on birth, allowed freedom of religion, mandated meritocracy, and protected private property.

National Assembly Transitional body established after the Tennis Court Oath in 1789 to replace the Estates General, act as a legislature, and write a new constitution. Replaced by the Constituent Assembly in 1791.

national self-determination The policy articulated by American president Wilson after World War I, which stated that a group considering itself a nation has the right to be ruled only by members of that nation.

nationalism An ideology, originating during the era of the French Revolution and the Napoleonic Wars, that stressed the importance of national identity and the nation-state.

nation-state The dominant form of political organization since the nineteenth century, consisting of a community of people who have a sense of unity based on belief in a common culture and shared interests.

natural law Understandable, rational laws believed to be inherent in nature rather than established by humans.

natural selection A key element in Darwin's theory of evolution, stating that forms of life with traits better suited to survival will reproduce in larger numbers, leading to the extinction of weaker ones.

nave From the Latin *navis* for ship, so named because the central space of a basilica-style or longitudinal church resembles the upside-down hull of a ship.

Nazism German variety of fascism led by Adolf Hitler and the National Socialist Party from the 1920s until 1945; stressed the supremacy of the Aryan race and preached fierce anti-Semitism.

neoclassicism Eighteenth-century artistic movement that drew inspiration from the classical art and architecture of ancient Greece and Rome.

neo-Europes Areas of the world settled and dominated by Europeans and their descendants, such as North America and Australia.

New Economic Policy (NEP) Lenin's economic policy after the Russian civil wars intended to stabilize the economy of the USSR. The NEP allowed Soviet citizens to own land and to sell goods in the private marketplace.

Night of the Broken Glass The anti-Semitic pogrom of November 9, 1938; a series of coordinated attacks on Jews and Jewish property backed by the Nazi government.

nominalism A scholastic philosophy that maintained that universals are mere names and have no real existence, held in particular by William of Ockham.

North Atlantic Treaty Organization (NATO) Alliance of western European states, the United States, Canada, and Turkey during the Cold War, founded in 1949. NATO began to include a few eastern European states after the fall of communism.

numina The vague divine forces that Iron Age Romans believed animated their world.

Nuremberg Trials Trial of high-ranking Nazis after World War II, resulting in the execution of twelve officials for crimes against humanity.

Old Regime(s) European society before the French Revolution; marked by absolutism and privileges for the nobles and the clergy.

oligarchy A form of government in which power lies with the powerful few, often propertied aristocrats or the wealthy.

Orange Revolution The successful protest movement in late 2004 in Ukraine, which resulted in the overturning of rigged election results.

ostracism An institution in classical Athens to expel dangerous individuals from Athens for up to ten years. The procedure was so called because citizens cast ostraka, broken pieces of pottery (shards) or prepared ceramic pieces, with the name of the person they wished to ostracize into a large urn.

Ottonian system The practice of the Ottonian rulers of Germany of treating the churches of the realm and their property (lands, buildings, and worldly revenues) as part of its royal or imperial operation.

pandemic An outbreak of communicable disease extending over many regions and involving high mortality.

papal plenitude of power The doctrine by which the high medieval papacy claimed that the pope had unlimited or absolute power.

parlements Provincial French law courts that acted as legal checks to the absolutist monarch's power.

paterfamilias The powerful head of the large Roman family was the extended family's nominal father or master of the house. He was generally the senior male member of the family, perhaps a grandfather or an uncle, and his powers and responsibilities were far reaching.

patria potestas The extensive paternal power exercised by the *paterfamilias* of the Roman family unit.

patricians Men from the oldest, most well-established, and distinguished Roman families.

Pax Romana The Roman peace fashioned by Augustus and extending over the Roman Empire between approximately 27 BCE and 180 CE.

Peace of Augsburg The 1555 treaty between Protestant and Catholic powers in the Holy Roman Empire that acknowledged that there were two permissible forms of religious observance, Protestant and Catholic.

Peace of God The injunction, formulated by tenth-century churchmen, to curb the violence of local lords against innocents (farmers, women, and children) by threatening to excommunicate violators.

Peloponnesian League A group of poleis committed to the interests of the Peloponnesus of Greece.

perestroika Term meaning "restructuring"; part of Soviet premier Mikhail Gorbachev's unsuccessful reform program in the late 1980s to decentralize and reform the Soviet economy.

Petrine authority Resting its authority in part on Christ's appointment of Peter as the rock upon which he would build his church, the church of Rome claimed that Peter, the first bishop of Rome, and his successors (the popes), had the right and obligation to govern the whole of the church.

phalanx A rectangular formation of infantry.

philosophes Leading French writers and thinkers of the Enlightenment.

Pietism A movement among Protestants that stressed simplicity, reading the Bible, and more emotional forms of worship.

plebeians Lower-class Roman citizens who can be divided roughly into two groups, the farmers and merchants, both of whom held a subordinate position within the Roman Republic.

pluralism The holding of several ecclesiastical offices at once as, for instance, when one man was bishop over several episcopal sees at the same time.

pogrom Organized persecution of the helpless, particularly Jews; often involving beatings and burning of Jewish property; more common in eastern Europe, especially in the Pale of Settlement.

polis (plural, poleis) The Greek city-state, which contained a surrounding territory.

Polish Home Army The main resistance group to German rule in Poland during World War II; loyal to the pro-western Polish government in exile in London.

polytheism The religious belief that many gods exist.

Pontifex Maximus High priest of Roman religion who controlled the calendar and exercised authority over the various colleges of priests.

pontiffs High priests of the Roman Republic and Empire.

Popular Front An alliance of leftist political parties forged in the 1930s, particularly in France, to defeat fascists on the right.

Portolan chart A chart showing navigable ports, landmarks, geographical features, and compass headings so that a pilot could plot his course with respect to the shoreline and his ship's present position.

positivism A nineteenth-century philosophy developed by Auguste Comte that held that scientific investigation and accumulation of data could enable thinkers to discover the laws of mankind and improve society.

postmodernism Umbrella term for artistic styles that reject objective reality, embrace relativism, and stress fragmentation.

praetor Magistrate dealing with military and foreign affairs.

Praetorian Guard A band of soldiers created by the emperor Augustus as his own imperial bodyguard. This guard continued throughout the imperial period.

prehistory The long period (200,000–3300 BCE) before the birth of writing in Mesopotamia, when humans lived in wandering groups that hunted and foraged.

primogeniture The practice, particularly in France, by which land and title passed to the eldest son, not to all heirs.

proletariat The industrial working class described by Marx.

Protestant One who adheres to one of the churches that emerged in the sixteenth century in opposition to the Catholic Church, its teachings, and its practices.

provisional government The interim government set up in Russia after the czar abdicated in spring 1917 and lasting until November 1917; headed by the democratic socialist Alexander Kerensky.

public sphere The virtual world in which individuals from different regions, status groups, and religious backgrounds speak to one another, and to society at large (often in print), on subjects of mutual interest.

purgatory A Catholic doctrine of an intermediate place or station between heaven and hell where after death humans await the Last Judgment.

Pyrrhic Victory Named after the experience of King Pyrrhus of Epirus, who waged a series of successful battles against Rome but found them too costly and withdrew. Hence, such a victory is one that comes at too great a cost.

quadrivium Mathematics, geometry, astronomy, and music; the material component of the seven liberal arts.

quaestor Magistrate and investigator of the Roman Republic.

rationalism The theory that the mind can ascertain truth through thinking, rather than through experimentation and observation; also, more generally, the idea that, through reason, humans can understand the world.

realism A nineteenth-century artistic movement that depicted contemporary objects and people as they appeared in objective reality.

Realpolitik The pragmatic practice of power politics based on realistic chances of success rather than ideals; associated with Bismarck's foreign policy.

Reign of Terror ("the Terror") The attempt to purge enemies of the revolution in 1793 and 1794, leading to arbitrary executions and general chaos as tens of thousands were executed.

relics The remains left behind by the saints such as their bones and objects they touched, which are called contact relics.

Renaissance humanism A set of beliefs and educational standards based on and formed by the mastery of ancient languages; the close, unmediated reading of ancient texts; and the emulation of ancient literary, artistic, and philosophical models.

Renaissance individualism The belief that human beings occupy a special place in the created world and are capable of extraordinary achievements.

revisionism (socialist) A moderate form of socialism, according to which increased equality and better working conditions could be obtained peacefully through parliamentary politics rather than through revolution.

Risorgimento An Italian term for "revival"; refers to the Italian unification movement in the nineteenth century.

robot The obligation of serfs to work the landlord's land for several days a week.

romanticism A cultural and literary movement in the first half of the nineteenth century that stressed feeling over reason.

salons Private gatherings in the Enlightenment, run mostly by aristocratic women, in which discussions of science, politics, economics, and literature took place.

sans-culottes Literally, "without breeches." Radical urban Parisians who demanded legislation such as the General Maximum, which would benefit Parisian workers.

satrap The governor of a satrapy or incorporated part of the Persian Empire who was directly subject to the great king.

Schengen Agreements Treaty signed in European Community nations in 1985 to eliminate internal border controls.

Schlieffen Plan The war plan designed in the German military by Count Alfred von Schlieffen that called for a swift defeat of France in six weeks before committing full forces against Russia; implemented by the Germans in 1914.

scholasticism The general term for the intellectual movement of university thinkers (the schoolmen) of the period between 1150 and 1350.

scramble for Africa The rapid imposition of European rule in Africa beginning in the 1870s and lasting until 1914.

Sea Raiders Unknown peoples who raided in the eastern Mediterranean Sea during the last centuries of the second millennium BCE.

second industrial revolution A new phase of industrialization beginning in the 1870s with breakthroughs in chemistry, electricity, and steel production.

second serfdom The gradual reimposition of serfdom in eastern Europe from the end of the sixteenth century until the middle of the nineteenth century.

Second Vatican Council (Vatican II) High-level meeting (1962–1965) of leaders of the Catholic Church, which resulted in reforms, including interfaith dialogue and the use of vernacular languages in the mass.

sedentism The settling of humans in communities, villages, and cities.

seigneurial dues Payments or services owed by the peasant to the landlord. In some places it continued until the nineteenth century.

Senate Technically a body of seniors or patricians, the Senate was made up of men from the oldest, most well-established, and distinguished Roman families, and represented the aristocratic or oligarchic element in Roman government. In the Republic it exercised control over foreign affairs and war, domestic peace and order, state finance, and religion.

separate spheres The theory that men were fit for the public world of business and politics and women were fit for the domestic sphere of raising children and managing the household.

sepoys South Asian soldiers serving in the armies of European powers and companies in India.

serfdom The legal condition of peasants in Europe beginning in the late Middle Ages, in which the peasant serfs were tied to the land, required to do work on the landlord's property, and needed permission to move or marry; serfdom lasted until the middle of the nineteenth century in portions of eastern Europe.

Shari'ah A code of sacred law determined by legal scholars based on the Qur'an, the traditions of Muhammad, community standards, and precedents.

shock therapy The rapid privatization of previously state-owned enterprises, withdrawal of state subsidies, and relinquishment of price controls. Attempted most notably in Russia and other former communist states in the early 1990s to engineer the rapid transition from a communist to a market economy.

show trial Highly publicized trial in which the outcome has been decided beforehand. Most prominently used in Stalin's regime in the 1930s and in eastern European satellite states in the late 1940s and early 1950s.

simony Named after Simon Magus; the buying or selling of church offices.

Skeptics Practitioners of Skepticism, a form of Hellenistic philosophy that doubted all knowledge.

social contract The idea that humans in their original state of nature agreed to give up some of their natural rights to a ruler in exchange for order and stability.

social Darwinism The late nineteenth- and twentieth-century application of Darwin's theory of evolution to human societies with an emphasis on "survival of the fittest."

social market economy Set of social and economic policies that embraced the capitalist marketplace but also tempered it with provisions guaranteeing social welfare. Characteristic of Western Europe after 1945.

socialist (socialism) An ideology that, in response to industrial capitalism, called for ownership of the means of production by the community, with the purpose of distributing wealth equally.

Society of Jesus (Jesuits) A Catholic holy order founded in the sixteenth century by Ignatius Loyola to convert Muslims and others to Christianity, and to teach.

society of orders The social hierarchy of the Old Regimes, based on birth and fixed in law; usually composed of three basic groups: the nobility, the clergy, and everyone else.

Socratic method A system of teaching named after Socrates that was based on asking students questions on the assumption that the questioned individuals already had the knowledge needed but by discovering it in this way, they would truly know the thing being taught and it would become part of their being.

Solidarity Polish trade union and political party established in 1980 that became the core around which resistance to the communist government formed.

sovereign debt crisis (Euro crisis) Financial crisis among European states since 2009 involving dangerously high levels of national debt accumulation, most notably in Greece and southern European countries.

soviets Workers' councils formed in factories, first during the 1905 revolution in Russia and then in the 1917 revolution; became the basis for government in the Soviet Union.

SPD (*Sozialdemokratische Partei Deutschlands*) Germany's socialist party; founded in the 1870s and banned until 1890.

spheres of influence The informal quasi-colonial division of a country such that others may exert significant political, economic, and cultural influence. Refers to the European division of China into various European zones (British, French, German, for example) in order to gain special privileges without having to take on the burden of administration.

"stab in the back" myth The false rumor circulating in Germany (Weimar Republic) after World War I that Germany had not lost the war but rather was betrayed, especially by Communists, Jews, and republicans operating on the home front.

Stakhanovite Heroicized model worker in the Soviet Union, based on the example of coal worker Alexei Stakhanov. Stakhanovites received perks such as telephones, apartments, or bicycles in exchange for their hard work and enthusiasm.

Stoics Practitioners of Stoicism, a form of Hellenistic philosophy that held that the material world and possessions were worthless, that all men should strive to do their best in all the things that they did or were forced to do, that it was virtuous activity that mattered, and that all should live in harmony with Nature.

stylites Pillar saints, such as Saint Simeon the Stylite (390–459), who lived atop poles or columns.

subsistence economy An agricultural economy that produces only enough food each year to meet its annual needs.

Sudetenland German name for the mountainous border lands of Czechoslovakia in the 1920s and 1930s containing a mostly German population; Nazi Germany demanded and received this territory in 1938.

suffragette Feminist movement in Britain in the early twentieth century seeking to obtain voting rights for women.

symbolism Artistic style of the late nineteenth century that rejected realism in favor of invoking symbols and mythological figures to represent and stir inner emotions.

syncretism The tendency to combine gods, religious beliefs, and practices.

T-4 Program Stands for Tiergarten 4, the address of the Berlin headquarters of the Nazi euthanasia program. Under the T-4 program, the Nazis began murdering mentally and physically handicapped people in 1939; officially stopped in Germany as a result of public pressure (though continued unofficially to 1945).

tabula rasa Literally, "blank slate." A theory favored by English intellectuals, such as John Locke, stating that individuals are born without innate knowledge and learn primarily through observation and experience.

taille The basic land tax imposed on peasants and nonnobles in France.

Tennis Court Oath A pledge by delegates of the Estates General, mostly the third estate, on June 20, 1789, not to disband until they had written a constitution for France. This declaration led to the formation of the National Assembly.

Tetrarchy The system of four rulers of the Roman Empire created by the emperor Diocletian, who appointed two Caesars to serve under the two emperors (Augusti).

Thermidorian reaction The overthrow of Robespierre and other radicals in 1794 as a reaction to the excesses of the Revolution, ending the Reign of Terror. The term refers to the month this occurred on the revolutionary calendar (July 1794).

third world Term used to describe countries not aligned with either the western (first world) or communist (second world) powers in the Cold War. The term has evolved to describe poorer countries.

tithe An obligatory contribution to the church, usually amounting to about 10 percent of earnings; a variety of taxes contained portions paid to the church as tithes.

Torah That part of the Hebrew Bible or Tanakh that contains Genesis, Exodus, Leviticus, Numbers, and Deuteronomy.

Tory Originally a derogatory term used to describe Catholic Irish bandits. It was applied to the faction supporting the king and the Anglican Church in the 1670s. This term stuck and the faction developed into a political party later known as the Conservatives.

total war A form of warfare in which all segments of society are mobilized for war and the distinction between soldier and civilian is blurred.

totalitarianism Authoritarian rule in which the state establishes and exercises complete domination over economic, political, cultural, and private matters, including religion.

Treaty of Brest-Litovsk Treaty between Germany and Bolshevik-controlled Russia in March 1918, in which most of the western Russian empire was ceded to Germany. These territories were taken away when Germany lost the war later that year.

Treaty of Versailles Peace treaty between Germany and the Allied powers that ended World War I.

treaty ports Certain ports in East Asia in which Europeans determined the trade and custom regulations and exempted themselves from local laws (see *extraterritoriality*).

tribune A representative of the Roman people or plebeians; one of ten such elected officers who presided over the Assembly of the People and had certain veto rights.

tribunes Leading magistrates of the Assembly of the People.

the Triumvirate Sometimes mistakenly called the Second Triumvirate; an alliance between Octavian (later Augustus), Marc Antony, and Lepidus that was officially sanctioned by the Roman Senate.

trivium Grammar, rhetoric, and logic; the language component of the seven liberal arts.

Truce of God Tenth-century churchmen extended the Peace of God to cover the violence done by knights and vassals to each other, forbidding violence on certain days of the week or times of the year.

Truman Doctrine U.S. president Harry Truman's policy initiated in 1947 stating that the United States would contain communism and offering military assistance to countries threatened by a communist takeover.

tympanum The curved space, often sculpted or painted, below an arch and above a lintel.

tyrants Autocrats in the Archaic Age of Greece who seized power by force.

Ummah In Islam the community of believers, the people of God.

Unam sanctam A bull issued by Pope Boniface VIII that declared the absolute supremacy of the papacy over all Christendom.

Ustasha Croatian fascists backed by Nazi Germany after the Germans conquered Yugoslavia; committed mass murder of Serbs and Jews during the war.

usury Charging interest on loans, a practice forbidden by the Catholic Church.

utilitarianism A nineteenth-century liberal philosophy that evaluated institutions on their social usefulness in order to achieve "the greatest good for the greatest number."

vassalage The institution or state of being a vassal, the sworn man of a more powerful individual.

velvet divorce The peaceful breakup of Czechoslovakia into the Czech Republic and the Republic of Slovakia in 1992.

velvet revolution Term for the nonviolent demonstrations at the end of 1989 that toppled the communist government of Czechoslovakia.

Versailles Palace built outside Paris and inhabited by Louis XIV. Its luxury and orderly design symbolized absolutism.

Vichy France French state established after France was defeated by Germany in 1940. It collaborated with the Germans until the Allies liberated France in 1944.

Victorian The era in Britain during which Queen Victoria reigned (1837–1901); associated with strict middle-class morality and values, such as patriarchal dominance, self-denial, self-improvement, deference, hard work, and separate spheres for women and men.

Vikings (or Northmen) Scandinavian (generally, Norse, Swedish, or Danish) raiders or pirates, so called from *vik*, meaning a bay or creek, from which their ships set out.

virtus A Latin term, meaning virtue or strength, which was part of the moral code of Rome's aristocratic elite.

volley-firing A military tactic developed during the military revolution, in which infantry would mass in lines, fire their muskets row by row, and repeat, allowing for a continuous line of fire.

war communism Economic system of the Bolsheviks during the Russian civil wars, involving nationalization of industry, state control of trade, collective farms, food rationing, and strict labor obligations.

war guilt clause Article in the Treaty of Versailles that placed the blame for World War I on Germany, creating bitter resentment among Germans.

Warsaw Pact Military alliance of eastern European communist regimes, led by the Soviet Union. It was founded in 1955 and disbanded after the fall of communism in eastern Europe.

welfare state Concept of the state as an institution responsible for the economic and social well-being of its citizens through governmental payments to the unemployed or disabled. Welfare states were also to provide public services such as health care and education.

Western (Papal) Schism A division, lasting from 1379 to 1449, between rival claimants as to who was the rightful pope.

Whig Originally a derogatory term used to describe fanatical Presbyterian Scottish bandits. This term was applied to the faction supporting parliamentary sovereignty and greater religious toleration. The Whigs became a major political faction in the eighteenth and nineteenth centuries, when they became known as the Liberals.

Ziggurat An elaborate temple structure erected by Ur-Nammu.

Zionism The Jewish nationalist movement started in the 1890s by Theodore Herzl; sought to establish an independent Jewish state in Palestine.

Zollverein The German customs union led by Prussia, which by 1834 contained the states that would make up the united Germany in 1871; it excluded Austria.

REFERENCES AND READINGS

Chapter 1

Anthony, David W. *The Horse, the Wheel, and Language: How Bronze-Age Riders from the Eurasian Steppes Shaped the Modern World.* Princeton, N.J.: Princeton University Press, 2007.

Kurht, A. *The Ancient Near East, c. 3000–330 BC*, 2 vols. London: Routledge, 1997.

Renfrew, Colin. *Prehistory: The Making of the Human Mind.* London: Weidenfeld & Nicolson, 2007.

Chapter 2

Bakker, Egbert J., Irene J. F. de Jong, and Hans van Wees, eds. *Brill's Companion to Herodotus.* Leiden/Boston: Brill, 2002.

Fontenrose, Joseph. *The Delphic Oracle: Its Responses and Operations with a Catalogue of Responses.* Berkeley: University of California Press, 1978.

Hornblower, Simon. *The Greek World, 479–323 BC.* London/New York: Methuen, 1983.

Osborne, Robin. *Greece in the Making, 1200–479 BC.* London/New York: Routledge, 1996.

Podlecki, A. J. *The Life of Themistocles: A Critical Survey of the Literary and Archaeological Evidence.* Montreal: McGill-Queen's University Press, 1975.

Samons II, Loren J., ed. *The Cambridge Companion to the Age of Pericles.* Cambridge/New York: Cambridge University Press, 2007.

Chapter 3

Archibald, Zofia H., John K. Davies, and Vincent Gabrielsen, eds. *Making, Moving and Managing: The New World of Ancient Economies, 323–31 BC.* Oxford: Oxbow Books, 2005.

Charboneaux, Jean, Roland Martin, and François Villard. *Hellenistic Art (330–50 B.C.),* Vol. 18: *Arts of Mankind.* New York: Braziller, 1973.

Havelock, Christine Mitchell. *Hellenistic Art: The Art from the Death of Alexander the Great to the Battle of Actium.* New York: Norton, 1981.

Walbank, F. W. *Cambridge Ancient History,* 2nd ed., Vol. 7.1: *The Hellenistic World.* Cambridge: Cambridge University Press, 2008.

Worthington, Ian. *Alexander the Great: Man and God.* Harlow, England/New York: Pearson/Longman, 2004.

Chapter 4

Bringmann, Klaus. *A History of the Roman Republic,* trans. W. J. Smyth. Cambridge: Polity, 2007.

Flower, Harriet I., ed. *The Cambridge Companion to the Roman Republic.* Cambridge: Cambridge University Press, 2004.

Scullard, H. H. *Festivals and Ceremonies of the Roman Republic.* London: Thames and Hudson, 1981.

Chapter 5

Galinsky, Karl, ed. *The Cambridge Companion to the Age of Augustus.* Cambridge: Cambridge University Press, 2005.

Hadot, Pierre. *The Inner Citadel: The Meditations of Marcus Aurelius,* trans. Michael Chase. Cambridge, Mass.: Harvard University Press, 1998.

Knapp, Robert. *Invisible Romans.* Cambridge, Mass.: Harvard University Press, 2011.

Polter, David S., ed. *A Companion to the Roman Empire.* Oxford: Blackwell, 2006.

Shelton, Jo-Ann. *As the Romans Did: A Sourcebook in Roman Social History,* 2nd ed. Oxford: Oxford University Press, 1998.

Zanker, Paul. *The Power of Images in the Age of Augustus,* trans. Alan Shapiro. Ann Arbor: University of Michigan Press, 1988.

Chapter 6

Bandinelli, Ranucci Binchi. *Rome: The Late Empire. Roman Art A.D. 200–400,* trans. Peter Green. New York: George Braziller, 1971.

Barnes, Timothy David. *The New Empire of Diocletian and Constantine.* Cambridge, Mass.: Harvard University Press, 1982.

Brown, Peter. *The World of Late Antiquity from Marcus Aurelius to Muhammad.* London: Thames and Hudson, 1971.

Ehrman, Bart D. *Lost Christianities: The Battle for Scripture and the Faiths We Never Knew.* Oxford: Oxford University Press, 2003.

MacMullen, Ramsay. *Corruption and the Decline of Rome.* New Haven and London: Yale University Press, 1988.

Ward-Perkins, Bryan. *The Fall of Rome and the End of Civilization.* Oxford: Oxford University Press, 2005.

Chapter 7

Brown, Peter. *The Cult of the Saints: Its Rise and Function in Latin Christianity.* Chicago: University of Chicago Press, 1981.

Cameron, Averil. *The Byzantines.* Malden, Mass.: Blackwell, 2006.

Donner, Fred M. *Muhammad and the Believers at the Origins of Islam.* Cambridge, Mass.: Harvard University Press, 2010.

Garver, Valerie L. *Women and Aristocratic Culture in the Carolingian World.* Ithaca, N.Y.: Cornell University Press, 2009.

Lapidus, Ira M. *A History of Islamic Societies.* Cambridge: Cambridge University Press, 2002.

McCormick, Michael. *Origins of the European Economy: Communications and Commerce, AD 300–900.* Cambridge: Cambridge University Press, 2001.

Treadgold, Warren T. *A Concise History of Byzantium.* New York: Palgrave, 2001.

Verhulst, Adriaan. *The Carolingian Economy.* Cambridge: Cambridge University Press, 2002.

Chapter 8

Abels, Richard. *Alfred the Great: War, Kingship, and Cultures in Anglo-Saxon England.* London and New York: Longman, 1998.

Allen, S. J., and Amt, Emilie, eds. *The Crusades: A Reader.* Toronto: University of Toronto Press, 2003.

The Complete Works of Liudprand of Cremona, trans. Paolo Squatriti. Washington, D.C.: The Catholic University of America Press, 2007.

Duby, Georges. *The Three Orders: Feudal Society Imagined,* trans. Arthur Goldhammer. Chicago: University of Chicago Press, 1980.

Chapter 9

Archambault, Paul J., trans. *A Monk's Confession: The Memoirs of Guibert of Nogent.* University Park: Pennsylvania State University Press, 1996.

Fichtenau, Heinrich. *Heretics and Scholars in the High Middle Ages, 1000–1200,* trans. Denise A. Kaiser. University Park: Pennsylvania State University Press, 1998.

Haskins, Charles Homer. *The Rise of Universities* (1923). Ithaca and London: Cornell University Press, 1957.

Kowaleski, Maryanne, ed. *Medieval Towns: A Reader.* Toronto: University of Toronto Press, 2006.

Moore, R. I. *The Formation of a Persecuting Society: Power and Deviance in Western Europe, 950–1250.* Oxford: Blackwell, 1990.

Mundy, John Hine. *Europe in the High Middle Ages*, 3rd ed. Harlow, England: Longman, 2000.

Southern, R. W. *Scholastic Humanism and the Unification of Europe,* Vol. 1: *Foundations.* Oxford: Blackwell, 1995.

Chapter 10

Brown, Neville. *History and Climate: A Eurocentric Perspective.* London: Routlege, 2001.

Fagan, Brian M. *The Little Ice Age: How Climate Made History, 1300–1850.* New York: Basic Books, 2000.

Herlihy, David. *The Black Death and the Transformation of the West,* ed. Samuel K. Cohn Jr. Cambridge, Mass.: Harvard University Press, 1997.

Jordan, William Chester. *The Great Famine: Northern Europe in the Early Fourteenth Century.* Princeton, N.J.: Princeton University Press, 1996.

Reyerson, Kathryn L. *Jacques Coeur: Entrepreneur and King's Bursar.* New York: Pearson Longman, 2005.

Waley, Daniel, and Peter Denley. *Later Medieval Europe, 1250–1520,* 3rd ed. New York: Pearson Longman, 2001.

Chapter 11

Burke, Peter. *The European Renaissance: Centres and Peripheries.* Oxford: Blackwell, 1998.

De Grazia, Sebastian. *Machiavelli in Hell.* Princeton, N.J.: Princeton University Press, 1989.

Pettegree, Andrew. *The Book in the Renaissance.* New Haven, Conn.: Yale University Press, 2010.

Ruggiero, Guido, ed. *A Companion to the Worlds of the Renaissance.* Malden, Mass.: Blackwell, 2002.

Schiffman, Zachary S. *Humanism and the Renaissance.* Boston and New York: Houghton Mifflin, 2002.

Snow, Edward. *Inside Bruegel: The Play of Images in "Children's Games."* New York: North Point Press, 1997.

Vasari, Giorgio. *Lives of the Artists,* 2 vols., trans. Geroge Bull. London: Penguin, 1987.

Chapter 12

Abulafia, David. *The Discovery of Mankind: Atlantic Encounters in the Age of Columbus.* New Haven and London: Yale University Press, 2008.

Bethencourt, Francisco, and Diego Ramada Curto, eds. *Portuguese Oceanic Expansion, 1400–1800.* Cambridge: Cambridge University Press, 2007.

Chiappelli, F., ed., with Michael J. B. Allen and Robert L. Benson. *First Images of America: The Impact of the New World on the Old.* Berkeley: University of California Press, 1976.

Elliott, J. H. *Empires of the Atlantic World: Britain and Spain in America, 1492–1830.* New Haven and London: Yale University Press, 2006.

Elliott, J. H. *The Old World and the New 1492–1650.* Cambridge: Cambridge University Press, 1970.

Newitt, M. D. D. *A History of Portuguese Overseas Expansion, 1400–1686.* London: Routledge, 2005.

Chapter 13

Collinson, Patrick. *The Reformation: A History.* New York: The Modern Library, 2004.

Goldstone, Lawrence, and Nancy Goldstone. *Out of the Flames: The Remarkable Story of a Fearless Scholar, a Fatal Heresy, and One of the Rarest Books in the World.* New York: Broadway Books, 2002.

Hsia, R. Po-chia, ed. *A Companion to the Reformation World.* Malden, Mass.: Blackwell, 2004.

MacCulloch, Diarmaid. *The Reformation.* New York: Viking, 2003.

O'Malley, John W. *Trent and All That: Reforming Catholicism in the Early Modern Era.* Cambridge, Mass.: Harvard University Press, 2000.

Rice, Eugene F., Jr., and Anthony Grafton. *The Foundations of Early Modern Europe, 1460-1559,* 2nd ed. New York: Norton, 1994.

Chapter 14

Blanning, Tim. *The Pursuit of Glory: The Five Revolutions That Made Modern Europe, 1648–1815.* New York: Penguin Books, 2007.

Clark, Christopher. *Iron Kingdom: The Rise and Downfall of Prussia, 1600–1947.* Cambridge, Mass.: Belknap/Harvard University Press, 2006.

Inalcik, Halil, and Donald Quataert, eds. *An Economic and Social History of the Ottoman Empire,* Vol. 2, 1600–1914. Cambridge: Cambridge University Press, 1994.

Kann, Robert A. *A History of the Habsburg Empire, 1526–1918.* Berkeley: University of California Press, 1974.

Kishlansky, Mark. *Monarchy Transformed: Britain 1603–1714.* New York: Penguin Books, 1997.

Parker, Geoffrey. *Europe in Crisis, 1598–1648,* 2nd ed. Oxford: Oxford University Press, 2001.

Roper, Lyndal. *Witch Craze: Terror and Fantasy in Baroque Germany.* New Haven, Conn.: Yale University Press, 2004.

Wilson, Peter H. *The Thirty Years' War; Europe's Tragedy.* Cambridge, Mass.: Belknap/Harvard University Press, 2009.

Chapter 15

Beales, Derek. *Enlightenment and Reform in Eighteenth-Century Europe.* New York: I. B. Tauris, 2005.

Beik, William. *A Social and Cultural History of Early Modern France.* Cambridge: Cambridge University Press, 2009.

Berg, Maxine. *Luxury and Pleasure in Eighteenth-Century Britain.* Oxford: Oxford University Press, 2005.

Blanning, Tim. *The Pursuit of Glory: The Five Revolutions That Made Modern Europe, 1648–1815.* New York: Penguin Books, 2007.

Darnton, Robert. *The Great Cat Massacre and Other Episodes in French Cultural History.* New York: Basic Books, 1984.

Davis, Natalie Zemon. *Women on the Margins: Three Seventeenth-Century Lives.* Boston, Mass.: Harvard University Press, 1995.

DeVries, Jan. *The Industrious Revolution: Consumer Behavior and the Household Economy, 1650 to the Present.* Cambridge: Cambridge University Press, 2008.

Doyle, William. *The Old European Order, 1660–1800.* Oxford: Oxford University Press, 1978.

Hochstrasser, Julie. *Still Life and Trade in the Dutch Golden Age.* New Haven, Conn.: Yale University Press, 2007.

Parker, Geoffrey, *The Military Revolution: Military Innovation and the Rise of the West, 1500–1800.* Cambridge: Cambridge University Press, 1988.

Shapin, Steven. *The Scientific Revolution.* Chicago: University of Chicago Press, 1996.

Szabo, Franz. *The Seven Years' War in Europe, 1756–1763.* New York: Pearson/Longman, 2008.

Chapter 16

Beales, Derek. *Enlightenment and Reform in Eighteenth-Century Europe.* London: I. B. Tauris, 2005.

Darnton, Robert. *The Literary Underground of the Old Regime.* Cambridge, Mass.: Harvard University Press, 1985.

Hufton, Olwen. *The Prospect before Her: A History of Women in Western Europe, 1500–1800.* New York: Vintage Books, 1998.

Israel, Jonathan. *Radical Enlightenment: Philosophy and the Making of Modernity, 1650–1750.* Oxford: Oxford University Press, 2002.

Koerner, Lisbeth. *Linnaeus: Nature and Nation.* Cambridge, Mass.: Harvard University Press, 2001.

Pinkard, Susan. *A Revolution in Taste: The Rise of French Cuisine, 1650–1800*. New York: Cambridge University Press, 2010.

Sheehan, James. *German History, 1770–1866*. Oxford: Oxford University Press, 1993.

Smith, Bernard. *European Vision and the South Pacific*, 2nd ed. New Haven, Conn.: Yale University Press, 1989.

Sorkin, David. *The Religious Enlightenment: Protestants, Jews, and Catholics from London to Vienna*. Princeton, N.J.: Princeton University Press, 2008.

Wulf, Andrea. *The Brother Gardeners: A Generation of Gentlemen Naturalists and the Birth of an Obsession*. New York: Vintage Books, 2010.

Chapter 17

Brown, Howard G. *Ending the French Revolution: Violence, Justice, and Repression from the Terror to Napoleon*. Charlottesville: University of Virginia Press, 2007.

Doyle, William. *The Oxford History of the French Revolution*, 2nd ed. Oxford: Oxford University Press, 2002.

Lieven, Dominic. *Russia against Napoleon: The True Story of the Campaigns of War and Peace*. New York: Allen Lane, 2010.

Rothenberg, Gunter. *The Napoleonic Wars*. London: Cassell, 2000.

Schama, Simon. *Citizens: A Chronicle of the French Revolution*. New York: Knopf, 1990.

Sutherland, Donald. *The French Revolution and Empire: The Quest for a Civic Order*. Malden, Mass.: Blackwell, 2003.

Tackett, Timothy. *When the King Took Flight*. Cambridge, Mass.: Harvard University Press, 2003.

Chapter 18

Abrams, M. H. *Natural Supernaturalism: Tradition and Revolution in Romantic Literature*. New York: Norton, 1971.

Brophy, James. *Capitalism, Politics and Railroads in Prussia, 1830–1870*. Columbus: Ohio State University Press, 1998.

Clark, Anna. *The Struggle for the Breeches: Gender and the Making of the British Working Class*. Berkeley: University of California Press, 1995.

Gideon, Siegfried. *Mechanization Takes Command: A Contribution to Anonymous History*. New York: Oxford University Press, 1969.

Hobsbaum, Eric. *The Age of Revolution, 1789–1848*. London: Weidenfeld and Nicolson, 1962.

Marcus, Steven. *Engels, Manchester and the Working Class*. New York: Vintage Books, 1975.

Mokyr, Joel. *The Enlightened Economy: An Economic History of Britain, 1700–1850*. New Haven, Conn.: Yale University Press, 2009.

Perkin, Harold. *The Age of the Railway*. London: Newton Abbot, David and Charles, 1971.

Sperber, Jonathan. *The European Revolutions, 1848–1851*. Cambridge: Cambridge University Press, 1994.

St. Clair, William. *Lord Elgin and the Marbles*, 3rd ed. Oxford: Oxford University Press, 1998.

Westwood, J. N. *Endurance and Endeavor: Russian History, 1812–1986*. Oxford: Oxford University Press, 1987.

Wilson, A. N. *The Victorians*. New York: Norton, 2003.

Chapter 19

Blackbourn, David. *The Conquest of Nature: Water, Landscape and the Making of Modern Germany*. New York: Norton, 2006.

Blackbourn, David. *The Long Nineteenth Century: A History of Germany, 1780–1918*. New York: Oxford University Press, 1998.

Flanders, Judith. *Inside the Victorian Home: A Portrait of Domestic Life in Victorian England*. New York: Norton, 2004.

Jordan, David P. *Transforming Paris: The Life and Labors of Baron Haussmann*. Chicago: University of Chicago Press, 1995.

Smith, Dennis Mack. *Cavour*. London: Methuen, 1984.

Sperber, Jonathan. *Europe, 1850–1914. Progress, Participation and Apprehension*. New York: Pearson Longman, 2009.

Wawro, Geoffrey. *The Franco-Prussian War: The German Conquest of France in 1870 and 1871*. Cambridge: Cambridge University Press, 2003.

Chapter 20

Colley, Linda. *Captives: Britain, Empire and the World*. New York: Pantheon Books, 2002.

Curtin, Philip D. *Disease and Empire: The Health of European Troops in the Conquest of Africa*. Cambridge: Cambridge University Press, 1998.

Hochschild, Adam. *King Leopold's Ghost: A Study of Greed, Terror, and Heroism in Colonial Africa*. Boston: Houghton Mifflin, 1998.

Judd, Dennis. *Empire: The British Imperial Experience from 1765 to the Present*. New York: Basic Books, 1998.

Kanfer, Stefan. *The Last Empire: De Beers, Diamonds, and the World*. New York: Farrar, Straus and Giroux, 1993.

Kiernan, V. G. *Colonial Empires and Armies, 1815–1960*. London: Fontana Paperbacks, 1998.

King, Charles. *The Ghost of Freedom: A History of the Caucasus*. Oxford: Oxford University Press, 2009.

Marlowe, John. *Cecil Rhodes: The Anatomy of Empire*. New York: Mason & Lipscomb, 1972.

Porter, Bernard. *The Absent-Minded Imperialists: Empire, Society and Culture in Britain*. Oxford: Oxford University Press, 2004.

Porter, Bernard. *The Lion's Share: A Short History of British Imperialism, 1850–2004*, 4th ed. Harlow, England: Pearson/Longman, 2004.

Said, Edward. *Orientalism*. New York: Pantheon Books, 1978.

Chapter 21

Bayly, C. A. *The Birth of the Modern World, 1780–1914: Global Connections and Comparisons*. Malden, Mass.: Blackwell, 2004.

Blackbourn, David. *Marpingen: Apparitions of the Virgin Mary in Bismarckian Germany*. Oxford: Oxford University Press, 1993.

Evans, Richard J. *Death in Hamburg: Society and Politics in the Cholera Years, 1830–1910*. Oxford: Oxford University Press, 1987.

Everdell, William R., *The First Moderns: Profiles in the Origins of Twentieth-Century Thoughts*. Chicago: University of Chicago Press, 1997.

Hermann, David. *The Arming of Europe and the Making of the First World War*. Princeton, N.J.: Princeton University Press, 1996.

Merriman, John. *A History of Modern Europe*, 1st ed. New York: Norton, 1996.

Miller, Michael B., *The Bon Marché*. Princeton, N.J.: Princeton University Press, 1994.

Ockman, Carol, Kenneth Silver, et al., *Sarah Bernhardt: The Art of High Drama*. New Haven, Conn.: Yale University Press, 2004.

Porter, Brian A. *When Nationalism Began to Hate: Imagining Modern Politics in Nineteenth-Century Poland*. New York: Oxford University Press, 2000.

Schorske, Carl. *Fin de Siècle Vienna: Politics and Culture*. New York: Vintage Books, 1980.

Teich, Mikulas, and Roy Porter, eds. *Fin de Siècle and Its Legacy*. Cambridge: Cambridge University Press, 1990.

Whiteside, Andrew. *The Socialism of Fools: Georg Ritter von Schönerer and Austrian Pan-Germanism*. Berkeley: University of California Press, 1975.

Chapter 22

Barry, John M. *The Great Influenza: The Story of the Deadliest Pandemic in History*. New York: Viking Books, 2004.

Bloxham, Donald. *The Great Game of Genocide. Imperialism, Nationalism, and the Destruction of the Ottoman Armenians.* Oxford: Oxford University Press, 2005.

Dobkin, Marjorie. *Smyrna: The Destruction of a City.* Kent, Ohio: Ohio State University Press, 1988.

Fitzpatrick, Sheila. *The Russian Revolution,* 2nd ed. Oxford: Oxford University Press, 1994.

Fussell, Paul. *The Great War and Modern Memory.* New York: Oxford University Press, 1975.

Glenny, Misha. *The Balkans: Nationalism, War, and the Great Powers, 1804–1999.* New York: Penguin Books, 1999.

Healy, Maureen. *Vienna and the Fall of the Habsburg Empire: Total War and Everyday Life in World War I.* New York: Cambridge University Press, 2004.

Horne, John, and Alastair Kramer. *German Atrocities 1914: A History of Denial.* New Haven, Conn.: Yale University Press, 2001.

Hull, Isabel V. *Absolute Destruction: Military Culture and the Practices of War in Imperial Germany.* Ithaca, N.Y.: Cornell University Press, 2005.

Keegan, John. *An Illustrated History of the First World War.* New York: Knopf, 2001.

Liulevicius, Vejas. *War Land on the Eastern Front: Culture, National Identity and German Occupation in World War I.* New York: Cambridge University Press, 2000.

MacMillan, Margaret. *Paris 1919: Six Months that Changed the World.* New York: Random House, 2002.

Strachan, Hew. *The First World War,* Vol. 1: *To Arms.* Oxford: Oxford University Press, 2001.

Whalen, Robert Weldon. *Bitter Wounds: German Victims of the Great War, 1914–1939.* Ithaca, N.Y.: Cornell University Press, 1984.

Chapter 23

Bosworth, R. J. B. *Mussolini.* London: Arnold, 2002.

Clark, Christopher M. *Iron Kingdom: The Rise and Downfall of Prussia, 1600–1947.* Cambridge, Mass.: Harvard University Press, 2006.

Farnsworth, Beatrice. *Aleksandra Kollontai: Socialism, Feminism and the Bolshevik Revolution.* Stanford, Calif.: Stanford University Press, 1980.

Fitzpatrick, Sheila. *Everyday Stalinism: Everyday Life in Extraordinary Times: Soviet Russia in the 1930s.* New York: Oxford University Press, 1999.

Glenny, Misha. *The Balkans: Nationalism, War, and the Great Powers, 1804–1999.* New York: Penguin Books, 1999.

Hobsbawm, E. J. *The Age of Extremes: A History of the World, 1914–1991.* New York: Pantheon Books, 1994.

Johnson, Lonnie. *Central Europe: Enemies, Neighbors, Friends.* New York: Oxford University Press, 1996.

Kotkin, Stephen. *Magnetic Mountain: Stalinism as a Civilization.* Berkeley: University of California Press, 1995.

Mazower, Mark. *Dark Continent: Europe's Twentieth Century.* New York: Knopf, 1999.

Tooze, Adam J. *Wages of Destruction: The Making and Breaking of the Nazi Economy.* New York: Viking, 2007.

Wasserstein, Bernard. *Civilization and Barbarism: A History of Europe in Our Time.* Oxford: Oxford University Press, 2007.

Weitz, Eric D. *Weimar Germany.* Princeton, N.J.: Princeton University Press, 2007.

Chapter 24

Aly, Götz. *Hitler's Beneficiaries: Plunder, Race War, and the Nazi Welfare State.* New York: Holt, 2007.

Bayly, C. A., and Tim Harper. *Forgotten Armies: The Fall of British Asia, 1941–1945.* Cambridge, Mass.: Harvard University Press, 2005.

Deák, István, Jan T. Gross, and Tony Judt., eds. *The Politics of Retribution in Europe: World War II and Its Aftermath.* Princeton, N.J.: Princeton University Press, 2000.

FitzGibbon, Constantine. *The Blitz.* London: Macdonald, 1970.

Gilbert, Martin. *Churchill: A Life.* New York: Holt, 1991.

Gilbert, Martin. *The Second World War: A Complete History.* New York: Holt, 1989.

Hastings, Max. *Winston's War: Churchill, 1940–1945.* New York: Knopf, 2010.

Herf, Jeffrey. *The Jewish Enemy: Nazi Propaganda during WWII and the Holocaust.* Cambridge, Mass.: Harvard University Press, 2006.

Herzog, Dagmar. *Sex after Fascism: Memory and Morality in Twentieth-Century Germany.* Princeton, N.J.: Princeton University Press, 2005.

Hilberg, Raul. *The Destruction of the European Jews.* Chicago: Quadrangle Press, 1961.

Mazower, Mark. *Hitler's Empire: How the Nazis Ruled Europe.* New York: Penguin Books, 2008.

Mazower, Mark. *Inside Hitler's Greece: The Experience of Occupation, 1941–1944.* New Haven, Conn.: Yale University Press, 1993.

Seib, Philip. *Broadcasts from the Blitz: How Edward R. Murrow Helped Lead America into War.* Washington, D.C.: Potomac Books, 2006.

Snyder, Timothy. *Bloodlands: Europe between Hitler and Stalin.* New York: Basic Books, 2010.

Tooze, Adam J. *Wages of Destruction: The Making and Breaking of the Nazi Economy.* New York: Viking Press, 2007.

Wasserstein, Bernard. *Barbarism and Civilization: A History of Europe in Our Time.* New York: Oxford University Press, 2007.

Chapter 25

De Grazia, Victoria. *Irresistible Empire: America's Advance through Twentieth-Century Europe.* Cambridge, Mass.: Harvard University Press, 2005.

Judt, Tony. *Postwar: A History of Europe since 1945.* New York: Penguin Press, 2006.

Kotkin, Stephen. *Armageddon Averted: The Soviet Collapse, 1970–2000.* Oxford: Oxford University Press, 2001.

Louis, William Roger. *Ends of British Imperialism: The Scramble for Empire, Suez and Decolonization.* London: I. B. Tauris, 2007.

Maier, Charles. *Dissolution: The Crisis of Communism and the End of East Germany.* Princeton, N.J.: Princeton University Press, 1997.

Sheehan, James J. *Where Have All the Soldiers Gone? The Transformation of Modern Europe.* Boston: Houghton Mifflin, 2008.

Zatlin, Jonathan. *The Currency of Socialism: Money and Political Culture in East Germany.* New York: Cambridge University Press, 2007.

Chapter 26

Glenny, Misha. *The Balkans: Nationalism, War, and the Great Powers, 1804–1999.* New York: Penguin Books, 2000.

Herzog, Dagmar. *Sexuality in Europe: A Twentieth-Century History.* New York: Cambridge University Press, 2011.

Judt, Tony. *Postwar: A History of Europe since 1945.* New York: Penguin Books, 2006.

Kotkin, Stephen. *Armageddon Averted: The Soviet Collapse, 1970–2000.* Oxford: Oxford University Press, 2001.

Rosenberg, Tina. *The Haunted Land: Facing Europe's Ghosts after Communism.* New York: Vintage Books, 1995.

Taras, Ray. *Europe Old and New: Transnationalism, Belonging, Xenophobia.* New York: Rowan & Littlefield, 2009.

Wegs, J. Robert, and Robert Ladrech. *Europe since 1945: A Concise History,* 5th ed. London: Palgrave-Macmillan, 2007.

NOTES

Chapter 1

1. See Andrew Robinson, *The Story of Writing: Alphabets, Hieroglyphs & Pictograms*, 2nd ed. (New York: Thames & Hudson, 2007), 72–79.

Chapter 2

1. M. H. Hasen and T. H. Nielsen, eds. *An Inventory of Archaic and Classical Poleis* (Oxford: Oxford University Press, 2004).

Chapter 4

1. See Ingrid D. Rowland, *The Scarith of Scornello: A Tale of Renaissance Forgery* (Chicago: University of Chicago Press, 2004).

Chapter 5

1. Walter Scheidel, "Quantifying the Source of Slaves in the Early Roman Empire," *Journal of Roman Studies* 87 (1997), 156–169; "The Slave Population of Roman Italy: Speculation and Constraints," *Topoi* 9.1 (1999), 129–144; "The Roman Slave Supply," in *The Cambridge History of Slavery*, Vol. 1: *The Ancient Mediterranean World*, ed. K. Bradley and P. Cartledge (Cambridge: Cambridge University Press, 2011), 287–310.
2. See Ramsay MacMullen, *Romanization in the Time of Augustus* (New Haven and London: Yale University Press, 2000), 124–137.

Chapter 6

1. See *The Nag Hammadi Scriptures: The International Edition*, ed. Marvin Miller (New York: HarperOne, 2007).

Chapter 7

1. See Michael McCormick, Paul Edward Dutton, and Paul A. Mayewski, "Volcanoes and the Climate Forcing of Carolingian Europe, A.D. 750–950," *Speculum* 82 (2007), 865–895.

Chapter 8

1. Elizabeth A. R. Brown, "The Tyranny of a Construct: Feudalism and Historians of Medieval Europe," *American Historical Review* 79:4 (1974), 1063–1088; Susan Reynolds, *Fiefs and Vassals: The Medieval Evidence Reinterpreted* (New York: Oxford University Press, 1994).
2. See Jean Claude Schmitt, *The Holy Greyhound: Guinefort, Healer of Children since the Thirteenth Century* (Cambridge and New York: Cambridge University Press, 1983).
3. See R. Howard Bloch, *A Needle in the Right Hand of God: The Norman Conquest of 1066 and the Making of the Bayeux Tapestry* (New York: Random House, 2006).

Chapter 9

1. Constant Mews, *The Lost Love Letters of Heloise and Abelard: Perceptions of Dialogue in the Twelfth Century*, trans. Neville Chiavaroli and Constant Mews, revised and updated ed. (New York: Palgrave Macmillan, 2008); Jan M. Ziolkowski, "Lost and Not Yet Found: Heloise, Abelard, and the *Epistolae duorum amantium, Journal of Medieval Latin* 14 (2004), 171–202; Constant J. Mews, "Discussing Love: The *Epistolae duorum amantium* and Abelard's *Sic et Non," Journal of Medieval Latin* 19 (2009), 130–147.

2. See Ivan Illich, *In the Vineyard of the Text: A Commentary to Hugh's Didascalicon* (Chicago: The University of Chicago Press, 1993).
3. See Reviel Netz and William Noel, *The Archimedes Codex* (London: Weidenfeld and Nicolson, 2007).

Chapter 10

1. See Eric Jager, *The Last Duel: A True Story of Crime, Scandal, and Trial by Combat in Medieval France* (New York: Broadway Books, 2004).
2. See Caroline Walker Bynum, *Wonderful Blood: Theology and Practice in Late Medieval Northern Germany* (Philadelphia: University of Pennsylvania Press, 2007).
3. See Marilyn Yalom, *Birth of the Chess Queen: A History* (New York: HarperCollins, 2004).

Chapter 11

1. See Peter Burke, *The Italian Renaissance: Culture and Society in Italy* (London: Polity Press, 1987).

Chapter 12

1. See Alfred W. Crosby Jr., *The Columbian Exchange: Biological and Cultural Consequences of 1492* (Westport, Conn.: Praeger, 2003).

Chapter 13

1. See R. W. Scribner, "The Printed Image as Historical Evidence," *German Life and Letters* 48.3 (1995), 324–337.
2. See Richard Marius, *Martin Luther: The Christian between God and Death* (Cambridge, Mass.: Harvard University Press, 1998), xii.

Chapter 14

1. Geoffrey Parker, "Crisis and Catastrophe: The World Crisis of the Seventeenth Century Reconsidered," in *The American Historical Review*, 113 (2008), 1053–1079.
2. Ibid., 1073.
3. Lyndal Roper, *Witch Craze: Terror and Fantasy in Baroque Germany* (New Haven, Conn.: Yale University Press, 2006), 222–246.
4. Tim Blanning, *The Pursuit of Glory: The Five Revolutions That Made Modern Europe, 1648–1815* (New York: Penguin Books, 2007), 559.
5. Quoted in Adam Nicolson, *God's Secretaries: The Making of the King James Bible* (New York: HarperCollins, 2003), 47.
6. Anon., *Conversations on the English Constitution* (London: 1828), Google ebooks, 180.
7. Mark Kishlansky, ed., *University of Chicago Readings in Western Civilization*, Vol. 6: *Early Modern Europe: Crisis of Authority* (Chicago: Chicago University Press, 1987), 371–380.

Chapter 15

1. Information on the life of Böttger comes from Janet Gleeson, *The Arcanum: The Extraordinary True Story* (New York: Little, Brown, 1998).
2. See Tim Blanning, *The Pursuit of Glory: The Five Revolutions That Made Modern Europe, 1648–1815* (New York: Penguin Books, 2007), 393–407.

3. Quoted in William Beik, *A Social and Cultural History of Early Modern France* (Cambridge: Cambridge University Press, 2009), 259.

4. On Esterhaza and Haydn's experience there, see Rebecca Gates-Coon, *The Landed Estates of the Esterhazy Princes: Hungary during the Reforms of Maria Theresa and Joseph II* (Baltimore, Md.: Johns Hopkins University Press, 1994).

5. Michael Kwass, "Big Hair: A Wig History of Consumption in Eighteenth-Century France," in *The American Historical Review* 111 (June 2006), 635.

6. Geoffrey Parker, *The Military Revolution: Military Innovation and the Rise of the West, 1500–1800* (Cambridge: Cambridge University Press, 1988), 115.

7. Franz Szabo, *The Seven Years' War in Europe, 1756–1763* (New York: Pearson/Longman, 2008), 428.

8. J. Z. Holwell, *A Genuine Narrative of the Deplorable Deaths of the English Gentlemen, and Others Who Were Suffocated in the Black-Hole in Fort-William, at Calcutta, in the Kingdom of Bengal, in the Night Succeeding the 20th Day of June, 1756* (London: A. Miller, 1758), 25–26.

Chapter 16

1. Abraham Anderson, *The Treatise of the Three Imposters and the Problem of Enlightenment: A New Translation of the Traité des trois Imposteurs*, 1777 ed. (Oxford: Oxford University Press, 1997), 26, 34.

2. Adam Smith, *An Inquiry into the Nature and Causes of the Wealth of Nations* (Chicago: University of Chicago Press, 1977), 2.

3. Quoted in Robert Darnton, *The Great Cat Massacre and Other Episodes in French Cultural History* (New York: Basic Books, 1984), 247.

4. Quoted in James Sheehan, *German History, 1770–1866* (Oxford: Oxford University Press, 1993), 67.

5. Quoted in Derek Beales, *Enlightenment and Reform in Eighteenth-Century Europe* (London: I. B. Tauris, 2005), 276–277.

6. This section draws on Robert Darnton, *The Literary Underground of the Old Regime* (Cambridge, Mass.: Harvard University Press, 1985).

7. Information in this section draws heavily on Andrea Wulf, *The Brother Gardeners: A Generation of Gentlemen Naturalists and the Birth of an Obsession* (New York: Vintage Books, 2010).

8. Quoted in Wulf, *The Brother Gardeners*, 93.

9. This section draws extensively on Susan Pinkard, *A Revolution in Taste: The Rise of French Cuisine, 1650–1800* (New York: Vintage Books, 2010).

10. On Menon and Massiolot, see Pinkard, *A Revolution in Taste.*

11. François Menon, *La cuisinière bourgeoise* (Paris: Libraires Associés, 1793), 147.

12. Quoted in Tim Blanning, *The Pursuit of Glory: Europe, 1648–1815* (New York: Penguin Books, 2007), 292.

Chapter 17

1. Emmanuel-Joseph Sieyès, "What Is the Third Estate?" in *University of Chicago Readings in Western Civilization*, Vol. 7: *The Old Regime and the French Revolution*, ed. Keith Baker (Chicago: University of Chicago Press, 1987), 157.

2. Material in this feature has been drawn from Timothy Tackett, *When the King Took Flight* (Cambridge, Mass.: Harvard University Press, 2003).

3. Tim Blanning, *The Pursuit of Glory: The Five Revolutions That Made Modern Europe* (New York: Penguin Books, 2007), 196.

4. Quoted in M. J. Syndenham, *The French Revolution* (New York: Putnam, 1965), 173.

5. Chaumette quoted in "Make Terror the Order of the Day," in *University of Chicago Readings in Western Civilization*, Vol. 7: *The Old Regime and the French Revolution*, ed. Keith Baker (Chicago: University of Chicago Press, 1987), 344.

6. Robespierre, "Report on the Principles of Political Morality (5 February 1794)," *University of Chicago Readings in Western Civilization*, Vol. 7: *The Old Regime and the French Revolution*, ed. Keith Baker (Chicago: University of Chicago Press, 1987), 374.

7. "Law of Suspects," in *University of Chicago Readings in Western Civilization*, Vol. 7: *The Old Regime and the French Revolution*, ed. Keith Baker (Chicago: University of Chicago Press, 1987), 353.

8. Quoted in William Doyle, *The Oxford History of the French Revolution*, 2nd ed. (Oxford: Oxford University Press, 2002), 254.

9. Howard G. Brown, *Ending the French Revolution: Violence, Justice, and Repression from the Terror to Napoleon* (Charlottesville: University of Virginia Press, 2007), 28.

10. Sayyid Badr al-Maqdisi, quoted in Juan Cole, *Napoleon's Egypt: Invading the Middle East* (New York: Palgrave Macmillan, 2007), 198–199.

11. Gunter Rothenburg, *The Napoleonic Wars* (London: Cassell, 2000), 37.

12. Thomas Nipperdey, *Deutsche Geschichte, 1800–1866: Bürgerwelt und starker Staat* (Munich: C. H. Beck Verlag, 1983), 1.

Chapter 18

1. Quoted in Steven Marcus, *Engels, Manchester and the Working Class* (New York: Vintage Books, 1975), 66.

2. This feature draws heavily on John Post, *The Last Great Subsistence Crisis in the Western World* (Baltimore, Md.: The Johns Hopkins University Press, 1977).

3. Niall Ferguson, "The European Economy, 1815–1914," in T. C. W. Blanning, ed., *The Nineteenth Century: Europe 1789–1914* (Oxford: Oxford University Press, 2000), 97.

4. Jonathan Sperber, *The European Revolutions, 1848–1851* (Cambridge: Cambridge University Press, 1994), 119–120.

5. Quoted in M. H. Abrams, *Natural Supernaturalism: Tradition and Revolution in Romantic Literature* (New York: Norton, 1971), 216.

6. Phillip Beauchamp [a.k.a. Jeremy Bentham], *Analysis of the Influence of Natural Religion on the Temporal Happiness of Mankind* (London: R. Carlile, 1822), 116.

7. Mill quoting Bentham in Michael St. John Packe, *The Life of John Stuart Mill* (London: Secker and Warburg, 1954), 16.

8. Siegfried Gideon, *Mechanization Takes Command: A Contribution to Anonymous History* (New York: Oxford University Press, 1969), 175.

9. Quoted in Anna Clark, *The Struggle for the Breeches: Gender and the Making of the British Working Class* (Berkeley: University of California Press, 1995), 79.

10. Quoted in Marcus, *Engels, Manchester and the Working Class*, 46.

11. Quoted in Pierre Goubert, *The Course of French History* (New York: F. Watts, 1988), 249.

Chapter 19

1. See David Blackbourn, *The Conquest of Nature: Water, Landscape, and the Making of Modern Germany* (New York: Norton, 2006).

2. Source for translations: http://en.wikipedia.org/wiki/La _Marseillaise); French modified slightly. The Watch on the Rhine, Tr. Suzanne Marchand 2012.

3. David P. Jordan, *Transforming Paris: The Life and Labors of Baron Haussmann* (Chicago: University of Chicago Press, 1995), 116.

4. This section draws extensively on Judith Flanders, *Inside the Victorian Home: A Portrait of Domestic Life in Victorian England* (New York: Norton, 2004).

5. James A. Secord, *Victorian Sensation: The Extraordinary Publication, Reception and Secret Authorship of the* Vestiges of the Natural History of Creation (Chicago: University of Chicago Press, 2000).

6. James Moore quoted in Secord, *Victorian Sensation*, 330, n. 81.

7. Bismarck quoted in David Blackbourn, *The Long Nineteenth Century: A History of Germany: 1780–1918* (New York: Oxford University Press, 1998), 252.

8. Denis Mack Smith, *Cavour* (London: Methuen, 1984), 216.

9. Material in this feature is drawn extensively from Geoffrey Wawro, *The Franco-Prussian War* (Cambridge: Cambridge University Press, 2003); quotation can be found on p. 100.

10. Quoted in Thomas Kohut, *Wilhelm II and the Germans: A Study in Leadership* (New York: Oxford University Press, 1991), 5.

Chapter 20

1. See Antony Thomas, *Rhodes: The Race for Africa* (New York: St. Martin's Press, 1997), quotations pp. 8, 31. See also John Marlowe, *Cecil Rhodes: The Anatomy of Empire* (New York: Mason & Lipscomb, 1972).

2. Quoted in Bernard Porter, *The Lion's Share: A Short History of British Imperialism, 1850–2004*, 4th ed. (Harlow, England: Pearson/Longman, 2004), 118.

3. Quoted in Benedict Anderson, *Imagined Communities* (New York: Verso Press, 1991), 91.

4. Quoted in Porter, *The Lion's Share*, 33.

5. Porter, *The Lion's Share*, 57.

6. Linda Colley, *Captives: Britain, Empire and the World* (New York: Pantheon Books, 2004), 303.

7. This feature draws on Matthew H. Edney, *Mapping an Empire: The Geographical Construction of British India, 1765–1843* (Chicago: University of Chicago, 1999); quotation, p. 248.

8. Alfred Crosby, *The Columbian Exchange: Biological and Cultural Consequences of 1492* (Westwood, Conn.: Greenwood, 1972).

9. Said's claim was advanced in his seminal work, *Orientalism* (New York: Pantheon Books, 1978).

10. Daniel R. Headrick, *The Tools of Empire: Technology and European Imperialism in the Nineteenth Century* (Oxford: Oxford University Press, 1981).

11. This feature draws on Stefan Kanfer, *The Last Empire: De Beers, Diamonds, and the World* (New York: Farrar, Straus and Giroux, 1993).

12. Quoted in Sara Friedrichsmeyer, Sara Lennox, and Susanne Zantop, "Introduction" in *The Imperialist Imagination: German Colonialism and Its Legacy*, eds. Friedrichsmeyer et al. (Ann Arbor: University of Michigan Press, 1998), 14.

Chapter 21

1. This section draws extensively on Carol Ockman et al., *Sarah Bernhardt: The Art of High Drama* (New Haven, Conn.: Yale University Press, 2004).

2. Alfred Crosby, *Ecological Imperialism: The Biological Expansion of Europe, 900–1900*, 2nd ed. (Cambridge: Cambridge University Press, 2004), 300.

3. Quoted in A. N. Wilson, *The Victorians* (New York: Norton, 2004), 525.

4. This feature is based on material from Michael Miller, *The Bon Marché* (Princeton: Princeton University Press, 1994).

5. Erwin Baelz, *Awakening Japan: The Diary of a German Doctor* (Bloomington: Indiana University Press, 1974), 385.

6. Statistics come from David Herrmann, *The Arming of Europe and the Making of the First World War* (Princeton: Princeton University Press, 1996), 237.

7. Wladyslaw Studnicki quoted in Brian Porter, *When Nationalism Began to Hate* (New York: Oxford University Press, 2000), 212.

Chapter 22

1. From W. A. Dolph Owings, ed., *The Sarajevo Trial*, Vol. 1 (Chapel Hill; North Carolina University Press, 1984), 54.

2. Moltke, quoted in Hew Strachan, *The First World War*, Vol. 1: *To Arms* (Oxford: Oxford University Press, 2001), 74.

3. Andreas Latzko, quoted in Strachan, *To Arms*, 109.

4. Moltke, quoted in John Keegan, *An Illustrated History of the First World War* (New York: Knopf, 2001), 107.

5. Cited in Paul Fussell, *The Great War and Modern Memory* (New York: Oxford University Press, 1975), 72.

6. R. W. Seton-Watson quoted in John Horne and Alan Kramer, "War between Soldiers and Enemy Civilians," in Roger Chickering, ed., *Great War, Total War: Combat and Mobilization on the Western Front, 1914–1918* (New York: Cambridge University Press, 2006), 161.

7. Ludwig Deppe, quoted in Strachan, *To Arms*, 571.

8. Frances Farmborough, *With the Armies of the Tsar: A Nurse at the Russian Front, 1914–1918* (New York: Stein and Day, 1975), 361.

9. Farmborough, *With the Armies of the Tsar*, 383.

10. Quoted in Keegan, *An Illustrated History of the First World War* (New York: A. A. Knopf, 2001), 393.

11. The data on which this map is based include approximate numbers of military and civilian deaths from all causes, including famine, flu, and other diseases. Russian losses in particular are difficult to gauge as many soldiers deserted or were captured and later released; also many documents were lost in the chaos of the revolution and civil wars. Finally, border shifts after the war make accounting difficult. The Ottoman numbers of civilian deaths include the approximately one million Armenians murdered during the war but not the population exchange after the war's end. *Sources:* Lonnie Johnson, *Central Europe: Enemies, Neighbors, Friends*, 2nd ed. (New York: Oxford University Press, 2001); Peter Simkins et al., *The First World War: The War to End All Wars* (New York: Routledge, 2003). Data compiled by Scott Berg.

12. For these and more details, see John M. Barry, *The Great Influenza: The Story of the Greatest Pandemic in History* (New York: Viking Books, 2004).

Chapter 23

1. This vignette draws on Beatrice Farnsworth, *Aleksandra Kollontai: Socialism, Feminism and the Bolshevik Revolution* (Stanford, Calif.: Stanford University Press, 1980).

2. Quoted in Lonnie R. Johnson, *Central Europe: Enemies, Neighbors, Friends* (New York: Oxford University Press, 1996), 195.

3. Quoted in Misha Glenny, *The Balkans: Nationalism, War, and the Great Powers, 1804–1999* (New York: Penguin Books, 1999), 401.

4. Quoted in Victoria De Grazia, *How Fascism Ruled Women: Italy, 1922–1945* (Berkeley:University of California Press, 1992), 41.

5. Robert Graves, *Goodbye to All That*, 2nd ed. (New York: Anchor Books, 1958), 228.

6. Quoted in Christopher Clark, *Iron Kingdom: The Rise and Downfall of Prussia, 1600–1947* (Cambridge, Mass.: Harvard University Press, 2006), 649.

7. Published in English under the title *I Will Bear Witness: A Diary of the Nazi Years, 1933–1941* (New York: Random House, 1998), and *I Will Bear Witness, 1942–1945: A Diary of the Nazi Years* (New York: Random House, 2001). Quotations in this feature come from the first of these volumes.

Chapter 24

1. Quoted in Max Hastings, *Winston's War: Churchill, 1940–1945* (New York: Knopf, 2010), 16.

2. For more on this plan, see Adam Tooze, *Wages of Destruction: The Making and Breaking of the Nazi Economy* (New York: Viking Press, 2007).

3. For a detailed discussion of Hitler's new order, see Mark Mazower, *Hitler's Empire: How the Nazis Ruled Europe* (New York: Penguin Books, 2008).

4. See Dagmar Herzog, *Sex after Fascism: Memory and Morality in Twentieth-Century Germany* (Princeton, N.J.: Princeton University Press, 2005).

5. Quoted in Martin Gilbert, *Churchill: A Life* (New York: Holt, 1992), 633.

6. This section draws on Constantine FitzGibbon, *The Blitz* (London: Macdonald, 1970).

7. Quoted in FitzGibbon, *The Blitz*, 91, 241.

8. Quoted in Philip Seib, *Broadcasts from the Blitz: How Edward R. Murrow Helped Lead America into War* (Washington, D.C.: Potomac Books, 2006), 116.

9. See Mark Mazower, *Inside Hitler's Greece: The Experience of Occupation, 1941–1944* (New Haven, Conn.: Yale University Press, 1993).

10. Bernard Wasserstein, *Barbarism and Civilization: A History of Europe in Our Time* (New York: Oxford University Press, 2007), 325.

11. Quoted in Richard Langworth, *Churchill by Himself: The Definitive Quotations* (New York: Public Affairs, 2008), 574.

12. This feature draws heavily on C. A. Bayly and Tim Harper, *Forgotten Armies: The Fall of British Asia, 1941–1945* (Cambridge, Mass.: Harvard University Press, 2005).

13. Götz Aly, *Hitler's Beneficiaries: Plunder, Race War, and the Nazi Welfare State* (New York: Holt Paperbacks, 2007).

14. Murrow, September 20, 1940 broadcast, quoted in Lynne Olson, *Citizens of London: The Americans Who Stood with Britain in Its Darkest, Finest Hour* (New York: Random House, 2010), 46; Archibald MacLeish quoted in Seib, *Broadcasts from the Blitz*, 148.

15. Quoted in Frederick Taylor, *Dresden: Tuesday, 13 February, 1945* (London: Bloomsbury, 2004), 295.

16. The numbers cited here and in Figure 24.2 are rough estimates because many borders and populations shifted during the war, and there continue to be significant disagreements between countries about the numbers of war dead. The totals for Poland include resistance fighters, nonethnic Poles, and Jews killed in the Holocaust. German totals include Austrian and ethnic Germans conscripted in the East and Germans killed in the postwar expulsion (estimates range widely, from 500,000 to 2 million). Deaths from Allied bombings are generally estimated at 600,000. The totals for Hungary and Romania include Holocaust victims (495,000 for Hungary and approximately 350,000 for Romania). For Japan, the numbers of civilians killed range from 500,000 to 1 million; military deaths include the 300,000 missing prisoners of war taken in Manchuria after the Soviet invasion. *Sources:* Rüdiger Overmans, *Deutsche militärische Verluste im Zweiten Weltkrieg* (Munich: R. Oldenburg Verlag, 1999); David Glantz, *Colossus Reborn: The Red Army at War, 1941–1943* (Lawrence, Kan., University of Kansas Press, 2005); David Glantz, *When Titans Clashed: How the Red Army Stopped Hitler* (Lawrence, Kan.: University of Kansas Press, 1998); Lonnie Johnson, *Central Europe: Enemies, Neighbors, Friends*, 2nd ed. (New York: Oxford University Press, 2001); and Jozo Tomasevich, *War and Revolution in Yugoslavia, 1941–1945: Occupation and Collaboration* (Stanford, Calif.: Stanford University Press, 2001). Data compiled by Scott Berg.

Chapter 25

1. This vignette draws on Jonathan Zatlin, *The Currency of Socialism: Money and Political Culture in East Germany* (New York: Cambridge University Press, 2007).

2. James J. Sheehan, *Where Have All the Soldiers Gone? The Transformation of Modern Europe* (Boston: Houghton Mifflin, 2008).

3. Khrushchev quoted in William Taubman, *Nikita Khruschev: The Man and His Era* (New York: Norton, 2003), 589.

4. Information in this feature is drawn from Victoria de Grazia, *Irresistible Empire: America's Advance through Twentieth-Century Europe* (Cambridge, Mass.: Harvard University Press, 2005).

5. Stephen Kotkin, *Armageddon Averted; The Soviet Collapse, 1970–2000* (Oxford: Oxford University Press, 2001).

Chapter 26

1. Quoted in Roy Taras, *Europe Old and New: Transnationalism, Belonging, Xenophobia* (New York: Rowan & Littlefield, 2009), 62.

2. Amy Knight, "The Mysterious End of the Soviet Union," *New York Review of Books*, April 5, 2012.

3. Anna Politkovskaya, *A Small Corner of Hell: Dispatches from Chechnya* (Chicago: University of Chicago Press, 2007).

4. Tony Judt, *Postwar: A History of Europe since 1945* (New York: Penguin Books, 2006), p. 691, note 17.

5. Dagmar Herzog, *Sexuality in Europe: A Twentieth-Century History* (New York: Cambridge University Press, 2011), 188.

6. Eurostat figures for 2010, appsso.eurostat.ec.europa.eu/nui/show.do?dataset=ilc_mddd11&lang=en.

7. Suzanne Daley and Nicholas Kulish, "Brain Drain Feared as German Jobs Lure Southern European," *New York Times*, April 29, 2012, 12.

8. Ian Morris, *Why the West Rules—For Now: The Patterns of History and What They Reveal about the Future* (New York: Farrar, Straus & Giroux, 2010), 593.

9. Thomas L. Friedman, "Russia: Sort of, but Not Really," in the *New York Times*, February 4, 2012, SR11.

CREDITS

Art Archive at Art Resource, NY; p. 518: © Alfredo Dagli Orti/ The Art Archive at Art Resource, NY.

Chapter 17   Opener: © Erich Lessing/Art Resource, NY; p. 526 (top): © Gianni Dagli Orti/Corbis; p. 526 (bottom left): © Réunion des Musées Nationaux/Art Resource, NY; p. 526 (bottom right): © The Gallery Collection/Corbis; p. 529: © Réunion des Musées Nationaux/Art Resource, NY; p. 531: © The Gallery Collection/ Corbis; p. 535: © Marc Charmet/The Art Archive at Art Resource, NY; p. 538: © Gianni Dagli Orti/Corbis; p. 540: © Bettmann/ Corbis; p. 541: © Gianni Dagli Orti/Corbis; p. 542: © Musée de la Ville de Paris, Musée Carnavalet, Paris, France/The Bridgeman Art Library; p. 545: © SuperStock/SuperStock; p. 547: © Peter Willi/SuperStock; p. 549: © Réunion des Musées Nationaux/Art Resource, NY; p. 550: © Geraldine Petrovic/Corbis; p. 553: © Fine Art Images/SuperStock; p. 555: © Musée de l'Armée/Dist. Réunion des Musées Nationaux/Art Resource, NY.

Chapter 18   Opener: © Imagno/Getty Images; p. 560: © Erich Lessing/Art Resource, NY; p. 562: © Art Resource, NY; p. 566: © Photos 12/Alamy; p. 568: © akg-images; p. 571: © SuperStock/ SuperStock; p. 572: © John Harper/Corbis; p. 575: © Bridgeman Art Library, London/SuperStock; p. 576: © akg-images/Newscom; p. 577: © Caspar David Friedrich/The Bridgeman Art Library/ Getty Images; p. 578: © Art Archive/SuperStock; p. 583: © Universal Images Group/Getty Images; p. 584: © Art Resource, NY; p. 586: © The Stapleton Collection/The Bridgeman Art Library; p. 587: © Universal History Archive/Getty Images; p. 590: © Marc Charmet/The Art Archive at Art Resource, NY.

Chapter 19   Opener: © Hulton Archive/Getty Images; p. 596: © Gianni Dagli Orti/De Agostini Picture Library/Getty Images; p. 599 (top): © Deutsches Historisches Museum, Berlin, Germany/ DHM/The Bridgeman Art Library; p. 599 (bottom): © Anton Alexander von Werner/The Bridgeman Art Library/Getty Images; p. 603: © Hulton Archive/Getty Images; p. 604: © De Agostini Picture Library/Getty Images; p. 609: © Haworth Art Gallery, Accrington, Lancashire, UK/The Bridgeman Art Library; p. 610: © V&A Images/ Alamy; p. 614: © Universal History Archive/Getty Images; p. 615: © Alfredo Dagli Orti/The Art Archive at Art Resource, NY; p. 616: © SSPL/Getty Images; p. 617: © Royalty-Free/Corbis; p. 619: © Hulton Archive/Getty Images; p. 622: © Anton Alexander von Werner/The Bridgeman Art Library/Getty Images; p. 623: © Corbis; p. 625: © The Stapleton Collection/The Bridgeman Art Library.

Chapter 20   Opener: © Marc Charmet/The Art Archive at Art Resource, NY; p. 633: © Baldwin H. Ward & Kathryn C. Ward/ Corbis; p. 634: © Werner Forman/Art Resource, NY; p. 635: © Eric Nathan/Gallo Images/Getty Images; p. 637: © Werner Forman/Art Resource, NY; p. 638: © AFP/Getty Images; p. 639: © Private Collection/The Bridgeman Art Library; p. 642 (top): © Fine Art Images/SuperStock; p. 642 (bottom): © National Army Museum, London/The Bridgeman Art Library; p. 645: © Adoc-photos/Art Resource, NY; p. 647: © AFP/Newscom; p. 648: © Alliance Images/ Alamy; p. 651: © Adoc-photos/Art Resource, NY; p. 653: Courtesy of KITLV/Royal Netherlands Institute of Southeast Asian and Caribbean Studies; p. 655: © Eric Nathan/Gallo Images/Getty Images; p. 656: © Universal Images Group/Getty Images; p. 659: © Van Hoepen/Hulton Archive/Getty Images.

Chapter 21   Opener: © akg-images/Newscom; p. 666 (top): © Bettmann/Corbis; p. 666 (bottom left): © AFP/Getty Images; p. 666 (bottom right), p. 668: © Time & Life Pictures/Getty Images; p. 673: © Bettmann/Corbis; p. 674: © The Art Gallery Collection/ Alamy; p. 675: © Kharbine-Tapabor/The Art Archive at Art Resource, NY; p. 676: © Erich Lessing/Art Resource, NY; p. 677: © AFP/Getty Images; p. 678: © Vanni/Art Resource, NY; p. 680: © Fine Art Images/SuperStock; p. 681: © Hemis/Alamy; p. 683:

© Time & Life Pictures/Getty Images; p. 687: © Buyenlarge/Getty Images; p. 690: © Musée Carnavalet/Roger-Viollet/The Image Works; p. 693: © Popperfoto/Getty Images.

Chapter 22   Opener: © SuperStock/SuperStock; p. 698 (top): AP Photo; p. 698 (bottom): © Archives Charmet/The Bridgeman Art Library; p. 699: © Eileen Tweedy/The Art Archive at Art Resource, NY; p. 703: © Hulton-Deutsch Collection/Corbis; p. 706: © The Art Archive at Art Resource, NY; p. 708: © Hulton Archive/Getty Images; p. 710: © The Art Archive at Art Resource, NY; p. 711: © akg-images/Jean-Pierre Verney/Newscom; p. 713: © The Art Archive at Art Resource, NY; p. 714: © Eileen Tweedy/The Art Archive at Art Resource, NY; p. 717: © akg-images/Newscom; p. 718: © Archives Charmet/The Bridgeman Art Library; p. 722 (top): © RIA Novosti/Alamy; p. 722 (bottom): © Paul Maeyaert/ The Bridgeman Art Library; p. 725: The Granger Collection, New York.

Chapter 23   Opener: © Fine Art Images/SuperStock; p. 730 (top): AP Photo; p. 730 (bottom left): © Alliance Images/Alamy; p. 730 (bottom right): © Hulton Archive/Getty Images; p. 731: © Corbis; p. 735: © Archives Charmet/The Bridgeman Art Library; p. 737: Courtesy of Special Collections, University of California Santa Cruz; p. 740: © Keystone/Getty Images; p. 742: © Hulton Archive/Getty Images; p. 743: © Alliance Images/Alamy; p. 745: © Keystone-France/Gamma-Keystone via Getty Images; p. 747: © Art Resource, NY; p. 748: © Banque d'Images, ADAGP/Art Resource, NY; p. 749: © Kharbine-Tapabor/The Art Archive at Art Resource, NY; p. 750: © Brent C. Brolin/Art Resource, NY; p. 755: © Corbis; p. 757, p. 759: © Bettmann/Corbis.

Chapter 24   Opener: © Dmitri Baltermants/The Dmitri Baltermants Collection/Corbis; p. 764 (top): AP Photo; p. 764 (bottom): © Yevgeny Khaldei/Agentur Voller Ernst/dpa/Corbis; p. 765: © Art Resource, NY; p. 768: © Universal Images Group/ Getty Images; p. 770: © United States Holocaust Memorial Museum; p. 772: © Science and Society/SuperStock; p. 773: © AFP/ Getty Images; p. 775: © Bettmann/Corbis; p. 776: © United States Holocaust Memorial Museum; p. 779: © Bettmann/Corbis; p. 781: © Itar-Tass Photos/Newscom; p. 782: © Art Resource, NY; p. 784: © Galerie Bilderwelt/Getty Images; p. 786: © Ullstein Bild/The Granger Collection, New York — All rights reserved.; p. 790: © Yevgeny Khaldei/Agentur Voller Ernst/dpa/Corbis; p. 791: © Bettmann/Corbis.

Chapter 25   Opener: © Bettmann/Corbis; p. 800 (top): © Regis Bossu/Sygma/Corbis; p. 800 (bottom): © Bettmann/Corbis; p. 801 (left): © Rolls Press/Popperfoto/Getty Images; p. 801 (right): © Robert Wallis/Corbis; p. 804: © Gamma-Keystone via Getty Images; p. 807: © Bettmann/Corbis; p. 808: © Arpad Hazafi/AP/ Corbis; p. 809: AP Photo; p. 810: AP Photo/Libor Hajsky/CTK; p. 815, p. 816: © Bettmann/Corbis; p. 819: © Frank Castoral/NY Daily News Archive via Getty Images; p. 820: © National Portrait Gallery, Smithsonian Institution/Art Resource, NY; p. 821: © Rolls Press/Popperfoto/Getty Images; p. 823: AP Photo/Peter Kemp; p. 824: Courtesy of The Advertising Archives; p. 826: AP Photo/ J. Scott Applewhite; p. 828: © Robert Wallis/Corbis.

Chapter 26   Opener: © Wim Robberechts/Photonews via Getty Images; p. 834 (top): © Anja Niedringhaus/EPA/Newscom; p. 834 (bottom): AP Photo/Petros Giannakouris; p. 835: AP Photo/Joerg Sarbach; p. 837: © Gideon Mendel/Corbis; p. 839: AP Photo/Peter Winkler; p. 842: AP Photo/Zoran Bozicevic; p. 845: AP Photo/Jerome Delay; p. 848: AP Photo/Pool; p. 850: AP Photo/Joerg Sarbach; p. 852: AP Photo/Agriculture Ministry press office; p. 853: © Cesar Manso/ AFP/Getty Images; p. 854: © Gideon Mendel/In Pictures/Corbis; p. 855: © Johannes Eisele/AFP/Getty Images; p. 857: AP Photo/ Sergei Chuzavkov; p. 861: AP Photo/Petros Giannakouris;

TEXT CREDITS

Chapter 1 p. 11: Jerry H. Bentley, Herbert F. Ziegler, and Heather E. Streets-Salter, *Traditions and Encounters: A Brief Global History,* 2nd ed., Table 1.1, p. 23. Copyright © 2010 by The McGraw-Hill Companies, Inc. Reprinted with permission.

Chapter 4 p. 111: Dennis Sherman and Joyce Salisbury, *The West in the World,* 4th ed., p. 112, Figure 4.3. Copyright © 2011 by The McGraw-Hill Companies, Inc. Reprinted with permission.

Chapter 5 p. 148: Dennis Sherman and Joyce Salisbury, *The West in the World,* 4th ed., Map 5.1, p. 144. Copyright © 2011 by The McGraw-Hill Companies, Inc. Reprinted with permission; p. 161: *Roman Civilization. Sourcebook II: The Empire,* ed. Naphtali Lewis and Meyer Reinhold (New York: Columbia University Press, 1955), pp. 9–11, 13–17, 19. Copyright 1955 Columbia University Press, copyright renewed 1983 by Naphtali Lewis and Meyer Reinhold. Reprinted with permission of Columbia University Press.

Chapter 7 p. 221: Dennis Sherman and Joyce Salisbury, *The West in the World,* 4th ed., Figure 7.8, p. 235. Copyright © 2011 by The McGraw-Hill Companies, Inc. Reprinted with permission; p. 229: Einhard, *The Life of Charlemagne* 18–19, trans. Paul Edward Dutton, in *Charlemagne's Courtier: The Complete Einhard* (Toronto: University of Toronto Press, 1998), pp. 27–29. © 1998 Paul Edward Dutton. Reprinted by permission of the University of Toronto Press.

Chapter 9 p. 291: Thomas Aquinas, *Summa Theologica* from *Basic Writings of Saint Thomas Aquinas,* ed. Anton C. Pegis, Vol. 1 (Indianapolis, IN: Hackett, 1997), pp. 21–24. Copyright © 1945 by Random House, Inc. Copyright renewed 1973 by Random House, Inc. Reprinted 1997 by Hackett Publishing Company, Inc. Reprinted by permission of Hackett Publishing Company, Inc. All rights reserved.

Chapter 13 p. 418: Translated by C. M. Jacobs and revised by Harold J. Grimm, from *Luther's Works,* Volume 31: *Career of the Reformer: I* by Martin Luther, edited by Grimm and Lehmann, pp. 25–33, copyright © 1957 Fortress Press, admin. Augsburg Fortress. Reproduced by permission. All rights reserved.

Chapter 15 p. 489: Excerpts from pp. 253–8 from *The Habsburg and Hohenzollern Dynasties in the 17th and 18th Centuries* by C. A. Macartney. Introduction, editorial notes, chronology, translations by the editor; and compilation copyright © 1970 by C. A. Macartney. Reprinted by permission of HarperCollins Publishers.

Chapter 16 p. 522: Jean-Jacques Rousseau, *Emile, or, On Education,* trans. Allan Bloom (New York: Basic Books, 1979), pp. 357–358, 364–365. English translation Copyright © 1979 by Basic Books. Reprinted by permission of Basic Books, a member of the Perseus Books Group.

Chapter 17 p. 557: Emmanuel-Joseph Sieyès, *What Is the Third Estate?* trans. M. Blondel, ed. S. E. Finer (New York: Praeger, 1964). Reproduced with permission of Praeger Publishing in the format Textbook via Copyright Clearance Center.

Chapter 19 p. 629: Translated by Nikola Iordanovski, in *Discourses of Collective Identity in Central and Southeast Europe (1770–1945): Texts and Commentaries,* vol. 2: *National Romanticism – The Formation of National Movements,* ed. Balázs Trencsényi and Michal Kopeček (Budapest: Central European University Press, 2007), pp. 484–485. Reprinted by permission of Central European University Press.

Chapter 26 p. 865: Daniel Hannan, "The European Project Is Now Sustained by Coup," blog for *The Telegraph,* 14 November 2011. © Telegraph Media Group Limited 2011. Reprinted with permission.

INDEX

Aachen (Germany), 214, 214 (map), 216, 224, 239

Abbasid Caliphate, 208 (illus.), 215–216

Abd al-Quadir, 639, 639 (illus.)

Abd al-Rahman I (Umayyad), 215–216

Abdul Karim, 603 (illus.)

Abelard, 261–263, 263 (illus.), 264–265, 267, 268

abolitionists, 617, 645

Abraham (Hebrew patriarch), 30, 32

Abrams, M. H., 579

absolutism, seventeenth-century
  Austrian Habsburgs and, 439–440, 439 (illus.)
  Dutch exception to, 445, 447
  English defeat of, 447–453, 450 (illus.), 450 (map), 452 (illus.)
  Enlightenment and, 495, 506
  family dynasties and ministers, 436–437
  famine and disease and, 424, 425
  France and, 420–421 (illus.), 421–423, 422 (illus.), 437–439, 438 (map)
  French Revolution and, 528
  monarchs and, 461–462, 461 (illus.)
  nobles and, 436–437
  origins of, 424, 426
  Ottoman Empire and, 446, 446 (illus.)
  Poland and, 443
  political philosophy and, 434–435
  Prussia and, 440
  Russia and, 440–442, 441 (map)
  Spain and, 443
  Sweden and, 443–444
  Thirty Years' War and, 424, 426–431, 427 (map), 428 (illus.), 430 (illus.)
  timeline of, 422–423 (illus.)
  Venetian exception to, 444–445, 444 (illus.), 445 (map)
  war and, 477

abstract expressionism, 820, 820 (illus.)

Abu Bakr, 208

Academy of Plato, 80

Academy of Sciences (Russia), 506

Aceh, Dutch conquest of, 653, 653 (illus.)

Achaean League, 103, 128

acropolis, 40, 47

Acropolis (Athens), 54, 64, 64 (illus.)

Act of Supremacy (1534; England), 401–402, 414

Act of Uniformity (1559; England), 414

Act of Union (1707; Britain), 498, 499

The Adages of Erasmus (printed by Manutius), 352, 352 (illus.), 388

Adamites, 451

The Address to the Christian Nobility of the German Nation (Luther), 394

Adenauer, Konrad, 807, 812

ad fontes, 344

Admad, Mehmed (al-Mahdi), 652

Adolf of Nassau, 300

The Adoration of the Magi (Botticelli), 333 (illus.)

The Adventures of Simplicius Simplicissimus (Grimmelshausen), 433

aedile, 135

Aegina, 53

Aelfgyva, 249, 249 (illus.)

Aeneid (Virgil), 150–151, 151 (illus.)

Aeschylus, 65

Aethelred, 248

Afghanistan
  Bactria, 86, 89–90, 89 (map)
  British in, 653
  in the Hellenistic world, 89
  Islam in, 207 (map)
  Soviets in, 816, 826

Africa. See also specific countries
  decolonization after World War II, 814 (map), 817–818
  European colonization of, 654–658, 655 (illus.), 656 (illus.), 657 (map)
  in the Great War, 704, 710–711, 711 (illus.)
  immigration into, 669
  migration of Homo sapiens sapiens from, 6
  Portuguese exploration of, 363, 364 (map)
  resistance to colonization by, 658–660, 659 (illus.)
  slave trade in, 363–365, 475–476, 476 (illus.), 497

afterlife, 21–22, 31

Agincourt, Battle of (1415), 315

Agnolo the Fat (Siena), 307, 309, 323 (source document)

agon, 43, 51

agora, 40, 47

Agricultural Revolution of Prehistory, 10

agriculture. See also peasants and serfs
  animal domestication, 8–10
  birth of, 9–10
  Carolingian, 220–221, 220 (illus.)
  in Carthage, 121
  collectivization of, in eastern Europe, 803
  collectivization of, in Soviet Union, 717, 734–735, 735 (illus.)
  Columbian Exchange, 369, 369 (illus.)
  in Egypt, ancient, 18–19, 19 (map)
  eighteenth-century changes in, 471–472, 472 (illus.)
  enclosure and, 471, 472 (illus.)
  encomienda system, 377–378
  in the fin de siècle, 679–680
  gardening, in the Enlightenment, 513–514, 514 (illus.)
  in Gaul, 205
  in the Great Depression, 753
  Great Famine and, 297–298, 297 (illus.)
  in Greece, ancient, 40, 47–48, 48 (illus.), 56

guest workers, 813, 848
  Hellenistic, 94
  in the High Middle Ages, 273–276
  irrigation, 13, 96
  Little Ice Age and, 296–297
  in Mesolithic Europe, 10–11
  in Mesopotamia, 5, 13
  plant domestication, 9–10, 19
  potatoes, introduction of, 469, 471
  in the Roman Empire, 156, 173, 175
  in the Roman Republic, 126
  in Russia, mid-nineteenth-century, 606
  slave, fourteenth-century, 364
  in western Europe, after World War II, 812–813

Agrippa, 147, 148

Ahmes-Nefertari statue, 59 (illus.)

Ahura Mazda (god), 52

airplanes, military, 712

Akhenaton, 22, 22 (illus.), 23, 25, 30

Akhmatova, Anna, 751

Akkadian empire, 16–17, 16 (illus.), 25

Alaric, 182, 183, 185

Alaska, Russians in, 640

Albania, 775, 822, 843

Albanians, in Yugoslavia, 844

Albert (prince of England), 576, 603

Albert the Great, 288

Albigensians, 277

Albrecht (archbishop of Magdeburg), 392

alchemy, 457–459, 484

Alcibiades, 63, 79

Alcuin (Carolingian), 214, 216, 219

Aldus Manutius, 352, 352 (illus.)

Alexander I (czar of Russia), 551, 554, 562

Alexander II (czar of Russia), 606, 685

Alexander III (czar of Russia), 606

Alexander the Great
  Aristotle as tutor of, 80
  Chaeronea, Battle of, 75 (map), 77
  chronology of, 82
  coins of, 90, 90 (illus.)
  conquest of Egypt by, 20
  death of, 86–87
  entombment in Alexandria, 71–72
  march to India, 83 (map), 85–86
  murder of Philip's wife and child by, 82
  Persian conquest by, 83–84, 83 (map)
  rise to power, 82–83

Alexander VI (Pope), 331–332, 334

Alexandria
  Alexander's burial in, 71–72
  Christianity in, 172
  library at, 97–98
  in the Ptolemaic kingdom, 88, 89 (map)
  urban plan of, 72, 84

Alexius I (Byzantine emperor), 254, 271–272

Alfonso VIII (king of Spain), 273

Alfonso XIII (king of Spain), 758

Alfred the Great (England), 241, 243
Algeria
    French colonization of, 604, 637, 639, 639
        (illus.)
    independence of, 814 (map), 817
    Islam in, 207 (map)
    war of independence, 604
Algerian War, 604
Ali (son-in-law of Muhammad), 208
Ali, Mehmed (khedive of Egypt), 651
Alice's Adventures in Wonderland (Carroll),
    611
alienation
    in the fin de siècle, 678
    in the Hellenistic Ages, 81
    in medieval universities, 287
Allied Powers, 772. See also specific countries
Alp Arslan, Sultan, 248
alphabets, 28, 29 (illus.), 41, 42, 126. See also
    writing
Alsace and Lorraine
    incorporation into Germany, 622, 624, 688
    return to France, 723, 724 (map)
Altar of Peace (Ara Pacis), 148–149, 149 (illus.)
alum, 361
Aly, Götz, 785
Amarna archive, 25
Ambrose (bishop; saint), 203–204, 203 (illus.)
Amenhotep III (Egyptian king), 23
Amenhotep IV (Egyptian king), 22, 22
    (illus.), 23, 25
American Civil War, 616–618, 617 (illus.)
Americanization, 853
American Relief Administration, 734
American War of Independence, 529,
    634–635
Americas. See also North America; South
        America; West Indies
    Columbus in, 368
    origin of name, 371, 371 (map)
    Spanish colonies in, 370, 375–380, 377
        (illus.), 657 (map)
Amon-Ra (god), 21, 23
Amorites, 28
amphorae, 48, 94
Amritsar Massacre (India), 739
Amyntas, 90
Anabaptists, 405–406, 406 (illus.)
Anabasis (Xenophon), 74
anarchism
    in the Cold War, 818
    in Europe, fin de siècle, 685, 686
    in Europe, 1870s, 669
    in France, 623
    the Great War and, 703
    in Russia, 606
    Spanish Civil War and, 758–759
    in Victorian England, 603
Anatolia. See Turkey
anatomical revolution, 484–485, 484 (illus.)
Anaximander of Miletus, 48–49
ancestor worship, 118
Ancus Marcius (legendary king), 118
al-Andalus, 215–216
Andronikos, Manolis, 76
Angevin Empire, 281
Angles, 167, 181, 181 (map), 187
Anglican Church (Church of England),
    401–402, 447, 448, 464

Anglo-Saxon kingdoms, 241–242, 241 (map),
    251
Anglo-Sikh Wars, 653
animals, domestication of, 8–10
Anne I (queen of England), 453
anomie, 678
Anschluss (Austria), 759
Anselm of Bec/Canterbury, 264
Anselm of Laon, 265
Anthony (hermit), 170
anthropology, 750
Anti-Comintern Pact, 758
Antigone (Sophocles), 65
Antigonid kingdom, 73 (illus.), 88, 89 (map)
Antigonus the One-Eyed, 88
Antikythera device, 156, 156 (illus.)
Antioch (Turkey), 255–256, 255 (map)
Antioch IV (Seleucid king), 99, 125
Antiochus III (Seleucid king), 123–124
Antiochus the Great, 89
Antipater, 88
anti-pope, 313
The Antiquities of Athens (Stuart and Revett),
    510
anti-Semitism
    in the Balkans, 776
    in Belarus, 858
    in Christian socialism, 685
    in the Crusades, 255, 269
    Disraeli and, 601
    in the Dreyfus affair, 689–690, 690 (illus.)
    in the fin de siècle, 685, 688–690, 690
        (illus.)
    in former Soviet countries, 844
    in France, 774
    in the Great Famine, 298
    Holocaust/Nazi Final Solution, 781,
        782–784, 782 (illus.), 783 (map), 784
        (illus.), 788
    in Nazi Germany, prewar, 742, 755–757,
        757 (illus.), 766, 769
    Night of the Broken Glass
        (Reichskristallnacht), 767–768, 768
        (illus.)
    during the plague, 308
    in Poland, 767 (map), 768, 770, 771–772
    in the Soviet Union, 780
Antoninus Pius (Roman emperor), 157, 158,
    159
Antony, Mark, 144–146
Anubis (god), 22
Apis (god), 22
Apollo (god), 43
apostates, 180
apotheosis, 151
appeasement, of Germany, 766–767, 767
    (map)
apprentices, 275, 468
Apuleius, Lucius, 166
Arabia
    Alexander's plans for, 86
    camels in, 9
    in the Great War, 710, 723
    Islam's spread in, 207–208, 207 (map)
    Muhammad in, 206–208
    Ottoman empire in, 340 (map), 693 (map),
        710
    in the 1920s–1930s, 739 (map)
Arab-Israeli War (1947–1949), 815

Aramaic language, 52
Ara Pacis, 148–149, 149 (illus.)
Arawak people, 376
Arc du Triomphe (France), 548
archaeology, 646, 648
Archaic Age of Greece. See Greece, Archaic
    Age
"Archaic Smile," 49, 49 (illus.)
Archidamus (king of Sparta), 62
Archilocus of Paros, 48
Archimedes of Syracuse, 96, 97, 123, 284, 284
    (illus.)
architecture
    Baroque, 431, 431 (illus.), 433, 463
    Byzantine, 189, 189 (illus.)
    Carolingian, 216–217, 217 (illus.)
    Christian, early, 177 (illus.)
    column design, 98–99
    Egyptian pyramids, 21
    Gothic, 260–261 (illus.), 267–268, 268
        (illus.), 269 (illus.), 273, 289, 289 (illus.)
    Greek, ancient, 49, 64, 64 (illus.)
    Hellenistic, 98–99, 98 (illus.)
    in the interwar years, 750, 750 (illus.)
    Islamic, 208 (illus.), 216 (illus.)
    Minoan, 25
    modernist, 677
    postmodernist, 855, 855 (illus.)
    Roman, 147–149, 148 (illus.), 155 (illus.),
        174 (illus.)
    Romanesque, 232–233, 232 (illus.), 233
        (illus.), 237, 237 (illus.), 244 (illus.), 250
Arch of Titus, 152, 152 (illus.)
Arcimboldo, Giuseppe, 404 (illus.)
Arditi, 741
Arendt, Hannah, 818
arête, 43
Argos (Greece), 54, 62 (map), 63
Arianism, 179, 183, 184, 186, 187
Aristagoras of Miletus, 52
Aristarchus of Samos, 96
Ariston of Paros, 49, 49 (illus.)
Aristophanes, 65–66, 78
Aristotle, 77, 80–81, 283, 288
Ark of the Covenant, 30, 31, 32
Arkwright, Richard, 582
Armenians
    in the Great War, 708, 709, 709 (map), 710
        (illus.)
    independence of, 840
    Ottoman massacre of, 692, 704
    Turkish massacre of, 725
arms race
    in the Cold War, 827
    prior to the Great War, 688, 690–691, 700
Arnold of Brescia, 277
Arnolfini Wedding Scene (van Eyck), 350
    (illus.)
Arnulf of Metz (Bishop), 206
Arsenal (Venice), 338
art. See also architecture; sculpture
    abstract expressionism, 820, 820 (illus.)
    of American exploration, 369 (illus.), 374
        (illus.), 377 (illus.), 379 (illus.), 385
        (illus.)
    Baroque, 409–410, 409 (illus.), 410 (illus.),
        431–432, 432 (illus.), 434 (illus.), 463
    cave paintings, 2–3 (illus.), 7, 9
    Egyptian, 20–21, 21 (illus.), 24, 24 (illus.)

Etruscan, 107 (illus.), 108, 108 (illus.), 109 (illus.)
European Renaissance, 350, 350 (illus.)
fakes, 127
in Gothic High Middle Ages, 266 (illus.), 270 (illus.), 271 (illus.), 274 (illus.), 281 (illus.), 286 (illus.), 287 (illus.)
Greek, Archaic, 49
Greek, Golden Age Athens, 64–65, 64 (illus.)
Hebrew, 31 (illus.)
Hellenistic, 98–99, 98 (illus.), 98 (illus.)
interwar, 748–750, 748 (illus.), 749 (illus.)
Italian Renaissance, 345–349, 346 (illus.), 347 (illus.), 348 (illus.)
Medici family and, 333–334, 333 (illus.)
modernism, 675–677, 675 (illus.), 677 (illus.), 678 (illus.)
neoclassicism, 509
Paleolithic Venus figurines, 35, 35 (illus.)
postmodernism, 855, 855 (illus.)
realism and Impressionism, 612–614, 614 (illus.)
in the Roman Empire, 151 (illus.), 155 (illus.), 167 (illus.)
in the Roman Republic, 117 (illus.)
in sixteenth century, 367 (illus.)
Artaxerxes II (king of Persia), 74
Art for All, 675
artisans, eighteenth-century, 468, 468 (illus.)
art nouveau, 675, 681, 681 (illus.)
Aryans, Nazis on, 11, 754
asceticism, 200, 277, 312
Asclepius, 81–82, 81 (illus.), 151
Asherah (goddess), 30
Asia. See also specific countries
    Boxer Rebellion in, 659
    British East India Company, 474, 480, 481, 635–637, 637 (illus.)
    Dutch trade with, 382, 447, 653, 653 (illus.)
    Enlightenment learning and, 496, 513, 515, 515 (illus.)
    French trade with, 423
    Genoese trade with, 361–362
    "the Great Game" in, 653–654, 654 (map)
    in the Great War, 711
    Ho Chi Minh in, 711, 740, 740 (illus.), 815
    imperial exchange and, 646, 648
    imperialism before the Great War, 641 (map)
    independence of colonies in, 813–817, 814 (map), 815 (illus.), 816 (illus.)
    missionaries in, 407, 407 (illus.), 644
    Mongol empire in, 279, 279 (illus.)
    Opium Wars in, 639–640
    plague in, 293, 304–306
    Portuguese trade with, 363–365, 364 (map), 380–382
    Russo-Japanese War, 686, 687, 687 (illus.)
    seventeenth-century trade with, 423
    seventeenth-century weather crisis in, 425, 425 (illus.)
    in World War II, 778–779, 779 (illus.), 780 (map), 786, 790, 792
Asia Minor. See Turkey (Anatolia)
Aspasia, 60, 61
Assassins, 248
assignat, 533–534, 535, 536, 543

Assur (god), 32
Assyrians, 32, 41, 51
Astralabe, 262
astrolabes, 366
astronomy, 96, 482–484
Atahualpa (emperor of Inca), 374, 374 (illus.)
Atala (Chateaubriand), 578
Atatürk (Mustafa Kemal), 710, 724–725, 725 (illus.)
Athanasius (Bishop of Alexandria), 169
Athens. See also Greece, ancient
    after the Peloponnesian War, 74
    art in, 64–65, 64 (illus.)
    Delian League in, 60–63, 64
    democracy in, 47, 58–59, 74
    Demosthenes and Isocrates in, 75–76
    Golden Age of, 63–66, 64 (illus.), 68 (source document)
    government of, 58–59
    in the Peloponnesian War, 61–63, 62 (map)
    Pericles in, 37, 61–63, 61 (illus.), 64
    in the Persian Wars, 53, 54–56, 54 (map)
    Plato, 50, 78, 79–80, 81
    pottery of, 49
    in the Roman Empire, 140
    slavery in, 59–60
    Socrates, 78–79, 79 (illus.), 101 (source document)
    surrender of empire by, 63, 65
Atlantic Charter, 792
Atlantis, 26
atomic weapons, 788, 792
Aton (god), 22, 23
Attila, 183
Attlee, Clement, 815
augury, 108, 118
August Decrees (France), 532, 533
Augustine, Saint, 175–176, 183, 326
Augustine of Canterbury, 202
Augustinians, 378
Augustus (Roman emperor)
    accomplishments of, 133–134, 147, 161 (source document)
    in Alexandria, 72
    ideology of, 147
    rebuilding Rome, 147–149, 148 (map), 149 (illus.)
    transformation of the Republic, 147
    in the Triumvirate, 144–146
Augustus the Strong (elector of Saxony), 458, 458 (illus.)
Aurelian (Roman emperor), 167
L'Aurore, 689
Auschwitz death camp, 782, 783 (map), 784, 784 (illus.), 788
auspicatus, 109
Austen, Jane, 511
Austerlitz, Battle of (1805), 551
Australia
    in the Great War, 710, 722
    immigration into, 669
Austria. See also Austro-Hungarian Empire
    absolutism, seventeenth-century, 439–440, 439 (illus.)
    Anschluss with Germany, 759
    Austro-Prussian War, 626
    Banking Crisis of 1873, 656, 668
    Bosnia Herzegovina annexation by, 652

Congress of Vienna and, 562, 564 (map)
    in the Crimean War, 616
    Enlightenment in, 508–509
    fascism in, 759
    French Revolution and, 545, 545 (illus.), 546
    German unification and, 620–621, 621 (map)
    in the Great Depression, 753
    Napoleon and, 551, 552 (map), 554
    peasants in, 508, 568
    Poland partition and, 507 (map)
    revolution of 1848, 589, 589 (map), 591
    Seven Years' War and, 477–479, 478 (map), 482
    Vienna, 439, 439 (illus.), 606, 679
    War of the Austrian Succession, 477, 478
Austrian Netherlands, 539–540, 543
Austro-Hungarian Empire. See also Habsburg Empire
    as dual monarchy, 626–627, 626 (map)
    Great War, eastern front, 707–708, 708 (illus.)
    Great War, entrance into, 701–702, 702 (map)
    Great War, peace treaties, 723, 724, 724 (map)
    Great War, southeastern fronts, 708–710, 709 (map)
    nationalism and end of, 691–692, 692 (map)
Austro-Prussian War, 626
authoritarianism, 732
Autobiography of a Sexually Emancipated Communist Woman (Kollontai), 731
The Autumn of the Middle Ages (Payton and Mammitzsch), 320
avant-garde, 674, 679
Averroists, 288
Avicenna (Ibn Sina), 288
Avignon
    papacy in, 299–300, 300 (illus.)
    plague in, 306 (map), 308
Axis Powers, 767. See also specific countries
Azerbaijan, 840, 841 (map)
Azores, 365
Aztec people, 358, 372–374, 377–379, 377 (illus.), 379 (illus.)

Baal (goddess), 30
Babel, Isaak, 751
babus, 637, 638
baby boom generation, 811–812, 820–821, 821 (illus.)
Babylon/Babylonians
    Alexander's conquest of, 84, 86
    attack on Israel, 32
    cuneiform writing from, 15
    Hebrew captivity in, 32
    in Persian Empire, 51
    in the Seleucid kingdom, 88–89, 89 (map)
"Babylonian Captivity of the Church," 300
The Babylonian Captivity of the Church (Luther), 394
Bacchants (Euripides), 77–78
Bach, Johann Sebastian, 433
Bachkarova, Yasha, 714
Bacon, Francis, 482

Bactria, 86, 89–90, 89 (map). See also
	Afghanistan
Baden-Powell, Robert, 660
Baelz, Erwin, 687
Baghdad, 207 (map), 215–216, 248
Baker, Josephine, 751
Baku (Azerbaijan), 718
"balance of power," 562
Balboa, Vasco Núñez de, 371–372
Balfour Declaration, 708, 738, 815
Bali, Dutch conquest of, 653, 653 (illus.)
balkanization, 360
Balkans
	after the Russo-Turkish Wars, 626–627,
		626 (map)
	Balkan Wars (1912–1913), 693–694, 693
		(illus.), 701
	in the Great War, 708–710, 709 (map)
	prior to the Great War, 701
	in World War II, 776, 776 (illus.)
Ball, John, 310–311
ballooning, 513, 513 (illus.)
Balzac, Honoré de, 611, 612
Bangladesh, formation of, 814 (map), 815
Banking Crisis (1873), 656, 668
Bank of Amsterdam, 474
Bank of England, 474
Bank of France, 546, 548
Banks, Joseph, 514
banks and finance. See also currency and
		money
	Banking Crisis of 1873 and, 656, 668
	British and Dutch banks, 474
	capital, in the Industrial Revolution,
		584–585
	European Central Bank, 850, 861, 862
	euros, 849–850, 850 (illus.), 860–862
	in the Great Depression, 753
	Medici family and, 333–334
	sovereign debt crisis, 860–862
	in Venice, 337–338
	World Bank, 805–806
Baptism, Protestants and, 405, 406
A Bar at the Folies-Bergère (Manet), 614
		(illus.)
barbarians, 180
Baroque culture
	architecture, 431, 431 (illus.), 433, 463
	devotionals, 431–432
	music, 433–434
	painting, 409–410, 409 (illus.), 432 (illus.),
		433, 434 (illus.)
	political philosophy, 434–435
	popular, 435
	sculpture, 410, 410 (illus.), 433
	theater, 432–433
	witch killing in, 424, 435–436, 436 (illus.)
Bartsiokas, Antonis, 76
Basayev, Shamil, 859
basilicas, 233
Basil II (Byzantine), 248
Basques, 215
bastard feudalism, 315
Bastille, assault on, 531–532, 531 (illus.)
Batavian Republic, 540
Bathsheba, 32
The Battleship Potemkin (Eisenstein), 749
Bauhaus school of architecture, 750
Bayam, Chilam, 376

Bayeux Tapestry, 249, 249 (illus.), 251 (illus.)
Bayle, Pierre, 495
Bazaine, Marshal Achille, 622
Beales, Derek, 519
The Beard-Hater (Julian), 179–180
Beatles, 819, 819 (illus.)
Beccaria, Cesare, 509
Beckett, Thomas, 281
Beer Hall Putsch (Germany), 744
bees, domestication of, 9
Beethoven, Ludwig van, 578
Behaeddin Shakir, 709
Behistun inscription, 15, 15 (illus.)
Behrens, Peter, 677
Belgium
	African colonies of, 656–657, 656 (illus.),
		657 (map), 711, 817
	formation of, 564 (map), 573–574, 574
		(map)
	government in, 847
	in the Great War, 702, 702 (map), 704–706,
		705 (map), 706 (illus.), 723
	in the Roman Empire, 142
	in World War II, 773
Belisarius, 189–190
Bellini, Gentile, 324–325 (illus.), 327, 345
Belorussia
	independence of, 841 (map)
	in the Russian civil wars, 733
	in the Soviet Union, 802 (map), 804–805
	in World War II, 785
Beneš, Eduard, 766–767
Benedictines, 199–201, 218–219
Benedict of Nursia (Saint), 198, 200
benefice, 234
Bentham, Jeremy, 579
Bergson, Henri, 678–679
Berlin
	airlift in, 807
	Berlin Wall, 807–808, 807 (illus.), 828, 828
		(illus.), 839, 839 (illus.)
	in the Cold War, 802 (map), 806–807
	in the fin de siècle, 670
	workers' uprising in, 808
	in World War II, 790, 790 (illus.)
Berlin Conference (1884), 656–658, 657 (map)
Berlin U-bahn, 672
Berlin Wall, 807–808, 807 (illus.), 828, 828
		(illus.), 839, 839 (illus.)
Berlusconi, Silvio, 847, 857
Bernadette Soubiros (of Lourdes), 676
Bernal, Martin, 50
Bernard (Frankish monk), 252
Bernard of Chartres, 264, 282–283
Bernard of Clairvaux, 268–269
Bernard of Italy (Carolingian), 223
Berners-Lee, Tim, 854
Bernhardt, Sarah, 665–667, 666 (illus.), 675,
		689
Bernini, Gianlorenzo, 410, 431, 431 (illus.)
Bernstein, Eduard, 685
Bessarion, Basilus, 341
Bethmann-Hollweg, Theobald von, 702
Beukels, Jan, 405–406, 406 (illus.)
Beyazit I Yilderim (the Lightning), 318
Bible
	Bishops', 448
	Carolingian, 218
	English, 313–314

Geneva, 448
Gutenberg, 351
King James, 448
Lutheran, 395–396
Septuagint, 92
Tyndale's English, 402
Vulgate, 218, 409
Bill of Rights (England), 453, 568
Bill of Rights (United States), 568
Bird in Space (Brancusi), 750
The Birth of the Clinic (Foucault), 820
Bishops' Bible, 448
Bismarck, Otto von
	on carving up Africa, 656
	Catholics and, 624
	Franco-Prussian War and, 621–623
	unification of Germany and, 616, 619–621,
		621 (map)
Bithynia (Turkey), 89 (map), 91, 123
Black Athena: The Afroasiatic Roots of Classical
		Civilization (Bernal), 50
Blackbourn, David, 596
Black Death, 305. See also plague
Black Hole of Calcutta, 480, 481, 481 (illus.),
		740
Black Shirts (Italy), 741
Blair, Tony, 847, 856
Blenheim, Battle of, 438, 438 (map)
The Blessings of Good Government
		(Lorenzetti), 274 (illus.)
Blitz, in Britain, 774
Blitzkrieg, 770, 772
Bloch, Marc, 236
blood cults, 312
blood-letting, 484
Bluehenge (England), 11
Blum, Léon, 758
Blumenbach, Johann Friedrich, 515
Boccaccio, Giovanni, 308, 309, 309 (illus.),
		343, 365
Boers, 637, 638, 655, 659–660, 659 (illus.)
Boethius, 187, 243
Bohr, Niels, 679, 750
Boleyn, Anne, 401
Bologna, University of, 283, 285–286, 285
		(map), 286 (illus.), 287
Bolsheviks
	in the Russian civil wars, 732–734, 733
		(map)
	in the Russian Revolution, 717–719, 717
		(illus.), 719 (illus.)
	in Russian socialist movement, 685
Bona Dea, 119
Bonaparte, Francois Charles Joseph, 554
Bonaventure, Saint, 288
Bonfire of the Vanities, 334–335
Boniface (Bishop), 212
Boniface VIII (Pope), 280, 299, 300
Le Bon Marche (Paris), 681
Bonnie Prince Charlie, 499 (map), 500, 500
		(illus.)
Bono (Paul David Hewson), 833–835, 834
		(illus.)
Book of Common Prayer (Cranmer), 402, 414,
		448
Book of Martyrs (Foxe), 435
Book of Prayer and Meditation (Luis de
		Granada), 432, 435
Book of the Dead (Egyptian), 22

books. *See also* literature
    Aldine, 352, 352 *(illus.)*
    banned by the Catholic Church, 409, 496, 502, 504–505
    for children, 674
    cookbooks, 517, 609
    in the Enlightenment, 505
    in the European Renaissance, 351–353, 352 *(illus.)*
    monasticism and, 201, 201 *(illus.)*
    palimpsests, 284, 284 *(illus.)*
    in the scientific revolution, 485
    small, portable, 283
    travel guides, 672
    Vatican library and, 331
    for women, 511
    for working-class readers, 674
Bora, Katharina von, 388–389, 388 *(illus.)*
Borgia, Cesare, 332
Borgia, Lucretia, 332
Boris (king of Bulgaria), 785
Bose, Subhas Chandra, 740
Bosnia Herzegovina. *See also* Serbia/Serbs
    Austrian annexation of, 652
    independence of, 626–627, 626 *(map)*, 844–846
    Princip in, 693, 697–699, 698 *(illus.)*
botany, 513–514, 646
Botswana, 814 *(map)*, 817
Böttger, Johann, 457–459, 458 *(illus.)*
Botticelli, Sandro, 333 *(illus.)*, 334, 336
Boulanger, Georges Ernest, 623
Bourbaki, Charles, 622
bourgeois, Enlightenment and, 495
The Bourgeois Cook (Menon), 517
bourgeoisie, French Revolution and, 528–529
Boxer Rebellion, 659
boyars, 441–442
Bracciolini, Poggio, 343
Bradley, Keith, 137
Bramah, Joseph, 582–583
Brancusi, Constantin, 750
Brandenburg, house of, 479
Brandt, Willy, 822
Braun, Eva, 769
Brazil, Treaty of Tordesillas and, 369
Breitenfeld, Battle of (1631), 429, 429 *(illus.)*
Brest-Litovsk, Treaty of (1918), 708, 718, 719–720, 732
Brethren of the Common Life, 312
Bretton Woods system, 805–806, 823
Brezhnev, Leonid, 800 *(illus.)*, 810–811, 816, 822
Brezhnev Doctrine, 810–811
bribery. *See* corruption
A Brief Account of the Destruction of the Indies (Las Casas), 380
Britain. *See also* England
    African colonies of, 631–633, 632 *(map)*, 633 *(illus.)*, 637, 656, 657 *(map)*, 711
    American War of Independence from, 529, 634–635
    appeasement of Germany by, 766–767, 767 *(map)*
    Boer Wars, 638, 659–660, 659 *(illus.)*
    in Burma, 779, 779 *(illus.)*
    Caribbean colonies, 479–480
    chartered companies of, 474, 480, 481, 636
    Chartism in, 575–576

    Christianization of, 202
    colonial independence from, 814–815, 814 *(map)*
    Crimean War and, 615–616
    Crystal Palace Exhibition of 1851, 610, 610 *(illus.)*
    devolution in, 847
    domestic service in, 609, 609 *(illus.)*
    Egypt as protectorate of, 652
    emigration from, 669, 670 *(illus.)*
    Great Depression in, 738
    in "the Great Game," in central Asia, 653–654, 654 *(map)*
    in the Great War, 702, 705, 710–711, 723
    India, colonization of, 636–637, 637 *(illus.)*, 641 *(map)*
    Indian Rebellion (1857), 642–643, 642 *(illus.)*
    Indo-European migration into, 11
    Industrial Revolution in, 580–588, 581 *(map)*, 583 *(illus.)*, 584 *(illus.)*, 586 *(illus.)*, 587 *(illus.)*
    interwar stability in, 738
    liberal modernization of, 601, 603, 603 *(illus.)*
    military build-up, pre–Great War, 691
    Opium Wars, 639–640
    railroads in, 581 *(map)*, 583–584, 584 *(illus.)*, 671 *(map)*
    reforms, after Napoleonic Wars, 567–568
    in the Roman Empire, 157, 159 *(map)*, 167
    social classes in, 607–608
    South African colony of, 632, 632 *(map)*, 637, 655, 655 *(illus.)*
    Suez Canal and, 650, 651–652, 651 *(illus.)*
    terrorist strikes in, 858
    textile industry in, 472–473, 568, 581
    as United Kingdom of Great Britain, 498
    Victorian life in, 607–611, 609 *(illus.)*, 610 *(illus.)*
    voting rights in, 575, 599, 601
    in World War II, 770, 773, 774–775, 775 *(illus.)*
Britain, Battle of (1940–1941), 774–775, 775 *(illus.)*
British Broadcasting Company (BBC), 787
British East India Company (BEIC), 474, 480, 481, 636–637, 637 *(illus.)*
British Museum, 646, 648
bronze, in Mesopotamia and Egypt, 24, 28
Bronze Age, 5 *(illus.)*, 7, 11, 24, 26–27
Brothers of the Common Life, 387
Brown, Elizabeth A. R., 236
Brown, Howard G., 544
Broz, Josef (Tito), 776, 804 *(illus.)*, 844
Bruegel, Pieter, the Elder, 353, 353 *(illus.)*
Bruges, 298, 349–350
Brühl (count of Saxony), 466
Bruni, Leonardo, 344
Brüning, Heinreich, 752
Brutus, 144
bubonic plague, 307–308. *See also* plague
Bucephala, 86
Bucolics (Virgil), 150
Bulgaria
    in the Balkan Wars, 693–694, 693 *(illus.)*
    in the Eastern bloc, 802 *(map)*, 803
    in the Great War, 702, 702 *(map)*, 708, 709 *(map)*, 723–724, 724 *(map)*

    independence of, 625–626, 625 *(illus.)*, 626 *(map)*, 841
    in the interwar years, 745
    material deprivation in, 851
    in World War II, 776, 785
Bulge, Battle of the, 789–790
bull, papal, 299
Bunyan, John, 435
Burckhardt, Jacob, 328
Burgundians, 181, 184, 188, 302 *(map)*
burials and death rituals
    Egyptian, 21–22
    Greek, ancient, 42
    Macedonian, 76
    Merovingian, 205, 205 *(illus.)*
    Mycenaean, 26–27
    in the Roman Republic, 117–118, 117 *(illus.)*
Burke, Edmund, 542, 567, 579
Burma, 777–779, 779 *(illus.)*, 780 *(map)*, 790
Burns, Robert, 500
Burton, Richard (explorer), 646
Bush, George W., 856
buttresses, 267
Buxtehude, Dieter, 433
Byblos (Lebanon), 28, 28 *(map)*
Byron, George Gordon, Lord, 571, 572, 573
Byzantine Empire. *See also* Constantinople
    fall of Constantinople, 318, 319, 319 *(illus.)*
    First Crusade and, 254
    formation of, 209–210, 209 *(map)*
    in the High Middle Ages, 278 *(map)*
    Islam and, 209–210
    Norman invasions of, 248
    Ottonian Empire and, 239, 240
    rise of Seljuk Turks in, 248
    translations of Islamic texts, 283
Byzantium, 179. *See also* Constantinople

Cabot, John, 375
Caesar, Julius, 142–144, 143 *(map)*, 145
Caesarian (Consular) Faction, 142
Cahiers de Doléances (Grievance Notebooks), 530, 532
Cajetan, Thomas (cardinal), 394
calculus, differential, 483
calendars
    Antikythera device, 156, 156 *(illus.)*
    French Revolution, 541, 542 *(illus.)*
    Julian, 144
    Nahua (Aztec), 379
    Roman Republic, 118–119
Caligula (Roman emperor), 157–158
Callimachus, 98
Calvin, John, 398, 402–404, 404 *(illus.)*
Calvinism
    churches, 431
    in England, 414
    in France, 411–412, 411 *(map)*, 412 *(illus.)*
    in the Netherlands, 413, 413 *(map)*
    in the Thirty Years' War, 426–428, 430
Cambodia, 652–653, 777, 815
Cambridge University, 285, 285 *(map)*
Cambyses (king of Egypt), 51
camels, 9, 94
Camillus, Marcus Furius, 113
campanilismo, 330
Campo Formio, Treaty of (1797), 545

Camus, Albert, 818
Canaan, 28, 30, 31
Canada
    in the French and Indian War, 480
    French attempt to colonize, 375
    in the Great War, 719
    immigration into, 669
Canary Islands
    Castile and, 365–366
    Columbus in, 368
    under Portugal, 361, 364
    resistance to colonization, 365
Candide (Voltaire), 503
Cannae, Battle of (216 BCE), 122
cannibalism, 25
cannons, 429, 477
Cantos (Pound), 751
Cape Colony, 631–633, 632 *(map)*, 633 *(illus.)*, 637
capitalism
    after the revolutions of 1848, 600–601
    "crony," 843
    Industrial Revolution and capital, 584–585
    liberalism and, 683
    Marx and Engels on, 565, 567
    mercantilism and, 474–475
    Trollope on, 607
    Victorian, 607
    welfare states and, 803, 812
    in western Europe, after World War II, 805–806
    "with a human face," 837
Capitoline gods, 109
capitularies, 214
captivity narratives, 481
Caracalla (Roman emperor), 167
Caravaggio, Michelangelo Merisi da, 409–410, 409 *(illus.)*
caravels, 366
Carbonari, 574
carbon-14 dating, 7
Carcassonne, walled city of, 227 *(illus.)*
Caribbean Islands. *See* West Indies
Carib people, 370
Carmelites, 408
Carol II (king of Romania), 745
Caroline Minuscule, 217, 217 *(illus.)*, 283
Carolingians. *See also* Charlemagne
    agriculture and commerce of, 220–221, 220 *(illus.)*, 221 *(illus.)*
    Charles the Bald and, 222, 223, 224 *(map)*, 226, 226 *(illus.)*
    Charles the Fat and, 227
    church under, 218–219
    cold climate during, 219
    culture of, 216–218, 217 *(illus.)*, 218 *(illus.)*
    division of the empire, 222–224, 224 *(map)*
    Louis the Pious, 215, 218, 222, 223, 223 *(illus.)*
    mayors of the palace, 210–211
    origin of line, 206
    papal approval of kingship, 213, 223
    Pepin the Short and, 211–213
    popular beliefs, 221–222
    in Spain, 215–216
    vassalage under, 235–236
    Viking raids on, 224–226, 224 *(illus.)*, 227
carracks, 366

Carroll, Lewis, 611
cartels, 679
Carter, Howard, 23
Carter, Jimmy, 823
Carthage
    Etruscans and, 113
    First Punic War, 120–123, 120 *(map)*, 121 *(illus.)*, 122 *(map)*
    Phoenicians in, 29, 41
    Roman destruction of, 128–129
    Roman Republic and, 115, 116, 119–123, 120 *(map)*, 122 *(map)*
    Second Punic War, 122–123
    surrender to, 123
Carthage, Battle of (255 BCE), 121
Cartier, Jacques, 375
Casablanca (film), 602, 788
Casement, Roger, 662 *(source document)*
Cassander, 88
Cassiodorus, 186
Cassius, 144
Castile, Canary Islands and, 365–366
castles, Romanesque, 237, 237 *(illus.)*
castrati, 510
Castro, Fidel, 809
Catalan Atlas (1375), 360 *(map)*
Çatalhüyük (Turkey), 10, 10 *(illus.)*, 19 *(map)*
Catanei, Vannozza, 332
Categories (Aristotle), 81
Catharism, 277
cathedrals
    Baroque, 431, 431 *(illus.)*, 433–434, 463
    in Christian Roman Empire, 189, 189 *(illus.)*, 318
    in the Early Middle Ages, 203–204, 203 *(illus.)*
    Gothic, 267–268, 268 *(illus.)*, 269 *(illus.)*, 273, 289, 289 *(illus.)*
    Romanesque, 230–231 *(illus.)*, 231–233, 232 *(illus.)*, 233 *(illus.)*, 256
cathedral schools, 264–266, 282–283
Catherine de' Medici, 411–412
Catherine II (the Great; czarina of Russia), 470, 479, 506, 506 *(illus.)*, 640–641
Catherine of Aragon, 401
Catherine of Siena, 312
Catholic Reformation, 406–410
    Baroque art and, 409–410, 409 *(illus.)*, 410 *(illus.)*
    chronology of popes in, 408
    Council of Trent, 408–409
    Jesuits in, 407–408, 407 *(illus.)*
    mysticism in, 408
Catiline, 141
Cato the Elder, 123, 126, 128, 136
cats, domestication of, 9
cattle, domestication of, 9
Catullus, 141–142
cave paintings, 2–3 *(illus.)*, 7, 9
Cavour, Camillo di, 616–619
Ceaușescu, Nicolae, 829
Cellini, Benvenuto, 345
cell phones, 853–854, 854 *(illus.)*
Central America. *See* North America
Central Middle Ages. *See* Romanesque Central Middle Ages
Central Powers (Great War), 702, 702 *(map)*. *See also specific countries*
Cereta, Laura, 326

Cervantes, Miguel de, 304, 433
Ceuta, Portuguese conquest of, 363
Chaeronea, Battle of, 75 *(map)*, 77
Chamberlain, Neville, 764, 766–767, 767 *(map)*
Chambers, Robert, 613
Champollion, Jean François, 20
Chardin, Jean, 517 *(illus.)*
"Charge of the Light Brigade" (Tennyson), 616
Charlemagne. *See also* Carolingians
    coronation of, 197–198, 198 *(illus.)*, 215
    culture and education, 216–218, 217 *(illus.)*, 218 *(illus.)*
    domestic life of, 229 *(source document)*
    empire of, 213–214, 214 *(map)*
    as father of Europe, 214–215
Charles Albert (king of Piedmont-Sardinia), 591
Charles Edward Stuart (Bonnie Prince Charlie; Scotland), 499 *(map)*, 500, 500 *(illus.)*
Charles I (king of England), 430, 449–450, 450 *(illus.)*, 450 *(map)*, 455 *(source document)*
Charles I (king of Spain), 372
Charles II (king of England), 451–452
Charles IV (king of France), 301
Charles IV (Wenceslas) of Bohemia, 300–301, 314
Charles IX (king of France), 411, 412
Charles Martel, Charles "the Hammer" (Carolingian), 211, 212, 214
Charles the Bald (Carolingian), 222, 223, 224 *(map)*, 226, 226 *(illus.)*, 237
Charles the Fat (Carolingian), 227
Charles V (Holy Roman emperor), 336, 394–395, 395 *(map)*, 398–399, 401
Charles V (the Wise; king of France), 313, 315
Charles VI (king of France), 315
Charles VII (the dauphin; king of France), 315–316
Charles VIII (king of France), 317, 334, 336
Charles X (king of France), 575
Charles XI (king of Sweden), 443
Charles XII (king of Sweden), 443–444
Charmides, 79
chartered (joint-stock) companies, 474, 474 *(illus.)*
Chartism (England), 576
Chartres cathedral, 267–268, 268 *(illus.)*, 269 *(illus.)*, 289
Chateaubriand, François-René de, 560, 578
Chauvet cave paintings (France), 2–3 *(illus.)*, 7, 9
Chechnya, 641, 840, 841 *(map)*, 842, 842 *(illus.)*, 859
Checkpoint Charlie (Berlin), 798–799 *(illus.)*, 839
Cheka (Russian secret police), 717, 734, 737, 771
Chelmno death camp, 784
Chernobyl nuclear reactor explosion, 826, 859
Chersonesus (Ukraine), 44 *(map)*, 45 *(illus.)*
chess, 317
chiaroscuro, 345, 347, 348
chickens, domestication of, 9
Childe Harold's Pilgrimage (Byron), 571, 572
Childeric (Frankish king), 164 *(illus.)*, 187

Childeric III (Merovingian), 211, 212
child labor, 682
children
    in Britain, in World War II, 774
    compulsory education for, 610, 672
    in domestic service, 609
    in the Great Famine, 299
    Nazis and, 768, 769–770
    in the Soviet Union, 737
    in Sparta, 56
Children's Games (Bruegel the Elder), 353
China
    Boxer Rebellion, 659
    Communist Revolution in, 809
    in the Great War, 711
    Indo-European migrations into, 11
    Japanese invasion of (1895), 652
    Japanese invasion of (1937), 777
    Jesuit missionaries in, 407, 407 *(illus.)*
    Opium Wars, 639–640
    plague in, 305
    Qing dynasty overthrow, 659
    rice domestication in, 10
    Sino-French War, 652
    Taiping Rebellion, 640, 652
    in World War II, 780 *(map)*
China Atlas (Richthofen), 646
Chios (Greece), 361
Chirico, Giorgi di, 748 *(illus.)*, 750
chivalry, 302–304, 303 *(illus.)*
chlorine gas, 704, 712
cholera, 643, 684
Chopin, Friedrich, 578
Chrétien de Troyes, 303
Christian Baptism (Menno), 406
Christian III (king of Denmark), 398
Christianity. *See also* Greek (Eastern)
        Orthodox Church; monasticism and
        monastic orders; Protestant
        Reformation; Roman Catholic Church
    Augustine and, 175–176
    bishops and hierarchy in, 172, 202–204
    Carolingians and, 212, 216–219
    chronology of, 175
    Clovis's conversion to, 187–188
    Cold War and, 821–822
    Council of Nicaea, 179
    desert and pillar fathers and mothers,
        170–171
    Donatism, 175–176
    early thinkers in, 170
    Great Schism, 245, 248, 253, 271
    Gregory the Great and, 201–202
    iconoclasm in, 209–210, 210 *(illus.)*
    institutional growth of, 180
    Investiture Controversy, 245–247, 246
        (illus.), 271
    life of Jesus in, 153
    millennium and the Second Coming,
        239, 241
    Nag Hammadi codices, 169
    from oral to authorized texts, 168–169,
        169 *(illus.)*
    orthodoxy in, 170
    Ottonian system, 239
    reforms to, Middle Ages, 244–247
    as Roman Empire state religion, 177–182
    Romanization of, 168–172, 171 *(map)*, 172
        (illus.)

Roman persecution of, 153, 168, 171,
        175–176
    Russian Orthodox Church, 442, 442
        (illus.), 506, 519, 576, 717, 822
    saints in, 203–204, 203 *(illus.)*
    spread of, 171 *(map)*
    spread of Islam and, 207–208
    Visigoths and, 183
Christian Socialist parties, 676, 685–686
Christina (queen of Sweden), 461, 485
A Christmas Carol (Dickens), 588
churches. *See* cathedrals
Churchill, Winston
    after World War II, 812
    in the Battle of Britain, 774
    on colonies, 814
    Dresden firebombing and, 791, 791
        (illus.)
    at Gallipoli, 710, 764
    in the Second Boer War, 660
    on war, 763–765, 764 *(illus.)*
Church of England (Anglican Church),
        401–402, 447, 448, 464
Cicero
    death of, 133–134, 134 *(illus.)*, 144
    Philippics, 144
    Renaissance scholars and, 341, 343, 344
    writings of, 126, 141–142, 150, 152
Cimon, 60, 61
Cinna (Roman consul general), 140
Circassians, 641, 642 *(illus.)*
circumcision, 30, 31
Cistercians, 268–269
cities and towns
    advantages of, 9, 12–13
    after the plague, 311
    birth of agriculture and, 9
    in the eastern Roman Empire, 191
    eighteenth-century, 467–468, 467 *(illus.)*,
        468 *(illus.)*
    emergence of, in Mesopotamia, 12–14, 14
        (map)
    in the fin de siècle, 670–672, 671 *(map)*,
        684, 685
    in the High Middle Ages, 274, 274 *(illus.)*
    poverty in, 468
    Protestant Reformation and, 399, 400
    transformed, in the nineteenth century,
        605–606
The City of God (Augustine), 176, 183
city-states
    in ancient Greece, 38, 39
    in Italian Renaissance, 330
    in Sumeria, 16
civic humanism, 343–344
Civil Constitution of the Clergy (France),
        533–534
civilization, characteristics of, 5–6, 12
Civil War, English, 449–450, 450 *(illus.)*, 450
        (map)
Civil War, Roman Republic, 142–144, 143
        (map)
Civil War, United States, 616–618, 617 *(illus.)*
Cixi (empress dowager of China), 659
Clarissa (Richardson), 510
classes. *See* social classes
Classical Age of Greece, 39, 56–66. *See also*
        Greece, ancient
Claudius (Roman emperor), 106

Claudius Pulcher, Publius, 118
cleanliness, 608
Cleisthenes, 58
Cleitus, 85
Clemenceau, Georges, 689
Clement II (Pope), 245
Clement V (Pope), 299
Clement VI (Pope), 308
Clement VII (Pope), 313, 401
Cleopatra VII (Egyptian queen), 143,
        144–146, 146 *(illus.)*
clergy. *See also* monasticism and monastic
        orders
    after Napoleon, 569–570
    in Bismarck's Germany, 624
    in the eighteenth century, 462–464, 463
        (illus.)
    in the French Revolution, 534, 539, 542
    Luther on, 396–397
    in the Old Regimes, 462–464, 463 *(illus.)*
clientage, 111, 112, 136
climate
    during Carolingian period, 219
    French Revolution and, 529, 530
    from ice core data, 219
    Little Ice Age, 295–297, 295 *(illus.)*, 296
        (illus.)
    Medieval Warm Period, 253, 273, 295
    seventeeth-century crises and, 425, 425
        (illus.)
    year without a summer (1816–1817),
        569
Clinton, Bill, 845
clocks, railroads and, 584
Clothar (Merovingian), 206
Clothar II (Merovingian), 206
The Clouds (Aristophanes), 78
Clovis (Franks), 187–188, 203
Cluniacs, 244–245
Cluny monastery, 244–245, 244 *(illus.)*
Cnut (king of Denmark, Norway, and
        England), 242, 248
coal
    air pollution from, 611
    in Britain, 580, 581 *(map)*, 586, 586 *(illus.)*,
        611
Code of Hammurabi, 17, 17 *(illus.)*
Codreanu, Cornelius, 745, 745 *(illus.)*
Coeur, Jacques, 316
co-evolution, domestication as, 8
coffee, in the Enlightenment, 516
coffee houses, in the Enlightenment, 497,
        497 *(illus.)*
coins. *See also* currency and money
    Archaic Greek, 48
    Hellenistic, 90, 90 *(illus.)*, 94
    from Italia, 139
    Roman, 125, 166
Colbert, Jean-Baptiste, 474–475, 485
Cold War, 799–830
    baby boom generation, 811–812, 820–821,
        821 *(illus.)*
    Berlin in, 806–808, 807 *(illus.)*, 828, 828
        (illus.)
    Brezhnev Doctrine, 810–811
    changes after World War II, 802–803
    Christianity and, 821–822
    communism's last years, 825–827, 826
        (illus.)

Cold War (continued)
  communist successes in, 809
  Conservatives in, 825
  culture in, 818–822, 819 (illus.), 820 (illus.), 821 (illus.)
  decolonialization in, 813–818, 814 (map), 815 (illus.)
  eastern Europe in, 803–805, 806–811, 808 (illus.), 810 (illus.)
  end of, 827–830, 828 (illus.)
  European Economic Community, 806 (map), 812–813, 823
  Greek civil war, 805, 813
  Hungarian uprising, 808–809, 808 (illus.)
  Iron Curtain in, 795, 802–803, 802 (map), 829
  map of Europe (1945–1949), 802 (map)
  NATO and Warsaw Pact in, 805, 806 (map)
  in 1968, 810, 810 (illus.), 821, 821 (illus.)
  nonaligned nations in, 817
  Prague Spring, 810, 810 (illus.)
  in the 1970s and 1980s, 822–825, 823 (illus.)
  sexual revolution, 823, 823 (illus.)
  Soviet bloc in, 803–805, 804 (illus.), 806 (map)
  space program in, 809
  timeline, 800–801 (illus.)
  Truman Doctrine, 805
  western Europe in, 805–806, 806 (map), 811–813, 822–825
Cole, Juan, 547
collectivization, Soviet, 734–735, 735 (illus.), 803
colonization. See also imperialism
  from 1650 to 1740, 473 (map)
  by Archaic Greek civilization, 44–45, 44 (map), 45 (illus.)
  criticism of, 378, 380
  decolonization after World War II, 814–818, 814 (map)
  by the Dutch, 447
  economic impact of, 377–378
  encomienda system, 377–378
  by England, 375, 451
  by Genoa, 361–362
  native narratives of, 379, 379 (illus.)
  pirates and, 475
  by Portugal, 364–365, 380–382
  religious conversion in, 378
  by Spain, 370, 375–380, 377 (illus.)
  by Venice, 339
colons, 639
Columbian Exchange, 369, 369 (illus.), 648
Columbus, Christopher, 362, 366–370, 367 (illus.)
Cominform (Communist Information Bureau), 803
Comintern, 742
commerce and trade
  from African colonies, 655, 657
  by Carolingians, 220
  by Carthage, 121
  chartered companies, 474, 474 (illus.)
  in the commercial revolution, 473–476, 473 (map), 474 (illus.), 476 (illus.)
  by Dutch, in Asia, 382, 447, 653, 653 (illus.)
  by Egypt, ancient, 19
  by English, in Asia, 382, 474, 480–481, 635–637, 637 (illus.)
  by Etruscans, 106–107, 108
  European Economic Community, 806 (map), 812–813
  in the European Renaissance, 349–350, 361
  by France, seventeenth-century, 437
  by Greece, ancient, 39–40, 48
  by Greece, Athens, 64
  Hebrews and, 32
  Hellenistic, 93–94
  in the High Middle Ages, 274–276, 275 (map)
  iron in, 28, 32
  in Italian Renaissance, 330–331, 330 (illus.)
  letters of credit in, 338
  map of (1650–1740), 473 (map)
  mercantilism, 474–475, 499
  Minoans and, 25
  Mycenaeans and, 26–27
  Phoenicians and, 28, 28 (map)
  political spectrum on (1815–1850), 564–567, 565 (illus.)
  by Portugal, 363–365, 364 (map), 380–382
  in the Restoration era, 568–569
  Roman Empire and, 166
  Roman Republic and, 125
  by Scotland, 498
  tariffs and, 474–475, 587–588
  by Venice, 337–339, 338 (map)
Committee of Public Safety, 538–539, 543
Commodus (Roman emperor), 159, 166, 167 (illus.)
Commonwealth of Independent States (CIS), 840
communes
  in the High Middle Ages, 276
  in medieval Italy, 330
  Paris Commune, 623–624, 623 (illus.), 668
communication technology
  in Europe, after 1989, 853–855
  in the Great War, 712–713
  imperialism and, 650
communism. See also Soviet Union
  in the Balkans, 776
  in Bulgaria, 734
  in China, 777, 778, 809
  collapse of, 825–830, 828 (illus.)
  Comintern, 742
  in Cuba, 809
  in eastern Europe, after the Great War, 744–746, 745 (illus.)
  in East Germany, 799–801, 829
  fascism vs., 742, 743–744, 754–755
  Great War and, 703
  Ho Chi Minh and, 740
  life under, 825–826
  Marx and Engels on, 565, 567, 589, 608, 611, 683–684
  national, 804–805, 804 (illus.)
  in the Paris Commune, 623 (illus.)
  Russian Revolution, 716–719, 717 (illus.)
  in Southeast Asia, 815
  in the Soviet bloc, 770, 802 (map), 803, 804–805, 804 (illus.), 808–811
  in the Soviet Union, 718, 719, 729–731, 734–738

in the Spanish Civil War, 758–759
  World War II and, 766
Communist Manifesto (Marx and Engels), 567, 589
Communist Youth League, 736
Comnena, Anna, 253
compasses, 366
computers
  modern, 853–855, 854 (illus.)
  Roman, 156, 156 (illus.)
Comte, Auguste, 611
concentration camps, 769, 769 (illus.), 782–784, 783 (map), 784 (illus.), 788
Concert of Europe, 561
conciliar movement, 313, 331
Conclusiones (Pico della Mirandola), 345
Concordat (France), 544, 548
Concordat (Germany), 755
The Condition of the Working Class in England (Engels), 565, 593 (source document)
Condorcet, Marquis de, 542
Confessions (Augustine), 176, 326
Confraternity of the Immaculate Heart of Mary, 676
Confutation (Eck), 403–404
Congo
  colonization of, 656–657, 656 (illus.), 657 (map), 662 (source document)
  independence of, 814 (map), 817
Congress of Vienna, 561–562, 564 (map)
conquistadors, 359, 372–374, 376–380
Conrad (Francia), 238–239
Conrad, Joseph, 657
conservatives
  after the revolutions of 1848, 597, 600
  in Britain, 643, 652, 686
  on capitalism, 600
  clergy as, 600
  Congress of Vienna and, 561–562, 564 (map)
  in the early nineteenth century, 565 (illus.), 567
  in eastern Europe, 600
  French Revolution and, 542, 544, 575, 623
  in Germany, 624, 744, 752, 754
  in Italy, 574
  nationalism and, 688
  in the political spectrum, 563, 565, 567
  in Russia, 600
  Tories renamed as, 598
  women's equality and, 747
Considerations on the Causes of the Greatness of the Romans and Their Decline (Montesquieu), 502
The Consolation of Philosophy (Boethius), 187
Constantine (Roman emperor), 175, 177–179, 178 (illus.), 181 (map), 194 (source document)
Constantine V (Byzantine emperor), 210
Constantine XI (Byzantine emperor), 318
Constantinople. See also Istanbul
  bubonic plague in, 191, 306, 306 (map)
  Byzantine Empire and, 209–210, 209 (map)
  Christianity in, 172
  conquest by Ottoman Turks, 318, 319, 319 (illus.)
  Constantine in, 178, 178 (illus.), 179
  First Crusade and, 255, 271
  Fourth Crusade attack on, 271–272

Hagia Sophia in, 189, 189 *(illus.)*, 318
iceberg in, 219
Justinian in, 188–192, 188 *(illus.)*, 189
    (illus.), 190 *(map)*
Latin Empire of, 272, 337
Liudprand of Cremona in, 240
in the tenth century, 240, 240 *(map)*
Viking attacks on, 226
Constantius II (Roman emperor), 179
Constitutent Assembly (France), 534, 535
constitutions
    in Austria-Hungary, 691
    in Belgium, 656
    in Britain, 280, 502, 603
    in the European Union (proposed), 848
    in France, 531, 532–535, 537–538, 543–544,
        560, 575
    in Germany, 589, 591, 624, 742–743, 752
    in Italy, 741
    in Japan, 640
    in Romania, 745
    in the Roman Republic, 110
    in Sicily, 588
    in Spain, 758
    in Sweden, 444
    in the United States, 497, 529, 568
    in Yugoslavia, 746
Constitutions (Loyola), 407
consul generals, Roman, 138–141
consuls, Roman, 109, 110, 111 *(illus.)*
consumer goods
    in the Cold War, 824, 824 *(illus.)*
    in eastern Europe, under Stalin, 804
    in Europe, after 1989, 851–853, 852 *(illus.)*
    in the fin de siècle, 664–665 *(illus.)*, 680,
        681, 681 *(illus.)*
    in the Old Regimes, 472–473
    in the Soviet Union, 809, 809 *(illus.)*
    in Victorian Britain, 608, 609–610
Contarini, Lorenzo, 340
Continental system, 551–552, 554
Convention (France), 537, 538–542
conversos, 367, 368
Cook, Captain James, 514
Cook, Thomas, 672
cookbooks, 517, 609
Cooking for Royalty and for the Bourgeois
    (Massialot), 517
Copernicus, Nicolaus, 482–483
Copper Age, 5 *(illus.)*, 7, 11
Le Corbusier, (Charles-Édouard Jeanneret),
    750
Corday, Charlotte, 538
Córdoba, 215–216, 216 *(illus.)*
Corinne, or Italy (de Staël), 526–527, 578
Corinth. *See also* Greece, ancient
    after the Peloponnesian War, 74
    coins in, 48
    culture of, 64
    Delian League and, 61, 63
    in the Persian Wars, 53, 54, 54 *(map)*
    Roman destruction of, 128
Corinthian War, 74
Corneille, Pierre, 432
Cornivus, Mattias (king of Hungary), 349
Corn Laws (England), 587–588, 601
Corpus of Civil Law (Justinian), 285
corruption
    in Europe, after 1989, 857–858, 857 *(illus.)*

religious, 244–247, 271
    in the Roman Republic, 136, 138
Cortés, Hernán, 358, 372–374, 377 *(illus.)*
corvée, 470
corvus, 121
cosmological revolution, 482–484
cottage industries, 274, 276, 472–473, 528,
    581, 586
cotton, Industrial Revolution and, 581, 582
Council for Mutual Economic Assistance
    (COMECON), 806, 806 *(map)*
Council of Basel, 313, 331, 342
Council of Constance, 313, 314 *(illus.)*
Council of Nicaea, 179
Council of Trent, 408–409, 426
Counter Reformation. *See* Catholic
    Reformation
The Count of Monte Cristo (Dumas), 578
Courbet, Gustave, 612
courtesans, 332. *See also* prostitutes
covenant, 29, 30, 32
Cranach, Lucas, 388 *(illus.)*, 391 *(illus.)*, 400
    (illus.)
Cranmer, Thomas, 401, 402
Crassus (Roman consul general), 141, 142
Crécy, Battle of (1346), 301, 302 *(illus.)*, 304
creoles, 634
Crete
    Greek uprisings in, 625
    Minoan civilization, 5 *(illus.)*, 25–26, 26
        (illus.), 26 *(map)*
Crimean War, 604, 615–616, 616 *(illus.)*
Critias, 79
Critique of Judgment (Kant), 508, 577
Critique of Practical Reason (Kant), 507–508
Critique of Pure Reason (Kant), 507
Croatia/Croatians
    in the Austro-Hungarian partition, 627
    Catholicism in, 838
    independence of, 844–845, 845 *(map)*
    in World War II, 776, 776 *(illus.)*
Croesus (king of Lydia), 52
Crompton, Samuel, 582
Cromwell, Oliver, 449–450, 451
Cromwell, Thomas, 401
"crony" capitalism, 843
Crosby, Alfred, 648, 669
crossbows, 301, 302 *(illus.)*
The Crowd (Le Bon), 695 *(source document)*
Crusades
    First, 254–256, 255 *(map)*, 256 *(illus.)*,
        258–259 *(source document)*
    Fourth, 271–272, 272 *(illus.)*
    Peasants', 255
    Second, 268–269
    Third, 269–270, 270 *(illus.)*
Crusoe, Robinson, 491–493, 492 *(illus.)*
Crystal Palace Exhibition (1851), 610, 610
    (illus.)
Cuba, communism in, 809
Culloden, Battle of (1746), 499 *(map)*, 500
Cult of the Supreme Being, 542
culture
    Baroque, 431–435, 434 *(illus.)*
    Carolingian, 216–218, 217 *(illus.)*, 218
        (illus.)
    Cold War, 818–822, 819 *(illus.)*, 820 *(illus.)*,
        821 *(illus.)*
    diversity in, 858

fin de siècle, 673–679, 674 *(illus.)*, 675
    (illus.), 677 *(illus.)*, 678 *(illus.)*
Greek, Archaic, 48–49
Greek, Athenian, 63–66, 64 *(illus.)*, 68
    (source document)
Hellenistic, 77–82, 78 *(illus.)*, 79 *(illus.)*, 81
    (illus.)
interwar, 748–752, 748 *(illus.)*, 749 *(illus.)*,
    750 *(illus.)*
mass, 674–675, 674 *(illus.)*
modernism, 675, 675 *(illus.)*, 677–678, 677
    (illus.), 678 *(illus.)*
Restoration, 576–580, 577 *(illus.)*, 578
    (illus.)
Roman Republic, 126–129
youth, 751–752
cuneiform writing, 5, 14–15, 14 *(illus.)*, 27, 52
Curchod, Suzanne, 525
Curie, Marie, 673
currency and money. *See also* banks and
    finance
    after the revolutions of 1848, 601
    in Berlin, in the Cold War, 806–807
    in the Carolingian empire, 220
    in the Central Middle Ages, 254
    euros, 849–850, 850 *(illus.)*, 860–862
    in the French Revolution, 533–534
    in the German reunification, 838
    in the Great Depression, 753
    in Greece, Archaic, 48
    Hellenistic, 90, 90 *(illus.)*, 94
    inflation, in the former Soviet Union,
        843
    inflation, in the Great War, 715
    inflation, in the Weimar Republic, 743,
        744
    International Monetary Fund, 805–806,
        862
    Roman Empire, 175
    Roman Republic, 125
    United States, off the gold standard, 823
    in Venice, 337
curule, 108
Curzio, 127
Cybele the Great Mother, 151
Cynics, 95–96
Cyprus, 9, 40
Cyrene (Libya), 44 *(map)*, 45
Cyrus (king of Persia), 51, 52
Cyrus the Younger, 74
Czechoslovakia. *See also* Prague
    church in, 314
    Czechs, in the Austro-Hungarian
        Empire, 691, 692 *(map)*
    German annexation of, 766–767, 767
        (map)
    independence of Slovakia from, 844
    in the interwar years, 746
    Prague Spring, 810, 810 *(illus.)*
    purging Communists in, 841
    in the Soviet bloc, 802 *(map)*, 803, 804,
        810, 810 *(illus.)*
    velvet revolution in, 829

Dachau, concentration camp at, 759
Dacia, in the Roman Empire, 159, 159 *(map)*
Dada, 748, 750
Dagestan, 641
Dagobert (Merovingian), 206

The Daily Mail (London), 674
Daladier, Edouard, 766
D'Alembert, Jean, 511
Dali, Salvador, 750
Damascus, 32, 207 *(map)*, 208 *(illus.)*
dance of death *(danse macabre)*, 312
Danes, in England, 241
Dante Alighieri, 288, 300, 338, 343
Darius (king of Persia), 51–54, 83 *(map)*,
    84–85, 85 *(illus.)*
Dark Age of Greece, 39–42, 40 *(illus.)*, 42
    (illus.). *See also* Greece, ancient
The Dark Night of the Soul (John of the
    Cross), 408
Darwin, Charles, 612, 613
David (king of Israel), 29, 31–32
David, Jacques Louis, 524 *(illus.)*, 538, 542,
    549 *(illus.)*
David Dances Naked before God, 218 *(illus.)*
Dawes, Arthur, 744
Dawes Plan, 744
Dayton Accords (1995), 846
D-Day, 789–790
dead reckoning, 366
Death in Hamburg (Evans), 684
death masks, Roman, 117–118, 117 *(illus.)*
Death of the Virgin (Caravaggio), 409–410,
    409 *(illus.)*
death rituals. *See* burials and death rituals
De Beers Diamond Company, 632, 636
Deborah (Hebrew), 30
Debussy, Claude, 678
Decameron (Boccaccio), 308, 309 *(illus.)*
Decembrist revolt (Russia), 576, 576 *(illus.)*
de Châtelet, Madame, 502, 503 *(illus.)*
Decius (Roman emperor), 167, 171
Declaration of Independence (United
    States), 529
Declaration of the Rights of Man (France),
    532–533, 563
Declaration of the Rights of Woman and the
    Female Citizen (France), 542
deconstructionism, 855
Defender of the Peace (Marsilius), 300
Defenestration of Prague, 426–427
Defoe, Daniel, 491, 510–511
de Gaulle, Charles, 773, 812, 817, 821
deism, 502, 518
Delacroix, Eugene, 571 *(illus.)*
Delftware, 472
Delian League, 60–63, 64
Del Medigo, Elijah, 342
Delos (Greece), 126
demes, 58
Demetrius I (ruler of Bactria), 89–90, 90
    (illus.)
demilitarized zone (DMZ; Korea), 815, 817
democracy
    Athenian, 47, 58–59, 74
    in the interwar years, 738, 741
    in the Weimar Republic, 741–742, 742
        (illus.)
    in western Europe, after 1989, 846–847
Democracy in America (Tocqueville), 560
Les Demoiselles d'Avignon (Picasso), 677
demos, 47, 58, 62
Demosthenes, 75–76, 77, 82, 86
demotic script, 20
denarius, 125, 166, 175, 198 *(illus.)*

Denis the Areopagite, 267
Denmark
    in the Thirty Years War, 428–430, 429
        (illus.)
    in World War II, 772
department stores, 664–665 *(illus.)*, 681, 681
    (illus.)
Derrida, Jacques, 855
Descartes, René, 482, 485
The Descent of Man (Darwin), 612, 613
de Staël, Madame (Anne-Louise-Germaine
    Necker), 525–527, 525 *(illus.)*, 548, 578
détente, 822
determinatives, 20
deutsche marks, 806–807
devotio moderna, 312
Dhuoda (Carolingian), 225
*Dialogue Concerning the Two Chief World
    Systems* (Galileo), 483
Dialogues (Gregory the Great), 202
diamonds, 632, 632 *(map)*, 654–655, 655
    (illus.)
*The Diary of an Austrian Middle-Class Woman
    1914–1924* (Eisenmenger), 727 *(source
    document)*
Diaspora, Hebrew, 32
Díaz del Castillo, Bernal, 357–359, 372, 377
Dickens, Charles, 587, 588, 612
Dictation of the Pope, 246, 247
Didascalicon (Hugh of St. Victor), 266
Diderot, Denis, 503–504, 511–512, 512 *(illus.)*
diet
    adulterated foodstuffs in, 670–671
    in Augustan Rome, 154
    Carolingian, 221
    in Egypt, ancient, 24
    in the Enlightenment, 516, 517, 517 *(illus.)*
    in the Great Famine, 299
    in the Great War, 714
    Jewish codes on, 31
    of sailors, 372
digital revolution, 853–855, 854 *(illus.)*
Dinocrates of Rhodes, 72
diocese, 202
Diocletian (Roman emperor), 166, 172–176,
    173 *(illus.)*, 174 *(illus.)*, 174 *(map)*
Diogenes, 95
Dionysus (god), 36 *(illus.)*, 65, 75, 77–78, 151
diplomacy, 25, 339
Directory (France), 543, 544, 545, 546
disabilities, Nazis and, 768, 769
Discalced Carmelites, 408
*Discourse on the Method of Rightly Conducting
    One's Reason . . .* (Descartes), 485
"Discourse on the Origin of Inequality"
    (Rousseau), 504
discrimination. *See also* anti-Semitism
    against Europeanized Africans, 638, 638
        (illus.)
    in the Hellenistic Ages, 92–93
    against immigrants, 848, 859
The Discus Thrower (Myron), 64 *(illus.)*
diseases. *See also* pandemics; plague
    in Africa, 637, 639
    in Americas after Columbus, 369, 374
        (illus.), 376
    cholera epidemic in Hamburg, 684
    in cities of the eighteenth century, 467
    in colonial soldiers, 643–644

    in Egypt, ancient, 24
    inoculations against, 484–485
    Justinian's Plague, 191
    mental illness as, 748, 771, 782
    in Peloponnesian War, 63
    smallpox, 369, 374 *(illus.)*, 376, 484–485
Disraeli, Benjamin, 601
The Dissolute Household (Steen), 433, 434
    (illus.)
Divine Comedy (Dante), 288, 300, 338, 343
divine right, 424
divorce
    in Augustan Rome, 154
    in the Byzantine Empire, 189
    of Henry VIII, 401–402, 402 *(illus.)*
    in Napoleonic Code, 548
Dix, Otto, 696–697 *(illus.)*
doge (Venice), 339
dogs, domestication of, 8
Dollfuss, Englebert, 759
Domesday Book, 250
domestic service, 609, 609 *(illus.)*
domestic violence, industrialization and,
    586–587
Dominic, Saint, 273, 277
Dominicans
    formation of, 273
    as mendicants, 277–278, 286
    Savonarola as, 334
    in Spanish colonies, 378, 380
    translation of Aristotle by, 288
Domitian, 157, 158
Donatello, 345, 346–347
Donation of Constantine, 212, 314, 344
Donation of Pepin, 212–213
Donatism, 175–176, 179
Don Giovanni (Mozart), 518
donkeys, domestication of, 9
Don Quixote de la Mancha (Cervantes), 304,
    433
Dorians, 27, 40, 56
Doric design, 49
Dostoyevsky, Fyodor, 677, 683
Dr. Strangelove (Kubrick), 818
Dr. Zhivago (Pasternak), 820, 826
Draco (Athenian ruler), 47
Drake, Sir Francis, 414, 475
drama. *See* theater
Drancourt, Michel, 307
Dresden, firebombing of, 791, 791 *(illus.)*
Dreyfus affair, 689–690, 690 *(illus.)*
Drouet, Jean-Baptiste, 535
Drowning of the Dummies, 119
Drumont, Édouard, 688–689, 690 *(illus.)*
Dubček, Alexander, 810
dueling, 466
Dumas, Alexandre, 578
Dunkirk beach, in World War II, 773
Duns Scotus, 313
Durkheim, Émile, 678
dust-veils, 190–191
Dutch East India Company, 382, 447, 474–475,
    474 *(illus.)*
Dutch East Indies, 447, 653, 653 *(illus.)*. *See
    also* Indonesia
Dutch Republic. *See also* Netherlands
    American colony of, 451
    banking in, 474
    commerce of, 451, 474–475, 474 *(illus.)*

cottage industries in, 472
Enlightenment in, 495–496, 496 (illus.)
formation of, 413, 413 (map)
in the French Revolution, 540
government in, 447
peasants, eighteenth-century, 470
in the Thirty Years' War, 430
Dutch Revolt, 413, 413 (map), 414, 426
Dutschke, Rudi, 820
Dylan, Bob, 819
dysentery, 643

Early Dynastic Egypt, 20
Early Middle Ages, 197–227. See also
      Carolingians
   al-Andalus, in Spain, 215–216, 216 (illus.)
   bishops in, 202–204
   Byzantine Empire in, 209–210, 209 (map)
   Carolingian culture, 216–222, 217 (illus.),
      218 (illus.), 221 (illus.)
   Carolingian empire division, 222–227,
      224 (map)
   Carolingian rise, 210–216, 214 (map)
   Gregory the Great in, 201–202, 201 (illus.)
   Islam in, 206–208, 207 (map)
   Merovingians in, 187–188, 202–206, 205
      (illus.), 211–213
   monasticism in, 199–201, 218–219
   saints in, 203–204, 203 (illus.)
   timeline of, 199–200 (illus.)
   Viking raids in, 224–226, 224 (illus.)
eastern bloc (eastern Europe)
   collapse of communism in, 827–830
   countries in, 806 (map)
   East Germany, 799–801, 800 (illus.), 802
      (map), 807–808, 807 (illus.), 828–829,
      828 (illus.)
   economy in, 803–804, 805
   Hungarian uprising (1956), 808–809, 808
      (illus.)
   Poland in, 802 (map), 803–804, 808, 811,
      828
   Prague Spring, 810, 810 (illus.)
   Soviet prison camps and, 803
Eastern Orthodox Church. See Greek
      (Eastern) Orthodox Church
Eastern Question, 616, 651
eastern Roman Empire, 185 (map). See also
      Byzantine Empire
   as Byzantine Empire, 209–210, 209 (map)
   Constantinople creation and, 179
   under Justinian, 188–192, 188 (illus.), 189
      (illus.), 190 (map)
East Germany, 799–801, 802 (map), 807–808,
      807 (illus.), 828–829, 828 (illus.). See
      also Germany
Eastlake, Charles L., 609
East-West Schism, 245, 248, 253, 271–272
Ebert, Friedrich, 719
Ebionite Christians, 170
Ebo Gospels, 218
Ecclesiastical Ordinances (Calvin), 403
Eck, Johann, 394, 403–404
eclecticism, 313
eclipse, lunar, 221–222
economy
   after the plague, 310
   capital, in the Industrial Revolution,
      584–585

in the Central Middle Ages, 253–254
command, 715
in eastern Europe, after World War II,
      803–804
Euro crisis, 860–862
in the fin de siècle, 679–682, 680 (illus.),
      681 (illus.), 682 (illus.)
in the French Revolution, 530, 533–534,
      539
in Gaul, 205–206
in the Great Depression, 738, 752, 753,
      753 (illus.)
during the Great War, 715
in Greece, Archaic, 47–48, 48 (illus.), 51
Hellenistic, 94–95
in the High Middle Ages, 272–276, 274
      (illus.), 275 (map)
mercantilism, 474–475
political spectrum on (1815–1850),
      564–567, 565 (illus.)
in the Restoration era, 568–569
in the Roman Empire, 173, 175, 191
in the Roman Republic, 125–126
Smith, Adam, on, 498–499, 501
social market, after 1989, 847
sovereign debt crisis, 860–862
Spanish colonization and, 377–378
tariffs and, 474–475, 587–588
in the Weimar Republic, 743
in western Europe, after World War II,
      805–806
ECSC (European Coal and Steel
      Community), 812
Ecstasy of Saint Teresa of Ávila (Bernini), 410
Edgar (king of England), 241
Edict of Milan (313), 177
Edict of Nantes (1598), 412, 438–439
Edict of Worms (1521), 395, 396, 398–399
Edison, Thomas Alva, 665
education
   in Athens, 68 (source document)
   cathedral schools, 264–266, 282–283
   under Charlemagne, 216–217
   compulsory, 610, 672
   Encyclopédie (Diderot) and, 504, 511–512,
      512 (illus.)
   in the fin de siècle, 672
   Luther on, 392
   monastic schools, 264, 266–267
   renaissance humanism and, 329, 343–344
   in Russia, under Alexander II, 606
   scholasticism and, 283, 287–288
   translating wisdom of the west, 283
   universal elementary, 508
   of women, 266, 511
Education of an Orator (Quintilian), 343
Edward, the Black Prince (England),
      301–303, 304
Edward I (king of England), 301
Edward III (king of England), 301, 304
Edward the Confessor (king of England), 248
Edward VI (king of England), 402, 413
EEC (European Economic Community), 806
      (map), 812–813, 823, 849. See also
      European Union
Egypt. See also Egypt, ancient
   as British protectorate, 652
   independence from Britain, 739, 739 (map)
   Islam in, 207 (map)

Mameluke rulers of, 380–381
Napoleon in, 545–546, 546 (map), 547, 547
      (illus.)
as nonaligned nation, 817
Suez Canal, 650, 651–652, 651 (illus.), 817
in World War II, 775–776, 789
Egypt, ancient, 18–24
   agriculture in, 18–19, 19 (map)
   Alexander in, 71–72, 83 (map), 84
   Alexandria in, 71–72, 84, 88, 89 (map),
      97–98
   Canaan invasion by, 30
   cats in, 9
   dynasties and kingdoms in, 20–22, 21
      (illus.)
   hieroglyphics in, 19–20
   Hyksos invasion, 19 (map), 22
   international relations of, 25
   life in, 23–24, 24 (illus.)
   Lower vs. Upper, 19, 19 (map), 20
   map of (1450 BCE), 26 (map)
   in Persian Empire, 51
   Ptolemaic kingdom of, 71–73, 88, 89
      (map), 143, 143 (map)
   religion in, 22–23
   Sea Raiders and, 27
   stability of, 18
Eichmann, Adolf, 782, 792–793, 818
Eichmann in Jerusalem (Arendt), 818, 820
eighteenth century. See Enlightenments;
      French Revolution; Old Regimes
      (seventeenth and eighteenth centuries)
eighth century. See Early Middle Ages
Einhard, 216, 229 (source document)
Einsatzgruppen, 780, 782, 782 (illus.)
Einstein, Albert, 679, 750, 754
Eisenmenger, Anna, 727 (source document)
Eisenstein, Sergei, 749
El (goddess), 30
Eleanor of Aquitaine, 281, 281 (illus.)
electricity, power from, 680
electrum, 48
Elements (Euclid), 97
eleventh century. See Romanesque Central
      Middle Ages
Elgin, Thomas Bruce, Lord, 572, 572 (illus.),
      640
Elgin marbles, 572, 648
El Greco, 443
Eliot, T. S., 751
Elisabeth (princess of Bohemia), 485
Elizabeth (czarina of Russia), 479
Elizabeth I (queen of England), 413–415, 414
      (illus.)
Ellington, Duke, 751
El Niño, seventeenth-century turmoil and,
      425, 425 (illus.)
Emancipation Proclamation (United States),
      617
emigration, fin-de-siècle, 669–670, 670 (illus.)
émigrés, 532, 535, 539–540, 544, 548
Emile (Rousseau), 504, 505, 522 (source
      document)
empiricism, 482
enclosure, 471, 472 (illus.)
encomienda system, 377–378
Encyclopédie (Diderot), 504, 511–512, 512
      (illus.)

endangered animals, 646
Ending the French Revolution (Brown), 544
Enfantin, Barthélemy Prosper, 566, 566 *(illus.)*
Engels, Friedrich, 565, 589, 593 *(source
  document),* 611, 683
England. *See also* Britain
  Anglo-Saxon kingdoms in, 241–242, 241
    (map), 251
  break with Roman Catholic Church, 398,
    401–402, 402 *(illus.)*
  Charles I and the Civil War, 449–450, 450
    (illus.), 450 *(map)*
  Christianization of, 202
  coffee houses, in the Enlightenment, 497,
    497 *(illus.)*
  cottage industries in, 472, 581
  Elizabeth I and the Spanish Armada,
    413–415, 414 *(illus.)*
  enclosure, 471, 472 *(illus.)*
  Enlightenment in, 496–498, 497 *(illus.)*
  French and Indian War and, 479–480
  Glorious Revolution in, 452–453, 498
  Great Famine in, 297–298
  in the High Middle Ages, 278 *(map),*
    280–281, 281 *(illus.)*
  under James I and IV, 447, 449
  Magna Carta and monarchy in, 273, 280
  Norman invasion of, 248, 250, 251
  North American colonies of, 375, 451,
    480, 814–815
  papal control over, 271
  Parliamentary powers in, 424, 426
  peasants, after the plague, 310–311
  peasants, eighteenth-century, 470
  plague in, 306 *(map),* 308
  Protestant Reformation in, 389
  Restoration in, 451–452, 452 *(illus.)*
  in the Roman Empire, 157, 159 *(map),* 167
  in the Seven Years' War, 439, 477–478,
    478 *(map),* 479, 480
  slavery and, 497
  in the Thirty Years' War, 428
  trade with Asia, 382, 474, 480, 481,
    635–637, 637 *(illus.)*
  under the Tudor kings, 317
  as United Kingdom of Great Britain, 498
  Viking raids and settlements in, 224,
    226, 241–242
  War of the Roses, 315, 317
  wool trade in, 275
English language, 241, 855–856
Enigma code, 772
enlightened absolutism, 506
The Enlightenment Bible (Sheehan), 519
Enlightenments, 491–520
  in Austria, 508–509
  as a cause of the French Revolution, 529
  in central Europe, 505–509
  diet in, 516, 517, 517 *(illus.)*
  in the Dutch Republic, 495–496, 496
    (illus.)
  education in, 504, 511–512, 512 *(illus.)*
  in England, 496–498, 497 *(illus.)*
  ethnography in, 515, 515 *(illus.)*
  in France, 490–491 *(illus.),* 501–505, 503
    (illus.), 504 *(illus.)*
  gardening in, 513–514, 514 *(illus.)*
  in Germany, 507–508, 507 *(map)*
  impacts of, 518–520

  in Italy, 509–510
  literature in, 497, 502–504, 510–512
  music in, 510, 516, 518, 518 *(illus.)*
  origins of, 494–495
  pornography in, 512
  religion in, 502–503, 505, 518–520
  Robinson Crusoe in, 491–493, 492 *(illus.)*
  in Russia, 506–507, 506 *(illus.)*
  salons in, 490–491 *(illus.)*
  in Scotland, 498–501, 499 *(map),* 500
    (illus.)
  in Spain and Portugal, 508
  timeline of, 492–493 *(illus.)*
  travel in, 509–510, 512–513, 513 *(illus.)*
  women in, 511
Enneads (Plotinus), 167–168
Ennius, 126
Entente (Allied Powers; Great War), 702, 702
  (map). See also specific countries
environmental issues. *See also* climate
  in cities, in the fin de siècle, 670–671, 684
  in Europe, after 1989, 859
  in the High Middle Ages, 273–274
Epaminondas, 74–75
Ephesus (Turkey), 52, 191
ephors, 56
The Epic of Gilgamesh, 16, 18
Epicureans, 95–96, 141
Epidaurus, Theater of, 98 *(illus.)*
epidemics. *See* diseases; pandemics
Epirus, under Roman rule, 125
equality
  in the American Revolution, 529
  in early nineteenth century, 563
  in the French Revolution, 532, 533,
    536–537, 538, 542
  liberals on, 563
  in the Napoleonic Code, 548
equestrians (Roman class), 138, 141
Erasmus, Desiderius, 351–352, 352 *(illus.),*
  387–388, 388 *(illus.)*
Eratosthenes of Cyrene, 96, 96 *(illus.)*
Eriugena (John the Scot), 226
Ernst, Max, 750
An Essay on Human Understanding (Locke),
  497
An Essay on the Principle of Population
  (Malthus), 579, 612
Essenes, 150
Estates General (France), 437, 439, 530–531,
  686
Esterhazy, Nicholas, 465, 465 *(illus.)*
Estonia
  independence of, 840, 841 *(map)*
  Soviet invasion and occupation of, 767
    (map), 771
  in the Soviet Union, 802 *(map),* 804–805
Ethical Policy (1901; Netherlands), 653, 659
Ethiopia, 658, 758
ethnic cleansing
  of Armenians, 706, 709, 710 *(illus.)*
  in the Balkans, 627, 844–845
  in the Caucasus, 641, 642 *(illus.)*
  in German Southwest Africa, 691
  Great War and, 700
  of Greeks in Turkey, 725
  of Jews in the Holocaust, 782–784, 782
    (illus.), 783 *(map),* 784 *(illus.)*
  in the Soviet Union breakup, 840

ethnography, 515, 515 *(illus.)*
Etruscans
  alphabet of, 29 *(illus.),* 105
  culture of, 105–109, 106 *(illus.),* 107 *(illus.),*
    108 *(illus.),* 109 *(illus.)*
  decline of, 113–114
  Greek trade with, 48, 108
Etrusco-Italic art, 108, 108 *(illus.)*
Eucharist, 399, 402, 409
Euclid, 97
Eugene Onegin (Pushkin), 578
eugenics, 613, 679, 747
Eugenius IV (Pope), 313, 331
EU Parliament, 850
Euphrates River, 13, 13 *(map),* 18
Euripides, 65, 77–78
Euro crisis, 860–862
Europa, 214
Europe
  after World War II, 802 *(map)*
  definitions of, 836–838, 837 *(illus.)*
  idea of, under Charlemagne, 214–215
  prehistoric, 6–11, 10 *(illus.)*
  railroads in, 671 *(map)*
Europe, after 1989, 833–863
  Bono in, 833–835, 834 *(illus.)*
  Chechen Wars, 840, 841 *(map),* 842, 842
    (illus.), 859
  consumerism in, 851–853, 852 *(illus.)*
  "crony" capitalism, 843
  cultural diversity in, 856, 858
  definitions of "Europe," 836–838, 837
    (illus.)
  democracy in western Europe, 846–847
  demographic challenges, 859–860, 860
    (illus.)
  digital revolution, 853–855, 854 *(illus.)*
  eastern bloc uncertainties, 840–841, 843
  English, as *lingua franca,* 855–856
  environmental pollution in, 859
  European Union, 838, 849–851, 851 *(map),*
    860–862
  football, 853, 853 *(illus.)*
  gender equality and gay rights in, 849
  German reunification, 838, 840–841
  minorities, toleration of, 848–849
  nationalism in former Soviet countries,
    843–844
  political corruption in, 857–858, 857
    (illus.)
  political violence in, 858–859
  pollution in, 859
  postmodernism in, 855, 855 *(illus.)*
  secularism in, 847–848
  social market economy, 847
  sovereign debt crisis, 860–862
  Soviet Union demise, 838, 840, 841 *(map)*
  terrorism in, 858–859
  timeline, 835–836 *(illus.)*
  United States and, 856–857
  Yugoslavia breakup, 844–846, 845 *(illus.),*
    845 *(map)*
European Central Bank, 850, 861, 862
European Coal and Steel Community
  (ECSC), 812
European Commission, 850
European Economic Community (EEC), 806
  (map), 812–813, 823, 849. *See also*
    European Union

European identity, 649, 649 (illus.), 835–838, 837 (illus.)

European Renaissance. See Renaissance, European

European Union (EU)
    chronology of formation, 851
    eastern European countries in, 850
    as "Europe," 836
    income inequalities in, 850–851, 851 (map)
    Maastricht Treaty and, 849
    reunified Germany in, 838
    Schengen Agreements, 849
    sovereign debt crisis, 860–862

euros, 849–850, 850 (illus.), 860–862

Eurozone, 849, 860–862

Eusebius of Caesarea, 175, 179, 194 (source document)

Evans, Arthur, 25

Evans, Richard, 684

Everest, George, 647, 647 (illus.)

évolués, 638, 638 (illus.)

evolution
    Christianity and, 613
    Darwin on, 612
    Hume on stage-theory of, 515
    Spencer on, 611

evolutionary change, 8

exceptionalism, 130 (source document)

Exclusion Crisis (England), 452, 497

The Existence of God (Thomas Aquinas), 291 (source document)

existentialism, 750, 818, 820

exploration, 357–384. See also colonization
    chronology, 363
    Columbian Exchange, 369, 369 (illus.)
    Columbus, 362, 366–370, 367 (illus.)
    Cortés and the Mexica Empire, 358, 372–374, 378
    European bias in, 359–360
    by France and England, 374–375
    by Genoa, 361–362
    life on ships, 372
    motivations for, 370–371
    Pizarro and the Inca Empire, 374, 374 (illus.), 378
    by Portugal, 363–365, 364 (illus.), 364 (map)
    by Spain, 364 (map), 365–366, 368–371, 372–374, 374 (illus.)
    technology for, 366
    timeline, 358–359 (illus.)
    travelers' tales, 361, 362, 362 (illus.)
    Vespucci, Amerigo, 371–372

Exsurge Domine (papal bull), 394

extraterritoriality, 640

fabianism, 122

Fabius (Roman dictator), 122

factories, 585–588, 586 (illus.), 587 (illus.), 673, 673 (illus.)

Fagus Factory (Gropius), 677, 678 (illus.)

Falange (Spain), 758

Falkland Islands, 825

Fallada, Hans, 751

families
    in Classical Athens, 58
    in the Dark Age of Greece, 40
    in early Rome, 108

Luther on, 397
    Nazi Party on, 747, 747 (illus.)
    in the Roman Republic, 111–112, 117–118, 117 (illus.)
    Victorian household, 608

Family of Love, 406

famines
    in 1816-1817, 569
    Great Famine, 297–298, 297 (illus.)
    in the Great War, 714
    in the Russian civil wars, 733
    in the 1840s, 588
    in the seventeenth century, 424
    in the Ukraine, under Stalin, 735

Fanon, Frantz, 817, 818

Farinati, Paolo, 385 (illus.)

Farmborough, Frances, 717

fasces, 108

fascism
    in Austria, 759
    communism, Nazism, and, 742
    in the interwar years, 738
    in Italy, 741–742, 742 (illus.)
    in Spain, 758

Faust (Goethe), 577–578

February Revolution (Russia), 716

Fedele, Cassandra, 326–327, 326 (illus.), 328, 343, 345

Federal Republic of Germany (FRG), 807–808, 807 (illus.)

Felix V (Anti-Pope), 313

Ferdinand II (Holy Roman emperor), 426–427

Ferdinand II (king of the Two Sicilies), 588

Ferdinand of Aragon (king of Spain), 317, 336, 367–368, 371

Fergusson, Niall, 569

Fersen, Axel, 535

Fertile Crescent, 19 (map)

feudalism, 234–236, 235 (illus.)

Ficino, Marsilio, 343, 344 (illus.), 345

Fielding, Henry, 511

FIFA (Fédération Internationale de Football Association), 853

fifteenth century. See exploration; Late Middle Ages; Renaissance, European; Renaissance, Italian

Fifth Crusade, 273

figs, domestication of, 10, 19

Final Solution, 769 (illus.), 782–784, 783 (map), 784 (illus.)

financiers. See banks and finance

fin de siècle (1880–1914), 665–695
    agriculture in, 679–680, 680 (illus.)
    anti-Semitism in, 688–690, 690 (illus.)
    arms race in, 688, 690–691, 700
    art, literature, and music in, 675–677, 675 (illus.), 677 (illus.), 678 (illus.)
    Austro-Hungarian Empire in, 691–692, 692 (map)
    Balkan Wars, 693–694, 693 (illus.)
    civil strife in, 686, 688
    consumer goods in, 664–665 (illus.), 680, 681, 681 (illus.)
    economies in, 679–682, 680 (illus.), 681 (illus.), 682 (illus.)
    liberalism in, 683–684
    mass culture in, 674–675, 674 (illus.)
    metropolis in, 670–672, 671 (map)

mobility in, 669–670, 670 (illus.), 676
    modern experience in, 667–669, 668 (illus.)
    modernism in, 675, 675 (illus.), 677–678, 677 (illus.), 678 (illus.)
    Ottoman Empire territorial losses, 692–694, 693 (map)
    political spectrum in, 683–686
    religion in, 676, 676 (illus.)
    Russian Revolution of 1905, 686
    Russo-Japanese War, 686, 687, 687 (illus.)
    Sarah Bernhardt in, 665–667, 666 (illus.), 675, 689
    sciences in, 678–679
    second industrial revolution, 680, 682
    social mobility in, 672
    timeline, 666–667 (illus.)
    women in, 672–673, 673 (illus.)
    workers in, 669, 682

Finland
    Congress of Vienna and, 562, 564 (map)
    in the Russian civil wars, 733, 733 (map)
    Soviets in, 772

First Bible of Charles the Bald, 218, 218 (illus.), 226 (illus.)

First Crusade, 254–256, 255 (map), 256 (illus.), 258–259 (source document)

First Estate, in the Old Regimes, 462–464, 463 (illus.)

First Punic War, 120–123, 120 (map), 121 (illus.), 122 (map)

First Triumvirate (Roman), 142

Fischer von Erlach, Johann Bernhard, 433

Five Pillars of Islam, 207

Flagellant movement, 311–312

Flaminius, 123

Flanders
    dikes in, 254
    Great Famine in, 298
    in the Hundred Years' War, 301, 302 (map)
    Renaissance in, 349–350, 350 (illus.)
    textile trade in, 274

Flanders (Dix), 696–697 (illus.)

Flanders, Judith, 608

Flaubert, Gustave, 612

Flavians, 157, 158

flax, domestication of, 19

Flemish art, 350, 350 (illus.)

flintlock muskets, 476

flood myths, 18, 300

Florence
    Bonfire of the Vanities, 334–335
    in the Enlightenment, 509
    General Council of Roman Catholic and Greek Orthodox Churches in, 336–337, 337 (illus.), 341
    government in, 332–333
    Machiavelli in, 335–336, 335 (illus.), 355
    Medici family in, 333–334, 333 (illus.)
    plague in, 306 (map), 308
    Renaissance in, 329 (map), 332–336, 334 (illus.), 335 (illus.)
    Savonarola in, 334–335, 335 (illus.)

Florentine Codex, 369 (illus.), 374 (illus.), 379, 379 (illus.)

flush toilets, 582, 610

flying buttresses, 267, 268, 269 (illus.), 289

food safety, 670–671

football, 853, 853 (illus.)

forest resources, in the Restoration era, 568–569

forgeries, art, 127

the Forty-Five (Scotland), 498, 499 (map), 500

Foshoda (Sudan), 652

Foster, Norman, 855

Foucault, Michel, 820, 855

Foundations of Christian Doctrine (Menno), 406

Fourier, Charles, 566, 683

1421: The Year China Discovered the World (Menzies), 381

1434: The Year a Magnificent Chinese Fleet Sailed to Italy and Ignited the Renaissance (Menzies), 381

Fourteen Points, 723

fourteenth century. *See* Late Middle Ages; Renaissance, Italian

Fourth Crusade, 271–272, 272 (illus.)

Fourth Lateran Council, 272, 273

Foxe, John, 435

fox tossing, 462

France. *See also* Carolingians; French Revolution; Napoleon Bonaparte; Paris; western Europe, after World War II

  African colonies of, 656, 657 (map)

  Algeria colonization by, 604, 637, 638, 639, 639 (illus.), 817

  American Revolution and, 529, 530

  cave paintings in, 2–3 (illus.), 7, 9

  in China, 652–653

  communes in, 276

  Concordat, 544, 548

  Congress of Vienna and, 561, 564 (map)

  Crimean War and, 615–616

  Crusades and, 255 (map), 268

  debt crisis in, 529, 530, 533–534, 548

  Dreyfus affair, 689–690, 690 (illus.)

  Enlightenment in, 501–505, 503 (illus.), 504 (illus.)

  Franco-Prussian War, 602, 604, 621–623, 686

  French Revolution in, 525–543

  Great Depression in, 738

  Great Famine in, 298

  in the Great War, 702, 702 (map), 705, 705 (illus.), 711, 711 (map), 723

  in the High Middle Ages, 278

  India, outposts in, 478, 478 (map), 480

  interwar stability in, 738

  invasions of Italy by, 336

  Jews in, 277, 567, 774

  July Revolution, 575, 575 (illus.)

  June Days, 590–591

  liberal modernization of, 603–606, 604 (illus.), 605 (map)

  under Louis IX, 282

  under Louis XIV and Louis XV, 437–439, 438 (map)

  The Marseillaise in, 539, 602

  Merovingians, 187–188, 202–206, 205 (illus.), 211–213

  minority populations in, 848–849

  monarchy in, 241–242, 242 (map), 280

  monasticism in, 201

  under Napoleon Bonaparte, 543–555

  Napoleonic Code, 548–549

  Napoleonic empire, 546–555, 552 (map)

  North American colonies of, 375, 437, 635

  Paris Commune, 623–624, 623 (illus.), 668

  peasants in, 274, 310–311, 311 (illus.), 470

  population growth in, 471

  reforms after Napoleon, 567–568

  religious wars in, 410–412, 412 (illus.)

  revolution of 1848, 588–591, 589 (map)

  Second Empire of, 603

  Second Republic of, 589–591, 603

  Seven Years' War, 439, 477–478, 478 (map), 480

  sister republics (1792–1799), 536 (map)

  standing army in, 477

  Third Republic, 622–624, 622 (illus.)

  in the Thirty Years' War, 430, 430 (illus.)

  Tunisia and, 652

  Vietnamese colony of, 815

  wine trade in, 275

  in World War II, 770, 773–774, 773 (illus.), 786, 789–790

Francis, Saint, 277

Franciscans

  in Asia, 382

  as mendicant orders, 273, 277–278

  in the Mongol court, 279

  in Spanish colonies, 378, 379

Francis I (king of France), 375, 402, 410

Francis II (king of France), 411

Franco, Francisco, 758–759, 813

Franco-Prussian War, 602, 604, 621–623, 686

Frankenstein (Shelley), 511

Franks, 181, 181 (map), 187–188

Franz Ferdinand (Austrian archduke), 698

Franz Joseph I (Austrian emperor), 591, 626, 691

fraternity, in the French Revolution, 537

Frederick Barbarossa (Frederick I; Holy Roman emperor), 270, 285

Frederick I (king of Denmark), 398

Frederick I (king of Prussia), 440, 462

Frederick II (king of Sicily; Holy Roman emperor), 271, 272, 273, 281–282

Frederick II (the Great; king of Prussia)

  on Christianity, 518

  conscription under, 477

  early life of, 440

  Enlightenment and, 507–508

  nobles and, 466

  peasants and, 471

  Seven Years' War and, 478, 479 (illus.), 480

Frederick III the Wise (Elector of Saxony), 392, 397

Frederick V (prince of the Palatinate), 426, 427

Frederick William (Great Elector), 440, 489 (source document)

Frederick William I (king of Prussia), 440

freedom of the press, 568, 627

Free French armies, 773–774, 778

The Free Word (Drumont), 688–689, 690 (illus.)

Freikorps, 743

French Academy of Sciences (Académie Royale des Sciences), 437, 485

French and Indian War, 478, 479–480. *See also* Seven Years' War

French East India Company, 437, 480

French Revolution, 525–543

  August Decrees, 532, 533

  Bastille, assault on, 531–532, 531 (illus.)

  chronology of, 534

  Civil Constitution of the Clergy, 534

  Committee of Public Safety, 538–539

  debt crisis in, 529, 530, 533–534, 548

  Declaration of the Rights of Man, 532–533

  Directory, 543, 544

  end of, 544

  execution of the king, 538, 538 (illus.)

  external wars in, 537, 539–540

  Haiti and, 540–541, 540 (illus.)

  long-term causes of, 528–529, 529 (illus.)

  Louis XVI in, 529–531, 533–535, 537–538, 538 (illus.)

  Moderate Revolution, 532–537

  Montagnards and Girondins in, 537–538, 542

  Napoleon's seizure of power, 546

  National Assembly and, 531–532

  outside France, 539–541, 540 (illus.)

  Radical Revolution, 537–543

  Reign of Terror, 538

  revolutionary culture, 541–542, 541 (illus.), 542 (illus.)

  sans-culottes, 536–537, 538–539, 541 (illus.)

  September Massacres, 537

  short-term causes of, 529–531

  sister republics in, 536 (map)

  Staël, Madame de, and, 525–527, 526 (illus.), 548

  Thermidorean reaction, 543

  timeline of, 526–527 (illus.)

  Vendée, 534, 536 (map)

French Wars of Religion, 410–412, 412 (illus.)

frescoes

  early Christian, 172 (illus.), 177 (illus.)

  Gothic, 271 (illus.)

  Minoan, 26 (illus.)

  Renaisssance, 347, 348–349, 348 (illus.)

Freud, Sigmund, 678

Friars Minor (Franciscans), 273

Friedrich, Caspar David, 577 (illus.), 578

Friedrich Wilhelm IV (king of Prussia), 591, 600

Fronde (France), 424, 437

Funeral Oration (Pericles), 62, 68 (source document)

funerals. *See* burials and death rituals

Fürtwangler, Wilhelm, 751

Futurism, 677

Gagarin, Yuri, 818

Galen, 484

Galeries Lafayette (Paris), 681, 681 (illus.)

Galerius, 175

Galileo Galilei, 483

galleys (ship), 338, 366

Gallipoli, Battle of (1915), 710, 722, 725, 764

Gama, Vasco de, 363, 372, 380

Gandhi, Mohandas, 638, 814

Ganshof, F. L., 236

Gapon, Father, 686

Gardeners Dictionary (Miller), 513–514

gardening, in the Enlightenment, 513–514, 514 (illus.)

Gare St. Lazare (Paris), 605, 605 (map)

Garibaldi, Giuseppi, 591, 619, 619 (illus.), 622

Gascony, in the Hundred Years' War, 301
Gaskell, Elizabeth, 610
gas warfare, 691, 704, 712
Gate of Paradise (Ghiberti), 346 *(illus.)*
Gaugamela, Battle of (331 BCE), 84, 85 *(illus.)*
Gauguin, Paul, 677
Gaul
    Carolingians in, 210–215, 214 *(map)*
    Christianity in, 180, 187–188
    Franks (Merovingians) in, 185 *(map)*,
      187–188, 204–206, 211–213
    Huns in, 183
    invasion and sack of Rome, 113, 114, 116
    in the Roman Empire, 142, 143 *(map)*, 145,
      147, 159 *(map)*
    Vandals in, 183
gay rights, 849
Gaza, Alexander's conquest of, 84
gender equality, 849
gender roles, 9
General Council of Roman Catholic and
    Greek Orthodox Churches, 336–337,
    337 *(illus.)*, 341
General History of the Things of New Spain
    (Sahagún), 378
General Maximum (France), 539
general strike
    in France (1968), 821
    in Russia (1905), 686
Genetic Adam, 6
genetics, 679
Geneva, Calvin in, 402–404, 404 *(illus.)*
Geneva Bible, 448
Geneva Conventions, 691, 781
Genghis Khan, 279
Genoa, trade and travel from, 361–362
genocide. *See* ethnic cleansing
Gentileschi, Artemisia, 410
geography, imperialism and, 646, 647, 647
    (illus.)
George (king of Greece), 685
George, Stefan, 677
George I (king of England), 453
George I (king of Greece), 573
George III (king of England), 461
Georgia, 709, 840, 841 *(map)*
Georgics (Virgil), 150
Gerard of Cremona, 283
German Atrocities, 1914 (Horne and Kramer),
    706
German Confederation, 562, 564 *(map)*. *See*
    also Germany
German Democratic Republic (GDR),
    799–801, 802 *(map)*, 807–808, 807
    (illus.), 828–829, 828 *(illus.)*
German Enlightenment, 507–508
Germanic kingdoms, 185–188, 185 *(map)*, 186
    (illus.)
Germanic tribes, 180–185, 181 *(map)*, 185
    (map)
Germany. *See also* Holy Roman Empire;
    western Europe, after World War II
    African colonies of, 656, 657 *(map)*,
      658–659
    appeasement of, 766–767, 767 *(map)*
    Berlin, in the Cold War, 802 *(map)*,
      806–807, 828–829, 828 *(illus.)*
    in the Carolingian empire, 214, 214 *(map)*
    colonies of, 636

Czechoslovakia annexation, 746, 766, 767
    (map)
division of, into east and west, 799–801,
    802 *(map)*, 807–808, 807 *(illus.)*,
    828–829, 828 *(illus.)*
Enlightenment in, 507–508, 507 *(map)*
Franco-Prussian War, 602, 604, 621–623,
    686
in the Great Depression, 752, 753
in the Great Famine, 298
Great War, eastern front, 707–708, 708
    (illus.)
Great War, entrance into, 701–702, 702
    (map)
Great War, peace treaties, 723–724, 724
    (map)
Great War, western front, 704–705, 705
    (illus.), 705 *(map)*, 707
Hamburg cholera epidemic, 684
Hitler-Stalin Pact (1939), 770
hyperinflation in, 743, 744
Iron Curtain in, 795, 802 *(map)*, 829
Kant, Immanuel, in, 494, 501, 507–508,
    515
Lutheranism in, 398–399, 398 *(illus.)*
military build-up, pre–Great War, 690
military build-up, pre–World War II, 757,
    766
national anthem in, 602
Nuremberg Nazi Party rally, 749, 754–755,
    755 *(illus.)*
Protestant Reformation in, 390–397
racial warfare in, 767–768, 768 *(illus.)*, 770
reparations from Great War, 723, 724,
    742, 752, 757
repatriating Germans, 768–769
reunification of, 838, 840–841
revolution of 1848, 589, 589 *(map)*, 591
Rhine River engineered, 595–597, 596
    (illus.), 596 *(map)*
Roman Empire and, 147
in the 1970s and 1980s, 822
second industrial revolution in, 680
in the Thirty Years' War, 426–430, 427
    (map), 428 *(illus.)*
unification of, 619–621, 621 *(map)*, 624
Weimar Republic, 742–744, 743 *(illus.)*
World War II, battle for Berlin, 790, 790
    (illus.)
World War II, in Europe and North
    Africa, 772
World War II, in Poland, 770–772
World War II, resistance within, 785–786,
    786 *(illus.)*
World War II aftermath, 801–802, 807–808,
    807 *(illus.)*
Gesellschaft für Erdkunde, 646
al-Ghazali, 248
ghettoes, Jews in, 342, 467, 771
Ghiberti, Lorenzo, 346, 346 *(illus.)*
Gibbon, Edward, 184
Gilbert of Poitiers, 268
Gilgamesh, 16, 18
Giovanni di Piano Carpini, 279
Girl Reading a Letter by an Open Window
    (Vermeer), 433
Girondins (France), 537–538, 542
Gislebertus, 230–231 *(illus.)*, 231–232, 232
    (illus.)

Glaber, Raoul, 239–240, 250
Gladstone, William Ewart, 599, 601, 603, 610,
    652
glasnost, 826–827, 838
glassware, Phoenician, 29
globalization, 836, 851–853, 852 *(illus.)*
gloria, 117–118, 117 *(illus.)*
Glorious Revolution (England), 452–453, 498
glossing, 282–283
Gnosticism, 169, 170, 180
Goa, 380
goats, domestication of, 10
God Dionysus Delivering Grapevines, 36 *(illus.)*
Godonuv, Boris (czar of Russia), 442
gods and goddessses
    Assyrian, 32
    Egyptian, 21–22, 21 *(illus.)*, 23, 97
    Greek, 43, 45–46, 81, 81 *(illus.)*
    Hebrew, 30, 31, 32
    Macedonian, 75
    Mesopotamian, 18, 30
    Minoan, 26
    Persian, 52
    Roman, 109, 113, 118–119, 151–152
"God Save the King," 602
Goebbels, Josef, 752, 754, 767, 785
Goethe, Johann Wolfgang von, 508, 510
    (illus.), 577–578
Gogh, Theo Van, 858
gold
    of Alexander the Great, 83, 84–85
    Carolingians and, 220
    in the Hellenistic Age, 91
    Portugal's quest for, 363
    in South Africa, 632, 632 *(map)*
Golden Ass (Lucius Apuleius), 166
Golden Bull, 300–301
Golden Psalter, 195 *(illus.)*
Golvin, Jean-Claude, 73 *(illus.)*
Gomułka, Władysław, 804, 808
Goodbye to All That (Graves), 751–752
Good Shepherd of the Catacombs (Rome),
    172 *(illus.)*
Gorbachev, Mikhail, 816, 825–827, 826 *(illus.)*,
    828, 838
Gordian knot, 84, 87
Gordon, George, 652
Göring, Hermann, 752, 754, 768, 773 *(illus.)*,
    790
Gospel of Silver Mark, 277
Gothic High Middle Ages, 261–291
    Abelard and Heloise in, 261–263, 263
      (illus.)
    architecture, 260–261 *(illus.)*, 267–268, 268
      (illus.), 269 *(illus.)*, 273, 289, 289 *(illus.)*
    cathedral schools in, 264–267, 282–283
    Church reforms in, 268–269, 271,
      272–273, 277
    Cistercians and repression of heretics,
      268–269, 277, 277 *(illus.)*
    Crusades in, 268–273, 270 *(illus.)*, 272
      (illus.)
    dissenting movements, 277, 277 *(illus.)*
    economy in, 272–276, 274 *(illus.)*, 275 *(map)*
    Fourth Lateran Council, 272, 273
    Gothic architecture, 267–268, 268 *(illus.)*,
      269 *(illus.)*
    Medieval Warm Period, 253, 273, 295
    Mongol relations in, 279, 279 *(illus.)*

Gothic High Middle Ages *(continued)*
   rulers in, 280–282, 281 *(illus.)*
   scholasticism, 283, 287–288, 289
   state development in, 278, 278 *(map)*, 280
   timeline, 262–263 *(illus.)*
   translation of ancient texts in, 283
   universities in, 283, 285–287, 285 *(map)*,
     286 *(illus.)*, 287 *(illus.)*
Goths, 167
Gouges, Olympe de, 542
government
   in Anglo-Saxon kingdoms, 241–242
   Carolingian, 210–211
   in the Dutch Republic, 447
   in England after the Glorious
     Revolution, 453
   Enlightenment thinkers on, 497–498,
     502, 504
   of the European Union, 850
   in Florence, Renaissance, 332–333
   in Greece, Classical, 56, 57–59, 68 *(source*
     document)
   in Greece, Dark Age of, 40–41
   in the High Middle Ages, 278, 280–281
   in Italy, medieval, 330
   in Mesopotamia, 16–17
   in the Persian Empire, 51–52
   political spectrum on (1815–1850),
     564–567, 565 *(illus.)*
   in the Roman Empire, 136, 138, 140, 173
   in the Roman Republic, 109–110, 111
     (illus.), 116, 135–136
   in the Soviet Union, 734–735
   in Venice, Renaissance, 339
   in western Europe after 1989, 846–847
Goya, Francisco, 553 *(illus.)*
Graaf, Laurens de, 475
Gracchus, Gaius, 136, 138
Gracchus, Tiberius, 136, 138
grain crops, domestication of, 10, 19
Granada, Luis de, 432, 435
Grande Armée, 549–551, 549 *(illus.)*, 554–555,
   555 *(illus.)*
The Graphic, 683 *(illus.)*
Grass, Günter, 855
Graves, Robert, 751–752
Great Depression
   in France and Britain, 738
   in Germany, 752, 753
   in Italy, 741
   in the Soviet Union, 738
Great Famine, 297–298, 297 *(illus.)*
Great Fear, 532
"the Great Game," 653–654, 654 *(map)*
Great Mosque of Córdoba, 216 *(illus.)*
Great Mosque of Damascus, 208 *(illus.)*
Great Northern War, 442, 443–444
great powers
   after the Seven Years' War, 480
   declarations of war and alliances,
     701–702, 702 *(map)*
   in the fin de siècle, 688
Great Reform Act (1832; England), 575, 587
Great (East-West) Schism, 245, 248, 253,
   271–272
Great Trigonometrical Survey (GTS), 647
Great War (World War I), 697–725
   alliances in, 701–702, 702 *(map)*
   armistice, 719–720

assassination of Franz Ferdinand, 698,
   701
   causes of, 700–701
   in the colonies, 710–711, 711 *(illus.)*
   eastern front, 707–708, 708 *(illus.)*
   economies in, 715
   fatality rates in, 699, 719, 720 *(illus.)*, 721
     (map)
   Greece and Turkey after, 724–725, 725
     (illus.)
   home front, 713–715, 714 *(illus.)*, 727
     (source document)
   peace treaties, 719–720, 723–724, 724 *(map)*
   Russian Revolution during, 716–719, 717
     (illus.), 718 *(illus.)*
   scale of, 699–700
   southeastern fronts, 708–710, 709 *(map)*,
     710 *(illus.)*
   Spanish flu, 720–721
   technology in, 711–713, 713 *(illus.)*
   timeline, 698–699 *(illus.)*
   as total war, 703–704, 703 *(illus.)*
   war memorials, 722, 722 *(illus.)*
   western front, 704–705, 705 *(illus.)*, 705
     (map), 707
   women in, 714–715, 714 *(illus.)*, 727 *(source*
     document)
Grebel, Conrad, 405
Greece. *See also* Greece, ancient; Greece,
   Archaic Age
   in the Balkan Wars, 693–694, 693 *(illus.)*
   in the Byzantine Empire, 209–210, 209
     (map)
   civil war in, 805, 813
   economic crisis in, 860–862
   in the Great War, 702, 702 *(map)*
   Istanbul, attempted conquest of, 724–725
   in the Ottoman Empire, 445, 445 *(map)*
   Soviet bloc and, 803
   in the Venetian Republic, 445, 445 *(map)*
   War of Independence, 570–573, 571
     (illus.), 572 *(illus.)*, 573 *(map)*
   in World War II, 775, 776
Greece, ancient. *See also* Athens; Corinth;
   Hellenistic Ages; Sparta
   after Alexander's death, 88
   after Mycenaean collapse, 39–40
   after Philip's assassination, 82–83
   agriculture in, 47–48, 48 *(illus.)*
   Archaic Age of, 42–51, 43 *(map)*
   Classical Age of, 39, 56–66
   colonization by (500 BCE), 44–45, 44
     (map), 45 *(illus.)*
   Corinthian War, 74
   Dark Age of, 39–42, 40 *(illus.)*, 42 *(illus.)*
   Delian League, 60–63, 64
   in Eastern Roman Empire, 185 *(map)*
   economy and culture of, 47–50, 48 *(illus.)*,
     49 *(illus.)*, 50 *(illus.)*
   First Hellenistic Age, 72 *(illus.)*, 73, 74–77,
     75 *(map)*
   Greek alphabet, 29 *(illus.)*, 42
   Hellenistic culture, 77–82, 78 *(illus.)*, 79
     (illus.), 81 *(illus.)*
   Herodotus, 37–39, 38 *(illus.)*, 50, 52, 54, 66
   Hesiod, 42, 45–46, 47–48, 51
   Homer, 27, 41–42, 42 *(illus.)*
   importance of, 59
   Indo-European migration into, 11

   Iron Age in, 40–41
   Lydians, 48, 51, 52, 52 *(illus.)*, 53 *(map)*
   major city-states in, 55–60, 57 *(map)*
   Mycenaean civilization, 5 *(illus.)*, 26–27,
     26 *(map)*, 39–40
   Near Eastern cultural influences on, 50
   Olympic Games, 42–43, 58
   Oracle at Delphi, 43–44, 43 *(illus.)*, 43
     (map), 51
   ostracism in, 53, 55, 55 *(illus.)*
   Pan-Hellenism *vs.* polis in, 51
   Peloponnesian War, 60–63, 62 *(map)*, 64
   Pericles in, 37, 61–63, 61 *(illus.)*, 64, 68
     (source document)
   Persian Wars, 51–56, 52 *(illus.)*, 53 *(map)*,
     54 *(map)*
   Philip of Macedon and, 74, 75–77, 75
     (map), 76 *(illus.)*
   in the Roman Empire, 143, 143 *(map)*, 159
     (map)
   slavery in, 46, 47, 56, 59–60
   in southern Italy, 115
   Thirty Tyrants in, 65, 74, 78, 79
   timeline of, 40–41 *(illus.)*
   tyrants and social reformers in, 46–47
   women in, 60, 66
Greece Expiring on the Ruins of Missolonghi
   (Delacroix), 571 *(illus.)*
Greek (Eastern) Orthodox Church
   in the Byzantine Empire, 209–210, 255
     (map)
   fall of Constantinople and, 318, 319
   General Council with Roman Catholic
     Church, 336–337, 337 *(illus.)*, 341
   Great Schism and, 245, 248, 271–272
   Vatican II and, 822
Greenland settlements, 296
Gregorian Chant, 218
Gregory IX (Pope), 278
Gregory of Tours, 202–204, 205
Gregory the Great (Pope), 201–202, 201
   (illus.)
Gregory VII (Pope), 245–247, 246 *(illus.)*, 254
Gregory XI (Pope), 312–313
The Grieving Parents (Kollwitz), 722, 722
   (illus.)
Grimm brothers, 574
Grimmelshausen, H. J. C. von, 433
Grimoald (Carolingian), 210
Gritti, Andrea, 340
Groote, Gerhard, 312
Gropius, Walter, 677, 678 *(illus.)*
Grotefend, Georg, 15
Grotius, Hugo, 434, 495
The Grouch (Menander), 78
Guanche people, 365, 375
Guarducci, Margherita, 127
guerrilla warfare, 553, 622, 704
Guèye, Lamine, 638, 638 *(illus.)*
Guibert of Nogent, 264
guilds, 274–275, 332, 468, 468 *(illus.)*, 472, 499
guillotine, 538, 538 *(illus.)*, 623
Guizot, François, 575
The Gulag Archipelago (Solzhenitsyn), 820,
   826
gulags, 734, 736
Gustavus Adolphus (king of Sweden),
   428–429, 429 *(illus.)*, 477
Gustavus Vasa (king of Sweden), 398

Gutenberg, Johann, 351
Gutians, 17
Gützlaff, Karl, 644–645
gymnasia (singular, *gymnasium*), 94
Gypsies, 776

Habsburg Empire. *See also* Austro-Hungarian
    Empire; Holy Roman Empire
    absolutism and, 439–440, 439 *(illus.)*
    Congress of Vienna and, 562, 564 *(map)*
    Enlightenment in, 508–509
    Ottoman attack on, 439, 439 *(illus.)*
    population growth in, 471
    in the Thirty Years' War, 426, 427–428,
        428 *(illus.)*, 430
hadiths, 207
Hadji Murad (Tolstoy), 641
Hadrian, 152, 157, 158, 159
Hadron Collider, 856
Haggard, Rider, 674
Hagia Sophia, 189, 189 *(illus.)*, 318
Hague Convention on Land Warfare (1899),
    691
Haiti (Saint Domingue), 437, 540–541, 540
    (illus.), 542
hajj, 207, 676
Halicarnassus (Turkey), 52
Hamburg, cholera epidemic in, 684
Hamilcar Barca, 121–122
Hamilton, William, 518 *(illus.)*
Hammurabi, 17, 17 *(illus.)*
Hancock, John, 475
Hannan, Daniel, 865 *(source document)*
Hannibal, 122–123, 122 *(map)*
Harald Hardrada (king of Norway), 248, 251
Hard Times (Dickens), 587
Hargreaves, John, 582
Harold (king of England), 248, 250, 251
Harris, Arthur, 791
Harris, Ruth, 676
Harrison, George, 819
Harry Potter (Rowling), 855
Harun al-Rasid (Abbasid), 215
haruspicy, 108
Harvey, William, 484, 484 *(illus.)*
Hasdrubal, 123
Hastings, Battle of (1066), 250, 251
Hathor (goddess), 20, 21 *(illus.)*
Hatshepsut (Egyptian queen), 23–24, 24
    (illus.)
Haussmann, Georges, Baron, 604–605, 604
    (illus.), 605 *(map)*
Havel, Václav, 810, 829, 841, 844, 856
Haydn, Joseph, 465
hazing, 287
Headrick, Daniel, 650
health care, 624, 812
Heart of Darkness (Conrad), 657
Hebrew Bible, 29–30, 31, 92
Hebrews
    alphabet of, 29 *(illus.)*
    Babylonian Captivity of, 32
    chronology of, 29–30
    Diaspora of, 32
    kings and kingdoms of, 29, 31–32
    language, 92
    monotheism of, 29
    Persian Empire and, 51
    temple of, 32, 51, 150

Hedin, Sven, 646, 672
Hegel, G. F. W., 579
Heidegger, Martin, 750, 818
height, sedentism and, 9
Heine, Heinrich, 595
Heisenberg, Werner, 750
Hejira, 207
Heliocentric theory, 96
Hellenic Confederacy, 77
Hellenistic Ages, 70–99
    Alexander the Great in, 82–87, 83 *(map)*,
        85 *(illus.)*
    Aristotle in, 77, 80–81
    art in, 98–99, 98 *(illus.)*
    culture in, 77–82, 78 *(illus.)*, 79 *(illus.)*, 81
        (illus.)
    currency in, 90, 90 *(illus.)*, 94
    Demosthenes and Isocrates in, 75–76, 77,
        82–83, 86
    discrimination in, 92–93
    economies in, 93, 94–95
    First, 72 *(illus.)*, 73, 74–77, 75 *(map)*
    Greek cities in Asia, 72, 84, 94
    kingdoms after Alexander's death,
        87–89, 89 *(map)*
    language in, 92, 92 *(illus.)*
    life in, 91
    literature in, 77–78, 97–98
    medicine in, 81–82, 81 *(illus.)*, 96–97
    outlier kingdoms, 89–91, 89 *(map)*
    Philip of Macedon and, 74, 75, 75 *(map)*,
        76–77, 76 *(illus.)*
    philosophy in, 95–96
    Plato in, 50, 78, 79–80, 81
    religion in, 97
    Second, 73, 73 *(illus.)*, 82–87, 83 *(map)*
    Socrates in, 78–79, 79 *(illus.)*, 101 *(source
        document)*
    technology and science in, 96–97, 96
        (illus.)
    timeline of, 72–73 *(illus.)*
    urban planning in, 71–72, 84
Hellenization, 92–93
Heloise, 261–263, 263 *(illus.)*, 265, 266, 267
helots, 56
henges, 10–11, 10 *(illus.)*
henotheism, 23, 30
Henrique (Henry the Navigator; king of
    Portugal), 362, 364, 365
Henry I (king of England), 243, 243 *(illus.)*
Henry II (king of England), 280–281, 281
    (illus.)
Henry II (king of France), 404, 411
Henry II (Ottonian Empire), 239
Henry III (Holy Roman emperor), 245
Henry IV (Holy Roman emperor), 246–247,
    246 *(illus.)*
Henry IV (king of France), 412
Henry of Flanders (Byzantium), 273
Henry the Fowler (Saxony), 239
Henry V (king of England), 315
Henry VI (Holy Roman emperor), 270
Henry VII (king of England), 317, 367, 375
Henry VIII (king of England), 389, 398,
    401–402, 402 *(illus.)*
Heraclitus of Ephesus, 49
Heraclius (Byzantine), 209
Herculaneum (Italy), 149
Herder, Johann Gottfried, 508

Herero rebellion, 658–659, 691
heretics, 253, 268–269, 272, 277, 314
Herman of Carinthia, 288
Hermeias, 80
Herodotus of Halicarnassus, 37–39, 38
    (illus.), 50, 52, 54, 66
Herod the Great (king of Judea), 147
Heron of Alexandria, 97
A Hero of Our Time (Lermontov), 641
Herophilus of Chalcedon, 97
Herzl, Theodor, 689, 690
Herzog, Dagmar, 769
Hesiod, 42, 45–46, 47–48, 51
Heutsz, J. B. van, 653, 653 *(illus.)*
Heydrich, Reinhard, 768
hieratic script, 20
Hieron II of Syracuse, 121
Highlanders (Scotland), 498, 499 *(map)*, 500,
    500 *(illus.)*
High Middle Ages. *See* Gothic High Middle
    Ages
highwaymen, 471
Hildebrand, 245
Hildegard of Bingen, 266, 266 *(illus.)*
Himmler, Heinrich, 752, 768, 769
Hindenburg, Paul von, 707, 719, 722, 752
Hints on Household Taste (Eastlake), 609
Hippocrates, 81 *(illus.)*, 82, 97
Hirohito (emperor of Japan), 777
Hiroshima, atomic bomb on, 788, 792
Historiai (Herodotus), 37–39, 50
historians
    of alternative history, 381
    on the Belgian atrocities in the Great
        War, 706, 706 *(illus.)*
    on the "Black Athena" controversy, 50
    on the Chinese in Australia, 381
    on climate effects, 415
    on the collapse of communism, 827
    Comnena, Anna, 253
    on the end of the French Revolution, 544
    on the Enlightenment, 519
    Eusebius of Caesarea, 175, 179, 194
        (source document)
    on the face of Philip of Macedon, 76
    on fakes and forgeries, 127
    on "feudalism," 236
    Gibbon, Edward, 184
    Herodotus of Halicarnassus, 37–39, 38
        (illus.), 50, 52, 54, 66
    historical classics, 320
    on Industrial Revolution in Europe *vs.*
        China, 582
    Livy, 110, 111, 118, 124
    Maitland, F. W., 236
    on the Michelangelo frescoes, 348, 348
        (illus.)
    Pirenne, Henri, 211
    Polybius, 103–104, 104 *(illus.)*, 109, 117,
        118, 130 *(source document)*
    on prehistoric ages, 7
    on Roman slavery, 137
    Sallust, 117, 136, 141
    on the Spanish Armada, 415
    Tacitus, 153
    Thucydides, 59, 61, 62–63, 66
Historical and Critical Dictionary (Bayle), 495
The History of Ancient Art (Winckelmann),
    510

The History of the Decline and Fall of the Roman Empire (Gibbon), 184
History of the Florentine People (Bruni), 344
History of the Franks (Gregory), 203
Hitler, Adolf. *See also* Germany; World War II
    in the Great War, 703, 703 (*illus.*), 743
    Mein Kampf, 744
    Nuremberg rally, 749, 754–755, 755 (*illus.*)
    rearmament of Germany, 757, 766
    rise to power, 743–744, 752, 754
    suicide of, 790
Hitler-Stalin Pact (1939), 770
Hittites, 17, 19 (*map*), 26 (*map*), 27
Hobbes, Thomas, 434–435
Ho Chi Minh, 711, 740, 740 (*illus.*), 815
Hohenzollerns, 392, 394
Hohle Fels Venus figurine, 35, 35 (*illus.*)
Hölderlin, Friedrich, 577
The Hollow Men (Eliot), 751
Holocaust, 782–784, 782 (*illus.*), 783 (*map*), 784 (*illus.*)
Holstein, 620
Holwell, J. Z., 481
Holy Alliance (1815), 562–563
Holy Roman Empire
    beginning of, 245
    Congress of Vienna and, 562, 564 (*map*)
    Crusades and, 255 (*map*), 268–269
    fragmentation of, 300–301
    in the High Middle Ages, 271–273, 278 (*map*), 281–282
    Lutheranism in, 398–399, 398 (*illus.*), 403–404, 411 (*map*)
    map of (1519–1558), 395 (*map*)
    map of (1721), 469 (*map*)
    under Napoleon, 551, 552 (*map*)
    religion in (1600), 411 (*map*)
    in the Thirty Years' War, 426–430, 427 (*map*)
Homer, 27, 41–42, 42 (*illus.*), 83
Homo sapiens, Linnaeus's classifications of, 515
Homo sapiens neanderthalensis, 6–7
Homo sapiens sapiens, 6–8, 8 (*map*)
homosexuals
    in the interwar years, 747, 748
    Nazis and, 754, 769, 769 (*illus.*)
    in western Europe, after 1989, 849
Honecker, Erich, 799–801, 800 (*illus.*), 829, 841
honor, in the Roman Republic, 117–118, 117 (*illus.*)
Honorius (Roman emperor), 185
Hoover, Herbert, 733–734
hoplites, 47, 47 (*illus.*), 53
Horace, 149–150, 151
Horatius Cocles, 108
Horne, John, 706
horses
    in agriculture, 273
    domestication of, 9, 11
    in the Great War, 713, 713 (*illus.*)
    in warfare, 32, 46
Horthy, Miklós, 745, 768, 785
Horus (goddess), 20, 21 (*illus.*), 22
hot-air balloons, 513, 513 (*illus.*)
House of Commons (England), 496
housing
    in Augustan Rome, 154, 155–156, 155 (*illus.*)

in Gaul, 206
    with sedentism, 9
hubris, 65, 66
Hugh Capet (Capetian), 242–243
Hugh of St. Victor, 266–267
Hugh the Great, 242
Hugo, Victor, 578
Huguenots, 411–412, 412 (*illus.*), 495
Huizinga, Johan, 320
Human Comedy (Balzac), 611, 612
humanism
    civic, 343–344
    classical literature and, 341–343
    in the European Renaissance, 349, 351, 352–353
    in the High Middle Ages, 266
    in the Italian Renaissance, 325–327, 326 (*illus.*), 341–344, 344 (*illus.*)
human population, 6–7. *See also* population growth
human rights, 434
Humbert (Cardinal), 245
Hume, David, 501, 515
Hundred Days (Napoleon's return), 555, 561
Hundred Years' War
    beginning of, 301–302, 302 (*illus.*), 304
    chivalry and, 304
    chronology of, 301
    final phase of, 315–316, 316 (*illus.*)
Hungary. *See also* Austro-Hungarian Empire
    communism ended in, 828
    economic crisis in, 862
    in the Great Depression, 752
    Great War peace treaties and, 723, 724, 724 (*map*)
    in the High Middle Ages, 278 (*map*)
    as Hungarian Soviet Republic, 745
    in the interwar years, 745
    Jews in, 757
    pollution in, 859
    revolution of 1848, 589, 589 (*map*), 590 (*illus.*), 591
    second serfdom in, 469–470, 469 (*map*)
    serfs in, 568
    in the Soviet bloc, 802 (*map*), 803, 804
    in the Treaty of Versailles, 723
    uprising and Soviet invasion (1956), 808–809, 808 (*illus.*)
    in World War II, 767, 767 (*map*), 776, 785
Hunger Plan (German), 781
Huns, 181 (*map*), 181, 183
hunter-gatherers, 7, 8–9, 10
hunting, monarchs and, 461 (*illus.*), 462
Hurrians, 27
Hus, Jan, 314, 314 (*illus.*), 394, 397
al-Husseini, Mohammed Amin, 785
Hussite churches, 314
Huth, Hans, 406
Hutter, Jacob, 406
Huxley, Thomas, 613
Hydaspes River, Battle of (326 BCE), 86
hydraulic press, 583
Hyksos invasion of Egypt, 19 (*map*), 22
Hyperides, 284
Hyperion (Hölderlin), 577

Ibn al-Wardi, Abu Hafs 'Umar Ibn, 305
Ibsen, Henrik, 677

Ice Age, 7
ice cores, climate history from, 219, 295–296
Iceland, 296, 861
iconoclasm, 210, 210 (*illus.*)
ideographs, 14, 20
Ides of March, 144
If This Be a Man (Levi), 784
Iliad (Homer), 27, 41–42, 42 (*illus.*)
Iliescu, Ion, 830, 841
illuminated manuscripts
    Carolingian, 196 (*illus.*), 217 (*illus.*), 218, 218 (*illus.*), 226 (*illus.*)
    Gothic, 271 (*illus.*)
    Romanesque, 235 (*illus.*), 238 (*illus.*), 239 (*illus.*), 243 (*illus.*), 246 (*illus.*)
Illyrians, 123, 125
Imitation of Christ (Thomas à Kempis), 312
imperator, 161
Imperia (courtesan), 332
imperialism. *See also* colonization
    Africa, scramble for, 654–658, 655 (*illus.*), 656 (*illus.*), 657 (*map*)
    after World War II, 813–818, 814 (*map*), 815 (*illus.*)
    in Algeria, 604, 637, 639, 639 (*illus.*)
    Athenian, 60, 62–63
    British East India Company and, 474, 480, 481
    in the Caucasus, 640–642, 641 (*map*), 642 (*illus.*)
    chartered companies in, 636
    in China, 639–640, 652–653
    civilizing mission of, 637, 638, 643, 644–645, 645 (*illus.*)
    colonial soldiers in, 643–644
    in the Congo, 656, 656 (*illus.*)
    decolonization after World War II, 814–818, 814 (*map*)
    Dutch and French in southeast Asia, 652–653, 653 (*illus.*)
    European identity and, 649, 649 (*illus.*)
    Europeanized natives, 638, 638 (*illus.*)
    "the Great Game," in central Asia, 653–654, 654 (*map*)
    Great War and, 710–711, 711 (*illus.*)
    Herodotus on, 39
    imperial exchange in, 648, 648 (*illus.*), 650
    independence of New World colonies, 529, 634–635
    in India, 636–637, 637 (*illus.*), 641 (*map*), 642–643, 642 (*illus.*)
    in Japan, 640
    mandates (mandate system), 723, 738
    motives for, 636, 637
    neo-Europes in, 633
    Opium Wars in, 639–640
    race and, 638, 638 (*illus.*), 650, 687
    resistance to, 658–660, 659 (*illus.*)
    revolts, in the interwar years, 738–741, 739 (*map*)
    of the Roman Republic, 114–115, 118, 119–125
    second wave of, 635–643
    self-determination and, 723, 738
    Suez Canal, 650, 651–652, 651 (*illus.*)
    technology and medicine and, 650–651
    third wave of, 650–658, 654 (*map*), 657 (*map*)
    timeline, 634–635 (*illus.*)

imperial papacy, 247, 254, 256, 271, 276, 278 (map), 280
Impressionism, 612–614, 614 (illus.)
inauguratio, 109
Inca Empire, 374, 374 (illus.), 378
The Incoherence of the Philosophers (al-Ghazali), 248
incunabula, 351
Index Librorum Prohibitorum, 409
India
    Alexander in, 86
    British colonization of, 636–637, 637 (illus.), 641 (map)
    French outposts in, 437, 478, 478 (map), 480
    in the Great War, 704
    in the Hellenistic Ages, 89, 90, 90 (illus.)
    independence of, 814–815, 814 (map), 815 (illus.)
    Indian Rebellion (1857), 642–643, 642 (illus.)
    opium in, 639–640
    plague in, 305
    railroads in, 643
    resistance to British control, 659, 739, 741
    Seven Years' War in, 478, 478 (map), 480
    survey of, 647, 647 (illus.)
The Indiscreet Jewels (Diderot), 503
individualism
    Renaissance, 341, 344–345, 349
    Socrates and, 78–79
Indo-European languages, 11
Indo-European migrations, 5 (illus.), 11, 12 (map)
Indonesia
    decolonization after World War II, 814 (map)
    Dutch control of, 447, 653, 653 (illus.)
    Japanese control of, 777
    in World War II, 780 (map)
inductive method of reasoning, 482
indulgences, 392–393, 393 (illus.), 400, 409
industrialization, 580–588. *See also* modernization
    capital in, 584–585
    cotton and, 581, 582
    in eastern Europe, under Stalin, 803–804
    Fourier on, 566
    gadgets in, 581–582
    reasons for, in Britain, 580–581, 581 (map)
    second wave of, 680, 682
    Tocqueville on, 560–561
    transportation and, 582 (map), 583–584, 584 (illus.)
    women and, 586–587, 586 (illus.)
    workers in, 585–588, 586 (illus.)
industries
    after the plague, 311
    cottage industries, 274, 276, 472–473, 581, 586
    factories, 585–588, 586 (illus.), 587 (illus.), 673, 673 (illus.)
    in the Great Depression, 753, 753 (illus.)
    in the High Middle Ages, 274–276, 275 (map)
    proto-industrialization, eighteenth-century, 472
infanticide, 91, 155
inflation
    in the former Soviet Union, 843

in the Great War, 715
in the Weimar Republic, 743, 744
Innocent III (Pope)
    Catharism and, 277
    Crusades and, 269–273
    Mongols and, 279
    papal politics of, 271, 271 (illus.)
Innocent X (Pope), 432 (illus.)
An Inquiry into the Nature and Causes of the Wealth of Nations (Smith), 499, 501
inquisitions
    French, 278
    Roman, 408
    Spanish, 317, 553
Inside the Victorian Home (Flanders), 608
Institutes (Calvin), 402, 403
intendants, 437
interdict, 271
International Monetary Fund (IMF), 805–806, 862
International War Crimes Tribunal, 845, 846
International Working Men's Organization, 683–685
interwar era (1918–1939), 729–759
    Austrian Anschluss, 759
    culture, 748–752, 748 (illus.), 749 (illus.), 750 (illus.)
    in eastern Europe, 744–746, 745 (illus.)
    in France and Britain, 731, 738–739, 739 (map)
    Great Depression, 738, 741, 752, 753, 753 (illus.)
    Italian fascism, 741–742, 742 (illus.), 757–758, 761 (source document)
    men in, 747–748
    Nazi rise to power in Germany, 743–744, 752, 754–757, 755 (illus.), 757 (illus.)
    opposition in colonies, 738–741, 739 (map), 740 (illus.)
    science, philosophy, and literature in, 750–751
    in the Soviet Union, 732–738, 733 (map), 735 (illus.), 737 (illus.)
    Spanish Civil War, 758–759, 758 (map), 759 (illus.)
    timeline, 730–731 (illus.)
    Weimar Republic (Germany), 742–744, 743 (illus.)
    women in, 729–731, 730 (illus.), 747, 747 (illus.)
Investiture Controversy, 245–247, 246 (illus.), 271, 390
Ioannes Myronas, 284
Ionia, 52, 53 (map), 60–61
Iphigenia (Racine), 665
Iran. *See also* Persian Empire
    cuneiform writing from, 15, 15 (illus.)
    Indo-European migration into, 11
    under Reza Shah Pahlavi, 739
Iraq. *See also* Babylon/Babylonians; Mesopotamia
    Abbasid Caliphate in, 208 (illus.), 215–216
    as British mandate, 739, 739 (map)
    Seljuk Turks in, 248
    United States war against, 856, 858
Ireland
    bank collapse in, 861, 862
    civil war with England, 430, 449, 451
    colonial soldiers from, 644

emigration from, 669, 670 (illus.)
in the French Revolution, 540
in the Great War, 703, 719
independence from England, 739
potato famine, 588
religious freedoms, after Napoleonic Wars, 567
Viking raids on, 224
Irenaeus of Lyons, 170
Irish Free State, 739
iron
    advantages of, 27–28
    in Greece, 39, 40–41
    Industrial Revolution and, 582, 584
    Israel and, 32
Iron Age, 5, 39, 40–41
Iron Cross (Prussian), 550
Iron Curtain, 795, 802 (map), 829
Iron Guard (Romania), 745
Iroquois people, 375
irrigation, 13, 96
Isaac (Hebrew patriarch), 30, 32
Isabella (queen of Spain), 317, 367–368
Ishtar (goddess), 32
Isis (goddess), 22, 97, 151
Islam/Islamic lands. *See also* Ottoman Empire
    Byzantine Empire and, 209–210
    Carolingians and, 211
    chronology of, 206
    in Europe, 822, 836
    First Crusade and, 254–256, 255 (map), 256 (illus.)
    Istanbul in, 318, 319, 319 (illus.)
    Muhammad and, 198–199, 206–208
    plague in, 305, 305 (illus.)
    Portuguese spice trade and, 380–381
    radical, 858
    schism in, 208
    Second Crusade and, 270, 270 (illus.)
    Seljuk Turks and, 248
    in Spain, 207 (map), 208, 215–216, 216 (illus.)
    spread of, 207 (map), 208
Islamism, 858
Ismail, Pasha (khedive of Egypt), 651
Isocrates, 75–76, 83
Israel
    formation of, by Hebrews, 32
    formation of modern, 814 (map), 815
    Samarian conquest of, 32
Israel, Jonathan, 519
Istanbul, 318, 319, 319 (illus.), 625
Italia, 139
Italian Renaissance. *See* Renaissance, Italian
Italian War (90–88 BCE), 139–140
Italy. *See also* Renaissance, Italian; Roman Empire; Roman Republic; western Europe, after World War II
    African colonies of, 657 (map)
    after World War II, 813
    in the Carolingian empire, 213 (map)
    colonies of, 376, 636
    Congress of Vienna and, 562, 564 (map)
    Crimean War and, 616
    economic crisis in, 862
    emigration from, 669, 670 (illus.)
    Enlightenment in, 509–510
    Ethiopian invasions by, 658, 758

Italy (continued)
 fascism in, 741–742, 742 (illus.), 761 (source document)
 Florence (See Florence)
 French and Spanish in, 336
 Genoa, 361–362
 Germanic tribes in, 181 (map), 183
 government in, after 1989, 847
 in the Great Famine, 298–299
 in the Great War, 702, 702 (map), 707, 723
 Greek colonies in, 115
 in the High Middle Ages, 278 (map)
 Huns in, 183
 Indo-European migration into, 11
 Jews in, 341, 342, 342 (illus.), 757
 Justinian in, 189–192, 190 (map)
 kingdoms and communes in, 330
 under the Lombards, 181, 181 (map), 201–202, 212–213
 maps of, 107 (map)
 Milan, 306 (map), 308, 329 (map), 336, 509
 Naples, 329 (map), 336, 509
 Napoleon in, 546, 552 (map)
 nationalist movements in, 574, 574 (map)
 Norman invasion of, 248
 Ostrogoths in, 185 (map), 186–187, 186 (illus.), 189–190, 191–192
 Padua, University of, 285 (map), 327, 328, 342, 345
 Papal States, 278 (map), 329 (map), 331–332
 plague in, 306 (map), 308
 political corruption in, 847, 857
 Ravenna, 182, 190
 revolution of 1848, 588, 589 (map), 590, 591
 under the Roman Republic, 115–117
 Rome (See Rome)
 unification of, 616, 618–619, 618 (map), 619 (illus.)
 Venice (See Venice)
 worker revolts, after the plague, 311
 in World War II, 775, 789
Ivanhoe (Scott), 578
Ivan III (the Great), 440, 442 (illus.)
Ivan IV (the Terrible; czar of Russia), 440–442, 441 (map)
ivory trade, 657
Iwo Jima, 780 (map), 790

al-Jabarti, Abd al-Rahman, 547
Jacob (Hebrew patriarch), 30
Jacobin Club, 533, 535, 537, 540
Jacobite revolution, 499 (map), 500
Jacquerie, 310, 311 (illus.)
James Edward Stuart (prince of Wales), 500
James I and VI (king of England), 427, 447–449
James II (king of England), 452, 452 (illus.), 500
Jameson, Leander Starr, 660
Janissaries, 446
Jansenism, 464
Japan
 atomic bombs dropped on, 788, 792
 defeat of China by (1895), 652
 in the Great War, 711
 Jesuit missionaries in, 382
 Russo-Japanese War, 686, 687, 687 (illus.)
 in World War II, 774, 777–779, 779 (illus.), 780 (map), 790, 792

Jardin des Plantes (Paris), 646
Jaruzelski, Wojciech, 811, 828
Jasenovać prison camp, 776, 776 (illus.)
Jaurès, Jean, 703
Jean de Meun, 283
Jefferson, Thomas, 529
Jenner, Edward, 485
Jeremiah (Hebrew prophet), 32
Jericho, 10, 19 (map), 30
Jerusalem
 Assyrian attack on, 32
 Babylonian conquest of, 32
 Christianity in, 177
 Crusades and, 255 (map), 256, 270
 divided between Israel and Palestine, 815
 Hebrew conquest of, 32
 Islam in, 207 (map), 208
 Roman looting of, 150, 152, 152 (illus.)
 Seljuk Turks in, 254
Jesuits, 382, 407–408, 407 (illus.), 624
Jesus of Nazareth, 153. See also Christianity
The Jewish State (Herzl), 690
Jewish Temple, Roman looting of, 150, 152, 152 (illus.)
Jews. See also anti-Semitism; Hebrews; Israel; Judaism
 Crusades and persecution of, 255, 269
 in the Enlightenment, 506, 508
 expelled from Spain, 317
 in the fin de siècle, 672, 688–690, 690 (illus.)
 in the French Revolution, 534
 in ghettoes, 467
 in Great Britain, 601
 in the Great Depression, 753
 in the Great Famine, 298
 in the Great War, 704, 708
 in Hellenistic Ages, 99
 in the High Middle Ages, 277
 in the Italian Renaissance, 341, 342, 342 (illus.)
 Jewish conspiracy myth, 743, 766
 Nazi Party on, before World War II, 755–757, 757 (illus.)
 in the Ottoman Empire, 339
 in the Pale of Settlement, 506, 570, 606, 744
 in the plague, 308
 in Poland, pre-war Nazi persecution of, 744, 757
 as pseudo-bankers, 473
 rabbis and, 464
 in the Restoration era, 567–568, 570
 Roman Empire and, 150
 in Romania, 745
 in Russia, 506, 688–689, 689 (map)
 signs required on, 277, 769 (illus.)
 in World War II, in France, 774
 in World War II, in Germany, 766, 767–768, 768 (illus.)
 in World War II, in Holocaust/Nazi Final Solution, 781, 782–784, 782 (illus.), 783 (map), 784 (illus.)
 in World War II, in medical experiments, 788
 in World War II, in Nazi sex laws, 769
 in World War II, in Poland, 767 (map), 768, 770, 771–772

 in World War II, in Reichskristallnacht, 767–768, 768 (illus.)
 in World War II, in the Balkans, 776
 in World War II, in the Soviet Union, 780
 on Zionism, 689, 690
jihad, 207–208, 547, 708, 710
Jinnah, Muhammad Ali, 814
Joan of Arc, 315–316, 316 (illus.)
João (John) I (king of Portugal), 364, 367
John I (king of England), 273, 280
John II (king of France), 302–303
John of Salisbury, 266, 280
John of the Cross, 408
John Paul II (Pope), 847–848, 848 (illus.)
John XII (Pope), 239
John XXIII (Pope), 333
joint-stock companies, 474, 474 (illus.)
Joseph (king of Spain), 552–553
Joseph II (Austrian emperor), 506, 508–509, 512, 518, 568
Josephine (consort of Napoleon Bonaparte), 554
Josephus, 150
Joshua, 30
The Joshua Tree (U2), 835
Journal des Dames, 511
A Journal of the Disasters in Afghanistan (Sale), 653
"Joy through Work" campaign, 754
Juan Diego Cuauhtlatoatzin, Saint, 378
Judaea, 147, 150
Judah, kingdom of, 32
Judaism. See also Jews
 Ark of the Covenant, 30, 31, 32
 in the Cold War years, 822
 covenant with one God, 29, 30, 32
 formative phase, 29–30
 in the Roman Empire, 152–153, 152 (illus.)
 scriptural basis of, 31
Judith and Her Maidservant with the Head of Holofernes (Gentileschi), 410
Jud Süss (film), 788
Jugurtha (king of Numidia), 138, 139
Julian (apostate), 179–180
Julie, or the Nouvelle Heloise (Rousseau), 504, 510–511
Julio-Claudian emperors, 157–158
Julius II (Pope), 349
July Ordinances (France), 575
July Revolution (France), 575, 575 (illus.)
June Days (Paris), 590–591
Junkers, 440
Jupiter (god), 109, 113, 118
Justin (Roman emperor), 187
Justinian (Roman emperor), 188–192, 188 (illus.), 189 (illus.), 190 (map), 285
Justin Martyr, 170
Juvenal, 156

Kandahar, Alexander in, 83 (map), 85
Kandinsky, Wassily, 677
Kant, Immanuel, 494, 501, 507–508, 515, 577
Das Kapital (Marx), 611
Karadžic, Radovan, 845, 846
Kara Mustapha, 439, 439 (illus.)
Karl Max-Hof (Vienna), 750
Karnak, temple at, 23
Katyn Forest massacre, 771

Kazakhstan, 841 (map)
keep, castle, 237
Kennedy, John F., 809
Kenya, 814 (map), 817
Kepler, Johannes, 482–483
Kerensky, Alexander, 716, 718
Ketuvim, 29
Kew Gardens (London), 514, 514 (illus.), 646
KGB (Soviet secret police), 717, 803
Kharijites, 208
Khartoum (Sudan), British invasion of, 652
Khayyam, Omar, 248
Khodorovsky, Mikhail, 857
Khrushchev, Nikita, 808–809, 809 (illus.)
Kimberley diamond mines, 632, 632 (map), 655, 655 (illus.)
King Death Triumphs, 312 (illus.)
Kingdom of Serbs, Croats, and Slovenes, 745–746. See also Yugoslavia
King James Bible, 448
King Solomon's Mines (Haggard), 674
Kipling, Rudyard, 650, 653
Kirch, Gottfried, 485
Kirch, Maria Winkelmann, 485, 487
Kirov, Sergei, 735, 737
Kish (Iraq), 16
"Kitchen Debate," 809 (illus.)
Kitchener, Horatio, 652
Klaus, Václav, 841
Klebemarks, 807
Klemperer, Victor, 756, 791
knighthood, 303–304
Knights Revolt, 396
Knights Templar, 299–300
Knossos, palace at, 25, 26 (illus.)
Kohl, Helmut, 825, 836, 838
koine, 92
Kollontai, Alexandra, 729–731, 730 (illus.)
Kollwitz, Käthe, 722, 722 (illus.)
Könsgen, Ewald, 265
Koprülü Mehmed (Ottoman grand vizier), 446
Koraes, Adamantios, 571
Korea, division of, 814 (map), 815, 817
Kosciuszko, Tadeusz, 540
Kosovo, 844, 846
Kossuth, Lajos, 589, 590 (illus.), 591
Kotkin, Steven, 827
kouroi, kore, 49, 49 (illus.)
Kramer, Alan, 706
Kremlin (Russia), 441, 442 (illus.)
Kruger, Paul, 660
Kubrick, Stanley, 818
Kuchma, Leonid, 857
kulaks, 735, 803
Kulturkampf, 624, 627
Kun, Bela, 745
Kursk, Battle at (1943), 789
Küyük Khan, 279, 279 (illus.)
Kwaśniewski, Aleksander, 856
Kyrgyzstan, 841 (map)

Lab'aya, 25
labor unions, 604, 684, 754
The Ladies Monthly, 511
The Ladies' Paradise (Zola), 681
Lafayette, Marquis de, 532
laissez faire, 499
Lake Trasimene, Battle of (217 BCE), 122

Lamarck, Jean-Baptiste, 613
land ownership
    in fascism, 742
    in Greece, ancient, 40–41, 46
    in the Hellenistic Age, 91
    manorialism, 220–221, 221 (illus.), 235
    in Norman England, 250
    in the Roman Empire, 138
    in the Roman Republic, 116, 136, 138
    in Soviet eastern Europe, 803
    in the Soviet Union, 734–735, 735 (illus.)
    vassalage and, 233, 234–236, 235 (illus.)
    in Victorian Britain, 609–610
land taxes, 467
Lang, Fritz, 749
Langland, William, 298
language
    Aramaic, 52
    in the Austrian empire, 508–509
    Chinese, 856
    English, 241, 855–856
    Etruscan, 105
    in German unification, 620
    Greek, modern, 571
    in the Hellenistic Age, 92, 92 (illus.)
    Indo-European, 11, 12 (map)
    in Italian unification, 618–619
    koine, 92
    Latin, 126, 179, 201, 217–218
    Romaic, 179
    Romance, 126
    Semitic (Akkadian), 17
    in Spanish colonies, 377
    vernacular, in the Renaissance, 343
Laon, commune of, 276
Laon Cathedral, 273
Laos, 652–653, 815
Las Casas, Bartolommeo de, 378, 380
Lascaux cave paintings (France), 7, 9
Last Judgment (Gislebertus), 230–231 (illus.), 232
Late Middle Ages (1300–1500), 293–321
    Avignon papacy, 299–300, 300 (illus.)
    chivalry in, 302–304, 303 (illus.)
    critics of the Church, 313–314, 314 (illus.)
    economy, after the plague, 310
    fall of Constantinople, 318, 319, 319 (illus.)
    fiscal pressures on monarchies after, 314–315
    Great Famine, 297–298, 297 (illus.)
    Holy Roman Empire fragmentation in, 300–301
    Hundred Years' War, 301–302, 302 (map), 315–316, 316 (illus.)
    Little Ice Age, 295–297, 295 (illus.), 296 (illus.)
    new monarchies in, 316–318, 317 (illus.), 318 (map)
    plague in, 293–294, 294 (illus.), 304–310, 305 (illus.), 306 (illus.), 307 (illus.), 309 (illus.)
    popular histories of, 320
    religion, after the plague, 311–313, 312 (illus.)
    social insurrection in, 310–311, 311 (illus.)
    timeline, 294–295 (illus.)
Lateran Accords, 741
Latin alphabet, 29 (illus.)
Latin Empire of Constantinople, 272, 337

Latin language, 126, 179, 201, 217–218
Latin League, 114
Latin peoples (Italy), 107, 112, 114, 139
Latvia
    independence of, 840, 841 (map)
    Soviet occupation of, 767 (map), 771
    in the Soviet Union, 802 (map), 804–805
Laud, William (archbishop of Canterbury), 449, 463
Law of Suspects (France), 539, 543
Law of Two-Thirds (France), 543
Lawrence, T. E. (Lawrence of Arabia), 710
Lawrence of Portugal, 279
Laws (Plato), 80
Laws of Burgos, 378
The Lawyer (Arcimboldo), 404 (illus.)
lay investiture, 246
League of Nations, 723, 757, 766
Lebanon, Phoenicians in, 28, 28 (map)
Lebensraum, 707, 778
Le Bon, Gustave, 678, 695 (source document)
Le Carré, John, 818
Le Chapelier, Isaac René Guy, 536
legal systems
    in ancient Greece, 46, 47
    Code of Hammurabi, 17, 17 (illus.)
    Code of Ur-Nammu, 17
    in the eastern Roman Empire, 189, 285
    Hebrew, 30, 31
    Islamic, 207–208
    jury trials, 280
    Napoleonic Code, 548–549
    in the Old Regimes, 460
    in the Restoration era, 567–568
    in the Roman Republic, 112
    in the Spanish colonies, 377–378
    trial by ordeal, 17, 251, 272, 280
Legion of Honor (France), 550, 550 (illus.)
legions, Roman, 114–115
legumes, domestication of, 10
leisure time, in Victorian Britain, 608
Lend-Lease Agreement, 775, 777
Lenin, Vladimir
    in forming the Soviet Union, 734
    in the Great War, 703
    in the Russian Revolution, 717–718, 717 (illus.)
    "What Is to Be Done?", 685
Leningrad, siege of (1941), 781, 781 (illus.)
Lennon, John, 819
Leo III (Byzantine), 209–210
Leo III (Pope), 197–198
Leo IX (Pope), 245
Leonardo da Vinci, 346, 347–348, 347 (illus.)
Leonidas (king of Sparta), 54
Leopold I (king of Belgium), 574
Leopold II (king of Belgium), 656–657, 656 (illus.), 662 (source document)
Leo X (Pope), 394, 402 (illus.)
Leo XIII (Pope), 685–686
Lepidus, 144, 145
Lermontov, Mikhail, 641
Lesseps, Ferdinand de, 566, 651–652
Lessing, Gotthold Ephraim, 508
"A Letter Concerning Toleration" (Locke), 497
letters of credit, 338
Letters on Sunspots (Galileo), 483
Letters to Atticus (Cicero), 341
Letters to the Ancient Dead (Petrarch), 341

Letter to the Corinthians (Paul), 153
Letter to the Grand Duchess Christina (Galileo), 483
Lettow-Vorbeck, Paul von, 710
le Vasseur, Marie-Thérèse, 505
levée en masse, 538–539, 549
Levelers, 451
Levi, Primo, 783–784
Leviathan (Hobbes), 434–435
Lewis of Bavaria, 300
Lex Gabinia, 141
Libby, Willard, 7
liberals (liberalism)
    after the revolutions of 1848, 598–600, 599 *(illus.)*
    anti-Semitism and, 688–689
    in Austria-Hungary, 691
    class society and, 607–608, 682
    command economies in the Great War and, 715
    in England, 575, 579–580, 587–588, 593, 601–603
    in the fin de siècle, 670, 683–684
    in France, 603–604, 605, 695
    in the French Revolution, 575, 575 *(illus.)*, 589–590, 668
    in Hamburg, 684
    India and, 637, 643
    Enlightenment and, 498, 504
    nationalism and, 570, 574
    positivism and, 611–612
    in the Restoration era, 563–565, 564 *(illus.)*, 567–568, 590, 591
    in Russia, 576, 576 *(illus.)*, 606
    in Spain, 553
    Tocqueville as, 559–561, 560 *(illus.)*
libraries
    at Alexandria, 97–98
    at Pergamum, 97
    at the Vatican, 331
La Libre Parole (*The Free Word*; Drumont), 688–689, 690 *(illus.)*
Libro dell'Oro (*Book of Gold*), 338–339
Libya
    Islam in, 207 *(map)*
    Italian conquest of, 693, 693 *(map)*
    Vandals in, 185, 185 *(map)*
    in World War II, 775
Licinius, 177
life
    in Augustan Rome, 153–154, 153 *(illus.)*
    in Benedictine monasteries, 200–201
    in the Blitz (Britain), 774–775, 775 *(illus.)*
    of clergy, eighteenth-century, 463 *(illus.)*, 463–464
    of colonial soldiers, 643–644
    in the Enlightenment, 516
    in Gaul, 205–206, 205 *(illus.)*
    in the Great Famine, 299
    in Greece, ancient, 47–48, 48 *(illus.)*, 59–60, 60 *(illus.)*
    in the Hellenistic Age, 91
    in the interwar years, 751–752
    in Justinian cities, 191–192
    in medieval universities, 287, 287 *(illus.)*
    of monarchs, eighteenth-century, 461–462, 461 *(illus.)*
    of nobles, eighteenth-century, 464–466
    in Norman England, 251

    on the road, 471
    on sea voyages, 372
    of serfs and peasants, eighteenth-century, 468–470, 469 *(illus.)*
    in the Soviet Union, 736–737, 737 *(illus.)*, 825–826
    in towns, eighteenth-century, 467–468, 467 *(illus.)*, 468 *(illus.)*
    in Victorian Britain, 607–611, 609 *(illus.)*, 610 *(illus.)*
    in World War II, in Europe, 780–789, 782 *(illus.)*, 784 *(illus.)*, 786 *(illus.)*, 787 *(illus.)*
life expectancy
    in Augustan Rome, 155
    in the eighteenth century, 470
    in Europe, after 1989, 860
    in the High Middle Ages, 273
lighthouse at Pharos, 73
lighting, artificial, 608
Lincoln, Abraham, 616–618, 617 *(illus.)*
Linear A script, 25
Linear B script, 26, 40
linear perspective, 345, 347
Linnaeus, Carolus, 514, 515, 612
Lin Zexu, 640
Lister, Joseph, 679
Liszt, Franz, 578, 578 *(illus.)*, 615 *(illus.)*
literature
    Alexandrian, 97–98
    Augustan, 149–151
    Baroque, 432–433, 435
    captivity narratives, 481, 481 *(illus.)*
    in Czechoslovakia, 810
    Enlightenment, 497, 502–504, 510–512
    in the fin de siècle, 677–678
    Hellenistic, 77–78
    Hittite, 27
    Latin and Greek classics, 341
    Mesopotamian, 18
    modernist, 675, 677–678
    postmodernist, 855
    realist, 612
    Renaissance, 341–343, 351–353, 352 *(illus.)*
    Romanesque, 237–238, 238 *(illus.)*
    Roman Republic, 126–128, 126 *(illus.)*, 141–142
    Romantic, 577–578
    Russian, 607
    for women, 511
Lithuania
    Catholic Church in, 822
    in the Great War, 707
    independence of, 840, 841 *(map)*
    Poland and, 744
    Soviet Union and, 767 *(map)*, 771, 802 *(map)*, 804–805
    in World War II, 785
The Little Commentary (Copernicus), 482
Little Ice Age, 295–297, 295 *(illus.)*, 296 *(illus.)*, 425 *(illus.)*
Little Man, What Now? (Fallada), 751
Little Peace of the Church (260–302), 171–172
Liudprand of Cremona, 239, 240
Livingstone, David, 630–631 *(illus.)*, 645
Livius Andronicus, 126
Livy, 110, 111, 118, 124
Lloyd, Marie, 674, 674 *(illus.)*
Locke, John, 495, 497–498, 563

logographs, 20
logos, 49
Lollards (idlers), 314
Lombards, 181, 181 *(map)*, 201–202, 212–213
London
    Crystal Palace Exhibition (1851), 610, 610 *(illus.)*
    in the Enlightenment, 497, 497 *(illus.)*, 514, 514 *(illus.)*
    fin de siècle, 670
    fire in, 467
    rapid transportation in, 606
    Spanish flu in, 720
    traffic in (1910), 668 *(illus.)*
London, Treaty of (1839), 574, 700
London Underground, 606, 672, 775 *(illus.)*
longbows, 301, 302 *(illus.)*, 304
longitude, 485
long peace (1815–1914), 643
Loos, Adolf, 677
The Lord of the Rings (Tolkien), 320
Lorenzetti, Ambrogio, 274 *(illus.)*, 330 *(illus.)*
Lorenzo Valla, 314, 344
The Lost Love Letters of Heloise and Abelard (Mews), 265
Lothar I (Carolingian), 222, 223, 224, 224 *(map)*
Louisiana Territory, 480, 635
Louis IV (king of France), 242
Louis IX (Saint Louis; king of France), 273, 282
Louis-Napoleon Bonaparte. *See* Napoleon III (French emperor)
Louis Philippe (king of France), 575, 575 *(illus.)*, 588–589
Louis the German (Carolingian), 222, 224 *(map)*
Louis the Pious, 215, 218, 222, 223, 223 *(illus.)*
Louis VI (the Fat; king of France), 267
Louis XI (Spider King; king of France), 316–317
Louis XII (king of France), 336, 410
Louis XIII (king of France), 428, 437
Louis XIV (Sun King; king of France)
    absolute monarchy of, 421–423, 422 *(illus.)*
    hunting by, 462
    palace at Versailles, 420–421 *(illus.)*, 437
    Protestantism banned by, 431
    wars and annexations of, 437–438, 438 *(map)*, 477
Louis XV (king of France), 430, 462, 501
Louis XVI (king of France)
    beheading of, 538, 538 *(illus.)*
    flight and return of, 534, 535
    governing by, 462
    indecision of, before the Revolution, 529, 530–531
    during the Revolution, 531–538
Louis XVIII (king of France), 555, 562, 575
Lourdes (Harris), 676
Lourdes pilgrimages, 676, 676 *(illus.)*
L'Ouverture, Toussaint, 540 *(illus.)*, 541
Louvre (Paris), 646, 648
"love-ins," 821, 821 *(illus.)*
Loyola, Ignatius, 407
Lucan, 157
Lucretius, 141
Luddites, 588
Ludendorff, Erich von, 707, 719

Lueger, Karl, 685
lugals, 16
Lukashenko, Alexander, 858
Lully, Jean-Baptiste, 434
Lumière, Auguste and Louis, 675
Lusitania, sinking of, 712
Luther, Martin
    Bible translation by, 395–396
    excommunication of, 394–395
    Indulgence Controversy and, 392–394,
        393 (*illus.*), 400
    Katherina von Bora and, 388–389
    Lutheran doctrines, 396–397
    as a monk, 391–392, 391 (*illus.*)
    Ninety-Five Theses, 392–393, 418–419
        (*source document*)
    on the Peasants' War, 398, 398 (*illus.*)
    spread of Lutheranism, 398–399
    Zwingli and, 399, 401
Lützen, Battle at (1632), 429
Luxemburg, Rosa, 684
Lycurgan code, 56
Lydia and Lydians, 48, 51, 52, 52 (*illus.*), 53
    (*map*), 105
Lysistrata (Aristophanes), 66

Maastricht Treaty (1992), 849
Ma'at, 22
Macao, Portuguese in, 380
MacArthur, Douglas, 815
Macaulay, Thomas, 637
Macedonia. *See also* Alexander the Great
    under Perseus, 124, 124 (*illus.*), 125
    under Philip, 74, 75–77, 75 (*map*), 76
        (*illus.*)
    Roman Republic conquest of, 123–125
    struggles for independence, 626, 626
        (*map*), 629 (*source document*)
Machiavelli, Niccolò, 335–336, 335 (*illus.*),
    355
machine guns, 650–651, 712
Macrinus (Roman emperor), 167
Madame Bovary (Flaubert), 612
Madeira Islands, 364–365
Madness and Civilization (Foucault), 820
Maecenas, 150
Maga, Hubert, 638
magazines, women's, 511, 609
Magdeburg, in the Thirty Years' War, 428,
    428 (*illus.*), 430
Magellan, Ferdinand, 372, 382
The Magic Mountain (Mann), 751
magistrates, 108
Magna Carta, 273, 280
Magritte, René, 750
Magyars, 226, 239, 626
al-Mahdi (Mehmed Ahmad), 652
Mahomet II (the Conqueror; Turkish
    sultan), 318, 319, 319 (*illus.*), 339
Maintenon, Madame de, 438
Maitland, F. W., 236
maize, domestication of, 10
Maji Maji Rebellion, 658
Malaya, Japanese control of, 777
Malevich, Kasimir, 748
La Malinche, 377 (*illus.*)
Mallarmé, Stephane, 678
*The Malleus Maleficarum (The Hammer of
    Witches)*, 435

Malplaquet, Battle of, 438, 438 (*map*)
Malthus, Thomas, 579, 612
Mamertines, 121
Mamluks, 545, 546 (*map*), 547
Mammitzsch, Ulrich, 320
Manchester, England, 560–561, 587–588, 587
    (*illus.*)
Manchuria
    in the Great War, 711
    in the Russo-Japanese War, 687, 687
        (*illus.*), 777
    in World War II, 780 (*map*)
mandates (mandate system), 723, 738
Mandela, Nelson, 848 (*illus.*)
Mandeville, John, 361, 362, 362 (*illus.*)
Manet, Edouard, 611, 612, 614 (*illus.*)
Manhattan Project, 788
Manheimer, Valentin, 599 (*illus.*)
Manichaeans, 176, 277
"Manifesto of the Temporary Government
    of Macedonia, March 23, 1881," 629
    (*source document*)
Mann, Thomas, 751, 754
manorialism, 220–221, 221 (*illus.*), 235
Mantinea, Battle of (362 BCE), 75
The Man without Qualities (Musil), 751
Mao Zedong, 809
maps and mapmaking
    fourteenth-century, 360 (*map*)
    nineteenth-century, 646, 647, 647 (*illus.*)
    Portuguese, 362
    Romanesque, 256 (*map*)
    sixteenth-century, 371 (*map*)
Marat, Jean Paul, 524 (*illus.*), 538, 541, 542
Maratha Confederacy, 637
Marathon, Battle of (490 BCE), 53, 54 (*map*)
Marcionite Christians, 170
Marcus Aurelius (Roman emperor), 157,
    159
Mari (Iraq), 17
Maria Theresa (Holy Roman emperor), 439,
    440, 508
marine insurance, 474
Marius, Gaius, 139
Marne, Battle of the (1914), 705, 705 (*map*)
marriage
    in ancient Egypt, 23
    in Augustan Rome, 154
    civil, 570
    domestic violence and, 586–587
    in the Hellenistic Age, 91
    Luther on, 397
    in the Roman Republic, 112
    same-sex, 849
    socialists on, 565, 566
The Marriage of Figaro (Mozart), 518
Marsalis, Wynton, 550 (*illus.*)
The Marseillaise, 539, 602
Marshall, George, 806
Marshall Plan, 806
Marsi, 139
Marsilius of Padua, 300
Martin, John, 578
Martin of Tours, 180
Martin V (Pope), 313, 331–332
The Martyrdom of Man, 632
Marx, Karl, 565, 589, 608, 611, 683–684
Marxism, in the Cold War, 818
Mary Barton (Gaskell), 619

Mary I (Bloody Mary; queen of England), 413
Mary II (queen of England), 452–453, 452
    (*illus.*)
Mary Stuart (queen of the Scots), 414
Masaccio, 347
Masaryk, Tomáš, 746
mass culture, 674–675, 674 (*illus.*)
Massialot, François, 517
mass transportation, 606, 671–672
matchlock muskets, 476
materfamilias, 112
*The Mathematical Principles of Natural
    Philosophy* (Newton), 483–484
mathematics, 49, 97
Matisse, Henri, 750
Matralia, 119
matrilineal societies, Paleolithic, 11
Matteotti, Giacomo, 741
Matthys, Jan, 405
Mauretania, 157, 159 (*map*)
Maurice and William of Nassau, 476–477
Maxim gun, 650–651
Maximian, 173
Max von Baden (German chancellor), 719
Maya Empire, 379
Mayakovsky, Vladimir, 751
Mayan codices, 379
Mazarin (Cardinal), 463 (*illus.*)
Mazzini, Giuseppe, 574, 589, 618
McCartney, Paul, 819
McCormick, Michael, 211
McDonald's, 852, 852 (*illus.*)
McLuhan, Marshall, 854
Mecca, 206–207
Medea (Euripides), 65
Medici, Catherine de', 411–412
Medici, Cosimo de', 333–334, 333 (*illus.*), 336,
    346, 347
Medici, Giovanni di Bicci de', 333–334, 333
    (*illus.*)
Medici, Lorenzo de' (the Magnificent), 327,
    333–334, 333 (*illus.*), 349
Medici, Piero de', 333 (*illus.*), 346
Medici family, 333–334, 333 (*illus.*), 483
medicine
    anatomical revolution, 484–485, 484
        (*illus.*)
    Asclepius and Hippocrates, 81–82, 81
        (*illus.*)
    bacteriology, 679
    concentration camp experiments, 788
    Hellenistic, 81–82, 81 (*illus.*), 96–97
    midwives, 487
    nurses, in wars, 616, 703
    penicillin, 788–789
    during the plague, 305, 305 (*illus.*), 307
        (*illus.*)
    quinine tablets, 650
    vaccinations, 484–485, 679
Medieval Warm Period, 253, 273, 295
Meditations (Marcus Aurelius), 159
Medvedev, Dmitry, 843
megaliths, 10–11, 10 (*illus.*)
Mehmed Ahmad (al-Mahdi), 652
Mehmed IV (Ottoman sultan), 446, 446 (*illus.*)
Meiji Restoration (Japan), 640
Mein Kampf (Hitler), 744
Melitus (Turkey), 52
Melos, Athenian conquest of, 63

men
    in the interwar years, 747–748
    in Sparta, 56
Menander, 78, 127, 128
Mendel, Gregor, 679
Mendelssohn, Moses, 508
mendicant orders, 273, 277–278, 286
Menelik II (Ethiopian emperor), 658
Mengele, Josef, 788, 792
menhirs, 11
Mennonites, 406
Menno Simons, 406
Menon, François, 517
Menotti, Ciro, 574
Menshevik, 685
mental illness, 748, 771, 782
Menuhin, Yehudi, 751
Menzel, Adolf, 612
Menzies, Gavin, 381
mercantilism, 474–475, 499
mercury, 362, 378, 611
Merian, Dorothea Marie, 486
Merian, Maria Sibylla, 486, 486 (illus.), 487, 495
meritocracy, 495
Merkel, Angela, 862, 864 (source document)
Merovingians, 187–188, 202–206, 205 (illus.), 211–213. See also Carolingians
Mersenne, Marin, 485
Mesolithic period, 4 (illus.), 7, 10–11, 10 (illus.)
Mesopotamia. See also Babylon/Babylonians
    appearance of cities in, 13–14, 13 (map)
    city-states and empires in, 16–17
    as civilization, 5, 5 (illus.)
    early agriculture in, 9
    Egyptian invasion in, 22
    in the Great War, 710
    map of (1450 BCE), 26 (map)
    in the Persian Empire, 51
    religion in, 17–18
    in the Seleucid kingdom, 89 (map)
    writing in, 14–16, 14 (illus.)
Mesopotamian model, 13
Messena, 56, 121
Metamorphoses (Ovid), 151
Metamorphoses of the Insects of Surinam (Merian), 486
Metellus Celer, 145
Methodism, 464, 570, 644
metics, 59
metric system, 541–542
Metropolis (Lang), 749
Metsys, Quentin, 388 (illus.)
Metternich, Klemens von, 561–562, 564 (map), 574, 589
Mews, Constant J., 265
Mexica (Aztec) Empire, 358, 372–374, 377–379, 377 (illus.), 379 (illus.)
Mexico
    in the Great War, 713
    maize in, 10
    Mexica (Aztec) Empire, 358, 372–374, 377–379, 377 (illus.), 379 (illus.)
    Mexico City, founding of, 373–374
    student massacre (1968), 821
Michael Romanov (czar of Russia), 442
Michelangelo Buonarotti, 346, 349

Middle Ages. See Early Middle Ages; Gothic High Middle Ages; Late Middle Ages; Romanesque Central Middle Ages
middle classes, in Victorian Britain, 608
Middle East. See also Mesopotamia; Persian Empire; specific countries
    Abbasid Caliphate, 208 (illus.), 215–216
    Alexander the Great in, 83–86, 83 (map)
    Bactria, 86, 89–90, 89 (map)
    birth of agriculture in, 9
    decolonization after World War II, 814 (map)
    in the interwar years, 739 (map)
    Seleucid kingdom, 73 (illus.), 88–89, 89 (map), 123–125
    spread of Islam in, 207–208, 207 (map)
Middle Kingdom, Egypt, 20, 21–22
middle passage, of African slaves, 475
Middle Republic (Roman), 118 , 119–125, 120 (map), 122 (map), 129. See also Roman Republic
Midway, Battle of (1942), 777, 780 (map)
midwives, 487
Mies van der Rohe, Ludwig, 750
migrant workers, 471
migrations
    Archaic Greek colonization as, 44–45, 44 (map), 45 (illus.)
    of Ashkenazi jews, 688
    into Europe after World War II, 836
    in the fin de siècle, 669–670, 670 (illus.)
    guest workers, 813, 848
    Hebrew Diaspora, 32
    of Homo sapiens sapiens, 6, 8 (map)
    Indo-European (after 2000 BCE), 26
    Indo-European (3500–1500 BCE), 5 (illus.), 11, 12 (map)
    internal European, in the fin de siècle, 669–670
Mi'kmaq people, 375
Milan
    in the Enlightenment, 509
    French seizure of, 336
    in the Italian Renaissance, 329 (map)
    plague in, 306 (map), 308
military
    in Carthage, 121
    colonial soldiers, 643–644
    in Greece, ancient, 56–57, 94–95
    in Hellenistic Ages, 94–95
    in Macedonia, 75
    medals, 550, 550 (illus.)
    under Napoleon, 549–551, 549 (illus.), 554–555, 555 (illus.)
    national draft, 538–539, 549
    in the Persian Empire, 52
    in the Roman Empire, 147, 166
    in the Roman Republic, 114–115, 136–137
    in the seventeenth and eighteenth centuries, 476–477
    standing armies, 477
Mill, James, 579–580
Mill, John Stuart, 580
millenarianism, 312, 405–406, 406 (illus.)
Millennium Declaration (EU), 837
Miller, Philip, 513–514
Milošević, Slobodan, 844, 846
Milton, John, 433

Milvian Bridge, Battle of (312), 177, 194 (source document)
mining
    diamonds, 632, 632 (map), 654–655, 655 (illus.)
    railroads and, 583
    silver, 220, 378, 443
    workers' conditions in, 378, 585–586, 586 (illus.)
Minoan civilization, 5 (illus.), 25–26, 26 (illus.), 26 (map)
Minos (king of Crete), 25
Minotaur, 25
Les Miserables (Hugo), 578
missi dominici, 214, 216
missionaries
    in Africa, 645, 657
    in Asia, 382, 644–645
    in China, 659
    Protestant, 644
    in Spanish colonies, 378, 379, 644
Missionary Travels and Researches in South Africa (Livingstone), 645
Miss Sarajevo beauty contestants, 845 (illus.)
Mitanni, 27
Mithraism, 176
Mithridates VI (rule of Pontus), 139–140, 141
Mitochondrial Eve, 6
Mitterrand, François, 825
Mladić, Radko, 845, 846
Moctezuma (emperor of Mexica), 373
modernism, 675, 675 (illus.), 677–678, 677 (illus.), 678 (illus.)
modernity, 667–669, 668 (illus.)
modernization
    of Great Britain, 601, 603, 603 (illus.)
    Rhine River engineering, 595–597, 596 (illus.), 596 (map)
    of Russia, 606
    of the Soviet Union, 737–738
Mohammed and Charlemagne (Pirenne), 211
Moll Flanders (Defoe), 510
Moltke, Helmuth von, 622, 701, 705
monarchies
    after the plague, 314–315
    Egyptian, 20–23, 20 (map), 21 (illus.)
    in England, after the Glorious Revolution, 452–453
    Hebrew, 29, 31–32
    Hellenistic, 88–91, 89 (map)
    in the High Middle Ages, 280
    Macedonian, 76
    Mesopotamian, 18
    origins of absolutism in, 424, 426
    Persian Empire, 51–52
    Spartan, 56
monasticism and ecclesiastical orders
    Augustinians, 378
    Benedictine, 199–201, 218–219
    Carolingians and, 218–219
    Cistercians, 268–269
    Cluniac reform of, 244–245, 244 (illus.)
    dissolved, in England, 401–402
    dissolved, in the French Revolution, 534
    Dominicans, 273, 277–278, 286, 288, 334, 378, 380
    eastern, 170
    in the Enlightenment, 519
    Franciscans, 273, 277–279, 378, 379, 382

Jesuits, 382, 407–408, 407 (illus.), 624
    monastic schools, 264, 266–267
    plague and, 311
    Protestant Reformation and, 387–389, 397
Monet, Claude, 613
money. See currency and money
Mongols, 279, 279 (illus.), 305
monophysite view of God, 179
monotheism, 23, 29. See also Hebrews;
        Judaism
Monroe Doctrine, 635
montage, 749
Montagnards (France), 537–538
Montagu, Mary Wortley, 484, 487
Montaigne, Michel de, 370
Montesquieu, Charles de Secondat, baron
        de, 501–502, 509
Monteverdi, Claudio, 434
Montgomery, Bernard, 789
Monti, Mario, 847, 862
More, Thomas, 351, 352, 401
Moreau, Gustave, 675, 675 (illus.)
Morocco, 688, 741, 758
mosaics
    Byzantine, 162–163 (illus.), 188 (illus.), 191
        (illus.)
    Roman, 167, 167 (illus.)
Moses, 29, 30
Mosse, Rudolf, 755
motion pictures
    in the Cold War, 818, 820
    in the fin de siècle, 675
    in the interwar years, 749, 749 (illus.)
    Nazi, 754–755
Motte-and-Bailey castles, 237, 237 (illus.)
Mozart, Wolfgang Amadeus, 516, 518, 518
        (illus.)
Mrs. Beeton's Book of Household Management,
        609
Muhammad, 198–199, 206–208
Muhammad al-Mahdi, 108
multitasking, 854 (illus.)
mummification, 22, 24, 97
mummy paintings, 98
municipal socialism, 685
Münster, millenarians in, 405–406, 406 (illus.)
Müntzer, Thomas, 398
Murat, Joachim, 552–553
Murrow, Edward R., 787–788, 792
music
    Baroque, 433–434
    Classical, 465, 465 (illus.)
    in the Cold War, 819, 819 (illus.), 820
    in the Enlightenments, 510, 516, 518, 518
        (illus.)
    interwar, 748, 751
    modernist, 678
    patriotic songs, 601, 602
    patronage and, 465, 465 (illus.)
    realist, 614–615, 615 (illus.)
    Romantic, 578–579, 578 (illus.)
music halls, 674, 674 (illus.)
Musil, Robert, 751
Muslims. See also Islam/Islamic lands
    in Arab lands, 207–208, 639
    in Chechnya, 641, 840, 859
    commerce by, 363, 380–381
    in Crete, 625
    in the European Union, 850, 858

meaning of word, 207
in the Philippines, 382
plague and, 305, 305 (illus.)
in Russia, 506
in Spain, 207 (map), 208, 215–216, 216
    (illus.), 272 (illus.), 273, 317, 317 (illus.),
    318 (map)
in Yugoslavia, 844–846
Mussolini, Benito
    defeat of, 789, 790
    Ethiopia invasion by, 758
    on Fascism, 761 (source document)
    rise to power, 741–742, 742 (illus.)
Mustafa II (Ottoman sultan), 446
Mustafa Kemal, 710, 724–725, 725 (illus.)
mustard gas, 712
Mycenaean civilization, 5 (illus.), 26–27, 26
    (map), 39–40
Myron (Athenian sculptor), 64, 64 (illus.)
Mysore Wars, 636–637
mystery religions, 97
Mystic Nativity (Botticelli), 336
Mytilene, 59, 63

Nabucco (Verdi), 578–579
Nagasaki, atomic bomb on, 788, 792
Nag Hammadi codices, 169
Nagy, Imre, 808–809
Nahua (Aztec) people, 372, 377, 378, 379, 379
    (illus.)
Namibia, 711
Nanjing, Treaty of (1842), 640, 652
Nansen, Fridtjof, 746
Nansen passport, 746
Naples
    in the Enlightenment, 509
    French invasion of, 336
    in the Italian Renaissance, 329 (map)
Napoleon Bonaparte, 543–555
    campaigns of, 551–553, 552 (map), 553
        (illus.)
    chronology of, 553
    Concordat, 544, 548
    Continental system, 551–552
    the Directory and, 543
    early life of, 543–545, 545 (illus.)
    in Egypt, 545–546, 546 (map), 547, 547
        (illus.)
    empire of, 546–555, 552 (map)
    exile, return, and death of, 555
    Grande Armée under, 549–551, 549
        (illus.), 554–555, 555 (illus.)
    Napoleonic Code, 548–549
    national bank and, 546, 548
    nationalism and, 554
    Russia's defeat of, 554–555, 555 (illus.)
    son of, 554
    stabilization of France, 546, 548
    Staël, Madame de, and, 526
Napoleonic Code, 548–549
Napoleonic empire, 546–555, 552 (map)
Napoleon III (French emperor)
    Catholic Church under, 600
    exile and death of, 623
    in the Franco-Prussian War, 622
    governing by, 603–604
    modernization of Paris by, 604–606, 605
        (illus.), 606 (map)
    Ottoman Empire and, 616

proclaimed as emperor, 591
    unification of Germany and, 621, 621 (map)
    unification of Italy and, 619
Napoleons (new franc), 546
Napoleon's Egypt (Cole), 547
Naram-Sin, 17
Narmer (Egyptian king), 20–21, 21 (illus.)
Nasser, Gamal Abdel, 817
Nathan the Wise (Lessing), 508
National Aeronautics and Space
        Administration (NASA), 809
National Assembly (France), 531–537, 603
national communism, 804–805, 804 (illus.)
nationalism, 570–574
    after the revolutions of 1848, 601
    Belgian, 564 (map), 573–574, 574 (map)
    Czech, 691
    in the fin de siècle, 688, 691–694, 692
        (map), 693 (map)
    in the former Soviet Union countries,
        843–844
    German, 620, 692
    Greek, 570–573, 571 (illus.), 572 (illus.),
        573 (map)
    Napoleon and, 546, 554, 570
    patriotic songs, 601, 602
    Slavic, 692
    Turkish, 692–693
    unification and, 620, 627
    Wilson's Fourteen Points and, 723, 738
national self-determination, 723, 738
National Socialism. See Nazism
National Socialist Workers' Party (NSDAP),
        744
Nations, Battle of the (1814), 555
nation-states, 601
Native Americans
    Aztec people, 358, 372–374, 377–379, 377
        (illus.)
    Carib people, 370
    Columbus and, 368, 369
    encomienda system and, 377–378
    European opinions of, 370
    in the French and Indian War, 479–480
    Inca people, 374, 374 (illus.), 378
    Iroquois people, 375
    map of (1500), 373 (map)
    Mi'kmaq people, 375
    pandemic among, 369, 374 (illus.), 376
    Taíno people, 368
NATO (North Atlantic Treaty
        Organization), 805, 806 (map), 836
Natura, 253
Natural History (Pliny the Elder), 361
natural history museums, 646
The Natural History of Religion (Hume), 501
naturalists, 486, 486 (illus.)
natural law, 434, 497
natural selection, 612, 613
nature, 486, 486 (illus.), 577, 577 (illus.)
naves, 233, 233 (illus.)
navies. See also military
    Chinese, 363, 381
    in the Great War, 704, 712
    Roman, 121–122, 121 (illus.)
    in the seventeenth and eighteenth
        centuries, 477
    in World War II, 778–779, 779 (illus.), 780
        (map), 790, 792

Navigation Acts (England), 451, 498
navigation technology, 366, 485
Nazism. *See also* fascism; World War II
    in Austria, 759
    Beer Hall Putsch, 744
    birth of, 743–744
    on euthanasia and sterilization, 768
    as fascism, 742
    Final Solution, 769 *(illus.)*, 782–784, 783
      (map), 784 *(illus.)*
    Hitler on, 744
    maternity homes, 769
    Night of the Broken Glass
      (Reichskristallnacht), 767–768, 768
      (illus.)
    Nuremberg rally (1934), 749, 754–755, 755
      (illus.)
    racial policy of, 742, 755, 756
    rise to power, 752, 754
    on sex, 769, 769 *(illus.)*
    women and, 747, 747 *(illus.)*
Neanderthals, 6–7
Near East, ancient
    Çatalhüyük (Turkey), 10, 10 *(illus.)*, 19
      (map)
    Egypt, 5 *(illus.)*, 18–24, 19 *(map)*, 20, 21
      (illus.), 25, 27
    Hebrews, 29–32
    Hittites, 17, 19 *(map)*, 26 *(map)*, 27
    iron and, 27–28
    Mesopotamia, 5, 9, 13–18, 13 *(map)*, 14
      (illus.), 22, 26 *(map)*
    Minoans, 5 *(illus.)*, 25–26, 26 *(illus.)*, 26
      (map)
    Mycenaeans, 5 *(illus.)*, 26–27, 26 *(map)*,
      39–40
    Phoenicians, 28–29, 28 *(map)*, 29 *(illus.)*,
      31, 32
    Sea Raiders, 24, 27, 31
Nebuchadnezzar (king of Babylon), 32
Necker, Jacques, 525, 530, 531–532
Nefertiti (Egyptian queen), 22 *(illus.)*, 23
Nehru, Jawaharlal, 815 *(illus.)*
Nelson, Admiral Horatio, 545, 551
neoclassicism, 509
neo-Europes, 634
Neolithic period, 4–5 *(illus.)*, 9–10, 19
Nero (Roman emperor), 153, 157–158
Nerva (Roman emperor), 157, 158
Nestorian Christians, 279, 382
Netherlandish Proverbs (Pieter Bruegel), 353,
    353 *(illus.)*
Netherlands. *See also* Dutch Republic
    Asia, trade with, 382, 447, 653, 653 *(illus.)*
    Austrian, 539–540, 543
    in China, 652–653, 653 *(illus.)*
    Congress of Vienna and, 573, 574 *(map)*
    dikes in, 254
    Dutch Revolt, 413, 413 *(map)*, 414, 426
    Ethical Policy, 653, 659
    in the French Revolution, 539–540
    in the Great Depression, 752
    in Indonesia, 653, 653 *(illus.)*
    Kingdom of the, 553, 562, 564 *(map)*
    Spanish, 413, 413 *(map)*, 438, 438 *(map)*
    United Provinces, 413, 413 *(map)*, 445, 447
    in World War II, 773
Neuilly, Treaty of, 723, 724, 724 *(map)*
Nev'im (Prophets), 29

New Astronomy (Kepler), 482–483
The New Book of Flowers (Merian), 486
Newcomen, Thomas, 581
New Economic Policy (NEP), 734, 736
Newfoundland, Scandinavians in, 296
New France, 437, 439
New Guinea, 711, 780 *(map)*
New Instrument of Science (Bacon), 482
New Kingdom, Egypt, 20, 22
New Poor Law (1834; England), 588
New Russia, 641
newspapers, 646, 674, 683 *(illus.)*, 737
New Testament, 168–169
Newton, Sir Isaac, 483–484
New Zealand, 669
Ngram Viewer (Google), 649, 649 *(illus.)*
Nicaean Creed, 179
Nicholas, Saint, 330
Nicholas I (czar of Russia), 568, 576, 576
    (illus.), 591, 606
Nicholas II (czar of Russia), 702, 702 *(map)*,
    716, 734
Nicholas II (Pope), 245, 248, 686
Nicholas V (Pope), 313, 331–332
Nichomachean Ethics (Aristotle), 288
Nicias peace accord, 63
Nicomedia, church of, 175
Niemöller, Martin, 755
Nietzsche, Friedrich, 669, 678, 679
Nightingale, Florence, 616 *(illus.)*
Night of the Broken Glass
    (Reichskristallnacht), 767–768, 768 *(illus.)*
Night of the Long Knives (Germany), 754
Nijinsky, Alexander, 678
Nile River, 18–19, 19 *(map)*, 24
1968, events in, 810, 810 *(illus.)*, 821, 821 *(illus.)*
nineteenth century (1850–1880), 595–627. *See*
    also fin de siècle (1880–1914); Napoleon
    Bonaparte; Restoration era (1815–1850)
    after the revolutions, 597–598
    Austro-Hungarian Empire formation,
      626–627, 626 *(map)*
    Britain in, 601, 603, 603 *(illus.)*, 607–611,
      609 *(illus.)*, 610 *(illus.)*
    capitalism in, 600–601
    conservatives in, 600
    Crimean War, 604, 615–616, 616 *(illus.)*
    Franco-Prussian War, 602, 604, 621–623,
      686
    German unification, 619–621, 621 *(map)*,
      624
    Italian unification, 616, 618–619, 618
      (map), 619 *(illus.)*
    liberalism in, 598–600, 599 *(illus.)*
    Napoleon III in, 591, 603–606, 616, 621, 623
    nationalism in, 601–602, 620, 627
    Paris, modernization of, 604–606, 605
      (map)
    Paris Commune, 623–624, 623 *(illus.)*, 668
    positivism in, 611–615, 614 *(illus.)*, 615
      (illus.)
    radicals in, 597, 599–600, 606, 623–624,
      623 *(illus.)*
    realism and Impressionism in, 612–615,
      614 *(illus.)*, 615 *(illus.)*
    Rhine River engineering in, 595–597, 596
      (illus.), 596 *(map)*
    Roman Catholic Church in, 600
    Russia in, 606–607

Russo-Turkish Wars, 625–626, 626 *(map)*,
    629 *(source document)*, 641
    timeline, 598–599 *(illus.)*
"Ninety-Five Theses" (Luther), 392–393,
    418–419 *(source document)*
Ninety-Seven Theses (Luther), 392
ninth century. *See* Early Middle Ages
Nixon, Richard M., 809 *(illus.)*, 822, 823
NKVD (Soviet secret police), 802, 803. *See*
    also KGB (Soviet secret police)
nobles and aristocrats
    in absolutist monarchies, 436–437, 528
    after the plague, 314–315
    in the Carolingian empire, 219
    in the Central Middle Ages, 254
    in Egypt, ancient, 23–24
    in the eighteenth century, 464–466
    in the French Revolution, 532, 535, 539,
      541
    gardens and landscaping by, 514
    in Greece, ancient, 46, 47, 58
    in the High Middle Ages, 276
    knighthood of, 303–304
    in Poland, 443
    in the Roman Republic, 110, 117–118, 117
      (illus.)
    in Russia, 441–442
    succession of kings and, 424
nominalism, 313
Nonsuch, Treaty of (1585), 414
Normandy, 225, 273, 301, 302 *(map)*
Normans
    castles of, 237, 237 *(illus.)*
    invasion of England by, 248, 250, 251
    invasion of Sicily and southern Italy by,
      245, 248, 253
North America. *See also specific countries*
    American War of Independence, 529,
      634–635
    Aztec people, 358, 372–374, 377–379, 377
      (illus.)
    British colonies in, 375, 451
    French and Indian War, 478, 479–480
    French colonies in, 375, 437, 635
    independence for colonies in, 635
    neo-Europes in, 634
    Spanish colonies in, 370, 375–380, 377
      (illus.), 635
North Atlantic Treaty Organization
    (NATO), 805, 806 *(map)*, 836
Northmen, 224. *See also* Vikings
Norway, 772, 859
Notre Dame Cathedral (Paris), 273
nouvelle cuisine, in the Enlightenment, 517,
    517 *(illus.)*
novels, 510–511, 751. *See also* literature
Nubia, 19 *(map)*, 20, 22, 91
nuclear weapons, 788, 792
numerals, Roman, 126
Numidia, 138
numina, 109, 118
Nuremberg Laws, 755–757, 757 *(illus.)*
Nuremberg Nazi Party rally (1934), 749,
    754–755, 755 *(illus.)*
Nuremberg Trials, 792
nurses, 616, 616 *(illus.)*, 703

Ockham's Razor, 313
O'Connell, Daniel, 567

Octavian. *See* Augustus (Roman emperor)
October (Eisenstein), 749
October Revolution (Russia), 718
Odo (France), 242, 244
Odovacar, 183, 186
Odyssey (Homer), 41
Oedipus Rex (Sophocles), 65
oil, 809, 823, 827
Okinawa, 780 *(map)*, 790
The Old Courtesan, 98 *(illus.)*
Old Kingdom, Egypt, 20, 21, 22
The Old Regime and the French Revolution
    (Tocqueville), 560
Old Regimes (seventeenth and eighteenth
        centuries)
    agricultural changes in, 471–472, 472
        (illus.)
    Böttger, Johann, in, 457–459, 458 *(illus.)*
    clergy, as first estate, 462–464, 463 *(illus.)*
    commercial revolution in, 473–476, 473
        (map), 474 *(illus.)*, 476 *(illus.)*
    industrialization in, 472–473
    legal inequalities in, 460
    military changes in, 475–478
    monarchs in, 461–462, 461 *(illus.)*
    music patronage in, 465, 465 *(illus.)*
    nobility, as second estate, 464–466
    piracy and smuggling in, 475
    scientific revolution in, 480–487, 484
        (illus.), 486 *(illus.)*
    serfs and peasants in, 468–471, 469 *(map)*,
        470 *(illus.)*, 471 *(illus.)*
    Seven Years' War in, 439, 477–478, 478
        (map), 480
    slave trade in, 475–476, 476 *(illus.)*
    taxes in, 466–467, 489 *(source document)*
    third estate in, 466–471
    timeline of, 458–459 *(illus.)*
    towns and townspeople in, 467–468, 467
        (illus.), 468 *(illus.)*
    urban poverty in, 468
    war costs in, 477–478
Old St. Peter's Basilica (Rome), 177, 177
    (illus.), 197
oligarchy, 57–58, 110, 136
Oliver Twist (Dickens), 587, 612
olives, 48 *(illus.)*
Olmütz, Treaty of, 620
Olympia (Manet), 612
Olympia (Riefenstahl), 749, 749 *(illus.)*
Olympias (mother of Alexander), 77
Olympic Games, 42–43, 58
On Christian Liberty (Luther), 394
On Crimes and Punishments (Beccaria), 509
ONE, 833–835
One Day in the Life of Ivan Denisovich
    (Solzhenitsyn), 820
On Germany (De Staël), 526
On Liberty (Mill), 580
On the Beach (Chirico), 748 *(illus.)*
On the Circulation of the Blood (Harvey), 484,
    484 *(illus.)*
On the Fabric of the Human Body (Vesalius),
    484, 496 *(illus.)*
On the Genealogy of Morals (Nietzsche), 679
On the Nature of Things (Lucretius), 141
On the Origin of Species (Darwin), 612, 613
On the Revolutions of the Heavenly Spheres
    (Copernicus), 482

OPEC (Organization of Petroleum
        Exporting Countries), 823
opera
    Baroque, 434, 465, 465 *(illus.)*, 466
    Enlightenment, 510, 516, 518
    Realist, 614–615, 615 *(illus.)*
    Romantic, 578–579
Operation Barbarossa, 778–780
Operation Michael (1918), 719
Operation Valkyrie, 786
Opium Wars, 639–640, 653
Oracle at Delphi, 43–44, 43 *(illus.)*, 43 *(map)*,
    51
oral cultures, 14, 16
Orange Free State, 655
Orange Revolution, 857, 857 *(illus.)*
Oration on the Dignity of Man (Pico della
    Mirandola), 345
Orban, Victor, 862
Order of the Garter, 304
Order of the Golden Fleece, 304
Oresteia trilogy (Aeschylus), 65
Organization of Petroleum Exporting
    Countries (OPEC), 823
Origen of Alexandria, 170
Origins of the European Economy
    (McCormick), 211
The Origins of Totalitarianism (Arendt), 818
Orpheus (Monteverdi), 434
Orsini, Clarice, 334
Orthodox Christian Church. *See* Greek
    (Eastern) Orthodox Church
Osiris (god), 22
ostracism, 53, 55, 55 *(illus.)*
Ostrogoths, 181, 181 *(map)*, 185 *(map)*, 186,
    186 *(illus.)*, 189–190, 192
Otto (king of Greece), 573
Otto I the Great (Ottonian emperor), 239,
    240
Otto II (Ottonian emperor), 239
Otto III (Ottonian emperor), 239
Ottoman Empire
    Armenian massacres by, 692, 709, 710
        (illus.)
    Balkan Wars, 693–694, 693 *(illus.)*
    conquest of Constantinople, 318, 319, 319
        (illus.)
    Crimean War, 616, 616 *(illus.)*
    cultural blending in, 339–340
    in the Great War, 702, 702 *(map)*, 708–710,
        709 *(map)*, 710 *(illus.)*, 723–724, 724
        (map)
    Greek independence from, 570–573, 571
        (illus.), 572 *(illus.)*, 573 *(map)*
    invasion of Holy Roman Empire, 439,
        439 *(illus.)*
    Jews in, 704
    pirates of, 475
    Renaissance in, 339–340
    Russo-Turkish Wars and, 625–626, 625
        (illus.), 641
    Serbian independence from, 626–627,
        626 *(map)*, 692, 692 *(map)*
    in the seventeenth century, 445 *(map)*, 446
    spread of, 340 *(map)*
    territorial losses (1800–1914), 692–694,
        693 *(map)*
Ottoman Public Debt Administration, 652
Ottonian system, 239

Ötzi (iceman), 3–5, 4 *(illus.)*, 10
Ovid, 149–150, 151
Owen, Robert, 584
Oxford University, 283, 285, 285 *(map)*

Pachomius, 170
Pacific Ocean, discovery of, 371–372, 382
Padua, University of, 285 *(map)*, 327, 328, 342,
    345
Paganini, Niccolò, 578
pagans, early Christianity and, 187
painting
    abstract expressionism, 820, 820 *(illus.)*
    Baroque, 409–410, 409 *(illus.)*, 432 *(illus.)*,
        433, 434 *(illus.)*
    interwar, 748–750, 748 *(illus.)*, 749 *(illus.)*,
        751
    modernist, 677, 677 *(illus.)*
    realist and Impressionist, 612–614, 614
        (illus.)
    Renaissance, 347–349, 347 *(illus.)*, 348
        (illus.)
    scientific illustration, 486, 486 *(illus.)*
    in sixteenth century, 367 *(illus.)*
    symbolist, 675, 675 *(illus.)*
Pakistan
    Alexander in, 83 *(map)*, 85
    formation of, 814 *(map)*, 815
    in the Hellenistic world, 89–90
    Islam in, 207 *(map)*
palace government, 205
Palach, Jan, 810, 829
Pale of Settlement, 506, 570, 606, 744
Paleolithic period, 4 *(illus.)*, 7–8, 35, 35 *(illus.)*
paleopathology, 307
Palermo (Sicily), 283
Palestine
    in the Antigonid kingdom, 89 *(map)*
    as British mandate, 739, 739 *(map)*, 815
    formation of Israel and, 814 *(map)*, 815
    in the Great War, 710
    in Persian Empire, 51
    in the Roman Empire, 159 *(map)*
    Zionism and, 690
Palette of Narmer, 20–21, 21 *(illus.)*
palimpsests, 284, 284 *(illus.)*
Palmieri, Matteo, 331
Pamela; Or, Virtue Rewarded (Richardson),
    510
pamphlets, 512, 530, 557 *(source document)*
pandemics. *See also* plague
    Justinian's, 191
    in Native Americans after Columbus,
        369, 374 *(illus.)*, 376
    plague, in the Middle Ages, 304–309, 305
        (illus.), 306 *(illus.)*, 307 *(illus.)*, 309
        (illus.)
    Spanish flu, 720–721
Pan-German League, 692
Pan-Hellenism, 51
pan-Islamic movement, 692
Pankhurst, Emmeline, 673
Pankhurst, Sylvia, 703
Pantheon, 148, 148 *(illus.)*
papacy
    in Avignon, 299–300, 300 *(illus.)*
    Carolingians and, 212–213, 215, 223
    in the Catholic Reformation, 408
    election of pope, 245

papacy (continued)
  in the eleventh century, 245
  fourteenth-century critics of, 313–314,
    314 (illus.)
  Gregory the Great and, 201–202
  imperial, 247, 254, 256, 271, 276, 278
    (map), 280
  Investiture Controversy and, 246–247,
    246 (illus.), 271
  in the Italian Renaissance, 331–332
  Otto I the Great and, 239
  papal plenitude of power, 271
  Western (Papal) Schism, 313
Papademos, Lucas, 847, 862
papal plenitude of power, 271
Papal States, 278 (map), 329 (map), 331–332
paper, 351
papyrus, 20, 28, 90
Paradise Lost (Milton), 433
parchment, 201
Parentalia, 119
Paris
  Bastille, assault on, 531–532, 531 (illus.)
  under the English, 315–316, 316 (illus.)
  in the Franco-Prussian War, 622–623, 686
  in the French Revolution, 532–533,
    535–537
  general strike (1968), 821
  June Days, 590–591
  modernization of, 604–606, 604 (illus.),
    605 (map)
  Paris Commune, 623–624, 623 (illus.),
    668
  Spanish flu in, 720
  University of, 282, 283, 285, 285 (map),
    286–287, 288
Paris Commune, 623–624, 623 (illus.), 668
Paris Métro, 672
Parkinson, Sydney, 514, 515 (illus.)
parlements, 437
Parliament of Women (Aristophanes), 78
parliaments, 424, 426, 831 (source document),
  850
Parmenides of Elea, 49
Parsifal (Wagner), 615
Parthenon (Athens), 62, 64, 64 (illus.)
Parthia, 146, 149
Pasternak, Boris, 751, 820, 826
Pasteur, Louis, 679
Pastoral Rule (Gregory the Great), 202
Patarines, 277
paterfamilias, 112, 220
patria potestas, 112
patriarchy, Roman, 111–112
patricians, 110–111, 112, 117–118, 117 (illus.)
patrilineal societies, Neolithic, 11
patriotism, 554, 601, 602. See also
  nationalism
Paul (Saul of Tarsus), 153
Paul III (Pope), 408
Pavarotti, Luciano, 845 (illus.)
Pavelić, Ante, 776, 785, 792
Pax Romana, 157
Payton, Rodney J., 320
Pazzi Conspiracy, 334
Peace of Augsburg (1530), 403–404, 426
Peace of God movement, 250, 252
Peace of Hubertusburg (1763), 479, 480
Peace of Nicias (421 BCE), 63

Peace of Westphalia (1648), 430–431, 437,
  438, 447, 463
Pearl Harbor, Japanese attack on, 777, 780
  (map)
Pearson, Lester B., 817
Peary, Robert, 646
peasants and serfs
  after the plague, 310–311, 311 (illus.)
  in Austria, 508, 568
  in the Carolingian empire, 220–221, 220
    (illus.), 221 (illus.)
  communism and, 567
  in Egypt, ancient, 23–24
  in England, 310–311
  in the Enlightenment, 516
  French Revolution and, 528–529, 529
    (illus.)
  in Germany, 398, 398 (illus.)
  in the High Middle Ages, 274
  Jacquerie, in France, 310, 311 (illus.)
  migrant, 471
  in Norman England, 251
  in Poland, 540
  in the Restoration era, 568–569
  revolts of, 310–311, 398, 470
  in Romania, 745
  in Russia, 470, 470 (illus.)
  in Russia, emancipation of, 606
  in the Russian civil wars, 733
  second serfdom, 469, 469 (map)
  in the seventeenth and eighteenth
    centuries, 468–471, 470 (illus.)
  in the Soviet Union, 734–735, 735 (illus.)
  taxes paid by, 466–467
  in the Thirty Years' War, 427–428
Peasants' Crusade, 255
Peasants' War (1524), 398, 398 (illus.)
Peisistratus (Greek tyrant), 46, 58, 64
Pelagians, 176
Peloponnesian League, 54, 56, 60–61
Peloponnesian War, 39, 60–63, 62 (map), 64
Peloponnesus, 57, 57 (map), 62 (map). See also
  Corinth; Sparta
penicillin, 788–789
Peninsular War, 553
pensions, 624
Peoples' Will, 606
Pepin of Heristal, 210
Pepin of Landen, 206
Pepin the Short, 211–213
Perdiccas, 88
Perestrelo, Bartolomeu, 364, 367
perestroika, 826–827, 838
Pergamum (Turkey), 70–71 (illus.), 81, 90–91,
  97, 99, 125
Pericles, 37, 61–63, 61 (illus.), 64, 68 (source
  document)
perioikoi, 56, 57
Periphyseon (Eriugena), 226
Perrissin, Jean, 386–387 (illus.)
Perry, Matthew, 640
Persepolis, 15, 84–85, 86. See also Persian
  Empire
Perses, 45–46
Perseus (king of Macedonia), 124, 124 (illus.),
  125
Persia
  Islam in, 207 (map), 208
  plague in, 305

  in the Roman Empire, 159, 159 (map), 167
  in the Seleucid kingdom, 88–89, 89 (map)
  Seljuk Turks in, 248
Persian Empire
  after the Peloponnesian War, 74
  Alexander's conquest of, 83–84, 83 (map)
  Delian League and, 60–61, 63
  in early sixth century, 185 (map)
  invasions of Greece by, 39, 51–56, 52
    (illus.), 53 (map), 54 (map)
  Ionia, reconquest of, 63
  Persepolis destruction and, 85
  on timeline, 41 (illus.)
The Persian Letters (Montesquieu), 502
Persians (Aeschylus), 65
Persian Wars, 51–56, 52 (illus.), 53 (map), 54
  (map)
Pétain, Philippe, 773, 773 (illus.)
Peter (Yugoslavian king), 776
Peter Damian, 245
Peter I (the Great; czar of Russia), 441 (map),
  442, 444, 477, 506
Peter III (czar of Russia), 479
Peterloo massacre (England), 588
Peters, Carl, 658
Petőfi, Sándor, 590 (illus.)
Petrarch (Francesco Petrarcha), 325–326,
  328, 341–343, 365
Petre, Robert James, 514
Petrine authority, 172
Petrograd (St. Petersburg), 506–507, 703
Petronius, 157
Phaedo (Plato), 81
Phaistos, palace at, 25
phalanxes, 47, 75, 110
Pharsalus, Battle of (48 BCE), 143, 144
Phidias, 62, 64
Philip II (king of Spain and Portugal), 382,
  413–415, 426, 443
Philip II Augustus (king of France), 270, 273
Philip III (king of Spain), 426
Philip III Arrhidaeus, 76
Philip IV (the Fair; France), 299–300, 301
Philip of Hesse, 396
Philip of Macedon, 74, 75, 75 (map), 76–77, 76
  (illus.)
Philippics (Cicero), 144
Philippics (Demosthenes), 75
Philippines
  Spanish religious war with, 382
  in World War II, 777, 780 (map), 790
Philip the Good (duke of Burgundy), 350
Philip V (king of Macedonia), 123–124
Philip V (king of Spain), 437–438, 443, 461
Philip VI (of Valois; king of France), 301
Philistines, invasion of Canaan by, 31
philosophes, 501, 511
Philosophy (William of Conches), 265–266
philosophy and philosophers
  in the age of absolutism, 434–435
  Aristotle, 77, 80–81
  Boethius, 187
  in the Cold War, 818, 820
  Descartes, 482, 507–508
  Enlightenment, 496, 497–498, 501–503,
    503 (illus.)
  in the fin de siècle, 678–679
  in Greece, Archaic, 48–49
  Hellenistic, 95–96

in the interwar years, 750
Persian, 248
Plato, 50, 78, 79–80, 81
positivism, 611–612
postmodernist, 855
in the Roman Republic, 141–142
Romanticism and, 579
scholasticism, 283, 287–288, 289, 313
Socrates, 78–79, 79 (illus.), 101 (source document)
Spinoza, 495, 496, 519
Phoenicians. See also Carthage
Alexander's conquest of, 84
alphabet of, 28, 29 (illus.), 32, 42, 106
colonization by, 44, 44 (map)
Greece and, 41
influence on the Hebrews, 32
trade by, 28–29, 48
phonetic literacy, 42
phonograms, 14, 20
photography, 613–614, 674–675
Phrasikleia (Ariston of Paros), 49, 49 (illus.)
Phrygian cap, 541, 541 (illus.)
Phrygians, 28
physics, 483–484, 679
physiocrats, 499
Piagnoni, 334
Picasso, Pablo, 677, 677 (illus.)
Pico della Mirandola, Giovanni, 334, 342, 344–345, 344 (illus.)
Picot, Georges, 711
pictographs, 19, 28
The Picture of Dorian Gray (Wilde), 675
Piers Plowman (Langland), 298
Pietism, 464, 507, 644
pigs, domestication of, 9
pikes, 75
pilgrimages
Christian, 252–253, 252 (illus.), 254, 676, 676 (illus.)
Crusades as, 254–256
Islamic, 207, 676
to Lourdes, 676, 676 (illus.)
Pilgrim's Progress (Bunyan), 435
Pindar, 58, 83
Piombo, Sebastiano del, 367 (illus.)
pirates
Ottoman, 475
Roman Empire and, 141
Spanish colonization and, 475
Vikings as, 224–226, 224 (illus.)
Pirenne, Henri, 211
Pisano, Andrea, 346
Piłsudski, Joseph, 741, 744–745
Pitt, William (British prime minister), 479–480, 543, 552
Pius II (Pope), 331
Pius IX (Pope), 588, 590
Pius VII (Pope), 548
Pizarro, Francisco, 374
placards affair, 402
plague. See also pandemics
in the Americas after Columbus, 376
arrival of, 304–306, 306 (map), 308
bubonic, pneumonic, and septicemic, 307–308
in eastern Roman Empire, 191
economy after, 310–311, 311 (illus.)
eyewitness account of, 323

in the fourteenth century, 293–294, 304–309, 305 (illus.), 306 (illus.), 307 (illus.), 309 (illus.)
immediate consequences of, 308–309
medical implications after, 309–310
religion after, 311–313, 312 (illus.)
in the seventeenth century, 424
transmission and symptoms of, 306–308
Planck, Max, 679
plant domestication, 9–10, 19
Plataea, battle of, 58
Plato, 50, 78, 79–80, 81, 283, 343
Platonic Academy, Florence, 343
Platonic Theology (Ficino), 343
Plautus, 127–128
plays. See theater
plebeians, 110–111, 112
Plethon, Georgius Gemistus, 341–343
Pliny the Elder, 361
Plotinus, 167–168
plows, 221
Plug Plot Riots (England), 588
pluralism, in the Church, 271
Plutus (Aristophanes), 78
pneumonic plague, 307. See also plague
Poetics (Aristotle), 288
poetry
Carolingian, 216, 223 (illus.)
in the fin de siècle, 677
Greek, ancient, 27, 41–42, 42 (illus.), 45–46, 48, 58
Hellenistic, 97–98
in the interwar years, 751
Italian Middle Ages, 288, 300, 338, 343
Roman, 126, 141, 151
Romanesque, 237–238, 238 (illus.)
Romantic, 577
pogroms, 255, 688, 767–768, 768 (illus.)
Poland
absolutist era in, 443
in the Austro-Hungarian Empire, 691, 692 (map)
Catholic Church in, 822, 848
communism ended in, 828, 841
Congress of Vienna and, 562, 564 (map)
expansion, in the interwar years, 744–745
German apology to, 822
German conquest of, 767, 767 (map), 770–772
in the Great War, 707–708
Jews in, 744, 757, 771
Katyn Forest massacre, 771
in late nineteenth century, 625
Napoleon in, 551, 552 (map)
partitions of (1772–1795), 507, 507 (map)
revolts during the French Revolution, 540
in the Russian civil wars, 733, 733 (map)
Seven Years' War and, 478
Solidarity in, 811, 828
in the Soviet bloc, 802 (map), 803, 804, 808, 811
Warsaw ghetto, 771–772
in World War II, 779, 782, 783 (map), 786, 790, 792
Poland-Lithuania, 432, 441
poleis (singular, polis). See also Athens; Corinth; Sparta
after the Peloponnesian War, 74

in Greece, Archaic, 46–47, 48
in Greece, Dark Age of, 40–41
identification with, 51
number of, 38
Pan-Hellenism and, 51
in Peloponnesian War, 61–63, 62 (map)
in Persian Wars, 52–56
slavery in, 59–60
Polish Home Army, 790
The Political and Social Doctrine of Fascism (Mussolini), 761 (source document)
Politics (Aristotle), 81, 288
Politkovskaya, Anna, 842
Poliziano, Angelo, 327, 344 (illus.)
Pollock, Jackson, 820, 820 (illus.)
Polo family, 279, 361
Pol Pot, 815
Polybius, 103–104, 104 (illus.), 109, 117, 118, 130 (source document)
polytheism
Egyptian, 22–23
Etruscan, 109
Hellenistic, 97
Mesopotamian, 17–18
Roman, 151–152
Poma, Guaman, 374 (illus.)
Pomeranz, Kenneth, 582
Pompadour, Madame de, 439
Pompeii (Italy), 149, 155 (illus.)
Pompey (Roman consul general), 140–141, 142, 143, 144, 150
Ponce de León, Juan, 371
Pont du Gard aqueduct (France), 132–133 (illus.)
Pontifex Maximus, 119
pontiffs, 109
Pontus (Turkey), 89 (map), 91, 140
Poor Law of 1796 (Britain), 585
Poor Men of Lyons, 277
Popillius, 125
popular culture. See also culture
in the Baroque, 435
in the Cold War, 818, 819, 819 (illus.)
in the fin de siècle, 673–675, 674 (illus.)
in the interwar years, 751–752
Popular Front (France), 738
population growth
after World War II, 811–812
in the Central Middle Ages, 154
in the eighteenth century, 471
at the end of the nineteenth century, 668
in Europe, after 1989, 859–860, 860 (illus.)
in Germany, 620
in the High Middle Ages, 272–273
Malthus on, 579
in the nineteenth century, 585, 606, 620
Porcari Conspiracy of 1453, 331
porcelain, 458 (illus.), 459, 472
pornography, 512
Portolan charts, 366
Portugal
African colonies of, 656, 657 (map), 711
after World War II, 813
Asian spice trade, 380–382
claims on Columbus's discoveries, 368–369
colonization by, 364–365, 364 (map), 376
economic crisis in, 861, 862
Enlightenment in, 509

Portugal *(continued)*
  exploration by, 363–365, 364 *(illus.)*, 364
    (map)
  independence from Spain, 430
  Napoleon in, 552
  slave trade by, 363–364
  Treaty of Tordesillas, 369
Porus (rule of Taxila), 86
positivism, 611–615
Postdam conference (1945), 792
postmodernism, 855, 855 *(illus.)*
potatoes, 469, 471, 588
Potemkin (Eisenstein), 749
Potosí silver mines, 378
pottery
  Athenian, 36 *(illus.)*, 55, 55 *(illus.)*
  eighteenth-century china, 472
  Greek, 43 *(illus.)*, 47 *(illus.)*, 48 *(illus.)*, 49,
    60 *(illus.)*
  Minoan, 25
  Mycenaean, 26
  prehistoric, 10
Pound, Ezra, 751
Pour le Mérite (Prussia), 550
Praeneste Fibula, 127, 127 *(illus.)*
praetor, 135
Praetorian Guard, 147, 157
Prague. *See also* Czechoslovakia
  under Charles IV, 301
  Defenestration of, 426–427
  Prague Spring, 810, 810 *(illus.)*
  in the Thirty Years' War, 427
The Praise of Folly (Erasmus), 351
predetermination, 403
prehistory, 6–11
  birth of agriculture, 9
  domestication of animals, 8–9, 10
  Indo-European migrations, 5 *(illus.)*, 11,
    12 *(map)*
  Mesolithic period, 4 *(illus.)*, 7, 10–11, 10
    (illus.)
  Ötzi, 3–5, 4 *(illus.)*
  slow pace of change in, 6
  timeline, 4–5 *(illus.)*
"Prelude to the Afternoon of a Faun"
    (Debussy), 678
Presbyterians, 447, 449
Prester John, 279
priesthood. *See also* clergy
  in ancient Egypt, 23
  in ancient Greece, 43
  in archaic Rome, 109
  in Judaism, 31
  in Mesopotamia, 18
Prima Porta statue of Augustus, 149, 149
    (illus.)
Primo de Rivera, Miguel, 741, 758
primogeniture, 223, 254
Prince (Machiavelli), 335, 355
Princip, Gavrilo, 693, 697–699, 698 *(illus.)*
Principia (Newton), 483–484
printing press
  in the French Revolution, 530, 557 *(source
    document)*
  Gutenberg and, 351
  pornography and, 512
  in the Protestant Reformation, 392, 394,
    400, 400 *(illus.)*
The Private Life of Louis XV, 512

privatization, 847
The Procession in St. Mark's Square (Bellini),
    324–325 *(illus.)*, 327
Procopius, 189
proletariat, 565, 567
propaganda
  motion pictures as, 749, 749 *(illus.)*
  in World War II, 754–755, 756, 787–788
property rights, 498, 504, 564–567, 565 *(illus.)*
Prosperity and Plunder (Beales), 519
prostitutes, 332, 849
prostration, Alexander and, 86
Protestant Reformation, 387–406
  Adamites, 451
  Anabaptists, 405–406, 406 *(illus.)*
  Bora, Katharina von and, 388–389, 388
    (illus.)
  "by faith alone" doctrine, 394, 397
  Calvin, John and, 398, 402–404, 404 *(illus.)*
  chronology of, 391
  Church of England and, 401–402
  declaration of "Protestant," 399
  deism, 502, 518
  Dutch revolt, 413, 413 *(map)*
  Edict of Worms (1521), 395, 396, 398–399
  Elizabeth I and the Spanish Armada,
    413–415, 414 *(illus.)*
  Erasmus, Desiderius and, 351–352, 352
    (illus.), 387–388, 388 *(illus.)*
  French Wars of Religion, 410–412, 412
    (illus.)
  in the Habsburg Empire, 426
  Jansenism, 464
  Knights Revolt, 396
  Luther, Martin and, 390–399, 391 *(illus.)*,
    393 *(illus.)*, 400, 401, 418–419 *(source
    document)*
  Mennonites, 406
  Methodism, 464, 570, 644
  millenarianism, 312, 405–406, 406 *(illus.)*
  Peace of Augsburg (1530) and, 403–404
  Peasants' War and, 398, 398 *(illus.)*
  Pietism, 464, 507, 644
  Presbyterians, 447, 449
  printing press and, 392, 394, 400, 400
    (illus.)
  Puritans, 447, 449, 451
  Schmalkaldic League and, 403–404
  spread of (1600), 411 *(map)*
  Thirty Years' War, 424, 426–431, 427
    (map), 428 *(illus.)*, 430 *(illus.)*
  timeline, 388–389 *(illus.)*
  Zwickau prophets and, 397, 405
  Zwingli, Huldrych and, 398, 399, 401
The Protocols of the Elders of Zion, 688–689
Proto Indo-European, 11
proto-industrialization, 472–473
Proust, Marcel, 678
provisional government (Russia), 716, 718
Prussia
  Congress of Vienna and, 562, 564 *(map)*
  conservatives in, 600
  consolidation of, 440
  Enlightenment in, 507–508, 507 *(map)*
  Kant in, 494, 501, 507–508, 515
  Napoleon and, 551, 552 *(map)*, 555
  Seven Years' War and, 477–479, 478
    (map), 480
  unification of Germany and, 620

Pseudo-Dionysius, 267
psychology, 678–679, 750
Ptah (god), 22
Ptolemaic kingdom, 71–73, 88, 89 *(map)*, 143,
    143 *(map)*
Ptolemy I, 71–72, 88, 89 *(map)*, 97
Ptolemy V, 123
public health, in fin-de-siècle cities, 671, 684
the public sphere, 495
Pugachev, Emelyan, 470, 470 *(illus.)*
Pulitzer, Joseph, 669
The Pumpkinification of Claudius the Clod
    (Seneca), 157
Punic Wars. *See* First Punic War; Second
    Punic War
Purgatory, 390, 392–393
Puritans, 447, 449, 451
Pushkin, Alexander, 578
Putin, Vladimir, 841, 843, 844, 857–858
Pynx, 58
Pyramids, Battle of the (1798), 545, 546 *(map)*
pyramids, Egyptian, 21
Pyrgi Tablets, 105, 106, 106 *(illus.)*
Pyrrhic Victory, 115
Pyrrhus of Epirus, 115, 121
Pythagoras of Samos, 49
Pythia, 43

Qingdao, 711
quadrivium, 264
quaestor, 135
quantum theory, 750
Quattrocento, 328
Queen Louise Medals (Prussia), 550
Quetzalcoatl (god), 373
quinine, imperialism and, 650
Quintilian, 343
Quisling, Vidkun, 772, 785
Qur'an (Koran), 207–208

Ra (god), 21, 22
Rabelais, Françoise, 351
race. *See also* anti-Semitism
  in football, 853
  in the Great War, 704
  imperialism and, 638, 638 *(illus.)*, 687, 723
  in Japan, in World War II, 777
  in Nazism, 742, 755, 768–770
Racine, Jean, 432 , 665
Radić, Stjepan, 746
Radical Enlightenment (Israel), 519
radicals. *See also* communism; socialism
  in Britain, 575–576, 588
  in the Enlightenment, 495–496, 501, 503,
    508, 511–512, 519
  in the French Revolution, 533–544, 538
    (illus.), 541 *(illus.)*
  nationalism and, 570, 574
  in the Paris Commune, 623–624, 623
    (illus.)
  in the political spectrum, 565–567, 565
    (illus.)
  in the revolutions of 1848, 589–590, 597,
    599–600
  in Russia, 606
radiocarbon testing, 7
radios, 712–713, 751
railroads
  in Britain, 581 *(map)*, 583–584, 584 *(illus.)*

in the fin de siècle, 671–672, 671 (map)
in India, 643
military use of, 616
in the Ottoman empire, 648, 650
in Paris, 605, 605 (map)
in South Africa, 655
travel by, 582 (map), 583–584
Rajah of Klungkung (Bali), 653
Raleigh, Sir Walter, 414
Ramses II (Egyptian king), 22, 27, 30
Ramses III (Egyptian king), 27
Rape of Nanjing, 777
Raphael, 345, 346, 349
Rasputin, Grigori, 716
rationalism, 482
Ravenna, 182, 190
Rawlinson, Henry, 15
Rayonnant style, 289, 289 (illus.)
Reagan, Ronald, 825, 826 (illus.), 827–828, 831
    (source document)
realism, 612–615, 614 (illus.), 615 (illus.)
Realpolitik, 620
Red Love (Kollontai), 731
Reflections on the Revolution in France
    (Burke), 542, 567
Reformation. See Catholic Reformation;
    Protestant Reformation
refractories, 534, 548
Reich Resettlement Office, 768–769
Reichsbank (Germany), 753
Reichstag building, restored, 855, 855 (illus.)
Reichstag fire, 754
Reign of Terror (France), 538
Reinhard, Anna, 399
relativity theory, 679, 750
relics, of saints, 203–204, 203 (illus.)
religion. See also Christianity; Islam/Islamic
    lands; Judaism
    ancestor worship, 118
    clergy, in the eighteenth century, 462–464,
        463 (illus.)
    in the Cold War, 821–822
    of Comte, 611
    Cult of the Supreme Being, 542
    deism, 502, 518
    Egyptian, 22–23
    Enlightenment and, 502–503, 505, 518–520
    Etruscan, 109, 109 (illus.)
    in Europe (1600), 411 (map)
    Hebrew, 29–30
    Hellenistic, 97
    Hittite, 27
    Macedonian, 75
    Mesopotamian, 17–18
    Minoan, 26
    Mithraism, 176
    monarchs and, 462
    Persian, 52
    political spectrum on (1815–1850),
        564–567, 565 (illus.)
    in the Restoration era, 569–570
    Roman Empire polytheism, 151–153, 152
        (illus.), 174–175, 180
    Roman Republic, 109, 109 (illus.), 113
        (illus.), 118–119, 147
    secularism, 847–848
The Religious Enlightenment (Sorkin), 519
religious toleration
    in Austria, 508

in the Dutch Republic, 447, 495–496
in England, 447, 449, 451, 453
innovative thinkers and, 495–496
Peace of Westphalia and, 430–431, 437,
    438, 447
in Russia, 506
Rembrandt van Rijn, 433, 496 (illus.)
Renaissance, European. See also
    Renaissance, Italian
    art in, 350, 350 (illus.)
    Bruges in, 349–350
    competitive spirit in, 360
    cosmopolitanism in, 340, 341
    humanism and individualism in, 349,
        351, 352, 353
    Ottoman Empire in the, 339–340, 340
        (map)
    print revolution in, 351–353, 352 (illus.)
    spread of, 349
    timeline, 326–327 (illus.)
Renaissance, Italian
    art of, 345–349, 346 (illus.), 347 (illus.), 348
        (illus.)
    classical literature in, 341–343
    in Florence, 329 (map), 332–336, 334
        (illus.), 335 (illus.)
    General Council of Roman Catholic and
        Greek Orthodox Churches, 336–337,
        337 (illus.), 341
    humanism in, 325–327, 326 (illus.),
        341–344, 344 (illus.)
    individualism in, 341, 344–345
    Jews in, 341, 342, 342 (illus.)
    Machiavelli in, 335–336, 335 (illus.), 355
    Medici family in, 333–334, 333 (illus.)
    papacy's return to Rome, 331–332
    Petrarch climbing Mont Ventoux,
        325–327
    reasons for, 329–331, 332 (illus.)
    Republics in, 329 (map)
    in Rome, 331–332, 336
    Savonarola in, 334–335, 335 (illus.)
    timeline, 326–327 (illus.)
    in Venice, 329 (map), 330 (illus.), 337–339,
        338 (map)
renaissance humanism, 325–327, 326 (illus.),
    341–344, 344 (illus.), 349, 351–353
renaissance individualism, 341, 344–345
Renoir, Pierre-Auguste, 612
Republic (Plato), 80
Republic of Letters, 485, 495
Requerimiento (1510), 377
Rerum Novarum (Of New Things) (Pope Leo),
    685–686
Restoration era (1815–1850). See also
    industrialization
    Belgian independence in, 564 (map),
        573–574, 574 (map)
    climate in, 569
    Concert of Europe in, 561–562
    Congress of Vienna, 561–563, 564 (map)
    culture, 576–580, 577 (illus.), 578 (illus.)
    economy in, 568–569, 568 (illus.)
    Greek independence in, 570–573, 571
        (illus.), 572 (illus.), 573 (map)
    Industrial Revolution in, 580–588, 581
        (map), 583 (illus.), 584 (illus.), 586
        (illus.), 587 (illus.)
    legal spectrum in, 567–568

nationalism in, 570–574, 571 (illus.), 573
    (map), 574 (map)
peasants in, 568–569
political spectrum in, 563–567, 565 (illus.)
religion in, 569–570
revolutions and reforms (1820s–1830s),
    574–576, 576 (illus.)
revolutions of 1848, 588–591, 589 (map),
    590 (illus.), 597
Romanticism in, 577–579, 577 (illus.), 578
    (illus.)
timeline, 562–563 (illus.)
Tocqueville in, 559–561, 560 (illus.), 589
utilitarianism in, 579–580, 587
utopian socialists in, 565, 566, 566 (illus.)
Revett, Nicholas, 510
revisionism (socialist), 685
Reza Shah Pahlavi (Shah of Iran), 739
Das Rheingold (Wagner), 596
Rhine River, 595–597, 596 (illus.), 596 (map)
Rhodes, Cecil, 631–633, 632 (map), 633 (illus.),
    655, 660
Rhodes, under Roman rule, 125
Rhodesia, 660
ribbed vaults, 267, 289
rice, domestication of, 10
Richard II (king of England), 311, 315
Richard of Aversa, 248
Richardson, Samuel, 510
Richard the Lionheart (king of England),
    270, 270 (illus.), 281
Richelieu, Cardinal, 437, 463
Richthofen, Ferdinand von, 646
Richthofen, Manfred Freiherr von, 712
Riefenstahl, Leni, 749, 754–755
rights. See also voting rights; women's rights
    in English law, 453, 496, 568
    in the French Revolution, 532–533
    gay, 849
    Locke on, 498
    property, 498, 504, 564–567, 565 (illus.)
    in the United States, 568
Rimbaud, Arthur, 677
Ring of Brodgar (Orkney Islands), 11
Ringstrasse (Vienna), 606
Risorgimento, 618
Rite of Spring (Stravinsky), 678
roads
    in the High Middle Ages, 276
    in Paris, 604–605
    in the Persian Empire, 52, 53 (map)
    Roman, 115, 116, 166
    tolls on, 276
Robert (Robertian king), 242
Robert Guiscard, 248
Roberval, Jean-François de la Roque de, 375
Robespierre, Maximilien, 533, 539, 541,
    542–543
Robinson Crusoe (Defoe), 491–493, 492 (illus.),
    510–511
robot labor, 470
Röhm, Ernst, 754
Romaic language, 179
Roman Catholic Church. See also
    Christianity; clergy; monasticism
    and monastic orders; papacy
    after the plague, 311–313, 312 (illus.)
    after the revolutions of 1848, 600
    in Asia, 382

Roman Catholic Church (continued)
    Avignon papacy, 299–300, 300 (illus.)
    Baroque art and, 409–410, 409 (illus.), 410 (illus.)
    in Bismarck's Germany, 624
    book banning by, 409, 496, 502, 504–505
    cathedral schools, 264–266, 268, 282–283
    Catholic Reformation, 406–410, 407 (illus.), 409 (illus.), 410 (illus.)
    chronology, thirteenth-century, 270
    in the Cold War, 822
    colonization and conversion to, 378
    conciliar movement in, 313
    corruption and reform in, 244–247
    Council of Trent, 408–409
    dissenting movements, 277, 277 (illus.)
    in England, Norman, 250
    England's break with, 398, 401–402, 402 (illus.)
    Enlightenment and, 509, 519
    in Europe (1600), 411 (map)
    in Europe (after 1989), 847–848, 848 (illus.)
    on evolutionary theory, 613
    in fascist Italy, 741–472
    in the fin de siècle, 676, 676 (illus.)
    First Crusade, 254–256, 255 (map), 256 (illus.), 258–259 (source document)
    fourteenth-century critics of, 313–314, 314 (illus.)
    Fourth Crusade, 271–273, 271 (illus.)
    Fourth Lateran Council, 272, 273
    in the French Revolution, 532, 534, 539, 542
    French Wars of Religion and, 411–412, 411 (map), 412 (illus.)
    fundamental tenets of, 390
    Galileo and, 483
    General Council with Greek Orthodox Church, 336–337, 337 (illus.), 341
    in the Great Famine, 298
    Great Schism and, 245, 248, 253, 271
    Indulgence Controversy, 392–394, 393 (illus.), 400, 409
    inquisitions, 278, 317, 408, 553
    Investiture Controversy, 245–247, 246 (illus.), 271, 390
    in Ireland, 567
    millennium and the Second Coming, 239, 241
    monarchs and, 462
    mysticism in, 408
    Napoleon and, 544, 548
    Nazis and, 755
    Ottonian system, 239
    Peace and Truce movements, 250, 252
    pilgrimages, 252–253, 252 (illus.), 254, 676, 676 (illus.)
    repression of heretics and, 253, 268–269, 272, 277–278, 277 (illus.)
    Second Crusade, 268–269
    Second Vatican Council (Vatican II), 822
    Third Crusade, 269–270, 270 (illus.)
    in the Thirty Years' War, 426–428
    Western (Papal) Schism, 313
Roman de la Rose (Jean de Meun), 283
Roman Empire, 133–160. See also eastern Roman Empire; Roman Republic
    Antony and Cleopatra in, 144–146, 146 (illus.)

Augustus's transformation of, 146–149, 148 (map), 149 (illus.)
Christianity, as state religion, 177–180
Christianity, Romanization of, 168–172, 171 (map), 172 (illus.)
Christian persecution in, 153, 171–172, 175–176
under Constantine, 175, 177–179, 178 (illus.), 181 (map)
Diocletian's renewal of, 172–176, 173 (illus.), 174 (illus.), 174 (map)
division into east and west, 173, 174 (map)
end of western empire, 183–185
external enemies of (350 BCE), 167–168, 168 (map)
Flavian emperors in, 157, 158, 159 (map)
Germanic kingdoms in the western part of, 185–188, 185 (map), 186 (illus.)
Germanic tribes entering, 180–185, 181 (map), 185 (map)
the good emperors in, 157, 158–159, 158 (illus.), 159 (map)
Judaism and, 152–153, 152 (illus.)
Julian in, 179–180
Julio-Claudian emperors in, 157–158, 159 (map)
Justinian in, 188–192, 188 (illus.), 189 (illus.), 190 (map)
late period of, 166–168, 168 (map)
life in, 153–154, 153 (illus.)
literature in, 149–151, 151 (illus.)
persecution of Christians in, 153, 168, 171, 175
social classes in, 155–157, 155 (illus.)
technology in, 156, 156 (illus.)
timeline of, 134–135 (illus.)
traditional religion in, 147, 151–153, 152 (illus.), 175, 179–180
women in, 154–155, 154 (illus.), 155 (illus.)
Romanesque Central Middle Ages (900–1100), 231–257
    Anglo-Saxon kingdoms in, 241–242, 241 (map)
    art and architecture in, 230–231 (illus.), 231–233, 232 (illus.), 237
    decentralized power and castles in, 236–237, 237 (illus.)
    delayed Second Coming in, 239, 241
    economy in, 253–254
    ethic of service in, 237–238, 238 (illus.)
    First Crusade, 254–256, 255 (map), 256 (illus.), 258–259 (source document)
    French kingdom in, 242–243, 242 (map)
    internal peace in, 250, 252
    Norman conquest of Sicily and southern Italy, 248
    Norman invasion of England, 248, 250, 251
    Ottonian rulers, 238–239, 239 (illus.)
    pilgrimages in, 252–253, 252 (illus.), 254
    religious corruption and reform, 244–247
    royal ideology of the three orders, 243–244, 243 (illus.)
    Seljuk Turks in the Byzantine Empire, 248
    timeline of, 234–235 (illus.)
    vassalage, 233, 234–238, 235 (illus.)

Roman exceptionalism, 130 (source document)
Roman Forum, 102–103 (illus.), 108, 148 (map)
Romania
    Ceaușescu overthrown in, 829–830
    "crony" capitalism in, 843
    independence of, 626, 626 (map), 841
    in the interwar years, 745, 745 (illus.)
    Jews in, 757
    pollution in, 859
    in the Soviet bloc, 802 (map), 803, 804
    in World War II, 785
Roman Inquisition (1542), 408
Roman Republic, 103–130. See also Roman Empire; Rome
    archaic religion in, 109, 109 (illus.)
    army of, 114–115, 116
    Caesar and, 142–144, 143 (map), 145
    Carthage and, 119–123, 120 (map), 122 (map), 128
    Civil War, 142–144, 143 (map)
    under the consul generals, 138–141
    consul generals in, 138–141
    control of eastern Mediterranean, 123–125
    corruption in, 136, 138
    defeat of Carthage, 123, 128
    dysfunction of late, 135–136
    early Rome, 107–109, 107 (map), 108 (illus.)
    Etruscans and, 105–109, 106 (illus.), 107 (illus.), 108 (illus.), 113–114
    First Punic War, 120–123, 120 (map), 121 (illus.), 122 (map)
    foundation myths, 105
    government in, 109–110, 111 (illus.), 116, 135–136
    Gracchi brothers's reforms in, 136, 138
    invasion and sack by Gauls, 113, 114, 116
    Italian War, 139–140
    literature in, 126–128, 126 (illus.), 141–142
    Mediterranean economy in, 125–126
    patriarchy in, 111–112
    pursuit of glory in, 117–118, 117 (illus.)
    reasons for territorial expansion, 115–117
    religion in, 109, 109 (illus.), 113 (illus.), 118–119
    Second Punic War, 122–123
    slavery in, 126, 136, 137
    social orders in, 110–111
    territorial expansion of, 112–115, 112 (map), 119–120, 120 (map)
    timeline, 104–105 (illus.)
    under The Triumvirate, 144
    virtues in, 117–118, 117 (illus.)
    war as religion in, 118
Romanticism, 577–579, 577 (illus.), 578 (illus.)
Rome. See also Etruscans; Roman Empire; Roman Republic
    annexed by Italy, 619
    archaic religion in, 109, 109 (illus.)
    Augustus's rebuilding of, 147–149, 148 (map), 149 (illus.)
    Aurelian's wall around, 167
    during the Avignon papacy, 331
    Christianity in, 172
    Constantinople moving from, 179
    in the Enlightenment, 509–510
    in the fifth and sixth centuries, 191–192
    Etruscans and, 105–109, 106 (illus.), 107 (illus.), 108 (illus.)

foundation myths, 105
Julius Caesar's entry into, 142–143, 143 (map)
Ostrogoths in, 186–187, 186 (illus.), 189–190, 192
Renaissance in, 331–332, 336
Republican government in, 110
Roman army under Sulla in, 140
sack of, by Gauls, 113, 114, 116
sack of, by Holy Roman Empire, 336
sack of, by Visigoths and Vandals, 183
settlement of, 107–109, 108 (illus.)
Rome-Berlin Axis Pact, 758
Rommel, Erwin, 775–776, 786, 789
Romulus (legendary Roman king), 108, 108 (illus.), 109
Romulus Augustulus, 183
Ronaldo, Cristiano, 853
Roosevelt, Franklin D., 777
Rosetta Stone, 20, 92 (illus.), 545–546
Rosselli, Cosimo, 344 (illus.)
round ships, 366
Rousseau, Jean-Jacques, 504–505, 504 (illus.), 510–511, 515, 522 (source document)
Rowling, J. K., 855
Roxane (wife of Alexander), 86, 88
Royal Geographical Society, 646, 647, 647 (illus.)
Royal Museums (Germany), 646, 648
Royal Society of London, 485
rubber trade, 657
Rubens, Peter Paul, 433
Rubicon River, 142, 145
Rudolf II (Holy Roman emperor), 432
Rudolf of Habsburg (Holy Roman emperor), 300
Rule of Saint Benedict, 199, 200–201, 218
Rus, 226
Rushdie, Salman, 855
Russia. See also Soviet Union
    after the revolutions of 1848, 600, 606–607
    Caucasus colonies, 640–642, 641 (map), 708
    Chechen wars, 840, 842–843, 842 (illus.)
    civil wars, 732–734, 733 (map)
    Congress of Vienna and, 562, 564 (map)
    Crimea War and, 616
    "crony" capitalism in, 843
    Decembrist revolt, 576, 576 (illus.)
    Enlightenment in, 506–507, 506 (illus.)
    in "the Great Game," in central Asia, 653–654, 654 (map)
    in the Great Northern War, 442, 444
    in the Great War, 702, 702 (map), 707–709, 708 (illus.), 718, 719
    on Greek independence, 573
    imperialism in, 640–642, 642 (illus.)
    independence from Soviet Union, 840
    invasion of Poland (1794), 540
    under Ivan the Great, 440, 442 (illus.)
    under Ivan the Terrible, 440–442, 441 (map)
    Jews in, 688–689, 689 (map), 704, 708
    military build-up, pre–Great War, 690
    Napoleon's defeat in, 554–555, 555 (illus.)
    under Peter the Great, 441 (map), 442
    Poland partition and, 507 (map)
    political corruption in, 857–858
    under Putin, 841, 843

Revolution of 1905, 686
Russian Revolution, 716–719, 717 (illus.), 718 (illus.)
Russo-Japanese War, 686, 687, 687 (illus.)
Russo-Turkish Wars, 625–626, 626 (map), 641
second industrial revolution in, 680
serfdom in, 470, 506, 568, 568 (illus.)
serf emancipation in, 606
Seven Years' War and, 478, 479
socialism in, 683–684
terrorist strikes in, 859
Viking settlements in, 226
under Yeltsin, 840
Russian Orthodox Church, 442, 442 (illus.), 506, 519, 576, 717, 822
Russian Revolution, 716–719, 717 (illus.), 718 (illus.)
Russo-Japanese War, 686, 687, 687 (illus.)
Russo-Turkish Wars, 625–626, 626 (map), 629 (source document), 641
Ruthenians, 691, 692 (map)

Sachs, Hans, 400 (illus.)
Sahagún, Bernardino de, 369 (illus.), 374 (illus.), 378, 379, 379 (illus.)
Sahara Desert, 19
Said, Edward, 649
Saint Bartholomew's Day Massacre (1572), 412, 412 (illus.)
Saint Domingue (Haiti), 437, 540–541, 540 (illus.), 542
saints, Roman Catholic, 203–204, 203 (illus.)
Sakuntala, 578
Saladin (ruler of Egypt and Syria), 270, 270 (illus.)
Salazar, Antonio, 813
Sale, Florentia, 653
Salerno, University of, 283, 285, 285 (map)
Sallust, 117, 136, 141
Salomé (Strauss), 678
salons, 490–491 (illus.), 501, 503, 527
salt, 298, 362, 475
SALT I/SALT II (Strategic Arms Limitation Treaties), 822–823
Samarkand, Russian conquest of. 653, 654 (map)
Samnites, 107, 107 (map), 114, 116, 139
Samoa, 711
Samuel (Hebrew judge), 31
Sanader, Ivo, 857
San Apollinae Nuovo mosaic, 191 (illus.)
sans-culottes (France), 536–537, 538–539, 541 (illus.)
Sanskrit, 11
San Stefan, Treaty of, 626, 626 (map)
Santangel, Luis de, 368
Santiago of Compostela, 253
Sappho of Lesbos, 48
Saracens, 226
Sarajevo, 844, 845 (illus.), 845 (map)
Sarapis (god), 97
Sarapis, temple of, 72
Sargon the Great, 16–17, 16 (illus.)
Sarkozy, Nicolas, 848, 862
Sartre, Jean-Paul, 750
The Satanic Verses (Rushdie), 855
satrapies, 51–52

Satyricon (Petronius), 157
Saudi Arabia. See also Arabia
    independence of, 739, 739 (map)
    Islam in, 206–208, 207 (map)
Saul (king of Israel), 29, 31
Savonarola, Giralamo, 334–335, 335 (illus.), 336, 342
Saxons, 167, 181, 181 (map), 187, 214, 214 (map)
Scandinavians. See also specific countries
    Luther and, 398
    Viking raids on Britain and France, 224–226, 224 (illus.)
Schacht, Hjalmar, 752, 766
Scheidel, Walter, 137
Schengen Agreements, 849
Schenk, Claus, 786
Schiller, Friedrich, 508, 577
Schleswig, 620
Schlieffen Plan, 704–705, 705 (map)
Schliemann, Heinrich, 26, 647
Schmalkaldic League, 403–404
Schmid, Catharina, 435–436
Schmitz, Philip C., 106
scholasticism, 283, 287–288, 289, 313
Scholl, Hans and Sophie, 785–786, 786 (illus.)
Schopenhauer, Arthur, 615 (illus.), 679
Schroeder, Gerhard, 847, 856–857
Schumann, Robert, 812
Schuschnigg, Kurt, 759
science
    anatomical revolution, 484–485, 484 (illus.)
    archaeology, 646, 648
    artisinal, 486–487
    botany, 513–514, 646
    cosmological revolution, 482–484
    geography, 646, 647, 647 (illus.)
    in Greece, Archaic, 48–49
    imperialism and, 645–648
    in the interwar years, 750
    modernism in, 678–679
    positivism and, 611
    Roman Catholic Church and, 483
    scientific academies, 437, 485
    scientific method, 482
    scientific revolution, 480–487, 484 (illus.), 486 (illus.)
    social life of, 485
    in the twelfth century, 266
    women in, 485–487, 486 (illus.), 673
    World War II and, 788–789
    zoology, 646
scientific method, 482
scientific socialism. See communism
Scipio Aemilianus, 128
Scipio Africanus, 122 (map), 123
"scorched-earth" tactic, 554, 708
Scotland
    Act of Union (1707) and, 498
    civil war with England, 430
    emigration from, 669, 670 (illus.)
    in the Enlightenment, 498–501, 499 (map), 500 (illus.)
    Highlanders Revolt, 498, 499 (map), 500, 500 (illus.)
    Hume, David, 501
    under James I and VI, 447
    resistance to England in, 280
    Smith, Adam, 498–499, 501
Scott, Sir Walter, 500, 578

scramble for Africa, 654–658, 655 (illus.), 656 (illus.), 657 (map)

sculpture
    in Archaic Greece, 49, 49 (illus.)
    Augustan, 148–149, 149 (illus.)
    Baroque, 410, 410 (illus.), 433
    Benin, 364 (illus.)
    Carolingian, 201 (illus.), 213 (illus.), 263 (illus.)
    in Golden Age Athens, 61 (illus.), 64–65, 64 (illus.)
    Hellenistic, 98, 98 (illus.), 98 (illus.)
    interwar, 750
    Late Middle Ages, 292–293 (illus.)
    late Roman, 167 (illus.), 173 (illus.), 178 (illus.), 182 (illus.)
    Minoan, 25
    Paleolithic Venus figurines, 35, 35 (illus.)
    Renaissance, 346–347, 346 (illus.)
    Roman Empire, 134 (illus.), 146 (illus.), 149 (illus.), 152 (illus.), 153 (illus.), 154 (illus.), 158 (illus.)
    Romanesque, 230–231 (illus.), 232 (illus.), 252 (illus.)
    Viking, 224 (illus.)
Scythians, 52 (illus.)
Sea Raiders (Sea Peoples), 24, 27, 31
Sebald, W. G., 855
Second Crusade, 268–269
Second Estate, 464–466, 528. See also nobles and aristocrats
Second Gulf War, 856
second industrial revolution, 680, 682
Second International Working Men's Organization, 684–685
Second Macedonian War, 123
Second Persian War, 54, 54 (map)
Second Punic War, 122–123, 122 (map)
second serfdom, 469, 469 (map)
Second Vatican Council (Vatican II), 822
Second World War. See World War II
Secord, James, 613
Secret History (Procopius), 189
secularism, 847–848
Sedan, Battle of, 594–595 (illus.)
sedentism, 9
seigneurial dues, 460
seignior, 274
Seleucid kingdom, 73 (illus.), 88–89, 89 (map), 123–125
Seleucus I, 88–89
self-determination, 723, 738
Seljuk Turks, 248, 254
Selkirk, Alexander, 492 (illus.)
Semitic alphabet, 28, 29 (illus.)
Senate
    Roman Empire, 147
    Roman Republic, 104, 109, 110, 111 (illus.), 116, 125–126, 138–139
Seneca, 157
Senghor, Leopold, 638 (illus.)
Sens Cathedral, 273, 289
separate spheres, of male and female virtue, 511
sepoys, 636–637, 642–643, 642 (illus.), 644
September Massacres (France), 537
septicemic plague, 307. See also plague
Septimius Severus (Roman emperor), 167
Septuagint, 92

Sepúlveda, Juan Ginés de, 380
Serbia/Serbs
    in the Balkan Wars, 693–694, 693 (illus.)
    in the breakup of Yugoslavia, 844–845, 845 (map), 846
    expansion of, 692, 692 (map)
    failed war for independence, 571
    in the Great War, 701–702, 702 (map), 708, 709 (map)
    independence of, 626–627, 626 (map)
    Princip, Gavrilo, 693, 697–699, 698 (illus.)
    in World War II, 776
    in Yugoslavia, 746
serfdom, 442, 468–471, 469 (map), 470 (illus.), 506, 568, 606. See also peasants and serfs
Serkin, Rudolf, 751
Servetus, Michael, 403
Servius Tullius (Etruscan king), 108
Set (god), 22
seventeenth century. See absolutism, seventeenth-century; Old Regimes
seventh century. See Early Middle Ages
Seven Years' War, 439, 477–478, 478 (map), 480
Sèvres, Treaty of, 724, 724 (map)
sewage systems, 156, 605, 684
sewing machines, 583, 648, 648 (illus.)
sex, Nazis and, 769
sexual revolution, 823, 823 (illus.)
Sforza, Ludovico, 336, 347
Shakespeare, William, 432
Shamil, 641, 840
Shari'ah, 207
Sheehan, Jonathan, 519
sheep, domestication of, 8, 10
Shelley, Percy Bysshe, 572
Shi'ism, 208
ships and shipbuilding
    cannons on, 477
    caravels, 366
    carracks, 366
    dreadnoughts, 688
    exploration and, 366
    galleys, 338, 366
    Phoenician, 29
    Roman, 121, 121 (illus.)
    round ships, 366
    steamships, 583
    submarines, 704, 712
    U-boats, 712
    Venetian, 338
shipwrecks, Hellenistic, 93–94
shire reeves, 241
shock therapy, 843
Shostakovich, Dmitri, 820
show trials, after World War II, 804
Siberia
    gulags in, 734, 736
    immigration into, 669
    Japanese invasion of, 711
Sibyl, 138
Sic et Non (Abelard), 265
Sicily
    Athenian attack on, 63
    in the Byzantine Empire, 209–210, 209 (map)
    Kingdom of the Two Sicilies, 564 (map), 588, 589 (map), 618, 618 (map)

Norman invasion of, 245, 248, 253
    plague in, 306, 306 (map)
    reforms of 1848, 588, 589 (map)
    slave revolt in, 136
Sickingen, Franz von, 396
Sidon (Lebanon), 28, 28 (map)
Sidonius Apollinaris, 164
Sieyès, Emmanuel Joseph, 466, 530, 543, 546, 557 (source document), 563
Sigismund III (king of Poland-Lithuania), 432, 443
Signoria, 332–333
Silesia, 478, 479, 480
silkworms, domestication of, 9
silver, 220, 378, 424, 443
Simeon the Stylite, Saint, 170
Simon IV de Montfort, 273, 277
simony, 245, 246
Singer Sewing Machines, 648, 648 (illus.)
Sino-French War, 652
Siraj al-Dawlah, 480, 481 (illus.), 481
Sistine Chapel, Michelangelo's frescoes for, 348, 348 (illus.), 349, 392
sixteenth century. See exploration; Protestant Reformation; Renaissance, European
sixth century. See Early Middle Ages
Sixtus IV (Pope), 331, 334
Six Varieties of Fart, 435
Skeptics, 95–96
Sketch for a Historical Picture of the Progress of the Human Spirit (Condorcet), 542
slave revolts
    in Haiti, 540–541, 540 (illus.)
    in the Roman Empire, 136, 140
slavery
    Aristotle on, 81
    by Boers in South Africa, 655
    of eastern Europeans, under Stalin, 803, 804
    in Egypt, ancient, 23
    encomienda system and, 377
    French Revolution and, 540–541, 540 (illus.), 542
    in Greece, ancient, 46, 47, 56, 59–60, 63
    in the Hellenistic Age, 91
    in Mesopotamia, 16
    as natural law, 380
    in the Renaissance, 340
    revolts of, 136, 140, 540–541, 540 (illus.)
    in the Roman Empire, 140–141, 155, 156–157
    in the Roman Republic, 126, 136, 137
    in South American silver mines, 378
    United States Civil War and, 617
    in World War II, 786
slave trade
    ban on, 637, 645
    by Dutch West India Company, 475
    by England, 497
    life and death in, 475–476, 476 (illus.)
    by Portugal, 363–364, 475
    by Spain, 365, 475
Slavs, 576, 691–692, 692 (map)
Slovakia, 844
Slovenia, 844, 845 (map)
smallpox, 369, 374 (illus.), 376, 484–485
Smith, Adam, 498–499, 501, 564, 682
smuggling, 475

Smyrna, 725
Sobibor death camp, 784
Sobieski, Jan, 439, 439 (illus.)
soccer, 853, 853 (illus.)
social classes. See also nobles and aristocrats;
    peasants and serfs; slavery
  artisans, in the eighteenth century, 468,
      468 (illus.)
  in Augustan Rome, 155–157, 155 (illus.)
  bourgeois, 495
  in the Central Middle Ages, 243–244, 243
      (illus.)
  clergy, in the Old Regimes, 462–464, 463
      (illus.)
  in communism and fascism, 735, 742
  in Egypt, ancient, 23
  in the eighteenth century, 460–471
  in England, Norman, 250
  in the fin de siècle, 682
  generational, 751–572
  in Greece, ancient, 46, 59–60
  in the Hellenistic Ages, 93 (illus.), 94
  in the interwar years, 751
  middle class, 608
  monarchs, in the Old Regimes, 461–462,
      461 (illus.)
  proletariat, 565, 567
  in the Roman Empire, 166
  in the Roman Republic, 110–111
  in towns and cities, in the eighteenth
      century, 467–468, 467 (illus.), 468 (illus.)
  in Victorian Britain, 607–608
The Social Contract (Rousseau), 504–505
social contracts, 498, 504–505
social Darwinism, 650, 679
socialism. See also communism
  Christian, 676, 685–686
  in the early nineteenth century, 565, 566,
      566 (illus.)
  in the fin de siècle, 683–685
  in the Great War, 691, 703
  International Working Men's
      Organization, 683–685, 684–685
  milestones in, 685
  municipal, 685
  national (See fascism)
  revolutionary vs. democratic, 684–685
  scientific, 565
  on trade unions, 684
  in unified Germany, 624
  utopian, 565, 566, 566 (illus.)
  welfare states as, 803, 812
  "with a human face," 810, 825, 826
social market economy, 847
social mobility, in the fin de siècle, 672
social question, 587–588, 682, 685
Social War (90–88 BCE), 139
Société de Geographie, 646
Society of Jesus (Jesuits), 407. See also Jesuits
society of orders, 460
Society of Righteous and Harmonious Fists
      (Boxers), 659
sociology, 678, 750
Socrates, 78–79, 79 (illus.), 101 (source
      document)
Socratic method, 79
Solidarity (Poland), 811, 828
Solomon (king of Israel), 29, 32
Solzhenitsyn, Alexander, 820, 826

Somme, Battle of the (1916), 707
The Song of Roland (Chanson de Roland),
      237–238, 238 (illus.), 303
Sophocles, 65
Sorkin, David, 519
source documents
  Agnolo the Fat and the Plague, 323
  Augustus on his accomplishments, 161
  "Broadcast to the People of the Soviet
      Union" (Stalin), 796
  "Charlemagne as Family Man"
      (Einhard), 229
  Condition of the Working Class in England
      (Engels), 593
  "Constantine's Dream" (Eusebius), 194
  Emile (Rousseau), 522
  The Existence of God (Thomas Aquinas),
      291
  Funeral Oration of Pericles, 68
  "Manifesto of the Temporary
      Government of Macedonia, March
      23, 1881," 629
  "Ninety-Five Theses" (Luther), 418–419
  Order Establishing a Consumption or Excise
      Tax . . . (Frederick William), 489
  Polybius on Roman Exceptionalism, 130
  A Pope Calls for Crusade (Robert the
      Monk), 258–259
  Reagan's address to the British
      Parliament, 831
  Socrates' speech at his trial, 101
  Trial of King Charles I, 1649, 455
  The Venus of Hohle Fels, 35 (illus.)
  "What Is the Third Estate?" (Sieyès), 557
South Africa
  Boer Wars, 638, 659–660, 659 (illus.)
  colonial, 631–633, 632 (map), 633 (illus.),
      637
  diamonds in, 632, 632 (map), 654–655,
      655 (illus.)
  Union of South Africa, 660
South America
  Brazil, Treaty of Tordesillas and, 369
  Inca Empire, 374, 374 (illus.), 378
  independence for colonies in, 635
  Spanish colonies in, 378
Southeast Asia. See also specific countries
  China and, 652
  Dutch trade in, 382, 447, 636, 652–653,
      653 (illus.)
  French Indochina, 652–653
  in the Great War, 711
  Ho Chi Minh in, 711, 740, 740 (illus.), 815
  independence of colonies in, 813, 814
      (map), 815–816, 816 (illus.)
  Japanese in, 777
  Seven Years' War in, 478 (map), 480
  United States war in, 815, 816, 816 (illus.)
  in World War II, 778–779, 779 (illus.), 780
      (map)
sovereign debt crisis (Euro crisis), 860–862
Soviet bloc. See eastern bloc (eastern
      Europe)
soviets, 686
Soviet Union. See also Russia
  in Afghanistan, 816, 826
  in Berlin, 802 (map), 806–807
  under Brezhnev, 800 (illus.), 810–811, 816,
      822

  chronology of, 736
  in the Cold War, 803
  collapse of, 838, 840, 841 (map)
  collectivization of agriculture in,
      734–735, 735 (illus.)
  Comintern, 742
  eastern Europe and, 770–771, 803–811,
      806 (map), 810 (illus.)
  economic policies in, 734
  in Finland, 772
  formation of, 718–719
  glasnost and perestroika in, 826–827, 826
      (illus.)
  under Gorbachev, 816, 825–827, 826
      (illus.), 828
  Great Terror in, 735–736
  Hitler-Stalin Pact (1939), 770
  Hungarian uprising and, 808–809, 808
      (illus.)
  under Khrushchev, 808–809, 809 (illus.)
  life in, 736–737, 737 (illus.), 825–826
  space program, 809
  Warsaw Pact, 805, 806 (map)
  in World War II, 778–780, 781, 781 (illus.),
      786, 789
space program, 809
Spain
  absolutist era in, 443
  African colonies of, 657 (map)
  after World War II, 813
  American colonies of, 370, 375–380, 377
      (illus.), 635
  armada against England, 414–415
  Canary Islands and, 365–366
  Civil War in, 758–759, 758 (map), 759
      (illus.)
  colonization by, 370, 375–380, 377 (illus.),
      657 (map)
  Columbus's claims for, 368–369
  economic crisis in, 862
  Enlightenment in, 509
  French and Indian War and, 480
  in the Great Famine, 298–299
  in the High Middle Ages, 278 (map)
  Inquisition, 317, 553
  invasions of Italy by, 336
  Islam in, 207 (map), 208, 215–216, 216
      (illus.), 318 (map)
  Jews expelled from, 317
  monarchy in, 280
  Muslims expelled from, 272 (illus.), 273,
      317, 317 (illus.)
  Napoleon in, 552–553, 552 (map), 553
      (illus.), 554
  native narrative of conquests of, 379, 379
      (illus.)
  in the Roman Empire, 123, 136, 142, 143
      (map), 147, 159 (map)
  Second Spanish Republic, 758
  serfs in, 470
  Seven Years' War and, 477–478, 478
      (map), 480
  Thirty Years' War and, 428–430, 443
  Tragic Week in Barcelona (1909), 686
  Treaty of Tordesillas, 369
  unification under Isabella and
      Ferdinand, 317, 318 (map)
  Vandals in, 183
  Visigoths in, 185, 185 (map)

Spain (continued)
  voyages of exploration, 371–374
  War of the Spanish Succession, 437–438, 477
Spanish Armada, 414–415
Spanish Civil War, 758–759, 758 (map), 759 (illus.)
Spanish flu, 720–721
Spanish Inquisition, 317, 553
Spanish Netherlands, 413, 413 (map), 438, 438 (map)
Spanish Road, 426, 427 (map), 437, 477, 595
Sparta. See also Greece, ancient
  after the Peloponnesian War, 74
  Lycurgan code in, 56
  militarization of, 56–57
  Peloponnesian League and, 54, 56
  in the Peloponnesian War, 57 (map), 62, 62 (map)
  in Persian Wars, 53, 54–56, 54 (map)
  under Philip of Macedon, 77
  slavery in, 59, 63
  women in, 60
Spartacus, 140–141
SPD (Sozialdemokratische Partei Deutschlands), 624
Species Plantarum (Linnaeus), 514
Speer, Albert, 749, 789, 792
Speke, John Hanning, 646
Spencer, Herbert, 611
spheres of influence, 640
The Sphinx (Moreau), 675, 675 (illus.)
Sphrantzes, George, 319
spice trade, 380–382, 447
spinning jenny, 582, 583 (illus.)
Spinoza, Baruch, 495, 496, 519
Spirit of the Laws (Montesquieu), 502
The Spiritual Canticle (John of the Cross), 408
Spitzweg, Carl, 612
sports, 669, 853, 853 (illus.)
Sputnik, 809
Srebrenica, 846
SS (Schutzstaffeln), 752, 770
St. Chapelle, 289, 289 (illus.)
St. Denis monastery (France), 206, 260–261 (illus.), 267
St. Lazare of Autun (France), 230–231 (illus.), 231, 233
St. Mark's Square (Venice), 444 (illus.)
St. Peter's Basilica, New, in Rome, 431 (illus.)
St. Petersburg (Petrograd), 506–507, 703, 716
"stab in the back" myth, 743, 766
stadtholder, 447
Staël, Madame de (Anne-Louise-Germaine Necker), 525–527, 525 (illus.), 548, 578
stained-glass windows, 260–261 (illus.), 267, 289, 289 (illus.)
Stakhanovites, 737
Stalin, Josef
  in the Cold War, 803–804, 808
  collectivization of agriculture, 734–735, 735 (illus.), 803
  eastern Europe and, 802, 802 (map)
  on national communism, 804–805
  as oil field worker, 684
  radio broadcast of invasion, 796 (source document)
  Soviet Union under, 734–738, 735 (illus.)
  in World War II, 779–780, 788, 792

Stanley, Henry Morton, 630–631 (illus.), 645, 646, 656
steam engines, 581, 583
steamships, 583
steel production, 680
Steen, Jan, 433, 434 (illus.), 495
stele, Akkadian, 17 (illus.)
Stephen (Pope), 213
Stephen I (king of Hungary), 252
Stephen of Bourbon, 238
Stilicho (Vandal general), 182, 182 (illus.)
Stinkpreussen, 627
Stobnicy, Jan ze, 371 (map)
stock market, seventeenth-century, 474, 474 (illus.)
Stock Market crash of 1929, 753
Stoics, 95–96, 159
Stonehenge (England), 10–11, 10 (illus.)
stone technology, 7, 10–11, 10 (illus.)
storm troopers (SA), 744, 752, 754
The Stranger (Camus), 818
strategos, 53, 62
Strauss, Richard, 678
Stravinsky, Igor, 678
Stuart, James, 510
Stuart kings of England, 452–453, 452 (illus.)
stylites, 170
submarines, 704, 712
subsistence economy, 220
subways, 606, 672
Sudan
  as British colony, 739, 739 (map)
  Nubia, 19 (map), 20, 22, 91
Sudetenland, 746, 766, 767 (map)
Suetonius, 157, 158
Suez Canal
  building of, 650, 651–652, 651 (illus.)
  in the Great War, 710
  in the interwar years, 739, 739 (map)
suffragettes, 673
sugarcane, 365, 475–476, 476 (illus.), 516
Suger (abbot), 267
Suicide (Durkheim), 678
Sulla (Roman dictator), 139, 140
Sumer, 13, 13 (map). See also Mesopotamia
Sumeria, 16
sumptuary laws, 473
sundials, 154
Sunnis, 208
surrealism, 750
Survival in Auschwitz (Levi), 784
Susa, 84–85, 86
Swann's Way (Proust), 678
Sweden
  absolutist era in, 443–444
  in the Great Northern War, 442, 443–444
  mobile army in, 429, 477
  in the Thirty Years' War, 428–430, 429 (illus.)
Switzerland
  Calvin in, 402–404, 404 (illus.)
  in the Great War, 705
  Zwingli in, 399, 401
Syllabus of Errors, 600
syllogisms, 79
Sylvester II (Pope), 245
symbolism, 675, 675 (illus.)
syncreticism, 97
Syracuse (Sicily), 63

Syria
  Amorites and Canaanites in, 28
  Islam in, 207 (map), 208
  Napoleon in, 545, 546 (map), 547
  in Persian Empire, 51
Systemae Naturae (Linnaeus), 514
Szabo, Franz, 479

T-4 Program, 768
tabula rasa, 497
Tacitus, 153, 158
Tagore, Rabindranath, 677
taille, 467
Taíno people, 368
Taiping Rebellion, 640, 652
Tajikistan, 841 (map)
Tamerlane (Timur the Lame), 318
Tanakh, 29
tanks, 712
Tannenberg, Battle of (1914), 707
Tanzania, 814 (map), 817
Tarentum (Italy), 115
Tarquinia, 114
Tarquin the Proud, 108
Tashkent, Russian conquest of, 653, 654 (map)
taxes
  in absolute monarchies, 461
  consumption, 489 (source document)
  Enlightenment thinkers on, 499
  Roman Republic and, 126
  on the third estate, 466–467
  tithing by churches, 463, 466
  on trade, 475
tea, 498, 640
technology
  after 1989, 712–713
  in the Central Middle Ages, 253–254
  in the fin de siècle, 669
  in the Great War, 711–713, 713 (illus.)
  Hellenistic, 96–97
  imperialism and, 650
  Roman, 156, 156 (illus.)
  stone, 7, 10–11, 10 (illus.)
  telegraph systems, 584, 616, 713
  water mills for grain, 221, 253
Temple of Athena (Athens), 64, 64 (illus.)
Temple of Luxor, 23
Temple of Mars the Avenger (Rome), 147–148
Temptation of Eve (Gislebertus), 223, 232 (illus.)
Ten Commandments, 30
Tennis Court Oath, 531
Tennyson, Alfred Lord, 616
Tenochtitlan, 358 (map), 372–374
Ten Oligarchs, 74
tenth century. See Romanesque Central Middle Ages
Terence, 128
Teresa of Ávila, 408
"the Terror" (France), 538
terrorism, 858–859
Tertullian, 170, 171
Tetrarchy, Roman, 173, 173 (illus.), 177
Tetzel, Johann, 392, 393, 393 (illus.)
textile trade
  in colonies, 636–637
  cottage industries in, 274, 472–473, 581, 586

cotton and, 581, 582
   Industrial Revolution in, 581
   in the Restoration era, 568
Thailand, Japanese control of, 777
Thales of Miletus, 48–49
Thatcher, Margaret, 823, 823 (illus.), 825, 827, 847
theater
   Baroque, 432–433
   Greek, Classical, 65–66
   Hellenistic, 77–78, 78 (illus.)
   modernist, 675, 677
   Roman Republic, 126–128, 126 (illus.)
   seventeenth-century, 432
Thebes (Greece)
   after the Peloponnesian War, 74–75
   Alexander's defeat of, 83
   in Athens and Sparta conflict, 61, 63
   under Philip of Macedon, 77
   as polis, 57–58, 57 (map)
thegns, 241
Themistocles, 53, 54, 55, 55 (illus.)
Theoderic (Ostrogoth), 186–187, 186 (illus.), 189, 191 (illus.)
Theodora (eastern Roman Empire), 162–163 (illus.), 163–164, 188–189
Theodosius (Roman emperor), 180, 182
Theogonis of Megara, 48
Theogony (Hesiod), 45
Theologico-Political Treatise (Spinoza), 496
Theophrastus, 96
Thera (Santorini), 26
Thermidorean reaction, 543
Thermopylae (Greece), 54, 54 (map), 56, 58, 124
Thessaly, under Roman rule, 125
Third Crusade, 269–270, 270 (illus.)
Third Estate. See also peasants and serfs
   French Revolution and, 528–529, 529 (illus.)
   National Assembly of, 531
   in the Old Regimes, 466–471, 467 (illus.), 468 (illus.), 470 (illus.)
Third Macedonian War, 125
Third Punic War, 128
third world, 817
thirteenth century. See Gothic High Middle Ages
Thirty Tyrants, 65, 74, 78, 79
Thirty Years' War, 424, 426–431, 427 (map), 428 (illus.), 430 (illus.)
Thomas à Kempis, 312
Thomas Aquinas, Saint ("Dumb Ox"), 280, 287–288, 291 (source document), 408
Thomas Christians, 382
Thoth (god), 22
Thoughts on the Education of Daughters (Wollstonecraft), 511
Thrace
   in the Ottoman Empire, 694
   Persian conquest of, 52, 53, 54 (map)
   in the Roman Empire, 157
   Seleucid invasion of, 123–124
Thucydides, 59, 61, 62–63, 66, 68 (source document)
Thus Spake Zarathustra (Nietzsche), 679
Thus Spake Zarathustra (Strauss), 678
Tianjin, Treaty of (1860), 640
Tiberius (Roman emperor), 153, 157

Tiberius Gracchus, 136, 138
Tiepolo, Giovan Battista, 509
Tigris River, 13, 13 (map), 18
Tillich, Paul, 750
Tilsit, Treaty of (1807), 551
Timaeus (Plato), 50, 283
timelines
   Cold War, 800–801 (illus.)
   Early Middle Ages, 199–200 (illus.)
   Enlightenments, 492–493 (illus.)
   Europe, after 1989, 835–836 (illus.)
   exploration age, 358–359 (illus.)
   fin de siècle (1880–1914), 666–667 (illus.)
   French Revolution, 526–527 (illus.)
   Gothic High Middle Ages, 262–263 (illus.)
   Great War (World War I), 698–699 (illus.)
   Greece, ancient, 40–41 (illus.)
   Hellenistic Ages, 72–73 (illus.)
   imperialism, 634–635 (illus.)
   interwar era (1918–1939), 730–731 (illus.)
   Italian Renaissance, 326–327 (illus.)
   Late Middle Ages (1300–1500), 294–295 (illus.)
   nineteenth century (1850–1880), 598–599 (illus.)
   Old Regimes (seventeenth and eighteenth centuries), 458–459 (illus.)
   prehistory, 4–5 (illus.)
   Protestant Reformation, 388–389 (illus.)
   Renaissance, European, 326–327 (illus.)
   Restoration era (1815–1850), 562–563 (illus.)
   Roman Empire, 134–135 (illus.)
   Romanesque Central Middle Ages (900–1100), 234–235 (illus.)
   Roman Republic, 104–105 (illus.)
   seventeenth-century absolutism, 422–423 (illus.)
   World War II, 764–765 (illus.)
Timoshenko, Yulia, 857, 857 (illus.)
Tipu Sultan, 637
Tiso, Jozef, 767, 785
tithes, 463, 466
Titian, 443
Tito (Josef Broz), 776, 804 (illus.), 844
Titoists, 804–805, 804 (illus.)
Titus (Roman emperor), 152, 152 (illus.), 157
Tocharian, Indo-European migrations into, 11
Tocqueville, Alexis de, 559–561, 560 (illus.), 589
Toghril Beg, 248
Toledo (Spain), 283
"Toleration of All Faiths" (Catherine the Great), 506
Tolkien, J. R. R., 320
Tolstoy, Leo, 641
Tomb of the Unknown Soldier, 722, 722 (illus.)
Tom Jones (Fielding), 511
Tone, Wolfe, 540
Topics (Aristotle), 81
Topkapi Palace (Istanbul), 446
Torah, 29, 31
Tordesillas, Treaty of (1494), 369, 382
Tories, 452, 598
Toscanini, Arturo, 751
totalitarianism, 732

total war, 703–704, 703 (illus.)
Totila (Ostrogoth), 190
Toussaint L'Ouverture, 540 (illus.), 541
trade. See commerce and trade
Trafalgar, Battle of (1805), 551, 552, 552 (map)
Trajan (Roman emperor), 157, 158, 158 (illus.), 159
Trajan's column, 158 (illus.)
Transjordan, as British mandate, 739 (map)
Transvaal, 655, 659–660
travel
   in the Enlightenment, 509–510, 512–513, 513 (illus.)
   in the fin de siècle, 672
   Genoa in, 361–362
   "the grand tour," 509–510
   in the interwar years, 751
   in the Middle Ages, 361
   pilgrimages, 252–253, 252 (illus.), 254, 676, 676 (illus.)
   by railroad, 582 (map), 583–584
   travelers' tales, 361, 362, 362 (illus.)
travel guides, 672
The Travels of Sir John Mandeville, 361, 362, 362 (illus.)
La Traviata (Verdi), 614
Treason Act (England, 1534), 401
treaties. See under specific treaties
A Treatise of Human Nature (Hume), 501
The Treatise of the Three Imposters, 496, 512, 519
treaty ports, 640
Treblinka death camp, 784
Trebonian, 189
trench warfare, 705, 705 (illus.), 707
Treschow, Hennig von, 786
Les Très Riches Heures du Duc de Berry, 295 (illus.)
trial by ordeal, 17, 251, 272, 280
Trianon, Treaty of, 723, 724, 724 (map), 745
tribunes, Roman, 110, 111 (illus.), 135
tribute, 52 (illus.)
Tridentine Index, 409
Tristan and Isolde (Wagner), 615
Triumph of the Will (Riefenstahl), 754–755
The Triumvirate (Roman), 144
trivium, 264
Trojan horse, 27
Trojan Wars, 27, 41–42, 42 (illus.), 65
Trollope, Anthony, 607, 609
Trotsky, Leon, 718, 732–733, 735, 737
Truce of God movement, 252
True History of the Conquest of New Spain (Díaz), 359
Truman, Harry, 792, 805
Truman Doctrine, 805
tuberculosis, 671
Tudjman, Franjo, 844, 857
tulip bulbs, 474
Tulla, Gottfried, 596
Tulp, Nicholaes, 496 (illus.)
Tunisia, French control of, 652
Turkestan, 653
Turkey (Anatolia). See also Ottoman Empire
   in the Antigonid kingdom, 89 (map)
   in the Byzantine Empire, 209–210, 209 (map)
   Çatalhüyük settlement, 10, 10 (illus.), 19 (map)

Turkey *(continued)*
  European Union and, 850
  Hittites, 17, 19 *(map)*, 26 *(map)*, 27
  Indo-European migrations into, 11, 12
    (map)
  Lydia and Lydians, 48, 51, 52, 52 *(illus.)*,
    53 *(map)*
  map of (1450 BCE), 26 *(map)*
  Mustafa Kemal in, 710, 724–725, 725
    (illus.)
  Neolithic agriculture in, 9
  Pergamum in, 70–71 *(illus.)*, 90–91, 97, 99
  in the Roman Empire, 159 *(map)*, 185
    (map)
  Trojan Wars, 27
Turkmenistan, 841 *(map)*
Turpin, Dick, 471
Tutankhaton (king of Egypt), 23, 27
Twain, Mark, 656 *(illus.)*
twelfth century. *See* Gothic High Middle
    Ages
Twelfth-Century Renaissance, 264. *See also*
    Gothic High Middle Ages
Twelve Tables (Roman), 112
twentieth century. *See* Cold War; Europe,
    after 1989; fin de siècle; Great War;
    interwar era; World War II
twenty-first century. *See* Europe, after 1989
Twenty One Demands (Japan), 711
Two Sicilies, Kingdom of the, 564 *(map)*,
    588–589 *(map)*, 618, 618 *(map)*
Two Treatises of Government (Locke), 497–498
Tyler, Wat, 310–311
tympanum sculptures, 232
typewriters, 673, 673 *(illus.)*
tyrants, in ancient Greece, 46–47
Tyre (Lebanon), 28, 28 *(map)*, 120

U2 (band), 833–835
U-boats, 712
Ugarit, 28, 28 *(map)*
Ukraine
  Chernobyl explosion in, 826, 859
  "crony" capitalism in, 843
  in the Great War, 708, 719
  independence of, 840, 841 *(map)*
  Poland and, 744
  political corruption in, 857, 857 *(illus.)*
  in the Russian civil wars, 733
  in the Soviet Union, 802 *(map)*, 804–805
  in World War II, 785
Ulbricht, Walter, 800–801, 807
Ulpian, 167
Ulrika (queen of Sweden), 444
Ulyanov, Alexander, 606
Umar, 208
Umayyad Caliphate, 208, 207 *(map)*, 215
Umberto I (king of Italy), 685
Ummah, 206
Unam sanctam (Boniface), 299
Union of Soviet Socialist Republics (USSR).
    See Soviet Union
United Kingdom of Great Britain, 498. *See
    also* Britain; England
United Nations
  in the breakup of Yugoslavia, 845
  formation of, 792
  mandates, 723, 738
  on Palestine, 815

Suez Canal and, 817
United Provinces (Netherlands), 413, 413
    (map), 445, 447
United States
  in Afghanistan, 816
  American War of Independence, 529,
    634–635
  atomic weapon development, 788
  in the breakup of Yugoslavia, 845
  Civil War in, 616–618
  consumerism in, 852, 852 *(illus.)*
  Cuban missile crisis, 809
  Dawes Plan, 744
  fin-de-siècle immigration into, 669
  in the Great War, 702, 707, 712, 715
  immigration restrictions in, 746
  Louisiana Territory, 480, 635
  Monroe Doctrine, 635
  second industrial revolution in, 680
  space program, 809
  Spanish flu in, 720
  Truman Doctrine, 805
  in Vietnam War, 815, 816, 816 *(illus.)*
  in World War II, 775, 777–778, 789–790
universities
  birth and spread of, 283, 285–287, 285
    (map), 286 *(illus.)*
  of Bologna, 283, 285–286, 285 *(map)*, 286
    (illus.), 287
  Cambridge University, 285, 285 *(map)*
  cathedral schools and, 282–283
  in the High Middle Ages, 282–289
  life in, 287, 287 *(illus.)*
  Oxford University, 283, 285, 285 *(map)*
  of Padua, 285 *(map)*, 327, 328, 342, 345
  of Paris, 282, 283, 285–287, 285 *(map)*, 288
  of Salerno, 283, 285, 285 *(map)*
  scholasticism and, 283, 287–288
  translations of collected wisdom and,
    283
Ur, 13 *(map)*, 17, 30
Urban II (Pope), 254–255, 258–259 *(source
    document)*, 271
urban planning
  of Alexandria, 72
  of Paris, 604–606, 605 *(illus.)*, 605 *(map)*
Urban VI (Pope), 313
Urban VIII (Pope), 483
Ur-Nammu, 17
Uruk (Iraq), 13, 13 *(map)*, 14, 16, 18, 19 *(map)*.
    See also Mesopotamia
USSR. *See* Soviet Union
Ustasha, 776, 776 *(illus.)*
usury, 276, 473
Uthman, 208
utilitarianism, 579–580, 587
Utopia (More), 351
utopian socialists, 565, 566, 566 *(illus.)*
Utrecht Psalter, 218
Uzbekistan, 841 *(map)*

vaccinations, 484–485, 679
Valens (Roman emperor), 181–182
Valerian (Roman emperor), 167, 171
Vandals, 181 *(map)*, 181, 183–186, 185 *(map)*,
    189
van der Weyden, Rogier, 350
Van Dyck, Anthony, 433
van Eyck, Jan, 350 *(illus.)*

Vasari, Giorgio, 328, 329, 345–346
vassalage, 233, 234–238, 235 *(illus.)*
Vatican Library, 331
Vega, Felix Arturo Lopé de, 432
Veii (Etruscan city), 113–114
Velázquez, Diego, 372, 432, 432 *(illus.)*
"velvet divorce," 844
Vendée, 534, 536 *(map)*
Venice
  under Austrians, 619
  colonies of, 339
  as commune, 330
  cosmopolitanism in, 340, 341
  Enlightenment in, 509
  Jews in, 341, 342, 342 *(illus.)*
  Renaissance in, 329 *(map)*, 330 *(illus.)*,
    337–339, 338 *(map)*
  as Venetian Republic, 444–445, 444
    (illus.), 445 *(map)*
Venizelos, Eleftherios, 725
Venus de Milo, 98
Venus figurine of Hohle Fels, 35, 35 *(illus.)*
Verdi, Giuseppe, 578–579, 614
Verdun, Treaty of (843), 222, 224 *(map)*
Vergerio, Pier Paolo, 343–344
Verlaine, Paul, 677
Vermeer, Jan, 433
Verrazzano, Giovanni da, 375
Versailles, palace at, 420–421 *(illus.)*, 437
Versailles, Treaty of, 723–724, 724 *(map)*,
    757
Vesalius, Andreas, 482, 484, 496 *(illus.)*
Vespasian (Roman emperor), 152, 157, 158
Vespucci, Amerigo, 371–372
Vesta, cult of, 119
Vestalia, 119
Vestal Virgins, 119, 138, 180
Vestiges of the Natural History of Creation
    (Chambers), 613
Vichy France, 773–774, 773 *(illus.)*
Victor Emmanuel II (king of Piedmont-
    Sardinia), 591, 618, 619
Victoria (queen of England), 575–576, 603,
    603 *(illus.)*
Vienna
  nineteenth-century transformation in,
    606
  Ottoman attack on, 439, 439 *(illus.)*
  stock market crash in (1873), 679
Vietnam
  French control of, 652
  Ho Chi Minh and, 711, 740, 740 *(illus.)*
  independence from French, 815
  Japanese control of, 777
  United States war in, 814 *(map)*, 815, 816,
    816 *(illus.)*
Vikings (Northmen)
  attacks on England, 241–242
  invasion of Francia, 224–226, 224 *(illus.)*,
    227
Ville de Paris, 681
Vimy Ridge, Battle of (1917), 719
Vindication of the Rights of Woman
    (Wollstonecraft), 511
Virgil, 149–151, 151 *(illus.)*
Virgin *(Parthenos)* Athena (Phidias), 64
Virgin Mary, 209, 570, 676, 676 *(illus.)*
Virgin of Guadalupe, 378
virtus, 117–118

Visigoths, 181 (map), 181–186, 185 (map), 188, 215
Vittorino da Feltre, 344
Vivaldi, Antonio, 434
Vivaldi brothers (travellers), 361
Vŭkov, Ivan, 745
volley-firing, 476–477
Voltaire (François Marie Arouet), 501–503, 503 (illus.), 507
Volterra family, 342
Vorontsov, Mikhail, 641
voting rights
    in France, 567, 575, 603
    in Germany, 620
    in the United Kingdom, 575, 599, 601
    for women, 673, 823
Vulgate Bible, 218, 409

Wagner, Richard, 596, 614–615, 615 (illus.), 678
Wagram, Battle of (1809), 554
Waldensians, 277
Waldseemüller, Martin, 371, 371 (map)
Wales, 280
Wałesa, Lech, 811, 841
Wallace, Alfred Russel, 613
Wallenstein, Albrecht von, 428, 430
Waning of the Middle Ages (Huizinga), 320
war communism, 734
war crimes, 706, 792–793
al-Wardi, Abu Hafs 'Umar Ibn, 305
warfare
    air wars, 712
    army mobility in, 429, 477
    Assyrian, 32
    bastions and walls for siege, 476
    Blitzkrieg, 770, 772
    boarding tactics, 121
    cannons and gunpowder, 304
    Crimean War and, 616
    dog tags in, 622
    elephants in, 122
    gas, 691, 704, 712
    Geneva Convention and, 691
    Greek hoplites, 47, 47 (illus.), 53
    guerrilla, 553, 622, 704
    knighthood and, 303–304
    legions, 114–115
    phalanxes, 47, 76, 110–111
    as religious rite, 118
    "scorched-earth" tactic, 554, 708
    submarine, 704
    trench, 705, 705 (illus.), 707
    volley-firing, 476–477
war guilt clause, 724, 742
war memorials, 722, 722 (illus.)
War of the Austrian Succession, 477, 478
War of the First Coalition, 537, 543
War of the Roses (England), 315, 317
War of the Second Coalition, 543, 551
War of the Spanish Succession, 437–438, 477
War of the Third Coalition, 548
Warsaw ghetto, 771–772
Warwaw Pact, 805, 806 (map)
washing machines, 824, 824 (illus.)
The Waste Land (Eliot), 751
"The Watch on the Rhine," 602
water clocks, 154
Waterloo, Battle of (1815), 555

water supply
    in Augustan Rome, 155
    in fin-de-siècle cities, 671, 684
    in Paris, 605
Watt, James, 581
The Way We Live Now (Trollope), 607
weapons
    airplanes, 712
    atomic, 788, 792
    bronze, 27
    cannons and gunpowder, 304, 429, 477
    Copper and Bronze age, 11
    crossbows and longbows, 301, 302 (illus.), 304
    in the Great War, 704
    imperialism and, 650–651
    iron, 27–28, 32
    javelins, 114
    machine guns, 650–651, 712
    matchlock and flintlock, 476
    nuclear disarmament, 822–823
    pikes, 75
    poison gas, 691, 704, 712
    pre–Great War arms race, 688, 690–691, 700
    quick-firing artillery, 690
    tanks, 712
    V-1 and V-2 rockets, 774
weather. See climate
Weber, Max, 678
Wedgewood china, 472
Weimar Republic, 742–744, 743 (illus.), 752
welfare states, 803, 812
Wellesley, Sir Arthur (duke of Wellington), 553, 555
Wellington, Arthur Wellesley, Duke of, 553, 555
Wells, H. G., 775
Weltschmerz, 577
Werner, Anton von, 599 (illus.)
Wesley, John, 464
western Europe, after World War II. See also Europe, after 1989
    baby boom in, 811–812
    countries in, 806 (map)
    economy in, 805–806
    European Economic Community, 806 (map), 812–813
    guest workers in, 813, 848
    in the 1970s and 1980s, 822–825, 823 (illus.)
    welfare state in, 803, 812
Western (Papal) Schism, 313
West Indies
    colonial soldiers in, 643–644
    Columbus in, 357
    Dutch trading in, 447
    in the French and Indian War, 480
    slave trade in, 475–476, 476 (illus.) (See also West Indies)
Westminster Abbey, 250
"What Is the Third Estate?" (Sieyès), 530, 543, 557 (source document)
"What Is to Be Done?" (Lenin), 685
wheat, 10, 19, 24 (illus.)
Whigs, 452, 598
"The White Man's Burden" (Kipling), 650
White on White (Malevich), 748
White Rose resistance group, 785–786, 786 (illus.)

Wilde, Oscar, 675, 678
Wilders, Geert, 859
Wilhelm I (German emperor), 621, 622
Wilhelm I (king of the Netherlands), 573
Wilhelm II (German emperor)
    arms race with British, 690–691
    in the Great War, 701–702, 702 (map), 719
    socialists under, 624
William, duke of Normandy, the Conqueror, 248–249, 251
William III (king of England), 452–453, 452 (illus.)
William IV (king of England), 575
William of Conches, 265–266, 268
William of Moerbeke, 288
William of Ockham, 300, 313
William the Silent (prince of Orange), 413
Wilson, Harold, 812
Wilson, Woodrow, 723, 740
Winged Victory of Samothrace, 98 (illus.)
witch killing, 403, 424, 435–436, 436 (illus.)
Władysław (king of Poland), 443
Wollstonecraft, Mary, 511
women. See also women's rights
    Carolingian, 217, 225
    in the Central Middle Ages, 243–244, 243 (illus.)
    in cottage industries, 472–473, 581, 586
    domestic violence and, 586–587
    education for, 266, 511
    in Egypt, ancient, 23–24
    in the Enlightenment, 498, 502, 503, 503 (illus.), 511
    in the fin de siècle, 672–673, 673 (illus.)
    in the French Revolution, 533, 542
    in the Great War, 703, 714–715, 714 (illus.), 727 (source document)
    in Greece, ancient, 47, 56, 60, 60 (illus.)
    in guilds, 468, 468 (illus.)
    in the Hellenistic Age, 91, 94
    in the High Middle Ages, 261–263, 266, 266 (illus.)
    industrialization and, 586–587, 586 (illus.)
    in the interwar years, 747, 747 (illus.), 751–752
    in the Italian Renaissance, 332
    under Napoleon, 548–549
    in Nazi Germany, 768
    as nurses, 616, 616 (illus.), 703
    Protestant Reformation and, 397
    religion and, 570
    in the Roman Empire, eastern, 189
    in the Roman Republic, 112, 119
    in Rome, Augustan, 154–155, 154 (illus.), 155 (illus.)
    science and, 485–487, 486 (illus.)
    sexual revolution, 823, 823 (illus.)
    in the Soviet Union, 729–731, 734, 736–737
    in Spanish colonies, 377, 377 (illus.)
    in Victorian Britain, 608–609
    in World War II, 786–787, 787 (illus.)
women's rights
    in the French Revolution, 542
    Great War and, 715
    Mill on, 580
    in the Napoleonic Code, 548–549
    in the Paris Commune, 623

women's rights (continued)
    in the 1970s and 1980s, 823, 823 (illus.)
    in the Soviet Union, 729–731, 730 (illus.),
        734, 737
    voting, 673, 823
    washing machines and, 824, 824 (illus.)
    in western Europe, post-1989, 849
Women's Social and Political Union, 673
Wonderful Transformation and Singular
    Flower-Food of Caterpillars . . .
    (Merian), 486, 486 (illus.)
workers/labor. *See also* peasants and serfs
    after the plague, 310
    in Benedictine monasteries, 200–201
    benefits to, in unified Germany, 624
    in the Central Middle Ages, 243–244, 243
        (illus.)
    child labor, 682
    domestic service, 609, 609 (illus.)
    in Egypt, ancient, 23
    in the fin de siècle, 669, 682
    in the French Revolution, 536–537
    in the Industrial Revolution, 585–588,
        586 (illus.)
    migrant, 471
    under the Nazis, 754
    in the political spectrum (1815–1850),
        564–567, 565 (illus.)
    as the proletariat, 565, 567
    in the Roman Empire, 173, 175
    in the Russian Revolution of 1905, 686
    in the Soviet Union, 736
    in Victorian Britain, 610–611
    wage work, 585–586
    women, 672–673, 673 (illus.), 714–715, 714
        (illus.)
    work hours and workweeks, 610
Works and Days (Hesiod), 45–46, 47
World Bank, 805–806
World Cup, 853, 853 (illus.)
World War I. *See* Great War
World War II, 763–795
    Balkans in, 776, 776 (illus.)
    Belgium and the Netherlands in, 773
    Britain in, 773, 774–775, 775 (illus.)
    chronologies of, 777, 778
    collaboration with Axis Powers in,
        784–785
    displaced persons after, 793–795
    in eastern Europe, 781, 785
    end of, 789–792, 790 (illus.), 791 (illus.)

Enigma code in, 772–773, 772 (illus.)
fatalities in, 793 (map), 794 (illus.)
France in, 770, 773–774, 773 (illus.), 786,
    789–790
German annexations before, 766–767, 767
    (map)
Holocaust/Nazi Final Solution, 781,
    782–784, 782 (illus.), 783 (map)
Italy in, 775, 789
Japan in, 774, 777–779, 779 (illus.), 780
    (map), 790, 792
Jews in, 766–772, 767 (map), 768 (illus.),
    774, 776, 781–784, 782 (illus.), 783
    (map), 784 (illus.), 788
Nazi racial war, 767–770, 768 (illus.)
in northern Africa, 775–776, 789
Norway and Denmark in, 771
Operation Barbarossa, 778–780
in the Pacific, 778–779, 779 (illus.), 780
    (map), 790, 792
Poland and, 767, 767 (map), 770–772, 779,
    782, 783 (map), 786, 790, 792
post-war agreements, 792–793, 793 (map)
propaganda in, 754, 756, 787–788
resistance in, 773–774, 785–786, 786 (illus.)
science and, 788–789
slave laborers in, 786
Soviet Union in, 770, 778–780, 781, 781
    (illus.), 786, 789
timeline, 764–765 (illus.)
war crimes trials, 792–793
women in, 786–787, 787 (illus.)
World Wide Web, 854
Worms, Concordat of, 247
The Wretched of the Earth (Fanon), 817
writing
    in ancient Egypt, 19–20
    Caroline Minuscule, 217, 217 (illus.), 283
    Etruscan, 105, 106, 106 (illus.)
    Gothic script, 283
    importance of, 14, 16
    Linear A, 25
    Linear B, 26, 40
    in Mesopotamia, 14–16, 14 (illus.)
    Phoenician, 28–29, 29 (illus.), 32, 42, 106
    Semitic, 28, 29 (illus.)
Wyclif, John, 313–314

Xanthippus, 121
Xavier, Francis, 382
Xenophon, 74, 78, 79

Xerxes (king of Persia), 54, 54 (map)

Yalta conference (1945), 792
Yeats, William Butler, 677
Yeltsin, Boris, 840, 843
Yersin, Alexandre, 307
Yersinia pestis bacteria, 293–294, 294 (illus.),
    304–308. *See also* bubonic plague
YHWH (Jehovah; Yah(weh)), 30
Young, Thomas, 20
Young Men's Christian Association
    (YMCA), 611, 676
Young Turks, 693, 725
Ypres
    Great Famine in, 298
    Second Battle of (1915), 704
Ypsilantis, Alexander, 571
Yugoslavia
    breakup of, 844–846, 845 (illus.), 845
        (map)
    Civil Wars in, 834, 834 (illus.)
    in the Cold War, 804
    in the interwar years, 745–746
    in World War II, 776, 776 (illus.)
Yuschenko, Victor, 857

Zadig (Voltaire), 503
Zambia, 814 (map), 817
Zarathustra (Zoroaster), 52
Zemsky Sobor, 441–442
zemstvos, 606
Zeno (Roman emperor), 186
Zenon, 93
Zeno of Citium, 95
Zerajić, Bogdan, 697
Zeus (god), 43, 45, 84
Zeus Ammon, oracle of (Libya), 84
Zheng He (Chinese Admiral), 363, 381
Zhirinovsky, Vladimir, 844
Ziggurat of Ur, 17
Zimmermann, Arthur, 713
Ziolkowski, Jan, 265
Zionism, 689, 690, 692, 723
Zola, Émile, 681, 689
Zollverein, 569, 585, 620
zoology, 646
Zoroastrianism, 52
Zwickau prophets, 397, 405
Zwingli, Huldrych, 399, 401, 405